P9-DZN-496

Contemporary Authors

NEW REVISION SERIES

Contemporary Authors

A Bio-Bibliographical Guide to
Current Writers in Fiction, General Nonfiction,
Poetry, Journalism, Drama, Motion Pictures,
Television, and Other Fields

ANN EVORY
LINDA METZGER
Editors

PETER M. GAREFFA
DEBORAH A. STRAUB
Associate Editors

NEW REVISION SERIES
volume 9

GALE RESEARCH COMPANY • THE BOOK TOWER • DETROIT, MICHIGAN 48226

EDITORIAL STAFF

Library of Congress Catalog Card Number 81-640179
ISBN 0-8103-1938-1
ISSN 0275-7176

Authors and Media People Featured in This Volume

John Ashbery—American poet, playwright, critic, editor, and professor; in an unprecedented sweep of the literary "triple crown" in 1976, his poetry collection *Self-Portrait in a Convex Mirror* won a Pulitzer Prize, National Book Award, and National Book Critics Circle Award. (Sketch includes interview.)

Jean L. Baer—American writer of self-help books for women, notably *Don't Say Yes When You Want to Say No,* coauthored with her husband, Herbert Fensterheim, and *How to Be an Assertive (Not Aggressive) Woman in Life, Love, and on the Job.* (Sketch includes interview.)

Charles Berlitz—American writer and linguist; formerly associated with the Berlitz Schools of Languages; known not only for his language books but also for several books on mysterious phenomena, such as *The Mystery of Atlantis, The Bermuda Triangle,* and *Without a Trace.* (Sketch includes interview.)

Doris Betts—American professor, novelist, and short-story writer; praised for her sensitive characterizations and her ability to describe human relationships; among her books are the short-story collections *The Gentle Insurrection* and *Beasts of the Southern Wild and Other Stories* and the novels *The River to Pickle Beach* and *Heading West.* (Sketch includes interview.)

William Peter Blatty—American novelist, screenwriter, and motion picture director and producer; his 1971 novel, *The Exorcist,* remained on the *New York Times* best-seller list for fifty-five weeks, and the screen adaptation, which Blatty wrote and produced, won an Academy Award and August Derleth Award.

John Cage—Influential and controversial American avant-garde composer who avoids structure in favor of spontaneity in his music; besides creating numerous musical compositions, he is a printmaker and author of several nonfiction books. (Sketch includes interview.)

Alistair Cooke—British-born American writer, journalist, and broadcaster; known for his efforts to explain America and Americans to the British through his popular essay collections, such as *Alistair Cooke's America,* and via the longest-running radio program in history, "Letters from America," which is heard throughout Britain and Europe; also host of the popular public television series "Masterpiece Theatre."

David Brion Davis—American history professor and writer; a leading expert on the history of slavery, he received a Pulitzer Prize in 1967 for *The Problem of Slavery in Western Culture* and a National Book Award in 1976 for *The Problem of Slavery in the Age of Revolution, 1770-1823.*

James T. Farrell—American novelist, short-story writer, and critic who died in 1979; considered a naturalistic writer, he portrayed the fragmented nature of life in Chicago's South Side, notably in his "Studs Lonigan" trilogy.

Dick Francis—Welsh-born mystery novelist, autobiographer, and former steeplechase jockey; his best-selling mystery novels—*For Kicks, Whip Hand, Twice Shy,* and *Banker,* for example—incorporate horses and racing in their plots. (Sketch includes interview.)

William Gibson—American playwright, poet, and critic; best known for his plays "The Miracle Worker," "Two for the Seesaw," and "Monday after the Miracle."

Joe Girard—American car salesman and motivational speaker; declared the world's greatest salesman in the *Guinness Book of World Records;* his books *How to Sell Anything to Anybody* and *How to Sell Yourself* are intended to help others reach his level of professional and personal success.

Erving Goffman—Canadian-born professor of anthropology and sociology who died in 1982; known for his observational approach in analyzing human interaction; author of *Behavior in Public Places, Gender Advertisements, Forms of Talk,* and other books in his field.

Edward Gorey—American writer and illustrator; his self-illustrated books include *The Unstrung Harp, The Beastly Baby,* and *The Gashlycrumb Tinies.*

Doris Grumbach—American professor, novelist, literary critic, and biographer; author of *The Company She Kept,* a controversial biography of author Mary McCarthy that was the subject of a threatened lawsuit, as well as the widely reviewed novels *Chamber Music* and *The Missing Person.* (Sketch includes interview.)

Marguerite Henry—Award-winning American writer of children's books; the author of many publications about animals, she is best known for horse stories, including *Misty of Chincoteague,* which received Boys' Clubs of America, Lewis Carroll Shelf, and Newbery Awards.

Eleanor Burford Hibbert—Prolific British author of best-selling Gothic romances and popular adventure and historical novels, notably those written under the pen names Victoria Holt, Eleanor Burford, and Jean Plaidy.

Paul Horgan—American novelist, biographer, and writer on national, regional, and church history; *Great River* and *Lamy of Santa Fe,* two of his books on America's Southwest, received Pulitzer Prizes in 1955 and 1976, respectively. (Sketch includes interview.)

William X. Kienzle—American best-selling mystery novelist; a former priest, he created amateur sleuth Father Robert Koesler, the protagonist in *The Rosary Murders, Death Wears a Red Hat, Shadow of Death,* and other mysteries.

Jerzy Kosinski—Polish-born American novelist, photographer, professor, and author of screenplays and nonfiction; his novels, in which many autobiographical elements are incorporated, include *The Painted Bird, Steps* (a National Book Award winner), *Passion Play,* and *Pinball;* his screenplay "Being There" received awards from the Writers Guild of America and the British Academy of Film and Television Arts.

James Laughlin—American publisher, editor, and poet; founder and publisher of New Directions Publishing Corp., which emphasizes quality books over commercial successes and has introduced many foreign authors in translation to American readers; his books of poetry include *Some Natural Things, The Wild Anemone, and Other Poems,* and *In Another Country;* also editor of "New Directions in Prose and Poetry" series.

Ursula K. Le Guin—Award-winning American novelist, short-story writer, and poet; author of *The Lathe of Heaven, The Dispossessed,* the Earthsea trilogy, and numerous other works; recipient of four Hugo Awards, three Nebula Awards, a National Book Award, and the Gandalf Award as "Grand Master of Fantasy."

Philip Levine—American professor and award-winning poet; his poetry concentrates on the plight of the American working class and pays tribute to the Spanish anarchist movement of the 1930s; in 1979 he received an American Book Award for *Ashes* and a National Book Critics Circle Award for *Ashes* and *7 Years from Somewhere.*

Dan Rather—American journalist; anchorman and managing editor of "CBS Evening News" and former co-anchorman of "60 Minutes"; known for his coverage of John F. Kennedy's assassination, the Vietnam War, and the White House during Richard M. Nixon's presidency; co-author of a nonfiction book, *The Palace Guard,* and his autobiography, *The Camera Never Blinks.* (Sketch includes interview.)

Rex Reed—American film critic and syndicated columnist; his books include *Do You Sleep in the Nude?, People Are Crazy Here,* and *Valentines and Vitriol.*

Andy Rooney—American writer, producer, and television narrator; his observations on everyday items, compiled from his essays on "60 Minutes" and his syndicated column, produced the best-selling books *A Few Minutes with Andy Rooney* and *And More by Andy Rooney.* (Sketch includes interview.)

Herbert A. Simon—American professor, computer specialist, political scientist, and author; received the 1978 Nobel Prize for economics for his pioneering work on the decision-making process within organizations, as outlined in such books as *Administrative Behavior, The New Science of Management Decision,* and *Models of Bounded Rationality, and Other Topics in Economics;* also known for his work in artificial intelligence modeling.

Thomas Szasz—Hungarian-born American psychiatrist who argues that psychiatry as practiced in the United States is "scientifically untenable and morally and socially indefensible," according to Edwin M. Schur in *Atlantic;* author of *The Myth of Mental Illness, The Age of Madness,* and *The Myth of Psychotherapy.*

Gay Talese—American pioneer of New Journalism, in which the techniques of fiction are employed in nonfiction; he has explored such topics as the *New York Times* in *The Kingdom and the Power,* the Mafia in *Honor Thy Father,* and sexuality in America in the controversial book *Thy Neighbor's Wife.* (Sketch includes interview.)

Peter Taylor—American professor, short-story writer, novelist, and playwright; a frequent contributor of short fiction to the *New Yorker,* he has published *Happy Families Are All Alike, In the Miro District and Other Stories,* and other collections. (Sketch includes interview.)

Diane Wakoski—American poet; written in the first person, her poems focus on intensely personal experiences, especially the failure of relationships; author of the poetry collections *The George Washington Poems, Thanking My Mother for Piano Lessons, The Motorcycle Betrayal Poems,* and *Saturn's Rings.* (Sketch includes interview.)

Alice Walker—American novelist, poet, and short-story writer; she received a Pulitzer Prize and American Book Award in 1983 for the novel *The Color Purple;* her other work includes the poetry collection *Revolutionary Petunias and Other Poems* and the short-story collections *In Love and Trouble* and *You Can't Keep a Good Woman Down.*

Tom Wolfe—American essayist, journalist, and artist; a leading chronicler of American trends, he is recognized as a flamboyant practitioner of New Journalism, as exhibited in the books *The Electric Kool-Aid Acid Test,* the American Book Award-winning *The Right Stuff,* and *From Bauhaus to Our House.* (Sketch includes interview.)

Preface

The *Contemporary Authors New Revision Series* provides completely updated information on authors listed in earlier volumes of *Contemporary Authors.* Entries for active individual authors from *any* volume of *CA* may be included in a volume of the *New Revision Series.* The sketches appearing in *New Revision Series* Volume 9, for example, were selected from more than ten previously published *CA* volumes.

As always, the most recent *Contemporary Authors* cumulative index continues to be the user's guide to the location of an individual author's listing.

Compilation Methods

The editors make every effort to secure information directly from the authors. Clippings of all sketches in selected *CA* volumes published several years ago are sent to the authors at their last-known addresses. Authors mark material to be deleted or changed, and insert any new personal data, new affiliations, new books, new work in progress, new sidelights, and new biographical/critical sources. All author returns are assessed, additional research is done, if necessary, and those sketches with significant change are published in the *New Revision Series.*

If, however, authors fail to reply, or if authors are now deceased, biographical dictionaries are checked for new information (a task made easier through the use of Gale's *Biography and Genealogy Master Index* and other volumes in the "Gale Biographical Index Series"), as are bibliographical sources, such as *Cumulative Book Index* and *The National Union Catalog.* Using data from such sources, revision editors select and revise nonrespondents' entries which need substantial updating. Sketches not personally reviewed by the authors are marked with a dagger (†) to indicate that these listings have been revised from secondary sources believed to be reliable, but they have not been personally reviewed for this edition by the authors sketched.

In addition, reviews and articles in major periodicals, lists of prestigious awards, and requests from *CA* users are monitored so that authors on whom new information is in demand can be identified and revised listings prepared promptly.

Comprehensive Revision

All listings in this volume have been revised and/or augmented in various ways, though the amount and type of change vary with the author. Revised entries include additions of or changes in such information as degrees, mailing addresses, literary agents, career items, career-related and civic activities, memberships, work in progress, and biographical/critical sources. They may also include the following:

1) Major new awards—Poets John Ashbery and Philip Levine and nonfiction and fiction writer Paul Horgan are only three of the numerous award-winning authors with updated entries in this volume. Ashbery's revised sketch, for example, lists over fifteen new awards. Included among them are a Pulitzer Prize, National Book Award, and National Book Critics Circle Award, all received in 1976 for *Self-Portrait in a Convex Mirror*—an unprecedented granting of the literary "triple crown" to one author in a single year. Added to Levine's revised entry are an American Book Award for *Ashes* and National Book Critics Circle Award for *Ashes* and *7 Years from Somewhere,* both received in 1979. Horgan's original entry, which listed his 1955 Pulitzer Prize and many other awards and honorary degrees, was updated for this volume to include, among other new items, yet another Pulitzer Prize as well as a Western Writers of America Award and Christopher Book Award, all received in 1976 for *Lamy of Santa Fe.*

2) Extensive bibliographical additions—To science fiction writer Kenneth Bulmer's already lengthy writings, senior assistant editor Thomas Wiloch added sixty-four new titles and noted the fifteen new pseudonyms under which Bulmer has published his work. Equally prolific, John Burke has written twenty-one new novels, fourteen travel books, and fifteen book adaptations of films and plays since his entry last appeared in *CA,* as noted by assistant editor Michaela Swart Wilson in Burke's revised listing.

3) Informative new sidelights—Numerous *CA* sketches contain sidelights, which provide personal dimensions to the listings, supply information about the critical reception the authors' works have received, or both. The sidelights for Jerzy Kosinski, for example, trace some of the autobiographical elements in his work, discuss major themes, and summarize the controversy about his alleged plagiarism. Kosinski's acting debut in the Warren Beatty film "Reds" is covered as well, and assistant editor Donna Olendorf quotes Kosinski's letter to *CA* on how an appeal "to go after a new experience" convinced him to take the part.

Avoiding the labels "science fiction" and "fantasy," Ursula K. Le Guin prefers to call her books simply "novels." The challenges of creating alien worlds and their accompanying histories, languages, and inhabitants and Le Guin's basic Taoist philosophy are topics assistant editor Kerry L. Lutz covers in sidelights.

Alice Walker's novels, short stories, and poems chronicle the American black woman's experiences and explore the possibilities for survival and ultimate triumph. In sidelights for this volume of *CA,* senior assistant editor Marian Walters writes about the general reception Walker's work has received and her characters' sense of hope even during adversity.

These sketches, as well as others with sidelights compiled by *CA*'s editors, provide informative and enjoyable reading.

Writers of Special Interest

CA's editors make every effort to include in each *New Revision Series* volume a substantial number of revised entries on active authors and media people of special interest to *CA*'s readers. Since the *New Revision Series* also includes sketches on noteworthy deceased writers, a significant amount of work on the part of *CA*'s editors goes into the revision of entries on important deceased authors. Some of the prominent writers, both living and deceased, whose sketches are contained in this volume are noted in the list headed "Authors and Media People Featured in This Volume" immediately preceding the preface.

Exclusive Interviews

CA provides exclusive, primary information on certain authors in the form of interviews. Prepared specifically for *CA,* the never-before-published conversations presented in the section of the sketch headed *CA INTERVIEW* give *CA* users the opportunity to learn the authors' thoughts, in depth, about their craft. Subjects chosen for interviews are, the editors feel, authors who hold special interest for *CA*'s readers.

Authors and journalists in this volume whose sketches include interviews are John Ashbery, Jean L. Baer, Charles Berlitz, Doris Betts, John Cage, Dick Francis, Doris Grumbach, Paul Horgan, Dan Rather, Andy Rooney, Gay Talese, Peter Taylor, Diane Wakoski, and Tom Wolfe.

Retaining *CA* Volumes

As new volumes in the series are published, users often ask which *CA* volumes, if any, can be discarded. Since the *New Revision Series* does not supersede any specific volumes of *CA,* all of the following must be retained in order to have information on all authors in the series:

- all revised volumes
- the two *Contemporary Authors Permanent Series* volumes
- *CA* Volumes 45-48 and subsequent original volumes

The chart on the following page is designed to assist users in keeping their collection as complete as possible.

Cumulative Index Should Always Be Consulted

The key to locating an individual author's listing is the *CA* cumulative index bound into the back of alternate original volumes (and available separately as an offprint). Since the *CA* cumulative index provides access to *all* entries in the *CA* series, the latest cumulative index should always be consulted to find the specific volume containing an author's original or most recently revised sketch.

(Preface continues on page following chart)

IF YOU HAVE:	**YOU MAY DISCARD:**
1-4 First Revision (1967)	1 (1962) 2 (1963) 3 (1963) 4 (1963)
5-8 First Revision (1969)	5-6 (1963) 7-8 (1963)
Both 9-12 First Revision (1974) AND *Contemporary Authors Permanent Series,* Volume 1 (1975)	9-10 (1964) 11-12 (1965)
Both 13-16 First Revision (1975) AND *Contemporary Authors Permanent Series,* Volumes 1 and 2 (1975, 1978)	13-14 (1965) 15-16 (1966)
Both 17-20 First Revision (1976) AND *Contemporary Authors Permanent Series,* Volumes 1 and 2 (1975, 1978)	17-18 (1967) 19-20 (1968)
Both 21-24 First Revision (1977) AND *Contemporary Authors Permanent Series,* Volumes 1 and 2 (1975, 1978)	21-22 (1969) 23-24 (1970)
Both 25-28 First Revision (1977) AND *Contemporary Authors Permanent Series,* Volume 2 (1978)	25-28 (1971)
Both 29-32 First Revision (1978) AND *Contemporary Authors Permanent Series,* Volume 2 (1978)	29-32 (1972)
Both 33-36 First Revision (1978) AND *Contemporary Authors Permanent Series,* Volume 2 (1978)	33-36 (1973)
37-40 First Revision (1979)	37-40 (1973)
41-44 First Revision (1979)	41-44 (1974)
45-48 (1974) 49-52 (1975) 53-56 (1975) 57-60 (1976) ↓ ↓ 107 (1983)	NONE: These volumes will not be superseded by corresponding revised volumes. Individual entries from these and all other volumes appearing in the left column of this chart will be revised and included in the *New Revision Series.*
Volumes in the *Contemporary Authors New Revision Series*	NONE: The *New Revision Series* does not replace any single volume of *CA*. All volumes appearing in the left column of this chart must be retained to have information on all authors in the series.

Those authors appearing in the *New Revision Series* are listed in the *CA* cumulative index with the designation **CANR-** in front of the specific volume number. For the convenience of those who do not have *New Revision Series* volumes, the cumulative index also notes the specific earlier volume of *CA* in which the sketch appeared. Below is a sample *New Revision Series* index citation:

Vonnegut, Kurt, Jr. 1922- CANR-1
Earlier sketch in CA 3R
See also CLC 1, 2, 3, 4, 5, 8, 12
See also AITN 1

For the most recent information on Vonnegut, users should refer to Volume 1 of the *New Revision Series,* as designated by "CANR-1"; if that volume is unavailable, refer to *CA* 1-4 First Revision, as indicated by "Earlier sketch in CA 3R," for his 1968 listing. (And if *CA* 1-4 First Revision is unavailable, refer to *CA* 3, published in 1963, for Vonnegut's original listing.)

Sketches not eligible for inclusion in a *New Revision Series* volume because the author or a revision editor has verified that no significant change is required will, of course, be available in previously published *CA* volumes. Users should always consult the most recent *CA* cumulative index to determine the location of these authors' entries.

For the convenience of *CA* users, the *CA* cumulative index also includes references to all entries in three related Gale series—*Contemporary Literary Criticism* (CLC), which is devoted entirely to current criticism of the works of today's novelists, poets, playwrights, short story writers, filmmakers, scriptwriters, and other creative writers, *Something About the Author* (SATA), a series of heavily illustrated sketches on authors and illustrators of books for young people, and *Authors in the News* (AITN), a compilation of news stories and feature articles from American newspapers and magazines covering writers and other members of the communications media.

As always, suggestions from users about any aspect of *CA* will be welcomed.

Contemporary Authors

NEW REVISION SERIES

† Indicates that a listing has been revised from secondary sources believed to be reliable, but has not been personally reviewed for this edition by the author sketched.

ABEL-SMITH, Brian 1926-

PERSONAL: Born November 6, 1926, in London, England; son of Lionel Abel (an army officer) and Genevieve (Walsh) Abel-Smith. *Education:* Clare College, Cambridge, B.A., 1951, M.A. and Ph.D., 1955. *Politics:* Labour Party. *Office:* London School of Economics and Political Science, University of London, Houghton St., London W.C.2, England.

CAREER: National Institute of Social and Economic Research, London, England, research fellow, 1953-55; University of London, London School of Economics and Political Science, London, lecturer, 1955-61, reader, 1961-65, professor of social administration, 1965—. Associate professor, Yale University, 1961. Member, Saintsbury Committee and Long-Term Study Group, British Ministry of Health; member, South West Regional Hospital Board, 1956-63; St. Thomas's Hospital, governor, 1957—, chairman of finance committee, 1963—; chairman of Chelsea and Kensington Hospital Management Committee, 1961-62; governor of Maudsley Hospital and the Institute of Psychiatry, 1963-67. Consultant to World Health Organization, 1957—, Social Affairs Division of United Nations, 1959, 1961, and Organization for Economic Cooperation and Development; senior advisor to British Secretary of State for Health and Social Security, 1968-70, 1974—. *Military service:* British Army, 1945-48; became captain. *Member:* Fabian Society (chairman, 1964-65; treasurer, 1965-68). *Awards, honors:* Received honorary M.D., 1981.

WRITINGS: (With R. M. Titmuss) *The Cost of the National Health Service in England and Wales,* Cambridge University Press, 1956; *A History of the Nursing Profession,* Heinemann, 1960; (with Titmuss) *Social Policy and Population Growth in Mauritius,* Methuen, 1961; *Paying for Health Services,* World Health Organization, 1963; *The Hospitals, 1800-1948,* Heinemann, 1964; (with Titmuss and others) *The Health Services of Tanganyika,* Pitman, 1964; (with Kathleen Gales) *British Doctors at Home and Abroad,* Codicote Press, 1964; (with Peter Townsend) *The Poor and the Poorest,* G. Bell, 1965; (with Robert Stevens) *Lawyers and the Courts,* Harvard University Press, 1967; *An International Study of World Health Expenditure,* World Health Organization, 1967; (with Stevens) *In Search of Justice: Society and the Legal System,* Penguin, 1968. (With Hilary Rose) *Doctors, Patients, and Pathology,* G. Bell, 1972; (with M. Zander and R. Brooke) *Legal Problems and the Citizen: A Study in Three London Boroughs,* Heinemann, 1973; (with others) *Accounting for Health,* King Edward's Hospital Fund for London, 1973; *People without Choice,* International Planned Parenthood Federation, 1973; (with T. Leynes) *Report on a National Pension Scheme for Mauritius,* Carl Achille (Mauritius), 1976; *Value for Money in Health Services,* Heinemann Educational Books, 1976; *Poverty Development and Health Policy,* World Health Organization, 1978; *National Health Service: The First Thirty Years,* H.M.S.O., 1978; (with P. Grandjeat) *Pharmaceutical Consumption,* Commission of the European Communities, 1978; (with A. Maynard) *The Organisation, Financing, and Cost of Health Care in the European Community,* Commission of the European Communities, 1979; *Sharing Health Care Costs,* U.S. Department of Health, Education, and Welfare, 1980. Also author of a number of reports published by the Fabian Society, 1953-66.

Contributor: *Conviction,* MacGibbon & Kee, 1958; M. Ginsberg, editor, *Law and Opinion in England in the Twentieth Century,* Stevens & Sons, 1959; *Aging and Social Health in the United States and Europe,* [Michigan], 1959; Clark Tibbitts and Wilma Donahue, editors, *Social and Psychological Aspects of Aging,* Columbia University Press, 1962; *The Changing Role of the Hospitals in a Changing World,* International Hospital Federation, 1963; Richard H. Williams, Tibbitts, and Donahue, editors, *Processes of Aging,* Volume II, Atherton, 1963; Peter Hall, editor, *Labour's New Frontiers,* Deutsch, 1964. Contributor of numerous articles to journals, including *New Statesman, New Society, Guardian, Times, Lancet,* and *Medical World.*

WORK IN PROGRESS: Research on the economics of health services.

SIDELIGHTS: As World Health Organization consultant on the costs of medical care, Brian Abel-Smith has traveled in Ceylon, Congo, Kenya, and other countries of Africa and Europe.

* * *

ADAMEC, Ludwig W(arren) 1924-

PERSONAL: Born March 10, 1924, in Vienna, Austria; U.S.

citizen; son of Ludwig and Emma (Kubitschek) Adamec; married Ena Vargas, June 9, 1962 (divorced May 8, 1975); children: Eric. *Education:* University of California, Los Angeles, B.A., 1960, M.A., 1961, Ph.D., 1966. *Home:* 3931 East Whittier, Tucson, Ariz. 85711. *Office:* Department of Oriental Studies, University of Arizona, Tucson, Ariz. 85721.

CAREER: University of California, Los Angeles, postdoctoral fellow, 1966, lecturer in history, 1966-67; University of Arizona, Tucson, assistant professor, 1967-69, associate professor, 1969-74, professor of Near Eastern studies and director of Near Eastern Center, 1974—. Research associate at University of Michigan, summer, 1967, and University of California, Los Angeles, 1968; Fulbright professor in Iran, 1973-74. Member of board of governors, American Research Center in Egypt, Center for Arabic Study Abroad, American Research Institute in Turkey, and American Research Institute in Yemen, 1974-81; vice-president, American Institute of Iranian Studies, 1979-81. Fulbright consultant, University of Baluchistan, Quetta, Pakistan, 1981-82.

MEMBER: Middle East Studies Association of North America (fellow), Middle East Institute, American Association of University Professors. *Awards, honors:* Fulbright-Hays award for research in India and Afghanistan, 1964-65; Social Science Research Council grant, summer, 1968, 1975, and 1979; Foundation for the Humanities grant, summer, 1978.

WRITINGS: *Afghanistan, 1900-1923: A Diplomatic History,* University of California Press, 1967; (editor with George L. Grassmuck and contributor) *Afghanistan: Some New Approaches,* Center for Near Eastern and North African Studies, University of Michigan, 1969.

(Editor) *Political and Historical Gazetteer of Afghanistan,* Akademische Druck-und Verlagsanstalt (Graz), Volume I: *Badakhshan and Northeastern Afghanistan,* 1972, Volume II: *Farah and Southwestern Afghanistan,* 1973, Volume III: *Herat and Northwestern Afghanistan,* 1975, Volume IV: *Mazar-i-Sharif and North-Central Afghanistan,* 1978, Volume V: *Kandahar and South-Central Afghanistan,* 1979; *Afghanistan's Foreign Affairs in the 20th Century: Relations with Russia, Germany, and Britain,* University of Arizona Press, 1974; (editor) *Who's Who in Afghanistan,* Akademische Druck-und Verlagsanstalt, 1975; *Historical Gazetteer of Iran,* Akademische Druck-und Verlagsanstalt, Volume I: *Tehran and Northwestern Iran,* 1976, Volume II: *Meshed and Northeastern Iran,* 1981; *Supplement to the Who's Who of Afghanistan: Democratic Republic of Afghanistan,* Akademische Druck-und Verlagsanstalt, 1979. Associate editor, *Afghanistan Journal,* 1974-76.

WORK IN PROGRESS: Editing additional volumes of *Political and Historical Gazetteer of Afghanistan* and *Historical Gazetteer of Iran.*

SIDELIGHTS: Ludwig W. Adamec has lived for periods in Afghanistan, India, Iran, Europe, and the Arab Middle East. He is competent in German, French, Spanish, Persian, Arabic, and cognate languages.

* * *

AIKEN, Michael Thomas 1932-

PERSONAL: Born August 20, 1932, in El Dorado, Ark.; son of William Floyd and Mary (Gibbs) Aiken; married 1969. *Education:* University of Mississippi, B.A., 1954; University of Michigan, M.A., 1955, Ph.D., 1964. *Office:* Department of Sociology, University of Wisconsin, Madison, Wis. 53706.

CAREER: University of Wisconsin—Madison, assistant professor, 1963-67, associate professor, 1967-70, professor of sociology, 1970—, associate dean, College of Letters and Sciences, 1980-82. Visiting associate professor, Columbia University, 1967-68; visiting professor, Universite Catholique de Louvain, Belgium, 1973, 1975, and Washington University, St. Louis, Mo., 1982-83. *Military service:* U.S. Army, Military Intelligence, 1956-59; became sergeant. *Member:* International Sociological Association, American Sociological Association.

WRITINGS: (With Louis A. Ferman and Harold L. Sheppherd) *Economic Failure, Alienation, and Extremism,* University of Michigan Press, 1968; (with Jerald Hage) *Social Change in Complex Organizations,* Random House, 1970; (editor with Paul E. Mott) *The Structure of Community Power: Readings,* Random House, 1970; (with N. Jay DeMeath and Gerald Maxwell) *The Dynamics of Idealism,* Jossey-Bass, 1971; (with Hage, R. Dewer, N. D. Tomaso, and G. Zeitz) *Coordinating Human Services,* Jossey-Bass, 1975; (with M. Ley-Ferrell) *Complex Organizations: Critical Perspectives,* Scott, Foresman, 1981.

* * *

AKERS, Alan Burt
See BULMER, (Henry) Kenneth

* * *

al-AZM, Sadik J. 1934-

PERSONAL: Born November 7, 1934, in Damascus, Syria; son of Jalal S. (a civil servant) and Naziha al-Azm; married Fawz Tuqan (a university teacher of English), July 2, 1957. *Education:* American University of Beirut, B.A. (with distinction), 1957; Yale University, M.A., 1959, Ph.D., 1961. *Religion:* No affiliation. *Address:* c/o Adib Ghanam, Assistant to the Minister, Ministry of Information, Damascus, Syria. *Office:* Department of Philosophy, Faculty of Letters, University of Damascus, Damascus, Syria.

CAREER: Hunter College of the City University of New York, New York, N.Y., instructor in department of philosophy, 1961-62; University of Damascus, Damascus, Syria, lecturer in department of philosophy, 1962-63; American University of Beirut, Beirut, Lebanon, assistant professor in department of philosophy, 1963-67, assistant professor in cultural studies program, 1967-68; University of Jordan, Amman, member of faculty of department of philosophy, 1968-69; author, lecturer, and critic; University of Damascus, professor of modern philosophy, 1977—.

WRITINGS—Surname alphabetized in some bibliographical sources under Azm: *Dirasat Fi al-Falsafa al-Gharbiyya al-Haditha* (title means "Studies in Modern Western Philosophy"), American University of Beirut Press, 1966; *Kant's Theory of Time,* Philosophical Library, 1967; (contributor) *Festival Book,* American University of Beirut Press, 1967; *Fi al-Hubb wa al-Hubb al-Uzri* (title means "Of Love and Arabic Courtly Love"), Kabbani Publications (Beirut), 1967.

Nagd al-Fikr al-Dini (title means "Critique of Religious Thought"), Tali'a Publications (Beirut), 1970; *The Origins of Kant's Arguments in the Antinomies,* Oxford University Press, 1972; *Dirasa Nagdiah Lil-Muga wamah al-Filistiniah* (title means "A Critical Study of the Palestinian Resistance Movement"), Al-Awdah Publications (Beirut), 1973; (contributor) *The Arabs Today: Alternatives for Tomorrow,* Forum Associates, 1973; *Al-Suhyuniah wa al-Sira' al Tabaki* (title means "Zionism and the Class Struggle"), Al-Awdah Publications, 1975; *Syasat Carter Wa Munasiru al-Hakabah al-Saudia* (title means "Carter's Policies and the Idealogues of the Saudi Era"), Tali'a Publications, 1977; *Ziarat al-Sadat Wa Bon's al-Salam al-Adel* (title means "Sadat's Visit and the Poverty of the Just Peace"), Tali'a Publications, 1978. Contributor of articles and reviews to journals in the Middle East, Europe, and North America. Editor, *Arab Studies Review,* 1969-73.

SIDELIGHTS: Sadik J. al-Azm told *CA* that "the Mufti of Lebanon declared *Nagd al-Fikr al-Dini* heretical, and the Lebanese authorities quickly banned the book. [I] was imprisoned for a week on charges of 'inciting confessional strife,' and then released on bail. A long trial followed, resulting in the dismissal of all charges against author, book, and publisher, turning the book into a *cause celebre,* the author into the 'official atheist' of the Arab World, and the trial into the most 'notorious' and protracted intellectual controversy that the Arab World has seen for many years."

Al-Azm says that he is interested in "furthering a critical reexamination and appraisal of Muslim and Arab thought in relation to the contemporary secular world and the forces shaping it."

* * *

ALBANESE, Catherine L(ouise) 1940-

PERSONAL: Born August 21, 1940, in Philadelphia, Pa.; daughter of Louis and Theresa (Spirizi) Albanese. *Education:* Chestnut Hill College, A.B. (summa cum laude), 1962; Duquesne University, M.A. (history), 1968; University of Chicago, M.A. (history of Christianity), 1970, Ph.D., 1972. *Office:* Department of Religion, Wright State University, Dayton, Ohio 45431.

CAREER: St. Xavier College, Chicago, Ill., instructor in history of Christianity, 1969-70; University of Chicago Extension, Chicago, Ill., instructor in medieval culture, 1970; Wright State University, Dayton, Ohio, assistant professor, 1972-76, associate professor, 1977-81, professor of religion, 1981—. Visiting associate professor at Pennsylvania State University, 1976-77. Lecturer; has presented papers at scholarly conferences and participated in panel discussions at professional seminars. Editorial referee for several publishing companies; consultant on church-state materials to Princeton University and Lilly Foundation, 1981.

MEMBER: American Academy of Religion, American Society of Church History, American Historical Association, American Studies Association, Organization of American Historians, American Society for Environmental History, American Catholic Historical Association, Ohio Academy of Religion (secretary-treasurer, 1973-74; vice-president, 1974-75; president, 1975-76), Phi Alpha Theta. *Awards, honors:* Wright State University grants, 1973-74, 1978-79, 1980-81; National Endowment for the Humanities, grants, 1975, 1977, fellowship for independent study and research, 1981-82; Fred Harris Daniels fellowship, American Antiquarian Society, 1977; American Philosophical Society grant, 1979.

WRITINGS: Sons of the Fathers: The Civil Religion of the American Revolution, Temple University Press, 1976; (contributor) R. Pierce Beaver, editor, *Papers of the American Society of Missiology,* William Carey Library, 1976; *Corresponding Motion: Transcendental Religion and the New America,* Temple University Press, 1977; (contributor with David L. Barr) Nicholas Peidiscalzi and William Collie, editors, *Teaching about Religion in Public Schools,* Argus Communications, 1977; (contributor) Beaver, editor, *American Missions in Bicentennial Perspective,* William Carey Library, 1977; (contributor) Joel Myerson, editor, *Dictionary of Literary Biography,* Volume III: *Antebellum Writers in New York and the South,* Gale, 1979.

America: Religions and Religion, Wadsworth, 1981; (contributor) Robert S. Ellwood, Jr., *Freedom of Religion in America: Historical Roots, Philosophical Concepts, and Contemporary Problems,* Transaction Books, 1982; (editor) *The American Transcendentalists,* Paulist Press, in press. Contributor of more than twenty articles and reviews to academic journals. Member of editorial board, *Environmental Review,* 1976-78, and *Journal of the American Academy of Religion,* 1979—; editorial referee for several journals, including *American Quarterly, Historian, Journal of American History,* and *Ohio Journal of Religious Studies.*

WORK IN PROGRESS: Nature Religion in America.

* * *

ALDING, Peter
See JEFFRIES, Roderic (Graeme)

* * *

AMAYA, Mario (Anthony) 1933-

PERSONAL: Born October 6, 1933, in New York, N.Y.; son of Mario A. and Maria Sophia (Garofalo) Amaya. *Education:* Brooklyn College (now Brooklyn College of the City University of New York), B.A., 1954; University of London Extension at the National Gallery, graduate study, 1960-62. *Home:* 229 East 79th St., New York, N.Y. 10028.

CAREER: Features writer and editor for International News Service, 1954-57; self-employed writer, editor, art critic, and exhibition organizer, London, England, 1956-68; Art Gallery of Ontario, Toronto, chief curator, 1969-72; Toronto Dominion Bank, Toronto, responsible for art purchase program, 1970-73; New York Cultural Center, New York City, director, 1972-75; Chrysler Museum, Norfolk, Va., director, 1976-78; National Academy of Design, New York City, director of development, 1980-81, member of advisory board, 1981—; art consultant and organizer of numerous art exhibits at museums, galleries, and institutes. Visiting professor, State University of New York at Buffalo, 1971; adjunct professor, Fairleigh Dickinson University, 1972-75. *Awards, honors:* William Copley Foundation award, 1969.

WRITINGS: Pop as Art, Viking, 1965; *Art Nouveau,* Dutton, 1966; *Tiffany Glass,* Walker & Co., 1967.

Catalogs: (Author of introduction) *Pre-Raphaelites: Art Nouveau,* Maas Gallery (London), 1964; *The Obsessive Image, 1960-68: The Opening Exhibition of the Institute of Contemporary Arts at Carlton House Terrace, 10 April-29 May, 1968,* Institute of Contemporary Arts, 1968; (author of introduction and notes) *The Sacred and Profane in Symbolist Art,* Art Gallery of Ontario, 1969.

(Author of introduction) *Edouard Vuillard, 1868-1940,* Art Gallery of Ontario, 1971; (editor) *A Tribute to Samuel J. Zacks from the Sam and Ayala Zacks Collection,* Art Gallery of Ontario, 1971; (author of introduction) *French 17th and 18th Century Master Drawings in North American Collections,* Art

Gallery of Ontario, 1972; *John Koch,* New York Cultural Center, 1973; *Art Deco, 1925-1975,* Rothmans of Pall Mall Canada Ltd., 1975; *Masterworks from the Chrysler Museum: Veronese to Franz Kline,* [Norfolk, Va.], 1978.

Member of advisory board and contributing editor, *Funk & Wagnalls Encyclopedia,* 1979—. Contemporary art critic, *Financial Times,* 1961-69; art critic, *Punch,* 1961-62. Contributor of art criticism to a number of periodicals, including *Vogue, Holiday, New Republic, Apollo, artscanada, London Sunday Time Color Supplement,* and *Nova.* Founding editor, *About the House* (Royal Opera House magazine), 1962-68, and *Arts and Artists,* 1965-69; member of editorial board, *Art in America,* 1969-72; American editor, *Connoisseur,* 1978—; contributing editor, *Architectural Digest,* 1979—.

* * *

AMOR, Amos
See HARRELL, Irene B(urk)

* * *

ANDERSON, George L(aVerne) 1905-1971

PERSONAL: Born February 27, 1905, in Blue Rapids, Kan.; died May 5, 1971; son of Anders (a miller) and Mary (Pittman) Anderson; married Caroline Miek, June 8, 1928; children: Marianne (Mrs. John E. Wilkinson), James LaVerne. *Education:* University of Kansas, A.B., 1926, M.A., 1930; University of Illinois, Ph.D., 1933. *Religion:* Lutheran. *Home:* 1702 University Dr., Lawrence, Kan. *Office:* Department of History, University of Kansas, Lawrence, Kan.

CAREER: Teacher and administrator in Kansas public schools, 1926-30; Colorado College, Colorado Springs, instructor, 1934-37, assistant professor, 1937-43, associate professor of history, 1943-45; University of Kansas, Lawrence, associate professor, 1945-49, professor of history, 1949-71, chairman of department, 1949-68. Visiting faculty member at Northern Montana College, 1934, and at New Mexico Highlands University, 1939, 1940, and 1942. Member of Board of Higher Education, United Lutheran Church in America (now Lutheran Church in America), 1946-62. *Member:* Agricultural History Society (president, 1958), Organization of American Historians, Kansas State Historical Society (president, 1961), Mississippi Valley Historical Association (member of board of editors, 1957-60), Phi Beta Kappa, Kiwanis Club (Lawrence; president, 1956).

WRITINGS: General William J. Palmer: A Decade of Colorado Railroad Building, 1870-1880, Colorado College Studies, 1936, 2nd edition, 1963; (editor) *Issues and Conflicts: Studies in Twentieth Century American Diplomacy,* University of Kansas Press, 1959; *General William Jackson Palmer: Man of Vision* (booklet), Colorado College, 1960; (editor) *A Petition Regarding the Conditions in the C.S.M. Prison at Columbia, S.C.,* University of Kansas Library, 1962; *Kansas West,* Golden West, 1963; *The Widening Stream: The Exchange National Bank of Atchison, 1858-1968,* Lockwood Co. (Atchison, Kan.), 1968.

Variations on a Theme: History as Knowledge of the Past, Coronado Press, 1970; *Essays on Public Lands: Problems, Legislation, and Administration,* Coronado Press, 1971; (contributor) John G. Clark, editor, *The Frontier Challenge: Responses to the Trans-Mississippi West,* University Press of Kansas, 1971; *Four Essays on Railroads in Kansas and Colorado,* Coronado Press, c.1971; *Essays on the History of Banking,* Coronado Press, 1972; (with Terry H. Harmon) *History of Kansas: Selected Readings by George L. Anderson and Terry H. Harmon,* University of Kansas, 1974; *Essays in Kansas History: In Memorium,* edited by Burton J. Williams, Coronado Press, 1977. Contributor to professional journals.†

* * *

ANDERSON, Joan Wester 1938-

PERSONAL: Born August 12, 1938, in Evanston, Ill.; daughter of Theodore (an electronics engineer) and Monica (Noesges) Wester; married William H. Anderson (an insurance agent), August 20, 1960; children: Christopher, Timothy, William, Brian, Nancy. *Education:* Attended Mount Mary College. *Religion:* Roman Catholic. *Home:* 811 North Hickory, Arlington Heights, Ill. 60004.

CAREER: Free-lance writer, 1973—; lecturer. WIND-Radio, Chicago, Ill., music librarian, 1959-61. Performed in local little theater productions and directed and performed in a quartet accompanying vocalists on record albums, both 1959-61.

WRITINGS: (With Ann Toland Serb) *Love, Lollipops and Laundry* (humor), Our Sunday Visitor Press, 1976; (with Serb) *Stop the World—Our Gerbils Are Loose* (humor), Doubleday, 1979; *The Best of Both Worlds: A Guide to Home-Based Careers,* Betterway Publications, 1982; *Dear World, Don't Spin So Fast . . .* (humor), Abbey Press, 1983; *Teen Is a Four-Letter Word* (inspirational), Betterway Publications, 1983. Author of a monthly humor column in *Marriage and Family Living* and a monthly health feature in *True Confessions.* Contributor of over three hundred articles and short stories to a variety of magazines and newspapers.

WORK IN PROGRESS: Developing a syndicated column on the "working-at-home movement."

SIDELIGHTS: Joan Wester Anderson told *CA:* "As a full-time housewife and mother, I believe that we are perhaps the most ignored minority group in society today. For this reason, I began my writing career by directing uplifting and humorous material to housewives, reinforcing their own feelings of self-worth. One of my current books, *The Best of Both Worlds: A Guide to Home-Based Careers,* goes a step farther and shows house-bound women how to put their talents to use in money-making capacities, thus being able to supplement the family income without sacrificing a strong family life. I have also developed a lecturing career, and my speeches follow the same theme, humorously advising women how they can develop their potential and personal interests within their family structure. If I can do this, any woman can!"

* * *

ANDERSON, Martin 1936-

PERSONAL: Born August 5, 1936, in Lowell, Mass.; son of Ralph and Evelyn Anderson; married Annelise Graebner, September 9, 1965. *Education:* Dartmouth College, A.B. (summa cum laude), 1957, M.S., 1958; Massachusetts Institute of Technology, Ph.D., 1962. *Office:* Hoover Institution, Stanford University, Stanford, Calif. 94305.

CAREER: Columbia University, Graduate School of Business Administration, New York, N.Y., assistant professor of finance, 1962-65, associate professor of business, 1965-68; special assistant and consultant to President Nixon, 1969-71; Stanford University, Hoover Institution, Stanford, Calif., senior fellow, 1971—. Director of research for Nixon presidential campaign, 1968; senior advisor to Reagan presidential campaign, 1976 and 1980. Public interest director, Federal Home Loan Bank of San Francisco, 1972-79. Member of Commission on Critical Choices for America, 1973-75, Council on Trends and Perspectives, 1974-76, and 1981—, Defense Manpower Commission, 1975-76, Committee on the Present Danger, 1977—, President's Economic Policy Advisory Board, 1982—, and President's Foreign Intelligence Advisory Board, 1982—. Assistant to President Reagan for policy development, 1981-82. *Military service:* U.S. Army, Security Agency; became second lieutenant. *Member:* American Finance Association, American Economic Association, Phi Beta Kappa.

WRITINGS—Published by Hoover Institution, except as indicated: *The Federal Bulldozer: A Critical Analysis of Urban Renewal, 1949-1962,* M.I.T. Press, 1964; (editor) *Conscription,* 1976; *Welfare: The Political Economy of Welfare Reform in the United States,* 1978; (editor) *Registration and the Draft,* 1982; (editor) *The Military Draft,* 1982.

SIDELIGHTS: In *Welfare: The Political Economy of Welfare Reform in the United States,* Martin Anderson utilizes his experiences within the Nixon and Reagan administrations to outline various attempts at welfare reform and to explain the reasons for the failure of these efforts. Writing in *National Review,* M. S. Evans calls attention to Anderson's "diligence in research and gift for clarifying issues." An *Atlantic* reviewer writes that *Welfare* is "clearly written and patiently argued. Anyone who can make economic analysis accessible to general readers, regardless of his doctrinal bias, deserves a respectful reading."

Robert Lekachman finds Anderson's "doctrinal bias" to be the book's major flaw. Lekachman comments in the *New York Times Book Review:* "Anderson argues this classic conservative case with rather more force than fairness. Thus he cites surveys concluding that large numbers of welfare beneficiaries are either ineligible or overpaid, and omits considerable evidence that even more people who are eligible receive either no benefits or less than the amounts to which they are legally entitled. . . . Mr. Anderson gives no sign of having ever visited a welfare center or of comprehending the hassles and humiliations of life on welfare. If this volume is, as the jacket blurbs declare, 'the most penetrating study ever written on the knottiest problem in U.S. politics' . . . then conservative thought is even more poverty-stricken than I had dared hope."

BIOGRAPHICAL/CRITICAL SOURCES: New York Times Book Review, July 9, 1978; *National Review,* July 23, 1978, November 10, 1978; *Atlantic,* September, 1978.

* * *

ANDERSON, Rachel 1943-

PERSONAL: Born March 18, 1943, in Hampton Court, Surrey, England; daughter of Donald Clive (a writer and military historian) and Verily (a writer; maiden name, Bruce) Anderson; married David Bradby (a university lecturer in French and drama), June 19, 1965; children: Hannah, Lawrence, Nguyen Thanh Sang (adopted son), Donald. *Education:* Attended Hastings School of Art, 1959-60. *Politics:* Socialist. *Religion:* "Church of England Christian." *Home:* Lower Damsells, Northrepps, Norfolk, England.

CAREER: Writer. Chatto & Windus Ltd., London, England, publicity assistant, 1963-64; worked for a brief period in editorial department of *Women's Mirror,* London, 1964, and for a very brief period (three days) in news department of British Broadcasting Corp., Bristol, England, 1966; these occupations "preceded, interspersed, and followed by jobs as nursemaid, cleaning woman, van driver, gardener, etc., etc., and freelance writer, and as broadcaster for BBC 'Woman's Hour.'"

WRITINGS: Pineapple (novel), J. Cape, 1965; *The Purple Heart Throbs* (survey of romantic fiction), Hodder & Stoughton, 1974; *Dream Lovers,* Hodder & Stoughton, 1978; *Moffatt's Road,* Hodder & Stoughton, 1978; *The Poacher's Son,* Oxford University Press, 1982; *Little Angel Comes to Stay,* Oxford University Press, 1983.

Also author of radio play, "Tomorrow's Tomorrow," 1970. Contributor of articles to *Observer, Good Housekeeping, Homes & Gardens, Times* (London), *Weekend Telegraph, Punch, Guardian,* and other magazines and newspapers in England. Children's book page editor, *Good Housekeeping,* 1979—.

WORK IN PROGRESS: Ching Ching Cukoo, a novel based on the earlier life of her adopted son, Nguyen Thanh Sang; *Bonding,* a survey of adoptive practices.

SIDELIGHTS: Rachel Anderson told *CA:* "[I was] brought up in a literary family. Am incapable of doing anything else so had to be a writer. Am [a] practicing Christian in an essentially heathen age. Speak French, Italian. Main interests are domestic bliss, travel, peace." In 1975, Anderson starred in "Fateful Eclipse," a television drama by Nigerian writer Loalu Oguniyi, broadcast on Western Nigerian Television.

* * *

ANDERSON, Roy Allan 1895-

PERSONAL: Born March 15, 1895, in Melbourne, Australia; son of Albert William and Margaret (Linklater) Anderson; married Myra Elsa Wendt, 1920; children: Allan W., Tui Myra, Hilary. *Education:* Studied at Australasian Missionary College, University of Melbourne, and University of Southern California. *Home:* 11486 Loma Linda Dr., Loma Linda, Calif. 92354. *Office:* Division of Religion, Loma Linda University, Loma Linda, Calif. 92354.

CAREER: Seventh-day Adventist Church, pastor and evangelist in South Australia Conference, 1918-20, North New Zealand Conference, 1920-26, Queensland Conference, 1926-30, South England Conference, 1930-36, and Southeast California Conference, 1936-38; La Sierra College, Riverside, Calif., teacher, 1938-41; General Conference of Seventh-day Adventists, Washington, D.C., editor of *Ministry,* 1941—; Andrews University, Berrien Springs, Mich., lecturer, 1958-66; Loma Linda University, Loma Linda, Calif., lecturer and instructor, 1967—. *Member:* Royal Geographical Society (fellow), Phi Chi Phi. *Awards, honors:* D.D. from University of Southern California, 1962.

WRITINGS: The Shepherd-Evangelist, Review & Herald, 1950; *Unfolding the Revelation,* Pacific Press Publishing Association, 1953, revised edition, 1974.

Preachers of Righteousness, Southern Publishing, 1963; *Secrets of the Spirit World,* Pacific Press Publishing Association, 1966; *Faith That Conquers Fear,* Southern Publishing, 1967; *Love Finds a Way,* Southern Publishing, 1967; *A Better World,* Southern Publishing, 1968.

The God-Man: His Nature and Work, Review & Herald, 1970; *Unfolding Daniel's Prophecies,* Pacific Press Publishing Association, 1975; *You Can Be Free: The Secret of Joy, Peace, and Power,* Pacific Press Publishing Association, 1977, published as *God's Unique Love for You: The Secret of Joy, Peace, and Power,* 1979; (with Jay M. Hoffman) *All Eyes on Israel,* Harvest Press, 1978.

Abandon Earth: Last Call, Pacific Press Publishing Association, 1982. Contributor of articles to magazines and journals, including *Review & Herald, Ministry, Signs of the Times, These Times, Australian Signs, Australasian Record, Scope, Advent Survey,* and *Messenger.*

AVOCATIONAL INTERESTS: Music, photography.

* * *

ANDERTON, David A(lbin) 1919-

PERSONAL: Born May 7, 1919, in Paterson, N.J.; son of John T. (a silk mill owner) and Helen (Smith) Anderton; married Katherine Meili, June 13, 1942; children: Bruce David, Craig Douglas. *Education:* Rensselaer Polytechnic Institute, B.A.E., 1941. *Home and office:* 30 South Murray Ave., Ridgewood, N.J. 07450.

CAREER: Free-lance writer and photographer. Grumman Aircraft, Bethpage, N.Y., engineer, 1941-46; General Electric Co., Schenectady, N.Y., project engineer, 1946-50; *Aviation Week,* New York, N.Y., technical editor, 1950-63. Has lectured on aerospace, travel, and jazz, and taught courses in aerodynamics. *Member:* American Society of Journalists and Authors, American Society of Magazine Photographers, Professional Photographers of America, American Institute of Aeronautics and Astronautics, Aviation/Space Writers Association.

WRITINGS: Strategic Air Command: Two-thirds of the Triad, Scribner, 1976; *Jet Fighters and Bombers,* Chartwell, 1976; *B-29 Superfortress at War,* Scribner, 1979; (with Bill Gunston) *Air Power: A Modern Illustrated Military History,* Phoebus Publishing, 1979; *Hellcat,* Crown, 1981; *The History of the U.S. Air Force,* Crescent, 1981; *Modern American Combat Aircraft,* Hamlyn Aerospace, 1982; *United States Fighters of World War II,* Hamlyn Aerospace, 1982; *Republic F-105 Thunderchief,* Anchor Books, 1983.

Author of a number of books published by the National Aeronautics and Space Administration, including *Sixty Years of Aeronautical Research, In This Decade: Mission to the Moon, Apollo 17 at Taurus-Littrow,* and *Laboratory in Space;* also author of "Bicentennial Symposium" series, published by NASA, 1976. Contributor of articles to journals.

WORK IN PROGRESS: Tactical Air Command.

SIDELIGHTS: David A. Anderton told *CA:* "I write for fun and I write for money, and as long as there is some of both on any given assignment, I'm happy. I approach my photographic assignments the same way. I like to believe in the subjects I write about, which tends sometimes to be limiting, but I sleep well." *Avocational interests:* Playing drums in and managing two bands, "one a big (seventeen-piece) swing-era band, and the other a traditional jazz octet"; building models (especially airplanes), collecting aviation classics and old books, collecting jazz records.

* * *

ANDONOV-POLJANSKI, Hristo 1927-

PERSONAL: Born September 21, 1927, in Dojran, Yugoslavia; son of George Andonov and Jordana (Bakalova) Andonova; married Jelica Mihailova (a professional adviser), February 16, 1958; children: Emil, Terezina. *Education:* University of Skopje, B.A., 1951, Ph.D., 1958. *Home:* Albert Ajnstein No. 1, Skopje, Yugoslavia. *Office:* Faculty of Philosophy, University of Skopje, Skopje, Yugoslavia.

CAREER: University of Skopje, Faculty of Philosophy, Skopje, Yugoslavia, assistant, 1953-59, lecturer, 1959-66, associate professor, 1966-70, professor, 1970—. Researcher for long periods at British Museum and in the Public Record Office. *Member:* Yugoslav Historical Association, Institute for History (Skopje). *Awards, honors:* Award of Republic of Macedonia, 1972, for *Gotze Delchev;* award for life achievement from Republic of Macedonia, 1981.

WRITINGS: (Contributor) *Prilog kon Bibliografijata po Arheologijata na Makedonija,* Institut za Nacionalna Istorija (Skopje), 1953; *Stranskiot pecat za Ilindenskoto vostanie,* [Skopje], 1953; (editor and author of preface) *Goce Delcev vo Spomenite na Sovremenicite,* Kultura (Skopje), 1963; *Makedonija vo Karti,* Institut za Nacionalna Istorija (Glasnik), 1965; (editor and author of preface) Karl Hron, *Narodnosta na Makedonskite Sloveni,* Arhiva na Makedonija (Skopje), 1966; *Britanska Bibliografija za Makedonija,* Arhiva na Makedonija (Skopje), 1966; (editor) *Krste Misirkov,* Institut za Makedonski Jazik, 1966; *Dramata vo Cer: Niz Zivotot i Deloto na Hristo Uzunov,* Kultura, 1968; (editor) *Britanski Dokumenti za Istorijata na Makedonskiot Narod* (title means "British Documents on the History of the Macedonian People"), Arhiva na Makedonija, Volume I: *1797-1839,* 1968, Volume II: *1840-1847,* 1977, Volume III: *1848-1866,* 1982; *Goce Delcev: ideolog i organizator na makedonskoto nacionalnooslobodltelno dvizenje,* Kultura, 1968; *Oddzivot na ilindenskoto vostanie vo svetot,* [Skopje], 1968; *San-Stefanska Bulgarija: Nenaucnoto tolkuvanje na makedonskata istorija,* Kultura, 1968; (editor) *Za Makedoncite* (poetry), Makedonska Kniga, 1969; (member of editorial board) *Istorija na makedonskiot narod,* three volumes, Institut za Nacionalna Istorija, 1969.

Goce Delchev, six volumes, Kultura, 1972, 2nd edition of Volume I, 1978; *Gotze Delchev: His Life and Time,* Misla (Skopje), 1973; *Velika Britanija i makedonskoto prasanje na Pariskata mirovna konferencija, 1919,* Arhiva na Makedonija, 1973; *Makedonija i Slovenija,* Kultura, 1978; *Selected Works,* five volumes, Misla, 1980-81; (editor) *Dokumenti za borbata na makedonskiot narod za samostojnost i za nacionalna drzava,* two volumes, Filozofski fakultet (Skopje), 1981; *Orations and Essays,* [Skopje], 1982; (editor) Tasko Arsov, *Zapiski,* [Skopje], in press; *Miss Stone,* [Skopje], in press. Contributor of article, in English, to *Macedonian Review.*

SIDELIGHTS: Hristo Andonov-Poljanski is competent in English, Russian, Bulgarian, Macedonian, Serbo-Croat, Slovenian, and has "literary" competency in French, German, and Italian.

* * *

ANDREW, J(ames) Dudley 1945-

PERSONAL: Born July 28, 1945, in Evansville, Ind.; son of James D. (an electronics engineer) and Lois J. (Zurlinden) Andrew; married Stephanie Phalen, February 1, 1969; children: Brigid Catherine, Ellen Jeannette, James Dudley. *Education:* University of Notre Dame, A.B., 1967; Columbia University, M.F.A., 1969; University of Iowa, Ph.D., 1972. *Religion:* Roman Catholic. *Home:* 1157 Court St., Iowa City, Iowa 52240.

Office: Division of Broadcasting and Film, University of Iowa, 102 Old Armory, Iowa City, Iowa 52242.

CAREER: University of Iowa, Iowa City, instructor, 1969-72, assistant professor, 1972-75, associate professor of English, speech and dramatic art, 1975—, head of Film Division, 1972—. Visiting professor at Colorado College, summers, 1970, 1974-76; director of summer seminar, National Endowment for the Humanities, 1977.

MEMBER: Council on International Educational Exchange (member of directorial board of Paris film program), Society for Cinema Studies, Speech Communication Association of America, American Film Institute, Committee on Institutional Cooperation (member of film panel), Midwest Modern Language Association (founder of film and literature section). *Awards, honors:* National Endowment for the Humanities fellowship for younger humanists, 1973-74; University of Iowa faculty scholar, 1981-84.

WRITINGS: The Major Film Theorists, Oxford University Press, 1976; *Andre Bazin,* Oxford University Press, 1978; (with Paul Andrew) *Kenji Mizoguchi,* G. K. Hall, 1981; *Concepts in Film Theory,* Oxford University Press, 1983; *Film in the Aura of Art,* Princeton University Press, 1984. Guest editor, *Quarterly Review of Film Studies;* member of editorial boards of *Quarterly Journal of Speech* and *Research in Film.*

* * *

ANDREWS, Bart 1945-

PERSONAL: Original name, Andrew Stephen Ferreri; name legally changed in 1964; born February 25, 1945, in Brooklyn, N.Y.; son of Joseph (a businessman) and Camille (Sollecito) Ferreri; divorced. *Education:* New York University, B.A., 1963. *Agent:* Andrews & Robb Agents, Sherry Robb, P.O. Box 727, Hollywood, Calif. 90028.

CAREER: Prospect House (resort hotel), Lake Bomoseen, Vt., social director, 1959-63; Columbia Broadcasting System (CBS), New York, N.Y., writer, 1963-64; free-lance television writer in Hollywood, Calif., 1964—; Andrews & Robb Agents, Hollywood, Calif., literary agent, 1982—. *Member:* American Society of Composers, Authors and Publishers, Authors Guild of Authors League of America, Writers Guild of America (West).

WRITINGS: Different Spokes for Different Folks (humor), Serendipity Press, 1973; *Official TV Trivia Quiz Book,* New American Library, 1975; *Yankee Doodle Dandies* (humor), New American Library, 1975; *Official Movie Trivia Quiz Book,* New American Library, 1976; *Official TV Trivia Quiz Book #2,* New American Library, 1976; (with Thomas J. Watson) *Lucy and Ricky and Fred and Ethel,* Dutton, 1976; *Star Trek Quiz Book,* New American Library, 1977; *TV or Not TV,* New American Library, 1977; *Star Wars Quiz Book,* New American Library, 1977; *Fabulous Fifties Quiz Book,* New American Library, 1978; *TV Addict's Handbook,* Dutton, 1978; *Official TV Trivia Quiz Book #3,* New American Library, 1978; *Tolkien Quiz Book,* New American Library, 1979; *TV Picture Quiz Book,* New American Library, 1979; *Super Sixties Quiz Book,* New American Library, 1979.

(With Brad Dunning) *The Worst TV Shows Ever,* Dutton, 1980; *TV Fun Book,* Scholastic Book Services, 1980; (with Watson) *Loving Lucy: An Illustrated Tribute to Lucille Ball,* St. Martin's, 1980; *I Love Lucy Quiz Book,* A. S. Barnes, 1981; *Double Lives,* Doubleday, 1983; *The Cat's Meow,* Dutton, 1984.

Also author of about 150 television comedy scripts, including material for Bob Newhart, Carol Burnett, Soupy Sales, Paul Lynde, and Phyllis Diller. Co-author of libretto for musical comedy "Ape over Broadway," first produced Off-Broadway at Bert Wheeler Theatre, March 12, 1975.

WORK IN PROGRESS: A novel.

* * *

ANTON, John P(eter) 1920-

PERSONAL: Born November 2, 1920, in Canton, Ohio; son of Peter C. and Christine (Giannopoulos) Anton; married Helen Vezos, November 26, 1955; children: James, Christopher, Peter. *Education:* College of Pedagogy, Tripolis, Greece, B.A., 1942; University of Athens, Certificate, 1945; Columbia University, B.S., 1949, M.A., 1950, Ph.D., 1954. *Politics:* Democrat. *Office:* New College, University of South Florida, 5700 North Tamiami Trail, Sarasota, Fla. 33580.

CAREER: Pace College (now University), New York, N.Y., instructor in history and philosophy, 1953-54; University of New Mexico, Albuquerque, visiting lecturer in philosophy, 1954-55; University of Nebraska, Lincoln, assistant professor of philosophy, 1955-58; Ohio Wesleyan University, Delaware, associate professor of philosophy, 1958-62; State University of New York at Buffalo, professor of philosophy, 1962-69, associate dean of Graduate School, 1967-69; Emory University, Atlanta, Ga., Fuller Callaway Professor of Philosophy and chairman of department, 1969-82; University of South Florida, New College, Sarasota, professor of philosophy and provost, 1982—. Visiting summer professor at Ohio State University, 1960, and Columbia University, 1966; research associate, University of California, Berkeley, 1971-72; distinguished visiting professor at Humboldt State University, 1979; Mary Woods Bennett Visiting Professor at Mills College, 1981. *Military service:* U.S. Army, Quartermaster Corps, 1946-47.

MEMBER: International Society for Neoplatonic Studies (chairman of executive committee), International Society for Metaphysics, American Philosophical Association, American Philosophical Society (fellow), American Philological Association, Society for the History of Philosophy, American Comparative Literature Association, Society for the Advancement of American Philosophy, American Classical League, American Society for Aesthetics (trustee), American Humanist Association, Society for Ancient Greek Philosophy (secretary-treasurer, 1971-80; president, 1980-82), Modern Greek Studies Association, Society for Macedonian Studies (honorary member), Hellenic Society for Philosophical Studies (honorary member), American Council of Learned Societies, American Association of University Professors, Phi Beta Kappa (honorary member), Phi Sigma Tau, Eta Sigma Phi. *Awards, honors:* Wurlitzer Foundation fellow, 1955-56; faculty research fellow, State University of New York at Buffalo; American Philosophical Society fellow, 1967, 1972, 1982; Outstanding Educator of America, 1970; Emory University Research Award, 1971, 1975.

WRITINGS: Meaning in Religious Poetry, New York Hellenic Society, 1954; *Aristotle's Theory of Contrariety,* Humanities, 1957; (editor, contributor, and compiler of bibliography) *Naturalism and Historical Understanding: Essays on the Philosophy of John Herman Randall, Jr.,* State University of New York Press, 1967; (translator from the Greek and editor) E. P. Papanoutsos, *Foundations of Knowledge,* State University of New York Press, 1968; *Philosophical Essays* (in Greek), Makrides & Co., 1969.

(Editor) *Essays in Ancient Greek Philosophy,* State University of New York Press, Volume I (with G. L. Kustas), 1971, Volume II (with A. Preus), in press; (editor with Craig Walton) *Philosophy and the Civilizing Arts: Essays Presented to Herbert W. Schneider on His Eightieth Birthday,* Ohio University Press, 1975; (editor with N. P. Diamantouros, John A. Petropulos, and Peter Topping) *Hellenism and the First Greek War of Liberation (1821-1830),* Institute for Balkan Studies, 1975; (editor) *Science and the Sciences in Plato,* Caravan Books, 1980; *Critical Humanism as a Philosophy of Culture,* North Central Publishing, 1981.

Contributor of numerous articles and reviews to journals, including *Athene, Journal of Philosophy, Western Humanities, Humanist,* and *Classical Journal.* Member of editorial boards, *Arethusa,* 1968-72, *Journal for Critical Analysis,* 1970—, *Neo-Hellenika,* 1970—; editorial consultant, *Journal of the History of Philosophy,* 1968—; co-editor, *Diotima,* 1972—; advisory editor, *Southern Journal of Philosophy,* 1974—.

WORK IN PROGRESS: Constantine Cavafy: His Poetry and Poetics.

BIOGRAPHICAL/CRITICAL SOURCES: Nea Estia (Athens), October 15, 1966.

* * *

ANTONACCI, Robert J(oseph) 1916-

PERSONAL: Born January 21, 1916, in Toluca, Ill.; son of Nick and Angeline (Matterelli) Antonacci; married second wife, Amaryllis Boyd (a bacteriologist), September 16, 1953; children: (first marriage) Robert J., Jr.; (second marriage) Clarissa. *Education:* Indiana University, B.S., 1941; University of Michigan, M.S., 1946, Ed.D., 1956.

CAREER: Oregon State University, Corvallis, assistant professor of health and physical education and wrestling coach, 1946-50; University of Chicago, Chicago, Ill., member of staff of department of physical education and guidance, 1950-53; Wayne State University, Detroit, Mich., associate professor of health and physical education, 1953-57; director of health, physical education, and safety for public schools, Gary, Ind., beginning 1957; member of staff of department of physical education, Temple University, Philadelphia, Pa. Member of Indiana board of directors, Health Funds for Medical Research, 1962-64; member of board of directors, United Fund of Gary, 1961-63, and Gary Youth Commission, 1960-64. *Military service:* U.S. Navy, 1941-45; became chief specialist.

MEMBER: American Association for Health, Physical Education and Recreation (chairman of Midwest association; vice-president of Indiana association), American Public Health Association, National Society for Study of Education, Phi Delta Kappa, Sigma Delta Psi, Phi Epsilon Kappa.

WRITINGS—Published by McGraw, except as indicated: (With others) *Sports Officiating,* Ronald, 1949; (with Jene Barr) *Baseball for Young Champions,* 1956, 2nd edition, 1977; (with Barr) *Football for Young Champions,* 1958, 2nd edition, 1976; (with Barr) *Basketball for Young Champions,* 1960, 2nd edition, 1979; (with Barr) *Physical Fitness for Young Champions,* 1962, 2nd edition, 1975; (with Gene Schoor) *Track and Field for Young Champions,* 1974; (with Anthony J. Puglisi) *Soccer for Young Champions,* 1978. Also editor of health and physical education teaching guides. Contributor to several books and to professional journals and newspapers.

WORK IN PROGRESS: Research on health habits and practices of elementary school children and on fitness status of boys and girls in secondary schools.

SIDELIGHTS: Robert J. Antonacci is a member of Indiana University's Hall of Fame as national collegiate wrestling champion.†

* * *

ANWEILER, Oskar 1925-

PERSONAL: Born September 29, 1925, in Rawicz, Poland; son of Sigmund (a head clerk) and Helene (Kolb) Anweiler; married Gerda Timmermann, June 4, 1949. *Education:* University of Hamburg, Dr.Phil., 1954. *Home:* Soldnerstrasse 10, Bochum, Germany D463. *Office:* University of Bochum, Bochum, Germany D463.

CAREER: University of Hamburg, Hamburg, Germany, lecturer, 1963-64; University of Bochum, Bochum, Germany, professor of comparative education, 1964—, dean of faculty of philosophy, education, and psychology, 1966-67, 1975-76. Visiting professor in New Zealand and Canada, 1973, 1979, 1981.

MEMBER: International Committee for Soviet and East European Studies (president, 1980—), Ostkolleg der Bundeszentrale fuer Politsche Bildung (member of governing board), Comparative Education Society in Europe (vice-president, 1973-77), Deutsch Gesellschaft fuer Osteuropakunde (vice-president, 1974—), Bundesinstitut fuer Ostwissenschaftliche und International Studien (member of governing board, 1982—).

WRITINGS: Die Raetebewegung in Russland, 1905-1921, E. J. Brill, 1958, translation by Ruth Hein published as *The Soviets: The Russian Workers, Peasants, and Soldiers Councils, 1905-1921,* Pantheon, 1975; (editor with Klaus Meyer) *Die Sowjetische Bildungspolitik seit 1917: Dokumente und Texte,* Quelle & Meyer, 1961, 2nd edition, 1973; *Geschichte der Schule und Paedogogik in Russland vom Ende des Zarenreiches bis zum Beginn der Stalin-Aera,* Quelle & Meyer, 1964, 2nd edition, 1978; *Die Sowjetpaedagogik in der Welt von Heute,* Quelle & Meyer, 1968; (editor) *Bildungsreformen in Osteuropa,* Kohlhammer, 1969.

(Editor with K. H. Ruffman) *Kulturpolitik der Sowjetunion,* Kroener, 1973; (editor with F. Kuebart and K. Meyer) *Die Sowjetische Bildungspolitik, 1958-1973: Dokumente und Texte,* [Berlin], 1976; (editor) *Erziehungs-und Socialisations-probleme in der Sowjetunion, der D.D.R. und Polen,* Schroedel, 1978; (editor) *Bildung und Erziehung in Osteuropa im 20sl Th.,* [Berlin], 1982; (editor with A. Hearden) *Sekundarschulbildung und Hochschule: Erfahrungen un Probleme in Grossbrittanien und der Bundesrepublik Deutschland,* Boehlau, 1982.

Contributor: Richard Pipes, editor, *Revolutionary Russia,* Harvard University Press, 1968; George Katkov and others, editors, *Russia Enters the Twentieth Century,* Temple Smith, 1971; Boris Meissner, editor, *Social Change in the Soviet Union,* University of Notre Dame Press, 1972; Hans Steffen, editor, *Bildung und Gesellschaft,* Vandenhoeck & Ruprecht, 1972; A. S. Makarenko, *Ein paedagogisches Poem,* Ullstein, 1972; Reginald Edwards and others, editors, *Relevant Methods in Comparative Education,* UNESCO Institute for Education (Hamburg), 1973, Unipub, 1974.

Co-editor, ''Erziehungswissenschaftliche Veroeffentlichungen des Osteuropa-Instituts an der Freien Universitaet Berlin'' series. Contributor to encyclopedias, including *Encyclopaedia*

Britannica, Lexikon der Paedagogik, and *Marxism, Communism, and Western Society: A Comparative Encyclopedia;* contributor to journals, including *Osteuropa Comparative Education* and *International Review of Education.* Co-editor, *Bildung und Erziehung.*

* * *

ARDEN, J. E. M.
See CONQUEST, (George) Robert (Acworth)

* * *

ARGYLE, Michael 1925-

PERSONAL: Born August 11, 1925, in Nottingham, England; son of George Edgar (a school teacher) and Phyllis (Hawkins-Ambler) Argyle; married Sonia Kemp (a lexicographer), June 24, 1949; children: Miranda, Nicholas, Rosalind, Ophelia. *Education:* Emmanuel College, Cambridge, M.A., 1952. *Religion:* Church of England. *Home:* 309 Woodstock Rd., Oxford, England. *Office:* Department of Experimental Psychology, Oxford University, South Parks Rd., Oxford, England.

CAREER: Oxford University, Oxford, England, university lecturer, 1952-69, reader in social psychology, 1969—, acting head of department of experimental psychology, 1978-80, fellow of Wolfson College, 1965—, a governor of Pusey House, 1976—. Fellow, Center for Advanced Study in the Behavioral Sciences, Stanford, Calif., 1958-59; visiting professor at a number of universities, including University of Michigan, University of Delaware, University of British Columbia, University of Ghana, University of Leuven, Hebrew University of Jerusalem, University of Bologna, and University of Adelaide; lecturer in Greece, Italy, Finland, New Zealand, Australia, and Egypt; director or participant in several professional conferences. Psychologist to Civil Service Selection Board, 1963-68; member of Royal Society Group on Non-Verbal Communication, 1968-71, and of Council for Academic Awards, 1974—. Member of advisory committee, British Sports Council, 1975-78. *Military service:* Royal Air Force, navigator, 1943-47; became flying officer.

MEMBER: British Psychological Society (fellow; chairman of Social Psychology Section, 1964-67, 1972-74), European Association for Social Psychology, American Society of Experimental Social Psychology (foreign member). *Awards, honors:* D.Sc., Oxford University and University of Brussels; D.Litt., University of Adelaide.

WRITINGS: The Scientific Study of Social Behaviour, Methuen, 1957; *Religious Behaviour,* Free Press of Glencoe, 1959; (with George Humphrey) *Social Psychology through Experiment,* Methuen, 1962; (with A. T. Welford and others) *Society: Problems and Methods of Study,* Routledge & Kegan Paul, 1962; (with M. Kirton and T. Smith) *Training Managers,* Action Society Trust, 1962; *Psychology and Social Problems,* Methuen, 1964.

The Psychology of Interpersonal Behaviour, Penguin, 1967, 4th edition, 1983; *Social Interaction,* Methuen, 1969, Aldine, 1970; *The Social Psychology of Work,* Taplinger, 1972; (editor) *Social Encounters: Readings in Social Interaction,* Aldine, 1973; *Bodily Communication,* Methuen, 1975; (with Benjamin Beit-Hallahmi) *The Social Psychology of Religion,* Routledge & Kegan Paul, 1975; (with M. Cook) *Gaze and Mutual Gaze,* Cambridge University Press, 1975; (with Peter Trower and B. Bryant) *Handbook of Social Skills,* Methuen, 1978, Volume I: *Social Skills and Mental Health,* Volume II: *Social Skills and Work;* (with Trower) *Person to Person,* Harper, 1979.

(With Adrian Furnham and Jean Ann Graham) *Social Situations,* Cambridge University Press, 1981. Editor of "Social Psychology Monographs" series, Penguin, 1967-74, and "International Series in Experimental Social Psychology," Pergamon, 1979—. Contributor to professional journals in Great Britain, Europe, and the United States. Member of editorial board or consulting editor to *British Journal of Social and Clinical Psychology, Journal of Applied Social Psychology, Journal for the Theory of Social Behaviour, Journal of Human Movement Studies, Journal of Nonverbal Behavior, Review of Personality and Social Psychology, Behaviour Research and Therapy, Language and Communication,* and *Journal of Social and Clinical Psychology.*

* * *

ARMSTRONG, William H(oward) 1914-

PERSONAL: Born September 14, 1914, in Lexington, Va.; son of Howard Gratton (a farmer) and Ida (Morris) Armstrong; married Martha Stone Street Williams, August 24, 1943 (died, 1953); children: Christopher, David, Mary. *Education:* Hampden-Sydney College, A.B. (cum laude), 1936; graduate study at University of Virginia. *Politics:* Independent. *Home:* Kimadee Hill, Kent, Conn. 06757.

CAREER: Kent School, Kent, Conn., history master, beginning 1945; farmer; writer. *Member:* Phi Beta Kappa, Omicron Delta Kappa. *Awards, honors:* National School Bell Award of National Association of School Administrators, 1963, for distinguished service in the interpretation of education; Lewis Carroll Book Shelf Award, 1970; John Newbery Medal from American Library Association, 1970, Mark Twain Award from Missouri Association of School Librarians, 1972, and Nene Award from Hawaii Association of School Librarians and Hawaii Library Association, all for *Sounder;* Jewish-Christian Brotherhood award, 1972; Sue Hedley Award.

WRITINGS: Study Is Hard Work, Harper, 1956, 2nd edition, 1967; *Through Troubled Waters,* Harper, 1957; (with Joseph W. Swain) *The Peoples of the Ancient World,* Harper, 1959; *87 Ways to Help Your Child in School,* Barron's, 1961; *Tools of Thinking,* Barron's, 1968, published as *Word Power in 5 Easy Lessons,* 1969; *Sounder,* Harper, 1969.

Barefoot in the Grass: The Story of Grandma Moses, Doubleday, 1970; (adapter) Hana Doskocilova, *Animal Tales,* translation from the Czechoslovakian by Eve Merriam, Doubleday, 1970; *Sour Land,* Harper, 1971; *The MacLeod Place,* Coward, 1972; *Hadassah: Esther the Orphan Queen,* Doubleday, 1972; *My Animals,* Doubleday, 1973; *The Mills of God,* Doubleday, 1973; *The Education of Abraham Lincoln,* Coward, 1974; *JoAnna's Miracle,* Broadman, 1978; *Tawny and Dingo,* Harper, 1979; *Study Tips: How to Improve Your Grades,* Barron's, 1981.

SIDELIGHTS: As a child, William H. Armstrong had a neighbor who entertained him with stories. One of his favorites was the saga of a loyal "coon dog" with an exceptional bark. When he became a writer, Armstrong drew on his recollection of this tale in producing *Sounder*—his award-winning novel, which the *New York Times Book Review* children's editor, George Wood, pronounced the best novel of 1969.

Set in the south, the story centers around Sounder, the dog, and the poor black sharecroppers who own him. One night, because there is no food in the house, the father sneaks out and steals a ham. When the sheriff comes to arrest him, Sounder tries to protect his master and is shot down in the road. The father is taken off to prison; the dog drags himself off into the forest and is assumed dead. But, writes June Meyer Jordan in the *New York Times Book Review,* "months later, he reappears, mutilated, prefiguring the eventual condition of his master." As the story unfolds to its end, the sound of the dog's bark is heard again "sad but strong," according to a *Times Literary Supplement* critic "and once again [the reader is] presented with that strange and age-old paradox, a tale whose ingredients are tragic and terrible but whose distillation is beauty."

Children's editor George Wood considers the book more than a dog story. "When I finished reading it," he wrote, "I could understand how the festering sores of past injustice among blacks have brought us the virulence of today." But not all critics agree that *Sounder* advances the goals of black Americans. Albert V. Schwartz in *The Black American in Books for Children: Readings in Racism* says that Armstrong's characterizations reinforce prejudicial stereotypes and questions why no one in the sharecropper's family, except the dog, is identified by name: "This would be an acceptable literary device in the hands of a Black author. For a white author to resort to it immediately raises the issue of white supremacy. Within the white world, deep-seated prejudice has long denied human individualization to the Black person." However John Rowe Townsend in his *Written for Children: An Outline of English Language Children's Literature* dismisses this charge as "misguided" and explains that Armstrong's intention was not to deny black characters individuality, but rather to make them "appear universal, not tied down to a local habitation and a name." Indeed, Armstrong himself told a *Hartford Courant* reporter that his story could just as well have been written about any family of any origin. "Except for one part of the book where the deputy sheriff makes a statement about being black, it could have been a poor white family," Armstrong said.

Several critics, including June Meyer Jordan, praise Armstrong's style in *Sounder*. She writes in the *New York Times Book Review* that "the author writes in details that glow alive. Examples: When the mother was troubled her lips were rolled inward and drawn long and thin. . . . But when she sang or told stories, her lips were rolled out, big and warm and soft." Although Jordan finds the story too violent for children, she recommends *Sounder* to "young and not so young adults. The deliberate cool of its telling," she concludes, "follows McLuhan's rule: We are urged into participation, a moral questioning and a moral wonder. When we stop reading, we want to hear the living voice, the distinctively human sound of this anonymous black family."

MEDIA ADAPTATIONS: A movie adapted from *Sounder* and nominated for an Academy Award was released by Twentieth Century-Fox in 1972.

AVOCATIONAL INTERESTS: "I raise purebred Corriedale sheep on a rocky hillside in Connecticut and live in a house built entirely by my own hands," Armstrong told *CA*. "I prefer stone masonry and carpentry to writing."

BIOGRAPHICAL/CRITICAL SOURCES: New York Times Book Review, October 26, 1969, November 9, 1969, February 13, 1972; *Horn Book,* December, 1969, August, 1970, June, 1971; *Saturday Review,* November 14, 1970; *Times Literary Supplement,* July 2, 1971, April 6, 1973; *Time,* December, 1971; Donnarae MacCann and Gloria Woodard, editors, *The Black American in Books for Children: Readings in Racism,* Scarecrow, 1972; *Hartford Courant,* November 25, 1973; John Rowe Townsend, *Written for Children: An Outline of English Language Children's Literature,* Lippincott, 1974; *Authors in the News,* Volume I, Gale, 1976; *Children's Literature Review,* Volume I, Gale, 1976.

* * *

ARNOLD, Emmy (von Hollander) 1884-1980

PERSONAL: Born December 25, 1884, in Riga, Latvia; died, 1980; daughter of Heinrich (a professor of law at University of Halle) and Monika (Otto) von Hollander; married Eberhard Arnold, December 20, 1909 (died November 22, 1935); children: Emi-Margret Zumpe, Eberhard, Johann Heinrich, Hans-Hermann (died, 1972), Monika E. Truempi. *Education:* Studied nursing in Halle/Saale, Germany, 1905-07. *Address:* Hutterion Society of Brothers, Woodcrest, Rifton, N.Y. 12471.

CAREER: Writer and editor. Served as housemother for Hutterion Society of Brothers (Bruderhof) communities, Rifton, N.Y., 1920-80. *Member:* Hutterion Society of Brothers.

WRITINGS: (Editor) *Sonnenlieder: Songs of Joy in Nature, Peace Among Men, and Communion with God* (German language), Eberhard Arnold Verlag, 1924; (editor) Ludwig von Zinzendorf, *Zinzendorf: Glaube und Leben* (songs and poems; subtitle means "Faith and Life"), Hochweg Verlag (Berlin), 1925; (editor and contributor) *Eberhard Arnold: A Testimony of Church Community from His Life and Writings,* Plough Publishing, 1953, 2nd edition, 1973; (compiler) *Inner Words for Every Day of the Year,* Plough Publishing, 1963; *Torches Together: The Beginning and Early Years of the Bruderhof Communities,* Plough Publishing, 1964, 2nd edition, 1971; (contributor) Eberhard Arnold, *When the Time Was Fulfilled,* Plough Publishing, 1965; (contributor) E. Arnold, *The Early Christians after the Death of the Apostles,* Plough Publishing, 1972; (with husband, E. Arnold) *Seeking from the Kingdom of God: Origins of the Bruderhof Communities,* Plough Publishing, 1974; (with E. Arnold) *The Heavens Are Opened,* Plough Publishing, 1974. Also author of poetry about religion.

SIDELIGHTS: With her husband, Emmy Arnold helped to found the Bruderhof, a religious community that derives its inspiration from the early Christians. The group, established in 1920 in Sannerz, near Frankfort-am-Main, Germany, was conceived as an act of "renunciation of normal middle class life in its totality, with its private property, its ambitions and injustices." Arnold recalled that "there was no financial basis of any kind either for our community settlement or for [our] proposed publishing house, when we decided to turn our backs on our past lives and to start afresh in full trust. Our well-meaning friends shook their heads; what an act of rash irresponsibility for a father of five little children to go into complete nothingness, just like that!" When Hitler came to power, the group moved first to England, then to Paraguay, and finally to the United States.

Arnold continued to assist with the work of the community and to consult with the editors of Plough Publishing, a Bruderhof establishment, concerning the posthumous publication of some of her husband's writings, until her death.

BIOGRAPHICAL/CRITICAL SOURCES: Chelsea, October, 1968.†

ARRINGTON, Leonard James 1917-

PERSONAL: Born July 2, 1917, in Twin Falls, Idaho; son of Noah Wesley (a farmer) and Edna (Corn) Arrington; married Grace Fort, April 24, 1943; children: James Wesley, Carl Wayne, Susan Grace (Mrs. Dean Madsen). *Education:* University of Idaho, B.S. 1939; Latter-day Saints Institute of Religion, Moscow, Idaho, graduate, 1939; University of North Carolina at Chapel Hill, Ph.D., 1952. *Politics:* Independent. *Religion:* Church of Jesus Christ of Latter-day Saints. *Home:* 2236 South 2200 East, Salt Lake City, Utah 84109. *Office:* Department of History, Brigham Young University, Provo, Utah 84601; and Historical Department, Church of Jesus Christ of Latter-day Saints, 50 East North Temple, Salt Lake City, Utah 84150.

CAREER: University of North Carolina at Chapel Hill, Kenan Teaching Fellow, 1939-40, teaching assistant in economics, 1940-41; North Carolina State College (now North Carolina State University at Raleigh), instructor in economics, 1941-42; economic analyst, North Carolina Office of Price Administration, 1942-43; North Carolina State College, assistant professor of economics, 1946; Utah State University, Logan, assistant professor, 1946-52, associate professor, 1952-58, professor of economic history, 1958-72; Brigham Young University, Provo, Utah, Lemuel H. Redd Professor of Western History, 1972—, director of Charles Redd Center for Western History, 1972-80. Professor of economics and history, Brigham Young University, 1956, 1958, 1966; Fulbright professor of American economics, University of Genoa and other Italian universities, 1958-59; lecturer in American civilization, University of Texas radio program, 1963; visiting professor of history, University of California, Los Angeles, 1966-67; instructor, Latter-day Saints Institute of Religion, Logan, Utah, 1969-70. Historian, Church of Jesus Christ of Latter-day Saints, 1972-80. Coordinator of social and economic planning, State of Utah, 1964-66. Member of advisory board, Jefferson Mint, 1969-72, Study Guild International, 1970-73, Mormon Trails Association, 1970-73, College of Business, Utah State University, 1975—, and Utah State Historical Records, 1976—. *Military service:* U.S. Army, 1943-46; allied representative, Central Institute of Statistics, Rome, Italy, 1944-45, and Committee for Price Control in Northern Italy, Milan, 1945; also served in Morocco, Tunisia, and Algeria.

MEMBER: American Historical Association (member of council, Pacific Coast Branch, 1963-66, president, 1981-82), Economic History Association (chairman of Western Section, 1957-59), Organization of American Historians, Agricultural History Society, Mormon History Association (president, 1965-66), Western Economic Association, Western History Association (president, 1968-69), Utah Historical Association (fellow), Utah Academy of Sciences, Arts, and Letters (member of council, 1960-63; member of board of fellows, 1973—; vice-president, 1974-75, president, 1975-76), Phi Beta Kappa, Rotary International, Sons of Utah Pioneers.

AWARDS, HONORS: Koonty Award, Pacific Coast Branch of American Historical Association, 1956, for best article published in *Pacific Historical Review;* Huntington Library fellow, 1957-58; awards of merit, American Association for State and Local History, and Pacific Coast Branch of American Historical Association, both 1959, for *Great Basin Kingdom: An Economic History of the Latter-day Saints, 1830-1900;* Charles Redd Humanities Award, Utah Academy of Sciences, Arts, and Letters, 1966; research grants from American Philosophical Society, 1966, American Council of Learned Societies, 1966-68, Roland Rich Woolley Foundation, 1970-75, and Nora Eccles Treadwell Foundation, 1970-72; David O. McKay Humanities Award, Brigham Young University, 1969; named Alumnus of the Year by Utah State University, 1975; D.H.L., University of Idaho, 1977.

WRITINGS: Great Basin Kingdom: An Economic History of the Latter-day Saints, 1830-1900, Harvard University Press, 1958; *Introduzione alla storia economica degli Stati Uniti,* Libraria Mario Bozzi (Genoa), 1959; (with Gary B. Hansen) *The Changing Economic Structure of the Mountain West, 1850-1950* (monograph), Utah State University, 1963; (with Hansen) *The Richest Hole on Earth: A History of the Bingham Copper Mine,* Utah State University Press, 1963; (with George Jensen) *The Defense Industry of Utah,* Utah State University Press, 1965; *Beet Sugar in the West: A History of the Utah-Idaho Sugar Company, 1891-1966,* University of Washington Press, 1966; (with Jensen) *Impact of Defense Spending on the Economy of Utah,* Utah State University, 1967; (with Anthony T. Cluff) *Federally Financed Industrial Plants Constructed in Utah during World War II,* Utah State University Press, 1969.

(With William L. Roper) *William Spry: Man of Firmness, Governor of Utah,* Utah State University Press, 1971; *Charles C. Rich: Mormon General and Western Frontiersman,* Brigham Young University Press, 1974; *David Eccles: Pioneer Western Industrialist,* Utah State University Press, 1975; *From Quaker to Latter-day Saint: Bishop Edwin D. Woolley,* Deseret, 1976; (with Feramorz Y. Fox and Dean L. May) *Building the City of God: Community and Cooperation among the Mormons,* Deseret, 1976; (with Davis Bitton) *The Mormon Experience: A History of the Latter-day Saints,* Knopf, 1979; *The Mormons in Nevada,* Las Vegas Sun, 1979; (with Bitton) *Saints without Halos: The Human Side of Mormon History,* Signature Books, 1981.

Contributor to periodicals. Member of editorial board, *Pacific Historical Review,* 1959-62, *Dialogue, Journal of Mormon Thought,* 1966-69, and *Arizona and the West,* 1973—; editor, *Western Historical Quarterly,* 1969-72; contributing editor, *Improvement Era,* 1969-70, and *Ensign,* 1971-76.

* * *

ASHBERY, John (Lawrence) 1927-
(Jonas Berry)

PERSONAL: Born July 28, 1927, in Rochester, N.Y.; son of Chester Frederick (a farmer) and Helen (a biology teacher at time of marriage; maiden name, Lawrence) Ashbery. *Education:* Harvard University, B.A., 1949; Columbia University, M.A., 1951; graduate study at New York University, 1957-58. *Agent:* Georges Borchardt, Inc., 136 East 57th St., New York, N.Y. 10022.

CAREER: Writer, critic, and editor. Worked as reference librarian for Brooklyn Public Library, Brooklyn, N.Y.; Oxford University Press, New York City, copywriter, 1951-54; McGraw-Hill Book Co., New York City, copywriter, 1954-55; New York University, New York City, instructor in elementary French, 1957-58; *New York Herald Tribune,* European Edition, Paris, France, art critic, 1960-65; *Art News,* New York City, Paris correspondent, 1964-65, executive editor in New York City, 1966-72; Brooklyn College of the City University of New York, Brooklyn, professor of English and co-director of Master of Fine Arts Program in Creative Writing, 1974—, distinguished professor, 1980—. Art critic for *Art International* (Lugano, Switzerland), 1961-64, *New York*, 1978-80, and *Newsweek*, 1980—. Has read his poetry at the Living Theatre, New York City, and at numerous universities, including Yale University, University of Chicago, and University of Texas.

AWARDS, HONORS: Discovery Prize co-winner, Young Men's Hebrew Association, 1952; Fulbright scholarship to France, 1955-56 and 1956-57; Yale Series of Younger Poets Prize, 1956, for *Some Trees;* Poets' Foundation grant, 1960 and 1964; Ingram-Merrill Foundation grant, 1962 and 1972; Harriet Monroe Poetry Award, *Poetry*, 1963; Union League Civic and Arts Foundation Prize, *Poetry*, 1966; National Book Award nomination, 1966, for *Rivers and Mountains;* Guggenheim fellowship, 1967 and 1973; National Endowment for the Arts grant, 1968 and 1969; National Institute of Arts and Letters Award, 1969; Shelley Memorial Award, Poetry Society of America, 1973, for *Three Poems;* Frank O'Hara Prize, Modern Poetry Association, 1974; Harriet Monroe Poetry Award, University of Chicago, 1975; Pulitzer Prize, National Book Award, and National Book Critics Circle Award, all 1976, all for *Self-Portrait in a Convex Mirror;* Levinson Prize, *Poetry*, 1977; Rockefeller Foundation grant in playwriting, 1978; D. Litt., Southampton College of Long Island University, 1979; Phi Beta Kappa Poet, Harvard University, 1979; English Speaking Union Poetry Award, 1979; American Book Award nomination, 1982, for *Shadow Train;* Academy of American Poets fellowship, 1982.

WRITINGS—Verse, except as indicated: *Turandot and Other Poems* (chapbook), Tibor de Nagy Gallery, 1953; *Some Trees*, foreword by W. H. Auden, Yale University Press, 1956, reprinted, Ecco Press, 1978; *The Poems*, Tiber Press, 1960; *The Tennis Court Oath*, Wesleyan University Press, 1962; *Rivers and Mountains*, Holt, 1966; *Selected Poems*, J. Cape, 1967; *Sunrise in Suburbia*, Phoenix Bookshop, 1968; *Three Madrigals*, Poet's Press, 1969; (with James Schuyler) *A Nest of Ninnies* (novel), Dutton, 1969; *Fragment* (also see below), Black Sparrow Press, 1969; *The Double Dream of Spring* (includes poem "Fragment," originally published in book form), Dutton, 1970; *The New Spirit*, Adventures in Poetry, 1970; (with Lee Hawood and Tom Raworth) *Penguin Modern Poets 19*, Penguin, 1971; *Three Poems*, Viking, 1972; (with Joe Brainard) *The Vermont Notebook*, Black Sparrow Press, 1975; *Self-Portrait in a Convex Mirror*, Viking, 1975; *Houseboat Days*, Viking, 1977; *As We Know*, Viking, 1979; *Shadow Train*, Viking, 1981.

Plays: "The Heroes" (one-act), first produced Off-Broadway at the Living Theater Playhouse, August 5, 1952, published in *Artists' Theater*, edited by Herbert Machiz, Grove, 1969; "The Compromise" (three-act), produced in Cambridge, Mass., at the Poet's Theater, 1956, published in *The Hasty Papers*, Alfred Leslie, 1960; "The Philosopher" (one-act), published in *Art and Literature*, No. 2, 1964; *3 Plays* (contains "The Heroes," "The Compromise," and "The Philosopher"), Z Press, 1978.

Editor of a number of volumes, including: (With others) *The American Literary Anthology*, Farrar, Straus, 1968; *Penguin Modern Poets 24: Kenward Elmslie, Kenneth Koch, James Schuyler*, Penguin, 1974; Richard F. Sknow, *The Funny Place*, O'Hara (Chicago), 1975; Bruce Marcus, *Muck Arbour*, O'Hara, 1975.

Also editor of art books with Thomas B. Hess, including: *Light*, Macmillan, 1969; *Painterly Painting*, Newsweek, 1971; *Art of the Grand Eccentrics*, Macmillan, 1971; *Avant-Garde Art*, Macmillan, 1971.

Work represented in numerous anthologies, including: *New American Poetry, 1945-1960*, Grove, 1960; Paris Leary and Robert Kelly, editors, *A Controversy of Poets*, Doubleday-Anchor, 1964; *L'Avant-Garde aujourd'hui*, [Brussels], 1965; *New Writing in the U.S.A.*, Penguin, 1966; *Poems of Our Moment*, Pegasus, 1968; *Anthology of New York Poets*, Random House, 1969; *N.Y. Amerikansk Poesi*, Gyldendal (Copenhagen), 1969; *Twentieth Century Poetry: American and British (1900-1970)*, McGraw, 1970; *Possibilities of Poetry: An Anthology of American Contemporaries*, Delta, 1970; *That Voice That Is Great within Us: American Poetry of the Twentieth Century*, Bantam, 1970; *Contemporary American Poetry*, Houghton, 1971; Louis Untermeyer, editor, *50 Modern American and British Poets, 1920-1970*, McKay, 1973; *Shake the Kaleidoscope: A New Anthology of Modern Poetry*, Simon & Schuster, 1973.

Collaborator with Joe Brainard on C Comic Books; collaborator with Elliott Carter on the musical setting "Syringa," first produced in New York at Alice Tully Hall, December, 1979; verse has been set to music by Ned Rorem, Eric Salzman, Paul Reif, and James Dashow. Poetry recordings include "Treasury of 100 Modern American Poets Reading Their Poems," Volume XVII, Spoken Arts, and "Poetry of John Ashbery," Jeffrey Norton. Translator, from the French, of the works of Jean-Jacques Mayoux, Jacques Dupin, Raymond Roussel, Andre Breton, Pierre Reverdy, Arthur Cravan, Max Jacob, Alfred Jarry, Antonin Artaud, and others. Also translator, under pseudonym Jonas Berry, of two French detective novels.

Contributor of poetry to periodicals, including *New York Review of Books, Partisan Review, Harper's*, and *New Yorker;* contributor of art criticism to periodicals, including *Art International* and *Aujourd'hui;* contributor of literary criticism to *New York Review of Books, Saturday Review, Poetry, Bizarre* (Paris), and other periodicals. Editor, *Locus Solus* (Lans-en-Vercors, France), 1960-62; co-founder and editor, *Art and Literature* (Paris), 1964-66; poetry editor, *Partisan Review*, 1976—.

WORK IN PROGRESS: Poems; a play; a translation of the literary works of Belgian surrealist painter Rene Magritte.

SIDELIGHTS: "Stop anywhere you happen to be in the underground and listen: that sound you hear is the sound of Ashbery's poetic voice being mimicked—a hushed, simultaneously incomprehensible and intelligent whisper with a weird pulsating rhythm that fluctuates like a wave between peaks of sharp clarity and watery droughts of obscurity and langour," Stephen Koch commented in a 1968 *New York Times Book Review* article. Poet John Ashbery's style, once considered avant-garde, has since become "so influential that its imitators are legion," Helen Vendler observes in the *New Yorker*. After suffering through a period of critical misunderstanding, Ashbery has entered the mainstream of American poetry, becoming, as James Atlas notes in the *New York Times Sunday Magazine*, "the most widely honored poet of his generation." Ashbery's position in American letters is confirmed by his unprecedented sweep of the literary "triple crown" in 1976, as his *Self-Portrait in a Convex Mirror* won the Pulitzer Prize, the National Book Award, *and* the National Book Critics Circle Prize. According to Howard Wamsley in *Poetry*, "The chances are very good that he will dominate the last third of the century as Yeats . . . dominated the first."

A key element of Ashbery's success is his openness to change; it is both a characteristic of his development as a writer and an important thematic element in his verse. "It is a thankless and hopeless task to try and keep up with Ashbery, to try and summarize the present state of his art,'' Raymond Carney writes in the *Dictionary of Literary Biography*. ''As [*As We Know*] shows, he will never stand still, even for the space (or time) of one poem. Emerson wrote that 'all poetry is vehicular,' and in the case of Ashbery the reader had better resign himself to a series of unending adjustments and movements. With each subsequent book of poetry we only know that he will never be standing still, for that to him is death.'' In a *Washington Post Book World* review of *Shadow Train,* David Young notes: ''You must enjoy unpredictability if you are to like John Ashbery. . . . We must be ready for anything in reading Ashbery because this eclectic, dazzling, inventive creator of travesties and treaties is ready to and eager to include anything, say anything, go anywhere, in the service of an esthetic dedicated to liberating poetry from predictable conventions and tired traditions.'' And in the *New York Times Book Review,* J. M. Brinnon observes that *Self-Portrait in a Convex Mirror* is ''a collection of poems of breathtaking freshness and adventure in which dazzling orchestrations of language open up whole areas of consciousness no other American poet has even begun to explore. . . . The influence of films now shows in Ashbery's deft control of just those cinematic devices a poet can most usefully appropriate. Crosscut, flashback, montage, close-up, fade-out—he employs them all to generate the kinetic excitement that starts on the first page of his book and continues to the last.''

As Brinnon's analysis suggests, Ashbery's verse has taken shape under the influence of films and other art forms. The abstract expressionist movement in modern painting, stressing nonrepresentational methods of picturing reality, is an especially important presence in his work. ''Modern art was the first and most powerful influence on Ashbery,'' Helen McNeil notes in the *Times Literary Supplement*. ''When he began to write in the 1950s, American poetry was constrained and formal while American abstract-expressionist art was vigorously taking over the heroic responsibilities of the European avant-garde. . . . Ashbery remarks that no one now thinks it odd that Picasso painted faces with eyes and mouth in the wrong place, while the hold of realism in literature is such that the same kind of image in a poem would still be considered shocking.''

True to this influence, Ashbery's poems, according to Fred Moramarco, are a ''verbal canvas'' upon which the poet freely applies the techniques of expressionism. Moramarco, writing in the *Journal of Modern Literature,* finds that Ashbery's verse, maligned by many critics for being excessively obscure, becomes less difficult to understand when examined in relation to modern art. ''*The Tennis Court Oath* is still a book that arouses passions in critics and readers [, some of whom have criticized] its purposeful obscurity. . . . For me it becomes approachable, explicable, and even down-right lucid when read with some of the esthetic assumptions of Abstract Expressionism in mind. . . . The techniques of juxtaposition developed by the Abstract painters, particularly [Mark] Rothko and [Adolph] Gottlieb, can be related to the verbal juxtaposition we find in *The Tennis Court Oath,* where words clash and interact with one another to invigorate our sense of the creative possibilities of language. . . . What we confront [in the title poem], it seems to me, is constantly shifting verbal perceptions. . . . [Jackson] Pollock's drips, Rothko's haunting, color-drenched, luminous, rectangular shapes, and Gottlieb's spheres and explosive strokes are here, in a sense, paralleled by an imagistic scattering and emotional and intellectual verbal juxtaposition.''

In the same article, Moramarco reviews ''Self-Portrait in a Convex Mirror,'' a long poem inspired by a work by the Renaissance painter Francesco Parmigianino, and is ''struck by Ashbery's unique ability to explore the verbal implications of painterly space, to capture the verbal nuances of Parmigianino's fixed and distorted image. The poem virtually resonates or extends the painter's meaning. It transforms visual impact to verbal precision. . . . It seems to me Ashbery's intention in 'Self-Portrait' is to record verbally the emotional truth contained in Parmigianino's painting. Visual images do not have to conform to verbal *thinking,* and it is this sort of universe that Ashbery's poetry has consistently evoked.'' And Jonathan Holden believes that ''Ashbery is the first American poet to successfully carry out the possibilities of analogy between poetry and 'abstract expressionist' painting. He has succeeded so well for two reasons: he is the first poet to identify the *correct* correspondences between painting and writing; he is the first poet to explore the analogy who has possessed the *skill* to *produce* a first-rate 'abstract expressionist' poetry, a poetry as beautiful and sturdy as the paintings of William de Kooning.'' In the *American Poetry Review,* Holden says that ''it is Ashbery's genius not only to be able to execute syntax with heft, but to perceive that syntax in writing is the equivalent of 'composition' in painting: it has an intrinsic beauty and authority almost wholly independent of any specific context. Thus, in Ashbery's poetry, the isolation of verse is analogous to the framing of a painting; and each sentence . . . is analogous to a 'brushstroke' . . . recorded in paint on a canvas.''

Ashbery's experience as an art critic has strengthened his ties to abstract expressionism and instilled in his poetry a sensitivity to the interrelatedness of artistic mediums. As he once commented in an essay on the American artist and architect Saul Steinberg: ''Why shouldn't a painting tell a story, or not tell it, as it sees fit? Why should poetry be intellectual and nonsensory, or the reverse? Our eyes, minds, and feelings do not exist in isolated compartments but are part of each other, constantly crosscutting, consulting and reinforcing each other. An art constructed to the above canons, or any others, will wither away since, having left one or more of the faculties out of account, it will eventually lose the attention of the others.''

Ashbery's verbal expressionism has attracted a mixed critical response. James Schevill, in a *Saturday Review* article on *The Tennis Court Oath,* writes: ''The trouble with Ashbery's work is that he is influenced by modern painting to the point where he tries to apply words to the page as if they were abstract, emotional colors and shapes. . . . Consequently, his work loses coherence. . . . There is little substance to the poems in this book.'' In the *New York Times Book Review,* X. J. Kennedy praises the book: '''I attempt to use words abstractly,' [Ashbery] declares, 'as an artist uses paint'. . . . If the reader can shut off that portion of the brain which insists words be related logically, he may dive with pleasure into Ashbery's stream of consciousness.'' And Moramarco believes Ashbery's technique has an invigorating effect: ''We become caught up in the rich, vitalized verbal canvas he has painted for us, transported from the mundane and often tedious realities of our daily lives to this exotic, marvelous world. . . . Literature and art can provide these moments of revitalization for us, and although we must always return to the real world, our esthetic encounters impinge upon our sensibilities and leave us altered.''

Many critics have commented on the manner in which Ashbery's fluid style has helped to convey a major concern in his poetry: the refusal to impose an arbitrary order on a world of flux and chaos. In his verse, Ashbery attempts to mirror the stream of perceptions of which human consciousness is composed. His poems move, often without continuity, from one image to the next, prompting some critics to praise his expressionist technique and others to accuse him of producing art which is unintelligible, even meaningless.

"Reality, for Ashbery, is elusive, and things are never what they seem to be. They cannot be separated from one another, isolated into component parts, but overlap, intersect, and finally merge into an enormous and constantly changing whole," Paul Auster writes in *Harper's*. "Ashbery's manner of dealing with this flux is associative rather than logical, and his pessimism about our ever really being able to know anything results, paradoxically, in a poetry that is open to everything. . . . His language is discursive, rhetorical, and even long-winded, a kind of obsessive talking *around* things, suggesting a reality that refuses to come forth and let itself be known."

In the *American Poetry Review,* W. S. Di Piero states: "Ashbery wonders at the processes of change he sees in people, in the seasons, in language, but his perception of the things about him also persuades him that nothing has ever really changed. . . . If all things, all thought and feeling, are subject to time's revisions, then what can we ever know? What events, what feelings can we ever trust? In exploring questions such as these, Ashbery has experimented with forms of dislocated language as one way of jarring things into order; his notorious twisting of syntax is really an attempt to straighten things out, to clarify the problems at hand." David Kalstone, in his book *Five Temperaments,* comments: "In his images of thwarted nature, of discontinuity between past and present, Ashbery has turned his agitation into a principle of composition. From the start he has looked for sentences, diction, a syntax which would make these feelings fully and fluidly available." "Robbed of their solid properties, the smallest and surest of words become part of a new geography," Kalstone writes of *The Double Dream of Spring* in the *New York Times Book Review*. To explore this "new geography," Kalstone notes, the reader must immerse himself in Ashbery's language and "learn something like a new musical scale."

Closely related to Ashbery's use of language as a "new musical scale" is his celebration of the world's various motions and drives. Under the poet's care, the most ordinary aspects of our lives leap into a new reality—a world filled with the joyous and bizarre. In his book *The Poem in Its Skin,* Paul Carroll finds that "one quality most of Ashbery's poems share . . . is something like the peculiar excitement one feels when stepping with Alice behind the Looking Glass into a reality bizarre yet familiar in which the 'marvelous' is as near as one's breakfast coffee cup or one's shoes. . . . His gift is to release everyday objects, experiences and fragments of dreams or hallucinations from stereotypes imposed on them by habit or preconception or belief: he presents the world as if seen for the first time." In a review of *Self-Portrait in a Convex Mirror* for *Harper's,* Paul Auster contends that "few poets today have such an uncanny ability to undermine our certainties, to articulate so fully the ambiguous zones of our consciousness. We are constantly thrown off guard as we read his poems. . . . The ordinary becomes strange, and things that a moment ago seemed clear are cast into doubt. Everything remains in place, and yet nothing is the same." Edmund White, appraising *As We Know* in *Washington Post Book World,* writes: "As David Shapiro has pointed out in his critical study, . . . all [of Ashbery's] long poems tend to end on a joyful note, though one harmonized with doubt and anguish. In [the conclusion of 'Litany'] the poet rejects the equation of life and text in order to acknowledge the rich messiness of experience. Like the familiar example of the bee which is aerodynamically impossible but doesn't know so and flies anyway, the poet—though faced with death, crushed under history and immersed in the fog of daily life—evinces a will to joy and thereby, becomes joyful."

Several critics have suggested that this joyful quality is sometimes contradicted by an intellectualism and obscurity present in Ashbery's verse. Victor Howes, reviewing *Houseboat Days* for the *Christian Science Monitor,* calls the poet "a kaleidoscope of Daffy Duck and Amadis de Gaul, of root beer stands and lines from Sir Thomas Wyatt and old Scotch ballads, or art-deco and scrimshaw," but, Howes asks, "does he touch the heart? Does he know the passions? My dear. My dear. Really, sometimes you ask too much." J. A. Avant of *Library Journal* argues that in *The Double Dream of Spring* "emotion has been intellectualized to the extent that it is almost nonexistent," while Pearl K. Bell comments in the *New Leader:* "Long stretches of 'Self-Portrait' read like the bland prose of an uninspired scholar, complete with references and quotations. Bleached of feeling and poetic surprise, the words gasp for air, stutter, go dead." In a *New York Review of Books* article on *The Double Dream of Spring,* Robert Mazzocco finds that "in Ashbery there has always been a catlike presence, both in the poems themselves and in the person these poems reveal: tender, curious, cunning, tremendously independent, sweet, guarded. Above all, like a cat, Ashbery is a born hunter: now prowling through deepest Africa; now chasing leaves or scraps of paper, rolling over and over, and then curling up, happily exhausted, beneath a bush. . . . But the one prime act of the cat—to spring, to pounce, to make the miraculous leap—Ashbery, for me, has yet to perform."

In *The Poem in Its Skin,* Carroll examines Ashbery's "Leaving the Atocha Station" and finds that "several close readings fail to offer a suspicion of a clue as to what it might be all about. I . . . feel annoyed: the poem makes me feel stupid. . . . [The] narrative skelton is fleshed out by skin and features made from meaningless phrases, images and occasional sentences. In this sense, 'Leaving the Atocha Station' out-Dadas Dada: it is *totally* meaningless. . . . The most obvious trait is the general sense that the reader has wandered into somebody else's dream or hallucination." After suggesting several ways to read the poem, Carroll concludes that "the reader should feel free to do whatever he wants with the words in this poem. . . . I also suspect some readers will respond to Ashbery's invitation that the reader too become a poet as rereads [the poem]." As Ashbery explains in an essay on Gertrude Stein in *Poetry,* a poem is "a hymn to possibility," "a general, all-purpose model which each reader can adapt to fit his own set of particulars." In the *New York Review of Books,* Irvin Ehrenpreis comments on Ashbery's assessment of the participatory nature of poetry: "The poem itself must become an exercise in re-examining the world from which the self has become alienated. We must confront its language with the same audacity that we want when confronting the darkened world within us and without. To offer a clear meaning would be to fix the reader in his place, to turn him away from the proper business of poetry by directing him to an apparent subject. . . . The act of reading must become the purpose of the poem. Consequently, the poem must stand by itself as the world stands by itself. It must change as the world changes. It must offer the same challenge as the world."

Carney contends that the possibilities inherent in an Ashbery poem often create confusion rather than interpretative freedom:

"Ashbery's poetry is a continuous criticism of all the ways in which literature would tidy up experience and make the world safe for poetry. But it must be admitted that the poetry that results is frequently maddening because of Ashbery's willingness to lose himself in a sea of details and memories even if it means losing the reader. Even [a judicious critic] can be baited into a fit of pique by Ashbery's randomness." In a review of *As We Know* for the *Chicago Tribune Book World,* Joseph Parisi grants that Ashbery's "'subject matter' remains incomprehensible, to be sure—the whole world of sensible objects, memories, and feelings, in all their profusion, variety, and flux," but nevertheless insists: "As these streams of everyday and extraordinary objects flow past us in no apparent order, but always in wondrously lyrical lines, the poems make their own curious kind of sense. After all, isn't this how we perceive 'reality'? . . . Ashbery's poems imply the improbability of finding ultimate significance amid the evanescence and transience of modern life. If however, in the process of these poems the old order is lost or irrelevant, the *longing* for it or some kind of meaning is not."

Di Piero describes the reaction of critics to Ashbery's style as "amusing. On the one hand are those who berate him for lacking the Audenesque 'censor' (that little editing machine in a poet's head which deletes all superfluous materials) or who accuse him of simply being willfully and unreasonably perverse. On the other hand are those reviewers who, queerly enough, praise the difficulty of Ashbery's verse as if difficulty were a positive literary value in itself, while ignoring what the poet is saying. I think that Ashbery's 'difficulty' (grammatical ellipses, misapplied substantives, fragmented verb phrases, etc.) is a function of his meaning. . . . Ashbery avoids generalized declarations of his vision of our fragmented, unpredictable world. Instead, he gives us a feel for the elusive processes of change." Vendler offers this summary in the *New Yorker:* "It is Ashbery's style that has obsessed reviewers, as they alternately wrestle with its elusive impermeability and praise its power of linguistic synthesis. There have been able descriptions of its fluid syntax, its insinuating momentum, its generality of reference, its incorporation of vocabulary from all the arts and sciences. But it is popularly believed, with some reason, that the style itself is impenetrable, that it is impossible to say what an Ashbery poem is 'about.' An alternative view says that every Ashbery poem is about poetry."

This alternative view emphasizes Ashbery's concern with the nature of the creative act, particularly as it applies to the writing of poetry. This is, Peter Stitt notes, a major theme of *Houseboat Days,* a volume acclaimed by Marjorie Perloff in *Washington Post Book World* as "the most exciting, most original book of poems to have appeared in the 1970s." Ashbery shares with the abstract expressionists of painting "a preoccupation with the art process itself," Stitt writes in the *Georgia Review.* "Ashbery has come to write, in the poet's most implicitly ironic gesture, almost exclusively about his own poems, the ones he is writing as he writes about them. The artist becomes his own theoretical critic, caught in the critical lens even at the moment of conception." Roger Shattuck makes a similar point in the *New York Review of Books:* "Nearly every poem in *Houseboat Days* shows that Ashbery's phenomenological eye fixes itself not so much on ordinary living and doing as on the specific act of composing a poem. Writing on Frank O'Hara's work, Ashbery defined a poem as 'the chronicle of the creative act that produces it.' Thus every poem becomes an *ars poetica* of its own condition." Ashbery's examination of creativity, according to Paul Breslin in *Poetry,* is a "prison of self-reference" which detracts from the poet's "lyrical genius." *New Leader*'s Phoebe Pettingell, however, argues that "Ashbery carries the saw that 'poetry does not have subject matter because it is the subject' to its furthest limit. Just as we feel we are beginning to make sense of one of his poems, meaning eludes us again. . . . Still, we are somehow left with a sense that the conclusion is satisfactory, with a wondering delight at what we've heard. And since a primary function of poetry is giving pleasure, Ashbery ranks very high. . . . *Houseboat Days* is evidence of the transcendent power of the imagination, and one of the major works of our time."

Ashbery's poetry, as critics have observed, has evolved under a variety of influences besides modern art, becoming in the end the expression of a voice unmistakably his own. Among the influences that have been discerned in his verse are the Romantic tradition in American poetry that progresses from Whitman to Wallace Stevens, the so-called "New York School of Poets," featuring contemporaries such as Frank O'Hara and Kenneth Koch, and the French surrealist writers with whom Ashbery has dealt in his work as a critic and translator. In *The Fierce Embrace,* Charles Molesworth traces Ashbery's development: "The first few books by John Ashbery contained a large proportion of a poetry of inconsequence. Borrowing freely from the traditions of French surrealism, and from his friends Frank O'Hara and Kenneth Koch, Ashbery tried out a fairly narrow range of voices and subjects. Subject matter, or rather the absence of it, helped form the core of his aesthetic, an aesthetic that refused to maintain a consistent attitude toward any fixed phenomena. The poems tumbled out of a whimsical, detached amusement that mixed with a quizzical melancholy. . . . With the exception of *The Tennis Court Oath,* Ashbery's first four commercially published books. . . . included some poems with interpretable meanings and recognizable structures. But reading the first four books together, one is struck by how precious are those poems that do make poetic sense, surrounded as they are by the incessant chatter of the poems of inconsequence. Slowly, however, it appears as if Ashbery was gaining confidence for his true project, and, as his work unfolds, an indulging reader can see how it needed those aggressively bland 'experiments' in nonsense to protect its frailty." Ashbery's "true project," Molesworth believes, is *Self-Portrait in a Convex Mirror.* Many reviewers agree with Molesworth that this volume, especially the long title poem, is Ashbery's "masterpiece."

Essentially a meditation of the painting "Self-Portrait in a Convex Mirror" by Parmigianino, the narrative poem focuses on many of the themes present in Ashbery's work. "I have lived with John Ashbery's 'Self-Portrait in a Convex Mirror' as with a favorite mistress for the past nine months," Laurence Lieberman declares in his book *Unassigned Frequencies.* "Often, for whole days of inhabiting *the room* of its dream, I have felt that it is the only poem—and Ashbery the only author—in my life. It is what I most want from a poem. Or an author." Lieberman finds that "when I put this poem down I catch myself in the act of seeing objects and events in the world as through different—though amazingly novel *other* eyes: the brilliantly varied other life of surfaces has been wonderfully revivified, and I take this transformation to be an accurate index of the impact of Ashbery's poetry upon the modus operandi of my perception." Like Molesworth, Lieberman believes that Ashbery's early work, though "unreadable," was an "indispensable detour that precipitated, finally, the elevated vision of Ashbery's recent work. . . . Following his many years of withdrawal and seclusion, a period of slow mellowing, this exactly appointed occasion has been granted to him. A reader feels he can bodily sense an immense weight lifting, as if Ashbery has been relieved, suddenly, of the burden of guilt and bewilderment that two decades of self-imposed ostracism that his choice of direction as an artist . . . had condemned him to, years of lonely waiting to connect with a viable audience, and to expedite human good fellowship with a widespread community of readers.''

Like other critics, Lieberman believes that Ashbery was once overly concerned with examining the nature of art and creativity, with escaping into his poems and ''producing forms that achieved a semblance of ideal beauty.'' In ''Self-Portrait,'' Lieberman contends, ''Ashbery forecloses irrevocably on the mortgage of an *ars poetica* which conceives the poem as 'exotic refuge,' and advances to an aesthetic which carries a full burden of mirroring the age's ills.'' Unlike Parmigianino, who retreated into his hermitage, Ashbery ventures out from ''the comfortable sanctuary of the dream'' to confront the world. ''His new art achieves a powerful re-engagement with the human community,'' Lieberman concludes. ''That is his honorable quest.''

CA INTERVIEW

CA interviewed John Ashbery on June 26, 1981, at his apartment in New York City.

CA: Each book of poems since your first, Some Trees, *has featured a long poem, but* Shadow Train *doesn't. Was that a conscious decision?*

ASHBERY: Well, I'm always trying not to repeat myself, and since most of my books *do* have a long poem, it occurred to me that one way of doing that would be to *not* have one this time, to just have short poems. Since I'm known for writing very long ones, I thought I'd just see what it's like if I don't. It's as simple as that really.

CA: Did the idea for poems of the same length come after you had written a few?

ASHBERY: I think I decided arbitrarily in advance that I would write fifty of them, and that they would be that length. That sounds sort of silly, but I think that's the way writing gets done in many cases. You start out with some rather arbitrary, schematic idea. When I wrote *Three Poems*—actually I hadn't decided to do that until I was well into writing the first one—but, I thought of them as sort of three empty boxes that I would fill with something or other. And then there were a few very vague notions of what I would write about. It wasn't planned.

CA: Was it the same with ''Litany?''

ASHBERY: I think so, but I can't really remember. It seems to me that I had begun writing it for some time before I was aware of it. I can't remember what I had in mind.

CA: Had you thought of putting two columns side by side before that?

ASHBERY: Yes. In fact there's a poem in *The Tennis Court Oath,* a short one, which does that. It's one that I never think of myself, and I had probably forgotten I'd done it when I thought I was doing it for the first time. I don't have total recall of my work.

CA: Another example of ''simultaneous but independent'' voices is your collaboration with Elliott Carter, ''Syringa.'' Were you happy with the result?

ASHBERY: Yes, I liked it very much. It was recently performed twice in New York—I heard it again with two different mezzos—and I'd been at the premier several years ago. I like his music very much; in fact, I think the idea of these parallel voices might have had something to do with my listening to his music a lot. There are these separate monologues which kind of interlock, but kind of don't, in much of his music. In particular, there's one piece he wrote for violin and piano which at the first performance had the violinist at one end and the pianist at the other end of this rather long stage. I think I must have heard that shortly before beginning to write ''Litany''.

CA: How do you feel about ''Litany'' now?

ASHBERY: I don't know. I'm quite puzzled by my work too, along with a lot of other people. I was always intrigued by it, but at the same time a little apprehensive and sort of embarrassed about annoying the same critics who are always annoyed by my work. I'm kind of sorry that I cause so much grief. Still, I thought that something interesting might happen just by the juxtaposition of the two monologues, and I think it does.

CA: What do you make of the criticism that the right column of ''Litany'' is much stronger than the left?

ASHBERY: This seems to be a theory that's gained some ground, though I don't know why that should be. When I wrote it I would write one column on a page of typewriter paper one day, and then the right-hand column the next, and then on to the next page. So it seems there should be no reason for any qualitative difference. That's the problem with criticism; you can't get anywhere unless you start with basic false premises, which you then build on and say true things.

CA: How much attention do you pay to what's written about you? And has that changed as you've become well known?

ASHBERY: Well, originally my books very seldom *got* reviewed, and I was greedy for any little mention anywhere. Now I tend not to read criticism, particularly if it's favorable. If it's unfavorable I'm more interested, although I often don't finish. I'm glad that it's there, but in a way it doesn't help me.

CA: In one of your own critical pieces, a review of the Picasso exhibition in New York last spring, you said that Picasso seemed to consider his art ''the mere by-product of the act of creation.'' The act is what counts. Does that apply to your own work?

ASHBERY: That's sort of how I feel about it, although I take the by-product fairly seriously. I fool around with it until it's . . .

CA: Just right?

ASHBERY: Well, just right as it can be. But in a way that's true because I usually start with very few preconceptions of what I'm writing, and not very much memory afterwards of what I was doing. It's a sort of attention that occasionally I feel I can bring to focus on what's happening right now. And then that stops, and something is there which I'd like to call a poem.

CA: Reading one of your reviews and then one of your poems, it's hard to believe they could come from the same person. Is it useful to your poetry, that ability in nonfiction to make perfectly lucid, unambiguous statements?

ASHBERY: Sure. Just as I do in my poetry. When I was living in Paris and writing for the *Herald Tribune* once or twice a week, it dawned on me that if I could produce this much writing for somebody else, I might very well be able to produce a little more for myself. The idea of having deadlines and being forced to write eventually made me less inhibited about sitting down and trying to write poetry.

CA: But those poems never seem to talk about being an art critic or a teacher. I'm wondering how your daily life relates to your poetry.

ASHBERY: I'm wondering too. It does relate in the sense that I'll often incorporate things that are close by, things on my desk, for instance. In fact it was a little embarrassing lately. Did you see this review of *As We Know* that just came out in the *Times Literary Supplement?* It uses a quotation from "Litany". [READS]:

. . . *I would soon again be the same man as before*—Meaning: *the same nausea when I heard cheerful talk, The same grief, the same deep and prolonged meditation, And almost the same frenzy and oppression.*

That actually is a bit of collage from Leopardi. When I was writing I had a xeroxed assignment for my students on the desk—a translation of a page from Leopardi's journals—and a page of some technical manual—the assignment was to somehow combine the two texts. I was thinking that if Leopardi's translator saw this review, there could be a new Jacob Epstein-Martin Amis controversy.

CA: Do you see yourself doing any more collaborations?

ASHBERY: I haven't written any in a long time. It's something that was sort of "in the air" twenty years ago. It was a perhaps puritanical notion that you shouldn't have any private property; therefore, if you wrote something with somebody else it would be collective and not yours. I was never entirely satisfied with any of the collaborations—except for *A Nest of Ninnies,* which I enjoy but it's kind of a trifle—yet I would come up with lines that I probably wouldn't have thought of on my own, and even though these were parts of a joint work, they could have resonances later on.

CA: How did you and James Schuyler work together on A Nest of Ninnies*?*

ASHBERY: We can't remember in a lot of cases who wrote what. We started writing it as a sort of pastime while we were riding in a car. We never expected that it would even be finished, much less published. This was almost thirty years ago, before we had a reputation or anything, and we'd sort of forget it for long periods and then do some more. It was just a game. Then I went away and lived mostly in France for ten years, during which we didn't work on it at all. When I got back I happened to mention it to an editor who said, "That sounds great, why don't you finish it?" So we put on a burst of energy and did.

CA: Would you go back to live in France?

ASHBERY: No. It's like a closed chapter in my life. I enjoy being there, but I don't feel drawn to it. I guess I do feel nostalgic when I'm there, a sad nostalgia.

CA: Do you think the mystique of being in Europe for ten years was a help to your career?

ASHBERY: It might have been, yes, because while my friends were becoming known here in New York—Kenneth Koch, Frank O'Hara, etc., etc.—I wasn't in the picture. I would get talked about and people would wonder who I was. A certain amount of curiosity built up, I guess.

CA: One critic thought popularity might be worrying you. Is it?

ASHBERY: It doesn't exactly worry me. I don't mind being popular but I do sometimes wonder, why? It doesn't seem as though this would be the kind of thing that becomes popular. I'm not sure that it is actually popular, but it's "talked about" a lot. I survived so long without any attention or feedback, I guess I became more resilient and self-sufficient. And then when it started to happen it was all very unexpected, and *nice* certainly—I guess I always wanted my work to become known. I just never thought it would.

CA: What have you been working on since Shadow Train*?*

ASHBERY: Last winter I wrote a prose piece of about twelve typescript pages called "Description of a Masque." The title comes from a work by Thomas Campion. Anyway, that will probably be coming out in limited edition with art work. I've also written a couple of prose poems, one of which will be appearing in the *Virginia Quarterly*. Besides that I haven't written much really—ten or twelve poems, maybe twenty at the most.

CA: With all your other commitments it's a wonder you have time to write. Is this a pace you can keep up?

ASHBERY: I don't know. I certainly hope so. I've come to the regrettable conclusion that I work best when I have too much to do. I mean, I can always write, there's always time enough to write. What I really need is time to sit around and do nothing, to think about nothing.

BIOGRAPHICAL/CRITICAL SOURCES—Books: William Packard, editor, *The Craft of Poetry,* Doubleday, 1964; Paris Leary and Robert Kelly, editors, *A Controversy of Poets,* Doubleday, 1965; Stephen Stepanchev, *American Poetry since 1945: A Critical Survey,* Harper, 1965; Richard Kostelanetz, editor, *The New American Arts,* Horizon Press, 1965; Paul Carroll, *The Poem in Its Skin,* Follett, 1968; John Bernard Meyers, editor, *The Poets of the New York School,* University of Pennsylvania Press, 1969; Richard Howard, *Alone with America: Essays on the Art of Poetry in the United States since 1950,* Athenuem, 1969; Kenneth Koch, *Rose, Where Did You Get That Red?,* Random House, 1973; Walter Sutton, *American Free Verse: The Modern Revolution in Poetry,* New Directions, 1973; Robert B. Shaw, editor, *American Poetry since 1960: Some Critical Perspectives,* Carcanet Press, 1973; Dore Ashton, *The New York School: A Cultural Reckoning,* Viking, 1973; *Contemporary Literary Criticism,* Gale, Volume II, 1974, Volume III, 1975, Volume IV, 1975, Volume VI, 1976, Volume IX, 1978; Volume XIII, 1980, Volume XV, 1980.

David K. Kermani, *John Ashbery: A Comprehensive Bibliography,* Garland Publishing, 1976; David Kalstone, *Five*

Temperaments: Elizabeth Bishop, Robert Lowell, James Merrill, Adrienne Rich, John Ashbery, Oxford University Press, 1977; Laurence Lieberman, *Unassigned Frequencies: American Poetry in Review, 1964-1977,* University of Illinois Press, 1977; Kostelanetz, *The Old Poetries and the New,* University of Michigan Press, 1979; Charles Molesworth, *The Fierce Embrace: A Study of Contemporary American Poetry,* University of Missouri Press, 1979; David Lehman, editor, *John Ashbery,* Cornell University Press, 1979; David Shapiro, *John Ashbery: An Introduction to the Poetry,* Columbia University Press, 1979; Lehman, editor, *Beyond Amazement: New Essays on John Ashbery,* Cornell University Press, 1980; *Dictionary of Literary Biography,* Gale, Volume V: *American Poets since World War II,* 1980, *Yearbook: 1981,* 1981.

Periodicals: *New York Times,* April 15, 1956; *Saturday Review,* June 16, 1956, May 5, 1962, August 8, 1970, July 8, 1972, September 17, 1977; *New Yorker,* September 1, 1956, March 24, 1969, March 16, 1981; *Poetry,* July, 1957, September, 1962, December, 1966, October, 1970, August, 1972, October, 1980; *New York Times Book Review,* July 15, 1962, February 11, 1968, May 4, 1969, June 8, 1969, July 5, 1970, April 9, 1972, August 2, 1975, November 13, 1977, January 6, 1980, September 6, 1981; *Christian Science Monitor,* September 6, 1962, March 9, 1970, October 12, 1977, December 3, 1979; *New York Review of Books,* April 14, 1966, December 14, 1973, October 16, 1975, March 23, 1978, January 24, 1980, July 16, 1981; *Nation,* December 12, 1966, April 14, 1969, September 3, 1977, November 11, 1978; *New Statesman,* June 16, 1967; January 4, 1980, April 24, 1981; *Times Literary Supplement,* September 14, 1967, July 25, 1975, September 1, 1978, March 14, 1980, June 5, 1981, October 8, 1982; *Contemporary Literature,* winter, 1968, spring, 1969; *Yale Review,* October, 1969, June, 1970, winter, 1981.

Library Journal, January 1, 1970; *Harper's,* April, 1970, November, 1975; *Hudson Review,* spring, 1970, autumn, 1975, autumn, 1976, spring, 1978, autumn, 1980, winter, 1981; *Virginia Quarterly Review,* autumn, 1970, winter, 1973, spring, 1976, spring, 1979, spring, 1980; *Western Humanities Review,* winter, 1971; *New York Quarterly,* winter, 1972; *Partisan Review,* fall, 1972, summer, 1976; *Parnassus,* fall-winter, 1972, fall-winter, 1977, spring-summer, 1978, fall-winter, 1979; *Commentary,* February, 1973; *American Poetry Review,* August-September, 1973, September-October, 1978, July-August, 1979, July-August, 1981; *Georgia Review,* winter, 1975, winter, 1978, summer, 1980; *Washington Post Book World,* May 11, 1975, October 30, 1977, December 11, 1977, November 25, 1979, June 7, 1981; *New Leader,* May 26, 1975, November 7, 1977, January 29, 1981; *New Republic,* June 14, 1975, November 29, 1975, November 26, 1977, December 29, 1979; *Spectator,* November 22, 1975; *Village Voice,* January 19, 1976, October 17, 1977, December 26, 1977; *Sewanee Review,* April, 1976, April, 1978, July, 1980; *Time,* April 26, 1976; *New York Times Sunday Magazine,* May 23, 1976, February 3, 1980; *Journal of Modern Literature,* September, 1976; *Listener,* August 18, 1977; *Newsweek,* September 26, 1977; *New York Arts Journal,* November-December, 1977; *Esquire,* January, 1978; *Southern Review,* April, 1978; *Poet and Critic,* Volume XI, number 3, 1979; *Observer,* December 9, 1979, December 16, 1979; *Chicago Tribune Book World,* January 27, 1980, July 26, 1981; *Encounter,* April, 1980; *Booklist,* May 1, 1981; *Village Voice Literary Supplement,* October, 1981.†

—Sketch by Stewart R. Hakola

—Interview by Dana Yeaton

ASHFORD, Jeffrey
See JEFFRIES, Roderic (Graeme)

* * *

ASHLEY, Leonard R(aymond) N(elligan) 1928-

PERSONAL: Born December 5, 1928, in Miami, Fla.; son of Leonard Saville (a lawyer) and Anne Constance (Nelligan) Ashley. *Education:* McGill University, B.A. (first class honors in English), 1949, M.A., 1950; Princeton University, A.M., 1953, Ph.D., 1956. *Religion:* Episcopalian. *Home:* 1901 Avenue H, Brooklyn, N.Y. 11230. *Office:* Department of English, Brooklyn College of the City University of New York, Brooklyn, N.Y. 11210.

CAREER: University of Utah, Salt Lake City, instructor in English, 1953-55; University of Rochester, Rochester, N.Y., instructor in English, 1958-61; New School for Social Research, New York, N.Y., lecturer, 1961-72; Brooklyn College of the City University of New York, Brooklyn, N.Y., instructor, 1961-64, assistant professor, 1964-67, associate professor, 1967-71, professor of English, 1971—. Has presented papers at a number of scholarly conferences in the United States and abroad. Founder and director of an experimental theater at University of Rochester. Reader and consultant for several publishing companies, including Harper & Row. *Military service:* Royal Canadian Air Force, 1955-58; stationed in Canada, England, and France; became flying officer.

MEMBER: International Linguistic Association (secretary-treasurer, 1980—), International Congress of Onomastic Sciences (member of executive council, 1980-81), Modern Language Association of America, American Association of University Professors (vice-president of Brooklyn College Chapter, 1970-72, president, 1972-74, member of executive council, 1974-75; secretary-treasurer of City University of New York Council, 1972-73, member of executive council, 1974-75), American Name Society (vice-president, 1976-78, president, 1979; member of board of managers, 1981-83), New England Modern Language Association, McGill Graduates' Society of New York (vice-president, 1970-71, president, 1971-75). *Awards, honors:* Shakespeare Gold Medal; three fellowships from Princeton University; research grants from three universities.

WRITINGS: (Contributor) F. F. Liu, *A Military History of Modern China,* Princeton University Press, 1956; (contributor) E.P.J. Corbett, *Classical Rhetoric for the Modern Student,* Oxford University Press, 1965; *Colley Cibber,* Twayne, 1965; *George Peele,* Twayne, 1966; (editor) *Nineteenth-Century British Drama: An Anthology of Representative Plays,* Scott, 1967; (editor with Stuart Astor) *British Short Stories: Classics and Criticism,* Prentice-Hall, 1967; *Authorship and Evidence in Renaissance Drama,* Droz (Geneva), 1968; (editor) *Other Peoples Lives: Thirty-Four Short Stories,* Houghton, 1970; *Mirrors for Man: Twenty-Six Plays of the World Drama,* Winthrop Publishing, 1974; *Tales of Mystery and Melodrama,* Barron's, 1977.

Also author of musical comedies, produced at McGill University and University of Rochester, of radio programs, and of television scripts. Contributing editor, "Enriched Classics" series and "Collateral Classics" series, both published by Simon & Schuster, and of "Papertexts" series; editor of books for Scholars' Facsimiles and Reprints, including *Phantasms of the Living, Shakespeare's Jest Book,* and *The Ballad Poetry of Ireland;* also editor of military history books, including *The Air Defence of North America.* Contributor to anthologies; contributor to a number of encyclopedias and reference books. Contributor of articles to journals, including *Shakespeare Newsletter, College English, Verbatim, Maledicta,* and *Dracula Journals,* of reviews to *Educational Theatre Journal, Names,* and other periodicals, of translations to magazines, including *Shenandoah,* and of poetry to *Western Humanities Review, Carleton Miscellany, Evidence,* and other journals.

WORK IN PROGRESS: Dozens of book and article projects in various stages of completion.

SIDELIGHTS: Leonard R.N. Ashley told *CA:* "As a reader for a number of university presses, I see many good books to recommend which do not reach print. As a reader for Harper & Row and other textbook publishers, I know how few proposals are actually marketed. Though I publish hundreds of pages of articles each year, I see that younger scholars are having an increasingly difficult time in the 'publish or perish' world of Academe (when they can find jobs at all). And I fear that, especially in the Humanities, opportunities are ever shrinking. With fewer electives and more unprepared graduate students, even senior professors find it more and more difficult to relate publication to teaching; moreover, the system requires those seeking promotion to slight the 'big book' (which takes years) and to churn out lots of smaller pieces, a habit which does not disappear when the top rank is reached.

"I am grateful for the Shakespeare Gold Medal, three Princeton fellowships, research grants from three universities, a full professorship in a municipal college with a distinguished fifty-year history and an exciting future under a vigorous and far-sighted president, but it is difficult to recommend the profession to would-be scholars just starting out. My own plans are to learn the new language (computers) and to adapt the old learning to new technologies (especially television), and I expect much of my future 'publication' to be in courses and materials for 'distance learning' and broadcasting.

"For some of us in academic pursuits, despite retrenchment and remediation and reduced income (the new Three R's), there is still the wonderful opportunity to study and write about whatever we like, and it is a marvel that a hard-pressed society is willing to pay even a favored few to do what they would do for nothing."

* * *

AULTMAN, Richard E(ugene) 1933-

PERSONAL: Born December 21, 1933, in Moline, Ill.; son of Chester Clyde and Margaret Augusta (Klouser) Aultman; married Marjorie Katherine Kirk, November 4, 1974; children: Kimberly Ann, Michael Stewart, Marjorie Katherine. *Education:* Northwestern University, B.A., 1956, M.S., 1957. *Religion:* Congregationalist. *Home:* 2 Cedar Lane, Weston, Conn. 06880.

CAREER: Decatur Herald-Review, Decatur, Ill., sports reporter, 1957-59; *Chicago Sun-Times,* Chicago, Ill., copy editor, 1959; *Golf Digest,* Norwalk, Conn., associate editor, 1959-61, executive editor, 1961-64, editor, 1964-73, contributing editor, 1973—. *Member:* Golf Writers Association of America, Beta Theta Pi. *Awards, honors:* MacGregor-Brunswick golf writers' award in magazine division from National Golf Writers Championship, 1963.

WRITINGS: (With Gary Player) *Golf Secrets,* Prentice-Hall, 1962; *Learn to Play Golf,* Rand-McNally, 1966.

Square-to-Square Golf Swing: Model Method for the Modern Player, Golf Digest, 1970; (with Bob Toski) *Touch System for Better Golf,* Golf Digest, 1971; (with Eddie Merrins) *Swing the Handle, Not the Clubhead,* Golf Digest, 1973; (with Jack Grout) *Play Golf As I Taught Jack Nicklaus,* Atheneum, 1975; (with Ken Bowden) *Methods of Golf's Masters,* Coward, 1975; (with Lee Trevino) *Groove Your Golf Swing My Way,* Atheneum, 1976; (with Sam Snead) *Golf Begins at Forty,* Dial, 1978; (with John Jacobs) *Quick Cures for Weekend Golfers,* Simon & Schuster, 1979; (with Paul Runyan) *The Short Way to Lower Scoring,* Golf Digest, 1979.

Better Golf in Six Swings, Golf Digest, 1981; *101 Ways to Better Golf,* Golf Digest, 1981. Co-author of syndicated column, "Golfing with Arnold Palmer," 1964—.

SIDELIGHTS: Richard E. Aultman has played golf since he was about four years old. He now teaches golf.

* * *

AXELSON, Eric 1913-

PERSONAL: Born July 11, 1913, in London, England; son of Charles Edmund and M.E.L. (Beddow) Axelson; married Hilda Mason (an artist, and associate of Royal College of Art), February 11, 1949; children: Ann Frances, Rafe Antony. *Education:* Natal University College (now University of Natal), B.A., 1932, M.A., 1934; graduate study at University of the Witwatersrand and King's College, London, 1935-37; University of the Witwatersrand, D.Litt., 1938. *Home address:* Box 15, Constantia, 7848, South Africa. *Office:* Brenthurst Press Ltd., Suite 19 Hyde Sq., Jan Smuts Ave., Hyde Park, Sandton, 2196, South Africa.

CAREER: Union War Histories section of the Prime Minister's Office, Pretoria, South Africa, assistant editor, 1946-49; Central African Archives, Salisbury, Southern Rhodesia (now Zimbabwe), editor, 1949-51; chief narrator, Union War Histories, 1952-54; Ernest Oppenheimer Institute of Portuguese Studies, Johannesburg, South Africa, research officer, 1955-62; University of Cape Town, Rondebosch, South Africa, professor of history and head of department, 1962-74, dean of the faculty of Arts, 1967-69, part-time assistant principal, 1972-74, full-time assistant principal, 1975-78; Brenthurst Press Ltd., Sandton, South Africa, general editor of "Brenthurst" series, 1975—. *Military service:* South African Land Forces, 1941-45; served in North Africa and Italy; became major.

MEMBER: Royal Historical Society (fellow), Royal Geographical Society (fellow), South African Historical Society (chairman, 1967-68), South African Association for the Advancement of Science (president, Section F, 1968), Academia Portuguesa da Historia, Academia de Marinha, Centro de Estudos Historicos Ultramarinos of Lisbon, Historical Society of Cape Town (co-founder and chairman, 1967), Owl Club (president, 1968). *Awards, honors:* Grant from Calouste Gulbenkian Foundation, 1960; travel grant from Carnegie Corp. of New York to study the teaching of African history at various American universities, 1966; comendador, Portuguese Order of Infante Dom Henrique, 1979; D.Litt. from University of Natal, 1980.

WRITINGS: South-East Africa, 1488-1530, Longmans, Green, 1940; (editor) *South African Explorers,* Oxford University Press, 1954; *Portuguese in South-East Africa 1600-1700,* Witwatersrand University Press, 1960; *Portugal and the Scramble for Africa, 1875-91,* Witwatersrand University Press, 1967; *Portuguese in South-East Africa, 1488-1600,* Witwatersrand

University Press, 1973; *Congo to Cape: Early Portuguese Explorers,* Faber, 1973; (co-editor and contributor) *Baines on the Zambezi, 1858-1859,* Brenthurst, 1982.

WORK IN PROGRESS: Portuguese in South-Africa, 1700-1800.

SIDELIGHTS: Eric Axelson explained that when he "became a research student at the University of the Witwatersrand in 1935, [I] was talked by Professor Leo Fouche into taking up study of Portuguese exploration and settlement in southeast Africa—a study which took [me] to archives and libraries in London, Paris, and Rome, and particularly Portugal. In Portugal the first problem was to find one's way around the National Archives; there were few aids, and short working hours: for fear of fire there was no electricity and the stack attendant had to use a candle.

"Incidental but exciting on return to South Africa was identifying the site of the farthest pillar raised by Dias in 1488, and excavating fragments. Years later [my wife Hilda and myself] recovered more fragments of a Dias pillar, at Luderitz; [we] made searches also for Vasco da Gama pillars on the south and east African coasts.

"Thanks to a grant from the Carnegie Corporation of New York, Central African Archives was able to send [me] to select documents in Europe on the early history of Mozambique and Rhodesia which were microfilmed by an accompanying photographer. Centro de Estudos Historicos Ultramarinos started transcribing, editing and publishing these documents in Portuguese and English.

"The University of the Witwatersrand made it possible for [me] to continue work on the Portuguese in southeast Africa. Valuable was a visit to Goa. At the University of Cape Town [I] introduced a separate course in African history—the first, [I] believe, to be offered in an African university."

* * *

AYRTON, Michael 1921-1975

PERSONAL: Surname originally Ayrton Gould; born February 20, 1921, in London, England; died November 17, 1975, in London, England; son of Gerald Gould (a poet and critic) and Barbara (a member of Parliament) Ayrton Gould; married Elisabeth Walshe (a writer), November, 1951. *Education:* Left school at fourteen to study art in Vienna and Paris. *Politics:* Labour. *Home:* Bradfields, Toppesfield, Halstead, Essex, England. *Agent:* International Literary Management Ltd., 2 Ellis St., Sloane Sq., London S.W.1, England.

CAREER: Novelist, essayist, art historian, illustrator, sculptor, painter, theatre designer, and film maker. Associated with the University of Essex. Paintings and sculpture have been exhibited at numerous galleries and art shows in Europe and the United States. Designer of three major theatre productions in London. Producer of documentary films, "The Drawings of Leonardo da Vinci," 1951, and "Greek Sculpture," 1959. *Military service:* Royal Air Force, 1941-43. *Member:* Savile Club (London). *Awards, honors:* Heinemann Award for Literature from Royal Society for Literature, 1968, for *The Maze Maker;* D.Litt. from University of Exeter, 1975.

WRITINGS: British Drawings, Collins, 1946; *Hogarth's Drawings,* Avalon, 1946; *Tittivulus,* Reinhardt, 1953; *Golden Sections,* Methuen, 1957; *The Testament of Daedalus,* Methuen, 1962; *Michael Ayrton: Drawings and Sculpture,* Cory, Adams & McKay, 1962, revised edition, 1966; *The Maze Maker* (novel), Holt, 1967; *Berlioz: A Singular Obsession,* BBC Publications, 1969; *Giovanni Pisano: Sculptor,* Weybright & Talley, 1969; *The Rudiments of Paradise,* Weybright & Talley, 1971; *Fabrications,* Secker & Warburg, 1972, Holt, 1973; *A Meaning to the Maze,* Abbey Press, 1974; *The Midas Consequence* (novel), Secker & Warburg, 1974, Doubleday, 1976; *Archilochos,* Secker & Warburg, 1977.

Also author of numerous art catalogs, television scripts, and introductions to art books. Illustrator of over twenty books. Contributor to *Spectator, New Statesman,* and other periodicals.

SIDELIGHTS: Michael Ayrton was "a well-known man of parts: painter, sculptor, illustrator, writer, mythraker," William Feaver remarked in *Listener*. "He identifie[d] strongly with Zobriel, a 19th-century French romantic composer and with Icarus, a classical golden boy whose wings came unstuck." Guy Davenport commented in the *National Review* that "admirers of good writing know Ayrton as a first-rate *raconteur* and the most literate theorist in the art of drawing since Wyndham Lewis."

As the son of the well-respected British writer Gerald Gould and former Labour Party chairman Barbara Ayrton Gould, Michael Ayrton grew up surrounded by famous and creative people, including close family friend William Yeats. At age fourteen, Ayrton dropped out of school and spent the next several years living with family members in Vienna and studying art in Paris before returning to London when England entered into World War II. Ayrton was designing the theatrical set and costumes for John Gielgud's production of "Macbeth" when he was drafted in 1941. Two years later, Ayrton was released from military service because of an injury, and he began to paint again.

Ayrton once explained in a *New Yorker* interview: "I achieved quite a reputation immediately after the war. This was embarrassingly easy to do, since we had been culturally isolated from the world for several years and a certain chauvinism gave me a temporary advantage. Subsequently, I went out of fashion as a painter, though I continue to paint and enjoy a modest success at it. I took up sculpture in earnest in the 1950s. . . . I've also done a number of essays and documentary films, and I finally sat down to write my novel."

Inspiration for much of his writing as well as the themes for his sculpture often stemmed from Ayrton's love of Greek mythology—so much so that he became known throughout the world for his interpretation of Greek legends. T. G. Rosenthal once wrote in *Encounter* of Ayrton's "preoccupation with myth. . . . All of his fiction, the two novels, the prose and verse fragment *The Testament of Daedalus* and his collection of illustrated short stories, *Fabrications,* . . . dealt largely with artists and their relationship to mythology. Once he had done the conventionally talented work on which his early reputation was built everything that followed was deeply rooted in mythology and antiquity."

According to a *New York Times* reviewer, "a long-standing interest in the Greek legend of Daedalus led to [Ayrton's] book *The Maze Maker*. Daedalus and his son, Icarus, who flew too high with man-made wings, appeared in many of Mr. Ayrton's works. His statue of Icarus stands near St. Paul's Cathedral in central London." In *The Maze Maker* "Ayrton most powerfully evokes the ancient world," wrote Alan Pryce-Jones in the *New York Times Book Review*. "His thesis is that 'the gods employ truths beyond fact and distort facts to fit these truths whereas man distorts the truth to fit his superstition.'" And a reviewer for the *Times Literary Supplement* viewed *The Maze Maker* as "an attempt to realize mythology in historical terms, and in the process to explicate the creative act and the creative temperament in clean, commonsense lines."

However, Guy Davenport suggested that this book is "something of an autobiography told in symbols and signs." He continued in the *National Review:* "It is a technical book about ancient sculpture, a psychology book about the ancient mind, a history book, and a book about the mind of the artist." A *Times Literary Supplement* critic wrote in a review of *The Maze Maker* that Ayrton had "surrendered his imagination so totally to his mythological persona as to produce in autobiographical detail a fascinatingly vivid evocation of the Minoan world, in all its ethnic and cultural complexity, and of a wry, cunningly sceptical but circumspect character whose attitude to his, or any, world holds something of the contradictory outlooks of Herodotus, Gulliver, or even at times Robinson Crusoe."

In addition to his own painting and sculpturing, Ayrton was very much interested in the works of other artists. As author of essays on art, numerous art catalogs, and art criticism, Ayrton was generally considered to be an enthusiastic and well-versed patron of the arts. Offering *The Rudiments of Paradise* as an example of what a critic for the *Times Literary Supplement* called Ayrton's ability "in communicating the excitement with which he has contemplated a number of extremely diverse masterpieces," R. L. Enequist wrote in the *Library Journal* that Ayrton's "criticisms are combined with a sense of wonder, and the combination makes the reader wish to delve further into each subject." Writing in *Saturday Review,* John White called *Giovanni Pisano: Sculptor* "the outcome of intense emotional experience as well as long and loving contemplation. It is a work of piety and personal homage. . . . The book confirms what is so evident in Ayrton's own sculpture: his concern not merely with human values but with the whole cultural context, the world of ideas as well as of institutions, which the artist helps to focus, to form, and to transform through his art." Finally, Paul West commented in the *Washington Post Book World:* "The English painter, sculptor, and film maker Michael Ayrton is a writer of unusual caliber. . . . [It is] clear that Ayrton's prose was no mere avocation but a belated delivery by a complete man whose creative output is all of a distinguished piece."

BIOGRAPHICAL/CRITICAL SOURCES: Punch, April 26, 1967; *Times Literary Supplement,* April 27, 1967, August 6, 1971; *Listener,* April 27, 1967, March 21, 1968; *New Statesman,* April 28, 1967, July 9, 1971; *New York Times,* November 4, 1967; *Washington Post Book World,* November 5, 1967, February 25, 1973; *New York Times Book Review,* November 5, 1967; *Saturday Review,* November 11, 1967, May 9, 1970, June 12, 1971; *National Review,* November 14, 1967; *New York Review of Books,* November 23, 1967; *New Yorker,* March 9, 1968; *Library Journal,* June 15, 1970, August, 1971; *Spectator,* November 25, 1972; *Books & Bookmen,* July, 1974; *Listener,* August 29, 1974; *Encounter,* June, 1976; *Contemporary Literary Criticism,* Volume VII, Gale, 1977.

OBITUARIES: New York Times, November 18, 1975; *AB Bookman's Weekly,* December 22-29, 1975.†

—Sketch by Margaret Mazurkiewicz

B

BAER, Jean L.

PERSONAL: Born in Chicago, Ill.; daughter of Fred Eugene (a journalist and public relations executive) and Helen (Roth) Baer; married Herbert Fensterheim (a clinical psychologist), June 20, 1968. *Education:* Cornell University, B.A. *Politics:* Democrat. *Home:* 151 East 37th St., New York, N.Y. 10016. *Agent:* Anita Diamant, 310 Madison Ave., New York, N.Y. 10017.

CAREER: Free-lance writer. Mutual Broadcasting Company, New York City, writer in press department, 1945-46; Air Features, Inc., New York City, publicist, 1946-49; Coll & Freedman Public Relations, New York City, member of staff, 1949-51; Voice of America, New York City and abroad, program information editor, 1951-53; *Seventeen,* New York City, director of public relations, 1953-68, senior editor and special projects director, 1968-74. *Member:* Overseas Press Club of America (member of board of governors, 1970—), Newswomen's Club of New York, Woman Pays Club (New York). *Awards, honors:* American Psychological Foundation award, 1975, for *Don't Say Yes When You Want to Say No.*

WRITINGS: Follow Me!, Macmillan, 1965; *The Single Girl Goes to Town,* Macmillan, 1968; *The Second Wife,* Doubleday, 1972; (with husband, Herbert Fensterheim) *Don't Say Yes When You Want to Say No,* McKay, 1975; *How to Be An Assertive (Not Aggressive) Woman in Life, in Love, and on the Job: A Total Guide to Self-Assertiveness,* Rawson, 1976; (with Fensterheim) *Stop Running Scared!,* Rawson, 1977; *The Self-Chosen: Our Crowd Is Dead, Long Live Our Crowd,* Arbor House, 1982. Contributor to women's magazines.

WORK IN PROGRESS: A book on marriage.

SIDELIGHTS: "Don't give me theories—tell me how people can use them." During the writing of *Don't Say Yes When You Want to Say No,* this was Jean Baer's advice to herself and to her husband and co-author Herbert Fensterheim, according to his introductory note to the book. In order to carry out this idea in *Don't Say Yes* and in Baer's entire series of self-help books aimed especially at the female reader, the author uses many case histories and stories from her own life to illustrate her major points. She also provides questions for self-review and games that allow readers to personally test her philosophy. *Don't Say Yes,* for example, offers laboratory exercises in thinking and communication as well as a guide to assertiveness on the job. *How to Be An Assertive (Not Aggressive) Woman* includes a "guide to speaking up on the job" and another on "climbing up the [corporate] ladder."

Critics find that these illustrative examples make Baer's self-help books more useful to the general reader than other volumes that merely state a problem without offering solutions. Mary Pradt Ziegler, for instance, states in her *Library Journal* review of *How to Be An Assertive (Not Agressive) Woman:* "Many valuable contributions distinguish Baer's assertion manual . . . from the plethora available." In particular, the critic praises the inclusion in the volume of Baer's own "self-disclosing anecdotes" and of reports on the problems other women (including literary agent Ann Buchwald and journalist Barbara Walters) have had with their own lack of assertiveness. Ziegler adds that these portions of the book contribute to its "authenticity." A *Publishers Weekly* reviewer also finds *How to Be An Assertive (Not Aggressive) Woman* a useful volume. The reviewer notes, "There are numerous questionnaires that will assist in . . . self-examination." Writing about *Don't Say Yes* in *Library Journal,* Denis Cogan notes that while there are numerous books that deal with specific psychological problems, Baer's "is the first I have read which deals with methods of altering the life style of the [troubled] individual."

In one chapter of *Don't Say Yes,* entitled "It Worked for Me—It Can Work for You," Baer relates her own evolution from what she refers to as "a female version of Caspar Milquetoast" into a "happy, nonneurotic" woman. Baer believes that her knowledge of assertiveness training, defined by the author in *Don't Say Yes* as a "scientific technique . . . through which by *changing your actions,* you can change *your attitudes and feelings about yourself,*" is responsible for this change. Because assertiveness became part of her life, claims Baer, she was able to survive and actually profit from being fired from the company for which she had worked for over twenty years (when her entire department at *Seventeen* was "disbanded in an economy measure"). "Before Assertiveness Training," she recalls in *How to Be An Assertive (Not Aggressive) Woman,* "I would have stayed passive and helpless in the face of . . . anxieties. . . . [But after this training] I felt like a winner—not because I had beaten anyone else but because I had had the courage to take a stand . . . and had accepted responsibility for my own decisions. I liked myself."

After the publication of *Stop Running Scared!,* Baer decided to alter her writing style. Failing in an attempt to produce a novel, the author set out to write *The Self-Chosen: Our Crowd Is Dead, Long Live Our Crowd,* a look at what Baer calls "Jewish Elite Persons" or JEPs. She tells *CA:* "I wanted to tell how the world of the Jewish elite has transformed itself since World War II. This was quite a change from writing how-to books. I became a reporter again." Bob Sokolsky of the *Camden Courier-Post* defines the book as "a case history of a changing strata of American society, especially Jewish society."

Baer (herself from a German Jewish family) began interviewing 254 prominent American Jews whom she felt could contribute to her study. Among those chosen for inclusion in Baer's book are Ambassador Sol M. Linowitz, cosmetics authority Adrien Arpel, president of the Bonwit Teller department store chain Helen Galland, and financial magnates Lester Crown and Laurence Tisch. They, along with Baer's other interviewees, fit the author's JEP classification. According to Helen Ganz Spiro of the *White Plains Reporter Dispatch,* Baer "used as a yardstick for inclusion in the book 'achievement, class, news value and openness.'" Commenting on the group interviewed by Baer, a *Jewish Week-American Examiner* reviewer notes that "the JEPs [are] a new generation of successful Jews to whom meritocracy matters more than background."

Critics, such as columnist John Barkham, praise the book for the insights it provides on this new group of Americans. Barkham writes in the *Youngstown Vindicator:* "Non-Jewish readers will find these gradations and social strata . . . unusually intriguing. . . . Jean Baer has produced a work of genuine significance on a small but highly influential segment of American people." A *West Coast Review of Books* critic says Baer "writes with warmth and enthusiasm which results in a most readable work." An *Association of Jewish Libraries Newsletter* reviewer terms the book "a gossipy, meaty compendium of family, feuds, fun and ambition concerning those who 'came over with a nickel in my pocket' and their children." And Bill Leff notes in a *Passaic Citizen* review, "It's a magnificently researched tome, one that every Jew should read and one that every Gentile should study to understand the Jewish rationale." Samuel Feinberg concurs in a *Women's Wear Daily* two-part feature: "To paraphrase an advertising message of Levy's rye bread, you don't have to be Jewish to enjoy *The Self-Chosen: Our Crowd Is Dead, Long Live Our Crowd.*"

Looking back on the writing of *The Self-Chosen,* Baer tells Sokolsky, "I worked on this for three years. It was the most difficult thing I ever did." On the same topic Baer comments to *CA:* "*The Self-Chosen* was a challenge. What a wonderful chance for a professional veteran to have the chance to do something new."

AVOCATIONAL INTERESTS: Travel, the theater, collecting antiques.

CA INTERVIEW

CA interviewed Jean Baer by phone December 1, 1981, at her home in New York City. Baer was taking a quick break from her work on *The Self-Chosen: Our Crowd Is Dead, Long Live Our Crowd.*

CA: When you were quite young, your father, a journalist and later a public-relations executive, taught you how to write a news story. Was that the beginning of your own career?

BAER: No, I was a stagestruck kid; I used to hang around all the stage doors. From the time I saw my first play at the age of nine I wanted to be an actress more than anything else in the world. But all the time I was very good in English. My father taught me how to write leads, and he told me (I remember so clearly), "Forget about the lead if you can't get it right away. Go ahead and write the story, and you'll come back and be able to write that lead." That's something I've always done. I never have a writer's block because I don't sit there staring at the typewriter. I just go on. For example, I'm doing a chapter right now on dynastic families for the new book, and I couldn't think of a lead. But that didn't stop me. I went on today and wrote twelve pages about two particular families. And at some point I'm going to find a great one-sentence opener, an anecdote or something, to begin it with. But at least I don't feel it was a lost day; I got a great deal done.

CA: Before you went to work for Seventeen, *you were in the press department at the Mutual Broadcasting Company and also worked as a program information editor for Voice of America.*

BAER: The job at MBC was my first real job. I worked on newspapers during the summer. Voice of America sent me abroad a great deal.

CA: Is that when you began to develop the wanderlust that resulted in the first book?

BAER: Yes, absolutely. I remember thinking on my first trip to Europe, I'll never go again. Well, I've been about forty times, and I've seen so many countries. You know, my interests and my work merge. I seem to turn one into the other.

CA: Were you doing any free-lance writing during those early jobs?

BAER: Occasionally here and there, a little thing.

CA: Tell me about your work at Seventeen. *That must have been quite an enviable job for a young woman to land when you began working there.*

BAER: People always think these magazine jobs are so marvelous. And many things about them are good: you meet interesting people, you get lots of trips—things like that. But I've always been sorry I didn't go out on my own earlier. You see, I wrote three books while I was at *Seventeen* (although only two of them were published while I was there). I got up at 5:30 in the morning to write. I wrote from 5:30 or 6:00 until 8:15; then I looked at the *Times,* had another cup of coffee, and took a taxi to my job, where I forgot about the writing and did my job all day long. Then I came home and ran the house.

CA: It sounds very difficult.

BAER: Yes. I think it's harder being a free lancer, though, because it's like Alice: you have to run twice as hard to stay in the same place. And of course, if you're any sort of professional at all, your standards for yourself get higher and higher.

CA: How did the first book, Follow Me!, *come about?*

BAER: While at *Seventeen* I was ghosting a free-lance column for which I got paid very little, and it was enormously successful. One day I was having lunch with a friend who happens to be a literary agent, and I was telling her how mad I was over this. I said, "You know, I think I could do an article on traveling alone." (I've always thought small.) She said, "Jean, will you do me a favor? Tonight just write a little outline, a presentation, and I'll send it to a magazine." I did it—I don't put things off. She called me up the next morning at 9:30 and said, "Did you do it?" I said, "Yes." And she said, "Good. I sold it to Macmillan as a book." She set up a lunch with Macmillan editor Cecil Scott, and suddenly I had signed a contract for a book! I lived in a state of terror for a year and a half, I was so afraid I wouldn't deliver that manuscript.

Cecil Scott gave me a wonderful lesson in writing. Before I started the book, I told him all my funny travel anecdotes—how I was serenaded by fifty naked men in Samarkand, and so on. But when I wrote the book, of course I didn't put myself in it—I'd never done that, never used the pronoun *I;* how could I? Mr. Scott said, "Jean, what happened to those stories you told me at lunch?" "But, Mr. Scott," I said (he was very British, very formal), "Those are about me. You don't want anything about *me*." He said, "I want the whole book to be about you. Go back and rewrite the book, and put all those stories in there." He made a small circle with his thumb and first finger. "Now look," he said. "Some anecdotes can be tiny." Then, expanding the circle, he said, "Some can be medium and some can be very big. Use that principle." I did a cut-and-paste job inserting all those stories, and even though nobody had even heard of me, the book became a best-seller.

As I said, I'd been rather frightened by Mr. Scott and had been very formal with him. About three or four weeks after *Follow Me*! came out, he called me up and said, "We're going to send you on a trip to the West Coast." He told me it had sold a thousand copies in Atlanta alone the week before. I asked, "Is that good?" because I didn't know anything. He said, "It's wonderful!" Then I said, "Gee, Cecil, I'm so glad." I immediately promoted myself to a first-name relationship, since things were going so well!

CA: Tell me more about the fifty naked men.

BAER: I'd gone to the U.S.S.R. on some sort of junket. But I didn't want to be just in Moscow, so I worked it out in advance through a Russian-oriented group in the United States to go to Tashkent and Samarkand and other places where nobody went at the time. In Samarkand I had a funny little room in what they called the first-rate hotel (it was like a tenth-rate hotel here). There was one light in the room, so I bought a copy of *The Bobbsey Twins and How They Grew;* that was the only English-language book I could find there. There was no other English-speaking person there except my guide, who went somewhere else at night. In the middle of the night—and it must have been 110 degrees—I heard this strange music, very oriental, and I couldn't figure out what it was. I looked out and saw all these naked men out there. In the morning my guide explained everything. Samarkand was an important city for the oriental-rug salesmen, who had come from the surrounding towns. They heard there was an American woman there, and they were serenading me as they settled down outside on their oriental rugs to go to sleep.

CA: Besides becoming a second wife yourself in 1968, what led you to write the book The Second Wife*?*

BAER: I had done two previous books about my own life, *Follow Me!,* of course, and *The Single Girl Goes to Town.* And here I was suddenly confronted with stepchildren and all the rest. The book is not a personal book, but it was certainly spurred by my own feelings. I think so much attention is paid to the first wife, no one realizes what the second wife takes on. I got enormous fan mail from it, absolutely enormous. And there's an interesting story in connection with it. In the book I quote a woman named Julia Perles, who is a very well known matrimonial lawyer. I was sent to her by a judge while I was gathering material for the book, and she was wonderful to me in the interview and told me to come back and clear the legal chapters with her, because she thought it likely I might get something twisted. (Which I did; there were several mistakes.) I'm very unassertive, despite the fact that I've written books about assertiveness. I can't make personal overtures. But this woman had just been so very nice, and she's so busy. So I sort of gathered my forces to call her up and ask her to lunch. When she answered the phone, I said, "Miss Perles, you probably don't remember me." She said, "Of course I remember you, Jean. Of the forty people I gave interviews to last year, you were the only one that sent me a thank-you note." We had lunch; we got along very well; she asked me to a cocktail party that Sunday. I said, "Well, I better not come because my husband's giving a speech and I'd be alone." And she said, "What's the difference? What time is his speech?" I said, "Five-thirty." She said, "Tell him we're serving dinner. Tell him to come when he's through." And he did. This couple have turned into close friends, and all because I made that gesture. It's been an interesting life experience for me, having held back so much.

CA: You collaborated with your husband, clinical psychologist Dr. Herbert Fensterheim, on two books: Don't Say Yes When You Want to Say No *and* Stop Running Scared!.

BAER: Never again! It's not that we don't get along—we get along beautifully. The thing is, each of us had written three books before we began *Don't Say Yes When You Want to Say No,* which was my idea because I was so fascinated by his work. So we had our own habits. I'm a morning person and he's a night person. All our weekends were spent working on that book. It got terribly difficult. At one point he heard me telling my stepmother, to whom I'm very close, "I'm doing seventy percent of the work." Then I heard him saying to someone, "She's trying to teach me how to write. I'm trying to teach her how to think."

On *Don't Say Yes,* every holiday we were working. We'd both been getting up at five o'clock—I really admired my husband so much for those long workdays. We'd been told we had to cut the manuscript by a hundred pages and have it in by the end of the Fourth of July weekend. Well, I had cut and cut and cut, and I ended up with eight pages that had no place to go but had to remain in the book. This was Saturday. I said, "I'm going to call Eleanor." (Eleanor Rawson, who was our editor on this book.) She wasn't home. Herb and I just sat there looking at each other; we couldn't do any more. Eleanor finally called the next morning. I told her the problem, and she said, "Have an eight-page chapter." I'd never heard of an eight-page chapter, but she said we could do it. I remember I went upstairs, typed in triplicate because no Xerox place was open, and fixed the eight-page chapter.

I remember when we finished *Don't Say Yes*. We finished at noon and I said, "We've got to celebrate." Herb said, "You want to go to a matinee?" I said, "No, the pressure to get there in time is too much." So we went to a movie, "That's Entertainment!" It was the perfect way to celebrate.

The Fourth of July work weekend happened again with *Stop Running Scared!* The manuscript was being put into galleys, and we decided we didn't like the chapter on "The Close Relationship." I begged Eleanor to let us rewrite it. She said, "If you get it to me by Monday at 8 A.M." So we spent the first weekend in our new country home rewriting. It worked. That chapter turned out to be the best in the book. You learn with every book and I think that's very important.

CA: Much of your very good advice on all the personal topics you've dealt with seems to boil down to the basic idea of setting clear and reasonable goals.

BAER: Setting good sub-goals. If I thought now of what I have to do in the next two months, I think I'd go kill myself. But I just say to myself, "Jean, get one chapter done by the end of the week. Then next week, you will do another chapter. On Sunday you'll do your clerical work." But I am disciplined. I do sit down every day; I don't put it off.

CA: Was that part of your upbringing?

BAER: Yes. My parents were born here, but I do come from a very Germanic background. To this day, I think I'd die if I were late. I write for five and a half hours every day, from 8:00 to 1:30. Then I have a decent lunch, because I've learned I can't go on if I don't. In the afternoon I do the interviews, the clerical work, the other things. But I've learned to let nothing get in the way of my writing in the morning. It's very lonely. I think many writers make the mistake of not structuring things so that they know they still have a voice. I set things up so that I can talk to somebody at the end of the day. (I should explain that my husband works until 9:00 on weekday nights.) It is lonely and it is physically wearing. Sometimes I can't get up from the chair at the typewriter because I'm sort of stuck in that position. But I give myself rewards. When I work on Saturday morning, then I feel it's all right for me to go to this very good butcher store near here and get myself steak tartare, which my mother brought me up not to eat. And I always spend a great deal of money when I'm writing a book. Last week I bought a fur coat; the week before that, two dresses. I go crazy at the end of the day.

But I'm not sympathetic to writers' blocks, I really am not. I think if you just stay in there and try, it may not be very good, but then you can go back and fix it. I do five drafts for every chapter, so the beginning one is never good. It's just a question of getting something down on paper.

I have another odd habit. I don't know if anybody else does it. I keep a copy of everything important—like all the original interviews—in the refrigerator. I'm always so afraid of fire. When we went away to Florida recently, I knew that there were copies of some of the chapters at the publishing house, so that was not a problem. But I keep one master set of the interviews, and I put that and the research for the next couple of chapters in the refrigerator. Eleanor Rawson said to me once, "This manuscript smells of turkey grease."

CA: Have you enjoyed working on The Self-Chosen*?*

BAER: I've enjoyed every minute, even when I think I'm going crazy with pressure from the publisher. It's a complete departure for me, and it's been such a learning experience. Sometimes I feel I shouldn't even have gotten an advance for it. The point of the book is that there's a whole new Jewish elite in which background doesn't matter but achievement does. This includes people like Dean Rosovsky of Harvard, who turned down the presidency of Yale, and Sylvia Porter and Roberta Peters—I've talked with so many people for this book, and they have been absolutely wonderful to me.

CA: You've written in several contexts about the importance of developing a social network. What do you think of the way women are networking now to better themselves and to help each other professionally?

BAER: I think it's very necessary. The men have had it easy for so long. But I do think the publishing world is one place where women have been equals; also in psychological work.

CA: You're known as a great hostess. Do you still find time to give parties?

BAER: Not when I'm finishing a book, but I assure you that the week after I get that manuscript in I'll be giving one. It's something I do well; I think it's because I feel very secure about it. My mother got sick when I was thirteen. She didn't die until some nine years later, but I had to run the house. And then I was single for many years, and I entertained a lot during that time. So it doesn't throw me. If you said to me, "In three hours I'm going to be there, and can you have dinner for me and six friends?" I could cope. I don't try that hard to be clever or elegant. I serve things I know how to do and I've done a million times, because I figure the people are what matter.

CA: You wrote one time about planning a novel. Is that still in your mind?

BAER: I failed. I've failed at two things in my life. The novel was one of them, and running a country house was the other. And I think that's why I failed at the novel: I was sitting there in that country house and I couldn't operate. I was just too lonely. But I might go back to the novel, because the idea was a very good one.

CA: Is there any advice you'd offer to aspiring writers?

BAER: I think the emphasis on goals is important, and I think you have to start small. I've written lots of little pieces on cooking and things like that, and all of it helped me to go further. All my years of interviewing as a reporter have helped me so much on this new book. I remember hearing Ralph Martin give a talk at the Overseas Press Club. He was flushed with the success of *Jennie* and he said something like, "I've written thirty-seven books and I never hit it big until now. You can all do it!" The thing is to be willing to put in the work.

BIOGRAPHICAL/CRITICAL SOURCES: Jean Baer and Herbert Fensterheim, *Don't Say Yes When You Want to Say No,* McKay, 1975; *Publishers Weekly,* March 3, 1975, August 9, 1976; *Library Journal,* May 15, 1975, November 1, 1976, June 4, 1982; Baer, *How to Be An Assertive (Not Aggressive) Woman in Life, in Love, and on the Job: A Total Guide to Self-Assertiveness,* Rawson, 1976; *Jewish Week-American Examiner,* July 11, 1982; *Youngstown Vindicator,* July 11, 1982; *Passaic Citizen,* July 28, 1982; *Belleville News-Democrat,* July 29, 1982; *Camden* (N.J.) *Courier-Post,* August 3, 1982; *Best Sellers,* September, 1982; *Chicago Sentinel,* September 16, 1982; *Association of Jewish Libraries Newsletter,* September/October, 1982; *West Coast Review of Books,* October, 1982; *White Plains Reporter Dispatch,* October 1, 1982; *St. Louis*

Jewish Light, October 20, 1982; *Women's Wear Daily,* November 17, 1982, November 19, 1982.

—*Sketch by Marian Walters*

—*Interview by Jean W. Ross*

* * *

BAHR, Robert 1940-

PERSONAL: Born October 29, 1940, in Newark, N.J.; son of Robert (an electrician) and Catherine (Kuebler) Bahr; married Alice Harrison (a librarian), 1971; children: Keith. *Education:* King's College, Briarcliff Manor, N.Y., B.A., 1964. *Agent:* Dominic Abel Literary Agency, 498 West End Ave., New York, N.Y. 10024. *Office:* 1104 Walnut St., Allentown, Pa. 18102.

CAREER: Rodale Press, Emmaus, Pa., editor, 1964-72; free-lance writer, 1972—. Lecturer. *Member:* National Association of Science Writers, American Society of Journalists and Authors, Society for the Scientific Study of Sex, American Society of Journalists and Authors, Authors League of America, Society of Children's Book Writers.

WRITINGS: (Compiler) *The Natural Way to a Healthy Skin,* Rodale Press, 1972; *The Virility Factor,* Putnam, 1976; *Healing and Hormones,* Dutton, 1977; *Least of All Saints,* Prentice-Hall, 1979; *The Blizzard,* Prentice-Hall, 1980; *The Great Blizzard* (juvenile), Dandelion, 1980; *Blizzard at the Zoo* (juvenile), Lothrop, 1982. Contributor to Reader's Digest General Books. Contributor to periodicals, including *Smithsonian, Sports Illustrated, Playboy, TV Guide,* and *Prevention.*

WORK IN PROGRESS: The Complete Book of Massage, for New American Library; *How to Have Fun Expanding Your Mind,* with Kreskin, for Doubleday.

SIDELIGHTS: Robert Bahr told *CA:* "I learned almost 20 years ago that the only way to survive as a writer is to do your best every day, to always give the boss a little more than you're being paid for. I tell my kid, 'Don't walk up to the starting line unless you mean to win the race,' and he tells me, 'Dad, you're so corny!' Well, sure. And I'm old-fashioned. But I've paid a hell of a lot of bills over the years, so it's not been such an impractical way to live."

* * *

BAILEY, Frederick George 1924-

PERSONAL: Born February 24, 1924, in Liverpool, England. *Education:* Oxford University, B.A., 1948, B.Litt., 1950; University of Manchester, Ph.D., 1954. *Office:* Department of Anthropology, University of California, San Diego, La Jolla, Calif. 92093.

CAREER: University of London, London, England, reader in Asian anthropology, 1960-63; University of Sussex, Brighton, England, professor of anthropology, 1964-71; University of California, San Diego, La Jolla, professor of anthropology, 1971—. *Military service:* British Army, 1943-46. *Member:* American Academy of Arts and Sciences (fellow). *Awards, honors:* S. C. Roy Gold Medal from Asiatic Society, 1961; Guggenheim fellow, 1977.

WRITINGS: Caste and the Economic Frontier, Manchester University Press, 1957; *Tribe Caste and Nation: A Study of Political Activity and Political Change in Highland Orissa,* Humanities, 1960; *Politics and Social Change: Orissa in 1959,* University of California Press, 1963; *Stratagems and Spoils: A Social Anthropology of Politics,* Schocken, 1969; (editor) *Gifts and Poisons: The Politics of Reputation,* Schocken, 1971; (editor) *Debate and Compromise: The Politics of Innovation,* Basil Blackwell, 1973; *Morality and Expediency: The Folklore of Academic Politics,* Aldine, 1977; *The Tactical Uses of Passion,* Cornell University Press, 1983.

WORK IN PROGRESS: Research into the politics of small groups.

SIDELIGHTS: Frederick George Bailey did field research in India, 1952-54, 1955, and 1959, and in Italy, 1963-72.

* * *

BAIRD, Martha (Joanna) 1921-1981

PERSONAL: Born June 10, 1921, in Dodge City, Kan.; died October 22, 1981; daughter of Harry Charles (a college professor) and Mary Lou (Jones) Baird; married Eli Siegel (founder and teacher of Aesthetic Realism), October 7, 1944 (died November 8, 1978). *Education:* Attended Kansas State College of Agriculture and Applied Science (now Kansas State University), 1939-40; State University of Iowa, B.A., 1943. *Politics:* "I lean towards the Left." *Home:* 67 Jane St., New York, N.Y. 10014. *Office:* Definition Press, 141 Greene St., New York, N.Y. 10012.

CAREER: WGN (radio station), Chicago, Ill., scriptwriter, 1943; American Guild of Variety Artists (AGVA), New York City, secretary, 1944-45; Society for Aesthetic Realism, New York City, secretary, 1946-81; Definition Press, New York City, editor, 1955-81. Teacher of music criticism, beginning 1973.

WRITINGS—Published by Definition Press, except as indicated: *Nice Deity* (poems), 1955; (with Sheldon Kranz and others) *Personal and Impersonal: Six Aesthetic Realists* (poems), Aesthetic Realism Foundation and Terrain Gallery, 1959; (editor) Eli Siegel (husband), *James and the Children: A Consideration of Henry James's "The Turn of the Screw,"* 1968; (editor with Ellen Reiss) *The Williams-Siegel Documentary,* 1970; (editor) Siegel, *Goodbye Profit System,* 1970, revised edition published as *Goodbye Profit System: Update,* 1982, three-act musical play adaptation of original edition (with Tom Shields) produced in New York City at Terrain Gallery, 1972; *Two Aesthetic Realism Papers,* 1971; (contributor) Vana Earle, *Big Day in Larned,* John Day, 1971; (editor with Reiss) *The Press Boycott of Aesthetic Realism: Documentation,* 1978; (contributor with Reiss) Raymond J. Corsini, editor, *Innovative Psychotherapies,* Wiley, 1981; (editor and author of introduction) Siegel, *Self and World: An Explanation of Aesthetic Realism,* 1981. Also composer of a music-drama, "Bilge Concerto," broadcast on WUWM-FM, Milwaukee, Wis., 1966.

Contributor to "Pageant of Literature" series, edited by M. T. Clare, Macmillan, 1965, "Reading Program" series, edited by Marion Gartler, Macmillan, 1965, and "New Basic Readers" series, edited by H. M. Robinson and others, Scott, Foresman, 1970. Work is represented in anthology *Poetry for Pleasure,* Doubleday, 1960. Contributor of poems and articles to periodicals, including *American Dialogue, New York Element,* and *Allegro.* Editor, *Definition: A Journal of Events and Aesthetic Realism,* 1961-67, and *Right of Aesthetic Realism to Be Known* (weekly newsletter), 1978-81.

WORK IN PROGRESS: Opposites in Music, a book of music criticism based on Aesthetic Realism.

SIDELIGHTS: Martha Baird was the wife of Eli Siegel, the founder of the philosophy of Aesthetic Realism. Based on Siegel's idea that "what makes a good poem is like what can make a good life,'' Aesthetic Realism teaches that ''the resolution of conflict in self is like the making one of opposites in art.'' (For a more detailed explanation of Aesthetic Realism, see Eli Siegel's sketch in this volume.) Baird spent most of her life studying her husband's philosophy; testing the principles of Aesthetic Realism in the fields of literature, music, and the mind; and writing her own poetry and music criticism according to those principles. She also served as secretary of the Society for Aesthetic Realism (''formed by students of Eli Siegel who think Aesthetic Realism is true and should be better known,'' Baird once explained) and as an editor at Definition Press, publisher of most of Siegel's pamphlets and books.

In her book *Two Aesthetic Realism Papers,* Baird described her introduction to Aesthetic Realism and her subsequent commitment to Siegel and his philosophy. Recounted the author: ''I was born in Dodge City, Kansas, in 1921, the place of the cowboys, Boot Hill, and Wild Bill Hickok. This, naturally, was before my time.

''I attended Kansas State College, in Manhattan, for a year and a half, but was graduated from the University of Iowa, where I started out to major in theatre, but switched to radio as more 'practical.'

''I worked for a while in Chicago as a radio writer for WGN, a big station owned by the *Chicago Tribune*. It was outward success, but not inward.

''I quit all this and came to New York in 1943. I used up all my money loafing around and going to movies, and finally, in desperation, took a job at the American Guild of Variety Artists (AGVA, a relative of Equity). I hated it at first, but grew to like it, and have, because of that experience, a little 'inside knowledge' of the labor movement.

''I do not know what would have happened to me if I had not met Eli Siegel and Aesthetic Realism at this time, but I did, and that changed everything. I began to study Aesthetic Realism in January 1944, after a period of cautiously looking it over. I came to feel this was the most important thing in the world—much more important, more exciting, than anything I had learned in college; the answer to the 'cultural gap' and how to get people so they could get along with each other. It just delighted me. It changed the way I felt inside, in a way I never dreamed anything could. I felt sure the whole world would agree with me as soon as it had a chance. This was an impersonal judgment but it had personal consequences, and I married Eli Siegel in October 1944.''

Baird further expressed her belief in the tenets of Aesthetic Realism in an unpublished autobiographical fragment written in 1972 and passed along to *CA* by Ellen Reiss, an editor at Definition Press. In this fragment, Baird maintained that ''the greatest and newest idea in the world is in the Aesthetic Realism of Eli Siegel, specifically in his statement 'All art is the making one of permanent opposites in reality' and in his showing that what art does is what we as people want. All my writing, prose and poetry, has been profoundly affected by this idea. I am passionately interested in Aesthetic Realism as a method for seeing whether something in art is good or not, particularly literature and music.''

BIOGRAPHICAL/CRITICAL SOURCES: Underground, November 2, 1966; Martha Baird and Ellen Reiss, editors, *The Williams-Siegel Documentary,* Definition Press, 1970; Baird, *Two Aesthetic Realism Papers,* Definition Press, 1971; *Right of Aesthetic Realism to Be Known,* April 25, 1979; Eli Siegel, *Self and World: An Explanation of Aesthetic Realism,* Definition Press, 1981.†

* * *

BANNISTER, Don
See BANNISTER, Donald

* * *

BANNISTER, Donald 1928-
(Don Bannister)

PERSONAL: Born May 7, 1928, in Birmingham, England; son of Charles Frederick (a coal miner) and Cissie (Fulford) Bannister; married Roma Scandolo, December 27, 1951 (separated); children: Simon Fulford, Shulie Jane, Lucy Ann Francesca, Piers Anthony. *Education:* University of Manchester, B.A., 1956; University of London, diploma in psychology, 1957, Ph.D., 1959. *Politics:* ''Anarcho-syndicalist.'' *Religion:* Atheist. *Office:* High Roads Hospital, Menston, Ilkley, West Yorkshire, England.

CAREER: Bexley Hospital, Bexley, Kent, England, head of department of psychology, beginning 1959; currently affiliated with High Roads Hospital, Menston, Ilkley, West Yorkshire, England. Member of external scientific staff of Medical Research Council (London), 1959—; visiting professor at University of Surrey, 1972—. Member of social effects of television advisory group to British Broadcasting Corp. *Member:* British Psychological Society, American Psychological Association.

WRITINGS: (With J.M.M. Mair) *The Evaluation of Personal Constructs,* Academic Press, 1968; (editor) *Perspectives in Personal Construct Theory,* Academic Press, 1970; (with Fay Fransella) *Inquiring Man,* Penguin, 1971; (editor) *Issues and Approaches in the Psychological Therapies,* Wiley, 1975. Contributor of over forty articles to psychology journals.

Under name Don Bannister; all novels; all published by Knopf: *Sam Chard,* 1979; *Long Day at Shiloh,* 1981; *Burning Leaves,* 1982.

WORK IN PROGRESS: A book on asylums; a study of self-construing in children; more novels.

SIDELIGHTS: Donald Bannister's *Long Day at Shiloh* is a fictionalized account of the Battle of Shiloh, one of the bloodiest and most controversial battles of the American Civil War. The fighting, which took place on April 6 and 7, 1862, in Hardin County, Tenn., involved more than 100,000 men and left almost 24,000 dead.

Although Shiloh has been the subject of numerous books—both fiction and nonfiction—Bannister, according to *Newsweek* reviewer Jean Strouse, has succeeded in taking a new look at the battle and ''uses the voices of Northern soldiers, officers and generals to create a vivid sense of the war in progress.'' Robert Hewison, writing in the *Times Literary Supplement,* says that Bannister's ''account has been built up from careful research into eye-witness reports and military histories, but the invented dialogue with its onomatopoeic spelling brings the material alive—and shows that concern for language absent from so many other historical novels. . . . As a battle-book, *Long Day at Shiloh* has an intellectual vigour which, for all their entertainment, most other history-novels lack.''

Donald Bannister told *CA* that he was ''a lazy and discontented and confused psychologist until 1957, when I read 'The Psychology of Personal Constructs' by George Kelly. This showed me that formal psychology could contain the fire, the twisted ingenuity, the personal feel of living. Now I am an energetic, contented, and confused psychologist.''

Bannister's *Inquiring Man* has been translated into German.

AVOCATIONAL INTERESTS: ''Fanatically concerned about canal sailing, the American Civil War, living in Yorkshire, and writing novels and psychological texts in roughly equal numbers.''

BIOGRAPHICAL/CRITICAL SOURCES: Newsweek, April 13, 1981; *Times Literary Supplement,* August 28, 1981, September 10, 1982.

* * *

BARBACH, Lonnie Villoldo 1946-

PERSONAL: Born October 6, 1946, in Newark, N.J.; daughter of Marvin M. (a salesman) and Temy (a purchasing coordinator; maiden name, Sokolow) Barbach. *Education:* Simmons College, B.S., 1967; Wright Institute, M.A., 1972, Ph.D., 1974. *Religion:* Jewish. *Home:* 60 Palm Way, Mill Valley, Calif. 94941. *Agent:* Rhoda Weyr, William Morris Agency, 1350 Avenue of the Americas, New York, N.Y. 10019. *Office:* Nexus, 1968 Green St., San Francisco, Calif.

CAREER: University of California, Medical Center, San Francisco, co-director of clinical training in Human Sexuality Program, 1973-78, member of clinical faculty, 1978—; Nexus (an institute for relationship training), San Francisco, psychologist, 1975—.

WRITINGS: For Yourself: The Fulfillment of Female Sexuality, Doubleday, 1975; *Women Discover Orgasm: A Therapist's Guide to a New Treatment Approach,* Free Press, 1980; (with Linda Levine) *Shared Intimacies: Women's Sexual Experiences,* Doubleday/Anchor, 1980; *For Each Other: Sharing Sexual Intimacy,* Doubleday/Anchor, 1982. Contributor to professional journals.

WORK IN PROGRESS: A book, *The New Super-Men,* with Linda Levine, on the evolving sexuality of the American male.

SIDELIGHTS: Lonnie Barbach told *CA:* ''My concern is basically to help women assume control over their lives on all levels, professional and personal. Sexual concerns provide one forum for accomplishing this.'' *Avocational interests:* Travel, different cultures, sports.

* * *

BARBER, Cyril J(ohn) 1934-

PERSONAL: Born May 18, 1934, in Pretoria, South Africa; naturalized U.S. citizen, 1976; son of Charles Stanley and Muriel Radford (Cook) Barber; married Aldyth Ayleen Aereboe, April 13, 1957; children: Allan Marlin, Stephen Marlin. *Education:* Attended University of Dublin, 1958-60; Dallas Theological Seminary, M.Th., 1967; Rosary College, M.A.L.S., 1971; graduate study at King's College, London, 1976, and New College, Oxford, 1976; Talbot Theological Seminary, D.Min., 1979. *Religion:* Independent Baptist. *Address:* P.O. Box 5181, Hacienda Heights, Calif. 91745.

CAREER: South Africa Mutual Life Insurance Society, Johannesburg, accountant, 1950-62; Dallas Theological Seminary, Dallas, Tex., acquisitions librarian, 1962, manager of bookstore, 1963-67; Winnipeg Bible College, Winnipeg, Manitoba, librarian and chairman of department of Bible exposition, 1967-69; Trinity Evangelical Divinity School, Deerfield, Ill., associate librarian, 1969, head librarian, 1970-72; Rosemead Graduate School of Psychology, Rosemead, Calif., assistant professor, 1972-74, associate professor of psychological bibliography and systematic theology, 1974-80, director of library, 1972-77; Talbot Theological Seminary, La Mirada, Calif., associate professor of practical theology, 1978-80, professor of bibliography and director of library, 1980-82. Consultant, lecturer, and counselor.

MEMBER: American Library Association, American Theological Library Association, Evangelical Theological Society, Christian Association for Psychological Studies, Society of Biblical Literature, Royal Society of Literature, Royal Geographical Society, Philosophical Society of Great Britain, P.E.N., California Library Association, California Writer's Guild, Beta Phi Mu, Kappa Tau Epsilon. *Awards, honors:* D.Lit. from University of London.

WRITINGS: (With Elmer Towns) *Successful Church Libraries,* Baker Book, 1970; *God Has the Answer . . . ,* Baker Book, 1974; *Love Unlimited,* Narramore Christian Foundation, 1974; *The Minister's Library,* Baker Book, 1974, Supplement I, 1976, Supplement II, 1978, Supplement III, 1980, Supplement IV, 1982; *Work: The Subtle Addiction,* Narramore Christian Foundation, 1974; *Searching for Identity,* Moody, 1975; *Read for Your Life,* Rosemead Graduate School of Psychology, 1975; *Nehemiah and the Dynamics of Effective Leadership,* Loizeaux Brothers, 1976, study guide, 1980; (with John Carter) *Always a Winner,* Regal Books, 1977; *Vital Encounter,* Here's Life Publishers, 1979; *How to Gain Life—Changing Insights from the Book of Books,* Brethren Missionary Herald Press, 1979.

(With Gary Strauss) *The Effective Parent,* Here's Life Publishers, 1980; (with wife, Aldyth Barber) *Your Marriage Has Real Possibilities,* Here's Life Publishers, 1981; *Dynamic Personal Bible Study,* Loizeaux Brothers, 1981; (with Strauss) *Leadership: The Dynamics of Success,* Attic Press, 1982; *Introduction to Theological Research,* Moody, 1982; *Ruth: The Grace of God in the Old Testament,* Moody, 1983.

Also author of *Twelve Keys to Spiritual Growth;* author with Aldyth Barber, *You Can Have a Happy Marriage*. Contributor of forewords to numerous books. Contributor to *Zondervan's Pictorial Encyclopedia of the Bible* and *Tyndale Family Bible Encyclopedia* and of articles and reviews to theology journals. Contributing editor of *Journal of Psychology and Theology,* 1972—.

WORK IN PROGRESS: What Parents Do to Their Kids, with Gary Strauss; *Judges.*

SIDELIGHTS: Barber writes *CA:* ''One man I worked under was noted for his slogans. Two deeply impressed me. 'The price of success is effort,' and 'Do it now.'''

* * *

BARNES, Jack 1940-

PERSONAL: Born January 30, 1940, in Dayton, Ohio. *Education:* Carleton College, B.A., 1961; graduate study at Northwestern University, 1961-63. *Politics:* Marxist. *Religion:* Atheist. *Office:* Socialist Workers Party, 14 Charles Lane, New York, N.Y. 10014.

CAREER: Young Socialist Alliance, New York City, national chairman, 1965-66; Socialist Workers Party, New York City, national organization secretary, 1969-72, national secretary, 1972—. *Member:* Phi Beta Kappa, Pi Delta Epsilon.

WRITINGS—All published by Pathfinder Press (New York, N.Y.): (With George Breitman, Derrick Morrison, Barry Sheppard, and Mary-Alice Waters) *Towards an American Socialist Revolution,* 1971; (with Joseph Hansen) *A Revolutionary Strategy for the '70's,* 1972; (with Waters, Sheppard, Tony Thomas, and Betsy Stone) *Prospects for Socialism in America,* 1976; (with Breitman, Michael Harrington, Peter Camejo, Stanley Aronowitz, and Carl Haessler) *The Lesser Evil,* 1977; *The Nicaraguan Workers' and Farmers' Government and the Revolutionary Leadership of the FSLN,* 1980; (with Waters) *Proletarian Leadership in Power,* 1980; (with Steve Clark) *The Changing Face of U.S. Politics,* 1981. Contributor to *Militant.*

WORK IN PROGRESS: Political writings on the economy and the political process.

* * *

BARTLETT, Elizabeth (Winters)

PERSONAL: Born in New York, N.Y.; married Paul Bartlett (an artist and novelist), April 19, 1943; children: Steven. *Education:* Columbia University, B.A., 1931, additional study in extension courses. *Residence:* San Diego, Calif. *Mailing address:* c/o Steven Bartlett, 7130 Maryland Ave., St. Louis, Mo. 63130.

CAREER: Writer. Southern Methodist University, Dallas, Tex., instructor in department of speech and theater, 1947-49; New School for Social Research, New York, N.Y., director of Creative Writers Association, 1955; San Jose State College (now University), San Jose, Calif., assistant professor of English, 1961-62; University of California, Santa Barbara, associate professor of English, 1962-64; *ETC: A Review of General Semantics,* San Francisco, Calif., poetry editor, 1964-76. Visiting lecturer at various universities in the United States and Canada, 1965—; professor of English, University of San Diego, 1979 and 1981; lecturer in creative writing, San Diego State University, 1980. Consultant at writers' conferences in California, New York, and other states. *Member:* International Society for General Semantics, Poetry Society of America.

AWARDS, HONORS: Huntington Hartford Foundation writing fellowships, 1959, 1960; Montalve Foundation writing fellowship, 1961; grants from National Institute of Arts and Letters and PEN International; National Endowment for the Arts poetry award, 1968-70; Yaddo and MacDowell writing fellowships, 1970.

WRITINGS—Poems, except as indicated: *Poems of Yes and No,* Editorial Jus (Mexico), 1952; *Behold This Dreamer,* Editorial Jus, 1959; *Poetry Concerto,* Vagrom Press, 1961; *It Takes Practice Not to Die,* Van Riper & Thompson, 1964; *Threads,* Unicorn Press, 1968; *Twelve-Tone Poems,* Sun Press, 1969.

Selected Poems, Carrefour Press, 1970; *The House of Sleep,* Autograph Editions, 1975; *Dialogue of Dust* (one-act play in verse), Autograph Editions, 1978; *In Search of Identity,* Autograph Editions, 1978; *A Zodiac of Poems,* Autograph Editions, 1979; *Address in Time,* Dufour, 1979; *Memory Is No Stranger,* Ohio University Press, 1981.

Also author of tape recordings for Library of Congress, several universities, and many FM radio stations. Contributor to poetry anthologies, including *The American Scene, New Voices, Poets West, Where Is Viet Nam?,* and *The Writing on the Wall.* Contributor of hundreds of poems to periodicals, including *Bitterroot, Commentary, Fiddlehead, Harper's, New York Times, Prairie Schooner, Shenandoah,* and *Voix de Paris;* also contributor of short stories, reviews, articles, and translations to periodicals.

WORK IN PROGRESS: This Side of the Fog, Hindsight, and *Heresy in Steel,* all books of poetry; "The Secret," a ballet script.

SIDELIGHTS: Elizabeth Bartlett is the creator of the "twelve-tone poem," a verse form in which poems are made up of twelve lines: six couplets of twelve syllables each. Bartlett told Pamela Camille, in a *Crosscurrents* interview, that the form "was inspired by [composer] Arnold Schoenberg's twelve-tone scale, and I use accented sounds to take the place of musical notes." The musical basis is no accident; she feels that music is central to all poems and that "poetry should never lose its identity as a musical form of expression."

In a *St. Louis Post-Dispatch* article, Charles Guenther says that the twelve-tone form "lends itself well to various uses as rhymed or free verse, in single lyrics, in multi-part poems, and even in narrative sequences. Ms. Bartlett handles the form gracefully and sensitively. This is smooth undulant and often brilliant poetry." Poet and literary critic Kenneth Rexroth, in the introduction to Bartlett's *Address in Time,* writes: "Elizabeth Bartlett's poems are good examples of the change, or one of the changes, in American poetry since World War II. They are poems of direct statement. They are poems of personal communication. They are overt judgments of life, of people, of value relations—judgments derived from her perception and contemplation of nature as a master symbol of human relations—simply, directly stated."

Bartlett told Camille that she lists no poets among her literary influences: "I was influenced by other kinds of writers, like Dostoevsky and his approach to life. His analysis of human emotions fits in with my own observations. Marx, Freud, Sir John Frazier, Charles Darwin . . . also, religious thinkers, those reaching for the humane. We can't dismiss these—Dostoevsky certainly didn't. The human, spiritual, and economic must always be taken into consideration. I've been an admirer of novelists like Joyce and Proust and Dorothy Richardson. All these I've mentioned tried to make the story of time and life meaningful, and they never leave out the spirituality of man."

Asked to comment on the state of contemporary poetry, Bartlett replied: "Language and lifestyle have changed; the computer has come into our lives. Before that, we had the staccato telegraph. We had the new kinds of rhythms that Gershwin introduced. Then we had music by composers like Arnold Schoenberg. . . . Today, we don't write like Shelley and Keats. We have expressive poets, like Ginsberg, with his *Howl* and *Kaddish.* We have the Jonathan Williams school in the East; we have the more sobering poetry of Howard Nemerov and Richard Wilbur; we have pop poetry, prose poetry such as that of Michael Benedict—all of these fit; they fit in with our widely varied lifestyles."

BIOGRAPHICAL/CRITICAL SOURCES: Elizabeth Bartlett, *Address in Time,* Dufour, 1979; *Crosscurrents,* spring, 1982; *St. Louis Post-Dispatch,* June 6, 1982.

* * *

BARTLETT, Irving H(enry) 1923-

PERSONAL: Born February 2, 1923, in Springfield, Mass.;

son of Lewis Irving and Carrie E. (Jones) Bartlett; married Virginia Kostulski (a television producer), November 30, 1944. *Education:* Ohio Wesleyan University, B.A., 1948; Brown University, M.A., 1949, Ph.D., 1952. *Home:* 5 Hinckley Rd., Milton, Mass. 02187. *Office:* University of Massachusetts, Boston, Mass. 02116.

CAREER: Assistant professor of history at Rhode Island College, Providence, 1953-54, and Massachusetts Institute of Technology, Cambridge, 1954-60; Cape Cod Community College, Hyannis, Mass., president, 1960-64; Carnegie-Mellon University, Pittsburgh, Pa., professor of history, beginning 1964, chairman of department, 1964-71; Harvard University, Cambridge, Charles Warren Fellow in American History, 1978-79; University of Massachusetts—Boston, John F. Kennedy Professor of American Civilization, 1980—. John Dorrance Visiting Professor, Trinity College, 1971. Vice-chairman of board of trustees, Allegheny County Community College, 1964-71. *Military service:* U.S. Army, Corps of Engineers, 1943-46; became captain. *Member:* American Historical Association, American Studies Association, American Academy of Political and Social Sciences, American Arbitration Association, Phi Beta Kappa. *Awards, honors:* Guggenheim fellowship, 1966-67.

WRITINGS: From Slave to Citizen: The Story of the Negro in Rhode Island, Providence Urban League, 1953; (editor and author of introduction) *William Ellery Channing: Unitarian Christianity and Other Essays,* Liberal Arts Press, 1957; *Wendell Phillips, Brahmin Radical,* Beacon, 1961; (contributor) Martin Duberman, editor, *The Antislavery Vanguard,* Princeton University Press, 1965; *The American Mind at the Mid-Nineteenth Century,* Crowell, 1967, 2nd edition, Harland Davidson, 1982; (with Edwin Fenton, David Fowler, and Seymour Mandelbaum) *A New History of the United States,* Holt, 1974; *Daniel Webster* (biography), Norton, 1978; *Wendell and Ann Phillips: The Community of Reform, 1840-1884,* Norton, 1980. Contributor to *Journal of Religion, Boston Public Library Quarterly,* and other journals.

WORK IN PROGRESS: A biography of John C. Calhoun.

* * *

BELL, Janet
See CLYMER, Eleanor

* * *

BELL, Winifred 1914-

PERSONAL: Born October 10, 1914, in Detroit, Mich.; daughter of Rupert A. (a corporation lawyer) and Elizabeth (Simmons) Bell. *Education:* University of Michigan, A.B., 1936, M.S.W., 1944; Columbia University, D.S.W., 1964. *Home:* 15700 Van Aken Blvd., Apt. 1, Shaker Heights, Ohio 44120. *Office:* Department of Social Services, Mather Hall, Cleveland State University, 1983 East 24th St., Cleveland, Ohio 44115.

CAREER: Michigan Child Guidance Clinic, Ann Arbor, psychiatric social worker, 1942-43; Family Service Society of Metropolitan Detroit, Detroit, Mich., district supervisor, 1944-48; Adult Psychiatric Clinic, Detroit, casework supervisor and acting director, 1948-59; U.S. Department of Health, Education, and Welfare, Washington, D.C., demonstration project specialist in Bureau of Family Services, 1962-66; University of Maryland at Baltimore, professor of social work, 1966-68; State University of New York at Albany, School of Social Welfare, professor of social policy, 1968-72; New York University, New York, N.Y., professor of social policy and co-director of Center for Study of Income Maintenance Policy, 1972-75; Comision sobre Sistema de Seguridad Social Integral, San Juan, Puerto Rico, associate director of research, 1975-76; Cleveland State University, Cleveland, Ohio, professor of social work, 1977—. Member of social service reorganization task force, U.S. Department of Health, Education and Welfare, 1968-69; member of New York State Committee on Children, 1972-75. Consultant to public welfare and mental health departments, and to model city programs. *Member:* American Sociological Association, Council on Social Work Education, American Civil Liberties Union, New York Civil Liberties Union (member of executive board, 1974-75).

WRITINGS: (With Elizabeth Wickenden) *Public Welfare: Time for a Change,* School of Social Work, Columbia University, 1961; *Aid to Dependent Children,* Columbia University Press, 1965; (with Robert Lekachman and Alvin L. Schorr) *Public Policy and Income Distribution,* Center for Studies in Income Maintenance Policy, School of Social Work, New York University, 1974; (with Dennis M. Bushe) *Neglecting the Many, Helping the Few: The Impact of the 1967 AFDC Work Incentives,* Center for Studies in Income Maintenance Policy, School of Social Work, New York University, 1975; (editor, with Schorr and Martha Ozawa, and contributor) *Taxation,* Center for Studies in Income Maintenance Policy, School of Social Work, New York University, 1975; (editor, with Schorr and Ozawa, and contributor) *Welfare Policy,* Center for Studies in Income Maintenance Policy, School of Social Work, New York University, 1975; *Contemporary Social Welfare,* Macmillan, 1983.

Contributor: Frank Loewenberg and Ralph Dolgoff, editors, *Social Intervention Practice,* F. E. Peacock, 1972; Patricia Stickney, editor, *Student Participation,* Council on Social Work Education, 1972; Schorr, editor, *Jubilee for Our Times: A Practical Program for Income Equality,* Columbia University Press, 1977; Betty L. Baer and Ronald C. Federico, editors, *Educating the Baccalaureate Social Worker: A Curriculum Development Resource Guide,* Ballinger, 1979. Contributor of articles to social work journals.

AVOCATIONAL INTERESTS: Music, cooking, gardening.

* * *

BELLAMY, Guy 1935-

PERSONAL: Born March 21, 1935, in Bristol, England; son of James Eric and Audrey Mary (Shern) Bellamy. *Education:* Attended school in Farnham, Surrey, England. *Home:* 28 Pilgrims Close, Farnham, Surrey, England. *Agent:* John Farquharson Ltd., Bell House, 8 Bell Yard, London WC2A 2JU, England.

CAREER: Former journalist; currently full-time writer. *Military service:* Royal Air Force; served in Germany.

WRITINGS—All novels, *The Secret Lemonade Drinker,* Holt, 1977; *I Have a Complaint to Make,* Secker & Warburg, 1979; *The Sinner's Congregation,* Secker & Warburg, 1982.

WORK IN PROGRESS: Another novel, "with a title that is so good that [I am] not prepared to reveal it in case a faster writer likes it too."

SIDELIGHTS: Guy Bellamy comments: "I have never been able to understand why British novels, aside from those of

Graham Greene, are so shoddily written alongside the contemporary American product.''

* * *

BENAGH, Jim 1937-

PERSONAL: Surname is pronounced *Benn*-aw; born October 10, 1937, in Flint, Mich.; son of William E., Sr. and Christine (Hoiland) Benagh; children: Jeffrey, Jason. *Education:* Attended University of Michigan, 1955-56, 1957-60. *Office address:* P.O. Box 1113, Englewood Cliffs, N.J. 07632.

CAREER: Cheboygan Daily Tribune, Cheboygan, Mich., sports editor and head photographer, 1953-55; *Ann Arbor News,* Ann Arbor, Mich., sports writer, 1960-61; *Sport* (magazine), New York City, associate editor, 1962-64; *Newsweek* (magazine), New York City, assistant sports editor, 1964-68, acting sports editor, 1968; free-lance writer and editor, 1968—. Public relations specialist for Mexican Olympic Committee, 1968; part-time sports editor, Random House, 1969; public relations writer for Fight of Champions, Inc., 1971. *Military service:* U.S. Army Reserve, sports editor of newspaper at Fort Knox, Ky., 1960-66. *Member:* Football Writers Association of America, Metropolitan Track and Field Writers Association (New York).

WRITINGS: Tom Harmon's Book of Sports Information (Teen-Age Book Club selection), J. Lowell Pratt, 1963, revised edition, 1965; *The Official Encyclopedia of Sports,* F. Watts, 1964; *1967 Pictorial Sports Annual,* Hammond, Inc., 1967; *Incredible Athletic Feats,* Hart Publishing, 1969.

(With Marv Albert) *Krazy about the Knicks,* Hawthorn, 1971, revised edition, 1973; *Watch It!: How to Watch Sports on T.V.,* Benjamin Co., 1971; *Official Ali-Frazier Fight Program,* Fight of the Century, Inc., 1971; *The Great Olympians,* StadiaSports, 1972; (and editor with Otto Penzler) *ABC's Wide World of Sports Encyclopedia,* StadiaSports, 1973; *Walt Frazier: Superguard of Pro Basketball,* Scholastic Book Services, 1973; *Incredible Football Feats,* Tempo Books, 1974; *Incredible Basketball Feats,* Tempo Books, 1974; *Incredible Baseball Feats,* Tempo Books, 1975; *Incredible Olympic Feats,* McGraw, 1976; *Making It to #1: How College Football and Basketball Teams Get There,* Dodd, 1976; *Terry Bradshaw: Superarm of Pro Football,* Putnam, 1976.

Picture Story of Wayne Gretsky, Messner, 1982. Contributor to *Encyclopedia Americana.* Contributor of more than three hundred articles and photographs to magazines, including *True, Argosy, Money, Boys' Life, Life,* and *Tennis,* and to newspapers, including *Washington Star* and *New York Times.* Cofounder and first editor of *Grid-iron;* former sports editor of *Michigan Daily.*

WORK IN PROGRESS: A novel about college sports.

SIDELIGHTS: Jim Benagh writes: ''Writing has allowed me to combine my two favorite pastimes—sports and travel—into a full-time profession. I've been to three summer Olympics, the Soviet Union, most major American cities and many intriguing smaller ones . . . and each time have managed to combine the trip with a sportswriting tie-in. But I also enjoy delving into the depths of sports and sports personalities and not just treat the fun and fames of sports as a vacation vehicle. I think that sports have a wide social impact in the nation and that needs to be studied beyond the day-to-day scores.''†

* * *

BENDER, Todd K. 1936-

PERSONAL: Born January 8, 1936, in Stark County, Ohio; son of Kenneth W. and Minnie (Hill) Bender; married Patricia Ann Minor, September 6, 1958; children: Kirsten Ann, Claire Elaine. *Education:* Kenyon College, B.A., 1958; University of Sheffield, graduate study, 1958-59; Stanford University, Ph.D., 1962. *Office:* Department of English, University of Wisconsin, Madison, Wis. 53706.

CAREER: Instructor in English at Stanford University, Stanford, Calif., 1961-62, and Dartmouth College, Hanover, N.H., 1962-63; University of Virginia, Charlottesville, assistant professor of English, 1963-66; University of Wisconsin—Madison, associate professor, 1966-73, professor of English, 1973—. Visiting professor at University of Athens, Athens, Greece, 1978-79. *Awards, honors:* Fulbright scholar at University of Sheffield, 1958-59; American Council of Learned Societies grant-in-aid for work at Oxford University, 1963, and fellowship at Bibliotheque Nationale, Paris, France, 1965-66; senior Fulbright scholar at University of Athens, 1978-79.

WRITINGS—Published by Garland Publishing, except as indicated: *Gerard Manley Hopkins: The Classical Background and Critical Reception of His Work,* Johns Hopkins Press, 1966; *A Concordance to Hopkins,* University of Wisconsin Press, 1970; *A Concordance to Heart of Darkness,* Southern Illinois University Press, 1973.

A Concordance to Lord Jim, 1975; *Modernism in Literature,* Holt, 1976; *A Concordance to Almayer's Folly,* 1978; *A Concordance to The Secret Agent,* 1979; *A Concordance to Victory,* 1979; *Concordance to The Shadow Line and Youth,* 1980; *Concordance to Pound's Cantos,* 1981; *Concordance to Nigger of the Narcissus,* 1981; *Concordance to Set of Six,* 1981; *Concordance to Arrow of Gold,* 1981; *Concordance to Jane Eyre,* 1981; *Concordance to The Good Soldier,* 1982; *Concordance to Keats,* 1982; *Concordance to Tales of Hearsay and Tales of Unrest,* 1982; *Concordance to Under Western Eyes,* 1983. Contributor to periodicals, including *Times Literary Supplement* and *Criticism.*

SIDELIGHTS: Todd K. Bender told *CA:* ''I am particularly interested in placing the analysis of literary language on a sounder footing by examining closely the vocabulary, sentence structure, and textual transmission of the work. The emergence of the computer and peripheral equipment in the last twenty years has revolutionized the tasks of the lexicographer, the editor, and the critic.

''Many of my books are concordances or verbal indexes, which simply list in alphabetical order all words used in a work and direct the reader to their contexts while revealing the frequency of each word's occurrence and the relative frequency of each type and token in the author's lexicon. These tables are reference works which can be used to improve the reader's understanding of the range of meaning of a given word, or the verbal habits of an author, or the likelihood that a passage has been contaminated in the process of textual transmission.''

* * *

BENGE, Eugene J(ackson) 1896-

PERSONAL: Born May 3, 1896, in Philadelphia, Pa.; son of Elmer (an accountant) and Ella Frances (Logan) Benge; married Grace Griffith, July 22, 1953; children: Jane (Mrs. Vincent J. Danielenko). *Education:* Teachers' College, B.S., 1917; Carnegie Institute of Technology (now Carnegie-Mellon University), additional study, 1919-20. *Politics:* Republican. *Religion:* Protestant.

CAREER: Atlantic Refining Co., Philadelphia, Pa., industrial relations manager, 1920-25; Philadelphia Rapid Transit Co., Philadelphia, chief statistician, 1926-29; American Oil Co., Baltimore, Md., personnel manager, 1930-35; training director, Firestone Tire Co., 1936-38; management consultant and director of self-developed management seminars in eleven foreign countries, 1939—. Former director of Sorg Paper Co.; director and member of executive committee of Council for International Progress in Management. *Military service:* U.S. Army, Psychological Examining Corps, 1971-18; became sergeant first class. *Member:* Society for the Advancement of Management (fellow; life member; international vice-president). *Awards, honors:* Received honor key from Society for the Advancement of Management, 1953, for a paper on industrial incentives.

WRITINGS: Standard Practice in Personnel Work, H. W. Wilson, 1920; *Cutting Clerical Costs,* McGraw, 1931; *Office Economies,* Ronald, 1937; (with S.L.H. Burk and E. N. Hay) *Manual of Job Evaluation,* Harper, 1941; *Manpower in Marketing,* Harper, 1945; *You, Triumphant!,* Harper, 1946; (with Jean Benge) *Win Your Man and Keep Him,* Windsor Books, 1948.

The Right Career for You, Funk, 1950; *Finding and Using Your Magic Emotion Power,* Prentice-Hall, 1958; *Salesmanship,* Alexander Hamilton Institute, 1958; *How to Become a Successful Executive,* Fell, 1960; *The Office: Nerve Center of Management,* Alexander Hamilton Institute, 1963; *Psychology Updated for Managers,* Assignments in Management, 1968.

How to Manage for Tomorrow, Dow Jones-Irwin, 1975; (with others) *Elements of Modern Management,* American Management Association, 1976; *How to Use Your Physical and Emotional Ability to Overcome Your Problems and Reach Your Goals,* Dow Jones-Irwin, 1977; *How to Lick Inflation before It Licks You,* Fell, 1981.

Management manuals; all published by Personnel Journal: *How to Reduce Administrative Overhead,* 1964; *A Performance Pay Plan for Salaried Employees,* 1964; *Statistics for Executives,* 3rd edition (Benge was not associated with earlier edition), 1965; *Techniques for Long Range Planning,* 1966; *Ten Top Management Problems,* 1967; *Appraising Key Man Performance,* 1967; *Planning and Control Methods for Managers,* 1973.

Also author of numerous management booklets. Author of monthly column in *American Bottler,* for seven years. Contributor of several hundred articles on business topics to various periodicals.

SIDELIGHTS: Eugene J. Benge once wrote *CA:* "I am particularly interested in the factors of success [and] have written and lectured on the subject. I believe, with the futurists, that we have already entered the post-industrial era, which will greatly alter our lives.

"I wrote a novel-length story, 'The Le Brun Cave Murders,' for one of the pulps which went out of business the next month; I have always hoped there was no connection!" Benge's books have been published in Japanese, Italian, Spanish, and Portuguese.†

* * *

BENWARD, Bruce (Charles) 1921-

PERSONAL: Born June 29, 1921, in Churubusco, Ind.; son of Charles Arthur and Maude (Jones) Benward; married Mary Gene Aishe, July 4, 1942; children: Cynthia, Tamara, Nadia. *Education:* Indiana University at Bloomington, B.Mus., 1942, M.Mus., 1943; University of Rochester, Ph.D., 1950. *Home:* 5602 Hammersley Rd., Madison, Wis. 53711. *Office:* School of Music, University of Wisconsin, Madison, Wis. 53706.

CAREER: University of Idaho, Moscow, instructor in music, 1945-46; University of Arkansas, Fayetteville, assistant professor, 1946-49, professor of music and chairman of department, 1951-65; University of Wisconsin—Madison, professor of music, 1965—, chairman of School of Music, 1969-74, director of graduate studies, 1975—. Member of Spokane Symphony Orchestra, 1945-46. *Member:* National Association of Schools of Music (chairman of graduate commission, 1976—), National Association of Music Executives of State Universities, Music Teachers National Association (regional officer), American Musicological Society, American Association of University Professors, Kappa Kappa Psi, Phi Eta Sigma, Phi Mu Alpha, Rotary Club. *Awards, honors:* Named Arkansas Traveler, 1965.

WRITINGS—All published by W. C. Brown, except as indicated: *Teacher's Dictation Manual in Ear Training* (includes workbook), 1961, 2nd edition published as *Workbook in Advanced Ear Training,* 1969, 3rd edition, 1974; *College Ear Training Applied* (records), 1961; (with Barbara Jackson) *Practical Beginning Theory,* 1963, 5th edition, 1982; (with Jackson) *Teacher's Key for Practical Beginning Theory* (includes recordings), 1963; *Sightsinging Complete,* 1965, 3rd edition, 1980; *Teacher's Dictation Manual in Advanced Ear Training and Sightsinging,* 1969.

Music in Theory and Practice, Volumes I-II, 1977, 2nd edition, 1981; *Ear Training: A Technique for Listening,* 1978, 2nd edition, 1983.

AVOCATIONAL INTERESTS: Color photography, photographic graphics, photographic silk screen, computer assisted instruction.

* * *

BERKMAN, Edward O(scar) 1914- (Ted Berkman)

PERSONAL: Born January 9, 1914, in Brooklyn, N.Y.; son of Samuel (a dentist) and Bertha (a legal secretary; maiden name, Holtzmann) Berkman; married Annahrae White, July, 1957 (divorced November, 1958). *Education:* Cornell University, A.B., 1933; also studied at Columbia University, 1934-35, Contemporary School of Music, 1953-54, and University of California, Los Angeles, 1955-56. *Politics:* "Exemplified by Chester Bowles, William O. Douglas." *Religion:* Jewish. *Residence:* Santa Barbara, Calif. *Agent:* Owen Laster, William Morris Agency, 1350 Avenue of the Americas, New York, N.Y. 10019.

CAREER: New York Daily Mirror, New York, N.Y., assistant city editor, foreign editor, and re-write man, 1933-36 and 1940-42; screenwriter for various film companies, 1938-40; American Broadcasting Co. and Overseas News Agency, foreign correspondent, 1945-46; United Nations Appeal for Children, worldwide director of information, 1947-48; screenwriter, 1950-60; author and television scriptwriter, 1960—. Lecturer, New School for Social Research, 1968, and Marymount College, 1972-75; instructor in screenwriting, Antioch College, 1979-80; instructor in screenwriting and biography, University of California, Santa Barbara, 1980-82; lecturer and workshop leader, Santa Barbara Writers Conference, 1982. Former member of board of directors of Trafalgar Hospital; member of board of directors of Center for Creative Learning. *Wartime service:* U.S. Foreign Broadcast Intelligence Service, Balkan-Middle East chief attached to U.S. Army, Psychological Warfare Branch, 1942-46; served in Cairo. *Member:* Writers Guild of America, Phi Beta Kappa.

AWARDS, HONORS: Best of show gold medals for non-theatrical films from Cleveland Film Festival, 1949, for "All I Need Is a Conference," and from Berlin Film Festival, 1955, for "Strangers in Paradise"; Christopher Award, 1957, for screenplay "Fear Strikes Out"; citation from American Jewish Congress, 1963, for "Cast a Giant Shadow"; fellowship from MacDowell Colony, 1969-70; Oppie award, 1972, naming *To Seize the Passing Dream* as best biographical novel.

WRITINGS—All under name Ted Berkman: *Cast a Giant Shadow* (biography of Colonel David Marcus), Doubleday, 1962, abridged edition, Jewish Publication Society, 1967; *Sabra* (on Israel's six-day war), Harper, 1969; *To Seize the Passing Dream* (biography of James McNeill Whistler), Doubleday, 1972; *The Lady and the Law* (on Fanny Holtzmann), Little, Brown, 1976; (with Janey Jimenez) *My Prisoner* (about Patty Hearst), Sheed, 1977.

Filmscripts: "The Squeaker," London Films, 1937; "The Green Cockatoo," London Films, 1939; "Bedtime for Bonzo," Universal, 1951; "Fear Strikes Out," Paramount, 1957; "Edge of Fury," United Artists, 1958; "Girl in the Night," Warner Brothers, 1960.

Author of television scripts for "Studio One," "Theater Guild of the Air," "This Proud Land," "Behind Closed Doors," and "Decision" (memoirs of Harry S Truman).

Contributing columnist, *Christian Science Monitor,* 1979-82; author of column for *Santa Barbara Magazine,* 1981-82; theatre critic, *Santa Barbara News and Review.* Writer of songs and lyrics published by Chappell. Contributor to popular magazines, including *New Republic, American Mercury, Coronet, Diplomat,* and *American Spectator;* contributor of book reviews to *Los Angeles Times,* 1978.

SIDELIGHTS: Ted Berkman gave the first eyewitness account of the King David Hotel explosion from Jerusalem in 1946, later served as informal adviser to Edward R. Murrow on Middle East affairs, and became a lecturer and appeared on national television and radio programs. His political involvement led him to work as campaign aide, speechwriter, and consultant to political figures including Averill Harriman and Chester Bowles. Berkman's film, "Bedtime for Bonzo," starring Ronald Reagan and a chimpanzee, regained popularity in 1980 when Reagan ran for and was elected president of the United States.

His life-long involvement with music (his songs were performed at the White House by Hildegarde in 1960) has taken him into jazz piano studies.

AVOCATIONAL INTERESTS: Swimming, table tennis, chess.

BIOGRAPHICAL/CRITICAL SOURCES: New York World-Telegram and Sun, October 9, 1962; *Miami News,* May 5, 1963; *Haaretz,* May 2, 1969; *New York Post,* March 11, 1972; *Santa Barbara News and Review,* October 23, 1980; *Santa Barbara News Press,* November 20, 1980; *People,* December 15, 1980; *Portal Magazine* (University of California, Santa Barbara), April 10, 1981.

BERKMAN, Ted
See BERKMAN, Edward O(scar)

* * *

BERKSON, Bill 1939-

PERSONAL: Born August 30, 1939, in New York, N.Y.; son of Seymour (a journalist) and Eleanor (Lambert) Berkson; married; children: one son. *Education:* Attended Brown University, 1957-59, Columbia University, 1959-60, and New School for Social Research, 1959-61. *Address:* P.O. Box 389, Bolinas, Calif. 94924.

CAREER: Art News, New York City, editorial associate, 1960-63; free-lance art critic in New York City, 1962-66; WNDT-TV, New York City, associate producer, "Art-New York" series, 1964-65; New School for Social Research, New York City, instructor in creative writing and literature, 1964-69; Yale University, New Haven, Conn., visiting fellow, 1969-70; Big Sky Books (publishers), Bolinas, Calif., editor, 1971—. Part-time writer, editor, and researcher, Museum of Modern Art, New York City, 1965-69; editor, Best & Co., 1969. *Awards, honors:* Dylan Thomas Memorial Award for Poetry, New School for Social Research, 1959; grant from Poets Foundation, 1968; resident at Yaddo, 1968; National Endowment for the Arts fellowship for creative writing in poetry, 1979-80.

WRITINGS: Saturday Night: Poems 1960-61, Tibor de Nagy, 1961; (editor) Frank O'Hara, *In Memory of My Feelings,* illustrated by 30 American artists, Museum of Modern Art, 1967; *Shining Leaves,* Angel Hair, 1969; *Recent Visitors,* Angel Hair, 1974; *Ants,* Arif, 1975; *100 Women,* Simon & Schuchat, 1975; *Enigma Variations,* Big Sky, 1975; *Blue Is the Hero: Poems 1960-74,* L Publications, 1976; (editor with Joe LeSueur) *Homage to Frank O'Hara,* Creative Arts, 1980; *Start Over,* Tombouctou, 1983.

Contributor to various anthologies. Contributor of poetry and articles to periodicals, including *Poetry, Big Table, Paris Review, Locus Solus, Mercure de France, Art and Literature, Art News, Arts, Kulchur,* and *Art in America.*

WORK IN PROGRESS: Parts of the Body.

BIOGRAPHICAL/CRITICAL SOURCES: Poetry, August, 1962; *The World,* Number 29, 1974.

* * *

BERLITZ, Charles (L. Frambach) 1914-
(Charles-Francois Bertin)

PERSONAL: Born November 22, 1914, in New York, N.Y.; son of Charles L. and Melicent (Berlitz) Frambach; Berlitz added to surname at request of grandfather, Maximilian D. Berlitz; married Valerie Ann Seary (an editor and writer), January 28, 1950; children: Lin Maria, Marc Daniel. *Education:* Yale University, A.B. (magna cum laude), 1936. *Politics:* Independent. *Religion:* Episcopal. *Home:* Glen Cove, Long Island, N.Y.; and 2816 Northeast 25th Ct., Ft. Lauderdale, Fla. 33305.

CAREER: Berlitz Schools of Languages, New York, N.Y., 1934-67, began as summer teacher at New York school while student at Yale, became assistant director of Chicago school, 1936, director of Berlitz schools in Brooklyn, N.Y., Baltimore, Md., Boston, Mass., 1936-40, language coordinator in Venezuela, 1941, vice-president of Berlitz Schools of Languages and president of Berlitz Publications, Inc., 1946-67. *Military service:* U.S. Army Reserve, twenty-five years of service in Intelligence, Counter Intelligence and Special Warfare; on active duty, 1941-46, 1947-49; became major; retired as lieutenant colonel, 1975. *Member:* Reserve Officers Association, Military Order of World Wars, Yale Club (New York).

WRITINGS—Published by Grosset, except as indicated: *The Berlitz Self-Teacher: Spanish,* 1949; *The Berlitz Self-Teacher: French,* 1950; *The Berlitz Self-Teacher: Italian,* 1950; *The Berlitz Self-Teacher: German,* 1951; *The Berlitz Self-Teacher: Russian,* 1951; *El Berlitz sin maestro: Ingles,* 1951; *The Berlitz Self-Teacher: Hebrew,* 1953; *The Berlitz Self-Teacher: Portuguese,* 1953; *French for Travelers,* 1954, 2nd edition, 1962; *Spanish for Travelers,* 1954, 2nd edition, 1962; *Italian for Travelers,* 1954, 2nd edition, 1962; *German for Travelers,* 1954; *Basic French Dictionary,* 1957; *Basic Spanish Dictionary,* 1957; *Basic Italian Dictionary,* 1957; *Basic German Dictionary,* 1957; (revisor) Maximilian Delphinus Berlitz, *English: First Book,* revised American edition (C. Berlitz was not associated with previous edition), Berlitz Publications, 1957; *Ingles para viajeros,* 1958; (revisor) M. D. Berlitz, *English: Book II,* revised American edition (C. Berlitz was not associated with previous edition), Berlitz Publications, 1958; *Scandinavian Languages for Travelers,* 1959, 2nd edition, 1962; *Russian Phrase Book,* 1959.

Diners' Dictionary, 1961; *World Wide Phrase Book,* 1962; *Hebrew Phrase Book,* 1964; *Japanese Phrase Book,* 1964; *Greek Phrase Book,* 1966; *The Mystery of Atlantis,* 1969.

Mysteries from Forgotten Worlds, photographs, drawings, and reports by J. Manson Valentine, Doubleday, 1972; (revisor) Rick Carrier and Barbara Carrier, *Dive: The Complete Book of Skin Diving,* revised edition, Crowell, 1973; *The Bermuda Triangle,* Doubleday, 1974; (revisor) C. O. Mason, *Dictionary of Foreign Terms,* 2nd edition (Berlitz was not associated with previous edition), Crowell, 1974; (with Valentine) *Without A Trace: New Information from the Triangle,* Doubleday, 1977; (with William Moore) *The Philadelphia Experiment: Project Invisibility,* Grosset, 1979.

The Roswell Incident, Grosset, 1980; *Doomsday: 1999 A.D.,* Doubleday, 1981; *Native Tongues,* Grosset, 1982.

With wife Valerie Berlitz; published by Grosset: *French for Children,* Book I, 1959, Book II, 1961; *Spanish for Children,* Book I, 1959, Book II, 1961; *German for Children,* Book I, 1959, Book II, 1962; *Italian for Children,* Book I, 1959; *Alphabet and Numbers: French,* 1963; *Alphabet and Numbers: Spanish,* 1963; *My First Spanish Book,* 1965; *My Second Spanish Book,* 1965; *My First French Book,* 1965; *My Second French Book,* 1965.

"Step-by-Step" series; published by Everest House: *French Step-by-Step,* 1979; *Spanish Step-by-Step,* 1979; *German Step-by-Step,* 1979; *Italian Step-by-Step,* 1979.

Under pseudonym Charles-Francois Bertin; "Passport" series; published by World Publishing, 1972; reprinted under author's real name by New American Library, 1974: *Passport to French; Passport to Spanish; Passport to German; Passport to Italian.*

Also author, under name Charles Berlitz, of "Berlitz Method" books, some revisions, some new editions; published by Berlitz Publications: *Primer libro, Segundo libro,* and *Escuela del aire,* in Spanish; *Premier livre, Deuxieme Livre,* and *Ecole de l'Air,* in French; *Erstes Buch* and *Zweites Buch,* in German; *Libro Italiano,* in Italian; and books in Afrikaana, Chinese, Greek, Hindi, Hungarian, two languages of Indonesia, Japanese, Korean, Malay, Swahili, and Urdu.

Author of "Ingles sin maestro" book and record course, for International Correspondence Schools; U.S. Army Training texts and tapes for Amharic, Hause, Khmer, Lao, Lingala, Somali, Swahili, and Urdu; texts and records for self-teaching record courses, in French, Spanish, German, Italian, and English for speakers of Spanish, published by Berlitz Publications; French, Spanish, and German film strip courses, published by Pathescope. Revisor of "Language Thirty," a collection of books and tapes for thirty different language courses, published by Dun Donnelly.

Author of column "Languages in the News," syndicated to seventy newspapers by Associated Press, 1961-64.

WORK IN PROGRESS: A book on Chinese for speakers of English.

SIDELIGHTS: "The force and excitement of learning a language," Charles Berlitz claims in the *Washington Post,* "is in the discovery of a whole new way of looking at the world. When we penetrate this different way of thinking, we have added another dimension to our personalities."

Although no longer associated with the Berlitz Schools of Languages, Berlitz is the grandson of the international chain's founder, Maximilian D. Berlitz. The author credits his grandfather with not only encouraging his study of languages, but also with fostering his interest in archeology. In a *Publishers Weekly* interview with Robert Dahlin, Berlitz notes that one of his grandfather's friends was linguist and Egyptologist Max Muller. Berlitz recalls: "I used to copy the Egyptian hieroglyphics when I was a child, thinking it was an alphabet just like any other." This interest in ancient civilizations led Berlitz to write *The Bermuda Triangle,* which explores the disappearances of planes and ships in an area of the Atlantic bounded by Bermuda, southern Florida, and a point southeast of Puerto Rico, as well as a series of later books dealing with Atlantis (the legendary lost continent) and other mysterious phenomena. Although several of his most recent books have dealt with such mysteries, Berlitz has never abandoned his interest in languages.

This interest in languages began at an early age when Berlitz's grandfather, who spoke fifty-eight languages, hung picture charts of animals, countries, fruits, and people in his grandson's bedroom. As the younger Berlitz grew up, his grandfather instructed members of the family to speak to the child in different languages and to explain these charts to the boy, each using a different tongue. His mother spoke to him in French, his father in English, his grandfather in German, and his cousin and the domestic help in Spanish. As a result, by the time Berlitz was four, he could speak four languages. "I didn't realize they were speaking different languages," Berlitz told Krucoff. "I thought each person had their own particular way of speaking. . . . I wanted my own language, too."

Berlitz began his formal affiliation with the Berlitz Schools of Languages while still a student at Yale University. For three summers, he taught courses at the New York Berlitz school. Eventually, he became vice-president of the entire U.S. Berlitz educational system and president of Berlitz Publications, Inc., the company's publishing house. During the time Berlitz held these positions (a period of more than twenty years), he oversaw the production of nearly fifty textbooks, tourist phrase books, and pocket dictionaries. Over 28 million copies of these books were sold during that same period. Berlitz was also instrumental in the development of record and tape language courses, and he set up special courses in various languages for employees of U.S. firms doing business overseas, as well as English courses for natives employed by these same companies.

In the mid 1960s, the publishing firm Crowell, Collier & Macmillan acquired control of Berlitz Schools of Languages and its subsidiary companies. Soon thereafter Berlitz left the schools entirely and attempted to establish a company bearing his own name, but Crowell, Collier & Macmillan obtained a temporary court order enjoining Berlitz from using his surname professionally. The company contended that the word "Berlitz" was a trademark and therefore Berlitz's use of his name on published material was illegal. Although Berlitz joked about the matter—in a *New York Times* article, Henry Ramont quoted the linguist as saying, "I am learning a rich new vocabulary of legal terms like 'injunction' and 'cross-motion,' which I expect to find very helpful for future translations"—it was a serious situation. During this period, material published by Berlitz either carried his name in very small print on the cover, or appeared under the pseudonym Charles-Francois Bertin, the name Berlitz had used in the French underground during World War II.

After a court fight of many years duration, the appellate division of the New York Supreme Court granted Berlitz the right to put his name on his work. Berlitz also recieved a $376,000 judgment for lost earnings. The decision, however, requires Berlitz to make clear to readers that he is no longer associated with the Berlitz schools. For this reason, all of his books now bear the notation: "Since 1967, Mr. Berlitz has not been connected with the Berlitz Schools in any way."

About this same time, Berlitz began to make frequent trips to Florida to research information for his book *The Bermuda Triangle*. His interest in the subject, he reports in the book, began when he was an investigative officer with the U.S. Air Force at the time of the disappearance in the Triangle of six Navy torpedo bombers. In *Publishers Weekly* Berlitz notes that while with the Air Force he "did a lot of investigating." And, he adds, "when I researched my books on Atlantis and the Bermuda Triangle, I approached them just as an investigator would." Besides delving into the disappearance of the Navy bombers, Berlitz also studies many other occurrences in the volume, including the story of the 425-foot freighter *Marine Sulphur Queen* which vanished off the Dry Tortugas in 1963 and the reported disappearance of the ocean racer *Revonoc* off the coast of Florida in 1967.

Despite Berlitz's efforts to document these cases, some critics view the book with skepticism. John Moorhead, in his review in the *Christian Science Monitor*, for example, writes: "The strange doings are described with relish. . . . [But Berlitz] leaves this reader feeling unconvinced and slightly manipulated." A *Time* reviewer notes: "*Triangle* takes off from established facts, then proceeds to lace its theses with a hodgepodge of half-truths, unsubstantiated reports and unsubstantial science." But Berlitz believes the theories expressed in *The Bermuda Triangle* are correct. According to Dahlin, Berlitz maintains "that the people and planes and ships that have reportedly disappeared in the Bermuda Triangle have been victims of some sort of electromagnetic disturbances that cause them to disintegrate and fall into the sea." Also, the author points out that *The Bermuda Triangle* is a popular success, if not a critical one. The book appeared on the *New York Times* best seller list for forty weeks, has been translated into twenty-two languages, and has sold approximately ten million copies worldwide.

The publication of Berlitz's book on the Triangle spawned numerous other books and articles about the same subject. In addition, so many people contacted Berlitz with stories of personal experiences within the Bermuda Triangle that he soon published *Without a Trace*, which included this additional information. Berlitz also organized research expeditions to explore his theories on the Triangle as well as on the existence of Atlantis. During one of his trips into the Caribbean, Berlitz reported the existence of a pyramid estimated to be 420 feet high with a base of 540 feet resting on the bottom of the ocean. He details this and other discoveries in *Without a Trace*.

Berlitz's love for collecting interesting facts, evident in *The Bermuda Triangle* and his other books exploring mysterious happenings, is also noted in *Native Tongues*, his first book about language itself rather than how to learn one. Dahlin refers to *Native Tongues* as "an agreeable hodgepodge of oddments and sundry bits of information about speech. Arranged in . . . chapters constructed of related facts and observations, the book is just the thing to poke about in for piquant revelations concerning the vagaries of words." In his *Chicago Tribune* article, Mike Winerup adds, "The book is brimming with the sort of tidbits you will read and say, "Now, I didn't know that.'" Berlitz's own explanation of the book appears in the *Washington Post*: "I have tried . . . to write an overview of how language has affected the people of the world all through history, to deal with curious linguistic customs and give readers a glimpse of how our neighbors on Planet Earth think."

Many of the facts Berlitz had gathered together in *Native Tongues* deal with the history of language, an area that fascinates the author. He observes, for instance, "The internationally-used Rx on prescriptions is an ancient Egyptian hieroglyph for the eye of Horus, an Egyptian god of medicine." He also notes that the Italian greeting *ciao* came from the word "slave," *schiavo*, or "I am your slave," and that English was selected over German as the official language of the United States by only one vote.

Asked about his plans for the future, Berlitz told Dahlin, "I don't know what I'll write about next, . . . but I'm always interested in languages." Although he knows many languages, the linguist continues studying them. His latest linguistic interests include Quechua (the language of the Incas), Navaho, Nahuatl (the language of the Aztecs), and Maya. He realizes that many do not share his own love of languages, but comments in the *Washington Post* that for him knowing just one language would be "like living in a huge, wonderful house and never leaving one room."

AVOCATIONAL INTERESTS: Underwater explorations, archaeology, ethnology, history.

CA INTERVIEW

CA interviewed Charles Berlitz by phone October 16, 1981, at his home in Fort Lauderdale, Florida.

CA: You've been traveling extensively to promote your new book, Doomsday: 1999 A.D. *What sort of response are you getting to the book so far?*

BERLITZ: I'm getting a very unusual response. It seems to have, perhaps on another level, excited as much interest as *The Bermuda Triangle,* because of a series of realizations on the part of the reading public that this time it isn't just a book about an unusual manifestation on the earth's surface, but it's something that probably affects the future of almost everyone on the earth.

CA: Did Doomsday *grow naturally out of your earlier interest in Atlantis and the whole idea of a lost world?*

BERLITZ: That's a good question. In a sense, yes, perhaps over my work of many years, because, as you know, I've been especially interested in the world of the sea bottom, particularly the possibility of there having been a world culture before ours, maybe on a series of islands in the Atlantic Ocean—more or less as the legend has it. I don't think there was necessarily one special island named Atlantis, which suddenly sank beneath the sea. But I think an island empire did exist, more or less toward the center of the ocean and on adjacent islands. And I believe most of this, just as the legend has it, perished over eleven thousand years ago with the rather sudden melting of the last glacier, which raised the ocean's water level up to a thousand feet. This much at least—the melting of the glaciers—is a fact; the rising of the waters is a fact; and I believe this fact is immortalized in the worldwide legend of the flood. I've always been very interested in that. In fact, I even tried to get an expedition up Mount Ararat to see if there was something left from the flood up there. When I was there, of course, the Turks were already very much opposed to any further research in the area, because people had been flying over it and taking pictures of something that seemed to be beneath the ice. And of course, with all this, I don't mean that there was just one Noah, because every nation, including every early tribe in the world, has its own legend of the enormous catastrophe that came thousands of years ago, which some people survived. In other words, all the Noahs have had different names, and even the animals that were put on board an ark or ship or raft or something of the sort have varied according to the parts of the world where the animals are found.

CA: You charted those legends in Doomsday.

BERLITZ: I've always been interested in the flood legends, and that led me to examine the question of whether something could happen to the earth that would be catastrophic enough to destroy civilization. That's largely what eventually brought on this book, although it also came out of my own studies of prehistoric civilization, which in turn has to do with the finds at the bottom of the Bermuda Triangle. So there is a theme that goes through all this. As I studied the possibility of cosmic collision or some disaster within the world, for the last six or seven years, I came to realize that many scientists and astronomers believe the earth is passing through a very difficult period at the present time because of the lineation of the planets. This sounds like science fiction, but however you interpret it, it seems that it is happening, because the number of earthquakes and seaquakes and the amount of general weakening of the earth's surface have been going on for the past five years, together with extensive activity within the sun itself, and apparently the effect of the planets piling up on the other side of the sun. This is just one element. Another thing, of course, is that the world is in great danger, not only from cosmic collision or cosmic influences on the world, but from what mankind is doing to it through overindustrialization and overpopulation.

The final thing is that in my studies of past religions and religious prophesies (which I have, of course, researched extensively in accord with my interest in ancient history), I found, when I figured prophecies out in terms of when they last coincided with our calendar at certain historical moments, that religious prophecies from all over the world coincide within the last five or ten years of this century in predicting destruction. At first I thought this was just an interesting coincidence. Then, as I went on calculating through all the different religions, including Hinduism, Buddhism, Christianity, Judaism, the very old ones of the Egyptians and the Babylonian-Assyrian group and the North and South American Indians, I saw that almost all races in the world put a common end to our present cycle of humanity, which comes within the end of our own twentieth century.

CA: You promote the exploration of space as a possible ''ark,'' an escape from a future catastrophe to earth on the scale of the great flood of Noah's time. Do you, like Timothy Leary, Frank Herbert, and others, advocate the colonization of space as soon as possible?

BERLITZ: I strongly recommend the expansion of the space program and perhaps a common effort on the part of all people of the earth, not just for the sake of military expediency or one-upmanship on a possible enemy, but for the general protection and possibility of escape. In the last couple of pages of *Doomsday,* I wrote that, while it's possible to construct some sort of a cosmic ''ark,'' as they are trying to do in Canada and some parts of the United States, the danger of a cosmic collision seems to be increasing at the present time. The main danger of cosmic collision occurs when the stretch between the planets gets to a certain level; the planetoids, which have an eccentric orbit to the earth, can get off their course a little bit and crash into the earth. The cooperation I recommended has aroused a great deal of interest in places that feel the planets are a menace to the earth, such as the West Coast of the United States, great parts of South America, and all of Europe. I think it would be possible to protect the earth from cosmic collision to a great extent.

It would also be possible, by the use of a world earthquake council, to mitigate the effects of earthquakes to some degree. Above all, the earth should be protected from man's destruction of it, especially in regard to the atom bomb; also overindustrialization; poisoning of the seas, lakes, rivers, and the air; and cutting down the world's forests, which control the production of most of the oxygen—this is taking place at a real runaway rate in several countries.

I don't know if I made it clear enough in my book that not only are these activities a threat to the natural beauty of the environment, but we are also in physical danger from the real lack of air to breathe, and water. With Brazil going ahead with industrialization of the Amazon basin within fifteen or twenty years, which comes close up to the cutoff point, we will actually be short of air to breathe, because fifty percent of all the oxygen produced by plants on the earth comes from this enormous forest in South America. The forests in Africa have been vanishing rather quickly with the great droughts they have been having because of climatic changes. And the forests of Southeast Asia are being consumed by overpopulation. But the greatest danger to our own supply of oxygen comes from the cutting out of great swaths of forest in the middle of Brazil, which isn't necessary; Brazil just has runaway industrialization.

CA: You collaborated with William L. Moore on The Philadelphia Experiment, *published in 1979, and* The Roswell Incident *in 1980, one dealing with Navy experimentation with invisibility, and the second with a 1947 UFO landing in New Mexico. One of the main difficulties you had in researching these topics came from the official cover-up by government and military agencies.*

BERLITZ: The cover-up is only on an official basis. You can understand that nobody in the air force or the army is willing to jeopardize his career to give out information, but privately, they will. Even Senator [Barry] Goldwater tried to get a look at what was going on at Wright-Patterson and they wouldn't let him in. A commission was formed at the time of the Roswell incident that had the last word about who would know about it. It's surprising that as many people know about it as do.

As far as the Philadelphia incident is concerned, although it has to do with Einstein's unified field theory, I don't think the main features of it are that unusual when you consider that, like the later successful experiment with the atom bomb, it was based on the idea of molecular disassembling through a series of impulses. The Philadelphia experiment wasn't really successful. In two of my books I had dealt with reports of its having happened, and Moore, who was a research writer himself, was extremely interested to find out if there were additional sources to those I had mentioned. In the course of his investigations he found several more sources. In some navy circles the experiment was well known. Whether the experiment took place exactly as Moore sketched it according to information from people who were there at the time, we don't know. All we have done is make a report about the possibility of its having really happened, which I believe it did.

CA: You dealt with the Bermuda Triangle in the book by that name and also in Without a Trace. *Have subsequent research and exploration bolstered the theories you outlined in those books?*

BERLITZ: Some of the theories I mentioned in the books are pretty far out, but that doesn't mean they couldn't happen. I put them together from the disappearances that had taken place. And since I wrote the book, three of my friends have disappeared in the Triangle; a neighbor has also disappeared. That's coming pretty close to home. And people write to me from all over the country asking me to find out what has happened to their son or brother of some other relative or friend who has disappeared within the Triangle. So many people have vanished that have not been reported. Of course, it doesn't mean that everyone who goes into the Triangle is going to disappear; some people in different parts of the world have asked me why so many big ships make it through. The truth is that there are influences there, perhaps influences we just haven't given a name to because we don't know enough about magnetism and electromagnetism and whatever other natural forces may explain what is taking place in that area. Some of the big ships have gotten into serious trouble within the Triangle fairly recently; one of the large freighters disappeared just a couple of months ago. Many cruise ships have stopped in the middle of the Triangle in a fog and couldn't get radio messages out. This happened to the *Queen Mary;* it happened several times to the *Rotterdam;* it happened to the refurbished *La France,* which is now called the *Norway.* For some reason the motors stop, you lose communication, you get in a very sudden fog, and then all sorts of things begin to happen. Within the last two years, since I wrote my books, some amazing things have happened within the Bermuda Triangle, some of which seem to relate to time itself.

CA: In the public mind, your name is associated with the teaching of languages, although you haven't been with the Berlitz schools for some time. Are you still teaching languages?

BERLITZ: I have recently written a number of books for self-instruction in languages and also teach languages on certain occasions. I separated from the schools on a question of policy in 1966, and actually it was quite fortunate for me, because it gave me time to pursue my real interests, which mainly had to do with underwater archaeology and the study of prehistory. I used to pursue these interests in my rare vacations and in conjunction with my other work. When I went to different countries for my Berlitz activities (which, besides writing books, had to do with setting up programs), I always had to find time to do a little excavating on my own. So my separation from the schools was really a godsend to me in a way; it gave me unlimited time to pursue my interests. And of course the languages that my grandfather insisted I learn as a child have been extremely helpful to me, because whenever I'm on tour for a book, I speak the language of the country I'm in. In Europe they generally think I'm a native of the country or my family is from the country.

CA: The accounts vary. How many languages do you actually know?

BERLITZ: I should qualify my most fluent languages as ''television languages''—in other words, languages in which I can defend myself on television and radio, because every time you're on a big radio or television show they will make traps to catch you in something. So, of the big European languages—the ones you have to speak fairly rapidly—I speak about ten. I can get along in about fifteen others, but not enough for television or press interviews, because you not only have to know the language—you have to be able to appreciate its nuances and even make jokes in it. But I do study a good many languages, so I'm really familiar with even more than that. That's probably where people get the idea I know thirty-five or something like that, which isn't true. I should say about twelve.

CA: Do you think Americans really lack an aptitude for language, or is that just a bad excuse for not learning them?

BERLITZ: I think Americans have a great background in languages that they don't want to take advantage of. That happened principally as a result of the First World War, when big influxes of immigrants came from Europe. They wanted to forget their native languages, the children especially. We should have an enormous language resurgence in this country with a great many varied languages—not just an obvious language like Spanish, which is now very important in the country, but with all the European languages. It is my hope that through my new language books many Americans will become interested enough in their linguistic background to learn the languages of their forbears, and other languages as well.

CA: Is there work in progress that you'd like to talk about?

BERLITZ: I'm presently writing a book to make it possible for English-speaking people to learn Chinese. I'm writing another general book on languages, which more or less deals with the thought and the spirit behind languages; and this involves all languages. And then I have my own two series of language books: one is the ''Step-by-Step'' series in French, German, Spanish, and Italian; and the other is a way to start using the language right away without studying it, which is called the ''Passport'' series. It has answers you show people to choose from when you ask them a question. It's based on frequency—rather unusual for a language book. The hope is to make people so interested they'll continue studying. But the book is very usable for traveling.

As you indicated in an earlier question, I do have difficulty sometimes because many people have known me for my language experience, and others know me for the sort of work I've been doing in archaeology and what might be called the aspect of my work in the investigation of natural and cosmic mysteries. Sometimes they think I'm a different person or a relative of the other one.

CA: Are you involved in any research that you'd like to talk about?

BERLITZ: I'm living in Florida principally for underwater research in the Caribbean. I work with other researchers down here, and we are not funded by anyone except ourselves. We are now finding ruins on the floor of the Atlantic Ocean and as far out as the Azores that I believe will change the concept of archaeology over the next few years. I hope we have time before Doomsday! I must say it's a little nerve-racking to see how Nostradamus's prophecy for 1999 coincides with the other prophecies I discuss in the recent book. All of the religions and practically all the serious prophecies of ancient and modern times have independently hit on 1999.

Many people are interested in this, but some of them take it lightly. For instance, I was in a restaurant in Chile recently, and I got a note from a lady at another table who said that she had heard the world was going to end on December 31, 1999. She wanted me to tell her at what time, because she wanted to give a farewell party. (She wrote for a newspaper, and she was there in the corner with friends waiting to see what I would say.) So I wrote back that I thought it would end about 10:30, and therefore, if she started the party at 5:00, she'd have enough time for it. I think that whether or not this cosmic disaster will be as serious as expected, we're still certainly in a period of great danger through our own fault. The atom bomb, which is only one of the threats, seems to get more serious day by day. It's calculated that within the next fifteen years forty to forty-two nations will have their own bombs ready to drop on their neighbors. One way to do something about this problem is to stop the bomb. Or we might even, as it's been suggested, use the bomb for protection against planetoids, asteroids, and comets, which would be a very interesting first step toward a world council on the bomb. So I'm really not as much of an alarmist as I seem. I'm trying to do something positive to combat what I consider a tremendous danger on several levels.

BIOGRAPHICAL/CRITICAL SOURCES: Saturday Evening Post, August 4, 1956, July, 1975; *New Yorker,* February 22, 1958; *Detroit News,* May 29, 1958; *Time,* June 21, 1963, January 6, 1975; *Wall Street Journal,* February 23, 1968, April 14, 1975, July 21, 1982; *New York Times,* January 3, 1970; Charles Berlitz, *The Bermuda Triangle,* Doubleday, 1974; *Newsweek,* December 16, 1974; *Christian Science Monitor,* December 27, 1974; *Punch,* August 20, 1975; *Washington Post,* March 6, 1979, June 28, 1982; *Publishers Weekly,* June 18, 1982; *Chicago Tribune,* July 12, 1982; *Los Angeles Times Book Review,* September 12, 1982.

—Sketch by Marian Walters

—Interview by Jean W. Ross

BERL-LEE, Maria
See LEE, Maria Berl

* * *

BERNE, Leo
See DAVIES, L(eslie) P(urnell)

* * *

BERRY, Adrian M(ichael) 1937-

PERSONAL: Born June 15, 1937, in London, England; married Marina Beatrice Sulzberger, January, 1967; children: two. *Education:* Christ Church, Oxford, graduate with honors in modern history, 1959. *Home:* 11 Cottesmore Gardens, London W.8, England. *Office: Daily Telegraph,* 135 Fleet St., London EC4P 4BL, England.

CAREER: Reporter, *Walsall Observer,* 1960-61; *Birmingham Post,* Birmingham, England, subeditor, 1961-62; financial analyst, *Investor's Chronicle,* 1962-63; *New York Herald Tribune,* New York City, reporter, 1964-65; *Time,* New York City, correspondent in Los Angeles and Washington, D.C., 1965-67; *Daily Telegraph,* London, England, member of science staff, 1968-70; *Sunday Telegraph,* London, journalist, beginning 1972; *Daily Telegraph,* science correspondent, 1977—. *Member:* Royal Astronomical Society (fellow), British Interplanetary Society (fellow and senior member).

WRITINGS: The Next Ten Thousand Years: A Vision of Man's Future in the Universe, Saturday Review Press, 1974; *The Iron Sun: Crossing the Universe through Black Holes,* Dutton, 1977; *From Apes to Astronauts,* Daily Telegraph, 1981; *Koyama's Diamond: A Novel of the Far Future,* Vantage, 1982; *The Super Intelligent Machine,* J. Cape, 1983.

SIDELIGHTS: Most of Adrian M. Berry's books deal with the distant future. In *The Next Ten Thousand Years* Berry writes of what man can expect thousands of years from now. He theorizes that the earth will not be able to provide for all of man's needs, so man will inhabit and industrialize all of the planets around the sun. Berry then looks beyond this solar system and explores the additional progress he feels man is destined to make. Robert Molyneux remarks in *Library Journal* that *The Next Ten Thousand Years* is "everything it promises to be: a vision, that all too rare thing, of what is foreseeable in man's future."

Brian Aldiss, however, finds Berry's work to be more science fiction than speculation based on fact. He explains in his review of *The Next Ten Thousand Years* published in *New Statesman* that "as a sort of science fiction, such brain-storming is something to be enjoyed for the breadth and bleakness of its vision. As factual speculation, it is too carelessly jittered with assumptions as unchallenged as Jupiter itself." And a critic for *Choice* writes: "Berry's science can't be faulted: however, some of his extrapolations rest on rather shaky theoretical and experimental ground."

Looking into the future again, Berry explains the nature and properties of black holes in *The Iron Sun: Crossing the Universe through Black Holes.* In this book, he suggests that man will be able to construct black holes and that space travel will take place by spaceships entering black holes and arriving at their destinations seconds later. "It will be feasible, probably within the next 250 years," Berry writes in *The Iron Sun,* "for a spaceship to vanish in one [black hole] and reappear the very next instant in another."

R. A. Sokolov believes that Berry presents his theory in an interesting and scientific manner. He writes in the *New York Times Book Review* that Berry "has worked out a highly plausible and gripping scenario, for spreading human civilization across immense distance. . . . Right or wrong, . . . Berry makes a readable case and, along the way, manages to explain the nuts and bolts of Einsteinian space-time, while giving the layman a clear account of the present state of cosmological thought."

However, a number of critics disagree with Sokolov and feel that Berry's work has little scientific merit. In his review of *The Iron Sun* for *Times Literary Supplement,* Derek Raine remarks that "if this book were intended merely as commercially oriented light entertainment, so be it. But what is claimed, amid learned references and explanatory appendixes, is that the light-barrier has been shown to be mythical. Sadly, for those who like their fantasies to be laced with a drop of reality, this claim has simply not been substantiated."

AVOCATIONAL INTERESTS: Skiing, chess.

BIOGRAPHICAL/CRITICAL SOURCES: Adrian M. Berry, *The Iron Sun: Crossing the Universe through Black Holes,* Dutton, 1974; *New Statesman,* May 17, 1974; *Library Journal,* July, 1974, September 1, 1977; *Choice,* November, 1974; *Times Literary Supplement,* July 29, 1977; *New York Times Book Review,* August 7, 1977; *Time,* August 15, 1977.

* * *

BERRY, Jonas
See ASHBERY, John (Lawrence)

* * *

BERTIN, Charles-Francois
See BERLITZ, Charles (L. Frambach)

* * *

BETTS, Doris (Waugh) 1932-

PERSONAL: Born June 4, 1932, in Statesville, N.C.; daughter of William Elmore and Mary Ellen (Freeze) Waugh; married Lowry Matthews Betts (an attorney), July 5, 1952; children: Doris LewEllyn, David Lowry, Erskine Moore II. *Education:* Attended Women's College of the University of North Carolina (now University of North Carolina at Greensboro), 1950-53, and University of North Carolina at Chapel Hill, 1954. *Politics:* Democrat. *Office:* Department of English, University of North Carolina, Chapel Hill, N.C. 27514. *Agent:* Timothy Seldes, Russell & Volkening, Inc., 551 Fifth Ave., New York, N.Y. 10017.

CAREER: Newspaper woman working part-time on the staff of *Statesville Daily Record,* 1950-51, and *Chapel Hill Weekly and News-Leader,* 1953-54; member of editorial staff of *Sanford Daily Herald,* Sanford, N.C., 1956-57, and *North Carolina Democrat,* Raleigh, N.C., 1960-62; editor of *Sanford News Leader* (weekly), Sanford, 1962; University of North Carolina at Chapel Hill, lecturer, 1966-74, associate professor, 1974-78, professor of creative writing, 1978—, director of Freshman-Sophomore English, 1972—, director of fellows program, 1975-76, assistant dean of honors program, 1979—. Visiting lecturer in creative writing, Duke University, spring, 1971. Member of staff of Indiana University Summer Writers Conference, 1972, 1973, and Squaw Valley Writers Conference, 1974. Member of literary panel of the National Endowment for the Arts, 1979. Member of North Carolina Tercentenary Commission, 1961-62; member of board of North Carolina Committee for Continuing Education in the Humanities, 1972—. *Member:* North Carolina Writers Association.

AWARDS, HONORS: Received short-story prize from *Mademoiselle* College Fiction Contest, 1953, for "Mr. Shawn and Father Scott"; G. P. Putnam-University of North Carolina Fiction Award, 1954, for *The Gentle Insurrection;* Sir Walter Raleigh Award for Fiction from Historical Book Club of North Carolina, 1957, for *Tall Houses in Winter,* and 1965, for *The Scarlet Thread;* Guggenheim fellowship in fiction, 1958-59; Tanner Award from University of North Carolina 1973; National Book Award finalist, 1974, for *Beasts of the Southern Wild and Other Stories.*

WRITINGS: The Gentle Insurrection (story collection), Putnam, 1954; *Tall Houses in Winter* (novel), Putnam, 1957; *The Scarlet Thread* (novel), Harper, 1964; *The Astronomer and Other Stories,* Harper, 1966; *The River to Pickle Beach* (novel), Harper, 1972; *Beasts of the Southern Wild and Other Stories,* Harper, 1973; *Heading West* (novel; Book-of-the-Month Club selection), Knopf, 1981.

Short stories, originally published in *Redbook, Rebel, Woman's Day, Mademoiselle, Cosmopolitan, Ms.,* and literary reviews, have been anthologized in *Best American Short Stories, North Carolina in the Short Story, A New Southern Reader, Young Writers at Work, Red Clay Reader, Best Little Magazine Fiction, Archetypes in the Short Story, Red Clay Anthology,* and other collections. Contributor of articles, poems, and short stories to literary magazines and journals.

WORK IN PROGRESS: A novel.

SIDELIGHTS: Although hailed by a large number of critics as one of America's best fiction writers, Doris Betts has not quite received the public recognition so many people feel she truly deserves. "Among those Southern women who have contributed so vigorously to postwar American fiction, Betts has never quite got her due," Jonathan Yardley points out in the *New York Times Book Review.* "She is a tough, wise and compassionate writer. . . . A writer with a firm hold on what we in the South call 'home truths.' She has a splendid prose style, and she deserves to be read."

Although she is described by Yardley and several other reviewers as a "Southern writer," some critics feel Betts' literature transcends geographic labeling. For example, in a review of *Beasts of the Southern Wild and Other Stories,* Sammy Staggs writes in the *Library Journal* that "while most of the stories have North Carolina settings, they are not mere 'regional' samples; despite the sometimes halting prose, Betts' stories have sound enough construction to survive well beyond the fabled boundaries of the literary South." Another critic who believes Betts should not be labeled strictly as a Southern writer is Michael Mewshaw. In the *New York Times Book Review,* Mewshaw explains his thoughts in a review of *Beasts of the Southern Wild and Other Stories:* "Although liberally laced with elements of the Southern gothic, the grotesque, black humor, surrealism and fantasy, the writing escapes categorization and remains very much an index of one woman's intriguing mind."

Nowhere is Betts' "intriguing mind" more evident than in her short-story collections. A writer for the *Virginia Quarterly Review* remarks that in *The Astronomer and Other Stories* "Betts once again reveals those qualifications which place her among the finest writers of contemporary fiction. For she continues to demonstrate not only her great powers of observation and imagination, her feeling for time, place, and character, but also a wonderful sense of form and structure.''

Reviewing *Gentle Insurrection and Other Stories* for the *New York Times,* Robert Tallant writes that in this ''collection of twelve short stories, Doris Betts . . . proves herself to be already a sturdy professional writer, a master of the short story form.'' And a *Publishers Weekly* critic calls the stories in *Beasts of the Southern Wild and Other Stories* ''extraordinary . . . for the writing itself and the human insights each and every one reveals. . . . Each tale, beautiful and deeply human, haunts, moves, enlightens by perception.''

Betts is generally considered a master at describing love, human relationships, and isolation in her stories. For example, Jonathan Yardley writes in the *Washington Post Book World* that all of ''Betts' stories are concerned with affairs of the heart. They occupy familiar terrain, but Betts elevates the familiar into the mysterious and fantastic. . . . The persistent quest in her stories is for love, and often the searcher is a misfit, a grotesque of sorts; sometimes love comes only in dreams and fantasies, sometimes it does not come at all, sometimes it comes tinged with loss.'' And H. T. Kane explains in the *Chicago Sunday Tribune* that Betts has ''a great deal to say about human relations, the gulf between young and old, and about love and understanding or the lack of it.'' Evelyn Easton remarks in the *Saturday Review* that Betts ''excels in the creation of charged atmospheres, subtle tensions, and unexpressed anxieties between well-meaning people who would like to understand one another, but are hopelessly divided by our human isolation.''

Another area of Betts' work that has received favorable critical attention is her sensitive characterizations. ''The author has created fascinating characters in this powerful book,'' a *Publishers Weekly* reviewer remarks of *The River to Pickle Beach,* while William Peden comments in *Sewanee Review* that ''Betts' people come to life with a few vivid, beautifully selective strokes.'' In a *New Republic* review, Doris Grumbach describes Betts' characters as ''living, suffering persons caught in sometimes ordinary situations (childbirth, approaching death, etc.) which her subtle, rapid prose renders distinctive and memorable.'' And Rita Estok writes in *Library Journal* that *The Astronomer and Other Stories* ''reveals Doris Betts' penetrating skill in character delineation. . . . Underlying the humor there is always compassion, a recognition that the situation or person depicts life and deserves understanding.''

Humor also is an important component in Betts' writings. While most of her readers acknowledge the seriousness of her stories, they also point to the element of comedy that is always presented in a sensitive and compassionate manner. Estok feels this is nowhere more apparent than in Betts' *The Astronomer and Other Stories*. She explains in a review published in *Library Journal* that ''these stories contain much wit and humor ranging from the very subtle to sheer slapstick. But, underlying the humor, there is always compassion, a recognition that the situation or person depicts life and deserves understanding.'' And Richard Sullivan points to *The Gentle Insurrection* as still another illustration of Betts' ability to write with both humor and sobriety. He remarks in the *Chicago Sunday Tribune* that all of these stories ''deserve attentive reading, as fine, quiet perceptive pieces, marked by a strong feeling for character, an enlivening strain of good humor, and an admirable technical control.''

AVOCATIONAL INTERESTS: Reading, camping, natural history, wilderness trips, birds.

CA INTERVIEW

CA interviewed Doris Betts by phone February 17, 1982, at her office at the University of North Carolina at Chapel Hill. *Heading West,* Mrs. Betts' fourth novel and seventh book of fiction, had recently been published by Alfred Knopf. It was a Book-of-the-Month Club selection for February, 1982.

CA: You said about ten years ago that you were a short-story writer rather than a novelist. Has Heading West *changed your feeling about that?*

BETTS: It would probably be more accurate to say *Heading West* represents my *attempt* to change, because I've spent a lot of time on it—more time than on the other novels. I have, I think, reached that age when the short story is no longer as aesthetically pleasing to me. The short story, like the lyric poem, may be the form of youth, when you still believe in the revelation and the isolated moment, and you do believe that people can change in twenty-four-hour periods. Well, you get older; you can't help seeing that the more things change, the more they stay the same, just the way your grandmother told you. And you do become interested then in longer structures and also in the things that abide. And so I have wanted to learn to be a novelist, a better novelist.

CA: Are you largely pleased with Heading West*?*

BETTS: Oh no, I'm not at all satisfied with it. When you write something you're satisfied with, you may retire.

CA: Some writers tend to get very smug about what they've done.

BETTS: Well now, don't you think our culture encourages that? I see people on TV who, regardless of what they have done, feel that they are ''selling'' their work and that it is necessary to pretend total confidence. I see pimply-faced sixteen-year-olds calling themselves artists. That title ought to be awarded when you've been dead five hundred years. It's such a cheap conceit. And it's very bad for the character. I believe somehow the universe will get you if you do things like that. It's self-aggrandizement. It's not healthy. What it really betrays is that you've forgotten how many magnificent things have been done—that you haven't read Dante lately or you haven't read Tolstoy at all. If you think you're great, you haven't been paying much attention.

CA: The plot of Heading West *goes a long way from the Southern settings of your previous novels.*

BETTS: And that was deliberate.

CA: Did your own travels lead you to the westward expansion in your fiction?

BETTS: Yes, in several ways. I should give the University of North Carolina credit for widening my world in general. I did a lot of travel for the university for a while in administrative positions, and then for the National Endowment for the Arts, and even for family vacations. Our family went twice to the Grand Canyon. Once we rode down the Colorado River on small rafts with a group for two weeks, and once we hiked into the Canyon and back out again. We also rafted down the Salmon River. We had a period there when the children were just the right age to backpack. So travel produced two experiences: one which is mental and takes you out of the Southern insular way of living (much as I value it), and the other, physical, revealing to the senses a different geography. The West *is* entirely different country from the Southeast. It is country that challenges your presuppositions.

CA: I've never been to the Grand Canyon, but reading about it in Heading West, *I felt as if I were there, seeing it.*

BETTS: Except when you go, you will do what I did: you will fall back, realizing there are no words to describe it and no way quite to convey that this, of all landscapes, is a philosophical landscape. It's the most terrifyingly beautiful landscape I ever expect to see. I imagine the sea was like that for Herman Melville. It has that same sense of eternal disregard and vastness . . . an implausible sight. I can still get chills thinking about it. Maybe landscape was like that for the astronauts who looked at the moon's surface and then stepped out on it. An alien landscape, and one that would just as soon kill you as look at you.

CA: You've said that you aren't from a bookish family. What gave you the interest in books and the urge to write?

BETTS: I was always interested in books, and I'm not sure why. I was writing and reading before I went to school. In a funny way that was the great gift the church gave me, because I was reading Bible stories early. It's not a bad idea to grow up with the King James Version of the Bible if you're at all interested in language. That's very vivid, very musical language. I grew up in a mill community and went to a mill school. I had good teachers, but I doubt they would be considered good by my children; they were old-fashioned, stern, believed in memory work, diagramming sentences, all of that—and they would pop your palm with a ruler if you didn't behave well. I thought they were wonderful. So I had a good, standard education, but loved books from the beginning. When I think of what life was like before people had free public libraries, I'm glad to have waited until this century to be born, because if you like books, the whole treasures of mankind are in small-town libraries. And they were for me.

CA: Your first collection of stories, The Gentle Insurrection, *was published in 1954, when you were barely into your twenties. How early did you start writing the stories in that collection?*

BETTS: They were all written during my freshman and sophomore years in college. We were in Columbia and expecting our first child when I submitted that book to the G. P. Putnam-University of North Carolina contest and also submitted one of the stories in it to the *Mademoiselle* College Fiction Contest. And all of a sudden, bang! bang!, we had a baby and two awards in one summer. We lived on that money for several years.

CA: Which story won the Mademoiselle *College Fiction Award?*

BETTS: "Mr. Shawn and Father Scott," which seems a dreadful story now. But it's a help to have available stories you wrote when you were a college student, because that saves you from feeling superior to the students you teach. Periodically I compare what I wrote with what they're writing, and I realize they're very much better than I was; so why am I sitting here nit-picking?

CA: You had several jobs on North Carolina newspapers, starting when you were quite young as a part-timer on the Statesville Daily Record *and finally working as a full-time editor on the* Sanford News Leader. *Did you consider a career in journalism?*

BETTS: Oh yes. I actually went to what is now UNC-Greensboro intending to major in journalism. (I wound up as an English major.)

But the opportunity to go to college at all developed from my newspaper work during high school. My family had very little money. And although I had won a Duke scholarship, the difference between the scholarship figure and the total cost was still more than we could afford. I was covering sports then for the *Greensboro News,* and one morning at 3 A.M. the guy there, who was bored, began asking if I was going to college, and I told him I couldn't afford to. And he began saying, "Well, maybe we could help you get a job on the news bureau at Woman's College [now UNC-Greensboro], here in Greensboro. Maybe there would be a way to pay part of the cost." Until then, I hadn't thought college possible.

And so, when I entered college, I was grateful to newspaper people, who had encouraged me to go, given references and introductions. I thought I would transfer to Chapel Hill my junior year and continue with journalism. I lacked the audacity to believe I could ever write fiction. I would have loved to be a poet, but that was a closet wish. Although I wrote a great deal of poetry, I didn't think you admitted to that in public.

CA: Have you written any poetry recently?

BETTS: Some. It's not good now, never will be good. It's useful for condensing an idea, and good training for being able to catch an essence quickly. The poem is close to the short story. But I lack poetic talent, and I'm so sorry. I agree with Faulkner—writing poetry is the higher calling.

CA: How did you become a teacher?

BETTS: Luck. The woman who was responsible for that Putnam Prize given to *The Gentle Insurrection* taught at UNC-Chapel Hill for eighteen years. Jessie Rehder *was* the creative writing program. In 1966 she asked if I would drive over from Sanford and sit in on their honors writing course one afternoon a week for three hours. I went and enjoyed it. At the end of that semester she suddenly died, quite unexpectedly. And so by horrible luck, for which I felt guilty, they hired me. Actually, they hired two to take her place: Max Steele, who still directs the program, and me part-time. (It's always the way, you know; when you've had someone's lifeblood, it takes two or three people to replace her.) First I taught one class a semester, and then two, but once they let me in under the tent, they had a leech on their hands and did not know it. I do love it here! The university has been so good for me, I cannot tell you.

CA: When your children were small, you've said, you learned to write whenever and wherever you got a chance. You told George Wolfe in his interview published in Kite Flying and Other Irrational Acts *that you "once wrote a very bad novel during lunch hours in the restaurant of a Chapel Hill shopping center."*

BETTS: Tall Houses in Winter. That's a lunch-hour novel if I ever saw one!

CA: Now that your children are grown, is it any easier really to find time for writing, since you do so many other things?

BETTS: It ought to be, in that you do not have the constant interruptions which keep you from finishing a sentence in your head, without the baby turning over in the high chair or something. It is easier in that you can pick a whole hour or two of uninterrupted time. But your life does fill up with other duties and tasks. One either advantage or disadvantage—I'm not sure which—is if you teach yourself to write by snatches, probably when you have unbroken time you will still write by snatches. You've formed the habit. I'm still the sort of person who carries a manuscript with her, who spends ten minutes in the dentist's office revising a page and then goes in to have a filling. I doubt I ever will become systematic or orderly.

CA: You seem to have worked very hard all your life.

BETTS: I like working. I would think I had died if I weren't working.

CA: Does it have a lot to do with the way you were brought up?

BETTS: Probably. Something to do with the 1930s, hard times, with a work ethic which was very strong at my house and which came also from rural ancestors. Laziness was unforgivable. But my working hard seems to me not solely from that kind of discipline, but also the result of an inexhaustible energy. My metabolism and thermostat are set high. If I didn't work and stay busy I probably would develop neuroses and psychosomatic illnesses, because that energy would have to go somewhere.

CA: You've mentioned getting some early advice from Katherine Anne Porter, and of course critics have compared you to Flannery O'Connor and Eudora Welty. Do you feel that you've been specifically influenced by certain writers, these or others?

BETTS: Probably you can't specify the influences if you are an omnivorous reader. When I was first compared to Flannery O'Connor I had never read a word she'd written. And when I read her, I thought, yes, there is an affinity, but it is the affinity of two people who have religious interests and who both live in a Southern, essentially secular, society, even though it claims to be religious. We have both been interested in the tensions between the claim and the fact. I think I would have liked her. I have since taught her work. One contemporary writer I also admire is Walker Percy, and probably for the same affinity, but his style is different from mine: his approach is different. Probably you'd better let others analyze your influences. It doesn't make much difference whether the list is accurate. That's a card game.

CA: You've been critical of academic criticism that makes such comparisons.

BETTS: I'm less critical now that I do some of it, because I see its usefulness. Literary categories are like colored pens on a map: they speed up comprehension. They produce classroom units. They organize the memory.

CA: My very favorite work of yours is the long story "The Astronomer." How do you feel about it?

BETTS: I like it, but it isn't a story most people single out. I wrote that while I was writing *The Scarlet Thread,* so "The Astronomer" was a rest from working on the larger novel, and I see ties between the two fictions. In the dedication to *Tall Houses in Winter* I named H. Lewis Patrick, a Presbyterian minister in Charlotte, probably the best preacher I ever heard. When he was pastor of my home church, First Associate Reformed Presbyterian in Statesville, North Carolina (I was in my early teens), he'd say things like, "I would like you to read T.S. Eliot now." He quoted Yeats in the pulpit and wouldn't oppose liquor stores, so in a conservative denomination, naturally he didn't last long. In the '40s he delivered a series of sermons on the book of Hosea which underlie "The Astronomer." That Old Testament story, too, is about a prophet who was asked to love an unlovely woman and thereby learned a great deal about himself and the possible love of God. I meant the end to be somewhat ambivalent; I didn't mean for him to go as far religiously as Eva did.

And I have this terrible habit (I'm trying to give it up now) of producing an ending that shimmers out past the book and foreshadows something beyond that somebody will notice. Nobody ever does. "The Astronomer" is supposed to end right before the Russians' *Sputnik* went up. In the final scene Mr. Beam was supposed to be looking at the stars seeking divine revelation; but you were supposed to know that the next thing to happen in the sky would be human and secular. I've got to quit doing that. I tried the same thing at the end of *The River to Pickle Beach*. Everybody's supposed to know that Foley Dickinson, the boy with the motorcycle, was really going on to the 1968 Democratic National Convention in Chicago where he was going to get the hell beat out of him. All his idealism, his views on nonviolence, were going to be ruined. But nobody else ever notices those things. It's just a little game you play with your left toe.

I do have a feeling for "The Astronomer" and *Pickle Beach* because both mark a turn toward what I have continued to do better since—to examine the yearning for religious faith and the difficulty of having one nowadays.

CA: In the George Wolfe interview you talked about the autobiographical nature of a marvelous story of yours, "The Spies in the Herb House." Dò you have problems in turning things that actually happened to you into fiction?

BETTS: No. For one thing I've learned to lie and be more skillful about lying. With time I also write fewer stories that have a direct autobiographical link; more likely they have an emotional link. Two stories in that collection—that one, and "All That Glisters Isn't Gold"—are just flat autobiography. I'd never lie about those two. They happened that way, and both were important to me. *Heading West* has very little to do with me autobiographically except for places, settings . . . except that you are always inside the characters to some degree. Nancy in *Heading West* is like me in some ways, not like me in many others, just as Bebe in *The River to Pickle Beach* is somewhat like me, but very much more like my mother, as she was meant to be. My mother is much gentler than I; I'm a little more like Nancy Finch.

CA: What kind of mail do you get from readers?

BETTS: Mostly good mail. I get some hate mail, but not much. It tends to be local or from this general area. The kind of mail I'm getting from *Heading West* I should have anticipated but didn't. I have friends who are homosexual and who are disturbed by what they take as an antihomosexual bias in the book. They won't often come right out and say it, but consistently their letters have dealt with that part of the book in ways that make me realize they feel damaged or mistreated in some way. That surprised me and I haven't even quite digested it yet. I hadn't thought of reading it that way. Most of the mail (I hate to say this) is "Dear Mrs. Betts: I have just read your novel. My unpublished novel is on the way to you under separate cover." I sometimes feel exasperated, but more often I feel like Miss Lonelyhearts, as if I owe something to those people. Writing is such a lonely business. And it's not all bad stuff they send, either. Some is good, and some may be publishable, but they have the illusion that I can get their work published, and that isn't true. Almost everybody I know seems to be a secret writer; nobody wants to be a magnificent reader—they all want to be magnificent writers.

CA: Some of your interests outside of writing have included motorcycles. Do you still ride a motorcycle?

BETTS: Not at the moment, simply because it broke down and we didn't fix it. But that was wonderful; I still would like to. Right now I'm taking horseback lessons, the current substitute for the motorcycle, and we square dance, so we get a little exercise.

CA: Your time at home, in the country, seems to be very important to you personally and perhaps important to your writing as well.

BETTS: Very, very. There's not enough of it. It's important to my life, because I really did want to have it all—a home, a family, a marriage that was satisfying, and work, and writing. The way I've done it (I'm not sure it's the best way, but it's the way that works) is to keep those things in pretty much airtight compartments. When I'm coming here to the university I close the door behind home, and when I go home I close it behind teaching and administration, and just do everything a hundred percent while I'm doing it. There's not much intermingling. I don't invite students to my house, for instance. Many would love to come, but you would never have a minute's privacy if you allowed drop-in visiting to start. And by the same token, my poor husband doesn't go and hear me give speeches. We've separated roles, and for us that's been the best way.

But you're right about the importance of home—the quietness, the chance to think instead of talk all the time. . . . I was thinking this morning (TV news will do this to you) that one reason for the kind of literature we get is because of where writers live. If I lived in New York City or Detroit or Newark, I would be more depressed about the future of human beings than I am, living in Pittsboro. That doesn't mean that I'm right and metropolitan writers are wrong, but they are affected by the fact that big-city living does something harsh to you. Rural and small-town living does something else—for good or ill; I think it can also make you insular, a boondocks person, can reduce your interest in big national changes that are taking place. I needed to be able to get away to urban centers, but I need to come home and sit in a little, quiet center, too.

CA: What's next for you?

BETTS: I am working on a long novel—well, it feels long. It's an attempt to deal with a foundling and the family that adopts him. The family has nine daughters, by gosh, so we're working with a crowd. I want to bring him from 1900 to the present time and to use his life as a way of watching this century get older. And because he will become (and perhaps fail as—I don't know yet) a Presbyterian preacher, I can deal through him with the decline of religion in American life. Its influence *has* declined, and I'm interested in why. I don't think of the Moral Majority as a resurgence of power but as a symptom of its lack. The central metaphor of the novel will be falconry, something I'm also very much interested in. There are wonderful manuals on falconry that go back to the twelfth century. A lot can be done with that metaphor if you reverse roles and assume that the falcon resembles the human spirit, that the falcon is the one who has flown far from the falconer, the divine spirit, and maybe can't come back, maybe will have to go wild in the universe.

BIOGRAPHICAL/CRITICAL SOURCES: Library Journal, June 1, 1954, February 1, 1965, January 1, 1966, June 1, 1972, October 1, 1973; *Saturday Review,* July 10, 1954, February 6, 1965; *Catholic World,* August, 1954; *Chicago Sunday Tribune,* September 5, 1954; *Kirkus Reviews,* February 1, 1957; *New York Herald Tribune Book Review,* March 3, 1957; *Virginia Quarterly Review,* Spring, 1966; *Publishers Weekly,* March 6, 1972, April 30, 1973, August 27, 1973; *New York Times Book Review,* May 21, 1972, October 28, 1973, January 17, 1982; *Choice,* September, 1972; *Washington Post Book World,* October 7, 1973; *New Republic,* November 10, 1973; *Sewanee Review,* Fall, 1974; *Contemporary Literary Criticism,* Gale, Volume III, 1975, Volume VI, 1976; *Chicago Tribune Book World,* November 22, 1981; *New York Times,* December 17, 1981; *Los Angeles Times Book Review,* December 20, 1981.†

—Sketch by Margaret Mazurkiewicz

—Interview by Jean W. Ross

* * *

BHATTACHARYA, Bhabani 1906-

PERSONAL: Born November 10, 1906, in India; son of Promotho (a judge) and Kiranbala Bhattacharya; married Salila Mukerji, June 14, 1935; children: Arjun (son), Ujjaini and Indrani (daughters). *Education:* Patna University, B.A. (with honors), 1927; University of London, B.A. (with honors), 1931, Ph.D., 1934. *Religion:* Hindu. *Home:* Godhuli, Bezonbagh, Nagpur 4, India; and c/o S. Khanderia, 460 Larkspur, Ann Arbor, Mich. 48105. *Agent:* Paul R. Reynolds, Inc., 12 East 41st St., New York, N.Y. 10017.

CAREER: Author and journalist. Embassy of India, Washington, D.C., press attache, 1949-50; *Illustrated Weekly of India,* Bombay, assistant editor, 1950-52. Participant in Harvard International Seminar, 1959, and Harvard-Japanese International Seminar at Tokyo, 1960; lecturer in New Zealand universities, 1962. Guest of the government of Australia, 1962, and of the German federal government and the British Council, 1963. Executive secretary, Tagore Commemorative Volume Society, 1959-60. *Awards, honors:* Prestige Award, University of New Zealand, 1962; National Academy of Letters (India) award, 1968, for *A Shadow from Ladakh.*

WRITINGS: Some Memorable Yesterdays, Pustak Bhandar (Patna), 1940; *Indian Cavalcade,* [Bombay], 1945; (contributor) *A Centenary Volume: Rabindranath Tagore, 1861-1961,* Sahitya Akademi, 1961; (editor) *Contemporary Indian Short Stories,* two volumes, Sahitya Akademi, 1967; *Gandhi the Writer,* National Book Trust (New Delhi), 1969; *Mahatma Gandhi,* Arnold-Heinemann, 1976; *Glimpses of Indian His-*

tory, Sterling (New Delhi), 1977; *Socio-Political Currents in Bengal: A 19th Century Perspective,* Vikas, 1980.

Novels, except as indicated: *So Many Hungers!,* Hind Kitabs (Bombay), 1947, Gollancz, 1948; *Music for Mohini,* Crown, 1952, 2nd edition, InterCulture Associates, 1976; *He Who Rides a Tiger,* Crown, 1954; *A Goddess Named Gold,* Crown, 1960; *A Shadow from Ladakh,* Crown, 1966; *Steel Hawk and Other Stories,* Hind Pocket Books (New Delhi), 1968; *A Dream in Hawaii,* Macmillan, 1980.

Translator: Rabindranath Tagore, *The Golden Boat,* Macmillan, 1932; (and editor) Tagore, *Towards Universal Man,* [New York], 1959.

Contributor to periodicals in India, England, the United States, and other countries.

WORK IN PROGRESS: America-India: Some Bridgeways of Thought.

SIDELIGHTS: Known for his warm and lively stories of Indian village life, Bhabani Bhattacharya is "a well-known figure on the Indian literary scene and has enjoyed a great reputation as an author for several years," as K. S. Narayana Ras states in *Books Abroad.*

Several reviewers comment that, because of the realism and detail in Bhattacharya's novels, the Western reader has the opportunity to learn much of Indian customs and practices from them. In *A Goddess Named Gold,* for example, Bhattacharya tells the story of a girl who is given a magic amulet that transforms copper into gold whenever she does a kind deed. Soon the people of her village are in a frenzy over the gold-producing power, and the result of their greed is a dangerous rending of their ties to family and friends.

"The story itself," Rosanne Archer writes in the *New York Herald Tribune Book Review,* "serves primarily to illumine the characters. Because they are very real, and very Indian, and very human, this novel will absorb and warm—and enlighten—those readers who want to know something more about other peoples and about themselves." The *Kirkus* reviewer finds the book ideal for "the American reader unfamiliar with India's customs, and eager to become acquainted with them." The *Chicago Tribune*'s Percy Wood concludes that the novel "is a most illuminating and satisfying reading experience, recommended without reservation. . . . It is hardly possible to overpraise this novel."

Bhattacharya's works have been translated into some 26 languages.

BIOGRAPHICAL/CRITICAL SOURCES—Periodicals: *New York Times,* June 15, 1952, October 24, 1954; *New York Herald Tribune Book Review,* October 24, 1954, August 28, 1960; *Kirkus,* July 15, 1960; *Christian Science Monitor,* September 8, 1960; *Chicago Tribune,* September 25, 1960; *Books Abroad,* spring, 1970.

Books: K. R. Chandrasekharan, *Bhabani Bhattacharya,* Arnold-Heinemann, 1974, InterCulture Associates, 1976; Dorothy B. Shimer, *Bhabani Bhattacharya,* Twayne, 1975; *Bhabani Bhattacharya: His Vision and Themes,* Abhinav, 1979; *Perspectives on Bhabani Bhattacharya,* Vimak, 1980.

* * *

BICKLEY, R(obert) Bruce, Jr. 1942-

PERSONAL: Born August 20, 1942, in New Rochelle, N.Y.; son of Robert Bruce (a realtor) and Jean (Wolcott) Bickley; married Karen Luce, July 2, 1966; children: Kathryn, David, John. *Education:* University of Virginia, B.A., 1964; Duke University, M.A., 1965, Ph.D., 1969. *Religion:* Protestant. *Home:* 3421 Robinhood Rd., Tallahassee, Fla. 32312. *Office:* Department of English, Florida State University, Tallahassee, Fla. 32306.

CAREER: Florida State University, Tallahassee, assistant professor, 1969-75, associate professor, 1975-79, professor of English, 1979—, associate dean of arts and sciences, 1983—. *Member:* South Atlantic Modern Language Association, College English Association, Phi Beta Kappa. *Awards, honors:* Woodrow Wilson II fellow, 1965-66; Danforth fellow, 1966-68; James B. Duke fellow, 1969-70.

WRITINGS: The Method of Melville's Short Fiction, Duke University Press, 1975; *Joel Chandler Harris: A Reference Guide,* G. K. Hall, 1978; *Joel Chandler Harris,* Twayne, 1978; *Critical Essays on Joel Chandler Harris,* G. K. Hall, 1978. Contributor to journals, including *American Literary Realism* and *Studies in American Humor.*

WORK IN PROGRESS: A book on the American Romantic short story.

SIDELIGHTS: R. Bruce Bickley, Jr. told *CA:* "Writing and publishing literary criticism and teaching undergraduate and graduate students are inextricably bound activities. Teaching *Bartleby the Scrivener, Benito Cereno,* and *Billy Budd,* and learning from my students in the process, helped sharpen and focus my ideas about Herman Melville's literary artistry, and fed directly into *The Method of Melville's Short Fiction.* And discussing some of Joel Chandler Harris's Uncle Remus tales and his local color story, 'Free Joe and the Rest of the World,' in a survey course whetted my interest in this underrated writer of the New South era. I got caught in Brer Rabbit's brier patch and wrote three books on Harris before I extricated myself (of course, like Brer Rabbit, I didn't really want to leave)."

* * *

BIELYI, Sergei
See HOLLO, Anselm

* * *

BIERMAN, Harold, Jr. 1924-

PERSONAL: Born June 17, 1924, in New York, N.Y.; son of Harold and Frieda (Zelezney) Bierman; married Florence Kelso, February 2, 1952; children: James Landon, Harold Scott, Donald Bruce, Jonathan David. *Education:* U.S. Naval Academy, B.S., 1945; University of Michigan, M.B.A., 1949, Ph.D., 1955. *Home:* 109 Kay St., Ithaca, N.Y. 14850. *Office:* Graduate School of Business Administration, Cornell University, Ithaca, N.Y. 14850.

CAREER: Instructor at Louisiana State University, Baton Rouge, 1950-51, and University of Michigan, Ann Arbor, 1953-55; University of Chicago, Chicago, Ill., assistant professor, 1955-56; Cornell University, Graduate School of Business Administration, Ithaca, N.Y., professor of accounting and managerial economics, 1956-69, Nicholas H. Noyes Professor of Business Administration, 1969—, associate dean, 1982—. Consultant to Ford Foundation. *Military service:* U.S. Navy, 1942-47, 1951-53; became lieutenant. *Member:* American Accounting Association, American Finance Association, Financial Management Association.

WRITINGS: Managerial Accounting, Macmillan, 1958, published as *Financial and Managerial Accounting,* 1963; (with Seymour Smidt) *The Capital Budgeting Decision,* Macmillan, 1960, 5th edition, 1980; (with Lawrence Fouraker and Robert Jaedicke) *Quantitative Analysis for Business Decisions,* Irwin, 1961, 6th edition (with Charles P. Bonini and Warren H. Houseman), 1981; (with Alan K. McAdams) *Management Decisions for Cash and Marketable Securities,* Cornell University, 1962; *Topics in Cost Accounting and Decisions,* McGraw, 1962; *Financial Accounting Theory,* Macmillan, 1965; (with Allan R. Drebin) *Financial Accounting: An Introduction,* Macmillan, 1968, 2nd edition, 1972; (with Drebin) *Managerial Accounting: An Introduction,* Macmillan, 1968, 2nd edition, 1972.

(With Houseman and Richard R. West) *Financial Policy Decisions,* Macmillan, 1970; (with Thomas R. Dyckman) *Managerial Cost Accounting,* Macmillan, 1971; (with Jerome E. Hass) *An Introduction to Managerial Finance,* Norton, 1973; *Decision Making and Planning,* Wiley, 1977; *Strategic Financial Planning,* Free Press, 1980; *Financial Management and Inflation,* Free Press, 1981. Contributor to professional journals.

SIDELIGHTS: Harold Bierman, Jr. writes, "I am attempting to close the gap between the business world and the academic community with my book writings."

* * *

BISHOP, Michael 1945-

PERSONAL: Born November 12, 1945, in Lincoln, Neb.; son of Lee Otis (in the U.S. Air Force) and Maxine (Mattison) Bishop; married Jeri Whitaker, June 7, 1969; children: Christopher James, Stephanie Noel. *Education:* University of Georgia, B.A., 1967, M.A., 1968. *Residence:* Pine Mountain, Ga. *Agent:* Howard Morhaim, 501 Fifth Ave., New York, N.Y. 10017.

CAREER: University of Georgia, Athens, instructor in English, 1972-74; freelance writer, 1974—. *Military service:* U.S. Air Force, 1968-72; became captain. *Member:* Science Fiction Writers of America, Science Fiction Poetry Association. *Awards, honors:* Phoenix Award, 1977; Clark Ashton Smith, 1978; Rhysling Award, Science Fiction Poetry Association, 1979; Nebula Award, Science Fiction Writers of America, 1982, for novelette "The Quickening".

WRITINGS—Science fiction novels, except as indicated: *A Funeral for the Eyes of Fire,* Ballantine, 1975, revised edition published as *Eyes of Fire,* Pocket Books, 1980; *And Strange at Ecbatan the Trees,* Harper, 1976, published as *Beneath the Shattered Moon,* DAW Books, 1977; *Windows and Mirrors* (poetry chapbook), Moravian Press, 1977; *Stolen Faces,* Harper, 1977; *A Little Knowledge,* Berkley Publishing, 1977; *Catacomb Years,* Berkley Publishing, 1979; (author of introduction) Philip K. Dick, *Ubik,* G. K. Hall, 1979; *Transfigurations,* Berkley Publishing, 1979; (with Ian Watson) *Under Heaven's Bridge,* Gollancz, 1981, Ace Books, 1982; *Blooded on Arachne* (short story collection), Arkham, 1982; *No Enemy But Time,* Timescape, 1982; (editor with Watson) *Changes* (anthology), Ace Books, 1982.

Work appears in anthologies, including: *Best Science Fiction: 1973,* edited by Harry Harrison and Brian W. Aldiss, Putnam, 1974; *Emphasis,* edited by David Gerrold, Ballantine, 1974; *World's Best Science Fiction, 1974,* edited by Donald A. Wollheim, DAW Books, 1974; *World's Best Science Fiction, 1975,* edited by Wollheim, DAW Books, 1975. Contributor to *Omni, Analog, Galaxy, Ellery Queen's Mystery Magazine, Isaac Asimov's Science Fiction Magazine,* and other publications.

WORK IN PROGRESS: Two novels, *Seraph* and *Who Made Stevie Crye?;* a short story collection, *One Winter in Eden;* editing *Cosmocopia* for Berkley.

SIDELIGHTS: Reviewing Michael Bishop's *No Enemy But Time* for the *Washington Post Book World,* John Clute finds the book a "strikingly intelligent new science fiction novel." The story concerns Joshua Kampa, a man who dreams of prehistoric Africa in surprisingly accurate detail. Enhanced by a newly-developed machine, Kampa's dreams become real, enabling him to explore the world of 2 million years ago and his own psyche. "In the world of dreams," Clute writes, "knowledge of the world and self-knowledge may be the same thing, but Bishop avoids any easy reduction of his complex, glowing, crystal-clear novel to a tale of self-delusion. In chapters that alternate the real past and the real present, *No Enemy But Time* gradually builds into a work of thrilling significance both as science fiction and as a study of character."

BIOGRAPHICAL/CRITICAL SOURCES: Authors in the News, Volume II, Gale, 1976; *Atlanta Journal & Constitution,* April 4, 1976; *New York Times Book Review,* May 23, 1976, June 26, 1977; *Science Fiction Review,* August, 1977; *Times Literary Supplement,* January 27, 1978; *Analog,* May, 1979, June, 1979; *Washington Post Book World,* January 24, 1982, April 25, 1982.

* * *

BLACKSTOCK, Walter 1917-

PERSONAL: Born January 22, 1917, in Atlanta, Ga.; son of Walter, Sr., and Lillian (Kennon) Blackstock; married Mary Louise Corder, January, 1946 (divorced, 1953); children: Lillian Louise, Walter, Juel Kennon. *Education:* University of Georgia, A.B., 1942; Vanderbilt University, A.M., 1944; Yale University, Ph.D., 1952. *Politics:* Independent.

CAREER: Fireman's Fund Insurance Co. and allied companies, Atlanta, Ga., clerk, stenographer, and claims adjuster, 1935-40; Scotch Woolen Mills, Atlanta, sometime salesman and agent, 1940-46; Georgia Institute of Technology, Atlanta, instructor in English, 1946-48; Florida State University, Tallahassee, assistant professor of English, 1948-56; Northeast Missouri State Teachers College (now Northeast Missouri State University), Kirksville, visiting English professor, 1957-58; Piedmont College, Demorest, Ga., professor of English, 1958; High Point College, High Point, N.C., professor of English and chairman of department, 1958-62; Lander College, Greenwood, S.C., professor of English, 1963-65; East Carolina College (now University), Greenville, N.C., associate professor of English, 1965-66; Methodist College, Fayetteville, N.C., professor of English and chairman of department, 1966-72; Elizabeth City State University, Elizabeth City, N.C., professor of English, beginning 1972.

MEMBER: Modern Language Association of America, Poetry Society of America, South Atlantic Modern Language Association, Poetry Council of North Carolina, Phi Beta Kappa. *Awards, honors:* Literary Achievement Award for Poetry, 1954, for *Call Back the Swallows;* Ford Foundation faculty fellowship for study with Archibald MacLeish at Harvard University, 1954-55; Oscar F. Young Memorial Award of Poetry Council of North Carolina, 1961, for *Miracle of Flesh.*

WRITINGS—Poetry; published by Wings Press, except as indicated: *Quest for Beauty*, Dorrance, 1942; *A Creed for Darkness*, 1946; *Delirium and Drums*, 1947; *Dreamer's Clay*, 1948; *The West Wind Blowing*, 1950; *Call Back the Swallows*, 1953; *The Deeper Bond*, 1955; *Miracle of Flesh*, Golden Quill, 1960; *Leaves before the Wind: New and Selected Poems from Two Decades*, Methodist College Press, 1967; *Not as Leaves Are Shaken*, Methodist College Press, 1969.

Editor: *The Selected Poems of James Larkin Pearson*, Rand McNally, 1960; *Word Gathers: Poems of the East Carolina University Poetry Forum*, East Carolina University Press, 1966. Contributor of articles to professional journals and poetry to periodicals. Originator and editor, *High Point College Studies*, 1960-62.

WORK IN PROGRESS: MacLeish and the American Proposition.†

* * *

BLAKE, Ken
See BULMER, (Henry) Kenneth

* * *

BLAKE, Robert
See DAVIES, L(eslie) P(urnell)

* * *

BLATTY, William Peter 1928-
(Terence Clyne)

PERSONAL: Born January 7, 1928, in New York, N.Y.; son of Peter (a carpenter) and Mary (Mouakad) Blatty; married Mary Margaret Rigard, February 18, 1950 (marriage annulled); married Elizabeth Gilman, 1950; married Linda Tuero (a professional tennis player), July 20, 1975; children: (previous marriage) Christine Ann, Michael Peter, Mary Joanne; (third marriage) two children. *Education:* Georgetown University, A.B., 1950; George Washington University, M.A., 1954; graduate study overseas. *Religion:* Roman Catholic. *Residence:* Georgetown, Washington, D.C. *Agent:* Brandt & Brandt Literary Agents, Inc., 1501 Broadway, New York, N.Y. 10036.

CAREER: Door-to-door Electrolux vacuum cleaner salesman, 1950; beer truck driver for Gunther Brewing Co., 1950; United States Information Agency, Beirut, Lebanon, editor of *News Review* (weekly magazine), 1955-57; University of Southern California, Los Angeles, publicity director, 1957-58; Loyola University of Los Angeles, Los Angeles, public relations director, 1959-60; full-time novelist and screenwriter, 1960—. Has produced and directed films, all based on his novels of the same titles, "The Exorcist," "The Ninth Configuration," and "Twinkle, Twinkle, 'Killer' Kane." Regular guest on "Tonight Show" television program. *Military service:* U.S. Air Force, Psychological Warfare Division, 1951-54; became first lieutenant. *Member:* Writers Guild of America. *Awards, honors:* Gabriel Award and Blue Ribbon, American Film Festival, 1969, for "Insight" television series script; Silver Medal, California Literature Medal Award, 1972, for *The Exorcist;* Academy Award ("Oscar") for best screenplay based on a work in another medium, Academy of Motion Picture Arts and Sciences, 1974, and August Derleth Award for best film, 1974, for "The Exorcist"; L.H.D., Seattle University, 1974.

WRITINGS—Novels, except as indicated: *Which Way to Mecca, Jack?*, Bernard Geis Associates, 1960; *John Goldfarb, Please Come Home!*, Doubleday, 1963; *I, Billy Shakespeare!*, Doubleday, 1965; *Twinkle, Twinkle, "Killer" Kane*, Doubleday, 1967; *The Exorcist*, Harper, 1971; *I'll Tell Them I Remember You* (informal biography of his mother, Mary Mouakad Blatty), Norton, 1973; *William Peter Blatty on "The Exorcist": From Novel to Film*, Bantam, 1974; *The Ninth Configuration*, Harper, 1978; *The Legion*, Simon & Schuster, 1983.

Screenplays: "The Man from the Diner's Club," Columbia, 1963; "John Goldfarb, Please Come Home!" (based on his novel of the same title), Twentieth Century-Fox, 1965; "A Shot in the Dark," United Artists, 1966; "What Did You Do in the War, Daddy?," United Artists, 1966; "Gunn," Paramount, 1967; "The Great Bank Robbery," Warner Bros., 1969; "Darling Lili," Paramount, 1970; (and producer) "The Exorcist" (based on his novel of the same title), Warner Bros., 1973; (and director and producer) "Twinkle, Twinkle, 'Killer' Kane" (based on his novel of the same title), United Film, 1980. Also author, "Promise Her Anything," 1962, (and director and producer) "The Ninth Configuration" (based on his novel of the same title), "The Baby Sitter," and "Insight" television series script. Contributor of articles to periodicals, including *Saturday Evening Post, Coronet*, and *This Week*.

SIDELIGHTS: William Peter Blatty achieved perhaps his greatest commercial success with *The Exorcist*, in both its novel and screen versions. Blatty states that he predicted the book's achievements even before penning the final chapters. "I knew it was going to be a success," he told Garry Clifford of *People*. "I couldn't wait to finish it and become famous."

The youngest son of Lebanese immigrants, Blatty vividly remembers his childhood. Raised primarily by his mother after his parents separated when he was six years old, Blatty recalls her determination to succeed. She strived to support the family by selling her homemade quince jelly along Park Avenue and in front of the Plaza Hotel in New York City. Blatty told Martha MacGregor of the *New York Post*, "My feeling was that if she couldn't come through with some kind of evidence of survival it couldn't be done." Despite his mother's efforts, however, Blatty still remembers their poverty and numerous evictions, explaining to Clifford: "I'd come home from school, . . . and all the furniture would be piled up in the street. It was pretty savage the way they did it—humiliating for a kid." A college scholarship to Georgetown University later provided his first real step away from New York City.

Although it was not until the publication of *The Exorcist* that Blatty became well-known, his second novel was the subject of a minor controversy. *John Goldfarb, Please Come Home!* chronicles the efforts of a captured American pilot to coach a team of Arabs to victory over the Notre Dame football team; the novel drew loud criticism from Notre Dame officials. University trustees protested that both book and film damaged the school's reputation, and they received an injunction blocking both from distribution. Upheld in New York State Supreme Court in 1964, the ruling was later overturned in 1965 after Blatty appealed the decision, explaining that he had meant no disrespect to Notre Dame. Once released, however, the movie failed to achieve major success.

After *John Goldfarb, Please Come Home!* Blatty experienced a disappointing period in his career. *I, Billy Shakespeare!* and *Twinkle, Twinkle, "Killer" Kane* both failed to impress critics. Numerous production changes in his screenplays combined with the sudden death of his mother in 1967 left Blatty emotionally drained. Reaction to these personal problems forced Blatty to retreat to a Lake Tahoe cabin for privacy and reevaluation of his beliefs. Once there, he drafted his first version of *The Exorcist,* a novel that would attain the number two position on the 1971 *Publishers' Weekly* best-seller list, and that would remain on the *New York Times*'s best-seller list for fifty-five weeks.

The Exorcist inspired varied critical reactions. Most critics acknowledge the sheer readability and mounting suspense of the novel, yet some question its validity, both in terms of literary value and intellectual appeal. Webster Schott of *Life* comments: "It's a page-turner *par excellence*. . . .Blatty writes and thinks sophisticated. . . . Faulkner, Blatty is not. But Poe and Mary Shelley would recognize him as working in their ambiguous limbo between the natural and the supernatural." The *New York Times Book Review*'s Newgate Callendar shares Schott's observations of the book, noting, "Well researched, written in a literate style, it comes to grips with the forces of evil incarnate, and there are not many readers who will be unmoved."

Newsweek's Peter S. Prescott admits the novel's wide attraction but denies higher merits, claiming, "I suspect [Blatty] wants his book to be interesting in an intellectual way, but it is not; nevertheless, it is wonderfully exciting." R. Z. Sheppard of *Time,* while decrying any literary and religious aspirations, nonetheless accurately predicts favorable public reaction to the work: "[*The Exorcist*] is a pretentious, tasteless, abominably written, redundant pastiche of superficial theology, comic-book psychology, Grade C movie dialogue and Grade Z scatology. In short [it] will be a bestseller and almost certainly a drive-in movie."

Warner Brothers paid over $400,000 for the film rights to the novel in 1971, allowing Blatty to retain complete control on the set. (He later demanded and was granted similar arrangements on the films "The Ninth Configuration" and "Twinkle, Twinkle, 'Killer' Kane," both based respectively on his novels of the same titles.) Blatty also wrote the film script and produced the movie himself. "The Exorcist"'s $10 million budget proved worth the investment in terms of revenues as the film grossed an average of $2 million per month during its original release.

Although *The Exorcist* is his first published novel dealing with demonic possession, Blatty has long been interested in the occult and the supernatural. His own informal research into case histories of "possessed" individuals revealed that, although most of the "victims" were probably mentally unbalanced, a small number of cases defied usual psychological and scientific explanations. Fascinated by these apparent anomalies, Blatty fashioned *Exorcist* character "Regan MacNeil" after one such case. He loosely based Regan on a Maryland patient, upon whom, owing to the failure of conventional medical and psychiatric therapies, Catholic priests resorted to the holy rite of exorcism. Blatty's interest in the supernatural continues in personal matters as well as in his writing. After his mother's death, he ultimately convinced himself that her spirit had transcended mortal boundaries, as detailed in the final chapters of *I'll Tell Them I Remember You.*

As a writer, Blatty works diligently, often selling film rights to production companies even before completion of a book. "When I write, I write," he comments to *People*'s Clifford. "From the time I've had enough coffee in the morning till the time I'm too tired at night. I'm compulsive." His seventh novel, *The Ninth Configuration,* took him four months to complete. He has adjusted to his wealth and recognition, owning at one time residences in Aspen, Malibu, and Los Angeles. But, he remains conscious of the fleeting nature of success, confessing to Clifford of *People,* "I'm always looking over my shoulder—I'm afraid someone will take it away."

BIOGRAPHICAL/CRITICAL SOURCES: Roy Newquist, *Counterpoint,* Simon & Schuster, 1964; *Life,* May 7, 1971, December 31, 1971; *Newsweek,* May 10, 1971; *Saturday Review,* June 5, 1971; *New York Times Book Review,* June 6, 1971, February 11, 1973, November 18, 1973; *Time,* June 7, 1971; *New York Post,* October 12, 1971, September 1, 1973; *Books and Bookmen,* April, 1972; *Harper's Bazaar,* August, 1972; William Peter Blatty, *I'll Tell Them I Remember You,* Norton, 1973; *New York Times,* October 6, 1973, August 8, 1980; *Contemporary Literary Criticism,* Volume II, Gale, 1974; *People,* March 4, 1974, October 9, 1978; *Washington Post,* April 4, 1974; *Times Literary Supplement,* April 19, 1974; R.L. Short, *Something to Believe In,* Harper, 1978.†

—Sketch by Michaela Swart Wilson

* * *

BLEDSOE, Thomas (Alexander) 1914-

PERSONAL: Born September 17, 1914, in Charleston, W. Va.; son of Thomas Alexander and Walker (Bradford) Bledsoe; married Bozenka Skrinar, May 14, 1964; children: (previous marriage) Elizabeth Page, Jane Byrd, Mary Walker, Elizabeth Carter, Margaret Randolph, Ann Alexander, Thomas Alexander IV; (stepchildren) Sonja Suzanne Huff, Charles Remmele Huff. *Education:* University of Louisville, A.B., 1937; University of Illinois, A.M., 1938. *Home:* 635 Connecticut St., San Francisco, Calif. 94107. *Agent:* Alex Jackinson, 156 Fifth Ave., New York, N.Y. 10010.

CAREER: University of Illinois at Urbana-Champaign, instructor in English, 1938-43; Rinehart & Co., New York City, editor of college department, 1946-54; Alfred A. Knopf, Inc., New York City, editor of college department, 1954-56; Beacon Press, Inc., Boston, Mass., director and editor-in-chief, 1956-58; Arlington Books, Cambridge, Mass., president and editor-in-chief, 1958-59; Council for Basic Education, Washington, D.C., executive director, 1959-61; American Printing House for the Blind, Louisville, Ky., textbook consultant, 1962-63; Macmillan Co., New York City, senior editor, 1963-64; Chandler Publishing Co., San Francisco, Calif., director of elementary and high school division, 1964-65. *Military service:* U.S. Naval Reserve, 1943-45; became lieutenant. *Member:* Authors League of America. *Awards, honors:* H.H.D. from University of Louisville, 1959.

WRITINGS: (With Robert J. Geist) *Current Prose,* Rinehart, 1953; (editor and author of critical and historical introduction) Hamlin Garland, *Main Travelled Roads,* Rinehart, 1954; *Dear Uncle Bramwell* (novel), A. Swallow, 1963; *Jane Austen: Pride and Prejudice* (study guide), Barnes & Noble, 1966; *The Story of Two Heroic Monasteries,* House of the Double Axe, 1966; *Great Expectations [by] Charles Dickens* (study guide), Barnes & Noble, 1966; *Meanwhile Back at the Henhouse* (novel), A. Swallow, 1966; *Charles Dickens: Hard Times* (study guide), Barnes & Noble, 1968; *William Dean Howells: The Rise of Silas Lopham,* Barnes & Noble, 1968; *Or We'll All Hang Separately: The Highlander Idea,* Beacon Press, 1969; (translator) Rodolfo Usigli, *Two Plays: Crown of Light and One of These Days,* Illinois University Press, 1971. Contributor of short stories, articles, and reviews to periodicals, including *Western Review, Trace, Accent, Anvil,* and *CEA Critic.*

WORK IN PROGRESS: Several novels.

SIDELIGHTS: Thomas Bledsoe once described his novels as "off-beat" and added candidly that he had more split decisions from publishers about them "than Bobo Olsen."

Bledsoe told *CA:* "My research is into the human interior, my effort [is] to keep writing novels that interpret the condition of modern man. That high-sounding phrase means that I am interested in people in the *now* in which they exist. To make both come alive is a rough job, almost as tough as trying to get the results published."

His viewpoint after almost twenty years as a professional editor: "I've settled on educational publishing because here I can introduce a lot of subversive (and important) ideas in books that will make money, or can, and might actually teach kids something important. . . . I am personally bitten by the bug of doing something that I consider important to make a living, but I am much impressed for the case for doing exactly the opposite. What I know for certain is that there is no middle ground between the two, for the writer at least. That ambivalence has been the fate of most of the many ad-men I have known, the majority of them aspiring writers at the bar at lunch.

"The years I have spent in publishing and my own experiences as a writer have left me both cynical and determined about the chances of a writer who follows no party line, neither square nor hip . . . and my advice to any young writer is that if you are good enough in your own terms, publication depends on a combination of energy and luck.

"The serious writer's task . . . is to enforce his art and his view of life on people who don't have the imagination to conceive it themselves. He has to believe in himself, start with the knowledge that he has nine strikes against him and be willing to erect a corpus that finally cannot be ignored. In short, he has to work.

"My chief avocations are music, sports, and books. But this doesn't get said in proper perspective. My single avocation is the marvelous, ribald, delicate, wonderful joy of life, and out of this all my writing comes as anyone's must."†

* * *

BLOOMFIELD, Harold H. 1944-

PERSONAL: Born October 8, 1944, in New York, N.Y.; son of Max (an accountant) and Fridl (Waldman) Bloomfield. *Education:* University of Pittsburgh, B.S. (cum laude), 1965; State University of New York, Downstate Medical Center, M.D. (honors in public health and psychiatry), 1969. *Religion:* Jewish.

CAREER: Kaiser Foundations Hospital, San Francisco, Calif., intern, 1969-70; Yale University, School of Medicine, New Haven, Conn., psychiatric resident, 1970-73; Institute of Psychophysiological Medicine, El Cajon, Calif., director of psychiatry, beginning 1974; Maharishi International University, Fairfield, Iowa, professor of psychiatry, beginning 1974; director, Age of Enlightenment Center for Holistic Health, San Diego, Calif. Mental health consultant to West Haven Board of Education, West Haven, Conn., 1972-73. *Member:* American Psychiatric Association, Association for the Advancement of Behavior Therapy.

WRITINGS: (Contributor) J. White, editor, *What Is Meditation?,* Anchor, 1974; (contributor) D. W. Orme-Johnson, and J. Farrow, editors, *Scientific Research on the Transcendental Meditation Program: Collected Papers,* Maharishi International University Press, Volume I, 1975; (with M. P. Cain, D. T. Jaffee, and R. B. Kory) *TM: Discovering Inner Energy and Overcoming Stress,* introduction by R. Buckminster Fuller, Delacorte, 1975; (with Robert B. Kory) *Happiness: The TM Program, Psychiatry, and Enlightenment,* Dawn Press, 1976; *How to Survive the Loss of a Love,* Bantam, 1977; *How to Enjoy the Love of Your Life: Over 100 Ways to Enrich Your Love Life,* Doubleday, 1979.

(With Kory) *The Holistic Way to Health and Happiness: A New Approach to Complete Lifetime Wellness,* Simon & Schuster, 1980; (with Kory) *Inner Joy: New Strategies to Put More Pleasure and Satisfactions in Your Life,* Wyden Books, 1980. Contributor to *Behavior Therapy, Psychotherapy, Medical Dimensions,* and other journals.

SIDELIGHTS: Harold H. Bloomfield studied with Maharishi Mahesh Yogi, the proponent of Transcendental Meditation, in 1973 and 1974. Bloomfield told *CA* that in 1973 he became the first American psychiatrist to be made a teacher of Transcendental Meditation and that he is currently involved with using Transcendental Meditation in conjunction with medical and psychiatric techniques.

Bloomfield has lectured throughout the U.S., Canada, and Europe. He is competent in German and Hebrew.

AVOCATIONAL INTERESTS: Tennis, swimming, basketball, and travel.†

* * *

BLUMBERG, Rhoda 1917-

PERSONAL: Born December 14, 1917, in New York; daughter of Abraham and Irena (Fromberg) Shapiro; married Gerald Blumberg (a lawyer), January 7, 1945; children: Lawrence, Rena, Alice, Leda. *Education:* Adelphi College, B.A., 1938. *Residence:* Yorktown Heights, N.Y. *Office:* 1 Rockefeller Plaza, New York, N.Y. 10020.

CAREER: Free-lance writer. Member of board of directors of Westchester Jewish Community Services and Federation of Jewish Philanthropy (Westchester County). *Member:* Authors Guild, Authors League of America.

WRITINGS—Published by F. Watts, except as indicated: *Simon & Schuster Travel Guides,* Cornerstone, 1974; *Firefighters,* 1975; *Sharks,* 1975; *UFO,* 1976; *First Ladies,* 1977; *Famine,* 1978; *Witches,* 1979; *Backyard Bestiary,* Coward, 1979.

Truth about Dragons, Four Winds, 1980; *First Travel Guide to the Moon,* Four Winds, 1980; *Southern Africa,* 1981; *Freaky Facts,* Wanderer, 1981; *Devils and Demons,* 1982; *First Travel Guide to the Bottom of the Sea,* Lothrop, 1983. Also author of scripts for radio interviews and documentary presentations. Contributor of articles to magazines.

* * *

BLUTIG, Eduard
See GOREY, Edward (St. John)

* * *

BOARMAN, Patrick M(adigan) 1922-

PERSONAL: Born April 23, 1922, in Buffalo, N.Y.; son of Marcus Daly (a lawyer) and Virginia (Madigan) Boarman; married Katharina Theresa Schumacher, December 12, 1953; children: Thomas, Christopher, Jesse, Barbara. *Education:* Fordham University, A.B., 1943; Columbia University, M.S. in Journalism, 1946; University of Geneva, Ph.D., 1965; also attended University of Amsterdam, 1949-50, University of Michigan, 1958, and University of Virginia, 1965.

CAREER: Columbia Broadcasting System, correspondent in Geneva, Switzerland, 1947-48; John Carroll University, Cleveland, Ohio, assistant professor of economics, 1948-49; National Catholic Welfare Conference, director of Office of Cultural Affairs in Bonn, Germany, 1951-55; University of Wisconsin—Milwaukee, assistant professor of economics, 1956-62; Bucknell University, Lewisburg, Pa., associate professor of economics, 1962-67; Long Island University, Greenvale, N.Y., professor of economics, 1967-72; Pepperdine University, Center for International Business, Los Angeles, Calif., director of research, 1972-75; Patrick M. Boarman Associates (international business consulting firm), Palos Verdes, Calif., president, 1975—.

Visiting professor of economics, University of Geneva, 1965-66. Director of research, U.S. House of Representatives Republican Conference, 1967-68; member of board of directors, Committee for Monetary Research and Education, New York City, 1970—; senior economist, World Trade Institute, New York City, 1971. Consultant, General Electric, 1964-65, American Telephone and Telegraph, 1969, and U.S. Secretary of the Treasury, 1970-71. *Military service:* U.S. Army, 1943. *Member:* American Economic Association, National Association of Business Economists, Royal Economic Society (fellow), Western Economic Association. *Awards, honors:* Distinguished Service Cross of Order of Merit, West German Federal Republic, 1956; Relm Foundation grant, 1966.

WRITINGS: (Editor) *Der Christ und die soziale Marktwirtschaft,* Kohlhammer (Stuttgart), 1955; (translator) Wilhelm Roepke, *Economics of the Free Society,* Regnery, 1963; *Union Monopolies and Antitrust Restraints,* Labor Policy Association, 1963; *Germany's Economic Dilemma—Inflation and the Balance of Payments,* Yale University Press, 1964; *The World's Money: Gold and the Problem of International Liquidity,* Bucknell University, 1965; (editor) *The Economy of South Vietnam: A New Beginning,* Center for International Business, Pepperdine University, 1973; (editor with Jayson Mugar) *Trade with China: Assessments by Leading Businessmen and Scholars,* Praeger, 1974; (editor with Hans Schollhammer) *Multinational Corporations and Governments: Business-Government Relations,* Praeger, 1975; (editor) *World Monetary Disorder: National Policies vs. International Imperatives,* Center for International Business, Pepperdine University, 1976. Contributor to *Modern Age, Challenge, Wall Street Journal,* and other journals and newspapers.

WORK IN PROGRESS: Research on international economic policy, on the theory and practice of the gold standard, and on capitalism and Christianity.†

* * *

BOBKER, Lee R(obert) 1925-

PERSONAL: Born July 19, 1925, in Belle Harbor, N.Y.; son of Harry and Theora (Katz) Bobker; married Kate Gene Russell (a businesswoman), April 5, 1950; children: Gene Ellen, Laurie Beth, Daniel Harry. *Education:* New York University, B.A., 1949. *Politics:* Liberal Democrat. *Religion:* Jewish. *Home:* 61 Sara Lane, New Rochelle, N.Y. 10804.

CAREER: Campus Film Productions, New York City, writer and director, 1949-52; Dynamic Films, Inc., New York City, vice-president, writer, director, producer, 1952-59; Vision Associates, New York City, president, 1959—. Instructor, New York University, 1956—. *Military service:* U.S. Army, 1943-46, served in Infantry; received Bronze Star Medal. *Member:* Screen Directors Guild. *Awards, honors:* Three Nominations for Academy Award from Motion Picture Academy of Arts and Sciences; has won about three hundred awards at national and international film festivals.

WRITINGS: Elements of Film, Harcourt, 1971, 3rd edition, 1979; *Making Movies: From Script to Screen,* Harcourt, 1973; *The Unicorn Group* (novel), Morrow, 1979; *Flight of a Dragon* (novel), Morrow, 1981.

Author of more than five hundred film scripts. Contributor to professional and popular periodicals.

WORK IN PROGRESS: A suspense novel, tentatively entitled *A Piece of String.*

AVOCATIONAL INTERESTS: Tennis, skiing, travel abroad, gourmet cooking (has rated restaurants for travel publications).

BIOGRAPHICAL/CRITICAL SOURCES: New York Times Book Review, April 8, 1979, March 1, 1981.

* * *

BOHLE, Bruce 1918-

PERSONAL: Born July 21, 1918, in St. Louis, Mo.; son of Edward F. (a postal employee) and Emma W. (Fricke) Bohle. *Education:* Washington University, St. Louis, Mo., B.A., 1939. *Politics:* "Normally Democratic." *Religion:* Protestant. *Home:* 260 Audubon Ave., New York, N.Y. 10033.

CAREER: St. Louis Star-Times, St. Louis, Mo., film critic, 1946-51, drama and music critic, 1950-51; St. Louis Symphony Orchestra, St. Louis, assistant manager, 1951-53; *Theatre Arts,* New York City, editor, 1953-61; Grolier, Inc., New York City, encyclopedia editor, 1960-64; American Heritage Publishing Co., New York City, usage editor, *American Heritage Dictionary,* beginning 1964. *Military service:* U.S. Army Air Forces, 1942-46. *Member:* Phi Beta Kappa.

WRITINGS: (Compiler) *The Home Book of American Quotations,* Dodd, 1967, published as *Apollo Book of American Quotations,* Apollo Editions, 1970; (editor with American Heritage editors) *Great Historic Places,* American Heritage Publishing Co., 1973; (editor with American Heritage editors) *Great Historic Places of Europe,* American Heritage Publishing Co., 1974; (editor with others) *The Written Word,* Houghton, 1977; (editor with others) *Usage,* Scholastic Magazines Press, 1979; (compiler and editor) *Human Life: Controversies and Concerns,* H. W. Wilson, 1979; (editor with others) *Roget's II: The New Thesaurus,* Houghton, 1980. Editor of 10th edition of *International Cyclopedia of Music and Musicians,* Dodd, 1975.

* * *

BOND, Nancy (Barbara) 1945-

PERSONAL: Born January 8, 1945, in Bethesda, Md.; daughter of William H. (a librarian) and Helen L. (an elementary school teacher; maiden name, Lynch) Bond. *Education:* Mount Holyoke College, B.A., 1966; College of Librarianship, Aberystwyth, Dyfed, Wales, Dip.Lib., 1972. *Politics:* Independent. *Religion:* "Informal." *Home:* 109 Valley Rd., Concord, Mass. 01742. *Office:* Center for the Study of Children's Literature, Simmons College, Boston, Mass. 02115.

CAREER: Oxford University Press, London, England, member of promotional staff, 1967-68; Lincoln Public Library, Lincoln, Mass., assistant children's librarian, 1969-71; Gardner Public Library, Gardner, Mass., director, 1973-75; Massachusetts Audubon Society, Lincoln, administrative assistant, 1976-77; Simmons College, Center for the Study of Children's Literature, Boston, Mass., instructor, 1978—; Barrow Book Store, Concord, Mass., salesperson, 1980—. *Member:* Library Association (England), National Audobon Society, Jersey Wildlife Preservation Trust. *Awards, honors: A String in the Harp* was named a Newbery honor book, a *Boston Globe—Horn Book* honor book, and received awards from the International Reading Association and the Welsh Arts Council, all 1976; *The Voyage Begun* was named a *Boston Globe—Horn Book* honor book, 1981.

WRITINGS—All juveniles; all published by Atheneum: *A String in the Harp,* 1976; *The Best of Enemies,* 1978; *Country of Broken Stone,* 1980; *The Voyage Begun,* 1981.

WORK IN PROGRESS: Writing juvenile and adult fiction.

SIDELIGHTS: Nancy Bond told *CA,* "Children's books are one of my greatest loves and always have been. I was much encouraged to find some fifteen years ago that I did not in fact ever have to outgrow them. But it took me rather a long time to realize I could do more than simply read them. There is a lot of very exciting fiction being written and published ostensibly for children! I wage a constant campaign to introduce it to other adults.

"My other deep interest is natural history. I am involved with organizations active in conservation, but more fundamental, I have a real conviction that men are only a part of the natural pattern and that much of what we do to the environment is senseless, thoughtless, and tragic. Only by pausing to look and make ourselves truly aware that all the parts fit, even though we may not understand how, can we preserve and protect the balance of the whole. It is therefore essential to me that we encourage by word and deed attention to minutiae, wonder at detail, and respect [for] life in all forms."

* * *

BONNER, James Calvin 1904-

PERSONAL: Born June 16, 1904, in Heard County, Ga.; son of William Allen (a farmer) and Sara Amanda (Moore) Bonner; married Ida Munro (a librarian), November 23, 1936; children: Page Bonner Craghear, James C., Jr., William Allen II. *Education:* University of Georgia, A.B.J., 1926, M.A., 1936; University of North Carolina, Ph.D., 1943. *Politics:* Democrat. *Religion:* Episcopalian. *Home:* 120 South Jackson St., Milledgeville, Ga. 31061. *Office:* Russell Hall, Georgia College, Milledgeville, Ga.

CAREER: Principal and athletic coach, Cave Spring High School, Cave Spring, Ga. 1926-27; Carrollton Agricultural and Mechanical School Carrollton, Ga., headmaster, 1927-33; West Georgia College, Carrollton, instructor, 1933-35, assistant professor of history, 1935-42; Randolph-Macon Woman's College, Lynchburg, Va., adjunct professor of history, 1942-44; Georgia College, Milledgeville, professor of history, 1944-69, professor emeritus, 1969—, chairman of department of history and political science, 1961-69. Visiting professor at Emory University, 1952; visiting scholar at Duke University. President of Georgia Council for the Social Studies, 1945. Secretary-treasurer of Lockerly Arboretum Foundation, 1960—. Consultant to Mississippi Park Commission, 1973-75. *Member:* American Historical Association, Agricultural History Society (member of executive council, 1948-50), Old Capital Historical Society (president, 1958-60), Southern Historical Association, Georgia Historical Society, Phi Kappa Phi, Pi Gamma Mu (governor of Georgia province, 1958-69). *Awards, honors:* West Georgia College Founders Award, 1945; Southern fellowship grant, 1958; research grant, American Association for State and Local History, 1961; Distinguished Service Award, Georgia College, 1970; named Georgia Author of the Year, Dixie Council of Authors and Journalists, 1972.

WRITINGS: (And editor with Lucien E. Roberts) *Studies in Georgia History and Government,* University of Georgia Press, 1940, reprinted, Reprint Co., 1974; (editor) Sarah Frances Williams, *Plantation Experiences of a New York Woman,* North Carolina Department of Archives and History, 1956; *The Georgia Story,* Harlow Publishing, 1958, 2nd edition, 1961; (contributor) Horace Montgomery, editor, *Georgians in Profile,* University of Georgia Press, 1958; *A Short History of Heard County,* privately printed, 1958, 2nd revised edition, Georgia College, 1967.

(Editor) Anna Maria Cook, *The Journal of a Milledgeville Girl, 1861-1867,* University of Georgia Press, 1964; *The Migration Pattern of the Descendants of Thomas Bonner,* [Milledgeville, Ga.], 1964; *A History of Georgia Agriculture, 1732-1860,* University of Georgia Press, 1964; (contributor) Arthur Link and Rembert W. Patrick, editors, *Writing Southern History,* Louisiana State University Press, 1965; *Georgia: A Student's Guide to Localized History* (juvenile), Teachers College Press, 1965; *Georgia's Last Frontier,* University of Georgia Press, 1972; *Atlas for Georgia History,* Miran Publishers, 1975; *Milledgeville: Georgia's Antebellum Capital,* University of Georgia Press, 1978; (with William I. Hair and Edward B. Dawson) *A History of Georgia College,* Georgia College, 1979; (with Oscar H. Joiner, Travis E. Smith and H. S. Shearouse) *A History of Public Education in Georgia,* Georgia State Board of Education, 1979. Contributor to *Encyclopaedia Britannica, Encyclopaedia of Southern History,* and *Dictionary of American History.* Contributor to journals, including *American Historical Review, Journal of Southern History, Agricultural History,* and *Georgia Review.* Editorial board member of *Journal of Southern History,* 1950-54, *Agricultural History,* 1963-65, and *Georgia Historical Quarterly.*

SIDELIGHTS: In an *Atlanta Journal and Constitution* review of James Calvin Bonner's *Milledgeville: Georgia's Antebellum Capital,* Gene Gabriel Moore writes that the book "is a fine and honorable effort. Once again [Bonner] shows his dedication to the historian's art and responsibility. He chooses the understatement but he is a gifted writer who constructs sentences that sing."

Bonner explained his early career change to *CA* in this manner: "Early in my career I made the transition from athletic coach to professor of history. I was led to this radical transition through my interest in and study of Greek (Hellenic) athletics. From the Greek athlete I moved to Greek architecture and then to classical history in general. I have always had an interest in architecture and its history and relationship to the lives of people."

AVOCATIONAL INTERESTS: Architecture and historical buildings (used hand-made bricks from historical structures to build his own eight room house in plantation classical style).

BIOGRAPHICAL/CRITICAL SOURCES: Journal of American History, June, 1965, June, 1979; *Civil War History,* June,

1967; *Atlanta Journal and Constitution*, September 24, 1978.

* * *

BORCHARDT, Dietrich Hans 1916-

PERSONAL: Born April 14, 1916, in Hanover, Germany; son of Max Noah (a physician) and Mina (Lewinski) Borchardt; married Janet Duff Sinclair, 1944; children: Sandra Helen, Ann Sinclair (deceased), Max William. *Education:* Received early education in Germany and Italy; Victoria University of Wellington, M.A. (with honors), 1946; New Zealand Library School, Diploma, 1947. *Home:* 57 Aylmer St., North Balwyn, Victoria 3104, Australia.

CAREER: Farm worker in Germany, Italy, and Spain, 1934-36; second-hand book dealer in Florence, Italy, 1936-39; farm worker and general laborer in New Zealand, 1939-43; book dealer in Wellington, New Zealand, 1943-46; University of Otago, Dunedin, New Zealand, acquisitions librarian, 1947-50; University of Tasmania, Hobart, deputy librarian, 1950-53, librarian, 1953-64; La Trobe University, Bundoora, Victoria, Australia, chief librarian, 1965-81. UNESCO library expert in Turkey, 1964-65; lecturer in bibliography at Graduate Library School, George Peabody College for Teachers (now George Peabody College for Teachers of Vanderbilt University), Nashville, Tenn., summers, 1968 and 1973. Member of council, Victoria College of the Arts; director of Blackwell Scientific Publications Ltd. (Australia). Member of Australian Advisory Council on Bibliographic Service, and chairman of Working Party on Bibliography; consultant in subject bibliography, National Library of Australia.

MEMBER: Library Association of Australia (fellow; past president of university and college libraries section; member of board of examiners, 1962-64, 1966-69), New Zealand Library Association, Library Association (United Kingdom), Bibliographical Society of Australia and New Zealand, Society of Indexers. *Awards, honors:* Carnegie grant to visit Europe and United States, 1958; H.C.L. Anderson Award, Library Association of Australia, 1979; Order of Australia, 1982.

WRITINGS: (Compiler, with B. Tilley, and author of introduction) *The Roy Bridges Collection in the University of Tasmania*, Cremorne, Stone, 1956; *Checklist of Royal Commissions, Select Committees of Parliament and Boards of Inquiry*, Part 1: *Commonwealth of Australia, 1900-1950*, Cremorne, Stone, 1958, Part 2: *Tasmania, 1956-1959*, Cremorne, Stone, 1960, Part 3: *Victoria, 1856-1960*, Wentworth Books, 1970, Part 4: *New South Wales, 1856-1960*, La Trobe University Library, 1975, Part 5: *Queensland, 1859-1960*, La Trobe University Library, 1978.

Australian Bibliography: A Guide to Printed Sources of Information, F. W. Cheshire, 1963, 3rd edition, Pergamon, 1979; *Senescence and Fertility* (La Trobe University inaugural lectures), F. W. Cheshire, 1967; *How to Find Out in Philosophy and Psychology*, Pergamon, 1968; *The Spread of Printing: Australia*, Hertzberger, 1968.

(With J. I. Horacek) *Librarianship in Australia, New Zealand, and Oceania*, Pergamon, 1975; *Australian Official Publications*, Longman, 1979; *A Bibliovision Splendid*, LaTrobe University, 1982. Contributor of more than sixty articles and reviews to library journals. Editor, *Australia Academic and Research Libraries*, 1970—, and *Australian Historical Bibliography Bulletin*, 1982—.

WORK IN PROGRESS: Checklist of Royal Commissions, 1960-1980; bibliography volume for *Australia, 1788-1988: A Bicentennial History;* a revision of *How to Find Out in Philosophy and Psychology*.

SIDELIGHTS: Dietrich Hans Borchardt told *CA:* "I have always believed that it is useless to try and remember everything. Better by far, as Samuel Johnson already stressed, to know where to find out. That is what bibliography is all about—it is the veritable and only key to knowledge, and those who hold it are the true powerbrokers of our age."

AVOCATIONAL INTERESTS: Gardening.

* * *

BORTON, Elizabeth
See TREVINO, Elizabeth B(orton) de

* * *

BOUCHER, Alan (Estcourt) 1918-

PERSONAL: Born January 3, 1918, in Frowlesworth, Leicestershire, England; son of Robin Estcourt (a civil servant) and Kathrine Veronica (Burns) Boucher; married Aslaug Thorarinsdottir, February 28, 1942; children: Alice Kristin, Robin Gunnar, Antony Leifur. *Education:* Attended Winchester College, England; Trinity College, Cambridge, B.A., 1939, M.A., 1942, Ph.D., 1951; University of Iceland, postgraduate study, 1948-50. *Religion:* Roman Catholic. *Home:* Tjarnargata 41, Reykjavik, Iceland. *Office:* Department of English, University of Iceland, Reykjavik, Iceland.

CAREER: Ampleforth School, York, England, assistant master in English, 1946-48; British Broadcasting Corporation, London, England, producer and program organizer in the schools broadcasting department, with special responsibilities in field of English literature and travel, 1951—; former supervisor in old Icelandic studies, Cambridge University, Cambridge, England; currently professor of English, University of Iceland, Reykjavik. *Military service:* British Army, Royal Artillery and Intelligence Corps, 1939-46; became captain. *Awards, honors:* Dame Bertha Phillpots Award for northern research, 1950, 1951; M.B.E., 1980.

WRITINGS: Iceland, Some Impressions, [Reykjavik], 1949; *The Runaways*, Nelson, 1959; *The Path of the Raven*, Constable, 1960; *Venturers North*, Nelson, 1962; *The Greenland Farers*, Constable, 1962; *The King's Men*, Doubleday, 1962; *The Empty Land*, Nelson, 1963; *The Wineland Venture*, Constable, 1963; *The Cottage in the Woods*, Nelson, 1963; *The Wild Ones*, Nelson, 1964; *Sea-Kings and Dragon Ships*, Walker, 1964; *The Land-Seekers*, Deutsch, 1964; *The Raven's Flight*, Constable, 1964; *The Hornstranders*, Constable, 1966; (compiler and translator) *Mead Moondaughter, and Other Icelandic Folktales*, Hart-Davis, 1967; *Stories of the Norsemen*, Burke, 1967; *The Sword of the Raven*, Scribner, 1969; *Modern Nordic Plays*, Universitets Forlag Oslo, 1973.

Translator from the Icelandic; all published by Iceland Review Books: *Poems of Today*, 1972; *Short Stories of Today*, 1973; *A Quire of Seven*, 1974; *Iceland's Folktales*, three volumes, 1977; O. J. Sigurdsson, *The Changing Earth and Selected Poems*, 1979; *A Tale of Icelanders*, 1980; *The Saga of Hallfred*, 1981; *Tales from the Eastfirth*, 1981.

In Icelandic: *Enskur Ordafordi Fyris Islandinga*, Prentfell, 1951; *Litil Synisbok Enskra Bokmennta*, Isafold, 1952; *Vid Sagnabrunninn*, Malog Menning, 1971.

Also author of play, "Delerium Bubonis," and of radio plays. Contributor to publications in Iceland.

WORK IN PROGRESS: Editing *Travellers in Iceland;* translating *The Saga of Gunnlaug Snake-Tongue.*

BIOGRAPHICAL/CRITICAL SOURCES: Young Readers Review, December, 1968; *Washington Post Book World,* February 9, 1969; *Books,* February, 1970.

* * *

BOULTON, Marjorie 1924- (Marguerite Mourier)

PERSONAL: Born May 7, 1924, in Teddington, England; daughter of Harry (a teacher) and Evelyn Maud (a teacher; maiden name, Cartlidge) Boulton. *Education:* Somerville College, Oxford, B.A., 1944, M.A., 1947, B.Litt., 1948, D.Phil., 1977. *Politics:* "Anti-totalitarian, whether right or left." *Home:* 36 Stockmore St., Oxford OX4 1JT, England. *Agent:* John Johnson, Clerkenwell House, 45-47 Clerkenwell Green, London ECIR OHT, England.

CAREER: Assistant English mistress in girls' high school, Westcliffe, England, 1944-46; Drake Hall Emergency Training College, Stafford, England, lecturer in English, 1948-50; Northern Counties College, Hexham, England, lecturer in English and speech training and librarian, 1950-62; Charlotte Mason College, Ambleside, England, vice-principal, 1955-62, principal, 1962-70. Professional examiner for public examinations. Jewelry designer and craftsperson. *Member:* Society of Authors, Esperanto Writers' Association, Universal Esperanto Association, British Esperanto Association, Esperanto Teachers Association, Esperanto Academy, Oxford Union Society, Cats' Protection League.

AWARDS, HONORS: Matthew Arnold prize, Oxford University, 1947; John Buchanan prize, Liverpool University, 1958; named Esperanto Author of the Year, 1958.

WRITINGS—In English: *Preliminaries* (poems), Fortune Press, 1949; *The Anatomy of Poetry* (critical study), Routledge & Kegan Paul, 1953, revised and enlarged edition, 1982; *The Anatomy of Prose,* Routledge & Kegan Paul, 1954; *Saying What We Mean,* Routledge & Kegan Paul, 1959, published as *The Anatomy of Language; The Anatomy of Drama,* Routledge & Kegan Paul, 1960.

Zamenhof, Creator of Esperanto, Routledge & Kegan Paul, 1960, Esperanto translation by the author, enlarged, Stafeto (La Laguna, Canary Isles), 1962; *Words in Real Life,* Macmillan, 1965; *Reading for Real Life,* Macmillan, 1971; *The Anatomy of the Novel,* Routledge & Kegan Paul, 1975; *The Anatomy of Literary Studies,* Routledge & Kegan Paul, 1980; *Julio Baghy* (criticism), Iltis (Saarbrucken, Netherlands), 1983.

In Esperanto: *Kontralte* (poetry), Stafeto, 1955; *Kvarpieda Kamarado* (autobiographical), privately printed, 1956; *Cent Gojkantoj* (poetry), privately printed, 1957; (author of introduction) *Angla Antologio* (anthology), Universala Esperanto-Associo, 1957; *Eroj* (poetry), Stafeto, 1959; *Virino ce La Landlimo* (one-act plays), Komuna Konversacia Klubo (Copenhagen), 1959; *Dekdu Piedetoj* (autobiographical), privately printed, 1964; *Okuloj* (short stories), Stafeto, 1967; *Nia Sango* (one-act play), British Esperanto Association, 1970; *Ni Aktoras* (three one-act plays), Dansk Esperanto-Forlag (Aabyhoj, Denmark), 1971; *Faktoj kaj Fantazioj,* Universala Esperanto-Associo, 1983; (with Paul Thorsen) *Du El* (poems), Stafeto, Kehlet (Antwerp), 1983.

In Polish: *List Zza Grobu* (fiction), translated from the English manuscript by Zofia Krajewska, Slask (Katowice, Poland), 1959; *Szantaz* (fiction), translation from the English manuscript by Krajewska, Slask, 1960.

Translator: (From the Hindi with R. S. Vyas) H. R. Bachchan, *The House of Wine,* Fortune Press, 1950; (from the French) Jules Supervielle, *The Shell and the Ear,* Lotus Press, 1951; Vlasta Ursic, *Wild Chestnuts* [and] *The House at the Toll-Gate,* privately printed, 1954; (from the Esperanto) Tibor Sekelj, *Window on Nepal,* R. Hale, 1959; (from the English) Charles Carter, *Pri Sentemo pri Cies Situacio,* Quaker Esperanto Society (Gloucester, England), 1972.

Contributor to *Encyclopaedia Britannica* and of articles, short stories, and poetry in English and Esperanto to magazines.

WORK IN PROGRESS: Translating poetry, ballads, and carols, including the Middle English poem "Pearl," into Esperanto.

SIDELIGHTS: Marjorie Boulton once told *CA:* "For some years my creative writing has been mostly in Esperanto, and in English I have written mostly simple books of literary criticism, intended to help relatively inexperienced students of literature. Now, however, that I hope to live, though frugally, as a full-time writer, or nearly so, I am anxious to write more imaginatively also in English." In addition to her knowledge of Esperanto, Miss Boulton knows French, Italian, and Latin, and a smattering of German, Swedish and Spanish.

Boulton designs, crafts, and markets necklaces under the name of Marguerite Mourier.

AVOCATIONAL INTERESTS: Cooking, "growing as much of my own food as possible," cats.

* * *

BOURAOUI, H(edi) A(ndre) 1932-

PERSONAL: Born July 16, 1932, in Sfax, Tunisia; immigrated to Canada, 1966; naturalized Canadian citizen, 1971. *Education:* University of Toulouse, licence es lettres, 1958; Indiana University, M.A., 1960; Cornell University, Ph.D., 1966. *Home:* 2911 Bayview Ave., Apt. 214J, Willowdale, Ontario, Canada M2K 1E8. *Office:* 314A Strong College, York University, 4700 Keele St., Downsview, Ontario, Canada M3J 1P3.

CAREER: Wells College, Aurora, N.Y., instructor, 1962-65, assistant professor of French, 1965-66; York University, Toronto, Ontario, assistant professor, 1966-68, associate professor, 1968-73, professor of French, 1973—, master of Strong College, 1978—. Consultant to Encyclopaedia Britannica Educational Corp., 1967-70; foreign language consultant to Rand McNally, 1972—. *Member:* Modern Language Association of America, American Association of Teachers of French (president of Toronto chapter, 1969-74), American Association of African Studies, Canadian Association of University Teachers, Association of Canadian University Teachers of French, Canadian Association of American Studies, Canadian Comparative Literature Association, Canadian Association of African Studies. *Awards, honors:* Canada Council grants, 1968, 1969, 1975, 1976; Polish Government grant, 1973.

WRITINGS: Musocktail (poems), Tower Associates (Wheaton, Ill.), 1966; *Tremble* (poems), Saint Germain des Pres, 1969; *Immensement croises* (dramatic poem; title means "Immensely Crossed"; produced in Toronto at York University Theatre, March, 1972), Saint Germain des Pres, 1969; *Creaculture I* (essays), Center for Curriculum Development (Philadelphia), 1971; *Creaculture II: Parole et action* (essays), Center for Curriculum Development, 1971; *Eclate module* (poems), Cosmos (Montreal), 1972.

Vesuviade (poems), Saint Germain des Pres, 1976; *Structure intentionnelle du Grand Meaulnes: Vers le poeme romance* (literary criticism; title means "Intentional Structure of Le Grand Meaulnes: Towards the Poem-Novel"), A. G. Nizet, 1976; *Sans Frontieres* (poems), Francite (St. Louis), 1979; *Haituvois* (poems), Editions Nouvelle Optique (Quebec), 1980; *Tales of Heritage* (poems), The Upstairs Gallery, 1981; *Vers et l'Envers* (poems), ECW Press, 1982; *Ignescent* (poems), Editions Silex (Paris), 1982; *The Critical Strategy* (literary criticism), ECW Press, 1983.

Contributor of critical articles in English to literary journals, including *French Review, Novel, Modern Fiction Studies, Contact* (Tunisia), and *Teatr* (Poland). Editor, *Waves,* 1968—; consultant to *Presence Francophone.*

WORK IN PROGRESS: L'Inconaison, a novel; *Interdiagonales,* a book of poems; *The Sexual Equation* and *Le Maghreb litteraire,* books of essays.

SIDELIGHTS: H. A. Bouraoui told *CA:* "I was born in North Africa, raised and educated in the south of France, and my graduate work took place in the United States. At present I live, write, and teach in Toronto. My situation as a Francophone writer living in an Anglophone society and my cosmopolitan background have been important to my career and my cast of thought. As a result of my breadth of cultural experience, I have attempted to disperse my publications in as wide a geographical sense as possible: the United States, Canada, France, Belgium, North Africa, Australia, Poland, etc.

"My criticism is mostly written in English, my creative work in French. I am primarily interested, however, in a world view which is not confined to a single language or nation. Thus I have written critical pieces on experimental theatre in Poland (also English and Italian experimental theatre), comparative culture in France and the United States, Francophone North African literature, the contemporary novel—the French nouveau roman, the American novel, Latin American, Egyptian, Moroccan, Algerian, Tunisian.

"Especially in my creative writing, I have tried to capture the ikons and images of a world exploding at the seams, revealed in the transmutations of my metaphors and in the explosion of my thematic explorations. As *Le Figaro litteraire* wrote, 'The striking power of these texts stuffed with puns, with deliberately grating sonorities, and with popular elements is undeniable. The poet utilizes it to denounce the faults of a pasteurized society.' I have been much concerned with the creation of new genres, trying to rejuvenate existing forms and to convert the *roman* into a *poeme romance,* the *poeme* into a *poeme-essai,* or a *poeme dramatique.*

"If I have an axe to grind, it is that both the public and critics have a tendency to catalogue artists by genre, politics, nationalism. If a writer rejects such categorization, he risks remaining somehow outside the structures of literary history. Since I have traveled extensively in Great Britain, Italy, Poland, Hungary, Germany, Australia, New Zealand, Switzerland, Belgium, Tunisia, Algeria, and Morocco, and speak four languages, French, English, Spanish, and Italian, I have come to believe in open spiritual frontiers, in democracy and, in a sense, universalism. To this end I have tried to promote fellow writers in countries outside their own whenever possible. I would like to break the barriers between nations, and between creation and criticism. I look towards a day of complete permeability to others whoever he/she is, of whatever nationality, color, race, creed, sex—all of those artificial barriers society has created in order to separate men. For this reason I strive to create and promote a notion of comparative culture—I invented the term 'Creaculture' to describe the creative interaction of man with his milieu—and especially to develop and encourage an art which crosses cultural boundaries."

BIOGRAPHICAL/CRITICAL SOURCES: Le Figaro litteraire, March 2-8, 1970; *Research Studies,* December, 1972; *Journal of Popular Culture,* summer, 1974.

* * *

BOYD, Neil
See DeROSA, Peter (Clement)

* * *

BOYLE, J(ohn) A(ndrew) 1916-1979

PERSONAL: Born March 10, 1916, in Worcester Park, Surrey, England; died in 1979, in England; son of William Andrew (a bookseller) and Florence May (Roberts) Boyle; married Margaret Elizabeth Dunbar, March 26, 1945; children: Fiona, Louise, Morag. *Education:* Attended University of Goettingen, 1935; University of Birmingham, B.A. (first class honors), 1936; graduate study at University of Berlin, 1936-39; University of London, Ph.D., 1947.

CAREER: Served with Royal Engineers, 1941; seconded to special department of Foreign Office, 1942-50; University of Manchester, Manchester, England, senior lecturer, 1950-59, reader, 1959-66, professor of Persian studies, beginning 1966. Visiting professor of Persian, University of California, Berkeley, 1959-60. Member of Gibb Memorial Trust, beginning 1970.

MEMBER: Royal Asiatic Society, British Institute of Persian Studies (member of governing council, beginning 1964), Iran-Shenasi (Tehran, Iran; member of advisory board, beginning 1969), British Society for Middle Eastern Studies (member of council, beginning 1973), Anglo-Mongolian Society (chairman, beginning 1970), Korosi Csoma Society (Hungary; honorary fellow, 1973), Folklore Society, Society of Authors. *Awards, honors:* Order and Decoration of Sepass, Iran, 1958, for translation of *The History of the World-Conqueror;* M.A. University of Manchester, 1970.

WRITINGS: A Practical Dictionary of the Persian Language, Luzac & Co., 1949, published as *Persian-English Dictionary, Romanized,* Saphrograph, 1978; (translator) Juvaini, *The History of the World-Conqueror,* Manchester University Press, 1958; *Modern Persian Grammar,* Harrassowitz, 1966; (editor and contributor) *Cambridge History of Iran,* Volume V: *The Saljuq and Mongol Periods,* Cambridge University Press, 1968.

(With Karl Jahn) *Rashid al-Din Commemoration Volume, 1318-1968,* Harrassowitz, 1970; (translator) Rashid al-Din, *The Successors of Genghis Khan,* Columbia University Press, 1971; (translator) Farid al-Din Attar, *The Ilahi-nama, or Book of God,* Manchester University Press, 1977; *The Mongol World Empire, 1206-1370,* Variorium Reprints, 1977; (editor) *Persia: History and Heritage,* Allen Unwin, 1978. Member of editorial board, "Cambridge History of Iran" series, Cambridge University Press.

OBITUARIES: AB Bookman's Weekly, February 5, 1979.†

* * *

BOYLE, Mark
See KIENZLE, William X(avier)

BRADFORD, Leland P(owers) 1905-

PERSONAL: Born July, 1905, in Chicago, Ill.; son of Theron Draper (a salesman) and Ivy (Powers) Bradford; married Martha Irene De Maeyer, October 12, 1933; children: David Lee. *Education:* University of Illinois, A.B., 1930, A.M., 1935, Ph.D., 1939. *Address:* P.O. Box 548, Pinehurst, N.C. 28374.

CAREER: University of Illinois at Urbana-Champaign, instructor in education psychology, 1936-42; U.S. government, chief of training for Works Progress Administration, Ill., 1939-43, for U.S. Immigration and Naturalization Service, Washington, D.C., 1943-44, and for Federal Security Agency, Washington, D.C., 1944-45; National Education Association, Washington, D.C., director of Division of Adult Education, 1946-62, director of National Training Laboratories, 1947-67, National Training Laboratories, Institute of Applied Behavioral Science, executive director, 1967-69, president, 1969-70; consultant on organizational development, 1970—. Diplomate in industrial psychology, American Board of Professional Psychology, 1970. Coordinator of research and training, Adult Education Association, 1951; member of U.S. Technical Assistance Team to Austria, 1954; delegate to UNESCO and other international conferences in Europe and Canada, 1955-60. Member of National Committee on Study Awards, Fund for Adult Education, 1952-54, and of National Screening Committee for Fulbright Awards, 1952-56; trustee, Lesley College, 1965—.

MEMBER: American Psychological Association (fellow), National Education Association, Society for the Psychological Study of Social Issues, American Association for the Advancement of Science, European Institute for Transnational Studies of Group and Organizational Development (fellow), New York Academy of Science, Kenwood Country Club (Bethesda, Md.), Pinehurst Club (Pinehurst, N.C.), Country Club of North Carolina. *Awards, honors:* Ford Foundation fellow, 1952-53; honored by Federation of Community Councils of Philadelphia, 1954, and National Association of Public School Adult Educators, 1959; L.H.D., Boston University, 1968, Lesley College, 1973; American Association of Training and Development award, 1969; first distinguished fellow, National Training Laboratories, 1970; LL.D., University of Cincinnati, 1976.

WRITINGS: (With Jack Gibb and Kenneth Benne) *T-Group Theory and Laboratory Method: Innovation in Re-Education,* Wiley, 1964; (contributor) A. J. Morrow, *The Failure of Success,* American Marketing Association, 1972; *National Training Laboratories: Its History, 1947-1970,* National Training Laboratories Institute, 1974; (with Benne, Gibb, and Ronald Lippitt) *Laboratory Method of Learning and Changing,* Learning Resources Corp., 1974; (editor) *Group Development,* University Associates, 1974, revised edition, 1978; *Making Meetings Work: A Guide for Leaders and Group Members,* University Associates, 1976; (with wife, Martha I. Bradford) *Retirement: Coping with Emotional Upheavals,* Nelson-Hall, 1979; *Preparing for Retirement: A Participant's Workbook,* University Associates, 1981; *Preparing for Retirement: A Trainer's Kit,* University Associates, 1981. Contributor of articles to magazines and journals in field of adult education, training, and group dynamics. Editor, *Adult Education Bulletin,* 1942-50.

* * *

BRADY, Frank 1934-

PERSONAL: Born March 15, 1934, in Brooklyn, N.Y.; son of James J. (a dispatcher) and Beatrice A. (Mignerey) Brady; married Roberta Lowe, March 1, 1954 (divorced December, 1962); married Maxine Kalfus (a writer and editor), March 31, 1963; children: (first marriage) Erin, Sean. *Education:* Rutgers University, B.A., 1954; Columbia University, M.F.A., 1976; New York University, M.A., 1980, doctoral candidate, 1980—. *Politics:* Democrat. *Home:* 175 West 72nd St., New York, N.Y. 10023. *Agent:* James Seligmann Agency, 60 East 20th St., New York, N.Y. 10009. *Office:* Department of Communications, St. Johns University, Jamaica, N.Y. 11432.

CAREER: Association of the Bar of the City of New York, New York City, librarian, 1956-58; *Chess Life* (magazine), Newburgh, N.Y., editor, 1958-61; *Eros* (magazine), New York City, associate publisher, 1961-63; *Chessworld* (magazine), New York City, editor, 1963-65; *Playboy* (magazine), Chicago, Ill., associate editor, 1965-69; *Avant-Garde* (magazine), New York City, publisher, 1969-70; writer and radio broadcaster, 1970—; member of English department faculty at Columbia University, New York University, and City University of New York, all in New York City, 1978-81; St. John's University, Jamaica, N.Y., assistant professor of communications, 1981—. Has done radio broadcasts for Pacific Radio Network, National Public Radio, Metromedia, Public Broadcast Service, and American Broadcasting Co. *Military service:* New York National Guard, Field Artillery, 1951-56. *Member:* P.E.N. American Center, Authors Guild, Authors League of America, Overseas Press Club, Sigma Delta Chi. *Awards, honors:* Nominated for Luther Mott Award, National Journalism Society, 1975.

WRITINGS: *Profile of a Prodigy* (biography of chess player Bobby Fischer), McKay, 1973; *Chess: How to Improve Your Technique,* F. Watts, 1974; *Hefner: An Unauthorized Biography,* Macmillan, 1974; *Barbra* (biography of Barbra Streisand), Grosset, 1977; *Favorite Bookstores,* Sheed Andrews, 1978; *Onassis* (biography), Prentice-Hall, 1978; *Orson Welles* (biography), Prentice-Hall, in press.

WORK IN PROGRESS: Researching the lives of several potential subjects, ranging from a famous painter to a great composer to a leading revolutionary.

SIDELIGHTS: Frank Brady told *CA:* "I am more than ever dedicated to the art of biography. I believe that in all biography there is a great deal of autobiography. As I study the life of a subject, I attempt to discover what is most human in his history or career and often emerge learning something about myself. Writing biographies, for me, therefore, becomes a looking glass into my own personality. Aspiring biographers might take note of Plutarch in that the smallest characteristic of a subject might be more revealing of his personality than his most imposing battles."

BIOGRAPHICAL/CRITICAL SOURCES: *Avant-Garde,* December, 1974; *People,* December 2, 1974; *New York Post,* December 14, 1974; *Los Angeles Times,* January 16, 1975.

* * *

BRAM, Elizabeth 1948-

PERSONAL: Born December 5, 1948, in New York, N.Y.; daughter of Joseph (a professor of anthropology) and Jean (a professor of classics; maiden name, Rhys) Bram. *Education:* Attended New York University, 1966-67, and Silvermine College of Art. *Home:* 4 Prospect St., Baldwin, N.Y. 11510.

CAREER: Artist (paints large murals) and writer. *Member:* Authors Guild, Authors League of America.

WRITINGS—All self-illustrated children's books: *The Door in the Tree,* Greenwillow Books, 1976; *A Dinosaur Is Too Big,* Greenwillow Books, 1977; *The Man on the Unicycle and Other Stories,* Greenwillow Books, 1977; *I Don't Want to Go to School,* Greenwillow Books, 1977; *One Day I Closed My Eyes and the World Disappeared,* Dial, 1978; *Saturday Morning Lasts Forever,* Dial, 1978; *There Is Someone Standing on My Head,* Dial, 1979; *Woodruff and the Clocks,* Dial, 1980.

AVOCATIONAL INTERESTS: Playing classical flute and piano; studying natural healing, nutrition, and agriculture; studying ballet.

* * *

BRANDON, Frank
See BULMER, (Henry) Kenneth

* * *

BRATT, John H(arold) 1909-

PERSONAL: Born August 23, 1909, in Holland, Mich.; son of Hero (a carpenter) and Jennie (Langejans) Bratt; married Gladys Buurma, August 15, 1941; children: Marcia Lynne (Mrs. Thomas Vander Woude), Evonne Alice (Mrs. Peter J. Kok), James Stuart. *Education:* Calvin College, A.B., 1934; Calvin Theological Seminary, Th.B., 1937; Columbia Theological Seminary, Decatur, Ga., Th.M., 1938; Harvard Divinity School, S.T.M., 1939; Union Theological Seminary in Virginia, Th.D., 1955. *Home:* 2238 Hall St. S.E., Grand Rapids, Mich. 49506. *Office:* Department of Theology, Calvin College, Grand Rapids, Mich. 49506.

CAREER: Ordained to ministry of Christian Reformed Church, 1942; Christian Reformed Church, Dorr, Mich., pastor, 1942-46; Calvin College, Grand Rapids, Mich., professor of religion and theology, 1946-81. *Member:* American Society of Church History, Evangelical Theological Society.

WRITINGS: New Testament Guide, Eerdmans, 1946, 2nd edition, 1958; *Life and Teachings of John Calvin,* Baker Book, 1957; (co-author) *The Rise and Development of Calvinism,* Eerdmans, 1958, 2nd edition, 1963; *Springboards for Discussion I,* Baker Book, 1970; (editor) *The Heritage of John Calvin,* Eerdmans, 1973; *Springboards for Discussion II,* Baker Book, 1974; *The Final Curtain,* Baker Book, 1980.

* * *

BRECK, Allen duPont 1914-

PERSONAL: Born May 21, 1914, in Denver, Colo.; son of Chesney Yales (an engineer) and Isabelle E. (Lee) Breck; married Alice Wolfe, September 7, 1944; children: Anne Rose Breck Peterson. *Education:* University of Denver, A.B., 1936; University of Colorado, M.A., 1939, Ph.D., 1950. *Politics:* Republican. *Religion:* Episcopalian. *Home:* 2060 South St. Paul, Denver, Colo. 80210. *Office:* Department of History, University of Denver, Denver, Colo. 80210.

CAREER: Instructor in social studies, Denver, Colo., public schools, 1936-42, 1946; University of Denver, Denver, 1946—, began as assistant professor, professor of history, 1966—, chairman of department, 1959-78. Member of Colorado Governor's Commission on Educational Standards, 1960-63; vice-chairman, Colorado State Commission on Social Studies, 1963—; member of American Council on Education Commission on the College Student. Lecturer, member of national advisory board, and chairman of regional selection committee of Danforth Foundation Associate Program. Lecturer, Phi Beta Kappa Associates, 1960—. Historiographer, Episcopal Diocese of Colorado. *Military service:* U.S. Army, Field Artillery, 1942-46.

MEMBER: American Historical Association, Mediaeval Academy of America, Renaissance Society of America, Society of American Archivists, English-Speaking Union of the United States (vice-chairman, Denver branch, 1963-64), Royal Historical Society of Great Britain (fellow), Western History Association, Rocky Mountain Social Science Association (president, 1963-64), Rocky Mountain Medieval and Renaissance Association (president, 1970—), Phi Beta Kappa (president, Denver chapter, 1963-64), Omicron Delta Kappa, Lambda Chi Alpha, Phi Alpha Theta. *Awards, honors:* L.H.D., University of Denver, 1973.

WRITINGS: A Centennial History of the Jews of Colorado, 1859-1959, Hirschfeld, 1960; *Johannis Wyclyf, Tractatus de Trinitate,* University of Colorado Press, 1962; *The Episcopal Church in Colorado, 1860-1960,* Big Mountain Press, 1964; *William Gray Evans, Western Executive, 1855-1924,* University of Denver Press, 1964.

(Editor) *Physics, Logic, and History,* Plenum Press, 1970; (editor with Wolfgang Yourgrau) *Biology, History, and Natural Philosophy,* Plenum Press, 1972; *John Evans of Denver: Portrait of a Twentieth-Century Banker,* Pruett, 1973; *Cosmology, History, and Theology,* Plenum Press, 1977; *The Methodist, Evangelical, and United Brethren Churches in the Rockies, 1850-1976,* Rocky Mountain Conference of the United Methodist Church, 1977; *Arnold Toynbee and the Nuisance of Spirit in a World of Matter* [and] *Arnold Toynbee and the Jews of the Middle East,* [Baghdad], 1978. Also author of articles and short monographs. Contributor to *American Archivist.* Editor, "The West in American History" series and "Studies in History" series, both University of Denver.

WORK IN PROGRESS: John Wyclyf, Tractatus de Tempore.

SIDELIGHTS: Allen duPont Breck told *CA* that he is concerned with the moral and intellectual dimension of historical study.†

* * *

BREMNER, Robert H(amlett) 1917-

PERSONAL: Born May 26, 1917, in Brunswick, Ohio; son of George L. (a lawyer) and Sue E. (Hamlett) Bremner; married Catherine Marting, March 18, 1950; children: Sue L., Ann R. *Education:* Baldwin-Wallace College, B.A., 1938; Ohio State University, M.A., 1939, Ph.D., 1943. *Home:* 33 Orchard Dr., Worthington, Ohio 43805. *Office:* Ohio State University, 230 West 17th Ave., Columbus, Ohio 43210.

CAREER: Ohio State University, Columbus, instructor, 1946-51, assistant professor, 1951-55, associate professor, 1956-60, professor of history, 1960-80, professor emeritus, 1980—. Research associate at University of Wisconsin, 1958-59, and Harvard University, 1966-69; visiting summer professor at University of Cincinnati, 1965, and University of Michigan, 1966. *Member:* Social Welfare History Group (chairman, 1966-68), Ohio Academy of History (president, 1965-66).

WRITINGS: From the Depths: The Discovery of Poverty in the United States, New York University Press, 1956; *American Philanthropy,* University of Chicago Press, 1960; (editor) *Essays on History and Literature,* Ohio State University Press,

1966; (editor) Anthony Comstock, *Traps for the Young,* Harvard University Press, 1967.

(Editor) *Children and Youth in America: A Documentary History,* Harvard University Press, 1970-74; (general editor) *U.S.A. 20121,* Ohio State University Press, 1980—; *Philanthropy and Social Welfare in the Civil War Era,* Knopf, 1981; *American Society and Institutions, 1945-1960,* Ohio State University Press, 1982.

* * *

BRICK, Michael 1922-1974

PERSONAL: Born March 27, 1922, in Brooklyn, N.Y.; died September 20, 1974; son of Abraham (an insurance agent) and Anna (Petrushka) Brick; married Barbara L. Rosen, June 19, 1949; children: Barrett Lee. *Education:* Brooklyn College (now Brooklyn College of the City University of New York), B.A., 1941; University of Pittsburgh, M.Litt., 1948; Columbia University, M.A., 1950, Ph.D., 1963. *Religion:* Hebrew.

CAREER: Journalist with *PM, New York Star,* and *Compass,* New York City, 1946-51; Orange County Community College, Middletown, N.Y., teacher of history and chairman of department, 1952-58; Dutchess Community College, Poughkeepsie, N.Y., dean of the college, 1958-60; Columbia University, Teachers College, New York City, instructor, 1960-63, associate professor, beginning 1963, professor of higher education and chairman of department. *Military service:* U.S. Army, 1943-46; became staff sergeant. *Member:* American Historical Association, American Association of Junior Colleges, Association for Higher Education, American Association of University Professors, Phi Delta Kappa, Kappa Delta Phi.

WRITINGS: Forum and Focus for the Junior College Movement: The American Association of Junior Colleges, Bureau of Publications, Teachers College, Columbia University, 1964; *An Analysis of Selected Business and Technology Programs in High Schools and in Two Year-Colleges and Institutes of New York,* Center for Urban Education, 1967; (with Earl J. McGrath) *Innovation in Liberal Arts Colleges,* Teachers College Press, 1969; *Collective Negotiations in Higher Education,* Community College Center, Teachers College, Columbia University, 1973.

WORK IN PROGRESS: A book on F.A.P. Barnard; a book on the faculty role in the governing of community colleges.†

* * *

BRIDGEMAN, Richard
See DAVIES, L(eslie) P(urnell)

* * *

BRISCO, Patty
See MATTHEWS, Clayton (Hartley) and MATTHEWS, Patricia (Anne)

* * *

BRISCOE, D(avid) Stuart 1930-

PERSONAL: Born November 9, 1930, in Millom, Cumberland, England; son of Stanley (a sales representative) and Mary (Wardle) Briscoe; married Jill Pauline Ryder, June 29, 1958; children: David Stanley Campbell, Judith Margaret, Peter Alan Stuart. *Religion:* Christian. *Home:* 2545 Eastwood Dr., Brookfield, Wis. 53005.

CAREER: District Bank Ltd., Spring Gardens, Manchester, England, member of inspection staff, 1955-60; Elmbrook Church, Brookfield, Wis., pastor, 1970—; secretary of Capernwray Missionary Fellowship, and evangelist and Bible teacher in over fifty countries. *Military service:* Royal Marine Commandos, 1948-50.

WRITINGS: The Fullness of Christ, Zondervan, 1965; *Living Dangerously,* Zondervan, 1968; *Where Was the Church When the Youth Exploded?,* Zondervan, 1972; *Discovering God,* Sowers of Seed, 1972; *Getting into God,* Zondervan, 1975; *Bound for Joy,* Regal Books, 1975; *What Works When Life Doesn't,* Victor Books, 1976; *All Things Weird and Wonderful,* Victor Books, 1977; *Let's Get Moving,* Regal Books, 1978; *Patterns for Power,* Zondervan, 1979; *Sound Sense for Successful Living,* Revell, 1979; *The Communicator's Commentary—Romans,* Word, Inc., 1982; *When the Going Gets Tough,* Regal Books, 1982.

* * *

BRODY, Jules 1928-

PERSONAL: Born March 6, 1928, in New York, N.Y.; son of Harry (a business executive) and Ida (Josephson) Brody; married Roxane Offner, July 26, 1953; children: Rachel, David, Jonathan. *Education:* Cornell University, B.A., 1948; Columbia University, M.A., 1949, Ph.D., 1956. *Home:* 62 Trenor Dr., New Rochelle, N.Y. 10804. *Office:* Department of Romance Languages, Queens College of the City University of New York, Flushing, N.Y. 11367.

CAREER: Columbia University, New York, N.Y., lecturer, 1950-53, instructor, 1953-56, assistant professor, 1956-59, associate professor of French, 1959-63; University of Rochester, Rochester, N.Y., professor of French and chairman of department of foreign and comparative literature, 1963-68; Queens College of the City University of New York, Flushing, N.Y., professor of French and associate dean of faculty, 1968—. Member of speakers bureau, United Jewish Welfare Fund, Rochester, N.Y.; trustee, Hillel School, Rochester, N.Y. *Member:* Modern Language Association of America, Society for French Studies (Oxford), American Association of Teachers of French, Societe d'Etudes du XVIIe Siecle (Paris), Phi Beta Kappa. *Awards, honors:* Fulbright research grant to Paris, 1961-62; Guggenheim fellow, 1961-62; recipient of L'Ordre des Palmes Academiques, France, 1968.

WRITINGS: Boileau and Longinus, Droz, 1958; (editor with N. Edelman and D. C. Cabeen) *Critical Bibliography of French Literature,* Volume III: *The 17th Century,* Syracuse University Press, 1961; (editor) *French Classicism: A Critical Miscellany,* Prentice-Hall, 1965; *Esthetique et societe chez Moliere,* Dramaturgie et Societe, 1968; (editor) *The Eye of the Beholder: Essays in French Literature by Nathan Edelman,* Johns Hopkins University Press, 1974; (contributor) *From Humanism to Classicism,* L'Espirt Createur, 1975; *Structures de personnalite et vision du monde dans les Memoires de Saint-Simon,* Cahiers Saint-Simon, 1976; *Boileau et la critique poetique,* Critique Creation Litteraires France, 1977; (contributor) *O un amy!: Essays on Montaigne in Honor of Donald M. Frame,* French Forum, 1977. Managing editor, *Romantic Review.*

AVOCATIONAL INTERESTS: Playing banjo and guitar, cabinetmaking.†

BROMELL, Henry 1947-

PERSONAL: Born September 19, 1947, in New York, N.Y.; son of W. B. and Mary M. (MacGaffin) Bromell. *Education:* Amherst College, B.A., 1970. *Agent:* Nan Blitman, 2228 22nd St., Santa Monica, Calif. 90405.

CAREER: Writer. Lecturer at Iowa Writer's Workshop, 1975; writer-in-residence at Amherst College, 1976. *Member:* Phi Beta Kappa. *Awards, honors:* Houghton Mifflin literary fellowship, 1974, for *The Slightest Distance.*

WRITINGS: The Slightest Distance (short stories), Houghton, 1974; *I Know Your Heart, Marco Polo* (short stories), Knopf, 1979; *The Follower* (novel), Simon & Schuster, 1982. Contributor of stories to anthologies. Contributor of short stories to *New Yorker* and *Atlantic Monthly* and of film articles to *Rolling Stone.*

SIDELIGHTS: In a *New York Times Book Review* article on Henry Bromell's *The Slightest Distance,* Annie Gottlieb writes: "A delicate nostalgia is the predominant mood of this collection of spare family miniatures, nine stories . . . about the various generations and branches of the Richardson family, all of whom share a common malaise-cum-philosophy: all are slightly out of register with the present moment so that they are almost always either longing or remembering. . . . Each of the stories laconically delineates the almost event-less surface of a moment in family life in counterpoint with . . . moments of numb reflection, or of memory, so seductive and elusive." William H. Pritchard, in the *Hudson Review,* says that "these stories, mostly published in the *New Yorker,* seemed when I read a couple of them there to be too quickly classifiable as made-to-order for the magazine; too quietly knowing about how well-bred stories ought to be written. But collected and read together they changed my mind." And Nolan Miller, writing in the *Antioch Review,* feels that Bromell's "crystal-clear, tightly spun stories . . . set in chronological order, add up to a surprisingly impressive [first book]. Henry Bromell has proved himself a writer to shout about."

In *I Know Your Heart, Marco Polo,* Bromell once again puts together a group of related stories about the Richardson family. Joyce Carol Oates, in a *New York Times Book Review* article, says that Bromell, "whose first collection of stories, *The Slightest Distance,* was an understated and highly promising achievement, seems to have come up with about 132 pages of inchoate material in this new collection. Some of it is clotted and burdened with extraneous detail; much of it is marred by inattentive observations . . . ; all of it is highly promising." Oates feels that *I Know Your Heart, Marco Polo,* "despite its presentation as a collection of stories, is really the first draft of what might have been a novel of more than ordinary worth. . . . First drafts are commonly 'organized' along an association-of-idea pattern, which results in lengthy, crammed, disjointed paragraphs later to be rearranged for dramatic effectiveness. Much of [the book] suffers from this kind of 'organization.'"

But Susan Wood, in a *Washington Post Book World* review, writes that although "the stories are not flawless," they "fill the reader with pleasure and remind us that, after all, one truly becomes oneself in relation to others." And William Logan, reviewing *I Know Your Heart, Marco Polo* for the *Chicago Tribune Book World,* states that "the sole criticism that can be made against this unusual collection—a better, deeper book than [Bromell's] first—is that the emotional response demanded from the reader has more the distance of pity than the intimacy of identification. Not often enough can we accept this family's problems as our own. It is more important to note that Bromell has graduated from a writer of description to a writer of perception."

BIOGRAPHICAL/CRITICAL SOURCES: Antioch Review, Volume XXIII, number 1, 1975; *New York Times Book Review,* January 5, 1975, April 1, 1979; *Hudson Review,* spring, 1975; *Contemporary Literary Criticism,* Volume V, Gale, 1976; *Chicago Tribune Book World,* March 11, 1979; *New York Times,* April 7, 1979; *Washington Post Book World,* May 6, 1979.

* * *

BROOKS, Janice Young 1943-
(Amanda Singer, Valerie Vayle)

PERSONAL: Born January 11, 1943, in Kansas City, Mo.; daughter of J. W. (a surgeon) and Louise (Jones) Young; married Lawrence E. Brooks, February 2, 1965; children: David Lawrence, Amy Louise. *Education:* University of Kansas, B.S.Ed., 1965; graduate study at University of Missouri—Kansas City, 1965-67. *Home:* 5410 Aberdeen, Shawnee Mission, Kan. 66205.

CAREER: Elementary teacher in the public schools of Turner, Kan., 1965-68; writer. Teacher at Avila College Writer's Conference. *Member:* Romance Writers of America, Mensa. *Awards, honors:* Thorpe Menn Award, American Association of University Women, 1982, for *Seventrees.*

WRITINGS: (Under pseudonym Amanda Singer) *Ozark Legacy,* Bouregy, 1975; *Kings and Queens: The Plantagenets of England,* Thomas Nelson, 1976; *In Love's Own Time,* Playboy Press, 1977; (co-author, under pseudonym Valerie Vayle) *Lady of Fire,* Dell, 1980; *Forbidden Fires,* Playboy Press, 1980; (under pseudonym Valerie Vayle) *Seaflame,* Dell, 1980; *Seventrees,* New American Library, 1980; (under pseudonym Valerie Vayle) *Oriana,* Dell, 1981; *Still the Mighty Waters,* Dell, 1983; *Our Lives, Our Fortunes,* Dell, 1984.

Contributor to *Fiction Writer's Market,* Writer's Digest Books, 1981, 1982. Contributor to periodicals, including *Writer's Digest, Mensa Bulletin, Woman's Day, Baby Talk, and Kansas City Star.*

WORK IN PROGRESS: A "double-romance, reverse-reincarnation" murder mystery; an historical novel dealing with the Fred Harvey Girls ("made famous a generation ago in a Judy Garland film").

SIDELIGHTS: Janice Young Brooks told *CA:* "Every book is my favorite while I'm writing it. I think writers have to feel that way or they'd never get through a single project. But looking back, my real favorite is *Seventrees,* partly because it's set in home territory, but mostly because I set out with one simple plan: to write exactly the sort of book I most love to read. It's a big family saga, with three generations, realistic characters and situations, lots of subplots and local flavor. Although it's far from the best selling book I've done, it's been the one that's provoked the most gratifying response from readers.

"I keep hearing that the historical novel is dead, its place in the women's fiction market taken by the sexy, short contemporary paperbacks, but I'm hanging in there anyway. Publishing trends change and I want to be there waiting with a big backlist when the historical readers come back to the fold. My dearest dream is to someday be classified with Anya Seton,

Susan Howatch, and Catherine Gaskin, the real greats in my field.''

* * *

BROOKS, John
See SUGAR, Bert Randolph

* * *

BROOKS, Stewart M. 1923-

PERSONAL: Born April 6, 1923, in Sidney, N.Y.; son of William Morris and Mabel (Elliott) Brooks; married Natalie Paynton, September 20, 1952; children: S. Marshall. *Education:* Albany College of Pharmacy, B.S. (cum laude), 1949; Philadelphia College of Pharmacy and Science, M.S., 1951. *Residence:* Waban, Mass.

CAREER: Muhlenberg Hospital School of Nursing, Plainfield, N.J., instructor in basic science, 1951-57; Lasell Junior College, Auburndale, Mass., science instructor, 1957-62. Boston City Hospital School of Nursing, Boston, Mass., instructor in basic science, 1962-65; full-time writer, 1965—. *Military service:* U.S. Army, Signal Corps, 1942-45; became sergeant. *Member:* American Pharmaceutical Association, Kappa Psi.

WRITINGS: Basic Facts of General Chemistry, Saunders, 1956; *Selected Experiments in General Chemistry,* Saunders, 1956; *Basic Facts of Pharmacology,* Saunders, 1957, 2nd edition, 1963; *Basic Facts of Medical Microbiology,* Saunders, 1958, 2nd edition, 1962; *Selected Experiments in Medical Microbiology,* Saunders, 1958, 2nd edition, 1962.

Body Water and Ions, Springer, 1960, 3rd edition, 1973; *Integrated Basic Science,* Mosby, 1962, 3rd edition, 1970, laboratory manual and workbook, 1964, 2nd edition, 1971; *Our Murdered Presidents: The Medical Story,* Fell, 1966; *Civil War Medicine,* C. C Thomas, 1966; *Basic Chemistry: A Programmed Presentation,* Mosby, 1966, 2nd edition, 1971; *A Programmed Introduction to Microbiology,* Mosby, 1968, 2nd edition, 1973; *The Sea inside Us,* Meredith, 1968; *McBurney's Point,* Barnes, 1969.

The World of the Viruses, Barnes, 1970; *Basic Biology,* Mosby, 1971; *The V.D. Story,* Barnes, 1971; *The Cancer Story,* Barnes, 1973; *Ptomaine,* Barnes, 1974; *Basic Science and the Human Body,* Mosby, 1975; *Going Metric,* Barnes, 1976; (editor) *Review of Nursing,* Little, Brown, 1978; (editor) *N.D.R.: Nurses Drug Reference,* Little, Brown, 1978; (with wife, Natalie Paynton-Brooks) *Turner's Personal and Community Health,* Mosby, 15th edition, 1979, 16th edition, 1983.

(With N. Paynton-Brooks) *The Human Body: Structure and Function in Health and Disease,* Mosby, 1980; (with N. Paynton-Brooks) *Handbook of Infectious Diseases,* Mosby, 1980.

Contributor to popular and professional journals.

AVOCATIONAL INTERESTS: Civil War, classical music, bird-watching, walking, gardening.

* * *

BROWER, David R(oss) 1912-

PERSONAL: Born July 1, 1912, in Berkeley, Calif.; son of Ross J. (an engineer) and Mary Grace (Barlow) Brower; married Anne Hus (a free-lance editor), May 1, 1943; children: Kenneth David, Robert Irish, Barbara Anne (Mrs. Harper McKee), John Stewart. *Education:* Attended University of California, Berkeley, 1929-31. *Office:* 124 Spear St., San Francisco, Calif. 94105.

CAREER: Sierra Club, San Francisco, Calif., editor, 1935-69, director of wilderness outings programs, 1939-56, executive director, 1952-69, honorary vice-president, beginning 1973; University of California Press, Berkeley, editor, 1941-52; Friends of the Earth Foundation, San Francisco and New York, N.Y., founder, president, and initiator of independent Friends of the Earth organizations in several countries, beginning 1969. Visiting scholar, Case Western Reserve University, 1974; representative and guest speaker at international and national environmental conferences.

Activist in wilderness preservation campaigns, including Saving Dinosaur National Monument, 1952-56, Saving Grand Canyon, 1952-68, Wilderness Act, 1952-64, North Cascades National Park, 1955-68, and Redwood National Park, 1963-68. Founder, Sierra Club Foundation, 1960, and Coleman Watershed Fund; John Muir Institute for Environmental Studies, co-founder, vice-president, 1968-72, director, 1969-71; chairman of academic advisory board and member of environmental sub-committee, International Center for Human Environment, beginning 1975; member of advisory council of University of California Water Resources Center and Save-the-Bay Association. *Military service:* U.S. Army, Mountain Troops, 1942-45; became lieutenant. U.S. Army Infantry Reserve, 1945-54; became major; received Combat Infantryman's Badge and Bronze Star.

MEMBER: Natural Resources Council of America (member of executive committee, 1954-59; chairman, 1955-57), Les Amis de la Terre (founder, 1970), Friends of the Earth Ltd. (founder and guarantor), Earth Island Ltd. (founder and chairman, beginning 1971), American Association for the Advancement of Science, American Alpine Club (Western vice-president, 1955-58), National Parks Association (honorary member), Mountaineers (honorary member), Trustees for Conservation (founder, 1954; secretary, 1960-61 and 1964-65; vice-president, 1962-63 and 1966-67; trustee), Rachel Carson Trust for the Living Environment (director, beginning 1966), League of Conservation Voters (founder and member of steering committee, beginning 1969), Jordens Vanner (founder, 1971), Oceanic Society (director, 1972-73), Wilderness Society, California Public Conservation Council (member of advisory council, 1958-60), Oregon Cascades Council (director, 1960-63), North Cascades Conservation Council (director, beginning 1957), Kern Plateau Association (director, beginning 1954).

AWARDS, HONORS: First class skier award from National Ski Association of America, 1942; conservation merit award from California Conservation Council, 1953; certificate of merit, Nash Conservation awards program, 1953; National Parks Association award, 1956; Leipzig International Book Fair honorary diploma, 1963, for ''Exhibit Format'' series book *In Wilderness Is the Preservation of the World;* Carey Thomas award for creative publishing, 1964, and awards from American Institute of Graphic Arts, Printing Industries of America, and Western Book Publishers Association, all for Sierra Club ''Exhibit Format'' series; Paul Bartsch award, Audubon Naturalist Society of the Central Atlantic States, 1967; D.Sc., Hobart and William Smith Colleges, 1967; D.H.L., Claremont Men's College Graduate School, 1971, Starr King School for the Ministry, 1971, and University of Maryland, College Park, 1973; Doctor of Philosophy, Ecology, University of San Francisco, 1973.

WRITINGS: Remount Blue: The Combat Story of the Third Battalion, Eighty-Sixth Mountain Infantry, University of California Press, 1948; *The De Facto Wilderness: What Is Its Place?,* Sierra Books, 1962; (author of foreword) Robert Wenkam, *Maui: The Last Hawaiian Place,* Friends of the Earth, 1970; (contributor) Harvey Manning, *Cry Crisis: Rehearsal in Alaska,* Friends of the Earth, 1974.

Editor; published by Sierra Books, unless otherwise indicated: *Manual of Ski Mountaineering,* 1942, 4th edition, 1969; *Going Light with Backpack or Burro,* 1951; *The Sierra Club: A Handbook,* 1957.

Eliot Porter, *The Place No One Knew: Glen Canyon on the Colorado,* 1963, revised edition, 1966, abridged edition, 1968; Francois Leydet, *Time and the River Flowing: Grand Canyon,* 1964; John Muir, *Gentle Wilderness: The Sierra Nevada,* 1964, revised edition, 1968; (and contributor) *Wildlands in Our Civilization,* 1964; *Not Man Apart,* 1965; Thomas F. Hornbein, *Everest: The West Ridge,* 1965; Porter, *Summer Island: Penobscot Country,* 1966, abridged edition, 1968; *The Sierra Club Wilderness Handbook,* Ballantine Books, 1967, 2nd revised edition, 1971; (and author of foreword) Mireille Johnston, *Central Park Country: A Tune within Us,* 1968; Harvey Manning, *The Wild Cascades: Forgotten Parklands,* Ballantine, 1969; *Wilderness: America's Living Heritage,* 1972.

Editor; all published by Friends of the Earth: (And author of foreword) Max Knight, *Return to the Alps,* 1970; (and author of foreword) Amory Bloch Lovings, *Eryri: The Mountains of Longing,* 1971; (and author of foreword) *Only A Little Planet,* 1972; Susanne Anderson, *Song of the Earth Spirit,* 1973; *Of All Things Most Yielding,* 1974.

Recordings: "Breaking the Species Barrier," Big Sur Recordings, 1971; "The Energy Crisis from an Environmentalist's Viewpoint," Phonotape, 1974.

Script writer and narrator for several wilderness films, 1940-58. General editor, "Exhibit Format" series, Sierra Books, twenty books, beginning 1960. Contributor to national magazines and professional publications. Editor, *Sierra Club Bulletin,* 1946-53, *Sierra Club Annual Magazine,* until 1968.

SIDELIGHTS: In 1939, David R. Brower led the first ascent of Shiprock Mountain in New Mexico. He has also made several other first ascents of mountains in the Sierra Nevada range. Through his work with the Sierra Club, Brower led some four thousand people on expeditions into remote wilderness areas between 1939 and 1956. Brower's influential conservation work includes the initiating of the National Wilderness Preservation system and the Outdoor Recreation Resources Review.

BIOGRAPHICAL/CRITICAL SOURCES: John McPhee, *Encounters with the Archdruid,* Farrar, Straus, 1971.†

* * *

BRUSHWOOD, John S(tubbs) 1920-

PERSONAL: Born January 23, 1920, in Glenns, Va.; son of John Benson (a retail merchant) and Evelyn (Stubbs) Brushwood; married Carolyn Norton, May 19, 1945; children: David Benson, Paul Darrach. *Education:* Randolph-Macon College, B.A., 1940; University of Virginia, M.A., 1942; National University of Mexico, summer study, 1943; Columbia University, Ph.D., 1950. *Religion:* Episcopalian. *Home:* 2813 Maine Ct., Lawrence, Kan. 66044. *Office:* University of Kansas, Lawrence, Kan. 66044.

CAREER: Virginia Polytechnic Institute (now Virginia Polytechnic Institute and State University), Blacksburg, instructor in Spanish, 1942-44; University of Missouri, Columbia, instructor, 1946-50, assistant professor, 1950-52, associate professor, 1952-57, professor of Spanish, 1957-67, chairman of department of Romance languages, 1953-57, 1958-59; University of Kansas, Lawrence, Roy A. Roberts Professor of Spanish American Literature, 1967—. Resident scholar, Bellagio Study and Conference Center, 1978.

MEMBER: Modern Language Association of America (chairman of contemporary Spanish American literature, 1966; chairman of 19th century Spanish American literature, 1972), American Association of Teachers of Spanish and Portuguese (president of state chapter, 1958), Instituto Internacional de Literatura Iberoamericana, American Association of University Professors, Midwest Modern Language Association (president, 1962-63; member of executive council, 1962-64), Phi Sigma Iota, Sigma Delta Pi.

AWARDS, HONORS: Grants from Fund for the Advancement of Education, 1951-52, American Philosophical Society, 1957, American Council of Learned Societies, 1961, Social Science Research Council, 1971, and National Endowment for the Humanities, 1976; Fulbright lectureship in Colombia, 1974; "Author of the Year" citation, University of Texas Press, 1975, for *The Spanish American Novel: A Twentieth-Century Survey;* Doctor of Letters, Randolph-Macon College, 1981; Balfour Jeffrey Research Award in Humanities and Social Sciences, 1982.

WRITINGS: The Romantic Novel in Mexico, University of Missouri Studies, 1954; (with Jose Rojas Garciduenas) *Breve historia de la novela mexicana,* Ediciones de Andrea, 1959; *Mexico in Its Novel: A Nation's Search for Identity,* University of Texas Press, 1966, revised edition published as *Mexico en su novela,* Fondo de Cultura Economica, 1973; (translator with wife, Carolyn Brushwood) Sergio Galindo, *The Precipice,* University of Texas Press, 1969; *Enrique Gonzales Martinez,* Twayne, 1969.

Los ricos en la prosa mexicana, Editorial Diogenes, 1970; (with Manuel Zapata Olivella) *Semanario: Literatura comparada,* Centro Colombo Americano, 1975; *The Spanish American Novel: A Twentieth-Century Survey,* University of Texas Press, 1975; (translator with C. Brushwood) Demeterio Aguilera Malta, *Don Goyo,* Humana Press, 1980; *Genteel Barbarism: New Readings of Nineteenth-Century Spanish-American Novels,* University of Nebraska Press, 1981.

Contributor: M. E. Johnson, editor, *Swan, Cygnets, and Owl,* University of Missouri Studies, 1956; *III Congreso latinoamericano de escritores,* Ediciones del Congreso de la Republica, 1971; *Investigaciones contemporaneas sobre la historia de Mexico,* Universidad Nacional Autonoma Mexicana and University of Texas, 1971; Andrew P. Dedicki and Enrique Pupo-Walker, editors, *Estudios de literatura hispanoamericana en honor a Jose J. Arrom,* International Book Service, 1974; Jaime Alazraki and others, editors, *Homenaje a Andres Iduarte,* American Hispanist Press, 1976; Wolodmyr T. Zyla and Wendell Aycock, editors, *Ibero-American Letters in a Comparative Perspective,* Texas Tech University Press, 1978; Aurora Ocampo, editor, *La critica de la novela hispano-americana contemporanea,* National University of Mexico, 1973; Donald Bleznick, editor, *Homenaje a Luis Leal,* Insula, 1978; Ocampo, editor, *La critica de la novela mexicana contemporanea,* National University of Mexico, 1980. Contributor to *Collier's Encyclopedia Yearbook;* contributor of articles, poems, and reviews to Hispanic studies journals, *Kansas City Star*, and other publications.

WORK IN PROGRESS: La novela mexicana, 1967-1982.

BIOGRAPHICAL/CRITICAL SOURCES: El Gallo Illustrado, April 26, 1964; *La Cultura en Mexico*, May 27, 1964; *Revista Mexicana de Cultura*, October 30, 1966; *Hispania*, March, 1971, December, 1976; *Americas*, February, 1976; *Cithara*, May, 1976.

* * *

BULL, Angela (Mary) 1936-

PERSONAL: Born September 28, 1936, in Halifax, Yorkshire, England; daughter of Eric Alexander (a company director) and Joyce (Benson) Leach; married Martin Wells Bull (a Church of England clergyman), September 15, 1962; children: Timothy Martin, Priscilla Emily. *Education:* University of Edinburgh, M.A. (with honors), 1959; St. Hugh's College, Oxford, graduate study, 1959-61. *Religion:* Church of England. *Home:* The Vicarage, Hall Bank Dr., Bingley, West Yorkshire BD16 4BZ, England.

CAREER: Writer. Casterton School, Kirkby Lonsdale, Westmorland, England, teacher of English, 1961-62; Bodleian Library, Oxford University, Oxford, England, assistant to keeper of western manuscripts, 1963.

WRITINGS—Published by Collins, except as indicated: *The Friend with a Secret*, 1965, Holt, 1966; (with Gillian Avery) *Nineteenth Century Children*, Hodder & Stoughton, 1965; *Wayland's Keep*, 1966, Holt, 1967; *Child of Ebenezer*, 1974; *Treasure in the Fog*, 1976; *Griselda*, 1977; *The Doll in the Wall*, 1978; *The Machine Breakers*, 1980; *The Bicycle Parcel*, Hamish Hamilton, 1981; *The Accidental Twins*, Faber, 1982.

WORK IN PROGRESS: A biography of Noel Streatfeild, for Collins.

* * *

BULMER, (Henry) Kenneth 1921-
(Alan Burt Akers, Ken Blake, Frank Brandon, Rupert Clinton, Ernest Corley, Arthur Frazier, Peter Green, Adam Hardy, Philip Kent, Bruno Krauss, Neil Langholm, Karl Maras, Manning Norvil, Charles R. Pike, Andrew Quiller, Chesman Scot, Nelson Sherwood, Richard Silver, H. Philip Stratford, Tully Zetford; Kenneth Johns, a joint pseudonym)

PERSONAL: Born January 14, 1921, in London, England; son of Walter Ernest (a chemist) and Hilda Louise (Corley) Bulmer; married Pamela Kathleen Buckmaster, March 7, 1953; children: Deborah Louise, Lucy-Ellen, Kenneth Laurence. *Education:* Attended schools in London, England. *Religion:* Congregational. *Home:* Waterdown House, 51 Front Rd., Tunbridge Wells, Kent TN2 5LE, England. *Agent:* Leslie Flood, E. J. Carnell Literary Agency, Rowneybury Bungalow, Sawbridgeworth, Nr. Old Harlow, Essex CM2O 2EX, England.

CAREER: Writer. Former editor, *Sword and Sorcery Magazine*. *Military service:* Royal Signal Corps., 1941-47. *Member:* Science Fiction Foundation (vice-president), British Science Fiction Association (honorary life member), British Fantasy Society (former president), Airship Association, Society of Ancients, Pike and Shot Society, Science Fiction Writers of America.

WRITINGS—All science fiction: (With A. V. Clarke) *Space Treason*, Panther Books, 1952; (with Clarke) *Cybernetic Controller*, Panther Books, 1952; *Encounter in Space*, Panther Books, 1952; *Space Salvage*, Panther Books, 1953; *The Stars Are Ours*, Panther Books, 1953; *Galactic Intrigue*, Panther Books, 1953; *Empire of Chaos*, Panther Books, 1953; *World Aflame*, Panther Books, 1954; *Challenge*, Curtis Warren, 1954; *City under the Sea* (bound with *Star Ways* by Poul Anderson), Ace Books, 1957, reprinted separately, Avon, 1980; *The Secret of ZI* (bound with *Beyond the Vanishing Point* by Ray Cummings), Ace Books, 1958 (published separately in England as *The Patient Dark*, R. Hale, 1969); *The Changeling Worlds* (bound with *Vanguard from Alpha* by Brian W. Aldiss), Ace Books, 1959.

The Earth Gods Are Coming (bound with *The Games of Neith* by Margaret St. Clair), Ace Books, 1960 (published separately in England as *Of Earth Foretold*, Digit, 1963); *Forschungskreuzer Saumarez*, Moewig, 1960, translation published as *Defiance*, Digit, 1963; *No Man's World* (bound with *Mayday Orbit* by Poul Anderson), Ace Books, 1961 (published separately in England as *Earth's Long Shadow*, Digit, 1962); *Beyond the Silver Sky* (bound with *Meeting at Infinity* by John Brunner), Ace Books, 1961; *The Fatal Fire*, Digit, 1962; *The Wind of Liberty*, Digit, 1962; *The Wizard of Starship Poseidon* (bound with *Let the Spacemen Beware!* by Poul Anderson), Ace Books, 1963; *The Million Year Hunt* (bound with *Ships to the Stars* by Fritz Leiber), Ace Books, 1964; *Demon's World* (bound with *I Want the Stars* by Tom Purdom), Ace Books, 1964 (published separately in England as *The Demons*, Compact, 1965); *Land Beyond the Map* (bound with *Fugitive of the Stars* by Edmond Hamilton), Ace Books, 1965; *Behold the Stars* (bound with *Planetary Agent X* by Mack Reynolds), Ace Books, 1965.

Worlds for the Taking, Ace Books, 1966; *To Outrun Doomsday*, Ace Books, 1967; *The Key to Irunium* (bound with *The Wandering Tellurian* by Allan Schwartz), Ace Books, 1967; *Cycle of Nemesis*, Ace Books, 1967; *The Doomsday Men*, Doubleday, 1968; *The Key to Venudine* (bound with *Mercenary from Tomorrow* by Mack Reynolds), Ace Books, 1968; *The Star Venturers* (bound with *The Fall of the Dream Machine* by Dean R. Koontz), Ace Books, 1969; *The Wizards of Senchuria* (bound with *Cradle of the Sun* by Brian M. Stableford), Ace Books, 1969; *Kandar*, Paperback Library, 1969; *The Ulcer Culture*, Macdonald, 1969, published as *The Stained-Glass World*, New English Library, 1976.

The Ships of Durostorum (bound with *Alton's Unguessable* by Jeff Sutton), Ace Books, 1970; *Blazon*, Curtis Books, 1970 (published in England as *Quench the Burning Stars*, R. Hale, 1970); *Star Trove*, R. Hale, 1970; *Swords of the Barbarians*, New English Library, 1970, Belmont-Tower, 1977; *The Hunters of Jundagai* (bound with *Project Jove* by John Glasby), Ace Books, 1971; *The Electric Sword Swallowers* (bound with *Beyond Capella* by John Rackham), Ace Books, 1971; *The Insane City*, Curtis Books, 1971; *The Chariots of Ra* (bound with *Earthstrings* by John Racjham), Ace Books, 1972; *On the Symb Socket Circuit*, Ace Books, 1972; *Roller Coaster World*, Ace Books, 1972.

Other: *Pretenders* (juvenile), New English Library, 1972; (editor) *New Writings in SF*, Volumes 22-30, Sidgwick & Jackson, 1973-76; (editor with John Carnell) *New Writings in SF Special*, Volume 1, Sidgwick & Jackson, 1975; (editor) *New Writings in SF Special*, Volumes 2-3, Sidgwick & Jackson, 1976-78; *Blind Run*, Severn House, 1980.

Contributor: Edward L. Ferman, editor, *Best from Fantasy and Science Fiction, #16,* Doubleday, 1967; Frederik Pohl, editor, *Nightmare Edge,* Ballantine, 1970; John Carnell, editor, *New Writings in SF,* Volume 19, Dobson, 1971; Richard Davis, editor, *Space Two,* Abelard Schuman, 1974; Christopher Carrell, editor, *Beyond This Horizon,* Ceolfrith Press, 1974; (under pseudonym Alan Burt Akers) Donald A. Wollheim, editor, *The DAW Science Fiction Reader,* DAW Books, 1976.

Under pseudonym Alan Burt Akers; "Dray Prescot" series; all science fiction novels; all published by DAW Books: *Transit to Scorpio,* 1972; *The Suns of Scorpio,* 1973; *Warrior of Scorpio,* 1973; *Swordships of Scorpio,* 1973; *Prince of Scorpio,* 1974; *Manhounds of Antares,* 1974; *Arena of Antares,* 1974; *Fliers of Antares,* 1975; *Bladesman of Antares,* 1975; *Avenger of Antares,* 1975; *Armada of Antares,* 1976; *The Tides of Kregen,* 1976; *Renegade of Kregen,* 1976; *Krozair of Kregen,* 1977; *Secret Scorpio,* 1977; *Savage Scorpio,* 1978; *Captive Scorpio,* 1978; *Golden Scorpio,* 1978; *A Life for Kregen,* 1979; *A Sword for Kregen,* 1979; *A Fortune for Kregen,* 1979; *A Victory for Kregen,* 1980; *Beasts of Antares,* 1980; *Rebel of Antares,* 1980; *Legions of Antares,* 1981.

Under pseudonym Ken Blake: *Where the Jungle Ends,* Severn House, 1978; *Stake Out,* Barker, 1978; *Hunter Hunted,* Barker, 1978; *Long Shot,* Severn House, 1979; *Fall Girl,* Sphere Books, 1979; *Dead Reckoning,* Sphere Books, 1980.

Under pseudonym Ernest Corley: *White-Out,* Jarrolds, 1960.

Under pseudonym Arthur Frazier; all published by New English Library: *Oath of Blood,* 1973; *The King's Death,* 1973; *A Flame in the Fens,* 1974; *An Axe in Miklagard,* 1975.

Under pseudonym Adam Hardy: *The Press Gang,* Pinnacle Books, 1973; *Prize Money,* Pinnacle Books, 1973; *Savage Siege,* Pinnacle Books, 1973 (published in England as *The Siege,* New English Library, 1973); *Treasure,* New English Library, 1973, published as *Treasure Map,* Pinnacle Books, 1974; *Powder Monkey,* New English Library, 1973, published as *Sailor's Blood,* Pinnacle Books, 1974; *Sea of Gold,* Pinnacle Books, 1974 (published in England as *Blood for Breakfast,* New English Library, 1974); *Court Martial,* Pinnacle Books, 1974; *Battle Smoke,* New English Library, 1974, Pinnacle Books, 1975; *Cut and Thrust,* New English Library, 1974, Pinnacle Books, 1975; *Boarders Away,* New English Library, 1975; *Fireship,* New English Library, 1975, Pinnacle Books, 1976; *Blood Beach,* New English Library, 1975; *Sea Flame,* New English Library, 1976; *Close Quarters,* New English Library, 1977.

Under pseudonym Philip Kent; all published by Pearson: *Mission to the Stars,* 1953; *Vassals of Venus,* 1954; *Slaves of the Spectrum,* 1954; *Home Is the Martian,* 1954.

Under pseudonym Bruno Krauss; all published by Sphere Books: *Steel Shark,* 1978; *Shark North,* 1978; *Shark Pack,* 1978; *Shark Hunt,* 1980.

Under pseudonym Neil Langholm: *The Dark Return,* Sphere Books, 1975; *Trail of Blood,* Sphere Books, 1976.

Under pseudonym Karl Maras: *Zhorani,* Comyns, 1954; *Peril from Space,* Comyns, 1954.

Under pseudonym Manning Norvil; all published by DAW Books: *Dream Chariots,* 1977; *Whetted Bronze,* 1978; *Crown of the Sword God,* 1980.

Under pseudonym Charles R. Pike: *Brand of Vengeance,* Mayflower Books, 1978.

Under pseudonym Andrew Quiller: *The Land of Mist,* Pinnacle Books, 1976; *Sea of Swords,* Pinnacle Books, 1976; *Hill of the Dead,* Chelsea House, 1981.

Under pseudonym Richard Silver: *By Pirate's Blood,* Pinnacle Books, 1975; *Jaws of Death,* Pinnacle Books, 1975.

Under pseudonym Tully Zetford; "Ryder Hook" series: *Whirlpool of Stars,* New English Library, 1974, Pinnacle Books, 1975; *The Boosted Man,* New English Library, 1974, Pinnacle Books, 1975; *Star City,* New English Library, 1974, Pinnacle Books, 1975; *The Virility Gene,* New English Library, 1975, Pinnacle Books, 1976.

With John Newman; under joint pseudonym Kenneth Johns: *The True Book about Space Travel,* Muller, 1960.

Contributor of short stories, some under pseudonyms, to *Magazine of Fantasy and Science Fiction, New Worlds, Science Fantasy,* and other publications.

SIDELIGHTS: "As I have been a freelance for over a quarter of a century," Kenneth Bulmer told *CA,* "it is inevitable that my work has altered a great deal over the years, and from a look back at early work the evident impression cannot be avoided that the genuine vision of those days was hampered by environment, editorial prejudices, and lack of data.

"At one time my life was centered around science fiction and the exploration of the excitement and challenges of what might lie in store and the investigation of the way people and individuals might react, leading to the order of insight necessary if we are to survive on this planet, let alone anywhere else. Some imperceptive reviewers have said that much of my work falls into the space opera category; but a reading of the texts will show this view untenable. Certainly, the challenge of the future, some of which has in a small way already spilled out into today, serves as a background to wider themes.

"The influence of science fiction in granting that ability to create imaginative worlds hitherto unknown has helped me in my historical novels, where the evocation of the conditions and human problems of Lord Nelson's navy bears a close relationship to the creation of logical and believable worlds present generations have not experienced. The outward trappings of Heroic Fantasy, somewhat richly clothing the 'Dray Prescot' novels, conceal underlying themes and preoccupations that, in the grand old cliche, illuminate the human condition, and bear a much closer relationship to reality than the majority of work in this area."†

* * *

BURACK, Sylvia K. 1916-
(Sylvia E. Kamerman)

PERSONAL: Born December 16, 1916, in Hartford, Conn.; daughter of Abraham and Augusta (Chermak) Kamerman; married Abraham S. Burack (an editor and publisher), November 28, 1940 (died June 28, 1978); children: Janet (Mrs. Alan D. Biller), Susan (Mrs. Chad A. Finer), Ellen (Mrs. Franklin Toker). *Education:* Smith College, B.A., 1938. *Home:* 72 Penniman Rd., Brookline, Mass. 02146. *Office:* Writer, Inc. and Plays, Inc., 8 Arlington St., Boston, Mass. 02116.

CAREER: Writer, Inc. and Plays, Inc. (publishers), Boston, Mass., associate editor, 1941-78, editor and publisher, 1978—. Massachusetts State College System, trustee, 1971-76, chairman of board, 1974-75; trustee of University of Massachusetts, 1976-81, and of Max C. Rosenfeld Fund. Member of Brookline

School Committee, 1949-69, and Massachusetts Board of Higher Education, 1973-75; Friends of the Libraries of Boston University, member of board of directors, 1978—, president, 1981—. *Member:* National Book Critics Circle, P.E.N. American Center, League of Women Voters, Phi Beta Kappa, Bostonian Society; also member of several other social, philanthropic, and civic associations.

WRITINGS—Editor under name Sylvia E. Kamerman, except as indicated; all published by Writer, Inc.: *Writing the Short Story,* 1942; *Book Reviewing,* 1978; (under name Sylvia K. Burack) *Writer's Handbook,* 1982; *Writing and Selling Fillers, Light Verse and Short Humor,* 1982.

All published by Plays: *Little Plays for Little Players,* 1952; *Blue Ribbon Plays for Girls,* 1955; *Blue Ribbon Plays for Graduation,* 1957; *A Treasury of Christmas Plays,* 1958; *Children's Plays from Favorite Stories,* 1959; *Fifty Plays for Junior Actors,* 1966; *Fifty Plays for Holidays,* 1969.

Children's Plays from Favorite Stories, 1970; *Dramatized Folk Tales of the World,* 1971; *A Treasury of Christmas Plays,* 1972; *Patriotic and Historical Plays for Young People,* 1975; *Space and Science Fiction Plays for Young People,* 1981; *Christmas Play Favorites for Young People,* 1982.

AVOCATIONAL INTERESTS: The theater, local politics, travel.

* * *

BURFORD, Eleanor
See HIBBERT, Eleanor Burford

* * *

BURKE, John (Frederick) 1922-
(Jonathan Burke, Owen Burke, Jonathan George, Joanna Jones, Robert Miall, Sara Morris, Martin Sands; Harriet Esmond, a joint pseudonym)

PERSONAL: Born March 3, 1922, in Rye, Sussex, England; son of Frederick Goode (a police officer) and Lilian Gertrude (Sands) Burke; married Joan Morris, September 13, 1941 (divorced, 1963); married Jean Williams, June 29, 1963; children: (first marriage) Bronwen, Jennifer, Sara, Jane, Joanna; (second marriage) David, Edmund. *Education:* Attended Holt School, Liverpool, England. *Politics:* Socialist. *Religion:* Agnostic. *Home and office:* 8 North Parade, Southwold, Suffolk IP18 6LP, England. *Agent:* Harold Ober Associates, Inc., 40 East 49th St., New York, N.Y., 10017; and David Higham Associates Ltd., 5-8 Lower John St., Golden Sq., London W1R 4HA, England.

CAREER: Writer. Museum Press Ltd., London, England, associate editor, 1953-56, production manager, 1956-57; Hamlyn Publishing Group Ltd., London, editorial manager of "Books for Pleasure" group, 1957-58; Shell International Petroleum, London, publicity media executive, 1959-63; Twentieth Century-Fox Productions, London, European story editor, 1963-65. Member, Royal Danish Embassy lecture panel in London. *Military service:* Royal Air Force, and Royal Electrical and Mechanical Engineers, 1942-47; became sergeant. *Member:* Society of Authors, Crime Writers Association, East Anglian Writers (member of council and honorary treasurer), Danish Club (London). *Awards, honors:* Rockefeller Foundation Atlantic Award in Literature, 1947, for *Swift Summer.*

WRITINGS—Novels, except as indicated: *Swift Summer,* Laurie, 1949; *Another Chorus,* Laurie, 1949; *These Haunted Streets,* Laurie, 1950; *The Outward Walls,* Laurie, 1951; *Chastity House,* Laurie, 1952; *The Poison Cupboard,* Secker & Warburg, 1956; (under pseudonym Sara Morris) *A Widow for the Winter,* Barker, 1961; *Only the Ruthless Can Play,* John Long, 1965; (editor) *Tales of Unease* (story anthology; also see below), Pan Books, 1966; *The Suburbs of Pleasure,* Dial, 1967; *Someone Lying, Someone Dying,* John Long, 1968; (editor) *More Tales of Unease* (story anthology), Pan Books, 1969.

(Under pseudonym Jonathan George) *The Kill Dog,* Doubleday, 1970; (under pseudonym Jonathan George) *Dead Letters,* Macmillan, 1972; *Expo 80,* Cassell, 1972; (editor) *New Tales of Unease* (story anthology), Pan Books, 1976; *The Devil's Footsteps,* Coward, 1976; *The Kama Sutra Tango,* Harper, 1977; *The Black Charade: A Dr. Caspian Story,* Coward, 1977; *Ladygrove: The Third Adventure of Dr. Caspian and Dronwen,* Coward, 1978; (under pseudonym Owen Burke) *The Figurehead,* Coward, 1979.

Under pseudonym Jonathan Burke; published by John Long, except as indicated: *The Dark Gateway,* Panther Books, 1954; *The Echoing Worlds,* Panther Books, 1954; *Twilight of Reason,* Panther Books, 1954; *Pattern of Shadows,* Museum Press, 1954; *Hotel Cosmos,* Panther Books, 1954; *Deep Freeze,* Panther Books, 1955; *Revolt of the Humans,* Panther Books, 1955; *Alien Landscapes* (short stories), Museum Press, 1955; *Pursuit through Time,* Ward, Lock, 1956; *Echo of Barbara,* 1959; *Fear by Installments,* 1960; *Deadly Downbeat,* 1962; *Teach Yourself Treachery,* 1962; *The Twisted Tongues,* 1964, published as *Echo of Treason,* Dodd, 1966; *The Weekend Girls,* 1966; *The Gossip Truth,* Doubleday, 1967 (published in England as *Gossip to the Grave,* John Long, 1967); *Rob the Lady,* 1969; *Four Stars for Danger,* 1970.

Under joint pseudonym Harriet Esmond: with wife, Jean Burke: *Darsham's Tower,* Delacorte, 1973 (published in England as *Darsham's Folly,* Collins, 1973); *The Eye Stones,* Delacorte, 1975; *The Florian Signet,* Fawcett, 1977.

Under pseudonym Joanna Jones: *Nurse Is a Neighbor,* M. Joseph, 1958; *Nurse on the District,* M. Joseph, 1959; *The Artless Flat-Hunter,* Pelham Books, 1963; *The Artless Commuter,* Pelham Books, 1965.

Under pseudonym Robert Miall; published by Pan Books: *UFO,* 1970; *UFO 2,* 1971; *Jason King,* 1972; *Kill Jason King!,* 1972; *The Protectors,* 1973; *The Adventurer,* 1973.

Travel books; under name John Burke; published by Batsford, except as indicated: (With William Luscombe) *The Happy Invaders: A Picture of Denmark in Springtime,* R. Hale, 1956; *Suffolk,* 1971; *England in Colour,* 1972; *Sussex,* 1974; *Illustrated History of England,* BCA Publications, 1974; *English Villages,* 1975; *South East England* (juvenile), Faber & Faber, 1975; *Czechoslovakia,* 1976; *Suffolk in Photographs,* 1976; *Beautiful Britain,* 1976; *Historic Britain,* 1977; *Life in the Villa in Roman Britain,* 1978; *Life in the Medieval Castle in Britain,* 1978; *Look Back on England,* Orbis, 1980; *The English Inn,* 1981.

Book adaptations from films and plays; under name John Burke, except as indicated; published by Pan Books, except as indicated: *The Entertainer,* Four Square Books, 1960; *Look Back in Anger,* Four Square Books, 1960; *The Three Hundred Spartans,* Signet, 1961 (published in England as *The Lion of Sparta,* Four Square Books, 1961); *Flame in the Streets,* Four Square Books, 1961; *The Angry Silence,* Hodder & Stoughton, 1961; *The Boys,* 1962; *Private Potter,* 1962; *The Man Who Finally Died,* 1963; *The World Ten Times Over,* 1963; *Guilty Party,*

Elek, 1963; *The System,* 1964; *A Hard Day's Night,* Dell, 1964.

Dr. Terror's House of Horrors, 1965; *Those Magnificent Men in Their Flying Machines,* Pocket Books, 1965 (published in England as *That Magnificent Air Race,* 1965); *The Trap,* 1966; *The Hammer Horror Omnibus,* 1966; *The Power Game,* 1966; *The Second Hammer Horror Omnibus,* 1967; *Privilege,* 1967; *Till Death Us Do Part,* 1967; (under pseudonym Martin Sands) *Maroc 7,* 1967; (under pseudonym Martin Sands) *The Jokers,* 1967; *Smashing Time,* 1968; *The Bliss of Mrs. Blossom,* 1968; *Chitty Chitty Bang Bang: The Story of the Film,* 1969; *The Smashing Bird I Used to Know,* 1969; *Moon Zero Two: The Story of the Film,* Signet, 1969; (under pseudonym Martin Sands) *The Best House in London,* Mayflower Books, 1969.

Strange Report, Hodder & Stoughton, 1970; *All the Right Noises,* Hodder & Stoughton, 1970; *Dad's Army,* Hodder & Stoughton, 1971; *Luke's Kingdom,* Fontana Books, 1976; *The Prince Regent,* Fontana Books, 1979.

Television plays: "Safe Conduct," produced on Granada TV, 1965; (adviser and contributor) "Tales of Unease" (based on anthology of same title, edited by Burke), produced by London Weekend TV, 1969; (story editor and contributor) "The Frighteners," produced by London Weekend TV, 1972. Also author of radio plays, all produced on British Broadcasting Corp. radio, including "The Prodigal Pupil," "The Man in the Ditch," and "Across Miss Desmond's Desk"; also author of screenplay, "Terror for Kicks"; also author of Reader's Digest/Automobile Association tourist publications. Also translator of two books from the French; also collaborator on three translations from the Danish.

WORK IN PROGRESS: Musical Landscapes, a study of composers in their environment in the British Isles, for publication by Webb & Bower.

SIDELIGHTS: John Burke told *CA* that he has "always had a strong sense of *place* and cannot write either fiction or historical/topographical works without personal knowledge of setting and background." He therefore travels widely throughout Britain to gain material for his writings. He mentioned that he relies "a great deal" on his wife, Jean, for her collaborative efforts under the joint pseudonym Harriet Esmond. Burke plays piano, harpsichord, and clarinet and knows French and Danish.

MEDIA ADAPTATIONS: Echo of Barbara was filmed by Independent Artists; *Nurse Is a Neighbor* was filmed as "Nurse on Wheels" by Anglo-Amalgamated; *Terror for Kicks* was filmed as "The Sorcerers."

AVOCATIONAL INTERESTS: Music.

* * *

BURKE, Jonathan
See BURKE, John (Frederick)

* * *

BURKE, Owen
See BURKE, John (Frederick)

* * *

BURKETT, David (Young III) 1934-

PERSONAL: Born July 7, 1934, in Pittsburgh, Pa.; son of David Young, Jr. and Faith (Espy) Burkett. *Education:* Northwestern University, B.S.J., 1956, M.S.J. (with highest distinction), 1957; graduate study at U.S. Department of State Foreign Service Institute, 1959. *Religion:* Lutheran. *Home and office:* 1235 East Mulberry, No. 302D, San Antonio, Tex. 78209.

CAREER: Valley Daily News, Tarentum, Pa., reporter, 1956-57; *Black Diamond* (magazine), Chicago, Ill., writer, 1957; Trinity University, San Antonio, Tex., public relations agent, 1960-70, instructor, 1960-70, assistant professor, 1970-75, associate professor of communication, 1975-80, consultant in managing-by-communicating, 1980—. Newscaster for KITE, San Antonio, Tex., 1965-69. Member of faculty of Short Course for Professional Writers, University of Oklahoma, 1973-75. Consultant to business and to Texas Commission on Alcoholism, and Office of Education Drug Rehabilitation Program. *Military service:* U.S. Air Force, chief of internal information, Air Training Command, 1957-60. U.S. Air Force Reserves, chief of information for Central Air Force Reserve Region, 1960-70; director of public affairs for 10th Air Force, 1970-80; currently in public affairs for Air University; present rank, colonel.

MEMBER: International Communication Association, International Association of Business Communicators, Association for Education in Journalism, American College Public Relations Association, American Management Association, Association for Humanistic Psychology, Reserve Officers Association of the United States, Alamo Business Communicators, Armed Forces Information Council of San Antonio, Sigma Delta Chi. *Awards, honors:* Reserve Information Officer of the Year in the United States, 1973.

WRITINGS: Declare Yourself: Discovering the Me in Relationships, Spectrum, 1975; *Very Good Management: A Guide to Managing by Communicating,* Prentice-Hall, 1983. Contributor to *San Antonio, Techniques, Quill, Spectrum, Airman, Mirage,* and public relations and journalism periodicals.

WORK IN PROGRESS: A book on the reexploration of creativity among high school and college students.

SIDELIGHTS: David Burkett told *CA:* "Writing is dangerous business; people tend to swallow whole what is in print. Good writing is not meant to settle things down but to stir them up. It is not to be believed but to be argued against. I think good readers are as difficult to find as are good writers. The reader for whom I write is one who will uncover my ideas and then discover his own. If he becomes a different person, it is his doing, not mine. Good writing makes good readers sweat."

* * *

BURKETT, Molly 1932-

PERSONAL: Born April 3, 1932, in England; daughter of John and Mary Preece; married John Burkett (an engineer); children: St. Joan, Sophie. *Education:* Goldsmiths College, London, teacher's diploma. *Home and office:* Animal Rehabilitation Centre, Hough-on-the-Hill, Grantham, Lincolnshire, England.

CAREER: Teacher, youth worker, and athletics coach, 1952—. Animal Rehabilitation Centre, Grantham, England, owner and operator, 1954—. Affiliated with National Wildlife Rescue Service.

WRITINGS: (With husband, John Burkett) *High Fly,* Pelham, 1968; *The Year of the Badger,* Lippincott, 1974; (with J. Burkett) *Foxes Three,* Lippincott, 1975; *Foxes, Owls and All: Lively Tales of an Animal-Crazy Household,* Allan Wingate,

1977; *Home for Animals,* W. H. Allen, 1979; *Take an Owl or Two: The Story of Boz and Owly,* Andre Deutsch, 1979. Contributor of more than a hundred articles and stories to magazines.†

* * *

BURTON, Maurice 1898-

PERSONAL: Born March 28, 1898, in London, England; son of William Francis and Jane Burton; married Margaret Rosalie Maclean, 1928; children: Richard Francis, Jane Mary, Robert Wellesley. *Education:* University of London, D.Sc., 1934. *Home:* Weston House, Albury, Guildford, Surrey GU5 9AE, England.

CAREER: Latymer Foundation, Hammersmith, London, England, biology master, 1924-27; British Museum of Natural History, London, 1927-58, began as assistant keeper, became deputy keeper in zoology department; free-lance writer, 1928—. *Member:* Zoological Society (fellow).

WRITINGS—Adult books: (Co-author) *The Science of Living Things,* Odhams, 1928; (co-editor and contributor) *Standard Natural History,* Warne, 1931; (editor) Jan Vlasak and Josef Seget, *Snow White: Story of a Polar Bear Cub,* Hodge, 1949, published as *Snowy: Story of a Polar Bear Cub,* Schuman, 1951; *The Story of Animal Life,* two volumes, Elsevier, 1949.

Curiosities of Animal Life, Ward Lock, 1952, R. M. McBride, 1956, revised edition, 1959; *Animal Courtship,* Hutchinson, 1953, Praeger, 1954; *Margins of the Sea,* Harper, 1954; *Living Fossils,* Thames & Hudson, 1954; *Animal Legends,* Muller, 1955, Coward, 1957; *Infancy in Animals,* Roy, 1956; *Phoenix Re-Born,* Hutchinson, 1959; *More Animal Legends,* Muller, 1959; *Sponges,* British Museum, 1959; *Under the Sea,* F. Watts, 1960; *Wild Animals of the British Isles: A Guide to the Mammals, Reptiles, and Batrachians of Wayside and Woodland,* Warne, 1960; (co-author) *The Glorious Oyster,* Sidgwick & Jackson, 1960; *Animal Senses,* Routledge & Kegan Paul, 1961; *The Elusive Monster: An Analysis of the Evidence from Loch Ness,* Hart-Davies, 1961; *Introducing Life under the Sea,* Spring Books, 1961; *Systematic Dictionary of Mammals of the World,* Crowell, 1962, published as *University Dictionary of Mammals of the World,* 1968 (2nd edition published in England as *Dictionary of the World's Mammals,* Sphere, 1970); (with K. Nixon) *Bird Families,* Warne, 1962; *A Revision of the Classification of the Calcareous Sponges,* British Museum of Natural History, 1963.

Meadows and the Forest Margin, Doubleday, 1965; *Nature in Motion,* Doubleday, 1966; (editor and contributor) *Nature: The Realm of Animals and Plants,* Grolier, 1966; *Weapons,* Doubleday, 1966; *Nature's Architects,* Doubleday, 1967; (co-editor and contributor) *Larousse Encyclopedia of Animal Life,* Hamlyn, 1967; *Wild Animals of the British Isles,* Warne, 1968; *The Hedgehog,* Deutsch, 1969, Transatlantic, 1970.

(Editor) *The Shell Natural History of Britain,* Rainbird, 1970; *Observer's Book of Wild Animals,* Warne, 1971; (editor) *World of Wildlife,* Orbis, 1971; (editor) *Encyclopedia of the Animal World,* Elsevier, 1972; (editor) *Encyclopedia of Animals in Colour,* Octopus, 1972; *The Sixth Sense of Animals,* Taplinger, 1973; *Animals of Europe: The Ecology of the Wildlife,* Holt, 1973; *The World of Reptiles and Amphibians,* Crown, 1973; (with daughter, Jane Burton) *The Colourful World of Animals,* Sundial, 1974.

How Mammals Live, Elsevier, 1975; *Maurice Burton's The Daily Telegraph Nature Book,* David & Charles, 1975; *Inside the Animal World,* Macmillan, 1977; *Just like an Animal,* Deut, 1978; *The Family of Animals,* Artus, 1978; (with son, Robert Burton) *The World's Disappearing Wildlife,* Marshall Cavendish, 1978; (with J. Burton) *Sealife,* Colour Library, 1978; *A Zoo at Home,* Dent, 1979; *British Wild Flowers,* Octopus Books, 1982.

Juveniles: *Animals and Their Behaviour,* Arnold, 1950; *The Elephant,* Gawthorn Press, 1951; *The Ox,* Gawthorn Press, 1951; *The Reindeer,* Gawthorn Press, 1951; *The Camel,* Gawthorn Press, 1951; *The Ass,* Gawthorn Press, 1951; *The Sheep,* Gawthorn Press, 1951; *When Dumb Animals Talk,* Hutchinson, 1955; *The True Book about Animals,* Muller, 1956; *Animal Families,* Routledge & Kegan Paul, 1958; *British Mammals,* Oxford University Press, 1958; *Life in the Deep,* Roy, 1958; *The True Book about the Seas,* Muller, 1959.

(Editor and contributor) *The Wonder Book of Animals,* Ward Lock, 1960; *In Their Element: The Story of Water Mammals,* Abelard, 1960; *Mammals of the Countryside,* Wheaton, 1960; *Wild Animals and Birds of the World,* Longacre Press, 1960; *Birds and Beasts of Field and Jungle,* Odhams, 1960; *The True Book about Prehistoric Animals,* Muller, 1961, 2nd edition published as *Prehistoric Animals,* International Publications Service, 1974; *The True Book about Deserts,* Muller, 1961, 2nd edition published as *Deserts,* International Publications Service, 1974; *More Mammals of the Countryside,* Wheaton, 1961; *Water Creatures,* Longacre Press, 1961; *Baby Animals,* Longacre Press, 1961; *Birds,* Gawthorn Press, 1961; *Mammals,* Gawthorn Press, 1961; (with E. W. Groves) *The Wonder Book of Nature,* Ward Lock, 1961; *Reptiles and Amphibians of the World,* Longacre Press, 1962, 2nd edition, 1971; *Birds of Britain,* Odhams, 1962, 2nd edition, 1971; *Mammals of Great Britain,* Odhams, 1962; *The True Book of the Seashore,* Muller, 1963; (with W. B. Shepherd) *The Wonder Book of Our Earth,* Ward Lock, 1963; *Young Animals,* Hamlyn, 1964.

The Zoo Book, Bancroft, 1966; (editor) *Animal World in Colour,* Odhams, 1966, Children's Press, 1969, Volume I: *Artists and Entertainers,* Volume II: *Explorers and Wanderers,* Volume III: *Animal Eccentrics,* Volume IV: *Animal Oddities,* Volume V: *Builders and Breakers,* Volume VI: *Comrades and Companions,* Volume VII: *Hunters: Mammals,* Volume VIII: *Hunters: Birds, Fish, and Amphibians,* Volume IX: *Hunters: Reptiles, Insects, and Invertebrates,* Volume X: *Animal Specialists,* Volume XI: *Unusual Feeders,* Volume XII: *Sleep and Hibernation; Animals,* Oxford University Press, 1966, F. Watts, 1968; *The Animal World: Birds, Fish, Reptiles* [and] *Insects,* F. Watts, 1968; *The Sea's Inhabitants,* Golden Press, 1968; *More Animals,* F. Watts, 1968; *Animal Partnerships,* Warne, 1969; *Animals of Australia,* Abedlard, 1969.

Maurice Burton's Book of Nature, Purnell, 1971, 3rd edition, 1974; *The Life of Birds,* edited by Angela Littler, Macdonald, 1972, Golden Press, 1974; *The Life of Fishes,* edited by Littler, Macdonald, 1972, Golden Press, 1974; *The Life of Insects,* Macdonald, 1972, Golden Press, 1974; *The Life of Meat Eaters,* Macdonald, 1973, Golden Press, 1974; *The Life of Reptiles and Amphibians,* Golden Press, 1974; *First Encyclopedia of Animals,* Purnell, 1974.

General editor, *Oxford Junior Encyclopaedia,* Volume II: *Natural History,* 1949; general editor with Robert Burton and contributor, *Purnell's Encyclopedia of Animal Life,* BPC Publishing, 1968-70, published as *The International Wildlife Encyclopedia,* 1970, four volume edition, Octopus, 1974; general editor, *The World Encyclopedia of Animals,* 1972. Nature correspondent for *Daily Telegraph,* 1949—. Contributor to *Junior*

Science Encyclopedia and to scientific journals. Science editor, *Illustrated London News,* 1946-64.

SIDELIGHTS: Maurice Burton's books have been translated into Dutch, Portuguese, Japanese, Spanish, Italian, French, German, Swedish, Finnish, Norwegian, Hindi, and Icelandic. *Avocational interests:* Gardening.

BIOGRAPHICAL/CRITICAL SOURCES: Observer, February 8, 1970.

* * *

BUSBY, F. M. 1921-

PERSONAL: Born March 11, 1921, in Indianapolis, Ind.; son of F.M., Sr. (a teacher) and Clara (a teacher; maiden name, Nye) Busby; married Elinor Doub (a medical secretary), April 28, 1954; children: Michele B. *Education:* Washington State University, B.Sc., 1946, B.Sc.E.E., 1947. *Politics:* "Eclectic; consider issues individually." *Religion:* "Much the same. . . ." *Home and office:* 2852 14th Ave. W., Seattle, Wash. 98119.

CAREER: Alaska Communication System Headquarters, Seattle, Wash., "trick chief" and project supervisor, 1947-53, telegraph engineer, 1953-70; writer, 1970—. *Military service:* National Guard, active duty, 1940-41. U.S. Army, 1943-45. *Member:* Science Fiction Writers of America (vice-president, 1974-76), Authors Guild, Authors League of America, Mystery Writers of America, Seattle Freelances.

WRITINGS—All science fiction: *Cage a Man* (Science Fiction Book Club selection; also see below), New American Library, 1974; *The Proud Enemy* (also see below), Berkley Publishing, 1975; *Rissa Kerguelen,* Putnam, 1976; *The Long View,* Putnam, 1976; *All These Earths,* Berkley Publishing, 1978; *Zeide M'Tana,* Dell, 1980; *The Demu Trilogy* (includes *Cage a Man, The Proud Enemy,* and *End of the Line),* Pocket Books, 1980.

Contributor to anthologies: *New Dimensions 3,* edited by Robert Silverberg, New American Library, 1973; *Best Science Fiction of the Year,* edited by Terry Carr, Ballantine, 1974; *Universe 5,* edited by Carr, Random House, 1974; *Golden Age,* second series, edited by Brian Aldiss, Futura (London), 1975; *Best Science Fiction of the Year,* edited by Lester del Rey, Dutton, 1976; *1979 Annual World's Best Science Fiction,* edited by Donald A. Wollheim, DAW Books, 1979; *Best of New Dimensions,* edited by Silverberg, Pocket Books, 1979.

Universe 10, edited by Carr, Doubleday, 1980; *Dream's Edge,* edited by Carr, Sierra Club Books, 1980; *Amazons II,* edited by Jessica Amanda Salmonson, DAW Books, 1982; *Heroic Visions,* edited by Salmonson, Ace Books, 1983.

Contributor of about forty stories to science fiction magazines.

WORK IN PROGRESS: The Alien Debt, The Star Rebel, Star Rebel's Quest, and *Slow Freight to Forever,* all science fiction novels; short stories.

SIDELIGHTS: F. M. Busby writes: "I 'played' with writing off-and-on for years before the chance came to take early retirement and try it in earnest. I like to deal with characters who are pushed hard by necessity and who generally manage to cope, more than not. Science fiction allows me to put characters into predicaments that could not exist in our own past and present; I like the challenge and enjoy working with it."

* * *

BUTLER, Joyce 1933-

PERSONAL: Born June 27, 1933, in Portland, Maine; daughter of Charles William Eaton (an accountant) and Dorothy (King) Kelley; married G. Robert Butler (in retail sales), March 22, 1954; children: Leslie Joyce, Stephanie Sydna, James Kelley. *Education:* Westbrook College, A.A., 1953; Boston University, A.B., 1955. *Politics:* Republican. *Religion:* Protestant. *Home address:* Durrell's Bridge Rd., Kennebunk, Me. 04043.

CAREER: Writer, historian, lecturer, archivist. Kennebunkport Historical Society, Kennebunkport, Me., curator, 1975-79; The Brick Store Museum, Kennebunk, Me., manuscript curator, 1980—. Participant in Bread Loaf Writers Conference, 1980, and in American Association for State and Local History Seminar on Publishing, 1981. Member of York County (Me.) Records Committee subcommittee to inventory contents of county courthouse, 1979—; research assistant to Thomas Hubka, professor at University of Oregon, on historical study, 1981-82. Advisor to collections committee, Maine Historical Society, 1980—; consultant on publishing and advisor, Maine Women Writers Collection, Westbrook College, 1981—. *Member:* International Women's Writing Guild, National Writers Club, Organization of American Historians, American Association for State and Local History, Authors Guild, Authors League of America, Maine Writers and Publishers Alliance, various state, regional, and national historic preservation societies.

AWARDS, HONORS: Hart Crane and Alice Crane Williams Memorial Fund Award from American Weave Press, 1969, for poem "Red Fox on Snow"; certificate of commendation, American Association for State and Local History, 1981, for research and writing of local history.

WRITINGS: Pages from a Journal, Mercer House Press, 1976; *Kennebunkport Scrapbook,* Volume I, Thomas Murphy Publisher, 1977; *Wildfire Loose: The Week Maine Burned,* Durrell Publications, 1978; (contributor) *Tilt: An Anthology of New England Women's Writing and Art,* New Victoria Publishers, 1978; (contributor) *Tales of Whales* (anthology), edited by Tim Dietz, Guy Gannett Publishing, 1982; (contributor) *Ladies Choice* (anthology), edited by Mavis Patterson, Thorndike Press, 1982. Also author of numerous monographs and exhibition catalogues, including *The South Congregational Church: An Architectural History,* South Congregational Church, 1973, *Abbott Fuller Graves, 1859-1936,* Brick Store Museum, 1979, *The Kennebunks: A Watering Place, the First Fifty Years, 1870-1920,* Brick Store Museum, 1980, and *Louis D. Norton, 1868-1940,* Brick Store Museum, 1982.

Also author of columns, "Pages from a Journal," 1969-79, and "Kennebunkport Scrapbook," 1974-78, for *York County Coast Star,* and "A Kennebunkport Album," 1978-80, and "Kennebunk-Kennebunkport Cameos," 1980, for *Tourist News* (Kennebunkport). Also contributor of articles to *Down East, Yankee, Maine Life, Bittersweet, Lady's Circle, Christian Science Monitor, Landmark Observer,* and *Magazine Antiques.* Trustee and advisor for *Salt* magazine, the Foxfire project of Kennebunk High School, 1976-79.

WORK IN PROGRESS: A book on a local ship master's letters, tentatively entitled *Under Neptune's Banner: The Life of Captain Ebenezer Mitchell, Kennebunk and Kennebunkport, Maine, 1845-1859;* research on Cochranism, a religious cult that flourished in southern Maine from 1817 to 1819.

SIDELIGHTS: Joyce Butler writes: "I am a writer who chose first to be a housewife/mother, with all the dedication, hard work, and community involvement that is a part of that vocation. My column ['Pages from a Journal' was] a recounting of my experiences in that job. Although 'Pages' was begun to fulfill my need and desire to be a writer, it soon became important to me as a positive statement about the everyday life of the American family, which is more often portrayed as emotionally unhealthy and foundering. The ordinariness of my subject matter is its strength; my readers delight in finding their own experiences mirrored in those of my family.

"My ambition is to write fiction: short stories and children's books about 'real' people as opposed to romantic figures and anthropomorphic animals. It is my wish that all my writing reflect my belief in the importance and dignity of the commonplace. My extensive work in state and local history confirms and I hope illustrates the validity of that belief.

"In 1974 research into one major aspect of local history led me into that wide-open, fascinating, demanding field. Now, almost ten years later, my writing efforts are almost wholly directed to local history. I believe not only in the value of collecting and publishing such material, but in the possibility for professionalism in the work of the non-academic historian."

During 1981-82, Joyce Butler aided in the research for a study of Maine's connected-form architecture and of a Maine farming community, Alewive District, Kennebunk, 1800-1900, for the book by Thomas Hubka, *Big House, Little House, Back House, Barn*.

AVOCATIONAL INTERESTS: Flower gardening, antiques, old houses, needlework.

* * *

BUTTACI, Sal(vatore) St. John 1941-

PERSONAL: Born June 12, 1941, in Corona, N.Y.; son of Michael S. (a welder) and Josephine (Amico) Buttaci; married Susan Linda Gerstle (a teacher and editor), March 9, 1974. *Education:* Seton Hall University, B.A. (cum laude), 1965; Montclair State College, teacher certification, 1970; Rutgers University, M.B.A., 1981. *Politics:* Democrat. *Religion:* Roman Catholic (Charismatic Christian). *Home:* 100 Maple St., Apt. 53, Garfield, N.J. 07026. *Office:* International Library for Business Research, 630 Third Ave., New York, N.Y. 10017.

CAREER: St. Anne's Elementary School, Fair Lawn, N.J., teacher of English and history, 1966-68, vice-principal, 1968-70, principal, 1970-71; public school teacher in Saddle Brook, N.J., 1971—; International Library for Business Research, New York City, research director, 1981—. President, Opening Night, Inc., Saddle Brook, 1982—.

MEMBER: International Platform Association, American Marketing Association, Association of Masters of Business Administration Executives, Committee of Small Magazine Editors and Publishers, New Jersey Poetry Society, Antique Auto Club of America.

WRITINGS—Poetry, published by New Worlds Unlimited: *Coming-Home Poems: Stops and Pauses on the Scrapbook Express,* 1974; (editor with wife, Susan Linda Gerstle) *Echoes of the Unlocked Odyssey,* 1974; (editor with S. L. Gerstle) *Shadows of the Elusive Dream,* 1975; (with S. L. Gerstle) *Reflections of the Inward Silence,* 1976; *Whispers of the Unchained Heart,* 1977; *Tracings of the Valiant Soul,* 1978; *Mirrors of the Wistful Dreamer,* 1979; *Visions of the Enchanted Spirit,* 1980; *Images of the Mystic Truth,* 1981; *Dreams of the Heroic Muse,* 1982.

Also author of "For Heaven's Sake, Sweeney," a three-act play, first produced in Paramus, N.J., 1970, "The Party," a two-act play, and of fifteen songs with Aldo Pecorelli and Alphonse Buttaci, 1980—. Contributor of poems to periodicals, including *English Journal, Gallery Series IV, The Archer, The Aquarian Weekly, The Writer,* and *Christian Science Moniter*.

WORK IN PROGRESS: Editing another poetry book, with wife, Susan Linda Gerstle.

SIDELIGHTS: Sal St. John Buttaci told *CA:* "Writing is only half the hitch in the writing talent: the other half is needing others to love you through your work. This is my reason for wanting to write. The need for someone—anyone!—to read me in a poem, find where my blood flows and my heart pounds, and in finding, love me in a few kind words."

After an automobile accident, Buttaci was paralyzed for several months, a condition that he reported as cured following healing by Evangelist Kathryn Kuhlman.

C

CADY, Jack A(ndrew) 1932-

PERSONAL: Surname rhymes with "lady"; born March 20, 1932, in Columbus, Ohio; son of Donald Victor (an auctioneer) and Pauline Lucille (a teacher and businesswoman; maiden name, Schmidt) Cady; married Betty Rex; married Patricia Distlehurst, March, 1966 (divorced January, 1972); married Deborah Robson (a writer and weaver), August, 1973 (divorced, 1976). *Education:* University of Louisville, B.S., 1961. *Politics:* "Every political system and form known is a catastrophe." *Religion:* Quaker ("not a good one"). *Home:* 933 Tyler St., Port Townsend, Wash. 98368.

CAREER: Auctioneer in Louisville, Ky., 1956-61; U.S. Department of Health, Education and Welfare, Corbin, Ky., Social Security claims representative, 1961-62; truck driver in the southeastern United States, 1962-65; tree high climber in Arlington, Mass., 1965-66; landscape foreman in San Francisco, Calif., 1966-67; University of Washington, Seattle, assistant professor of English, 1968-72; Knox College, Galesburg, Ill., visiting writer, 1973; Clarion State College, Clarion, Penn., visiting writer, 1974; Cady-Robson Landscaping, Port Townsend, Wash., in landscape construction, beginning 1974; *Port Townsend Journal,* Port Townsend, editor and publisher, 1974-76; Sitka Community College, Sitka, Alaska, visiting writer, 1977-78; free-lance writer, 1978—. Has lectured at numerous colleges in the western United States. Landscape consultant. *Military service:* U.S. Coast Guard, 1952-56; became petty officer 2nd class.

AWARDS, HONORS: "First" Award from *Atlantic Monthly,* 1965, for short story "The Burning"; National Literary Award from National Council of the Arts, 1971, for story "The Shark"; Washington Governor's Award and Iowa Award for Short Fiction from University of Iowa Press, both 1972, for *The Burning and Other Stories.*

WRITINGS: The Burning and Other Stories, University of Iowa Press, 1973; *Tattoo and Other Stories,* Circinatum, 1978; *The Well* (novel), Arbor House, 1980; *Singleton* (novel), Madrona, 1981; *The Jonah Watch* (novel), Arbor House, 1982; *McDowell's Ghost,* Arbor House, 1982; *The Man Who Could Make Things Vanish,* Arbor House, 1983.

Work anthologized in *Best American Short Stories,* edited by Martha Foley, Houghton, 1966, 1969, 1970, 1971, and *American Literary Anthology No. 3,* edited by George Plimpton and Peter Ardery, Viking, 1971. Columnist, *Port Angeles Daily News.* Contributor of stories to literary magazines, including *Atlantic Monthly, Twigs, Carolina Quarterly, Overdrive,* and *Yale Review.*

WORK IN PROGRESS: Research on the moral and religious origins of the United States, for a book tentatively entitled *Voices.*

SIDELIGHTS: Jack Cady writes: "Art and writing, when it attains to the condition of literature, is non-secular. Politics, religion, economies have nothing to do with good writing. The writer has nothing to sell. All he does is try to discover a true thing and then say it truly. That is the whole job. Art allows humans to be humane in human affairs. It sustains. It seeks not idealism but rather, continues to discover and bring to light the ideal. To do this one must assume the highest standards and pursue them relentlessly. Writing is only one of the arts. It is not greater or substantially different from painting, sculpture, teaching, acting, or the composition of music. The guy who works at it is not an artist. Instead, he works as hard as he can at what he's doing and it may be that the result attains to a condition greater than himself."

* * *

CAGE, John (Milton, Jr.) 1912-

PERSONAL: Born September 5, 1912, in Los Angeles, Calif.; son of John M. and Lucretia (Harvey) Cage; married Xenia Andreyevna Kashevarcff, June 7, 1935 (divorced, 1945). *Education:* Attended Pomona College, 1928-30; studied music and composition privately with Richard Buhlig, Adolph Weiss, Henry Cowell, and Arnold Schoenberg. *Home:* 101 West 18th St., No. 5B, New York, N.Y. 10011.

CAREER: Composer, author, and printmaker. Free-lance library researcher, 1934-35; Cornish School, Seattle, Wash., accompanist and teacher, 1936-38; School of Design, Chicago, Ill., faculty member, 1941-42; Merce Cunningham and Dance Co., New York City, musical director, 1944-66; New School for Social Research, New York City, teacher of composition, 1955-60; Wesleyan University, Center for Advanced Studies, Middletown, Conn., research professor and associate, 1960-61; University of Cincinnati, Cincinnati, Ohio, composer-in-residence, 1967; University of Illinois at Urbana-Champaign, Center for Advanced Studies, research professor, 1967-69.

Member of summer faculty, Mills College, 1938-39, and Black Mountain College, 1950-52. Directed concert of percussion music sponsored by Music of Modern Art and League Composers, 1943. Organized group of musicians and engineers for recording music directly on magnetic tape, 1951. Art director for Jack Lenor Larson (textile company), circa 1956-57.

MEMBER: National Institute of Arts and Letters, American Academy of Arts and Sciences, American Society of Composers, Authors and Publishers, American Federation of Musicians, Foundation for Contemporary Performance Arts, Cunningham Dance Foundation (past president and member of board of directors), New York Mycological Society (founding honorary member).

AWARDS, HONORS: Guggenheim fellowship, 1949; award from National Academy of Arts and Letters, 1949, for "extending the boundaries of musical art"; Woodstock Art Film Festival First Prize, 1951, for the score of "Works of Calder"; award for contributions to amateur mycology, 1964, from subcommittee on fungi of People-to-People Program; Thorne Music Fund grant, 1967-69; Commandeur de l'ordre des Arts et Lettres, French Ministry of Culture, 1982.

WRITINGS: (With Kathleen Hoover) *Virgil Thomson: His Life and Music,* Yoseloff, 1959, reprinted, Books for Libraries, 1970; *Silence: Selected Lectures and Writings,* Wesleyan University Press, 1961, revised edition, 1973; *A Year from Monday: New Lectures and Writings,* Wesleyan University Press, 1967, excerpted edition published as *Diary: How to Improve the World (You Will Only Make Matters Worse) Continued, Part 3,* Something Else Press, 1967; (with Alison Knowles) *Notations,* Something Else Press, 1969.

(Contributor) Robert Fillison, *Teaching and Learning as Performing Arts,* Wittenhorn, 1970; (contributor) Ihab Hassan, editor, *Liberations: New Essays on the Humanities in Revolution,* Wesleyan University Press, 1971; (with Lois Long and Alexander H. Smith) *Mushroom Book,* Hollanders Workshop, 1972; (contributor) *Biology and the History of the Future,* Edinburgh University Press, 1972; *M: Writings, '67-'72,* Wesleyan University Press, 1973; (contributor) *The Drawings of Morris Graves,* New York Graphic Society, 1974; *Pour les oiseaux: entretiens avec Daniel Charles,* Editions Pierre Belfond (Paris), 1976, translation published as *For the Birds,* Marion Boyars, 1981; *Writing through Finnegans Wake,* University of Tulsa, 1978; *Writings through Finnegans Wake,* Printed Editions, 1979; *Empty Words: Writings, '73-'78,* Wesleyan University Press, 1979; (contributor) *Poets' Encyclopedia,* Unmuzzled Ox, 1980; *Another Song,* Callaway Editions, 1981; *Themes and Variations,* Station Hill Press, 1982.

Musical compositions; all published by Henmar Press: *First Construction (in Metal),* 1939; *Amores,* 1943; *Dance,* 1944; *Sonatas and Interludes,* 1946-48; *The Seasons,* 1947; *Imaginary Landscape, No. 4,* 1951; *Imaginary Landscape, No. 5,* 1952; *4'33'',* 1952; *William Mix,* 1952; *Music of Changes,* 1952; *Music for Carillon, No. 2,* 1954; *34'46.766,* 1954; *Winter Music,* 1957; *Fontana Mix,* 1958; *Aria,* 1958; *Variations,* 1958-68; *Theatre Piece,* 1960; *Imaginary Landscape, No. 1,* 1960; *Atlas Eclipticalis,* 1961-62; *The Shape of Time,* 1962; *Correspondence and Notes re Rozart Mix for Magnetic Tape,* 1965; *How to Pass, Kick, Fall, and Run,* 1967; *Musicircus,* 1967; *HPSCHD,* 1967-69; *Cheap Imitations,* 1972.

Also composer of "A Valentine Out of Season," 1944, "Water Music," 1952, "Music for Amplified Toy Pianos," 1960, "Cartridge Music," 1960, "Reunion," 1968, "Renga" with "Apartment House 1776" (for two synchronized orchestral groups), 1976, "32 Etudes Australes," and numerous other works.

Also author of graphic works "Not Wanting to Say Anything about Marcel," with Calvin Sumsion, 1969, "Seven Day Diary," 1978, "Score without Parts," 1978, "17 Drawings by Thoreau," 1978, "Signals," 1978, "Changes and Disappearances," 1979-82, "On the Surface," 1980-82, and "Dereau," 1982.

Recordings: "Sonatas and Interludes," Avakian, 1946; "25-Year Retrospective Concert of the Music of John Cage," Avakian, 1958; "Fontana Mix," Studio di Fonologia (Milan), 1958; "Sounds of New Music," Folkways, 1958; "Indeterminacy" (two record set), Folkways, 1959; "Concert Percussion for Orchestra," Mainstream, 1961; "John Cage/Christian Wolff," Mainstream, 1962; "New Music for Solo Clarinet," Advance, 1964; "New Music for Violin and Piano," Mainstream, c. 1971; "John Cage: Three Dances/Steve Reich: Four Organs," Angel, 1973; "The Dial-a-Poem Poets," Giorno Poetry Systems, 1974; "10 + 2 = 12: American Text Sound Pieces," 1750 Arch, 1974; "John Cage Talking to Hans G. Helms on Music and Politics," S Press, 1975; "The Dial-a-Poem Poets: Biting Off the Tongue of a Corpse," Giorno Poetry Systems, 1975; "Jan Steele/John Cage: Voices and Instruments," Antilles, 1976; "The Dial-a-Poem Poets: Totally Corrupt," Giorno Poetry Systems, 1976; "Breathingspace '77," Watershed Tapes, 1977; "John Cage" (two record set), Tomato Music, 1977-78; "Tapesongs," Chiaroscuro, 1977; "The Nova Convention," Giorno Poetry Systems, 1979; "John Cage: Etudes Australes, Books 1 & 2," Tomato Music, 1979; "American Composer's Orchestra: Cage; The Season/Wuorinen, 2-Part Symphony," Composer's Recordings, 1979; "Sugar, Alcohol, and Meat: The Dial-a-Poem Poets," Giorno Poetry Systems, 1980; "John Cage: Chorals and Cheap Imitation," CP^2, 1981.

Other recordings: "John Cage: Music for Keyboard, 1935-1948," Columbia; "New Electronic Music from Leaders of the Avant-Garde," Columbia; "Piano Space," CP^2; "Nova Musicha Series," Cramps Records; "John Cage: Sonatas and Interludes for Prepared Piano, 1946-48," Composer's Recordings; "La Salle Quartet," Deutsche Grammophon; "Variations IV: John Cage with David Tudor" (two record set), Everest; "Wound and Winter Music," Finnadar; "Viola Today," Finnadar; "Prepared Piano: The First Four Decades," Musical Heritage Society; "The Contemporary Contrabass," Nonesuch Records; "Extended Voices," Odyssey; "The Blackearth Percussion Group," Opus One; "Electronic Music," Turnabout; "Concord Quartet," Turnabout; "20th Century Music for Voice and Guitar," Turnabout; "Magnificathy," Wergo; "The San Francisco Conservatory New Music Ensemble," Wergo; "John Cage," Wergo.

Contributor to museum catalogs and to periodicals. Co-editor, *New Music,* 1943-54.

SIDELIGHTS: A major figure in American music for some forty-five years, controversial avant-garde composer John Cage has, according to David Bither of *Horizon,* "pioneered the development of the percussion orchestra; experimented with the use of noise; invented the prepared piano; acted as the earliest American proponent of electronic and taped music; originated the multi-discipline, multi-media 'happening'; initiated the use of chance and indeterminate methods in composition; and pursued, almost alone, the notion of extended silence as musical material." Cage's novel musical concepts and methods have been widely used by other avant-garde composers, serving as an impetus for further experimentation in the field. "Two generations of younger composers," Tom Johnson writes, "now look to Cage almost as a father figure." Cage has "not only influenced the kind of music today's up-to-date composers write," Samuel Lipman explains in *Music after Modernism,* "but also our very idea of what it means to be an avant-garde composer."

The first of Cage's innovations to attract widespread attention was his "prepared piano" in 1938. This was a piano with various wood, metal, and rubber objects placed on the piano strings to alter the sound and produce a whole new range of tonal possibilities. When played, the piano sounded unlike any other musical instrument and could, with the rearranging or replacement of objects, be adjusted to create an almost endless variety of new sounds. "For the first time," Paul Griffiths writes in *A Concise History of Avant-Garde Music,* "[the musician] could experiment at first hand with sounds in a way that was to become commonplace in the electronic studio." Cage experimented with screws and bolts, weather stripping, and a myriad of other objects on the piano strings. His prepared piano concerts in America and Europe caused a sensation, and a number of other composers adopted his method until the modification of musical instruments has today become an accepted tool of the avant-garde musician.

In the following years, Cage's innovations continued to set the pace for avant-garde music while outraging more conservative members of the musical establishment. He was the first American composer, for example, to explore the possibility of using electronic sounds in music. His "Imaginary Landscape, No. 1," dating from 1939, is considered to be the first electronic musical composition ever written. Spurred by an intense interest in the music and philosophy of the Orient, Cage wrote "Music of Changes" in 1951, a composition written according to the dictates of the I Ching, a Chinese book of wisdom used as an oracle and consulted by tossing yarrow sticks or coins. To determine each note in the work—and its duration, pitch, loudness, and tempo—Cage consulted the I Ching and allowed the chance operations to answer all of his aesthetic questions.

In 1952, Cage wrote a decidedly different piece—again based on his study of Eastern thought—which caused him to reach "a level of public notoriety granted to few artistic creators in our time," as Lipman states. Entitled "4'33''," this work consists of four minutes and thirty-three seconds of silence. Pianist David Tudor first performed the work in concert by sitting quietly at the piano for the indicated length of time. Cage explains that the noises around us are interesting and that the random sounds in an auditorium during the performance of "4'33''"—coughing, shuffling of programs, clearing of throats—are just as valid as anything created by a composer. With this composition Cage wanted, as he states, to "let sounds be themselves in a space of time."

By the 1960s, Cage was creating complex performances involving taped sound sequences, video material, lights, scenery, and electric eyes. These multi-media performances were minimally structured and relied on random factors. As dancers moved through a field of criss-crossed electric eyes, their steps triggered off lights, taped sounds, video displays, and other phenomena, creating the performance. "Instead of composing according to chance operations," writes Griffiths, "[Cage] was now leaving as much as possible unfixed until the moment of performance." Again Cage's work proved influential, giving birth to a host of similar performances by other artists, and the term "happening" was coined to describe this multi-media form of creation. Speaking of several Cage works from this period, Lipman writes that "as music this makes no impression at all. But as a sonic environment it conjures up a world without plan, purpose, meaning, or value. The sounds suggest a Rorschach test devised and administered by a Dada psychologist; its meaning is in the eye (ear) of the beholder (listener), and its wit can be fully appreciated only by those who are hostile to the idea of organized social life."

"When I've found that what I'm doing has become pleasing, even to one person," Cage says, explaining the changes his music has taken, "I have redoubled my efforts to find the next step." It is in attempting to find that "next step" that Cage has studied Zen Buddhism, the works of Buckminster Fuller, Henry David Thoreau, and anarchism, and applied ideas from each of these studies to his composition of music. In his many books, Cage discusses his influences and how they have affected his work.

One of Cage's primary goals throughout his career was shaped by a statement by Zen Buddhist Ananda K. Coomaraswamy: "The responsibility of the artist is to imitate nature in her manner of operation." Accordingly Cage has strived to remove himself from his music in order to "liberate sounds from abstract ideas about them . . . to let them be physically, uniquely themselves." Cage writes in *For the Birds* that his early music was expressive and tried to say something. "When I discovered India," he writes, "what I was saying started to change. And when I discovered China and Japan, *I changed the very fact of saying anything:* I said nothing anymore. Silence: since everything already communicates, why wish to communicate?" "The problem," writes Joseph McLellan of the *Washington Post,* "is to find silence, to strip away form and content, and above all the personality that imperialistically imposes such things on the raw matter of music."

Cage has confronted this problem in the structure of his compositions, using random factors, spontaneity, and the role of chance—anything necessary to remove the composer's presence from the music and allow the sounds to exist on their own. "I try to arrange my composing means," Cage has written, "so that I won't have any knowledge of what might happen."

This quest to allow the music to exist on its own, unchanged by the composer, also reflects Cage's anarchistic ideals. The seeming chaos of his works pleases him. "I think that being able to understand something," he explains, "to be able to know what is happening, is on the side of law and order and organization rather than on the side of poetry and chaos and anarchy." "Music, for those who accept the Cage hypothesis," McLellan claims, "can be any kind of sound."

The radical nature of Cage's work has long been a source of controversy in music circles, and a performance of his music is as likely to cause people to walk out as to applaud. Some critics have attacked Cage's work. Aaron Copland, for example, doesn't believe the random nature of Cage's music can "hold the continuing interest of the rational mind." An early supporter, Virgil Thomson, now sees Cage heading down "a one-way tunnel to the gadget fair," a reference to Cage's use of electronic devices.

But the overwhelming critical response to Cage's musical innovations has been favorable. The *New York Times* notes that "as a result of the Cage group's work, many observers of the music scene agree, the tide of ideas is running from America to Europe for the first time in musical history." Music critic

Peter Yates believes Cage has been "the most influential composer, worldwide, of his generation." Cage "has become," writes McLellan, "a prominent part of the musical landscape—perhaps, as is now being said, the most influential composer in the history of American music."

CA INTERVIEW

CA interviewed John Cage by phone October 28, 1981, at his home in New York City.

CA: In a 1970 interview just published in your new book, For the Birds, *you said, "I value the faculty for inventing more than anything." Do you consider yourself more an inventor than a musician or an artist?*

CAGE: Well, I'm the son of my father, and he was an inventor. I've always felt that in anything I do there should be, if possible, that quality of discovery.

CA: Thoreau and Buckminster Fuller have been major influences on your life and your work, as have the writings of James Joyce and Gertrude Stein. Are there current writers or innovators besides Fuller whose work you consider significant?

CAGE: I'm very devoted to the work of Norman O. Brown, especially his books *Life against Death* and *Love's Body*. I have also found the work of Marshall McLuhan very relevant.

CA: You've told some good stories about your mother in your books. I especially like the one about when you mother was watching teenagers dancing to rock-and-roll on TV. You asked her how she liked the new music, and she said, "Oh, I'm not fussy about music," and then she went on to say, "You're not fussy about music either." Was she one of the earliest champions of your work?

CAGE: She was always devoted, and so was Dad. There's a lovely story that I haven't published yet in which my father said to me, "Son John, remember, your mother's always right, even when she's wrong!"

CA: In everything you've chosen to do in your life, you seem to combine great seriousness of purpose with a sense of fun, and the two seem perfectly compatible in your outlook. Is this true?

CAGE: I think people are inclined toward optimism or toward pessimism, and I'm inclined toward optimism. And so I prefer, as I said once, laughter to tears. I have the feeling that even in a very bad situation there are elements that turn toward the good. I keep my attention, insofar as I can, positive rather than negative.

CA: You do seem to enjoy things so much, the hard work as well as the leisure activities like hunting for mushrooms. Have you always been able to enjoy whatever you were doing at a given time?

CAGE: Right.

CA: Performances of your music have consistently brought a mixed response from the audience, and that doesn't appear to bother you. Have you ever been disturbed by an audience response or by a criticism that you thought was unjust?

CAGE: There was a rather bad audience situation in Zagreb, Yugoslavia, once. I think it was the worst. The concert was given at midnight in a festival of modern music, and the hall was completely filled with people. But the moment I walked out on the stage to conduct a small ensemble of players, there was such an uproar from the audience that it was impossible to hear the music, and it lasted up until the intermission. I went to my room to rest a moment during the intermission, and there was a knock on the door. A young girl was there. I thought, "Well, that's good. There's at least one person who enjoys the work." I said, "Are you enjoying the work?" And she said, "Certainly not. When are you going to kill the cat?" It turned out that a pianist in Rome some time before that had given a piano recital of new music, and it had been reviewed by a German critic as being equivalent to killing a cat. So they had the idea that, in a concert of this kind of music, a cat was to be killed. And all those people came that night expecting something horrible. That was very shocking.

CA: Accounts of your appearance and performances on the Italian television quiz shows indicate that you had an unusually receptive audience there.

CAGE: I was very popular, yes.

CA: What's the most receptive audience you can remember?

CAGE: I think an audience doesn't have a character of its own; it's made up of individuals. You never can tell what each person is thinking and feeling and whether they're enjoying it or not. Very often the ones who don't enjoy it are more vocal than the ones who do.

CA: You spent about eighteen months in Europe at the beginning of the 1930s, but you weren't in Paris long. What was your impression of Paris and of the experimentation in the arts going on there at that time?

CAGE: It was such that I became actively interested in modern painting and modern music. It was there that I came into contact with both, and it gave me the feeling that if such things were possible in the arts, I too could become an artist. I began writing music, and I began painting pictures. It's only recently that I've returned to visual art in the making of etchings at the Crown Point Press.

CA: Are these the etchings based on Thoreau illustrations?

CAGE: I use Thoreau a good deal. In the last series only the title refers to Thoreau. There are no images from Thoreau in it, but it's called "On the Surface," and what I'm referring to is Thoreau's remark that silence is a sphere and sounds are bubbles on its surface.

CA: Are those etchings on exhibit now?

CAGE: I made them in California and you can see them in the Crown Point Gallery there in Oakland. I think there may be shows arranged this next year here in the East and in Europe.

CA: Do you find New York City the best place to work, or can you work equally well anywhere?

CAGE: I take my work with me when I go on tour. Because I've traveled with the Cunningham Dance Company, I've had to learn how to use my time whether I'm home or not at home.

CA: Are you able then to work on any kind of fixed schedule? Do you try to?

CAGE: No, I don't follow a fixed schedule. I now have 175 plants, and the first thing I do in the morning is take care of the plants. When that's done I look at the mail, and if there's something urgent I answer it. And then I start to work.

CA: Do you consider New York, San Francisco, and other major cities the best places for someone to do experimental work in the arts?

CAGE: Either there or in the universities. The universities are very interested in the latest developments, for the most part, and they're aware of them through the media. As I travel around it seems to me that there's advanced work going on just about everywhere.

CA: You've enjoyed teaching and been highly regarded as a teacher. Are you able to do any teaching now with your other activities?

CAGE: If I do teach I take it quite seriously and it takes up all my time, so I prefer not to teach. I like to think of my work, my writing and my music, as, in a sense, my form of teaching.

CA: From your own experience, what do you think is the best thing a teacher can do for his students?

CAGE: To find out what they're capable of and to enlarge their horizons, but from their own point of view rather than from the teacher's point of view. Not to teach *something,* but to facilitate the student's development of himself. It takes a lot of time; it's almost like psychoanalysis. That's why I don't like to do it too much.

CA: Is that what you found most helpful to you in your relationships with your own teachers?

CAGE: I studied for two years with Schoenberg, and he didn't take that attitude at all. My attitude is extremely permissive and exploratory, whereas his attitude was very much that of a disciplinarian. He said at one point, "My purpose in teaching you is to make it impossible for you to write music." And the moment I heard that I determined to be obstinate, to devote myself to the writing of music. That was his way, but my way is quite different.

CA: You once said that "logic, organization, government should all be forgotten inasmuch as they begin themselves by making us forget the essential." Have you changed your feelings about that at all?

CAGE: I think that at present my greatest trouble with government is that there are different governments, and so we bring about the struggles for power between governments. I think the first thing to do would be to have, instead of several governments, only one for the whole earth; that one should be intelligent rather than seeking for power, and its intelligence should lie in its bringing about a balance between human needs (as R. Buckminster Fuller puts it) and world resources. At present we have nations senselessly at each other's throats, each one, for instance, wanting a little bit more oil than the other. And we shouldn't want the oil in the first place because it's polluting the atmosphere and, furthermore, coming to an end. We think it's important to solve the problem of employment, whereas we've invented a technology that will do most of our work for us. We should learn to live without working. That would mean we would have to live creatively; we would have to create our own work rather than doing foolish work that someone else asks us to do, work that isn't necessary.

Already the Olivetti Company in Italy retires it workers at the age of forty-five. Therefore, they have to educate them during employment in how to use their leisure time once they're retired. You can take vacations up to a point, but after that there's a kind of energy in each person that makes him want to do something. The Olivetti Company used to teach people to do gardening, but now they're beginning to teach the practice of the arts. It's a very advanced company, a very enlightened company.

CA: Does this work for most people? Are they able then to retire at forty-five and enjoy the rest of life?

CAGE: Of course.

CA: Do you think the kind of world government that you've described is possible within any time we can conceive of?

CAGE: I think that what will happen before the use of intelligence comes into play, unfortunately, is some catastrophe of a nearly global proportion. We've become so callous through the TV that we can see some disaster on the other side of the globe and simply think to ourselves that we're no less comfortable than we were before. But if the sense of real pain and disaster is large enough, the people who survive will feel that they should come to their senses. And then, I think, we might expect some play of intelligence. We have a great deal of intelligence in the form of books and advice, not only contemporary but down through the ages, but we pay no attention.

CA: Writing about boredom and its connection to the ego, you said that if we can break with the ego, "everything is endlessly reborn," and then we're not even in danger of boredom. Until we put machines to work on menial jobs instead of people, do you think it's possible for assembly-line workers and garbage collectors and people in similar jobs to avoid boredom in some way?

CAGE: It's possible, but I don't know that they search for the means. It's hard to say. Probably some do, but many don't. I'm afraid that most people connect their employment not with the enjoyment of life but with the receipt of a check.

CA: You mentioned the etchings you've been working on recently. Would you tell me more about them?

CAGE: I'm still in the process of making two series, one called "Changes and Disappearances" and the other, as I said earlier, called "On the Surface." Each series will be finished when I get to the number thirty-five, and they're prints of which only two copies are made of each image. I'm keeping one set of all thirty-five images together and, hopefully, that will go to some museum. The others are distributed through individual sales. I'm at number thirty in the series called "Changes and Disappearances," and about twenty or twenty-one with "On the Surface." In January I'll go to Oakland for two weeks and, hopefully, finish both series.

CA: You've been writing for piano and violin recently also?

CAGE: Yes. I wrote the *Etudes Australes* for Grete Sultan for piano, and I'm still working on the *Freeman Etudes* for violin for Paul Zukovsky. At the moment I'm writing a piece called *Dance/Four Orchestras*—it's one orchestra divided into four groups—for the conductor Dennis Russell Davies.

CA: Are there any more books planned?

CAGE: This year there was *For the Birds,* and then there's been a limited edition of one called *Another Song* with photographs by Susan Barron. There'll be another limited edition called *Mud Book,* which I wrote years ago with Lois Long. It's going to be rather elegantly printed, like a collector's item; it's really a children's book on how to make mud pies and cakes. It's being printed in Japan right now and will be available through Callaway Editions in New York. There's a book called *Themes and Variations* that's being published by the Station Hill Press at Barrytown, New York. And then there'll be another collection like *Empty Words* and *M* and *A Year From Monday* and *Silence*. It will be called *X,* and it will come from Wesleyan University Press.

CA: Do you still find time to hunt mushrooms?

CAGE: I do, but less time than when I lived in the country. I love to hunt mushrooms, but I don't own a car, and so it's a question of my circumstances, whether I have to make a trip that carries me into the country—for instance, when we went out to Purchase near here to see the exhibition called "Soundings," I drove with my friends Bill Anastasi and Dove Bradshaw and Merce Cunningham, and on the way out I noticed mushrooms. So after we'd seen the exhibition (we had brought a kind of picnic supper with us because we were going to go to a performance that evening in the city) we stopped and hunted the mushrooms and had a picnic supper.

CA: You seem to thrive on the city. I can hear those noises in the background as we talk.

CAGE: I love them!

CA: Did you miss the noises when you lived out in the country?

CAGE: Well, you have others there. You have the birds, and they're very noisy. And in the community, children crying and dogs barking and so on.

CA: And you like all of those noises, too?

CAGE: Surely.

CA: You said one time, "If you want to know the truth of the matter, the music I prefer, even to my own and everything, is what we hear if we are just quiet." Do you continue to hear sounds that you've never heard before?

CAGE: Oh yes.

CA: It's just a matter of turning off everything and listening?

CAGE: No, I listen all the time, whether I'm doing something else or not. I enjoy it all. I keep talking about it and writing about it. Many people tell me that they're following suit and enjoying their lives too, what they see and what they hear.

BIOGRAPHICAL/CRITICAL SOURCES—Books: John Cage, *Silence: Selected Lectures and Writings,* Wesleyan University Press, 1961; Robert Dunn, compiler, *John Cage* (bibliography), Henmar Press, 1962; Gilbert Chase, editor, *American Composers Speak,* Louisiana State University Press, 1966; Cage, *A Year from Monday: New Lectures and Writings,* Wesleyan University Press, 1967; David Ewen, *The World of Twentieth Century Music,* Prentice-Hall, 1968; Calvin Tomkins, *The Bride and the Bachelors,* Viking, 1968; Richard Kostelanetz, *Master Minds,* Macmillan, 1969; Kostelanetz, editor, *John Cage,* Praeger, 1970; Cage, *M: Writings, '67-'70,* Wesleyan University Press, 1973; Cage, *Pour les oiseaux,* Editions Pierre Belfond (Paris), 1976, translation published as *For the Birds,* Marion Boyars, 1981; Paul Griffiths, *A Concise History of Avant-Garde Music from Debussy to Bouley,* Oxford University Press, 1978; Samuel Lipman, *Music after Modernism,* Basic Books, 1979; Griffiths, *Modern Music: The Avant-Garde since 1945,* Braziller, 1981.

Periodicals: *Quarterly Journal of Speech,* April, 1962; *New Yorker,* November 28, 1964; *New York Times,* January 15, 1967; *Saturday Evening Post,* October 19, 1968; *Studio,* July, 1969; *Nation,* December 22, 1969; *New York Review of Books,* April 23, 1970; *Village Voice,* November 8, 1973; *Music Journal,* December, 1976; *Craft Horizon,* February, 1979; *Art News,* March, 1979; *Antioch Review,* fall, 1979; *New York Times Book Review,* December 2, 1979; *Spectator,* June 28, 1980; *Sewanee Review,* July, 1980; *Times Literary Supplement,* December 5, 1980; *Horizon,* December, 1980; *Washington Post,* October 3, 1981.

—*Sketch by Thomas Wiloch*

—*Interview by Jean W. Ross*

* * *

CALLAHAN, John
See GALLUN, Raymond Z(inke)

* * *

CAMERON, Ian
See PAYNE, Donald Gordon

* * *

CAMPBELL, Beatrice Murphy
See MURPHY, Beatrice M.

* * *

CAMPBELL, Ian 1942-

PERSONAL: Born August 25, 1942, in Lausanne, Switzerland; son of Donald (a clergyman) and Mary (a school teacher; maiden name, Cruickshank) Campbell. *Education:* University of Aberdeen, M.A., 1964; University of Edinburgh, Ph.D., 1970. *Politics:* "Unaligned." *Religion:* Presbyterian. *Home:* 12A St. Catherine's Pl., Edinburgh EH9 1NU, Scotland. *Office:* Department of English, University of Edinburgh, Edinburgh EH8 9JX, Scotland.

CAREER: University of Edinburgh, Edinburgh, Scotland, lecturer, 1967-81, reader in English literature, 1981—. Visiting professor, University of Guelph, summer, 1973; British Council visiting lecturer, Hamburg, summer, 1971, Caen, 1980, and Aix-en-Provence, 1981. *Member:* Association of Scottish Literary Studies (council member), Universities' Committee of Scottish Literature (council member), Scottish Association for the Speaking of Verse (chairman), Carlyle Society (chairman), English Association (Edinburgh; council member), University of Edinburgh Graduates' Association, Saltire Society. *Awards, honors:* Carnegie Research Fellowship in Switzerland, 1978.

WRITINGS: (Editor with R. D. S. Jack) Robert McLellan, *Jamie the Saxt,* J. Calder, 1970; (editor with C. R. Sanders, K. J. Fielding, and others) *The Duke-Edinburgh Edition of the Letters of Thomas and Jane Welsh Carlyle,* Duke University Press, Volumes I-IV, 1970, Volumes V-VII, 1977, Volumes VIII-IX, 1981, Volumes X-XI, in press; (editor) Thomas Carlyle, *Reminiscences,* Everyman, 1971; (editor) Carlyle, *Selected Essays,* Everyman, 1972; *Thomas Carlyle,* Hamish Hamilton, 1974, Scribner, 1975.

Carlyle and Europe, Carlyle Society, 1978; *Thomas Carlyle,* Longmans, 1978; (editor) *Nineteenth Century Scottish Fiction: Critical Essays,* Carcanet New Press, 1979; *Billy Budd* (notes on the novel by Herman Melville), Longmans, 1980; *Dr. Jeykyll and Mr. Hyde* (notes on the novel by Robert Louis Stevenson), Longmans, 1980; *Selected Short Stories of Robert Louis Stevenson,* Ramsay Head, 1980; (editor) *Thomas and Jane,* Edinburgh University Library, 1980; (contributor) *Writers and Their Works IV,* Scribners, 1981; *Kailyard: A New Assessment,* Ramsay Head, 1981; *The Speak of the Mearns,* Ramsay Head, 1982.

Also contributor to numerous festschrifts and collections of essays. Contributor of papers to literary journals, including *Studies in Scottish Literature, Dickens Studies Annual, Scottish Literary Journal, Victorian Poetry, Carlyle Newsletter, Criticism,* and *Extrapolation;* contributor of articles to science periodicals, including *ISIS;* contributor to British Broadcasting Corp. and to independent television in the United Kingdom. Co-editor, *Carlyle Newsletter,* 1979-81; review editor, *Edinburgh University Journal;* editor of annual publications, Carlyle Society.

WORK IN PROGRESS: Articles on English and Scottish literature, on Scottish-Swiss relationships in the nineteenth century, and on history of science; additional volumes of *Duke-Edinburgh Edition of the Letters of Thomas Carlyle and Jane Welsh Carlyle;* editing the letters of Lewis Grassic Gibbon; conference papers on Scottish influences; papers for Edinburgh Univesity Quartercentenary, 1983.

SIDELIGHTS: Ian Campbell writes: "Being born in Switzerland, I find it a healthy widening of interests for a Scottish academic teaching English (British) literature to have an awareness of Europe. As Scotland's political consciousness widens, we have a unique opportunity as university teachers to inform that consciousness by the critical study of past and present materials with as wide a perspective as possible."

AVOCATIONAL INTERESTS: Railed transport "of any kind," music (organist), travel.

* * *

CARPENTER, John R. 1936-

PERSONAL: Born April 14, 1936, in Cambridge, Mass.; son of Frederic Ives (a writer) and Lillian (a psychologist; maiden name, Cook) Carpenter; married Bogdana Chetkowska (a professor), April 15, 1963; children: Michael, Magdalena. *Education:* Harvard University, B.A. (cum laude), 1958; Sorbonne, University of Paris, Dr. d'universite, 1964. *Politics:* Independent. *Residence:* Ann Arbor, Mich.

CAREER: Poet, translator, critic, and teacher. Co-organizer of "Seattle Poetry," a series of readings. Member of Berkeley Civic Arts Commission, 1968-73; artist-in-residence for Seattle Arts Commission, 1975. *Military service:* U.S. Air Force Reserve, 1960-62. *Awards, honors:* National Endowment for the Arts fellowships, 1976-77 and 1980-81; Witter Bynner Poetry Translation Award, 1979, and second prize of Islands and Continents Translation Award, both for *Selected Poems* by Zbigniew Herbert.

WRITINGS: *Historie de la litterature francaise sur la Louisiane, 1683-1763* (title means "History of the French Literature of Louisiana, 1683-1763"), Nizet, 1965; *Putting the Loon Together* (poems), Seattle Arts Commission, 1975; (translator, editor, and author of introduction) Zbigniew Herbert, *Selected Poems,* Oxford University Press, 1977; *Poetry, Space and Children,* University of Washington Press, 1983.

Editor of anthologies of children's work; published by Seattle Public Schools: *The Dreamer on His Back,* 1978; *Chimineys, the Wind and the Three Giants,* 1978; *Stealing the Moon and Stars,* 1979; *The Birth of the World,* 1979; *Scowler,* 1979.

Poems and translations have been anthologized in *The New York Times Book of Verse,* edited by Thomas Lask, Macmillan, 1972, *Selected Poems of Czeslaw Milosz,* Seabury Press, 1974, and *Anthology of Washington State Writers,* Washington State Arts Commission, 1979. Contributor of poems, translations, and articles to literary journals, including *Poetry, London, The Seventies, Encounter, Modern Poetry in Translation, Poetry Northwest, Epoch,* and *Perspective,* and to newspapers.

WORK IN PROGRESS: Two collections of poems; a novel based on the Equity Funding Scandal; a critical work on the poetry written between 1940 and 1956, focusing on Eastern European poetry, and accompanied by an anthology of poetry; translations of poetry by Zbigniew Herbert, *Report from the Besieged City,* for Oxford University Press.

SIDELIGHTS: John R. Carpenter told *CA:* "Despite a variety of writing projects that are quite different from one another, at present I have a major concern overriding all others. This is the desire to find a new manner of writing that will 'write the world,' that will manage to render experience the way it happens, and the world the way it really is. This will involve a mix of lack of punctuation and of certain punctuation forms. It will probably not be 'poetry,' at least not the way poetry is generally understood, nor will it be 'prose.' I have put this project off for far too long. I have no illusions that I or anyone could succeed at this—to attempt it, and to sustain the attempt honestly, will be enough."

* * *

CARR, Philippa
See HIBBERT, Eleanor Burford

* * *

CARTER, Lonnie 1942-

PERSONAL: Born October 25, 1942, in Chicago, Ill.; son of Harold and Evelyn (Lipsey) Carter; married Marilyn Smutko, 1966 (divorced, 1972). *Education:* Marquette University, B.A., 1964, M.A., 1966; Yale University, M.F.A., 1969. *Home:* Cream Hill Rd., West Cornwall, Conn. 06796.

CAREER: Playwright, 1966—. Teacher of playwriting, Yale University School of Drama, 1974-75, New York University

Dramatic Writing Program, 1979—, and Marquette University, Rockland Community College, and University of Connecticut.

AWARDS, HONORS: Molly Kazan Award for best original play, Yale Drama School, 1967, for "Another Quiet Evening at Home"; Schubert fellowship, 1968-69; Peg Santvoord fellowships, Yale Repertory Theatre, 1970, 1971, 1973; Berkshire Theatre Festival prize, 1971, for "Plumb Loco"; Guggenheim fellowship, 1971-72; National Endowment for the Arts grant, 1974; CBS Foundation grant, 1974-75; Connecticut Commission on the Arts grant, 1976; P.E.N. grant, 1978; Open Circle Theater Award, Goucher College, 1978.

WRITINGS—All plays: "Adam" (two-act), first produced in Milwaukee, Wis., at Marquette University, March, 1966; "Another Quiet Evening at Home" (one-act), first produced in New Haven, Conn., at Yale University, May, 1967; "If Beauty's in the Eye of the Beholder, Truth Is in the Pupil Somewhere, Too" (one-act), first produced in New Haven, at Yale University, March, 1969.

"Workday" (two-act), first presented as reading in New Haven, at Yale University, January, 1970; "Iz She Izzy or Iz He Ain'tzy or Iz They Both" (one-act; music by Robert Montgomery), first produced in New Haven, at Yale Repertory Theatre, March, 1970, produced in New York at St. Clement's Theatre, April, 1972; "More War in Store with Peace as Chief of Police" (one-act) [and] "If Time Must Have a Stop, Space Is Where It's at Here at Dead Center of America" (one-act), first produced in New York at Old Reliable, September, 1970; "Plumb Loco" (one-act), first presented as reading in Stockbridge, Mass., at Berkshire Theatre, December, 1970; "The Big House" (two-act), first produced in New Haven, at Yale Repertory Theatre, October, 1971; "Smoky Links" (two-act), first presented as reading in New York at American Place Theatre, December, 1972; "Watergate Classics" (three sketches), first produced in New Haven, at Yale Repertory Theatre, November, 1973; "Cream Cheese" (two-act), first produced in New York at American Place Theatre, March, 1974.

"Trade-Offs" (three-act), first presented as reading in New Haven, at Yale Repertory Theatre, March, 1976; "Bleach," first produced in Chicago, Ill., at The Body Politic, 1977; "Bicicletta," first presented as a staged reading in New York at The Public Theatre, presented at Lincoln Center, 1981; "Victoria Fellows," first produced in Towson, Md., at Goucher College, 1978.

"Sirens," first produced in New York on WNYU-FM (New York University radio), November 30, 1981; "Certain Things about the Trombone," first produced on WNYU-FM, April 19, 1982, produced Off-Off-Broadway at Soho Repertory Theatre, 1982; "Lulu," first produced on WNYU-FM, January 10, 1983.

Also author of television script "From the Top," for Public Broadcasting System, 1976. Contributor to *Yale Theatre Tri-Quarterly,* and *Scripts.*

WORK IN PROGRESS: A stage adaptation of *The Odd Women* by George Gissing; a script about actress Louise Brooks, "The Girl in the Shiny Black Helmet."

* * *

CASHIN, Edward J(oseph, Jr.) 1927-
(Edward L[awrence] Cashin)

PERSONAL: Born July 22, 1927, in Augusta, Ga.; son of Edward Joseph (a cotton broker) and Margaret (O'Leary) Cashin; married Mary Ann Klug; children: Edward Lawrence, Milette. *Education:* Marist College, B.A., 1952; Fordham University, M.A., 1956, Ph.D., 1962. *Politics:* Independent. *Religion:* Roman Catholic. *Home:* 3412 Woodstone Pl., Augusta, Ga. 30909. *Office:* Augusta College, Augusta, Ga. 30904.

CAREER: Member of Roman Catholic religious community, the Marist Brothers, 1946-68; name in religion, Edward L. Cashin. Teacher of history at Mount St. Michael Academy, Bronx, N.Y., and Christopher Columbus High School, Miami, Fla.; Marist College, Poughkeepsie, N.Y., assistant professor of history and academic vice-president, 1963-68; New York State Education Department, Office of Planning in Higher Education, consultant, 1969; Augusta College, Augusta, Ga., professor of history, 1970—, chairman of department of history, political science, and philosophy, 1975—. Vice-president of board of directors, Dutchess County Committee for Economic Opportunity, 1966-67. *Member:* Georgia Historical Society (curator, 1978-81), Georgia Association of Historians (president, 1975-76), Richmond County Historical Society (president, 1974-76), Historic Augusta (treasurer, 1979-81). *Awards, honors:* Freedoms Foundation Award, 1959; E. Merton Coulter Award from Georgia Historical Society, 1975; Augusta College Alumni Town-Gown Award, 1982.

WRITINGS: (Under name Edward L. Cashin) *Your Calling as a Brother,* Rosen, 1966; *Higher Education in the Mid-Hudson Region,* New York State Education Department, 1969; (with Heard Robertson) *Augusta and the American Revolution,* Ashantilly Press, 1975; *A History of Augusta College 1783-1975,* State Printing Co. (Columbia, S.C.), 1976; (contributor) *An Uncivil War: The American Revolution in the Southern Backcountry,* University of Virginia Press, 1983; (contributor) *Proceedings of Georgia's Semisesquitenial Symposium,* University of Georgia Press, 1983. Contributor to *Worldmark Encyclopedia, Dictionary of Georgia Biography, Proceedings of Georgia Association of Historians Annual Meeting, Catholic Youth Encyclopedia for School and Home,* and *Collier's Encyclopedia Yearbook;* also to *Georgia Historical Quarterly, Georgia Review,* and *Richmond County History.*

SIDELIGHTS: Edward J. Cashin told *CA:* "When I joined the Marist Brothers, a Roman Catholic teaching order, in 1946, it was customary to select a new name. I decided to use the name Lawrence, instead of Joseph as my middle name. When I withdrew from the Marists in 1968, I resumed [using] my original name, Edward Joseph. I had grown rather fond of the name I [had] used for twenty years and bestowed it upon my son. I hope for his sake that he will not be mistaken for me. Since I have returned to my native town [after living in New York], I have focused my research and writing on local history, a task which I enjoy."

* * *

CASHIN, Edward L(awrence)
See CASHIN, Edward J(oseph, Jr.)

* * *

CASPARY, Vera 1899-

PERSONAL: Born November 13, 1899, in Chicago, Ill.; daughter of Paul (a department store buyer) and Julia (Cohen) Caspary; married I. G. Goldsmith (a film producer), October 5, 1949 (deceased). *Education:* Educated in Chicago public schools. *Politics:* Independent Democrat. *Home:* 55 East Ninth St., New

York, N.Y. 10003. *Agent:* Mitch Douglas, International Creative Management, 40 West 57th St., New York, N.Y. 10019.

CAREER: Free-lance writer of books, plays, and films. *Dance* (magazine), New York, N.Y., editor, 1925-27. *Member:* Authors Guild, Authors League of America, Dramatists Guild, Writers Guild of America West. *Awards, honors:* Awards from Screen Writers Guild for "A Letter to Three Wives" and "Les Girls."

WRITINGS: The White Girl, Sears, 1929; *Ladies and Gents,* Century, 1929; *Music in the Street,* Sears, 1930; *Thicker than Water,* Liveright, 1932; *Laura,* Houghton, 1942; *Bedelia,* Houghton, 1944; *Stranger than Truth,* Random House, 1946.

The Weeping and the Laughter, Little, Brown, 1950; *Thelma,* Little, Brown, 1952; *The Husband,* Harper, 1957; *Evvie,* Harper, 1960; *A Chosen Sparrow,* Putnam, 1964; *The Man Who Loved His Wife,* Putnam, 1966; *The Rosecrest Cell,* Putnam, 1967; *Final Portrait,* W. H. Allen, 1971; *The Dreamers,* Pocket Books, 1975; *Elizabeth X,* Pocket Books, 1978; *The Secrets of Grown-Ups* (autobiography), McGraw, 1979.

Films: "Scandal Street," Paramount, 1931; "The Night of June 13," Paramount, 1932; "I'll Love You Always," Columbia, 1935; "Easy Living," Paramount, 1937; "Lady from Louisiana," Republic, 1941; "Claudia and David," Twentieth Century-Fox, 1946; "Bedelia" (based on her novel of the same title), General Film Distributors, 1946; "Out of the Blue," Eagle Lion, 1947; "A Letter to Three Wives," Twentieth Century-Fox, 1949; "Three Husbands," United Artists, 1950; "I Can Get It for You Whole-Sale," Twentieth Century-Fox, 1951; "The Blue Gardenia," Warner Bros., 1953; "Give a Girl a Break," Metro-Goldwyn-Mayer, 1954; "Les Girls," Metro-Goldwyn-Mayer, 1957; "Bachelor in Paradise," Metro-Goldwyn-Mayer, 1961. Also author of "Such Women Are Dangerous."

Author of plays "Blind Mice," with Winifred Lenihan, 1931, "Laura" (based on her novel of the same title), with George Sklar, "Wedding in Paris," and "Geraniums in My Window."

WORK IN PROGRESS: The Lady Lies, a novel.

SIDELIGHTS: In her autobiography, *The Secrets of Grown-Ups,* Vera Caspary looks back on more than fifty years of free-lance writing. *Washington Post Book World* reviewer Faiga Levine calls Caspary's life "a Baedeker of the 20th century. An independent woman in an unliberated era, she collided with or was touched by many of its major historical and cultural events: wars, the Depression, the Spanish Civil War, the Leopold-Loeb/Bobby Frank murder case, Hollywood in its romantic heyday, Hollywood in the grip of McCarthyism, the footloose life of the artistic rich, publishing, Broadway." A *New York Times Book Review* critic writes that "despite the coy title, this is a lively, tough account of how a woman born into a conservative Jewish family broke conventions by plunging into the world of journalism and screenwriting at a time when women's liberation was still a faint rumble from the underground." Mary Ann Callan, in a *Los Angeles Times Book Review* article, says that "against stifling odds, [Caspary] breaks from tradition, defies prejudice," and achieves remarkable success. "To do this," Callan continues, "she also prostitutes her talents for hack work in advertising and sometimes in film, all for the purpose of buying time to write what she wants. 'Without conviction,' [Caspary] says, 'it is agony to write anything worth the paper it is printed on.'"

Caspary's 1942 novel, *Laura,* is probably her best known work, and it may have been the first book to be promoted as a "psychothriller" by a publisher. At the time of its publication, *Books* reviewer Will Cuppy said, "If you have no room for 'psychothriller' in your vocabulary, just think of it as a superior mystery, done with a novel twist and much skill." A *Springfield Republican* critic called *Laura* "a difficult book to classify; it carries a triple threat as a mystery, a love story, and a character study." And Isaac Anderson of the *New York Times* concluded that, whatever label is applied to the book, "it is something quite different from the run-of-the-mill detective story, and Vera Caspary deserves thanks for providing it."

Although *Laura* was quite successful when it was first published, the book achieved even greater popularity when, in 1944, it was produced as a film starring Dana Andrews, Gene Tierney, and Clifton Webb. Joseph LaShelle won an Academy Award for his outstanding cinematography on the picture, which also garnered Oscar nominations for supporting actor Webb, director Otto Preminger, and screenplay writers Jay Dratler, Samuel Hoffenstein, and Betty Reinhardt. The movie has become something of a cult classic, and its notoriety has been further enhanced by the fact that Preminger claims "Laura" as his first work, refusing to recognize his five earlier films.

BIOGRAPHICAL/CRITICAL SOURCES: Books, January 31, 1943; *New York Times,* January 31, 1943; *Springfield Republican,* February 7, 1943; *Washington Post Book World,* August 18, 1979; *Los Angeles Times Book Review,* December 23, 1979; *New York Times Book Review,* January 20, 1980.

* * *

CASSERLEY, H(enry) C(yril) 1903-

PERSONAL: Born June 12, 1903, in London, England; son of Edward and Sarah Casserley; married wife, Kathleen Mary, July, 1931; children: one son. *Education:* Attended Emanuel College, London. *Politics:* Conservative. *Religion:* Church of England. *Residence:* Berkhamsted, Hertfordshire, England.

CAREER: In insurance business, 1920-64; free-lance journalist and photographer on railway history, 1964—. *Military service:* British Army, 1942-44. *Member:* Stephenson Locomotive Society (general secretary, 1944-62).

WRITINGS: Locomotive Calvalcade: A Comprehensive Review Year by Year of the Changes in Steam Locomotive Development and Design which Have Taken Place on the Railways of the British Isles between the Years 1920 and 1951, Herts, 1952; (editor) *Service Suspended: A Pictorial Souvenir of British Passenger Services that Are No Longer in Operation,* Ian Allan, 1952; (with L. L. Asher) *Locomotives of British Railways: London, Midland, and Scottish Group* (also see below), A. Dakers, 1955; (with Asher) *Locomotives of British Railways: London and North Eastern Group* (also see below), A. Dakers, 1957; (with Asher) *Locomotives of British Railways: Great Western Group* (also see below), A. Dakers, 1958; (editor) *The Observer's Book of Railway Locomotives of Britain,* revised edition (Casserley not associated with earlier edition), Warne, 1958, 5th edition, 1966.

The Historic Locomotive Pocketbook: From the "Rocket" to the End of Steam, Batsford, 1960; *British Locomotive Names of the Twentieth Century,* Ian Allan, 1963, revised edition, 1967; (with Asher) *Locomotives of British Railways: A Pictorial Record,* Spring Books, 1963, published as *Steam Locomotives of British Railways* (also includes *Locomotives of British Railways: London, Midland, and Scottish Group, . . . London and North Eastern Group,* and . . . *Great Western Group*), Hamlyn, 1973; (with Stuart W. Johnston) *Locomotives at the Grouping,* Ian Allan, 1965; *Britain's Joint Lines,* Ian Allan, 1968; (with C. C. Dorman) *Midland Album,* Ian Allan, 1967, published as *Railway History in Pictures: The Midlands,* A. M. Kelley, 1969; *Preserved Locomotives,* Ian Allan, 1968, 4th edition, 1976.

Railway History in Pictures: Wales and the Welsh Border Counties, David & Charles, 1970; *London & South Western Locomotives,* Ian Allan, 1971; *Railways between the Wars,* David & Charles, 1971; *Famous Railway Photographers: H. C. Casserley,* David & Charles, 1972; *Railways since 1939,* David & Charles, 1972; *Outline of Irish Railway History,* David & Charles, 1974; *LMSR Steam, 1923-1948,* Barton, 1975; *Wessex,* David & Charles, 1976; *LMSR Locomotives, 1923-1948,* three volumes, Barton, 1976; *LNER Steam, 1923-1948,* Barton, 1976; *LNER Locomotives, 1923-1948,* Barton, 1976; *Recollections of the Southern Railway between the Wars,* Barton, 1976; *Welsh Railways in the Heyday of Steam,* Barton, 1977; *Irish Railways in the Heyday of Steam,* Barton, 1979; *Scottish Railways in the Heyday of Steam,* Barton, 1979; *Light Railways of Britain: Standard Gauge and Narrow Gauge,* Barton, 1979.

Observer's Directory of British Steam Locomotives, Warne, 1980; *Later Years of Metropolitan Steam,* Barton, 1981.

SIDELIGHTS: Many of H. C. Casserley's books are illustrated with his photographs.

BIOGRAPHICAL/CRITICAL SOURCES: H. C. Casserley, *Famous Railway Photographers: H. C. Casserley,* David & Charles, 1972.

* * *

CASTEL, J(ean) G(abriel) 1928-

PERSONAL: Born September 17, 1928, in Nice, France; son of Charles (a businessman) and Simone (Ricour) Castel; married Jane Jewett (a music and art history teacher), September 5, 1953; children: Christopher, Maria, Marc. *Education:* University of Aix-Marseille, B.Sc. and Phil., 1947; University of Paris, LL.B. and LL.M., 1950; University of Michigan, J.D., 1953; Harvard University, S.J.D., 1958. *Religion:* Roman Catholic. *Home:* 658 Hillsdale Ave. E., Toronto, Ontario, Canada. *Office:* Osgoode Hall Law School, York University, Toronto, Ontario, Canada.

CAREER: United Nations, Department of Economic Affairs, New York City, legal research assistant, 1952; worked for Dewey, Ballantine, Busby, Palmer, & Wood (law firm), New York City, 1953; McGill University, Montreal, Quebec, assistant professor, 1954-55, associate professor of law, 1955-59; York University, Osgoode Hall Law School, Toronto, Ontario, professor of law, 1959—; barrister and solicitor, Toronto, 1960—. Visiting professor at Laval University, and University of Montreal, both 1959-68, University of Mexico, 1963, University of Lisbon, 1964, University of Nice, 1968, University of Puerto Rico, 1973, University of Montreal, 1979, University of Ottawa, 1980, McGill University, 1981, University of Aukland, 1981, and University of Paris I (Sorbonne), 1982. President of Committee on Private International Law of the Office for the Revision of the Civil Code (Quebec). Consultant to Department of External Affairs, Canadian Government, and to Canada Law Reform Commission, 1978-80. *Military service:* Served with French resistance, 1944-45.

MEMBER: Canadian Bar Association (council, 1957—), Canadian Institute of International Affairs, Association of Canadian Law Teachers, International Law Association, International Faculty of Comparative Law. *Awards, honors:* Fulbright scholar, 1950; British Commonwealth fellow, 1962; Confederation Medal and Jubilee Medal, both from Queen's Counsel.

WRITINGS: Foreign Judgments: A Comparative Study, McGill University Press, 1956; *Private International Law,* Canada Law Book, 1960; *Cases, Notes and Materials on the Conflict of Laws,* Butterworth, 1960, 3rd edition published as *Conflict of Laws,* 1974; *Civil Law System of Quebec,* Butterworth, 1962; *International Law, Chiefly As Interpreted and Applied in Canada,* University of Toronto Press, 1965; *Canadian Conflict of Laws,* two volumes, Butterworth, 1975; (with S. A. Williams) *International Criminal Law,* York University, 1975; *Introduction to Conflict of Laws,* Butterworth, 1978; *Droit International Prive Quebecois,* Butterworth, 1980; (with Williams) *Canadian Criminal Law: International and Transnational Aspects,* Butterworth, 1981. Contributor to periodicals. Editor, *Canadian Bar Review,* 1957—.

WORK IN PROGRESS: A textbook on international business transactions.

SIDELIGHTS: J. G. Castel writes: "There are no shortcuts to scholarship." *Avocational interests:* Travel, riding, swimming, music, and painting.

* * *

CATE, Curtis 1924-

PERSONAL: Born May 22, 1924, in Paris, France; son of Karl Springer (a businessman) and Josephine Savilla (Wilson) Cate; married Helena Bajanova, October, 1965. *Education:* Harvard University, graduate (magna cum laude), 1947; Ecole des Langues Orientales, diploma in Russian, 1949; Magdalen College, Oxford, graduate study, 1949-52. *Agent:* Wallace & Sheil, 177 East 70th St., New York, N.Y. 10021.

CAREER: Atlantic Monthly, Boston, Mass., European editor, 1958-65; biographer and literary critic. *Military service:* U.S. Army, 1943-46. *Awards, honors:* Grand Prix Litteraire from l'Aero-Club de France, 1974, for *Antoine de Saint-Exupery: His Life and Times.*

WRITINGS: Antoine de Saint-Exupery: His Life and Times, Putnam, 1970; *George Sand,* Houghton, 1975; *Ides of August: The Berlin Wall Crisis—1961,* M. Evans, 1978; (with Boris Goldovsky) *My Road to Opera,* Houghton, 1979. Has contributed to many popular magazines, including *Horizon, National Review, Tour d'Horizon, Cornhill,* and *New York Times Book Review.*

SIDELIGHTS: An American raised in Paris, Curtis Cate frequently combines the roles of biographer and historian in his subjective studies of European people and events. His first book, *Antoine de Saint-Exupery: His Life and Times,* won the 1974 Grand Prix Litteraire in France and reflects what *Life* reviewer John Phillips calls Cate's "lasting infatuation for this extraordinary man" who was an aviator, moralist, storyteller, and popular philosopher. It also provides a background of France in the twenties, thirties, and forties—the troubled times during which Saint-Exupery lived.

Calling it a "handsome volume which will be of special interest to Francophiles and to those who were touched, however briefly, by the magnetism of 'Saint-Ex,'" the *Atlantic* reviewer commends Cate "for having written a volume which is at once dedicated and definitive." In the view of Nona Balakian, writing in the *New York Times,* Cate's panoramic approach is appropriate "since Saint-Exupery's life touched the life of his country at so many significant points.'' But other reviewers express reservations. ''Were the book leaner, a rushed reviewer could perhaps have extracted a clearer picture of this individualist and non-conformist,'' writes Edward Gannon in his *Best Sellers* review. ''But the book is about the 'Times' of Saint-Ex too, and there is therefore no world or national event touching Saint-Ex on which the reader is not filled in, and when Cate can, he gives generous biographies of even the minor characters walking through Saint-Ex's life.'' So much detail, much of it repetitive, ''clogs the narrative and adds nothing to his delineation of Saint-Ex's character and account of his life,'' according to Lewis Galantiere in the *New York Times Book Review.* ''For all this,'' Galantiere concludes, ''he has written the fullest and most reliable, indeed the best book we have on Saint-Ex and one that is not likely soon to be superseded.''

In his second biography, *George Sand,* Cate investigates the life of that nineteenth-century French novelist who is today more widely remembered for her flamboyant lifestyle than for the books she wrote. Then, as now, reports LeAnne Schreiber in *Time,* ''her public image was that of a cigar-smoking iconoclast in top hat and trousers, an unabashed libertine of dubious sexual inclinations. . . . Trying to disentangle the woman who was born Aurore Dupin in 1804, from the legendary creature known as George Sand could easily have proved a biographer's undoing. But Curtis Cate . . . approaches the task with both the patience of a scholar and the relish of a storyteller. He manages to puncture the myth without deflating the life.''

Among the legends he lays to rest are rumors of nymphomania, frigidity, and lesbianism according to Selden Rodman who writes in the *National Review* that Cate ''treats her not as a simplistic stereotype, but as a highly complex, compelling individual. . . . Motivated by intense feeling rather than passion, stirred by compassion and romanticism rather than sensuality,'' Sand was a victim of what Cate calls ''nympholepsy—a frenzied pursuit of ecstatic rapture, a mystic yearning for the unattainably sublime, a desperate craving for the ineffably tender.''

Though the book runs over 700 pages, ''it is not one of those computer affairs where, at the touch of a button marked with a date, every fact and name tumbles out of information storage,'' observes James R. Mellow in the *New Leader.* ''The reader is aware of a shaping hand and gets a feeling for the passage of time. The nineteenth century grows old with its subject; tastes shift, morals change, the romantic ardor of youth is trimmed to a steadier flame. Cate is particularly good at sketching in the tangled political and social issues of the period.'' *George Sand,* he concludes, ''is a vivid achievement, a lively and readable book.''

A far more controversial publication is Cate's *Ides of August: The Berlin Wall Crisis—1961.* In this detailed political narrative, Cate not only chronicles the construction of the east-west barrier, but also, in the opinion of *Time* reviewer Edwin Warner, ''strongly implies that the Wall would never have been built if the Western Allies had shown a little more sophistication and a little less fear.''

Cate believes that President Kennedy was intimidated by Soviet leader Nikita Khrushchev, who had been making what Warner calls ''grim references to a nuclear holocaust'' if the West did not meet Soviet demands in Berlin. Communists, particularly East German party boss Walter Ulbricht, were anxious to gain control of the entire city in order to stop the massive exodus of East Germans, who, by the hundreds and later by the thousands, were crossing over to West Berlin to be flown to freedom and a new life in West Germany. As William Manchester reports in the *New York Times Book Review:* ''East Germany was hemorrhaging talent; 22,000 doctors, scientists and engineers had left it for good. And the more obvious it became that Mr. Ulbricht must act, the heavier the swell of refugees became.'' The exodus spelled the failure of Ulbricht's regime. But construction of the Wall was a flagrant violation of international law, and Cate believes that it would never have been erected if the West had reacted forcefully and intelligently. ''There is considerable evidence that if American tanks had knocked down the Wall as soon as it was started, it never would have been completed,'' Warner writes in *Time.*

Furthermore, Cate argues, it was this capitulation that encouraged further Soviet adventurism, including the placement of nuclear missiles in Cuba. Because Cate's book sees the Wall in this historical context, Manchester concludes that it is ''invaluable. . . . Coming after the Bay of Pigs and the Vienna summit, where Premier Khrushchev had bullied President Kennedy, [the Berlin crisis] convinced Moscow that the young President was a weakling who could be pushed around. Mr. Kennedy said at the time: 'I've got a terrible problem. If he thinks I . . . have no guts, until we remove those ideas we won't get anywhere with him. So we have to act.' The place to act tough, the President decided, was Vietnam.''

BIOGRAPHICAL/CRITICAL SOURCES: Best Sellers, November 1, 1970; *Life,* November 13, 1970; *Atlantic,* December, 1970; *New York Times,* December 5, 1970, October 15, 1975; *New York Times Book Review,* December 27, 1970, August 24, 1975, November 26, 1978, April 22, 1979; *Books and Bookmen,* March, 1971; *Horn Book,* April, 1971; Curtis Cate, *George Sand,* Houghton, 1975; *Saturday Review,* August 23, 1975; *Time,* September 15, 1975, February 19, 1979; *Times Literary Supplement,* November 21, 1975; *New Leader,* December 22, 1975; *National Review,* January 23, 1976, November 10, 1978; *New Statesman,* February 23, 1979; *Washington Post,* May 7, 1979.

—Sketch by Donna Olendorf

* * *

CHADWICK, Henry 1920-

PERSONAL: Born June 23, 1920, in Bromley, Kent, England; son of John (a barrister) and Edith (Horrocks) Chadwick; married Margaret Elizabeth Brownrigg, 1945; children: Priscilla, Hilary, Juliet. *Education:* Magdalene College, Cambridge, B.A. and Mus.B., 1941. *Home:* Magdalene College, Cambridge University, Cambridge, England. *Office:* Divinity School, Cambridge University, St. John's St., Cambridge, England.

CAREER: Ordained priest, Church of England, 1943; Wellington College, Berkshire, England, assistant master, 1945; Cambridge University, Queens' College, Cambridge, England, fellow and chaplain, 1946-58, dean, 1950-55; Oxford University, Christ Church, Oxford, England, Regius Professor of Divinity and canon, 1959-69, dean, 1969-79; Cambridge University, Divinity School, Regius Professor of Divinity, 1979-82. Visiting professor, University of Chicago, 1957; Forwood Lecturer, University of Liverpool, 1961; Hewett Lecturer, Union Theological Seminary, 1962; Gifford Lecturer, University of St. Andrews, 1962-64; Burns Lecturer, University of Otago, 1971. Delegate, Oxford University Press, 1960-79. *Member:* British Academy (fellow), American Academy of Arts and Sciences, American Philosophical Society. *Awards, honors:* D.D. from University of Glasgow, 1957, and Yale University, 1970; D.Teol. from University of Uppsala, 1967; D.H.L. from University of Chicago, 1978.

WRITINGS: (Editor and translator) Origen, *Contra Celsum,* Cambridge University Press, 1953, revised edition, 1980; (editor with John E. L. Oulton) *Alexandrian Christianity,* Westminster, 1954; (editor and translator) *Lessing's Theological Writings,* A. & C. Black, 1956, Stanford University Press, 1957; (editor) Wilfred Lawrence Knox, *Sources of the Synoptic Gospels,* Volume II, Cambridge University Press, 1957; (editor) *The Sentences of Sextus: A Contribution to the History of Early Christian Ethics,* Cambridge University Press, 1959.

(Editor) *St. Ambrose on the Sacraments,* Loyola University Press, 1960; *The Vindication of Christianity in Westcott's Thought,* Cambridge University Press, 1961; (contributor) M. Black and H. H. Rowley, editors, *Peake's Commentary on the Bible,* Thomas Nelson, 1962; *Early Christian Thought and the Classical Tradition,* Oxford University Press, 1966; *The Early Church,* Penguin, 1967, published as *The Early Christian Church,* Eerdmans, 1969.

Die Kirche in der antiken Welt, de Gruyter, 1973; *Priscillian of Avila: The Occult and the Charismatic in the Early Church,* Oxford University Press, 1976; *Boethius: The Consolations of Music, Logic, Theology and Philosophy,* Oxford University Press, 1981; *History and Thought of the Early Church,* Variorum, 1982.

General editor of Harper's "New Testament Commentaries," 1958—. Contributor to professional journals. Editor of *Journal of Theological Studies,* 1954—.

SIDELIGHTS: Henry Chadwick's book *Boethius: The Consolations of Music, Logic, Theology and Philosophy* is considered by some critics to be one of the finest works on the respected Roman philosopher. "Chadwick has given us not only the first complete intellectual portrait, and a wholly convincing one: he has also allowed its subject to emerge from his pages enhanced in stature, in interest and importance," R. A. Markus writes in the *Times Literary Supplement.*

Markus continues "It is the outstanding achievement of Chadwick's biography to allow us to see Boethius's career and his thought as a unified whole. Political and theological alignments were never, perhaps, more closely intertwined than in his lifetime. During the long-drawn-out conflicts among the clergy, the aristocracy and the people of Rome over the papacy, conflicts which had their roots in, among other things, doctrinal differences between the Western Church and the court at Constantinople, the Gothic king could not fail to become involved in the struggles in the City."

AVOCATIONAL INTERESTS: Music.

BIOGRAPHICAL/CRITICAL SOURCES: Times Literary Supplement, January 8, 1982.

* * *

CHAI, Winberg 1932-

PERSONAL: Born October 16, 1932, in Shanghai, China; came to United States in 1951; U.S. citizen; son of Ch'u (a college professor) and Ruth (Tsao) Chai; married Carolyn Everett; children: May-lee (daughter), Jeffrey. *Education:* Wittenberg University, B.A., 1955; New School for Social Research, M.A., 1958; New York University, Ph.D., 1968; postdoctoral study, Virginia Polytechnic and State University, 1970, Western Behavioral Science Institute, summer, 1971, and Harvard University, summer, 1980. *Politics:* Independent. *Religion:* Lutheran. *Home address:* P.O. Box 472, Vermillion, S.D. 57069.

CAREER: New School for Social Research, New York City, lecturer in history and philosophy, 1957-61; University of Redlands, Redlands, Calif., 1965-73, began as assistant professor, became associate professor of political science, chairman of department of government, coordinator of Asian and international studies programs; City College of the City University of New York, New York City, professor, 1973-79, chairman of department of Asian studies, 1973-79, chairman of division of humanities, 1978-79, coordinator of CCNY-Chiba University (Japan) Exchange Program; University of South Dakota, Vermillion, S.D., professor of political science, 1979-81, distinguished professor of international studies and humanities, 1981—, vice-president for academic affairs, 1979-80, special assistant to president, 1980-81. Visiting assistant professor of political science, Drew University, 1961-62; visiting lecturer in politics, California State University, spring, 1967; part-time professor of politics, New York University, 1975-79; research associate, Columbia University, 1974-1983. Consultant to numerous organizations and companies, including Asia Society, China Institute of America, Software Systems Technology, Inc., and Jewish Community Council of Greater New York.

MEMBER: International Studies Association, American Association of Chinese Studies (president, 1978-80), American Association for the Advancement of Science, American Association of University Professors, American Political Science Association (Asian scholars, co-chair), Association of Asian Studies, National Committee on U.S.-China Relations, Inc., New York Academy of Sciences, Museum of Modern Art.

AWARDS, HONORS: Grants from World Law Fund, 1966, Ford Foundation, 1968, 1969, National Science Foundation, 1970, Hubert Eaton Memorial Fund, 1972-73, City College Fund, 1973, Field Foundation, 1973, 1975, Saudi Arabia government, 1975, Pacific Cultural Foundation, 1978, 1981, Henry Luce Foundation, 1978, South Dakota Humanities Committee, 1980; Haynes Foundation fellowship, 1967, 1968.

WRITINGS: (With father, Ch'u Chai) *The Story of Chinese Philosophy,* Washington Square Press, 1961; (with C. Chai) *The Changing Society of China,* New American Library, 1962, revised edition, 1969; (editor) *I Ching: Book of Changes,* University Books (New Hyde Park, N.Y.), 1964; (editor) *Essential Works of Chinese Communism,* Pica Press, 1969, revised edition, Bantam, 1972.

(Editor and author of introduction) *The Foreign Relations of the "People's Republic of China,"* Putnam, 1972; *The New Politics of Communist China: Modernization Process of a Developing Nation,* Goodyear Publishing, 1972; (with C. Chai) *Confucianism: A Short History,* Barron's, 1973; *The Search for a New China: A Capsule History, Ideology, and Leadership of the Chinese Communist Party, 1921-1974,* Putnam, 1975; (editor with James C. Hsiung) *Asia and U.S. Foreign Policy,* Praeger, 1981; (editor with Hsiung and contributor) *The Republic of China on Taiwan: The First Thirty Years,* Praeger, 1981.

Editor and translator with C. Chai: *A Treasury of Chinese Literature: A New Prose Anthology, Including Fiction and Drama,* Appleton-Century-Crofts, 1965; *The Humanist Way in Ancient China: Essential Works of Confucianism,* Bantam, 1965; (and author of introduction) *The Sacred Books of Confucius, And Other Confucian Classics,* University Books, 1965; *Li Chi: Book of Rites,* two volumes, University Books, 1966.

Contributor: *Asian Man,* Encyclopaedia Britannica Educational Corp., 1977; *The Future of Taiwan: A Difference of Opinion,*

M. E. Sharpe, 1980. Contributor to journals, including *American Political Science Review, Asian Society and Thought, Chinese Culture Quarterly, World Affairs,* and *Business Review*.

WORK IN PROGRESS: Asians in America: A History; Sino-American Relations: A Documentary History.

* * *

CHAMPION, Larry S(tephen) 1932-

PERSONAL: Born April 27, 1932, in Shelby, N.C.; son of Flay Oren (an oil distributor) and Mary (Helms) Champion; married Nancy Ann Blanchard, December 22, 1956; children: Mary Katherine, Rebecca Jane, Larry Stephen, Jr. *Education:* Davidson College, B.A. (cum laude), 1954; University of Virginia, M.A., 1955; University of North Carolina, Ph.D., 1961. *Politics:* Democrat. *Religion:* Presbyterian. *Home:* 5320 Sendero Dr., Raleigh, N.C. 27612. *Office:* Department of English, North Carolina State University, Raleigh, N.C. 27650.

CAREER: Instructor in English, Davidson College, Davidson, N.C., 1955-56, and University of North Carolina at Chapel Hill, 1959-60; North Carolina State University at Raleigh, instructor, 1960-61, assistant professor, 1961-65, associate professor, 1965-68, professor of English, 1968—, associate head, 1968-71, head of department, 1971—. Editorial consultant to Canada Council, Prentice-Hall, Inc., University of Georgia Press, University of Kentucky Press, Pennsylvania State Press, and Princeton University Press. *Military service:* U.S. Army, 79th Army Band, 1956-58; served in Canal Zone, Panama.

MEMBER: Modern Language Association of America, Shakespeare Association of America, Renaissance Society of America, National Council of Teachers of English, South Atlantic Modern Language Association, Southeastern Renaissance Conference, North Carolina English Teachers Association, Phi Beta Kappa, Phi Kappa Phi. *Awards, honors:* Academy of Outstanding Teachers award, 1966; selected as academic administration intern by American Council on Education, 1967-68.

WRITINGS: Ben Jonson's "Dotages": A Reconsideration of the Late Plays, University of Kentucky Press, 1967; *The Evolution of Shakespeare's Comedy,* Harvard University Press, 1970; (editor) *Quick Springs of Sense: Studies in the Eighteenth Century,* University of Georgia Press, 1974; *Shakespeare's Tragic Perspective: The Development of His Dramatic Technique,* University of Georgia Press, 1975; *Tragic Patterns in Jacobean and Caroline Drama,* University of Tennessee Press, 1977; *Perspective in Shakespeare's English Histories,* University of Georgia Press, 1980; (editor) *King Lear: An Annotated Bibliography,* two volumes, Garland Publishing, 1980. Contributor to literary and scholarly journals. Editorial consultant to *Papers on Language and Literature* and *PMLA*.

WORK IN PROGRESS: A study of Thomas Dekker's drama.

* * *

CHANDLER, Jennifer (Westwood) 1940-
(Jennifer Westwood)

PERSONAL: Born May 1, 1940, in England; daughter of Wilfrid James and Beatrice Fulcher; married Trevor Frank Westwood in 1958 (divorced, 1966); married Brian Herbert Chandler (a management consultant), 1968; children: (first marriage) Jonathan James. *Education:* St. Anne's College, Oxford, B.A., 1963, M.A., 1970; New Hall, Cambridge, B.A., 1965, M.A., 1972, M.Litt., 1973. *Religion:* Church of England. *Home:* 133 Shepherdess Walk, London, N.1, England.

CAREER: Cambridge University, Cambridge, England, conductor of university classes and tutorials in Old Norse and Anglo-Saxon, 1965-68; free-lance editor and publishing adviser, 1969—. *Member:* Viking Society for Northern Research, Folklore Society.

WRITINGS—Under name Jennifer Westwood, except as indicated: (Adaptor and translator) *Medieval Tales,* Hart-Davis, 1967, Coward, 1968; *Gilgamesh and Other Babylonian Tales,* Bodley Head, 1968, Coward, 1970; *The Isle of Gramarye,* Hart-Davis, 1970; *Tales and Legends,* Coward, 1971; *Stories of Charlemagne,* Bodley Head, 1972, S. G. Phillip's, 1976; (contributor) Kevin Crossley-Holland, editor, *Faber Book of Northern Legends,* Faber, 1977; *Alfred the Great,* Wayland, 1978; (adaptor) Oscar Wilde, *The Star Child: A Fairy Tale,* illustrated by Fiona French, Four Winds Press, 1979; (contributor under name Jennifer Chandler) *The Book of London,* St. Michael, 1979; *Fat Cat,* illustrated by French, Abelard, in press; *Albion: A Gazetteer of British Myths, Legends, and Folktales,* Granada, in press. Reviewer of children's books, under name Jennifer Chandler, for *Times Literary Supplement,* 1975-78. Contributor to *British Heritage*.

SIDELIGHTS: "I began writing whilst still at university, for the amusement of my son Jonathan," Jennifer Westwood Chandler told *CA*. "What he liked most in the world was stories, and it so happened that—after reading Old and Middle English language and literature at Oxford, and the Anglo-Saxon Tripos at Cambridge—stories was what I knew. I realized that I had access to a fund of stories in dead languages that were either unavailable to children or available only in Victorian retellings long since out of print. I set about trying to retell some of these in intelligible modern English whilst keeping the flavor and style of the originals—particularly in *Gilgamesh,* where a semi-liturgical style was aimed at.

"One thing has led to another: I now write also on Dark Age history and archaeology for children (*Alfred the Great* and contributions on the Anglo-Saxons and Vikings to *British Heritage*), and on legends and folktales for adults. . . . A most exciting development in my career has been to work with the British illustrator Fiona French, with whom I have long been close friends. Our abridged picture-book version of Oscar Wilde's fairytale *The Star Child* is now published in several languages, including Japanese. . . . *Fat Cat,* a classic Danish folktale, [is] virtually the first piece of Danish I ever managed to read. I stayed in Denmark for a time as a child, living in a Danish family, and again as a student, and the book is a token of the gratitude I feel for those good times.

"As a student I've also lived in Sweden and Iceland, and with my family have lived for a year each in Iran (1976-77) and the United States (1978-79). My interest in ancient monuments has led to extensive travels in Europe and the Middle East, and of course my own country.

"I speak French, and much less Danish and Icelandic than I used to do; on the other hand, I have learned to read and write in Farsi (Persian). Of the dead languages, I can get by in Latin, Anglo-Saxon (Old English), Old Norse and Old French."

* * *

CHAPIN, Kim 1942-

PERSONAL: Born July 18, 1942, in Bay City, Mich.; son of

Wendell Phillips (a printer) and Roberta (a realtor; maiden name, Cameron) Chapin; married Anne R. Constable (a journalist), April 20, 1979; children: Alexander Burnet. *Education:* Attended Vanderbilt University, 1960-64. *Home:* 6223 Utah N.W., Washington, D.C. 20015.

CAREER: Free-lance writer. *Atlanta Journal,* Atlanta, Ga., reporter, 1964-66; *Sports Illustrated,* New York, N.Y., member of staff, 1966-68, staff writer, 1968-69; *Santa Fe Reporter,* Santa Fe, N.M., sports editor, 1974. *Military service:* U.S. Army Reserve, 1965-69.

WRITINGS: (With Billie Jean King) *Tennis to Win,* Harper, 1970; (with King) *Billie Jean,* Harper, 1974; (with Gayle Barron) *The Beauty of Running,* Harcourt, 1980; *Fast as White Lightning: The Story of Stock Car Racing,* Dial, 1981. Co-author of "The Speed Merchants," a documentary filmscript, 1972. Contributor to magazines, including *True, Car and Driver, World Tennis, American Home, Sports Illustrated,* and *Southern Living.*

SIDELIGHTS: In his book *Fast as White Lightning: The Story of Stock Car Racing,* Kim Chapin chronicles the history of Grand National stock car racing, from its beginnings in Georgia bootleg country in the late 1940s and early 1950s to its status as a multi-million-dollar sport in the 1980s. Janet Guthrie writes in *Washington Post Book World* that "Chapin's research has been thorough," and that he has "incorporated a yeasty mixture of strong and outrageous characters into a book that even knowledgeable racing fans will find revealing and informative."

AVOCATIONAL INTERESTS: Travel.

BIOGRAPHICAL/CRITICAL SOURCES: Washington Post Book World, July 19, 1981; *Newsweek,* July 20, 1981.

* * *

CHAPMAN, Hester W(olferstan) 1899-1976

PERSONAL: Born November 26, 1899, in London, England; died April 6, 1976; daughter of T. and E. (Thomas) Pellatt; married Nigel K. Chapman, 1926 (deceased); married R. L. Griffin, 1938 (deceased). *Education:* Privately educated. *Home:* 13 Conway St., London W.1, England. *Agent:* Hughes Massie Ltd., 21 Southampton Row, London WC1B 5HL, England.

CAREER: Historical novelist and biographer. Mannequin in Paris, France, in early years, then, intermittently, telephone operator, secretary, governess, schoolmistress, and literary agent, in London, England. During World War II worked for Fighting French and American Red Cross.

WRITINGS: She Saw Them Go By (novel), Houghton, 1933; *To Be a King: A Tale of Adventure,* Gollancz, 1934; *Long Division* (novel), Secker & Warburg, 1943; *I Will Be Good* (novel), Secker & Warburg, 1945, Houghton, 1946; (editor with Princess Romanovsky-Pavlovsky) *Diversion,* introduction by Rebecca West, Collins, 1946, reprinted, Arden Library, 1977; *Worlds Apart* (novel), Secker & Warburg, 1947; *Great Villiers: A Study of George Villiers, Second Duke of Buckingham, 1628-1687,* Secker & Warburg, 1949.

Ivor Novello's King's Rhapsody (novel based on the musical romance by Novello), Harrap, 1950, published as *King's Rhapsody,* Houghton, 1951; *Ever Thine* (novel), J. Cape, 1951; *Mary II: Queen of England* (biography), J. Cape, 1953, reprinted, Greenwood Press, 1976; *Falling Stream* (novel), J. Cape, 1954, reprinted, Hutchinson, 1976; *Queen Anne's Son: A Memoir of William Henry, Duke of Gloucester, 1689-1700,* Deutsch, 1954; *The Stone Lily* (novel), J. Cape, 1957; *The Last Tudor King: A Study of Edward VI, October 12th, 1537-July 6th, 1553,* J. Cape, 1958, Macmillan, 1959.

Two Tudor Portraits: Henry Howard, Earl of Surrey, and Lady Katherine Grey, J. Cape, 1960, Little, Brown, 1963; *Eugenie* (novel), Little, Brown, 1961; *Lady Jane Grey, October, 1537-February, 1554,* J. Cape, 1962, Little, Brown, 1963; *The Tragedy of Charles II in the Years 1630-1660,* Little, Brown, 1964; *Lucy,* J. Cape, 1965; *Privileged Persons: Four Seventeenth-Century Studies* (includes biographies of Louis XIII, Electress Sophia, Hortense Mancini, Duchess Mazarin, and Thomas Bruce, Earl of Ailesbury), Reynal, 1966; *Fear No More* (historical novel), Reynal, 1968; *The Sisters of Henry VIII: Margaret Tudor, Queen of Scotland (November, 1489-October, 1541), Mary Tudor: Queen of France and Duchess of Suffolk (March, 1496-June, 1533),* J. Cape, 1968, published as *The Thistle and the Rose,* Coward, 1971.

Caroline Matilda: Queen of Denmark, 1751-1775, J. Cape, 1971, Coward, 1972; *Limmerston Hall,* Coward, 1972; *The Challenge of Anne Boleyn,* Coward, 1974; *Four Fine Gentlemen,* Constable, 1977, University of Nebraska Press, 1978.

SIDELIGHTS: Hester W. Chapman's biographies were frequently praised by reviewers, who cited her accuracy, in-depth research, and vivid characterizations as reasons for the success of her books. Christopher Hill, writing in *Spectator,* called her "a biographer of competence, industry and imagination." *Canadian Historical Review*'s H. C. Porter labelled her style "imaginative, but always distinguished and controlled." Reviewing *The Last Tudor King,* a *Times Literary Supplement* critic commented: "She writes well, has a gift for lucid narrative, considerable powers of observation and description, a balanced judgment, a sensitive imagination, an eye for the picturesque, and a serious sense of the responsibilities of a biographer."

Chapman's biographies attracted a large readership. She had a talent for making historical events interesting. "Chapman is both scholarly and readable and shows great insight into the vagaries of human temperament," remarked J. H. Plumb in the *New York Times Book Review.* Plumb found Chapman's rendition of Charles II "believable. He could have been like that." A *Times Literary Supplement* critic commented that her "knowledge of seventeenth-century history . . . is both detailed and accurate. She approaches her subjects with a sympathetic understanding, and her style of writing is never anything but lively and readable."

Chapman's attention to details, her unpretentious writing style, and her vivid characterizations are also present in her novels. Reviewing *She Saw Them Go By* in *Books,* Iris Barry wrote: "There is an unusual simplicity, almost ordinariness, about the telling of this eventful and vivid tale which is extremely striking. One is utterly convinced that these things all happened. . . . The writing is good and unaffected, the characterization lucid, and to have met and known the heroine herself is both an education and a delight." A *Boston Transcript* critic pointed to what may have been Chapman's greatest literary talent: "It is the characterization that gives [Chapman's novels their] distinction, that and the unusual charm of narration, qualities that are seldom found in a tale of adventure."

AVOCATIONAL INTERESTS: Theatre, interior decorating, travel.

BIOGRAPHICAL/CRITICAL SOURCES: Books, October 8, 1933; *Boston Transcript,* November 1, 1933; *New York Times,*

November 12, 1933; *Spectator,* December 19, 1958; *Kirkus Reviews,* August 1, 1959; *Canadian Historical Review,* September, 1959; *Times Literary Supplement,* February 8, 1963, November 17, 1966, April 12, 1974, October 14, 1977; *New York Times Book Review,* December 20, 1964; *Observer,* February 24, 1974, August 7, 1977; *Historian,* February, 1980.

OBITUARIES: AB Bookman's Weekly, May 31, 1976.†

* * *

CHAPMAN, Samuel Greeley 1929-

PERSONAL: Born September 29, 1929, in Atlanta, Ga.; son of Calvin C. (a stock broker) and Jane (Greeley) Chapman; married Patricia Hepfer, June 19, 1949 (died December 13, 1978); children: Lynn Randall, Deborah Jane. *Education:* University of California, Berkeley, B.A., 1951, M.A., 1959. *Politics:* Republican. *Religion:* Protestant. *Home:* 2421 Hollywood, Norman, Oklahoma 73069. *Office:* Department of Political Science, University of Oklahoma, Norman, Okla. 73069.

CAREER: Berkeley Police Department, Berkeley, Calif., undercover agent in Vice Division, 1950-51, patrolman, 1951-56; Public Administration Service, Chicago, Ill., police consultant, 1956-59; Michigan State University, East Lansing, assistant professor, School of Police Administration and Public Safety, 1959-63; Multnomah County Sheriff's Police Department, Portland, Ore., chief, 1963-65; U.S. Department of Justice, Washington, D.C., assistant director, President's Commission on Law Enforcement and Administration of Justice, 1965-67; University of Oklahoma, Norman, professor of political science, 1967—, director of law enforcement administration degree program. Norman City Council, councilman, 1972—, mayor pro-tempore, 1975-76 and 1979-80. Member, Oklahoma Crime Commission, 1968-71; Oklahoma University Athletics Council, member, 1969-72 and 1977-80, chairman, 1970-72 and 1979-80; Salvation Army of Norman, member of board, 1979—, president, 1981—; member of board, Norman Community Playhouse, 1981—; member of by-laws committee, United Way of Norman, 1981—. Consultant on police service, fire protection, and other matters of municipal government to more than eighty cities in United States and Canada; consulting editor, John Wiley and Sons, Holbrook Press, Prentice-Hall, Inc., Basic Books, Inc., and Harper & Row, Publishers.

MEMBER: International Association of Chiefs of Police, American Society for Public Administration, Oklahoma Association of Criminal Justice Educators (vice-president, 1979—), Lambda Alpha Epsilon, Alpha Phi Sigma.

WRITINGS: Dogs in Police Work: A Summary of Experience in Great Britain and the United States, Public Administration Service (Chicago), 1960; (contributor) *Municipal Police Administration,* 5th edition (Chapman was not associated with earlier editions), International City Managers' Association, 1961, 7th edition, 1971; (with Sir Eric Johnson) *The Police Heritage in England and America,* Michigan State University, 1962; (editor) *Police Patrol Readings,* C. C Thomas, 1964, 2nd edition, 1970; (contributor) William Hewitt, *British Police Administration,* C. C Thomas, 1965; (with Donald E. Clark) *A Forward Step: Educational Backgrounds for Police,* C. C Thomas, 1966.

(Contributor) Johnston, Savitz, and Wolfgang, editors, *The Sociology of Punishment and Correction,* 2nd edition (Chapman was not associated with earlier editions), Wiley, 1970; (contributor) C. R. Hormachea, editor, *Confrontation: Violence and the Police,* Holbrook, 1971; (author of introduction) Leonhard Felix Fulk, *Police Administration,* Patterson Smith Reprint Series, 1971; (with others) *Perspectives on Police Assaults in the South Central United States,* University of Oklahoma Bureau of Government Research, 1974; (author of foreword) William H. Hewitt, *New Directions in Police Personnel Administration,* Lexington Books, 1975; (with George D. Eastman) *Short of Merger: Countywide Police Resource Pooling,* Lexington Books, 1976; *Police Murders and Effective Countermeasures,* Davis Publishing, 1976; *Police Dogs in America,* University of Oklahoma Bureau of Government Research, 1979.

Contributor to professional journals in United States and abroad, including *International Criminal Police Review* (Paris), *Criminologist* (London), and *Police Chief.*

AVOCATIONAL INTERESTS: Bridge, fly fishing, and softball.

* * *

CHAPMAN, Stanley D(avid) 1935-

PERSONAL: Born January 31, 1935, in Nottingham, England; son of Horace (a tool-room engineer) and Dulcie (Woodward) Chapman; married Audrey Palmer (a teacher), July, 1960; children: Julian Robert, Timothy David. *Education:* London School of Economics and Political Science, B.Sc. (honors), 1956; University of Nottingham, M.A., 1960; University of London, part-time external student, 1963-65, Ph.D., 1966. *Politics:* "Floating voter." *Religion:* Methodist. *Home:* 35 Park Lane, Sutton, Bonington, Loughborough, Leichestershire, England.

CAREER: Schoolmaster in Nottingham, England, 1957-60, and Wigan, Lancashire, England, 1960-62; Dudley College of Education, Dudley, England, lecturer in history, 1962-66; University of Aston, Birmingham, England, lecturer in economic history, 1966; University of Nottingham, Nottingham, England, Pasold Lecturer in Textile History, 1968-73, reader, 1973—.

WRITINGS: (With C. Aspin) *James Hargreaves and the Spinning Jenny,* Helmshore Historical Society, 1964; *The Early Factory Masters,* David & Charles, 1967; (author of introduction) William Felkin, *History of the Hosiery and Lace Manufacturers,* centenary edition, David & Charles, 1967; (with J. D. Chambers) *The Beginnings of Industrial Britain,* University Tutorial Press, 1968; (editor) *The History of Working Class Housing: A Symposium,* David & Charles, 1971; *The Cotton Industry in the Industrial Revolution,* Macmillan, 1972; *Jesse Boot of Boots the Chemists,* Hodder & Stoughton, 1974.

(With S. Chassagne) *European Textile Printers in the Eighteenth Century: A Study of Peel and Oberkampf,* Heinemann, 1981; *Stanton and Staveley: A Business History,* Woodhead Faulkner, 1981; *The Rise of Merchant Banking in Britain,* Allen & Unwin, 1983. Contributor to journals in Britain and the United States. Co-editor, *Textile History,* 1971—.

WORK IN PROGRESS: Kleinwort Benson in the History of Merchant Banking.

* * *

CHARLWOOD, D(onald) E(rnest) 1915- (Don Charlwood)

PERSONAL: Born September 6, 1915, in Melbourne, Victoria, Australia; son of Ernest Joseph (a clerk) and Emily F. (Cameron) Charlwood; married Nell East (a teacher and librarian), June 8, 1944; children: Jan, Susan, Doreen, James. *Education:*

Attended Frankston High School, 1927-32. *Politics:* "No affiliations—independent views." *Religion:* Church of England. *Home:* Qualicum, Mount View Rd., Templestowe, Victoria 3106, Australia.

CAREER: Australian Department of Civil Aviation, Melbourne, employed in Air Traffic Control, 1945-75, in charge of selecting and training controllers throughout Australia, 1953-75. *Military service:* Royal Australian Air Force, 1941-45; trained as navigator in Canada; served in Royal Air Force Bomber Command and Pacific Ferry Group; became flight lieutenant. *Member:* P.E.N., Fellowship of Australian Writers, Australian Society of Authors (Victorian representative).

WRITINGS—Published by Angus & Robertson, except as indicated: *No Moon Tonight* (memoirs), 1956; *All the Green Year* (novel), 1965; *An Afternoon of Time* (story collection), 1967; *Take-Off to Touchdown,* 1967; *The Wreck of the "Loch Ard": End of A Ship, End of An Era* (regional history), 1971; *Wrecks and Reputations* (regional history), 1977; *Flight and Time* (short stories), Neptune Press, 1979; (under name Don Charlwood) *The Long Farewell: Settlers under Sail,* Allen Lane, 1982. Work represented in several anthologies including *Classic Australian Short Stories,* edited by Judah Waten and Stephen Murray-Smith, Wren Publishing, 1974, and *Festival and Other Stories,* edited by Brian Buckley and Jim Hamilton, Wren Publishing, 1974. Contributor to *Blackwood's Magazine.*

WORK IN PROGRESS: An autobiographical novel.

BIOGRAPHICAL/CRITICAL SOURCES: London Times, March 4, 1982.

* * *

CHARLWOOD, Don
See CHARLWOOD, D(onald) E(rnest)

* * *

CHARTERS, Ann (Danberg) 1936-

PERSONAL: Born November 10, 1936, in Bridgeport, Conn.; daughter of Nathan (a contractor) and Kate (Schultz) Danberg; married Samuel Barclay Charters (an ethnomusicologist and writer), March 14, 1959; children: Mallay, Nora Lili. *Education:* University of California, Berkeley, B.A., 1957; Columbia University, M.A., 1959, Ph.D., 1965. *Office:* Department of English, University of Connecticut, Storrs, Conn. 06268.

CAREER: Colby Junior College, New London, N.H., teacher of creative writing, 1961-63; Random House-Knopf (publishers), New York City, assistant editor, 1965; Columbia University, New York City, instructor in literature, 1965-66; New York City Community College of Applied Arts and Sciences of the City University of New York, Brooklyn, N.Y., assistant professor of English, 1967-70; University of Connecticut, Storrs, associate professor, 1974—. Pianist featured on records, "Essay in Ragtime," issued by Folkways, and "A Scott Joplin Bouquet" and "Treemonisha: The First Negro Folk Opera," both issued by Portents. *Member:* International P.E.N., Phi Beta Kappa.

WRITINGS: The Ragtime Songbook, Oak Publications, 1965; (editorial assistant) Perry Bradford, *Born with the Blues,* Oak Publications, 1965; (compiler) *A Bibliography of Works by Jack Kerouac,* Phoenix Bibliographies, 1967, revised edition, Phoenix Book Shop, 1975; *Olson/Melville: A Study in Affinity,* Oyez, 1968; *Melville in the Berkshires: A Construct,* Portents, 1969.

Charles Olson: The Special View of History, Oyez, 1970; (with Allen Ginsberg) *Scenes Along the Road: Photographs of the Desolation Angeles* (photographs, text, and poems), Gotham Book Mart, 1970; (editor) *Scattered Poems by Jack Kerouac,* City Lights, 1971; *Nobody: The Story of Bert Williams,* Macmillan, 1970; *Kerouac: A Biography,* Straight Arrow Books, 1973; (with husband, Samuel Charters) *I Love: The Story of Vladimir Mayakovsky and Lili Brik,* Farrar, Straus, 1979.

SIDELIGHTS: Ann Charters' book *I Love: The Story of Vladimir Mayakovsky and Lili Brik* is a biography of the well-known Russian poet Vladimir Mayakovsky that focuses on what A. Bernard Stein describes in the *Chicago Tribune Book World* as "the *menage a trois* formed by Mayakovsky, Lili Brik, and her husband, Osip, and the salons, the literary wars, the polemics as to the relationship and obligations of art to society, the adventures and misadventures that roiled about them."

Just before the Russian revolution, Mayakovsky met and fell in love with the strong-willed Lili Brik who was married to literary critic and editor, Osip Brik. Soon the three formed a strong relationship that would last more than fifteen years; Mayakovsky would compose poetry, Osip would aid in the publication, the advertising, the arranging and organizing Mayakovsky's lectures and readings, and Lili would help print posters and distribute them. "The Charters describe, convincingly and with great sensitivity, the love story of Lili Brik and Mayakovsky, using well-chosen selections from Mayakovsky's poetry for emphasis," remarks J. S. Toomre in *Library Journal.* John Fludas explains in *Saturday Review* that Charters and her co-author/husband Samuel also recount the "tension between artistic freedom and political obedience in a seismic era, the last few czarist years and the early Soviet state, and they tell how a maverick Futurist poet came to be accepted even by the prosey Stalin."

BIOGRAPHICAL/CRITICAL SOURCES: Newsweek, April 2, 1973; *Choice,* July/August, 1973; *Library Journal,* May 1, 1979; *Saturday Review,* July 7, 1979; *New York Times Book Review,* July 15, 1979; *Time,* July 30, 1979; *Chicago Tribune Book World,* September 2, 1979; *New York Times,* September 6, 1979; *Times Literary Supplement,* November 23, 1979.

* * *

CHARTERS, Samuel (Barclay) 1929-

PERSONAL: Born August 1, 1929, in Pittsburgh, Pa.; son of Samuel and Lillian (Kelley) Charters; married Ann Danberg, March 14, 1959; children: Mallay, Nora Lili. *Education:* Sacramento City College, A.A., 1949; attended Tulane University, 1954; University of California, Berkeley, A.B., 1956.

CAREER: Ethnomusicologist, writer, and poet. Folkways Records, New York, N.Y., recording director, 1956-63; Prestige Records, Bergenfield, N.J., recording editor, beginning 1963. *Military service:* U.S. Army, 1951-53.

WRITINGS: Jazz: New Orleans, 1885-1957, W.C. Allen, 1958, revised edition, Oak Publications, 1963; *The Country Blues,* Rinehart, 1959, reprinted with new introduction, Da Capo Press, 1975; *Eight Poems in the Imagist Manner,* Tunnel Town Press, 1960; (with Leonard Kunstadt) *Jazz: A History of the New York Scene,* Doubleday, 1962; *The Poetry of the Blues,* Oak Publications, 1963; *Heroes of the Prize Ring* (poems), Portents, c.1964; *Looking for Michael McClure at the Corner of Haight and Ashbury,* privately printed, 1967; *Days; or, Days as Thoughts in a Season's Uncertainties* (poems), Oyez, 1967; *The Bluesmen: The Story and the Music of the Men Who Made the Blues,* Oak Publications, 1967; *Some Poems Against the War,* Portents, 1968; *To This Place,* Oyez, 1969.

As I Stand at this Window, Oyez, 1970; *Some Poems and Some Poets,* photographs by wife, Ann Charters, Oyez, 1971; (author of introduction) *Country Joe and the Fish: The Life, The Times, and the Songs,* Quick Fox, 1971; (editor) Larry Eigner, *Selected Poems,* Oyez, 1972; *From a Swedish Notebook,* Oyez, 1972; *From a London Notebook,* Portents, 1973; *In Lagos, Ereko Street, Nine p.m. 1976,* Oyez, 1976; *The Legacy of the Blues: The Art and Lives of Twelve Great Bluesmen,* Da Capo Press, 1977; *Sweet as the Showers of Rain,* Music Sales Corp., 1977; (with wife, Ann Charters) *I Love: The Story of Vladimir Mayakovsky and Lili Brik,* Farrar, Straus, 1979.

The Roots of the Blues: An African Search, Merrimack Book Service, 1980; *Of Those Who Died,* Oyez, 1980.

WORK IN PROGRESS: The Jug Band Book, for Holzman; *The Music of the Bahamas,* for Oak.

SIDELIGHTS: "[Samuel] Charters is . . . a storyteller, a scholar, a sensitive observer of folkways and folk wisdom," remarks Ben Reuven of the *Los Angeles Times.* Although Charters has written a number of other books (including several works of poetry), the majority of his literary endeavors concern the history, the life, and the makers of music, with the blues and jazz being a special interest. A reviewer for *Choice* states that in his opinion Charters is "one of the most prolific and important writers on the blues."

In his *The Roots of the Blues* Charters explores the influence of Africa and African music on American jazz. As Tony Russell points out in the *Times Literary Supplement:* "Traces have drawn Charters to the trail of the blues-singer and those characteristics of his music that might have come from a distantly remembered African background. The trail leads back to Gambia, source of many of the slaves who were brought to the southern states."

In preparation for this book, "Charters set off on a trek through West Africa, armed with notebook and tape recorder; he hoped to discover the African origins of a form of music we regard as purely American—the blues," Reuven explains. The critic calls *The Roots of the Blues* an "intoxicating experience, a rich blend of music and folklore and history that captures rhythms of life in exotic lands."

Charles Keil reports in the *New York Times Book Review* that Charters is "aware that the label 'blues' characterizes only a small portion of the larger African-American song, dance and narrative continua. [He] examines the social histories and ongoing social relations that generate these cultural manifestations, and [he] discovers much of interest."

But as Gordon Lutz observes in *Library Journal,* the music Charters looks for and finds in Africa "only vaguely resembles the American blues styles" and that the African "origins of the blues have been obscured by ages of overlying musical and cultural influences."

One of Charters' literary departures from the subject of music that received much critical attention is the biography he coauthored with his wife, Ann Charters, entitled *I Love: The Story of Vladimir Mayakovsky and Lili Brik.* Living and writing in Russia during an explosive and politically unstable period (which included the Russian Revolution of 1917), Vladimir Mayakovsky was a well-known poet who fell in love with the married Lili Brik. A. Bernard Stein explains in the *Chicago Tribune Book World* that this is the "biography of the *menage a trois* formed by Mayakovsky, Lili Brik, and her husband, Osip, and the salons, the literary wars, the polemics as to the relationship and obligations of art to society, the adventures and misadventures that roiled about them." (For more information on *I Love: The Story of Vladimir Mayakovsky and Lili Brik* see Ann Charters' sketch in this volume.)

Charters has done much of his research for his books on music in field, with documentary recording in the American South, British Isles, Mexico, and the Bahamas.

BIOGRAPHICAL/CRITICAL SOURCES: Poetry, July, 1968; *Library Journal,* May 1, 1979, January 1, 1981; *Saturday Review,* July 7, 1979; *Time,* July 30, 1979; *Chicago Tribune Book World,* September 2, 1979; *New York Times,* September 6, 1979; *Choice,* November, 1979, July/August, 1981; *Times Literary Supplement,* November 23, 1979, January 15, 1982; *Los Angeles Times,* August 8, 1982.†

* * *

CHASE, Ilka 1905-1978

PERSONAL: Born April 8, 1905, in New York, N.Y.; died February 15, 1978, in Mexico City, Mexico; daughter of Francis Dane Chase (a hotel manager) and Edna (an editor of *Vogue* magazine; maiden name, Allaway) Woolman Chase; married Louis Calhern (an actor), 1926 (divorced); married William B. Murray (a radio executive), July 13, 1935 (divorced); married Norton Sager Brown (a doctor), 1946. *Education:* Attended private schools in New York and France. *Residence:* Long Island, N.Y.; and Cuernavaca, Mexico.

CAREER: Actress and author. Appeared in more than twenty Broadway plays, including "The Women," 1936, and "Present Laughter," 1975, in motion pictures, including "Fast and Loose," 1930, and "Now Voyager," 1940, and on radio and television programs; host of radio interview program, "Penthouse Party" (formerly called "Luncheon at the Waldorf"), 1938-45, and "The Ilka Chase Show."

WRITINGS—Published by Doubleday, except as indicated; novels: *In Bed We Cry,* 1943, abridged edition, Avon, 1947; *I Love Miss Tilli Bean,* 1946; *New York 22: That District of the City which Lies between Fiftieth and Sixtieth Streets, Fifth Avenue, and the East River,* 1951, reprinted, Greenwood Press, 1971; *The Island Players,* 1956; *Three Men on the Left Hand,* 1960; *The Sounds of Home,* 1971; *Dear Intruder,* 1976.

Biographical: *Past Imperfect* (autobiography), 1942; *Free Admission* (autobiography), 1948; (with mother, Edna Woolman Chase) *Always in Vogue,* 1954.

Travel: *The Carthaginian Rose,* 1961; *Elephants Arrive at Half-Past Five,* 1963; *Second Spring and Two Potatoes,* 1965; *Fresh from the Laundry,* 1967; *The Varied Airs of Spring,* 1969; *Around the World and Other Places,* 1970; *Worlds Apart,* 1972.

Other: "In Bed We Cry" (play; adaptation of her novel of same title), first produced on Broadway at Belasco Theatre, November 14, 1944; *The Care and Feeding of Friends* (entertaining guide), 1973.

Author of syndicated weekly newspaper column.

SIDELIGHTS: Ilka Chase explained her ideas on writing to Roy Newquist in an interview appearing in *Counterpoint*. Chase commented: "The older I grow, the more I write, the more I strive for simplicity, clarity, and precision. However, I think anyone who is recounting something in a book—I'm speaking now of nonfiction—if you're relating something that's happened you're sometimes faced with a problem. I think as a matter of fact I spoke of it in *Past Imperfect* because that's when I was first confronted with it. Should you tell *exactly* what happened or should you make it interesting? Sometimes by a tiny omission, a wee addition, you can add a fillip and a flourish to what might in actuality have been on the drab side. It is in moments like these that an author and his conscience are alone in a quiet room wrestling it out to the ultimate throw."

BIOGRAPHICAL/CRITICAL SOURCES: Roy Newquist, *Counterpoint,* Rand McNally, 1964.

OBITURARIES: New York Times, February 16, 1978; *Washington Post,* February 16, 1978; *Newsweek,* February 27, 1978; *Time,* February 27, 1978.†

* * *

CHAVES, Jonathan 1943-

PERSONAL: Born June 8, 1943, in Brooklyn, N.Y.; son of Aaron David (a doctor) and Frieda (Perskey) Chaves; married Anna Caraveli (a Ph.D. candidate), November 27, 1974; children: Ian, Colin, Rachel. *Education:* Brooklyn College of the City University of New York, B.A., 1965; Columbia University, M.A., 1966, Ph.D., 1971. *Office:* Department of East Asian Languages and Literatures, George Washington University, Washington, D.C. 20052.

CAREER: Brooklyn College of the City University of New York, Brooklyn, N.Y., instructor, 1970-71, assistant professor of Chinese language and literature, 1971-73; State University of New York at Binghamton, assistant professor of classical Chinese language and literature, Chinese art, and Japanese literature, 1973-77; Cornell University, Ithaca, N.Y., visiting assistant professor, 1977-79; George Washington University, Washington, D.C., associate professor, 1979—. *Member:* Association for Asian Studies. *Awards, honors:* American Council of Learned Societies grant, summer, 1973, for study in Taiwan; Asian Literature Program grant from Asia Society, 1976; nominee in translation, National Book Award, 1979, for *Pilgrim of the Clouds: Poems and Essays from Ming Dynasty China by Yiian Hung-tao and His Brothers;* National Endowment for the Humanities grant, 1981-83, for new courses in Chinese literature.

WRITINGS: (Contributor) Tseng Yu-ho Ecke, editor, *Chinese Calligraphy,* Philadelphia Museum of Art, 1971; (contributor) Liu Wu-chi and Irving Yucheng Lo, editors, *Sunflower Splendor,* Indiana University Press, 1975; (translator and author of introduction) *Heaven My Blanket, Earth My Pillow: Poems from Sung Dynasty China by Yang Wanli,* Weatherhill, 1975; *Mei Yao-ch'en and the Development of Early Sung Poetry,* Columbia University Press, 1976; (translator) *Pilgrim of the Clouds: Poems and Essays from Ming Dynasty China by Yiian Hung-tao and His Brothers,* Wetherhill, 1978. Also author of poetry. Contributor of articles and translations to art and literature journals.

WORK IN PROGRESS: Studying Chinese poetry and poetic theory.

SIDELIGHTS: Jonathan Chaves has studied in India and Japan. His specialty is *Shih* poetry of the Sung dynasty. He is also interested in Japanese literature, and the "literatures of the primitive world."

* * *

CH'EN, Jerome 1921-

PERSONAL: Born October 2, 1921, in Chengtu, China; became British citizen; son of K'o-ta (an office clerk) and Hui-chih (Ma) Ch'en; married Mary B. Sheridan, 1968; children: Barbara, Rosemary. *Education:* Southwest Associated University, Kunming, China, B.A., 1943; Nankai Institute of Economics, M.A., 1945; University of London, Ph.D., 1956. *Office:* Department of History, York University, 4700 Keele St., Downsview, Toronto, Ontario, Canada M3J 1P3.

CAREER: University of Leeds, Leeds, England, senior lecturer in history, 1963-71; York University, Toronto, Ontario, professor of history, 1971—. Visiting lecturer, Australian National University, 1971; Centenary Visiting Professor, University of Adelaide, 1974. *Member:* Canadian Society for Asian Studies, Royal Society of Canada (fellow).

WRITINGS: (Translator from the Chinese with Michael Bullock) *Poems of Solitude,* Abelard, 1960, 2nd edition, Tuttle, 1970; *Yuan Shih-k'ai,* Stanford University Press, 1961, 2nd edition, 1972 (first edition published in England as *Yuan Shin-k'ai, 1859-1916: Brutus Assumes the Purple,* Allen & Unwin, 1961); (translator) *Mao and the Chinese Revolution* (with thirty-seven poems by Mao Tse-tung), Oxford University Press, 1967; (compiler) *Mao,* Prentice-Hall, 1969.

(Editor) *Mao Papers: Anthology and Bibliography,* Oxford University Press, 1970; (editor with Nicholas Tarling) *Studies in the Social History of China and Southeast Asia,* Cambridge University Press, 1970; *China and the West: Society and Culture, 1815-1937,* Hutchinson, 1979, Indiana University Press, 1980; *The Military-Gentry Coalition,* [Toronto], 1980; *State Economic Policies of the Ch'ing Government, 1840-1895,* Garland Publishing, 1980. Contributor of essays to *Twentieth Century, China Quarterly, T'oung Pao,* and other periodicals.

* * *

CHEN, Nai-Ruenn 1927-

PERSONAL: Born March 1, 1927, in Foochow, China; married Catherine Tien-pai Yang, July 1, 1961; children: Jerome, Tina. *Education:* National Taiwan University, B.A., 1950; University of Illinois, M.S., 1955, Ph.D., 1960. *Home:* 9615 Byeforde Rd., Kensington, Md. 20895. *Office:* Office of the People's Republic of China and Hong Kong, U.S. Department of Commerce, Washington D.C. 20230.

CAREER: University of Chicago, Chicago, Ill., economist in Laboratories for Applied Science, 1960-62; lecturer in economics at University of California, Berkeley, and research economist, Social Science Research Council Committee on the Economy of China, Berkeley, 1962-66; Cornell University, Ithaca, N.Y., assistant professor, 1966-69, associate professor of economics, 1969-73; U.S. Department of Commerce, Office of the People's Republic of China and Hong Kong, Washington D.C., international economist, 1973—.

WRITINGS: The Economy of Mainland China, 1949-1963: A Bibliography of Materials in English, Committee on the Economy of China, Social Science Research Council, 1963; *Chinese Economic Statistics,* Aldine, 1967; (with Walter Galenson) *The Chinese Economy under Communism,* Aldine, 1969; *China's*

Economy Post-Mao, Government Printing Office, 1978; *China's Economy and Foreign Trade, 1978-79,* Government Printing Office, 1979; *China's Economy and Foreign Trade, 1979-81,* Government Printing Office, 1981; *China under the Four Modernizations,* Government Printing Office, 1982.

Contributor: John P. Hardt, editor, *China: A Reassessment of the Economy,* Government Printing Office, 1975; Shao-Chuan Leng, editor, *Post-Mao China and United States-China Trade,* University Press of Virginia, 1977; C. M. Hou and T. S. Yu, editors, *Modern Chinese Economic History,* University of Washington Press, 1979; S. Kim, editor, *China in the Global Community,* Praeger, 1980.

WORK IN PROGRESS: Research on China's inflation.

* * *

CHESTER, Laura 1949-

PERSONAL: Born April 13, 1949, in Cambridge, Mass.; daughter of George Miller (a lawyer) and Margaret (Sheftall) Chester; married Geoffrey M. Young (a writer and editor), August 28, 1969; children: Clovis Chester Young, Ayler Chester Young. *Education:* Attended Skidmore College, 1967-69; University of New Mexico, B.A., 1972. *Home:* 2016 Cedar, Berkeley, Calif. 94709.

CAREER: Stooge (magazine), Albuquerque, N.M., co-editor, 1969-74; The Figures (small press), Berkeley, Calif., co-editor, 1975—. *Awards, honors:* Steloff Poetry Prize from Skidmore College, 1969; Kappa Alpha Theta poetry award from University of New Mexico, 1970.

WRITINGS—Poetry, with occasional journal entries and other prose: *Tiny Talk,* Roundhouse, 1972; (with husband, Geoffrey M. Young) *The All Night Salt Lick,* Tribal Press, 1972; (editor with Sharon Barba) *Rising Tides: Twentieth Century American Women Poets,* Simon & Schuster, 1973; *Nightlatch,* Tribal Press, 1974; *Primagravida,* Christopher Books, 1975; (editor with Barba) *Proud and Ashamed,* Christopher Books, 1977; *Chunk Off and Float,* Cold Mountain, 1978; *Watermark,* Figures, 1978. Also author of *My Pleasure,* Figures. Contributor of more than a hundred articles and poems to literary magazines. Co-editor of *Best Friends.*

WORK IN PROGRESS: We Heart; Lupus Notes.

SIDELIGHTS: Laura Chester told *CA:* "Being a bride of the sixties, I was influenced by feminism, and yet my writing has never been one of statement. Though I've worked from an intimate perspective, where the intuitive is a formative force, I've also wanted my writing to have a life of its own, word for word's sake, beyond gender, personal history, or explanation.

"My writing often feels similar to the semi-conscious linking of the twilight reverie, what we go to sleep on, the prickling of memory, of audial and surface phenomenon, each unit moving on, yet all held together, as mixed motion in time, like the day in the life of any nurturer. A peopled poetry, an inclusive poetry, taking us beyond the isolation of 'I' familiar to poetic vision.

"I've always understood that a poem, or any piece of writing, has something of its own life, its own force, but now I see that it can also become part of a greater upward or downward spiral. I do not want to limit myself to the perpendicular of intellectualism, nor the squiggles of siren stuff, but I do want to be receptive to the unpredictable curve, letting a wholeness come through me, thought, word and feeling inseparable, inspiration firmly linked to the craft-work of shaping. Writing for me has got to be grand."

* * *

CHODES, John 1939-

PERSONAL: Born February 23, 1939, in New York, N.Y.; son of Ralph Jay (an editor) and Henrietta (Jonas) Chodes. *Education:* Hunter College of the City University of New York, B.A., 1963; Germain School of Photography, commercial photography certificate, 1965. *Politics:* Free Libertarian Party. *Religion:* Jewish. *Agent:* Charles Ryweck, 67-48 212nd St., Bayside, N.Y. 11364; and David Gordon Productions, 405 Strand, London WC2, England. *Home and office:* 411 East 10th St., New York, N.Y. 10009.

CAREER: Full-time writer, 1965-67; *Business Week* (magazine), New York City, sales promotion copywriter, 1967-70; *Forbes* (magazine), New York City, sales promotion copywriter, 1970-71; *Fortune* (magazine), New York City, sales promotion copywriter, 1971-72; *New York Times,* New York City, sales promotion copywriter, 1972-75; *Cue* (periodical), New York City, sales promotion copywriter, 1976-77; freelance writer and playwright, 1977—. Technical advisor to "Marathon Man," Paramount, 1975. Past New York State communications director, Free Libertarian Party. *Awards, honors:* Journalistic Excellence Award, Road Runners Club of America, 1975, for *Corbitt.*

WRITINGS: "Avenue A Anthology" (play), first produced in New York at Federal Theatre, 1967; *The Myth of America's Military Power,* Branden Press, 1972; *Corbitt* (biography), Tafnews, 1974; *Bruce Jenner* (biography for young adults), Grosset, 1976; "Molineaux" (play), first produced in New York at Playwrights' Horizons, 1979.

WORK IN PROGRESS: A biography of Frederick II (1194-1250), in play form.

SIDELIGHTS: John Chodes told *CA:* "'Molineaux' was a play about a famous nineteenth-century sports figure who had been a slave. Tom Molineaux killed himself because he did not like being free. I wrote about him because I believe most of hate being free." Critic John Corry of the *New York Times* states, "In 'Molineaux,' John Chodes has heaped cliches, historic and otherwise, high atop one another, and somehow has written an interesting play." Apart from the play's biographical elements, Corry adds, "'Molineaux' is also about race, the lure of the big time and illusory freedom."

About some of his other works, Chodes also told *CA:* "*Corbitt* was a biography of a friend who converted me into a marathon runner and had a tremendous influence on my life. In *The Myth of America's Military Power,* I tried to show that our excessive reliance on sophisticated military hardware, air power, and all the other hugely expensive devices of twentieth-century war, have had no effect whatever on our various enemies."

BIOGRAPHICAL/CRITICAL SOURCES: New York Times, July 28, 1979.

* * *

CHURCHMAN, C(harles) West 1913-

PERSONAL: Born August 29, 1913, in Philadelphia, Pa.; son of Clarke Wharton and Norah (Fassitt) Churchman; married Gloria King, September 27, 1950; children: Daniel. *Education:*

University of Pennsylvania, A.B., 1935, M.A., 1936, Ph.D., 1938. *Address:* P.O. Box 553, Bolinas, Calif. 94924. *Office:* Department of Business Administration, University of California, Berkeley, Calif.

CAREER: University of Pennsylvania, Philadelphia, instructor in philosophy, 1937-42; U.S. Ordnance Laboratory, Frankfort Arsenal, head of mathematics section, 1942-45; University of Pennsylvania, assistant professor of philosophy and head of department, 1945-48; Wayne University (now Wayne State University), Detroit, Mich., associate professor of philosophy, 1948-51; Case Institute of Technology (now Case Western Reserve University), Cleveland, Ohio, professor of engineering administration, 1951-58; University of California, Berkeley, visiting professor, 1957-58, professor of business administration, 1958—. Adjunct professor, Wharton School of Finance and Commerce, University of Pennsylvania, 1971. Co-founder, Institute for Experimental Method, Philadelphia, 1945-48; director of research, System Development Corp., 1962-63. Fellow, Western Behavioral Sciences Institute, 1981. *Member:* American Association for the Advancement of Science (fellow), Philosophy of Science Association, American Philosophical Association, Institute of Management Sciences (president, 1962), American Statistical Association (fellow). *Awards, honors:* Dr. Sci. from Washington University, 1974.

WRITINGS: Elements of Logic and Formal Science, Lippincott, 1940; (editor with R. L. Ackoff and M. Wax) *Measurement of Consumer Interest,* University of Pennsylvania Press, 1947; *Theory of Experimental Inference,* Macmillan, 1948; (with Ackoff) *Methods of Inquiry: An Introduction to Philosophy and Scientific Theory,* Educational Publishers, 1950; (with Ackoff and E. L. Arnoff) *Introduction to Operations Research,* Wiley, 1957; (editor with P. Ratoosh) *Measurement: Definitions and Theories,* Wiley, 1959.

Prediction and Optimal Decision, Prentice-Hall, 1961; *Challenge to Reason,* McGraw, 1968; *The Systems Approach,* Delacorte, 1968, 2nd edition, 1979; *Design of Inquiring Systems,* Basic Books, 1972; (with L. Auerbach and S. Sadan) *Thinking for Decisions,* Scientific Research Associates, 1975; *The Systems Approach and Its Enemies,* Basic Books, 1979.

Thought and Wisdom, Intersystems Publications, 1982. Contributor to *Management Science* and *Operations Research.* Editor of *Philosophy of Science,* 1948-57, and *Management Science,* 1954-60.

WORK IN PROGRESS: Natural Resource Administration: Introducing a New Methodology for Management Development; Statistics.

* * *

CLARK, David Ridgley 1920-

PERSONAL: Born September 17, 1920, in Seymour, Conn.; son of Ridgley Colfax (a superintendent of schools) and Idella May (Hill) Clark; married Mary Adele Matthieu, July 10, 1948; children: Rosalind Elizabeth, John Bradford, Matthew Ridgley, Mary Frances. *Education:* Wesleyan University, Middletown, Conn., B.A., 1947; Yale University, M.A., 1950, Ph.D., 1955; also studied at Reed College, 1940-41, Indiana University, 1948-50, and Kenyon School of English, 1949. *Politics:* Citizens' Party. *Religion:* Society of Friends. *Home:* 330 Market Hill Rd., Amherst, Mass. 01002. *Office:* Department of English, University of Massachusetts, Amherst, Mass. 01003.

CAREER: Instructor in English at Mohawk College, Utica, N.Y., 1947, and University of Massachusetts, Amherst, 1951-56; Smith College, Northampton, Mass., lecturer in English, 1956-57; University of Massachusetts, Amherst, assistant professor, 1958, associate professor, 1958-65, professor of English, 1965—, chairman of department, 1975-76. Fulbright Lecturer at University of Iceland, Reykjavik, 1960-61, and University College, Dublin, Ireland, 1965-66; lecturer at Yeats International Summer School, Ireland, 1960; visiting associate professor, University of Michigan, summer, 1966; visiting professor at Syracuse University, 1968, University of Victoria, 1971-72, 1975, and 1977, Sir George Williams University, 1972, and State University of New York at Stoneybrook, 1977; visiting fellow, University of Cambridge, 1978. *Wartime service:* Civilian Public Service as conscientious objector. *Member:* American Committee for Irish Studies, Canadian Association for Irish Studies.

AWARDS, HONORS: Bollingen Foundation fellowship, 1957, 1961, 1962, 1963; Eugene Saxton and American Philosophical Society fellowships, 1957 and 1976; American Council of Learned Societies grant-in-aid, 1958, 1965, 1977, and 1981; Modern Language Association of America grant, 1958; National Endowment for the Humanities grant, 1969 and 1978.

WRITINGS: (With Stanley Koehler, Leon Barron, and Robert Tucker) *A Curious Quire* (poems), University of Massachusetts Press, 1962; *W. B. Yeats and the Theatre of Desolate Reality,* Dufour, 1965; (editor with Robin Skelton) *Irish Renaissance,* Dolmen Press (Dublin), 1965; *Dry Tree* (poems), Dolmen Press, 1965; (with Fred B. Millett and Arthur W. Hoffman) *Reading Poetry,* Harper, 1968.

John Millington Synge, Riders to the Sea, Merrill, 1970; *Studies in the Bridge,* Merrill, 1970; (editor) *Twentieth Century Interpretations of Murder in the Cathedral,* Prentice-Hall, 1971; (with George R. Mayhew) *A Tower of Polished Black Stones,* Dolmen Press, 1971; (with Mayhew and Michael J. Sidnell) *Druid Craft: The Writing of the Shadowy Waters,* University of Massachusetts Press, 1971; *Lyric Resonance,* University of Massachusetts Press, 1972.

That Black Day, Dolmen Press, 1980; (editor) *Critical Essays on Hart Crane,* G. K. Hall, 1982; *Yeats at Songs and Choruses,* University of Massachusetts Press, 1982. Poetry has appeared in *Kenyon Review, Poetry, Folio, Voices, Transatlantic Review, Dublin Magazine,* and other publications; contributor of more than thirty articles to literary journals. Contributing editor, *Massachusetts Review;* member of editorial board, *Cornell Yeats.*

WORK IN PROGRESS: Studies in the manuscripts of William Butler Yeats; editing *The Complete Plays* volume of *The Collected Edition of the Works of W. B. Yeats,* for Macmillan.

* * *

CLARK, Eric 1911-

PERSONAL: Born June 22, 1911, in Belfast, Ulster, Northern Ireland; married Margaret Thompson McKee, August 4, 1947; children: Robin, Hilary. *Education:* Larkfield College, D.L.T.C., 1947; Queens University of Belfast, Dip. Ed., 1960. *Home:* Thornleigh House, Kincora Ave., Belfast BT4 3DW, Northern Ireland.

CAREER: Galleon Press, Belfast, Northern Ireland, managing editor, 1949—. Contemporary painter, whose work has been exhibited in Europe and in the Indies. *Military service:* British Army, Royal Corps of Signals, 1940-46; received Burma Star. *Member:* British Society of Commerce (fellow), P.E.N., Ulster Academy.

WRITINGS—Published by Galleon Press, except as indicated: *Morse,* 1941; *Ulster Quizbook,* three volumes, 1944-48; *Ulster Soccer Quiz,* 1947; (editor) *Greenwood Anthology* (poems), Muller, 1950; *Sleeves Up,* 1950; *Stark Passage,* 1950; *Don a Green Battledress,* 1951; *Laugh with Ulster,* 1955; *The Troopship Was Bound for Bombay,* 1958.

Learning to Paint, 1965; *Everybody's Guide to Survival,* Collins, 1969; *Corps Diplomatique,* Allen Lane, 1973, published as *Diplomat: The World of International Diplomacy,* Taplinger, 1974; *Black Gambit,* Morrow, 1978; *The Sleeper,* Hodder & Stoughton, 1979, Atheneum, 1980.

Send in the Lions, Atheneum, 1981. Also author of television scripts for British Broadcasting Corp. and other television services. Contributor of articles and poems to journals and newspapers. Editor, *Ulster Weekend.*

WORK IN PROGRESS: Jungle Adventures and *Burma Green,* both war stories; *Water Color Experiments; Art for Art's Sake;* and poems.†

* * *

CLARKE, Brenda (Margaret Lilian) 1926-
(Brenda Honeyman)

PERSONAL: Born July 30, 1926, in Bristol, England; daughter of Edward (an insurance agent) and Lilian Rose (Brown) Honeyman; married Ronald John Clarke (a civil servant), March 5, 1955; children: Roger Stephen, Gwithian Margaret. *Education:* Cambridge University, school certificate, 1942. *Politics:* Socialist. *Religion:* Methodist. *Home:* 25 Torridge Rd., Keynsham, Bristol, Avon BS18 1QQ, England. *Agent:* David Grossman Literary Agency Ltd., 12-13 Henrietta St., Covent Garden, London WC2E 8LH, England.

CAREER: British Civil Service, Ministry of Labour, Bristol, England, clerical officer, 1942-55; writer, 1968—. Section leader for British Red Cross, 1941-45. *Member:* Society of Authors, Wessex Writers' Association.

WRITINGS: The Glass Island, Collins, 1978; *The Lofty Banners,* Fawcett, 1979; *The Far Morning,* Fawcett, 1982; *All through the Day,* Hamlyn Paperbacks, 1983.

Under name Brenda Honeyman; published by R. Hale, except as indicated: *Richard by Grace of God,* 1968; *The Kingmaker,* 1969; *Richmond and Elizabeth,* 1970, Pinnacle, 1973; *Harry the King,* 1971, published as *The Warrior King,* Pinnacle, 1972; *Brother Bedford,* 1972; *Good Duke Humphrey,* 1973; *The King's Minions,* 1974; *The Queen and Mortimer,* 1974; *Edward the Warrior,* 1975; *All the King's Sons,* 1976; *The Golden Griffin,* 1976; *At the King's Court,* 1977; *A King's Tale,* 1977; *Macbeth, King of Scots,* 1977; *Emma, the Queen,* 1978; *Harold of the English,* 1979.

SIDELIGHTS: Brenda Clarke told *CA:* "Acquiring an agent changed the course of my writing career. Instead of 'factional' novels about the Middle Ages and Saxon England, [my agent] persuaded me to turn my attention to romantic fiction." *Avocational interests:* Theatre, reading, history, music.

* * *

CLARKE, Robin Harwood 1937-

PERSONAL: Born October 19, 1937, in Bedford, England; son of Leonard Harwood (a schoolmaster) and Dorothy (Hawkins) Clarke; married Janine Hill (an actress), February 8, 1962. *Education:* Cambridge University, B.A. (with honors), 1960. *Home:* Criftin House, Wenthor, Near Bishops Castle, Shropshire, England.

CAREER: Encyclopaedia Britannica, London, England, scientific subeditor, 1960-61; *Discovery,* London, assistant editor, 1961-63, editor, 1963-64; *Science Journal,* London, editor, 1964-69. Science writer and broadcaster, British Broadcasting Corp., Overseas Service. *Member:* Association of British Science Writers (secretary).

WRITINGS: The Diversity of Man, Roy, 1964; (editor) Germaine and Arthur Beiser, *Story of Cosmic Rays,* Phoenix House, 1964; *We All Fall Down: The Prospect of Biological and Chemical Warfare,* Allen Lane, 1968, Penguin, 1969; *The Silent Weapons: The Realities of Chemical and Biological Warefare,* McKay, 1968.

The Great Experiment: Science and Technology in the Second United Nations Development Decade, United Nations, 1971; *The Science of War and Peace,* J. Cape, 1971, McGraw, 1972; (with Geoffrey Hirdley) *The Challenge of the Primitives,* McGraw, 1975; (editor) *Notes for the Future: An Alternative History of the Past Decade* (anthology), Thames & Hudson, 1975, Universe Books, 1976; *Technological Self-Sufficiency,* Faber & Faber, 1976; *Building for Self-Sufficiency: Tools, Materials, Building, Heat, Insulation, Solar Energy, Wind Power, Water and Plumbing, Waste and Compost, Methane, Transport, Food,* Universe Books, 1977. Contributor of articles to periodicals, including *Listener, Daily Telegraph Magazine, New Scientist,* and *Elizabethan.* Editor, "World of Science Library Series."

SIDELIGHTS: We All Fall Down has been translated into Spanish, French, and German.†

* * *

CLINTON, Rupert
See BULMER, (Henry) Kenneth

* * *

CLOUD, Patricia
See STROTHER, Pat Wallace

* * *

CLUTTERBUCK, Richard 1917-
(Richard Jocelyn)

PERSONAL: Born November 22, 1917, in London, England; son of Lewis St. John Rawlinson (a colonel in the British Army) and Isabella (Jocelyn) Clutterbuck; married Angela Barford, May 15, 1948; children: Peter, Robin, Julian. *Education:* Cambridge University, M.A. (mechanical sciences), 1939; attended British Army Staff College, 1948, Imperial Defence College, 1965, and University of Singapore, 1966-68; University of London, Ph.D. (politics), 1971. *Office:* Department of Politics, University of Exeter, Exeter, England.

CAREER: British Army, officer, 1937-72, became Engineer-in-Chief of the Army, with rank of major general; served in more than fifteen countries around the world, including France, Belgium, Ethiopia, Egypt, Algeria, Palestine, Malaya, and the United States; University of Exeter, Exeter, England, reader in political conflict, 1972-83. Member of General Advisory Council of the British Broadcasting Corp., 1975-81. *Member:* Institute of Civil Engineers (London; fellow).

AWARDS, HONORS—Literary: George Knight Clowes Prize of *Army Quarterly,* 1954; Bertrand Stewart Prize of Ministry of Defence; Toulmin Medal of Society of American Military Engineers, 1963. Military: Officer of Order of the British Empire, 1958, for services in Malaya; Companion of the Order of the Bath, 1972, for services as Engineer-in-Chief of the Army.

WRITINGS: (Under pseudonym Richard Jocelyn) *Across the River,* Constable, 1957; *The Long, Long War,* Praeger, 1966.

Riot and Revolution in Singapore and Malaya, 1945-1963, Faber, 1973; *Protest and the Urban Guerrilla,* Cassell, 1973, Abelard, 1974; *Living with Terrorism,* Faber, 1975; (contributor) Anthony Deane-Drummond, editor, *Riot Control,* Royal United Services Institute for Defence Studies, 1975; *Guerrillas and Terrorists,* Faber, 1977, Ohio University Press, 1980; *Kidnap and Ransom,* Faber, 1978; *Britain in Agony: The Growth of Political Violence,* Faber, 1978, Penguin, 1980; (contributor) Jennifer Shaw and others, editors, *Ten Years of Terrorism,* Royal United Services Institute for Defence Studies, 1979.

The Media and Political Violence, Macmillan, 1981; (contributor) Paul Wilkinson, editor, *British Perspectives on Terrorism,* Allen & Unwin, 1981; (contributor) David Watt, editor, *The Constitution of Northern Ireland,* Heinemann, 1981.

Also author of play, "A Means to an End," broadcast by Radio Malaya, 1958. Contributor of more than sixty articles to British and American periodicals.

WORK IN PROGRESS: Research for two books, tentatively entitled *The British Disease and the Microelectronic Revolution* and *Conflict and Violence in Singapore and Malaya, 1945-1982.*

SIDELIGHTS: Described by Laurie Taylor in the London *Times* as a "soldier turned expert in political violence turned academic," Richard Clutterbuck has written several books on terrorism and political violence. A thirty-five-year veteran of the British Army, he has experienced and researched the various forms of urban violence in modern societies. Although John Deedy believes that Clutterbuck's "views are strongly Union Jack . . . and occasionally arbitrary," the critic adds in his *New Republic* review of *Protest and the Urban Guerrilla* that Clutterbuck's "conclusions about Ireland are inescapable." Reviewing the same book, a critic for *Choice* remarks: "Clutterbuck writes as a committed and sensible member of the liberal-democratic camp and his book is both a useful corrective to the writings of the revolutionaries and a warning to democrats everywhere."

In two of his recent books, *The Media and Political Violence* and *Britain in Agony: The Growth of Political Violence,* Clutterbuck explores the influence of the media, particularly television, on political violence. In a *Times Literary Supplement* review of *The Media and Political Violence,* Paul Johnson writes that Clutterbuck "demonstrates, pretty convincingly I think, that certain groups in our society do have an interest in promoting hostility . . . and that television . . . makes it much easier for them to accomplish their object. . . . [This] book shows that television, and especially the BBC, is far more likely to fall for . . . propaganda than the press." Taylor comments that Clutterbuck's "argument is that political violence in Britain between 1971 and 1977 reached its highest peak since 1911 [and] that television and the press did much to arouse antagonism to those who were said to have perpetrated it." Johnson concludes, however, that in "light of Clutterbuck's own evidence, the media are only one of the various factors which tend to stimulate or aggravate violence, trade-union extremists and fringe political groups being rather more important."

AVOCATIONAL INTERESTS: Canoeing at sea (led a canoe party of twenty-four soldiers across the English Channel to France in 1960).

BIOGRAPHICAL/CRITICAL SOURCES: New Republic, November 2, 1974; *Choice,* May, 1975; London *Times,* March 1, 1980; *Times Literary Supplement,* July 31, 1981.

* * *

CLYMER, Eleanor 1906-
(Janet Bell, Elizabeth Kinsey)

PERSONAL: Born January 7, 1906, in New York, N.Y.; daughter of Eugene (an engineer) and Rose (Fourman) Lowenton; married Kinsey Clymer (a former newspaperman and social worker), 1933; children: Adam. *Education:* Attended Barnard College, 1923-25; University of Wisconsin, B.A., 1928; additional study at Bank Street College of Education and New York University. *Home:* 11 Nightingale Rd., Katonah, N.Y. 10536.

CAREER: During early 1930's, worked for a publisher and a social work agency, and taught young children; writer of children's books, 1943—. *Member:* Authors Guild (former chairman of children's book committee), Wilderness Society, Native American Rights Fund.

AWARDS, HONORS: Zyra Lourie Book Award, Woodward School, 1968, for *My Brother Stevie;* Juvenile Literature Award, Border Regional Library Association, Texas, 1971, for *The Spider, the Cave and the Pottery Bowl;* Children's Book Award, Child Study Association of America, 1975, for *Luke Was There;* Sequoyah Award, Oklahoma Library Association, for *The Get-Away Car.*

WRITINGS: A Yard for John (Junior Literary Guild selection), Dodd, 1943; *Here Comes Pete* (Junior Literary Guild selection), Dodd, 1944; *The Grocery Mouse* (Junior Literary Guild selection), Dodd, 1945; *Little Bear Island,* Dodd, 1945; *The Country Kittens,* Dodd, 1947; *The Trolley Car Family,* McKay, 1947; *The Latch-Key Club,* McKay, 1949.

Treasure at First Base, Dodd, 1950; *Tommy's Wonderful Airplane,* Dodd, 1951; *Thirty-Three Bunn Street,* Dodd, 1952; *Make Way for Water,* Messner, 1953; (with Lilliam Gilbreth) *Management in the Home* (adult book), Dodd, 1954; *Chester,* Dodd, 1955; *Not Too Small After All,* F. Watts, 1955; *Sociable Toby,* F. Watts, 1956; (with Lillian Erlich) *Modern American Career Women,* Dodd, 1959.

Mr. Piper's Bus, Dodd, 1961; *The Case of the Missing Link,* Basic Books, 1962, revised edition, 1968; *Benjamin in the Woods,* Grosset, 1962; *Now That You Are Seven* (part of six-book series), Association Press, in cooperation with Child Study Association of America, 1963; *Search for a Living Fossil: The Story of the Coelacanth,* Holt, 1963 (published in England as *Search for a Fossil,* Lutterworth, 1965); *Harry, the Wild West Horse,* Atheneum, 1963; (with Ralph C. Preston) *Communities at Work* (textbook), Heath, 1964; *The Tiny Little House,* Atheneum, 1964; *Chipmunk in the Forest,* Atheneum, 1965; *The Adventure of Walter,* Atheneum, 1965; *Wheels: A Book to Begin On,* Holt, 1965; *My Brother Stevie,* Holt, 1967; *The Big Pile of Dirt,* Holt, 1968; *Horatio,* Atheneum, 1968; *The Second Greatest Invention: Search for the First Farmers,* Holt, 1969;

Belinda's New Spring Hat (Junior Literary Guild selection), F. Watts, 1969.

We Lived in the Almont, Dutton, 1970; *The House on the Mountain,* Dutton, 1971; *The Spider, the Cave and the Pottery Bowl,* Atheneum, 1971; *Me and the Eggman,* Dutton, 1972; *How I Went Shopping and What I Got,* Holt, 1972; *Santiago's Silver Mine,* Atheneum, 1973; *Luke Was There,* Holt, 1973; *Leave Horatio Alone,* Atheneum, 1974; *Take Tarts as Tarts Is Passing,* Dutton, 1974; *Engine Number Seven,* Holt, 1975; *Hamburgers—and Ice Cream for Dessert,* Dutton, 1975; *Horatio's Birthday,* Atheneum, 1976; *Horatio Goes to the Country,* Atheneum, 1978; *The Get-Away Car,* Dutton, 1978.

Horatio Solves a Mystery, Atheneum, 1980; *A Search for Two Bad Mice,* Atheneum, 1982; *My Mother Is the Smartest Woman in the World,* Atheneum, 1982.

Under pseudonym Janet Bell: *Monday-Tuesday-Wednesday Book,* McBride, 1946; *Sunday in the Park,* McBride, 1946.

Under pseudonym Elizabeth Kinsey: *Teddy,* McBride, 1946; *Patch,* McBride, 1946; *Sea View Secret,* F. Watts, 1952; *Donny and Company,* F. Watts, 1953; *This Cat Came to Stay!,* F. Watts, 1955.

WORK IN PROGRESS: Books on the American Southwest, Ireland, Nova Scotia, the Indians of the Northeast, and autobiographical fiction.

SIDELIGHTS: Eleanor Clymer writes: "At New York University, I studied story writing, but it wasn't till I was married and had a child that I discovered my real interest: children's books. I had worked with children at camps and settlement houses, telling stories and writing about children. Then I went to Bank Street College and studied with Lucy Sprague Mitchell, who was revolutionizing children's literature. She urged her students not to keep repeating time-worn fairy stories but to listen to the children themselves, watch their play, and find out what made sense to them, in other words to be guided by their interests and capacities. Since then I have written realistic fiction for the most part, based on the interests of the children I knew—baseball, airplanes, photography, pets, and so on. I have also written non-fiction dealing with my earlier interest in science: archaeology, anthropology, and biology.

"About ten years ago I began to feel I had things I really wanted to say, but I hadn't settled on a way to say them. That was when I wrote *My Brother Stevie*. In that book I tried to write what a real child, living in the inner city, might have said in her own words if she had been telling the unvarnished truth about her life. The book had some sad parts, but it had some funny parts, too, because life is like that—sad and funny. After that, I wrote a number of books about children in the city, based on my recollections of city life. By that time we had moved to a country village, where I found a very different environment. I have taken part in local activities and have also traveled a good deal. Both of these things gave me material for books about places other than New York City. Some are serious, but others, like *The Get-Away Car,* were written just for fun. *My Mother Is the Smartest Woman in the World* is about local grassroots politics because I think children need to know how exciting and important politics can be.

"My feelings about books for children is that even the lightest and simplest must have something to say, because when one writes for children one is telling them something about the world."

MEDIA ADAPTATIONS: Luke Was There was adapted for a film.

CLYNE, Terence
See BLATTY, William Peter

* * *

COCCIOLI, Carlo 1920-

PERSONAL: Born May 15, 1920, in Leghorn, Italy; son of Attilio and Anna (Duranti) Coccioli. *Education:* University of Naples and University of Rome, D.Sc. *Religion:* Roman Catholic. *Address:* Apartado Postal 27.529, Mexico City 7 D.F., Mexico.

CAREER: Author, primarily of novels, 1946—. *Military service:* Italian Army, officer; employed by Allied Forces in Psychological Warfare Branch, 1944-45; received Medaglia d'Argento al V.M. (star medal) for activities in anti-fascist Resistance. *Awards, honors:* Charles Veillon Prize, 1950, for *Il Giuoco;* Selezione Campiello Prize and Basilicata Prize, both 1976, for *Memoires du Roi David;* Scanno Prize, 1978, for *Fabrizio Lupo;* Grand Prix du Rayonnement de la Langue Francaise, 1982.

WRITINGS: Il Migliore e l'Ultimo (novel), Vallecchi, 1946; *La Difficile speranza,* La Voce, 1947; *La Piccola Valle di Dio* (novel), Vallecchi, 1948, translation by Campbell Nairne published as *The Little Valley of God,* Heineman, 1956, Simon & Schuster, 1957.

Il cielo e la terra, Vallecchi, 1950, reprinted, Rusconi, 1977, translation by Frances Frenaye published as *Heaven and Earth,* Prentice-Hall, 1952; *Il Giuoco* (novel), Garzanti, 1950; *Le Bal des egares* (novel), Flammarion, 1951; *Fabrizio Lupo* (novel), Table Ronde (Paris), 1952, reprinted, Rusconi, 1978, translation by Bernard Frechtman published as *The Eye and the Heart,* Heinemann, 1960, published as *Fabrizio's Book,* Shorecrest, 1966; *L'Immagine e le stagioni* (novel), Vallecchi, 1954; *La Ville et le sang* (novel), Flammarion, 1955, translation by Mary McLean published as *Daughter of the Town,* Heinemann, 1957; *Manuel le Mexicain* (novel), Plon, 1956, translation by Hans Koningsberger published as *Manuel, the Mexican,* Simon & Schuster, 1958; *Journal,* Table Ronde, 1957; *Le Caillou blanc* (novel), Plon, 1958, translation by Elizabeth Sutherland and Vera Bleuer published as *The White Stone,* Simon & Schuster, 1960; *Un Suicide* (novel), Flammarion, 1959; *Florence que j'aime,* Editions Sun (Paris), 1959, translation published as *The Florence I Love,* Tudor, 1960.

Ambroise (novel), Flammarion, 1961; *Soleil* (novel), Plon, 1961; *Omeyotl: Diario messicano,* Vallecchi, 1962; *L'Aigle Azteque est tombe* (novel), Plon, 1964; *L'erede di Montezuma,* Vallecchi, 1964; *Le corde dell'arpa* (novel), Longanesi, 1967.

Documento 127, Club degli autori, 1970; *Le tourment de Dieu,* Fayard, 1971; *Hommes en fuite: la grande aventure des Alcooliques Anonymes,* Fayard, 1972; *Memoires du Roi David,* Table Ronde, 1976; *Requiem per un cane,* Rusconi, 1977.

Le case del lago (novel), Rusconi, 1980; *La casa di Tacubaya,* Editorial Nuova, 1982. Also author of plays, "Los Fanaticos," "La Colline de la Lune," and "El Esperado." Author of column for *Excelsior* (Mexico City). Regular contributor to Italian periodicals.

* * *

COHEN, Warren I. 1934-

PERSONAL: Born June 20, 1934, in Brooklyn, N.Y.; son of

Murray and Fay (Phillips) Cohen; married Janice Prichard, June 22, 1957; children: Geoffrey Scott, Anne Leslie. *Education:* Columbia University, A.B., 1955; Fletcher School of Law and Diplomacy, A.M., 1956; University of Washington, Seattle, Ph.D., 1962. *Home:* 1233 Tanager Lane, East Lansing, Mich. 48823.

CAREER: University of California, Riverside, lecturer in history, 1962-63; Michigan State University, East Lansing, assistant professor, 1963-67, associate professor, 1967-71, professor of history, 1971—, director of Asian Studies Center, 1979—. Visiting professor, National Taiwan University, Taipei, 1964-66; Fulbright lecturer, Tokyo, 1969-70. Foreign policy consultant. *Military service:* U.S. Navy, 1956-59; became lieutenant.

WRITINGS: (Editor) *Intervention, 1917: Why America Fought,* Heath, 1966; *The American Revisionists,* University of Chicago Press, 1967; *America's Response to China,* Wiley, 1971, 2nd edition, 1980; *The Chinese Connection,* Columbia University Press, 1978; *Dean Rusk,* Cooper Square, 1980; (editor) *New Frontiers in American-East Asian Relations,* Columbia University Press, 1983. Contributor of articles and reviews to *Journal of Asian Studies, Orbis, Journal of American History,* and other history and political science journals. Editor, *Diplomatic History,* 1979-82.

WORK IN PROGRESS: With wife Janice P. Cohen, *East Asian Art and American Culture.*

* * *

COLE, Jackson
See SCHISGALL, Oscar

* * *

COLEMAN, William V(incent) 1932-

PERSONAL: Born January 27, 1932, in Waterbury, Conn.; son of William V. and Ethel (Brennan) Coleman; married Patricia Register (a writer), November 27, 1975. *Education:* Saint Bernard College, Rochester, N.Y., B.A., 1953; Saint Bernard's Seminary, B.D., 1955, M.Div., 1957; Fairfield University, M.A., 1965; Florida State University, Ph.D., 1976. *Office:* 22 Willow St., Mystic, Conn. 06355.

CAREER: Writer. Ordained Roman Catholic priest, 1957; Catholic Diocese of Savannah, Ga., rector of St. John's Seminary, 1958-68, director of education, 1968-74; left priesthood, 1974; Growth Associates, Mystic, Conn., president, 1975—. *Member:* American Education Association, National Association for the Advancement of Colored People, National Association of Public Continuing Adult Education.

WRITINGS—Published by Twenty-Third Publications, except as indicated: (With Patricia McLemore) *Personal Morality* (monograph), 1974; *Mine Is the Morning,* twenty volumes, 1974-77; *God Believes in Me,* five volumes, Ave Maria Press, 1975; *The Way of the Cross,* 1975; *Finding a Way to Follow: Values for Today's Christian,* Morehouse, 1977.

All with wife, Patricia R. Coleman; published by Twenty-Third Publications, except as indicated: *Confirmed to Courage,* 1976; *The Saints: Heroes to Follow,* 1976; *Daybreak,* ten volumes, 1976-77; *The Church,* 1977; *God's Own Child,* 1977; *Jesus, Our Brother,* 1977; *Rediscovering Lent,* 1977; *Morality,* 1977; *Parish Youth Ministry,* 1977; *Renewing Your Family's Covenant,* 1978; *Planning Tomorrow's Parish,* 1978; *Only Love Can Make It Easy,* two volumes, 1979; *Together with Jesus,* eight volumes, 1979; *Together in Prayer,* eight volumes, 1979; *A Time for Comfort and Hope,* 1979; *Catholic Prayers and Devotions,* 1979; *Make Friends with God,* Growth Associates, 1980; *A Confirmation Journal,* 1980; *A Junior High Prayerbook,* 1980; *Awakening to Jesus,* 1981; *Sex Today,* Growth Associates, 1981; *The Youth Ministry Handbook,* Growth Associates, 1981; *Prayer Talk,* Ave Maria Press, 1982; *The Mass Today,* Growth Associates, 1982; *No-Pain Learning,* Growth Associates, 1982; *You, Your Life and Jesus,* Growth Associates, 1982; *Confirm: Renew,* two volumes, Growth Associates, 1982; *Be Reconciled,* Growth Associates, 1982.

Also author of scripts for numerous filmstrips produced by Twenty-Third Publications and over fifty cassette tapes produced by Twenty-Third Publications, National Catholic Reporter, and Growth Associates. Author of column, "Update," published in *Today's Parish.* Publisher of *Southern Cross, Catholic Youth Ministry, Parish Communication,* and *Synthesis.*

SIDELIGHTS: William V. Coleman told *CA* that he is "in the process of opening a retreat center in Weston, Vt. called 'The Mustard Seed' where Patty and I will give retreats and conferences including some on writing." Coleman continues: "I am searching for language in which to communicate religious truth. This springs from the conviction that the traditional language no longer means what it did. I am also convinced that mere reading without some interaction with other people leads the ordinary person into shallow, usually useless knowledge."

* * *

COLLINS, Clark
See REYNOLDS, Dallas McCord

* * *

CONQUEST, (George) Robert (Acworth) 1917-
(J. E. M. Arden, Ted Pauker)

PERSONAL: Born July 15, 1917, in Great Malvern, England; son of Robert Folger W. and Rosamund A. (Acworth) Conquest; married Joan Watkins, 1942 (divorced, 1948); married Tatiana Mihailova, 1948 (divorced, 1962); married Caroleen Macfarlane, April 4, 1964; married Elizabeth Neese, 1979; children: (first marriage) John Christopher Arden, Richard Charles Pleasanton. *Education:* Attended University of Grenoble, 1935-36; Magdalen College, Oxford, B.A., 1939, M.A., 1972. *Home:* 52 Peter Coults Cir., Stanford, Calif. 94305.

CAREER: Writer. H. M. Foreign Service, 1946-56, served in Sofia, Bulgaria, as first secretary, was member of United Kingdom delegation to United Nations; London School of Economics and Political Science, London, England, research fellow, 1956-58; University of Buffalo (now State University of New York at Buffalo), Buffalo, N.Y., lecturer in English, 1959-60; Columbia University, New York, N.Y., senior fellow, 1964-65; Woodrow Wilson International Center for Scholars, Smithsonian Institution, Washington, D.C., fellow, 1976-77; Hoover Institution, Stanford, Calif., senior research fellow, 1977-79; distinguished visiting scholar, Heritage Foundation, Washington, D.C., 1980-81; Hoover Institution, senior research fellow and scholar curator of Russian and East European collection, 1981; Harvard University, Ukrainian Research Institute, Cambridge, Mass., research associate, 1981—. *Military service:* Oxfordshire and Buckinghamshire Light Infantry, 1939-46. *Member:* Science Fiction Writers of America, Royal

Society of Literature (fellow), Society for the Advancement of Roman Studies, British Interplanetary Society, Travellers Club. *Awards, honors:* P.E.N. prize, 1945, for poem "For the Death of a Poet"; Festival of Britain verse prize, 1951; Officer, Order of British Empire, 1955.

WRITINGS: A World of Difference (novel), Ward, Lock, 1955, new edition, Ballantine, 1964; *Poems,* St. Martins, 1955; (under pseudonym J. E. M. Arden) *Where Do Marxists Go from Here?,* Phoenix House, 1958; *Common Sense about Russia,* Macmillan, 1960; *Soviet Deportation of Nationalities,* St. Martins, 1960, revised edition published as *The Nation Killers: The Soviet Deportation of Nationalities,* Macmillan, 1970; *Power and Policy in the U.S.S.R.: The Study of Soviet Dynastics,* Macmillan, 1961, St. Martins, 1962, published as *Power and Policy in the U.S.S.R.: The Struggle for Stalin's Succession, 1945-60,* Harper, 1967; *Courage of Genius: The Pasternak Affair,* Collins, 1961, published as *The Pasternak Affair: Courage of Genius,* Lippincott, 1962, reprinted, Octagon Books, 1979; *Between Mars and Venus* (poems), St. Martins, 1962; *The Last Empire,* Ampersand Books, 1962; *The Future of Communism,* Today Publications, 1963; *The Soviet Succession Problems,* 1964; *Marxism Today,* Ampersand Books, 1964; *Russia after Khrushchev,* Praeger, 1965; (with Kingsley Amis) *The Egyptologists* (novel), J. Cape, 1965, Random House, 1966.

The Great Terror: Stalin's Purge of the Thirties, Macmillan, 1968, revised edition, Macmillan, 1973; *Arias from a Love Opera, and Other Poems,* Macmillan, 1969; *Where Marx Went Wrong,* T. Stacey, 1970; *V. I. Lenin,* Viking, 1972; (translator from the Russian) Aleksandr Isaevich Solzhenitsyn, *Prussian Nights: A Narrative Poem,* Collins, Harvill Press, 1978; *Kolyma: The Arctic Death Camps,* Viking Press, 1978; *Forays* (poems), Chatto, 1979; *The Abomination of Moab* (collection of essays), M. T. Smith, 1979; *Present Danger—Towards a Foreign Policy: Guide to the Era of Soviet Aggression,* Hoover Institution Press, 1979; *We and They: Civic and Despotic Cultures,* M. T. Smith, 1980.

Editor: (With others) *New Poems: A P.E.N. Anthology,* Transatlantic, 1953; *New Lines: An Anthology,* Macmillan (London), 1956, St. Martins, 1957; *Back to Life: Poems from behind the Iron Curtain,* Hutchinson, 1958, St. Martins, 1960; *New Lines, 2,* Macmillan (London), 1963; (and author of introduction) Petr Ionovich Iakir, *A Childhood in Prison,* Macmillan (London), 1972; (and author of introduction) *The Robert Sheckley Omnibus,* Gollancz, 1973; (and author of introduction) Tibor Szamuely, *The Russian Tradition,* Secker & Warburg, 1974.

Editor with Kingsley Amis: *Spectrum: A Science Fiction Anthology* (annual), Volume I, Gollancz, 1961, Harcourt, 1962, Volume II, Gollancz, 1962, Harcourt, 1963, Volume III, Gollancz, 1963, Harcourt, 1964, published as *Spectrum: A Third Science Fiction Anthology,* Berkley Publishing, 1965, Volume IV, Harcourt, 1965, Volume V, Gollancz, 1966, Harcourt, 1967.

Editor of "Soviet Studies" series, seven volumes, published by Praeger: *Industrial Workers in the U.S.S.R.,* 1967; *Soviet Nationalities Policy in Practice,* 1967; *The Politics of Ideas in the U.S.S.R.,* 1967; *Religion in the U.S.S.R.,* 1968; *The Soviet Police System,* 1968; *The Soviet Political System,* 1968; *Justice and the Legal System in the U.S.S.R.,* 1968; *Agricultural Workers in the U.S.S.R.,* 1968.

Literary editor, *Spectator,* 1962-63; editor, *Soviet Analyst,* 1971-73.

WORK IN PROGRESS: N.K.V.D.—Politics of Political Police, 1936-1939; The Peasant Genocide; A Greater Union; Tyrants and Typewriters.

SIDELIGHTS: Although he is also a poet and a novelist, Robert Conquest is most widely known as a specialist on Russian political and cultural affairs. In his numerous volumes dealing with the U.S.S.R., Conquest attempts to illuminate for Western readers various events in recent Russian history with particular emphasis on the dictatorship of Soviet leader Joseph Stalin.

Conquest's books have received positive reviews from critics, who note in particular the exhaustive research that precedes the actual writing of each volume. In his *Nation* review of *The Pasternak Affair,* Conquest's study of the events surrounding Russian novelist's Boris Leonidovich Pasternak's publication of *Dr. Zhivago,* Sidney Monas calls Conquest's book an "intelligent, terse, well-documented summary which recapitulates everything of importance." A *Times Literary Supplement* reviewer refers to the same important documentation apparent in *The Nation Killers,* which deals with Stalin's deportation of whole nations of people from their homelands to Siberian exile during World War II. The critic states that the book "will be recognized as a distinguished work of scholarship. . . . The scale and thoroughness of research which have gone to produce this . . . comparatively slim volume could easily be underestimated. . . . Although the grim story is clearly still not complete, it is difficult to imagine that Mr. Conquest has overlooked any significant detail."

One of Conquest's most widely praised books is *The Great Terror: Stalin's Purge of the Thirties,* the author's survey of the nearly twenty million deaths caused by Stalin during one four-year period. According to Alexander Gerschenkron in the *New York Review of Books,* "It is an immense and splendid effort in research. Based on a painstaking scrutiny of the available material, it offers a comprehensive, skillfully organized critical summary of that material." John Gross presents a similar view in his *New Statesman* review. The work, he writes, is "impressive in its narrative sweep, its meticulous scholarship and the clarity with which Mr. Conquest has organised and presented an immense mass of highly complex material." Perhaps the highest praise comes from an *Economist* reviewer who calls *The Great Terror* "a masterpiece in historical detection."

Combining his interest in the U.S.S.R. with his love of poetry, Conquest has edited a volume of poems from Russia and several Eastern European countries, *Back to Life: Poems from behind the Iron Curtain.* It was another collection of poems, *New Lines,* which originally made Conquest known among literary circles. This collection, edited by Conquest, contains the work of nine British poets of the early 1950s, including Kingsley Amis and John Wain, who were recognized by Conquest as having common themes and techniques. According to a *Poetry* review, this group came to be known as the "Movement" and represented "a reaction against the excesses of the 1940's."

BIOGRAPHICAL/CRITICAL SOURCES: Times Literary Supplement, September 30, 1955, July 13, 1956, January 9, 1959, June 10, 1960, June 9, 1961, December 1, 1961, December 14, 1962, September 2, 1965, October 3, 1968, August 7, 1969, September 4, 1970, May 12, 1978; *Spectator,* July 20, 1956, June 3, 1960, May 4, 1962; *Poetry,* November, 1957, December, 1960; *New Statesman,* December 20, 1958, May 21, 1960, June 9, 1961; November 24, 1961, May 27, 1968; *Guardian,* November 17, 1961; *San Francisco Chronicle,* June 24, 1962; *Nation,* August 11, 1962, September 28, 1969; *Yale Review,* October, 1962; *Saturday Review,* October 13, 1962,

May 8, 1965, November 9, 1968; *New York Times Book Review,* April 4, 1965, October 27, 1968, June 18, 1978; *New York Review of Books,* August 5, 1965, June 19, 1969; *American Political Science Review,* September, 1965; *Economist,* October 19, 1968; *National Review,* May 4, 1971; *New York Times,* May 26, 1978.

* * *

CONROY, Michael R(alph) 1945-

PERSONAL: Born April 20, 1945, in Gallipolis, Ohio; son of Joseph Ralph (a deputy sheriff in Dallas, Tex.) and Fayma Beatrice (a secretary; maiden name Cowan) Conroy; married Jerrie Lee Payne (a journalist), September 6, 1969 (divorced December 4, 1973); children: Janie Faye. *Education:* Attended South Texas Junior College, 1966, Corpus Christi Junior College, 1969, Los Angeles Valley College, 1970, and Lee College, 1973; Sam Houston State University, B.B.A., 1980. *Politics:* Non-partisan. *Religion:* Baptist. *Home:* 18110 East 4th St., Tulsa, Okla. 74108.

CAREER: Owner of Contract Drafting Service, beginning 1969, Mike Conroy & Associates, Architects and Engineers, beginning 1970, and Mike Conroy Drafting Service, beginning 1970, all Houston, Tex.; author. *Military service:* U.S. Marine Corps., 1963-69; served in South Vietnam; received Vietnam Service Medal with one star, Purple Heart with star, Vietnamese Cross of Gallantry with device. *Member:* Veterans of Foreign Wars.

WRITINGS—All published by Yellow Jacket, except as indicated: *Truong Oi Mai,* Mandala Press, 1968; *The Green Ghosts of Vietnam,* 1974; *Mission at San y Sydro,* 1975; *Crusaders,* 1975; *Bong Sai,* 1976; *Susurrations,* 1976; *Fourth Down and Bedroom to Go,* 1976; *Knight Flight!,* 1977; *Summon the Brave,* 1980; *The Phrenetic,* 1981.

WORK IN PROGRESS: Khe Sahn Stands; Death in Hue; Tham Biet Tri; Operation Taylor Common; People's Soldier; Canvasback; The Girl He Left Behind; The Isle of Palms; The Priapist.

AVOCATIONAL INTERESTS: Distance-running, boxing, photography, theatre (designs sets).

BIOGRAPHICAL/CRITICAL SOURCES: Houston Post, November 1, 1970.

* * *

COOK, Melva Janice 1919-

PERSONAL: Born August 1, 1919, in Texas; daughter of Ancel and Irene (Frazier) Cook. *Education:* North Texas State University, B.S., 1940; additional study at Southwestern Baptist Theological Seminary. *Home:* 2802 Valley Rd., Nashville, Tenn. 37215. *Office:* 127 Ninth Ave. N., Nashville, Tenn. 37234.

CAREER: Director of children's work, Baptist Convention of Texas, 1950-54; First Baptist Church, Muskogee, Okla., director of children's work, 1954-56; Baptist Sunday School Board, Nashville, Tenn., editorial coordinator, program consultant in family ministry, 1975—.

WRITINGS—Published by Broadman, except as indicated: *I Know God Loves Me,* 1960; *Christmas at Kyle's House,* 1964; *The Thinking Book,* 1966; (with A. V. Washburn) *Administering the Bible Teaching Program of a Church,* Convention Press, 1969; (with Joseph W. Hinkle) *How to Minister to Families in Your Church,* 1978; *Thirty Plus and Single,* Convention Press, 1979; (with Richard Brown) *The Special Occasion Cook Book for Home and Church,* 1983; *Cassie's Busy Day,* in press. Also author of *Bible Teaching for Fours and Fives,* published by Convention Press. Editor, "Beginner Lesson Courses," Baptist Sunday School Board, 1957-64.

* * *

COOKE, (Alfred) Alistair 1908-

PERSONAL: Born November 20, 1908, in Manchester, England; came to United States in 1937, naturalized in 1941; son of Samuel (a Wesleyan preacher) and Mary Elizabeth (Byrne) Cooke; married Ruth Emerson, August 24, 1934 (divorced); married Jane White Hawkes, April 30, 1946; children: (first marriage) John Byrne; (second marriage) Susan Byrne. *Education:* Jesus College, Cambridge, B.A. (summa cum laude), 1930, diploma in education, 1931; graduate study at Yale University, 1932-33, and Harvard University, 1933-34. *Home:* Nassau Point, Cutchogue, Long Island, N.Y. 11935; and 1150 Fifth Ave., New York, N.Y. 10028.

CAREER: British Broadcasting Corp. (BBC), London, England, film critic, 1934-37, commentator on American affairs, 1938—, broadcaster of "Letters from America," 1946—. London correspondent for National Broadcasting Co., 1936-37; special correspondent for *London Times,* 1938-40; American feature writer for *London Daily Herald,* 1941-43; *Manchester Guardian* (now *Guardian*), United Nations correspondent, 1945-48, chief U.S. correspondent, 1948-72. Master of ceremonies for Ford Foundation weekly television series on National Broadcasting Corp., Columbia Broadcasting Corp., and American Broadcasting Corp. networks, "Omnibus," 1952-61; host for United Nations television series, "International Zone," 1961-67, and for Public Broadcasting Services television series "Masterpiece Theatre," 1971—; writer and narrator of television series "America: A Personal History of the United States," 1972-73. *Member:* National Press Club (Washington, D.C.), Athenaeum Club (London), Royal and Ancient Golf Club (St. Andrews).

AWARDS, HONORS: Commonwealth Fund fellow, 1932-33, and 1933-34; Peabody Award for International News Reporting, 1952; National Academy of Television Arts and Sciences Emmy awards, 1958, for "Omnibus" and, 1973, for "America"; LL.D. from University of Edinburgh, 1969, and University of Manchester, 1973; Benjamin Franklin medal of the Royal Society of Arts, 1973; Knight Commander, Order of the British Empire, 1973; Litt.D. from University of St. Andrews, 1975.

WRITINGS: (Compiler and editor) *Garbo and the Night Watchmen: A Selection from the Writings of British and American Film Critics,* J. Cape, 1937, new edition, Secker & Warburg, 1971, published as *Garbo and the Night Watchmen: A Selection Made in 1937 from the Writings of British and American Film Critics,* McGraw-Hill, 1971; *Douglas Fairbanks: The Making of a Screen Character,* Museum of Modern Art, 1940.

A Generation on Trial: U.S.A. v. Alger Hiss, Knopf, 1950, 2nd edition, 1952, enlarged 2nd edition, Penguin, 1968; (contributor) John Gehlmann, editor, *Challenge of Ideas,* Odyssey, 1950; *Letters from America* (adapted from "Letters from America" radio series), Hart-Davis, 1951, published as *One Man's America,* Knopf, 1952; *Christmas Eve* (short stories), Knopf, 1952; *A Commencement Address,* Knopf, 1954; (compiler) *Vintage Mencken,* Vintage, 1955; *Around the World in*

Fifty Years: A Political Travelogue, limited edition, Field Enterprises Educational Corp., 1966; *Talk about America* (adapted from "Letters from America" radio series), Knopf, 1968.

(Author of introduction) *General Eisenhower on the Military Churchill: A Conversation with Alistair Cooke,* edited by James Nelson, Norton, 1970; *Alistair Cooke's America,* Knopf, 1973; *Six Men,* Knopf, 1977; *The Americans: Fifty Talks on Our Life and Times* (adapted from "Letters from America" radio series; Literary Guild alternate selection), Knopf, 1979, published in England as *The Americans: Letters from America on Our Life and Times,* Penguin, 1980; (author of introduction) Richard Kenin, *Return to Albion: Americans in England, 1760-1940,* Holt, 1979; (author of text) Robert Cameron, *Above London: Photographs,* Bodley Head, 1980; *Masterpieces: A Decade of Masterpiece Theatre,* Knopf, 1981. Contributor to periodicals, including *Theatre Arts Monthly, New Republic, Encore, Fortnightly Review, Spectator,* and *New Yorker.*

SIDELIGHTS: Commenting on Alistair Cooke in the *New York Times Book Review,* James Reston writes, "Reading him is like spending the evening with him: you may have heard it all before, but never told with such grace and sparkle." Reston praises Cooke's distinctive narrative style, cultivated during the author's long career as a radio commentator for the British Broadcasting Corp. Although Cooke is a broadcaster and a journalist (for nearly a quarter-century he served as U.S. correspondent for the British newspaper *Guardian*), the basis for his popularity is a role that encompasses both these professions: his role of interpreter. Cooke is not, however, a traditional interpreter who translates one language to another; instead he is one whose "duties require him to explain to the Old World the behavior of the Americans," according to John Skow in the *New York Times.* In this, his self-appointed role of interpreter, Cooke has achieved his biggest success and, as William Noble states in a *Pittsburgh Press* article, "for . . . years he has made a . . . living interpreting America for the British."

Fulfilling his "duties," the British-born U.S. citizen has performed a variety of tasks—filing newspaper reports about U.S. events for *Guardian* readers, writing the commentaries making up his weekly, 15-minute B.B.C. broadcast "Letters from America," and introducing British television programs to American audiences as host of National Educational Television's "Masterpiece Theater"—but, however varied the task, Cooke is always involved with explaining one side of the Atlantic to the other. Reviewing Cooke's interpretive work, many critics hold the opinion voiced by Katherine Winton Evans in the *Washington Post Book World,* "You couldn't ask for a more civilized, fair-minded fellow to explain us to the outside world—and maybe to ourselves."

Cooke first came to the United States in 1932 on a Commonwealth Fund fellowship. Although the purpose of his visit was to study drama at Yale University, he soon abandoned his formal theatrical investigations. Wanting originally to be a theater director, Cooke had helped found the Cambridge University Mummers (the first university dramatic society admitting women as members) during his college years and had spent part of his time in the United States on his fellowship doing research in drama. According to Michiko Kakutani's account in the *New York Times,* Cooke thus recalls this period in his life, "My interest in the theater began to wane . . . as I discovered that the continental United States itself was much more dramatic than anything on Broadway." In a *Parade* interview with George Michaelson, Cooke explains the impact of this first look at the land that would become his home. He remarks: "That trip was an absolute eye-opener for me. . . . Even then, even in the Depression, there was a tremendous energy and vitality to America. The landscape and the people were far more gripping and dramatic than anything I had ever seen. It truly changed me."

This change in thinking that Cooke noticed on his first trip to America eventually led to a career change for him at the British Broadcasting Corp. From his position as film critic, he became full-time observer of the American scene. Cooke came to be, writes J. W. Savage in the *Chicago Tribune Magazine,* "a sort of human trans-oceanic bridge between the United States and the rest of the world." Cooke's new focus of interest is also evident in his writings. His first books—*Garbo and the Night Watchmen* and *Douglas Fairbanks,* for example—reflect his early interest in the performing arts. His later books—*Alistair Cooke's America* and the three volumes of *One Man's America, Talk about America,* and *The Americans,* for example—are collections of radio and television essays in which Cooke gives his personal views on his adopted home and its citizens.

Savage points out that originally the idea of talking about the United States on radio seemed unlikely even to the future broadcaster. According to the critic, Cooke's first reaction upon hearing of the idea was astonishment. "What would I talk about?," he wondered. The B.B.C. executive who suggested the program reminded Cooke of the stories about America that the journalist constantly told his friends. The executive believed that these items of interest—merely topics of conversation to Cooke—would hold the attention of the B.B.C.'s listeners, and so he scheduled the show to run for thirteen weeks. The talk show first broadcast in March, 1946, has been heard weekly ever since.

In a *New York Times Book Review* article Moira Hodgson remarks: "It is a mammoth task to explain America to foreigners, particularly to those who have never been here. Alistair Cooke has been telling the British about the Americans with enormous success for over forty years. His weekly radio program for the British Broadcasting Corporation, 'Letters from America,' has run longer than any other in history." And, Savage notes, the program is listed in *The Guinness Book of World Records* as the longest-running talk show in the world. Only heard in the United States on shortwave radios, "Letters from America" boasts listeners in countries all over the world, including Ethiopia, Australia, Israel, Germany, India, and Central America.

"Although [he] occasionally consults his 3,000-book library," notes Kakutani, "and frequently picks up ideas from newspapers, Mr. Cooke maintains that he never thinks out a talk in advance. He simply allows his 'unconscious to talk to the typewriter.'" Cooke explains: "This is the proper psychological condition for composing a talk. . . . We do not go out to dinner with a little agenda in our pockets of what the evening's conversation is to be about." Cooke's method of writing these talks, according to Anatole Broyard of the *New York Times,* is as casual as his speaking manner. The critic observes: "Once a week . . . [Cooke] sits down at his typewriter and improvises. He writes on whatever comes to his mind, a couple of thousand words, the equivalent of thirteen and a half minutes of broadcasting. The talk is then taped, sent to London and relayed all over the world."

"Letters from America" has maintained through the years a steady and enthusiastic listening audience as well as a complement of critics who continue to praise Cooke's abilities as a writer. Many reviewers particularly comment on Cooke's conversational approach to broadcasting, the same approach that James Reston and other critics find in Cooke's books. Commenting on talks from the radio program, for example, Winton Evans writes: "Alistair Cooke's talks . . . are like the best of after-dinner conversation—agreeable rambling, informative and evanescent." Barry Siegel of the *Los Angeles Times Book Review* similarly notes, "These talks are at all times literate, charming, and informative"; and, Benny Green, in *Spectator,* calls Cooke's "Letters," "those deceptively relaxed broadcasting masterpieces."

Cooke's radio program became the basis for the author's first book of personal glimpses of America, *One Man's America.* Again, a skeptical note was sounded when the idea was first mentioned, but this time the skepticism came not from Cooke, but from his publisher, Alfred A. Knopf. Although Cooke's better-known books are collections of essays, he was originally warned against this type of book by Knopf. In an interview with Judy Klemesrud of the *New York Times Book Review,* Cooke recalls, "He warned me that books of pieces never sold very well." However, Cooke went on to publish the manuscript, which subsequently became a best-seller. Over twenty years later, Cooke became a millionaire due to the popular success of *Alistair Cooke's America*—another book of "pieces" (based on his television series "America: A Personal History"). This volume sold more than two million copies in the United States and England. Published in 1973, the profusely illustrated volume was still on the best-seller list in mid-1974. Cooke's third book of talks adapted from his radio program, *The Americans,* made the best-seller list too, with more than 80,000 hard-cover copies in print.

Even those reviewers of *The Americans* who are critical of the volume's spoken tone—Winton Evans, for example, calls Cooke's work "better said than read"—praise Cooke's work in general. As Evans points out, Cooke "warns us from the outset [in the book's introduction] that these 'talks' were written to be spoken, not read." Joy Gerville-Reache comments in the *Christian Science Monitor:* "Cooke is an extraordinarily gifted commentator. . . . His tributes [in *The Americans*] to famous Americans . . . are penetrating, instructive, and compassionate. . . . The conversational style [, however,] is not always so successful in print as it is on the radio. But it is a tribute to the skill of the author that each letter is woven into a consistent and well-founded whole." And Hodgson notes: "In these letters Mr. Cooke looks at the Americans with the eye of a stern but kindly headmaster addressing a recalcitrant schoolboy. . . . He emerges as a witty, urbane man with a remarkable knowledge of history. . . . [However] the talks in *The Americans* were meant to be heard, not read. And indeed, the suddenness and order of the ideas suggest speaking, not writing."

From a different perspective, Green states: "Thousands of other professional broadcasters have . . . attempted the adjustment of the spoken into the written word, without the slightest success, a fact which suggests that Cooke is as unique as the hippogriff [a legendary animal having the foreparts of a griffin and the body of a horse]. He is, in fact, one of the most gifted and urbane essayists of the century, a supreme master of that form of literary work. . . . The book [is] . . . the most readable, informative and engaging collection of essays on literate subjects to be published this year."

Although *Alistair Cooke's America* received similar praise, some reviewers find Cooke's interpretations of American history to be lacking in substance. A *Times Literary Supplement* reviewer, for instance, notes: "The structure of his narrative has been preserved and the intonations of a familiar voice will be audible to many a reader. . . . [The book] is grandiose in intent but deficient in substance. . . . It is difficult to conceive what understanding . . . a reader [with little knowledge of U.S. history] will possess of such crises [as the Revolution and the Civil War] after digesting Mr. Cooke's descriptions; it will certainly be only partial and almost certainly confused." And J. B. Priestly in *Books & Bookmen* comments: "What [the book's] author has undertaken to do, he does very well. Any reservations I may have will be concerned not with what has gone into the book but what has been left out." In a similar vein, John Skow writes in a *Time* review: "The author's knowledge and his generosity of spirit are evident throughout. Still, a complaint must be made. Obviously Cooke assumes that his readers have no solid grasp of U.S. history. In this he is certainly correct. His solution, though, is to cover the whole subject in a chalk-talk. . . . [However,] what Cooke does include is very good indeed. He is not simply an urbane purveyor of condensed data, but a reporter, with a gift for getting down on paper the human content of what he sees."

Noting the difficulties of being an interpretive reporter, Cooke writes in *The Americans:* "A foreign correspondent is both an interpreter and a victim of his subject matter. He must be aware of his own changing view of the country he's assigned to." In order to help retain a foreigner's perspective on U.S. events, Cooke periodically returns to England. These visits, however, may be unnecessary. Bearing in mind George Bernard Shaw's observation that England and America are two countries separated by the same language, Cooke tells Kakutani: "I find life congenial in both England and America. After all these years here, I'm bilingual."

AVOCATIONAL INTERESTS: Golf, photography, playing the piano, listening to jazz recordings, motion pictures, beachcombing, the American West, travel, chess.

BIOGRAPHICAL/CRITICAL SOURCES: New York Times, September 24, 1950, November 14, 1979; *New Republic,* September 25, 1950; *New York Herald Tribune Book Review,* October 1, 1950; *San Francisco Chronicle,* October 8, 1950; *Nation,* November 4, 1950; *Saturday Reveiw of Literature,* November 18, 1950; *New Yorker,* December 23, 1950, October 28, 1968; *New York Herald Tribune,* April 20, 1952; *Washington Post,* November 28, 1968; *New York Times Book Review,* December 8, 1968, September 25, 1977, November 11, 1979, January 27, 1980.

Newsweek, November 27, 1972, September 19, 1977; *Pittsburgh Post,* March 25, 1973; *Christian Science Monitor,* April 26, 1973, October 5, 1977, November 14, 1979; *New York Post,* November 6, 1973; *Times Literary Supplement,* November 30, 1973, March 18, 1982; *Time,* December 3, 1973; *Atlantic,* January, 1974; *National Review,* March 1, 1974; *Parade,* March 3, 1974; *Books & Bookmen,* April, 1974, May, 1974; *Authors in the News,* Volume I, Gale, 1976; *Chicago Tribune Magazine,* July 1, 1979; *Spectator,* November 10, 1979; *Washington Post Book World,* December 23, 1979; *Detroit News,* January 20, 1980; *Los Angeles Times Book Review,* February 3, 1980.

—Sketch by Marian Walters

* * *

COOKE, Bernard J. 1922-

PERSONAL: Born May 31, 1922, in Norway, Mich.; son of

John Michael (a dentist) and Eleanor (Crevier) Cooke. *Education:* St. Louis University, A.B., 1944, M.A., 1946; St. Mary's College, St. Mary's, Kan., S.T.L., 1953; Institut Catholique de Paris, S.T.D., 1956.

CAREER: Entered Society of Jesus (Jesuits), 1939, ordained Roman Catholic priest, 1952, requested release from order, 1970; Marquette University, Milwaukee, Wis., professor and chairman of department of theology, 1958-70; University of Windsor, Windsor, Ontario, professor of religious studies, 1970-76; University of Calgary, Calgary, Alberta, professor of religious studies, beginning 1976. Resident fellow, Yale Divinity School, 1969-70; visiting professor of theology, University of Santa Clara, 1973-74. Member of board of directors of National Liturgical Conference. Consultant to North Central Association of Colleges and Secondary Schools. *Military service:* U.S. Army, auxiliary chaplain, 1954-56.

MEMBER: Religious Education Association (national board of directors, 1963—), Society for the Scientific Study of Religion, Academy of Religion and Mental Health, Catholic Theological Society, Catholic Biblical Society of America, Society of Catholic College Teachers of Sacred Doctrine (president, 1960-62). *Awards, honors:* D.Litt., University of Detroit, 1968.

WRITINGS: Christian Sacraments and Christian Personality, Holt, 1965; *Formation of Faith,* Loyola University Press, 1965; *The Challenge of Vatican II,* Argus, 1966; *Christian Involvement,* Argus, 1966; *New Dimensions in Catholic Life,* Dimension Books, 1968; *The God of Space and Time,* Holt, 1969; *The Eucharist: Mystery of a Friendship,* G. A. Pflaum, 1969; *Beyond Trinity,* Marquette University Press, 1969.

Christian Community: Response to Reality, Holt, 1970; *Theology in an Age of Revolution,* Dimension, 1971; *Rethinking Your Faith,* Claretian, 1972; *Ministry to Word and Sacraments: History and Theology,* Fortress, 1976.

Contributor: R. Pelton, editor, *The Church as the Body of Christ,* University of Notre Dame Press, 1963; Hofinger and Stone, editors, *Pastoral Catechetics,* Herder, 1964; R. Ryan, editor, *Contemporary New Testament Studies,* Liturgical Press, 1965; Keller and Armstrong, editors, *Apostolic Renewal in the Seminary,* Christopher, 1965; Albert Schlitzer, editor, *The Spirit and Power of Christian Secularity,* University of Notre Dame Press, 1969; James Michael Lee and Patrick C. Rooney, editors, *Toward a Future for Religious Education,* Pflaum Press, 1970. Contributor to religion and theology journals.

WORK IN PROGRESS: Research and preliminary work on books on the theology of priesthood, on imagination, and on American culture.†

* * *

COOKSON, Catherine (McMullen) 1906- (Catherine McMullen; Catherine Marchant, a pseudonym)

PERSONAL: Born June 20, 1906, in Tyne Dock, South Shields, England; mother's name, Catherine Fawcett; married Thomas H. Cookson (a schoolmaster), June 1, 1940. *Home:* Bristol Lodge, Langley on Tyne, Northumberland. *Agent:* Anthony Sheil Associates Ltd., 2-3 Morwell St., London WC1B 3AR, England.

CAREER: Writer. Lecturer for women's groups and other organizations. *Member:* Society of Authors, P.E.N. (England), Authors Guild (U.S.A.), Women's Press Club (London). *Awards, honors:* Winifred Holtby Award for Best Regional Novel, Royal Society of Literature, 1968, for *The Round Tower;* recipient of Freedom of the County Borough of South Shields in recognition of her services to the city.

WRITINGS: Kate Hannigan, Macdonald & Co., 1950, reprinted, Macdonald & Jane's, 1979; *Fifteen Streets* (also see below), Macdonald & Co., 1952, reprinted, Corgi Books, 1979; *Colour Blind,* Macdonald & Co., 1953, reprinted, Macdonald & Jane's, 1975, published as *Color Blind,* New American Library, 1977; *Maggie Rowan,* Macdonald & Co., 1954, New American Library, 1975; *Rooney,* Macdonald & Co., 1957, reprinted, Macdonald & Jane's, 1974; *The Menagerie,* Macdonald & Co., 1958, reprinted, Macdonald & Jane's, 1974; *Slinky Jane,* Macdonald & Co., 1959, reprinted, Macdonald & Jane's, 1979.

Fenwick Houses, Macdonald & Co., 1960, reprinted, Macdonald & Jane's, 1979; *The Garment,* Macdonald & Co., 1962, New American Library, 1974; *The Blind Miller* (also see below), 1963, reprinted, Heinemann, 1979; *Hannah Massey,* Macdonald & Co., 1964, New American Library, 1973; *The Long Corridor,* Macdonald & Co., 1965, New American Library, 1976; *The Unbaited Trap,* Macdonald & Co., 1966, New American Library, 1974; *Katie Mulholland,* Macdonald & Co., 1967, reprinted, Macdonald & Jane's, 1980; *The Round Tower* (also see below), Macdonald & Co., 1968, New American Library, 1975; *The Nice Bloke,* Macdonald & Co., 1969, published as *The Husband,* New American Library, 1976; *Our Kate: An Autobiography,* Macdonald & Co., 1969, Bobbs-Merrill, 1971, published as *Our Kate: Catherine Cookson, Her Personal Story,* Macdonald & Jane's, 1974.

The Glass Virgin, Macdonald & Co., 1970, Bantam, 1981; *The Invitation,* Macdonald & Co., 1970, New American Library, 1974; *The Dwelling Place,* Macdonald & Jane's, 1971; *Feathers in the Fire* (also see below), Macdonald & Co., 1971, Bobbs-Merrill, 1972; *Pure as the Lily,* Macdonald & Co., 1972, Bobbs-Merrill, 1973; *The Mallen Streak* (first novel in trilogy; also see below), Heinemann, 1973; *The Mallen Girl* (second novel in trilogy; also see below), Heinemann, 1974; *The Mallen Lot,* Dutton, 1974 (published in England as *The Mallen Litter* [third novel in trilogy; also see below], Heinemann, 1974); *The Invisible Cord* (also see below), Dutton, 1975; *The Gambling Man* (also see below), Morrow, 1975; *The Tide of Life,* Morrow, 1976; *The Girl* (also see below), Morrow, 1977; *The Cinder Path* (also see below), Morrow, 1978; *Tilly Trotter,* Heinemann, 1978, published as *Tilly,* Morrow, 1980; *Selected Works,* Heinemann/Octopus, Volume I (contains *Fifteen Streets, The Blind Miller, The Round Tower, Feathers in the Fire,* and *A Grand Man* [also see below]), 1978, Volume II (contains *The Mallen Streak* [also see below], *The Invisible Cord, The Gambling Man, The Girl,* and *The Cinder Path*), 1980; *The Mallen Novels* (trilogy, contains *The Mallen Streak, The Mallen Girl,* and *The Mallen Litter*), Heinemann, 1979; *The Man Who Cried,* Morrow, 1979.

Tilly Wed, Morrow, 1981 (published in England as *Tilly Trotter Wed,* Heinemann, 1981); *Tilly Alone,* Morrow, 1982 (published in England as *Tilly Widowed,* Heinemann, 1982); *The Whip,* Summit Books, 1982. Also author of *Fanny McBride,* 1959, reprinted, Macdonald & Jane's, 1980.

"Mary Ann" series: *A Grand Man,* Macdonald & Co., 1954, Macmillan, 1955, reprinted, Morrow, 1975; *The Lord and Mary Ann,* Macdonald & Co., 1956, reprinted, Macdonald & Jane's, 1974, Morrow, 1975; *The Devil and Mary Ann,* Macdonald & Co., 1958, Morrow, 1976; *Love and Mary Ann,* Macdonald & Co., 1961, Morrow, 1976; *Life and Mary Ann,*

Macdonald & Co., 1962, Morrow, 1977; *Marriage and Mary Ann,* Macdonald & Co., 1964, Morrow, 1978; *Mary Ann's Angels,* Macdonald & Co., 1965, Morrow, 1978; *Mary Ann and Bill,* Macdonald & Co, 1966, Morrow, 1979; *Mary Ann Omnibus* (contains all novels in "Mary Ann" series), Macdonald & Jane's, 1981.

Juvenile novels: *Matty Doolin,* Macdonald & Co., 1965, New American Library, 1976; *Joe and the Gladiator,* Macdonald & Co., 1968; *The Nipper,* Bobbs-Merrill, 1970; *Blue Baccy,* Macdonald & Jane's, 1972, Bobbs-Merrill, 1973; *Our John Willie,* Morrow, 1974; *Mrs. Flanagan's Trumpet,* Macdonald & Jane's, 1977, Lothrop, 1980; *Go Tell It to Mrs. Golightly,* Macdonald & Jane's, 1977, Lothrop, 1980; *Lanky Jones,* Lothrup, 1981.

Under pseudonym Catherine Marchant: *Heritage of Folly,* Macdonald & Co., 1963, reprinted, Macdonald & Jane's, 1980; *Evil at Roger's Cross,* Lancer Books, 1965, revised edition published as *The Iron Facade,* Heinemann, 1976, Morrow, 1980; *The Fen Tiger,* Macdonald & Co., 1963, Morrow, 1979; *House of Men,* Macdonald & Co., 1964, Macdonald & Jane's, 1980; *Miss Martha Mary Crawford,* Heinemann, 1975, Morrow, 1976; *The Slow Awakening,* Heinemann, 1976, Morrow, 1977.

WORK IN PROGRESS: Thorman's Moth and *The Black Velvet Gown,* both for Summit Books.

SIDELIGHTS: Catherine Cookson enjoys a large following of "loyal readers," according to Anne Duchene writing in the *Times Literary Supplement.* Duchene notes: "These days there are never fewer than fifty Cookson titles in print in English at any time; they are translated into fifteen languages; and new books are still steadily produced."

The critic believes that Cookson's popularity is due to the fact that many readers can easily identify with the characters in her novels. Other reviewers make similar observations. Riley Hughes, for example, commenting on *The Grand Man* in *Catholic World,* states: "Miss Cookson's characters are vivid and believable; her locale . . . is a fresh and . . . fruitful one." Writing about the same book, a *Times Literary Supplement* critic remarks: "The character-drawing is excellent, Mary Ann [the main character] herself is a real joy, and one senses the truth of the background. In fact, a touching and amusing short novel." Duchene concludes: "[Cookson] writes stories in which her readers can gratefully recognize experiences and emotions of their own—heightened, to be sure, by greater comedy or greater violence than their own lives normally vouchsafe, but based on all their own affections, furies, aspirations and reactions."

BIOGRAPHICAL/CRITICAL SOURCES: New York Times, January 7, 1955; *Times Literary Supplement,* January 7, 1955, June 19, 1969, July 24, 1981; *Catholic World,* June, 1955; *Our Kate: An Autobiography,* Macdonald & Co., 1969, Bobbs-Merrill, 1971, published as *Our Kate: Catherine Cookson, Her Personal Story,* Macdonald & Jane's, 1974; *New York Times Book Review,* October 20, 1974.

* * *

COOPER, Bruce M(ichael) 1925-

PERSONAL: Born September 6, 1925, in Shrewsbury, England; son of Frederick Joseph (a business executive) and Myrtle (Horey) Cooper; married Maud Helena Martennson, June 11, 1954; children: Kristina, Crispin, Joanna, Barbara, Susan. *Education:* Attended Ratcliffe College, Leicester, England; University of Edinburgh, M.A. (honors), 1952; Peterhouse, Cambridge, Certificate of Education, 1953. *Politics:* Liberal. *Religion:* Roman Catholic. *Office:* Ulster Polytechnic, Shore Rd., Newtonabbey, County Antrim BT37 0QB, Northern Ireland.

CAREER: Workers' Educational Association, Suffolk, England, tutor and organizer, 1954-56; Hatfield College of Technology, Hatfield, England, lecturer in communication, 1956-61; Stockton Billingham Technical College, Billingham, England, head of department of liberal studies, 1961-65; head of management training, Imperial Chemical Industries Ltd., Agricultural Division, 1966-71; Ulster Polytechnic, Jordanstown, Newtonabbey, dean of management and continuing education, 1971—. Broadcaster on British Broadcasting Corp. programs, often as spokesman for Roman Catholic viewpoint on birth control and contraception issues. Consultant on report writing. *Military service:* British Army, Royal Artillery, 1943-47; served in India, 1945-47.

WRITINGS: (Co-author) *Writing Technical Reports,* Penguin, 1964, 5th edition, 1964; (with A. F. Bartlett) *Industrial Relations: A Study in Conflict,* Heinemann, 1976. Also author of *Group Discussion Leading,* 1969, and co-author of *Structuring the Church for Missions,* 1969. Contributor to education and industrial journals, and to *Spectator, Sunday Telegraph, Listener,* and *Times Educational Supplement.*

WORK IN PROGRESS: Writing the Project; compiling a series of essays by authorities in the field for *Modern Thought in Technical Education.*

AVOCATIONAL INTERESTS: Penal reform.†

* * *

COOPER, John C(harles) 1933-

PERSONAL: Born April 3, 1933, in Charleston, S.C.; son of Chauncey Miller (in U.S. Navy) and Margarete Anna (Gerard) Cooper; married Clelia Ann Johnston, June 6, 1954; children: Martin Christopher, Catherine Marie, Cynthia Ann, Paul Conrad. *Education:* University of South Carolina, B.A. (cum laude), 1955; Lutheran Theological Southern Seminary, B.D. (cum laude), 1958; Lutheran School of Foreign Missions, certificate, 1959; Chicago Lutheran Theological Seminary, S.T.M., 1960; University of Chicago, M.A., 1964, Ph.D., 1966. *Home:* Apt. 29-A, Countryside Village, Selinsgrove, Pa. 17870. *Office:* Susquehanna University, Selinsgrove, Pa. 17870.

CAREER: Ordained minister of The Lutheran Church in America, 1958; Thiel College, Greenville, Pa., lecturer in English and Bible, 1959-60; pastor in Tampa, Fla., 1960-61; Newberry College, Newberry, S.C., assistant professor of Bible and philosophy, 1961-63, associate professor, 1965-66, professor of philosophy, 1968, head of department, 1966-68; Eastern Kentucky University, Richmond, professor of philosophy and chairman of department, 1968-71; Winebrenner Theological Seminary, Findlay, Ohio, professor of systematic theology and dean of academic affairs, 1971-82; Susquehanna University, Selinsgrove, Pa., professor of religion, 1982—. Member of Commission on Youth Activities, The Lutheran Church in America, 1967-72; supply pastor, St. John's Lutheran Church, McComb, Ohio, 1971-82. Trustee, Wittenberg University, 1976-80. *Military service:* U.S. Marine Corps, 1950-52; served in Korea and Japan; became sergeant; retired for combat injuries; received Presidential Unit Citation. *Member:* American Academy of Religion, American Philosophical Association, MENSA, Phi Beta Kappa.

WRITINGS: The Roots of the Radical Theology, Westminster Press, 1967; (editor with Charles Sauer) *Wine in Separate Cups,* Commission on Youth Activities, Lutheran Church, 1967; *The Christian and Politics* (pupil's books and teacher's book), Lutheran Church Press, 1968; *Radical Christianity and Its Sources,* Westminster Press, 1968; *The New Mentality,* Westminster Press, 1969.

The Turn Right, Westminster Press, 1970; (with Carl Skrade) *Celluloid and Symbols,* Fortress, 1970; *Religion in the Age of Aquarius,* Westminster Press, 1971; *Paul for Today,* Lutheran Church Press, 1971; *A New Kind of Man,* Westminster Press, 1972; *Getting It Together,* Lutheran Church Press, 1972; *The Recovery of America,* Westminster Press, 1973; *Religion after Forty,* Pilgrim Press, 1973; *Finding a Simpler Life,* Pilgrim Press, 1974; *Fantasy and the Humane Spirit,* Seabury, 1975; *Your Exciting Middle Years,* Word, Inc., 1976; *Amos, Prophet of Justice,* Lutheran Church Press, 1976; *Living, Loving, and Letting Go,* Word, Inc., 1977; *Why We Hurt and Who Can Heal,* Word, Inc., 1978.

(With Una McManus) *Not for a Million Dollars,* Impact Books, 1980; *The Joy of the Plain Life,* Impact Books, 1981; *Religious Pied Pipers,* Judson, 1981; (contributor) J. R. Royce and L. P. Mos, editors, *Humanistic Psychology,* Plenum, 1981; *Dealing with Destructive Cults,* Zondervan, 1982; (contributor) M. M. Gentz, editor, *Writing to Inspire,* Writer's Digest, 1982; *Coping with Rejection,* Prentice-Hall, 1983. Contributor of poetry, reviews, and more than two hundred articles to periodicals.

SIDELIGHTS: John C. Cooper reads French, German, Spanish, and Italian; he has a working knowledge of classical Greek and Biblical languages. *Avocational interests:* Travel (has been to Europe, North Africa, the Middle East, the Far East, and to islands in the Caribbean and the Pacific), wilderness camping, hiking, exploring, rafting, swimming.

* * *

CORBETT, Edward P(atrick) J(oseph) 1919-

PERSONAL: Born October 29, 1919, in Jamestown, N.D.; son of John T. (a maintenance man) and Adrienne (Beaupre) Corbett; married Sylvia M. Mikkelsen, November 4, 1944; children: Mary Elizabeth, James, John, Catherine and Maureen (twins), Peter, Thomas. *Education:* Attended Venard College, Clark Summit, Pa., 1938-42; University of Chicago, M.A., 1948; Loyola University, Chicago, Ill., Ph.D., 1956. *Politics:* Democrat. *Religion:* Roman Catholic. *Office:* Department of English, Ohio State University, Columbus, Ohio 43210.

CAREER: Instructor in English at Creighton University, Omaha, Neb., 1948-50, and Loyola University, Chicago, Ill., 1952-53; Creighton University, assistant professor, 1953-56, associate professor, 1956-61, professor of English, 1961-66, director of freshman English, 1953-66; Ohio State University, Columbus, professor of English, 1966—, vice-chairman of department and director of freshman English, 1966-70. Trustee of St. John Vianney Seminary, Elkhorn, Neb., 1960-66; chairman, Conference on College Composition and Communication, 1971. Appears in national television and radio commercials and acts in community theater. Advisor, English Association of Ohio, 1973-79; consultant to Educational Testing Service, 1980-81. *Military service:* U.S. Marine Corps, 1944-46; became staff sergeant.

MEMBER: Modern Language Association of America (member of delegate assembly, 1974-76; member of executive committee of Division on the Teaching of Writing, 1976-79), National Council of Teachers of English, Conference on College Composition and Communication, Rhetoric Society of America (chairman, 1973-77; executive secretary, pro tem, 1980—), Speech Association of America, American Association of University Professors, English Association of Ohio (president, 1971).

WRITINGS: Classical Rhetoric for the Modern Student, Oxford University Press, 1965, 2nd edition, 1971; (contributor) Gary Tate, editor, *Reflections on High School English,* University of Tulsa Press, 1966; (contributor) Robert M. Gorrell, editor, *Rhetoric: Theories for Application,* National Council of Teachers of English, 1967; (editor with Tate) *Teaching Freshman Composition,* Oxford University Press, 1967; (editor with James Golden) *The Rhetoric of Blair, Campbell, and Whately,* Holt, 1968; *Rhetorical Analyses of Literary Works,* Oxford University Press, 1969; (editor with Tate and contributor) *Teaching High School Composition,* Oxford University Press, 1970; (editor with Virginia Burke) *The New Century Composition-Rhetoric,* Appleton, 1971; *The Little English Handbook: Choices and Conventions* (also see below), Wiley, 1973, 3rd edition, 1981; *The Essay: Subject and Stances,* Prentice-Hall, 1974.

(Contributor) Tate, editor, *Teaching Composition: Ten Bibliographical Essays,* Texas Christian University Press, 1976; *The Little Rhetoric* (also see below), Wiley, 1977; *The Little Rhetoric and Handbook* (includes *The Little English Handbook: Choices and Conventions* and *The Little Rhetoric*), Wiley, 1977, 2nd edition, 1982; (with James B. Bell) *The Little English Handbook for Canadians* (adaptation of *The Little English Handbook: Choices and Conventions*), Wiley, 1977, 2nd edition, 1982; (editor with Tate) *A Writing Teacher's Sourcebook,* Oxford University Press, 1982.

General editor, "Literary Casebook" series, twenty-two volumes, Charles E. Merrill, 1968-71. Contributor to *Commonweal, America,* and professional journals. Member of editorial board, *Philosophy and Rhetoric,* 1973—, *Style,* 1979—, and *Rocky Mountain Review of Language and Literature,* 1979—; associate editor, *Quarterly Journal of Speech,* 1972-74; editor, *College Composition and Communication,* 1974-79; member of publications committee, Conference on College Composition and Communication Studies in Writing and Rhetoric, 1980—.

* * *

CORLEY, Ernest
See BULMER, (Henry) Kenneth

* * *

CORREY, Lee
See STINE, G(eorge) Harry

* * *

COULSON, Juanita (Ruth) 1933-
(John Jay Wells)

PERSONAL: Surname is pronounced *Col*-son; born February 12, 1933, in Anderson, Ind.; daughter of Grant Elmer (a tool and die maker) and Ruth Margaret (Oemler) Wellons; married Robert Stratton Coulson (a writer), August 21, 1954; children: Bruce Edward. *Education:* Ball State University, B.S., 1954, M.A., 1961. *Politics:* Independent. *Religion:* Unitarian Universalist. *Home address:* Route 3, Hartford City, Ind. 47348. *Agent:* Jim Allen, Virginia Kidd Literary Agency, 538 East Harford St., Milford, Pa. 18337.

CAREER: Writer; art editor and publisher of *Yandro* (science fiction magazine), 1953—. Elementary school teacher, 1954-55; collator, Heckman's Bookbindery, North Manchester, Ind., 1955-57. *Member:* Science Fiction Writers of America.

AWARDS, HONORS: Joint nominee with husband, Robert S. Coulson, for Hugo Award, 1960-64, 1966-67, for best amateur science fiction magazine, *Yandro,* joint winner with R. S. Coulson, Hugo Award, 1965, for *Yandro,* and co-Fan Guest of Honor, with R. S. Coulson, 30th World Science Fiction Convention, 1972, all from World Science Fiction Society; Ralph Holland Memorial Award from Fan Art Show, Hartford City, Ind., 1962.

WRITINGS: Crisis on Cheiron, Ace Books, 1967; *The Singing Stones,* Ace Books, 1968; *The Secret of Seven Oaks,* Berkley Publishing, 1972; *Door into Terror,* Berkley Publishing, 1972; (contributor) Richard A. Lupoff and Don Thompson, editors, *The Comic-Book Book,* Arlington House, 1973; *Stone of Blood,* Ballantine, 1975; *Unto the Last Generation,* Laser Books, 1975; *Space Trap,* Laser Books, 1976; *Fear Stalks the Bayou,* Ballantine, 1976; (contributor) Sandra Marshak and Myrna Culbreath, editors, *Star Trek: The New Voyages,* Bantam, 1976; *Dark Priestess,* Ballantine, 1977; *Web of Wizardry,* Del Rey Books, 1978; *Fire of the Andes,* Ballantine, 1979; *The Death God's Citadel,* Del Rey Books, 1980.

"Children of the Stars" series; published by Del Rey Books: *Tomorrow's Heritage,* 1981; *Outward Bound,* 1982; *Legacy of the Earth,* 1983.

Contributor to *If, Fantastic,* and with Marion Zimmer Bradley to *Fantasy and Science Fiction* under pseudonym John Jay Wells. Art editor and publisher of Science Fiction Writers of America's *Forum* magazine, 1971-72.

WORK IN PROGRESS: The Past of Forever, fourth book in "Children of the Stars" series; *World He Never Made; What Do You Mean, We?*

SIDELIGHTS: Juanita and Robert S. Coulson's publication, *Yandro,* is referred to as a "fanzine" by science fiction enthusiasts. Although it is one of the longest-running large fanzines, *Yandro* is only one of many published throughout the world. A fanzine is an amateur science fiction magazine published by those interested in the genre. Each issue of *Yandro* includes science fiction pieces, as well as columns, letters, and reviews on other topics.

BIOGRAPHICAL/CRITICAL SOURCES: Science Fiction Review, November, 1981.

* * *

COULSON, Robert S(tratton) 1928- (Thomas Stratton, a joint pseudonym)

PERSONAL: Surname is pronounced *Col*-son; born May 12, 1928, in Sullivan, Ind.; son of Springer (a house painter) and Mary (Stratton) Coulson; married Juanita Wellons (a writer and artist), August 21, 1954; children: Bruce Edward. *Education:* International Correspondence Schools, completed course in electrical engineering, 1960. *Politics:* "Political liberal, economic conservative." *Religion:* Agnostic. *Home address:* Route 3, Hartford City, Ind. 47348.

CAREER: Writer; text editor of *Yandro* (science fiction magazine), 1953—. Factory hand, Heckman's Bookbindery, North Manchester, Ind., 1947-57; Honeywell, Inc., Wabash, Ind., draftsman, 1957-59, technical writer, 1959-65; Overhead Door Co., Hartford City, Ind., lead draftsman, 1965-68, head draftsman, 1968-75. President of Filk Foundation, Inc., 1978—.

AWARDS, HONORS: Joint nominee with wife, Juanita Coulson, for Hugo Award, 1960-64, 1966-67, for best amateur science fiction magazine, *Yandro,* joint winner with J. Coulson, Hugo Award, 1965, for *Yandro,* and co-Fan Guest of Honor, with J. Coulson, 30th World Science Fiction Convention, 1972, all from World Science Fiction Society.

WRITINGS—With Gene DeWeese, except as indicated: *Gates of the Universe,* Laser Books, 1975; *Now You See Him/It/Them,* Doubleday, 1975; (sole author) *To Renew the Ages,* Laser Books, 1976; (with Piers Anthony) *But What of Earth?,* Laser Books, 1976; (contributor) Sandra Ley, editor, *Beyond Time,* Pocket Books, 1976; *Charles Fort Never Mentioned Wombats,* Doubleday, 1977.

With DeWeese under joint pseudonym Thomas Stratton: *The Invisibility Affair: Man from U.N.C.L.E., No. 11,* Ace Books, 1967; *The Mindtwisters Affair: Man from U.N.C.L.E., No. 12,* Ace Books, 1967; (contributor) L. Sprague DeCamp and George Scithers, *The Conan Grimoire: Essays in Swordplay and Sorcery,* Mirage Press, 1972.

Contributor to *Dictionary of Literary Biography.* Book reviewer for *Amazing Stories,* 1983—. Regular contributor to *Empire Fantasy* magazine; also contributor, with DeWeese, of short stories to magazines, including *Amazing Stories* and *Fantasy and Science Fiction.* Text editor of Science Fiction Writers of America's *Forum* magazine, 1971-72.

WORK IN PROGRESS: Several novels.

* * *

COWAN, Gregory M(ac) 1935-1979

PERSONAL: Born August 17, 1935, in Seattle, Wash.; died July 2, 1979; son of Walter G. (a physician) and Pearl (Ramsey) Cowan; married Elizabeth Wooten (a college professor), 1975. *Education:* Whitman College, B.A., 1957; University of Washington, Seattle, M.A., 1960; graduate study at Washington State University, 1957-60, Portland State University, 1960-61, and New School for Social Research, 1974-76. *Home:* 2608 Melba Cir., Bryan, Tex. 77801. *Office:* Department of English, Texas A & M University, College Station, Tex. 77843.

CAREER: Clark College, Vancouver, Wash., 1960-67, began as instructor, became assistant professor of English; Forest Park Community College, St. Louis, Mo., assistant professor, 1967-69, associate professor, 1969-71, professor of English, 1971-74; Empire State College of State University of New York at Saratoga Springs, associate professor, 1975-76; Texas A & M University, College Station, associate professor, 1976-79. National Junior College Committee, representative, 1969-75, chairman, 1972-74. Consulting editor on junior and community college texts, Random House Publishers, Inc., 1967-74.

MEMBER: American Association of University Professors, Association of Humanistic Psychology, Conference on College Composition and Communication (member of executive committee, 1969-75; chairman of Committee to Develop Guidelines for Junior College English Teacher Training Programs, 1969-70), Modern Language Association of America, National Council of Teachers of English, Midwest Regional Conference on English in the Two-Year College (member of executive committee, 1969-75), Pacific Northwest Regional Conference on English in the Two-Year College, Southeast Regional Conference on English in the Two-Year College.

WRITINGS: (With Elizabeth McPherson) *Making the Most of It,* [Vancouver, Wash.], 1965; (with McPherson) *Plain English Please: A Rhetoric,* Random House, 1966, 4th edition, 1980; (with McPherson) *Background for Writing,* Random House, 1967; (with McPherson) *Exercising Plain English,* Random House, 1970; (with McPherson) *Plain English Rhetoric and Reader,* Random House, 1970, 3rd edition, 1980; (with McPherson) *English in Plain Words,* five volumes, Random House, 1971; *Guidelines for Junior College English Teacher Training Programs* (monograph), National Council of Teachers of English, 1971; *Three for Show: A Visual Approach to the Short Story,* Random House, 1973; (compiler) *An Annotated List of Programs for Community College English Teachers: A CCCC Report,* ERIC Clearinghouse on Reading and Communication Skills, 1977; (with wife, Elizabeth Cowan) *Writing,* Wiley, 1980. Also author of directories of graduate programs for junior and community college teachers, 1977 and 1978. Contributor to journals in his field.

AVOCATIONAL INTERESTS: Cooking, sailing, jogging, carpentry, folk music, politics of issue campaigning, democratization of education, traveling.†

* * *

COWAN, Peter (Walkinshaw) 1914-

PERSONAL: Born November 4, 1914, in Perth, Western Australia; son of Norman Walkinshaw and Marie (Johnson) Cowan; married Edith Howard, June 18, 1941; children: Julian Walkinshaw. *Education:* University of Western Australia, B.A., 1941, Diploma in Education, 1946. *Home:* 149 Alfred Rd., Mount Claremont, Western Australia. *Office:* English Department, University of Western Australia, Nedlands, Western Australia.

CAREER: Clerk, farm laborer, and casual worker in Australia, 1930-39, and teacher, 1941-42; University of Western Australia, Nedlands, part-time teacher, 1946-50; Scotch College, Swanbourne, Western Australia, senior English master, 1950-62; University of Western Australia, senior tutor in English, 1964—. *Military service:* Royal Australian Air Force, 1943-45. *Member:* Australian Society of Authors.

AWARDS, HONORS: Commonwealth literary fellowship, 1963, to write *Seed;* Australian Council for the Arts fellowship, 1975 and 1980; honorary research fellow, University of Western Australia Department of English, 1982.

WRITINGS: Drift (short stories), Reed & Harris, 1944; *The Unploughed Land* (short stories), Angus & Robertson, 1958; *Summer* (novel), Angus & Robertson, 1964; (editor) *Short Story Landscape* (anthology), Longmans, Green, 1964; *The Empty Street* (short stories), Angus & Robertson, 1965; *Seed* (novel), Angus & Robertson, 1966.

(Editor with Bruce Bennett) *Spectrum One: Narrative Short Stories,* Longman, 1970; (editor with Bennett) *Spectrum Two: Modern Short Stories,* Longman, 1970; (editor) *Today* (short stories), Longman, 1971; (contributor) *This Is Australia,* Hamlyn, 1975; *The Tins and Other Stories* (short stories), University of Queensland Press, 1973; (editor) *A Faithful Picture: The Letters of Eliza and Thomas Brown at York in the Swan River Colony, 1841-1852,* Fremantle Arts Centre Press, 1977; (editor) *A Unique Position* (biography), University of Western Australia Press, 1978; *Mobiles* (short stories), Fremantle Arts Centre Press, 1979; (editor with Bennett and Hay) *Spectrum Three: Experimental Short Stories* (anthology), Longman Cheshire, 1979; (contributor) Bennett, editor, *The Literature of Western Australia,* University of Western Australia Press, 1979. Contributor of short stories to anthologies.

WORK IN PROGRESS: Short stories; a biography; articles on the environment and on Western Australian literature.

AVOCATIONAL INTERESTS: Nature and wild life conservation, particularly in Australia.

BIOGRAPHICAL/CRITICAL SOURCES: Meanjin Quarterly, number 2, 1960, number 2, 1966; Evan Jones, editor, *Commonwealth Literary Fund Lectures,* Australian National University Press, 1961; Dorothy Hewett, editor, *Sandgropers,* University of Western Australia Press, 1973; *Westerly,* number 3, 1973; John Barnes, *An Australian Selection,* Angus & Robertson, 1974; Bruce Bennett, *The Literature of Western Australia,* University of Western Australia Press, 1979.

* * *

COWIE, Evelyn E(lizabeth) 1924-

PERSONAL: Born September 17, 1924, in Peterborough, England; daughter of Robert (a civil servant) and Edith (Scott) Trafford; married Leonard Wallace Cowie (a clerk in holy orders, senior lecturer at Whitelands College, and author), August 9, 1949; children: Alan Leonard. *Education:* University College, London, M.A., 1948. *Politics:* Conservative. *Religion:* Church of England. *Home:* 38 Stratton Rd., Merton Park, London SW19 3JG, England. *Office:* King's College, University of London, London, England.

CAREER: University of London, London, England, senior lecturer in history at Goldsmiths' College, 1957-65, lecturer in education at King's College, 1965—.

WRITINGS: Breakfasts (juvenile), Jenkins, 1958; *Left-Overs* (juvenile), Jenkins, 1959; *Man and Roads* (juvenile), Hamish Hamilton, 1963; *Man and Shops* (juvenile), Hamish Hamilton, 1964; *Man and the Crusades* (juvenile), Hamish Hamilton, 1969; (with husband, Leonard W. Cowie) *Great Ideas in Education,* Pergamon General Books, 1971; *Education:* Methuen, 1973; (author of text with L. W. Cowie) *Environment through Photographs,* Volume III: *Architecture,* Cassell, 1974; *History and the Slow-Learning Child,* Historical Association, 1979.

"Living through History" series, Cassell, Volume I: *Homes,* 1967, Volume II: *Villages,* 1967, Volume III: *Towns,* 1967, Volume IV: *The Land,* 1967, Volume V: *Industry,* 1968, Volume VI: *Leisure,* 1968, Volume VII: *Transport,* 1969, Volume VIII: *Communications,* 1969, Volume IX: *Discovery,* 1970, Volume X: *Costume,* 1975, Volume XI: *War,* 1975, Volume XII: *Government,* 1975.

* * *

COWIE, Leonard W(allace) 1919-

PERSONAL: Born May 10, 1919, in Brighton, Sussex, England; son of Reginald George (a clerk in holy orders) and Ella Constance (Peerless) Cowie; married Evelyn Elizabeth Trafford (a writer and lecturer at University of London), August 9, 1949; children: Alan Leonard. *Education:* Pembroke College, Oxford, M.A., 1941; University of London, Ph.D., 1954.

Politics: Conservative. *Home:* 38 Stratton Rd., Merton Park, London SW19 3JG, England.

CAREER: Clergyman, Church of England. Assistant curate, High Wycombe, Buckinghamshire, England; history master at Royal Grammar School, High Wycombe, 1943-45; College of St. Mark and St. John, Chelsea, London, England, principal lecturer in history, 1945-68; Whitelands College, Putney, London, England, senior lecturer in history, 1969-82.

WRITINGS: Henry Newman: An American in London, 1708-43, S.P.C.K., 1956; *The True Book about the Bible,* Muller, 1959.

Seventeenth-Century Europe, G. Bell, 1960, Ungar, 1964; *The New Outlook History,* Hamish Hamilton, Volume I: *English Social History to 1603,* 1961, Volume II: *English Social History, 1603 to Modern Times,* 1962, Volume III: *From Empire to Commonwealth,* 1963, Volume IV: *Britain, 1837 to Modern Times,* 1963, Volume V: *British Social and Economic History from 1900,* 1965; *The March of the Cross,* McGraw, 1962; *Eighteenth-Century Europe,* G. Bell, 1963, Ungar, 1964; *English History, 55 B.C.-A.D. 1485,* Hamish Hamilton, 1964; *From the Peace of Paris to World War I: British History, 1763-1914,* Thomas Nelson, 1966; *Hanoverian England, 1714-1837,* Humanities, 1967; (editor) *Documents and Descriptions in European History, 1714-1815,* Oxford University Press, 1967; *Luther: Father of the Reformation,* Weidenfeld & Nicolson, 1968, published as *Martin Luther: Leader of the Reformation,* Praeger, 1969; *The Reformation,* John Day, 1968, 2nd edition, Hart-Davis, 1974; *Europe, 1789-1939,* Thomas Nelson, 1969.

Industrial Evolution: 1750 to the Present Day, Thomas Nelson, 1970; *The Pilgrim Fathers,* Wayland, 1970, Putnam, 1972; *Plague and Fire: London, 1665-66,* Putnam, 1970; *The Reformation of the Sixteenth Century,* Putnam, 1970; *The Age of Feudalism,* P. Hamlyn, 1971; *The Superpowers,* Thomas Nelson, 1971; (with wife, Evelyn E. Cowie) *Great Ideas in Education,* Pergamon General Books, 1971; *The Age of Drake,* Wayland, 1972; *Bell and Lancaster,* Methuen, 1972; *The Black Death and the Peasants' Revolt,* Putnam, 1972; *The Trial and Execution of Charles I,* Putnam, 1972; *A Dictionary of British Social History,* G. Bell, 1973, revised edition published as *Life in Britain: A Junior Encyclopaedia of Social History,* Bell & Hyman, 1980; *Religion,* Methuen, 1973; *The Trade Unions: 1750 to the Present Day,* Thomas Nelson, 1973; *Discovering History,* Oliver & Boyd, Volume III: *From the Renaissance to the Industrial Revolution,* 1973, Volume IV: *From the Industrial Revolution to Modern Times,* 1973; (with John Selwyn Gummer) *The Christian Calendar,* Merriam, 1974; (author of text with E. E. Cowie) *The Environment through Photographs:* Volume III: *Architecture,* Cassell, 1974; *Louis XIV,* Methuen, 1975; *Decisive Battles,* G. Bell, 1976; *Sixteenth-Century Europe,* Longman, 1977; *The Railway Age,* Macdonald & Co., 1978.

History in Close-up: Britain and Europe, Cassell, 1981.

* * *

COX, Constance 1915-

PERSONAL: Born October 25, 1915, in Sutton, Surrey, England; daughter of J. Frederick (an educator) and Anne E. (Vince) Shaw; married Norman C. Cox (a Royal Air Force pilot), June 7, 1933 (deceased). *Education:* Attended schools in England. *Home:* 2 Princes Ave., Hove, Sussex, England. *Agent:* Eric Glass Ltd., 28 Berkeley Sq., London W1X 6HD, England.

CAREER: Playwright and adapter of classics for stage, 1942—; writer and adapter for television, 1955—. Former racing and competition driver; amateur actress and producer at Brighton Little Theatre Co. and New Venture Theatre, both Brighton, England. *Member:* Sussex Playwrights' Club (honorary treasurer), West Sussex Writer's Club.

AWARDS, HONORS: News Chronicles award for best television play of the year, 1956; Television and Screenwriters' Guild Special Award for adaptations of the classics, 1964; Prix Jeunesse International (second place) for thirteen-part television serial, "The Old Curiosity Shop," 1964; Television and Screenwriters' Guild Award, 1967, for television serial "The Forsyte Saga."

WRITINGS—Published plays: *Vanity Fair* (adapted from the novel by William Makepeace Thackeray), Samuel French, 1947; *The Picture of Dorian Gray* (adapted from the novel by Oscar Wilde), Fortune Press, 1948; *Madame Bovary* (adapted from the novel by Gustave Flaubert), Fortune Press, 1948; *Northanger Abbey* (adapted from the novel by Jane Austen), Fortune Press, 1950; *Mansfield Park* (adapted from the novel by Jane Austen), Evans Brothers, 1950, reprinted, Hub Publications, 1977; *The Count of Monte Cristo* (adapted from the novel by Alexander Dumas), Fortune Press, 1950; *Spring at Marino* (adapted from Ivan Turgenev's novel *Fathers and Sons*), Samuel French, 1951; *The Desert Air,* English Theatre Guild, 1951; *Because of the Lockwoods,* Evans Brothers, 1953; *Three Knaves of Normandy* (adapted from the medieval comedy "The Farce of the Worthy Master Pierre Patelin"), Evans Brothers, 1958; *Jane Eyre* (adapted from the novel by Charlotte Bronte), J. Garnet Miller, 1959.

Pride and Prejudice (adapted from the novel by Jane Austen), J. Garnet Miller, 1960, reprinted, 1972; *The Caliph's Minstrel,* Evans Brothers, 1961; *Lord Arthur Saville's Crime* (adapted from the short story by Oscar Wilde), Samuel French, 1963; *A Miniature 'Beggar's Opera'* (adapted from the play by John Gay), Evans Brothers, 1964; *The Three-Cornered Hat* (adapted from the play by Juan Ruiz Alarcon y Mendoza), Evans Brothers, 1966; *Trilby* (adapted from the novel by George du-Maurier), Evans Brothers, 1967; *The Woman in White* (adapted from the novel by Wilkie Collins), Evans Brothers, 1967; *Everyman* (adapted from the anonymous medieval morality play), Samuel French, 1967; *Maria Marten; or Murder in the Red Barn,* Samuel French, 1969; *Miss Letitia,* Samuel French, 1970; *Wuthering Heights* (adapted from the novel by Emily Bronte), English Theatre Guild, 1974; *The Murder Game,* Samuel French, 1976; *Lady Audley's Secret,* Samuel French, 1976.

Also author of unpublished, produced plays, "The Romance of David Garrick," 1942, "The Nine Days' Wonder," 1944, "Remember Dick Sheridan," 1944, "The Hunchback of Notre Dame," 1944, "Elizabeth and Darcy," 1945, "Sleeping Dogs," 1947, "Georgia Story," 1949, "The Enemy in the House," 1951, "The Woman in White," 1953, "Heathcliff," 1959, and "Nightmare," 1963.

Author of librettos for musical plays, "Vanity Fair," with Julian Slade, 1967, "Two Cities," 1969, and "Smiling Through," with John Hanson, 1974.

Author of plays produced on television, "The Trial of Admiral Byng," "Trilby," "Heathcliff," "Lord Arthur Saville's Crime," "Georgia Story," "The Nine Days' Wonder," "Spring at Marino," and "Miss Letitia."

Author of television serials, "Jane Eyre," "Vanity Fair," "Precious Bane," "The History of Mr. Polly," "The Lost

King," "Champion Road," "Thunder in the West," "The Golden Spur," "Pride and Prejudice," "Little Women," "Good Wives," "Jo's Boys," "Bleak House," "Angel Pavement," "Oliver Twist," "The Old Curiosity Shop," "Lorna Doone," "Martin Chuzzlewit," "Rogue Herries," "Silas Marner," "Judith Paris," "A Tale of Two Cities," "John Halifax, Gentleman," "Jane Eyre" (new version), "The Master of Ballantrae," "The Franchise Affair," "The House under the Water," "Katy, and What Katy Did at School," "The Forsyte Saga," parts four, five, and seven, and "Rebecca of Sunnybrook Farm."

Author of radio series, "The Herries Chronicle," 1969, "War and Peace," 1971, and "The Barchester Chronicles," 1974.

AVOCATIONAL INTERESTS: Music, motoring, and croquet.

* * *

CRAIG, David
See TUCKER, James

* * *

CRAMER, Clarence H(enley) 1905-1982

PERSONAL: Born June 23, 1905, in Eureka, Kan.; died March 15, 1982 in Cleveland, Ohio; son of David H. (a minister) and Irma (Henley) Cramer; married Elizabeth Garman, December 30, 1949. *Education:* Ohio State University, A.B. and B.Sc. in Education, 1927, M.A., 1928, Ph.D., 1931. *Politics:* Democrat. *Religion:* Presbyterian. *Home:* 11424 Cedar Glen Pkwy., Cleveland, Ohio 44106.

CAREER: Southern Illinois Normal University (now Southern Illinois University at Carbondale), associate professor of history, 1931-42; Case Western Reserve University, Cleveland, Ohio, 1949-82, began as associate professor of business and history, became professor emeritus of history, 1973-82, chairman of department, 1963-67, associate, later acting dean of School of Business Administration, 1949-54, dean of Adelbert College, 1954-69, university historian, 1973-82. Visiting professor of history, University Oklahoma, 1936 and 1940. *Wartime Service:* Served with National War Labor Board, 1943-44, United Nations Relief and Rehabilitation Administration, Germany, 1944-47, and International Refugee Organization, 1947-48. *Member:* American Historical Association, Organization of American Historians, Ohio Academy of History, Phi Beta Kappa. *Awards, honors:* Cleveland Arts Prize for Writing, Woman's City Club of Cleveland, 1973, for *Open Shelves and Open Minds: A History of the Cleveland Public Library* and *American Enterprise: Free and Not So Free.*

WRITINGS: Royal Bob: The Life of Robert G. Ingersoll, Bobbs-Merrill, 1952; *Newton D. Baker: A Biography,* World Publishing, 1961, reprinted, Garland Publishing, 1979; *Open Shelves and Open Minds: A History of the Cleveland Public Library,* Press of Case Western Reserve University, 1972; *American Enterprise: Free and Not So Free,* Little, Brown, 1972 (published in England as *American Enterprise: The Rise of U.S. Commerce,* Elek, 1973); *Case Western Reserve University: A History of the University, 1826-1976,* Little, Brown, 1976; *The Law School at Case Western Reserve University, 1892-1977,* Law School, Case Western Reserve University, 1977; *The School of Library Science at Case Western Reserve University: Seventy-Five Years, 1904-79,* School of Library Science, Case Western Reserve University, 1979. Also author of history of Engineering School, Case Western Reserve University, 1980.

WORK IN PROGRESS: A history of the dental school at Case Western Reserve University.

OBITUARIES: Case Western Reserve University Alumni Bulletin, summer, 1982.

* * *

CRAWFORD, Ann Fears 1932-

PERSONAL: Born August 26, 1932, in Beaumont, Tex.; daughter of Thaddeus Alvin (a physician) and Dorothy (Huey) Fears; married Frank B. Crawford, Jr., September 19, 1953 (divorced, 1957); children: Kevin Brooks. *Education:* University of Texas, B.F.A., 1953, Ph.D., 1976; Los Angeles State College of Applied Arts and Sciences (now California State University, Los Angeles), M.A., 1956. *Politics:* Democratic. *Religion:* Episcopalian. *Agent:* Bertha Klausner International Literary Agency, Inc., 71 Park Ave., New York, N.Y. 10016. *Office address:* Sam Houston Memorial Museum, Sam Houston State University, P.O. Box 2054, Huntsville, Tex. 77341.

CAREER: Steck-Vaughn Co. (publishers), Austin, Tex., editor, 1958-62; Texas Butane Dealers Association, Austin, magazine editor, 1965; Institute of Texan Cultures, Austin, research associate, 1966-68; *Austin People Today,* Austin, editor, 1973-74; currently director of Sam Houston Memorial Museum, Sam Houston State University, Huntsville, Tex. Free-lance writer and editor. Professor at Southwestern University and University of Texas at San Antonio. *Member:* National Organization for Women, Women in Communications, Texas State Historical Society, Austin Heritage Society, Texas Women's Political Caucus, Phi Kappa Phi.

WRITINGS: (With Norman Schacter) *Experience,* Books 1-3, Steck, 1965-66; *A Boy Like You,* Pemberton, 1966; (editor with William D. Wittliff) *The Eagle: The Autobiography of Santa Anna,* Pemberton, 1967; *Experience* (high school text), Steck, 1968; (editor) June Rayfield Welch, *Texas: New Perspectives* (high school text), Steck, 1973; (with Jack Keever) *John Connally: Portrait in Power,* Jenkins Publishing, 1973; *Viva: The Story of Mexican Americans,* Steck, 1976; (with Crystal Ragsdale) *Women in Texas,* Eakins, 1982.

WORK IN PROGRESS: A biography of Governors Jim and Mirian Ferguson of Texas, for Pemberton; a history of O'Connor ranch.

SIDELIGHTS: Ann Fears Crawford told *CA:* "Although most of my work has been in the field of political writing, I began to concentrate on women and women's studies as early as 1976. Few books concerning women were available in the field, and particularly in Texas was there a lack of books concerning women.

"Working with a colleague, Crystal Ragsdale, I began researching women in Texas. What a wealth of material there was! Our book *Women in Texas* remains one of the definitive sources on women in the Lone Star State."

* * *

CRAWFORD, Richard (Arthur) 1935-

PERSONAL: Born May 12, 1935, in Detroit, Mich.; son of Arthur Richard (a foundryman) and Mary Elizabeth (Forshar) Crawford; married Sophie Shambes, December 27, 1958 (divorced, 1965); married Penelope Ball (a musician), April 26, 1967; children: (first marriage) Lynn E., William J.; (second marriage) Amy E., Anne L. *Education:* University of Michigan, B.Mus., 1958, M.Mus., 1959, Ph.D., 1965. *Religion:* Protestant. *Home:* 1158 Baldwin, Ann Arbor, Mich. 48104. *Office:* Burton Tower, University of Michigan, Ann Arbor, Mich. 48109.

CAREER: University of Michigan, Ann Arbor, instructor, 1962-66, assistant professor, 1966-69, associate professor, 1969-75, professor of music history and musicology, 1975—. Visiting professor and senior research fellow at Brooklyn College of the City University of New York, 1973-74; consultant to National Endowment for the Humanities and Rockefeller Foundation. *Member:* American Musicological Society (president, 1982-84), Society for Ethnomusicology, Music Library Association, American Antiquarian Society. *Awards, honors:* Kinkeldey Award from American Musicological Society, 1976; Guggenheim Foundation fellowship, 1977-78.

WRITINGS: Andrew Law: American Psalmodist, Northwestern University Press, 1968; (with David P. McKay) *William Billings of Boston: Eighteenth-Century Composer,* Princeton University Press, 1975; *American Studies and American Musicology,* Institute for Studies in American Music, Brooklyn College of the City University of New York, 1975; (editor) *The Civil War Songbook: Complete Original Sheet Music for Thirty-seven Songs,* Dover, 1977; *A Historian's Introduction to Early American Music,* American Antiquarian Society, 1980. Contributor to biographical dictionaries and of articles and reviews to music journals.

WORK IN PROGRESS: The Core Repertory of Early American Psalmody; A Bibliography of Sacred American Music: 1698-1840.

AVOCATIONAL INTERESTS: Camping.

* * *

CREDLE, Ellis 1902-

PERSONAL: Surname pronounced "Cradle"; born August 18, 1902, in North Carolina; daughter of Zach (a planter) and Bessie (Cooper) Credle; married Charles de Kay Townsend (a photographer; died, 1974); children: Richard Fraser Townsend. *Education:* Louisburg Junior College, graduated, 1922; attended New York School of Interior Decoration, 1925, Art Students League, and Beaux Arts Architectural Institute. *Home:* Apdo. 26 Zapopan, Jalisco, Mexico.

CAREER: Taught school in Blue Ridge Mountains for two years; held a variety of jobs, including that of salesclerk, librarian, guitarist, soap distributor, usher in Carnegie Hall, and governess; artist with American Museum and Brooklyn Children's Museum; author and illustrator, mainly of books for children. *Awards, honors:* Cheshire Cat Award, for *Down, Down the Mountain.*

WRITINGS—Author and illustrator; published by Thomas Nelson, except as indicated: *Down, Down the Mountain* (Junior Literary Guild selection; Weekly Readers Book Club selection), 1934, reprinted, 1978; *Pig-O-Wee,* Grosset, 1935; *Across the Cotton Patch,* 1935; *Little Jeemes Henry,* 1936; *Pepe and the Parrot,* 1937; *The Goat That Went to School,* Grosset, 1940; *Here Comes the Show Boat,* 1940; *Janie's Shoes,* Grosset, 1941; *Adventures of Tittletom,* Oxford University Press, 1949; *Big Doin's on Razar Back Ridge,* 1956; *Little Fraid, Big Fraid,* 1964; *Monkey See, Moneky Do: A Folktale Retold by Ellis Credle,* 1968; *Andy and the Circus,* 1971. Also author and illustrator of *Don't Wash My Ears,* Cadmus.

Author: *The Flop-Eared Hound,* Oxford University Press, 1938; *Johnny and His Mule,* Walck, 1946; *My Pet Peepelo,* Oxford University Press, 1948; *Tall Tales from the High Hills,* Thomas Nelson, 1957; *Little Pest Pico,* illustrations by son, Richard Fraser Townsend, Thomas Nelson, 1969; *Mexico: Land of Hidden Treasure* (nonfiction), Thomas Nelson, 1971.

Illustrator: Emma Gamboa, *El sombrero aventurero de la nina Rosaflor,* Casa Grafica (San Jose, Costa Rica), 1969.

WORK IN PROGRESS: A book about the boy who claimed to see the first flight at Kitty Hawk; a trilogy of adult novels about plantation life in South Carolina, the first titled *Mist on the Marshes;* a novel for young people, *A Mare in the Mist.*

SIDELIGHTS: Ellis Credle told *CA:* "If I had to choose the circumstance that was most important in turning me toward a career of writing and illustrating for children, I should say that it was the fact that I saw myself running out of money during the year that I had chosen to study art in New York. To piece out my foundering financial situation I got a job as part-time governess for two children. One of my duties was to read to them from their library of a hundred or more books for children. This gave me a background in the subject, and I soon discovered that the children much preferred the stories I made up myself. These were based on things that had happened to me on my grandfather's tobacco plantation and also adventures on the Carolina outer islands. I began to write these tales down with the idea of finding a publisher. I never succeeded with any of these casual sketches, but after a serious study of what *was* being published at the time, reading perhaps every book in the New York Public Library—not many in those early days—I produced *Down, Down the Mountain,* writing and rewriting, doing and redoing the pictures. This was the first picture book of the Blue Ridge Mountaineers and the Appalachian country. The *New York Herald Tribune* gave it two columns with illustrations included. Other principal newspapers followed suit. It's still in print after forty-seven years.

"I find that books for little children seem to require well-plotted stories. I sometimes wonder how one can find a plot that hasn't been used time and again. Fortunately, children like the same old thing over and over again. They don't mind if the plot is time-worn; their experience doesn't include many plots. But they do lose interest if one wanders from the main line and begins dillying and dallying with words. Unfortunately, editors do demand fresh plots and that makes it hard.

"I began the adult novel I am [working on] now, *Mist on the Marshes,* with no plot at all. I could not think of one. I began with a romantically melancholy background, the Carolina rice-growing low-country that I knew as a child, with its decaying mansions and plantation houses surrounded with gnarled live-oaks hung with sadly swaying beards of gray Spanish moss. I wrote what happened to an imaginary family, with only day-to-day, short-term objectives. Finally I thought up what seems to me a logical ending for these particular characters. After I had the ending, it was easy to go back, motivate the people a little more, rearrange the chapters to maintain suspense and lead on to the desired end. I am using the same method in a novel for young people, *The Mare in the Mist.* It is a wasteful and time consuming way to write a book and I don't recommend it; it means that a lot of chapters have to be left out, a lot of writing done for nothing. It is not as profitable as having a plot at the ready and heading directly for it, especially if you are good at thinking up plots. But so far, it's the best I have been able to do. But it rather seems to me a lot of lives are lived that way—on a trial and error method with finally an objective in sight and a rearrangement to get there. So maybe, with all its defects it's a sound way to write a novel, one of many ways, perhaps."

* * *

CROUCH, Steve 1915-

PERSONAL: Born February 25, 1915, in Anson, Tex.; son of Stephen Dallas (a clergyman) and Esther (Poindexter) Crouch; married Mary Mayginnes, March 3, 1937 (divorced, 1937); married Ethlyn Douglas (a painter), June 6, 1939 (divorced, 1979); children: (second marriage) Stephen D. III. *Education:* University of Oklahoma, B.A., 1938; graduate study at University of Chicago, 1943-44. *Home and office address:* Box 2113, Carmel, Calif. 93921.

CAREER: U.S. Army, Artillery, 1938-47, leaving service as a major; photographer and writer. Member of board of trustees, Monterey Peninsula Museum of Art, 1965-80, Friends of Photography, 1973-76. Field instructor in photography, University of California, Santa Cruz, 1974—. *Awards, honors*—Military: Bronze Star Medal. Civilian: Silver Medal from Commonwealth Club of California, 1974, for *Steinbeck Country*.

WRITINGS: Peninsula Pictorial, G. C. Beaman, 1950; *Steinbeck Country,* American West, 1973; *Desert Country,* Crown, 1976; *Fog and Sun, Sea and Stone: The Monterey Coast,* Graphic Arts Center Press, 1980; *Numbered Days,* Graphic Arts Center Press, 1983.

WORK IN PROGRESS: A book on Mexico; a book on the Spanish land grant cattle ranches of California; a book of short stories on the people of Monterey and Cannery Row.

SIDELIGHTS: Steve Crouch told *CA:* "When in college, I had every intention of becoming a writer of fiction—maybe even good fiction. Somehow, as the years passed, that intention faded and disappeared. Instead I became a photographer.

"When I was approached by a publisher who was interested in bringing out a book of my photographs on the land where John Steinbeck lived and wrote, we agreed that a friend of mine should write the text. Unfortunately, my friend and I battled long because to me the photographs were paramount, to him they were only illustrations of his text. Eventually, the publisher settled the argument by asking me to write my own text, which I did—a text that paralleled the photographs, each able to stand alone, yet each reinforcing the other.

"This method has worked well enough for all of my books to have attracted a satisfying degree of critical approval."

AVOCATIONAL INTERESTS: Travel, classical music.

* * *

CROWLEY, Daniel J(ohn) 1921-

PERSONAL: Born November 27, 1921, in Peoria, Ill.; son of Michael Bartholomew (a plumbing contractor) and Elsie (Schnebelin) Crowley; married Pearl Ramcharan (a teacher), February 4, 1958; children: Peter Mahendranath Njoya, Eve Lakshmi Lueji, Magdalene Lilawati Balchis. *Education:* Northwestern University, A.B., 1943, Ph.D., 1956; Bradley University, M.A., 1948. *Politics:* Democrat. *Religion:* Roman Catholic. *Home:* 726 Peach Lane, Davis, Calif. 95616. *Office:* 224 Young Hall, University of California, Davis, Calif. 95616.

CAREER: Bradley University, Peoria, Ill., instructor in art history, 1948-50; University of the West Indies, Port-of-Spain, Trinidad, tutor in anthropology, 1953-56; Northwestern University, Evanston, Ill., instructor in anthropology, 1956-57; University of Notre Dame, Notre Dame, Ind., assistant professor of sociology, 1958-59; University of California, Davis, assistant professor, 1961-62, associate professor, 1962-67, professor of anthropology and art, 1967—. Field research in Bahama Islands, 1952, 1953, Trinidad, Tobago, and Santa Lucia, 1953-56, 1958, 1966, 1972, 1973-74, 1980, Congo, Angola, Zambia, and Tanzania, 1960, Mexico, 1962, Ghana, Togo, and Dahomey, 1969-71, and Brazil, 1978-79, 1981, 1982. Member of executive board, Davis Art Center, 1966-68. *Military service:* U.S. Naval Reserve, active duty, 1942-47; became lieutenant junior grade.

MEMBER: American Anthropological Association (fellow), Society for Ethnomusicology (councillor, 1961-65, 1967-69), American Folklore Society (member of executive board, 1963-65; president, 1969-71), American Society for Aesthetics (president of California division, 1964-65), African Studies Association, Royal Anthropological Institute (fellow), Southwestern Anthropological Association (fellow), Trinidad Ethnographic Society, California Folklore Society (Northern regional vice-president, 1971-73; president, 1979-80), Sigma Xi. *Awards, honors:* Jo Stafford Prize in American Folklore, 1952; Ford Foundation fellow, 1959-61; centennial citation from University of California, Santa Cruz, 1976.

WRITINGS: I Could Talk Old-Story Good: Creativity in Bahamian Folklore, University of California Press, 1966; (editor and author of preface) *African Folklore in the New World,* University of Texas Press, 1977; (translator with wife, Pearl Ramcharan-Crowley) *Congolese Sculpture,* Human Relations Area File Press, 1982.

Contributor: Richard M. Dorson, editor, *Folklore Research around the World,* Indiana University Press, 1961; D. K. Wilgus, editor, *Folklore International: Essays in Traditional Literature, Belief, and Custom in Honor of Wayland Hand,* Folklore Association, 1967; Gwendolyn M. Carter and Ann Paden, editors, *Expanding Horizons in African Studies,* Northwestern University Press, 1969.

John F. Szwed, editor, *Black Americans,* Basic Books, 1970; Carol F. Jopling, editor, *Art and Aesthetics in Primitive Societies,* Dutton, 1971; Douglas Fraser and Herbert M. Cole, editors, *African Art and Leadership,* University of Wisconsin Press, 1972; Warren L. d'Azevedo, editor, *The Traditional Artist in African Societies,* Indiana University Press, 1973; *Folktales Told around the World,* University of Chicago Press, 1975; Linda Degh, Henry Glassie, and Felix Oinas, editors, *Folklore Today: A Festschrift in Honor of Richard M. Dorson,* Indiana University Press, 1976; Mabel H. Ross and Barbara K. Walker, editors, *Tales Told among the Nkundo of Zaire,* Shoe String, 1979.

Nikolai Buliakoff and Carl Lindahl, editors, *Folklore on Two Continents: Essays in Honor of Linda Degh,* Trickster Press, 1980; Susan Vogel, editor, *For Spirits and Kings: African Art from the Paul and Ruth Tishman Collection,* Metropolitan Museum of Art, 1981; John Povey and Arnold Rubin, editors, *Observations and Interpretations: 2000 Years of Nigerian Art,* African Studies Center, University of California, Los Angeles, 1981; Simon Ottenberg, editor, *African Religious Groups and Beliefs,* Sahakar Publications, 1981.

Also contributor to *Encyclopaedia Britannica, Encyclopedia International, International Encyclopedia of the Social Sciences, Catholic Encyclopaedia,* and also to journals. Book review editor, *Journal of American Folklore,* 1961-64; contributing editor of *Research in African Literature,* 1970—, *African Arts,* 1971—, and *Journal of African Studies,* 1974—.

WORK IN PROGRESS: Preparing a collection of Caribbean folktales; monograph on Trinidad Creole culture; monograph comparing the carnivals of Trinidad, Rio de Janeiro, Salvador da Bahia, and Recife, Brazil.

* * *

CRUICKSHANK, C(harles) G(reig) 1914-

PERSONAL: Born June 10, 1914, in Fyvie, Aberdeenshire, Scotland; son of George Leslie and Annie (Duncan) Cruickshank; married Maire Kissane, June 16, 1943; children: Christopher, Charles, Matthew. *Education:* University of Aberdeen, M.A., 1936; Hertford College, Oxford, D.Phil., 1940; postdoctoral study at University of Edinburgh, 1940-41. *Home:* 15 McKay Rd., Wimbledon Common, London SW20 OHT, England.

CAREER: British Civil Service, principal in Ministry of Supply, 1941-45, and for Board of Trade, 1945-51, both London, England, trade commissioner in Colombo, Ceylon (now Sri Lanka), 1951-55, and Ottawa, Ontario, Canada, 1955-58, senior trade commissioner, Wellington, New Zealand, 1958-62, director of Commodities Division of Commonwealth Secretariat, London, 1965-68, regional export director for Board of Trade, London, 1969-71, inspector for Foreign and Commonwealth Office, London, 1971-72, assigned to Civil Aviation Authority, 1972-73, assistant secretary for Department of Trade and Industry, London, 1973—. *Member:* Royal Wimbledon Golf Club.

WRITINGS: Elizabeth's Army, Oxford University Press, 1946, revised and enlarged edition, Clarendon Press, 1966; *Army Royal: Henry VIII's Invasion of France, 1513,* Clarendon Press, 1969; *The English Occupation of Tournai,* Clarendon Press, 1971; (co-editor) *A Guide to the Sources of British Military History,* University of California Press, 1971; *The German Occupation of the Channel Islands,* Oxford University Press, 1975; *Greece 1940-41,* Davis-Poynter, 1975; *The V-Mann Papers* (spy novel), R. Hale, 1976; *The Tang Murders,* R. Hale, 1976; *The Fourth Arm: Psychological Warfare, 1938-45,* Davis-Poynter, 1977; *The Deceivers,* R. Hale, 1978; *The Ebony Version,* R. Hale, 1978; *Deceptions in World War II,* Oxford University Press, 1981. Contributor to periodicals, including *English Historial Review, Army Quarterly, Punch, Men Only,* and *History Today.*

WORK IN PROGRESS: The British official history, *SOE in the Far East,* for Oxford University Press; *Annus Mirabilis: 1759,* for Oxford University Press.

SIDELIGHTS: C. G. Cruickshank's accounts of sixteenth-century military expeditions won him such admiration that he was asked to write the official history of the German occupation of the Channel Islands during World War II. Cruickshank's account, *The German Occupation of the Channel Islands,* is "a meticulous, superbly organized monograph on the war years . . . [that] will answer all questions of the military scholar," according to one *Choice* reviewer. C. Northcote Parkinson observes in *Books and Bookmen* that *The German Occupation of the Channel Islands* is "a fascinating and well documented study of a previously neglected subject. The work has been done extremely well and more is now known of this than any other period of Channel Island history."

Cruickshank himself has commented on his transition from chronicler of sixteenth-century battles to historian of twentieth-century wars. In a letter to *CA* he wrote: "A historian who, like me, has time-warped himself from sixteenth to twentieth century faces a problem. Henry VIII cannot sue for libel, but every survivor of a 'contemporary history' can. Queues may form in attorneys' offices even before the book is printed.

"For me the transition from 'pure paper' to 'paper and people' raw material came when I wrote the official history, *The German Occupation of the Channel Islands,* my qualifications being that I had written *The English Occupation of Tournai*—by Henry VIII in the sixteenth century. I was now faced by two gospels: one according to the contemporary papers; one according to the many survivors. Where they agreed, perhaps there *was* the whole truth, pure and simple. Where they conflicted—which to believe? The papers, risking the wrath of the survivors? The survivors, putting scholarly virtue at risk? The official historian, with privileged access to secret papers not to be released under any arrangement, has a further problem. If his readers disbelieve his conclusions, he cannot in his defense lay before them the secret papers.

"There is a simple remedy: Stay with Henry VIII. The ink on his papers may have faded, but their message remains unaltered; he cannot be conjured up (at least by the ordinary critic) to demolish some pet theory of the historian, or to give evidence for the plaintiff in an action for libel."

BIOGRAPHICAL/CRITICAL SOURCES: Economist, June 14, 1969, May 24, 1975, January 14, 1978; *Choice,* September, 1969, October, 1975; *Times Literary Supplement,* July 2, 1971, July 11, 1975, May 28, 1976, December 2, 1977, December 14, 1979; *Observer,* May 11, 1975; *New Statesman,* May 23, 1975; *Encounter,* January, 1979.

* * *

CRUMP, Spencer (M., Jr.) 1933-

PERSONAL: Born November 25, 1933, in San Jose, Calif.; son of Spencer M. (a dentist) and Jessie (Person) Crump; married Mary Dalgarno, January 12, 1963 (divorced, 1975); children: John Spencer, Victoria Elizabeth Margaret. *Education:* University of Southern California, B.A., 1960, M.Sc. (education), 1962, M.A. (journalism), 1969, doctoral studies, 1974—. *Politics:* Democrat. *Religion:* Unitarian Universalist. *Office address:* P.O. Box 38, Corona del Mar, Calif. 92625.

CAREER: Long Beach Independent, Long Beach, Calif., picture editor, 1952-56; *Los Angeles Times,* Los Angeles, Calif., editor of suburban sections (South Bay and Orange County), 1959-62; Trans-Anglo Books, Los Angeles, editorial director, 1962—; Orange Coast College, Costa Mesa, Calif., chairman of communications department, 1966—. Managing director, Person-Crump Development Co., Lubbock, Tex., 1951—; director of Cottonwood Square and of Briarwood Associates, both Dallas, Tex. Elected member, Los Angeles Democratic Central Committee, 1960-61. Consultant to Flying Spur Press and Queen Beach Press, 1976—, Southern Pacific Railroad, 1979-80, and Trans-Anglo/Interurban Press, 1981—. *Member:* Railway and Locomotive Historical Society, Society of Professional Journalists, American Civil Liberties Union, Fellowship of Reconciliation, California Historical Society, Book Publishers Association of Southern California, Orange County Press Club, Masons.

WRITINGS—Published by Trans-Anglo, except as indicated: *Ride the Big Red Cars,* 1962; *Redwoods, Iron Horses, and the*

Pacific, 1963; *Western Pacific: The Railroad That Was Built Too Late*, 1963; *California's Spanish Missions Yesterday and Today*, 1964; *252 Historic Places You Can See in California*, 1964; *Black Riot in Los Angeles*, 1966; *Henry Huntington and the Pacific Electric*, 1970; *Fundamentals of Journalism*, McGraw, 1974; *California's Spanish Missions: An Album of Their Yesterdays and Todays*, 1975; *The Stylebook for News Writing*, 1979; *Newsgathering and Reporting for the 1980's and Beyond*, Beta Publishers, 1981.

AVOCATIONAL INTERESTS: Collecting western books.

* * *

CUNLIFFE, Barrington Windsor 1939-
(Barry Cunliffe)

PERSONAL: Born December 10, 1939, in Portsmouth, England; son of George (a naval officer) and Beatrice (Mersh) Cunliffe. *Education:* St. John's College, Cambridge, B.A., 1961, M.A., 1963, Ph.D., 1966, Litt.D., 1976. *Residence:* Oxford, England. *Agent:* Curtis Brown Ltd., 1 Craven Hill, London W2 3EW, England. *Office:* Institute of Archaeology, Oxford University, 36 Beaumont St., Oxford, England.

CAREER: University of Bristol, Bristol, England, lecturer in classics, 1963-66; University of Southampton, Southampton, England, professor of archaeology, 1966-72; Oxford University, Institute of Archaeology, Oxford, England, professor of European archaeology and fellow of Keble College, 1972—. *Member:* British Academy (fellow), Society of Antiquaries (fellow), Royal Archaeological Institute, Prehistoric Society, Medieval Society, Society for the Promotion of Roman Studies, *Antiquity* Trust, *Vindolanda* Trust.

WRITINGS—Under name Barry Cunliffe: *Excavations at Richborough*, Volume V, Society of Antiquaries, 1968; (editor and contributor) *Roman Bath*, Society of Antiquaries, 1969; *Excavations at Fishbourne: 1961-1969*, Society of Antiquaries, 1971; *Fishbourne: A Roman Palace and Its Gardens*, Johns Hopkins Press, 1971; *Roman Bath Discovered*, Routledge & Kegan Paul, 1971; *The Cradle of England*, British Broadcasting Corp., 1972; *The Making of the English*, British Broadcasting Corp., 1973; *The Regni*, Duckworth, 1974; *Iron Age Communities in Britain*, Routledge & Kegan Paul, 1974, 2nd edition, 1978.

Rome and the Barbarians, Walck, 1975; (with Trevor Rowley) *Oppida: The Beginnings of Urbanisation in Barbarian Europe*, State Mutual Book and Periodical Service, 1976; *Hengistbury Head*, Merrimack Book Service, 1978; *Rome and Her Empire*, McGraw, 1978; *The Celtic World*, McGraw, 1979; (editor) *Antiquity and Man*, Thames & Hudson, 1982.

Also author of television scripts for British Broadcasting Corp., "Cradle of England" (six programs), 1972, "Making of the English" (six), 1973, "Pompeii," 1974, and "Throne of Kings" (six), 1975. Contributor to archaeological journals, and contributor of reviews to *Times Literary Supplement*, *Nature*, and *New Scientist*. Executive editor of *World Archaeology*.

WORK IN PROGRESS: Results of archaeological excavations in Great Britain; research on Europe during the thousand years before the Romans invaded it.

AVOCATIONAL INTERESTS: Travel (East Europe, Mediterranean), Tunisian sun and life style, food, Chinese pottery.

CUNLIFFE, Barry
See CUNLIFFE, Barrington Windsor

* * *

CUNNINGHAM, Aline

PERSONAL: Married James L. Cunningham; children: five. *Education:* Washington University, St. Louis, Mo., B.F.A. *Home:* 225 Highland, St. Louis, Mo. 63122.

CAREER: Self-employed commercial artist.

WRITINGS—Self-illustrated juveniles; all published by Concordia: *Gifts*, 1973; *My Counting Book*, 1973; *My House*, 1973; *Who Am I?*, 1973; *Getting Ready*, 1973; *New Friends*, 1974; *Christmas Is a Birthday*, 1975; *Green Frog*, 1975; *I Talk to God*, 1975; *The Tree and Four Friends*, 1975; *The Surprise*, 1975; *Today*, 1976. Also author of *Christmas Creche Craft*, Concordia, 1979.

Illustrator; published by Concordia, except as indicated: Thomas Smith, *All Aboard, Mouse*, Dent, 1973; Smith, *No Home for Sandy*, Dent, 1973; Smith, *One Cold Day*, Dent, 1973; Smith, *A Ride for Samson*, Dent, 1974; Smith, *Hold a Shell to Your Ear*, Dent, 1974; Dorothy Van Woerkom, *Let Us Go to Bethlehem!*, 1976; Joan Lowery Nixon, *Who Is My Neighbor?*, 1976; Nixon, *Five Loaves and Two Fishes*, 1976; Sibyl Hancock, *An Ark and a Rainbow*, 1976; Mary Blount Christian, *When Time Began*, 1976; Christian, *Jonah, Go to Nineveh!*, 1976; Joan Chase Bowden, *Something Wonderful Happened*, 1977; Christian, *Daniel, Who Dared*, 1977; Carol Greene, *Seven Baths for Naaman*, 1977; Hancock, *Climbing up to Nowhere*, 1977; Jeannette McNeely, *Led by a Star*, 1977; Nixon, *The Son Who Came Home Again*, 1977.

WORK IN PROGRESS: More preschool books.

* * *

CURE, Karen 1949-

PERSONAL: Born June 17, 1949, in Chicago, Ill.; daughter of Charles William (a physician) and Eloise (Greer) Cure. *Education:* Brown University, A.B., 1971; Columbia University, 1976-77. *Home and office:* 365 West End Ave., New York, N.Y. 10024.

CAREER: *Holiday* (magazine), Indianapolis, Ind., associate editor, 1971-73; free-lance writer, 1973—. Counselor for students planning careers as free-lance writers, Brown University. *Member:* American Society of Journalists and Authors.

WRITINGS: *Mini-Vacations U.S.A.*, Follett, 1976; *The Travel Catalogue*, Holt, 1978; *Official Guide to Walt Disney World*, Houghton, 1982; (contributor) *Official Guide to Disneyland*, Houghton, 1983. Editor, "Steve Birnbaum Travel Guide" series, Houghton. Contributor to magazines and newspapers, including *Better Homes and Gardens*, *Apartment Life*, *Diversion*, *Travel and Leisure*, *Newsday*, *Amoco Traveller*, *Fairlanes*, *Sojourn*, *New York*, *Harper's*, *American Health*, and *Passages*. Contributing editor, *TWA Ambassador* and *Disney News*.

WORK IN PROGRESS: A novel about Southern Indiana.

SIDELIGHTS: Karen Cure told *CA:* "For my many service-oriented travel pieces, I have always tried to motivate people to go out and explore places that I've enjoyed, to give them enough information to keep [them] from running down too many blind alleys, and to make sure that they don't miss anything they ought to see.

"Recently I have been working at broadening the scope of my writing to include subjects besides travel and types of articles besides service-oriented pieces. The novel in progress is another attempt in the same direction."

Cure notes of her career as a free-lance writer, "[It is] a career which I should add has been very kind to me if not always as well-paying as I would wish."

* * *

CURLEY, Arthur 1938-

PERSONAL: Born January 22, 1938, in Boston, Mass.; son of Alphonsus M. and Lillian (Norton) Curley. *Education:* Harvard University, A.B., 1959; Simmons College, M.L.S., 1962. *Office:* The Research Libraries, New York Public Library, Fifth Ave. and 42nd St., New York, N.Y. 10018.

CAREER: Boston Public Library, Boston, Mass., adult services librarian, 1959-61; library director, Avon Public Library, Avon, Mass., 1961-64, Palatine Public Library, Palatine, Ill., 1964-68, Montclair Public Library, Montclair, N.J., 1968-75, Cuyahoga County Library System, Cleveland, Ohio, 1975-76; Detroit Public Library, Detroit, Mich., public services director, 1977-80, deputy director, 1978-80; New York Public Library, New York, N. Y., deputy director of Research Libraries, 1980—. Part-time circulation and stack supervisor, Widner Library, Harvard University, 1960-61. Adjunct instructor in management, Graduate School of Library and Information Science of Rutgers University, 1972-75, and of University of Michigan, 1979-80; director and chairman of standards committee, Study of Statewide Library Needs, Mass., 1962-64; planning director, Governor's Conference on Libraries, Mass., 1963-64, and Governor's Conference on Regional Library Development, Ill., 1965; executive director, National Library Week, Mass., 1963-64; member of executive board, Illinois Regional Processing Center, 1965-67; member of executive board and planning coordinator, Regional Library System, Ill., 1966-68; chairman, Committee to Develop a New State Plan for Library Development, N.J., 1972-75; member, Inter-library Document Delivery Task Force, Mich., 1977-80; president and chairman of board, Harvard Library in New York, 1982.

MEMBER: Academic and Research Libraries Association, Association of Specialized and Cooperative Library Agencies, Library Administration and Management Association, Library and Information Technology Association, Special Libraries Association, American Society for Information Science, American Library Association (councillor-at-large, 1970-74; delegate to legislation assembly, 1971-74; member of President's Commission, 1976-78), Public Library Association (legislation chairman, 1971-74). *Awards, honors:* Avon Public Library received the American Library Association Book-of-the-Month Club Library Award for 1964; *Modern Romance Literatures* was included in *Library Journal* citation of outstanding reference books of 1967.

WRITINGS: (With Dorothy Curley) *Modern Romance Literatures,* Ungar, 1967; (contributor) Melvin Voigt, editor, *Advances in Librarianship,* Volume IV, Academic Press, 1974; (contributor) Bill Katz, editor, *The Best of Library Literature: 1974,* Scarecrow, 1975; (contributor) John Wakeman, editor, *World Authors,* H. W. Wilson, 1975; (with Jana Varlejs) *Aker's Simple Library Cataloging,* 6th edition (Curley was not associated with earlier editions), Scarecrow, 1977; (contributor) *Recurring Library Issues,* Scarecrow, 1979; (contributing editor) *Serials for Libraries,* American Bibliographical Center/Neal Schumann, 1980; *Library Personnel Management,* Neal Schumann, 1980; *Best of Library Literature, 1979,* Scarecrow, 1980. Also editor of *Collection Building: Studies in the Development and Effective Use of Library Resources,* 1978. Contributor to *Encyclopedia of Library and Information Sciences,* 1968—, and to *Dictionary of American Library Biography.* Author of "Viewpoint" column for *Library Journal,* 1972. Contributor of book reviews and articles to professional journals, including *Library Journal.* Editor, *New Jersey Libraries,* 1971-74.

WORK IN PROGRESS: Building Library Collections, for Scarecrow.

* * *

CUTLER, Irving H. 1923-

PERSONAL: Born April 11, 1923, in Chicago, Ill.; son of Zelig (a newsman) and Frieda (Wopner) Cutler; married Marian Horovitz, August 31, 1951; children: Daniel, Susan. *Education:* Herzl Junior College, Chicago, Ill., A.A., 1942; University of Chicago, M.A., 1948; Northwestern University, Ph.D., 1964. *Home:* 3217 Hill Lane, Wilmette, Ill. *Office:* Department of Geography, Chicago State University, 95th St. and King Dr., Chicago, Ill. 60628.

CAREER: U.S. Department of Labor, Chicago, Ill., regional labor and housing investigator, 1946-47; Crane Junior College, Chicago, instructor in social science, 1954-59; U.S. Army, Corps of Engineers, Chicago, transportation geographer, 1957; Chicago State University, Chicago, professor of geography, 1961—, chairman of department, 1974—. Member of Wilmette Human Relations Committee, 1967-70. Consultant to Ginn & Co., 1964-65, U.S. Office of Economic Opportunity, 1965-66, Journal Films, 1967-68, and Governor's Task Force on the Future of Illinois, 1979-80. *Military service:* U.S. Navy, 1943-46; became lieutenant junior grade.

MEMBER: International Geographical Union, Association of American Geographers, National Council for Geographic Education, Illinois Geographical Society, Geographic Society of Chicago (member of board of directors, 1977—; vice-president, 1982—), Chicago Jewish Historical Society (member of board of directors, 1977—), Chicago Historical Society, Save the Dunes Council. *Awards, honors:* Haas research grant.

WRITINGS: The Chicago-Milwaukee Corridor: A Geographic Study of Intermetropolitan Coalescence, Northwestern University Studies in Geography, 1965; (with John Beck and John Hobgood) *Pembroke Township: A Research Report on Problems and Possibilities,* U.S. Office of Economic Opportunity, 1966; (editor) *The Chicago Metropolitan Area: Selected Geographic Readings,* Simon & Schuster, 1970; *Chicago: Metropolis of the Mid-Continent,* Geographic Society of Chicago, 1973, 3rd edition, 1982; *Urban Geography,* C. E. Merrill, 1978; (co-author) *Urban Communities,* C. E. Merrill, 1982.

Contributor: Harold Mayer, editor, *1967 Conference on Mass Transportation,* Brotherhood of Railroad Trainmen, 1968; Herbert Gross, editor, *A Modern City: Its Geography,* National Council for Geographic Education, 1970; Ronald E. Nelson, editor, *Illinois: Land and Life in the Prairie State,* Kendall/Hunt, 1976; Brian J.L. Berry, editor, *Chicago: Transformation of an Urban System,* Ballinger, 1976; Peter d'A Jones and Melvin G. Holli, editors, *Ethnic Chicago,* Eerdmans, 1981. Contributor to geography and transportation journals.

WORK IN PROGRESS: Jewish Chicago, for University of Illinois Press.

CUTLER, Ivor 1923-
(Knifesmith)

PERSONAL: Born in 1923. *Home:* 21 Laurier Rd., London NW5 1SD, England.

CAREER: Humorist, composer, writer, cartoonist, painter, poet, singer, actor, free-form jazz pianist, and teacher of movement and drama as a psychological catharsis for children. Featured in British Broadcasting Corp. radio programs "Monday Night at Home," 1959-62, "Don't Look Now," 1962-63, "The I. C. Snow," 1964, and "This Time of Day," 1965; television appearances include "Acker Bilk Show," 1962, "Albert Channel Too," 1964, "Diary of a Nobody" (composed the music), 1964, "Off-Beat," 1964, and "Pure Gingold," 1965-66; has performed on stage at the Establishment, 1961-62, Players Theatre, 1961—, and has starred in "Get Up and Gruts," Edinburgh Festival, 1962, and "An Evening of British Rubbish," Comedy Theatre, 1963. Toured with the Van Morrison performance, 1979, and on university, college, and festival circuits. Worked with the Beatles on the film, "Magical Mystery Tour," 1967. *Military service:* Royal Air Force Volunteer Reserve. *Member:* Equity, EXIT (society for voluntary euthanasia). *Awards, honors:* Pye Radio Award, 1980, for comedy scripts.

WRITINGS: Gruts, Museum Press, 1962; *Cock-a-doodle Don't,* Dobson, 1966; *Meal One,* Heinemann, 1971; *Many Flies Have Features* (poetry), Trigram, 1973; *Balooky Klujypop* (juvenile), Heinemann, 1975, published as *The Elephant Girl,* Morrow, 1976; *The Animal House* (juvenile), Heinemann, 1976, Morrow, 1977; *A Flat Man,* Trigram, 1977; *Private Habits* (poetry), Arc, 1981. Also author of plays, "The Blasted Circle," and "The Fleas," and of over fourteen additional plays and comedy scripts for the British Broadcasting Corp. Author of material for extended-play records, "Who Tore Your Trousers?," "Get Away from the Wall," "Ivor Cutler of Y'hup, O.M.P.," "Ludo," "Dandruff," "A Great Grey Grasshopper," "Velvet Donkey," "Jammy Smears," and "Life in a Scotch Sitting Room." Contributor of cartoons to *Observer, Private Eye, Sunday Times, International Times,* and of poetry to *Sunday Times, New Statesman,* and *Tribune.*

WORK IN PROGRESS: An album of poems for Caedomon Records.

SIDELIGHTS: Ivor Cutler told *CA:* "From nine till twelve years old, my teacher, Mr. Smith, hit me with a leather belt twice a week for bad writing. I used, therefore, to write essays averaging eleven words, to avoid being hit, but in vain. I composed music from fifteen years old, a habit that has stuck. I started painting at twenty-three. At thirty, having taught for six years, I wanted to be a full-time painter, so I thought I'd sell my funny songs. No one would sing them, so I decided to sing them myself. A radio producer asked if I did anything else. I said I had written stories and went home quickly, wrote three, went back and read them to him. He laughed, and I wrote for him for four years. There was a big fight about me. Lots of people hated my stories; an equal number liked them. That's the way it's always been, I'm glad to say. Most of the people who don't like my work, I don't like, so it's quite useful. I don't like it when people I don't like like my work. I started writing poetry in 1965, but it took eight years for it to be good enough to publish. Writing poetry is like being in love. You get so excited trying to put two words together.

"I never know what I'm going to write beforehand, so, having written something, I am always pleased and curious to see what I have written, and, if I'm lucky, it's good enough to read to audiences. I always perform with the lights on, so that I can see the audience's faces when they laugh and can make sure that everyone is paying attention, particularly, young lovers. It's a lovely way to earn a living, except I hate trains and hotels. Humorists are sad people, and I am no exception. You have to be sad to be any good at being funny."

D

DANIELS, Les(lie Noel III) 1943-

PERSONAL: Born October 27, 1943, in Danbury, Conn.; son of Leslie Noel, Jr. (a copywriter) and Eva (Ruppaner) Daniels. *Education:* Brown University, B.A., 1965, M.A., 1968. *Address:* Box 814, Providence, R.I. 02901. *Agent:* Max Gartenberg, 15 West 44th St., New York, N.Y. 10036.

CAREER: Musician, composer, and writer. Formerly associated with the musical group "Soop."

WRITINGS: Comix: A History of Comic Books in America, Outerbridge & Dienstfrey, 1971; *Living in Fear: A History of Horror in the Mass Media,* Scribner, 1975; (editor) *Dying of Fright: Masterpieces of the Macabre,* Scribner, 1976; (editor) *Thirteen Tales of Terror* (textbook), Scribner, 1976; *The Black Castle* (novel), Scribner, 1978; *The Silver Skull* (novel), Scribner, 1979; *Citizen Vampire* (novel), Scribner, 1981. Film critic for *Providence Eagle.*

* * *

DARDIS, Tom 1926-

PERSONAL: Born August 19, 1926, in New York, N.Y.; son of Michael Gregory (an accountant) and Josephine Coletta (O'Hara) Dardis; married Jane Buckelew (a nurse), October 25, 1947 (divorced, 1982); children: Anthony, Anne, Francis. *Education:* New York University, A.B., 1949; Columbia University, M.A., 1952, Ph.D., 1979. *Agent:* John Cushman Associates, 25 West 43rd St., New York, N.Y. 10036.

CAREER: Avon Books, New York City, associate editor, 1952-55; Berkley Publishing Corp., New York City, executive editor, 1955-60, editor-in-chief, 1960-72; free-lance writer, 1972-74; Adelphi University, Garden City, N.Y., adjunct professor of English, 1974-80; John Jay College of Criminal Justice of the City University of New York, New York City, assistant professor, associate professor of English, 1982—. *Military service:* U.S. Army, 1943-46; became sergeant.

WRITINGS: Some Time in the Sun: The Hollywood Years of Fitzgerald, Faulkner, Nathanael West, Aldous Huxley and James Agee (nonfiction), Scribner, 1976, revised edition, Penguin, 1981; *Keaton: The Man Who Wouldn't Lie Down* (biography), Scribner, 1979; *Lloyd: The Man on the Clock* (biography), Viking, 1983.

Editor: *Daughters of Eve,* Berkley Publishing, 1958; *Banned!,* Berkley Publishing, 1961; *Banned #2,* Berkley Publishing, 1962.

SIDELIGHTS: "Tom Dardis is a genuine film historian and not just a putter-together of Hollywood books for the fast buck," writes Ralph Tyler in *Chicago Tribune Book World.* Acclaimed for their willingness to reexamine common myths and misconceptions about various Hollywood figures, Dardis's books are among the most highly regarded in their field.

Some Time in the Sun is a study of the Hollywood years of several of America's brightest literati. Novelists William Faulkner, F. Scott Fitzgerald, Aldous Huxley, and Nathanael West, and critic James Agee, all served as studio screenwriters during the 1930s and 1940s. Rather than asking what Hollywood did to these talented writers, as do most writers on the subject, Dardis asks what did these writers "do to Hollywood when they had to work there?" says *New York Times*'s John Leonard. According to Benny Green in *Spectator,* "Tom Dardis's book about the tribulations of creative writers in pre-war Hollywood is a wonderful read for anyone who has ever seen a lousy movie and then rushed home to read [F. Scott Fitzgerald's] *The Last Tycoon* in search of an explanation."

Some Time in the Sun seeks to dispell the common assumption that life in Hollywood destroyed these writers both morally and artistically. As Leonard comments, "We are more accustomed to hearing about what Hollywood did to them, a morality tale in which Hollywood usually plays the part of a venereal disease." Rather than relating tales of personal downfall, such as Faulkner's bouts of drunkenness or of Fitzgerald's affair with gossip columnist Sheilah Graham, Dardis instead concentrates on what his subjects actually accomplished in Hollywood and on the fact that not only did their studio work allow them to earn desperately needed money, but also to gain time to renew their creative forces and to return to the genres in which they began. As examples, Dardis cites Fitzgerald's unfinished *The Last Tycoon,* often regarded as his best work, and West's celebrated *The Day of the Locust.* Of *Some Time in the Sun,* Gavin writes in *Books and Bookmen:* "Dardis disposes of the myth that Hollywood 'destroyed' writers. He makes it clear that all his subjects were able to earn money that they vitally needed, and that if anyone destroyed Fitzgerald and Agee, it was Fitzgerald and Agee."

Gore Vidal in *New York Review of Books* considers Dardis to be "at his best when he shows his writers taking seriously their various 'assignments'" and in the way he "catches the ambivilence felt by the writers who had descended (but only temporarily) from literature's Parnassus to the swampy marketplace of the movies." However, most critics consider the chief value of Dardis's book to lie in its attempt to verify, "as far as anyone can," as Green notes, "which lines of dialogue they did and didn't write." *Some Time in the Sun,* says Lambert, "is full of fascinating incidental research, of things I never knew and doubt that many other people did—especially concerning the movies on which these writers worked, at one stage or another, without receiving credit."

Dardis's biography of silent film star Buster Keaton contains what is considered the most detailed and definitive analysis of Keaton's career. *Keaton: The Man Who Wouldn't Lie Down* is, says Dwight McDonald in *New York Review of Books,* "the definitive life. I don't think it will ever be superceded except in the unlikely event someone discovers a new cache of important documentary material Dardis has overlooked. It is scholarly yet readable, the fullest, most objective and factually detailed book on virtually every aspect of Buster's career and personality: artistic, financial, and psychological." *Chicago Tribune Book World*'s Clarence Peterson calls the book "a valuable reassessment of the great comic and an absorbing night's reading."

In preparation for *Keaton,* Dardis viewed all of the actor's films (the only biographer thought to have done so), spoke with one of Keaton's close friends, a sister, and an ex-wife, and poured over studio records of Keaton's career, digging up much information other film historians missed or ignored. Praised for his handling of sensitive material and for his insightful analysis, Dardis is, says McDonald, "no great respecter of *idees recues*: He's a genial iconoclast who doesn't hesitate to reverse (always with solid evidence) many of the most common assumptions about Buster's personal and professional life." Three years of preparation and "his careful research and skilled narration pay off in this biography of the master comedian with the tragic mask," comments Ralph Tyler in *Chicago Tribune Book World.* "Dardis's biography whets the appetite for a look at all of Keaton's movies."

BIOGRAPHICAL/CRITICAL SOURCES: New York Times, June 25, 1976; *Newsweek,* July 19, 1976; *New Yorker,* September 13, 1976; *New York Review of Books,* November 25, 1976, October 9, 1980; *Books and Bookmen,* August, 1977; *Spectator,* October 16, 1977; *Chicago Tribune Book World,* August 12, 1979, December 14, 1980; *Washington Post Book World,* January 11, 1981; *New York Times Book Review,* January 18, 1981.

* * *

DAVIDSON, Glen W(illiam) 1936-

PERSONAL: Born July 26, 1936, in Wendell, Idaho; son of W. Dean (a rancher and teacher) and Grace (a teacher; maiden name, Barnum) Davidson; married Shirlee Proctor (a registered nurse), November 26, 1971; children: Heather Ann, Kristin Lynne. *Education:* University of the Pacific, A.B. (magna cum laude), 1958; Drew University, B.D., 1961, M.Div. (cum laude), 1961; Claremont Graduate School, Ph.D. 1964; postdoctoral study at University College, Oxford, 1968, at University of Chicago and Newberry Library, 1967-68, and at University of Iowa, 1970-72. *Religion:* Methodist. *Home:* 13 Pinehurst Dr., Springfield, Ill. 62704. *Office:* School of Medicine, Southern Illinois University, P.O. Box 3926, Springfield, Ill. 62708.

CAREER: Colgate University, Hamilton, N.Y., instructor, 1964-66, assistant professor of philosophy and religion, 1966-67, assistant chaplain, 1964-67; University of Chicago, Chicago, Ill., research fellow-in-residence, 1967-68, assistant professor of history of religions, 1968-70, associate director and coordinator of professional degrees programs, 1968-70; University of Iowa, Iowa City, research fellow-in-residence, 1970-72; Southern Illinois University, School of Medicine, Springfield, associate professor, 1972-76, professor of psychiatry, 1976—, chief of thanatology, 1972-76, associate professor, 1974-76, professor of culture and medicine, and chairman of department, 1974-76, chairman of department of medical humanities, 1976—. Lecturer at Mount Saint Vincent University, summer, 1971, and at Chapman College, World Campus Afloat, spring, 1972; adjunct professor for Program in Human Development Counseling and Gerontology, Sangamon State University, 1976—. Staff member of Memorial Medical Center, Springfield, and St. John's Hospital, Springfield. Member, Springfield Committee for Research Involving Human Subjects, 1973-77, and Behavioral Science Task Force, 1973-82; director of investigative team on primary care of chronic disease, India, 1978; coordinator of United States-India team on comparative medical education, 1978-80. Consultant to Mountain States Tumor Institute, 1972—; member of board of advisors, Project X: Health/Medicine and the Faith Traditions, 1980—.

MEMBER: American Association of Marriage and Family Therapists, Society for Health and Human Values, Institute of Society, Ethics, and the Life Sciences, Society for Values in Higher Education (fellow), Foundation of Thanatology (member of national professional advisory board, 1970—), Gypsy Lore Society. *Awards, honors:* Research grants from Glide Foundation, 1964-65, Colgate Research Council, 1965-67, Newberry Library, 1967, 1972, Illinois Humanities Council, 1978, National Endowment for the Humanities, 1980, Illinois Medical Society Foundation, 1981, and United Ministries in Education, 1982; named outstanding alumnus, Claremont Graduate School, 1982.

WRITINGS: King Mohammed V of Morocco (monograph), College of the Pacific, 1958; *The Pound Fishers: A Photographic Essay,* privately printed, 1966.

(Contributor) Sallie TeSelle, editor, *The Rediscovery of Ethnicity: Its Implications for Culture and Politics in America,* Harper, 1973; (contributor) Robert B. Reaves, Jr. and others, editors, *Ministering to the Dying Patient,* Health Science Publishing, 1973; (author of foreword) Nancy C. Andreasen, *Understanding Mental Illness: A Layman's Guide,* Augsburg, 1974; (author of foreword) David Belgum, *What Can I Do about the Part of Me I Don't Like?,* Augsburg, 1974.

Living with Dying, Augsburg, 1975; (author of foreword) George Paterson, *Helping Your Handicapped Child,* Augsburg, 1975; (contributor) J. Donald Bane and others, editors, *Death and Ministry: Pastoral Care of the Dying and the Bereaved,* Seabury, 1975; (contributor) Bernard Schoenberg and others, editors, *Bereavement: Its Psychosocial Aspects,* Columbia University Press, 1975; (contributor) Frank Reynolds and Earle H. Waugh, editors, *Encounters with Death: Essays in the History and Anthropology of Religion,* Pennsylvania State University Press, 1976; (contributor) *Human Values Teaching Programs for Health Professionals Catalogue,* Institute for Values in Medicine, 1976; (contributor) Terrill Mast, editor, *Curriculum Objectives,* Southern Illinois University School of Medicine,

1976, 2nd edition, 1980; (author of foreword) John J. Dawson, *The Cancer Patient,* Augsburg, 1978; (author of foreword) George Paterson, *The Cardiac Patient,* Augsburg, 1978; *The Hospice: Development and Administration,* Hemisphere Publishing, 1978, 2nd edition, 1983; *Understanding Death of the Wished-for Child,* OGR Service, 1979; (contributor) Hannelore Wass, editor, *Dying: Facing the Facts,* McGraw, 1979.

(With Richard Dayringer, Rosalia E.A. Paiva, and Nancy Pistorius) *Ethical Issues in the Practice of Medicine: A 1980 Study of the Behavior and Opinion of Eight Hundred Illinois Physicians,* Department of Medical Humanities, Southern Illinois University School of Medicine, 1981; (with wife, Shirlee P. Davidson) *A Training Manual for SIDS Parent Counselors and Public Health Nurses,* State of Illinois Department of Public Health, 1981; (contributor) Thomas K. McElhinny, editor, *Human Values Teaching Programs for Health Professionals,* Whitmore, 1981; (contributor) Wass, editor, *Childhood and Death,* Hemisphere Publishing, 1982; (contributor) Edmund Pellegrino and McElhinney, editors, *Teaching Ethics, the Humanities and Human Values in Medical Schools: A Ten Years Overview,* Society for Health and Human Values, 1982; (author of foreword) Judy Stigger, *Coping with Infertility,* Augsburg, 1983; (author of foreword) Paul Maves, *A Place for Us: Where to Live in Our Later Years,* Augsburg, 1983.

Also author of film, radio, and television scripts. General editor, "Religion and Medicine" series, Augsburg, 1973—; series editor, "Medical Humanities" series, Southern Illinois University, 1979—; editor, monograph series, Pearson Museum, 1980—. Contributor to *Proceedings of the SIDS Pathologists and Coroners Conference,* State of Illinois Department of Public Health, 1981. Also contributor of articles and reviews to medical and professional journals, including *Journal of Pediatrics, Illinois Medical Journal, Journal of the American Medical Association,* and *Death Education.* Associate editor, *Death Education,* 1976—.

WORK IN PROGRESS: From the Healer's Hand: The Pearson Museum; Making Clinical Judgements; Religion and Medical Education.

* * *

DAVIDSON, Roger H(arry) 1936-

PERSONAL: Born July 31, 1936, in Washington, D.C.; son of Ross Wallace (a botanist) and Mildred (Younger) Davidson; married Nancy Dixon (an editorial assistant at Brookings Institution), September 29, 1961; children: Douglas Ross, Christopher Reed. *Education:* University of Colorado, B.A. (magna cum laude), 1958; Columbia University, Ph.D., 1963. *Office:* Congressional Research Service, U.S. Library of Congress, Washington, D.C. 20540.

CAREER: Fort Collins Coloradoan, Fort Collins, Colo., municipal reporter, summers, 1957-59; Brookings Institution, Washington, D.C., research assistant, 1960; Dartmouth College, Hanover, N.H., assistant professor of government, 1962-68; University of California, Santa Barbara, associate professor, 1968-71, professor of political science, 1971-82; U.S. Library of Congress, Congressional Research Service, Washington, D.C., senior specialist on American government, 1980—. Staff associate, W. E. Upjohn Institute for Employment Research, Washington, D.C., 1965-66; chairman, Upper Valley Human Rights Council, Hanover, N.H., 1967-68; scholar-inresidence, National Manpower Policy Task Force, 1970-71; professional staff member, Select Committee on Committees of U.S. House of Representatives, 1973-74, and of U.S. Senate, 1976-77. Member of Gioleta Valley Citizens Planning Group, Santa Barbara, Calif., 1974-75.

MEMBER: National Academy of Public Administration, American Political Science Association, American Association of University Professors, Western Political Science Association, Phi Beta Kappa, Delta Sigma Rho. *Awards, honors:* Faculty fellowship, Dartmouth College, 1965-66.

WRITINGS: (With D. M. Kovenock and M. K. O'Leary) *Congress in Crisis: Politics and Congressional Reform,* Wadsworth, 1966; (with J. F. Bibby) *On Capitol Hill: Studies in Legislative Politics,* Holt, 1967, 2nd edition, 1972; (with Sar A. Levitan) *Antipoverty Housekeeping: The Administration of the Economic Opportunity Act,* Institute of Labor and Industrial Relations, University of Michigan/Wayne State University, 1968; *The Role of the Congressman,* Pegasus, 1969; *The Politics of Comprehensive Manpower Legislation,* Johns Hopkins University Press, 1972; (with W. J. Oleszek) *Congress against Itself,* Indiana University Press, 1977; (with Samuel Charles Patterson and Randall B. Ripley) *A More Perfect Union: Introduction to American Government,* Dorsey, 1972, 2nd edition, 1982; (with Oleszek) *Congress and Its Members,* Congressional Quarterly Press, 1981. Contributor to *American Behavioral Scientist, American Journal of Politics, Western Political Quarterly,* and other journals.

WORK IN PROGRESS: Continuing research into public opinion and attitudes of the public toward legislative bodies.

* * *

DAVIES, L(eslie) P(urnell) 1914- (Leo Berne, Robert Blake, Richard Bridgeman, Morgan Evans, Ian Jefferson, Lawrence Peters, Thomas Philips, G. K. Thomas, Leslie Vardre, Rowland Welch)

PERSONAL: Born October 20, 1914, in Cheshire, England; son of Arthur (a gardener) and Annie (Sutton) Davies; married Wynne Tench, November 13, 1940. *Education:* Manchester College of Science and Technology, University of Manchester, qualified as optometrist (F.B.O.A.), 1939. *Home:* El Botanico, Puerto de la Cruz, Tenerife, Canary Islands. *Agent:* Howard Moorepark, 444 East 82nd St., New York, N.Y. 10028; and Carl Routledge, Charles Lavell Ltd., Mowbray House, 176 Wardour St., London W1V 3AA, England.

CAREER: Assistant dispensing pharmacist in Crewe, England, 1930-39; optometrist in private practice, 1939—; free-lance writer. Professional artist in Rome, Italy, 1945-46; postmaster in Birmingham, England, 1947-57. *Military service:* British Army, Royal Army Medical Corps, World War II; served in France, and with 8th Army in North Africa and Italy; became staff sergeant.

WRITINGS: The Paper Dolls, Jenkins, 1964, Doubleday, 1966; *Man Out of Nowhere,* Jenkins, 1965, published as *Who Is Lewis Pinder?,* Doubleday, 1966; *The Artificial Man,* Jenkins, 1965, Doubleday, 1967; *Psychogeist,* Jenkins, 1966, Doubleday, 1967; *The Lampton Dreamers,* Jenkins, 1966, Doubleday, 1967; (under pseudonym Leslie Vardre) *Tell It to the Dead,* Long, 1966, published as *The Reluctant Medium,* Doubleday, 1967; *Twilight Journey,* Jenkins, 1967, Doubleday, 1968; (under pseudonym Leslie Vardre) *The Nameless Ones,* Jenkins, 1967, published as *A Grave Matter,* Doubleday, 1968; *The Alien,* Jenkins, 1968; *Dimension A,* Doubleday, 1969; *Stranger to Town,* Doubleday, 1969.

Adventure Holidays, Ltd., Doubleday, 1970; *Genesis Two*, Doubleday, 1970; *The White Room*, Barrie & Rockliff, 1970; *The Shadow Before*, Doubleday, 1970; *Give Me Back Myself*, Doubleday, 1971; *What Did I Do Tomorrow*, Barrie & Jenkins, 1971, Doubleday, 1973; *Assignment Abacus*, Doubleday, 1975; *Possession*, Doubleday, 1976; *The Land of Leys*, Doubleday, 1979; *Morning Walk*, Hale, 1982.

Author of more than 250 short stories published under various pseudonyms in United Kingdom and abroad.

MEDIA ADAPTATIONS: The Artificial Man was filmed with title "Project X," Paramount, 1968, and *The Alien* was filmed as "The Groundstar Conspiracy," Universal, 1970. The film rights to *Psychogeist* have been sold.

AVOCATIONAL INTERESTS: Reading about the unusual; painting.

* * *

DAVIS, David Brion 1927-

PERSONAL: Born February 16, 1927, in Denver, Colo.; son of Clyde Brion (a writer) and Martha (a writer and painter; maiden name, Wirt) Davis; married Frances Warner, October 22, 1948 (divorced, 1971); married Toni Hahn (a psychiatric social worker), September 9, 1971; children: (first marriage) Jeremiah, Martha, Sarah; (second marriage) Adam, Noah. *Education:* Dartmouth College, A.B., 1950; Harvard University, A.M., 1953, Ph.D., 1956. *Politics:* Democrat. *Home:* 733 Lambert Rd., Orange, Conn. 06477. *Office:* 226 Hall of Graduate Studies, Yale University, New Haven, Conn. 06520.

CAREER: Dartmouth College, Hanover, N.H., instructor in history and Fund for the Advancement of Education intern, 1953-54; Cornell University, Ithaca, N.Y., assistant professor, 1955-58, associate professor, 1958-63, Ernest I. White Professor of History, 1963-69; Yale University, New Haven, Conn., professor of history, 1969-72, Farnham Professor of History, 1972-78, Sterling Professor of History, 1978—. Fulbright lecturer in India, 1967, and at Universities in Guyana and the West Indies, 1974; Harold Vyvyan Harmsworth Professor of American History, Oxford University, 1969-70; lecturer at fourth International Symposium, Smithsonian Institution, 1970; Benjamin Rush Lecturer, American Psychiatric Association, 1976; lecturer at George Washington University, 1977, and at University of Wyoming and Center for Study of Southern Culture and Religion, Tallahassee, Fla., 1979; Pierce Lecturer, Oberlin College, 1979; French-American Foundation Chair in American Civilization, Ecole des Hautes Etudes en Sciences Sociales, Paris, 1980-81; Patten Foundation Lecturer, Indiana University, 1981; public lecturer at Universities of Paris, Leiden, Amsterdam, Utrecht, Tel Aviv, and Beer Shiva, and at Hebrew University, Jerusalem, 1981; has presented papers to professional conferences and learned societies. Commissioner, Orange, Conn., Public Library Commission, 1974-75; associate director, National Humanities Institute, Yale University, 1975. *Military service:* U.S. Army, 1945-46.

MEMBER: American Historical Association (member of Pulitzer Prize and Beveridge Prize committees), Organization of American Historians, Society of American Historians, American Antiquarian Society, Institute of Early American History and Culture (member of council), American Academy of Arts and Sciences, Phi Beta Kappa.

AWARDS, HONORS: Guggenheim fellow, 1958-59; Anisfield-Wolf Award, 1967; Pulitzer Prize, 1967, for *The Problem of Slavery in Western Culture;* National Mass Media Award from National Conference of Christians and Jews, 1967; Center for Advanced Study in the Behavioral Sciences fellow, 1972-73; Beveridge Prize from American Historical Association, 1975; National Book Award for history, 1976, for *The Problem of Slavery in the Age of Revolution, 1770-1823;* Bancroft Prize, 1976; Huntington Library fellow, 1976; Litt.D., Dartmouth College, 1977; National Endowment for the Humanities research grants 1980 and 1981; Fulbright traveling fellow, 1980-81.

WRITINGS: Homicide in American Fiction, Cornell University Press, 1957; *The Problem of Slavery in Western Culture*, Cornell University Press, 1967; (editor) *Ante-bellum Reform*, Harper, 1967; *The Slave Power Conspiracy and the Paranoid Style*, Louisiana State University Press, 1969; *Was Thomas Jefferson an Authentic Enemy of Slavery?*, Clarendon Press, 1970; (editor) *The Fear of Conspiracy: Images of Un-American Subversion from the Revolution to the Present*, Cornell University Press, 1971; *The Problem of Slavery in the Age of Revolution, 1770-1823*, Cornell University Press, 1975; (with others) *The Great Republic: A History of the American People*, Little, Brown, 1977, revised edition, 1981; (editor) *Antebellum American Culture: An Interpretive Anthology*, Heath, 1979.

Contributor: Alfred Kazin and Charles Shapiro, editors, *The Stature of Theodore Dreiser*, Indiana University Press, 1955; Shapiro, editor, *Twelve Original Essays on Great American Novels*, Wayne State University Press, 1958; Martin Duberman, editor, *The Antislavery Vanguard*, Princeton University Press, 1965; C. Vann Woodward, editor, *The Comparability of American History*, Basic Books, 1967; Samuel Klausner, editor, *Why Man Takes Chances*, Anchor Books, 1968.

Richard Blum, editor, *Surveillance and Espionage in a Free Society*, Praeger, 1972; Sidney Mintz, editor, *Slavery, Colonialism, and Racism*, Norton, 1974; Harry Owens, editor, *Perspectives and Irony in American Slavery*, University of Mississippi Press, 1976; David Reiss, editor, *The American Family*, Plenum, 1979; Max Skidmore, editor, *Viewpoints, U.S.A.*, Heinemann (New Delhi), 1979; Christine Bolt and Seymour Drescher, editors, *Religion, Anti-Slavery, and Reform*, Dawson, 1980; Erich Angermann and Marie-Luise Frings, editors, *Oceans Apart?: Comparing Germany and the United States*, Klett Cotta (Stuttgart), 1981. Contributor to professional journals and other periodicals, including *New York Times Book Review, Times Literary Supplement, American Historical Review, Journal of American History, New England Quarterly, Yale Review*, and *Reviews in American History*.

WORK IN PROGRESS: Slavery and Human Progress and *The Problem of Slavery in the Age of Emancipation, 1815-1890*, both for Oxford University Press.

SIDELIGHTS: David Brion Davis is widely regarded as a leading expert on the history of slavery in the United States and throughout the world. His books on the subject have been praised for their scholarship, lucidity, and especially for their new insights into a much-analyzed institution.

In a *New York Times Book Review* article, J. H. Plumb calls the Pulitzer Prize-winning *The Problem of Slavery in Western Culture* "one of the most scholarly and penetrating studies of slavery" and says that here Davis displays "his mastery not only of a vast source of material, but also of the highly complex, frequently contradictory factors that influenced opinion on slavery." In this book, according to George M. Fredrickson in the *New York Review of Books*, Davis is concerned "mainly with the changes that had to occur in Western views of the nature of man and his relationship to society and authority before antislavery ideas could emerge.'' For example, he discusses ''the role of original sin as a justification for slavery and how the modification and dilution of this traditional Christian doctrine in the eighteenth century had raised troublesome questions about black servitude.''

In *The Problem of Slavery in the Age of Revolution, 1770-1823,* Davis continues this analysis with, Fredrickson writes, a study of ''how ideas antithetical to slavery could win acceptance and become the basis of practical policies that served the broader needs of dominant groups.'' To do this, Davis compares the American antislavery movement with that in Great Britain and other countries at the same time. Fredrickson feels that it is clear from Davis's account ''that the British antislavery movement had much greater success in this period than the American, even though both countries legislated against the international slave trade in the same year (1807).'' To account for this dichotomy, ''Davis undertakes a detailed analysis of the relationship of antislavery to dominant ideologies in both the United States and Great Britain.'' The result, according to Plumb is ''a rich and powerful book [that] will, I am sure, stand the test of time—scholarly, brilliant in analysis, beautifully written.''

BIOGRAPHICAL/CRITICAL SOURCES: New York Times Book Review, February 9, 1975; *Nation,* April 26, 1975; *New York Review of Books,* October 16, 1975.

* * *

DAVIS, George 1939-

PERSONAL: Born November 29, 1939, in West Virginia; son of Clarence (a clergyman) and Winnie Davis; married Mary Cornelius (a secretary), August 31, 1963; children: Pamela, George. *Education:* Colgate University, B.A., 1961; Columbia University, M.F.A., 1971. *Home:* 327 Claremont Ave., Mt. Vernon, N.Y. 10552. *Office:* Rutgers University, New Brunswick, N.J. 08903.

CAREER: U.S. Air Force, 1961-68, became captain; *Washington Post,* Washington, D.C., staff writer, 1968-69; *New York Times,* New York, N.Y., deskman, 1969-70; Bronx Community College of the City University of New York, Bronx, N.Y., assistant professor, 1974-78; Rutgers University, New Brunswick, N.J., assistant professor, 1978—. President of Contemporary Communications (marketing firm). *Member:* Authors Guild, Authors League of America. *Awards, honors*—Military: Air Medal. Other: Awards from New York State Council on the Arts, America the Beautiful Fund, and National Endowment for the Humanities.

WRITINGS: Coming Home (novel), Random House, 1972; *Love, Black Love,* Doubleday, 1978; (with Glegg Watson) *Black Life in Corporate America,* Doubleday, 1982. Contributor of articles and short stories to numerous periodicals, including *Black World, Essence, National Observer, Smithsonian, New York Times Magazine, Black Enterprise,* and *Beauty Trade.*

SIDELIGHTS: George Davis's book *Black Life in Corporate America* explores the status of black people in management positions in business today. For three years Davis and his coauthor Glegg Watson researched this project, interviewing well over 150 managers—both black and white—and talking with numerous experts in the field of blacks in the business world. Wente Bowen writes in the *Los Angeles Times* that after analyzing all of the data, Davis and Watson point out in their book that ''on the surface, most blacks and whites get along quite well in most corporate settings, but many black managers find the corporate environment to be 'living hell' for them. Their suggestions are ignored, and they invariably end up being second in charge behind a white guy. 'Even if he's dumb, they will trust him more.' In short, racism holds back the progress of the black manager inside corporate America.''

BIOGRAPHICAL/CRITICAL SOURCES: Newsweek, April 6, 1970; *Los Angeles Times,* September 9, 1982; *New York Times Book Review,* October 24, 1982.

* * *

DAVIS, Maggie (Hill)

PERSONAL: Born in Norfolk, Va.; daughter of George Blair and Dorothy (Mason) Hill; children: four sons. *Education:* Attended schools in New York, N.Y. *Religion:* Quaker.

CAREER: Writer. Formerly radio and television script writer and producer, public relations agent, and newspaper feature writer; formerly assistant director of promotion at television stations in Atlanta, Ga.; Yale University, New Haven, Conn., research assistant to chairman of psychology department; currently director of corporate public relations, Snelling and Snelling International, Sarasota, Fla. Lecturer on writing at Emory University, University of Georgia, and Yale University; lecturer at writing seminars at Yale University, 1973, 1974, and 1975. Visiting artist-writer, International Cultural Center, Tunisia, 1965. Conducted research in Ireland, 1978. Volunteer member of Georgia Governor's Committee to Improve Education, 1964. *Member:* Authors Guild, Public Relations Society of America, Authors League of America. *Awards, honors:* Named ''Georgia Writer of the Year,'' Georgia Writers Association, 1964.

WRITINGS—Novels: *The Winter Serpent,* McGraw, 1958; *The Far Side of Home* (Literary Guild selection), Macmillan, 1963; *Rommel's Gold,* Lippincott, 1971; *The Sheik,* Morrow, 1977; *Eagles,* Morrow, 1980. Contributor of stories and articles to *Ladies' Home Journal, Holiday, Georgia Review, Cosmopolitan, Holiday,* and *Venture.*

WORK IN PROGRESS: A novel.

SIDELIGHTS: Maggie Davis told *CA:* ''Count on everything being a thousand times more difficult if you're a woman. I've been told I 'write like a man.' Which means, I suppose, that I'm placed somewhere outside the tedious preciosities of a Joyce Carol Oates, the talentless vulgarities of a Judith Krantz, and [am] four thousand times removed from Harlequin Romances.''

Davis lived in Spain for one year. Her books have been translated into Japanese, Spanish, Dutch, and Portuguese.

BIOGRAPHICAL/CRITICAL SOURCES: New York Times Book Review, May 30, 1971; *Times Literary Supplement,* February 24, 1978.

* * *

DAVIS, Suzanne
See SUGAR, Bert Randolph

* * *

DAY, John R(obert) 1917-

PERSONAL: Born June 26, 1917, in Enfield, Middlesex, England; son of Robert Henry (a railway officer) and Annie (Barker) Day; married Helen Irene Merrell, June 11, 1949; children: Peter John, Martin Christopher. *Education:* Attended London School of Economics and Political Science, London, 1938, 1951-52, and North-West Polytechnic, 1950-54. *Home:* "Four Winds," Plough Rd., Great Bontley, Colchester, England.

CAREER: London & North Eastern Railway, London, England, 1935-51, started in locomotive running department, advanced through commercial manager's and chief civil engineer's departments to purchasing officer's department; Railway Executive and British Transport Commission, London, member of headquarters staff, 1951-54; *Railway Gazette,* London, member of editorial staff, 1954-57; London Transport, London, head of technical press section, 1957-64, senior assistant to press officer, 1964-74, manager of Collection of Historical Vehicles, 1974-78. Member, Chartered Institute of Transport; associate of Institution of Railway Signal Engineers. Consultant, London Transport Museum. *Military service:* British Army, Royal Engineers, 1940-46; Army Emergency Reserve, 1948-60; became captain. *Member:* Movement Control Officers' Club, Association of British Transport Museums. *Awards, honors:* Modern Transport Award, honours graduate, Institute of Transport.

WRITINGS: (With B. G. Wilson) *Famous Railways of the World,* Muller, 1957; (with Wilson) *Unusual Railways,* Macmillan, 1957; (with B. K. Cooper) *Railway Signalling Systems,* Muller, 1958, 2nd revised edition, 1963.

(With Cooper) *Railway Locomotives,* Muller, 1960; *More Unusual Railways,* Macmillan, 1960; *Railways of Southern Africa,* Arthur Barker, 1963; *The Story of London's Underground,* London Transport, 1963, revised edition, 1979; *Railways of Northern Africa,* Arthur Barker, 1964; *Railways under the Ground,* Arthur Barker, 1964; (contributor) *Railway Enthusiast's Bedside Book,* Batsford, 1966; (with P. Duff and M. Hill) *Transport Today and Tomorrow,* Lutterworth, 1967; *The Story of the Victoria Line,* London Transport, 1969, 2nd edition, 1972; *Trains,* Hamlyn, 1969, Grosset, 1970.

(With William Fenton) *The Last Drop: The Steam Age on the Underground from 1863 to 1971,* London Transport, 1971, revised edition, 1973; *The Story of the London Bus,* London Transport, 1973; *London's Trams and Trolleybuses,* London Transport, 1977.

Engines, Hamlyn, 1980; *Source Book of Underground Railways,* Ward, Lock, 1980; *Source Book of London Transport,* Ward, Lock, 1982.

Author of column, "Railways To-Day," published in *Railway Engineering* for many years. Contributor to *Horizon Book of Railways,* to encyclopedias, and to periodicals, including *Country Life, Modern Transport, Railway World, Times* (London), *Guardian, Irish Times,* and *Birmingham Mail.*

WORK IN PROGRESS: Long-term research for possible book on Fritz Bernhard Behr.

SIDELIGHTS: John R. Day carries his firm belief in lasting importance of properly modernized, automated railroads into his home, where he tries out signaling and electrical ideas on a model railroad in the attic. His writing is usually done between 10 p.m. and 1 a.m. *Avocational interests:* Chess, organ-playing.

* * *

de CAMP, Catherine C(rook) 1907-

PERSONAL: Born November 6, 1907, in New York, N.Y.; daughter of Samuel (a lawyer) and Mary E. (Beekman) Crook; married Lyon Sprague de Camp (an author under name of L. Sprague de Camp), August 12, 1939; children: Lyman Sprague, Gerard Beekman. *Education:* Barnard College, B.A. (magna cum laude), 1933; graduate study at Western Reserve (now Case Western Reserve) University, Columbia University, and Temple University, 1934-38. *Politics:* "Uncommitted." *Religion:* Episcopalian. *Home:* 278 Hothrope Lane, Villanova, Pa. 19085.

CAREER: Oxford School, Harford, Conn., teacher of English, 1934-35; teacher of English and history at Laurel School, Shaker Heights, Ohio, 1935-37, and Calhoun School, New York, N.Y., 1937-39; Temple University, Philadelphia, Pa., instructor in child development, 1949; editor of books and radio scripts for husband, L. Sprague de Camp, 1949-62; writer in collaboration with husband, 1962—; business manager for husband, L. Sprague de Camp. Lecturer on science fiction, business side of writing, and family finance. Has worked as social worker with the handicapped, tutor, and substitute teacher.

MEMBER: Academy of Natural Sciences (Philadelphia), University Museum of University of Pennsylvania, Historical Society of Pennsylvania, Fellows in American Studies (fellow), Phi Beta Kappa, Cum Laude Society, Barnard Club of Philadelphia (president, 1956-59). *Awards, honors:* Eighth Drexel Citation for Distinguished Contribution to Literature for Young People, 1978.

WRITINGS: The Money Tree: A Guide to Successful Personal Finance, New American Library, 1972; *Teach Your Child to Manage Money,* U.S. News & World Report, 1975; (editor) *Creatures of the Cosmos,* Westminster, 1977.

With husband, L. Sprague de Camp: *Ancient Ruins and Archaeology,* Doubleday, 1964, published as *Citadels of Mystery,* Ballantine, 1973; *Spirits, Stars and Spells,* Canaveral, 1966; *The Story of Science in America,* Scribner, 1967; *The Day of the Dinosaur,* Doubleday, 1968; *Darwin and His Great Discovery,* Macmillan, 1972; *Three Thousand Years of Fantasy and Science Fiction,* Lothrop, 1972; *Tales beyond Time,* Lothrop, 1973; *Science Fiction Handbook, Revised: How to Sell and Write Imaginative Stories,* Owlswick, 1975; *Footprints on Sand,* Advent, 1981; (also with Lin Carter) *Conan the Barbarian,* Bantam, 1982.

Writer of scripts on developments in science for Voice of America, 1949-50. Contributor to *Time* and *South.*

WORK IN PROGRESS: Dark Valley Destiny: The Life of Robert E. Howard, with L. Sprague de Camp.

SIDELIGHTS: Catherine C. de Camp told *CA:* "Although I wrote poetry as a teenager and taught English as a young high-school teacher, I became a professional writer in self-defense. You see, I married an author, a man so dedicated to his writing that he was not even present in spirit most of the day and all of the evening seven days a week. Dutifully, I learned to pay the bills, tend our two little sons, stretch the dollars, cope with plumbers and publishers, and bat my head against the wall—silently, of course.

"One day I realized that a successful writer needs a well-organized business office and a competent person to run it. That day I became a liberated woman. No longer a mute wraith doing Cinderella's chores, overworked and undervalued, I became a respected business woman who sold my husband's works, managed the income, invested the surplus, handled the publicity and answered the fan mail.

"I enjoyed my job as dragon at the gates of the ivory tower for a while; but dragons seldom gain fame or even a pat on the ego. So one day I decided to write a book of my own, instead of merely acting as editor and rewrite girl on the books that came out in my husband's name. It took five years to write *The Money Tree: A Guide to Successful Personal Finance;* but I loved every minute of the hours I spent on the book. After that, I was hooked. I've been writing ever since.

"I still handle the growing piles of contracts, tax returns, and correspondence with lawyers, literary agents and devoted readers. I still rewrite many a manuscript for the senior author of the de Camp team, but when I do my half of the work, I get my billing as a collaborator. I have to sneak down late at night often to do a bit of original writing during the darkling hours when no phones ring. But I wouldn't trade my occupation for any other on earth. Besides, my husband seems happy with our arrangements: he says he's still in love with me after forty-three years of marriage. What's more, he takes me everywhere with him and treats me like a princess."

AVOCATIONAL INTERESTS: Modern dance, genealogical and historical research, travel, lecturing, gardening, interior decoration, and antique hunting.

BIOGRAPHICAL/CRITICAL SOURCES: Philadelphia Sunday Bulletin, December 6, 1964; *Main Line Times,* March 3, 1966; *Night Voyages,* fall, 1979.

* * *

de CAMP, L(yon) Sprague 1907-
(Lyman R. Lyon, J. Wellington Wells)

PERSONAL: Born November 27, 1907, in New York, N.Y.; son of Lyon and E. Beatrice (Sprague) de Camp; married Catherine A. Crook (a writer), August 12, 1939; children: Lyman Sprague, Gerard Beekman. *Education:* California Institute of Technology, B.S., 1930; attended Massachusetts Institute of Technology, 1932; Stevens Institute of Technology, M.S., 1933. *Politics:* Democrat. *Home:* 278 Hothorpe Lane, Villanova, Pa.

CAREER: Inventors Foundation, Inc., Hoboken, N.J., editor and instructor, 1933-36; International Correspondence Schools, Scranton, Pa., principal, 1936-37; Fowler-Becker Publishing Co., New York City, editor, 1937-38; American Society of Mechanical Engineers, New York City, editor, 1938; free-lance writer. Member of board of elections, Nether Providence Township, Pa., 1955-60. *Military service:* U.S. Navy, World War II; became lieutenant commander. *Member:* History of Science Society, Society for the History of Technology (member of advisory board), Association Phonétique Internationale, Bread Loaf Writers Conference (fellow), University of Pennsylvania Museum, Trap Door Spiders Club, Hyborian Legion, Philadelphia Academy of Natural Science.

AWARDS, HONORS: International Fantasy Award, 1953, for *Lands Beyond;* Cleveland Science Fiction Association award, 1953, for *Tales from Gavagan's Bar;* fiction award, Athenaeum of Philadelphia, 1958, for *An Elephant for Aristotle;* Grand Master (Gandalf Award), World Science Fiction Convention, 1976; Eighth Drexel Citation for Distinguished Contribution to Literature for Young People, 1978; Nebula Grand Master, Science Fiction Writers of America, 1979.

WRITINGS—Science fiction and fantasy: *Lest Darkness Fall,* Holt, 1941, reprinted, Remploy, 1973; (with Fletcher Pratt) *The Incomplete Enchanter,* Holt, 1941, reprinted, Sphere Books, 1979; (with Pratt) *The Land of Unreason,* Holt, 1942, reprinted, Ballantine, 1970; (with Pratt) *The Carnelian Cube,* Gnome, 1948, reprinted, Lancer Books, 1967; *Divide and Rule,* Fantasy Press, 1948; *The Wheels of If, and Other Science Fiction,* Shasta, 1948, reprinted, Berkley Publishing, 1970; (with Pratt) *The Castle of Iron,* Gnome, 1950, reprinted, Pyramid Publications, 1962; (with P. Schuyler Miller) *Genus Homo,* Fantasy Press, 1950; *The Undesired Princess,* Fantasy Press, 1951; *Rogue Queen,* Doubleday, 1951; *The Continent Makers, and Other Tales of the Viagens,* Twayne, 1953; (with Pratt) *Tales from Gavagan's Bar,* Twayne, 1953, enlarged edition, Owlswick Press, 1978; *The Tritonian Ring, and Other Pusadian Tales,* Twayne, 1953, reprinted, Ballantine, 1977; *Cosmic Manhunt,* Ace, 1954; *Solomon's Stone,* Avalon, 1957; *The Tower of Zanid,* Avalon, 1958.

The Glory That Was, Avalon, 1960; (with Pratt) *Wall of Serpents,* Avalon, 1960; *The Search for Zei,* Avalon, 1962; *A Gun for Dinosaur* (short stories), Doubleday, 1963; *The Hand of Zei,* Avalon, 1963, reprinted, Owlswick Press, 1981; (editor) *Swords and Sorcery,* Pyramid Publications, 1963; (editor) *The Spell of Seven,* Pyramid Publications, 1965; (editor) *The Fantastic Swordsmen,* Pyramid Publications, 1967; *The Goblin Tower,* Pyramid Publications, 1968; *The Reluctant Shaman and Other Fantastic Tales,* Pyramid Publications, 1970; (editor) *Warlocks and Warriors,* Putnam, 1970; *The Clocks of Iraz,* Pyramid Publications, 1971; (author of introduction) Abdul Alhazred, *Al Azif (The Necronomicon),* Owlswick Press, 1973; *The Fallible Fiend,* New American Library, 1973; (with Pratt) *The Compleat Enchanter: The Magical Misadventures of Harold Shea,* Doubleday, 1975; *The Hostage of Zir,* Putnam, 1977; *The Best of L. Sprague de Camp,* Doubleday, 1978; *The Great Fetish,* Doubleday, 1978; *The Purple Pterodactyls: The Adventures of W. Wilson Newberry, Ensorcelled Financier,* Phantasia Press, 1979; *The Enchanter Completed,* with foreword by wife Catherine C. de Camp, Sphere Books, 1980.

"Conan" series; all published by Lancer Books, except as indicated: (With Robert E. Howard) *Tales of Conan,* Gnome, 1955; (with Bjoern Nyberg) *The Return of Conan,* Gnome, 1957; (with Howard) *Conan the Adventurer,* 1966; (with Lin Carter and Howard) *Conan,* 1967; (with Howard) *Conan the Warrior,* 1967; (with Howard) *Conan the Usurper,* 1967; *The Conan Reader,* Mirage Press, 1968; (with Howard and Nyberg) *Conan the Avenger,* 1968; (editor) Howard, *Conan the Conquerer,* 1968; (with Howard and Carter) *Conan the Wanderer,* 1968; (with Carter) *Conan of the Isles,* 1968; (editor with George H. Scithers) *The Conan Swordbook,* Mirage Press, 1969; (with Howard and Carter) *Conan of Cimmeria,* 1969; (with Carter) *Conan the Buccaneer,* 1971; (editor with Scithers) *The Conan Grimoire,* Mirage Press, 1972; (with Carter) *Conan of Aquilonia,* 1977; (with Carter) *Conan the Swordsman,* Bantam, 1978; (with Carter) *Conan the Liberator,* Bantam, 1979; *Conan and the Spider God,* Bantam, 1982.

Nonfiction: (With Alf K. Berle) *Inventions and Their Management,* International Textbook Company, 1937, reprinted, Van Nostrand, 1959; *The Evolution of Naval Weapons,* U.S. Government Printing Office, 1947; (with Willy Ley) *Lands Beyond,* Rinehart, 1952; *Lost Continents: The Atlantis Theme in History, Science, and Literature,* Gnome, 1954, reprinted, Dover, 1970; *Engines: Man's Use of Power from the Water Wheel to the Atomic Pile* (juvenile), Golden Press, 1959, revised edition, 1961; *Man and Power: The Story of Power from the Pyramids to the Atomic Age* (juvenile), Golden Press, 1961; *The Heroic Age of American Invention,* Doubleday, 1961; *Energy and Power: How Man Uses Animals, Wind, Water, Heat, Electricity, Chemistry, and Atoms to Help Him in His Daily*

Living (juvenile), Golden Press, 1962; *The Ancient Engineers,* Doubleday, 1963, reprinted, Ballantine, 1980; *Elephant,* Pyramid Publications, 1964; *The Great Monkey Trial,* Doubleday, 1968; *Scribblings,* NESFA Press, 1972; *Great Cities of the Ancient World,* Doubleday, 1972; *Lovecraft: A Biography,* Doubleday, 1975; *The Miscast Barbarian: A Biography of Robert E. Howard, 1906-1936,* Gerry de la Ree, 1975; *Literary Swordsmen and Sorcerers: The Makers of Heroic Fantasy,* Arkham, 1976; *The Ragged Edge of Science,* Owlswick Press, 1980.

With wife, Catherine C. de Camp: *Science Fiction Handbook,* Hermitage, 1953, revised edition, Owlswick Press, 1975; *Ancient Ruins and Archaeology,* Doubleday, 1964, published as *Citadels of Mystery,* Ballantine, 1973; *Spirits, Stars, and Spells,* Canaveral, 1967, 2nd edition published as *Spirits, Stars, and Spells: The Profits and Perils of Magic,* Owlswick Press, 1980; *The Story of Science in America* (juvenile), Scribner, 1967; *The Day of the Dinosaur,* Doubleday, 1968; *Darwin and His Great Discovery* (juvenile), Macmillan, 1972; (co-editors) *Three Thousand Years of Fantasy and Science Fiction,* Lothrop, 1972; (co-editors) *Tales Beyond Time: From Fantasy to Science Fiction,* Lothrop, 1973; *Science Fiction Handbook, Revised: How to Write and Sell Imaginative Stories,* McGraw, 1977; *Footprints on Sand: A Literary Sampler,* Advent, 1981.

Historical fiction: *An Elephant for Aristotle,* Doubleday, 1958; *The Bronze God of Rhodes,* Doubleday, 1960; *The Dragon of the Ishtar Gate,* Doubleday, 1961; *The Arrows of Hercules,* Doubleday, 1965; *The Golden Wind,* Doubleday, 1969.

Verse: *Demons and Dinosaurs,* Arkham, 1970; *Phantoms and Fancies,* Mirage Press, 1972; *Heroes and Hobgoblins,* Heritage Press, 1978.

Contributor to *Visual Encyclopedia of Science Fiction.* Contributor of over 350 short stories and articles to periodicals. Author of 76 radio scripts for "Voice of America" on scientific topics.

WORK IN PROGRESS: Dark Valley Destiny: The Life and Death of Robert E. Howard, with Catherine C. DeCamp and Jane W. Griffin; *The Bones of Zora; The Knights of Zinjaban; The Fringe of the Unknown.*

SIDELIGHTS: William Mattathias Robins in *Dictionary of Literary Biography* notes that L. Sprague de Camp's works of fiction are "concerned purely with entertaining and the reader" and do not attempt to achieve "the psychological or sociological depths of the greatest science fiction novels; however, he is a master of the humorous tales, and his stories are always fast paced and satisfying."

The details in de Camp's books are very exact and never reach beyond scientific possibilities. For example, his space travellers must live within the perimeters set by the theory of relativity, a theory in which he believes, and he ignores the concept of hyperspace, a theory in which he does not believe. De Camp also "has the ability to visualize his characters, settings, and actions, and to impress these vividly upon the reader," Robins notes. "He believes that the creative mind recombines elements that it has received through the senses into new, meaningful, and useful combinations."

Among the most successful of de Camp's work are the Conan books, based upon the character created by the late fantasy writer, Robert E. Howard. Conan is a muscular barbarian who lives in an ancient, untamed land and overcomes all obstacles with a well-placed sword. Howard created Conan for the pulp magazines of the thirties, but it wasn't until the sixties when de Camp reworked much of Howard's writings into novels and completed Howard's unfinished manuscripts that the character's popularity soared. Conan now appears successfully in several media.

BIOGRAPHICAL/CRITICAL SOURCES: Horn Book, April, 1965; *Classical World,* November, 1965; Sam Moskowitz, *Seekers of Tomorrow,* World, 1966; *New York Times Book Review,* November, 1967, February 24, 1974; *Natural History,* February, 1969; *Quarterly Journal of Speech,* April, 1969; *Scientific American,* December, 1969; *Science Fiction Review,* August, 1970; *American Historical Review,* June, 1971; *New York Review of Books,* June 3, 1971; *New York Times,* January 29, 1975; *Atlantic,* March, 1975; *Times Literary Supplement,* March 26, 1976; *Magazine of Fantasy and Science Fiction,* July, 1976, September, 1978; *Analog,* November, 1977; *Book World,* March 5, 1978; *Night Voyages,* fall, 1979; *Dictionary of Literary Biography,* Volume VIII: *Twentieth-Century Science Fiction Writers,* Gale, 1981.

*   *   *

DELEAR, Frank J. 1914-

PERSONAL: Surname is pronounced Dee-*leer;* born January 21, 1914, in Boston, Mass.; son of Joseph F. (an architectural sculptor) and Adelaide (von der Luft) Delear; married Marion Robertsen, September 3, 1940; children: Susan (Mrs. Richard Noel), David, Betsy (Mrs. Fred Voight), James, Janet. *Education:* Boston College, B.A., 1936. *Religion:* Episcopalian. *Home:* 308 Patriot Way, Centerville, Mass. 02632.

CAREER: Quincy Patriot Ledger, Quincy, Mass., assistant sports editor, 1936-37; *Bridgeport Post Telegram,* Bridgeport, Conn., reporter, aviation editor, 1937-42; Chance Vought Aircraft, Stratford, Conn., publicity representative, 1942-47; United Aircraft Corp., East Hartford, Conn., assistant to public relations director, 1947-48; Socony-Vacuum Oil Co., New York, N.Y., writer in public relations department, 1948-52; Hamilton Standard (division of United Aircraft Corp.), Windsor Locks, Conn., assistant public relations director, 1952-57; Sikorsky Aircraft (division of United Aircraft Corp.), Stratford, Conn., public relations manager, 1957-77; free-lance writer specializing in aviation. *Member:* Aviation/Space Writers Association (chairman of National Writing Awards Committee), American Aviation Historical Society, Professional Writers of Cape Cod (president). *Awards, honors:* Aviation/Space Writers Association writing award citation, 1970, for *Igor Sikorsky.*

WRITINGS: Wings for the Navy, Chance Vought Aircraft, 1944; *Miracle of the Helicopter,* Sikorsky Aircraft, 1961; *The New World of Helicopters,* Dodd, 1967; *Igor Sikorsky: His Three Careers in Aviation,* Dodd, 1969; *Helicopters and Airplanes of the U.S. Army,* Dodd, 1977; *Famous First Flights across the Atlantic,* Dodd, 1979; *Airplanes and Helicopters of the U.S. Navy,* Dodd, 1982. Writer of scripts for company-produced movies. Contributor to *Yankee,* to newspapers and aviation magazines.

SIDELIGHTS: As a boy, Frank J. Delear built model planes and worked at an airport; he later learned to fly, but poor eyesight prevented a pilot's career. He has followed at first hand the development of the helicopter since its beginnings in 1939. Delear states: "The twentieth century is the most dangerous and barbaric yet known to man and if man's intellect does not soon prevail over his emotions and prejudices the twenty-first century will be the quietest ever known."

Regarding a career in writing, Delear told *CA:* "To all aspiring writers: look askance at all publishers and believe the words of Terri Schultz in the October, 1982 issue of *Quill:* 'Writers are the migrant workers of the publishing industry.' To authors: don't expect a publisher's 'salesmen' to get out and sell your work. They don't and they won't. Despite the foregoing, I am generally happy to have had five books published and pleased to think that on library shelves, somewhere, they are going to outlive me—a sort of minor league immortality, if you will."

* * *

De MARINIS, Rick 1934-

PERSONAL: Born May 3, 1934, in New York, N.Y.; son of Alphonse and Ruth (Siik) De Marinis; married Carole Joyce Bubash (an artist and writer); children: Richard Michael, Suzanne Louise, Naomi Anna. *Education:* Attended San Diego State College (now University), 1952-54; University of Montana, B.A., 1961, M.A., 1967. *Politics:* Independent. *Residence:* Missoula, Mont. *Agent:* Jane Schwenger, Box 5992, Grand Central Station, New York, N.Y. 10017. *Office:* University of Montana, Missoula, Mont. 59801.

CAREER: University of Montana, Missoula, instructor in English, 1967-69; San Diego State University, San Diego, Calif., assistant professor of English, 1969-76; member of faculty, University of Montana, Missoula. *Military service:* U.S. Air Force, 1954-58.

WRITINGS: A Lovely Monster: The Adventures of Claude Rains and Dr. Tellenbeck (novel), Simon & Schuster, 1976; *Scimitar: A Novel,* Dutton, 1977; *Cinder,* Farrar, Straus, 1978; *Jack and Jill: Two Novellas and a Short Story,* Dutton, 1979. Contributor of short stories to numerous publications, including *Esquire, Atlantic Monthly, Iowa Review, Malahat Review, Cavalier,* and *Colorado State Review.*

SIDELIGHTS: Rick De Marinis's *Jack and Jill* "will certainly please readers of Vonnegut, although his often witty tangling of theme and form may irritate a reader who had come to like such tangles when tied by Nabokov," according to Susan Fromberg Schaeffer in the *Chicago Tribune Book World.* She adds, "His characters often fail to come alive," concluding, "nevertheless, this is an innovative, interesting, and highly imaginative book."

BIOGRAPHICAL/CRITICAL SOURCES: Chicago Tribune Book World, January 21, 1979.

* * *

DEMONE, Harold W(ellington), Jr. 1924-

PERSONAL: Born July 23, 1924, in Arlington, Mass.; son of Harold Wellington and Elsie R. (Timlick) Demone; married Marguerite F. Reilly, August 20, 1949; children: Deborah Jan. *Education:* Tufts University, A.B., 1948, A.M., 1949; postgraduate study at Boston University, 1951-54; Brandeis University, Ph.D. *Office:* Graduate School of Social Work, Rutgers University, 536 George St., New Brunswick, N.J. 08903.

CAREER: Tufts University, Medford, Mass., 1949-54, began as instructor, became assistant professor in department of sociology; New Hampshire Department of Health, Concord, executive director of Division of Alcoholism, 1954-56; Commonwealth of Massachusetts, Boston, commissioner on alcoholism, 1956-59, assistant to commissioner of public health, 1959-60; Medical Foundation, Inc., Boston, executive director, 1960-67; executive director, United Community Services of Metropolitan Boston, Inc., 1967-73; executive vice-president, United Community Planning Corp., 1974-77; Rutgers University, New Brunswick, N.J., professor of sociology, 1979—, distinguished professor and dean of Graduate School of Social Work, 1977—.

Lecturer in social medicine, Boston University, 1962-78; lecturer in social welfare, Harvard University School of Public Health, 1966-67; special lecturer in planning, School of Social Work, Simmons College, 1973-74. Associate clinical professor of social welfare in department of psychiatry, Harvard Medical School, 1965-78. Part-time professor, Center of Alcohol Studies, Rutgers University, 1978—. Faculty member of Yale University Summer School of Alcohol Studies, 1959-61. Director of Massachusetts Mental Retardation Planning Project, 1964-67. Member of board of Tuberculosis and Health League, 1960-63, United Health Foundations, and Massachusetts Mental Health Planning Project, 1963-65. Senior consultant, Massachusetts Vocational Rehabilitation Planning Commission, 1966-68; consultant to U.S. Department of Health and Human Services. Member of numerous advisory committees and commissions studying mental health. *Military service:* U.S. Army, Infantry, 1943-45; awarded three battle stars and Bronze Star.

MEMBER: International Association of Schools of Social Workers, National Association of Social Workers, American Association for the Advancement of Science, American Public Health Association (fellow), American Sociological Association (fellow; chairman of committee on issues of public policy, 1968-71), American Public Welfare Association, Society for the Study of Social Problems, Professional Association on Alcoholism (president, 1959), American School Health Association, World Future Society, Massachusetts Public Health Association (president, 1963-64), Alpha Kappa Delta, Pi Gamma Mu. *Awards, honors:* Received awards from the Massachusetts Psychological Association, 1966, Massachusetts Association for Mental Health, 1966, and Massachusetts Association of Retarded Children, 1967; Lemuel Shattuck Award from Massachusetts Public Health Association, 1975.

WRITINGS: (With Morris E. Chafetz) *Alcoholism and Society,* Oxford University Press, 1962; (with Dwight Harshbarger) *The Planning and Administration of Human Services,* Behavioral Publications, 1973; (editor with Harshbarger) *A Handbook of Human Service Organizations,* Behavioral Publications, 1974; *Stimulating Human Services Reform,* Aspen Systems Corp., 1978; (with M. Gibelman) *A Manual for Human Service Administrators,* Human Services, 1983.

Contributor: Raymond G. McCarthy, editor, *Alcohol Education for Classroom and Community,* McGraw, 1964; Jack Mendelson, editor, *Alcoholism,* Little, Brown, 1966; H. Grunebaum, editor, *The Practice of Community Mental Health,* Little, Brown, 1970; Harshbarger and R. Maley, editors, *Behavioral Analysis and System Analysis: An Integrative Approach to Mental Health Programs,* Behaviordelia, 1975; Jack Zusman and Elmer F. Bertsh, editors, *The Future Role of the State Hospital,* Lexington Books, 1975; Milton Greenblatt and Mare Schuchet, editors, *Alcoholism Problems in Women and Children,* Grune, 1976; C. C. Attkisson, W. A. Hargeaves, M. J. Horowitz, and J. E. Sorenson, editors, *Evaluation of Human Service Programs,* Academic Press, 1978.

Curran, McGarry, and Petty, editors, *Modern Legal Medicine, Psychiatry, and Forensic Science,* F. A. Davis, 1980; R. Bell, M. Sundel, J. F. Aponte, S. A. Murrell, and E. Linn, editors, *Assessing Health and Human Service Needs,* Human Sciences,

1982; E. Mansell Pattison and Edward Kaufman, editors, *The Encyclopedia Handbook of Alcoholism,* Gardner Press, 1982; H. C. Schulberg and M. Killilea, editors, *Principles and Practices in Community Mental Health,* Jossey-Bass, 1982; F. Baker, D. Bartlett, and B. Miller, editors, *Programs Evaluation on Trial,* Human Sciences, 1982.

Also author of numerous monographs, reports, and brochures. Contributor of over one hundred book reviews and articles to various periodicals. Associate editor of *Journal of Health and Human Behavior,* 1960-66; consulting editor of *Community Mental Health Journal,* 1974—. Editorial consultant to *Journal of Psychiatric Opinion,* 1965-75; editorial referee of *Journal of Studies on Alcohol,* 1978—. Member of editorial board of *Health Policy Quarterly,* 1979—.

WORK IN PROGRESS: "A book on the purchase of human services, continued research on adolescent drinking and work on human resources (manpower)."

* * *

DENNISON, A(lfred) Dudley, Jr. 1914-

PERSONAL: Born January 6, 1914, in Johnstown, N.Y.; son of Alfred Dudley and Marguerite (France) Dennison; married Virginia Lee Beers, October 24, 1940; married Gloria Moreno; children: (first marriage) Wayne, Norman, Melanie. *Education:* Hamilton College, B.A., 1935; Cornell University Medical College, M.D., 1939. *Home:* 6832 Granero, El Paso, Tex. 79935. *Agent:* (Speaking) Redpath Bureau, 343 South Dearborn St., Chicago, Ill. 60604.

CAREER: Diplomate, American Board of Internal Medicine, 1950, Subspecialty Board of Cardiovascular Diseases, 1951; Indiana University Medical School, Indianapolis, associate in medicine, 1953—; consulting cardiologist, Indianapolis, Ind., 1953-68; Methodist Hospital, Indianapolis, chief of cardiology, 1964-68; Milligan College, Milligan, Tenn., dean, 1968-69; Veteran's Administration Hospital, Johnson City, Tenn., staff member, 1969-70; Veteran's Administration Hospital, Des Moines, Iowa, chief of cardiology and assistant chief of medicine, 1970-72; Texas Tech University Medical School, El Paso, professor of medicine and chief of cardiology, 1975—; medical director, Security Southwest Life Insurance Co., El Paso. Member of faculty, New York University Postgraduate Medical School, 1948-52. Fellow in pediatric cardiology, Victoria Heart Foundation; trustee, Taylor University. Ordained to ministry, Christian Church, 1977. Consultant in cardiology to numerous hospitals in Indiana, Iowa, and New Jersey. *Military service:* U.S. Naval Reserve, 1942-45; became lieutenant commander.

MEMBER: American College of Physicians (fellow), American College of Chest Physicians (fellow; past governor of Indiana chapter; member of board of governors, 1957—), American College of Cardiology (fellow; past governor of Indiana chapter; member of board of governors, 1957-60), American College of Angiology (fellow), American Heart Association (fellow; member of Council on Clinical Cardiology), American Scientific Affiliation, Polk County Heart Association (member of board of directors, 1971-73), Essex County Heart Association (president, 1950-51), Nu Sigma Nu, Alpha Phi Omega, Theta Delta Chi, Masonic Order (32nd Degree), Blue Lodge, Scottish Rite, Shrine, York Rite.

WRITINGS—Published by Zondervan, except as indicated: (With James Hefley) *Biblical World,* Baker Publishing, 1966; *Shock It to Me, Doctor,* 1970; *Give It to Me Straight, Doctor,* 1972; (contributor) J. Allen Peterson, editor, *For Men Only,* 1973; *Prescription for Life,* 1975; *Windows, Ladders, and Bridges,* 1976; *Contemporary Illustrations for Speakers and Teachers,* 1979. Contributor to periodicals, including *Indiana State Medical Journal, Christian Life,* and *Christianity Today.* Member of editorial advisory board, *Emergency Medicine,* 1969—; health editor, *Christian Life,* 1970—.

* * *

DENZER, Ann Wiseman
See WISEMAN, Ann (Sayre)

* * *

DePAUW, Linda Grant 1940-

PERSONAL: Born January 19, 1940, in New York, N.Y.; daughter of Phillip and Ruth (Marks) Grant; married John W. DePauw (a social science analyst), October 23, 1960 (divorced January, 1973); children: Jolie Diane, Benjamin Grant. *Education:* Swarthmore College, B.A., 1961; Johns Hopkins University, Ph.D., 1964. *Home:* 1101 South Arlington Ridge Rd., Arlington, Va. 22202. *Office:* Department of History, George Washington University, Washington, D.C. 20052.

CAREER: University of Virginia, Fairfax, assistant professor of history, 1964-65; National Historical Publications Commission, Washington, D.C., assistant editor of First Federal Congress project, 1965; George Washington University, Washington, D.C., assistant professor, 1966-69, associate professor, 1969-75, professor of American history, 1975—. Lecturer on women's rights, women's history, and military history to colleges and universities and to organizations, including American Bar Association, National Organization for Women, Women's Equity Action League, U.S. Army Military History Institute, Colonial Dames, American Women in Radio and Television, Smithsonian Institute, and National Park Service; speaker on television and radio in United States and Europe.

Member of Columbia University Seminar on Early American History and Culture, Inter-University Seminar on Armed Forces and Society, and Coordinating Committee on Women in the Historical Profession; member of board of Women's Coalition for the Third Century; former chairperson of Columbia University seminar on early American history and culture. Concept developer and chief historian of museum exhibit, "Remember the Ladies," which travelled to six cities in 1976-77 under auspices of Pilgrim Society. Developer, with *Ms.* magazine, of educational board game, "Herstory," for Coach House Games. Consultant to many civic and historical groups, including National Archives, National Park Service, Stanton Project, National Public Radio, American Bibliographical Center, American Revolution Bicentennial Administration, and National Endowment for the Humanities.

MEMBER: American Military Institute, Association for Documentary Editing (member of original steering committee; author of constitution), Authors Guild, Authors League of America, National Women's Studies Association, U.S. Naval Institute, American Historical Association, Southern Historical Association. *Awards, honors:* American Historical Association Albert J. Beveridge Award, 1964, for *The Eleventh Pillar: New York State and the Federal Constitution; Founding Mothers: Women of America in the Revolutionary Era* was named "notable book" by American Library Association, and "best book of the year" by *School Library Journal.*

WRITINGS: The Eleventh Pillar: New York State and the Federal Constitution, Cornell University Press, 1966; (editor-in-chief) *Documentary History of the First Federal Congress, 1789-1791,* three volumes, Johns Hopkins Press, 1972-77; *Founding Mothers: Women of America in the Revolutionary Era,* Houghton, 1975; (contributor) James Kirby Martin and Karen R. Strubaus, editors, *American Revolution: Whose Revolution?,* Krieger, 1976; (contributor) *Legacies of the American Revolution,* University of Utah Press, 1978; (contributor) *The American Revolution: New Perspectives,* Northeastern University Press, 1979; *Seafaring Women,* Houghton, 1982.

Also author of pamphlets, "Four Traditions: Women of New York in the Era of the American Revolution," 1974, and "Fortunes of War: New Jersey Women and the American Revolution," 1976. Contributor to scholarly journals and periodicals, including *New York History, Prologue, Maryland Historical Magazine, Ms., Washington Post, Armed Forces and Society,* and *Human Rights.*

WORK IN PROGRESS: Editing last fifteen volumes of *Documentary History of the First Federal Congress, 1789-1791,* for Johns Hopkins Press; an eighth grade history textbook, entitled *Young America;* a novel about a female officer in a space navy, entitled *Baptism of Fire.*

* * *

DERFLER, (Arnold) Leslie 1933-

PERSONAL: Born January 11, 1933, in New York, N.Y.; son of David (a salesman) and Ruth (Zarelnik) Derfler; married Gunilla Akesson, June 24, 1962; children: Ingrid, Linnea, Astrid, Elin. *Education:* City College (now City College of the City University of New York), B.A., 1954; University of Chicago, graduate study, 1956; Columbia University, M.A., 1957, Ph.D., 1962. *Office:* Department of History, Florida Atlantic University, Boca Raton, Fla. 33432.

CAREER: City College of the City University of New York, New York, N.Y., lecturer, 1960-62; Carnegie-Mellon University, Pittsburgh, Pa., 1962-68, began as assistant professor, became associate professor; University of Massachusetts—Amherst, associate professor, 1968-69; Florida Atlantic University, Boca Raton, professor of history, 1969—, chairman of department, 1978—. *Military service:* U.S. Army, 1954-56. *Member:* American Historical Association, Societe d'Histoire Moderne, Society for French Historical Studies. *Awards, honors:* Carnegie Falk grant-in-aid; Fulbright travel grant; American Council of Learned Societies grant; American Philosophical Society grant; Koren Prize of the Society for French Historical Studies, 1964; National Endowment for the Humanities fellowship, 1971-72.

WRITINGS: The Dreyfus Affair: Tragedy of Errors, Heath, 1963; *The Third French Republic: 1870-1940,* Van Nostrand, 1966; *Socialism since Marx: A Century of the European Left,* Macmillan, 1973; (editor) *Alexandre Millerand: The Socialist Years,* Mouton, 1977; *President and Parliament: A Short History of the French Presidency,* University Presses of Florida, 1983. Contributor to journals, including *International Review of Social History, Revue d'Histoire Moderne,* and *Historical Abstracts.*

WORK IN PROGRESS: A biography of Paul LaFangue, Marx's disciple and son-in-law, who helped introduce Marxism to France.

DeROSA, Peter (Clement) 1932- (Neil Boyd)

PERSONAL: Born November 12, 1932, in London, England; son of Louis Leopold and Ruby (Read) DeRosa; married, 1972; children: Francis, Daniel. *Education:* Attended Jesuit College of St. Ignatius, London, England, St. Edmund's College of Divinity, 1950-56, and Gregorian University, Rome, Italy, 1956-59. *Home:* High Valley, Ashford, County Wicklow, Ireland.

CAREER: Former priest in London, England; lecturer, St. Edmund's College of Divinity; Corpus Christi College, London, lecturer in philosophy, 1960-65, vice-principal, 1965-71; radio producer for British Broadcasting Corp.; currently full-time writer. Assistant director, National Catechetical Center, London.

WRITINGS: (With H. J. Richards) *Christ in Our World,* Bruce, 1966; *Christ and Original Sin,* Bruce, 1967; *God Our Saviour: A Study of the Atonement,* Bruce, 1967; (editor) *Introduction to Catechetics,* Bruce, 1968; *Jesus Who Became Christ,* Dimension, 1974, revised edition, Collins, 1975; *The Bee and the Rose,* Argus Communications, 1975; *Not I, Not I, But the Wind that Blows through Me: About the Life of God in the Life of Men,* Argus Communications, 1975; *Cloud Cuckoo Land: The Impossible Dream,* Argus Communications, 1975; *Come Holy Spirit: The Life of God in the Life of Men,* Collins, 1975; *The Best of All Possible Worlds,* Argus Communications, 1975; *A Bible Prayerbook for Today,* Collins, 1976, published as *Prayers for Pagans and Hypocrites,* Morrow, 1979. Also author of *Destiny,* the first novel in a proposed trilogy about the life of Jesus.

Under pseudonym Neil Boyd: *Bless Me, Father,* St. Martin's, 1977; *A Father Before Christmas,* M. Joseph, 1978; *Father in a Fix,* M. Joseph, 1979, Morrow, 1980; *Father under Fire,* M. Joseph, 1980, Morrow, 1981; *Bless Me Again, Father,* M. Joseph, 1981.

Also author of scripts for London Weekend Television series "Bless Me, Father," based on his book of the same title. Contributor to the *Sunday Express* and to theology journals in England and the United States.

SIDELIGHTS: Under the pseudonym Neil Boyd, Peter DeRosa is the author of several semi-autobiographical works that recount the sometimes humorous, sometimes touching events in London's fictional St. Jude's parish. The books' principal characters are Father Neil, the young priest who relates the stories of life at St. Jude's, Father Charles Duddleswell, the crafty and often irreverent senior pastor, and Mrs. Pring, the kindly housekeeper whose peppery exchanges with Father Duddleswell make for "the funniest dialogue I have read in ages," according to a *Best Sellers* critic.

DeRosa's lighthearted approach reminds many readers of James Herriot, author of *All Creatures Great and Small* and other best-sellers chronicling the experiences of a Yorkshire veterinarian. Herriot, in fact, was the first to urge the former priest to write about St. Jude. As DeRosa recalled in a William Morrow & Co. publicity release: "I started to write after meeting James Herriot, I was producing [for the British Broadcasting Corp.] in Yorkshire, and he explained to me how he had written his novels. It immediately struck me that I could make use of my memories of the priestly life. People have written about the priesthood before, but always in a very dramatic way, and it was to get away from this that I wrote my book. If you ever see a priest in a film, he is always shown in a confessional while someone is confessing a murder. I thought this was ludicrous. . . . Most lives are superficially tedious, but if you look below the surface there is always something interesting if you can only find the right angle to it.''

AVOCATIONAL INTERESTS: Literature, especially the great French and Russian novelists; travel; sports; ''educating my two sons.''

BIOGRAPHICAL/CRITICAL SOURCES: Best Sellers, April, 1978.

* * *

Des GAGNIERS, Jean 1929-

PERSONAL: Born February 4, 1929, in St. Joseph de-la-Rive, Quebec, Canada. *Education:* University of Montreal, B.A., 1949; College Jean de Brebeuf, graduate study, 1951-53; Laval University, Licencie en philosophie, 1953; Ecole du Louvre, diploma in art history and archaeology, 1956. *Religion:* Roman Catholic. *Office:* University Museum, Laval University, Quebec, Quebec, Canada.

CAREER: Laval University, Quebec, Quebec, assistant professor, 1952-62, professor of archaeology, 1962—, director of classics department, beginning 1967, head of Museum and Collections, 1976—, director of excavations in Laodikeia, Turkey, 1961-64, and in Soli, Cyprus, 1964—. Lecturer on Greek art. Member of Art Council of Canadian Scholars, 1956—; member of board of trustees of National Museums of Canada, 1972-76. *Member:* Canadian Classical Association, Societe Royale du Canada.

WRITINGS: (Author of text) *Objects d'art grec du Louvre,* Musee du Quebec, Ministere des affaires culturelles, 1967; (with others) *Laodicee du Lycos: Le Nymphee, campagnes 1961-63,* Presses de l'Universite Laval, 1969; *L'Ile-aux-Coudres,* Lemeac, 1969; *L'Acropole d'Athenes,* Presses de l'Universite Laval, 1971; *J. M. Morrice,* Pelican, 1971; (with Vassos Karageorghis) *La ceramique chypriote de style figure,* three volumes, Edizione dell'Ateneo, 1974-79; (with Karageorghis) *Vases et figurines de l'age du Bronze a Chypre,* Presses de l'Universite Laval, 1976; *La Conservation du patrimoine museologique du Qubec,* Ministere des Affaires Culturelles, 1981.

WORK IN PROGRESS: Soloi: Dix campagnes de fouilles, with Tran Tam Tinh and R. Ginouves, for Presses de l'Universite Laval.

* * *

DETHIER, Vincent Gaston 1915-

PERSONAL: Born February 20, 1915, in Boston, Mass.; son of Jean Vincent and Marguerite Frances (Lally) Dethier; married Lois Evelyn Check, January 23, 1960; children: Jehan Vincent, Paul. *Education:* Harvard University, A.B. (cum laude), 1936, A.M., 1937, Ph.D., 1939. *Home:* 331 Strong St., Amherst, Mass. 01002. *Office:* Department of Zoology, University of Massachusetts, Amherst, Mass. 01002.

CAREER: Clark University, Worcester, Mass., fellow in biology, 1937; G. W. Pierce Laboratory, Franklin, N.H., entomologist, 1937-38; John Carroll University, Cleveland, Ohio, instructor, 1939-41, assistant professor of biology, 1941-42; professor of zoology and entomology, Ohio State University, 1946-47; Johns Hopkins University, Baltimore, Md., associate professor, 1947-51, professor of biology, 1952-58; University of Pennsylvania, Philadelphia, professor of zoology and psychology and associate of Neurological Institute, all 1959-67; Princeton University, Princeton, N.J., professor of biology, 1967-75; University of Massachusetts—Amherst, professor of zoology, 1975—. Harvard fellow at Atkins Institute of Arnold Arboretum (Soledad, Cuba), 1939-40; Hixon Lecturer at California Institute of Technology, 1949. Director of research at International Centre for Insect Physiology and Ecology (Kenya). President of board of trustees of Chapin School, 1971-74; vice-president of board of trustees, Kneisel Hall School of Chamber Music, 1978-80. Consultant to Canadian Defence Board and Office of the U.S. Surgeon General. *Military service:* U.S. Army Air Forces, research physiologist in Chemical Corps, 1942-45. U.S. Army Reserve, Office of the Surgeon General, 1948-62; became lieutenant colonel.

MEMBER: American Philosophical Society, National Academy of Science (fellow), American Academy of Arts and Sciences (fellow), American Association for the Advancement of Science (fellow), American Society of Zoologists (president, 1967), Society of General Physiologists, American Society of Naturalists, Royal Entomological Society (fellow; honorary member), Royal Society of Arts (fellow), Southern California Academy of Sciences (fellow).

AWARDS, HONORS: Belgian-American Educational Foundation fellow in the Belgian Congo, 1952; Fulbright senior research scholar at London School of Hygiene and Tropical Medicine, 1954; Sc.D. from Providence College, 1964, and Ohio State University, 1970; Guggenheim fellow in the Netherlands, 1964-65, and at University of Sussex, 1972-73.

WRITINGS: Chemical Insect Attractants and Repellents, Blakiston, 1947; (contributor) K. D. Roeder, editor, *Insect Physiology,* Wiley, 1953; (with Eliot Stellar) *Animal Behavior: Its Evolutionary and Neurological Basis,* Prentice-Hall, 1961, 3rd edition, 1970; *To Know a Fly* (partially self-illustrated), Holden-Day, 1962; *The Physiology of Insect Senses,* Wiley, 1963.

Fairweather Duck (juvenile; self-illustrated), Walker & Co., 1970; *Topics in the Study of Life: The BIO Source Book,* Harper, 1971; (with Claude Alvin Villee) *Biological Principles and Processes,* Saunders, 1971, 2nd edition, 1976; *Buy Me a Volcano,* Vantage, 1972; *The Hungry Fly,* Harvard University Press, 1976; *Man's Plague,* Darwin Press, 1976; *The Ant Heap,* Darwin Press, 1979; *The World of the Tent-Makers,* University of Massachusetts Press, 1980; *Newberry: The Life and Times of a Maine Clam* (juvenile), Down East Books, 1981.

Short stories anthologized in *Best American Short Stories,* edited by H. Calisher, Houghton, 1981, and in *Best of Kenyon Review.* Contributor to scientific journals; contributor of short stories to periodicals, including *Kenyon Review* and *Texas Quarterly.* Member of editorial board of *Journal of Comparative Physiology* and *Journal of Experimental Biology.*

AVOCATIONAL INTERESTS: Boating, skiing.

* * *

de TREVINO, Elizabeth B.
See TREVINO, Elizabeth B(orton) de

* * *

DeWEESE, Gene
See DeWEESE, Thomas Eugene

DeWEESE, Jean
See DeWEESE, Thomas Eugene

* * *

DeWEESE, Thomas Eugene 1934-
(Gene DeWeese; Jean DeWeese, a pseudonym; Thomas Stratton, a joint pseudonym)

PERSONAL: Born January 31, 1934, in Rochester, Ind.; son of Thomas Jacob and Alfreda (a print shop worker; maiden name, Henning) DeWeese; married Beverly Joanne Amers (a librarian), May, 1955. *Education:* Valparaiso Technical Institute, associate degree in electronics, 1953; also attended University of Wisconsin—Milwaukee, Indiana University, and Marquette University. *Politics:* Independent. *Religion:* None. *Home and office:* 2718 North Prospect, Milwaukee, Wis. 53211. *Agent:* Scott Meredith Literary Agency, Inc., 845 Third Ave., New York, N.Y. 10022.

CAREER: Delco Radio, Kokomo, Ind., technician, 1954-59; Delco Electronics, Milwaukee, Wis., technical writer, 1959-74; free-lance writer, 1974—. *Member:* Science Fiction Writers of America, Mystery Writers of America. *Awards, honors:* Award for best novel, 1976, for *Jeremy Case,* and award for best juvenile book, 1979, for *Major Corby and the Unidentified Flapping Object,* both from Council for Wisconsin Writers.

WRITINGS—Under name Gene DeWeese: (With Gini Rogowski) *Making American Folk Art Dolls,* Chilton, 1975; (with Robert Coulson) *Gates of the Universe* (science fiction), Laser Books, 1975; (with Coulson) *Now You See It/Him/Them* (science fiction), Doubleday, 1975; *Jeremy Case* (science fiction), Laser Books, 1976; (with Coulson) *Charles Fort Never Mentioned Wombats* (science fiction), Doubleday, 1977; *Major Corby and the Unidentified Flapping Object* (juvenile science fiction), Doubleday, 1979.

The Wanting Factor (horror), Playboy Press, 1980; *Nightmares from Space* (juvenile science fiction), F. Watts, 1981; *A Different Darkness* (horror), PBJ Books, 1982; *Something Answered* (horror), Pinnacle Books, 1983; *Adventures of a Two-Minute Werewolf* (juvenile science fiction), Doubleday, 1983.

Under pseudonym Jean DeWeese: *The Reimann Curse* (Gothic fantasy), Ballantine, 1975; *The Moonstone Spirit* (Gothic fantasy), Ballantine, 1975; *The Carnelian Cat* (Gothic fantasy), Ballantine, 1975; *Web of Guilt* (Gothic novel), Ballantine, 1976; *Cave of the Moaning Wind* (Gothic fantasy), Ballantine, 1976; *The Doll with Opal Eyes* (romantic suspense), Doubleday, 1976; *Nightmare in Pewter* (Gothic fantasy), Doubleday, 1978.

Hour of the Cat (mystery), Doubleday, 1980; *The Backhoe Gothic* (Gothic mystery), Doubleday, 1981.

Science fiction; with Coulson under joint pseudonym Thomas Stratton: *The Invisibility Affair: Man from U.N.C.L.E., No. 11,* Ace Books, 1967; *The Mindtwisters Affair: Man from U.N.C.L.E., No. 12,* Ace Books, 1967; (contributor) L. Sprague de Camp and George Scithers, *The Conan Grimoire: Essays in Swordplay and Sorcery,* Mirage Press, 1972.

Science fiction reviewer, *Milwaukee Journal.*

SIDELIGHTS: "The first thing I remember writing was in grade school, something about Mickey Mouse, I think, inspired by one of his science fictional adventures in Walt Disney comics," Gene DeWeese told *CA.* "The first thing actually printed was probably an account of an ice storm in the high school paper, which was printed as an insert in the *Rochester News Sentinel.* The first money I ever got for anything I wrote was for a series of articles on local people and businesses and a science fiction column for the same *News Sentinel.* I was still in high school, and I got the magnificent sum of a nickel per column inch. Between that and my first 'professional fiction' sale were lots of 'payment-in-contributor's-copies' contributions to science fiction amateur magazines (fanzines) such as *Yandro, Indiana Fantasy, Fan-Fare,* and the *Chigger Patch of Fandom.*

"That first professional sale was a 'Man from U.N.C.L.E.' novel, a collaboration with Robert Coulson under the name Thomas Stratton. It was made primarily because the editor of the series happened to subscribe to a fanzine Coulson and his wife published and because she (Juanita Coulson, who had already sold a couple of sf novels) didn't really want to do an 'U.N.C.L.E.' novel when said editor offered her the chance. All of which partially explains why the dedication page reads, 'To Serendipity.'

"Incidentally, that book, *The Invisibility Affair,* may have the distinction of being the only book for which the text was accepted but the title, author's names and dedication were all rejected. The original title, *The Invisible Dirigible Affair,* was too long for their cover format (though it was restored in the French translation). Using two names was considered too confusing, no explanation given. Then, with only one author's name appearing on the cover, the original dedication, 'To my wives and child,' was considered too racy for the intended preteen audience, which I suppose shows how things have changed in the last fifteen years.

"Since then I've plowed through twenty-odd books of various sorts and varying quality, with *Major Corby, Hour of the Cat, Jeremy Case, The Wanting Factor,* and *Something Answered* at the top of my own personal list of favorites. As you can tell from the books listed above, I've written in a number of fields, but one book, *The Doll with Opal Eyes,* may have established a record of sorts on its own, having been published in the U.S. as 'romantic suspense,' in England as a straight crime novel, and in France and Argentina as a romance.

"The only 'advice' I've ever gotten that has been consistently helpful (and consistently difficult to follow) is simply, 'If you want to be a writer, sit down and *write*!' Don't dream about it or talk about it or read about it—do it. (Having a spouse with a steady job doesn't hurt, either.)"

* * *

DIAMOND, Edwin 1925-

PERSONAL: Born June 18, 1925, in Chicago, Ill.; son of Louis Joseph (a journalist) and Jessie (Isaacson) Diamond; married Adelina Lust, December 5, 1948; children: Ellen, Franna, Louise. *Education:* University of Chicago, Ph.B., 1947, M.A. (with honors), 1949. *Home:* 20 Waterside Pl., New York, N.Y. *Office: Adweek,* 820 Second Ave., New York, N.Y.

CAREER: City News Bureau and *Chicago Herald American,* Chicago, Ill., reporter, 1953; International News Service, Chicago and Washington, D.C., science writer, 1953-57; *Newsweek,* New York City, science editor, 1958-62, senior editor, 1962-69; *New York Magazine,* New York City, contributing editor, 1970-78; *Esquire* magazine, New York City, contributing editor, 1978-80; *New York Daily News,* New York City, associate editor of *Tonight* edition, 1980-81; associated with *Adweek*, New York City, 1981—. Massachusetts Institute of Technology, senior lecturer in political science, 1970—, founder of News Study Group, 1972—. Commentator, *Washington Post-Newsweek* Stations, Inc., 1970-79, and "Spectrum" series for Columbia Broadcasting System, 1974-75. Participant in Karl Taylor Compton Seminar on the Mass Communication of Complicated Issues, 1971; group study leader, Institute of Politics, Kennedy School of Government, Harvard University, 1974-78. Member of Alumni Cabinet, University of Chicago. *Military service:* U.S. Army, 1943-46, 1951-53; became first lieutenant; received Bronze Star Medal with oak leaf cluster, Purple Heart, and three Battle Stars. *Member:* American Federation of Television and Radio Artists.

AWARDS, HONORS: Lowell Mellett Award for Media Criticism, 1978; Award of Excellence, *Communications Arts Magazine;* Page One Awards from Chicago and Washington Newspaper Guilds; Science Writers Award, Westinghouse-American Association for Advancement of Science.

WRITINGS: The Science of Dreams, Doubleday, 1962; *The Rise and Fall of the Space Age,* Doubleday, 1964; (contributor) *The Media and the Cities,* University of Chicago, 1966; (contributor) Alfred Balk and James Boylen, editors, *Our Troubled Press,* Little, Brown, 1971; (contributor) Michael Emery and Ted Smythe, editors, *Readings in Mass Communication: Concepts and Issues in the Mass Media,* W. C. Brown, 1974; *The Tin Kazoo: Television, Politics, and the News,* M.I.T. Press, 1975; *Good News, Bad News,* M.I.T. Press, 1978; (with Bruce Mazlish) *Jimmy Carter: A Character Portrait,* Simon & Schuster, 1980; *Sign-Off: The Last Days of Television,* M.I.T. Press, 1982.

Contributor to *Esquire, Columbia Journalism Review, New York Magazine, New York Times Magazine, TV Guide, Harpers, Washington Journalism Review, American Film,* and other periodicals. Member of board of advisors, *Technology Review.*

WORK IN PROGRESS: A study of changes in American nuclear policy since 1945; further studies of television coverage of political news; an analysis of political advertising.

SIDELIGHTS: In three of his books on television in America—*The Tin Kazoo: Television, Politics, and the News, Good News, Bad News,* and *Sign-Off: The Last Days of Television*—Edwin Diamond argues against the popular belief that television has had a powerful effect on Americans' perceptions of the world and thus a strong influence on the United States' political process. In a review of *The Tin Kazoo,* the *New York Times*'s John Leonard writes that Diamond is the "quiet man at the end of the table [who] bangs his spoon on a glass, declares that the conventional wisdom happens to be balderdash, produces a sheaf of statistics from his inside coat pocket and thumps your pieties into a concussion. . . . [*The Tin Kazoo*] argues that if TV commercials and news programs alter our attitudes in any significant way, nobody can prove it and there is hard evidence to the contrary." *Publishers Weekly* calls Diamond "a lambaster of news hype and sham . . . [who] faults TV news coverage for its safe, neutral stance."

The Tin Kazoo, says Michael J. Robinson in *Chronicle of Higher Education,* presents "a report card about the quality of journalism we have been getting from our major [television] sources of news during the late 1960s and early 70s." Of that same book, Kevin McAuliffe writes in *New Republic:* "With Diamond, the problem is not journalism, it is journal*ists;* the profession, far from being inherently defective, suffers from problems caused by individuals and correctable by them. . . . Too much flip psychojournalism in Nixon's last days and not enough tough, hard reporting when it counted, too few blacks in broadcasting and too many quack 'show doctors' peddling the latest audience research surveys."

Although the central thesis of *The Tin Kazoo* is that television does not have profound effects on Americans' thinking, it is the tangential points Diamond covers—such as psychojournalism, coverage of Watergate, and the future of television news—that are most interesting, says Leonard. "Nevertheless," Leonard concludes, "the basic point is worth pondering." Writes McAuliffe: "Loosely writing up semi-scholarly findings, complete with graphs, tables and demographics, in an informal, overly conversational-style, [Diamond] delivers his knocks with the savvy of an insider's prism."

Good News, Bad News, notes Robinson, "offer[s] the same basic conclusions [as *The Tin Kazoo*]: The quality of American journalism isn't great, and various forces may be cutting the quality; the political impact of television—and all media—is vastly overplayed and exaggerated; the public is smarter than you think when it comes to politics; and the press should clean up its act or face the consequences." A *Choice* critic comments that Diamond, "a member of the school of thought that discounts the influence of the press in politics, . . . is most effective when he addresses himself to [that] theme." Gaye Tuchman in *Public Opinion Quarterly,* while praising Diamond's style, finds *Good News, Bad News* less than satisfactory: "In both style and substance, Edwin Diamond's *Good News, Bad News* is breezy. But that very panache . . . masks a somewhat conventional rendition of standard ideas of newsworkers and researchers. *Good News, Bad News* doesn't have much news." Still, contends Robinson, who points out that a third of the book is devoted to political aspects of entertainment programming, "for those who want an interesting description of press coverage and press business since Watergate, *Good News*[, *Bad News*] can be recommended."

Diamond's third book on the news media, *Sign-Off,* presents a "lively discussion of television in what Diamond calls its prime-time—now," says Frank Mankiewicz in the *Washington Post Book World.* Abraham Z. Bass comments in *Library Journal* that the study provides "a good presentation for the lay person of underlying and ongoing problems in TV." Unlike *The Tin Kazoo* and *Good News, Bad News, Sign-Off* examines more than television journalism and delves into advertising, soap operas, and non-news programming. However, writes Mankiewicz, despite the book's claims to examine these facets of television, "except for an exegetic minute-by-minute study of sex on soap opera, . . . there is no analysis of what might be called non-news television . . . in shaping our political and social attitudes." The reviewer concludes: "This book would be a more complete study if its ambit included more than the news/public affairs side of TV. . . . Diamond touches on [the] phenomenon of life's imitating art in his discussion of TV news coverage of the 1980 campaign. Even without placing it in the broader context of 'entertainment,' this book is worth reading and pondering for these sections alone. I wish only that he had devoted more time to the question of whether television doesn't shape that society in large part, and then reflect it. We can look forward to . . . Ed Diamond's next report."

While most critics praise *The Tin Kazoo* and *Sign-Off,* many concur with a *Choice* reviewer's assessment that *Good News, Bad News* "just misses the mark." A major criticism of *Good News, Bad News* is, as Robinson points out, "that Diamond presents almost no hard data of his own [to substantiate claims made in the book]—especially if we equate hard data with quantitative data. Diamond and his staff at M.I.T. have conducted interviews . . . and analysed 600 hours of videotape. But one finds no systematic presentation of those data." Further, Robinson asserts, Diamond "practically ignores the professional literature about TV, mass media, elections, and public opinion," and therefore *Good News, Bad News* "gives us little but intuition to support [Diamond's] theory of minimal effects [of the news media]. His book really focuses on the realities of the news business. His theories about effects are tossed in, unsupported."

Tuchman and Benjamin DeMott, who writes in *Politics Today*, each criticize *Good News, Bad News* for lack of substance. Says Tuchman: "Potentially exciting insights are marred by a lack of sustained argument and a refusal to ask about the theoretical importance of the phenomena being described. That refusal is a pity, because it's very clear that Diamond . . . is a very bright man." DeMott calls Diamond "a breezy writer, not uninterested in celebrifying the characters he interviews." "I'm afraid this book doesn't really qualify as a penetrating probe," DeMott comments, but also adds that "here and there *Good News, Bad News* offers a shade more than informational snippets and remnants of old nightmares [of television newscasting]. The discussion of the impact of exit-interview techniques developed by the networks during the primaries—in-depth sessions with voters as they left the polling place—is useful. So, too, is the inquiry into the intricacies of media perception of that ultimate grail of mystery in election campaigns, namely, 'momentum.'"

Breaking away from his role as media critic, Diamond coauthored *Jimmy Carter: A Character Portrait*. The biography, written with historian Bruce Mazlish, "attempts to provide . . . an analytical view of the man by examining his background and character," states Donne Raffat in the *Los Angeles Times Book Review*. Alternately subtitled "An Interpretive Biography" on the title page, *Jimmy Carter* "manages to capture a character in motion—in the process of change and development," Raffat adds. "Ever since Jimmy Carter defied all political sense by going from near anonymity to the presidency, a common complaint has been that he is a hard man to understand," comments Steven Stark in *Politics Today*. "Starting from that premise, [the authors] have written a biography that purports to explain the president's character to the American people. . . . Their findings may presage a series of revisionist appraisals that conclude that [Carter] has not been such a poor president after all."

Many critics argue with Diamond and Mazlish's use of a psychoanalytic approach to Carter's biography. George B. Forgie in *Nation* says, "The air of quackery that unfortunately surrounds the use of psychoanalytic concepts in historical and biographical writing is unlikely to be dispelled by this warily admiring new study of President Carter." Diamond and Mazlish "do not do much to forward the cause of psychohistory—an academic field not held in particularly high esteem among historians in the first place—with their analysis of why Carter has a deep and abiding love for the underdog," observes Eleanor Randolph in the *Washington Post Book World*. "It is not primarily because he is a Christian, we are told, nor is it because battling for the underdog has been a tradition in American politics ever since it become apparent that the underdogs had all the votes. Instead the authors concluded that Carter has a deep respect for the little man primarily because he is short."

BIOGRAPHICAL/CRITICAL SOURCES: Publishers Weekly, July 7, 1975, April 30, 1982; *New York Times*, October 11, 1975; *New Republic*, July 3, 1976, January 26, 1980; *Chronicle of Higher Education*, November 13, 1978; *Politics Today*, March/April, 1979, November/December, 1979; *Choice*, September, 1979; *Psychology Today*, January, 1980; *Washington Post Book World*, January 13, 1980, July 4, 1982; *Los Angeles Times Book Review*, February 10, 1980; *Nation*, March 22, 1980; *Public Opinion Quarterly*, spring, 1980; *People*, April 7, 1980; *Library Journal*, April 1, 1982.

—*Sketch by Heidi A. Tietjen*

* * *

DICK, Bernard F(rancis) 1935-

PERSONAL: Born November 25, 1935, in Scranton, Pa.; son of Jacob Nelson and Anita (Sarambo) Dick; married Katherine M. Restaino (a college administrator), July 31, 1965. *Education:* University of Scranton, B.A. (summa cum laude), 1957; Fordham University, M.A., 1960, Ph.D., 1962. *Religion:* Roman Catholic. *Home:* 989 Wilson Ave., Teaneck, N.J. 07666. *Office:* Department of English, Fairleigh Dickinson University, Teaneck, N.J. 07666.

CAREER: Iona College, New Rochelle, N.Y., instructor, 1960-64, assistant professor, 1964-67, associate professor of classics, 1967-70, chairman of department, 1967-70; Fairleigh Dickinson University, Teaneck, N.J., associate professor, 1970-73, professor of English, and chairman of department, 1973-79, professor of English and comparative literature, 1979—. Adjunct lecturer in Latin, College of New Rochelle, 1962-63. *Member:* Modern Language Association of America, American Association of University Professors, American Comparative Literature Association, Society for Cinema Studies.

WRITINGS: William Golding, Twayne, 1967; *The Hellenism of Mary Renault*, Southern Illinois University Press, 1972; *The Apostate Angel: A Critical Study of Gore Vidal*, Random House, 1974; *Anatomy of Film*, St. Martin's, 1978; *Billy Wilder*, Twayne, 1981; (editor) *Dark Victory*, University of Wisconsin Press, 1981; *Hellman in Hollywood*, Fairleigh Dickinson University Press, 1982; *Joseph L. Mankiewicz*, Twayne, 1983.

WORK IN PROGRESS: The Depiction of World War II in the American Film, 1939-1970.

SIDELIGHTS: Bernard F. Dick writes: "Trained as a classicist, with a doctorate in classics, I deplore the demise of the classics, since my classical background has enabled me to move into comparative literature and film. There is no better preparation for a career in academics than the classics." *Avocational interests:* Opera, music, theater, film, World War II.

* * *

DICKENS, Roy S(elman), Jr. 1938-

PERSONAL: Born March 16, 1938, in Atlanta, Ga.; son of Roy Selman (a government worker) and Edith (Metcalf) Dickens; married Carol McClendon (a historian), August 13, 1961; children: David. *Education:* Georgia State University, B.A., 1963; University of Alabama, M.A., 1966; University of North Carolina, Ph.D., 1970. *Office:* Department of Anthropology, University of North Carolina, Chapel Hill, N.C. 27514.

CAREER: California State College, San Bernardino, assistant professor, 1970-71; Georgia State University, Atlanta, assistant professor, 1971-76, associate professor of anthropology,

1976-82; University of North Carolina at Chapel Hill, associate professor of anthropology, 1982—.

MEMBER: American Anthropological Association, Society for American Archaeology, American Association for the Advancement of Science, Sigma Xi.

WRITINGS: Cherokee Prehistory: The Pisgah Phase in the Appalachian Summit Region, University of Tennessee Press, 1976; (with Carole E. Hill) *Cultural Resources: Planning and Management,* Westview, 1978; (contributor) Duane H. King, editor, *The Cherokee Indian Nation: A Troubled History,* University of Tennessee Press, 1979; (with James L. McKinley) *Frontiers in the Soil: The Archaeology of Georgia,* Frontiers Publishing, 1979; *Archaeology of Urban America: The Search for Pattern and Process,* Academic Press, 1982. Also contributor to *Mississippian Settlement Patterns,* Academic Press. Contributor of articles to *American Antiquity,* and various regional journals.

WORK IN PROGRESS: Research on American urban culture and Southeastern Indian cultures through archaeology.

* * *

DIGGORY, James C(lark) 1920-

PERSONAL: Born November 4, 1920, in Philadelphia, Pa.; son of Benjamin James (a real estate appraiser) and Alice Adeline (Clark) Diggory; married Daisy Elliot (a teacher), September 3, 1944; married second wife, Sylvia Farnham (a psychologist), June 6, 1961; married third wife, Carlanne H. Cronin, June 9, 1977; children: (first marriage) Terence, Edith. *Education:* King's College, New Castle, Del., B.A., 1942; University of Pennsylvania, M.A., 1943, Ph.D., 1948. *Politics:* "Mixed, usually Democratic." *Religion:* None. *Home:* 5719 Woodmont St., Pittsburgh, Pa. 15217. *Office:* Department of Psychology, Chatham College, Pittsburgh, Pa. 15232.

CAREER: University of Pennsylvania, Philadelphia, assistant professor, 1948-56, associate professor of psychology, 1956-66; Chatham College, Pittsburgh, Pa., professor of psychology and chairman of department, 1966—. *Member:* American Psychological Association (fellow), American Association for the Advancement of Science, American Association of University Professors, New York Academy of Sciences, Sigma Xi.

WRITINGS: Self-Evaluation: Concepts and Studies, Wiley, 1966; (contributor) E. S. Schneidman, editor, *Essays in Self-Destruction,* Science House, 1967; (contributor) H.L.P. Resnik, editor, *The Diagnosis and Management of the Suicidal Individual,* Little, Brown, 1968; (contributor with N. L. Farberow, W. Breed, W. E. Bunney, D. J. Lettieri, P. May, G. E. Murphy, and F. J. Sullivan) Resnik and B. C. Hathorne, editors, *Suicide Prevention in the Seventies,* National Institute of Mental Health, 1973; (contributor) A. T. Beck, Resnik, and Lettieri, editors, *The Prediction of Suicide,* Charles Press, 1974; (contributor) Schneidman, editor, *Current Developments in Suicidology,* Grune, 1976. Contributor to professional journals.

WORK IN PROGRESS: Continuing research on self-evaluation; studies of suicidal behavior.

SIDELIGHTS: James C. Diggory reads German, French, Spanish, and has some speaking ability in those languages; he can decipher Italian and a little Dutch and studied Arabic, Hebrew, classical Greek, and Russian ("cannot read them now for any practical use"). *Avocational interests:* Singing, baroque music, playing the guitar, painting, sculpturing in wood and clay, designing and making furniture, growing bonsai trees, and the study of history.

* * *

DILTZ, Bert Case 1894-

PERSONAL: Born February 10, 1894, in Port Credit, Ontario, Canada; son of Charles Elisha and Martha Jane (Case) Diltz; married Agnes Marcella Brown, August 7, 1926; children: Charles Herbert, David Alexander, Douglas Graden. *Education:* Queen's University, B.A. (with honors), 1921, M.A. (with gold medal in English), 1922; University of Toronto, specialist's teaching certificate, 1923; additional study at Columbia University, summers, 1923-25. *Religion:* Presbyterian. *Home:* 92 Colin Ave., Toronto, Ontario, Canada.

CAREER: Lindsay Collegiate Institute (secondary school), Ontario, teacher of English, 1923-28, head of department, 1923-28, vice-principal, 1926-28; University of Toronto, Toronto, Ontario, instructor, 1928-31, professor of methods in English and history, 1931-58, dean of college, 1958-63; writer, 1963—. *Military service:* Canadian Expeditionary Forces, Signal Section of Infantry Brigade, 1916-19; served in France and Belgium. *Awards, honors:* LL.D. from Queen's University, 1960.

WRITINGS: Models and Projects for English Composition, Clarke, Irwin (Toronto), 1932; (with Honora M. Cochrane) *Sense and Structure in English Composition,* Clarke, Irwin, 1933; (with Cochrane) *Aim and Order in English Composition,* Clarke, Irwin, 1934; (with H. E. Cavell) *Living English,* Clarke, Irwin, 1939; *Poetic Pilgrimage: An Essay in Education,* Clarke, Irwin, 1942; *Pierian Spring: Reflections on Education and the Teaching of English,* Clarke, Irwin, 1946; *New Models and Projects for Creative Writing,* three parts, Clarke, Irwin, 1949-51; *The Sense of Wonder,* McClelland & Stewart (Toronto), 1953; (editor) *New Horizons: An Anthology of Short Poems for Senior Students,* McClelland & Stewart, 1954; *Poetic Experience,* McClelland & Stewart, 1955; (editor) *Word Magic: An Anthology of Poems for Grades Nine and Ten,* McClelland & Stewart, 1957.

Patterns of Surmise, Clarke, Irwin, 1962; (editor with R. J. McMaster) *Many Minds: An Anthology of Prose,* McClelland & Stewart, Book 1, 1963, Book 2, 1965; (editor) *Frontiers of Wonder: Prose and Poetry for the Intermediate Levels,* Books 1 and 2, McClelland & Stewart, 1968; *Stranger Than Fiction,* McClelland & Stewart, 1969; *Sense or Nonsense: Contemporary Education at the Crossroads,* McClelland & Stewart, 1972; *A Flurry of Verses in Seven Flutters,* The Printery, 1978; *Fleeting Fantasies for Fellow Travellers,* Coach House Press, 1981; *Barnado Boy,* Initiative Publishing, 1982.

WORK IN PROGRESS: A collection of stories, sketches, and verses, *Whittlings of Current Concerns;* a teacher's story, *In Pursuit of Survival.*

SIDELIGHTS: Bert Case Diltz told *CA:* "When I was about twelve years old, the wild life of the countryside fascinated me. Birds, bees, butterflies, and beetles thrived, and so did my collecting instinct.

"At that time books on nature study were not commonly available. My mother searched the big stores and libraries without success. It was then that I began recording in old scribblers some of my observations, such as the discovery of a whippoorwill's nest of chips and a hummingbird's shallow abode glued to the upperside of a low, horizontal bough of a large oak tree.

"When my teacher . . . discovered my interests and hobbies, she allotted me on several occasions . . . a portion of school-time to tell the story of my experience in the out-of-doors, such as the pressing of leaves and wild flowers, the mounting of butterflies and the bottling of snakes.

"If later I ever developed any talent for writing, it was at that time that my skill in communication began."

AVOCATIONAL INTERESTS: Reading, writing, gardening.

* * *

DINER, Hasia R(ena) 1946-

PERSONAL: Born October 7, 1946, in Milwaukee, Wis.; daughter of Morris (a teacher) and Ita (Eichenbaum) Schwartzman; married Steven Diner (a college professor), July 12, 1970; children: Shira Miriam, Eli. *Education:* University of Wisconsin—Madison, B.A., 1968; University of Chicago, M.A.T., 1970; University of Illinois at Chicago Circle, Ph.D., 1975. *Religion:* Jewish. *Home:* 3825 Veazey St. N.W., Washington, D.C. 20016. *Office:* American University, Washington, D.C. 20016.

CAREER: University of Maryland, College Park, instructor in history, beginning 1975; Radcliffe College, Bunting Institute, Cambridge, Mass., research associate, 1978-80; currently affiliated with Washington Semester in the Arts and Humanities, American University, Washington, D.C. Instructor at Federal City College, 1975-76; visiting assistant professor, George Washington University, 1976-77, and Goucher College, 1977-78. Director of employment discrimination counseling, Women's Legal Defense Fund, 1975—.

MEMBER: American Historical Association, Organization of American Historians, American Studies Association, National Capitol Labor Historians, American Jewish Committee, Chesapeake Area Women Historians.

WRITINGS: (Contributor) Arthur Schlesinger and Roger Bruns, editors, *Congress Investigates,* Chelsea House, 1975; *In the Almost Promised Land: American Jews and Blacks, 1915-1935,* Greenwood Press, 1977; *Women in Urban Society: An Annotated Bibliography,* Gale, 1979; *New Homes, New Lives, New Women: Irish Female Migration to Urban America,* Johns Hopkins University Press, in press.

* * *

DINNERSTEIN, Leonard 1934-

PERSONAL: Born May 5, 1934, in New York, N.Y.; son of Abraham and Lillian (Kubrik) Dinnerstein; married Myra Rosenberg, August 20, 1961; children: Andrew, Julie. *Education:* City College (now City College of the City University of New York), B.A., 1955; Columbia University, M.A., 1960, Ph.D., 1966. *Politics:* Democratic. *Religion:* Jewish. *Home:* 5821 East 7th St., Tucson, Ariz. 85711. *Office:* Department of History, University of Arizona, Tucson, Ariz. 85721.

CAREER: New York Institute of Technology, New York City, instructor in American history, 1960-65; Brooklyn College of the City University of New York, Brooklyn, N.Y., lecturer, 1965; City College of the City University of New York, New York City, lecturer in American history, 1966-67; Fairleigh Dickinson University, Teaneck, N.J., assistant professor of American history, 1967-70; University of Arizona, Tucson, professor of history, 1970—. Adjunct assistant professor at Columbia University, summers, 1969, 1972, 1974, 1981, and at New York University, 1969-70. Lecturer at Hunter College in the Bronx (now Herbert H. Lehman College of the City University of New York), 1966. Director of summer seminar for the National Endowment for the Humanities, 1980. *Member:* American Historical Association, Organization of American Historians. *Awards, honors:* Anisfield-Wolf Award from *Saturday Review,* 1969, for *The Leo Frank Case;* National Endowment for the Humanities summer fellowship, 1970 and 1977, research fellowship, 1978; research grants from the University of Arizona, 1971, 1972, 1979, Immigration History Research Center, 1975, Harry S Truman Library, 1976, Eleanor Roosevelt Institute, 1977, University of Arizona Foundation, 1979, Herbert Hoover Library, 1979, and American Philosophical Society, 1979.

WRITINGS: The Leo Frank Case, Columbia University Press, 1968; (with David M. Reimers) *Ethnic Americans: A History of Immigration and Assimilation,* Dodd, 1975, 2nd edition, Harper, 1982; (with Roger L. Nichols and Reimers) *Natives and Strangers: Ethnic Groups and the Building of Modern America,* Oxford University Press, 1979; *America and the Survivors of the Holocaust,* Columbia University Press, 1982.

Editor: (With Fred Jaher) *The Aliens: A History of Ethnic Minorities in America,* Appleton, 1970, 2nd edition published as *Uncertain Americans,* Oxford University Press, 1977; (with Kenneth T. Jackson) *American Vistas,* Oxford University Press, 1971, 3rd edition, 1979; *Antisemitism in the United States,* Holt, 1971; (with Mary Dale Palsson) *Jews in the South,* Louisiana State University Press, 1973; (with Jean Christie) *Decisions and Revisions: Interpretations of Twentieth-Century American History,* Praeger, 1975; (with Christie) *America Since World War II: Historical Interpretation,* Praeger, 1976.

Contributor: Jaher, editor, *The Age of Industrialism in America,* Free Press, 1968; Leon Friedman and Fred L. Israel, editors, *The Justices of the United States Supreme Court, 1789-1969: Their Lives and Major Decisions,* four volumes, Bowker, 1969; A. M. Schlesinger, editor, *History of American Presidential Elections,* four volumes, McGraw, 1971; Schlesinger, editor, *History of United States Political Parties,* four volumes, Chelsea House, 1973; (with George Lankevich) *The Study of American History,* two volumes, Dushkin, 1974; Bernard J. Weiss, editor, *American Education and the European Immigrant: 1840-1940,* University of Illinois Press, 1982.

Also author of papers presented at historical association conferences across the country. Contributor of articles to *American Jewish Historical Quarterly, Jewish Social Studies, American Jewish Archives, Alabama Review, Virginia Magazine of History and Biography, New York History,* and other periodicals. Contributor of book reviews to *American Jewish Historical Quarterly, Arizona and the West, American Journal of Sociology, International Migration Review, Jewish Social Studies, Journal of American History, New Jersey History, New York History,* and other periodicals.

BIOGRAPHICAL/CRITICAL SOURCES: Spectator, July 5, 1968; *Chicago Tribune Book World,* September 26, 1982.

* * *

DiORIO, Al(bert John) 1950-

PERSONAL: Born June 20, 1950, in Philadelphia, Pa.; son of Albert J. (a tailor) and Martha (Breve) DiOrio. *Education:* Glassboro State College, B.A. *Religion:* Roman Catholic. *Home:* 21 Green Tree Rd., Stratford, N.J. 08084. *Agent:* Mitch Douglas, International Creative Management, 40 West 57th St., New York, N.Y. 10019.

CAREER: N. W. Ayer ABH International, New York, N.Y., budget-cost control administrator/contract specialist, beginning 1971; member of staff, Ted Bates, New York; supervisor of budgets and contracts, U.S. Navy. *Member:* Authors League of America.

WRITINGS: Little Girl Lost: The Life and Hard Times of Judy Garland, Arlington House, 1974; *Borrowed Time: The Thirty-Seven Years of Bobby Darin,* Running Press, 1981.

WORK IN PROGRESS: A biography of actress Barbara Stanwyck, for publication by Coward.

SIDELIGHTS: About his books, Al DiOrio told *CA:* "My intention in writing biographies of such entertainers as Judy Garland and Bobby Darin is to explain to the public what it is that gives these performers the ability to electrify an audience as they do. Everyone draws from personal experience in their work, and those in show business do so more than anyone else. When Judy Garland sang 'Over the Rainbow' she moved her audience to tears, and when Darin sang 'Mack the Knife' he turned on an entire generation. Only by understanding the man or woman behind these performances can we begin to understand the excitement we, the public, feel while watching them. Show business is not all glamour and glitter, tuxedos and furs. There is an undercurrent that few people know of, and this is epitomized by Garland, the woman who gave more love than anyone else but demanded more than anyone could give, and by Darin—a boy from the Bronx who knew his time could run out any day and intended to make the most of it while he could."

MEDIA ADAPTATIONS: Borrowed Time: The Thirty-Seven Years of Bobby Darin is being filmed by Reno/Metz, for scheduled release in 1983.

* * *

DITSKY, John (Michael) 1938-

PERSONAL: Born March 9, 1938, in Detroit, Mich.; son of John George (an automotive worker) and Elizabeth (a bookseller and buyer; maiden name, Brestovansky) Ditsky; married Claire Suzette Ponka, June 16, 1962; children: Katherine. *Education:* University of Detroit, Ph.B., 1958, M.A., 1961; New York University, Ph.D., 1967. *Home:* 18235 Oak Dr., Detroit, Mich. 48221. *Office:* Department of English, University of Windsor, Windsor, Ontario, Canada.

CAREER: University of Detroit, Detroit, Michigan, instructor in English, 1964-66; Wayne State University, Detroit, instructor in English, 1966-67; University of Windsor, Windsor, Ontario, assistant professor, 1967-71, associate professor, 1971-75, professor of English, 1975—. Poet and critic. *Member:* Modern Language Association of America, Steinbeck Society, Canadian Association for American Studies, Kyushu American Literature Society.

WRITINGS: The Katherine Poems, Killaly Press (London, Ontario), 1975; *Essays on "East of Eden,"* Steinbeck Society of America, 1977; *Scar Tissue,* Vesta (Cornwall, Ontario), 1978; *The Onstage Christ,* Vision (London, England), 1980; *Friend and Lover,* Ontario Review Press, 1981.

Work represented in anthologies: *Soundings,* edited by Andy Wainright and Jack Ludwig, Anansi Press (Toronto), 1970; *Windsor Salt,* edited by Marty Gerudis, Black Moss Press (Toronto), 1970; *Contraverse: Nine Poets,* edited by Dorothy Farmiloe, Corcorde Press (Windsor), 1971.

Staff reviewer, *Fanfare* and *Choice*. Contributor of over seven hundred poems, reviews, and articles to over three hundred journals and periodicals, including *Modern Poetry Studies, Southern Humanities Review, Ariel, Canadian Forum, North American Review, Georgia Review,* and *Epoch.* Member of the editorial board of *Steinbeck Quarterly;* poetry editor of *University of Windsor Review.*

WORK IN PROGRESS: Poems and articles.

SIDELIGHTS: John Ditsky told *CA:* "I enjoy trying to say things well; lust after print. It all helps in the classroom."

* * *

DOGYEAR, Drew
See GOREY, Edward (St. John)

* * *

DONNE, Maxim
See DUKE, Madelaine (Elizabeth)

* * *

DONNER, Joern 1933-

PERSONAL: Born February 5, 1933, in Helsinki, Finland; son of Kai and Greta (von Bonsdorff) Donner; married Inga-Britt Wik, 1954 (divorced, 1962); children: Johan, Jakob. *Education:* Helsinki University, Mag. Phi., 1961. *Politics:* Left. *Home:* Svartmangatan 24, Stockholm C, Sweden; and Pohjoisranta 12, SF-00170 Helsinki, Finland. *Office:* Northern Film Production Establishment, Vaduz, Liechtenstein.

CAREER: Writer. *Dagens Nyheter,* Stockholm, Sweden, literary critic, 1951—; AB Sandrew Film, Stockholm, under contract as scriptwriter and feature film director, 1963—. Cofounder, Finnish Film Archive, Helsinki, Finland, 1957. *Member:* Union of Finnish Journalists, Union of Writers in Finland. *Awards, honors:* Venice Film festival, opera prima prize, 1963; Coppa Volpi, 1964; Finnish State Prize for Literature, 1972, for *Sommar av kaelek och sorg.*

WRITINGS—Published by Soederstroem & Co., except as indicated: *Valsignade liv* (short stories), 1951; *Sla dej inte till ro,* 1952; *Brev,* 1954; *Jag, Erik Anders* (novel), 1955; *Bordet* (novel), 1957; *Rapport fran Berlin,* Albert Bonnier (Stockholm), 1958, translation published as *Report from Berlin,* Indiana University Press, 1961; *Berliini-arkea ja uhkaa,* Werner Soderstrom (Helsinki), 1958.

Paa ett sjukhus: dagbok foer vuxna, 1960; *Helsingfors-Finlands ansikte,* 1960; *Djavulens ansikte* (monograph on Ingmar Bergman), Aldus Publishers (Stockholm), 1962, translation published as *The Personal Vision of Ingmar Bergman,* Indiana University Press, 1964, published as *The Films of Ingmar Bergman: From "Torment" to "All These Women,"* Dover, 1972; *Rapport fran Donau* (travel book), Albert Bonnier, 1962; *Maailmankirja,* Otava, 1968; *Vaerldsboken,* 1968; *Suomen kuva maailmalla,* Helsinki, 1969.

Sommar av kaelek och sorg, 1971.

All published by Wahlstroem & Widstrand: *Nya boken om vaart land,* 1967; *Marina Maria,* 1972; *Sverigeboken,* 1973; *Nu Maaste du,* 1974; *Angelas Krig,* 1976; *Sagt och gjort,* 1976; *Jakob och friheten,* 1978; *Jag, Jorn Donner* (diaries), 1980.

Also author and director of films: "En sondag i september" (title means "Sunday in September"), 1963; "Att alska" (title means "To Love"), 1964.†

* * *

DORSETT, Lyle W(esley) 1938-

PERSONAL: Born April 17, 1938, in Kansas City, Mo.; son of Albert Wesley (a sales executive) and Eda Rose (Hilderbrand) Dorsett; married Mary Ann Hayes, July 9, 1970. *Education:* Junior College of Kansas City, A.A., 1958; University of Missouri, B.A., 1960, M.A., 1962, Ph.D., 1965. *Home:* 2185 Goddard Pl., Boulder, Colo. 80303. *Office:* Department of History, University of Denver, Denver, Colo. 80210.

CAREER: University of Missouri—St. Louis, assistant professor of history, 1965-66; University of Southern California, Los Angeles, assistant professor of history, 1966-68; University of Missouri—St. Louis, associate professor of history, 1968-71; University of Colorado, Denver Center, associate professor of history, 1971-72; University of Denver, Denver, professor of history, 1972—. *Member:* American Historical Association, Organization of American Historians, Southern Historical Association. *Awards, honors:* American Philosophical Society grant; National Endowment for the Humanities summer fellowship.

WRITINGS: The Pendergast Machine, Oxford University Press, 1968; (editor) *The Challenge of the City, 1860-1910,* Heath, 1968; *The Early American City,* Forum Press, 1973; *Bosses and Machines in Urban America,* Forum Press, 1974; *The Queen City: A History of Denver,* Pruett, 1977; *Franklin D. Roosevelt and the City Bosses,* Kennikat, 1977; (with A. T. Brown) *K. C.: A History of Kansas City, Mo.,* Pruett, 1978; *Joy: A Biography of Mrs. C. S. Lewis,* Macmillan, 1983. Contributor to periodicals, including *Arizona and the West, New England Quarterly, Journal of Southern History, Pacific Northwest Quarterly,* and *Colorado Magazine.*

SIDELIGHTS: Lyle W. Dorsett told *CA:* "For years I have loved history. Peeking into old diaries, letters, and newspapers to get a feeling for bygone eras is a joy. Once I have reconstructed a slice of the past, I can't rest until I communicate my findings in writing.

"During the 1960's and 1970's, most of my writing was on the subject of urban history. Gradually my interests have been turning to people rather than cities. The fascination with people emerges in the books I wrote on Denver and Roosevelt, and is manifested in the biography of Joy Davidman Lewis (Mrs. C. S. Lewis).

"Human motivation interests me as much as anything now that I'm in middle life. I am especially fond of studying the lives of people who have a personal relationship with God—people who are motivated by a love for Christ. This is why I chose to write about Joy Davidman Lewis. Certainly I will pry into this field of Christian biography in the years to come."

* * *

DOWDY, Mrs. Regera
See GOREY, Edward (St. John)

* * *

DOXEY, William S(anford, Jr.) 1935-

PERSONAL: Born January 20, 1935, in Miami, Fla.; son of William S. (a pilot) and Elizabeth (a teacher; maiden name, Latham) Doxey; married Lyndall Blackburn, August 22, 1959; children: William S. III, Beth, Charles Latham. *Education:* Florida State University, A.B., 1961, M.A., 1963; University of North Carolina, Ph.D., 1970. *Politics:* Democrat. *Religion:* Baptist. *Home:* 550 North White, Carrollton, Ga. 30117. *Agent:* Julie Fallowfield, McIntosh & Otis, Inc., 475 Fifth Ave., New York, N.Y. 10017. *Office:* Department of English, West Georgia College, Carrollton, Ga. 30117.

CAREER: West Georgia College, Carrollton, assistant professor, 1968-70, associate professor, 1971-75, professor of English, 1976—. Has also worked as a lifeguard, roofer, and land surveyor. *Military service:* U.S. Army, 1957-58.

WRITINGS—Novels, except as indicated; published by Tower, except as indicated: *A Winter in the Woods* (poems), Windless Orchard Press, 1975; *ESPionage,* 1979; *Dead Wrong,* 1980; *Bye-Bye, Lonesome Blues,* 1981. Contributor of stories and poems to literary journals and magazines, including *Carolina Quarterly, Southern Review, Descant, Quartet, Four Quarters, Esquire, Galaxy, Amazing Stories,* and *Alfred Hitchcock Mystery Magazine.* Founder and co-editor of *Notes on Contemporary Literature.*

WORK IN PROGRESS: Star Poem, "an epic novel/poem of science fiction dealing with found artifact inducing universal consciousness."

SIDELIGHTS: William S. Doxey explains to *CA* that he is "perhaps best known as Father of Ludistic Philosophy (based on idea that if God exists He is a comedy writer); am devoted to LSD (long slow distance) running and manage to cover eight to ten miles a day; have competence in the language of dreams; love a good fight; hate fatness and professional patriots; believe S. Dali is best artist of the century." He adds: "If I had known at fifteen what I know now, I would've killed myself."

* * *

DOYLE, Robert V(aughn) 1916-

PERSONAL: Born June 5, 1916, in Madison, Wis.; son of William V. (a textile merchant) and Frances E. (White) Doyle; married Margaret Serdahely (a registered nurse), March 15, 1941; children: Kathleen M. (Mrs. Paul Mayer). *Education:* Studied at University of Wisconsin—Milwaukee. *Politics:* "Registered Democrat, independent philosophy." *Home:* 1209 Fairweather Dr., Sacramento, Calif. 95833.

CAREER: Worked in home furnishing industry in Wisconsin, 1936-39; Sears Roebuck, New Orleans, La., salesman, 1940-42; Cutler-Hammer, Milwaukee, Wis., supervisor, 1942-44; interior designer for Barker Brothers furniture stores in California, 1944-54; R. V. Doyle Interiors, Bakersfield, Calif., owner, 1954-57; John Breuner Co., Sacramento, Calif., interior designer, 1957-72. Educational consultant in interior design, 1951-72; teacher of interior design, Bakersfield College (now California State University, Bakersfield), 1952-55. Freelance writer of radio drama, 1945-52, of magazine articles, 1957—; author, 1967—; *South Natomas News,* Sacramento, Calif., executive editor, 1980—. Member of board of trustees, Stanford Settlement, 1981—, and American River College, 1981—; member of board of directors, South Natomas Community Association, 1981—. *Military service:* 1939-40.

WRITINGS: Your Career in Interior Design, Simon & Schuster, 1969, 2nd edition, 1975; *Careers in Elective Government,* Simon & Schuster, 1976; *Working and Living with Appropriate*

Technology, Simon & Schuster, 1980. Reporter and editorial writer for *South Natomas News.*

WORK IN PROGRESS: Research for a novel set in 1793; a contemporary novel dealing with politics and land-use; a book on the restoration of Tudor mansions.

SIDELIGHTS: Robert V. Doyle told *CA:* "My career as a writer, with all its classic fits and starts, has opened doors for me; I have discovered an acceptance that could not have occurred through any other skills at my disposal.

"Research in appropriate technology showed me certain truths. I wanted to share these truths with others. Through writing, I feel I have awakened in people a keener sense of awareness in their community. As my own community—South Natomas—became aroused, so did a new philosophy, founded in fairness: fairness to the community as a whole and to its future; fairness to its progeny, to its needy, to its policymakers, to its land developers; and, most important, fairness to the land itself.

"I can only hope that the interaction inaugurated in the South Natomas community, as part of the City of Sacramento and the State of California, will grow with the tenacity of the wild mustard that greens our fields each winter.

"Is this the dream-wish for immortality hauntingly shared by all writers?"

* * *

DRAPER, Hastings
See JEFFRIES, Roderic (Graeme)

* * *

DRESNER, Samuel H(ayim) 1923-

PERSONAL: Born November 7, 1923, in Chicago, Ill.; son of Julius (a salesman) and Maude (Handmacher) Dresner; married Ruth Rapp, June 16, 1951; children: Hannah, Miriam, Nehama. *Education:* Attended Northwestern University and Hebrew Union College—Jewish Institute of Religion; University of Cincinnati, B.A., 1945; Jewish Theological Seminary of America, Rabbi, 1951, Doctor of Hebrew Letters, 1954. *Politics:* Republican. *Home:* 115 Eastwood Dr. Deerfield, Ill. 60015. *Office:* Moriah Congregation, 200 Hyacinth Lane, Deerfield, Ill. 60015.

CAREER: City College (now City College of the City University of New York), New York, N.Y., director of Hillel Foundation, 1951-53; Har Zion Temple, Philadelphia, Pa., associate rabbi, 1953-56; Beth El Temple, Springfield, Mass., rabbi, 1957-69; Beth El Congregation, Highland Park, Ill., rabbi, 1969-77; Moriah Congregation, Deerfield, Ill., rabbi, 1977—. Chairman of Springfield Committee for the Improvement of Mass Media and Springfield Human Relations Commission. *Awards, honors: The Jew in American Life* chosen by U.S. Information Agency as one of 75 best books on American life, 1963.

WRITINGS: Prayer, Humility, and Compassion, Jewish Publication Society, 1957; *The Jewish Dietary Laws,* Burning Bush Press, 1959, 2nd revised edition, 1966; *The Zaddik,* Abelard, 1960, reprinted, Schocken, 1974; *Three Paths of God and Man,* Harper, 1960; *The Jew in American Life,* Crown, 1963; *God, Man and Atomic War,* Living Books, 1966.

The Sabbath, Burning Bush Press, 1970; *Between the Generations: A Jewish Dialogue,* Hartmore, 1971; *Polnoy,* Schocken, 1974; *Levi Yitzhak of Berditchev: Portrait of a Hasidic Master,* Hartmore, 1974; (with Byron Sherwin) *Judaism: The Way of Sanctification,* United Synagogue Book Service, 1978.

Contributor to numerous periodicals including *Judaism, Commentary, Forum,* and *Jewish Digest.* Editor, *Conservative Judaism,* 1959-69.

WORK IN PROGRESS: Editing *Herchel: A Selection from His Writings* and *The Circle of the Baal Shem Tov: Essays in Hasidism.*

* * *

DREYFACK, Raymond

PERSONAL: Born in New York, N.Y.; son of Marcus (a manufacturer) and Frances (Wagner) Dreyfack; married Tess Karlitz (a special assistant to a psychiatrist); children: Kenneth, Madeleine. *Education:* Attended City College (now City College of the City University of New York), Columbia University, and New York University, 1945-55. *Home:* 0-57 Pine Ave., Fair Lawn, N.J. 07410.

CAREER: Henry Kelly Importing and Distributing Co., New York, N.Y., data processing manager, 1947-52; Faberge Perfumes, Inc., Ridgefield, N.J., systems director, 1953-63; freelance writer and public relations consultant, 1963—. Former lecturer at New York University. *Member:* American Society of Journalists and Authors.

WRITINGS: Twelve Psychic Selling Strategies That Will Multiply Your Income, Parker Publishing, 1975; *Sure Fail: The Art of Mismanagement,* Morrow, 1976; *How to Boost Company Productivity and Profits,* Dartnell, 1976; *The Image Makers* (novel), Major, 1976; *Zero-Base Budgeting: Pros and Cons,* Dartnell, 1977; *The Complete Book of Walking,* Farnsworth Publishing, 1979.

Profitable Salesmanship in the '80s, Chilton, 1980; *Making It in Management the Japanese Way,* Farnsworth Publishing, 1982; *Profitable Customer Service,* Dartnell, 1983.

Ghost writer of books and articles. Contributor of chapters of books and articles to business and management journals. Special projects editor, *Plant Engineering;* contributing editor, *Supervision* and *American Salesman;* former editor and copublisher, *Profit Improvement News.*

WORK IN PROGRESS: The Malek Manual, a novel; an untitled book on computers.

* * *

DRUKS, Herbert 1937-

PERSONAL: Born April 1, 1937, in Vienna, Austria; son of Charles Druks (a businessman). *Education:* City University of New York (now City College of the City University of New York), B.A., 1958; Rutgers University, M.A., 1959; New York University, Ph.D., 1964. *Address:* c/o Robert Speller & Sons, 30 East 23rd St., New York, N.Y. 10010.

CAREER: Works as college professor of history and international relations.

WRITINGS—Published by Robert Speller: *Harry S Truman and the Russians,* 1967, 2nd edition published as *Truman and the Russians,* 1981; *From Truman through Johnson,* two volumes, 1971; *Cities in Civilization,* Volume I, 1971; *The Failure to Rescue,* 1977; *The U.S. and Israel, 1945-1973: A Diplomatic History,* 1979.

WORK IN PROGRESS: The U.S. and Israel, 1945-83.

SIDELIGHTS: Herbert Druks told *CA:* "I seek out the facts, the truth, and then try to write it clearly. Both collecting data and writing requires much patience, detective work, and time. Nothing comes easy. And even after the work is done, I am never completely satisfied. The reason? The primary sources are seldom complete. In writing U.S. diplomatic history, one has to confront such obstacles as the State Department and CIA unwillingness to make their papers available. There is the Freedom of Information Act, but we are still severely limited to the primary sources, and such agencies as CIA and State like to play favorites. Other sources of contemporary history, like the *New York Times* and TV-Radio major networks, often distort the facts till it sounds more like political propaganda and it becomes more and more impossible to rely on these sources for information. So, after all is done, one feels rather frustrated. The full story cannot be told because the materials have not been made available."

* * *

Du BROFF, Sidney 1929-

PERSONAL: Born July 18, 1929, in Chicago, Ill.; son of Harry (a proofreader) and Anna (Rubin) Du Broff; married Nedra Geiser (a psychologist), October 30, 1954. *Education:* Attended Los Angeles City College, one year. *Politics:* Free enterprise. *Religion:* "None. Culture: Jewish." *Home:* 7, The Corner, Grange Rd., London W.5, England.

CAREER: Writer and free-lance journalist. *Member:* British Society of Authors. *Awards, honors:* Recipient of Golden Hedgehog international literary contest award for stories, "After All" and "The Happy Birthday."

WRITINGS: Woe to the Rebellious Children (novel), Geiser Productions, 1967; *Black Fuse* (novel), Everest, 1975; *Shooting, Fishing, and Gun Book I,* Spur Publications, 1976; *Fly Fishing on Still Water,* Moonraker, 1981; *Still-Water Fly Fishing for Young People,* Heinemann, 1982; *The English Lakes,* Longman, 1983. Also author of radio and television scripts. Former correspondent for several German publications. Contributor of articles, short stories, and reviews to over a hundred periodicals published in twenty-three countries.

WORK IN PROGRESS: Come Fly Fishing with Me Again; The Couples' Fly Fishing Handbook; America: Israel's Friend or Enemy?

SIDELIGHTS: "It has been a hard twenty-year journey making the trip from that of a committed socialist to a profound believer in free enterprise," Sidney Du Broff writes to *CA*. "Amongst the reasons for this change, after having visited every European socialist country (except Albania—[but] I'm published there, too) is that socialism does not work—at least not very well. True, any ten year old could have told me this in the beginning, and I could have been saved that hard journey; that is what is so disturbing.

"In the beginning I found America too conservative, and now I find it too radical. I suppose that we have both changed. But at either end of the scale, I have found life there somewhat tedious. Consequently [my wife and I] have lived in England since 1960. Is it better? No, but it's different. Europe—and I have visited and reported on every country—is essentially a mucky place.

"What, in fact, was really required, was America. There was one somewhere—a place that rejected all that was mucky about Europe. Sheltered from the rest of the world, enjoying our wonderful isolation, we have emerged rather naive, allowing ourselves to be dragged into a holy war in Vietnam, which we lost. Are we so short of capable individuals that we had a Nixon for a president? (I'm not knocking anybody—I supported him.) And then there was Carter—I voted for him by absentee ballot—and I shudder. He had to be better than Ford—but wasn't. And then things were so bad that even Ronald Reagan looked good—so I voted for him. Hope is a fire that burns brightly—at times—and then is doused soon afterwards.

"And what of England? Since 1960 I have had occasion to make some observations: The two best things about it are the National Health Service and the trout fishing. In that respect at least, Britain can serve as a beacon of light in creating a National Health Service on which the rest of the world could model itself.

"Far from European residence making me European, it has, on the contrary, made me more American every day. We [Americans] have our faults and our flaws—but the rest have more."

* * *

DUBROVIN, Vivian 1931-

PERSONAL: Born March 24, 1931, in Chicago, Ill.; daughter of Ross (a school superintendent) and Emilie (a teacher; maiden name, Robert) Herr; married Kenneth P. Dubrovin (a director of agricultural research), September 5, 1954; children: Kenneth R., Darryl, Diana, Laura, Barbara. *Education:* University of Illinois, B.S., 1953. *Religion:* Episcopalian. *Home:* 1901 Arapahoe Dr., Longmont, Colo. 80501.

CAREER: Cuneo Press, Chicago, Ill., editor of "Cuneo Topics," 1953; U.S. Savings & Loan League, Chicago, staff writer for *News,* 1954; University of Wisconsin Press, Madison, editor, 1955-56; free-lance writer, 1971—. Director of numerous writing conferences. Consultant, lecturer, and participant in writing programs and workshops. *Member:* National League of American Penwomen (president, Central Colorado branch, 1978-80), American Association of University Women (member of executive board and chapter editor, 1978-79), Society of Children's Book Writers (Rocky Mountain chapter, vice-president, 1978-79, president, 1979-80).

WRITINGS—Juveniles; "Summer Fun/Winter Fun" series, published by EMC Corp., 1974: *Baseball Just for Fun; The Magic Bowling Ball; The Track Trophy; Rescue on Skis.* Also author of other books and tapes in the series.

"Saddle Up!" series, published by EMC Corp., 1975: *A Better Bit and Bridle; A Chance to Win; Trailering Troubles; Open the Gate.* Also author of other books in the series.

Contributor of stories and articles to periodicals, including *Curriculum Review, Instructor, Jack and Jill, Wee Wisdom, Crusader, Adventure,* and *Humpty Dumpty.*

WORK IN PROGRESS: A third-grade novel; a high interest/low reading level romance for children.

BIOGRAPHICAL/CRITICAL SOURCES: Longmont Times-Call, October 31, 1974; *Boulder Town and Country,* December 25, 1974; *Loveland Reporter-Herald,* April 19, 1975.

* * *

DUCHE, Jean 1915-

PERSONAL: Born March 17, 1915, in Chabanais, Charente,

France; son of Joseph and Berthe (Jaulin) Duche; married Nathalie Epstein (a writer under the name Natache Duche), March 20, 1946; children: Caroline. *Education:* Attended Ecole Montalembert, Limoges, and Lycee Louis le Grand, Paris; Faculte de Droit de Paris, licence en droit, 1936; Faculte des Lettres de Paris (Sorbonne), licence es-lettres, 1940.

CAREER: Free-lance journalist, 1944—. Editorial writer, *Elle,* 1951—. *Military service:* Armee francaise, 1936-38, 1939-40. *Awards, honors:* Prix de l'Humour (premium of one franc), 1951, for *Elle et lui;* Chevalier de la Legion d'honneur.

WRITINGS: Liberte europeenne, Flammarion, 1949; *Elle et lui,* Flammarion, 1951, translation by Virginia Graham published as *I Said to My Wife,* Deutsch, 1953; *Trois san toit,* Flammarion, 1952, translation by Diana Athill published as *Not at Home,* Deutsch, 1955; *L'Histoire de France racontee a Juliette,* Presses de la Cite, 1954, revised edition, 1968, translation by R. H. Stevens published as *The History of France as Told to Juliette,* Burke Publishing, 1958, Roy, 1960; *L'Histoire de France racontee a Francois et Caroline,* Editions G.P., 1955, revised edition, Flammarion, 1970; *Les Grandes heures de Lyon,* Amiot-Dumont, 1956; *On s'aimera toute la vie,* Amiot-Dumont, 1956; *L'Histoire du monde,* Flammarion, Volume I: *L'Animal vertical,* 1958, Volume II: *Le Feu de Dieu,* 1960, Volume III: *L'Age de raison,* 1963, Volume IV: *Le Grand tournant,* 1966.

Le Coeur a l'ouvrage, Livre Contemporain, 1960; *Pourquoi Jaccoud a-t-il tue?,* Flammarion, 1960; (with F. A. Roulhec) *Deux siecles d'histoire de France par la caricature, 1760-1960,* Le Pont Royal, 1961; (with wife, Natache Duche) *Des Jeunes filles parlent,* Flammarion, 1965; *Les Grandes routes du Commerce,* Flammarion, 1969, translation published as *The Great Trade Routes,* McGraw, 1969; *Rever des Iles britanniques,* Editions Vilo, 1969.

Pecus, R. Laffont, 1970; (with Anne-Marie Bryan) *Pour parler: Manuel de conversation francaise,* Prentice-Hall, 1970, 2nd edition, 1977; *La Premier sexe,* R. Laffont, 1971; *L'Enlevement de M. Remi-Potel,* R. Laffont, 1975; *La Mythologie racontee a Juliette,* R. Laffont, 1977; *Cortes: Ou, L'Affrontement des dieux,* Ramsay, 1978.

WORK IN PROGRESS: More volumes in series *L'Histoire du monde.*

SIDELIGHTS: Jean Duche once told *CA:* "I live as little as possible in Paris and as much as possible in the country. If I don't have books to write, I participate every day in the hunt."

BIOGRAPHICAL/CRITICAL SOURCES: Books and Bookmen, January, 1970; *Library Journal,* June 15, 1970.†

* * *

DUKE, Madelaine (Elizabeth) 1925-
(Maxim Donne, Alex Duncan)

PERSONAL: Born August 21, 1925, in Geneva, Switzerland; daughter of Richard and Federica Duke; married Alexander Macfarlane (a physician), August, 1946. *Education:* University of St. Andrews, B.Sc., 1945; University of Edinburgh, M.B., Ch.B., 1955. *Address:* c/o Mondial Books Ltd., Norman Alexander & Co., 19 Bolton St., Piccadilly, London W1Y 8HD, England.

CAREER: Author, novelist, and part-time medical psychotherapist. Part-time teacher of creative writing at University of Sussex. *Member:* P.E.N., Society of Authors, Royal Society of Medicine. *Awards, honors:* Huntington Hartford Foundation fellow, 1962.

WRITINGS: Top Secret Mission, Evans Brothers, 1954, Criterion, 1955; *Slipstream: The Story of Anthony Duke,* Evans Brothers, 1955, published as *Slipstream,* Panther Books, 1979; *No Passport: The Story of Jan Felix,* Evans Brothers, 1957; *Beyond the Pillars of Hercules: A Spanish Journey,* Evans Brothers, 1957; *Azael and the Children* (Book Society selection), J. Cape, 1958; (contributor of short fiction) John Pudney, editor, *Pick of Today's Short Stories* (anthology), Putnam, Volume XI, 1958, Volume XII, 1960; *No Margin for Error,* J. Cape, 1959, Walker & Co., 1963.

A City Built to Music, J. Cape, 1960; *Ride the Brooding Wind,* Walker & Co., 1961; *Thirty Pieces of Nickel,* J. Cape, 1962; *The Sovereign Lords,* J. Cape, 1963; (under pseudonym Maxim Donne) *Claret, Sandwiches, and Sin: A Cartoon,* Heinemann, 1964, Doubleday, 1966; *Sobaka,* Heinemann, 1965; *This Business of Bomfog: A Cartoon,* Heinemann, 1967, Doubleday, 1969; *The Secret People,* Brockhampton Press, 1967, Doubleday, 1969; *The Lethal Innocents,* M. Joseph, 1968; *The Sugarcube Trap* (for young adults), Brockhampton Press, 1969.

Death of a Holy Murderer, M. Joseph, 1974; *Death at the Wedding* (sequel to *Death of a Holy Murderer*), M. Joseph, 1975; *Death of a Dandie Dinmont,* M. Joseph, 1978; *Flashpoint,* M. Joseph, 1982.

Under pseudonym Alex Duncan: *It's a Vet's Life,* M. Joseph, 1961; *The Vet Has Nine Lives,* M. Joseph, 1962, large print edition, Ulverscroft, 1969; *Vets in the Belfry,* M. Joseph, 1964; *The Best of Vets,* W. H. Allen, 1977; *Vets in Congress,* W. H. Allen, 1978; *Vet among the Pigeons,* Star Books, 1978; *Vet on Vacation,* Star Books, 1979; *Vet among the Pigeons* [and] *Vet in the Manger* (omnibus), W. H. Allen, 1980; *Vet in a State* [and] *Vet on Vacation* (omnibus), W. H. Allen, 1980; *To Be a Country Doctor,* W. H. Allen, 1980. Also author, under pseudonym Alex Duncan, of *Vet's Choice, God and the Doctor,* and *The Diary of a Country Doctor.*

Also contributor to anthologies. Contributor to medical journals and to literature periodicals, including *Books and Bookmen.*

SIDELIGHTS: Madelaine Duke, who holds the title Baroness de Hartog, is competent in German and knows French and Italian. She told *CA:* "I prefer writing novels to producing nonfiction because the novel can be more truthful than, for instance, biography. All one can give as a writer is a personal vision and the sum total of one's experience of life." She is a registered silversmith.

MEDIA ADAPTATIONS: Top Secret Mission was adapted for television by Irving G. Neiman and broadcast on "U.S. Steel Hour," 1958.

AVOCATIONAL INTERESTS: Geology, silversmithing, world travel.

* * *

DUKES, Paul 1934-

PERSONAL: Born April 5, 1934, in Wallington, England; son of James Albert (an electrical contractor) and Margaret (Newman) Dukes; married Sara Dodd, March 28, 1966 (divorced December 6, 1972); married Rosemary Ann Mackay, May 6, 1974; children: (second marriage) Daniel, Ruth. *Education:* Peterhouse, Cambridge, B.A. (honors), 1954; University of Washington, Seattle, M.A., 1956; University of London, Ph.D.,

1964. *Politics:* Socialist (Labour Party). *Religion:* Atheist. *Home:* 74 Whitehall Rd., Aberdeen, Scotland. *Office:* History Department, Taylor Building, King's College, University of Aberdeen, Aberdeen, Scotland.

CAREER: University of Maryland, Overseas Program, lecturer, 1959-64; University of Aberdeen, King's College, Aberdeen, Scotland, lecturer, 1964-71, senior lecturer in history, 1972—, reader, 1975—. *Military service:* British Army, 1956-58. *Member:* Historical Association, British Universities Association of Slavists, National Association of Soviet and East European Studies.

WRITINGS: Catherine the Great and the Russian Nobility, Cambridge University Press, 1967; *The Emergence of the Super-Powers,* Harper, 1970; *A History of Russia,* McGraw, 1974; *Russia under Catherine the Great,* Oriental Research Partners, Volume I, 1977, Volume II, 1978; *October and the World,* Macmillan, 1979; *The Making of Russian Absolutism, 1613-1801,* Longman, 1982.

WORK IN PROGRESS: A History of Europe, 1648-1984.

SIDELIGHTS: Paul Dukes is competent in French, Russian, and German.

* * *

DUNCAN, Alex
See DUKE, Madelaine (Elizabeth)

* * *

DUNDES, Alan 1934-

PERSONAL: Surname is pronounced *Dun*-deez; born September 8, 1934, in New York, N.Y.; son of Maurice (an attorney) and Helen (Rothschild) Dundes; married Carolyn Browne, September 8, 1958; children: Alison, Lauren, David. *Education:* Yale University, B.A., 1955, M.A.T., 1958; Indiana University, Ph.D., 1962. *Home:* 1590 La Vereda, Berkeley, Calif. 94708. *Office:* Department of Anthropology, University of California, Berkeley, Calif. 94720.

CAREER: University of Kansas, Lawrence, instructor in English, 1962-63; University of California, Berkeley, assistant professor of anthropology, 1963-65, associate professor, 1965-68, professor of anthropology and folklore, 1968—. *Military service:* U.S. Navy, 1955-57; became lieutenant. *Member:* American Folklore Society, American Anthropological Association, California Folklore Society. *Awards, honors:* Second place in Chicago Folklore Prize competition for *The Morphology of North American Indian Folktales;* Guggenheim fellowship, 1966-67; senior fellowship, National Endowment for the Humanities, 1972-73.

WRITINGS: The Morphology of North American Indian Folktales, Academic Scientarium Fennica, 1964; (editor) *The Study of Folklore,* Prentice-Hall, 1965; (editor) *Every Man His Way: Readings in Cultural Anthropology,* Prentice-Hall, 1968.

(Editor) *Mother Wit from the Laughing Barrel: Readings in the Interpretation of Afro-American Folklore,* Prentice-Hall, 1973; (with Alessandro Falassi) *La Terra in Piazza: An Interpretation of the Palio of Siena,* University of California Press, 1975; (with Carl R. Pagter) *Urban Folklore from the Paperwork Empire,* American Folklore Society, 1975; *Analytic Essays in Folklore,* Mouton, 1975; (compiler) *Folklore Theses and Dissertations in the United States,* University of Texas Press, 1976.

Interpreting Folklore, Indiana University Press, 1980; (editor) *The Evil Eye: A Folklore Casebook,* Garland Publishing, 1981; (editor with Wolfgang Mieder) *The Wisdom of Many: Essays on the Proverb,* Garland Publishing, 1981; (with Claudia A. Stibbe) *The Art of Mixing Metaphors: A Folkloristic Interpretation of the "Netherlands Proverbs," by Pieter Bruegel the Elder,* Academia Scientiarum Fennica, 1981; (editor) *Cinderella: A Folklore Casebook,* Garland Publishing, 1982. Contributor to professional journals.

BIOGRAPHICAL/CRITICAL SOURCES: California Monthly, Volume LXXVI, number 1, October, 1965.

* * *

DUNLOP, Agnes M. R. (?)-1982
(Elisabeth Kyle, Jan Ralston)

PERSONAL: Born in Ayr, Scotland; died February 23, 1982, in Ayr, Scotland; daughter of James (a lawyer) and Elizabeth (Riddell) Dunlop. *Education:* Educated privately. *Religion:* Presbyterian. *Address:* c/o Tait, Dunlop, Hillhouse & Co., Solicitors, 2 Wellington Sq., Ayr, Scotland. *Agent:* Brandt & Brandt Literary Agents, Inc., 1501 Broadway, New York, N.Y. 10036.

CAREER: Writer.

WRITINGS—Under pseudonym Elisabeth Kyle, except as indicated; published by P. Davies, except as indicated: *The Begonia Bed,* Bobbs-Merrill, 1934; *Orangefield,* Bobbs-Merrill, 1938; *Broken Glass,* 1940; *The White Lady,* 1941; *But We Are Exiles,* 1942; *The Pleasure Dome,* 1943; *The Skaters' Waltz,* 1944; *Carp Country,* 1946; *Mally Lee,* Doubleday, 1947; *A Man of Talent,* 1948.

A Little Fire, Appleton, 1950 (published in England as *Douce,* P. Davies, 1950); *The Tontine Bell,* 1951; *Conor Sands,* 1952; *The Regent's Candlesticks,* 1954; *Caroline House: A Mystery,* Thomas Nelson, 1955; *The Other Miss Evans,* 1959.

Return to the Alcazar, 1962; *Love Is for the Living,* Holt, 1967; *High Season,* 1968; *Duet: The Story of Clara and Robert Schumann,* Holt, 1968; *Great Ambitions: A Story of the Early Years of Charles Dickens,* Holt, 1968; *Queen's Evidence,* 1969.

Mirror Dance, 1970, Holt, 1971; *The Scent of Danger,* 1971, Holt, 1972; *The Silver Pineapple,* 1972.

Juveniles: *The Mirrors of Versailles,* Constable, 1939; *Visitors from England,* 1941; *Vanishing Island,* 1942, published as *Disappearing Island,* Houghton, 1944; *Behind the Waterfall,* 1943; *The Seven Sapphires,* 1944; *Lost Karin,* 1947, published as *Lost Karin: A Mystery,* 1948; *The Mirrors of Castle Doone,* 1947, published as *The Mirrors of Castle Doone: A Mystery for Boys and Girls,* Houghton, 1950; *Holly Hotel: A Mystery,* Houghton 1947; *West Wind,* 1948, Houghton, 1950; *The House on the Hill,* 1949.

The Provost's Jewel, 1950, Houghton, 1951; (under pseudonym Jan Ralston) *Mystery of the Good Adventure,* Dodd, 1950; *The Lintowers,* 1951; *The Captain's House,* 1952; Houghton, 1953; *Forgotten as a Dream,* 1953; *Reiver's Road,* Thomas Nelson, 1953, published as *On Lenox Moor,* 1954; *The House of the Pelican,* Thomas Nelson, 1954; *A Stillness in the Air,* 1956; *Maid of Orleans: The Story of Joan of Arc,* Thomas Nelson, 1957; *Queen of Scots: The Story of Mary Stuart,* Thomas Nelson, 1957; *Run to the Earth,* Thomas Nelson, 1957; *The Money Cat,* Hamish Hamilton, 1958; *Oh Say, Can You See?,* 1959.

The Eagles' Nest, Thomas Nelson, 1961; *The Story of Grizel,* Thomas Nelson, 1961; *Girl with an Easel,* Evans Brothers, 1962; *Portrait of Lisette,* Thomas Nelson, 1963; *Girl with a Pen,* Evans Brothers, 1963, published as *Girl with a Pen: Charlotte Bronte,* Holt, 1964; *Victoria: The Story of a Great Queen,* Thomas Nelson, 1964; *Girl with a Song: The Story of Jenny Lind,* Evans Brothers, published as *The Swedish Nightingale: Jenny Lind,* Holt, 1965; *Girl with a Destiny: The Story of Mary of Orange,* Evans Brothers, 1965, published as *Princess of Orange,* Holt, 1966; *The Boy Who Asked for More: The Early Life of Charles Dickens,* Evans Brother, 1966.

Song of the Waterfall: The Story of Edvard and Nina Grieg, Holt, 1970; *The Stilt Walkers,* Heinemann, 1972; *The Key of the Castle,* Heinemann, 1976; *The Burning Hill,* 1977.

WORK IN PROGRESS: A novel.

AVOCATIONAL INTERESTS: European travel, history, music, collecting antiques, and art.

* * *

DURAND, John Dana 1913-1981

PERSONAL: Born July 24, 1913, in Washington, D.C.; died October 27, 1981; son of Walter Yale (a teacher and economist) and Sara (Watson) Durand; married Dorothy Martin, February 21, 1942; children: Mark. *Education:* Attended George Washington University, 1929-30, and University of North Carolina, 1930-31; Cornell University, A.B., 1933; Princeton University, Ph.D., 1939. *Office:* Population Studies Center, University of Pennsylvania, 3718 Locust Walk, Philadelphia, Pa. 19174.

CAREER: U.S. Bureau of the Census, Washington, D.C., demographer, 1933-36, 1939-47; United Nations, Population Division, New York, N.Y., demographer, 1948-65; University of Pennsylvania, Philadelphia, professor of economics and sociology, beginning 1965. *Member:* Population Association of America (former president), International Union for Scientific Study of Population, American Statistical Association (fellow; former member of board of directors).

WRITINGS: The Labor Force in the United States, 1890-1960, Social Science Research Council, 1948, reprinted, Gordon and Breach, 1972; (with Karen C. Holden) *Methods for Analyzing Components of Change in Size and Structure of the Labor Force with Application to Puerto Rico, 1950-60,* Population Studies Center, University of Pennsylvania, 1969; *Historical Estimates of World Population: An Evaluation,* Population Studies Center, University of Pennsylvania, 1974; *The Labor Force in Economic Development: A Comparison of International Census Data, 1946-66,* Princeton University Press, 1975. Contributor of articles to journals in his field, including *Population Studies, American Journal of Sociology, Proceedings of the American Philosophical Society,* and *Annals of the American Academy of Political and Social Science.*

WORK IN PROGRESS: Research in world demographic history.†

E

EAGLE, Dorothy 1912-

PERSONAL: Born March 10, 1912, in Newcastle upon Tyne, England; daughter of Edwin (keeper of National Gallery, London) and Eva (Postance) Glasgow; married Charles Henry Eagle, April 29, 1941; children: Roger Charles, Martin Swinburne, John Richard. *Education:* Bedford College, University of London, B.A., 1934. *Home:* 25 Linkside Ave., Oxford, England.

CAREER: London County Council, London, England, children's care (medical) organizer, 1936-38; city almoner (social worker), Oxford, England, 1938-42; Clarendon Press, Oxford, England, member of editorial staff, 1953-78. Director, Mary Glasgow Publications Ltd. (language magazines for schools). *Member:* National Council of Women (Oxford committee, 1966-69).

WRITINGS—All published by Oxford University Press: (Editor with J. Coulson, C. T. Carr, and L. M. Hutchinson) *The Oxford Illustrated Dictionary,* 1962, 2nd edition (sole editor), 1975; (editor) *The Oxford Companion to English Literature,* 4th edition (Eagle was not associated with earlier editions), 1967; (editor) *The Concise Dictionary of English Literature,* 2nd edition (Eagle was not associated with first edition), 1970; (assistant to editor) *The Oxford Companion to Art,* 1970; (assistant to editor) *The Oxford English-Arabic Dictionary,* 1972; (compiler and editor with Hilary Carnell) *The Oxford Literary Guide to the British Isles,* 1977, revised edition, 1978; (editor) *The Oxford Illustrated Literary Guide to Great Britain and Ireland,* 1981. Assistant to editor, *Review of English Studies,* 1963-78.

BIOGRAPHICAL/CRITICAL SOURCES: London Times, June 18, 1981; *Sunday Telegram* (Worcester, Mass.), December 6, 1981.

* * *

ECCLES, John Carew 1903-

PERSONAL: Born January 27, 1903, in Melbourne, Australia; son of William James (a teacher) and Mary (a teacher; maiden name, Carew) Eccles; married Irene Frances Miller, July 3, 1928 (divorced April 10, 1968); married Helena Taborikova (a medical scientist), April 27, 1968; children: (first marriage) Rosamund Margaret (Mrs. Richard Mason), Peter James, Alice Catherine, William, Mary Rose (Mrs. Brian Mennis), John Mark, Judith Clare, Frances Joan, Richard Aquinas. *Education:* University of Melbourne, M.B. (first class honors) and B.S., both 1925; Magdalen College, Oxford, graduate study, 1925-27; Exeter College, Oxford, M.A. and D.Phil., both 1929. *Religion:* Unaffiliated Christian. *Home:* Ca' a la Gra', CH 6611 Contra (Ticino), Switzerland.

CAREER: Oxford University, Magdalen College, Oxford, England, tutorial fellow and demonstrator in physiology, 1934-37; Sydney Hospital, Sydney, Australia, director of Kanematsu Memorial Institute of Pathology, 1937-43; University of Otago, Dunedin, New Zealand, professor of physiology, 1944-51; Australian National University, Canberra, professor of physiology, 1952-66; American Medical Association, Institute for Biomedical Research, Chicago, Ill., head of research laboratory group, 1966-68; State University of New York at Buffalo, distinguished professor of physiology and biophysics and Dr. Henry C. and Bertha H. Buswell Research Fellow, both 1968-75. Waynflete Lecturer at Magdalen College, Oxford, 1952; Herter Lecturer at Johns Hopkins University, 1955; Ferrier Lecturer at Royal Society of London, 1959; Sherrington Lecturer at University of Liverpool, 1966; Patten Lecturer at Indiana University, 1972; Gifford Lecturer, University of Edinburgh, 1977-79. Chairman of committees on vision, hearing, and airsickness for Australian Armed Forces Organization, 1941-43.

MEMBER: Muscular Dystrophy Association of America (member of advisory board, 1966-71), American Philosophical Society (honorary member), National Academy of Science (foreign associate), American Physiological Society (foreign honorary member), American Academy of Arts and Sciences (foreign honorary member), American College of Physicians (honorary member), American Neurological Association, Electroencephalographic Society (honorary member), Australian Academy of Sciences (fellow; president, 1957-61), Physiological Society of Great Britain (honorary member), Accademia Nazionale dei Lincei (foreign honorary member), Indian Academy of Sciences (foreign associate), Royal Belgian Academy, Deutsche Akademie der Naturforschung, Leopoldina, Royal Society of New Zealand (fellow), Pontifical Academy of Science, New York Academy of Science (honorary life member), Royal Society of London (fellow).

AWARDS, HONORS: Rhodes scholar, 1925; junior research fellow at Exeter College, Oxford, 1927-32, Staines medical fellowship, 1932-34; Rolleston Memorial Prize from Oxford University, 1932; named knight bachelor, 1958; honorary degrees include S.D. from Cambridge University, 1960, University of Tasmania, 1964, University of British Columbia, 1966, Gustavus Adolphus College, 1967, Marquette University, 1967, and Loyola University of Chicago, 1969; LL.D. from University of Melbourne, 1965; M.D. from Charles University, Prague, 1969, Yeshiva University, 1969, and Oxford University, 1974; Doctor Honoris Causa from Universite de Fribourg, 1980; Baly Medal from Royal College of Physicians, 1961; Royal Medal from Royal Society of London, 1962; joint winner of Nobel Prize for Medicine and Physiology, 1963; Cothenius Medal from Deutsche Akademie der Naturforschung Leopoldina, 1963; honorary fellow of Exeter College, Oxford, 1961, and Magdalen College, Oxford, 1964; special award from Parkinson's Disease Foundation, 1972.

WRITINGS: (With Richard Stephen Creed and others) *Reflex Activity of the Spinal Cord,* Clarendon Press, 1932; *The Neurophysiological Basis of Mind: The Principles of Neurophysiology,* Clarendon Press, 1953; *The Physiology of Nerve Cells,* Johns Hopkins Press, 1957.

The Physiology of Synapses, Academic Press, 1964; *The Brain and the Unity of Conscious Experience,* Cambridge University Press, 1965; *The Brain and the Person,* Australian Broadcasting Commission, 1965; (editor) *Brain and Conscious Experience,* Springer-Verlag, 1966; (with Masao Ito and Janos Szentagothai) *The Cerebellum as a Neuronal Machine,* Springer-Verlag, 1967; *The Inhibitory Pathways of the Central Nervous System,* C. C Thomas, 1969.

Facing Reality: Philosophical Adventures by a Brain Scientist, Springer-Verlag, 1970; (editor with A. G. Karczmar) *The Brain and Human Behavior,* Springer-Verlag, 1972; *The Understanding of the Brain,* McGraw, 1973, 2nd edition, 1976; (with K. R. Popper) *The Self and Its Brain,* Springer-Verlag, 1976; *The Human Mystery,* Springer-Verlag, 1979; *The Human Psyche,* Springer-Verlag, 1980; (with W. C. Gibson) *Sherrington: His Life and Thought,* Springer-Verlag, 1980.

Contributor of more than five hundred papers to scientific journals.

SIDELIGHTS: John Carew Eccles received the Nobel Prize in 1963 for establishing a relationship between inhibition of nerve cells and repolarization of a cell's membrane. *Avocational interests:* Walking, European travel, art, archaeology, classical music.

BIOGRAPHICAL/CRITICAL SOURCES: Sarah R. Riedman and Elton T. Gustafson, *Portraits of Nobel Laureates in Medicine and Physiology,* Abelard, 1963; Donald Robinson, *One Hundred Most Important People in the World Today,* Putnam, 1970; *Newsweek,* June 21, 1971.

* * *

ECKES, Alfred Edward, Jr. 1942-

PERSONAL: Born July 11, 1942, in North Conway, N.H.; son of Alfred Edward and Virginia (Marshall) Eckes. *Education:* Washington and Lee University, B.A., 1964; Christ's College, Cambridge, graduate study, 1964-65; Fletcher School of Law and Diplomacy, M.A., 1966; University of Texas at Austin, Ph.D., 1969. *Office:* U.S. International Trade Commission, 701 E St., N.W., Washington, D.C. 20436.

CAREER: Ohio State University, Columbus, assistant professor, 1969-75, associate professor of history, 1975-79; U.S. House of Representatives, Washington, D.C., executive director of House Republican Conference, 1979-81; U.S. International Trade Commission, Washington, D.C., commissioner, 1981—, chairman, 1982—. Research assistant to U.S. Representative Samuel L. Devine, 1974-77; editorial page editor, *Columbus Dispatch,* 1977-79. *Member:* Organization of American Historians, Society for Historians of American Foreign Relations, Phi Beta Kappa. *Awards, honors:* Fulbright fellowship, 1964-65; Woodrow Wilson fellowship, 1965-66.

WRITINGS: A Search for Solvency: Bretton Woods and the International Monetary System, 1941-1971, University of Texas Press, 1975; *The United States and the Global Struggle for Minerals,* University of Texas Press, 1979; (with Eugene H. Roseboom) *A History of Presidential Elections: From George Washington to Jimmy Carter,* Macmillan, 1979. Author of news analysis column in *Columbus Dispatch,* 1971-74.

WORK IN PROGRESS: Research on U.S. international trade and tariffs.

SIDELIGHTS: Alfred Eckes told *CA:* "Yes, I do look forward to resuming academic writing when my government tour concludes. In my view, all writers—especially, historians—might benefit from government service where theories mingle with practical realities. I would encourage other academics to leave the campus periodically to rejuvenate in the operational world. Such an exposure sharpens one's own teaching skills and professional knowledge."

* * *

EDDLEMAN, H(enry) Leo 1911-

PERSONAL: Born April 4, 1911, in Morgantown, Miss.; son of Richard Aaron (a minister), and Lucille (Power) Eddleman; married Sarah Fox, September 7, 1937; children: Sarah Enfield (Mrs. Donald Duvall), Evelyn Lucille (Mrs. John Gordinier). *Education:* Mississippi College, A.B., 1932; Southern Baptist Theological Seminary, Th.M., 1935, Ph.D., 1942. *Office:* Criswell Center for Biblical Studies, 525 North Ervay, Dallas, Tex. 75201.

CAREER: Southern Baptist Convention, ordained minister, 1931, missionary in Middle East, 1935-41; New Orleans Baptist Theological Seminary, New Orleans, La., teacher of Old Testament and Hebrew, 1941-42; Parkland Baptist Church, Louisville, Ky., pastor, 1942-52; Southern Baptist Theological Seminary, Louisville, teacher of Old Testament and Hebrew, 1950-54; Georgetown College, Georgetown, Ky., president, 1954-59; New Orleans Baptist Theological Seminary, president, 1959-70; Baptist Sunday School Board, Nashville, Tenn., doctrinal reader, 1970-72; Criswell Center for Biblical Studies, Dallas, Tex., president, 1972-75, professor of Hebrew, biblical history, and Semitic languages, 1975—. *Member:* National Association of Professors of Hebrew of America, International Platform Association, American Association of Independent Colleges and Universities, Rotary. *Awards, honors:* D.D., Georgetown College, 1949.

WRITINGS: To Make Men Free, Broadman, 1954; *The Teachings of Jesus* (Matthew 5-7), Convention Press, 1955; *Missionary Task of a Church,* Convention Press, 1961; *Mandelbaum Gate,* Convention Press, 1963; (compiler) *The Second Coming,* Broadman, 1963; *Trustees and Higher Education,* Christ for the World Publishers, 1967; (editor) *Last Things: A Symposium of Prophetic Messages,* Zondervan, 1969; *An Ex-*

egetical and Practical Commentary on Acts: A Verse-by-Verse Study of the Fifth Book of the New Testament, Books of Life, 1974; *By Life or by Death: A Practical Commentary on Paul's Letter to the Philippians,* Exposition Press, 1981.

AVOCATIONAL INTERESTS: Tennis, swimming, fishing.†

* * *

EDDY, John P(aul) 1932-

PERSONAL: Born January 18, 1932, in Glencoe, Minn.; son of Paul Lewis (a businessman) and Berneice (Greenslit) Eddy; married Elizabeth Ann Hobe, May 17, 1958; children: Mark, Mary, Matthew, Michael. *Education:* University of Minnesota, B.S., 1954; Garrett Theological Seminary, M.Div., 1959; Northwestern University, M.A., 1960; Southern Illinois University, Ph.D., 1968. *Home:* 1320 Heather Ln., Denton, Tex. 76201. *Agent:* Porter, Dierks & Porter-Lent, Authors' Agents, 215 West Ohio St., Chicago, Ill. 60610. *Office:* 163 Wooten Hall, North Texas State University, Denton, Tex. 76203.

CAREER: Central Mindanao Colleges (now University), Musuan, Budkidnon, Philippines, instructor, 1954; worked for United Methodist Church, 1954-68; ordained minister of United Methodist Church, 1960; Johnson State College, Johnson, Vt., assistant professor and dean of students, 1968-69; New Mexico Institute of Mining and Technology, Socorro, professor of psychology and education, 1969-70; Loyola University of Chicago, Chicago, Ill., professor of guidance and counseling, beginning 1970; member of faculty, North Texas State University, Denton. Instructor, Scarritt College for Christian Workers, and Mankato State College (now University), both 1961-65; visiting professor at Rust College, 1963—; adjunct professor of education, University of Albuquerque, 1970. Member of board of trustees of Wesley Foundation, Mankato State College (now University), 1960-65. *Military service:* National Guard, 1964-65.

MEMBER: International Association of Educators for World Peace (world president, 1972-73; North and South American president, 1974-78), World Peace Academy (vice-president, 1974-75), Society for World Service Federation (vice-president, 1975-76), American Personnel and Guidance Association (peace commission chairperson).

AWARDS, HONORS: Television citation, KEYC-TV, Mankato, Minn., 1965; distinguished service award, International Association of Educators for World Peace of Romania, 1974; World Citizen award and citation for humanitarian service, both Society for World Service Federation, both 1975; Peace Scholar award, World Peace Academy, 1975; Bicentennial Counselor award, Bicentennial Crusade for World Peace, 1975; World Peace Center award, Felician College, 1975; Asians for Unity award, Asians for Unity of Chicago, 1975.

WRITINGS: Education and Inquiry, Johnson State College, 1968; *Campus Religious Affairs,* Simon & Schuster, 1969; *Principles of Marketing,* Collier, 1972; *Action and Careers in a New Age,* American Personnel & Guidance Association, 1973; *The Teacher and the Drug Scene,* Phi Delta Kappa, 1973; *A Career Education Primer for Educators,* ERIC Press, 1975.

Peace Education and Human Relations Training, Stipes, 1976; *College Student Personnel Development, Administration and Counseling,* 2nd edition, University Press of America, 1980; *Counseling Theories,* University Press of America, 1981; *Counseling Methods,* University Press of America, 1981; *Crisis Intervention Counseling,* University Press of America, 1983. Contributor to twenty television scripts.

Member of editorial board, *Dialog on Campus,* 1968-70, *Science Activities,* 1969-76, *World Circulation Newsletter* (of International Association of Educators for World Peace), 1973-76, *International Educational Foundations Quarterly,* 1974-76, *Peace Progress,* 1975-78, *Peace Digest,* 1975-76, and *Journal of Peace Education.*

WORK IN PROGRESS: Research on career education in the schools and society, peace education in the schools and society, and drug education that saves people.

AVOCATIONAL INTERESTS: Travel, conservation.

* * *

EDELSTEIN, Arthur

PERSONAL: Born in Brooklyn, N.Y.; son of Harry (a trumpeter) and Miriam (Stewart) Edelstein; married Eleanor Frances Steiner, September 10, 1957 (divorced September 1, 1963); children: Michael Stewart. *Education:* Brooklyn College (now of the City University of New York), B.A., 1956; graduate study, Columbia University, 1956-57; Stanford University, M.A., 1962, Ph.D., 1976. *Home:* 2 Dale St., Wellesley, Mass. 02181. *Office:* Department of Humanities and Social Sciences, Wentworth Institute of Technology, Boston, Mass. 02115.

CAREER: Ford Instrument Co., New York City, machine operator, 1941-43, 1947-55; Fernandez Bilingual Institute, New York City, instructor in English, 1956-57; Stanford University, Stanford, Calif., instructor in creative writing, 1962-63; Hunter College of the City University of New York, New York City, lecturer in literature, 1963-66; Brandeis University, Waltham, Mass., visiting assistant professor, 1966-71, assistant professor of English, 1971-76, director of writing program, 1971-74; College of William and Mary, Williamsburg, Va., visiting associate professor of English, 1977-78; Wellesley College, Wellesley, Mass., visiting professor of English, 1981-82; Wentworth Institute of Technology, Boston, Mass., visiting professor of humanities, 1982-83. Lecturer at universities. Consultant to Massachusetts Foundation for the Humanities and Public Policy, 1979—. *Military service:* U.S. Army, 1942-46; served in Pacific theater; became sergeant.

MEMBER: Modern Language Association of America. *Awards, honors:* Wallace Stegner Creative Writing fellowship, 1961-62; National Endowment for the Humanities fellowship, 1972-73.

WRITINGS: (Editor) Theodore Dreiser, *Sister Carrie,* Harper, 1965; (editor with Jonathan Baumbach) *Moderns and Contemporaries* (anthology of short stories), Random House, 1968, revised edition, 1978; (editor) Stephen Crane, *Three Great Novels,* Fawcett, 1970; *Contemporary World Literature,* Brandeis National Women's Committee, 1975; (editor and contributor) *Images and Ideas in American Culture: The Functions of Criticism,* Brandeis University Press, 1979.

Contributor of articles and stories to professional and popular journals, including *Southern Review, Commentary, Modern Occasions, Saturday Review, New Leader,* and *National Observer,* and to newspapers. East Coast editor of *Per Se: An International Quarterly,* 1964-67.

WORK IN PROGRESS: A novel, *Going Down.*

SIDELIGHTS: Arthur Edelstein writes: "During my years as a factory worker, I came to literature through the works of American literary realists (Dreiser, Crane, Howells, et al). Since they wrote mainly of workers and the poor, I saw my childhood and youth in their writings.'' *Avocational interests:* American politics.

* * *

EDEN, Alvin N(oam) 1926-

PERSONAL: Surname originally Edelstein; legally changed, 1946; born March 21, 1926, in Brooklyn, N.Y.; son of Emmanuel M. (an educator) and Rae (Taran) Edelstein; married Elaine Jaffe (an interior designer), November 20, 1952; children: Robert, Elizabeth. *Education:* Columbia University, B.A., 1948; Boston University, M.D., 1952. *Agent:* Emilie Jackson, Curtis Brown Ltd., 575 Madison Ave., New York, N.Y. 10022. *Office:* 107-21 Queens Blvd., Forest Hills, N.Y. 11375.

CAREER: Bellevue Hospital, New York, N.Y., intern, 1952-53, resident in pediatrics in University Hospital-Bellevue Medical Center, 1953-55; private practice in pediatrics in Forest Hills, N.Y., 1955—. Diplomate of American Board of Pediatrics; director of department of pediatrics at Wyckoff Heights Hospital, 1958—; New York University Medical Center, instructor, 1955-60, assistant professor, 1960-68, associate professor, 1968—. *Military service:* U.S. Navy, Hospital Corps, 1944-46.

MEMBER: Pan-American Medical Association, American Medical Association, American Academy of Pediatrics (fellow), Leo Taran Foundation (vice-president), New York Pediatric Society (past president), Queens Pediatric Society (past president).

WRITINGS: (With Joan Rattner Heilman) *Growing Up Thin,* McKay, 1975; *Handbook for New Parents,* Berkley Publishing, 1979; *Positive Parenting,* Bobbs-Merrill, 1980; *Dr. Eden's Diet and Nutrition Program for Children,* Dutton, 1980. Author of ''Visit with a Pediatrician,'' a monthly column in *American Baby,* 1973—. Contributor to medical journals for professionals and laymen.

* * *

EDGY, Wardore
See GOREY, Edward (St. John)

* * *

EDLIN, Herbert Leeson 1913-1976

PERSONAL: Born January 29, 1913, in Manchester, England; died December 25, 1976; son of Herbert Ebenezer (a doctor) and Nellie (Leeson) Edlin; married Betty Margaret Pritchard, June 11, 1941; children: two sons. *Education:* University of Edinburgh, B.Sc., 1933; Oxford University, Dip.For., 1934. *Home:* 15 Howard Rd., Coulsdon, Surrey, England.

CAREER: Tropical agriculturist in Malaysia, 1935-40; Forestry Commission of Great Britain, London and Edinburgh, district officer at New Forest, Hampshire, England, 1940-45, publications officer, 1945-76. Extra-mural lecturer in conservation at University of London, 1950-76.

WRITINGS: British Woodland Trees, Batsford, 1944, 3rd edition, 1949; *Forestry and Woodland Life,* Batsford, 1947; *Woodland Crafts in Britain: An Account of the Traditional Uses of Trees and Timbers in the British Countryside,* Batsford, 1949, 2nd edition, David & Charles, 1973.

British Plants and Their Uses, Batsford, 1951; *The Changing Wild Life of Britain,* Batsford, 1952; *The Forester's Handbook,* Thames & Hudson, 1953; (with Maurice Nimmo) *Tree Injuries: Their Causes and Their Prevention,* Thames & Hudson, 1956; (with Nimmo) *Treasury of Trees,* Countrygoer Books, 1956; *Trees, Woods and Man,* Collins, 1956, 4th edition, 1974; *England's Forests: A Survey of the Woodlands Old and New in the English and Welsh Counties,* Faber, 1958; *The Living Forest: A History of Trees and Timbers,* Thames & Hudson, 1958.

Wild Life of Wood and Forest, Hutchinson, 1960; (reviser) Edward Step, *Wayside and Woodland Trees,* Warne, 1964, revised edition published as *Wayside and Woodland Trees: A Guide to the Trees of Britain and Ireland,* 1964; *Know Your Conifers,* H.M.S.O., 1965, 2nd edition, 1970; *Forestry,* R. Hale, 1966; *Man and Plants,* Aldus Books, 1967, published as *Plants and Man: The Story of Our Basic Food,* Natural History Press, 1969; *Know Your Broadleaves,* H.M.S.O., 1968; *Timber! Your Growing Investment,* H.M.S.O., 1969; *Forests of Central and Southern Scotland,* H.M.S.O., 1969; *What Wood Is That: A Manual of Wood Identification,* Viking, 1969; new edition, Stobart, 1977.

Collins Guide to Tree Planting and Cultivation, Collins, 1970, 3rd edition, 1975; *The Public Park,* Routledge & Kegan Paul, 1971; (with Anthony Huxley) *Atlas of Plant Life,* John Day, 1973; *Trees and Timbers,* Routledge & Kegan Paul, 1973; (with Nimmo) *The World of Trees,* Bounty Books, 1974; *The Observer's Book of Trees,* Warne, 1975, Scribner, 1979; *Forests of North-East Scotland,* H.M.S.O., 1976, 2nd edition, 1978; *Trees and Man,* Columbia University Press, 1976 (published in England as *The Natural History of Trees,* Weidenfield & Nicolson, 1976); (compiler and contributor) *The Tree Key: A Guide to Identification in Garden, Field, and Forest,* Scribner, 1978; (with Nimmo and others) *The Illustrated Encyclopedia of Trees, Timbers and Forests of the World,* Harmony Books, 1978.

Editor; all published by H.M.S.O. for Forestry Commission of Great Britain: *Guide to the Argyll National Forest Park,* 1938, 5th edition published as *Argyll Forest Park,* 1976; *Hardknott,* 1949; *The Queen Elizabeth Forest Park Guide,* 1954, 2nd edition published as *Queen Elizabeth Forest Park: Ben Lomond, Loch Ard and the Trossachs,* 1973; *Dean Forest and Wye Valley,* 2nd edition, 1956, 4th edition, 1974; *Cambrian Forests,* 1959, 2nd edition, 1975; *Glen Trool,* 1959, 3rd edition, 1965; *Glamorgan Forests,* 1961; *Snowdonia,* 3rd edition, 1963, 4th edition, 1969; *New Forest,* 2nd edition, 1961, 4th edition, 1969; *North Yorkshire Forests,* 1963, 3rd edition, 1972; *Forestry Practice: A Summary of Methods of Establishing Forest Nurseries and Plantations with Advice on Other Forestry Questions for Owners, Agents, and Foresters,* 8th edition, 1964; *East Anglian Forests,* 1972; *Galloway Forest Park,* 4th edition, 1974.

Also author of numerous pamphlets and park guides, including *Forestry,* Pilot Press, 1947, *Forest Parks,* H.M.S.O., 1961, 2nd edition, 1969, *Short Guide to Snowdonia National Forest Park,* H.M.S.O., 1962, *Short Guide to the Dean and Wye Valley Forest Park,* H.M.S.O., 1963, *Forestry in Great Britian: A Review of Progress to 1964,* H.M.S.O., 1964, *Checklist of Forestry Commission Publications, 1919-65,* H.M.S.O., 1966, and *Forestry in Great Britian: A Review of Progress to 1973,* Great Britian Forestry Commission, 1973. Contributor to *Encyclopaedia Britannica.* Also contributor to journals, including *Forestry, Quarterly Journal of Forestry, Scottish Forestry, Commonwealth Forestry Review,* and *The Young Farmer.*

SIDELIGHTS: *The Tree Key* is a transatlantic identification book, featuring American trees planted in Europe, and European trees naturalized in America. *Avocational interests:* Mountaineering, wandering in wild places, swimming in rough seas; photographing all these.†

* * *

EGAN, E(dward) W(elstead) 1922-
(Eamon MacAodhagain)

PERSONAL: Born March 26, 1922, in New York, N.Y.; son of Edward Bulger (a railroad executive) and Irene (Welstead) Egan. *Education:* Hamilton College, B.A., 1947; University of Paris, graduate study, 1948-49. *Politics:* "Enrolled Republican but vote as I please." *Religion:* "Catholic by background but non-religious." *Home:* 105 East 15th St., New York, N.Y. 10003.

CAREER: U.S. Department of State, Washington, D.C., technical assistance project analyst for Economic Cooperation Administration, Mutual Security Agency, and then Foreign Operations Administration in Paris, France, 1949-56; free-lance writer, 1956-67; Sterling Publishing Co., Inc., New York, N.Y., 1967-81, began as reference book editor, became senior editor; free-lance writer and editor, 1981—. Theatre in Education, Inc., consultant, 1956—, member of board, 1964—, vice-president, 1965—. *Military service:* U.S. Army Air Forces, 1942-46. *Member:* Editorial Freelancers Association.

WRITINGS—Published by Sterling, except as indicated: *France in Pictures,* 1965, 2nd revised edition, 1972; *Italy in Pictures,* 1966, revised edition, 1972; *Belgium and Luxembourg in Pictures,* 1966; *Ceylon in Pictures,* 1967; *Brazil in Pictures,* 1967; (editor with Leonard F. Wise) *Kings, Rulers, and Statesmen,* 1967; *Argentina in Pictures,* 1967; (adapter) Stenuit, *The Dolphin: Cousin to Man,* translation by Catherine Osborne, 1968.

(Adapter) J. M. Guilcher and R. H. Noailles, *A Fern Is Born,* translation by Rhea Rollin, 1971; (translator and adapter) J. P. Vanden Eeckhoudt, *The Secret Life of Small Animals,* 1972; (translator and adapter) E. Bosiger and P. Faucher, *Birds That Fly in the Night,* 1973; (contributing editor) Norris McWhirter and Ross McWhirter, *Dunlop Illustrated Encyclopedia of Facts,* Doubleday, 1973; (translator and adapter) Gerard Majax, *Secrets of the Card Sharks,* 1977; (coordinating editor) *The Middle East: The Arab States,* 1978; (contributing editor) Norris McWhirter, *Guinness Book of Essential Facts,* 1979. Also author, under pseudonym Eamon MacAodhagain, of "unpublished and/or rejected verse."

Translator: Robert Girard, *Learn Art in One Year,* 1968; J. M. Guilcher and R. H. Noailles, *The Hidden Life of Flowers,* 1971; (with Rhea Rollin) Guilcher and Noailles, *A Tree Grows Up,* 1972; Edouard Cauvin, *Tiny Living Things,* 1973; Marie-Claude Riviere, *Pin Pictures,* 1975; Francois Cherrier, *Fascinating Experiments in Chemistry,* 1978; Cherrier, *Fascinating Experiments in Physics,* 1978; George Fronval and Daniel Dubois, *Indian Signs and Signals,* 1978.

SIDELIGHTS: E. W. Egan says that he does not "disbelieve in saints, angels, and flying saucers, but suspends belief in them pending actual confrontation. However if such beliefs help others to refrain from killing one another (or me) I am all for them." He is competent in French, reads Latin, and knows a smattering of Italian, German, Bengali, Russian, and Greek.

AVOCATIONAL INTERESTS: Travel (has been to Europe, Australia, India, and the Middle East), language, literature, arts, history, natural sciences, reading, television, cycling, gardening, walking.

* * *

EISENBERG, Lee 1946-

PERSONAL: Born July 22, 1946, in Philadelphia, Pa.; son of George M. (a microbiologist) and Eve (Blonsky) Eisenberg. *Education:* University of Pennsylvania, A.B. (cum laude), 1968, M.A., 1970. *Residence:* New York, N.Y. *Office: Esquire,* 2 Park Ave., New York, N.Y. 10016.

CAREER: Esquire (magazine), New York, N.Y., 1970—, senior editor, 1974-76, editor-in-chief, 1976-77, vice-president for development, 1981—. Founding partner, Eisenberg, McCall & Okrent, Inc. (book producers), 1978—. Lecturer at New York University, 1974-75, and Rice University, 1979. Consultant to New York Times Co., 1977, and Warner Bros., 1978. *Member:* American Society of Magazine Editors, Authors Guild. *Awards, honors:* One-Man Show award, Art Directors Club, 1974.

WRITINGS: (With Tom Ferrell) *Sneaky Feats,* Sheed, 1975; *More Sneaky Feats,* Sheed, 1977; *Atlantic City,* Clarkson, 1980; (editor with DeCourcy Taylor) *The Ultimate Fishing Book,* 1981. Contributor to popular magazines, including *Rolling Stone, New York Times Book Review,* and *National Review.*

SIDELIGHTS: The Ultimate Fishing Book, edited by Lee Eisenberg and DeCourcy Taylor, "proves conclusively that not all anglers' tales are malarky," comments a *New York Times Book Review* critic. A collection of nine essays by well-known writers is combined with art portraying the sport of fishing as well as some famous fishermen. A *Washington Post Book World* reviewer noted *Esquire* founder Arnold Gingrich's wisdom that "fishing itself is often the least important thing about fishing." Adds the critic: "Gingrich also observed that some of the best fishing is done in print, and he has been proven right again."

BIOGRAPHICAL/CRITICAL SOURCES: Washington Post Book World, December 6, 1981; *MacLeans,* December 14, 1981; *New York Times Book Review,* February 7, 1982.

* * *

ELFORD, Homer J. R. 1912-

PERSONAL: Born June 15, 1912, in Rochester, Minn.; son of Jonathan Rodney (a mail carrier and farmer) and Mida E. (Dean) Elford; married Margaret Mann, June 15, 1937; children: Cary Mann, Mary Margaret Elford Price. *Education:* Attended Rochester State Junior College, 1930-32; Hamline University, A.B., 1934; Boston University, S.T.M., 1937. *Politics:* Republican. *Home:* 3453 Sandalwood Ct., Youngstown, Ohio 44511.

CAREER: United Methodist clergyman, serving churches in Stillwater, Minn., 1937-40, Grand Forks, N.D., 1940-45, Minneapolis, Minn., 1945-47, and St. Paul, Minn., 1947-51; Trinity United Methodist, Youngstown, Ohio, senior minister, 1952-77; interim pastor at various churches, 1977—. Member of board of trustees, Mahoning County-Youngstown Public Library; Penn-Ohio College, former chairman of board of trustees, currently member of board of trustees. Delivered sermons on patriotism for Freedom Foundation, 1964 and 1972. *Member:* American Association of Retired Persons, Masons. *Awards, honors:* D.D., Wesley College (Grand Forks, N.D.), 1942, and Hamline University, 1950; honorary doctor of laws degree, Mount Union College, 1960.

WRITINGS: I Will Uphold the Church, Tidings, 1949, 2nd edition, 1968; *A Guide to Church Ushering,* Abingdon, 1961, 2nd edition, 1982; *A Layman's Guide to Protestant Worship,* Abingdon, 1963; *A Manual on Church Finance,* Postal Church Service, 1978. Sermons anthologized in *Ministers' Manual,* edited by Charles Wallis, Harper, 1969-82. Contributor of sermons to *Pulpit Digest* and to booklets.

* * *

ELLER, Vernard (Marion) 1927-

PERSONAL: Born July 11, 1927, in Everett, Wash.; son of Jay Vernard (a professor) and Geraldine (Crill) Eller; married Phyllis Kulp, July 9, 1955; children: Sander Mack, Enten Vernard, Rosanna Kathryn. *Education:* La Verne College (now University of La Verne), B.A., 1949; Bethany Theological Seminary, Oak Brook, Ill., B.D., 1955; Northwestern University, M.A., 1958; Pacific School of Religion, Th.D., 1964. *Politics:* Democratic. *Home:* 2448 Third St., La Verne, Calif. 91750. *Office:* Department of Religion, University of La Verne, La Verne, Calif. 91750.

CAREER: Clergyman, Church of the Brethren. Church of the Brethren, Elgin, Ill., editor of youth publications, 1950-56; University of La Verne, La Verne, Calif., assistant professor, 1958-63, associate professor, 1963-68, professor of religion, 1968—. Adjunct professor, Fuller Theological Seminary; member of faculty, Pacific School of Religion, summer, 1971. *Member:* American Academy of Religion, American Society of Christian Ethics, American Society of Church History, Brethren Journal Association, Swenson-Kierkegaard Foundation (fellow). *Awards, honors:* Named Alumnus of the Year, La Verne College, 1970.

WRITINGS: Kierkegaard and Radical Discipleship: A New Perspective, Princeton University Press, 1968; *His End Up,* Abingdon, 1969; *The Promise: Ethics in the Kingdom of God,* Doubleday, 1970; *The MAD Morality or the Ten Commandments Revisited,* Abingdon, 1970; *The Sex Manual for Puritans,* Abingdon, 1971; *In Place of Sacraments: A Study of Baptism and the Lord's Supper,* Eerdmans, 1972; *King Jesus' Manual of Arms for the 'Armless: War and Peace from Genesis to Revelation,* Abingdon, 1973, enlarged edition, Herald Press, 1981; *The Simple Life: The Christian Stance toward Possessions,* Eerdmans, 1973; *The Most Revealing Book of the Bible: Making Sense out of Revelation,* Eerdmans, 1974.

Cleaning Up the Christian Vocabulary, Brethren Press, 1976; *A Study Guide to the Most Revealing Book of the Bible,* La Verne College Press, 1977; *The Outward Bound: Caravaning as the Style of the Church,* Eerdmans, 1980; *Thy Kingdom Come: A Blumhardt Reader,* Eerdmans, 1981; *The Language of Canaan and the Grammar of Feminism,* Eerdmans, 1982; *A Pearl of Christian Counsel for the Brokenhearted,* University Press of America, 1982; *Towering Babble: God's People without God's Word,* Brethren Press, 1983.

Contributor: Donald Durnbaugh, editor, *The Church of the Brethren Past and Present,* Brethren Press, 1971; Paul M. Robinson, editor, *Call the Witnesses,* Brethren Press, 1974; Christians and Van Hook, editors, *Jacques Ellul: Interpretive Essays,* University of Illinois Press, 1981. Regular contributor to *Christian Century* and periodicals of Church of the Brethren; occasional contributor to other religious journals.

SIDELIGHTS: Vernard Eller told *CA:* "Undoubtedly there will be more books (there always are), but at this point I am rejecting rather than accepting ideas. It is not that I mind writing books; but I would like to find some way of being successful without being so slam-bang controversial."

* * *

ELLIOTT, William Douglas 1938-

PERSONAL: Born January 13, 1938, in Bemidji, Minn.; son of Alfred M. (a zoologist) and Lulu (a school teacher; maiden name, Maynard) Elliott; married Gwendolyn Warren (a librarian), July 19, 1960; children: Sharon Elizabeth, Douglas Warren. *Education:* Miami University, Oxford, Ohio, B.A., 1960; University of Michigan, M.A., 1961, Ed.D., 1967; University of Iowa, M.F.A., 1962; postdoctoral study at Australian National University, 1974, Cambridge University, 1978, Simon Fraser University and University of Toronto, both 1981. *Home:* 3308 Cedar Lane, Bemidji, Minn. 56601. *Agent:* Ann Elmo Agency, Inc., 60 East 42nd St., New York, N.Y. 10017. *Office:* Department of English, Hagg-Sauer 393, Bemidji State University, Bemidji, Minn. 56601.

CAREER: Ohio University, Zanesville, instructor in English, 1964-65; Washtenaw Community College, Ann Arbor, Mich., instructor in English, 1966-67; Bemidji State University, Bemidji, Minn., assistant professor, 1967-68, associate professor, 1968-79, professor of English, 1980—, director of creative writing, 1969—, acting director, Canadian studies program, 1980—. Instructor at Muskingum College, 1964-65. Co-founding director of Upper Midwest Writers' Conference, 1969, 1970, 1980—; Poets Exchange of Minnesota, founder, director, 1973-81; Minnesota Arts Board, panel member, 1976-78, chairman, Region II arts and humanities, 1980-82. Has given readings from his poetry and fiction; has also presented scholarly papers to professional organizations.

MEMBER: Modern Language Association of America, Midwest Modern Language Association, Minnesota Council of Teachers of English, Phi Kappa Phi.

AWARDS, HONORS: Jule and Avery Hopwood Awards in Creative Writing from University of Michigan, 1959, 1961, and 1962; scholarship from Breadloaf Writers' Conference, 1961; humanities award in shorter fiction from McKnight Foundation, 1968, for novella "Stopping Off in Switzerland"; Martha Foley award of distinction, 1970, for short story "People Are Too Sentimental"; grants from Minnesota State University, 1972, 1976, 1977, 1978, American Philosophical Society, 1974, Minnesota State Arts Board, 1980, Bemidji State University, 1981, Canadian Embassy, 1981, and Bush Foundation, 1982-83; Pulitzer Prize nomination for poetry, 1974; fellowships from Minnesota State Arts Council, 1975, and from National Endowment for the Humanities, 1980-81.

WRITINGS: European Sketches and Other Poems (chapbook), New Concord Press, 1964; *Pine and Jack Pine* (poetry chapbook), Northwoods Press, 1973; *Winter in the Rex* (poetry chapbook), Kendall Press, 1973; *Flood* (broadsheet), Sceptre Press, 1973; *Minnesota* (broadsheet), Smith-Park Poets, 1975; *Henry Handel Richardson* (criticism), Twayne, 1975.

Published by Bemidji State University Press: *Eco-Catastrophe* (poetry chapbook), 1973; *Bird Sermon,* 1976; *Timber Drive: New and Selected Poems,* 1978; *Blue River,* 1978; *The Paul Bunyan Poems,* 1979; *Fishing the Offshore Island: New and Selected Poems,* 1980.

Contributor to anthologies: *New Generation: Poets,* edited by Frederick Wolven, Ann Arbor Review Press, 1971; *Minnesota Poetry Anthology,* edited by William Meissner, St. Cloud State University, 1972; *Mid-America,* Michigan State University Press, 1977; *Dacotah Territory Ten Year Anthology,* Moorhead State University Press, 1982.

Plays: "This Night in Sleep" (one-act), first produced in Bemidji, Minn. at Community Arts Council, May 31, 1968; "The Replacement" (one-act), first produced in Bemidji, Minn. at Community Arts Council, May 31, 1968.

Contributor of hundreds of articles, plays, poems, stories, and reviews to literary journals, including *Poetry Review, Partisan Review, New Orleans Review, Kansas Quarterly, Red Cedar Review,* and *Fiddlehead.* Co-founder and literary editor, *North Country Anvil,* 1970-71; founder and editor-advisor, *North Country,* 1972-82; co-founder and poetry editor, *Leatherleaf, A Northwoods Journal,* 1972-74; founder and editor, *Loonfeather: Minnesota North Country Art,* 1979—.

WORK IN PROGRESS: Novels include *Catastrophe* (science fiction), *Stopping Off in Switzerland, Community College, Moving Out, Charlene, Charlene, Blue River,* and *The Last Pines of Jacob Riley* (historical logging novel of northern Minnesota); books of poetry include *Crossing the Borders, Late March Blizzard, By the Mississippi, The Eastern Bird Wars,* and *Middle River;* nonfiction includes *Genre into Form* (a text), and *This Summer, the Frail Sea,* on the ecological crisis; research on Australian literature, especially poetry of contemporary living authors, and contemporary Canadian literature, especially the poetry and fiction of Robert Kroetsch.

SIDELIGHTS: William Douglas Elliott told *CA:* "I began as a fiction writer in Michigan, Ohio, and at the Iowa Writers' Workshop and returned to northern Minnesota after a twenty-year absence to write the 'definitive' journey-and-return novel (I was nine when I left!). Instead, influenced by Robert Bly and others, my published output has been the deep image poem of the woods and lakes north country, while novel writing continues energetically but unpublished. My advice to young writers would be: go home again, but take it as just another experience—ordering life for writing ultimately deflates itself. The novel I returned to write has undergone several transformations in form and content and point of view. Chapters have been published in *New Orleans Review, Kansas Quarterly, Red Cedar Review,* and *Great River Review.* While like a lifenovel, it metamorphosizes—now it is a mystery novel, where it may remain!

"Yet I have always been of the Midwestern consciousness and see my role still as a fiction writer of Mid-America. This role may evolve sideways into either a reluctant poet of the Minnesota north country or an energetic organizer of writers' conferences, creative writing programs, and scholarly undertakings in the new Canadian literary explosion to the north of us and the literature of the Australian outback—two academic specialties I pursue with more excitement than I should."

* * *

ELMSLIE, Kenward 1929-

PERSONAL: Born April 27, 1929, in New York, N.Y.; son of William Gray (a speculator) and Constance (Pulitzer) Elmslie. *Education:* Harvard University, B.A., 1950. *Home:* Poets Corner, Calais, Vt.

CAREER: Writer. Composer/librettist panel member, National Endowment for the Arts, 1973-76. Publisher of Z Press; editor of *Z Magazine. Member:* Dramatists Guild, American Society of Composers, Authors and Publishers (ASCAP), American Guild of Authors and Composers, Authors League of America. *Awards, honors:* National Endowment for the Arts award, 1967, for poem, "The Power Plant Sestina"; Frank O'Hara Award for poetry, 1971; librettist grant, National Endowment for the Arts, 1980.

WRITINGS—Poems: *Pavilions,* Tibor de Nagy Editions, 1961; *The Baby Book,* Boke Press, 1965; *Power Plant Poems,* C Press, 1967; *The 1967 Gamebook Calendar,* Boke Press, 1967; *The Champ,* Black Sparrow Press, 1968; *Album,* Kulchur Press, 1969.

Girl Machine, Angel Hair, 1971; *Circus Nerves,* Black Sparrow Press, 1971; *Motor Disturbance,* Columbia University Press, 1971; *Tropicalism,* Z Press, 1975; *Topiary Trek,* Topia Press, 1977; *The Alphabet Work,* Titanic Books, 1977; *Communications Equipment,* Burning Deck, 1979; *Moving Right Along,* Z Press, 1980.

Opera libretti: *Miss Julie* (music by Ned Rorem; produced by New York City Opera, 1965), Boosey & Hawkes, 1965; *Lizzie Borden* (music by Jack Beeson; produced by New York City Opera, 1965), Boosey & Hawkes, 1965; *The Sweet Bye and Bye* (music by Beeson; produced by Julliard Opera Co., 1956), Boosey & Hawkes, 1966; *The Seagull* (music by Thomas Pasatieri; produced by Houston Grand Opera, 1973), Belwin-Mills, 1973; *Washington Square* (music by Pasatieri; produced by Michigan Opera Theatre, 1976), Belwin-Mills, 1977; "Three Sisters," music by Pasatieri, commissioned by the National Endowment for the Arts librettist program, 1980.

Plays: *The Grass Harp* (musical; based on the novel by Truman Capote; produced on Broadway at the Martin Beck Theatre, 1971), Samuel French, 1972; "City Junket," produced off-Broadway by the Eye and Ear Theatre, April, 1980; "Lola" (musical), first produced off-Broadway by the York Theatre Company, April, 1982.

Anthologies: *An Anthology of New York Poets,* edited by Ron Padgett and David Shapiro, Random House, 1970; *Another World,* edited by Anne Waldman, Bobbs-Merrill, 1971; *The Ruins of Earth,* edited by Thomas M. Disch, Berkley Publishing, 1972; *Penguin Modern Poets 24: Kenward Elmslie, Kenneth Koch, James Schuyler,* edited by John Ashbery, Penguin, 1974; *Angels of the Lyre,* edited by Winston Leyland, Panjandrum, 1975; *Homage to Frank O'Hara,* edited by Bill Berkson and Joe Lesueur, Creative Arts, 1980; *Knock Knock,* edited by Vicki Hudspith and Medeleine Keller, Bench Press, 1981; *Poets' Theatre,* edited by Michael Slater and Cynthia Savage, Ailanthus Press, 1981.

Others: *The Orchid Stories* (novel), Doubleday, 1973; *Bimbo Dirt,* illustrations by Ken Tisa, Z Press, 1982; (with Tisa) *Palais Bimbo Snapshots* (postcard series), Alternative Press, 1982. Art critic, *Art News,* 1966-67.

AVOCATIONAL INTERESTS: Attending rehearsals of something he has written, cooking, weeding, walking, tennis, movies, reading newspapers, seeing friends.

BIOGRAPHICAL/CRITICAL SOURCES: New York Times, April 27, 1980.

* * *

ELSTAR, Dow
See GALLUN, Raymond Z(inke)

EMRICH, Duncan (Black Macdonald) 1908-197(?) (Blackie Macdonald)

PERSONAL: Born April 11, 1908, in Mardin, Turkey; son of Richard Stanley Merrill (a missionary) and Jeannette (a missionary; maiden name, Wallace) Emrich; married Sally Richardson Selden, November 20, 1955. *Education:* Brown University, A.B., 1932; Columbia University, M.A., 1933; University of Madrid, Doctor en Letras, 1934; Harvard University, Ph.D., 1937; postdoctoral study at Sorbonne, University of Paris, University of Aix-en-Provence, University of Nancy, University of Cologne, and Escuela de Estudios Arabes. *Home:* 2029 Connecticut Ave. N.W., Washington, D.C. 20008. *Agent:* John Cushman Associates, 25 West 43rd St., New York, N.Y. 10036. *Office:* Department of Literature, American University, Washington, D.C. 20016.

CAREER: Columbia University, New York, N.Y., instructor in English literature, 1937-40; University of Denver, Denver, Colo., assistant professor of English, 1940-42; Library of Congress, Washington, D.C., chief of archives of American folksong, 1945-46, chief of folklore section, 1946-55; U.S. Department of State, cultural attache at American embassy in Athens, Greece, 1955-58, cultural affairs officer and consul at American Consulate General in Calcutta, India, 1959-62, public affairs officer at American embassy in Lome, Togo, West Africa, 1963-66; U.S. Information Agency, Washington, D.C., desk officer for former French West African countries, 1966-69; American University, Washington, D.C., professor of folklore, beginning 1969.

Fulbright lecturer on American civilization at universities of Rome, Naples, Messina, and Palermo, 1948-49. U.S. representative, International Folk Music Council, London, and International Folklore Conference, Paris, both 1948. Weekly radio broadcaster on folklore, on National Broadcasting Co. program "Weekend," 1953-55. *Military service:* U.S. Army, 1942-45; served with Military Intelligence in Washington, D.C., also served in England, France, and Germany; named American historian to General Eisenhower; became major; received Croix de guerre. *Member:* Helenic-American Union (founder), Indo-American Society (founder), Parnassos Society (Athens; honorary member), National Council on Religion in Higher Education, American Folklore Society, Zeta Psi.

AWARDS, HONORS: Hicks Prize in English and Preston Gurney Literary Prize, both from Brown University, 1932; Shattuck Scholar, 1935-36, and Edward Austin fellow, 1936-37, both at Harvard University; Guggenheim fellow, 1949; *The Nonsense Book* was named Children's Book of Library of Congress, 1970, Best Book of the Year by *School Library Journal,* 1970, American Library Association Notable Book, 1970, Top Honor Book of Chicago Book Clinic, 1971, Children's Book of the Year by Child Study Association of America, and received the Lewis Carroll Shelf Award, 1971; *The Hodgepodge Book* was named Outstanding Children's Book by the *New York Times Book Review,* 1972.

WRITINGS—Juveniles: *The Cowboy's Own Brand Book,* Crowell, 1954; (compiler) *The Nonsense Book of Riddles, Rhymes, Tongue Twisters, Puzzles and Jokes from American Folklore,* Four Winds Press, 1970; (compiler) *The Book of Wishes and Wishmaking,* American Heritage Press, 1971; (compiler) *The Hodgepodge Book: An Almanac of American Folklore, Containing All Manner of Curious, Interesting, and Out-of-the-Way Information Drawn from American Folklore, and Not to Be Found Anywhere Else in the World; As Well as Jokes, Conundrums, Riddles, Puzzles, and Other Matter Designed to Amuse and Entertain—All of It Most Instructive and Delightful,* Four Winds Press, 1972; *The Whim-Wham Book,* Four Winds Press, 1975; *Riddles & Jokes & Foolish Facts,* Scholastic Paperbacks, 1976.

Adult books; compiler, except as noted: *Who Shot Maggie in the Freckle and Other Ballads of Virginia City,* privately printed, 1940; *Casey Jones, and Other Ballads of the Mining West,* W. H. Kistler Stationery Co. (Denver), 1942; *It's an Old Wild West Custom,* Vanguard, 1949; *Comstock Bonanza: Western Americana of J. Ross Browne, Mark Twain, Sam Davis, Bret Harte, James W. Gally, Dan de Quille, Joseph T. Goodman [and] Fred Hart,* Vanguard, 1950; (editor with Charles Clegg) *The Lucius Beebe Reader,* Doubleday, 1967; *The Folklore of Love and Courtship: The Charms and Divinations, Superstitions and Beliefs, Signs and Prospects of Love, Sweet Love,* American Heritage Press, 1970; *The Folklore of Weddings and Marriage: The Traditional Beliefs, Customs, Superstitions, Charms, and Omens of Marriage and Marriage Ceremonies,* American Heritage Press, 1970; (author) *Folklore on the American Land,* Little, Brown, 1972; *American Folk Poetry: An Anthology,* Little, Brown, 1974.

Contributor to folklore journals, and to *Saturday Review, Reader's Digest, Library of Congress Quarterly, Holiday, Moslem World, American Heritage,* and other periodicals; contributor of articles, under pseudonym Blackie Macdonald, to *Police Gazette.*

SIDELIGHTS: Duncan Emrich once wrote *CA:* "I like people, I like folklore, I like to collect, I like to write. The English language is a wonderful thing—from the polished purity of the 18th century to the superb mangling of the present day Bronx. A phrase can make a day: from Montana: 'Well, there goes a ten-dollar Stetson on a five-cent head.' Worth living to read or hear that."

A *Choice* reviewer called *American Folk Poetry: An Anthology* as close to "pure folk" as one can come to in a printed source and representative of "American poetry at its best, this volume well demonstrates the special aesthetics, as well as the wondrous language those anonymous creators knew so well. . . ." Of Emrich's *Folklore on the American Land,* a *Christian Science Monitor* reviewer said, "[It is] a glad and moving book, one which will deeply touch any man or woman who cherishes the wit, the gladness, the imagination, the bravado, the vision, the earthiness, the insight, and the power, which have grown up around and characterize the American land."

BIOGRAPHICAL/CRITICAL SOURCES: Horn Book, October, 1970, August, 1971, February, 1972, April, 1973; *Christian Science Monitor,* April 27, 1972; *New York Times Book Review,* December 19, 1972; *Choice,* December, 1974.†

* * *

ENDLER, Norman S(olomon) 1931-

PERSONAL: Born May 2, 1931, in Montreal, Quebec, Canada; son of Elie (a cutter of men's clothing) and Pearl (Segal) Endler; married Beatrice Kerdman, June 26, 1955; children: Mark, Marla. *Education:* Attended Bet Berl College, Kfar Saba, Israel, 1950-51; McGill University, B.Sc., 1953, M.Sc., 1954; University of Illinois, Ph.D., 1958. *Religion:* Jewish. *Home:* 52 Sawley Dr., Willowdale, Ontario, Canada. *Office:* York University, Toronto, Ontario, Canada M3J 1P3.

CAREER: University of Illinois at Urbana-Champaign, clinical intern in Student Counseling Service and Psychological Clinic, 1957-58; Pennsylvania State University, Division of Counseling, University Park, psychologist, 1958-60; York University, Toronto, Ontario, research associate and lecturer, 1960-62, assistant professor, 1962-65, associate professor, 1965-68, professor of psychology, 1968—, director of graduate program, 1968-71, chairman of department, 1974-79. University of Illinois, clinical counselor, summer, 1958, research assistant professor, summer, 1964, research associate professor of psychology, summers, 1965-67. Visiting professor, University of Stockholm, 1974; distinguished university scholar at various British universities, including Oxford, Sheffield, and London School of Economics, May-June, 1978; visiting scholar, Stanford University, 1979-80.

Research fellowships from York University, National Research Council of Canada, National Institutes of Mental Health, Joseph E. Atkinson Foundation, Laidlaw Foundation, Canada Council, and from various other organizations. Leave fellowships from Canada Council, 1973-74, British Council, Oxford University, 1977-80, Social Sciences and Humanities Research Council, 1979-80. Member of advisory board of Integra Foundation, 1971-74, Addiction Research Foundation, 1977—, and board of Jewish education task force on teacher recruitment, training, and welfare, 1971-73. Also member of various committees and councils on addiction research, suicide prevention, and other aspects of social and clinical psychology. Has served in various capacities on committees for selection of fellowships. Consulting psychologist, Clarke Institute of Psychiatry, 1972—.

MEMBER: American Psychological Association (fellow), Society for the Psychological Study of Social Issues (fellow), Society of Experimental Social Psychology, Society for Research in Child Development, Canadian Association of University Teachers, Canadian Psychological Association (fellow), Eastern Psychological Association, Midwestern Psychological Association, Ontario Psychological Association (member of board of directors, 1968-70, education and training board, 1970-73, 1979-82, chairman, 1972-73), New York Academy of Sciences, Sigma Xi. *Awards, honors:* Canada Council senior fellowship, 1967-68; Canadian Silver Jubilee Medal from Governor General, 1978.

WRITINGS: (Editor with L. R. Boulter and H. Osser) *Contemporary Issues in Developmental Psychology,* Holt, 1968, 2nd edition, 1976; (with E. J. Shipton and F. D. Kemper) *Maturing in a Changing World,* Prentice-Hall, 1971; (editor with David Magnusson) *Interactional Psychology and Personality,* Hemisphere, 1976; (editor with Magnusson) *Interactional Psychology: Current Issues in Theory and Research,* Halsted, 1976; (editor with Magnusson) *Personality at the Crossroads: Current Issues in Interactional Psychology,* Lawrence Erlbaum Associates, 1977; *Holiday of Darkness,* Wiley, 1982; (editor with J. Hunt) *Personality and the Behavioral Disorders,* 2nd edition (Endler was not associated with 1st edition), Wiley, in press.

Contributor: J. A. Dyal, editor, *Readings in Psychology: Understanding Human Behavior,* 2nd edition, McGraw, 1967; J. G. Snider and C. E. Osgood, editors, *Semantic Differential Technique: A Sourcebook,* Aldine, 1969; H. C. Lindgren, editor, *Contemporary Research in Social Psychology,* Wiley, 1969; E. McGinnes and C. B. Forster, editors, *The Reinforcement of Social Behavior: Selected Readings,* Houghton, 1971; R. A. Baron and R. M. Liebert, editors, *Human Social Behavior,* Dorsey, 1971; H. Mischel and W. Mischel, editors, *Readings in Personality,* Holt, 1973; J. W. Gaebelein and P. A. Santoro, editors, *Readings in Introductory Psychology,* M.S.S. Information Corp., 1975; C. D. Spielberger and R. Diaz-Guerrero, editors, *Cross-cultural Anxiety,* Hemisphere Publishing, 1976; I. C. Uzgiris and F. Weizmann, editors, *The Structuring of Experience,* Plenum, 1977; D. M. Landers and R. W. Christina, editors, *Psychology of Motor Behavior and Sport-1977,* Human Kinetics, 1978; L. A. Pervin and M. Lewis, editors, *Perspectives in Interactional Psychology,* Plenum, 1978; O. Buros, editor, *The Eighth Mental Measurements Yearbook,* Gryphon, 1978.

I. L. Kutash and L. B. Schlesinger, editors, *Handbook on Stress and Anxiety: Contemporary Knowledge, Theory, and Treatment,* Jossey-Bass, 1980; A. I. Rabin, J. Aronoff, R. M. Barclay, and R. A. Zucker, editors, *Further Explorations in Personality,* Wiley, 1981; Magnusson, editor, *Toward a Psychology of Situations: An Interactional Perspective,* Lawrence Erlbaum Associates, 1981; M. P. Zanna, E. T. Higgins, and C. P. Herman, editors, *Consistency in Social Behavior: The Ontario Symposium,* Volume II, Lawrence Erlbaum Associates, 1982; A. Furnham and M. Argyle, editors, *Social Behavior in Context,* Allyn & Bacon, 1982; L. Goldberger and S. Breznitz, editors, *Handbook of Stress,* Free Press, 1982; M. M. Page and R. Dienstbier, editors, *Nebraska Symposium on Motivation 1982: Personality—Current Theory and Research,* University of Nebraska Press, in press.

Contributor of numerous articles on anxiety, social conformity, and hostility to professional journals, including *Journal of Personality, Journal of Social Psychology,* and *Canadian Journal of Behavioural Science.* Advisory editor, *Journal of Consulting and Clinical Psychology,* 1969-79; editorial consultant, *Journal of Personality,* 1975—, and *Journal of Research in Personality,* 1977—; member of editorial board, *Canadian Journal of Behavioural Science,* 1978-79.

WORK IN PROGRESS: Research in anxiety and the interaction model of personality.

* * *

ENGGASS, Robert 1921-

PERSONAL: Surname sounds like *En*-gis; born December 20, 1921, in Detroit, Mich.; son of Clarence and Helen (Strasburger) Enggass; married Catherine Cavanaugh (a translator), June 27, 1949. *Education:* Harvard University, A.B., 1946; University of Michigan, M.A., 1950, Ph.D., 1955. *Politics:* Democrat. *Home:* 340 West Lake Dr., Athens, Ga. 30606. *Office:* Department of Art, University of Georgia, Athens, Ga. 30606.

CAREER: Bryn Mawr College, Bryn Mawr, Pa., instructor in art history, 1955-56; Williams College, Williamstown, Mass.. assistant professor of art history, 1956-57; University of Buffalo (now State University of New York at Buffalo), Buffalo, N.Y., associate professor of art history, 1957-58; Pennsylvania State University, University Park, professor of art history, 1958-71; University of Kansas, Lawrence, professor of art history, 1971-78; University of Georgia, Athens, Callaway Professor of Art, 1979—.

MEMBER: College Art Association of America, American Association of University Professors, American Society for Eighteenth-Century Studies, Royal Society of Arts (London), Instituto di Studi Romani (Rome). *Awards, honors:* American Council of Learned Societies grants-in-aid, 1958, 1970, and

1976; Fulbright research scholar, Rome, 1963-64; Kress Foundation grants, 1966, 1967, 1969, and 1970; University of Kansas research grants, 1971-78; Borghese Prize for best book on a Roman topic, 1977, for *Early Eighteenth Century Sculpture in Rome: An Illustrated Catalogue Raisonne*.

WRITINGS: The Painting of Baciccio, Pennsylvania State University Press, 1964; (author of foreword) Filippo Baldinucci, *The Life of Bernini,* Pennsylvania State University Press, 1964; (contributor) Frederick Cummings, editor, *Art in Italy, 1600-1750,* Detroit Institute of Arts, 1965; (author of foreword) G. B. Bellori, *The Lives of Annibale and Agostino Carracci,* Pennsylvania State University Press, 1967; (with Jonathan Brown) *Sources and Documents in the History of Art: Italy and Spain, 1600-1750,* Prentice-Hall, 1970; (editor with Marilyn Stokstad) *Hortus Imaginum: Essays in Western Art,* University of Kansas, 1975; *Early Eighteenth Century Sculpture in Rome: An Illustrated Catalogue Raisonne,* two volumes, Pennsylvania State University Press, 1976; (translator and author of introduction with wife, Catherine Enggass) Nicola Pio, *Vite di Pittori,* Vatican Library, 1977; (translator and author of introduction with C. Enggass) *Malvasia's Life of Guido Reni,* Pennsylvania State University Press, 1980.

Contributor to *Dizionario biografia degli Italiana,* [Rome]. Contributor to *Burlington* (London), *Art Bulletin, Gazette des Beaux Arts* (Paris), *Paragone* (Florence), *Bollettino d'Arte* (Rome), *Apollo* (London), *Storia Dell'arte* (Rome), *Revue de l'art* (Paris), and other art journals.

WORK IN PROGRESS: Book length essay on stylistic concepts in eighteenth century Italian art; an annotated English language edition of Emile Male's *Religious Art after the Council of Trent,* with Giuseppe Scavizzi, for Princeton University Press.

SIDELIGHTS: Robert Enggass and his wife and collaborator Catherine Enggass spend part of every year in Rome where they keep a *pied-a-terre*. Engass told *CA:* "For me, Rome is where the stuff is."

* * *

ENGSTROM, Ted W.
See ENGSTROM, Theodore W(ilhelm)

* * *

ENGSTROM, Theodore W(ilhelm) 1916-
(Ted W. Engstrom)

PERSONAL: Born March 1, 1916, in Cleveland, Ohio; son of David W. (an engineer) and Ellen E. (Olson) Engstrom; married Dorothy E. Weaver, November 3, 1939; children: Gordon, Donald, Jo Ann (Mrs. Michael Bengel). *Education:* Taylor University, A.B., 1938. *Politics:* Republican. *Religion:* Congregationalist. *Home:* 3205 La Encina Way, Pasadena, Calif. 91107. *Office:* World Vision International, 919 West Huntington Dr., Monrovia, Calif. 91016.

CAREER: Taylor University, Upland, Ind., director of promotion, 1938-40; Zondervan Publishing House, Grand Rapids, Mich., editorial director, 1940-51; Youth for Christ International, Wheaton, Ill., president, 1951-63; World Vision International, Monrovia, Calif., executive vice-president and chairman of hunger task force, 1963-82, president; 1982—. Member of board of directors of World Vision International, Tom Skinner Associates, American Institute of Church Growth, African Enterprise, and George Fox College; former chairman of board of directors of Taylor University and honorary lifetime trustee; co-director of "Managing Your Time," a management seminar series. *Military service:* U.S. Army, 1943-45; became sergeant.

MEMBER: Arcadia Rotary Club. *Awards, honors:* D.H.L. from Taylor University, 1955; named evangelical layman of the year by National Association of Evangelicals, 1970; Order of Civil Merit (Korea), 1973.

WRITINGS—Under name Ted W. Engstrom; published by Zondervan, except as indicated: (Editor) *Victorious and Fruitful Living, and Other Sermons: A Compilation of Sermons Written by Leading Teachers, Preachers and Evangelists in the Holiness Movement,* 1942; (editor) *Sermon Outlines and Illustrations,* 1942; (editor) *Great Sermons by Great American Preachers,* 1943; (editor) *Golden Nuggets,* Volume IV: *The Gospels,* 1944; (editor) *Treasury of Gospel Gems,* five volumes (Volume IV originally published as *Golden Nuggets,* Volume IV), 1944; *Bible Stories for Boys and Girls,* 1948; (editor) *Two Hundred Twenty-Seven Heart-Reaching Illustrations,* 1949; (editor) Frederic William Farrar, *Life of Christ* (condensed edition), 1949.

Fifty-Two Workable Young People's Programs, 1950; *One Hundred Eighty-Eight Heart-Reaching Outlines* (sermons), 1950; (editor) *Bedtime Stories for Boys and Girls,* 1951; (editor) *Great Sermons from Master Preachers of All Ages,* First Series, 1951; (editor) *One Hundred Thirty-Two Heart-Reaching Poems,* 1952; *The Real McKoy,* 1953; *Workable Prayer Meeting Programs,* 1955; *Ten Talks to Teens,* 1958.

(With Warren M. Wiersbe) *Fifty-Two Workable Junior High Programs,* 1960; (with R. Alec Mackenzie) *Managing Your Time: Practical Guidelines on the Effective Use of Time,* 1967.

The Making of a Christian Leader, 1976; (with Ed Dayton) *Strategy for Living,* Regal Books, 1976; (with Dayton) *The Art of Management for Christian Leaders,* Word, 1976; *What in the World Is God Doing?,* Word, 1978; (with D. J. Juroe) *The Work Trap,* Revell, 1979.

The Most Important Thing a Man Needs to Know about the Rest of His Life, Revell, 1981; *The Pursuit of Excellence,* 1982. Contributor of several hundred articles to religious magazines. Publisher of *World Vision;* editor of *Christian Digest,* 1941-53.

SIDELIGHTS: Theodore W. Engstrom has made more than one hundred trips abroad, to one hundred different countries, in the interest of his mission work. World Vision International, with which he is presently associated, was founded mainly to work in Korea, but now is actively involved in ministries in more than forty countries. In addition to child care, emergency relief, and community development, the organization supports evangelistic activities of national churches and carries on a program of mission education in the United States.

AVOCATIONAL INTERESTS: Golf, music, reading.

* * *

EPAFRODITO
See WAGNER, C(harles) Peter

* * *

EPSTEIN, Perle S(herry) 1938-

PERSONAL: Born August 21, 1938, in New York; daughter of Jacob A. (a retired labor union organizer) and Lillian (a volunteer worker with children; maiden name, Tobachnick) Besserman; married Gerald Epstein (a psychiatrist), June 7, 1958. *Education:* Brooklyn College (now Brooklyn College of the City University of New York), B.A., 1959; Columbia University, M.A., 1961, Ph.D., 1967. *Agent:* Elizabeth Darhansoff, 1220 Park Ave., New York, N.Y. 10028.

CAREER: Assistant to ambassador of Korean mission to United Nations, summers, 1961-62; Kingsborough Community College, Brooklyn, N.Y., instructor in English, 1963-64; Jersey City State College, Jersey City, N.J., assistant professor of English, 1964-66; New York University, Washington Square College, New York, N.Y., lecturer in humanities and Eastern philosophy, 1966-79; writer. Assistant professor at Briarcliff College, 1970-72, 1976-77.

WRITINGS: The Private Labyrinth of Malcolm Lowry: Under the Volcano and the Cabbala, Holt, 1969; *Kabbalah: The Way of the Jewish Mystic,* Doubleday, 1978; *Pilgrimage: Adventures of a Wandering Jew,* Houghton, 1979.

For young adults: *Individuals All,* Macmillan, 1972; *The Way of Witches,* Doubleday, 1973; *Monsters: Their Histories, Homes, and Habits,* Doubleday, 1974; *Oriental Mystics and Magicians,* Doubleday, 1975.

Contributor to *Encyclopedia Americana* and to journals, including *Transatlantic Review, Present Tense, University of British Columbia Literary Review, Village Voice,* and *Jersey Journal.*

SIDELIGHTS: Perle S. Epstein writes: "My parents revered the written word—my brother and I started to read when we were two, were members of the local library at age four. It was always taken for granted that we'd go the academic route—but there is also a strong mystical and spiritual family tradition that kept life—which was frequently, materially speaking, hard—from becoming a grind. . . . We're all a bit eccentric—even other-worldly sometimes."

One form Epstein's other-worldliness has assumed is an obsession with the Cabbala (also spelled Cabala and Kabbalah), which figures in all her adult books. Defined by J.M. Edelstein in the *New Republic* as "anything of an occult, mystical, or theosophical nature," the term has come to encompass all mystery and magic. "There is," notes Edelstein "a 'Jewish Cabbala' and a 'Christian Cabbala'; both are esoteric systems based on the assumption that every word, letter and number of the Scriptures, to begin with, has an occult meaning."

In her first book, *The Private Labyrinth of Malcolm Lowry: Under the Volcano and the Cabala,* Epstein discusses the Cabala's influence on Lowry's fictive masterpiece *Under the Volcano;* in her second, *Kabbalah: The Way of the Jewish Mystic,* she explains the Kabbalah to lay readers; and in her third book, *Pilgrimage: Adventures of a Wandering Jew,* she describes her personal attempts to unravel this ancient mystical truth. In *Pilgrimage* her goal, according to *Publishers Weekly,* was to "attain the direct knowledge of God known to Jewish mystics, to make the Kabbalah [a] reality." *Library Journal* critic Marcia G. Fuchs describes *Pilgrimage* as "absolutely captivating," but Elinor Langer is less enthused. "As poignant as her religious passion might be, it is rarely adequately evoked in the book," she writes in the *New York Times Book Review.* "Anecdotal, descriptive, far better at capturing surfaces than depths, the book has the form of a pilgrim's progress without content," she concludes.

AVOCATIONAL INTERESTS: Travel, music.

BIOGRAPHICAL/CRITICAL SOURCES: Library Journal, July 1969, August, 1969; *New Republic,* August 2, 1969; *Publishers Weekly,* August 20, 1979; *New York Times Book Review,* October 14, 1979.

* * *

ESMOND, Harriet
See BURKE, John (Frederick)

* * *

ESTEP, W(illiam) R(oscoe), Jr. 1920-

PERSONAL: Surname is pronounced *Eas*-tep; born February 12, 1920, in Williamsburg, Ky.; son of William Roscoe and Rhoda Mae (Snyder) Estep; married Edna McDowell, December 23, 1942; children: William Merl, Rhoda Elaine, Mary Morgan, Lena Gipson, Martin Andrew (died, 1969). *Education:* Berea College, B.A., 1942; Southern Baptist Theological Seminary, Th.M., 1945; Southwestern Baptist Theological Seminary, Th.D., 1951; additional study at Union Theological Seminary, 1958, La Escuela de Idiomas, Costa Rica, 1959, University of Basel, 1967, University of Zurich, 1967-68, Concordia Seminary, 1970, and Oxford University, 1974. *Home:* 1 York Ave., Fort Worth, Tex. *Office address:* P.O. Box 22037, Fort Worth, Tex. 76122.

CAREER: Baptist minister; pastor of churches in Kentucky, Oklahoma, and Texas. Los Angeles Baptist Seminary, Los Angeles, Calif., professor of church history, 1946-47; Union Baptist Seminary, Houston, Tex., professor of church history, 1951-53; Southwestern Baptist Theological Seminary, Fort Worth, Tex., professor of church history, 1954—. Teacher, extension department, Baylor University, 1952-53; guest teacher, Seminario Bautista Internacional Teologico, Cali, Colombia, 1959-60, Southern Baptist Theological Seminary, Ruschlikon Baptist Seminary, 1967-68, and Spanish Baptist Seminary, Madrid, 1975; lecturer at numerous schools and professional conferences in the United States, Central America, and South America. *Member:* American Society of Church History, Southern Baptist Historical Society, Verein fuer Reformationgeschichte (Heidelberg, Germany), Delta Phi Alpha.

WRITINGS: La Fe de Los Apostoles, Editorial Verdad, 1962; *The Anabaptist Story,* Broadman, 1963, revised edition, Eerdmans, 1975; (contributor) *Baptist Advance,* Broadman, 1964; *Baptists and Christian Unity,* Broadman, 1966; *Colombia: Land of Conflict and Promise,* Convention Press, 1968.

And God Gave the Increase: A Centennial History of the First Baptist Church of Beaumont, 1872-1972, First Baptist Church of Beaumont, 1972; *Anabaptist Beginnings: 1523-1533,* de Graaf (Netherlands), 1976; (editor) *The Lord's Free People in a Free Land,* School of Theology, Southwestern Baptist Theological Seminary, 1976; (editor) *Balthasar Hubmaier, Anabaptist Theologian and Martyr,* Judson, 1978; (editor) *The Reformation: Luther and the Anabaptists,* Broadman, 1979; *The Reformation and Protestantism,* Caribe Press, 1981.

Contributor to *Encyclopedia of Southern Baptists,* 1956, 1970, 1971, and 1981, *The Concept of the Believer's Church,* 1969, *God and Caesar: Case Studies in the Relationship between Christianity and the State,* 1971, *Adult Life and Work Lesson Annual,* 1973, and *Baptist Relations with Other Christians,* 1974. Contributor of numerous articles to religious periodicals and professional journals. Editor, *Southwestern Journal of Theology,* 1963-67.

SIDELIGHTS: W. R. Estep told *CA:* "For me, writing is hard work. I never would have gone into it simply from the sheer joy of literary production. Recognizing, however, that the pen is not only 'mightier than the sword' but longer lasting than the spoken word and that books outlast classroom lectures, I began to write in order to convey a message which I felt my discipline had to offer to a twentieth-century audience.

"My serious attempt at writing history was motivated by a desire to let the message found particularly in sixteenth-century Anabaptism speak to my own generation. Subsequently, I became involved in all sorts of writing projects as editor, translator, and contributor to encyclopedias, as well as author. However, there has always been the desire that my writing would help the reader to achieve a greater degree of self-understanding in translating the proven values of the past into positive action in the present. As I reflect upon my writing career, perhaps the overall motivation has been to challenge the reader to live a more meaningful life. Perhaps my goals have been too ambitious and my purpose has not been fully attained. In short, I suppose I have attempted to extend my teaching career by writing."

Commenting on the state of contemporary literature, Estep writes: "I feel that the book shelves are cluttered with trash. I also feel that we are doing the students in high schools and universities a terrible disservice by neglecting the great masters of the past for contemporary fads which major on sexual fantasies. It is time that we were getting back to the classic examples of literary excellence for the sake of our students."

Estep speaks Spanish and German and has a reading knowledge of Greek, Hebrew, Latin, French, and Portuguese. Some of his books have been translated into Portuguese, Spanish, Italian, Serbo-Croate, and Korean.

MEDIA ADAPTATIONS: The Anabaptist Story is being produced as a motion picture in Switzerland.

AVOCATIONAL INTERESTS: Photography, electronics, music, golf, fishing, gardening.

* * *

ETTINGHAUSEN, Richard 1906-1979

PERSONAL: Born February 5, 1906, in Frankfurt-on-Main, Germany; came to the United States in 1934, naturalized in 1938; died of cancer, April 2, 1979, in Princeton, N.J.; son of Edmund S. and Selma (Stern) Ettinghausen; married Basia Gruliow, 1934 (died, 1935); married Elizabeth Sgalitzer, September 22, 1945; children: (second marriage) Stephen Edmund, Thomas Andrew David. *Education:* University of Frankfurt, Ph.D., 1931; postdoctoral study at University of Munich and Cambridge University. *Home:* 24 Armour Rd., Princeton, N.J. 08540. *Office:* 1 East 78th St., New York, N.Y. 10021.

CAREER: American Institute of Persian Art and Archaeology, New York City, research associate, 1934-37; Institute of Advanced Study, Princeton, N.J., member, 1937-38; University of Michigan, Ann Arbor, associate professor of Islamic art, 1938-44; Smithsonian Institution, Freer Gallery of Art, Washington, D.C., associate in Near Eastern art, 1944-58, curator, 1958-61, head curator, 1961-67; Los Angeles County Museum of Art, Los Angeles, Calif., adjunct curator, 1967-69; Metropolitan Museum of Art, New York City, consultive chairman of Islamic Department, 1969-79. Research professor, University of Michigan, 1949-79; New York University, Institute of Fine Arts, adjunct professor, 1961-67, professor, 1967-79. Trustee of Phillips Gallery, Washington, D.C.; trustee, member of the executive committee, and chairman of the accessions committee of the Textile Museum, Washington, D.C. Member of the Permanent Committee for the Preparation of a New History of Iran.

MEMBER: College Art Association of America, Iran-America Society (president of New York branch, 1975-79), American Oriental Society, Asia House, American Research Center in Egypt, International Society of Oriental Research, Archaeological Institute of America (president, 1960-61, 1963-64), Institut d'Egypte (associate), German Archeological Institute (honorary member), French Academie des Inscriptions et Belles Lettres, British Academy (honorary member). *Awards, honors:* Order of the Imperial Crown of Iran; Pour le Merite, German Federal Republic, 1976, for achievements as a scholar and teacher.

WRITINGS: The Unicorn, Smithsonian Institution Press, 1950; (editor) *A Selected and Annotated Bibliography of Books and Periodicals in Western Languages Dealing with the Near and Middle East, with Special Emphasis on Mediaeval and Modern Times,* Middle East Institute, 1952, supplement, 1954; *Early Realism in Islamic Art,* Instituto per l'oriente (Rome), 1956; *The "Wade Cup" in the Cleveland Museum of Art: Its Origins and Decorations,* [Washington], 1957; (editor) *Aus der Welt der Islamaischen Kunst: Festschrift fur Ernst Kuehuel zum 75 Geburtstag am 26. 10. 1957,* Gebr. Mann (Berlin), 1959.

Medieval Near Eastern Ceramics in the Freer Gallery of Art, Smithsonian Institution Press, 1960; *Persian Miniatures in the Bernard Berenson Collection,* Officine Grafiche Ricordi (Milan), 1961; (with Grace Dunham Guest) *The Iconography of a Kashan Luster Plate,* [Washington], 1961; *Paintings of the Sultans and Emperors of India in American Collections,* William Heinman, 1961; *Islamic Art,* World Publishing, 1962; *Arab Painting,* World Publishing, 1962; *Ancient Glass in the Freer Gallery of Art,* Smithsonian Institution Press, 1962; *Turkish Miniatures from the Thirteenth to the Eighteenth Century,* New American Library, 1965; *Masterpieces from Turkey,* Skira (Geneva), c. 1966; (with Ekrem Akurgal and Cyril Mango) *Treasures of Turkey,* Skira, 1966; *The Immanent Features of Persian Art,* Iran-America Society, 1966.

(Editor) Leo Ary Mayer, *Mamluk Playing Cards,* Brill, 1971; (editor) *Islamic Art in the Metropolitan Museum of Art,* [New York], 1972; *From Byzantium to Sasanian Iran and the Islamic World: Three Modes of Artistic Influence,* Brill, 1972; (with others) *Prayer Rugs,* Textile Museum, 1974; *Originality and Conformity in Islamic Art,* O. Harrassowitz, 1977.

Highlights of Persian Art, Allanheld & Schram, 1982. Also author of *The Splendor of Turkish Weaving,* 1973, and of proceedings of New York University Near East Round Table, 1973, and Dumbarton Oaks Colloquium, 1974. Editor, *Ars Islamica,* 1938-50; Near Eastern editor, *Ars Orientalis,* 1954-57, and member of editorial board, 1957-61; member of editorial board, *Artibus Asiae,* 1971-79, and *Art Bulletin;* coeditor, *Kunst des Orients,* 1968-79.

OBITUARIES: New York Times, April 3, 1979; *Washington Post,* April 4, 1979.†

* * *

EVANS, Alan

See STOKER, Alan

EVANS, Luther Harris 1902-1981

PERSONAL: Born October 13, 1902, in Sayers, Tex.; died December 23, 1981, in San Antonio, Tex.; son of George Washington (a railway section foreman) and Lillie (Johnson) Evans; married Helen Murphy, September 12, 1925; children: Gill Cofer. *Education:* University of Texas, A.B., 1923, A.M., 1924; Stanford University, Ph.D., 1927. *Politics:* Democrat. *Religion:* Methodist. *Office:* World Federalists, U.S.A., 777 United Nations Plaza, New York, N.Y. 10017.

CAREER: Instructor at Stanford University, Stanford, Calif., 1924-27, New York University, New York City, 1927-28, Dartmouth College, Hanover, N.H., 1928-30; Princeton University, Princeton, N.J.; assistant professor of politics, 1930-35; U.S. Works Progress Administration, Washington, D.C., national director of Historical Records Survey, 1935-39; Library of Congress, Washington, D.C., director of Legislative Reference Service, 1939-40, chief assistant librarian, 1940-45, Librarian of Congress, 1945-53; UNESCO, member of U.S. National Commission, 1946-52, 1959-63, director-general, Paris, France, 1953-58; Brookings Institution, Washington, D.C., director of survey of federal departmental libraries, 1959-61; National Education Association, Washington, D.C., director of project on the educational implications of automation, 1961-62; Columbia University, New York City, director of international and legal collections, 1962-71. Director, Popular Printing, Inc., 1963-81. Visiting professor, University of Puerto Rico, 1972. Chairman of United States delegation, Washington Conference on Copyrights, 1946, and UNESCO Copyright Conference, 1952. Member of board of trustees, Fisk University, 1950-53; chairman of board of directors, United States Committee on refugees, 1963-67; member of national board, American Civil Liberties Union, 1963-69, and American Association for the United Nations. Consultant to president of University of Texas, 1956, to United States Department of State, 1961, and to University Microfilms, 1963-71.

MEMBER: American Library Association, American Documentation Institute (president, 1951-52), American Political Science Association, American Society of Information Science, World Federalists, U.S.A. (president, 1971-81), Society for International Development, American Society of the French Legion of Honor, Archons of Colophon. *Awards, honors:* Honorary degrees from twelve universities, including Columbia University, Yale University, Brown University, Dartmouth College, University of British Columbia, and National University of Nicaragua; decorated by governments of Brazil, France, Japan, Lebanon, and Peru.

WRITINGS: The Virgin Islands from Naval Base to New Deal, Edwards, 1945, reprinted, Greenwood, 1975; *Documentation for the Meeting of the Committee on Educational Interchange Policy,* New York Committee on Educational Interchange Policy, 1962; (joint editor) *Automation and the Challenge to Education,* National Education Association, 1962; (principal author) *Federal Departmental Libraries,* Brookings Institution, 1963; *Background Book, Tenth National Conference of U.S. National Commission for UNESCO,* and *Supplement,* U.S. National Commission for UNESCO, 1965, revised edition published as *The Decade of Development: Problems and Issues,* Oceana, 1966; *The United States and UNESCO,* Oceana, 1971. Chairman of report, *Working Group on Publishing and Printed Materials,* [Washington, D.C.], 1961. Contributor to *Saturday Review* and professional journals. Editor, *American Documentation* (quarterly), 1961.

WORK IN PROGRESS: An autobiography.

OBITUARIES: New York Times, December 24, 1981; *AB Bookman's Weekly,* February 22, 1982; *Library Journal,* May 15, 1982.†

* * *

EVANS, Morgan
See DAVIES, L(eslie) P(urnell)

* * *

EVSLIN, Bernard 1922-

PERSONAL: Born April 9, 1922, in Philadelphia, Pa.; son of Leo (an inventor) and Tillie (Stalberg) Evslin; married Dorothy Shapiro (a writer and teacher), April 18, 1942; children: Thomas, Lee, Pamela, Janet. *Education:* Attended Rutgers University. *Home:* 158 Sutton Manor, New Rochelle, N.Y. 10805.

CAREER: Full-time professional writer and producer of documentaries filmed in United States and various parts of Europe and Asia. *Military service:* U.S. Army, 1942-45. *Awards, honors:* "Face of the Land" was named best television film of 1959 in *Variety* poll; National Education Association Award, 1961, for best television documentary on an educational theme; *The Green Hero* was nominated for a National Book Award, 1975.

WRITINGS: Merchants of Venus, Fawcett, 1964; *The Greek Gods* (also see below), Scholastic Book Services, 1966; *Heroes and Monsters of Greek Myth* (also see below), Scholastic Book Services, 1967; *Heroes, Gods and Monsters of the Greek Myths* (includes *The Greek Gods* and *Heroes and Monsters of Greek Myth*), Four Winds, 1967; *Adventures of Ulysses* (also see below), Scholastic Book Services, 1969; *The Trojan War* (also see below), Scholastic Book Services, 1971; *Gods, Demigods and Heroes,* Scholastic Book Services, 1975; *The Green Hero,* Four Winds, 1975; *The Dolphin Rider,* Scholastic Book Services, 1976; *Greeks Bearing Gifts* (includes *Adventures of Ulysses* and *The Trojan War*), Four Winds, 1976; *Heraclea,* Four Winds, 1978; *Signs and Wonders: Tales from the Old Testament,* Bantam, 1979.

Also author of two plays, "Step on a Crack," first produced on Broadway at Ethel Barrymore Theatre, October, 1962, and "Geranium Hat," first produced off Broadway at Orpheum Theatre, March 17, 1969. Author of scripts for many documentaries and shorts.

WORK IN PROGRESS: Serving the Goddess, a novel.

SIDELIGHTS: Several of Bernard Evslin's books have been translated into Japanese.

* * *

EYRE, Annette
See WORBOYS, Anne(tte Isobel) Eyre

F

FADIMAN, Clifton (Paul) 1904-

PERSONAL: Born May 15, 1904, in Brooklyn, N.Y.; son of Isidore Michael (a pharmacist) and Grace Elizabeth (a nurse) Fadiman; married Pauline Elizabeth Rush (an editor), 1927 (divorced, 1949); married Annalee Whitmore Jacoby (a writer), 1950; children: Jonathan, Kim, Anne. *Education:* Columbia University, A.B., 1925. *Home:* 3222 Campanil Dr., Santa Barbara, Calif. 93109.

CAREER: Ethical Culture (now Fieldston) High School, New York City, teacher of English, 1925-27; People's Institute, New York City, lecturer, 1925-33; Simon & Schuster (publishers), New York City, assistant editor, 1927-29, general editor, 1929-35; *New Yorker* magazine, New York City, book editor, 1933-43; master of ceremonies or host of radio and television programs, including "Information, Please!," 1938-48, "Conversation," 1954-57, "Mathematics," "What's in a Word?," "This Is Show Business," "Quiz Kids," and "Alumni Fun"; free-lance writer and lecturer, 1957—; Encyclopaedia Britannica Educational Corp., consultant in humanities, writer and general editor, "Humanities Film Series," 1963-81.

Teacher of great books classes in New York, Chicago and San Francisco; Regents Lecturer, University of California, Los Angeles, 1967; instructor, Santa Barbara Writers Conference, 1973-81; Woodrow Wilson Foundation Lecturer, Pomona College, 1974. Member of editorial committee, Book-of-the-Month Club, 1944—, and National Book Award for Children's Books, 1974; member of board of directors, Council for Basic Education; former consultant to Fund for the Advancement of Education, Academy for Educational Development, National Advisory Council for the National Humanities Series, and Center for the Study of Democratic Institutions. *Awards, honors: Saturday Review of Literature* award for distinguished service to American Literature, 1940, for radio program "Information, Please!"; American Library Association Clarence Day Award, 1969.

WRITINGS: Party of One: The Selected Writings of Clifton Fadiman, World Publishing, 1955; *Any Number Can Play* (essays and criticism), World Publishing, 1957; *The Voyages of Ulysses* (juvenile), Random House, 1959.

The Adventures of Hercules (juvenile), Random House, 1960; *The Lifetime Reading Plan* (essays and criticism), World Publishing, 1960; *The Story of Young King Arthur* (juvenile), Random House, 1961; *Appreciations: Essays,* Hodder & Stoughton, 1962; *Enter, Conversing* (essays), World Publishing, 1962; *Wally the Word Worm* (juvenile), Macmillan, 1964, revised edition, 1982.

The Literature of Childhood (lecture), University of Denver Graduate School of Librarianship, 1971; (with Sam Aaron) *The Joys of Wine,* Abrams, 1975; (with Aaron) *The Wine Buyer's Guide,* Abrams, 1977; (with James Howard) *Empty Pages: A Search for Writing Competence in School and Society,* Pitman Learning, 1979.

Translator: Friedrich Nietzsche, *Ecce Homo* [and] *The Birth of Tragedy,* Modern Library, 1926; (with William A. Drake) Franz Werfel, *The Man Who Conquered Death,* Simon & Schuster, 1927; Desider Kostolanyi, *The Bloody Poet: A Novel about Nero,* Macy-Masius, 1927.

Editor: *Living Philosophies,* Simon & Schuster, 1931; *The Voice of the City and Other Stories by O. Henry,* Limited Editions Club, 1935; (and author of introduction and biographical notes) W. H. Auden and others, *I Believe: The Personal Philosophies of Certain Eminent Men and Women of Our Time,* Simon & Schuster, 1939 (published in England as *I Believe—The Personal Philosophies of 23 Eminent Men and Women of Our Time,* Allen & Unwin, 1940, revised edition, 1962).

(And author of prologue and commentary) *Reading I've Liked: A Personal Selection from Two Decades of Reading and Reviewing,* Simon & Schuster, 1941; *The Three Readers: An Omnibus of Novels, Stories, Essays and Poems,* Press of the Readers Club, 1943; (and author of introduction) Henry James, *The Short Stories of Henry James,* Random House, 1945; (and author of introduction) Charles Dickens, *The Posthumous Papers of the Pickwick Club,* Simon & Schuster, 1949.

(With Charles Van Doren) *The American Treasury, 1945-1955,* Harper, 1955; *Fantasia Mathematica; being a Set of Stories, Together with a Group of Oddments and Diversions, All Drawn from the Universe of Mathematics,* Simon & Schuster, 1958.

Clifton Fadiman's Fireside Reader, Simon & Schuster, 1961; (and author of introduction) *Dionysus: A Case of Vintage Tales about Wine,* McGraw, 1962; *The Mathematical Magpie; being More Stories, Mainly Transcendental, plus Subsets of Essays, Rhymes, Music, Anecdotes, Epigrams, and Other Prime Oddments and Diversions, Rational and Irrational, All Derived from the Infinite Domain of Mathematics,* Simon & Schuster, 1962; (and author of introduction) *Party of Twenty: Informal Essays from Holiday Magazine,* Simon & Schuster, 1963; (with Allan A. Glatthorn and Edmund Fuller) *Five American Adventures,* Harcourt, 1963; (and author of introduction) *Fifty Years; being a Retrospective Collection of Novels, Novellas, Tales, Drama, Poetry, and Reportage, and Essays,* Knopf, 1965.

(And compiler with Jean White) *Ecocide—and Thoughts toward Survival,* Center for the Study of Democratic Institutions, 1971; (with Marianne Carus) *Cricket's Choice,* Open Court, 1974.

Author of introductions to more than forty books, including works by Edith Wharton, Leo Tolstoy, Herman Melville, Sinclair Lewis, John P. Marquand, Stendhal, Joseph Conrad, and others, 1931—. Contributor of article on children's literature to *Encyclopaedia Britannica;* also contributor to *Signature* magazine. Member of board of editors, *Transatlantic,* 1943-45, *Encyclopaedia Britannica,* 1955—, and Open Court Publishing Co.; associate editor, *Gateway to the Great Books;* member of advisory board, *Cricket: The Magazine for Children,* 1972—.

WORK IN PROGRESS: A large-scale world anthology of children's literature.

AVOCATIONAL INTERESTS: Wine and "the avoidance of exercise."

* * *

FARMER, Penelope (Jane) 1939-

PERSONAL: Born June 14, 1939, in Westerham, Kent, England; daughter of Hugh Robert MacDonald and Penelope (Boothby) Farmer; married Michael John Mockridge (a lawyer), August 16, 1962 (divorced, 1977); children: Clare Penelope, Thomas. *Education:* St. Anne's College, Oxford, Degree in History (with second-class honors), 1960; Bedford College, London, Diploma in Social Studies, 1962. *Politics:* "Left-wing." *Home:* 39 Mount Ararat Rd., Richmond, Surrey, England. *Agent:* Deborah Owen, 78 Narrow St., London E14, England.

CAREER: Writer. Teacher for London County Council Education Department, London, England, 1961-63. *Member:* Society of Authors.

WRITINGS—Children's books, except as indicated: *The China People,* Hutchinson, 1960; *The Summer Birds,* Harcourt, 1962; *The Magic Stone,* Harcourt, 1964; *The Saturday Shillings,* Hamish Hamilton, 1965; *Emma in Winter,* Harcourt, 1966; *Seagull,* Harcourt, 1967; *Charlotte Sometimes,* Harcourt, 1969.

A Castle of Bone, Atheneum, 1972; *William and Mary,* Atheneum, 1974; *Year King* (young adult novel), Atheneum, 1976; *Beginnings* (collection of myths), Atheneum, 1977; (translator) Amos Oz, *Soumchi,* Harper, 1980. Also author of short stories and of television and radio scripts.

WORK IN PROGRESS: Two adult novels, one tentatively entitled *Mothers.*

AVOCATIONAL INTERESTS: Collecting early children's books; cinema, listening to music, playing the piano.

* * *

FARRELL, James T(homas) 1904-1979 (Jonathan Titulescu Fogarty, Esq.)

PERSONAL: Born February 27, 1904, in Chicago, Ill.; died August 22, 1979, of a heart attack in New York, N.Y.; son of James Francis and Mary (Daly) Farrell; married Dorothy Patricia Butler, 1931 (divorced); married Hortense Alden (divorced September, 1955); re-married Dorothy Butler Farrell, September, 1955 (separated, 1958); children: (with second wife) Kevin. *Education:* Attended night classes at De Paul University, one semester, 1924-25; attended University of Chicago, eight quarters, until 1929; attended New York University, one semester. *Home:* 310 East 44th St., New York, N.Y.

CAREER: Writer. Worked wrapping shoes in a chain store in Chicago, Ill., as a clerk for the American Railway Express Co. in Chicago, a filling-station attendant, a cigar store clerk in New York City, an advertising salesman for Donnelly's *Red Book* in Queens, New York, in an undertaking parlor in Chicago, was a campus reporter for the *Chicago Herald Examiner,* and, for two weeks, was a scenario writer in Hollywood, Calif. Served as chairman of the national board, Workers Defense League, New York City, and as a member of the Spanish Refugee Aid Committee. *Member:* National Institute of Arts and Letters, Authors League of America, American Civil Liberties Union, Overseas Press Club. *Awards, honors:* Guggenheim fellowship for creative writing, 1936; Book-of-the-Month Club prize, 1937, for *Studs Lonigan: A Trilogy;* Messing Award, St. Louis University Library Association; honorary degrees from Miami University, Oxford University, Ohio State University, Columbia University, University of Chicago, and Glassboro State College.

WRITINGS: Young Lonigan: A Boyhood in Chicago Streets (also see below), Vanguard, 1932, with new introduction, World Publishing, 1943, published as *Young Lonigan: The Studs Lonigan Story,* Avon, 1972; *Gas-House McGinty,* Vanguard, 1933; *Calico Shoes, and Other Stories* (also see below), Vanguard, 1934 (published in England as *Seventeen, and Other Stories,* Panther, 1959); *The Young Manhood of Studs Lonigan* (also see below), Vanguard, 1934, with new introduction, World Publishing, 1944, reprinted, Avon, 1973; *Judgment Day,* Vanguard, 1935, with new introduction, World Publishing, 1945, reprinted, Avon, 1973; *Studs Lonigan: A Trilogy* (contains *Young Lonigan, The Young Manhood of Studs Lonigan,* and *Judgment Day*), Vanguard, 1935, with new introduction, Modern Library, 1938, published with an introduction and a new epilogue by the author, Vanguard, 1978; *Guillotine Party, and Other Stories* (also see below), Vanguard, 1935.

A World I Never Made, Vanguard, 1936, with new introduction, World Publishing, 1947; *A Note on Literary Criticism,* Vanguard, 1937; *Fellow Countrymen: Collected Stories,* Vanguard, 1937; *Can All This Grandeur Perish?, and Other Stories* (also see below), Vanguard, 1937; *The Short Stories of James T. Farrell* (contains *Calico Shoes, and Other Stories, Guillotine Party, and Other Stories,* and *Can All This Grandeur Perish?, and Other Stories*), Vanguard, 1937; *No Star Is Lost,* Vanguard, 1938, with new introduction, World Publishing, 1947, reprinted, Popular Library, 1961.

Father and Son, Vanguard, 1940, with new introduction, World Publishing, 1947 (published in England as *Father and His Son,* Routledge & Kegan Paul, 1943), reprinted, Arno, 1976; *Ellen Rogers,* Vanguard, 1941; *Short Stories,* Blue Ribbon Books, 1941; *$1000 a Week, and Other Stories* (also see below), Vanguard, 1942; *My Days of Anger,* Vanguard, 1943, with new introduction, World Publishing, 1947; *Fifteen Selected Stories,* Avon, 1943; *To Whom It May Concern, and Other Stories,* Vanguard, 1944 (also see below), published as *More Stories,* Sun Dial Press, 1946; *Twelve Great Stories,* Avon, 1945; *The*

League of Frightened Philistines, and Other Papers, Vanguard, 1945; *When Boyhood Dreams Come True,* Vanguard, 1946, published as *Further Short Stories,* Sun Dial Press, 1948; *More Fellow Countrymen,* Routledge & Kegan Paul, 1946; *Bernard Clare,* Vanguard, 1946, published as *Bernard Carr,* New American Library, 1952; *The Fate of Writing in America,* New Directions, 1946; *The Life Adventurous, and Other Stories* (also see below), Vanguard, 1947; *Literature and Morality,* Vanguard, 1947; *A Hell of a Good Time, and Other Stories,* Avon, 1947; *Yesterday's Love, and Eleven Other Stories,* Avon, 1948; *The Road Between,* Vanguard, 1949; *A Misunderstanding,* House of Books, 1949.

An American Dream Girl, and Other Stories, Vanguard, 1950; (under pseudonym Jonathan Titulescu Fogarty, Esq.) *The Name Is Fogarty: Private Papers on Public Matters,* Vanguard, 1950; *This Man and This Woman,* Vanguard, 1951; (contributor of "The Frontier and James Whitcomb Riley") *Poet of the People,* Indiana University Press, 1951; *Yet Other Waters,* Vanguard, 1952; *The Face of Time,* Vanguard, 1953; *Reflections at Fifty, and Other Essays,* Vanguard, 1954; *French Girls Are Vicious, and Other Stories,* Vanguard, 1955; (author of introduction) Theodore Dreiser, *Best Short Stories,* World Publishing, 1956; *An Omnibus of Short Stories* (contains *$1000 a Week, and Other Stories, To Whom It May Concern, and Other Stories,* and *The Life Adventurous, and Other Stories*), Vanguard, 1956; *My Baseball Diary,* A. S. Barnes, 1957; *A Dangerous Woman, and Other Stories,* Vanguard, 1957; *Saturday Night, and Other Stories,* Hamish Hamilton, 1958; *It Has Come to Pass,* T. Herzl Press, 1958; (editor) H. L. Mencken, *Prejudices,* Vintage, 1958; *The Girl at the Sphinx* (collection of short stories previously published by Vanguard), Hamish Hamilton, 1959; (with others) *Dialogue on John Dewey,* edited by Corliss Lamont and Mary Redmer, Horizon, 1959.

Boarding House Blues, Paperback Library, 1961; *Side Street, and Other Stories,* Paperback Library, 1961; *Sound of a City* (short stories), Paperback Library, 1962; *The Silence of History* (first of a projected 29-volume series), Doubleday, 1963; *Selected Essays,* edited by Luna Wolf, McGraw, 1964; *What Time Collects,* Doubleday, 1964; *The Collected Poems of James T. Farrell,* Fleet, 1965; *Lonely for the Future,* Doubleday, 1966; *When Time Was Born* (prose poem), The Smith, 1966; *The Letters to Theodore Dreiser,* The Smith, 1966; *New Year's Eve, 1929,* The Smith, 1967; *A Brand New Life* (novel), Doubleday, 1968; *Childhood Is Not Forever,* Doubleday, 1969; *Judith* (also see below), Duane Schneider Press, 1969.

Invisible Swords, Doubleday, 1971; (contributor) Ray Boxer and Harry Smith, editors, *The Smith-Fourteen,* The Smith, 1972; *Judith, and Other Stories,* Doubleday, 1973; *The Dunne Family,* Doubleday, 1976; *Literary Essays, 1954-1974,* edited by Jack Alan Robbins, Kennikat Press, 1976; *Olive and Maryanne,* Stonehill Publishing, 1977; *The Death of Nora Ryan,* Doubleday, 1978; *Eight Short Stories and Sketches,* Arts End, 1981. Also author of *Tommy Gallagher's Crusade,* 1939, and editor of *A Dreiser Reader,* 1962. Contributor to magazines and to the Asian press.

WORK IN PROGRESS: A novel, *Native's Return;* further volumes in his "A Universe of Time" cycle.

SIDELIGHTS: In 1941, Joseph Warren Beach described James T. Farrell's writing as "perhaps the plainest, soberest, most straightforward of any living novelist," thus citing the basis of both the criticism and praise of Farrell's work. Farrell was most often recognized as a naturalistic writer, a school to which he adhered even during the thirties when symbolism was increasingly popular. In *Reflections at Fifty,* Farrell wrote: "I have been called a naturalist and I have never denied it. However, my own conception of naturalism is not that which is usually attributed to me. By naturalism I mean that whatever happens in this world must ultimately be explainable in terms of events in this world, . . . in terms of natural origins rather than of extranatural or supernatural origins." In *The Modern Novel in Britain and the United States,* Walter Allen wrote: "James T. Farrell, for all his indebtedness to Joyce, began as a naturalist and has remained one, unrepentant and defiant. He is the true heir of Dreiser. If he lacks Dreiser's tragic sense, he has an icily relentless passion that transforms his best work into a formidable indictment of society."

In *American Fiction, 1920-1940,* Beach wrote: "Farrell's type of naturalism is not a kind to appeal to the common run of readers. It has little to offer those who go to fiction for light entertainment, the glamour of the stage, or the gratification of their bent for wishful thinking. There is no reason why the squeamish or tender-minded should put themselves through the ordeal of trying to like his work. But there will always be a sufficient number of those whom life and thought have ripened and disciplined, who have a taste for truth, however unvarnished, provided it be honestly viewed, deeply pondered, and imaginatively rendered. For many such it may well turn out that James T. Farrell is the most significant of American novelists writing in 1940."

Farrell's ambition and direction as a writer, as well as his thematic material, sprang directly from his own youth in Chicago's South Side. Blanche Housman Gelfant noted in *The American City Novel* that, although the South Side was a slum, without variety, beauty, or surprise, "it provided Farrell with the substance of his art and his purpose as a city novelist. . . . Few city writers are as much the insider as he; and of the writers who have the same kind of inmost knowledge of manners, none has exploited his material to such powerful effect." Beach added: "His literary performance is determined by his pity and loathing for all that was mean, ugly, and spiritually poverty stricken in the *mores* and culture to which he was born. All his work is a representation, patient, sober, feeling, tireless, pitiless, of a way of living and a state of mind which he abhors, and from which he has taken flight as one flees from the City of Destruction."

Beach contended that "the main theme of all this writing is a state of mind widely diffused in the world [Farrell] knows best—a social state of mind highly unfavorable to the production of full and happy lives, to beauty of thought and sentiment, or any of those spiritual values that characterize human civilization at its best." The state of mind is the product of the environment; the environment, in turn, is "defined in its effect upon the inner man," wrote Gelfant. The development of the individual is thus shown as a cumulative process of assimilating these environmental influences. Gelfant noted that Farrell once said: "The conditions of American life create alienated and truncated personalities" because the individual is forced to rely on himself in the face of chaos and "his inner experience becomes one of loneliness, alienation, and unfulfillment." It was Farrell's purpose, according to Gelfant, to utilize the novel to "establish communication between people who in real life had become lost in their private inner worlds and were no longer able to reach out towards each other." And although "the emotional drive behind Farrell's art was anger," he proceeded by *objectively* considering those problems which are characteristically rooted in emotional involvement. His method was to develop a cinematic sequence of self-contained episodes (each "significant as a revelation of individual character, as well as of a total way of life," noted Gelfant) that would best portray the lack of orientation and the fragmented nature of life in the South Side.

Beach said of the novels: "These are linguistic documents, as they are social documents, of high seriousness and value, but not slavishly photographic. Farrell is obviously more concerned with the spirit than the letter of truth. . . . The documentation is really prodigious, but it did not require the author's going beyond the limits of experience and memory. . . . [Scenes] spring like geysers from the seething burdened depths of the author's being. . . . The appeal is first to the imagination, and only in retrospect to the mind and conscience. In so far as anything is lacking it is some principle of relief." Gelfant stated: "And in the vision of life projected in Farrell's novels this lack of relief is an essential and fundamental quality." Without this relief the world created by Farrell becomes a dynamic oppressive force with which the individual must unsuccessfully contend. Gelfant summarized: "Although Farrell's style has been severely criticized, it is an effective medium through which milieu and character come to life. As a city novelist, Farrell was keenly aware of the inappropriateness of a lyrical manner to the materials of everyday urban life. He adopted the language of his characters as his aesthetic medium, and his versatility as a stylist is revealed in the variety of distinctive speech patterns he recreated."

During the 1930's, Farrell decided that certain literary critics were "perpetrating error and should be exposed before they could do further damage," noted Walter B. Rideout in *The Radical Novel in the United States, 1900-1954*. In 1936 Farrell published *A Note on Literary Criticism,* which, according to Rideout, was the "only extended discussion of Marxist aesthetics written from a Marxist standpoint in the United States during the thirties." Rideout contended that "the book constitutes a simultaneous attack and defense. The attack is directed against both 'revolutionary sentimentalism,' as represented by [Michael] Gold, and 'mechanical Marxism,' as represented by [Granville] Hicks. Since each of these two 'Leftist' tendencies in literary criticism has, in its extreme emphasis on the functional ('use-value') aspect of literature, ignored the aesthetic aspect, they have together, Farrell argued, kept Marxist criticism weak, because they substitute measurement for judgement. Hence, the critic's task, which is ultimately one of judgement, of evaluation, has been avoided." Rideout added later: "If Farrell's own statement of the critic's function is not strikingly original, if his dissection of the deficiencies of proletarian literature and criticism is, stylistically speaking, performed as much with a meat ax as with a scalpel, still the dissection itself was a thorough one." Farrell, in fact, aroused so much critical feeling with this work that *The New Masses* summarized his comments, and those of his supporters, with the arguments of his opponents under the heading "The Farrell Controversy."

Rideout believed that Farrell was prompted, to some extent, to write the criticism by the demands of "several extremist reviewers [who] had called for the display of more 'class-consciousness' in the un-class-conscious characters of whom he wrote." But Farrell also believed that critics were essentially re-defining literature as a socially effective instrument. Gelfant wrote: "Farrell's definition of literature as an 'instrument of social control,' makes clear his belief that fiction could not be directly a 'means of solving problems' within society. Rather it was 'a means of helping people to discover more about themselves and about the condition of life about them.' As literature brought the reader to a sharper awareness, it was, however, instrumental in social reform, for it is awareness that produces the pressing sense of concern that moves man finally to act. In order to make the reader more sensitive to his world, literature must exploit fully its aesthetic potentialities." And in 1967 Farrell told the *New York Times:* "I don't think literature should include partisan thinking. . . . I don't believe in things like political commitment in novels." He admitted that he had been in "political campaigns of all kinds" though, and he once bought Trotsky a typewriter. "Why? Because he needed it."

Farrell's was not a simple separation of art from propaganda, however. Gelfant noted: "He distinguished between the two by defining literature as a form of revelation, and propaganda as a form of political action. . . . The implicit assumption underlying Farrell's theory is that knowledge will make us free. Whatever the artist has to add to our experience and understanding of the world about us, of any part of it, can be of social consequences."

Many critics believed that the Studs Lonigan trilogy was extremely successful as a work of "social consequence." Rideout contended that Farrell was the only writer who succeeded in chronicling "with great zest and passion the slow downward spiral of what [was then] considered both a dull and ideologically unimportant class. [Farrell succeeded] because setting down the minutely detailed degradation of Studs Lonigan represented for [Farrell] an angry act of catharsis." Rideout believed that the Studs Lonigan trilogy was one of the "most durable achievements of the radical novel of the thirties."

Farrell's later work, however, received less critical acclaim. James R. Frakes wrote of *Lonely for the Future:* "At this late date Farrell's style reads like vicious self-parody. . . . In this world of human wrecks and pointless waste, James T. Farrell continues to chronicle his bleak Chicago inferno like a bleeding Virgil." Although the *Time* reviewer called Farrell "the most heroic figure in modern American letters," he wrote in his review of *When Time Was Born:* "Farrell calls his latest literary enterprise a prose poem. It is neither prose nor poem, but it appears to be an attempt to rewrite the first chapters of the *Book of Genesis*. The first sentence blithers and blathers and blunders along for five pages and 1,390 words. Reading it can only be likened to the experience of a man who, having lost an election bet, has undertaken to eat a pad of Brillo and is wondering which is the more unpalatable—the steel-wool structure or the pink soapy filling." But Beach summarized: "The best single test for a writer of fiction is the creation of characters that live in the imagination. Farrell has brought to life an unusual number of such living characters. Studs Lonigan, Jim O'Neill, Al O'Flaherty, Aunt Margaret, and grandmother O'Flaherty are among the memorable people in English fiction."

To comment on his life's work, Farrell borrowed a line from Yeats: "I, too," said Farrell, "spit into the face of time, even though I am aware that this is merely a symbolic expression of a mood: Time slowly transfigures me. . . . Joy and sadness, growth and decay, life and death are all part of the transfiguration of time. To look into the Face of Time, and to master its threat to us—this is one of the basic themes and purposes of art and literature."

Farrell told *CA* that his works have been translated into about 25 languages. A Farrell archive is maintained at the University of Pennsylvania.

MEDIA ADAPTATIONS: "Studs Lonigan" was filmed by United Artists in 1960.

AVOCATIONAL INTERESTS: Baseball.

BIOGRAPHICAL/CRITICAL SOURCES—Books: Joseph Warren Beach, *American Fiction, 1920-1940,* Macmillan, 1941; Alfred Kazin, *On Native Grounds,* Harcourt, 1942; James T. Farrell, *Reflections at Fifty, and Other Essays,* Vanguard, 1954; Blanche Housman Gelfant, *The American City Novel,* University of Oklahoma Press, 1954; Walter B. Rideout, *The Radical Novel in the United States, 1900-1954,* Harvard University Press, 1956; Edgar Marquess Branch, *A Bibliography of James T. Farrell's Writings, 1921-1957,* University of Pennsylvania Press, 1959; Edgar M. Branch, *James T. Farrell,* University of Minnesota Press, 1963; Walter Allen, *The Modern Novel in Britain and the United States,* Dutton, 1965; *Contemporary Literary Criticism,* Gale, Volume I, 1973, Volume IV, 1975, Volume VIII, 1978, Volume XI, 1979; Charles Child Walcutt, editor, *Seven Novelists in the American Naturalist Tradition,* University of Minnesota Press, 1974; A. M. Wald, *James T. Farrell,* New York University Press, 1978; *Conversations with Writers,* Volume II, Gale, 1978; *Dictionary of Literary Biography,* Volume IV: *American Writers in Paris, 1920-1939,* Gale, 1980.

Periodicals: *Harper's,* October, 1954; *New York Times Book Review,* August 12, 1962, January 7, 1968, July 14, 1968, January 19, 1969, November 25, 1973, September 16, 1979; *Esquire,* December, 1962; *Saturday Review,* June 20, 1964; *National Observer,* June 29, 1964; *Literary Times,* April, 1965; *New York Herald Tribune Book Week,* February 27, 1966; *Time,* May 27, 1966; *Prairie Schooner,* spring, 1967; *American Book Collector,* May, 1967; *New York Times,* December 3, 1967; *Nation,* June 3, 1968, October 16, 1976; *Washington Post,* September 11, 1968; *Best Sellers,* May 15, 1971; *New Yorker,* March 18, 1974; *Twentieth Century Literature,* February, 1976; *American Quarterly,* winter, 1977; *People,* March 12, 1979.

OBITUARIES: Washington Post, August 23, 1979; *Chicago Tribune,* August 23, 1979, August 28, 1979; *New York Times,* August 23, 1979; *Detroit News,* August 26, 1979; *Time,* September 3, 1979; *Newsweek,* September 3, 1979; *New Republic,* October 6, 1979.†

*   *   *

FARWELL, Byron E. 1921-

PERSONAL: Born June 20, 1921, in Manchester, Iowa; son of E. L. and Nellie (Sheldon) Farwell; married Ruth Saxby, December 15, 1941; children: Joyce, Byron, Lesley. *Education:* Attended Ohio State University, 1939-40; University of Chicago, student, 1946-49, M.A., 1968; *Address:* P.O. Box 81, Hillsboro, Va. 22132. *Agent:* Russell & Volkening, Inc., 551 Fifth Ave., New York, N.Y. 10176.

CAREER: Writer. Chrysler International, Geneva, Switzerland, director of public relations, 1959-65, director of administration, 1965-71; mayor of Hillsboro, Va., 1977-81. Chairman of board of governors, College du Leman, 1967-68; member of editorial board, Small Town Institute. *Military service:* U.S. Army, 1940-45, 1950-51; became captain. *Member:* Royal Society of Literature (fellow), Royal Geographical Society (fellow).

WRITINGS: The Man Who Presumed: A Biography of Henry M. Stanley, Longmans, Green (London), 1953, Henry Holt, 1957, reprinted, Greenwood Press, 1974; *Let's Take a Trip* (juvenille), Grosset, 1955; *Burton: A Biography of Sir Richard Francis Burton,* Longmans, Green (London), 1963, Henry Holt, 1964, reprinted, Greenwood Press, 1975; *Prisoners of the Mahdi,* Harper, 1967.

Queen Victoria's Little Wars, Harper, 1972; *The Great Anglo-Boer War,* Harper, 1976 (published in England as *The Great Boer War,* Allen Lane, 1977); *Mr. Kipling's Army,* Norton, 1981 (published in England as *For Queen and Country,* Allen Lane, 1981); *Here Come the Gurkhas!,* Norton, 1982. Contributor to *Colliers Encyclopedia.*

WORK IN PROGRESS: Eminent Victorian Soldiers.

SIDELIGHTS: Byron Farwell has consistently earned critical praise for his books on British history and for his biographies. In a *Detroit News* article, William Boozer says that Farwell "is a military historian and Virginian who got his own close-up look at the British military as an American Army captain of engineers with the Mediterranean Allied Air Force in the British Eighth Army area of World War II. Then and since, he has done his homework in giving us [a] captivating look at 19th-century British society."

In a *Commonweal* review of Farwell's *The Man Who Presumed: A Biography of Henry M. Stanley,* John Cournos writes: "Mr. Farwell has done a splendid job. He has written a biography which is nearly always interesting and at times wildly exciting." R.W. Henderson, in a *Library Journal* article, says that the story of this famed British explorer "is one that has enduring appeal. Although Farwell adds little, if anything new, he has handled his material expertly, presenting it with freshness and vigor." *San Francisco Chronicle* reviewer Marc Rivette feels that "Mr. Farwell makes [Stanley] live, even though Stanley was too shy to be universally appealing. He makes him a figure of respect and even love. It is a neat and telling job of illuminating the life of a man, once on the tip of fame, but who in this day and age is remembered mostly for his one immortal question. [Dr. Livingstone, I presume?]"

Farwell's second biographical study, *Burton: A Biography of Sir Richard Francis Burton,* tells the story of the British writer, linguist, and explorer, best known as the translator of the sixteen-volume classic *Arabian Nights.* In a *Harper's* review, Paul Pickrel writes: "Farwell has written a scholarly and judicious biography. He has visited many of the places Burton visited, read all his extant works, tried to clear up the conflicting testimony and to fill in the gaps in information left by earlier writers, including Burton himself." *A Times Literary Supplement* critic says that Farwell "has approached this wonderful but pathetic figure with sensible diligence . . . He is eminently fair to everybody. His dates, we may be sure, are unimpeachable. If you know nothing about Richard Burton, Mr. Farwell's work is now unquestionably the place to start learning." And an *Economist* reviewer concludes that Farwell has "made a most entertaining book out of one of the most entertaining, improbable and outrageous of nineteenth-century characters. . . . Mr. Farwell does nothing to gloss over [Barton's] faults, even the most unattractive of them. . . . Yet as we close the book, we find ourselves positively liking this intolerable man—and feeling not a little sorry for him."

Farwell's historical studies have been as well received as his biographies, with reviewers particularly impressed by his ability to focus on the human side of the British military. A *Choice* critic calls *The Great Anglo-Boer War* "by far the best general history" of that conflict. "Farwell, an American, has successfully written a history that graphically describes all elements of the war—military, political, and social—in a manner that holds the attention of the reader.'' Neal Ascherson, writing in the *New York Review of Books,* notes that ''Mr. Farwell hasn't tried to write a political history of the war, to approach it from any novel angle, or to base his book on original research. . . . He is simply concerned to tell the chronicle of the war from its start to its finish with all the human detail he can muster.'' In *Library Journal,* J.A. Casada says that Farwell ''captures the human rhythms of the war in all their inherent drama. He has given us the single best account of the war in its full scope.''

One of Farwell's most widely reviewed books is *Mr. Kipling's Army,* an overall look at the British military during the nineteenth and early twentieth centuries. A *Choice* critic calls the book ''a fascinating and often amusing portrait of life in the British Army during the reigns of Queen Victoria and King Edward VII,'' covering such topics as education, training, discipline, medical care, and dependent families. ''It is essentially accurate,'' writes the reviewer, ''pointing out the many idiosyncrasies of the army without turning it into a caricature.'' Charles Champlin of the *Los Angeles Times* says that the title of the book ''seems absolutely appropriate. Kipling illuminates its pages; its descriptions in a real sense verify everything Kipling had to say.'' Champlin also feels that *Mr. Kipling's Army* ''is alternately amusing and horrifying, obviously the result of an astonishing amount of digging (said to have taken 15 years).''

New Republic writer John Keegan believes ''it was an excellent idea of Byron Farwell's to provide the still densely ranked host of Kipling's admirers with a documentary study of the principal institution from which he drew his cast of characters, the long-service, volunteer army of the Widow of Windsor, enlisted for drink and ruled by the lash, as the old saw had it. . . . The author knows a great deal about the regiments, the Fifth Fusiliers, the East Lancashires, the Rifle Brigade, the Scarlet Lancers, and he conveys to us something of their secret.'' Nicholas Best, in a *Times Literary Supplement* review, says that ''instead of war, [Farwell] looks at the army in peace, at its character, opinions, prejudices and way of life, at its methods of recruitment and training, both for officers and other ranks, and above all at its insularity at a time when Britain dominated forty per cent of the world's land mass.'' Best points out that although ''much of the story has been told before, there is much that bears retelling,'' especially in light of the fact that ''many of the Victorian army's customs and attitudes are very much alive today and, unfortunately, still flourishing.''

Byron Farwell lived in Europe and Africa for fourteen years. In the course of researching some of his books, he has visited more than one hundred countries.

BIOGRAPHICAL/CRITICAL SOURCES: New York Times, September 8, 1957; *Saturday Review,* September 14, 1957; *Time,* September 23, 1957, February 28, 1964; *Commonweal,* October 18, 1957; *Times Literary Supplement,* October 25, 1963, January 29, 1982; *New Statesman,* November 22, 1963; *Economist,* December 21, 1963; *Library Journal,* January 15, 1964, June 15, 1976; *Harper's,* March, 1964; *New York Review of Books,* April 16, 1964, July 15, 1976; *Choice,* December, 1976, June, 1981; *New Republic,* December 27, 1980; *Los Angeles Times,* February 13, 1981; *Washington Post Book World,* February 22, 1981; *Detroit News,* March 29, 1981.

—Sketch by Peter M. Gareffa

FEDDER, Norman J(oseph) 1934-

PERSONAL: Born January 26, 1934, in New York, N.Y.; son of Abraham Herbert (a rabbi) and Harriet (Solomon) Fedder; married Deborah Pincus, November 24, 1955; children: Jordan Michael, Tamar Beth. *Education:* Attended Johns Hopkins University, 1950-52; Brooklyn College (now Brooklyn College of the City University of New York), B.A., 1955; Columbia University, M.A., 1956; New York University, Ph.D., 1962. *Religion:* Jewish. *Home:* 1309 Nichols St., Manhattan, Kan. 66502.

CAREER: Trenton State College, Trenton, N.J., assistant professor of English, 1960-61; Indiana State College (now Indiana University of Pennsylvania), Indiana, Pa., associate professor of English, 1961-64; Florida Atlantic University, Boca Raton, associate professor of English, 1964-67; University of Arizona, Tucson, associate professor of drama, 1967-70; Kansas State University, Manhattan, associate professor, 1970-80, professor of speech-theatre program, 1980—. Judge at American College Theatre Festival; theatre consultant to B'nai B'rith, Hillel Foundation, and American Baptist Church; director of religious theatre project for American Theatre Association; developed Kansas Heritage Theatre to perform original plays throughout the state, 1976-77; developed the Jewish Heritage Theatre, a touring company, 1978.

MEMBER: American Theatre Association, American Association of University Professors, Kansas Association of the Religious Communities, the Arts, and the American Revolution (president), Association of Kansas Theatre (chairman of religious theatre division). *Awards, honors:* Honorable mention in Charles H. Sergel Drama Competition, University of Chicago; winner of Sacramento State College National Drama Competition; National Foundation for Jewish Culture grant, 1978, to develop the Jewish Heritage Theatre.

WRITINGS: The Influence of D. H. Lawrence on Tennessee Williams, Mouton & Co., 1966; (contributor) *Tennessee Williams: A Tribute,* University Press of Mississippi, 1977; (contributor) *Tennessee Williams: 13 Essays,* University Press of Mississippi, 1980.

Plays: ''The Eternal Kick,'' produced at Indiana State College, 1963; ''My Old Room,'' produced at University of Arizona, 1968; ''The Planter May Weep,'' first produced at University of Arizona, 1968; ''A Thousand at the Branches,'' produced at University of Arizona, fall, 1969.

''Some Events Connected with the Early History of Arizona,'' first produced by Arizona Pioneers Historical Society, 1970; ''Earp!'' (musical), produced in Abilene at Kansas State Historical Theatre, 1971; ''Monks'' (musical), produced at Kansas State University, 1972; ''PUBA,'' produced at University of North Carolina, 1973; ''The Betrayal'' (one act), produced in Baptist churches throughout Kansas, 1974, published in *Baker's Plays,* [Boston], 1978; ''The Decision,'' produced in Colby at Kansas Baptist Conference, 1974; ''The Kansas Character'' and ''No Place Like Kansas'' (both one acts), both first produced in various communities throughout Kansas, 1976; ''A Jew in Kansas'' (one act) and ''Next Thing to Kinfolk,'' both produced in New York City at the First National Jewish Festival, 1980.

Also author of Readers Theatre scripts, ''Proud to Be a Baptist,'' ''Tevye in the Golden Land,'' and ''The Matter with Kansas,'' produced on tour throughout Kansas, 1975; author of television script, "We Can Make Our Lives Sublime," produced by Columbia Broadcasting System, Inc., 1970. Contributor of articles to *Kansas Speech Journal* and *Arts in Society*. Religious theatre editor, *Dramatics Magazine*.

WORK IN PROGRESS: "The Buck Stops Here," a musical about Harry S Truman; editing *Wrestling with God: An Anthology of Contemporary Religious Drama,* for Anchorage Press.

SIDELIGHTS: Norman J. Fedder writes that his play "The Matter with Kansas" was designated an official bicentennial project.

* * *

FEEGEL, John R(ichard) 1932-

PERSONAL: Born November 16, 1932, in Middletown, Conn.; son of Fred B. (a member of the state police) and Eva (Lillian) Feegel; married Elaine Blanchet, February, 1959 (divorced, 1973); children: John, Jr., Mark Robert, Catherine, Elizabeth, Tom. *Education:* College of the Holy Cross, B.S., 1954; University of Ottawa, M.D., 1960; University of Denver, J.D., 1964. *Politics:* Republican. *Religion:* Roman Catholic. *Home:* 3002 Waverly Ave., Tampa, Fla. 33609. *Office:* Mitzel, Mitzel & Feegel, 701 East Washington St., Tampa, Fla. 33602.

CAREER: Licensed to practice medicine in Colorado, Florida, North Carolina, and Georgia; certified by the Medical Council of Canada, 1965; certified diplomate by the American Board of Pathology, 1966; admitted to the Bar of Colorado, 1964, and Florida, 1967. St. Mary's Hospital, West Palm Beach, Fla., intern, 1960-61; Denver General Hospital, Denver, Colo., resident in pathology, 1961-64; Plantation General Hospital, Plantation, Fla., associate pathologist, 1967; Tampa General Hospital, Tampa, Fla., associate pathologist, 1967-76; South Florida Baptist Hospital, Plant City, chief pathologist, 1969-76, chief of staff, 1974-75; Memorial Hospital of North Carolina, Chapel Hill, member of staff, 1976-77; Emory University, School of Medicine, Atlanta, Ga., director of forensic pathology residency program, 1978—; Mitzel, Mitzel & Feegel (law firm), Tampa, partner, 1980—.

Deputy coroner, Denver, Colo., 1961-65; deputy medical examiner, Dade County, Fla., 1967; Hillsborough County, Fla., medical examiner, 1967-69, chief medical examiner, 1973-77; associate chief medical examiner, State of North Carolina, 1976-77, Atlanta, Ga., 1977—. Associate clinical professor of pathology, College of Medicine, University of South Florida, 1973-77, University of North Carolina, 1976-77, Emory University, 1978—, and Morehouse College, 1979—. Lecturer on forensic pathology and related topics at a variety of institutions, including University of Denver, University of Georgia, and North Carolina Justice Academy. Consultant in forensic pathology to the state attorneys of Hillsborough, Pasco, Desoto, Manatee, Polk, and Pinellas counties, all in Fla., all 1973-77. Also consultant to Attorney General's Office, State of Florida, 1973-77. *Military service:* U.S. Public Health Service, 1965-67; became commander.

MEMBER: American Medical Association, American College of Clinical Pathologists, College of American Pathologists, American Academy of Forensic Sciences, Georgia Medical Association, Florida Bar Association. *Awards, honors:* Recognition award, American Medical Association, 1975-78; Edgar Award, Mystery Writers of America, 1976, for *Autopsy;* nominee, Jim Townsend Award for fiction, 1982.

WRITINGS: Legal Aspects of Laboratory Medicine, Little, Brown, 1973; (contributor) *Legal Medicine Annual,* Appleton, 1973; (contributor) J. Henry, editor, *Legal Aspects of Laboratory Medicine, Part VI,* Todd & Sanford, 1978.

Fiction: *Autopsy,* Avon, 1975; *Death Sails the Bay,* Avon, 1978; *The Dance Card,* Dial, 1981; *Malpractice,* New American Library, 1981.

Contributor to *Yankee* and to scientific journals. *Hillsborough County Medical Bulletin,* editorial associate, 1971-75, contributor of monthly column, "Medical-Legal Notes," 1972-74.

WORK IN PROGRESS: A detective novel.

SIDELIGHTS: Pathologist John R. Feegel uses his experience as chief examiner for several southern states to write graphic spy novels with clinical expertise. "Cloak and scalpel" is the term that Alan Cheuse uses to describe Feegel's writing in the *New York Times Book Review.* Of Feegel's 1980 thriller, *The Dance Card,* Cheuse observes, "There are an abundance of corpses and enough cutting . . . to make even the most jaded reader wince." Though he regards it as "far less subtle" than a novel by John le Carre, Cheuse maintains *The Dance Card* "will keep most aficionados of the genre turning pages through the night."

AVOCATIONAL INTERESTS: Sailing, Mayan architecture, pistol shooting, fishing.

BIOGRAPHICAL/CRITICAL SOURCES: People, July 28, 1975; *New York Times Book Review,* February 8, 1981; *Chicago Tribune Book World,* February 15, 1981; *Los Angeles Times Book Review,* March 1, 1981; *Tampa Bay Magazine,* April, 1981.

* * *

FEHREN, Henry 1920-

PERSONAL: Surname originally Foehrenbacher; born August 19, 1920, in St. Cloud, Minn.; son of Henry and Martha (Engel) Foehrenbacher. *Education:* St. John's University, Collegeville, Minn., B.A., 1944; St. John's Seminary, Collegeville, Minn., seminarian, 1944-48; Moorhead State College (now University), M.S.Ed., 1964. *Politics:* Democrat. *Home:* 371 Seventh Ave., New York, N.Y. 10001.

CAREER: Roman Catholic priest, ordained 1948. St. Donatus Church, Brooten, Minn., pastor, 1953-60; St. Thomas Church, Kent, Minn., pastor, 1960-65; St. Joseph Church, Foxhome, Minn., pastor, 1960-69; free-lance writer and editor. Involved in parish work. Adjunct instructor in English, Bernard M. Baruch College of City University of New York, 1980—.

WRITINGS: Christ Now, Kenedy, 1966; *God Spoke One Word,* Kenedy, 1967; (contributor) G. S. Sloyan, editor, *Secular Priest in the New Church,* Herder & Herder, 1967; *Never Quite Ready for Heaven,* Claretian, 1972; *That's the Spirit,* Claretian, 1974; *Prayers of the Bible,* Pueblo, 1977; *Prayers of the Faithful,* Pueblo, 1977; *A New Look at Some Old Sins,* Claretian, 1978.

Author of booklets; contributor of articles and reviews to *Encyclopedia Americana, Encyclopedia International, Worship, Ave Maria, My Sunday Visitor, Continuum, Liturgical Arts, Preaching, My Daily Visitor, Today's Family, Pastoral Life, National Catholic Reporter,* and other magazines and thirty diocesan weekly papers; columnist, *U.S. Catholic,* 1965—. Formerly editor, Benzinger's Sunday bulletins and *Liturgical Prayer* magazine.

WORK IN PROGRESS: Booklet on pastoral care of the sick; a prayer book.

SIDELIGHTS: Henry Fehren told *CA:* "I did not intend to become a writer. Except for two articles, all my writing has been done at the request of editors and publishers. When the first article was requested of me nineteen years ago, I decided that I could write as badly as anyone else and sent the article in. Since then there has been no stopping. I especially enjoyed my work as religious technical advisor on script, props, settings, locations, customs, costumes, and actual filming for the movie *True Confessions,* with Robert DeNiro and Robert Duvall.

"My writing habits are chaotic—I can write only for a deadline. Advice to aspiring writers? Read good writers. I love to read Shakespeare, Samuel Johnson, Jonathan Swift, Jane Austen and Charles Dickens, among others. They are not contemporary, but they knew the language.

"Books and articles of mine have been burned by outraged readers. Writing is difficult, lonely work; I prefer teaching college English and editing."

AVOCATIONAL INTERESTS: Travel, including trips to all fifty states of America, all countries of North Africa, the Middle East, South and Central America, the Caribbean, Mexico, Canada, the Soviet Union, and Europe.

* * *

FELDMAN, Gerald D(onald) 1937-

PERSONAL: Born April 24, 1937, in New York, N.Y.; son of Isadore and Lillian (Cohen) Feldman; married Philippa Blume, June 22, 1958 (divorced, 1982); children: Deborah Eve, Aaron. *Education:* Columbia University, B.A. (magna cum laude), 1958; Harvard University, M.A., 1959, Ph.D., 1964. *Politics:* Democrat. *Religion:* Jewish. *Residence:* Berkeley, Calif. *Office:* Department of History, University of California, Berkeley, Calif. 94720.

CAREER: University of California, Berkeley, assistant professor, 1963-68, associate professor, 1968-70, professor of history, 1970—, Institute of International Studies, member of advisory and program committees, 1969-70, member of executive committee, 1979-82, acting chairman of committee on Advanced Industrial Societies and West European Studies, 1971-72. Delegate to Council for European Studies, 1971-72; member of Curatorium for State and the Economy in the Weimer Republic conference, 1973; co-chairman of conference on twentieth-century capitalism, 1974; participant in consultation program, Historische Kommission zu Berlin, summer, 1976; appointee to the Historisches Kolleg, Munich, 1982-83. *Member:* American Historical Association, Phi Beta Kappa.

AWARDS, HONORS: American Council of Learned Societies fellowships, 1966-67, 1970-71; Social Science Research Council grant, 1966-67; honorary mention, Conference Group on Central European History, 1970, for best article; Guggenheim fellowship, 1973-74; National Endowment for the Humanities fellowship, 1977-78; Lehrman Institute fellowship, 1981-82; German Marshall Fund fellowship, 1981-82.

WRITINGS: *Army, Industry and Labor in Germany, 1914-1918,* Princeton University Press, 1966; (editor) *German Imperialism, 1914-1918: The Development of a Historical Debate,* Wiley, 1972; (editor with Thomas G. Barnes) *A Documentary History of Modern Europe,* Little, Brown, 1972, Volume I: *Renaissance, Reformation, and Absolutism, 1400-1660,* Volume II: *Rationalism and Revolution, 1660-1815,* Volume III: *Nationalism, Industrialization, and Democracy, 1814-1914,* Volume IV: *Breakdown and Rebirth, 1914 to the Present; Iron and Steel in the German Inflation, 1916-1923,* Princeton University Press, 1977; (with Heidrun Homburg) *Industrie und Inflation: Studien und Dokumente zur Politik der deutschen Unternehmer 1916 bis 1923,* Hoffmann und Campe, 1977; (editor with Otto Buesch) *Historische Prozesse der deutschen Inflation 1914-1924,* Colloquium-Verlag, 1978; (editor with Carl-Ludwig Holtfrerich, Gerhard A. Ritter, and Peter-Christian Witt) *The German Inflation: A Preliminary Balance,* [New York and Berlin], 1982.

Contributor: Ritter, editor, *Entsehung und Wandel der modernen Gesellschaft: Festschrift fur Hans Rosenberg zum 65. Geburtstag,* De Gruyter, 1970; I. Geiss and B. Wendt, editors, *Deutschland in der Weltpolitik des 19. und 20 Jahrhunderts: Fritz Fischer zum 65. Geburtstag,* Bertelsmann Universitasverlag, 1973; Hans-Ulrich Wehler, editor, *Sozialgeschichte heute: Festschrift fur Hans Rosenberg zum 70. Geburtstag,* Vandenhoeck & Ruprecht, 1974; Henrich Winkler, editor, *Organisierter Kapitalismus: Voraussetzunger und Anfange,* Vandenhoeck & Ruprecht, 1974. Contributor to proceedings and historical journals in the United States and Germany. Member of editorial board, *Journal of Social History, Central European History,* 1973-75, and *Journal of Modern History,* 1973-75.

WORK IN PROGRESS: *A Social and Political History of the German Inflation, 1914-1923,* for Oxford University Press; *Vom Weltkrieg zur Weltwirtschaftskrise: Studien zur Wirtschafts-und Sozialgeschichte 1914-1932,* for Vandenhoeck & Ruprecht; *Die ueberforderte Arbeitsgemeinschaft: Studien und Dokumente zur schichte der Zentralarbeitsgemeinschaft.*

* * *

FIELD, Stanley 1911-

PERSONAL: Born May 20, 1911, in the Ukraine; son of Henry (a merchant) and Nina (Zibulski) Field; married Joyce S. Stillman (an artist and editor), December 7, 1935; children: Jeffrey Michael, Constance Elyse. *Education:* Brooklyn College (now Brooklyn College of the City University of New York), B.A., 1934. *Home:* 3520 Duff Dr., Falls Church, Va. 22041.

CAREER: Radio announcer for WLTH, WNYC, and WMCA, New York City, 1934-36; Emil Mogul Advertising Agency, New York City, copywriter, 1936-38; National Broadcasting Co., New York City, contract writer, 1938-40; U.S. Department of Defense, Washington, D.C., radio-television information specialist, 1942-75. Adjunct professor of broadcasting, American University, Washington, D.C., 1952-68. Instructor at Graduate School, U.S. Department of Agriculture, Mt. Vernon College, and Adult Education Services, Fairfax County, Va. *Member:* Poets and Writers, Author's Guild, Broadcast Education Association, Associated Writing Programs. *Awards, honors:* Special award for script writing from YMCA International.

WRITINGS: *Television and Radio Writing,* Houghton, 1959; *Guide to Scholarships, Fellowships and Grants,* Public Affairs Press, 1967; *Bible Stories for Adults Only,* Jonathan David, 1967; *Professional Broadcast Writer's Handbook,* TAB Books, 1974; *The Making of the Mini-Documentary,* TAB Books, 1975; *Creative Writing and Successful Selling,* Jonathan David, 1983.

Television scripts: "Life in Washington" (series of documentaries), broadcast by WRC; "Womanpower" (hour-long documentary starring Helen Hayes), broadcast by National Broadcasting Co.; "Fond Recollections" (hour-long musical), broadcast by National Broadcasting Co. Also author of special material for Tallulah Bankhead and Ray Milland.

Radio scripts: "Shakespeare's England" (series of weekly dramas); "Words at War"; "Your Rights and Mine"; "Together We Live"; "Legend of the Great Hope"; "This Small World"; "The Masterpiece"; "She Ran for President"; and other dramas; also author of transcribed series for Veterans of Foreign Wars and American National Red Cross.

Film scripts; all produced by Stuart Finley Productions: "Cash for Trash"; "Recycling,"; "Garbage Is a Dirty Word"; "Realities of Recycling." Contributor of poetry to *Northwoods Journal, Cameo, Hyacinths and Biscuits, Touchstone,* and other periodicals; contributor of short stories and articles to *Green's Magazine, Woman's Life, Home Life, Pollution Control Journal, Friar, Live, Northern Virginia, Journal of Broadcasting,* and other periodicals.

WORK IN PROGRESS: A Woman Is a Foreign Land, a novel; *The Pursuit of Rosa Casandra,* a historical novel; *She Ran for President,* a novelized biography.

SIDELIGHTS: Stanley Field wrote *CA:* "My own experience is that of the part-time creative writer and that raises a dilemma I can pose but cannot guarantee to resolve. Is it more courageous, if you believe you have the talent, to devote yourself fully to writing despite any obligations: a well-paying job, a family to support, kids to send through college? Do you consider Paul Gauguin a genius? Do you sympathize with his giving up a prosperous banking career to devote himself completely to art? Would you? Or would you say, why couldn't he keep his wealth-producing job and paint nights and Sundays? Why couldn't a writer maintain his creative activities on a part-time basis?

"There are two descriptive words for a writer: compulsive drive. And I think they spell it out for myself and for all other creative people, part-time or full-time."

* * *

FIELDS, Rick 1942-

PERSONAL: Born May 16, 1942, in Manhattan, N.Y.; son of Allen D. (a publicist) and Reva (Freed) Fields. *Education:* Attended Harvard University, 1960-62, 1963-64, and University of New Mexico, 1965. *Politics:* "Interdependence of all sentient beings." *Religion:* Buddhist. *Office address:* c/o *New Age Magazine,* Box 1200, Allston, Mass. 02134.

CAREER: Has worked as an English teacher for Berlitz in Guadalajara, Mexico, as an apple picker, a street theatre writer and actor, a warehouse worker, a reporter, an editor, a plumber's helper, a furniture mover, and a teacher at University of Colorado, Naropa Institute, and at Loretto College. Special projects editor, *New Age Magazine.*

WRITINGS: Loka: A Journal from Naropa Institute, Doubleday, 1974; *Loka II,* Doubleday, 1975; *How the Swans Come to the Lake: A Narrative History of Buddhism in America,* Shambhala Publications, 1981; *On the Path: A Guide to Spirtuality and Everyday Life,* J.P. Tarcher, 1983.

SIDELIGHTS: In *How the Swans Came to the Lake: A Narrative History of Buddhism in America,* Rick Fields documents the rise of Buddhism in the modern west. According to *Washington Post Book World* reviewer Nancy Wilson Ross, the book is "literally crammed with the sort of lively and accurate information in its special field which I had for years been longing to find assembled in an orderly manner. . . . Not only has [Fields] thoroughly researched the rich lode of material at his disposal . . . , but he also possesses first-hand knowledge of how Buddhist practice 'works,' and further, he is blessed with a flair for characterization and the perceptive turn of phrase which give his unusual material all the elements of a 'good read.'"

BIOGRAPHICAL/CRITICAL SOURCES: Washington Post Book World, April 25, 1982.

* * *

FIFIELD, William 1916-

PERSONAL: Born April 5, 1916, in Chicago, Ill.; son of Lawrence Wendell (a Congregational minister) and Juanita (Sloan) Fifield; married Donna Hamilton (an actress); children: John Lawrence, Donna Lee and Brian Robert (twins). *Education:* Whitman College, A.B. (magna cum laude), 1937. *Politics:* None. *Religion:* None. *Agent:* Brandt & Brandt Literary Agents, Inc., 1501 Broadway, New York, N.Y. 10036.

CAREER: Writer. Began radio work while an undergraduate and returned to it (and later television) as an announcer, writer, actor, producer-director, for CBS and NBC, in Chicago, New York, and Hollywood at various short intervals, 1937-60; left radio originally to freelance as a short-story writer, living and traveling abroad most of the time since 1940; international representative for Bordeaux Wines, 1955-58; former bullfighter. *Member:* Phi Beta Kappa. *Awards, honors:* O. Henry Memorial Award for short story "Fishermen of Patzcuaro"; Huntington Hartford Foundation award for creative writing.

WRITINGS: The Devil's Marchioness (novel), Dial, 1957; *The Sign of Taurus* (novel), Holt, 1960; *Matadora* (novel), Weidenfield & Nicolson, 1960; (with Alexis Lichine) *Encyclopaedia of Wines and Spirits,* Knopf, 1967, revised edition, Cassell, 1979; *Jean Cocteau par Jean Cocteau: Entretiens* (interviews), Stock (Paris), 1973; *Jean Cocteau,* Columbia University Press, 1974; *Modigliani,* Morrow, 1976.

Also author of over one hundred radio and television plays. Contributor of short stories to anthologies and to periodicals, including *Harper's, Paris Review, American Mercury, Yale Review, Argosy,* and *Tomorrow.*

WORK IN PROGRESS: A tetralogy on the Florentine Renaissance period.

SIDELIGHTS: The much-traveled William Fifield prefers not to be called an expatriate. "I'm an outlander," he says, "just as Lawrence Durrell is." Born in Chicago, raised in Seattle, he has lived abroad intermittently for some forty years, settling in Mexico, Haiti, Martinique, Austria, London, Portugal, Spain, Florence, the Italian Riviera, Paris, and Provence. His activities and interests have included a spell as an amateur bullfighter and a continuing concern with psychic phenomena, including the crystal ball, hypnotism, the seance, and clairvoyance.

When he is writing, he begins working at 4 a.m. and writes for about ten hours at a stretch, composing directly onto a typewriter at the rate of 80 or 90 words per minute. He is interested in achieving a new novel form, one which "will keep it within readable length without loss of breadth or depth."

BIOGRAPHICAL/CRITICAL SOURCES: Atlantic, July, 1957; *New Statesman,* January 25, 1958; *Times Literary Supplement,* February 7, 1958, May 22, 1959; *New York Times Book Review,* May 8, 1960, May 29, 1960; *Chicago Daily News,* May

14, 1960; *New York Herald Tribune Book Review,* June 5, 1960; *Kansas City Star,* June 28, 1960.†

* * *

FIGUEROA, Loida
See FIGUEROA-MERCADO, Loida

* * *

FIGUEROA-MERCADO, Loida 1917-
(Loida Figueroa)

PERSONAL: Born October 6, 1917, in Yauco, Puerto Rico; daughter of Agustin (a cane cutter) and Emeteria (Mercado) Figueroa; married third husband, Jose Nelson Castro, November 14, 1953 (divorced, 1957); children: Eunice, Maria Antonia, Rebeca, Avaris (daughter). *Education:* Polytechnic Institute, San German, P.R., B.A. (magna cum laude), 1941; Columbia University, M.A., 1952; Universidad Central de Madrid, Ph.D., 1963. *Politics:* Independent. *Religion:* Protestant. *Address:* Entrega General, Estacion Salud, Mayaguez, Puerto Rico 00708.

CAREER: Teacher in elementary and high schools, 1942-57; Guanica High School, Guanica, P.R., acting principal, 1947, 1955; University of Puerto Rico, Mayaguez, professor of Puerto Rican history, 1957-74; Brooklyn College of the City University of New York, Brooklyn, N.Y., professor of Puerto Rican history, 1974-77; writer and lecturer. *Member:* P.E.N. Club de Puerto Rico, Association of Caribbean Historians, Asociacion de Historiadores Latinoamericanos y del Caribe, Sociedad de Autores Puertorriquenos, Phi Alpha Theta. *Awards, honors:* Yale University fellow, autumn, 1975.

WRITINGS: Acridulces (poems), Rodriquez Lugo, 1947; *Arenales* (novel), Ediciones Rumbos, 1961; *Breve Historia de Puerto Rico,* Editorial Edil, Volume I: *Desde sus comienzos hasta 1800,* 1968, Volume II: *Desde 1800 a 1892,* 1969, 4th edition of Volumes I and II published together as *Breve Historia de Puerto Rico,* Part I, 1971, Part II: *Desde 1892-1900,* 1976, translation of Part I published as *History of Puerto Rico from the Beginning to 1892,* Anaya Book Co., 1972; *Tres puntos claves: Lares, idioma, soberania,* Editorial Edil, 1972; *La Historafia de Puerto Rico,* Ediciones Paraninfo (Madrid), 1975; *El Caso de Puerto Rico a Nivel International;* Editorial Edil, 1980. Editor of *Atenea* (journal).

WORK IN PROGRESS: Una Isla en el Mar de los Caribes y otros Ensayos; Conociendo a Vieques, a travel chronicle.

SIDELIGHTS: Loida Figueroa-Mercado wrote *CA:* "A speech by the late Juan B. Soto, Chancellor of the University of Puerto Rico, given during my high school commencement exercises in 1934 induced me to change my purpose to be a nurse, prompting me instead to continue studying all the way to Ph.D. The aim was attained in 1963.

"I wrote poems when I was young, but I have abandoned this genre since 1958. I have written one novel, but others rumble in my brain. I cannot direct my pen to write them on account of my involvement in historical writings. I have continued in this track because the majority of our people do not know their own history, and historians in Puerto Rico are few.

"I do not have scheduled hours for writing. As a matter of fact, apart from the many lectures I am asked to deliver, there are long spells when I do not investigate or write; but, when I decide to do it, I concentrate on my purpose and leave everything else aside. For example, I began to write *Brevè Historia de Puerto Rico* (not so brief now) because there was no adequate textbook for the course I was asked to teach in the University. I continued writing it and will continue again soon, because even persons on the street ask me when I am going to publish the next volume.

"In regard to historical writing, my advice is that great care be taken in the collecting of data and more care still in the selection of relevant events. The reader should be provided with a tracing of the causes and effects of specific trends, and with comparisons to other nations and periods. Objectiveness is a must, but a telephone guide book should be avoided. Opinions can be given, but based on facts. Nevertheless, one has to remember that perfect objectiveness is impossible."

* * *

FINCH, Robert (Duer Claydon) 1900-

PERSONAL: Born May 14, 1900, in Freeport, Long Island, N.Y.; son of Edward and Ada Finch. *Education:* University of Toronto, B.A., 1925; attended University of Paris, 1928. *Address:* 4 Devonshire Place, Toronto, Ontario, Canada M5S E21.

CAREER: University of Toronto, University College, Toronto, Ontario, lecturer, 1928-30, assistant professor, 1931-42, associate professor, 1942-51, professor of French, 1952-68, professor emeritus, 1970—, writer-in-residence, 1970-71. Poet, literary critic, painter. Member of board of trustees, Massey College, University of Toronto, and Leonard Foundation. *Member:* Royal Society of Canada (fellow). *Awards, honors:* Jardine Memorial Prize, 1924, for poetry; Governor General's Awards, 1946, for *Poems,* and 1961, for *Acis in Oxford;* Lorne Pierce Gold Medal, 1968; LL.D., University of Toronto, 1973.

WRITINGS: Poems, Oxford University Press, 1946; *The Strength of the Hills* (poems), McClelland & Stewart, 1948; *A Century Has Roots* (masque), University of Toronto Press, 1953; (editor with C. R. Parsons) Chateaubriand, *Rene,* University of Toronto Press, 1957; *Acis in Oxford, and Other Poems,* privately printed, 1959, University of Toronto Press, 1961; *Dover Beach Revisited, and Other Poems,* Macmillan, 1961; *Silverthorn Bush, and Other Poems,* Macmillan, 1966; *The Sixth Sense: Individualism in French Poetry, 1686-1760,* University of Toronto Press, 1966.

(Editor with Eugene Joliat) *French Individualist Poetry, 1686-1760: An Anthology,* University of Toronto Press, 1971; (contributor) Alan Jarvis, editor, *Douglas Duncan: A Memorial Portrait,* University of Toronto Press, 1974; (contributor) Arnold Edinborough, editor, *The Enduring Word: A Centennial History of Wycliffe College,* University of Toronto Press, 1978; (editor with Joliat) Saint-Evremond, *Sir Politick Would-Be,* Droz, 1978; (editor with Joliat) Saint-Evremond, *Les Opera,* Droz, 1979; *Variations and Theme* (poems), Porcupine's Quill, 1980; *Has and Is* (poems), Porcupine's Quill, 1981. Contributor to periodicals.

SIDELIGHTS: Robert Finch is a poet, essayist, musician, painter, and literary critic who writes elegant, controlled verse. "At its best," writes L. A. MacKay in *Saturday Night,* his poetry "has a mannered dexterity, an ornate lucidity, and a studiously restrained tone that is capable alike of light grace and poignant though delicately phrased emotion." Writing in *Canadian Literature,* George Woodcock observes that Finch "writes with poise and self-consciousness. The Dionysic fury never leads him where his reason would not have him go, and his craftsmanship is controlled and accurate. Thus, one imagines, Flaubert might write if another incarnation made him a Canadian poet instead of a French novelist.''

BIOGRAPHICAL/CRITICAL SOURCES: Saturday Night, May, 1949; *Canadian Literature,* summer, 1962; *The Canadian Forum,* December, 1967; *Comparative Literature,* winter, 1968; *Contemporary Literary Criticism,* Volume XVIII, Gale, 1981.

* * *

FINCHER, Ernest B(arksdale) 1910-

PERSONAL: Born March 21, 1910, in Mescalero, N.M.; son of Elijah B. (a clergyman) and Catherine (a teacher; maiden name, Arvin) Fincher. *Education:* Texas Technological College (now Texas Tech University), B.A., 1931; Columbia University, M.A., 1934; New York University, Ph.D., 1950. *Politics:* 'McCarthy-type Democrat.'' *Religion:* Society of Friends (Quakers). *Home:* Deerpath Farm, Asbury, N.J. 08802.

CAREER: Social science teacher in public schools in Amarillo, Tex., 1931-33; Columbia University Press, New York, N.Y., member of editorial staff, 1934-35; high school social science teacher in Westwood, N.J., 1935-42; New Jersey State College at Montclair (now Montclair State College), assistant professor, 1946-49, associate professor, 1949-55, professor of political science, 1955-70; free-lance writer, 1970—. *Wartime service:* Alternative service with American Friends Service Committee, 1942-46. *Member:* American Academy of Political and Social Science, New York Historical Society.

WRITINGS: (With W. G. Kimmel and Russell Fraser) *Democracy at Work,* Winston, 1939, 2nd edition, 1941; (with John Ferguson and Dean McHenry) *American Government Today,* McGraw, 1951; *The President of the United States,* Abelard, 1955; *The Government of the United States,* Prentice-Hall, 1967, 3rd edition, 1976.

(With Merle Prunty) *Lands of Promise,* Macmillan, 1971, 2nd edition, 1973; *In a Race with Time,* Macmillan, 1972, 2nd edition, 1974; *Spanish Americans as a Political Factor in New Mexico, 1912-1950,* Arno, 1974; *The Presidency: An American Invention,* Abelard, 1977; *The Bill of Rights: Safeguard of Freedom,* F. Watts, 1978; *The American Legal System,* F. Watts, 1980; *The Vietnam War,* F. Watts, 1980; *The War in Korea,* F. Watts, 1981.

SIDELIGHTS: Ernest B. Fincher, who is competent in Spanish, writes: ''My outlook on the world is colored by the fact that I am a pacifist—a conscientious objector in World War Two—but a political activist who believes that the world can survive only if drastic changes are made in social, economic, and political institutions. My dissatisfaction with the present order has been heightened by extensive travel in Latin America and by taking part in seminars involving radical students in that part of the world.'' In addition to Latin America, he has also spent time in Europe and Asia.

AVOCATIONAL INTERESTS: Conservation, international affairs, ballet and other arts.

BIOGRAPHICAL/CRITICAL SOURCES: New York Times Book Review, April 26, 1981.

* * *

FINKEL, Donald 1929-

PERSONAL: Born October 21, 1929, in New York, N.Y.; son of Saul Aaron (an attorney) and Meta (Rosenthal) Finkel; married Constance Urdang (a writer), August 14, 1956; children: Liza, Thomas Noah, Amy Maria. *Education:* Columbia University, B.S., 1952, M.A., 1953. *Office:* Washington University, St. Louis, Mo. 63130.

CAREER: University of Iowa, Iowa City, instructor, 1957-58; Bard College, Annandale-on-Hudson, N.Y., instructor, 1958-60; Washington University, St. Louis, Mo., poet-in-residence, 1960—. Visiting professor, Bennington College, 1966-67. *Member:* Antarctican Society, Author's Guild, Authors League of America, Phi Beta Kappa. *Awards, honors:* Helen Bullis Prize, 1964, for *Simeon;* Guggenheim fellow, 1967; *The Garbage Wars* was nominated for a National Book Award, 1970; Ingram Merrill Foundation grant, 1972; National Endowment for the Arts grant, 1973; Theodore Roethke Memorial Award, 1974, for *Adequate Earth; A Mote in Heaven's Eye,* and *What Manner of Beast* were nominated for National Book Critics Circle awards, 1975 and 1981; Morton Dauwen Zabel Award, 1980, for *Going Under and Endurance.*

WRITINGS—Poetry; published by Atheneum, except as indicated: *The Clothing's New Emperor,* edited by John Hall Wheelock, Scribner, 1959; *Simeon,* 1964; *A Joyful Noise,* 1966; *Answer Back,* 1968; *The Garbage Wars,* 1970; *Adequate Earth,* 1972; *A Mote in Heaven's Eye,* 1975; *Going Under and Endurance,* 1978; *What Manner of Beast,* 1981. Contributor to *Poetry, New Yorker,* and other publications.

SIDELIGHTS: Donald Finkel's poetic method has been compared to collage because he frequently interweaves ''found'' poems and quoted material with his own unpunctuated free verse. His forte, according to *Nation* reviewer Mary Kinzie, is ''finding eloquent and credible language for the speechless and alien''—a feat accomplished by ''extraordinary leaps of insight,'' Kinzie maintains. *Saturday Review* critic Chad Walsh praises Finkel's ''impressive sense of poetic architecture,'' noting that ''an unsolemn but not frivolous vitality charges through much of his verse.''

This vitality is evident in Finkel's 1966 publication, *A Joyful Noise,* which reveals the author to be ''a creator of comic extravagance, of an imagination which responds to the seemingly chance, grotesque and unreal nature of present-day life in its own terms,'' according to *Poetry* reviewer R. J. Mills. Finkel's poems are grimly and outrageously funny, bawdy, satirical, and dreamlike. His characters comprise ''a Jewish-French-Irish stew whose chefs might be Isaac Singer, Andre Breton, and Samuel Beckett,'' Mills says. Joseph Bennett adds in the *New York Times Book Review,* however, that Finkel is ''so gifted he does not need subjects for his poems. . . . He has, above all, the gift of wonderment.'' In the end, Bennett concludes, Finkel makes a joyful noise indeed.

In *Answer Back,* his 1968 volume of poems, Finkel is ''T. S. Eliot reborn, so far as much of the technique is concerned,'' writes Chad Walsh. The book is actually one long poem which, ''zig-zagging between the neolithic past and the napalm present, creates a sense of the human condition in which all times are blended into a dimension of eternal experience. This poet is worthy grist for the scholarly commentators, but meanwhile I pause to celebrate his extraordinary sense of language and acuteness of observation,'' Walsh says.

More recently, Finkel has been inspired by challenges to the view that language is the divine right of human beings and that the power to name sets man apart. In *What Manner of Beast,* Finkel explores what Mary Kinzie calls ''the fearful ease of permeating the boundary between the human realm and the merely animal. [The book] has a dual subject: the 'humanity' (that is the shared intelligence, the need for affection and the ability to 'play') of primitives and lesser animals, and the 'animality' (the shared bewilderment, the darkness, the resort to instinct) of modern men and women." In depicting characters such as Victor, the wild boy of Aveyron, or Washoe, the first of the "talking" chimpanzees, who struggles to express emotion through a language designed to ask for things, "a man less sure of his purpose might rely too much on the pathos of this predicament," Phoebe Pettingell observes in *New Leader*. But Finkel, she believes "uses his compassion and humor to poke our sensitive spots and our loneliness, binding us closer to our fellow inhabitants on this earth."

BIOGRAPHICAL/CRITICAL SOURCES: New York Times Book Review, December 20, 1964, September 4, 1966, November 22, 1970, September 7, 1975; *Saturday Review,* January 2, 1965; *Poetry,* November, 1966, February, 1969, September, 1973, February, 1976; *New Republic,* February 3, 1973; *Parnassus,* fall/winter, 1973, spring/summer, 1979; *Nation,* May 19, 1979, December 12, 1981; *Times Literary Supplement,* January 18, 1980, July 2, 1982; *New Leader,* March 8, 1982.

* * *

FINN, Ralph L(eslie) 1912-

PERSONAL: Born January 17, 1912, in London, England; son of Alec (an architect) and Leah (a schoolmistress; maiden name, Platt) Finn; married Freda Nathanson, June 15, 1937; children: Alan Hugh, Andrea Anne. *Education:* Oxford University, A.B., 1933, diploma in Modern Literature, University Extension, 1945. *Religion:* Jewish. *Home:* 22 Overton Rd., London N. 14, England.

CAREER: R. S. Caplin Ltd. (advertising), London, England, chief executive, 1941-46; Muse Arts Ltd. (publishers and impresarios), London, director, 1946-52; Max Factor, London, advertising manager, 1952-54; Legget Nicholson (advertising), London, idea-man, 1954-57; Everetts Advertising, London, copy chief, beginning 1957. *Member:* Institute of Arts and Letters (fellow), Institute of the Practitioners of Advertising (associate member), Institute of Journalists. *Awards, honors:* Voted "one of the world's six best creative men," Australian Advertising Convention, 1960.

WRITINGS: Out of the Depths, Royal Air Force Benevolent Fund, 1941; *Down Oxford Street,* Hutchinson, 1942; *Return to Earth,* Hutchinson, 1943; *He Said What's Blue,* Hutchinson, 1944; *Twenty-Seven Stairs,* Hutchinson, 1944; *The Lunatic, the Lover and the Poet,* Hutchinson, 1945; *Time Marches Sideways,* Hutchinson, 1945; *And All Is Mist,* Hutchinson, 1946; *Waiting Room,* Hutchinson, 1946; *Everyday Cameos,* Rich & Cowan, 1946; *I Sent You Red Roses,* Panther, 1947; *Death of a Dream,* Panther, 1948; *Indiscreet Guide to East End,* Muse Arts, 1948; *And the Ants Came,* Panter, 1949; *After the Sickness,* Panther, 1950; *The Peephole,* Panther, 1951; *Captive on the Flying Saucers,* Gaywood Press (London), 1951; *Freaks against Supermen,* Gaywood Press, 1951; *My Greatest Game,* Saturn Press, 1953; *World Cup, 1954,* Panther, 1954; *Champions Again, Manchester United,* Hale, 1957.

Spurs Supreme: A Review of Soccer's Greatest-ever Side 1960-61, R. Hale, 1961; *Spurs Go Marching On,* R. Hale, 1963; *No Tears in Aldgate* (biography), R. Hale, 1963; *England, World Champions, 1966,* R. Hale, 1966; *London's Cup Final, 1967,* R. Hale, 1967; *Spring in Aldgate,* R. Hale, 1968; *Arsenal: Chapman to Mee,* R. Hale, 1969; *A History of Chelsea Football Club,* Pelham, 1969; *World Cup, 1970,* R. Hale, 1970; *Spurs Again: The Story of the League Cup Season, 1970-71,* R. Hale, 1971; *Romansgate in Thanet,* 2nd edition, W. E. White, 1972; *Tottenham Hotspur, F.C.: The Official History,* R. Hale, 1972.

Contributor of over one thousand short stories to *People, Sunday Dispatch, Evening News, Lilliput, Reynolds News, Courier, Birmingham Evening News,* and other publications, and of articles on copywriting to professional journals.

SIDELIGHTS: Ralph L. Finn speaks German, French, Italian, and Spanish. *Avocational interests:* Sports (particularly soccer), chess, music.†

* * *

FISCHER, Fritz 1908-

PERSONAL: Born March 5, 1908, in Ludwigsstadt, Germany; son of Max (a railroad inspector) and Emilie (Schreider) Fischer; married Margarete Lauth, March 25, 1942; children: Anke (Mrs. Kersten Hochbaum), Jan-Hinrich. *Education:* Attended University of Erlangen, 1926-28; University of Berlin, Dr.theol., 1934, Dr.phil., 1937. *Politics:* "Sympathizing with Social Democrats." *Religion:* Lutheran. *Home:* Frenssenstrasse 19 a, 2 Hamburg 55 (Blankenese), West Germany. *Office:* Historisches Seminar der Universitaet, Von-Melle-Park 6 IX, 2 Hamburg 13, West Germany.

CAREER: University of Berlin, Berlin, Germany, assistant professor of church history, 1934-39, assistant professor of history, 1939-42; University of Hamburg, Hamburg, Germany, associate professor, 1942-48, professor of history, 1948-73, professor emeritus, 1973—, director of history seminars, 1948-73. Visiting professor at universities in United States, 1952-53, 1964; guest professor, University of Notre Dame, 1954, St. Antony's College, Oxford, 1969-70; lecturer at universities in Austria, Belgium, Canada, Denmark, England, France, Holland, Japan, Poland, and Switzerland, 1961—; participant in history symposium in London and Oxford, 1950. *Military service:* German Air Force, 1939-45; became first lieutenant; prisoner of war with American army, 1945-47. *Member:* P.E.N., Mitarbeiter des Internationalen Schulbuchinstituts (Brunswick, West Germany), British Academy (corresponding member), Verband der Historiker Deutschlands, Kommission fuer Geschichte der politischen Parteien und des Parlamentarismus (Bonn), Mitarbeiter der Friedrich Ebert-Stiftung (Bonn). *Awards, honors:* Fellow, Institute for Advanced Study, 1964-65; Bundesverdienstkreuz der Bundesrepublik Deutschland, 1974, D. Litt., University of Sussex, 1974, University of East Anglia, 1981, Oxford University, 1983.

WRITINGS: Moritz August von Bethmann-Hollweg und der Protestantismus: Religion, Rechts- und Staatsgedanke (title means "Moritz August von Bethmann-Hollweg and Protestantism: His Religion and His Ideas of State and Law"), Verlag dr. Emil Ebering (Berlin), 1938, Kraus Reprint, 1965; *Ludwig Nicolovius: Rokoko, Reform, Restauration* (biography of Ludwig Nicolovius), Verlag W. Kohlhammer (Stuttgart), 1939; (contributor) Alfred Herrmann, editor, *Festschrift Ludwig Bergstraesser,* Droste Verlag, 1954; *Deutsche Kriegsziele Revolutionierung und Separatfrieden im Osten, 1914-1918,* R. Oldenbourg Verlag, 1959.

Griff nach der Weltmacht: Die Kriegszielpolitik des Kaiserlichen Deutschland, 1914/18, Droste Verlag, 1961, 4th edition, 1970, translation published as *Germany's Aims in the First*

World War, Norton, 1967; *Weltmacht oder Niedergang,* Europaeische Verlagsanstalt (Frankfurt), 1965, translation by Lancelot L. Farrar, Robert Kimber, and Rita Kimber published as *World Power or Decline: The Controversy over Germany's Aims in the First World War,* Norton, 1974; *Krieg der Illusionen: Die deutsche Politik von 1911 bis 1914,* Droste Verlag, 1969, 2nd edition, 1970, translation by Marion Jackson published as *War of Illusions: German Policies from 1911 to 1914,* Norton, 1975.

Der Erste Weltkrieg und das Deutsche Geschichtsbild, Droste Verlag, 1977; *Buendnis der Eliten: Zur Kontinuitaet der Machtstrukturen in Deutschland 1871-1945,* Droste Verlag, 1979; (contributor) *Crisis Diplomacy,* Deakin University (Victoria, Australia), Volume IV: *The End of the Concert,* 1982; *Juli 1914: Wir sind nicht hineingeschlittert. Das Staatsgeheimnisum die Riezler-Tagebuecher,* Rowohlt Verlag (Hamburg), 1983.

Contributor to *Historische Zeitschrift.* Editor, *Hamburger Studien zur neueren Geschichte,* 1965-68; co-editor, *Studien zur modernen Geschichte,* 1971—.

SIDELIGHTS: Fritz Fischer told *CA:* "After World War II historical research was, naturally enough, mostly concentrated on this war and on the dark characteristics of Nazi Germany. Looking back critically at the events which led up to the Third Reich, I felt it was impossible for me to accept the assumption that this was an isolated phenomenon but rather that there were conditions—spiritual, psychological, economic, social, and constitutional—which made the seizure of power by Hitler possible. This consideration led me back to the spirit and aims of Wilhelminian Germany and thus to the elements of continuity in German history from 1890 to 1945."

The resulting book caused a resounding scandal. "When the German edition of [*Germany's Aims in the First World War*] first appeared in 1961," writes Bernard D. Williams in *Best Sellers,* "it naturally caused a bitter reaction within Germany since Professor Fischer has uncovered many unpublished documents from various archives that reveal how the industrial and intellectual circles, as well as the military, supported the aggressive policy of making Germany a great world power." Describing the book as "a blow of almost lethal destructiveness," Geoffrey Barraclough reasons in the *New York Review of Books* that it is "no wonder that Fischer's book . . . has been the subject of violent controversy. . . . His arguments were too destructive of orthodox German mythology, his documentation too solid simply to be brushed aside. It is good that there should be controversy, because the questions Fischer raises transcend the normal disputes of academic history. What is at issue is not simply the validity of the specific evidence he cites, or of the conclusions he draws from it, but the character of an epoch. . . . Fischer shows beyond all reasonable doubt that the so-called 'war-guilt clause' which attributed 'responsibility' to Germany was essentially correct. This is why his book produced such an uproar in the Federal Republic."

Since the appearance of Fischer's book in Germany, historians have digested its contents and followed up with a number of new books. Barraclough contends that "it may be said of all this work . . . that its effect has been to confirm, rather than impair, the 'Fischer thesis.' It is possible that Fischer overshoots his mark at certain points; but few, if any, foreign historians have rejected his interpretation, and even in Germany it is remarkable how closely Fischer's leading opponent, Gerhard Ritter, came to adopting Fischer's views in the last volume of *Staatskunst und Kriegshandwerk* which appeared before his death."

Writing in the *New York Times Book Review,* George L. Mosse suggests that "Fischer has . . . written a prophetic book about the ambitions of nations—the 'Great Power complex,' as it might be called. . . . The Germany example shows how self-confidence led to a quest for domination, war and ultimate destruction through an excessive faith in the nation's power and might. This seems to be the moral of this important book, and as such it is relevant far beyond that period with which it deals and that nation whose particular war aims it analyzes."

BIOGRAPHICAL/CRITICAL SOURCES: Ernst W. Graf Lynar, editor, *Deutsche Kriegsziele, 1914-1918: Eine Diskussion,* Ullstein Buecher (Frankfurt), 1964; *Best Sellers,* December 1, 1967; *New York Times Book Review,* December 24, 1967; *Times Literary Supplement,* February 22, 1968; *New York Review of Books,* March 14, 1968; John A. Moses, *The War Aims of Imperial Germany: Professor Fritz Fischer and His Critics,* University of Queensland Papers, 1968; George W. Hallgarten, *Deutsche Selbstschau nach 50 Jahren: Fritz Fischer, seine Gegner und Vorlaeufer,* Europaeische Verlagsanstalt, 1969; Imanuel Geiss, *Studien ueber Geschichte und Geschichtswissenschaft,* Suhrkamp Verlag, 1972; Geiss and B J. Wendt, editors, *Festschrift fuer Fritz Fischer: Deutschland in der Weltpolitik des 19. und 20. Jahrhunderts,* Bertelsmann Universitaetsverlag, 1973; Moses, *The Politics of Illusion: The Fischer Controversy in German Historiography,* Harper, 1975; Dirk Stegmann, Wendt, and P.-Chr. Witt, editors, *Festschrift fuer Fritz Fischer: Industrielle Gesellschaft und politisches System,* Verlag Neve Gesellschaft, 1978.

* * *

FISCHER, George 1923-

PERSONAL: Born May 5, 1923, in Berlin, Germany; U.S. citizen by birth; son of Louis and Bertha (Markoosha) Fischer; married Elinor Halsted, 1958 (divorced, 1972); children: Sara, Mark. *Education:* University of Wisconsin, B.A., 1947; Harvard University, Ph.D., 1952. *Office:* Ph.D. Program in Sociology, Graduate School and University Center, City University of New York, 33 West 42nd St., New York, N.Y. 10036.

CAREER: Harvard University, Cambridge, Mass., associate of Russian Research Center, 1947-61; Brandeis University, Waltham, Mass., assistant professor, 1953-58, associate professor of history, 1958-60; Cornell University, Ithaca, N.Y., professor of political science, 1961-65; Columbia University, New York City, lecturer in sociology, 1965-69, faculty member of Russian Institute; City University of New York, professor of sociology at Richmond College (now College of Staten Island), Staten Island, N.Y., 1969-73, and Graduate School and University Center, New York City, 1969—. *Military service:* U.S. Army, 1942-46; became captain. *Member:* Movement for a New Society, New Jewish Agenda, Phi Beta Kappa. *Awards, honors:* Harvard University Society of Fellows junior fellowship, 1949-53; Center for Advanced Study in the Behavioral Sciences fellow, 1958-59; Social Science Research Council faculty research fellowship, 1959-60; Guggenheim fellowship, 1964.

WRITINGS: Russian Emigre Politics (monograph), East European Fund, Ford Foundation, 1951; *Soviet Opposition to Stalin,* Harvard University Press, 1952, published as *Soviet Opposition to Stalin: A Case Study in World War II,* Greenwood Press, 1970; (editor with Hugh McLean) *Russian Thought and Politics,* Books for Libraries, 1957; *Russian Liberalism: From Gentry to Intelligentsia,* Harvard University Press, 1958; *The Personal Papers of Leon Trotsky* (monograph), Harvard University Library, 1959.

Science and Politics: The New Sociology in the Soviet Union (monograph), Center for International Studies, Cornell University, 1964; (editor) *The Soviet Union, Arms Control, and Disarmament: Background Materials on Soviet Attitudes* (monograph), School of International Affairs, Columbia University, 1965; *American Research on Soviet Society: Guide to Specialized Studies since World War II by Sociologists, Psychologists, and Anthropologists in the United States,* New York State Education Department, 1967; (editor) *Science and Ideology in Soviet Society,* Atherton, 1967; *The Soviet System and Modern Society: Career Patterns versus Western Theories,* Atherton, 1968; *Ideology and Opinion Making* (monograph), Bureau of Applied Social Research, Columbia University, 1969.

(With Walter Schenkel) *Social Structure and Social Change in Eastern Europe: Guide to Specialized Studies Published in the West since World War II in English, French, and German,* Foreign Area Materials Center (New York), 1970; (editor) *The Revival of American Socialism: Selected Papers of the Socialist Scholars Conference,* Oxford University Press, 1971; *What's What on Staten Island: Guide to Community Services* (monograph), Richmond College of the City University of New York, 1971; *Urban Higher Education in the United States: A Study for the Chancellor of the City University of New York* (monograph), Central Office of the City University of New York, 1974; *Ways to Self-Rule: Beyond Marxism and Anarchism,* Exposition Press, 1978.

* * *

FISCHER, Gerald C(harles) 1928-

PERSONAL: Born April 11, 1928, in Buffalo, N.Y.; son of Charles Arthur and Ivalo Fischer; married Janice Everingham, August 29, 1953; children: Alyson Beth. *Education:* University of Buffalo (now State University of New York at Buffalo), B.S., 1952; Columbia University, M.S., 1953, Ph.D., 1960. *Politics:* Republican. *Religion:* Episcopalian. *Home:* 7616 Huron St., Philadelphia, Pa. 19118. *Office:* 1432 Philadelphia National Bank Building, Philadelphia, Pa. 19107.

CAREER: Marine Midland Corp., Buffalo, N.Y., portfolio analyst, 1954-56; Jamestown Community College, Jamestown, N.Y., instructor in economics and banking, 1956-57; Canisius College, Buffalo, assistant professor of banking and finance, 1957-58, 1960-62; Indiana University, Graduate School of Business, Bloomington, 1962-67, began as assistant professor, became associate professor of finance; Temple University, Philadelphia, Pa., research professor of business administration, 1967—. Consultant to American Bankers Association, 1964-65, Robert Morris Associates, 1967—, and other corporations. *Military service:* U.S. Army, 1945-48; became staff sergeant. *Member:* American Finance Association. *Awards, honors:* Ford Foundation faculty research grant, 1964-65.

WRITINGS: Bank Holding Companies, Columbia University Press, 1961; *American Banking Structure,* Columbia University Press, 1968; (editor) *Commercial Banking 1975 and 1980: A First Step in Long-Range Planning,* Robert Morris Associates, 1970; (co-author) *Economic Power of Commercial Banks,* American Bankers Association, 1971; *The Future of the Registered Bank Holding Company,* Association of Registered Bank Holding Companies, 1972; (co-author) *Credit Unions and the Credit Union Industry,* New York Institute of Finance, 1977; (co-author) *Credit Department Management,* Robert Morris Associates, 1980; *The Prime: Myth and Reality,* Temple University, 1982. Contributor to financial journals.

WORK IN PROGRESS: A book on bank holding company developments from 1956-1981.

* * *

FLUMIANI, Carlo M(aria) 1911-

PERSONAL: Born August 15, 1911, in Trieste, Italy; son of Aurelio and Irma Flumiani; married Cristina Capprelli, 1937; children: Victor, Leo. *Education:* University of Milan, Ph.D., 1934; London School of Economics and Political Science, postdoctoral study, 1936. *Religion:* Roman Catholic. *Home:* 22 Western Ave., Gloucester, Mass. *Office:* Department of Finance, Boston College, Chestnut Hill, Mass. 02167.

CAREER: Harvard University fellow in France, 1938; University of Santa Clara, Santa Clara, Calif., assistant professor of political science and head of department, 1946-53; St. Joseph's College, Albuquerque, N.M., dean of School of Business Administration, 1953-56; Boston College, Chestnut Hill, Mass., associate professor of finance, 1956—. Director of Institute for Economic and Financial Research. Originator of cylinder theory for investment measurement. *Member:* American Economic Association.

WRITINGS—Published by Library of Wall Street, except as indicated: *The Cylinder Theory,* 1961, 2nd revised edition, 1967; *The Warning Signals,* 1963; *How to Read the Wall Street Journal for Pleasure and for Profit,* 1964; *The Technical Wall Street Encyclopedia,* 1964.

Stock Market Charting for Fun and Profit, 1965; *The Stock Market Trading Secrets of the Late Jesse Livermore,* 1965; *Teenager's Guide to the Stock Market,* 1965; *The Wall Street Diet and Reducing Guidebook,* 1965; *The Wall Street Cook Book,* 1966; *Stock Market Games People Play to Win,* 1967; *Young People Introduction to the World of Wall Street,* 1967; *How to Develop the Creative Powers of Your Imagination,* Library of Science, 1967; *I Was a Teenage Bankrupt, and How I Recouped My Losses and Made a Fortune in the Stock Market,* 1968. Also author of a number of shorter works, most of them on the subjects of finance and stock market analysis, published by Library of Wall Street.

All published by American Classical College Press: *Stock Market Manual for Teenagers,* 1973; *Teenager's Guide to Economics and Finance,* two volumes, 1973; *The Wall Street Manual for Teenagers,* 1973; *History's Key to Stock Market Profits,* 1974; *How to Protect Your Money from the Destructive Powers of Inflation, Business Depressions, Political Turmoil, Wars, Revolutions and How to Double Your Patrimony Safely Every Five Years,* 1974; *Dominating the Business and Political World,* 1974; *Seven Unusual Business Careers: Guaranteed Maximal Profit Potential for the Intelligent College Graduate and the Daring Businessman,* 1974; *Silver, Gold, and the Approaching Revolution in the International Monetary System,* 1974; *The Work Efficiency Organizer and Life Perfector,* 1974.

The Chart Encyclopedia of Wall Street Technical Action, 1975; *Elliott Wave Theory in Projection Charts,* two volumes, 1975; *The Collapse of Gold and the Tragic Dilemma of the Swiss Banks,* 1976; *The Decline and Decay of American Education,* 1976; *The New Dictionary of Strange and Ingenious Stock*

Market Tricks the Experts Follow in Their Search for Wealth, 1976; *The Historical Function of the Large Corporation,* two volumes, 1976; *Three Ways for an Investor with Very Little Money to Make a Killing in the Stock Market,* 1976.

The Large Corporation, the Perversion of the Democratic Order, and the Corporate State, 1977; *The Laws of History and the Caprice of Men,* 1977; *The Method,* 1977; *The New Expanded Dictionary of Stock Market Charts,* 1977; *The Subtle Art of Reading Stock Market Charts as a Guide to Successful Scalping Operations,* 1977; *The Subtle Operative Techniques on How to Make a Fortune in a Bear Market When Prices Decline Sharply and May Prepare the Ground for a Robust Advance,* 1977; *Managing the Large Corporation in a World of Conflicting and Antagonistic Forces,* 1977; *The Survival of the Leadership Corporation and the Corporate State,* 1977; *The Winning Power of Stock Market Charts,* 1977; *Economics: The Essential Knowledge Which Everybody, but Absolutely Everybody Ought to Possess of Economics and Economic Forecasting,* 1978; *Stock Market and Wall Street: The Essential Knowledge Which Everybody, but Absolutely Everybody Ought to Have of the Stock Market and Wall Street,* 1978; *Stock Market Charts: The Essential Knowledge of Stock Market Charts, How to Interpret and Apply Them Which Everybody, but Absolutely Everybody Who Is Interested in Speculation Ought to Know,* 1978.

(Editor) *Collection of the Best Critical Studies Which Have Appeared in the "Catholic Activist,"* 1980; *The Dynamic Substance and Power of the Theory of Inventiveness,* 1982. Also author of dozens of shorter works, most of them on the subjects of finance and stock market analysis, published by American Classical College Press.

All published by Institute for Economic and Financial Research: *The Logical Powers of Stock Market Action,* 1977; *The Wave Theory Flow of Speculative Matter into the Active Cylinder Theory Stream,* 1980; *The Lessons of a Famous Course in the Techniques of Stock Market Charts,* 1981; *The Physiology and Psychology of Stock Market Charts,* 1981; *The Theory of Inventiveness in Schematic Representations,* 1982. Also author of several shorter works, most of them on the subjects of finance and stock market analysis, published by Institute for Economic and Financial Research.

SIDELIGHTS: Carlo M. Flumiani told *CA* that he believes "all human events and the course of history have a divine origin and a divine goal."†

* * *

FLYNN, George L. 1931-

PERSONAL: Born November 2, 1931, in Chicago, Ill.; son of Clifford Joseph (a traffic manager) and Louise (Maloney) Flynn; married Jill Gilbert, October 12, 1957; children: Kathleen, George Thomas, William Clifford. *Education:* University of Detroit, B.S., 1953. *Politics:* Independent. *Religion:* Roman Catholic. *Home:* 97 Minnehaha Blvd., Oakland, N.J. 07436.

CAREER: Prentice-Hall, Inc., Englewood Cliffs, N.J., 1957-67, began as field representative, became editor; Simon & Flynn, Inc., New York, N.Y., vice-president, 1967-71; freelance writer, editor, and film producer, 1971—. *Military service:* U.S. Air Force, 1954-56; became first lieutenant. *Awards, honors:* Award from Council on International Nontheatrical Events and Ohio State award, both 1971, for television documentary "A Man Named Lombardi."

WRITINGS: Vince Lombardi on Football, two volumes, New York Graphic Society, 1973, revised edition, distributed by Van Nostrand, 1981; *The Vince Lombardi Scrapbook,* Grosset, 1976; *Commitment to Excellence* (also see below), American Telephone & Telegraph, 1978; (with Ernest M. Vandeweghe) *Growing with Sports: A Parent's Guide to the Young Athlete,* Prentice-Hall, 1979.

Television production: "Vince Lombardi's The Art and Science of Football" (a series of twelve half-hour films), CBS-TV, 1969-70; "A Man Named Lombardi," NBC-TV, 1971; "The Rivals," pilot production, 1972; "This Was Boxing," 1974; "Boxing's Biggest Showdown," 1981.

Also author of *The Expert's Sports Quiz Book, The Schenley Football Annuals,* 1977, 1978, 1979, and two film productions, "Commitment to Excellence" (sales motivational film), 1976, and "The Equitable Life Sportsmedicine Series" (sixteen half-hour video tapes), 1981-82.

SIDELIGHTS: George L. Flynn played varsity basketball in college and has worked with many well-known sports figures, including Vince Lombardi, Red Smith, and Howard Cosell, in the production of his films and books.

* * *

FOGARTY, Jonathan Titulescu, Esq.
See FARRELL, James T(homas)

* * *

FOGARTY, Michael P(atrick) 1916-

PERSONAL: Born October 3, 1916, in Maymyo, Burma; son of Philip Christopher and Mabel (Pye) Fogarty; married Phyllis Clark, September 11, 1939; children: Sally Margaret, Priscilla Mary, Bernard Michael Charles, Kieran Patrick. *Education:* Christ Church, Oxford, B.A. (with first class honors), 1938, M.A., 1941. *Politics:* Labour, 1934-59; Liberal, 1959—. *Religion:* Roman Catholic. *Home:* Red Copse, Foxcombe Rd., Boars Hill, Oxford, England. *Office:* Institute for Family and Environmental Research, 1/2 Castle Lane, London SW1E 6DR, England.

CAREER: Oxford University, Nuffield College, Oxford, England, research staff, 1941-44, fellow, 1944-51; University of Wales, University College, Cardiff, Montague Burton Professor of Industrial Relations and head of department, 1951-66; Political and Economic Planning (independent social research institute), London, England, consultant, 1966-68; Economic and Social Research Institute, Dublin, Ireland, professor and director, 1968-72; Centre for Studies in Social Policy, London, deputy director, 1973-78; Policy Studies Institute, London, deputy director, 1978-82; Institute for Family and Environmental Research, London, director, 1981—. Research officer, Ministry of Town and Country Planning, London, 1944-45; research associate, National Institute of Economic and Social Research, London, 1950-51; visiting professor, University of Notre Dame, 1956; professor associate, Brunel University, and Administrative Staff College, 1973—. Former chairman of Oxford City Labour Party, and municipal and parliamentary candidate. Liberal party, vice-president, 1964-66, parliamentary candidate, 1964, 1966, 1974. County councillor, Oxfordshire and district councillor, Vale of White Horse. *Military service:* British Army, Royal Artillery, 1939-41; discharged as lieutenant after being wounded at Dunkirk.

MEMBER: British Institute of Management, Association of University Teachers (vice-president, 1964-66), Newman Association (president, 1957-59; honorary president, 1966—), Catholic Social Guild (chairman, 1959-63). *Awards, honors:* Doctor of Political and Social Science, University of Louvain, 1964.

WRITINGS: Prospects of the Industrial Areas of Great Britain, Methuen, 1944; (editor) *Further Studies in Economic Organisation,* Methuen, 1947; *Plan Your Own Industries* (regional planning), Basil Blackwell, 1947; *Town and Country Planning,* Hutchinson, 1948; *Economic Control,* Routledge & Kegan Paul, 1955; *Personality and Group Relations in Industry,* Longmans, Green, 1956; *Christian Democracy in Western Europe, 1820-1953,* University of Notre Dame Press, 1957.

The Just Wage, Geoffrey Chapman, 1961; *Under-Governed and Over-Governed,* Geoffrey Chapman, 1962; *The Rules of Work,* Geoffrey Chapman, 1964; *Company and Corporation—One Law?,* Geoffrey Chapman, 1965; *Wider Business Objectives: American Thinking and Experience,* Political and Economic Planning, 1966; *A Companies Act 1970?,* Political and Economic Planning, 1967; (with Rhona Rapoport and Robert Rapoport) *Women and Top Jobs: The Next Move,* Political and Economic Planning, 1967.

(With others) *Women in Top Jobs: Four Studies in Achievement,* Allen & Unwin, 1971; (with Rhona Rapoport and Robert Rapoport) *Sex, Career and Family,* Sage Publications, 1971; *Irish Entrepreneurs Speak for Themselves,* Economic and Social Research Institute (Dublin), 1973; *Company Responsibilities and Participation,* Political and Economic Planning, 1975; *Forty to Sixty: How We Waste the Middle-Aged,* Bedford Square Press, 1975; *Work and Industrial Relations in the European Community,* Political and Economic Planning, 1975.

Retirement Age and Retirement Costs, Policy Studies Institute, 1980; (with Eileen Reid) *Differentials for Managers and Skilled Manual Workers,* PSI Press, 1980; (with Isobel Allen and Patricia Walters) *Women in Top Jobs, 1968-1979,* Heinemann, 1981; (editor) *Retirement Policy: The Next Fifty Years,* Heinemann, 1982; (editor with Robert Rapoport and Rhona Rapoport) *Families in Britain,* Routledge & Kegan Paul, 1982.

Author of monographs on industrial and social topics; also author of scripts for British Broadcasting Corp. and independent television. Contributor to professional journals in England, western Europe, and the United States. Former British correspondent for *Commonweal;* deputy editor, *Economist,* 1946-47.

WORK IN PROGRESS: Research on the social role of the churches in northwestern Europe, and on the problem of the older worker and retirement.

SIDELIGHTS: Michael P. Fogarty speaks French and German, reads Spanish, Italian, Dutch, and Latin, and is learning Russian. *Avocational interests:* Swimming, walking.

* * *

FOGARTY, Robert S(tephen) 1938-

PERSONAL: Born August 30, 1938, in Brooklyn, N.Y.; son of Michael and Gretta Fogarty; married Geraldine Wolpman, December 30, 1961; children: David, Suzanne. *Education:* Fordham University, B.S.S., 1960; University of Denver, M.A., 1962, Ph.D., 1968. *Home:* 216 Fairfield Pike, Yellow Springs, Ohio 45387. *Office: Antioch Review,* Antioch College, Yellow Springs, Ohio 45387.

CAREER: Michigan State University, East Lansing, assistant professor of American studies, 1963-68; Antioch College, Yellow Springs, Ohio, 1968—, began as associate professor, currently professor of history, chairman of department, 1970—. Director, ACM/GLCA program in the humanities, Newberry Library, 1978-79. Guest lecturer at various institutions, including Ball State University, Hope College, University of Michigan, and University of the Pacific. Commentator on historical topics for Organization of American Historians and American Political Science Association. Has delivered papers to professional organizations. Consultant to various educational projects, including National Endowment for the Humanities, Film Project, 1977, and Cooperative Education Training Center, 1980. *Member:* Organization of American Historians, American Studies Association (member of executive board of Ohio-Indiana chapter, 1979-81), National Historic Sites Association (member of executive committee, 1975-80), Society for Editors of Scholarly Journals.

AWARDS, HONORS: Under Fogarty's editorship, *Antioch Review* received grants from the Coordinating Council of Literary Magazines, Ohio Arts Council, and National Endowment for the Arts; Michigan Historical Commission research grant, 1970; Antioch Ford Foundation Humanities grant, 1972; American Philosophical Society travel grant, 1975; *Dictionary of American Communal and Utopian History* was named Outstanding Reference Book of 1980 by the American Library Association, 1981; M. K. Cooper Award for Literary Excellence, Ohio Library Association, 1981, for *Antioch Review;* Coordinating Council of Literary Magazines, editor's fellowship, 1981.

WRITINGS: (Contributor) Kerry Smith, editor, *In Search of Leaders,* Association for Higher Education, 1967; (editor) *American Utopianism,* F. T. Peacock, 1972, 2nd edition, 1974; (editor with Lawrence Grauman) *Letters from a Self-Made Merchant to His Son,* Outerbridge & Dientsfrey, 1974; (contributor) Robert Walker, editor, *American Studies: Topics and Sources,* Greenwood Press, 1976; (contributor) *Simple Gifts,* William Benton Museum of the Arts, 1980; *Dictionary of American Communal and Utopian History,* Greenwood Press, 1980; *The Righteous Remnant: The House of David,* Kent State Press, 1981. Consulting editor for nineteen-volume "American Utopian Adventure," Porcupine Press, 1975. Contributor to history and American studies journals. Editor of *Antioch Review,* 1977—; member of editorial board, *Alternative Issues,* 1977—.

WORK IN PROGRESS: The Communal World: 1865-1914.

BIOGRAPHICAL/CRITICAL SOURCES: New York Times Book Review, January 31, 1982; *Times Literary Supplement,* November 5, 1982.

* * *

FONSECA, Aloysius Joseph 1915-

PERSONAL: Born January 16, 1915, in Karachi, India; son of Alex (a printer) and Mary (Raymond) Fonseca. *Education:* University of Madras, M.A.; Economische Hogeschool, Ph.D.; Gregorian University, Rome, Italy, Th. and L.Ph. *Office: La Civilta Cattolica,* Via di Porta Pincianal, 00187 Rome, Italy.

CAREER: Roman Catholic priest, member of Society of Jesus (Jesuits). Writer; former editor of *Social Action* (monthly), Indian Social Institute, New Delhi; member of editorial board, *La Civilta Cattolica.* Professor of industrial relations in several Jesuit colleges in India; professor of economics at Pontifical Gregorian University, Rome. Member of delegation of the Holy See to F.A.O., Rome. *Member:* Indian Economic Association.

WRITINGS: The Citizen and the State, 3rd edition, Indian Institute of Social Order, 1955; *A Textbook of Civics and Indian Administration,* Orient Longmans, 1961; *Wage Determination and Organized Labour in India,* Oxford University Press, 1964; (editor) *Trade and Development,* Indian Social Institute, 1968; (editor) *Challenge of Poverty in India,* Vikas, 1971; *Labour Problems in the Economic and Social Development of India,* International Institute for Labour Studies (Geneva), 1970; *Wage Issues in a Developing Economy: The Indian Experience,* Oxford University Press (Bombay), 1975; (editor) *The Marxian Dilemma: Transformation of Values to Prices,* South Asia Books, 1980. Contributor to *La Civilta Cattolica.*

* * *

FORD, D(ouglas) W(illiam) Cleverley 1914-

PERSONAL: Born March 4, 1914, in Sheringham, England; son of Arthur James (a clerk) and Mildred (Cleverley) Ford; married Olga Mary Gilbart-Smith, June 28, 1939. *Education:* University of London, A.L.C.D. (with first class honors) and B.D., 1936, M.Th., 1941. *Home:* Rostrevor, Lingfield, Surrey RH7 6BZ, England.

CAREER: Ordained Anglican priest, 1937; London College of Divinity, London, England, tutor, 1936-39; curate in Bridlington, England, 1939-42; vicar in Hampstead, London, 1942-55, and in Kensington Gore, England, 1955-74; senior chaplain to Archbishop of Canterbury, England, 1975-80. Director of College of Preachers, 1960-73; chairman, Queen Alexandra's House Association, 1965-74; governor, Westminster City School, 1965-74; rural dean of Westminster, 1965-74; prebendary of St. Paul's Cathedral, London, 1968; canon of York, 1969; chaplain to Queen Elizabeth II, 1973—; tutor, Southwark Ordination course, 1980—; lecturer, Wey Institute of Religious Studies, 1980—; Six Preacher of Canterbury Cathedral, 1982—. *Member:* Athenaeum Club (London).

WRITINGS: Why Men Believe in Jesus Christ, Lutterworth, 1950; *An Expository Preacher's Notebook,* Hodder & Stoughton, 1960, Harper, 1961; *A Theological Preacher's Notebook,* Hodder & Stoughton, 1962; *A Pastoral Preacher's Notebook,* Hodder & Stoughton, 1965; *A Reading of Saint Luke's Gospel,* Lippincott, 1967; *Preaching at the Parish Communion,* Mowbray, Volume I, 1967, Volume II, 1968, Volume III, 1969, Volume VII, 1975; *Preaching Today,* Epworth, 1969.

Preaching through the Christian Year, Mowbray, 1971; *Praying through the Christian Year,* Mowbray, 1973; *Have You Anything to Declare?,* Mowbray, 1973; *Preaching on Special Occasions,* Mowbray, Volume I, 1975, Volume II, 1982; *New Preaching from the Old Testament,* Mowbray, Volume I, 1976, Volume II, 1983; *New Preaching from the New Testament,* Mowbray, Volume I, 1977, Volume II, 1982; *The Ministry of the Word,* Hodder & Stoughton, 1979, Eerdmans, 1980; *Preaching through the Acts of the Apostles,* Mowbray, 1980. Contributor to *Expository Times.*

SIDELIGHTS: D. W. Cleverley Ford told *CA* that he began his writing career as a result of people wishing to read what he had said in lectures and sermons. "Since my spoken word had always been carefully prepared, having been written and rewritten, this was not difficult. Writing for speaking is different from writing for reading, but it is good training in the art of clarity. I believe that a writer's work will be flat if it pays attention only to conveying information couched in a good literary style; it also needs to move the reader. This implies a sense of drama. I suppose a person either has or has not this sense. A rough and ready test of a good piece of writing is whether or not the reader is sorry when he has come to the end."

AVOCATIONAL INTERESTS: Languages, music, gardening, maintaining a country cottage.

* * *

FORD, Elbur
See HIBBERT, Eleanor Burford

* * *

FORREST, Richard S(tockton) 1932-
(Stockton Woods)

PERSONAL: Born May 8, 1932, in Orange, N.J.; son of Williams Kraemer and Georgia (Muller) Forrest; married Frances Anne Reese, December 20, 1952 (divorced May, 1955); married Mary Brumby (an office manager), May 11, 1955; children: (first marriage) Richard; (second marriage) Christopher, Remley, Katherine, Mongin, Bellamy. *Education:* Attended New York Dramatic Workshop, 1950, and University of South Carolina, 1953-55. *Politics:* Democrat. *Religion:* Unitarian Universalist. *Residence:* Old Saybrook, Conn. *Agent:* Harold Ober Associates, 40 East 49th St., New York, N.Y. 10017.

CAREER: Playwright, 1955-58; Lawyers Title Insurance Corp., Richmond, Va., state manager, 1958-68; Chicago Title Insurance Co., Chicago, Ill., vice-president, 1969-72; free-lance writer, 1972—. Vice-president of Connecticut Board of Title Underwriters. *Military service:* U.S. Army, Rangers, 1951-53; served in Korea; became staff sergeant. *Member:* Mystery Writers of America, Authors Guild, Authors League of America. *Awards, honors:* Nominated for Edgar Award from Mystery Writers of America, 1975.

WRITINGS—Mystery novels: *Who Killed Mr. Garland's Mistress,* Pinnacle Books, 1974; *A Child's Garden of Death,* Bobbs-Merrill, 1975; *The Wizard of Death,* Bobbs-Merrill, 1977; *Death through the Looking Glass,* Bobbs-Merrill, 1978; *The Death in the Willows,* Holt, 1979; *The Killing Edge,* Belmont, 1980; *Death at Yew Corner,* Holt, 1981.

Under pseudonym Stockton Woods: *The Laughing Man,* Fawcett, 1980; *Game Bet,* Fawcett, 1981.

Plays: "Cry for the Spring"; "The Meek Cry Loud"; "The Sandhouse."

WORK IN PROGRESS: Fool's Errand, a suspense novel.

SIDELIGHTS: Richard S. Forrest writes that he "spent early years as a playwright until growing family made business a necessity. Resigned position as vice-president of major insurance company on fortieth birthday to write full time—why not?"

BIOGRAPHICAL/CRITICAL SOURCES: Publishers Weekly, December 12, 1980; *Washington Post Book World,* January 18, 1981; *New York Times Book Review,* March 8, 1981; *Chicago Tribune Book World,* April 19, 1981.

* * *

FOSTER, M(ichael) A(nthony) 1939-

PERSONAL: Born July 2, 1939, in Greensboro, N.C.; son of Maurice G. and Helen Anthony (Voltz) Foster; married Judith Ann Forsythe, May 29, 1965; children: Matthew, Eugene.

Education: Attended Syracuse University, 1957-60, and University of Maryland in Europe, Karamursel, Turkey, 1961-62; University of Oregon, B.A., 1964. *Politics:* "Republican; economic conservative, civil rights liberal." *Religion:* Eastern Orthodox. *Home and office:* 5409 Amberhill Dr., Greensboro, N.C. 27405.

CAREER: U.S. Air Force, 1957-62, 1965-76, became captain; held positions as Russian linguist, 1957-62, intelligence officer, 1965-71, missile launch officer, 1971-75, and weapons director, 1975-76; currently affiliated with Piedmont Welding Supply Co., Greensboro, N.C.

WRITINGS—Science fiction; published by DAW Books, except as indicated: *The Warriors of Dawn,* 1975; *Gameplayers of Zan,* 1977; *Day of the Klesh,* 1979; *Waves,* 1980; *The Morphodite,* 1981; (contributor) George R.R. Martin, editor, *New Voices 4,* Berkley Publishing, 1981; *Transformer,* in press.

WORK IN PROGRESS: The Hallucinations of Holden Czelewski, a collection of stories; *Candastara,* a novel.

SIDELIGHTS: M. A. Foster writes: "I have been a science-fiction reader since about age twelve. . . . I would now like to see a greater emphasis in SF be placed on more tradition . . . such as characterization, motivation, depth of backgrounds, subtle emotional effects. SF seems to be headed toward wooden characters and high-technology backgrounds. Since I worked in that kind of environment for fifteen years, I am well acquainted with its limitations, and do not consider the general run of modern SF either inspiring or instructive." Several of Foster's books have been translated into German, Italian, French, and Portuguese.

* * *

FOSTER, Paul 1931-

PERSONAL: Born October 15, 1931, in Salem, N.J.; son of Eldridge M. and Mary (Manning) Foster. *Education:* Rutgers University, B.A., 1954; attended St. John's University Law School, 1955, 1957-58. *Religion:* Protestant. *Home:* 242 East Fifth St., New York, N.Y. 10003.

CAREER: Playwright. La Mama Experimental Theatre Club, New York, N.Y., president and co-founder, 1962—. Foreign lecturer on American theater for Department of State in Europe and South America, 1978, 1980. Taught dramatic writing at University of California, San Diego, 1981, and at New York University, 1982. *Military service:* U.S. Naval Reserve, Judge's Advocate General Corps, 1955-57. *Member:* P.E.N., Dramatist's Guild, Authors League of America, Societe des Auteurs et Compositeurs (Paris), Eugene O'Neill Theatre Foundation.

AWARDS, HONORS: Rockefeller Foundation fellowship for playwriting, 1967, 1968; New York Drama Critics Award, 1968, for *Tom Paine; Elizabeth I* was nominated for a Tony Award, 1972; Creative Artists Public Service grants, 1972, 1974; National Endowment for the Arts fellowship, 1973, 1975; British Arts Council award, 1973, for *Elizabeth I;* Guggenheim literature fellowship, 1974.

WRITINGS: Minnie the Whore, The Birthday, and Other Stories, Ediciones Zodiaco (Caracas), 1962.

Plays: *Hurrah for the Bridge* (one-act; first produced Off-Off Broadway at Caffe Cino, 1963), Canal Ramirez, 1963; *Balls and Other Plays* (contains "Balls," first produced Off-Off Broadway at Cafe La Mama, 1965; "The Recluse," first produced Off-Off Broadway at Cafe La Mama, 1964; "Hurrah for the Bridge," [see above]; "The Hessian Corporal," first produced Off-Off Broadway at Cafe La Mama, 1966), Calder & Boyars, 1967, Samuel French, 1968; *Tom Paine* (full-length; first produced Off-Off Broadway at Cafe La Mama, May 15, 1967; produced on the West End at the Vaudeville Theatre, 1967; produced Off-Broadway at Stage 73, 1968), Calder & Boyars, 1967, Grove Press, 1968; "The Madonna in the Orchard" (full-length; first produced Off-Off Broadway at Cafe La Mama, 1965), published in Germany as *Die Madonna im Apfelhag,* S. Fischer Verlag, 1968, published as *The Madonna in the Orchard,* Breakthrough Press, 1971.

Heimskringla; or, The Stoned Angels (written for television in order to utilize the videospace electronic technique; first produced by National Education Television for "Theatre America" series, 1969), Calder & Boyars, 1970, Samuel French, 1971; "Satyricon" (first produced Off-Broadway at La Mama Theatre, 1972), published in *The Off-Off Broadway Book,* edited by Bruce Mailman and Albert Poland, Bobbs-Merrill, 1972; *Elizabeth I* (first produced on Broadway at the Lyceum Theatre, 1972), Samuel French, 1972; *Silver Queen Saloon* (first produced Off-Broadway at La Mama Theatre, 1973), Samuel French, 1975; *Marcus Brutus* (first produced at Stage West, Springfield, Mass., 1975), Calder & Boyars, 1975.

Unpublished works: "Mellon" (filmscript), first produced by Francis Thompson, Inc. for Exxon Corp., 1981; "The Cop and the Anthem" (filmscript), first produced by Learning Corp. of America, 1982; "When You're Smiling" (filmscript), first produced by Learning Corp. of America, 1982; "A Kiss Is Just a Kiss" (play), first produced at Manhattan Punchline Theatre, February, 1983. Also author of "The House on Lake Geneva," a play, as yet neither published nor produced.

WORK IN PROGRESS: A new musical, book, and lyrics concerning Rasputin.

SIDELIGHTS: Of playwright Paul Foster, Leonard Harris of Columbia Broadcasting System, Inc. comments: "Foster's thinking is original. Here is a man born to write for the theater." William Raidy of the Newhouse National News Service believes, "[*Elizabeth I*] has a vitality and a zest and it is truly an inventive and inspired piece of theater."

In a review of *Marcus Brutus,* Clive Barnes of the *New York Times* writes, "Foster is an important playwright. He wants to push theater beyond its conventionally realistic bounds and to use it as an arena for philosophic and historic thought." Raidy calls *Marcus Brutus* "a compelling fascinating, unusual drama . . . his characters are divinely human." Charles Smith of the *Boston Advocate* writes, "[*Marcus Brutus* is a] play that will leave your mind gasping for air. It is an excellent work."

Foster speaks French and German.

BIOGRAPHICAL/CRITICAL SOURCES: New Statesman, October 27, 1967; *Listener,* November 2, 1967; *Village Voice,* March, 1968; *New Yorker,* April 6, 1968; *Newsweek,* April 8, 1968; *Hudson Review,* summer, 1968; *Los Angeles Free Press,* November 22, 1968; *Long Island Press,* April 6, 1972; *Boston Advocate,* January 12, 1975; *New York Times,* January 20, 1975, June 24, 1978.

* * *

FRANCIS, Dick 1920-

PERSONAL: Born October 31, 1920, in Tenby, Wales; son of George Vincent and Molly (Thomas) Francis; married Mary

Brenchley, June 21, 1947; children: Merrick, Felix. *Education:* Attended Maindenhead County School. *Home:* Penny Chase, Blewbury, Berkshire, England. *Agent:* John Johnson, 45/47 Clerkenwell Green, London, England.

CAREER: Amateur steeplechase rider, 1946-48; professional steeplechase jockey, 1948-57; *Sunday Express,* London, England, racing correspondent, 1957-73; writer. Exercises racehorses in winter; judges hunters at horse shows in summer. *Military service:* Royal Air Force, 1940-46; became flying officer (pilot). *Member:* Crime Writers Association. *Awards, honors:* Steeplechase jockey championship, 1954; Silver Dagger award, Crime Writers Association, 1965, for *For Kicks;* Edgar Allen Poe award, Mystery Writers of America, 1969, for *Forfeit,* and 1980, for *Whip Hand;* Gold Dagger award, Crime Writers Association, 1980, for *Whip Hand.*

WRITINGS—Mystery novels, except as indicated; published by Harper, except as indicated: *The Sport of Queens* (racing autobiography), M. Joseph, 1957, Harper, 1969; *Dead Cert,* Holt, 1962; *Nerve,* 1964; *For Kicks,* 1965; *Odds Against,* M. Joseph, 1965, Harper, 1966; (compiler with John Welcome) *Best Racing and Chasing Stories* (anthology), Faber, 1966; *Flying Finish,* M. Joseph, 1966, Harper, 1967; *Blood Sport,* 1967; *Forfeit,* 1968; *Enquiry,* 1969.

Rat Race, 1970; *Bonecrack,* 1971; *Smokescreen,* 1972; *Slayride,* 1973; *Knock Down,* 1974; *High Stake,* 1975; *In the Frame,* 1976; *Risk,* 1977; *Trial Run,* 1978; *Whip Hand,* 1979; *Reflex,* M. Joseph, 1980, Putnam, 1981; *Twice Shy,* M. Joseph, 1981, Putnam, 1982; *Banker,* M. Joseph, 1982, Putnam, 1983. Contributor to *Horseman's Year, In Praise of Hunting, Stud and Stable,* and other magazines.

WORK IN PROGRESS: Additional mystery novels.

SIDELIGHTS: When steeplejockey Dick Francis retired from horseracing at age thirty-six, he speculated in his autobiography that he would be remembered as "the man who didn't win the National"—England's prestigious Grand National steeplechase. If he hadn't turned to fiction, his prediction might have been correct, but with the publication of his first novel, *Dead Cert,* in 1962, Francis launched a second career that was even more successful than his first. He became a mystery writer. Since that time, Francis has averaged a thriller a year, astounding critics with the fecundity of his imagination and garnering awards such as Britain's Silver Dagger (in 1965 for *For Kicks*) and two Edgars (for *Forfeit* in 1969 and *Whip Hand* in 1980). Since all of his books concern horses, racing still figures in his life, and his affinity for the racetrack actually enhances his prose, according to Julian Symons who writes in the *New York Times Book Review* that "what comes most naturally to [Francis] is also what he does best—writing about the thrills, spills and chills of horse racing."

Before he began writing, Francis experienced one of racing's most publicized "spills" firsthand. In 1956, when he was already a veteran jockey, Francis had the privilege of riding Devon Loch—the Queen Mother's horse—in the annual Grand National. Fifty yards from the finish line, with the race virtually won, the horse inexplicably faltered. Later examination revealed no physical injury and no clue was ever found. "I still don't have the answer," Francis told Pete Axthelm of *Newsweek.* "Maybe he was shocked by the noise of 250,000 people screaming because the royal family's horse was winning. But the fact is that with nothing wrong with him, ten strides from the winning post he fell. The other fact is," he added, "if that mystery hadn't happened, I might never have written all these other ones."

Though each of his novels deals with what many consider a specialized subject, Francis's books have broad appeal. One explanation, offered by Judith Rascoe in the *Christian Science Monitor,* is that "you needn't know or care anything about racing to be his devoted reader." And, writing in the *New York Times,* book reviewer John Leonard agrees: "Not to read Dick Francis because you don't like horses is like not reading Dostoyevsky because you don't like God. . . . Race tracks and God are subcultures. A writer has to have a subculture to stand upon."

Francis's ability to make this subculture come alive for his reader—to create what Rascoe calls "a background of almost Dickensian realism for his stories"—is what sets him apart from other mystery writers, critics say. "In particular," observes Charles Champlin in the *Los Angeles Times,* "his rider's view of the strains and spills, disappointments and exultations of the steeplechase is breathtaking, a far cry from the languid armchair detecting of other crime solvers." Writing in the *London Magazine,* John Welcome expresses similar admiration, praising especially Francis's ability to infuse his races with a significance that extends beyond the Jockey Club milieu: "One can hear the smash of birch, the creak of leather and the rattle of whips. The sweat, the strain, the tears, tragedies and occasional triumphs of the racing game are all there, as well as its seductive beauty. In this—as in much else—no other racing novelist can touch him. He has made racing into a microcosm of the contemporary world."

While critics initially speculated that Francis's specialized knowledge would provide only limited fictional opportunities, most have since changed their minds. "It is fascinating to see how many completely fresh and unexpected plots he can concoct about horses," marvels Anthony Boucher in the *New York Times Book Review.* Philip Pelham takes this approbation one step further, writing in *London Magazine* that "Francis improves with every book as both a writer of brisk, lucid prose and as a concocter of ingenious and intricately worked-out plots." His racetrack thrillers deal with such varied storylines as crooks transporting horses by air (*Flying Finish*), stolen stallions (*Blood Sport*), and a jockey who has vanished in Norway (*Slayride*). To further preserve the freshness of his fiction, Francis creates a new protagonist for each novel and often develops subplots around fields unrelated to racing. "His books," notes Axthelm, "take him and his readers on global explorations as well as into crash courses in ventures like aviation, gold mining and, in *Reflex,* amateur photography."

Notwithstanding such variations in plot and theme, Francis is known as a formula writer whose novels, while well-written, are ultimately predictable. In all the Francis novels, writes John Welcome, "the hard-done-by chap [is] blindly at grips with an unknown evil, the threads of which he gradually unravels. Frequently—perhaps too frequently—he is subjected to physical torture described in some detail. His heroes are hard men used to injury and pain and they learn to dish it out as once they had to learn to take it. Racing has made them stoics."

Barry Bauska, writing in *The Armchair Detective,* offers a more detailed version of the "typical" Francis thriller: "At the outset something has happened that looks wrong (a jockey is set down by a board of inquiry that seemed predetermined to find him guilty; a horse falls going over a final hurdle it had seemed to clear; horses perfectly ready to win consistently fail to do so). The narrator protagonist (usually not a detective, but always inherently curious) begins to poke around to try to discover what has occurred. In so doing he inevitably pokes too hard and strikes a hornets' nest. The rest of the novel then centers on a critical struggle between the searcher-after-truth and the mysterious agent of evil, whose villainy had upset things in the first place.''

While a number of Francis's books include a love story, a much more pressing theme, according to Peter Axthelm, is that of pain. ''Again and again,'' he writes in *Newsweek,* ''his villains probe the most terrifying physical or psychic weakness in his heroes. A lifetime's most treasured mementos are destroyed by mindless hired thugs; an already crippled hand is brutally smashed until it must be amputated. The deaths in Francis novels usually occur 'off-camera.' The tortures are more intimate affairs, with the reader forced to watch at shudderingly close range.''

The prevalence of such violence, coupled with Francis's tendency to paint the relationship between hero and villain as a confrontation between Good and Evil, makes some reviewers uneasy. In his *Times Literary Supplement* review of *Risk,* for example, Alex de Jong comments that ''characterization is sometimes thin and stylized, especially the villains, out to inflict pain upon the accountant who has uncovered their villainy, crooked businessmen and trainers, all a little too well dressed, florid and unexpectedly brutal bullies, created with a faint hint of paranoia.'' Francis, however, justifies the punishment he metes out to his characters as something his fans have come to expect. ''Somehow the readers like to read about it,'' he told Judy Klemesrud in the *New York Times Book Review.* ''But I don't subject them to anything I wouldn't put up with myself. This old body has been knocked around quite a bit.''

While the violence of his early novels is largely external, his later novels emphasize more internal stress, according to critics who believe that this shift has added a new dimension to Francis's work. *London Magazine*'s John Welcome, for instance, comments that in *Reflex,* a 1980 publication, Francis's lessened emphasis on brutality has enabled him to ''flesh out his characters. The portrait of Philip Nore, the mediocre jockey nearing the end of his career, is created with real insight; as is the interpretation of his relations with the horses he rides.'' And, writing in *The Armchair Detective,* Barry Bauska expresses a similar view: ''In recent years, though the plots may run along similar lines, Francis' focus has been increasingly directed at the protagonist himself, and at considering what goes into the making not so much of a 'hero' as of a good man. This line . . . seems plainly the direction of Francis' future development as a novelist. In such works survival is still a key concept—'everyone lives on a precipice'—but it is no longer the ability/capacity to endure the villain's tortures, but rather the strength to prevail over one's own self doubts and private fears. Surely it is not mere coincidence that as a focus of tension physical pain is being supplanted by psychological strains as Mr. Francis himself grows farther and farther away from his riding days. The result of course is that Dick Francis is becoming less a writer of thrillers and more a creator of literature.''

MEDIA ADAPTATIONS: Dead Cert was filmed by United Artists in 1973. *Odds Against* was the basis for a 1979 Yorkshire Television series called ''The Racing Game.''

AVOCATIONAL INTERESTS: Boating, fox-hunting.

CA INTERVIEW

CA interviewed Dick Francis by phone January 22, 1982, at his winter home in Fort Lauderdale, Florida.

CA: You came to writing in a rather unusual way, beginning as a racing columnist after you retired from your career as a jockey. Had you ever considered writing before that?

FRANCIS: I'd half done my autobiography before I started on my newspaper work. I was talked into writing my autobiography by my agent. He got an introduction to me in the summer of 1956, and he thought I had a peg on which to hang an autobiography. That was the summer after the 1956 Grand National, when the Queen Mother's horse, Devon Loch, nearly won but inexplicably collapsed very near the finish line. Then when I had to retire from riding in January, 1957, I was interviewed by different media—television, radio, the press. I suppose I was news because I was the Queen Mother's jockey and I'd been a champion jockey and because of the unusual occurrence in the last Grand National; I was interviewed quite frequently. And they all said, ''What are you going to do, Dick, now you are retired?'' I said I didn't really know. I didn't think I wanted to train, because I'd rather get up on horses myself than give someone else a leg up on them. I said I'd half written my autobiography, and I'd try and finish it off and see what developed. I suppose the sports editor of the *London Sunday Express* thought, ''Well, perhaps this fellow can put one or two words together.'' He got an introduction to me, took me out to lunch, and asked if I would consider writing half a dozen articles on the British racing scene for the *Sunday Express.* I agreed to do this, and after I'd written about three of them, they wanted me to join the staff full-time. But I didn't think I was a newspaper man; I didn't think I was a writer by nature. It was six months after I'd started writing these weekly articles that I eventually agreed to sign on the dotted line as a newspaper man. Those weekly articles went on for sixteen years. That no doubt helped me in finding the right words for stories, and it kept me very much in the racing scene.

But the carpets were getting a little bit thin and the car wanted renewing and two sons needed to be educated, and my wife said to me, ''Go on. You always said you were going to write a novel. Now's the time to do it.'' I started on *Dead Cert* in 1961, finished it in 1962, and it was published in 1962—the first novel. Michael Joseph had first refusal of it because when they published my autobiography, *The Sport of Queens,* in 1957, one of the clauses in the contract was that they should have first refusal of anything else I wrote. Well, I sent the manuscript to them in the hope that they might say yea or nay and thought I'd wait a few months. And—I couldn't get over it—within ten days or two weeks I heard back from them by my agent that they'd publish *Dead Cert* straightaway. Hardly a word was changed. Then another two years went by before *Nerve* was published in 1964.

Dead Cert and *Nerve* had both been published in the early spring, but when I was writing my fourth book, *For Kicks,* the publishers said, ''Come on. We want two books from you this year, because we want to get you on the autumn sale list for the Christmas sales.'' I told them, ''I can't possibly do two. You keep *For Kicks* until the autumn instead of bringing it out in the spring.'' ''Oh no, your readers will be looking for a book early on in the year and they'll be disappointed if they don't get another one.'' So 1965 was a very hard year. I wrote *For Kicks* and *Odds Against* that year, and there's been one in the autumn ever since.

CA: How did you happen to choose mysteries?

FRANCIS: Chiefly because my wife and I like reading mysteries and we used to love going to the theater and the cinema, especially to see mysteries. We don't go to the cinema too much now because of television. We also, on discussion, thought it was a good field to branch out into, because mysteries are on sale everywhere—airports, railway stations, shops. So we thought perhaps there was a market there and that's proven to be right.

CA: Does your wife still help you with editing and spelling and research?

FRANCIS: Yes, she does.

CA: You said in your autobiography that you didn't enjoy school—in fact, you dropped out of high school—and you don't indicate that you did a lot of reading. But you write like a man who grew up with books. Were there some literary influences?

FRANCIS: No, I don't think so. But, especially during the war when I was abroad, I used to like to read Edgar Wallace and Conan Doyle; they're both English who-dun-it writers! I still like that sort of book. I like reading my colleagues on the Crime Writers Association here. Some of them are friends of mine, and we read each other's books.

CA: What other current writers do you read?

FRANCIS: Of the English writers I like Desmond Bagley, and there's Gavin Lyall. I used to like reading Alistair MacLean, but although I still read him now, I don't get the same enjoyment out of him as I used to. Michael Underwood I like reading. He was, until he retired about three years ago, Director of Public Prosecution of the Law Courts in London. He writes thrillers, and I like reading them because one learns so much about British law.

CA: Most of your plots involve the world of racing, but they've also dealt with aviation, gold mining, art, and photography. When you're planning to write about a field that you don't know, or even a place you don't know, you make a point of learning about it first-hand. Has this led you into some adventures?

FRANCIS: Yes, it has. For the research, my wife and I have traveled all around the world. Before I wrote *In the Frame,* my publishers wanted me to go to Australia to do a promotion campaign, and I said, "If I'm going that far I want to see some of the rest of the world." We had nine weeks. We went to Hawaii—spent two or three days in Honolulu—then on to Fiji, then we spent five weeks going round and round Australia, then two weeks in New Zealand, two or three days in Hong Kong, and two or three days in Singapore on our way home. It was fascinating. And we've been to Norway, Italy, and South Africa. I'd spent some time in South Africa during the war. Then I was asked to go out to Johannesburg to judge the National Horse Show, and that stay lasted for nearly three weeks. We went down a gold mine and through the Kruger National Park game reserve. Just recently I've been to Canada, so I think I shall have to bring Canada into a novel.

CA: Does your mail indicate that you have readers who aren't primarily interested in racing but enjoy your books anyway?

FRANCIS: Yes, I'm glad to say it does. In fact, I think more readers of that kind write to me than those who are primarily interested in racing. Racing people don't like writing!

CA: Do you work out the plots in great detail before you begin writing each book?

FRANCIS: No. I like to know my main characters—I like to know them as well as I know my own family—and I like to know well in advance the crime or the event on which I'm going to base the main intrigue of the story.

CA: But then it takes shape as you write?

FRANCIS: Yes, a lot of the minor plots I incorporate as I go along.

CA: Have your fictional characters ever gotten you in trouble with real people who might have thought you were modeling characters on them?

FRANCIS: No, they haven't. In my first book, *Dead Cert,* I did find that the actual character whom I was thinking about was inclined to run away with my pen. I was thinking about a certain person whom I knew and I incorporated his image into the story. Then, reading it through, I thought, "Gosh, this is too much like the chap I am actually thinking about." One would have to give the fictitious characters one or two characteristics unlike the real caracters they were built on.

CA: In The Sport of Queens, *which was first published in 1957, you commented on the difference in attitude between the sports press here and the sports press in England, where the writers, you said, were on better personal terms with jockeys and less likely to smear them in the press. Is that still true?*

FRANCIS: I won't say one hundred percent, but for ninety-eight or ninety-nine percent of the press in England it is true. If they are talking to a jockey or trainer who happens to drop something he doesn't want to appear in the press and asks the newsmen not to print it, usually it won't be printed. But there are one or two—I won't name them—who are real mudslingers, and one has to be very careful when one is talking to them. I like to think that I did a lot for the way the press is received in racing now, myself and John Oaksey, Lord Oaksey, who used to write as John Lawrence. We both rode, and we knew how the press were received by the racing people. I think we did a lot to help.

CA: How about book reviewing in the two countries? Do you think it's done better in England than it is here?

FRANCIS: No, I don't think so. They might be a little bit more accurate with some of the facts in England, because they know them and they know the scene which I'm writing about a little bit more than the American book reviewers. It's difficult writing about the English scene if you are an American. But no, I find the press in both countries very accurate, and I like to think they've all been very kind to me.

CA: Odds Against, *which was published in 1965 in England and 1966 here, was made into a television series called "The Racing Game." Did you write the television scripts?*

FRANCIS: No, I didn't. But the scriptwriters had a lot of discussions with me—they came to see me and telephoned me—and the producer sent me the scripts before they started shooting so that I could check to see if the facts were right. Actually, only the first episode of the series was an adaptation of *Odds Against*. The following episodes were based on story lines which I gave them.

CA: Is there more television in the offing?

FRANCIS: Not at the moment, I'm afraid. They only made six episodes of "The Racing Game." They *were* going to make more, but there was a ruction within the production company, Yorkshire Television, and every series on the books got scrapped. It's rather a pity. "The Racing Game" was well received in England, in this country, and even in Australia—I went to Australia for the initial showings there. A lot of people in Scandinavia have seen it, and in other countries in Europe. But no one's going to change their minds.

CA: You liked the way the series was done?

FRANCIS: Yes. I was delighted with the way Mike Gwilym played the main character, Sid Halley. He learned to ride and he really immersed himself in the story. That pleased me one hundred percent. And I was happy with the producer, Jacky Stoller; she did wonders in getting the facts right.

CA: Have you thought about doing any writing for the movies?

FRANCIS: No. They did make a movie of *Dead Cert,* and, oh, it was ghastly. The main evil character I had in the book, Uncle George, didn't appear in the film at all. The main character in this film was a policeman. It was wrong, all wrong. They did have a royal command performance for the initial showing. Princess Anne went to see it in London. I sat next to her. I thought she was going to enjoy it, but I'm sure she didn't. She didn't comment on it. I saw a lot of the prerelease runs being shown, and I thought it was going to be all right. But when it came to the actual showing, Tony Richardson, who had been responsible for making it, thought it was just too long and he cut the first ten minutes off. The first ten minutes had helped to unfold the story and tell the viewer what was actually happening. But the viewer didn't see it because it was just cut off. The Russians pirated *Dead Cert* many years ago. When I went to Russia about four or five years ago, the chap I went with arranged for a private viewing of the film the Russian television company had made of *Dead Cert.* Well, I couldn't understand a word of it, but I could follow the story far better in the Russian edition than I could in the English edition.

CA: Do you follow the races closely in this country?

FRANCIS: Not closely. I haven't been this year because I've been too busy. Hialeah is just a little bit far away. I went to Gulfstream last year four or five times, I think. But I am going to Hialeah next week or the week after.

CA: Do you get to ride very often yourself?

FRANCIS: Not over here. I haven't ridden over here in some years. But I ride quite a lot at home. I judge in horse shows, and in Britain the judges ride all the horses in the ring. I judge the hunters and riding horses in horse shows quite a lot, and I have a few days' hunting a year. My son has a training stable at Lambourn, about twenty miles away from where I am. I often go over and ride out at his place early in the morning, then come back and sit and work on the book.

CA: You seem to be quite happy writing mysteries.

FRANCIS: Well, it's hard work, but it has made me happy enough.

CA: Have you thought about trying any other kind of book?

FRANCIS: Very briefly I have thought about it. I did discuss it with my English publisher, Mrs. Anthea Joseph, a few years ago, and she said, "Oh, we will publish anything you write, but we would rather you keep horses in the background because you are known now to write books with a horse background." She felt that if I didn't, a lot of my readers would be disappointed. She was a woman whose word was well worth listening to, and I've listened.

BIOGRAPHICAL/CRITICAL SOURCES—Books: Dick Francis, *The Sport of Queens,* M. Joseph, 1957; *Contemporary Literary Criticism,* Gale, Volume II, 1974, Volume XXII, 1982.

Periodicals: *New York Times Book Review,* March 21, 1965, March 10, 1968, March 16, 1969, June 8, 1969, July 26, 1970, May 21, 1972, July 27, 1975, September 28, 1975, June 13, 1976, July 10, 1977, May 20, 1979, June 1, 1980, March 29, 1981, April 25, 1982; *New York Times,* March 6, 1969, April 7, 1971, March 20, 1981; *New Yorker,* March 15, 1969; *Christian Science Monitor,* July 17, 1969; *Family Circle,* July, 1970; *Washington Post Book World,* April 30, 1972, February 18, 1973, April 19, 1980, April 18, 1982; *Time,* March 11, 1974, July 14, 1975, May 31, 1976, July 7, 1978, May 11, 1981; *London Magazine,* February-March, 1975, March, 1980, February-March, 1981; *Times Literary Supplement,* October 28, 1977, October 10, 1980, December 10, 1982; *The Armchair Detective,* July, 1978; *Los Angeles Times,* March 27, 1981, April 9, 1982; *Newsweek,* April 6, 1981.

—Sketch by Donna Olendorf

—Interview by Jean W. Ross

* * *

FRANCIS, Dorothy Brenner 1926-
(Ellen Goforth)

PERSONAL: Born November 30, 1926, in Lawrence, Kan.; daughter of Clayton (a district judge) and Cecile (Goforth) Brenner; married Richard M. Francis (a professional musician), August 30, 1950; children: Lynn Ann Francis Tank, Patricia Louise Francis Pocius. *Education:* University of Kansas, Mus.B., 1948. *Politics:* Republican. *Religion:* Methodist. *Home:* 1505 Brentwood Ter., Marshalltown, Iowa 50158.

CAREER: Band and vocal instructor in Orange, Calif., 1948-50, Pleasant Hill, Mo., 1950-51, Cache, Okla., 1951-52, and Gilman, Iowa, 1961-62; former teacher of piano and trumpet and director of a Methodist junior high choir; correspondence teacher for Institute of Children's Literature, Redding Ridge, Conn. Member of board of community Chamber Orchestra, Marshalltown, 1967. *Member:* P.E.O. Sisterhood, Marshalltown Tuesday Music Club (former president), Mu Phi Epsilon.

WRITINGS: Adventure at Riverton Zoo, Abingdon, 1966; *Mystery of the Forgotten Map,* Follett, 1968; *Laugh at the Evil Eye,* Messner, 1970; *Another Kind of Beauty,* Criterion, 1970; *Hawaiian Interlude,* Avalon, 1970; *Studio Affair,* Avalon, 1972; *Nurse on Assignment,* Avalon, 1972; *A Blue Ribbon for Marni,* Avalon, 1973; *Nurse under Fire,* Avalon, 1973; *Nurse in the Caribbean,* Avalon, 1973; *Murder in Hawaii,* Scholastic Book Services, 1973; *Nurse in the Keys,* Avalon, 1974; *Golden Girl,* Scholastic Book Services, 1974.

Nurse at Spirit Lake, Avalon, 1975; *Allamanda House,* Avalon, 1975; *The Flint Hills Foal,* Abingdon, 1976; *Two against the Arctic,* Pyramid, 1977; *Run of the Sea Witch,* Abingdon, 1978; *The Boy with the Blue Ears,* Abingdon, 1979; *Shoplifting: The Crime Everybody Pays For,* Elsevier/Nelson, 1979, 3rd edition, 1982; (under pseudonym Ellen Goforth) *Path of Desire,* Silhouette Press, 1980; *New Boy in Town,* Silhouette Press, 1981; *Special Girl,* Silhouette Press, 1981; *Treasure of the Heart,* Silhouette Press, 1982; *A New Dawn,* Silhouette Press, 1982; *Say Please,* Silhouette Press, 1982; *Secret Place,* Silhouette Press, 1982; *Captain Morgana Mason,* Dutton, 1982; *A Blink of the Mind,* Dell, 1982. Contributor of short stories to Augsburg publications; contributor of light verse to magazines.

WORK IN PROGRESS: A book on vandalism, for Dutton.

SIDELIGHTS: Dorothy Brenner Francis told *CA*, "In all my books for children, I've tried to show different lifestyles which I hope will make the reader wonder and think and continue to read." Several of Francis's books have been translated into foreign languages.

* * *

FRANCO, Jean 1924-

PERSONAL: Born March 31, 1924, in England; daughter of William (a shopkeeper) and Ella (Newton) Swindells; formerly married to Juan Antonio Franco; children: Alexis Parke. *Education:* University of Manchester, B.A. (first class honors), 1944, M.A., 1946; King's College, London, first class honors degree in Spanish, 1960, Ph.D., 1964. *Home:* 440 Riverside Dr., New York, N.Y. 10027. *Office:* Department of Spanish and Portuguese, Columbia University, New York, N.Y. 10027.

CAREER: University of London, London, England, lecturer at Queen Mary College, 1960-64, reader at King's College, 1964-68; University of Essex, Colchester, England, professor of Latin American literature, 1968-72; Stanford University, Stanford, Calif., professor of Spanish, 1972-82; Columbia University, New York, N.Y., professor of Spanish, 1982—. *Member:* Society for Latin American Studies (founder-member; treasurer, 1965-67; vice-chairman, 1967-68).

WRITINGS: (Editor) *Cuentos americanos de nuestros dias,* Harrap, 1965; (editor) *Short Stories in Spanish,* Penguin, 1966; *The Modern Culture of Latin America: Society and the Artist,* Praeger, 1967, revised edition, Penguin, 1970; (editor) Horacio Quiroga, *Cuentos escogidos,* Pergamon, 1968; *An Introduction to Spanish-American Literature,* Cambridge University Press, 1969; *A Literary History of Spain,* Volume VII: *Spanish-American Literature since Independence,* Harper, 1973; *Cesar Vallejo: The Dialectics of Poetry and Silence,* Cambridge University Press, 1976. Editor of Latin American section, *Penguin Companion to Literature,* Volume III: *United States and Latin America.* Contributor to *Times Literary Supplement* and *Spectator.* Editor of *Tabloid,* 1980—.

WORK IN PROGRESS: The Absent Bourgeois, a series of essays on the relation between literature, popular and mass culture in Latin America.

SIDELIGHTS: Jean Franco told *CA:* "I have helped edit and run a small journal called *Tabloid* which deals with mass culture and mass culture criticism. Although my main critical work continues to be on Latin America (whose literature, despite the 'boom' is still not familiar to U.S. readers), I have found it stimulating to move into this new field, especially [because] it has given me the opportunity to work with graphics as well as with words."

Franco's *Cesar Vallejo: The Dialectics of Poetry and Silence* is the first full-length study in English of this major Peruvian poet.

BIOGRAPHICAL/CRITICAL SOURCES: Modern Language Journal, September, 1978; *New York Review of Books,* December 21, 1978; *Hispanic American Historical Review,* May, 1979.

* * *

FRANDA, Marcus F. 1937-

PERSONAL: Born August 16, 1937, in Nassawaupee Township, Wis.; son of Simon John and Esther Mary (Schallie) Franda; married Vonetta Jane Pedlow, August 9, 1959; children: Charles Arthur, Stephanie Jane. *Education:* Beloit College, B.A., 1959; University of Chicago, A.M., 1960, Ph.D., 1966. *Home:* Cooper Hill Rd., Salisbury, Conn. 06068. *Office:* Institute of World Affairs, Salisbury, Conn. 06068.

CAREER: Colgate University, Hamilton, N.Y., assistant professor, 1965-71, associate professor of political science, 1971-77; Institute of World Affairs, Salisbury, Conn., academic director, 1982—. Associate, American Universities Field Staff; member of executive board, United States Educational Foundation. *Member:* Association for Asian Studies, American Political Science Association, American Academy of Political and Social Science. *Awards, honors:* Shell Oil Co. award for excellence in teaching, 1967-68; Rotary Club award for international committee work.

WRITINGS: West Bengal and the Federalizing Process in India, Princeton University Press, 1968; (co-author) *State Politics in India,* Princeton University Press, 1968; (translator from the Bengali with S. K. Chatterjee) Narendranath Mitra, *Mahanagar,* Jaico, 1968.

Political Development and Political Decay in Bengal, Firma K.L. Mukhopadhyay (Calcutta), 1971; *Radical Politics in West Bengal,* M.I.T. Press, 1971; (translator with Chatterjee) Tarasankar Banerjee, *Panchagram,* Manohar, 1973; (with Paul R. Brass) *Radical Politics in South Asia,* M.I.T. Press, 1973; (with John Osgood Field) *The Communist Parties of West Bengal: An Electoral Profile,* Manohar, 1974; (editor) *Responses to Population Growth in India: Changes in Social, Political and Economic Behavior,* Praeger, 1975; *India in an Emergency,* American Universities Field Staff, 1976; *Small Is Politics,* Wiley, 1978.

India's Rural Development: An Assessment of Alternatives, Indiana University Press, 1980; *Voluntary Associations and Local Development in India,* Young Asia, 1981; *The Seychelles: Unquiet Islands,* Westview, 1982; *Bangladesh: The First Decade,* South Asia, 1982; *Punjabis, War and Women: The Short Stories of Gulzar Singh Sandhu,* Heritage Publishers, 1983. Also author of numerous monographs on Indian social and environmental subjects, the Indian Ocean, Southeast Asia, and the gulf states.

* * *

FRANKLIN, H. Bruce 1934-

PERSONAL: Born February 28, 1934, in Brooklyn, N.Y.; son of Robert and Florence (Cohen) Franklin; married Jane Morgan, February 11, 1956; children: Karen, Gretchen, Robert. *Education:* Amherst College, B.A., 1955; Stanford University, Ph.D., 1961; College of San Mateo, certificate in environmental horticulture, 1974. *Office:* Department of English, Rutgers University, Newark, N.J.

CAREER: Tugboat deckhand and mate in New York Harbor, 1955-56; Stanford University, Stanford, Calif., assistant professor of English and American literature, 1961-64; Johns Hopkins University, Baltimore, Md., assistant professor of English and American literature, 1964-65; Stanford University, Stanford, Calif., associate professor of English and American literature, 1965-72; Rutgers University, Newark, N.J., professor, 1975-80, distinguished professor of English, 1980—. Visiting lecturer, Free University of Paris, France, 1967, Venceremos College, 1971, Yale University Graduate School, 1974-75; visiting associate professor, Wesleyan University, 1974-75. National chairman, Conference of the Advanced Placement Program in English, 1963. Commentator on radio station KPFA in Berkeley, Calif., 1970-74. Member of executive board, Palo Alto Fair Play Council, 1962-64; scientific writing consultant, Stanford Research Institute, 1962-64. *Military service:* U.S. Air Force, 1956-59; became captain.

AWARDS, HONORS: American Council of Learned Societies fellow, 1968-69; Center for the Humanities fellow, Wesleyan University, 1974; Rockefeller Foundation Humanities fellow, 1975-76; Alexander Cappon Prize for the Essay, 1978; Merit Award, Rutgers University, 1979; Eaton Award, 1981, for *Robert A. Heinlein: America as Science Fiction.*

WRITINGS: The Wake of the Gods: Melville's Mythology, Stanford University Press, 1963; *Future Perfect: American Science Fiction of the Nineteenth Century,* Oxford University Press, 1966, expanded and revised edition, 1978; (editor) Herman Melville, *The Confidence Man* (annotated edition), Bobbs-Merrill, 1967; (editor) Nathaniel Hawthorne, *The Scarlet Letter, and Other Writings,* Lippincott, 1967; (co-author) *Who Should Run the Universities?,* American Enterprise Institute for Public Policy Research, 1969.

From the Movement: Toward Revolution, Van Nostrand, 1971; (editor) *The Essential Stalin,* Doubleday, 1972; *Back Where You Came From: A Life in the Death of the Empire* (political autobiography), Harper's Magazine Press, 1975; *The Victim as Criminal and Artist: Literature from the American Prison,* Oxford University Press, 1978, expanded and revised edition, Lawrence Hill, 1982; *Robert A. Heinlein: America as Science Fiction,* Oxford University Press, 1980; (author of introduction) T. J. Reddy, *Poems in One/Part Harmony,* Carolina Wren Press, 1980; (editor) Jack London, *The Iron Heel,* Lawrence Hill, 1980; *American Prisoners and Ex-Prisoners: An Annotated Bibliography of Published Works, 1798-1981,* Lawrence Hill, 1982.

Contributor: *Melville's Benito Cereno: A Text for Guided Research,* Heath, 1965; Thomas J. Rountree, editor, *Studies in Moby Dick,* C. E. Merrill, 1969; *The Mirror of Infinity,* Harper, 1970; *Studies in Billy Budd,* C. E. Merrill, 1970; *Science Fiction: The Other Side of Realism,* Bowling Green University Popular Press, 1971; *Studies in Pierre,* C. E. Merrill, 1971; *Critics on Melville,* University of Miami Press, 1972; *The Politics of Literature,* Pantheon, 1972; *A Casebook for Research,* Kendall/Hunt, 1973; *Why Teach the Humanities to Adult Basic Education Students,* Center for Resource Development in Adult Education (Kansas City, Missouri), 1975; *Weapons of Criticism,* Ramparts, 1976; *Science-Fiction Studies: Selected Articles,* Gregg, 1976; *Turning Points: Essays on the Art of Science Fiction,* Harper, 1977; *Amerikanische Literaturkritik im Engagement,* Akademie-Verlag, 1978; *The Encyclopedia of Science Fiction,* Doubleday, 1979; *English Literature: Opening Up the Canon,* Johns Hopkins University Press, 1981; *The Slave's Narrative as Literature and History,* Oxford University Press, 1982.

Contributor to *Encyclopedia Americana,* 1971. Also contributor to numerous literary journals, including *Nineteenth-Century Fiction, Minnesota Review, Saturday Review of the Arts,* and *New England Quarterly*. Referee for numerous academic presses, including Northwestern University Press, University of California Press, Oxford University Press, Ramparts Press, Duke University Press, and Yale University Press, 1966—. Editorial consultant, *Science-Fiction Studies,* 1973—.

SIDELIGHTS: H. Bruce Franklin first made headlines in 1972 when he became the only tenured professor ever to be fired from Stanford University for his political ideology. While his academic credentials were impeccable, Franklin's radical views on the Vietnam war were unacceptable to the administration, and when he urged students to protest secret military research in universities, he lost his job. After three years of unemployment, the Melville scholar reentered the academic community as an English professor at Rutgers University. His attitude, however, has not changed. "The main thing that has happened since 1968 is not that those of us who had certain views that were considered radical in '68 have changed our views," he told Paul Wilner in the *New York Times,* "but that the majority of American people now hold the views that I held. They don't seem now to be so radical." Nonetheless, critics still consider many of Franklin's writings revolutionary, and because they are also well-documented and thoroughly researched, he has earned a reputation as a writer who successfully combines the roles of scholar and activist.

In *The Victim as Criminal and Artist: Literature from the American Prison,* Franklin focuses on the literary contributions of society's victims, particularly blacks. While scholars and literary critics have traditionally dismissed prison writing as insignificant or valueless, Franklin argues that it is actually one of the main lines of American literature. "In the several years I spent on [the book,] I never ceased to be amazed at the richness of prison and slave writing and how it has been utterly ignored or misinterpreted by the academy," Franklin told David W. McCullough in a *Book of the Month Club News* interview. His thesis, according to Francis X. Kroncke writing in the *San Francisco Bay Guardian,* is that "prison and slave artists have created and preserved, through poems, working songs, spirituals and novels, a tradition of protest against America as prison and a vision for an alternative revolutionary future."

The book opens with an examination of slave narratives—which Franklin calls "the first genre the U.S. contributed to the written literature of the world"—then moves to a discussion of Herman Melville, whom Franklin considers a classic example of an author who has been misunderstood. After studying Melville for years, Franklin came to realize, as he told *Publishers Weekly,* "that the single most formative event in his life was the committing of a crime and his imprisonment." Furthermore, as a sailor, Melville lived a life of bondage and was thus able to understand the oppressions of capitalism. Thus, in Franklin's view, Melville's artistic imagination was "shaped by his experience of work, oppression, and resistance" and not some abstract creed of symbolism as the academy maintains.

Arranged in roughly chronological order, the book proceeds to a study of more recent, but still largely forgotten, prison literature, including the violent narratives of Chester Himes and Malcolm Braly. The 1971 rebellion at Attica State Prison is also included, analyzed from Franklin's rather unique perspective which Kroncke explains: "The ill-fated uprising . . . occurred, in part, because of the education young blacks obtained from their cultural heritage of songs and stories. Their political education, though formed by contemporary intellectual analysis, had an emotional, cultural basis that few non-blacks share." The crux of Franklin's argument, according to Ronald D. Cohen, is "that the black experience and the prison experience have been and are the same." This, Cohen writes in *In These Times,* "gives blacks a profound insight into the basic flaws of a society that is a prison for all."

Unlike some earlier studies of the "underground," the victim, and the deviant, Franklin's book "does not romanticize and explode with self pity," according to Terence M. Ripmaster writing in the *Negro History Bulletin*. Nor does its author suggest that one must be oppressed to be a good writer. Instead Franklin's message is that "in societies divided into social classes much of the most signficant art has come from the misery of the oppressed classes." Because his book provides a framework for interpreting these neglected but truly American documents, Kroncke concludes that *The Victim as Criminal and Artist* merits the description of "a seminal work."

BIOGRAPHICAL/CRITICAL SOURCES: London Times, June 5, 1966; *Publishers Weekly,* March 17, 1975, August 22, 1977; *New York Times,* February 5, 1978; *Los Angeles Times,* February 19, 1978; *Book of the Month Club News,* March, 1978; *Review: The Chronicle of Higher Education,* March 6, 1978; *New York Times Book Review,* April 30, 1978; *San Francisco Bay Guardian,* May 11-19, 1978; *In These Times,* May 17-23, 1978; *Los Angeles Times Book Review,* May 28, 1978; *Negro History Bulletin,* September-October, 1978; *American Literature,* November, 1978; *Minnesota Review,* fall, 1978.

* * *

FRANKLIN, R(alph) W(illiam) 1937-

PERSONAL: Born August 20, 1937, in Ojus, Fla.; son of John Bryan and Lillie May (Perry) Franklin. *Education:* University of Puget Sound, B.A., 1959; Northwestern University, M.A., 1960, Ph.D., 1965; University of Chicago, M.A., 1968. *Office:* The Beinecke Rare Book and Manuscript Library, 1603A Yale Station, New Haven, Conn. 06520.

CAREER: University of Wisconsin—Madison, lecturer, 1964-65, assistant professor of English, 1965-66; Tacoma (Wash.) public schools, instructor, 1966-67; Middlebury College Library, Middlebury, Vt., curator of special collections, 1968-70; Washington State Library, Olympia, assistant chief of technical services and development, 1970-71, consultant, 1971-74, bibliographic systems consultant, 1974-76; University of Chicago, Graduate Library School, Chicago, Ill., assistant professor and dean of students, 1971-74; Whitworth College Library, Spokane, Wash., director, 1977-82; Yale University, The Beinecke Rare Book and Manuscript Library, New Haven, Conn., director, 1982—. *Member:* Bibliographical Society of America, American Library Association.

WRITINGS: The Editing of Emily Dickinson: A Reconsideration, University of Wisconsin Press, 1967; *The Manuscript Books of Emily Dickinson,* Harvard University Press, 1981. Contributor to literature and library journals.

SIDELIGHTS: "R. W. Franklin's facsimile edition of *The Manuscript Books of Emily Dickinson* has brought us one step closer to a full understanding of her work," M. L. Rosenthal writes in the *Times Literary Supplement*. Largely unpublished during her lifetime, Dickinson penned some 1,800 poems and, while most were collected into a three-volume variorum edition in 1955, there were too many for critics to deal with appropriately. Over time scholars realized that Dickinson had grouped her own poems into fascicles—folded sheets of paper which she stitched together and then used for organizing her work. Franklin's book reproduces the manuscripts of the separate fascicles, showing how Dickinson wrote out her poems and indicating variant phrasing she was considering. "Franklin's labours in rearranging the poems within each fascicle and in arranging the fascicles in chronological order (as well as correcting earlier portable mistakes in the placing of a number of poems in the wrong fascicles) have been indispensable," Rosenthal observes. "*The Manuscript Books* comes to us now as tangible proof of the importance of the fascicles for an understanding of Emily Dickinson's art."

AVOCATIONAL INTERESTS: Mountain climbing, hiking, camping, skiing, water sports, music.

BIOGRAPHICAL/CRITICAL SOURCES: Times Literary Supplement, March 26, 1982.

* * *

FRANZWA, Gregory M. 1926-

PERSONAL: Born February 27, 1926, in Glidden, Iowa; son of Frederick W. (a postmaster) and Mabel (Henderson) Franzwa; married second wife, Laura Brockmeyer Goehri, November 22, 1966; children: (first marriage) Theodore, Christian, Patrice; Scott (stepchild). *Education:* University of Iowa, B.A., 1950. *Politics:* Republican. *Religion:* None. *Home address:* P.O. Box 42, Gerald, Mo. 63037.

CAREER: Formerly self-employed as owner of Gregory M. Franzwa Public Relations, St. Louis, Mo.; Patrice Press, Gerald, Mo., owner, 1966—. *Military service:* U.S. Naval Reserve, 1943-46; became lieutenant junior grade.

WRITINGS—Published by Patrice Press, except as indicated: *The Old Cathedral,* Archdiocese of St. Louis, 1965; *The Story of Old Ste. Genevieve,* 1967; *The Oregon Trail Revisited,* 1972; *History of the Hazelwood School District,* 1977; *Legacy,* 1978; *Leif Sverdrup,* 1980; *Maps of the Oregon Trail,* 1982.

WORK IN PROGRESS: The California Trail Revisited, completion expected in 1984.

AVOCATIONAL INTERESTS: Jazz musician.

BIOGRAPHICAL/CRITICAL SOURCES: St. Louis Magazine, June, 1967.

* * *

FRASER, Amy Stewart 1892-

PERSONAL: Born December 23, 1892, in Ballater, Scotland; daughter of James Anderson (a clergyman) and Agnes (Smart) Lowe; married Mark Stewart Fraser (a physician), July 24, 1914 (died, 1966); children: James, Mark, Elspeth, Sheila (Mrs. Thomas Newlands), Jean (Mrs. Peter Forbes). *Education:* Attended Dunfermline College of Hygiene and Physical Education, 1911-13. *Politics:* Conservative. *Religion:* Church of Scotland. *Home:* Hillcrest House, Harraby Grove, Carlisle, Cumbria CA1 2QN, England.

CAREER: Organizer for physical education, Perthshire Education Committee, Scotland, 1913-14; organized Women's Voluntary Services, 1938-66. Member of Carlisle City Council, 1937-46. *Member:* Electrical Association for Women (national chairman, 1961-66), Cumberland National Society for Prevention of Cruelty to Children (past president), National Council of Women (life president). *Awards, honors:* Member of Order of British Empire; award from Scottish Arts Council, 1974, for literary merit of *The Hills of Home*.

WRITINGS—All published by Routledge & Kegan Paul: *The Hills of Home*, 1973; (editor) *Da Ye Min Langsyne*, 1975; *In Memory Long*, 1977; *Roses in December: Edwardian Recollections*, 1981.

BIOGRAPHICAL/CRITICAL SOURCES: Times Literary Supplement, August 21, 1981.

* * *

FRASSANITO, William A(llen) 1946-

PERSONAL: Born September 28, 1946, in New York, N.Y.; son of Americo Anthony (a jeweler) and Edythe (Totten) Frassanito. *Education:* Gettysburg College, B.A., 1968; State University of New York at Oneonta, M.A., 1969. *Politics:* Independent. *Religion:* Protestant. *Home and office:* 333 Baltimore St., Gettysburg, Pa. 17325.

CAREER: National Park Service, licensed guide at Gettysburg (Pa.) Battlefield, 1966-68; Frassanito Bros., Huntington, N.Y., jeweler, 1973-75; self-employed historian, lecturer, and writer, 1975—. Chief photographic consultant for the National Historical Society's six-volume series, *The Image of War: 1861-1865*, and for Time-Life Books' forthcoming twenty-four volume series, *The Civil War*. *Military service:* U.S. Army Intelligence, 1969-71; became first lieutenant; received Bronze Star. *Member:* National Stereoscopic Association, Animal Protection Institute of America, Photographic Historical Society of New York, The Company of Military Historians.

AWARDS, HONORS: Pennsylvania Commandery and War Library and Museum Award, 1968, for research in military history; *Gettysburg* was named a notable book of the year by the American Library Association, 1975; Photographic Historical Society of New York Award, 1976, for distinguished achievement in the field of photographic history; *Antietam* was named a "choice" book of 1978-79 by the Detroit Public Library; Museum of the Confederacy's Founders Award, Confederate Memorial Literature Society, 1979, for distinguished research and writing on the period of the Confederate States of America; *Gettysburg* was chosen by a panel of Civil War scholars as one of the best books ever written on the Civil War, 1981.

WRITINGS: Gettysburg: A Journey in Time (Book of the Month Club selection), Scribner, 1975; *Antietam: The Photographic Legacy of America's Bloodiest Day* (Book of the Month Club selection; History Book Club selection), Scribner, 1978; (contributor) *The Image of War: 1861-1865*, Volume III: *The Embattled Confederacy*, Doubleday, 1982; *Grant and Lee: The Virginia Campaigns* (History Book Club selection), Scribner, 1983.

WORK IN PROGRESS: Gettysburg: The Community and the War, an in-depth anatomy of the society and culture of Gettysburg, based largely on letters, diaries, and local newspaper accounts.

SIDELIGHTS: At the age of nine, William A. Frassanito saw a collection of Civil War pictures in *Life* magazine and a lasting interest was born. "The photographs made the war come alive for me," he told *Studio Photography* interviewer Barry Sparks. Since that time, Frassanito has developed his hobby into a profession, becoming a Civil War historian who uses old photographs to reconstruct important battle scenes. His meticulous research of several hundred Gettysburg and Antietam photographs has brought to light new information while dispelling some old misconceptions about the war. In his two award-winning books, *Gettysburg: A Journey in Time* and *Antietam: The Photographic Legacy of America's Bloodiest Day*, Frassanito discusses his findings. A third book, *Grant and Lee: The Virginia Campaigns*, completes the trilogy.

Although old photographs have long accompanied Civil War narratives, Frassanito is the first to use them as historical documents. "Many people see Civil War photos as mere illustrations, but they are our visual record," he explains to Sparks. "While many more books will be written about the conflict, there can be no more photographs taken. The photographers allow us to relive the experience." Frassanito sees himself as a detective, trying to piece together clues. "I [want] to know who, what, and where. I [want] to put myself in the photographer's shoes."

Among the conclusions Frassanito has reached is that Civil War photographers were more interested in effect than in accuracy. In the case of one famous Gettysburg photo, for example, Frassanito discovered that photographers had moved a dead soldier forty yards, placed his head on a knapsack, and propped up a rifle in the background. "The result was one of the most memorable Gettysburg photographs," Sparks explains. In two other Gettysburg photos, several doctors are shown surveying a group of dead soldiers. In both pictures, the bodies are lying on a large boulder. "At first glance," Sparks notes, "the scenes appear to be authentic. But to Frassanito the trick was thinly disguised. Live soldiers were posed as dead." The first clue was the boulder in the background, which was identical in both pictures even though the bodies had been changed. Other evidence was the robust appearance of the corpses and the absence of leaves on the trees. Sparks explains that "the photos were most likely taken in the late fall of 1863 when the Soldiers Cemetery was formally dedicated on November 19. The Weavers [who photographed the pictures] were known to have attended the dedication and probably coaxed several participating soldiers into posing for them."

While Gettysburg is better known than Antietam, Frassanito believes the latter may be more significant. Not only was Antietam the first battlefield in history to be photographed before the dead were buried, it also produced the largest number of casualties in American military history. Writing in the *New Republic*, a critic observes, "The corpses, bloated and stacked along the wave of the battle, evoke the bravery and terror of the great civil war." And *Chicago Tribune Book World* reviewer Jack Hurst suggests that by "investigating photographs made after the battle . . . Frassanito develops a clear picture of how it must have been to be there."

BIOGRAPHICAL/CRITICAL SOURCES: Publishers Weekly, April 28, 1975, August 7, 1978; *Newsday*, May 2, 1975; *Atlantic*, October, 1978; *New Republic*, October 14, 1978; *Chicago Tribune Book World*, December 10, 1978; *Studio Photography*, February, 1981.

* * *

FRAZIER, Arthur
See BULMER, (Henry) Kenneth

FREND, W(illiam) H(ugh) C(lifford) 1916-

PERSONAL: Born January 11, 1916, in Shottermill, Surrey, England; son of Edwin George (a clerk in holy orders) and Edith (Bacon) Frend; married Mary Crook, June 2, 1951; children: Sarah Anne, Simon William Clifford. *Education:* Keble College, Oxford, B.A. (with first class honors), 1937, D.Phil., 1940. *Politics:* Unionist. *Religion:* Episcopalian. *Home:* Marbrae, Balmaha, Glasgow, Scotland. *Office:* University of Glasgow, Glasgow, Scotland.

CAREER: Civil servant in British War Office and in Cabinet Office, 1940-42; member of editorial board, Allied German War Documents Project, 1947-51; University of Nottingham, Nottingham, England, research fellow, 1951-52; Cambridge University, Cambridge, England, S. A. Cook bye-fellow at Gonville and Caius College, 1952-56, fellow of Gonville and Caius College and university lecturer in divinity, 1956-69, university proctor, 1957-59, Birkbeck lecturer in ecclesiastical history, 1967-68; University of Glasgow, Glasgow, Scotland, professor of ecclesiastical history, 1969—, dean of divinity, 1972-75. Ordained deacon in the Episcopal Church in Scotland, July, 1982. Visiting professor at Rhodes University, 1964, University of South Africa, 1976, and John Carroll University, 1981. Associate director of excavations of Egypt Exploration Society at Qasribrim, Nubia, 1964. Chairman of Cambridge City Liberal Party, 1968-69. *Military service:* British Army, Political Intelligence Service, 1942-46; received Gold Cross of Merit with Swords (Poland). Commissioned in the Territorial Army, Brigade Intelligence Officer (retired, 1967).

MEMBER: European Commission for Comparative Study of Ecclesiastical History (vice-president, 1964, president, 1980), Society of Antiquaries (fellow), Royal Historical Society (fellow), Society for Promotion of Roman Studies (member of council, 1966), Association of University Teachers (Scotland; chairman, 1976-78), Royal Society of Edinburgh (fellow, 1979). *Awards, honors:* B.D., Cambridge University, 1964; D.D. from Oxford University in recognition of contribution to historical theology, 1966, and University of Edinburgh, 1974.

WRITINGS: *The Donatist Church,* Oxford University Press, 1952; *Martyrdom and Persecution in the Early Church,* Basil Blackwell, 1965, Doubleday, 1967, reprinted, Baker Book (Grand Rapids, Mich.), 1981; *The Early Church,* Lippincott, 1965, reprinted, Fortress Press, 1981; (contributor) Arthur J. Arberry, editor, *Religion in the Middle East,* two volumes, Cambridge University Press, 1969.

The Rise of the Monophysite Movement, Cambridge University Press, 1972; *Religion Popular and Unpopular in the Early Christian Centuries,* Variorum (London), 1976; *Town and Country in Early Christianity,* Variorum, 1980; *The Rise of Christianity,* Fortress Press, 1983. Contributor to *Journal of Theological Studies, Journal of Ecclesiastical History,* and other journals. Editor, *Modern Churchman,* 1963-82.

WORK IN PROGRESS: *Saints and Sinners in the Early Church,* for Seabury; reports on archaeological work done at Qasribrim, Nubia, 1972-74.

SIDELIGHTS: W.H.C. Frend wrote to *CA:* "I'm basically a bridge subject man with an interest in archaeology, history, and theology. Am against narrow specialization, believe that the proper study of man is man. Am interested in politics from a national rather than a party point of view. Believe in seeing things on the spot and have a deep dislike of any policy which places creative workers in the hands of administrators."

BIOGRAPHICAL/CRITICAL SOURCES: *Journal of Roman Studies,* Volume LVI, 1966.

* * *

FRESE, Dolores Warwick 1936-
(Dolores Warwick)

PERSONAL: Born April 9, 1936, in Baltimore, Md.; daughter of Charles Carroll and Mary (Keeler) Warwick; married John Jerome Frese, September 6, 1958; children: Paul Joseph, Christopher Sean, John Matthew. *Education:* College of Notre Dame of Maryland, B.A., 1958; State University of Iowa (now University of Iowa), M.A., 1962, Ph.D., 1972. *Religion:* Roman Catholic. *Home:* 533 East Angela Blvd., South Bend, Ind. 46617. *Office:* Department of English, University of Notre Dame, Notre Dame, Ind. 46556.

CAREER: University of Notre Dame, Notre Dame, Ind., associate professor of English, 1973—. Social worker, Associated Catholic Charities, Baltimore, Md., 1958; assistant house mother, St. Mary's Villa, Baltimore. Consultant on youth grants, National Endowment for the Humanities, 1978—. *Member:* International Arthurian Society, International Society of Anglo-Saxonists, Modern Language Association of America, Chaucer Society, Midwest Modern Language Association. *Awards, honors:* First prize for poetry, National Catholic Press Association competition, 1957, 1958; first prize for poetry from *Atlantic,* 1957.

WRITINGS: *Promised Spring,* Dodd, 1960; *Learn to Say Goodbye,* Farrar, Straus, 1971; (co-editor and contributor) *Anglo-Saxon Poetry: Essays in Appreciation,* University of Notre Dame Press, 1975; (editor) Steve Katz, *Moving Parts,* Fiction Collective, 1977; *Virgins and Martyrs,* Juniper Press, 1978. Contributor of poetry to *America, Critic, Commonweal,* and other publications.

WORK IN PROGRESS: *Didn't We Have Fun Yesterday?,* a novel.

* * *

FRIEDLANDER, Albert H(oschander) 1927-

PERSONAL: Born May 10, 1927, in Berlin, Germany; came to United States in 1940; son of Alex (a textile broker) and Sali (Hoschander) Friedlander; married Evelyn Philipp (a pianist), July 9, 1961; children: Ariel Judith, Michal Sali, Noam Ilana. *Education:* University of Chicago, Ph.B., 1946; Hebrew Union College—Jewish Institute of Religion, Cincinnati, Ohio, B.H.L., 1950, Rabbi, 1952, D.D., 1977; Columbia University, Ph.D., 1966. *Politics:* Democrat. *Home:* Kent House, Rutland Gardens, London S.W. 7, England. *Office:* Leo Baeck College, 33 Seymour Pl., London, England.

CAREER: Rabbi in Fort Smith, Ark., 1952-57, Wilkes-Barre, Pa., 1957-61, and Easthampton, Long Island, N.Y., 1961-65; Columbia University, New York, N.Y., religious counselor, 1961-66; Wembley Liberal Synagogue, Harrow, Middlesex, England, rabbi, 1966-71; Westminster Synagogue, London, England, rabbi, 1971—; Leo Baeck College, London, lecturer, 1966-71, director, 1971-82, dean, 1982—. Visiting professor at Emory University, 1975, and at University of Berlin, summers, 1981, 1982. *Member:* World Union for Progressive Judaism (member of American board, 1964-66; member of European board, 1967—; vice-president, 1975—), Central Conference of American Rabbis (chairman of committee on art and literature, 1961-66), B'nai B'rith.

WRITINGS: Early Reform Judaism in Germany: An Introduction, published in two parts, Union of American Hebrew Congregations, 1954-55; *Isaac M. Wise: The World of My Books,* American Jewish Archives, 1954; (translator) Leo Baeck, *This People Israel* (original title, *Dieses Volk*), Holt, 1965; *Leo Baeck: Teacher of Theresienstadt,* Holt, 1968; *Leo Baeck: Leben und Lehre,* Deutsche Verlags-Anstalt, 1973; *Glaube nach Auschwitz,* Kaiser Verlag, 1980.

Editor: *The Words They Spoke: Statements from the Speeches and Writings of Early Leaders of Reform Judaism,* Union of American Hebrew Congregations, 1954; *Never Trust a God Over 30: New Styles in Campus Ministry,* introduction by Paul Goodman, McGraw, 1967; *Out of the Whirlwind: A Reader of Holocaust Literature,* Doubleday, 1968; *Meir Gertner: An Anthology,* [London], 1977; *G. Salsberger: Leben und Werk,* [Frankfurt], 1982; (and translator) *The Five Megillot,* Central Conference of American Rabbis, 1983.

Libretti: "The Two Brothers," 1971; "The Harp and the Lovers," 1974; "The Burning City," 1975; "The Five Scrolls," 1975; "Wedding Song," 1981; "Children of Theresienstadt," 1982.

Also author of *The Misuse of the Holocaust: Post-Auschwitz Theology,* 1983. Author of monographs, including *Jews and God,* 1972, *Jewish View of Suffering,* 1974, and *Leo Baeck's Theology of Suffering,* 1974. Contributing editor, *Jews from Germany in the United States,* 1955. Contributor of reviews, articles, and notes to *Saturday Review, Dimensions, American Judaism, Encounter, Reconstructionist,* and other journals in the United States and Germany. *European Judaism,* member of editorial board, editor, 1979—.

WORK IN PROGRESS: Contemporary Theology; Anthology of Holocaust Poetry; Shared Paths: Towards a Joint Autobiography, with Paul Oestreicher; liturgy for "Scroll of Fire," with Elie Wiesel.

SIDELIGHTS: "It is to Albert Friedlander's credit that, despite his profound love for his late teacher, he does not permit emotion to interfere with objective scholarly appraisal," according to Alan W. Miller reviewing *Leo Baeck: Teacher of Theresienstadt* in *Saturday Review.* He further describes Friedlander's work as a "sensitive and thoughtful exploration of the tension between the mind and the man."

Friedlander told *CA* his motivation encompasses "the need to communicate, to preserve and to transmit the past, to enlarge the role of the rabbi in contemporary life."

BIOGRAPHICAL/CRITICAL SOURCES: Saturday Review, January 11, 1969; *New Republic,* March 15, 1969; *Christian Century,* September 3, 1969.

* * *

FRUMKIN, Robert M. 1928-

PERSONAL: Born March 20, 1928, in Newark, N.J.; son of Solomon and Anna (Gruber) Frumkin; married Miriam Zisenwine, 1950 (divorced, 1964); married Beverly Crouch Babcock, 1964 (divorced, 1966); married Grace Butcher, 1970 (divorced, 1973); children: (first marriage) Judith. *Education:* Upsala College, B.A., 1948; New School for Social Research, graduate student, 1948-49; Ohio State University, M.A., 1951, Ph.D., 1961; postdoctoral study at Syracuse University, 1963-64, Case Western Reserve University, 1967-68, and Kent State University, 1969-72. *Home:* 339 Radel Ter., South Orange, N.J. 07079.

CAREER: Ohio State Department of Mental Hygiene and Correction, Columbus, social research analyst, 1952-54; State University of New York College for Teachers at Buffalo (now State University of New York at Buffalo), instructor in sociology and psychology, 1954-57; State University of New York at Oswego, 1957-63, began as assistant professor, became associate professor of sociology and anthropology; Benjamin Rose Institute, Cleveland, Ohio, research associate in gerontology, 1964-65; director of research for Community Action for Youth, Cleveland, 1965-66, and Cleveland Society for the Blind, 1966-67; Kent State University, Kent, Ohio, associate professor of rehabilitation counseling, 1967-75; Beacon Hill Clinic, Southfield, Mich., psychotherapist, 1976; Northville State Hospital, Northville, Mich., chief psychologist, 1976-77; Shaw College, Detroit, Mich., associate professor of psychology, sociology, and cultural anthropology, 1977-81; *Jewish Horizon* (weekly newspaper), Union, N.J., assistant editor, 1982—. Lecturer, Cuyahoga Community College, 1965; research consultant, Cleveland Psychiatric Institute, 1966. Licensed psychologist, State of Ohio, 1974-76; certified rehabilitation counselor, 1974-78. *Military service:* U.S. Navy, Hospital Corps, 1946-47.

MEMBER: American Humanist Association, American Art Therapy Association, Middle East Friendship League (founder), Society for the Scientific Study of Sex (fellow), American Sociological Association (fellow), American Psychological Association, American Civil Liberties Union, Mensa, National Rehabilitation Association, New Jewish Agenda, Social Activist Professors Defense Foundation.

AWARDS, HONORS: Fellowships from Ericsson Society of New York, in science, 1945-46, and State University of New York Research Foundation, summer, 1963; research grants from National Institutes of Mental Health, 1965-66, and Cleveland Foundation, 1966; first prize for nonfiction writing, Sigma Tau Delta literary competition, 1965.

WRITINGS: The Measurement of Marriage Adjustment, Public Affairs, 1954; *The Meaning of Sociology,* University of Buffalo, 1956; *The Patient as a Human Being,* University of Buffalo, 1956; *Freedom to Love,* Paine Press, 1956; *Hospital Nursing: A Sociological Interpretation,* University of Buffalo, 1956; *The Nurse as a Human Being,* University of Buffalo, 1956; *Social Problems, Pathology and Philosophy: Selected Essays and Studies,* Frontiers Press, 1962; *The Kent State Coverup,* two volumes, Frontiers Press, 1980. Also author of "Kangaroo Court" (play), 1974.

Contributor: *Mental Health and Mental Disorder: A Sociological Approach,* edited by A. M. Rose, Norton, 1955; *Contemporary Sociology,* edited by J. S. Roucek, Philosophical Library, 1961; *Encyclopedia of Sexual Behavior,* edited by A. Ellis and A. Abarbanel, Hawthorn, 1961; *The Heritage of American Education,* edited by R. E. Gross, Allyn & Bacon, 1962; *The Unusual Child,* edited by Roucek, Philosophical Library, 1965; *Life in Families,* edited by H. M. Hughes, Allyn & Bacon, 1970; *New Developments in Modern World Sociology,* edited by D. Martindale and R. Mohan, Greenwood Press, 1975.

Contributor of more than 200 articles and reviews to sociology, psychology, education, religious, literary, medical, nursing, and other journals. Abstractor, *Psychological Abstracts,* 1954-63; editor, *Heritage* (literary magazine), 1949-51, and *Ethos* (literary magazine), 1955-58; reserach editor, *Journal of Human Relations,* 1958-70; *Zedek,* associate editor, 1980-82, editor, 1982—.

WORK IN PROGRESS: The Anatomy of a Kent State Conspiracy and Assassination; The Sexual Potential of the Handicapped; Social Psychological Aspects of Disability; Open Relationships; "The Measure of Love," a play; *Thunder in the Snow,* a novel; *You Can Come Home Again,* a novel.

SIDELIGHTS: Robert M. Frumkin writes *CA:* "From the very beginning my motivation to write has been prompted by a desire to express what I think and/or feel about significant, often controversial, issues which have caught my attention and interest. My first writing prize was for an essay on world peace and brotherhood in a statewide competition in New Jersey. I was fifteen at the time.

"A genuine interest and delight in writing—all kinds of writing—was fired in me by a gifted freshman English teacher, Leon Ormond, at Arts High School in Newark, N.J.

"I have been influenced by a number of writers, including Francis Bacon, Thomas Paine, Jessica Mitford, James Baldwin, Albert Camus, Robert Frost, Langston Hughes, and Henrik Ibsen. What I admire in almost all of these writers is the power and relative simplicity with which they communicate vital issues to their readers.

"While there are legitimately many possible purposes to writing, for me, writing is a way of educating, informing, getting people to think and act upon crucial issues of our times. In this period of our world's history, it is the responsibility of serious writers to be involved, at least to some degree, in helping to save life on earth from total destruction. While it is important for all people to relax and enjoy life, it is also important that the survival of life on this earth be among the writer's primary commitments. If all life on earth is destroyed, then there will be neither writers to write nor readers to read. I spend much of my time working for world peace and nuclear disarmament. We must do something to prevent a nuclear holocaust."

AVOCATIONAL INTERESTS: Drawing, painting, sculpture, wood carving, piano, tennis, table tennis, track and field, hiking, rowing, ice skating, and other forms of outdoor recreation.

* * *

FRY, Christopher 1907-

PERSONAL: Name originally Christopher Fry Harris; born December 18, 1907, in Bristol, England; son of Charles John (an architect and later a church lay reader) and Emma Marguerite Fry (Hammond) Harris; married Phyllis Marjorie Hart (a journalist), December 3, 1936; children: one son. *Education:* Attended Bedford Modern School, Bedford, England, 1918-26. *Religion:* Church of England. *Home:* The Toft, East Dean, Chichester, Sussex, England.

CAREER: Master of a Froebel school and tutor, 1926-27; Citizen House, Bath, England, actor, 1927; Hazelwood Preparatory School, Limpsfield, Surrey, England, schoolmaster, 1928-31; director of Tunbridge Wells Repertory Players, 1932-35; director of Oxford Repertory Players, 1940 and 1944-46; Arts Theatre, London, England, director, 1945, staff dramatist, 1947. Playwright and translator. *Military service:* Pioneer Corps, 1940-44. *Member:* Dramatists Guild, Royal Society of Literature (fellow).

AWARDS, HONORS: Shaw Prize Fund award, 1948, for *The Lady's Not for Burning*; William Foyle Poetry Prize, 1951, for *Venus Observed;* New York Drama Critics Circle Award, 1951, for *The Lady's Not for Burning,* 1952, for *Venus Observed,* and 1956, for *Tiger at the Gates;* Queen's Gold Medal for Poetry, 1962; Heinemann Award for Literature, 1962, for *Curtmantle;* Writers Guild Best British Television Dramatization award nomination, 1971, for "The Tenant of Wildfell Hall."

WRITINGS—Plays: (Author of script) *Thursday's Child* (first produced in London, 1939), music by Martin Shaw, Girl's Friendly Press (London), 1939; *The Boy with a Cart: Cuthman, Saint of Sussex* (also see below; first produced in Coleman's Hatch, Sussex, England, 1937; produced in New York, 1953), Oxford University Press, 1939, 2nd edition, Muller, 1956; *A Phoenix Too Frequent* (comedy; first produced in London at Mercury Theatre, 1946; produced in Cambridge, Mass., 1948), Hollis & Carter, 1946, Oxford University Press, 1949; *The Firstborn* (also see below; tragedy; first produced at Edinburgh Festival, Scotland, 1948; produced in New York, 1958), Cambridge University Press, 1946, Oxford University Press, 1950, 3rd edition, Oxford University Press, 1958; *The Lady's Not for Burning* (also see below; spring comedy; first produced in London at Arts Theatre, 1948; produced in New York, 1950), Oxford University Press, 1949, 2nd edition, 1950; *Thor, with Angels* (also see below; first produced at Canterbury Festival, England, 1948; produced in Washington, D.C., 1950), Oxford University Press, 1949.

Venus Observed (also see below; autumn comedy; first produced in London at St. James Theatre, 1950; produced in New York, 1952), Oxford University Press, 1950; *A Sleep of Prisoners* (also see below; first produced in London at St. James Church, 1951; produced in New York, 1951), Oxford University Press, 1951; *The Dark Is Light Enough: A Winter Comedy* (also see below; first produced on the West End at Aldwych Theatre, 1954; produced in New York, 1955), Oxford University Press, 1954; *Curtmantle* (also see below; first produced in Tilburg, Holland, 1961), Oxford University Press, 1961, 2nd edition, 1965; *A Yard of Sun: A Summer Comedy* (first produced at Nottingham Festival, England, July 11, 1970; produced in Cleveland, Ohio, at Cleveland Playhouse, October 13, 1972), Oxford University Press, 1970.

Unpublished plays: "Open Door," first produced in London, 1935; "The Tower," (pageant), first produced at Tewkesbury Festival, England, 1939. Also author of radio plays for "Children's Hour" series, 1939-40, and of television plays, "The Canary," 1950, "The Tenant of Wildfell Hall," 1968, "The Brontes of Haworth" (four plays; also see below), 1973, "The Best of Enemies," 1976, and "Sister Dora," 1977.

Translator: Jean Anouilh, *Ring Around the Moon* (first produced on the West End at Globe Theatre, 1950), Oxford University Press, 1950; Jean Giraudoux, *Tiger at the Gates* (also see below; first produced on the West End at Apollo Theatre, 1955), Oxford University Press, 1955, 2nd edition, Methuen, 1961; Anouilh, *The Lark* (first produced on the West End at Lyric Theatre, 1955), Methuen, 1955, Oxford University Press, 1956; Giraudoux, *Duel of Angels* (also see below; first produced on the West End at Apollo Theatre, 1958), Methuen, 1958, Oxford University Press, 1959; Giraudoux, *Judith* (also see below; first produced on the West End at Her Majesty's Theatre, 1962), Methuen, 1962; Sidonie Gabrielle Colette, *The Boy and the Magic,* Dobson, 1964, Putnam, 1965; Henrik

Ibsen, *Peer Gynt,* Oxford University Press, 1970; Edmond Rostand, *Cyrano de Bergerac* (first produced at the Chichester Festival Theatre, 1975), Oxford University Press, 1975.

Other writings: (With W. A. Darlington and others) *An Experience of Critics and the Approach to Dramatic Criticism,* Perpetua, 1952, Oxford University Press, 1953; *The Boat that Mooed* (juvenile), Macmillan, 1965; *The Brontes of Haworth,* Davis-Poynter, 1975; *Can You Find Me: A Family History,* Oxford University Press, 1978; *Death Is a Kind of Love* (lecture), Tidal Press, 1979; *Charlie Hammond's Sketch Book,* Oxford University Press, 1980.

Omnibus volumes: *Three Plays: The Firstborn; Thor, with Angels; A Sleep of Prisoners,* Oxford University Press, 1960; (translator) Jean Giraudoux, *Plays* (contains *Judith, Tiger at the Gates,* and *Duel of Angels*), Methuen, 1963; *Plays* (contains *Thor, with Angels* and *The Lady's Not for Burning*), Oxford University Press, 1969; *Plays* (contains *The Boy with a Cart, The Firstborn,* and *Venus Observed*), Oxford University Press, 1970; *Plays* (contains *A Sleep of Prisoners, The Dark Is Light Enough,* and *Curtmantle*), Oxford University Press, 1971.

Filmscripts: "A Queen Is Crowned," Universal, 1953; "The Beggar's Opera," Warner Brothers, 1953; "Ben Hur," Metro-Goldwyn-Mayer, 1959; "Barabbas," Dino de Laurentis Productions, 1961; "The Bible: In the Beginning," Twentieth Century-Fox, 1966, published as *The Bible: An Original Screenplay,* Pocket Books, 1966.

Work appears in anthologies, including: *Representative Modern Plays: Ibsen to Tennessee Williams,* edited by Robert Warnock, Scott, Foresman, 1964; *The Modern Theatre,* edited by Robert W. Corrigan, Macmillan, 1964; *The Drama Bedside Book,* edited by H. F. Rubinstein, Atheneum, 1966.

SIDELIGHTS: A British dramatist best known for his elegant verse plays, Christopher Fry is also a critic and translator who branched into nonfiction in 1978 with *Can You Find Me: A Personal History.* As Fry explains in the book, the project began when someone suggested that he write a childhood memoir; it developed into a history when he realized that he was less interested in the details of his youth than in "what led up to those years, the story of my parents and my grandparents, aunts and uncles, the network of events and characters out of which I had emerged."

For information about his ancestors Fry turned to the diary of Ada Louise, his maiden aunt, supplementing her detailed lifelong account with family letters and personal memories. The title he took from a postcard his mother sent Ada in 1906: "Thought this sheep-shearing photo would interest you. Can you find me." It is a good title, Patricia Beer of the *Times Literary Supplement* reports, because "the absence of the question mark . . . evokes from the start the literate but not highly educated members of the middle class who are to be the main characters."

While Fry finds his family remarkable, critics say they were ordinary folk, made interesting through Fry's portrayal. "They were," says Beer, "people with talents, problems, and peculiarities that were only occasionally more dramatic than anybody elses. Mr. Fry makes them memorable by portraying them precisely as they were, with no descent to the picturesque." And, writing in the *New Republic,* Marc Granetz echoes this sentiment: "Family trees, photographs and actual letters help [retrieve the past,] but the author of a family history's most important resources are his skillfulness with language and a strong sense of perspective. Christopher Fry has both."

Though *Can You Find Me* was well-received, Fry's literary reputation still rests on his plays—an unorthodox mixture of verse and prose which, according to David Daiches in *The Present Age in British Literature,* have "restored to English drama something of the verbal sprightliness and the relish of the exploratory and suggestive use of language that we get in the Elizabethans." While some critics maintain that Fry's popularity is linked to his language skills, others such as Derek Stanford believe it stems from a combination of qualities. "In a universe often viewed as mechanic," Stanford writes in *Christopher Fry,* "he has posited the principle of mystery; in an age of necessitarian ethics, he has stood unequivocally for ideas of free-will. In theatre technique, he has gaily ignored the sacrosanct conventions of naturalistic drama; and in terms of speech he has brought back poetry onto the stage with undoctored abandon."

Fry's plays have been translated into French, German, Spanish, Dutch, Norwegian, Finnish, Italian, Swedish, Danish, Greek, Serbo-Croat, Hungarian, Tamil, Portuguese, Flemish, Czech, and Polish.

BIOGRAPHICAL/CRITICAL SOURCES: Derek Stanford, *Christopher Fry: An Appreciation,* Nevill, 1951; David Daiches, *The Present Age in British Literature,* Indiana University Press, 1958; Kenneth Muir, *Contemporary Theatre,* Edward Arnold, 1962; Stanley M. Wiersma, *Christopher Fry: A Critical Essay,* Eerdmans, 1970; Derek Stanford, *Christopher Fry,* Longman Group, revised edition, 1971; *Contemporary Literary Criticism,* Gale, Volume II, 1974, Volume X, 1979, Volume XIV, 1980; Christopher Fry, *Can You Find Me,* Oxford University Press, 1978; *Times Literary Supplement,* October 20, 1978; *New Republic,* December 2, 1978; *New York Times Book Review,* January 21, 1979.

* * *

FULLER, John (Leopold) 1937-

PERSONAL: Born January 1, 1937, in Ashford, Kent, England; son of Roy Broadbent (a poet and lawyer) and Kathleen (Smith) Fuller; married Cicely Prudence Martin, July 20, 1960; children: Sophie Claire, Louisa Charlotte, Emily Renira Alice. *Education:* New College, Oxford, B.A., 1960, M.A., 1964, B.Litt., 1965. *Home:* 4 Benson Place, Oxford, England. *Office:* Magdalen College, Oxford, England.

CAREER: State University of New York at Buffalo, visiting lecturer in English, 1962-63; University of Manchester, Manchester, England, assistant lecturer, 1963-66; Magdalen College, Oxford, England, fellow and tutor in English, 1966—. *Awards, honors:* Newdigate Prize, 1960; Richard Hillary Award, 1961; E. C. Gregory Award, 1965; Geoffrey Faber Memorial Prize, 1974, for *Cannibals and Missionaries* and *Epistles to Several Persons;* Southern Arts Literature Prize, 1980.

WRITINGS—Poetry: *Fairground Music,* Chatto & Windus, with Hogarth Press, 1961; *The Tree That Walked,* Chatto & Windus, with Hogarth Press, 1967; *The Art of Love,* The Review (Oxford, England), 1968; *The Labours of Hercules: A Sonnet Sequence,* Manchester Institute of Contemporary Arts, 1970; *The Wreck,* limited edition, Turret Books, 1970; *Cannibals and Missionaries,* Secker & Warburg, 1972; *Boys in a Pie,* Steam Press (London), 1972; *Hut Groups,* limited edition, Cellar Press (Hertfordshire, England), 1973; (with Adrian Mitchell and Peter Levi) *Penguin Modern Poets 22,* Penguin, 1973; *Epistles to Several Persons,* Secker & Warburg, 1973; *Poems and Epistles,* David R. Godine, 1974; *Squeaking Crust,*

Chatto & Windus, 1974; *A Bestiary*, Sycamore Press, 1974; *The Mountain in the Sea*, Secker & Warburg, 1975; *Lies and Secrets*, Secker & Warburg, 1979; *The Illusionists*, Secker & Warburg, 1980; *Waiting for the Music*, Salamander, 1982; *The Beautiful Inventions*, Secker & Warburg, 1983.

Libretti: *Herod Do Your Worst: A Nativity Opera* (produced in Thame, Oxfordshire, England, 1967; music by Bryan Kelly), Novello (London), 1968; *Three London Songs*, music by Kelly, Novello, 1969; *Half a Fortnight* (produced in Leicestershire, England, 1970; music by Kelly), Novello, 1973; *The Spider Monkey Uncle King* (produced in Cookham, Berkshire, England, 1971; music by Kelly), Novello, 1974.

Unpublished libretti: "Fox-Trot" (music by Kelly), produced in Leicestershire, 1972; "The Queen in the Golden Tree" (music by Kelly), produced in Edinburgh, 1974; "How Did You Get Here, Jonno?" (music by Kelly), produced in Wolverchampton, Staffordshire, England, 1975; "The Ship of Sounds" (music by Kelly), produced in Leicestershire, 1975; "Adam's Apple" (music by Kelly), produced in Abingdon, Berkshire, England, 1975; "Linda" (music by Kelly), produced in Reading, Berkshire, England, 1977; "St. Francis of Assissi" (music by Kelly), produced in London, 1981.

Editor: (With J. Mitchell and others) *Light Blue Dark Blue*, Macdonald & Co., 1960; *Oxford Poetry 1960*, Fantasy Press, 1960; *Poetry Supplement*, Poetry Book Society (London), 1962; (with Harold Pinter and Peter Redgrove) *New Poems 1967: A P.E.N. Anthology of Contemporary Poetry*, Hutchinson, 1968; *Poetry Supplement*, Poetry Book Society, 1970; *Dramatic Works of John Gay*, Oxford University Press, 1982; *New Poetry 8*, Hutchinson, 1982.

Criticism: *A Reader's Guide to W. H. Auden*, Farrar, 1970.

Fiction: *The Last Bid* (novel), Deutsch, 1975; *The Extraordinary Wool Mill and Other Stories*, Deutsch, 1980.

Other: *The Sonnet*, Methuen, 1972.

Editor of *Nemo's Almanac*, an annual.

SIDELIGHTS: David Harsent of *Spectator* commented: "John Fuller is a poet of formidable intelligence and skill; he is also rewardingly susceptible to the oddities of experience: the strange lesions in our lives around which lines of poetry accrete. His two . . . collections, *Fairground Music* and *The Tree That Walked*, are books one goes back to repeatedly for their wit, their depth and their sheer entertainment value. *Cannibals and Missionaries* displays all those qualities." Peter Porter of the *Observer* noted in reference to *Epistles to Several Persons:* "These enormously resourceful poems are a pleasure to read—only one doubt remains with me: is this stanza a little light for what are often serious matters? Burns, writing in dialect, made it surprisingly tough. Fuller is sometimes too bland. His rhyming is prodigious but not cumbrous, his marshalling of proper names always apt, and his syntax gives the necessary lift to the metre. One is always being delighted by the touch of a master."

BIOGRAPHICAL/CRITICAL SOURCES: Observer, November 12, 1961; *Poetry Review*, summer, 1967; Ian Hamilton, *A Poetry Chronicle: Essays and Reviews*, Harper, 1973; *Poetry*, March, 1977; *The New Republic*, May 28, 1977; *London Review of Books*, January 24, 1980; *Times Literary Supplement*, March 28, 1980, December 19, 1980; *Quarto*, November, 1980.

FURTADO, Celso 1920-

PERSONAL: Born July 26, 1920, in Pombal, Paraiba, Brazil; son of Mauricio Medeiros and Maria Alice (Monteiro) Furtado; married Lucia Tosi (a chemist), September 15, 1948 (divorced, 1975); children: Mario, Andre. *Education:* University of Brazil, M.A., 1944; University of Paris, Ph.D., 1948; Cambridge University, postdoctoral study, 1957-58. *Home:* 11, rue Guy de la Brosse, 75005 Paris, France. *Office:* Ecole de Hautes Etudes en Sciences Sociales, Paris, France.

CAREER: United Nations Economic Commission for Latin America, economist, 1949-57; Development Bank of Brazil, director, 1959-60; Superintendency for the Development of the Northeast of Brazil, executive head, 1959-64; Brazilian government, minister of planning, 1962-63; Yale University, New Haven, Conn., research fellow, 1964-65; Universite Pantheon, Sorbonne, Paris, France, professor of economics, 1965-79; Ecole de Hautes Etudes en Sciences Sociales, Paris, directeur d'Etudes Associe, 1980—. Visiting professor, American University, Washington, D.C., 1972, Cambridge University, 1973-74, and Columbia University, 1977.

WRITINGS: The Economic Growth of Brazil, University of California Press, 1963; *Development and Underdevelopment*, University of California Press, 1964; *Diagnosis of the Brazilian Crisis*, University of California Press, 1965; *Economic Development of Latin America*, Cambridge University Press, 1970; *Obstacles to Development in Latin America*, Doubleday, 1970; *Analise do Modelo brasileiro*, Civilizacao Brasileira, 1972; *O Mito do Desenvolvimento Economico*, Paz e Terra, 1974; *Prefacio a Nova Economia Politica*, Paz e Terra, 1976; *Criatividade e Dependencia*, Paz e Terra, 1978; *Pequena Introducao ao Desenvolvimento*, Editora Nacional, 1980; *O Brasil pos-"milagre"*, Paz e Terra, 1981; *A Nova Dependencia*, Paz e Terra, 1982.

* * *

FUSS, Peter 1932-

PERSONAL: Surname rhymes with "goose"; born February 11, 1932, in Berlin, Germany; naturalized U.S. citizen; son of Ernest Martin and Ruth (Sonnemann) Fuss; married Carol Ann Wimsatt, November 25, 1961 (divorced, January 14, 1976); married Barbara Harrington, May 1, 1982; children: (first marriage) Tobin, Jenna. *Education:* Fordham University, B.S., 1954; Harvard University, M.A., 1956, Ph.D., 1962. *Home:* 761 Radcliffe, St. Louis, Mo. 63130. *Office:* Department of Philosophy, University of Missouri, St. Louis, Mo. 63121.

CAREER: University of Michigan, Ann Arbor, lecturer in philosophy, 1960-61; University of California, Riverside, lecturer, 1961-62, assistant professor, 1962-68, associate professor of philosophy, 1968-69; University of Missouri—St. Louis, associate professor, 1969-75, professor of philosophy, 1975—. Visiting associate professor, University of Washington, Seattle, 1966-67. Consultant to Yale University Press and Humanities Press. *Member:* Society for the Study of the History of Philosophy, Society for Phenomenology and Existential Philosophy, Hegel Society of America, American Philosophical Association, American Association of University Professors. *Awards, honors:* Humanities Institute fellowship, University of California, 1968-69; summer faculty fellowship, University of Missouri, 1973; curriculum development grant, University of Missouri, 1978.

WRITINGS: (Editor and translator with Philip Wheelwright) *Five Philosophers,* Odyssey, 1963; *The Moral Philosophy of Josiah Royce,* Harvard University Press, 1965; (editor and translator with Henry L. Shapiro) *Friedrich Nietzsche: A Self-Portrait from His Letters,* Harvard University Press, 1971; *God in Contemporary Thought,* Nauwelaerts, 1977.

Contributor: *Conscience,* Alba House, 1973; Terence Ball, editor, *Political Theory and Praxis,* University of Minnesota Press, 1977; Robert W. Shahan and Kenneth R. Merrill, editors, *American Philosophy from Edwards to Quine,* University of Oklahoma Press, 1977; Melvyn A. Mill, editor, *Hannah Arendt: The Recovery of the Public World,* St. Martin's Press, 1979. Also contributor of essays and reviews to professional journals, including *Idealistic Studies* and *Clio*. Editorial consultant, *Journal of History of Philosophy*.

WORK IN PROGRESS: A translation of and critical commentary on Hegel's *Phenomenology of Spirit,* with John Dobbins; a commentary on Rousseau's *Second Discourse*.

G

GAEDEKE, Ralph M(ortimer) 1941-

PERSONAL: Born May 25, 1941, in East Prussia; son of Horst F. and Margot (Boltz) Gaedeke; married Johanna V. House (an administrative assistant), June 19, 1965; children: Jolene R., Michael C. *Education:* University of Washington, Seattle, B.A., 1964, M.A., 1965, Ph.D., 1969. *Home:* 237 Hartnell Pl., Sacramento, Calif. 95825; and P.O. Box 46, Anchor Point, Alaska 99556 (summer address). *Office:* School of Business and Public Administration, California State University at Sacramento, 6000 J. St., Sacramento, Calif. 95819.

CAREER: University of Saskatchewan, Saskatoon, Canada, instructor in business administration, 1965-66; University of Washington, Seattle, instructor, 1967-69; California State University, Sacramento, associate professor of marketing and international business, 1969-71; University of Alaska, Anchorage, associate professor of business administration, 1971-73; California State University, Sacramento, associate professor, 1973-74, professor of marketing and international business, 1974—. Summer professor at University of Alaska, 1974. Consultant to Small Business Administration and private corporations in Anchorage, 1971-72 and 1974-75, and Sacramento, 1973-74 and 1974-75; consultant to Community Economic Development Corp., Anchorage, 1974-75. Also consultant to various savings and loan associations, Campbell-Hausfeld, and Detwiler Corporation. *Member:* Academy of International Business, American Marketing Association (president, Sacramento Valley Chapter, 1974-75), Beta Gamma Sigma, Delta Sigma Pi.

WRITINGS: (With Guy Gordon, John Wheatley, John Hallag, and D. McNabb) *The Impact of a Consumer Credit Limitation Law—Washington State: Initiative 245* (monograph), University of Washington Press, 1970; (with Warren W. Etcheson) *Consumerism: Viewpoints from Business, Government and the Consumer Interest,* Canfield Press, 1972; (with Dean F. Olson and Jack W. Peterson) *A Study of the Impact of Ten Rural Consumer Cooperative Stores* (monograph), Office of Economic Opportunity, 1973; (with Eugene Eaton) *Dimensions of Relevant Markets: The Case of Urethane Building Insulation in Alaska* (monograph), Upjohn, 1975; *Village Development Alternatives for Old Chitina* (monograph), AHTNA Regional Corp., 1975; *Marketing in Private and Public Nonprofit Organizations,* Goodyear Publishing, 1977; (with Dennis H. Tootelian) *Small Business Management: Operations and Profiles,* Goodyear Publishing, 1978, 2nd edition, Scott, Foresman, 1984.

(With Tootelian) *Small Business Management,* Goodyear Publishing, 1980, 2nd edition, Scott, Foresman, 1984; (with Tootelian and Leete A. Thompson) *Marketing Management: Cases and Readings,* Goodyear Publishing, 1980, 2nd edition, Scott, Foresman, 1984; (with Tootelian) *Marketing: Principles and Applications,* West Publishing, 1983. Also contributor to *Encyclopedia of Professional Management,* 1979, and American Institute for Decision Sciences *Proceedings and Abstracts,* 1979, 1980. Contributor of book reviews and articles to professional journals.

* * *

GALINSKY, Ellen 1942-

PERSONAL: Born April 24, 1942, in Pittsburgh, Pa.; daughter of Melvin H. (a businessman) and Leora (a businesswoman; maiden name, Osgood) May; married Norman Galinsky (an artist), August 15, 1965; children: Philip Andrew, Lara Elizabeth. *Education:* Vassar College, A.B., 1964; Bank Street College of Education, M.S.Ed., 1970. *Home address:* Lawrence Lane, Palisades, N.Y. 10964. *Agent:* Virginia Barber, 353 West 21st St., New York, N.Y. 10011. *Office:* Bank Street College of Education, 610 West 112th St., New York, N.Y. 10025.

CAREER: Bank Street College of Education, New York, N.Y., teacher, researcher, and project director of the work and family life study and family matters, 1964—. *Member:* Authors Guild, Authors League of America.

WRITINGS: *Catbird* (juvenile; with own photographs), Coward, 1971; *The Baby Cardinal* (juvenile; with own photographs; Junior Literary Guild selection), Putnam, 1976; *Beginnings* (nonfiction), Houghton, 1976; (with William H. Hooks) *The New Extended Family,* Houghton, 1977; *Between Generations: The Six Stages of Parenthood,* Times Books, 1981. Contributor to magazines, including *Parents' Magazine* and *Redbook.*

WORK IN PROGRESS: Two practical books for parents, answering their questions with the expertise of professionals and parents, for Times Books.

SIDELIGHTS: Ellen Galinsky writes: "I am interested in nature, in how natural forces wear away at and shape each other;

I am interested in how the natural world relates to the human one; I am interested in people and how they change; I am interested in how institutions affect people; and I am interested in myths and realities. I write and photograph to probe the dualities that lie at the end of every search."

In *Between Generations: The Six Stages of Parenthood,* Galinsky, an early-childhood specialist, focuses on the relationship between parent and child. "The result," writes Anthony Astrachan in the *New York Times Book Review,* "is a book that is useful and important but not truly innovative, a hybrid of Benjamin Spock/Jean Piaget/Berry Brazelton on the one hand and Daniel Levinson/Roger Gould/Gail Sheehy on the other." Nonetheless, *Between Generations,* which contains anecdotes and interviews, should be helpful to "both parents needing guidelines and the general reader interested in . . . human development," the *Library Journal* reviewer concludes.

BIOGRAPHICAL/CRITICAL SOURCES: New York Times Book Review, February 12, 1978, June 28, 1981; *Library Journal,* December 15, 1980; *Los Angeles Times,* February 12, 1981.

* * *

GALLAGHER, Charles A(ugustus) 1927-

PERSONAL: Born August 18, 1927, in New York, N.Y.; son of Charles A. (a newspaperman and union president) and Therese (Farrell) Gallagher. *Education:* Loyola University, Chicago, Ill., B.A., 1951, P.H.L., 1952; Woodstock College, S.T.L., 1959. *Office:* Pastoral and Matrimonial Renewal Center, 567 Morris Ave., Elizabeth, N.J. 07208.

CAREER: Entered Society of Jesus (Jesuits), 1945; teacher of Latin, mathematics, and religion, and basketball coach at Roman Catholic high school in Buffalo, N.Y., 1952-55; ordained Roman Catholic priest, 1958; involved in spiritual training in Port Townsend, Wash., 1959-60; Xavier High School, New York, N.Y., assistant headmaster, 1960-62; Gonzaga Retreat House, Monroe, N.Y., youth retreat master, 1962-67; Marriage Encounter Resource Community, Great Neck, N.Y., executive secretary priest, 1968-74, director, 1974-81; Pastoral and Matrimonial Renewal Center, Elizabeth, N.J., executive director, 1981—.

WRITINGS: Marriage Encounter: As I Have Loved You, Doubleday, 1975; (with Joseph McDonald and Judith McDonald) *Jesus Invites Us to Love,* Sadlier, 1976; (with Lyman Coleman) *Evenings for Parents,* Sadlier, 1976; (with Coleman) *Evenings for Couples,* Sadlier, 1976; (with Coleman) *More Evenings for Parents,* Sadlier, 1977; (with Coleman) *More Evenings for Couples,* Sadlier, 1977.

One Flesh, Veritas Family Resources (Dublin, Ireland), 1980; (with Peter Davis and Cathy Davis) *How to Bring Up Children Today,* Veritas Family Resources, 1982; *Call to Healing,* Sadlier, 1982; (with Oliver Crilly and John Doherty) *Prayer, Saints, Scriptures and Sharing,* Pastoral and Matrimonial Renewal Center, in press; (with John Colligan and Kathy Colligan) *Building Extended Family,* Pastoral and Matrimonial Renewal Center, in press.

WORK IN PROGRESS: Celebrating Advent; Working at Lent; Enjoying Feast Days; Preparing Engaged Couples for the Sacrament of Matrimony; Reconciliation of Priests with Their People.

SIDELIGHTS: Charles A. Gallagher told *CA* that "all sorts of lip service is being paid to marriage and the family and to parents. The basic problem in the western world is alienation. The answer is not fundamentally in the field of economics or education, but in relationship. Marriage is the core relationship in human experience. We are a society that is technologically highly developed and personally impoverished. Marriage Encounter, a movement of the Catholic Church, offers real hope for human progress and development."

* * *

GALLUN, Raymond Z(inke) 1911-
(John Callahan, Dow Elstar, E. V. Raymond)

PERSONAL: Surname is accented on last syllable; born March 22, 1911, in Beaver Dam, Wis.; son of Adolph (a farmer) and Martha (Zinke) Gallun; married Frieda Ernestine Talmey (a high-school foreign language teacher), December 26, 1959 (died May 19, 1974); married Bertha Erickson Backman, February 24, 1978. *Education:* Attended University of Wisconsin, Madison, 1929-30, Alliance Francaise, Paris, France, 1938-39, and San Marcos University, Lima, Peru, 1960. *Politics:* "No party affiliation." *Religion:* Agnostic. *Home:* 110-20 71st Ave., Forest Hills, N.Y. 11375. *Agent:* Robert P. Mills, 333 Fifth Ave., New York, N.Y. 10016.

CAREER: Science-fiction writer. Prior to 1942, worked as a laborer in a cannery, a shoe factory, and a hemp mill. Construction worker for U.S. Army Corps of Engineers, 1942-43; marine blacksmith at Pearl Harbor Navy Yard, 1944; technical writer on sonar equipment for EDO Corp., College Point, N.Y., 1964-75. *Member:* Science Fiction Writers of America. *Awards, honors:* First Fandom Hall of Fame Award, 1979.

WRITINGS—Science fiction: *People Minus X,* Simon & Schuster, 1957; *The Planet Strappers,* Pyramid Press, 1961; *The Eden Cycle,* Ballantine, 1974; *The Best of Raymond Z. Gallun,* edited by J. J. Pierce, Del Ray Books, 1977; *Skyclimber,* Tower Books, 1981.

Contributor to anthologies: *The Best of Science Fiction,* edited by Groff Conklin, Crown, 1946; *Adventures in Time and Space,* edited by J. Healy and J. Francis McComas, Random House, 1946, published as *Famous Science-Fiction Stories,* Modern Library, 1957; *Imagination Unlimited,* edited by Everett F. Bleiler and T. E. Dikty, Farrar, Straus & Young, 1951; *Possible Worlds of Science Fiction,* edited by Conklin, Vanguard Press, 1951; *Space Service,* edited by Andre Norton, World Publishing, 1953; *Space Pioneers,* edited by Norton, World Publishing, 1954; *Thinking Machines,* edited by Conklin, Vanguard Press, 1954; *Escales dans l'infini,* edited by Georges Gallet, Hachette, 1954.

Coming of the Robots, edited by Sam Moscowitz, Collier, 1963; *Five Unearthly Visions,* edited by Conklin, Gold Medal Books, 1965; *Tomorrow's Worlds,* edited by Robert Silverberg, Meredith Press, 1969; *The Astounding-Analog Reader,* edited by Harry Harrison and Brian W. Aldiss, Doubleday, 1972; *Jupiter,* edited by Carol Pohl and Frederik Pohl, Ballantine, 1973; *Before the Golden Age,* edited by Isaac Asimov, Doubleday, 1974; *History of the Science-Fiction Magazine,* edited by Michael Ashley, Pitman Press, 1974; *The Best of Planet Stories,* edited by Leigh Brackett, Ballantine, 1975; *Earth Is the Strangest Planet,* edited by Robert Silverberg, Thomas Nelson, 1977; *Science Fiction of the Forties,* edited by Frederik Pohl, Avon, 1978; *Analog Readers' Choice,* edited by Stanley Schmidt. Dial Press, 1981.

Also author of unpublished novels *Gemi the Finder, Ormund House* (autobiographical fiction), *The Magnificent Mutation,* and *Legend Seed.* Contributor of several hundred stories, sometimes under pseudonyms John Callahan, Dow Elstar, and E. V. Raymond, to science fiction magazines and other popular periodicals, including *Astounding Stories, Collier's,* and *Family Circle*.

SIDELIGHTS: Most of Raymond Z. Gallun's stories were published in the 1930s, a period of science-fiction writing presently being revived and gaining considerable popularity among fans of the genre. In a letter to *CA,* Gallun comments upon the current science-fiction scene: "Almost by definition, science fiction should be forward-looking, backward-looking, inward-looking, every-which-way-looking—innovative of possibly useful ideas as it used to be, not so often tedious and repetitious. Sorcerers and swordplay, pseudo-medieval settings and improbable, super-muscular heroes and anti-heroes, tired socio-political themes rehashed on planets of distant stars, still far out of the reach of our present reality. These things have their place, of course. Yet in such over-muchness? Is the readership truly scared into that degree of escape from what is actual? Or away from solid technology, which is still the best available approach to problem-solving?

"We are at the edge of a historic fledging from the Earth into the wider frontier of the universe. The first real steps are possible now—while we also listen for intelligent signals from the stars. So why isn't more attention paid to what is on our true horizon? Manned and womaned exploration of Mars and the first habitations there. Probes into local gas giants (Jupiter, Saturn, etc.) or down into their moons. Mysterious Io and its active sulphur-volcanoes; the dense, cryogenic nitrogen atmosphere of Titan. Probes onto Venus and the asteroids. Maybe the possible refurbishing of our own moon. . . .

"And as for the other—non-spatial—fields: How about, for instance, probing into ourselves? Isn't it obvious that our bodies know more than our conscious minds, controlling and monitoring, as they do, thousands of intricate processes, including the very existence of our conscious minds, which are like mere bubbles floating on top of all of that physical bio-complexity? Yes, we get a free ride through life atop a wonderful bio-machine about which our understanding remains very limited. As a very small example of the superiority of bodily knowledge, bodies (animal before human) recognized the existence of and successfully fought disease germs a billion years before Pasteur. But what if, by some minor mutation in the nervous system of some person, the barrier between body know-how and conscious mind were broken down, so that all that knowledge became available by means of an introspective sense?

"In other areas of science-fiction writing—instead of so much patterning from the historically dismal, louse-ridden, bigotry-pervaded Middle Ages, why not, for variation at least, draw from the cultures of Ancient Rome, Mesopotamia, Egypt, or from some possible first civilization of the latest ice age, in the then half-dry Mediterranean basin? Ready-made there would even be the menace of a great flood when the polar glaciers dwindled and much of their water went back into the oceans.

"You see, I—along with other forward- and outward-looking writers and readers—have had my differences with what publishers have been putting out lately. Of course the publishers should know better than I what kind of yarns have had the best sales figures in the last couple of years. To a certain extent publishers lead and guide their readership and, in return, are influenced by reader feedback—some of which undoubtedly calls for yet more of the same. But where is the end of this except in dull monotony, which must adversely affect sales more and more, as more and more readers feel cheated when flowery blurbs and publicity fall flat while the books are being read?

"I don't think the fault is with the writers, who are pretty flexible people generally, nor do I think it is with the editors, who must conform to commands from higher up. I hope the time will soon return when book manuscripts will again be selected on the basis of their individual merit, instead of being picked, packaged, and marketed by name-trademark and category, as if they were detergents, pet-food, or sugary breakfast cereals."

BIOGRAPHICAL/CRITICAL SOURCES: Michael Ashley, *The History of the Science Fiction Magazine,* Part I: *1926-1935,* Pitman, 1974; *Foundation: The Review of Science Fiction,* Number 22, 1981.

* * *

GARB, Solomon 1920-

PERSONAL: Born October 19, 1920, in New York, N.Y.; son of Gerson and Fanny (Smith) Garb; married Hildreth Rose; children: James, Gordon, Richard. *Education:* Cornell University, A.B., 1940, M.D., 1943.

CAREER: Cornell University, Medical College, New York, N.Y., research fellow, 1949-50, instructor in pharmacology, 1950-53, assistant professor of clinical pharmacology, 1953-56, assistant professor of pharmacology, 1956-57; Albany Medical College, Albany, N.Y., associate professor of pharmacology, 1957-61; University of Missouri, Medical School, Columbia, associate professor, 1961-66, professor of pharmacology and associate professor of community health, 1966-70; American Medical Center, Denver, Colo., scientific director, beginning 1970; University of Colorado, Denver Medical Center, Denver, associate clinical professor of medicine, beginning 1974. Cancer researcher. Consultant to American Medical Association Council on Drugs; vice-chairman of Civil Defense advisory committee, Boone County, Mo.; member of Columbia Civil Defense advisory committee. *Military service:* U.S. Army, Medical Corps, 1944-46; became captain.

MEMBER: American Medical Association, American College of Clinical Pharmacology (fellow), American Association for the Advancement of Science, Society for Experimental Biology and Medicine, American Society for Pharmacology and Experimental Therapeutics, Association of Hospital Directors of Medical Education, American Federation for Clinical Research, New York Academy of Sciences, Missouri Medical Society, Boone County Medical Society. *Awards, honors:* Polk Prize for research, Medical College, Cornell University, 1943; Henry M. Moses Prize for research, Montefiore Hospital (New York), 1949; research fellowships from New York Heart Association, 1949, and American Heart Association, 1953; U.S. Public Health Service, senior research fellowship, 1957, career research development award, 1962.

WRITINGS—All published by Springer Publishing Co.: *Laboratory Tests in Common Use,* 1956, 6th edition, 1976; *Essentials of Therapeutic Nutrition,* 1958; (with Betty J. Crim) *Pharmacology and Patient Care,* Springer, 1962, 3rd edition (with Garf Thomas) 1970; (with Evelyn Eng) *Disaster Handbook,* 1964, 2nd edition, 1969; *Cure for Cancer: A National Goal,* 1968; *Clinical Guide to Undesirable Drug Interactions and Interferences,* 1971, revised edition published as *Undesirable Drug Interactions,* 1974; (with Eleanor Krakauer and Carson Justice) *Abbreviations and Acronyms in Medicine and Nursing,* 1975; *Food: High Nutrition, Low Cost,* 1975. Also author of *The Physician in Civil Defense,* c. 1961. Contributor to *World Book Encyclopedia* and contributor of more than fifty articles to medical journals.

WORK IN PROGRESS: A book on drug advertising and its effects on the public; a book on moondoggling.†

* * *

GARBINI, Giovanni 1931-

PERSONAL: Born October 8, 1931, in Rome, Italy; son of Vittorio and Margherita (Virgili) Garbini; married Maria Enrica Mognaschi (a teacher), August 23, 1956; children: Paolo, Enrica. *Education:* Attended University of Rome, 1950-54. *Religion:* Roman Catholic. *Home:* Via Piave 41, Rome, Italy 00187.

CAREER: University of Rome, Rome, Italy, associate professor of Semitic epigraphy, 1957-68; professor of Semitic philology, Oriental Institute, Naples, Italy, 1964-67, Superior Normal School, Pisa, Italy, 1977-82, University of Rome, 1982—. Has taken part in archaeological expeditions at Ramat Rahel (Jerusalem), Tas Silg (Malta), Motya (Sicily), Monte Sirai (Sardinia), and in northern Yemen. *Military service:* Italian Army, officer, 1955-56.

WRITINGS: Il Semitico di Nord-Ovest, Oriental Institute (Naples), 1960; *Le Origini della Statuaria Sumerica,* University of Rome Press, 1962; *The Ancient World,* McGraw, 1966; *Le Lingue semitiche: Studi di storia linguistica,* Oriental Institute, 1972; *Storia e problemi dell 'epigrafia semitica,* Oriental Institute, 1979; *I Fenici: Storia e religione,* Oriental Institute, 1980.

WORK IN PROGRESS: Studies in Semitic historical linguistics; a philological commentary to the *Song of Songs.*

* * *

GARBO, Norman 1919-

PERSONAL: Born February 15, 1919, in New York, N.Y.; son of Maximillian W. and Fannie (Deitz) Garbo; married Rhoda Locke, April 15, 1942; children: Mickey. *Education:* Attended City College (now City College of the City University of New York), 1935-37, and New York Academy of Fine Art, 1937-41. *Residence:* Sands Point, Long Island, N.Y.

CAREER: Portrait painter, 1941—; writer, lecturer. *Military service:* U.S. Army Air Forces, 1941-45; became lieutenant.

WRITINGS: Pull Up an Easel, A. S. Barnes, 1955; (with Howard Goodkind) *Confrontation,* Harper, 1966; *The Movement* (novel), Morrow, 1969; *To Love Again* (nonfiction), McGraw, 1977; *The Artist* (novel), Norton, 1978; *Cabal* (novel), Norton, 1979; *Spy* (novel), Norton, 1980; *Turner's Wife* (novel), Norton, in press.

Author of syndicated column, "Pull Up an Easel," for *Chicago Tribune* and New York News Syndicate, 1953-60; contributor of short stories to *Saturday Evening Post* and other periodicals.

BIOGRAPHICAL/CRITICAL SOURCES: New York Times Book Review, May 7, 1978, September 7, 1980; *Los Angeles Times Book Review,* March 25, 1979, September 21, 1980.

* * *

GARDINER, Judy 1922-

PERSONAL: Born May 18, 1922, in London, England; daughter of Godfrey (a major in the British Army) and Millicent (a former chorus girl) Collier; married George Gardiner (an engineer), April 6, 1946; children: David Mills, Angela Sarah-Louisa. *Education:* Educated in England. *Politics:* "Have none." *Religion:* "Have none." *Home:* Poplar Cottage, High Easter, Chelmsford, Essex, England. *Agent:* Rupert Crew Ltd., King's Mews, Gray's Inn Rd., London WC1N 2JA, England.

CAREER: Writer of fiction. *Military service:* Women's Auxiliary Air Force, 1940-43.

WRITINGS—Novels, except as indicated: *The Power of Sergeant Mettleship* (three novellas), M. Joseph, 1967; *The Dimbug,* M. Joseph, 1969; *My Love, My Land,* Hamlyn, 1980; *The Quick and the Dead,* Hamlyn, 1981, St. Martin's, 1982; *Who Was Sylvia?,* Severn House, 1982; *The Big Goodnight,* Hamlyn, 1982.

Also author of television plays including "Anniversary" and "You and Your Old German." Short stories have been published in *Argosy, Housewife, Good Housekeeping, Woman's Journal, She, Woman's Realm,* and other popular magazines in Britain.

WORK IN PROGRESS: A big novel covering the years between the two world wars, with a strong background of Liverpool.

SIDELIGHTS: Judy Gardiner wrote *CA:* "I began writing when I was very small, the stories evolving from a series of imaginary companions—I was an only child and probably a bit lonely. I think my writing life has been divided into two halves: the first belongs to the days when I wrote from an emotional compulsion. To scribble things down that had thrilled me, horrified me, etc. was always a great pleasure to me—a bit like having a drink or a cigarette. The second half dates from the time I began to write professionally. Learning the trade was a long and arduous business; there was no information available about what publishers and editors wanted; it just had to be trial and error and, being of a humble disposition, I always took it for granted that manuscripts were returned because they were bad and not merely unsuitable for that particular market.

"Eventually I got going and grabbed at every offer of an introduction to another editor or publisher, working very hard to produce the kind of work they wanted. In my time I've written practially everything except romance and porn (both tend to make me giggle). These days I count it as an extra bonus if I get the old kind of thrill from writing, but I do find a profound pleasure in the craft of writing itself. I'm very proud of being a professional writer and if my work entertains people—I've certainly no messages to offer!—then I count myself one of the happiest of mortals."

* * *

GARDNER, Howard 1943-

PERSONAL: Born July 11, 1943, in Scranton, Pa.; son of Ralph (a businessman) and Hilde (Weilheimer) Gardner; married Judith Krieger (a psychologist), June 9, 1966 (divorced); married Ellen Winner, November 23, 1982; children: (first marriage) Kerith, Jay, Andrew. *Education:* Harvard University, A.B. (summa cum laude), 1965, Ph.D., 1971; graduate study at London School of Economics and Political Science, 1966. *Home:* 15 Lancaster St., Cambridge, Mass. 02140.

CAREER: Harvard University, Cambridge, Mass., research associate, 1971—, co-director, Project Zero, 1973—; Boston Veteran's Administration Hospital, Boston, Mass., research psychologist, 1972—. Associate professor of medicine, Boston

University School of Medicine, 1979—. *Member:* Society for Research in Child Development, Academy of Aphasia, Phi Beta Kappa. *Awards, honors:* Claude Bernard Journalism Award from National Society for Medical Research, 1975, for "Brain Damage: Gateway to the Mind"; MacArthur Prize fellowship, 1981.

WRITINGS: (With Martin Grossack) *Man and Men,* Intext, 1970; *The Quest for Mind,* Knopf, 1973; *The Arts and Human Development,* Wiley, 1973; *The Shattered Mind: The Person after Brain Damage* (selection of *Psychology Today* Book Club and Quality Paperback Book Club), Knopf, 1975; *Developmental Psychology,* Little, Brown, 1978; *Artful Scribbles: The Significance of Children's Drawings,* Basic Books, 1980; *Art, Mind, and Brain,* Basic Books, 1982. Editor of "Classics in Psychology" and "Classics in Child Development," both for Arno. Contributor to professional journals. Contributing editor, *Psychology Today.*

WORK IN PROGRESS: A book on intelligence; a history of cognitive science.

SIDELIGHTS: Howard Gardner writes: "I am trained as a developmental psychologist. At present I conduct basic research on the development and breakdown of the capacity to use various kinds of symbols (words, pictures, gestures, and the like). I work with normal and gifted children and with once normal adults who have suffered brain damage. . . . I enjoy the challenge of trying to make my research, and that of other social scientists, accessible to the interested layman."

In one of his books, *Artful Scribbles: The Significance of Children's Drawings,* Gardner investigates the flowering of creativity in young children, its subsequent decline as they mature, and the questions that this developmental sequence raises. Why, he asks, does artistic expressiveness decline when children enter school? Should the work they produce be considered "real art"—or the domain of anthropologists? And what connection exists between children's spontaneous expressions and the deliberate work of mature artists? Writing in the *New York Times Book Review,* Marie Winn characterizes *Artful Scribbles* as "one of those studies that raises more questions than it can answer."

In his study, Gardner traces the artistic development of his own son and daughter over a period of months, and then years, sounding, to use Winn's words, "a poignant note that underlies much of this book—a note of diminishment and loss." For as the children mature, their drawings become more realistic, but less compelling. In his daughter's case, "dramatic scenes give way to placid bucolic compositions," which Gardner deems "predictable." But, unlike those who attribute this artistic decline to the oppressive atmosphere of schools, Gardner sees it as a natural step in development. Winn explains: "As language skills develop toward the end of early childhood, Mr. Gardner suggests, the child is able to rely more on linguistic resources for expression and no longer feels the deep need to communicate through the nonverbal medium of drawing."

While much of his discussion is theoretical, Gardner also deals with some educational issues, including "the vexed question of the value of copying," *Times Literary Supplement* critic Peter Fuller reports. "Copying," he continues, "has been out of favour in art education in recent years, but Gardner argues that, if it is introduced at a certain stage of development, and not over-rigidly imposed, it can provide an important bridge between drawing as a 'natural' expressive activity and participation in the pictorial tradition of one's own culture."

While he does not see any real "progress" in art from one generation to the next, Gardner does draw a parallel between the artistry of young children and that of great artists. Winn explains: "Gardner points out the similar pleasure each takes in the actual, sensual process of drawing, the similar willingness of each to flout convention, the similarly infallible sense of natural balance . . . and, perhaps most important, the identical need shared by young children and all great artists, to find a unique means of expression through the graphic medium." Writing in *Saturday Review,* Joyce Milton concludes that the book should be of interest to "anyone curious about the difference between the youngster who has not yet learned the rules of seeing and the master artist who has learned how to break them."

BIOGRAPHICAL/CRITICAL SOURCES: New York Times, February 14, 1975; *New York Times Book Review,* March 2, 1975, April 6, 1980; *Times Literary Supplement,* January 20, 1978, September 19, 1980; *Saturday Review,* May, 1980.

* * *

GARFIELD, Evelyn Picon 1940-

PERSONAL: Born August 23, 1940, in Newark, N.J.; daughter of Sol and Edith (Haskell) Picon; married former spouse Louis Garfield (a businessman), November 3, 1961; married Ivan Schulman (a professor); children: (first marriage) Gene Douglas, Audrey Suzanne. *Education:* University of Michigan, A.B., 1963; Washington University, St. Louis, Mo., M.A., 1967; Rutgers University, Ph.D., 1972. *Office:* Department of Romance and Germanic Languages, Wayne State University, Detroit, Mich. 48202.

CAREER: Montclair State College, Upper Montclair, N.J., assistant professor of Spanish language and literature, 1970-74; University of Massachusetts—Boston, co-director of Affirmative Action, in the office of the vice-chancellor for academic affairs, 1974-76; Brown University, Providence, R.I., assistant professor of Spanish and Latin American literature, 1976-80; Wayne State University, Detroit, Mich., associate professor of Spanish, 1980—. *Member:* Modern Language Association of America, American Association of University Professors, National Organization for Women, Women's Equity Action League, Phi Sigma Iota, Sigma Delta Pi. *Awards, honors:* Grant from American Philosophical Society, 1973, for travel to France; National Endowment for the Humanities grant, 1973; co-director, National Endowment for the Humanities summer seminar, 1982.

WRITINGS: Julio Cortazar, Ungar, 1975; *Es Julio Cortazar un surrealista?* (title means "Is Julio Cortazar a Surrealist?"), Editorial Gredos (Madrid), 1975; *Cortazar por Cortazar,* Centro de Investigaciones Linguistico-Literarias, Universidad Veracruzana (Mexico), 1978, 2nd edition, 1981.

Contributor: Jaime Alazarki and Ivar Ivask, editors, *The Final Island: The Fiction of Julio Cortazar,* University of Oklahoma Press, 1978; *In Honor of Boyd G. Carter,* University of Wyoming, 1981; *Nuevos asedios al modernismo,* Taurus, 1983; E. Dale Carter, editor, *Otro round: Estudios sobre la obra de Julio Cortazar,* California State University Press, 1983. Contributor to supplement of *Encyclopedia of World Literature in the Twentieth Century.* Contributor to numerous journals, including *Nueva Revista de Filologia Hispanica* (Mexico), *Hispanic Review, Revista Iberoamericana, Journal of Latin American Lore, Eco* (Bogota), and *Zona Franca* (Caracas).

WORK IN PROGRESS: Las entranas del vacio: Ensayos sobre la modernidad hispanoamericana, a theoretical investigation of Spanish American modernity, written in collaboration with husband, Ivan Schulman; *Women's Voices from Latin America: Interviews with Six Contemporary Authors,* critical essays, interviews, and bio-bibliography; *Introduccion a los estudios literarios: Espana e Hispanoamerica,* written in collaboration with Schulman.

BIOGRAPHICAL/CRITICAL SOURCES: Hispania, December, 1976.

* * *

GARNET, Eldon 1946-

PERSONAL: Born June 20, 1946, in Toronto, Ontario, Canada; son of Samuel and Sylvia (Goodman) Garnet. *Education:* University of Toronto, B.A., 1969; York University, M.A., 1972. *Agent:* Sydney Coin, 473 Brunswick Ave., Toronto, Ontario, Canada.

CAREER: Editor, poet, photographer, filmmaker. *Awards, honors:* Grants from Canada Council and the Arts and Ontario Arts Council.

WRITINGS: Angel (poems), Press Porcepic, 1971; *Asparagus* (poems), Rumblestill Press, 1973; (editor) *The Book of Process,* Rumblestill Press, 1974; (editor with Brian Trevers) *Plastic Bag,* Rumblestill Press, 1974; *The Last Adventure* (poems), Oberon, 1975; (editor) *The Other Canadian Poetry,* Press Porcepic, 1975; *The Martyrdom of Jean de Brebeuf* (a long poem), Press Porcepic, 1978; *JFM 232/Spiraling* (photography), IWI Communications, 1979; *Cultural Connections* (photography), Image Nation, 1982.

* * *

GATENBY, Rosemary 1918-

PERSONAL: First syllable of surname rhymes with "late"; born October 8, 1918, in Muncie, Ind.; daughter of Samuel Orr (an automotive engineer) and Edna (Cooper) White; married William Hal Gatenby (an executive), September 14, 1945; children: Halley, Jane. *Education:* Wellesley College, B.A., 1940; graduate study at Columbia University, 1940-41, and University of Toledo, 1948. *Politics:* Republican. *Religion:* Presbyterian. *Residence:* Weston, Conn.

CAREER: Sperry Gyroscope Co., Long Island, N.Y., secretary, 1942-45; free-lance writer.

WRITINGS—Mystery novels: *Evil Is as Evil Does,* Mill, 1967; *Aim to Kill,* Mill, 1968; *Deadly Relations,* Morrow, 1970; *Hanged for a Sheep,* Dodd, 1973; *The Season of Danger,* Dodd, 1974; *The Fugitive Affair,* Dodd, 1976; *The Nightmare Chrysalis,* Dodd, 1977; *Whisper of Evil,* Dodd, 1978; *The Third Identity,* Dodd, 1979.

Contributor: A. S. Burack, editor, *Techniques of Novel Writing* (text), Writer, Inc., 1973; Burack, editor, *Writing Suspense and Mystery Fiction* (text), Writer, Inc., 1977; Alice Laurance and Isaac Asimov, editors, *Who Done It?* (short stories), Houghton, 1980.

WORK IN PROGRESS: One straight novel; one mystery novel set in Washington, D.C.

* * *

GAUCH, Patricia Lee 1934-

PERSONAL: Born January 3, 1934, in Detroit, Mich.; daughter of William Melbourne (an investor) and Muriel (Streng) Lee; married Ronald Raymond Gauch (a scientist and administrator), August 21, 1955; children: Sarah, Christine, John. *Education:* Miami University, Oxford, Ohio, B.A., 1956; Manhattanville College, M.A.T., 1970. *Residence:* Basking Ridge, N.J. *Agent:* Dorothy Markinko, McIntosh & Otis, Inc., 18 East 41st St., New York, N.Y. 10017.

CAREER: Reporter for *Louisville Courier-Journal,* Louisville, Ky.; teacher; Coward-McCann & Geoghegan, New York, N.Y., publisher-writer, 1969—. Book reviewer for the *New York Times.*

WRITINGS—Published by Coward: *A Secret House,* 1970; *Christina Katerina and the Box,* 1971; *Aaron and the Green Mountain Boys,* 1972; *Christina Katerina and the First Annual Grand Ballet,* 1973; *Grandpa and Me,* 1973; *This Time, Tempe Wick?,* 1974; *Thunder at Gettysburg,* 1975.

Published by Putnam: *The Impossible Major Rogers,* 1977; *Once upon a Dinkelsbuhl,* 1977; *On to Widecombe Fair,* 1978; *The Green of Me,* 1978; *Fridays,* 1979; *Kate Alone,* 1980; *The Little Friar that Flew,* 1980; *Morelli's Game,* 1981.

SIDELIGHTS: Patricia Lee Gauch told *CA:* "I stumbled onto writing when I was in college and discovered that college newspapers attracted people as excited about ideas and possibilities as I was. As a reporter I grew more and more curious, a trait which eventually carried me into children's literature where I explore, with unending curiosity, character. Plot, for me, is challenging, but to spend hours at a typewriter pitting the drives and sensitivities and personality of one character against those of other characters is fascinating; more, it's compelling."

BIOGRAPHICAL/CRITICAL SOURCES: Publishers Weekly, November 6, 1978; *New York Times Book Review,* February 17, 1980, February 8, 1981.

* * *

GAVER, Jessyca (Russell) 1915-

PERSONAL: Surname rhymes with "favor"; born August 18, 1915, in New York, N.Y.; daughter of Nathan and Molly (Baron) Levine; married Kimon Patrick Russell, November 23, 1938 (divorced, 1945); married Jack Gaver (a drama critic and amusement editor with United Press International), March 24, 1945 (died December 16, 1974); children: Claudia (Mrs. James Walter Grace; an adopted daughter). *Politics:* None. *Religion:* Baha'i.

CAREER: Free-lance magazine and book writer for more than thirty years; publisher-editor-writer of "Writers Newsletter" and its supplement for distributors and wholesalers of magazines and paperback books.

WRITINGS: Round Trip to Nowhere (novel), Dell, 1963; *The Baha'i Faith: Dawn of a New Day,* Hawthorn, 1965; *Diamond Acres* (novel), Award Books, 1969; *A Complete Directory of Medical and Health Services,* Award Books, 1970; *Pentecostalism,* Award Books, 1971; *Vitamin C: The Protective Vitamin,* Award Books, 1971; *Birth Defects and Your Baby,* Lancer Books, 1972; *Sickle Cell Disease: Its Tragedy and Its Treatment,* Lancer Books, 1972; *"You Shall Know the Truth": The Baptist Story,* Lancer Books, 1973.

How to Help Your Doctor Help You, Pinnacle Books, 1975; *How Deep the Cup,* Leisure Books, 1975; *The Golden Dozen,* Leisure Books, 1976; *A Guide Book for Widows and Widowers:*

All the Wise and Wherefores!, Belmont-Tower, 1976; *Shadow of a Love* (novel), Manor Books, 1977; *The Faith of Jimmy Carter*, Manor Books, 1977; *How to Help Your Pharmacist Help You*, Manor Books, 1978; *The Hungry Years*, Manor Books, 1978. More than four hundred articles have been published in magazines, some under a variety of pseudonyms.

WORK IN PROGRESS: "Always researching one or two books and working on various free-lance articles."

* * *

GAVRONSKY, Serge 1932-

PERSONAL: Born August 16, 1932, in Paris, France; brought to United States in 1940, naturalized citizen in 1956; son of Victor and Anne (Minor) Gavronsky; married, 1960; children: Adriane. *Education:* Columbia University, B.A., 1954, M.A., 1955, Ph.D., 1965. *Home:* 525 West End Ave., New York, N.Y. 10024. *Office:* Department of French, Barnard College, Columbia University, 606 West 120th St., New York, N.Y. 10027.

CAREER: Columbia University, Barnard College, New York, N.Y., lecturer, 1960-63, instructor, 1963-65, assistant professor, 1965-69, associate professor, 1969-74, professor of French, 1974—, chairman of department, 1975—. *Awards, honors:* Fulbright travel grant, 1958-59; French Government fellow, 1958-59, 1970-71, summer, 1975; National Endowment for the Humanities pilot grant, 1978, implementation grant, 1982; John Simon Guggenheim Foundation fellow and Carmago Foundation fellow, both 1979; French Government grant, 1979; Chevalier dans l'Ordre des Palmes Academiques, 1981.

WRITINGS: The French Liberal Opposition and the American Civil War, Humanities, 1968; (editor and translator) *Poems and Texts: Eight Contemporary French Poets*, October House, 1969; *Lectures et compte-rendu, poemes* (title means "Readings and Accounts"), Flammarion, 1973; *Le Moyen Age* (title means "The Middle Ages"), Macmillan, 1974; (editor with Patricia Terry and translator) *Modern French Poetry: A Bilingual Anthology*, Columbia University Press, 1975; *Francis Ponge: The Sun and Other Texts*, Sun Books, 1976; *Frances Ponge and the Power of Language*, University of California Press, 1979; (translator) Arakawa and Gins, *Le Mecanisme du sens*, Editions Maeght, 1979; *The German Friend* (novel), SUN, 1983; *Culture/Ecriture*, Bulzoni, 1983. Contributor to scholarly journals. Co-founder and American editor of *Two Cities*, 1960-65; New York representative of *El Corno Emplumado*, 1965-68.

SIDELIGHTS: Poems and Texts: Eight Contemporary French Poets, edited and translated by Serge Gavronsky, is "a grab bag of gems and rotten apples," according to Eric Sellin in *Books Abroad*. While praising Gavronsky's choice of poems and some of his interviews with the poets, Sellin finds the descriptions of decor or situation that precede each dialogue "downright embarrassing." For Anthony Hartley, however, it is not the introductions to the interviews, but the introduction to the book itself—an essay entitled "From Surrealism to Structuralism"—that seems out of place. "The difficulty with the present vogue of structuralism," he writes in his *Washington Post Book World* review, "is that it means all things to all men. . . . Until there is a more ambitious attempt to define the latest climate of French intellectual fashion it is better to refer poets to their literary (rather than philosophical) sources." Nonetheless, Hartley concludes that Gavronsky "gives us some excellent poems with helpful translations and comments in his interviews with the poets themselves."

BIOGRAPHICAL/CRITICAL SOURCES: Washington Post Book World, October 26, 1969; *Books Abroad*, summer, 1970.

* * *

GEARHEART, B(ill) R. 1928-

PERSONAL: Born September 5, 1928, in Wichita, Kan.; son of H. Floyd (a decorator) and Lucille (Hooker) Gearheart; married Jean Wood, June 4, 1950 (divorced); married Carol Kozisek, May 14, 1976; children: (first marriage) Mark, Leslie Jean, Susan. *Education:* Friends University, Wichita, Kan., B.A., 1949; Wichita State University, M.Ed., 1955; Colorado State College (now University of Northern Colorado), Ed.D., 1963. *Religion:* Methodist. *Home:* 2209 20th Street Rd., Greeley, Colo. 80631.

CAREER: Wichita (Kan.) public schools, teacher of mathematics and science, 1949-51, principal, 1953-59; Cedar Rapids (Iowa) public schools, director of special services and assistant superintendent, 1960-66; University of Northern Colorado, Greeley, 1966—, began as associate professor, currently professor of special education. *Military service:* U.S. Naval Reserve, 1951-53; served in the Atlantic and with Sixth Fleet; became lieutenant junior grade.

WRITINGS: Administration of Special Education, C. C Thomas, 1967; (with E. Willenberg) *Application of Pupil Assessment Information: For the Special Education Teacher*, Love Publishing, 1970, revised edition, 1980; (editor and contributor) *Education of the Exceptional Child: History, Present Practices and Trends*, International Textbook, 1972; *Learning Disabilities: Educational Strategies*, Mosby, 1973, revised edition, 1981; *Organization and Administration of Programs for the Exceptional Child*, C. C Thomas, 1974; (with F. Litton) *The Trainable Retarded: A Foundations Approach*, Mosby, 1975; (with M. Weishahn) *The Handicapped Child in the Regular Classroom*, Mosby, 1976; *Teaching the Learning Disabled: A Combined Task/Process Approach*, Mosby, 1976; (with G. Marsh and wife, Carol Gearheart) *The Learning Disabled Adolescent*, Mosby, 1978; *Special Education for the Eighties*, Mosby, 1980; (contributor) M. Gottlieb, editor, *Concise Textbook of Developmental Pediatrics*, Medical Examination Publishing, 1983.

SIDELIGHTS: B. R. Gearheart told *CA:* "I enjoy professional writing, and I particularly enjoy attempting to make new areas of interest simple and readable for college students. I dislike reading professional work in which the author attempts to make a given topic more complex, either through style or the use of ten-dollar words where simpler words will do. In the past several years I have been particularly interested in 'launching' new authors from among my doctoral students, and have had a modest degree of success."

Learning Disabilities: Educational Strategies has been translated into Japanese; *Teaching the Learning Disabled: A Combined Task/Process Approach* has been translated into Spanish.

* * *

GELLINEK, Christian 1930-

PERSONAL: Surname is accented on first syllable, and pronounced with hard "g"; born May 5, 1930, in Potsdam, Germany; son of Christian (a professor) and Margaretha (Lorenzen)

Gellinek; married Jose E. Schellekens, June 27, 1975; children: Else, Saskia. *Education:* Attended University of Goettingen, 1953-57; University of Toronto, B.A, 1959; Yale University, M.A., 1963, Ph.D., 1964. *Religion:* "Calvinist-reformed." *Home:* 401 Southwest 42nd St., Gainesville, Fla. 32607. *Office:* German Department, University of Florida, Gainesville, Fla. 32611.

CAREER: Pickering College, Newmarket, Ontario, head of German and Latin department, 1959-61; Yale University, New Haven, Conn., instructor, 1964-66, assistant professor, 1966-68, associate professor of German, 1968-70; Connecticut College, New London, associate professor of German, 1970-71; University of Florida, Gainesville, professor of German, 1971—. *Member:* Modern Language Association of America, Mediaeval Academy of America, American Association of Teachers of German, Anglo-Norman Text Society. *Awards, honors:* Morse fellow, 1965-66, Fulbright fellow, 1980-81.

WRITINGS: Koenig Rother: Studie zur literarischen Deutung, Francke (Berne), 1968; *Programmed German Dictionary,* Prentice-Hall, 1968; *Kaiserchronik,* Athenaeum-Verlag (Frankfurt), 1971; *Leuchtsignale,* Blaeschke (Austria), 1979; *Elementare Linguistik,* Lang (Switzerland), 1980; *Herrschaft im Hochmittelalter,* Lang, 1980; *Der Friedenssaal,* Westfaelische Vereinsdruckerei (Muenster), 1982; *Hugo Grotius,* Twayne, 1982.

* * *

GEMMING, Elizabeth 1932-

PERSONAL: Born December 27, 1932, in Glen Cove, N.Y.; daughter of Alexander Henry (a teacher and school principal) and Ruth (a secretary; maiden name, Smith) Prinz; married Klaus Gemming (a book designer), July 3, 1957; children: Marianne, Christina. *Education:* Wellesley College, B.A., 1954; University of Munich, graduate study, 1954-55. *Home:* 49 Autumn St., New Haven, Conn. 06511.

CAREER: Teacher of English in secondary schools in Munich, Germany, 1954-55; Pantheon Books, Inc., New York, N.Y., assistant editor and member of promotion staff, 1955-57; free-lance writer, editor, and translator, 1957—. *Member:* Phi Beta Kappa. *Awards, honors:* Fulbright scholarship, University of Munich, 1954-55.

WRITINGS—Juveniles, except as indicated: *Huckleberry Hill: Child Life in Old New England,* Crowell, 1968; (with husband, Klaus Gemming) *Learning through Stamps,* Barre, Volume I: *The World of Art,* 1968, Volume II: *Around the World,* 1968, Volume III: *Portraits of Greatness,* 1969.

Getting to Know New England, Coward, 1970; *Blow Ye Winds Westerly: The Seaports and Sailing Ships of Old New England,* Crowell, 1972; *Block Island Summer* (adult book; photographs by K. Gemming), Chatham Press, 1972; *Getting to Know the Connecticut River,* Coward, 1974; *Born in a Barn: Farm Animals and Their Young* (photographs by K. Gemming), Coward, 1974; *Maple Harvest: The Story of Maple Sugaring,* Coward, 1976; *Wool Gathering: Sheep Raising in Old New England,* Coward, 1979.

Lost City in the Clouds: The Discovery of Machu Picchu, Coward, 1980; *The Cranberry Book,* Coward, 1983.

Translator from the German; all juveniles: Renato Rascel, *Piccoletto: The Story of the Little Chimney Sweep,* Pantheon, 1958; Max Bolliger, *Sandy at the Children's Zoo,* Crowell, 1967; Alfons Weber, *Elizabeth Gets Well,* Crowell, 1970.

SIDELIGHTS: Many of Elizabeth Gemming's juvenile works are set in New England. Readers are introduced to this region by way of such Gemming books as *Huckleberry Hill: Child Life in Old New England, Wool Gathering: Sheep Raising in Old New England, Maple Harvest: The Story of Maple Sugaring,* and *Blow Ye Winds Westerly: The Seaports and Sailing Ships of Old New England.*

Not only do these books relive the various colorful historical aspects of this area, they also give the reader an opportunity to learn about the people of New England and the work that often separates them from the rest of the country. For instance, Elizabeth Gillis writes in *Library Journal* that *Getting to Know New England* "captures the character of New England." Gillis goes on to remark that Gemming not only writes about the historical traditions of the area, she also "describes farming, fishing, and manufacturing."

Many reviewers acknowledge Gemming's ability to reflect her obvious love of and attraction to New England in such a manner that she also attracts and captures the interest of her young readers. While writing in *Washington Post Book World* that *Huckleberry Hill* is a "serene, vivid, loving account of country life," Jean Baron praises Gemming's talent for writing "direct, clear, uncluttered sentences [that] offer rich experiences." And J. W. Paul writes in *School Library Journal* that Gemming's "topics are interestingly present, in just enough detail for a [young reader.]"

Another reason for Gemming's success in writing for children is offered by Judith K. Miller. In a review of *Getting to Know the Connecticut River* for *Library Journal,* she states that Gemming's "broad, accurate coverage" of the New England region and its people is "interspersed with anecdotes that make interesting reading." And almost echoing Miller's thoughts, Elizabeth Gillis writes in another issue of *Library Journal* that *Blow Ye Winds* is a "very colorful, anecdotal [and] . . . lively account."

AVOCATIONAL INTERESTS: Travel (Europe, especially Italy), American cultural history, medieval history and art, knitting, family history, birdwatching.

BIOGRAPHICAL/CRITICAL SOURCES: New York Times Book Review, November 3, 1968, March 19, 1972; *Washington Post Book World,* November 3, 1968; *Library Journal,* April 15, 1971, May 15, 1972, May 15, 1974; *School Library Journal,* April, 1980.

* * *

GENSZLER, G(eorge) William II 1915-

PERSONAL: Born November 2, 1915, in Columbia, Pa.; son of George W. (a clergyman) and Stella K. (Hunsicker) Genszler; married Dorothy Helen Mezinis, June 15, 1940; children: Sandra Joy (Mrs. John Knutson), George William III, David Garrett. *Education:* Carthage College, B.A., 1937; Northwestern Lutheran Theological Seminary, M.Div., 1940. *Home and office:* 1126 Wedgewood Dr., Waukesha, Wis. 53786.

CAREER: Ordained Lutheran minister, 1940; pastor in Killdeer, N.D., 1940-44, and in Wisconsin Dells, Wis., 1944-51; First United Lutheran Church, Sheboygan, Wis., pastor, 1951-79; St. Luke's Lutheran Church, Waukesha, Wis., pastor, 1979-82. Lutheran Church in America, member of executive board of Wisconsin-Upper Michigan Synod, 1969-76, management committee, Office of Communication, 1978—, and Board of Publications. President of Ecumenical Dialogue Society, 1966-

68, Sheboygan Human Rights Committee, 1967, and Sheboygan Ministerial Association, 1969; member of board of directors of Sheboygan Family Service Association, 1954-62, Sheboygan Boy Scouts, 1958-62, Sheboygan United Way, 1969-77, and Sheboygan Red Cross, 1975-79; member of Wisconsin Council of Church Broadcast Ministry, 1968-84; state chairman of Lutheran World Relief, 1968—. Member of board of trustees, Carthage College, Kenosha, Wis. 1978-84. *Awards, honors:* D.D., Carthage College, 1967; thirty years service citation from Lutheran World Federation, 1981, for service through Lutheran World Relief.

WRITINGS: Don't Fall Flat on Your Faith, C.S.S. Publishing, 1973; *Hay, Harmony, Hallelujah,* C.S.S. Publishing, 1974; *Questions around the Cross,* Fortress, 1978.

WORK IN PROGRESS: A stewardship book, *Pay or Burn.*

SIDELIGHTS: G. William Genszler told *CA:* "One of the glories of the Christian ministry is that I have found an outlet for every creative talent I possess from sign painting, architecture, carpentry, building, together with the joy of preaching, writing (poems, plays, articles and books) and lecturing across the country and abroad. Even though I have retired from an active pastorate, I have greater opportunity to share ideas and thoughts with a wider audience. I look at preaching and writing as good stewardship."

* * *

GEORGE, Jonathan
See BURKE, John (Frederick)

* * *

GEORGESCU-ROEGEN, Nicholas 1906-

PERSONAL: Born February 4, 1906, in Constanza, Romania; son of Stavru (an army officer) and Maria (a high school teacher; maiden name, Niculescu) Georgescu; married Etilia Busuioc, September 2, 1934. *Education:* University of Bucharest, M.A., 1926; University of Paris, D.Stat., 1930; University College, London, postdoctoral research, 1930-31. *Religion:* Orthodox. *Home:* 2614 Hemingway Dr., Nashville, Tenn. 37215. *Office:* Vanderbilt University, Nashville, Tenn. 37235.

CAREER: University of Bucharest, Bucharest, Romania, professor of statistics, 1932-46; Harvard University, Cambridge, Mass., lecturer and research associate in econometrics, 1948-49; Vanderbilt University, Nashville, Tenn., professor of economics and statistics, 1949-69, Distinguished Professor of Economics, 1969-76, Distinguished Professor of Economics Emeritus, 1976—. Rockefeller visiting professor in Japan, 1962-63; Ford Foundation visiting lecturer and consultant in Brazil, 1964; visiting professor at University of Sao Paulo, 1966, adviser, 1966-67; Fulbright lecturer in France, 1976-78. Posts in Romania included assistant director of Central Statistical Institute, Bucharest, 1932-39, economic adviser to Treasury Department, 1938-39, delegate to Committee on Peaceful Change, League of Nations, 1938, and secretary-general of the Romanian Armistice Commission, 1944-45. Member of Committee on Mineral Resources and the Environment, National Research Council, 1973-75, and Technology Assessment Task Force, 1977-79.

MEMBER: Econometric Society (fellow), International Institute of Sociology (fellow), International Institute of Statistics (fellow), American Economic Association (distinguished fellow), American Academy of Arts and Sciences (fellow), American Association for the Advancement of Science, Atlantic Economic Association (distinguished associate), Southern Economic Association, Societe de Statistique de Paris, Accademia della Columbaria (fellow), Phi Beta Kappa (honorary member). *Awards, honors:* Rockefeller fellowship in United States, 1934-36; Guggenheim fellow and Fulbright scholar in Italy, 1958-59; Harvie Branscomb Distinguished Professor Award, 1967; Earl Southerland Prize, 1976; Doctor Honoris Causa, Strasburg, 1976, Florence, 1981.

WRITINGS: Methoda Statistica, Institutul Central de Statistica (Bucharest), 1933; *Un quantum-index pentru comertul exterior al Romaniei,* Institutul Central de Statistica, 1938; (associate editor and contributor of three chapters) *Activity Analysis of Production and Allocation,* edited by T. C. Koopmans, Wiley, 1951; *Analytical Economics: Issues and Problems,* Harvard University Press, 1966.

La Science economique: Ses Problemes et ses difficultes, Dunod, 1970; *The Entropy Law and the Economic Problem,* University of Alabama Press, 1971; *The Entropy Law and the Economic Process,* Harvard University Press, 1971; *Analisi economica e processo economico,* Sansoni (Italy), 1973; *Energy and Economic Myths: Institutional and Analytical Economic Essays,* Pergamon, 1976; *Demair la decroissance,* Pierre-Marcel Favre (Paris), 1979; *Entropy and Economic Myths,* Science Council of Canada, 1980; *Economics of Natural Resources: Myths and Facts* (in Japanese), Koyo Keysai, 1981; *Alguns problemas de orientacao con economia,* Edicoes Multiplic (Brazil), 1981; *Energia e miti economici,* Boringheri, 1982.

Contributor: Jean Mary Bowman, editor, *Expectations, Uncertainty, and Business Behavior,* Social Science Research Council, 1958; *Essays on Econometrics and Planning, Presented to Professor P. C. Mahalanobis,* Pergamon, 1964; C. Eicher and L. Witt, editors, *Agriculture in Economic Development,* McGraw, 1964; R. E. Kuenne, editor, *Monopolistic Competition: Studies in Impact,* Wiley, 1967; U. Papi, editor, *Economic Problems of Agriculture in Industrial Societies,* Macmillan, 1969; C. R. Wharton, Jr., editor, *Subsistence Agriculture and Economic Development,* Aldine, 1969.

G. M. Meier, editor, *Leading Issues in Economic Development,* Oxford University Press, 1970; Paul M. Sweezy and others, editors, *La Teoria dello sviluppo capitalistico,* Boringheri (Italy), 1970; H. Daly, editor, *Toward a Steady-State Economy,* W. H. Freeman, 1973; R. E. Neel, *Readings in Price Theory,* Southwestern Co., 1973; Jiri Zeman, editor, *Entropy and Information in Science and Philosophy,* Elsevier-North Holland, 1975; M. Buescu, editor, *A Moderna Historia Economica,* APED (Brazil), 1976; K. D. Wilson, editor, *Prospects for Growth,* Praeger, 1977; Louis Junker, editor, *The Political Economy of Food and Energy,* University of Michigan, 1977; M. Pfaff, editor, *Grenzen des Umverteilung,* Dumker & Humbolt (Berlin), 1978; Gerhard Schwodiauer, editor, *Equilibrium and Disequilibrium in Economic Theory,* Reidel, 1978; Camilo Dagum, editor, *Methodolgia y critica economica,* Fondo de Cultura (Mexico), 1978; Stephen Lyons, editor, *Sun! A Handbook for the Solar Decade,* Friends of the Earth, 1978; V. Kerry Smith, editor, *Scarcity and Growth Reconsidered,* John Hopkins University Press, 1979; P. M. Nemetz, editor, *Energy Policy: The Global Challenge,* Butterworths, 1979.

L. E. St-Pierre and R. G. Brown, editors, *Future Sources of Organic Raw Materials,* Pergamon, 1980; R. K. Pachauri, editor, *International Energy Studies,* Wiley, 1980; E. Malinvaud and J. P. Fitoussi, editors, *Unemployment in Western Countries,* Macmillan, 1980; H. Daly and A. Umana, editors,

Energy, Economics and the Environment: Toward a Comprehensive Perspective, Lexington Books, 1982; W. C. Schieve and P. M. Allen, editors, *Self-Organization and Dissipative Structures,* University of Texas Press, 1982.

Editor and contributor, *Enciclopedia Romaniei,* four volumes, [Bucharest], 1938-43. Contributor to *International Encyclopedia of Social Sciences, Dictionary of the History of Ideas, Encyclopedia of Economics,* and to economic journals in England, France, Italy, Romania, Brazil, Switzerland, Mexico, Japan, and the United States. Associate editor, *Econometrica,* 1951-68.

SIDELIGHTS: Nicholas Georgescu-Roegen told *CA:* "I must hold the conditions of Romania, where I was brought up, responsible for my methodology and my direct interests. My perhaps unusual tendency of probing the veracity of even what is regarded as obvious is due to the able mathematical school of that country during my learning years. The economic conditions of Romania, where one oil well after another reached bottom with the result that the once-famous oil field of Ploesti is now dry, made me aware of the gravity of the economic role of natural resources. Because I have exposed many fallacies in economic theory and also the now-popular fallacy of an endless ecological Jerusalem, I have drawn a great deal of interested adversity. But this is a cross I must bear, just as many writers, I am sure, must."

In addition to his native language, Georgescu-Roegen speaks French, Italian, and German.

BIOGRAPHICAL/CRITICAL SOURCES: Business Week, March 24, 1975; *Science,* October 31, 1975; *Le Monde,* May 31, 1981.

* * *

GERMANY, (Vera) Jo(sephine)
(Josie King)

PERSONAL: Born in Cambridge, England; daughter of Arthur (a warehouse foreman) and Jessie (a postmistress; maiden name, Garner) Savidge; married Leslie Germany (a chartered electrical engineer), October 28, 1944. *Education:* Attended secondary schools and technical college in England. *Religion:* "Agnostic, but have recently acquired an interest in anomalous phenomena." *Residence:* Cambridge, England.

CAREER: Writer. Has worked as office clerk and concert party artist. Past chairman of St. John's Players. *Member:* Society of Women Writers and Journalists, Writers' Guild of Great Britain, Romantic Novelists Association, English Folklore Society. *Awards, honors:* Special merit award from Romantic Novelists Association, 1974, for *Bride for a Tiger.*

WRITINGS—Gothic novels; *Bride for a Tiger,* Hurst & Blackett, 1973, Pocket Books, 1975; *Candles Never Lie,* Hurst & Blackett, 1974; *Black Moonlight,* Hurst & Blackett, 1975; *Devil Child,* Hurst & Blackett, 1977, St. Martin's, 1978; *City of Golden Cages,* St. Martin's, 1978; *Bride for the Guillotine,* Piatkus Press, 1979.

Modern romance novels: (Under pseudonym Josie King) *Dance at Your Wedding,* Silhouette Books, 1983. Contributor of short stories to women's magazines and of articles on English folklore to periodicals.

WORK IN PROGRESS: Researching American history with a view to writing several historical romances set there.

SIDELIGHTS: Jo Germany writes: "I am insatiably curious about the way people lived and behaved during the eighteenth and nineteenth centuries, and I also find their customs and beliefs fascinating. Therefore the majority of my published works have historical backgrounds.

"Life as a novelist gives one a wonderful freedom to work where and when one pleases, and the research involved adds fascinating interest when visiting various countries of the world. Over the years I have travelled widely, visiting not only America and many western European countries, but also exotic countries such as China, Thailand, Hong Kong, Bali, Russia, Turkey, etc., where the life style is so unlike my own."

BIOGRAPHICAL/CRITICAL SOURCES: Cambridge Evening News, May 11, 1973; *Pye World,* August, 1973; *Cambridge Independent Press,* May 15, 1975; *Writer,* December, 1975.

* * *

GEWE, Raddory
See GOREY, Edward (St. John)

* * *

GIBSON, William 1914-
(William Mass)

PERSONAL: Born November 13, 1914, in New York, N.Y.; son of George Irving (a bank clerk) and Florence (Dore) Gibson; married Margaret Brenman (a psychoanalyst), September 6, 1940; children: Thomas, Daniel. *Education:* Attended College of City of New York (now City College of the City University of New York), 1930-32. *Politics:* Democrat. *Religion:* None. *Residence:* Stockbridge, Mass. *Agent:* Flora Roberts, 157 West 57th St., New York, N.Y. 10022.

CAREER: Author and playwright. Piano teacher at intervals in early writing days to supplement income. President and cofounder of Berkshire Theatre Festival, Stockbridge, Mass., 1966—. *Member:* P.E.N., Authors League of America, Dramatists Guild. *Awards, honors:* Harriet Monroe Memorial Prize, 1945, for group of poems published in *Poetry;* Topeka Civic Theatre award, 1947, for "A Cry of Players"; Sylvania Award, 1957, for television play "The Miracle Worker."

WRITINGS—Plays: *I Lay in Zion* (one-act; first produced in Topeka, Kan., at Topeka Civic Theatre, Easter, 1943), Samuel French (acting edition), 1947; (under pseudonym William Mass) *The Ruby* (one-act lyrical drama), with libretto (based on Lord Dunsany's *A Night at an Inn*) by Norman Dello Joio, Ricordi, 1955; *The Miracle Worker* (three-act; originally written as a television drama; produced by Columbia Broadcasting System for "Playhouse 90" in 1957 and by National Broadcasting Company in 1979; rewritten for stage and first produced on Broadway at Playhouse Theatre, October 19, 1959; rewritten for screen and produced by United Artists in 1962; also see below), Knopf, 1957.

Dinny and the Witches [and] *The Miracle Worker* (the former first produced Off-Broadway at Cherry Lane Theatre, December 9, 1959; also see below), Atheneum, 1960; *Two for the Seesaw* (three-act comedy; copyrighted in 1956 as "After the Verb to Love"; first produced on Broadway at Booth Theatre, January 16, 1958; also see below), Samuel French, 1960; *Dinny and the Witches: A Frolic on Grave Matters,* Dramatists Play Service, 1961; (with Clifford Odets) *Golden Boy* (musical adaptation of Odet's original drama, with lyrics by Lee Adams, and music by Charles Strouse; first produced on Broadway at

Majestic Theatre, October 20, 1964), Atheneum, 1965; *A Cry of Players* (three-act; first produced in Topeka, Kan., at Topeka Civic Theatre, February, 1948; produced on Broadway at the Vivian Beaumont Theatre, November 14, 1968), Atheneum, 1969.

"John and Abigail" (three-act drama; first produced in Stockbridge, Mass., at Berkshire Theatre Festival, summer, 1969, produced in Washington, D.C., at Ford's Theatre, January 9, 1970), published as *American Primitive: The Words of John and Abigail Adams Put into a Sequence for the Theater, with Addenda in Rhyme,* Atheneum, 1972; *The Body and the Wheel* (first produced in Lenox, Mass. at Pierce Chapel, April 5, 1974), Dramatists Play Service, 1975; *The Butterfingers Angel, Mary and Joseph, Herod the Nut, and the Slaughter of 12 Hit Carols in a Pear Tree* (first produced in Lenox, Mass. at Pierce Chapel, December, 1974), Dramatists Play Service, 1975; *Golda* (first produced on Broadway at the Morosco Theatre, November 14, 1977), Samuel French, 1977.

"Goodly Creatures," first produced in Washington, D.C. at the Round House Theatre, January, 1980; "Monday after the Miracle," first produced in Charleston, S.C. at the Dock Street Theatre, May, 1982, produced on Broadway at the Eugene O'Neill Theatre, December 14, 1982.

Other publications: *Winter Crook* (poems), Oxford University Press, 1948; (under pseudonym William Mass) *The Cobweb* (novel), Knopf, 1954; *The Seesaw Log* (a chronicle of the stage production, including the text of *Two for the Seesaw*), Knopf, 1959; *A Mass for the Dead* (chronicle and poems), Atheneum, 1968; *A Season in Heaven* (chronicle), Atheneum, 1974; *Shakespeare's Game* (criticism), Atheneum, 1978.

SIDELIGHTS: While William Gibson has published poetry, plays, fiction, and criticism, he is best known for his 1957 play "The Miracle Worker." Originally written and performed as a television drama, adapted in later years for both stage and screen, "The Miracle Worker" remains Gibson's most widely revived piece. It was refilmed for television in 1979 and also formed the basis for Gibson's 1982 play, "Monday after the Miracle," which picks up the characters almost twenty years later. Writing in the *Dictionary of Literary Biography,* Stephen C. Coy calls it "a classic American play—and television play, and film—the full stature of which has yet to be realized."

The story, which is based on real people and actual events, concerns the relationship between Helen Keller, a handicapped child who has been deaf and blind since infancy, and Annie Sullivan, the formerly blind teacher who has been called in to instruct her. When Annie arrives, she finds that Helen has been utterly spoiled by well-intentioned parents who, in their sympathy, allow her to terrorize the household. Annie's efforts to civilize Helen and Helen's resistance result in a fierce, and frequently physical, struggle that forms the central conflict of the play. The "miracle" occurs when, after months of frustration, Annie is finally able to reach the child. Coy explains: "Just as the struggle appears to be lost, Helen starts to work the pump in the Keller yard and the miracle—her mind learning to name things—happens before the audience as she feels the water and the wet ground. Annie and others realize what is happening as Helen, possessed, runs about touching things and learning names, finally, to their great joy, 'Mother' and 'Papa.' The frenzy slows as Helen realizes there is something she needs to know, gets Annie to spell it for her, spells it back, and goes to spell it for her mother. It is the one word which more than any other describes the subject of *The Miracle Worker:* 'Teacher.'"

Praising the play's "youthfulness and vigor," the *New York Times* reviewer Bosley Crowther described the tremendous concentration of energy apparent in the battle scenes between Helen and Annie: "The physical vitality and passion are absolutely intense as the nurse, played superbly by Anne Bancroft . . . moves in and takes on the job of 'reaching the soul' of the youngster, played by Patty Duke. . . . When the child, who is supposed to be Helen Keller in her absolutely primitive childhood state, kicks and claws with the frenzy of a wild beast at the nurse who is supposed to be Annie Sullivan, the famous instructor of Miss Keller, it is a staggering attack. And when Annie hauls off and swats her or manhandles her into a chair and pushes food into her mouth to teach her habits, it is enough to make the viewer gasp and grunt."

The Broadway production of the play was so well-received that a film version with the same stars was made in 1962 and enjoyed similar success. Later revivals have not fared so well. When "The Miracle Worker" was filmed for television in 1979 (with Patty Duke playing Annie Sullivan), Tom Shales commented in the *Washington Post* that "the only point in doing 'The Miracle Worker' again was to give Patty Duke Astin a chance on the other side of the food." His objections range from what he calls "careless casting" to the inappropriateness (almost an insult, he calls it) of making a television movie from a screenplay written for live television. For the writing itself, however, Shales has nothing but praise. "William Gibson's play . . . remains, even when not perfectly done, a nearly perfect joy, one of the most assuredly affirmative dramatic works to come out of the optimistic '50s."

MEDIA ADAPTATIONS: The Cobweb was filmed by Metro-Goldwyn-Mayer in 1957; "Two for the Seesaw" was filmed by United Artists in 1962.

BIOGRAPHICAL/CRITICAL SOURCES: Cosmopolitan, August, 1958; *Newsweek,* March 16, 1959, July 27, 1970; *Tulane Drama Review,* May, 1960; *New York Times,* May 24, 1962, May 27, 1962, June 3, 1962, November 16, 1977, December 9, 1980, May 26, 1982, December 15, 1982; *Saturday Review,* March 23, 1968; *New York Times Book Review,* April 14, 1968; *New Yorker,* November 23, 1968; *Nation,* December 2, 1968; *New Leader,* December 16, 1968; *New England Theatre,* spring, 1970; *Variety,* February 21, 1971; *Washington Post,* October 13, 1979, January 20, 1980, January 26, 1980, November 27, 1981, December 3, 1981, October 3, 1982, October 14, 1982; *Dictionary of Literary Biography,* Volume VII: *Twentieth Century American Dramatists,* Gale, 1981; *Los Angeles Times,* October 19, 1982; *Contemporary Literary Criticism,* Volume XXIII, Gale, 1983.

* * *

GIDDINGS, Robert (Lindsay) 1935-

PERSONAL: Born June 29, 1935, in Worcester, England; son of Arthur Wesley (a cabinetmaker) and Stella Mary (McCallum) Giddings; married Marie Ethel Matthews, December 8, 1963; children: James Nield (adopted son), Giles. *Education:* Attended College of Commerce, Bristol, England, 1954-55; University of Bristol, B.A., 1958, M.A., 1960, Dip.Ed., 1961, M.Litt., 1967; University of Keele, Ph.D., 1974. *Politics:* Labour. *Religion:* None. *Home:* 49 Buxton Rd., Weymouth, Dorsetshire, England. *Agent:* Bolt & Watson Ltd., 26 Charing Cross Rd., Suite 8, London WC2H 0DG, England. *Office:* Department of English and Media Studies, Dorset Institute of Higher Education, Cranford Ave., Weymouth, Dorsetshire, England.

CAREER: Master at various schools in England, 1961-64; City of Bath Technical College, Bath, England, lecturer in English and communication studies, 1964-82; Dorset Institute of Higher Education, Weymouth, England, senior lecturer in English and media studies, 1982—. Tutor at Open University, Milton Keynes, England, 1972-80; associate tutor at Postgraduate School of Education, University of Bath, Bath, 1972-82; Fulbright exchange professor at St. Louis Community College, St. Louis, Mo., 1975-76; guest lecturer at Cheltenham Festival of Literature, 1978, and at many other British and American universities. Regular radio correspondent, scriptwriter, and reporter for British Broadcasting Corp., Bristol, England; literary adviser to Radio West, Bristol, England; classic serials consultant to HTV. *Member:* Society of Authors, Dickens Society (United States), Conservation Society, Donizetti Society, National Association of Teachers in Further and Higher Education, Association of University Teachers.

WRITINGS: The Tradition of Smollett, Methuen, 1967; *British Trade Unions,* Bristol Tutor Group, 1968; *You Should See Me in Pyjamas* (autobiography), Hamish Hamilton, 1981; (with Elizabeth Holland) *J.R.R. Tolkien: The Shores of Middle-Earth,* Junction Books, 1981; (contributor) Alan Bold, editor, *Smollett: Author of the First Distinction,* Barnes & Noble, 1982.

Author of six-volume programmed course, "British History 1660-1763," Bristol Tutor Group, 1967; author of television scripts, including "Sitting Target," produced by British Broadcasting Corp., June, 1967, and of radio anthology, "Mincepiety," broadcast by British Broadcasting Corp., December, 1976. Regular columnist for *Tribune* and *Music and Musicians.* Contributor to periodicals, including *Sunday Times, New Statesman, Prediction, Vancouver Sun, Western Daily Press,* and *Music and Letters.*

WORK IN PROGRESS: A Dictionary of Literary Originals, with Alan Bold, and *A Book of Musical Quotations,* both for Longman; *The Changing World of Charles Dickens* and *J.R.R. Tolkien: This Far Land,* both for Barnes & Noble; "Sir Walter Scott and Romantic Opera" for an anthology of critical essays, edited by Alan Bold; "Yesteryear in Parliament," radio documentary on eighteenth-century political satire, for British Broadcasting Corp.

AVOCATIONAL INTERESTS: Travel (has traveled widely in Europe and United States), Wagner, conservation.

* * *

GIERTZ, Bo H(arald) 1905-

PERSONAL: Born August 31, 1905, in Rapplinge, Sweden; son of Knut Harald (a professor) and Anna (Ericsson) Giertz; married Ingrid Andren, October 24, 1932 (died July 2, 1942); married Elisabeth af Heurlin, September 17, 1945 (died July 3, 1968); children: (first marriage) Lars, Birgitta Hemstrom, Ingrid Giertz Martenson, Martin. *Education:* University of Uppsala, B.A. (classic linguistics), 1928, B.A. (theology), 1931. *Home:* Tandasgatan 15, 41266 Gothenburg, Sweden.

CAREER: Evangelical-Lutheran clergyman. Diocese of Linkoping, Sweden, pastor in various congregations, 1934-38, vicar of Torpa, 1938-49; Bishop of Gothenburg, 1949-70. Lutheran World Federation, vice-president, 1957-63, member of executive committee, 1957-70, chairman of National Committee in Sweden, 1963-72; member of board of Church of Sweden Mission, 1964-70. *Awards, honors:* D.Div., University of Lund, Sweden, 1974.

WRITINGS—Published by Verbum, except as indicated: *Kristi Kyrka* (title means "The Church of Christ"), 1939; *Kyrkofromhet* (title means "Living in the Church"), 1939; *Stengrunden,* 1941, translation by Clifford Ansgar Nelson published as *The Hammer of God: A Novel about the Cure of Souls,* Augustana Press, 1960; *Grunden* (title means "The Foundation"), 1942; *Tron allena* (title means "By Faith Alone"), 1943; *Den stora loegnon och den stora sanningen* (title means "The Big Lie and the Great Truth"), 1945; *Kampen om maenniskan* (title means "Struggle for Man"), 1947; *Med egna oegon,* 1948, translation by Maurice Michael published as *With My Own Eyes: A Life of Jesus,* Macmillan, 1960; *Herdabrev* (title means "Pastoral Letter"), 1949; *The Message of the Church in a Time of Crisis and Other Essays,* translation by Nelson, Augustana Book Concern, 1958; *Brytningstider* (title means "Times of Change"), Pro Caritate, 1957; *Vad saeger Guds Ord?,* 1957, translation by Nelson published as *Preaching from the Whole Bible: Background Studies in the Preaching Texts for the Church Year,* Augsburg, 1967; *23 teser om skriften kvinnan och praestaembetet,* Diakonistyrelsens Bokfoerlag, 1958.

Raett och oraett i sexuallivet, 1960; *Afrikanska oeverraskningar* (title means "African Surprises"), 1961; *Folkvandring* (title means "Migration"), Pro Caritate, 1962; *I smaeltdegeln* (title means "In the Melting Pot"), Pro Caritate, 1967; *Trons ABC* (title means "ABC of Faith"), 1971; *Riddarna pa Rhodos* (title means "The Knights of Rhodes"; novel), Askild & Karnekull, 1972; *Att kunna laesa sin Bibel* (title means "How to Read the Bible"), 1973; *Att tro pa Kristus* (title means "Faith in Christ"), 1973; *Att leva med Kristus* (title means "Life with Christ"), 1974; (translator) *Nya Testamentet oversatt av Bo Giertz* (title means "New Testament Translated by Bo Giertz"), Verbum and Pro Caritate, 1982.

Translator and author of commentary: *Five Letters of Paul,* 1976; *Corinthians,* 1977; *Romans,* Pro Caritate, 1977; *Mark,* Pro Caritate, 1978; *Matthew,* 1978; *Luke,* 1979; *John,* Pro Caritate, 1979; *Acts,* Pro Caritate, 1980; *Revelation,* Pro Caritate, 1980; *Thessalonians and Pastoral Letters,* Pro Caritate, 1981; *Hebrews,* 1982; *Catholic Letters,* Pro Caritate, 1982.

SIDELIGHTS: For a number of years Bo H. Giertz served a small parish, giving him the opportunity, he says, "to do a lot of writing—novels and essays on Christian items. I suppose these books were the reason why I was elected bishop of Gothenburg." His writings have been translated into German, Norwegian, Danish, Finnish, Icelandic, Hungarian, Tamil, and Zulu. He speaks German and English fluently, and can read six other languages. In addition to five trips to the United States, he has made several visits to Africa and Asia, and one trip to South America. His friends honored him on his sixtieth birthday, 1965, with a festschrift in Swedish, *Till Bo Giertz.*

* * *

GIES, Frances 1915-

PERSONAL: Born June 10, 1915, in Ann Arbor, Mich.; daughter of Robert John (a professor) and Frances (Gibson) Carney; married Joseph Gies (a writer and editor), February 16, 1940; children: Charles Robert, Frances Jane, Paul Joseph. *Education:* University of Michigan, A.B., 1937, A.M., 1938. *Politics:* Democrat. *Religion:* Episcopalian. *Residence:* Ann Arbor, Mich.

CAREER: Twentieth Century-Fox, New York, N.Y., reader, 1942-54. Writer. *Member:* American Historical Association,

Mediaeval Academy of America, Phi Beta Kappa, Phi Kappa Phi.

WRITINGS—With husband, Joseph Gies; published by Crowell, except as indicated: *Life in a Medieval City,* Harper, 1966; *Leonard of Pisa and the New Mathematics of the Middle Ages,* 1970; *Merchants and Moneymen,* 1972; *Life in a Medieval Castle,* 1974; *The Ingenious Yankees,* 1976; *Women in the Middle Ages,* 1978. Contributor of short stories and articles to various magazines.

SIDELIGHTS: One of several publications written jointly by Frances and Joseph Gies, *Women in the Middle Ages* portrays what life was like for seven medieval women of varying social ranks and occupations. An abbess, a reigning queen, a great lady, a textile worker, an Italian merchant's wife, a fifteenth-century gentlewoman, and a "typical" nameless peasant are depicted in what the *Library Journal* calls "rich detail drawn from household records, letters, and secondary sources."

Because so little information about individual women is available for this time period, "the Gieses, in choosing their seven women have not been able to muster a representative selection," Caroline Davidson suggests in her *Washington Post* review. Thus the abbess they describe is no ordinary nun, but the Abbess Hildegarde of Bingen, author of two books in Latin at a time when few women could read or write. "To compensate for the unusual qualities of the women they describe, the Gieses do try to place them in perspective," Davidson continues. "For example, the chapter on [the] thirteenth-century Flemish cloth maker, includes a fascinating discussion of women working in cities and their frequent exploitation by male entrepreneurs."

Under medieval conditions, "feminine wiles" became indispensable for female survival, as the *New York Times*'s reviewer Anatole Broyard explains: "Denied so many basic human rights, women had to become ingenious improvisors, had to develop indirectness to a high art, had to think harder, in many cases, than their husbands." Broyard maintains that this was especially true of upper class women whose "lives seem to have been passed in ceaseless political maneuvering and bickering, which were the lot of powerful people in those days." He finds it "a relief, after them, to read of women who were employed as ale-tasters because they were 'sad and discrete persones' or those who ran comfortable homes for their husbands without the aid of machines and still found time to whisper good advice to them in business and endearment in bed."

So lively are these subjects that Broyard credits them for much of the book's appeal. It is, however, for different reasons that Davidson endorses *Women in the Middle Ages:* "Given the obscurity of the subject and the paucity of soundly based work on it, this new book is welcome. Its unpretentious style and the felicity with which the illustrations complement the text both deserve praise."

BIOGRAPHICAL/CRITICAL SOURCES: Publishers Weekly, April, 1978; *Library Journal,* May 15, 1978; *New York Times,* June 29, 1978; *Washington Post,* July 15, 1978; *Antioch Review,* fall, 1978; *Choice,* December, 1978; *New York Times Book Review,* September 23, 1979; *Chicago Tribune Book World,* September 30, 1979.†

* * *

GIES, Joseph (Cornelius) 1916-

PERSONAL: Born October 8, 1916, in Ann Arbor, Mich.; son of Charles George and Jane (Sturman) Gies; married Frances Carney (a writer), February 16, 1940; children: Charles Robert, Frances Jane, Paul Joseph. *Education:* University of Michigan, B.A., 1939; Columbia University, graduate study. *Politics:* Democrat. *Residence:* Ann Arbor, Mich.

CAREER: This Week, New York City, staff member in copy department, 1942, copy chief, 1946-65; Doubleday & Co., Inc., New York City, editor-in-chief, Nelson Doubleday Division, 1965-67; Encyclopaedia Britannica, Chicago, Ill., senior technology editor for *Britannica III,* 1967-72; Association of Governing Boards of Universities and Colleges, Washington, D.C., director of publications, 1974—. *Military service:* U.S. Army, 1944-46; served in France and Germany with 42nd Infantry Division; became staff sergeant.

WRITINGS: They Never Had It So Good (novel), Harper, 1949; *A Matter of Morals* (novel), Harper, 1951; *Adventure Underground* (nonfiction), Doubleday, 1962; *Bridges and Men* (nonfiction), Doubleday, 1963; (with Robert H. Shoemaker) *Stars of the World Series,* Crowell, 1964; *Wonders of the Modern World,* Crowell, 1966; *Harry S Truman, a Pictorial Biography,* Doubleday, 1968; *Franklin D. Roosevelt, Portrait of a President,* Doubleday, 1971; *Crisis 1918,* Norton, 1974; *The Colonel of Chicago,* Dutton, 1979; (with Melvin Kranzberg) *By the Sweat of Thy Brow,* Putnam, 1975.

With wife, Frances Gies; published by Crowell, except as indicated: *Life in a Medieval City,* Harper, 1966; *Leonard of Pisa and the New Mathematics of the Middle Ages,* 1970; *Merchants and Moneymen,* 1972; *Life in a Medieval Castle,* 1974; *The Ingenious Yankees,* 1976; *Women in the Middle Ages,* 1978.

Contributor of articles on technology to *Encyclopaedia Britannica* and other encyclopedias. Contributor of articles, mostly on technology and social science subjects, to *Columbia Journalism Review, This Week, Engineer,* and other publications; has also written fiction for periodicals.

WORK IN PROGRESS: A novel about the technological side of the Civil War.

SIDELIGHTS: Joseph Gies told *CA:* "My most rewarding writing experiences have been the collaborations with my wife. Some of our books have provided us with memorable travel in Europe and America, but in the work itself there is an added richness from two people, in close touch with each other, giving mutual help at all stages of planning, research, and writing. With books on which my byline alone appears, this has been true, too. 'This chapter doesn't quite work.' 'You are assuming too much on the reader's part.' 'Too long—they'll all fall asleep.' Such critiques have been invaluable, but even better is, 'I didn't quite like this sentence (or paragraph, or passage),' with a new version attached, 'is this better?'" (For a critical overview of *Women in the Middle Ages,* one of the Gieses' joint publications, see the *Sidelights* section of Frances Gies's sketch.)

BIOGRAPHICAL/CRITICAL SOURCES: Publishers Weekly, April, 1978; *Library Journal,* May 15, 1978; *New York Times,* June 29, 1978; *Washington Post,* July 15, 1978; *Antioch Review,* fall, 1978; *Choice,* December, 1978; *New York Times Book Review,* September 23, 1979; *Chicago Tribune Book World,* September 30, 1979.

* * *

GIFFORD, Barry (Colby) 1946-

PERSONAL: Born October 18, 1946, in Chicago, Ill.; son of

Adolph Edward (a pharmacist) and Dorothy (a model; maiden name, Colby) Stein; married Mary Lou Nelson, 1970; children: Phoebe Lou, Asa Colby. *Education:* Attended University of Missouri, 1964, and Cambridge University, 1966. *Address:* 1213 Peralta Ave., Berkeley, Calif. 94706.

CAREER: Poet, novelist, and biographer. Visiting lecturer at State University of New York at Buffalo, 1974. Has worked as a merchant seaman, musician, journalist, and truck driver. *Awards, honors:* Silverthorne Award for Poetry from Silverthorne Press, 1967, for *The Blood of the Parade;* American Library Association Notable Book Award, 1978, for *Jack's Book: An Oral Biography of Jack Kerouac;* National Endowment for the Arts fellowship, 1982.

WRITINGS: The Blood of the Parade (poems), Silverthorne Press, 1967; *A Boy's Novel* (short stories), Christopher's Books, 1973; *Kerouac's Town* (essay with photographs), Capra, 1973; *Coyote Tantras* (poems), Christopher's Books, 1973.

Persimmons: Poems for Paintings, Shaman Drum Press, 1976; *The Boy You Have Always Loved* (poems), Talon Books, 1976; (translator) *Selected Poems of Francis Jammes,* Utah State University Press, 1976; (editor) *The Portable Curtis: Selected Writings of Edward S. Curtis,* Creative Arts, 1976; *Living in Advance* (lyrics and music), Open Reading Books, 1976; *A Quinzaine in Return for a Portrait of Mary Sun* (poems), Workingmans Press, 1977; *Horse Hauling Timber out of Hokkaido Forest* (poems), Christopher's Books, 1978; (with Lawrence Lee) *Jack's Book: An Oral Biography of Jack Kerouac,* St. Martin's, 1978; *Lives of the French Impressionist Painters* (poems), Donald S. Ellis, 1978.

Landscape with Traveler: The Pillow Book of Francis Reeves (novel), Dutton, 1980; *Port Tropique* (novel), Creative Arts, 1980; *The Neighborhood of Baseball* (memoirs), Dutton, 1981; *Francis Goes to the Seashore* (novella and short stories), St. Martin's, 1982; (co-author) *Saroyan: A Biography,* Harper, 1984.

Contributor of stories, poems, articles, and reviews to numerous periodicals, including *New York Times, Rolling Stone, Beloit Poetry Journal, Esquire, Western American Literature,* and *San Francisco Examiner.*

WORK IN PROGRESS: Giotto's Circle, poems, for Tombouctou Books; *Chinese Notes,* poems, for Louisiana State University Press; a novel, *An Unfortunate Woman.*

SIDELIGHTS: Barry Gifford told *CA:* "I grew up in Chicago where my father's friends were racketeers. He ran an all-night drugstore on the corner of Chicago and Rush, and I would stay up late listening to their talk and dunking doughnuts with the organ grinder's monkey. Afternoons I spent watching showgirls rehearse at the Club Alabam next door.

"I was always interested in language; I always listened. After my father died (I was twelve) there was no money, so my mother and I went to work. I began to read everything: influences were Jack London, Jack Kerouac, B. Traven; later Pound, Emily Dickinson, Jean Rhys, Proust, and Flaubert."

AVOCATIONAL INTERESTS: Travel (has been to Europe, South and Central America, Japan, and North Africa).

BIOGRAPHICAL/CRITICAL SOURCES: Saturday Review, August, 1978; *Washington Post Book World,* October 22, 1978, June 29, 1980, December 26, 1980, May 2, 1982; *New York Times Book Review,* January 18, 1981; *Chicago Tribune Book World,* June 14, 1981; *Los Angeles Times Book Review,* October 24, 1982.

GILBERT, Arthur 1926-1976

PERSONAL: Born June 4, 1926, in Philadelphia, Pa.; died May, 1976; son of Harry Robert (a textile manufacturer) and Esther (Glaser) Gilbert; married Jean Kroeze (a sportswear buyer), November 6, 1959; children: Karen, Amy, Lisa, Hillary. *Education:* New York University, B.A., 1947; Jewish Institute of Religion, M.H.L. and Rabbi, 1951; National Psychological Association for Psychoanalysis, certification, 1953. *Home:* 50 Riverside Dr., New York, N.Y. *Office:* 43 West 57th St., New York, N.Y. 10019.

CAREER: Rabbi. Temple B'nai Jeshurun, Newark, N.J., assistant rabbi, ending 1954; Anti-Defamation League of B'nai B'rith, New York, N.Y., director of Department of Interreligious Cooperation, 1954-61; director of Religious Freedom and Public Affairs Project, National Conference of Christians and Jews, 1961-65; director of Department of Religious Curriculum Research, Anti-Defamation League of B'nai B'rith, 1965-76; Reconstructionist Rabbinical College, Philadelphia, Pa., dean, 1968-72. Temple Adas Israel, Sag Harbor, Long Island, N.Y., rabbi. Adjunct professor of religion and psychology at Marymount Manhattan College.

MEMBER: Central Conference of American Rabbis, National Association of Inter-group Relations Officials, Religious Education Association (vice-president, New York chapter, 1966), American Civil Liberties Union, National Association for the Advancement of Colored People, New York Board of Rabbis (executive board, 1964-66). *Awards, honors:* Award from Catholic Press Association for best nonfiction article, 1961; D.D., Iowa Wesleyan College, 1967; Mass Media Brotherhood Award of the National Conference of Christians and Jews, 1969, for *The Vatican Council and the Jews.*

WRITINGS: (With Oscar Tarcov) *Your Neighbor Celebrates,* Friendly House, 1957; (contributor) Philip Scharper, editor, *American Catholics: A Protestant-Jewish Viewpoint,* Sheed & Ward, 1960; *Meet the American Jew,* Broadman, 1961; *Religion and the Public Order,* University of Chicago Press, 1964; *Currents and Trends in Contemporary Jewish Thought,* Ktav, 1965; (editor) *The Passover Seder,* Ktav, 1965; *A Jew in Christian America,* Sheed, 1966; (contributor) *Torah and Gospel,* Sheed, 1966; (contributor) *The Star and the Cross,* Bruce, 1966; *Religion and Public Education: Resources and Reactions,* Anti-Defamation League of B'nai B'rith, 1967; *The Vatican Council and the Jews,* World Publishing, 1968; (compiler with W. M. Abbott, R. L. Hunt, and J. C. Swain) *The Bible Reader: An Interfaith Interpretation,* Bruce, 1969.

Prime Time: Children's Early Learning Years, School Book Service, 1973; *Homework for Jews: Preparing for Jewish-Christian Dialogue,* National Conference of Christians and Jews, 1973; *Your Neighbor Worships,* Anti-Demamation League of B'nai B'rith, in press. Editor of "Background Reports," a series of studies issued by National Conference of Christians and Jews, 1961-65; editor of Central Conference of American Rabbis *Journal,* 1960-65, and *Reconstructionist,* beginning 1960; member of editorial board, *Journal of Ecumenical Studies,* beginning 1966.

OBITUARIES: New York Times, May 16, 1976.†

* * *

GILBERT, Harriett 1948-

PERSONAL: Born August 25, 1948, in London, England;

daughter of Michael (a lawyer and novelist) and Roberta (Marsden) Gilbert. *Education:* Attended Rose Bruford College of Speech and Drama. *Residence:* London, England. *Agent:* Richard Scott Simon, 32 College Cross, London N1 1PR, England.

WRITINGS—Novels; published by Harper, except as indicated: *I Know Where I've Been,* 1972; *Hotels with Empty Rooms,* 1973; *An Offence against the Persons,* Hodder & Stoughton, 1974, Harper, 1975; *Given the Ammunition,* 1976; *Tide Race,* Constable, 1977; *Running Away,* 1979. Contributor of articles, stories, and reviews to *Girl about Town, Washington Post, New Statesman, Flair, Time Out,* and *Guardian*. Book editor, *City Limits.*

WORK IN PROGRESS: A novel.

AVOCATIONAL INTERESTS: Reading, bicycling, walking, talking.

* * *

GILDER, George F. 1939-

PERSONAL: Born November 29, 1939, in New York, N.Y.; son of Richard Watson and Anne (Alsop) Gilder; married Cornelia Brooke (an historic preservationist), 1976; children: Louisa Ludlow, Mary Ellen Tiffany. *Education:* Harvard University, A.B., 1962. *Politics:* Republican. *Home:* The Red House, Tyringham, Mass. 02164. *Office:* Manhattan Institute for Policy Research, 20 West 40th St., New York, N.Y. 10018.

CAREER: Advance (magazine), editor and co-founder in Cambridge, Mass., 1961-62, and in Washington, D.C., 1962-64; *New Leader,* New York City, associate editor, beginning 1965; legislative assistant to Senator Charles McC. Mathias, Washington, D.C., 1968-70; Manhattan Institute for Policy Research, New York City, program director, 1981—. Speech writer for Nelson A. Rockefeller, 1964, Richard M. Nixon, 1968, Ben C. Toledano, 1972, and Robert Dole, 1976. *Military service:* U.S. Marine Corps Reserve, 1958-64. *Awards, honors:* Kennedy Institute of Politics fellow, Harvard University, 1971-72.

WRITINGS: (With Bruce K. Chapman) *The Party That Lost Its Head,* Knopf, 1966; *Sexual Suicide,* Quadrangle, 1973; *Naked Nomads: Unmarried Men in America,* Quadrangle, 1974; *Visible Man,* Basic Books, 1978; *Wealth and Poverty,* Basic Books, 1981. Contributor to *Playboy, Harper's, National Review, Commentary, True, Wall Street Journal,* and other periodicals. Editor, *Ripon Forum,* 1971-72.

WORK IN PROGRESS: The Spirit of Enterprise, for Simon & Schuster.

SIDELIGHTS: George Gilder has created controversy with his conservative commentary on everything from the biological basis of women's roles as housewives to the moral basis of the capitalist system. For example, he was named "the nation's leading male-chauvinist-pig author" by *Time* magazine in 1974, and M. J. Sobran of the *National Review* says he is "a man of free and fresh mind and genial temper whose ideas have a way of making people want to scratch his eyes out." Probably best known for his views on the women's movement and on supply-side economics, Gilder has appeared on numerous television talk shows and at public lectures to discuss his unique brand of social philosophy.

Gilder's book *Sexual Suicide* concerns the biological and anthropological bases of sexual behavior in our culture, and how, in his view, contemporary American society is courting cultural disaster by its deviation from the norms established by primitive man. In using the term "sexual suicide," Gilder claims that every impulse we have as social animals is tied closely to our sexual instincts and behaviors that depart from the norm, including homosexuality, the enjoyment of pornography, and promiscuity, are all "indices of sexual frustration." In fact, Gilder continues in the book, these types of behavior "all disclose a failure to achieve profound and loving sexuality. When a society deliberately affirms these failures—contemplates legislation of homosexual marriage, celebrates the women who denounce the family, and indulges pornography as a manifestation of sexual health . . .—the culture is promoting a form of erotic suicide. For it is destroying the cultural preconditions of profound love and sexuality: the durable heterosexual relationships necessary to a community of emotional investments."

The "women who denounce the family"—or feminists—says Gilder, are collectively "promoting in the United States an epidemic of erotic and social disorders. . . . They are . . . subverting . . . and undermining civilized society. . . . [Along with] sexologists . . . and pornographers . . . [they are] collaborators in a Sexual Suicide Society." In an interview with Richard K. Rein in *People* magazine, Gilder re-emphasizes his stance against the feminist movement. "All the cliches about oppressed women are baloney," he says. "Women have the opportunity of motherhood, time to be creative and be individuals, and less pressure to submit their lives to a wretched career. You read these feminist books and you'd think every man is a U.S. senator. The fact is most men work for other men."

"The beauty of Gilder's reasoning" in *Sexual Suicide,* says Isa Kapp in the *New Leader,* "is that it is so persevering and complete. Yet it rests on the somewhat questionable first premise that because woman's responsibility in procreation is more important and more sensuously satisfying than man's, men feel emotionally deprived. To compensate for this male disadvantage, women must hew to their role and reinforce men in theirs; if they falter, we tumble into social disarray. . . . In real life, few males minimize their part in conceiving babies, and most seem content to remain fond spectators in the process of bearing and nursing them. That men feel in any way inferior is not clear."

"One reads this elaborate, Freud-haunted apology for patriarchy with a depressing sense of deja vu," says Judith Adler Hennessee in the *New York Times Book Review.* "Whether men invent a mythology that makes women superior or inferior, the end result is likely to be the same—women belong in the home." Hennessee also remarks that there are "dozens of statements in this book that are preposterous, as well as oversimple generalizations that contain a germ of truth but veer off wildly into fantasy. One searches in vain for some understanding of the individual need for self-fulfillment."

In 1977, *Playboy* included George Gilder on that magazine's "enemies list." A *Playboy* writer elaborates on Gilder's philosophy concerning women's roles: "Fortunately, Gilder says, most women aren't really interested in careers. Their low wages prove that. They aren't suffering from discrimination; they just aren't paying much attention. Anyway, women have a natural sense of filing." Commenting in *American Anthropologist* on Gilder's views, Eugenia Shanklin says that, "curiously, the women's movement has a natural ally in Gilder; they might consider subsidizing him. When he attempts to make a case for women receiving less money than men for the same work, the absurdities emerge far more readily than when the refutation is presented by rhetoric and polemics."

In his 1981 book, *Wealth and Poverty,* which he calls a "theology" for capitalism, Gilder attempts to establish a moral basis for the capitalist system, using examples from the economies of primitive tribal societies to illustrate the relationship between gift-giving and the spirit of capitalism. In an article in the *Washington Post Book World* on *Wealth and Poverty,* James K. Glassman says, "If you don't understand the wave of new conservative ideas that has swept this country during the past four or five years—or if you consider those ideas window dressing for jingoism and bigotry—then this is the book to read." *Wealth and Poverty* has been publicly endorsed by President Ronald Reagan and proclaimed "Promethean in its vision" by Reagan's budget adviser David Stockman, as quoted in a *New York Times* article.

"The ultimate strength and crucial weakness of both capitalism and democracy are their reliance on individual creativity and courage, leadership and morality, intuition and faith," writes Gilder in *Wealth and Poverty.* "Capitalist production entails faith—in one's neighbors, in one's society, and in the compensatory logic of the cosmos. Search and you shall find, give and you will be given unto, supply creates its own demand. It is this cosmology, this sequential logic, that essentially distinguishes the free from the socialist economy."

In the *National Review,* conservative critic Irving Kristol, writing of Gilder's belief in the fundamental morality of capitalism, disagrees with what he calls Gilder's "pseudo-anthropological analysis of economic activity as inherently and inelectably giving birth to a viable morality. . . . Successful commercial activity . . . [does] not add up to a complete moral code that a society can base itself on." Similarly, Andrew Klaven, discussing *Wealth and Poverty* in the *Saturday Review,* claims that the book "is rendered nonsensical not by its methodical defense of what is known as conservative, supply-side economics, but by the moral hogwash on which that defense is based." Gilder's particular brand of economics, says Ann Crittenden in the *New York Times,* "comes in an ideological fruitcake that many find hard to swallow."

Yet some critics praise Gilder for his social vision. "For all his inflammatory generalizations . . . and intellectual U-turns," says Hazlett, Gilder "is a writer with a fine sense of what America has become—and what it still might be." Similarly, Sobran maintains that Gilder is a "dauntlessly original thinker, who is unabashed at reaching traditional conclusions. He says things that were never before necessary to say, and it may be a long time before anyone else says them as well."

BIOGRAPHICAL/CRITICAL SOURCES: George Gilder, *Sexual Suicide,* Quadrangle, 1973; *New York Times Book Review,* December 9, 1973; *New Leader,* December 10, 1973; *Contemporary Sociology,* September, 1974; *Time,* December 9, 1974; *Washington Star-News,* December 13, 1974; *National Review,* May 9, 1975, August 18, 1978, April 17, 1981; *Authors in the News,* Volume I, Gale, 1976; *American Anthropologist,* number 4, 1976; *Playboy,* October, 1977; Gilder, *Wealth and Poverty,* Basic Books, 1981; *Saturday Review,* January, 1981; *Washington Post Book Review,* February 8, 1981; *Newsweek,* February 16, 1981; *Los Angeles Times Book Review,* April 19, 1981; *New York Times,* April 26, 1981, May 16, 1981; *People,* May 18, 1981; *Commentary,* July, 1981; *Commonweal,* December 4, 1981; *Contemporary Issues Criticism,* Volume I, Gale, 1982; *Nation,* February 26, 1983.†

—Sketch by Kerry L. Lutz

GILFOND, Henry

PERSONAL: Son of Louis and Vera Gilfond; married Edythe (a costume designer); children: Michael, Pamela. *Home and office address:* P.O. Box 357, Hampton Bays, N.Y. 11946. *Agent:* Bertha Case, 345 West 58th St., New York, N.Y. 10019.

CAREER: Writer. Teacher in New York (N.Y.) schools for a number of years. *Member:* American National Theatre and Academy, Dramatists Guild of the Authors League of America.

WRITINGS—Published by F. Watts, except as indicated: *Journey without End,* Philosophical Library, 1958; *How to Run for School Office,* Hawthorn, 1969; *Heroines of America,* Fleet Press, 1971; *The Reichstag Fire, February, 1933: Hitler Utilizes Arson to Extend His Dictatorship,* 1973; *Black Hand at Sarajevo,* Bobbs-Merrill, 1975; *Voodoo,* 1976; *The New Ice Age,* 1977; *Genealogy: How to Find Your Roots,* 1978; *Syria,* 1978; *Water: A Scarce Resource,* 1978; *How to Give a Speech,* 1980; *Afghanistan,* 1980; *Gambia, Ghana, Liberia, Sierra Leone,* 1981; *Countries of the Sahara,* 1981; *The Executive Branch,* 1981; *Disastrous Earthquakes,* 1981.

With Gene Schoor; juveniles; published by Messner: *The Jim Thorpe Story,* 1952; *The Story of Ty Cobb,* 1952; *Red Grange,* 1952; *Christy Mathewson,* 1953; *Casey Stengel,* 1953; *The Jack Dempsey Story,* 1954; *The Ted Williams Story,* 1954; *The Stan Musial Story,* 1955.

Editor; published by Walker & Co.: *Plays for Reading,* 1966; *American Plays for Reading,* 1966; *Holiday Plays for Reading,* 1967; *Plays for Today,* 1967; *Mythology Plays,* 1967; *African Plays for Reading,* 1967; *Latin-American Plays for Reading,* 1967; *Favorite Short Stories,* 1967; *Asian Plays for Reading,* 1968.

Ghost-writer on subjects ranging from pediatrics to politics. Author of radio and television scripts and a full-length play, "The Wick and the Tallow," recorded by Folkways, 1967. Contributor to *Reader's Digest* compendiums, 1972-80, and to *New York Times Book Review.* Former editor, *New World Monthly* (literary magazine) and *Dance Observer.*

WORK IN PROGRESS: Northern Ireland: Turmoil and Strife; Poems: 1962-1982.

SIDELIGHTS: Henry Gilfond told *CA:* "Ask me to write anything from a letter to an introduction to *Hamlet* (which in fact I have done) and much more than likely I'll do it, for money or, as often as not, for the love of writing. I've written everything from a fifty-year history of a small church to brochures for artists, for love and for the gratification that comes with a work appreciated. Actually there is little I enjoy more than hitting the keys of a typewriter, and with good reason. After all, it is the act of creating that may well be equated with the art of living."

* * *

GILPATRICK, Eleanor G(ottesfocht) 1930-

PERSONAL: Born October 29, 1930, in Brooklyn, N.Y.; daughter of Murry and Essie (Hirsch) Gottesfocht; married Jerome Gilpatrick, September 8, 1956 (divorced August, 1959). *Education:* Brooklyn College (now Brooklyn College of the City University of New York), B.A., 1951; New School for

Social Research, M.A., 1959; Cornell University, Ph.D., 1964. *Home:* 302 West 12th St., New York, N.Y. 10014.

CAREER: Boni Watkins Jason & Co., New York City, junior research analyst, 1959-60; United Furniture Workers of America, New York City, assistant research director and secretary to president, 1960-61; University of Illinois at Urbana-Champaign, assistant research professor, Bureau of Economic and Business Research, 1964-66; Skill Advancement, Inc., New York City, senior research associate, 1966-67; City University of New York, New York City, director of Health Services Mobility Study, Research Foundation, 1967-78, professor of health science in School of Health Sciences, Hunter College, 1968—, designer and coordinator of master's program in allied health science admininstration. *Member:* American Public Health Association, American Economic Association, Industrial Relations Research Association, American Association of University Professors, Metropolitan Economic Association, Phi Beta Kappa.

WRITINGS: Structural Unemployment and Aggregate Demand, Johns Hopkins Press, 1966; *Use of Job Vacancies to Select Promising Industries for Training Programs,* Skill Advancement, Inc., 1967; *Aspects of Manpower Supply in Illinois Regions, 1940, 1950 and 1960,* Department of Business and Economic Development, State of Illinois, 1967; (with Paul K. Corliss) *The Occupational Structure of New York City Municipal Hospitals,* Praeger, 1970.

Published by Research Foundation, City University of New York: *Train Practical Nurses to Become Registered Nurses: A Survey of the PN Point of View,* 1968; (with Christina Gullion) *The Design Guidelines for Educational Ladders Using Task Data,* 1973; *Task Descriptions in Diagnostic Radiology,* four volumes, 1976; *Using Task Data in Diagnostic Radiology,* two volumes, 1977; *The Technologist Function in Fields Related to Radiology: Tasks in Radiation Therapy and Diagnostic Ultrasound,* 1977; *Relating Technologist Tasks in Diagnostic Radiology, Ultrasound, and Radiation Therapy,* 1977; *The Health Services Mobility Study Method of Task Analysis and Curriculum Design,* four volumes, 1977.

Contributor to *Proceedings of the Inaugural Convention of the Eastern Economic Association,* 1975, *The Annals* of the American Academy of Political and Social Science, 1975, and to *Proceedings of the National Conference for Evaluating Competence in the Health Professions,* 1976.

WORK IN PROGRESS: Fairy tales with mental health themes.

* * *

GIRARD, Joe 1928- (Joe Girardi)

PERSONAL: Real name, Joe Girardi; uses shortened form of name for business purposes; born November 1, 1928, in Detroit, Mich.; son of Antony (an automobile assembly worker) and Grace (Stabile) Girardi; married June Krantz, June 2, 1951; children: Joe, Grace. *Education:* Attended high school in Detroit, Mich. *Politics:* Independent. *Religion:* Roman Catholic. *Residence:* Grosse Pointe Shores, Mich. *Office address:* P.O. Box 358, East Detroit, Mich. 48021.

CAREER: Building contractor in Detroit, Mich., 1949-63; Merollis Chevrolet, East Detroit, Mich., new car and truck salesman, 1963-78; professional motivational speaker, 1978—. *Military service:* U.S. Army, 1947. *Awards, honors:* Golden Plate Award from American Academy of Achievement, 1975.

WRITINGS: How to Sell Anything to Anybody, Simon & Schuster, 1978; *How to Sell Yourself,* introduction by Norman Vincent Peale, Simon & Schuster, 1980. Also author of sales-technique film series and sales-training program.

WORK IN PROGRESS: Stop the World I Want to Get On, for Simon & Schuster.

SIDELIGHTS: In 1966, investigators from the *Guinness Book of World Records* undertook an eight-month study to officially determine if Joe Girard, salesman at Merollis Chevrolet of East Detroit, Michigan, was indeed the world's greatest salesperson. After consulting sales figures from corporations around the world, checking retail sales generated by salespeople involved with "big ticket" items (such as automobiles, boats, or houses), the *Guinness* people declared Girard the "world's greatest" at the job of selling. His record-breaking total of 1,425 cars and trucks sold retail in 1973 has never been equalled.

By 1977, according to a report in *Forbes,* Girard was "spending only sixty percent of his working time selling cars." The rest of his time was devoted to promoting training programs aimed at helping others achieve the same level of success in their lives as Girard was able to achieve in his. In an effort to reach an even wider audience, Girard soon published his first book, *How to Sell Anything to Anybody.* After the book's publication, he left his sales position in order to devote full attention to telling others about his book and about his ideas on selling.

In *How to Sell Anything to Anybody,* as a *Business Week* reviewer notes, Girard develops two separate but inter-related stories. "The first is a series of thoughtful suggestions on the art of selling," writes the critic. "The second, more engaging story, is that of Joe Girard."

Among Girard's selling tips are ways salespeople can organize their time and business, how they can appear honest and down-to-earth to their clients, and (most important in the Girard credo) how to develop a positive mental attitude. Other Girard hints include having distinctive business cards printed, sending former customers birthday and holiday greetings, and getting the customer to feel "obliged" to the salesperson. One way Girard used to carry out this last hint was to keep several different brands of cigarettes in his desk. When he saw a customer patting his pockets looking for a cigarette, Girard would offer his client a smoke and let him keep the entire pack. Sometimes, he would even offer "the shirt off his back" to satisfy a customer and used to keep a spare shirt in his office just in case someone took him up on his offer.

A major portion of *How to Sell Anything to Anybody* is devoted to the story of Girard's life; according to Vicky Billington in a *Detroit News* article, his story "has a definite rags-to-riches theme." Girard gives a capsulized autobiography in the introduction of the book and also his explanation of why he wrote it. He says: "For the first thirty-five years of my life I was the world's biggest loser. I got thrown out of about forty different jobs. I lasted only ninety-seven days in the U.S. Army. I couldn't even make it as a crook. . . . How I got from there to here is what this book is about."

An idea of where "here" is for Girard appears in the last chapter of the book. The author writes: "I never forget . . . the nights I slept in freight cars in the railroad yard. Now I sleep in a beautiful home in Grosse Pointe Shores, just a few blocks from where members of the Henry Ford II family live. As a present for my wife, I had a spectacular bathroom built with a marble tub and a sauna and columns . . . that . . . cost me $32,000. That's more money than I ever made in any two years before I got into the selling profession.''

In his second book, *How to Sell Yourself*, the salesman details what a *Publishers Weekly* reviewer calls Girard's ''strategy of personal salesmanship.'' According to Girard, the first step in selling ourselves to others is selling ourselves to ourselves. Girard reveals how individuals can take stock of their strengths and weaknesses and take charge of their lives.

Contained in the volume's introduction by Norman Vincent Peale (author of the best-selling self-help book *The Power of Positive Thinking*) is one of the reviews of Girard's work of which he is most proud. In Peale's introductory comments, he includes the following statement: ''This book . . . is one of the best books in [the motivational] field. In my opinion, it will become a classic in the success literature of our time. . . . Joe Girard can help you. I know, for he has helped me.''

BIOGRAPHICAL/CRITICAL SOURCES: Newsweek, July 2, 1973; *Forbes*, November 1, 1977; *Adcrafter*, November 4, 1977; Joe Girard, *How to Sell Anything to Anybody*, Simon & Schuster, 1978; *Detroit News*, January 19, 1978; *West Coast Review of Books*, March, 1978; *Business Week*, May 1, 1978; *Publishers Weekly*, December 10, 1979, August 14, 1981; Girard, *How to Sell Yourself*, Simon & Schuster, 1980.

* * *

GIRARDI, Joe
See GIRARD, Joe

* * *

GITTELL, Marilyn 1931-

PERSONAL: Born April 3, 1931, in New York, N.Y.; daughter of Julius and Rose (Meyerson) Jacobs; married Irwin Gittell (a certified public accountant), August 20, 1950; children: Amy, Ross. *Education:* Brooklyn College (now Brooklyn College of the City University of New York), A.B., 1952; New York University, M.P.A., 1953, Ph.D., 1960. *Home:* 110-21 73rd Ave., Forest Hills, N.Y. 11375. *Office:* Graduate School and University Center of the City University of New York, New York, N.Y. 10036.

CAREER: Tax Foundation, New York City, research assistant, 1952-55; Government Affairs Foundation, Albany, N.Y., research associate, 1955-60; Queens College of the City University of New York, Flushing, Long Island, N.Y., instructor, 1960-62, assistant professor, 1962-65, associate professor, 1965-67, professor of political science, 1967-71, professor of urban studies and chairman of department, 1971-73, director of Institute for Community Studies and director of honors program, 1967-73; Brooklyn College of the City University of New York, Brooklyn, N.Y., professor of political science, 1973-78, assistant vice-president and associate provost, 1973-78; Graduate School and University Center of the City University of New York, New York City, professor of political science, 1978—.

Visiting distinguished professor, University of Texas at Arlington, 1981. Consulting editor, Praeger Publishers, 1968-73. Chairperson, Citizens Committee for Robert Kennedy, Queens County, N.Y., 1968; member of planning committee, White House Conference on Children and Youth, 1970; member of Task Force on Democratic Forms for New Towns, Twentieth Century Fund, 1970-71, Associate Task Force on Manpower, U.S. Department of Labor, 1970-74, community committee for New York Metropolitan Museum of Art, 1971-78, New York State Task Force on Post Secondary Education, 1971—, National Study Commission on Undergraduate and Teacher Education, 1972-76, and of New York State Regents Committee on Examinations, 1974-78; member of board of trustees, Interface, 1975—; member of board of directors, Research Foundation of the City University of New York, 1980—. Member of advisory board, Legal Research and Services for the Elderly, 1969-73, Puerto Rican Research Center, 1971-75, and Queens Lay Advocate Service, 1972-78; member of New York State Advisory Committee for Resource Center for Women, 1975-77; consultant to numerous organizations, including New York State Constitutional Revision Commission, 1958-59, United Nations, 1966, Ford Foundation, 1967, and to New Jersey Chancellor of Higher Education, 1978-79. Conductor of series of forty radio programs, ''Megalopolis: U.S.A.,'' for WNYC, 1960.

MEMBER: American Political Science Association, American Society for Public Administration, Northeastern Regional Political Science Association (member of executive committee, 1972), New York State Political Science Association (member of executive board, 1966-67), Phi Beta Kappa. *Awards, honors:* Grants from Ford Foundation, 1967-70, 1975-76, City University of New York, 1970-71, New York Foundation, 1971, New World Foundation, 1971-72, Carnegie Foundation, 1972-74, 1981, and from several other public and private sources.

WRITINGS—Published by Praeger, except as indicated: (Co-author) *Metropolitan Communities: A Bibliography*, Public Administration Service, 1956; (co-author) *Metropolitan Surveys: A Digest*, Public Administration Service, 1958; (editor) *Educating an Urban Population*, Sage Publications, 1967; *Participants and Participation: A Study of School Policy in New York City*, 1967; (with T. E. Hollander) *Six Urban School Systems: A Comparative Study of Institutional Response*, 1968; (editor with Alan Hevesi) *The Politics of Urban Education*, 1969; (editor with Maurice Berube) *Confrontation at Ocean Hill-Brownsville*, 1969.

(With Mario Fantini and Richard Magat) *Community Control and the Urban School*, 1970; *Local Control in Education*, 1972; (with Fantini) *Decentralization: Achieving Reform*, 1973; *School Boards and School Policy*, 1973; (editor with Ann Cook and Herb Mack) *City Life: A Documentary History of the American City*, 1973; (editor with Cook and Mack) *What Was It Like: When Your Grandparents Were Your Age*, Knopf, 1976; *Limits of Participation: The Decline of Community Organizations*, Sage Publications, 1980.

Monographs: *Megalopolis, U.S.A.: A Radio Course*, Queens College Press, 1960; (with William Fredericks) *State Technical Assistance to Local Government*, Council of State Governments, 1962; *Governing the Public Schools*, Temporary Commission on City Finances (New York), 1966; (with Hollander and William Vincent) *Investigation of Fiscally Independent and Dependent City School Districts*, U.S. Office of Education, 1967.

The Community School in the Nation, Institute for Community Studies, Queens College of the City University of New York, 1970; *School Decentralization and School Policy in New York City*, Institute for Community Studies, Queens College of the City University of New York, 1971; *An Evaluation of the Impact of the Emergency Employment Act in New York City*, National Manpower Task Force, 1972; *Citizen Organizations: Citizen Participation in Educational Decision-making*, two volumes, Institute for Responsive Education, 1979.

Contributor: Louis Masotti and Dan Bowen, editors, *Civil Violence in the Urban Community,* Sage Publications, 1968; Alan Rosenthal, editor, *Governing Education: A Reader on Politics, Power and Public School Policy,* Doubleday, 1969; H. R. Mahodd and Edward L. Angus, editors, *Urban Politics and Problems,* Scribner, 1969.

Needs of Elementary and Secondary Education for the Seventies, U.S. Government Printing Office, 1970; Henry M. Levin, editor, *Community Control of Schools,* Brookings Institution, 1970; Annette Rubinstein, editor, *Schools against Children: The Case for Community Control,* Monthly Review Press, 1970; Jewel Bellush and Stephen David, editors, *Race and Politics in New York City: Six Case Studies in Decentralization,* Praeger, 1971; *Freedom, Bureaucracy and Schooling,* National Education Association, 1971; Susan Fainstein and Norman Fainstein, editors, *The View from Below: Urban Politics and Social Policy,* Little, Brown, 1972; Allan Gartner, Colin Greer, and Frank Riessman, editors, *What Nixon Is Doing to Us,* Harrow Books, 1974; Sar A. Levitan and Robert Taggart, editors, *Emergency Employment Act,* Olympus, 1974.

(With Bruce Dollar) Antonia Pantoja, Barbara Blourock, and James Bowman, editors, *Badges and Indicia of Slavery: Cultural Pluralism Redefined,* Study Commission on Undergraduate Education and the Education of Teachers, 1975; Maynard C. Reynolds, editor, *Special Education in School System Decentralization,* Leadership Training Institute, University of Minnesota, 1975; Frederick B. Rough, editor, *Milliken vs. Bradley: Implication for Metropolitan Desegregation,* U.S. Government Printing Office, 1975; Carl A. Grant, editor, *Community Participation in Education: What Is/What Should Be,* Pendell, 1976; Charles Brecher and Raymond D. Horton, editors, *Setting Municipal Priorities, 1981,* Allanheld, Osmun, 1980.

Author of *Studying the Community: A Research Handbook,* with Constancia Warren, 1980; author of *Final Evaluation Report on Syracuse Youth Community Service* and *Final Evaluation Report on Syracuse Youth Community Service: Ethnographic Research,* both with Marguerite Beardsley and Marsha Weissman, 1981. Contributor to *Hearings of 92nd Congress,* U.S. Government Printing Office, 1971; contributor to *Encyclopedia Americana,* 1964, *Proceedings of the Academy of Political Science,* 1968, and *Encyclopedia of Education,* 1971. Contributor of articles to professional journals, including *Change, Social Policy, Public Administration Review, Journal of Negro Education, New Generations,* and *American Behavioral Scientist.* Editor, *Urban Affairs Quarterly,* 1965-70; member of editorial advisory board, *Urban Affairs Annual Review,* 1966-74, and *Journal of Education,* 1977-79; member of editorial board, *Social Policy,* 1969—.

* * *

GITTINGS, John 1938-

PERSONAL: Born September 24, 1938, in London, England; son of Robert William Victor and Katherine (Cambell) Gittings; married Aelfthryth Georgina Buzzard (a social worker); children: Daniel John, Thomas Fidel, Joseph Russell, Max Benjamin. *Education:* School of Oriental and African Studies, Civil Service Diploma (Chinese), 1958; Corpus Christi College, Oxford, Oriental studies, 1958-61 (with first honors). *Politics:* Socialist. *Religion:* Atheist. *Home:* 7 Aberdeen Park, London NS 2AN, England. *Office:* School of Languages, Polytechnic of Central London, 309 Regent St., London WIR 8AL, England.

CAREER: Royal Institute of International Affairs, London, England, Chinese specialist, 1963-66; Instituto de Estudios Internacionales, Santiago, Chile, specialist in Asian studies, 1966-67; affiliated with *Far Eastern Economic Review,* Hong Kong, 1968-69; *The Guardian,* London, China specialist, 1971—; Polytechnic of Central London, School of Languages, London, senior lecturer, 1976—.

WRITINGS: The Role of the Chinese Army, Oxford University Press, 1967; *Survey of the Sino-Soviet Dispute: A Commentary and Extracts from the Recent Polemics, 1963-67,* Oxford University Press, 1968; *A Chinese View of China,* Pantheon, 1973; *The World and China, 1922-1972,* Harper, 1974; (editor) *The Lessons of Chile,* Spokesman Books, 1975; *How to Study China's Socialist Development,* University of Sussex, 1976; (with Noam Chomsky and Jonathan Steele) *Superpowers in Collision,* Penguin, 1982.

* * *

GLEASON, Judith 1929-

PERSONAL: Born December 9, 1929, in Pasadena, Calif.; married William Gleason (a lawyer), September 24, 1953; children: Maud, William, Esther, Richard, Helen. *Education:* Radcliffe College, B.A., 1951; Columbia University, M.A., 1954, Ph.D., 1963. *Politics:* "Usually vote Democratic." *Religion:* "Santeria." *Home and office:* 26 East 91st St., New York, N.Y.

CAREER: Writer. Sarah Lawrence College, Bronxville, N.Y., lecturer in literature, 1960-63; New York University, New York, N.Y., adjunct associate professor of African arts, 1970-76; writer and choreographer with Educational Theater, 1976—. Conductor of private creative writing workshops and individual therapy sessions.

WRITINGS: This Africa, Northwestern University Press, 1964; *Agotime: Her Legend,* Grossman, 1970; *Orisha: The Gods of Yorubaland* (juvenile), Atheneum, 1971; *A Recitation of Ifa, Oracle of the Yoruba,* Grossman, 1973; *Santeria, Bronx* (juvenile), Atheneum, 1975; *Leaf and Bone* (poems), Viking, 1980. Contributor to *Parnassus.*

WORK IN PROGRESS: A book on the divinities of the Niger River.

SIDELIGHTS: Judith Gleason's novel *Agotime: Her Legend* tells the story of Agotime, the nineteenth-century African queen who was sold by her stepson into slavery and sent to Brazil. Gleason traces Agotime's historical journey to Latin America and her influence in Brazil as the leader of a cult devoted to water spirits and adds fictionalized descriptions of the events that shaped her life. From the research she conducted in Africa and Brazil, Gleason has woven "a tapestry of fact and legend," according to David Rosenthal in a *Nation* article, "a strange and powerful book which re-creates both the reality and the surrounding mythological and spiritual aura of 19th-century [Africa] and Brazil. . . . *Agotime* is history, odyssey and myth. When I finished reading it, I wanted to enter its magic circle, to dance and be haunted by the gods myself."

AVOCATIONAL INTERESTS: Travel, ethnic dance, "rivers wherever they may be, preferably hot climates."

BIOGRAPHICAL/CRITICAL SOURCES: Library Journal, February 1, 1970; *New York Times Book Review,* August 16, 1970; *Nation,* March 15, 1971.

GLUECK, Eleanor T(ouroff) 1898-1972

PERSONAL: Surname rhymes with "book"; born April 12, 1898, in New York, N.Y.; died September 25, 1972; daughter of Bernard L. (an industrialist) and Anna (Wodzislawski) Touroff; married Sheldon Glueck (a criminologist and Roscoe Pound Professor Emeritus of Law, Harvard University), April 16, 1922 (died March 10, 1980); children: Joyce Glueck Rosberg (died, 1956). *Education:* Barnard College, A.B., 1920; New York School of Social Work, diploma, 1921; Harvard University, Ed.M., 1923, Ed.D., 1925. *Politics:* Independent. *Religion:* Jewish. *Office:* Westengard House, 3 Garden St., Cambridge, Mass. 02138.

CAREER: Dorchester Welfare Center, Dorchester, Mass., head social worker, 1921-22; Harvard University, Cambridge, Mass., researcher in criminology in department of social ethics, 1925-28, Law School, research assistant on crime survey, 1928-30, research assistant in criminology, 1930-53, research associate in criminology, 1953-64, co-director of research project into the causes, treatment and prevention of juvenile delinquency, 1929-64. Member of delinquency committee, American Medical Association Conference on Mental Health, 1961; member, Massachusetts State Committee on Action for Mental Health, 1962; trustee and member of executive committee, Judge Baker Guidance Center, Boston, Mass. Technical consultant, White House Conference on Children and Youth, 1960.

MEMBER: International Society of Criminology, International Conference of Social Work, International Society of Social Defense, World Federation for Mental Health, American Association for the Advancement of Science, American Academy of Arts and Sciences (fellow), American Society of Criminology, National Association of Social Workers, National Conference of Social Welfare, American Association of University Women, Medical Correctional Association, United Prison Association (member of corporation), German Society of Criminology, Massachusetts Conference on Social Welfare, League of Women Voters, Association of Alumnae of Barnard College.

AWARDS, HONORS—All except honorary degree and Distinguished Alumna Award are shared with husband, Sheldon Glueck: Herbert C. Parsons Memorial Award, United Prison Association of Massachusetts, 1946; Distinguished Service Award, Boston Juvenile Court, 1952; Big Brother of the Year Award, Big Brothers of America, 1957; Sc.D., Harvard University, 1958; August Vollmer Award, American Society of Criminology, 1961; gold medal, Institute of Criminal Anthropology, University of Rome, 1964; First Beccaria Gold Medal, German Society of Criminology, 1964; Distinguished Alumna Award, Association of Alumnae of Barnard College, 1969.

WRITINGS: The Community Use of Schools, Williams & Wilkins, 1927; *Extended Use of School Buildings,* U.S. Government Printing Office, 1927; *Evaluative Research in Social Work,* Columbia University Press, 1936; *The Glueck's Adventure in Japan,* Obun (Japan), 1962.

With husband, Sheldon Glueck: *Five Hundred Criminal Careers,* Knopf, 1930, reprinted, Kraus Reprint, 1965; *Five Hundred Delinquent Women,* Knopf, 1934, reprinted, Kraus Reprint, 1965; *One Thousand Juvenile Delinquents,* Harvard University Press, 1934, reprinted, Kraus Reprint, 1965; (editors) *Preventing Crime: A Symposium,* McGraw, 1936, reprinted, Kraus Reprint, 1966; *Later Criminal Careers,* Commonwealth Fund, 1937, reprinted, Kraus Reprint, 1966. *Juvenile Delinquents Grown Up,* Commonwealth Fund, 1940, reprinted, Kraus Reprint, 1966; *Criminal Careers in Retrospect,* Commonwealth Fund, 1943, reprinted, Kraus Reprint, 1966; *After-Conduct of Discharged Offenders,* Macmillan (London), 1944, reprinted, Kraus Reprint, 1976.

Unraveling Juvenile Delinquency, Harvard University Press, 1950; *Delinquents in the Making,* Harper, 1952; *Physique and Delinquency,* Harper, 1956; *Predicting Delinquency and Crime,* Harvard University Press, 1959.

Research in Juvenile Delinquency, [Cambridge, Mass.], 1961; *Family Environment and Delinquency,* Houghton, 1962, reprinted, Fred B. Rothman, 1982; *Ventures in Criminology,* Tavistock Publications, 1964; (and Franco Farracuti) *Replication of "Unraveling Juvenile Delinquency" in Puerto Rico,* Harvard University, 1966; *Delinquents and Non-Delinquents in Perspective,* Harvard University Press, 1968.

Toward a Typology of Juvenile Offenders: Implications for Therapy and Prevention, Grune, 1970; (editors) *Identification of Pre-Delinquents,* Intercontinental Medical Book Corp., 1972; *Of Delinquency and Crime: A Panorama of Years of Search and Research,* C. C Thomas, 1974; *Lives of Labor—Lives of Love: Fragments of Friendly Autobiographies,* Exposition Press, 1977.

Contributor of monographs and articles to professional journals. Former member of editorial advisory board, *International Journal of Social Psychiatry* and *Psychiatric Opinion.*

BIOGRAPHICAL/CRITICAL SOURCES: Saturday Review, April 6, 1963; *U.S. News and World Report,* April 25, 1965; *Pictorial Living* (Sunday supplement to *Boston Advertiser),* June 13, 1965.†

* * *

GLUECK, Sheldon 1896-1980

PERSONAL: Born August 15, 1896, in Warsaw, Poland; brought to the United States in 1903, naturalized in 1920; died March 10, 1980, in Cambridge, Mass.; buried in Brooklyn, N.Y.; son of Charles and Anna (Steinhardt) Glueck; married Eleanor Touroff (a research criminologist), April 16, 1922 (died Spetember 25, 1972); children: Joyce Glueck Rosberg (died, 1956). *Education:* Attended Georgetown University, 1914-15; George Washington University, A.B., 1920; National University, L.L.B., L.L.M., 1920; Harvard University, A.M., 1922, Ph.D., 1924. *Politics:* Independent. *Religion:* Hebrew. *Office:* Langdell Hall, Law School, Harvard University, Cambridge, Mass. 02138.

CAREER: Harvard University, Cambridge, Mass., instructor in criminology and penology in department of social ethics, 1925-29, Law School, assistant professor, 1929-31, professor of criminology, 1931-50, Lowell Lecturer, 1935, Roscoe Pound Professor of Law, 1950-63, Roscoe Pound Professor of Law Emeritus, 1963-80, co-director of research project into the causes, treatment and prevention of juvenile delinquency, beginning 1925. Admitted to New York State Bar. Member of advisory committee on rules of criminal procedure and advisory committee on revision of the rules, U.S. Supreme Court; member of committee on youth correction authority and the model penal code, American Law Institute; member of advisory board, Psychiatry and the Law Foundation; member of board of overseers, Center for the Study of Violence, Brandeis University. Official delegate of U.S. Government to International Prison Congress, Prague, 1930, and Paris, 1950; advisor to Justice

Robert H. Jackson on the law governing war criminals. *Military service:* U.S. Army, American Expeditionary Forces, World War I; became sergeant.

MEMBER: International Society of Criminology, International Academy of Law and Sciences (member of council), World Union of Organizations for the Safeguard of Youth (member of scientific committee), American Bar Association (member of committee on juvenile delinquency), American Society of Criminology, American Academy of Arts and Sciences (fellow), American Association for the Advancement of Science, American Psychiatric Association (honorary fellow), National Council on Crime and Delinquency (member of professional council), Harvard Faculty Club.

AWARDS, HONORS: Recipient with wife, Eleanor T. Glueck, of Herbert C. Parsons Memorial Award, United Prison Association of Massachusetts, 1946, Distinguished Service Award, Boston Juvenile Court, 1952, Big Brother of the Year Award, Big Brothers of America, 1957, August Vollmer Award, American Society of Criminology, 1961, gold medal, Institute of Criminal Anthropology, University of Rome, 1964, and First Beccaria Gold Medal, German Society of Criminology, 1964; LL.D., University of Thessalonika, 1948; Sc.D., Harvard University, 1958; Isaac Ray Award, American Psychiatric Association, 1961; S.S.D., George Washington University, 1963.

WRITINGS: Mental Disorder and the Criminal Law, Little, Brown, 1925, reprinted, Kraus Reprint, 1966; (editor) *Probation and Criminal Justice: Essays in Honor of Herbert C. Parsons,* Macmillan, 1933, reprinted, Arno, 1974; *Crime and Justice,* Little, Brown, 1936, reprinted, Kraus Reprint, 1966; (with Livingston Hall) *Cases and Materials on Criminal Law,* West Publishing, 1940; *War Criminals,* U.S. War Department, 1944; *War Criminals: Their Prosecution and Punishment,* Knopf, 1944, reprinted, Kraus Reprint, 1966; *What Shall Be Done with the War Criminals?,* U.S. Government Printing Office, 1944; *The Nuremberg Trial and Aggressive War,* Knopf, 1946, reprinted, Kraus Reprint, 1966; (with Hall) *Cases on Criminal Law and Its Enforcement,* West Publishing, 1951, 2nd edition, 1958; (editor) *The Welfare State and the National Welfare,* Addison-Wesley, 1952; *Crime and Correction: Selected Papers,* Addison-Wesley, 1952; (editor) *The Problem of Delinquency,* Houghton, 1959; *Law and Psychiatry: Cold War or Entente Cordiale?,* Johns Hopkins Press, 1962; (editor) *Roscoe Pound and Criminal Justice,* Oceana, 1965; *Continental Police Practice: In the Formative Years,* C. C Thomas, 1974.

With wife, Eleanor T. Glueck: *Five Hundred Criminal Careers,* Knopf, 1930, reprinted, Kraus Reprint, 1965; *Five Hundred Delinquent Women,* Knopf, 1934, reprinted, Kraus Reprint, 1965; *One Thousand Juvenile Delinquents,* Harvard University Press, 1934, reprinted, Kraus Reprint, 1965; (editors) *Preventing Crime: A Symposium,* McGraw, 1936, reprinted, Kraus Reprint, 1966; *Later Criminal Careers,* Commonwealth Fund, 1937, reprinted, Kraus Reprint, 1966.

Juvenile Delinquents Grown Up, Commonwealth Fund, 1940, reprinted, Kraus Reprint, 1966; *Criminal Careers in Retrospect,* Commonwealth Fund, 1943, reprinted Kraus Reprint, 1966; *After-Conduct of Discharged Offenders,* Macmillan (London), 1944, reprinted, Kraus Reprint, 1976.

Unraveling Juvenile Delinquency, Harvard University Press, 1950; *Delinquents in the Making,* Harper, 1952; *Physique and Delinquency,* Harper, 1956; *Predicting Delinquency and Crime,* Harvard University Press, 1959.

Research in Juvenile Delinquency, [Cambridge, Mass.], 1961; *Family Environment and Delinquency,* Houghton, 1962, reprinted, Fred B. Rothman, 1982; *Ventures in Criminology,* Tavistock Publications, 1964; (and Franco Farracuti) *Replication of "Unraveling Juvenile Delinquency," in Puerto Rico,* Harvard University, 1966; *Delinquents and Nondelinquents in Perspective,* Harvard University Press, 1968.

Toward a Typology of Juvenile Offenders: Implications for Therapy and Prevention, Grune, 1970; (editors) *Identification of Pre-Delinquents,* Intercontinental Medical Book Corp., 1972; *Of Delinquency and Crime: A Panorama of Years of Search and Research,* C. C Thomas, 1974; *Lives of Labor—Lives of Love: Fragments of Friendly Autobiographies,* Exposition Press, 1977.

Also author of book and lyrics for a musical, *Mr. Littlefellow,* Dorrance, 1976, and of two plays, "American Occupational Zone" and "Prisoner's Progress."

Contributor to professional publications. Member of editorial advisory board, *International Journal of Social Psychiatry;* consulting editor, *Community Mental Health Journal.*

WORK IN PROGRESS: A book reporting on the 500 delinquents and 500 non-delinquents of *Unraveling Juvenile Delinquency;* several legal articles; plays.

SIDELIGHTS: A noted authority on criminology and penology, Sheldon Glueck was best known for his pioneering studies on the causes and possible prevention of juvenile delinquency. In collaboration with his wife, Eleanor, Glueck developed "social prediction tables" for the early detection of potential delinquents. According to J. Y. Smith of the *Washington Post,* these tables "have been used with a degree of accuracy ranging up to 90 percent to identify potential criminals while they are still young children."

Laurie Johnston of the *New York Times* explained that "the Gluecks identified 40 'highly decisive' factors in forecasting the existence and level of criminal behavior, five of them in the family and social background: Discipline by the father, supervision by the mother, the father's affection, the mother's affection and the cohesiveness of the family." The Gluecks concluded that "these factors . . . have more bearing on whether a child becomes delinquent than poverty, surroundings and even the lack of a father in the family," Smith wrote.

Some critics maintained that such early detection methods, if abused, would result in the premature "labeling" of an individual. Nevertheless, Johnston reported, "the studies had wide impact and produced hopes that, with adequate financing, the theoretical science of criminology would continue to emerge into an applied science, with accurate prognostic techniques."

AVOCATIONAL INTERESTS: Theatre (directing, acting, and writing), travel.

BIOGRAPHICAL/CRITICAL SOURCES: Books, February 2, 1930; *Harvard Law Review,* June, 1930, December, 1934, April, 1944; *Christian Century,* July 9, 1930; *Nation,* August 27, 1930, January 12, 1963, December 3, 1964; *Columbia Law Review,* June, 1934, February, 1941; *New York Times,* November 11, 1934, December 30, 1934, November 28, 1943, August 4, 1946.

Yale Law Journal, March, 1941, March, 1944; *American Journal of Public Health,* February, 1944; *American Sociological Review,* October, 1944, December, 1969; *Weekly Book Review,* January 7, 1945; *New Republic,* August 26, 1946; *Saturday Review of Literature,* September 21, 1946.

Times Literary Supplement, July 6, 1962; *Harvard Educational Review,* spring, 1963.

OBITUARIES: Washington Post, March 12, 1980; *New York Times,* March 13, 1980; *Newsweek,* March 24, 1980; *Time,* March 24, 1980.†

* * *

GODECHOT, Jacques Leon 1907-

PERSONAL: Born January 3, 1907, in Luneville, France; son of Georges and Therese (Lazard) Godechot; married Lambert Arlette, September 13, 1933; children: Didier, Thierry, Yves, Eveline (Mrs. Dominique Mouries). *Education:* University of Nancy, licence es lettres, 1927; Sorbonne, University of Paris, Doctorat, 1938. *Home:* 17 rue A Mercie, Toulouse 31000, France. *Office:* Universite de Toulouse-Le Mirail, Toulouse 31058, France.

CAREER: Lycee Kleber, Strasbourg, France, history teacher, 1933-35; Ecole Navale, Brest, France, professor of maritime history, 1935-40; University of Toulouse, Toulouse, France, professor of contemporary history, 1945-74, director of history department, 1956-76, dean of School of Literature and Humanities, 1961-71. *Military service:* French Army, Infantry, 1929-30 and 1939-45; became captain.

MEMBER: International Committee on the French Revolution (president, 1975—), Societe des etudes robespierristes (president, 1926—), Societe d'histoire moderne (president, 1974-75), Societa di storia del Risorgimento (honorary member), American Historical Association, Societe d'histoire de la revolution de 1848 (president, 1961-79), French Committee on Economic and Social History of the French Revolution (president, 1975—), Socio straniero dell' academia razionale dei Lincei (Rome). *Awards, honors:* Officier de la Legion d'honneur, 1962; chevalier du merite italien, 1963.

WRITINGS: La Propagande royaliste aux armees sous le Directoire, Mellottee (Paris), 1933; *Les Commissaires aux armees sous le Directoire: Contribution a l'etude des rapports entre les pouvoirs civils et militaires,* Fustier (Paris), 1937; *Histoire de l'Atlantique,* Bordas (Paris), 1947; (editor) *La Revolution de 1848 a Toulouse et dans la Haute-Garonne,* Prefecture de la Haute-Garonne (Toulouse), 1949; *Les Institutions de la France sous la Revolution et l'Empire,* Presses Universitaires de France (Paris), 1951, 2nd edition, 1968; *Histoire de Malte,* Presses Universitaires de France, 1952, 3rd edition, 1981; *La Grand Nation: L'Expansion revolutionnaire de la France dans le monde de 1789 a 1799,* Aubier (Paris), 1956, revised edition, 1983.

La Contre-revolution: Doctrine et action, 1789-1804, Presses Universitaires de France, 1961, translation by Salvator Attanasio published as *The Counter-Revolution: Doctrine and Action, 1789-1804,* Fertig, 1971, revised edition, Princeton University Press, 1981; (with others) *Babeuf [et] Buonarroti: Pour le deuxieme centenaire de leur naissance,* Thomas (Nancy), 1961; *Les Revolutions, 1770-1799,* Presses Universitaires de France, 1963, 3rd edition, 1970, translation by Herbert H. Rowen published as *France and the Atlantic Revolution of the Eighteenth Century, 1770-1799,* Free Press, 1965; (editor and author of introduction) *La Pensee revolutionnaire en France et en Europe, 1780-1799,* A. Colin (Paris), 1964.

La Prise de la Bastille, 14 juillet 1789, Gallimard, 1965, translation by Jean Stewart published as *The Taking of the Bastille, July 14th, 1789,* Scribner, 1970; (with Suzanne Moncassin) *Demographie et subsistances en Languedoc [du XVIII au debut du XIXe-siecle],* Bibliotheque Nationale, 1965; (author of introduction) *La Presse ouvriere, 1819-1850: Angleterre, Etats-Unis, France, Belgique, Italie, Allemagne, Tchecoslovaquie, Hongrie,* Societe d'histoire de la revolution de 1848 (Bures-sur-Yvette), 1966; *L'Europe et l'Amerique a l'epoque napoleonienne, 1800-1815,* Presses Universitaires de France, 1967, translation with Beatrice Hyslop and David Dowd published as *The Napoleonic Era in Europe,* Holt, 1971; (contributor) *L'Abolition du regime feodal dans le monde occidental,* Societe des etudes robespierristes (Paris), 1969; *Napoleon,* A. Michel (Paris), 1969; *L'Epoca delle rivoluzioni,* Unione tipograficoeditrice torinese, 1969; (with Claude Bellanger, Claude Levy, and others) *Histoire general de la presse francaise,* five volumes, Presses Universitaires de France, 1969-76.

(Editor) *Les Constitutions de la France depuis 1789,* Garnier-Flammarion (Paris), 1970; (contributor) *L'Abolition de la feodalite dans le monde occidental,* two volumes, Editions du Centre national de la recherche scientifique (Paris), 1971; *Les Revolutions de 1848,* A. Michel (Paris), 1971; (with M. Vaussard) *Histoire de l'Italie moderne,* two volumes, Hachette (Paris), 1972; *Un Jury pour la Revolution,* R. Laffont (Paris), 1974; (with Philippe Wolff and others) *Histoire de Toulouse,* Edouard Privat (Toulouse), 1974; *La Vie quotidienne en France sous le Directoire,* Hachette, 1977; *Regards sur l'epoque revolutionnaire,* [Toulouse], 1980.

WORK IN PROGRESS: L'Europe de Napoleon, with Jean Tulard; *La Revolution dans la region Toulousaine;* editing *Considerations sur la Revolution francaise* by Mme. de Stael.

* * *

GOFFMAN, Erving 1922-1982

PERSONAL: Born June 11, 1922, in Canada; died November 19, 1982, in Philadelphia, Pa.; son of Max and Anne Goffman; widower; children: one son. *Education:* University of Toronto, B.A., 1945; University of Chicago, M.A., 1949, Ph.D., 1953. *Office:* University of Pennsylvania, Philadelphia, Pa. 19104.

CAREER: University of Chicago, Division of Social Sciences, Chicago, Ill., assistant, 1952-53, resident associate, 1953-54; National Institute of Mental Health, Bethesda, Md., visiting scientist, 1954-57; University of California, Berkeley, assistant professor, 1958-59, associate professor, 1959-62, professor of sociology, 1962-68; University of Pennsylvania, Philadelphia, Benjamin Franklin Professor of Anthropology and Sociology, 1968-82. *Member:* American Sociological Association (president, 1981-82). *Awards, honors:* LL.D., University of Manitoba, 1976; Guggenheim fellowship, 1977-78; *In Medias Res,* International Prize for Communicating, 1978; D.H.L., University of Chicago, 1979; Mead-Cooley Award in social psychology; *Forms of Talk* was nominated for a National Book Critics Circle award, 1981.

WRITINGS: The Presentation of Self in Everyday Life (monograph), University of Edinburgh Social Sciences Research Centre, 1956, revised and expanded edition, Anchor Books, 1959; *Encounters: Two Studies in the Sociology of Interaction,* Bobbs-Merrill, 1961; *Asylums: Essays on the Social Situation of Mental Patients and Other Inmates,* Anchor Books, 1961; *Stigma: Notes on the Management of Spoiled Identity,* Prentice-Hall, 1963; *Behavior in Public Places: Notes on the Social Organization of Gatherings,* Free Press of Glencoe, 1963; *Interaction Ritual: Essays on Face-to-Face Behavior,* Doubleday, 1967; *Strategic Interaction,* University of Pennsylvania Press, 1969; *Relations in Public: Micro-Studies of the Public Order,* Basic Books, 1971; *Frame Analysis: Essays on the Organization of Experience,* Harper, 1974; *Gender Advertise-*

ments, Harper, 1979; *Forms of Talk,* University of Pennsylvania Press, 1981. Contributor to such periodicals as *Psychiatry* and the *American Journal of Sociology.*

SIDELIGHTS: A sociologist well-known for his analyses of human interaction, Erving Goffman relied less on formal scientific method than on observation to explain contemporary life. He wrote on subjects ranging from the way people behave in public to the different "forms" of talk, and always from the point of view that every facet of human behavior is "significant in the strategy and tactics of social struggle," a *Times Literary Supplement* critic says. Roy Harris, in another *Times Literary Supplement* review, calls Goffman "a public private-eye. . . forever on the lookout for candid-camera evidence which might lead to divorce proceedings between ourselves and our social images." And, because Goffman communicated so vividly the "horror and anguish—as well as some of the absurd comedy—of everyday life," *New York Times Book Review* critic Marshall Berman dubs him "the Kafka of our time."

In *Gender Advertisements,* his 1979 publication, Goffman investigated the way that commercial advertising both reflects and helps shape our concept of ''masculine'' and ''feminine'' behavior. After examining a selection of advertising pictures from magazines, Goffman concluded that women are consistently subordinated to men in a variety of situations, relating to them not as equals but as children to parents. Writing in the *New York Times,* Anatole Broyard explains: ''Like children, . . . women are allowed to cop out of reality because the men beside them take responsibility for it. Like children, they 'are saved from seriousness,' allowed to look and behave childishly, assuming physically inefficient and clowning postures.'' Furthermore, notes Anne Hollander in the *New York Times Book Review,* ''it is women who are permitted to burst into tears, to stare absently into space while men speak earnestly to them, or to hide their mouths with their hands when startled. . . . And because of the general understanding that gender displays are natural to human behavior, portrayals along such lines in the social interplay of the sexes must be taken as 'both shadow and substance': They show not only what we wish or pretend to be, but what we are.''

While critics herald the truth of Goffman's interpretations, they do question some of the assumptions from which his conclusions were drawn. Hollander, for one, suggests that the way male-female relationships are depicted in photographs may be more a reflection of pictorial conventions than a reflection of the status of women today. Some thematic images of female subordination are ironic, she argues, ''invoking a detached understanding of established pictorial rituals as well as an engagement with current social ones.'' And Anatole Broyard articulates a similar view: ''Increasingly today, it seems that advertising is not only read as parody, but intended as parody as well. Much of the humor of advertising depends on this double meaning, which is a play on the oversimplification being depicted.'' Broyard's stated intention is not to discredit what he considers a valuable study, but rather, as he puts it, ''to show that men and women are more complicated than they are advertised to be.''

BIOGRAPHICAL/CRITICAL SOURCES: American Journal of Sociology, November, 1962; *American Anthropologist,* December, 1962; *American Sociological Review,* June, 1964; *Times Literary Supplement,* December 31, 1971, December 18, 1981; *New York Times Book Review,* December 3, 1972, February 27, 1972, June 4, 1972, April 29, 1979; *New York Review of Books,* November 1, 1973; *New York Times,* April 18, 1979; *Choice,* September, 1979, September, 1981.

* * *

GOFFSTEIN, M(arilyn) B(rooke) 1940-

PERSONAL: Born December 20, 1940, in St. Paul, Minn.; daughter of Albert A. (an electrical engineer) and Esther (Rose) Goffstein; married Peter Schaaf (a photographer), August 15, 1965. *Education:* Bennington College, B.A., 1962. *Home:* 697 West End Ave., New York, N.Y. 10025.

CAREER: Author and illustrator; has had several one-woman exhibitions of pen and ink and watercolor drawings in New York, N.Y., and St. Paul, Minn.

AWARDS, HONORS: Sleepy People, Across the Sea, My Noah's Ark, and *An Artist* were selected for American Institute of Graphic Arts' Children's Book Shows; *The Gats!* was an honor book in *Book Week*'s Children's Spring Book Festival, 1966; *Across the Sea, Goldie the Dollmaker,* and *Me and My Captain* were named *New York Times'* Outstanding Children's Books in 1968, 1969, and 1974; *A Little Schubert, Natural History,* and *An Artist* were named *New York Times'* Best Illustrated Children's Books, 1972, 1978, and 1980; *Fish for Supper, Family Scrapbook,* and *My Noah's Ark* were named American Library Association Notable Books in 1976, 1978, and 1978; *Fish for Supper* was also a Caldecott Honor Book, 1977; Jane Adams Peace Award Special Certificate, 1979, for *Natural History; An Artist* was a National Book Award nominee, 1980.

WRITINGS—All self-illustrated: *The Gats!* (also see below), Pantheon, 1966; *Sleepy People* (also see below), Farrar, Straus, 1966, revised edition, 1979; *Brookie and Her Lamb* (also see below), Farrar, Straus, 1967, revised edition, 1981; *Across the Sea* (also see below), Farrar, Straus, 1968; *Goldie the Dollmaker* (also see below), Farrar, Straus, 1969.

The Two Piano Tuners (also see below), Farrar, Straus, 1970; *The Underside of the Leaf* (novel; also see below), Farrar, Straus, 1972; *A Little Schubert* (also see below), Harper, 1972; *Me and My Captain,* Farrar, Straus, 1974; *Daisy Summerfield's Style* (novel), Delacorte, 1975; *Fish for Supper,* Dial, 1976; *My Crazy Sister,* Dial, 1976; *Family Scrapbook,* Farrar, Straus, 1978; *My Noah's Ark,* Harper, 1978; *Natural History,* Farrar, Straus, 1979; *Neighbors,* Harper, 1979; *The First Books* (trade paperback collection; includes *The Gats!, Sleepy People, Brookie and Her Lamb, Across the Sea, Goldie the Dollmaker, The Two Piano Tuners, The Underside of the Leaf,* and *A Little Schubert*), Avon, 1979.

An Artist, Harper, 1980; *Laughing Latkes,* Farrar, Straus, 1980; *Lives of the Artists,* 1982.

SIDELIGHTS: ''It is not simple to simplify. M. B. Goffstein is a miniaturist recording different aspects of the world, large and little. Like a whittler she eliminates excess in order to extract an essence,'' Karla Kuskin writes in the *New York Times Book Review.* Goffstein, a prolific artist, has written and illustrated fourteen picture books in thirteen years, during which time she also produced two young adult novels. Writing in the *Washington Post Book World,* Maggie Stern calls her ''one of the finest illustrator/writers of our time. Like porcelain, there is more to her work than meets the eye. Beneath the delicacy and fragility is a core of astounding strength.''

BIOGRAPHICAL/CRITICAL SOURCES: Childrens Literature Review, Volume III, Gale, 1978; *Washington Post Book World,* September 9, 1979; *New York Times Book Review,* December

16, 1979, January 11, 1981; *Kirkus Reviews,* September 15, 1980.

* * *

GOFORTH, Ellen
See FRANCIS, Dorothy Brenner

* * *

GOLD, Don 1931-

PERSONAL: Born March 13, 1931, in Chicago, Ill.; son of Sidney and Bess (Seidler) Gold; married Joan Gallagher, March 24, 1954 (divorced, 1968); children: Tracy, Paul. *Education:* Northwestern University, B.S.J., 1952, M.S.J., 1953. *Home:* 3000 N. Sheridan Rd., Chicago, Ill. 60657.

CAREER: Down Beat (magazine), Chicago, Ill., managing editor, 1956-59; *Playboy,* Chicago, associate editor, 1959-62; *Saturday Evening Post,* New York City, associate editor, 1962-64; *Ladies' Home Journal,* New York City, assistant managing editor, 1964-65; *Holiday* (magazine), New York City, managing editor, 1965-68; William Morris Agency (literary agency), New York City, head of literary department, 1968-73; writer, 1973-75; *Travel and Leisure* (magazine), New York City, managing editor, 1975-77; *Playboy,* managing editor, 1980—. *Military service:* U.S. Army, Intelligence, 1953-55; became sergeant. *Member:* International P.E.N., Authors Guild, Authors League of America.

WRITINGS: (Editor) *The Human Commitment* (anthology), Chilton, 1967; *Letters to Tracy* (nonfiction), McKay, 1972; *Bellevue* (nonfiction), Harper, 1975; *The Park* (mystery), Harper, 1977; *Until the Singing Stops* (nonfiction), Holt, 1980; *The Priest* (nonfiction), Holt, 1981. Contributor to popular magazines, including *Harper's, Playboy, Ladies' Home Journal, Cosmopolitan, Reader's Digest,* and *Travel and Leisure.*

SIDELIGHTS: The Priest, Don Gold's journalistic portrayal of the everyday life of New York City parish priest Brian O'Connor, documents the problems as well as the positive aspects of a career devoted to the Catholic Church and its people. A *Detroit News* reviewer, who characterizes Gold as a journalist "who has written sensitively and well on a number of subjects," feels that *The Priest* is "the best book on the Church I've read in years, a report valuable to Catholics and non-Catholics alike on the situation inside today." The critic goes on to praise the book as a "fully realized and perfectly edited *cinema verite* documentary." Joseph Nocera, writing in *Washington Post Book World,* finds that, although the book is limited with respect to the depth of Gold's inquiry and the extent of his objectivity, "most importantly . . . we get . . . a penetrating look at the current state of relations between parish priests . . . and the bishops and other chancery officials."

BIOGRAPHICAL/CRITICAL SOURCES: New York Times Book Review, July 6, 1975, March 26, 1978; *Choice,* February, 1976; *Washington Post Book World,* July 5, 1981; *Detroit News,* August 16, 1981; *Los Angeles Times Book Review,* August 23, 1981.

* * *

GOLD, Doris B. 1919-

PERSONAL: Born November 21, 1919, in New York, N.Y.; daughter of Saul and Gertrude (Reiss) Bauman; married Wilson Branch, February, 1947; married Bernard George Gold (a bakery foreman), August, 1953; children: (second marriage) Albert, Michael. *Education:* Brooklyn College (now Brooklyn College of the City University of New York), B.A., 1946; Washington University, St. Louis, Mo., M.A., 1955; attended Pratt Institute and University of Kansas. *Religion:* Jewish. *Office:* Associated Young Men's-Young Women's Hebrew Associations of New York, 130 East 59th St., New York, N.Y. 10022.

CAREER: Writer. University of Kansas, Lawrence, instructor in English, 1946-47; evening instructor in English at State University of New York at Farmingdale, and for Levittown (N.Y.) adult education program, 1958-60; substitute teacher of English and art in secondary schools of New York City, 1953, 1960-64, and in Levittown, 1956-60; *Young Judaean* (magazine), New York City, editor, 1964-72. Teacher of English to new Americans for Young Men's Hebrew Association and Young Women's Hebrew Association, St. Louis, Mo., 1950, and for New York Association for New Americans, 1962. East coast coordinator of Volunteerism Task Force, National Organization for Women, 1972-75. *Awards, honors:* American Scene Poetry Award, Poetry Society of Colorado, 1945; Carruth Poetry Award, University of Kansas, 1947; Allan Tate poetry scholarship at Indiana University, 1949; citation from Mid-Island Young Men's-Young Women's Hebrew Associations, 1963; New York State Council on the Arts grant, 1970-73, for work on astronomy education program.

WRITINGS: (Editor, and adapter of twenty stories) *Stories for Jewish Juniors,* Jonathan David, 1967; (contributor) Vivian Gornick and B. K. Moran, editors, *Woman in Sexist Society: Studies in Power and Powerlessness,* Basic Books, 1971; *Volunteerism Bibliography,* Council of Planning Librarians, 1979; *Honey in the Lion: Collected Poems,* Bibliography Press, 1979; (editor with Jack N. Porter) *Jews and the Cults,* Bibliography Press, 1981. Also author of plays, including "Golden Land," "Lincoln and Liberty Too," and others produced by synagogue and church groups, and "Time Out of Joint," a Shakespearean burlesque; also dramatized sections of Mary Antin's *The Promised Land.* Contributor of poetry to *Tiger's Eye, Experiment,* and *Writer,* feature stories to *Levittown Tribune* and *Newsday,* book reviews to *New York Times* and *Kansas City Star,* and feature articles to *Jerusalem Post, The Jewish Week,* and *Woman's Day.*

WORK IN PROGRESS: Poems on Judaica themes; a feminist essay on Jewish women poets.

* * *

GOLDBERG, Herb 1937-

PERSONAL: Born July 14, 1937, in Berlin, Germany; son of Jacob and Ella (Nagler) Goldberg. *Education:* City College (now City College of the City University of New York), B.A., 1958; Adelphi University, Ph.D., 1963. *Office:* 1100 Glendon Ave., No. 939, Los Angeles, Calif. 90024.

CAREER: California State University, Los Angeles, professor of psychology, 1965—; licensed psychologist in private practice of psychotherapy with individuals, couples, and families. *Member:* American Psychological Association, American Academy of Psychotherapists, California State Psychological Association, Phi Beta Kappa.

WRITINGS: (With George R. Bach) *Creative Aggression,* Doubleday, 1974; *The Hazards of Being Male,* Signet, 1976; (with Robert T. Lewis) *Money Madness,* Morrow, 1978; *The New*

Male: From Self-Destruction to Self-Care, Morrow, 1979; *The New Male-Female Relationship,* Morrow, 1983. Contributor to *American Psychologist, Journal of Abnormal Psychology, Professional Psychology, Clinical Psychologist, Voices,* and *International Journal of Social Psychiatry.*

SIDELIGHTS: In his books, psychologist Herb Goldberg interprets and explains for the lay reader the phenomena that he deals with as a professional, the psycho-sociological crises that plague contemporary experience.

Goldberg told *CA:* "I write because I believe that psychological exploration is a key to altering the course of the human experience in positive and dramatic ways. It is the one tool that has never been effectively used to mine the human potential. I feel that, once clarified and understood, the human experience can be dramatically transformed."

In *The New Male: From Self-Destruction to Self-Care,* Goldberg explores the psychological crisis that he believes men face as male-female roles in society undergo drastic change. The contemporary male, claims Goldberg in the book, "has become a hyperactive, hypercerebral, hypermechanical, rigid, self-destructive machine out of control." According to James A. Levine in *Psychology Today,* Goldberg's book serves as a "guide to interpersonal relationships at a time of change." A *Publishers Weekly* reviewer says that Goldberg "offers a wealth of worthwhile suggestions that will help lead . . . to more constructive behavior" within male-female relationships.

BIOGRAPHICAL/CRITICAL SOURCES: Herb Goldberg, *The New Male: From Self-Destruction to Self-Care,* Morrow, 1979; *Publishers Weekly,* July 16, 1979; *New York Times Book Review,* September 16, 1979; *Psychology Today,* November, 1979.

* * *

GOLDBERG, Reuben L(ucius) 1883-1970 (Rube Goldberg)

PERSONAL: Born July 4, 1883, in San Francisco, Calif.; died of cancer December 7, 1970, in New York, N.Y.; son of Max (a moneylender and land speculator) and Hannah (Cohn) Goldberg; married Irma Seeman, October 17, 1916; children: Thomas Reuben, George Warren. *Education:* University of California, B.S., 1904. *Home:* 317 West 75th St., New York, N.Y. *Office:* 140 West 57th St., New York, N.Y.

CAREER: Cartoonist, writer, and sculptor. *San Francisco Chronicle,* San Francisco, Calif., sports cartoonist, 1905-06; *San Francisco Bulletin,* San Francisco, cartoonist, 1906-07; *New York Evening Mail,* New York City, sports cartoonist, 1907-25; cartoonist with McNaught Syndicate, 1916-30; *New York Sun,* New York City, editorial and political cartoonist, beginning 1938; *New York Journal American,* New York City, cartoonist, beginning 1950; King Features Syndicate, New York City, cartoonist, beginning 1950; sculptor, 1964-70. Worked as political cartoonist for *New York Journal* and *New York World Journal Telegram.* Worked in vaudeville as stand-up comedian, cartoonist, and fortune-teller, 1911. Creator of cartoon characters "Boob McNutt," "Mike and Ike," and "Professor Lucifer Gorgonzola Butts." Sculpture exhibited at Smithsonian National Museum of History and Technology, entitled "Do It the Hard Way: Rube Goldberg and Modern Times," 1970. Director of cartoon courses in Famous Artists' School. *Military service:* U.S. National Guard; became sergeant.

MEMBER: National Cartoonist Society (past president; honorary president), Artists and Writers Association, Society of Illustrators (president), Dutch Treat Club, The Lambs, Coffee House. *Awards, honors:* Pulitzer Prize, 1948, for best editorial cartoon; Freedoms Foundation Award; Banshees Award; Page One Award; Sigma Chi Award; National Museum of History and Technology award, 1970, for cartoon designs.

WRITINGS—Under name Rube Goldberg: *Is There a Doctor in the House?,* Day, 1929; *The Rube Goldberg Plan for the Post-War World,* F. Watts, 1944; (with Sam Boal) *Rube Goldberg's Guide to Europe,* Vanguard, 1954; (with others) *Famous Artists' Cartoon Course,* [Westport, Conn.], 1956, new edition, 1965; *How to Remove Cotton from a Bottle of Aspirin,* Doubleday, 1959.

I Made My Bed, Doubleday, 1960; *Rube Goldberg versus the Machine Age: A Retrospective Exhibition of His Work, with Memoirs and Annotations by Rube Goldberg,* edited by Clark Kinnaird, Hastings House, 1968; *Do It the Hard Way,* National Museum of History and Technology, 1970; *Bobo Baxter: The Complete Daily Strip, 1927-28,* Hyperion Press (Westport, Conn.), 1977; *The Best of Rube Goldberg* (cartoons), compiled by Charles Keller, Prentice-Hall, 1979.

Filmscripts; produced by Universal Film Corp., except as indicated: "There's a Will," 1927; "Whose Wife?," 1927; "Women Chasers," 1927; "No Blondes Allowed," 1927; "Oh, Mabel!," 1927; "What a Party!," 1927; "Take Your Pick," 1928; "She's a Pippin," 1928; "Husbands Won't Tell," 1928; "Hold Your Horses," 1928; "Just Wait," 1928; "Just the Type," 1929; "Good Skates," 1929; "This Way Please," 1929; "Soup to Nuts," Fox Film Corp., 1930. Also author of *Chasing the Blues,* 1915; also author of song lyrics, essays, plays, and short stories. Contributor of articles and stories to periodicals, including *Cosmopolitan, Redbook, Saturday Evening Post, Collier's,* and *Vanity Fair.*

SIDELIGHTS: Rube Goldberg was best known for his zany humor, which manifested itself in his comic creations. Among his most loved cartoon characters were "Boob McNutt," "Bobo Baxter," and "Mike and Ike." Goldberg achieved success with his daily comic strips as well as with gag items. In addition, he gained popularity from his intricate drawings of complex contraptions designed to perform very simple functions. His work was so widely recognized that dictionaries added his name as an adjective. For example, *Webster's New Collegiate Dictionary* defines "Rube Goldberg" as "accomplishing by complex means what seemingly could be done simply." In his cartoon work, Goldberg's character "Professor Lucifer Gorgonzola Butts" invented these impossible mechanisms.

Goldberg's background prepared him for his career. By the age of twelve, he had already become a sign painter. His father later discouraged him from pursuing art on a professional basis, yet Goldberg continued his artistic expression while a university student at the University of California, Berkeley, where he drew cartoons for the campus yearbook and humor magazine. Upon graduation, he joined the staff of the *San Francisco Chronicle* as a sports cartoonist. A number of other jobs later, he finally found a $50 per week position with the *New York Evening Mail,* again as a sports cartoonist. His career took off with the subsequent syndication of his work back in San Francisco, followed by other locations.

Goldberg's comic strips were often popular but enjoyed erratic life spans. Sometimes public boredom set in, as in the case of "Brad and Dad" (1939-41), but often Goldberg simply tired of a strip during its success, as with "Boob McNutt" (1916-33) and ended it. Frequently, he introduced new characters that the public virtually ignored but that satisfied him, such as the sexy do-gooder "Lala Palooza" (1935-39). Inherited wealth from his father allowed Goldberg the freedom to experiment and to indulge his fancies without the fear of financial ruin.

Rube Goldberg's style differed from that of his peers. His cartoons lacked a precise line, which sometimes led to confusion in his drawings. His original humor and narrative ability proved his main talents, garnering him tremendous popular appeal. Despite his commercial successes, however, Rube Goldberg himself was probably better known than many of his comic strip characters. The annual award given by the National Cartoonist Society for outstanding cartoonist of the year is called the "Reuben" in Goldberg's honor.

MEDIA ADAPTATIONS: Numerous films were based on Rube Goldberg's cartoons, including "The Campus Flirt," Famous Players-Lasky Corp., 1926, "Dates for Two," Universal Film Corp., 1927, "Taking the Count," Universal Film Corp., 1927, "Cash Customers," Universal Film Corp., 1927, "And Morning Came," Universal Film Corp., 1928, "Chaperons," Universal Film Corp., 1929, "Finishing School," Universal Film Corp., 1929, and "Early to Wed," Universal Film Corp., 1929. His sports-page cartoon, "I'm the Guy," was the basis for one of the first hit songs based on a newspaper cartoon, 1912.

AVOCATIONAL INTERESTS: Golf, sculpture.

BIOGRAPHICAL/CRITICAL SOURCES: Editor and Publisher, May 8, 1949, July 22, 1950; *Newsweek,* November 16, 1959; Rube Goldberg, *Rube Goldberg versus the Machine Age: A Retrospective Exhibition of His Work, with Memoirs and Annotations by Rube Goldberg,* edited by Clairk Kinnaird, Hastings House, 1968; *Washington Post,* November 25, 1970; *Webster's New Collegiate Dictionary,* Merriam, 1980.

OBITUARIES: Variety, December 9, 1970.†

* * *

GOLDBERG, Rube
See GOLDBERG, Reuben L(ucius)

* * *

GOLDFARB, Ronald L. 1933-

PERSONAL: Born October 13, 1933, in Jersey City, N.J.; son of Robert S. and Aida Goldfarb; married Joanne Jacob (an architect), June 9, 1957; children: Judy Anne, Nicholas, Maximilian. *Education:* Syracuse University, A.B., 1954, LL.B., 1956; Yale University, LL.M., 1960, J.S.D., 1962. *Home:* 7312 Rippon Rd., Alexandria, Va. 22307. *Office:* 918 16th St. N.W., Washington, D.C. 20006.

CAREER: Admitted to practice before District of Columbia, New York, and California Bars, and Bar of U.S. Supreme Court. Commission on Law and Social Action, New York City, staff counsel, 1960-61; U.S. Department of Justice, Washington, D.C., special prosecutor, Organized Crime and Racketeering Section, 1961-64; Twentieth Century Fund, New York City, research director, 1964-65; Kurzman and Goldfarb (law firm), Washington, D.C., partner, 1965-70; Goldfarb, Singer and Austern (law firm), Washington, D.C., partner, 1970—. Chairman of board, The Writing Co. Member, President's Task Force for the War against Poverty, 1964; chairman, Special Review Committee, U.S. District Court, District of Columbia, 1975-76. Member, board of trustees, Syracuse University Library Associates, 1965-70; vice-president, Washington Service Bureau, 1966-79; president, D.C. Citizens' Council for Criminal Justice, 1971-72; chairman of board of several non-profit organizations, including Law Science Council; member of governing board, American Jewish Committee and National Alliance for Safer Cities. Consultant to many institutions, public and private, including Ford Foundation, Westinghouse Broadcasting Co., Brookings Institution, and President's Advisory Commission on Civil Disorders. *Military service:* U.S. Air Force, staff judge advocate, 1957-60. U.S. Air Force Reserve, 1960-64; became captain.

MEMBER: American Bar Association, American Trial Lawyers Association (faculty), Federal Bar Association, New York State Bar Association, California State Bar Association, Yale Law School Association (president, 1974), Cosmos Club (Washington, D.C.). *Awards, honors:* Federal Bar Association prize for best work in field of constitutional law, 1965-66, for *Ransom: A Critique of the American Bail System;* award from New Jersey Education Association, 1966; Woodrow Wilson fellow, 1974—.

WRITINGS: The Contempt Power, Columbia University Press, 1963; *Ransom: A Critique of the American Bail System,* Harper, 1965; (with Alfred Friendly) *Crime and Publicity: The Impact of News on the Administration of Justice,* Twentieth Century Fund, 1967; (contributor) *Administration of Criminal Justice,* University of North Carolina, 1967; (contributor) *How to Try a Criminal Case,* American Trial Lawyers Association, 1967; (with Linda Singer) *After Conviction: A Review of the American Correction System,* Simon & Schuster, 1973; *Conspiracy: The Harrisburg Trial and the Democratic Tradition,* Harper, 1973; *Jails: The Ultimate Ghetto of the Criminal Justice System,* Doubleday, 1975.

Migrant Farm Workers: A Caste of Despair, Iowa State University Press, 1981; (with James Raymond) *Clear Understandings: A Guide to Legal Writing,* Random House, 1982. Contributor of articles to numerous law journals, newspapers, and magazines, including *New York Times, Modern Law Review, Commonweal, Psychology Today, Michigan Law Review,* and *Washington Post.*

* * *

GOLDHABER, Gerald Martin 1944-

PERSONAL: Born January 23, 1944, in Brookline, Mass.; son of Robert (a restauranteur) and Ruth (a realtor; maiden name, Steinman) Goldhaber; married Marylynn Blaustein (a clinical social worker), August 17, 1969; children: Michelle Beth, Marc David. *Education:* University of Massachusetts, B.A., 1965; University of Maryland, M.A., 1966; Purdue University, Ph.D., 1970. *Politics:* Democrat. *Religion:* Jewish. *Home:* 48 Jamstead Ct., Williamsville, N.Y. 14221. *Office:* Department of Communication, State University of New York at Buffalo, 535 Baldy Hall, Buffalo, N.Y. 14260.

CAREER: University of New Mexico, Albuquerque, assistant professor in department of speech communication, 1970-74; State University of New York at Buffalo, associate professor of communication, 1974—, associate chairman of department, 1974-75, chairman of department, 1979—. Director, Southwest Institute for Transactional Analysis, 1972-74, International Communication Associations Communication Audit Project, 1972-79, and State University of New York Communication Research Team, 1976, 1980. President, Goldhaber Research Associates (pollsters), 1978—. Political commentator on various radio and television programs in Canada and New York. Lecturer, University Speakers Bureau; has presented scholarly papers and lectures at various communication symposiums. Co-organizer, University-wide Organization Studies Group, 1978-81. Member of Industrial Communications Council. Has served on advisory council of State University of New York Communication Research Center, Institute for Human Resources, and Center for Policy Studies. Consultant to numerous business, government, and educational institutions, including American Institute of Banking, United States Atomic Energy Commission, Hooker Chemical Company, *New York Times,* University of South Florida, and University of Texas-San Antonio.

MEMBER: International Communication Association (vice-president, 1974-76), International Sociological Research Association (life fellow), International Society for Social Network Analysis, International Transactional Analysis Association (special fields advanced member, provisional teaching member, both 1972-79), American Association for Public Opinion Research, American Marketing Association, Marketing Research Association, Speech Communication Association, Academy of Management, Western Speech Communication Association (legislative assembly delegate, 1970-72, member of nominating committee, 1973).

AWARDS, HONORS: Research grants from Purdue Research Foundation, 1968, 1969, University of New Mexico Research Allocations Committee, 1971, 1972, 1973, Office of Economic Opportunity, 1973, State University of New York at Buffalo, 1974, Council on Higher Education, 1976; University of New Mexico Student Government Award, 1972, for excellence in teaching; State University of New York at Buffalo award, 1975, for innovative teaching techniques.

WRITINGS: Organizational Communication, W. C. Brown, 1974, 3rd edition, 1983; (editor with Brent Peterson and R. Wayne Pace, and contributor) *Communication Probes,* Science Research Associates, 1974, 3rd edition, 1982; (with Lawrence Rosenfeld and Val Smith) *Experiments in Human Communication,* Holt, 1975; (editor with wife, Marylynn Goldhaber, and contributor) *Readings and Principles in Transactional Analysis,* Allyn & Bacon, 1976; (with E. Zannes) *Stand Up and Speak Out,* Addison-Wesley, 1978, 2nd edition, 1983; (editor and contributor) *Improving Institutional Communication,* Jossey-Bass, 1978; (with H. Dennis, G. Richetto, and O. Wiio) *Information Strategies: New Pathways to Corporate Power,* Prentice-Hall, 1979, 2nd edition, Ablex Publishing, 1983; (with D. Rogers) *Auditing Organizational Communication Systems: The ICA Communication Audit,* Kendall-Hunt, 1979.

Contributor: Dorothy Jongeward, editor, *Everybody Wins: Transactional Analysis Applied to Organizations,* Addison-Wesley, 1973; Sam Duker, editor, *Time-Compressed Speech,* Scarecrow, 1974; W. Arnold and J. Buley, editors, *Urban Communication,* Winthrop Publishing, 1977; David Gootnick, editor, *Handbook of Teaching Business Communication,* Communication Dynamics Press, 1979. Also contributor to *Communication Yearbook II,* 1978, and *Communication Yearbook IV,* 1980.

Also author of numerous monographs. Contributors of scholarly articles and book reviews to professional journals, including *Journal of College Science Teaching, Human Communication Research,* and *Journal of Business Communication,* and of popular articles to magazines. Member of editorial board, *Organizational Communications Abstracts,* 1974—; review editor, *Western Journal of Communication,* 1978-82, and *Human Communication Research,* 1978-81.

WORK IN PROGRESS: The Charisma Factor, with Wanda Knoer, for Grosset and Dunlop; *The Communication Factor,* with Knoer.

SIDELIGHTS: Gerald Martin Goldhaber has good reading capability in French, Latin, Spanish, Hebrew, and German. *Avocational interests:* Sunshine, good exercise, proper diet, water skiing, paddleball, travel.

* * *

GOLDMAN, Albert 1927-

PERSONAL: Born April 15, 1927, in Dormont, Pa.; son of Harry Benjamin and Marie (Levenson) Goldman. *Education:* Attended Carnegie Institute of Technology (now Carnegie-Mellon University), 1944-45, 1946-47; University of Chicago, A.M., 1950; Columbia University, Ph.D., 1961. *Residence:* New York, N.Y. *Agent:* Paul R. Reynolds, Inc., 12 East 41st St., New York, N.Y. 10017.

CAREER: Writer. Columbia University, New York, N.Y., associate professor of English, 1963-72. Moderator and writer of "Wednesday Review," weekly television cultural program, WNDT, New York. Pop music critic, *Life* magazine, 1970-73. *Military service:* U.S. Navy, 1945-46. *Member:* Phi Beta Kappa.

WRITINGS: (Editor with Everet Sprinchorn) *Wagner on Music and Drama,* Dutton, 1964; *The Mine and the Mint: Sources for the Writings of Thomas De Quincey,* Southern Illinois University Press, 1965; *Freakshow: The Rocksoulbluesjazzsickjewblackhumorsexpoppsych Gig and Other Scenes from the Counterculture,* Atheneum, 1971; *Ladies and Gentlemen—Lenny Bruce!!,* Random House, 1974; *Carnival in Rio,* Hawthorn, 1978; *Grass Roots: Marijuana in America Today,* Harper, 1979; *Disco,* Hawthorn, 1979; *Elvis,* McGraw, 1981. Editor-in-chief, *Cultural Affairs.*

WORK IN PROGRESS: A biography of John Lennon, for Morrow.

SIDELIGHTS: Elvis, Albert Goldman's best-selling biography of the late Elvis Presley, is "undeniably the most ambitious, the most comprehensive, and the most grotesquely fascinating picture to emerge of the man and the myth," according to Lynn Van Matre of the *Chicago Tribune Book World.* The book has generated controversy ever since its appearance in late 1981, not only because of the fame of its subject, but because of what many critics see as Goldman's unfair treatment of Presley's life and work. As Blake Morrison comments in the *Times Literary Supplement,* "reviewers on both sides of the Atlantic have been quick to point out [that] Goldman's [book] is one of the most vengeful and cannibalistic biographies ever written." A *London Times* reviewer says that "critics have fallen over themselves to get at [Goldman]. . . . Even critics whose normal aloofness from popular culture suggests they'd be hard-pressed to tell a hound dog from a blue suede shoe have scrambled through the crowd" to attack the book.

Commenting on this criticism, Goldman tells Tim Grobaty in a *Chicago Tribune* interview: "What was particularly terrible was that the people who were really out to get me were not the fans. . . . The real grim reapers were your 35- or 38-year-olds, you know, with an M.A. in American Studies from Berkeley, rock and roll intellectual types. They really had the knife out." Greil Marcus writes in a *Village Voice* article about

Goldman's motives, maintaining that Goldman meant "to entirely discredit Elvis Presley, the culture that produced him, and the culture he helped to create—to altogether dismiss and condemn, in other words, not just Elvis Presley, but the white working-class South from which Presley came, and the pop world which emerged in Presley's wake." Furthermore, says Marcus, "what is at stake is this: any book that means to separate a people from the sources of its history and its identity, that means to make the past meaningless and the present incomprehensible, is destructive of that people's ability to know itself as a people, to determine the things it might do as a people, and to discover how and why those things might be done. This is precisely the weight of the cultural genocide he wishes to enact."

"Greil went nuts," Goldman tells Grobaty. "He accused me of ethnogenocide! Try that one out. Ethnogenocide! It's what Hitler did, right? Wiping out whole peoples, right? . . . If I respected [my critics] as writers or people of intelligence, I guess I would go out and cut my throat. The truth, though, is most of them are morons. I respect very few of them."

Many critics find the amount and type of detail revealed about Elvis in the book to be excessive. Morrison believes that "it is the graphic portrait of Presley's last years . . . that makes *Elvis* so offensive." The information Goldman gathered from his more than six hundred interviews with Presley's friends and acquaintances "often gleefully [crosses] the bounds of good taste into a posthumous invasion of privacy," says Van Matre. "One gets the distinct impression that it's the sleaze that really sets [Goldman] off." Jim Miller writes in *Newsweek* that because Goldman "avers that 'there is absolutely no poignance in this history,' . . . he savors the sheer vulgarity of Presley's long decline."

Goldman reacts to this kind of criticism in an interview with Carol Lawson in the *New York Times Book Review*. "It's absurd to believe that I wanted to trash Elvis," says Goldman. "One of the greatest problems was trying to find something positive to say about this man. Every time I started investigating a given area, even one that promised to make him look good, it always ended up making him look bad."

In a *Washington Post Book World* review, Jonathan Yardley acknowledges Goldman's attempt to present a balanced picture of Presley's life. "Though Goldman makes a halfhearted effort to argue to the contrary, the Elvis Presley who emerges from this book is a person wholly without redeeming virtue. He was selfish, greedy, stupid and lazy. That he was so widely and passionately adored says more about us than it does about him, and what it says is not good. . . . Because [Goldman] is a conscientious biographer he tries to like his subject, or at least to pity him, and to make the reader feel the same, but all the evidence that he so forthrightly presents damns the effort; what he demonstrates is that there was scarcely enough art in Presley to justify the contemptible life."

In spite of the revelations about Elvis that Goldman's book provides, some critics believe it does little to mar Elvis's image in the public eye. "When Goldman finishes his juicy recounting of Elvis Presley's life," says J. D. Reed in *Time*, "the mystery of the King's fascination remains. For that, fans and readers should rejoice." Similarly, Morrison writes that "harsh things might be said, then, but Goldman vents his spleen in the wrong place, on the suffering man rather than on the artist, and at the end of his book Elvis Presley's reputation is as secure as ever." Miller points out that "Elvis Presley was, after all, the most exciting pop singer of his generation—even if Albert Goldman can't figure out why."

Yet some critics find *Elvis* both entertaining and useful. "Goldman has perhaps had an unduly hard time of it," says Morrison. "However unpleasant this book, it makes vivid and compelling reading." In the *New York Times Book Review*, Roy Blount, Jr. calls the book a "morbidly fascinating biography." Writing in the *New York Times*, Christopher Lehmann-Haupt says that Goldman's "analysis of Presley's music is really quite brilliant, especially when he comes to explaining its sources, its techniques and the reasons for its appeal. He has constructed a convincing profile of Presley's deep characterological faults."

BIOGRAPHICAL/CRITICAL SOURCES: New York Times Book Review, May 26, 1974, October 25, 1981, December 13, 1981; *Washington Post Book World*, October 18, 1981; *Time*, November 2, 1981; *Newsweek*, November 2, 1981; *New York Times*, November 2, 1981; *Chicago Tribune Book World*, November 15, 1981; *Village Voice Literary Supplement*, December, 1981; *London Times*, December 23, 1981; *Times Literary Supplement*, January 29, 1982; *Chicago Tribune*, March 23, 1982.

—Sketch by Kerry L. Lutz

* * *

GOLDSTEIN, Sidney 1927-

PERSONAL: Born August 4, 1927, in New London, Conn.; son of Max (a dairy manager) and Bella (Hoffman) Goldstein; married Alice Dreifus (a part-time statistical researcher), June 21, 1953; children: Beth Leah, David Louis, Brenda Ruth. *Education:* University of Connecticut, B.A., 1949, M.A., 1951; University of Pennsylvania, Ph.D., 1953. *Religion:* Jewish. *Home:* 95 Kiwanee Rd., Warwick, R.I. 02888. *Office:* Brown University, Providence, R.I. 02912.

CAREER: University of Pennsylvania, Philadelphia, instructor in sociology, 1953-55, research associate, Wharton School of Finance and Commerce, 1955-58; Brown University, Providence, R.I., assistant professor, 1955-57, associate professor, 1957-60, professor of sociology, 1960-77, George Hazard Crooker University Professor, 1977—, chairman of department of sociology and anthropology, 1963-70, director of population studies and training center, 1966—. Member of ad hoc committee of experts on demographic aspects of urbanization, United Nations; member of advisory committee on 1970 Census, U.S. Bureau of the Census. Member of board of directors, Bureau of Jewish Education. Consultant to Institute for Neurological Diseases and Blindness, 1960-71, National Institutes of Health, 1960-61, Ford Foundation and Rockefeller Foundation, 1971-81, United Nations Economic and Social Commission for Asia and the Pacific, 1971-82, Urban Institute, and RAND Corp., 1974—.

MEMBER: International Union for the Scientific Study of Population, Committee on International Cooperation in Research and Demography (member of governing bureau, 1981—), Social Science Research Council, American Sociological Association (fellow), Population Association of America (president, 1975-76), American Statistical Association, Association for Jewish Demography and Statistics (member of board of directors, 1965—), Eastern Sociological Association, Sociological Research Association, Institute of Contemporary Jewry (Jerusalem), Rhode Island Jewish Historical Society (member of board of directors), Phi Beta Kappa. *Awards, honors:* Social Science Research Council grant, 1956-57, and fellowship, 1961-

62; Guggenheim fellowship, 1961-62; Fulbright research scholarship to Denmark, 1961-62; Alexander Dushkin fellowship from Hadassah, 1965-66; Chulalongkorn University (Bangkok) medal for distinguished service, 1968; Committee on Scholarly Communication with People's Republic of China distinguished scholar, 1981.

WRITINGS: Patterns of Mobility, 1910-1950: A Method for Measuring Migration and Occupational Mobility in the Community, University of Pennsylvania Press, 1958; *Consumption Patterns of the Aged,* University of Pennsylvania Press, 1960; *The Norristown Study: An Experiment in Interdisciplinary Research Training,* University of Pennsylvania Press, 1961; (contributor) William Gomberg and Arthur B. Shostak, editors, *Blue Collar World,* Prentice-Hall, 1964; (with Calvin Goldscheider) *Jewish-Americans: Three Generations in a Jewish Community,* Prentice-Hall, 1968; *A Population Survey of the Greater Springfield Jewish Community,* Springfield Jewish Community Council, 1968.

(With Alden Speare, Jr. and William H. Frey) *Residential Mobility, Migration, and Metropolitan Change,* Ballinger, 1975; (editor with David F. Sly) *Working Paper I: Basic Data Needed for the Study of Urbanization,* International Union for the Scientific Study of Population, 1975; (editor with Sly) *Working Paper II: The Measurement of Urbanization and the Projection of Urban Population,* International Union for the Scientific Study of Population, 1975; (editor with Sly) *Patterns of Urbanization: Comparative Country Studies,* two volumes, International Union for the Scientific Study of Population, 1976; *Circulation in the Context of Total Mobility in Southeast Asia,* East-West Population Institute, 1978; (with wife, Alice Goldstein) *Surveys of Migration in Less Developed Countries: A Methodological Review,* East-West Population Institute, 1981.

All with Kurt B. Mayer: *Migration and Economic Development in Rhode Island,* Brown University Press, 1958; *The First Two Years: Problems of Small Business Growth and Survival,* U.S. Small Business Administration, 1961; *Metropolitanization and Population Change in Rhode Island,* Rhode Island Development Council, 1962; *Residential Mobility, Migration, and Commuting in Rhode Island,* Rhode Island Development Council, 1963; *The People of Rhode Island, 1960,* Rhode Island Development Council, 1963.

Contributor of about seventy articles to *Gerontology, Sales Management, Vanderbilt Law Review,* and sociology, demography, and history journals.

WORK IN PROGRESS: Writing on problems of urbanization, fertility, and population redistribution in developing countries in conjunction with earlier work with the Population Division of the United Nations and recent research in Thailand; also writing on differential fertility and mortality by religious identification; further research in social and demographic aspects of the Rhode Island population.

SIDELIGHTS: Sidney Goldstein has traveled extensively in Europe and Australia, has made several trips to the Far East, including a sabbatical year at Chulalongkorn University in Bangkok, Thailand, 1968-69, and research trips to the People's Republic of China, 1981 and 1983. Goldstein speaks and reads French and German.

* * *

GOLIARD, Roy
See SHIPLEY, Joseph T(wadell)

GOMORI, George 1934-

PERSONAL: Born April 3, 1934, in Budapest, Hungary; son of Lajos and Rosalie (Fein) Gomori; married second wife, Mari Markus, January 10, 1981; children: (first marriage) Beata Csilla, Anna Serena, Peter. *Education:* Attended University of Eotvos Lorand, Budapest, 1953-56; University of London, B.A. (with honors), 1958; Oxford University, B.Litt., 1962; Cambridge University, M.A., 1969. *Home:* 46 Grantchester Rd., Cambridge, England. *Office:* Department of Slavonic Studies, Cambridge University, Cambridge, England.

CAREER: University of California, Berkeley, lecturer in Polish and Hungarian, 1963-64; Harvard University, Cambridge, Mass., research fellow in Polish studies at Russian Research Center, 1964-65; University of Birmingham, Birmingham, England, Centre for Russian and East European Studies, research associate, 1965-67, senior research associate and librarian, 1967-69; Cambridge University, Cambridge, England, assistant lecturer, 1969-73, lecturer in Slavonic studies, 1973—. Fellow, Darwin College, 1970—. *Member:* International Hungarian Philological Society, British University Association of Slavists, P.E.N. *Awards, honors:* Jurzykowski Award for Translation, 1972; Artisjus Award for Translation, 1981.

WRITINGS: Virag-bizonysag (poems), Otthom Kiado (London), 1958; *Hajnali uton* (poems), Poets' and Painters' Press, 1963; (translator with Vince Sulyok) Boris Pasternak, *Karacsonyi csillag* (poems), Occidental, 1965; *Hungarian and Polish Poetry, 1945-1956,* Clarendon Press, 1966; (editor with C. H. Newman) *New Writing of East Europe,* Quadrangle, 1968; *Atvaltozasok* (poetry), Szepsi Csombor Kor (London), 1969; *Cyprian Norwid,* Twayne, 1974; (editor with James Atlas) Attila Jozsef, *Selected Poems and Texts,* Carcanet Press, 1974; (editor) Laszlo Nagy, *Love of the Scorching Wind,* translation by T. Connor and K. McRobbie, Oxford University Press, 1974; *Level hanyatlo birodalombol* (poems), Aurora (Munich), 1976; (editor and translator with Clive Wilmer) Miklos Radnoti, *Forced March: Selected Poems,* Carcanet Press, 1979; (editor with R. Burns) *Homage to Mandelstam* (poems), Cambridge University Press, 1981.

Work anthologized in *Norwid zywy,* edited by W. Gunther, Swiderski (London), 1962, *Histoire du soulevement hongrois 1956,* edited by G. Gosztony, Editions Horvath, 1966, and in *Vandorenek,* [Budapest], 1981. Contributor of essays, poems, and articles to Hungarian journals. Editor of special eastern European literature edition of *Tri-Quarterly* (published in Evanston, Ill.), spring, 1967.

WORK IN PROGRESS: A study of Anglo-Hungarian cultural connections in the sixteenth and seventeenth centuries; a study of H. Morsztyn, a poet of the early Polish Baroque period; a study of Mickiewicz and Norwid.

SIDELIGHTS: George Gomori is fluent in English and Polish. He also speaks Russian, French, German, and Indonesian.

BIOGRAPHICAL/CRITICAL SOURCES: Polish Review, Volume XXII, number 4, 1977; *Jewish Quarterly,* summer/autumn, 1980.

* * *

GOODMAN, Roger B. 1919-

PERSONAL: Born May 18, 1919, in New York, N.Y.; son of

Henry (a teacher) and Mollie (Bernstein) Goodman; married Laura S. Rosenblum (a teacher of library science), November 14, 1942; children: Peter W., David W. *Education:* City College (now City College of the City University of New York), B.S.S., 1940; Columbia University, M.A., 1946. *Religion:* Jewish. *Home:* 2005 Pearson St., Brooklyn, N.Y. 11234.

CAREER: New York (N.Y.) Board of Education, teacher of English, 1948-75, chairman of department of English at Grover Cleveland High School, 1960-63, chairman of department of English at Stuyvesant High School, 1963-75. Assistant to New York Board of Examiners. Actor and reader with semi-professional companies for more than ten years, including New York's Roundabout Theatre and Brooklyn Public Library Reading Ensemble. Free-lance writer. *Military service:* U.S. Army, 1940-46, 1948-51; became first lieutenant. *Member:* Council of Supervisory Associations, Association of Chairmen of English of New York.

WRITINGS: (Editor) *Just for Laughs,* Oxford Book Co., 1955; (with David Lewin) *New Ways to Greater Word Power,* Dell, 1955; (editor) *Short Masterpieces of the World's Greatest Literature,* Bantam, 1957; *A Concise Handbook of Better English,* Bantam, 1960; (editor) *The World's Best Short Short Stories,* Bantam, 1965; (editor) *World Wide Short Stories,* Globe Book, 1966; *Cast of Characters* (poems), Pequod Press, 1970; (with Charles Spiegler) *Matter for Judgement,* Globe Book, 1980; (with Robert Potter) *The World Anthology,* Globe Book, 1982; *The Twin Lights of Navesink,* Pulitzer Communications, 1982. Author of "Sharpen Your Word Sense" in *Coronet,* 1955-58.

SIDELIGHTS: Roger B. Goodman told *CA:* "As a free-lance writer, I find it almost impossible to resist the seductive lure of the 'easy-to-do, fast-to-write, quick-return' project. As a result, I always manage to be diverted from the writing I feel I *really* want to do—principally poetry. But that (to my shame, I must confess) is just my own fault. And, since truth must be told, these easy projects frequently become more onerous and time-consuming than the work I—or any writer—feel I want to really come to grips with. Maybe—some day!"

AVOCATIONAL INTERESTS: Reading modern poetry and writing poetry.

* * *

GORDIS, Robert 1908-

PERSONAL: Born February 6, 1908, in Brooklyn, N.Y.; son of Hyman and Lizzie (Engel) Gordis; married Fannie Jacobson, February 5, 1928; children: Enoch, Leon, David. *Education:* Yeshiva University, diploma, 1923; City College (now City College of the City University of New York), B.A. (cum laude), 1926; Dropsie College, Ph.D., 1929; Jewish Theological Seminary of America, Rabbi (with distinction), 1932. *Home:* 150 West End Ave., New York, N.Y. 10023. *Office:* Jewish Theological Seminary of America, 3080 Broadway, New York, N.Y. 10027.

CAREER: Temple Beth-El, Rockaway Park, N.Y., rabbi, 1931-69, rabbi emeritus, 1969—; Jewish Theological Seminary of America, New York, N.Y., professor of Bible, 1937-67; Temple University, Philadelphia, Pa., professor of religion, 1967-74; Jewish Theological Seminary of America, Rapaport Professor of the philosophies of religion, 1974—. Adjunct professor of religion, Columbia University, 1948-57; visiting professor of Old Testament, Union Theological Seminary, 1953-54; visiting professor of Bible, Hebrew University, 1970; teacher at Jewish institutions. Rabbinical Assembly of America, member of executive council, 1935, president, 1944-46; president, Synagogue Council of America, 1948-49. Member of national advisory committee on freedom and religious affairs, National Conference of Christians and Jews. Member of board of directors, Villanova University Institute of Church and State. Member of national council, Boy Scouts of America. Public lecturer on contemporary American issues, the status and problems of religion, and on Jewish life and culture. Consultant and associate to Center for Study of Democratic Institutions, 1960—. *Awards, honors:* D.D. from Jewish Theological Seminary of America, 1940; National Jewish Book Award, 1979, for *Love and Sex: A Modern Jewish Perspective.*

WRITINGS: The Biblical Text in the Making, Dropsie College Press, 1937, augmented edition, Ktav, 1971; *The Jew Faces a New World,* Behrman, 1941; *The Wisdom of Ecclesiastes,* Jewish Publication Society, 1945; *Conservative Judaism—An American Philosophy,* Behrman, 1945; *Koheleth: The Man and His World,* Bloch, 1955, 3rd revised edition, Schocken, 1968; *Judaism for the Modern Age,* Farrar, Straus, 1957; *Religion and International Responsibility,* Council on Religion & International Affairs, 1959.

A Faith for Moderns, Bloch, 1960, revised and augmented edition, 1971; *The Song of Songs,* Jewish Theological Seminary Press, 1961, revised and augmented edition published as *The Song of Songs and Lamentations: A Study, Modern Translation and Commentary,* Ktav, 1974; *The Root and the Branch: Judaism and the Free Society,* University of Chicago Press, 1962; *The Book of God and Man: A Study of Job,* University of Chicago Press, 1965; *Sex and the Family in the Jewish Tradition,* Burning Bush Press, 1967; *Leave a Little to God,* Bloch, 1967; (editor) *Encounters with Job,* Department of Religion, Temple University, 1969; *Poets, Prophets, and Sages: Essays in Biblical Interpretation,* Indiana University Press, 1971; (editor with Ruth B. Waxman) *Faith and Reason: Essays in Judaism,* Ktav, 1973; (editor with Moshe Davidowitz) *Art in Judaism: Studies in the Jewish Artistic Experience,* National Council on Art in Jewish Life, 1975; *The Word and the Book: Studies in Biblical Language and Literature,* Ktav, 1976; (editor) *Megillat Esther: The Mascretic Hebrew Text with Introduction, New Translation and Commentary,* Ktav, 1977; *The Book of God and Man,* University of Chicago Press, 1978; *Understanding Conservative Judaism,* The Rabbinical Assembly, 1978; *Love and Sex: A Modern Jewish Perspective,* Farrar, Straus, 1978; (editor) *The Book of Job: Commentary, New Translation, and Special Studies,* Jewish Theological Seminary of America, 1978.

Author of sound recording, *The Universal Implications of Judaism,* for Center for the Study of Democratic Institutions, 1976. Contributor to Judaism Pamphlet Series, B'nai B'rith Youth Organization; contributor of articles to journals and magazines in the United States, Great Britain, and Israel, including *Saturday Review, New York Times Book Review, Hadassah Magazine, Commentary, Journal of Semitic Studies,* and *Tarbitz.* Associate editor, *Universal Jewish Encyclopedia;* contributing editor, *Menorah Journal, Reconstructionist, Conservative Judaism, Jewish Forum;* founder, and member of board of editors, *Judaism;* member of publications committee, Jewish Publication Society.

* * *

GORDON, Donald
See PAYNE, Donald Gordon

GOREY, Edward (St. John) 1925-
(Eduard Blutig, Drew Dogyear, Mrs. Regera Dowdy, Wardore Edgy, Raddory Gewe, Roy Grewdead, Redway Grode, O. Mude, Edward Pig, Ogdred Weary, Dreary Wodge, Dogear Wryde)

PERSONAL: Born February 22, 1925, in Chicago, Ill.; son of Edward Leo and Helen (Garvey) Gorey. *Education:* Harvard University, A.B., 1950. *Home:* 36 East 38th St., New York, N.Y. 10016; and 149 Mill Way, Barnstable, Mass. 02630.

CAREER: Writer, illustrator, and designer. Employed in art department of Doubleday & Co., Inc., New York, N.Y. 1953-60. Gorey's illustrations have been shown in museums and galleries, including Graham Gallery, New York, N.Y., and Yale University Library, both 1974. *Military service:* U.S. Army, 1943-46. *Awards, honors:* Best Illustrated Book of the Year award, *New York Times,* 1969, for illustrations of *The Dong with the Luminous Nose,* by Edward Lear, and 1971, for illustrations of *The Shrinking of Treehorn,* by Florence Parry Heide; *The Shrinking of Treehorn* was named best picture book at the Bologna Children's Book Fair, 1977; Antoinette Perry (''Tony'') Award, 1978, for the costume design of the Broadway revival of ''Dracula.''

WRITINGS—All self-illustrated: *The Unstrung Harp* (also see below), Duell, Sloan & Pearce, 1953; *The Listing Attic* (also see below), Duell, Sloan & Pearce, 1954; *The Doubtful Guest* (also see below), Doubleday, 1957, reprinted, Dodd, 1978; *The Object-Lesson* (also see below), Doubleday, 1958; (compiler) *The Haunted Looking Glass: Ghost Stories,* Looking Glass Library, 1959.

The Bug Book (also see below), Epstein & Carroll, 1960; *The Fatal Lozenge* (also see below), Obolensky, 1960; *The Hapless Child* (also see below), Obolensky, 1961, reprinted, Dodd, 1980; (under pseudonym Ogdred Weary) *The Curious Sofa,* Obolensky, 1961, reprinted, Dodd, 1980; (under pseudonym Ogdred Weary) *The Beastly Baby,* Fantod Press, 1962; *The Willowdale Handcar* (also see below), Bobbs-Merrill, 1962, reprinted, Dodd, 1979; *The Vinegar Works* (includes *The Gashlycrumb Tinies, The Insect God,* and *The West Wing;* also see below), Simon & Schuster, 1963; *The Wuggly Ump* (also see below), Lippincott, 1963; *15 Two: Or, the Nursery Frieze,* Fantod Press, 1964; *The Sinking Spell* (also see below), Obolensky, 1965; *The Remembered Visit* (also see below), Simon & Schuster, 1965; *The Inanimate Tragedy,* Fantod Press, 1966; *The Gilded Bat,* Simon & Schuster, 1966; (under pseudonym Eduard Blutig) *The Evil Garden,* Fantod Press, 1966; (under pseudonym Mrs. Regera Dowdy) *The Pious Infant,* Fantod Press, 1966; *The Utter Zoo Alphabet,* Dutton, 1967; (with Victoria Chess) *Fletcher and Zenobia,* Meredith Corp., 1967; *The Other Statue,* Simon & Schuster, 1968; *The Blue Aspic,* Meredith Corp., 1968; *The Epipleptic Bicycle,* Dodd, 1968; *The Secrets,* Simon & Schuster, 1968; *The Deranged Cousins: Or, Whatever,* Fantod Press, 1969; *The Iron Tonic: Or, a Winter Afternoon in Lonely Valley,* Albondonaci Press, 1969; (under pseudonym Raddory Gewe) *The Eleventh Episode,* Fantod Press, 1969.

The Osbick Bird, Fantod Press, 1970; *The Chinese Obelisks: Fourth Alphabet,* Fantod Press, 1970; *The Sopping Thursday,* Gotham Book Mart, 1970; (with Peter F. Neumeyer) *Donald Has a Difficulty,* Fantod Press, 1970; (with Neumeyer) *Why We Have Day and Night,* Young Scott Books, 1970; *Fletcher and Zenobia Save the Circus,* Dodd, 1971; *The Disrespectful Summons,* Fantod Press, 1971; (translator) Alphonse Atlais, *Story for Sara,* Albondocani Press, 1971; (under pseudonym Edward Pig) *The Untitled Book,* Fantod Press, 1971; *The Awdrey-Gore Legacy,* Dodd, 1972; *Leaves from a Mislaid Album,* Gotham Book Mart, 1972; *The Abandoned Sock,* Fantod Press, 1972; *Amphigorey* (includes *The Unstrung Harp, The Listing Attic, The Doubtful Guest, The Object-Lesson, The Bug Book, The Fatal Lozenge, The Hapless Child, The Curious Sofa, The Willowdale Handcar, The Gashlycrumb Tinies, The Insect God, The West Wing, The Wuggly Ump, The Sinking Spell,* and *The Remembered Visit*), Putnam, 1972.

The Lavender Leotard: Or, Going a Lot to the New York City Ballet, Gotham Book Mart, 1973; *A Limerick,* Salt-Works Press, 1973; *Category: Fifty Drawings,* Gotham Book Mart, 1973; *The Lost Lions,* Fantod Press, 1973; *The Glorious Nosebleed: Fifth Alphabet,* Dodd, 1974; *The Listing Attic* [and] *The Unstrung Harp,* Abelard-Schuman, 1975; *Amphigorey Too,* Putnam, 1975; *L'Heure Bleue,* Fantod Press, 1975; *The Broken Spoke,* Dodd, 1976; *Gorey x 3: Drawings by Edward Gorey,* Addison-Wesley, 1976; *The Loathsome Couple,* Dodd, 1977; *The Fantod Words,* ten volumes, Diogenes (Zurich), 1978; *Gorey Endings: A Calendar for 1978,* Workman, 1978; *The Green Beads,* Albondocani Press, 1978; (with Larry Evans) *Gorey Games,* Troubadour Printing, 1979; *Dracula: A Toy Theatre,* Scribner, 1979; *Gorey Posters,* Abrams, 1979.

Dancing Cats and Neglected Murderesses, Workman, 1980; *The Gashlycrumb Tinies,* Dodd, 1981; *The Dwindling Party,* Random House, 1982; *The Water Flowers,* Congdon & Weed, 1982; *The Prune People,* Albondocani Press, 1983; *The Eclectic Abecedarium,* Bromer, 1983; *Amphigorey Also,* Congdon & Weed, 1983.

Illustrator: Rex Warner, *Men and Gods,* Farrar, Straus, 1959; John Ciardi, *The Man Who Sang the Sillies,* Lippincott, 1961; Walter De La Mare, *Die Orgie—eine Idylle,* Diogenes, 1965; Eric Protter, editor, *Monster Festival,* Vanguard Press, 1965; Frank Jacobs, *Alvin Steadfast on Vernacular Island,* Dial, 1965; Felicia Lamport, *Cultural Slag,* Houghton, 1966; Hyacinthe Phypps, *The Recently Deflowered Girl,* Diogenes, 1966; John Buchan, *Die neunundreissig Stufen,* Diogenes, 1967; Ennis Rees, *Brer Rabbit and His Tricks,* Young Scott Books, 1967; Jane Trahey, *Son of the Martini Cookbook,* Clovis Press, 1967; Muriel Spark, *The Very Fine Clock,* Knopf, 1968; Jan Wahl, *Cobweb Castle,* Holt, 1968; Rees, *More of Brer Rabbit's Tricks,* Young Scott Books, 1968; Edward Lear, *The Jumblies,* Young Scott Books, 1968; Rhoda Levine, *He Was There from the Day We Moved In,* Harlin Quist, 1968; Lear, *The Dong with the Luminous Nose,* Young Scott Books, 1969; Neumeyer, *Donald and the . . . ,* Addison-Wesley, 1969; Doris Orgel, *Merry, Rose, and Christmas-Tree June,* Knopf, 1969.

Ciardi, *Someone Who Could Win a Polar Bear,* Lippincott, 1970; Edward Fenton, *Penny Candy,* Holt, 1970; Felice Holman, *At the Top of My Voice and Other Poems,* Norton, 1970; Florence Parry Heide, *The Shrinking of Treehorn,* Holiday House, 1971; Rees, *Lions and Lobsters and Foxes and Frogs,* Young Scott Books, 1971; Donald Nelsen, *Samuel and Emma,* Parents' Magazine Press, 1971; Jacob David Townsend, *Miss Clafooty and the Demon,* Lothrop, 1971; Beatrice Schenk de Regniers, reteller, *Red Riding Hood,* Atheneum, 1972; John Bellairs, *The House with a Clock in Its Walls,* Dial, 1973; Edith Tarcov, *Rumpelstiltskin,* Four Winds Press, 1973; *Jack the Giant Killer,* Scholastic Magazines, 1973; Howard Moss, *Instant Lives,* Saturday Review Press, 1974; Jacob Grimm,

Rotkappchen: ein Maarchen der Bruder Grimm, Diogenes-Verlag, 1974; Edmund Wilson, *The Rats of Rutland Grange,* Gotham Book Mart, 1974; Terence Winch, *Nuns: Poems,* Wyrd Press, 1976; Heide, *Treehorn's Treasure,* Holiday House, 1981; T. S. Eliot, *Old Possum's Book of Practical Cats,* Harcourt, 1982. Illustrator of over fifty other books; also illustrator of title sequence animation for television series "Mystery" for Public Broadcasting Service and of numerous book jackets, posters, and magazines.

Author of film, *The Black Doll,* Gotham Book Mart, 1973; also author of *The Fantod Pack of Edward Gorey,* Owl Press. Designer of album cover for recording of his stories for Watt 4; designer of sets for two productions of "Les Ballets Trockadero de Monte Carlo," 1977; designer of set and costumes for musical "Dracula," 1978, and for production of "Gorey Stories," 1978; designer of shower curtain for Metropolitan Opera catalogue. Contributor of cartoons to periodicals, including *New York Times, Sports Illustrated,* and *Esquire.*

SIDELIGHTS: In 1959, Edward Gorey's four small volumes, *The Unstrung Harp, The Listing Attic, The Doubtful Guest,* and *The Object-Lesson,* were reviewed by literary critic Edmund Wilson in the *New Yorker.* Wilson said that Gorey "has been working quite perversely to please himself, and has created a whole little personal world, equally amusing and sombre, nostalgic at the same time as claustrophobic, at the same time poetic and poisoned." Since writing those first four books, Gorey has expanded his "personal world" through the odd characters and antique settings that appear in subsequent works and represent the eccentric view of life that makes Gorey such a unique literary figure.

And since those remarks were made by Wilson, other critics have repeatedly cited Gorey's work for both its style and effect. David Ansen, for example, describes Gorey's books in a *Newsweek* article as stories in which "the subterranean awfulness of life emerges in images at once witty and macabre, fey and ferocious." In *New Republic,* Gerald Weales says that Gorey's illustrated tales give "off an emanation of horror, a suggestion of the unnatural, a whiff of rot. This is not to be taken seriously, of course, but the *frisson* is supposed to be there, just under the laugh." Colin Covert, writing in the *Detroit Free Press,* believes that Gorey's work "is in a genre that defies classification: spooky little editions that are not children's books, comic books, nor fine art, but something in a league all its own."

Edward Gorey himself defies classification, according to those who have visited his one-room Manhattan apartment (which Gorey describes as a "ghastly" place he has had for over thirty years). Physically, says Covert, "Gorey the man cuts a distinctive figure. . . . He stands 6-foot-2, sports a flowing snow-white beard and habitually dresses in a large fur coat, a long ski scarf, a quail-stalker's cap and tennis shoes." Interviewers often note Gorey's passion for the New York City Ballet, whose performances he attended almost daily between 1956 and 1976.

While he claims in *People* magazine that many of his books are "intended for children primarily," children are very often the targets of Gorey's unique sense of humor. D. Keith Mano writes in *People* that Gorey "would make W. C. Fields sound like Father of the Year. . . . In his work the infant mortality rate is higher than it was in 1556." Gorey's book *The Beastly Baby,* for example, begins "Once upon a time there was a baby. It was worse than other babies. . . . Dangerous objects were left about in the hope that it would do itself an injury, preferably fatal."

Gorey has written several alphabet books that critic Elizabeth Janeway, in the *New York Times Book Review,* describes as "jovially grisly." *The Gashlycrumb Tinies,* for instance, which "turns into a grimly amusing catalog of infant mortality," according to Ansen, offers such lessons as "A is for Amy who fell down the stairs / B is for Basil assaulted by bears. . . . K is for Kate who was struck with an axe / L is for Leo who swallowed some tacks."

In the *People* magazine interview, Gorey says, by way of explanation, "I've never known any babies. I don't have any relationship to children. . . . They are pathetic and quite frequently not terribly likable." In *Conversations with Writers,* Gorey recalls his own childhood, which might provide some insight into his approach to children: "Of course, I was a very precocious reader as a child. I learned to read by myself when I was 3½ or something. I can remember reading *Dracula* when I was about seven, and it scared me to death. . . . I remember reading all the novels of Victor Hugo when I was about eight. . . . They couldn't get me to put [his books] down."

Peter Andrews analyzes Gorey's work in a *Horizon* article, claiming that the writer "has staked out for his special province the virtually lost art of the illustrated novella, which flourished in the Victorian era. Like Victorian authors, he besieges his characters with one unspeakable calamity after another, . . . [and] in the most comic rendering of Gorey's mock-Gothic sagas there is the hint of real terror lurking near the surface." Janeway points out that the "Gorey canon is a type of speech unique to itself. The content handled is the kind of Victorian literature which the passage of a century has turned into pure camp. Not that Gorey is writing camp, he isn't."

Martin Gottfried explores Gorey's artistic concerns, writing in the *Saturday Review* that Gorey's work "presents the great cliche of our day—'style versus content'—extended to its ultimate absurdity. For Gorey . . . bases his humor on the contrast between perfect manners (the *style* of behavior) and immorality, sexual perversion, and sadism (a somewhat extreme *content* of behavior). His description of an orgy is exquisitely discreet: 'unusually well-endowed' people doing 'the oddest things' on 'a curious sofa.'"

Gorey's illustrations also evoke the Victorian era, according to critics who compare his pen-and-ink drawings to the work of such nineteenth-century artists as Wilhelm Busch and Aubrey Beardsley. In *Harper's,* John Hollander characterizes Gorey's artwork as "parodic adaptation of nineteenth-century wood engraving." A *Newsweek* reviewer calls Gorey a "draftsman whose grotesques are curiously endearing. The care he has lavished upon his gory creatures serves to diminish the terror." Janeway asserts that "Gorey's messages to the reader . . . are conveyed by his style. . . . Because they are conscious, designed comments on life made by a subtle and powerful mind," Gorey's drawings "transmute mere representation into art; minor art, perhaps, but authentic and totally individual."

Characterizing Gorey's effect on his audience, Brendan Gill says in the *New Yorker* that "we stand staring in awe at his world, which has little to do with the conventional ordering of the world in which the rest of us wake and eat and drink and fall asleep. Sunlight and time passing and the force of gravity are trifles that Gorey dismisses out of hand . . . for in Gorey country it is nearly always dusk . . . and time is suspended, and the air is so thin that one is hard put to it not to be incessantly somersaulting." Gorey himself, however, sees his "little personal world" in an entirely different way. "What

I'm really interested in,'' he says in *Newsweek,* ''is everyday life. It's dreadfully hazardous. I never could understand why people always feel they have to climb up Mount Everest when you know it's quite dangerous getting out of bed.''

Many of Gorey's books have been translated into German.

MEDIA ADAPTATIONS: Several of Gorey's tales were adapted by Stephen Currens for the stage and produced as ''Gorey Stories,'' which opened at the Booth Theater on October 30, 1978.

AVOCATIONAL INTERESTS: Cats, movies, opera, concerts, country cooking, ballet, book collecting.

BIOGRAPHICAL/CRITICAL SOURCES: New Yorker, December 26, 1959, November 6, 1978; *Newsweek,* August 26, 1963, October 30, 1972, October 31, 1977; *New Republic,* November 26, 1966; *Harper's,* February, 1970; *New York Times Book Review,* October 29, 1972; *Commentary,* January, 1973; *Conversations with Writers,* Volume I, Gale, 1977; *Horizon,* November, 1977; *People,* July 3, 1978; *Saturday Review,* January 6, 1979; *Detroit Free Press,* October 29, 1982.

—Sketch by Kerry L. Lutz

* * *

GORSLINE, Douglas (Warner) 1913-

PERSONAL: Born May 24, 1913, in Rochester, N.Y.; son of Henry W. (a real estate broker) and Sarah (Warner) Gorsline; married Elisabeth Evarts Perkins, September 26, 1936 (divorced); married S. Marie Carson, November, 1977; children: (first marriage) John Warner, Jeremiah Evarts. *Education:* Attended Yale University, 1931-32, and Art Students League, New York City, 1932-35. *Home:* 21150 Bussy Le Grand, Les Laume, France. *Agent:* Ted Riley, 215 East 31st St., New York, N.Y. 10016.

CAREER: Artist and free-lance illustrator. Work represented in numerous private and public collections, including Butler Institute of American Art, Library of Congress, National Academy of Design, St. Paul Art Gallery, and Houghton Library, Harvard University; has had one-man shows in galleries and institutions in United States and Europe, most recently at Pearl Fox Gallery, Philadelphia, Pa., Memorial Art Gallery, Rochester, N.Y., and Bodley Gallery, New York, N.Y. Art instructor, Art School of the National Academy, 1960-62. *Member:* National Academy of Design. *Awards, honors:* Purchase awards from American Academy of Arts and Letters, 1962, National Academy of Design, 1963, St. Paul Gallery, and Springfield Museum; Tiffany Foundation grant, 1963; and about a dozen other awards from groups and organizations, including American Watercolor Society, Audubon Artists, and National Arts Club.

WRITINGS—Self-illustrated: *Farm Boy,* Viking, 1950; *What People Wore: A Visual History of Dress from Ancient Times to Twentieth-Century America,* Viking, 1952, reprinted, Crown, 1977.

Illustrator: Izaak Walton, *The Compleat Angler,* Limited Editions Club, 1948; Marian King, *Young Mary Stuart, Queen of Scots,* Lippincott, 1954; Florence W. Rowland, *Jade Dragons,* Walck, 1954; Bernardine Kielty, *Marie Antoinette,* Random House, 1955; Anne Molloy, *Captain Waymouth's Indians,* Hastings, 1956; Louisa May Alcott, *Little Men,* Grosset, 1957; Fred Reinfeld, *Trappers of the West,* Crowell, 1957; Catherine O. Peare, *Charles Dickens: His Life,* Harper, 1959; Bernardine Kielty, *Jenny Lind Sang Here,* Houghton, 1959. Louise D. Rich, *First Book of the Early Settlers,* F. Watts, 1960; Walter D. Edmonds, *They Had a Horse,* Dodd, 1962; Paul Horgan, *Citizen of New Salem,* Farrar, Straus, 1962; Jeanne L. Gardner, *Sky Pioneers: The Story of Wilbur and Orville Wright,* Harcourt, 1963; James P. Wood, *Hound, Bay Horse and Turtle Dove,* Simon & Schuster, 1963; Clyde R. Bulla, *Viking Adventure,* Crowell, 1963; James P. Wood, *Trust Thyself: A Life of Emerson for the Young Reader,* Pantheon, 1964; Nina B. Baker, *Nickels & Dimes: The Story of F. W. Woolworth,* Harcourt, 1966; John and Patricia Beatty, *At the Seven Stars,* Macmillan, 1967; Rosemary S. Nesbitt, *Great Rope,* Lothrop, 1968; Ruth Loomis, *Valley of the Hawk,* Dial, 1969.

Dale Eunson, *The Day They Gave Babies Away,* Farrar, Straus, 1970; Ferdinand Monjo, *Vicksburg Veteran,* Simon & Schuster, 1971; Ferdinand Monjo, *Me and Willie and Pa: A Story of Abraham Lincoln and His Son Tad,* Simon & Schuster, 1973; Clement C. Moore, *The Night Before Christmas,* Random House, 1975; Peggy Mann and Katisa Prusina, *A Present for Yanya,* Random House, 1975; *Nursery Rhymes,* Random House, 1976; *North American Indians,* Random House, 1977; *Cowboys,* Random House, 1978; *Pioneers,* Random House, 1979. Also illustrator of *Story of Good Queen Bess,* Grosset.

AVOCATIONAL INTERESTS: Travel in Europe and Asia.

* * *

GOTTSCHALK, Louis (Reichenthal) 1899-1975

PERSONAL: Born February 21, 1899, in Brooklyn, N.Y.; died June 24, 1975; son of Morris Frank and Anna (Krystall) Gottschalk; married Laura Riding (a writer), 1920 (divorced, 1925); married Fruma Kasdan (an associate professor at University of Chicago), December 16, 1930; children: (second marriage) Alexander, Paul. *Education:* Cornell University, A.B., 1919, A.M., 1920, Ph.D., 1921. *Home:* 5551 University Ave., Chicago, Ill. 60637. *Office:* 1126 East 59th St., Chicago, Ill. 60637.

CAREER: University of Illinois, Urbana, instructor in history, 1921-22; University of Louisville, Louisville, Ky., assistant professor, 1923-25, associate professor of history, 1925-27; University of Chicago, Chicago, Ill., associate professor, 1927-35, professor of history, 1935-59, department chairman, 1937-42, Swift Distinguished Service Professor, 1959-64, professor emeritus, 1964-75. Visiting professor, University of Illinois, Chicago Circle, 1966-74. B'nai B'rith Hillel Commission, chairman, 1963-69, honorary chairman, 1969-75. Consultant, U.S. Army Air Forces, 1943-44. *Military service:* U.S. Naval Reserve, 1918.

MEMBER: American Historical Association (president, 1953), Conference on Jewish Relations, American Friends of Lafayette, American Philosophical Society, American Academy of Arts and Sciences, Societe d'Historire Moderne, American Council of Learned Societies (vice-chairman, 1965), Social Science Research Council, American Society for Eighteenth-Century Studies (president, 1971), Phi Beta Kappa, Zeta Beta Tau, Quadrangle Club.

AWARDS, HONORS: Guggenheim fellowship, 1928-29, 1954-55; Anciens Combattants de France, medal of merit, 1938; Princeton Bicentennial Medal, 1946; Newberry Library fellow, 1946; James H. Hyde prize, 1948; University of Louisville Sesquicentennial Award, 1948, and LL.D., 1970; Legion d'Honneur, 1953; Center for Advanced Studies in the Behavioral Sciences fellow, 1957-58; D.Litt., Augustana College, 1954; Dr. honoris causa, University of Toulouse, 1957; D.H.L.,

Hebrew Union College, 1963; Fulbright Distinguished Lecturer to Japan, 1968.

WRITINGS: Jean Paul Marat: Study in Radicalism, Greenberg, 1927, revised edition, University of Chicago Press, 1967; *Era of the French Revolution,* Houghton, 1929; *Lafayette Comes to America,* University of Chicago Press, 1935, revised edition, 1965; *Lafayette Joins the American Army,* University of Chicago Press, 1937, reprinted, 1974; *Lady-in-Waiting: The Romance of Lafayette and Aglae de Hunolstein,* Johns Hopkins Press, 1939; *Lafayette and the Close of the American Revolution,* University of Chicago Press, 1942, revised edition, 1965; (editor) *Letters of Lafayette to Washington, 1777-1799,* privately printed, 1944, 2nd revised edition, American Philosophical Society, 1976; (with others) *The Use of Personal Documents in History, Anthropology, and Sociology,* Social Science Research Council, 1945; *The Place of the American Revolution in the Causal Pattern of the French Revolution: An Address at the Seventeenth Annual Meeting of the American Friends of Lafayette,* American Friends of Lafayette, 1948.

Lafayette between the American and the French Revolution, University of Chicago Press, 1950, reprinted, 1974; *Understanding History: A Primer of Historical Method,* Knopf, 1950, 2nd edition, 1969; (with D. F. Lach) *Europe and the Modern World,* Scott, Foresman, Volume I: *The Rise of Modern Europe,* Volume II: *The Transformation of Modern Europe,* 1951-54, last eleven chapters of Volume II published as *Europe and the Modern World Since 1870,* 1954; *The Era of the French Revolution,* Houghton, 1957; (editor) *Generalization in the Writing of History: A Report to the Committee on Historical Analysis, Social Science Research Council,* University of Chicago Press, 1963; (with Loren C. MacKinney and Earl H. Pritchard) *UNESCO History of Mankind,* Harper, 1969; (with Margaret Maddox) *Lafayette in the French Revolution: Through the October Days,* University of Chicago Press, 1969; (with Maddox) *Lafayette in the French Revolution: From the October Days through the Federation,* University of Chicago Press, 1973; (with Lach and S. A. Bill) *Toward the French Revolution: Europe and America in the Eighteenth Century World,* Scribner, 1973; *Lafayette in America, 1777-1783,* L'Esprit de Lafayette Society (Arveyres, France), 1975; (editor with others) *Lafayette: A Guide to the Letters, Documents, and Manuscripts in the United States,* Cornell University Press, 1975.

Assistant editor, *Journal of Modern History,* 1929-43, acting editor, 1943-45.

WORK IN PROGRESS: Lafayette in the French Revolution: From July, 1790 to August, 1792, for University of Chicago Press; *Reflections on Revolution,* a collection of autobiographical anecdotes.

BIOGRAPHICAL/CRITICAL SOURCES: Richard Herr and H. T. Parker, editors, *Ideas in History: Essays Presented to Louis Gottschalk by His Former Students,* Duke University Press, 1965.

OBITUARIES: New York Times, June 25, 1975; *AB Bookman's Weekly,* August 4, 1975.†

* * *

GOULD, Cecil (Hilton Monk) 1918-

PERSONAL: Born May 24, 1918, in England; son of R. T. (a lieutenant commander in the Royal Navy) and Muriel Hilda (Estall) Gould. *Education:* Attended Westminster School, England, 1931-36; educated privately in Germany, 1936-37, and at Courtauld Institute of Art, University of London, 1937-39. *Home:* Jubilee House, Thorncombe, Dorsetshire, England.

CAREER: National Gallery, London, England, assistant keeper, 1946-62, deputy keeper, 1962-73, keeper, 1973-78. Consultant to Timken Art Gallery, San Diego, Calif., 1982—. *Military service:* Royal Air Force, 1940-46; served in France, Middle East, Italy, Belgium, and Germany. *Member:* Royal Society of Arts (fellow).

WRITINGS: An Introduction to Italian Renaissance Painting, Phaidon, 1957; *Trophy of Conquest: The Musee Napoleon and the Creation of the Louvre,* Faber, 1965; *Early Renaissance: Fifteenth-Century Italian Painting,* McGraw, 1965; *Leonardo: The Artist and the Non-Artist,* New York Graphic Society, 1974; *The Paintings of Correggio,* Faber, 1977; *Bernini in France,* Weidenfeld & Nicolson, 1982.

Compiler of National Gallery catalogs, including: *The Sixteenth-Century Venetian School,* 1959; *The Sixteenth-Century Italian Schools Excluding the Venetian,* 1962; (and author of introduction and notes) *Corot,* 1965; *Michelangelo: Battle of Cascina* (Charlton Lecture), 1966; *The Raising of Lazarus, by Sebastiano del Piombo,* 1967; *The Studio of Alfonso d'Este and Titian's Bacchus and Ariadne: A Re-examination of the Chronology of the Bacchanals and of the Evolution of One of Them,* 1969; *Titian,* 1969; (with Martin Davies) *French School: Early 19th Century, Impressionists, Post-Impressionists,* 1970; *Raphael's Portrait of Pope Julius II: The Re-emergence of the Original,* 1970; *"The School of Love" and Correggio's Mythologies,* 1970; (with Kenneth Clark) *The Leonardo Cartoon,* 1972; *The Draped Figure,* 1972; *Failure and Success: 150 Years of the National Gallery, 1874-1974,* 1974; *Space in Landscape,* 1974; *Rival of Nature: Renaissance Painting in Its Context,* 1975.

Contributor to *Encyclopaedia Britannica, Chambers's Encyclopaedia,* and *Dizionario Biografico degli Italiani;* contributor to *Burlington Magazine, Art Quarterly, Art Bulletin,* and other journals in American and Europe.

SIDELIGHTS: As former keeper of the prestigious British National Gallery, Cecil Gould has established himself as "one of the leading English scholars," whose work shows him to have the "highest standards of accuracy and thoroughness," according to Kenneth Clark in *Spectator*.

Critics repeatedly praise Gould for his scholarship, especially in reference to *The Paintings of Correggio*. This study of the early sixteenth-century Italian artist, which includes an extensive catalog of Correggio's work, is hailed by a *Choice* reviewer as a "work of impeccable scholarship [which] must necessarily establish itself as the standard work on Correggio." Clark asserts that, from "the point of view of information, it seems unlikely that anyone will have to write a book on Correggio again."

Gould speaks French, German and Italian.

AVOCATIONAL INTERESTS: Travel, music, skiing.

BIOGRAPHICAL/CRITICAL SOURCES: Library Journal, November 1, 1975, January 15, 1977; *New York Times Book Review,* December 7, 1975; *Choice,* April, 1976, April, 1977; *Spectator,* February 12, 1977; *Times Literary Supplement,* March 19, 1982.

* * *

GRAEME, Roderic

See JEFFRIES, Roderic (Graeme)

GRAVES, John (Alexander III) 1920-

PERSONAL: Born August 6, 1920, in Fort Worth, Tex.; son of John Alexander and Nancy (Kay) Graves; married Jane Cole, 1958; children: Helen, Sally. *Education:* Rice University, B.A., 1942; Columbia University, M.A., 1948. *Residence:* Hard Scrabble Ranch, Somervell County, Tex.

CAREER: Free-lance writer. University of Texas at Austin, instructor in English, 1948-50; Texas Christian University, Fort Worth, adjunct professor of English, 1958-65; employed with U.S. Department of Interior, 1965-68. *Military service:* U.S. Marine Corps, 1941-45; became captain; received Purple Heart. *Member:* P.E.N., Nature Conservancy, Audubon Society, Texas Institute of Letters, Phi Beta Kappa. *Awards, honors:* Collins Award of Texas Institute of Letters, 1961, for *Goodbye to a River;* Guggenheim fellow, 1963; Rockefeller fellow, 1972; Parkman Prize of Texas Institute of Letters, 1974, for *Hard Scrabble: Observations on a Patch of Land.*

WRITINGS: Goodbye to a River, Knopf, 1960; (with Robert Boyle and others) *The Water Hustlers,* Sierra Club, 1971, revised edition, 1973; (with others) *Growing Up in Texas,* Encino Press, 1972; *The Last Running,* Encino Press, 1974; *Hard Scrabble: Observations on a Patch of Land,* Knopf, 1974; (with Jim Bones, Jr.) *Texas Heartland: A Hill Country Year,* Texas A&M University Press, 1975.

From a Limestone Ledge: Some Essays and Other Ruminations about Country Life in Texas, Knopf, 1980; (illustrator) *Landscapes of Texas,* Texas A&M University Press, 1980; (editor) Gail W. Starr, *Mall,* Envision Commission, 1980; *Blue and Some Other Dogs,* Encino Press, 1981. Contributor of short stories to *Prize Stories: The O'Henry Awards,* 1955 and 1962, and *Best American Short Stories,* 1960. Contributor to numerous magazines.

SIDELIGHTS: A native Texan naturalist, John Graves writes primarily of his home state and of his experiences as the owner of Hard Scrabble Ranch, four hundred acres of arid land near Fort Worth. According to a reviewer in the *Atlantic, Hard Scrabble: Observations on a Patch of Land,* a book of essays, is "a rumination tinctured with [Graves's] love of history, his inquisitiveness about his neighbors, and his shrewd knowledge of the natural world." A *New Yorker* critic finds that Graves's subjects, which include everything from "hired help [to] armadillos, . . . come to us reshaped and reenlivened by his agreeably individual . . . notions." Edward Hoagland calls the book "galloping [and] spontaneous" in the *New York Times Book Review* and points out that "what the best [naturalists], like Graves, do have . . . and what can give their books exceptional staying power, is a tone that suits the book . . . a life, a grace, an impetus [that] is lent to their efforts" by their unique perspective.

Referring to *From a Limestone Ledge: Some Essays and Other Ruminations about Country Life in Texas,* Susan Wood of the *Washington Post* says that Graves "writes about Texas and Texans with full attention to the complex peculiarities that distinguish the region; but because he so lovingly particularizes, rather than generalizes, his thoughts come to us in larger terms, made universal by the art of language and feeling. Although permeated with a sense of place, Graves's writing translates Texas as though it were Anywhere." Bill Marvel, reviewing the book in the *Detroit News,* claims that the "ruminative essay on country life is a tradition in American letters, . . . and it is [here] that John Graves's *From a Limestone Ledge* takes its place."

AVOCATIONAL INTERESTS: Natural history, the outdoors.

BIOGRAPHICAL/CRITICAL SOURCES: New York Times Book Review, May 19, 1974; *Atlantic,* August, 1974; *New Yorker,* August 19, 1974, December 29, 1980; *Washington Post,* December 27, 1980; *Detroit News,* January 25, 1981.

* * *

GRAVES, Richard Perceval 1945-

PERSONAL: Born December 21, 1945, in Brighton, England; son of John Tiarks Ranke (a teacher) and Mary (a teacher; maiden name, Wickens) Graves; married Anne Katharine Fortescue, April 4, 1970; children: David John Perceval, Philip Macartney, Lucia Mary. *Education:* St. John's College, Oxford, B.A., 1968, M.A., 1972. *Politics:* Social Democrat. *Religion:* Church of England. *Home:* Pen-Y-Bryn House, Boot St., Whittington, Oswestry, Shropshire SY11 4DG, England. *Agent:* Andrew Best, Curtis Brown Academic Ltd., 1 Craven Hill, London W2 3EP, England.

CAREER: Writer. Teacher of English, history, and Latin at private schools in England, 1968-73. Whittington parish councillor, 1973-76; chairman of Whittington Youth Club, 1974-79, Oswestry borough councillor, 1977-83. *Member:* United Oxford and Cambridge University Club, Society of Authors.

WRITINGS: Lawrence of Arabia and His World, Scribner, 1976; *A. E. Housman: The Scholar-Poet,* Routledge & Kegan Paul, 1979, Scribner, 1980; *The Brothers Powys,* Scribner, 1983. Editor of *Housman Society Journal,* 1977-80.

WORK IN PROGRESS: A family view of Robert Graves, for Routledge & Kegan Paul; an historical novel about William Rufus.

SIDELIGHTS: In his book *A. E. Housman: The Scholar-Poet,* Richard Perceval Graves "presents a portrait of not only the sad artist and acerbic scholar, but what Housman's contemporaries were prevented from seeing: the kind, sensuous, many-sided human being," writes Joseph Parisi in the *Chicago Tribune Book World.* "With a minimum of amateur psychologizing, Graves . . . humanizes a deceptively haughty figure." Housman himself, says Parisi, "could have approved Graves' labors and care. His biography is not only definitive but oddly inspiring." Graves's "realistic, honest, admiring approach is the best thing that could have happened to Housman's reputation," says a *New Yorker* critic.

BIOGRAPHICAL/CRITICAL SOURCES: New York Times Book Review, May 25, 1980; *Atlantic,* June, 1980; *Chicago Tribune Book World,* June 15, 1980; *Time,* July 28, 1980; *New Yorker,* August 18, 1980.

* * *

GRAY, Anne 1931-

PERSONAL: Born October 26, 1931, in London, England; came to the United States in 1947, naturalized in 1948; daughter of Joseph (a jeweler) and Clara (an accountant; maiden name, Laub) Gray; married, August 7, 1966; children: two sons. *Education:* Hunter College (now Hunter College of the City University of New York), B.A. (cum laude), 1953; San Diego State College (now University), M.A., 1968; La Jolla University, Ph.D., 1982. *Politics:* Conservative. *Religion:* Protestant. *Residence:* La Jolla, Calif.

CAREER: Passenger Service Agent for American Airlines, 1955-56; elementary school teacher in San Diego, Calif., 1960-64; junior high school teacher of music, speech, and drama, 1964-68; junior college teacher of English in San Diego, 1968-69; private piano instructor, 1970-80; currently private speech instructor and free-lance writer. Fund raiser for the San Diego Symphony Orchestra. *Member:* Penwomen of America (La Jolla Branch), La Jolla Republican Women's League, Toastmasters of La Jolla (past president), La Jolla Auxiliary of the San Diego Symphony Orchestra Association (president).

WRITINGS: Donald Duck, Television Star, Western Publishing, 1974; *The Wonderful World of San Diego,* Pelican, 1975, 2nd edition, 1975; (co-editor) *Concert de Cuisine,* [San Diego], 1983. Also author of material for "Walt Disney Foreign Comics." Contributor to *Holistic Living News, Bike World, La Jolla Sun, San Diego Union,* and *Health & Strength.*

WORK IN PROGRESS: Where Have You Been All Your Life?, a nonfiction motivational book; *The Kitten without a Tail, Neeta and the Litterbugs,* juvenile books; "His Name Shall Be Called Emmanuel," a TV script; *How to Hang onto Your Husband,* a humor-motivational book.

AVOCATIONAL INTERESTS: International travel, concert-going, organizing musicales to benefit the San Diego Symphony.

* * *

GREEN, Jonathan (William) 1939-

PERSONAL: Born September 26, 1939, in Troy, N.Y.; son of Alan Singer (a rabbi) and Frances (Katz) Green; married Louise Lockshin (an artist and musician), September 16, 1962; children: Raphael Michael, Benjamin Ethan. *Education:* Attended Massachusetts Institute of Technology, 1958-60, and Hebrew University of Jerusalem, 1960-61; Brandeis University, B.A. (magna cum laude), 1963, doctoral study, 1964-67; Harvard University, M.A., 1967. *Home:* 1430 South Galena Rd., Galena, Ohio 43021. *Office:* University Gallery of Fine Art, Hopkins Hall, Ohio State University, Columbus, Ohio 43210.

CAREER: Free-lance architectural and advertising photographer, 1966—; Ezra Stoller Associates, Mamaroneck, N.Y., associate photographer, 1967-69; Massachusetts Institute of Technology, Cambridge, instructor, 1968-69, assistant professor, 1969-73, associate professor of photography, 1973-75, project director of Visible Language Workshop, 1973-75, acting director of Creative Photography Laboratory and Gallery, 1974-76; Ohio State University, Columbus, associate professor of photography and cinema, 1976—, director of Silver Image Gallery, 1978-81, director of University Gallery of Fine Art, 1981—. Proposal reviewer for National Endowment for the Humanities, 1975-76.

Photographs are included in numerous permanent collections, including Bell System Collection, Cleveland Museum of Art, Museum of Fine Arts (Boston), and Moderna Museet (Stockholm); photographs have been included in over thirty exhibitions; has made photomurals for installation in Boston, Rochester, N.Y., and Chicago; producer of exhibition panels for American Institute of Architects award exhibitions, 1968-76; official exhibition photographer for Alfred Stieglitz Center of the Philadelphia Museum of Art, 1969-76. Member of organizational committee and juror for "New England Photo Vision '72"; visiting critic at Worcester Museum of Art, 1972; initiated Boston Photography Survey, 1972; member of organizational committee for children's show at Boston Center for the Arts, 1972; advisor and juror for "Photography/Maine 1973." Consultant and review panelist for National Endowment for the Arts, 1975-76; consultant to Polaroid Corp., 1976, and to Columbus Museum of Art, 1978.

MEMBER: International Center of Photography, International Museum of Photography, Society for Photographic Education, Friends of Photography (Carmel), Visual Studies Workshop (Rochester), Center for Creative Photography (Tucson), Phi Beta Kappa. *Awards, honors:* Grants from National Endowment for the Arts and Florence V. Burden Foundation, 1972-73, and art publishing award from Art Librarians Society of North America, 1973, all for *Camera Work: A Critical Anthology;* award from New York Type Directors Club, 1974, for *The Snapshot;* National Endowment for the Arts photographer's fellow, 1978; Bell System grant, 1979.

WRITINGS: (Editor and author of introduction) *Camera Work: A Critical Anthology,* Aperture, 1973; (with Minor White) *Celebrations,* Aperture, 1974; (editor and author of introduction) *The Snapshot,* Aperture, 1974; (contributor) Petruck, editor, *The Camera Viewed: Writings on Twentieth-Century Photography,* Dutton, 1979; *The Continuity of American Photography,* Abrams, 1983.

Contributor of photographs: Renato Danese, editor, *American Images: New Work by Twenty Contemporary Photographers,* McGraw, 1979; *Twenty-Five Years of Record Houses,* McGraw, 1981.

Author of book jacket copy; author of advertising copy for *Aperture.* Contributor of articles and photographs to architecture and photography journals and popular magazines, including *Architectural Record, Afterimage, Aperture, Travel and Leisure, Popular Mechanics,* and *New Yorker. Aperture,* editorial consultant, 1972-73, associate editor, 1974-76; associate editor of *Boston Photographic Survey,* 1974-76.

SIDELIGHTS: Two of Jonathan Green's best-known works, *Camera Work: A Critical Anthology* and *The Snapshot,* deal with photographers and photography as a major force in the history of modern art.

Green's first book, *Camera Work: A Critical Anthology,* serves as a guide to the history of the early twentieth-century periodical *Camera Work.* Edited by Alfred Stieglitz, one of the most important figures in modern photography, the journal sought to present the best in literature and aesthetic criticism, as well as the work of the most avant-garde photographers of the period. Green's book preserves both textual and photographic contributions to the journal, including those of Bernard Shaw, Gertrude Stein (whose work appeared there for the first time anywhere), Edward J. Steichen, and Clarence H. White.

Hilton Kramer of the *New York Times Book Review* praises the anthology as being "exemplary in every respect." Green's introduction to the collection, he says, "and his lengthy notes, together with his painstaking indexes and other editorial apparatus, are a model of what a book of this sort should be." Douglas Davis, writing in *Newsweek,* calls the book "beautiful and invaluable."

In *The Snapshot,* Green explores the informal, spontaneous medium of the snapshot through photographic examples, interviews, and essays. Contributors include several famous photographers, such as Lisette Model, Paul Strand, Emmet Gowin, and Robert Frank. In an article in *Saturday Review,* Margaret R. Weiss describes the book as a "provocative anthology."

A writer for *Newsweek* recognizes it as "a major new book" on the basis of its thorough documentation of "the symbiotic link between the work of our finest photographers and their first experience of photography."

BIOGRAPHICAL/CRITICAL SOURCES: New York Times Book Review, April 21, 1974, December 1, 1974; *Newsweek,* April 29, 1974, October 21, 1974; *Saturday Review,* April 5, 1975; *Choice,* July, 1975; *New York Times,* February 8, 1976; *New Yorker,* April 26, 1976; *Village Voice,* February 4, 1980.

* * *

GREEN, Martin (Burgess) 1927-

PERSONAL: Born September 21, 1927, in London, England; son of Joseph William Elias (a shopkeeper) and Hilda (Brewster) Green; married Carol Elizabeth Hurd, 1967; children: Martin Michael, Miriam. *Education:* St. John's College, Cambridge, B.A. (with English honours), 1948, M.A., 1952; King's College, London, teachers' diploma, 1951; Sorbonne, University of Paris, Certificat d'Etudes Francaises, 1952; University of Michigan, Ph.D., 1957. *Politics:* Labour. *Religion:* Roman Catholic. *Office:* Department of English, Tufts University, Medford, Mass. 02155.

CAREER: Teacher at College Moderne, Fourmies, France, 1951-52, and at Konya Koleji, Konya, Turkey, 1955-56; Wellesley College, Wellesley, Mass., instructor in modern literature, 1957-61; Tufts University, Medford, Mass., assistant professor of American literature, 1963-65; University of Birmingham, Birmingham, England, lecturer in American literature, 1965-68; Tufts University, professor of English, 1968—. *Military service:* Royal Air Force, 1948-50; became sergeant. *Awards, honors:* Three major Avery and Jule Hopwood Creative Writing Awards, University of Michigan, 1954.

WRITINGS: Mirror for Anglo-Saxons, Harper, 1960; *Reappraisals,* Hugh Evelyn, 1963, Norton, 1965; *Science and the Shabby Curate of Poetry,* Norton, 1965; *The Problem of Boston,* Norton, 1966; *Yeats's Blessings on von Hugel: Essays in Literature and Religion,* Longmans, Green, 1967, Norton, 1968.

Cities of Light and Sons of the Morning, Little, Brown, 1972; *The von Richthoffen Sisters: The Triumphant and the Tragic Modes of Love,* Basic Books, 1974; (editor with Philip C. Ritterbush) *Technology as Institutionally Related to Human Values,* Acropolis Books, 1974; *The Labyrinth of Shakespeare's Sonnets: An Examination of Sexual Elements in Shakespeare's Language,* C. Skilton, 1974; *Children of the Sun: A Narrative of "Decadence" in England after 1918,* Basic Books, 1976, revised edition, Constable, 1977; *Transatlantic Patterns: Cultural Comparisons of England with America,* Basic Books, 1977; *The Earth again Redeemed: May 26 to July 1, 1984* (science fiction), Basic Books, 1977.

"The Lust for Power" trilogy; published by Basic Books: *The Challenge of the Mahatmas,* 1978; *Dreams of Adventure, Deeds of Empire,* 1979; *Tolstoy and Gandhi: Men of Peace,* 1983.

WORK IN PROGRESS: Study of the American adventure narrative.

SIDELIGHTS: Scholar Martin Green is, according to Jonathan Raban in the *New York Times Book Review,* a "merchant-venturer in the commerce of ideas, a wickedly clever cultural historian at whose approach disciplinary frontiers seem to melt into thin air. He has the gift of making himself appear equally at home in literature, anthropology, social history, politics and gossip."

Green, a British expatriate, has written several books on English cultural and social history, often using literary figures to illustrate his point. In *Children of the Sun: A Narrative of "Decadence" in England after 1918,* for example, Green explores the post-World War I cultural phenomenon of dandyism among the young, wealthy socialites and artists of the period. Focusing on such writers as Evelyn Waugh, Christopher Isherwood, and Harold Acton, Green sets out "to describe the imaginative life of English [high] culture after 1918 and to trace the prominence within it, the partial dominance over it, established by men of one intellectual temperament," as he is quoted in a *World Literature Today* article.

Hilton Kramer says in the *New York Times Book Review* that "among much else that Mr. Green's book accomplishes, it gives us a new and vivid understanding of what the concept of the Establishment in England truly signified. . . . He has . . . written a very important book."

In *Transatlantic Patterns: Cultural Comparisons of England with America,* Green discusses the contemporary cultural differences between the two countries on the basis of their literature. Examining writers as diverse as Dorothy Sayers and John D. MacDonald, Norman Mailer and Doris Lessing, Green tries "to define the difference between England and America in terms of attitudes toward marriage, humor, detective stories, Marx and Freud. . . . What he is after is extremely subtle and pertinent—not cultural—caricature," according to Christopher Lehmann-Haupt in the *New York Times.* Lehmann-Haupt goes on to say that this book "will not come as much of a surprise to anyone who has followed Mr. Green's lively and original intellectual career."

Dreams of Adventure, Deeds of Empire is a survey of the tradition of adventure stories in Western literature, from the work of Daniel DeFoe to that of contemporary writers. In this book, which Raban cites as a "fine professorial performance," Green proposes that the adventure novel—such as *Robinson Crusoe, The Adventures of Huckleberry Finn,* or *Kim*—should be recognized as serious literature rivalling the domestic novels of such writers as Jane Austen, Tolstoy, and D. H. Lawrence. This book "bubbles with notes and parentheses, debating-points and essay subjects, new ideas about well-known writers and engaging introductions to the less known," says D.A.N. Jones in the *Times Literary Supplement.*

BIOGRAPHICAL/CRITICAL SOURCES: New York Times Book Review, January 25, 1976, August 7, 1977, May 27, 1979; *New York Review of Books,* April 15, 1976; *World Literature Today,* spring, 1977; *Spectator,* June 4, 1977; *New York Times,* June 29, 1977; *Times Literary Supplement,* July 18, 1980.

* * *

GREEN, Peter
See BULMER, (Henry) Kenneth

* * *

GREENBURG, Dan 1936-

PERSONAL: Born June 20, 1936, in Chicago, Ill.; son of Samuel (an artist) and Leah (Rozalsky) Greenburg; married Nora Ephron (a journalist), April 9, 1967 (divorced); married Suzanne O'Malley (a writer and editor), June 28, 1980. *Education:* University of Illinois, B.F.A., 1958; University of California, Los Angeles, M.A., 1960. *Politics:* Democrat. *Religion:* Jewish. *Home and office:* 323 East 50th St., New York,

N.Y. 10022. *Agent:* Morton Janklow, Morton Janklow Associates, 598 Madison Ave., New York, N.Y.

CAREER: Writer. Lansdale Co. (advertising agency), Los Angeles, Calif., copywriter, 1960-61; Carson/Roberts (advertising agency), Los Angeles, Calif., copywriter, 1961-62; *Eros* Magazine, New York City, managing editor, 1962-63; Papert, Koenig, Lois (advertising agency), New York City, copywriter, 1963-65. *Member:* Authors Guild, Authors League of America, Mystery Writers of America, Dramatists Guild, Writers Guild of America West. *Awards, honors: Playboy* Magazine prize for best humorous piece published in 1964, for condensation of *How to Be a Jewish Mother;* Advertising Writers Association of New York Silver Key Awards, 1964 and 1972.

WRITINGS: How to Be a Jewish Mother, Price/Stern/Sloan, 1964; *Kiss My Firm But Pliant Lips,* Grossman Publishers, 1965; (with Marcia Jacobs) *How to Make Yourself Miserable: Another Vital Training Manual,* Random House, 1966; *Chewsday: A Sex Novel,* Stein & Day, 1968; *Jumbo the Boy and Arnold the Elephant* (children's book), Bobbs-Merrill, 1969; *Philly* (novel), Simon & Schuster, 1969; *Porno-Graphics: The Shame of Our Art Museums* (humor), Random House, 1969.

Scoring: A Sexual Memoir, Doubleday, 1972; *Something's There: My Adventures in the Occult,* Doubleday, 1976; *Love Kills* (novel), Harcourt, 1978; *What Do Women Want?* (novel), Simon & Schuster, 1982; (with wife, Suzanne O'Malley) *How to Avoid Love and Marriage,* Simon & Schuster, 1982.

Plays: "How to Be a Jewish Mother" (adapted from his book), first produced in New York at Hudson Theatre, December 28, 1967; "Arf" and "The Great Airplane Snatch" (both one-act), first produced in New York at Stage 73 Theatre, May 27, 1969; (contributor with others) Kenneth Tynan, compiler, *Oh! Calcutta!* (first produced in New York at Eden Theatre, June 18, 1969), Grove, 1969.

Also author of screenplays, "Live a Little, Love a Little" (adapted from *Kiss My Firm But Pliant Lips*), "Chewsday," "Philly," "California Safari," "I Could Never Have Sex with Any Man Who Has So Little Regard for My Husband," and "Private Lessons."

Work represented in many anthologies, including *Twentieth Century Parody: American and British, Twelfth Anniversary Playboy Reader,* and *Esquire's World of Humor.* Contributor to *Playboy, Esquire, Monocle,* and *Eros.*

WORK IN PROGRESS: A play; a novel; and a screenplay.

SIDELIGHTS: Dan Greenburg's novel *Love Kills* is a "very savvy Manhattan chiller" that "induces genuine, sweaty panic," according to *Newsweek*'s Walter Clemons. The story follows the movements of a maniacal killer who calls himself the Hyena and a psychic victim-to-be who collaborates with the police to prevent her own murder. Greenburg has written what a *West Coast Review of Books* critic describes as "an unusual type of mystery, perhaps a bit too gory, but how can you have murder without blood and violence?" Although "one suspects that [his] commitment to this novel began and ended in his checkbook," notes Christopher Dickey in the *Washington Post Book World,* Greenburg "is a skilled and funny writer with a nice eye for personal (if not police) detail and a formula well-proven long before he came to it. Even if he has given us garbage, things are sometimes found there . . . that, in their curious way, bring pleasure."

AVOCATIONAL INTERESTS: Travel (has been to Israel, Europe, Africa, and Guatemala).

BIOGRAPHICAL/CRITICAL SOURCES: Playboy, February, 1965; *Newsweek,* August 14, 1978; *Washington Post Book World,* August 14, 1978, April 23, 1982; *New Yorker,* September 4, 1978; *West Coast Review of Books,* November, 1978; *New York Times,* December 8, 1978; *New York Times Book Review,* May 16, 1982; *Los Angeles Times,* May 18, 1982; *National Review,* July 9, 1982.

* * *

GREENE, Adam
See SCOTT, Peter Dale

* * *

GREENE, Wilda 1911-

PERSONAL: Born January 25, 1911, in Falkville, Ala.; daughter of Frank T. and Ida Dixie (Lovelady) Witt; married Wallace S. Greene, Jr., March 2, 1936 (died May, 1982); children: Donna (Mrs. William T. Miller). *Education:* Attended public schools. *Religion:* Baptist. *Home and office:* 155 Boxwood Dr., Franklin, Tenn. 37064.

CAREER: Writer. *Member:* National League of American Pen Women, National Federation of Press Women, Authors Guild, Authors League of America, Tennessee Woman's Press and Authors Club, Nashville Woman's Press and Authors Club.

WRITINGS: Visitation Evangelism, Moody, 1955; *The Disturbing Christ* (devotional study of Hebrews), Broadman, 1968; *24 Hours with Jesus,* Abingdon, 1978; *Hebrews,* Baptist Sunday School Board, 1981; *James,* Baptist Sunday School Board, 1981. Contributor to *Broadman Devotional Annual,* 1973. Contributor of articles, biblical background material, and curriculum materials to religious publications, including *Open Windows.*

WORK IN PROGRESS: The Eight Most Interesting Women in the Bible.

SIDELIGHTS: Wilda Greene explains the purpose of *The Eight Most Interesting Women in the Bible:* "Until we have seen the women of biblical times plugging down the tents in which their families dwelled, squatting in pain to bear their children, and surviving the tumult of a court system filled with brutality, cruelty, and jealousy, we have not really understood them at all. I chose eight women who lived between the time of the patriarch [Abraham] and the kingship period. Although each of the women was strongly influenced by the political, social, and economic turmoil of the period in which she lived, each survived with dignity, beauty, and great faith in God."

* * *

GREENFIELD, Patricia Marks 1940-

PERSONAL: Born July 18, 1940, in Newark, N.J.; daughter of David Marks, Jr. (a life insurance salesman) and Doris (Pollard) Marks; married Sheldon Greenfield (a physician), March 13, 1965; children: Lauren. *Education:* Radcliffe College, A.B. (summa cum laude), 1962; attended University of Dakar, 1963-64; Harvard University, Ph.D., 1966. *Office:* Department of Psychology, University of California, Los Angeles, Calif. 90024.

CAREER: Syracuse University, Syracuse, N.Y., investigator at Research and Development Center in Early Childhood Education, 1967, research associate, 1967-68; Harvard University, Cambridge, Mass., research fellow in psychology, Center for Cognitive Studies, 1968-72, lecturer on social relations, 1970; Stanford University, Stanford, Calif., acting assistant professor of psychology, 1972-73; University of California, Santa Cruz, associate professor, 1973-74; University of California, Los Angeles, associate professor, 1974-78, professor of psychology, 1978—. Visiting lecturer, Clark University, 1971; collaborating scientist, Yerkes Regional Primate Center, Emory University, 1980—. Program advisor, Bromley-Heath Infant Daycare Center, 1969-70; National Institute of Education, member of literacy grant review panel, 1978, member of unsolicited grant review panel, 1979. Consultant to numerous institutions, including Education Development Center, Cambridge, Mass., 1972, University of California, Los Angeles, School of Medicine, 1972-73, and Health Services Research Center, 1976, and to Northwest Regional Educational Laboratory, 1978-80; member of international advisory board, International Congress on Early Childhood Education, Israel.

MEMBER: International Association for Cross-Cultural Psychology (member of executive committee, 1972-74), American Association for the Advancement of Science (fellow), Phi Beta Kappa. *Awards, honors:* First Award of Sixth Annual Creative Talent Awards Program of American Institute for Research, 1967, for dissertation, "Culture, Concepts, and Conservation: A Comparative Study of Cognitive Development in Senegal"; grants from Spencer Foundation, 1975-81, Society for the Psychological Study of Social Issues, 1978, and National Institute of Education, 1979-81.

WRITINGS: (Editor with Jerome S. Bruner, R. R. Olver, and others) *Studies in Cognitive Growth,* Wiley, 1966; (with F. Tronick) *Infant Curriculum: The Bromley-Heath Guide to the Care of Infants in Groups,* Media Projects, 1973, 2nd edition, Goodyear Books, 1980; (with J. Smith) *The Structure of Communication in Early Language Development,* Academic Press, 1976.

Contributor: D. Goslin, editor, *Handbook of Socialization Theory,* Rand McNally, 1963; D. Price-Williams, editor, *Cross-Cultural Studies: Selected Readings,* Penguin, 1969; R. Cancro, editor, *Intelligence: Genetic and Environmental Influences,* Grune, 1971; Bruner, editor, *The Relevance of Education,* Norton, 1971; P. Adams, editor, *Language in Thinking,* Penguin, 1972; V. P. Clark, P. A. Escholz, and A. F. Rosa, editors, *Language: Introductory Readings,* St. Martin's, 1972; Bruner, editor, *Beyond the Information Given,* Norton, 1973.

M. Haehr and W. M. Stallings, editors, *Culture, Child, and School: Socio-Cultural Influences on Learning,* Brooks/Cole Publishing, 1975; H. C. Lindgren, editor, *Child Behavior,* National Press Books, 1975; K. F. Reigel and J. A. Meacham, editors, *The Developing Individual in a Changing World,* Volume I: *Historical and Cultural Issues,* Mouton, 1976; D. O. Walter, L. Rogers, and J. M. Finzi-Fried, editors, *Human Brain Function,* UCLA Brain Information Service/Brain Research Institute, 1976; G. Steiner, editor, *Piaget and Beyond: The Psychology of the 20th Century,* Volume VII, Kindler, Verlag (Zurich), 1977; P. Dasen, editor, *Cross-Cultural Contributions,* Gardner Press, 1977; A. Lock, editor, *Action, Symbol, and Gesture: The Emergence of Language,* Academic Press, 1978; N. Waterson and C. Snow, editors, *Development of Communication: Social and Pragmatic Factors in Language Acquisition,* Wiley, 1978; E. O. Keenan, editor, *Studies in Developmental Pragmatics,* Academic Press, 1978; K. Nelson, editor, *Children's Language,* Gardner Press, Volume I, 1978, Volume II, 1980; P. French, editor, *The Development of Meaning,* Bunka Hyoron Press (Japan), 1979.

D. Olson, editor, *The Social Foundations of Language and Thought: Essays in Honor of J. S. Bruner,* Norton, 1980; N. Warren, editor, *Studies in Cross-Cultural Psychology,* Volume II, Academic Press, 1980; G. Forman, editor, *Action and Thought: From Sensorimotor Schemes to Symbolic Operations,* Academic Press, 1981; D. Wagner and H. Stevenson, editors, *Cultural Perspectives on Child Development,* W. H. Freeman, 1982.

Also author, with Bruner and Allegra M. May, of filmscript, "Early Words: Language and Action in the Life of a Child," and of cassette tape, "What Can We Learn from Cultural Variation in Child Care?" Contributor to *Readings in Developmental Psychology Today,* 2nd edition, 1977. Contributor to *Proceedings of the Inaugural Meeting of the International Association for Cross-Cultural Psychology,* 1975, and to *Papers and Reports on Child Language Development,* 1978 and 1979. Contributor of articles and reviews to professional journals, including *Journal of Child Language, Recherche Pedagogie et Culture, Journal of Cross-Cultural Psychology, Journal of Psycholinguistic Research, Contemporary Psychology,* and *Child Behavior.* Member of editorial board, *Child Development,* 1969-71; corresponding associate commentator, *The Behavioral and Brain Sciences,* 1979—.

WORK IN PROGRESS: Contributions to two books, *Children's Language,* Volume II, and *The Sociogenesis of Language and Human Conduct.*

SIDELIGHTS: Patricia Marks Greenfield is competent in French and in Wolof, a major Senegalese language. *Avocational interests:* Travel, skiing, "social action."

* * *

GREENHAW, H(arold) Wayne 1940-

PERSONAL: Born February 17, 1940, in Colbert County, Ala.; son of Harold Reed (a salesman) and Lee (Able) Greenhaw; married Faye Berry, September, 1965 (divorced August, 1967); married Sarah Virginia Maddox, August, 1972. *Education:* Attended Instituto Allende, San Miguel, Mexico, summer, 1959; University of Alabama, B.S. in Ed., 1966. *Residence:* Montgomery, Ala. *Agent:* Charles D. Taylor, Books and Production East, 24 Elm St., Manchester, Mass. 02144. *Office:* 3239 Lexington Rd., Montgomery, Ala. 36106.

CAREER: Tuscaloosa News, Tuscaloosa, Ala., part-time sports reporter, 1958-62; Tuscaloosa Country Club, Tuscaloosa, assistant manager, 1960-63; *Graphic Weekly,* Tuscaloosa, sports columnist, 1963-64; Draper Correctional Center, Elmore, Ala., writer for experimental educational project, 1964-65; *Alabama Journal,* Montgomery, general assignment reporter, 1965-76; Maxwell Federal Prison Camp, Montgomery, Ala., director of creative writing program; instructor in journalism at Alabama State University, Montgomery, and at Troy State University, Troy, Ala. *Awards, honors:* First place in investigative reporting and second place in feature writing, Alabama Associated Press Awards, 1966; Nieman fellow, Harvard University, 1972-73.

WRITINGS: The Golfer, Lippincott, 1967; *The Making of a Hero: Lt. William Calley and the My Lai Massacre,* Touchstone Publishing, 1971; *Watch Out for George Wallace,* Prentice-Hall, 1976; *Elephant in the Cottonfields: Ronald Reagan and the New Republican South,* Macmillan, 1982.

Writer of two six-part series for Alabama Educational Television. Contributor of more than 200 articles to magazines.

WORK IN PROGRESS: A novel about childhood in the South; a film on the early history of Alabama.

SIDELIGHTS: H. Wayne Greenhaw told *CA:* "I am continuously faced with the problem of moving on to new vistas, and I believe that teaching in college and in prison keeps my juices flowing. Every week I have to come up with something new to tell my students, because they are anxious to *know*. Teaching is creating. I am still a journalist although I no longer work for a newspaper. I think there is true creation in reporting the facts in interesting and fascinating ways."

* * *

GREENWOOD, Gordon 1913-

PERSONAL: Born September 17, 1913, in Terowie, South Australia; son of R. O. and L. A. (Hales) Greenwood; married Thora J. Smeal, February 16, 1939; children: Helen (Mrs. Geoffrey Derrick), David, Stephen, Andrew. *Education:* University of Sidney, B.A. (first class honors), 1935, M.A. (first class honors), 1937; University of London, Ph.D., 1939. *Home:* 164 Victoria St., Chelmer, Brisbane, Queensland, Australia. *Office:* University of Queensland, St. Lucia, Brisbane, Queensland, Australia.

CAREER: New England University College, Armidale, Australia, lecturer in history, 1939-41; University of Sydney, Sydney, Australia, lecturer, 1942-43, senior lecturer, 1944-46, acting professor of history, 1947-49; University of Queensland, Brisbane, Australia, professor of history, 1949—, dean of Faculty of Arts, 1951-55, member of senate, 1953—. Member of Commonwealth Advisory Committee on Advanced Education. *Member:* Australian Institute of International Affairs (Commonwealth president, 1961-65), Social Science Research Council of Australia, Australian Humanities Research Council, University of Queensland Football Club (president). *Awards, honors:* Carnegie and Commonwealth fellow, 1956; United States Leader Award, 1964; named Companion of the Order of St. Michael and St. George, 1981.

WRITINGS: Early American-Australian Relations, Melbourne University Press, 1944; *The Future of Australian Federalism,* Melbourne University Press, 1946; (contributor) C. Hartley Grattan, editor, *Australia,* University of California, 1947; (contributor) *Federalism in Australia,* Wadley & Ginn, 1949; (editor and contributor) *Australia: A Social and Political History,* Angus & Robertson, 1955, Praeger, 1956; (editor with Norman Harper, and contributor) *Australia in World Affairs,* F. W. Cheshire, Volume I, 1957, Volume II, 1963, Volume III, 1968, Volume IV, 1974; (editor and co-author) *Brisbane 1859-1959,* Oswald Ziegler, 1959.

The Modern World, Volume I, Angus & Robertson, 1964; *Approaches to Asia: Australian Postwar Policies and Attitudes,* McGraw, 1974; (co-editor and contributor) *Design for Diversity: Library Services for Higher Education and Research in Australia,* Queensland University Press, 1977; (co-editor and contributor) *Documents on Australian International Affairs, 1901-14,* Nelson, 1977. Contributor to professional journals. Editor of *Australian Journal of Politics and History*.

AVOCATIONAL INTERESTS: Literature, drama, sports, travel (has traveled in Europe, Asia, and the United States).

* * *

GREWDEAD, Roy
See GOREY, Edward (St. John)

GRIFALCONI, Ann 1929-

PERSONAL: Surname is pronounced "*Grih*-fal-koh-nee"; born September 22, 1929, in New York, N.Y.; daughter of Joseph and Mary Hays (a writer; maiden name, Weik) Grifalconi. *Education:* Cooper Union Art School, certificate in advertising art, 1950; attended University of Cincinnati, 1951; New York University, B.S., 1954. *Home:* 124 Waverly Pl., New York, N.Y. 10011.

CAREER: Artist and designer in advertising and display, 1950-54; High School of Fashion Industry, New York City, teacher of art and display, 1954-65; full-time free-lance artist and illustrator, largely in children's book field, 1965—; Media Plus, Inc., New York City, owner and president, 1968—; owner and producer, Grey Falcon House, New York City. *Awards, honors: New York Times* Best Illustrated Book of 1968 and Newbery Award Honor Book, both for *The Jazz Man; New York Times* citation and Ad Club Best Designed Book award, both for *The Ballad of the Burglar of Babylon*.

WRITINGS—Juveniles, except as indicated; author and illustrator: (With Ruth Jacobsen) *Camping through Europe by Car, with Maximum Fun at Minimum Cost* (travelogue), Crown, 1963; *City Rhythms,* Bobbs-Merrill, 1965; *The Toy Trumpet: Story and Pictures,* Bobbs-Merrill, 1968; *The Matter with Lucy: An Album,* Bobbs-Merrill, 1973.

Illustrator: Rhoda Bacmeister, *Voices in the Night,* Bobbs-Merrill, 1965; Ina B. Forbus, *Tawny's Trick,* Viking, 1965; Gladys Tabor, *Still Meadow Cookbook,* Lippincott, 1965; O. Arnold, *Hidden Treasures of the Wild West,* Abelard, 1966; Margaret Embry, *Peg-Leg-Willy,* Holiday House, 1966; Edwin Palmer Hoyt, *American Steamboat Stories,* Abelard, 1966; De Luca, editor, *Italian Poetry Selections,* Harvey House, 1966; Mary Hays Weik (Grifalconi's mother), *The Jazz Man,* Atheneum, 1966; N. Zimmelman, *Pepito,* Reilly & Lee, 1967; Tillie S. Pine and Joseph Levine, *The Africans Knew,* McGraw, 1967; Johanna Johnston, *A Special Bravery,* Dodd, 1967; E. S. Lampman, *Half-Breed,* Doubleday, 1967; Louise A. Steintorf, *The Treasure of Tolmec,* John Day, 1967; Barbara Reid, *Carlo's Cricket,* McGraw, 1967.

Pine and Levine, *The Incas Knew,* McGraw, 1968; Pine and Levine, *The Maya Knew,* McGraw, 1968; B. Byars, *Midnight Fox,* Viking, 1968; John and Sara Westbrook Brewton, compilers, *America Forever New,* Crowell, 1968; Bronson Potter, *Antonio,* Atheneum, 1968; Chekov, *Shadows and Light,* translated by M. Morton, Doubleday, 1968; Elizabeth Bishop, *The Ballad of the Burglar of Babylon,* Farrar, Straus, 1968; Anne Norris Baldwin, *Sunflowers for Tina,* Doubleday, 1969; Ruby Zagoren, *Venture for Freedom,* World Publishing, 1969; Lois Kalb Bouchard, *The Boy Who Wouldn't Talk,* Doubleday, 1969; Langston Hughes, *Don't You Turn Back: Poems,* edited by Lee Bennett Hopkins, Knopf, 1969.

Hopkins, *This Street's for Me!,* Crown, 1970; Lorenz B. Graham, *David He No Fear,* Crowell, 1971; Walter Dean Myers, *The Dragon Takes a Wife,* Bobbs-Merrill, 1972; Toby Talbot, *The Night of the Radishes,* Putnam, 1972; Weik, *A House on Liberty Street,* Atheneum, 1972; John Lonzo Anderson, *The Day the Hurricane Happened,* Scribner, 1974; Lucille Clifton, *Everett Anderson's Year,* Holt, 1974; Ann McGovern, *The Secret Soldier,* Four Winds Press, 1975; Letta Schatz, *Banji's Magic Wheel,* Follett, 1975; Clifton, *Everett Anderson's Friend,* Holt, 1976; Clifton, *Everett Anderson's 1 2 3,* Holt, 1977; Clifton,

Everett Anderson's Nine Month Long, Holt, 1978; Genevieve S. Gray, *How Far, Felipe?,* Harper, 1978.

Also author of screenplays, "The House on Liberty Street" series (based on her mother's book, *A House on Liberty Street,* which Grifalconi illustrated), and "The Jazz Man" (based on her mother's book of the same title, which Grifalconi illustrated). Also illustrator of other books.

WORK IN PROGRESS: Illustrating books.

AVOCATIONAL INTERESTS: Singing, playing the guitar, photography, archaeology.

BIOGRAPHICAL/CRITICAL SOURCES: Lee Bennett Hopkins, *Books Are by People,* Citation Press, 1969.

* * *

GRIFFIN, A(rthur) H(arold) 1911-

PERSONAL: Born January 15, 1911, in Liverpool, England; son of James Arthur (a decorator) and Annie Elizabeth (Jackson) Griffin; married Mollie Barker, October 23, 1937; children: Robin M. M., Sandra E. *Education:* Attended Barrow Grammar School. *Home:* Cunswick End, Plumgarths, Kendal, Cumbria, England.

CAREER: Journalist in England on weekly newspapers, 1928-32, *Lancashire Evening Post,* 1932-37, *Daily Mail,* Manchester, and other papers, 1937-46, and *Lancashire Evening Post,* Kendal, 1946-76. Free-lance journalist and writer for radio and television; authority on English Lake District. *Military service:* British Army, 1940-46; became lieutenant colonel. *Member:* Rotary Club of Kendal (past president), various climbing and skiing clubs.

WRITINGS—Published by R. Hale, except as indicated: *Inside the Real Lakeland,* Guardian Press, 1961; *In Mountain Lakeland,* Guardian Press, 1963; *Pageant of Lakeland,* 1966; *The Roof of England,* 1968; *Still the Real Lakeland,* 1970; *Long Days in the Hills,* 1974; *A Lakeland Notebook,* 1975; *A Year in the Fells,* 1976; *Freeman of the Hills,* 1978; *Adventuring in Lakeland,* 1980. Contributor to "Country Diary" in *Guardian* for more than thirty years (*Pageant of Lakeland* is based on these contributions); also contributor to other newspapers, and climbing, skiing, and other outdoor magazines.

AVOCATIONAL INTERESTS: Travel and exploration, particularly in mountain areas, mountaineering, skiing, music.

* * *

GRIFFIN, Gerald G(ehrig) 1933-

PERSONAL: Born April 13, 1933, in Flint, Mich.; son of Jasper Cokelen (a tool and die setter) and Lillian (O'Toole) Griffin; married Sally Atkinson, August 10, 1951 (divorced, 1959); married Patricia A. Wilbur (a marriage and family counselor), July 23, 1965; children: (first marriage) Gregory, John, Diane (stepdaughter). *Education:* General Motors Institute, B.B.A., 1956; Flint Junior College, A.S., 1959; Michigan State University, M.A., 1963, Ph.D., 1966. *Home and office:* 2260 Powers Ferry Dr. N.E., Marietta, Ga. 30067.

CAREER: Fuller Brush Co., Saginaw, Mich., field manager, 1960-61; Ionia State Hospital, Ionia, Mich., clinical psychologist, 1963-65; private practice as consulting psychologist, 1966—. Member of board of directors, Pro Data, Inc., 1955-56. Consultant to Bobby Dodd Workshop, 1967-72, and Walden University, 1972—. *Member:* National Rehabilitation Association, American Psychological Association, American Association of Marriage and Family Counselors, American Psychologists in Private Practice, Georgia Psychological Association, Georgia Psychologists in Private Practice, Alabama Psychological Association.

WRITINGS: The Silent Misery: Why Marriages Fail, C. C Thomas, 1974; (contributor) Richard Hardy and John Cull, editors, *Deciding on Divorce,* C. C Thomas, 1974; *The Corruptors,* Condor Publishing, 1977; (with Robin Moore) *The Death Disciple,* Condor Publishing, 1978; (with Moore) *The Last Coming,* Condor Publishing, 1978. Contributor to *Detroit Free Press, American Personnel and Guidance Journal,* and *Highway Magazine.*

WORK IN PROGRESS: Comin' To: And Making Your Next Marriage a Success; a novel, *The Conversation Piece.*†

* * *

GRIMSHAW, Allen Day 1929-

PERSONAL: Born December 16, 1929, in New York, N.Y.; son of Austin (a professor) and Elizabeth (Thompson) Grimshaw; married Polly Ann Swift (a librarian), June 3, 1952; children: Gail Elizabeth (deceased), Andrew Swift, Adam Thompson. *Education:* Attended Purdue University, 1946-48; University of Missouri, A.B., 1950, M.A., 1952; University of Pennsylvania, Ph.D., 1959. *Home:* 4001 Morningside Dr., Bloomington, Ind. 47401. *Office:* Department of Sociology, Indiana University, Bloomington, Ind. 47401.

CAREER: Indiana University, Bloomington, instructor, 1959-61, assistant professor, 1961-65, associate professor, 1965-69, professor of sociology, 1969—, director of Institute for Comparative Sociology, 1966-69. Visiting associate professor at University of California, Berkeley, 1968-69. Consultant to numerous institutions, including American Council of Learned Societies, National Endowment for the Humanities, National Institute for Mental Health, National Institute for Child Health and Development, National Science Foundation, and Social Science Research Council. *Military service:* U.S. Air Force Reserve, 1952-54.

MEMBER: International Sociological Association, Linguistic Association of Canada and the U.S., American Sociological Association (fellow), American Anthropological Association (fellow), Association for Asian Studies (life member), Linguistic Society of America, American Association for the Advancement of Science (fellow), Peace Research Society, American Association of University Professors (president of Indiana University, Bloomington chapter, 1970-71), North Central Sociological Association, Pacific Sociological Association, Phi Beta Kappa, Alpha Pi Zeta, Alpha Kappa Delta. *Awards, honors:* American Institute of Indian Studies faculty research fellow, 1962-63; National Institute of Mental Health research grant, 1964-66; National Science Foundation research grant, 1975.

WRITINGS: (Editor and contributor) *Racial Violence in the United States,* Aldine, 1969; (editor with J. Michael Armer, and contributor) *Comparative Social Research: Methodological Problems and Strategies,* Wiley, 1973; (editor) *Language as Social Resource,* Stanford University Press, 1981.

Contributor: Raymond J. Murphy and Howard Elison, editors, *Problems and Prospects of the Negro Movement,* Wadsworth Publishing, 1961; Kimball Young and Ray Mack, editors, *Principles of Sociology: A Reader in Theory and Research,* 3rd edition (Grimshaw was not associated with earlier editions), American Book Co., 1965; Stanley Lieberson, editor, *Explorations in Sociolinguistics,* Indiana University Research Center in Anthropology, Folklore, and Linguistics, 1966; Louis H. Massotti and Don R. Bowen, editors, *Riots and Rebellion: Civil Violence in the Urban Community,* Sage Publications, 1968; Simon Dinitz and others, editors, *Deviance: Studies in the Process of Stigmatization and Social Reaction,* Oxford University Press, 1969; Doris Y. Wilkinson, editor, *Black Revolt: Strategies of Protest,* McCutchan, 1969.

Dell Hymes, editor, *Pidginization and Creolization of Languages,* Cambridge University Press, 1971; Joshua A. Fishman, editor, *Advances in the Sociology of Language,* Mouton & Co., 1971; James F. Short and Marvin E. Wolfgang, editors, *Collective Violence,* Aldine, 1972; Bernhard Badura and Klaus Gloy, editors, *Soziologie der Kommunikation* (title means "Sociology of Communication"), F. F. Verlag Gunther Holzboog, 1972; Roger W. Shuy, editor, *Twenty-Third Annual Round Table, Monograph Series on Language and Linguistics,* Georgetown University Press, 1973; Wilbur Schramm, Ithiel Pool, Nathan Maccoby, Edwin Parker, Frederick Frey, and Leonard Fein, editors, *Handbook of Communication,* Rand McNally, 1973; Richard A. Bauman and Joel Sherzer, editors, *Explorations in the Ethnography of Speaking,* Cambridge University Press, 1974; Catherine Snow and Charles A. Ferguson, editors, *Talking to Children: Language Input and Acquisition,* Cambridge University Press, 1977; Uta Quasthoff, editor, *Sprachstruktur-Sozialstruktur: Zur Linguistischen Theorienbildung,* Skriptor, 1978.

Paul Werth, editor, *Conversation, Speech and Discourse,* Croom-Helm, 1981; Morris Rosenberg and others, editors, *Sociological Perspectives on Social Psychology,* Basic Books, 1981. Contributor of more than fifty articles and reviews to professional journals. Editor, *American Sociologist,* 1976-78; associate editor, *Journal of Conflict Resolution,* 1967-71, *American Sociological Review,* 1970-73, *Language in Society,* 1971—, and *Sociometry,* 1974-75.

WORK IN PROGRESS: Sociolinguistics: An Introduction; research on conflict theories, on continuing language socialization, and on analytic frames for verbal interaction.

AVOCATIONAL INTERESTS: Squash.

* * *

GRODE, Redway
See GOREY, Edward (St. John)

* * *

GROSS, Bertram M(yron) 1912-

PERSONAL: Born December 25, 1912, in Philadelphia, Pa.; son of Samuel and Regina Gross; married Nora Faine, September 4, 1938 (divorced, 1979); married Kusum Singh, March 10, 1979; children: (first marriage) David, Larry, Samuel, Theodore. *Education:* University of Pennsylvania, B.A., 1933, M.A., 1935. *Office:* Urban Affairs Department, Hunter College of the City University of New York, New York, N.Y. 10021.

CAREER: U.S. Government, Washington, D.C., 1938-53, held various posts, including research and hearings director, Senate Committee on Small Business, 1942-43, staff director, Senate Military Affairs Subcommittee on War Contracts, 1943-44, economic adviser, Senate Banking and Currency Committee, 1945-46, executive secretary, Council of Economic Advisers to the President, 1946-51, chairman of National Capital Regional Planning Council, 1952-53; economic adviser to government of Israel, Jerusalem, 1953-56; Hebrew University of Jerusalem, Jerusalem, external lecturer, 1955-56, visiting professor of administration, 1956-60; Syracuse University, Maxwell School of Citizenship and Public Affairs, Syracuse, N.Y., professor of administration, 1960-68; Wayne State University, Detroit, Mich., director of Urban Studies Center, 1968-69; Hunter College of the City University of New York, New York, N.Y., Distinguished Professor of Urban Affairs, 1970—. Visiting professor at University of California, Berkeley, 1962, and at Harvard University, 1962-63. Member and vice-chairman of Arlington County Planning Commission, 1950-52. Consultant to United Nations Korean Reconstruction Administration, 1952-53, El Al (Israel national airlines), 1956-57, 1959, Ford Foundation and Indian Institute of Public Administration, 1961, secretary of Department of Health, Education, and Welfare, 1966-67.

MEMBER: American Political Science Association (chairman, committee on political parties), American Society for Public Administration. *Awards, honors:* Woodrow Wilson Foundation Award for best book of the year in the field of government and democracy, 1953, for *The Legislative Struggle: A Study in Social Combat;* Center for Advanced Study in the Behavioral Sciences fellowship, 1961-62; Social Science Research Council faculty research fellow, 1961-62; Mosher Award for best article in 1971, for "Planning in an Era of Social Revolution."

WRITINGS: The Home That Jack's Building (marionette play; produced at Philadelphia Federal Theatre), U.S. Housing Authority, 1939; (with others) *Toward a More Responsible Two-Party System,* Rinehart, 1950; *The Legislative Struggle: A Study in Social Combat,* McGraw, 1953; (with Will Lumer) *The Hard Money Crusade,* Public Affairs Press, 1954; (contributor) Richard W. Taylor, editor, *Life, Language, Law: Essays in Honor of Arthur E. Bentley,* Antioch Press, 1957.

(Contributor) Lewis A. Dexter and David M. White, editors, *People, Society and Mass Communications,* Free Press of Glencoe, 1964; (contributor) Jesse Burkhead, *Public School Finance: Economics and Politics,* Syracuse University Press, 1964; *The Managing of Organizations: The Administrative Struggle,* two volumes, Free Press of Glencoe, 1964, condensed edition published in one volume as *Organizations and Their Managing,* Free Press, 1968; *The State of the Nation: Systems Accounting,* Tavistock Press, 1966; *The Administration of Economic Development Planning: Principles and Fallacies* (booklet), United Nations, 1966; *Friendly Fascism: The New Face of Power in America,* M. Evans, 1980.

Editor: *Action under Planning: The Guidance of Economic Development,* McGraw, 1967; *A Great Society?,* Basic Books, 1968; *Social Intelligence for America's Future: Explorations in Societal Problems,* Allyn & Bacon, 1969; (with Herman Mertins) *Symposium on Changing Styles of Planning in Post-Industrial America,* American Society for Public Administration, 1971.

Also author of legislation, "Employment Act of 1946" and original "Humphrey-Hawkins Full Employment Act of 1978"; author of *Mutsre ha-minhal,* 1964, and *Planning against Poverty: Guided Development in Poor Nations,* 1965. Editor of National Planning Series, Syracuse University, 1965-68; special editor of *The Annals,* American Academy of Political and Social Science, 1967 and 1970. Contributor to *Encyclopedia of the Social Sciences;* contributor to periodicals, including

American Political Science Review, Challenge, Public Administration, Social Policy, and *Nation.*

WORK IN PROGRESS: People against Charisma, with wife, Kusum Singh; *Full Employment Planning from the Bottom Sideways.*

SIDELIGHTS: In *Friendly Fascism: The New Face of Power in America,* Bertram M. Gross explores "the interpenetration of Big Business and Big Government" in the United States, according to J. Hoberman in the *Village Voice.* Richard Streicker, writing in the *Los Angeles Times Book Review,* says that Gross's "central thesis is elegant, comprehensive and alarming: Control of our national life is increasingly in the hands of a big business-big government partnership that does our planning, defines our jobs, creates (or destroys) our environment . . . and defines our political choices." In the *New York Review of Books,* Jason Epstein finds *Friendly Fascism: The New Face of Power in America* "interesting in so far as it reflects what seems to be a widespread feeling among liberals as well as conservatives that democracy in America has played itself out: that soon Americans won't be able to govern themselves."

BIOGRAPHICAL/CRITICAL SOURCES: New York Times Book Review, June 8, 1980, August 3, 1980; *Washington Post Book World,* July 20, 1980; *Village Voice,* July 30, 1980; *Los Angeles Times Book Review,* August 17, 1980; *New York Review of Books,* October 23, 1980.

* * *

GROSSKURTH, Phyllis 1924-

PERSONAL: Born March 16, 1924, in Toronto, Ontario, Canada; daughter of Milton Palmer (an actuary) and Winifred (Owen) Langstaff; married Robert A. Grosskurth (a naval commander); married Mavor Moore, May, 1968 (divorced February, 1980); children: (first marriage) Christopher, Brian, Ann. *Education:* University of Toronto, B.A., 1946; University of Ottawa, M.A., 1960; University of London, Ph.D., 1962. *Religion:* Church of England. *Home:* 147 Spruce St., Toronto, Ontario, Canada M5A 26J. *Agent:* David Higham Associates Ltd., 5-8 Lower John St., London W1R 4HA, England. *Office:* Department of English, University College, University of Toronto, Toronto, Ontario, Canada M5S 1A8.

CAREER: Carleton University, Ottawa, Ontario, lecturer, 1964-65; University of Toronto, Toronto, Ontario, assistant professor of English, 1965—. Honorary research fellow, University College, University of London. *Member:* P.E.N. *Awards, honors:* Governor General's Literary Award for nonfiction and University of Columbia Medal for Biography, both for *John Addington Symonds: A Biography.*

WRITINGS: John Addington Symonds: A Biography, Longmans, Green, 1964, published as *The Woeful Victorian,* Holt, 1965; *Notes on Browning's Works,* [Toronto], 1967; *Leslie Stephen,* Longmans, Green, for National Book League and British Council, 1968; *Gabrielle Roy,* edited by William French, Forum House, 1969; *Havelock Ellis: A Biography,* Knopf, 1980. Contributor to periodicals, including *New York Review of Books* and *Times Literary Supplement.* Literary editor of *Canadian Forum,* 1975-76.

WORK IN PROGRESS: A biography of Melanie Klein.

SIDELIGHTS: In *Havelock Ellis: A Biography,* Phyllis Grosskurth documents the life of this pioneer in the study of human sexuality. Havelock Ellis (1859-1939) is best known for his six-volume work, *Studies in the Psychology of Sex,* written between 1897 and 1910, which was, according to Steven Marcus in a *New York Times Book Review* article, "the first relatively successful serious and scholarly effort in English to achieve the open-minded, liberal, tolerant, positive and encouraging view of human sexual behavior" characteristic of the modern attitude toward the subject.

Grosskurth based this biography on extensive research, which included reading more than 20,000 letters written by Ellis himself. Stuart Hampshire reviews the book in the *Times Literary Supplement,* commenting on the amount of Grosskurth's work: "The author's research and documentation are formidably complete. . . . Here one has the whole of Havelock Ellis, known and knowable, and the story of his life is told in a lively and engaging style, with excellent descriptions of the persons . . . who played a part in the life of this withdrawn, but far from solitary, thinker."

"Professor Grosskurth's biography is indispensable and . . . provides the reader with all the information necessary to make a private judgement" of Ellis, says Robert Kirsch in the *Los Angeles Times.* "Yet, for all the careful research, the massive detail which has gone into this work, there is, at times, a lack of sympathy for Ellis . . . which makes the portrait of [him] . . . seem cool and cerebral." Marcus, however, stresses the significance of Grosskurth's biography. "When one finishes her book," he says, "one has a strongly renewed sense of what heroic efforts were involved in the passage of Western culture from the 19th century into modernity. Ellis was an important figure in this evolutionary transformation, and it is right that his work should not be forgotten."

BIOGRAPHICAL/CRITICAL SOURCES: New York Times, May 8, 1980; *Los Angeles Times,* May 12, 1980; *Chicago Tribune Book World,* May 25, 1980; *New York Times Book Review,* June 22, 1980; *London Times,* July 17, 1980; *Washington Post Book World,* July 20, 1980; *Times Literary Supplement,* November 28, 1980.

* * *

GRUBER, Gary R. 1940-

PERSONAL: Born November 19, 1940, in New York, N.Y.; married; two children. *Education:* City College of the City University of New York, B.S. (with honors), 1962; Columbia University, M.A., 1964; Yeshiva University, Ph.D., 1969. *Address:* P.O. Box 657, Mill Valley, Calif. 94941.

CAREER: Author; developer and producer of research, learning, and testing programs. Cambridge University Press, New York, N.Y., chief editor in physics and mathematics, 1969; Hofstra University, Hempstead, Long Island, N.Y., assistant professor of physics and astronomy and director of astronomy and mathematical physics, 1969-73, senior research scientist, 1973-74. Director of public affairs and the public understanding of science, New York Academy of Sciences, 1973-74. Senior projects director, Center for the Study of Instruction, Harcourt, Brace, Jovanovich, Inc., 1976-77. Consultant to Prentice-Hall, John Wiley & Sons, and Oxford University Press, 1969—. Has developed and conducted Scholastic Aptitude Test preparation courses. Lecturer on education and science to seminars, universities, and research institutes. Has appeared on numerous radio and television programs.

MEMBER: American Physical Society, American Association for the Advancement of Science, American Mathematical Society, American Astronomical Society, American Association of Physics Teachers, American Association of University Professors, National Association of Science Writers. *Awards, honors:* Research fellowship, University of Glasgow, 1966-68; National Science Foundation grant, 1971-72.

WRITINGS—Published by Simon & Schuster, except as indicated: *Physics,* Monarch, 1971; *High School Equivalency Examination Test,* 1971, 3rd updated edition, 1976; *General Mathematical Ability,* 1971; *Correctness and Effectiveness of Expression,* 1971; *Reading Interpretation in the Natural Sciences and Literature,* 1971; (with Edward C. Gruber) *Graduate Record Examination Aptitude Test: A Complete Review for the Verbal and Math Parts of the Test,* 1971, 3rd updated edition, 1976; (with E. C. Gruber) *Test of English as a Foreign Language,* Monarch, 1973, 6th updated edition, 1982; *College-Level Examination Program,* Monarch, 1973, 2nd updated edition, 1979; *Standard Written English Test,* 1974; *American College Testing Programs for College Entrance,* 1974; *Graduate Management Admissions Test,* 1975; *Professional and Administrative Career Program for the Federal Government,* 1976; *New Medical College Admission Test,* Contemporary Books, 1977; (with E. C. Gruber and Barry S. Willdorf) *Law School Admission Test,* Monarch, 1977, 2nd updated edition, 1979; *Scholastic Aptitude Test,* Contemporary Books, 1978.

Math Review for the Graduate Management Admission Test, Monarch, 1982; *Shortcuts and Strategies for the Graduate Management Admission Test,* Monarch, 1982; *Shortcuts and Strategies for the Graduate Record Examination,* Monarch, 1982; *Inside Strategies for the SAT,* Educational Design, 1982. Contributor of articles to journals.

WORK IN PROGRESS: "I am presently working on a project which I believe will necessitate the restructuring of all learning and thinking educational methods, nationally."

SIDELIGHTS: Recognized as an expert in the field of educational testing, Gary R. Gruber is the author of over twenty examination preparation manuals and of special examination review courses. Arville Finacom, writing in the *Daly City Record,* explains that "Gruber's activities today involve preparing high school and college students to confront and conquer the battery of aptitude tests challenging them on successive steps of the academic ladder."

In his book *Inside Strategies for the SAT* Gruber writes that the Scholastic Aptitude Test, "which is supposed to measure verbal and math aptitude, is perhaps the most important exam anyone can take: This one test can determine a person's future career and his or her goals for a lifetime. The SAT is supposed to be an indicator of the intelligence and aptitude of the nation's young people, just as the Dow Jones Average is an indicator of the nation's economic health. . . . With colleges now increasing their standards, it is extremely important for a student to do well on this exam."

According to *Independent Journal*'s Mark Whittington, "Gruber gives the students an overview of the tests and teaches them strategies and shortcuts. But the key is practicing those techniques. The kids who improve the most are those who practice at home." However, Finacom believes that Gruber's strategies do more than just prepare students for a single test. He points out that "the skills Gruber teaches are those of critical thinking, analytical methods applicable easily to any number of problem solving situations in home or business as well as school. In effect, students who master Gruber's modes find themselves well prepared for the conditions and transactions they must approach objectively as they move through academic, career and personal futures."

Noting that average SAT scores have declined steadily over the past two decades, Gruber believes that the average scores would be even lower if the Educational Testing Service had not revised the exam over the years to make it simpler. As Gruber told the *Pacific Sun:* "Actually, I'll bet if you took a ten-year-old exam and used it instead of today's exam, the average score would be 300 instead of 400. . . . The verbal scores are low because kids don't read that much anymore. The math scores are declining because kids have been memorizing the math; then when they take the SAT and haven't had algebra or geometry for two years they're in trouble." Gruber continues: "The ironic thing is I think today's kids are as bright if not brighter than [their parents]. They're more alert, more aware of politics. The kids today seem to want to be entertained more than ever. . . . What kids don't realize—and here is the tragedy—is that work isn't necessarily tedious . . . that the process can be enjoyable. The kids are missing out on the enjoyment of working."

BIOGRAPHICAL/CRITICAL SOURCES: Daly City Record, July 23, 1980; *San Francisco Chronicle,* February 21, 1981; *Independent Journal,* March 21-22, 1981; *Pacific Sun,* August 21-27, 1981; *Chicago Tribune,* September 29, 1981; *Los Angeles Times,* November 29, 1981; *Detroit News,* October 3, 1982; *Houston Chronicle,* October 3, 1982; Gary R. Gruber, *Inside Strategies for the SAT,* Educational Design, 1982.

* * *

GRUMBACH, Doris (Isaac) 1918-

PERSONAL: Born July 12, 1918, in New York, N.Y.; daughter of Leonard William and Helen Isaac; married Leonard Grumbach (a professor of physiology), October 15, 1941 (divorced, 1972); children: Barbara, Jane, Elizabeth, Kathryn. *Education:* Washington Square College, A.B., 1939; Cornell University, M.A., 1940. *Home:* 2748 Stephenson Lane N.W., Washington, D.C. 20015. *Agent:* Maxine Groffsky, 2 Fifth Ave., New York, N.Y. 10011. *Office:* Department of English, American University, Washington, D.C. 20016.

CAREER: Metro-Goldwyn-Mayer, New York City, title writer, 1940-41; *Mademoiselle,* New York City, proofreader, copy editor, 1941-42; Time Inc., associate editor of *Architectural Forum,* 1942-43; Albany Academy for Girls, Albany, N.Y., English teacher, 1952-55; College of Saint Rose, Albany, instructor, 1955-58, assistant professor, 1958-60, associate professor, 1960-69, professor of English, 1969-73; *New Republic,* Washington, D.C., literary editor, 1973-75; American University, Washington, D.C., professor of American literature, 1975—. Visiting University fellow, Empire State College, 1972-73; adjunct professor of English, University of Maryland, 1974-75. Critic; book reviewer, "Morning Edition," National Public Radio, 1982—. *Military service:* U.S. Navy, W.A.V.E.S., 1941-43. *Member:* American Association of University Professors, P.E.N., Phi Beta Kappa.

WRITINGS: The Spoil of the Flowers (novel), Doubleday, 1962; *The Short Throat, the Tender Mouth* (novel), Doubleday, 1964; *The Company She Kept,* Coward, 1967; (contributor) James O'Gara, editor, *The Postconcilor Parish,* Kenedy, 1967; (contributor) Silvia E. Kameran, editor, *Book Reviewing,* Writer, Inc., 1978; *Chamber Music* (novel), Dutton, 1979; *The Missing Person* (novel), Putnam, 1981.

Columnist for *Critic,* 1960-64, and *National Catholic Reporter,* 1968—; author of nonfiction column for *New York Times Book Review,* 1976—, column, "Fine Print," for *Sat-*

urday Review, 1977-78, and fiction column, for *Chronicle of Higher Education*, 1979—. Contributor of reviews and criticism to periodicals, including *New York Times Book Review*, *Chicago Tribune*, *Commonweal*, *Los Angeles Times*, *Nation*, *Washington Post*, *Washington Star*, and *New Republic*. Contributing editor, *New Republic*, 1971-73.

WORK IN PROGRESS: A novel, *The Magician's Girl;* a literary biography of Willa Cather.

SIDELIGHTS: Doris Grumbach, a respected literary critic, made a splash in the publishing world with her book on author Mary McCarthy. *The Company She Kept*, Grumbach's literary biography of the acerbic novelist, became the subject of a threatened lawsuit before its publication and of a volatile critical debate after its release.

The Company She Kept parallels events and characters in McCarthy's novels with those in her life. "The fiction of Mary McCarthy is autobiographical to an extraordinary degree, in the widest sense of autobiography," Grumbach explains in the foreword to her book. "In the case of Mary McCarthy there is only a faint line between what really happened to her, the people she knew and knows, including herself, and the characters in her fictions." To prepare the biography, Grumbach spent a year reading McCarthy's work and criticism of it and interviewed the author extensively at her Paris home.

Difficulties with McCarthy arose, Grumbach says, when McCarthy, who suggested she read the galleys of the book to catch any factual errors, protested against some of the information Grumbach had included in the manuscript. In a *New York Times Book Review* article on her dispute with McCarthy, Grumbach reports that McCarthy had voluntarily provided her with intimate biographical details in conversation and in a detailed memorandum. McCarthy's anger over their inclusion therefore came as a surprise, says Grumbach. "I was unprepared for the fury of her response when she saw the galleys . . . and realized that I had used the autobiographical details she had, as she said, given me," commented Grumbach. "She had said, once, that it felt strange to have a book written about one, 'a book that includes you as a person, not just a critical analysis of your writings.' Now she insisted that the *curriculum vitae* had been sent to be 'drawn upon,' not used, although just how this was to be done continues to be a mystery to me. . . . [McCarthy's] feeling was that the tapes and her letters to me had been intended solely for 'your own enlightenment.'"

For all the attendant publicity, however, *The Company She Kept* was not well received by the literary establishment. Writes Stephanie Harrington in *Commonweal:* "To anyone who has read *The Company She Kept*, . . . the newspaper stories that followed the book's publication must have seemed too preposterous to be anything but a desperate attempt by the publisher's publicity department to drum up business for a clinker."

A *Times Literary Supplement* reviewer, who describes *The Company She Kept* as "sparkily written and often critically sharp," feels that Grumbach falls short of her stated goal of "weaving one fabric of [the] diverse threads of McCarthy's biography and her fiction." Grumbach, says the critic, "never fully succeeds in dramatizing the complex interactions that go into such a process; [therefore, *The Company She Kept*] is likely to end up as required reading for gossips." Ellen Moers in *New York Times Book Review* does not argue the validity of Grumbach's attempt to find the fact in Mary McCarthy's fiction—the process of "set[ting] out to name names," as Moers calls it—but instead claims that Grumbach misreads McCarthy and thus arrives at erroneous conclusions. To Grumbach's statement that "there is only a faint line" between fact and fiction for McCarthy, Moers responds: "This simply cannot be true. The husbands in McCarthy fiction . . . are such dreary mediocrities, her artist colonies and political oases are so bare of talent or distinction, her suites of college girls are so tediously third-rate—only a powerful imagination could have made such nonentities out of the very interesting company that Mary McCarthy actually kept."

Harrington considers Grumbach's autobiographical approach to McCarthy's fiction "a cliche." Grumbach, says Harrington, "deals with the body of critical writing about Mary McCarthy through a disturbingly superficial cataloguing technique, juxtaposing bits and snatches from critics who fall into the over-enthusiastic category with those in the over-critical category. Her own comments, which add little to the analytical dialogue, seem to be there because she realizes that she is supposed to do *something* besides quote other critics and give us biographical information we have already gotten from the books by, articles about, and interviews of, Mary McCarthy."

However, *Saturday Review* critic Granville Hicks does not find Grumbach's approach to her subject objectionable and approves of her straightforward manner in tackling it. "Although there is nothing novel about finding Miss McCarthy in her books, critics are usually cautious about identifying characters in fiction with real people, and I am grateful for Mrs. Grumbach's refusal to beat around that particular bush," Hicks says.

Hicks also notes that he is glad that *The Company She Kept* is free of "academic jargon," but adds that he wishes some of the "machinery of scholarship—a bibliography, certainly, and at least a few notes to identify the less obvious sources of information"—were included in the McCarthy biography. Other critics also comment on the omission of footnotes and bibliography, and Moers claims that their absence vitiates the value of *The Company She Kept* as a "sympathetic chronological reading of the McCarthy opus and a [source of] a little information about the circumstances of composition." In addition, Moers calls Grumbach's justification of her heavy reliance on McCarthy herself as her source of information "the familiar nonsense of the lazy biographer . . . that her subject 'is her own best researcher, her own most honest biographer.'" In the *New York Times Book Review* article, Grumbach states that "not one whit of [the information] was the result of underhanded scurrying about to friends, underhanded questioning of former husbands or lovers or enemies." This statement, claims Harrington, causes Grumbach to convict "herself out of her own mouth of gross negligence as a biographer-critic." "Her scruples about being 'underhanded' and 'scurrying about' to obtain information from others besides her subject may be admirable in the context of a personal relationship, but they are certainly inimical to the kind of scholarship that produces first-rate biography or serious literary criticism when that criticism, as in this case, rests on the premise that the work under discussion 'is autobiographical to an extraordinary degree,'" writes Harrington.

In the wake of the harsh reviews *The Company She Kept* received, Grumbach tried to deflect some of that criticism from herself by explaining the circumstances leading to her decision to write the McCarthy biography. Explaining in the *New York Times Book Review* that she was asked to write the book on McCarthy, rather than instigating the project herself, Grumbach states, "An editor asks, somewhere in the inner room of a dim New York restaurant, would you do a book on Her?

And because you do not ordinarily eat and drink such sumptuous lunches in the proximate company of so many successful-looking people, and because you need the money, and because after all, She *is* a good writer (you've *always* thought this) and apparently a *fascinating* woman, you say yes, I will." Comments Harrington: "Mrs. Grumbach's apologia in the *Times* . . . [indicates] that it was foolhardy to expect a serious piece of work in the first place when she only decided to take on Mary McCarthy because an editor asked 'somewhere in the inner room of a dim New York restaurant, would you do a book on Her?'"

Recognizing the shortcomings of *The Company She Kept,* Grumbach summarizes her difficulties with the book in *New York Times Book Review:* "The value of the whole experience lies, for me," she says, "in the recognition of how difficult, even well-nigh impossible, it is to write a book that deals with a living person. It does not matter in the least that the living person is willing to assist the writer (beware the Greeks bearing . . .) in conversation or letter; the fact remains, the law being what it is, the subject can give with one hand, take back with the other, and in this process of literary Indian-giving the writer is virtually helpless."

Ten years after publishing *The Company She Kept* and fifteen years after writing her novels, *The Short Throat, the Tender Mouth* and *The Spoil of the Flowers,* Grumbach returned to fiction. Her first novel after the hiatus was *Chamber Music,* written as the memoirs of ninety year-old Caroline MacLaren, widow of a famous composer and founder of an artists' colony in his memory. Released with a 20,000 copy first printing and a $20,000 promotional campaign, *Chamber Music* won the popular and critical acclaim that eluded Grumbach's earlier books. Peter Davison in *Atlantic Monthly* calls the book "artful, distinctive, provocative, [and] compassionate." *Chamber Music,* writes Victoria Glendinning in *Washington Post Book World,* "is a book of originality and distinction."

Chamber Music is the story of "the chamber of one heart," says Caroline MacLaren in the introduction to her memoirs. The novel's plot revolves around the subjugation of Caroline to her husband Robert and to Robert's music. Their marriage is a cold and barren one and *Chamber Music* charts its course through Robert's incestuous relationship with his mother, his homosexual affair with a student, and, finally, to his agonizing death in the tertiary stage of syphilis. Especially noted for its sensitive handling of its delicate subject matter and for its characterizations, *Chamber Music* is called by *New York Times*'s John Leonard, "one of those rare novels for adults who listen." The characters in *Chamber Music,* Leonard continues, "are all stringed instruments. The music we hear occurs in the chamber of Caroline's heart. It is quite beautiful." With her third novel, Grumbach "makes us hear the difficult music of grace," says Nicholas Delbanco in *New Republic.*

Although *Chamber Music*'s "revelations of sexuality are meant to shatter," as one *Publishers Weekly* critic comments, and the passage on Robert's illness gives "a clinical description so simply precise, so elegantly loathsome, that it would do nicely either in a medical text or in a book on style," as Edith Milton observes in *Yale Review,* it is the contrast between *Chamber Music*'s action and its language that gives the novel its impact. While much of the material in *Chamber Music* is meant to shock, the language is genteel and full of Victorian phrases. "What gives the main part of this book its polish and flavor is the contrast between matter and manner," says Glendinning. "Clarity and elegance of style account . . . for the distinction of *Chamber Music,*" writes Eleanor B. Wymard in *Commonweal,* and other critics have high praise for Grumbach's writing. A *Washington Post Book World* reviewer claims the book's language is "as direct and pure as a Hayden quartet" and Abigail McCarthy in *Commonweal* states that *Chamber Music* has "the classical form, clarity, and brilliance of a composition for strings." Because it is Caroline's story, the novel adopts her voice—a voice that is "slightly stilted, slightly vapid, of the genteel tradition," one *Atlantic* critic observes. Asserts Milton: "The novel is wonderfully written in [Caroline's] voice to evoke a time gone by, an era vanished. . . . The prose, understated, beautiful in its economies, supports a story of almost uncanny bleakness."

The use of a first person narrator is disturbing to some of *Chamber Music*'s reviewers. These critics find that Caroline's voice mars rather than enhances her story. Frances M. Esmonde de Usabel states in *Library Journal* that while "this poignant tale . . . is well and simply told, its retrospective tone and lack of drama lessen the reader's involvement in Caroline's long, lonely life." Writing in *Nation,* Vivian Gornick finds that Caroline's lack of self-understanding limits the depth to which the motives and personalities in *Chamber Music* can be explored. "Grumbach made [Caroline] a first-person narrator and then proceeded to write as though she herself knew no more than the character knew," states Gornick. "As the character was both a Victorian and a remarkably childish woman, insufficient in perception, depth, or self-understanding, much of what she 'knew' was banal, and when she thought she was being most revealing it was as though she were writing a letter to the editor: her confession remained buried inside the sealed surface of what often read like public prose."

Eleanor Wymard also finds that *Chamber Music*'s readers "experience and know only what Caroline herself does" and that because "Grumbach's point of view is so patently and consistently that of Caroline MacLaren[,] . . . the novel is essentially bankrupt." "By using diary form," Wymard continues, "Caroline MacLaren believes that she is drawing us into the mysterious territory of 'inner lives,' but, on the contrary, she seldom does. . . . By writing in the first person, Grumbach continually weakens the psychorealism of Caroline MacLaren. As narrator, [Caroline] simply does not probe the complexity of the subject matter which is herself."

Katha Pollitt, however, believes Caroline's narration to be less confining than do some of Grumbach's other critics. "The lush romanticism of her scenes—artistic self-destruction, late-awakened passion—is given an odd and provocative twist by the voice in which it is expressed: the dry, sad tones of a woman who has been in mourning for nigh on fifty years," Pollitt writes in *Ms.* "This is the point of the emotional deadness of her prose, which is full of words like 'murine' and 'inunction' and 'haptic.'" Paul Ableman in *Spectator* comments that Caroline's characteristic delicacy saves *Chamber Music* from the "exhibitionism and sensationalism that is almost ubiquitous, and usually artistically otiose, in fiction today." Ableman adds that "perhaps for this very reason, Miss Grumbach's book seems more real than much modern realism. . . . *Chamber Music* tells us all we need to know about the sexual behavior of its characters and yet . . . seems decorous." Says *Listener*'s John Naughton: "The spartan freshness of tone in *Chamber Music*—its air of having been written, longhand, in one sitting—is extremely effective."

The tone of Caroline's narration changes in the final third of the novel when Robert dies and she begins her love affair with

Robert's nurse. Described by David Evanier in *National Review* as a "paean to Sapphic love," *Chamber Music* "slides gently down into sentimentality," says Glendinning, with the beginning of Caroline and Anna's love affair. "The result is an odd, haunting composition," writes a *Time* reviewer. "But the love that dare not speak its name eventually tends to drown out the delicate strains of Grumbach's musical prose." A *Times Literary Supplement* critic's assessment is even harsher: "It is surprising that a writer so free from the usual sentimentalities when writing about music and its practitioners should allow herself to speak of the 'soft spring rain,' of her lover's tenderness and to talk swooningly of fireside breastbarings and shared joy in growing things. Lesbianism is no excuse for this."

Because of the lesbian affair between Caroline and Anna and the theme of Caroline's repression by her husband, many reviewers have been prompted to add *Chamber Music* to "the growing genre of women's fiction," as Gerald M. Knoll comments in *America*. "With insight and compassion, Grumbach recreates the inner life of a woman who typifies the life-role of American women at the turn of the century—a life role that lingers . . . today," Knoll continues. Writing in *New Statesman,* Nicholas Shrimpton observes, "The novel's chief concern is with the repression, and eventual restoration, of a woman's sensibility."

Although many critics agree that a thorough reading of *Chamber Music* necessitates a discussion of feminism, not all agree on the success of *Chamber Music*'s feminist themes. Rather than seeing Caroline as "a character of memorable beauty and strength," as she is described by Knoll, other reviewers, such as Peter Davison in *Atlantic Monthly,* consider her "a victim, . . . a pliant, pathetic slave to illusion." Pollitt writes in *Ms.* that she is "baffled by Caroline's life." "Grumbach's point is that before being sexually awakened by Anna, Caroline had no self at all," says Pollitt. "But, in fact, there is no such thing as a human being without an ego, there are only direct and indirect ways of gratifying it. This was as true for the most submissive Victorian wife as for today's most ardent feminist. A woman who devotes herself to her husband's genius has some very strong reasons for doing so, even if it's just a wish to be Mrs. Genius, and a novelist should tell us what they are."

The love affair between Caroline and Anna has garnered considerable critical comment. In describing the romance, "Grumbach is at her most poignant and gentle," notes a *Publishers Weekly* reviewer. Paul Ableman observes that *Chamber Music* depicts "the most lyrical, and ultimately moving, [lesbian love story] I have read." On the other hand, there are those critics who find Caroline's rapturous descriptions of her life with Anna jarring and thus detrimental to the novel as a whole; *Yale Review*'s Milton comments, "[Here] the novel falls on its nose and does not recover."

"*Chamber Music* is about Woman Abused," writes Evanier in *National Review*. "There is no line drawn here between feminism and lesbianism. They conjoin—it's the same 'liberation.' The novel is a wooden tract, about as surprising as a Soviet poster depicting workers joyfully stoking a furnace." The correlation between Caroline's love for another woman and her ability to lift herself out of the meek and self-effacing despair forced upon her by her marriage to Robert is pointed out by a number of critics, including one for *New Yorker*. "At this point," says the reviewer, "Doris Grumbach apparently feared that the theme of Man's Oppression of Women in Love and Art had been too subtly drawn, . . . for she has tacked on an implausible ending that reduced the memoirs to a feminist parable."

In her short preface to *Chamber Music,* Grumbach states that the novel's characters "are based vaguely upon persons who were once alive" but stresses that the book is fiction. "*Chamber Music* is a thinly, and strangely, fictionalized variation on the life of Marian MacDowell, [composer] Edward MacDowell's widow, who . . . founded an artist's colony in New Hampshire. . . . The names are changed; though not by much considering what else changes with them," says Milton. Gail Godwin, writing in *New York Times Book Review,* suspects that the parallels between the MacDowells and the MacLarens "handicap . . . [Grumbach's] own possibilities for creating a fictional hero who might have come to life more vividly." However, other critics, including Glendinning, find that "the illusion of authenticity is strengthened by the inclusion of real people." "Robert MacLaren himself is given a semihistorical glamor by the parallels between his career and that of . . . Edward MacDowell—the two share teachers, musical styles, even a Boston address, and MacDowell's widow did indeed found an artist's colony in his name," writes Katha Pollitt. "Such details give Caroline's memoirs the piquancy of a historical novel."

Franny Fuller, the protagonist of Grumbach's novel *The Missing Person,* is also patterned after an actual figure. Franny, a 1930s movie star and sex symbol, closely resembles actress Marilyn Monroe. Written as a series of vignettes interweaving the events of Franny's career with an ongoing commentary by a gossip columnist, *The Missing Person* traces the actress's life from her sad beginnings in Utica, New York, through her rise to stardom, and finally to her disappearance from both Hollywood and the public consciousness. "Here, with certain sympathetic changes, is quite visibly another tale about the sad life of Marilyn Monroe," observes *New York Times*'s Herbert Mitgang.

"Missing person," says Cynthia Propper Seton in *Washington Post Book World,* refers to "this sense that one is all facade, that there is no self inside." Franny is supposed to serve as a prototype for all the "missing persons" who are, "above all, missing to themselves," claims Herbert Gold in *New York Times Book Review*. "There seems evidence," Abigail McCarthy writes in *Commonweal,* "that Doris Grumbach may initially have thought of Franny Fuller's story as a feminist statement in that women like Franny whom America 'glorifies and elevates' are sex objects made larger than life. But if so, as often happens in the creative process, she has transcended the aim in the writing. The creatures of the Hollywood process she gives us, men as well as women, are all victims."

Grumbach, in a prefatory note to the novel, comments on the nature of the book. "This novel is a portrait, not of a single life but of many lives melded into one, typical of the women America often glorifies and elevates, and then leaves suspended in their lonely and destructive fame," she says. Still, comments Richard Combs in *Times Literary Supplement,* "there is no prize for guessing that the novel's heroine is Marilyn Monroe."

The close correlation between Marilyn Monroe's and Franny's lives is disturbing to many critics. "The question that poses itself about a book like this is, Why bother? If you must write about Marilyn Monroe then why not do so in fiction or otherwise?" asks James Campbell in *New Statesman*. "Real names thinly disguised are a bore." Combs believes Grumbach's reliance on the facts of Marilyn Monroe's life hinders her ability to substantiate the point she makes in the preface. "The more the real Hollywood shows through [in the novel], the less satisfying the portrait becomes," Combs says. "The author's assumption . . . seems to be that since Hollywood put fantasy on an anonymous, mass-production basis, the results can be freely arranged by the inspired do-it-yourselfer. . . . But in re-fantasizing the fantasy factory, Mrs. Grumbach allows herself the license of fiction without taking on the responsibility . . . to find revised truth in the revised subject."

Even with Grumbach's forewarning that Franny is the symbolic lost child of Hollywood, Seton claims *The Missing Person* does not meet its implied purpose of explaining why that phenomenon occurs. "So it seems that *The Missing Person* is meant to be a hypothetical explanation of the phenomenon of Marilyn Monroe," the critic comments. "And the question is whether Doris Grumbach's intrusion is a worthy attempt to bring a clearer lens, a fresher, more insightful understanding, to the lives of people, who, in all their aspects, have become cliches. . . . An underlying weakness in this story is that the inner person in Franny Fuller was already missing before she left Utica. Franny isn't ruined by Hollywood, or even touched by it." Gold holds a similar opinion: "Despite the deftness and delicacy of Miss Grumbach's touch, and the credible projection of a Marilyn Monroe aura, Franny does not offer us the sense of surprise that we expect of a fully created fictional character," he says. "[Anyhow,] Franny the star is just plain, dim Franny."

"It is hard for [Franny] to have a separate imaginary existence in the mind of the reader," states Abigail McCarthy. "But this flaw, if it is one, is more than compensated for by the writer's evocation of the scene against which Franny moves—tawdry, wonderful Hollywood at its peak." Indeed, Grumbach is praised for her fine writing and for "the adroit structure of the novel," as Gold calls it. "There is in this prose a certain leanness, a sparseness that separates most of the characters into a chapter each, surrounded by an implied emptiness. Instead of the usual crowded Hollywood narrative, [*The Missing Person*] has the melancholy air . . . of an underpopulated landscape," writes Combs. Seton comments on Grumbach's ability to capture the tone and feeling of old Hollywood films and newsreels in her writing. "Doris Grumbach's special gift lies in her ability to suit the style and structure of her novels to the world in which she writes," McCarthy says. "*The Missing Person* is itself like a motion picture—a pastiche of scenes centered on the star, complete with flashbacks, close-ups and fade-outs."

CA INTERVIEW

CA interviewed Doris Grumbach by phone December 9, 1981, at her home in Washington, D.C.

CA: You've been a teacher, writer, editor, and critic. Was your education directed toward a career in writing or publishing?

GRUMBACH: No, not really. I was a philosophy major in college and then I was a medievalist in graduate school. I really didn't think about being a writer until later on.

CA: After college you worked briefly as a title writer for Metro-Goldwyn-Mayer in New York, then went to Time *as an associate editor. Did these jobs lead you in the direction of a writing career?*

GRUMBACH: I've always had jobs that involved some journalistic writing of a kind. I suppose that's how I came to it. As a young child I thought I might like to write fiction, but, you know, many young children think that.

CA: You wrote in a 1964 Commentary *essay, "On Women Novelists," about the time and energy many women writers must devote to family, and speculated that this might account for their excellence in the short story rather than the novel. Did you struggle to write while your own children were young?*

GRUMBACH: I've never struggled to write, honestly. My children, for some reason, were never that much of a problem—perhaps because I had a very good husband. I think I wrote as late as I did mainly because I wasn't ready to do very much before. I don't think that I illustrate the current theory that women are silenced by marriage and family.

CA: In that same article you contended that there have been very few first-rate women novelists as compared to men. Did this bring a lot of response from readers?

GRUMBACH: Oh yes. And I made some good friends through those letters. Michele Murray wrote an essay on the subject for *Commonweal*. She's now dead, but she was a very good friend. I think what I said in the article is true, but I don't think it's because there weren't a lot of first-rate women out there, only that the culture encouraged them to do other things. And I don't think it's just that they were married and had children. After all, many men have to earn livings as bank clerks and such and had problems providing for a family which are parallel to the problems women have in bearing and raising children. But the culture just smiled at women who thought they might want to write—put it in the same category as painting on china or house decorating. There have been first-rate women writers. Jane Austen was a first-rate writer, as was Virginia Woolf, and there are many others. Edith Wharton was a good writer, though probably not as great as her friend Henry James. But I think there are going to be more and more now. The culture is hospitable to the idea. At the moment I'm writing a book on Willa Cather. And while I don't put her in the same class as Jane Austen and Virginia Woolf, she was a very good writer. Her Nebraska novels are sort of epic in a way for anybody who studies the settlement of the West. It's now the Midwest, of course, but then it was the frontier.

CA: You are known in part for what John Leonard has called "the intelligence and sinew" of your literary criticism. How did you become interested in doing reviews and criticism?

GRUMBACH: Accidentally. When my children were very small I wrote a short essay on the subject of faith and religion for a magazine that the Jesuits edit, called *America*. It was the first place I think I was ever published in any sort of national way. The literary editor of the magazine was a well-known Catholic critic named Father Harold Gardiner, who is now dead. He wrote to me after that essay and said, "Would you like to review occasionally for *America*?" And I said I would. It seemed the sort of thing you could do while you were folding diapers. From there I got requests from other magazines, mainly Catholic magazines, and I began to review quite regularly.

CA: Was it difficult at first, or were you used to reading with a kind of critical eye?

GRUMBACH: I had taken some excellent courses in college with James Burnham, Edwin Berry Burgum, Margaret Schlauch, and other people who taught me something about literary criticism. So it wasn't too difficult to make the move into more journalistic criticism.

CA: In 1975, you wrote in the New York Times *"Guest Word" about the "sullen craft of literary editorship," about your time in that capacity at the* New Republic. *How does a literary editor decide on the books to allot space to?*

GRUMBACH: I've discovered that every editor is different and you can't generalize. I was just talking to Brigitte Weeks at the *Washington Post* yesterday about her choices. My own way was simply to look at the books that were coming out and decide first which interested me and then which I thought would interest the readers of the *New Republic,* who were on the whole rather political people. The literary books were chosen because either the authors were people I thought worthy of notice or their former works had been notable or I just happened to have liked them. I think it's a very personal thing; each editor makes that decision. In the *New York Times,* for example, there are many reasons, including very commercial reasons, why books are reviewed. In the *New Republic* that wasn't true. We didn't have any advertising worth talking about, so the advertisers weren't a factor in the decision. I was a one-man show and I just picked what interested me.

CA: What were the worst pressures on you as a literary editor?

GRUMBACH: I had two years of rather Camelot-like perfection in that job. I had a wonderful editor, a man named Gilbert Harrison, who also owned the magazine. He put no pressures on me at all. He gave me a free hand in the job, allowed me to choose the reviewers without even a suggestion. So until the magazine was sold and I worked under the new owner and found that there were extreme difficulties then, I never felt any pressure. Once I decided to leave, it was simply because the pressures were personal and political.

CA: Did your experience as a literary editor help you in any way as a free-lance reviewer?

GRUMBACH: Oh yes. Once I left, many people asked me to review, and for a year and a half I made a living as a reviewer—until I got tired of it. I had always thought I should go back and write fiction. So I did. I'm very grateful, really, in a way, to the *New Republic* because, first, it made it possible for me to make enough money to work on a novel, and second, leaving there opened up that area of life which I thought I'd never go back to, writing fiction.

CA: Your first two novels, The Spoil of the Flowers *[1962] and* The Short Throat, the Tender Mouth *[1964] are very difficult to find.*

GRUMBACH: They are. In a book Bowker published recently about book collecting, Peter Howard says that they're the two most difficult works in the 1960s to find. I think it's because Doubleday trashed them; since they sold so badly, most of the copies must have been destroyed. I don't feel badly about it, because I don't think they're extremely good. I think the first one is better than the second, but I don't think either of them is notable.

CA: The first two novels were followed by The Company She Kept *in 1967. You described in a* New York Times *article the difficulties you had with Mary McCarthy over that book. How much changing had to be done when she saw the galleys and objected to your using material she'd freely given you when you were preparing to write the book?*

GRUMBACH: It wasn't so much changing; it was cutting. And there was no arguing with her: it had to go. So the book has suffered from being truncated in that way. Somebody came to see me recently who has Mary McCarthy's permission to write a biography of her, and I found myself living through those agonizing times again.

CA: In the last two books, Chamber Music *and* The Missing Person, *your main characters resemble actual people who were more or less recognizable. Did you find it tricky to work with such characters in fiction?*

GRUMBACH: In the first book, *Chamber Music,* I don't think too many people knew the characters. They knew them vaguely, maybe, but nobody knows very much about Marian and Edward MacDowell. Actually, I knew very little about them, too. I simply made a lot of guesses about what their lives might have been like. In *The Missing Person* I perhaps made an error relying so heavily upon the outline of a life. I really was not writing about Marilyn Monroe, as everybody assumed, but simply about someone who might have been almost anyone. I erred in staying too closely to the biographical facts, and people decided the novel was all about her. Actually I knew nothing about her except this broad outline, and again I tried to do the same thing I had done in *Chamber Music*. I think that had its difficulties. In England, where much less is known about Monroe, the book was read, I think, properly. There are some excellent reviews, including one in the *London Review of Books,* which is really an understanding review of what I was trying to do. In America the book was misread in many cases. Some of the reviews were good, but other critics misread the book.

CA: For a number of years now you've been both a writer and a teacher. Have the two jobs meshed well for you?

GRUMBACH: Yes. I have a very understanding university. It allows me a great deal of leeway to write. I enjoy seeing students. I only go in one day a week at the moment, because I can do all my work at the university in one day. So it has meshed really well. My chairman and the dean support me in my writing habit; they've given me much more leeway than I have any right to expect. They're wonderful people.

CA: Your teaching career has spanned some years of real change in education. Much of what we read and hear and see of education currently is gloomy. What are your feelings about the situation, and about your own students?

GRUMBACH: I should say that I don't teach undergraduates anymore. What I see are the survivors, really, the people who are relatively good, and I don't think they are worse than graduate students used to be. For many years I taught at an undergraduate college, the College of Saint Rose in Albany, New York, and I never saw graduate students. I had no idea what they were like then. Now I see almost entirely graduate students, and I think that the people who go on to do graduate work in literature are about the way they were. I'm not one of these people who thinks the whole enterprise has gone to pot. I think we're educating many more people, and that naturally lowers the standards. We may not get the classically educated people who came to us from the high schools years ago, but I think I get good students and I'm not pessimistic that the world of literature is going to collapse because we are educating them badly.

CA: Do you have time to do much reading?

GRUMBACH: At this moment I'm working on two books, the Cather biography and a novel I'm finishing, so I have almost no time to read. I'm not doing any reviewing, just teaching my one day a week and then working the rest of the time on these two books. I don't read very much, except late at night. Then I try to keep up a little with current fiction, which is partly what I read, but so little at the moment that it's hardly worth mentioning. I've read the new Updike novel, *Rabbit Is Rich,* and I admire what Updike has done in those three Rabbit books; they're quite an accomplishment. I've read the Nabokov lectures on literature. They're wonderful lectures for a teacher. It's particularly edifying to see the kind of thinking and broad scholarship that go into a lecture like that. Nabokov's way of looking at books is always fresh, always new. It's not what other critics have been saying. I have spent a lot of time reading those. But mostly I'm just reading for Cather.

CA: Are you interested in writing for television or movies?

GRUMBACH: Not really. Television is an art I came upon too late. I'm not interested in watching it most of the time. The movies are a great art, but I have enough trouble mastering one craft, and I don't think I could manage another.

CA: Is there any kind of writing you'd like to try that you haven't done yet?

GRUMBACH: I'd like to write a play, but I have in mind two novels beyond the one I'm doing now, and it strikes me that maybe if I write those, I'll be done. I don't know that I'll have that much more to say. I started late and I can't plan too much beyond the book at hand. I think it would be interesting to try the form of a play, but I haven't thought enough really about it to know whether I could do it.

BIOGRAPHICAL/CRITICAL SOURCES: Doris Grumbach, *The Company She Kept,* Coward, 1967; *New York Times Book Review,* June 11, 1967, March 25, 1979, March 29, 1981; *Commonweal,* October 6, 1967, June 22, 1979, January 15, 1982; *Times Literary Supplement,* December 7, 1967, November 30, 1979, September 11, 1981; Grumbach, *Chamber Music,* Dutton, 1979; *Publishers Weekly,* January 15, 1979, February 13, 1981; *Atlantic Monthly,* March, 1979; *Library Journal,* March 1, 1979; *New Republic,* March 10, 1979; *New York Times,* March 13, 1979, July 20, 1981; *Washington Post Book World,* March 18, 1979, February 10, 1980, April 5, 1981; *Newsweek,* March 19, 1979; *Ms.,* April, 1979; *Time,* April 9, 1979; *New Yorker,* April 23, 1979; *America,* June 2, 1979; *National Review,* June 8, 1979; *Listener,* August 9, 1979; *Spectator,* August 11, 1979; *Observer,* August 12, 1979; *New Statesman,* August 17, 1979, August 28, 1981; *Yale Review,* autumn, 1979; *Contemporary Literary Criticism,* Gale, Volume XIII, 1980, Volume XXII, 1982; Grumbach, *The Missing Person,* Putnam, 1981; *Nation,* March 28, 1981; *American Spectator,* January, 1982.

—Sketch by Heidi A. Tietjen

—Interview by Jean W. Ross

* * *

GUENTHER, John (Lewis)

PERSONAL: Born in Ann Arbor, Mich.; son of Roy Roland (a manufacturer) and Lillian (Rohsenberger) Guenther; married Catherine Macrae, August 27, 1938; children: Ian, Colin, Hector. *Education:* Attended University of Illinois, 1930-32, and Harvard University, 1943. *Home:* 16 Hix Ave., Rye, N.Y. 10580. *Agent:* Curtis Brown Ltd., 575 Madison Ave., New York, N.Y. 10022. *Office:* 304 East 42nd St., New York, N.Y. 10017.

CAREER: Writer for Scripps-Howard newspapers in Evansville and Indianapolis, Ind., 1933-38; writer for United Press, Chicago, Ill., 1941-42; *Newsweek,* New York City, editor and writer, 1942-43, 1946-47; Lockheed Aircraft Corp., New York City, public relations executive, 1947-54; public relations consultant, New York City, 1954-59; General Foods Corp., White Plains, N.Y., assistant to director of public relations, 1959-67; public relations executive in New York City, 1967—. *Military service:* U.S. Army Air Forces, 1943-46; served in European theater, 1944-45; became captain. *Member:* P.E.N., Academy of American Poets, National Press Club (Washington, D.C.), Overseas Press Club (New York), Air Force Association.

WRITINGS: The Stone Land (poems), privately printed, 1933; *The English Boys* (poem), Riverside Press, 1941; (with A. W. Levier) *Pilot* (biography), Harper, 1954; (with Frank K. Everest, Jr.) *The Fastest Man Alive* (biography), Dutton, 1958, reprinted, Arno, 1980.

Time and Place (poems), Fortune Press, 1961; (contributor) *A Garland for Dylan Thomas,* edited by George Firmage, Clarke & Way, 1963; *Sidney Keyes: A Biographical Inquiry,* London Magazine Editions, 1967; *Elegies* (poems), Fortune Press, 1967; *In Love, In Paris,* Pinnacle Books, 1974; *A Modern Hamlet: A Play in Blank Verse,* Home Planet Publications, 1976; *Cihuateteo: New and Selected Poems,* Celli Press, 1979; *Pearl Harbor: A Narrative Poem,* Purchase Press, 1980.

WORK IN PROGRESS: Marthe, "a novel about Rilke in Paris."

* * *

GUEST, Harry
See GUEST, Henry Bayly

* * *

GUEST, Henry Bayly 1932-
(Harry Guest)

PERSONAL: Born October 6, 1932, in Penarth, Wales; son of Walter Howard and Elsie (Matthews) Guest; married Lynn Doremus Dunbar (a writer and translator), December 28, 1963; children: Natalie Doremus, Nicholas Bayly Dunbar. *Education:* Trinity Hall, Cambridge, B.A., 1954; Sorbonne, University of Paris, D.E.S., 1955. *Religion:* Church of England. *Home:* 1 Alexandra Ter., Exeter, Devonshire EX4 6SY, England.

CAREER: Teacher of French, German, and English literature at private schools in Essex, England, 1955-61, and Sussex, England, 1961-66; Yokohama National University, Yokohama, Japan, lecturer in English literature, 1966-72; Exeter School, Exeter, England, teacher of French and head of department, 1972—. *Member:* Poetry Society (member of general council, 1972-75).

WRITINGS—Under name Harry Guest: *Arrangements* (poems), Anvil Press, 1968; *The Cutting-Room* (poems), Anvil Press, 1970; *Another Island Country* (textbook), Eikosha, 1970; (with wife, Lynn Guest, and Kajima Shozo) *Post-War Japanese Poetry,* Penguin, 1972; *The Achievements of Memory* (visual poem), Sceptre, 1974.

The Enchanted Acres (poems), Sceptre, 1975; *Mountain Journal* (poem), Rivelin, 1975; *A House against the Night* (poems), Anvil Press, 1976; *English Poems,* Words Press, 1976; *The Hidden Change* (poems), Greylag, 1978; *Zeami in Exile* (long poem), Sceptre, 1978; *Days* (novel), Anvil Press, 1978; (co-editor) *Elek Book of Oriental Verse,* Elek, 1979; *Elegies* (poems), Pig Press, 1980; (translator) Victor Hugo, *The Distance, The Shadows* (poems), Anvil Press, 1981; *Lost and Found* (poems), Anvil Press, 1983. Author of "The Emperor of Outer Space," a poem for four voices, first broadcast on British Broadcasting Corp. (BBC) Radio, February 3, 1976.

WORK IN PROGRESS: A novel.

AVOCATIONAL INTERESTS: Playing the piano, "going for long walks in remote areas, particularly to visit Stone Age sites."

BIOGRAPHICAL/CRITICAL SOURCES: Times Literary Supplement, August 21, 1981.

* * *

GULLIVER, Lemuel
See HASTINGS, Macdonald

* * *

GUNN, Thom(son William) 1929-

PERSONAL: Born August 29, 1929, in Gravesend, England; son of Herbert Smith (a journalist) and Ann Charlotte (Thomson) Gunn. *Education:* Trinity College, Cambridge, B.A., 1953, M.A., 1958; attended Stanford University, 1954-55, 1956-58. *Religion:* Atheist. *Residence:* 1216 Cole St., San Francisco, Calif. 94117.

CAREER: University of California, Berkeley, 1958-66, began as lecturer, became associate professor of English. Full-time writer, 1966—. *Military service:* British Army, National Service, 1948-50. *Awards, honors:* Levinson Prize, 1955; Somerset Maugham Award, 1959; American Institute of Arts and Letters grant, 1964; National Institute and American Academy Awards in Literature, 1964; Guggenheim fellowship, 1971; W. H. Smith Award, 1980.

WRITINGS: (Editor) *Poetry from Cambridge,* Fortune Press, 1953; *Fighting Terms,* Fantasy Press, 1954, revised edition, Faber, 1962; *The Sense of Movement,* Faber, 1957, University of Chicago Press, 1959; *My Sad Captains* (also see below), University of Chicago Press, 1961; (with Ted Hughes) *Selected Poems,* Faber, 1962; (editor with Ted Hughes) *Five American Poets,* Faber, 1963; *A Geography,* Stone Wall Press, 1966; (with Ander Gunn) *Positives,* Faber, 1966, University of Chicago Press, 1967; *Touch,* Faber, 1967, University of Chicago Press, 1968; *The Garden of the Gods,* Pym-Randall Press, 1968; (editor and author of introduction) Fulke Greville Brooke, *Selected Poems of Fulke Greville,* University of Chicago Press, 1968; *Poems, 1950-1966: A Selection,* Faber, 1969; *The Explorers,* R. Gilbertson, 1969; *The Fair in the Woods,* Sycamore Press, 1969; *Sunlight,* Albondoncani Press, 1969; *Moly* (also see below), Faber, 1971; *Moly* [and] *My Sad Captains,* Farrar, Straus, 1973; *To the Air,* David R. Godine, 1974; *Jack Straw's Castle,* Farrar, Straus, 1976; *Selected Poems 1950-1975,* Farrar, Straus, 1979; *The Passages of Joy,* Farrar, Straus, 1982; *The Occasions of Poetry,* edited by Clive Wilmer, Farrar, Straus, 1982.

Work represented in many anthologies, including: *Springtime,* edited by G. S. Fraser and I. Fletcher, Peter Owen, 1953; *Mark in Time,* edited by R. Johnson and N. Harvey, Glide Publications, 1971. Poetry reviewer, *Yale Review,* 1958-64. Contributor to *Encounter, New Statesman, Poetry,* and other publications.

SIDELIGHTS: An English poet long resident in California, Thom Gunn combines a respect for traditional poetic forms with an interest in popular topics, such as the Hell's Angels and LSD. While Gunn wrote most of his early verses in iambic pentameter, his more recent poems assume a variety of forms, including syllabic stanzas and free verse. The course of his development is recorded in *Selected Poems 1950-1975,* in which "the language begins as English and progresses toward American," according to *Nation* reviewer Donald Hall.

Gunn's masterful fusion of "modern" and "traditional" elements has brought him critical acclaim. Writing in the *New York Times Book Review,* M. L. Rosenthal praises *Selected Poems 1950-1975,* noting that "Gunn has developed his craft so that by now even his freest compositions have a disciplined music." And, echoing this sentiment, *New York Review of Books* critic Stephen Spender suggests that the contradiction between the "conventional form" of Gunn's poems and their "often Californian 'with it' subject matter" is what distinguishes his work. "It is," Spender elaborates, "as though A. E. Housman were dealing with the subject matter of *Howl,* or Tennyson were on the side of the Lotus Eaters."

In a *Poetry* article, Robert B. Shaw speculates that Gunn's fluctuation between metrical poems and free verse reflects an internal struggle: "On the one hand, the poet feels the attraction of a life ruled by traditional, even elitist values, and by purely individual preferences—a private life in the classic sense, the pursuit of happiness. On the other hand, he feels a visionary impulse to shed his isolated individuality and merge with a larger whole."

Selected Poems 1950-1975 features examples of both verse styles, prompting M. L. Rosenthal to conclude that it is "fortunate that American readers now have a single volume of Thom Gunn's selected poems. With their undemonstrative virtuosity, their slightly corrupt openness, their atmosphere of unfathomable secrets and their intimacy, so like that of a reticent friend who has something crucial to confess, these poems strike a chord at once insinuatingly familiar and infinitely alien."

AVOCATIONAL INTERESTS: Reading, films, drinking.

BIOGRAPHICAL/CRITICAL SOURCES: New York Review of Books, September 20, 1973; *Poetry,* May, 1974, September, 1975; *New York Times Book Review,* June 16, 1974, January 20, 1980; *Contemporary Literary Criticism,* Gale, Volume III, 1975, Volume VI, 1976, Volume XVIII, 1981; *Nation,* November 10, 1979.

* * *

GURNEY, Gene 1924-

PERSONAL: Born July 5, 1924, in Fremont, Ohio; son of Jacob and Josephine (Mange) Gurney; married 1951, wife's name, Clare (divorced, 1977). *Education:* University of Maryland, B.S., 1954; George Washington University, M.A., 1966; Pacific Western College, Ph.D., 1980. *Home:* 4654 South 34th St., Arlington, Va. 22206.

CAREER: U.S. Air Force, 1943-73, retired as colonel. *Awards, honors:* Aviation/Space Writers Association Award, 1963, for *The War in the Air* and 1965, for *Private Pilot's Handbook of Weather;* Silver Anvil Award, Public Relations Society of

America, 1964, for his part in creating more than five hundred aviation books as director of the Air Force Book Program; Republic of Vietnam Gold Medal of Honor, 1971, for his public relations productions.

WRITINGS: (With Mark P. Friedlander) *Five Down and Glory: A History of the American Air Ace,* Putnam, 1959; *Journey of the Giants,* Coward, 1961; (with Carroll V. Glines) *Minutemen of the Air,* Random House, 1961; *Americans into Orbit: The Story of Project Mercury,* Random House, 1962; (editor) *Test Pilot,* F. Watts, 1962; *The War in the Air,* Crown, 1962; *The B-29: The Plane That Won the War,* Fawcett, 1963; *Great Air Battles,* F. Watts, 1963; *The Pentagon,* Crown, 1964; (with Joseph A. Skier) *Private Pilot's Handbook of Weather,* Aero Publishers, 1964, 2nd edition, 1974; *Rocket and Missile Technology,* F. Watts, 1964; *The Smithsonian Institution,* Crown, 1964; *Flying Aces of World War I,* Random House, 1965; *Arlington National Cemetery,* Crown, 1965; *Chronology of World Aviation,* F. Watts, 1965; *Library of Congress,* Crown, 1966, revised edition, 1981; *Pictorial History of the United States Army,* Crown, 1966; *Walk in Space: The Story of Project Gemini,* Random House, 1967; (with James C. Elliott) *Private Pilot's Handbook of Navigation,* Aero Publishers, 1967; *P-38 Lightning,* Arco, 1969; *Beautiful Washington, D.C.: A Picture Story of the Nation's Capital,* Crown, 1969.

Americans to the Moon: The Story of Project Apollo, Random House, 1970; *The United States Coast Guard: A Pictorial History,* Crown, 1973; (with Friedlander) *Higher, Faster and Farther,* Aero Publishers, 1973; *How to Save Your Life on the Nation's Highways and Byways,* Crown, 1974; (with Nick P. Apple) *The Air Force Museum,* Crown, 1975, revised edition, 1983; *America in Wax,* Crown, 1977; (with Harold Wise) *The Official Washington, D.C. Directory: A Pictorial Guide,* Crown, 1977; (with Brian Sheehan) *Educational Guide to U.S. Service and Maritime Academies,* Van Nostrand, 1978; *Space Technology Spinoffs,* F. Watts, 1979; (with Friedlander) *Handbook of Successful Franchising,* Van Nostrand, 1981; (with Friedlander) *Kingdoms of Europe,* Crown, 1982; (with Kurt Willinger) *The Jeep in War and Peace,* Crown, 1983.

With Clare Gurney; published by F. Watts, except as indicated: *Mount Vernon,* 1965; *Monticello,* 1966; *F.D.R. and Hyde Park,* 1970; *Unidentified Flying Objects,* Abelard, 1970; *The Colony of Maryland,* 1972; *Cosmonauts in Orbit: The Story of the Soviet Manned Space Program,* 1972; *North and South Korea,* 1973; *The Launching of Sputnik, October 4, 1957: The Space Age Begins,* 1975; *Women on the March,* Abelard, 1975; *The United States Treasury: A Pictorial History,* Crown, 1978; *Agriculture Careers,* 1978.

* * *

GUTHEIM, Frederick 1908-

PERSONAL: Born March 3, 1908, in Cambridge, Mass.; son of August George and Augusta (Meiser) Gutheim; married Mary Purdon, June 8, 1935; children: Nicholas. *Education:* University of Wisconsin, B.A., 1931; University of Chicago, graduate study, 1933-36; additional study at Ecole des Hautes Etudes Urbaines, London School of Economics and Political Science, and University of Heidelberg. *Address:* 2372D Mount Ephraim, Dickerson, Md. 20842.

CAREER: Brookings Institution, Washington, D.C., junior staff member of Institute for Government Research, 1931-33; Illinois Housing Association, Chicago, executive secretary, 1933-34; assistant editor for architecture, Federal Writer's Project Federal Guide Series, 1936-37; U.S. Housing Authority, Division of Research and Information, Washington, D.C., assistant director, 1938-40; U.S. Federal Works Agency, Washington, D.C., consultant, 1940-41; National Housing Agency, Hampton Roads, Va., area representative, 1941-43; French Mission for Urbanism and Reconstruction, Washington, D.C., assistant chief, 1945-46; National Housing Agency, Land and Public Services Division, Washington, D.C., principal urban development specialist, 1946-47; *New York Herald Tribune,* New York City, staff and editorial writer, 1947-50.

American Institute of Architects, Washington, D.C., assistant executive director, 1950-52; Galaxy, Inc., Washington, D.C., in private practice as consultant in city and regional planning, 1953-59; U.S. Congress, Washington, D.C., staff director of Joint Committee on Metropolitan Problems, 1959-60; Washington Center for Metropolitan Studies, Washington, D.C., president, 1960-65; in independent practice as consultant on urban affairs, Washington, D.C., 1965—; Williams College, Williamstown, Mass., assistant professor, 1968-69; Central Washington State College, Ellensburg, distinguished visiting professor, 1970; George Washington University, Washington, D.C., professor of history, 1971-74, professor of American studies, 1974—, director of graduate program in historic preservation, 1976-79, consultant on research in American civilization, 1979—.

Chairman of Washington Regional Planning Council, 1950-52; commissioner of Upper Montgomery County Planning Commission, 1950-57; member of National Capital Regional Planning Council, 1952-57; National Capital Transportation Agency, member of advisory board, 1961-65, chairman, 1961-63; member of President's Council on Pennsylvania Avenue, 1962-65; chairman of Joint Committee on the National Capital, 1963—; member of Interior Department Task Force on the Potomac, 1965-66. Director of U.S. government exhibitions at New York and San Francisco World's Fairs, 1939; director of exhibitions at Museum of Modern Art, New York City, 1939, Grand Palais, Paris, France, 1946, Marshallhaus, Berlin, West Germany, 1952, Edinburgh Festival, Edinburgh, Scotland, 1956, and at National Gallery of Art, London, England, 1956; director of numerous circulating exhibitions for U.S. Information Agency, American Institute of Architects, and others. Chairman of Washington Arts Council, 1962-64; chairman of Neighborhood Commons, Inc., 1963-65. Member of visitors committee of schools of architecture at Princeton University, 1950-53, Harvard University, 1950-55, and Carnegie-Mellon University, 1964—.

Producer of films, television, and radio programs, including "A Fatal Beauty," with Robert Cole, 1981, "American Reflections: The Potomac," with Cole, 1982, and "Chesapeake Bay," with Cole and Russell Nichols, 1982. Consultant to Habitat, 1976, and to United Nations on environmental problems, 1982; consultant to colleges and universities, including Williams College, Central Washington State College, and George Washington University. *Military service:* U.S. Army, 1943-45. *Awards, honors:* Guggenheim fellowship, 1965-66; Calvert Prize, Maryland Historical Trust, 1976; D.P.S., George Washington University, 1979.

WRITINGS: (Editor and author of introduction) *Frank Lloyd Wright, Selected Writings, 1894-1940,* Duell, Sloan & Pearce, 1941, published as *Frank Lloyd Wright on Architecture: Houses for Family Living,* Women's Foundation, 1948; *The Potomac,* Rinehart, 1949, revised edition, Grosset, 1969; (with Coleman Woodbury) *Rethinking Urban Redevelopment,* Public Administration Service (Chicago), 1949; *Planning for the Future in the Potomac River Basin,* Interstate Commission on the Potomac River Basin, 1950; *One Hundred Years of Architecture in America, 1857-1957: Celebrating the Centennial of the American Institute of Architects,* Reinhold, 1957.

Alvar Aalto, Braziller, 1960; *Urban Space and Urban Design,* Washington Center for Metropolitan Studies, 1962; (contributor) Lowden Wingo, editor, *Cities and Space,* Johns Hopkins Press, 1963; (contributor) Roger Revelle and Hans H. Landsberg, editors, *America's Changing Environment,* Houghton, 1970; (author of introduction) Alexander Papageorgiou, *Continuity and Change: Preservation in City Planning,* Pall Mall, 1971; (editor and author of introduction) *In the Cause of Architecture: Frank Lloyd Wright,* McGraw, 1975; *Planning Washington, 1924-1976: An Era of Planning for the National Capital and Environs,* U.S. Government Printing Office, 1976; *The Federal City: Plans and Realities,* Smithsonian Institution Press, 1976; *Worthy of the Nation: The History of Planning for the National Capital,* Smithsonian Institution Press, 1977.

Also author of *Housing as Environment,* 1953. Architectural critic, *Washington Post,* 1960-62. Contributor to professional journals, including *Architectural Record* and *Journal of the American Institute of Architects.* Advisory editor, *Magazine of Art,* 1935-40; corresponding editor, *Urbanistica,* 1950-58, and *Progressive Architecture,* 1954-59.

SIDELIGHTS: Alvar Aalto has been translated into French, German, and Italian.

* * *

GUTTERIDGE, Don(ald George) 1937-

PERSONAL: Born September 30, 1937, in Point Edward, Ontario, Canada; son of William and Margaret Grace (McWatters) Gutteridge; married Anne Barnett (a teacher), June 30, 1961; children: John, Catherine. *Education:* University of Western Ontario, B.A. (with honors), 1962. *Home:* 114 Victoria St., London, Ontario, Canada N6A 2B5. *Office:* Faculty of Education, University of Western Ontario, 1137 Western Rd., London, Ontario, Canada.

CAREER: English teacher at a school in Elmira, Ontario, 1960-62; teacher and head of English department in Ingersoll, Ontario, 1963-64, and London, Ontario, 1964-68; University of Western Ontario, London, assistant professor, 1968-74, associate professor, 1975-77, professor of English, 1977—. *Member:* League of Canadian Poets, Canadian Association of University Teachers. *Awards, honors:* President's Medal from University of Western Ontario, 1972, for the poem "Death at Quebec"; Canada Council travel grant, 1973.

WRITINGS: Riel: A Poem for Voices, Fiddlehead, 1968, revised edition, Van Nostrand, 1972; *The Village Within: Poems toward a Biography,* Fiddlehead, 1970; *Death at Quebec and Other Poems,* Fiddlehead, 1971; *Perspectives* (poems), Pennywise Press, 1971; *Language and Expression: A Modern Approach,* McClelland & Stewart, 1971; *Saying Grace: An Elegy* (poems), Fiddlehead, 1972; *Coppermine: The Quest for North* (poems), Oberon, 1973; *Bus-Ride* (novel), Nairn Publications, 1974; *Borderlands* (poems), Oberon, 1975; *Tecumseh: Dreams and Visions* (poems), Oberon, 1976; *A True History of Lambton County* (poems), Oberon, 1977; *All in Good Time* (novel), Black Moss Press, 1981; *God's Geography* (poems), Brick Books, 1982.

WORK IN PROGRESS: Poems: New and Selected.

SIDELIGHTS: Don Gutteridge's poetry reaches into Canada's past, to help establish for Canadians a sense of time and place, to give them roots which he feels are presently lacking. *Media adaptations: Riel: A Poem for Voices* and *Borderlands* have been dramatized for radio by Canadian Broadcasting Corp.

BIOGRAPHICAL/CRITICAL SOURCES: Edge Nine, summer, 1969; Margaret Atwood, *Survival: Themes in Canadian Literature,* House of Anansi, 1971; Leslie Monkman, *A Native Heritage,* University of Toronto Press, 1981.

H

HAAS, Carolyn Buhai 1926-

PERSONAL: Born January 1, 1926, in Chicago, Ill.; daughter of Michael (a manufacturer) and Tillie (a social worker; maiden name, Weiss) Buhai; married Robert G. Haas (an advertising executive), June 29, 1947; children: Andrew, Mari, Betsy, Thomas, Karen. *Education:* Smith College, B.Ed., 1947; also attended National College of Education and Chicago Art Institute. *Politics:* Democrat. *Religion:* Jewish. *Home:* 280 Sylvan Rd., Glencoe, Ill. 60022. *Agent:* Marilyn Marlow, Curtis Brown Ltd., 575 Madison Ave., New York, N.Y. 10022. *Office address:* CBH Publishing, Inc., P.O. Box 236, Glencoe, Ill. 60022.

CAREER: Elementary school teacher in Chicago, Ill., 1947-49; art teacher in public schools of Glencoe, Ill., 1969-70; Parents As Resources Project, Northfield, Ill., co-founder and partner, 1970-81; CBH Publishing, Glencoe, president, 1979—. Has presented conferences on parenting to various associations and conducted eduational workshops in Colorado, Illinois and other states. Member of Chicago chapter of American Jewish Committee and Frank Lloyd Wright Bridge Restoration Committee; member of board of directors of Glencoe Family Counseling Service, Glencoe Human Relations Committee, and Northwestern Women's Board. Consultant to WWTW-Television's series "Look at Me!," 1974-76, and "Look at Me II," 1978-80, and to various educational organizations, including Hawaii Head Start, Chicago Board of Education, and Office of Riverside County Superintendent of Schools.

MEMBER: Society of Children's Book Writers, Scholarship and Guidance Association (Chicago; president), Chicago Reading Roundtable, Friends of the Glencoe Public Library (president; member of board), Smith College Club.

WRITINGS—All juveniles: (With Ann Cole and Betty Kiralfy Weinberger) *Recipes for Fun,* six volumes, Parents As Resources Project, 1970-76; (with Faith Bushnell, Cole, and Weinberger) *I Saw a Purple Cow,* Little, Brown, 1972; (with Elizabeth Heller, Cole, and Weinberger) *A Pumpkin in a Pear Tree,* Little, Brown, 1976; (with Heller, Cole, and Weinberger) *Children Are Children Are Children,* Little, Brown, 1978; *The Big Book of Recipes for Fun,* CBH Publishing, 1979; (with Cole and Barbara Naftzger) *Backyard Vacation,* Little, Brown, 1980; (with Cole and Weinberger) *Purple Cow to the Rescue,* Little, Brown, 1982; (with Cole and Weinberger) *Recipes for Fun and Learning,* CBH Publishing, 1982. Co-author of "Recipes for Fun," a newspaper column syndicated by *Des Moines Register and Tribune,* 1970-76. Contributor to education journals and magazines for parents.

WORK IN PROGRESS: Read to Me, Just Fifteen Minutes a Day; revised editions of the *Recipes for Fun* books.

* * *

HAERING, Bernhard 1912-

PERSONAL: Given name listed in some biographical and bibliographical sources as Bernard; born November 10, 1912, in Tuttlingen, Germany (now West Germany); son of Johannes N. and Franziska (Flad) Haering. *Education:* Theologische Hochschule, B. and Theology, 1939; University of Tuebingen, D.S.T., 1947. *Home:* Via Merulana 31, C.P. 2458, 00100 Rome, Italy. *Office:* Academia Alfonsiana, Pontifical Lateran University, Rome, Italy.

CAREER: Ordained Roman Catholic priest. Maor Seminary of the Redemptorists, Gars am Inn, Bavaria, Germany (now West Germany), professor of moral theology and sociology, 1939-40, 1947-57; Pontifical Lateran University, Academia Alfonsiana, Rome, Italy, lecturer, 1949-53, professor of systematic moral theology, 1957—. Lecturer, International Catechetical Institute, Lumen Vitae, Brussels, Belgium, 1957—; part-time professor of the sociology of the family, Lateran University, Rome, 1960—; summer professor, University of San Francisco, 1965, 1968, 1971, 1974, and 1977; visiting professor, Brown University, 1966, Yale University, 1966-67, Union Theological Seminary, New York, 1967-68, Kennedy Institute of Bioethics, Georgetown University, 1974-75, and Fordham University, 1977; lecturer in Third World countries. Consultor to Preparatory Theological Commission of the Second Vatican Council, and peritus and secretary for Schema 13 at the Council; also consultor to Catholic Academy of Bavaria. *Military service:* German Army, 1939-45. *Member:* German Society for Sociology, Catholic Centre of Sociological Research for Germany.

AWARDS, HONORS: LL.D., St. Joseph's College, Rensselaer, Ind., 1962, University of Notre Dame, 1966, St. Francis College, Biddeford, Me., 1966, and La Salle College, 1967; D.H.L., Wagner College, 1967, and College of Our Lady of the Elms, 1980; National Catholic Book Award, 1970, for *A*

Theology of Protest; Wlodzimierz Pietrzak Award, Poland, 1973; Bundesverdienstkreuz first class, Bundesrepublik Deutschland, 1973; named honorary citizen, City of Baltimore, 1975; Verdienstmedalle des Landes Baden-Wuerttemberg, 1980.

WRITINGS: Das Helige und das Gute: Religion und Sittlichkeit in ihrem gegenseitigen Bezug, Erich Wewel (Munich), 1950; *Das Gesetz Christi: Moraltheologie dargestelli fuer Priester und Laien,* three volumes, Erich Wewel, 1954, 7th edition, 1963, translation by Edwin G. Kaiser published as *The Law of Christ: Moral Theology for Priests and Laity,* Newman, Volume I, 1961, Volume II, 1963, Volume III, 1967; *Soziologie der Familie: Die Familie und ihre Umwelt,* Otto Mueller (Salzburg), 1954, translation by Meyrich Booth published as *The Sociology of the Family,* Mercier Press, 1959.

Macht und Ohnmacht der Religion: Religionssoziologie als Anruf, Otto Mueller, 1956; *Der Christ und die Obrigkeit,* Winfried Werk (Augsburg), 1956, translation by Patrick O'Shaughness published as *The Liberty of the Children of God,* Alba House, 1967; *Frohes Beichten,* Seelsorger Verlag (Vienna), 1956; *Christ in einer neuen Welt,* Erich Wewel, 1958, translation by Lucidia Haering published as *Christian Renewal in a Changing World,* Desclee (Tournai), 1964, revised edition, Image Books, 1968.

Ehe in deiser Zeit, Otto Mueller, 1960, translation by Geoffrey Stevens published as *Marriage in the Modern World,* Newman, 1964; *Gabe und Auftrag der Sakramente,* Otto Mueller, 1962, translation by R. A. Wilson published as *A Sacramental Spirituality,* Sheed, 1965, published as *The New Covenant,* Burns & Oates, 1966; *Das Konzil im Zeichen der Einheit,* Herder (Freiburg), 1963, translation by Kaiser published as *The Johannine Council: Witness to Unity,* Herder & Herder (New York), 1963; *Die Gegenwaertige Heilsstunde,* Erich Wewel, 1964, translation by Arlene Swidler published in two volumes as *This Time of Salvation* and *Christian Maturity,* Herder & Herder, 1967; *Meditations on the Sacraments and Christian Life for Priests and Seminarians,* New Migne Press, 1964; *The Priest: Teacher of Morality,* Sacred Heart Seminary, 1964; *Der Christ und die Ehe,* Haus der katholischen Frauen (Duesseldorf), 1964, translation published as *Married Love: A Modern Christian View of Marriage and Family Life,* Argus Communications, 1970.

Il Matrimonio nelle prospettive del Vaticano II, Favero (Vicenza), 1966; *Il concilio comincia adesso,* Edizioni Paoline (Rome), 1966, translation published as *Road to Renewal: Perspectives of Vatican II,* Alba House, 1966; *Moralverkuendigung nach dem Konzil,* Kaffke (Frankfurt), 1966, translation by Hilda Graeft published as *Road to Relevance: Present and Future Trends in Catholic Moral Teaching,* Alba House, 1970; *Toward a Christian Moral Theology,* University of Notre Dame Press, 1966; *Bernhard Haering antwortet: Aktuelle moraltheologie Problems unserere Zeit,* Verlag der St. Paulus-Mission (Remscheid), 1966, translation by the Society of St. Paul published as *Bernard Haering Replies: Answers to Fifty Moral and Religious Questions,* Alba House, 1967; *Confession and Happiness,* St. Paul Publications, 1966; *Mit dem Konzil in eine neue Zeit,* Verlag der St. Paulus-Mission, 1966; *The Transformation of Man: A Study of Conversion and Community,* Geoffrey Chapman, 1967; *La morale del discorso della montaga,* Edizioni Paoline, 1967, translation by Albert Wimmer published as *What Does Christ Want?,* Alba House, 1968; *Dinamica da Renovacao,* Ediciones Paulinas (Sao Paulo), 1967.

Shalom: Peace: The Sacrament of Reconciliation, Farrar, Straus, 1968, revised edition, Image Books, 1969; *The Christian Existentialist: The Philosophy and Theology of Self-Fulfillment in Modern Society,* New York University Press, 1968; *Die Freude verkuenden,* Ars Sacra (Munich), 1968, translation by Edward Quinn published as *Celebrating Joy,* Herder & Herder, 1970 (published in England as *Proclaiming Joy,* Burns & Oates, 1970); *Brennpunkt Ehe: Heutige Probleme und Perspektiven in Tradition and Lehramt,* Kaffke, 1968, translation by D. White published as *Love Is the Answer,* Dimension, 1970; *Acting on the Word,* Farrar, Straus, 1968; *New Horizon for the Church in the Modern World,* Ave Maria Press, 1968; *Zusage an die Welt,* Kaffke, 1968, translation published as *The Church on the Move,* Alba House, 1970; *Krise um Humanae Vitae,* Kaffke, 1968; *Liebe ist mehr als Gebot: Lebenserneuerung aus dem Geist der Bergpredigt,* Erich Wewel, 1968; *Teologie moral en camino: Situacion y perspectivas nuevas,* El Perpetuo Socorro (Madrid), 1969; (with Karl Rahner) *A propos de l'encyclique Humanae vitae,* Editions Pauline, 1969.

Die grosse Versoehnung: Neue Perspektiven des Bussakramentes, Otto Mueller, 1970; *A Theology of Protest,* Farrar, Straus, 1970, revised edition published as *Theologie im Protest: Die Kirche im Konflikt,* Otto Mueller, 1971; *Vita cristiana nella luce dei sacramenti,* Favero, 1970, translation published as *The Sacraments and Your Everyday Life,* Liguori Publications, 1976 (published in England as *The Sacraments in a Secular Age: A Vision in Depth of Sacramentality and Its Impact on Moral Life,* St. Paul Publications, 1976); *Paternita responsabile,* A.V.R. (Rome), 1970; *Morality Is for Persons: The Ethics of Christian Personalism,* Farrar, Straus, 1971; *Hope Is the Remedy,* St. Paul Publications, 1971, Doubleday, 1972; (with Piet Fransen) *Pastoral Problems Today in a Changing Church and a Changing World,* [Pretoria], 1972; *Heilender Deist: Ethische Probleme der modernen Medizen,* Matthias-Gruenewald Verlag (Mainz), 1972, translation published as *Medical Ethics,* edited by Gabrielle L. Jean, St. Paul Publications, 1972, Fides/Claretian, 1973; *Etica cristiana in un'epoca di secolarizzazione,* Edizione Paoline, 1972, translation published as *Faith and Morality in a Secular Age,* Doubleday, 1973; *Prospettive e problemi ecumenici di teologia morale,* Edizioni Paoline, 1973; *Morale e evangelizzazione del mondo di oggi: La morale dell'evangelizzazione e l'evangelizzazione della morale,* Edizioni Paoline, 1974, translation by Albert Kuuire published as *Evangelization Today,* Fides/Claretian, 1974; *Suende im Zeitalter der Saekularisation,* Verlag Styria (Graz), 1974, translation published as *Sin in the Secular Age,* Doubleday, 1974.

Gebet Gewinn der Mitte, Verlag Styria, 1975, translation published as *Prayer: The Integration of Faith and Life,* Fides/Claretian, 1975; *Ethics of Manipulation: Issues in Medicine, Behavior Control and Genetics,* Seabury, 1975 (published in England as *Manipulation: Ethical Boundaries of Medical, Behavioural and Genetic Manipulation,* St. Paul Publications, 1975); *Beatitudini: Testimonianza e impegno sociale,* Edizioni Paoline, 1975, translation published as *The Beatitudes: Their Personal and Social Implications,* St. Paul Publications, 1976, published as *Blessed Are the Pure in Heart: The Beatitudes,* Seabury, 1977; *Embattled Witness: Memories of a Time of War,* Seabury, 1976; *Un mese mariano: 31 brevi meditazioni bibliche,* Edizioni Paoline, 1977, translation by the Society of St. Paul published as *Mary and Your Everyday Life: A Book of Meditations,* Liguori Publications, 1978 (published in England as *The Song of the Servant: Biblical Meditations on Mary the Mother and Model of the Church,* St. Paul Publications, 1978); *The Eucharist and Our Everyday Lives,* St. Paul Publications, 1978, Seabury, 1979; *Free and Faithful in Christ:*

Moral Theology for Priests and Laity, Seabury, Volume I: *General Moral Theology,* 1978, Volume II: *The Truth Will Set You Free,* 1979, Volume III: *Light to the World,* 1981.

Discovering God's Mercy: Confession Helps for Today's People, Liguori Publications, 1980 (published in England as *Reconciliation,* St. Paul Publications, 1980); *In Pursuit of Holiness,* Liguori Publications, 1982 (published in England as *Called to Holiness,* St. Paul Publications, 1982); *Commentario sulla "Familiaris Consortio" di Giovanni Pablo II,* Edizioni Paoline, 1982; *Jesus lieben lernen,* Herder & Herder, 1982.

Editor: (With H. S. Brechter and others, and contributor) *Lexikon fuer Theologie und Kirche: Das Zweite Vatikanische Konzil: Dokumente und Kommentare,* Herder (Freiburg), 1968; (with Rahner and G. Kaffke, and contributor) *Wort in Welt: Studien zur Theologie der Verkuendigung,* Kaffke, 1968; (with Rahner, and contributor) *Palabra en el mundo,* Ediciones Sigueme (Salamanca), 1972.

Author of introduction: B. Schlegelberger, *Rapporti sessuali prima e fuori del matrimonio,* Edizioni Paoline, 1973; E. Hillman, *Polygamy Reconsidered: African Plural Marriage and the Christian Churches,* Orbis, 1975; M. Cucco, editor, *Il peccato dei fidanzati,* Edizioni Paoline, 1976.

Contributor: V. Redlich, editor, *Moralprobleme im Umbruck der Zeit,* M. Hueber Verlag (Munich), 1957; G. Wuest, editor, *Familie in Volk und Kirche: Handbuch fuer Familienarbeit,* Winfried Werk, 1960; K. Rudolf, editor, *Der Christ und die Wirklichkeit: Moralprobleme der Zeit,* Seelsorger Verlag, 1960; *Kirch und Ueberlieferng,* Herder (Freiburg), 1960; P. Delhaye and others, editors, *Pastorale du peche,* Desclee (Tournai), 1961; *Mitteilungen fuer Seelsorge und Lainarbeit,* Bischoefliche Kanzlei (Mainz), 1961; G. Poage and G. Lievin, editors, *Today's Vocation Crisis,* Mercier Press, 1962; *Quaderni dell'Ufficio Catechistico,* [Torino], 1963; G. Bauer, editor, *Die zehn Gebote Gottes,* Kreuz Verlag (Stuttgart), 1963; *Vocazioni religiose e mondo moderne,* Sacra Congregazione dei Religiosi, Pontificia Opera delle Vocazioni Religiose (Milan), 1963; G. Thils and K. V. Truhlar, editors, *Laiecs et vie chretienne parfaite,* Herder (Rome), 1963; F. Bourdeau and A. Danet, *Introduzione alla Legge di Christo,*Morcelliana (Brescia), 1963; P. Schmilden, editor, *Religioese Erziehung im Heim,* Lambertus Verlag (Freiburg), 1963; *Mario von Galli, Kraft und Ohnmacht,* Knecht (Frankfurt), 1963; E. McDonagh, editor, *The Meaning of Christian Marriage,* Gill & Son (Dublin), 1963; *The Problem of Population: Moral and Theological Considerations,* University of Notre Dame Press, 1964; F. Boeckle and F. Groner, editors, *Moral zwischen Anspruch und Verantwortung,* Patmos (Duesseldorf), 1964; *Gott in Welt, Festgabe fuer Karl Rahner,* Herder (Freiburg), 1964; P. Bormann, editor, *Liturgie in der Gemeinde,* Meinwerk (Salzkotten), 1964; *Probleme der Beichterziehung,* Veroeffentlichungen des Katechetischen Instituts, Universitaet Graz, 1964; M. Schmaus and A. Laeple, editors, *Wahrheit und Zeugnis,* Patmos, 1964.

M. Marx, editor, *Protestants and Catholics on Spiritual Life,* Liturgical Press, 1965; *Apostolic Renewal in the Seminary in Light of Vatican Council II,* The Christopores (New York), 1965; F. Schoelsser, *Kirche; Anspruch und Aegernis,* Pustet (Regensburg), 1965; *Laien und christliche Vollkommenheit,* Herder (Freiburg), 1966; *Perche non credo?,* Cittadella (Assisi), 1966; J. H. Miller, editor, *Theological Issues of Vatican II,* University of Notre Dame Press, 1966; *Obedience, the Greater Freedom,* St. Paul Editions (Boston), 1966; *Politics and the Kingdom,* B.B.C. Publications, 1966; *First Step in Christian Renewal,* Dimension, 1967; Thomas E. Bird, editor, *Modern Theologians, Jews and Christians,* Association Press, 1967; R. W. Gleason, editor, *Contemporary Spirituality,* Fordham University Press, 1967; *Chiesa e mondo universitario,* Edizioni Ares (Milan), 1967; *Riflessioni sull' "Humanae Vitae,"* Edizioni Paoline, 1968; D. Callaghan, *The Catholic Case for Contraception,* Macmillan, 1968; G. H. Outka and P. Ramsey, editors, *Norm and Context in Christian Ethics,* Scribner, 1968; G. Blandino, *Una discussione su l'etica della felicita,* Edizioni di Ethica (Bologna), 1968; *Eglise et communaute humaine,* Desclee (Paris), 1968; L. K. Shook, editor, *Theology of Renewal,* Palm Publishers, 1968; *La theologie du renouveau,* Pontifical Institute of Medieval Studies (Toronto), 1968; F. X. Arnold and others, editors, *Handbuch der Pastoraltheologie,* Herder (Freiburg), 1968; Rahner and A. Darlap, editors, *Sacramentum mundi,* Herder (Freiburg), 1969; C. Curran, editor, *Contraception: Authority and Dissent,* Herder & Herder, 1969; *La violenza dei cristiani,* Cittadella, 1969; *Liberazione dell'uomo: Realta di oggi e storia della salvezza,* Edizioni Paoline, 1969; *La poverta evangelica e l'apostolato sacrodotale,* Centro Studio O.N.A.R.M.O. (Rome), 1969.

D. Ciotta, editor, *Educarsi alla responsabilita,* Cittadella, 1970; L. M. Colonnese, editor, *Human Rights and the Liberation of Man in the Americas,* University of Notre Dame Press, 1970; J. T. Noonan, Jr., editor, *The Morality of Abortion: Legal and Historical Perspectives,* Harvard University Press, 1970; E. L. Long and R. T. Handy, editors, *Theology and Church in Times of Change,* Westminster, 1970; J. Papin, editor, *The Dynamic in Christian Thought,* Villanova University Press, 1970; *Ateismo contemporaneo,* Societa Editrice Internazionale (Torino), 1970; *La vida religiosa en nuestros dias,* Ediciones Paulinas (Madrid), 1970; *Magistero e morale,* Edizioni Dehoniane (Bologna), 1970; *Il matrimonio,* Edizioni Paoline, 1971; *Rapporti prematrimoniali,* Edizioni Paoline, 1972; *Kirche und Publizistik,* Schoeningh (Paderborn), 1972; *Die Zukunft des Oekumenismus,* Knecht, 1972; A. Santini, editor, *Le chiese e la guerra,* Napoleone Editore (Rome), 1972; S. Holm and N. Thulstrup, editors, *Ethisk Antologi,* Universitetsforlaget (Copenhagen), 1972; *Manipulacion del hombre y moral,* Instituto Superior de Scienias Morales (Madrid), 1973; L. Wrenn, editor, *Divorce and Remarriage in the Catholic Church,* Paulist/Newman, 1973; G. Zizola, editor, *Religione e mondo moderno,* Morcelliana, 1974; J. Huettenbuegel, editor, *Gott-Mensch-Universum,* Verlag Styria, 1974; *Vita e Pensiero,* [Milan], 1974; *Aspetti della teologia del sacerdozio dopo il Concilio,* Citta Nuova Editrice (Rome), 1974.

Praktisches Handbuch der Pastoral-Anthropologie, Herder (Freiberg), 1975; *Papsttum heute und morgen,* Pustet, 1975; *Los religiosos, frente a los graves problemas de la evangelizacion: Justicia, liberacion, promocion humana, compromiso social y politico,* Instituto teologico de Vida Religiosa (Madrid), 1975; P. Beretta, editor, *Si o no all'aborto?,* Edizioni Paoline, 1976; J. Feiner and M. Loehr, editors, *Mysterium Salutis,* Benzinger (Zurich), 1976; K. Demmer and B. Schueller, editors, *Christlich glauben und handeln,* Patmos, 1977; Beretta, editor, *Morire si, ma quando?,* Edizioni Paoline, 1977; Schoelsser, editor, *Warum ich so lebe: Christen Ueber den Weg im Orden,* Katholisches Bibelwerk (Stuttgart), 1977; F. Herraez, *La opcion fundamental,* Ediciones Sigueme, 1978; S. de Fiores and T. Goffi, editors, *Nuova Dizionario di spiritualita,* Edizioni Paoline, 1980.

Contributor to proceedings of Catholic Theological Society, 1963, Society of Catholic College Teachers of Sacred Doctrine, 1965, National Sunday School Conference, 1965, and Institute on Problems That Unite Us, 1965; contributor to *Dizionario enciclopedico di teologia morale,* 1973. Contributor of more than 325 articles to journals in the United States, Germany, Italy, and France, including *Commonweal, Paulus, Masses Ouvieres, Digest Cattolico, Anima e Corpi, Pentecostes,* and *Dialog.*

SIDELIGHTS: Recognized as one of the foremost Roman Catholic moral theologians and an expert on questions of sexual morality, Bernhard Haering "has been on the field of battle for a more human, a more fully Christian ethical norm for a long time," according to *Commonweal*'s Albert L. Schlitzer. "His efforts to free moral decision-making from the shackles of legalism predate Vatican II and continue unabated."

Haering's book *The Law of Christ,* David Hollenbach notes in *America,* was "an early indication" of the great change in moral thinking occuring within the Catholic Church. During the Second Vatican Council of the early 1960s, the new ideas that Haering advocated were formally recognized, and the wave of liberalization that has since swept across the Church has created, as Merle Longwood observes in *Commonweal,* "a flood of articles delineating the renewal of Catholic moral theology, and an even greater number of articles and books focusing on particular moral issues." However, Longwood continues, "there have been few books which have attempted to present systematically the basic principles of moral theology in light of these recent developments." Haering's *Free and Faithful in Christ,* Longwood adds, fills the need for "sustained, comprehensive, internally consistent works that express the current thinking being done in this discipline."

In *Morality Is for Persons,* Haering "presents a critique of the traditional Catholic approach to morality, which he regards as legalistic and the product of a false understanding of 'natural law' as an alleged source of self-evident principles by which man should live," writes John Gaskell in *Books and Bookmen.* Haering "directs the reader back to a dynamic view of morality which he sees as more consonant with Christian revelation. The general tone is one of great openness to other viewpoints and ideas." "He defends a 'natural law,' but not the rigid, timeless and impersonal kind upheld by the Schoolmen of the past," Schlitzer remarks. "[Haering] argues that accepted moral principles are always historically and culturally conditioned. Natural law is not a code with ready and certain answers for every situation." And in an *Encounter* review of *Shalom,* J. Robert Nelson says Haering "insists that the whole purpose [of priests] is not to exercise ecclesiastical discipline, but to bestow upon each person a sense of peace and joy in the realization that he has been forgiven and reconciled by God."

BIOGRAPHICAL/CRITICAL SOURCES: Encounter, summer, 1969; *Best Sellers,* June 15, 1971, June 1, 1976; *America,* September 11, 1971, September 2, 1972, March 3, 1973, December 2, 1978; *Commonweal,* December 17, 1971, February 28, 1975, February 1, 1980; *Critic,* January, 1973, May 15, 1979; *Books and Bookmen,* January, 1973; *Choice,* October, 1973, April, 1980; *Times Literary Supplement,* July 26, 1974; *Christian Century,* February 25, 1976, December 1, 1976, April 16, 1980; *Journal of Religion,* July, 1977, October, 1977; *Theology Today,* July, 1980.

* * *

HALACY, D(aniel) S(tephen), Jr. 1919-

PERSONAL: Born May 16, 1919, in Charleston, S.C.; son of Daniel Stephen and Pearl (Edwards) Halacy; married Beth Ann Debolt, June 2, 1946; children: Jessie Ann, Deirdre Jean. *Education:* Phoenix College, A.A., 1956; Arizona State University, B.A., 1957. *Religion:* Methodist. *Home:* 12761 West Alameda Dr., Lakewood, Colo. 80228.

CAREER: Free-lance writer. Convair Corp., San Diego, Calif., foreman, 1952-54; AiResearch Manufacturing Co., Phoenix, Ariz., engineering writer, 1957-58; Goodyear Aircraft, Litchfield Park, Ariz., chief editor, 1958-60; Motorola Corp., Phoenix, manager, Technical Information Center, 1961-62; Arizona state senator, 1967-70; assistant to U.S. Senator Paul Fannin, 1975-76; member of staff, Arizona Solar Energy Commission, 1977-78; Solar Energy Research Institute, Golden, Colo., senior information officer, 1979—. Teacher of creative writing, Phoenix College. *Military service:* U.S. Army Air Forces, 1943-46; became second lieutenant. U.S. Air Force, 1951-52; became first lieutenant; received Air Medal with oak leaf clusters. *Member:* Association for Applied Solar Energy, Adult Education Association, Authors League of Authors Guild of America (state senator), Toastmasters International, Arizona Soaring Association.

WRITINGS: Fabulous Fireball: The Story of Solar Energy, Macmillan, 1957, revised edition, 1967; *Fun with the Sun,* Macmillan, 1959; *America's Major Air Disasters,* Monarch, 1961; *Computers: The Machines We Think With,* Harper, 1962, revised edition, 1969; *Encyclopedia of the World's Great Events: 1936,* Monarch, 1963, reprinted, Arlington House, 1974; *The Coming Age of Solar Energy,* Harper, 1963, revised edition, 1973; *Encyclopedia of the World's Great Events: 1932,* Monarch, 1964; *Nine Roads to Tomorrow,* Macrae Smith, 1964; *The Robots Are Here,* Norton, 1965; *Bionics,* Holiday House, 1965; *Beyond Tomorrow,* Macrae Smith, 1965; *Cyborg: Evolution of the Superman,* Harper, 1965; *Encyclopedia of the World's Great Events: 1964,* Monarch, 1965; *Theodor Von Karman, Father of Supersonic Flight,* Messner, 1965.

Fuel Cells, World Publishing, 1966; *The Shipbuilders,* Lippincott, 1966; *33 Miles a Minute: The Story of Air Transport,* Messner, 1966; *The Water Crisis,* Dutton, 1966; *Radiation, Magnetism and Living Things,* Holiday, 1966; *The "In" Sports,* Macrae Smith, 1966; *They Gave Their Names to Science,* Putnam, 1967; *Science and Serendipity,* Macrae Smith, 1967; *Energy and Engines,* World, 1967; *Century Twenty-One: Your Life in the Year 2001 and Beyond,* Macrae Smith, 1968; *Colonization of the Moon,* Van Nostrand, 1968; *The Weather Changers,* Harper, 1968; *X-Rays and Gamma Rays,* Holiday House, 1969; *Experiments with Solar Energy,* Norton, 1969.

Charles Babbage, Father of the Computer, Crowell-Collier, 1970; *Habitat: Man's Universe and Ecology,* Macrae Smith, 1970; *Man Alive: Life and Man's Physical Nature,* Macrae Smith, 1970; *Man and Memory: Breakthrough in the Science of the Human Mind,* Harper, 1970; *Feast and Famine,* Macrae Smith, 1971; *Now or Never: The Fight against Pollution,* Four Winds Press, 1971; *Social Man,* Macrae Smith, 1972; *The Geometry of Hunger,* Harper, 1972; *Soaring,* Lippincott, 1972; *Your City Tomorrow,* Four Winds Press, 1973; *Government by the States: A History,* Bobbs-Merrill, 1973; *What Makes a Computer Work?,* Little, Brown, 1973; *Genetic Revolution: Shaping Life for Tomorrow,* Harper, 1974; *On the Move: Man and Transportation,* Macrae Smith, 1974; *Earthquakes: A Natural History,* Bobbs-Merrill, 1974; (with James Martin) *Arizona and Tomorrow's Solar Power Plants,* Arizona State Fuel and Energy Office, 1974; (with Heinz R. Hink and Bruce Mason) *Arizona: People and Government,* H.M.H. Book Co., 1975; *The Sky Trap,* Elsevier-Nelson, 1975; *The Energy Trap,* Four Winds Press, 1975; *Survival in the World of Work,* Scribner, 1975; *With Wings as Eagles: The Story of Soaring,* Bobbs-Merrill, 1975; *The Complete Book of Hang Gliding,* Hawthorn, 1975.

Earth, Water, Wind and Sun: The Energy Alternatives, Harper, 1977; *How to Improve Your Memory,* F. Watts, 1977; *Ice or Fire?: Surviving Climatic Change,* Harper, 1978; (with wife, Beth Halacy) *The Solar Cookery Book,* Peace Press, 1978; *Nuclear Energy,* F. Watts, 1978; *Census: One Hundred Ninety Years of Counting America,* Elsevier-Nelson, 1980; *The Charlie Brown Encyclopedia of Energy,* Random House, 1982.

Fiction for young people: *Star for a Compass,* Macmillan, 1956; *High Challenge,* Macmillan, 1957; *Whale Spotters,* Macmillan, 1958; *Duster Pilot,* Chilton, 1961; *Ripcord,* Whitman, 1962; *'Copter Cowboy,* Chilton, 1963; *Surfer,* Macmillan, 1965; *Sky on Fire!,* Macmillan, 1965; *Dive from the Sky!,* McGraw, 1967; *The Adventures of Ethan Strong,* McGraw, 1967, published as *Ethan Strong: Strike and Fight Back,* McGraw, 1968; *Rocket Rescue,* Norton, 1968; *Master Spy,* McGraw, 1968; *Return from Luna,* Norton, 1969; *Ethan Strong: Watch by the Sea,* McGraw, 1969; *The Secret of the Cove,* Lion Press, 1969.

Contributor of about three hundred stories and articles, and about the same number of pieces of light and humorous verse, to magazines; some of his magazine work has been anthologized.

WORK IN PROGRESS: The New Producing Your Own Power Book, for Rodale Press.

* * *

HALEY, Jay 1923-

PERSONAL: Born July 19, 1923, in Midwest, Wyo.; son of Andrew J. and Mary (Sneddon) Haley; married Elizabeth Kuehn (a musician), December 25, 1950 (divorced, 1971); children: Kathleen, Andrew, Gregory. *Education:* University of California, Los Angeles, B.A., 1948; University of California, Berkeley, B.L.S., 1951; Stanford University, M.A., 1953. *Home:* 8707 Burning Tree Rd., Bethesda, Md. 20034. *Office:* Family Therapy Institute, 4602 North Park Ave., Chevy Chase, Md. 20815.

CAREER: Project for Study of Communication (Veterans Administration and Stanford University), Palo Alto, Calif., research associate, 1953-62; Mental Research Institute, Palo Alto, director of family experimentation, 1962-67; Philadelphia Child Guidance Clinic, Philadelphia, Pa., director of family research, 1967-74; Family Therapy Institute, Chevy Chase, Md., director, 1974—.

WRITINGS: Strategies of Psychotherapy, Grune, 1963; (editor) *Advanced Techniques of Hypnosis and Therapy,* Grune, 1967; (with Lynn Hoffman) *Techniques of Family Therapy,* Basic Books, 1967; *The Power Tactics of Jesus Christ: And Other Essays,* Grossman, 1969; (editor) *Changing Families,* Grune, 1971; *Uncommon Therapy,* Norton, 1972; *Leaving Home,* McGraw, 1981; *Reflections on Therapy,* Family Therapy Institute, 1982.

* * *

HALL, B(axter) C(larence) 1936-

PERSONAL: Born June 9, 1936, in Buckhorn, Ark.; son of B. C. and Hattie (Younger) Hall; married Daphna Haviland Knight (a singer and teacher), June 6, 1959; children: B. C. III, Joseph Nathan. *Education:* Henderson State University, B.A., 1959; University of Iowa, M.F.A., 1961. *Religion:* "Apostasy." *Home:* 1971 West Brichta Dr., Tucson, Ariz. 85705. *Agent:* Charles Neighbors, Inc., 240 Waverly Pl., New York, N.Y. 10014.

CAREER: Log Cabin Democrat, Conway, Ark., reporter and editor, 1958-59; Arkansas Polytechnic College, Russellville, professor of English, 1961-74; University of Arizona, Tucson, professor of English, beginning 1974. Reporter for *Arkansas Gazette,* 1963-67.

WRITINGS: (Editor) *Writings from the Lower Sonoran Region* (anthology), Aware Press, 1972; *The Burning Season* (novel), Putnam, 1974; *The Weight Training Book,* Ace Books, 1979; *Keepers of the Feast,* Seaview, 1980; (with Bob Lancaster) *Judgement Day,* Playboy Press, 1982.

SIDELIGHTS: B. C. Hall writes: "I once served on a censorship-of-film board during which time no films whatsoever were censored. I was later impeached." He adds: "I consider hardly anything vital except for wife, my sons, my dogs, and some bourbon. I learned vocabulary from listening to Harry Caray broadcast St. Louis Cardinal baseball games; I learned something about life from watching my brother ride horses and shoot pool."

BIOGRAPHICAL/CRITICAL SOURCES: Iowa Review, February, 1975.†

* * *

HALL, Brian P(atrick) 1935-

PERSONAL: Born December 29, 1935, in London, England; son of Leonard (a clerk) and Elsie (Ross) Hall; married Diane Ellis Jones (a physical therapist and value conference facilitator), May 6, 1961; children: Martin, Christine. *Education:* University of London, certificate in chemistry and mathematics, 1958; University of British Columbia, B.A., 1962; University of Western Ontario, M.Div., 1965; Centro de Investigaciones Culturales, further graduate study, 1966; Clermont Graduate School, Dr.Rel., 1969. *Home:* 1324 Redwood Dr., Santa Cruz, Calif. 95060. *Office:* Director of Pastoral Counseling, University of Santa Clara, 224 Bannan Hall, Santa Clara, Calif. 95053.

CAREER: Rogers Sugar Refinery, Vancouver, British Columbia, research chemist, 1959-60; part-time chemist, 1960-63; Anglican World Mission, Canadian Mission Board, Overseas Mission, researcher on the possibilities of social services in Venezuela, 1963-66, 1966-68; ordained Episcopal priest, 1966; priest in charge of mission parish in Barrio Cuba, San Jose, Costa Rica, 1966-68; Salvation Army Family Service, Los Angeles, Calif., director of family service, 1968-69; Catholic Family Service, Gary, Ind., director of family and community programs, 1969-71; Center for Exploration of Values and Meaning, Indianapolis, Ind., co-founder and member of board of directors, 1971-73, executive director and president, 1973-78, chairman of board of directors, 1973-75; University of Santa Clara, Graduate Division of Counseling, Psychology, and Education, Santa Clara, Calif., director of pastoral counseling, 1978—. Licensed psychologist in State of Indiana. Adjunct professor at St. Louis University. Fund raiser for Family Institute (Costa Rica); chairman of board of Indianapolis Omega Project, 1975. Consultant to Dendron Publishing. *Member:* American Association of Pastoral Counselors (fellow), American Association of Family Counselors (clinical member).

WRITINGS—Published by Paulist/Newman, except as indicated: *Learning to Live with Change,* two volumes, with tape recording, Argus Communications, 1969; *Values: Exploration and Discovery,* with kit, Argus Communications, 1971; *Value Clarification as Learning Process,* Volume I: *A Sourcebook,* Volume II: *A Guidebook,* Volume III (with Maury Smith): *A Handbook for Christian Educators,* 1973; (with Joseph Osburn) *Nog's Vision,* 1973; *The Development of Consciousness: A Confluent Theory of Values,* 1975; *The Chrysalis Child,* 1975; *The Wizard of Maldoone,* 1975.

The Personal Discernment Inventory, Paulist Press, 1980; *God's Plans for Us: A Practical Strategy for Discernment of Spirits,* Paulist Press, 1980; *Leadership through Values: An Approach to Personal and Organizational Development,* Paulist Press, 1980; *Shepherds and Lovers,* Paulist Press, 1982.

Also author, with Hendrix and Smith, of five volumes in the "Wonder" series for Paulist/Newman, 1974; author and designer of four video films in "Leadership Development Program" series for Franciscan Communications; author of tape scripts on teaching. Contributor to church publications.

AVOCATIONAL INTERESTS: Sailing, fencing with foils, chess, painting, art history, hiking.

BIOGRAPHICAL/CRITICAL SOURCES: U.S. News and World Report, March 17, 1975.

* * *

HALL, Lynn 1937-

PERSONAL: Born November 9, 1937, in Lombard, Ill.; daughter of Raymond Edwin (a city official) and Alice (a high school teacher; maiden name, Seeds) Hall; married Dean W. Green, May 1, 1960 (divorced September, 1961). *Education:* Attended schools in Iowa. *Religion:* Protestant. *Home:* Touchwood, Route 2, Elkader, Iowa 52043.

CAREER: Writer. Secretary in Fort Worth, Tex., 1955-57; secretary and veterinarian's assistant in Des Moines, Iowa, 1957-66; affiliated with Ambro Advertising Agency, Des Moines, Iowa, 1966-68. Member of Garnavillo Library Board. *Member:* Collie Club of America, Cedar Valley Collie Club, Dubuque Kennel Club. *Awards, honors:* Charles W. Follett award, 1971, for *A Horse Called Dragon;* Netherlands' Silver Quill Award, 1976; Edgar Allan Poe Award, 1979; Best Book for Young Adults award, American Library Association, 1980, for *The Leaving;* Boston Globe/Horn Book Award, 1981; Tennessee Children's Choice Award, 1981.

WRITINGS—Juveniles; published by Follett, except as indicated: *The Shy Ones,* 1967; *The Secret of Stonehouse,* 1968; *Ride a Wild Dream,* 1969; *Too Near the Sun* (Junior Literary Guild selection), 1970; *Gently Touch the Milkweed* (Junior Literary Guild selection), 1970; *A Horse Called Dragon,* 1971; *The Famous Battle of Bravery Creek,* Garrard, 1972; *The Siege of Silent Henry,* 1972; *Sticks and Stones,* 1972; *Lynn Hall's Dog Stories,* 1972; *Flash, Dog of Old Egypt,* Garrard, 1973; *Barry, the Bravest St. Bernard,* Garrard, 1973; *Riff, Remember,* 1973; *To Catch a Tartar,* 1973; *Stray,* 1974; *Bob, Watchdog of the River,* Garrard, 1974.

Troublemaker, 1975; *Kids and Dog Shows,* 1975; *New Day for Dragon,* 1975; *Captain: Canada's Flying Pony,* Garrard, 1976; *Flowers of Anger,* 1976; *Owney, the Traveling Dog,* Garrard, 1977; *Dragon Defiant,* 1977; *Shadows,* 1977; *Careers for Dog Lovers,* 1978; *Mystery of Pony Hollow,* Garrard, 1978; *Mystery of the Lost and Found Hound,* Garrard, 1979; *Mystery of the Schoolhouse Dog,* Garrard, 1979; *Dog of Bondi Castle,* 1979; *The Leaving,* Scribner, 1980; *Dragon Delight,* 1980; *Mystery of the Stubborn Old Man,* Garrard, 1980; *Mystery of the Plum Park Pony,* Garrard, 1980; *The Horse Trader,* Scribner, 1980; *The Haunting of the Green Bird,* 1980; *The Disappearing Grandad,* 1980; *The Mysterious Moortown Bridge,* 1980; *The Ghost of the Great River Inn,* 1980; *The Mystery of the Caramel Cat,* Garrard, 1981; *Danza!,* Scribner, 1981; *Half the Battle,* Scribner, 1982; *Tin Can Tucker,* Scribner, 1982.

WORK IN PROGRESS: The Somethin' Special Horse, for Golden Press; *The Mystery of Megan's Mare,* for Scribner.

SIDELIGHTS: "The loves of my life, horses and dogs, provide the impetus for my writing," Lynn Hall told *CA.* "The truth is that I write not so much to provide books for children as to relish the sheer fun of a good horse story or a good dog story. When I've read all the horse stories I can find, then there's nothing to do but make up some new ones. I consider myself singularly lucky to have made a life's work out of a life-long love."

AVOCATIONAL INTERESTS: Breeding and exhibiting border collies; playing the piano; remodeling her house; exploring woods.

* * *

HALL, Richard (Seymour) 1925-

PERSONAL: Born July 22, 1925, in Margate, Kent, England; son of Douglas Beecroft and Gladys (Alcock) Hall; married Barbara Taylor (a journalist), July 10, 1947 (divorced, 1975); married Caroline E. Cattley (a journalist); children: (first marriage) Robin, Nicolas, Simon, Crispin, Jeremy. *Education:* Keble College, Oxford, M.A. (with honors), 1948. *Politics:* "Radical but non-party." *Religion:* Agnostic. *Home:* 21 Earls Ter., London W.8, England; and The Old School, Ufton, Oxfordshire, England. *Agent:* A. D. Peters & Co. Ltd., 10 Buckingham St., London WC2N 6BU, England.

CAREER: Daily Mail, London, England, sub-editor, 1948-50, 1955-56; *Illustrated,* London, sub-editor, 1950-54; *Mufulira Magazine,* Mufulira, Zambia, editor, 1956-58; Government Information Services, Zambia, managing editor, 1958-60; *African Mail,* Lusaka, Zambia, managing editor, 1960-65; *Times of Zambia,* Ndola, Zambia, editor-in-chief, 1965-68; founder and editor, *African Development* (magazine), 1968-70; *Observer,* London, editor of colour magazine, 1970-73; *Financial Times,* London, syndication director, 1974-79; *Observer,* columnist, 1980-82, Commonwealth correspondent, 1982—. Correspondent for *Newsweek* and *Daily Mail. Military service:* British Navy, 1943-45. *Member:* Royal Geographical Society.

WRITINGS: Kaunda, Founder of Zambia, Longmans, Green, 1964; *Zambia,* Pall Mall, 1965, Praeger, 1966; *The High Price of Principles: Kaunda and the White South,* Hodder & Stoughton, 1969, African Publishing, 1970, revised edition, Penguin, 1973; *Discovery of Africa,* Grosset, 1970; *Stanley: An Adventurer Explored* (Book-of-the-Month Club selection), Collins, 1974, Houghton Mifflin, 1975; *Explorers in Africa,* Usbourne Publishing Ltd., 1975; (with Hugh Peyman) *The Great Uhuru Railway: China's Showpiece in Africa,* Gollancz, 1976; *Zambia, 1890-1964: The Colonial Period,* Longman, 1977; *Lovers on the Nile: The Incredible Adventures of Sam and Florence Baker* (Book-of-the-Month Club selection), Collins, 1980, Random House, 1981.

SIDELIGHTS: British journalist Richard Hall, who spent twelve years living in central Africa, has written several books dealing with the history of the continent, particularly the British exploration and subsequent colonization of the land in the nineteenth century, as well as the British presence in Africa today.

Stanley: An Adventurer Explored and *Lovers on the Nile: The Incredible Adventures of Sam and Florence Baker* both focus on the lives of famous British explorers from the Victorian era, when Africa, the "Dark Continent," was a subject of great interest in England. In *Stanley: An Adventurer Explored,* Hall tells the story of Henry Morton Stanley (the man who found the lost explorer David Livingstone in 1871), drawing on material from what Edward Weeks in *Atlantic* calls "Stanley's cryptic diaries, . . . an immense correspondence, . . . an unfinished biography, . . . and from his own remarkable skill in solving the riddles" about the adventurer's life. "Through this detailed study" of Stanley's career, says a reviewer in *Publishers Weekly,* "we acquire a much fuller, more human perspective of the man."

Victorian adventurer Samuel Baker and his wife, Florence (whom he purportedly bought at a slave market in the Turkish Balkans), made two long journeys to the lake regions of central Africa in search of the unknown sources of the Nile. *Lovers on the Nile: The Incredible Adventures of Sam and Florence Baker,* the story of those travels, will "fulfill the appetite of exploration buffs," according to Wendy Law-Yone in *Washington Post Book World.* "It reveals more than the surface details of quest and discovery, and uncovers the attitudes behind the endeavors. . . . Happily, . . . [Hall gives us] the images we crave: lumbering elephants and hungry crocodiles, waterfront caravans and street scenes that resonate like the names of their cities—Khartoum, Constantinople, Zanzibar—all suggesting, as the Nile does, both menace and magic." Anatole Broyard writes in the *New York Times* that "it is the profound social history" Hall presents "that makes *Lovers on the Nile* such good reading."

The High Price of Principles: Kaunda and the White South is an account, according to a *Times Literary Supplement* critic, "of the political and economic development of Zambia" since the country gained independence from Britain in 1964. The critic feels that Hall, "a realistic, informed and by no means uncritical observer of the Zambian scene . . . at first hand," has written "a disturbing book [that] should be obligatory reading for all concerned in British policy towards Africa."

BIOGRAPHICAL/CRITICAL SOURCES: Times Literary Supplement, January 15, 1970, April 11, 1980; *Atlantic,* March, 1975; *New York Times,* March 19, 1980; *Washington Post Book World,* April 20, 1980.

* * *

HALLIE, Philip P. 1922-

PERSONAL: Born May 4, 1922, in Chicago, Ill.; son of William and Nettie (Leibowitz) Hallie; married Doris Ann Gabrielle, September 19, 1954; children: Michelena Louise, Louis Gabriel. *Education:* Grinnell College, B.A., 1946; Harvard University, M.A., 1948, Ph.D., 1951; Oxford University, B.Litt., 1950. *Home:* 137 Highland Ave., Middletown, Conn. *Office:* Wesleyan University, Wesleyan Station, Middletown, Conn. 06457.

CAREER: Vanderbilt University, Nashville, Tenn., assistant professor, 1952-56, associate professor, 1956-59, professor, 1959-62; Wesleyan University, Middletown, Conn., Griffin Professor of Philosophy and Humanities, 1962—. Member of national screening board, Fulbright graduate scholarships to Britain; represented United States at International Congress of Philosophy, Mysore, India, 1959. *Military service:* U.S. Army, Field Artillery, 1944-45; received three battle stars.

MEMBER: American Philosophical Association, Mind Association, American Association of University Professors, Phi Beta Kappa. *Awards, honors:* Midwest Poetry Conference Prize, 1946; Fulbright scholar, 1948-50; Guggenheim fellow, 1958-59; senior fellow, Center for Advanced Study, 1961-62; M.A., Wesleyan University, 1965; American Council of Learned Societies fellow, 1966-67; National Endowment for the Humanities fellow, 1981-82; D.Litt., Grinnell College.

WRITINGS: Maine de Biran: Reform of Empiricism, Harvard University Press, 1959; (editor) *Scepticism, Man, and God,* Wesleyan University Press, 1965; *The Scar of Montaigne,* Wesleyan University Press, 1967; *The Paradox of Cruelty,* Wesleyan University Press, 1967; *Lest Innocent Blood Be Shed: The Story of the Village of Le Chambon and How Goodness Happened There,* Harper, 1979. Contributor to *Encyclopedia of Philosophy* and to philosophy journals. Member of editorial board, *American Scholar,* 1964-66.

WORK IN PROGRESS: A study of a German officer who saved many French lives during World War II.

SIDELIGHTS: In his book *Lest Innocent Blood Be Shed,* Philip P. Hallie tells the story of a remote village in France that sheltered over 2,500 Jews during World War II. The people of Le Chambon, along with their Protestant minister Andre Trocme, organized a network of resistance to the Nazi occupation of France, hiding Jews in their homes and helping them reach safety in Switzerland. Hallie spent three years researching this story, interviewing the survivors of the war still living in Le Chambron, "talking at great length *with* them," as Terrence Des Pres writes in *Harper's,* "getting to know them as individuals, as friends, allowing himself to abandon the scholar's detachment so that . . . he might come to understand" them and their remarkable story.

Subtitled *The Story of the Village of Le Chambon and How Goodness Happened There,* the book is "an absorbing contribution to the study of being good—a subject that is fascinating because it is difficult," according to Naomi Bliven in a *New Yorker* article. "*Goodness.* When was the last time anyone used that word in earnest, without irony, as anything more than a doubtful cliche?" asks Des Pres. "*Lest Innocent Blood Be Shed* is one of the rarest of books, the kind that can change the way we live. It is conceived and written on a modest scale, but Philip Hallie knows full well the wisdom of starting small—that is one of the book's themes—and among other large accomplishments he has restored to the word *goodness* its rightful moral beauty. We can begin again to use it with confidence. We can—with the example of Le Chambon to remind us—begin again to believe that decency is possible."

BIOGRAPHICAL/CRITICAL SOURCES: New York Times Book Review, April 15, 1979; *Harper's,* May, 1979; *Saturday Review,* May 12, 1979; *Time,* May 21, 1979; *Washington Post Book World,* June 1, 1979; *New Yorker,* January 21, 1980.

* * *

HALPERIN, Mark (Warren) 1940-

PERSONAL: Born February 19, 1940, in New York, N.Y.; son of George W. (a dentist) and Minna (Scherzer) Halperin; married Barbara Scott (a painter), July 15, 1966; children: Noah. *Education:* Bard College, B.A., 1960; New School for

Social Research, graduate study, 1962-64; University of Iowa, M.F.A., 1966. *Home address:* Route 4, Box 279A, Ellensburg, Wash. 98926. *Office:* Department of English, Central Washington State College, Ellensburg, Wash. 98926.

CAREER: Machlett Laboratories, Inc., Stanford, Conn., junior physicist, 1960-62; Rockefeller Institute, New York, N.Y., electron microscope technician, 1963; University of Iowa, Iowa City, electron microscope technician, 1964-66; Central Washington State College, Ellensburg, assistant professor of English, 1966—. *Member:* Yakima River Conservancy (president, 1969-74), Alpine Lakes Protection Society (trustee, 1968-71). *Awards, honors:* U.S. Award from International Poetry Forum, 1975, for *Backroads*.

WRITINGS—All poetry: *Backroads,* University of Pittsburgh Press, 1976; *Gomer,* Sea Pen Press, 1979; *The White Coverlet,* Jawbone Press, 1979; *A Place Made Fast,* Copper Canyon Press, 1982. Contributor to literary magazines, including *Iowa Review, North American Review, Yale Review, Porch,* and *Poetry Northwest.*

WORK IN PROGRESS: A new book of poems.

SIDELIGHTS: Mark Halperin writes: "At this point, I want the kind of balance in my poems that I think of as formal, whether I work in traditional forms or so-called free ones. I would like my poetry to go out to the world rather than in to myself, though this is a matter of emphasis more than exclusion. Without being dour about it, I believe poems are important and the making of them serious. Thus, I expect to be unsure of what it is I'm after, to learn to live in and from that dis-ease."

* * *

HAMLET, Ova
See LUPOFF, Richard A(llen)

* * *

HAMM, Jack 1916-

PERSONAL: Born March 5, 1916, in Elkhart, Kan.; son of Ted Beaumont and Hazel (Trotter) Hamm; married Dorisnel Alexander, August 29, 1943; children: Dawna, Monty, Charlotte, Jerry. *Education:* Studied at Wichita Art Association, 1932, Frederic Mizen Academy of Art, 1936, and University of Colorado, 1947; Baylor University, B.A., 1948. *Politics:* Republican. *Religion:* Baptist.

CAREER: Mizen Academy of Art, Chicago, Ill., teacher for two years; Baylor University, Waco, Tex., instructor in art for six years, extension teacher in Dallas, Tex., 1962; artist and cartoonist for *Baptist Standard,* Texas Alcohol-Narcotic Education, Inc., and Religious Drawings Syndicate, Inc. Illustrator for Albert Edward Wiggam's column, "Let's Explore Your Mind," National Newspaper Service, for more than five years; artist and cartoonist for Newspaper Enterprise Association, one year; television artist, "Jack Hamm Show," KBTV, Dallas, one year, for KPRC-TV, Houston, Tex., for two years. *Awards, honors:* Freedoms Foundation Award for best cartoon of 1953 promoting American freedom, six additional Honor Medals, 1957-63; National American Legion annual editorial award for most patriotic drawing of 1954.

WRITINGS: Cartoons That Live, Van Kampen, 1954; *Kompas,* Christliches Verlagshaus, 1955; *The Living Scriptures,* Kregel, 1958; *He Will Answer,* Doubleday, 1961; *Saints Alive,* Kregel, 1961; *Drawing the Head and Figure,* Grosset, 1963; *Cartooning the Head and Figure,* Grosset, 1967, 2nd edition published as *How to Draw Cartoons,* Coles, 1979; *Drawing Toward God,* Droke, 1968; *How to Draw Animals,* Grosset, 1969; *Drawing Scenery: Landscapes and Seascapes,* Grosset, 1972; (with John W. Drakeford) *Pornography,* Thomas Nelson, 1973; *Still-Life Drawing and Painting,* Grosset, 1976.

WORK IN PROGRESS: Drawing methods.

SIDELIGHTS: Jack Hamm's editorial drawings are syndicated abroad as well as in this country; the text is translated into thirteen languages and dialects for foreign publication.

BIOGRAPHICAL/CRITICAL SOURCES: Time, May 28, 1951; *Guideposts,* December, 1951; *American,* September, 1952; *Pic,* November, 1952; *Newsweek,* February 2, 1953; *American Press,* January, 1961.†

* * *

HANSON, Anthony Tyrrell 1916-

PERSONAL: Born November 24, 1916, in London, England; son of Philip Herbert (a civil servant) and Deena (Tyrrell) Hanson; married Miriam Joselin, September 25, 1945; children: Philip, Andrew. *Education:* Attended Cheltenham College; Trinity College, University of Dublin, B.D., 1942, D.D., 1953. *Home:* Orchard Villa, Melbourne Place, Topcliffe Rd., Sowerby Y07 1QY, England. *Office:* Department of Theology, University of Hull, Hull, Humberside, England.

CAREER: Clergyman of Anglican Church. Curate in County Down, Ireland, 1941-43; Student Christian Movement, London, England, secretary, 1943-46; Andhra United Theological College, Dornakal, Andhra Pradesh, South India, tutor, 1947-55; United Theological College, Bangalore, South India, tutor, 1955-59; St. Anne's Cathedral, Belfast, Northern Ireland, canon theologian, 1959-62; University of Hull, Hull, England, professor of theology, 1963-82. Helped to organize interdenominational theology department (Roman Catholic, Reformed, Anglican) at Lesotho, South Africa; also helped to obtain affiliation of Irish School of Ecumenics, Dublin, to the University of Hull.

WRITINGS: (With R. H. Preston) *Revelation of St. John the Divine,* S.C.M. Press, 1949; (with wife, Miriam Hanson) *The Book of Job,* S.C.M. Press, 1953, revised edition, 1970; *Jonah and Daniel,* Madras, 1955; *The Wrath of the Lamb,* S.P.C.K., 1957; *The Pioneer Ministry,* S.C.M. Press, 1961; *The Church of the Servant,* S.C.M. Press, 1962; *St. Paul's Understanding of Jesus,* University of Hull Press, 1963; *Beyond Anglicanism,* Longman & Todd, 1965; *Jesus Christ in the Old Testament,* S.P.C.K., 1965; (editor) *The Pastoral Letters,* Cambridge University Press, 1966; (editor) *Vindications,* S.C.M. Press, 1966; *Studies in the Pastoral Epistles,* S.P.C.K., 1968.

(Editor) *Teilhard Reassessed,* Longman & Todd, 1970; *Studies in Paul's Technique and Theology,* Eerdmans, 1974; *Grace and Truth,* S.P.C.K., 1975; *Church, Sacraments, and Ministry,* Mowbrays, 1975.

The New Testament Interpretation of Scripture, S.P.C.K., 1980; *The Pastoral Epistles: New Century Bible,* Eerdmans, 1982; *The Image of the Invisible God,* S.C.M. Press, 1982.

WORK IN PROGRESS: Further study of Paul's writing against Rabbinic background.

HANSON, R(ichard) P(atrick) C(rosland) 1916-

PERSONAL: Born November 24, 1916, in London, England; son of Sir Philip (a civil servant) and Lady (maiden name, Tyrrell) Hanson; married Mary Dorothy Powell, August 29, 1950; children: Catherine Mary, Daniel Alexander, Monica Brigid, Simon John. *Education:* Trinity College, Dublin, B.A. in classics and in ancient history (both degrees with first class honors), 1938, B.D., 1941, D.D., 1950, M.A., 1962. *Home:* 24 Styal Rd., Wilmslow, Cheshire SK9 4AG, England.

CAREER: Clergyman of Church of Ireland, 1941—; pastoral work as priest in Dublin and County Down, Ireland, 1941-45; Queen's College, Birmingham, England, vice-principal, 1945-50; St. John's, Shuttleworth, Bury, England, vicar, 1950-52; University of Nottingham, Nottinghamshire, England, lecturer, 1952-58, senior lecturer, 1958-61, reader in theology, 1961-62; University of Durham, Durham, England, Lightfoot Professor of Divinity, 1962-64; University of Nottingham, professor of Christian theology and head of department, 1964-70; bishop of Clogher (Ireland), 1970-73; University of Manchester, Manchester, England, professor of historical and contemporary theology, 1973-82. Honorary canon of Southwell Cathedral, 1965—, and Coventry Cathedral, 1967—; assistant bishop of Manchester, 1973-83. Chairman of Council of Christians and Jews (Manchester area), 1975-82. *Member:* Royal Irish Academy, Society for the Study of Theology, Society of Authors.

WRITINGS—Published by S.C.M. Press, except as indicated: (With R. H. Fuller) *The Church of Rome: A Dissuasive,* 1948; *II Corinthians,* 1954; *The Summons to Unity,* Edinburgh House Press, 1954; *Origen's Doctrine of Tradition,* S.P.C.K., 1954; *Allegory and Event,* 1959; *God: Creator, Saviour, Spirit,* 1960; *Tradition in the Early Church,* 1962; (translator and abridger) *Justin Martyr's Dialogue with Trypho,* World Christian Books, 1963; *Clarendon Commentary on Acts,* Oxford University Press, 1965, revised edition published as *The Acts: A New Clarendon Commentary,* 1967; (editor) *Difficulties for Christian Belief,* Macmillan (London), 1967; (editor with M. W. Barley) *Christianity in Britain 300-700,* Leicester University Press, 1968; *Saint Patrick: His Origins and Career,* Oxford University Press, 1968; (editor) *The Pelican Guide to Modern Theology,* two volumes, Penguin, 1969-70.

The Attractiveness of God, S.P.C.K., 1973; *Mystery and Imagination: Reflections on Christianity,* S.P.C.K., 1976; (editor with Cecile Blanc) *St. Patrick: Confession, Lettre a Corotrius* (in Latin), Du Cerf (Paris), 1978; *Christian Priesthood Examined,* Letterworth Press, 1980; *The Continuity of Christian Doctrine,* Seabury, 1981; *The Life and Writings of the Historical St. Patrick,* Seabury, 1983.

Contributor: Alfred Robert C. Leaney, editor, *A Guide to the Scrolls,* 1958; N. Ehrenstrom and W. G. Muelder, editors, *Institutionalism and Church Unity,* Association Press, 1963; W. Browning, editor, *The Anglican Synthesis,* Derby, 1964; R.J.W. Bevan, *The Christian Way Explained,* Mowbray, 1964; A. T. Hanson, editor, *Vindications,* 1966; *Lambeth Conference 1968: Preparatory Essays,* S.P.C.K., 1968; *Eucharistic Agreement,* S.P.C.K., 1975; *Theology and Change* (memorial to Alan Richardson), 1975.

Contributor to *Studia Patristica,* Volumes III, XII, and XIII, 1961, 1976, *The Cambridge History of the Bible,* 1970, 1975, and *Latin Script and Letters* (festschrift to Ludwig Bieler), 1976. Contributor to *Vigiliae Christianae, Expository Times, Times Literary Supplement, London Times, Irish Theological Quarterly, Zeitschrift fuer Kirchengeschichte,* and other theology and denominational journals.

WORK IN PROGRESS: An edition of the Greek text of Hermias's *Irrisio Gentilium Philosophorum;* a book on the search for the Christian doctrine of God in the fourth century A.D.

SIDELIGHTS: R.P.C. Hanson reads ancient Hebrew, ancient Greek, Latin, French, German, and Italian; he speaks a little French.

* * *

HARBINSON, W(illiam) A(llen) 1941-

PERSONAL: Born September 9, 1941, in Northern Ireland; son of Alfred (a welder) and Martha (a stitcher; maiden name, Allen) Harbinson; married Ursula Mayer, November 5, 1969; children: Shaun, Tanya. *Education:* Attended Belfast College of Technology, 1956-57, and Liverpool College of Building, 1958-61. *Home:* 44 Rosebery Rd., Muswell Hill, London N10 2LJ, England. *Agent:* Writers House, Inc., 21 West 26th St., New York, N.Y. 10010.

CAREER: Writer. Apprentice textile engineer in Belfast, Northern Ireland, 1955-57; apprentice gas fitter in Liverpool, England, 1958-61; free-lance writer in London, England, 1967-68; Stonehart Publications, London, subscriptions clerk, 1968-69; *Knave and Fiesta,* London, assistant editor, 1970-71; *Scorpio,* London, assistant editor, 1971-72; chief associate editor in London of *Men Only* and *Club International,* and London office of *Club U.S.A.,* 1972-76. *Military service:* Royal Australian Air Force, medical clerk, 1961-67. *Member:* International P.E.N., British Film Institute, Society of Authors, Arts Club.

WRITINGS—Novels: *Two Gentlemen of Pleasure,* Horwitz, 1967; *The Gentlemen Rogues,* Horwitz, 1967; *The Running Man,* Horwitz, 1967, Award Books, 1970; *Guide for the Single Man,* Horwitz, 1968; *Death of an Idol,* Horwitz, 1969; *Our Girl Friday,* Horwitz, 1969.

Instruments of Death, Corgi Books, 1973, published as *None But the Damned,* Pinnacle Books, 1974; *Knock,* Intergroup, 1975; *Meat,* Panther, 1975; (with Lindsay Galloway) *The MacKinnons* (novelization of television series), Panther House, 1977; *No Limit for Charlie,* Panther House, 1977; *The Oil Heist,* Corgi Books, 1978; *Stryker's Kingdom,* Corgi Books, 1979; *Genesis,* Corgi Books, 1979, Dell, 1982.

Deadlines, New English Library, 1981; *Revelation,* Corgi Books, 1982, Dell, 1983.

Biographies: *Bronson!,* Pinnacle Books, 1975; *Elvis Presley: An Illustrated Biography,* M. Joseph, 1975, Grosset, 1976, revised edition published as *The Life and Death of Elvis Presley,* M. Joseph, 1977; (editor and compiler of photographs) Colin Wilson, *Ken Russell: A Director in Search of a Hero,* Intergroup, 1975; *George C. Scott: The Man, the Actor, and the Legend,* Pinnacle Books, 1977; *Evita: A Legend for the Seventies,* Star Publishing, 1977.

Author of "Astronaut," a radio play, for BBC, 1972; author of script material for television series "The Explorers," for BBC-TV, 1974. Contributor of stories and articles to men's magazines in the United States, England, and Australia.

WORK IN PROGRESS: Otherworld, a novel.

HARDIN, Garrett James 1915-

PERSONAL: Born April 21, 1915, in Dallas, Tex.; son of Hugh (a businessman) and Agnes (Garrett) Hardin; married Jane Swanson, September 7, 1941; children: Hyla, Peter, Sharon, David. *Education:* University of Chicago, Sc.B., 1936; Stanford University, Ph.D., 1941. *Politics:* Republican. *Religion:* Unitarian Universalist. *Home:* 399 Arboleda Rd., Santa Barbara, Calif. 93110.

CAREER: Writer and lecturer. Carnegie Institution of Washington, staff member in Division of Plant Biology, Stanford, Calif., 1942-46; University of California, Santa Barbara, assistant professor, 1946-50, associate professor of biology, 1950-56, professor of human ecology, 1956-78, professor emeritus, 1978—; The Environmental Fund, Washington, D.C., chief executive officer, 1980-81. Visiting professor at University of California, Los Angeles, University of California, Berkeley, Dartmouth College, and at University of Chicago; endowed lecturer at numerous universities; visiting national lecturer for Phi Beta Kappa and Sigma Xi. *Member:* American Association for the Advancement of Science, American Philosophical Society, American Academy of Arts and Sciences, Sigma Xi.

WRITINGS: Biology: Its Principles and Implications, W. H. Freeman, 1949, fifth edition (with Carl Bajema), 1978; *Nature and Man's Fate,* Holt, 1959; (editor) *Population, Evolution and Birth Control,* W. H. Freeman, 1964.

Birth Control, Bobbs-Merrill, 1970; *Exploring New Ethics for Survival,* Viking, 1972; *Stalking the Wild Taboo,* Kaufmann, 1973; *Mandatory Motherhood: The True Meaning of "Right to Life,"* Beacon Press, 1974; (editor with John Baden) *Managing the Commons,* W. H. Freeman, 1977; *The Limits of Altruism,* Indiana University, 1977; *Promethean Ethics: Living with Death, Competition and Triage,* University of Washington, 1980. Author of essay, "The Tragedy of the Commons," included in over fifty anthologies. Contributor of more than 200 scholarly articles to numerous periodicals.

SIDELIGHTS: Human ecologist Garrett Hardin told *CA:* "From my earliest school years I was interested in writing; but I early concluded that it was important to have something to write about. . . . When I became interested in science, I saw this as an area in which I could exercise my writing abilities to good effect, because the level of competence in explaining science to the public was, and is, low.

"In trying to explain the discoveries of others, I sometimes find that the muddled accounts previously given accurately reflect muddled thinking. In wrestling with such material I have often been able to throw new light on old problems. Analyzing 'Gause's principle' in population biology, I found that things became clearer if it was rechristened the 'competitive exclusion principle.' I coined this term in 1959 in the course of writing my popular account of Darwinian evolution, *Nature and Man's Fate,* and the term has since become standard.

"A more striking example of creation through exposition is found in the success of my essay 'The Tragedy of the Commons.' . . . It is one of the most cited scientific papers of the past decade, and it has been included as a classic in economics in a series published by Bobbs-Merrill. I find this fact amusing, for I have never taken a course in economics.

"This honor is also significant. Divisions between academic disciplines are rather artificial. To most academicians the conventional boundaries are as restrictive of vision as the blinders on a drayhorse. One shouldn't complain: such academic blinders present an opportunity to the outsider whose eyes are not so blinded. He can discover new truths at the interfaces of old disciplines. To do so he must free his mind of taboos; my attempts to help others do so have been brought together in a collection of essays under the title *Stalking the Wild Taboo.*

"The iconoclastic work of the scholar who stands outside the various academic establishments is sometimes a bit lonely—but it *is* fun!"

AVOCATIONAL INTERESTS: Music (playing violin in a string quartet).

* * *

HARDIN, J. D.
See RIEFE, Alan

* * *

HARDWICK, Richard Holmes, Jr. 1923-
(Rick Holmes)

PERSONAL: Born June 28, 1923, in Atlanta, Ga.; son of Richard Holmes (an insurance executive) and Caroline (Shivers) Hardwick; married Margaret Wilkins (a secretary), March 14, 1951; children: Amy, Caroline, Lynn. *Education:* Attended Emory University, 1940-42; University of Georgia, B.S., 1947. *Politics:* Independent. *Religion:* Episcopalian. *Agent:* Scott Meredith Literary Agency, Inc., 845 Third Ave., New York, N.Y. 10022.

CAREER: Owner of forty-foot ketch, sailing and chartering in the Caribbean, 1946-48; Peachtree Trust Co., Atlanta, Ga., assistant cashier, 1948-50; Lockheed Aircraft, Marietta, Ga., industrial engineer, 1950-51; Cutter's Inc. (boat company), Atlanta, vice-president, 1951-55; Surfside Motel, Saint Simon Island, Ga., co-owner, 1955-60; free-lance writer, 1960—. Vice-president of Hardwick Co., Inc., 1967—. *Military service:* U.S. Army, 1942-46; Japanese-English interpreter; also trained as pilot in Air Corps Reserve. *Member:* Mystery Writers of America, Authors Guild.

WRITINGS: Skin and Scuba Diving, Monarch, 1963; *The Plotters,* Doubleday, 1965; *The Season to Be Deadly,* Doubleday, 1966; *Flipper: The Mystery of the Black Schooner* (juvenile), Whitman Publishing, 1966; *Charles Richard Drew: Pioneer in Blood Research,* Scribner, 1967; (with C. S. Reynolds) *The Mortality Merchants,* McKay, 1968; (with R. W. Youngblood) *Twenty Years in the Secret Service,* Simon & Schuster, 1974. Also author of *Candy Mossler: Her Life and Trial.*

Novels; under name Rick Holmes; all published by Monarch: *Tropic of Cleo,* 1962; *New Widow, Love under Capricorn,* 1963; *Man Crazy,* 1965; *Child Woman,* 1965; *Riverfront Girl,* 1965.

Contributor to *Alfred Hitchcock Mystery Magazine, Yachting, Man's Magazine, Toronto Star Weekly, Manhunt, Saint Mystery Magazine, Mister,* and many other periodicals.

WORK IN PROGRESS: A mystery novel; several nonfiction books; short stories and magazine articles.

AVOCATIONAL INTERESTS: Sailing, golf, fishing, bridge.†

* * *

HARDY, Adam
See BULMER, (Henry) Kenneth

HARDY, Stuart
See SCHISGALL, Oscar

* * *

HARING, Bernard
See HAERING, Bernhard

* * *

HARMON, Maurice 1930-

PERSONAL: Born June 21, 1930, in Dublin, Ireland; son of Patrick and Mary (Owens) Harmon; married Maura Lynch, October 17, 1951; children: Diarmaid, Maura. *Education:* University College, Dublin, B.A., 1951, H.D.E., 1953, M.A., 1955, Ph.D., 1961; Harvard University, A.M., 1957. *Home:* 20 Sycamore Rd., Mount Merrion, Dublin, Ireland. *Office:* University College, National University of Ireland, Dublin 2, Ireland.

CAREER: Lewis and Clark College, Portland, Ore., assistant professor of English and Anglo-Irish literature, 1958-60; University of Notre Dame, Notre Dame, Ind., assistant professor, 1961-64; National University of Ireland, University College, Dublin, lecturer in English and Anglo-Irish literature, 1964—. Visiting professor at University of Massachusetts, 1967. Executive secretary of Swift Tercentenary Committee, 1967, and of J. M. Synge Centenary Committee, 1971. *Member:* International Association for the Study of Anglo-Irish Literature (chairman, 1979-82), Royal Irish Academy, American Committee for Irish Studies (Irish representative).

WRITINGS: Sean O'Faolain: A Critical Introduction, University of Notre Dame Press,1967; *Modern Irish Literature, 1800-1967,* Dolmen Press, 1967; (editor) *Fenians and Fenianism: Centenary Essays,* Scepter Publishers, 1968, University of Washington Press, 1970; *The Celtic Master,* Dolmen Press, 1969, Dufour, 1970; *J. M. Synge Centenary Papers, 1971,* Humanities, 1972; (editor) William Shakespeare, *Coriolanus,* Education Co. of Ireland, 1972; *The Poetry of Thomas Kinsella,* Wolfhound Press, 1974, Humanities, 1975; (editor with Patrick Rafroidi) *The Irish Novel in Our Time,* University of Lille, 1976; (editor) *Richard Murphy: Poet of Two Traditions,* Wolfhound Press, 1977; *Selective Bibliography for the Study of Anglo-Irish Literature and Its Backgrounds: An Irish Studies Handbook,* P. D. Meany, 1977; (editor) *Image and Illusion: Anglo-Irish Literature and Its Contexts,* Wolfhound Press, 1979; (editor and author of introduction) *Irish Poetry after Yeats: Seven Poets,* Little, Brown, 1979; (with Roger McHugh) *Short History of Anglo-Irish Literature from Its Origins to the Present Day,* Barnes & Noble, 1982.

Also editor of Shakespeare's *King Lear, King Richard II,* and *Romeo and Juliet*. Contributor to journals, including *University of Massachusetts Review, Northwest Review, Eire-laeland, R'Herne,* and *Studell.* Editor of *Irish University Review* and *Journal of Irish Studies.*

* * *

HARRELL, Irene B(urk) 1927-
(Amos Amor, Mildred Waylan)

PERSONAL: Born March 10, 1927, in Montcalm County, Mich.; daughter of Howard Lofton (a builder) and Marguerite (Weatherby) Burk; married Allen Waylan Harrell (a District Court judge), June 22, 1952; children Thomas Burk, Alice Elizabeth, James Britton, Susan Irene, Marguerite Owens, Maria Weatherby. *Education:* Ohio State University, B.A. (summa cum laude), 1948; University of North Carolina, B.S., 1949; Famous Writers School, graduate, 1965. *Religion:* First Assembly of God. *Home:* 408 Pearson St., Wilson, N.C. 27893.

CAREER: Free-lance writer. Westerville Public Library, Westerville, Ohio, librarian, 1949-52; University of North Carolina at Chapel Hill, librarian in Sociology, Anthropology and City Planning Library, 1952-53; Halifax County Library, Halifax, N.C., director, 1953-54; Atlantic Christian College, C.L. Hardy Library, Wilson, N.C., 1958-64, began as cataloger, became librarian; Logos International, Plainfield, N.J., editor and writer, 1970-79. *Member:* Phi Beta Kappa.

WRITINGS—All published by Word Books: *Prayerables: Meditations of a Homemaker,* 1967; *Good Marriages Grow: A Book for Wives,* 1968; (editor) James Buckingham, *Some Gall: And Other Reflections on Life,* 1970; (compiler) *God Ventures: True Accounts of God in the Lives of Men,* 1970; *Ordinary Days with an Extraordinary God: Prayerables II,* 1971; (with husband, Allen W. Harrell) *The Opposite Sex,* 1972; *Security Blankets—Family Size,* 1973; *The Windows of Heaven: Prayerables III,* 1975; (with Nora Lam) *China Cry,* 1980.

All published by Logos International: *Lo, I Am with You: Prayersteps to Faith,* 1970, published as *Miracles through Prayer,* 1970; (with Floyd Miles) *Black Tracks: A Junkie Turns to God and Kicks the Habit,* 1972; (with John Herbert and Lucille Walker) *God's Living Room,* 1972; (with Michael Esses) *Phenomenon of Obedience,* 1973; (with Harold Hill) *How to Live Like a King's Kid,* 1974; (with Esses) *Jesus in Genesis,* 1975; (with Iverna Tompkins) *How to Be Happy in No Man's Land,* 1975; (with Hill) *From Goo to You by Way of the Zoo?,* 1976; (with Sid Roth) *Something for Nothing,* 1976; (with Esses) *Next Visitor to Planet Earth,* 1976; (with Hill) *How to Be a Winner,* 1976; (with Tompkins) *How to Live with Kids and Enjoy It,* 1977; (with Esses) *Jesus in Exodus,* 1977; (with Hill) *How to Live in High Victory,* 1977; (with Tompkins) *God and I: A Book about Faith and Prayer,* 1978; (with Hill and Gretchen Black) *Instant Answers for King's Kids in Training,* 1978; (with Hill and Black) *How to Flip Your Flab—Forever!,* 1979.

Other: (Editor) Lucy Gray, *Diary of Hope,* Baker Book, 1970; *Muddy Sneakers and Other Family Hassles,* Abingdon, 1974; *Multiplied by Love: Lessons Learned through the Holy Spirit,* Abingdon, 1976; (editor) Ernst Schmidt, *Make It Happen!,* Abingdon, 1976; *Super-Prayerables: To Add a Glow to Your Life,* Acton House, 1977; (with Kay Golbeck) *Lord, How Will You Get Me Out of This Mess?,* Chosen Books, 1978; (with Colleen Townsend Evans) *The Vine Life,* Chosen Books, 1980; (editor) Hill, *How to Live the Bible Like a King's Kid,* Revell, 1980; (with Golbeck) *Hopeless? Never!,* G.R. Welch, 1981; (with Charlene Curry) *The General's Lady,* Tyndale, 1981; (with Hill) *God's in Charge Here,* Revell, 1982; (with Tommy Lewis) *Isn't It Amazin'?: A Book about the Love of God,* FGBMFI Gift Publications, 1982.

Contributor of poems, articles, and stories to numerous magazines, incuding *Jack and Jill, Guideposts, Christian Life, Logos Journal,* and *Faith at Work.*

WORK IN PROGRESS: Call Me Ishi, with B.J. Smith; *Singing Waters,* with Golbeck; *How to Get More for Your Money,* with

Hill; a novel; a composite Bible; editing works for Gloria Phillips, Janice Gravely, Erma Schlecht, Ziva Beckman, Judy Fiorientino, Petti Wagner, and Pat and Al Moehring.

* * *

HARRINGTON, Charles (Christopher) 1942-

PERSONAL: Born January 14, 1942, in New York, N.Y.; son of William Treanor and Lucette (Van Limbeek) Harrington; married Giselle Nemeth (a college teacher), June 3, 1962; children: Christopher, Jonathan. *Education:* Syracuse University, A.B., 1962; Harvard University, Ph.D., 1968. *Religion:* Unitarian Universalist. *Residence:* Ancram, N.Y. 12502. *Office address:* Box 95, Teachers College, Columbia University, New York, N.Y. 10027.

CAREER: Columbia University, Teachers College, New York, N.Y., assistant professor, 1967-71, associate professor, 1971-78, professor of anthropology and education, 1978—, deputy director of Institute for Urban and Minority Education, 1975—. *Member:* American Anthropological Association (fellow), Society for Applied Anthropology (fellow), Council on Anthropology and Education, American Sociological Association.

WRITINGS: Errors in Sex Role Behavior, Teachers College Press, 1970; (co-author) *The Learning of Political Behavior,* Scott, Foresman, 1970; (editor) *Readings in Anthropology and Education,* Mss Information, 1971; (editor) *Cross-Cultural Approaches to Learning,* Mss Information, 1973; *Psychological Anthropology and Education,* AMS Press, 1979; (co-editor) *Readings in Equal Education,* AMS Press, 1982; (co-editor) *Desegregation in Public Education,* AMS Press, 1983. Contributor of reviews to *American Record Guide.* Editor of *Anthropology and Education Quarterly,* 1977-82.

WORK IN PROGRESS: Two books reporting the results of a large-scale empirical study of the life histories of successful forty- to fifty-five-year-olds who come from backgrounds of low educational achievement and low social class.

* * *

HARRIS, Leonard 1929-

PERSONAL: Born September 27, 1929, in New York, N.Y.; son of Saul B. (a businessman) and Frances (Paley) Harris; children: Sally, David. *Education:* City College (now City College of the City University of New York), B.S.S., 1950. *Agent:* Sterling Lord Agency, Inc., 660 Madison Ave., New York, N.Y. 10021. *Office:* Goodson-Todman, 375 Park Ave., New York, N.Y. 10022.

CAREER: Writer, actor, and critic. *Hartford Courant,* Hartford, Conn., reporter, editor, and rewrite man, 1958-60; *New York World-Telegram and Sun,* New York City, critic, feature writer, and reporter, 1960-66; WCBS-Television, New York City, arts editor, critic, and correspondent, host of talk show "Gateway," and producer and writer for documentary series "Eye on New York," 1966-74; free-lance writer and actor, 1974—. Adjunct associate professor at Fordham University, 1969-74, and Hunter College of the City University of New York, 1975.

Host of "In Conversation," a live interview series produced at 92nd St. Y, intermittently, 1972-74; co-host of magazine news program, "The Fifty-First State," January-August, 1975; television appearances include guest host of "Midday Live," panelist on "What's My Line?" and "To Tell the Truth," and host and writer of "Bravo Magazine" and "HBO Sneak Preview" cable programs; writer and spot producer for "That's My Line," 1980; co-star of feature films, "Taxi Driver," 1976, and "Hero at Large," 1978. *Member:* Phi Beta Kappa.

WRITINGS: The Masada Plan (suspense novel), Crown, 1976; *Don't Be No Hero* (novel), Crown, 1978; *The Hamptons* (novel), Simon & Schuster, 1981. Writer for revival of "Omnibus" series, ABC-TV, 1980. Theater critic for *The Hollywood Reporter,* 1982—. Contributor to theater journals.

WORK IN PROGRESS: A novel and a screenplay.

* * *

HARRIS, Marilyn
See SPRINGER, Marilyn Harris

* * *

HARRISON, (Thomas) Ross 1943-

PERSONAL: Born September 26, 1943, in Belfast, Northern Ireland; son of John Geoffrey (a university professor) and Patricia (a psychologist; maiden name, Foster) Harrison; married Gillian Davies, August 17, 1968; children: Sophie, Thomas, Jonathan. *Education:* Cambridge University, B.A., 1964, Ph.D., 1968; Oxford University, graduate study, 1965-66. *Politics:* Labour. *Religion:* "Nothing orthodox." *Home:* 21 Millington Rd., Cambridge, England. *Office:* Department of Philosophy, King's College, Cambridge University, Cambridge, England.

CAREER: Cambridge University, St. John's College, Cambridge, England, research fellow, 1967-70; University of Bristol, Bristol, England, lecturer in philosophy, 1970-74; Cambridge University, King's College, lecturer in philosophy, 1975—. *Member:* Aristotelian Society.

WRITINGS: On What There Must Be, Oxford University Press, 1974; (contributor) E. Pivcevic, editor, *Phenomenology and Philosophical Understanding,* Cambridge University Press, 1975; (editor and contributor) *Rational Action,* Cambridge University Press, 1979; (contributor) Godfrey Vesey, editor, *Idealism Past and Present,* Cambridge University Press, 1982; *Bentham,* Routledge & Kegan Paul, 1983.

* * *

HARRISON, William 1933-

PERSONAL: Born October 29, 1933, in Dallas, Tex.; son of Samuel Scott and Mary Etta (Cook) Harrison; married Merlee Kimsey, February 2, 1957; children: Laurie, Sean, Quentin. *Education:* Texas Christian University, B.A., 1955; Vanderbilt University, M.A., 1959; graduate study at University of Iowa, 1962. *Agent:* Owen Laster, William Morris Agency, 1350 Ave. of the Americas, New York, N.Y. 10019. *Office:* Department of English, University of Arkansas, Fayetteville, Ark. 72701.

CAREER: University of Arkansas, Fayetteville, member of English department faculty, 1964—. *Awards, honors:* Guggenheim fellowship, 1973-74; National Endowment for the Arts grant, 1977; Christopher Award, 1979, for work in television.

WRITINGS—Novels, except as indicated: *The Theologian,* Harper, 1965; *In a Wild Sanctuary,* Morrow, 1969; *Lessons in Paradise,* Morrow, 1971; *Roller Ball Murder and Other Stories* (short stories), Morrow, 1974; *Africana,* Morrow, 1977;

Savannah Blue, Richard Marek, 1981; *Burton and Speke,* Richard Marek, 1982.

Also author of screenplay for film "Rollerball," Norman Jewison Production for United Artists, 1975. Author of additional screenplays for television and films. Contributor of short stories to magazines and anthologies.

WORK IN PROGRESS: A novel, *Pack of Dogs;* an original screenplay, "Arsons of Desire."

SIDELIGHTS: Many of William Harrison's writings focus on the lives of the alienated and the disaffected. The themes of several of his novels and of his screenplay for "Rollerball" concern the struggle of individuals against society and its traditional mores and values. In some of Harrison's novels, such as *The Theologian,* the characters create their own tortured worlds. In other of his works—"Rollerball," for example—it is the world itself that has gone awry, and the heroes are left to challenge the established powers.

The protagonist of *The Theologian,* Randle Fast, is a seminarian in the rural South. Increasingly obsessed with the occult and with the wife of his mentor, Fast moves further and further from conventional mores until he breaks completely with orthodox religious and moral values. Ultimately, Fast, whose life is "colored by peyote dreams and desperate desires" as Martin Levin observes in *New York Times Book Review,* emerges as a psychopathic murderer. According to J. S. Phillipson in *Best Sellers,* Fast is "amoral" and thus becomes "in the traditional Judaeo-Christian view, something less than human. . . . Using the standards of an amoral society, [Harrison] has produced another anti-hero of the sort common in present-day literature."

The four misfit graduate students of *In a Wild Sanctuary* are also at odds with a society that they see as corrupt and unbearable but cannot seem to transcend. The four—"linked not by mutual sympathy so much as by this personal understanding of each other's solitude," as a *Times Literary Supplement* critic comments—make a pact to commit suicide one by one and to leave no clue of the pact or the motive. When three of the four friends begin to waver, they are driven on by Clive, who is "no mere misfit," according to Levin, "but a gaudy psychopath in the Leopold-Loeb tradition." "Yes, it strains the credulity at first," writes *New York Times*'s John Leonard, but as the four students "wound one another and drink poisonous abstractions, and fail to connect private despairs with public violence (Vietnam)—the attitudinizing achieves a mad logic of its own." A twist in the plot reveals the finally ordered suicides to not be suicides at all, but rather murders perpetrated by Clive and then discovered by the father of one of the dead students. The final confrontation between Clive and the father is, says Leonard, "a shouting into the wind across a generational, and moral divide, [that turns] suicide into murder, and opens a hole in our conceptual world beyond which ideas have become monsters."

In *Africana,* Leo and his band of mercenaries troop across Africa, crossing countries in societal and political upheaval and fighting wars wherever they can find them, in order to avoid their internal "civilization," or what E. S. Duvall calls in *Atlantic,* "the bitter truth . . . , [the] mundanity of spirit [that] lies behind their violent self-assertion." *Africana,* says Robert Brian in *Times Literary Supplement,* is a pastiche of fable, philosophy, poetry, and adventure story in which the crazed, "uncivilized" Leo and his mercenaries are contrasted with such historical figures as United Nations Secretary General Dag Hammerskjold. As the two visions of reality—the uncivilized and the civilized—are brought to confront one another, there is a stalemate. Hammerskjold, Brian notes, dies as he dreams "of ordering chaos in Africa," two of the mercenaries fade into the domesticity of suburban London, and Leo perishes as he machine-guns bathers on a Mombasa beach, unable to find peace in any country or culture. Comments Brian: "Violence is set against tameness, the wild against the domestic, war against peace, the individual against the group, man against woman. Leo tells his men: 'We fight—not for the . . . material necessity and comforts—and not to save our bleeding homes and families—but for poetry! Domesticity is not civilization, it is the bloody enemy.'"

Harrison again emphasizes the contrast between the "civilized" and the "uncivilized" in *Savannah Blue,* when he pits American businessmen and the CIA against Quent Clare, second-generation colonialist in Africa. When Clare's mother dies of a disease transmitted by some visiting Americans, Clare becomes "obsessed with the collision of cultures in the modern world [and then] goes on a one-man spree of savage civil disobedience," writes Eric Zorn in *Chicago Tribune Book World.* *Savannah Blue* pits Clare against not only the American agents sent to apprehend him, but also against, as Zorn observes, "the influences of American ways on the savage purity of African culture."

The film "Rollerball" also examines the clash between the individual and society. In "Rollerball," *Time*'s Jay Cocks writes, Harrison "champion[s] nonconformity and the glories of individuality against a faceless state." The film is set in 2018, and the brutal game of rollerball is designed to be "the bloodletter of mankind's aggressive instinct, . . . the cure for war, and the emblem of a unified world that . . . has mysteriously rid [itself] of opinion, poverty, and every foreseeable physical distress," comments Penelope Gilliatt in *New Yorker.* The game, meant to demonstrate to spectators that individual effort is futile, succeeds as a cultural pacifier until one rollerball player manages to remain so long in the sport that he becomes a national hero, thus challenging the corporate state's power and authority. "'Rollerball' isn't a movie," says Arthur Cooper in *Newsweek,* "it's a protest demonstration . . . [against] the increasing sterility of modern life." Unfortunately, notes Colin Westerbeck, Jr. in *Commonweal,* "attempting to deliver a roundhouse punch to all civilization, ['Rollerball'] misses and socks itself right in the puss instead."

BIOGRAPHICAL/CRITICAL SOURCES: Library Journal, September 1, 1965, January 15, 1970, March 15, 1971, March 1, 1981; *Best Sellers,* October 15, 1965, November 1, 1969, July 7, 1977; *New York Times Book Review,* October 24, 1965, November 30, 1969; *Publishers Weekly,* August 11, 1969, October 12, 1970, January 11, 1971, March 7, 1977, December 12, 1980; *New York Times,* October 30, 1969, February 7, 1981; *Newsweek,* November 3, 1969, July 7, 1975; *Time,* December 19, 1969, July 7, 1975; *Times Literary Supplement,* December 11, 1970, December 2, 1977; *New Yorker,* July 7, 1975; *Commonweal,* July 18, 1975; *New Republic,* July 26, 1975; *Saturday Review,* August 9, 1975; *Atlantic,* June, 1977; *Chicago Tribune Book World,* May 10, 1981; *Washington Post Book World,* November 23, 1982.

—Sketch by Heidi A. Tietjen

* * *

HARTMAN, Patience
See ZAWADSKY, Patience

HARWOOD, Lee 1939-

PERSONAL: Born June 6, 1939, in Leicester, England; son of Wilfrid Travers Lee (a teacher) and Grace (Ladkin) Harwood; married Judith Walker. *Education:* Queen Mary College, London, B.A., 1961. *Politics:* Socialist. *Religion:* None. *Home:* 21 Chatsworth Rd., Brighton, Sussex, England.

CAREER: Held various jobs including stonemason's mate, library assistant, bookshop assistant, forester, and bus conductor, 1961-69; writer in residence, Aegean School of Fine Arts, Paros, Greece, 1971-72; post office clerk, 1974—. Writer, mainly of poetry. Has given readings of his poetry in the United States, in London, and at English universities. *Awards, honors:* Poets Foundation (New York) annual award, 1967; Alice Hunt Bartlett Prize, Poetry Society (London), 1976.

WRITINGS: title illegible, Writers Forum, 1965; (with William Burroughs) *Darazt,* Lovebooks, 1965; *The Man with Blue Eyes,* Angel Hair Books, 1966; *The White Room,* Fulcrum Press, 1968; *Landscapes,* Fulcrum Press, 1969; *The Beautiful Atlas,* Kavanagh, 1969; (translator) Tristan Tzara, *Cosmic Realities Vanilla Tobacco Dawnings,* ARC Publications, 1969.

(Translator) Tristan Tzara, *Destroyed Days,* Voiceprint Editions, 1971; (with John Ashbery and Tom Raworth) *Penguin Modern Poets,* Volume XIX, Penguin, 1971; *The Sinking Colony,* Fulcrum Press, 1971; *Captain Harwood's Log of Stern Statements and Stout Sayings,* Writers Forum, 1973; (compiler) *Tristan Tzara: A Bibliography,* Aloes Books, 1974; (translator) Tristan Tzara, *Selected Poems,* Trigram, 1975; *Freighters,* Pig Press, 1975; *H.M.S. Little Fox,* Oasis Books, 1975; *Old Bosham Bird Watch and Other Stories,* Pig Press, 1977; *Boston-Brighton,* Oasis Books, 1977; (with Antony Lopez) *Wish You Were Here,* Transgravity Press, 1979; *All the Wrong Notes,* illustrations by wife, Judith Walker, Pig Press, 1981.

Poems anthologized in *Children of Albion,* edited by Michael Horowitz, Penguin, 1969, *British Poetry Since 1945,* edited by Edward Lucie-Smith, 1970, *Twenty-three Modern British Poets,* edited by John Matthias, Swallow Press, 1971, and *English and American Surrealist Poetry,* edited by Edward B. Germain, Penguin, 1978. Contributor of poetry to magazines and journals, including *Art and Literature, Paris Review, Angel Hair, Poetry Review* (London), *London Magazine,* and *Six Pack.* Former editor of *Tzarad* and *Boston Eagle.*

* * *

HASTINGS, Graham
See JEFFRIES, Roderic (Graeme)

* * *

HASTINGS, Macdonald 1909-1982
(Lemuel Gulliver)

PERSONAL: Born October 6, 1909, in London, England; died October 4, 1982; son of Basil Macdonald (a playwright, author, and essayist) and Wilhelmina Harriet (White) Hastings; married Anne Scott-James (an author, editor, and journalist), 1944 (marriage dissolved); married Anthea Hodson Joseph (deputy chairman of Michael Joseph Ltd., publishers), 1963; children: (first marriage) Max Hugh Macdonald, Clare Selina; (second marriage) Susan Harriet Selina. *Education:* Educated in England. *Home:* Brown's Farm, Old Basing, Hampshire RG24 0DE, England. *Agent:* James Brown Associates, Inc., 25 West 43rd St., New York, N.Y. 10036; and Curtis Brown Ltd., 1 Craven Hill, London W2 3EW, England.

CAREER: Picture Post, London, England, war correspondent and feature writer, 1939-45; *Strand Magazine,* London, editor, 1946-49; *Country Fair,* London, founder and editor, 1951-58; free-lance writer, 1951-82. Broadcaster, beginning in early 1940s; television commentator for the British Broadcasting Corp., beginning in 1950s. *Member:* Detection Club, Savage Club (member of board of trustees), Beefsteak Club, Saintsbury Club, Thursday Club (all London).

WRITINGS—Mystery novels, except as indicated: *Cork on the Water,* Random House, 1951, reprinted, Tom Stacey Reprints, 1971; *Cork in Bottle,* M. Joseph, 1953, Knopf, 1954, revised edition, M. Joseph, 1956, reprinted, Tom Stacey Reprints, 1972; *Cork and the Serpent,* M. Joseph, 1955, reprinted, Severn House, 1975; *Cork in the Doghouse,* M. Joseph, 1957, Knopf, 1958, reprinted, Tom Stacey Reprints, 1972; *A Glimpse of Arcadia* (historical novel), M. Joseph, 1960, Coward-McCann, 1961, revised edition, M. Joseph, 1974; *Cork on the Telly,* M. Joseph, 1966, published as *Cork on Location,* Walker & Co., 1967.

Nonfiction: *Passed as Censored* (war reminiscences), Harrap, 1941; *Rolls Royce: The Story of a Name* (monograph), Rolls Royce Ltd., 1950; *Macdonald Hastings' Country Book: A Personal Anthology,* George Newnes, 1961; *The Other Mr. Churchill: A Lifetime of Shooting and Murder* (biography), Harrap, 1963, Dodd, 1965; (editor) Robert Churchill, *Game Shooting: A Textbook on the Successful Use of the Modern Shotgun,* M. Joseph, 1963, Stackpole, 1967, revised edition published as *Robert Churchill's Game Shooting,* M. Joseph, 1970, published as *Churchill's Game-Shooting,* Stackpole, 1972, new revised edition published as *Robert Churchill's Game Shooting,* Arms & Armour, 1979; (author of commentary) John Gay, *London Observed,* John Day, 1964; *How to Shoot Straight: A Manual for Newcomers to the Field,* Pelham, 1967, A. S. Barnes, 1970; *English Sporting Guns and Accessories,* Ward, Lock, 1969.

Jesuit Child (autobiography), M. Joseph, 1971, St. Martin's, 1972; *Mary Celeste: A Centenary Record,* M. Joseph, 1972; (with Carole Walsh) *Wheeler's Fish Cookery Book,* M. Joseph, 1974; *Diane: A Victorian,* M. Joseph, 1974; *After You, Robinson Crusoe: A Practical Guide for a Desert Islander,* Pelham, 1975; *Shooting: Why We Miss,* Pelham, 1976, McKay, 1977; *Game Book: Sporting Round the World,* M. Joseph, 1979; *The Shotgun: A Social History,* David & Charles, 1981.

Books for young readers: *Eagle Special Investigator,* M. Joseph, 1953; *Adventure Calling,* Hulton Press, 1955; *The Search for the Little Yellow Men,* Knopf, 1956; *Men of Glory,* Hulton Press, 1958; *More Men of Glory,* Hulton Press, 1959; *Sydney the Sparrow,* Ward, Lock, 1973.

Also author of television series, "Call the Gun Expert," "Riverbeat," "Voyage into England," and "In Deepest Britain"; author of television program, "The Hated Society: The Jesuits," and of a feature film commissioned by the government of Iran, "Flame of Persia," 1973. Contributor to *Lilliput* magazine under pseudonym Lemuel Gulliver, 1940-45; regular contributor to various British periodicals and newspapers.

SIDELIGHTS: Although many critics have praised him for his interesting mystery novels, Macdonald Hastings has also written a number of works of nonfiction, including books on game shooting and several biographies. One of his more famous books is his autobiography, *Jesuit Child.* In this work Hastings writes of his years studying at the Jesuit-run boarding school, Stonyhurst College, and of the Jesuit influence on its students. E. B. Hill explains in *Best Sellers* that "this memoir-history is absorbing, chiefly because the author is urbane, uninhibited, frank, and . . . gifted with a nice use of language. He is a 'Jesuit child' in the sense that he attended Jesuit schools for several years. . . . [He] makes comparisons . . . between his experiences and those of some great Jesuits, and puts the whole thing together into a work that is very pleasant reading. . . . Jesuits will howl at some of the incidents and analogies." And P. P. Read remarks in the *New York Times Book Review* that "the early reminiscences are to me the most interesting part of [*Jesuit Child*.] The Jesuit method of education seems in some ways so savage and in others so humane."

Hastings once explained his writings to *CA* in this manner: "Mine is a coat of many colours. Successful authors write the same book again and again. From book to book my own taste is to write something different. It seems to me that is what life is about. I am consistent in my love of the open air. Most of my work is about green places in Britain. . . . I shoot, I fish. I hunt, I garden."

Hastings' books have been translated into Italian, German, French, Dutch, and Japanese.

BIOGRAPHICAL/CRITICAL SOURCES: Macdonald Hastings, *Jesuit Child,* M. Joseph, 1971; *Times Literary Supplement,* November 26, 1971; *Best Sellers,* May 1, 1972; *New York Times Book Review,* June 18, 1972.†

* * *

HATCH, Richard A(llen) 1940-

PERSONAL: Born August 18, 1940, in Anderson, Ind.; son of Clarence Wilbur (a clergyman) and Mildred (Sutton) Hatch; married Ann Marie Menchinger, August 27, 1960. *Education:* Attended Anderson College, Anderson, Ind., 1957-59; Boston University, B.S., 1961; University of Illinois, Ph.D., 1969. *Home:* 5375 Wellesley St., La Mesa, Calif. *Office:* Department of Information Systems, San Diego State University, San Diego, Calif.

CAREER: Illinois State Legislature, Springfield, intern, 1966-67; University of Illinois at Urbana-Champaign, assistant to director of public information, 1966, instructor in business and technical writing, 1967-69; Western Michigan University, Kalamazoo, associate professor and coordinator of communication studies in business, 1969-75; San Diego State University, San Diego, Calif., 1975—, began as assistant professor of communications study, became associate professor of information systems. *Member:* American Business Communication Association (vice-president, 1974-75), Association for Computing Machinery.

WRITINGS: (Compiler) *Some Founding Papers of the University of Illinois,* University of Illinois Press, 1967; (editor) *An Early View of the Land-Grant Colleges,* University of Illinois Press, 1967; (with Francis W. Weeks) *Business Writing Cases and Problems,* Stipes, 1972; (with Irene S. Caldwell and Beverly Welton) *Basics for Communication in the Church,* Warner Press, 1971; *Communicating in Business,* Science Research Associates, 1977.

(With Norman E. Sondak) *Using BASIC on the CYBER,* Science Research Associates, 1982; *Business Communication: Theory and Practice,* Science Research Associates, 1983; *Business Writing,* Science Research Associates, 1983; (contributor) David E. Gootnick and Margaret M. Gootnick, editors, *The Standard Handbook of Business Communication,* Free Press, 1983. Associate editor, *Bostonia* (Boston University), 1960-61.

WORK IN PROGRESS: Introduction to Business Data Processing, with Sondak, for Science Research Associates.

* * *

HAUGEN, Einar (Ingvald) 1906-

PERSONAL: Born April 19, 1906, in Sioux City, Iowa; son of John Ellingsen (a cabinetmaker) and Kristine (Gorset) Haugen; married Eva Lund, June 18, 1932; children: Anne Margaret Littlefield, Camilla Christine Cai. *Education:* Attended Morningside College, 1924-27; St. Olaf College, B.A. (summa cum laude), 1928; University of Illinois, M.A., 1929, Ph.D., 1931. *Politics:* Independent ("usually Democratic"). *Religion:* ("Mildly") Unitarian Universalist. *Office:* 146 Widener Library, Harvard University, Cambridge, Mass. 02138.

CAREER: University of Wisconsin—Madison, assistant professor, 1931-36, associate professor, 1936-38, Thompson Professor of Scandinavian Languages, 1938-62, Vilas Research Professor of Scandinavian and Linguistics, 1962-64, director of Linguistic Institute, 1943-44; Harvard University, Cambridge, Mass., Victor S. Thomas Professor of Scandinavian and Linguistics, 1964-75, professor emeritus, 1975—. University of Oslo, visiting lecturer, 1938, Fulbright research professor, 1951-52; visiting summer lecturer at universities, including University of Michigan, 1949, and Georgetown University, 1954; U.S. Department of State lecturer at University of Iceland, 1956, Kiel University, 1968, and at Uppsala University, 1976. Cultural Officer at U.S. Embassy, Oslo, Norway, 1945-46; consultant to English Language Educational Council, Tokyo, Japan, 1958-60. President of Ninth International Linguistic Congress, 1962; Permanent International Council of Linguists, president, 1966-72, life member, 1972—.

MEMBER: American Academy of Arts and Sciences, Linguistic Society of America (president, 1950), American Dialect Society (president, 1965, 1966), Modern Language Association of America, Norwegian-American Historical Association, Society for Advancement of Scandinavian Society (president, 1938), Oslo Academy of Science (corresponding member), Icelandic Academy of Science (corresponding member).

AWARDS, HONORS: Order of St. Olaf, first class, Norway, 1940; Guggenheim fellowship, 1942-43; Center for Advanced Study in the Behavioral Sciences fellowship, 1963-64; Litt.D., University of Michigan, 1953; Ph.D., St. Olaf College, 1958, University of Oslo, 1961, University of Wisconsin, 1969, University of Reykjavik, 1971, University of Trondheim, 1972, University of Uppsala, 1975; Commander, Order of the North Star, Sweden, 1970; Nausen prize, Oslo, 1970; Jancke prize, 1976.

WRITINGS: Beginning Norwegian, Appleton, 1937, 3rd edition, 1975; *Norsk i Amerika,* Cappelen (Oslo), 1938, 2nd edition, 1975; *Reading Norwegian,* Appleton, 1938; *Norwegian Word Studies,* two volumes, University of Wisconsin Press, 1941; *Voyages to Vinland,* Knopf, 1941, 2nd edition, 1942; *Spoken Norwegian,* Holt, 1945, 3rd edition, 1982.

First Grammatical Treatise, Linguistic Society of America, 1950, 2nd edition, Longman, 1972; *The Norwegian Language in America,* two volumes, University of Pennsylvania Press, 1953, 2nd edition, Indiana University Press, 1969; *Bilingual-*

ism in the Americas, American Dialect Society, 1956; (translator and editor) *Beyer's History of Norwegian Literature,* New York University Press, 1957; (editor) *Norwegian-English Dictionary,* University of Wisconsin Press, 1965; *Language Conflict and Language Planning,* Harvard University Press, 1966; (translator and editor) *Fire and Ice: Three Icelandic Plays,* University of Wisconsin Press, 1967; *The Norwegians in America,* Columbia University Press, 1967.

(Translator) Guomundur Kamban, *We Murderers,* University of Wisconsin Press, 1970; (translator) H. Koht, *Life of Ibsen,* Benjamin Blom, 1971; *The Ecology of Language: Essays by Einar Haugen,* edited by Anwar S. Dil, Stanford University Press, 1972; (contributor) T.A. Sebeok, editor, *Current Trends in Linguistics,* Volume X, Mouton & Co., 1973; (editor) Georges Dumezil, *Gods of the Ancient Northmen,* University of California Press, 1973; *A Bibliography of Scandinavian Languages and Linguistics, 1900-1970,* Olso University Press, 1974; (editor with Morton Bloomfield) *Language as a Human Problem,* Norton, 1974; *The Scandinavian Languages: An Introduction to Their History,* Harvard University Press, 1976; (with wife, Eva Lund Haugen) *Land of the Free: Bjornson's America Letters 1880-1881,* Norwegian-American Historical Association, 1978; *Ibsen's Drama: Author to Audience,* University of Minnesota, 1979.

(Editor with J.D. McClure and D.S. Thomson) *Minority Languages Today,* Edinburgh University Press, 1981; *Oppdalsmalet* (title means "The Oppdal Dialect of Norwegian"), Tanum-Norli (Oslo), 1982; *Scandinavian Language Structures,* University of Minnesota, 1982; *Ole Edvart Rolvaag,* Twayne, 1983.

WORK IN PROGRESS: A Bibliography of Scandinavian Dictionaries, with E.L. Haugen; *Han Ola og han Per, a Norwegian-American Comic Strip,* with Joan Buckley; 2nd edition of *Norwegian-English Dictionary;* German translation of *The Scandinavian Languages.*

SIDELIGHTS: Einar Haugen told *CA:* "My purpose in writing has nearly always been connected with my profession—to promote understanding and knowledge of the language, literature, and culture of the Scandinavian countries, especially Norway. Welcome digressions have included stays in Germany, Romania, Japan, and Australia in connection with my work in linguistics. The science of language is truly a universal branch of knowledge, and today it has many houses, some too esoteric for me. When I work with language, I prefer to deal with empirical data, synchronic or diachronic, and to find out its mechanisms rather than speculate on its theory. My purposes have been primarily practical, as shown by my several textbooks and surveys of the field.

"I like to see the human beings behind the language, which has attracted me to the new field of sociolinguistics. Within this, my specialty has been bilingualism, an interest that goes back to a bilingual childhood, growing up in a Norwegian-speaking family within a midwestern English-speaking community. This background has also given me an understanding for minority groups wherever they are, and consideration for what kind of language planning can help to preserve their identity, a form of what I have called 'language ecology.'"

BIOGRAPHICAL/CRITICAL SOURCES: Einar Haugen, *The Ecology of Language,* introduction by Anwar S. Dil, Stanford University Press, 1972; *Studies by Einar Haugen,* Mouton, 1972; *Studies for Einar Haugen,* Mouton, 1972.

HAUGH, Richard (Stanley) 1942-

PERSONAL: Born May 4, 1942, in Boston, Mass.; son of Victor Stanley (a businessman) and Marion Haugh; married Vera Verhovskoy (a translator), June 26, 1965; children: Alexandra, Andrew, Peter. *Education:* University of Massachusetts, B.A., 1965; Andover Newton Theological School, M.A., 1968; Fordham University, Ph.D., 1973. *Religion:* Greek Orthodox.

CAREER: High school teacher of German and English in Boston, Mass., 1966, and in Brookline, Mass., 1966-68; Academy of Aeronautics, Flushing, N.Y., assistant professor of literature, 1968-71; Iona College, New Rochelle, N.Y., assistant professor of religious studies, 1971-75, visiting professor of humanities, 1975-76; Harvard University, Cambridge, Mass., National Endowment for Humanities fellow in residence, 1976-77; Falmouth Academy, Falmouth, Mass., founder and president, beginning 1977. Associate professor of humanities, Tuskegee Institute, 1977-78; visiting professor of church history, Rice University, 1978-79. *Member:* Mediaeval Academy of America, Society for the Scientific Study of Religion, Society of American Orthodox Theologians, Association of Russian-American Scholars (member of board of directors, 1970—), Norwegian-American Historical Association.

WRITINGS: (Editor with John B. Dunlop and Alexis Klimoff, and contributor) *Aleksandr Solzhenitsyn: Critical Essays and Documentary Material,* Volume I, Nordland, 1973, enlarged edition, Macmillan, 1975; *Dostoevsky's Vision of the Golden Age,* Association of Russian-American Scholars, 1973; *Photius Encyclical: Translation and Introduction,* Transaction Books, 1974; *Photius and the Carolingians: The Trinitarian Controversy,* Nordland, 1975; (co-translator) George P. Fedotov, *St. Filipp: Metropolitan of Moscow,* Nordland, 1975; (editor) *The Political, Social and Religious Thought of Russian Samizdat: An Anthology,* Nordland, 1977; *The Correspondence between Leo Tolstoy and American Shakers,* Transaction Press, 1977. Also author of *St. Vladimir and Olaf Tryggyason,* 1974, and of *Dostoevsky and Hawthorne.* Contributor to journals in his field. Editor, *Transactions,* 1970—.

WORK IN PROGRESS: John Cassian and Augustine; Augustine and Eastern Christianity; The "Libri Carolini".†

* * *

HAWKINS, A. Desmond
See HAWKINS, (Alec) Desmond

* * *

HAWKINS, (Alec) Desmond 1908-
(A. Desmond Hawkins)

PERSONAL: Born October 20, 1908, in East Sheen, Surrey, England; married Barbara Skidmore; children: two sons, two daughters. *Home:* 2 Stanton Close, Blandford Forum, Dorset DT11 7RT, England. *Agent:* David Higham Associates Ltd., 5-8 Lower John St., Golden Sq., London W1R 4HA, England.

CAREER: Free-lance writer, critic, and broadcaster, 1935-45; British Broadcasting Corp. (BBC), Bristol, England, features producer of West region, 1945-55, program director, 1955-66, founder of natural history unit, 1959, regional controller, 1966-69; free-lance writer, critic, and broadcaster, 1970—. London correspondent, *Partisan Review,* prior to 1940. *Member:* BBC

Club. *Awards, honors:* Silver medal from Royal Society for the Protection of Birds, 1959; Officer of the Order of the British Empire, 1963; LL.D., Bristol University, 1974.

WRITINGS: Hawk among the Sparrows (novel), Knopf, 1939; *Lighter than Day* (novel), Longmans, Green, 1940; *Thomas Hardy,* Alan Swallow, 1950, new edition published as *Hardy the Novelist,* David & Charles, 1966; *Sedgemoor and Avalon: A Portrait of Lowland Somerset,* R. Hale, 1954; *Wildlife of the New Forest,* Russell & Co., 1972; *Avalon and Sedgemoor,* David & Charles, 1973; *Hardy: Novelist and Poet,* Barnes & Noble, 1976; *Cranborne Chase,* Gollancz, 1980; *Concerning Agnes,* Sutton, 1981; *Hardy's Wessex,* Macmillan, 1983.

Editor: (Under name A. Desmond Hawkins, and author of introduction) *Poetry and Prose of John Donne,* Thomas Nelson, 1938; (and author of introduction) D. H. Lawrence, *Stories, Essays, and Poems,* Dent, 1939; (with Donald Boyd, Frank Gillard, and Chester Wilmot) *War Report: A Record of Dispatches Broadcast by the BBC's War Correspondents with the Allied Expeditionary Force, 6 June 1944—5 May 1945,* Oxford University Press, 1946; *BBC Naturalist Book,* Rathbone Books, 1957; *The Second BBC Naturalist,* Adprint, 1960.

Literary editor, *New English Weekly,* 1935-40, and *Purpose* (quarterly), 1936-40; fiction critic, *Criterion,* 1936-39.

BIOGRAPHICAL/CRITICAL SOURCES: Times Literary Supplement, May 2, 1980.

* * *

HAY, John 1915-

PERSONAL: Born August 31, 1915, in Ipswich, Mass.; son of Clarence Leonard (an archaeologist) and Alice (Appleton) Hay; married Kristi Putnam, February 14, 1942; children: Susan, Katherine, Rebecca (deceased), Charles. *Education:* Harvard University, A.B., 1938. *Religion:* Episcopalian. *Home:* Red Top Rd., Brewster, Mass. 02631.

CAREER: Writer. *Charleston News & Courier,* Charleston, S.C., Washington correspondent, 1939-40. Dartmouth College, visiting professor, 1972-81, adjunct professor of environmental studies, 1982—. President of board of directors of Cape Cod Museum of Natural History, 1956-79; chairman of Brewster Conservation Commission, 1964-71. *Military service:* U.S. Army, 1940-45. *Member:* Phi Beta Kappa. *Awards, honors:* John Burroughs Medal, 1964, for *The Great Beach;* named conservationist of the year by Massachusetts Wildlife Federation, 1970.

WRITINGS: A Private History (poems), Duell, Sloan & Pearce, 1947; *The Run,* Doubleday, 1959, revised edition, 1965; *Nature's Year: The Seasons of Cape Cod,* Doubleday, 1961; (with Arline Strong) *A Sense of Nature,* Doubleday, 1962; *The Great Beach,* Doubleday, 1963; (with Peter Farb) *The Atlantic Shore: Human and Natural History from Long Island to Labrador,* Harper, 1966; *Sandy Shore,* Chatham Press, 1968; *Six Poems,* privately printed, 1969.

In Defense of Nature, Little, Brown, 1970; *Spirit of Survival: A Natural and Personal History of Terns,* Dutton, 1974; (with Richard Kauffman) *The Primal Alliance: Earth and Ocean,* edited by Kenneth Brower, Friends of the Earth, 1974; *The Undiscovered Country,* Norton, 1982. Contributor of poems, articles, and reviews to magazines.

SIDELIGHTS: John Hay tells *CA* that his travels "have to do principally with my writing and interest in nature: Hudson Bay for birds of the tundra, Cape Cod Bay for a possible whale, Florida for pelicans, Britain for terns, and Maine for its ravens and herons." In his book *In Defense of Nature,* Hay shares his observations of wildlife along the Atlantic seashore, noting the effects of pollution on animal and plant life there. In the *New York Times Book Review,* Thomas Foster calls Hay "a gifted and perceptive reporter of the many fascinating, complex and interdependent forms of life he's been encountering from eastern Canada to Cape Cod." According to Donald Gropman in the *Christian Science Monitor,* Hay "dramatizes our isolation from the rest of life" in this book. "He reports back to us from his travels—near journeys to distant lands, for all he does is go out-of-doors, stop, look, and listen. The creatures and plants he sees and hears have become alien to most of us, and so his delicate reports carry the air of the esoteric." A *Publishers Weekly* critic characterizes the nature writer as "more than a staunch conservationist, . . . a man with an almost religious sense of nature."

AVOCATIONAL INTERESTS: "I enjoy climbing hills in New Hampshire, swimming in Maine and Cape Cod, growing vegetables, and splitting oak logs in the wintertime."

BIOGRAPHICAL/CRITICAL SOURCES: Publishers Weekly, May 5, 1969; *Christian Science Monitor,* September 18, 1969; *New York Times Book Review,* December 21, 1969; *Library Journal,* March 1, 1970.

* * *

HAYDEN, Dolores 1945-

PERSONAL: Born March 15, 1945, in New York, N.Y.; daughter of J. Francis and Katharine (McCabe) Hayden. *Education:* Mount Holyoke College, B.A. (magna cum laude), 1966; Girton College, Cambridge, diploma, 1967; Harvard University, M.Arch., 1972. *Office:* Graduate School of Architecture and Urban Planning, University of California, Los Angeles, Calif. 90024.

CAREER: University of California, Berkeley, lecturer in architecture, 1973; Massachusetts Institute of Technology, Cambridge, assistant professor, 1973-76, associate professor, 1977-79; University of California, Los Angeles, associate professor, 1979-81, professor of urban planning, 1981—. *Awards, honors:* Farrand fellow, 1972; National Endowment for the Humanities fellow, 1976-77; Radcliffe Institute fellow, 1976-77; Rockefeller fellow, 1979-80; Guggenheim fellow, 1981.

WRITINGS: Seven American Utopias: The Architecture of Communitarian Socialism, 1790-1975, M.I.T. Press, 1976; *The Grand Domestic Revolution: A History of Feminist Designs for American Homes, Neighborhoods and Cities,* M.I.T. Press, 1981; *Redesigning the American Dream,* Norton, 1983.

WORK IN PROGRESS: Essays on architecture and politics.

SIDELIGHTS: Dolores Hayden's book *The Grand Domestic Revolution: A History of Feminist Designs for American Homes* explores American architectural history in light of the work of material feminists in the late nineteenth and early twentieth centuries. Hayden focuses on little-known plans designed to reorganize not only the physical structures of homes and communities, but their socio-cultural structures as well. Architectural critic Paul Goldberger writes in the *New York Times Book Review* that "this is a book that is full of things I have never seen before, and full of new things to say about things I thought I knew well. It is a book about houses and about culture and about how each affects the other, and it must stand as one of the major works on the history of modern housing. . . . Feminists, obviously, will want to read [this book]; they will find within it many figures, both women and men, who . . . are too little known in our time. But it is perhaps more important that planners and architects, feminist or not, read it. The issues are ones that architecture, that permanent mirror of our values, often chooses to ignore. Granted, it is not the role of architects to design society—it is more their responsibility to provide the physical settings that society requires of them. But they will understand that role better after reading . . . Hayden's book."

BIOGRAPHICAL/CRITICAL SOURCES: New York Times Book Review, July 5, 1981.

* * *

HAYES, Geoffrey 1947-

PERSONAL: Born December 3, 1947, in Pasadena, Calif.; son of Philip Dutton (a waiter) and Juliette (a secretary; maiden name, Dante) Hayes. *Education:* Attended John O'Connell Institute, San Francisco Academy of Art, and New York School of Visual Arts. *Home:* 316 East 83rd St., New York, N.Y. 10028. *Office:* Harper & Row Publishers, Inc., 10 East 53rd St., New York, N.Y. 10022.

CAREER: Harcourt, Brace, Jovanovich, Inc., New York City, clerk, 1966-69; Dun & Bradstreet, New York City, clerk, 1969-72; Merling, Marx & Seidman (advertising agency), New York City, in art department, 1972-73; Kajima International, New York City, interior designer, 1973-75; Harper & Row Publishers, Inc., New York City, artist and designer, 1975—. *Awards, honors: When the Wind Blew* was chosen by the *New York Times* as one of the ten best illustrated books of the year in 1977.

WRITINGS—All self-illustrated juveniles; all published by Harper: *Bear by Himself,* 1976; *The Alligator and His Uncle Tooth,* 1977; *Patrick Comes to Puttyville and Other Stories,* 1978; *The Secret Inside,* 1980; *Elroy and the Witch's Child,* 1982.

Illustrator: Margaret Wise Brown, *When the Wind Blew,* Harper, 1977.

WORK IN PROGRESS: Patrick and Ted.

SIDELIGHTS: Geoffrey Hayes comments: "Writing and drawing have always come naturally to me. My brother and I, being only two years apart, channeled our creative energies into stories and books which we gave to one another. All the writing I do now is an extension and development of those early works. Many authors relive their past in their fiction, but while some (such as Proust) do so in autobiographical novels, I find fantasy not only the best form for expressing my feelings, but as viable as any literary genre."

* * *

HAYTER, William Goodenough 1906-

PERSONAL: Born August 1, 1906, in Oxford, England; son of Sir William Goodenough (an adviser to the Egyptian Government) and Alethea (Slessor) Hayter; married Iris Hoare, October 19, 1938; children: Teresa Margaret. *Education:* Attended Winchester College; New College, Oxford, M.A., 1929. *Home:* Bassetts House, Stanton St. John, Oxford OX9 1EX, England.

CAREER: Entered British Diplomatic Service, 1930, and served abroad in Vienna, Moscow, and China prior to World War II; postwar posts included assistant undersecretary of state, 1948, H. M. minister in Paris, 1949, ambassador to Soviet Union, 1953-57, and deputy undersecretary of state, 1957-58; Oxford University, New College, Oxford, England, warden, 1958-76. Trustee, British Museum, 1960-70. *Awards, honors:* Companion of St. Michael and St. George, 1948; Knight Commander of St. Michael and St. George, 1953.

WRITINGS: The Diplomacy of the Great Powers, Hamish Hamilton, 1959, Macmillan, 1961; *The Kremlin and the Embassy,* Hodder & Stoughton, 1967; *Russia and the World: A Study of Soviet Foreign Policy,* Secker & Warburg, 1970; *William of Wykeham, Patron of the Arts,* Chatto & Windus, 1970; *A Double Life* (memoirs), Hamish Hamilton, 1974; *Spooner: A Biography,* W. H. Allen, 1976. Contributor to *Observer.*

BIOGRAPHICAL/CRITICAL SOURCES: New Leader, May 22, 1967; *Times Literary Supplement,* August 24, 1967, May 24, 1974, March 4, 1977.

* * *

HEAD, Sydney W(arren) 1913-

PERSONAL: Born October 9, 1913, in England; came to the United States in 1920, naturalized citizen; married Dorothy Mack. *Education:* Stanford University, A.B., 1936, M.A., 1937; New York University, Ph.D., 1952. *Office:* Communication Department, University of Miami, Coral Gables, Fla. 33124.

CAREER: University of Miami, Coral Gables, Fla., 1938-61, began as instructor, became professor of radio-television-film; African American Institute, Addis Ababa, Ethiopia, regional representative and media consultant, 1962-64; RTV International, Addis Ababa, Ethiopia, chief of government media advisory team, 1964-69; Temple University, Philadelphia, Pa., professor of communications, 1970-80. Fulbright Professor at University of Ghana, 1976-77; visiting professor at University of Miami, 1981—. Broadcasting consultant in Ethiopia and the Sudan. *Military service:* U.S. Army, 1942-45. *Member:* International Institute of Communications, Association for Education in Journalism, Broadcasting Education Association.

WRITINGS: Broadcasting in America, Houghton, 1956, 4th revised edition, 1982; *Broadcasting in Africa,* Temple University Press, 1974; (with S. Eastman and L. Klein) *Broadcast Programming,* Wadsworth, 1981; *Comparative World Broadcasting,* Wadsworth, 1984. General editor of "Comparative and International Broadcasting" series, Temple University Press.

* * *

HEDLEY, (Gladys) Olwen 1912-

PERSONAL: Born April 28, 1912, in London, England; daughter of Osborne Janion and Sarah Gladys Patricia (Shelby-Jones) Hedley. *Home:* 15 Denny Crescent, London SE11 4UY, England. *Agent:* John Johnson, Clerkenwell House, 45-47 Clerkenwell Green, London EC1R 0HT, England.

CAREER: Windsor, Slough and Eton Express (Berkshire County newspaper), Windsor, England, member of editorial staff and editor of women's page, 1932-39; British Red Cross, assistant organizer of hospitals library and V.A.D. nurse in Windsor, during World War II and until 1947; Royal Library, Windsor Castle, Windsor, part-time assistant, 1948-52, librarian, research assistant, and member of Her Majesty's Household, 1952-64. *Awards, honors:* Elected Fellow of Royal Society of Literature, 1975.

WRITINGS—Published by Pitkin Pictorials, except as indicated: *Round and about Windsor,* Oxley & Son, 1948; *Round and about Windsor and District,* Oxley & Son, 1948, revised edition, 1950; *Windsor Castle,* International Publications Service, 1967, 2nd edition, 1972; *Buckingham Palace,* 1968, published as *The Pictorial History of Buckingham Palace,* British Book Centre, 1974; *Fountains Hall,* 1968; *City of London,* 1969, published as *London in Pictures,* British Book Centre, 1974, revised edition, in press; *Charles, Twenty-First Prince of Wales,* 1969.

Lichfield Cathedral, 1970; *"Mayflower" and the Pilgrim Fathers,* 1970; *Cambridge: The City and the Colleges,* 1971; *Hampton Court Palace,* 1971; *Prisoners in the Tower,* 1972; *Royal Places,* R. Hale, 1972; *London in Pictures,* 1973; *Queen Charlotte,* John Murray, 1975; *The Princes of Wales,* 1975; *Her Majesty's Tower of London,* 1976; *The Queen's Silver Jubilee,* 1977; *A Child's Guide to Windsor Castle,* Beric Tempest, 1979.

Kensington Palace, 1980; (contributor) *The Royal Wedding Official Souvenir,* 1981; *Royal Palaces,* 1982; *Historic Windsor and Runnymede,* 1982. Contributor to annual, *Report of the Society of the Friends of St. George's and the Descendants of the Knights of the Garter,* and to *First Windsor Literary Arts Festival,* 1977. Contributor of historical acticles to numerous periodicals, including *Homes and Gardens, The Berkshire Archaeological Journal, History Today, The Illustrated London News, Times* (London), and *Country Life.*

WORK IN PROGRESS: Editing court journals of Fanny Burney for McGill University and New York Public Library; *The Old Royal Household.*

SIDELIGHTS: Olwen Hedley was a resident of Windsor Castle for 18 years, the same castle where 300 years earlier Sir John Owen, one of her Welsh ancestors, was imprisoned with King Charles I during the civil war. She told *CA* that "a collateral ancestor was General Isaac Shelby, who took a prominent part on the American side in the War of Independence, became first governor of Kentucky and was, I believe, honoured by having Shelbyville in Indiana named after him."

Hampton Court Palace, London in Pictures, and *Her Majesty's Tower of London* have all been translated into French and German.

* * *

HEILMAN, Robert Bechtold 1906-

PERSONAL: Born July 18, 1906, in Philadelphia, Pa.; son of Edgar James (a clergyman) and Mary Alice (Bechtold) Heilman; married Elizabeth Wiltbank, 1927 (divorced, 1934); married Ruth Delavan Champlin, July 31, 1935; children: (second marriage) Champlin. *Education:* Lafayette College, A.B., 1927; Tufts University, graduate study, 1927-28; Ohio State University, M.A., 1930; Harvard University, M.A., 1931, Ph.D., 1935. *Politics:* "Swing voter." *Religion:* Lutheran. *Home:* 4554 45th Ave. N.E., Seattle, Wash. 98105. *Office:* Department of English, GN-30, University of Washington, Seattle, Wash. 98195.

CAREER: University of Maine, Orono, instructor in English, 1930-33, 1934-35; Louisiana State University, Baton Rouge, instructor, 1935-36, assistant professor, 1936-42, associate professor, 1942-46, professor of English, 1946-48; University of Washington, Seattle, professor of English, 1948-76, professor emeritus, 1976—, chairman of department, 1948-71. Arnold Professor of English, Whitman College, 1977. *Member:* International Association of University Professors of English, International Shakespeare Association, Modern Language Association of America (member of national executive council, 1966-69), National Council of Teachers of English (distinguished lecturer, 1968), American Association of University Professors (member of national executive council, 1962-65), Shakespeare Association of America (trustee, 1977-80), Philological Association of Pacific Coast (president, 1958), Phi Beta Kappa (senator, 1967; member of executive committee, 1973—).

AWARDS, HONORS: Arizona Quarterly Essay Prize, 1956, for an essay on *Othello; Explicator* Award (for criticism), 1957, for *Magic in the Web: Action and Language in Othello;* Huntington Library grant, 1959; Longview Award, 1960, for essay in *Texas Quarterly;* Guggenheim fellowship, 1964-65, and 1975-76; D.Litt., Lafayette College, 1967; National Endowment for the Humanities senior fellow, 1971-72; LL.D., Grinnell College, 1971; L.H.D., Kenyon College, 1973; HH.D., Whitman College, 1977; Litt.D., University of the South, 1978; Christian Gauss Prize of Phi Beta Kappa, 1979, for *The Ways of the World: Comedy and Society.*

WRITINGS: America in English Fiction, 1760-1800, Louisiana State University Press, 1937; *This Great Stage: Image and Structure in King Lear,* Louisiana State University Press, 1948; *Magic in the Web: Action and Language in Othello,* University Press of Kentucky, 1956; *Tragedy and Melodrama: Versions of Experience,* University of Washington Press, 1968; *The Iceman, the Arsonist, and the Troubled Agent: Tragedy and Melodrama on the Modern Stage,* University of Washington Press, 1973; *The Ghost on the Ramparts and Other Essays in the Humanities,* University of Georgia Press, 1973; *The Ways of the World: Comedy and Society,* University of Washington Press, 1978.

Editor and author of critical introduction: Jonathan Swift, *Gulliver's Travels,* Modern Library, 1950, revised edition, 1969; Swift, *A Tale of a Tub* [and] *The Battle of the Books,* Modern Library, 1950; *An Anthology of English Drama Before Shakespeare,* Rinehart, 1952; Joseph Conrad, *Lord Jim,* Rinehart, 1957; Thomas Hardy, *The Mayor of Casterbridge,* Riverside, 1962; George Eliot, *Silas Marner,* Riverside, 1962; William Shakespeare, *Cymbeline,* Pelican, 1964; Euripides, *Alcestis,* Chandler, 1965; Hardy, *Jude the Obscure,* Harper, 1966; Shakespeare, *The Taming of the Shrew,* Signet, 1966; Hardy, *Tess of the D'Urbervilles,* Bantam, 1971.

Editor: *Aspects of Democracy,* Louisiana State University Press, 1941; *Aspects of a World at War,* Louisiana State University Press, 1943; (with Cleanth Brooks) *Understanding Drama* (textbook), Henry Holt, 1945, enlarged edition, 1948; *Modern Short Stories: A Critical Anthology* (textbook), Harcourt, 1950.

Contributor: T. A. Kirby and N. M. Caffee, editors, *Studies for W. A. Read,* Louisiana State University Press, 1941; Allen Tate, editor, *A Southern Vanguard,* Prentice-Hall, 1947.

Louis Rubin and Robert Jacobs, editors, *Southern Renascence,* Johns Hopkins Press, 1953; Robert Rathburn and Martin Steinman, editors, *From Jane Austen to Joseph Conrad,* University of Minnesota Press, 1958.

James G. McManaway, editor, *Shakespeare 400,* Holt, 1964; Edward A. Bloom, editor, *Shakespeare 1564-1964,* Brown University Press, 1965; Gerald W. Chapman, editor, *Essays on Shakespeare,* Princeton University Press, 1966; Kenneth

Muir, editor, *Shakespeare Survey 19,* Cambridge University Press, 1966.

Kirby and W. Olive, editors, *Essays in Honor of E. L. Marilla,* Louisiana State University Press, 1970; David Madden, editor, *American Dreams, American Nightmares,* Southern Illinois University Press, 1970; Brom Weber, *Sense and Sensibility in 20th Century Writings,* Southern Illinois University Press, 1970; John Halperin, editor, *The Theory of the Novel: New Essays,* Oxford University Press, 1974; Halperin, editor, *Jane Austen: Bicentenary Essays,* Cambridge University Press, 1975; Lewis P. Simpson, editor, *The Possibilities of Order: Cleanth Brooks and His Work,* Louisiana State University Press, 1976; Walter Edens and others, editors, *Teaching Shakespeare,* Princeton University Press, 1976; William H. New, editor, *A Political Art: Essays and Images in Honour of George Woodcock,* University of British Columbia Press, 1978; Anne Smith, editor, *The Novels of Thomas Hardy,* Vision Press (London), 1979; Peggy W. Prenshaw, editor, *Eudora Welty: Critical Essays,* University Press of Mississippi, 1979.

Also author of *The Charliad* (verse), 1973. Contributor to *English Institute Annual,* Columbia University Press, 1949, and *The Range of English: NCTE Distinguished Lectures,* National Council of Teachers of English, 1968; contributor of essays and reviews to journals. Member of editorial board, *Poetry Northwest,* 1962—, *Studies in the Novel,* 1966—, *Shakespeare Studies,* 1966—, *Modern Language Quarterly,* 1973-77, *Sewanee Review,* 1974—, and *Mississippi Studies in English,* 1981—. Regular reviewer for Phi Beta Kappa *Key Reporter,* 1959—.

WORK IN PROGRESS: A book-length study of farce and its relation to other dramatic forms.

AVOCATIONAL INTERESTS: Watching football games; doing chores at a hideaway shack on a high bank overlooking Puget Sound.

*   *   *

HENRY, Marguerite

PERSONAL: Born in Milwaukee, Wis. *Address:* P.O. Box 385, Rancho Santa Fe, Calif. 92067.

CAREER: Full-time professional writer.

AWARDS, HONORS: Newbery Honor Award, Junior Scholastic Gold Seal Award, and Award of the Friends of Literature, 1948, for *Justin Morgan Had a Horse;* Newbery Medal, 1949, for *King of the Wind;* William Allen White Award, 1956, for *Brighty of the Grand Canyon;* Sequoyah Children's Book Award, 1959, for *Black Gold,* 1969, for *Mustang, Wild Spirit of the West;* Society of Midland Author's Clara Ingram Judson Award, 1961, for *Gaudenzia: Pride of the Palio,* 1973, for *San Domingo: The Medicine Hat Stallion;* Western Heritage Award, 1967, for *Mustang, Wild Spirit of the West;* Boys' Clubs of America Award, Lewis Carroll Shelf Award, and Newbery Honor Award for *Misty of Chincoteague;* Society of Midland Authors Award for *San Domingo: The Medicine Hat Stallion;* Literature for Children Award, Southern California Council, 1973; Kerlan Award, University of Minnesota, 1975; named Author of the Diamond Jubilee Year by Illinois Association of Teachers of English, 1982.

WRITINGS—Published by Rand McNally, except as indicated: *Auno and Tauno: A Story of Finland,* Albert Whitman, 1940; *Dilly Dally Sally,* Saalfield, 1940; *Birds at Home,* Donohue, 1942, revised edition, Hubbard Press, 1972; *Geraldine Belinda,* Platt, 1942; (with Barbara True) *Their First Igloo on Baffin Island,* Albert Whitman, 1943; *Boy and a Dog,* Follett, 1944; *Little Fellow* (Junior Literary Guild selection), Winston, 1945, revised edition, Rand McNally, 1975; *Robert Fulton: Boy Craftsman,* Bobbs-Merrill, 1945; *Sea Star: Orphan of Chintoteague,* 1949; *Muley-Ears, Nobody's Dog* (Junior Literary Guild selection), 1959.

Gaudenzia: Pride of the Palio, 1960; *Misty, the Wonder Pony, by Misty, Herself,* 1961; *Mustang, Wild Spirit of the West,* 1966; *Dear Readers and Riders,* 1969; *San Domingo: The Medicine Hat Stallion,* 1972; *Pictorial Life Story of Misty,* 1976; *One Man's Horse,* 1977; *The Illustrated Marguerite Henry,* 1980; *Marguerite Henry's Misty Treasury,* 1982.

With illustrations by Wesley Dennis: *Justin Morgan Had a Horse,* Follett, 1945, revised edition, Rand McNally, 1954; *Misty of Chincoteague* (Junior Literary Guild selection), 1947; *Benjamin West and His Cat, Grimalkin,* Bobbs-Merrill, 1947; *Always Reddy,* McGraw, 1947; *King of the Wind,* 1948; *Little-or-Nothing from Nottingham,* McGraw, 1949; *Born to Trot,* 1950; *Album of Horses* (Junior Literary Guild selection), 1951, reprinted, 1979; *Portfolio of Horses,* 1952; *Brighty of the Grand Canyon* (Junior Literary Guild selection), 1953; *Wagging Tails: An Album of Dogs,* 1955; *Cinnabar: The One O'Clock Fox,* 1956; *Black Gold,* 1957; *All about Horses,* Random House, 1962, revised edition, 1967; *Five O'Clock Charlie,* 1962; *Stormy, Misty's Foal,* 1963; *White Stallion of Lipizza,* 1964; *Portfolio of Horse Paintings,* 1964.

"Pictured Geographies" series; published by Albert Whitman: *Alaska in Story and Pictures,* 1941, 2nd edition, 1942; *Argentina . . . ,* 1941, 2nd edition, 1942; *Brazil . . . ,* 1941, 2nd edition, 1942; *Canada . . . ,* 1941, 2nd edition, 1942; *Chile . . . ,* 1941, 2nd edition, 1942; *Mexico . . . ,* 1941, 2nd edition, 1942; *Panama . . . ,* 1941, 2nd edition, 1942; *West Indies . . . ,* 1941, 2nd edition, 1942; *Australia . . . ,* 1946; *Bahamas . . . ,* 1946; *Bermuda . . . ,* 1946; *British Honduras . . . ,* 1946; *Dominican Republic . . . ,* 1946; *Hawaii . . . ,* 1946; *New Zealand . . . ,* 1946; *Virgin Islands . . . ,* 1946.

Contributor to *World Book Encyclopedia.* Contributor of articles to magazines, including *Nations' Business, Saturday Evening Post, Reader's Digest,* and *Forum.*

SIDELIGHTS: "As far as children are concerned, Marguerite Henry is the poet laureate of horses," says May Hill Arbuthnot in *Children's Reading in the Home.* While Henry has written stories about dogs, foxes, and other animals, as well as numerous picture histories of countries around the world, she is best known for her horse stories. Writing in *Children and Books,* Arbuthnot explains why Henry is "probably the most successful writer of horse stories we have ever had[:] Her success rests on a sound basis. Every book represents careful research, the stories are well told, the animal heroes are true to their species, and the people in her books are as memorable as the animals."

When asked why she writes so prolifically about horses, Henry explains: "It is exciting to me that no matter how much machinery replaces the horse, the work it can do is still measured in horsepower . . . even in this space age. And although a riding horse often weighs half a ton and a big drafter a full ton, either can be led about by a piece of string if he has been wisely trained. This to me is a constant source of wonder and challenge."

Many of Henry's stories are based on the lives of legendary horses. The background for one of her most successful books,

Misty of Chincoteague, for example, came from the history surrounding a herd of wild ponies living on an island off the coastline of the eastern United States. Henry relates that in 1946 she received a telephone call from editor Mary Alice Jones suggesting she write a story based on the legend of the Spanish moor ponies that were washed into the sea, centuries ago, when a Spanish galleon was wrecked on a hidden reef. Preliminary research revealed that the ponies swam, unhurt, for the nearest shore, which happened to be Assateague Island off the coasts of Virginia and Maryland. Today, descendants of these ponies still run wild on that island. One day a year, called Pony Penning Day, oystermen and clam diggers from Chincoteague Island nearby turn cowboy. They round up the wild ponies, drive them into the sea, swim them over to their own island, and sell the colts in a big auction. With illustrator Wesley Dennis, Henry went to Pony Penning Day in search of a story. She returned with the story and a colt named Misty.

This was the beginning of *Misty of Chincoteague,* a book that M. G. King, in the *Chicago Sun Book Week,* calls "one of the finest horse stories you'll find for the eight to 12-year-olds." Miriam E. Wilt says of *Misty of Chincoteague* in *Elementary English* that "it is one of the finest horse stories ever written. Chincoteague is a way of life. The salt air of the Atlantic is in it. The fine sense of values, the feeling of drama, the deft characterization all blend together to give us *Misty,* . . . our introduction to a magical land of fact, phantasy, and legend woven into stories that entwine around our heart like ivy clinging to a wall."

King of the Wind tells the story of the eighteenth-century Arabian stallion Sham, one of the three horses to sire the thoroughbred line, whose descendants include the famous Man o' War. The figure of Sham is the "most romantic horse to appear in literature for youth for some time" according to Gladys Crofoot Castor in the *New York Times Book Review.* "In *King of the Wind,*" says the *New York Herald Tribune Weekly Book Review* critic, "Marguerite Henry stirs the reader's imagination, holds his interest, makes him laugh a little and cry a little—satisfies him."

Another Henry book, *Brighty of the Grand Canyon,* is based on the life of a burro named Bright Angel and his adventures in the prospecting days of the Old West. Henry has "built an enchanting story" on the legend of Brighty, says a critic in *Virginia Kirkus' Bookshop Service.* "Brighty was a little grey burro, a wild creature with a more than human faculty for picking friends and making enemies—and getting into and out of scrapes. There's adventure and mystery here, set against the superb backdrop of the Grand Canyon, where Brighty made the trail that others follow." Wilt describes *Brighty of the Grand Canyon* as "wild, free, lovable. A story of adventure, mystery, beauty, and human-animal companionship. A bond stronger than ropes, chains, or distance that existed between a man and a burro."

In the acceptance paper she wrote for *Newbery Medal Books: 1922-1955,* Marguerite Henry speaks of the children who come to visit her in her writing study. They often ask, she says, "'Will you write a book for me? Not for any other boy. Just for me?' I'm a long time answering. How can I tell him that is what I am trying to do? How can I say, 'Johnny, I'm trying! I'm trying to write a book that you can crawl into as snugly as you do into your own bed, a book about which you can say, "This is mine. It fits around me. I fit into it. It fits under and over and around me. It warms me. It is mine, mine, *mine*!"'"

Fourteen of Henry's books have been translated into several languages, including German, Swedish, Danish, French, Italian, Japanese, Urdu, Arabic, and Afrikaans.

MEDIA ADAPTATIONS: Misty of Chincoteague was filmed by Twentieth Century-Fox in 1961; *Brighty of the Grand Canyon* was filmed by Paragon Productions in 1966; *Justin Morgan Had a Horse* was filmed by Walt Disney Productions in 1972; *San Domingo: The Medicine Hat Stallion* was adapted for television as "Peter Lundy and the Medicine Hat Stallion" in 1977.

BIOGRAPHICAL/CRITICAL SOURCES: Chicago Sun Book Week, October 18, 1947; *New York Times,* November 16, 1947, November 15, 1953, December 22, 1957; *New York Herald Tribune Weekly Book Review,* November 14, 1948; *New York Times Book Review,* November 14, 1948; *Virginia Kirkus' Bookshop Service,* October 15, 1953; *Elementary English,* November, 1954, January, 1967; Bertha Mahoney Miller and Elinor Whitney Field, editors, *Newbery Medal Books: 1922-1955,* Horn Book, 1955; *Chicago Sunday Tribune,* November 17, 1957; *Saturday Review,* February 15, 1958; Marguerite Henry, *Dear Readers and Riders,* Rand McNally, 1969; May Hill Arbuthnot, *Children's Reading in the Home,* Scott, Foresman, 1969; Arbuthnot and Zena Sutherland, *Children and Books,* 4th edition, Scott, Foresman, 1972; *Los Angeles Times,* November 11, 1979; Marguerite Henry, *The Illustrated Marguerite Henry,* Rand McNally, 1980; "Story of a Book," Pied Piper Productions, 1980; *Children's Literature Review,* Volume IV, Gale, 1982.

—Sketch by Kerry L. Lutz

* * *

HERBERT, Jean (Daniel Fernand) 1897-1980

PERSONAL: Born July 27, 1897, in Paris, France; died August 21, 1980, in Geneva, Switzerland; son of Fernand and Laurence (Mury) Herbert; married May Anbuhl, 1920; married second wife, Josette Perelli, February 18, 1964; children: (first marriage) Janine Yates, Yvette Renoux. *Education:* University of Paris, M.A., 1914, LL.B., 1920. *Religion:* Christian. *Home:* La Luciole, 1253 Vandoeuvres, Geneva, Switzerland.

CAREER: Writer, editor, and translator. Albin Michel (publishers), Paris, France, editor-in-chief of *Spiritualities vivantes,* 1944-80; United Nations, New York, N.Y., chief interpreter, 1945-49; Derain (publishers), Lyon, France, editor-in-chief of *Dieux hindous,* and *Les Trois Lotus,* 1950-80; University of Geneva, Geneva, Switzerland, privat-docent, 1955-80; Elsevier Publishing Co., Amsterdam, Netherlands, editor-in-chief of *Glossaria Interpretum* and *Lexica,* 1956-80. Chairman of the boards of examiners in schools for interpreters, Universities of Paris and Trieste, 1955-80; adviser on interpretation to many international organizations. *Military service:* French Army, reserve officer, active duty in World Wars I and II; awarded Croix de Guerre.

MEMBER: International Association of Conference Interpreters (Paris; president), Societe des Gens de Lettres (Paris), Societe Mexicaine d'Archeologie et de Statistique (honorary member). *Awards, honors:* Corona d'Italia, 1920; Laureat de l'Academie Francaise, 1965; gold medal of the Royal Linguists' Society (London), 1971.

WRITINGS: Lexique francais-anglais-americain des termes d'artillerie et de balistique, Ministere de la Guere, 1918; (with Georges Mathieu) *La Grande-Bretagne au travail,* Roger, 1919.

(With P. G. Wilson) *Through French Eyes* (senior level), Pitman, 1933; *Through French Eyes: Questions and Answers,* Pitman, 1934; (with Wilson) *Through French Eyes* (intermediate level), Pitman, 1934; (with Wilson and father, Fernand Herbert) *La Vie commerciale,* Pitman, 1934; *La Sabiduria hindu,* Ercilla, 1939; *Bibliographie de l'oeuvre de Swami Vivekananda dans les langues europeennes,* Adrien-Maisonneuve, 1939.

Etudes sur Ramana Maharshi, Adrien-Maisonneuve, 1940; *L'Enseignement de Ramakrishna,* Adrien-Maisonneuve, 1941, new edition, Albin Michel, 1972; *Vedantisme et vie pratique,* Adrien-Maisonneuve, 1942; (with Lizelle Reymond) *Etudes et Portraits,* Adrien-Maisonneuve, 1943; *Comment se preparer a la meditation,* Derain, 1943; *La Notion de la vie future dans l'hindouisme,* Adrien-Maisonneuve, 1944, new edition, Albin Michel, 1945; *Lexique Ramakrishna-Vivekananda,* Ophrys, 1945; *Spiritualite hindoue,* Albin Michel, 1947, reprinted, 1972.

Les yogas hindous, Adyar, 1950; *Le Message de la mythologie hindoue,* Derain, 1950; *Le Yoga de Shri Aurobindo,* Derain, 1951; *Wege zum Hinduismus,* Rascher, 1951; *Manuel de l'Interprete,* Georg, 1952, English language edition published as *The Interpreter's Handbook,* Georg, 1952, 2nd English language edition, revised and enlarged, published as *The Interpreter's Handbook: How to Become a Conference Interpreter,* Librairie de l'Universite (Geneva), 1968; *La Mythologie Hindoue: Son message,* Albin Michel, 1953; *Indischer Mythos als geistige Realitaet,* Barth, 1953; (with H. Ghaffar) *Premier album de mythologie hindoue,* Derain, 1955; (with others) *Conference Terminology,* Elsevier, 1957, new augmented edition, 1962; *Asie,* Migros, 1957, new edition, Albin Michel, 1958; *L'Enseignement de Shivananda,* Albin Michel, 1958; (with Huguette Herbert) *Dans l'Inde: L'Accueil des dieux,* Aubier, 1959; *Asien, Denken und Lebensformen der oestilichen Welt,* Piper Verlag, 1959.

Introduction a l'Asie, Albin Michel, 1960, translation published as *An Introduction to Asia,* Oxford University Press, 1965; *Aux sources du Japon: Le Shinto,* Albin Michel, 1964; *Les Dieux nationaux du Japon,* Albin Michel, 1965; *Dieux et sectes populaires du Japon,* Albin Michel, 1966; *Shinto: At the Fountainhead of Japan,* Stein & Day, 1967; *Bibliographie du Shinto et des sectes shintoistes,* Brill, 1968; *Ce que Gandhi a vraiment dit,* Stock, 1969.

Le Yoga de l'amour, Albin Michel, 1973; *Le Bouddhisme en Asie au XXe siecle,* de Tartas, 1974; *Les grands courants spirituels modernes dans l'Hinduoisme,* de Tartas, 1974; *L'Hindouisme vivant,* Laffont, 1975; *A Yoga do Amor,* Artenova, 1976; *Reflexions sur la Bhagavad-Gita vue dans son contexte,* Dervy-Livres, 1976; *La Cosmogonie japonaise,* Dervy-Livres, 1977; *Table analytique de la Bhagavad-Gita,* Vandoevres, 1978; *L'India confina con Dio,* Elvetica, 1978; *Le Yoga de la Vie quotidienne: Karma-Yoga,* Dervy-Livres, 1978; *Qu'est-ce que l'Hindouisme?,* Journal de Bord (Nice), 1978; *How to Use the Bhagavad-Gita,* The British Wheel of Yoga, 1978; *L'objet et la methode des etudes mythologiques dans l'Hindouisme,* Cahiers internationaux du Symbolisme, 1978; (contributor) *La mort est une autre naissance,* Seghers, 1979.

L'interpretation psychologique du Veda selon Shri Aurobindo, Dervy-Livres, 1980; *La sagesse de l'Inde et le Pantheon hindou,* Rose-Croix AMORC, 1980; (contributor) *Le Soufisme,* l'Originel, 1980; *La Religion d'Okinawa,* Dervy-Livres, 1981. Also author of *Mon Maitre Autobindo.*

Translator: (With Ester Levy) Edwyn Bevan, *Histoire des Lagides,* Payot, 1934; (and author of preface) Mahatma Gandhi, *Lettres a l'ashram,* Albin Michel, 1937; (with others) Shri Rama-krishna, *Les Paroles du maitre,* Adrien-Maisonneuve, 1937; (with Pierre Sauvageot) Adams Beck, *A la decouverte du yoga,* Attinger, 1938; (and author of preface; translator with Sauvageot) Adams Beck, *Zenn,* Attinger, 1938; (and author of preface) Rabindranath Tagore, *Sadhana,* Albin Michel, 1940; (and author of preface; translator with Alice Prudhomme) Swami Vijoyananda, *Ainsi parlait Christ,* Jeheber, 1940; (with Camille Rao) *Bhagavad-Gita,* Adrien-Maisonneuve, 1941; (and author of preface; translator with Rao) *La Bhagavad-Gita interpretee par Shri Aurobindo,* Adrien-Maisonneuve, 1942, new edition, Albin Michel, 1947; (and author of preface; translator with Odette de Saussure) Swami Brahmananda, *Disciplines monastiques,* Adrien-Maisonneuve, 1943; (with Prudhomme) Swami Ramdas, *Carnet de pelerinage,* Volume I, Ophrys, 1943, new edition including Volume II, Albin Michel, 1953; (and author of preface) Ananda Moyi, *Aux sources de la joie,* Ophrys, 1943; (and author of preface and notes) Shankaracharya, *Hymnes a Shiva,* Derain, 1944; Swami Yatiswarananda, *Commentaries sur la discipline monastique de Swami Brahmananda,* Derain, 1949.

(And author of preface) Swami Sivananda, *La Pratique de la meditation,* Albin Michel, 1950; (with Rose Rigaud) Nivedita, *Vivekananda tel que je l'ai vu,* Albin Michel, 1952; (and author of preface; translator with H. Gharrar) S. V. Yesudian and E. Haich, *Sport et Yoga,* Santoza, 1953; (with others) D. T. Suzuki, *Essais sur le Bouddhisme Zen,* Albin Michel, Volume I, 1954, Volume II, 1956, Volume III, 1958; (with others) Swami Ramdas, *Presence de Ram,* Albin Michel, 1956; (with Huguette Herbert) Mulk Raj Anand, *Kama-kala,* Nagel, 1958; (with Charles Andrieu) Lama Anagarika Govinda, *Les Fondements de la mystique tibetaine,* Albin Michel, 1960; (with wife, Josette Herbert, and Antoinette Perelli) Lama Anagarika Povinole, *Le Chemin des Nueges blouis,* Albin Michel, 1969.

Dalai-lama, *Introduction au Bouddhisme tibetain,* Dervy-Livres, 1972; (with J. Herbert) *L'Enseignement de Ma Ananda Moyi,* Albin Michel, 1974; *Enseignement du Dalai Lama,* Albin Michel, 1976; John Blofeld, *Le Taoisme Vivant,* Albin Michel, 1977; Mohammad Iqbal, *l'Aile de Gabriel,* Albin Michel, 1977; Lama Anagarika Govinda, *Meditation creatrice et conscience multidimensionnelle,* Albin Michel, 1978; Seyyed Hossein Nasr, *Essais sur le Soufisme,* Albin Michel, 1980; (with Isabelle da Prato) *Choisis la Vie,* Toynbee/Ikeda, 1980; (with J. Herbert) Blofeld, *le Yoga de la Compassion,* Albin Michel, in press.

Translator of works by Swami Vivekananda: (And author of preface) *Mon Maitre,* Adrien-Maisonneuve, 1935; (and author of preface) *Jnana-Yoga,* Adrien-Maisonneuve, 1936; (and author of preface) *Le Yoga de la connaissance,* Adrien-Maisonneuve, 1936; (and author of preface) *Karma-Yoga,* Adrien-Maisonneuve, 1937; (and author of preface) *Entretiens inspires,* Adrien-Maisonneuve, 1937; (and author of preface; translator with Reymond) *Bhakti-Yoga,* Adrien-Maisonneuve, 1937; *Commentaires sur les aphorismes de Patanjali,* Adrien-Maisonneuve, 1938; (and author of preface; translator with Reymond) *Conferences sur Bhakti-Yoga,* Adrien-Maisonneuve, 1939; *Au coeur des choses,* Adrien-Maisonneuve, 1940; (and author of preface; translator with others) *Les Yogas pratiques,* Albin Michel, 1950.

Translator of works by Shri Aurobindo: (And author of preface; translator with Reymond) *Lumieres sur le yoga,* Adrien-Maisonneuve, 1938; *L'Isha Upanishad,* Adrien-Maisonneuve, 1939; (with Rene Daumal and Rao) *La Kena Upanishad,* Adrien-Maisonneuve, 1944; (with others) *La Vie divine,* Albin Michel,

Volume I, 1949, Volume II, 1956, Volume III, 1958, Volume IV, 1959; (with others) *Trois Upanishads,* Albin Michel, 1949; *Lettres,* Adyar, Volume I, 1950, Volume II, 1952, Volume III, 1958; (with D. Bonarjee) *Heraclite,* Derain, 1951; (and author of preface; translator with others) *Guide du Yoga,* Albin Michel, 1951; *De la Grece a l'Inde,* Albin Michel, 1976; (and author of preface) *Metaphysique et Psychologie,* Albin Michel, 1976; *La Pratique du Yoga integral,* Albin Michel, 1976; *Experiences psychiques dans le Yoga,* Albin Michel, 1977; *Reponses,* Albin Michel, 1977; *Brahman et Maya dans les Upanishads,* Dervy-Livres, 1980.

SIDELIGHTS: Jean Herbert's books *Manuel de l'Interprete* and *Conference Terminology* have been published in six other languages.†

* * *

HERRICK, William 1915-

PERSONAL: Born January 10, 1915, in Trenton, N.J.; son of Nathan and Mary (Saperstein) Horvitz; married Jeannette Esther Wellin, August 31, 1948; children: Jonathan, Michael, Lisa. *Education:* Educated in public schools, New York, N.Y. *Home:* Rider Mills Rd., Old Chatham, N.Y. 12136. *Agent:* Roberta Pryor, International Creative Management, 40 West 57th St., New York, N.Y. 10019.

CAREER: Writer. Court reporter, 1943-69.

WRITINGS—All novels: *The Itinerant,* McGraw, 1967; *Strayhorn,* McGraw, 1968; *Hermanos!,* Simon & Schuster, 1969; *The Last to Die,* Simon & Schuster, 1971; *Golcz,* Columbia Publishing, 1976; *Shadows and Wolves,* New Directions, 1980; *Love and Terror,* New Directions, 1981.

WORK IN PROGRESS: Another novel, *Kill Memory,* for New Directions.

* * *

HERZ, Martin F(lorian) 1917-

PERSONAL: Born July 9, 1917, in New York, N.Y.; son of Gustave L. and Edith (Flammerschein) Herz; married Elisabeth Kremenak (a gynecologist), April 6, 1957. *Education:* Columbia University, B.S., 1937, graduate study, 1939-41. *Home:* 4207 Cathedral Ave. N.W., Washington, D.C. 20016. *Office:* Institute for Study of Diplomacy, Georgetown University, Washington, D.C. 20057.

CAREER: Wessel, Duval & Co., New York, N.Y., junior executive, 1940-41; U.S. Department of State, Foreign Service officer, 1946-77, assigned to Vienna, 1946-48, officer in charge of Austrian cultural and information affairs, Washington, D.C., 1949-50, second secretary, U.S. Embassy, Paris, France, 1950-54, second secretary, then first secretary of U.S. Embassy, Phnom Penh, Cambodia, 1955-57, first secretary of U.S. Embassy, Tokyo, Japan, 1957-59, political-military adviser, Bureau of African Affairs, Washington, D.C., 1960-61, special assistant for planning, Bureau of African Affairs, 1961-63, counselor for political affairs, U.S. Embassy, Tehran, Iran, 1963-67, country director, Bureau of East Asian Affairs, 1967-68, minister-counselor for political affairs, Saigon, Vietnam, 1968-70, deputy assistant secretary of state, Washington, D.C., 1970-74, ambassador to the People's Republic of Bulgaria, Sofia, 1974-77; Georgetown University, Washington, D.C., Oscar Idea Professor of diplomacy and director of Institute for Study of Diplomacy, 1978—. *Military service:* U.S. Army, 1941-46; served in Europe; became major; received Purple Heart and Bronze Star.

MEMBER: American Foreign Service Association (board member, 1961-63, 1967-68; vice-chairman of board, 1963). *Awards, honors:* Commendable Service Award, U.S. Department of State, 1961; Superior Honor Award, 1970; Grand Medal of Honor with Silver Star, Austria, 1973; Horseman of Madara, First Class, Bulgaria, 1977.

WRITINGS: (With Zack Hanle) *The Golden Ladle,* Ziff-Davis Publishing, 1943; *A Short History of Cambodia,* Praeger, 1958; *Beginnings of the Cold War,* Indiana University Press, 1966; *How the Cold War Is Taught,* Ethics and Public Policy Center (Washington, D.C.), 1978; *Decline of the West?: George Kennan and His Critics,* Ethics and Public Policy Center, 1978; *The Prestige Press and the Christmas Bombing, 1972,* Ethics and Public Policy Center, 1980; *215 Days in the Life of an American Ambassador,* Georgetown University, 1981. Contributor to *Foreign Service Journal, Army Digest, Public Opinion Quarterly,* and *Military Review.*

WORK IN PROGRESS: Two novels.

SIDELIGHTS: Martin F. Herz speaks French, German, Italian, Spanish, Japanese, and Farsi (Persian).

BIOGRAPHICAL/CRITICAL SOURCES: Daniel Lerner, *Psywar,* George W. Stewart, 1949; Morris Janowitz and William E. Daugherty, editors, *Psychological Warfare Casebook,* Johns Hopkins Press, 1958.

* * *

HERZOG, Arthur (III) 1927-

PERSONAL: Born April 6, 1927, in New York, N.Y.; son of Arthur, Jr. and Elizabeth (Dayton) Herzog; divorced; children: Matthew. *Education:* Attended University of Arizona, 1946; Stanford University, B.A., 1950; Columbia University, M.A., 1956. *Politics:* Democrat. *Religion:* None. *Address:* P.O. Box 1012, Cooper St., New York, N.Y. 10003. *Agent:* Candida Donadio, 111 West 57th St., New York, N.Y. 10017.

CAREER: Fawcett Publications, Greenwich, Conn., editor, 1954-57; full-time free-lance writer, 1957—. *Military service:* U.S. Navy, 1945-46.

WRITINGS: (Co-author) *Smoking and the Public Interest,* Consumers Union, 1963; *The War-Peace Establishment,* Harper, 1965; *The Church Trap,* Macmillan, 1968; *McCarthy for President,* Viking, 1969.

The B.S. Factor, Simon & Schuster, 1973; *The Swarm,* Simon & Schuster, 1974, movie edition, New American Library, 1978; *Earthsound,* Simon & Schuster, 1975; *Orca,* Simon & Schuster, 1976; *Heat,* New American Library, 1976; *I.Q. 83,* Berkley Publishing, 1977; *Make Us Happy,* Crowell, 1978; *Glad to Be Here,* Crowell, 1979.

Aries Rising, Richard Marek, 1980; *The Craving,* Dell, 1982. Contributor of articles to *Harper's, Esquire, New York Times,* and other publications.

WORK IN PROGRESS: A novel on "business takeovers and an aphrodisiac."

SIDELIGHTS: "To connoisseurs of disaster, Arthur Herzog is a familiar name," Joseph McLellan writes in the *Washington Post,* referring to Herzog's reputation as a writer of disaster novels. *The Swarm,* one of Herzog's most popular books, concerns a swarm of killer bees that attacks New York City. The novel, says McLellan, brings "a chilling sense of reality to a most unpromising subject."

In *I.Q. 83,* Herzog writes about a virus that drastically reduces the intelligence of its victims, leaving them virtually incapable of performing even ordinary tasks. "Once seeded in the imagination," writes Donald Goddard in a *New York Times Book Review* article, "Arthur Herzog's vision of a world lapsing into imbecility roots itself at a deeper layer of unease than most armchair catastrophe-lovers are used to. Those frightened by the idea of killer sharks or fires in high buildings can still safety swim in backyard pools or live at peace in ranch-style homes. But what precautions can they take against an invisible virus, spread like the common cold, that causes the mind to wrinkle up like a leaky balloon?" Similarly, McLellan asserts, "one can't help feeling that in this vision of catastrophe Arthur Herzog has produced a kind of terror impossible to attain with killer bees, sharks, earthquakes or towering infernos."

MEDIA ADAPTATIONS: The Swarm was filmed in 1978.

BIOGRAPHICAL/CRITICAL SOURCES: Washington Post, June 20, 1978, December 22, 1978; *New York Times Book Review,* July 2, 1978.

* * *

HESS, Beth B(owman)

PERSONAL: Born in Buffalo, N.Y.; daughter of Albert A. (an advertising executive) and Yetta (a social worker; maiden name, Lurie) Bowman; married Richard C. Hess (a businessman), April 26, 1953; children: Laurence Albert, Emily Frances. *Education:* Radcliffe College, B.A. (magna cum laude), 1950; Rutgers University, M.A., 1966, Ph.D., 1970. *Politics:* Democrat. *Religion:* Jewish. *Home:* 17 Pepperidge Rd., Morristown, N.J. 07960. *Office:* Department of Social Sciences, County College of Morris, Dover, N.J. 07801.

CAREER: County College of Morris, Dover, N.J., assistant professor, 1969-73, associate professor, 1973-79, professor of social sciences, 1979—. Adjunct professor at Graduate Center, City University of New York, 1979; visiting professor at Gerontology Center, Boston University, 1980-81; lecturer at Douglass College, 1981. *Member:* American Sociological Association, Sociologists for Women in Society, National Council on Family Relations, Society for the Study of Social Problems (director, 1981-83), Gerontological Society (fellow), Eastern Sociological Society (executive secretary, 1978-81). *Awards, honors:* Peter I. Gellman Distinguished Service Award from Eastern Sociological Society, 1982.

WRITINGS: (With Matilda White Riley and Anne Foner) *Aging and Society,* Volume I, Russell Sage Foundation, 1968; (editor) *Growing Old in America,* Transaction Books, 1976, 2nd edition, 1980; (with Elizabeth W. Markson) *Aging and Old Age: An Introduction to Social Gerontology,* Macmillan, 1980; (editor with Kathleen Bond) *Leading Edges: Recent Research on Psychosocial Aging,* U.S. Government Printing Office, 1981; (with Markson and Peter J. Stein) *Sociology,* Macmillan, 1982; (with Myra Marx Ferree) *The New Feminism,* G. K. Hall, 1983.

Contributor: (With Riley, Toby, and Foner) D. Goslin, editor, *Handbook of Socialization Theory and Research,* Rand McNally, 1969; Riley, Foner, and Marilyn Johnson, editors, *Aging and Society,* Volume III, Russell Sage Foundation, 1971; (with Joan Waring) Richard Lerner and Graham Spanier, editors, *Child Influences on Marital and Family Interaction,* Academic Press, 1978; *Older Women in the City,* Arno, 1979; Markson and G. R. Batra, editors, *Public Policies for an Aging Population,* Lexington Books, 1980; M. Haug, editor, *Communications Technology and the Elderly: Issues and Forecasts,* Springer Publishing Co., 1982; (with Waring) Markson, editor, *The World of Older Women,* Lexington Books, 1982; R. Genovese, editor, *Families and Change: Social Needs and Public Policies,* J. F. Bergin, 1982; (with Paula Dressel) E. Macklin and R. Rubin, editors, *Contemporary Family and Alternative Life Styles: Handbook on Research and Theory,* Sage Books, 1982; (with Beth Soldo) W. J. Sauer and R. T. Coward, editors, *Social Support Networks and the Care of the Elderly,* Springer Publishing Co., 1983.

Contributor to *Proceedings of Association for Gerontology in Higher Education,* 1975, and to *New Encyclopedia,* 1983. Contributor of reviews and articles to scholarly journals, including *Contemporary Sociology, The Gerontologist,* and *Social Policy.* Associate editor of *Society, Research on Aging,* and *Contemporary Sociology.*

WORK IN PROGRESS: Women and the Family, with Marvin Sussman, for Haworth.

SIDELIGHTS: Beth B. Hess writes: "It seems that the theme which best describes my adulthood, as for so many older women today, is 'balance'; that is, managing the demands of scholarship, teaching, parenthood and marriage. This has been a richly rewarding mix; one which I hope will increasingly characterize the lives of both men and women.

"I have also sought to balance my commitment to sociology with an obligation to social activism. My biography in this respect is no doubt similar to that of most academics my age: active involvement at the community level in the major movements of the last two decades: civil liberties, civil rights, antiwar, and, most significantly, the feminist movement.

"Admittedly, this balancing act can strain one's abilities and energies; to achieve all one wishes in all these roles is perhaps impossible. So, while there is much that I regret not doing better, there is little to which I would not commit myself again."

* * *

HIBBARD, Howard 1928-

PERSONAL: Born May 23, 1928, in Madison, Wis.; son of Benjamin Horace (a professor) and Margaret (a home economist; maiden name, Baker) Hibbard; married Shirley Irene Griffith, September 14, 1951; children: Claire Alexandra, Susan Giulia, Carla Costanza. *Education:* University of Wisconsin, B.A., 1949, M.A., 1952; Columbia University, graduate study, 1952-53, postdoctoral study, 1967-70; Harvard University, Ph.D., 1958. *Politics:* Democrat. *Religion:* Atheist. *Home:* 176 Brewer Rd., Scarsdale, N.Y. 10583. *Office:* Department of Art History and Archeology, 815 Schermerhorn Hall, Columbia University, New York, N.Y. 10027.

CAREER: Columbia University, New York, N.Y., assistant professor, 1959-62, associate professor, 1962-66, professor of art history, 1966—. *Member:* College Art Association of America, Society of Architectural Historians (member of board of directors, 1963-65), American Academy in Rome (fellow), Renaissance Society of America, American Academy of Arts and Sciences (fellow), American Association of University Professors. *Awards, honors:* American Council of Learned Societies fellowship, 1962-63; Guggenheim fellowships, 1965-

66, 1972-73; National Foundation for the Humanities senior fellowships, 1967, 1979-80.

WRITINGS: The Architecture of the Palazzo Borghese, American Academy in Rome, 1962; *Bernini,* Penguin, 1965, 4th edition, 1974; (editor with Douglas Fraser and Milton J. Lewine) *Essays in the History of Art Presented to Rudolph Wittkower,* Phaidon, 1967; (editor with Fraser and Lewine) *Essays in the History of Architecture Presented to Rudolph Wittkower,* Phaidon, 1967; *Bernini e il barocco* (title means "Bernini and Baroque Sculpture"), Fratelli Fabbri, 1968; (with Joan Nissman) *Florentine Baroque Art from American Collections,* Metropolitan Museum of Art, 1969.

Carlo Maderno and Roman Architecture: 1580-1630, A. Zwemmer, 1971, Pennsylvania State University Press, 1972; *Poussin: The Holy Family on the Steps,* Viking, 1974; *Michelangelo,* Harper, 1974; *Masterpieces of Western Sculpture: From Medieval to Modern,* Thames & Hudson, 1977; *Michelangelo: Painter, Sculptor, Architect,* Vendome Press, 1978; *The Metropolitan Museum of Art,* Harper, 1980; *Caravaggio,* Harper, 1982.

Co-editor of "Studies in Architecture" series, A. Zwemmer, 1971-80; member of board of advisors, "Princeton Essays in the Arts" series, Princeton University Press, 1974-79. Contributor of articles and reviews to scholarly journals. *Art Bulletin* (of College Art Association of America), book review editor, 1961-65, associate editor, 1963-64, editor-in-chief, 1974—.

WORK IN PROGRESS: Research on Italian sculpture of the later sixteenth century.

SIDELIGHTS: Since 1955, Howard Hibbard has spent about half his time in Italy, especially in Rome, where he works in the libraries and archives.

Hibbard is described as "a scholar as sound as they come," by critic John Canaday in *New Republic,* who comments on *Michelangelo: Painter, Sculptor, Architect:* "Without romanticizing or other concessions to popularization, [Hibbard] writes as if the whole story [of Michelangelo] were new."

A reviewer for the *Times Literary Supplement* praises Hibbard's *Poussin: The Holy Family on the Steps,* saying that "altogether the book is a beautiful presentation of much that is essential in Poussin's art."

AVOCATIONAL INTERESTS: Chinese cooking.

BIOGRAPHICAL/CRITICAL SOURCES: Times Literary Supplement, May 24, 1974; *New York Times Book Review,* December 4, 1977; *New Republic,* December 9, 1978.

* * *

HIBBERT, Eleanor Burford 1906-
(Eleanor Burford; pseudonyms: Philippa Carr, Elbur Ford, Victoria Holt, Kathleen Kellow, Jean Plaidy, Ellalice Tate)

PERSONAL: Born 1906, in London, England; daughter of Joseph and Alice (Tate) Burford; married G. P. Hibbert. *Education:* Privately educated. *Agent:* A. M. Heath & Co., Ltd., 35 Dover St., London W. 1, England.

CAREER: Full-time writer.

WRITINGS—Under name Eleanor Burford: *House at Cupid's Cross,* Jenkins, 1949; *Passionate Witness,* Jenkins, 1949; *Believe the Heart,* Jenkins, 1950; *Love Child,* Jenkins, 1950; *Saint or Sinner?,* Jenkins, 1951; *Dear Delusion,* Jenkins, 1952; *Bright Tomorrow,* Jenkins, 1952; *Leave Me My Love,* Jenkins, 1953; *When We Are Married,* Jenkins, 1953; *Castles in Spain,* Jenkins, 1954; *Heart's Afire,* Jenkins, 1954; *When Other Hearts,* Jenkins, 1955; *Two Loves in Her Life,* Jenkins, 1955; *Begin to Live,* Mills & Boon, 1956; *Married in Haste,* Mills & Boon, 1956; *To Meet a Stranger,* Mills & Boon, 1957; *Pride of the Morning,* Mills & Boon, 1958; *Dawn Chorus,* Mills & Boon, 1959; *Red Sky at Night,* Mills & Boon, 1959; *Blaze of Noon,* Mills & Boon, 1960; *Night of the Stars,* Mills & Boon, 1960; *Now That April's Gone,* Mills & Boon, 1961; *Who's Calling?,* Mills & Boon, 1962.

Under pseudonym Philippa Carr; all published by Putnam: *The Miracle at St. Bruno's,* 1972; *The Lion Triumphant,* 1973; *The Witch from the Sea,* 1975; *Saraband for Two Sisters,* 1976; *Lament for a Lost Lover,* 1977; *The Love Child,* 1978; *Song of the Siren,* 1979; *Will You Love Me in September,* 1980; *The Adulteress,* 1981.

Under pseudonym Elbur Ford: *Poison in Pimlico,* Laurie, 1950; *Flesh and the Devil,* Laurie, 1950; *Bed Disturbed,* Laurie, 1952; *Such Bitter Business,* Heinemann, 1953, published as *Evil in the House,* Morrow, 1954.

Under pseudonym Victoria Holt; published by Doubleday, except as indicated: *Mistress of Mellyn,* 1960; *Kirkland Revels,* 1962; *Bride of Pendorric,* 1963, included in *Three Great Romantic Stories,* Collins, 1972; *The Legend of the Seventh Virgin,* 1965; *Menfreya in the Morning,* 1966 (published in England as *Menfreya,* Collins, 1966); *The King of the Castle,* 1967; *Queen's Confession: A Biography of Marie Antoinette,* 1968, published as *The Queen's Confession,* Fawcett, 1974; *The Shivering Sands,* 1969; *The Secret Woman,* 1970; *The Shadow of the Lynx,* 1971; *On the Night of the Seventh Moon,* 1972; *The Curse of the Kings,* 1973; *The House of a Thousand Lanterns,* 1974; *Lord of the Far Island,* 1975; *Pride of the Peacock,* 1976; *The Devil on Horseback,* 1977; *My Enemy the Queen,* 1978; *The Spring of the Tiger,* 1979; *The Mask of the Enchantress,* 1980; *The Judas Kiss,* 1981; *The Demon Lover,* 1982.

Under pseudonym Kathleen Kellow; all published by R. Hale: *Danse Macabre,* 1952; *Rooms at Mrs. Olivers',* 1953; *Lilith,* 1954; *It Began in Vauxhall Gardens,* 1955; *Call of the Blood,* 1956; *Rochester, the Mad Earl,* 1957; *Milady Charlotte,* 1959; *The World's a Stage,* 1960.

Under pseudonym Jean Plaidy; published by R. Hale, except as indicated: *Beyond the Blue Mountains,* Appleton, 1947, new edition, R. Hale, 1964; *Murder Most Royal,* 1949, Putnam, 1972, published as *Kings Pleasure,* Appleton, 1949.

The Goldsmith's Wife, Appleton, 1950; *Madame Serpent* (also see below), Appleton, 1951; *Italian Woman* (also see below), 1952; *Daughter of Satan,* 1952, Putnam, 1973; *Queen Jezebel* (also see below), Appleton, 1953; *The Spanish Bridegroom,* 1953, Macrae Smith, 1956; *St. Thomas's Eve,* 1954, Putnam, 1970; *The Sixth Wife,* 1954, Putnam, 1969; *Gay Lord Robert,* 1955, Putnam, 1972; *Royal Road to Fotheringay,* 1955, Fawcett, 1972, published as *Royal Road to Fotheringay: A Novel of Mary, Queen of Scots,* Putnam, 1968; *The Wandering Prince* (also see below), 1956, Putnam, 1971; *Health unto His Majesty* (also see below), 1956, published as *A Health unto His Majesty,* Putnam, 1972; *Flaunting, Extravagant Queen,* 1957; *Here Lies Our Sovereign Lord* (also see below), 1957, Putnam, 1973; *Madonna of the Seven Hills,* 1958, Putnam, 1974; *Triptych of Poisoners,* 1958; *Light on Lucrezia,* 1958; *Louis, the Well-*

Beloved, 1959; *Rise of the Spanish Inquisition* (also see below), 1959; *Road to Compiegne,* 1959.

Castile for Isabella (also see below), 1960; *Growth of the Spanish Inquisition* (also see below), 1960; *Spain for the Sovereigns* (also see below), 1960; *Daughters of Spain* (also see below), 1961; *The Young Elizabeth,* Roy, 1961; *Meg Roper: Daughter of Sir Thomas More,* Constable, 1961, Roy, 1964; *The End of the Spanish Inquisition* (also see below), 1961; *Katharine, the Virgin Widow* (also see below), 1961; *King's Secret Matter* (also see below), 1962; *The Young Mary, Queen of Scots,* Parrish, 1962, Roy, 1963; *The Shadow of the Pomegranate* (also see below), 1962; *The Captive Queen of Scots,* 1963, Putnam, 1970; *The Thistle and the Rose,* 1963, Putnam, 1973; *Mary, Queen of France,* 1964; *The Murder in the Tower,* 1964, Putnam, 1974; *Evergreen Gallant,* 1965, Putnam, 1973; *The Three Crowns,* 1965; *The Haunted Sisters,* 1966; *The Queen's Favourites,* 1966; *Lilith* (originally published under pseudonym Kathleen Kellow), 1967; *Queen in Waiting,* 1967; *The Princess of Celle,* 1967; *The Prince and the Quakeress,* 1968; *Caroline, the Queen,* 1968; *It Began in Vauxhall Gardens* (originally published under pseudonym Kathleen Kellow), 1968; *The Scarlet Cloak* (originally published under pseudonym Ellalice Tate), 1969; *The Third George,* 1969; *Perdita's Prince,* 1969.

Sweet Lass of Richmond Hill, 1970; *Indiscretions of the Queen,* 1970; *The Regent's Daughter,* 1971; *Goddess of the Green Room,* 1971; *The Captive of Kensington Palace,* 1972; *Victoria in the Wings,* 1972; *The Queen's Husband,* 1973; *The Queen and Lord M,* 1973; *The Widow of Windsor,* 1974; *The King's Mistress,* Pyramid Publications, 1974; *Uneasy Lies the Head,* 1982.

Trilogies; under pseudonym Jean Plaidy: *The Spanish Inquisition: Its Rise, Growth, and End* (includes *The Rise of the Spanish Inquisition, The Growth of the Spanish Inquisition,* and *The End of the Spanish Inquisition*), Citadel, 1967; *Katharine of Aragon* (includes *Katharine, the Virgin Widow, The Shadow of the Pomegranate,* and *The King's Secret Matter*), R. Hale, 1968; *Catherine de Medici* (includes *Madame Serpent, The Italian Woman,* and *Queen Jezebel*), R. Hale, 1969; *Isabella and Ferdinand* (includes *Castile for Isabella, Spain for the Sovereigns,* and *Daughters of Spain*), R. Hale, 1970; *Charles II* (includes *The Wandering Prince, Health unto His Majesty,* and *Here Lies Our Sovereign Lord*), R. Hale, 1972.

Under pseudonym Ellalice Tate; all published by Hodder & Stoughton: *Defenders of the Faith,* 1956; *Scarlet Cloak,* 1957; *Queen of Diamonds,* 1958; *Madame du Barry,* 1959; *This Was a Man,* 1961.

Contributor to newspapers and magazines, at times under a number of undisclosed pseudonyms.

SIDELIGHTS: Eleanor Burford Hibbert, who reportedly earns $300,000 a book, told the Woman's News Service: "I don't care about the critics. I write for the public. It's nicer to be read than to get nice reviews. I don't say my books are profound, they're pure entertainment."

"I think people want a good story and this I give them," she told *CA.* "They like something which is readable and you can't really beat the traditional for this. I write with great feeling and excitement and I think this comes over to the reader."

Doubleday has kept the Victoria Holt pseudonym a well-guarded secret since it first appeared. Many believed that Victoria Holt was in reality Daphne du Maurier. "I have heard her name mentioned in connection with mine," Hibbert told *CA,* "and I think it is because we have both lived in Cornwall and have written about this place. *Rebecca* is the atmospheric suspense type of book which mine are, but I don't think there is much similarity between her others and mine." In a Woman's News Service release she said: "My American publishers got the idea of making me into a mystery woman with the new name of Victoria Holt. People began to ask, 'Who is she?,' but they wouldn't say."

The critics have been generous to the Gothic tales bearing the Holt name. Genevieve Casey says of *Kirkland Revels* in the *Chicago Sunday Tribune*: "Murder, intrigue, threats of insanity, family skeletons rattling in closets and ghosts who walk in the moonlight keep the reader credulous and turning pages fast in this absorbing story." Reviewing *The Legend of the Seventh Virgin* for *Best Sellers,* Casey writes: "Among the clamour of novels by angry young men, among the probings and circumlocution of psychological novels, the works of Victoria Holt stand out, unpretentious, sunny, astringent, diverting."

In the *New York Times Book Review,* Anthony Boucher says of *Menfreya in the Morning:* "It's hard to say objectively, just why . . . [this] is so intensely readable and enjoyable. . . . It is Holt's weakest and slightest plot to date, and equally certainly nothing much happens in the way of either action or character development for long stretches. But somehow the magic . . . is still there."

"Dickens, Zola, Brontes (particularly), and nearly all the Victorians" have influenced her writings, Hibbert says. "I write regularly every day. I think this is important. As in everything else, practice helps to make perfect. Research is just a matter of reading old records, letters, etc., in fact everything connected with the period one is researching. I can only say that I love writing more than anything else. I find it stimulating and I never cease to be excited about it."

Hibbert has traveled widely. She has been around the world and plans to go to Australia and the Pacific Islands.

MEDIA ADAPTATIONS: Mistress of Mellyn, Hibbert's first novel under her pseudonym Victoria Holt, was adapted for the stage by Mildred C. Kuner, and *Daughter of Satan,* written under the pseudonym of Jean Plaidy, is being filmed.

BIOGRAPHICAL/CRITICAL SOURCES: Chicago Sunday Tribune, January 14, 1962; *Best Sellers,* February 1, 1965, July 1, 1971, August 15, 1974; *New York Times Book Review,* April 17, 1966; *Atlanta Journal-Constitution,* July 4, 1966; *Contemporary Literary Criticism,* Volume VII, Gale, 1977; *Washington Post Book World,* November 7, 1982.

* * *

HICKS, Clifford B. 1920-

PERSONAL: Born August 10, 1920, in Marshalltown, Iowa; son of Nathan LeRoy and Kathryn Marie (Carson) Hicks; married Rachel G. Reimer, May 12, 1945; children: David, Douglas, Gary. *Education:* Northwestern University, B.A. (cum laude), 1942.

CAREER: Popular Mechanics, Lombard, Ill., member of editorial staff, 1945-60, editor, 1960-63, special projects editor, 1963—. *Military service:* U.S. Marine Corps Reserve, 1942-45, became major; received Silver Star. *Member:* Sigma Delta Chi. *Awards, honors: First Boy on the Moon* was named Best

Juvenile Book of the Year by Friends of American Writers, 1960.

WRITINGS—Published by Holt, except as indicated: *Do-It-Yourself Materials Guide,* Popular Mechanics Press, 1955; *First Boy on the Moon,* Winston, 1959; *Marvelous Inventions of Alvin Fernald,* 1960; *Alvin's Secret Code,* 1963; *The World Above,* 1965; *Alvin Fernald, Foreign Trader,* 1966; *Alvin Fernald, Mayor for a Day,* 1970; *Peter Potts,* Dutton, 1971; *Alvin Fernald, Superweasel,* 1974; *Alvin's Swap Shop,* 1976; *Alvin Fernald, TV Anchorman,* 1980; *The Wacky World of Alvin Fernald,* 1981. Editor of *Popular Mechanics Do-It-Yourself Encyclopedia.* Contributor of fiction and nonfiction to magazines.

* * *

HIRSCHHORN, Clive 1940-

PERSONAL: Born February 20, 1940, in Johannesburg, South Africa; son of Colin Kalman (a hotelier) and Pearl (Rabinowitz) Hirschhorn. *Education:* University of the Witwatersrand, Johannesburg, B.A., 1960. *Politics:* Conservative. *Religion:* Jewish. *Home:* 42d South Audley St., Mayfair, London W.1, England. *Office: Sunday Express,* Fleet St., London E.C.4, England.

CAREER: Empire Films, Johannesburg, South Africa, publicist, 1960-62; American Broadcasting Companies (ABC-TV), Teddington, England, story editor, 1962-63; *Sunday Express,* London, England, feature writer and film and theater critic, 1964—.

WRITINGS: Gene Kelly, W. H. Allen, 1974, Regnery, 1975; *The Films of James Mason,* L.S.P. Books, 1975; *The Warner Bros. Story,* Crown, 1979; *The Hollywood Musical,* Crown, 1981. Also author of a play, "A State of Innocence," first produced at Library Theatre, Johannesburg, 1958.

SIDELIGHTS: Film and theater critic Clive Hirschhorn has parlayed his knowledge of the entertainment industry into books that document the history of motion pictures in America. *The Warner Bros. Story* is an encyclopedic work covering the films made by the Hollywood studio from 1918 through the 1970s. Hirschhorn's comments on the more than 1,800 movie stills that illustrate the book are described in *Choice* as "frequently witty and even critical; . . . they are reviews as much as they are narratives." Richard Christiansen of the *Chicago Tribune Book World* calls *The Warner Bros. Story* a "bounteous treasure trove of information and entertainment, . . . often a dazzling souvenir of the . . . crisp, contemporary style of Warner Bros. at its best."

The Hollywood Musical traces the history of the musical film from 1927, when "The Jazz Singer" (the first musical and the first motion picture to use sound) was produced, until 1980. Critic Peter S. Prescott comments on the scope of the book in *Newsweek:* "Hirschhorn . . . aims at a kind of completeness entirely in keeping with the grandiosity of his subject." In the *New York Times Book Review,* Seymour Peck says that Hirschhorn "sets himself the goal of absolute completeness" in describing more than 1,300 films "and seems to have achieved it."

AVOCATIONAL INTERESTS: Music.

BIOGRAPHICAL/CRITICAL SOURCES: Chicago Tribune Book World, March 30, 1980; *Choice,* May, 1980; *New York Times Book Review,* November 15, 1981; *Los Angeles Times Book Review,* December 20, 1981; *Newsweek,* December 21, 1981.

HOCKABY, Stephen
See MITCHELL, Gladys (Maude Winifred)

* * *

HODGART, Matthew (John Caldwell) 1916-

PERSONAL: Born September 1, 1916, in Paisley, Scotland; son of Matthew (an engineer) and Katherine (Gardner) Hodgart; married Margaret Patricia Elliott (a writer), August 3, 1949; children: Matthew Stephen, Suzanne Louise, Jane Katherine. *Education:* Pembroke College, Cambridge, B.A., 1938, M.A., 1945. *Office:* 13 Montpelier Villas, Brighton BNI 3DG, England.

CAREER: Cambridge University, Cambridge, England, assistant lecturer, 1945-49, university lecturer, 1949-64, fellow of Pembroke College, 1949-64; University of Sussex, Brighton, Sussex, professor of English, 1964-70; Concordia University, Montreal, Quebec, professor of English, 1970-77. Visiting professor at Cornell University, 1961-62 and 1969, University of California, Los Angeles, 1977-78, Stanford University, 1979, La Trobe University, 1979-80, and Johns Hopkins University, 1982. *Military service:* British Army, World War II, became major; awarded Croix de Guerre, French Legion d'Honneur (Chevalier), mentioned in dispatches. *Member:* Oxford and Cambridge Club, Pall Mall (London).

WRITINGS: The Ballads, Hutchinson, 1950, revised edition, 1962; (with Mabel Worthington) *Song in the Work of James Joyce,* Temple University Press, 1959; *Samuel Johnson,* Arco, 1962; (editor) Horace Walpole, *Memoirs and Portraits,* Batsford, 1963; (editor) *The Faber Book of Ballads,* Faber, 1965; *Satire,* Weidenfeld & Nicolson, 1969; *A New Voyage to the Country of the Houyhnhnms,* Putnam, 1969; *James Joyce: A Student's Guide,* Routledge & Kegan Paul, 1978. Editor of a selection of work by John Ruskin, 1972. Contributor to periodicals, including *Spectator, New Statesman, Cambridge Journal, Cambridge Review,* and *Guardian.*

SIDELIGHTS: Matthew Hodgart's *Satire,* a scholarly study of the genre, is "very well done," according to a *Times Literary Supplement* reviewer, who goes on to say that the book is "of considerable scope written in an agreeable style which easily accommodates information, attitude, and illustration." John Gross, critiquing the work in *Observer Review,* feels that Hodgart "makes an admirable guide" to the history of satire in literature and that "he has the knack of condensing without over-simplifying, and generalising without sinking into platitude. The result is a model of its kind, lucid, vigorously written and succinct."

Hodgart again explores satire in *A New Voyage to the Country of the Houyhnhnms,* a fictional work disguised in the subtitle as the "Fifth Part of the Travels into Several Remote Parts of the World by Lemuel Gulliver." This so-called "newly discovered manuscript," posing as a continuation of Jonathan Swift's *Gulliver's Travels,* is actually Hodgart's own satirical commentary on the student protest movement of the 1960s in the United States, which he observed as a visiting professor at Cornell University in 1969.

Speaking of Hodgart's skill in imitating Swift's style, John Hollander writes in *Harper's* that the author "has maintained throughout this book the elegance of almost perfect pastiche, even to the spelling and typography." A *Times Literary Sup-*

plement critic, however, asserts that Hodgart's "pastiche succeeds at the expense of his satire; there are times in the course of his brilliant and extended parody when the reader may well lose touch with the reality that is its raison d'etre." In *Library Journal,* Keith Cushman writes that Hodgart "wields the satirist's whip quite well," and finds "*A New Voyage* amusing and effective."

BIOGRAPHICAL/CRITICAL SOURCES: Observer Review, July 6, 1969; *Times Literary Supplement,* July 24, 1969, March 12, 1970; *Life,* April 10, 1970; *Library Journal,* May 15, 1970; *Harper's,* June, 1970; *Choice,* January, 1979.

* * *

HOFFMAN, William 1925-

PERSONAL: Born May 16, 1925, in Charleston, W.Va.; son of Henry William and Julia (Beckley) Hoffman; married Alice Sue Richardson, April 17, 1957; children: Ruth Beckley, Margaret Kay. *Education:* Hampden-Sydney College, B.A., 1949; graduate study at Washington and Lee University, 1949-50, University of Iowa, 1951. *Religion:* Presbyterian. *Address:* P.O. Box 382, Charlotte Courthouse, Va. 23923. *Agent:* Curtis Brown Ltd., 575 Madison Ave., New York, N.Y. 10022.

CAREER: Writer. Hampden-Sydney College, Hampden-Sydney, Va., assistant professor, 1952-59, writer in residence, 1966-70. Breeder of horses at Wynyard farm in Charlotte County, Va.; director of Elk Grocery Co., Elk Storage and Warehouse Co., and Kay Co. *Military service:* U.S. Army, 1943-46. *Member:* Authors Guild, Authors League of America. *Awards, honors:* D.L., Hampden-Sydney College, 1980.

WRITINGS—Novels, except as indicated; published by Doubleday, except as indicated: *The Trumpet Unblown,* 1955; *Days in the Yellow Leaf,* 1958; *A Place for My Head,* 1960; *The Dark Mountains,* 1963; *Yancey's War,* 1966.

A Walk to the River, 1970; *A Death of Dreams,* 1973; *Virginia Reels* (short stories), University of Illinois Press, 1979; *The Land That Drank the Rain,* Louisiana State University, 1982.

Also author of play "The Love Touch." Contributor of short stories to *Playboy, Cosmopolitan, Virginia Quarterly Review, Carleton Miscellany, Sewanee Review, McCall's, Gentlemen's Quarterly,* and *Scholastic.*

WORK IN PROGRESS: Another novel.

SIDELIGHTS: Although William Hoffman "might be classified as a Southern writer," says Sylvia Shorris in *Nation,* "most of his stories move beyond their settings. . . . [His] sophistication should win him a wider audience."

J. L. McManus, reviewing *Virginia Reels* in the *Chicago Tribune,* finds that, while the stories all take place in Virginia, they appeal to more than a purely regional readership. The book, says McManus, "is imaginative and powerful . . . [and] compellingly written, its stories worth knowing."

BIOGRAPHICAL/CRITICAL SOURCES: Chicago Tribune, January 7, 1979; *Nation,* February 10, 1979; *New York Times Book Review,* February 25, 1979.

* * *

HOFMAN, Anton
See HOLLO, Anselm

HOFSOMMER, Donovan Lowell 1938-

PERSONAL: Born April 10, 1938, in Fort Dodge, Iowa; son of Vernie G. and Helma J. (Schager) Hofsommer; married Sandra L. Rusch (a high school teacher), June 13, 1964; children: Kathryn Anne, Kristine Beret, Knute Lars. *Education:* University of Northern Iowa, B.A., 1960, M.A., 1966; Oklahoma State University, Ph.D., 1973. *Religion:* Presbyterian. *Home and office:* 1010 Zephyr, Plainview, Tex. 79072.

CAREER: High school history teacher in Fairfield, Iowa, 1961-65; Lea College, Albert Lea, Minn., instructor in history, 1966-70; Wayland College, Plainview, Tex., associate professor of history, 1973-81, head of department, 1973-81; special representative and historical writer for Southern Pacific Transportation Co., 1981—. *Military service:* Iowa National Guard, 1960-66.

MEMBER: Organization of American Historians, Western History Association, Railway and Locomotive Historical Association, National Railway Historical Association, Lexington Group, State Historical Society of Iowa, Texas Historical Society, Phi Alpha Theta, Phi Delta Kappa. *Awards, honors:* Award from American Association for State and Local History, 1976, for *Prairie Oasis;* Muriel H. Wright Heritage Endowment Award from Oklahoma Historical Society, 1979.

WRITINGS: Prairie Oasis: The Railroads, Steamboats, and Resorts of Iowa's Spirit Lake Country, Waukon & Mississippi Press, 1975; (editor) *Railroads of the Trans-Mississippi West: A Selected Bibliography of Books,* Llano Estacado Museum, 1976; *Katy Northwest: The Story of a Branch Line Railroad,* Pruett, 1976; (editor) *Railroads in Oklahoma,* Oklahoma Historical Society, 1977; (editor) *Railroads in the West,* Sunflower University Press, 1978. Contributor of more than thirty articles to history and transportation journals and to newspapers. Editor of *Lexington Newsletter;* member of editorial board of *Railroad History, Journals of the West,* and *Annals of Iowa.*

WORK IN PROGRESS: Quit Arguing and Push: A History of the Quanah, Acme & Pacific Railway, for Pruett; *A History of the Southern Pacific, 1901-1983,* for Southern Pacific Transportation Co.

* * *

HOLLAND, Cecelia (Anastasia) 1943-

PERSONAL: Born December 31, 1943, in Henderson, Nev.; daughter of William Dean (an executive) and Katharine (Schenck) Holland. *Education:* Pennsylvania State University, student, 1961-62; Connecticut College, B.A., 1965. *Politics:* Anarchist. *Religion:* Atheist. *Residence:* Fortuna, Calif.

CAREER: Writer. Visiting professor of English at Connecticut College, 1979—. *Awards, honors:* Guggenheim fellowship, 1981-82.

WRITINGS—Adult novels; published by Knopf, except as indicated: *The Firedrake,* Atheneum, 1966; *RaKossy,* Atheneum, 1967; *The Kings in Winter,* Atheneum, 1968; *Until the Sun Falls,* Atheneum, 1969; *Antichrist,* Atheneum, 1970; *The Earl,* 1971; *The Death of Attila,* 1973; *Great Maria,* 1974; *Floating Worlds,* 1976; *Two Ravens,* 1978; *City of God,* 1979; *Home Ground,* 1981; *The Sea Beggars,* 1982.

Juveniles: *Ghost on the Steppe,* Atheneum, 1970; *The King's Road,* Atheneum, 1971.

WORK IN PROGRESS: Research into the Carolingian Byzantine world of 800 A.D.

SIDELIGHTS: In her novel *City of God,* Cecelia Holland "proves that there can be more to historical thrillers than swordplay and seduction," according to a *Time* critic. *City of God* is set in the Rome of the Borgias, between 1500 and 1503, and is told from the point of view of Nicholas, a secretary to the Florentine ambassador to Rome. Holland "convincingly pictures Renaissance Rome, the sumptuousness of the costumes and furnishings, the squalor and menace of the streets,'' notes Audrey Foote in the *Washington Post Book World.* Furthermore, she ''adroitly leads the reader through the tangle of dynastic ambitions and shifting alliances. Best of all, she creates a fascinating focal character in Nicholas.''

BIOGRAPHICAL/CRITICAL SOURCES: Atlantic, June, 1977; *Spectator,* October 22, 1977; *Chicago Tribune Book World,* February 25, 1979; *Washington Post Book World,* March 12, 1979; *Time,* April 9, 1979; *New York Review of Books,* September 27, 1979.

* * *

HOLLO, Anselm 1934-
(Sergei Bielyi, Anton Hofman)

PERSONAL: Born April 12, 1934, in Helsinki, Finland; son of Juho A. (a translator and university professor) and Iris (Walden) Hollo; married Josephine Wirkus (a poet and translator), December 23, 1957; children: Hannes, Kaarina, Tamsin. *Education:* Attended Helsinki University and Tuebingen University, 1952-56. *Address:* 2624-A 21st St., San Francisco, Calif. 94110.

CAREER: Worked as a journalist doing book and film reviews and interviews for the Finnish press in Germany, Sweden, and Austria, 1950-58; British Broadcasting Corp., London, England, radio producer, 1958-66; State University of New York at Buffalo, visiting professor of English, 1967; University of Iowa, Iowa City, visiting professor in Poetry Workshop, 1968-73; Hobart and William Smith Colleges, Geneva, N.Y., professor of English, 1973-75; University of Maryland Baltimore County, Baltimore, professor of English, 1975-77; Southwest State University, Marshall, Minn., visiting writer, 1977-78; Sweet Briar College, Sweet Briar, Va., Margaret Banister Distinguished Writer in Residence, 1978-81; New College of California, San Francisco, lecturer in poetics and associate in residence, 1981—. Instructor at Naropa Institute, Boulder, Colo., winter, 1981, spring, 1984.

WRITINGS—Poetry: *Sateiden Valilla* (title means ''Rainpause''), Otava (Helsinki), 1956; *Loverman,* the dead language press (New York), 1961; *St. Texts and Finnpoems,* Migrant Press (Birmingham, England), 1961; (with David Ball) *We Just Wanted to Tell You,* Writers Forum (England), 1963; *And What Else Is New,* New Voice (Kent, England), 1963; *History,* Matrix Press (England), 1963; (with eight German poets) *Zwischenraume,* Limes Verlag (Wiesbaden), 1963; *Trobar: Loytaa,* Otava, 1964; *And It Is a Song,* Migrant Press, 1965; *Faces and Forms,* Ambit Books (London), 1965; *Here We Go,* Stranger's Press, 1965.

The Claim, Goliard Press (London), 1966; *The Going-On Poem,* Writers Forum, 1966; *Isadora and Other Poems,* Writers Forum, 1967; *Poems/Runoja* (bilingual edition), Otava, 1967; *The Man in the Treetop Hat,* Turret Books (London), 1968; *The Coherences,* Trigram Press, 1968; *Maya: Works, 1959-69,* Grossman, 1971; *Sensation 27,* Institute of Further Studies (New York), 1973; *Black Book No. 1,* Bowling Green State University Writing Program, 1975.

Heavy Jars, Toothpaste Press, 1976; *Sojourner Microcosms,* Blue Wind Press, 1977; *With Ruth in Mind,* Station Hill, 1979; *Finite Continued,* Blue Wind Press, 1980; *No Complaints,* Toothpaste Press, 1982.

Editor and translator: Allen Ginsberg, *Kaddisch* (poems), Limes Verlag, 1962; Yevgeni Yevtushenko, Andrei Voznesensky, and Semyon Kirsanov, *Red Cats* (poems), City Lights, 1962; *Some Poems by Paul Klee,* Scorpion Press, 1963; Gregory Corso, *In der Fluechtigen Hand der Zeit* (poems), Limes Verlag, 1963; Ginsberg, *Huuto ja Muita Runoja* (poems), Tajo, 1963; (co-translator) Ginsberg, *Kuolema van Goghin Korvalle* (poems), Tajo, 1963; *Idan ja Lannen Runot* (anthology of modern American poetry), Weilin & Goos, 1963; Voznesensky, *Selected Poems,* Grove, 1964; (with Matti Rossi) *Nain Ihminen Vastaa* (anthology of modern Latin American poetry), Tajo, 1964.

Rolf-Gunter Dienst, *Five Feet Two* (poems), Tarasque Press, 1965; *Word from the North: New Poetry from Finland,* Screeches Press, 1965; (with Gunnar Harding) *New Poetry from Sweden,* University of Minnesota Press, 1979.

Translator: Vladimir Maximov, *A Man Survives* (novel), Grove, 1963; *John Lennon Panee Omiaan* (translation of *John Lennon in His Own Write*), Otava, 1964; Veijo Meri, *Das Manilaseil* (novel), Carl Hanser Verlag, 1964; Lars Gorling, *491* (novel), Grove, 1966; Matti Rossi, *The Trees of Vietnam* (poems), El Corno Emplumado, 1966; Lars Ullerstam, *The Erotic Minorities* (essays), Grove, 1966; Bertolt Brecht, *Jungle of Cities* (plays), Grove, 1966; John Lennon, *Hispanjalainen Jakovainaa* (prose), Otava, 1966; Pentti Saarikoski, *Helsinki* (poems), Rapp & Carroll, 1967; Paavo Haavikko, *Selected Poems,* Cape Goliard, 1968.

Jean Genet, *Querelle* (novel), Grove, 1975; Emmanuelle Arsan, *Emmanuelle II* (novel), Grove, 1975; Franz Innerhofer, *Beautiful Days* (novel), Urizen Books, 1976; Francois Truffaut, *Small Change* (novel), Grove, 1977; Tillmann Moser, *Apprenticeship on the Couch,* Urizen Books, 1977; Wolfgang Schiwelbusch, *The Railroad Journey,* Urizen Books, 1981; Pentti Saarikoski, *Poems 1958-1980,* Toothpaste Press, 1983.

Others: (With Gregory Corso and Tom Raworth) *The Minicab War* (satire), Matrix Press, 1961; (editor) *Jazz Poems* (anthology of modern English poetry), Vista Books, 1963; (editor) *Negro Verse* (anthology), Vista Books, 1964. Also author of numerous radio scripts for British Broadcasting Corp. and for Finnish and German broadcasts (some under pseudonym Anton Hofman).

SIDELIGHTS: Anselm Hollo writes: ''Milton's *Paradise Lost,* first edition, sold forty copies. I have been doing rather better than that, these past fifteen years. Yet I think I know, by face and voice, seventy per cent of my readers: love them well and wish them luck. Not a guru, not a politician, I welcome anyone reading this entry to the world—increasingly occult—where the above-mentioned books can be found and, hopefully, enjoyed, encountered. It is as friendly and undoubtedly real as those proposed (and shared, by me and you) by Pharoah Sanders and Ed Sanders.''

* * *

HOLMES, Rick
See HARDWICK, Richard Holmes, Jr.

HOLT, Victoria
See HIBBERT, Eleanor Burford

* * *

HONE, Ralph E(merson) 1913-

PERSONAL: Born July 27, 1913, in Toledo, Ohio; son of Henry Ralph and Ethel (Skeldon) Hone; married Harriet Crawford, December 27, 1944; children: Beth (Mrs. Robert Melonuk), Hannah (Mrs. James Leckman), Martha, Philip. *Education:* Ohio State University, B.A., 1943, M.A., 1945; New York University, Ph.D., 1955. *Home:* 229 Anita Ct., Redlands, Calif. 92373.

CAREER: Associate professor of English at Gordon College, Boston, Mass., 1949-54, and Wheaton College, Wheaton, Ill., 1954-56; University of Redlands, Redlands, Calif., associate professor, 1956-59, professor of English and Latin, 1959-78, director of Division of Language and Literature, 1960-78, director of Redlands in Europe, Salzburg, Austria, 1961-62, dean of humanities, 1972-78. Visiting professor, University of California, Los Angeles, summer, 1959; Fulbright professor at University of Helsinki, 1965-66; International Professor, Waseda University, Tokyo, 1979-80. *Member:* Modern Language Association of America, Renaissance Society of America, Milton Society of America, California Writers Guild, Omicron Delta Kappa, Redlands Fortnightly Club, Pi Delta Phi, Phi Beta Kappa (honorary member). *Awards, honors:* Mortar Board Distinguished Teacher Award, 1964; Edgar Allan Poe Award (''Edgar'') for Best Critical Biographical Study, Mystery Writers of America, 1979, for *Dorothy L. Sayers: A Literary Biography*.

WRITINGS: The Voice out of the Whirlwind: The Book of Job, Chandler Publishing, 1960, revised edition, 1972; (editor) John Milton, *Samson Agonistes: The Poem and Materials for Analysis,* Chandler Publishing, 1965; *Dorothy L. Sayers: A Literary Biography,* Kent State University Press, 1979; (with G. H. Armacost and E. Mertins) *The Seventy-Fifth Anniversary of the University of Redlands,* privately printed, 1982. Staff reviewer, *Los Angeles Times*. Contributor to *Huntington Library Quarterly, Studies in Philology,* and *Notes and Queries* (London).

SIDELIGHTS: Ralph E. Hone's *Dorothy L. Sayers: A Literary Biography,* which received an Edgar Award in 1979, is, according to Robin Winks in *New Republic,* an ''affectionate, careful, and entertaining'' study. Dorothy Leigh Sayers (1893-1957) is regarded as one of the greatest mystery writers of the twentieth century for her detective novels of the twenties and thirties. Among the first women to receive a degree from Oxford University, Sayers spent the last twenty years of her life as a medieval scholar and theologian, translating the works of Dante and writing plays and essays as an apologist for Christianity.

Barbara Grizzuti Harrison in the *New York Times Book Review* writes that, in presenting Sayers' life story, Hone includes descriptions ''in great detail [of] her wartime work, her volatile association with the BBC, her lecture schedule, . . . previously unpublished letters to her friends and her antagonists, fragments of her *Sunday Times* columns, reviews of her work, . . . her early poetry and an occasional vivid anecdote from a friend.''

Although Harrison claims that Hone's writing is ''plodding and pedagogic'' at times, Winks believes that ''we do learn quite a bit'' from the book, on account of the ''great accuracy and perceptiveness'' of Hone's scholarship. And M. L. Mastro, writing in *Library Journal,* feels that Hone ''offers a living picture of a complex woman'' with both ''integrity and good craftsmanship.''

BIOGRAPHICAL/CRITICAL SOURCES: New York Times Book Review, July 15, 1979; *Time,* August 13, 1979; *Library Journal,* September 1, 1979; *Los Angeles Times Book Review,* September 16, 1979; *Choice,* November, 1979; *New Republic,* February 16, 1980.

* * *

HONEYMAN, Brenda
See CLARKE, Brenda (Margaret Lilian)

* * *

HONG, Edna H. 1913-

PERSONAL: Born January 28, 1913, in Thorpe, Wis.; daughter of Otto (a farmer) and Ida (Nordby) Hatlestad; married Howard V. Hong (a professor of philosophy at St. Olaf College), June 8, 1938; children: Irena (Mrs. Roy Elveton), Erik, Peder, Rolf, Mary (Mrs. Tom Loe), Judith, Theodore, Nathaniel. *Education:* St. Olaf College, B.A., 1938. *Politics:* Independent. *Religion:* Lutheran. *Home address:* P.O. Box 64, Route 5, Northfield, Minn. 55057.

CAREER: Homemaker and writer. *Awards, honors:* Co-recipient, with husband, Howard V. Hong, of National Book Award, 1968, for *Kierkegaard's Journals and Papers,* Volume I; D.H.L., St. Olaf College, 1977.

WRITINGS—Published by Augsburg, except as indicated: (Translator with husband, Howard V. Hong) Soeren Aabye Kierkegaard, *For Self Examination,* 1940; (with H. V. Hong) *Muskego Boy,* 1943; *The Boy Who Fought with Kings,* 1946; *Paving Block Stories,* Northfield News, 1955; (with Mary Hinderlie) *Festival of Christmas,* 1957; *Clues to the Kingdom,* 1968; *Turn over Any Stone,* 1970; *The Gayety of Grace,* 1970; *From This Good Ground,* 1974; *Bright Valley of Love,* 1976; (contributor with H. V. Hong and daughter, Mary Hong Loe) Chester G. Anderson, editor, *Growing Up in Minnesota,* University of Minnesota Press, 1976; *The Downward Ascent,* 1979; *A Nostalgic Almanac,* 1980; *The Way of the Sacred Tree,* 1983.

Editor and translator with H. V. Hong: Kierkegaard, *Works of Love,* Harper, 1962; *Kierkegaard's Journals and Papers,* Indiana University Press, Volume I, 1967, Volume II, 1970, Volumes III-VII, 1975-76; Kierkegaard, *Armed Neutrality* [and] *An Open Letter,* Indiana University Press, 1968; G. Malantichuk, *Kierkegaard's Thought,* Princeton University Press, 1971; *Kierkegaard's Writings,* Princeton University Press, Volume XIV: *Two Ages: The Age of Revolution and the Present Age,* 1978, Volume VII: *The Concept of Anxiety,* 1980, Volume XIX: *The Sickness unto Death: A Christian Psychological Exposition for Upbuilding and Awakening,* 1980, Volume XIII: *The Corsair Affair and Articles Related to the Writings,* 1981.

* * *

HONG, Howard V(incent) 1912-

PERSONAL: Born October 19, in 1912, in Wolford, N.D.; son of Peter B. (a businessman) and Ada J. (Cooper) Hong; married Edna Hatlestad (a writer), June 8, 1938; children: Irena (Mrs. Roy Elveton), Erik, Peder, Rolf, Mary (Mrs. Tom Loe),

Judith, Theodore, Nathaniel. *Education:* St. Olaf College, B.A., 1934; State College of Washington (now Washington State University), graduate study, 1934-35; University of Minnesota, Ph.D., 1938; University of Copenhagen, postdoctoral study, 1938-39. *Politics:* Independent. *Religion:* Lutheran. *Home address:* P.O. Box 64, Route 5, Northfield, Minn. 55057. *Office:* Department of Philosophy, St. Olaf College, Northfield, Minn. 55057.

CAREER: St. Olaf College, Northfield, Minn., instructor, 1938-40, assistant professor of philosophy and English, 1940-46, associate professor of philosophy and psychology, 1946-49, professor of philosophy and chairman of department, 1949—, director of Kierkegaard Library, 1972—. Visiting lecturer at University of Minnesota, 1954, and Pacific Lutheran Theological Seminary, 1956. World Young Men's Christian Association, Geneva, Switzerland, field secretary for war prisoners' aid in Germany, Scandinavia, and United States, 1943-46; senior field officer in Germany, Refugee Division, World Council of Churches, 1947-48. Senior representative in Europe, Lutheran World Federation Service to Refugees, 1947-49; director of Christian Service Institute, 1957-60. *Member:* American Philosophical Association, Phi Beta Kappa.

AWARDS, HONORS: American-Scandinavian Foundation fellowship, 1938-39; American Council of Learned Societies fellowship, 1951-52; J.A.O. Preus Award, 1953; Rockefeller Foundation grant, 1958-59; Fulbright grant to Denmark, 1959-60, 1968; co-recipient, with wife, Edna H. Hong, of National Book Award, 1968, for translation of *Kierkegaard's Journals and Papers,* Volume I; National Endowment for the Humanities, senior scholar, 1970-71, research scholar, 1972-73.

WRITINGS—Published by Augsburg, except as indicated: (Translator with wife, Edna H. Hong) Soeren Aabye Kierkegaard, *For Self Examination* 1940; (with E. H. Hong) *Muskego Boy,* 1943; *This World and the Church,* 1955; (editor and contributor) *Integration and the Christian Liberal Arts College,* St. Olaf College Press, 1956; (contributor) *Christian Social Responsibility,* Muhlenberg, 1957; (editor and contributor) *Christian Faith and the Liberal Arts,* 1960; (translator and reviser) Kierkegaard, *Philosophical Fragments,* Princeton University Press, 1962; (contributor with E. H. Hong and daughter, Mary Hong Loe) Chester G. Anderson, editor, *Growing Up in Minnesota,* University of Minnesota Press, 1976.

Editor and translator with E. H. Hong: Kierkegaard, *Works of Love,* Harper, 1962; *Kierkegaard's Journals and Papers,* Indiana University Press, Volume I, 1967, Volume II, 1970, Volumes III-VII, 1975-76; Kierkegaard, *Armed Neutrality* [and] *an Open Letter,* Indiana University Press, 1968; G. Malantschuk, *Kierkegaard's Thought,* Princeton University Press, 1971; *Kierkegaard's Writings,* Princeton University Press, Volume XIV: *Two Ages: The Age of Revolution and the Present Age,* 1978, Volume VII: *The Concept of Anxiety,* 1980, Volume XIX: *The Sickness unto Death: A Christian Psychological Exposition for Upbuilding and Awakening,* 1980, Volume XIII: *The Corsair Affair and Articles Related to the Writings,* 1981.

General editor of "Kierkegaard's Writings" series, Princeton University Press, 1975—.

* * *

HONIG, Donald 1931-

PERSONAL: Born August 17, 1931, in Maspeth, Long Island, N.Y.; son of George and Mildred (Elson) Honig; divorced; children: Catherine Rose. *Residence:* Cromwell, Conn. *Agent:* Theron Raines, 475 Fifth Ave., New York, N.Y. 10017.

CAREER: Professional writer. *Member:* Dramatists Guild, Authors League of America. *Awards, honors:* New York State Council of the Arts grant, 1972; Connecticut Commission on the Arts grant, 1974, 1981.

WRITINGS: Sidewalk Caesar (novel), Pyramid Books, 1958; *Walk Like a Man* (novel), Morrow, 1961; *Divide the Night* (novel), Regency Books, 1961; (editor) *Blue and Gray: Great Writings of the Civil War,* Avon, 1961; *No Song to Sing* (novel), Morrow, 1962; (editor) *Short Stories of Stephen Crane,* Avon, 1962, McGraw, 1967; *The Adventures of Jed McLane,* McGraw, 1967; *Jed McLane and the Stranger,* McGraw, 1969.

In the Days of the Cowboy, Random House, 1970; *Up from the Minor Leagues,* Cowles, 1970; *Dynamite,* Putnam, 1971; *Johnny Lee,* McCall Publishing, 1971; *Judgment Night,* Belmont Books, 1971; *The Journal of One Davey Wyatt,* F. Watts, 1972; *The Love Thief,* Belmont Books, 1972; *An End of Innocence,* Putnam, 1972; *Way to Go Teddy,* F. Watts, 1973; *The Severith Style,* Scribner, 1972; *Illusions,* Doubleday, 1974; *Playing for Keeps,* F. Watts, 1974; *Breaking In,* F. Watts, 1974; *The Professional,* F. Watts, 1974; *Coming Back,* F. Watts, 1974; *Fury On Skates,* Four Winds Press, 1974.

With the Consent of the Governed: Conversations with Eight U.S. Senators, Dell, 1975; *Baseball: When the Grass Was Real,* Coward, 1975; *Running Harder,* F. Watts, 1976; *Going the Distance,* F. Watts, 1976; *Baseball between the Lines,* Coward, 1976; *The Man in the Dugout,* Follett, 1977; *I Should Have Sold Petunias,* Jove, 1977; *The Last Great Season,* Simon & Schuster, 1979; *The October Heroes,* Simon & Schuster, 1979; *The Image of Their Greatness,* Crown, 1979.

Marching Home, St. Martin's, 1980; *The 100 Greatest Baseball Players of All Time,* Crown, 1981; *The Brooklyn Dodgers: An Illustrated Tribute,* St. Martin's, 1981; *The New York Yankees: An Illustrated History,* Crown, 1981; *Baseball's 10 Greatest Teams,* Macmillan, 1982; *The Los Angeles Dodgers: An Illustrated Tribute,* St. Martin's, 1983; *The National League: An Illustrated History,* Crown, 1983; *The American League: An Illustrated History,* Crown, 1983.

Author with Leon Arden of play, "The Midnight Ride of Alvin Blumm," first produced in 1966. Contributor of 200 stories and articles to various trade publications.

* * *

HONIGMANN, E(rnst) A(nselm) J(oachim) 1927-

PERSONAL: Born November 29, 1927, in Breslau, Germany; son of H. D. (a physician) and U. M. (Heilborn) Honigmann; married Elsie M. Packman, July 1, 1958; children: Elaine, Paul, Richard. *Education:* University of Glasgow, M.A., 1948; Oxford University, B.Litt., 1950. *Religion:* Protestant. *Office:* University of Newcastle upon Tyne, Newcastle upon Tyne NE1 7RU, England.

CAREER: Shakespeare Institute, Stratford-upon-Avon, England, fellow, 1951-54; University of Glasgow, Glasgow, Scotland, lecturer, 1954-66, senior lecturer in English, 1966-67; University of Newcastle upon Tyne, Newcastle upon Tyne, England, reader, 1968-70, Joseph Cowen Professor of English Literature, 1970—. Visiting professor at University of Washington, summer, 1967. *Awards, honors:* D.Litt., University of Glasgow, 1966.

WRITINGS: (Editor) *King John,* Harvard University Press, 1954; *The Stability of Shakespeare's Text,* University of Nebraska Press, 1965; (editor) *Milton's Sonnets,* St. Martin's, 1966; (editor) William Shakespeare, *Richard III,* Penguin, 1968; (editor) Shakespeare, *Twelfth Night,* Macmillan, 1971; *Shakespeare: Seven Tragedies,* Macmillan, 1976; (co-editor) *The Revels Plays,* Manchester University Press, 1976—; *Shakespeare's Impact on His Contemporaries,* Macmillan, 1982. Coeditor of *Anglistica,* 1981—.

* * *

HOOD, (Martin) Sinclair (Frankland) 1917-

PERSONAL: Born January 31, 1917, in Queenstown, Ireland; son of Martin (a lieutenant commander, Royal Navy) and Frances (Winants) Hood; married Rachel Simmons, March 5, 1957; children: Martin, Mary, Dictynna. *Education:* Magdalen College, Oxford, M.A., 1939; University of London, Diploma in Prehistoric Archaeology, 1947; attended British School of Archaeology, Athens, 1947-48, 1951-53, and British Institute of Archaeology, Ankara, 1948-49. *Politics:* Liberal-Conservative. *Religion:* Church of England. *Home:* Old Vicarage, Great Milton, Oxford, England.

CAREER: British School of Archaeology, Athens, Greece, assistant director, 1949-51, director, 1954-62. Archaeological work has been mainly centered in Greece and Turkey; took part in excavations in England at Dorchester, Oxford, 1937, Compton, 1946-47, and Southwark, 1946, in Turkey, at Smyrna, 1948-49, Atchana, 1949-50, Sakca-Gozu, 1950, in Greece at Mycenae, 1950-52, in Palestine, at Jericho, 1952; in charge of excavations at Emporio in Chios, 1952-55, and Knossos in Crete, 1950-61. *Wartime service:* Conscientious objector, serving with British Civil Defence, 1939-46. *Member:* Society of Antiquaries, Athenaeum Club (London).

WRITINGS: (With D. Smollett and P. de Jong) *Archaeological Survey of the Knossos Area,* Oxford University Press, 1958; *The Home of the Heroes: The Aegean before the Greeks,* McGraw, 1967; (editor with Mark Cameron) Sir Arthur Evans, *Knossos Fresco Atlas,* Gregg, 1968; *The Minoans: Crete in the Bronze Age,* Thames & Hudson, 1971; *The Arts in Prehistoric Greece,* Pelican, 1978; (with D. Smyth) *Archaeological Survey of the Knossos Area,* 2nd edition, Thames & Hudson, 1981; (with W. Taylor) *The Bronze Age Palace at Knossos,* Thames & Hudson, 1981; *Excavations in Chios 1938-1955: Prehistoric Emporio and Ayio Gala,* two volumes, Thames & Hudson, 1981-82.

Contributor to *Annual of the British School at Athens;* contributor to scholarly journals, including *Anatolian Studies, Antiquity, Kadmos,* and *Journal of Hellenic Studies.*

WORK IN PROGRESS: Reports on archaeological excavations at Knossos.

SIDELIGHTS: Sinclair Hood writes to *CA:* "Began to take a serious interest in history and archaeology after reading Gibbon's *Decline and Fall of the Roman Empire* and Baikie's *Sea Kings of Crete* when about sixteen. Much interested in problems of dating prehistoric periods, and skeptical of the value of results so far obtained by scientific methods of dating." Hood speaks modern Greek, French, and German; he can read some Italian and Spanish.

HOPF, Alice L(ightner) 1904- (A. M. Lightner)

PERSONAL: Born October 11, 1904, in Detroit, Mich.; daughter of Clarence Ashley (a lawyer) and Frances (McGraw) Lightner; married Ernest J. Hopf (an artist), April 29, 1935; children: Christopher. *Education:* Vassar College, B.A., 1927. *Home:* Box 174, Birch Rd., Upper Black Eddy, Pa. 18972. *Agent:* Larry Sternig, 742 Robertson St., Milwaukee, Wis. 53213.

CAREER: Grey Advertising, Inc., New York, N.Y., editorial secretary, retired 1973. Free-lance writer. *Member:* Xerxes Society. *Awards, honors:* Best science book awards from National Association of Science Teachers, 1972, for *Biography of a Rhino,* 1973, for *Misunderstood Animals,* 1975, for *Wild Cousins of the Cat,* 1976, for *Biography of an Armadillo* and *Biography of an American Reindeer,* and 1980, for *Biography of a Snowy Owl.*

WRITINGS—Nonfiction about nature: *Monarch Butterflies,* Crowell, 1965; *Wild Traveler: The Story of a Coyote,* Norton, 1967; *Earth's Bug-Eyed Monsters,* Norton, 1968; *Butterfly and Moth,* Putnam, 1969; *Carab, the Trap-Door Spider,* Putnam, 1970; *Wild Cousins of the Dog,* Putnam, 1973; *Misunderstood Animals,* McGraw, 1973; *Wild Cousins of the Cat,* Putnam, 1975; *Misplaced Animals,* McGraw, 1975; *Wild Cousins of the Horse,* Putnam, 1977; *Life Spans of Animals and Plants,* Holiday House, 1978; *Nature's Pretenders* (Junior Literary Guild selection), Putnam, 1979; *Animals That Eat Nectar and Honey,* Holiday House, 1979; *Pigs Wild and Tame,* Holiday House, 1979; *Whose House Is It?,* Dodd, 1980; *Bugs Big and Little,* Messner, 1980; *Strange Sex Lives in the Animal Kingdom,* McGraw, 1981; *Chickens and Their Wild Relatives,* Dodd, 1982.

"Biography" series; published by Putnam: *Biography of an Octopus,* 1971; . . . *of a Rhino,* 1972; . . . *of an Ant,* 1974; . . . *of an Ostrich,* 1974, new edition, 1975; . . . *of an Armadillo,* 1975; . . . *of an American Reindeer,* 1976; . . . *of a Giraffe,* 1978; . . . *of a Snowy Owl,* 1979; . . . *of a Komodo Dragon,* 1981.

Under name A. M. Lightner: *The Pillar and the Flame* (poem), H. Vinal, 1928; *The Rock of Three Planets,* Putnam, 1963; *The Planet Poachers,* Putnam, 1965; *Doctor to the Galaxy,* Norton, 1965; *The Galactic Troubadours,* Norton, 1965; *The Space Plague,* Norton, 1966; *The Space Olympics,* Norton, 1967; *The Space Ark,* Putnam, 1968; *The Walking Zoo of Darwin Dingle,* Putnam, 1969; *The Day of the Drones,* Norton, 1969; *The Thursday Toads,* McGraw, 1971; *Star Dog,* McGraw, 1973; *Gods or Demons,* Four Winds, 1973; *The Space Gypsies,* McGraw, 1974; *Star Circus,* Dutton, 1977.

Contributor of articles and short stories to periodicals, including *Argosy, New York Daily News,* and *IF.*

WORK IN PROGRESS: A book about the hyena.

* * *

HOPPER, Robert 1945-

PERSONAL: Born November 2, 1945, in Schenectady, N.Y.; son of Jack Hicks (an engineer) and Olga (a teacher and psychologist; maiden name, Butler) Hopper; married Kathryn Quammen, June 10, 1967; children: Brian, Christine. *Education:* Bowling Green State University, B.A., 1966, M.A.,

1967; University of Wisconsin—Madison, Ph.D., 1970. *Home:* 2601 Bend Cove, Austin, Tex. 78704. *Office:* Department of Speech Communication, University of Texas at Austin, Austin, Tex. 78712.

CAREER: University of Texas at Austin, assistant professor, 1970-75, associate professor, 1975-80, professor of speech, 1980—, senior staff research associate at Center for Communication Research, 1973—. Visiting scholar at Oxford University, 1983. *Member:* International Communication Association, Speech Communication Association.

WRITINGS: (With Rita C. Naremore) *Children's Speech: A Practical Introduction to Communication Development,* Harper, 1973; *Human Message Systems,* Harper, 1976; (with Frederick Williams and Diana Natalicio) *The Sounds of Children,* Prentice-Hall, 1977; (with Jack Whitehead) *Human Communication Concepts and Skills,* Harper, 1979; (with D. F. Gundersen) *Communication in Law Enforcement,* Harper, in press; *Talk at Work,* Scott, Foresman, in press. Contributor to speech and communication journals.

SIDELIGHTS: Robert Hopper writes: "I write because it acts as a tonic for depression. I find writing about myself quite spooky, though in reality I write about nothing else—I usually veil it some." *Avocational interests:* Gardening, songwriting, hiking.

* * *

HORAN, James David 1914-1981

PERSONAL: Born July 27, 1914, in New York, N.Y.; died after open-heart surgery, October 13, 1981, in New York, N.Y.; son of Eugene (a newspaperman) and Elizabeth (Schaub) Horan; married Gertrude Dorrity, September 4, 1938; children: Patricia, Brian Boru, Gary, James C. *Education:* Attended Drake College, New Jersey, two years. *Politics:* Independent. *Religion:* Catholic.

CAREER: Novelist and historian. *New York Journal-American,* New York, N.Y., 1930-66, assistant city editor, 1936, war correspondent, 1942-45, special events editor, 1955, assistant managing editor, 1961, Sunday editor, 1964-66. Co-producer of television series, "Turnpike"; story editor and technical adviser and scriptwriter, "The D.A.'s Man"; story editor of television series, "The Black Cat"; commentator, "Armstrong-Circle Theatre Hour" and "Assignment, Teen-age Junkie."

MEMBER: Western Writers of America, New York Civil War Round Table (president, 1956-57), New York City Reporters Association, Westerners (co-founder, New York Corral; sheriff, 1952-53).

AWARDS, HONORS: Pulitzer Prize for public service, 1944; Edgar Allan Poe Award ("Edgar") of Mystery Writers of America, 1957; New York Posse Buffalo Award, Westerners, 1960, for *The Great American West,* and 1970, for *The Life and Art of Charles Schreyvogel;* special award, New Jersey Association of Teachers of English, 1960, 1962, 1978, 1979, and 1980; Western Heritage Award for best novel of the year, 1961, for *The Shadow Catcher;* New York Reporters Association Gold Typewriter Award, 1961; American Newspaper Guild Page One Citation, 1961.

WRITINGS—Published by Crown, except as indicated: (Editor with Gerold Frank) *Out in the Boondocks: Marines in Action in the Pacific, 21 U.S. Marines Tell Their Stories,* Putnam, 1943; (with J. M. Eckberg and Frank) *U.S.S. Seawolf: Submarine Raider of the Pacific,* Putnam, 1945; *Action Tonight: The Story of the Destroyer O'Bannon in the Pacific,* Putnam, 1945; *Desperate Men: Revelations from the Sealed Pinkerton File,* Putnam, 1949, revised edition, Doubleday, 1962.

(With Howard Swiggett) *The Pinkerton Story,* Putnam, 1951; *Desperate Women,* Putnam, 1952; *King's Rebel* (novel), 1953; *Confederate Agent: A Discovery in History,* 1954; (with Paul Sann) *Pictorial History of the Wild West,* 1954, new edition, Spring Books, 1961; *Mathew Brady: Historian with a Camera,* 1955, 11th revised edition, 1974; *Across the Cimarron,* 1956; (with Harold R. Danforth) *The D.A.'s Man,* 1957; *Seek out and Destroy* (novel), 1958; *The Wild Bunch,* New American Library, 1958, revised edition, 1970; *The Great American West: A Pictorial History from Coronado to the Last Frontier,* 1959; *The Mob's Man,* 1959.

(With Danforth) *Big City Crimes,* Permabooks, 1960; (editor) James Iredell Waddell, *C.S.S. Shenandoah,* 1960; *The Shadow Catcher* (novel), 1961; *The Desperate Years: A Pictorial History of the Thirties,* 1962; *The Seat of Power* (novel), 1965; *Timothy O'Sullivan: American's Forgotten Photographer,* Doubleday, 1966; *The Right Image* (novel), 1967; *The Pinkerton's: The Detective Dynasty That Made History,* 1967.

The Life and Art of Charles Schreyvogel, 1970; *The Blue Messiah* (novel), 1971; *The McKenney-Hall Portrait Gallery of American Indians,* 1972; *Portraits of American Indians,* 1973; *The New Vigilantes* (novel), 1975; *The Authentic Wild West: The Gunfighters,* 1976; *The Authentic Wild West: The Outlaws,* 1977; (editor with wife, Gertrude Horan) *The Jinglebob Press,* 1977; *The Trial of Frank James for Murder,* 1977; *The Dalton Brothers,* 1977; *The Life of Tom Horn,* 1977; *Ginerva* (novel), 1978.

The Authentic Wild West: The Lawmen, 1980; *The Peking Agent* (novel), 1982.

WORK IN PROGRESS: A trilogy of novels.

SIDELIGHTS: James David Horan told *CA:* "I began writing in the 1930s when I was a young general assignment reporter for a New York City afternoon newspaper with the press room of the famous West Side Court as my base. It had a battered old Remington typewriter in it, and rather than become part of the constant card game, I began writing. In the depth of the Great Depression I was amazed to discover there were publishers willing to pay as much as a hundred dollars for my articles!"

BIOGRAPHICAL/CRITICAL SOURCES: New York Times Book Review, September 12, 1982.

OBITUARIES: New York Times, October 14, 1981; *Chicago Tribune,* October 14, 1981; *Publishers Weekly,* October 30, 1981; *AB Bookman's Weekly,* December 21, 1981.

* * *

HORGAN, Paul 1903-

PERSONAL: Born August 1, 1903, in Buffalo, N.Y.; son of Edward Daniel and Rose Marie (Rohr) Horgan. *Education:* Attended New Mexico Military Institute, 1920-23. *Religion:* Roman Catholic. *Home:* 77 Pearl St., Middletown, Conn. 06457. *Office:* Wesleyan University, Middletown, Conn. 06457.

CAREER: Novelist, biographer, and writer on national, regional, and church history. Eastman Theatre, Rochester, N.Y., member of production staff, 1923-26; New Mexico Military Institute, Roswell, librarian, 1926-42, assistant to president,

1947-49; Wesleyan University, Middletown, Conn., fellow of Center for Advanced Studies, 1959, 1961, director of Center, 1962-67, adjunct professor of English, 1967-71, professor emeritus and author-in-residence, 1971—. Visiting lecturer at University of Iowa, 1946, and Yale University, 1969; Saybrook College of Yale University, Hoyt fellow, 1965, associate fellow, 1966—; Aspen Institute for Humanistic Studies, scholar-in-residence, 1968, 1971, 1973, fellow, 1973—; Pierpont Morgan Library, fellow, 1974—, member of council of fellows, 1975-79, 1982—, life fellow, 1977—.

President of board of directors, Roswell Museum, 1948-55; member of board of directors, Roswell Public Library, 1958-62, and Witter Bynner Foundation, 1972-79; chairman of board of directors, Santa Fe Opera, 1958-71; School of American Research, member of board of managers, 1959—, fellow, 1978; member of advisory board, John Simon Guggenheim Foundation, 1961-67; lay trustee, St. Joseph's College, West Hartford, Conn., 1964-68; Book-of-the-Month Club, member of board of judges, 1969-72, associate, 1972-73; trustee, Associates of Yale University Library, 1976-79; founding trustee, Lincoln County (N.M.) Heritage Trust, 1976—; member of national advisory board, Center for the Book, Library of Congress, 1978—. *Military service:* U.S. Army, chief of Army Information Branch, 1942-46; became lieutenant colonel; received Legion of Merit; recalled for temporary active duty with U.S. Army general staff, 1952. *Member:* American Catholic Historical Association (president, 1960), American Academy of Arts and Sciences (fellow), National Institute of Arts and Letters, Connecticut Academy of Arts and Sciences (fellow), Phi Beta Kappa, Athenaeum Club (London), Century Club, Yale Club (New York).

AWARDS, HONORS: Harper Prize Novel Award ($7,500), 1933, for *The Fault of Angels;* Guggenheim fellow, 1945 and 1959; Pulitzer Prize in history, 1955, for *Great River,* and 1976, for *Lamy of Santa Fe;* Carr P. Collins Award, Texas Institute of Letters, 1955, for *Great River,* and 1976, for *Lamy of Santa Fe;* Bancroft Prize, Columbia University, 1955, for *Great River;* Campion Award for eminent service to Catholic letters, Catholic Book Club, 1957, for *The Centuries of Santa Fe;* created Knight of St. Gregory, 1957; National Catholic Book Award in fiction, Catholic Press Association, 1965, for *Things as They Are,* and 1969, for *Everything to Live For;* Jesse H. Jones Award, Texas Institute of Letters, 1971, for *Whitewater;* Western Writers of America Award and Christopher Book Award, both 1976, for *Lamy of Santa Fe;* Laetare Medal, University of Notre Dame, 1976; Baldwin Medal, Wesleyan University, 1982; library at New Mexico Military Institute, and Art Center and gallery of Roswell Museum all named for Horgan.

Honorary degrees include Litt.D. from Wesleyan University, 1956, Southern Methodist University, 1957, University of Notre Dame, 1958, Boston College, 1958, New Mexico State University, 1961, College of the Holy Cross, 1962, University of New Mexico, 1963, Fairfield University, 1964, St. Mary's College, 1976, and Yale University, 1977; D.H.L. from Canisius College, 1960, Georgetown University, 1963, Lincoln College, 1968, Loyola College, Baltimore, 1968, D'Youville College, 1968, Pace University, 1968, St. Bonaventure University, 1970, La Salle University, 1971, and Catholic University of America, 1973.

WRITINGS: A Tree on the Plains: A Music Play for Americans (score by Ernst Bacon; first produced in Spartanburg, S.C., May, 1942; produced in New York, 1943), A. L. Williams, 1942; *Songs after Lincoln* (poems), Farrar, Straus, 1965.

Nonfiction: (Self-illustrated) *Men of Arms* (juvenile), McKay, 1931; *From the Royal City of the Holy Faith of St. Francis of Assissi: Being Five Accounts of Life in That Place* (sketches originally published in *Yale Review*), Rydal, 1936; (author of preface) Robert Hunt, editor, *Selected Poems by Witter Bynner,* Knopf, 1936; (editor with Maurice Garland Fulton) *New Mexico's Own Chronicle: Three Races in the Writing of Four Hundred Years,* Upshaw, 1937; (author of biographical introduction) *Diary and Letters of Josiah Gregg,* University of Oklahoma Press, Volume I, 1941, Volume II, 1943; (with the editors of *Look* magazine) *Look at America: The Southwest,* Houghton, 1947.

Great River: The Rio Grande in North American History (Book-of-the-Month Club alternate selection), two volumes, Rinehart, 1954, limited edition with Horgan's watercolor illustrations, 1954, published in a single volume, Holt, 1960; (self-illustrated) *The Centuries of Santa Fe,* Dutton, 1956, reprinted, Gannon, 1976; *Rome Eternal,* Farrar, Straus, 1959; *Citizen of New Salem* (biography; Book-of-the-Month Club selection), Farrar, Straus, 1961 (published in England as *Abraham Lincoln, Citizen of New Salem,* Macmillan, 1961); *Conquistadors in North American History,* Farrar, Straus, 1963 (published in England as *Conquistadors in North America,* Macmillan, 1963); *Andrew Wyeth: An Exhibition of Watercolors, Temperas, and Drawings,* Art Gallery, University of Arizona, 1963; *Peter Hurd: A Portrait Sketch from Life,* University of Texas Press, 1965; *Memories of the Future,* Farrar, Straus, 1966; (contributor) Bessie A. Stuart, compiler, *And Yet, Entirely Different,* Dearborn Public Schools, 1968.

The Heroic Triad: Essays in the Social Energies of Three Southwestern Cultures, Holt, 1970; (editor and author of introduction and commentary) *Maurice Baring Restored: Selections from His Work,* Farrar, Straus, 1970; *Encounters with Stravinsky: A Personal Record,* Farrar, Straus, 1972; *Approaches to Writing,* Farrar, Straus, 1973; *Ernst Bacon: A Contemporary Tribute,* [Orinda, Calif.], 1974; *Lamy of Santa Fe: His Life and Times,* Farrar, Straus, 1975; *Josiah Gregg and His Vision of the Early West,* Farrar, Straus, 1979.

Fiction: *The Fault of Angels,* Harper, 1933; *No Quarter Given,* Harper, 1935; *Main Line West* (also see below), Harper, 1936; *The Return of the Weed* (short stories), Harper, 1936 (published in England as *Lingering Walls,* Constable, 1936), reprinted, Northland Press, 1980; *A Lamp on the Plains,* Harper, 1937, reprinted, Popular Library, 1964; *Far from Cibola* (also see below), Harper, 1938, reprinted, University of New Mexico Press, 1974; *The Habit of Empire,* Rydal, 1938; *Figures in a Landscape* (short stories), Harper, 1940; *The Common Heart* (also see below), Harper, 1942.

The Devil in the Desert (also see below), Longmans, Green, 1952; *One Red Rose for Christmas* (also see below), Longmans, Green, 1952; *Humble Powers* (contains *The Devil in the Desert, One Red Rose for Christmas,* and "To the Castle"), Macmillan (London), 1954, Image Books, 1956; (self-illustrated) *The Saintmaker's Christmas Eve,* Farrar, Straus, 1957, reprinted, Paperback Library, 1971; *A Distant Trumpet,* Farrar, Straus, 1960; *Mountain Standard Time* (contains *Main Line West, Far from Cibola,* and *The Common Heart*), Farrar, Straus, 1962; *Toby and the Nighttime* (juvenile), Ariel Books, 1963; *Things as They Are,* Farrar, Straus, 1964; *The Peach Stone: Stories from Four Decades* (includes *The Devil in the Desert*), Farrar, Straus, 1967; *Everything to Live For,* Farrar, Straus, 1968.

Whitewater (Reader's Digest Condensed Book Club selection; Book-of-the-Month Club and Literary Guild alternate selection), Farrar, Straus, 1970; *The Thin Mountain Air,* Farrar, Straus, 1977; *Mexico Bay* (Book-of-the-Month Club alternate selection), Farrar, Straus, 1982.

Short stories represented in many anthologies, including: *Folk-Say: A Regional Miscellany,* four volumes, edited by B. A. Botkin, University of Oklahoma Press, 1929-32; *O. Henry Memorial Award Prize Stories of 1931,* edited by Blanche Colton Williams, Doubleday, 1931; *Prose, Poetry and Drama for Oral Interpretation,* edited by W. J. Forma, Harper, 1936; *O. Henry Memorial Award Prize Stories of 1936,* edited by Harry Hansen, Doubleday, 1936; *Short Stories from the "New Yorker,"* Simon & Schuster, 1940.

Author of play "Yours, A. Lincoln," first produced in New York, July 9, 1942. Contributor of stories, articles, and essays to periodicals, including *Harper's, Atlantic, Yale Review, North American Review, Direction, America, Good Housekeeping, Ladies' Home Journal, Southwest Review, Theatre Arts, Horizon, Vanity Fair, Saturday Evening Post,* and *Collier's.*

SIDELIGHTS: Though a prolific writer exercising his talents in a wide variety of genres, Paul Horgan is known "primarily [as] a novelist and historian of the West," writes Jonathan Yardley in the *Washington Post Book World.* "His is not the West of Zane Grey and Louis L'Amour," Yardley explains, "but that of Willa Cather: a West of pioneers and settlers, of priests and ranchers, of ordinary people set down in an extraordinary landscape." Horgan's works on the land and people of the West, particularly the Southwest, have received much praise and many awards—including two Pulitzer Prizes in history—because of his knowledge of the region and his solid craftsmanship. "Few men know the Southwest as well as Paul Horgan," says J. F. Bannon in *America,* "[but] fewer still can write of it, its history and its peoples, with [the] same feeling and understanding." Horgan's success also stems from the larger concerns in his works. "Horgan is at once regional and transcontinental," notes Robert Gish in the *Chicago Tribune Book World,* for he is preoccupied with "the great American themes of the East's contact with the West." He has become, according to *Publishers Weekly* editor John F. Baker, "one of the Grand Old Men of American literature."

Much of Horgan's fiction is set in the Southwest, the region he has spent over half his life in since moving to New Mexico at the age of twelve. The characters are often descendants of the Indians and Spaniards who first tried to control the land as well as Anglo-Americans of a later generation who impose new ways and traditions upon the old. "For both groups Horgan shows infinite understanding and sympathy," states James M. Day in his critical study *Paul Horgan.* "Having lived in New Mexico for so many years himself, he could hardly escape the mingling of the two traditions and the effect they have on the people. Although a historian of stature, it is less his grasp of the facts of the Southwestern past than his absorption of the atmosphere of the place that distinguishes his fiction."

Horgan's greatest mark of success as a Southwestern fiction writer is, according to Day, his ability to capture the spirit of both the Indian-Spanish and the Anglo-American cultures without judging either. Specifically, Day cites Horgan's expression of their radically different approaches to the land itself: "Unlike those descended from Indians and Spaniards, [the Anglo-Americans who are the main characters in Horgan's novels] do not merely accept their place as part of the land, but they must consciously adopt a relationship to it. For them it is almost a matter of will to accept the land, while for the native the relationship simply *is.* For the Indian, his entire life is part of a great whole, encompassing past, present, and future in the eternal face of the land itself, about which there is no necessity to think. . . . Horgan's recognition of the distinction between these two modes of thought marks the depth of his understanding of the people of the Southwest."

A characteristic of Horgan's fiction "remarked upon most frequently," claims Day, "is his descriptive power, particularly when writing of the land itself." Also illustrator for several of his books and many of the jackets, Horgan has been widely praised for his capacity to evoke a scene through words as well as through watercolors. Nevertheless, "the heart of Horgan's books is not the land or what it represents," concludes Day, "but the people who inhabit it. . . . Set against the unchanging background of the plains and mountains of the Southwest, this [approach] is particularly effective."

Horgan's characteristic focus on the people who inhabit the Southwest is also evident in his nonfiction works, particularly in *Great River* and *Lamy of Santa Fe,* both winners of the Pulitzer Prize in history. *Great River* is an account of the Rio Grande and the people who have lived beside it through two thousand years of history. Divided chronologically by the four cultures that dominate the river valley—Indian, Spanish, Mexican, and Anglo-American—the book includes chapters on the elements of belief, custom, group behavior, and social energy that give each culture its unique style. Writing in *Saturday Review,* Walter Prescott Webb claims "these chapters on social history may in time prove to be the most valuable portions of the work because [Horgan brings] to bear here a keen insight into the lives of those who have lived on and near the river's bank. . . . His acquaintance with the sources, and with individuals along the river and away from it that know them, is amazing."

The expertise Horgan acquired for *Great River* did not come quickly or easily. Traveling the river's full length of 1,800 miles three times and making dozens of shorter trips, he spent ten years researching and writing the two-volume opus. Moreover, Webb says, "Horgan tells us that [*Great River* had] been in the making since he came to Albuquerque at the age of [twelve]. I for one understand what he means. I doubt that anyone can really know an arid land who has not lived long in it, lived there when young to absorb its spirit before he can convey its charm and mystery."

In praising *Great River,* reviewers single out not only Horgan's knowledge of the subject but also his ability to effectively, and often poetically, communicate that knowledge. William deBuys, who in the *New Republic* calls the book "as good a digest of the American frontier experience as one may hope to find," believes that what "sets *Great River* apart [from other histories] and is its finest virtue is Horgan's ability to inspirit human events with the flavor and feeling of the land that spawned them. The stage he sets is broad, permanent. In the background one feels the pulse of the land and its river; they endure." "Paul Horgan is an artist," states J. Frank Dobie in the *New York Times Book Review,* "which means that he is a master of proportions, perspective, and details. [*Great River*] is an unfoldment of life with stretches of narrative as vivid as 'Livy's pictured page' and essays as bold as the divagations of Henry Fielding." Orville Prescott comments in the *New York Times:* "Horgan writes about [each culture and its way of life] with harsh realism and every appearance of objective judgment. But he writes so well, with such skill in capturing the typical emotion of the past, that *Great River* seems almost a romantic book in spite of his best efforts—which is only fitting and proper, for all history, if regarded correctly as the amazing story of men, is romantic."

James M. Day states that *Great River* has been charged with weakness in bibliography and questionable statements of historical interpretation, but he defends Horgan against all these charges: "Horgan suffers the inevitable fate of any man who tries to combine the discipline of history and the imagination of literature. The historians condemn him for sacrificing facts for a personal interpretation of truth, and the critics condemn him for sacrificing literary design to the undisciplined pattern of man's past. Both are right, in a sense, though the criticism is somewhat unjustified because it attacks the writer on grounds of not accomplishing what he has no intention of doing to begin with."

One of Horgan's intentions for *Great River* was to include a sketch he had written on the life of Jean Baptiste Lamy, first bishop of Santa Fe and the inspiration for Willa Cather's novel *Death Comes for the Archbishop*. But Horgan decided to withdraw it from *Great River* and keep it for later expansion. A few years later he began detailed research for a biography of the priest, after gaining access to the archives of the Catholic Church in the Vatican. Containing correspondence dealing with church affairs and missions around the world, the archives "gave him a great deal of hitherto unavailable information about Lamy's early life," notes John F. Baker. Horgan also utilized the archives of American church history at the University of Notre Dame and traveled to Mexico in his quest for information. "'Writing this one man's life,'" Horgan told Baker, "'took even more research than writing the whole history and geography of a river spanning thousands of miles.'" But as with *Great River,* Horgan's efforts were rewarded with a Pulitzer Prize in history and much critical acclaim.

Reviewing *Lamy of Santa Fe* in the *Washington Post Book World,* Jonathan Yardley believes that in Horgan, "Lamy has found his fit biographer, a man devoted as he to the Southwest and as firm in thought and language." "Horgan does better than serve his subject," insists Dennis Halac in *Commonweal.* "This illuminating study," continues Halac, "rises out of its regional interest, not only because of its associations with Cather and Horgan, but as a work of biographical art. The reader is given an excursion into Lamy's life . . . to express a biography with the finest literary standards and, thus, the greatest possible satisfaction." Colman McCarthy, writing in the *New Republic,* also praises Horgan's technique: "Horgan's scholarship avoids heaviness, and he also stays clear of the candlestick prose that all too often drips the wax of piety whenever the life of a holy man is recounted. Solid and detached biographies of the saintly are uncommon, [and] the excellence of Horgan's work is not accidental."

Lamy of Santa Fe separates much fact about the archbishop from the fiction of Cather's novel, *Death Comes for the Archbishop,* according to Michael Rogin in the *New York Times Book Review.* "Cather invented Lamy's relationship to Indian culture," notes Rogin, "along with the vignettes and Indian friendships to sustain it. . . . Lamy's opposition to the reservation policy is also fiction, not history. So, too, apparently, his criticism of slavery. . . . The historical Lamy promoted the railroad and other instruments of Yankee progress; newcomers blamed him for changing the traditional Southwest. Nostalgia for the architecture and life of old New Mexico, Horgan warns, reads twentieth-century attitudes back into Lamy's time."

Yet, as Halac points out, *Lamy of Santa Fe* contains some improvisations of its own: "the ceremony of Lamy's investiture derived from the ordinals; a sidetrip by young French missionaries to Niagara Falls where they reflect upon Chateaubriand's impressions, which were popular then; Lamy's pious view of Rome contrasted by a contemporary account of Henry James." Halac considers "these inspired innovations" to be the "finest touches in the book," because they "flesh out a story that, in less sensitive hands, could become tedious or spotty. I cannot recall a biography that uses its material so suggestively, not with distortion or as mere embellishment but to knit it into one piece."

"From Mr. Horgan's pages," surmises F. D. Reeve in the *Yale Review,* "emerges a portrait of a wise, patient, tolerant, self-sacrificing, faithful administrator whose design was to improve the physical and moral conditions of all men in the society in which he served. Mr. Horgan's affectionate re-creation of Archbishop Lamy, splendidly documented in rich detail yet portrayed with a master novelist's skill, shows that the West was won in a final sense not by the guns that killed the Indians but by the faith that directed the conquerors' labors." "The life of Lamy," concludes Jonathan Yardley, "with its beguiling mixture of deep spirituality and frontier courage, seems to epitomize the characteristics that Horgan admires, in the desert setting with which he is most comfortable."

MEDIA ADAPTATIONS: Horgan's novel *One Red Rose for Christmas* was adapted into a one-act play, *One Red Rose,* by Sister Mary Olive O'Connell, which was published by Longmans, Green in 1954 and produced on television in 1958. In other television presentations of *One Red Rose* at Christmastime, Helen Hayes appeared twice, and a later dramatic reading was given by Horgan and Ruth Hill on ABC-TV. *A Distant Trumpet* was filmed by Warner Bros. in 1964, and the movie starred Troy Donahue.

CA INTERVIEW

CA interviewed Paul Horgan by phone August 12, 1981, at his home in Middletown, Conn.

CA: You're talented not only in writing but in music, painting, and stage design.

HORGAN: Those began early in my extreme youth. I had a knack for all these things and had to decide which to follow as a life's work, as a career. I decided on writing because all the other arts which I was familiar with and had some experience in fed writing very directly, and the reverse is not true, in my view. A writer can use all the sensibilities of the painter, the musician, the actor—the novelist has to be an impersonator. It's pretty obvious. So I decided, I think at about twenty or twenty-one, to concentrate on writing without losing interest in all the other things. I have done a great deal of watercolor drawing and painting to supplement information for my work, chiefly for the histories I've written. It's important to me to make visual records of places that I want to recall, and what I draw or paint tells me what I saw and felt at the time. It may not tell anybody else, but it tells me.

CA: Is your painting on exhibit anywhere?

HORGAN: No. There are well over a hundred small paintings for *Great River,* and I think probably for *Lamy of Santa Fe,* a biography of Archbishop Lamy, there were close to that. But they're all in my archives at the Beinecke Rare Book and

Manuscript Library at Yale, which is the depository of all my manuscript material. They show some there occasionally.

CA: In Approaches to Writing *you describe those first novels that never found publishers.*

HORGAN: Apprenticeship novels.

CA: What gave you the fortitude to keep writing novels through the long apprenticeship period in which five attempts went unpublished.

HORGAN: I don't think it's a matter of will, actually. I think it's a matter of possession—one is possessed by the necessity, the intention. And I learned something from each one of those early five unpublished efforts. They had to be endured. I think any apprenticeship has to be taken affirmatively, not viewed as a disappointment every time something fails. Of course, it is to a degree, but it should not be ultimately discouraging. At least it wasn't to me.

CA: You wrote about it in a marvelously humorous way. Did that perspective come much later? Weren't you at all frustrated at the time?

HORGAN: Not really, no. As I think I indicated, many of these early works were imitative of other writers, and so one went on to something else until one's own voice appeared—and then off to the races!

CA: And you advise your writing students to look for their own voices also. Are you able to help many of them actually get started writing?

HORGAN: I've taken so very few. I've never had more than three in one year, and often fewer. That way I can work all year on a project with a student and see it intensively week by week—usually it's a novel the young person is writing. I don't believe writing itself can be taught; you can't insert talent into anyone. The chief function of the teacher, as I said in *Approaches to Writing,* is to help the student find his own voice, and when he's done that, nobody can do anything more for him. He's got to go on and develop the technical skills himself. That does take time, and youngsters are impatient the first time out.

CA: How early did you acquire the habit of jotting down ideas and notes?

HORGAN: That's very hard to say. I think it must have been in my twenties, and at first I put random notes down on stray pieces of paper, some of which were salvaged. Later on I did it in a more orderly way by keeping a blank book which I wrote in. You never know the life of a note. It's very mysterious. Some of them die and some of them prosper tremendously in, I suppose, the subconscious. The valuable ones are those to which something is added every time you look at them, that grow into something.

CA: You've worked in many genres—the novel, the short story, juvenile books, history, biography, even plays. Do you enjoy one more than the others?

HORGAN: No, I don't think so. That's an interesting question; it comes up all the time. The fact is that the form is dictated by the material. Whether it's to be a novel or a work of fact—history, nonfiction, whatever—is entirely determined by what's appropriate to the subject. When I have an idea that is strong enough imaginatively to hook me day after day—in many cases year after year—until it's done, then I'm completely involved in it and gratified to be dealing with it. I don't think I have a preference. It makes it awfully difficult for reviewers to categorize me, because it's easier for them to speak of a *novelist* or a *historian* or this or that, but I believe that the act of writing cannot always be specialized. So I've been interested in every kind of form, of statement.

CA: How do you feel about being labeled a Catholic writer?

HORGAN: I said long before Graham Greene said it, I'm a writer who happens to be Catholic, not the other way around. To say a "Catholic writer" implies that one is, in a sense, an apologist for the Catholic faith or viewpoint. Since it is a true thing to me, everything I do is informed by it to a degree, but that doesn't mean that I'm a propagandist.

CA: Your career falls naturally into two parts, the earlier fiction from 1933 to 1942 and the remainder of your work to date beginning with the publication of Great River *in 1954. During the twelve-year hiatus between these parts, you served in the army and worked on short fiction and* Great River. *Did it bother you not to have a major work coming out during that time?*

HORGAN: I would have liked, of course, to see a book coming along fairly often, but the fact is I was completely absorbed in *Great River*—a huge historical venture, two volumes originally and nearly half a million words—and it took a great amount of travel and research. So, occasionally, when I would come to the end of a research phase, I would write a short story that would appear in a periodical. I didn't actually miss my presence as a book author, book presenter, during that time. I was ready soon after *Great River* to make books regularly. Of course, during the army period it was impossible to think about anything except my job.

CA: With the works that involve massive research, such as Great River, Lamy of Santa Fe *and* The Centuries of Santa Fe, *is it a problem to know when to stop researching and begin the actual writing?*

HORGAN: Yes, it is a problem. It calls finally for an act of decision and will to say, *now;* this could go on for ten more years. Is there enough already accumulated and authenticated and ready to go with so there is a complete arc of historical experience, or does one need more? Sometimes it's tempting to go on researching, but you've got to say, better stop, better get on with it. So it really is an act of deliberate conclusion of that research time, and one invariably feels, well, I must have missed a good deal, but still what I have here fulfills a design I've had in mind all along and it's time to go. It's a very interesting problem.

CA: And each one, I'm sure, is different. I read that with Lamy of Santa Fe *you went farther and did much more travel than originally you thought you might.*

HORGAN: Indeed I did, yes. Luckily I was able to find wonderful material in Rome, in the archives there. Everywhere Lamy went I had to go, in any case. He had traveled widely and worked in many places, and I had to see them before I could describe them. So there was an enormous amount of travel involved in this, all very interesting and very rewarding. One curious and interesting thing: Father Hesburgh gave me great resources at Notre Dame University, and then I was allowed to stay there for six weeks or so in the winter time. They had a fine Lamy archive, including letters that had been written *to him* which were originally at Santa Fe and were later moved to the Notre Dame archives. But I found the other end of the correspondence in Rome—his letters to the Vatican—so I was able to put together letters *from him* and the answers. It was a nice conclusion both ways.

CA: The Time *reviewer said there was a particular problem separating fact from fiction in Lamy's case. Did you find that so?*

HORGAN: Not at all. I'd known Willa Cather's novel *Death Comes for the Archbishop* years and years before. It presents a very perceptive character portrait of him, but she invented most of it; it's a novel, a piece of fiction, so that's entirely legitimate. But I deliberately did not reread her book while I was working through the many years—really a quarter of a century—getting *Lamy* ready. Cather has a seductive style, and I didn't want to have any unconscious overlaps. I dealt entirely with documentation, whereas she drew factual material from one single source and she embroidered it very widely with fancy—remaining true to his nature, I'd say. She gave an attractive portrait of him, but it wasn't historical in every respect, and I like to think that mine is. I had no real problem with the fictional tradition that Miss Cather established.

CA: You moved from Buffalo, New York, to New Mexico as a twelve-year-old. Did that have a rather stunning immediate effect on you that later influenced your writing?

HORGAN: Very distinctly so, decidedly. I felt very much displaced at first, a youngster without his old friends and his old familiar things. But like most people who move to the Southwest, I found the place absorbing and I finally came to terms with it. I became an absolute *devote* of the region, the landscape, particularly, and the historical aspects. That's what led me to the Rio Grande in later years, because even as a child, I sensed that it was a marvelous natural resource. So I spent a tremendous amount of time along the river and thinking about the river. I didn't know then that I was possibly going to try to own it in a literary way, but the sense of it really was lodged quite deeply. I've really been a Southwesterner, a New Mexican, for much more than half my life. I still consider myself a New Mexican, slightly displaced.

CA: There seem to be many autobiographical elements in the "Richard novels," [Things as They Are, Everything to Live For, *and* The Thin Mountain Air]. *Do you find personal experience tricky to work with in fiction?*

HORGAN: No, I don't. I don't deliberately exclude it nor do I invoke it. The events and most of the characters are actually inventions, but they're supported by strong recollection of certain places and certain people. I'm sure there is a grain of something from life in all fiction, something that isn't pure fantasy. I think it's a great mistake always to confuse what sounds like an autobiographical experience in fiction with the real life of the author. Most of it is intuitive, and it's made up of a mosaic from many different observations of very different people, different kinds of events. It's awfully hard to describe the process, but things seem to flow together as if you took a palmful of mercury and threw it on a flat surface: the beads separate, and then mysteriously they come together again in a pattern to make the whole again, attracted to the central energy. Really, the physical backgrounds of the Richard books are places that I know because I lived in them, and I took great delight in trying to recapture the sense of them. What took place there, the kinds of people, the kinds of events come from many sources. I can't separate, if I try, the things that I actually went through myself and what I have the people in my fiction go through.

CA: You have commented on the popular speech and how it is so heavily influenced now by show-business style as we hear it on TV and film and radio. How do you feel about what's happening to our language, not only from television but also from the kind of jargon that comes from the social sciences and technology?

HORGAN: I think the language is being battered on all sides. There are some current pop usages that will survive. After all, the dictionary finally is created by the popular talk. But the lack of discrimination that occurs in much writing nowadays is disturbing, because what is fugitive and pop is used quite recklessly. I group everything that seems of a transitory nature, like advertising jargon, which I think is the chief villain. Children grow up hearing these things and that frames a kind of idiom. It's a strange thing to say, and of course elitist (though I have no objection to elitism when it's perfectly free choice and well earned), but I think the layers of the language can now be discerned as a kind of high English and a low English. And the comic strip language, I don't think that kind of talk is rich enough for serious writing. Young people are missing the grand inheritance of the language. How many of them could possibly get through Henry James now? He's taught a good deal in university literature courses, and I suppose what they focus on is the psychology and the subtlety of the events and so forth. But I'm sure the language must be very difficult reading for them. And certainly it's never imitated, never adopted by the young.

CA: You also have mentioned the lack of scope in much of our fiction now. You've called recent years "the age of the put-on. All periods," you wrote, "have had put-ons—but when have they ever become models for success?" Do you think we'll return to fiction that has a broader scope?

HORGAN: I think so, but I think this is undoubtedly a kind of cycle. Social modes, as you know, repeat themselves, but at some distance. There are phases in every area, in art and architecture even, certainly in dress. Styles have a way of being revived later when they are adapted by persons in different circumstances. I think the fugitive itself will fall away and the richer expression will return and survive. It's going on all the time, actually. There are contemporary writers working who aren't affected by the put-on or the let-down.

CA: Did you enjoy working as a selection judge for the Book-of-the-Month Club?

HORGAN: I did; it was very interesting. I don't share the down-the-nose view of the general, overall history of the Book-of-the-Month Club. If you look at the fifty-year accumulation of titles, it's extraordinary how many are absolutely first-rate. I took the job at the request of Mr. Harry Scherman, who was then head of it, and I served about two-and-a-half years. I found it very, very interesting, and I had remarkable colleagues on the board, but it just became too much work to allow me to do my own work, both teaching and writing, so I had to resign. It's very amazing the volume of reading one had to do every month. It was an enormous job—to do it thoroughly, to do justice to the material.

CA: You are reputed to have been quite a musician at one time.

HORGAN: That is misleading. I don't know how it ever got lodged so firmly in my tiny mythology that I'm a musician. At one time, as a very young person, I studied singing at the Eastman School of Music in Rochester, but I didn't continue it for more than a couple of years. I got derailed into these other interests, as I mentioned earlier. I can't live without music. I somewhat pompously call myself a virtuoso listener, which means music is really essential to me and I really love it and may listen with some discernment—I don't know. But that's the extent of it. I've conducted in a gratifying but comic way a symphony orchestra in rehearsal. The Dallas Symphony Orchestra allowed me to do this in rehearsal one day and it was pure paradise. But that doesn't mean I'm a musician. I'm much more of a painter in practice than I am a musician in my own way, although painting is not my right arm.

CA: I know you don't like to discuss very specifically what you're working on, but do you plan to try anything absolutely new, anything you haven't tried before?

HORGAN: The only new form that I haven't assailed is screen-writing, but that's a technique that I think would require a great deal of study and much more time than I feel I can afford now with the other things I want to do. There are notes for two, perhaps three, novels, and first drafts of almost fifty short stories waiting to be rewritten and winnowed for a collected book. All this may be interrupted for some autobiographical writing. In any case, work goes on.

BIOGRAPHICAL/CRITICAL SOURCES: Saturday Review of Literature, August 26, 1933, February 9, 1935, March 21, 1936, April 9, 1937, January 2, 1943; *Books,* August 27, 1933, February 3, 1935, March 22, 1936, March 21, 1937, April 21, 1940; *New York Times,* August 27, 1933, February 3, 1935, March 22, 1936, March 14, 1937, March 6, 1938, April 21, 1940, November 22, 1942, March 23, 1952, October 11, 1954, December 18, 1955, October 7, 1956, September 22, 1957, July 10, 1969, September 1, 1970, September 26, 1970, May 8, 1976; *New York Herald Tribune Book Review,* January 30, 1935, October 10, 1954, October 24, 1954, May 5, 1957, April 17, 1960; *Times Literary Supplement,* July 25, 1935, March 26, 1971, December 22, 1972; *Spectator,* August 9, 1935; *Commonweal,* June 19, 1936, June 24, 1960, October 23, 1970, March 26, 1976; *New Republic,* March 23, 1938, December 21, 1942, February 7, 1976.

Saturday Review, September 16, 1954, October 16, 1954, December 8, 1956, October 5, 1957, April 23, 1960, August 8, 1964, August 12, 1967, August 31, 1968, October 3, 1970, August 9, 1975, September 17, 1977; *New York Times Book Review,* October 10, 1954, May 5, 1957, April 17, 1960, April 23, 1961, August 2, 1964, June 19, 1966, May 14, 1967, August 25, 1968, August 27, 1970, September 27, 1970, July 2, 1972, October 5, 1975, September 11, 1977, January 18, 1981, March 28, 1982; *Christian Science Monitor,* October 14, 1954, January 24, 1963, October 1, 1970, June 28, 1972; *Newsweek,* November 29, 1954, September 12, 1977; *New Yorker,* December 4, 1954, September 12, 1977; *Time,* January 24, 1955, May 2, 1960, October 12, 1970, November 10, 1975; *San Francisco Chronicle,* September 23, 1957.

Atlantic, April, 1961, October, 1970, October, 1975; *Reporter,* April 25, 1963; *Best Sellers,* September 1, 1964, August 1, 1970, October 1, 1970; James M. Day, *Paul Horgan,* Steck-Vaughn, 1967; *Washington Post Book World,* September 8, 1968, January 31, 1971, June 18, 1972, August 17, 1975, October 23, 1977, February 21, 1982.

Life, October 9, 1970; *America,* October 10, 1970, October 11, 1975; *Nation,* November 2, 1970; *New York Review of Books,* November 5, 1970; Paul Horgan, *Encounters with Stravinsky: A Personal Record,* Farrar, Straus, 1972; *Saturday Review of the Society,* July 29, 1972; *Yale Review,* winter, 1973, winter, 1976; *Critic,* winter, 1975; *Publishers Weekly,* July 14, 1975; *Contemporary Literary Criticism,* Volume IX, Gale, 1978; *Washington Post,* December 1, 1979; *Los Angeles Times,* March 4, 1982.

—Sketch by James G. Lesniak

—Interview by Jean W. Ross

* * *

HORNE, Alistair (Allan) 1925-

PERSONAL: Born November 9, 1925, in London, England; son of Sir James Allan and Auriel Camilla (Hay) Horne; married Renira Margaret Hawkins, November 28, 1953 (divorced, 1982); children: Camilla, Alexandra, Vanessa. *Education:* Jesus College, Cambridge, M.A., 1949. *Politics:* "Nonconformist but anti-Communist." *Religion:* Church of England. *Agent:* A. D. Peters & Co., Ltd., 10 Buckingham St., London WC2N 6BU, England.

CAREER: Cambridge Daily News, Cambridge, England, journalist, 1950-51; *Daily Telegraph,* London, England, staff correspondent in Germany, 1952-55; free-lance writer, 1955—. Director of Mombasa Investment Trust, Ltd. *Military service:* Royal Air Force, 1943; British Army, Coldstream Guards, 1944-47, attached to Counter-Intelligence; became captain. *Member:* Royal Institute of International Affairs, Garrick Club (London). *Awards, honors:* Hawthornden Prize, 1963, for *The Price of Glory;* Yorkshire Post Book of the Year Prize and Wolfson Literary Award, both 1978, both for *A Savage War of Peace: Algeria 1954-1962.*

WRITINGS: Back into Power, Parrish, 1955, published as *Return to Power,* Praeger, 1956; *The Land Is Bright,* Parrish, 1958; *Canada and the Canadians,* Macmillan, 1961; *The Price of Glory: Verdun, 1916* (first book in trilogy), St. Martin's, 1962; *The Fall of Paris: The Seige and the Commune, 1870-1871* (second book in trilogy), St. Martin's, 1965; *To Lose a Battle: France, 1940* (third book in trilogy), Little, Brown, 1969; *Death of a Generation: From Neuve and Chapelle to Verdun and the Somme,* Heritage Press, 1970; *The Terrible Year: The Paris Commune 1871,* Viking, 1971; *Small Earthquake in Chile: Allende's South America,* Viking, 1972 (published in England as *Small Earthquake in Chile: A Visit to Allende's South America,* Macmillan, 1972); *A Savage War of Peace: Algeria 1954-1962,* Macmillan, 1977, Viking, 1978; *Napoleon, Master of Europe 1806-1807,* Morrow, 1979. Also author of script, "The Terrible Year," based on book of same title, for B.B.C. "Chronicle," 1971. Contributor to periodicals, including *Times Literary Supplement, Observer, Spectator, New York Times, Time and Tide,* and *Sunday Telegraph.*

WORK IN PROGRESS: An official biography of Harold Macmillan, former Prime Minister of England.

SIDELIGHTS: Alistair Horne is a "distinguished historian whose trilogy on Franco-German conflict from 1870 to 1940 could hardly be bettered," John Leonard writes in the *New York Times*. Horne's studies of revolutionary movements, especially his award-winning analysis of the Algerian insurrection, have also received critical acclaim. Horne's books, critics have observed, are marked by a balanced presentation of warring parties, strong narrative hold, extensive research, and, as John Ardagh notes in *Washington Post Book World,* "a passionate flair for exploring the human detail of military history."

The Price of Glory, the first volume of Horne's trilogy, is "a battle saga which rises above mere narrative to achieve the status of veritable drama," according to L. F. Eliot in the *National Review*. It is "one of the most scrupulously documented war (or anti-war) books of our time," Leon Wolff says in the *New York Times Book Review*. "No historian of our times has so poignantly recaptured the malignancy of war on the Western Front." Barbara Tuchman similarly praises *The Fall of Paris,* the trilogy's second volume. In a *New York Times Book Review* article, she finds that "Horne tells the story . . . with such vivid verisimilitude that the reader feels he is inside the beleaguered city and turns the pages anxiously to learn what will be his fate. . . . As a historian, [Horne] is honest, meticulous, consistently interesting and readable, with an eye for the colorful and informative detail, the telling picture and dramatic episode."

The third volume of the trilogy, *To Lose a Battle,* chronicles the six-week rout of France by the German Army in 1940 and examines the reasons behind the collapse of the French Army, regarded at the time as the strongest military unit in Europe. "Horne's superbly readable narrative explores this question in its political, military, economic, and moral ramifications," Jack Beatty comments in the *New Republic*. "Horne's pen gives instant life to everything in its path; like the German army, he sweeps easily before him the political contortions of the Third Republic, with its giddy succession of premiers, its government by crony and mistress, and its deep and virulent social divisions between left and right." An *Economist* critic observes: "All the details are there: the small, fleeting triumphs, the cowardice, the stupidity and the intelligence. Horne's great gift is his ability to hold his readers in the grip of such feelings, constantly shifting his focus . . . without mystifying or fatiguing them." And Keith Eubank of *Library Journal* believes *To Lose a Battle* "should become one of the great classic accounts of this terrible disaster which befell France. . . . It is a magnificent book."

Horne's study of the "savage war of peace" in Algeria has been called "as full and objective a history of the Algerian war as we are likely to see" by James Joll in the *New York Times Book Review*. On November 4, 1954, the Algerian revolutionary army *Front de Liberation Nationale* (F.L.N.) attacked a police station in the city of Biskra to begin its campaign against French colonial rule. Eight years later the French withdrew and the undeclared war ended, with two million soldiers and civilians dead or exiled.

"The terror, mutilation, counterterror, torture and murder took place on both sides. There was no middle," Leonard writes in the *New York Times*. "The criminal difference between the 19th century and the 20th," Leonard adds, "is that in the 20th there are no civilians." "It is a frightful story—begotten in the blood of innocents," Priscilla L. Buckley says in the *National Review*. "[The war has been] much written about but never as skillfully or even-handedly as in this book." And in *Spectator,* Raymond Carr comments: "Occasionally an epic subject encounters a fine historian. This was the case with the Algerian war and Mr. Horne. The result is a book of compelling power, written with compassion and understanding." *A Savage War of Peace* "is a magnificent book," Carr continues. "It has the poetic sense of place without which no great work of history can be written. It is more than a narrative, skillfully distilled from a mountain of sources, often difficult to follow because of its complexity, but which nevertheless holds the reader."

Several reviewers have commented on the fairness of Horne's account of the conflict, a great achievement "given that the sources are so polemical, that the passions of the participants have not died down, and that so many indeed still refuse to say much about their roles," Theodore Zeldin observes. Writing in *Listener,* Zeldin notes that Horne "tells his story—and it is a gripping story—not quite with detachment, because he is too appalled by the cruelty of it all, but with fairness and lucidity, showing that horrific violence was used by almost all the parties involved." "For Mr. Horne, after talking to everybody he could find and reading everything he could get his hands on, nobody is a hero. He merely does his considerable best to understand," Leonard observes. And Richard Cobb writes in the *New Statesman:* "Horne's book is quite unsurpassed, and is likely to remain so. . . . He has a word of understanding for all the protagonists, even the most fanatical and cruel. . . . Added to the sheer force of an implacable narrative is the author's ability to *see* the situation on the ground and to describe . . . the dramatic topography of Algiers and its neighbouring beaches. . . . Here is a historian who has been over the ground, and who, ten years after Independence, can still read through the dilapidated buildings . . . in order to decipher the lost messages. . . . Such a repetitive account of daily killings, of mindless violence, could be merely sickening; yet, thanks to the author's ever-alert compassion, to his eye for each pathetic detail, it attains a sort of sombre beauty and a dignity that illuminates the whole book." *A Savage War of Peace,* Cobb concludes, is "a work of great beauty and insight."

AVOCATIONAL INTERESTS: Skiing, painting, shooting, fishing, travel.

BIOGRAPHICAL/CRITICAL SOURCES: Time, February 22, 1963, May 22, 1978; *National Review,* February 26, 1963, July 1, 1969, June 23, 1978; *New York Times Book Review,* April 7, 1963, January 30, 1966, July 20, 1969, March 19, 1978; *New Statesman,* June 21, 1963, May 2, 1969, November 18, 1977; *Economist,* April 19, 1969; *Times Literary Supplement,* May 8, 1969, April 21, 1978; *Library Journal,* May 15, 1969; *Washington Post Book World,* July 20, 1969, July 16, 1978; *Christian Science Monitor,* July 26, 1969; *Nation,* August 27, 1973, April 29, 1978; *Spectator,* October 22, 1977; *Listener,* January 26, 1978; *New York Times,* March 23, 1978; *Harper's,* August, 1978; *New Republic,* January 19, 1979.

—Sketch by Stewart R. Hakola

* * *

HORNUNG, Clarence Pearson 1899-

PERSONAL: Born June 12, 1899, in New York, N.Y.; son of Jules S. (a candy merchant) and Caroline (Pfaelzer) Hornung; married Sara Stoff, June 3, 1923; children: Richard Sanford, Donald Gilbert. *Education:* City College (now City College of the City University of New York), B.A., 1920; studied art at

Cooper Union, 1921, and advertising design at New York University, 1921-22. *Home:* 12 Glen Rd., West Hempstead, N.Y. 11552.

CAREER: Industrial designer and illustrator, specializing in trademarks, packaging, and product identification; Collectors' Prints, Inc. (publishers of prints in limited editions), New York, N.Y., president, 1964-72. Founder and co-publisher of *Automobile Quarterly,* 1961-62. An exhibition of his watercolors has been shown in a number of libraries. *Military service:* U.S. Army, Infantry, 1918-19; became second lieutenant. *Member:* American Institute of Graphic Arts, Typophiles.

WRITINGS: Bookplates of Harold Nelson, Caxton Press (New York), 1929; *Trade-Marks,* Caxton Press (New York), 1930; *Handbook of Designs and Devices,* Harper, 1932, 2nd edition, Dover, 1946; *Lettering from A to Z,* Ziff-Davis, 1946, 2nd edition, William Penn Publishing, 1954; *Handbook of Early Advertising Art,* two volumes, Dover, 1947, 3rd revised edition, 1956; *Wheels across America,* A. S. Barnes, 1959; *Pictorial Archives of American Business and Industry,* Dover, 1959.

(Art editor) *Book of the American West,* Messner, 1963; *Gallery of the American Automobile,* Collectors' Prints, 1965; *Portrait Gallery of Early Automobiles,* Abrams, 1968; *Antiques and Jewelry Designs,* Braziller, 1968; *An Old Fashioned Christmas in Illustration and Decoration,* Dover, 1970; *Antique Automobile Coloring Book,* Dover, 1971; *Treasury of American Design,* two volumes, Abrams, 1972; *Will Bradley: His Graphic Work,* Dover, 1974; *Allover Patterns for Designers and Craftsmen,* Dover, 1975; *Oldtime Automobile Advertisements,* Dover, 1975; (with Fridolf Johnson) *Two Hundred Years of American Graphic Art,* Braziller, 1975; *American Antiques, Arts, and Crafts,* Abrams, 1975; *The Way It Was: New York, 1850-1890,* Schocken, 1977; *The American Eagle in Art and Design,* Dover, 1978; *The Way It Was in the U.S.A.,* Abbeville Press, 1978; *Primer of Japanese Patterns,* Dover, 1982. Contributor to *New York Times* and to trade publications.

WORK IN PROGRESS: The Italian Sketchbook; Geometrix; The Infinity of Design; The Great Book of Poster Masters.

SIDELIGHTS: Clarence Pearson Hornung's *Treasury of American Design,* on which he estimates he spent "four solid years," is a two-volume survey of the more than 17,000 watercolor drawings in the *Index of American Design.* The *Index,* kept in the National Gallery of Art in Washington, D.C., was a project completed by American artists under the Works Progress Administration (WPA), from 1935 to 1941. It represents the country's folk art and design as found in such artifacts as toys, ceramics, and furniture. A *Choice* reviewer finds that Hornung's anthology possesses "a scope and quality that will stimulate the awakening interest and pride in American craftsmanship" and calls the book a "fascinating, informative, highly recommended publication."

In *The Way It Was: New York, 1850-1890,* Hornung has selected over two hundred engravings, including work done by such artists as Winslow Homer and Charles Graham for popular nineteenth-century periodicals, to re-create the feel of New York City in its heyday. The woodcuts are accompanied by comments on the times by well-known contemporary writers, Walt Whitman and Herman Melville among them. Alden Whitman writes in the *New York Times* that this "collection of woodcuts—which can be read as an archaeologist reads the shards of a bygone civilization—is a splendid tribute to a lost art and a lost city."

AVOCATIONAL INTERESTS: Hornung told *CA* that he is "an avid collector of books, posters, and printed ephemera" that overflow his garage, basement, and attic; he sketches and paints in watercolor on frequent trips to Europe and the Orient.

BIOGRAPHICAL/CRITICAL SOURCES: Publishers Weekly, October 9, 1972, October 20, 1975, June 13, 1977; *Choice,* March, 1973, October, 1976, December, 1977; *Library Journal,* April 15, 1976, October 1, 1977; *New York Times,* August 4, 1977.

* * *

HOROWITZ, Morris A(aron) 1919-

PERSONAL: Born November 19, 1919, in Newark, N.J.; son of Samuel and Ann (Litwin) Horowitz; married Jean Ginsburg, July 12, 1941; children: Ruth, Joel. *Education:* New York University, B.A., 1940; Harvard University, Ph.D., 1954. *Home:* 5 Riedesel Ave., Cambridge, Mass. 02138. *Office:* Department of Economics, Northeastern University, Boston, Mass. 02115.

CAREER: U.S. Department of Labor, Washington, D.C., labor economist, 1941-42; Office of Defense Transportation, Washington, D.C., labor economist, 1942-44; National War Labor Board, Washington, D.C., labor economist and director of Shipbuilding Commission's Case Analysis Division, 1944-46; University of Illinois at Urbana-Champaign, research assistant professor of economics at Institute of Labor and Industrial Relations, 1947-51; Wage Stabilization Board, Washington, D.C., director of Office of Case Analysis, 1951-52, vice-chairman of review and appeals committee, 1952-53; Harvard University, Cambridge, Mass., research associate in law, 1953-54, research associate in labor economics, 1954-56; Northeastern University, Boston, Mass., associate professor, 1956-59, professor of economics, 1959—, chairman of department, 1959—, research associate in Bureau of Business and Economic Research, 1956-59. Lecturer at Northeastern University, 1953-56; visiting professor at Massachusetts Institute of Technology, 1968-69, 1973. Ford Foundation manpower specialist for Argentina, 1961-62; member of labor arbitrators' panel of Federal Mediation and Conciliation Service; labor arbitrator and mediator; vice-chairman of Massachusetts Joint Labor-Management Committee for Municipal Police and Fire, 1979—.

MEMBER: American Economic Association, Industrial Relations Research Association, American Arbitration Association (member of labor panel), Latin American Studies Association, Association of Evolutionary Economics, National Academy of Arbitrators, Phi Beta Kappa, Phi Kappa Phi, Pi Mu Epsilon.

WRITINGS: (Contributor) Joseph S. Rancek, editor, *The Challenge of Science Education,* Philosophical Library, 1959; *The New York Hotel Industry: A Labor Relations Study,* Harvard University Press, 1960; *Structure and Government of the Carpenters' Union,* Wiley, 1962; (with Miguel A. Almada and Eduardo A. Zalduendo) *Los Recursos Humanos de Nivel Universitario y Tecnico en La Republica Argentina* (title means "High Level Manpower in the Republic of Argentina"), Instituto Torcuato di Tella, 1963; (contributor) Frederick Harbison and Charles A. Myers, editors, *Manpower and Education,* McGraw, 1964; (contributor) *Employment Impact of Technological Change,* Appendix Volume II, National Commission on Technology, Automation, and Economic Progress, 1966.

(Contributor) G. L. Mangum and R. T. Robson, editors, *Metropolitan Impact of Manpower Programs: A Four City Com-*

parison, Olympus, 1973; *Manpower and Education in Franco Spain,* Archon, 1974; (with Harold M. Goldstein) *Entry-Level Health Occupations: Development and Future,* Johns Hopkins Press, 1977; (with Goldstein) *Health Personnel: Meeting the Explosive Demand for Medical Care,* Aspen Press, 1977; (with Goldstein) *Utilization of Health Personnel: A Five Hospital Study,* Aspen Press, 1978; (contributor) Sar A. Levitan and Garth L. Mangum, editors, *CETA Training: A National Review and Eleven Case Studies,* Upjohn, 1981; (with Joanne Loscalzo) *Private Sector On-the-Job Training for Disadvantaged Workers: An Industry-Wide Approach,* Northeastern University, 1982.

Author of about thirty research reports for Institute of Labor and Industrial Relations at University of Illinois, Bureau of Business and Economic Research at Northeastern University, and other private and government institutions. Contributor to professional journals.

WORK IN PROGRESS: Research on manpower planning in Italy.

* * *

HORWOOD, Harold 1923-

PERSONAL: Born November 2, 1923, in St. John's, Newfoundland, Canada; son of Andrew (a businessman) and Vina (Maidment) Horwood. *Education:* Attended Prince of Wales College and took special courses at Memorial University College. *Politics:* New Democratic Party (social-democrat). *Residence:* Annapolis Royal, Nova Scotia, Canada.

CAREER: Evening Telegram, St. John's, Newfoundland, Canada, reporter, columnist, then editorial page editor, 1952-58; free-lance writer, 1958—; *The Examiner,* St. John's, managing editor, 1960-61; *Evening Telegram,* St. John's, associate editor, 1968-70. Member of Newfoundland House of Assembly (provincial parliament), for District of Labrador, 1949-51. Teacher of creative writing, Memorial University, 1969; writer-in-residence at University of Western Ontario, 1976-77, and University of Waterloo, 1980-82. Has assisted organized labor in planning, organizing and writing briefs. *Member:* Writers' Union of Canada (chairman, 1981), Association of Canadian Television and Radio Artists.

WRITINGS: Tomorrow Will Be Sunday (novel), Doubleday, 1966; *Foxes of Beachy Cove* (nonfiction), Doubleday, 1967; *Newfoundland,* St. Martin's, 1969; *White Eskimo* (novel), Doubleday, 1972; (editor) *Voices Underground* (poetry), New Press, 1972; (with Cassie Brown) *Death on the Ice,* Doubleday, 1972; *Beyond the Road,* Van Nostrand, 1976; *The Colonial Dream,* McClelland & Stewart, 1978; *Bartlett, the Great Canadian Explorer,* Doubleday, 1978; *Only the Gods Speak* (fiction), Breakwater, 1979; *Tales of the Labrador Indians,* Harry Cuff Publications, 1981; *Canada, a History,* Bison Books, 1982; *Pirates and Outlaws of Early Canada,* Doubleday, in press. Author of television and radio documentaries for Canadian Broadcasting Corp. Contributor of articles and historical sketches to magazines.

WORK IN PROGRESS: Remembering Summer, a novel; *Corner Brook, a History.*

* * *

HOSTETLER, Marian 1932-

PERSONAL: Born February 9, 1932, in Ohio; daughter of M. Harry (a grocer; in insurance) and Esther (Hostetler) Hostetler. *Education:* Goshen College, B.A., 1954; Goshen Biblical Seminary, graduate study, 1957-58; Indiana University, M.S., 1973. *Religion:* Mennonite. *Home:* 1910 Morton, Elkhart, Ind. 46516.

CAREER: Mennonite Board of Missions, Elkhart, Ind., editorial assistant, 1958-60, teacher in Algeria, 1960-70; Concord Community Schools, Elkhart, Ind., elementary teacher, 1971—. Member of Mennonite Publication Board. *Member:* National Education Association, Indiana State Teachers Association.

WRITINGS—All published by Herald Press: *African Adventure,* 1976; *Foundation Series Curriculum,* Grade 3, Quarter 2, 1977; *Journey to Jerusalem,* 1978; *Fear in Algeria,* 1979; *Secret in the City,* 1980.

WORK IN PROGRESS: A mystery for children, *Mystery at the Mall.*

SIDELIGHTS: Marian Hostetler writes: "The years I spent in North Africa were important in giving me the occasion to begin writing as well as giving me background useful in most of what I've written. My more recent travels in Chad, Nepal, Egypt, and Cyprus have been helpful as well."

AVOCATIONAL INTERESTS: Painting, reading, archaeology.

* * *

HOWARTH, David (Armine) 1912-

PERSONAL: Born July 18, 1912, in London, England; son of Osbert J. R. and Eleanor (Paget) Howarth; married Nanette Smith; children: Clare, Virginia, Stephen, Joanna. *Education:* Cambridge University, B.A., 1933. *Residence:* Blackboys, Sussex, England. *Agent:* Curtis Brown Ltd., 575 Madison Ave., New York, N.Y. 10022.

CAREER: Free-lance writer. Baird Television Co., London, England, researcher, 1933-34; British Broadcasting Corp., London, assistant talks editor, 1934-40, war correspondent, 1939-40. *Military service:* Royal Naval Volunteer Reserve, World War II; became lieutenant commander.

WRITINGS: The Shetland Bus, Nelson, 1951, published as *Across to Norway,* Sloane, 1952, reprinted, Fontana, 1974; *Thieves' Hole,* Rinehart, 1954; *We Die Alone,* Macmillan, 1955, published as *Escape Alone,* Fontana, 1971; *Sledge Patrol,* Macmillan, 1958; *D-Day,* McGraw, 1959.

The Shadow of the Dam, Macmillan, 1961; (editor) Ngawang Lobsang Yishey Tenzing Gyatso, *My Land and My People: The Autobiography of His Holiness the Dalai Lama,* Weidenfeld & Nicolson, 1962; *The Desert King: Ibn Saud and His Arabia,* McGraw, 1964, new edition, Quartet Books, 1980; (contributor) *Three Great Escape Stories from the Second World War,* Collins, 1965; *Panama: Four Hundred Years of Dreams and Cruelty,* McGraw, 1966 (published in England as *The Golden Isthmus,* Collins, 1966); *Waterloo: Day of Battle,* Atheneum, 1968 (published in England as *A Near Run Thing: The Day of Waterloo,* Collins, 1968); *Trafalgar: The Nelson Touch,* Atheneum, 1969; (editor) *Great Escapes,* David White, 1969.

Sovereign of the Seas: The Story of British Sea Power, Collins, 1974; *The Greek Adventure: Lord Byron and Other Eccentrics in the War of Independence,* Atheneum, 1976; *1066: The Year of Conquest,* Collins, 1977, Viking Press, 1978; *Dhows,* Quartet Books, 1977; *Great Britons,* British Broadcasting Corp., 1978; *The Men-of-War,* Time-Life, 1978.

Woolsthorpe Manor, Lincolnshire, National Trust, 1980; *Famous Sea Battles,* Little, Brown, 1981; *The Voyage of the Armada: The Spanish Story,* Viking Press, 1981.

Also author of *Group Flashing Two,* 1952, and *One Night in Styria,* 1953. Contributor of articles and serials to American and British periodicals.

SIDELIGHTS: British military historian David Howarth is a "brilliant" writer, according to a *New Yorker* critic, "full of grace and wit and solid common sense." Other reviewers hold similar opinions of Howarth and find his historical accounts both well-researched and entertaining.

Referring to *Waterloo: Day of Battle,* historian John Toland says in the *New York Times Book Review* that Howarth "has written the most balanced, realistic and valuable account of the struggle I have yet read. . . . By recreating the [battle] as a dramatist rather than as a military analyst he has evoked an exciting panorama." By virtue of the book's "excellent descriptive and narrative writing," notes Elbridge Colby in *Best Sellers,* "the story . . . really lives."

"Howarth's way of writing history is fun," says Christopher Lehmann-Haupt in a *New York Times* review of *1066: The Year of Conquest,* a book that tells the story of the Norman invasion of England. "[It is] not that he eschews the scholarly issues, . . . but it is the sense [he] creates of being there that is the signal accomplishment" of the book. A *New Yorker* critic affirms that, although Howarth's "approach is rational, and his assumptions are confirmed by the accepted sources, . . . the familiar story loses nothing of its power to haunt and stir and strangely mystify."

David Quinn, writing in the *Times Literary Supplement,* asserts that Howarth "is at home in writing about the sea and does so effectively" in *The Voyage of the Spanish Armada: The Spanish Story.* In the *New York Times Book Review,* Neal Johnston calls the book a "brief, elegant and entirely absorbing study of the most satisfying David and Goliath saga of our millenium. Using materials lost in the Spanish archives for centuries, David Howarth retells the legendary confrontation from the Spanish perspective." In his skillful use of detail concerning the ships, the lack of provisions, and the soldiers' physical condition, Howarth has, according to Phoebe-Lou Adams in *Atlantic,* "combined research, historical imagination, common sense, and narrative skill to produce a fascinating tale."

We Die Alone has been translated into Swedish and Spanish; *Panama: Four Hundred Years of Dreams and Cruelty* has been translated into German.

BIOGRAPHICAL/CRITICAL SOURCES: New York Times Book Review, October 20, 1968, April 2, 1978, September 27, 1981; *Best Sellers,* November, 1968; *New York Review of Books,* June 10, 1976; *Time,* July 26, 1976; *New Yorker,* August 16, 1976, February 20, 1978; *New York Times,* February 14, 1978; *Atlantic,* November, 1981; *Times Literary Supplement,* December 18, 1981; *Washington Post Book World,* December 20, 1981.†

* * *

HOWELL, John C(hristian) 1924-

PERSONAL: Born February 24, 1924, in Miami, Fla.; son of Heman M. and Laura (Andersen) Howell; married Doris D. Dooley, March 8, 1947; children: Michael Christian, John Mark. *Education:* Stetson University, B.A. (magna cum laude), 1949; Southwestern Baptist Theological Seminary, B.D., 1952, Th.D., 1960. *Home:* 5621 North Doniphan, Kansas City, Mo. 64118. *Office:* Midwestern Baptist Theological Seminary, Kansas City, Mo.

CAREER: Baptist minister in Crowley, Tex., 1950-56, and Bradenton, Fla., 1956-60; Midwestern Baptist Theological Seminary, Kansas City, Mo., professor of ethics, 1960—, academic dean, 1976-82. Associate counselor, Midwest Christian Counseling Center. *Military service:* U.S. Army, 1943-46. *Member:* American Society of Christian Ethics, National Council on Family Relations, American Association of Pastoral Counselors, Missouri Council on Family Relations, Kansas City Society for Theological Studies, Kansas City Association for Mental Health. *Awards, honors:* Ph.D., Southern Baptist Theological Seminary, 1975; D.D., Stetson University, 1979.

WRITINGS: Teaching about Sex: A Christian Approach, Broadman, 1966; (contributor) Ross Coggins, editor, *The Gambling Menace,* Broadman, 1966; (contributor) H.C. Brown, Jr., editor, *The Cutting Edge,* Volume I, Word, 1969; *Growing in Oneness,* Convention Press, 1972; (contributor) E.S. West, editor, *Extremism Left and Right,* Eerdmans, 1972; *Teaching Your Children about Sex,* Broadman, 1973; *Equality and Submission in Marriage,* Broadman, 1979; *Senior Adult Family Life,* Broadman, 1979; (contributor) William Pinson, Jr., editor, *An Approach to Christian Ethics,* Broadman, 1979. Contributor to publications in his field.

* * *

HOWELLS, John G(wilym) 1918-

PERSONAL: Born June 24, 1918, in Amlwch, Wales; son of Richard David and Mary (Hughes) Howells; married Ola Harrison, December 11, 1943; children: David John Barry, Richard Keith, Cheryll Mary, Roger Bruce. *Education:* University of London, B.S. and M.B., 1943, M.D., 1951; L.R.C.P. (London), 1943; M.R.C.S., 1943; D.P.M., 1947; University of Goettingen, graduate study, 1947; F.R.C. Psych., 1971. *Office:* Institute of Family Psychiatry, 23 Henley Rd., Ipswich, England.

CAREER: Charing Cross Hospital, London, England, house physician and senior house surgeon, 1943; University of London, London, England, registrar, Institute of Psychiatry and Institute of Neurology, 1947-49; consulting psychiatrist, 1949—; Institute of Family Psychiatry, Ipswich, England, director, 1949—. World Health Organization, fellow in United States, 1961, and consultant; University of Nebraska, visiting professor, 1962. Originator of family psychiatry system of practice and organizer of first hospital department of family psychiatry. *Member:* World Psychiatric Association, Royal Society of Medicine, British Medical Association, American Psychiatric Association (distinguished fellow).

WRITINGS: Family Psychiatry, Oliver & Boyd, 1963; *Theory and Practice of Family Psychiatry,* Oliver & Boyd, 1968; *Remember Maria,* Butterworth, 1974; (editor) *World History of Psychiatry,* Brunner/Mazel, 1974; *Contemporary Issues in Psychiatry,* Butterworth, 1974; *Principles of Family Psychiatry,* Brunner/Mazel, 1975; (editor) *Advances in Family Psychiatry,* two volumes, International Universities Press, 1980-81; (with W. Guirguis) *Family and Schizophrenia,* International Universities Press, 1983; (with M. L. Osborn) *Labyrinths of the Mind,* Greenwood Press, 1983. Editor of "Modern Perspectives in Psychiatry" series, nine volumes, 1965-81. Deviser, with J. R. Lickorish, of psychological test, "Family

Relations Indicator.'' Contributor of about 100 articles to medical journals. Editor of *International Journal of Family Psychiatry,* 1980—.

WORK IN PROGRESS: Continued work on ''Modern Perspectives in Psychiatry'' series; research in family psychiatry.

AVOCATIONAL INTERESTS: Growing roses; music, art, poetry, ''rumination.''

* * *

HOY, John C. 1933-

PERSONAL: Born December 5, 1933, in Yonkers, N.Y.; married Marie Vance (vice president of Notre Dame College). *Education:* Wesleyan University, B.A., 1955, M.A., 1960; graduate study in psychology and higher education at University of Chicago and University of Pennsylvania. *Home:* Cape Deer Farm, Pepperell, Mass. 01463. *Office:* New England Board of Higher Education, 47 Temple Place, Boston, Mass.

CAREER: St. Louis Country Day School, St. Louis, Mo., teacher of English and history, 1955-56; Wesleyan University, Middletown, Conn., assistant director of admissions, 1956-59; Morgan Park Academy, Chicago, Ill., director of development and guidance, and teacher of English, 1959-60; Lake Forest College, Lake Forest, Ill., director of admissions, 1960-62; Swarthmore College, Swarthmore, Pa., dean of admissions, 1962-64; Wesleyan University, dean of admissions and assistant to president, 1964-67, dean of admissions and freshmen, 1967-69, dean of special academic affairs, 1968-69; University of California, Irvine, vice-chancellor of university and student affairs, 1969-78; New England Board of Higher Education, Boston, Mass., president, 1978—. National Scholarship Service and Fund for Negro Students, member of advisory board, 1964-66, trustee, 1966—; member of Commission on Tests, College Entrance Examination Board and College Scholarship Service, 1966-69; African Scholarship Program of American Universities, trustee, 1966-71, and member of selection committee; member of scholarship selection committees of various foundations and corporations; trustee of Independent Day School, Middletown, 1964-67; member of executive committee, New England Loan Marketing Board, 1982—.

MEMBER: National Association of College Admissions Counselors (member of executive board, 1962-65), Center for the Study of the Presidency (member of board of educators), New England Association of Colleges and Secondary Schools (member of commission on higher education).

WRITINGS: Choosing a College: The Test of a Person, Delacorte, 1967; (contributor) Asa S. Knowles, editor, *Handbook of College and University Administration,* McGraw, 1970; (editor) *The Effective President,* Palisades, 1976; (editor) *Business and Academics,* University Press of New England, 1981; (editor) *New England's Vital Resource,* American Council on Education, 1982; (editor) *Financing Higher Education: The Public Investment,* Auburn House, 1982.

Author of syndicated column distributed through Newspaper Enterprise Association. Contributor of articles and reviews to professional journals and newspapers, including *Christian Science Monitor, New York World Telegram and Sun,* and *Saturday Review;* also contributor of poetry to *Approach, Beloit Poetry Journal,* and other periodicals. Chairman of editorial board, Association of College Admissions Counselors (now National Association of College Admissions Counselors) *Journal,* 1961-63; member of editorial board, American Council on Education, *The Educational Record,* 1979—.

WORK IN PROGRESS: A book on education aid and productivity—comparing international models and their effectiveness.

* * *

HSU, Cho-yun 1930-

PERSONAL: Born July 10, 1930, in China; son of Fengtsao and Ying (Tsang) Hsu; married Man-Li; children: Leo Lo-pung Hsu (son). *Education:* National Taiwan University, B.A., 1953, M.A., 1956; University of Chicago, Ph.D., 1961. *Home:* 5427 Hobart St., Pittsburgh, Pa. 15217. *Office:* Department of History, University of Pittsburgh, Pittsburgh, Pa. 15260.

CAREER: National Taiwan University, Taipei, Taiwan (Formosa), China, 1963-70, began as associate professor, became professor of history of ancient China, chairman of department of history, 1965-70; University of Pittsburgh, Pittsburgh, Pa., professor of history, 1970—. Research fellow of Academia Sinica, Taipei. *Member:* Chinese Historians Association, Ethnological Society of China, American Historical Society, Association for Asian Studies, American Sociological Association. *Awards, honors:* Named one of ten outstanding young men of China, 1964; elected member of Academia Sinica, 1980.

WRITINGS: The Journey Within (in Chinese), Book World Press (Taipei), 1964; *Ancient China in Transition: A Study of Social Mobility, 722-222 B.C.,* Stanford University Press, 1965; *Introduction to Historical Studies* (in Chinese), Commercial Press (Taipei), 1966; *Han Agriculture,* University of Washington Press, 1980; *Studies on Ancient China,* Lien-Chin Press, 1982; *Essays on Current Issues,* China Times, 1982. Contributor to *Comparative Studies of History and Society* and *Bulletin of the Institute of History and Philology.*

WORK IN PROGRESS: History of the Western Chou; editing a series of monographs on the history of ancient China.

* * *

HUFFORD, Susan 1940-

PERSONAL: Born December 15, 1940, in Cincinnati, Ohio; daughter of William, Jr. and Helen (Berger) Hufford. *Education:* DePauw University, B.A., 1960; Temple University, M.A., 1961; also studied in Austria. *Home:* 270 West End Ave., New York, N.Y. 10023. *Agent:* Jane Jordan Browne, Multimedia Product Development, Inc., 410 South Michigan Ave., Room 828, Chicago, Ill. 60605.

CAREER: Writer. Actress and singer; appeared in Broadway production of ''Fiddler on the Roof,'' 1970-72, in Broadway musical production ''Billy,'' on television, and with theatrical touring companies.

WRITINGS—Gothic novels: *Midnight Sailing,* Popular Library, 1975; *Devil's Sonata,* Popular Library, 1975; *Melody of Malice,* Popular Library, 1979; *Going All the Way,* New American Library, 1980; *Reflections,* Seaview, 1981.

WORK IN PROGRESS: A motion picture screenplay about contemporary relationships.

SIDELIGHTS: Susan Hufford writes: ''I've become quite intrigued with the gothic novel, . . . its history and its potential for modern women. I reject the notion that the gothic revolves around a weak, ineffectual female. In the past, many of these books have been written by men, using women's names, but as elsewhere in their lives, women are demanding more for themselves. As a feminist, I was at first in conflict over the fact that I was writing gothic novels—a traditionally unliberated form. But now I feel quite differently."†

*   *   *

HUGHES, Colin A(nfield) 1930-

PERSONAL: Born May 4, 1930, on Harbour Island, Bahamas; son of John Anfield (a civil servant) and Byrle (Johnson) Hughes; married Gwen Glover, August 6, 1955; children: John Anfield. *Education:* Attended George Washington University, 1946-48; Columbia University, B.A., 1949, M.A., 1950; London School of Economics and Political Science, Ph.D., 1952. *Home:* 2 Ambalindum St., Hawker, Australian Capital Territory 2614, Australia. *Office:* Australian National University, Box 4, Canberra, Australian Capital Territory 2600, Australia.

CAREER: McKinney, Bancroft & Hughes (attorneys), Nassau, Bahamas, counsel and attorney, 1954-56; University of Queensland, St. Lucia, Australia, lecturer, 1956-59; McKinney, Bancroft & Hughes, counsel and attorney, 1959-61; Australian National University, Canberra, Australian Capital Territory, fellow, 1961-65; University of Queensland, professor of political science, 1965-74; Australian National University, professorial fellow, 1975—.

WRITINGS: (Editor with David G. Bettison and Paul W. van der Veur) *The Papua-New Guinea Elections, 1964,* Australian National University, 1965; (with John S. Western) *The Prime Minister's Policy Speech,* Australian National University Press, 1966; (editor) *Readings in Australian Government,* University of Queensland Press, 1968; (with B. D. Graham) *A Handbook of Australian Government and Politics 1890-1964,* Australian National University Press, 1968; *Issues and Images,* Australian National University Press, 1969.

(Editor with D. J. Murphy and R. B. Joyce) *Prelude to Power,* Jacaranda Press, 1970; (with John S. Western) *The Mass Media in Australia,* University of Queensland Press, 1971, 2nd edition, 1982; (with Graham) *Voting for the Australian House of Representatives, 1901-1964,* Australian National University Press, 1974; *Mr. Prime Minister: Australian Prime Ministers, 1901-1972,* Oxford University Press, 1976; *A Handbook of Australian Government and Politics 1965-74,* Australian National University Press, 1977.

(Editor with Murphy and Joyce) *Labor in Power: The Labor Party and Governments in Queensland 1915-57,* University of Queensland Press, 1980; *The Government of Queensland,* University of Queensland Press, 1980; *Race and Politics in the Bahamas,* St. Martin's, 1981; (editor with Brian Costar) *Labor to Power: Victoria 1982,* Drummond, in press. Editor of *The Australian University,* 1975-77.

*   *   *

HULET, Claude Lyle 1920-

PERSONAL: Born December 22, 1920, in Pontiac, Mich.; son of Arno Lincoln (a teacher) and Grace (a teacher; maiden name, Johnson) Hulet; married Norma Christine Bennett, May 30, 1942; children: Claude, Roger, Richard. *Education:* Attended Universidad Autonoma de Mexico, 1941, and English Language Institute, 1942; University of Michigan, B.A., 1942, M.A., 1947, Ph.D., 1954. *Religion:* Protestant. *Home:* 4601 Hampton Rd., La Canada, Calif. 91011. *Office:* Department of Spanish and Portuguese, University of California, Los Angeles, Calif. 90024.

CAREER: Washington University, St. Louis, Mo., instructor, 1951-54, assistant professor of Spanish and Portuguese, 1954-58; University of California, Los Angeles, assistant professor, 1958-64, associate professor, 1964-70, professor of Spanish and Portuguese, 1970—, assistant coordinator of Brazil Student Leader Seminar, 1963-66, coordinator of Seminar, 1966-73, chairman of Romance Linguistics and Literature program, 1974-76. Director of Instituto Guatemalteco Americano, 1946. *Military service:* U.S. Army Air Forces, 1942-45; became technical sergeant.

MEMBER: Modern Language Association of America, American Association of Teachers of Spanish and Portuguese, Instituto Internacional de Literatura Iberoamericana, Philological Association of Pacific Coast, Pacific Coast Council on Latin American Studies, Modern and Classical Language Association of Southern California, Phi Kappa Phi.

AWARDS, HONORS: Organization of American States fellowship to Brazil, 1960; Fulbright-Hays fellowship to Brazil, 1964; Machado de Assis Medal from Brazilian Academy of Letters, 1968; Order of Rio Branco, rank of cavaleiro, from Brazilian Government, 1969; Instituto de Alta Cultura fellowship to Portugal, 1972; Fulbright-Hays travel grant to Portugal, 1972.

WRITINGS: Algumas reminiscencias do Brazil em Carlos Guido y Spano, International Institute of Iberoamerican Literature, 1962; *El sustituto: Interpretacion filosofico literario,* Atenea, 1963; *Latin American Prose in English Translation: A Bibliography,* Pan American Union, 1964; *A beata Maria do Egito: Uma nova tragedin por Rachel de Queiroz,* International Institute of Iberoamerican Literature, 1965; *Latin American Poetry in English Translation: A Bibliography,* Pan American Union, 1965; (editor) *Brazilian Literature,* four volumes, Georgetown University Press, 1974. Associate editor of *Hispania,* 1963-81.

WORK IN PROGRESS: Anthologies of Spanish-American literature and of Brazilian literature in English translation; studies on Spanish-American and Brazilian culture; a study of popular ballads in Northeast Brazil.†

*   *   *

HUNT, Dave
See HUNT, David C(harles Hadden)

*   *   *

HUNT, David C(harles Hadden) 1926- (Dave Hunt)

PERSONAL: Born September 30, 1926, in Riverside, Calif.; son of Albert E. (a chiropractor) and Lillian M. (Wilkins) Hunt; married Ruth E. Klassen (a teacher), June 24, 1950; children: David, Janna, Karen, Jon. *Education:* Oregon State University, student, 1947-48; University of California, Los Angeles, B.A., 1951. *Politics:* Conservative. *Religion:* Christian. *Residence:* Southern California.

CAREER: Writer. Thomas & Moore (certified public accountants), Los Angeles, Calif., staff accountant, 1951-54; David C. Hunt, Beverly Hills, Calif., certified public accountant, 1954-56; United Properties of America, Beverly Hills, vice-president and general manager, 1956-66; Amerige Convalescent Hospital, Fullerton, Calif., owner and administrator, 1967-72. *Military service:* U.S. Naval Reserve, 1944-45; served in South Pacific. U.S. Army, 1946-47; served in Japan.

WRITINGS—All under name Dave Hunt: (Editor) William Law, *The Power of the Spirit,* Christian Literature Crusade, 1970; *Confessions of a Heretic* (autobiography), Logos International, 1972, published in paperback as *On the Brink,* 1975; (with Hershel Smith) *The Devil and Mr. Smith* (biography), Revell, 1974; (with Hans Kristian) *Mission: Possible* (biography), Revell, 1975; *God of the Untouchables,* Revell, 1976; (with Rabindranath R. Maharaj) *Death of a Guru,* A. J. Holman, 1977; *The Cult Explosion,* Harvest House, 1980; *Study Guide to the Cult Explosion,* Harvest House, 1981.

Also author of *Science and God,* a book that was secretly published in Eastern European languages and smuggled behind the Iron Curtain in 1977, and of *Russia and the Coming Holocaust.*

WORK IN PROGRESS: Assignment: Life, a companion to the film of the same title; a revised edition of *Russia and the Coming Holocaust; Fear No Man;* two filmstrips with Tom McMahon.

SIDELIGHTS: David C. Hunt writes: "My interest is in presenting the validity of Christian experience to the contemporary public, as well as exposing the deceptive and growing influence of Eastern mysticism in the West.

"I have a series of books and films in mind involving the return of Christ and the end of the world, almost science fiction but more realistic. I am also interested in writing a definitive dramatized history of the persecution of believers in the Soviet Union, and have visited there twice and interviewed a number of people.

"I believe that current events prove the failure of the psychological-sociological-political methods to cure the ills of society, and want to present man's return to God as the only solution."

AVOCATIONAL INTERESTS: International travel, skiing, backpacking, tennis, fishing.

* * *

HUNT, Robert C(ushman) 1934-

PERSONAL: Born May 30, 1934, in Binghamton, N.Y.; son of Robert Cushman (a psychiatrist) and Fanny (Cassidy) Hunt; married Eva Verbitsky (an anthropologist), September 21, 1960 (died February 29, 1980); married Irene J. Winter (an art historian and archaeologist), October 18, 1982; children: (first marriage) Melissa Gabriela. *Education:* Hamilton College, B.A., 1956; University of Chicago, M.A., 1959; Northwestern University, Ph.D., 1965. *Office:* Department of Anthropology, Brandeis University, Waltham, Mass. 02154.

CAREER: Northwestern University, Evanston, Ill., instructor, 1964-65, assistant professor of anthropology, 1965-66; University of Illinois at Chicago Circle, Chicago, assistant professor of anthropology, 1966-69; Brandeis University, Waltham, Mass., associate professor of anthropology, 1969—, chairman of department, 1980—. Visiting assistant professor of anthropology at Northwestern University, 1968-69. *Member:* American Anthropological Association (fellow), American Ethnological Society (fellow), Current Anthropology (associate), American Association for the Advancement of Science (fellow).

WRITINGS: (Editor) *Personalities and Cultures,* Natural History Press, 1967; *The Local Social Organization of Irrigation Systems: Policy Implications of Its Relationship to Production and Distribution,* Agency for International Development, 1978.

Contributor; with Eva Hunt, except as indicated: P. Bock, editor, *Peasants in the Modern World,* University of New Mexico Press, 1969; John Middleton, editor, *From Child to Adult,* Natural History Press, 1970; (sole contributor) Hsu, editor, *Kinship and Culture,* Aldine, 1971; Abrahams and Troike, editors, *Language and Cultural Diversity in American Education,* Prentice-Hall, 1972; (sole contributor) Byars and Love, editors, *Quantitative Social Science Research on Latin America,* University of Illinois Press, 1973; Downing and Gibson, editors, *Irrigation's Impact on Society,* University of Arizona Press, 1974; Service and Cohens, editors, *Origins of the State: A Symposium,* ISHI Press, 1978.

Contributor to proceedings of the American Ethnological Society, 1965. Contributor of articles and reviews to periodicals in his field, including *American Anthropologist, Current Anthropology, Midway Magazine, Anales, America Indigena,* and *Science.* Editor of American Anthropological Association *Newsletter;* associate editor of *American Anthropologist,* 1971-73.

WORK IN PROGRESS: Social Organizational Correlates of the Shift from Self-Sufficient Food Production; Water Work: Community and Centralization in Canal Irrigation.

* * *

HUNTER, J(ames) Paul 1934-

PERSONAL: Born June 29, 1934, in Jamestown, N.Y.; son of Paul Wesley (a clergyman) and Florence (Walmer) Hunter; married Kathryn Montgomery, July 1, 1971; children: Debra, Lisa, Paul III, Anne. *Education:* Indiana Central College, A.B., 1955; Miami University, Oxford, Ohio, M.A., 1957; Rice University, Ph.D., 1963. *Home:* 215 Melrose St., Rochester, N.Y. 14619. *Office:* Department of English, University of Rochester, Rochester, N.Y. 14627.

CAREER: Instructor in English at University of Florida, Gainesville, 1957-59, and Williams College, Williamstown, Mass., 1962-64; University of California, Riverside, assistant professor of English, 1964-66; Emory University, Atlanta, Ga., associate professor, 1966-68, professor of English, 1968-80, department chairman, 1973-79; University of Rochester, Rochester, N.Y., professor of English, 1981—, dean of arts and science, 1981—. *Member:* Modern Language Association of America, American Society of Eighteenth Century Studies. *Awards, honors:* Guggenheim fellow, 1976-77.

WRITINGS: The Reluctant Pilgrim: Defoe's Emblematic Method and Quest for Form in "Robinson Crusoe," Johns Hopkins Press, 1966; (editor) Daniel Defoe, *Moll Flanders* (critical edition), Crowell, 1970; (editor) *Norton Introduction to Literature,* Norton, 1973, 3rd edition, 1981; *Norton Introduction to Poetry,* Norton, 1973, 2nd edition, 1981; *Occasional Form: Henry Fielding and the Chains of Circumstance,* Johns Hopkins University Press, 1975. Contributor to *Philological Quarterly, Review of English Studies, Journal of English and Germanic Philology, Novel,* and *Scriblerian.*

WORK IN PROGRESS: A book on the origins of the English novel.

* * *

HURD, Clement 1908-

PERSONAL: Born January 12, 1908, in New York, N.Y.; son of Richard M. (a mortgage banker) and Lucy (Gazzam) Hurd;

married Edith Thacher (a writer), June 24, 1939; children: John Thacher. *Education:* Yale University, Ph.B., 1930; studied painting in Paris with Fernand Leger, 1931-33. *Home:* 30 Mountain Lane, Mill Valley, Calif. 94941. *Agent:* Curtis Brown Ltd., 575 Madison Ave., New York, N.Y. 10022.

CAREER: Illustrator and writer. *Military service:* U.S. Army, 1942-46.

WRITINGS: Town, W. R. Scott, 1939; *Country,* W. R. Scott, 1939; *The Race,* Random House, 1940, published as *The Race Between the Monkey and the Duck,* Wonder Books, 1946; *The Merry Chase,* Random House, 1941; *Run, Run, Run,* Harper, 1951.

Illustrator: Margaret Wise Brown, *Bumble Bugs and Elephants,* W. R. Scott, 1938, revised edition, 1941; Gertrude Stein, *The World Is Round,* limited autographed edition, W. R. Scott, 1939; Brown, *Runaway Bunny,* Harper, 1942; Brown, *Goodnight Moon,* Harper, 1947; Brown, *The Bad Little Duckhunter,* W. R. Scott, 1947; Morrell Gipson, *Hello Peter,* Doubleday, 1948; Brown, *My World,* Harper, 1949; Brown, *The Peppermint Family,* Harper, 1950; Jane Siepmann, *Lion on Scott Street,* Oxford University Press, 1952; Brown, *Little Brass Band,* Harper, 1955; Brown, *Diggers,* Harper, 1960; May Garelick, *Winter's Birds,* W. R. Scott, 1965; Edna Mitchell Preston, *Monkey in the Jungle,* Viking, 1968; G. Cowles, *Nicholas,* Seabury, 1975.

All written by wife, Edna Thacher Hurd; published by Lothrop, except as indicated: *Hurry, Hurry,* W. R. Scott, 1938, published as *Hurry Hurry: A Story of What Happened to a Hurrier,* 1947, enlarged edition published as *Hurry Hurry,* Harper, 1960; *Engine, Engine, No. 9,* 1940; *Sky High,* 1941; *The Annie Moran,* 1942; *Speedy, the Hook and Ladder Truck,* 1942; *Benny the Bulldozer,* 1947, E. M. Hale, 1956; *Toughy and His Trailer Truck,* 1948; *Willy's Farm,* 1949.

Caboose, 1950; *Old Silversides,* 1951; *St. George's Day in Williamsburg, Va.,* Colonial Williamsburg, 1952; *Somebody's House,* 1953; *Nino and His Fish,* 1954; *The Devil's Tail: Adventures of a Printer's Apprentice in Early Williamsburg,* Doubleday, 1954; *The Cat from Telegraph Hill,* 1955; *Mr. Charlie's Chicken House,* Lippincott, 1955; *Mr. Charlie's Gas Station,* Lippincott, 1956; *Windy and the Willow Whistle,* Sterling, 1956; *Mary's Scary House,* Sterling, 1956; *It's Snowing,* Sterling, 1957; *Mr. Charlie's Camping Trip,* Lippincott, 1957; *Johnny Littlejohn,* 1957; *Fox in a Box,* Doubleday, 1957; *Mr. Charlie, the Fireman's Friend,* Lippincott, 1958; *The Faraway Christmas: A Story of the Farallon Islands,* 1958; *Mr. Charlie's Pet Shop,* Lippincott, 1959; *Last One Home Is a Green Pig,* Harper, 1959.

Published by Harper, except as indicated: *Mr. Charlie's Farm,* Lippincott, 1960; *Stop, Stop,* 1961; *Come and Have Fun,* 1962; *Christmas Eve,* 1962; *No Funny Business,* 1962; *Follow Tomas,* Dial, 1963; *The Day the Sun Danced,* 1965; *Johnny Lion's Book,* 1965; *The So-So Cat,* 1965; *What Whale? Where?,* 1966; *Little Dog Dreaming,* 1967; *The Blue Heron Tree,* Viking, 1968; *Rain and the Valley,* Coward, 1968; *This Is the Forest,* Coward, 1969.

Johnny Lion's Bad Day, 1970; *Catfish,* Viking, 1970; *The Mother Beaver,* Little, Brown, 1971; *Wilson's World,* 1971; *The Mother Deer,* Little, Brown, 1972; *Johnny Lion's Rubber Boots,* 1972; *The Mother Whale,* Little, Brown, 1973; *Catfish and the Kidnapped Cat,* 1974; *The Mother Owl,* Little, Brown, 1974; *The Mother Kangaroo,* Little, Brown, 1976; *Look for a Bird,* 1977; *The Mother Chimpanzee,* Little, Brown, 1977; *Dinosaur My Darling,* 1978.

The Black Dog Who Went into the Woods, 1980; *Under the Lemon Tree,* 1980.

BIOGRAPHICAL/CRITICAL SOURCES: Charlotte S. Huck and D. A. Young, *Children's Literature in the Elementary School,* Holt, 1961; *The Children's Bookshelf,* Bantam, 1965; *Publishers Weekly,* February 7, 1966.

* * *

HURD, Edith (Thacher) 1910-
(Juniper Sage, a joint pseudonym)

PERSONAL: Born September 14, 1910, in Kansas City, Mo.; daughter of Hamilton John and Edith (Gilman) Thacher; married Clement Hurd (an artist and illustrator), June 24, 1939; children: John Thacher. *Education:* Radcliffe College, A.B., 1933; attended Bank Street College of Education, 1934. *Politics:* Democrat. *Home:* 30 Mountain Lane, Mill Valley, Calif. 94941. *Agent:* Marilyn Marlow, Curtis Brown Ltd., 575 Madison Ave., New York, N.Y. 10022.

CAREER: Writer. Taught four years at the Dalton School, New York, N.Y.; U.S. Office of War Information, San Francisco, Calif., news analyst, 1942-45.

WRITINGS: The Wreck of the Wild Wave, Oxford University Press, 1942; *Jerry, the Jeep,* Lothrop, 1945; *The Galleon from Manila,* Oxford University Press, 1949; *Mr. Shortsleeves' Great Big Store,* Simon & Schuster, 1952; *The Golden Hind,* Crowell, 1960; *Sandpipers,* Crowell, 1961; *Starfish,* Crowell, 1962; *Sailors, Whalers and Steamers,* Lane, 1964; *Who Will Be Mine?,* Golden Gate, 1966; *Come with Me to Nursery School,* Coward, 1970; *The White Horse,* Harper, 1970; *I Dance in My Red Pajamas,* Harper, 1982.

With Margaret Wise Brown: (Under joint pseudonym Juniper Sage) *The Man in the Manhole and the Fix-it Men,* W. R. Scott, 1946; *Five Little Firemen,* Simon & Schuster, 1948; *Two Little Miners,* Simon & Schuster, 1949; *The Little Fat Policeman,* Simon & Schuster, 1950.

All illustrated by husband, Clement Hurd; published by Lothrop, except as indicated: *Hurry, Hurry,* W. R. Scott, 1938, published as *Hurry Hurry: A Story of What Happened to a Hurrier,* 1947, enlarged edition published as *Hurry Hurry,* Harper, 1960; *Engine, Engine, No. 9,* 1940; *Sky High,* 1941; *The Annie Moran,* 1942; *Speedy, the Hook and Ladder Truck,* 1942; *Benny the Bulldozer,* 1947, E. M. Hale, 1956; *Toughy and His Trailer Truck,* 1948; *Willy's Farm,* 1949.

Caboose, 1950; *Old Silversides,* 1951; *St. George's Day in Williamsburg, Va.,* Colonial Williamsburg, 1952; *Somebody's House,* 1953; *Nino and His Fish,* 1954; *The Devil's Tail: Adventures of a Printer's Apprentice in Early Williamsburg,* Doubleday, 1954; *The Cat from Telegraph Hill,* 1955; *Mr. Charlie's Chicken House,* Lippincott, 1955; *Mr. Charlie's Gas Station,* Lippincott, 1956; *Windy and the Willow Whistle,* Sterling, 1956; *Mary's Scary House,* Sterling, 1956; *It's Snowing,* Sterling, 1957; *Mr. Charlie's Camping Trip,* Lippincott, 1957; *Johnny Littlejohn,* 1957; *Fox in a Box,* Doubleday, 1957; *Mr. Charlie, the Fireman's Friend,* Lippincott, 1958; *The Faraway Christmas: A Story of the Farallon Islands,* 1958; *Mr. Charlie's Pet Shop,* Lippincott, 1959; *Last One Home Is a Green Pig,* Harper, 1959.

Published by Harper, except as indicated: *Mr. Charlie's Farm,* Lippincott, 1960; *Stop, Stop,* 1961; *Come and Have Fun,* 1962;

Christmas Eve, 1962; *No Funny Business,* 1962; *Follow Tomas,* Dial, 1963; *The Day the Sun Danced,* 1965; *Johnny Lion's Book,* 1965; *The So-So Cat,* 1965; *What Whale? Where?,* 1966; *Little Dog Dreaming,* 1967; *The Blue Heron Tree,* Viking, 1968; *Rain and the Valley,* Coward, 1968; *This Is the Forest,* Coward, 1969.

Johnny Lion's Bad Day, 1970; *Catfish,* Viking, 1970; *The Mother Beaver,* Little, Brown, 1971; *Wilson's World,* 1971; *The Mother Deer,* Little, Brown, 1972; *Johnny Lion's Rubber Boots,* 1972; *The Mother Whale,* Little, Brown, 1973; *Catfish and the Kidnapped Cat,* 1974; *The Mother Owl,* Little, Brown, 1974; *The Mother Kangaroo,* Little, Brown, 1976; *Look for a Bird,* 1977; *The Mother Chimpanzee,* Little, Brown, 1977; *Dinosaur My Darling,* 1978.

The Black Dog Who Went into the Woods, 1980; *Under the Lemon Tree,* 1980. Contributor of poetry to *Grade Teacher.*

BIOGRAPHICAL/CRITICAL SOURCES: Charlotte S. Huck and D. A. Young, *Children's Literature in the Elementary School,* Holt, 1961; *The Children's Bookshelf,* Bantam, 1965; *Books for Children, 1960-1965,* American Library Association, 1966; Nancy Larrick, *A Parent's Guide to Children's Reading,* 3rd edition, Doubleday, 1969; *New York Times Book Review,* July 27, 1980.

* * *

HUSEN, Torsten 1916-

PERSONAL: Born March 1, 1916, in Lund, Sweden; son of Johan S. (an executive director) and Betty Maria (Prawitz) Husen; married Ingrid Joensson (a language teacher), April 10, 1940; children: Sven-Torsten, Mats O., Goerel. *Education:* University of Lund, B.A., 1937, M.A., 1938, Fil.lic., 1941, Ph.D., 1944. *Home:* Armfeltsgatan 10, S-11534 Stockholm, Sweden. *Office:* University of Stockholm, S-10691 Stockholm, Sweden.

CAREER: University of Stockholm, Stockholm, Sweden, reader, 1947-52, professor of educational psychology, 1953-56, professor of education and director of Institute of Educational Research, 1959-71, professor of international education, 1971-81, professor emeritus, 1982—. Visiting professor, University of Chicago, 1959, University of Hawaii, 1968, Ontario Institute for Studies in Education, 1971, and Stanford University, 1981. Chairman of governing board, International Institute for Educational Planning, 1970-80. Member of panel of scientific advisers to Swedish Government, 1963-69. Adviser to Minister of Education on Swedish school reform, 1957-65. Consultant to Organization for Economic Co-operation and Development, 1968—. *Military service:* Swedish Armed Forces, senior psychologist, 1944-51.

MEMBER: International Association for the Evaluation of Educational Achievement (chairman), National Academy of Education (United States; foreign associate), Swedish Royal Academy of Sciences.

AWARDS, HONORS: Prize for educational authorship, Swedish Literary Foundation, 1961; fellow, Center for Advanced Study of the Behavioral Sciences, 1965-66 and 1973-74; medal for distinguished service, Teachers College, Columbia University, 1969; honorary degrees from University of Chicago, 1967, Brunel University, 1974, University of Glasgow, 1974, University of Rhode Island, 1975, University of Joensuu, 1979, and University of Amsterdam, 1982; fellow, National Center for the Humanities, 1978-79.

WRITINGS: *Psykologisk krigfoering,* C.W.K. Gleerup, 1942; *Adolescensen: Undersoekningar roerande manlig svensk ungdom i aaldern 17-20 aar,* Almqvist & Wiksell, 1944; *Studier roerande de eidetiska fenomenen,* C.W.K. Gleerup, Volume I, 1946, Volume II, 1952; *Begavning och miljo: Studier i begavningsutvecklingens och begavningsurvalets psykologisk-pedagogiska och sociala problem,* H. Geber, 1948; *Om innerborden av psykologiska matningar: Nagra bidrag till psykometrikens metodlara,* C.W.K. Gleerup, 1949; *Anders Berg under folkskolans pionjaeraar,* Erlanders Bookstore, 1949.

Raettstavningsfoermagans psykologi: Nagra experimentella bidrag, Svensk Lararetidnings Forlag, 1950; *Testresultatens prognosvarde: En Undersokning av den teoretiska skolningens inverkan pa testresultaten, intelligenstedens prognosvarde och de sociala faktorernas inverkan pa urvalet till hogre laroanstalter,* H. Geber, 1950; (with Sven-Eric Henricson) *Some Principles of Construction of Group Intelligence Tests for Adults: A Report on Construction and Standardization of the Swedish Induction Test (the I-test),* Almqvist & Wiksell, 1951; *Tvillingstudier: Undersoekningar roerande begavningsforhallanden, skolprestationer, intraparrelationer, antropometriska matt, handstilslikhet samt diagnosproblem m.m. inom e reprensentativ population likkonade tvillingar,* Almqvist & Wiksell, 1953; *Psykologi,* Svenska Bokforlaget, 1954, 5th edition with Lars Larsson, 1966.

(With others) *Betyg och standardprov: En orientering for foraldrar och larare,* Almqvist & Wiksell, 1956; (with others) *Standardproven: En redogoerelse foer konstruktion och standardisering,* Almqvist & Wiksell, 1956; *Militart och civilt,* Norstedt, 1956; *Ur psykologisk synvinkel,* Almqvist & Wiksell, 1957; *Pedagogisk psykologi,* Svenska Bokforlaget, 1957, 4th edition, 1968; (with Artur Olsson) *Akademiska studier: Studieteknik for studenter,* Svenska Bokforlaget, 1958; *Psychological Twin Research: A Methodological Study,* Almqvist & Wiksell, 1959; *Att undervisa studenter,* Almqvist & Wiksell, 1959; (editor with Sten Henrysson) *Differentiation and Guidance in the Comprehensive School: Report on the Sigtuna Course Organized by the Swedish Government under the Auspices of the Council of Europe, August, 1958,* Almqvist & Wiksell, 1959.

(With Urban Dahllof) *Matematik och modersmaalet i skola och yrkesliv: Studier av kunskapskrav, kunskapsbehallning och undervisningens upplaggning,* Studieforbundet Naringsliv och Samhalle, 1960, translation published as *Mathematics and Communication Skills in School and Society: An Empirical Approach to the Problem of Curriculum Contest,* Industrial Council for Social and Economic Studies, 1960; *Psykologi, introduktion til psykologien af i dag,* A. Busck, 1960; *Skolan i ett foranderligt samhalle,* Almqvist & Wiksell, 1961, 2nd edition, 1963; *De Farliga psykologerna,* Raben & Sjogren, 1961; *Studieteknik foer gymnasiet,* Svenska Bokforlaget, 1961; (with Elvy Johanson) *Fysik och kemi i skola och yrkesliv,* Studienfoerbundet Naaringsliv och Samhalle, 1961; *School Reform in Sweden,* U.S. Department of Health, Education and Welfare, 1961; *Tonaaringarna i utbildningssamhaelle: Nagra maenniska ocho miljoe: Studier i Amerikansk pedagogik,* Almqvist & Wiksell, 1962; (with Gosta Ekman) *Att studera psykologi och pedagogik,* Svenska Bokforlaget, 1962; *Problems of Differentiation in Swedish Compulsory Schooling,* Svenska Bokforlaget, 1962; (with Malcolm Shepherd Knowles) *Erwachsene lernen,* E. Klett, 1963; *Skola foer 60-talet,* Almqvist & Wiksell, 1963; (with Gunnar Boalt) *Skolans sociologi,* Almqvist & Wiksell, 1964, 3rd edition, 1967; *Det nya gymnasiet: Information och debatt,* Almqvist & Wiksell, 1964.

(With Karl-Erik Warneryd) *Psykologi for fackskolan,* Svenska Bokforlaget, 1966; *Skola i foervandling,* Almqvist & Wiksell, 1966; (editor with Ingvar Carlson) *Tonaringarna och skolan,* Almqvist & Wiksell, 1966; (editor) *International Study of Achievement in Mathematics: A Comparison of Twelve Countries,* Wiley, 1967; (with Boalt) *Educational Research and Educational Change: The Case of Sweden,* Wiley, 1968; *Skola foe 80,* Almqvist & Wiksell, 1968; (compiler) *Livsaaskaadning och religion,* Svenska Bokforlaget, 1968; *Talent, Opportunity and Career: A Twenty-six Year Follow-Up of 1500 Individuals,* Almqvist & Wiksell, 1969; (compiler with Sune Askaner) *Litteratur: Konst och musik,* Laromedelsforlaget, 1969.

(Compiler with Ulf Hard af Segerstad) *Samhaallsfraagor: Planering ocho miljoe,* Laromedelsforlaget, 1971; *Present Trends and Future Developments in Education: A European Perspective,* Ontario Institute for Studies in Education, 1971; *Utbildning ar 2000,* Bonniers, 1971; *Social Background and Educational Career: Research Perspectives on Equality of Educational Opportunity,* Organization for Economic Co-operation and Development, 1972; *Skolans kris ocha andra uppsatser om utbildning,* Almqvist & Wiksell, 1972; *Svensk skola i internationell belysning: Naturorienterande amnen,* Almqvist & Wiksell, 1973; *Talent, Equality and Meritocracy,* Nijhoff, 1974; *The Learning Society,* Methuen, 1974; *Social Influences on Educational Attainment,* Organization for Economic Co-operation and Development, 1975; *Universiteten och forskningen,* Natur och Kultur, 1975; *The School in Question,* Oxford University Press, 1979.

The Future of Formal Education, Almqvist & Wiksell, 1980; *En obotlig akademiker* (memoirs), Natur och Kultur, 1981, translation published as *An Incurable Academic,* Pergamon, 1982.

Co-editor-in-chief, *International Encyclopedia of Education: Research and Studies;* editor, *Scandinavian Encyclopedia of Psychology and Education;* member, international board of consultants, *World Book Encyclopedia.*

WORK IN PROGRESS: The Relationships between Researchers and Policymakers in Education.

SIDELIGHTS: In an article entitled "Marriage to Higher Education" in the *Journal of Higher Education,* Torsten Husen writes: "I can hardly think of any other group in society to which the principle of lifelong learning applies more adequately than to academics involved in advanced teaching and research. In essence, to be involved in research means that one constantly has to revise ideas and restructure models of reality and incessantly move into new intellectual territory. A university professor is never 'fully prepared' or 'competent.' One has to prove oneself continuously. The most salient feature of the professorial role is that of a permanent student who is involved in continuous learning, not least from one's own students of whom the more able often are the initiators of new paradigms of thinking in the discipline."

Utbildning ar 2000 has been translated into Polish, Russian, Arabic and Hindi; *The Learning Society* has been translated into Dutch, Italian, and Spanish; *The School in Question* has been translated into Swedish, Danish, German, Spanish, and Japanese.

AVOCATIONAL INTERESTS: Collecting old books.

BIOGRAPHICAL/CRITICAL SOURCES: Journal of Higher Education, Volume LI, number 6, 1980; Torsten Husen, *An Incurable Academic,* Pergamon, 1982.

HUSSEY, David Edward 1934-

PERSONAL: Born June 28, 1934, in London, England; son of Walter and Alma (Pearl) Hussey; married Evelyn Dorothy Wilson, April 23, 1960; children: Dorothy Anne, Susan Catherine. *Education:* Chartered Institute of Secretaries, A.C.I.S., 1957; University of South Africa, B.Com., 1966. *Religion:* Methodist. *Home:* 44 Forestfield, Horsham, Sussex, England. *Office:* Harbridge House Europe, 3 Hanover Sq., London W1R 9RD, England.

CAREER: Employed by Government of Rhodesia and Nyasaland, 1951-64; Union Carbide, London, England, project analyst, 1964-67; Fyffs Group (United Fruit), London, planning manager, 1967-69; planning manager at Wander Ltd. and Sandoz Ltd., 1969-72; Otis Elevator Co. Ltd., London, planning and personnel manager, 1972-75; Harbridge House Europe (management consultants), London, senior vice-president and managing partner, 1976—. *Military service:* Rhodesian Territorials, 1952-64. *Member:* Society for Long Range Planning (past vice-chairman; member of executive committee, 1967—). *Awards, honors:* Co-winner, John Player Management Author of the Year award, 1974, for *Corporate Planning: Theory and Practice.*

WRITINGS—Published by Pergamon, except as indicated: *Introducing Corporate Planning,* 1971, 2nd edition, 1979; *Corporate Planning for Distribution,* International Journal of Physical Distribution, 1973; *Corporate Planning: Theory and Practice,* 1974, 2nd edition, 1982; (editor) *Corporate Planner's Yearbook,* 1974, 2nd edition, 1979; *Inflation and Business Policy,* Longman, 1976; (with M. J. Langham) *Corporate Planning: The Human Factor,* 1978; *Corporate Planning in Inflationary Conditions: A Guide for Accountants,* Institute of Cost and Management Accountants, 1980; (editor with Bernard Taylor) *The Realities of Planning,* 1981; *Corporate Planning: An Introduction for Accountants,* Institute of Chartered Accountants in England and Wales, 1981. Also author of *Corporate Planning: The Research.*

Contributor: Martin Christopher and Gordon Wills, editors, *Marketing Logistics and Distribution Planning,* Allen & Unwin, 1972; Philip Sadler and Alan Robson, editors, *Corporate Planning,* Institute of Cost and Management Accountants, 1973; Peter Baynes, editor, *Case Studies in Corporate Planning,* Pitman, 1973; Subhash Jain and Surendra Singhvi, editors, *Essentials of Corporate Planning,* Planning Executives Institute, 1973; Stanley Oliver, editor, *Accountant's Guide to Management Techniques,* Gower Press, 1975; Taylor and David Farmer, editors, *Corporate Planning and Procurement,* Halsted Press, 1975; H. Steinmann, editor, *Plannung und Kontrolle,* Verlag Vahlen, 1981; J. Worsley, editor, *Business Matters,* Cassell and BBC Publications, in press.

Author of column "Brief Case," in *Long Range Planning.* Contributor of more than twenty-five articles to scholarly journals, including *Accountant, Long Range Planning, Director, Financial Times, International Journal of Physical Distribution,* and *Works Management.*

WORK IN PROGRESS: A book on social responsibility in business decision-making, with Lyn Wilson; "sporadic research, as time permits," on smuggling activities in Sussex during the eighteenth century.

SIDELIGHTS: When the Rhodesian Federation broke up, it dissolved what was to David Edward Hussey a worthwhile experiment in racial partnership, so he went to England to live.

Introducing Corporate Planning has been translated into French, Spanish, and Hungarian.

AVOCATIONAL INTERESTS: His family, the countryside, gardening, antique maps, reading, history, travel (has been to Australia, New Zealand, Jamaica, Singapore, and to much of Africa and Europe).

BIOGRAPHICAL/CRITICAL SOURCES: Financial Times, February 19, 1971; *International Management,* March, 1971, April, 1972; *Bulawayo Chronicle,* May, 1971; *Business International Money Report,* January 5, 1979; *Professional Administration,* April, 1979.

* * *

HUTTON, Warwick 1939-

PERSONAL: Born July 17, 1939; son of John (an artist) and Helen (Blair) Hutton; married Elizabeth Mills, August 26, 1965; children: Hanno, Lily. *Education:* Colchester Art School, N.D.D., 1961. *Politics:* None. *Religion:* None. *Residence:* Cambridge, England.

CAREER: Illustrator, painter, and glass engraver. Visiting lecturer, Cambridge College of Art and Technology, 1972—, and Morley College, 1973-75. *Awards, honors: The Nose Tree* was chosen by the *New York Times* as one of the ten best picture books of the year in 1981.

WRITINGS: Making Woodcuts, St. Martin's, 1974; (reteller and illustrator) *Noah and the Great Flood,* Atheneum, 1977; (reteller and illustrator) *Sleeping Beauty,* Atheneum, 1979; (reteller and illustrator) *The Nose Tree,* Atheneum, 1981.

WORK IN PROGRESS: A book about Jonah.

SIDELIGHTS: Warwick Hutton told *CA:* "I am a full-time artist. Although I am primarily a painter, the large-scale glass engraving technique which my father invented has been passed on to me. When I am not occupied with painting and woodcuts, I carry out commissioned glass engravings for civic buildings, churches, homes, etc."

The story of *The Nose Tree,* a German folktale about three soldiers and a wicked princess, is "brought to life" by Warwick Hutton's illustrations, according to Karla Kuskin in the *New York Times Book Review.* "Painting with unusual grace, he sketches figures as convincingly as he lays out a far-reaching landscape or delineates a castle chamber."

BIOGRAPHICAL/CRITICAL SOURCES: New York Times Book Review, November 29, 1981; *New York Times,* November 30, 1981.

* * *

HYMAN, Ronald T. 1933-

PERSONAL: Born October 16, 1933, in Chicago, Ill.; son of Maurice H. (a salesman) and Matilda (Grossman) Hyman; married Suzanne Linda Katz, February 13, 1958; children: Jonathan, Elana, Rachel. *Education:* University of Miami, Coral Gables, Fla., B.A., 1955; Vanderbilt University and George Peabody College for Teachers, M.A.T., 1956; Columbia University, Ed.D., 1965. *Politics:* Liberal. *Religion:* Jewish. *Home:* 227 Lincoln Ave., Highland Park, N.J. 08904. *Office:* Graduate School of Education, Rutgers University, New Brunswick, N.J. 08903.

CAREER: Public school teacher, 1956-62; Columbia University, New York, N.Y., research assistant, 1962-64; Queens College of the City University of New York, Flushing, N.Y., assistant professor, 1964-66; Rutgers University, New Brunswick, N.J., associate professor, 1966-74, professor of education, 1974—, chairperson of department of science and humanities education in Graduate School of Education, 1977-80. Visiting summer professor at Hofstra University, 1965 and 1966. Member of State Advisory Council for Gifted and Talented Education. Conductor of workshops on teaching strategies and teacher supervision and evaluation. *Member:* Association for Supervision and Curriculum Development, American Educational Research Association, National Society for the Study of Education, National Council for the Social Studies, American Association of University Professors, Curriculum Theory Network, Association of Teacher Educators, New Jersey Association for Supervision and Curriculum Development (member of executive board).

WRITINGS: The Principles of Contemporary Education, Monarch, 1966; (with A. A. Bellack, H. M. Kliebard, and F. L. Smith) *The Language of the Classroom,* Teachers College Press, 1966; (editor) *Teaching: Vantage Points for Study,* Lippincott, 1968, 2nd edition, 1974; *Ways of Teaching,* Lippincott, 1970, 2nd edition, 1974; (editor) *Contemporary Thought on Teaching,* Prentice-Hall, 1971; (editor with Maurie Hillson) *Change and Innovation in Elementary and Secondary Organization,* 2nd edition (Hyman was not associated with previous edition), Holt, 1971; (editor) *Approaches in Curriculum,* Prentice-Hall, 1973; (editor with Samuel L. Baily and contributor) *Perspectives on Latin America,* Macmillan, 1974.

School Administrator's Handbook of Teacher Supervision and Evaluation Methods, Prentice-Hall, 1975; (with Alan Teplitsky) *Walk in My Shoes,* Prentice-Hall, 1976; *Paper, Pencils, and Pennies: Games for Learning and Having Fun,* Prentice-Hall, 1977; (with Allan Pessin) *The Securities Industry,* New York Institute of Finance, 1977; (with Kevin Goldstein-Jackson and Norman Rudnick) *Experiments with Everyday Objects: Science Activities for Children, Parents, and Teachers,* Prentice-Hall, 1978; *Simulation Gaming for Values Education: The Prisoner's Dilemma,* University Press of America, 1978; *Strategic Questioning,* Prentice-Hall, 1979; *Improving Discussion Leadership,* Teachers College Press, 1980.

Co-general editor of "Latin America Social Studies" series for Macmillan, 1974-75; advisory editor of "Spectrum Series in Applied Education" for Prentice-Hall. Contributor of articles and reviews to education journals, including *Contemporary Education, Elementary School Journal, Journal of Teacher Education, Media and Methods, Notre Dame Journal of Education,* and *Teachers College Record.*

I

INGE, M(ilton) Thomas 1936-

PERSONAL: Surname rhymes with "fringe"; born March 18, 1936, in Newport News, Va.; son of Clyde Elmo and Bernice Lucille (Jackson) Inge; married Betty Jean Meredith, December 28, 1958 (divorced, April 20, 1977); married Tonette Long Bond, June 12, 1982; children: (first marriage) Scott Thomas; (stepchildren) Michael Gordon Bond. *Education:* Randolph-Macon College, B.A., 1959; Vanderbilt University, M.A., 1960, Ph.D., 1964. *Home address:* P.O. Box 1298, 332 Stony Creek Dr., Clemson, S.C. 29633. *Office:* Department of English, 101 Strode Tower, Clemson University, Clemson, S.C. 29631.

CAREER: Irby Studio, Richmond, Va., free-lance commercial artist, 1953-55; Virginia State Department of Highways, Richmond, traffic technician, summers, 1956-58; Vanderbilt University, Nashville, Tenn., instructor in English, 1962-64; Michigan State University, East Lansing, 1964-69, began as assistant professor, became associate professor of American thought and language; Virginia Commonwealth University, Richmond, 1969-80, began as associate professor, became professor of English, chairman of department, 1974-80; Clemson University, Clemson, S.C., professor of English and head of department, 1980—. Fulbright lecturer in American literature, University of Salamanca, Spain, 1967-68, Buenos Aires, Argentina, 1971, and Moscow State University, 1979; visiting associate professor, Vanderbilt University, summer, 1969.

MEMBER: American Studies Association, Modern Language Association of America, American Humor Studies Association, Children's Literature Association, South Atlantic Modern Language Association, Society for the Study of Southern Literature, Popular Culture Association, The Ellen Glasgow Society, The Melville Society, Phi Beta Kappa, Omicron Delta Kappa, Pi Delta Epsilon, Lambda Chi Alpha.

WRITINGS: (With Thomas Daniel Young) *Donald Davidson: An Essay and a Bibliography,* Vanderbilt University Press, 1965; (editor) George Washington Harris, *Sut Lovingood's Yarns,* College and University Press, 1966; *Publications of the Faculty of the University College: A Bibliography,* Michigan State University, 1966; (editor) Harris, *High Times and Hard Times, Sketches and Tales,* Vanderbilt University Press, 1967; (editor) *Agrarianism in American Literature,* Odyssey Press, 1969; (editor) John Donald Wade, *Augustus Baldwin Longstreet: A Study of the Development of Culture in the South,* revised edition, University of Georgia Press, 1969; (editor) *Honors College Essays 1967-68,* Michigan State University Honors College, 1969; (editor with others) *The Black Experience: Readings in Afro-American History and Culture from Colonial Times through the Nineteenth Century,* Michigan State University Press, 1969.

(Editor) William Faulkner, *A Rose for Emily,* C. E. Merrill, 1970; (editor) Richmond Croom Beatty, *William Byrd of Westover,* Archon Books, 1970; (editor) *The Merrill Studies in "Light in August,"* C. E. Merrill, 1971; (with Young) *Donald Davidson,* Twayne, 1971; (editor) *Virginia Commonwealth University Self-Study,* Virginia Commonwealth University, 1972; (editor) *The Frontier Humorists: Critical Views,* Archon Books, 1975; (editor) *Ellen Glasgow: Centennial Essays,* University Press of Virginia, 1976; (editor with Maurice Duke and Jackson R. Bryer) *Black American Writers: Bibliographical Essays,* two volumes, St. Martin's, 1978; (editor and contributor) *Handbook of American Popular Culture,* three volumes, Greenwood Press, 1978-81; (editor) *Bartelby the Inscrutable: A Collection of Commentary on Herman Melville's Tale,* Archon Books, 1979.

(Editor and contributor) *Concise Histories of American Popular Culture,* Greenwood Press, 1982; (editor with Edgar E. MacDonald) *James Branch Cabell: Centennial Essays,* Louisiana State University Press, 1982; (editor with Duke and Bryer) *American Women Writers: Bibliographic Essays,* Greenwood Press, 1983.

Contributor: Donald Davidson, editor, *Concise American Composition and Rhetoric,* Scribner, 1964, fifth edition, 1968; Louis D. Rubin, Jr., and C. Hugh Holman, editors, *Southern Literary Study: Problems and Possibilities,* University of North Carolina Press, 1975; Peter Marzio, editor, *A Nation of Nations,* Harper, 1976; (author of introduction) George Herriman, *Baron Bean: A Complete Compilation,* Hyperion Press, 1977; James Vinson, editor, *Great Writers of the English Language: Novelists and Prose Writers,* St. Martin's, 1979.

General editor of "American Critical Tradition" series for Burt Franklin & Co., 1973-79, research guide series for St. Martin's, 1975-76, and reference guide series in popular culture for Greenwood Press, 1978—. Contributor to *The Lovingood Papers 1963, 1964, and 1965,* edited by Ben Harris McClary,

University of Tennessee Press, *American Literary Scholarship: An Annual 1970, 1971, 1972, and 1973,* edited by J. Albert Robbins, Duke University Press, *Southern Writers: A Biographical Dictionary,* edited by Robert Bain and others, Louisiana State University Press, 1979, and *Dictionary of Literary Biography,* Volume XI: *American Humorists, 1800-1950,* edited by Stanley Trachtenberg, Gale, 1982. Book reviewer for *Nashville Tennessean, Richmond Times-Dispatch, Menomonee Falls Gazette, Choice,* and *Books for Children.* Contributor of essays, articles, and reviews to numerous scholarly journals, including *American Literature, Journal of Ethnic Studies, Journal of Popular Culture, Tennessee Studies in Literature, Georgia Review,* and *Encounter.* Founding editor of *Resources for American Literary Study,* 1971-79, and of *American Humor: An Interdisciplinary Newsletter,* 1974-80.

WORK IN PROGRESS: American Comic Art: A Reference Guide and a revised edition of *Handbook of Popular Culture,* both for Greenwood Press; editing *Encyclopedia of Southern Culture* for University of North Carolina Press; contributions to *History of Southern Literature,* Louisiana State University Press; other projects on the critical reception of William Faulkner, Faulkner in the Soviet Union, the history and development of the comic book, comic art, Walt Disney, and American humor.

SIDELIGHTS: M. Thomas Inge told *CA:* "I consider myself primarily a literary and cultural historian with strong interests in editing, bibliography, and criticism. Clarifying events, ascertaining the facts, and establishing the bibliographic record are essential preliminary steps in understanding and appreciating our cultural heritage. My interests range widely through nineteenth- and twentieth-century American literature and culture with specific focuses on American humor, Southern and ethnic writing, twentieth-century fiction, American literature abroad, popular culture, comic art, biography, and intellectual history."

* * *

IPCAR, Dahlov (Zorach) 1917-

PERSONAL: Born November 12, 1917, in Windsor, Vt.; daughter of William (a sculptor) and Marguerite (a painter; maiden name, Thompson) Zorach; married Adolph Ipcar (a dairy farmer), September 29, 1936; children: Robert William, Charles. *Education:* Attended Oberlin College, 1933-34. *Home and office:* Robinhood Farm, Star Route 2, Bath, Me. 04530. *Agent:* McIntosh & Otis, Inc., 475 Fifth Ave., New York, N.Y. 10017.

CAREER: Artist; author and illustrator of children's books. Had first one-woman show, 1939, in Museum of Modern Art's Young People's Gallery; since then her oils, collages, and cloth sculptures have been exhibited at more than forty one-woman shows, six of them in New York City, and included in group shows at Corcoran Gallery of Art, Carnegie Institute, Boston Art Festival, and elsewhere; oils are in the permanent collections of Metropolitan Museum, Whitney Museum, Brooklyn Museum, Newark Museum, Colby College, University of Maine, Westbrook College, and other private and public collections; work also includes two murals for U.S. Treasury Department, Washington, D.C. *Member:* American Civil Liberties Union, Citizens for Safe Power (director), Bath-Brunswick Regional Arts Council (director, 1971-73). *Awards, honors:* Maine State Award, Maine Commission of Arts and Humanities, 1972; D.H.L., University of Maine, 1978; Deborah Morton Award, Westbrook College, 1978; D.F.A., Colby College, 1980.

WRITINGS—Juveniles; self-illustrated: *Animal Hide and Seek,* Scott, 1947; *One Horse Farm,* Doubleday, 1950; *World Full of Horses,* Doubleday, 1955; *The Wonderful Egg,* Doubleday, 1958; *Ten Big Farms,* Knopf, 1958; *Brown Cow Farm,* Doubleday, 1959.

I Like Animals, Knopf, 1960; *Stripes and Spots,* Doubleday, 1961; *Deep Sea Farm,* Knopf, 1961; *Wild and Tame Animals,* Doubleday, 1962; *Lobsterman,* Knopf, 1962; *Black and White,* Knopf, 1963; *I Love My Anteater with an A,* Knopf, 1964; *Horses of Long Ago,* Doubleday, 1965; *Calico Jungle,* Knopf, 1965; *Bright Barnyard,* Knopf, 1966; *The Song of the Day Birds and the Night Birds,* Doubleday, 1967; *Whisperings and Other Things,* Knopf, 1967; *Wild Whirlwind,* Knopf, 1968; *The Cat at Night,* Doubleday, 1969.

The Marvelous Merry-go-round, Doubleday, 1970; *Sir Addlepate and the Unicorn,* Doubleday, 1971; *The Cat Came Back,* Knopf, 1971; *The Biggest Fish in the Sea,* Viking, 1972; *A Flood of Creatures,* Holiday House, 1973; *The Land of Flowers,* Viking, 1974; *Bug City,* Holiday House, 1975; *Hard Scrabble Harvest,* Doubleday, 1976; *Lost and Found,* Doubleday, 1981.

Young adult fiction: *General Felice,* illustrations by Kenneth Longtemps, McGraw, 1967; *The Warlock of Night,* Viking, 1969; *The Queen of Spells,* Viking, 1973; *A Dark Horn Blowing,* Viking, 1978.

Illustrator: Margaret Wise Brown, *The Little Fisherman,* Scott, 1945; Evelyn Beyer, *Just Like You,* Scott, 1946; John G. McCullough, *Good Work,* Scott, 1948.

Contributor of adult short stories to *Texas Quarterly, Yankee,* and *Argosy;* also contributor to *Hornbook.*

SIDELIGHTS: Dahlov Ipcar discusses her approach to writing and art with *CA:* "I illustrated my first children's book in 1945, and after illustrating two others, I went on to write my own stories for children and illustrate them myself. I have always loved animals, and most of my stories as well as my art reflect this. My animal subject matter is not always realistically treated—my ideas are often fanciful. I love to paint complex, exotic jungles.

"As a small child I rejected stories of the 'here and now'; I preferred fantasy and had a very active imagination. All my art is done from imagination, even the 'realistic' works. I feel that reality is more meaningful when transmuted through the artist's mind rather than copied directly, so I have trained my visual memory, and it has freed me to do animals in action, zebras running, antelopes leaping: things one cannot see if one depends on models or on photographs which freeze the action in awkward and ugly shapes.

"I love the marvelous and intricate diversity of nature, and I try to treat it with respect. I try to do the best art I can in my illustrations without shortcuts or playing down to children. I feel even the youngest children deserve the best in art, and while I may stylize animal forms I dislike the present trend of turning everything into cartoons. I believe children should be offered beauty to delight them and ideas to expand their minds.

"I am primarily a visual person; I usually think of pictures first. I pick a subject I would enjoy exploring in pictures, such as coral reef fish, brightly colored bugs, or merry-go-round horses, and then the idea for the written story follows.

"My writing of adult short stories led me into writing novels for teen-agers. This is very different from writing for young children, but in both sorts of writing the poetic feeling of the words, the flow and rhythm, are very important to me. The writing I do for young children is usually cheerful and open; there are no dark, hidden meanings. My writing for older children and adults, however, is different. It is full of strange, grim things, but there is beauty there as well, for I write fantasies and the visual side of me creates beautiful settings for my stories.

"Each of my novels seems to have been written under a strong compulsion, or inspiration. I seem to be writing to fulfill a very personal need to express something, perhaps something inexpressible but nevertheless very important to me emotionally. Symbols reoccur: talking ravens, black bulls, war dogs. To me their meaning is completely mysterious, and I prefer to keep it that way. I transform ordinary reality into a reality that has special meaning to me. I hope it will also have meaning to others."

AVOCATIONAL INTERESTS: Old folk songs, chess, gardening.

BIOGRAPHICAL/CRITICAL SOURCES: Lee Bennett Hopkins, *Books Are by People,* Citation Press, 1969.

* * *

ISAACS, Neil D. 1931-

PERSONAL: Born August 21, 1931, in New York, N.Y.; son of Maurice B. (a wholesale appliance dealer) and Florence (Braun) Isaacs; married Esther Reece Karmazine, December 21, 1953; children: Ian Mark, Jonathan Dean, Daniel Reece, Anne Braun. *Education:* Dartmouth College, A.B., 1953; University of California, Berkeley, A.M., 1956; Brown University, Ph.D., 1959. *Politics and religion:* Secular Humanism. *Home:* 208 Pewter Lane, Colesville, Md. 20904. *Office:* Department of English, University of Maryland, College Park, Md.

CAREER: College of New York (now City College of the City University of New York), New York, N.Y., instructor in English, 1959-63; University of Tennessee, Knoxville, assistant professor, 1963-65, associate professor of English, 1965-71; University of Maryland, College Park, professor of English, 1971—. Has lectured and presented papers throughout the United States; has appeared on television and radio shows. *Member:* Popular Culture Association, South Atlantic Modern Language Association.

WRITINGS: (Editor with Louis H. Leiter) *Approaches to the Short Story,* Chandler Publishing, 1963; *Structural Principles of Old English Poetry,* University of Tennessee Press, 1968; (editor with R. A. Zimbardo and contributor) *Tolkien and the Critics,* University of Notre Dame Press, 1968; *Eudora Welty,* Steck, 1969.

(With Rachel Maddux and Stirling Silliphant) *Fiction into Film: A Walk in the Spring Rain,* University of Tennessee Press, 1970; *All the Moves: A History of College Basketball,* Lippincott, 1975; *Checking Back: A History of N.H.L. Hockey,* Norton, 1977; (editor with Robert J. Higgs) *The Sporting Spirit: Athletes in Literature and Life,* Harcourt, 1977; *Jock Culture, U.S.A.,* Norton, 1978; (with Gerald Strine) *Covering the Spread: How to Beat Pro Football,* Random House, 1978; (with Dick Motta) *Sports Illustrated Basketball,* Harper, 1981; (editor with Zimbardo and contributor) *Tolkien: New Critical Perspectives,* University of Kentucky Press, 1981.

Contributor: *Old English Poetry,* Brown University Press, 1967; Burton Raffel, translator, *Sir Gawain and the Green Knight,* New American Library, 1970; *John McGalliard Festschrift,* University of Notre Dame Press, 1975; *Sport and the Humanities,* Bureau of Educational Research and Service (Knoxville), 1980; *Sports in American Culture,* American Studies Press, 1980; *Modern European Filmmakers and the Art of Adaptation,* Ungar, 1981; *The Short Stories of F. Scott Fitzgerald: Critical Perspectives,* University of Wisconsin Press, in press; *The Contemporary American Novel,* Max Huebler Verlag, in press.

Also author of ten brief items in *Columbia Encyclopedia,* third edition. Also contributor to *Professors on Sports,* edited by Melvin Friedman, in press. Author, with Dick Penner, of song, "Otis, Janis, Jimi, and Me," MusicMusicMusic, Inc., 1972. Author of columns in *Baltimore Sun, Boston Globe, New York Times, Washington Post,* and *Washington Star.* Contributor of poetry, articles, and reviews to periodicals, including *Literature and Psychology, Notes and Queries, Sewanee Review, Victorian Poetry, Mississippi Review, English Studies,* and *Poetry Journal.* Editor, with Eric W. Stockton, of *Tennessee Studies in Literature,* Volume XI: *Medieval Literature,* 1966; consulting editor for film books, University of Tennessee Press, 1973-80; member of editorial board, *Literature/Film Quarterly,* 1973—.

WORK IN PROGRESS: The Great Molinas: A Fictional Memoir; Inventing Myself, a collection of short fiction and other pieces.

BIOGRAPHICAL/CRITICAL SOURCES: National Review, June 17, 1969; *New York Times,* August 7, 1978.

* * *

ISRAEL, Elaine 1945-

PERSONAL: Born January 24, 1945, in New York, N.Y.; daughter of Otto (in electrical devices business) and Kate (Mendle) Israel. *Education:* Bronx Community College of the City University of New York, A.A., 1964; University of Rhode Island, B.A., 1966. *Office:* Scholastic Magazines, 50 West 44th St., New York, N.Y. 10036.

CAREER: Long Island Star Journal, Long Island, N.Y., reporter, 1966-68; Scholastic Magazines, New York, N.Y., writer and associate editor of *Newstime,* 1968—.

WRITINGS—All juveniles; all published by Messner: *The Great Energy Search,* 1974; (with Essie E. Lee) *Alcohol and You,* 1975; *The Hungry World,* 1977; *Up, Over, Under and Around: The New Explorers,* 1980.

SIDELIGHTS: Elaine Israel comments: "Loving to write has been the one constant in my life. There was never a time when I didn't do some kind of writing. As a child, I wrote rather melodramatic short stories. At home I used reams of paper for a newspaper only a few understanding friends were allowed to read. My first ambition was to be a great reporter, like the late war correspondent Marguerite Higgins. I kept diaries and wrote endless letters to friends in anticipation of such writings being useful when I became famous!

"I still haven't written fiction for publication, which is something I'd really like to do. But I have worked as a reporter on a city newspaper. I now write for a national children's magazine, *Newstime.* It is work that is fulfilling and fun.

"The . . . nonfiction books I've had published were written after work and on weekends. I'm lucky to live in New York

City, which is one big library. I'm also lucky to live in surroundings that are conducive to creativity. My apartment is in a rambling old building that looks very much like a castle. My windows face a walled garden full of big old trees.

"It would be wonderful if something I've written—or will write—becomes as important and permanent as those trees."

AVOCATIONAL INTERESTS: Travel, photography.†

* * *

IVERSON, Genie 1942-

PERSONAL: Born November 10, 1942, in Newport News, Va.; daughter of Elmer Victor (a naval officer) and Willa (a writer and journalist; maiden name, Okker) Iverson. *Education:* Attended New York University, 1964-65; University of California, Berkeley, B.A., 1966. *Address:* P.O. Box 405, San Mateo, Calif. 94401.

CAREER: Contra Costa Times, Walnut Creek, Calif., staff reporter and youth editor, 1968-71; Lesher News Bureau, Martinez, Calif., reporter, 1971-72; Iverson Game Bird Calls, San Mateo, Calif., promotion director, 1971—.

WRITINGS—All juveniles: *Jacques Cousteau* (biography), Putnam, 1976; *Louis Armstrong* (biography), Crowell, 1976; *I Want to Be Big* (fiction), Dutton, 1979; *Margaret Bourke-White* (biography), Creative Education, 1980; *The Goose That Laid Gold Eggs* (play), Ginn, 1982; *The Robbers and the Fig Tree* (play), Ginn, 1982.

WORK IN PROGRESS: Researching a biography and a history for children.

SIDELIGHTS: Genie Iverson told *CA:* "I write because I enjoy it. So far I have worked on profiles and biography because I am interested in people, human behavior, and history interpreted through individual lives."

J

JACOBS, Lou(is), Jr. 1921-

PERSONAL: Born July 24, 1921, in Dayton, Ohio; son of Louis R. (a salesman) and Clara (Beigel) Jacobs; married Barbara Mills, September 24, 1965; children: Jordan, Kevin, Barry, Ethan. *Education:* Carnegie Institute of Technology (now Carnegie-Mellon University), B.A. in Industrial Design, 1942; attended Art Center College of Design, 1947-50. *Home:* 293 Avenida Andorra, Cathedral City, Calif. 92234. *Agent:* Ann Elmo Agency, Inc., 60 East 42nd St., New York, N.Y. 10017.

CAREER: Free-lance writer and photographer. Peter Muller-Munk Associates, Pittsburgh, Pa., industrial designer, 1942-43, 1946. *Military service:* U.S. Army, Corps of Engineers, 1943-46; served in European and Pacific theaters; became sergeant. *Member:* American Society of Magazine Photographers (president, Southern California chapter, 1956-58; member of board, 1958-64, 1974—; national second vice-president, 1982—).

WRITINGS—Juveniles; self-illustrated with photographs: *Wonders of an Oceanarium,* Golden Gate, 1965; *Duncan the Dolphin,* Follett, 1966; *SST: Plane of Tomorrow,* Golden Gate, 1967; *Oil, U.S.A.,* Elk Grove Press, 1967; *Airports, U.S.A.,* Elk Grove Press, 1967; *Four Walruses: From Arctic to Oceanarium,* W. R. Scott, 1968; *Shamu: The Killer Whale,* Bobbs-Merrill, 1968; (photographs with wife, Barbara Jacobs) *Beautiful Junk,* Little, Brown, 1968; *Aircraft, U.S.A.,* Elk Grove Press, 1968; *Jumbo Jets,* Bobbs-Merrill, 1969; *Truck Cargo, Air Cargo,* Elk Grove Press, 1970; *The Shapes of Our Land,* Putnam, 1970; *You and Your Camera,* Lothrop, 1971; *Space Station '80,* Hawthorn, 1974; *By Jupiter!: The Remarkable Journey of Pioneer 10,* Hawthorn, 1975.

Photography texts; published by Amphoto, except as indicated: *How to Use Variable Contrast Papers,* 1960, 3rd edition, 1970; *The ABC's of Lighting,* 1961; *Electronic Flash,* 1962, 2nd edition, Chilton, 1971; *Free-lance Magazine Photography,* 1965; *Petersen's Basic Guide to Photography,* Petersen, 1973; *How to Take Great Pictures with Your SLR,* H. P. Books, 1974; *The Konica Auto-Reflex Manual,* 1974; *Photography Today,* Goodyear Publishing, 1976; *Amphoto Guide to Selling Photographs,* 1979; *Amphoto Guide to Lighting,* 1979; *The Photography Workbook,* 1980.

Illustrator: Marilyn Gould and George Gould, *Skateboards, Scooterboards, and Seatboards You Can Make,* Lothrop, 1977; M. Gould, *Playground Sports: A Book of Ball Games,* Lothrop, 1978; Carole Barkin and Elizabeth James, *A Place of Your Own,* Dutton, 1981.

* * *

JAFFEE, Mary L.
See LINDSLEY, Mary F(rances)

* * *

JAZAYERY, M(ohammad) Ali 1924-

PERSONAL: Born May 27, 1924, in Shushtar, Iran; son of S. Kazim (an accountant) and Batul (Jazayery) Jazayery. *Education:* University of Tehran, License, 1950; National Teachers College, Tehran, License, 1950; University of Texas, Ph.D., 1958. *Home:* 705 Laurel Valley Rd., Austin, Tex. 78746. *Office:* Department of Oriental and African Languages and Literature, University of Texas, Austin, Tex. 78712.

CAREER: Anglo-Iranian Oil Co., Ahwaz, Iran, employee, 1944-45; co-editor of *Jahan-e Pak* (daily newspaper), 1945-46, and *Daftarha-ye-Mahaneh* (journal), 1945-50, both published in Tehran, Iran; Iranian Ministry of Education, Ahwaz, high school teacher of English, 1950-51; University of Texas at Austin, teaching assistant, 1953-54; American Council of Learned Societies, Washington, D.C., textbook writer (English-Persian), 1954-55; University of Texas at Austin, lecturer in English, 1955-58; University of Tehran, Tehran, associate professor of English, 1958-59, also concurrently assistant to U.S. cultural attache at American Embassy, Tehran; University of Michigan, Ann Arbor, lecturer in Persian, 1959-62; University of Texas at Austin, associate professor, 1962-68, professor of linguistics, 1968-70, professor of Persian linguistics and literature, 1970—, Center for Middle Eastern Studies, assistant director, 1966-73, director, 1980—, department of Oriental and African languages and literature, acting chairman, 1974, chairman, 1976—.

Summer lecturer in Persian at Johns Hopkins University, 1957, Harvard University, 1958, and Princeton University, 1967; visiting summer professor at New York University, 1968, and Portland State University, 1972. Affiliated with Voice of America, 1954-56; Peace Corps, director of Iran Training Language Program, summer, 1962, language coordinator for Training

Project in Iran, 1965, senior consultant and language coordinator for Training Project in Afghanistan, 1965, and senior consultant and language coordinator, Iran, 1966. Chairman of Committee on Persian Language Instruction in North America, 1972—. Consultant to University of Michigan, University of Miami Desegregation Assistance Center, Jefferson County (Kentucky) School System, and State of Alabama Office of Education.

MEMBER: Linguistic Society of America (life member), American Oriental Society, Modern Language Association of America, National Council of Teachers of English, American Association of University Professors, Middle East Studies Association of North America (life member), American Council on the Teaching of Foreign Languages, Society for Iranian Studies (member of council, 1978—), Middle East Institute, Dictionary Society of North America.

WRITINGS: Aludegiha-ye Ejtema' e Ma (title means "The Abuses of Our Society"), Sepehr (Tehran), 1947; (contributor) M. K. Azadeh, editor, *Why Was Kasravi Assassinated?*, Peyman Press (Tehran), 1947; (with H. H. Paper) *English for Iranians,* American Council of Learned Societies, 1955; (with Paper) *The Writing System of Modern Persian,* American Council of Learned Societies, 1955.

(Editor with M. Farzan and others) *Modern Persian Reader,* three volumes, University of Michigan Press, 1963; (contributor) E. B. Atwood and A. A. Hill, editors, *Studies in Language, Literature, and Culture of the Middle Ages and Later,* University of Texas Press, 1969; (contributor) *American Oriental Society Middle West Branch Semi-Centennial Volume,* Indiana University Press, 1969; (contributor) J. Duchesne-Guillemin, editor, *Acta Iranica,* E. J. Brill (Leiden), 1974; (contributor) *Studies in Descriptive and Historical Linguistics: Festschrift for Winfred P. Lehmann,* John Benjamins (Amsterdam), 1977; (contributor) *Kasravi's Writings in the Field of Language and Linguistics,* Sepehr, 1978; (editor with E. C. Polome and W. Winter) *Linguistic and Literary Studies in Honor of Archibald A. Hill,* four volumes, Mouton (The Hague), 1978-79; *Le Farhangestan: Academia Irania de la Lengua,* Press of the Autonomous National University of Mexico, 1979.

Also author of *Elementary Lessons in Persian,* 1965, *Persian Anecdotes and Proverbs: An Introductory Reader for Foreigners,* 1965, and *Drills in Reading and Writing Persian,* 1965. Contributor to *Sepehr Yearbook I,* 1948, *Sepehr Yearbook II,* 1949, and *Sepehr Yearbook III,* 1950; also contributor to *Proceedings of the Tenth International Congress of Linguists,* 1970, to *The Concise Encyclopedia of the Middle East,* Public Affairs Press, 1975, and to *The Encyclopaedia of Islam,* E. J. Brill, 1976. Translator of "Practical Psychology in Plain Language" series, seven volumes, Sepehr, 1947-50.

Contributor of articles and reviews to scholarly journals, including *Review of National Literatures, International Journal of Middle Eastern Studies, Rahnema-ye Ketab* (Tehran), *Texas Studies in English, Bulletin of School of Oriental and African Studies,* and *Journal of Persian Studies. Literature East and West,* member of editorial board, 1970—, acting editor, 1974-75; member of editorial board, *Kherad-o-Kushesh* (Iran), 1975—.

WORK IN PROGRESS: Three books, tentatively entitled *The Arabic Element in Contemporary Persian, The French Element in Contemporary Persian,* and *English Loanwords in Contemporary Persian;* a book about the life and work of Ahmad Kasravi (1890-1946), Iranian historian, linguist, and social reformer; *Language Reform in Iran: A History and an Appraisal;* research on various aspects of contemporary Persian grammar.

SIDELIGHTS: M. Ali Jazayery told *CA:* "My life's motivation, since about 1941, has been to do something, in however small a way, to help society improve itself, which I consider a debt we all owe all human beings. My writings have so far dealt mostly with language as it reflects Iranian society—its history and its current condition. My major ambition, however, is to complete a definitive work on the life and teachings of Ahmad Kasravi, who was assassinated in Tehran in 1946 by religious fanatics, with the blessing of the religious establishment, and with only token efforts by the government to punish the assassins. Kasravi was an internationally recognized historian of Iran, a jurist (judge and attorney), and for a brief period a university professor. Around 1932, he began writing on the ills of Iranian society, showing the many faults in almost all of its cultural institutions, especially its religion, political and economic systems, literature, language, and its treatment of women. He also boldly attacked blind westernization and man's loss of control to machines. While much of his writing relates to his native Iran, his horizon was much broader, covering the whole world.

"I am convinced that introducing him and his ideas in a widely-used language such as English would be a very useful service, and I hope to devote much more time to this effort than I have in the past. Such an effort will more directly and more satisfyingly serve my lifelong motive of being more useful to society than just 'earning my keep' through a job—however respectable the job may be."

* * *

JEAL, Tim 1945-

PERSONAL: Born January 27, 1945, in London, England; son of Clifford Freeman and Norah (Pasley) Jeal. *Education:* Christ Church, Oxford, M.A. *Home:* 29 Willow Rd., London N.W.3, England.

CAREER: Writer. British Broadcasting Corp., London, England, work on production of television documentaries, 1966-70. Member of Arts Council Bursary, 1970. *Member:* Writers Guild of Great Britain. *Awards, honors:* John Llewelyn Rhys Memorial Prize, 1974, for *Cushing's Crusade.*

WRITINGS—Novels, except as indicated: *For Love or Money,* McGraw, 1967; *Somewhere beyond Reproach,* Macmillan (London), 1968, McGraw, 1969; *Livingstone* (biography), Putnam, 1973; *Cushing's Crusade,* Heinemann, 1974; *Until the Colours Fade,* Delacorte, 1976; *A Marriage of Convenience,* Simon & Schuster, 1979; *Carnforth's Creation,* Collins, 1983.

SIDELIGHTS: Novelist Tim Jeal, who "knows his way around Victorian England as well as Stanley knew the Congo," according to Martin Levin in the *New York Times Book Review,* is often praised by critics for his ability to portray life in that period of English history. Of Jeal and his novel *A Marriage of Convenience,* for example, Nicholas Shrimpton says in the *New Statesman* that the writer "does not merely write [an] historical [novel] set in Victorian England, he tries to recreate the broad scope and narrative urgency of the genuine article." Reviewer Stephen Vaughan feels that the novel is a particularly well-written example of the historical genre, commenting in the *Observer* that "it is rare . . . to meet the realities of passion" in a narrative which must necessarily try to capture the overly emotional flavor of Victorian romance, and that "when this combines with rich historical details, . . . the result is outstanding."

AVOCATIONAL INTERESTS: Travel, reading.

BIOGRAPHICAL/CRITICAL SOURCES: New York Times Book Review, November 7, 1976; *Washington Post Book World,* July 19, 1979; *New Statesman,* July 20, 1979; *Observer,* August 5, 1979.

* * *

JEFFERSON, Ian
See DAVIES, L(eslie) P(urnell)

* * *

JEFFRIES, Roderic (Graeme) 1926-
(Peter Alding, Jeffrey Ashford, Hastings Draper, Roderic Graeme, Graham Hastings)

PERSONAL: Born October 21, 1926, in London, England; son of Graham Montague (a writer) and Lorna (Louch) Jeffries; married Rosemary Powys Woodhouse, March 13, 1958; children: Xanthe Kathleen, Crispin John. *Education:* University of Southampton, navigation studies, 1942-43; Gray's Inn, Barrister-at-Law, 1953. *Home:* Ca Na Paiaia, Pollensa, Mallorca, Spain.

CAREER: Writer. British Merchant Navy, 1943-49, went to sea as apprentice, became second mate; began part-time writing and study of law, 1950; practiced law, 1953-54. Former part-time dairy farmer. *Member:* Paternosters.

WRITINGS: Evidence of the Accused, Collins, 1961, British Book Center, 1963; *Exhibit No. Thirteen,* Collins for the Crime Club, 1962; *Police and Detection,* Brockhampton Press, 1962, published as *Against Time!,* Harper, 1963; *The Benefits of Death,* Collins for the Crime Club, 1963, Dodd, 1964; *An Embarrassing Death,* Collins for the Crime Club, 1964, Dodd, 1965; *Dead against the Lawyers,* Dodd, 1965; *Police Dog,* Harper, 1965; *Death in the Coverts,* Collins for the Crime Club, 1966; *A Deadly Marriage,* Collins, 1967; *Police Car,* Brockhampton Press, 1967, published as *Patrol Car,* Harper, 1967; *A Traitor's Crime,* Collins for the Crime Club, 1968; *River Patrol,* Harper, 1969.

Dead Man's Bluff, Collins, 1970; *Police Patrol Boat,* Brockhampton Press, 1971; *Trapped,* Harper, 1972; *Mistakenly in Mallorca,* Collins for the Crime Club, 1974; *Two Faced Death,* Collins, 1976; *The Riddle in the Parchment,* Hodder & Stoughton, 1976; *The Boy Who Knew Too Much,* Hodder & Stoughton, 1977; *Troubled Deaths,* Collins, 1977; *Murder Begets Murder,* St. Martin's, 1978; *Eighteen Desperate Hours,* Hodder & Stoughton, 1979; *The Missing Man,* Hodder & Stoughton, 1980; *Just Deserts,* St. Martin's, 1980; *Unseemly End,* St. Martin's, 1981; *Voyage into Danger,* Hodder & Stoughton, 1981.

Under pseudonym Peter Alding: *The C.I.D. Room,* John Long, 1967, published as *All Leads Negative,* Harper, 1967; *Circle of Danger,* John Long, 1968; *Murder among Thieves,* John Long, 1969, McCall Publishing Co., 1970; *Guilt without Proof,* John Long, 1970, McCall Publishing Co., 1971; *Despite the Evidence,* John Long, 1971, Saturday Review Press, 1972; *Call Back to Crime,* John Long, 1972; *Field of Fire,* John Long, 1973; *The Murder Line,* Walker & Co., 1974; *Six Days to Death,* Walker & Co., 1975; *Murder Is Suspected,* Walker & Co., 1978; *Ransom Town,* Walker & Co., 1979; *A Man Condemned,* Walker & Co., 1981.

Under pseudonym Jeffrey Ashford: *Counsel for the Defence,* John Long, 1960, Harper, 1961; *Investigations Are Proceeding,* John Long, 1961, published as *The D.I.,* Harper, 1962; *The Burden of Proof,* Harper, 1962; *Will Anyone Who Saw the Accident . . . ,* Harper, 1963; *Enquiries Are Continuing,* John Long, 1964; *The Superintendent's Room,* John Long, 1964, Harper, 1965; *The Hands of Innocence,* John Long, 1965, Walker & Co., 1966; *Consider the Evidence,* Walker & Co., 1966; *Hit and Run,* Arrow Books, 1966; *Forget What You Saw,* Walker & Co., 1967; *Grand Prix Monaco,* Putnam, 1968; *Prisoner at the Bar,* Walker & Co., 1969.

Grand Prix Germany, Putnam, 1970; *To Protect the Guilty,* Walker & Co., 1970; *Bent Copper,* Walker & Co., 1971; *Grand Prix United States,* Putnam, 1971; *A Man Will Be Kidnapped Tomorrow,* Walker & Co., 1972; *Grand Prix Britain,* Putnam, 1973; *The Double Run,* Walker & Co., 1973; *Dick Knox at Le Mans,* Putnam, 1974; *The Color of Violence,* Walker & Co., 1974; *Three Layers of Guilt,* John Long, 1975; *Slow Down the World,* Walker & Co., 1976; *Hostage to Death,* Walker & Co., 1977; *The Anger of Fear,* Walker & Co., 1978; *A Recipe for Murder,* Walker & Co., 1979; *The Loss of the Culion,* Walker & Co., 1981.

Under pseudonym Hastings Draper: *Wiggery Pokery,* W. H. Allen, 1956; *Wigged and Gowned,* W. H. Allen, 1958; *Brief Help,* W. H. Allen, 1961.

Under pseudonym Roderic Graeme: *Brandy Ahoy!,* Hutchinson, 1951; *Concerning Blackshirt,* Hutchinson, 1952; *Where's Brandy?,* Hutchinson, 1953; *Blackshirt Wins the Trick,* Hutchinson, 1953; *Blackshirt Passes By,* Hutchinson, 1953; *Salute to Blackshirt,* Hutchinson, 1954; *Brandy Goes a Cruising,* Hutchinson, 1954; *Blackshirt Meets the Lady,* Hutchinson, 1956; *Paging Blackshirt,* John Long, 1957; *Blackshirt Helps Himself,* John Long, 1958; *Double for Blackshirt,* John Long, 1958; *Blackshirt Sets the Pace,* John Long, 1959.

Blackshirt Sees It Through, John Long, 1960; *Blackshirt Finds Trouble,* John Long, 1961; *Blackshirt Takes the Trail,* John Long, 1962; *Blackshirt on the Spot,* John Long, 1963; *Call for Blackshirt,* John Long, 1963; *Blackshirt Saves the Day,* John Long, 1964; *Danger for Blackshirt,* John Long, 1965; *Blackshirt at Large,* John Long, 1966; *Blackshirt in Peril,* John Long, 1967; *Blackshirt Stirs Things Up,* John Long, 1969.

Under pseudonym Graham Hastings: *Twice Checked,* R. Hale, 1959; *Deadly Game,* R. Hale, 1961.

AVOCATIONAL INTERESTS: Shooting, training gun dogs, vintage Bentleys, travel.

* * *

JEFKINS, Frank William 1920-

PERSONAL: Born June 27, 1920, in Norbury, Croydon, Surrey, England; son of Frederick and Edith Rhoda (Harmer) Jefkins; married Frances Kee, September 13, 1952; children: John Malcolm, Valerie Edith. *Education:* London University, BSc (Econ); Open University, BA (Hons). *Home and office:* 84 Ballards Way, South Croydon, Surrey CR2 7LA, England.

CAREER: Llandudno Publicity Association, Llandudno, Wales, publicity manager, 1949-51; Advertising Association, London, England, assistant general secretary, 1951-52; Amalgamated Press Ltd., London, copywriter, 1953-54; Odhams Press Ltd., London, group executive, 1954-58; George Newnes Ltd., London, senior copywriter-executive, 1958-59; Rentokil Group Ltd., London, public relations officer, 1959-63; Scientific Public Relations Ltd., London, director and general manager, 1963-68; Frank Jefkins School of Public Relations, Frank Jefkins School of Communication, and Frank Jefkins PR Services, Surrey, England, principal, 1968—. Chief examiner in advertising, marketing, and public relations for London Chamber of Commerce and Industry; external examiner for Hong Kong Polytechnic.

MEMBER: International Public Relations Association, International Association of Business Communicators, Institute of Public Relations (fellow; member of council), C.A.M. Society, Institute of Marketing, British Association of Industrial Editors, Croydon Advertising Association.

WRITINGS: Copywriting and Its Presentation, Crosby Lockwood, 1958; *Wanted on Holiday* (novel), Hodder & Stoughton, 1960; *Public Relations in World Marketing,* Crosby Lockwood, 1966; *Press Relations Practice,* Intertext, 1968; *Planned Public Relations,* Intertext, 1969.

Advertising Today, Intertext, 1973, 3rd edition, 1983; *Advertising Made Simple,* Heinemann, 1973, 3rd edition, 1982; *Dictionary of Marketing and Communication,* Intertext, 1973, 2nd edition, 1983; *Marketing and PR Media Planning,* Pergamon, 1974; *Advertisement Writing,* Macdonald & Evans, 1976; *Planned Press and Public Relations,* Intertext, 1977; *Effective Press Relations and House Journal Editing,* Frank Jefkins School, 1977, 2nd edition, 1980; *Public Relations for Marketing Management,* Macmillan, 1978.

Public Relations, Macdonald & Evans, 1980, 2nd edition, 1983; *Effective PR Planning,* Frank Jefkins School, 1980; *Effective Publicity Writing,* Frank Jefkins School, 1981; *Public Relations Made Simple,* Heinemann, 1982; *Effective Marketing Strategy,* Frank Jefkins School, 1982; *Introduction to Marketing, Advertising and Public Relations,* Macmillan, 1982; *Modern Marketing,* Macdonald & Evans, 1983.

AVOCATIONAL INTERESTS: Travel and motor touring, gardening, photography, philately, classical music, literature.

* * *

JENNINGS, Gary (Gayne) 1928-

PERSONAL: Born September 20, 1928, in Buena Vista, Va.; son of Glen Edward (a printer) and Vaughnye May (Bays) Jennings; married Glenda Kay Clarke (a hospital administrator), 1972. *Education:* New York Art Students League, student, 1949-51. *Residence:* Mexia, Tex. *Agent:* McIntosh & Otis, Inc., 475 Fifth Ave., New York, N.Y. 10017.

CAREER: Writer. Copywriter and account executive for advertising agencies, New York, N.Y., 1947-58; newspaper reporter in California and Virginia, 1958-61; managing editor, *Dude* and *Gent,* 1962-63. *Military service:* U.S. Army, Infantry, 1952-54; served as correspondent in Korea; awarded Bronze Star, citation from Republic of Korea Ministry of Information. *Member:* P.E.N. International, International Society for Philosophical Enquiry.

WRITINGS: Personalities of Language, Crowell, 1965; *The Treasure of the Superstition Mountains* (nonfiction), Norton, 1973; *The Terrible Teague Bunch* (novel), Norton, 1975; *Sow the Seeds of Hemp* (novel), Norton, 1976; *Aztec* (novel; Literary Guild selection), Atheneum, 1980.

Young adult; nonfiction, except as indicated: *March of the Robots,* Dial, 1962; *The Movie Book,* Dial, 1963; *Black Magic, White Magic,* Dial, 1964; *Parades!,* Lippincott, 1966; *The Killer Storms,* Lippincott, 1970; *The Shrinking Outdoors,* Lippincott, 1972; *The Earth Book,* Harper, 1974; *March of the Heroes,* Association Press, 1975; *March of the Gods,* Association Press, 1976; *The Rope in the Jungle* (novel), Lippincott, 1976; *March of the Demons,* Association Press, 1978.

Contributor to numerous anthologies and textbooks. Contributor of articles, short stories, and essays to periodicals, including *Cosmopolitan, Fantasy & Science Fiction, Harper's, National Geographic, Redbook,* and *Ellery Queen's Mystery Magazine.*

WORK IN PROGRESS: Marco, a novel based on the hitherto untold adventures of Marco Polo.

SIDELIGHTS: "In rubbing the myths of each race to their common bones, Gary Jennings has produced in *Aztec* a monumental novel" about the Spanish conquest of Mexico in the sixteenth century, says Nicholas Shakespeare in the *London Times. Aztec,* according to Judith Matloff in the *Saturday Review,* is a "gripping piece of historical fiction" that tells the story through the voice of Mixtli, an Aztec warrior.

New York Times reviewer Christopher Lehmann-Haupt observes that "*Aztec* has everything that makes a story vulgarly appealing, in the best sense of the phrase. It has sex . . . , it has violence . . . , and the story is filled with revenge." Lehmann-Haupt believes the "revenge provides much of the fuel for the drama of Mixtli's history. The violence usually serves a constructive storytelling purpose. . . . And the sexual passages almost always relate to the book's most fascinating and subtle aspect, which is the way the hero, Mixtli, unconsciously re-enacts the life of the Indian god Quetzalcoatl."

In a *Publishers Weekly* interview with Jennings, John F. Baker details the ten years of research the author did before writing *Aztec,* commenting that Jennings "read many existing fictions about Mexico's ancient Indian tribes, . . . [and] he traveled extensively among Mexican Indians, studying their languages, getting a sense of their traditions, visiting their ancient sites." This travel was often in remote parts of Mexico where the native Indians were hostile to Jennings. The research paid off, though, as Matloff comments: "In this vivid epic, Jennings conveys 16th-century Aztec daily life—hieroglyphic classes, magic mushroom preparations, sacrificial rituals, [and] sophisticated plumbing technology."

Writing in the *Washington Post Book World,* Thomas M. Disch maintains that "historical novels are most often praised or dismissed as novels, but surely it is their power as narrative history that is their main strength, the power to evoke the *feel* of ages lost to memory. . . . So it is with Gary Jennings' *Aztec.* . . . [It is] a story of unfailing . . . power to bind a spell."

Aztec has been translated into Mexican Spanish.

BIOGRAPHICAL/CRITICAL SOURCES: Saturday Review, November, 1980; *Chicago Tribune Book World,* November 30, 1980; *Washington Post Book World,* November 30, 1980; *Publishers Weekly,* December 12, 1980; *Atlantic,* January, 1981; *New York Times,* February 5, 1981; *London Times,* July 9, 1981.

* * *

JENSON, Robert W(illiam) 1930-

PERSONAL: Born August 2, 1930, in Eau Claire, Wis.; son of Martin Thomas (a clergyman) and Valborg (Tiller) Jenson;

married Blanche A. Rockne, August 6, 1954; children: Kari Elizabeth. *Education:* Luther College, B.A., 1951; University of Minnesota, graduate study, 1951-54; Luther Theological Seminary, B.D., 1955; Ruprecht-Karl University, Th.D., 1959; University of Basel, advanced study, 1959; Heidelberg University, Dr.Th., 1959. *Office:* Lutheran Theological Seminary, Gettysburg, Pa. 17325.

CAREER: Decorah Lutheran Congregation, Decorah, Iowa, assistant pastor, 1955-56; Luther College, Decorah, instructor, 1955-59, assistant professor of philosophy, 1960-63, associate professor of religion and philosophy, 1963-66, chairman of department of philosophy, 1961-66; Oxford University, Mansfield College, Oxford, England, lecturer in theology, 1966-68; Lutheran Theological Seminary, Gettysburg, Pa., professor of systematic theology, 1968—. *Member:* American Theological Society, American Association of University Professors (president, local chapter, 1961), Iowa Philosophical Society.

WRITINGS: Alpha and Omega: A Study of the Theology of Karl Barth, Nelson, 1963; *Seven Days of Creation* (poems), privately printed, 1964; *A Religion against Itself,* John Knox, 1967; *God after God: The God of the Past and of the Future as Seen in the Work of Karl Barth,* Bobbs-Merrill, 1969; *The Knowledge of Things Hoped For: The Sense of Theological Discourse,* Oxford University Press, 1969.

(With Carl E. Braaten) *The Futurist Option,* Newman Press, 1970; *Story and Promise: A Brief Theology of the Gospel about Jesus,* Fortress, 1973; (with Eric W. Gritsch) *Lutheranism: The Theological Movement and Its Confessional Writings,* Fortress, 1976; *Visible Words: The Interpretation and Practice of Christian Sacraments,* Fortress, 1978; *The Triune Identity: God According to the Gospel,* Fortress, 1982. Contributor to *Faculty Papers in Memoriam Karl Barth,* Theological Seminary of United Lutheran Church in America, 1969. *Dialog,* associate editor, 1961-75, editor, 1975—. Contributor to professional journals.†

* * *

JIANOU, Ionel 1905-

PERSONAL: Born October 23, 1905, in Bucharest, Rumania; son of Leon and Charlotte Susan Stark; married Margaret Grosswald, March 29, 1931; children: Ion-Alexander. *Education:* University of Paris, master's degree. *Politics:* "No." *Home:* 10, Avenue Stephane Mallarme, Paris 75017, France.

CAREER: Gallery Caminul Artei, Bucharest, Rumania, artistic manager, 1942-47; Editura de Stat Pentru Literatura si Arta (ESPLA) and Meridiane Publishing House, Bucharest, manager of artistic section, 1951-61; Popular University, Fine Arts Institute, Bucharest, professor of history of art, 1954-61; Arted, Editions d'Art, Paris, France, president, 1962-81. *Member:* Association Internationale des Critiques d'Art, P.E.N. (Paris), Societe des Gens de Lettres.

WRITINGS—Published by Editura de Stat Pentru Literatura si Arta, except as indicated: *P. Iorgulescu-Yor,* Arta si Technica Grafica, 1938; *T. Pallady,* Caminul Artei, 1944; *N. Tonitza,* Caminul Artei, 1945; *G. Petrascu,* Editura Fundatilor Regale, 1945; *Luchian,* Caminul Artei, 1947; *I. Negulici,* 1951; *C. Rosenthal,* 1951; *B. Iscovescu,* 1953; (with Ion Frunzetti) *Maestrii Picturii Romanesti in Muzeul de Arta al Republicii Populare Romane,* 1953; *St. Dumitrescu,* 1954; *N. Grigorescu,* Editions de l'Etat pour les Langues Etrangeres, 1955; (with Petru Comarnescu) *Stefan Luchian,* 1956; (with M. Popescu) *Maestrii Picturii Romanesti,* 1957; (with W. Benes) *Marturii despre N. Grigorescu,* 1957; *Iser,* 1957; (with Comarnescu) *Les Maitres de la Peinture Roumaine au XX siecle,* Editions de l'Etat pour les langues etrangeres, 1958; *A. Ciucurencu,* 1958.

Published by Arted-Editions d'Art, except as indicated: *Brancusi,* 1963, translation by Anette Michelson published under same title, Tudor, 1963; *Zadkine,* 1964, translation published under same title, New York Graphic Society, 1965; (with Michel Dufet) *Bourdelle,* 1965, translation by Kathleen Muston and Bryan Richardson published under same title, Tudor, 1966; *La Sculpture et les sculpteurs, de la prehistoire a nos jours et dans le monde entier,* F. Nathan, 1966; (with Cecile Goldscheider) *Rodin,* 1967, translation by Muston and Geoffrey Skelding published under same title, Tudor, 1967; (with Mircea Eliade and Comarnescu) *Temoignages sur Brancusi,* 1967; *Lardera,* 1968; (with Waldemar George) *Henri Georges Adam,* 1968; *Henry Moore,* 1968, translation by Skelding published under same title, Tudor, 1968; *Valentine Prax,* 1968; *Couturier,* 1969.

Cinq mille ans d'architecture, F. Nathan, 1970; (with George) *Dimitrios Demou,* 1970; (with Helene Lassalle) *Gilioli,* 1971; *Etienne Hajdu,* 1972; *Jean Arp,* 1973; (with Annick Pely) *Marta Pan,* 1974; (with Enzo Carli) *Vittorio Tavernari,* 1975; *Antoine Poncet* (text in French and English; English translation by Annie Samuelli), 1975; (with Constantin Noica) *Introduction a la sculpture de Brancusi,* 1976; *Froso Eftimiadi,* 1977; *Ladis Schwartz,* 1977; *Andras Beck,* 1978; *Alice Sfintesco,* 1979; (with Nicola Micieli) *Lia Godano,* 1979; *Moshe Ziffer* (text in French and English), 1980; (with Eliade, Comarnescu, and Noica) *Brancusi-Temoignages-Introduction,* 1981.

Also author of *La Sculpture moderne en France depuis 1950,* with G. Xuriguera and Aube Lardera, Arted-Editions d'Art. Contributor to *Dictionnaire Universel des Arts et des Artistes,* 1969, *Dictionary of Modern Sculpture,* 1970, and *Le Petit Larousse de la Peinture,* 1979. Contributor to periodicals in Rumania and France.

SIDELIGHTS: N. Grigorescu has been translated into four languages, *Rodin* has been translated into German, and *Lia Godano* contains both French and the Italian translation.

* * *

JOCELYN, Richard
See CLUTTERBUCK, Richard

* * *

JOHNPOLL, Bernard K(eith) 1918-

PERSONAL: Born June 3, 1918, in New York, N.Y.; son of I. Joseph and Rachel (Elkin) Johnpoll; married Lillian Kirtzman, 1944; children: two daughters. *Education:* Boston University, A.B. (magna cum laude), 1959; Rutgers University, A.M., 1963; State University of New York, Ph.D., 1966. *Politics:* Independent. *Religion:* None. *Home:* 6600 Pond Apple Rd., Boca Raton, Fla. 33433. *Office:* Department of Communication, Florida Atlantic University, Boca Raton, Fla. 33431.

CAREER: Boston Record-American, Boston, Mass., news editor, 1950-60; Rutgers University, New Brunswick, N.J., lecturer in political science, 1962-63; Hartwick College, Oneonta, N.Y., assistant professor of political science, 1963-65; University of Saskatchewan, Regina, visiting assistant professor, 1965-66; State University of New York at Albany, associate professor, 1966-71, professor of political science, 1971-82, professor emeritus, 1982—; Florida Atlantic University, Boca Raton, professor of communication, 1982—.

WRITINGS: Canadian News Index, University of Saskatchewan Press, 1966; *The Politics of Futility: The General Jewish Workers Bund of Poland, 1917-1943,* Cornell University Press, 1967; *Pacifist's Progress: Norman Thomas and the Decline of Socialism,* Quadrangle, 1970; (editor and author of introduction) Norman Thomas, *Norman Thomas on War: An Anthology,* Garland Publishing, 1974; (editor with Mark Yerburgh) *The League for Industrial Democracy: A Documentary History,* three volumes, Greenwood Press, 1980; *The Impossible Dream: Rise and Demise of the American Left,* Greenwood Press, 1981.

WORK IN PROGRESS: "The American Diary," a thirteen-part television series for American National Enterprises; "Years to Remember," a television series for Berkshire Productions.

SIDELIGHTS: Bernard K. Johnpoll has a good knowledge of Yiddish and German. He can read Russian, Swedish, Norwegian, Danish, Spanish, and Portuguese.

* * *

JOHNS, Kenneth
See BULMER, (Henry) Kenneth

* * *

JOHNSON, B(ryan) S(tanley William) 1933-1973

PERSONAL: Born February 5, 1933, in London, England; died by his own hand, November 13, 1973; son of Stanley Wilfred and Emily Jane Johnson; married Virginia Ann Kimpton; children: two. *Education:* King's College, London, B.A. (with honors in English), 1959. *Home:* 9 Dagmar Ter., London N1 2BN, England. *Agent:* Michael Bakewell Assoc., 118 Tottenham Court Rd., London W1, England.

CAREER: Writer; film and television director and producer. *Member:* Writer's Guild, Equity, Society of Authors. *Awards, honors:* Gregory Awards for *Travelling People* and *Poems;* Somerset Maugham Award, 1967, for *Trawl*; Grand Prix, Tours International Short Film Festival, and Melbourne International Short Film Festival, both 1968, for "You're Human Like the Rest of Them"; First Gregynog Arts fellow, University of Wales, 1970.

WRITINGS: Travelling People (novel), Constable, 1963; *Poems,* Constable, 1964, Chilmark, 1964; *Albert Angelo* (novel), Constable, 1964; (with Zulfikar Ghose) *Statement against Corpses* (short stories), Constable, 1964; (author of text) *Street Children,* illustrated with photographs by Julia Trevelyan Oman, Hodder & Stoughton, 1964; *Trawl* (novel), Secker & Warburg, 1966; (editor) *The Evacuees* (personal narratives; also see below), Gollancz, 1968; *The Unfortunates* (novel; also see below), Panther House, 1969.

House Mother Normal: A Geriatric Comedy (novel), limited edition, Trigram Press, 1971, Collins, 1971; (with Margaret Drabble) *Consequences: A Novel,* Greater London Arts Association, 1972; *Poems Two,* Trigram Press, 1972; *Christie Malry's Own Double-Entry* (novel), Viking, 1973; (editor) *All Bull: The National Servicemen,* Quartet Books, 1973; *A Dublin Unicorn,* Byron Press, 1973; *Everybody Knows Somebody Who's Dead,* Covent Garden Press, 1973; *Aren't You Rather Young to Be Writing Your Memoirs?* (selected short prose), Hutchinson, 1973; (editor) *You Always Remember the First Time,* Quartet Books, 1975; *See the Old Lady Decently* (novel), Viking, 1975.

Plays: "Whose Dog Are You?" (also see below), first produced in London at Quipu Basement Theatre, January, 1971; "B. S. Johnson versus God" (includes "Whose Dog Are You?" and "You're Human Like the Rest of Them"; also see below), first produced in London at Basement Theatre, January 18, 1971.

Radio play: "Entry," produced on BBC Third Programme, 1965.

Films: "You're Human Like the Rest of Them," produced by British Film Institute, 1967, published in *New English Dramatists 14,* Penguin, 1970; "Up Yours Too, Guillaume Apollinaire!," produced by British Film Institute, 1968; "Paradigm," produced by Elisabeth Films, 1969.

Television films: "The Evacuees," (based on his book of the same title), first produced on BBC 2, October, 1968; "The Unfortunates" (based on his book of the same title), produced on BBC 2, February, 1969; "Charlie Whildon Talking, Singing, and Playing" (documentary), produced on BBC 2, March, 1969; "Bath" (documentary on architecture of city), produced on BBC 2, June, 1969; "The Smithsons on Housing" (architectural documentary), produced on BBC 2, July, 1970; "On Reflection: Sam Johnson" (documentary), produced by London Weekend Television, January, 1971; "On Reflection: Alexander Herzen," produced by London Weekend Television, April, 1971; "Not Counting the Savages," produced on BBC-TV, January, 1972; "Hafod a Henref," produced by Harlech Television, April, 1972.

Also author of play, "One Sodding Thing After Another," commissioned by Royal Court Theatre, 1967. Contributor to anthologies. Contributor to *Times, Observer, New Statesman, Spectator, Times Literary Supplement, Encounter,* and other periodicals. Poetry editor, *Transatlantic Review,* 1965-73.

SIDELIGHTS: B. S. Johnson, generally regarded as an experimental writer, utilized his art to probe the structure of the novel by creating new forms of prose and by manipulating the basic conventions of the medium to suit his own avant-garde vision. "For ten years," wrote Robert S. Ryf in *Critique: Studies in Modern Fiction,* "in seven novels and a number of short pieces, Johnson single-mindedly and belligerently pushed at the frontiers of the novel and prowled the shifting and nebulous borders between fiction and fact. He was centrally concerned with the relationships of the writer to his material as well as to his readers."

Called a "caricature . . . of the classical novelist . . . who sees through the fiction game and its weary conventions" by D. Keith Mano in the *New York Times Book Review,* Johnson believed the traditional form of the novel was outdated and the structure of the modern novel had to be extended to reflect modern man's expanded perception of reality. A critic for the *Times Literary Supplement* asserted that Johnson was "against narrative, against fictions of all kinds, against novels which require effort to appreciate, and balefully serious about his conception of the way his medium should develop."

In *Travelling People,* his first novel, Johnson employed many different manipulative techniques designed to transform the novelistic medium. According to Ryf, the book contains "a collection of styles, including that of ironic detached expository narrative, extreme fragmentation with suggested headlines in the manner of [part of James Joyce's] *Ulysses,* sections of interior monologue, quotations, scraps of conversation, and letters." This novel, which "showed that Johnson had unusual talent and some disconcerting and provocative ideas" about the medium, as Bernard Bergonzi suggested in his book *The Situation of the Novel,* also revealed what Johnson had learned from reading James Joyce, Samuel Beckett, and Laurence Sterne. Bergonzi believed that the "typographical eccentricities" found in the novel, such as the instance "when one character has a heart-attack and Johnson illustrates its effect with a blank page printed entirely in black," can be traced to the influence of the eighteenth-century novelist Sterne. Critic Julian Barnes argued in the *New Statesman* that Johnson's artistic devices did not, in fact, "go very far beyond Sterne."

Ryf quoted Johnson as defining the form of his novel *Trawl* as "all interior monologue, a representation of the inside of my mind but at one stage removed; the closest one can come in writing." Here Johnson's obsession with truth in fiction emerged in a work that is "one of the early and most important instances in the contemporary novel of the author's use of himself as his own principal character," according to Ryf. Although Johnson was attempting to present autobiographical reality—truth—in the novel, the work, ironically, "reads like a fairly conventional novel of recall," wrote Ryf, "in which the central character tries to come to terms with his present situation in the light of his past." Furthermore, while Johnson tried to represent the workings of his own mind, processes which are often considered to be randomly ordered, Ryf found that "one's final impression of the novel is that it is . . . highly and artfully patterned."

Johnson's concern with the randomness of human experience and thought surfaced again in *The Unfortunates,* a book which was issued in a box and held together by a removable paper wrapper. Johnson's motive in using this highly unusual form was to create an alternative to what he called the "enforced consecutiveness of the conventionally bound novel." By utilizing twenty-seven loose sections, or chapters, which could be rearranged to the reader's liking, he felt, as Ryf quoted him, that the "whole novel reflected the randomness of the material; it was itself a physical tangible metaphor for randomness." Patrick Parrinder, writing in *Critical Quarterly,* believed that the novel's theme, which deals with the narrator's feelings toward his friend's death by cancer, "contrasts sharply with the whimsical randomness that results from putting the novel into a box. . . . Johnson's idea is to allow the reader to participate in his own uncertainties about structuring the novel; but in fact the demonstration is pointless because it makes one feel that the structure does not matter."

In the *Listener,* Mary Sullivan explained the structure of *House Mother Normal: A Geriatric Comedy* as "an attempt to make the reader register the experience of nine persons as nearly as possible simultaneously. The . . . thoughts . . . and . . . words of each of eight old men and women are presented in turn, as each lives through an evening in an old people's home; finally their heartless and obscene housemother has her say." These nine interior monologues, each of which covers the same span of time within the plot's framework, comprise what Parrinder called a "technical *tour de force,*" which was "handled with such ingenuity that we can identify with each of the inmates in turn, while putting together the complex jigsaw of events" of the plot. "The novel," said Parrinder, "has a powerful *momento mori* effect, not least through Johnson's use of blank spaces to indicate periods of pain, mental confusion and unconsciousness. . . . *House Mother Normal,* I believe, will stand as Johnson's finest work."

Johnson completed the novel *See the Old Lady Decently* just a few weeks before committing suicide. It was to be the first part of his projected "Matrix" trilogy, and parts two and three were to be entitled *Buried Although* and *Amongst Those Left Are You.* In this, his last novel, Johnson was still experimenting. The book's themes, which center around the concepts of motherhood, are represented, according to a *New Yorker* critic, in "documents, imaginings, fragments, concrete poems—enough verbal games to fill a compact volume. . . . The book is clever, playful, and spirited." While the novel is "about mother, mother country, great earth mother," noted Mano, "it's as much about the possibilities inherent in fiction. . . . This is an extraordinary novel, full of agonized, half-articulate emotions. B. S. Johnson could not have confronted himself with a more harrowing challenge. May he rest in peace."

Ryf concluded that although Johnson was "stubborn and unregenerate, . . . these very qualities help make his work significant. For he was not satisified with the form he inherited. He rejected what to him was an outworn legacy, and he stretched the form to accommodate and give voice to the stuff of the contemporary world. He never let us forget how important the novel is."

BIOGRAPHICAL/CRITICAL SOURCES: Bernard Bergonzi, *The Situation of the Novel,* University of Pittsburgh Press, 1970; *Times Literary Supplement,* June 11, 1971, November 9, 1973; *Listener,* June 17, 1971; *New York Times Book Review,* September 23, 1973, August 10, 1975; *New Statesman,* May 2, 1975; *New Yorker,* September 22, 1975; *Contemporary Literary Criticism,* Gale, Volume VI, 1976, Volume IX, 1978; *Critical Quarterly,* summer, 1977; *Critique: Studies in Modern Fiction,* Volume XIX, number 1, 1977.

OBITUARIES: Times, November 15, 1973; *AB Bookman's Weekly,* July 15, 1974; *Transatlantic Review,* summer, 1974.†

—Sketch by Kerry L. Lutz

* * *

JOHNSON, Benjamin A. 1937-

PERSONAL: Born June 29, 1937, in Melby, Minn.; son of Ben Arvid (an insurance agent) and Ruth Ulrika (Werner) Johnson; married Suzanne Wasgatt, May 13, 1960; children: Samuel Perry, Jennie Ruth, Krister Davis, Jesse Jerome. *Education:* Gustavus Adolphus College, B.A., 1959; Lutheran School of Theology, Chicago, Ill., B.D., 1961; Harvard Divinity School, Th.D., 1966; attended Oxford University, 1971-72. *Politics:* Independent. *Home:* 264 South Broadmoor Blvd., Springfield, Ohio 45504. *Office:* Salem at Riverside, 211 First St. S.E., St. Cloud, Minn. 56301.

CAREER: Ordained minister of Lutheran Church in America, 1965; Wittenberg University, Hamma School of Theology, Springfield, Ohio, 1965-78, began as associate professor, became professor of New Testament and dean; Trinity Seminary, Columbus, Ohio, professor, 1978-80; Salem at Riverside, St. Cloud, Minn., senior pastor, 1980—. *Member:* Society for Religion in Higher Education, Society of Biblical Literature.

WRITINGS: (Editor with Herbert T. Neve) *The Maturing of American Lutheranism,* Augsburg, 1968; *The Church in the New Testament,* Lutheran Church in America, 1968; (with Daniel B. Stevick) *Proclamation—Holy Week: Aids for Interpreting the Lessons of the Church Year,* Fortress, 1973; *The Mark of the Christian Community,* C.S.S. Publishing, 1975; *Matthew,* C.S.S. Publishing, 1978; *Blueprint for Sainthood,* C.S.S. Publishing, 1980.

SIDELIGHTS: Benjamin A. Johnson is competent in Greek, German, and French, and has some competence in Hebrew, Aramaic, and Latin.

* * *

JOHNSON, James L. 1927-

PERSONAL: Born February 26, 1927, in Dollar Bay, Mich.; son of Eric R. (a laborer) and Anna (Backman) Johnson; married Rosemary Lorts, June 7, 1952; children: Jay. *Education:* Attended Suomi College, 1947-49; Moody Bible Institute, B.Th., 1959; University of Michigan, B.A. in Journalism, 1963. *Politics:* Liberal Republican. *Home:* 1209 Tall Oaks Lane, Wheaton, Ill. 60187. *Office:* Department of Journalism, Wheaton College, Wheaton, Ill. 60187.

CAREER: Baptist minister. *Africa Challenge* (magazine), Lagos, Nigeria, editor, 1956-59; minister of Bible church in Chicago, Ill., 1959-61; Evangelical Literature Overseas, Wheaton, Ill., director, 1963—; Wheaton College, Wheaton, Ill., 1968—, special instructor in journalism, coordinator of journalism department, founder of communications department. Christian Writers Institute, former staff instructor, currently consultant; partner in Johnson/Johnson Literary Agency. Director of resource development, World Relief Corp., Wheaton. *Military service:* U.S. Navy, 1944-45. *Member:* Sigma Delta Chi, Kappa Tau Alpha. *Awards, honors:* Prize for essay, "Take the Fear Out of Integration," from *Christian Herald,* 1967.

WRITINGS—Fiction: *Code Name Sebastian,* Lippincott, 1967; *The Nine Lives of Alphonse,* Lippincott, 1968; *A Handful of Dominoes,* Lippincott, 1970; *The Death of Kings,* Doubleday, 1974; *A Piece of the Moon Is Missing,* A. J. Holman, 1974; *The Last Train from Canton,* Lippincott, 1980.

Nonfiction: *The Nine to Five Complex,* Zondervan, 1972; (with Eugene B. McDaniel) *Before Honor,* Lippincott, 1973; *What Every Woman Should Know about a Man,* Zondervan, 1974; *Loneliness Is Not Forever,* Zondervan, 1977; *How to Enjoy Life and Not Feel Guilty,* Harvest House, 1980; *Coming Back,* Harvest House, 1981.

WORK IN PROGRESS: Love Is a River, for Zondervan.

SIDELIGHTS: James L. Johnson speaks Yoruba, a Nigerian language, and German. *Avocational interests:* Reading, sports.

BIOGRAPHICAL/CRITICAL SOURCES: Decision, June, 1967.

* * *

JOHNSON, W(alter) R(alph) 1933-

PERSONAL: Born July 9, 1933, in Trinidad, Colo.; married Sabina Thorne (a writer), March 2, 1962 (divorced 1979); children: Nicholas, Leatrice. *Education:* Attended San Diego State College (now University), 1951-53; University of California, Berkeley, B.A., 1961, M.A., 1963, Ph.D., 1966. *Residence:* Chicago, Ill. *Office:* Department of Classics, University of Chicago, Chicago, Ill. 60637.

CAREER: University of California, Berkeley, assistant professor, 1966-72, associate professor of classics and comparative literature, 1972-74; Cornell University, Ithaca, N.Y., associate professor, 1974-76, professor of classics, 1976-82; University of Chicago, Chicago, Ill., professor of classics and comparative literature, 1982—. *Military service:* U.S. Army, 1953-58. *Member:* American Philological Association.

WRITINGS: A Messenger of Satan, Janus Press, 1957; *Luxuriance and Economy: Cicero and the Alien Style,* University of California Press, 1971; (author of foreword) Horace, *Selected Odes, Epodes, Satires, Epistles,* translation by Burton Raffel, New American Library, 1973; (author of afterword) Horace, *The Art of Poetry,* translation by Raffel, State University of New York Press, 1974; *Darkness Visible: A Study of Vergil's Aeneid,* University of California Press, 1976; *From Actium,* Janus Press, 1977; *The Idea of Lyric,* University of California Press, 1982; (contributor) *Ancient Writers,* Scribner, 1982. Contributor of essays to journals in his field

WORK IN PROGRESS: A book on the early German Romantics and the classics, *The Dreams of Ardinghell.*

* * *

JONES, Joanna
See BURKE, John (Frederick)

* * *

JORDAN, Terry G(ilbert) 1938-

PERSONAL: Born August 9, 1938, in Dallas, Tex.; son of Gilbert John (a college professor) and Vera Belle (Tiller) Jordan; married Marlis Anderson, August 18, 1962; children: Tina, Sonya, Eric. *Education:* Southern Methodist University, B.A., 1960; University of Texas, M.A., 1961; University of Wisconsin, Ph.D., 1965. *Home:* 6305 Augusta National Dr., Austin, Tex. 78746. *Office:* Department of Geography, University of Texas, Austin, Tex. 78712.

CAREER: Arizona State University, Tempe, assistant professor of geography, 1965-69; North Texas State University, Denton, professor of geography and chairman of department, 1969-82; University of Texas at Austin, Walter Prescott Webb Professor of Geography, 1982—. *Member:* Association of American Geographers, American Geographical Society, Pioneer America Society, Texas State Historical Association, Texas Folklore Society, Phi Beta Kappa. *Awards, honors:* Woodrow Wilson fellow; Tullis Award, Texas State Historical Association, 1979; Honors Award, Association of American Geographers, 1982.

WRITINGS: German Seed in Texas Soil: Immigrant Farmers in Nineteenth-Century Texas, University of Texas Press, 1966; *The European Culture Area: A Systematic Geography,* Harper, 1973; *The Human Mosaic: A Thematic Introduction to Cultural Geography,* Harper, 1976, 3rd edition, 1982; *Texas Log Buildings: A Folk Architecture,* University of Texas Press, 1978; *Trails to Texas: Southern Roots of Western Cattle Ranching,* University of Nebraska Press, 1981; *Texas Graveyards: A Cultural Legacy,* University of Texas Press, 1982.

WORK IN PROGRESS: Work on the European antecedents of American folk architecture.

K

KAGAN, Donald 1932-

PERSONAL: Born May 1, 1932, in Lithuania; naturalized U.S. citizen; son of M. and Leah (Benjamin) Kagan; married Myrna Dabrusky (a teacher), January 13, 1955; children: Robert William, Frederick Walter. *Education:* Brooklyn College (now Brooklyn College of the City University of New York), A.B., 1954; Brown University, M.A., 1955; Ohio State University, Ph.D., 1958; American School of Classical Studies in Athens, postdoctoral study, 1958-59. *Politics:* Democrat. *Religion:* Jewish. *Office:* Department of Classical Languages, Yale University, New Haven, Conn. 06520.

CAREER: Instructor in history at Capital University, Columbus, Ohio, part-time, 1957-58, and at Pennsylvania State University, University Park, 1959-60; Cornell University, Ithaca, N.Y., assistant professor, 1960-63, associate professor, 1964-67, professor of ancient history, 1967-69; Yale University, New Haven, Conn., professor of history and classics, 1969-78, Richard M. Colgate Professor, 1978—, chairman of classics department, 1972-75, master of Timothy Dwight College, 1976-78. *Awards, honors:* Fulbright grant to Greece, 1958-59; American Philosophical Society research grant and New York University summer seminar grant, 1960; fellowship to Center for Hellenic Studies, 1966-67; National Endowment for the Humanities senior fellowship, 1971-72.

WRITINGS: (Editor) *The Decline and Fall of the Roman Empire in the West,* Heath, 1962, 2nd edition, 1978; *The Great Dialogue: A History of Greek Political Thought from Homer to Ploybius,* Free Press, 1965; (editor) *Readings in Greek Political Thought,* Free Press, 1965; (editor) *Problems in Ancient History,* two volumes, Macmillan, 1966, 2nd edition, 1975; (editor with L. P. Williams and Brian Tierney) *Great Issues in Western Civilization,* two volumes, Random House, 1967, 3rd edition, 1976; *The Outbreak of the Peloponnesian War,* Cornell University Press, 1969; *The Archidamian War,* Cornell University Press, 1974; (with S. Ozment and F. Turner) *The Western Heritage,* Macmillan, 1979; *The Peace of Nicias and the Sicilian Expedition,* Cornell University Press, 1981. Contributor to professional journals.

* * *

KAKAPO, Leilani 1939-

PERSONAL: Born August 11, 1939, in Kalano, Hawaii; daughter of Caldwell and Martha (Loki) Kiilehau; married Arnold Kakapo (a migrant worker), June 24, 1961 (divorced, 1964); children: Carter, Semantha, Arnold, Jr. *Education:* Attended Kalano Junior College, 1957-58; extension courses at Zug Island University, 1960; City and State University, B.A., 1972. *Politics:* Reaganist. *Home and office:* 221 Lewiston Rd., Grosse Pointe Farms, Mich. 48236.

CAREER: Free-lance writer and "busy little housewife"; distributor, Buy-America Corp., 1981—. Lecturer at libraries and grade schools. Organizer of annual "Waakiki-Monte Carlo" night, New Age Bethlehem Christ Church, 1976—. *Member:* Ethnic Writers of America, Old Hawaiians League of Southeastern Michigan. *Awards, honors:* Certificate of merit, 1965, for *Uki-Buki-Wuki;* gold medal, Northeast Kalano Library Association, 1966.

WRITINGS: Kowa Bengay, Sandwich Islands Press, 1959; *The Pagans of Porter Bay,* Sandwich Islands Press, 1960; *The Revolt of Kamana Kow,* Vishlag Press, 1962; *Hang Twelve,* Anton, 1963; *Meeska Mooska Mousketeer,* Sandwich Islands Press, 1964; *Uki-Buki-Wuki,* Vishlag Press, 1965; *How Uki-Buki-Wukis Are Made,* Vishlag Press, 1965; *From Here to Michigan,* Anton, 1966; *Art and Archeology of Hawaiian Tikis,* Sandwich Islands Press, 1969; (editor) Nan Russini, *My Hawaiian Vacation,* Pineapple Press, 1975; *Honoluee Luau* (teenage novel), Spinster Publications, 1977; *Pineapple Juice in Michigan* (autobiography), Sundusk, 1979; *Sugarcane Summer* (novel), Sundusk, 1981; *A Pig Roast for Poouala* (juvenile), Surf's Up Press, 1982. Contributor to numerous periodicals.

SIDELIGHTS: Writing in the *Hawaii Tattler,* Ralph B. Kouana, Jr. calls Leilani Kakapo's book *Sugarcane Summer* "one of the most outstanding books of the year—and possibly one of the best books from a Hawaiian in the last century. This book has it all: romance, heroes, villains, suspense, beautiful women, mystery, sex, violence, and a terrific sense of humor." *Pineapple Juice in Michigan,* says Dora Schapp in *Library Reader Review,* "is surely a winner. Mrs. Kakapo's grace and style is certainly a credit to her tropical upbringing."

BIOGRAPHICAL/CRITICAL SOURCES: Kalano Post Advertiser, November 12, 1959; *Milani Times Register,* May 1, 1963; *Library Reader Review,* November 19, 1979; *Hawaii Tattler,* December 19, 1981; *Kokapi News,* January 28, 1982.

KAMERMAN, Sylvia E.
See BURACK, Sylvia K.

* * *

KARPIN, Fred L(eon) 1913-

PERSONAL: Born March 17, 1913, in New York, N.Y.; son of Solomon and Clara (Jabrow) Karpin; married Nettie Cantor (an assistant to a hotel manager), September 26, 1944; children: Carolyn, Rita. *Education:* Brooklyn College (now Brooklyn College of the City University of New York), B.S., 1934. *Religion:* Jewish. *Home and office:* 9814 Cottrell Ter., Silver Spring, Md.

CAREER: Statistician and economist for U.S. Government, 1934-42, 1946-49; free-lance economist, 1950-62; writer and lecturer on contract bridge, 1962—. *Military service:* U.S. Army Air Forces, 1943-45. *Member:* American Contract Bridge League.

WRITINGS: The Point Count System, Kaufman Press, 1948; *Contract Bridge: The Play of the Cards,* Bridge Quarterly, 1958, reprinted, M. Hardy, 1981; *Psychological Strategy in Contract Bridge,* Harper, 1960, reprinted, Dover, 1977; *How to Play (and Misplay) Slam Contracts,* Harper, 1962, published as *How to Play Slam Contracts,* Collier, 1965; *Winning Play in Contract Bridge: Strategy at Trick One,* Dell, 1964, 2nd edition published as *Bridge Strategy at Trick One,* Dover, 1976; (with Norman Kay and Sidney Siloder) *The Complete Book of Duplicate Bridge,* Putnam, 1965; *Winning Play in Tournament and Duplicate Bridge: How the Experts Triumph,* Dover, 1968, 2nd edition, 1976.

The Finesse: How to Win More Tricks More Often, Prentice-Hall, 1972; *The Art of Card Reading,* Harper, 1973; *The Drawing of Trumps and Its Postponement,* M. Hardy, 1981.†

* * *

KASH, Don E(ldon) 1934-

PERSONAL: Born May 29, 1934, in Macedonia, Iowa; son of Albert (a businessman) and Blanche (Smith) Kash; married Beverly Ann Brendes; children: Kelli Denise, Jeffrey Paul. *Education:* University of Iowa, B.A., 1959, M.A., 1960, Ph.D., 1963. *Office:* Science and Public Policy Program, University of Oklahoma, 432 Physical Science Bldg., Norman, Okla. 73019.

CAREER: Texas Technological College (now Texas Tech University), Lubbock, instructor, 1960-61; Arizona State University, Tempe, assistant professor of political science, 1963-65; University of Missouri at Kansas City, assistant professor of political science, 1965-66; Purdue University, Lafayette, Ind., associate professor of political science and director of Program in Science and Public Policy, 1966-70; University of Oklahoma, Norman, professor of political science and director of Science and Public Policy Program, 1970-78; U.S. Geological Survey, assistant director for regulation, 1978, chief of Conservation Division, 1978-81; University of Oklahoma, George Lynn Cross Research Professor of Political Science and research fellow in Science and Public Policy Program, 1981—. Member of review committee on energy and environmental systems, Argonne Universities Association, 1970-78; chairman of Office of Technology Assessment, Review of Energy Research and Development Administration Program, 1977. National Research Council, member of Marine Board, 1974-77, member of Committee on Gas Production Opportunities, 1977—, member of Assembly of Engineering, 1977-81, chairman of National Dredging Study, 1981—. *Military service:* U.S. Army, 1954-56. *Member:* American Association for the Advancement of Science, American Political Science Association, American Association of University Professors.

WRITINGS: The Politics of Space Cooperation, Purdue University Press, 1967; (with others) *Energy under the Ocean: A Technology Assessment,* University of Oklahoma Press, 1973; (with others) *North Sea Oil and Gas: Implications for Future U.S. Development,* University of Oklahoma Press, 1973; (with others) *Energy Alternatives: A Comparative Analysis,* U.S. Government Printing Office, 1975; (with others) *Our Energy Future: The Role of Research, Development, and Demonstration in Reaching a National Consensus on Energy Supply,* University of Oklahoma Press, 1976; (with others) *Energy Policy-Making: A Selected Bibliography,* University of Oklahoma Press, 1977. Contributor to numerous professional journals.

WORK IN PROGRESS: A book on the evolution of U.S. energy policy.

* * *

KASTENBAUM, Robert (Jay) 1932-

PERSONAL: Born August 8, 1932, in New York, N.Y.; son of Sam and Anne (Einson) Kastenbaum; married Barbara Elizabeth Brown, January 18, 1958; married Beatrice Schaberg, June 17, 1971; children: David Samuel, Cynthia Holly. *Education:* East Los Angeles College, A.A., 1952; Long Beach State College (now California State University, Long Beach), B.A., 1954; University of Southern California, Ph.D., 1959. *Home:* 1149 East Vinedo Lane, Tempe, Ariz. 85284. *Office:* Adult Development and Aging Program, Arizona State University, Tempe, Ariz. 85284.

CAREER: Worked through college years in California as newspaperman, including editor of community weeklies; Cushing Hospital (geriatric institution), Framingham, Mass., head of psychology department and co-principal investigator of U.S. Public Health Service project on working with the aged and dying, 1961-67; Wayne State University, Detroit, Mich., professor of psychology and director of Center for Psychological Studies of Dying, Death, and Lethal Behavior, 1967-72; University of Massachusetts—Boston, professor of psychology, 1972-77; Cushing Hospital, director, 1977-81; Arizona State University, Tempe, professor of gerontology and director of Adult Development and Aging Program, 1981—. Research associate of Institute on Gerontology, University of Michigan, 1967-72.

MEMBER: American Psychological Association (fellow; past president of Division of Adult Development and Aging), American Association of Suicidology (fellow; past president), Gerontological Society of America (fellow; chairperson-elect of Section on Behavioral and Social Sciences). *Awards, honors:* National Institute of Mental Health research fellow at Clark University, 1959-61.

WRITINGS: (Contributor) H. Feifel, *The Meaning of Death,* McGraw, 1959; (editor and contributor) *New Thoughts on Old Age,* Springer, 1964; (editor and contributor) *Contributions to the Psychobiology of Aging,* Springer, 1965; (with Avery D. Weisman) *The Psychological Autopsy: A Study of the Terminal Phase of Life,* Community Mental Health Journal, 1968.

(With Ruth B. Aisenberg) *The Psychology of Death,* Springer, 1972, abridged edition, 1976; (editor with D. P. Kent and

S. Sherwood) *Research Planning and Action for the Elderly,* Behavioral Publications, 1972; *Death, Society, and Human Experience,* Mosby, 1977, revised edition, 1981; *Growing Old: Years of Fulfillment,* Harper, 1979; *Humans Developing: A Lifespan Perspective,* Allyn & Bacon, 1979; (editor and contributor) *Between Life and Death,* Springer, 1979; (with Brian L. Mishara) *Alcohol and Old Age,* Grune, 1980; (editor and contributor) *Old Age on the New Scene,* Springer, 1981; (with T. X. Barber, C. Wilson, B. Ryder, and L. B. Hathaway) *Old, Sick, and Helpless,* Ballinger, 1981.

Also author of play ''All Fall Down: A Celebration of Love and Death,'' 1971, of one-act plays ''Why Does the Fireman?,'' 1980, and ''A Month of Sundays,'' 1980, and of three-act play ''The Spanish Armada, Part II,'' 1982; author of cycle of poems *Is Music Enough?,* 1980. Editor of ''Death and Dying'' series, Springer, 1979—, and ''Cushing Hospital'' series on aging and terminal care, Ballinger, 1980; co-editor, with Jon Hendricks, of ''Foundations of Gerontology'' series, Little, Brown, 1981—. Editor of and contributor to special edition of *Journal of Social Issues,* ''Old Age as a Social Issue,'' 1966.

Contributor to periodicals, including *Journal of Human Relations, Psychology Today,* and *Genetic Psychology Monographs*. Founder and editor of *International Journal of Aging and Human Development* and *Omega, Journal of Death and Dying,* both 1970—.

WORK IN PROGRESS: None of the Above, a trilogy in which the ''three plays pursue the same moral questions in various guises and disguises through all the hiding places of time, place and person''; a book examining the survival of death hypothesis from both a historical and contemporary standpoint, for Multimedia Productions; *Critical Problems in the Psychology of Aging,* for Little, Brown; *Time, Aging, and the Perfection of Being,* for Basic Books; research on ''time perspective and communication across the life-span, on terminal care and the hospice as a social movement, and on the early development of 'old behaviors.'''

SIDELIGHTS: ''As a student of psychology about a quarter of a century ago,'' writes Robert Kastenbaum, ''I was puzzled to see that both love and death were considered either out of bounds or somehow irrelevant to the understanding of human behavior and experience. The same was very nearly true for normal adult development (Was there really life after adolescence?), the meaning of time, the creative process and other topics that intrigued me. I bumbled along my own road, discovering something of both the pleasures and the sorrows of the aged, learning about dying from the dying, and writing articles and books myself because there were so few available on these topics at that time. Now, both the study of aging and the death awareness movement are attracting many resourceful clinicians, researchers, and educators.

''Without stepping back from my own continued professional and scientific interest in these areas, I am gradually giving in to the impulse to explore human experience through other media—and so it is that a wild play or a cycle of poetry will now rush forth in the place of the scientific article or book I am supposed to be writing. A moment in a play or a line of poetry occasionally seems to capture what I have been after for years while wearing my scientist, clinician, or administrator suit. I also am making increased use of the creative writing of others to supplement scientific materials when introducing students and other newcomers to the mysteries of aging and death.''

BIOGRAPHICAL/CRITICAL SOURCES: Newsweek, April 6, 1970.

KATZ, William Loren 1927-

PERSONAL: Born June 2, 1927, in New York, N.Y.; son of Bernard (a researcher) and Madeline (Simon) Katz. *Education:* Syracuse University, B.A., 1950; New York University, M.A., 1952. *Home:* 231 West 13th St., New York, N.Y. 10011. *Office:* New School for Social Research, New York, N.Y. 10011.

CAREER: Writer. New York City public schools, teacher of American history, 1955-60; Greenburgh District 8 School System, Hartsdale, N.Y., high school teacher of American history, 1960-68; New School for Social Research, New York City, instructor in U.S. history, 1977—. Scholar-in-residence and research fellow, Columbia University, 1971-73; lecturer on American Negro history at teacher institutes; teacher of black history at Tombs Prison; producer of audio-visual materials on minorities for classrooms. Has testified before U.S. Senate on Negro history; has appeared on numerous television and radio programs in United States and England, including ''Today Show'' on NBC-TV. Consultant to President Kennedy's Committee on Juvenile Delinquency and Youth Development, Smithsonian Institution, U.S. Air Force schools in England, Belgium, and Holland, 1974-75, Inner London Educational Authority, 1982, British House of Commons, *Life* Magazine, *New York Times,* and CBS-TV. *Military service:* U.S. Navy, 1945-46. *Member:* United Federation of Teachers. *Awards, honors:* Gold Medal Award for nonfiction from National Conference of Christians and Jews, and Brotherhood Award, both 1968, for *Eyewitness: The Negro in American History; The Black West: A Documentary and Pictorial History* received an Oppie Award in 1971 and was named a Book-of-the-Month Club bonus book.

WRITINGS: Eyewitness: The Negro in American History, Pitman, 1967, 3rd edition, 1974; *Five Slave Narratives,* Arno/New York Times, 1968; *Teachers' Guide to American Negro History,* Quadrangle, 1968, revised edition, 1971; (with Warren J. Halliburton) *American Minorities and Majorities: A Syllabus of United States History for Secondary Schools,* Arno, 1970; *The Black West: A Documentary and Pictorial History,* Doubleday, 1971, revised edition, 1973; (with Halliburton) *A History of Black Americans,* Harcourt, 1973; *An Album of Reconstruction,* F. Watts, 1974; *An Album of the Civil War,* F. Watts, 1974; (with Bernard Gaughran) *The Constitutional Amendments,* F. Watts, 1974; *Minorities in American History,* six volumes, F. Watts, 1974-75; (with Jacqueline Hunt) *Making Our Way* (Junior Literary Guild selection), Dial, 1975; *Black People Who Made the Old West,* Crowell, 1977; *The Great Depression,* F. Watts, 1978; *Nazis,* F. Watts, 1979.

General editor, ''The American Negro: His History and Literature'' series, 147 volumes, Arno, 1968-71, ''Minorities in America: Picture Histories'' series, 1972—, ''Teaching Approaches to Black History in the Classroom,'' 1973; editor, ''The Anti-Slavery Crusade in America'' series, 70 volumes, Arno/New York Times, ''Pamphlets in American History'' series, Microfilm Corp. of America/New York Times, 1978-82, ''Vital Sources in American History for High School Students'' series, 179 volumes, 1980. Contributor of articles to periodicals and professional journals, including *Reader's Digest, Journal of Negro History, Journal of Black Studies, Teachers College Record, Freedomways,* and *Southern Education Report*. Member of editorial board, *Black Studies,* 1970—.

WORK IN PROGRESS: A history of the Klu Klux Klan; a screenplay on Seminole Indians who served as scouts for the U.S. Army after the Civil War in Texas; editing Kenneth Wiggins Porter manuscript collection on blacks in the West.

SIDELIGHTS: William Loren Katz told *CA:* "Since I agree with the idea that the historian who condoned a crime was perpetuating it throughout history—his guilt was greater than that of the original perpetrator of the crime, not only because the effect of his sin was more enduring, but also because his motive was less pressing—I have attempted to offer a history that enables us to look at the past intelligently and shape our future with the knowledge of the past in mind. My concentration on minorities has been pursued because I believe that society is only as strong as its weakest members, and that the responsibility of our nation is to spread justice to all within its borders. The first line of defense of all of us is protection for the least of us."

BIOGRAPHICAL/CRITICAL SOURCES: Reader's Digest, July 1969.

* * *

KAUFMAN, Roger (Alexander) 1932-

PERSONAL: Born June 4, 1932, in Washington, D.C.; son of Joseph (an engineer) and Naomi (Greenhouse) Kaufman; married Janice E. Carron (a puppeteer), October 13, 1963; children: Richard J., Nancy Joy, Jac Damon. *Education:* George Washington University, B.A., 1950; Johns Hopkins University, M.A., 1956; University of California, Berkeley, graduate study, 1956-59; New York University, Ph.D., 1963. *Home:* 8011 Prospect Way, La Mesa, Calif. 92041. *Office:* Graduate School of Human Behavior, U.S. International University, San Diego, Calif. 92124.

CAREER: Diplomate of American Board of Professional Psychology, 1970. Martin Co., Baltimore, Md., head of personnel and training, 1960-61; U.S. Industries, New York City, manager, training system analyst, 1961-62; Bolt Beranek & Newman, Inc., New York City, senior consultant in education and training, 1962-64; Douglas Aircraft Co., Long Beach, Calif., assistant to vice-president for engineering and assistant to the vice-president for research and development, 1964-66; Chapman College, Orange, Calif., professor of education, 1966-70; U.S. International University, Elliott Campus, San Diego, Calif., professor of psychology and human behavior at Graduate School of Human Behavior, 1970—. Adjunct professor at University of Southern California, 1967-70. Chairman of planning, management, and educational evaluation panel, National Center for Educational Research and Development of National Institute of Education, 1972—; member, Secretary of the U.S. Navy's Advisory Board on Education and Training (SABET), 1972-76; consultant to numerous state and local education agencies, industrial organizations, military agencies, and to secretary of U.S. Department of Health, Education, and Welfare, 1969-70.

MEMBER: American Psychological Association, American Educational Research Association, National Society for Performance and Instruction (secretary, 1962-63; vice-president, 1963-64; president, 1974-75), Human Factors Society, Phi Delta Kappa. *Awards, honors:* Presidential citation, National Society for Programmed Instruction.

WRITINGS: System Approach to Education: Derivation and Definition, University of Oregon, 1970; (with Leon Lessinger and Dale Parnell) *Accountability: Policies and Procedures,* Croft Educational Service, 1971; *Educational System Planning,* Prentice-Hall, 1972; (with Fenwick W. English) *Needs Assessment: A Focus for Curriculum Development,* Association for Supervision and Curriculum Development, 1975; *FORTRAN Coloring Books,* MIT Press, 1978; *Identifying and Solving Problems: A System Approach,* 2nd edition, University Associates, 1979; (with English) *Needs Assessment: Concept and Application,* Educational Technology Publications, 1979. Contributor to journals in his field.†

* * *

KELLING, George W(alton) 1944-

PERSONAL: Born April 7, 1944, in Philadelphia, Pa.; son of Harold D. (an English professor) and Dora (Walton) Kelling; married second wife, Rosemarie (a teacher), December, 1972; married third wife, Lisa Springer (a writer), June, 1982; children: (stepchildren) Annette, Michael, Kenneth. *Education:* University of Colorado, B.A., 1965, M.A., 1971, Ph.D., 1972. *Politics:* "I do not vote." *Religion:* Society of Friends (Quaker). *Home and office:* 255 West 75th St., New York, N.Y. 10023.

CAREER: Columbia University, Barnard College, New York, N.Y., assistant professor of psychology, 1972-81; full-time writer, 1981—. Subject matter consultant to Professional Examination Service, 1979—.

WRITINGS: Language: Mirror, Tool, and Weapon, Nelson-Hall, 1975; (contributor) Desmond S. Cartwright, Barbara Tomson, and Hershey Schwartz, editors, *Gang Delinquency,* Brooks-Cole, 1975; (translator with Lisa Springer) Ludwig Paneth, *The Meaning of Numbers in the Unconscious,* Samuel Weiser, 1979; *Blind Mazes: A Study of Love,* Nelson-Hall, 1980.

Author, with L. Springer, of four filmstrip scripts, "A History of Dreams," "Research on Sleep and Dreams," "The Interpretation of Dreams," and "Facts about Dreams," for Avna Productions and Barbara Castro Productions, all 1981. Also author of a pamphlet, *Guidelines for Item Writers,* Professional Examination Service, 1981; also author of numerous papers presented to organizations. Contributor of articles and short stories to numerous publications, including *Forms, Insight, Newsday, Psychoanalytic Review, Criminology, Psychological Reports,* and *Runner's World.*

WORK IN PROGRESS: A book on the perception of people; another book on love; a novel; a book on the problems faced by the aged.

* * *

KELLOW, Kathleen
See HIBBERT, Eleanor Burford

* * *

KELLY, George W. 1894-

PERSONAL: Born May 8, 1894, in Scotch Ridge, Ohio; son of Alfred Nathan (an evangelist) and Flora (a teacher; maiden name, Lepard) Kelly; married Jane Cleveland (deceased); married Augusta Zientara, May 16, 1952; children: Winston. *Education:* Attended Valparaiso University, 1910, and Dickson College, 1911. *Politics:* "The best man." *Religion:* "My own philosophy." *Home:* 15126 County Rd. G, Cortez, Colo. 81321.

CAREER: Writer. Grew up in Ohio and wilderness highlands of Tennessee; worked for Union Pacific railroad for five years;

worked as a grower, orchardist and landscape architect, 1919-30; established Arapahoe Acres Nursery in Littleton, Colo., 1930; director of Horticulture House in Denver, Colo., 1944-45; conducted radio and television programs entitled "Green Thumb," 1951-56; operated Cottonwood Garden Shop in Littleton, 1955-66; designed Denver Garden Show, 1964-70; bought 100 acres of desert in McElmo Canyon, Colo., in 1966, and experiments with landscape materials and native plants. Co-founder of Rocky Mountain Horticultural Publishing Co.

MEMBER: American Horticultural Council (founding member), Garden Writers Association of America (fellow), Colorado Forestry and Horticulture Association. *Awards, honors:* American Horticultural Council award, 1957; American Horticulture Society award, 1959; National Council of State Garden Clubs award, 1959; American Rose Society award, 1975.

WRITINGS: Rocky Mountain Horticulture Is Different, privately printed, 1950, expanded edition published as *How to Have Good Gardens in the Sunshine States,* Pruett, 1967, published as *Rocky Mountain Horticulture,* Pruett, 1967; *Sort Guide to the Perennial Garden Flowers,* Crown, 1964.

A Guide to the Woody Plants of Colorado, Pruett, 1970; *A Way to Beauty,* Pruett, 1976; *Trees for the Rocky Mountains,* privately printed, 1976; *Shrubs for the Rocky Mountains,* Rocky Mountain Horticultural Publishing, 1979.

Ground Covers for the Rocky Mountains, Rocky Mountain Horticultural Publishing, 1980; *Useful Native Plants of the Four-Corner States,* Rocky Mountain Horticultural Publishing, 1980; *Flowers for the Rocky Mountains,* Rocky Mountain Horticultural Publishing, 1981; *These Are the Things I Prize,* Rocky Mountain Horticultural Publishing, 1982. Also author of pamphlets *Good Gardens with Less Water in Colorado,* 1981, and *Grow Your Own Food,* 1982. Contributor of several hundred short stories to magazines and newspapers. Editor, *Green Thumb* magazine, 1944-55.

WORK IN PROGRESS: A simplified study of Colorado wildflowers.

SIDELIGHTS: "For thirty years or so," George W. Kelly told *CA,* "my whole effort and ambition has been to furnish horticultural literature fitted for this arid alkaline area of the Rocky Mountains which has been almost completely neglected by the garden writers of the East and California."

* * *

KENDRICK, David Andrew 1937-

PERSONAL: Born November 14, 1937, in Gatesville, Tex.; son of Andrew Greene (a banker) and Nina (a librarian; maiden name, Murray) Kendrick; married Gail Tidd, July 4, 1964; children: Ann Murray, Colin Andrew. *Education:* University of Texas, B.A., 1960; Massachusetts Institute of Technology, Ph.D., 1965, postdoctoral study, 1965-66. *Home:* 7209 Lamplight Lane, Austin, Tex. 78731. *Office:* Department of Economics, University of Texas, Austin, Tex. 78712.

CAREER: Harvard University, Cambridge, Mass., assistant professor of economics, 1966-70; University of Texas at Austin, professor of economics, 1970—. Visiting scholar, Stanford University, 1969-70; visiting professor, Massachusetts Institute of Technology, 1978-79. Consultant to World Bank and to U.S. Bureau of the Budget. *Military service:* U.S. Army Reserve, active duty, 1960-61; present rank, captain. *Member:* Econometric Society, Society for Economic Dynamics and Control (president, 1980-81), Phi Beta Kappa, Pi Tau Sigma.

WRITINGS: Programming Investment in the Process Industries, M.I.T. Press, 1967; *Notes and Problems in Economic Theory,* Markham, 1970; (editor with M. Intriligator) *Frontiers of Quantitative Economics,* North-Holland Publishing, 1975; (with Ardy Stoutjesdijk) *The Planning of Industrial Investment Projects,* Johns Hopkins University Press, 1978; (with P. Dixon and S. Bowles) *Notes and Problems in Microeconomic Theory,* North-Holland Publishing, 1980; *Stochastic Control for Economic Models,* McGraw, 1981. Founding editor, with Edison Tse, of *Journal of Economic Dynamics and Control.*

* * *

KENNEDY, Gavin 1940-

PERSONAL: Born February 20, 1940, in Wetherby, Yorkshire, England; son of Robert (a motor mechanic) and Anne (Kennedy) Plenderleith; married Patricia Anne Millar (a college lecturer), July 2, 1973; children: Florence, Beatrice, Gavin, Jr. *Education:* University of Strathclyde, B.A., 1969, M.Sc., 1972; University of Brunel, Ph.D., 1974. *Politics:* "Member of Scottish National Party—I'm a kind of radical democrat drifting towards right of centre." *Religion:* "Protestant (my wife and children are Roman Catholic)." *Home:* 33 Midmar Gardens, Edinburgh EH10 6DY, Scotland. *Agent:* Colin Haycraft, Duckworth, 43 Gloucester Crescent, London N.W.1, England. *Office:* Business School, University of Strathclyde, George St., Glasgow, Scotland.

CAREER: University of Brunel, Uxbridge, England, lecturer in economics, 1971-73; University of Strathclyde, Glasgow, Scotland, senior lecturer in economics, 1974—. Director of Blair, Kennedy & Associates (management and economic consultants). *Member:* British Institute of Management, Association of Teachers of Management, Writers Guild of Great Britain, Navy Records Society, Society for Nautical Research, Hakluyt Society. *Awards, honors:* Two NATO research fellowships; *Yorkshire Post* Book of the Year Award, 1978, for *Bligh.*

WRITINGS: The Military in the Third World, Scribner, 1974; *The Economics of Defence,* Faber, 1975; (editor and contributor) *The Radical Approach: Papers on an Independent Scotland,* Palingenesis Press, 1976; *The Death of Captain Cook,* Duckworth, 1978; *Bligh* (biography), Duckworth, 1978; (editor) R. T. Gould, *Captain Cook,* Duckworth, 1978; *Burden Sharing in NATO,* Holmes & Meier, 1979; (co-author) *Managing Negotiations,* Business Books, 1980, published as *Managing Negotiations: A Guide for Managers, Labor Workers, and Everyone Else Who Wants to Win,* Prentice-Hall, 1982; (editor, author of introduction, and contributor of captions for illustrations) Sir John Barrow, *The Mutiny of the Bounty,* Godine, 1980; (editor with George Mackaness and contributor) *A Book of the Bounty: William Bligh and Others,* Dent, 1981; *Mathematics for Innumerate Economists,* Holmes & Meier, 1982; *Everything Is Negotiable!,* Hutchinson, 1982; *The Compleat International Business Negotiator,* Hutchinson, 1983; *Defense Economics,* Duckworth, in press; *Invitation to Statistics,* Martin Robertson, in press.

WORK IN PROGRESS: Myopic Visionaries, a book "about how the left in NATO countries rationalise the existence and activities of socialist militarism."

SIDELIGHTS: "My first two books," writes Gavin Kennedy, "were extensions of my academic work. I next wrote on Captain Cook and Captain Bligh out of interest in the historical controversies associated with both men. The Bligh biography is probably too long (it defends Bligh and criticises Fletcher Christian), but I enjoyed the research work. Subsequent invitations to edit and introduce two other *Bounty* books created the opportunity to update and modify the assertions made in my *Bligh*. I still receive correspondence from all over the world on the *Bounty* story, including letters from descendants of the mutineers. I hope to return to the subject with a book in a year or two.

"My other books can be divided neatly by style and subject: those that are written with a touch of humour and those in a more serious vein, and those that reflect my role as an economics teacher and those that are the product of my consultancy work in business negotiation. On writing as a vocation, I do not recommend a too early or too ambitious goal of relying on book royalties—unless the author has either a disposition in favour of poverty or a generous benefactor. Writing is hard though agreeable work and is best practiced rather than thought about. I believe my writing is improving (slowly), and while much of this is the result of increasing experience, I think also my switching from a typewriter to a word processor had something to do with it. Endless revision is a daunting task, but the word processor makes this much easier."

Reviewing Kennedy's *Bligh* in the *Washington Post Book World,* Alfred Friendly calls the biography "surely the finest produced to date, a monument of prodigious research, skilled organization and argument as tight as a Euclidean proposition. His thesis, presented with compelling evidence, is that the mutiny derived from 'the coincidence of the collapse in the authority of the commander and an emotional storm in an immature and possibly mentally unstable young man.' (Christian was only twenty-four.)" Friendly maintains that Kennedy clearly shows "it was [Fletcher] Christian and his companions' subsequent behavior in the South Pacific, not Bligh's, that was of unrivaled brutality, bloodiness, and insanity."

MEDIA ADAPTATIONS: "The Art of Negotiation," a thirty-minute filmed adaptation of *Managing Negotiations,* was produced by Rank-Aldis in 1982.

AVOCATIONAL INTERESTS: Reading, travel (largely on the seminar and lecture circuit).

BIOGRAPHICAL/CRITICAL SOURCES: Washington Post Book World, January 28, 1979; *New York Times Book Review,* March 1, 1981.

* * *

KENNEDY, Paul Michael 1945-

PERSONAL: Born June 17, 1945, in Wallsend, England; married; children: three. *Education:* University of Newcastle-upon-Tyne, M.A. (first class honors), 1966; Oxford University, D.Phil., 1970. *Politics:* "Wobbly." *Religion:* Roman Catholic. *Office:* School of English and American Studies, University of East Anglia, Norwich NR4 7TJ, England.

CAREER: University of East Anglia, Norwich, England, lecturer, 1970-75, reader, 1975-82, professor of history, 1982—. *Member:* Royal Historical Society (fellow). *Awards, honors:* Fellow of Alexander von Humboldt Foundation, 1972; fellow at Institute for Advanced Study, Princeton University, 1978-79.

WRITINGS: Pacific Onslaught, Ballantine, 1972; *Pacific Victory,* Ballantine, 1973; *The Samoan Tangle,* Barnes & Noble, 1974; *The Rise and Fall of British Naval Mastery,* Scribner, 1976; (editor with J. A. Moses) *Germany in the Pacific and Far East, 1870-1914,* University of Queensland Press, 1977; (editor) *The War Plans of the Great Powers, 1880-1914,* Allen & Unwin, 1979; *The Rise of the Anglo-German Antagonism, 1860-1914,* Allen & Unwin, 1980; *The Realities behind Diplomacy: Background Influences on British External Policy, 1865-1980,* Allen & Unwin, 1981. Contributor to history journals in England, Germany, Australia, Canada, and the United States.

WORK IN PROGRESS: Strategy and Diplomacy, 1850-1945 (essays); *The Dynamics of World Power, 1500-2000,* for Fontana.

SIDELIGHTS: Paul M. Kennedy's *The Rise of the Anglo-German Antagonism, 1860-1914* is an "exceptionally well-researched account," writes James Joll in the *Times Literary Supplement.* "Kennedy has provided both a clear political narrative . . . and a detailed analysis of the economic and social factors which led to the new nationalism which made war possible. He provides an admirable synthesis of the current historiographical debate about the influence of domestic factors on foreign policy and the role of pressure groups in both England and Germany. He refuses to fall into the error common among many historians, especially in Germany, where the discussion of these questions has a much more polemical tone than in England, of thinking that everything can be explained in terms of a single cause or at least a single analytical model."

BIOGRAPHICAL/CRITICAL SOURCES: Economist, January 17, 1981; *Times Literary Supplement,* January 30, 1981, May 22, 1981.

* * *

KENT, Philip
See BULMER, (Henry) Kenneth

* * *

KETCHAM, Orman W(eston) 1918-

PERSONAL: Born October 1, 1918, in Brooklyn, N.Y.; son of Walter S. (a sales manager) and Arline (Weston) Ketcham; married Anne Phelps Stokes (a teacher), December 22, 1947; children: Anne W., Helen L. P., Elizabeth M., Susan S. *Education:* Princeton University, B.A. (cum laude), 1940; Yale University, LL.B., 1947. *Religion:* Congregational. *Home:* 2 East Melrose St., Chevy Chase, Md. 20015. *Office:* Washington College of Law, American University, Massachusetts and Nebraska Aves. N.W., Washington, D.C. 20016.

CAREER: Admitted to the Bar of U.S. District Court, 1948, of U.S. Court of Appeals, 1948, and of Supreme Court of the United States, 1952. Covington & Burling, Washington, D.C., associate attorney, 1947-52; Fund for the Republic, Washington, D.C., executive assistant, 1953; U.S. Foreign Operations Administration, Washington, D.C., assistant general counsel, 1953-55; U.S. Department of Justice, Washington, D.C., trial attorney in Antitrust Division, 1955-57; Juvenile Court of the District of Columbia, Washington, D.C., judge, 1957-70; Superior Court of the District of Columbia, Washington, D.C., associate judge, 1970-77; National Center for State Courts, Williamsburg, Va., senior staff attorney, 1977-81; American University, Washington College of Law, Washington, D.C., senior fellow and adjunct professor of law, 1981—.

Adjunct professor of law at Georgetown University, 1963-67, University of Virginia, 1971-77, and William and Mary College, 1978-80; member of faculty, Salzburg Seminar in American Studies, 1976. National Council on Crime and Delinquency, member of council of judges, 1959-74, member of board of directors, 1973—; member of Coordinating Committee for Effective Justice, 1965-69; member of U.S. delegation, United Nations Congress on Prevention of Crime and Treatment of Offenders, 1965 and 1975; member of visiting committee to Brookings Institute, 1971-77. Advisor to President's Commission on Law Enforcement and Administration of Justice, 1966-67, and National Committee on Secondary Education, 1970-74; chairman of advisory board, Ford Foundation's "Lawyer in Juvenile Court" project, 1966-68; member of advisory committee, National Legal Resource Center, American Bar Association, 1978—; member of advisory board, Crime Stoppers, U.S.A., 1980—. *Military service:* U.S. Naval Reserve, active duty in Atlantic and Pacific theaters, 1941-46; became lieutenant commander.

MEMBER: International Association of Youth Magistrates (vice-president, 1966-74), American Bar Association, National Council of Juvenile Court Judges (president, 1965-66), American Law Institute, District of Columbia Bar Association, Phi Delta Phi, Cosmos Club, Chevy Chase Club. *Awards, honors:* Elliott/Winant fellow of British-American Associates, 1981.

WRITINGS: (Contributor) Margaret Rosenheim, editor, *Justice for the Child,* Free Press of Glencoe, 1962; (with Monrad G. Paulsen) *Cases and Materials Relating to Juvenile Courts,* Foundation Press, 1967; (with others) *The Changing Faces of Juvenile Justice,* New York University Press, 1978. Contributor to *U.N. International Year of the Child* and to periodicals, including *Crime and Delinquency, Northwestern University Law Review, Virginia Law Review, Cornell Law Review, Social Science Review, George Washington Law Review, Rutgers Law Review,* and *Boston University Law Review.*

SIDELIGHTS: Orman W. Ketcham told *CA* that legal writing "can be both informative and interesting. There is no reason to assume that all legal and judicial written expressions are obfuscation or legalese. I believe that legal writing must adhere to an outline and structure, but it need not be dull and pedantic or filled with professional legalisms."

* * *

KIENZLE, William X(avier) 1928-
(Mark Boyle)

PERSONAL: Born September 11, 1928, in Detroit, Mich.; son of Alphonzo and Mary Louise (Boyle) Kienzle; married Javan Herman (an editor and researcher), 1974. *Education:* Sacred Heart Seminary College, B.A., 1950; also attended St. John's Seminary, 1950-54, and University of Detroit, 1968. *Politics:* Independent. *Religion:* Roman Catholic. *Residence:* Southfield, Mich.

CAREER: Ordained Roman Catholic priest, 1954; left priesthood, 1974; Roman Catholic Archdiocese of Detroit, Detroit, Mich., archdiocesan priest in five parishes, 1954-74; *MPLS.* magazine, Minneapolis, Minn., editor-in-chief, 1974-77; Western Michigan University, Kalamazoo, associate director of Center for Contemplative Studies, 1977-78; University of Dallas, Irving, Tex., director of Center for Contemplative Studies, 1978-79; writer 1979—. *Member:* Authors Guild, Authors League of America, Crime Writers Association. *Awards, honors:* Michigan Knights of Columbus journalism award, 1963, for general excellence; honorable mention from Catholic Press Association, 1974, for editorial writing.

WRITINGS—Mystery novels; all published by Andrews & McMeel: *The Rosary Murders* (Mystery Guild selection; Literary Guild and Doubleday Book Club alternate selection), 1979; *Death Wears a Red Hat* (Mystery Guild selection; Literary Guild and Doubleday Book Club alternate selection), 1980; *Mind over Murder* (Mystery Guild selection; Literary Guild and Doubleday Book Club alternate selection), 1981; *Assault with Intent* (Mystery Guild selection; Literary Guild and Doubleday Book Club alternate selection), 1982; *Shadow of Death* (Mystery Guild, Literary Guild, and Doubleday Book Club selection), 1983. Contributor under pseudonym Mark Boyle to *MPLS.* magazine. Editor-in-chief of *Michigan Catholic,* 1962-74.

WORK IN PROGRESS: Two mystery novels for Andrews & McMeel, *Kill and Tell* and *Murder on 3.*

SIDELIGHTS: Though he no longer delivers the sermons that captivated his parishioners, William X. Kienzle is still telling stories. After leaving the priesthood in 1974, he "exchanged his pulpit for a typewriter," to use Bill Dunn's words, and began writing the tales that have made him a best-selling mystery author. The twenty years he spent in the clergy now provide the raw material for his books. "I set my mysteries in the church because that's what I know best," he explained to Dunn in a *Publishers Weekly* interview. And the phenomenal success of his first novel attests to his broad appeal. *The Rosary Murders* spent ten weeks on the B. Dalton bestseller list, sold an estimated 35,000 hardback copies in the United States, and had an initial paperback run of 325,000 copies. Foreign rights have been purchased in the Netherlands, Great Britain, Denmark, Brazil, Germany and Spain. And the accomplishment is all the more impressive because Kienzle works without the assistance of an agent.

A native Detroiter, Kienzle uses the city and its Catholic parishes as a backdrop for his fiction, reportedly drawing many of his characters from people he has known. His work is so finely tuned to the ambience of Detroit that he returned to the area after accepting a teaching post at the University of Dallas. "I had to get back because all of my books were involved with Detroit," he told Dunn. "The city was changing. I wanted to be there."

According to *Detroit News Magazine* writer Andrea Wojack, Kienzle's choice of genres was "an afterthought. His original idea was to tell stories of the parish life of Detroit clergymen." In an interview with *Detroit Free Press* writer Dave Zurawik, Kienzle explained: "My real intent was to write about fundamentally my experiences in the seminary and mostly my twenty years in the priesthood, because I span from the time of Bing Crosby in 'Going My Way' in '54. At that time when I was ordained, the image of a priest was so firm. All the big actors in Hollywood—Gregory Peck and Humphrey Bogart, big men—were playing priests. In '74 by the time I left there was no image left. . . . I wanted to write about the strong image."

During this period, Kienzle was working full time. Having spent the last twelve years of his priesthood editing the *Michigan Catholic,* Kienzle was able to secure a position as editor-in-chief of *MPLS.*—Minneapolis's city magazine. Overworked and underpaid, he left that position for the opportunity to teach contemplative studies at first one, then another, university. But, "all that time," Kienzle told Zurawik, "the strong image of a priest had been in my mind." He contacted a publisher about writing his memoirs but was informed that there was no readership for that type of book. "And then somebody suggested there is a market, there are people who are interested in mystery books, and then on the back of an envelope I just put down these names that would correspond to the ten commandments and that was the skeleton of *Rosary Murders*.''

For his main character, Kienzle created Father Robert Koesler, an amateur sleuth and sharply defined priest, who resembles Kienzle in several ways. ''The fictitious Father Koesler divides his time between his pastoral duties within the Detroit archdiocese and his journalistic duties as an editor of the area's Catholic newspaper, just as Kienzle spent his time during the 1960's,'' Wojack observes. Despite these similarities, Wojack does not envision Koesler as Kienzle in disguise. Rather, she sees him as a product of both Kienzle's background and ''the tradition of clerical detectives in fiction, like Chesterton's Father Brown and Harry Kemelman's Rabbi Small.'' And, writing in the *Los Angeles Times Book Review,* Andrew M. Greeley makes a similar observation: ''William Kienzle is the Harry Kemelman of Catholicism, and his priest detective, Robert Koesler . . . is the Detroit response to Rabbi Small. . . . I am not suggesting that Kienzle is consciously imitating Kemelman—though there would be nothing wrong with such imitation. Rather I am arguing that religio-ethnic subcultures are fertile seedbeds for mystery stories. Kienzle's sensitivity to pathos and foolishness, shallow fads and rigid ideologies, mindless nonsense and deep faith of the contemporary Catholic scene compares favorably with Kemelman's vivid description of suburban Jewish life.''

Despite Kienzle's assertion that his novels are, as Dunn reports, ''first of all thrillers,'' many critics find a deeper meaning in his work. In his review of *Mind over Murder,* for example, *Free Press* managing editor Neal Shine observes: ''There has always been the sense that there's as much message as mystery in Kienzle's books. Kienzle is a former Detroit priest whose feelings about some of the ways in which the Catholic Church deports itself can hardly be called ambivalent. In *Mind over Murder* he goes to the heart of the matter for a lot of Catholics—marriage and the Church. The people with the clearest motives for rubbing out the monsignor [Thomas Thompson, director of the Tribunal, the archdiocesan matrimonial court,] are those who have run up against his incredibly inflexible rulings on marriage.''

While Kienzle acknowledges that he left the priesthood because he disagreed with the Church laws banning divorce and remarriage, he remains a practicing Catholic with fond memories of his years as a clergyman. He writes not to retaliate against Church authority but because, as he told *CA,* ''I have abundant stories to tell.''

MEDIA ADAPTATIONS: Take One Productions has purchased the film rights to *The Rosary Murders.*

BIOGRAPHICAL/CRITICAL SOURCES: Best Sellers, July, 1979, July, 1981, July, 1982; *Detroit Free Press,* February 22, 1980, April 26, 1981; *Detroit News Magazine,* March 16, 1980; *Publishers Weekly,* April 18, 1980; *New York Times Book Review,* June 15, 1980, June 21, 1981, May 23, 1982; *Los Angeles Times Book Review,* June 22, 1980, May 23, 1982; *Times Literary Supplement,* October 3, 1980; *Detroit News,* April 5, 1981; *Los Angeles Times,* April 24, 1981; *Chicago Tribune Book World,* July 11, 1982.

—Sketch by Donna Olendorf

* * *

KILBY, Clyde Samuel 1902-

PERSONAL: Born September 26, 1902, in Johnson City, Tenn.; son of James L. (a carpenter) and Sophronia C. (Miller) Kilby; married Martha Harris, June 11, 1930. *Education:* University of Arkansas, B.A., 1929; University of Minnesota, M.A., 1931; New York University, Ph.D., 1938. *Religion:* Presbyterian. *Home:* 620 North Washington St., Wheaton, Ill. *Office:* Department of English, Wheaton College, Wheaton, Ill. 60187.

CAREER: John Brown College (now University), Siloam Springs, Ark., registrar, 1927-30, superintendent of education and chairman of department of English, 1931-34; Rochester State Junior College, Rochester, Minn., registrar, 1934-35; Wheaton College, Wheaton, Ill., assistant professor, 1935-38, associate professor, 1938-45, professor of English, 1945-77, professor emeritus, 1977—, chairman of Division of Language and Literature, 1945-46 and 1952-58, chairman of department of English, 1951-66, assistant dean of men, 1935-38, curator, C. S. Lewis Collection, 1973-76, curator, Marion E. Wade Collection, 1976-81, curator emeritus, 1981—. Extension instructor, University of Arkansas, Fayetteville, 1934-35. *Member:* Modern Language Association of America, Near East Archeological Society (vice-president, 1958), Conference on Christianity and Literature (president, 1956-59), Johnsonian Circle, Lambda Iota Tau (international executive secretary, 1958-60). *Awards, honors:* Alumni grant, Wheaton College, 1948-49; Senior Teacher of the Year Award, Wheaton College, 1964; Illinois Author of the Year, Illinois Association of Teachers of English, 1973.

WRITINGS: Poetry and Life, Odyssey, 1953, reprinted, Books for Libraries, 1975; *Minority of One,* Eerdmans, 1959; *Christianity and Aesthetics,* Inter-Varsity, 1961; *The Christian World of C. S. Lewis,* Eerdmans, 1964; (editor) *A Mind Awake: An Anthology of C. S. Lewis,* Harcourt, 1967; (editor) C. S. Lewis, *Letters to an American Lady,* Eerdmans, 1967; (contributor) M. R. Hillegas, editor, *Shadows of Imagination,* Southern Illinois University Press, 1969.

(Contributor) Carolyn Keefe, editor, *C. S. Lewis: Speaker and Teacher,* Zondervan, 1971; (with Douglas Gilbert) *C. S. Lewis: Images of His World,* Eerdmans, 1973; (contributor) *Imagination and the Spirit,* Eerdmans, 1971; *Tolkien and the Silmarillion,* Harold Shaw, 1976; *Image of Salvation in the Fiction of C. S. Lewis,* Harold Shaw, 1978; (editor with Marjorie L. Mead) *Brothers and Friends: The Diaries of Major Warren Hamilton Lewis,* Harper, in press. Contributor of book reviews to *New York Herald-Tribune;* contributor of articles to *Explicator, Studies in Philology, Word Study, Christianity Today,* and *Illinois State Historical Journal.* Contributing editor, *Christianity Today,* 1956—; consulting editor, *His* (magazine), 1958—, and *Eternity* (magazine).

WORK IN PROGRESS: Purposive Beauty, a manuscript dealing with the Christian aspects of aesthetics.

* * *

KING, Josie
See GERMANY, (Vera) Jo(sephine)

* * *

KINSEY, Elizabeth
See CLYMER, Eleanor

* * *

KIRK, Ruth (Kratz) 1925-

PERSONAL: Born May 7, 1925, in Los Angeles, Calif.; daughter of Reginald Patrick (an engineer) and Esther Clarice (a physician; maiden name Cumberland) Kratz; married Louis Gladwin Kirk (a former National Park Service naturalist), September 3, 1945; children: Bruce Gladwin, Wayne Louis. *Education:* Attended Occidental College, 1943-44, and Tennessee State University, 1946. *Residence:* Tacoma, Wash.

CAREER: Writer, photographer, and natural historian. Peninsula College, Port Angeles, Wash., instructor in photography, 1962-65; Canadian Broadcasting Corp. (CBC-TV), Vancouver, British Columbia, writer and narrator of documentary films, beginning 1966; University of Washington Press, Seattle, co-producer with husband, Louis Kirk, of films and filmstrips of natural history, beginning 1968. Member of board of managers, Washington State Congress P.T.A., 1966-68; trustee, Washington State Nature Conservancy, beginning 1970. Adviser to International Commission on National Parks, 1963-64. *Member:* National Audubon Society, Wilderness Society, Delta Kappa Gamma. *Awards, honors:* Kenneth Boyle Award, Northwest Booksellers, 1967; Governor's award, State Festival of Arts, 1967 and 1971; award from Washington Pen Women, 1969; Children's Book Award (shared with co-author Richard D. Daugherty), New York Academy of Science, 1975, for *Hunters of the Whale*.

WRITINGS: (With Ansel Adams and Nancy Newhall) *Death Valley*, Five Associates (San Francisco), 1954; *The Olympic Seashore*, Olympic Natural History Association, 1962, 2nd edition, 1969; *Sigemi, A Japanese Village Girl* (juvenile), Harcourt, 1965; *The Olympic Rain Forest*, University of Washington Press, 1966; *Japan: Crossroads of East and West* (Junior Literary Guild selection), Nelson, 1966; *David, Young Chief of the Quileutes: An American Indian Today*, Harcourt, 1967; *Laura of Mexico*, Singer, 1969; (with Robert Reynolds and Archie Satterfield) *California: Its Coast and Desert*, C. H. Belding, 1974; *Badlands*, Badlands Natural History Association, 1976; (with Richard D. Daugherty) *Exploring Washington Archaeology*, University of Washington Press, 1978; *Snow*, Morrow, 1978.

Illustrated with photographs by the author and husband, Louis Kirk: *Exploring Death Valley*, Stanford University Press, 1956, 3rd edition, 1977; *Exploring the Olympic Peninsula*, University of Washington Press, 1964, 3rd edition, 1980; *Exploring Mount Rainier*, University of Washington Press, 1968, revised edition, 1973; *The Oldest Man in America: An Adventure in Archaeology*, Harcourt, 1970; *Desert Life*, Natural History Press, 1970; *Exploring Yellowstone*, University of Washington Press, 1972; *Desert: The American Southwest*, Houghton, 1973; *Yellowstone: The First National Park*, Atheneum, 1974; (with Daugherty) *Hunters of the Whale: An Adventure of Northwest Coast Archaeology*, Morrow, 1974; *Washington State National Parks, Historic Sites, Recreation Areas, and Natural Landmarks*, University of Washington Press, 1974; *Exploring Crater Lake Country*, University of Washington Press, 1975.

Also author of filmscripts produced by CBC-TV and PBS-TV.

SIDELIGHTS: Having lived at ranger stations from the Mexican to the Canadian borders in such varied areas as Death Valley, Calif., Organ Pipe Cactus, Ariz., Olympic National Park, Wash., and the Badlands of South Dakota, Ruth Kirk and her husband, Louis, traveled to England, Scotland, and Wales in 1963, and to Southeast Asia and Japan in 1964, as advisers on national park development for the International Commission on National Parks. Kirk told *CA* that she and her husband now spend their time making documentaries that share a common theme: "Man in relation to the land—past, present, and future."

BIOGRAPHICAL/CRITICAL SOURCES: Occidental College Alumnus, January, 1965; *New York Times*, January 23, 1978.

* * *

KLINE, George L(ouis) 1921-

PERSONAL: Born March 3, 1921, in Galesburg, Ill.; son of Allen Sides and Wahneta (Burner) Kline; married Virginia Harrington Hardy (a registration supervisor at Pennsylvania Institute of Technology), April 17, 1943; children: Brenda Marie, Jeffrey Allen, Christina Hardy (Mrs. Francis C. Hanak). *Education:* Attended Boston University, 1938-41; Columbia College, A.B. (with honors), 1947; Columbia University, M.A., 1948, Ph.D., 1950. *Home:* 632 Valley View Rd., Ardmore, Pa. 19003. *Office:* Thomas Library, Bryn Mawr College, Bryn Mawr, Pa. 19010.

CAREER: Columbia University, New York, N.Y., instructor in philosophy, 1950-52; University of Chicago, Chicago, Ill., visiting assistant professor of philosophy, 1952-53; Columbia University, instructor, 1953-54, assistant professor of philosophy, 1954-59; Bryn Mawr College, Bryn Mawr, Pa., lecturer in philosophy and Russian, 1959-60, associate professor, 1960-66, professor of philosophy, 1966—, Milton C. Nahm Professor of Philosophy, 1981—, chairman of department, 1977-82. Visiting professor at University of Puerto Rico, summer, 1957, Swarthmore College, 1959-60, 1981-82, Johns Hopkins University, 1968-69, and University of Pennsylvania, 1980-81; lecturer at London School of Economics and Political Science, Oxford University, Trinity College, University of Dublin, Free University (West Berlin, West Germany), University of Heidelberg, University of Marburg, University of Zagreb, University of Belgrade, Mid-East Technical University (Ankara, Turkey), and Queens University (Belfast, Northern Ireland). Consultant to U.S.S.R. research program, 1952-55, Foreign Area Fellowship program, 1959-64, National Endowment for the Humanities, 1972-77, 1982—, and Council for International Exchange of Scholars, 1980-82. *Military service:* U.S. Army Air Forces, 1942-45; became first lieutenant; received Distinguished Flying Cross.

MEMBER: Internationale Hegel-Vereinigung, International Society for Metaphysics, P.E.N. American Center, Metaphysical Society of America (councillor, 1969-71, 1978-82), American Association for the Advancement of Slavic Studies (member of board of directors, 1972-75), Hegel Society of America (councillor, 1968-70, 1974-78; vice-president, 1971-73), Philosophy Education Society (member of board of directors, 1966—), Society for the Philosophy of Creativity (chairman of Eastern division, 1976-79), Society for the Advancement of American Philosophy, Society for the Study of the History of Philosophy, Society for Phenomenology and Existential Philosophy, Society for Ancient Greek Philosophy, Phi Beta Kappa.

AWARDS, HONORS: Cutting fellowship for study in Paris, 1949-50; Fulbright fellowships, 1950 and 1979; Ford Foundation fellowship to Paris, 1954-55; Rockefeller fellowship to the Soviet Union and other East European countries, 1960; Emerson Prize nomination, 1969, for ***Religious and Anti-Religious Thought in Russia;*** National Endowment for the Humanities senior fellowship, 1970-71; Guggenheim fellowship, 1978-79.

WRITINGS: Spinoza in Soviet Philosophy, Humanities, 1952, reprinted, Hyperion Press, 1981; (editor) *Soviet Education,* Columbia University Press, 1957; (editor and author of introduction) *Alfred North Whitehead: Essays on His Philosophy,* Prentice-Hall, 1963; (editor and contributor) *European Philosophy Today,* Quadrangle, 1965; (editor with James M. Edie, James P. Scanlan, and Mary-Barbara Zeldin, and contributor) *Russian Philosophy,* three volumes, Quadrangle, 1965, revised edition, 1969; *Religious and Anti-Religious Thought in Russia,* University of Chicago Press, 1968.

Contributor: Ernest J. Simmons, editor, *Continuity and Change in Russian and Soviet Thought,* Harvard University Press, 1955; H. H. Fisher, editor, *American Research on Russia,* Indiana University Press, 1959; C. E. Black, editor, *The Transformation of Russian Society,* Harvard University Press, 1960; W. Reese and E. Freeman, editors, *Process and Divinity: The Hartshorne Festschrift,* Open Court, 1964; P. L. Horecky, editor, *Russia and the Soviet Union: A Bibliographic Guide to Western-Language Publications,* University of Chicago Press, 1964.

A. T. Tymieniecka and C. Parsons, editors, *Contributions to Logic and Methodology in Honor of J. M. Bochenski,* North-Holland Publishing, 1965; N. Lobkowicz, editor, *Marx and the Western World,* University of Notre Dame Press, 1967; E. N. Lee and M. Mandelbaum, editors, *Phenomenology and Existentialism,* Johns Hopkins Press, 1967, revised edition, 1969; John P. Anton, editor, *Naturalism and Historical Understanding: Essays on the Philosophy of John Herman Randall, Jr.,* State University of New York Press, 1967; G. Tagliacozzo and H. V. White, editors, *Giambattista Vico: An International Symposium,* Johns Hopkins Press, 1969; C. Jelavich, editor, *Language and Area Studies: East Central and Southeastern Europe—A Survey,* University of Chicago Press, 1969; Edie, editor, *New Essays in Phenomenology: Studies in the Philosophy of Experience,* Quadrangle, 1969; M. Hayward and W. C. Fletcher, editors, *Religion and the Soviet State: A Dilemma of Power,* Praeger, 1969; Frederick J. Adelman, editor, *Demythologizing Marxism,* Nijhoff, 1969.

Darrel E. Christensen, editor, *Hegel and the Philosophy of Religion,* Nijhoff, 1970; Richard H. Marshall, Jr., Thomas E. Bird, and Andrew Q. Blane, editors, *Aspects of Religion in the Soviet Union, 1917-1967,* University of Chicago Press, 1971; Mary Warnock, editor, *Sartre: A Collection of Critical Essays,* Anchor Books, 1971; Suzanne Massie, editor, *The Living Mirror: Five Young Poets from Leningrad,* Doubleday, 1972; K. W. Algozin, J. J. O'Malley, and F. G. Weiss, editors, *Hegel and the History of Philosophy,* Nijhoff, 1974; Craig Walton and Anton, editors, *Philosophy and the Civilizing Arts: Essays Presented to Herbert W. Schneider on His Eightieth Birthday,* Ohio University Press, 1974.

Rudolf L. Tokes, editor, *Dissent in the U.S.S.R.: Politics, Ideology, and People,* Johns Hopkins University Press, 1975; Fred Moody, editor, *Ten Bibliographies of Twentieth-Century Russian Literature,* Ardis, 1977; Siegfried Hessing, editor, *Speculum Spinozanum, 1677-1977,* Routledge & Kegan Paul, 1977; Anthony M. Mlikotin, editor, *Western Philosophical Systems in Russian Literature: A Collection of Critical Studies,* University of Southern California Press, 1979; Edward Allworth, editor, *Ethnic Russia in the U.S.S.R.: The Dilemma of Dominance,* Pergamon, 1980.

Translator: V. V. Zenkovsky, *A History of Russian Philosophy,* two volumes, Columbia University Press, 1953; *Boris Pasternak: Seven Poems,* Unicorn Press, 1969, 2nd edition, 1972; (and author of introduction) *Joseph Brodsky: Selected Poems,* foreword by W. H. Auden, Penguin (London), 1973, Harper, 1974.

Contributor of translations: P. A. Schilpp, editor, *The Philosophy of Karl Jaspers,* Tudor, 1957; Rene Wellek, editor, *Dostoevsky: A Collection of Critical Essays,* Prentice-Hall, 1962; Simmons, editor, *Leo Tolstoy: Short Stories,* Modern Library, 1964; Peter Spackman and Lee Ambrose, editors, *Forum Anthology,* Atheneum, 1968; Leopold Tyrmand, editor, *Explorations in Freedom: Prose, Narrative, and Poetry from Kultura,* Free Press, with State University of New York at Albany, 1970; Daniel Wiessbort, editor, *Post-War Russian Poetry,* Penguin, 1974; Donald Junkins, *The Contemporary World Poets,* Harcourt, 1976; Robin Milner-Gulland and Martin Dewhirst, editors, *Russian Writing Today,* Penguin, 1977; Valentina Sinkevich, *The Coming of Day,* Crossroads, 1978; John Bayley, editor, *The Portable Tolstoy,* Viking, 1978; Joseph Brodsky, *A Part of Speech,* Farrar, Straus, 1980; Ruth Miller and Robert Greenberg, editors, *Poetry: An Introduction,* St. Martin's, 1981.

Contributor to *Dictionary of Russian Literature, Encyclopedia of Morals, Encyclopedia of Russia and the Soviet Union, Encyclopedia of Philosophy, Modern Encyclopedia of Russian and Soviet Literature,* and *Columbia Dictionary of Modern European Literature,* 2nd edition. Member of editorial board, *Encyclopedia of Philosophy,* 1962-67. Contributor of articles, reviews, and translations to periodicals, including *New Leader, New Yorker, Vogue, Humanist, Journal of Philosophy, Ethics, Partisan Review, Antaeus, Russian Review, Slavic Review, Problems of Communism, Review of Metaphysics, Philosophy Forum, Southern Journal of Philosophy,* and *Philosophy and Phenomenological Research.* Editor of philosophy section, *American Bibliography of Slavic Studies,* 1957-67; *Journal of Philosophy,* co-editor, 1959-64, consulting editor, 1964-78; consulting editor, *Current Digest of the Soviet Press,* 1961-64, *Studies in Soviet Thought,* 1962—, *Journal of Value Inquiry,* 1967—, *Process Studies,* 1970—, *Philosophy Research Archives,* 1975—, *Soviet Union,* 1975-80, *Journal of the History of Ideas,* 1976—, and *Slavic Review,* 1977-79.

WORK IN PROGRESS: Further studies of Spinoza, Vico, Hegel, Marx, and Whitehead, and of Russian philosophy, especially ethics and social philosophy; further translations of Russian poetry.

SIDELIGHTS: George Kline, who reads Russian, German, Spanish, Italian, and French, has translated into English the Russian poetry of Boris Pasternak and Joseph Brodsky. "There are two contrasting theories as to how Russian poetry should be put into English," writes Kline in *Bryn Mawr Now.* "The first . . . holds that Russian poetry is best rendered in free verse, using a vigorous and 'uncluttered' contemporary idiom. Partisans of the opposing theory (including Brodsky and myself) hold, not that English versions of Russian poetry should be 'cluttered' or unvigorous, but that they should at all costs reproduce the regular meter of the original and, wherever possible, the rhymes or slant-rhymes as well."

BIOGRAPHICAL/CRITICAL SOURCES: Bryn Mawr Now, spring, 1974.

* * *

KNIFESMITH
See CUTLER, Ivor

KOERTGE, Ronald 1940-

PERSONAL: Surname is pronounced *Kur*-chee; born April 22, 1940, in Olney, Ill.; son of William Henry and Bulis Olive (Fiscus) Koertge; married Cheryl Vasconcellos (a teacher). *Education:* University of Illinois, B.A., 1962; University of Arizona, M.A., 1965. *Home:* 1121 Grevelia, South Pasadena, Calif. 91030. *Agent:* William Reiss, Paul R. Reynolds, Inc., 12 East 41st St., New York, N.Y. 10017. *Office:* Department of English, Pasadena City College, 1560 Colorado Blvd., Pasadena, Calif. 91106.

CAREER: Pasadena City College, Pasadena, Calif., assistant professor of English, 1965—.

WRITINGS: Meat: Cherry's Market Diary, Mag Press, 1973; *The Father Poems,* Sumac Press, 1974; *The Hired Nose,* Mag Press, 1974; *My Summer Vacation,* Venice Poetry Co., 1975; *Men under Fire,* Duck Down Press, 1976; *Twelve Photographs of Yellowstone,* Red Hill Press, 1976; *How to Live on Five Dollars a Day,* Venice Poetry Co., 1976; *Cheap Thrills,* Wormwood Review Press, 1976; *Sex Object,* Little Caesar Press, 1979; *The Boogeyman* (novel), Norton, 1980; *The Jockey Poems,* Maelstrom Press, 1980; *Diary Cows,* Little Caesar Press, 1982.

* * *

KOSINSKI, Jerzy (Nikodem) 1933-
(Joseph Novak)

PERSONAL: Born June 14, 1933, in Lodz, Poland; came to United States in 1957, naturalized in 1965; son of Mieczyslaw (a classicist) and Elzbieta (a concert pianist; maiden name, Liniecka) Kosinski; married Mary Hayward Weir (an art collector), 1962 (died, 1968). *Education:* University of Lodz, B.A., 1950, M.A. (history), 1953, M.A. (political science), 1955; Ph.D. candidate in sociology at Polish Academy of Sciences, 1955-57, and at Columbia University, 1958-63; graduate study at New School for Social Research, 1962-66. *Office:* c/o Scientia-Factum, Inc., Hemisphere House, 60 West 57th St., New York, N.Y. 10019.

CAREER: Writer and photographer. Ski instructor in Zakopane, Poland, winters, 1950-56; assistant professor (aspirant) of sociology, Polish Academy of Sciences, Warsaw, 1955-57; researcher at Lomonosov University, Moscow, 1957; on first arriving in the United States, variously employed as a paint scraper on excursion-line boats, a truck driver, chauffeur, and cinema projectionist; resident fellow in English at Center for Advanced Studies, Wesleyan University, 1967-68; visiting lecturer in English and resident senior fellow of the Council of Humanities, Princeton University, 1969-70; professor of English and resident fellow of Davenport College and School of Drama, Yale University, 1970-73. Has also worked as a screen actor, portraying Grigory Zinoviev in "Reds," a Paramount Pictures film produced and directed by Warren Beatty, 1981. Has had one-man photographic exhibitions at the State's Crooked Circle Gallery in Warsaw, 1957, and has exhibited his photographs throughout the world.

MEMBER: P.E.N. (president, 1973-75), International League for Human Rights (director, 1973-79), Authors Guild, Authors League of America, American Federation of Television and Radio Artists, American Civil Liberties Union (chairman, artists and writers committee), Screen Actors Guild, Century Association.

AWARDS, HONORS: Ford Foundation fellowship, 1958-60; Prix du Meilleur Livre Etranger (France), 1966, for *The Painted Bird;* Guggenheim fellowship in creative writing, 1967-68; National Book Award, 1969, for *Steps;* National Institute of Arts and Letters and the American Academy of Arts and Letters award in literature, 1970; John Golden fellowship in playwriting, 1970-72; Brith Sholom Humanitarian Freedom Award, 1974; American Civil Liberties Union First Amendment Award, 1978; best screenplay of the year award from Writers Guild of America, 1979, and from the British Academy of Film and Television Arts, 1981, both for *Being There;* Polonia Media National Achievement Perspectives Award, 1980; Spertus College of Judaica International Award, 1982.

WRITINGS—Fiction: *The Painted Bird,* abridged edition, Houghton, 1965, complete edition, Modern Library, 1970, complete and revised 10th anniversary edition, with an introduction by the author, Houghton, 1976; *Steps,* Random House, 1968; *Being There* (also see below), Harcourt, 1971; *The Devil Tree,* Harcourt, 1973, revised and expanded edition, St. Martin's, 1981; *Cockpit,* Houghton, 1975; *Blind Date,* Houghton, 1977; *Passion Play* (also see below) St. Martin's, 1979; *Pinball,* Bantam, 1982.

Screenplays; both based on his novels of the same titles: *Being There* (filmed by Lorimar; released by United Artists, 1979), Scientia-Factum, 1977; *Passion Play,* Scientia-Factum, 1982.

Nonfiction: (Under pseudonym Joseph Novak) *The Future Is Ours, Comrade: Conversations with the Russians,* Doubleday, 1960; (under pseudonym Joseph Novak) *No Third Path: A Study of Collective Behavior,* Doubleday, 1962; (editor) *Socjologia Amerykanska: Wybor Prac, 1950-1960* (title means "American Sociology: Translations of Selected Works, 1950-1960"), Polish Institute of Arts and Sciences (New York), 1962; *Notes of the Author on "The Painted Bird,"* Scientia-Factum, 1965; *The Art of the Self: Essays a propos "Steps,"* Scientia-Factum, 1968.

All of Kosinski's books have been translated into numerous languages, including German, French, Italian, and Spanish.

WORK IN PROGRESS: Autofocus, a novel; *Selected Essays, 1958-83.*

SIDELIGHTS: A controversial novelist, Jerzy Kosinski first stunned the literary world in 1965 with *The Painted Bird*—a graphic account of an abandoned child's odyssey through war-torn Eastern Europe—which some critics consider the best piece of literature to emerge from World War II. Kosinski's second novel, *Steps,* was equally successful and won a National Book Award in 1969. Other novels, all part of an elaborate fictional cycle, followed; though Kosinski labels them fiction, his books parallel his real-life experiences, earning him the reputation of a writer who mingles art and life.

The only child of Jewish intellectuals, Kosinski enjoyed a sheltered childhood until he was six years old. Then Hitler invaded Poland, disrupting the young boy's family and irrevocably altering the shape of his life. As Jews, Kosinski's parents were forced into hiding, and eventually the child was entrusted to a stranger's care. Though he was soon placed with a foster mother, she died within two months of his arrival, and, until the end of the war when he was reunited with his parents, young Kosinski wandered from one remote peasant village to another, living by his wits. By the time he was nine, Kosinski had been so traumatized by his experience that he was struck mute. "Once I regained my speech after the war, the trauma began," he told Barbara Leaming of *Penthouse.* "The Stalinist [system in Poland] went after me, asking questions I didn't want to hear, demanding answers I would not give."

When the State refused to grant him and his family permission to emigrate to the West, Kosinski used the deceptive techniques he had mastered as a runaway to plot his escape. He was twenty-four, a doctoral student at the Polish Academy of Sciences in Warsaw, when he undertook an elaborate and dangerous ruse. Inventing four academicians in four different branches of learning, Kosinski contrived to have them sponsor him for a research project in the United States. It took him over two years to obtain the passport and the necessary travel documents, but by the winter of 1957, he was ready. He arrived in New York City a few days before Christmas—friendless, penniless, and with only a rudimentary knowledge of the spoken American idiom.

Since that time, Jerzy Kosinski has become an American success story. Quickly mastering the language, he enrolled in a Ph.D. program, launched a writing career, and married the rich widow of an American steel baron. A prize-winning photographer, Kosinski is also an amateur athlete and, according to the *New York Times Magazine,* "a polo-playing pet of the jet set." In 1981, he added a screen debut to his list of accomplishments, earning critical praise for his portrayal of the Soviet bureaucrat Grigory Zinoviev in Warren Beatty's film "Reds." Despite the tremendous variety that characterizes both his personal and professional life, Kosinski remains deeply committed to writing: "Fiction is the center of my life," he told Margaria Fichtner in a *Chicago Tribune* interview. "Anything I do revolves around what I write and what I write very often revolves around what I do."

To gather material Kosinski frequently prowls the streets of New York and other cities, sometimes traveling in disguise. "I like to go out at night," he told Ron Base in the *Washington Post.* "I like to see strange things, meet strange people, see people at their most abandoned. I like people who are driven. The sense of who they are is far greater."

Though Kosinski cloaks these experiences under a fictive mask, critics say the autobiographical elements of his writing are unmistakable. "Mostly, in his novels," writes Barbara Gelb in the *New York Times Magazine,* "he describes actual events as a newspaper reporter would, altering details only slightly to fictionalize them." *Detroit News* staff writer Ben Brown agrees, delineating the following similarities between Kosinski and his characters: "Like the boy wanderer in *The Painted Bird* (1965), Kosinski was an abandoned child, wandering alone through the rural villages of Eastern Europe during World War II. Like the emigrant photographer-social scientist in *Cockpit* (1975), Kosinski, also a photographer-social scientist, escaped from [Poland] by creating a hole in the post-Stalinist bureaucracy through which he could slide to freedom in the West. By view of his marriage . . . Kosinski was surrounded by the kind of vast inherited wealth he gave Jonathan Wahlen in *The Devil Tree* (1973). And like Fabian in . . . *Passion Play* [1979] . . . Kosinski is an expert horseman [and] an avid polo player." In fact, according to Ron Base, Kosinski "never strays far from his own life in order to discover his novels' protagonists, and given the life he leads, who can blame him? Everything including his past and present seems calculated to yield a novel every three years or so."

But Ross Wetzsteon believes it is not calculation, but necessity which motivates Kosinski's pen: "He [was] fated to become a writer in order to survive. To admit his past is real would be to allow it to cripple him; to admit his fiction is autobiographical would be to allow himself to be devastated by the horror of its experiences. 'I am not the person who experienced those horrors,' Kosinski is saying, but rather, 'I am the one who conquered them.'" And Kosinski, writing in *Notes of the Author on "The Painted Bird,"* reinforces this point of view: "We fit experiences into molds which simplify, shape and give them an acceptable emotional clarity. *The remembered event becomes a fiction, a structure made to accomodate certain feelings.* If there were not these structures, art would be too personal for the artist to create, much less for the audience to grasp. *There is no art which is reality; rather, art is the using of symbols by which an otherwise unstateable subjective reality is made manifest.*"

The "subjective reality" that is "made manifest" in Kosinski's fiction is the ability of the individual to survive. "The whole didactic point of my novels is how you redeem yourself if you are pressed or threatened by the chances of daily life, how you see yourself as a romantic character when you are grotesque, a failure," Kosinski told Ben Brown in a *Detroit News* interview. Though the theme is recurrent, Kosinski approaches it differently in each book as Lawrence Cunningham explains in *America:* "At times, as in *The Painted Bird,* the individual is the victim of society, while in *Cockpit,* a Kafkaesque secret agent named Tarden wages a one-man war against the whole of society and those members of it who epitomize the brutality of that society. In *Being There* . . . the hero of the novel betrays the whole of American society not because of his power or viciousness, but because of his simplicity, naivete and sheer ignorance of how the culture game is played." Notwithstanding these differences, Cunningham believes the novels share the same moral ambivalence: "In Kosinski's . . . universe there is, at the same time, grand moral testimony to the worth of the individual and a curious shrinking from the common bonds of trusting humanity. . . . Kosinski is a survivor. If his experience has not permitted him to teach us much about human relationships, it has been, nonetheless, a vade mecum [or manual] of making it in this very tough world."

And what makes this "alien world" of Kosinski's so frightening, according to Elizabeth Stone, is the sharp chill of recognition it causes the reader to feel. "In the lives of Kosinski's characters, there is something of ourselves," she writes in *Psychology Today.* "Kosinski's novels pierce the social skin and go deeper. They are all accounts of the self in extreme psychological peril, and they make sense the way dreams make sense. Whatever they say to the rational mind—about police states, political prisoners, and social evil—to the anarchic primitive troubled sleeper in all of us, the novels recreate the aura of nightmare paranoia, rouse fears of psychic petrification, depersonalization, engulfment. . . . His characters chronicle not only what, at its worst, the world is like, but also what, at *our* worst, it feels like. His thematic preoccupations are the dangerous deceitfulness of appearances: isolation, loneliness, anxiety, and violence in a Hobbesian world. . . . And what each novel probes is: given an infinitude of dangers—many of them dangers of our own perceptions—by what strategies can we survive?"

Not surprisingly, the survival techniques his characters employ are similar to tactics Kosinski himself has used. One, according to Stone, is giving voice to experience—as Kosinski does in his writing, and as the nameless protagonist of *The Painted Bird* does when he regains his speech. Another, Stone continues, is by cultivating invisibility and turning it into an advantage—which Kosinski does when he travels in disguise and which Levanter of *Blind Date* does when he rapes a girl from behind, thus preventing her from identifying him. Though Kosinski has said repeatedly that he has never seen himself as a victim, critics maintain that his characters—and even Kosinski himself—are obsessed with revenge. While he prefers to view revenge as a "defense rather than an obsession," Kosinski does not disagree. "My characters often defend themselves against entrapments by oppressive societies," he told Barbara Leaming. "I see revenge as the last vestige of the eminently threatened self. When I was a student at the Stalinist university and the party threatened me with prison unless I would reform or openly perform an act of self-criticism and repent, I warned them, 'Don't forget, if I go down, some of you will go with me.' Revenge can be a positive force—the victim's final dignity."

In Kosinski's case, retaliation for the injustices he had suffered under the Communist system came with the publication of his first book, a nonfiction collection of essays, written when he had been a student in the United States for about two years. Described by Barbara Gelb as "a strongly anti-communist tract," *The Future Is Ours, Comrade: Conversations with the Russians* became an instant best seller and was serialized by the *Saturday Evening Post* and *Reader's Digest*. It was the first of two books that Kosinski would write on communism and, like the subsequent *No Third Path: A Study of Collective Behavior,* it was published pseudonymously. Kosinski's reasons for taking a pen name remain unclear. Kosinski told Ron Base, "I didn't think my spoken English was good enough [to publicly defend my sociological methods, my ethics and philosophy, he added in a note to *CA*.] So I published it under the pen name Joseph Novak." But earlier Kosinski had offered *Washington Post Book World* interviewer Daniel J. Cahill a different explanation: "When you're a student you're supposed to read serious books—not publish them. The pen name allowed me to conduct my studies uninterrupted by the controversy that my books triggered among my fellow students and professors. A side benefit of a pen name is that it allows you to recommend your own books, to those who don't know you've written them, as the very best on the subject—without ever feeling immodest."

One of the people who read the first Novak book was Mary Weir, the thirty-one year old widow of steel magnate Ernest Weir. More than fifty years her senior, Ernest died leaving his wife a fortune. "In addition to a Park Avenue apartment, there were houses in Hobe Sound and Southampton, a permanently reserved floor at the Ritz in Paris and a large suite at the Connaught in London, as well as a villa in Florence," reports Barbara Gelb. Mary Weir read *The Future Is Ours, Comrade* shortly after a trip she had taken to Russia and agreed so wholeheartedly with Kosinski's observations that she wrote him a fan letter. Kosinski, in a characteristic blending of fact and fiction, recounts the event in his novel *Pinball*. "Long ago," says Domostroy, one of its protagonists and, Kosinski told *CA,* an obvious stand-in for the author, "when I had received enough fan letters to know how similar they all were, I received one unusual one. The writer, a woman, said she knew me only from my work, . . . but her analysis . . . was so acute, as were her perceptions of . . . the undercurrents of my life, . . . that I was flat-out enthralled."

They arranged a meeting, but Mary, knowing that Kosinski had envisioned her as a frail, elderly widow, impersonated her own secretary to put him at ease. Himself a master of disguise, Kosinski was charmed when he discovered her trick, and the couple was married in 1962. In the Cahill interview, Kosinski described their life together and how it enhanced his art: "During my marriage, I had often thought that it was Stendhal or F. Scott Fitzgerald, both preoccupied with wealth they did not have, who deserved to have had my experience. I wanted to start writing fiction and, frankly, was tempted to begin with a novel that . . . would utilize my immediate experience, the dimension of wealth, power and high society that surrounded me, not the poverty I had seen and experienced so shortly before. But during my marriage I was too much a part of Mary's world to extract from it the nucleus of what I saw, of what I felt. And as a writer, I perceived fiction as the art of imaginative extraction. So instead, I decided to write my first novel *The Painted Bird* about a homeless boy in the war-torn Eastern Europe, an existence I've known but also one that was shared by millions of Europeans, yet was foreign to Mary and our American friends. The novel was my gift to Mary, and to her world."

Although the book initiated Kosinski's career as a novelist, it came at a time of personal tragedy. Mary died of an incurable illness in 1968. "In a curious way," writes Ron Base, "her death provided him with the ultimate freedom. Now he could draw on all the possibilities of his life without worrying about embarrassing wives and children." Though he did pursue these themes in a number of later books, his next novel is similar in setting and theme to *The Painted Bird*. "The protagonist-narrator of *Steps* is alternately the dark-complected boy of Kosinski's first novel . . . and that same boy as an adult," observes William Plummer in the *Village Voice*. A series of seemingly unconnected, and often brutal, episodes, the book, according to Stanley Kauffmann in the *New Republic,* "is a piercing view of [Kosinski's] past as part of the world's present. For me, the title does not signify progress from one place to another or from one state to another, but simply action about experience: steps taken to accommodate experience and continuing reality to the possibility of remaining alive. . . . The book says finally: 'Hell. Horror. Lust. Cruelty. Ego. Buy *my* hell and horror and lust and cruelty and ego. Life is—just possibly—worth living if we can imagine it better and imagine it worse.'"

Steps won a National Book Award in 1969; however, since that time Kosinski thinks the attitude of the publishing world toward literature has changed. "Today that book would not win," he told Carol Lawson in a 1979 interview for the *New York Times Book Review*. "There is a heavy sentimental climate in the book community in New York." His assessment appears to have been correct: When, as an experiment, a young reporter retyped *Steps* and submitted it under a different name, he found that it went unrecognized and rejected by every major publishing house—including the one that had originally printed it. Undaunted, Kosinski reworked the incident and included it in his 1982 novel, *Pinball*.

Even at the time it was published, *Steps* aroused controversy. While critics generally agree that the book is beautifully written, several, including Geoffrey Wolff writing in *New Leader,* question its morality: "Kosinski's power and talent are not in doubt. I can think of few writers who are able to so persuasively describe an event, set a scene, communicate an emotion. Nonetheless, the use he has set his power to is in doubt. His purpose is serious, I am sure, but he misreads our tolerance. He has created what never was on land or sea and arrogantly expects us to take his creations, his self-consuming octopus, his other monsters, as emblems." Echoing this sentiment, Robert Alter writes in the *New York Times Book Review* that *Steps* "is scarcely a novel at all but rather a series of discontinuous erotic jottings, sometimes brutal, generally deficient in feeling, and finally repetitious." According to *New York Times* reviewer

Christopher Lehmann-Haupt, the problem is not just what Kosinski writes, but how he writes it: "Lacking a sense of the language, and thus lacking any style of his own, the author gropes for any passable cliche. It is just what happens in bad pornography."

Kosinski bridles at such comparisons. "Pornography views sex as physical, not spiritual," he told Barbara Leaming. "It does to sex what totalitarianism does to politics: it reduces it to a single dimension. But for me, as for all my fictional characters, sex is a spiritual force, a core of their being, indeed, the procreative basis for self-definition." Those critics who find his heavy doses of sex and violence gratuitous don't understand what he's trying to do, Kosinski maintains. "I am astonished again and again at how superficially people read books," he told Ben Brown of the *Detroit News*. "I know what I write. I know why I do it the way that I do it. There's no greater sense of responsibility than (my own). But I have a certain vision of literature I will not sacrifice for sentimental critics brought up on *Fiddler on the Roof*."

Among those critics who do appreciate Kosinski's writing is Arnost Lustig, who writes in the *Washington Post Book World* that "Kosinski develops his own style and technique, trying to avoid the classical plot and trying not to get lost in a limitless and chaotic jungle without beginning, middle and end. His style is in harmony with his need to express new things about our life and the world we do live in, to express the inexpressible. Sometimes his way of writing and the structure of [*Blind Date*] reminds one of a steam engine where energy grows to the point where it either explodes or moves forward. Accumulating stories of different, sometimes ambiguous meaning, giving to himself as well as to the reader the same chance for interpretation, he traces the truth in the deepest corners of our outdoor and indoor lives, of our outer appearance and our inner reality."

A perfectionist about his work, Kosinski writes slowly and rewrites extensively, averaging two to three years per book. For example, he rewrote *Passion Play*, his 1979 novel, almost a dozen times and then further altered it in three different sets of galleys and two page-proofs, where he condensed the text by one-third. Above his ten percent publisher's allowance, Kosinski must bear the cost of such corrections. He does not, however, complain. "When I face the galley-proofs I feel as though my whole life was at stake on every page and that a messy paragraph could mess up my whole life from now on," he told Daniel J. Cahill. "As I have no children, no family, no relatives, no business or estate to speak of, my books are my only *spiritual* accomplishment, my life's most private frame of reference, and I would gladly pay all I earn to make it my best."

To that end Kosinski has regularly and, he told *CA*, "openly" employed free-lance editors to help him review his manuscripts. The types of alterations his assistants make (collating corrections, checking galleys against retyped manuscripts, and watching for the inadvertant repetition of an action or a word) are purely mechanical activities in Kosinski's opinion. But Geoffrey Stokes and Eliot Fremont-Smith of the *Village Voice* disagree, charging in the June 22, 1982 issue that "Kosinski's ethics and his very role as author have been seriously challenged." While the *Village Voice* allegations cover a broad spectrum, ranging from complaints that Kosinski lied about his past to charges that his first two books were actually written and financed by the Central Intelligence Agency, the most serious accusations concern Kosinski's unacknowledged dependence on his assistants. Fremont-Smith and Stokes allege that Kosinski not only wrote *The Painted Bird* in Polish and had it secretly translated into English but, in his later novels, depended upon his free-lance editors for "the sort of *composition* that we usually call writing."

As proof, the reporters offer the testimony of several free lancers formerly in Kosinski's part-time employ, including John Hackett, now professor of English at the University of Texas, Barbara Mackey, now assistant director at the Denver Arts Center, and Richard Hayes, a former professor of drama at New York University and the University of California, Berkeley. While none of these people see themselves as Kosinski's "collaborators," both Hackett, who worked on *Cockpit,* and Hayes, who assisted with a draft of *Passion Play,* insist they were more than "mere" proofreaders, the former noting that he helped with the manuscript, the latter saying that he "invested [Kosinski's] language with a certain Latinate style." However when Mackey, the assistant who worked on *The Devil Tree,* was contacted by the *Washington Post Book World* for a follow-up story, she insisted, "I did *nothing* but editing," and went on to criticize what she calls the *Village Voice*'s "shoddy journalism." Furthermore, she continued, Stokes asked her "leading questions" and assured her that their discussion was off the record and that he would get back to her about permission to use her name.

A number of Kosinski's publishing house editors have also come to his defense. In a *Publishers Weekly* article, Les Pockell, the editor of *Passion Play* and *The Devil Tree,* says that the charges are "totally ludicrous. It's clear no one in the article is asserting that he or she wrote the book." Because Kosinski is "obsessive" about his writing, Pockell continues, "he retained people to copy edit. It's always a situation of submitting recommendations to an author to approve or not approve, and the recommendations are always a reaction to the author's material." And Pockell told the *Los Angeles Times Calendar* that he felt Stokes and Fremont-Smith "played upon the ignorance of the general public about the conventions of publishing" and added that "to turn Kosinski's working methods into something sinister makes one wonder about their motives."

In a letter to the *Village Voice,* Austen Olney, editor in chief of Houghton Mifflin, says: "I have been marginally involved with the three Kosinski novels published by Houghton Mifflin and can attest to the fact that he is a difficult and demanding author who makes endless (and to my way of thinking often niggling) corrections in proof. I have been sometimes overwhelmed by his flamboyant conceits and his artful social manipulations, but I have never had any reason to believe that he has ever needed or used any but the most routine editorial assistance. The remarkable consistency of tone in all his novels seems to me sufficient evidence that they all come from his hands alone."

But perhaps the strongest reaction to the *Village Voice* charges comes from Kosinski himself. While affirming the reporters' first amendment right to print the piece, Kosinski told the *Washington Post Book World* that "there is not a single factual thing in that article." Furthermore, he informed the *Village Voice* reporters: "Not a single comma, not a single word is not mine—and not the mere presence of the word but the reasons why as well. This goes for manuscript, middle drafts, final draft, and every f——ing galley—first page proofs, second and third, hardcover editions and paperback editions." Nonetheless, the controversy has taken its toll. Comparing himself to an injured victim, Kosinski told the *Washington Post Book World,* "Like any other assassination, the damage has been done."

In the aftermath of the controversy the *New York Times* published a 6,000 word feature article by John Corry, examining the origin as well as the nature of the various charges made against the author. "Jerzy Kosinski," he writes, "has become a man defined by rumors. . . . His works are being discredited by rumors because his life is being discredited by rumors. That he is a writer is almost incidental. He is an intellectual, a creative person, under ideological attack. The ideology was born in Eastern Europe, and so were the most damaging rumors. They have been around for seventeen years, only now they have grown more insistent."

Despite the shadow that Stokes and Fremont-Smith have cast on his writing career, Kosinski's acting debut remains an unqualified success. Critics were delighted by Kosinski's portrayal of the Soviet bureaucrat Grigory Zinoviev in "Reds." Observes the *Time* magazine critic: "As [journalist John] Reed's Soviet nemesis, novelist Jerzy Kosinski acquits himself nicely—a tundra of ice against Reed's all-American fire." *Newsweek* compliments Kosinski's "delightfully abrasive" performance, comparing him to "an officious terrier gnawing on the bone of Marxist-Leninist dogma."

In a London *Times* interview, Kosinski explains how Warren Beatty, who not only directed but also starred in the film as John Reed, elicited the performance: "[Beatty] hired as extras for members of Zinoviev's committee recent Soviet emigres who had moved to Spain. They hadn't learnt foreign languages yet. They spoke only Russian. Being Soviet, they didn't like me because I was a Pole and I've lived in America for 25 years. They thought I was a very bad actor. And they regard Zinoviev in the blind way of Soviet propaganda as a Jewish cosmopolitan who, although he helped Lenin to power, was executed by Stalin in the 1930s purges, probably justly. [In such an atmosphere] I was thrown back on my Soviet past; I felt frightened and disillusioned. And Warren Beatty/John Reed would come in with his naivete and his sweet American smile telling me, as Reed, that he wanted to see his wife and, as Beatty, about the problems he was having with the film. And I, both as Zinoviev and as Kosinski, sat there saying: What do you know of the troubles of life? What do you know of authentic pain and grief and anguish. . . . The hostility transferred itself to my acting."

Ironically, Kosinski's initial reaction to Beatty's invitation was to turn the offer down. "But then," Kosinski told *CA*, "Barry Diller, the head of Paramount called me and asked me about my decision. He said, 'You used to be known to seek new exploits, and to go after a new experience so you'll have something to write about. You have never played in a movie. Why don't you want to do it?' I mumbled something about being uncertain about portraying someone else—without creative control, which as a novelist I retain in my own work. Then Barry said, 'Well, think again. As an actor you can certainly afford to turn such a chance down. But should you—as a novelist?' I reflected. 'Tell Warren I'll be on the set tomorrow,' I said, mentally already packing my bags."

MEDIA ADAPTATIONS: Kosinski recorded "Selected Readings from *The Painted Bird*" for CMS Records in 1967. Scenes from *Steps* were performed on the television show "Critique," in 1969.

AVOCATIONAL INTERESTS: Horseback riding (polo and jump), skiing, photography.

BIOGRAPHICAL/CRITICAL SOURCES—Books: Jerzy Kosinski, *Notes of the Author on "The Painted Bird,"* Scientia-Factum, 1965; John Watson Aldridge, editor, *The Devil in the Fire: Retrospective Essays on American Literature and Culture, 1951-71,* Harper's Magazine Press, 1972; *Contemporary Literary Criticism,* Gale, Volume I, 1973, Volume II, 1974, Volume III, 1975, Volume VI, 1976, Volume X, 1979, Volume XV, 1980; Joe D. Bellamy, editor, *The New Fiction: Interviews with Innovative American Writers,* University of Illinois Press, 1974; Jerome Klinkowitz, *Literary Disruptions: The Making of a Post-Contemporary American Fiction,* University of Illinois Press, 1975; Lawrence L. Langer, *Holocaust and the Literary Imagination,* Yale University Press, 1975; Sepp Tiefenthaler, *Jerzy Kosinski,* Bouvier Publishers (Bonn), 1980; George Plimpton, editor, *Writers at Work: The "Paris Review" Interviews,* Volume V, Penguin, 1981; Jack Hicks, *In the Singer's Temple: The Romance of Terror and Jerzy Kosinski,* University of North Carolina Press, 1981; Norman Lavers, *Jerzy Kosinski,* G. K. Hall, 1982; Daniel Cahill, *The Fiction of Jerzy Kosinski,* Iowa State University Press, 1982; Byron L. Sherwin, *Jerzy Kosinski: Literary Alarmclock,* Cabala Press, 1982.

Periodicals: *New York Times Book Review,* May 22, 1960, October 31, 1965, October 20, 1968, February 11, 1973, August 10, 1975, October 21, 1979; *Manchester Guardian,* October 21, 1960; *New Statesman,* October 22, 1960; *Harper's,* October, 1965, March, 1969; *Saturday Review,* November 13, 1965, April 17, 1971, April 24, 1971, March 11, 1972; *Nation,* November 29, 1965; *National Review,* February 8, 1966; *Times Literary Supplement,* May 19, 1966; *Commentary,* June, 1966; *Commonweal,* July 1, 1966; *New York Times,* December 12, 1966, September 13, 1979, February 25, 1982, November 7, 1982; *New Leader,* October 7, 1968; *Time,* October 18, 1968, April 26, 1971, October 31, 1977, September 17, 1979, December 7, 1981; *New Republic,* October 26, 1968, June 26, 1971; *New York Review of Books,* February 27, 1969; *Listener,* May 8, 1969; *Denver Quarterly,* autumn, 1969, spring, 1971, winter, 1973; *New York Post,* August 21, 1969, February 19, 1973.

Newsweek, April 26, 1971, February 19, 1973, September 10, 1979, December 7, 1981; *Publishers Weekly,* April 26, 1971, July 9, 1982; *Washington Post,* August 30, 1971, March 25, 1973, November 27, 1977, September 16, 1979, February 4, 1980, February 21, 1982; *Paris Review,* summer, 1972; *Centennial Review,* winter, 1972; *Denver Post,* February 11, 1973, September 7, 1979; *Philadelphia Inquirer,* February 18, 1973; *North American Review,* spring, 1973, March, 1980; *Los Angeles Times Calendar Magazine,* April 22, 1973, August 1, 1982; *Guardian,* June 25, 1973; *Fiction International,* fall, 1973; *Media & Methods,* April, 1975; *Village Voice,* August 11, 1975, October 31, 1977, June 22, 1982, July 6, 1982; *Third Press Review,* September/October, 1975; *Washington Post Book World,* November 27, 1977, September 16, 1979, February 21, 1982, July 11, 1982; *Psychology Today,* December, 1977; *San Francisco Review of Books,* March, 1978; *America,* November 11, 1978; *U.S. News and World Report,* January 8, 1979; *Christian Science Monitor,* March 1, 1979; *Detroit News,* October 7, 1979; *Polo,* December, 1979.

Chicago Tribune, January 19, 1980; *American Photographer,* June, 1980; *Chicago Review,* summer, 1980; *Critique,* Volume XXII, number 2, 1981; *New York Times Magazine,* February 21, 1982; *Philadelphia Inquirer,* February 21, 1982; *Times* (London), March 10, 1982; *Penthouse,* July, 1982.

—Sketch by Donna Olendorf

KRAUSS, Bruno
See BULMER, (Henry) Kenneth

* * *

KROLL, Steven 1941-

PERSONAL: Born August 11, 1941, in New York, N.Y.; son of Julius (a diamond merchant) and Anita (a business executive; maiden name, Berger) Kroll; married Edite Niedringhaus (a children's book editor), April 18, 1964 (divorced, 1978). *Education:* Harvard University, B.A., 1962. *Politics:* "Committed to change." *Religion:* Jewish. *Home and office:* 64 West 11th St., New York, N.Y. 10011. *Agent:* Joan Daves, 59 East 54th St., New York, N.Y. 10022.

CAREER: Transatlantic Review, London, England, associate editor, 1962-65; Chatto & Windus Ltd., London, reader and editor, 1962-65; Holt, Rinehart & Winston, New York, N.Y., acquiring editor in trade department, 1965-69; full-time writer, 1969—. Instructor in English, University of Maine at Augusta, 1970-71. *Member:* Author's Guild, Author's League of America, Harvard Club.

WRITINGS—Juveniles, except as indicated; published by Holiday House, except as indicated: *Is Milton Missing?,* 1975; *The Tyrannosaurus Game,* 1976; *That Makes Me Mad!,* Pantheon, 1976; *Sleepy Ida and Other Nonsense Poems,* Pantheon, 1977; *Gobbledygook,* 1977; *If I Could Be My Grandmother,* Pantheon, 1977; *Santa's Crash-Bang Christmas,* 1977; *T. J. Folger, Thief,* 1978; *Fat Mack,* 1979; *Space Cats,* 1979; *The Candy Witch,* 1979.

Monster Birthday, 1980; *Amanda and the Giggling Ghost,* 1980; *Dirty Feet,* Parents' Magazine Press, 1980; *Giant Journey,* 1981; *Friday the 13th,* 1981; *Bathrooms,* Avon, 1982; *Banana Bits,* Avon, 1982; *The Big Bunny and the Easter Eggs,* 1982; *Are You Pirates?,* Pantheon, 1982; *One Tough Turkey,* 1982; *Toot! Toot!,* 1983; *The Hand-Me-Down Doll,* 1983; *The Goat Parade,* Parents' Magazine Press, 1983; *Otto,* Parents' Magazine Press, 1983; *Woof! Woof!,* Dial, 1983; *Take It Easy* (young adult), Four Winds, 1983.

WORK IN PROGRESS: Happy Mother's Day, for Holiday House.

SIDELIGHTS: Steven Kroll told *CA:* "Language—what we say and what we write—defines us. But no one is taught that truth in school, and through the mass media language has been everywhere debased. If we are to escape our current confusion, we must regain some sense of our use of language. I have always felt this way, was drawn to writing for that reason as well as by the need to tell stories. I also play a lot of tennis and squash, walk all over New York, and travel wherever I can. Sometimes I think languid thoughts about cruising down the Mississippi on a riverboat."

* * *

KRUTILLA, John Vasil 1922-

PERSONAL: Born February 13, 1922, in Tacoma, Wash.; married, 1954; children: two sons, one daughter. *Education:* Reed College, B.A., 1949; Harvard University, M.A., 1951, Ph.D., 1952. *Office:* Resources for the Future, 1755 Massachusetts Ave. N.W., Washington, D.C. 20036.

CAREER: Tennessee Valley Authority, industrial economist, 1952-53, economist in Office of the General Manager, 1953-54, acting chief economist, 1954-55; Resources for the Future (foundation for research and education in conservation and development of natural resources), Washington, D.C., research associate, 1955-60, associate director of Water Resources Research Program, 1961-63, senior staff member, 1963-68, director of Natural Environments Program, 1968-75, senior fellow, 1975—. Visiting professor at University of Colorado, summer, 1959, National University of Mexico, summer, 1960, University of Michigan, 1969, and Natural Resources Institute, Oregon State University, summer, 1969; professorial lecturer at George Washington University, 1960-61. National Academy of Sciences, member of advisory committee on interrelation of agricultural land use and wildlife resources, 1967-68, member of Assembly of Life Sciences, 1974-75. Consultant to United Nations Economic Commission for Latin America, 1959, United Nations Economic Commission for Asia and the Far East, 1961-62, United Nations Development Program, 1969-72, and United Nations Environmental Program, 1980; also consultant to U.S. Department of Commerce, U.S. Department of the Interior, U.S. Department of Agriculture, and Bureau of the Budget. *Military service:* U.S. Coast Guard, 1942-46.

MEMBER: Association of Environmental and Resource Economists (president, 1980), Wilderness Society (treasurer, 1974-76). *Awards, honors:* American Motors Conservation Award, 1977; honorary doctor of laws, Reed College, 1978.

WRITINGS—Published by Johns Hopkins University Press, except as indicated: (With Otto Eckstein) *Multiple Purpose River Development: Studies in Applied Economic Analysis,* 1958; *Sequence and Timing in River Basin Development with Special Application to Columbia River Development* (monograph), 1960; *The Columbia River Treaty: An International Evaluation* (monograph), Resources for the Future, 1963; *The Columbia River Treaty: The Economics of an International River Basin Development,* 1967.

Natural Environments: Studies in Theoretical and Applied Analysis, 1972; (with Anthony C. Fisher) *The Economics of Natural Environments: Studies in the Valuation of Commodity and Amenity Resources,* 1975; (with V. Kerry Smith) *The Structure and Properties of a Wilderness Travel Simulator,* 1976; (with Fisher) *The Regional Economic and Fiscal Impacts of Energy Resource Development: A Case Study of Northern Great Plains Coal,* 1978; (with Constance M. Boris) *Water Rights and Energy Development in the Yellowstone River Basin: An Integrated Analysis,* 1980; (editor with Smith and contributor) *Explorations in Natural Resource Economics,* 1982. Co-author of *Unemployment, Idle Capacity, and Public Expenditure Criteria,* 1968; also co-author of government reports on water resource development, flood loss management, and cost analysis of conservation programs.

Contributor: *TVA: The First Twenty Years,* University of Alabama Press, 1956; *Land and Water: Planning for Economic Growth,* University of Colorado Press, 1961; *Economics and Public Policy in Water Resource Development,* Iowa State University Press, 1964; *Regional Development and Planning,* M.I.T. Press, 1964; *Water Research,* 1966; *Economic Aspects of Anti-Trust,* Random House, 1969.

America's Changing Environment, Houghton, 1970; *Environmental Quality Analysis: Research Studies in the Social Sciences,* 1972; *Benefit-Cost and Policy Analysis,* Aldine, 1973; *Pollution, Resources and the Environment,* Norton, 1973; *The Governance of Common Property Resources,* 1974; Robert Calter, editor, *Energy Supply and Government Policy,* Cornell University Press, 1976; Vernon L. Smith, editor, *Economics of Natural and Environmental Resources,* Gordon & Breach, 1977; V. Kerry Smith, editor, *Scarcity and Growth Reconsidered,* 1979. Contributor to economic and natural resource journals.

* * *

KUNTZ, J(ohn) Kenneth 1934-

PERSONAL: Born January 20, 1934, in St. Louis, Mo.; son of John Frederick (principal of an elementary school) and Zula (a teacher; maiden name, Reed) Kuntz; married Ruth Stanley (a teacher), July 7, 1962; children: David Kenneth, Nancy Ruth. *Education:* Grinnell College, B.A., 1956; Yale University, B.D., 1959; Union Theological Seminary, New York, N.Y., Ph.D., 1963. *Politics:* Democrat. *Home:* 321 Koser Ave., Iowa City, Iowa 52240. *Office:* School of Religion, University of Iowa, Iowa City, Iowa 52242.

CAREER: Ordained minister of United Methodist Church, 1959; member of Iowa Conference. Union Theological Seminary, New York, N.Y., tutor in Old Testament, 1961-63; Wellesley College, Wellesley, Mass., instructor, 1963-65, assistant professor of Biblical history, literature, and interpretation, 1965-67; University of Iowa, Iowa City, assistant professor, 1967-70, associate professor, 1970-76, professor of religion, 1976—. *Member:* Society of Biblical Literature, American Academy of Religion, Catholic Biblical Association, American Schools of Oriental Research, American Association of University Professors, Chicago Society of Biblical Research, Phi Beta Kappa (president of local chapter, 1977-78). *Awards, honors:* Huber Award (faculty research grant), Wellesley College; Old Gold Award (faculty research grant), University of Iowa; National Endowment for the Humanities grant; Alexander von Humboldt Award for study in Germany, 1971-72, 1973, 1979.

WRITINGS: The Self-Revelation of God, Westminster, 1967; *The World of the Old Testament,* University of Iowa, 1968; *The World of the New Testament,* University of Iowa, 1969; *The People of Ancient Israel: An Introduction to the Old Testament,* Harper, 1974; *Religion and Women: Images of Women in the Bible,* University of Iowa, 1978. Contributor to *Dictionary of the Bible and Religion,* Abingdon.

WORK IN PROGRESS: Research in the Psalms and wisdom literature of the Old Testament; engaging in rhetorical criticism of Pentateuchal narrative in the Old Testament.

SIDELIGHTS: J. Kenneth Kuntz is competent in Biblical Hebrew and has a working knowledge of Greek, Aramaic, Ugaritic, and Akkadian. *Avocational interests:* Music (plays organ and occasionally serves as church organist), photography, woodworking.

* * *

KUP, Alexander Peter 1924-

PERSONAL: Born March 26, 1924, in Ryde, Isle of Wight, England; son of Robert Laurence (a company director) and Dorothy (Woodhead) Kup; married Philippa Warwick, February 14, 1958; children: Alexander Timothy Neville, Katherine. *Education:* University of St. Andrews, M.A., 1948, Ph.D., 1952. *Office:* Department of History, Simon Fraser University, Burnaby, British Columbia, Canada.

CAREER: H. M. General Register House, Edinburgh, Scotland, assistant keeper of manuscripts, 1951-53; assistant archivist to Archbishop of York, York, England, 1953-54; University of Sierra Leone, Fourah Bay College, Freetown, professor of modern history, 1954-67; Simon Fraser University, Burnaby, British Columbia, professor of history, 1967—. Vice-chairman of Sierra Leone Museum; member of Sierra Leone Monuments and Relics Commission.

WRITINGS: (With P. Gouldesborough) *Printed Sources of Scottish History,* British Records Association, 1954; *A History of Sierra Leone 1400-1787,* Cambridge University Press, 1961; *The Story of Sierra Leone,* Cambridge University Press, 1964; (editor) Adam Afzelius, *Sierra Leone Journal, 1795-1796,* Uppsala Institute (Africa), 1967; *Sierra Leone: A Concise History,* St. Martin's, 1975; *Sir Charles MacCarthy: Soldier and Administrator,* University Library of Manchester, 1978. Editor, *Sierra Leone Studies,* 1954-61. Contributor to *Man, West African Review,* and to other journals.†

* * *

KYLE, Elisabeth
See DUNLOP, Agnes M. R.

L

LABER, Jeri 1931-

PERSONAL: Born May 19, 1931, in New York, N.Y.; daughter of Louis (an engineer) and Mae (Zias) Lidsky; married Austin Laber (an attorney), October 3, 1954 (divorced, 1978); children: Abigail, Pamela, Emily. *Education:* New York University, B.A., 1952; Columbia University, M.A., 1954. *Home:* 257 West 86th St., New York, N.Y. 10024.

CAREER: Current Digest of Soviet Press, New York City, foreign editor, 1954-56; Institute for Study of U.S.S.R., New York City, publications director, 1961-70. Free-lance writer and editor, 1970-75; Association of American Publishers, New York City, executive director of International Freedom to Publish Committee, 1975—; Helsinki Watch Committee, New York City, executive director, 1979—. *Member:* Amnesty International, Index on Censorship (member of board), Fund for Free Expression (member of board).

WRITINGS: Czechoslovakia: Some Soviet People Protest, Radio Liberty Committee, 1968; (with Milly Finn) *Cooking for Carefree Weekends,* Simon & Schuster, 1974; (author and editor) *Woman's Day Cookbook for Two,* Random House, 1976; (author and editor) *Gifts from Your Kitchen,* Simon & Schuster, 1976; *Cooking for One,* Random House, 1977; *The Hamburger Cookbook,* Random House, 1978; (editor and contributor) *The Fannie Farmer Cookbook,* Knopf, 1979; (editor) *The Corning Cookbook,* Random House, 1982. Contributor to journals and newspapers, including *The New Republic, Commentary, Worldview, House and Garden, New York Times,* and *Wall Street Journal.*

SIDELIGHTS: Jeri Laber told *CA:* "Holding two jobs in the human rights field is demanding, especially because of the nature of the work itself, since there is no end to what can and must be done. Nevertheless it is rewarding work to which I am deeply committed. My writings these days are mainly Op Ed articles and articles about my experiences travelling in Eastern Europe. I also review books on human rights and Soviet and East European affairs. One of these days I hope to publish a collection of my interviews with dissenters in Eastern Europe, and my photographs from these meetings."

* * *

LaHAYE, Tim 1926-

PERSONAL: Born April 27, 1926, in Detroit, Mich.; son of Francis T. (an electrician) and Margaret (a fellowship director; maiden name, Palmer) LaHaye; married Beverly Jean Ratcliffe (a writer and lecturer), July 5, 1947; children: Linda (Mrs. Gareld Murphy), Larry, Lee, Lori. *Education:* Bob Jones University, B.A., 1950; Western Conservative Baptist Seminary, D.Min., 1977. *Religion:* Baptist. *Home:* 2447 Camino Monte Sombra, El Cajon, Calif. 92021.

CAREER: Pastor of Baptist churches in Pickens, S.C., 1948-50, and in Minneapolis, Minn., 1950-56; Scott Memorial Baptist Church, El Cajon, Calif., senior pastor, 1956-81. Host, with wife, of weekly thirty-minute television program "LaHayes on Family Life," 1982—. President of Christian Heritage College, 1970-76; lecturer for Family Life Seminars, 1972—. *Military service:* U.S. Army Air Forces, 1944-46; became sergeant. *Awards, honors:* D.D. from Bob Jones University, 1962.

WRITINGS: Spirit-Controlled Temperaments, Tyndale, 1966; *How to Be Happy Though Married,* Tyndale, 1968; *Transformed Temperaments,* Tyndale, 1971; *The Beginning of the End,* Tyndale, 1972; *How to Win Over Depression,* Zondervan, 1973; *Revelation Illustrated and Made Plain,* Zondervan, 1973.

The Act of Marriage, Zondervan, 1976; *How to Study the Bible for Yourself,* Harvest House, 1976; *The Bible's Influence on American History,* Creation-Life Publishers, 1976; *The Battle for the Mind,* Revell, 1980; *The Battle for the Family,* Revell, 1981; *The Battle for the Public Schools,* Revell, 1982; *Anger Is a Choice,* Zondervan, 1982.

WORK IN PROGRESS: How to Manage Your Pressures before They Manage You, for Zondervan.

AVOCATIONAL INTERESTS: Flying his own twin-engine plane, skiing, football.

* * *

LAL, P. 1929-

PERSONAL: Born August 28, 1929, in Kapurthala, Punjab, India; son of Parmeshwar (a medical practitioner) and Jagdish (Devi) Lal; married Shyamasree Nag (a teacher), January 31, 1955; children: Amanda, Srimati. *Education:* St. Xavier's College, Calcutta, India, B.A., 1950; Calcutta University, M.A., 1952. *Religion:* Hindu. *Home:* 162/92 Lake Gardens, Calcutta 700045, Bengal, India.

CAREER: St. Xavier's College, Calcutta, India, 1953—, began as lecturer, became professor, honorary professor of English, 1972—. Secretary of Writers Workshop, Calcutta, 1958—.

WRITINGS—Published by Writers Workshop (Calcutta), except as indicated: *The Art of the Essay,* Atma Ram, 1950; (editor with Raghavendra Rao) *Modern Indo-Anglian Poetry,* Kavita, 1958; *The Parrot's Death, and Other Poems,* 1959, 3rd edition, 1968.

Love's the First (poems), 1962; (editor) *T. S. Eliot: Homage from India,* 1965; *"Change!" They Said: New Poems,* 1966; (compiler and editor) *The First Workshop Story Anthology,* 1967; *Draupadi & Jayadratha & Other Poems,* 1967; *The Annotated Mahabharata Bibliography,* 1967; *Creations and Transcreations,* Dialogue (Calcutta), 1968; *The Concept of an Indian Literature: Six Essays,* 1968; (compiler and editor) *Modern Indian Poetry in English,* 1969; *Yakshi from Didarganj: Poems,* 1969; (compiler) Manmohan Ghose, *Selected Poems,* 1969.

(With P. N. Shastri) *A Handbook of Assamese Literature,* 1972; (with Shastri) *A Handbook of Gujarati Literature,* 1973; *Transcreations: Two Essays,* 1973; *The Lemon Tree of Modern Sex* (essays), 1974; *The Man of Dharma and the Rasa of Silence* (poems), 1974; *Calcutta: A Long Poem,* 1978.

Translator; published by Writers Workshop (Calcutta), except as indicated: Rehbar, *Premchand: His Mind and Art,* Atma Ram, 1952; (with Jai Ratan) Premchand, *Godan,* Jaico, 1956.

(And editor) *Great Sanskrit Plays,* New Directions, 1964; Rgveda Vedas, *The Golden Womb of the Sun,* 1965; Bhagavadgita Mahabharata, *The Bhagavad Gita,* 1965; *Sanskrit Love Lyrics,* 1966; Dhammapada, *The Dhammadpada,* Farrar, Straus, 1967; Adi-Granth, *The Jap-ji: Fourteen Religious Songs,* 1967; Upanishads, *The Isa Upanisad,* 1968; Mahabharata, *The Mahabharata,* 120 volumes, 1968-80; Mahendra Vikrama Varma, King of Kashi, *The Farce of the Drunk Monk,* 1968; Adi-Granth, *More Songs from the Jap-ji,* 1969; Upanishads, *The Avyakta Upanisad,* 1969; Upanishads, *The Mahanarayana Upanisad,* 1969.

(With Shyamasree Devi) Rabindranath Tagore, *Tagore's Last Poems,* 1972, 3rd edition, 1980; (with Devi) Tarapada Roy, *Where to, Tarapada-babu,* 1974; Upanishads, *Brhadaranyaka Upanisad,* 1974; (with Nandini Nopany) Premchand, *Twenty-four Stories by Premchand,* Vikas, 1980; Vyasa, *The Mahabharata of Vyasa,* Vikas, 1980; Valmiki, *The Ramayana of Valmiki,* Vikas, 1981.

Editor with Alfred Schenkman, *Orient Review and Literary Digest,* 1954-58; editor, *Writers Workshop Miscellany,* 1958.

SIDELIGHTS: "When asked for an opinion," writes P. Lal, "I invariably apply three criteria to verse by young poets: newness of image, which is hard to achieve without concentrated feeling—and wide reading, so as to avoid the already achieved; rhythmic memorability, which is impossible without a firm grounding in prosody and awareness of the difference between strict verse, free verse, and loose verse; and 'moral idealism,' by which now-unfashionable phrase I mean that a self-respecting poet should at least refrain from expressing his lyrical pains and ecstasies until he has found a coherent culture pattern or set of myth values in whose context alone they can have their true meaning. I would like my poems to be read with these three qualities in mind, since [I write] with those qualities very much in my conscious and unconscious mind. They make a pretty mantra—the three M's—Metaphor, Music, and 'Morality.'

"The three uses of poetry make another attractive mantra: poetry as prescription, poetry as propaganda, poetry as prayer. Much adolescent poetry is therapeutic, serving to heal the nervous fevers that afflict its creator's sensitive personality. Medicinal poems, like medical prescriptions, should preferably be destroyed after they have plucked out one's deep-rooted sorrows. Poetry can also help spread a useful or required social message; time gently assigns such verse to the mercy of undiluted oblivion or the other oblivion of pedantic footnotes and bewhiskered bibliographies. Strictly speaking, lyrical poetry is truly itself only when it begins to possess some of the qualities of prayer. I will not try to define prayer, but I agree with the cliche that prayer is most likely to be effective when it is for and about others, not for oneself.

"Some readers may wonder why I have written so many elegies on Gandhiji. . . . The news of Gandhiji's assassination in 1948—I was then nineteen—was a traumatic shock of such magnitude that for many days suicidal guilt feelings overpowered me and many of my college friends. Recovery was possible only through confessional declaration: I actually wrote over a hundred long poems in an elegy-sequence. As for sonnets, they poured out cornucopiously. They are not the best examples of versecraft, but I have let them be represented in my collected poems because I feel that, in certain areas of human experience, extra-esthetic considerations applied to artistic creations are perfectly in order. I am not suggesting that mine was an area of such experience; only that the assassination of Bapu made many of us grow up very suddenly by giving us a cruel glimpse of real tragedy, not the literary kind our learned professors so earnestly communicated to us. Sometimes, to have a literary standard as the sole criterion to judge the quality of a literary work can be as self-limiting as to have a sole political, social, or psychological standard; catharsis in art and catharsis in life are two very valuable but very different experiences.

"A small confession: I never write for the printed page only; all my poems [are] composed to be read aloud. The melodic pattern, such as it is, is to me all-important and should at least partly bring out the 'meaning' wherever the meaning is not self-evident. All my poems are recorded on two stereo . . . cassettes in the Writers Workshop 'Sunbird' series of Indian poets reading their own work."

BIOGRAPHICAL/CRITICAL SOURCES: K.R.S. Iyengar, *Indian Writing in English,* Asia Publishing House, 1962; Desai Naik and Amur Naik, editors, *Critical Essays on Indian Writing in English,* Macmillan, 1968; S. Mokashi-Punekar, *P. Lal: An Appreciation,* Writers Workshop, 1968; Iyengar, editor, *Indian Literature since Independence,* Sahitya Akademi, 1973; Meenakshi Mukherjee, editor, *Considerations,* Allied Publishers (New Delhi), 1977.

* * *

LAMPLUGH, Lois 1921-

PERSONAL: Surname is pronounced "Lamploo"; born June 9, 1921, in Barnstaple, Devonshire, England; daughter of Aubrey Penfound and Ruth (Lister) Lamplugh; married Lawrence Carlile Davis (a sales representative), September 24, 1955; children: Susan Ruth, Hugh Lawrence. *Education:* B.A. (with honors), Open University, 1978. *Home:* Springside, Bydown, Swimbridge, Devonshire EX32 0QB, England. *Agent:* A. P. Watt Ltd., 26/28 Bedford Row, London WC1R 4HL, England.

CAREER: Writer. Jonathan Cape Ltd., London, England, member of editorial staff, 1946-57; former part-time teacher at school for maladjusted boys. *Wartime service:* Served in Auxiliary Territorial Service, World War II. *Member:* Society of Authors, West Country Writers Association.

WRITINGS—Juveniles, except as indicated: *The Stream Way* (adult book), Golden Galley Press, 1948; *Nine Bright Shiners,* J. Cape, 1955; *The Pigeongram Puzzle,* J. Cape, 1955, Verry, 1960; *Vagabonds' Castle,* J. Cape, 1957, Verry, 1965; *Rockets in the Dunes,* J. Cape, 1958; *The Sixpenny Runner,* J. Cape, 1960; *Midsummer Mountains,* J. Cape, 1961; *The Rifle House Friends,* Deutsch, 1965; *The Linhay on Hunters's Hill,* Deutsch, 1966; *The Fur Princess and Fir Prince,* Dent, 1969; (with Peter Dickinson) *Mandog,* BBC Publications, 1972; *Sean's Leap,* Deutsch, 1979; *The Winter Donkey,* Deutsch, 1980. Also author of *Falcon's Tor.* Author of half-hour documentary "Coleridge," Harlech Television, 1966, and of over 300 five-minute stories for television, including "Honeyhill" series, Harlech Television, 1967-70.

SIDELIGHTS: Lois Lamplugh told *CA:* "It is possible that I became a writer simply because I happened to spend the first eighteen years of my life in or near the village of Georgeham [where] in the 1920s Henry Williamson was living—for part of the time in a cottage he rented from my grandmother. (He wrote most, if not all, of *Tarka the Otter* in that cottage.)"

A country child, Lamplugh still prefers country living, adding "for all that, I wrote my first children's books when I was living and working in London—perhaps a form of escape, since they were set in North Devon." She wrote a great deal of unpublished work, mainly novels and verse, in her teens and had a book accepted for publication by Faber in 1942. It was an account of her experiences in the Auxiliary Territorial Service, and the War Office withheld approval of publication on the grounds that it would discourage recruiting. The manuscript remains unpublished.

Sean's Leap arose from Lamplugh's experience of teaching at a school for maladjusted boys and was written "at intervals between courses [she was taking at the Open University] on 'Renaissance and Reformation,' 'The Nineteenth Century Novel,' and 'Twentieth Century Poetry.'" Lamplugh believes "the outlook for children's books in England is poor at present, with the cuts in spending affecting the buying of books for schools and children's libraries, and this is why I've been at work on a book about the past of Barnstaple. However, I hope that a novel for older children, *Falcon's Tor,* . . . may see the light one day."

AVOCATIONAL INTERESTS: Listening to music (especially Italian opera), gardening, walking.

* * *

LAMSA, George M(amishisho) 1892-1975

PERSONAL: Born circa August 5, 1892, in Kurdistan, Turkey; came to United States in 1916, naturalized in 1923; died in 1975; son of Jando Peshah and Sarah Peshah (Yokhanan) Lamsa. *Education:* Archbishop of Canterbury's College, Urmiah, Persia (now Reza'iyeh, Iran), A.B. equivalent, 1907; Archbishop of Canterbury's College, Turkey, Ph.D. equivalent in theology, 1908; studied at University of Pennsylvania, 1918, Episcopal Theology Seminary in Virginia, 1918-21, and Dropsie College, 1942-44. *Home:* 8603 Crownhill St., San Antonio, Tex. 78209.

CAREER: Writer, translator, and lecturer. Left Turkey at beginning of World War I and migrated to South America; served in British Merchant Marine for a time, and worked on railroads, in mines, and later in printing shops in United States; field secretary of Archbishop of Canterbury's Assyrian Mission in United States, 1925-31; Aramaic Bible Society, Inc., St. Petersburg Beach, Fla., founder, 1943, and chairman of the board. *Member:* Authors League, American Oriental Society, American Geographical Society, Royal Society of Arts (London; fellow), Christian Jewish Mohammedan Society (founding member, 1923).

WRITINGS: The Secret of the Near East: Slavery of Women, Social, Religious and Economic Life in the Near East, Ideal Press, 1923; (with William C. Emhardt) *The Oldest Christian People,* Macmillan, 1926, reprinted, AMS Press, 1970; *The Origin of the Gospel,* Winston, 1927.

Key to the Original Gospels, Winston, 1931; *My Neighbor Jesus: In the Light of His Own Language, People, and Time,* Harper, 1932, 12th edition, Aramaic Bible Society, 1973; *Gospel Light: Comments on the Teachings of Jesus from Aramaic and Unchanged Eastern Customs,* A. J. Holman, 1936, reprinted, 1962; *Shepherd of All: The Twenty-Third Psalm,* A. J. Holman, 1939; *Modern Wisdom,* Association Press, 1939.

Second Reader in Aramaic, A. J. Holman, 1942; *New Testament Commentary from the Aramaic and the Ancient Eastern Customs,* A. J. Holman, 1945; *New Testament Origin,* Ziff-Davis, 1947; (editor) *The Short Koran: Designed for Easy Reading,* Ziff-Davis, 1949.

A Brief Course in the Aramaic Language, Aramaic Bible Society, 1961; *Old Testament Light: A Scriptural Commentary Based on the Aramaic of the Ancient Peshitta,* Prentice-Hall, 1964, 3rd edition, A. J. Holman, 1978; *The Kingdom on Earth,* Unity, 1966; *Gems of Wisdom,* Unity, 1966; *And the Scroll Opened,* Doubleday, 1967; *The Hidden Years of Jesus,* revised edition, Unity, 1968, 3rd revised edition, 1978; *More Light on the Gospel,* Doubleday, 1968; *Roses of Gulistan* (poetry), Aramaic Bible Society, 1968.

The Man from Galilee: A Life of Jesus, Doubleday, 1970; *Idioms in the Bible Explained,* Aramaic Bible Society, 1971, 3rd edition, 1978; *Pearls of Wisdom,* De Vorss, 1978.

Translator from the Aramaic; all published by A. J. Holman: *The Four Gospels,* 1933; *Book of Psalms, According to the Eastern Version,* 1939; *New Testament According to the Eastern Text,* 1940; *The Old Testament,* 1955; *The Holy Bible from the Peshitta,* 1957, 5th edition, 1961.

SIDELIGHTS: George M. Lamsa spent more than thirty years laboring on his translation of the Bible from ancient Aramaic, a project conceived while he was also trying to learn the idioms of the English language. Besides Aramaic, he was competent in Hebrew, Turkish, Arabic, and Spanish.†

* * *

LANCE, Derek (Paul) 1932-

PERSONAL: Born October 1, 1932, in Norwich, Norfolk, England; son of Joseph Bertram (a shopkeeper) and Florence Mary (Hunt) Lance. *Education:* Queens' College, Cambridge, M.A., 1957, Certificate of Education, 1958; seminary studies, 1973-75. *Religion:* Catholic. *Home and office:* 60 Spinney Hill Rd., Northampton NN3 1DN, England.

CAREER: Becket School, Nottingham, England, head of history department, 1958-65; St. Thomas Aquinas Grammar School, Birmingham, England, deputy headmaster and head of religious education, 1965-73; ordained Catholic priest in diocese of Northampton, England, 1975; chaplain in Northampton, 1977—. Part-time religious instructor at Borstal Institution (for delinquents), 1964-65; member of committee, Cheshire Homes; member of School Council, 1969-71; member of governing board, Corpus Christi College, 1969-71. *Military service:* British Army, Intelligence Corps, 1952-54; became sergeant. *Member:* Catholic Teachers Association (president, Nottingham branch, 1963), Catholic Colleges Conference, Historical Association, Newman Association (vice-president, Nottingham branch, 1964).

WRITINGS: Till Christ Be Formed: Teaching Religion as the History of Salvation, Burns & MacEachern, 1964, revised edition published as *Teaching the History of Salvation: An Introduction for Teachers,* Paulist Press, 1964; *A Christian View of Life,* Living Parish, 1965; *Eleven to Sixteen: A Complete Course for Religious Education at the Secondary School Level,* Darton, Longman & Todd, 1967; *What Is Christianity?,* Darton, Longman & Todd, 1970; *What's the Point?,* Darton, Longman & Todd, 1971. Consulting editor of "Insight" series, Paulist Press, and "Where We Stand" series, Darton, Longman & Todd. Editor of *Good News,* 1978-81, and *Sower,* 1979—.

SIDELIGHTS: Derek Lance speaks French and Italian. *Avocational interests:* Social work among delinquents and youth, music (classical and light), camping, oil painting (landscapes and portraits).

* * *

LANE, Mary (Lois) B(eauchamp) 1911-

PERSONAL: Born March 7, 1911, in Edwardsburg, Mich.; daughter of Hugh Dunning (a farmer) and Bea (Scott) Beauchamp; married Howard A. Lane, February 28, 1958 (deceased). *Education:* Northeast Missouri State Teachers College (now Northeast Missouri State University), B.A., 1930; Northwestern University, M.A., 1945; New York University, Ed.D., 1950. *Politics:* Democrat.

CAREER: Teacher in La Plata and Webster Groves, Mo.; curriculum consultant in Minneapolis (Minn.) public schools, 1945-48; New York University, Center for Human Relations Studies, New York, N.Y., instructor in elementary education and member of staff, 1951-58; San Francisco State University, San Francisco, Calif., beginning 1962, began as instructor, became professor of education. Part-time instructor in educational psychology, University of California, Berkeley, 1958-59. Director of summer workshops at University of Florida, 1951, and University of Kansas City, 1956-59. Director, Cross Cultural Family Center. Consultant in early childhood education, group dynamics, and human relations. *Member:* Association for Childhood Education International, Association for Supervision and Curriculum Development, National Association for Young Children, American Civil Liberties Union, YWCA.

WRITINGS: (With Ardelle Llewellyn and Vivienne S. Worley) *Building Brotherhood: What Can Elementary Schools Do?,* edited by Franklin Patterson, National Conference of Christians and Jews, c. 1954; (with husband, Howard A. Lane) *Human Relations in Teaching,* Prentice-Hall, 1956; (with H. A. Lane) *Understanding Human Development,* Prentice-Hall, 1959; (editor) H. A. Lane, *On Educating Human Beings* (essays), Follett, 1964; (with Freeman F. Elzey and Mary S. Lewis) *Nurseries in Cross-Cultural Education: A Final Report,* San Francisco State College, 1971; *Learning about Life: A Child-Centered Approach to Sex Education,* Evans Brothers, 1973; *Education for Parenting,* National Association for the Education of Young Children, 1975. Contributor to education journals.

AVOCATIONAL INTERESTS: Outdoor living, gardening, camping, travel.†

* * *

LANG, T. T.
See TAYLOR, Theodore

* * *

LANGHOLM, Neil
See BULMER, (Henry) Kenneth

* * *

LANGLOIS, Walter G(ordon) 1925-

PERSONAL: Born May 27, 1925, in Springfield, Mass.; son of Walter E. (a businessman) and Ann Mae (Doyle) Langlois; married Sheila Wood, May 30, 1959; children: Walter Rawson, Rebecca Ann. *Education:* Yale University, B.A., 1950, M.A., 1952, Ph.D., 1955; University of Paris, Certificat (with honors), 1949; additional study at University of Florence, 1952-53, and Harvard University, 1960-61. *Office:* Department of Modern and Classical Languages, University of Wyoming, Laramie, Wyo. 82071.

CAREER: University of Wisconsin—Madison, instructor in French and Italian, 1954-56; Lycee Sisowath, Pnom-Penh, Cambodia, Smith-Mundt Professor, 1956-57; Boston College, Boston, Mass., assistant professor of French and Asian studies, 1957-64; University of Kentucky, Lexington, associate professor, 1964-67, professor of French literature, 1967-74; University of Wyoming, Laramie, professor of modern languages, 1974—. *Military service:* U.S. Army, 1943-46; received Bronze Star and Croix de Guerre. *Member:* Modern Language Association of America, American Association of Teachers of French, Manuscript Society (vice-president, 1982—), Phi Beta Kappa. *Awards, honors:* Fulbright scholar in Italy, 1952-53; Harvard University postdoctoral fellow, 1960-61; Guggenheim fellow in France, 1967-68; American Council of Learned Societies fellow, 1971-72; National Endowment for the Humanities fellow, 1980-81.

WRITINGS—Published by Lettres Moderne, except as indicated: *Andre Malraux: The Indochina Adventure,* Praeger, 1966, augmented edition published in French as *Andre Malraux: L'Aventure indochinoise,* Mercure de France, 1967; (editor) *The Persistent Voice: Hellenism in French Literature since the Eighteenth Century,* New York University Press, 1971; (editor) *Andre Malraux: Du 'farfelu' aux Antimemoires,* 1972; *Essai di bibliographie des etudes en langue anglaise consacrees a Andre Malraux, 1924-1970,* 1972; (editor) *Andre Malraux: Visages du romancier,* 1973; (editor) *Malraux: Influences et affinites,* 1975; *Malraux et l'art,* 1978; *Malraux et l'histoire,* 1982. Contributor to literary journals. Editor, *Melanges Malraux Miscellany.*

WORK IN PROGRESS: Malraux et la croixade espagnole (1936-37), for Mercure de France.

AVOCATIONAL INTERESTS: Collecting books and manuscripts.

LARKIN, Emmet 1927-

PERSONAL: Born May 19, 1927, in New York, N.Y.; son of Emmet Joseph and Annabell (Ryder) Larkin. *Education:* New York University, B.A., 1950; Columbia University, M.A., 1951, Ph.D., 1957; graduate study at London School of Economics and Political Science, London, 1955-56. *Home:* 5021 South Woodlawn Ave., Chicago, Ill. 60615. *Office:* Department of History, University of Chicago, 5801 South Ellis Ave., Chicago, Ill. 60637.

CAREER: Brooklyn College (now Brooklyn College of the City University of New York), Brooklyn, N.Y., part-time instructor, 1954-55, instructor in history, 1955-60; Massachusetts Institute of Technology, Cambridge, assistant professor of history, 1960-66; University of Chicago, Chicago, Ill., associate professor, 1966-71, professor of history, 1971—. Executive secretary of Labor Seminar at Columbia University, 1956-60. *Military service:* U.S. Army, 1944-46. *Member:* American Committee for Irish Studies (treasurer, 1961-75; vice-president, 1975-78; president, 1978-81).

AWARDS, HONORS: Fulbright scholar at University of London, 1955-56; grants-in-aid from American Philosophical Society, 1958, 1959, 1963, Social Science Research Council, 1958, 1961, American Council of Learned Societies, 1962, and Massachusetts Institute of Technology, 1964 and 1965; Dominion fellow at Massachusetts Institute of Technology, 1962-63; Howard Foundation fellow at Brown University, 1964-65; National Endowment for the Humanities fellow at Newberry Library, 1976-77; John Gilmary Shea Prize, Catholic Historical Association, 1976, for *The Roman Catholic Church and the Creation of the Modern Irish State, 1878-1886*.

WRITINGS: (Contributor) Ray B. Browne, William J. Roscelli, and Richard J. Loftus, editors, *The Celtic Cross: Studies in Irish Culture and Literature,* Purdue University Studies, 1964; *James Larkin: Irish Labour Leader, 1876-1947,* M.I.T. Press, 1965; *The Roman Catholic Church and the Creation of the Modern Irish State, 1878-1886,* American Philosophical Society, 1975; *The Historical Dimensions of Irish Catholicism* (essays previously published in the *American Historical Review,* with a new introduction), Arno, 1976; *The Roman Catholic Church and the Plan of Campaign in Ireland, 1886-1888,* Cork University Press, 1978; *The Roman Catholic Church in Ireland and the Fall of Parnell, 1888-1891,* University of North Carolina Press, 1979; *The Making of the Roman Catholic Church in Ireland, 1850-1860,* University of North Carolina Press, 1980. Contributor to *Victorian Studies, Church History, Review of Politics, Irish Historical Studies, American Historical Review,* and other periodicals.

WORK IN PROGRESS: A History of the Roman Catholic Church in Ireland in the Nineteenth Century.

SIDELIGHTS: In *The Roman Catholic Church in Ireland and the Fall of Parnell, 1888-1891,* Emmet Larkin argues that during the ascendancy of Irish Nationalist leader Charles Parnell, the foundations of the modern Irish state were laid on the basis of an alliance between the Roman Catholic Church and Parnell's Irish parliamentary party. F.S.L. Lyons, writing in the *Times Literary Supplement,* considers this thesis "a little too glib for comfort, [because] it oversystematizes a situation which was always confused and complex. To make it fit all the circumstances Professor Larkin sometimes has to squeeze history into shapes which don't quite correspond with the facts." Nevertheless, Lyons believes "when Professor Larkin is exploring the inner mind of the Irish Church it would be a bold man who would challenge him. No one has a better knowledge than he both of the episcopal archives in Ireland and of the relevant sources in Rome, and that knowledge has never been more powerfully deployed than in this book."

BIOGRAPHICAL/CRITICAL SOURCES: Times Literary Supplement, February 15, 1980.

* * *

LARRISON, Earl J(unior) 1919-

PERSONAL: Born May 11, 1919, in Mabton, Wash.; son of Earl (an accountant) and Anna Marie (an educator; maiden name, Kuble) Larrison. *Education:* University of Washington, Seattle, B.S., 1941, M.S., 1946; additional graduate study at University of Michigan, 1946-49. *Politics:* Independent. *Religion:* Unitarian. *Home:* 803 Residence St., Moscow, Idaho 83843. *Office:* Department of Zoology, University of Idaho, Moscow, Idaho 83843.

CAREER: Metallurgical chemist for Washington Iron Works, 1942-46; University of Idaho, Moscow, 1949—, currently professor of bird and mammal ecology. *Member:* American Association for the Advancement of Science (fellow), American Society of Mammalogists, Wildlife Society, National Audubon Society, Ecological Society of America, Cooper Ornithological Society, American Ornithologists Union, American Association of University Professors, American Federation of Teachers, Northwest Scientific Association, Idaho Academy of Science (founder), Palouse Audubon Society (founder; president, 1971-73), Phi Beta Kappa, Phi Delta Kappa, Sigma Xi, Phi Sigma.

WRITINGS: (With Harry W. Higman) *Pilchuck: The Life of a Mountain,* Superior, 1949; (with Higman) *Union Bay: The Life of a City Marsh,* University of Washington Press, 1951; *Field Guide to the Birds of Puget Sound,* Seattle Audubon Society, 1952; *Owyhee: The Life of a Northern Desert,* Caxton, 1957.

Wildlife of the Northern Rocky Mountains, Naturegraph, 1961; (with Edward M. Francq) *Field Guide to the Birds of Washington State,* Seattle Audubon Society, 1962; (with Jerry L. Tucker and Malcomb Jollie) *Guide to Idaho Birds,* Idaho Academy of Science, 1967; *Guide to Idaho Mammals,* Idaho Academy of Science, 1967, revised edition (with Donald R. Johnson) published as *Mammals of Idaho,* University Press of Idaho, 1981; (with Klaus G. Sonnenberg) *Washington Birds: Their Location and Identification,* Seattle Audubon Society, 1968; *Washington Mammals: Their Habits, Identification and Distribution,* Seattle Audubon Society, 1970, revised edition published as *Mammals of the Northwest: Washington, Oregon, Idaho, and British Columbia,* 1976; (editor with others) *Washington Wildflowers,* Seattle Audubon Society, 1974; (with John W. Weber) *Birds of Southeastern Washington,* University Press of Idaho, 1977.

Birds of the Pacific Northwest, University Press of Idaho, 1981. Editor of *Idaho Academy of Science Bulletin,* 1965-70.

WORK IN PROGRESS: An autobiography, *Trails of a Mouse Trapper;* research on chipmunk behavior, bird and mammal faunistics, and winter animal behavior.

AVOCATIONAL INTERESTS: Photography, camping, expeditions, organ playing, music, travel (Canada, Alaska, Africa, Central America).†

LARSON, George C(harles) 1942-

PERSONAL: Born March 31, 1942, in New Jersey; son of George Lester (an architect) and Mildred (Frehner) Larson; married Valarie Thompson, July 7, 1971. *Education:* Harvard University, A.B., 1964. *Home and office address:* The Wordworks, P.O. Box 2780, Hendersonville, N.C. 28793.

CAREER: Medical World News, New York City, junior editor, beginning 1966; *Scholastic* (magazine), New York City, staff writer, beginning 1971; *Flying,* New York City and California, managing editor and senior editor, 1971-78; free-lance and technical editor for *Business and Commercial Aviation* (magazine), 1978—. Worked briefly for *Mother Earth News,* 1978. *Military service:* U.S. Army, 1966-70; became captain; received Bronze Star. *Member:* Aerospace Writers Association.

WRITINGS: (Editor) *I Learned About Flying from That,* Delacorte, 1976; *The Blimp Book,* Squarebooks, 1979; *Fly on Instruments,* Doubleday, 1980. Contributor to *Flieger* magazine (Munich).

SIDELIGHTS: George C. Larson is rated as a commercial single- and multi-engine instrument pilot.

* * *

LARSON, Muriel 1924-

PERSONAL: Born February 9, 1924, in Orange, N.J.; daughter of Eugene Louis and Helen (Fretz) Koller; children: Gay (Mrs. Charles Hazelrigs), Lori. *Education:* South River Bible Institute, diploma, 1957; Bob Jones University, additional study, 1967-69. *Politics:* Independent. *Religion:* Baptist. *Home:* 10 Vanderbilt Cir., Greenville, S.C. 29609.

CAREER: Stenographer with printing company in Dunellen, N.J., 1955-57, and with Tennessee Valley Authority, Chattanooga, S.C., 1962-63; Bob Jones University, Greenville, S.C., public relations writer, 1967-69; full-time writer, 1969—. Lecturer on creative writing. Has also served as a piano teacher, choir director, substitute teacher, home missionary, church organist, and instructor at writers' conferences.

WRITINGS: Devotions for Women's Groups, Baker Book, 1967; *How to Give a Devotion,* Baker Book, 1967; (contributor) James R. Adair, editor, *God's Power to Triumph,* Moody, 1968; *Devotionals for Children's Groups,* Baker Book, 1969.

(Contributor) Adair, editor, *Unhooked,* Baker Book, 1971; *Living Miracles,* Warner Press, 1973; *It Took a Miracle,* Warner Press, 1974; *You Are What You Think,* Bible Voice, 1974; *God's Fantastic Creation,* Moody, 1975; *The Bible Says Quiz Book,* Moody, 1976; *Are You Real, God?,* Bible Voice, 1976; (contributor) Grace Fox, editor, *The Hairy Brown Angel,* Victor Books, 1977; *I Give Up, God,* Bible Voice, 1978; *Joy Every Morning,* Moody, 1979; *What Happens When Women Believe,* Bible Voice, 1979.

(Contributor) Ted Miller and Adair, editors, *Escape from Darkness,* Victor Books, 1982. Also prepares crossword puzzles for several publishers. Also author of play, "Miracles," and of gospel hymns and choruses. Contributor of numerous articles, stories, devotionals, and poems to *Good News Broadcaster, War Cry, Christian Life, Woman's Touch, Living with Children,* and many other periodicals. Editor, *Reinhearter* (monthly church paper), Dallas, Tex., 1966-67.

WORK IN PROGRESS: Living by Faith.

SIDELIGHTS: Muriel Larson wrote *CA:* "I have always been interested in writing and started while in high school by writing for the school paper and preparing the social column for my town for a weekly paper.

"I began my career as a writer while a minister's wife. When I attended a national conference with my husband, a woman writer addressed us women and inspired me to start writing. The two stories I wrote on the way home from that conference were accepted eventually by two periodicals, and I was in business. Since then I have had more than 3,300 first and reprint right writings accepted for publication by about 150 periodicals, as well as my twelve books, twelve gospel songs, and one play for radio.

"My main purpose in writing is to glorify God and point other people to Him, for I have found a wonderful life in serving and trusting the Lord. The purpose behind all my writings is to help others find the truth of God that leads to the abundant life He promised those who commit their way unto Him.

"The most important advice I give to aspiring writers at the conferences at which I teach is to keep trying. Persistence, perseverance, and self-discipline are necessary for success. Also, when you start submitting your work to editors, send two to four articles out to several places. Then if one is accepted, it encourages you to continue on. If you just send one out and it is rejected, you tend to lose heart and fall by the wayside."

AVOCATIONAL INTERESTS: Music (plays piano, organ, accordian, clarinet, and sings), gardening, camping.

* * *

LATNER, Pat Wallace
See STROTHER, Pat Wallace

* * *

LAUGHLIN, James 1914-

PERSONAL: Born October 30, 1914, in Pittsburgh, Pa.; son of Henry Hughart and Marjory (Rea) Laughlin; married Margaret Keyser, 1942 (divorced, 1952); married Ann Clark Resor, May 19, 1957; children: (first marriage) Paul, Leila; (second marriage) Robert, Henry. *Education:* Harvard University, A.B., 1939. *Politics:* Republican. *Religion:* Presbyterian. *Home:* Mountain Rd., Norfolk, Conn. 06058. *Office:* New Directions Publishing Corp., 333 Avenue of the Americas, New York, N.Y. 10014.

CAREER: New Directions Publishing Corp., New York City, founder, 1936, editor and publisher, 1936—; Intercultural Publications, Inc., New York City, president, 1952-69; University of Iowa, Iowa City, Ida Bean Visiting Lecturer, 1981-82; Brown University, Providence, R.I., adjunct professor of English, 1983. Lecturer at over twenty colleges and universities; member of visiting committee to department of German at Princeton University and Harvard University; member of U.S. National Commission for UNESCO, 1962-63, and U.S. National Commission for International Cooperation Year, 1966. Alta Lodge Co., vice-president, 1948-58, president, 1958-59; vice-president, Alta Ski Lifts Co., 1950—. Trustee, Merton Legacy Trust; agent, Ezra Pound Literary Property Trust and estate of William Carlos Williams. Consultant to Indian Southern Languages Book Trust, 1956-58. *Member:* P.E.N., American Academy of Arts and Sciences, Authors League of America; Century Association and Harvard Club (both New York).

AWARDS, HONORS: Prize for short story published in *Atlantic;* Chevalier, Legion of Honor, for cultural service in publishing translations of French literature; D.Litt., Hamilton College, 1970, and Colgate University, 1973; American Academy of Arts and Letters Award, 1977, for distinguished service to the arts; D.H.L., Duquesne University, 1981, and Yale University, 1982.

WRITINGS—Published by New Directions, except as indicated: (Editor with Albert M. Hayes) *A Wreath of Christmas Poems,* 1942, reprinted, 1972; *Some Natural Things* (poems), 1945; *A Small Book of Poems,* 1948; *The Wild Anemone, and Other Poems,* 1957; *Selected Poems,* 1959 (published in England as *Confidential Report, and Other Poems,* Gaberbocchus, 1959); *The Pig* (poems), Perishable Press, 1970; *In Another Country: Poems 1935-1975,* selected by Robert Fitzgerald, City Lights, 1978. Translator of other books of poetry for publication abroad.

Editor of "New Directions in Prose and Poetry" series, forty-five volumes, New Directions, 1936—. Also editor of various numbers of *Perspectives USA* and "Perspectives" supplements to *Atlantic,* 1952-58. Contributor of articles on skiing to *Town and Country, Harper's, Ski, Sports Illustrated, Ski Annual,* and other publications.

SIDELIGHTS: While a sophomore on leave of absence from Harvard University, James Laughlin met Ezra Pound in Rapallo, Italy and was invited to attend the "Ezuversity"—Pound's term for the private tutoring he gave Laughlin over meals, on hikes, or whenever the master paused in his labors. "I stayed several months in Rapallo at the 'Ezuversity,' learning and reading," recalls Laughlin in an interview with Linda Kuehl for the *New York Times Book Review,* "until Pound said it was time for me to go back to Harvard and do *something useful.* Being useful meant that I should publish books, because at that time publishing was still suffering from the Depression and none of [Pound's] friends, except Hemingway, had steady publishers." "Never has advice been better followed," surmises poet and critic Donald Hall in the *New York Times Book Review,* for after returning to Harvard from Italy, Laughlin founded New Directions, a company dedicated to publishing quality works with little regard to their chances for commercial success.

With his own money (Laughlin's well-to-do father had given him $100,000 when he graduated from college), Laughlin initially set out to publish and thereby recognize experimental and avant-garde writers of merit. His first New Directions book, an anthology containing the work of such authors as Pound, Gertrude Stein, E. E. Cummings, William Carlos Williams, Elizabeth Bishop, and Henry Miller, appeared in 1936. "At the time," reports Hall, "the 22-year-old editor-publisher . . . loaded his Buick with 600 unpaginated copies [of *New Directions in Prose and Poetry*], became a traveling salesman, and persuaded bookstores to stock a few volumes—out of pity, he believes."

During the 1940s, according to Hall, Laughlin's company provided the first lengthy publication of Randall Jarrell, John Berryman, Karl Shapiro, Tennessee Williams, Paul Goodman, Jean Garrigue, John Frederick Nims, and Eve Merriam. The list of New Directions authors eventually grew to include George Oppen, Carl Rakosi, Charles Reznikoff, Robert Creeley, Lawrence Ferlinghetti, Gregory Corso, Gary Snyder, Kenneth Rexroth, Denise Levertov, Thomas Merton, and Robert Duncan. "For the most part," writes Hall, "the list represented the new," which initially meant limited commercial success. "When I started doing the books," Laughlin told Edwin McDowell of the *New York Times Book Review,* "they were way out ahead of the public taste. Nobody could understand them and nobody wanted to buy them. . . . But a younger generation of professors matured and became interested in using them in college courses, and that's what put us on our feet."

Though, as Hall points out, New Directions "started in the service of verbal revolution," it made other, equally impressive contributions to our literature in print. It published F. Scott Fitzgerald's *The Crack Up* when other publishers would not; when *The Great Gatsby* was out of print, New Directions brought it back; the company also reprinted the works of Henry James, E. M. Forster, Ronald Firbank, and Evelyn Waugh when no one else would. Hall believes that in these instances, the decision to publish established authors was governed by the same assumptions underlying the publication of new writers: "the assumption of quality and the assumption that these books would not sell in the marketplace."

But New Directions may have made its most important contribution, suggests Hall, in bringing foreign authors to American readers in translation: "not only the obvious Rimbaud, Baudelaire, Rilke, Valery, Kafka and Cocteau, but the less known and the unknown: Montale, Neruda, Queneau, Cardenal, Lorca, Pasternak, Paz, Borges, Mishima, Lihn, Vittorini, Parra, Guillevic." The first American publisher of Vladimir Nabokov, New Directions made available Nabokov's critical work on Gogol, a group of short stories, and some translations of classic Russian poetry, as well as his second novel in English, *The Real Life of Sebastian Knight.*

After years of being subsidized by the money of Laughlin's family, New Directions is now a profit-making venture. Aided by the million-copy sale of Lawrence Ferlinghetti's *Coney Island of the Mind,* the hundreds of thousands of reprints of Herman Hesse's *Siddhartha,* the academic acceptance of writers like Pound, and the popularity of younger authors like Gary Snyder, Denise Levertov, and John Hawkes, the company has been making money for over twenty years. Laughlin, who emphasizes in the *New York Times Book Review* that New Directions has always been an intimate group venture and that the profits have been "small," modestly gives others credit for the company's critical and commercial success: "I am only a happenstance catalyst who started publishing because Ezra said I had to 'do something useful.' The credit, whatever there may be, belongs to the writers we published and to the long-suffering people who actually saw that the books got printed, proofread, and sold. Without all of them, New Directions would have been just an amateur's hobby."

BIOGRAPHICAL/CRITICAL SOURCES: Time, January 16, 1950; *Newsweek,* May 1, 1967; *New York Times Book Review,* February 25, 1973, August 23, 1981, February 28, 1982; *Conjunctions,* winter, 1982.

—Sketch by James G. Lesniak

* * *

LAW, Janice
See TRECKER, Janice Law

* * *

LEAR, Martha Weinman 1930-

PERSONAL: Born March 11, 1930, in Malden, Mass.; daughter of Joseph and Kenia (Pugach) Weinman; married Harold Alexander Lear (a physician), May 28, 1961 (died September 13, 1978). *Education:* Boston University, B.S., 1950.

CAREER: Writer. *Collier's,* New York City, associate editor, 1951-56; *Woman's Home Companion,* New York City, associate editor, 1956; National Broadcasting Co. Television, New York City, staff writer, 1957; *New York Sunday Times Magazine,* New York City, writer and editor, 1957-61. *Member:* Authors League of America, Society of Magazine Writers, American Newspaper Guild.

WRITINGS: The Child Worshippers, Crown, 1963; *Heartsounds,* Simon & Schuster, 1979. Contributor to *McCall's, Pageant,* and other publications.

SIDELIGHTS: In August of 1973, writer and magazine editor Martha Weinman Lear was in Europe on assignment when she received word that her physician-husband, Harold Lear, had suffered a massive heart attack in their New York apartment. Dr. Lear had not fully recovered from this first heart attack when he suffered a second attack several months later, which left him in severe pain and unable to resume a normal life. After he was given an angiograph (an X-ray of the heart), open-heart surgery requiring a double bypass was performed. Complications following the operation prevented Dr. Lear from recovering fully.

One of the many friends who visited the ailing Dr. Lear was Lewis Bergman, the editor of the *New York Times Magazine*. Bergman felt Dr. Lear's experience as a doctor and patient would make for a good article, so he commissioned the doctor to write his story of medical treatment for the magazine. Although Dr. Lear approached the project enthusiastically, he soon became too ill to continue and asked his wife Martha to undertake the major responsibility for the venture.

Martha Lear conducted daily discussion sessions with her husband and took detailed notes of his treatment, condition, and emotional state. It soon became apparent to the Lears that they had assembled more than enough material for an article and that they really should tell their story in book form. From his hospital bed, Dr. Lear predicted that this accumulation of work would be a best seller—a prediction Lear never lived to see fulfilled. After a painful five-year battle with heart disease and eleven lengthy hospitalizations, Dr. Lear died on September 13, 1978. *Heartsounds,* the book chronicling this battle, was published almost a year and a half later.

Heartsounds has been described by reviewers as one of the most moving and sensitive accounts of a couple's fight against death. A reviewer for the *New Yorker* feels that Martha Lear writes of her ordeal "with passion" and describes her book as a "sustained and clinically detailed study of a man's descent from full well-being, through an ordeal of pain, helplessness, and mental disarray, to death." And Christopher Lehmann-Haupt is impressed with what he calls in the *New York Times* "the extraordinary sense of reality that Martha Lear somehow brings to her account."

Apart from describing the deep emotional torture she and her husband experienced during the years covered in *Heartsounds,* Martha Lear recorded much of Dr. Lear's medical regimen and, in some cases, what she felt was mistreatment. Although his treatment was mentally and physically painful to bear, Lear was shocked and disturbed by what he felt was the uncaring and occasionally unprofessional treatment he received. "Much of the anguish which Hal and Martha suffered was caused not by his heart disease but by the doctors who were supposed to be treating him," explains William A. Nolen in the *Washington Post Book World.* "Both he and his wife were often misled, mistreated and ignored. . . . I wish I could say that Martha Lear has painted a distorted portrait of medical care in the United States, but I can't." Christopher Lehmann-Haupt observes in the *New York Times* that Dr. Lear was "subjected to the shortcomings of the medical profession, which, to judge from *Heartsounds,* are probably no greater or less than those of, say, lawyers or glassblowers. It's just that one expects more from doctors. Hal Lear certainly did, being one himself; and he was made to agonize by his experience over how many patients he himself had failed in the past."

Martha Lear told Judy Klemesrud of the *New York Times Book Review* that "pointing the finger of blame was never one of my motives in writing the book." Maggie Scarf, however, points out in another issue of the *New York Times Book Review* that "whether or not Ms. Lear intended to write an indictment of present-day medical care, as it is practiced on *people,* she has indeed written one. One sees not only that there are inadequacies in the health-care system, but occasional acts of callousness that leave one breathless, speechless with rage."

Although *Heartsounds* is about the slow loss of human life and a person's control over that life, most reviewers seem to agree that the main theme weaving through *Heartsounds* is love. Scarf reports that "this is an awesome and gripping book. It is about loving as much as about dying. [It is] about rage and dependence, and quarrels and jokes, and need and empathy. This is honest, tough, frightening, . . . but it is, finally, about two people who touch and unite at the very center of their shared being."

BIOGRAPHICAL/CRITICAL SOURCES: Martha Weinman Lear, *Heartsounds,* Simon & Schuster, 1979; *Washington Post Book World,* March 9, 1980; *New York Times Book Review,* March 16, 1980, June 29, 1980, May 31, 1981; *Newsweek,* March 24, 1980; *New York Times,* April 17, 1980; *New Yorker,* April 28, 1980.†

* * *

LEAVER, Robin Alan 1939-

PERSONAL: Born May 12, 1939, in Aldershot, Hampshire, England; son of Robert James and Violet Hester (Hack) Leaver; married Patricia Joyce Gooding (a nurse), June 30, 1962; children: Martin, Joanna, Kathryn. *Education:* Attended Royal Aircraft Establishment Technical College and Farnborough Technical College, 1954-60, Brasted Place College, Kent, 1960-62, and Clifton Theological (now Trinity) College, Bristol, 1962-64. *Home:* The Priory, Cogges, Witney, Oxfordshire OX8 6LA, England.

CAREER: Royal Aircraft Establishment, Farnborough, Hampshire, England, apprentice, 1954-60; ordained into the ministry of the Church of England, deacon, 1964, priest, 1965; curate of church in London, England, 1964-67; curate in charge of church in Essex, England, 1967-71; St. Mary's Church, Castle Street, Reading, England, incumbent, 1971-77; Latimer House, Oxford, England, associate librarian, 1976—; St. Mary's Church, Cogges, Oxfordshire, England, incumbent, 1977—. Honorary member, Reimenschneider Bach Institute, Berea, Ohio, 1973—; chaplain of Luckley-Oakfield School, 1973-75.

MEMBER: International Heinrich Schuetz Society, Internationale Arbeitsgemeinschaft fuer Hymnologie (member of Vorstand, 1981—), Internationale Arbeitsgemeinschaft fuer Theologische Bachforschung, Hymn Society of America, Hymn

Society of Great Britain and Ireland (member of executive committee, 1981—), Luther Gesellschaft, Neue Bach Gesellschaft, Group for Renewal of Worship. *Awards, honors:* Winston Churchill fellowship, 1971, for research on Johann Sebastian Bach.

WRITINGS: *Luther on Justification,* Concordia, 1975; *A Thematic Guide to the Anglican Hymn Book,* Church Book Room Press, 1975; *The Liturgy and Music: A Study of the Use of the Hymn in Two Liturgical Traditions,* Grove Books, 1976; *The Work of John Marbeck,* Sutton Courtenay Press, 1978; *Catherine Winkworth: The Influence of Her Translations on English Hymnody,* Concordia, 1978; *The Doctrine of Justification in the Church of England,* Latimer House, 1979.

A Hymn Book Survey, 1962-80, Grove Books, 1980; (contributor) Stanley Sadie, editor, *The New Grove Dictionary of Music and Musicians,* Macmillan, 1980; (contributor) C. O. Buchanan and others, editors, *Anglican Worship Today,* Collins & World, 1980; *Hymns with the New Lectionary,* Grove Books, 1980; *Bibliotheca Hymnologica,* S.P.C.K., 1981; *English Hymns and Hymn Books: Catalogue of an Exhibition Held in the Bodleian Library, Oxford,* Bodleian Library, 1981; (with Malcolm Harper) *Churchman Index, 1965-1980,* Latimer House, 1982; *Marbeck's Book of Common Prayer Noted, 1550,* Sutton Courtenay Press, 1982; *Bachs Theologische Bibliothek,* Haenssler (Stuttgart), 1982; *Music as Preaching: Bach, Passions and Music in Worship,* Latimer House, 1982.

Contributor to *Organ Yearbook.* Contributor of articles and reviews to periodicals, including *Bach, Churchman, Hymn Society Bulletin, Internationale Arbeitsgemeinschaft fuer Hymnologie Bulletin, Bach-Jahrbuch, Jahrbuch fuer Liturgik und Hymnologie, Concordia Theological Monthly, Hymn, Music in Worship, News of Liturgy, Expository Times, Musik und Kirche,* and *American Organist.*

WORK IN PROGRESS: Editing the English translation of Guenther Stiller's *Johann Sebastian Bach und das Leipziger gottesdienstlichen Leben seiner Zeit;* research into the early and parallel development of English and Dutch metrical psalters in the sixteenth century.

* * *

LeBARON, Charles W. 1943-

PERSONAL: Born November 4, 1943, in New York, N.Y.; son of James Wade (in advertising) and Doris (Davison) LeBaron. *Education:* Princeton University, A.B., 1965; Harvard University, M.A.T., 1966, student, 1978—. *Home:* 107 Ave. Louis Pasteur, Boston, Mass. 02115. *Agent:* Roslyn Targ, 250 West 57th St., New York, N.Y. 10107.

CAREER: San Francisco General Hospital, San Francisco, Calif., social worker (alternate service as conscientious objector), 1969-73; Manhattan Developmental Services, New York, N.Y., social worker, 1974-78.

WRITINGS: *The Diamond Sky* (novel), Dial, 1975; *Gentle Vengeance: An Account of the First Year at Harvard Medical School* (nonfiction), Richard Marek, 1981.

SIDELIGHTS: Charles LeBaron's book *Gentle Vengeance* is based on the journals he kept during his first year as a student at Harvard Medical School. His purpose in writing it, he tells Christopher Lehmann-Haupt in the *New York Times,* was to exact what he calls a "revenge of gentleness" from the callous indifference to suffering he found in the medical field, to fight his own kind of war against disease and poverty. Subtitled *An Account of the First Year at Harvard Medical School,* the book seeks to reveal the rigors of Harvard's grueling curriculum and what LeBaron regards as its "disdain for the practical business of dispensing medicine to sick people," according to Lehmann-Haupt.

Elizabeth Morgan writes in the *Washington Post Book World* that LeBaron "conveys convincingly the feeling of a medical student intimidated by being part of a great medical school, yet disappointed in his colleagues and faculty." LeBaron's writing, however, eventually falters, says Morgan. "He tries to explain in cozy terms and at length thermo-dynamic flux, and later fungal cultures, in a doomed attempt to make physiology and microbiology light reading. They aren't."

Lehmann-Haupt, on the other hand, cites what he terms LeBaron's "raw writing talent" in his praise of *Gentle Vengeance,* describing it as a gift for "getting characters and incidents down on paper, and for recapturing the sense of wonder that the school's curriculum very nearly killed: wonder at the power of evolution to defy entropy, for instance. Or wonder at the [complexity of] the human brain."

BIOGRAPHICAL/CRITICAL SOURCES: *New York Times Book Review,* April 11, 1976; *New York Times,* March 5, 1981; *Washington Post Book World,* March 8, 1981.

* * *

LEE, Barbara (Moore) 1934-
(Barbara Moore)

PERSONAL: Born April 29, 1934, in Tulsa, Okla.; daughter of Prentiss Thomas (an oil journalist) and Edna (Swaggerty) Moore; married John Lee (a writer and professor of journalism), April 14, 1957. *Education:* University of Arizona, B.A. (magna cum laude), 1971, M.A., 1972. *Politics:* Democrat. *Religion:* None. *Home address:* Route 2, Hunter's Glen, Box 109, San Marcos, Tex. 78666. *Agent:* Don Congdon, Harold Matson Co., Inc., 276 Fifth Ave., New York, N.Y. 10001.

CAREER: Reporter on newspapers in Fort Worth, Tex., 1955-57, Denver, Colo., 1958-60, and San Antonio, Tex., 1963-65. *Member:* Phi Beta Kappa, Phi Kappa Phi.

WRITINGS—Under name Barbara Moore: *Hard on the Road,* Doubleday, 1974; (with husband, John Lee) *Monsters Among Us* (nonfiction), Pyramid Publications, 1975; *The Fever Called Living* (novel about Edgar Allan Poe), Doubleday, 1976; *Something on the Wind,* Doubleday, 1978; *The Doberman Wore Black,* St. Martin's, 1983.

* * *

LEE, John (Darrell) 1931-

PERSONAL: Born March 12, 1931, in Indiahoma, Okla.; son of John Henry (a barber) and Lealiu (Prince) Lee; married Barbara Moore (a writer), April 14, 1957. *Education:* Texas Technological College (now Texas Tech University), B.A., 1952; West Virginia University, M.S.J., 1965. *Politics:* Democrat. *Home address:* Route 2, Hunter's Glen, Box 109, San Marcos, Tex. 78666. *Agent:* Don Congdon, Harold Matson Co., Inc., 276 Fifth Ave., New York, N.Y. 10001.

CAREER: *Fort Worth Star-Telegram,* Fort Worth, Tex., reporter-photographer, 1952-57; *Denver Post,* Denver, Colo., reporter-photographer, 1958-60; Goodyear Tire & Rubber Co., Akron, Ohio, member of public relations staff, 1960-62; American University, Washington, D.C., assistant professor of journalism, 1965-67; University of Arizona, Tucson, associate professor, 1967-69, professor of journalism, 1969-71; New York University, New York, N.Y., professor of journalism, 1972-76; full-time writer. Washington (D.C.) Journalism Center, assistant director, 1966-67, consultant, 1967—. *Member:* Association for Education in Journalism, Sigma Delta Chi, Kappa Tau Alpha. *Awards, honors:* More than twenty local, state, and national photography awards.

WRITINGS: Expatriate Press, West Virginia University Press, 1965; *Caught in the Act* (novel), Morrow, 1968; (editor) *Diplomatic Persuaders: New Role of the Mass Media in Internal Relations,* Wiley, 1968; *Assignation in Algeria* (novel), Walker & Co., 1971; (with wife, Barbara Moore) *Monsters Among Us* (nonfiction), Pyramid Publications, 1975; *The Ninth Man* (novel), Doubleday, 1976; *The Thirteenth Hour* (novel), Doubleday, 1978; *Lago* (novel), Doubleday, 1980.

Photographs have appeared in more than one hundred magazines and one thousand newspapers throughout the world; also contributor of articles to magazines.

WORK IN PROGRESS: Olympia '36, a novel.

* * *

LEE, Maria Berl 1924-
(Maria Berl-Lee)

PERSONAL: Born July 30, 1924, in Vienna, Austria; came to United States, 1941; naturalized, 1948; daughter of Arthur C. (a judge and lawyer) and Gunda (a teacher; maiden name, Weisel) Berl; married Ray E. Lee, Jr. (a financial analyst and writer), October 13, 1951. *Education:* Nazareth College, B.A. (magna cum laude), 1946; Fordham University, M.A., 1949. *Home:* 68-46 Ingram St., Forest Hills, N.Y. 11375. *Agent:* Ruth Cantor, 156 Fifth Ave., Suite 1005, New York, N.Y. 10010. *Office:* International Institute of Rural Reconstruction, 1775 Broadway, New York, N.Y. 10019.

CAREER: Eastman Kodak, Rochester, N.Y., bilingual secretary, 1946-48; U.S. Embassy, Vienna, Austria, translator and interpreter for Uniformed Services Contingency Option Act, 1949-51; Georgetown University, Washington, D.C., assistant placement director, 1951-53; John F. Fleming (rare-book seller), New York City, assistant, 1953-59; Jacobus F. Frank & Co. (importer), New York City, assistant head of Indonesian imports, 1965-69; International Institute of Rural Reconstruction, New York City, assistant to director of public affairs and to U.S. resident director, 1969-77, assistant to chairman and to vice-president, 1977—. Bilingual free-lance writer, 1942—. Lecturer for Austrian Forum, 1972-75, and Social Science Society for Intercultural Relations, 1975, and at colleges and universities, including Nazareth College, 1974, Austrian Institute, 1975, and Queens College of the City University of New York, 1975-76; representative at First Austrian Writers' Congress, 1981. *Member:* P.E.N. (Austria), National Writers Club, Austrian Forum (director, 1981), Society of German-American Studies, Verband deutsch-amerikanische Autoren in Amerika, Kappa Gamma Pi, Nazareth College of Rochester Alumni Association.

AWARDS, HONORS: Many short story and poetry prizes from organizations and publications, including National Writers Club, 1967, 1969, 1971, *Writer's Digest,* 1970, *Tempo,* 1970, *North American Mentor,* 1974, and *Poetry Parade;* Society of German-American Studies citation of merit, 1973; Society of German-American Authors first prize, 1975, for novella "Postskript fuer Lydia"; Outstanding Alumni Award, Nazareth College, 1979; *North American Mentor* certificate of merit, 1980 and 1981.

WRITINGS: Don't Rock the Waterbed (play; produced in the United States, 1975), Performance Publishing, 1975; *The Case in Question* (play; produced in the United States, 1977), Performance Publishing, 1977. Also author of three novels as yet unpublished, "Late Days in March," "A Force in Motion," and "The Town That Would Allow No Crime." Short story included in anthology *Beginnings,* Sheed, 1956. Collaborator for U.S. Department of the Interior's "Immigrants on Tape" program, 1973. Book reviewer for *Rochester Catholic Courier,* 1944-45, and for *Long Island Poetry Collective,* 1977-80; author of literary criticism column "Literary Accolade," in *Spafaswap* magazine, 1974—, and of column in *Echos,* 1980-81. Contributor of articles, short stories, and poetry to popular and literary magazines, including *North American Mentor, Expecting, Bitterroot, Second Coming, Poet Lore, Erehwon, Poesie-USA, Car Exchange, Kappa Gamma Pi, Austrian Information,* and *Skylark* (India).

Under name Maria Berl-Lee: *Ein Tag der Ueberaschungen* (play; produced in Bavaria, 1967), W. Koehler Verlag (Munich), 1966; *Bombe im Tor* (play; produced in Bavaria, 1970), W. Koehler Verlag, 1970; (contributor) Mimi Grossberg, editor, *Oesterreichisches aus Amerika,* Bergland Verlag (Vienna), 1973; *Schaumwein aus meinem Kurg* (collection of short stories, poetry, and drama), Bergland Verlag, 1974; (contributor) Grossberg, editor, *Amerika im Austro-Amerikanischen Gedicht 1938-1978,* Bergland Verlag, 1978; (contributor) Lisa Kahn, editor, *Reisegepaeck: Sprache,* Fink Verlag (Munich), 1979; (contributor) Gerhard Friesen, editor, *Nachrichten aus den Staaten,* Wilfrid Laurier University, 1982; *Lieder einer Doppelzunge* (poetry and essay), Blaeschke Verlag (Austria), 1982. Also author of unpublished novella "Postskript fuer Lydia." Contributor of short stories and poetry to German language periodicals in Germany, Austria, and the United States, including *Lyrik und Prosa, Literatur und Kritik, Aufbau, New Yorker Staats-Zeitung, Deutsche Welt-USA,* and *Lyrica Germanica.*

WORK IN PROGRESS: Translating *Adventures and Travels of the Baron of Muenchhausen,* for Westburg Associates; a trilogy on ancient Persia, Greece, and Egypt, of which the first two volumes are completed.

SIDELIGHTS: Maria Lee began creating stories in cartoon style before she could write. She told *CA:* "My studies in three languages—first in German, then in French, finally in English, with Spanish, Latin and smatterings of other languages thrown in—have given me an abiding love of words and how they are used, and a deep interest in experimenting with different languages and the connections between them.

"Most people, in my experience, are passionately interested in where the writer hooks his ideas and how a literary work is actually created. In many of my lectures, particularly before college students, I have tried to explain the interrelationship of fiction and fact—that fiction is based upon and entwined with fact, but that to be spellbinding and gripping it needs another dimension which confers meaning, the power to move deeply, and relevance to the reader."

AVOCATIONAL INTERESTS: Travel, music, theatre, hiking, swimming.

LEE, Mary Price 1934-

PERSONAL: Born July 10, 1934, in Philadelphia, Pa.; daughter of Llewellyn and Elise (Mirkil) Price; married Richard Lee (a copywriter), May 12, 1956; children: Richard, Barbara, Monica. *Education:* University of Pennsylvania, B.A., 1956, M.S. in Ed., 1967. *Residence:* Flourtown, Pa.

CAREER: Author of young people's books. Teacher for short period; employed in public relations department at Westminster Press, Philadelphia, Pa., 1973-74. Has tutored foreign students in English. *Member:* Children's Reading Roundtable, Phi Beta Kappa, Philadelphia Athenaeum.

WRITINGS—Juveniles; published by Westminster, except as indicated: *Money and Kids: How to Earn It, Save It, and Spend It,* 1973; *Ms. Veterinarian,* 1976; *The Team That Runs Your Hospital,* 1980; *Your Name: All about It,* 1980; *A Future in Pediatrics: Medical and Non-medical Careers in Child Health Care,* Messner, 1982; *Your Future in Research and Development in Industry,* Richards Rosen, 1983.

Columnist, *Chestnut Hill Local,* 1970-72. Contributor to *Philadelphia Magazine* and *Philadelphia Inquirer.* Contributing editor, *Today's Girl,* 1972-73.

WORK IN PROGRESS: A student traveler's guide to Boston, for Richards Rosen.

SIDELIGHTS: Mary Price Lee once wrote *CA:* "My children provide great incentive to write for their teenage group and serve both as guinea pigs and critics. I am a travel enthusiast and particularly a Francophile."

* * *

LEES, Francis A(nthony) 1931-

PERSONAL: Born January 19, 1931, in Brooklyn, N.Y.; son of Roy A. (a banker) and Mary A. (Oszuscowitz) Lees; married Kathryn Veronica Murphy, June 6, 1959; children: Veronica, Francis, Daniel, Jeanette Marie. *Education:* Brooklyn College (now Brooklyn College of the City University of New York), B.A., 1952; St. Louis University, M.A., 1953; New York University, Ph.D., 1961. *Religion:* Roman Catholic. *Home:* 192 Coolidge Dr., East Meadow, N.Y. 11554.

CAREER: Fordham University, New York, N.Y., instructor in economics and finance, 1956-60; St. John's University, Jamaica, N.Y., assistant professor, 1960-61, associate professor, 1962-65, professor of economics and finance, 1965—. *Military service:* U.S. Army, 1953-56. *Member:* American Association of University Professors, American Finance Association, Academy of International Business, Eastern Finance Association.

WRITINGS: (With Nicholas K. Bruck) *Foreign Investment, Capital Controls, and the Balance of Payments* (monograph), Institute of Finance, New York University, 1968; *International Banking and Finance,* Macmillan, 1974; (with Maximo Eng) *International Financial Markets,* Praeger, 1975; *Foreign Banking and Investments in the United States,* Macmillan, 1976; (with Hugh Brooks) *Economic and Political Development of the Sudan,* Macmillan, 1977; (with Eng and A. Angelini) *International Lending, Risk, and the Euromarkets,* Macmillan, 1979; *Reporting Transnational Business Operations,* Conference Board, 1980; *Public Disclosure of Corporate Earnings Forecasts,* Conference Board, 1981; *Corporate Debt: Changing Perceptions of Financial Risk,* Conference Board, 1982. Contributor to economics, business, and banking journals.

WORK IN PROGRESS: Study of international banking; analysis of country risk and political risk; analysis of corporate stock repurchasing.

SIDELIGHTS: In addition to the professional interests indicated by his books, Francis A. Lees is concerned with the place of the United States in world politics. He has traveled in the Sudan, Egypt, and Europe.

* * *

LEES, Gene 1928-

PERSONAL: Born February 8, 1928, in Hamilton, Ontario, Canada; son of Harold (a musician, later a construction engineer) and Dorothy (Flatman) Lees; married Carmen Lister, 1951; married Micheline A. Ducreux, July, 1955; married Janet Suttle, 1971; children: (second marriage) Philippe. *Education:* Attended Ontario College of Art, Toronto, for one year. *Home and office address:* P.O. Box 240, Ojai, Calif. 93023.

CAREER: Reporter for Canadian newspapers, 1948-55, first for *Hamilton Spectator,* later for *Toronto Telegram* and *Montreal Star; Louisville Times,* Louisville, Ky., classical music critic, and film and drama editor, 1955-58; studied the performing arts in Europe under Reid fellowship, 1958-59; *Down Beat* (jazz magazine), Chicago, Ill., editor, 1959-61; *Hi Fi/Stereo Review,* New York City, contributing editor, 1962-65; columnist for *High Fidelity,* 1965-79; *Jazzletter,* Ojai, Calif., founder and principal writer, 1981—. Lyricist, composer, and collaborator with other composers on songs; toured Latin America under the auspices of U.S. Department of State as manager of jazz sextet, 1962; thirty songs with his lyrics, among them "Waltz for Debby," "Song of the Jet," "Paris Is at Her Best in May," and "Someone to Light Up My Life," were released in a Richmond Organization portfolio, 1968. Radio and television writer and singer for the Canadian Broadcasting Corp. and various independent Canadian radio stations. *Member:* Composers, Authors, and Publishers Association of Canada. *Awards, honors:* ASCAP-Deems Taylor Award, American Society of Composers, Authors, and Publishers, 1978, for articles in *High Fidelity.*

WRITINGS: And Sleep until Noon (novel), Simon & Schuster, 1966; *The Modern Rhyming Dictionary: How to Write Lyrics,* Cherry Lane, 1981. Contributor of articles and short stories to the *New York Times, Los Angeles Times, Saturday Review, American Film,* and other periodicals in the United States, Canada, and Europe.

WORK IN PROGRESS: Collected essays from the *Jazzletter.*

SIDELIGHTS: A distinguished lyricist known for his words to "Quiet Nights" and other bossa nova songs, Gene Lees helped introduce the bossa nova in America and has translated the Portuguese lyrics of many Brazilian songs into English. His songs have been recorded by Frank Sinatra, Tony Bennett, and others, and he has collaborated with such composers as Charles Aznavour of France, Antonio Carlos Jobim of Brazil, and Lalo Schifrin of Argentina. In 1976, Lees collaborated with Roger Kellaway on the musical score for the film "The Mouse and His Child."

Lees told *CA* that he used to consider himself primarily a lyricist and composer but now that perception has changed. "Increasingly," he writes, "I see jazz not only as a unique American contribution to the arts, but as profoundly significant, and since

I have been deeply involved in it, both as observer and participant, a responsibility as chronicler seems to have devolved on me. I'm taking it very seriously. Some of the great masters, such as Arte Shaw and Benny Carter, are still with us, and I carry a lot of the music's unwritten history in my head. I think it matters to get as much of it as possible on paper for the sake of future generations; hence, the *Jazzletter*. Together with writing my own songs, that's what I intend to do in the next few years. I have finally come to accept nonfiction as art. Increasingly I see that what the sea was to Conrad, the world of jazz is to me."

BIOGRAPHICAL/CRITICAL SOURCES: BMI (publication of Broadcast Music, Inc.), November, 1967; *Los Angeles Times Book Review,* January 17, 1982.

* * *

LeFEVRE, Robert (Thomas) 1911-

PERSONAL: Surname is pronounced "luh-*fave*"; born October 13, 1911, in Gooding, Idaho; son of Daniel Griffin (a teacher and salesman) and Ethel Adeline (Thomas) LeFevre; married Peggy Tapp, 1930 (divorced, 1943); married Lois K. Reuling, April 9, 1944; children: (first marriage) Robert, Jr., David T.; (second marriage) Thomas R. *Education:* Attended Hamline University, 1931-32. *Politics:* Independent. *Address:* c/o Pine Tree Press, Box 2353, Orange, Calif. 92669.

CAREER: Writer and producer of radio scripts, and free-lance magazine writer; *Gazette Telegraph,* Colorado Springs, Colo., editorial editor, 1954-65, editor-in-chief, 1960-65; Rampart College, Santa Ana, Calif., founder, 1957, president, 1957-74, president emeritus, 1974—; independent lecturer, 1974—. *Military service:* U.S. Army Air Forces, 1942-45; served in Europe; became captain. *Awards, honors:* LL.D., Burton College, 1959.

WRITINGS: The Nature of Man and His Government, Caxton, 1959; *This Bread Is Mine,* ALP Publications, 1960; *Constitutional Government Today in Soviet Russia,* Exposition, 1962; (with Edmund A. Opitz) *Must We Depend upon Political Protection?,* Freedom School, 1962; *The Philosophy of Ownership,* Rampart College, 1966; *The Libertarian,* Bramble Minibooks, 1973; *Limited Government: Hope or Illusion?,* Society for Libertarian Life, 1975; *Does Government Protection Protect Society?,* Society for Libertarian Life, 1976; *Fundamentals of Liberty,* Pine Tree Press, 1976; *The Power of Congress (as Congress Sees It): The Congressional Correspondence of Robert LeFevre,* edited by R. S. Radford, Pine Tree Press, 1976; *Lift Her up, Tenderly,* Pine Tree Press, 1977; *Raising Children for Fun and Profit,* Pine Tree Press, 1979. Weekly columnist for Freedom Newspapers, 1976—. Publisher of *Rampart College Newsletter,* 1964-72, *Rampart Journal,* 1965-68, and *LeFevre's Journal,* 1973-78.

SIDELIGHTS: "I am invariably asked about my attitude toward government," writes Robert LeFevre. "With minor exceptions, everything I have written relates to it. To me, human society passes through three ages: infantile, adolescent, and adult. A government is probably necessary in the first of these periods. Early humans are like children; the clever and strong take control of them. In the adolescent period we are called barbarians. The government in its own character gives ample demonstration. But as we mature and stand on the threshold of adulthood, the problem reverses. In an effort to become truly civilized, we must shed the trappings of barbarism and at last become reasonable. The real question of our time is this: Can we survive government long enough to learn to live without it?"

BIOGRAPHICAL/CRITICAL SOURCES: California Sun, July, 1971; *The Lady and the Tycoon,* Caxton, 1973; *Franklin Auditor,* August, 1974; *Libertarian Review,* April, 1981.

* * *

Le GUIN, Ursula K(roeber) 1929-

PERSONAL: Born October 21, 1929, in Berkeley, Calif.; daughter of Alfred Louis (an anthropologist) and Theodora (a writer; maiden name, Kracaw) Kroeber; married Charles Alfred Le Guin (a historian), December 22, 1953; children: Elisabeth, Caroline, Theodore. *Education:* Radcliffe College, B.A., 1951; Columbia University, M.A., 1952. *Residence:* Portland, Ore. *Agent:* Virginia Kidd, 538 East Hartford St., Milford, Pa. 18337.

CAREER: Writer. Part-time instructor in French at Mercer University, 1954-55, and University of Idaho, 1956; has run writing workshops at University of Washington, Portland State University, University of California, San Diego, University of Reading, England, and for the Arts Council of Australia. Creative consultant to Public Broadcasting Service in 1979 on the production of "The Lathe of Heaven," adapted for television from her novel of the same title. *Member:* Authors League, Writers Guild, P.E.N., Science Fiction Research Association, Science Fiction Poetry Association, National Organization for Women, National Abortion Rights Action League, Women's International League for Peace and Freedom, Phi Beta Kappa.

AWARDS, HONORS: Fulbright fellowship, 1953; *Boston Globe-Horn Book* Award, 1969, for *A Wizard of Earthsea;* Nebula Award for best novel, 1969, and Hugo Award for best novel, 1970, both for *The Left Hand of Darkness;* Newbery Silver Medal Award, 1972, for *The Tombs of Atuan;* National Book Award, 1973, for *The Farthest Shore;* Hugo Award for best novella, 1973, for *The Word for World Is Forest;* Hugo Award nomination, Nebula Award nomination, and *Locus* Award, all 1973, for *The Lathe of Heaven;* Hugo Award for best short story, 1974, for "The Ones Who Walk Away from Omelas"; Nebula Award for best novel, Hugo Award for best novel, Jupiter Award for best novel, and Jules Verne Award, all 1975, all for *The Dispossessed: An Ambiguous Utopia;* Nebula Award for best short story and Jupiter Award for best short story, both 1975, for "The Day before the Revolution"; Nebula Award nomination and Jupiter Award, both 1976, for short story "The Diary of the Rose"; Gandalf Award nomination, 1978; Gandalf Award as "Grand Master of Fantasy," 1979; Balrog Award nomination for best poet, 1979.

WRITINGS—Novels, except as indicated: *Rocannon's World* (also see below; bound with *The Kar-Chee Reign* by Avram Davidson), Ace Books, 1966; *Planet of Exile* (also see below; bound with *Mankind under the Lease* by Thomas M. Disch), Ace Books, 1966; *City of Illusions* (also see below), Ace Books, 1967; *A Wizard of Earthsea* (first volume of Earthsea trilogy; also see below), Parnassus, 1968; *The Left Hand of Darkness,* Ace Books, 1969; *The Tombs of Atuan* (second volume of Earthsea trilogy; also see below), Atheneum, 1971; *The Lathe of Heaven,* Scribner, 1971; *The Farthest Shore* (third volume of Earthsea trilogy; Junior Literary Guild selection; also see below), Atheneum, 1972; *From Elfland to Poughkeepsie* (lecture), Pendragon Press, 1973; *Wild Angels* (poems), Capra, 1974; *The Dispossessed: An Ambiguous Utopia,* Harper, 1974.

The Wind's Twelve Quarters (short stories), Harper, 1975; *Dreams Must Explain Themselves* (critical essays), Algol Press, 1975; *The Word for World Is Forest* (novella; originally published in collection *Again, Dangerous Visions;* also see below), Berkley Publishing, 1976; *Very Far Away from Anywhere Else,* Atheneum, 1976; *Orsinian Tales* (short stories), Harper, 1976; (editor) *Nebula Award Stories XI* (anthology), Harper, 1977; *The Earthsea Trilogy* (includes *The Wizard of Earthsea, The Tombs of Atuan,* and *The Farthest Shore*), Gollancz, 1977; *The Language of the Night* (critical essays), Putnam, 1978; *Three Hainish Novels* (contains *Rocannon's World, Planet of Exile,* and *City of Illusions*), Doubleday, 1978; *Malafrena,* Putnam, 1979; *Leese Webster* (juvenile), Atheneum, 1979; *The Beginning Place,* Harper, 1980 (published in England as *Threshold,* Gollancz, 1980); (editor with Virginia Kidd) *Interfaces* (short stories), Grosset, 1980; (editor with Kidd) *Edges* (short stories), Pocket Books, 1980; *Hard Words* (poems), Harper, 1981; *The Compass Rose* (short stories), Harper, 1982; *The Eye of the Heron* (novella; originally published in collection *Millennial Women;* also see below), Harper, 1983.

Contributor: Damon Knight, editor, *Orbit 5,* Putnam, 1969; Harry Harrison and Brian Aldiss, editors, *Best SF: 1969,* Putnam, 1970; Terry Carr and Donald A. Wollheim, editors, *World's Best Science Fiction,* Ace Books, 1970; Robin Scott Wilson, editor, *Those Who Can,* Mentor, 1970; Knight, editor, *Orbit 6,* Putnam, 1970; James Blish, editor, *Nebula Award Stories 5,* Doubleday, 1970; Samuel R. Delaney and Marilyn Hacker, editors, *Quark #1,* Paperback Library, 1970; editors of *Playboy* magazine, editors, *The Dead Astronaut,* Playboy Press, 1971; Robert Silverberg, editor, *New Dimensions I,* Doubleday, 1972; Wilson, editor, *Clarion II,* Signet, 1972; Harlan Ellison, editor, *Again, Dangerous Visions,* Volume I, Doubleday, 1972.

Silverberg, editor, *New Dimensions III,* Doubleday, 1973; editors of *Playboy* magazine, editors, *The Best from Playboy,* number 7, Playboy Press, 1973; Wilson, editor, *Clarion III,* Signet, 1973; Knight, editor, *Orbit 14,* Harper, 1974; Carr, editor, *Universe 5,* Random House, 1974; editors of *Galaxy* magazine, editors, *The Best from Galaxy,* Volume II, Award, 1974; Michel Parry, editor, *Dream Trips,* Panther, 1974; Silverberg and Roger Elwood, editors, *Epoch,* Berkley Publishing, 1975; Silverberg, editor. *The New Atlantis and Other Novellas of Science Fiction,* Hawthorn, 1975; Edward Blishen, editor, *The Thorny Paradise,* Kestrel Books, 1975; Pat Rotter, editor, *Bitches and Sad Ladies,* Harper's Magazine Press, 1975; James Baen, editor, *The Best from Galaxy,* Volume III, Award, 1975; James Gunn, editor, *Nebula Award Stories X,* Harper, 1975.

Pamela Sargent, editor, *More Women of Wonder,* Vintage, 1976; Carr, editor, *The Best Science Fiction of the Year #5,* Ballantine, 1976; Peter Nicholls, editor, *Science Fiction at Large,* Gollancz, 1976, Harper, 1977; Jack Dann and Gardner Dozois, editors, *Future Power,* Random House, 1976; Lee Harding, editor, *The Altered I: An Encounter with Science Fiction,* Norstrilia Press (Carlton, Australia), 1976, Berkley Windhover, 1978; Kaye Webb and Treld Bicknell, editors, *Puffin's Pleasure,* Puffin, 1976; Dozois, editor, *Best Science Fiction Stories of the Year,* Sixth Annual Collection, Dutton, 1977; Kenneth Melvin, Stanley Brodsky, and Raymond Fowler, Jr., editors, *Psy Fi One,* Random House, 1977; R. V. Cassill, editor, *The Norton Anthology of Short Fiction,* Norton, 1978; Kidd, editor, *Millennial Women,* Delacorte, 1978; Alice Laurance, editor, *Cassandra Rising,* Doubleday, 1978; Robert Boyer and Kenneth Zahorski, editors, *Dark Imaginings,* Delta, 1978.

Author of postcard short story, Post Card Partnership, 1975, and of short story, *The Water Is Wide,* Pendragon Press, 1976; author of recordings for Alternate World Recordings, 1976, and Caedmon Records, 1977. Contributor to *Sword & Sorcery Annual,* 1975. Contributor of short stories, novellas, essays, and reviews to numerous science fiction, scholarly, and popular periodicals, including *Fantastic, Science-Fiction Studies, Western Humanities Review, New Republic, Redbook, Playgirl, Playboy, New Yorker, Foundation,* and *Omni.*

WORK IN PROGRESS: The Valley, a large and long-term novel.

SIDELIGHTS: Critics often find it difficult to characterize Ursula Le Guin's writing; while some classify it as science fiction/fantasy, others discount such categorization by emphasizing that her work exceeds such narrow limits, and many critics avoid using any labels at all. George Edgar Slusser, writing in his book *The Farthest Shores of Ursula Le Guin,* claims that "there is little doubt that Le Guin is one of the best writers currently working in the science fiction and fantasy genres." Yet Slusser maintains that "what is happening, and will probably continue to happen in Le Guin's fiction, is an interesting merger of genres—the literature of speculation, science fiction and fantasy, with that of personal relationships and manners, the so-called 'mainstream' novel."

In his essay on Le Guin in the *Dictionary of Literary Biography,* Brian Attebery writes that the author "has brought to science fiction a new sensitivity to language, a powerful set of symbols and images, and a number of striking and sympathetic characters. She has purposely avoided most technical details in order to concentrate on human problems and relationships. Writers of fantasy . . . tend to view literature as a way not merely of seeing reality but of coming to terms with it. By altering elements and changing rules, a fantasist tries to explore the patterns that lie beneath the surface of observable fact. Consequently Le Guin's fiction is extraordinarily risky: it is full of hypotheses about morality, love, society, and ways of enriching life expressed in the symbolic language found in myth, dream, or poetry. However, the greater the risk, the greater the reward, and for the reader, . . . the reward is a glimpse of something glowing, something very much like truth."

Similarly, Joseph D. Olander and Martin Harry Greenberg say in their introduction to *Ursula K. Le Guin* that, while "Le Guin's fiction may be filled with wizards, aliens, and clones, . . . the vision contained in her stories and novels is, above all, concerned with what is most permanent about the human condition. When one enters the world of her fiction, one encounters a distinctive universe of discourse."

Le Guin herself points out in a *Publishers Weekly* interview that "'science fiction' is a label, very much like 'Yankee' or 'Middle Westerner'—useful in pointing to a region and hinting at certain probable qualities; useless when used as a definition; and tiresome when used as a put-down." In an essay entitled "The View In," Le Guin comments: "I write science fiction because that is what publishers call my books. Left to myself, I should call them novels."

Le Guin's novels present realities based on a wide variety of settings and characters, located on many different planets and in many different time spans. Some, like the books of the Earthsea trilogy, take place wholly outside of space and time as we know it, much as do J.R.R. Tolkien's *Lord of the Rings* and C. S. Lewis's "Narnia" series. Her other novels adhere to their own spatial and temporal structures set within the framework of human history. The works which form Le Guin's "Hainish cycle," for example (including *Rocannon's World, Planet of Exile, City of Illusions, The Left Hand of Darkness, The Dispossessed: An Ambiguous Utopia,* and many of her short stories), are bound by a common historical context—their characters and cultures originated with a race called the Hain—which embraces Earth and its history as well.

Le Guin has invented a great diversity of beings to inhabit the alien worlds of her fiction and has endowed them with physical and mental characteristics in just as great a diversity. The Athsheans of *A Word for World Is Forest,* for instance, are an intelligent, ape-like species covered with green fur and capable of perceiving reality through daydreams. The inhabitants of the planet Gethen in *The Left Hand of Darkness,* while very human in appearance, are an androgynous race, capable of either fathering or mothering a child. Several different species live on the planet called *Rocannon's World,* including a large winged creature much like an angelic robot; the Liuar, a feudal society of very tall, lordly people with yellow hair and dark skin; the Clayfolk, short, pale, intelligent troglodytes; and the Fiia, simple-minded, elvish humanoids.

In her introduction to the 1977 edition of *Rocannon's World,* Le Guin comments on the complexities of literary invention: "When I set out to write my first science fiction novel, . . . I had written several novels, but I had never before invented a planet. It is a mysterious business, creating worlds out of words. I hope I can say without irreverence that anyone who has done it knows why Jehovah took Sunday off. . . . Even in science fiction, all that wonderful freedom to invent worlds and creatures and sexes and devices has . . . become strangely limited. You have to be sure all the things you invented, even if you haven't mentioned them or even thought of them yet, hang together; or they will all hang separately. As freedom increases, so, alas, does responsibility."

Le Guin has occasionally been accused of shirking her responsibility as a female writer by ignoring the issue of feminism in her writing. As Derek de Solla Price points out in the *New Republic,* she has also been "attacked by radical feminists for not going far enough, for using male protagonists, as she does even in *The Left Hand of Darkness,* and for putting other issues, both political and environmental, ahead of feminism." Yet, according to Price, the major effect of *The Left Hand of Darkness,* with its androgynous characters, "is to force us to examine how sexual stereotyping dominates actual human concepts of personality and influences all human relationships. . . . I know of no single book likely to raise consciences about sexism more thoroughly and convincingly than this one."

Le Guin discusses her own discovery of feminist values and her reaction to feminism in an essay entitled "Is Gender Necessary?": "In the mid-1960s the women's movement was just beginning to move again. . . . There was a groundswell gathering. I felt it, but I didn't know it was a groundswell; I just thought it was something wrong with me. I considered myself a feminist; I didn't see how you could be a thinking woman and not be a feminist; but I had never taken a step beyond the ground gained for us by Emmeline Pankhurst and Virginia Woolf.

"Along about 1967, I began to feel a certain unease. . . . I began to want to define and understand the meaning of sexuality and the meaning of gender, in my life and in our society. Much had gathered in the unconscious—both personal and collective—which must either be brought up into consciousness, or else turn destructive. It was that same need . . . that had led Beauvoir to write *The Second Sex,* and Friedan to write *The Feminist Mystique,* and that was, at the same time, leading Kate Millett and others to write their books, and to create the new feminism. But I was not a theoretician, a political thinker or activist, or a sociologist. I was and am a fiction writer. The way I did my thinking was to write a novel. That novel, *The Left Hand of Darkness,* is the record of my consciousness, the process of my thinking."

Most of the protagonists in Le Guin's earlier fictions are men; women appear, for the most part, in supporting roles, such as the figure of Rolery in *Planet of Exile* or that of Irene in *The Beginning Place.* When asked why she does not consistently adopt the female viewpoint in her work, Le Guin explains, as quoted in the *Milwaukee Journal:* "I don't want to write autobiographies. I want to distance myself from my books. That's one of the reasons I write science fiction. I write about aliens. Men are aliens, too. I like the alien point of view." Moreover, as Le Guin writes in the introduction to the 1978 edition of *Planet of Exile:* "it's ever so much easier to write about men doing things, because most books about people doing things are about men, and that is one's literary tradition . . . and because, as a woman, one probably has not done awfully much in the way of fighting, raping, governing, etc., but has observed that men do these things . . . and because, as Virginia Woolf pointed out, English prose is unsuited to the description of feminine being and doing, unless one to some extent remakes it from scratch. It is hard to break from tradition; hard to invent; hard to remake one's mother tongue. One drifts along and takes the easy way. Nothing can rouse one to go against the stream . . . but . . . an angry conscience."

Le Guin goes on to emphasize the importance she places on other issues besides that of feminism: "I am often very angry, as a woman," she says. "But my feminist anger is only an element in, a part of, the rage and fear that possess me when I face what we are all doing to each other, to the earth, and to the hope of liberty and life. I still 'don't care' whether people are male or female, when they are all of us and all our children. One soul unjustly imprisoned, am I to ask which sex it is? A child starving, am I to ask which sex it is?"

This humanistic outlook pervades all of Le Guin's work. In the *New Republic,* Price discusses the subject within the larger context of the science fiction genre, claiming that "a significant amount of science fiction has been profoundly thoughtful about the situation of contemporary humanity in the light of its possible futures and its imaginable alternatives. In recent years, no [writer] inside the field of science fiction or outside of it [has] done more to create a modern conscience than . . . Ursula K. Le Guin." Le Guin, however, "is not competing with Orwell or Hemingway," according to Slusser. "Her social analysis is acute, but its purpose is not indignation or reform. She has no social program, offers no panaceas. Nor does she, at the other extreme, give us characters who turn their backs on seemingly hopeless social chaos, and go off to the wilderness to carve some private relationship out of confrontation with the elements."

Writing in *Ursula K. Le Guin,* John H. Crow and Richard D. Erlich suggest that Le Guin's particular form of humanism springs from her unique artistic vision. "Le Guin's work demands to be taken seriously," they claim. "Even in her early work, it is impossible not to respect the keen intelligence and mature vision. Her vision is essentially one of integration.

Whether she develops a political theory, a philosophical perspective, or offers insights into human psychology, she depicts the possibility of unification if not its necessity. Regardless of how many worlds she creates, she remains a firm proponent of the oneness of the world, and it is this vision that unifies her work."

This vision of integration, say many critics and scholars, can be traced to the influence of Taoism, an ancient Chinese philosophy, on Le Guin and her work. According to the Taoist philosophy, there is one, universal way, or *tao,* from which all things originate and toward which all things return. In their book *Tao: The Eastern Philosophy of Time and Change,* Philip Rawson and Laszlo Legeza describe Tao as an absolute, cosmic force, governing time, space, change, and all of human life and perception—a force which has at its core the concept of harmonious balance between the elements of the universe.

According to Slusser, Le Guin's best work "examines the possibility of balance between the individual and his world. Le Guin has always believed strongly in such balance, in the dynamics of polarity. Taoism is not an interlude; it is and has always been the strongest single force behind her work, the mold that shapes novel after novel, and binds them one to another in a coherent pattern of human history. Her use of oriental wisdom is highly personal, the creative adaptation of a philosophical system to a literary genre long dominated by a harshly western vision of evolution and technological progress."

The Earthsea trilogy, considered by Le Guin herself to be among her best work, exemplifies her holistic perspective of the universe, a perspective shaped by Taoist philosophy. As Robert Scholes suggests in a *Hollins Critic* article, "What Earthsea represents, through its world of islands and waterways, is the universe as a dynamic, balanced system, not subject to the capricious miracles of any deity, but only to the natural laws of its own working, which include a role for magic and for powers other than human, but only as aspects of the great Balance or Equilibrium, which is the order of this cosmos. . . . Le Guin works not with a theology but with an ecology, a cosmology, a reverence for the universe as a self-regulating structure."

The theme of equilibrium between opposing forces works on several levels within the trilogy to present a unified system of meaning. On the most immediate and recognizable level, the integration of man with himself is the subject of the books. The individual's journey toward maturity and self-knowledge represents the struggle for balance. In *The Wizard of Earthsea,* the young maze, or wizard, Ged is the one who undertakes this journey; in *The Tombs of Atuan,* it is the girl-priestess, Tenar; and in *The Farthest Shore,* it is Ged's apprentice Arren. Writing in *Ursula K. Le Guin,* Margaret P. Esmonde suggests that "all of these journeys symbolize the journey every human being must make, one through pain and fear . . . to the acceptance of mortality."

Secondary to the theme of maturation in the trilogy, according to Crow and Erlich, is the "pattern of movement from social disorder to social order," a theme which depends on that of the development of the individual for its ultimate meaning. In Le Guin's schema, "society is beyond hope if the individual remains undeveloped as a human being." The individuals of the trilogy achieve psychological integration as they come to recognize the significance of balance between light and dark, good and evil, and man and nature.

The darkness or "shadow" lurking within Earthsea, which the mage Ged ultimately subdues, is symbolic of the discontent and alienation faced in modern life, according to Rollin A. Lasseter in *Ursula K. Le Guin: Voyager to Inner Lands and to Outer Space:* "The shadow of Earthsea is the shadow of Western, European, mankind; and even more pressingly the shadow of each and every one of us individually as well as collectively. It is my shadow. It is the backside, the mocking opposite of the meaningful and ordered cosmos we inherited from the Ages of Faith." T. A. Shippey writes in *MOSAIC X/2* that Earthsea "resembles America in the aftermath of Vietnam: exhausted, distrustful, uncertain."

In a *Horn Book* article, Eleanor Cameron analyzes the success of *The Wizard of Earthsea.* "Like all the great fantasies," she says, it "leaves an echoing in our minds, that sense of having experienced something we can never quite put into words. . . . [It] is a work which, though it is fantasy, continually returns us to the world about us, its forces and powers; returns us to ourselves, to our own struggles and aspirations, to the very core of human responsibility."

Another striking feature that unifies the Earthsea trilogy, and all of Le Guin's fiction, for that matter, is the extent to which the author invents names, terms, even whole languages, and, as many critics observe, invents them in order to evoke both the fantastic and the realistic modes of experience. Cameron, for example, comments on this aspect of *A Wizard of Earthsea:* "As for the little names . . . of plants and birds and fish and places and people, it would seem . . . Le Guin must herself be a wizard at naming." While in J.R.R. Tolkien's books, Cameron points out, "when it comes to birds and animals and plants, we do not find strange names. In Walter de la Mare's *The Three Royal Monkeys,* we find, on the contrary, all names to be strange." Le Guin, however, "combines known names with strange ones," inventing terms such as "rushwash tea," "turbies," small silver fish, "corly-root," used by witches to heal the sick, "harrekki," a little lizard; characters' names such as Serret, Ogion, and Pechvarry; and place names such as Roke Island, Havnor, Atuan, Selidor, and Iffish. "Do you feel what I feel in those syllables?" asks Cameron. "The sound of these names falls upon my ear with ease and sense of complete appropriateness, given the nature and atmosphere of Earthsea."

"People often ask how I think of names in fantasies, and again I have to answer that I find them, that I hear them," says Le Guin in her essay "Dreams Must Explain Themselves." "These are words, like rushwash tea, for which I can offer no explanation. They simply drink rushwash tea there [in Earthsea]; that's what it's called, like lapsang soochong or Lipton's here. Rushwash is a Hardic word, of course. If you press me, I will explain that it comes from the rushwash bush, which grows both wild and cultivated everywhere south of England, and bears a small round leaf which when dried and steeped yields a pleasant brownish tea. I did not know this before I wrote the foregoing sentence. Or did I know it, and simply never thought about it? What's in a name? A lot, that's what."

Writing in *Ursula K. Le Guin: Voyage to Inner Lands and to Outer Space,* scholar John R. Pfeiffer believes that the emphasis in the Earthsea trilogy on names and on language "[underscores] the principal statement of the work: words and speech—the genesis, discipline, and creative power of language—make the world." Merely reading the work, says Pfeiffer, "is not at all enough. It was made to be heard. It was made to be heard very much in the way the Anglo-Saxon heroic epic *Beowulf* was made to be heard. Moreover, the special purpose'' of Le Guin's epic ''is to tell us that speech and language . . . act much as metaphysics.''

The language of fantasy, according to Le Guin, is as valuable as that of any other discipline. Discussing the subject in her National Book Award acceptance speech, she says that ''The fantasist, whether he uses the ancient archetypes of myth and legend or the younger ones of science and technology, may be talking as seriously as any sociologist—and a good deal more directly—about human life as it is lived, and as it might be lived, and as it ought to be lived. For after all, as great scientists have said and all children know, it is above all by the imagination that we achieve perception, and compassion, and hope.''

''Can one find a common denominator in the work and thought of Ursula K. Le Guin?'' asks author Theodore Sturgeon in a *Los Angeles Times* article. ''Probably not; but there are some notes in her orchestrations that come out repeatedly and with power. A cautionary fear of the development of democracy into dictatorship. Celebrations of courage, endurance, risk. Language, not only loved and shaped, but investigated in all its aspects; call that, perhaps, communication. But above all, in almost un-earthly terms Ursula Le Guin examines, attacks, unbuttons, takes down and exposes our notions of reality.''

MEDIA ADAPTATIONS: The Lathe of Heaven was filmed for television by the Public Broadcasting Service in 1979; ''The Ones Who Walk Away from Omelas'' was performed as a drama with dance and music at the Portland Civic Theatre in 1981.

BIOGRAPHICAL/CRITICAL SOURCES—Books: Philip Rawson and Laszlo Legeza, *Tao: The Eastern Philosophy of Time and Change,* Avon, 1973; Robert Scholes, *Structural Fabulation: An Essay on Fiction of the Future,* University of Notre Dame Press, 1975; George Edgar Slusser, *The Farthest Shores of Ursula Le Guin,* Borgo, 1976; *Authors in the News,* Volume I, Gale, 1976; *Contemporary Literary Criticism,* Gale, Volume VIII, 1978, Volume XIII, 1980, Volume XXII, 1982; *Children's Literature Review,* Volume III, Gale, 1978; Joseph Olander and Martin Harry Greenberg, editors, *Ursula K. Le Guin,* Taplinger, 1979; Joe DeBolt, editor, *Ursula K. Le Guin: Voyager to Inner Lands and to Outer Space,* Kennikat, 1979; *Dictionary of Literary Biography,* Volume VIII, Part 1: *Twentieth-Century American Science Fiction Writers,* Gale, 1981; Ursula K. Le Guin, *The Language of the Night: Essays on Fantasy and Science Fiction,* Berkley Publishing, 1982.

Periodicals: *Horn Book,* April, 1971; *Hollins Critic,* April, 1974; *Milwaukee Journal,* July 21, 1974; *New Republic,* February 7, 1976, October 30, 1976; *Publishers Weekly,* June 14, 1976; *MOSAIC X/2,* Winter, 1977; *Horizon,* January, 1980; *Los Angeles Times,* September 5, 1982.

—Sketch by Kerry L. Lutz

* * *

LEHNUS, Donald James 1934-

PERSONAL: Born November 7, 1934, in Lyons, Kan.; son of Carl Henry (a machinist) and Maude (Proffitt) Lehnus. *Education:* University of Kansas, B.A., 1956; University of California, Berkeley, M.L.S., 1957; Case Western Reserve University, Ph.D., 1973. *Religion:* Protestant.

CAREER: Queens Borough Public Library, Jamaica, N.Y., assistant librarian, 1957-58; Franklin Square Public Library, Franklin Square, N.Y., assistant director, 1958-62; San Leandro Community Library Center, San Leandro, Calif., librarian, 1962-63; University of Antioquia, Medellin, Colombia, professor of cataloging, 1964-66; Western Michigan University, Kalamazoo, assistant professor of cataloging, 1967-70; University of Puerto Rico, Graduate School of Library Science, Rio Piedras, associate professor of cataloging, 1973—. Visiting professor at University of Washington, Seattle, 1969. *Member:* Sociedad de Bibliotecarios de Puerto Rico, American Library Association (life member), Association of American Library Schools, American Association of University Professors, American Society for Information Science.

WRITINGS: Who's on Time: A Study of Time's Covers from March 3, 1923 to January 3, 1977, Oceana, 1980; *Book Numbers: Their History, Principles, and Application,* American Library Association, 1980; *Angels to Zeppelins: A Guide to the Persons, Objects, Topics and Themes on United States Postage Stamps,* Greenwood Press, 1982.

Monographs: *Principios de catalogacion y clasificacion para bibliotecas pequenas* (title means ''Fundamentals of Cataloging and Classification for Small Libraries''), Editorial Universidad de Antioquia, 1966; *How to Determine Author and Title Entries According to Anglo-American Cataloging Rules: An Interpretive Guide with Card Examples,* Oceana, 1971; *Catalogacao descritiva: manual pratico contendo 225 modelos de fichas exemplificativas das Regras de Catalogacao Descritiva* (title means ''Descriptive Cataloging: A Practical Manual Containing 225 Examples of Cards Illustrating the Rules of Descriptive Cataloging''), Editora e Distribuidora VIPA, 1971; *A Comparison of Panizzi's Ninety-One Rules and the Anglo-American Cataloging Rules of 1967,* Graduate School of Library Science, University of Illinois, 1972; *Milestones in Cataloging: Famous Catalogers and Their Writings, 1835-1969,* Libraries Unlimited, 1974.

Contributor to *Journal of the American Society for Information Science, Journal of Education for Librarianship, Wilson Library Bulletin,* and other periodicals.

WORK IN PROGRESS: An anthology of cataloging articles.

AVOCATIONAL INTERESTS: Travel.

* * *

LEINWAND, Gerald 1921-

PERSONAL: Born August 27, 1921, in Brooklyn, N.Y.; son of Louis (a merchant) and Rose (Simonoff) Leinwand; married Selma Fienberg (a teacher), August 26, 1945; children: Roberta Barrie, Adrienne Sue. *Education:* New York University, B.A., 1941, M.S., 1942, Ph.D., 1962; Columbia University, M.A., 1945. *Home:* 325 Green Dunes Rd., West Hyannisport, Mass. 02672.

CAREER: Abraham & Strauss, New York City, executive trainee, 1941-42; teacher of social studies in New York City, 1942-45, and in Bennington, Vt., 1945-51; New York City Board of Education, junior high school teacher, 1954-57, senior high school teacher, 1957-62, television teacher, ''Highlights of World History,'' 1962; City College of the City University of New York, New York City, assistant professor, 1963-65, associate professor of education, 1965-71, assistant dean, 1967-68; Bernard M. Baruch College of the City University of New York, New York City, professor and dean of school of education, 1968-77; Western Oregon State College, Monmouth, president, 1977-82. Owner and operator of furniture retail business, 1952-63. Senior consultant, American

Association of State Colleges and Universities, 1982—. *Member:* National Council for Social Studies, American Association for Higher Education, American Historical Association, Association of Teachers of Social Studies of City of New York (member of executive board; chairman of scholarship and textbook committees).

WRITINGS—Published by Washington Square Press, except as indicated: *The Pageant of World History,* Allyn & Bacon, 1962, new revised edition, 1977; *The American Constitution,* Doubleday, 1964; (with D. M. Feins) *Teaching History and the Social Studies in Secondary School,* Pitman, 1967; (editor) *Civil Rights and Civil Liberties,* 1969; (editor) *Negro in the City,* 1969; (editor) *Poverty and the Poor,* 1969; (compiler) *Crime and Juvenile Delinquency,* 1969; (editor) *Air and Water Pollution,* 1969; *The Traffic Jam,* 1969.

(Compiler) *The Draft,* 1970; (with others) *The Slums,* 1970; *The City as a Community,* 1970; (compiler) *The Consumer,* 1970; (compiler) *Minorities All,* 1971; *Governing the City,* Pocket Books, 1971; (compiler) *The Police,* Pocket Books, 1972; (compiler) *Prisons,* Pocket Books, 1972; *The Pageant of American History,* Allyn & Bacon, 1975; *Teaching World History,* National Council for the Social Studies, 1978. Contributor to journals.

* * *

LEITCH, Patricia 1933-

PERSONAL: Born July 13, 1933, in Paisley, Renfrewshire, Scotland; daughter of James Ritchie (an engineer) and Anna (Mitchell) Leitch. *Education:* Craigie College of Education, primary teacher's diploma, 1967. *Home:* 11 Argyll Ter., Dunoon, Argyll, Scotland. *Agent:* A. M. Heath & Co. Ltd., 40-42 William IV St., London WC2N 4DD, England.

CAREER: Library assistant in Glasgow Corporation libraries and Renfrewshire County Library, Scotland, 1954-59; instructor at Kilmacolm Riding School, 1960-61; shop assistant in various bookshops, 1962-63; Troon Primary School, Ayrshire, Scotland, teacher, 1968-70; typist for various employers, 1971-73; writer, 1974—.

WRITINGS—Juveniles: *A Pony of Our Own,* Blackie & Son, 1960; *To Save a Pony,* Hutchinson, 1960; *Rosette for Royal,* Blackie & Son, 1963; *Janet Young Rider,* Constable, 1963, published as *Last Summer to Ride,* Funk, 1965; *The Black Loch,* Collins, 1963, Funk, 1968; *Highland Pony Trek,* Collins, 1964; *Riding Course Summer,* Collins, 1965; *Cross Country Pony,* Blackie & Son, 1965; *Treasure to the East,* Gollancz, 1966; *Jacky Jumps to the Top,* Collins, 1973; *First Pony,* Collins, 1973; *Afraid to Ride,* Collins, 1973; *Rebel Pony,* Collins, 1973; *Pony Surprise,* Collins, 1974; *Dream of Fair Horses,* Collins & World, 1975; *The Adventures of Robin Hood,* Collins & World, 1979.

"Jinny" series; published by Collins & World: *For Love of a Horse,* 1976; *A Devil to Ride,* 1976; *The Summer Riders,* 1977; *Night of the Red Horse,* 1978; *Gallop to the Hills,* 1979; *Horse in a Million,* 1980; *The Magic Pony,* 1982; *Red Horse Rescue,* 1983.

WORK IN PROGRESS: The Lordly Ones, a juvenile novel.

SIDELIGHTS: "I have always had a vivid imagination, being typical of the Jungian category of introverted intuitive," writes Patricia Leitch. "I have neither a visual nor an aural imagination. It is something else. Most of my books are 'pony books,' some are fantasies, but really they all say the same thing—'Sin is Behovely, but all shall be well, and all manner of thing shall be well.'" Leitch adds she is "a vegetarian and am enthused by the growing synthesis of Eastern and Western cultures."

BIOGRAPHICAL/CRITICAL SOURCES: Young Readers' Review, September, 1968.

* * *

LEMAY, J(oseph) A(lberic) Leo 1935-

PERSONAL: Born January 7, 1935, in Bristow, Va.; son of Joseph Albert (a steelworker) and Valencia L. (Winslow) Lemay; married Muriel Ann Clarke (a real estate broker), August 11, 1965; children: John, Lee, Kate. *Education:* University of Maryland, A.B., 1957, A.M., 1962; University of Pennsylvania, Ph.D., 1964. *Politics:* Republican. *Religion:* Unitarian Universalist. *Home:* 4828 Kennett Pike, Greenville, Del. 19807. *Office:* Department of English, University of Delaware, Newark, Del. 19711.

CAREER: George Washington University, Washington, D.C., assistant professor of English, 1963-65; University of California, Los Angeles, assistant professor, 1965-70, associate professor, 1970-75, professor of English, 1975-77; University of Delaware, Newark, H. F. du Pont Winterthur Professor of English, 1977—. *Military service:* U.S. Army, 1957-59.

MEMBER: Modern Language Association of America, American Studies Association, American Antiquarian Society, Institute for Early American History and Culture (council member, 1978-81), Maryland Historical Society, Pennsylvania Historical Society, Virginia Historical Society, Hakluyt Society. *Awards, honors:* Grants from American Philosophical Society and Colonial Williamsburg; Guggenheim fellow; Institute for Advanced Research fellow, University of Delaware, 1980-81.

WRITINGS: Ebenezer Kinnersley: Franklin's Friend, University of Pennsylvania Press, 1964; *Men of Letters in Colonial Maryland,* University of Tennessee Press, 1972; *A Calendar of American Poetry in Colonial Newspapers and Magazines through 1765,* American Antiquarian Society, 1972; (editor) *The Oldest Revolutionary: Essays on Benjamin Franklin,* University of Pennsylvania Press, 1976; (editor) *Essays in Early Virginia Literature Honoring Richard Beale Davis,* Burt Franklin, 1977; (editor) *The Autobiography of Benjamin Franklin: A Genetic Text,* University of Tennessee Press, 1981. Contributor to periodicals, including *American Literature, New England Quarterly,* and *Virginia Magazine of History and Biography.*

WORK IN PROGRESS: The Ideology of Early American Humor; New England's Annoyances: America's First Folk Song; The Art of Poe's "Murders in the Rue Morgue."

* * *

LeMOND, Alan 1938-
(David Tahlaquah)

PERSONAL: Born February 27, 1938, in Evansville, Ind.; son of Jesse Roy and Dorothy E. (Taylor) LeMond; married Mary Anne Hirsch, July 19, 1969 (divorced); children: Lisa Anne, Nicole Christina. *Education:* Oakland City College, B.A., 1965. *Home address:* Box 65, Velpen, Ind. 47590. *Agent:* Owen Laster, William Morris Agency, 1350 Avenue of the Americas, New York, N.Y. 10019.

CAREER: *Esquire* (magazine), New York City, copywriter, 1965-67; *Cavalier* (magazine), New York City, associate editor, 1967-68, editor, 1968-70; New Earth, Inc. (editorial consulting and packaging firm), New York City, president, beginning 1970; Marvel Comics, Inc., New York City, editor, 1974-76; editor and publisher of *Patoka Valley Citizen,* 1981—. *Military service:* U.S. Army, 1961-63.

WRITINGS: (With May Acton and Parker Hodges) *Mug Shots: Who's Who in the New Earth,* New American Library, 1972; (with Acton) *Ralph Nader: A Man and a Movement,* Paperback Library, 1972; (with Ron Fry) *No Place to Hide: Bugs, Computers, Informers, and Dossiers and What to Do about Them,* St. Martin's, 1975; (with Mark Spitz) *The Mark Spitz Complete Book of Swimming,* Crowell, 1976; *Bravo Baryshnikov,* Grosset, 1978; (with James LaForte) *Men's Hair: The Long and Short of It,* Contemporary Books, 1979. Contributor of articles and fiction, under pseudonym David Tahlaquah, to *Cavalier, Nugget, Celebrity,* and to movie fan books. Co-founder and editor of *Your Land,* 1972.

* * *

LETTAU, Reinhard 1929-

PERSONAL: Born September 10, 1929, in Erfurt, Germany; naturalized U.S. citizen; son of Reinhard F. and Gertrude (Felsberg) Lettau; married Mary Gene Carter, September 4, 1954; children: Karen, Kevyn, Catherine. *Education:* Attended University of Heidelberg; Harvard University, Ph.D., 1960. *Home:* 1150 Cuchara Dr., Del Mar, Calif. *Office address:* Department of Literature, University of California, San Diego, P.O. Box 109, La Jolla, Calif. 92037.

CAREER: Smith College, Northampton, Mass., instructor, 1957-59, assistant professor, 1959-63, associate professor of German literature and language, 1963-67; University of California, San Diego, La Jolla, Calif., professor of German literature and creative writing, 1967—. Guest lecturer at University of Massachusetts, 1958, and Mt. Holyoke College, 1960; Hanser Verlag, Munich, Germany, scout, 1965—. *Member:* P.E.N., Modern Language Association of America, German Academy of Performing Arts, Group 47. *Awards, honors:* Prize for best German radio play, 1978.

WRITINGS: *Schwierigkeiten beim Haeuserbauen* (short stories; also see below), Hanser Verlag, 1962, translation by Ursule Molinaro published as *Obstacles,* Pantheon, 1965; *Auftritt Manigs* (short prose), Hanser Verlag, 1963, translation by Molinaro and Ellen Sutton published, with Molinaro's translation of *Schwierigkeiten beim Haeuserbauen,* in England as *Obstacles,* Calder & Boyars, 1966; (editor) *Lachen mit Thurber,* Rowohlt, 1963; *Gedichte,* Colloquium, 1967; *Handbuch der Gruppe 47,* Luehterhand, 1967; *Feinde,* Hanser Verlag, 1968, translation by Agnes Book published as *Enemies,* Calder & Boyars, 1973.

Taglicher Faschismus, Hanser Verlag, 1971; *Immer kuerzer werdende Geschichten und Gedichte und Portraets,* Hanser Verlag, 1973; (editor) Franz Kafka, *Die Aeroplane in Brescia und andere Texte,* Fischer Verlag, 1977; (co-editor) *Karl Marx Love Poems,* City Lights, 1977; *Fruehstueckgespraeche in Miami* (comedy; first produced in Giessen, West Germany, 1978), Hanser Verlag, 1977, translation by Lettau and Julie Pradi published as *Breakfast in Miami,* Riverrun Press (New York), 1981.

Zerstreutes Hinausschaun: vom Schreiben ueber Vorgaenge in direkter Naehe oder in d. Entfernung von Schreibtischen (essays), Hanser Verlag, 1980; *Schwieriskeikh-Manig,* Ullskin, 1982. Also author of "Oscar Wilde's Trials," produced on German television, 1966.

WORK IN PROGRESS: *Zur Frage der Himmelsrichtunjen* (prose).

SIDELIGHTS: Translations of Reinhard Lettau's books have appeared in France, England, Spain, Italy, Poland, Sweden, Denmark, Norway, Finland, and China.

* * *

LEVI, Anthony H(erbert) T(igar) 1929-

PERSONAL: Born May 30, 1929, in Ruislip, England; son of Herbert Simon (a merchant) and Edith Mary (Tigar) Levi. *Education:* Studied philosophy for three years in Munich, modern languages for three years at Oxford University, and theology for four years; Oxford University, B.A., 1958, D.Phil., 1963; Heythrop College, S.T.L., 1963. *Home:* East Castlemount, North Castle St., St. Andrews, Fife, Scotland. *Office:* Department of French, Buchanan Building, University of St. Andrews, St. Andrews, Fife, Scotland.

CAREER: Engaged in business in England, 1946-49; member of Society of Jesus (Jesuits), 1949-71; Oxford University, Christ Church, Oxford, England, lecturer in French, 1966-71; University of St. Andrews, St. Andrews, Fife, Scotland, Buchanan Professor of French Language and Literature, 1971—. University of Warwick, reader in French, 1966, personal chair in French, 1970.

WRITINGS: *French Moralists: The Theory of the Passions, 1585-1649,* Oxford University Press, 1964; *Religion in Practice,* Harper, 1966; (editor and contributor) *Humanism in France at the End of the Middle Ages and in the Early Renaissance,* Manchester University Press, 1970; (author of introduction and notes) Desiderius Erasmus, *The Praise of Folly,* Penguin, 1971; (editor with Francis Haskell and Robert Shackleton) *The Artist and the Writer in France: Essays in Honour of Jean Seznec,* Oxford University Press, 1974; *The Satires of Erasmus,* Toronto University Press, in press. Also editor of *Complete Works of Erasmus in English,* two volumes.

Contributor: James Walsh, editor, *Spirituality through the Centuries,* Burns & Oates, 1964; G. Richard-Molard, editor, *L'homme devant Dieu,* Droguet Ardant, 1964; Terence C. Cave, editor, *Ronsard the Poet,* Methuen, 1973; N. Strasbourg, editor, *Heroisme et creation litteraire,* Klincksieck, 1973; R. R. Bolgar, editor, *Classical Influences on European Culture, A.D. 1500-1700,* Cambridge University Press, 1976; Peter Sharratt, editor, *French Renaissance Studies, 1540-70: Humanism and the Encyclopedia,* Edinburgh University Press, 1976. Contributor to periodicals, including *Heydrop Journal, Dublin Review,* and *Month.*

WORK IN PROGRESS: *La Rochefoucauld;* a new *Oxford Companion to French Literature.*

* * *

LEVIN, Betty 1927-

PERSONAL: Born September 10, 1927, in New York, N.Y.; daughter of Max (a lawyer) and Eleanor (a musician; maiden name, Mack) Lowenthal; married Alvin Levin (a lawyer), 1947; children: Katherine, Bara, Jennifer. *Education:* University of Rochester, A.B., 1949; Radcliffe College, M.A., 1951; Harvard University, A.M.T., 1951. *Home:* Old Winter St., Lincoln, Mass. 01773. *Office:* Center for the Study of Children's Literature, Simmons College, Boston, Mass. 02115.

CAREER: Museum of Fine Arts, Boston, Mass., assistant in research, 1952; Pine Manor Open College, Chestnut Hill, Mass., instructor in literature, 1970-75; Simmons College, Center for the Study of Children's Literature, Boston, Mass., member of faculty, 1975—. Instructor at Emmanuel College, 1975, and Radcliffe College, beginning 1976. *Member:* Authors Guild, Authors League of America. *Awards, honors:* Fellowship in creative writing at Radcliffe Institute, 1968-70.

WRITINGS: The Zoo Conspiracy (juvenile fiction), Hastings House, 1973; *The Sword of Culann* (young adult fiction), Macmillan, 1973; *A Griffon's Nest* (young adult historical fiction), Macmillan, 1975; *The Forespoken* (young adult historical fiction), Macmillan, 1976; *Landfall,* Atheneum, 1979; *A Beast on the Brink,* Avon, 1980; *The Keeping-Room,* Greenwillow, 1981. Contributor of articles to education journals and to *Horn Book.*

WORK IN PROGRESS: A biography; a children's novel; a novel for young adults.

* * *

LEVIN, Marlin 1921-

PERSONAL: Born October 21, 1921 in Harrisburg, Pa.; son of Isadore R. and Rose (Hoffman) Levin; married Betty Florence Schoffman (a teacher); children: Sara, Oren, Don. *Education:* Temple University, B.Sc. (with honors). *Office:* Time-Life News Service, 19B Keren Hayessod, 94188 Jerusalem, Israel.

CAREER: Women's Wear Daily, New York, N.Y., staff member, 1947; *Jerusalem Post,* Jerusalem, Israel, diplomatic correspondent and news editor, 1947-59; Time-Life News Service, Jerusalem correspondent for *Time* and *Life,* 1958-76, 1980—, Boston correspondent for *Time,* 1976-80. Jerusalem correspondent for United Press International, 1949-51, and for American Broadcasting Corp. (ABC-TV) and Radio, 1952-67; Israel correspondent for London *Daily Mail,* 1956-62. Former instructor in journalism at Hebrew University of Jerusalem. *Military service:* U.S. Army, cryptographer in Signal Corps, 1943-46; served in European and Pacific theaters; became sergeant. *Member:* Overseas Press Club, Israel Foreign Press Association (chairman, 1973).

WRITINGS—Contributor, except as indicated; published by Time-Life, except as indicated: *Israel,* 1962, new edition, 1968; (author) *Balm in Gilead,* Schocken, 1973; *The Sea Traders,* 1974; *The Israelites,* 1975; *Soldiers of Fortune,* 1981; *Fighting Jets,* 1983; *Armies of the World,* Greenwood Press, 1983. Levin's bylines have appeared in magazines and newspapers in England and the United States, including *Discover* and other Time, Inc., periodicals.

SIDELIGHTS: Marlin Levin has covered Israel from its founding to the Palestine War, Sinai Campaign, Eichmann trial, Six-Day War, Yom Kippur War, and the Cyprus Civil War. Other notable assignments include coverage of the Sadat peace mission to Jerusalem and the 1982 war in Lebanon.

* * *

LEVINE, Philip 1928-

PERSONAL: Born January 10, 1928, in Detroit, Mich.; son of A. Harry (a businessman) and Esther (a bookseller; maiden name, Priscoll) Levine; married Frances Artley (a gardener), July 4, 1954; children: Mark, John, Theodore Henri. *Education:* Wayne University (now Wayne State University), A.B., 1950, A.M., 1954; University of Iowa, M.F.A., 1957. *Politics:* Anarchist. *Religion:* Anarchist. *Home:* 4549 North Van Ness Ave., Fresno, Calif. 93704. *Office:* Department of English, California State University, Fresno, Calif. 93710.

CAREER: Poet. Worked at "vastupid jobs" in Detroit, Mich. during the early 1950s, including assemblyman for Ford Motor Co. and railroad shipper; University of Iowa, Iowa City, member of faculty, 1955-57; California State University, Fresno, professor of English, 1958—. Elliston Professor of Poetry, University of Cincinnati, 1976; post-in-residence, National University of Australia, Canberra, summer, 1978; teacher at Squaw Valley Writers Community. Has read his poetry at the Library of Congress, Poetry Center of San Francisco, Pasadena Art Gallery, Guggenheim Museum, Princeton University, Massachusetts Institute of Technology, University of Michigan, University of California, Stanford University, Wayne State University, University of Iowa, San Francisco State University, and other schools. Former advisor to the affiliated societies of the Academy of American Poets.

AWARDS, HONORS: Stanford University poetry fellowship, 1957; Joseph Henry Jackson Award, San Francisco Foundation, 1961, for manuscript "Berenda Slough and Other Poems" (later published as *On the Edge*); Chaplebrook Foundation grant, 1969; National Endowment for the Arts grants, 1969, 1970 (refused), 1976-81; named outstanding lecturer, California State University, Fresno, 1971; named outstanding professor, California State University System, 1972; Frank O'Hara Memorial Prize, *Poetry,* 1973; National Institute of Arts and Letters grant, 1973; award of merit, American Academy of Arts and Letters, 1974; Guggenheim fellowships, 1974, 1981; Harriet Monroe Memorial Prize for Poetry, University of Chicago, 1976; Lenore Marshall Award for Best American Book of Poems, 1976, for *The Names of the Lost;* American Book Award for Poetry, 1979, for *Ashes;* National Book Critics Circle Prize, 1979, for *Ashes* and *7 Years from Somewhere;* notable book award, American Library Association, 1979, for *7 Years from Somewhere.*

WRITINGS—Poems: *On the Edge,* Stone Wall Press, limited edition, 1961, 2nd edition, 1963; *Silent in America: Visas for Those Who Failed,* limited edition, Shaw Avenue Press (Iowa City), 1965; *Not This Pig,* Wesleyan University Press, 1968; *5 Detroits,* Unicorn Press, 1970; *Thistles: A Poem Sequence,* limited edition, Turret Books (London), 1970; *Pili's Wall,* Unicorn Press, 1971, revised edition, 1980; *Red Dust,* illustrated with prints by Marcia Mann, Kayak, 1971; *They Feed They Lion,* Atheneum, 1972; *1933,* Atheneum, 1974; *New Season* (pamphlet), Graywolf Press (Port Townsend, Wash.), 1975; *On the Edge and Over: Poems Old, Lost, and New,* Cloud Marauder, 1976; *The Names of the Lost,* limited edition, Windhover Press (Iowa City), 1976, 2nd edition, Atheneum, 1976; *7 Years from Somewhere,* Atheneum, 1979; *Ashes: Poems New and Collected,* Atheneum, 1979; *One for the Rose,* Atheneum, 1981. Also narrator of sound recording, "The Poetry and Voice of Philip Levine," Caedmon, 1976.

Other: (Editor with Henri Coulette) *Character and Crisis: A Contemporary Reader,* McGraw, 1966; (editor and translator with Ernesto Trejo) *Tarumba: The Selected Poems of Jaime Sabines,* Twowindows Press, 1979; *Don't Ask* (collection of interviews with Levine), University of Michigan Press, 1979.

Contributor of poems to anthologies: P. Engle and others, editors, *Midland*, Random House, 1961; D. Hall, editor, *New Poets of England and America*, Meridian, 1962; Engle and J. T. Langland, editors, *Poet's Choice*, Dial, 1962; J. F. Kessler, editor, *American Poems*, Southern Illinois University Press, 1964; S. Berg and R. Mezey, editors, *Naked Poetry*, Bobbs-Merrill, 1969. Contributor to numerous other anthologies. Contributor of poems to periodicals, including *New Yorker, Poetry, New York Review of Books, Hudson Review, Paris Review*, and *Harper's*.

WORK IN PROGRESS: Sweet Will, a collection of new and selected poems, for Atheneum; editor and translator, with Ada Long, of a book of Spanish poems by Gloria Fuertes; fiction, "for the first time in twenty years."

SIDELIGHTS: While working in the auto plants of Detroit during the 1950s, poet Philip Levine resolved "to find a voice for the voiceless," he told *CA*. "I saw that the people that I was working with . . . were voiceless in a way," he explains in *Detroit Magazine*. "In terms of the literature of the United States they weren't being heard. Nobody was speaking for them. And as young people will, you know, I took this foolish vow that I would speak for them and that's what my life would be. And sure enough I've gone and done it. Or I've tried anyway. . . . I just hope I have the strength to carry it all the way through."

In *Hudson Review*, Vernon Young finds that Levine "has never acknowledged the claim of any society save that of the blue-collar dispossessed, the marginal and crunched for whom he has elected to be the evangelist and spokesman." "His poems are personal, love poems, poems of horror, poems about the experiencing of America," Stephen Spender writes in the *New York Review of Books*. "Reading [*They Feed They Lion*] one feels in the presence of a strange, alarming and irrefutable way of seeing things." And Joyce Carol Oates says in the *American Poetry Review*, "He is one of those poets whose work is so emotionally intense, and yet so controlled, so concentrated, that the accumulative effect of reading a number of his related poems can be shattering." "I really think he is extraordinary," Oates concludes, "a visionary of our dense, troubled mysterious time."

Herbert Leibowitz, in a *New York Times Book Review* article on *Ashes*, comments: "A child of the working class who grew up in Detroit during the Depression, Mr. Levine has returned again and again in his poems to the lives of factory workers trapped by poverty and the drudgery of the assembly line, which breaks the body and scars the spirit. The lurid fires of the foundries serve as a backdrop to the prevailing greyness." According to Leibowitz, Levine has become "the elegist of lost souls beaten down by forces they could not understand or control." "Levine cries out for explanations, a sense of moral justice, really, to compensate for . . . tragedies," Ira Sadoff asserts in the *Antioch Review*. Sadoff believes that the poems in *The Names of the Lost* "are often melancholy, powerful, though occasionally a little sentimental. . . . It is the memory of the poet's own Detroit childhood, where political realities take on a haunting particularity, that calls forth his greatest powers, his descriptions of the nobility and harsh realities of urban life."

In addition to concentrating on the working class in his work, Levine has paid tribute to the Spanish anarchist movement of the 1930s, especially in *The Names of the Lost*. "From the beginning of his poetic career, Philip Levine has focused on two themes with ritual consistency: the tribulations of the powerless and the Spanish Civil War," Leibowitz summarizes. "Though he was too young to fight in that war, it embodies for him the historical exemplum: a people's uprising that succeeded, quixotically, for a few rare days in hinting at what a genuine egalitarian society might be." And in *The Fierce Embrace*, Charles Molesworth writes: "The almost mystical brooding of his stay in Barcelona has merged with the abrasive gratings of his Detroit childhood. Both cities are built on the backs of sullen, exploited workers, and the faded revolution in one smolders like the blunting, racist fear in the other." As Leibowitz sums up, "the poet's 'Spanish self,' as he calls it, is kin to his Detroit self. Both bear witness to the visionary ideal destroyed."

Levine's obsession with the "voiceless" makes for "a daunting, brooding art, often without solace," Robert Mazzocco observes in the *New York Review of Books*. "He is particularly sensitive to lack, absence, finality," Denis Donoghue summarizes in another *New York Review of Books* article. And Joan Taylor writes in the *Dictionary of Literary Biography:* "Levine met his enemy in the gray arenas of industrialism, . . . of factory hum and stink, vacant lots, junkyards, and railroad tracks. . . . Levine's hero is the lonely individual who tries and often fails within this big industrial machine." "His speakers are guerrillas," Paul Gray says in *Time*, "trapped in an endless battle long after the war has been lost."

Molesworth describes Levine's poetic world as one "of harsh consequence and fierce limitations, . . . but throughout every poem we sense that someone, no matter how bleary-eyed the dawn, is looking hard at hard facts." In *Cry of the Human*, Ralph J. Mills, Jr., asserts that Levine struggles "to view life stripped of the vestiges of illusory hope or promise, a type of hard spiritual conditioning which helps to engender his fundamental responsiveness to the dilemmas of the poor, embittered, failed lives of the 'submerged population' . . . in modern society, a responsiveness that accounts for much of both the energy and the deep humaneness of all his work. A firm grip on existence itself takes priority for Levine from the start, though with it necessarily comes an acceptance of pain and the admission that failure, defeat, and imperfection—but not surrender!—are unavoidable." Concludes Mills: "Committed to a fallen, unredeemable world, finding no metaphysical consolations, Levine embraces it with an ardor, anguish, and fury that are themselves religious emotions."

Despite its painful quality, Levine's verse displays a certain joyfulness, a sense of victory-in-defeat, Marie Borroff contends. Writing in the *Yale Review*, Borroff describes the title poem of *They Feed They Lion* as "a litany celebrating, in rhythms and images of unflagging, piston-like force, the majestic strength of the oppressed, rising equally out of the substances of the poisoned industrial landscape and the intangibles of humiliation." And Richard Hugo comments in the *American Poetry Review:* "Levine's poems are important because in them we hear and we care. They call us back to the basic sources of despair: the dispossession, the destitution, the inadequacy of our love for each other. And they call back again that we can triumph over our sad psychic heritage through language and song." "Levine has remained a child and kept alive the impulse to sing," Hugo continues. "The dawn that drenched him awake, still burns in him, on his tongue, in his words. . . . Whatever we are, hopeful, hurt, angry, sad, happy, we should least of all forget Philip Levine's poems. They attend us and our lives in profound, durable ways. I believe he is destined to become one of the most celebrated poets of the time." Mazzocco asserts that Levine is "affectionate in his hate, hard in his compassion,'' and fully aware of ''the twilit other world where the negative and the positive seem to be twins of the same coin, where the poet is both victor and victim, and at times blessed because he is both.'' ''Here is exaltation made manifest,'' Borroff concludes, ''a hymn for a godforsaken time.''

Levine's poetry for the common man is distinguished by simple diction and a rhythmic narrative style, by ''the strength of a living syntax,'' Robert Pinsky writes in the *New York Times Book Review*. In an *American Poetry Review* appraisal of *Ashes* and *7 Years from Somewhere,* Dave Smith notes that in Levine's poems ''the language, the figures of speech, the narrative progressions are never so obscure, so truncated as to forbid less sophisticated readers. Though he takes on the largest subjects of death, love, courage, manhood, loyalty, etc., he brings the mysteries of existence down into the ordinarily inarticulate events and objects of daily life.'' ''Levine's poetic world values reality above all else,'' Robert D. Spector remarks in the *Saturday Review,* ''a reality that is reinforced by his earthy language, colloquial syntax, and natural rhythms.'' Molesworth believes that Levine ''often implies that he, or at least the people of and for whom he speaks, considers words a form of mystification; as is often the case with laborers and other people whose lives are filled with pressured actions, there is a mistrust of too-glib talk, of a speech that doesn't know when to shut up or to say the simple thing that will leave everyone alone with their own feelings. This accounts . . . for the near-dominance of the narrative mode in Levine's work, for most of his narratives point simply to observed and irreducible events.'' Levine himself, in an interview with Calvin Bedient in *Parnassus,* defines his ''ideal poem'' as one in which ''no words are noticed. You look through them into a vision of . . . the people, the place.''

''If a poem's primary interest is with characters and events outside its surface—not just with the pattern created by words themselves—the poet runs the risk of producing prose,'' Taylor writes. As Taylor points out, several critics have commented on this consequence of Levine's narrative style, of his pursuit of the ''ideal poem.'' In the *New York Review of Books,* Helen Vendler states: ''Often Levine seems to me simply a memoir-writer in prose who chops up his reminiscent paragraphs into short lines.'' In her appraisal of *One for the Rose,* Vendler asks, ''Is there any compelling reason why it should be called poetry?'' Taylor asserts that this ''formal problem'' is created by ''the primarily narrative nature'' of Levine's poems. She concludes that ''Levine may now be approaching the solution more closely than ever in his growing concern with his language and his lines as they reflect his poetic vision. This is an exciting development; Levine's reader has come to know the poet's public self, his sympathy for the oppressed, and his reverence for human dignity. But the reader expects and desires in the poem an exploration of Levine's idiosyncratic shaping imagination, his passion for the word as it enables him, in the present, to perceive people and place. This revelation will inform Levine's [poems] with even greater lyric power and precision.''

Levine has also been criticized, as Leibowitz puts it, for ''digging for gold in a nearly exhausted vein.'' ''The business of sharing the deprivations of one's fellow man, and then discovering in a poem that one has thereby become the fellow man's brother—this seems to me such a commonplace,'' Robley Wilson, Jr. contends in the *Carleton Miscellany*. ''Sometimes,'' writes Stephen Yenser in a *Yale Review* article on *7 Years from Somewhere,* ''I wish he were less like that farmer who must keep on plowing the same field.''

''Some have said he has written the same poem for years, that he lacks variety and vision,'' Smith comments. ''True, his vision is such a relentless denunciation of injustice that he has occasionally engaged in reductive oversimplifications.'' Smith believes that in spite of this objection and others, Levine's poetry is ''nearly a national treasure. . . . It might be said that Mr. Levine has a formula and I would answer that we should all be so fortunate, for what he has is a style patiently developed to fit his need to speak the hurt and the joy that in all of us remains unshaped and embryonic.''

W. S. Di Piero asserts that Levine's polemical bent sometimes ''risks a kind of melodrama'' which tends to weaken the impact of his verse. Writing in *Commonweal,* Di Piero, however, believes ''that in Levine's case this is a flaw of a high order, commensurate with his high ambition.'' Similarly, Pinsky says that ''it must be admitted that Levine's work is uneven and that its failing is the maudlin, . . . the locking of tone into a flaw or groove, running there without the capacity for modulation of emotion: a single, sustained whine, piercing but not penetrating.'' In his review of *The Names of the Lost,* Pinsky qualifies his criticism, stating that ''Levine has earned and undertaken the hardness of high standards.'' And Yenser, appraising Levine's work for *Parnassus,* raises the question of whether Levine's identification with suffering ''does not trivialize the experience it means to bring home, whether the technique has not subverted the subject.''

According to Jack Anderson in *Prairie Schooner,* ''Levine achieves a calm resolution, . . . one devoid of easy sentimentality and consonant with his flinty perceptions.'' ''When he focuses on the private pains and social ills of others, his best poems oblige us to cry with him,'' Alan Helms states in the *Partisan Review*. ''*They Feed They Lion* is not a comforting experience. More important, in its compassion, its skill, and its rare power to disturb our dulled attentions, it is a necessary and valuable one.'' Finally, Smith concludes that Levine ''risks the maudlin, the sentimental, the banal, and worse because he cannot live in the world fully enough; because the world is so much with us all we must sing or die of its inexpressible presence.''

BIOGRAPHICAL/CRITICAL SOURCES—Books: *Contemporary Literary Criticism,* Gale, Volume II, 1974, Volume IV, 1975, Volume V, 1976, Volume IX, 1978, Volume XIV, 1980; Ralph J. Mills, Jr., *Cry of the Human,* University of Illinois Press, 1975; Philip Levine, *Don't Ask,* University of Michigan Press, 1979; Charles Molesworth, *The Fierce Embrace: A Study of Contemporary American Poetry,* University of Missouri Press, 1979; *Dictionary of Literary Biography,* Volume V: *American Poets since World War II,* Gale, 1980.

Periodicals: *New York Review of Books,* April 25, 1968, September 20, 1973, April 3, 1975, December 17, 1981; *Saturday Review,* June 1, 1968, March 11, 1972, September 7, 1977; *Carleton Miscellany,* fall, 1968; *Shenandoah,* summer, 1972; *Poetry,* July, 1972, March, 1975, August, 1977, December, 1980; *New York Times Book Review,* July 16, 1972, February 20, 1977, October 7, 1979, September 12, 1982; *Yale Review,* autumn, 1972, autumn, 1980; *Western Humanities Review,* autumn, 1972; *Virginia Quarterly Review,* autumn, 1972; *Parnassus,* fall/winter, 1972, fall/winter, 1974, fall/winter, 1977, spring/summer, 1978; *American Poetry Review,* November, 1972, May, 1973, March, 1974, May, 1974, May, 1977, November, 1979.

Prairie Schooner, winter, 1974; *Sewanee Review,* spring, 1976; *New Leader,* January 17, 1977, August 13, 1979; *Antioch*

Review, spring/summer, 1977; *Detroit Magazine,* February 26, 1978; *Time,* June 25, 1979; *Commonweal,* October 12, 1979; *Hudson Review,* winter, 1979-80; *Harper's,* January, 1980; *Nation,* February 2, 1980; *New York Times Magazine,* February 3, 1980; *Georgia Review,* spring, 1980; *Village Voice Literary Supplement,* May, 1982; *Times Literary Supplement,* July 2, 1982.

—*Sketch by Stewart R. Hakola*

* * *

LEWIS, Richard S. 1916-

PERSONAL: Born January 8, 1916, in Pittsburgh, Pa.; son of S. Morton (a dentist) and Mary (a building contractor; maiden name, Lefstein) Lewis; married Louise Silberstein (a teacher), June 8, 1938; children: Jonathan, David. *Education:* Pennsylvania State University, B.A., 1937. *Politics:* Independent. *Home and office:* 3114 Isabella St., Evanston, Ill. 60201.

CAREER: Cleveland Press, Cleveland, Ohio, reporter, 1937-43; *Indianapolis Times,* Indianapolis, Ind., reporter, critic, and city editor, 1946-49; *St. Louis Star-Times,* St. Louis, Mo., investigator-reporter, 1949-51; *Chicago Sun-Times,* Chicago, Ill., reporter, assistant city editor, and science editor, 1951-68; editor of *Science and Public Affairs* and *Bulletin of the Atomic Scientists,* 1968-74; writer. Member, Illinois Board of Mental Health Commissioners. *Military service:* U.S. Army, 1943-46; served in European theater. *Member:* National Press Club, National Association of Science Writers, Quadrangle Club.

WRITINGS: The Other Child: The Brain-Injured Child, Grune, 1951, revised edition, 1960.

A Continent for Science, Viking, 1965; *Appointment on the Moon,* Viking, 1968, revised edition, 1969; (editor with Eugene I. Rabinowitch) *Man on the Moon: The Impact on Science, Technology, and International Cooperation,* Basic Books, 1969 (published in England as *Men in Space: . . . ,* Chiltern, 1970).

(Editor with Jane Wilson and Rabinowitch) *Alamogordo Plus Twenty-Five Years,* Viking, 1970; *The Nuclear-Power Rebellion: Citizens vs the Atomic Power Establishment,* Viking, 1972; (editor with Bernard I. Spinrad) *The Energy Crisis,* Educational Foundation for Nuclear Science, 1972; (editor with P. M. Smith) *Frozen Future: A Prophetic Report from Antarctica,* Quadrangle, 1972; (editor) *The Environmental Revolution,* Educational Foundation for Nuclear Science, 1973; *The Voyages of Apollo: The Exploration of the Moon,* Quadrangle, 1974; *From Vinland to Mars: A Thousand Years of Exploration,* Quadrangle, 1976; *The Other Child Grows Up,* Times Books, 1977; *The Coming of the Ice Age,* Putnam, 1979.†

* * *

LEWIS, W(alter) David 1931-

PERSONAL: Born June 24, 1931, in Towanda, Pa.; son of Gordon C. (a correctional official and Episcopal clergyman) and Eleanor E. (Tobias) Lewis; married Carolyn Wyatt Brown, June 12, 1954 (divorced May, 1980); children: Daniel Kent, Virginia Lorraine, Nancy Ellyn. *Education:* Attended Juniata College, 1948-49; Pennsylvania State University, B.A., 1952, M.A., 1954; Cornell University, Ph.D., 1961. *Religion:* Episcopalian. *Home:* 218 Patio Apartments, Auburn, Ala. 36830. *Office:* 7030B, Haley Center, Auburn University, Auburn, Ala. 36849.

CAREER: Hamilton College, Clinton, N.Y., instructor in public speaking, 1954-57; University of Delaware, Newark, part-time instructor, 1959-61, lecturer in history, 1961-65; Eleutherian Mills-Hagley Foundation, Wilmington, Del., fellowship coordinator, 1959-65; State University of New York at Buffalo, associate professor, 1965-71, professor of history, 1971; Auburn University, Auburn, Ala., Hudson Professor of History and Engineering, 1971—. Director of Auburn Project on Technology, Human Values, and the Southern Future, 1974-79. Organist and music director at Holy Trinity Episcopal Church, Auburn. *Member:* Society for the History of Technology (program chairman, 1973), Lexington Group of Transportation Historians, Phi Beta Kappa, Phi Kappa Phi, Delta Sigma Rho, Phi Delta Theta.

AWARDS, HONORS: Three grants from National Endowment for the Humanities; summer grants from State University of New York Research Foundation, Eleutherian Mills Historical Library, and Auburn University Research Foundation; fellow at National Humanities Center, University of Chicago, 1978-79.

WRITINGS: From Newgate to Dannemora: The Rise of the Penitentiary in New York, 1796-1848, Cornell University Press, 1965; (editor with David T. Gilchrist) *Economic Change in the Civil War Era,* Eleutherian Mills-Hagley Foundation, 1965; *Iron and Steel in America,* Hagley Museum, 1976; (editor with B. Eugene Griessman) *The Southern Mystique: The Impact of Technology on Human Values in a Changing Region,* University of Alabama Press, 1977; (with Wesley Phillips Newton) *Delta: The History of an Airline,* University of Georgia Press, 1979.

Contributor: Kenneth S. Lynn, editor, *The Professions in America,* Houghton, 1965; Melvin Kranzberg and Carroll W. Pursell, editors, *Technology in Western Civilization,* Oxford University Press, 1967; Stanley Coben and Lorman Ratner, editors, *The Development of an American Culture,* Prentice-Hall, 1970; Edward T. James and others, editors, *Notable American Women,* Harvard University Press, 1971. Contributor to *Dictionary of American Biography, Encyclopedia of American History,* and *Encyclopedia of Southern History.* Contributor of articles and reviews to periodicals, including *Technology and Culture, Pennsylvania Magazine of History and Biography,* and *Business History Review.*

WORK IN PROGRESS: A history of All American Aviation, a predecessor of U.S. Air, from 1937 to 1948.

* * *

LIGHTNER, A. M.
See HOPF, Alice L(ightner)

* * *

LINDSLEY, Mary F(rances)
(Mary L. Jaffee)

PERSONAL: Born in New York, N.Y.; daughter of Guy Robert (an actor) and Florence (Everett) Lindsley; married Irving Lincoln Jaffee (a writer), January 26, 1963. *Education:* Hunter College (now Hunter College of the City University of New York), A.B., 1929; Columbia University, M.A., 1932. *Politics:* Independent. *Religion:* Roman Catholic. *Home:* 13361 El Dorado, Apt. 201H, Seal Beach, Calif. 90740.

CAREER: Hunter College (now Hunter College of the City University of New York), New York, N.Y., instructor, 1930-

55, assistant professor, 1955-68, associate professor of English literature and creative writing, 1968-71; writer, 1971—. Conducted weekly radio talk show, "Prose and Poetry," California State University, Long Beach, 1978-80; trustee and acting vice-president, World University, Tucson, Ariz., 1982—.

MEMBER: International Biographical Society (fellow), International Institute of Community Service (fellow), United Poets Laureate International, World Poetry Society, Poetry Society of America, Accademia Leonardo da Vinci (honorary representative; member of board of directors), Dickens Fellowship, New York Poetry Forum (California representative; life member), California Federation of Chaparral Poets (president of Orpheus chapter, 1974-76), Sherlock Holmes Society of Los Angeles.

AWARDS, HONORS: Accademia Leonardo da Vinci, bronze medal, 1965, silver medal, 1966; President Marcos Medal from the Philippines, 1968; golden laurel crown from United Poets Laureate International, 1968, 1969, 1973, 1975; D.H.L. from Free University of Asia, 1969; trophy from California Olympiad of the Arts, 1972, 1976; medal from Chinese Poetry Society, 1973; Order of Merit of Eight Chinese Virtues from World University, Hong Kong, 1973; D.L.A. from Great China Arts College of World University, 1973; Order of Merit of Six Chinese Arts, 1974; American Song Festival prize, 1981, for song lyrics; D.Litt., World University, 1982.

WRITINGS—Poetry books, except as indicated; published by Accademia Leonardo da Vinci, except as indicated: *The Uncensored Letter and Other Poems,* Island Press Cooperative, 1949; *Grand Tour and Other Poems,* Philosophical Library, 1952; *Promenade,* 1965; *Pomp and Circumstance,* 1966; *Pax Romana,* 1967; *Selected Poems,* Gaus, 1967; *Atma,* 1968; *Rosaria,* 1969.

Work Day of Pierre Toussaint, 1970; *Circe and the Unicorn,* 1971; *The Masquers,* 1972; (under name Mary L. Jaffee, with husband, Irving Lincoln Jaffee) *Beyond Baker Street* (short stories), Pontine, 1973; *One Life,* 1974; *Anarch's Hand,* 1974; *Night on the Saxon Shore,* 1975; *American Cavalcade,* Dorrance, 1975; *Wasp in Amber,* 1976; *Marvelous Boy,* 1977; *Song of Mr. Cibber,* 1978; *Age of Reason,* Triton Press, 1979; *A Narrow Mind,* 1980; *Dr. Burney's Daughter,* 1981; *Crisis in Counterpoint,* Happy Publishers, 1982; *Georgina,* Happy Publishers, 1982.

Author, with Christine Solomon, of three-act play "The Flimflammers," produced in Seal Beach, Calif., 1974; also author, with Solomon, Laura Steele, and Ethol Pullen, of Bicentennial program "California under Nine Flags," produced in Seal Beach, 1976. Editor of column "Magic Casements," *Seal Beach Journal,* 1979-80.

WORK IN PROGRESS: Centennial Child, a novel about life on the stage in the late 1800s and early 1900s.

SIDELIGHTS: Mary F. Lindsley writes: "I believe that an author has under all his humor the obligation to present the truth as he sees it; to ridicule and oppose what is evil, and to inspire his readers to ideals, constructive action, compassion, and, above all, hope." *Avocational interests:* Play production, photography, cartooning, travel (Europe and Asia).

* * *

LIPPINCOTT, David (McCord) 1925-

PERSONAL: Born June 17, 1925, in New York, N.Y.; son of William Jackson (a banker) and Dorothy (McCord) Lippincott; married Joan Bentley, October 16, 1959; children: Christopher Bentley. *Education:* Yale University, B.A., 1949. *Politics:* Independent. *Religion:* Episcopalian. *Home and office:* 655 Park Ave., New York, N.Y. 10021; and Birch Mill Rd., Old Lyme, Conn. 06371. *Agent:* Jane Rotrosen Agency, 318 East 51st St., New York, N.Y. 10022.

CAREER: McCann-Erickson, Inc. (advertising firm), New York, N.Y., copywriter, 1950-53, television head, 1953-58, vice-president and associate creative director, 1958-63, senior vice-president, 1963-69 and 1969-70, executive director of McCann-Erickson Ltd. in England, 1965-66; Erwin-Wasey, Ruthrauf & Ryan (advertising firm), Los Angeles, Calif., vice-chairman of the board of directors, 1967-68. Novelist, composer-lyricist, and television writer, 1950—. Managing director of Center for Advanced Practices, Interpublic Group of Companies, 1963-66. *Military service:* U.S. Army Intelligence, 1943-45; received Bronze Star. *Member:* American Society of Composers, Authors, and Publishers, American Guild of Authors and Composers, The Players (New York City).

WRITINGS—Novels: *E Pluribus Bang!,* Viking, 1971; *Voice of Armageddon,* Putnam, 1974; *Tremor Violet,* Putnam, 1975; *Blood of October,* W. H. Allen, 1977; *Savage Ransom,* Rawson Wade, 1978; *Salt Mine,* Viking, 1979; *Dark Prism,* W. H. Allen, 1980; *Unholy Mourning,* Dell, 1982.

Author of television plays for Columbia Broadcasting System, Inc., "Peter Who Wished" and "The Dog." Composer-lyricist of the Liberty record album, *The Body in the Seine.* Also author of material for the Broadway revue, "Pleasure Dome" and of songs for "Poor Little Lambs," an Off-Broadway production.

WORK IN PROGRESS: The Nursery, The Home, and *Skin of the Snake,* all for Dell.

BIOGRAPHICAL/CRITICAL SOURCES: New York Times Book Review, November 22, 1970, July 7, 1974, August 10, 1975, May 13, 1979; *Times Literary Supplement,* July 2, 1971; *Observer,* April 9, 1978; *Time,* April 16, 1979.

* * *

LOBEL, Anita (Kempler) 1934-

PERSONAL: Born June 3, 1934, in Cracow, Poland; came to United States in 1952; married Arnold Stark Lobel, 1955; children: Adrianne, Adam. *Education:* Pratt Institute, B.F.A. *Home and office:* 603 Third St., Brooklyn, N.Y. 11215.

CAREER: Free-lance textile designer, 1957-64; writer and illustrator of books for children, 1964—.

AWARDS, HONORS: Sven's Bridge was named among the best-illustrated picture books of 1965 by *New York Times; Under a Mushroom* appeared on Child Study Association book list, 1971; *Book World* Children's Spring Book Festival Award, 1973, for *Little John; A Birthday for the Princess* was a Children's Book Showcase title, 1974; *On Market Street* was named a Caldecott Honor Book, received *Boston Globe/Horn Book* award, and was nominated for an American Book Award, all 1982.

WRITINGS—Self-illustrated; published by Harper, except as indicated: *Sven's Bridge,* 1965; *The Troll Music,* 1966; *Potatoes, Potatoes,* 1967; *The Seamstress of Salzburg,* 1970; *Under a Mushroom,* 1971; *A Birthday for the Princess,* 1973; *King Rooster, Queen Hen,* Greenwillow, 1975; *The Pancake,* Greenwillow, 1978.

Illustrator: Paul Kapp, *Cock-A-Doodle Doo! Cock-A-Doodle Dandy!*, Harper, 1966; Meindert de Jong, *Puppy Summer*, Harper, 1966; *The Wishing Penny, and Other Stories* (anthology), Parents Magazine Press, 1967; F. N. Monjo, *Indian Summer*, Harper, 1968; Alice Dalgliesh, *The Little Wooden Farmer*, Macmillan, 1968; Benjamin Elkin, *The Wisest Man in the World*, Parents Magazine Press, 1968; Barbara Borack, *Someone Small*, Harper, 1969.

Doris Orgel, *Uproar*, McGraw, 1970; Mirra Ginsburg, editor, *Three Rolls and One Doughnut: Fables from Russia*, Dial, 1970; Elkin, *How the Tsar Drinks Tea*, Parents Magazine Press, 1971; Theodore Storm, *Little John*, retold by Orgel, Farrar, Straus, 1972; John Langstaff, *Soldier, Soldier, Won't You Marry Me*, Doubleday, 1972; Cynthia Jameson, *One for the Price of Two*, Parents Magazine Press, 1972; Arnold Lobel, *How the Rooster Saved the Day*, Greenwillow, 1977; Janet Quin-Harkin, *Peter Penny's Dance*, Dial, 1976; Arnold Lobel, *A Treeful of Pigs*, Greenwillow, 1979.

Penelope Lively, *Fanny's Sister*, Elsevier-Dutton, 1980; Arnold Lobel, *On Market Street*, Greenwillow, 1981; Jane Hart, editor, *Singing Bee!: A Collection of Favorite Children's Songs*, Lothrup, 1982.

SIDELIGHTS: Anita Lobel's harsh childhood, spent in Poland during the thirties and forties, stands out in sharp contrast to the bright colors that she uses to illustrate her own and others' books for children. Although she and her brother were separated from their parents at the outbreak of World War II and together spent several months in a Nazi concentration camp in Germany, Lobel notes that the love and protection of their nanny enabled the children to successfully overcome these experiences. In a *Washington Post Book World* interview conducted by John F. Berry, the author-illustrator comments, "I really feel Nanny's affection colors my work, because I don't feel I have to portray the awful bleakness of the time."

In 1945, Lobel and her brother were rescued from the camp by the Swedish Red Cross and, two years later, were reunited with their parents through the assistance of a relief organization based in Stockholm. Lobel lived in Sweden until 1952, when her parents, who hoped to locate some of their relatives, decided to move to the United States. Although she had received some encouragement to become an artist, Lobel was interested in theatrical arts. Once settled in her new home, she began to participate in school play productions at Pratt Institute. Soon, she met and married her author-illustrator husband, Arnold Lobel. After graduating from Pratt, she started her own textile design business, which eventually developed into her present writing and illustrating career.

Reviewers have written favorably about her books, but, according to Berry, only with her later production have her "talents as a superb illustrator . . . finally [gotten] recognition." However, a sampling of reviews of her early books includes praise for both her writing and drawing abilities. A *Times Literary Supplement* reviewer, for example, comments on *Potatoes, Potatoes*, "[The book] is . . . beautifully executed by its author/artist." The critic adds: "It is so skillfully told that it holds the attention." Barbara Wersba, reviewing the same volume in the *New York Times Book Review*, remarks: "Mrs. Lobel's illustrations . . . [are] excellent picture-book fare; finely drawn and colored."

Although, as Lobel tells Berry, she and her husband used to work constantly from nine in the morning until late afternoon and then, after spending the evening with their two children, would go back to work and continue at their tasks until about 2 a.m., their growing reputations as writers and illustrators gives them more free time with which to pursue other activities. Lobel, for instance, has taken up acting again and has appeared in several Off-Broadway productions. "My ideal day now," she says in the interview, "is to work from nine until two in the afternoon at my drawing desk, then go to a rehearsal—if I'm lucky enough to have a part."

BIOGRAPHICAL/CRITICAL SOURCES: New York Times Book Review, October 1, 1967; *Times Literary Supplement*, June 26, 1969; *Washington Post Book World*, June 13, 1982.

* * *

LOESCHER, Ann Dull 1942-

PERSONAL: Born November 11, 1942, in New Jersey; daughter of Floyd N. (an insurance agent) and Ann (a craft teacher; maiden name, Spence) Dull; married Gilburt Damian Loescher (a professor of international relations), September 25, 1971; children: Margaret Madeline, Claire Helen. *Education:* Colby-Sawyer College, A.A., 1962; University of Connecticut, B.A., 1965; Southern Connecticut State College, M.A., 1968. *Residence:* South Bend, Ind., and London, England. *Agent:* Marilyn Marlow, Curtis Brown Ltd., 575 Madison Ave., New York, N.Y. 10022.

CAREER: Elementary school teacher in Niantic, Conn., 1965-68; American Community School, London, England, elementary school teacher, 1968-75, assistant principal, 1973-75.

WRITINGS—All with husband, Gil Loescher: *The Chinese Way*, Harcourt, 1974; *Human Rights: A Global Crisis*, Dutton, 1978; *China: Pushing toward the Year 2000*, Harcourt, 1981; *The World's Refugees: A Test of Humanity*, Harcourt, 1982.

AVOCATIONAL INTERESTS: Travel (has travelled in western Europe, Rumania, Hungary, Yugoslavia, the Soviet Union, Mongolia, and the People's Republic of China), photography, hiking, reading, cooking.

* * *

LOESCHER, Gil(burt Damian) 1945-

PERSONAL: Born March 7, 1945, in San Francisco, Calif.; son of Burt G. (a rancher) and Helene (Aachen) Loescher; married Ann Dull (a teacher), September 25, 1971; children: Margaret Madeline, Claire Helen. *Education:* St. Mary's College of California, B.A., 1967; Monterey Institute of Foreign Studies, M.A., 1969; London School of Economics and Political Science, Ph.D., 1975. *Religion:* Roman Catholic. *Residence:* South Bend, Ind., and London, England. *Agent:* Marilyn Marlow, Curtis Brown Ltd., 575 Madison Ave., New York, N.Y. 10022. *Office:* Department of Government, University of Notre Dame, Notre Dame, Ind. 46556.

CAREER: American Community School, London, England, principal, 1969-71; University of Notre Dame, professor of international relations in Notre Dame, Ind. and in Notre Dame Program, London, England, 1975—, assistant dean, College of Arts and Letters. Research associate, Catholic Institute for International Relations, London, 1982—. Free-lance photographer. *Member:* Amnesty International U.S.A. (member of board of directors), Royal Institute of International Affairs, International Studies Association, American Political Science Association, Association for Asian Studies.

WRITINGS: (With wife, Ann Dull Loescher) *The Chinese Way*, Harcourt, 1974; (with A. D. Loescher) *Human Rights: A Global*

Crisis, Dutton, 1978; (with Donald Kommers) *Human Rights and American Foreign Policy,* University of Notre Dame Press, 1978; (with A. D. Loescher) *China: Pushing toward the Year 2000,* Harcourt, 1981; (with A. D. Loescher) *The World's Refugees: A Test of Humanity,* Harcourt, 1982. Also special co-editor of *World Refugees,* annals of the American Academy of Political and Social Science. Contributor to *Yearbook of World Affairs.* Contributor of articles to numerous periodicals, including *The World Today, Survey, Political Science Quarterly,* and *Round Table;* contributor of photographs to newspapers and magazines, including *New York Times, London Times, Newsweek,* and *Nova.*

WORK IN PROGRESS: U.S. Refugee Admissions Policy: 1945-1982, with John Scanlan.

SIDELIGHTS: Gil Loescher writes: "As an academic whose professional field is international relations, I feel a responsibility to acquaint young people and general readers, as well as specialists, with the complexities of international issues. In today's interdependent world, young readers in particular need to understand intercultural issues."

AVOCATIONAL INTERESTS: Travel (has travelled in western and eastern Europe, the Soviet Union, Cuba, North Africa, and the People's Republic of China), reading, hiking, theater, most sports.

* * *

LOEWENBERG, Gerhard 1928-

PERSONAL: Born October 2, 1928, in Berlin, Germany; became U.S. citizen; son of Walter (a physician) and Anne-Marie (Cassirer) Loewenberg; married Ina Perlstein, August 22, 1950; children: Deborah, Michael. *Education:* Cornell University, A.B., 1949, A.M., 1950, Ph.D., 1955. *Religion:* Jewish. *Home:* 6 Brickwood Knoll, Iowa City, Iowa 52240. *Office:* Department of Political Science, University of Iowa, Iowa City, Iowa 52242.

CAREER: Mount Holyoke College, South Hadley, Mass., instructor, 1953-56, assistant professor, 1956-62, associate professor, 1962-68, professor of political science, 1968-69, chairman of department, 1963-69, acting academic dean, 1968-69; University of Iowa, Iowa City, professor of political science, 1970—, chairman of department, 1982—, director of Comparative Legislative Research Center, 1971—. Visiting lecturer at Smith College, spring, 1956, and Columbia University, fall-winter, 1966-67; member of visiting faculty at Holyoke Junior College, 1958-60, and University of Massachussetts Summer Session in Bologna, Italy, 1967; visiting associate professor at University of California, Los Angeles, summer, 1966, and Cornell University, spring, 1968. Board of trustees of Mount Holyoke College, member, 1971—, chairman, 1979—.

MEMBER: International Political Science Association, American Political Science Association, (executive council, 1971-73), American Association of University Professors, Inter-University Consortium for Political Research (council member, 1971-74; chairman, 1973-74), Midwest Political Science Association, Phi Beta Kappa.

AWARDS, HONORS: Fulbright grant for advanced Guggenheim fellowship, 1969-70; National Science Foundation grants, 1971-72, 1975-79, 1981-83; Ford Foundation grants, 1974-80.

WRITINGS: Parliament in the German Political System, Cornell University Press, 1967; *Modern Parliaments: Change or Decline?,* Aldine-Atherton, 1971; (with Samuel C. Patterson) *Comparing Legislatures,* Little, Brown, 1979.

Contributor: J. L. Finkle and R. W. Gable, editors, *Political Development and Social Change,* Wiley, 1966; Richard Rose and Mattei Dogan, editors, *European Politics: A Reader,* Little, Brown, 1971; Henry Steele Commager and others, editors, *Festschrift fur Karl Loewenstein,* Tubinger J.C.B. Mohr, 1971; Donald Schoonmake, editor, *German Politics,* Heath, 1971; S. C. Patterson and John C. Wahlke, editors, *Comparative Legislative Behavior: Frontiers of Research,* Wiley, 1972; Allan Kornberg, editor, *Legislatures in Comparative Perspective,* McKay, 1973; Karl H. Cerny, editor, *Germany at the Polls,* American Enterprise Institute, 1978.

Contributor to journals, including *Legislative Studies Quarterly, Social Science History, British Journal of Political Science, Comparative Politics,* and *Midwest Journal of Political Science.* Member of editorial board of *American Journal of Political Science,* 1973-76; managing editor of *Legislative Studies Quarterly,* 1976—.

WORK IN PROGRESS: How Political Leaders Cope with Conflict: The Influence of the Parliamentary Setting on Leaders in Belgium, Italy, and Switzerland.

AVOCATIONAL INTERESTS: Music, hiking, bicycling.

* * *

LOGAN, Jake
See RIEFE, Alan

* * *

LORANT, Stefan 1901-

PERSONAL: Born February 22, 1901, in Budapest, Hungary; came to United States in 1940, naturalized in 1948; married Laurie Jean Robertson (a lecturer), August, 1963 (divorced, 1978); children: Christopher Stefan, Mark Imre. *Education:* Attended Academy of Economics, Budapest, Hungary; Harvard University, M.A., 1961. *Home:* Farview, Lenox, Mass. 01240.

CAREER: Director, cameraman, and editor of films in Vienna, Austria, and in Berlin, Germany, 1920-25; *Das Magazin,* Leipzig, Germany, editor, 1925; *Munchner Illustrierte Presse,* Munich, Germany, editor-in-chief, 1926-33; *Weekly Illustrated* (pictorial magazine), London, England, founder and editor, 1934; *Lilliput,* London, editor-in-chief, 1937-40; *Picture Post,* London, editor-in-chief, 1938-40; writer and photojournalist in the United States, 1940—. *Member:* Authors Guild, P.E.N., American History Society. *Awards, honors:* Carey-Thomas Award, 1946, for *The New World;* LL.D., Knox College, 1958; Literary Award (Man of the Year), Pittsburgh, 1965; selected as one of "The 1000 Who Made the 20th Century" by *Sunday Times Magazine,* 1969.

WRITINGS: I Was Hitler's Prisoner, Putnam, 1935; *Lincoln: His Life in Photographs,* Duell, Sloan & Pearce, 1941; *The New World,* Duell, Sloan & Pearce, 1946, revised and enlarged edition published as *The New World: The First Pictures of America* (Book-of-the-Month Club selection), 1965; *F.D.R.: A Pictorial Biography,* Simon & Schuster, 1950; *The Presidency,* Macmillan, 1951; *Lincoln: A Picture Story of His Life,* Harper, 1952, revised and enlarged edition, Norton, 1969; *The Life of Abraham Lincoln,* McGraw, 1954, published as *The Life of Abraham Lincoln: A Short, Illustrated Biography,* New

American Library, 1961; *The Life and Times of Theodore Roosevelt,* Doubleday, 1959.

(Editor) *Pittsburgh: The Story of An American City,* Doubleday, 1964, revised, enlarged, and updated Bicentennial edition, Authors Edition, 1975; *The Glorious Burden: The American Presidency,* Harper, 1968, new edition published as *The Glorious Burden: The History of the Presidency and Presidential Elections from George Washington to James Earl Carter, Jr.* (Book-of-the-Month Club selection), Authors Edition, 1976; *Sieg Heil! (Hail to Victory): An Illustrated History of Germany from Bismarck to Hitler* (Book-of-the-Month Club selection), Norton, 1974; *Pete: The Life of Peter F. Flaherty,* Authors Edition, 1978. Also author of *My Years in England: Fragment of an Autobiography,* 1982; also author of filmscript, "Life of Mozart," 1920. Contributor of articles to periodicals, including *Life, Look, Saturday Evening Post,* and *New York Times.*

WORK IN PROGRESS: Four volumes of his autobiography, entitled *My Six Lives.*

SIDELIGHTS: In the United States, Stefan Lorant is perhaps best known for his books on the American presidential system. He has devoted his life to literary and artistic expression. His photojournalistic talents put him in the forefront of the field, and Duane LaFleche of the *Knickerbocker News* has dubbed him "the dean of American pictorial history."

Lorant's early career, like his later endeavors, involved the arts. In the 1920s he worked behind the camera in the Vienna and Berlin film industries. "Life of Mozart," appearing when he was nineteen years old, was his first major success. Twenty-two films in Berlin followed his career in Vienna, including the still-available "Life of Paganini." In 1921, he gave actress Marlene Dietrich her first screen test and later described the experience to a *New York Times* reporter: "I loved her on first sight, but I had to tell her sadly: 'Go home, darling, and get married; you have too little talent.' I'm glad we've remained good friends ever since I began to write."

Lorant's interest in American presidents began with Abraham Lincoln in 1933. While in Germany, the Hungarian-born Lorant was editor of the popular illustrated weekly *Munchner Illustrierte Presse* at the same time that Adolf Hitler was editor of the competing *Illustrierter Boebachter*. "Hitler was furious with me because I would not print anything about him," Lorant recalled to Tony Burton of the *Knickerbocker News*. Hitler's anger against Lorant surfaced in March of 1933 upon the Nazi invasion of Bavaria. Hitler ordered Lorant seized and thrown in jail for what the Germans termed "protective custody." A guard distributed reading material to inmates, and Lorant obtained a collection of Lincoln's works. He explained to a *New York Times* reviewer: "It was a German translation of Lincoln's letters and speeches, published around 1880. . . . It was the sort of book that many Germans would discard and give to prisons so that the prisoners can read it." Lorant commented to Mary Wiegers of the *Washington Post,* "You can imagine what a tremendous effect [the Lincoln book] had on me, reading words like 'with malice towards none, with charity towards all' in my situation." He further explained to Burton: "I was fascinated. In Hitler's Germany, it was like finding Jesus Christ when you're walking in the wilderness . . . when you need Him most."

While imprisoned, Lorant had the support of both the Hungarian government and the Hungarian Press Association. Their combined efforts to gain his release proved successful, and he left the jail six and one-half months after entering it. His experiences under the Nazi regime, recorded in a diary while an inmate, led to his subsequent book, *I Was Hitler's Prisoner.* The book, described by *New York Herald Tribune Book Review* critic Dorothy Thompson as one of "the most valuable first-hand reports which have come out of Germany since April, 1933," achieved much success throughout Europe and the United States. Thompson continues, "Lorant's book is the record of a bourgeois intellectual, of no strong political feelings, who presents in his terse narrative simply an array of case histories." She adds: "He is pre-eminently the journalist, the reporter, the born bystander and recorder. Faced with complete uncertainty, contemplating possible death, one thing excites him, one thing gives the whole horrible experience a purpose: that he is on the inside of one of the great stories of the world." England's edition sold approximately one million copies, the first record paperback sale for Penguin. The book was considered such a realistic portrayal of Nazi life that it was issued to the British military so they would be better acquainted with the enemy.

From Germany, Lorant traveled to England, where he continued in the field of journalism. He created three of the country's most popular pictorial magazines: *Weekly Illustrated, Lilliput,* and *Picture Post.* Each depended greatly upon Lorant's discerning eye for strong, evocative photographs. His philosophy about pictures demanded that they be natural and unposed, and that they should, as realistically as possible, reflect everyday life. His insistence upon realism and his instinctive ability to select meaningful photographs contributed to the popularity of his British publications.

Lorant came to the United States in 1940, where he immediately pursued his interest in Abraham Lincoln. He searched through the Library of Congress, public libraries, and photography studios and emerged with what soon became *Lincoln: His Life in Photographs.* The collection, containing unique photographs and historical material on the past president, elevated Lorant to the position of "Lincoln expert." He expressed his concern about this opinion to Burton: "It disturbed me very much because I felt it was superficial. . . . I didn't think I deserved the success." His subsequent efforts to validate the label led to his second and third Lincoln volumes. Of the 1969 revised and enlarged edition of his second Lincoln pictorial essay, Lorant commented to Wiegers: "Now I think there will be nothing new that can be added to the Lincoln biography. . . . It is relatively complete." For his Lincoln research, Lorant received an honorary doctorate from Knox College in Illinois on the 100th anniversary of the Lincoln-Douglas debates on the college's campus.

En route to increasing his knowledge of Lincoln, Lorant became enthralled with the entire American presidential past. He also published books on Franklin Delano Roosevelt and Theodore Roosevelt; his research culminated in a definitive volume entitled *The Glorious Burden: The History of the Presidency and Presidential Elections from George Washington to James Earl Carter, Jr.* This "truly impressive volume," according to the *Knickerbocker News*'s LaFleche, chronicles the life, times and issues of all the presidents' tenures.

Lorant counts among his admirers many famous individuals. His house contains what he calls his "Vanity Wall." Photographs adorning this wall show Lorant with Winston Churchill, H. G. Wells, John Kennedy, and Marilyn Monroe, among others. He especially treasures a shot of Marilyn Monroe, a Lincoln fan herself, holding his second Lincoln volume.

BIOGRAPHICAL/CRITICAL SOURCES: Stefan Lorant, *I Was Hitler's Prisoner,* Putnam, 1935; *New York Herald Tribune Book Review,* July 28, 1935, December 1, 1946; *Time,* July 15, 1940; *Picture Post* (London), October 2, 1948; *Knickerbocker News* (Albany, N.Y.), March 5, 1960, January 18, 1969; *Saturday Review,* March 1, 1969, February 14, 1970; *Sunday Times Magazine,* August 3, 1969, October 25, 1970; *New York Times,* October 6, 1969; *Washington Post,* December 26, 1969; *Hartford Courant* (Hartford, Conn.), April 19, 1974; *Authors in the News,* Volume I, Gale, 1976; *Listener,* September 1, 1977; *Creative Camera* (London), August, 1982.

—Sketch by Michaela Swart Wilson

* * *

LORD, Vivian
See STROTHER, Pat Wallace

* * *

LUBIN, Bernard 1923-

PERSONAL: Born October 15, 1923, in Washington, D.C.; son of Israel Harry (a businessman) and Anna (Cohen) Lubin; married Alice Weisbord, August 8, 1958. *Education:* George Washington University, B.A., 1952, M.A., 1953; Pennsylvania State University, Ph.D., 1958. *Office:* Department of Psychology, University of Missouri, Kansas City, Mo. 64110.

CAREER: U.S. Merchant Marine, 1943-48; intern at St. Elizabeth's Hospital, Washington, D.C., 1952-53, Roanoke V.A. Hospital, 1954, and Wilkes-Barre V.A. Hospital, 1955; University of Wisconsin—Madison, postdoctoral fellow in psychology at University Hospital, 1957-58; Indiana University, School of Medicine, Indianapolis, instructor in clinical psychology and chief psychologist to adult psychiatric and consultation services, 1958-62, assistant professor, 1962-64, associate professor of clinical psychology, 1964-67; Indiana Department of Mental Health, Indianapolis, director of psychological services, 1962-64, director of research and training, 1964-67; director of Division of Psychology, Mental Health Center, Kansas City, and professor at University of Missouri School of Medicine, 1967-74; University of Houston, Houston, Tex., professor of psychology and director of clinical training program, 1974-76; University of Missouri—Kansas City, professor of psychology, medicine, and education and chairman of department of psychology, 1976—. Diplomate of American Board of Examiners in Professional Psychology, and American Board of Examiners in Psychological Hypnosis. President, Midwest Group for Human Resources, 1966-69; president-elect, Indiana Public Health Foundation, 1967-68.

MEMBER: American Psychological Association (fellow), American Group Psychotherapy Association (fellow), National Training Laboratories (fellow), American Association for the Advancement of Science (fellow), Association for the Advancement of Mental Health Research and Education (secretary, 1962-67), Indiana Psychological Association (president, 1967-68), Missouri Psychological Association (fellow). *Awards, honors:* N. T. Veatch Award for distinguished research and creative activity, 1981.

WRITINGS: (Contributor) *Readings in Counseling and Guidance,* Macmillan, 1965; (with wife, Alice W. Lubin) *Group Psychotherapy: A Bibliography of the Literature from 1956 through 1964,* Michigan State University Press, 1966; (editor with E. E. Levitt) *The Clinical Psychologist: Background, Roles, and Functions,* Aldine, 1967; (with Levitt) *Depression: Concepts, Controversies and Some New Facts,* Springer Publishing, 1975, 2nd edition (with J. Brooks), Erlbaum, in press; (contributor) *Clinical Methods in Psychology,* Wiley, 1976, 2nd edition, in press; (editor with L. D. Goodstein and A. W. Lubin) *Organizational Change Source Book,* University Associates, 1979, Volume I: *Case Studies in Organizational Development,* Volume II: *Case Studies in Conflict Management;* (with W. O'Connor) *Ecological Models: Contributions to Clinical and Community Psychology,* Wiley, in press. Also author of two psychological tests. Contributor of more than 130 articles and reviews to professional journals.

* * *

LUDINGTON, (Charles) Townsend 1936-

PERSONAL: Born January 31, 1936, in Bryn Mawr, Pa.; son of Charles Townsend (an aeronautical engineer) and Constance (Cameron) Ludington; married Harriet Jane Ross, February 22, 1958; children: David Townsend, Charles Cameron, James Ross, Sarah Ross. *Education:* Yale University, B.A., 1957; Duke University, M.A., Ph.D., 1967. *Politics:* Independent. *Home:* 713 Shady Lawn Rd., Chapel Hill, N.C. 27514. *Agent:* Carol Brandt, Brandt & Brandt Literary Agents, Inc., 1501 Broadway, New York, N.Y. 10036. *Office:* Department of English, University of North Carolina, Chapel Hill, N.C. 27514.

CAREER: English and history teacher in Miami, Fla., 1960-62; University of North Carolina at Chapel Hill, instructor, 1966-67, assistant professor, 1967-72, associate professor, 1972-78, professor of English, 1978-82, Boshamer Professor of English and American Studies, 1982—. Fulbright lecturer at University of Lyon, 1971-72. *Military service:* U.S. Marine Corps, 1957-60; became captain. *Member:* Modern Language Association of America, American Studies Association, Southeastern Modern Language Association. *Awards, honors:* Awarded Mayflower Cup, Society of Mayflower Descendants in North Carolina, 1981, for *John Dos Passos: A Twentieth Century Odyssey.*

WRITINGS: (Editor with James Woodress and Joseph Arpad) *Essays Mostly on Periodical Publication in America,* Duke University Press, 1973; (editor) *The Fourteenth Chronicle: Letters and Diaries of John Dos Passos,* Gambit, 1973; *John Dos Passos: A Twentieth Century Odyssey,* Dutton, 1980.

WORK IN PROGRESS: A biography of the American painter Marsden Hartley.

SIDELIGHTS: Townsend Ludington's books *The Fourteenth Chronicle: Letters and Diaries of John Dos Passos* and *John Dos Passos: A Twentieth Century Odyssey* explore the life and writings of the famous American novelist John Dos Passos. *The Fourteenth Chronicle* is a collection of letters written by Dos Passos from 1910 to 1970. This compilation includes beautifully styled correspondence to literary friends such as Ernest Hemingway, tender, almost poetic statements of love to his first wife, and bold and spirited political expressions. A reviewer for *Choice* believes that *The Fourteenth Chronicle* is special "both in its easy delineation of Dos Passos's intellectual passage and in its poignant depiction of an eventful period of social change." And Peter Meinke writes in *New Republic* that this volume of letters "should help in fleshing out Dos Passos for his readers. . . . The main impression one gets from reading it is that of a decent and generous man of boundless enthusiasm and energy; if a satirist is a romantic with 20/20 vision, Dos Passos fits the description."

Ludington's second work on Dos Passos is a biography assembled after examining the novelist's writings, interviewing his family members and friends, and, of course, scrutinizing his correspondence. In *John Dos Passos: A Twentieth Century Odyssey,* Ludington explores both the public and private life of the great author, the growth of and changes in his literary style, and the drastic shifts in his political thought and involvement.

Daniel Aaron writes of this book in a *New Republic* review: "Untendentious and grounded on a generation of scholarship and newly opened collections of literary memorabilia [*John Dos Passos*] provides the fullest and most detailed record to date of Dos Passos's public and private life." And W. A. Swanberg remarks in the *Washington Post Book World* that Ludington "shows in full color Dos Passos the paradox, the self-contradiction, the eccentric of such proportions that the mere facts of his life would make arresting reading even had he no particular genius. . . . As biographer, [Ludington's] view is steady, informed, tolerant and researched in depth."

In his biography of Dos Passos, Ludington introduces the reader to a very young boy who was born out of wedlock and then sent with his mother to live in Belgium and England so as not to be an embarrassment to his father, who was a rich, successful, and married Washington lawyer. When John Randolph Dos Passos's wife died, he sent for and married Dos Passos's mother. As Daniel Aaron explains in the *New Republic:* "[Ludington] is particularly good on the childhood of Dos Passos. Without resort to psychoanalytic probing, he shows the mark of the bar sinister on the personality of a boy denied a proper father until he was fourteen."

Many critics agree that this lack of "psychoanalytic probing" makes the book unique. John Leonard writes in the *New York Times* that "Ludington is a conscientious biographer, a mole in the archives, so old fashioned as to be fusty. . . . He is steadfast in his refusal to psychologize. . . . He merely reports the facts, and quotes the reviews, and acquaints us with the incredibly busy itineraries . . . and moves on." Writing in *Saturday Review,* Donald Newlove remarks that Ludington is "world-minded, deft at memorable characterization of Dos Passos's parents and his many friends, alive both to social context and poetic detail, always fair toward but never inflating the writer's accomplishments. You care for Dos Passos in these pages." And finally, in a review published in the *Chicago Tribune Book World,* Clancy Sigal comments that the "great value of this restrained, calmly factual biography is that it may lead to a fresh assessment of a writer who had enormous influence in his time."

Ludington employs this same reporter-narrative style while discussing Dos Passos's political activities and the changes in his literary style over his lifetime. "An early darling of the proletariat," Donald Newlove comments in *Saturday Review,* "Dos Passos was bitterly disillusioned both by communism and his later 'chosen country' of capitalism." And of this aspect of Dos Passos's life Alfred Kazin writes in the *New York Times Book Review* that "the radical novelist arrested . . . outside Charlestown Prison for protesting the death sentence of Sacco and Vanzetti . . . ended up in Westmoreland County, Va., as a supporter of Barry Goldwater and a contributor to the *National Review.*" In a review of *John Dos Passos* published in the *Los Angeles Times Book Review* Herbert Gold remarks that Ludington's book is an "honest work, and enough of the evidence comes through to enable the reader to make his or her own judgment. That the biographer clearly likes his subject, is sympathetic to his career, is not a disadvantage."

Concerning Dos Passos's literary career, Gold explains further in the *Los Angeles Times Book Review* that Dos Passos "was a *writing* writer, one of the writingest of a generation that included Hemingway, Fitzgerald and Edmund Wilson." And Alfred Kazin comments in the *New York Times Book Review* that "without Dos Passos's inventiveness and social curiosity, without his daring to unite history and fiction, without his brilliant sense of the momentum carrying us along in our industrial mass society, a good deal of our present sophistication in fiction, in the classy new journalism, in even the formal writing of American history, would not exist. . . . Ludington brings all this out with clarity, exactness, moderation. Dos Passos emerges from his biography not a great man but an original. It is impossible to imagine his like today."

AVOCATIONAL INTERESTS: Travel in Europe.

BIOGRAPHICAL/CRITICAL SOURCES: Library Journal, August, 1973, October 1, 1980; *New Republic,* September 22, 1973, November 8, 1980; *Choice,* October, 1973; *New York Review of Books,* November 29, 1973; *National Review,* December 7, 1973; *Saturday Review,* October, 1980; *Los Angeles Times Book Review,* October 19, 1980; *New York Times,* October 23, 1980; *New York Times Book Review,* October 26, 1980; *Chicago Tribune Book World,* October 26, 1980; *Washington Post Book World,* November 16, 1980.

—Sketch by Margaret Mazurkiewicz

* * *

LUPOFF, Dick
See LUPOFF, Richard A(llen)

* * *

LUPOFF, Richard A(llen) 1935-
(Dick Lupoff; Ova Hamlet, Pascal Pascudniak, Addison Steele II; Dick O'Donnell, joint pseudonym)

PERSONAL: Born February 21, 1935, in Brooklyn, N.Y.; son of Sol J. (an accountant) and Sylvia (Feldman) Lupoff; married Patricia Loring, August 27, 1958; children: Kenneth Bruce, Katherine Eve, Thomas Daniel. *Education:* University of Miami, Coral Gables, Fla., B.A., 1956. *Politics:* None. *Religion:* Jewish. *Home:* 3208 Claremont Ave., Berkeley, Calif. 94705. *Agent:* Henry Morrison, Inc., 58 West Tenth St., New York, N.Y. 10011.

CAREER: Remington Rand Univac, New York City, technical writer, 1958-63; International Business Machines Corp., New York City and Poughkeepsie, N.Y., writer and director of technical films, 1963-70; full-time writer, 1970-82; various office positions, 1982—. *Military service:* U.S. Army, 1956-58; became first lieutenant.

AWARDS, HONORS: World Science Fiction Society, joint winner, with wife, Patricia Lupoff, of Hugo Award, for amateur science fiction magazine *Xero,* 1962, nominee for Hugo Award, 1975, for novelette "After the Dreamtime," and 1976, for short story "Sail the Tide of Mourning"; nominee for Nebula Award from Science Fiction Writers of America, 1972, for novella "With the Boomer Boys on Little Old New Alabama," 1975, for short story "Sail the Tide of Mourning," and, 1978, for novel *Sword of the Demon.*

WRITINGS—Nonfiction: *Edgar Rice Burroughs: Master of Adventure,* Canaveral, 1965, revised edition, Ace Books, 1974;

(editor with Don Thompson) *All in Color for a Dime*, Arlington House, 1969; (editor with Thompson under real name and contributor with Thompson under joint pseudonym Dick O'Donnell) *The Comic-Book Book*, Arlington House, 1973; *Barsoom: Edgar Rice Burroughs and the Martian Vision*, Mirage, 1976.

Fiction: *One Million Centuries*, Lancer Books, 1967; *Sacred Locomotive Flies*, Ballantine, 1971; *Into the Aether* (adaptation of his comic strip "The Amazing Adventures of Professor Thintwhistle and His Incredible Ether Flyer"; also see below), Dell, 1974; *The Crack in the Sky*, Dell, 1976; *The Triune Man*, Berkley Publishing, 1976; *Sandworld*, Berkley Publishing, 1976; *Lisa Kane: A Novel of Supernatural* (juvenile novel), Bobbs-Merrill, 1976; (with Robert E. Howard) *The Return of Skull-Face*, Fax, 1977; *Sword of the Demon*, Harper, 1977; *Space War Blues*, Dell, 1978; *The Ova Hamlet Papers* (contains material originally published under pseudonym Ova Hamlet), Pennyfarthing Press, 1979; *Stroka Prospekt*, Toothpaste Press, 1982.

Editor of *What If?: Stories That Should Have Won the Hugo* (anthology), Pocket Books, Volume I, 1980, Volume II, 1981; also editor of five volumes of previously unpublished miscellaneous writings of Edgar Rice Burroughs, 1963-64. Contributor to anthologies, including *Again, Dangerous Visions*, edited by Harlan Ellison, Doubleday, 1972, and *New Dimensions, 4*.

Author, occasionally under pseudonym Pascal Pascudniak, with Stephen W. Stiles, of comic strips, including "The Amazing Adventures of Professor Thintwhistle and His Incredible Ether Flyer," *Horbib*, 1964-65, "The Adventures of Isidore," *Jive Comics*, 1969, and "Professor Thintwhistle" (adaptation of his *Into the Aether*), *Heavy Metal*, 1980-81.

Science fiction book reviewer for *San Francisco Chronicle*, 1979-81. Contributor of short stories and articles to newspapers and magazines; contributor with Michael Kurland of short story "The Square Root of Dead" to *Mike Shayne's Mystery Magazine;* contributor under pseudonym Addison Steele II of short story "The Wedding of Ova Hamlet" to *Fantastic*. Co-editor with wife, Patricia Lupoff, of *Xero*, 1960-63. Book editor and reviewer, *Starship* (formerly *Algol*), 1968-79; west coast editor, *Crawdaddy*, 1970-71, and *Changes*, 1971-72; contributing editor of *Organ*, 1972.

WORK IN PROGRESS: Lovecraft's Book, for Arkham House; *Circumpolar!*, for Simon & Schuster; a novel, *Sun's End;* third and fourth volumes of *What If?: Stories That Should Have Won the Hugo*.

SIDELIGHTS: Richard A. Lupoff tells *CA:* "I've spent most of my intellectual life trying to become a 'good' writer (in the artistic sense) and a successful one (in the sense of making a living at it). I made my first sale (as a sports reporter) while still in my teens, sold my first book in 1965, and became a full-time author in 1970.

"In all modesty, I feel that I am at the peak of my career—artistically—but the market has been tending steadily downward for the past couple of years. After hanging on as long as I could, I've finally given up on full-time authorship and returned to an office job. For the first time in twelve years! Maybe I'll get back to full-time writing some day, or maybe this is how it's going to be from here on out. In any case, it was fun while it lasted!"

BIOGRAPHICAL/CRITICAL SOURCES: Analog: Science Fiction/Science Fact, July, 1977, February 2, 1981; *Magazine of Fantasy and Science Fiction*, summer, 1981; *Science Fiction Review*, November, 1981.

* * *

LUSSIER, (Joseph) Ernest 1911-1979

PERSONAL: Born February 21, 1911, in Fall River, Mass.; died March 9, 1979; son of Louis (an operative) and Victoria (Labonte) Lussier. *Education:* Angelicum, S.T.L., 1938; Ecole Biblique and Pontifical Biblical Commission, S.S.L., 1952.

CAREER: Ordained Roman Catholic priest of Congregation of Blessed Sacrament Fathers (S.S.S.), 1938; Blessed Sacrament Seminary, Cleveland, Ohio, professor of biblical literature, languages, and archeology, 1938-67; St. Mary of the Lake Seminary, Mundelein, Ill., professor of New Testament, 1968-74; Eymard Seminary, Hyde Park, N.Y., research professor, beginning 1974. *Member:* Catholic Biblical Association of America, American Schools for Oriental Research, Society for Biblical Literature and Exegesis, Catholic Biblical Association of England.

WRITINGS—Published by Alba House, except as indicated: *Commentary on Proverbs and Sirach*, Liturgical Press, 1965; *Getting to Know the Eucharist*, 1974; *Christ's Priesthood According to the Epistle to the Hebrews*, Liturgical Press, 1975; *Living the Eucharistic Mystery*, 1975; *The Eucharist: The Bread of Life*, 1977; *God Is Love: According to St. John*, 1977; *Christ's Farewell Discourse*, 1979; *Adore the Lord: Adoration Viewed through the Old Testament*, 1979; *Jesus Christ Is Lord: Adoration Viewed through the New Testament*, 1979.

Contributor to *New Catholic Encyclopedia* and to religion journals. Book review editor for *Emmanuel*, beginning 1965.

WORK IN PROGRESS: Priestly Living; Christian Living; Biblical Prayer.†

* * *

LUTZ, John (Thomas) 1939-

PERSONAL: Born September 11, 1939, in Dallas, Tex.; son of John Peter and Jane (Gundelfinger) Lutz; married Barbara Jean Bradley, March 25, 1958; children: Steven, Jennifer, Wendy. *Education:* Attended Meramec Community College, 1965. *Politics:* "Reasonable." *Home and office:* 880 Providence Ave., Webster Groves, Mo. 63119. *Agent:* Barbara Lowenstein, 250 West 57th St., New York, N.Y. 10019.

CAREER: Writer. Has worked in construction and as a truck driver. *Member:* Mystery Writers of America, Private Eye Writers of America. *Awards, honors:* Mystery Writers of America scroll, 1981, for short story "Until You Are Dead."

WRITINGS—Mystery novels: *The Truth of the Matter*, Pocket Books, 1971; *Buyer Beware*, Putnam, 1976; *Bonegrinder*, Putnam, 1976; *Lazarus Man*, Morrow, 1979; *Jericho Man*, Morrow, 1980; *The Shadow Man*, Morrow, 1981. Contributor of about one hundred fifty stories to magazines.

Contributor to anthologies: *Ellery Queen's Mystery Bay*, edited by Ellery Queen, World Publishing, 1972; *Ellery Queen's Murdercade*, edited by Queen, Random House, 1975; *Best Detective Stories*, edited by E. Hoch, Dutton, 1976; *Tricks and Treats*, edited by J. Gores and B. Pronzini, Doubleday, 1976; *Tales to Take Your Breath Away*, edited by Eleanor Sullivan, Dial, 1977; *Alfred Hitchcock's Tales to Make Your Blood Run Cold*, edited by Sullivan, Dial, 1978; *Tales to Scare You Stiff*, edited by Sullivan, Dial, 1978; *Dark Sins, Dark Dreams,* edited by Barry Malzberg and Pronzini, Doubleday, 1978; *Midnight Specials,* edited by Pronzini, Bobbs-Merrill, 1978; *Tales to Be Read with Caution,* edited by Sullivan, Dial, 1979.

Tales to Make Your Teeth Chatter, edited by Sullivan, Dial, 1980; *Ellery Queen's Circumstantial Evidence,* edited by Queen, Dial, 1980; *Tales to Make You Weak in the Knees,* edited by Sullivan, Dial, 1981; *Arbor House Treasury of Mystery and Suspense,* edited by Pronzini, Malzberg, and Martin Greenberg, Arbor House, 1981; *Arbor House Treasury of Horror and the Supernatural,* Arbor House, 1981; *Creature,* edited by Pronzini, Arbor House, 1981.

WORK IN PROGRESS: Short stories; a novel.

SIDELIGHTS: John Lutz writes: "It would be difficult for me to say exactly what motivated me to begin writing; it's possible that the original motivation is gone, much as a match that starts a forest fire is consumed in the early moments of the fire. I continue writing for selfish reasons. I thoroughly enjoy it."

* * *

LUZA, Radomir 1922-

PERSONAL: Born October 17, 1922, in Prague, Czechoslovakia; came to United States, 1953, naturalized U.S. citizen, 1959; son of Vojtech (a five-star army general) and Milada (Vecera) Luza; married Libuse Podhrazska, February 5, 1949; children: Radomir V., Sabrina. *Education:* Masaryk University, Ju.Dr., 1948; New York University, M.A., 1957, Ph.D., 1959. *Home:* 839 Roseland Pkwy., New Orleans, La. 70118. *Office:* Department of History, Tulane University, New Orleans, La. 70118.

CAREER: A member of the Czechoslovakia Resistance, Luza was jailed by the Gestapo in 1941 and lived underground during the rest of World War II; became deputy commanding officer of the Partisan Brigade and later headed the Social Democratic Youth in Czechoslovakia; escaped to France after the Communist take-over in 1948 and remained in Paris until 1953, when he came to the United States; M.L. Annenberg Foundation, Philadelphia, Pa., research associate, 1960-62; Educational Fund, Inc., Detroit, Mich., European representative, 1963-66; Louisiana State University, New Orleans, associate professor of modern European history, 1966-67; Tulane University, New Orleans, professor of history, 1967—. Visiting professor, University of Hamburg, 1969-70. Member of Council of Free Czechoslovakia, Washington, D.C., 1960—. *Member:* American Historical Association, Association for the Advancement of Slavic Studies, and numerous American historical associations. *Awards, honors:* Received award from Theodor Koerner Foundation, 1965; grants from Social Research Council, 1969, American Philosophical Society, 1971, 1975, and American Council on Learned Societies, 1972, 1977.

WRITINGS: Odsun: Prispevek k historii ceskonemeckych vztahu v letech 1918-1952, Nase Cesta, 1952; *The Transfer of the Sudeten Germans: A Study of Czech-German Relations, 1933-62,* New York University Press, 1964; *History of the International Socialist Youth Movement,* Sijthoff, 1970; (editor with Victor S. Mamatey) *A History of the Czechoslovak Republic, 1918-1948,* Princeton University Press, 1973; *Austro-German Relations in the Auschluss Era,* Princeton University Press, 1975; *Oesterreich in der NS-Zeit,* Boehlau, 1977. Member of editorial board of *Svedectvi,* an exile Czechoslovak political review, and of *IUSY Bulletin.*

LUZI, Mario 1914-

PERSONAL: Born October 20, 1914, in Florence, Italy; son of Margherita (Papini) Luzi; married Elena Monale (a teacher), June 20, 1942; children: Gianni. *Education:* University of Florence, D.Ph., 1936. *Religion:* Catholic. *Home:* Bellariva 20, Florence, Italy 50136.

CAREER: Poet. University of Florence, Florence, Italy, professor of French literature, 1938—. *Awards, honors:* Premio Marzotto Narrative o Poesia, 1957, for *Onore del vero;* Premio Taormina, 1964, for *Nel magma.*

WRITINGS: Un'illusione platonica e altri saggi (essays), Edizioni di Rivoluzione (Florence), 1941, enlarged edition, M. Boni (Bologna), 1972; *Biografia a Ebe,* Vallecchi (Florence), 1942; *Un brindisi* (poetry), G. C. Sansoni (Florence), 1946; *L'inferno e il limbo* (essays; title means "Hell and Limbo"), Marzocco (Florence), 1949, enlarged edition, Casa editrice Il Saggiatore (Milan), 1964.

Primizie del deserto (poetry; title means "First Fruits of the Desert"), Schwarz (Milan), 1952; *Studio su Mallarme,* G. C. Sansoni, 1952; *Aspetti della generazione napoleonica: e Ed altri soggi di litteratura francese* (essays), Guanda (Parma), 1956; *Onore del vero* (poetry; title means "Honor of Truth"), N. Pozza (Venice), 1957; (editor) *L'idea simbolista,* Garzanti (Milan), 1959.

Il giusto dell vita (poetry; title means "What Is Right in Life"), Garzanti, 1960, 2nd edition, 1971; *Lo stile di Constant,* Il Saggiatore, 1962; *Nel magma* (poetry; title means "In the Magma"), Garzanti, 1963, 2nd edition, All'Insegna del Pesce d'Oro (Milan), 1964, enlarged edition, Garzanti, 1966; *Dal fondo delle campagne* (poetry; title means "From the Bottom of the Field), Einaudi (Torino), 1965; *Tutto in questione* (essays), Vallecchi, 1965; (editor) *Faraoni* (memoirs of Enzo Faraoni), Galleria Pananti (Florence), 1969.

(Author of text with Mario de Micheli) *Cento opere di Carlo Carra,* Galleria d'arte moderna Fratelle Falsetti (Prato), 1971; *Su fondamenti invisibili* (poetry), Rizzoli (Milan), 1971; (with Carolo Cassola) *Poesia e Romanzo* (poetry), Rizzoli, 1973; *Ipazia* (one-act play), Scheiwiller, 1973, enlarged edition, Rizzoli, 1979; *Vicissitudine e forma* (essay), Rizzoli, 1974; *In the Dark Body of Metamorphosis and Other Poems,* translation by Isidore Lawrence Salomon, Norton, 1975; *Al fuoco della controversia,* Garzanti, 1978; *Tutte le poesie,* two volumes, Garzanti, 1979.

Trame, Rizzoli, 1982. Contributor to *Corriere della Sera* and *Il Giornale Nuovo.*

SIDELIGHTS: Mario Luzi is considered to be among the major Italian poets of the twentieth century, an artist who has "always been at the centre of modern Italian poetry," as Bruce Merry comments in the *Modern Language Review.*

Luzi's style, his poetic tone, according to Robert Mazzocco in the *New York Review of Books,* is primarily meditative, and he "conceives his themes generally against the coming of night, the break of day, silhouettes at noon; cherishes signs of Fate, Time, Woman, the Mother Church, of fire, smoke, dust, of rivers caught 'between thunder and lightning,' the exigencies of the Florentine flood; mythologizes the penalties of the day, spiritual and cultural unease."

"For Luzi," says Radcliffe Squires in *Michigan Quarterly Review,* "all experience alters, alters profoundly, yet the alteration alters only to lead the self into the self. . . . Luzi is a wonderful poet, so sure of his truth that he has no use for glitter.''

BIOGRAPHICAL/CRITICAL SOURCES: Modern Language Review, April, 1973; *Michigan Quarterly Review,* winter, 1975; *Times Literary Supplement,* January 24, 1975; *New York Review of Books,* April 17, 1975; *Contemporary Literary Criticism,* Volume XIII, Gale, 1980.

* * *

LYNNE, Becky
See ZAWADSKY, Patience

* * *

LYON, Lyman R.
See de CAMP, L(yon) Sprague

M

MABEY, Richard (Thomas) 1941-

PERSONAL: Born February 20, 1941, in Berkhamsted, England; son of Thomas Gustavus (a bank official) and Nelly (Moore) Mabey. *Education:* St. Catherine's College, Oxford, B.A. (honors), 1963, M.A., 1971. *Politics:* "Green." *Agent:* Richard Simon, 32 College Cross, London N.1, England.

CAREER: Dacorum College of Further Education, Hemel Hempstead, Hertfordshire, England, lecturer in social studies, 1963-65; Penguin Books Ltd., Education Division, Harmondsworth, Middlesex, England, senior editor, 1966-73; free-lance writer and broadcaster, 1973—. Visiting associate, St. Catherine's College, Oxford, 1982—. *Member:* London Wildlife Trust (president), Nature Conservancy Council, Green Alliance. *Awards, honors: Times Educational Supplement* Information Book Award, 1977, for *Street Flowers;* Leverhulme research fellowship, 1983.

WRITINGS: (Editor) *Class: A Symposium,* Anthony Blond, 1967, Dufour, 1969; *Behind the Scene,* Penguin, 1968; *The Pop Process,* Hutchinson, 1969; *Food for Free: Guide to Edible Wild Plants of Britain,* Collins, 1972; *Children in Primary School,* Penguin, 1972; *The Unofficial Countryside,* Collins, 1973; *The Roadside Wildlife Book,* David & Charles, 1974; *The Pollution Handbook,* Penguin, 1974; *Street Flowers,* Kestrel, 1976; (editor) Gilbert White, *The Natural History of Selborne,* Penguin, 1977; *Plants with a Purpose,* Collins, 1977; *The Common Ground,* Hutchinson, 1980; (with Tony Evans) *The Flowering of Britain,* Hutchinson, 1980; (co-author) *Back to the Roots,* Hutchinson, 1983; (editor) *Selected Prose of Richard Jefferies,* Penguin, 1983. Also author of frequent broadcasts for BBC-TV. Contributor to numerous periodicals, including London *Times, Punch, Illustrated London News, New Society, New Scientist,* and *Nature.*

WORK IN PROGRESS: Editing a collection of essays and articles, for Hutchinson; preparing biography and editing collected works of Gilbert White.

* * *

MacAODHAGAIN, Eamon
See EGAN, E(dward) W(elstead)

MACDONALD, Blackie
See EMRICH, Duncan (Black Macdonald)

* * *

MacDONALD, Craig 1949-

PERSONAL: Born September 26, 1949, in Oakland, Calif.; son of Franklin (an English professor) and Jane (Curry) MacDonald. *Education:* San Jose State College (now University), B.A. (with distinction), 1971.

CAREER: San Diego Union, San Diego, Calif., reporter, beginning 1972. Guest lecturer at San Jose State University, beginning 1971. *Military service:* U.S. Army Reserve, 1972—. *Member:* California Writers Club, San Diego Historical Society, San Jose State University Alumni Association, San Diego Press Club, Phi Alpha Theta, Sigma Delta Chi, Phi Kappa Phi. *Awards, honors:* McCormick journalism scholarship, 1972, for feature articles published in *Spartan;* Copley newspaper editorial fellowship, 1972; second place in J. C. Penney-University of Missouri Newspaper Journalism Awards and Pulitzer Prize nomination, both 1974, for six-part series on energy crisis.

WRITINGS: Cockeyed Charley Parkhurst: The West's Most Unusual Stagewhip (biography), Filter Press, 1973; *Ghost Town Glimpses,* Anthelion, 1975; *Leather'n Lead: An Anthology of Desperadoes in the Far West, 1820-1920,* Branden Press, 1976; *At Your Leisure,* Beta Book, 1980.

Contributor to *Ebony, Quill, Desert Magazine, Friends* (Chevrolet magazine), *California Highway Patrolman,* and *California Today.*

WORK IN PROGRESS: Books on western transportation and on the western migration of relatives.

SIDELIGHTS: Craig MacDonald crossed the Sierra Nevada range in a covered wagon and in a stage coach. He also swam the American River rapids in an effort to capture the flavor of early pioneers who ventured west.†

* * *

MACKEY, J(ames) P(atrick) 1934-

PERSONAL: Born February 9, 1934, in Dungarvan, County

Waterford, Ireland; son of Peter (an estate agent) and Esther (Morrissey) Mackey; married Noelle Quinlan, August 25, 1973; children: Ciara, James. *Education:* National University of Ireland, B.A. (with first class honors), 1954; Pontifical University, Maynooth, Ireland, B.Ph., 1955, B.D. (first place), 1957, S.T.L., 1959, D.D., 1960; Queen's University, Belfast, Ph.D., 1965; also attended University of London, Oxford University, Univrsity of Strasbourg, Institut Catholique, University of Heidelberg, and University of Vienna. *Office:* Faculty of Divinity, New College, University of Edinburgh, Mound Place, Edinburgh EH1 2LX, Scotland.

CAREER: Pontifical University, Maynooth, Ireland, assistant lecturer in Hebrew and Old Testament, 1959; Queen's University, Belfast, Northern Ireland, assistant lecturer, 1960-63, lecturer in philosophy, 1963-66; St. John's College, Waterford, Ireland, lecturer in philosophical theology and theology, 1966-69; University of San Francisco, San Francisco, Calif., associate professor, 1969-73, professor of philosophy of religion and theology, 1973-79; University of Edinburgh, New College, Edinburgh, Scotland, Thomas Chalmers Professor of Theology, 1979—. Visiting professor at Catholic University of America, summer, 1968, and University of California, Berkeley, autumn, 1974; lecturer at Belmont Abbey College, summer, 1970; has lectured in South Africa. Member of Center for Hermeneutical Studies, 1974—. *Member:* Irish Theological Association, College Theology Society. *Awards, honors:* British Academy research scholarship, 1964-65.

WRITINGS: The Modern Theology of Tradition, Darton, Longman & Todd, 1962, Herder, 1963; *Life and Grace,* Gill, 1966, published as *The Grace of God: The Response of Man,* Magi Books, 1967; (contributor) Donal Flanagan, editor, *The Meaning of the Church,* Gill, 1966; (contributor) Denis O'Callaghan, editor, *Sin and Repentance,* Gill, 1967; *Tradition and Change in the Church,* Pflaum, 1968; *Contemporary Philosophy of Religion,* Magi Books, 1968; (editor) *Morals, Law, and Authority: Sources and Attitudes in the Church,* Pflaum, 1969.

The Church: Its Credibility Today, Bruce Books, 1970; *The Problems of Religious Faith,* Franciscan Herald, 1972; (contributor) Paul Surlis, editor, *Faith: Its Nature and Meaning,* Macmillan, 1973; (contributor) Patrick Corcoran, editor, *Looking at Lonergan's Method,* Talbot Press, 1975; *Jesus: The Man and the Myth,* Paulist/Newman, 1979.

The Christian Experience of God as Trinity, Crossroads Press, 1983. Contributor to *Encyclopedic Dictionary of Christian Doctrine.* Contributor of articles and reviews to theology journals.

SIDELIGHTS: J. P. Mackey's books have been published in Spanish, French, Polish, German, and Italian.

* * *

MACMILLAN, William Miller 1885-1974

PERSONAL: Born October 1, 1885, in Aberdeen, Scotland; died October 23, 1974; son of John (a minister and teacher) and Elizabeth (Lindsay) Macmillan; married Jean Sutherland; married Mona Constance Mary Tweedie (a writer), 1934; children: Elizabeth Lindsay Macmillan Dow, John Duncan, Hugh William, Catriona Mary Miller. *Education:* Merton College, Oxford, B.A., 1906, M.A., 1920; graduate study at University of Aberdeen, 1907-09, and University of Berlin, 1910. *Religion:* Church of Scotland. *Home:* Long Wittenham, Abingdon, Berkshire, England.

CAREER: Rhodes University, Grahamstown, South Africa, lecturer in history and economics, 1911-16; University of the Witwatersrand, Johannesburg, South Africa, professor of history, 1917-34; University of London, London, England, Heath Clark Lecturer, 1938-39; British Broadcasting Corp., London, acting director of Empire intelligence, 1941-43; British Council, senior representative in West Africa, 1943-46; University of St. Andrews, St. Andrews, Scotland, director of colonial studies, 1947-54; University College of the West Indies, Kingston, Jamaica, acting professor of history, 1954-55. Hoernle Memorial Lecturer in South Africa, 1949. Chairman of Johannesburg Joint Council of Europeans and Africans, 1931-32; member of Advisory Committee on Education in the Colonies, 1938-41, and Colonial Labour Advisory Committee, 1946-52; served on official missions to Tanganyika (now Tanzania), 1950, to Bechuanaland Protectorate (now Botswana), 1951, and to other parts of Africa.

MEMBER: Institut Colonial International, Royal Society of International Affairs, Royal Commonwealth Society, Royal African Society, African Studies Association of the United Kingdom, Anti-Slavery and Aborigines Protection Society (honorary vice-president), Royal and Ancient Golf Club of St. Andrews. *Awards, honors:* Rhodes scholar at Oxford University; Chevalier, Royal Belgian Order of the Lion; Coronation Medal, 1953; D.Litt. from Oxford University, 1957, University of Natal, 1962, and University of Edinburgh, 1974.

WRITINGS: Economic Conditions in a Non-Industrial South Africa Town, [Grahamstown], 1915; *The Place of Local Government in the Union of South Africa,* W. E. Horton, 1918; *The South African Agrarian Problem and Its Historical Development,* Central News Agency, 1919, reprinted, State Library (Pretoria), 1974; *A South African Student and Soldier: Harold Edward Howse, 1894-1947,* T. M. Miller, 1920; *The Cape Colour Question: A Historical Survey,* Faber & Gwyer, 1927, reprinted, Balkema (Cape Town), 1968, Humanities, 1969; *Bantu, Boer and Briton: The Making of the South African Native Problem,* Faber & Gwyer, 1929, revised and enlarged edition, Clarendon Press, 1963, reprinted, Greenwood Press, 1979.

Complex South Africa: An Economic Footnote to History, Faber, 1930; *Warning from the West Indies: A Tract for Africa and the Empire,* Faber, 1936, reprinted, Books for Libraries, 1971, revised edition, Penguin, 1938; *Africa Emergent: A Survey of Social, Political, and Economic Trends in British Africa,* Faber, 1938, revised edition, Penguin, 1949; (with Charles Kingsley Meek and E.R.J. Hussey) *Europe and West Africa: Some Problems and Adjustments,* Oxford University Press, 1940; *Democratise the Empire: A Policy of Colonial Reform,* Universal Distributors, 1941.

The Road to Self-Rule: A Study in Colonial Evolution, Faber, 1959, Praeger, 1960; *My South African Years: An Autobiography,* D. Philip (Cape Town), 1975. Regular contributor to *New Statesman,* 1922-36, and to British Broadcasting Corp. program "Colonial Commentary," 1946-52; contributor to periodicals.

SIDELIGHTS: William Miller Macmillan based his South African historical writings on the previously unknown collected papers of John Philip, a controversial nineteenth-century missionary. Philip's papers were later destroyed by fire in the University of Johannesburg Library in 1931.

Macmillan's *The Road to Self-Rule: A Study in Colonial Evolution* has been translated into Italian.

OBITUARIES: AB Bookman's Weekly, December 2, 1974.†

* * *

MADISON, Arnold 1937-

PERSONAL: Born November 28, 1937, in Bayport, N.Y.; son of Arnold Alfred (a lithographer) and Jeanette (Tonder) Madison. *Education:* State Teachers College (now State University of New York College at Plattsburgh), B.Sc., 1958. *Home:* R.D. 3, Swart Hill Rd., Amsterdam, N.Y. 12010.

CAREER: Writer for young people. Public school teacher in Bethpage, N.Y., 1958-68; State University of New York at Albany, instructor, 1975-76; Institute of Children's Literature (home study school), Redding Ridge, Conn., instructor, 1976—. Actor at Wingspread Summer Theatre, Colon, Mich., 1957, and director of community theater productions. Instructor at writer's conferences, including St. Davids (Wayne, Pa.), League of Utah Writers, and Cape Cod Writers (Craigville, Mass.). *Member:* Mystery Writers of America, Authors League of America.

AWARDS, HONORS: Danger Beats the Drum was runner-up for Edgar Allan Poe (Edgar) Award of Mystery Writers of America as best juvenile mystery of 1966; *Pocket Calculators: How to Use and Enjoy Them* was selected by *Library Journal* as one of the best adult science and technical books, 1978; Golden Kite Award from Society of Childrens Book Writers, 1980, for *Runaway Teens: An American Tragedy; Carry Nation* and *Lost Treasures of America* were selected by Children's Book Council as "notable children's trade books in the field of social studies."

WRITINGS—Young adult fiction: *Danger Beats the Drum,* Holt, 1966; *Think Wild!,* Holt, 1968; *The Secret of the Carved Whale Bone,* McKay, 1969; *Fast Break to Danger,* Pyramid Publications, 1973; *It Can't Happen to Me,* Scholastic Book Services, 1981; *But This Girl Is Different,* Scholastic Book Services, 1982; *We'll Never Be the Same,* Scholastic Book Services, 1983.

Nonfiction: *Vandalism: The Not-so-Senseless Crime,* Clarion Books, 1970; *Drugs and You,* Messner, 1971; *Vigilantism in America,* Clarion Books, 1973; *Treasure Hunting,* Hawthorn, 1974; *Smoking and You,* Messner, 1975; *Carry Nation* (biography), Lodestar Books, 1977; *Aviation Careers,* F. Watts, 1977; *American Global Diplomacy,* F. Watts, 1977; *Lost Treasures of America,* Rand McNally, 1977; *Suicide and Young People,* Clarion Books, 1978; (with David L. Drotar) *Pocket Calculators: How to Use and Enjoy Them,* Lodestar Books, 1978; *Don't Be a Victim!: Protect Yourself and Your Belongings,* Messner, 1978; *Great Unsolved Cases,* F. Watts, 1978; *Arson!,* F. Watts, 1978; *Lacrosse,* McKay, 1978; *Runaway Teens: An American Tragedy,* Lodestar Books, 1979; *Surfing: Basic Techniques,* McKay, 1979.

Mummies in Fact and Fiction, F. Watts, 1980; *How the Colonists Lived,* McKay, 1980; *Polish Greats,* McKay, 1980; (revisor) Lee Wyndham, *Writing for Children and Teenagers,* Writer's Digest Books, 1980; *How to Play Girls' Softball,* Messner, 1981; *Transplanted and Artificial Body Organs,* Beaufort Book Co., 1981; (with Kevin Fredericks) *Born on the Edge* (dramatized autobiography), Clarion Books, 1983.

Also co-author of Institute of Children's Literature's "Writing for Magazines" course and author of three of the Institute's "Talk Abouts" concerning writing. Contributor of more than sixty articles, serials and short stories for children and adults to magazines, including *The Writer, Health, Teacher,* and *Treasure.*

SIDELIGHTS: Arnold Madison told *CA* that "theme is just as necessary to a mystery as to a straight novel. By choosing your characters and setting, you make a statement. Many juvenile mysteries are thin, mere fluff, because their only purpose is pure entertainment. My theme for *Danger Beats the Drum* was how hate can destroy you if you let it. In *The Secret of the Carved Whale Bone,* I wanted to say to the reader that we should open ourselves to progress and be prepared to capitalize on the positive aspects of change and combat the negative results. Although they are cloaked as mysteries, I think they are stated as validly as they would have been in an ordinary novel."

BIOGRAPHICAL/CRITICAL SOURCES: Writer, August, 1972.

* * *

MAGDOL, Edward 1918-

PERSONAL: Born September 14, 1918, in Brooklyn, N.Y.; married Miriam Sper; children: one son, one daughter. *Education:* University of Michigan, B.A., 1939; Columbia University, M.A., 1949; University of Rochester, Ph.D., 1971. *Home:* 3100 Lake Mendota Dr., Madison, Wis. 53705. *Office:* Department of History, University of Wisconsin, Madison, Wis. 53706.

CAREER: Viking Press, New York City, copy editor, 1946-48; high school teacher in New York City, 1949-52; free-lance copy editor and proofreader, 1952-56; *New York Times,* New York City, proofreader, 1958-59; Credit Union National Association, Madison, Wis., editor and feature writer for credit union publications, 1959-68, editor of *Everybody's Money* (magazine), 1964-68; State University of New York College at Potsdam, assistant professor, 1971-74, associate professor of history and chairman of department, 1974-81; University of Wisconsin—Madison, honorary fellow in department of history, 1981—. *Military service:* U.S. Naval Reserve, active duty, 1942-45; became ensign.

WRITINGS: Owen Lovejoy: Abolitionist in Congress, Rutgers University Press, 1967; (with John R. Prindle, Paul Butler, and Jerome Belanger) *It's Not Just Money,* Credit Union National Association International, 1967; *A Right to Land,* Greenwood Press, 1977; (editor with Jon L. Wakelyn) *The Southern Common People,* Greenwood Press, 1980; (contributor) Alan M. Kraut, editor, *Abolitionism in American Politics, 1830-1860,* Greenwood Press, 1982.

WORK IN PROGRESS: A collection of the speeches of Thaddeus Stevens; social composition of the American antislavery movement.

* * *

MAGUIRE, John David 1932-

PERSONAL: Born August 7, 1932, in Montgomery, Ala.; son of John Henry (a clergyman) and Clyde (Merrill) Maguire; married Lillian Louise Parrish, August 29, 1953; children: Catherine Merrill, Mary Elizabeth, Anne King. *Education:* Washington and Lee University, A.B. (magna cum laude), 1953; University of Edinburgh, graduate study, 1953-54; Yale University, B.D. (summa cum laude), 1956, Ph.D., 1960; postdoctoral research at Yale University, University of Tuebingen, both 1964-65, and at University of California, Berkeley, 1968-69. *Politics:* Democrat. *Home:* 709 North Harvard Ave., Claremont, Calif. 91711. *Office:* Office of the President, Harper East 105, Claremont University Center, Claremont, Calif. 91711.

CAREER: International Student Center of New Haven, Inc., New Haven, Conn., acting director, 1956-58; Yale University, Divinity School, New Haven, assistant instructor in systematic theology, 1958-59; Wesleyan University, Middletown, Conn., assistant professor, 1960-66, associate professor of religion, 1966-70, associate provost, 1967-68; State University of New York College at Old Westbury, president, 1970-80; Claremont Colleges, Claremont Graduate School and Claremont University Center, Clarmont, Calif., president, 1981—. Visiting lecturer at Pacific School of Religion, 1968-69; visiting professor of humanities, Silliman University, Republic of the Philippines, and Chinese University of Hong Kong, 1976-77.

Ordained Baptist clergyman; acting chaplain at Washington and Lee University, 1952-53. Permanent trustee and director, Martin Luther King Center for Social Change, Atlanta, Ga., 1968—; member of board of directors, 1971-81, and president of board, Nassau County Health and Welfare Council, 1974-76; president, Long Island Regional Advisory Council on Higher Education, 1970-80, and Long Island Community Foundation, 1977-81; director, National Association for the Advancement of Colored People Legal Defense and Educational Fund (West Coast), 1982. Trustee of United Board for Christian Higher Education in Asia, 1974-81, and Institute of International Education, 1981. Member of Connecticut Advisory Committee to U.S. Commission on Civil Rights, 1961-67; advisor, China Institute in America, 1974-81.

MEMBER: American Academy of Religion, Association of American Colleges (member of board of directors, 1981—), American Committee on East-West Accord (president, 1981—), Society for Values in Higher Education (fellow; president of board of directors, 1974-81), Phi Beta Kappa, Omicron Delta Kappa.

AWARDS, HONORS: Fulbright Scholarship to Scotland, 1953-54; Julia A. Archibald High Scholarship award, Yale Divinity School, 1956; Day fellowship, Yale Graduate School, 1956-57; lifetime Kent fellowship, 1957; Howard Foundation fellowship for postdoctoral study, and Fulbright travel grant to Germany, 1964-65; E. Harris Harbison Award for distinguished teaching, Danforth Foundation, 1967; selected by American Council on Education and *Change* magazine as one of 100 young leaders in American higher education, 1978; Litt.D., Washington and Lee University, 1979.

WRITINGS: Family Relocation under Urban Renewal in Connecticut, Connecticut Advisory Committee to the U.S. Commission on Civil Rights, 1963; *The Dance of the Pilgrim: A Christian Style of Life for Today,* Association Press, 1967; (principal author and general editor) *Reports from the Study of Educational Policies and Programs at Wesleyan,* 1967-68, three volumes, Wesleyan University, 1968.

Contributor: Wayne H. Cowan, editor, *Witness to a Generation,* Bobbs-Merrill, 1966; Ruth Shinn, editor, *Campus 70: The New Feel of Things,* CPCU Printers (Washington), 1970; Harold Hodgkinson, *The Identity Crisis of Higher Education,* Jossey-Bass, 1970; George Plimpton and Jean Stein, editors, *An American Journey: The Life and Times of Robert F. Kennedy,* Harcourt, 1970; Owen Gingerich, editor, *The Nature of Scientific Discovery,* Smithsonian Press, 1975; William Lovell, editor, *Religion and the Future of America,* National Council of Churches, 1975; Samuel Magill, editor, *The President as Educational Leader,* Association of American Colleges, 1976; *Asian and American Universities: Common Challenges, Mutual Contributions,* Riverside Press, 1977.

Contributor to numerous journals, including *Christianity and Crisis, Civil Rights Bulletin, Wesleyan Alumnus, Intercollegian,* and *Foundations: A Journal of History and Theology.* Member of editorial board of *Christianity and Crisis.*

SIDELIGHTS: An original "freedom rider," John David Maguire was imprisoned briefly in 1961 in his native city, Montgomery, Ala., for challenging segregated terminal facilities.

* * *

MAHER, Ramona 1934-
(Agatha Mayer)

PERSONAL: Surname is pronounced May-er; born October 25, 1934, in Phoenix, Ariz,; daughter of Raymond E. (a meteorologist and writer) and Josephine (Allan) Maher; married A. Roberto Martinez (a clinical psychologist), February 11, 1955 (divorced, 1957); married Tim Weeks (a lawyer and judge), June 16, 1960 (divorced, 1971); children: (first marriage) Ramon Esteban. *Education:* Texas Christian University, B.A., 1954; additional study at University of New Mexico, 1954-61 (intermittently), University of Washington, Seattle, 1964-66, and Arizona State University, 1968-69. *Politics:* Democrat. *Religion:* Methodist. *Home:* 326 West Dobbins Rd., Phoenix, Ariz. 85401.

CAREER: Writer. Fort Worth Youth Employment Service, Fort Worth, Tex., director, 1951-54; University of New Mexico Press, Albuquerque, editor, 1955, 1956-61; Kirtland Air Force Base, Shock Tube Facility, Albuquerque, technical editor, 1961-62; University of Alaska, College, assistant to academic vice-president, 1962-63; University of Washington Press, Seattle, managing editor, 1963-67; Arizona Historical Foundation, Tempe, editor, 1967-69; Arizona Education Association, Phoenix, editor, 1970-76. Founder with Joy Harvey, Baleen Press (private publishing house). Poetry readings at colleges, universities, and conferences. *Member:* Authors Guild, Romance Writers of America.

AWARDS, HONORS: First prize in *Seventeen* Short Story Contest, 1954; runner-up in Samuel French Playwriting Contest, 1954, for "When the Fire Dies"; *The Abracadabra Mystery* was winner of *Calling All Girls* Prize Competition (also sponsored by Dodd, Mead), 1961; Spur Award of Western Writers of America for best western juvenile, 1961, for *Their Shining Hour;* National Endowment for the Arts grant, 1969, and creative writing fellowship, 1974-75.

WRITINGS: When the Fire Dies (play), Samuel French, 1955; *Their Shining Hour* (juvenile western), Day, 1960; *The Abracadabra Mystery,* Dodd, 1961; *A Dime for Romance,* Day, 1963; (under pseudonym Agatha Mayer) *Secret of the Dark Stranger,* Dell, 1964; (with Tim Weeks) *Ice Island,* Day, 1965; *Secret of the Sundial,* Dodd, 1966; *Shifting Sands: The Story of Sand Dunes,* Day, 1968; *Mystery of the Stolen Fish Pond,* Dodd, 1969; *The Blind Boy and the Loon, and Other Eskimo Myths,* Day, 1969; (contributor) *A Part of Space: Ten Texas Writers,* Texas Christian University Press, 1969.

Secret of Grasshopper Hill, Dodd, 1971; *About Armadillos and Others* (poems), Baleen Press, 1972; *Lincoln County Poems,* Konocti, 1973; *The Glory Horse,* Coward, 1974; (contributor) Gary Elder, editor, *The Far Side of the Storm,* San Marcos

Press, 1975; *When Windwagon Smith Came to Westport,* Coward, 1977; *Alice Yazzie's Year,* Coward, 1977; (contributor) Lou Halsell Rodenberger, editor, *Her Work: Stories by Texas Women,* Shearer Publishing, 1982.

Poems represented in anthologies, including: *American Literary Anthology No. 2,* Random House, 1969; *From the Belly of the Shark,* Doubleday, 1973; *For Neruda, For Chile,* edited by Walter Lowenfels, Beacon Press, 1974; *The Indian Rio Grande,* San Marco Press, 1977; *Southwest: A Contemporary Anthology,* Red River Press, 1977; *Traveling America with Today's Poets,* Macmillan, 1977; *The Windflower Home Almanac of Poetry,* Windflower Press, 1980; *Dacotah Territory: A Ten-Year Retrospective,* North Dakota Institute of Regional Studies, 1982.

Also author of play, "Princess Scribble-Scrawl," distributed by National Association of Junior Leagues, and of plays produced by Dallas Little Theatre, Texas Christian University Players, and Columbia University. Author of monthly review column on juvenile books, *Arizona Republic,* 1969-71. Contributor of numerous poems, reviews, and juvenile stories to journals, magazines, and newspapers, Guest editor, *Mademoiselle,* 1954; co-founder and editor, *Inscape,* 1957-59, 1969-77; book review editor, *New Mexico Quarterly,* 1959-61, and *Arizona Teacher,* 1967-69.

WORK IN PROGRESS: A collection of new poems, for Konocti; short stories; a novel.

* * *

MALLORY, Mark
See REYNOLDS, Dallas McCord

* * *

MANNING, Bayless Andrew 1923-

PERSONAL: Born March 29, 1923, in Bristow, Okla.; son of Raphael Andrew and Helen Mahala (Guffy) Manning; married Marjorie Jolivette, July 10, 1945 (divorced, 1972); married Donna Dillon, March 7, 1972; children: (first marriage) Bayless Andrew, Jr., Elizabeth Jane, Lucia, Matthew Dexter. *Education:* Yale University, A.B., 1943, LL.B., 1949. *Home:* 345 Park Ave., New York, N.Y. 10022.

CAREER: Member of District of Columbia, Ohio, and Connecticut bars. Law clerk to Supreme Court Justice Stanley F. Reed, 1949-50; Jones, Day, Cockley & Reavis, Cleveland, Ohio, attorney, 1950-56; Yale University, School of Law, New Haven, Conn., associate professor, 1956-60, professor, 1960-64, chairman of Latin American studies program, 1958-60; Stanford University, School of Law, Stanford, Calif., professor and dean, 1964-71; president of Council on Foreign Relations, 1971—. Special assistant to U.S. under secretary of state, 1962-63; member of President's Advisory Panel on Ethics and Conflict of Interest in Government, 1961, President's Emergency Mediation Panel, 1967, and President's Commission on Campus Unrest, 1970. Member of board of directors, Aetna Life & Casualty Co., Scovill Manufacturing Co., J. Henry Schroder Banking Corp., and Schroder Trust Co. Consultant to Senate Committee on Government Operations, 1960, Peace Corps, U.S. Department of Commerce, 1961-62, and to Connecticut and California legislatures. *Military service:* U.S. Army, Signal Corps, Intelligence, Japanese translator, 1943-46; became first lieutenant. *Member:* American Society of International Law, American Academy of Arts and Sciences, American Bar Association, Phi Beta Kappa, Order of the Coif.

WRITINGS: (Staff director) *Conflict of Interest and Federal Service,* Harvard University Press, 1960; *Federal Conflict of Interest Law,* Harvard University Press, 1964; *American Legal Education: Evolution and Mutation* (monograph), Stanford University, 1969; *The Conduct of United States Foreign Policy in the Nation's Third Century,* Claremont University Center for the Claremont Colleges, 1975; *A Concise Textbook on Legal Capital,* Foundation Press, 1977, 2nd edition, 1981. Contributor to law journals, mainly articles on aspects of corporation law. Editor-in-chief, *Yale Law Journal,* 1949.†

* * *

MARAS, Karl
See BULMER, (Henry) Kenneth

* * *

MARCHANT, Catherine
See COOKSON, Catherine (McMullen)

* * *

MARINACCI, Barbara 1933-

PERSONAL: Surname is pronounced Mar-ee-notch-ee, the first syllable rhymes with "far"; born September 19, 1933, in San Jose, Calif.; daughter of Karl W. (an importer and writer) and Eleanor (Williams) Kamb; married Rudy Marinacci (an art director), August 30, 1958; children: Michael, Christopher, Ellen. *Education:* Attended Reed College, 1950-52, Stanford University, 1952, and University of California, Berkeley, 1953. *Politics:* Democrat. *Religion:* Unitarian Universalist. *Home:* 234 Twelfth St., Santa Monica, Calif. 90402.

CAREER: Dodd, Mead & Co., New York, N.Y., editor, 1955-60; founder and consultant, The Bookmill (editorial and graphic service), 1975—; Windsor Publications, Inc., Woodland Hills, Calif., editor-in-chief of history book division, 1980-82.

WRITINGS: *Leading Ladies* (collection of biographies of famous actresses), Dodd, 1961; *They Came from Italy* (collection of biographies of Italian-Americans in various fields), Dodd, 1967; *O Wondrous Winger: An Introduction to Walt Whitman,* Dodd, 1970; (with others) *California's Spanish Place-Names,* Presidio Press, 1980; *Take Sunset Boulevard,* Presidio Press, 1981; *Commodity Speculation for Beginners,* Macmillan, 1982.

WORK IN PROGRESS: A dramatization of New England's anti-slavery movement; a novel about a seven-generation California family with a Hispanic past; a collection of biographies of women in Los Angeles history; a biography of anthropologist Louis Leakey.

SIDELIGHTS: Barbara Marinacci told *CA:* "I have always been attracted to both writing and editing and cannot readily separate the two functions, whether working on my own books or on someone else's. This often confuses others when I refuse to be put in an either/or position. I have found that the editor's procedural and organizational skills can be highly useful and beneficial when writing, if I can suspend my almost automatic overcritical tendencies when doing a first draft. Then, when involved with other people's projects—which is largely how I earn a living—I usually find that my particular disposition and instincts as a writer, including intensity, absorption, playful phrasing, synthesizing concepts, evolving patterns, a creative word flow, and a convenient ability to become interested in and knowledgeable about almost anything, can assist me considerably, especially when I must rewrite, complement, or complete the author's own work."

* * *

MARRANCA, Bonnie 1947-

PERSONAL: Born April 28, 1947, in Elizabeth, N.J.; daughter of Angelo Joseph (a small businessman) and Evelyn (Mirabelli) Marranca; married Gautam Dasgupta (a critic), August 1, 1975. *Education:* Montclair State College, B.A., 1969; attended University of Copenhagen, 1969; graduate study at University Center of the City University of New York, 1973—; Hunter College of the City University of New York, M.A., 1976. *Politics:* Independent. *Religion:* Roman Catholic. *Home:* 238 East 9th St., New York, N.Y. 10003. *Office: Performing Arts Journal,* 325 Spring St., Rm. 318, New York, N.Y. 10013.

CAREER: Assistant to Broadway press agent Max Eisen in New York City, 1968; Theatre in Education, New York City, administrative assistant, 1970; assistant to playwright-producer Irv Bauer in New York City, 1970-71; New York City Department of Cultural Affairs, New York City, assistant in Street Theatre Division, 1973; Herbert H. Lehman College of the City University of New York, Bronx, N.Y., instructor in theater, spring, 1974; *Soho Weekly News,* New York City, theatre critic, 1975-77; publisher and editor with husband, Gautam Dasgupta, of Performing Arts Journal Publications, 1976—. Instructor in theatre, Richmond College of the City University of New York, summer, 1976. *Member:* P.E.N., New Drama Forum.

WRITINGS: (Editor) Richard Foreman and others, *The Theatre of Images,* Drama Book Specialists, 1977; *Theatre of the Ridiculous,* Performing Arts Journal Publications, 1979; *Animations: A Trilogy for Mabou Mimes,* Performing Arts Journal Publications, 1979; *American Dreams: The Imagination of Sam Shepard,* Performing Arts Journal Publications, 1981; (with husband, Gautam Dasgupta) *American Playwrights: A Critical Survey,* two volumes, Drama Book Specialists, 1981.

Contributor of essays and reviews to journals and magazines, including *Nation, Art in Society, Educational Theatre Journal, Margins, Village Voice, Viva, Rolling Stone,* and *Changes.* Co-editor of *Performing Arts Journal,* 1975—.

WORK IN PROGRESS: A book of essays on performance and drama.

SIDELIGHTS: Bonnie Marranca writes: "Whenever I am dealing with American theatre I try to emphasize its American roots, not out of patriotic feelings, but because I feel that critics have too often overlooked our American artistic heritage in favor of praising European influences. Over the last dozen years American experiments in art, dance, film, and theatre have synthesized in a truly American aesthetic that now makes New York the most exciting, innovative center of the arts in the world. It's time American institutions and the government realized this and started supporting the arts and our artists. Performing Arts Journal Publications is a special project of my husband's and mine. We started [it] simply because there was no public forum for good, solid, analytical writings on the performing arts."

AVOCATIONAL INTERESTS: Travel, visiting museums, browsing in book stores.

MARSHALL, James Vance
See PAYNE, Donald Gordon

* * *

MARTIN, Philip (John Talbot) 1931-

PERSONAL: Born March 28, 1931, in Melbourne, Victoria, Australia; son of Henry Martin (a public servant) and Lorna (Talbot) Martin. *Education:* University of Melbourne, B.A., 1958. *Religion:* Roman Catholic. *Office:* Department of English, Monash University, Clayton, Victoria 3168, Australia.

CAREER: University of Melbourne, Melbourne, Victoria, Australia, publications officer, 1956-60, tutor in English, 1960-62; Australian National University, Canberra, Australian Capital Territory, lecturer in English, 1963; Monash University, Clayton, Victoria, lecturer, 1964-70, senior lecturer in English, 1971—. Visiting lecturer at University of Amsterdam, 1967; visiting lecturer in Australian literature, University of Venice, 1976. Broadcaster for Australian Broadcasting Commission, 1962—. *Member:* Poets' Union of Australia.

WRITINGS: Voice Unaccompanied (poems), Australian National University Press, 1970; *Shakespeare's Sonnets: Self, Love and Art* (criticism), Cambridge University Press, 1972; *A Bone Flute* (poems), Australian National University Press, 1974; (translator and editor) *From Sweden* (pamphlet; poems), Monash University, 1979; *A Flag for the Wind* (poems), Longman Cheshire, 1982.

Poetry represented in anthologies, including: *Modern Australian Poetry,* edited by Douglas Stewart, Angus & Robertson (Sydney), 1963; *Australian Poetry,* edited by C. W. Crabbe, Angus & Robertson, 1972; *Dimensions,* edited by Bruce Dawe, [Sydney], 1973; *Antologia della poesia australiana contemporanea* (title means "Anthology of Contemporary Australian Poetry"), edited by Bernard Hickey, Nuova Accademia (Milan), 1977.

Author of book-length collection of translations "Selected Poems of Lars Gustafsson"; also author of numerous radio and television scripts. Contributor of poetry, articles, and reviews to Australian, British, and American journals.

WORK IN PROGRESS: A book-length poem on an orchestra conductor.

SIDELIGHTS: Philip Martin writes that he "regards broadcasting and translating as extensions" of his roles of poet and university professor. "My poetry," he says, "is modern-traditional rather than avant-garde and is concerned with love and death, with relationships between people, and with the continuity of past and present."

* * *

MARTIN, Ralph 1942-

PERSONAL: Born December 12, 1942, in New York, N.Y.; son of Ralph C. (a salesman) and Mary (Murray) Martin; married Anne Chapman; children: John, Mary, Elizabeth, Catherine, Rachel. *Education:* University of Notre Dame, B.A., 1964; Princeton University, additional study, 1964. *Address:* Renewal Ministries, P.O. Box 7712, Ann Arbor, Mich. 48107.

CAREER: National Secretariat for the Cursillo, Lansing, Mich., member, 1964-70; Word of God (Christian community), Ann Arbor, Mich., coordinator, 1970—; Renewal Ministries, Ann Arbor, director, 1980—. Member of Catholic Charismatic Renewal Service Committee, 1970—; director of International Communication Office of Charismatic Renewal Services, 1972-80.

WRITINGS: Unless the Lord Build the House, Ave Maria Press, 1971; *Hungry for God: Practical Help in Personal Prayer,* Doubleday, 1974, revised edition, Collins, 1975; *Fire in the Earth,* Word of Life, 1975; (editor and compiler) *New Wine, New Skins,* Paulist Press, 1976; (editor and compiler) *Sent by the Spirit,* Paulist Press, 1976; (editor and compiler) *The Spirit and the Church,* Paulist Press, 1976; *Husbands, Wives, Parents, Children,* Servant Publications, 1978.

A Crisis of Truth: The Attack on Faith, Morality and Mission in the Catholic Church, Servant Publications, 1982. Consulting editor of *New Covenant.*

* * *

MARTIN, Ralph P(hilip)

PERSONAL: Born in Liverpool, England; came to United States in 1969; married Lily Nelson; children: Patricia Ruth Losie, Elizabeth Joan Knode. *Education:* Attended Manchester Baptist College; University of Manchester, B.A., 1949, M.A., 1956; King's College, London, Ph.D., 1963. *Office:* Department of New Testament, Fuller Theological Seminary, 135 North Oakland Ave., Pasadena, Calif. 91101.

CAREER: Ordained Baptist minister, 1949; pastor of Baptist churches in Gloucester, England, 1949-53, and Dunstable, England, 1953-59; London Bible College, London, England, lecturer in theology, 1959-65; University of Manchester, Manchester, England, lecturer in New Testament, 1965-69; Fuller Theological Seminary, Pasadena, Calif., professor of New Testament, 1969—, director of graduate studies program, 1979—. Visiting professor at Bethel College and Seminary, St. Paul, Minn., 1964-65, and Fuller Theological Seminary, 1968; visiting lecturer at Institute of Holy Land Studies, Jerusalem, 1978, New College, Berkeley, 1979, Moore Theological College, Sydney, Australia, 1981, and Ridley Theological College, Melbourne, Australia, 1981. *Member:* Society of Biblical Literature and Exegesis, Institute for Biblical Research, Studiorum Novi Testamenti Societas.

WRITINGS: The Epistle of Paul to the Philippians: An Introduction and Commentary, Eerdmans, 1959; *An Early Christian Confession: Philippians II, 5-11 in Recent Interpretation,* Tyndale Press, 1960; (editor) *Vox Evangelica: Biblical and Historical Essays,* Epworth, Volume I, 1962, Volume II, 1963; *Worship in the Early Church,* Revell, 1964, revised edition, Eerdmans, 1975; *Acts,* Scripture Union, 1967, Eerdmans, 1968; *Carmen Christi: Philippians II, 5-11 in Recent Interpretation and in the Setting of Early Christian Worship,* Cambridge University Press, 1967, revised edition, 1983; *First and Second Corinthians, Galatians,* Eerdmans, 1968.

(Editor with W. Ward Gasque) *Apostolic History and the Gospel: Biblical and Historical Essays,* Eerdmans, 1970; *Commentary on Ephesians,* Broadman, 1971; *Colossians: The Church's Lord and the Christian's Liberty—An Expository Commentary with a Present-Day Application,* Paternoster Press, 1972, Zondervan, 1973; *Mark: Evangelist and Theologian,* Paternoster Press, 1972; *Colossians and Philemon,* Attic Press, 1974, revised edition, Eerdmans, 1981; *New Testament Foundations: A Guide for Christian Students,* Eerdmans, Volume I, 1975, Volume II, 1978; *Philippians,* Attic Press, 1976, revised edition published as *Commentary on Philippians,* Eerdmans, 1980; *Where the Action Is: Mark's Gospel Today,* Regal Books, 1976; *The Family and the Fellowship: New Testament Images of the Church,* Eerdmans, 1980; (editor with Peter Toon) *The Church in the Theology of the Reformers,* John Knox, 1981; (editor with Toon) *A Divine Sovereignty and Human Responsibility: Biblical Perspectives in Tension,* John Knox, 1981; *Mark,* John Knox, 1981; (editor with Toon) *Reconciliation: A Study of Paul's Theology,* John Knox, 1981; *The Worship of God,* Eerdmans, 1982; *Understanding the New Testament: Acts,* Broadman, 1982; *Understanding the New Testament: First Corinthians-Galatians,* Broadman, 1982.

Contributor: Carl F.H. Henry, editor, *Jesus of Nazareth, Saviour and Lord,* Eerdmans, 1965; C. A. Joyce, editor, *My Call to Preach,* Marshall, Morgan & Scott, 1966; F. L. Cross, editor, *Studia Evangelica,* Volume II, Akademie Verlag, 1964; Cross, editor, *Studia Patristica,* Volume VI, Akademie Verlag, 1966; I. H. Marshall, editor, *New Testament Interpretation,* Eerdmans, 1978. Also contributor to *A History of Christianity,* 1977.

Contributor to *New Bible Dictionary, New Bible Commentary, Baker's Dictionary of Christian Ethics, New International Dictionary of the Christian Church, Interpreter's Dictionary of the Bible, New International Dictionary of New Testament Theology, Illustrated Bible Dictionary, International Standard Bible Encyclopedia,* and *Zondervan Pictorial Bible Dictionary.* Contributor to theology journals.

* * *

MARTZ, William J. 1928-

PERSONAL: Born December 5, 1928, in Yonkers, N.Y.; son of Maurice H. and Mary (Hazel) Martz; married Nedra Dee Linville, June 20, 1953. *Education:* University of Rochester, B.A., 1950; Northwestern University, M.A., 1951; Yale University, Ph.D., 1957. *Office:* Department of English, Ripon College, Ripon, Wis. 54971.

CAREER: Middlebury College, Middlebury, Vt., instructor in English, 1955-58; Ripon College, Ripon, Wis., assistant professor, 1958-63, associate professor, 1963-65, professor of English, 1966—, Ralph Hale Ruppert Distinguished Professor, 1981. *Member:* Modern Language Association of America, Midwest Modern Language Association.

WRITINGS—Published by Scott, Foresman, except as indicated: (Compiler) *Beginnings in Poetry,* 1965, 2nd edition, 1973; *The Distinctive Voice,* 1966; *The Achievement of Theodore Roethke,* 1966; *The Achievement of Robert Lowell,* 1966; *Shakespeare's Universe of Comedy,* David Lewis, 1971; (editor) William Shakespeare, *Hamlet,* 1970; *The Place of "The Merchant of Venice" in Shakespeare's Universe of Comedy,* Revisionist Press, 1976; *The Place of "The Tempest" in Shakespeare's Universe of Comedy,* Coronado Press, 1978; *The Place of "Measure for Measure" in Shakespeare's Universe of Comedy,* Coronado Press, 1982. Author of pamphlet, *John Berryman,* University of Minnesota, 1969. General editor of "Modern Poets" series, for Scott, Foresman.

* * *

MASS, William

See GIBSON, William

* * *

MATTESSICH, Richard V(ictor) 1922-

PERSONAL: Born August 9, 1922, in Trieste, Italy; naturalized

Canadian citizen; son of Victor (a ship purser) and Gerda (Pfaundler) Mattessich; married April 12, 1952; wife's name, Hermine. *Education:* Attended Engineering College, Vienna, Austria, 1936-40; Vienna School of Economic and Business Administration, Dipl. Kfm., 1944, Dr. rer. pol., 1945; additional study at University of St. Gall, McGill University, Sir George William University, University of Michigan, and University of California, Berkeley. *Home:* 1807 Knox Rd., Vancouver, British Columbia, Canada. *Office:* Faculty of Commerce and Business Administration, University of British Columbia, Vancouver, British Columbia, Canada.

CAREER: Research associate, Austrian Institute for Economic Research, 1945-47; instructor at Rosenberg College, 1947-52, and McGill University, Montreal, Quebec, 1952-53; Mount Allison University, Sackville, New Brunswick, professor and head of department of commerce, 1953-59; University of California, Berkeley, associate professor of business administration, 1959-67; Ruhr University, Bochum, West Germany, professor, 1966-67; University of British Columbia, Vancouver, professor of business administration, 1967-80, Distinguished Arthur Andersen & Co. Professor, 1980—, Killam Senior Fellow, 1971-72. Chartered Accountant. Visiting professor, Free University of Berlin, 1965, Institute of Business Administration, University of Economics and Social Sciences, St. Gall, Switzerland, 1965-66, and Austrian Academy of Management, 1971-73; Erskine Visiting Fellow, University of Canterbury, Christchurch, New Zealand, 1970; guest lecturer, University of Osaka, Japan, 1972. Founder and director of Institute of Industrial Administration and Methodology, University of Technology, Vienna, Austria, 1976-78; member of board of governors, School of Chartered Accountancy, Institute of Chartered Accountants of British Columbia, 1981-82. Corresponding adviser to University of Punjab-Lahore, Pakistan, 1958.

MEMBER: American Accounting Association, Canadian Association of Administration Sciences, Philosophy of Science Association, Schmalenbach Gesellschaft, Academia Italiana di Ecomonia Aziendale (fellow). *Awards, honors:* Ford Foundation fellow, 1961-62; International Literature Award, American Institute of Certified Public Accountants, 1972.

WRITINGS: Accounting and Analytical Methods—Measurement and Projection of Income and Wealth in the Micro- and Macro-Economy, Irwin, 1964, reprinted, Scholars Book Co., 1977; *Simulation of the Firm through a Budget Computer Program,* Irwin, 1964, reprinted, University Microfilms, 1979; (editor with W. Busse von Colbe) *Der Computer im Dienste der Unternehmungsfuehrung,* Bertelsmann Universitaetsverlag, 1968; (editor and translator) R. N. Anthony, editor, *Harvardfaelle aus der Praxis des betrieblichen Rechnungswesens,* Bertelsmann Universitaetsverlag, 1969; (with others) *Matrix Accounting* (in Japanese), translation by S. Koshimura, Daisan Shuppan Ltd. (Tokyo), 1969.

Die wissenschaftlichen Grundlagen des Rechnungswesens, Bertelsmann Universitaetsverlag, 1970; (editor) *Topics in Accounting and Planning,* Faculty of Commerce and Business Administration, University of British Columbia, 1971; *Instrumental Reasoning and Systems Methodology: An Epistemology of the Applied and Social Sciences,* D. Reidel, 1978; (with Laurent Picard and others) *University Management Education and Research: A Developing Crisis,* [Ottawa], 1980; (editor and contributor) *Modern Accounting Research: A Survey and Guide,* Canadian Certified General Accountants Research Foundation, 1983. Editor of "Monograph and Reprint" series, Faculty of Commerce and Business Administration, University of British Columbia, 1967-71, 1973-74.

Contributor: Karl Devine, editor, *Readings in the Theory of Accounting,* University of Djakarta, 1962; T. H. Williams and C. H. Griffin, editors, *The Mathematical Dimensions of Accountancy,* South-Western, 1964; N. L. Enrick, *Management Operations Research,* Holt, 1965; Morton Backer, *Handbook of Modern Accounting Theory,* 2nd edition, Prentice-Hall, 1965; Williams and Griffin, editors, *Management Information: A Quantitative Accent,* Irwin, 1967; William E. Thomas, editor, *Readings in Cost Accounting, Budgeting and Control,* 3rd edition, South-Western. 1968; H. Kloidt, editor, *Betriebswirtschaftliche Forschung in internationaler Sicht,* Duncker & Humblot (Berlin), 1969.

Erich Kosiol, editor, *Handwoerterbuch des Rechnungswesens,* C. E. Poeschel Verlag (Stuttgart), 1970; C. J. Gibson, G. G. Meredith, and R. Peterson, editors, *Accounting Concepts,* Cassel (Melbourne), 1972; E. Grochla, editor, *Handwoerterbuch der Betrievswirtschaftslehre,* C. E. Poeschel Verlag, 1974; Grochla and N. Szyperski, editors, *Information Systems and Organization Structure,* De Gruyter, 1975; M. Schweitzer, editor, *Auffassungen und Wissenschaftsziele der Betrievswirtschaftslehre,* Wissenschaftliche Buchgemeinschaft, 1978; H. Mueller-Merbach, editor, *Quantitative Ansaetze in der Betriebswirtschaft,* Vahlen (Munich), 1978; G. Duglos, *Unternehmungsbezogene Konfliktforschung: Methodologische und forschungsprogrammatische Grundfragen,* C. E. Poeschel Verlag, 1979; R. R. Sterling and A. L. Thomas, *Accounting for a Simplified Firm Owning Depreciable Assets: Seventeen Essays and a Synthesis Based on a Common Case,* Scholars Book Co., 1979; J. J. Davies, editor, *1978 Accounting Research Convocation,* University of Alabama, 1979.

M. Gaffikin and M. Aitken, editors, *The Development of Accounting Theory: Significant Contributors to Accounting Thought in the 20th Century,* Garland Publishing, 1982; Stephen Zeff, editor, *The Accounting Postulates and Principles Controversy of the 1960s,* Garland Publishing, 1982; Fritz Machlup and Una Mansfield, editors, *The Study of Information: Interdisciplinary Messages,* Wiley, 1983. Contributor to several other books and to proceedings of professional organizations and conferences.

Contributor of articles and reviews to professional journals, including *Accounting Review, Management International, Quarterly Review of Economics and Business, Journal of Accounting Research,* and *American Economic Review.* Member of editorial board, *Economia Aziendale.*

SIDELIGHTS: Richard V. Mattessich was photographer, producer, and director of two 16 mm. films, "White City at the Golden Gate" and "Between Pacific and Sierra Nevada."

* * *

MATTHEWS, Clayton (Hartley) 1918- (Patty Brisco, a joint pseudonym)

PERSONAL: Born October 24, 1918, in Waurika, Okla.; son of Virgil and Mittie Jane Matthews; married Patricia Anne Brisco (a writer), November 3, 1972. *Education:* Attended John Tarleton Junior College, 1937. *Politics:* Democrat. *Religion:* None. *Home and office:* 3783 Latrobe St., Los Angeles, Calif. 90031. *Agent:* Jay Garon, Jay Garon-Brooke Associates, Inc., 415 Central Park W., New York, N.Y. 10025.

CAREER: Writer. Has worked as a surveyor, animal trainer in a carnival, carnival barker, and truck driver. *Member:* Mystery Writers of America (vice-president of Southern California chapter, 1968-69), Writers Guild of America (Western division).

WRITINGS: A Rage of Desire, Monarch Books, 1960; *The Strange Ways of Love,* Monarch Books, 1961; *The Promiscuous Doll,* Monarch Books, 1962; *Faithless,* Monarch Books, 1962; *Nude Running,* Monarch Books, 1963; *The Corrupter,* Monarch Books, 1963; *Hypnotism for the Millions,* Sherbourne, 1968; *Secret and Psychic Organizations for the Millions,* Sherbourne, 1969; *Dive into Death,* Sherbourne, 1969.

The Mendoza File, Powell Publications, 1970; *Nylon Nightmare,* Powell Publications, 1970; *Hager's Castle,* Powell Publications, 1970; (contributor) Allen J. Hubin, editor, *Best Detective Stories of the Year* (anthology), Dutton, 24th edition, 1970, 25th edition, 1971; (contributor) Edward D. Hoch, editor, *Dear Dead Days* (anthology), Walker & Co., 1972; (with Gary Brandner) *Saturday Night in Milwaukee,* Curtis Books, 1973; *Bounty Hunt at Ballarat,* Pinnacle Books, 1973; *141 Terrace Drive,* Berkley Publishing, 1974; *River Falls,* Berkley Publishing, 1974; (with Arthur Moore) *Las Vegas,* Pocket Books, 1974; *The Big Score,* Brandon Books, 1974; *New Orleans,* Pocket Books, 1975; *The Negotiator,* Pyramid Publications, 1975; *Hong Kong,* Pocket Books, 1976; *Dallas,* Pocket Books, 1976; *The Power Seekers,* Pinnacle Books, 1978; *The Harvesters,* Pinnacle Books, 1979.

The Birthright (first novel in trilogy), Pinnacle Books, 1980; (with wife, Patricia Matthews) *Midnight Whispers,* Bantam, 1981; (with P. Matthews) *Empire,* Bantam, 1982; *The Disinherited* (second novel in trilogy), Bantam, 1983.

With wife, Patricia Matthews; under joint pseudonym Patty Brisco; gothics, except as indicated: *Merry's Treasure* (juvenile), Avalon Books, 1969; *Horror at Gull House,* Belmont-Tower, 1972; *House of Candles,* Manor, 1973; *The Crystal Window,* Avon, 1973; *Mist of Evil,* Manor, 1976.

Contributor of about thirty stories to mystery magazines and adventure publications, including *Alfred Hitchcock's Mystery Magazine, Mike Shayne Mystery Magazine,* and *Manhunt.*

* * *

MATTHEWS, Patricia (Anne) 1927- (Patty Brisco; Laurie Wylie)

PERSONAL: Born July 1, 1927, in San Fernando, Calif.; daughter of Roy Oliver and Gladys (Gable) Ernst; married Marvin Owen Brisco, December 21, 1946 (divorced); married Clayton Hartley Matthews (a writer), November 3, 1972; children: (first marriage) Michael Arvie, David Roy. *Education:* Attended Pasadena Junior College, 1942-45, Mt. San Antonio Junior College, 1953, and Los Angeles State College of Applied Arts and Sciences (now California State Univeristy, Los Angeles), 1960. *Home:* 3783 Latrobe St., Los Angeles, Calif. 90031.

CAREER: Writer. California State University, Los Angeles, secretary to general manager of Associated Students, 1959-1977. *Member:* Mystery Writers of America, P.E.N., Writers Guild of America, Authors League of America, Romance Writers of America, Friends of the Theatre (member of board of directors).

WRITINGS—Romances, except as indicated; published by Pinnacle Books, except as indicated: (Under name Patty Brisco) *The Other People* (science fiction), Powell Publications, 1970; (under name Patty Brisco) *The Carnival Mystery* (juvenile), Scholastic Book Services, 1974; (under name Patty Brisco) *The Campus Mystery* (juvenile), Scholastic Book Services, 1977; *Love's Avenging Heart,* 1977; *Love's Wildest Promise,* 1977; *Love, Forever More,* 1977; *Love's Daring Dream,* 1978; *Love's Pagan Heart,* 1978; *River of Fear,* Scholastic Book Services, 1978; (under name Patty Brisco) *Raging Rapids* (juvenile), Bowmar, 1978; (under name Patty Brisco) *Too Much in Love* (juvenile), Scholastic Book Services, 1979; *Love's Golden Destiny,* 1979; *Love's Magic Moment,* 1979; (under pseudonym Laurie Wylie) *The Night Visitor* (occult), 1979; *Love's Many Faces* (poetry), 1979.

Love's Bold Journey, 1980; *Love's Raging Tide,* 1980; *Love's Sweet Agony,* 1980; *Tides of Love,* Bantam, 1981; (with husband Clayton Matthews) *Midnight Whispers,* Bantam, 1981; (with C. Matthews) *Empire,* Bantam, 1982; *Embers of Dawn,* Bantam, 1982; *Flames of Glory,* Bantam, 1983; *Dancer of Dreams,* Bantam, 1983.

With husband, Clayton Matthews; under joint pseudonym Patty Brisco; gothics, except as indicated: *Merry's Treasure* (juvenile), Avalon Books, 1969; *Horror at Gull House,* Belmont-Tower, 1972; *House of Candles,* Manor, 1973; *The Crystal Window,* Avon, 1973; *Mist of Evil,* Manor, 1976.

Short stories represented in *Action,* edited by Dolly Hasinbiller, Scholastic Book Services, 1977. Contributor of short stories to *Ladies' Home Journal, Escapade, Dude, Alfred Hitchcock's Mystery Magazine,* and *Mike Shayne's Mystery Magazine;* contributor of poetry to *American Bard, Oregonian,* and *Poetry.*

SIDELIGHTS: Patricia Matthews told *CA:* "People ask us what it is like being married to another writer—and for us it has been great. We have not only worked together on several books, but we each are available for ideas, advice, editing, and other input for the books that we do separately. Talking over ideas with each other often engenders *new* ideas, and triggers the creative process. We live a relatively quiet life with our large, spoiled Burmese cat, Pyewacket (who is also my familiar, as I am very interested in the occult)."

* * *

MAXWELL, Grover (Edward) 1918-1981

PERSONAL: Born June 21, 1918, in Rockvale, Tenn.; died June 14, 1981; son of John Edward and Jane Ashby (Jackson) Maxwell; married Mary Lou Canton, October 28, 1960; children: Russell, Stephen. *Education:* University of Tennessee, B.S., 1941, Ph.D., 1950; University of Minnesota, advanced study in philosophy, 1954-57. *Home:* 2011 Kenwood Pkwy., Minneapolis, Minn. 55405. *Office:* Minnesota Center for Philosophy of Science, University of Minnesota, Minneapolis, Minn. 55455.

CAREER: Tennessee Valley Authority, Florence, Ala., chemist, 1941-43; University of Minnesota, Minneapolis, instructor in chemistry, 1950-51; University of Connecticut, Storrs, instructor in chemistry, 1951-52; Adelphi College, Garden City, N.Y., professor of chemistry, 1954; University of Minnesota, Minneapolis, professor of philosophy of science, 1957-81, professor of philosophy, 1961-81, research professor at Minnesota Center for Philosophy of Science, 1957-71, director of Minnesota Center for Philosophy of Science, 1971-81. Visiting professor, University of California, Berkeley, 1965-66, London School of Economics, 1966-67, and University of Hawaii, 1970. Peace candidate for U.S. Congress, 1968. Consultant, National Science Foundation, 1962-64. *Military service:* U.S. Navy, 1943-46; became lieutenant junior grade. *Member:* American Philosophical Association, American Association for the Advancement of Science, American Association of University Professors, Sigma Xi. *Awards, honors:* National Science Foundation grant, 1964-67, 1972, 1974.

WRITINGS: (Editor with Herbert Feigl and M. Scriven) *Minnesota Studies in the Philosophy of Science,* University of Minnesota Press, Volume II, 1958, Volume III, 1962; (editor with Feigl, and contributor) *Current Issues in the Philosophy of Science,* Holt, 1961; (with Feigl) *Scientific Explanation, Space, and Time,* University of Minnesota Press, 1962; (editor with Paul K. Feyerabend) *Mind, Matter, and Method: Essays in Honor of Herbert Feigl,* University of Minnesota Press, 1966.

The Nature and Function of Scientific Theories, University of Pittsburgh Press, 1970; (editor with Robert M. Anderson, Jr.) *Induction, Probability, and Confirmation,* University of Minnesota Press, 1975. Also contributor to *The Philosophy of Karl R. Popper,* Open Court, and *Pittsburgh Studies in Philosophy of Science,* University of Pittsburgh Press; contributor to anthologies. Contributor of articles to chemistry and philosophy journals.

WORK IN PROGRESS: A book, *Introduction to Induction and Scientific Method.*†

* * *

MAXWELL, Vicky

See WORBOYS, Anne(tte Isobel) Eyre

* * *

MAYER, Agatha

See MAHER, Ramona

* * *

MAYER, Thomas 1927-

PERSONAL: Born January 18, 1927, in Vienna, Austria; son of Felix (a businessman) and Helen (Pollatschek) Mayer; married Dorothy Harmison, April 7, 1963. *Education:* Queens College (now Queens College of the City University of New York), B.A., 1948; Columbia University, M.A., 1949, Ph.D., 1953. *Politics:* Democratic. *Home:* 3054 Buena Vista Way, Berkeley, Calif. 94708. *Office:* Department of Economics, University of California, Davis, Calif. 95616.

CAREER: U.S. Government, Washington, D.C., economist with Department of Treasury, 1951-52, Office of Price Stabilization, 1952, and Department of Interior, 1953; West Virginia University, Morgantown, visiting assistant professor of economics, 1953-54, research associate, 1956; University of Notre Dame, Notre Dame, Ind., assistant professor of finance, 1954-56; Michigan State University, East Lansing, 1956-61, began as assistant professor, became professor of economics; University of California, Berkeley, visiting associate professor, 1961-62; University of California, Davis, professor of economics, 1962—. *Military service:* U.S. Army, 1945-46. *Member:* American Economic Association, Royal Economic Society (Britain), Econometric Society, Western Economic Association (vice-president, 1976-77; president-elect, 1977-78; president, 1978-79), American Finance Association.

WRITINGS: Monetary Policy in the United States, Random House, 1968; *Elements of Monetary Policy,* Random House, 1968; *Permanent Income, Wealth and Consumption,* University of California Press, 1971; (with D. C. Rowan) *Intermediate Macroeconomics,* Norton, 1972; *The Structure of Monetarism,* Norton, 1978; *Money, Banking and the Economy,* Norton, 1981.

Contributor: *Consumer Loans of West Virginia Banks,* Bureau of Business Research, West Virginia University, 1957; (with T. Gies and E. Ettin) *Private Financial Institutions,* Prentice-Hall, 1964; (with M. Bronfenbrenner) G. Mueller, editor, *Readings in Macroeconomics,* Holt, 1966; Richard Thorn, editor, *Contemporary Monetary Theory and Policy,* Random House, 1966; G. Horwich, editor, *Monetary Process and Policy,* Irwin, 1967; Lawrence S. Ritter, editor, *Money and Economic Activity,* 3rd edition, Houghton, 1967; Paul F. Jessup, compiler, *Innovations in Bank Management,* Holt, 1969.

Sid Mittra, compiler, *Money and Banking,* Random House, 1970; Jonas Prager, editor, *Monetary Economics,* Random House, 1971; T. Gies and V. Apilado, *Banking Markets and Financial Institutions,* Irwin, 1971; Karl Brunner, editor, *Government Credit Allocation,* Institute of Contemporary Studies, 1975; (with K. Scott) James J. White, *Teaching Materials on Banking Law,* Western Publishing, 1976; T. Havrilesky and J. Boorman, *Current Issues in Monetary Theory and Policy,* AHM Publishing, 1976; Havrilesky and Boorman, *Current Perspectives in Banking,* AHM Publishing, 1976; Jerome Stein, editor, *Monetarism,* North Holland Publishing, 1976; R. Teigen, *Readings in Money, National Income, and Stabilization Policy,* Irwin, 1978; Michael Claudon and Richard Cornwall, editors, *Incomes Policies for the United States: A New Approach,* Martinus Nijhoff, 1981; Brunner, editor, *Contemporary Views of the Great Depression,* Martinus Nijhoff, 1981; Paul Wachtel, editor, *Crises in the Economic and Financial Structure,* Lexington Books, in press.

Also contributor to A. B. Atkinson, *Wealth, Income and Inequality;* contributor to numerous studies and compendiums prepared for U.S. congressional committee hearings and for Federal Reserve System. Member of editorial board, "Studies of Monetary Economics" series, North Holland Publishing, 1976—, and "Cambridge Surveys of Economic Literature" series, Cambridge University Press, 1977—. Contributor to *American Academic Encyclopedia* and to *Papers and Proceedings* of American Economic Association. Contributor of articles to magazines, newspapers, and professional journals, including *New York Times, National Review,* and *American Banker.* Member of editorial board, *Journal of Finance,* 1967-70, *Western Economic Journal,* 1969-72, *Journal of Money, Credit and Banking,* 1970-74, *Journal of Monetary Economics,* 1974-80, *Journal of Economic Literature,* 1975-77, *Journal of Macroeconomics,* 1977—.

WORK IN PROGRESS: A study of the efficacy of monetary policy.

* * *

McCALL, George J(ohn) 1939-

PERSONAL: Born April 11, 1939, in Monterey Park, Calif.; son of Weldon George (a truck driver) and Nina Faye (Callahan) McCall; married Michal Moses (a sociologist), June 8, 1964 (divorced May, 1977), married Nancy Shields (a sociologist), May 5, 1979; children: (first marriage) Sarah Jane; (second marriage) Grant Shields. *Education:* University of Iowa, B.A., 1961; Indiana University, graduate study, summer, 1961; Harvard University, M.A., 1963, Ph.D., 1965. *Politics:* Democrat. *Religion:* Unitarian Universalist. *Home:* 8250 Glen Echo Dr., St. Louis, Mo. 63121. *Office:* Department of Sociology and Anthropology, University of Missouri—St. Louis, 8001 Natural Bridge Rd., St. Louis, Mo. 63121.

CAREER: University of Iowa, Iowa City, instructor in sociology, 1963-64; University of Illinois at Urbana-Champaign, instructor, 1964-65, assistant professor, 1965-67, associate professor, 1967-68; University of Illinois at Chicago Circle, Chicago, associate professor, 1967-70, professor of sociology, 1970-72, graduate coordinator, 1967-70; University of Missouri—St. Louis, professor of sociology, 1972—, chairman of department, 1972-74, 1977, director of Social and Behavioral Sciences Laboratory, 1974-81. Visiting lecturer, University of Wisconsin—Madison, summer, 1971; visiting scientist, Center for Studies of Crime and Delinquency, National Institute of Mental Health, 1975-76. Consultant to Graduate Record Exam in Sociology, 1969, 1972, National Academy of Sciences, 1976, and National Institute of Mental Health, 1976—.

MEMBER: American Sociological Association, Society for the Study of Social Problems, Midwest Sociological Society, Phi Beta Kappa, Alpha Delta Sigma. *Awards, honors:* Woodrow Wilson fellowship, 1961-64; National Science Foundation fellowship, 1961-64; program director of National Institute of Mental Health training grant in evaluation research, 1977-81.

WRITINGS: (With J. L. Simmons) *Identities and Interactions,* Free Press, 1966, revised edition, 1978; (with Simmons) *Issues in Participant Observation,* Addison-Wesley, 1969; (editor) *Social Relationships,* Aldine, 1970; *Observing the Law: Applications of Field Methods to the Study of the Criminal Justice System,* National Institute of Mental Health, 1975; *Observing the Law: Field Methods in the Study of Crime and the Criminal Justice System,* Free Press, 1978; (editor with George H. Weber) *Social Scientists as Advocates: Views from the Applied Disciplines,* Sage Publications, 1978; (with Simmons) *Social Psychology: A Sociological Approach,* Free Press, 1982.

Contributor: Howard S. Becker, editor, *The Other Side: Perspectives on Deviance,* Free Press, 1964; L. A. Dexter and D. M. White, editors, *People, Society, and Mass Communications,* Free Press, 1964; G. P. Stone and H. A. Farberman, editors, *Social Psychology Through Symbolic Interaction,* Ginn, 1970; *Society Today,* CRM Books, 1971; Kenneth Thompson and Jeremy Tunstall, editors, *Sociological Perspectives,* Penguin, 1971; James M. Henslin, editor, *Down to Earth Sociology,* Free Press, 1972; Alan Dundes, editor, *Mother Wit from the Laughing Barrel: Readings in the Interpretation of Afro-American Folklore,* Prentice-Hall, 1973; Ted L. Huston, editor, *Foundations of Interpersonal Attraction,* Academic Press, 1974; Theodore Mischel, editor, *The Self: Psychological and Philosophical Issues,* Basil Blackwell, 1977; D. L. Sills, editor, *International Encyclopedia of the Social Sciences,* Macmillan and Free Press, 1979; Howard Robboy, Sidney L. Greenblatt, and Candace Clark, editors, *Social Interaction: Introductory Readings in Sociology,* St. Martin's, 1979; Gordon E. Misner, editor, *Criminal Justice Studies: Their Transdisciplinary Nature,* C. V. Mosby, 1981; Stuart S. Nagel, editor, *Encyclopedia of Policy Studies,* Marcel Dekker, 1982; William Ickes and Eric S. Knowles, editors, *Personality, Roles, Social Behavior,* Springer-Verlag, 1982; Steven W. Duck, editor, *Dissolving Personal Relationships,* Academic Press, in press.

External book reviewer for journals, including *Social Psychology Quarterly, Journal for the Theory of Social Behavior, American Psychological Reports, Sociologist,* and *Social Forces.* Contributor to journals, including *Social Problems, Public Opinion Quarterly, Psychological Reports,* and *Perceptual and Motor Skills.* Associate editor, *Sociological Quarterly,* 1968-73, *Social Problems,* 1969-74, *Sociometry,* 1972-74, *American Sociological Review,* 1974-78, *Sociological Methods and Research,* 1975—, and *Journal for the Theory of Social Behavior,* 1975-77; advisory editor, *Urban Life,* 1971—.

WORK IN PROGRESS: Social Sciences and Public Policy.

AVOCATIONAL INTERESTS: Animal behavior (especially wolves and primates), folklore (Negro blues, Russian, Finnish), neuropsychology, ecology, sports, camping, fishing.

* * *

McCAULEY, Michael F(rederick) 1947-

PERSONAL: Born April 12, 1947, in Chicago, Ill.; son of George Lawrence (a stationary engineer) and Virginia (Johnson) McCauley; married Gabrielle Goder, May 29, 1971; children: Megan Colleen. *Education:* Loyola University, Chicago, Ill., A.B., 1969. *Residence:* Oak Park, Ill.

CAREER: Taught high school English at Woodlands Academy, Lake Forest, Ill., briefly, beginning c. 1969; Thomas More Association, Chicago, Ill., 1970-81, began as editor, became managing editor of newsletters, including *Overview, Markings, You,* and *Stress;* American Hospital Association, Chicago, editorial consultant for *Cross-Reference,* 1981; free-lance editorial consultant, 1982—.

WRITINGS: (Editor) *On the Run: Spirituality for the Seventies,* Thomas More Press, 1974; *A Contemporary Meditation on Doubting,* Thomas More Press, 1976; *The Jesus Book,* Thomas More Press, 1978; *In the Name of the Father,* Thomas More Press, 1983. Contributor of book reviews to *Critic* and *Commonweal.*

* * *

McCORD, Guy
See REYNOLDS, Dallas McCord

* * *

McHANEY, Thomas L(afayette) 1936-

PERSONAL: Born October 17, 1936, in Paragould, Ark.; son of Thomas L. (a lawyer) and Maxine (Brown) McHaney; married Karen Honigmann (a cartographer), May 30, 1962; children: Sudie Ann, Jessie Wynne, Molly Josephine. *Education:* Attended Christian Brothers College, 1954-56; Mississippi State University, B.A., 1959; University of North Carolina at Chapel Hill, M.A., 1963; University of South Carolina, Ph.D., 1968. *Politics:* Democrat. *Home:* 985 Courtenay Dr., Atlanta, Ga. 30306. *Office:* Department of English, Georgia State University, University Plaza, Atlanta, Ga. 30303.

CAREER: University of Mississippi, Oxford, instructor in English, 1963-65; Georgia State University, Atlanta, assistant professor, 1968-73, associate professor of English, 1973—. Fulbright lecturer, University of Bonn, 1976. *Member:* Modern Language Association of America, American Association of University Professors, Southern Humanities Conference, South Atlantic Modern Language Association. *Awards, honors:* Woodrow Wilson fellowship, 1960; fiction awards from *Reflections,* 1965, *Atlanta,* 1969, and *Prairie Schooner,* 1973; special award for fiction from Henry Bellaman Foundation, 1970, for short stories.

WRITINGS: (Contributor) Matthew J. Bruccoli, editor, *The Chief Glory of Every People,* Southern Illinois University Press, 1973; *William Faulkner's The Wild Palms: A Study,* University

Press of Mississippi, 1975; *William Faulkner: A Reference Guide,* G. K. Hall, 1976.

"Last of the Civil War Orphans" (play), produced in Atlanta, Ga., by Atlanta New Play Project, 1981; "A Place Where They Cried" (play), produced in Atlanta by Alliance Theatre Company, 1983. Contributor of articles and short stories to journals, including *PMLA, Mississippi Quarterly, Transatlantic, Prairie Schooner, Georgia Review,* and *Cimarron Review.* Member of editorial board of *Costerus: A Journal of English and American Literature,* 1972—.

* * *

McINTYRE, Kenneth E. 1918-

PERSONAL: Born May 8, 1918, in Wolbach, Neb.; son of Morris and Anna Elizabeth (Gerlach) McIntyre; married Eleanor McNeel, June 9, 1940; children: Mary Jean (Mrs. Jay C. Davis), Douglas, Robert. *Education:* Hastings College, Hastings, Neb., A.B., 1940; University of Nebraska, M.A., 1943, Ph.D., 1948. *Religion:* Methodist. *Home:* 4017 Greenhill Pl., Austin, Tex. 78759. *Office:* University of Texas, Austin, Tex. 78712.

CAREER: High school teacher of English and history in Nebraska, 1940-43; superintendent of schools in St. Paul, Neb., 1943-45; University of South Dakota, Vermillion, assistant professor, 1948-50, associate professor of education, 1950-51; University of Tennessee, Knoxville, associate professor of education, 1951-52; University of Texas at Austin, associate professor, 1952-57, professor of educational administration, 1957—. *Member:* National Association of Secondary School Principals, Phi Delta Kappa.

WRITINGS: (With L. D. Haskew) *Foundations in Educational Administration,* Southwestern Cooperative Program in Educational Administration, University of Texas, 1954; *Group Processes: A Breakthrough in the Preparation of Educational Administrators,* Southwestern Cooperative Program in Educational Administration, University of Texas, 1955; *Recruiting and Selecting Leaders for Education,* Southwest School Administration Center, University of Texas, 1956; *Learning in a Block-of-Time Program,* Southwest School Administration Center, University of Texas, 1957; *Selection and On-the-Job Training of School Principals,* Bureau of Laboratory Schools, University of Texas, 1960; (with Ben M. Harris and Wailand Bessent) *In-Service Education: A Guide to Better Practice,* Prentice-Hall, 1969; (with Harris and Bessent) *In-Service Education: Materials for Laboratory Sessions,* Prentice-Hall, 1969.

(Editor) *The Principalship in the 1970's,* University of Texas Press, 1971; *McIntyranny,* Foundations in Educational Administration Association, 1975; (with Walter F. Beckman, Larry L. Smiley, and Scott D. Thomson) *Rolling Hills High School In-Basket,* with discussion guide, National Association of Secondary School Principals, 1975; (with Richard A. Gorton) *The Senior High School Principalship: The Effective Principal,* National Association of Secondary School Principals, 1978; (with Harris, Vance C. Littleton, and Daniel F. Long) *Personnel Administration in Education,* Allyn & Bacon, 1979; *McIntyranny II,* Foundations in Educational Administration Association, 1979. Also author of a number of shorter works, including technical reports, monographs, and instruction manuals.

Contributor: *Rural Education: A Forward Look,* Department of Rural Education, National Education Association, 1955; (with Roy M. Hall) *Administrative Behavior in Education,* Harper, 1957; E. W. Bessent, editor, *Designs for In-Service Education,* University of Texas, 1967; Dale L. Bolton, editor, *The Use of Simulation in Educational Administration,* C. E. Merrill, 1971; (with Kenneth St. Clair) Luvern L. Cunningham and William J. Gephart, editors, *Leadership: The Science and the Art Today,* F. E. Peacock, 1973; Jack A. Culbertson, Curtis Henson, and Ruel Morrison, editors, *Performance Objectives for School Principals,* McCutchan, 1974; Kenneth H. Hansen, editor, *Learning: An Overview and Update,* [San Diego], 1976; Charles A. Reavis and Karolyn J. Snyder, editors, *Perspectives on Teacher Performance,* Texas Association for Supervision and Curriculum Development, 1982. Contributor to yearbooks and professional journals.

WORK IN PROGRESS: Research on selection of school administrators, on training programs for school administrators, and on the evaluation of teacher and administrator performance.

* * *

McKUSICK, Marshall Bassford 1930-

PERSONAL: Born January 13, 1930, in Minneapolis, Minn.; son of James G. Blaine (a lawyer) and Marjorie (Chase) McKusick: married Charity Koeper, August 21, 1954; children: Blaine, Lucy. *Education:* University of Minnesota, B.A., 1952, M.A., 1954; Yale University, Ph.D., 1960. *Religion:* Unitarian Universalist. *Office:* Department of Anthropology, University of Iowa, Iowa City, Iowa 52242.

CAREER: University of California, Los Angeles, lecturer in anthropology and research archaeologist, 1958-60; University of Iowa, Iowa City, assistant professor, 1960-64, associate professor of anthropology, 1964—. State archaeologist of Iowa. *Member:* American Anthropological Association, Society for American Archaeology. *Awards, honors:* National Endowment for the Humanities fellow, 1971-73.

WRITINGS: *Men of Ancient Iowa; As Revealed by Archaeological Discoveries,* Iowa State University Press, 1964; (editor and author of introduction) Ellison Orr, *Reminiscences of a Pioneer Boy,* [Iowa City], 1971; *The Davenport Conspiracy,* Office of the State Archaeologist (Iowa City), 1970; (editor) *Prehistoric Investigations,* Office of the State Archaeologist (Iowa City), 1971; *The Grant Oneota Village,* University of Iowa, 1973; *The Iowa Northern Border Brigade,* Office of the State Archaeologist (Iowa City), 1975. Also author of evaluation and index for *Iowa Archaeological Reports, 1934-1939,* Society for American Archaeology, 1963.†

* * *

McMULLEN, Catherine
See COOKSON, Catherine (McMullen)

* * *

MEAD, Frank Spencer 1898-1982

PERSONAL: Born January 15, 1898, in Chatham, N.J.; died June 16, 1982; son of Frank and Lillie (Spencer) Mead; married Judy Duryee, October 24, 1927; children: Donald Duryee, Judy Spencer. *Education:* University of Denver, A.B., 1922; studied at Episcopal Theological Seminary of Virginia, 1922-23; Union Theological Seminary, New York, N.Y., B.D., 1927. *Politics:* Independent. *Home:* 6 McKinley St., Nutley, N.J. 07110. *Office:* Fleming H. Revell Co., 184 Central Ave., Old Tappan, N.J. 07675.

CAREER: Young Men's Christian Association, New York City, secretary, 1923-24; ordained Methodist minister, 1927, holding pastorates in Newark, N.J., 1927-31, and Kearny, N.J., 1931-34; *Homiletic Review,* New York City, editor, 1934; *Baptist Leader,* Philadelphia, Pa., editor, 1935-37; free-lance writer, 1938-41; *Christian Herald,* New York City, executive editor, 1942-48; Fleming H. Revell Co., New York City and Westwood, N.J., editor-in-chief, beginning 1949, and a director of the firm. *Military service:* U.S. Army, 1917-18. *Member:* Phi Beta Kappa, Beta Theta Pi. *Awards, honors:* Litt.D., Dickinson College, 1950.

WRITINGS: The March of Eleven Men, Bobbs-Merrill, 1932; *Who's Who in the Bible,* Harper, 1934; *See These Banners Go,* Bobbs-Merrill, 1935; *Ten Decisive Battles of Christianity,* Bobbs-Merrill, 1937; *Right Here at Home,* Friendship, 1939; *Tales from Latin America,* Friendship, 1942; *On Our Own Doorstep,* Friendship, 1948.

Handbook of Denominations in the U.S., Abingdon, 1951, 7th edition, 1980; *The Baptists,* Broadman, 1954; (with Iona Henry) *Triumph over Tragedy,* Revell, 1957; *Joshua the Warrior,* Doubleday, 1959; (with Roy Rogers) *My Favorite Christmas Story,* Revell, 1960; (editor) *Communion Messages,* Revell, 1961; *Reaching beyond Your Pulpit,* Revell, 1962; *Rebels with a Cause,* Abingdon, 1964; *The Encyclopaedia of Religious Quotations,* Revell, 1965.

(With Dale Evans Rogers) *Let Freedom Ring!,* G. K. Hall, 1976; (editor) *Talking with God: Prayers for Today,* Holman, 1976; (with D. E. Rogers) *Hear the Children Crying,* Revell, 1978. Editor of *Tarbell's Teacher's Guide* (annual), Revell, 1949-82. Contributor to magazines.

AVOCATIONAL INTERESTS: Golf.

OBITUARIES: Publishers Weekly, July 9, 1982.†

* * *

MEISTER, Robert 1926-

PERSONAL: Born February 19, 1926, in Budapest, Hungary; son of Leopold (a doctor) and Anna (de Murai) Meister; children: Christine, Anna. *Education:* Cornell University, B.A., 1950; University of Erlangen, graduate study. *Home:* 15 West 72nd St., New York, N.Y. 10023. *Agent:* Harvey Klinger, 301 West 53rd St., New York, N.Y. 10019.

CAREER: Free-lance writer, editor, and translator, 1950-58; Libra Publishers, New York, N.Y., editor-in-chief, 1958-70; free-lance writer, 1970—.

WRITINGS: A Jovo Emlekei (title means "Memories of the Future"), Franklin, 1945; *Die Tucke der Dingen* (title means "The Meanness of Objects"), Mendelssohn, 1947; (editor and author of foreword) *A Literary Guide to Seduction,* Stein & Day, 1963; (translator from the German) Peter Fuchs, *African Decameron,* Astor-Honor, 1964; (translator from the French) Pierre Biner, *The Living Theatre,* Avon, 1971; *Hypochondria: Towards a Better Understanding,* Taplinger, 1980; *Fathers,* Richard Marek, 1981; *Without Heroes* (novel), St. Martin's, 1983.

* * *

MELLERSH, H(arold) E(dward) L(eslie) 1897-

PERSONAL: Born May 28, 1897, in London, England; son of F. H. (an insurance secretary) and Florence (Parker) Mellersh; married Margot Sadler, August, 1921; children: Jacqueline (Mrs. Tony Nayman), Sally, Nicholas, Angela (Mrs. Robert Myers). *Education:* University of London, B.Sc., 1921. *Religion:* Church of England. *Home:* 6 Hill St., Stogumber, Taunton, England. *Agent:* Peter Janson-Smith Ltd., 31 Newington Green, Islington, London N16 9PU, England.

CAREER: Civil servant with Ministry of Supply until 1957; author. *Military service:* British Army, 1915-19; served in France; became lieutenant. *Member:* Linnean Society of London (fellow), West Country Writers' Association.

WRITINGS: Let Loose (novel), Selwyn & Blount, 1926; *Ill Wind* (novel), Chapman & Hall, 1930; *The Salt of the Earth,* Chapman & Hall, 1931; *The World and Man: A Guide to Modern Knowledge,* Hutchinson, 1952; *The Story of Life,* Hutchinson, 1957, Putnam, 1958; *The Story of Man: Human Evolution to the End of the Stone Age,* Hutchinson, 1959, published as *The Story of Early Man: Human Evolution to the End of the Stone Age,* Viking, 1960.

From Ape Man to Homer: The Story of the Beginnings of Western Civilization, R. Hale, 1962, Taplinger, 1963; *Soldiers of Rome,* R. Hale, 1964, published as *The Roman Soldier,* Taplinger, 1965; *Archaeology: Science and Romance,* Wheaton, 1966; *Minoan Crete,* Putnam, 1967; *FitzRoy of the Beagle,* Hart-Davis, 1968, Mason & Lipscomb, 1974; *The Destruction of Knossos: The Rise and Fall of Minoan Crete,* Weybright, 1970; *Chronology of the Ancient World, 10,000 B.C. to A.D. 799,* Barrie & Jenkins, 1976.

Children's books: *Finding Out about Ancient Egypt,* Muller, 1960, Lothrop, 1962; *Finding Out about Stone Age Britain,* Muller, 1961; *Saxon Britain,* Weidenfeld & Nicolson, 1961; *Finding Out about the Trojans,* Muller, 1962; *Carthage,* Weidenfeld & Nicolson, 1963; *Charles Darwin: Pioneer of the Theory of Evolution,* Arthur Barker, 1964, published as *Charles Darwin: Pioneer in the Theory of Evolution,* Praeger, 1969; *The Boys' Book of the Wonders of Man and His Achievements,* Roy, 1964; *Imperial Rome,* John Day, 1964, 3rd edition, Hart-Davis, 1974; *Sumer and Babylon,* Wheaton, 1964, Crowell, 1965; *The Discoverers: The Story of the Great Seafarers,* Wheaton, 1969; *The Explorers: The Story of the Great Adventurers by Land,* Wheaton, 1969; *Schoolboy into War,* Kimber, 1978.

Contributor to *Wheaton's Atlas of British and World History,* 1972. Also contributor to *Reader's Digest Dictionary* and to *New Statesman, Fortnightly,* and *Contemporary Review.*

WORK IN PROGRESS: A short history of Peru.

SIDELIGHTS: H.E.L. Mellersh once wrote: "Having gone straight into the Army in the first world war—and having luckily survived, though wounded three times—I went and got myself married to a girl more lovely than I deserved. She had almost equally delightful young niece and nephews and to these I found myself telling stories, or, rather, one long story that went on and on until I had my own children and then my grandchildren to tell it to.

"But I had also come out of the war remarkably ignorant and I set about re-educating myself. Particularly I had to do so in things that they hadn't taught me much about at school, such as ancient history. That subject fascinated me; Stone Age man, the Sumerian, the boy or girl in ancient Rome. They had really lived in a world different from ours and yet, no doubt, feeling that their world was as modern as we think our own. I began to write about them for grownups.

"Then my literary agent approached a publisher of a series of books that not only covered the ancient history of people, but also sought to show how that history had been discovered. So they let me write, *Finding Out about Ancient Egypt*.

"I really knew very little about ancient Egypt, and I, too, had to 'find out.' I think my ignorance was almost an advantage. I could, perhaps, make things more easily clear for others who didn't know much about the subject either—not that I recommend ignorance as a good recipe for writing!

"Since then, I have gone on writing for children. Some books have been less successful than *Finding Out about Ancient Egypt*, but what makes one book successful and another not, I cannot tell. I have at any rate tried never to write down to children, assuming that they were just as intelligent as their seniors, if not more so. That has always seemed a good idea.

"To have visited the country whose ancient people one is going to write about certainly helps, though I have not always managed it. For the rest, it is a matter of reading and reading. I live in the country now, but I get my books from and pretty often go to visit the London Library, a wonderful institution that always seems to have what I want. When looking for the right book I don't mind 'skipping,' nor do I persevere if the book seems too dull for words; I may have missed something, but I should probably not have taken it in anyway."†

* * *

MESZAROS, Istvan 1930-

PERSONAL: Born December 19, 1930, in Budapest, Hungary; son of Istvan and Ilona (Kocsis) Meszaros; married Donatella Morisi (a teacher), February 15, 1956; children: Laura, Susan, George. *Education:* Attended Eotvos College, 1949-50; Budapest University, B.A. (first class honors), 1953; Friedrich Schiller University, Dr.Phil., 1955. *Politics:* Socialist.

CAREER: Budapest University, Budapest, Hungary, assistant professor, 1951-55, associate professor of philosophy, 1956; University of Turin, Turin, Italy, assistant professor of philosophy, 1956-59; University of London, London, England, research fellow of Bedford College, 1959-61; St. Andrews University, St. Andrews, Scotland, associate professor of philosophy, 1961-66; Sussex University, Brighton, Sussex, England, associate professor of philosophy, 1966-72; York University, Toronto, Ontario, professor of social science, beginning 1972. *Member:* International Sociological Association, Societe Europeenne de Culture, Toronto Society for the Study of Social and Political Thought. *Awards, honors:* Attila Jozsef Prize, 1951, for an essay; Issac Deutscher Memorial Prize, 1970, for *Marx's Theory of Alienation*.

WRITINGS: Marx's Theory of Alienation, Merlin, 1970, 4th edition, 1975; *The Necessity of Social Control,* Merlin, 1971; (editor and contributor) *Aspects of History and Class Consciousness,* Routledge & Kegan Paul, 1971; *Lukacs' Concept of Dialectic,* Merlin, 1972; (editor with Eva Foldes) *Comemius and Hungary: Essays,* Akademiai Kiado, 1973; (with Renato Constantino) *Neo-Colonial Identity and Counter-Consciousness: Essays in Cultural Decolonisation,* Merlin, 1978; *The Work of Sartre,* Humanities Press, Volume I: *Search for Freedom,* 1979, Volume II: *The Challenge of History,* 1979.

In Hungarian: *Szatira es valosag: Adalekok a szatira elmeletehez* (title means "Satire and Reality: Contributions to the Theory of Satire"), SZKK (Budapest), 1955; *La rivolta degli intellettuali in Ungheria* (title means "Revolt of the Intellectuals in Hungary"), Einaudi (Turin), 1958; *Attila Jozsef e l'arte moderna* (title means "Atilla Jozsef and Modern Art"), Lerici (Milan), 1964; *Kisfilm az osztalyfonoki oran,* Tankonyvkiado (Budapest), 1968; *A magyar neveles tortenete, 1790-1849,* Tankonyvkiado, 1968; *Nepoktatasunk, 1553-1777,* Akademiai Kiado (Budapest), 1972; *A Szalkai-kodex es a XV,* Akademiai Kiado, 1972; *Iskolai jegyzetonyv a XVI-XVIII,* Akademiai Kiado, 1976.

SIDELIGHTS: Reviewing Istvan Meszaros's book, *Marx's Theory of Alienation,* a *Times Literary Review* critic states that "in recent years there have been a good many discussions of the concept of alienation. . . . But [*Marx's Theory of Alienation*] differs from these in two major respects. In the first place it is firmly centered on Marx's own writings and yet comprehensive in its application of the concept of alienation to economics, politics, aesthetics, and eventually to contemporary educational upheaval. In the second place, it is an account which self-consciously asserts its own place in the mainstream of Marxist thought." The critic judges the book to be "immensely learned and well-read."

BIOGRAPHICAL/CRITICAL SOURCES: Times Literary Supplement, July 20, 1970.†

* * *

METZGER, Norman 1924-

PERSONAL: Born December 21, 1924, in New York, N.Y.; son of Murray (a shoe designer) and Evelyn (Goldstein) Metzger; married Marcia Averack, August 25, 1946; children: Bart. *Education:* School of Business and Civic Administration of the City College (now Bernard M. Baruch College of the City University of New York), B.B.A., 1948; Columbia University, M.A., 1954. *Home:* 250 East 87th St., New York, N.Y. 10028. *Office:* Department of Health Care Management, Mount Sinai Medical Center, 100th St. and Fifth Ave., New York, N.Y. 10029.

CAREER: Employed as assistant to controller for Hillman Periodicals, 1948-49, production manager for Coronet Handballs, Inc., 1949-52, and personnel director for Norden-Ketay Corp., 1952-59; Bernard M. Baruch College of the City University of New York, New York City, adjunct instructor, 1957-67, adjunct professor of health care administration, 1967—; Mount Sinai Medical Center, New York City, vice-president for labor relations, 1960—, professor at Mount Sinai School of Medicine, 1966—. Adjunct professor of health care administration, New School for Social Research, 1978—. *Military service:* U.S. Navy, 1943-46.

MEMBER: American Society for Hospital Personnel Administration, Association of Hospital Personnel Administrators, Commerce and Industry Association, League of Voluntary Hospitals and Homes of New York (member of board of directors). *Awards, honors:* Editorial award from *Hospital Management,* 1965, for article "The Challenge Ahead: The Effects of Union Organizing Efforts on Hospital Administration"; four annual awards for outstanding contribution to hospital personnel administration literature, from Association of Hospital Personnel Administrators and American Hospital Association, 1972-1982.

WRITINGS: Men and Molecules, American Chemical Society, 1972; *Labor-Management Relations in the Health Services Industry,* Science & Health, 1972; *Personnel Administration in Hospitals and Homes,* Spectrum, 1975, revised edition, 1979; *The National Labor Relations Act: A Guidebook for Health Care Administrators,* Spectrum, 1975; *Personnel Management and Labor Relations: A Guide for the Nursing Home Admin-*

istrator, American Nursing Home Association, 1975; *Personnel Administration in the Health Services Industry: Theory and Practice,* Spectrum, 1975; *The Health Care Supervisor's Handbook,* Aspen Systems Corp., 1978; (with Harry Munn) *Effective Communication in Health Care,* Aspen Systems Corp., 1981; (editor) *Handbook of Health Care Human Resources Management,* Aspen Systems Corp., 1981. Also author of *Labor Relations and Personnel Management in Long-Term Health Care Facilities.*

Contributor of numerous articles to hospital journals, including *Hospital Management, Hospitals: Journal of the American Hospital Association, Medical Laboratory Observer, Nursing Care, Executive Housekeeper,* and *Journal of the Association of Hospital Personnel Administrators.* Member of editorial board of *Hospital Supervision.*

* * *

MEUDT, Edna Kritz 1906-

PERSONAL: Born September 14, 1906, in Wyoming Valley, Wis.; daughter of John William (a farmer) and Kristin (Neilsen) Kritz; married Peter J. Meudt (a farmer), October 10, 1924 (died May 2, 1972); children: Richard, Howard, Kathleen (Mrs. George Ott), Christine (Mrs. Daniel Parkinson). *Education:* Attended rural schools in Wisconsin and Sacred Heart Academy. *Politics:* Predominantly Democrat. *Religion:* Roman Catholic. *Home:* Rural Route 3, Dodgeville, Wis. 53533.

CAREER: Poet. Teacher, Rhinelander Seminar and Festival of Arts, sponsored by University of Wisconsin extension; conductor of poetry workshop at Deep South Writer's Conference, Lafayette, La., 1965, and in Wisconsin high schools; judge in state and national poetry contests; lecturer on poetry to colleges and writers' conferences; participant in Poets-in-the-Schools projects.

MEMBER: International Poetry Society, Academy of American Poets, National Federation of State Poetry Societies (president, 1963-64; now vice-president), Catholic Poetry Society of America, Wisconsin Fellowship of Poets (president, 1952-54, 1960-61), Wisconsin Regional Writers Association (member of board of directors, 1950-54), Wisconsin Arts Board (chairman of creative writers panel), Wisconsin State Historical Society, Wisconsin Academy of Sciences, Arts and Letters.

AWARDS, HONORS: Wisconsin Regional Writers Association bard's chair and jade ring award, 1958; American Poetry League first prize, 1959; National League of American Pen Women honors award, 1963, for *Round River Canticle;* Wisconsin Writer's Cup Award, Theta Sigma Phi, 1965, for *In No Strange Land;* Wisconsin Arts Council Governor's Award, 1970; American Revolution Bicentennial grant, 1976; National League of American Pen Women prize, 1976, for *The Ineluctable Sea;* Council for Wisconsin Writers prize, 1977, for *Promised Land;* University of Wisconsin award of distinction, 1978; *North American Mentor* prize.

WRITINGS—Poetry: *Round River Canticle,* Wake-Brook, 1960; *In No Strange Land,* Wake-Brook, 1964; *No One Sings Face Down,* Wisconsin House, 1970; *The Ineluctable Sea,* Wake-Brook, 1975; *Plain Chant for a Tree,* Wake-Brook, 1980; *Promised Land: Life and Times of Henry Dodge,* Westburg Associates, 1981.

Also author of play, "A Case of Semantics." Poetry included in anthologies published by Wisconsin Fellowship of Poets. Contributor of poems to *American Weave, Beloit Poetry Journal, National Wildlife, American Forests, Sign, Christian Century, Creative Wisconsin,* and other journals. Co-editor, *Hawk & Whippoorwill Recalled;* editorial consultant, *Orbis.*

SIDELIGHTS: Edna Kritz Meudt told *CA:* "I am a comfort to late starters. My first poem was published in 1944, written out of pain and shock when a second son was reported 'lost at sea.' It was written for self-solace and not intended for publication. The report was false and afterwards the poem was sent to a national magazine where it was published. Beginner's luck? Not really. It represented what in later years I tell others who wish to write, the three 'Rs' of writing: Relevancy, Restraint, Revision. Unknowingly all were practiced, probably because the situation was authentic. The poem had emotional impact. I learned a valuable lesson. For me, at that time, a poem to be worth the writing had to be a wrenching up of deep and often terrible concerns. And today, still, above all else it must be honest. Nothing weakens a poem so much as falsity to fact—either in the emotion or the means of describing it."

BIOGRAPHICAL/CRITICAL SOURCES: Capital Times, May 17, 1965.

* * *

MEYENDORFF, John 1926-

PERSONAL: Born February 17, 1926, in Neuilly-sur-Seine, France; son of Theophile (a painter) and Catherine (Schidlovsky) Meyendorff; married Marie Mojaysky, January 26, 1950; children: Paul, Serge, Elizabeth, Ann. *Education:* University of Paris, B.Ph., B.D., and Licencie-es-Lettres, 1948, Diplome d'etudes superieres, 1949, Diplome de l'Ecole Partique des Hautes Etudes, 1954, and Docteur-es-Lettres, 1958. *Office:* St. Vladimir's Orthodox Theological Seminary, 575 Scarsdale Rd., Tuckahoe, N.Y. 10707.

CAREER: Priest of Eastern Orthodox Church. Orthodox Theological Institute, Paris, France, 1950-59, began as lecturer, became assistant professor of church history; St. Valdimir's Orthodox Theological Seminary, Tuckahoe, N.Y., professor of church history and patristics and editor of *St. Vladimir's Seminary Quarterly,* 1959—. Harvard University, Dumbarton Oaks Research Library and Collection, lecturer in Byzantine theology, 1959-67, and acting director of studies, 1977. Adjunct professor in department of religion, Columbia University, 1962-67; professor of Byzantine history, Fordham University, 1967. World Council of Churches, former chairman of Faith and Order Commission, currently member of central committee. *Member:* British Academy (fellow). *Awards, honors:* LL.D., University of Notre Dame, 1966.

WRITINGS: Introduction a l'etude de Gregoire Palamas, Editions du Seuil, 1959, translation by George Lawrence published as *A Study of Gregory Palamas,* Faith Press, 1964; *St. Gregoire Palamas et la mystique orthodoxe,* Editions du Seuil, 1959, translation published as *St. Gregory Palamas and Orthodox Spirituality,* St. Vladimir's Seminary Press, 1974; (translator from the Greek, and author of commentary and critical notes) Gregory Palamas, *Defense des saints hesychastes,* two volumes, [Louvain], 1959, 2nd edition, 1974, translation published as *Gregory Palamas,* Paulist Press, 1982.

L'Eglise Orthodoxe hier et aujourd'hui, Editions du Seuil, 1960, 2nd edition, 1969, translation by John Chapin published as *The Orthodox Church: Its Past and Its Role in the World Today,* Pantheon, 1962, revised edition with additions by author, Darton, Longman, & Todd, 1962; *Orthodoxie et catholicite,* Editions du Seuil, 1965, translation published as *Or-*

thodoxy and Catholicity, Sheed, 1966; *Le Christ dans la theologie byzantine,* Editions du Cerf, 1969, translation published as *Christ in Eastern Christian Thought,* Corpus Books, 1969, 2nd edition, St. Vladimir's Seminary Press, 1975.

Marriage: An Orthodox Perspective, St. Vladimar's Seminary Press, 1970; *Byzantine Hesychasm: Historical and Theological Problems,* Variorum, 1973; (editor with Joseph McLelland) *The New Man: An Orthodox and Reformed Dialogue,* Agora Books, 1973; *Byzantine Theology,* Fordham University Press, 1974; *Living Tradition,* St. Valdimir's Seminary Press, 1976.

The Legacy of Byzantium in the Orthodox Church, St. Vladimir's Seminary Press, 1981; *Byzantium and the Rise of Russia,* Cambridge University Press, 1981. Editorial advisor and contributor, *Encyclopaedia Britannica.*

SIDELIGHTS: The Orthodox Church has also been published in Italian, Spanish, Dutch, and German editions.

BIOGRAPHICAL/CRITICAL SOURCES: Times Literary Supplement, March 13, 1981.

* * *

MEYER, John Robert 1927-

PERSONAL: Born December 6, 1927, in Pasco, Wash.; son of Philip Conrad and Cora (Kempter) Meyer; married Helen Lee Stowell, December 17, 1949; children: Leslie Karen, Ann Elizabeth, Robert Conrad. *Education:* Attended Pacific University, Forest Grove, Ore., 1945-46; University of Washington, Seattle, A.B., 1950; Harvard University, Ph.D., 1955. *Home:* 138 Brattle St., Cambridge, Mass. 02138. *Office:* Morgan Hall 322, Graduate School of Business Administration, Harvard University, Boston, Mass. 02163.

CAREER: Harvard University, Boston, Mass., junior fellow, 1953-55, assistant professor, 1955-58, associate professor, 1958-59, professor of economics, 1959-68, 1973—; National Bureau of Economic Research, president, 1967-77; Yale University, New Haven, Conn., professor of economics, 1968-73. Director of Dun & Bradstreet, Union Pacific Corp., Mutual of New York, and AMCA International. *Military service:* U.S. Navy, 1946-48. *Member:* American Economic Association, American Statistical Association, Econometric Society, American Academy of Arts and Sciences, Economic History Association, Phi Beta Kappa. *Awards, honors:* Guggenheim fellow, 1958-59; Ford Foundation research professorship, 1962-63.

WRITINGS: (With Edwin Kuh) *The Investment Decision: An Empirical Inquiry,* Harvard University Press, 1957; (with M. J. Peck, C. Zwick, and J. Stenason) *Economics of Competition in the Transportation Industries,* Harvard University Press, 1959.

(With Robert Glauber) *Investment Decisions, Economic Forecasting and Public Policy,* Harvard University Press, 1964; (with A. Conrad) *The Economics of Slavery and Other Essays on the Qualitative Studies of Economic History,* Aldine, 1964; (with M. Wohl and J. F. Kain) *The Urban Transportation Problem,* Harvard University Press, 1965; (with Conrad) *Studies in Econometric History,* Chapman & Hall, 1965; (with David Denoon) *Technological Change, Migration Patterns and Some Issues of Public Policy,* Harvard University, 1967; (with Kain) *Interrelationships of Transportation and Poverty,* Harvard University, 1968; (with Paul O. Roberts) *An Analysis of Investment Alternatives in the Colombian Transport System,* Harvard University, 1968.

(With Donald Eugene Farrar) *Managerial Economics,* Prentice-Hall, 1970; (with Mahlon R. Straszheim) *Pricing and Project Evaluation,* Brookings Institution (Washington), 1971; (with Gerald Kraft) *The Role of Transportation in Regional Economic Development,* Lexington Books, 1971; (compiler with Kain) *Essays in Regional Economics,* Harvard University Press, 1971; (editor) *Techniques of Transport Planning,* Brookings Institution, 1971.

(With Robert Wilson, Alan Baughcum, Ellen Burton, and Louis Caouette) *The Economics of Competition in the Telecommunications Industry,* Oelgoschlager, 1980; (with Clinton Oster, Ivor Morgan, Benjamin Benson, and Diana Strassmann) *Airline Deregulation,* Auburn House, 1981; (with J. A. Gomez-Ibanez) *Autos, Transit and Cities,* Harvard University Press, 1981.

Contributor: *The Public Stake in Union Power,* University of Virginia Press, 1959; *Technological Change and the Future of the Railways,* Northwestern University Press, 1961; *Digital Computers and Their Applications,* Harvard University Press, 1962; (with Kuh) *Impacts of Monetary Policy,* Prentice-Hall, 1964. Contributor of articles to economics journals in the United States and abroad.

* * *

MIALL, Robert
See BURKE, John (Frederick)

* * *

MICKIEWICZ, Ellen Propper 1938-

PERSONAL: Surname is pronounced Mits-*Keh*-vich; born November 6, 1938, in Hartford, Conn.; daughter of George K. and Rebecca (Adler) Propper; married Denis Mickiewicz (a professor), June 2, 1963; children: Cyril. *Education:* Wellesley College, B.A., 1960; Yale University, M.A., 1961, Ph.D., 1965. *Home:* 1555 Rainier Falls Dr., Atlanta, Ga. 30329. *Office:* Graduate School of Arts and Sciences, Emory University, Atlanta, Ga. 30322.

CAREER: Yale University, New Haven, Conn., lecturer in political science, 1965-67; Michigan State University, East Lansing, assistant professor, 1967-69, associate professor, 1969-73, professor of political science, 1973-80, associate professor in Computer Institute for Social Science Research, 1972-73, academic administrative intern in Office of Provost, 1976-77; Emory University, Atlanta, Ga., professor of political science and dean of Graduate School of Arts and Sciences, 1980—. Kathryn W. Davis Visiting Professor of Wellesley College, 1978; associate at Harvard University Russian Research Center, 1978. Founder and first chairman of the board of directors, Opera Guild of Greater Lansing. *Member:* International Studies Association (vice-president for North America, 1983—), American Political Science Association, American Association for the Advancement of Slavic Studies (member of board of directors, 1978-81). *Awards, honors:* Guggenheim fellowship, 1973-74; Sigma Xi grant, 1973-74; Ford Foundation grant, 1979-83.

WRITINGS: Soviet Political Schools, Yale University Press, 1967; (contributor with Frederick C. Barghoorn) *Communication in International Politics,* University of Illinois Press, 1972; (editor and contributor) *Handbook of Soviet Social Science Data,* Free Press, 1973; *Media and the Russian Public,* Praeger, 1981.

Contributor to Grolier's *Encyclopedia International,* 1969 and 1979. Contributor of articles and reviews to newspapers and journals, including *New York Times, Slavic Review,* and *Problems of Communism.* Editor of *Soviet Union,* 1980—.

WORK IN PROGRESS: Studies of the feedback loop in the Soviet Union.

* * *

MILES, (Louise) Bebe 1924-1980

PERSONAL: Born March 18, 1924, in New York, N.Y.; died June 21, 1980; daughter of Philip J. (an insurance executive) and Louise (a nurse; maiden name, Stephan) Priore; married Robert T. Miles (a safety engineer), August 29, 1946; children: Diane, Victoria (Mrs. Richard Smith), Robin. *Education:* Syracuse University, B.A. (magna cum laude), 1945. *Politics:* Republican. *Religion:* Christian. *Home address:* Philip Circle, R.D. 4, Doylestown, Pa. 18901.

CAREER: Binghamton Sun, Binghamton, N.Y., reporter, 1945-46; Syracuse University, Syracuse, N.Y., editor of alumni magazine, 1946-47; free-lance writer, 1947-65; Bryn Mawr Hospital, Bryn Mawr, Pa., in public relations, 1965-66; Bucks County Bar Association, Doylestown, Pa., in public relations, beginning 1966. Employed in public relations by W. Atlee Burpee, 1972-73; member of staff of Bowman's Hill State Wildflower Preserve.

MEMBER: Garden Writers Association of America (member of executive board, 1974-76), Pennsylvania Horticultural Society, Bucks County Audubon Society, Bucks County Historical Society, Doylestown Nature Club (member of executive board), Bowman's Hill State Wildflower Preserve (member of executive committee), Phi Beta Kappa, Alpha Chi Omega, Syracuse University Alumnae Association. *Awards, honors:* Award from Garden Federation of Pennsylvania, 1971, for *Bluebells and Bittersweet.*

WRITINGS: The Wonderful World of Bulbs, Van Nostrand, 1963; *Bluebells and Bittersweet,* Van Nostrand, 1970; *Designing with Natural Materials,* Van Nostrand, 1975; *Bulbs for the Home Gardener,* Grosset, 1976; *Wildflower Perennials for Your Garden: A Detailed Guide to Years of Bloom from America's Long-Neglected Native Heritage,* Hawthorn, 1976. Contributor to gardening magazines and to *Ranger Rick* (children's nature magazine).†

* * *

MILLER, Lillian B(eresnack) 1923-

PERSONAL: Born February 15, 1923, in Boston, Mass.; daughter of Samuel M. and Ida Frances (Curland) Beresnack; married Nathan Miller (a professor of history), November 3, 1948; children: Hannah E. Lieberman, Joel A., Rebecca S. *Education:* Radcliffe College, A.B. (magna cum laude), 1943; Columbia University, A.M., 1948, Ph.D., 1962. *Office:* National Portrait Gallery, Smithsonian Institution, Washington, D.C. 20560.

CAREER: Bard College, Annandale-on-Hudson, N.Y., instructor in literature, 1946-49; University of Wisconsin—Milwaukee, instructor, 1961-62, lecturer, 1962-67, associate professor of history, 1967-71; Smithsonian Institution, National Portrait Gallery, Washington, D.C., historian, 1971-74, historian of American culture, 1974—. Caroline Werner Gannett Professor of the Humanities, Rochester Institute of Technology, 1981-82. Commissioner, Commission on Artistic Properties for the State of Maryland, 1973-76. *Member:* American Historical Association, Organization of American Historians, Eighteenth-Century Studies Association, Institute of Early American History and Culture (member of council, 1982-85), Dunlap Society (member of advisory board, 1980—), Phi Beta Kappa.

WRITINGS: Patrons and Patriotism: The Encouragement of the Fine Arts in the United States, 1790-1860, University of Chicago Press, 1966; *"If Elected . . .": Unsuccessful Candidates for the Presidency, 1796-1968,* Smithsonian Institution Press, 1972; *The Lazzaroni: Science and Scientists in Mid-19th Century America,* Smithsonian Institution Press, 1972; *In the Minds and Hearts of the People: Prologue to the American Revolution, 1760-1774,* New York Graphic Society, 1974; *The Dye Is Now Cast: The Road to American Independence, 1774-1776,* Smithsonian Institution Press, 1975; (editor and author of foreword) *Charles Fenderich, Lithographer,* University of Chicago Press, 1978; (editor) *The Collected Papers of Charles Willson Peale and His Family,* three volumes, Kraus Microform, 1980; (contributor) *The Best of the Smithsonian,* Smithsonian Institution Press, 1982; (author of introduction) Wendy C. Wick, *The Eighteenth Century Graphic Portraits,* Barra Foundation, 1982; (contributor) *Charles Willson Peale and His World,* Abrams, 1982.

Also contributor to *Indiana Historical Society Lectures for 1972-1973,* 1974, 1976, 1977, and to *Meaning in American Art,* 1976. Editor of the Charles Willson Peale papers for the National Portrait Gallery. Contributor to *American Magazine of Art, American Art Journal,* and to historical journals. Member of editorial advisory board, *Winterthur Portfolio.*

WORK IN PROGRESS: The Fine Arts in American Civilization, two volumes, for University of Chicago Press; *Selected Papers of Charles Willson Peale and His Family,* eight volumes, for Yale University Press; *The Puritan Portrait; The Great American Collectors.*

* * *

MILLER, Marshall Lee 1942-

PERSONAL: Born October 18, 1942, in Chattanooga, Tenn.; son of W. Landon (a clergyman) and Katherine (Rankin) Miller; married Marlene Siskin (a journalist), June 21, 1970. *Education:* Harvard University, B.A., 1964; Yale University, J.D., 1970; also attended Oxford University and University of Heidelberg, 1964-67.

CAREER: Arnold & Porter, Washington, D.C., attorney, 1970-71; U.S. Environmental Protection Agency, Washington, D.C., special assistant to the administrator, 1971-73; U.S. Department of Justice, Washington, D.C., associate deputy attorney general, 1973-74; Jones, Day, Reavis & Pogue, Washington, D.C., attorney, 1974-75; U.S. Department of Labor, Washington, D.C., deputy administrator of Occupational Safety and Health Administration, beginning 1974. Lecturer at Yale University and Government Institute Seminars on the Environment. Member of National Academy of Sciences' advisory panel on government regulation of chemicals in the environment.

WRITINGS—Editor, except as indicated; published by Government Institutes, except as indicated: (Author) *Bulgaria during the Second World War,* Stanford University Press, 1975; *Environmental Law Handbook,* 1975; *Toxic Substances Law and Regulations, 1977,* 1977; *Toxic Substances Control II,*

1978; *Toxic Substance Control III: Implementing the Regulatory Program,* 1979; *Occupational Health and Safety Regulation,* 1980; *Toxic Control in the Eighties,* 1980.†

* * *

MITCHELL, Gladys (Maude Winifred) 1901- (Stephen Hockaby, Malcolm Torrie)

PERSONAL: Born April 19, 1901, in Cowley, Oxford, England; daughter of James and Annie Julia Maude (Simmonds) Mitchell. *Education:* Attended Goldsmith's College, 1919-21; University of London, diploma in history, 1926. *Politics:* Conservative. *Religion:* Agnostic. *Home:* 1 Cecil Close, Corfe Mullen, Dorsetshire BH21 3PW, England. *Agent:* Curtis Brown Ltd., 1 Craven Hill, London W2 3EW, England.

CAREER: Author of mystery novels. Teacher of English and history, 1921-61. *Member:* Society of Authors, Crime Writers' Association, Ancient Monuments Society (fellow), Detection Club. *Awards, honors:* Silver Dagger Award from Crime Writers' Association, 1976.

WRITINGS—All mystery novels; published by M. Joseph, except as indicated: *Speedy Death,* Dial, 1929; *The Mystery of a Butcher's Shop,* Gollancz, 1929, Dial, 1930.

The Longer Bodies, Gollancz, 1930; *The Saltmarsh Murders,* Gollancz, 1932, Macrae Smith, 1933; (with Anthony Berkeley, Milward Kennedy, John Rhode, Dorothy Sayers, and Helen Simpson) *Ask a Policeman,* Arthur Barker, 1933; *Death in the Wet,* Macrae Smith, 1934 (published in England as *Death at the Opera,* Grayson & Grayson, 1934); *The Devil at Saxon Wall,* Grayson & Grayson, 1935; *Dead Men's Morris,* 1936; *Come Away, Death,* 1937; *St. Peter's Finger,* 1938; *Printer's Error,* 1939.

Brazen Tongue, 1940; *Hangman's Curfew,* 1941; *When Last I Died,* 1941, Knopf, 1942; *Laurels Are Poison,* 1942; *The Worsted Viper,* 1943; *Sunset over Soho,* 1943; *My Father Sleeps,* 1944; *The Rising of the Moon,* 1945; *Here Comes a Chopper,* 1946; *Death and the Maiden,* 1947, reprinted, Lythway Press, 1973; *The Dancing Druids,* 1948, reprinted, Severn House, 1975; *Tom Brown's Body,* 1949.

Groaning Spinney, 1950; *The Devil's Elbow,* 1951, reprinted, Sheldon House, 1977; *The Echoing Strangers,* 1952, reprinted, Severn House, 1975; *Merlin's Furlong,* 1953, reprinted, Hutchinson, 1972; *Faintly Speaking,* 1954, reprinted, Magna Print Books, 1979; *Watson's Choice,* 1955, reprinted, Dell, 1981; *Twelve Horses and the Hangman's Noose,* 1956, reprinted, Magna Print Books, 1977; *The Twenty-Third Man,* 1957; *Spotted Hemlock,* 1958; *The Man Who Grew Tomatoes,* 1959, London House, 1960, reprinted, Severn House, 1976.

Say It with Flowers, 1960; *The Nodding Canaries,* 1961; *My Bones Will Keep,* 1962, reprinted, Magna Print Books, 1978; *Adders on the Heath,* London House, 1963; *Death of a Delft Blue,* 1964, London House, 1965; *Pageant of Murder,* London House, 1965; *The Croaking Raven,* 1966; *Skeleton Island,* 1967; *Three Quick and Five Dead,* 1968; *Dance to Your Daddy,* 1969.

Gory Dew, 1970; *Lament for Leto,* 1971; *A Hearse on May-Day,* 1972; *The Murder of Busy Lizzie,* 1973; *A Javelin for Jonah,* 1974; *Winking at the Brim,* McKay, 1974; *Convent on Styx,* 1975; *Late, Late in the Evening,* 1976; *Noonday and Night,* 1977; *Fault in the Structure,* 1977; *Wraiths and Changelings,* 1978; *Mingled with Venom,* 1978; *Nest of Vipers,* 1979; *The Mudflats of the Dead,* 1979.

Uncoffin'd Clay, 1980; *The Whispering Knights,* 1980; *The Death-Cap Dancers,* 1981; *Lovers, Make Moan,* 1981; *Here Lies Gloria Mundy,* 1982; *Death of a Burrowing Mole,* 1982; *The Greenstone Griffins,* 1983; *Cold, Lone and Still,* 1983.

Children's books: *The Three Fingerprints,* Heinemann, 1940; *Holiday River,* Evans Brothers, 1948; *The Seven Stones Mystery,* Evans Brothers, 1949; *The Malory Secret,* Evans Brothers, 1950; *Pam at Storne Castle,* Evans Brothers, 1951; *Caravan Creek,* Blackie & Son, 1954; *On Your Marks,* Heinemann, 1954, new revised edition, Parrish, 1964; *The Light Blue Hills,* Bodley Head, 1959.

Under pseudonym Stephen Hockaby: *Marsh Hay,* Grayson & Grayson, 1933; *Seven Stars and Orion,* Grayson & Grayson, 1934; *Gabriel's Hold,* Grayson & Grayson, 1935; *Shallow Brown,* M. Joseph, 1936; *Outlaws of the Border,* Pitman, 1936; *Grand Master,* M. Joseph, 1939.

Under pseudonym Malcolm Torrie; all published by M. Joseph: *Heavy as Lead,* 1966; *Late and Cold,* 1967; *Your Secret Friend,* 1968; *Churchyard Salad,* 1969; *Shades of Darkness,* 1970; *Bismarck Herrings,* 1971.

SIDELIGHTS: Gladys Mitchell has long been recognized as one of England's most famous and entertaining mystery novelists. Will Cuppy offers *Saltmarsh Murders* as a typical example of Mitchell's work, calling the novel in *Books* "a most unusual combination of horror, fun, and honest-to-goodness brainwork." A *Saturday Review of Literature* critic believes that *Death in the Wet* is still another one of Mitchell's successes with its "grand background, excellent characterizations, engrossing puzzle all built up to solution that goes pop!"

Many critics attribute Mitchell's popularity to her ever-present master sleuth, the colorful Dame Beatrice Lestrange Bradley. "Possibly the most fascinating and maddening female sleuth ever created" is the way Anthony Boucher describes her in the *New York Times Book Review.* And James Sandoe writes in a review of *Spotted Hemlock* published in the *New York Herald Tribune Book Review* that Dame Bradley, "that formidable, bright-eyed old speculator, gives us a fine time as she probes among the suspects."

However, Mitchell's writing, which has spanned over fifty years, is not without its detractors. While many reviewers and readers praise her writing, others find it somewhat annoying. As Boucher explains in the *New York Times Book Review,* "There are no moderate attitudes on the work of Gladys Mitchell; either you love her (as I do) or you plain can't read her."

The general point of disagreement centers around Mitchell's tendency to base her plots on outrageous and irregular happenings, with an occasional event taxing the belief of some readers. While many critics agree with Ralph Partridge's statement in the *New Statesman* that "Mitchell's powerful prose and even more powerful imagination surmounts all trivial inconsistencies of time and place," others side with E. R. Punshon who comments in the *Manchester Guardian* that "Mitchell has on occasion tried her readers a little highly by allowing mystery to become too much like confusion." A writer for the *Times Literary Supplement* remarks that "Mitchell's plot, her characters and her easy style are alike excellent, though she occasionally disregards an improbability that no professional detective would overlook."

A number of reviewers point to Mitchell's efforts to frequently change her style, an apparent attempt to update her fiction, as still another reason for her success and her ability to keep her readers coming back for more. While her attempts at change have not always met with approval, Mitchell's followers have remained loyal. According to Patricia Craig, Mitchell's "detective fiction has undergone quite a few changes since it began with *Speedy Death* in 1929, even though each of her novels features the same central character, the redoubtable Mrs. Bradley (later Dame Beatrice)." As Craig explains in an article published in the *Times Literary Supplement:* "In the formal construction of her stories and in the articulate sedateness of her dialogues, Mitchell's work is coming more and more to resemble Ivy Compton Burnett's. Like Compton Burnett, too, she refuses to differentiate between comedy and tragedy, and this is one reason why her books are so memorable. But Mitchell's basic traits are all her own: she is a writer who can absorb influences without being overwhelmed by them."

AVOCATIONAL INTERESTS: Athletics, swimming, architecture (from Roman to eighteenth-century English).

BIOGRAPHICAL/CRITICAL SOURCES: Books, April 2, 1933, February 4, 1934; *Saturday Review of Literature,* February 10, 1934; *Times Literary Supplement,* March 29, 1934, August 8, 1980, April 17, 1981, October 29, 1982; *New Statesman,* August 30, 1958, December 3, 1960; *Manchester Guardian,* October 9, 1958; *New York Herald Tribune Book Review,* December 7, 1958; *New York Times Book Review,* December 11, 1960; *Washington Post Book World,* February 15, 1981.

* * *

MITCHELL, J(ames) Clyde 1918-

PERSONAL: Born June 21, 1918, in Pietermaritzburg, South Africa; son of George S. and Rose K. (Jones) Mitchell; married Edna Grace Maslen, 1943 (died, 1962); married Hilary Ward-Hancock Flegg (a medical sociologist), August 24, 1963 (died, 1976); children: (first marriage) Donald, Gillian, Kerr, Alan; (stepchildren) Erica Flegg. *Education:* Natal University College, B.A., 1941; University of South Africa, B.A. (honors), 1948; Oxford University, D.Phil., 1950. *Home:* 25 Staunton Rd., Oxford, England. *Office:* Nuffield College, Oxford University, London, England.

CAREER: Rhodes-Livingstone Institute, Lusaka, Zambia, assistant anthropologist, 1946-50, sociologist, 1950-52, director, 1953-55; University College of Rhodesia and Nyasaland, Salisbury, South Rhodesia, professor of African studies, 1955-64, professor of sociology, 1964-65, vice-principal, 1961-62; University of Manchester, Manchester, England, professor of urban sociology, 1966-74; Oxford University, Nuffield College, London, England, fellow, 1974—. Simon research fellow, University of Manchester, 1953; visiting professor, Johns Hopkins University School of International Studies, 1960. Participant in United Nations and UNESCO conferences in London, Paris, Uganda, Ethiopia, Egypt, and Nigeria. Associate member, Scientific Council for Africa. *Military service:* South African Air Force, navigator, 1942-45; became lieutenant.

MEMBER: British Sociological Association, American Sociological Association, Association of Social Anthropologists of the Commonwealth, International Population Union, Africa Studies Association (United States), other organizations in Rhodesia. *Awards, honors:* Rivers Memorial Medal, Royal Anthropological Institute, 1960, for distinguished field work in central Africa.

WRITINGS: (With J. A. Barnes) *The Lamba Village,* School of African Studies, University of Cape Town, 1950; *The Yao Village,* Manchester University Press, 1956; *The Kalela Dance,* Rhodes-Livingstone, 1957; *Tribalism and the Plural Society* (lecture), Oxford University Press, 1960; *The Sociological Background to African Labour,* Ensign Publications, 1961; (editor) *Social Networks in Urban Situations,* Manchester University Press, 1969; (editor with J. Boissevain) *Network Analysis,* Mouton, 1973; (editor) *Numerical Techniques in Social Anthropology,* Institute for the Study of Human Issues, 1980.

Contributor: E. Colson and M. Gluckman, editors, *Seven Tribes of British Central Africa,* Oxford University Press, 1951; W. V. Brelsford, *The Tribes of Northern Rhodesia,* Government Printer (Lusaka), 1956; *The Development of a Middle Class in Tropical and Sub-Tropical Countries,* [Brussels], 1956; W. V. Brelsford, editor, *Handbook of Rhodesia and Nyasaland,* Cassell, 1960; K. M. Barbour and R. M. Prothero, editors, *Essays on African Population,* Routledge & Kegan Paul, 1961.

Also contributor to other books. Contributor of papers to published proceedings of international and African conferences. Contributor of forty articles to journals, including *Civilisations, African Studies, Africa, Human Problems, British Journal of Sociology,* and *Central African Journal of Medicine.*

WORK IN PROGRESS: Studies of urbanization in Zambia, 1950-53, based on social surveys; studies of occupational prestige among Africans; study of attitudes to urban living in Zimbabwe; network analysis.

* * *

MODRAS, Ronald E(dward) 1937-

PERSONAL: Born August 23, 1937, in Detroit, Mich.; son of Edward and Anne (Adamowicz) Modras. *Education:* St. Mary's College, Orchard Lake, Mich., B.A., 1959; Catholic University of America, S.T.B., 1963; University of Tuebingen, Ph.D., 1972. *Address:* 20955 Whitlock Dr., Dearborn Heights, Mich. *Office:* St. Louis University, 3634 Lindell, St. Louis, Mo. 63108.

CAREER: Ordained Roman Catholic priest, Archdiocese of Detroit, Detroit, Mich., 1963; parish priest in Detroit, 1963-67; Institute for Continuing Education, Detroit, professor of ecumenical studies, 1966-68; Marygrove College, Detroit, chaplain, 1967-68; Pius XII Institute for Religious Education, Detroit, visiting professor, 1969-71; St. John's Provincial Seminary, Plymouth, Mich., assistant professor of systematic theology, 1972-78; Harvard University, Divinity School, Cambridge, Mass., visiting scholar, 1979; St. Louis University, St. Louis, Mo., associate professor, 1979—. Adjunct professor at University of Detroit, 1972-78, Madonna College and St. Mary's College, 1974-78. Vice-chairman, Detroit Archdiocesan Commission for Ecumenical Affairs, 1966-68; chairman, National Workshop for Christian Unity, 1968; member of a taskforce for Polish-American and Jewish-American relations; member of advisory committee for Catholic-Jewish relations. *Member:* Catholic Society of America, American Academy of Religion, North American Paul Tillich Society.

WRITINGS: Paths to Unity, Sheed, 1968; (contributor) H. Kung and W. Kasper, editors, *Polarization in the Church,* Herder & Herder, 1973; *Tillich's Theology of the Church,* Wayne State University Press, 1976; (with A. Kosnik and others) *Human Sexuality: New Directions in American Catholic Thought,* Paulist/Newman, 1977; (contributor) Kung and J. Moltmann, editors, *An Ecumenical Confession of Faith,* Seabury, 1979. Editor-in-chief of a number of printed materials for the Archdiocese of Detroit, including fifty-four pamphlets. Contributor of articles to *Commonweal, Theological Studies, Modern School-*

man, and *Currents in Theology and Mission.* Member of editorial board, *Concilium* and *Currents in Theology and Mission.*

WORK IN PROGRESS: Theological Anthropology; The Philosophy and Writings of Pope John Paul II.

SIDELIGHTS: Human Sexuality: New Directions in American Catholic Thought has been translated into Italian and Spanish.

* * *

MOERI, Louise 1924-

PERSONAL: Surname rhymes with "story"; born November 30, 1924, in Klamath Falls, Ore.; daughter of Clyde (a farmer) and Hazel (Simpson) Healy; married Edwin Albert Moeri (a civil servant), December 15, 1946; children: Neal Edwin, Rodger Scott, Patricia Jo Ann. *Education:* Stockton Junior College, A.A., 1944; University of California, Berkeley, B.A., 1946. *Religion:* Protestant. *Home:* 18262 South Austin Rd., Manteca, Calif. 95336.

CAREER: Writer. Manteca Branch Library, Manteca, Calif., library assistant, 1961-78.

WRITINGS: Star Mother's Youngest Child, Houghton, 1975; *A Horse for XYZ,* Dutton, 1977; *How the Rabbit Stole the Moon,* Houghton, 1977; *The Girl Who Lived on the Ferris Wheel,* Dutton, 1979; *Save Queen of Sheba,* Dutton, 1981; *Unicorn and the Plow,* Dutton, 1982; *First the Egg,* Dutton, 1982.

WORK IN PROGRESS: Down Wind, a juvenile novel.

SIDELIGHTS: "I began writing poetry as a very small child," Louise Moeri told *CA,* "and continued over a long period of time to struggle to get something down on paper. I have received innumerable rejection slips. The thing that kept me going is a picture I have in my mind. I see myself as a very old lady in a rest home with a blanket over my knees with a choice of two statements to make: 'I tried very hard to write—gave it everything I had' and 'how I wish I had tried harder'."

* * *

MOIR, Alfred 1924-

PERSONAL: Surname is pronounced Moy-er; born April 14, 1924, in Minneapolis, Minn.; son of William Wilmerding (a physician) and Blanche (Kummer) Moir. *Education:* Harvard University, A.B., 1948, M.A., 1949, Ph.D., 1953; University of Rome, graduate study, 1950-52. *Home:* 1460 Cantera Ave., Santa Barbara, Calif. 93110. *Office:* Department of Art History, University of California, Santa Barbara, Calif. 93106.

CAREER: Harvard University, Harvard College, Cambridge, Mass., proctor, 1949-50; Tulane University of Louisiana, Newcomb College, New Orleans, instructor, 1952-54, assistant professor, 1954-59, associate professor of art history, 1959-63; University of California, Santa Barbara, associate professor, 1963-65, professor of art history, 1965—, chairman of department, 1963-69, director of Education Abroad Program in Italy, 1978-80. Consultant, Isaac Delgado Museum of Art, New Orleans, 1954-57. Art historian in residence, American Academy in Rome, 1969-70. *Military service:* U.S. Army, 1943-46; became master sergeant. *Member:* College Art Association, Society of Architectural Historians, Mediaeval Academy of America, Renaissance Society of America, Southern California Art Historians. *Awards, honors:* Fulbright fellow in Italy, 1950-51; honorary alumnus, Tulane University.

WRITINGS: (Contributor) *Art in Italy, 1600-1700,* Detroit Institute of Arts, 1965; *The Italian Followers of Caravaggio,* Harvard University Press, 1967; (editor) *Seventeenth-Century Italian Drawings from the Collection of Janos Scholz,* University of California, 1973; *Caravaggio and His Copyists,* College Art Association of America, 1975; *European Drawings in the Santa Barbara Museum of Art,* [Santa Barbara, Calif.], 1976; (editor) *Regional Styles of Drawing in Italy,* [Santa Barbara], 1977; *Caravaggio,* Abrams, 1982. Contributor to art journals.

* * *

MONTAGUE, John (Patrick) 1929-

PERSONAL: Born February 28, 1929, in New York, N.Y.; son of James Terence and Mary (Carney) Montague; married Madeleine de Brauer, October 18, 1956 (divorced, 1972); married Evelyn Robson; children: (second marriage) Oonogh, Silylle. *Education:* University College, Dublin, B.A., 1949, M.A., 1953; Yale University, postgraduate studies, 1953-54; University of Iowa, M.F.A., 1955. *Agent:* A. D. Peters & Co., 10 Buckingham St., Adelphi, London WC2N 6BU, England. *Office:* Department of English, University College, National University of Ireland, Cork, Ireland.

CAREER: Author, poet, editor, and translator. *Standard* (newspaper), Dublin, Ireland, film critic, 1949-52; Bord Failte (Irish tourist board), Dublin, Ireland, executive, 1956-59; *Irish Times,* Paris correspondent, beginning 1961; currently lecturer in poetry, University College, University of Dublin. Visiting lecturer at University of California, Berkeley, 1964, 1965, University of Dublin, 1967 and 1968, and University of Vincennes, 1968. *Member:* Irish Academy of Letters. *Awards, honors:* Fulbright fellowship; May Morton Memorial Award for poetry; Arts Council of Northern Ireland grant, 1970; Irish American Cultural Institute prize, 1976; Marten Toonder Award, 1977.

WRITINGS: Forms of Exile (poetry), Dolmen Press, 1958; *The Old People,* Dolmen Press, 1960; *Poisoned Lands, and Other Poems,* MacGibbon & Kee, 1961, Dufour, 1963, revised edition, Humanities, 1977; (with Thomas Kinsella and Richard Murphy) *Three Irish Poets* (pamphlet), Dolmen Press, 1961; (editor with Kinsella) *The Dolmen Miscellany of Irish Writing,* Dolmen Press, 1962; *Death of a Chieftain, and Other Stories,* MacGibbon & Kee, 1964, Dufour, 1968.

Old Mythologies: A Poem, privately printed, c. 1965; *All Legendary Obstacles,* Oxford University Press, 1966; *Patriotic Suite,* Dufour, 1966; (editor with Liam Miller) *A Tribute to Austin Clarke on His Seventieth Birthday,* Dufour, 1966; *A Chosen Light* (poetry), MacGibbon & Kee, 1967, Swallow Press, 1969; *Home Again,* Festival Publications (Belfast), 1967; *Hymn to the New Omagh Road,* Dolmen Press, 1968; *The Bread God* (pamphlet), Dolmen Press, 1968; *A New Siege* (poetry), Dolmen Press, 1969.

(With John Hewitt) *The Planter and the Gael,* Arts Council of Northern Ireland, 1970; *Tides* (poetry), Dolmen Press, 1970, Swallow Press, 1971; *The Rough Field* (poetry), Dolmen Press, 1971, Swallow Press, 1972, revised edition, Wake Forest University Press, 1979; (editor and translator) *The Faber Book of Irish Verse,* Faber, 1972, published as *The Book of Irish Verse,* Macmillan, 1974; (translator) *A Fair House: Versions of Irish Poetry,* Cuala Press, 1973; *The Cave of Night* (poetry), Stone Press, 1974; *A Slow Dance* (poetry), Dolmen Press, 1975; *O'Riada's Farewell* (poetry), Golden Stone Press, 1975; (translator with wife Evelyn Robson) Andre Frenaud, *November,*

Golden Stone Press, 1977; *The Great Cloak* (poetry), Wake Forest University Press, 1978.

Selected Poems, Wake Forest University Press, 1982. Also author of dramatization, "The Rough Field," produced in London, 1973. Contributor to *Paris Review.*

SIDELIGHTS: Although John Montague was born in Brooklyn, he has lived most of his life in Ireland. His parents, strict Catholics, were born and raised in Northern Ireland. In 1920 Montague's father, James Terence Montague, came to the United States seeking a better life for himself and his family. Eight years later he sent for his wife, Mary, and their two sons. A year later, John was born. Mary Montague had a difficult time adjusting to her new home in America and, since times were very hard during this period in the United States, the three boys were sent to Northern Ireland to live with relatives. While his older brothers were raised by their maternal grandmother, Montague lived with his two maiden aunts on the family farm in rural Garvaghey.

It has been suggested that it was this early and traumatic separation from his parents and his brothers, coupled with a boyhood in rural Northern Ireland, that has most influenced Montague's writing. As a result, the attempt and pains of loving, political and religious dilemmas, and the vanishing simple country life are recurring themes in many of his works, especially his poetry. For example, in 1976 a reviewer for the *New York Times Book Review* comments that Montague for some time has "been working with large sequences that relate his personal life and psyche to his family's background in rural Ulster and to the whole of Ireland's catastrophic history."

Writing in the *Malahat Review,* Derek Mahon describes Montague as "the best Irish poet of his generation. . . . Montague is not a metaphysician: he is a historian and autobiographer." Montague has long been appreciated and admired for his deep feeling for Ireland—the people and the landscape—and his ability to reflect these emotions in his poetry. A reviewer for *Choice* points out that Montague's "best poems have always been those poems about himself, full of the intensity of feeling, the power of experience."

These intense feelings that Montague mirrors in his writings are especially evident in his collection *The Rough Field.* For example, in his review published in *Hollins Critic,* Benedict Kiely writes that this is Montague's most remarkable book and "one of the most interesting statements made in this century about Ireland past and present. . . . It is a unity, a movement and sequence of poems as strong and steady as the mountain stream descending on the lowlands to define a world, taking with it the past and present of that one small backward place, but a place over-burdened with history. . . . Family history and his own personal agony, and the history of the place over three and a half centuries . . . are all twisted together, strands in a strong rope." And M. L. Rosenthal points out in *Nation* that Montague's "poems come out of a deeply human speaking personality for whom language and reality are more than just a source of a plastic design of nuances. . . . [The author] tells a story, paints a picture, evokes an atmosphere, suggests the complexities and torments of adult love and marriage—all in the most direct, concrete, involving way."

Montague's editing of the anthology *The Book of Irish Verse* is another example of his commitment to Ireland and his involvement in its heritage. Victor Howes remarks in the *Christian Science Monitor* that this collection of poetry written by other Irish authors "is rich in its translations of mythological early poems. It is similarly rich in its presentation of the 20th-century poets. [The] anthology conveys the sense that Irish poets are again finding a voice that is national, unique and as significant as it was in the days of 'Eire of high recital / Recital skillfully done,' the days of an Ireland known for its 'Kings and queens and poets a-many.'" And a critic writes in a *Choice* review of *The Book of Irish Verse* that Montague's "winnowing results in an anthology having the vibrancy and understated qualities of fineness that mark all that is best in the Irish tradition."

Despite his interest in Ireland's heritage, Montague is a very contemporary Irish poet in that he writes about current issues and topics. However, not everyone feels Montague performs a service to his homeland by publicizing some of Ireland's troubles and problems. Derek Mahon writes in the *Malahat Review* that "Montague has been criticized for 'using' the present crisis in Ulster as raw material for his poetry. (His critics do not, however, accuse Yeats of doing the same thing at an earlier period.) The criticism seems to me at best an injustice founded in misunderstanding—at worst a cheap jibe. The implication, an essentially philistine one, is that something as frivolous as poetry has no business concerning itself with something as serious as human suffering. . . . Ireland is central to Montague's myth, and has been since his first booklet . . . was published."

Still another respected and admired feature of Montague's work is his craftsmanship. "Montague has always been a fastidious craftsman," W. J. McCormack writes in the *Times Literary Supplement.* And M. L. Rosenthal explains in a review published in *Nation* that "Montague does have a highly developed sense of the craft; he is a real poet, who works at his desk and drinks of the tradition. But he brings all his engagement with his art directly to bear on the world of our common life . . . and thus makes immediate contact with his readers. He thinks and talks like a grown-up man, and that fact alone makes him better literary company than most of his poetic contemporaries."

BIOGRAPHICAL/CRITICAL SOURCES: Times Literary Supplement, January 5, 1967, November 9, 1967, March 19, 1976, August 11, 1978, July 16, 1982; *New Statesman,* August 18, 1967; *Punch,* January 3, 1968; *New York Times,* March 23, 1968; *Library Journal,* June 1, 1968, August, 1970, July, 1977; *Spectator,* December 5, 1970; *Nation,* May 17, 1971; *Malahat Review,* July, 1973; *New York Times Book Review,* September 19, 1976; *Choice,* May, 1977, December, 1978; *Christian Science Monitor,* June 9, 1977; *Hollins Critic,* December, 1978; *Stand,* Volume XX, number 1, 1978-79; *Contemporary Literary Criticism,* Volume XIII, Gale, 1980; *Village Voice Literary Supplement,* February, 1983.

—Sketch by Margaret Mazurkiewicz

* * *

MONTAGUE, Lisa

See SHULMAN, Sandra (Dawn)

* * *

MOONEY, Elizabeth C(omstock) 1918-

PERSONAL: Born February 8, 1918, in Rome, N.Y.; daughter of Edward Hulett (a lumber dealer) and Elizabeth (Baker) Comstock; married Booth Mooney (a writer), March 9, 1946 (died, 1977); children: Edward, Joan. *Education:* Smith College, B.A., 1939. *Politics:* Democrat. *Religion:* Episcopal. *Home:* 5709

Overlea Rd., Washington, D.C. 20016. *Agent:* Paul R. Reynolds, Inc., 12 East 41st St., New York, N.Y. 10017.

CAREER: Employed in war-related secretarial positions, 1939-43; *Utica Press and Observer-Dispatch,* Utica, N.Y., reporter, 1943-45, bureau chief, 1945-46; free-lance writer, 1946—. *Member:* Washington Independent Writers, Kenwood Golf Club (Washington, D.C.).

WRITINGS—Juveniles, except as indicated: *Jane Addams,* Follett, 1968; *The Mystery of the Narrow Land,* Follett, 1969; *The Sandy Shoes Mystery,* Lippincott, 1970; *In the Shadow of the White Plague* (adult nonfiction), Crowell, 1979; (co-author) *Not My Daughter: Facing Up to Adolescent Pregnancy* (adult nonfiction), Prentice-Hall, 1979; *Alone: Surviving as a Widow* (adult nonfiction), Putnam, 1981. Author of "The Land and People of Asia," a film strip, National Geographic Society, and "Rats in the Suburbs," a television script adapted from one of her own published stories, Multimedia, 1974. Contributor, especially of travel articles, to magazines, including *Smithsonian, Ladies' Home Journal, Yankee, Washingtonian, Maryland,* and *Redbook.*

SIDELIGHTS: In *Alone: Surviving as a Widow,* Elizabeth C. Mooney tells how she coped with the loneliness that filled her life after the sudden death of her husband. But, Mooney's book is not "a guide to living alone," writes Webster Schott in the *Washington Post Book World.* "Rather it's a journal of self-discovery. And like much of art, it tells us what we knew but what we may have forgotten." The critic continues: "It is not a unique story that Mooney has to tell. What is remarkable about it is the intimacy of the telling. . . . What confirms the vitality of her work . . . is the surprising range of social as well as personal observation, and [Mooney's] formidable literary skills."

Explaining how she began her career as a writer, Mooney comments: "I went into writing quite naturally from newspaper reporting. When I married and the children were young I wrote children's books because I understood young people. When they grew up and started making their telephone calls upstairs, I went back to freelance journalism which took me out into the world again and kept me in contact with people."

BIOGRAPHICAL/CRITICAL SOURCES: Elizabeth C. Mooney, *Alone: Surviving as a Widow,* Putnam, 1981; *Washington Post Book World,* August 9, 1981.

* * *

MOORE, Barbara
See LEE, Barbara (Moore)

* * *

MORGAN, Bryan S(tanford) 1923-1976

PERSONAL: Born July 23, 1923, in London, England; died July, 1976, in England; son of Charles Leslie and Winifred (Lock) Morgan. *Education:* St. Catharine's College, Cambridge, B.A., 1944. *Politics:* Tory. *Religion:* Anglo-Catholic.

CAREER: Free-lance author, journalist, and editor. *Awards, honors:* Atlantic Award in Literature; scholarship to Salzburg Seminar in American Studies.

WRITINGS: Vain Citadels (novel), Heinemann, 1947; *Rosa,* Hodder & Stoughton, 1949; *Men and Discoveries in Electricity,* J. Murray, 1952; *The Business at Blanche Capel* (novel), Hamish Hamilton, 1953; *The End of the Line,* Cleaver-Hume, 1955; (editor) *Golden Milestone,* Newman Neame, 1955; *Apothecary's Venture,* Newman Neame, 1959.

Fastness of France, Cleaver-Hume, 1962; *Men and Discoveries in Chemistry,* J. Murray, 1962; (editor) *The Railway-Lover's Companion,* Eyre & Spottiswoode, 1963; *Express Journey, 1864-1964: A Centenary History of the Express Dairy Company,* Newman Neame, 1964; *Andorra: The Country in Between,* Ray Palmer, 1964; *Playing with History,* Newman Neame, 1965; *Electrons at Work,* Macmillan (London), 1965, St. Martin's, 1966; (with Joan Morgan) *Pepe's Island,* Oliver & Boyd, 1965, Criterion, 1966; *Acceleration,* Newman Neame, 1965; (editor) William Plenderbeith Knowles, *New Life through Breathing,* Allen & Unwin, 1966; *Sermons in Stone,* Newman Neame, 1966; *Explosions and Explosives,* Macmillan (London), 1967; (editor) Louis Rose, *Faith Healing,* Gollancz, 1968; *Railway Relics,* Ian Allen, 1969.

Civil Engineering: Railways, Longman, 1971; *The Rolls and Royce Story,* Collins, 1971; *Men and Discoveries in Mathematics,* J. Murray, 1972; *The Great Trains,* Stephens, 1974; *Navigation,* Viking, 1974; (editor) *Crime on the Lines: An Anthology of Mystery Short Stories with a Railway Setting,* Routledge & Kegan Paul, 1975; *Stories of the Railway,* Routledge & Kegan Paul, 1977.

Also author of *The Sacred Nursery,* 1951, *Total to Date,* 1953, and *Early Trains,* 1973. Author of television and radio scripts. Contributor to journals.

AVOCATIONAL INTERESTS: Travel, small boats, chess.

OBITUARIES: AB Bookman's Weekly, October 4, 1976.†

* * *

MORRIS, Sara
See BURKE, John (Frederick)

* * *

MOURIER, Marguerite
See BOULTON, Marjorie

* * *

MUDE, O.
See GOREY, Edward (St. John)

* * *

MURPHY, Beatrice M. 1908-
(Beatrice Murphy Campbell)

PERSONAL: Born June 25, 1908, in Monessen, Pa.; children: Alvin H. *Education:* Attended public schools in Washington, D.C. *Politics:* Democrat. *Religion:* Roman Catholic. *Home:* 2737 Devonshire Pl. N.W., Apt. 222, Washington, D.C. 20008.

CAREER: Has held secretarial positions at Catholic University of America, U.S. Office of Price Administration, and Veterans Administration, all Washington, D.C.; Negro Bibliographic and Research Center, Washington, D.C., founder, 1965, managing editor and director, 1965-71; Minority Research Center, Washington, D.C., managing editor and director, 1971-77; Beatrice M. Murphy Foundation, Washington, D.C., executive director, 1977—. Member of board of directors, Center City Community Development Corp.; president of Emery Community Center Senior Citizens; member of D.C. Committee on the Aging; publicity chairman for Blind Action Forum; volunteer worker with the blind. *Member:* Pen and Brush Club (former president), Women's National Book Association, D.C. Press Club, Political Study Club (president).

WRITINGS: (Editor) *Negro Voices,* Exposition, 1938; (editor) *Ebony Rhythm,* Exposition, 1948, 2nd edition, 1968; *Catching the Editor's Eye,* Hobson, 1949; *Love Is a Terrible Thing,* Hobson, 1949; (with Nancy L. Arnez) *The Rocks Cry Out,* Broadside Press, 1969; (editor) *Today's Negro Voices,* Messner, 1970; *Get With It, Lord,* privately printed, 1977.

Contributor to anthologies: *The Light of Day,* Henry Harrison Publishers, 1929; *Parnassian,* Laurel Publishing, 1930; *Galaxy,* Garden Press, 1933; *Spring,* Cornwall House, 1935; *Contemporary American Women Poets: 1937,* Henry Harrison Publishers, 1937; *Crown Anthology of Verse,* Crown, 1938; Arna Bontemps, editor, *Golden Slippers,* Harper, 1939; Langston Hughes and Bontemps, editors, *Poetry of the Negro,* Doubleday, 1949, reprinted, 1970.

Author of feature column, "Think It Over," *Washington Tribune,* 1933-35, and of poetry column for Associated Negro Press, 1940-41. Contributor of poems and reviews to *Afro-American, Christian Herald, Easterner, Interracial Review, New York Times, Pulse,* and *Tan Confessions.* Feature and children's editor, *Washington Tribune,* 1935-37; editor of *Bibliographic Survey: The Negro in Print,* 1965-72.

SIDELIGHTS: Beatrice M. Murphy began to lose her eyesight in 1967, and she has undergone numerous operations since 1969 in a futile effort to save her sight. Though legally blind and physically handicapped, she is still actively engaged in writing and speaking.

BIOGRAPHICAL/CRITICAL SOURCES: Negro Digest, August, 1969; *Best Sellers,* April 1, 1970.

* * *

MUSOLF, Lloyd D(aryl) 1919-

PERSONAL: Surname is pronounced Mew-solf; born October 14, 1919, in Yale, S.D.; son of William Ferdinand and Emma Marie (Pautz) Musolf; married Dorothy Berdyne Peet, June 30, 1944; children: Stephanie, Michael, Laura. *Education:* Huron College, B.A., 1941; University of South Dakota, M.A., 1946; Johns Hopkins University, Ph.D., 1950. *Politics:* Democrat. *Office:* Institute of Governmental Affairs, University of California, Davis, Calif. 95616.

CAREER: Vassar College, Poughkeepsie, N.Y., instructor, 1949-50, assistant professor, 1950-55, associate professor of political science, 1955-59; Michigan State University, East Lansing, associate professor and chief of MSU advisory group, Saigon, Vietnam, 1959-61, professor of political science, 1961-63; University of California, Davis, Institute of Governmental Affairs, professor of political science and director, 1963—. Visiting professor, University of Michigan, 1955-56, Johns Hopkins University, and University of Delaware. Consultant to New York State Commission on a Constitutional Convention, 1957-58, California State Personnel Board, 1963-65, United Nations Seminar on Public Enterprise, Geneva, 1966, and to United Nations Public Administration Division, 1968. Member of U.S. delegation to International Congress of Administrative Sciences, Paris, 1965. *Military service:* U.S. Navy, 1942-45; became lieutenant; received Presidential Unit Citation.

MEMBER: American Political Science Association, American Society for Public Administration (member of council, 1967-70), Conference of University Bureaus of Governmental Research (chairman, 1965-67), American Association of University Professors, National Association of Schools of Public Affairs and Administration (member of executive council, 1972-74), Council on Graduate Education for Public Administration, Western Political Science Association, Western Governmental Research Association (member of executive board, 1966-68), California Conference on Education for Public Administration, Pi Gamma Mu, Pi Sigma Alpha.

WRITINGS: Federal Examiners and the Conflict of Law and Administration, Johns Hopkins Press, 1953; *Public Ownership and Accountability: The Canadian Experience,* Harvard University Press, 1959; (editor with Samuel Krislov) *The Politics of Regulation,* Houghton, 1964; *Government and the Economy,* Scott, Foresman, 1965; (editor) *Communications Satellites in Political Orbit,* Chandler, 1968.

(Editor with Allan Kornberg) *Legislatures in Developmental Perspective,* Duke University Press, 1970; (with others) *American National Government: Policies and Politics,* Scott, Foresman, 1971; *Mixed Enterprise in a Developmental Perspective,* Heath, 1972; *Legislatures, Environmental Protection, and Developmental Goals: British Columbia and California,* Sage, 1974; (contributor) *Public Enterprise in Asia: Studies on Coordination and Control,* Asian Centre for Development Administration, 1976; (editor with J. Fred Springer) *Malaysia's Parliamentary System: Representative Politics and Policymaking in a Divided Society,* Westview Press, 1979; (editor with Joel Smith, and contributor) *Legislatures in Development: Dynamics of Change in New and Old States,* Duke University Press, 1979; (with Howard G. Schutz and Lawrence Shepard) *Regulating Occupations in California,* Institute of Governmental Studies, 1980. Also contributor to *Public Enterprise and Public Interest,* Institute of Public Administration of Canada. Contributor to *Asian Survey* and political science and public administration journals.

WORK IN PROGRESS: Uncle Sam's Private, Profitseeking Corporations.

SIDELIGHTS: Lloyd D. Musolf told *CA:* "It's stimulating and somewhat unnerving to try to keep up with three rapidly changing research fields: public enterprise, comparative legislatures, and economic regulation."

N

NABOKOV, Peter (Francis) 1940-
(Peter Towne)

PERSONAL: Born October 11, 1940, in Auburn, N.Y.; son of Nicolas (a writer and composer) and Constance (Holladay) Nabokov. *Education:* Attended St. Johns College; Columbia University, B.S., 1965; Goddard College, M.S., 1973. *Home:* 147 Caledonia St., Pacific Grove, Calif. 93950.

CAREER: Worked on Navaho, Sioux, and Crow reservations in Montana, 1962, and later sailed with the Merchant Marine; *New Mexican,* Santa Fe, N.M., staff reporter, 1967-68; Monterey Peninsula College, Monterey, Calif., instructor in American Indian studies, 1970-73, 1977-78; Human Resources Research Organization, Carmel, Calif., research associate, 1972-75; University of California, Berkeley, Calif., instructor, 1979, 1982. Research associate, Museum of the American Indian, Heye Foundation, 1962-82, and Santa Barbara Museum of Natural History, 1978-82. Lecturer at Center for the Study of Indian History, Haskell Indian Junior College, University of California, Berkeley, University of California, Santa Barbara, College of the Virgin Islands, Colorado College, and University of North Dakota. *Member:* Society for the Prevention of Cruelty to Children. *Awards, honors:* Albuquerque Press Club awards, two first prizes, and New Mexico Press Association, first prize in editorial writing, all 1967.

WRITINGS: Two Leggings: The Making of a Crow Warrior, Crowell, 1967; *Tijerina and the Courthouse Raid,* University of New Mexico Press, 1970, revised edition, Ramparts, 1971; (contributor) *Solving "The Indian Problem": The White Man's Burdensome Business,* New York Times, 1975; (under pseudonym Peter Towne) *George Washington Carver,* Crowell, 1975; (contributor) Chester Klevens, editor, *Methods and Materials of Continuing Education,* Klevens Publishing, 1976; (contributor) *Shelter II,* Shelter Publications, 1978; (editor) *Native American Testimony: An Anthology of Indian and White Relations,* Volume I: *First Encounter to Dispossession,* Crowell, 1978; *Indian Running,* Capra, 1981. Contributor to *Nation, Co-Evolution Quarterly, New West, New York Times Magazine,* and other publications.

SIDELIGHTS: In his books on the American Indian, Peter Nabokov presents a sympathetic and compelling view of their history and traditions.

Nabokov's *Two Leggings: The Making of a Crow Warrior* is "a crisp, unexaggerated re-creation of the life of a nineteenth-century Plains Indian warrior," as Meredith Brown of *Saturday Review* states. A detailed biography that also examines Indian society of the time, H. E. Smith of *Library Journal* finds the book "a unique record of a vanished culture," while Brown judges it "a handbook to the values and patterns of leadership in a culture that flourished less than 100 years ago."

In similar terms, E. Z. Friedenberg writes in the *New York Review of Books* that *Tijerina and the Courthouse Raid* is "even more valuable as sociology than as history, because it shows so clearly how things work, and on the basis of such carefully and quite literally painfully gathered evidence, both by observation and documentation." The value of *Native American Testimony,* according to N. S. Momaday of the *New York Times Book Review,* is its "keen insight into the mind and spirit of the American Indian."

In *Indian Running,* Nabokov successfully presents his study of Indian ceremonial running, Kenneth Funston of the *Los Angeles Times Book Review* believes, "in a most Indian way [that] tells you much more than it actually says." "Nabokov's shyness," Funston states, "his hesitation about sticking his nose where it's not wanted, is probably the best route. [Through] his retiring journalism, Nabokov [reflects] a whole system of Native American etiquette, a way of being—and a way of letting others be."

BIOGRAPHICAL/CRITICAL SOURCES: Library Journal, June 15, 1967; *Saturday Review,* September 9, 1967; *New York Review of Books,* December 18, 1969; *New York Times Book Review,* January 11, 1970, April 30, 1978; *New Leader,* February 16, 1970; *Yale Review,* June, 1970; *Nation,* June 1, 1970; *Commonweal,* November 10, 1978; *Los Angeles Times Book Review,* November 29, 1981.

* * *

NARVESON, Jan F(redric) 1936-

PERSONAL: Born June 15, 1936, in Erskine, Minn.; son of Carl Robert and Sophie (Krbechek) Narveson; children: Kaja Lee. *Education:* University of Chicago, B.A., 1955, B.A., 1956; Harvard University, M.A., 1957, Ph.D., 1961; Oxford University, graduate study, 1959-60. *Politics:* "Mildly libertarian." *Religion:* None. *Home:* 57 Young St. W., Waterloo,

Ontario, Canada N2L 2Z4. *Office:* Department of Philosophy, University of Waterloo, Waterloo, Ontario, Canada N2L 3G1.

CAREER: University of New Hampshire, Durham, instructor, 1961-62, assistant professor of philosophy, 1962-63; University of Waterloo, Waterloo, Ontario, assistant professor, 1963-66, associate professor, 1966-69, professor of philosophy, 1969—. Visiting professor at Johns Hopkins University, 1967, Stanford University, 1968, and University of Calgary, 1976. Founder and president, Kitchener-Waterloo Chamber Music Society. Member of board, Kitchener-Waterloo Symphony Orchestra, Kitchener-Waterloo Philharmonic Choir, Kitchener-Waterloo Community Orchestra, and Chamber Music Institute. *Member:* American Philosophical Association, Canadian Philosophical Association, Canadian Civil Liberties Union, Phi Beta Kappa. *Awards, honors:* Woodrow Wilson fellow, 1956-57; Frank Knox Memorial fellow at Oxford University, 1959-60.

WRITINGS: Morality and Utility, Johns Hopkins Press, 1967; *Thinking about Ethics,* Graphics Department, University of Waterloo, 1967; *Thinking about Politics,* Graphics Department, University of Waterloo, 1968; (editor) *Moral Issues,* Oxford University Press (Toronto), in press.

Contributor: S. Gorovetz, editor, *Mill's Utilitarianism: Text and Commentary,* Bobbs-Merrill, 1971; J. Rachels, editor, *Moral Problems,* Harper, 1971, 2nd edition, 1975; M. Bayles, editor, *Ethics and Population,* Schenkman, 1976; W. Shea and John King-Farlow, editors, *Contemporary Issues in Political Philosophy,* Science History Publications, 1976; W. Aiken and H. LaFollette, editors, *World Hunger and Moral Obligation,* Prentice-Hall, 1977; *Obligations to Future Generations,* Temple University Press, 1978; *Limits of Utilitarianism,* University of Minnesota Press, 1982; *Ethics and Animals,* Humana Press, 1982; E. Regis, editor, *Gewirth's Ethical Rationalism,* University of Chicago Press, 1983. Contributor to *Ethics, Analysis, Mind, Canadian Journal of Philosophy,* and other publications.

AVOCATIONAL INTERESTS: "Major passion for music and audio equipment; minor passion for photography and motor cars."

* * *

NAYLOR, Harriet H. 1915-

PERSONAL: Born December 4, 1915, in White Plains, N.Y.; daughter of Arthur Leslie and Henrietta (Bedford) Core; married George Naylor (a professor), July 31, 1939 (deceased); children: Margery Bedford (Mrs. Peter van Inwagen), Elizabeth Beekman, George Dustin. *Education:* Columbia University, A.B., 1937, graduate study in social work, 1937-39, M.A., 1963. *Politics:* Independent. *Religion:* Congregational. *Home address:* R.R. 1, Box 381, Staatsburg, N.Y. 12580.

CAREER: United Charities and Housekeeping Service, Chicago, Ill., staff member, 1939-40; Girl Scouts of America, New York City, training adviser in personnel department, 1960-62; Young Women's Christian Association (YWCA), New York City, training consultant in Bureau of Personnel and Training, 1962-66; director of volunteer services, New York State Department of Mental Hygiene, 1967-71; National Center for Voluntary Action, Washington, D.C., consultant, 1970, regional director, 1971, director of education and training, 1971-74; U.S. Department of Health, Education, and Welfare, Washington, D.C., director of volunteer development, 1974-80; trainer and consultant in volunteer development, 1980—. Instructor, Virginia Commonwealth University, 1973-74. Volunteer worker in various organizations for more than twenty-five years; member of board, Volunteer Development Task Force; member of national board, YWCA. *Member:* Adult Education Association of the U.S.A., Association of Volunteer Bureaus, Association of Volunteer Administration (life member), National School Volunteer Program.

WRITINGS: Volunteers Today: Finding, Training and Working with Them, Association Press, 1967; (contributor) *Social Work Practice,* Columbia University Press, 1969; (contributor) J. C. Cull and R. E. Hardy, editors, *Volunteerism: An Emerging Profession,* C. C Thomas, 1973; *Leadership through Volunteering,* Dryden, 1976; *Volunteers: Resource for Human Development,* Project SHARE, 1979. Contributor of articles on development through education to *Girl Scout Leader, Adult Leadership,* and other journals.

SIDELIGHTS: Harriet Naylor has lived in Greece, Indonesia, Thailand, and East Pakistan, where her husband served with the United Nations.

* * *

NEWLOVE, John (Herbert) 1938-

PERSONAL: Born June 13, 1938, in Regina, Saskatchewan, Canada; son of Thomas Harold (a lawyer) and Mary Constant (Monteith) Newlove; married Susan Mary Phillips (a teacher), August 9, 1966; stepchildren: Jeremy Charles Gilbert, Tamsin Elizabeth Gilbert. *Education:* Attended school in Saskatchewan, Canada. *Address:* c/o McClelland & Stewart, 25 Hollinger Rd., Toronto, Ontario, Canada M48 3G2.

CAREER: Poet. Poet-in-residence at Loyola College, 1974-75, University of Western Ontario, 1975-76, and University of Toronto, 1976-77. *Awards, honors:* Koerner Foundation award, 1964; Canada Council grant, 1965, 1967, 1977; Governor General's award for poetry, 1972; Deep Springs College Arts Award.

WRITINGS: Grave Sirs, privately printed by R. Reid and T. Tanabe (Vancouver), 1962; *Elephants, Mothers and Others,* Periwinkle Press, 1963; *Moving in Alone,* Contact Press (Toronto), 1965, new edition, Oolichan Books, 1977; *Notebook Pages,* Charles Pachter (Toronto), 1966; *What They Say,* Weed/Flower Press, 1967; *Four Poems,* It, 1967; *Black Night Window,* McClelland & Stewart, 1968; *The Cave,* McClelland & Stewart, 1970; *Lies,* McClelland & Stewart, 1972; (editor) Joe Rosenblatt, *Dream Craters,* Press Porcepic, 1974; (editor) *Canadian Poetry: The Modern Era,* McClelland & Stewart, 1977; *The Fat Man: Selected Poems, 1962-1972,* McClelland & Stewart, 1977; (with John Metcalf) *Dreams Surround Us,* Bastard Press, 1977; *The Green Plain,* Oolichan Books, 1981.

WORK IN PROGRESS: A book of poems.

SIDELIGHTS: John Newlove's poetry is "enormously well crafted, subtly controlled in tone, and richly various in style," writes Robin Skelton in *Canadian Literature,* "even while remaining consistent to what emerges as an over-all purpose to portray the human tragedy with an economy and elegance." Reviewing *Lies* for *Canadian Forum,* Stephen Scobie sees a similar objective in Newlove's poetry: "*Lies* deals with masks, illusions, self-deception; but in the end the most grotesque masks are true, and the dreams all turn into nightmares."

"Newlove's vision," Skelton believes, "is indeed dark. His universe is one of solitude, failure, ugliness, and nausea. The only driving forces of life are desire, which is always thwarted, and dreams which are never fulfilled. . . . Newlove has . . . created a place where no other poet has yet had the courage to go.'' Scobie finds ''strange, surrealistic images'' in *Lies* which ''arrange themselves in shapes which tease meaning towards the reader without ever declaring themselves fully.'' He also finds ''outright pictures of human misery'' and a ''deep pervading pessimism.''

What relieves Newlove's pessimism, Scobie believes, ''is Newlove's attitude of acceptance rather than outrage.'' Skelton sees Newlove's work ultimately praising the resilience of man. He calls *The Fat Man: Selected Poems, 1962-1972* ''a tribute to courage and a statement of the awesome spiritual strength of man.'' The book, Skelton states, is ''one of the most impressive [poetry collections] to have been published in the English speaking world in the last twenty years.'' ''Newlove,'' writes George Bowering in *Canadian Forum,* ''is one of our dozen really good poets.''

BIOGRAPHICAL/CRITICAL SOURCES: Canadian Forum, May, 1968, November, 1968, November, 1970, March, 1974; *Fiddlehead,* summer, 1968; *Poetry,* February, 1970; *Open Letter,* spring, 1973, fall, 1974; *Canadian Literature,* winter, 1978; *Contemporary Literary Criticism,* Volume XIV, Gale, 1980.

* * *

NEWMAN, Barclay M., Jr. 1931-

PERSONAL: Born February 22, 1931, in Princeton, W.Va.; son of Barclay M. (a biologist) and Lillie Mae (Whitman) Newman; married Jean Butler, May 30, 1953; children: Tina, Dana. *Education:* Union University, Jackson, Tenn., B.A., 1953; Southern Baptist Theological Seminary, B.D., 1956, Ph.D., 1960; also attended Hebrew Union Jewish School of Religion, fall, 1958, Summer Institute of Linguistics, University of Oklahoma, 1960, and Hartford Seminary Foundation, fall, 1966. *Office:* American Bible Society, 1865 Broadway, New York, N.Y. 10023.

CAREER: Baptist clergyman. William Jewell College, Liberty, Mo., assistant professor of religion, 1960-63, associate professor of religion and Greek, 1963-66; American Bible Society, New York, N.Y., translations consultant, 1966—. *Member:* Society of Biblical Literature, Baptist Professors of Religion.

WRITINGS: The Meaning of the New Testament, Broadman, 1966; *Rediscovering the Book of Revelation,* Judson Press, 1968; *A Concise Greek-English Dictionary of the New Testament,* United Bible Societies, 1971; (author of introduction) Claude A. Frazier, editor, *What Did the Bible Mean?,* Broadman Press, 1971; (contributor) *The Student,* Broadman Press, 1972; (with Eugene A. Nida) *A Translator's Handbook on the Acts of the Apostles,* United Bible Societies, 1972; (contributor) Claude A. Frazier, editor, *Should Preachers Play God?,* Independence Press, 1973; (with Nida) *A Translator's Handbook on Paul's Letter to the Romans,* United Bible Societies, 1973; (contributor) *Commentary on Genesis,* Broadman Press, 1973; (contributor) *Understanding and Translating the Bible,* American Bible Society, 1974; (with Nida) *A Translator's Handbook on the Gospel of John,* United Bible Socities, 1975; *Pedoman Singkat Menterjamahkan Alkitab* (title means ''A Brief Guide for Translating the Bible''), Indonesian Bible Society, 1976; (contributor) *The Interpreter's Dictionary of the Bible,* Abingdon, 1976.

Translator: *Between the Woman and the Prophet,* Universiti Malaya, 1976; *Modern Malaysian Stories,* Dewan Bahasa, 1977; *Prize-Winning Malay Poems, 1971-76,* Dewan Bahasa, 1980; Alias Ali, *Crisis* (novel), Dewan Bahasa, 1980.

Contributor to *New Testament Studies, Bible Translator,* and *Asian Beacon.*

SIDELIGHTS: Barclay M. Newman, Jr. is competent in Greek, Hebrew, German, Malay, and Indonesian.

* * *

NEWMAN, Jay Hartley 1951-

PERSONAL: Born December 20, 1951, in New York, N.Y.; son of Jack (a businessman) and Thelma (an author and educator; maiden name, Siegel) Newman. *Education:* Attended London School of Economics and Political Science, University of London, 1971-72; Yale University, B.A., 1973; Columbia University, J.D., 1976; New York University, L.L.M., 1981. *Home:* 1101 Prospect St., Westfield, N.J. 07090. *Office:* Cravath, Swaine & Moore, 1 Chase Manhattan Plaza, 57th Floor, New York, N.Y. 10005.

CAREER: Admitted to Bar of New Jersey, 1976, of New York, 1977, of Washington, D.C., 1978; law clerk to Judge Francis L. Van Dusen, U.S. 3rd Circuit Court of Appeals, Philadelphia, Pa., 1976-77; associate, Cravath, Swaine & Moore (law firm), New York, N.Y.; writer. *Member:* American Bar Association, Lawyers for the Arts, Phi Delta Phi.

WRITINGS—All published by Crown: (With brother, Lee Scott Newman) *Plastics for the Craftsman,* 1972; (with L. S. Newman and mother, Thelma R. Newman) *Paper as Art and Craft: The Complete Book of the History and Processes of the Paper Arts,* 1973; (with L. S. Newman and T. R. Newman) *The Frame Book: Contemporary Design with Traditional and Modern Methods and Materials,* 1974; (with L. S. Newman) *Kite Craft,* 1974; (with L. S. Newman) *Wire Art: Metals, Techniques, Sculpture, Collage, Jewelry, Mixed Media,* 1975; (with L. S. Newman and T. R. Newman) *The Lamp and Lighting Book: Design, Elements, Materials, Shades for Standing Lamps, Ceiling and Wall Fixtures,* 1976; (with T. R. Newman) *The Container Book: Basic Processes for Making Bags, Baskets, Boxes, Bowls, and Other Container Forms with Fibers, Fabrics, Leather, Wood, Plastics, Metal, Clay, Glass, and Natural Materials,* 1977; (with T. R. Newman) *The Mirror Book,* 1978; (with L. S. Newman) *Electroplating and Electroforming for Artists and Craftsmen,* 1979; (with L. S. Newman and T. R. Newman) *Machine Embroidery,* 1981.

Contributor to professional journals. Notes and comments editor, *Columbia Law Review,* 1974-76.

SIDELIGHTS: Some of Jay Hartley Newman's books have been translated into French and Portuguese. *Avocational interests:* Travelling.

* * *

NG, Larry K. Y. 1940-

PERSONAL: Surname is pronounced Ing; born August 6, 1940, in Singapore; son of Khuan Seak (a goldsmith) and Poh Hiang (Tan) Ng. *Education:* Stanford University, A.B., 1961; Columbia University, M.D., 1965. *Religion:* Methodist. *Home:* 2026 R St. N.W., Washington, D.C. *Office:* National Institutes of Health, 9000 Rockville Pike, Bethesda, Md. 20010.

CAREER: Mount Sinai Hospital, Los Angeles, Calif., intern, 1965-66; University of Pennsylvania, Philadelphia, resident in neurology, 1966-69; National Institutes of Health, Bethesda, Md., neurologist with National Institute of Mental Health, 1969-72, with National Institute on Drug Abuse, 1972—.

Member: Society of Biological Psychiatry, World Academy of Art and Science, World-Man Fund (president), Phi Beta Kappa. *Awards, honors:* S. Weir Mitchell Award, American Academy of Neurology, 1971; A. E. Bennett Award, Society of Biological Psychiatry, 1972; award for research in acupuncture, American Society of Chinese Medicine, 1975; commendation medal, Commission Corps, U.S. Public Health Service, 1981.

WRITINGS: (Associate editor) *The Population Crisis and Use of World Resources,* Indiana University Press, 1964; (editor) *The Population Crisis: Implications and Plans for Action,* Indiana University Press, 1965; (editor) *Alternatives to Violence: A Stimulus to Dialogue,* Time-Life, 1968; (editor) *Strategies for Public Health,* Van Nostrand, 1981; (editor) *Pain, Discomfort, and Humanitarian Care,* Elsevier-North Holland, 1981; (editor) *New Approaches to Treatment of Chronic Pain,* U.S. Government Printing Office, 1981.

* * *

NICOLSON, James R(obert) 1934-

PERSONAL: Born July 10, 1934, in Shetland Islands, Scotland; son of Frank Huggins (a customs officer) and Helen (Tait) Nicolson; married Violet Sinclair, September 6, 1965; children: Eileen, Margaret, Robert. *Education:* University of Aberdeen, M.A., 1956, B.Sc., 1961. *Home:* Fairhaven, Castle St., Scalloway, Shetland Islands ZE1 0TP, Scotland.

CAREER: Mining geologist for Sierra Leone Development Co., Marampa mine, 1961-67; fisherman in the Shetland Islands, Scotland, 1969-72; member of Blacksness Pier Trust, 1973-76. *Member:* Royal Geographical Society, Geological Society of London.

WRITINGS: Shetland, David & Charles, 1972, revised edition, 1979; *The Tent and the Simbek* (nonfiction), William Luscombe, 1974; *Beyond the Great Glen* (nonfiction), David & Charles, 1975; *Shetland and Oil,* William Luscombe, 1975; *Lerwick Harbour,* Lerwick Harbour Trust, 1977; *Traditional Life in Shetland,* R. Hale, 1978; *Food from the Sea,* Cassell, 1979; *Shetland Folklore,* R. Hale, 1981. Contributor to Scottish magazines and newspapers. Editor, *Shetland Life.*

SIDELIGHTS: James R. Nicolson writes that his special interests are working people, "such as West African peasants, Scottish crofters and fisherman," and life in the north of Scotland, especially the Shetland Islands.

BIOGRAPHICAL/CRITICAL SOURCES: Times Literary Supplement, September 18, 1981.

* * *

NIDEFFER, Robert M(orse) 1942-

PERSONAL: Born February 6, 1942, in Oxnard, Calif.; son of Richard G. (a farmer) and Mary (executive director of Campfire Girls; maiden name, Morse) Nideffer; married Lilly Dauenhauer, July, 1963 (divorced, 1970); married Peggy Johnson (a psychiatric nurse), May 29, 1971; children: Robert F., James A., Julie A. *Education:* Lewis and Clark College, B.S., 1967; Vanderbilt University, M.A., 1969, Ph.D., 1971. *Home:* 12468 Bodega Way, San Diego, Calif. 92120. *Office:* California School of Professional Psychology, San Diego, Calif.

CAREER: University of Oregon, Eugene, intern in medical psychology, 1971; University of Rochester, Rochester, N.Y., assistant professor, 1971-75, associate professor of psychology and psychiatry, 1976-77, director of Biofeedback Laboratory, 1975-77; senior clinical psychology associate, Strong Memorial Hospital, 1975-77; faculty member, National Academy of Professional Psychologists, 1975-77; California School of Professional Psychology, San Diego, Calif., professor, 1977—. President, Enhanced Performance Associates, 1977—. Member of advisory board of Pretrial Services and of executive board of Monroe County Sports Medicine Committee. ABPP diplomate in clinical psychology, 1977. *Military service:* U.S. Army, Security Agency, 1959-62; served in Japan.

MEMBER: American Psychological Association, Society for Psychophysiological Research, Society for Clinical and Experimental Hypnosis, National Register of Health Services Providers in Psychology, North American Society for the Psychology of Sport and Physical Activity.

WRITINGS: The Inner Athlete, Crowell, 1976; *A.C.T.: Attention Control Training,* Wyden Books, 1978; *How to Put Anxiety behind You,* Stein & Day, 1978; *The Ethics and Practice of Applied Sport Psychology,* Mouvement Publications, 1981; *An Athlete's Guide to Attention Control Training,* Human Kinetics Publishers, 1983. Also author of *Predicting Human Behavior,* 1980, and *Taking Care of Business,* 1982.

Contributor to psychology journals and to *Coach and Athlete, Redbook, Gentleman's Quarterly,* and *Sundancer.*

SIDELIGHTS: Robert M. Nideffer comments: "A combination of the study of Aikido and the martial arts in Japan and the study of psychology and the disorganization associated with psychotic processes led to the development of a theory of human performance. Research in both areas (athletics and schizophrenia) seemed to support the theory and led to application of techniques designed to help individuals function under stress. In addition a test was developed to be used as a diagnostic and selection tool to identify individuals who function effectively under stress."

* * *

NOBLE, Elizabeth Marian 1945-

PERSONAL: Born January 2, 1945, in Adelaide, Australia; came to the United States in 1973; daughter of Richard Neetlee (a civil servant) and Phyllis (Heggaton) Bagot; married Geoffrey Noble (an energy consultant), December 19, 1970; children: Julia. *Education:* University of Adelaide, diploma, 1965; University of Western Australia, B.A., 1972. *Politics:* "Member of no political party." *Religion:* None. *Home address:* P.O. Box 405, Forestdale, Mass. 02644. *Office:* Maternal and Child Health Center, 2464 Massachusetts Ave., Cambridge, Mass. 02140.

CAREER: Private physical therapy practitioner and childbirth educator, 1966—; Maternal and Child Health Center (physical therapy services), Cambridge, Mass., 1980—. Lecturer in United States and abroad on physical therapy in obstetrics and gynecology, physiology of labor, and philosophy of childbirth preparation. Member of delegation on maternal and child health to Peoples Republic of China, 1982. Consultant for Marie Osmond's video tape on exercises for pregnant women, 1983. *Member:* American Physical Therapy Association (founder and chairwoman of Obstetrics-Gynecology Section, 1976—). *Awards, honors:* American Field Service exchange scholarship, 1961-62.

WRITINGS: Essential Exercises for the Childbearing Year, Houghton, 1976, 2nd edition, 1980; *Having Twins,* Houghton, 1980; "Essential Childbearing Year" (film), Polymorph Films,

1981; *Childbirth with Insight,* Houghton, 1983. Contributor to *Journal of Nurse Midwifery.*

WORK IN PROGRESS: A research project "involving female pelvic floor function evaluation through the childbearing year, objectively measured with Kegel's perineometer with attention to women instructed in exercise and who do not have an episiotomy"; research on separation of the abdominal muscles (diastis recti) and the value of early exercise in this regard; research for a book on artificial insemination.

AVOCATIONAL INTERESTS: Travel to Europe ("lived two years in the Netherlands and speak Dutch") and to the Middle East, Asia, and North and South America.

* * *

NORMAN, Alexander Vesey Bethune 1930-
(Vesey Norman)

PERSONAL: Born February 10, 1930, in Delhi, India; son of Alexander Maximilian Bethune (a lieutenant colonel in the British Army) and Shiela Maude (Maxwell) Norman; married Catherine Margaret Barne (a researcher), December 10, 1954; children: Andrew Fion Bethune. *Education:* University of London, B.A., 1958. *Office:* The Armouries, H. M. Tower of London, London EC3N 4AB, England.

CAREER: Scottish United Services Museum, Edinburgh, Scotland, assistant curator, 1957-63; Wallace Collection (museum of fine and applied arts), London, England, assistant to director, 1963-76; The Armouries, H. M. Tower of London, London, Master of Armouries and inspector of armouries of Wallace Collection, 1977—. Honorary curator of armoury at Abbotsford. *Military service:* British Army, Scottish Horse Royal Armoured Corps, 1951-55; became second lieutenant. *Member:* International Society for the Study of Church Monuments (vice-president), Society of Antiquaries of Scotland (fellow), Society of Antiquaries of London (fellow), Museums Association, Arms and Armour Society (vice-president), Society for Army Historical Research, Meyrick Society.

WRITINGS: (Under name Vesey Norman) *Arms and Armour,* Weidenfeld & Nicolson, 1964, published as *Arms and Armor,* Putnam, 1966; (with Don Pottinger) *Warrior to Soldier, 449 to 1660: A Brief Introduction to the History of English Warfare,* Weidenfeld & Nicolson, 1966, published as *A History of War and Weapons, 449 to 1660: English Warfare from the Anglo-Saxons to Cromwell,* Crowell, 1966; *Small-Swords and Military Swords,* Arms & Armour Press, 1967; (under name Vesey Norman) *The Medieval Soldier,* Crowell, 1971; *Arms and Armour in the Royal Scottish Museum,* H.M.S.O., 1972; *Gold Boxes,* Trustees of the Wallace Collection (London), 1975; *Wallace Collection Catalogue of Ceramics,* Volume I: *Pottery, Majolica, Faience, Stoneware,* Trustees of the Wallace Collection, 1976; *The Rapier and Small-Sword 1460-1820,* Arms & Armour Press, 1980.

SIDELIGHTS: In a *Times Literary Supplement* review of Alexander Norman's *The Rapier and Small-Sword 1460-1820,* G. M. Wilson comments: "This is a work of great scholarship which distils the author's lifetime of interest in and study of his subject into a form it is difficult not to find addictive."

BIOGRAPHICAL/CRITICAL SOURCES: Times Literary Supplement, March 13, 1981.

* * *

NORMAN, Vesey
See NORMAN, Alexander Vesey Bethune

* * *

NORVIL, Manning
See BULMER, (Henry) Kenneth

* * *

NOVAK, Joseph
See KOSINSKI, Jerzy (Nikodem)

O

O'BRIEN, James J. 1929-

PERSONAL: Born October 20, 1929, in Philadelphia, Pa.; son of Sylvester J. (a doctor) and Emma (Filer) O'Brien; married Carmen Hiester, June 9, 1952; children: Jessica, Michael, David. *Education:* Cornell University, B.C.E., 1952; University of Houston, M.E., 1958. *Residence:* New Hope, Pa.

CAREER: Rohm & Haas, Bristol, Pa., and Houston, Tex., engineer, 1955-59; Radio Corp. of America, Moorestown, N.J., and Alaska, engineer, 1959-62; affiliated with Manohly Associates, 1962-65; Meridian Engineering, Haddonfield, N.J., executive vice-president, 1965-68; president, MDC Systems, 1968-72; president, O'Brien, Kreitzberg & Associates, 1972—. *Military service:* U.S. Navy, Korean War; became lieutenant. *Member:* Society of CPM Consultants (director), Project Management Institute (national secretary; vice-president; president, chairman), Construction Specification Institute, American Society of Civil Engineers (fellow), American Association of Cost Engineers, Society of American Value Engineers, American Institute of Industrial Engineers, Cornell Society of Engineers, Tau Beta Pi, Chi Epsilon. *Awards, honors:* Professional Manager Award, 1969; honorary doctorate, World Open University, 1975; National Construction Management Award, American Society of Civil Engineers, 1976.

WRITINGS: CPM in Construction Management, McGraw, 1965, 2nd edition, 1971; *Scheduling Handbook,* McGraw, 1969; *Management Information Systems,* Van Nostrand, 1970; *Management with Computers,* Van Nostrand, 1971; (editor) *Contractor's Management Hand Book,* McGraw, 1971; *Construction Inspection Hand Book,* Van Nostrand, 1974; *Construction Delay,* Cahners, 1976; *Value Analysis in Design and Construction,* McGraw, 1976; *Construction Management,* McGraw, 1978. Contributor of forty articles to professional journals.

* * *

O'DONNELL, Dick
See LUPOFF, Richard A(llen)

* * *

OFFNER, Eric D(elmonte) 1928-

PERSONAL: Born June 23, 1928, in Vienna, Austria; came to United States, 1941, naturalized, 1949; son of Sigmund G. (a businessman) and Kathe (Delmonte) Offner; married Julie Cousins, 1955 (died, 1959); married Barbara Shotton (a painter), June 4, 1961. *Education:* City College (now City College of the City University of New York), B.B.A., 1949; Cornell University, LL.B., 1952. *Religion:* Ethical Culture. *Office:* 1412 Broadway, New York, N.Y. 10018.

CAREER: Admitted to bar of State of New York, 1952; Langner, Parry, Card & Langner, New York City, attorney, 1952-57; Haseltine, Lake & Waters (firm specializing in foreign patents and trademarks), New York City, partner, beginning 1957; currently partner, Offner & Kuhn, New York City. President, Riverdale-Yonkers Society for Ethical Culture, 1964-67. Vice-president and member of board of directors, Riverdale Mental Health Clinic. *Member:* Association Internationale pour la Protection de la Propriete Industrielle, American Bar Association, U.S. Trademark Association, American Patent Law Association, New York Patent Law Association (member of board of governors), Bar Association of City of New York.

WRITINGS: International Trademark Protection, Fieldston Press, 1965; *International Trademark Service,* five volumes, Fieldston Press, 1970, 2nd edition, 1981; *Protection of Trademarks,* Law Association of Canada, 1972; *Comparative U.S.-European Common Market Patent Service,* Fieldston Press, 1978. Contributor to periodicals and to professional journals. Editor-in-chief, *Cornell Law Forum,* 1950-51; associate editor, *Bulletin of New York Patent Law Association,* 1961-66; member of editorial board, *Trademark Reporter,* 1961-64.

AVOCATIONAL INTERESTS: Soccer, New Orleans jazz, publishing.

* * *

OGATA, Sadako (Nakamura) 1927-

PERSONAL: Born September 16, 1927, in Tokyo, Japan; daughter of Toyoichi and Tsuneko (Yoshizawa) Nakamura; married Shijuro Ogata (a banker), January 21, 1961; children: Atsushi, Akiko. *Education:* University of the Sacred Heart, Tokyo, Japan, B.A., 1951; Georgetown University, M.A., 1953; Tokyo University, graduate research study, 1953-56; University of California, Berkeley, Ph.D., 1963. *Religion:* Roman Catholic. *Home:* 3-29-18 Denenchotu, Otaka, Tokyo, Japan. *Office:* Institute of International Relations, Sophia University, Tokyo, Japan.

CAREER: University of the Sacred Heart, Tokyo, Japan, lecturer in international relations, 1953-56; International Christian University, Tokyo, lecturer, 1965-73, associate professor of international relations and Japanese diplomatic and political history, 1974-76; Permanent Mission of Japan to the United Nations, New York, N.Y., minister, 1976-78, envoy extraordinary and minister plenipotentiary, 1978-79, Japanese representative to the United Nations Human Rights Commission, 1982—; Sophia University, Institute of International Relations, Tokyo, professor. Member of Japanese delegation to the United Nations General Assembly, 1968, 1970, 1975. *Member:* Political Science Association and Association for American Studies (both Japan), Japan Association of International Relations. *Awards, honors:* Walter A. Haas International Alumnus Award, University of California, 1978; Doctor of Laws, Cedar Crest College, 1978, Smith College, 1980.

WRITINGS: Defiance in Manchuria—The Making of Japanese Foreign Policy, 1931-32, University of California Press, 1964; *Manshu jihen to seisaku no keisei katei* (title means "Decision-Making Process of the Manchurian Affair Foreign Policy"), Hara Shobo, 1966; (contributor) Dorothy Borg and others, editors, *Pearl Harbor as History,* Columbia University Press, 1973; (contributor) *The Foreign Policy of Modern Japan,* University of California Press, 1977; *Vantage Point from the United Nations,* Asahi Evening News Publications, 1980; *Survey of International Organization Studies in Japan,* N.I.R.A., 1982.

* * *

OLIVA, Leo E. 1937-

PERSONAL: Born November 5, 1937, in Woodston, Kan.; son of E. I. (a farmer) and Lela (Miller) Oliva; married Marlene Causey, August 31, 1958 (divorced, 1975); married Bonita M. Pabst, February 14, 1976; children: (first marriage) Eric, Stephanie, Rex. *Education:* Fort Hays Kansas State College, A.B., 1959; University of Denver, M.A., 1960, Ph.D., 1964. *Address:* R.R. 1, Woodston, Kan. 67675.

CAREER: Texas Wesleyan College, Fort Worth, assistant professor of history, 1962-64; Fort Hays Kansas State College, Hays, assistant professor, 1964-67, associate professor, 1967-69, professor of history, 1969-78, acting chairman of department, 1966-67, chairman of department, 1967-75; self-employed farmer and free-lance writer. *Member:* Kansas State Historical Society, Kansas Corral of the Westerners (sheriff, 1972), Phi Kappa Phi, Phi Alpha Theta, Pi Gamma Mu.

WRITINGS: Soldiers on the Santa Fe Trail, University of Oklahoma Press, 1967; *Fort Hays,* Kansas State Historical Society, 1980; *Fort Larned,* Kansas State Historical Society, 1982. Contributor of articles and book reviews to magazines and journals.

WORK IN PROGRESS: A military history of the Smoky Hill Trail; a study of the Indian in American literature; histories of Kansas frontier forts; a literary biography of Martin Litvin; a centennial history of Ash Rock Church in Kansas.

* * *

OLIVER, Mary 1935-

PERSONAL: Born September 10, 1935, in Cleveland, Ohio; daughter of Edward William (a teacher) and Helen M. (Vlasak) Oliver. *Education:* Attended Ohio State University for one year, and Vassar College for one year. *Home address:* Box 338, Provincetown, Mass. 02657.

CAREER: Poet. Worked at "Steepletop," the estate of Edna St. Vincent Millay, as secretary to the poet's sister, Norma Millay. Chairman of writing department, Fine Arts Work Center, Provinceton, Mass., 1972-73; Mather Visiting Professor, Case Western Reserve University, 1980, 1982. *Member:* Poetry Society of America, P.E.N. *Awards, honors:* Poetry Society of America, first prize, 1962, for poem "No Voyage"; Devil's Advocate Award, 1968, for poem "Christmas, 1966"; Shelley Memorial Award, 1970; National Endowment for the Arts fellow, 1972-73; Alice Fay di Castagnola Award, 1973; Guggenheim fellow, 1980-81.

WRITINGS: No Voyage, and Other Poems, Dent, 1963, expanded edition, Houghton, 1965; *The River Styx, Ohio, and Other Poems,* Harcourt, 1972; *The Night Traveler,* Bits Press, 1978; *Twelve Moons,* Little, Brown, 1978; *Sleeping in the Forest,* Ohio Review Chapbook, 1979; *American Primitive,* Atlantic-Little, Brown, 1983. Contributor of poetry to periodicals in England and the United States.

SIDELIGHTS: Mary Oliver's "intuitive sense of nature's dark forces is wedded to a keen sense of the real," writes Anthony Manousos in the *Dictionary of Literary Biography*. Reviewing *No Voyage, and Other Poems* in *Commonweal,* Carl Johnson writes: "There is no vanity, no pretentiousness and no false sense of urgency about its transactions with the truths of nature and of consciousness. In the moderation of her stanzas there is residual strength, and in her simplicity the discretion of a mature mind."

Oliver writes most often of the mythic quality of nature. "Her vision of nature," Manousos maintains, "is celebratory and religious in the deepest sense." Manousos sees *Twelve Moons* as "the most integrated and ambitious vision that Oliver has yet attempted" and finds the poems in this collection "spare, subtle, and dynamic hymns to the natural forces within and without us [that] testify to Mary Oliver's ability to sing in the wilderness and make us listen."

BIOGRAPHICAL/CRITICAL SOURCES: New Statesman, September 27, 1963; *Commonweal,* March 19, 1965; *Christian Science Monitor,* April 15, 1965; *Minnesota Review,* May-July, 1965; *Virginia Quarterly Review,* summer, 1965; *New York Times Book Review,* November 21, 1965, October 21, 1979; *New Republic,* December 9, 1978; *Western Humanities Review,* spring, 1979; *Los Angeles Times Book Review,* August 26, 1979; *Dictionary of Literary Biography,* Volume V: *American Poets since World War II,* Gale, 1980; *Contemporary Literary Criticism,* Volume XIX, Gale, 1981.

* * *

OLSEN, Jack
See OLSEN, John Edward

* * *

OLSEN, John Edward 1925-
(Jack Olsen, Jonathan Rhoades)

PERSONAL: Born June 7, 1925, in Indianapolis, Ind.; son of Rudolph O. (a salesman) and Florence (Drecksage) Olsen. *Education:* Attended University of Pennsylvania, 1945-46. *Agent:* Scott Meredith Literary Agency, 845 Third Ave., New York, N.Y. 10022. *Office:* 7954 Northeast Baker Hill Rd., Bainbridge Island, Wash. 98110.

CAREER: Reporter for *San Diego Union Tribune* and for *San Diego Journal,* San Diego, Calif., 1947-50, *Washington Daily*

News, Washington, D.C., 1950-51, *New Orleans Item,* New Orleans, La., 1952-53, and *Chicago Sun-Times,* Chicago, Ill., 1954-55; WMAL-TV, Washington, D.C., television news editor and broadcaster, 1950-51; *Time,* New York City, correspondent, 1956-58, chief of Midwest bureau, 1959; *Sports Illustrated,* New York City, senior editor, 1960-74. *Military service:* U.S. Army, Office of Strategic Services, 1943-44. *Member:* Authors Guild, Authors League of America, National Audubon Society. *Awards, honors:* National Headliner Award from Press Club of Atlantic City; Page One Award from Chicago Newspaper Guild; citations from Indiana University and Columbia University.

WRITINGS—All under name Jack Olsen, except as indicated: *The Mad World of Bridge,* Holt, 1960; (under pseudonym Jonathan Rhoades) *Over the Fence Is Out,* Holt, 1961; *The Climb Up to Hell,* Harper, 1962; (with Charles Goren) *Bridge Is My Game,* Doubleday, 1965; *Black Is Best: The Riddle of Cassius Clay,* Putnam, 1967; *Silence on Monte Sole,* Putnam, 1968; *The Black Athlete: A Shameful Story,* Time-Life, 1968; *Night of the Grizzlies,* Putnam, 1969; (with Fran Tarkenton) *Better Scramble than Lose,* Four Winds Press, 1969.

The Bridge at Chappaquiddick, Little, Brown, 1970; *Aphrodite: Desperate Mission,* Putnam, 1970; *Slaughter the Animals, Poison the Earth,* Simon & Schuster, 1971; *The Girls in the Office,* Simon & Schuster, 1972; *The Girls on the Campus,* Pocket Books, 1974; *Sweet Street,* Ballantine, 1974; *The Man with the Candy,* Simon & Schuster, 1974; *Alphabet Jackson,* Playboy Press, 1974; *Massy's Game,* Playboy Press, 1974; *The Secret of Fire Five,* Random House, 1977; *Night Watch,* Times Books, 1979; *Missing Persons,* Atheneum, 1981; *Have You Seen My Son?,* Atheneum, 1982.

Contributor of over 300 stories and articles to *Life, Reader's Digest, Fortune, This Week, Nouvelle Candide, Playboy, Daily Sketch,* and other periodicals. Also contributor to anthologies.

SIDELIGHTS: Jack Olsen told *CA:* "I have spent 30 years telling it like it is."

* * *

OLSON, Toby 1937-

PERSONAL: Name at birth, Merle Theodore Olson; born August 17, 1937, in Berwyn, Ill.; son of Merle T. Olson and Elizabeth (Skowbo) Olson Potokar (a telephone company supervisor); married Ann Yeomans, September 10, 1963 (divorced, 1965); married Miriam Meltzer (a social worker), November 27, 1966. *Education:* Occidental College, B.A., 1965; Long Island University, M.A., 1967. *Home:* 329 South Juniper St., Philadelphia, Pa. 19107. *Office:* Department of English, Temple University, Philadelphia, Pa. 19122.

CAREER: Long Island University, Brooklyn, N.Y., assistant professor of English, 1966-74; Friends Seminary, New York, N.Y., writer-in-residence, 1974-75; Temple University, Philadelphia, Pa., associate professor of English, 1975—. Member of faculty at New School for Social Research, 1967-75; poet-in-residence at State University of New York College at Cortland, 1972. Associate director and instructor at Aspen Writers' Workshop, 1964-67; has given poetry readings all over the United States. *Military service:* U.S. Navy, surgical technician, 1957-61. *Member:* Coordinating Council of Literary Magazines, Poets and Writers, P.E.N.

AWARDS, HONORS: Award from Creative Artists Public Service Program of New York State Council on the Arts, 1975; nominated for Pennsylvania Governor's Award, 1980, and for Faulkner Award, P.E.N., 1983, for *Seaview.*

WRITINGS: The Hawk-Foot Poems, Abraxas Press, 1968; *Maps* (poems), Perishable Press, 1969; *Worms Into Nails* (poems), Perishable Press, 1969; *The Brand* (poems), Perishable Press, 1969; *Pig's Book* (poems), Dr. Generosity Press, 1969; *Vectors* (poems), Membrane Press, 1972; (author of introduction) Carl Thayler, *Goodrich,* Capricorn Books, 1972; *Fishing* (poems), Perishable Press, 1974; *The Wrestlers and Other Poems,* Barlenmir House, 1974; *City* (poems), Membrane Press, 1974; (author of introduction) Helen Saslow, *Arctic Summer,* Barlenmir House, 1974.

Changing Appearance: Poems 1965-1970, Membrane Press, 1975; *The Life of Jesus* (fiction), New Directions, 1976; *Home* (poems), Membrane Press, 1976; (author of introduction) Annette Hayn, *One Armed Flyer,* Poets Press, 1976; *Four Poems,* Perishable Press, 1976; *Three and One* (poems), Perishable Press, 1976; *Doctor Miriam* (poems), Perishable Press, 1977; *The Florence Poems,* Permanent Press, 1978; *Aesthetics* (poems), Membrane Press, 1978; *Birdsongs* (poems), Perishable Press, 1980; *Two Standards* (poems), Salient Seedling Press, 1982; *Seaview* (fiction), New Directions, 1982; *Still/Quiet,* Landlocked Press, 1982.

Also author of numerous poetry broadsides, including *Cold House,* Perishable Press, 1970, *Tools,* Dr. Generosity Press, 1970, *Shooting Pigeons,* Perishable Press, 1972, and *From Home,* Wine Press, 1972. Also editor of *Margins 1976.*

Poems and stories represented in anthologies, including *Inside Outer Space,* edited by Robert Vas Dias, Doubleday, 1970; *New Directions-25,* edited by J. Laughlin, New Directions, 1972; *Loves, Etc.,* edited by Marguerite Harris, Doubleday, 1973; and *Active Anthology,* edited by George Quasha, Sumac Press, 1974. Also contributor to *New Directions 29, 35,* and *40.*

Contributor of articles, stories, poems, and reviews to more than one hundred journals, including *Nation, New York Quarterly, Choice, Confrontation, Ohio Review, American Poetry Review,* and *Poetry Now.*

WORK IN PROGRESS: A book of poems, *Truro;* a novel.

BIOGRAPHICAL/CRITICAL SOURCES: Los Angeles Times Book Review, June 13, 1982.

* * *

O'MEARA, Thomas F(ranklin) 1935-

PERSONAL: Born May 15, 1935, in Des Moines, Iowa; son of Joseph M. (a salesman) and Frances C. (Rock) O'Meara. *Education:* Attended Loras College, 1953-55; Aquinas Institute of Philosophy, River Forest, Ill., M.A., 1959, Lic.Phil., 1959; Aquinas Institute of Theology, Dubuque, Iowa, M.A., 1963; University of Munich, Ph.D., 1967. *Office:* Department of Theology, University of Notre Dame, Notre Dame, Ind. 46556.

CAREER: Ordained Roman Catholic priest, member of Dominican Order of Preachers, 1962. Aquinas Institute of Theology, Dubuque, Iowa, professor of systematic theology, beginning 1966; currently teaching at University of Notre Dame, Notre Dame, Ind. Visiting professor, Notre Dame University, Weston College School of Theology, Boston Theological Institute, and Seminary of S.S. Peter and Paul (Nigeria). Member of executive board, Catholic Committee on Urban Ministry. *Member:* Catholic Theological Society of America (president).

WRITINGS: (With C. D. Weisser) *Paul Tillich in Catholic Thought,* Priory, 1964; *Mary in Protestant and Catholic Theology,* Sheed, 1966; (editor) *Rudolf Bultmann in Catholic Thought,* Herder & Herder, 1968; (editor) Thomas Aquinas, *Summa theologiae,* McGraw, 1968; *Holiness and Radicalism in Religious Life,* Herder & Herder, 1970; (editor) *Projections: Shaping an American Theology for the Future,* Doubleday, 1970; *Paul Tillich's Theology of God,* Dubuque, 1971; *Loose in the World,* Paulist Press, 1974; *Romantic Idealism and Roman Catholicism,* University of Notre Dame Press, 1982; *Theology of Ministry,* Paulist Press, 1983. Contributor of articles to *Harvard Theological Review, Theology Today,* and other periodicals.

* * *

O'MORRISON, Kevin

PERSONAL: Born in St. Louis, Mo.; son of Sean E. and Dori (Adams) O'Morrison; married Linda Soma (a theatrical secretary), April 30, 1966. *Education:* Tutored privately for university equivalent. *Home and office:* 20 East 9th St., New York, N.Y. 10003.

CAREER: Playwright; stage, film, television, and radio actor. Playwright-in-residence at more than thirty colleges and universities, including University of Minnesota, 1966, Trinity University, 1974, State University of New York College at Brockport, and member colleges of Kansas City Regional Council for Higher Education; visiting professor of professional theater, University of Missouri—Kansas City, 1976; adjucator for New Plays Program, American College Theatre Festival, 1979-80. Drama consultant, under aegis of Office for Advanced Drama Research, 1966. *Military service:* U.S. Army Air Forces, three years. *Member:* Dramatists Guild, Writers Guild of America, Authors League of America, O'Neill Playwrights, Actors Equity, Screen Actors Guild, American Federation of Radio and Television Artists, Players Club.

AWARDS, HONORS: O'Neill Playwrights Selection, O'Neill National Playwrights' Conference, 1971, for "The Morgan Yard," and 1976, for "Ladyhouse Blues"; Creative Artists Public Service fellowship, 1975; National Endowment for the Arts playwriting fellowship, 1980; first prize, National Repertory Theatre National Playwriting Contest, 1981, for "A Party for Lovers"; "Ladyhouse Blues" was chosen as an American Playwrights Theatre "Offering."

WRITINGS—Plays: "The Long War," first produced Off-Broadway at Chelsea Theatre Centre, 1965, as "Three Days Before Yesterday," produced Off-Broadway at Triangle Theatre, 1969, published in *Playwrights for Tomorrow,* Volume IX, edited by A. H. Ballet, University of Minnesota Press, 1967; *The Morgan Yard* (first produced in Cleveland, Ohio, at Cleveland Playhouse, 1973), Samuel French, 1975; "The Realist," first produced in San Antonio, Tex. at Trinity University, October 16, 1974; *Ladyhouse Blues* (first produced Off-Broadway at Phoenix Theatre and in Dallas, Tex. at Dallas Theatre Center, both October 28, 1976; produced Off-Broadway at St. Peter's Church, 1979), Samuel French, 1977; "Requiem," first produced in Missoula, Montana, at Montana Summer Theatre, 1977; "Dark Ages" (includes one-act plays, "On Line" and "On Ice"), first produced Off-Off-Broadway at Impossible Ragtime Theater, January 4, 1980.

Television screenplays: "The House of Paper," produced on NBC-TV, February 15, 1959; "And Not a Word More," produced on CBS-TV, July 3, 1960; "A Sign for Autumn," produced on NBC-TV, March 11, 1962.

Author of radio adaptation of "Ladyhouse Blues," broadcast by Public Radio Network; also author of play, "A Party for Lovers," and of book and music for musical, "Report to the Stockholders," with music by Larry Grossman. Author of screenplay, "Next Time, Dynamite, and Honey"; author of unpublished novel, "Something Perfect."

WORK IN PROGRESS: A full-length play, tentatively entitled "Something in the Air."

SIDELIGHTS: The opening of Kevin O'Morrison's "Ladyhouse Blues" at St. Peter's Church in Manhattan was surrounded by much "huffery and puffery," writes Stanley Kauffmann in *Saturday Review,* and was "gossetted by grants, conference workshops, and previous productions." The play, a selection at the O'Neill National Playwrights' Conference in 1976 and one of the most noted Off-Broadway offerings of 1979, received international attention after its St. Peter's Church run and has since been produced throughout the United States and in Europe. Set in St. Louis on a hot summer's day in 1919, "Ladyhouse Blues" is a "period piece that exactly captures a time, an environment and a mood," comments *New York Times*'s Mel Gussow.

Critics have praised O'Morrison's ability to capture the ambience of the World War I period in "Ladyhouse Blues." *Time* reviewer T. E. Kalem notes that the play "has a sparse plot, [one that is] downright anemic. Yet, O'Morrison fleshes it out with the wondrous detail of by-gone commonplaces." The play is, says Gussow, "an album of photographs of women in white —in chemises and nightgowns—posing as if for a portrait of pioneers. The photographs are still, the album is comprehensive."

It is the play's effect of a *tableaux* that is important in "Ladyhouse Blues," states Gussow. "The play moves with the slowness of life—at first glance it seems too slow," writes the critic. "Having introduced the characters and confirmed their personalities, the playwright circles his situation until we are saturated with atmospheric detail. By the second act, having watched the women bake cornbread, wash laundry, light kerosene lamps and wilt in the heat, we realize that in 'Ladyhouse,' atmosphere is the essense." Concurs Kalem: "Mood, rather than action, dominates the evening."

Other critics, however, find the play's deliberately slow pace and reenactment of early twentieth-century life a drawback. *Saturday Review*'s Kauffmann terms "Ladyhouse Blues" a "kitchen sink opus" and contends that the play is "just a recital of 'realities.'" "If it had been written in 1919, . . . it might have been revived as a modestly rewarding example of early American naturalism," writes Kauffmann. "Today it's dramatically, socially, psychologically comatose. . . . Absolutely nothing is intended in this play except to show us what these people were, and that simply is not enough." *New York*'s John Simon calls "Ladyhouse Blues" a "well-nigh perfectly produced play," but then adds: "The only question is why was it done? [The play] is a pile of prosaic, shopworn conflicts. . . . The real trouble is that the language, thought, and sensibility of the play, despite low-level proficiency, do not rise above daytime-serial stature."

New York Times's Walter Kerr disagrees. The play, says Kerr, is "a very good one." Kerr asserts that "Ladyhouse Blues" could have "been languid, drowsy with mood and bog-soft with self-pity [but] has been provided—in the writing—with built in energies. . . . O'Morrison is someone to know: his sense of place, his flair for attractively differentiated people, his cunning command of a casual but often cracking vernacular are exemplary."

Information on O'Morrison's work is on file at the Library for the Performing Arts, Lincoln Center, New York City, at the Walter Hampden Library, The Players, New York City, and at the Eugene O'Neill Memorial Library, Waterford, Conn.

BIOGRAPHICAL/CRITICAL SOURCES: Evening Herald (Dublin, Ireland), October 1, 1974; *Irish Independent,* October 1, 1974; *Irish Times,* October 2, 1974; *San Antonio Express,* October 18, 1974; *New York Times,* April 10, 1979, October 18, 1979, November 16, 1979, January 10, 1980; *New York,* October 29, 1979; *New Yorker,* October 29, 1979; *Time,* October 29, 1979; *Nation,* November 10, 1979; *Saturday Review,* January 5, 1980.

* * *

O'NEILL, Charles Edwards 1927-

PERSONAL: Born November 16, 1927, in New Orleans, La.; son of John Henry (a public health engineer) and Albion (Edwards) O'Neill. *Education:* Spring Hill College, A.B., 1950; Institut St.-Louis, Chantilly, France, S.T.L., 1958; Gregorian University, Rome, Italy, Ph.D., 1963. *Office:* Jesuit Historical Institute, Via Penitenzieri 20, Rome 00193, Italy.

CAREER: Ordained Roman Catholic priest, 1957; member of Society of Jesus (Jesuits). Instructor in history at Jesuit High School, New Orleans, La., 1951-54, Loyola University, New Orleans, 1961-62, and St. Charles College, Grand Cocteau, La., 1964; Loyola University, New Orleans, assistant professor, 1965-67, associate professor, 1967-71, professor of history, 1971-76, research professor, 1977-82; Jesuit Historical Institute, Rome, Italy, director, 1977—. *Member:* Organization of American Historians, American Catholic Historical Association, Louisiana Historical Association, Delta Epsilon Sigma, Alpha Pi Omicron. *Awards, honors:* Chevalier des Palmes Academiques, 1968; award of merit, Outstanding Educators of America, 1970.

WRITINGS: Church and State in French Colonial Louisiana, Yale University Press, 1966; (editor with E. J. Burrus, J. de la Pena, and M. T. Garcia) *Catalogo de documentos sobre la epoca espanola de Luisiana: Seccion de Gobierno del Archivo General de Indias,* Loyola University (New Orleans) and Spanish Archives, 1968.

(Contributor) *Sacrae Congregationist de Propaganda Fide Memorial Rerum, 1622-1972,* Freiburg, Volume I, 1972, Volume II, 1974; (author of foreword) Rodolphe L. Desdunes, *Our People and Our History,* translation by D. O. McCants, Louisiana State University Press, 1973; (contributor) *Span and the Mississippi Valley,* University of Illinois Press, 1974; (editor) *Charlevoix's Louisiana,* Louisiana State University Press, 1977; (contributor) *Louisiana's Black Heritage,* Louisiana State Museum, 1979.

Contributor to *Dictionary of Canadian Biography* and *Dizionario degli Istituti di Perfezione.* Contributor to *Louisiana History* and *America.*

WORK IN PROGRESS: Research on the history of Jesuits and on French and Spanish colonial Louisiana.

SIDELIGHTS: Charles O'Neill speaks French, Spanish, and Italian. He reads Latin, Greek, German, and Portuguese.

OPPENHEIM, Joanne 1934-

PERSONAL: Born May 11, 1934, in Middletown, N.Y.; daughter of Abe P. (an electrical engineer) and Helen (Jassem) Fleischer; married Stephen Oppenheim (a lawyer), June 27, 1954; children: James, Anthony, Stephanie. *Education:* Sarah Lawrence College, B.A., 1960; Bank Street College of Education, M.S., 1980. *Address:* Sackett Lake Rd., Box 29, Monticello, N.Y. *Office:* Publications Department, Bank Street College of Education, 610 West 112th St., New York, N.Y. 10025.

CAREER: Teacher in primary grades, Monticello, N.Y., 1960-80; Bank Street College of Education, New York, N.Y., member of Writer's Laboratory, 1962—, associate editor in publications department, 1980—. *Awards, honors:* Outstanding Teachers of America award, 1973.

WRITINGS—Juveniles, except as indicated: *Have You Seen Trees?,* W. R. Scott, 1967; *Have You Seen Birds?,* W. R. Scott, 1968; (with G. Nook) *Have You Seen Roads?,* W. R. Scott, 1969; *Have You Seen Boats?,* W. R. Scott, 1971; *On the Other Side of the River,* F. Watts, 1972; *Have You Seen Houses?,* W. R. Scott, 1973; *Mrs. Peloki's Snake,* Dodd, 1980; (contributor) *Pleasure of Their Company* (adult book), Chilton, 1980; *James Will Never Die* (Literary Guild selection), Dodd, 1982; *Mrs. Peloki's Cinderella,* Dodd, 1983; *Parents and Kids and Play* (adult book), Ballantine, 1983. Contributor to "Bank Street Readers" series, Macmillan, 1965. Contributor of articles to magazines.

* * *

ORDISH, George 1908-

PERSONAL: Born March 25, 1908, in London, England; son of Francis Prior and Lilian (Edmonds) Ordish; married Olive Harvey-James (a writer); children: Caron Jennifer, Roger, Pamela Meliora. *Education:* University of London, Dip.Hort., 1937, B.Sc. (Econ.), 1945. *Home:* Bohemia, Nancledra, Penzance, Cornwall TR20 8BP, England. *Agent:* Mrs. D. Owen, 78 Narrow Street, London E14 8BP, England.

CAREER: Imperial Chemicals Industries Ltd., London, England, pest control expert, 1938-59; Foreign and Commonwealth Office, Ministry of Overseas Development, London, pest control expert, 1956-62; *Tropical Science* (magazine), London, editor, 1966-72. Pest control expert for United Nations in New York and Mexico, and for Food and Agriculture Organization in Rome, Italy, 1957-60. *Member:* International Organization for Biological Control, Association of Applied Biologists, Guild of Agricultural Journalists, Circle of Wine Writers, Baconian Club, English Vineyards Association. *Awards, honors:* New York Secondary Education Board Book Award, 1961, for *The Living House.*

WRITINGS: Untaken Harvest, Constable, 1952; *Wine Growing in England,* Hart Davis, 1953; *Garden Pests,* Hart Davis, 1956; *The Living House,* Lippincott, 1959.

(With Ed Hyams) *The Last of the Incas,* Simon & Schuster, 1964; *Man, Crops, and Pests in Central America,* Pergamon, 1964; (with Pearl Binder) *Pigeons and People,* Dobson, 1967; *Biological Methods in Crop Pest Control,* Constable, 1967.

(With Binder) *Ladies Only* (novel), Dobson, 1972; *The Great Wine Blight,* Scribner, 1972; *John Curtis: Pioneer of Pest Control,* Osprey, 1974; *The Year of the Butterfly,* Scribner,

1975; *The Constant Pest,* Scribner, 1976; *Vineyards in England and Wales,* Faber, 1977; *The Year of the Ant,* Scribner, 1978; *The Living American House,* Morrow, 1981.

Translator: Jose Maria Tey, *Hong Kong to Barcelona in the Junk 'Rubia',* Harrap, 1962; Roger Callois, *The Mask of Medusa,* Gollancz, 1964; Remy Chauvin, *Animal Societies,* Gollancz, 1968; Alfred Metraux, *The History of the Incas,* Pantheon, 1968; Remy Chauvin, *The World of Ants,* Gollancz, 1970; (with Caron Shipton) Richard Armand, Robert Iattes, and Jacques Lesbourne, *The Management Revolution,* Macdonald, 1970. Editor, *PANS* (Pest Articles and News Summary), 1960-66.

SIDELIGHTS: George Ordish "can do," writes Edward Hyams in *New Statesman,* "what not one scientist in 10,000 can do, express himself with simple clarity and a touch of sardonic humor and, while instructing in a subject which affects all of us, entertain."

BIOGRAPHICAL/CRITICAL SOURCES: New York Times Book Review, August 21, 1960, April 12, 1981; *New Statesman,* July 14, 1967, July 7, 1972; *Economist,* June 24, 1972; *Times Literary Supplement,* August 18, 1972.

* * *

ORLOVSKY, Peter 1933-

PERSONAL: Born July 8, 1933, in New York, N.Y.; son of Oleg (a silk screen printer for neckties) and Katherine (Schworten) Orlovsky. *Education:* Attended San Francisco Junior College for two and one half years. *Politics:* Pacifist. *Religion:* Buddhist. *Address:* P.O. Box 582, Stuyvesant Station, New York, N.Y. 10009.

CAREER: Poet, singer, ambulance attendant, mental hospital attendant, farmer's helper, dishwasher in a hospital, secretary for Allen Ginsberg (whom he claims to have "married, Crismiss 1954", and with whom he has traveled in India, Morocco, Spain, France, England, Holland, Istanbul, Greece, East Africa, Pakistan, Yugoslavia, and Bulgaria); collater and sweeper at Peace Eye Bookstore, New York City, 1963; adviser to League for Sexual Freedom, and to LEMAR (a society supporting the legalization of marijuana); singer and walker for peace in New York City, San Francisco, Calif., and Washington, D.C. *Military service:* U.S. Army, "bed pan medic," November, 1953-July, 1954.

WRITINGS—All poetry: (Contributor) *The Beat Scene,* edited by E. Wilentz, Centaur Press, 1960; (contributor) *New American Poetry: 1945-1960,* edited by Donald M. Allen, Grove, 1960; *Dear Allen, Ship Will Land Jan. 23, '58,* Intrepid Press, 1971; *Lepers Cry,* Phoenix Book Shop, 1972; *Clean Asshole Poems & Smiling Vegetable Songs: Poems, 1957-1977,* City Lights Books, 1978; (with Allen Ginsberg) *Straight Hearts' Delight: Love Poems and Selected Letters, 1947-1980,* Gay Sunshine, 1981.

Also contributor to *Beatitude Anthology,* 1965. Contributor of poems to *Yugen, Outsider,* and *F--- You: A Magazine of the Arts.*

SIDELIGHTS: "Embracing both comic buffoonery and lyric tenderness," writes Kenneth Funston of *Library Journal* about *Clean Asshole Poems,* "[Peter] Orlovsky's playful style reveals a traditional literary character, an 'uncouth swain' celebrating sex (both homo- and heterosexual), plant life, and the beat-beatitude-beauty of all humankind." The love relationship between Orlovsky and poet Allen Ginsberg is frankly presented in *Straight Hearts' Delight,* "a record of that love," writes Gary Steele in the *Los Angeles Times Book Review,* "in immediate and almost unmediated letters, poems, and photos."

Orlovsky once told *CA* that his activities include distributing "countless birth poems all over, trying to learn Indian Raggs, [and] careing for 2 [of my] brothers who have been partly cattle treeted driven into state Mental Hospitals, one brother for almost 13 years & my younger brother for 2½ years."

Writing in *The New American Poetry,* Orlovsky says of himself: "Trouble in school: always thinking dreaming sad mistry problems. . . . Love pretzles & cant remember dreams anymore. . . . Did weight lifting with bus stops. Got to enjoy burnt bacon with mothers help. Stare at my feet to much & need to undue paroniac suden clowds. Enjoy mopping floors, cleaning up cat vommit. Enjoy swimming underwater. . . . Getting to enjoy blank mind state, especially in tub. . . . got to like flies tickleing nose & face. . . . I.Q. 90 in school, now specialized I.Q. is thousands."

Orlovsky has appeared in two films, Andy Warhol's "Couch," 1965, and "Me and My Brothers," 1969.

BIOGRAPHICAL/CRITICAL SOURCES: Donald M. Allen, editor, *The New American Poetry: 1945-1960,* Grove, 1960; *Library Journal,* May 1, 1979; *Los Angeles Times Book Review,* March 1, 1981.†

* * *

OSBORNE, Chester G. 1915-

PERSONAL: Born September 18, 1915, in Portsmouth, N.H.; son of James Chester (a pianist and composer) and Viola (a musician; maiden name, Cofman) Osborne; married Mary Rooney, April 26, 1943; children: Maureen (Mrs. Frank Pagano), Patricia (Mrs. Donald Feiler), Virginia (Mrs. Mark Mesiano), James, Kevin. *Education:* New England Conservatory of Music, Mus.B., 1937; Northwestern University, Mus.M., 1950. *Home address:* Box 517, Center Moriches, Long Island, N.Y. 11934.

CAREER: Boston Symphony Orchestra and other orchestras, Boston, Mass., trumpeter, 1935-38; Center Moriches High School, Center Moriches, N.Y., member of faculty, 1938-42, 1946-70. Writer of children's books. Curator of manuscripts, Manor of St. George (museum), Mastic, N.Y., 1955-76. Founder of Center Moriches Music Award Association. *Military service:* U.S. Army, 1942-46; became staff sergeant. *Member:* American Society of Composers, Authors, and Publishers, Music Educators National Conference (life member), New York State School Music Association (adjudicator). *Awards, honors:* Gold Medal, Boys' Clubs of America, for *The First Lake Dwellers.*

WRITINGS: The First Bow and Arrow, Follett, 1951; *The First Puppy,* Follett, 1953; *The First Lake Dwellers* (Junior Literary Guild selection), Follett, 1956; *The First Wheel,* Follett, 1959; *The Wind and the Fire,* Prentice-Hall, 1959; *The Silver Anchor,* Follett, 1967.

Musical compositions: *The British Eighth* (march), National Educational Music, 1943; *Christmas Cards* (suite), Daugherty, 1945; *Treasure Island* (overture), Mills, 1946; *I See the Moon,* Elkan-Vogel, 1973; *Dumb, Dumb, Dumb,* Elkan-Vogel, 1973; *Connemara Sketches* (suite), William Allen, 1975; *Aisling,* Pro Art Publications/Belwin Mills, 1977; *Lowlands,* Pro Art Publications/Belwin Mills, 1977; *Diversions for Drummers,* Elkan-Vogel, 1978; *The Silver Anchor* (overture), William Allen,

1978; *The Piper and the Captain* (suite), Southern Music, 1981; *The Heathery Mountain* (suite), Southern Music, 1982; *Fancy That!*, Studio Press, in press; *Captain Flint*, Studio Press, in press; *The Twenty-Fourth Candle* (play with music), Studio Press, in press.

Contributor to *Encyclopedia Americana*. Contributor of articles, stories, and plays to *Children's Playmate, Instructor, Junior Natural History, Long Island Forum*, and other publications.

WORK IN PROGRESS: The Memory String, a novel; *Mozart's Magic Ring*, a play with music.

SIDELIGHTS: In a review of Chester Osborne's musical composition *Connemara Sketches*, the reviewer for *Instrumentalist* finds the piece "simple and attractive, nicely flattering, and not overarranged" and believes "listeners will probably become entranced with the beauty of each melody."

BIOGRAPHICAL/CRITICAL SOURCES: New York Times Book Review, August 5, 1956; *New York Sunday News*, October 4, 1964; *Choral Journal*, February, 1974; *School Musician*, November, 1976; *Instrumentalist*, November, 1976.

* * *

OSBORNE, Milton Edgeworth 1936-

PERSONAL: Born April 17, 1936, in Sydney, Australia; son of George Davenport (a university professor) and Gwynneth J. (Love) Osborne; married Rhondda M. McGown, March 18, 1959. *Education:* University of Sydney, B.A. (first class honors), 1958; Cornell University, graduate study in Southeast Asia Program. *Home:* 8 Karuah Rd., Turramurra, New South Wales, Australia.

CAREER: Australian Diplomatic Service, 1958-62, serving on embassy staff in Phnom Penh, Cambodia, 1959-61. Writer. *Member:* Australian Institute of International Affairs, Association for Asian Studies.

WRITINGS: Singapore and Malaysia, Cornell University Press, 1964; *Strategic Hamlets in South Viet-Nam*, Cornell University Press, 1965; *Southeast Asian Reactions to Possible Alternative American Policies in Asia* (monograph), Institute of Advanced Studies, Australian National University, 1968; *The French Presence in Cochinchina and Cambodia: Rule and Response (1859-1905)*, Cornell University Press, 1969.

Region of Revolt: Focus on Southeast Asia, Pergamon, 1970; *Politics and Power in Cambodia*, Longman, 1974; *River Road to China: The Mekong River Expedition, 1866-1873*, Liveright, 1975; *From Conviction to Anxiety: The French Self-Image in Vietnam* (monograph), School of Social Sciences, Flinders University of South Australia, 1976; *Southeast Asia: An Introductory History*, Allen & Unwin, 1979; *Before Kampuchea: Preludes to Tragedy*, Allen & Unwin, 1979. Contributor to scholarly journals.†

P

PAPE, D. L.
See PAPE, Donna (Lugg)

* * *

PAPE, Donna (Lugg) 1930-
(D. L. Pape)

PERSONAL: Surname is pronounced Poppy; born June 21, 1930, in Sheboygan, Wis.; daughter of Arthur Phillip and Ruth (Fenninger) Lugg; married William Pape (a carpet mechanic), June 16, 1951; children: Diane Ruth, Jan Lynn, Jean Carol. *Home:* 1734 South 15th St., Sheboygan, Wis. 53081.

CAREER: Free-lance writer, 1960—; photo-journalist, 1960-64; writes verse for various greeting card companies. *Member:* National Writers Club, Society of Children's Book Writers, Wisconsin Regional Writers' Association, Sheboygan County Writers' Club, Children's Reading Round Table of Chicago. *Awards, honors:* First Prize in Wisconsin Regional Writers' Association juvenile writing contest, 1965.

WRITINGS: The Best Surprise of All, Whitman Publishing, 1961; *Splish, Splash, Splush,* Whitman Publishing, 1962; *Tony Zebra and the Lost Zoo,* Whitman Publishing, 1963; *I Play in the Snow,* Whitman Publishing, 1967; *Mary Lou, the Kangaroo,* E. M. Hale, 1967; *The Seal Who Wanted to Ski,* E. M. Hale, 1967; *Catch That Fish,* L. W. Singer, 1969.

Handy Hands, Standard Publishing, 1973; *A Special Way to Travel,* Standard Publishing, 1973; *Big Words for Little People,* Standard Publishing, 1973; *A Gerbil for a Friend,* Prentice-Hall, 1973; (with daughter, Jan Pape, and Jeanette Grote) *Puzzles and Silly Riddles,* Scholastic Book Service, 1973; *Promises Are Special Words,* Moody, 1975; (with Grote) *Pack of Puzzles,* Scholastic Book Service, 1975.

(With Grote) *Puzzle Panic,* Scholastic Book Service, 1976; (with Grote) *Fun Puzzles for One,* Xerox Education Publications, 1976; (with Grote and Carol Karle) *Puzzle Party,* Reader's Digest Press, 1977; (with Grote) *All Kinds of Puzzles,* Scholastic Book Service, 1978; *The Peek-a-Boo Book,* Golden Press, 1978; (with Grote) *A Turn for the Words,* Grosset & Dunlap, 1979; (with Grote) *Puzzle Parade,* Xerox Education Publications, 1979.

(With Virginia Mueller) *Think-Pink Solve and Search Puzzles,* Xerox Education Publications, 1980; (with Mueller and Karle) *Bible Activities for Kids,* Bethany House, Books 1-6, 1980-82; *The Mouse at the Show,* Elsevier/Nelson, 1981; *Jack Jump Under the Candlestick,* Albert Whitman, 1982.

All published by Garrard: *Leo Lion Looks at Books,* 1972; *Mrs. Twitter, the Sitter,* 1972; *Mr. Mogg in the Log,* 1972; *Count on Leo Lion,* 1973; *The Kangaroo Who Leaped in Her Sleep,* 1973; *A Bone for Breakfast,* 1974; (with John McInnes) *Taffy Finds a Halloween Witch,* 1975; (with McInnes) *The Big White Thing,* 1975; *Snowman for Sale,* 1977; *Where Is My Little Joey?,* 1978; *Dog House for Sale,* 1979; *The Snoino Mystery,* 1980; (with Leonard Kessler) *Play Ball, Joey Kangaroo,* 1980.

"Pape Series of Speech Improvement and Reading"; all published by Oddo; all 1965: *The Three Thinkers of Thay-Lee; Professor Fred and the Fid-Fuddlephone; Scientist Sam; King Robert, the Resting Ruler; Liz Dearly's Silly Glasses; Shoemaker Fooze.* Also author, with Grote, of *Puzzling Pastimes* and *Packet of Puzzles,* 1973. Contributor to speech therapy workbooks for Word-Making Productions, and of stories to Whitehaven Game Co. Contributor to *Humpty Dumpty Magazine, Jack and Jill, Highlights, Our Little Messenger, Junior World,* and other juvenile magazines.

AVOCATIONAL INTERESTS: Music, art.

* * *

PARENT, David J(oseph) 1931-

PERSONAL: Born May 31, 1931, in Hamlin, Me.; son of Patrick D. (a navy-yard worker) and Yvonne Marie (Violette) Parent; married Ana Maria Ferran (a Spanish professor), May 2, 1971; children: David Alberto, Michael Joseph, Robert Rafael. *Education:* Marist College, B.A., 1953; University of Heidelberg, certificate, 1960; University of Cincinnati, M.A., 1965, Ph.D., 1967. *Politics:* "Democratic far left." *Home:* 1422 Hanson Dr., Normal, Ill. 61761. *Office:* Department of German, Illinois State University, Normal, Ill. 61761.

CAREER: Orford High School, Orford, N.H., teacher of English and French, 1963; College of Mount St. Joseph, Cincinnati, Ohio, instructor in German, 1963-65; Boston College, Boston, Mass., assistant professor of German, 1965-68; Illinois State University, Normal, 1968—, began as associate professor, currently professor of German. Member of Joint Publications Research Service. *Military service:* U.S. Army,

1954-56. *Member:* International Education Association, Modern Language Association of America, American Association of University Professors, American Association of Teachers of German (president of southern Illinois chapter, 1971).

WRITINGS—Translator, except as indicated; published by Applied Literature Press, except as indicated: (Author) *Werner Bergengruen's Das Buch Rodenstein: A Detailed Study,* Mouton & Co., 1974; (author) *Werner Bergengruen's Ungeschriebene Novelle,* Bouvier, 1974; Michael Landmann, *Philosophical Anthropology,* Westminster, 1974; Landmann, *Reform of the Hebrew Alphabet,* 1976; Juan Garcia Ponce, *Entry into Matter: Modern Literature and Reality,* 1976; Landmann, *Philosophy: Its Mission and Its Disciplines,* 1977; Jorge Millas, *The Intellectual Challenge of Mass Society,* 1977; *Alienatory Reason,* 1978; Gustav Landauer, *For Socialism,* Telos Press, 1978; *De Homine: Man in the Mirror of His Thought,* 1979.

Editor, "Medieval Studies" series and "Illinois Language and Culture" series, both Applied Literature Press. Contributor to periodicals, including *German Quarterly, Essays in Literature,* and *Filologia Moderna.* Associate editor and translator, *TELOS.*

WORK IN PROGRESS: Studies in German literature; translations of philosophical works; studies in structuralism/post-structuralism.

SIDELIGHTS: David J. Parent told *CA:* "Since 1975 I have been engaged mainly in translating. One focus of this activity has been the philosophical anthropology of Michael Landmann, whose view of man is infused with the Bible, the ancient Greeks, and the anti-positivistic flowering of the 1920s; a second focus is the social-philosophy journal *TELOS,* published by Paul Piccone in St. Louis, Mo. I was active in the anti-war protests in 1968 and have struggled in vain for a democratization of university life. My overriding concern, however, which I would like to realize in future writing, is for a humanization of the world order in the direction of some form of democratic socialism. The current system of capitalism fails miserably to provide a decent and just living for the people of the world."

BIOGRAPHICAL/CRITICAL SOURCES: Christian Century, July 31, 1974; *Choice,* November, 1974.

* * *

PARKER, Donn B(lanchard) 1929-

PERSONAL: Born October 9, 1929, in San Jose, Calif.; son of Donald W. (a salesman) and Miriam (Blanchard) Parker; married Lorna Schroeder, August 16, 1952; children: Diane, David. *Education:* University of California, Berkeley, B.A., 1952, M.A., 1954. *Religion:* Lutheran. *Home:* 265 Vernal Court, Los Altos, Calif. 94022. *Office:* Stanford Research Institute, Menlo Park, Calif. 94025.

CAREER: General Dynamics Corp., San Diego, Calif., senior research engineer, 1954-62; Control Data Corp., Palo Alto, Calif., manager, 1962-69; Stanford Research Institute, Menlo Park, Calif., researcher and senior management systems consultant, 1969—. Instructor, University of California, San Diego, 1955.

MEMBER: Association for Computing Machinery (member of board of directors, 1957—), American Federation of Information Processing Societies (member of board of directors and chairman of professional standards, 1970-75), American Society of Industrial Security. *Awards, honors:* National Science Foundation research grants, 1973-79; U.S. Department of Justice research grants, 1979—.

WRITINGS: Crime by Computer, Scribner, 1976; *Ethical Conflicts in Computer Science and Technology,* AFIPS Press, 1977; *Computer Security Management,* Reston, 1981; *Fighting Computer Crime,* Scribner, 1983. Contributor to *Encyclopedia of Computer Science, Encyclopaedia Britannica,* and *Encyclopedia of Criminal Justice.* Contributor of articles to *New York Times* and to professional journals.

WORK IN PROGRESS: Research on computer abuse and security.

SIDELIGHTS: Donn B. Parker told *CA:* "Writing my books on nights and weekends and holding down a full-time research and consulting job is a tough life. A book takes about two years, and fortunately most of the research and sources come from my professional work. My thirty years in the computer field, mostly programming computers, has been excellent experience for organizing and producing a book. Writing a large computer program or a book manuscript require the same thoughts, organization, management, and logic. But in the end, it's all worthwhile. When I travel around the world lecturing and consulting, it's always a delight to see copies of my books, even in Portuguese and Japanese languages, on the shelves of strangers. My hope is that my books will facilitate the beneficial use of computers worldwide and mitigate the harmful results derived from such powerful technology."

* * *

PARKER, Harold T(albot) 1907-

PERSONAL: Born December 26, 1907, in Cincinnati, Ohio; son of Samuel Chester (a college professor) and Lucile (Jones) Parker; married Louise Salley Parker, 1980. *Education:* University of Chicago, Ph.B., 1928, Ph.D., 1934; Cornell University, graduate study, 1929-30. *Home:* 2211 Arrington St., Durham, N.C. 27707. *Office:* Department of History, Duke University, Durham, N.C. 27706.

CAREER: Duke University, Durham, N.C., instructor, 1939-42, assistant professor, 1946-51, associate professor, 1951-57, professor of modern European history, 1957-77. Visiting professor, University of Alabama in Huntsville, 1978, 1979-81; Brown Education fellow, University of the South, 1979. *Military service:* U.S. Army Air Forces, 1942-45; became staff sergeant. *Member:* American Historical Association, Society for French Historical Studies (president, 1957-58).

WRITINGS: The Cult of Antiquity and the French Revolutionaries, University of Chicago Press, 1937; *Three Napoleonic Battles,* Duke University Press, 1943; (editor with Theodore Ropp) *Historical Synopsis of the World Today,* Duke University Press, 1946; (editor with Richard Herr) *Ideas in History,* Duke University Press, 1965; (with Marvin Brown) *Major Themes in Modern European History,* Moore Publishing, 1974; *The Bureau of Commerce in 1781,* Carolina Academic Press, 1979; (editor with Georg Iggers) *International Handbook of Historical Studies,* Greenwood Press, 1979; (editor) *Problems in European History,* Moore Publishing, 1979; (editor with Iggers) *Theory and Social History,* Social Research Associates, 1980.

WORK IN PROGRESS: The French Central Government and French Industry: An Administrative History, 1781-1818; The Personality of Napoleon; A Visual History of Europe.

PASCUDNIAK, Pascal
See LUPOFF, Richard A(llen)

* * *

PATENT, Dorothy Hinshaw 1940-

PERSONAL: Born April 30, 1940, in Rochester, Minn.; daughter of Horton Corwin (a physician) and Dorothy (Youmans) Hinshaw; married Gregory Joseph Patent (a professor of zoology), March 21, 1964; children: David Gregory, Jason Daniel. *Education:* Stanford University, B.A., 1962; University of California, Berkeley, M.A., 1965, Ph.D., 1968; also attended University of Washington, Friday Harbor, 1965-67. *Home:* 5445 Skyway Dr., Missoula, Mont. 59801.

CAREER: Sinai Hospital, Detroit, Mich., post-doctoral fellow, 1968-69; Stazione Zoologica, Naples, Italy, post-doctoral researcher, 1970-71; University of Montana, Missoula, faculty affiliate in department of zoology, 1975—, acting assistant professor, 1977. Member of board of directors, Missoula Farmers' Market. *Member:* American Institute of Biological Sciences, American Society of Zoologists, Society of Children's Book Writers.

AWARDS, HONORS: The National Science Teachers Association has cited twelve of Patent's works as outstanding science trade books, including *Weasels, Otters, Skunks and Their Family,* 1973, *How Insects Communicate,* 1975, *Plants and Insects Together,* 1976, *The World of Worms,* 1978, *Animal and Plant Mimicry,* 1978, *Beetles and How They Live,* 1978, *Butterflies and Moths: How They Function,* 1979, *Sizes and Shapes in Nature: What They Mean,* 1979, and *Raccoons, Coatimundis and Their Family,* 1979; Golden Kite Award in nonfiction, Society of Children's Book Writers, 1977, for *Evolution Goes On Every Day,* and 1980, for *The Lives of Spiders.*

WRITINGS—Juvenile nonfiction, except as indicated; published by Holiday House, except as indicated: *Weasels, Otters, Skunks and Their Family,* 1973; *Microscopic Animals and Plants,* 1974; *Frogs, Toads, Salamanders and How They Reproduce,* 1975; *How Insects Communicate,* 1975; *Fish and How They Reproduce,* 1976; *Plants and Insects Together,* 1976; *Evolution Goes On Every Day,* 1977; *Reptiles and How They Reproduce,* 1977; (with Paul C. Schroeder) *Beetles and How They Live,* 1978; *Animal and Plant Mimicry,* 1978; *The World of Worms,* 1978; *Butterflies and Moths: How They Function,* 1979; *Raccoons, Coatimundis and Their Family,* 1979; *Sizes and Shapes in Nature: What They Mean,* 1979.

Bacteria: How They Affect Other Living Things, 1980; *Bears of the World,* 1980; *The Lives of Spiders,* 1980; *Horses and Their Wild Relatives,* 1981; *Hunters and the Hunted: Surviving in the Animal World,* 1981; *Horses of America,* 1981; *Arabian Horses,* 1982; *Spider Magic,* 1982; *A Picture Book of Cows,* 1982; (with Diane Bilderback) *Garden Secrets* (adult nonfiction), Rodale Press, 1982.

Contributor to gardening and farming magazines and to scientific journals.

WORK IN PROGRESS: For children, a book on germs and a book on ponies, both for Holiday House, and a book on bald eagles, for Clarion Books; for adults, a book on fruit-growing, with Diane Bilderback, for Rodale Press, and a zoology textbook, with husband, Gregory J. Patent, for C. E. Merrill.

AVOCATIONAL INTERESTS: Gardening, travel, racquetball.

BIOGRAPHICAL/CRITICAL SOURCES: San Rafael Independent-Journal, January 26, 1974; *Missoulian,* December 19, 1981.

* * *

PAUKER, Ted
See CONQUEST, (George) Robert (Acworth)

* * *

PAWLIKOWSKI, John T. 1940-

PERSONAL: Surname is pronounced Paw-lee-*cow*-ski; born November 2, 1940, in Chicago, Ill.; son of Thaddeus John (a cork molder) and Anna (Mizera) Pawlikowski. *Education:* Attended Mount St. Philip, Milwaukee, Wis., 1958-60, and Servite Priory, Benburb, Northern Ireland, 1960-62; Loyola University, Chicago, Ill., A.B., 1963, graduate study, 1963-66; also attended Stonebridge Priory, Lake Bluff, Ill., 1963-66, and University of Wisconsin, 1965-67; College of Jewish Studies, Chicago, diploma, 1967; St. Mary of the Lake Seminary, Mundelein, Ill., S.T.B., 1967; University of Chicago, Ph.D., 1970. *Politics:* "Generally Democratic." *Home:* 1420 East 49th St., Chicago, Ill. 60615. *Office:* Catholic Theological Union, 5401 South Cornell Ave., Chicago, Ill. 60615.

CAREER: Ordained Roman Catholic priest of Servite Fathers (O.S.M.), 1967; University of Chicago, Chicago, Ill., chaplain's assistant at Calvert House (Newman Club), 1967—; Catholic Theological Union, Chicago, 1968—, began as assistant professor, currently professor of ethics and acting president. Seminarian-Lay Apostolate Conference, executive chairman, 1964-65, member of executive committee, 1965-66; chairman of National Council of Churches' Faith and Order Study Commission on Israel, 1972-73, and Chicago Institute for Inter-religious Research, 1973; fellow, International Institute of Community Service, 1975; member of United States Holocaust Memorial Council, 1980—; member of national board, Americans for Democratic Action, 1981—; also affiliated with Anti-Defamation League of B'nai B'rith, Inter-Seminary Movement, and Southern Christian Leadership Conference. Member of advisory Committee, Secretariat for Catholic-Jewish Relations, National Conference of Catholic Bishops, 1971-73. *Member:* American Society of Christian Ethics, Catholic Theological Society of America, American Academy of Religion. *Awards, honors:* Fellowship to Institute of Jewish Studies, Wheeling College; Men of Achievement Award, 1973; Inter-faith Award, American Jewish Committee, 1973; Founder's Citation, National Catholic Conference Interracial Justice.

WRITINGS: Epistle Homilies, Bruce Publishing, 1966; *Catechetics and Prejudice: How Catholic Teaching Materials View Jews, Protestants, and Racial Minorities,* Paulist/Newman, 1973; *What Are They Saying about Christian-Jewish Relations?,* Paulist/Newman, 1980; *Christ: In Light of the Christian-Jewish Dialogue,* 1982; *The Challenge of the Holocaust for Christian Theology,* Anti-Defamation League of B'nai B'rith, in press. Also author of *Proposals for Church-Sponsored New Housing,* 1971, *Sinai and Calvary, Social Ethics: Biblical and Theological Foundations,* and of *Church-State Relations: A Contemporary Catholic Perspective.*

Contributor: Walter Wagoner, *The Seminary,* Sheed, 1966; Michael Zeik and Martin Siegel, editors, *Root and Branch,* Roth, 1973; Robert Heyer, editor, *Jewish/Christian Relations,* Paulist/Newman, 1975; Clyde L. Manschreck and Barbara Brown

Zikmund, editors, *The American Religious Experiment: Piety and Practicality,* Exploration Press, 1976; Alan T. Davies, editor, *Antisemitism and the Foundations of Christianity,* Paulist/Newman, 1979; Harry James Cargas, editor, *When God and Man Failed: Non-Jewish Views of the Holocaust,* Macmillan, 1981; Henry Friedlander and Sybil Milton, editors, *The Holocaust: Ideology, Bureaucracy, and Genocide,* Kraus Reprint, 1981; Eugene J. Fisher and Daniel F. Polish, editors, *Formation of Social Policy in the Catholic and Jewish Traditions,* University of Notre Dame Press, 1982. Also contributor to *Auschwitz: Beginning of a New Era,* edited by Eva Fleischner, Ktav, and to *Selected Papers 1979: The American Society of Christian Ethics,* edited by Max L. Stackhouse. Contributor to journals, including *Furrow, Today, Journal of Ecumenical Studies, Cross Currents, Journal of Religion,* and *Ecumenist.*

SIDELIGHTS: John T. Pawlikowski speaks Polish and some German, modern Hebrew, and French; he reads Latin, French, German, Hebrew (Biblical and modern), and Greek (classical and modern).

* * *

PAYNE, Donald Gordon 1924-
(Ian Cameron, Donald Gordon, James Vance Marshall)

PERSONAL: Born January 3, 1924, in London, England; son of Francis Gordon and Evelyn (Rogers) Payne; married Barbara Back, August 20, 1947; children: Christopher, Nigel, Adrian, Alison, Robin. *Education:* Corpus Christi College, Oxford, M.A., 1949. *Religion:* Church of England. *Home:* Pippacre, Westcott Heath, near Dorking, Surrey, England. *Agent:* David Higham Associates Ltd., Golden Square, London W. 1, England; and Harold Ober Associates, Inc., 40 East 49th St., New York, N.Y. 10017.

CAREER: Christopher Johnson Publishers Ltd., London, England, trainee, 1949-52; Robert Hale Ltd. (publishers), London, editor, 1952-56; full-time writer. *Military service:* Royal Naval Volunteer Reserve, Fleet Air Arm pilot, 1942-46; became lieutenant.

WRITINGS—Under pseudonym Ian Cameron: *The Midnight Sea,* Hutchinson, 1958; *Red Duster, White Ensign* (story of Malta convoys), Muller, 1959, Doubleday, 1960; *The Lost Ones,* Hutchinson, 1961, Morrow, 1968; *Wings of the Morning* (story of Fleet Air Arm in World War II), Hodder & Stoughton, 1962, Morrow, 1963; *Lodestone and Evening Star* (history of sea exploration), Hodder & Stoughton, 1965, Dutton, 1966; *The Island at the Top of the World,* Avon, 1970; *The Impossible Dream: Building of the Panama Canal,* Morrow, 1971; *The Mountains at the Bottom of the World: Novel of Adventure,* Morrow, 1972; *Magellan and the First Circumnavigation of the World,* Saturday Review Press, 1973; *Antarctica: The Last Continent,* Little, Brown, 1974; *The Young Eagles,* St. Martin's, 1980; *To the Farthest Ends of the Earth,* Dutton, 1980.

Under pseudonym Donald Gordon: *Star-Raker,* Morrow, 1962; *Flight of the Bat,* Hodder & Stoughton, 1963, Morrow, 1964; *The Golden Oyster,* Hodder & Stoughton, 1967, Morrow, 1968; *Leap in the Dark,* Morrow, 1971.

Under pseudonym James Vance Marshall: (Co-author) *The Children,* M. Joseph, 1959, published as *Walkabout,* Doubleday, 1961; *A River Ran Out of Eden,* Morrow, 1963; *My Boy John that Went to Sea,* Hodder & Stoughton, 1966, Morrow, 1967; *A Walk to the Hills of the Dreamtime,* Morrow, 1970; *The Wind at Morning,* Morrow, 1973, new edition, G. K. Hall, 1974.

WORK IN PROGRESS: Still Waters, a novel.

MEDIA ADAPTATIONS: The film "Walkabout" was produced by Twentieth Century-Fox in 1971 and "Island at the Top of the World" by Walt Disney Productions in 1974.

* * *

PAYNE, Ernest A(lexander) 1902-1980

PERSONAL: Born February 19, 1902, in London, England; died January 14, 1980, in Oxford, England; son of Alexander William and Mary Catherine (Griffiths) Payne; married Winifred Mary Davies, October 28, 1930; children: Elizabeth Ann (Mrs. Antony Fergus Prain). *Education:* King's College, London, B.A., 1921; Regent's Park College, Oxford, B.D., 1925; Mansfield College, Oxford, B.Litt., 1927, M.A., 1944; University of Marburg, additional study, 1927-28. *Office:* 4 Southampton Row, London W.C.1, England.

CAREER: Ordained to Baptist ministry, 1928, with first pastorate in Bugbrooke, Northampton, England, 1928-32; Baptist Missionary Society, London, England, young people's secretary and editor, 1932-40; Oxford University, Oxford, England, senior tutor, Regent's Park College, 1940-51, lecturer in comparative literature and history of modern missions, 1946-51; Baptist Union of Great Britain and Ireland, London, general secretary, 1951-67, vice-president, 1976-77, president, 1977-78. World Council of Churches, vice-chairman of Central Committee, 1954-68, president, 1968-75. British Council of Churches, vice-president, 1960, chairman of executive committee, 1962-71; vice-president, Baptist World Alliance, beginning 1965. Examiner in Oxford University, Universities of Wales, Edinburgh, and Bristol. Director of Baptist Insurance Co. Ltd.

MEMBER: Baptist Historical Society (president), United Society for Christian Literature (vice-president), Athenaeum Club (London). *Awards, honors:* D.D., University of St. Andrews, 1951; LL.D., McMaster University, 1961; Grand Medaille d'argent de la cite de Paris, 1962; Companion of Honour, Great Britain, 1968.

WRITINGS: The Saktas: An Introductory and Comparative Study, H. Milford, 1933, reprinted, Garland Publishing, 1980; *Freedom in Jamaica: Some Chapters in the Story of the Baptist Missionary Society,* Carey Press, 1933; *The First Generation: Early Leaders of the Baptist Missionary Society in England and India,* Carey Press, 1936; *Marianne Lewis and Elizabeth Sale: Pioneers of Missionary Work among Women,* Carey Press, 1937; *The Great Succession: Leaders of the Baptist Missionary Society during the Nineteenth Century,* Carey Press, 1938, 2nd edition, 1946; *Henry Wyatt of Shansi, 1895-1938,* Carey Press, 1939, 2nd edition, 1946.

The Church Awakes: The Story of the Modern Missionary Movement, Livingston Press, 1942; (with Katleen Margaret Shuttleworth) *Missionaries All: A Pageant of British History,* Carey Press, 1942; *Before the Start: Steps Towards the Founding of the L.M.S.,* E. & S. Livingstone, 1942; (editor) *Studies in History and Religion,* Lutterworth, 1942; *The Free Church Tradition in the Life of England,* S.C.M. Press, 1944, revised edition, Hodder & Stoughton, 1965; *The Fellowship of Believers: Baptist Thought and Practice Yesterday and Today,* Carey Kingsgate Press, 1944, enlarged edition, 1952, reprinted, Arno, 1980; *South-East from Serampore: More Chapters in the Story of the Baptist Missionary Society,* Carey Kingsgate Press, 1945; *Henry Wheeler Robinson, Scholar, Teacher, Principal: A Memoir,* Nisbet, 1946; *College Street Church, Northampton, 1697-1947,* Carey Kingsgate Press, 1947; *The Baptist Movement in the Reformation and Onwards,* Carey Kingsgate Press, 1947; (translator) Karl Barth, *The Teaching of the Church Regarding Baptism,* S.C.M. Press, 1948; *The Anabaptists of the 16th Century and Their Influence in the Modern World,* Carey Kingsgate Press, 1949; *The Bible in English,* Epworth, 1949.

The Baptists of Berkshire: Through Three Centuries, Carey Kingsgate Press, 1951; *The Excellent Mr. Burls,* Carey Kingsgate Press, 1951; *The Free Churches and Episcopacy,* Carey Kingsgate Press, 1952; *The Free Churches and the State,* Carey Kingsgate Press, 1952; *The Baptist Union and Its Headquarters: A Descriptive Record,* Carey Kingsgate Press, 1953; *James Henry Rushbrooke, 1870-1947: A Baptist Greatheart,* Carey Kingsgate Press, 1954; *The Baptists of the World and Their Overseas Missions,* Carey Kingsgate Press, 1955; *The Growth of the World Church: The Story of the Modern Missionary Movement,* Macmillan, 1955; *The Meaning and Practice of Ordination among Baptists,* Carey Kingsgate Press, 1957; (with David G. Moses) *Why Integration?: An Explanation of the Proposal before the World Council of Churches and the International Missionary Council,* Edinburgh House Press, 1957; (translator) Johannes Schneider, *Baptism and Church in the New Testament,* Carey Kingsgate Press, 1957; (contributor) G. R. Elton, editor, *New Cambridge Modern History,* Cambridge University Press, 1958; *The Baptist Union: A Short History,* Attic Press, 1959.

(Compiler with Stephen F. Winward) *Orders and Prayers for Church Worship: A Manual for Ministers,* Carey Kingsgate Press, 1960, 2nd edition, 1962, published (with Winward and James W. Cox) as *Minister's Worship Manual: Orders and Prayers for Worship,* World Publishing, 1969; (author of introduction) William Carey, *An Inquiry into the Obligation of Christians to Use Means for the Conversion of the Heathens,* Carey Kingsgate Press, 1961; *Roger Williams (1603-1683),* Independent Press, 1961; (with Norman S. Moon) *Baptists and 1662,* Carey Kingsgate Press, 1962; *Veteran Warrior: Memoir of B. Grey Griffith,* Carey Kingsgate Press, 1962; (contributor) G. F. Nuttall and Owen Chadwick, editors, *From Uniformity to Unity, 1662-1962,* S.P.C.K., 1962; (contributor) R.J.W. Bevan, editor, *The Churches and Christian Unity,* Oxford University Press, 1963; *Baptists and Church Relations,* Baptist Union of Great Britain and Ireland, 1964; *Free Churchmen, Unrepentant and Repentant, and Other Papers,* Carey Kingsgate Press, 1965; *Thomas Helwys and the First Baptist Church in England,* 2nd edition (Payne was not associated with previous edition), Baptist Union of Great Britain and Ireland, 1966; (contributor) A. M. Motter, editor, *Preaching on Pentecost and Christian Unity,* Fortress, 1966; *Some Recent Happenings in the Roman Church,* Baptist Union, 1966; (contributor) Leonard George Champion, editor, *Outlook for Christianity,* Lutterworth, 1967.

The World Council of Churches, 1948-69, Baptist Union, 1970; *Violence, Non-Violence and Human Rights,* Baptist Union, 1971; *Thirty Years of the British Council of Churches, 1942-72,* British Council of Churches, 1972; (contributor) R. H. Fischer, editor, *A Palette for a Portrait: Franklin Clark Fry,* Lutheran Quarterly, 1972; *The Free Churches: Today's Challenges,* Free Church Federal Council, 1973; *Venerable Dissenting Institution,* Dr. Williams's Trust, 1979.

(Contributor) Edwin S. Gaustad, editor, *British Baptists: An Original Anthology,* Arno, 1980. Also author of *Out of Great Tribulation: Baptists in the U.S.S.R.,* 1974 and *The Struggle for Human Rights,* 1974. Contributor to festschriften honoring Martin Nemoeller and W. A. Visser't Hooft, to *Dictionary of National Biography,* and to *Upper Room Disciplines.* Editor, *Baptist Quarterly,* 1944-50.

SIDELIGHTS: Ernest A. Payne was one of the more active participants in the British and international ecumenical movements. Influenced early by his Baptist parents, Payne later studied under such men as Old Testament scholar Wheeler Robinson and King's College instructor W. R. Matthews. In 1951, after working for the Baptist Missionary Society for eight years and joining the theological departments at Regent's Park College and Oxford University, Payne was chosen to fill the post of general secretary of the Baptist Union of Great Britain and Ireland.

During his tenure, Payne quickly earned great respect from his fellow churchmen and three years later accepted the appointment to vice-chairman of the central committee of the World Council of Churches. In this position Payne traveled extensively and was introduced to various Christian denominations all over the world. After fourteen years he was elected to the presidency at the Fourth Assembly of the World Council of Churches, becoming the first English Freechurchman ever to occupy this office.†

* * *

PEARLMAN, Daniel (David) 1935-

PERSONAL: Born July 22, 1935, in New York, N.Y. *Education:* Brooklyn College (now Brooklyn College of the City University of New York), B.A., 1957; Columbia University, M.A., 1958, Ph.D., 1968. *Office:* Department of English, University of Rhode Island, Kingston, R.I. 02881.

CAREER: Brooklyn College (now Brooklyn College of the City University of New York), Brooklyn, N.Y., instructor in English, 1958-60; University of Arizona, Tucson, instructor in English, 1960-62; Brooklyn College of the City University of New York, instructor in English, 1962-67; Monmouth College, West Long Branch, N.J., assistant professor of English, 1967-69; Mercer Community College, Trenton, N.J., professor of English and chairman of department, 1969-71; Columbus International College, Seville, Spain, director of academic affairs, 1972-73; Universidad de Sevilla, Seville, Spain, visiting professor of English, 1973-74; Herbert H. Lehman College of the City University of New York, Bronx, N.Y., assistant professor of academic skills, 1974-76; University of Idaho, Moscow, professor of English and chairman of department, 1976-80; University of Rhode Island, Kingston, professor of English and chairman of department, 1980—. *Member:* Modern Language Association of America. *Awards, honors:* American Philosophical Society research grants, 1968 and 1971-72; American Council of Learned Societies research fellowship, 1971-72, for literary research abroad; National Endowment for the Arts grant, 1979; Idaho Research Foundation/University of Idaho Foundation grant, 1979; University of Rhode Island grant, 1981-82.

WRITINGS: Guide to Rapid Revision, Odyssey, 1965, 3rd edition, Bobbs-Merrill, 1982; *The Barb of Time: On the Unity of Ezra Pound's Cantos,* Oxford University Press, 1969; (contributor) Grace Schulman, editor, *Ezra Pound: A Collection of Criticism,* McGraw, 1974; (translator with Luisa Campos) *Do caos a ordem: Visoes de sociedade nos Cantares de Ezra Pound,* Assirio e Alvim (Portugal), 1983; *The Complete Correspondence between Ezra Pound and Senator William E. Borah,* Black Swan, 1984.

Also author of a discussion guide to accompany film "Ezra Pound: Poet's Poet," 1971; author of unpublished novels *Astrobal, The Interview,* and *Look-out Man.* Contributor of articles and reviews to literary journals. Associate editor, *Paideuma* (journal of Ezra Pound scholarship).

WORK IN PROGRESS: Contributing to Volume II of *Index to the Cantos of Ezra Pound,* for University of Maine Press; *Robert Frost and the New Deal.*

BIOGRAPHICAL/CRITICAL SOURCES: Virginia Quarterly Review, spring, 1970; *Criticism,* fall, 1970.

* * *

PELLOWSKI, Anne 1933-

PERSONAL: Born June 28, 1933, in Pine Creek, Wis.; daughter of Alexander (a farmer) and Anna (Dorava) Pellowski. *Education:* College of St. Teresa, B.A., 1955; Columbia University, M.S.L.S. (with honors), 1959; additional graduate study at University of Minnesota, summer, 1955, University of Munich, 1955-56, and New School for Social Research, 1965. *Religion:* Roman Catholic.

CAREER: College of St. Teresa, Winona, Minn., instructor in English, 1956-57; Winona Public Library, Winona, children's librarian, 1957; New York Public Library, New York City, children's librarian, 1957-59, researcher, 1960-65, senior children's librarian, 1961-62, assistant story-telling and group work specialist in Office of Children's Services, 1963-65; University of Maryland, Overseas Branch, Munich, Germany, instructor in English, 1959-60; U.S. Committee for UNICEF, New York City, director of Information Center on Children's Cultures, 1967-82; freelance writer, 1982—. Adjunct lecturer, University of Maryland, 1965-66; summer lecturer, University of Wisconsin, 1966, Columbia University, 1967, and University of Pennsylvania, 1980. Records stories for children under CMS label. United States representative at numerous international conferences, including International Film Festival, Moscow, 1973, and conference on film production and distribution of films for young people, Teheran, 1974. Consultant to UNESCO, Biblioteca Nacional de Venezuela, Childraft, and other groups. *Member:* American Library Association, Educational Film Library Association, Friends of the International Board on Books for Young People. *Awards, honors:* Fulbright fellow in Germany, 1955-56; Grolier Foundation Award, American Library Association, 1979; Constance Lindsay Skinner Award, Women's National Book Association, 1980.

WRITINGS: The World of Children's Literature, Bowker, 1968; (editor) *Have You Seen a Comet?,* John Day, 1971; (author of introduction) Isabelle Jan, *On Children's Literature,* Schocken, 1974; *The World of Storytelling,* Bowker, 1978; *The Nine Crying Dolls,* Philomel Books, 1979; *Made to Measure: Children's Books in Developing Countries,* UNESCO, 1980.

"Four Farms" series; all published by Philomel Books: *Willow Wind Farm: Betsy's Story,* 1981; *Stairstep Farm: Anna Rose's Story,* 1981; *Winding Valley Farm : Annie's Story,* 1982; *First Farm in the Valley: Anna's Story,* 1982.

Contributor of chapters to books and of articles to professional publications.

WORK IN PROGRESS: Additional titles in the "Four Farms" series; a book on storytelling.

SIDELIGHTS: Commenting on her "Four Farms" novels, a series (based on her own family's history) that traces five generations of Polish-American children on a Wisconsin farm, Anne Pellowski told *CA:* "A number of sociologists (Merle Curti in particular) have pointed out the difficulty in studying the history of movements and re-settlements from the point of view of the 'little people,' the ordinary folk. Since my great-grandfather was part of a pre-Civil War immigrant group of Kashubian Poles who settled in the Midwest, and his great- and great-great-grandchildren have spread out over the entire country, I decided to attempt writing a series of historical fiction tracing the lives of various descendants as they appeared in succeeding generations. I hope to show how some customs have survived through all those years, whereas others lasted only a generation or two and have now been supplanted by the American way."

* * *

PENTZ, Croft Miner

PERSONAL: Born in Waynesboro, Pa.; son of F. Daniel and Edna F. (Miner) Pentz; married Frances Cook, December 25, 1952. *Education:* Attended Central Bible Institute, Springfield, Mo., two years. *Home:* 1371 O'Mara Dr., Union, N.J. 07083.

CAREER: Minister to the deaf, 1952—. Instructor in sign language, Northeast Bible Institute, Green Lane, Pa., 1955-63; chaplain, New Jersey School for the Deaf, 1958—. Youth director, Metropolitan Section, Assemblies of God, New Jersey, 1959-65. *Member:* Young Men's Christian Association (Elizabeth, N.J.).

WRITINGS—Published by Baker Book, except as indicated: *1001 Sentence Sermons for Every Need,* Zondervan, 1962; *175 Simple Sermon Outlines,* 1963; (compiler) *Speaker's Treasury of 400 Quotable Poems,* Zondervan, 1963; *48 Simple Sermon Outlines,* 1965; (editor) *Preaching Poems for Sermons and Addresses,* 1966; *The Christian Worker,* privately printed, 1966; *Sermon Outlines from Acts,* 1978; *Outlines on Revelation,* 1978; *Outlines on the Holy Spirit,* 1978; *Outlines for Growing Christians,* 1978; *Sermon Outlines for Special Days,* 1979; *Expository Outlines from Romans,* 1980; *Outlines on the Parables of Jesus,* 1980. Also author of *Expository Outlines on Hebrews.*

Contributor to *Sermon Builder, Gospel Herald,* and other denominational periodicals. Contributing editor, *Shepherd's Staff.*

BIOGRAPHICAL/CRITICAL SOURCES: TV Guide, January 9, 1960; *Silent Worker,* January, 1962; *Christian Life,* May, 1962; *Presbyterian Life,* April 15, 1963.†

* * *

PERRY, Lloyd M(erle) 1916-

PERSONAL: Surname originally Perrigo; born May 24, 1916, in Hodgdon, Me.; son of Percy (a storekeeper) and Medston (Smith) Perrigo; married Elva Grace Wilson, June 19, 1943; children: Rixson Merle, Gregg Chandler, Cynthia Jean. *Education:* Gordon College of Theology and Missions, A.B., 1939; Gordon Divinity School, B.D., 1943; Columbia University, M.A., 1946; Northern Baptist Theological Seminary, Th.D., 1948; Northwestern University, Ph.D., 1961; McCormick Seminary, D.Min., 1978. *Home:* 16850 West Orchard Valley Dr., Gurnee, Ill. 60031. *Office:* Trinity Evangelical Divinity School, 2065 Half Day Rd., Deerfield, Ill. 60015.

CAREER: Farm and Trades School, Boston, Mass., chaplain, 1938-40; pastor of Baptist churches in Hampton, N.H., 1940-43, and Brooklyn, N.Y., 1943-46; ordained Baptist minister, 1943; Aurora College, Aurora, Ill., associate professor of speech, 1946-47; Northern Baptist Seminary, Chicago, Ill., professor of public speaking and homiletics, 1947-51; Gordon Divinity School, Beverly Farms, Mass., professor of practical theology, 1951-62; Central Baptist Church, Indianapolis, Ind., pastor, 1962-64; Trinity Evangelical Divinity School, Deerfield, Ill., professor of speech and homiletics and chairman of department, 1964—, director of Doctor of Ministry Program, 1977—. Lyman Steward Lecturer, Talbot Theological Seminary, 1972; Staley Lecturer, Fort Wayne Bible College, 1973; speaker at Moody Pastors Conference, 1977-81. Pastor of Baptist churches in Wheaton, Ill., 1949-51, Beverly Farms, Mass., 1953-55, and Everett, Mass., 1958-59. *Member:* American Speech, Language, and Hearing Association, Association of Seminary Professors in the Practical Fields, National Association of Teachers of Speech, Phi Alpha Chi, Kappa Delta Pi.

WRITINGS: (With Faris D. Whitesell) *Variety in Your Preaching,* Revell, 1954; (with Howard) *How to Study Your Bible,* introduction by Billy Graham, Revell, 1957; (with Howard and Strickland) *Introducing the Bible,* Powell Publishing Co., 1957; (with Whitesell and Wilson) *Seven Sermon Structures,* Powell Publishing Co., 1958; (with Whitesell and Wilson) *Preaching Biblical Sermons,* Powell Publishing Co., 1959; (with Strickland) *Variety in Biblical Preaching,* Powell Publishing Co., 1959.

(With Edward John Lias) *A Manual of Pastoral Problems and Procedures,* Baker Book, 1960; *A Manual for Biblical Preaching,* Baker Book, 1965; (with Robert D. Culver) *How to Search the Scriptures,* Baker Book, 1967, published as *How to Get More from Your Bible,* Baker Book, 1979; (contributor) Ralph G. Turnbull, editor, *Baker's Dictionary of Practical Theology,* Baker Book, 1967; (contributor) Roy C. Irving and Roy B. Zuck, editors, *Youth and the Church,* Moody, 1968.

Biblical Sermon Guide, Baker Book, 1970; *Biblical Preaching for Today's World,* Moody, 1973; (with Eidenire) *Biblical Preaching: Learning to Present God's Message,* with recordings, Moody, 1975; *Getting the Church on Target,* Moody, 1977; (with J. R. Strubhar) *Evangelistic Preaching: A Step-by-Step Guide to Pulpit Evangelism,* Moody, 1979.

(With Ericson) *John: A New Look at the Fourth Gospel,* Tyndale, 1981; (with Gilbert Peterson) *Churches in Crisis,* Moody, 1981; (with Norman Shawchuck) *Revitalizing the Twentieth-Century Church,* Moody, 1982; (with Calvin Hanson) *Romans: A Model for Bible Study Method,* Moody, 1982; (with Sell) *Speaking to Life's Problems: A Source Book for Preaching and Teaching,* Moody, 1983.

Contributor to *Christianity Today* and *Church Advocate.*

WORK IN PROGRESS: The History of Preaching: A Source of Illustrations, with Wiersbe; *Acts: A Sourcebook for Study and Sermonizing,* with Osborne; *The Science of Sermonizing: An Introduction to Sermon Construction.*

* * *

PETERS, Lawrence
See DAVIES, L(eslie) P(urnell)

* * *

PETERSEN, William J. 1929-

PERSONAL: Born August 19, 1929, in Chicago, Ill.; son of Elmer N. (a farmer) and Edna (McAlpine) Petersen; married Ardythe Ekdahl (a teacher), December 20, 1952; children: Kenneth, Randall, Kathryn. *Education:* Wheaton College, Wheaton, Ill., B.A., 1950. *Religion:* Baptist. *Home:* 613 Clearview Ave., Woodbury Heights, N.J. 08097. *Office: Eternity,* 1716 Spruce St., Philadelphia, Pa. 19103.

CAREER: Chain o'Lakes Guide (weekly newspaper), Waupaca, Wis., editor, 1949; *Gideon* (magazine), Chicago, Ill., assistant editor, 1950-51; *Fort Sheridan Tower,* Fort Sheridan, Ill., editor, 1952-53; *Christian Life* (magazine), Chicago, Ill., editorial director, 1953-57; *Eternity* (magazine), Philadelphia, Pa., executive editor, 1957-75, editor, 1975—. *Member:* Evangelical Press Association (president). *Military service:* U.S. Army, 1951-53.

WRITINGS: Another Hand on Mine, McGraw, 1967; *Astrology and the Bible,* Victor, 1972; *Those Curious New Cults,* Keats Publishing, 1973; *What You Should Know about Gambling,* Keats Publishing, 1974; *How to Be a Saint while Lying Flat on Your Back,* Zondervan, 1974; *Two Stars for God,* Warner Paperback, 1974; *TM: Ado about Nothing,* Keats Publishing, 1976; *The Last Days of Man,* Warner Paperback, 1977; *Meet Me on the Mountain,* Victor Books, 1979; *The Discipline of Timothy,* Victor Books, 1980. Editor of "Shepherd Illustrated Classic" series, Keats Publishing. Contributor to religious periodicals.

WORK IN PROGRESS: Martin Luther Had a Wife, for Tyndale; *The Other Side of Jeremiah,* for Victor Books.

SIDELIGHTS: William J. Petersen did research in the Congo, Uganda, and Kenya for his book *Another Hand on Mine.*

* * *

PETTY, Walter T. 1918-

PERSONAL: Born June 18, 1918, in St. Paul, Kan.; married Dorothy C. Hart, July 30, 1940; children: Walter T., Jr., Roy A., Claire. *Education:* Central Missouri State College (now University), A.B., B.S., and B.S. in Ed., 1940; University of Iowa, M.A., 1950, Ph.D., 1955; additional graduate study at Washington University, St. Louis, Mo., 1945, and Drake University, 1951. *Home:* 8 Pine Trail Rd., Route 9, Rogers, Ark. 72756.

CAREER: Teacher and principal in Blairstown, Mo., 1940-42; chemist, Atlas Powder Co., 1942-44; teacher in Webster Groves, Mo., 1945-46; principal of high school in Leon, Iowa, 1946-48; superintendent of schools, Decatur County, Iowa, 1948-53; Sacramento State College (now California State University, Sacramento), professor of education, 1955-66, chairman of department of elementary education, 1958-61; State University of New York at Buffalo, professor of education, 1966-82, professor emeritus, 1983—, acting dean of faculty of educational studies, 1975-78. *Military service:* U.S. Army, Infantry, 1944-45. *Member:* International Reading Association, National Council of Teachers of English, National Conference on Research in English (president, 1969), National Education Association (life member).

WRITINGS: (Editor) *Meeting Individual Needs through Reading,* Sacramento State College Press, 1958; (with Harry A. Greene) *Developing Language Skills in the Elementary Schools,* Allyn & Bacon, 1959, 5th edition, 1975; *Improving Your Spelling Program,* Chandler Publishing, 1959.

The Language Arts in the Elementary School, Center for Applied Research in Education (New York), 1962; (with Mary

Bowen) *Slithery Snakes and Other Aids to Children's Writing,* Appleton, 1967; (with Paul Herold and Earline Stoll) *Research in the Teaching of Vocabulary,* National Council of Teachers of English, 1967; (editor) *Issues and Problems in the English Language Arts: A Book of Readings,* Allyn & Bacon, 1967.

(With wife, Dorothy C. Petty, and Marjorie Becking) *Experiences in Language,* Allyn & Bacon, 1973, 3rd edition, 1980; *Curriculum for the Modern Elementary School,* Rand McNally, 1976; (with Julie Jensen) *Developing Children's Language,* Allyn & Bacon, 1980.

Also author, with Gus Plessas, of "You Can Spell" series of thirty books for grades one through eight, with teacher's manuals and workbooks, Allyn & Bacon, 1964-65.

SIDELIGHTS: "Basically I'm a teacher rather than a writer," Walter T. Petty told *CA.* "I simply try to put on paper ideas about good teaching. My goal is to make a small gain in the effectiveness of teaching in our schools."

* * *

PETULLA, Joseph M. 1932-

PERSONAL: Born September 29, 1932, in Oil City, Pa.; son of Louis (a shoe repairer) and Jennie (Ruby) Petulla. *Education:* St. Bonaventure University, B.A., 1954; University of Notre Dame, M.A., 1959; Graduate Theological Union, Berkeley, Calif., Ph.D., 1971. *Politics:* Democrat. *Home:* 1230 Colusa Ave., Berkeley, Calif. 94707. *Office:* University of San Francisco, San Francisco, Calif. 94117.

CAREER: Cathedral Prep School, Erie, Pa., member of staff, 1958-63; Gannon College, Erie, Pa., instructor in theology, 1963-67; Laney College, Oakland, Calif., instructor in urban studies, 1971-72; University of California, Berkeley, lecturer in conservation and resource studies, 1972-78; University of San Francisco, San Francisco, Calif., director of Graduate Program in Environmental Studies and Management, 1978—. *Awards, honors:* National Science Foundation interdisciplinary grant, 1982-83.

WRITINGS: The Friendship of Christ, Sadlier, 1967; *Faith on Monday* (textbook), Sadlier, 1968; *All Over the World,* Sadlier, 1968; *Where Is Your Brother?* (adult education), Sadlier, 1969; (contributor) *Where Do We Go from Here?* (adult education), Sadlier, 1969; *Christian Political Theology: A Marxian Guide,* Orbis, 1972; *American Environmental History,* Boyd & Fraser, 1977; *American Environmentalism: Values, Tactics, Priorities,* Texas A&M University Press, 1980. Contributor to *America, Nation, Cross Currents,* and other periodicals.

WORK IN PROGRESS: Studies in environmental philosophy, history writing, and research.

* * *

PETZOLD, Paul 1940-

PERSONAL: Born September 12, 1940, in Epsom, Surrey, England; son of Max Leo and Iris (Hopps) Petzold. *Education:* Attended Polytechnic Film School, London, 1958-61. *Home:* 4A Alexandra Mans., West End Lane, London NW6 1LU, England. *Office:* Paul Petzold Ltd., 60-62 London Rd., Kingston-upon-Thames, Surrey, England.

CAREER: Free-lance filmmaker, 1961-62; Focal Press, London, England, book editor, 1962-78, publishing director, 1978-81; Paul Petzold Ltd., Kingston-upon-Thames, England, publisher, 1981—. Co-director of screenplay "Background to Ballet," British Broadcasting Corp. (BBC), 1962.

WRITINGS: All in One Cine Book, Focal Press, 1969, 4th edition, 1979, published as *All in One Movie Book,* Amphoto, 1969, 4th edition, 1979; *Light on People in Photography,* Amphoto, 1971; (with Freddie Young) *The Work of the Motion Picture Cameraman,* Hastings House, 1972; *Effects and Experiments in Photography,* Amphoto, 1972; *Photoguide to Moviemaking,* Amphoto, 1975; *Photoguide to Low Light Photography,* Amphoto, 1976; (with A. A. Englander) *Filming for Television,* Hastings House, 1976; *Photoguide to Lighting,* Amphoto, 1977; *Focal Book of Practical Photography,* Pitman, 1980.

WORK IN PROGRESS: A book on video technique.

* * *

PFALTZGRAFF, Robert L., Jr. 1934-

PERSONAL: Born June 1, 1934, in Philadelphia, Pa.; son of Robert L. and Mary (Warriner) Pfaltzgraff; married Diane A. Kressler (an associate professor of political science), May 20, 1967; children: Suzanne Diane, Robert Louis III. *Education:* Swarthmore College, B.A., 1956; University of Pennsylvania, M.B.A., 1958, M.A., 1959, Ph.D., 1964. *Home:* 663 Wallace Dr., Strafford, Pa. 19087. *Office:* Institute for Foreign Policy Analysis, Inc., Central Plaza Bldg., Tenth Floor, 675 Massachusetts Ave., Cambridge, Mass. 02139.

CAREER: University of Pennsylvania, Philadelphia, research assistant, 1959-63, assistant professor of political science, 1964-71, Foreign Policy Research Institute, research associate, 1964-71, deputy director, 1971-73, director, 1973-76; Tufts University, Fletcher School of Law and Diplomacy, Medford, Mass., associate professor, 1971-78, professor of international politics, 1978—; Institute for Foreign Policy Analysis, Inc., Cambridge, Mass., president, 1976—. Visiting lecturer, Foreign Service Institute, U.S. Department of State, 1970-71; George C. Marshall Professor, College of Europe, 1971-72; guest professor, National Defense College, Tokyo, 1981. President, U.S. Strategic Institute, 1977-79. *Member:* International Institute for Strategic Studies (London), Council on Foreign Relations. *Awards, honors:* Guggenheim fellowship, 1968-69; Relm fellow, 1969.

WRITINGS: (Contributor) *Building the Atlantic World,* Harper, 1963; *Britain Faces Europe: 1957-1967,* University of Pennsylvania Press, 1969; *The Atlantic Community: A Complex Imbalance,* Van Nostrand, 1969; (editor) *Politics and the International System,* Lippincott, 1969, 2nd edition, 1972.

(Co-author) *Contending Theories of International Relations,* Lippincott, 1971, 2nd edition, Harper, 1981; (co-editor and contributor) *SALT: Implications for Arms Control in the 1970s,* University of Pittsburgh Press, 1973; (co-editor and contributor) *The Superpowers in a Multinuclear World,* Heath, 1974; (editor and contributor) *Contrasting Approaches to Strategic Arms Control,* Heath, 1974; (co-editor and contributor) *New Technologies and Non-Nuclear Conflict: The Other Arms Race,* Heath, 1975; *The Study of International Relations,* Gale, 1977; (co-author) *The Cruise Missile: Bargaining Chip or Defense Bargain?,* Institute for Foreign Policy Analysis, 1977; (co-author) *Soviet Theater Strategy in Europe: Implications for NATO,* U.S. Strategic Institute, 1978; (co-editor and contributor) *Arms Transfers to the Third World: The Military Buildup in Less Industrial Countries,* Westview, 1978; (co-editor and contributor) *The Atlantic Community in Crisis: Redefining the*

Atlantic Relationship, Pergamon, 1979; (co-author) *SALT II and U.S.-Soviet Strategic Forces,* Institute for Foreign Policy Analysis, 1979.

Energy Issues and Alliance Relationships: The United States, Western Europe and Japan, Institute for Foreign Policy Analysis, 1980; (co-editor and contributor) *Intelligence Policy and National Security,* Macmillan, 1981; (co-author) *Power Projection and the Long-Range Combat Aircraft: Missions, Capabilities, and Alternative Designs,* Institute for Foreign Policy Analysis, 1981; (co-editor and contributor) *Projection of Power: Perspectives, Perceptions and Problems,* Archon, 1982; (co-editor and contributor) *The U.S. Defense Mobilization Infrastructure: Problems,* Archon, 1982.

Special editor and contributor, *Annals of the American Academy of Political and Social Science,* September, 1981. Contributor to *American Behavioral Scientist, Journal of Common Market Studies, New Republic, European Review, Air University Review, American Spectator, Arms Control and Security, Astronautics and Aeronautics, Atlantic Community Quarterly, Current History, Europa-Archiv, Europe-America Letter, Intercollegiate Review, International Affairs, International Security, International Studies Quarterly, International Security Review, Spettatore Internazionale, Orbis, Political Science Quarterly, Politique Internationale,* and *Strategic Review.* Editor, *Orbis,* beginning 1973.

WORK IN PROGRESS: Research on American foreign policy since World War II, on West European perspectives on deterrence, defense, and strategy, on international security dimensions of space, and on U.S. alliance policies in the 1980s.

*   *   *

PHILIPS, Thomas
See DAVIES, L(eslie) P(urnell)

*   *   *

PHILLIPS, Dewi Zephaniah 1934-

PERSONAL: Born November 24, 1934, in Swansea, Wales; son of D. O. and A. F. (Davies) Phillips; married Margaret Monica Hanford; children: Aled Huw, Steffan John, Rhys David. *Education:* University College of Swansea, University of Wales, B.A. (first class honors in philosophy), 1956, M.A., 1958; St. Catherine's Society, Oxford, B.Litt., 1961. *Politics:* Welsh Nationalist. *Religion:* Congregationalist. *Home:* 45 Queen's Rd., Sketty, Swansea, Glamorganshire, Wales. *Office:* Department of Philosophy, University College of Swansea, University of Wales, Singleton Park, Swansea SA2 8PP, Wales.

CAREER: University of St. Andrews, St. Andrews, Scotland, assistant lecturer in philosophy, 1961-62, lecturer, 1962-63; University of Wales, University College of North Wales, Bangor, lecturer in philosophy, 1962-65, University College of Swansea, Swansea, Wales, lecturer, 1965-67, senior lecturer, 1967-70, professor of philosophy, 1971—. *Member:* Aristotelian Society, Welsh Philosophical Society.

WRITINGS: The Concept of Prayer, Schocken, 1965; *Faith and Philosophical Enquiry,* Routledge & Kegan Paul, 1970, Schocken, 1971; *Death and Immortality,* St. Martin's, 1970; (with H. O. Mounce) *Moral Practices,* Schocken, 1970; (with Ilham Dilman) *Sense and Delusion,* Humanities Press, 1971; *Religion without Explanation,* Basil Blackwell, 1976; *Through a Darkening Glass,* University of Notre Dame Press, 1982.

Editor: *Religion and Understanding,* Macmillan, 1967; J. L. Stocks, *Morality and Purpose,* Routledge & Kegan Paul, 1969; *Studies in Ethics and the Philosophy of Religion,* Schocken, 1968-74; John Anderson, *Education and Inquiry,* Basil Blackwell, 1980; Jakob Fries, *Dialogues on Morality and Religion,* Basil Blackwell, 1982.

Contributor: I. T. Ramsey, editor, *Christian Ethics and Contemporary Philosophy,* Collier, 1966; A. Godlin, editor, *Du Cri a la parole,* Editions de Lumen Vitae, 1967; Judith J. Thomson and Gerald Dworkin, editors, *Ethics,* Harper, 1968; J. E. Caerwyn Williams, editor, *Ysgrifau Beirnindol,* Volume IV, Gee & Sons, 1969; J. H. Gill, editor, *Philosophy Today,* Macmillan, 1969; W. D. Hudson, editor, *The Is/Ought Question,* Macmillan, 1969.

B. Mitchell, editor, *The Philosophy of Religion,* Oxford University Press, 1971; *Problems of Moral Philosophy,* Dickenson, 1972; G. Vesey, editor, *Philosophy and the Arts,* Macmillan, 1973; Ingolf U. Dalferth, editor, *Sprachlogik des Glaubens,* Chr. Kaiser Verlag (Munich), 1974; Malcolm L. Diamond and Thomas V. Litzenburg, editors, *The Logic of God,* Bobbs-Merrill, 1975; John King-Farlow and William Shea, editors, *The Challenge of Religion Today,* Science History Publications, 1976; S. Brown, editor, *Reason and Religion,* Cornell University Press, 1977.

Frederick Crosson, editor, *The Autonomy of Religious Belief,* University of Notre Dame Press, 1981; Paul Helm, editor, *Divine Commands and Morality,* Oxford University Press, 1981; Irving Block, editor, *Perspectives on the Philosophy of Wittgenstein,* Basil Blackwell, 1981.

Also editor of *Saith Ysgrif Ar Grefydd,* 1967; author of *Athronyddu Am Grefydd,* 1974, and *Dramau Gwenlyn Parry,* 1982. General editor, *Values and Philosophical Inquiry,* Basil Blackwell, 1978—. Contributor to proceedings of philosophy societies and to professional journals.

WORK IN PROGRESS: Belief, Change and Forms of Life; a study of Kierkegaard's *Purity of Heart.*

*   *   *

PIG, Edward
See GOREY, Edward (St. John)

*   *   *

PIKE, Charles R.
See BULMER, (Henry) Kenneth

*   *   *

PILPEL, Robert H(arry) 1943-

PERSONAL: Born February 16, 1943, in New York, N.Y.; son of Robert Cecil (a lawyer) and Harriet (a lawyer; maiden name, Fleischl) Pilpel. *Education:* Stanford University, B.A. (with great distinction), 1963; Yale University, J.D., 1966; additional study at University of Rome, 1970-72. *Home and office:* 322 West 57th St., New York, N.Y. 10019. *Agent:* Timothy Seldes, Russell & Volkening, Inc., 551 Fifth Ave., New York, N.Y. 10017.

CAREER: Lawyer with U.S. Air Force, 1967-70, became captain; judge advocate with U.S. Air Force Reserve, Rome, Italy, beginning 1972, became major; currently full-time writer. *Member:* Phi Beta Kappa. *Awards, honors:* Fulbright fellow, 1970-71.

WRITINGS: (With Joel Rosenman and John Roberts) *Young Men with Unlimited Capital,* Harcourt, 1974; *Churchill in America,* Harcourt, 1976; *To the Honor of the Fleet* (historical novel), Atheneum, 1979; *Between Eternities* (novel), Harcourt, 1984. Contributor to *Harper's, Harper's Bookletter,* and *New York Sunday Times.*

SIDELIGHTS: Described by author Robert H. Pilpel as an attempt "to say something about the relationship between history and individual moral choice," *To the Honor of the Fleet* is a fictional account of an elaborate espionage scheme (concocted by an advisor to President Woodrow Wilson) designed to end World War I in its early stages and thus preserve American neutrality. Because the scheme involves sabotaging British naval operations, Pilpel's main characters, two U.S. Navy officers assigned to observe the combatants' forces and carry out the sabotage, must decide what is more important to them: their sense of personal honor and integrity or their loyalty to their country and their superiors.

Though he finds the plot somewhat "improbable," Richard F. Shepard declares in his *New York Times* review of *To the Honor of the Fleet* that it is "a well-told story, a novel that handles [its subject] with knowledge and a good sense of narrative. . . . [Pilpel] writes clearly and with feelings intent on unfolding the action. . . . [The book] makes good, attractive and informative reading."

Commenting in the *New York Times Book Review,* Anton Myrer remarks that the novel "is scrupulously researched and deftly plotted. . . . Historical figures move credibly across this broad canvas. The naval battles are rendered vividly. Mr. Pilpel's enthusiasm occasionally leads him into excessive historical or technical analyses. . . . Nonetheless, he has given us an interesting study in perversities."

Best Sellers reviewer Ingeborg C. Langer also has words of praise for *To the Honor of the Fleet.* Calling it a "fine first novel," Langer notes that Pilpel deals with "the large questions that have continued to haunt the twentieth century." And "as in war," concludes the reviewer, "betrayal and murder coexist with nobility and sacrifice in this immensely readable and vivid history."

AVOCATIONAL INTERESTS: Bicycling ("have bicycled from Italy to Frankfurt, around Corsica, around Sardina, and from Italy to Hungary"), flying (has commercial pilot license with instrument rating).

BIOGRAPHICAL/CRITICAL SOURCES: Library Journal, June 15, 1979; *New York Times,* August 7, 1979; *New York Times Book Review,* August 26, 1979; *Best Sellers,* October, 1979.

* * *

PINSON, William M(eredith), Jr. 1934-

PERSONAL: Born August 3, 1934, in Fort Worth, Tex.; son of William M. (a businessman) and Ila (Jones) Pinson; married Bobbie Judd, June 4, 1955. *Education:* North Texas State College (now University), B.A., 1955; University of Edinburgh, graduate study, 1956-57; Southwestern Baptist Seminary, B.D., 1959, Th.D., 1963. *Home:* 1714 Creekhaven, Duncanville, Tex. 75137. *Office:* Baptist General Convention of Texas, 511 North Akard, Dallas, Tex. 75201-3355.

CAREER: Ordained clergyman of Baptist Church, 1956; Christian Life Commission, Dallas, Tex., associate director, 1957-63; Southwestern Baptist Seminary, Fort Worth, Tex., professor of ethics, 1963-75; First Baptist Church, Wichita Falls, Tex., pastor, 1975-77; Golden Gate Baptist Seminary, Mill Valley, Calif., president, 1977-82; Baptist General Convention of Texas, Dallas, executive director, 1982—. *Member:* American Society of Christian Ethics. *Awards, honors:* Lilly Foundation scholarship, 1964; named one of the outstanding young men in America by U.S. Junior Chamber of Commerce, 1965; named distinguished alumnus of Southwestern Baptist Seminary, 1979, and North Texas State University, 1980.

WRITINGS: Ambassadors and Christian Citizenship, Brotherhood Commission, 1963; *How to Deal with Controversial Issues,* Broadman, 1966; *Resource Guide to Current Social Issues,* Broadman, 1968; *No Greater Challenge,* Convention Press, 1969.

(With T. B. Maston) *Right or Wrong,* revised edition, Broadman, 1971; (editor with Clyde Fant) *Twenty Centuries of Great Preaching,* thirteen volumes, Word, Inc., 1971; *A Program of Application for the Local Church,* Christian Life Commission, 1972; *Don't Blame the Game,* Word, Inc., 1972; *Contemporary Christian Trends,* Word, Inc., 1972; *The Local Church in Ministry,* Broadman, 1973; *The Five Worlds of Youth,* Convention Press, 1974; *Applying the Gospel: Suggestions for Christian Social Action in a Local Church,* Broadman, 1975; (with Nolan P. Howington and Alton H. McEachern) *Growing Disciples through Preaching,* Broadman, 1976; *Families with Purpose,* Broadman, 1979; (editor and contributor) *An Approach to Christian Ethics: The Life, Contribution and Thought of T. B. Maston,* Broadman, 1979.

The Word Topical Bible of Issues and Answers, Word, Inc., 1981; *The Biblical View of the Family,* Convention Press, 1982.

Contributor: C. W. Scudder, editor, *Crisis in Morality,* Broadman, 1965; R. Coggins, editor, *The Gambling Menace,* Broadman, 1966; F. Valentine, editor, *Peace! Peace!,* Word, Inc., 1967.

WORK IN PROGRESS: A source book on biblical ethics; a book on decision making; an ethics text.

* * *

PITZ, Henry C(larence) 1895-1976

PERSONAL: Born June 16, 1895, in Philadelphia, Pa.; died November 26, 1976, in Philadelphia, Pa.; son of Henry William (a manufacturer) and Anna (Stiffel) Pitz; married Mary Wheeler Wood, June 10, 1935; children: Julia Leaming (Mrs. Thomas H. Barringer), Henry William II. *Education:* Attended Philadelphia Museum College of Art, 1914-18, and Spring Garden Institute, Philadelphia, 1917 and 1920. *Politics:* Independent. *Religion:* Episcopalian. *Home:* 3 Cornelia Pl., Philadelphia, Pa. 19118.

CAREER: Artist and illustrator, 1920-76. Philadelphia Museum College of Art, Philadelphia, Pa., professor of illustration and decoration and director of department, 1937-60, professor emeritus, 1960-76. Instructor in watercolors, Pennsylvania Academy of Fine Arts, Philadelphia, 1939-46; visiting critic, Bryn Mawr Art Center, 1939; visiting lecturer in fine arts, University of Pennsylvania, 1941, and Carnegie Institute of Technology (now Carnegie-Mellon University), 1964; visiting instructor, Cleveland Institute of Art; visiting lecturer, University of Utah, 1971.

Work has been displayed in numerous national and international exhibitions, including shows at the Pennsylvania Academy of Fine Arts, 1930-69, American Watercolor Society, 1946-68, National Academy of Design, 1950-72, National

Gallery of Art, 1970, and Phoenix Art Museum; work is represented in many permanent collections of museums, schools, and libraries in the United States, including the Library of Congress, Philadelphia Museum of Art, Cleveland Museum of Art, and National Gallery of Art. Painted three murals for Smithsonian Institution exhibit at Chicago World's Fair; official artist, NASA Apollo 10 Space Project, 1969, and U.S. Environmental Protection Agency, 1972. Member of board of editors, American Artist Book Club, beginning 1968. *Military service:* U.S. Army, American Expeditionary Forces, 1918-19.

MEMBER: National Academy of Design (academician), American Watercolor Society (director), Society of Illustrators (life member), Newcomen Society, Audubon Artists, Philadelphia Art Alliance (vice-president, 1938-61; member of board of directors, beginning 1942), Philadelphia Sketch Club (vice-president, 1938-40; president, 1940-42), Philadelphia Water Color Club (director), Woodmere Art Gallery (member of board of trustees, beginning 1968), Philobiblon Club, Salmagundi Club (New York), Franklin Inn Club (Philadelphia).

AWARDS, HONORS: Recipient of numerous awards, including: Bronze Medal, International Print Exhibition, 1932; Dana Gold Medal, Pennsylvania Academy of Fine Arts, 1934; Bronze Medal, Paris International Exhibition, 1938; Hans Obst Prize, American Watercolor Society Annual, 1952; Obrig Prize, National Academy, 1953 and 1956; Alumni Gold Medal, Philadelphia Museum College of Art, 1956, Silver Star Cluster, 1957; National Academy Prize for Water Color, 1962; Pennational Artists Gold Medal, 1968; Philadelphia Athenaeum Literary Award, 1969, for *The Brandywine Tradition;* D.lett., Ursinus College, 1971.

WRITINGS: (Author and illustrator with Edward Warwick) *Early American Costume,* Century Co., 1929, revised edition (with Warwick and Alexander Wyckoff) published as *Early American Dress: The Colonial and Revolutionary Periods,* Benjamin Blom, 1965; (editor) *A Treasury of American Book Illustration,* Watson-Guptill, 1947; *The Practice of Illustration,* Watson-Guptill, 1947; *Pen, Brush and Ink,* edited by Arthur L. Guptill, Watson-Guptill, 1949.

(Editor) Norman Kent and others, *Watercolor Methods,* Watson-Guptill, 1955; *Drawing Trees,* Watson-Guptill, 1956, revised and enlarged edition published as *How to Draw Trees,* 1972; *Ink Drawing Techniques,* Watson-Guptill, 1957; *Sketching with the Felt-Tip Pen: A New Artist's Tool,* Studio Publications, 1959.

(Editor and reviser) Arthur L. Guptil, *Drawing with Pen and Ink,* revised edition, Reinhold, 1961; *Illustrating Children's Books: History, Technique, Production,* Watson-Guptill, 1963; *Drawing Outdoors,* Watson-Guptill, 1965; *How to Use the Figure in Painting and Illustration,* Reinhold, 1965; *The Brandywine Tradition,* Houghton, 1969.

Charcoal Drawing, Watson-Guptill, 1971; (editor and author of introduction) *Frederic Remington: 173 Drawings and Illustrations,* Dover, 1972; *Howard Pyle: Writer, Illustrator, Founder of the Brandywine School,* C. N. Potter, 1975; *Two Hundred Years of American Illustration,* Random House, 1977.

Illustrator: John Bennett, *Master Skylark,* Century Co., 1922; Arthur Conan Doyle, *Micah Clarke,* Harper, 1922; Robert Shackleton, *The Book of Washington,* Penn Publishing, 1923; Allen French, *The Story of Rolf and the Viking's Bow,* Little, Brown, 1924; Bertha Evangeline Bush, *A Prairie Rose,* Little, Brown, 1925; Francis S. Drake, *Indian History for Young Folks,* Harper, 1927; Ula Echols, *Knights of Charlemagne,* Longmans, Green, 1928; John Buchan, *Prester John,* Houghton, 1928; Robert Leighton, *Olaf, the Glorious,* Macmillan, 1929.

Robert W. Chambers, *Cardigan,* Harper, 1930; El Cid (pseudonym of Rodrigo Diaz de Bivar), *The Tale of the Warrior Lord,* translated by Merriam Sherwood, Longmans, Green, 1930; Washington Irving, *Voyages of Columbus,* Macmillan, 1931; *The Story of Beowulf,* adapted by Strafford Riggs, Appleton-Century-Crofts, 1933; Ernest P. Mitchell, *Deep Water: The Autobiography of a Sea Captain,* Little, Brown, 1933.

Charles J. Finger, *The Distant Prize,* Appleton-Century-Crofts, 1935; Finger, *Dog at His Heel,* Winston, 1936; Geoffrey Household, *Spanish Cave,* Little, Brown, 1936; Daniel Defoe, *The Life and Strange Surprising Adventures of Robinson Crusoe,* adapted for young readers by Edward L. Thorndike, Appleton-Century-Crofts, 1937; Paul L. Anderson, *Pugnax the Gladiator,* Appleton-Century-Crofts, 1939.

Ursula Moray Williams, *Peter and the Wanderlust,* Lippincott, 1940; Elizabeth Jane Coatsworth, *You Shall Have a Carriage,* Macmillan, 1941; Phyllis Reid Fenner, compiler, *There Was a Horse: Folktales from Many Lands,* Knopf, 1941.

Albert L. Stillman, *Jungle Haven,* Winston, 1942; Sydney Greenbie, *Three Island Nations: Cuba, Haiti, Dominican Republic,* Row, Peterson, 1942; Frederic A. Krummer, *For Flag and Freedom,* Morrow, 1942; Fenner, editor, *Time to Laugh: Funny Tales from Here and There,* Knopf, 1942; Patricia F. Ross, *In Mexico They Say,* Knopf, 1942, reprinted, 1961; Catherine Cate Coblentz, *Falcon of Eric the Red,* Longmans, Green, 1942; Robert Davis, *Hudson Bay Express,* Holiday House, 1942.

Hope Brister, *Cunning Fox and Other Tales,* Knopf, 1943; Finger, *High Waters in Arkansas,* Grosset, 1943; Fenner, compiler, *Giants and Witches, and a Dragon or Two,* Knopf, 1943; Fenner, compiler, *Princesses and Peasant Boys: Tales of Enchantment,* Knopf, 1944; Mildred A. Jordan, *Shoo-fly Pie,* Knopf, 1944; Mary Regina Walsh, *Molly, the Rogue,* Knopf, 1944; Mildred A. Jordan, *Apple in the Attic: A Pennsylvania Legend,* Grosset, 1944; David Loring MacKaye and J.J.G. MacKaye, under joint pseudonym Loring MacKay, *Twenty-Fifth Mission,* Longmans, Green, 1944.

William W. Theisen and G. L. Bond, compilers, *Living Literature for Supplementary Reading,* five books, Macmillan, 1945-48; Fenner, compiler, *Adventure, Rare and Magical,* Knopf, 1945.

Rosita Torr Forbes, *Henry Morgan: Pirate,* McKay, 1946 (published in England as *Henry Morgan: Pirate and Pioneer,* Cassell, 1948); Andre Maurois, *Washington: The Life of a Great Patriot,* translated by Eileen Lane Kinney, Oxford University Press, 1946; David W. Moore, *The End of Long John Silver,* Crowell, 1946; Walsh, *The Mullinger Heifer,* Knopf, 1946; Elizabeth Hough Sechrist, editor, *One Thousand Poems for Children* (based on the selections of Roger Ingpen), new edition, Macrae, 1946; Charlie May Simon, *Joe Mason, Apprentice to Audubon,* Dutton, 1946; Fenner, compiler, *Demons and Dervishes: Tales with More-than-Oriental Splendor,* Knopf, 1946.

Mildred Houghton Comfort, *Children of the Mayflower,* Beckley-Cardy, 1947; Fenner, compiler, *Fools and Funny Fellows: More "Time to Laugh" Tales,* Knopf, 1947; D. L. MacKaye and J.J.G. MacKaye, under joint pseudonym Loring MacKaye, *John of America,* Longmans, Green, 1947.

Kathleen Monypenny, *Young Traveler in Australia,* Phoenix House, 1948, Dutton, 1954; Charlie May Simon, *Royal Road,* Dutton, 1948; Comfort, *Children of the Colonies,* Beckley-Cardy, 1948; Enid LaMonte Meadowcroft, *By Secret Railway,* Crowell, 1948; Margaret Carver Leighton, *Judith of France,* Houghton, 1948; Georgii Skrebitskii, *White Bird's Island,* translated from the Russian by Zina Voynow, Knopf, 1948; Fenner, compiler, *With Might and Main: Stories of Skill and Wit,* Knopf, 1948; Jeanette Eaton, *That Lively Man, Ben Franklin,* Morrow, 1948.

Walsh, *The Widow Woman and Her Goat,* Knopf, 1949; David W. Moore, *End of Black Dog,* Crowell, 1949; Jan Juta, *Look Out for the Ostriches: Tales of South Africa,* Knopf, 1949; Mary Macleod, editor, *Book of King Arthur and His Noble Knights* (adapted from *Morte d'Arthur* by Sir Thomas Malory), Lippincott, 1949.

Mrs. Stockton V. Banks, *Washington Adventure,* Whittlesey House, 1950; David W. Moore, *Scarlet Jib,* Crowell, 1950; David W. Moore, *Sacramento Sam,* Crowell, 1951; Fenner, compiler, *Magic Hoofs: Horse Stories from Many Lands,* Knopf, 1951; Opal Wheeler, *Hans Andersen: Son of Denmark,* Dutton, 1951; Elizabeth Hall Janeway, *Vikings,* Random House, 1951; Nathan Reinherz, *Quest of the Sage's Stone,* Crowell, 1951.

(Contributor) *Evergreen Tales,* Limited Editions Club, 1952; Armstrong Sperry, *River of the West,* Winston, 1952; Betty Peckham, *Tangle-Britches,* Aladdin Books, 1954; Mabel Watts, *Over the Hills to Ballypog,* Aladdin Books, 1954; Robert Louis Stevenson, *Treasure Island,* Doubleday, 1954.

Donald E. Cooke, *Valley of Rebellion,* Winston, 1955; Charles Dickens, *Dombey and Son,* Heritage Press, 1957; Jules Verne, *Mysterious Island,* World Publishing, 1957; Catherine Owens Peare, *William Penn,* Lippincott, 1957.

Henry Frith, *King Arthur and His Knights,* Doubleday, 1963; James Fenimore Cooper, *The Spy,* Limited Editions Club, 1963; Thomas Fall, *Edge of Manhood,* Dial, 1964; Fall, *Wild Boy,* Dial, 1965.

Contributor of articles to *Encyclopaedia Britannica* and *American Artist, Horn Book, Studio, Print, American Heritage,* and other periodicals; contributor of illustrations to *Scribner's, Cosmopolitan, Harper's, Saturday Evening Post, Gourmet, Jack and Jill, Reader's Digest,* and other national magazines. Associate editor, *American Artist,* beginning 1942.

BIOGRAPHICAL/CRITICAL SOURCES: Ernest W. Watson, *Forty Illustrators,* Watson-Guptill, 1946; Richard Ellis, *Book Illustration,* Kingsport Press, 1952; Norman Kent, *Watercolor Methods,* Watson-Guptill, 1955; David Bland, *A History of Book Illustration,* World Publishing, 1958; *Illustrators of Children's Books: 1946-1956,* Horn Book, 1958, supplement, *1957-1966,* 1968; Walter Reed, *The Illustrator in America,* Reinhold, 1966; Diana Klemin, *The Illustrated Book,* C. N. Potter, 1970.

OBITUARIES: New York Times, December 1, 1976.†

* * *

PLAIDY, Jean
See HIBBERT, Eleanor Burford

* * *

PLEYDELL, Susan
See SENIOR, Isabel J(anet Couper Syme)

PORTER, Bern(ard Harden) 1911-

PERSONAL: Born February 14, 1911, in Porter Settlement, Me.; son of Lewis Harden and Etta Flora (Rogers) Porter; married Helen Elaine Hendren (a poet), 1946 (divorced August, 1947); married Margaret Eudine Preston (a writer), August 27, 1955 (died April 17, 1975); married Lula Mae Blom, September 9, 1976. *Education:* Colby College, Sc.B., 1932; Brown University, Sc.M., 1933; special courses at Da Vinci School, 1937, Convair School, 1957, University of Maine, 1960, and Federal School, 1963. *Politics:* Republican. *Religion:* Methodist. *Agent:* William Rutledge, 5228 Irvine Ave., North Hollywood, Calif. *Office:* 22 Salmond Rd., Belfast, Me. 04915.

CAREER: Bern Porter (publishing company), Belfast, Me., president, 1929—; physicist with Acheson Colloids Corp., Port Huron, Mich., 1935-40, and with Manhattan District Engineers, Princeton, N.J., Berkeley, Calif., and Oak Ridge, Tenn., 1940-45; Bern Porter, Inc., Belfast, chairman of board, 1945—; Bern Porter International, Belfast, president, 1974—. Artist and illustrator; exhibited in Maine, New York, San Francisco, Japan, and Tasmania. Director of Contemporary Gallery, West Coast Design Guild, and Fund for Contemporary Expression, 1947-50. Chairman of the board, Institute of Advanced Thinking, 1959—. Consulting physicist, 1945—. Republican candidate for governor of Maine, 1969.

MEMBER: International Poetry Society (fellow), International Platform Association, International Academy of Poets (founder), Society for International Development, Technical Publishing Society (fellow), American Astronautical Society (associate fellow), Society of Technical Writers and Publishers (associate member), American Physical Society, Institute of Radio Engineers, American Rocket Society (associate member), American Society of Emeriti, National Society of Programmed Instruction, Phi Beta Kappa, Sigma Xi, Kappa Phi Kappa, Chi Gamma Sigma, Xi Epsilon Mu, Fenway Club (Boston), Algonquin Club, St. Andrew's Club. *Awards, honors:* Sc.D., Institute of Advanced Thinking, 1959; recipient of awards from P.E.N., 1975, 1976, and 1977, and from Authors League, 1977; Carnegie Author, 1975; diploma merit, Centro Studi E Scambi Internazionale, Rome, 1976; National Endowment for the Arts literary award, 1979.

WRITINGS—Published by Bern Porter, except as indicated: *Colloidal Graphite: Its Properties and Applications,* Acheson, 1939; *Map of Physics,* Cenco, 1939; *Map of Chemistry,* University of Pennsylvania, 1941; (self-illustrated) *Doldrums,* Al Press, 1941; *Me,* 1943; *Henry Miller: A Bibliography,* 1943, revised edition, 1969; *Map of Joyceana,* Circle Editions, 1946; *Art Techniques,* Gillick Press, 1947; *The Union of Science and Art,* Greenwood Press, 1948; *Schillerhaus: 1947-1950,* 1955; *Drawings: 1954-1955,* 1956; *Commentary on the Relationship of Art and Science,* Stanford University, 1956; *Rocket Data Book,* Convair, 1956; *Dictionary of Rocket Terminology,* Convair, 1956; *H. L. Mencken: A Bibliography,* 1957; *Drawings: 1955-1956,* 1959.

F. Scott Fitgerald: A Bibliography, 1960; *Aphasia,* 1961; *The Waste-Maker, 1926-1961,* 1961; *Scandinavian Summer,* 1961; *Circle: Reproductions of Art Work, 1944-1947,* Circle Editions, 1963, reprinted, 1978; *Reporting and Preventive Maintenance Forms for the 465L Program,* Federal Electric Corp., 1963; *Charcoal Drawings, 1935-1937,* 1963; *I've Left* (autobiographical essays), Marathon, 1963, reprinted, University Microfilms, 1978, 2nd edition, Marathon, 1969; *Assorted Art,*

1928-1963, 1963; *Applicable 465L Publications,* Federal Electric Corp., 1963; *Day Notes for Mother,* 1964; *Native Alphabet,* 1964; *Scigraffiti,* 1964; *AL0110,* 1964; *What Henry Miller Said and Why It Is Important* (booklet), D. Turrell, 1964, 2nd edition, Bern Porter, 1969; *Dynamic Test Vehicle Instrumentation and Data System Criteria,* Boeing, 1965; *Dynamic Test Vehicle Data Reduction and Correlation Requirements,* Boeing, 1965; *The First Publication of F. Scott Fitzgerald* (booklet), Quality Books, 1965; *Dynamic Test Program Requirements,* Boeing, 1965; *Mathematics for Electronics,* Prentice-Hall, 1965; *Art Productions: 1928-1965,* D. Turrell, 1965; *468B,* 1966; *Captive Firing of Flight State Reliability Study,* Boeing, 1966; *System Methodologies and Their Utilization,* Boeing, 1966; *Moscow,* 1966; *Founds,* Contemporary, 1966; *Cut Leaves,* 1966; *The Box,* 1968; *Summary Report of the Knox County Regional Comprehensive Plan: Phase III,* [Rockland, Me.], 1969; *Dieresis,* 1969; *Artifacts,* 1969; *scda 19,* 1969.

Oraison funebres de Bossuet, 1970; *OEye,* 1970; *Reminiscences, 1927-1970,* 1970; *PER Book,* 1970; *Enry One,* 1970; *Enry 2-5,* 1970; *ULA,* 1971; *Assorted Cuts, 1965-1970,* five volumes, 1971; *b.p.,* 1971; *NEXA 914,* 1971; *Found Poems,* Something Else Press, 1972; *The 14th of February,* 1972; *Trattoria Due Fermi,* 1973; *Hand-Fashioned Chocolates,* 1974; *Eighty-Nine Offenses,* Abyss Publications, 1974; *Selected Founds,* Croissant Pamphlet No. 2, 1975; *Run-On,* 1975; *Where to Go/What to Do/When in New York/Week of June 22, 1972,* 1975; *The Last Acts of Saint FY,* 1975; *American Strange,* 1979; *I Ricordi di Firenze,* 1981; *Isla Vista,* Turkey Press, 1981; *The Book of Do's,* Dog Ear Press, 1982.

Editor: Henry Miller, *The Plight of the Creative Artist in the U.S.A.,* 1944; Miller, *Henry Miller Miscellanea,* 1945; Miller, *Echolalia,* 1946; *Seashore Brochures,* Christian F. Ver Becke, 1947; *Robert Carleton Brown,* 1956; Harry Kiakis, *The Watts Towers,* 1959; Kiakis, *Venice: Beatnik Capitol,* 1961; Dieter Rot, *Cutcards,* 1963; Ray Johnson, *A Book about Death,* 1963; Jack Roth, *The Exciting, Igniting World of Art,* 1964; William B. Faulkner, Jr., *Man,* 1965; *Bay-Area Creators: 1945-1965,* 1965; *B. P. at Schillerhaus,* 1966; *Harry Bowden: His Studio and Work,* 1966; *Wernher von Braun: A Bibliography and Selected Papers,* 1966; *Art Scrapbook,* 1967; *Art Prints,* 1967; *Selected Articles by R. Buckminster Fuller,* 1968; *The Private Papers of Wilhelm Reich, 1942-1954,* 1969; Philip Lloyd Ely, *Bernard Langlaïs,* 1969; *Contemporary Italian Poets,* 1973; *Vestigia: Notes on the Life and Work of Janelle Viglini,* 1975; *The Viglini Letters,* two volumes, 1975; *Gee Whizzels,* 1977.

Editor and illustrator: Miller, *Semblance of a Devoted Past,* 1944; *The Happy Rock: A Book about Henry Miller,* 1945, reprinted, Walton Press, 1970; John Hoffman, *Journey to the End,* 1956; John G. Moore, *The Latitude and Longitude of Henry Miller,* Marathon, 1962; William B. Faulkner, Jr., *Henry: An Anthology by World Poets,* 1970.

Illustrator of more than twenty books, including: A. L. Blackwood, *General Physics Text,* 1943; Leonard Wolfe, *Hamadryad Hunted,* 1947; Antoine Artaud, *Judgement,* 1955; Dick Higgins, *What Are Legends,* 1960; Stephen Berry Kimble, *Henry Miller,* 1965; Michael Fraenkel, *Genesis,* 1970; James Joyce, *Poems Pennyeach,* 1970; Alfred, Lord Tennyson, *Lover's Tale,* Walton Press, 1971; James Erwin Schevill, *Breakout,* 1974; Higgins, *City with All the Angels: A Radio Play,* Unpublished Editions, 1974. Also illustrator of *Die Fabelhafte Getraume von Taifen,* by Higgins, 1970, and *Origins, Initiations,* by Kirk Robertson, 1980. Illustrator of maps and posters; illustrator for more than twenty magazines and newspapers, 1926-82.

Also author of numerous booklets and pamphlets on art, technology, and literature. Editor of magazines, including *Colby White Mule,* 1929-32, *The Leaves Fall,* 1942-45, *Circle,* 1944-45, and *Broadside,* 1954-56.

WORK IN PROGRESS: Resume of Physics, three volumes; *Here Comes Everybody's Don't Book; The Book of Death; Holy Smokes; The Bern Book; Porter's Book.*

SIDELIGHTS: Bern Porter writes: "Travels in remote areas like Newfoundland, Tasmania, Russia, Venezuela, with extended living periods among cultures like the Laplanders, Ulithians, Guamanians, Balinese, and others, force me into a continuing search for ways the science of physics can promote a better life. My experiences with the development of the A-bomb and later pilgrimage to Hiroshima have already given rise to many creative forms like sciarch, sciart, et. al., discussed in my autobiographical work, *I've Left.* I enjoy a large correspondence with creative workers from all over the world. Current interests are centered on techniques and procedures for programed instruction, learning 'by machine' and experiments in visual expression of language structure. Additional and prolonged travels [include trips to] South America, Canada, Nepal, and Greenland."

BIOGRAPHICAL/CRITICAL SOURCES: James Erwin Schevill, *The Roaring Market and the Silent Tomb* (biography), Abbey Press, 1957; Bern Porter, *I've Left* (autobiographical essays), Marathon, 1963, reprinted, University Microfilms, 1978, 2nd edition, Marathon, 1969; Schevill, *Lovecraft's Follies* (theater version), Swallow Press, 1971; *Maine Times,* August 22, 1980; Margaret Dunbar, *Bern! Porter! Interview!,* Dog Ear Press, 1982.

* * *

POWLEDGE, Fred 1935-

PERSONAL: Born February 23, 1935, in Nash County, N.C.; son of Arlius Raymond (an auditor) and Pauline (Stearns) Powledge; married Tabitha Morrison, December 21, 1957; children: Pauline Stearns. *Education:* University of North Carolina, B.A., 1957. *Home and office:* 271 Degraw St., Brooklyn, N.Y. 11231. *Agent:* Virginia Barber, 353 West 21st St., New York, N.Y. 10011.

CAREER: Associated Press, editor-writer in New Haven, Conn., 1958-60; *Atlanta Journal,* Atlanta, Ga., reporter, 1960-63; *New York Times,* New York, N.Y., reporter, 1963-66; freelance writer, 1966—. Lecturer, New School for Social Research, 1968-69. *Military service:* U.S. Army Reserve, 1957-63.

WRITINGS: Black Power—White Resistance: Notes on the New Civil War, World Publishing, 1967; *To Change a Child,* Quadrangle, 1968; *Model City, A Test of American Liberalism: One Town's Efforts to Rebuild Itself,* Simon & Schuster, 1970; *Mud Show: A Circus Season,* Harcourt, 1975; *Born on the Circus,* Harcourt, 1976; *The Backpacker's Budget Food Book,* McKay, 1977; *Journeys through the South,* Vanguard Press, 1979; *So You're Adopted: A Book about the Experience of Being Adopted,* Scribner, 1982; *Water: The Nature, Uses, and Future of Our Most Precious and Abused Resource,* Farrar, Straus, 1982. Contributor to periodicals, including *New Yorker, Esquire, Penthouse,* and *Nation.*

WORK IN PROGRESS: Research and writing on food and the environment.

SIDELIGHTS: Fred Powledge's interest in race relations and upheaval stems, he says, from being a white Southerner exposed to the ideas of both democracy and racism. His more recent interest in environmental matters grew out of the realization that "air, water, and earth need recognition of their rights, just as people do."

BIOGRAPHICAL/CRITICAL SOURCES: *New York Review of Books,* February 29, 1968; *New York Times Book Review,* August 12, 1979.

* * *

PRICE, Alfred 1936-

PERSONAL: Born August 3, 1936, in Cheam, Surrey, England; son of Lewis (a building contractor) and Augustine (Gefall) Price; married Jane Beaven, March 14, 1964; children: Fiona, Clare. *Education:* Educated at schools in Surrey, England. *Religion:* Church of England. *Agent:* Campbell Thomson & McLaughlin Ltd., 31 Newington Green, London N16 9PU, England.

CAREER: Royal Air Force, 1952-74, specialized in electronic warfare, aircraft weaponry, and modern air fighting tactics; currently full-time writer. *Member:* Royal Historical Society (fellow). *Awards, honors:* L. G. Groves Memorial Prize for aircraft safety, 1963.

WRITINGS: *Instruments of Darkness: The Struggle for Radar Supremacy,* Kimber & Co., 1967, revised edition published as *Instruments of Darkness: The History of Electronic Warfare,* Macdonald & Jane's, 1977, Scribner, 1978; *German Air Force Bombers of World War II,* Volume I, Doubleday, 1968, 2nd edition, Hylton-Lacey, 1971, Volume II, Hylton-Lacey, 1969.

Luftwaffe: Birth, Life, and Death of an Air Force, Macdonald & Co., 1970; *Aircraft versus Submarine: The Evolution of the Anti-Submarine Aircraft, 1912-1972,* Kimber & Co., 1973, U.S. Naval Institute, 1974; *Battle over the Reich,* Ian Allan, 1973, Scribner, 1974; *Spitfire at War,* Ian Allan, 1974, Scribner, 1977; *World War II Fighter Conflict,* Macdonald & Jane's, 1975, Hippocrene, 1979; *The Bomber in World War II,* Macdonald & Jane's, 1976, Scribner, 1979; *Blitz on Britain: The Bomber Attacks on the United Kingdom, 1939-1945,* Ian Allan, 1977; *Focke-Wulf 190 at War,* International Publications Service, 1977; *Spitfire: A Documentary History,* Macdonald & Jane's, 1977; *Luftwaffe Handbook, 1939-1945,* Scribner, 1977; *Battle of Britain: The Hardest Day—August 18, 1940,* Macdonald & Jane's, 1979, published as *The Hardest Day: 18 August 1940—The Battle of Britain,* Scribner, 1980.

(With Jeff Ethell) *The German Jets in Combat,* Jane's Publishing Co., 1980; (with Ethell) *Target Berlin: Mission 250, 6 March 1944,* Jane's Publishing Co., 1981; *Luftwaffe: 1933-1945,* two volumes, Arms & Armour Press, 1981, Stackpole, 1982; *The Spitfire Story,* Jane's Publishing Co., 1982.

WORK IN PROGRESS: A detailed history of electronic warfare in the United States.

SIDELIGHTS: Alfred Price told *CA:* "I never cease to be enthralled with the research for my books. There are so many fascinating people around, all one has to do is to ask the right questions. And if one looks around the various archives carefully enough, the required documentary evidence can usually be found. Fortunately other people seem to find my historical research interesting too and buy my books, thus enabling me to continue in my chosen profession."

PROCTER, Ben H. 1927-

PERSONAL: Born February 21, 1927, in Temple, Tex.; son of Leslie C. (a teacher) and Hazel (Barnes) Procter; married, 1951; children: Ben Rice. *Education:* University of Texas, B.A., 1951, M.A., 1952; Harvard University, Ph.D., 1961. *Politics:* Democrat. *Religion:* Protestant. *Home:* 2506 Boyd, Fort Worth, Tex. *Office:* Department of History, Texas Christian University, Fort Worth, Tex. 76129.

CAREER: Austin Recreation Department, Austin, Tex., baseball supervisor, 1948-55; Texas Christian University, Fort Worth, 1957—, began as instructor, professor of history, 1968—, Piper Professor, 1973. Consultant, St. Mark's School, Dallas, Tex., 1962. *Military service:* U.S. Navy Reserve, 1945-46. *Member:* American Historical Association, Organization of American Historians, American Association of University Professors, Southwestern Social Science Association, Western Historical Society, Southern Historical Society, Texas State Historical Society, Tarrant County Historical Society, Phi Beta Kappa, Pi Sigma Alpha, Phi Alpha Theta. *Awards, honors:* Summerfield G. Roberts Award for best book of the Republic period in Texas, 1963, for *Not without Honor.*

WRITINGS: *Not without Honor: The Life of John H. Reagan,* University of Texas Press, 1962; (with Sam Kinch) *Texas under a Cloud,* Jenkins Publishing, 1972; (with Jim Berry Pearson) *Texas: The Land and Its People,* Hendrick-Long Publishing Co., 1972, 2nd edition, 1978; (editor with Archie P. McDonald) *The Texas Heritage,* Forum Press, 1980.

Contributor; published by Texian Press, except as indicated: *Heroes of Texas,* 1964; *Six Missions of Texas,* 1965; *Frontier Forts of Texas,* 1966; *Rangers of Texas,* 1969; *Reflections by Western Historians,* University of Arizona, 1969; *The Mexican-Americans: An Awakening Minority,* Glencoe, 1969; *Capitols of Texas,* 1970. Contributor to encyclopedias and professional publications. Member of editorial board, *Texana.*†

* * *

PROKOP, Phyllis Stillwell 1922-

PERSONAL: Born December 5, 1922, in Weleetka, Okla.; daughter of Albert and Dora (Woodward) Stillwell; married Charles L. Prokop (a technical adviser for Exxon), June 5, 1944; children: Charles Kent, Bert Kimball. *Education:* University of Oklahoma, B.A., 1944; University of Houston, M.A., 1972. *Residence:* Houston, Tex.

CAREER: Speaker and book reviewer. Formerly employed as a teacher. *Awards, honors:* Religion in Media Angel Award finalist, 1981, for *A Kind of Splendor;* Golden Pen Award, Southwest Writers Conference, for unpublished novel "The Trees Are A-Singing, Buddy Boy."

WRITINGS: *Conversations with Giants,* Concordia, 1964; *Conversations with Prophets,* Concordia, 1966; *Sunday Dinner Cookbook,* Broadman, 1969; *Heavenscope,* Broadman, 1975; *How to Wake Up Singing,* Broadman, 1979; (with Jacques Goettsche) *A Kind of Splendor,* Broadman, 1980; *The Sword and the Sundial,* David Cook, 1981; (with others) *The Three Ingredient Cookbook,* Broadman, 1981. Also author of unpublished novel "The Trees Are A-Singing, Buddy Boy."

SIDELIGHTS: Phyllis Stillwell Prokop told *CA:* "Every day presents ideas for several books since there is more of life in every day than can be held between two covers. Writing skill lies in finding the form to preserve the day as it was without too much distortion and the leisure to capture it quickly, before it has a chance to drift off into vague memory.''

BIOGRAPHICAL/CRITICAL SOURCES: Ivanell Elder, editor, *Gentle Giants of Texas,* Eakin Publications (Burnet, Texas), 1983.

* * *

PRUYSER, Paul W(illem) 1916-

PERSONAL: Born May 28, 1916, in Amsterdam, Netherlands; son of Herman J. and Elizabeth (van Dingstee) Pruyser; married Jansje M. Fontijn, April 17, 1946; children: Henriette, Herman, Pauline. *Education:* University of Amsterdam, candidate in psychology, 1948; Boston University, Ph.D., 1953. *Religion:* Presbyterian. *Home:* 3337 Northwest 35th St., Topeka, Kan. 66618. *Office address:* Menninger Foundation, P.O. Box 829, Topeka, Kan. 66601.

CAREER: Staff clinical psychologist at National Veterans Epilepsy Center, 1950-54, and Topeka State Hospital, Topeka, Kan., 1954-55; Menninger Foundation, Topeka, staff clinical psychologist, 1956-62, associate director of department of education, 1961-62, director of department of education, 1962-71, Henry March Pfeiffer Professor, 1972—, director of interdisciplinary studies program, 1977—. Chairman of committee on research and education, Kansas Neurological Institute, Topeka, 1960-65. Lecturer in psychology, McCormick Theological Seminary, Chicago, Ill., 1959-75; professorial lecturer in pastoral psychology, School of Divinity, St. Louis University, 1964-65; Lyman Beecher Lecturer, Yale Divinity School, 1968. *Military service:* Netherlands Army, 1939-40.

MEMBER: American Psychological Association, American Association for the Advancement of Science, American Society of Psychopathology of Expression (vice-president), Society for the Scientific Study of Religion (member of council, 1963-65; vice-president, 1964-65; president, 1974-75), Kansas Psychological Association.

WRITINGS: (With Karl A. Menninger and M. Mayman) *A Manual for Psychiatric Case Study,* 2nd edition (Pruyser was not associated with earlier edition), Grune, 1962; (with Menninger and Mayman) *The Vital Balance,* Viking, 1963; (member of editorial committee) B. H. Hall, editor, *A Psychiatrist for a Troubled World: Selected Papers of William C. Menninger, M.D.,* Viking, 1967; *A Dynamic Psychology of Religion,* Harper, 1968.

Between Belief and Unbelief, Harper, 1974; *The Minister as Diagnostician,* Westminster, 1976; (editor) *Diagnosis and the Difference It Makes,* Jason Aronson, 1977; *The Psychological Examination,* International University Press, 1979.

Contributor: S. Doniger, editor, *Know Thyself,* Association Press, 1962; Menninger and S. Hiltner, editors, *Constructive Aspects of Anxiety,* Abingdon, 1963; Robert Dentler, editor, *Major American Social Problems,* Rand McNally, 1967; James W. Lapsley, editor, *The Concept of Willing,* Abingdon, 1967; Joseph Havens, editor, *Psychology and Religion: A Contemporary Dialogue,* Van Nostrand, 1968.

Contributor to *Encyclopedia of Mental Health,* F. Watts, 1963, and to medical, pastoral psychology, and other journals. Member of editorial board, *Journal for the Scientific Study of Religion,* 1961-66; member of editorial advisory board, *Pastoral Psychology,* 1967—. *Bulletin of Menninger Clinic,* member of editorial board, 1958-78, editor-in-chief, 1978—.

BIOGRAPHICAL/CRITICAL SOURCES: Pastoral Psychology, Number 121, 1962; *Christian Century,* September 25, 1968.

* * *

PURVES, Alan C(arroll) 1931-

PERSONAL: Born December 14, 1931, in Philadelphia, Pa.; son of Edmund Randolph and Mary Carroll (Spencer) Purves; married Anita Woodruff Parker, June 18, 1960 (died, 1975); married Anne H. Nesbitt, July 14, 1976; children: (first marriage) William C., Theodore R. *Education:* Harvard University, A.B., 1953; Columbia University, M.A., 1956; Ph.D., 1960. *Office:* Curriculum Laboratory, University of Illinois at Urbana-Champaign, Urbana, Ill. 61801.

CAREER: Hofstra University, Hempstead, N.Y., lecturer in English, 1956-58; Columbia University, New York City, instructor in English, 1958-61; Barnard College, New York City, assistant professor of English, 1961-65; Educational Testing Service, Princeton, N.J., associate examiner, 1965-68; University of Illinois at Urbana-Champaign, associate professor, 1968-70, professor of English, 1970-73, professor of English education, 1973—. *Military service:* U.S. Army, 1953-55. *Member:* Modern Langauge Association of America, National Council of Teachers of English, National Conference on Research in English, American Educational Research Association.

WRITINGS: (Editor) Theodore Spencer, *Selected Essays,* Rutgers University Press, 1967; (with Victoria Rippere) *Elements of Writing about a Literary Work,* National Council of Teachers of English, 1968; (with Richard Beach) *Literature and the Reader,* National Council of Teachers of English, 1972; *How Porcupines Make Love: Notes on a Response-Centered Curriculum,* Wiley, 1972; (editor) *Responding,* eighteen volumes, Ginn, 1973; *Literature Education in Ten Countries,* Wiley, 1973; (editor with Daniel U. Levine) *Education Policy and International Assessment,* McCutchan, 1975; *Assessment in Literature,* Pergamon, 1977; *Achievement in Reading and Literature: The United States in International Perspective,* Pergamon, 1981; *An International Perspective on the Assessment of Composition,* Pergamon, 1982. Contributor to professional journals. Associate editor, *Odyssey Review,* 1961-64; editor, *Research in the Teaching of English,* 1973—.

WORK IN PROGRESS: A book on children's literature.

Q

QUILLER, Andrew
See BULMER, (Henry) Kenneth

* * *

QUINNEY, Richard 1934-

PERSONAL: Born May 16, 1934, in Elkhorn, Wis.; son of Floyd and Alice (Holloway) Quinney; married Valerie Yow (a professor of history), 1958; children: Laura, Anne. *Education:* Carroll College, B.S., 1956; Northwestern University, M.S., 1957; University of Wisconsin, Ph.D., 1962. *Home address:* Route 2, Elkhorn, Wis. 53121. *Office:* Department of Sociology, Northern Illinois University, De Kalb, Ill. 60115.

CAREER: St. Lawrence University, Canton, N.Y., instructor in anthropology and sociology, 1960-62; University of Kentucky, Lexington, assistant professor of sociology, 1962-65; New York University, New York, N.Y., associate professor, 1965-67, professor of sociology, 1967-72, on leave for research and writing at University of North Carolina, 1972-74; Brown University, Providence, R.I., visiting professor, 1975-78, adjunct professor of sociology, 1978-83; Boston College, Chestnut Hill, Mass., distinguished visiting professor, 1978-79, adjunct professor of sociology, 1980-83; Northern Illinois University, De Kalb, professor of sociology, 1983—. Visiting professor, Brooklyn College and the Graduate Center of the City University of New York, 1974-75, and University of Wisconsin—Milwaukee, 1980. Has given numerous guest lectures. Has been research director and chairperson of numerous grants and studies. Has presented papers at numerous annual meetings; photography has been exhibited in North Carolina, New York, and Rhode Island.

MEMBER: American Sociological Association (member of executive council of criminology section, 1972-74, chairperson, 1977-78; member of committee on committees, 1974-76), Society for the Study of Social Problems (chairperson of Crime and Juvenile Delinquency Division, 1975-77), American Academy of Religion, Midwest Sociological Society, Eastern Sociological Society, Rhode Island Historical Society, State Historical Society of Wisconsin.

WRITINGS: Social and Cultural Profile of Lexington and Fayette County, Kentucky (pamphlet), City-County Planning Commission of Lexington and Fayette County, 1963; (with Marshall Clinard) *Criminal Behavior Systems: A Typology,* Holt, 1967, 2nd edition, 1973; (editor) *Crime and Justice in Society,* Little, Brown, 1969; *The Social Reality of Crime,* Little, Brown, 1970; (with Clinard) *The Problem of Crime,* Dodd, 1970, 2nd edition (with John Wildeman) published as *The Problem of Crime: A Critical Introduction to Criminology,* Harper, 1977; (author of introduction) Nicholas M. Regush, *The Drug Addiction Business: A Denunciation of the Dehumanizing Politics and Practices of the So-Called Experts,* Dial, 1971; *Critique of Legal Order: Crime Control in Capitalist Society,* Little, Brown, 1974; (editor) *Criminal Justice in America: A Critical Understanding,* Little, Brown, 1974.

Criminology: Analysis and Critique of Crime in America, Little, Brown, 1975, 2nd edition published as *Criminology,* 1979; (author of foreword) James A. Inciardi, *Careers in Crime,* Rand McNally, 1975; *Class, State, and Crime: On the Theory and Practice of Criminal Justice,* Longman, 1977, 2nd edition published as *Class, State, and Crime,* 1980; *Capitalist Society: Readings for a Critical Sociology,* Dorsey, 1979; *Providence: The Reconstruction of Social and Moral Order,* Longman, 1980; (editor with Piers Beirne) *Marxism and Law,* Wiley, 1982; *Social Existence: Metaphysics, Marxism and the Social Sciences,* Sage, 1982.

Contributor: Walter C. Reckless, *The Crime Problem,* Appleton-Century-Crofts, 1967; Reckless and Simon Dinitz, *Critical Issues in the Study of Crime,* Little, Brown, 1968; Harwin L. Voss, editor, *Society, Delinquency, and Delinquent Behavior,* Little, Brown, 1970; Anthony L. Guenther, editor, *Criminal Behavior and Social Systems: Contributions of American Sociology,* Rand McNally, 1970, 2nd edition, 1976; Bernard Haring, *The Church on the Move,* Alba House, 1970; Voss and David M. Petersen, *Ecology, Crime and Delinquency,* Appleton-Century-Crofts, 1971; Jack D. Douglas, editor, *Crime and Justice in American Society,* Bobbs-Merrill, 1971; Erwin O. Smigel, editor, *Handbook on the Study of Social Problems,* Rand McNally, 1971; Douglas and Robert A. Scott, editors, *Theoretical Perspectives on Deviance,* Basic Books, 1972; Peter Woll, editor, *American Government: Readings and Cases,* Little, Brown, 1972, new edition, 1978.

Erich Goode and Harvey A. Faberman, editors, *Social Reality,* Prentice-Hall, 1973; Charles M. McCaghey and R. Serge Denisoff, editors, *Deviance, Conflict, and Criminality,* Rand McNally, 1973; Regush, editor, *Visibles and Invisibles: A Primer for a New Sociological Imagination,* Little, Brown, 1973; Jack Sussman, *Crime and Justice,* AMS Press, 1974; Israel Drapkin and Emilio Viano, editors, *Victimology,* Lexington Books, 1974; Ronald L. Akers and Richard Hawkins, editors, *Law and Control in Society,* Prentice-Hall, 1974; Charles E. Reasons, editor, *The Criminologist: Crime and the Criminal,* Goodyear Publishing, 1974; Abraham S. Blomberg, editor, *Current Perspectives on Criminal Behavior: Original Essays in Criminology,* Knopf, 1974, 2nd edition published as *Current Perspectives on Criminal Behavior: Essays on Criminology,* 1981.

James A. Inciardi, Jr., and Harvey A. Segal, *Emerging Social Issues,* Praeger, 1975; Richard L. Hensel and Robert A. Silverman, editors, *Perception in Criminology,* Columbia University Press, 1975; Stuart H. Traub and Craig B. Little, editors, *Theories of Deviance,* F. E. Peacock, 1975, 2nd edition, 1980; Silverman and James J. Teevan, Jr., *Crime in Canadian Society,* Butterworth & Co., 1975; F. James Davis and Richard Stivers, editors, *The Collective Definition of Deviance,* Free Press, 1975; Klaus Lunderssen and Fritz Sack, *I Die selektiven Normen der Gesellschaft,* Suhrkamp Verlag (Frankfurt), 1975; Joe Hudson and Burt Galaway, editors, *Considering the Victim,* C. C Thomas, 1975; Ian Taylor, Paul Walton, and Jock Young, editors, *Critical Criminology,* Routledge & Kegan Paul, 1975; Derrall Cheatwood and Therold Lindquist, *The Human Image: Sociology and Photography,* State University of New York Press, 1976; Leon Radzinowicz and Marvin E. Wolfgang, editors, *Crime and Justice,* Volume I, Basic Books, 1977; Timothy J. Curry and Alfred C. Clarke, *Introducing Visual Sociology,* Kendall/Hunt, 1977; Arthur B. Shostak, editor, *Our Sociological Eye: Personal Essays on Society and Culture,* Alfred Publishing, 1977.

Leonard D. Savitz and Norman Johnson, editors, *Crime in Society,* Wiley, 1978; M. David Ermann and Richard Lundman, editors, *Corporate and Governmental Deviance,* Oxford University Press, 1978; Saul D. Feldman, editor, *Deciphering Deviance,* Little, Brown, 1978; Ronald A. Farrell and Victoria Lynn Swigert, editors, *The Substance of Social Deviance,* Alfred Publishing, 1978; Delos H. Kelly, editor, *Deviant Behavior: Readings in the Sociology of Deviance,* St. Martin's, 1979; Lord Lloyd of Hampstead, *Introduction to Jurisprudence,* 4th edition, Stevens & Sons, 1979; Scott G. McNall and Gary N. Howe, editors, *Current Perspectives in Social Theory: A Research Annual,* Volume II, Jai Press, 1981; William E. Thornton, Jr., Jennifer James, and William G. Doerner, editors, *Delinquency and Justice,* Scott, Foresman, 1982.

Contributor of articles, book reviews, and photography to numerous periodicals, including *Social Forces, American Journal of Sociology, Infinity, Rural Sociology, Mirror, American Sociological Review, Social Problems, Contemporary Crises,* and *American Behavioral Scientist.* Associate editor, *Victimology,* 1976—, (and member of board of directors) *The Insurgent Sociologist,* 1977—, *Contemporary Crises,* 1977—, and *California Sociologist,* 1977—; advisory editor, *Offender Rehabilitation,* 1976—, and *Qualitative Sociology,* 1978—; contributing editor, *Crime and Social Justice: A Journal of Radical Criminology,* 1974-78; corresponding editor, *Theory and Society,* 1974-77; member of editorial board, *Criminology,* 1978-81.

WORK IN PROGRESS: An autobiographical work, *Midwest Landscape.*

SIDELIGHTS: About the body of Richard Quinney's work, David O. Friedrichs comments in *Radical Criminology: The Coming Crisis*: "Quinney's contributions to criminology to date might be classified, theoretically and chronologically, as conventional, conflict oriented, critical, neo-Marxist, and most recently prophetic. This singular intellectual career over a period of approximately two decades may be virtually without parallel in the discipline. But whatever direction his work now takes, Quinney has undeniably made a fundamental contribution to the development of radical criminology." Friedrichs concludes: "With rare intellectual courage, immense scholarly erudition, awesome imagination, and remarkable productiveness, Quinney has explored the outer reaches of the criminological frontier. Even if Quinney is 'wrong' or 'one-sided' in many instances, the conviction remains that his work and thought will continue to be discussed, will continue to inspire and provoke, long after his more timid if technically more 'correct' criminological brethren are forgotten or relegated to obscure footnotes."

As Friedrichs points out, Quinney's more recent work is thought-provoking and prophetic. In the prologue to *Providence: The Reconstruction of Social and Moral Order,* Quinney expresses his belief that the advanced capitalist society is rapidly approaching its demise, primarily because its attendant secularism alienates humanity from itself by extinguishing the spiritual dimension of existence. "Now in these days," he writes, "the word of God is seldom heard, and visions are not often granted. We are reaching the end of an age; the advanced capitalist society with its highly secular and utilitarian sensibility is coming to an end. The contradictions of the existing social and moral order and the personal and collective struggle are bringing about a new human history."

"The task ahead," he suggests in *Social Existence: Metaphysics, Marxism and the Social Sciences,* "is to create the symbols that will allow us as human social beings to find our place in the world. The contemporary crisis is both material and symbolic: a social existence cannot be constructed without attending to both the conditions of material existence and the symbols for social and spiritual existence. Our hope is for a social existence filled with a meaning that relates to an order in the universe. Our immediate work is in the reconstruction of symbols in the struggle for social existence.

"Throughout contemporary discourse we continue to draw from the symbolism of the prophetic Judeo-Christian tradition. This is the symbolism that has formed the basis of Western intellectual and spiritual existence. However much this symbolism has been repressed in the academy and in everyday life, an alternative symbolism has not developed. This is a major crisis in our thought and in our lives. The traditional metaphysic, with the emphasis on the God-question, while addressing the essential problems of social existence, does not seem to be entirely appropriate for the contemporary sensibility. The two-world theory of reality—the earthly world opposed to the world beyond—is in need of revision. There remains the need for a symbolism that gives depth to our existence. The answer is not to think and live without symbols, but to reconstruct a symbolic system that returns meaning to our existence."

BIOGRAPHICAL/CRITICAL SOURCES: Issues in Criminology, spring, 1971; Marshall B. Clinard and Robert F. Meier, *Sociology of Deviant Behavior,* 5th edition, Holt, 1979; Richard Quinney, *Providence: The Reconstruction of Social and Moral Order,* Longman, 1980; James A. Inciardi, editor, *Radical Criminology: The Coming Crisis,* Sage, 1980; Allen E. Liska, *Perspectives on Deviance,* Prentice-Hall, 1981; Quinney, *Social Existence: Metaphysics, Marxism and the Social Sciences,* Sage, 1982.

QUIRIN, G(eorge) David 1931-

PERSONAL: Born March 29, 1931, in Calgary, Alberta, Canada; son of George Edward and Helen (Welsh) Quirin; married Jean McNamee, March 2, 1957; children: John Jacob, Kathleen Ann, James Joseph. *Education:* University of Alberta, B.A., 1952, M.A., 1958; Princeton University, A.M., 1960, Ph.D., 1961. *Home:* 173 Inglewood Dr., Toronto, Ontario, Canada. *Office:* Faculty of Management Studies, University of Toronto, Toronto, Ontario, Canada.

CAREER: Imperial Oil Ltd., Calgary, Alberta, various positions, 1952-56; Hubert Harries & Associates, Calgary, economist, 1956-58; Canadian Government, Department of Northern Affairs and National Resources, Ottawa, Ontario, economic consultant, 1960-61; University of British Columbia, Vancouver, associate professor of finance, 1961-66; University of Toronto, Toronto, Ontario, associate professor, 1966-68, professor of economics and finance, 1969—. Visiting professor at University of Malaya, 1963, and University of Singapore, 1963-64. Research director, Royal Commission on Automobile Insurance, Victoria, 1966-68.

WRITINGS: The Economics of Oil and Gas Exploration in Northern Canada, Queen's Printer, 1962; *The Capital Expenditure Decision,* Irwin, 1967; (with F. F. Matthewson) *Fiscal Transfer Pricing in Multinational Corporations,* University of Toronto Press, 1979; (with J. C. Wiginton) *Expenditures: Public and Private Perspectives,* Irwin, 1981; (with B. A. Kalzman) *Pricing Canadian Oil,* Fraser Institute (Vancouver), 1982.

R

RALSTON, Jan
See DUNLOP, Agnes M. R.

* * *

RAMSEY, G(ordon) C(lark) 1941-

PERSONAL: Born May 28, 1941, in Hartford, Conn.; son of Clark McNary and Virginia A. (Childs) Ramsey. *Education:* Yale University, B.A., 1963; private organ and choral studies. *Politics:* Republican. *Religion:* Christian Science. *Home:* 58 Mountain View Rd., Avon, Conn. 06001. *Office:* Avon Old Farms School, Avon, Conn. 06001.

CAREER: Worcester Academy, Worcester, Mass., instructor in English, assistant to the headmaster, and alumni director, 1963-69, director of glee club, 1964-65; Yale Alumni Fund, New Haven, Conn., assistant director, 1969-71; Association of Yale Alumni, New Haven, assistant executive director, 1972-77; Avon Old Farms School, Avon, Conn., director of financial development, 1978-80; writer, fund-raiser for nonprofit organizations, and historical researcher, 1980—. Historian, Yale Alumni Fund, 1973-77, and Avon Old Farms School, 1982—. Technical expert for 1938 Chevrolet, Vintage Chevrolet Club of America, 1975-80. Trustee and member of executive committee, Barlow School, 1975-80. Church organist. *Member:* Association of Yale Alumni (member of assembly and committee chairman, 1977-80). *Awards, honors:* Research grant from Dodd, Mead & Co., for work in Great Britain on Agatha Christie book; honorary graduate, Avon Old Farms School, 1980.

WRITINGS: Agatha Christie: Mistress of Mystery, Dodd, 1967; *These Fields and Halls* (prayerbook), Council for Religion in Independent Schools, 1974; *An Undertakeing Sett Forward* (history of Yale Alumni Fund), Yale University, 1976.

Contributor of articles and reviews to newspapers and magazines, including *HiFi Stereo Review,* and *New York Times,* Record critic, *American Organist,* 1966-68; editor of newsletter "Stovebolts," Southern New England Region, Vintage Chevrolet Club of America, 1975-79.

WORK IN PROGRESS: History of Avon Old Farms School.

RATHER, Dan (Irvin) 1931-

PERSONAL: Born October 31, 1931, in Wharton, Tex.; son of Irvin (an oil pipeliner) and Byrl (a waitress; maiden name, Page) Rather; married Jeannie Grace Goebel (a painter), April 21, 1957; children: Dawn Robin, Daniel Martin. *Education:* Sam Houston State Teachers College (now Sam Houston State University), B.A. in journalism, 1953; attended University of Houston Law School, 1957-59, and South Texas School of Law, 1959. *Politics:* Independent. *Religion:* Protestant. *Residence:* New York, N.Y., and Washington, D.C. *Office:* CBS News, 555 West 57th St., New York, N.Y. 10019.

CAREER: KSAM-Radio, Huntsville, Tex., writer, reporter, and broadcaster, 1950-54; reporter for Associated Press, 1951-52, and for United Press International, 1953, both in Huntsville; Sam Houston State Teachers College (now Sam Houston State University), Huntsville, member of faculty in department of journalism, 1953-54; part-time writer and reporter for *Huntsville Item,* Huntsville, and *Houston Chronicle,* Houston, Tex., mid-1950s; KTRH-Radio, Houston, reporter, writer, and news director, 1954-59; KHOU-Television, Houston, director of news and public affairs, 1960-61; Columbia Broadcasting System (CBS) News, reporter and journalist in Dallas, Tex., and New Orleans, La., 1961-63, White House correspondent in Washington, D.C., 1964, bureau chief in London, England, 1965-66, correspondent in Vietnam, 1966, White House correspondent in Washington, D.C., 1966-74, anchorman-correspondent for "CBS Reports" on CBS-TV, 1974-75, co-anchorman for "60 Minutes" on CBS-TV, 1975-81, anchorman for "Dan Rather Reporting" on CBS-Radio, beginning 1977, anchorman and managing editor for "CBS Evening News" on CBS-TV, 1981—. *Military service:* U.S. Marine Corps, 1954. *Member:* Sigma Delta Chi. *Awards, honors:* Recipient of National Headliners award, Overseas Press Club award, and five Emmy Awards from National Academy of Television Arts and Sciences.

WRITINGS: (With Gary P. Gates) *The Palace Guard* (nonfiction), Harper, 1974; (with Mickey Herskowitz) *The Camera Never Blinks: Adventures of a TV Journalist* (autobiography), Morrow, 1977. Occasional contributor of articles to *Newsday* and other publications.

SIDELIGHTS: In February, 1980, CBS executives made an announcement that marked the end of one era and the beginning of another: veteran reporter Dan Rather had accepted the network's multi-million-dollar offer to succeed Walter Cronkite as anchorman and managing editor of the evening news. It was a momentous occasion for Rather, who described himself as "humbled and astounded" at the thought of inheriting the most coveted post in the CBS news operation. It was also a momentous occasion for the network. "By choosing Rather," a writer for *Time* observed, "CBS is gambling that the time has come for an electrifying anchorman rather than an avuncular one, a younger, more dynamic personality to replace an old familiar face." Yet as the *Time* writer went on to point out, "the network really did not dare let Rather go." Audience surveys conducted by several television-news consultant firms indicated that he alone equaled or surpassed Walter Cronkite for communicating honesty, warmth, and compassion. In short, concluded the *Time* writer, Rather had become "the one man in television who, working for a competitor, could conceivably demolish the house that Cronkite built."

In his autobiography, *The Camera Never Blinks,* Dan Rather recalls that being a reporter "was all I could ever remember wanting to do." He attributes his passion for news to his father, a "voracious reader" who impulsively subscribed to newspapers from all over the United States. The elder Rather was also, according to his son, "a man of sudden angers who would leap from his chair and cancel whichever paper had offended him. . . . Out of that cycle, somehow, grew my interest in the news, how it was gathered and reported and in what form it reached our home."

Though he had always dreamed of working for a newspaper, Rather's first major reporting job was with a 250-watt radio station in Huntsville, Tex., while he was still a journalism student at Sam Houston State Teachers College. For forty cents an hour, he was a jack-of-all-trades, putting together newscasts, doing the play-by-play for local junior high, high school, and college football games, and even answering the phone, repairing the equipment, and mowing the lawn. "Nothing was closed to me," Rather says. "I could do anything I was big enough to try. This led to some comic crises, but it was the richest kind of training."

After becoming what he calls "sidetracked" for a year or so following graduation from college, Rather moved on to part-time writing and reporting assignments for the *Houston Chronicle,* then joined the news staff of KTRH, a 50,000-watt radio station owned by the *Chronicle*. It was while working at KTRH that Rather first had a sense that he was doing "the one thing I had always visualized myself doing. Not the broadcast part, but the reporting, covering City Hall, the courts, the police station. I was learning." Before long he was broadcasting KTRH's late-night news program, taking advantage of the opportunity to improve his announcing style.

Six years later, in 1960, the twenty-nine-year-old Rather became news director and anchorman for KHOU-TV, the CBS affiliate in Houston. Within a year after his arrival, the station moved from third place to first place in the ratings. When Hurricane Carla struck the Texas Gulf Coast in September, 1961, Rather headed a news team that provided unprecedented live coverage of the storm for nearly three days from the offices of the Galveston Weather Bureau. His adroit handling of the situation captured the attention of CBS executives in New York who had monitored the reports from Texas, and soon Rather was offered a job with the network—an offer he promptly turned down. Remarks the newsman in *The Camera Never Blinks:* "The idea [of working for CBS] did not exactly overwhelm me. . . . It wasn't a case of my being timid or without ambition. But at that moment I was right where I wanted to be, doing what I wanted to do. . . . I had been in local television only two years. I still found myself thinking, I have to get out of broadcasting and get back to what I set out to do, which was print journalism, the newspaper business."

Several months later, however, CBS came up with an offer Rather found impossible to refuse. In an unusual move, the network agreed to make him a correspondent rather than a reporter, the customary entry level position. Thus, in February, 1962, Rather left Houston for New York and the promise of at least a six-month-long trial period as a correspondent.

Rather's subsequent rise through the ranks at CBS was decidedly meteoric. As a *Time* writer observes, he was simply "more aggressive and tenacious than the competition, working as many hours a day as his assignment called for and then adding a few more for good measure." Within six weeks after his arrival in New York, he was chosen to head a new domestic bureau in Dallas. (It was later consolidated with the Atlanta bureau and moved to New Orleans with Rather still in charge.) Over the next two years, he covered the civil rights movement in the South, reporting on such stories as the rioting that followed James Meredith's enrollment at the University of Mississippi in 1962 and the assassination of Medgar Evers in 1963.

On November 22, 1963, Rather was in Dallas to coordinate CBS's coverage of President Kennedy's visit to the city and to conduct an interview with former vice-president John Nance Garner (who was celebrating his ninety-eighth birthday) for use as a possible filler piece on the evening news. When the crew assigned to film and report on the presidential motorcade found they were short one man, Rather, having completed his interview, volunteered to stand at the last post along the route, a point only four or five blocks from the building that housed the network's Dallas affiliate. As soon as he noticed a police car and what he believed to be the president's limousine suddenly and inexplicably break away from the rest of the motorcade and speed off in the wrong direction, Rather instinctively ran to the affiliate's offices and began monitoring local police communications. Among the confusing messages he heard was a reference to a nearby hospital. Within minutes Rather was on the phone. In separate conversations with the hospital's switchboard operator, a physician, and a Catholic priest, he learned that the president had been shot and was dead. Though in retrospect he wishes he had "exercised more care," Rather passed along these unofficial reports to network radio and television editors. CBS Radio soon became the first to announce that Kennedy had been assassinated. Recalls the newsman in his autobiography: "I felt a chill. It dawned on me that it was possible I had committed a blunder beyond comprehension, beyond forgiving. . . . At no time did we stop and tell ourselves, in some smaller way what we said and what we did would become a part of the history of that week. . . . You can't call the story back but you think about it."

For the next five days Rather filed numerous live reports and helped coordinate CBS's coverage of the assassination and subsequent events, including the president's funeral and the murder of the man suspected of shooting him, Lee Harvey Oswald. His work so impressed network executives that he was immediately promoted to Washington correspondent, an assignment that required him to report on the new Johnson administration. He remained in that post until after the 1964 election, when it was decided that he needed some overseas experience. Though Rather would have preferred to go to Vietnam, London became his base. From there he traveled throughout Europe, the Middle East, and parts of Asia, covering the Greek and Turkish civil war on Cyprus and Pakistan's invasion of India. He nevertheless remained steadfast in his determination to someday report from Vietnam on what he sensed would become "the most important story of this generation."

In November, 1965, Rather's persistence finally paid off. Despite the misgivings of family and friends, he began lobbying for a correspondent position in Vietnam. This time, CBS agreed to send him to Saigon for a three-month stint. He ended up staying a year, ignoring the official press briefings (which emphasized the political aspects of the war) in favor of venturing out into the field to report on actual combat. Reflecting on the impact of this decision to concentrate on battles rather than words, Rather notes: "For the first time . . . war was coming into our homes. For the first time people could watch actual combat scenes while they ate dinner. I don't say that is necessarily a good thing. But the war changed the way we think about television. And TV changed the way we think about war."

Rather returned to the United States in November, 1966, and once again was assigned to cover the White House. He stayed on in Washington even after the 1968 election, despite the fact that the networks customarily rotate correspondents when a new president takes office. As a result, Rather's years as Washington correspondent encompassed the entire Watergate era. His aggressive coverage of President Nixon, conducted in a manner some regarded as hostile, made him a nationally-recognized figure; it also earned him the nickname "the Reporter the White House Hates."

Rather, who maintains in *The Camera Never Blinks* that as far as he is concerned "in our system no citizen has to face any leader on bended knee," insists that his only intention during his confrontations with the president was "to draw out answers to questions I thought needed to be asked. I was not baiting the president or promoting myself. But some people wanted to read into it more than was there." Nevertheless, he adds, "by being drawn into the fevers of Watergate I felt I had in some ways failed at my job. My job is to inform, not persuade. At the same time I don't want to come across as some kind of Pollyanna. I do not subscribe to the idea of the reporter-as-robot. I can't walk into a room and say to you look, every day that I went into the White House I left my emotions behind me. But one test of the professional is how hard he tries and how well he succeeds in keeping his own feelings out of a story. I tried."

Rather was transferred from the White House beat to New York in August, 1974, shortly after President Nixon resigned and Gerald Ford took office. The transfer was neither sudden nor unexpected, but the newsman could not help but be suspicious about the timing. In fact, he spent an agonizing ten days wondering if CBS was finally caving in to pressure generated by those who felt Rather embodied the media's "liberal" politics and antagonistic attitude towards President Nixon. (Audience surveys later demonstrated that public confidence in Rather and other "liberal" newsmen increased dramatically as more and more of the Watergate story became known.) He finally decided that the new job his superiors had offered him—anchorman-correspondent for the documentary-style "CBS Reports"—might very well be the "golden opportunity" they promised it was. In addition to this position, unfilled since the days of Edward R. Murrow, Rather was also chosen to serve as anchor for CBS's Saturday and Sunday evening newscasts. Acknowledging in *Newsweek* that "coming to New York was best for [CBS] and for me," Rather accepted the network's offer, welcoming the opportunity, as he later phrased it in his autobiography, "to treat in depth subjects that left an imprint on the American condition."

During his two years with "CBS Reports," Rather wrote and narrated numerous wide-ranging documentaries, including several highly-acclaimed ones on the assassinations of John Kennedy, Robert Kennedy, and Martin Luther King, Jr., the attempt to assassinate George Wallace, the environmental causes of cancer, and the influence of special-interest groups on congressional elections. Commenting on one of these programs in *Newsday,* Marvin Kitman observed: "Rather is the only person whom the network news system has produced since Edward R. Murrow who can conceivably supply the conscience missing from television news."

In 1976, Rather left "CBS Reports" to join the anchor team of Mike Wallace and Morley Safer on "60 Minutes." Described by Rather in *The Camera Never Blinks* as a show that "falls between the banzai charge of daily journalism and the thoughtful, reflective, one-hour-to-do-it of 'CBS Reports,'" "60 Minutes" further enhanced the veteran correspondent's reputation. In fact, maintains at least one television news consultant quoted in *Newsweek,* co-anchoring "60 Minutes" is what gave Rather the "stature" he needed to be considered a serious candidate for Walter Cronkite's job. Explained the consultant: "[On '60 Minutes'] the audience saw [Rather] going one-on-one and not just sitting behind a desk reading the news."

Alarmed by the defection of many members of the CBS news staff to rivals ABC and NBC during the late 1970s, the network approached Rather about signing a long-term contract in the fall of 1979. But their offer did not include any mention of replacing Cronkite. Rather then began to contact ABC and NBC about a possible anchor spot, thus touching off what *Newsweek* refers to as "the hottest bidding war in the history of broadcast journalism" and "an executive-suite shoot-out worthy of Hollywood's star wars." After six weeks of intense negotiations, the forty-eight-year-old newsman made his decision: he would stay with CBS. "The attraction of ABC and NBC was getting a fresh start under conditions I never dreamed were possible," Rather remarked at the time of the announcement, according to *Newsweek.* "But I want to be the best there is in my time, and CBS is still the leader. And the symbolism of that anchor chair is so heavy."

Rather is not, however, the type of man to indulge in fantasies of achieving celebrity status—especially when it might interfere with his professional responsibilities. "The good journalist does *not* become a part of the story he covers," he declares in his autobiography. "A newsman does not make news. The idea of the reporter as *pop media star* is offensive to me. . . . That way is simply not compatible with the vision Ed Murrow had of the scholar-correspondent, a vision still good enough for me." In short, as he told the *Detroit Free Press*'s Hugh McCann, becoming a celebrity only makes "you forget what you're about—if what you're about is being a reporter."

It would indeed seem that being a reporter *is* all Dan Rather has ever wanted to do. "I am a fellow who has been happy at every job he has ever had, who would be happy if he were still doing the drive-time news on radio in Houston," he says in *The Camera Never Blinks.* Several years before Cronkite's pending retirement necessitated a search for a successor, Rather pondered his future in journalism in light of the goals he had long ago set for himself. "People, mostly TV columnists, keep asking who will be the next Walter Cronkite,'' the newsman began. ''The answer is easy. No one. It would be foolish to believe there is going to be another Cronkite or Eric Sevareid. My job is to make myself a pretty good Dan Rather. Sure, I have fantasized at one time or another about anchoring the evening news, socking away the money for a few years and then returning to what I do best—reporting.'' After all, concluded Rather, evoking an image of the ''scholar-correspondent'' who comes closest to being his hero, ''I have to believe that if Ed Murrow were alive he would not be doing the news at seven o'clock.''

AVOCATIONAL INTERESTS: Watching basketball games, playing tennis, fishing, studying sculpture.

CA INTERVIEW

CA interviewed Dan Rather by phone October 20, 1981, at his office in New York City.

CA: In your 1977 autobiography, The Camera Never Blinks, *you wrote, ''Sure, I have fantasized at one time or another about anchoring the Evening News. . . .'' Now that it's a reality, how do you like it?*

RATHER: I love it. I enjoy it greatly. It's a new challenge, it's new wind and water for me. And I think any time you go into new wind and water, there are moments of anxiety; I'd be less than candid if I didn't say I've had those and I *have* those, but I do enjoy it terrifically.

CA: Are you getting a lot of encouraging mail?

RATHER: Yes, I do get a lot of encouraging mail, but I should say that I'm not much of a believer in mail for two reasons. One, a great deal of mail can be orchestrated either for or against, and that's one of the things I've learned in covering politics over the years. Also, many people never write. People who write tend to be people who have time on their hands. I think I've gotten pretty good at discerning mail that comes from the heart and mail that is just written offhandedly. Mail that comes from the heart, whether pro or con, critical or complimentary, I tend to take seriously.

CA: As anchorman for ''The CBS Evening News,'' how much do you participate in the selection, writing, and editing of the show?

RATHER: Totally, completely. I wouldn't want to do it if I didn't. Being managing editor of the broadcast is more important to me than being the anchorman. That was, frankly, something I had to fight to get, but I did fight to get it because I knew how important it was to me and my own sense of satisfaction. Many of the decisions are shared with others. In an organization this large, I can't make every single decision; but the final decisions as to what we cover, how we cover it, what goes into the broadcast, those decisions are mine—for better or for worse.

CA: Television has been so much criticized lately—from within as well as by viewers and professional critics—for its emphasis on what makes the most visual impact. Do you think the charge is warranted?

RATHER: I wouldn't argue with that criticism. I would just caution that it's a little too simple to say that television only cares about pictures. Television *does* care about pictures and other visual things because it is a visual medium. We shouldn't be apologetic or defensive about that. But it also is a medium of the ear. One tends to forget that the television box, in addition to having a screen, also has a speaker. The writing of our broadcast, for example, gets more attention than the visual elements in the broadcast. That may not be widely believed, but it is true. We spend a great deal of our time each day worrying about what's visually going to be in the broadcast. But we spend *more* of our time worrying about what is going to be written for the broadcast.

CA: Actors talk about the nightmare in which they come on the stage and find they've forgotten all their lines. What's the newscaster's greatest worry?

RATHER: I can't speak for others, but my greatest concern is to have it right. This is a humbling job in a lot of ways. Last night we had a broadcast in which three names were misspelled. I almost literally beat my head against the doorfacing; I go home feeling really punk about things like that. Mind you, there aren't many days when we misspell *any* names, much less *three*—we can't stay in business if we do that very often. But accuracy is extremely important to us. The performing end of it has never consumed that much of my thought and effort (though it did more in the beginning than it does now). I might have been better off if I had spent more time on that, but it's not what interests me.

CA: Do you think there are times when television should downplay coverage of such things as riots in an effort not to incite further chaos or violence? Would that be legitimate censorship?

RATHER: It's certainly a legitimate concern, and it is a continuing and increasingly deep concern with me and with all of us here. When there's a story, one's journalistic instinct is to get on it, climb all over it, swarm it, and to tell and show people what you know. The other side of the question is, when does the story begin to feed on itself? We can no longer say that television is in its infancy—it isn't. It's somewhere around puberty now, and it's going through a lot of the difficulties of puberty. But we learned enough from what happened during the '60s and some of the early '70s to know that's at least one of the questions we ought to be asking ourselves pretty regularly. I don't have an answer to it.

I don't want to fall into the trap of believing that one should just put out good news. It gets down to a definition of news. Somebody says, ''Well, you're always talking about what's wrong with the world,'' and that's one definition of news. If you walk outside your house and start talking with your neighbor and your neighbor says, ''What went on today?'' and you say, ''Well, Jim Jones down the street paid his taxes, and Mrs. Smith took the children to school this morning,'' nobody would call that news. If you say, ''Jim Jones *didn't* pay his taxes and the IRS is out there arresting him, and Mrs. Smith was hit by a bus this morning,'' it's not *good* news but it's part of what is news. You can't say, ''The Ford Pintos do not explode when hit from the rear.'' Is that a story? No. So we don't want to fall into that trap. On the other hand, I do have that nagging feeling, particularly when we don't put things such as a riot into some context, when we deal with it only on the surface, that there certainly is a sociological danger and a great danger of our being irresponsible.

CA: It must be very hard to put things into a context immediately when important news is breaking. It's got to be covered at the time if it's to be covered.

RATHER: I think so, partly because we know how quickly rumors spread. One of the things we do pretty well is serve as a kind of national clearinghouse for information in times of crisis or perceived crisis. For example, let's take the assassination attempt on the president. There are some people who'd say, "Don't go on the air with that right away." I don't agree, because very quickly rumors begin to spread, and while there are dangers with live, as-it-happens coverage, the one problem you don't have is people believing that something is being kept from them, which is very dangerous indeed.

CA: As a veteran of "60 Minutes," how do you feel about the criticism that show has come under recently, primarily the charge of deceptive editing?

RATHER: Number one, I'm very proud of "60 Minutes" and I think we have a right to be proud of it. Part of the show's difficulty is that it's been successful. Any time you're successful, you're going to take shots, there's no question. Number two, "60 Minutes" is the only program that regularly—week in, week out; year in, year out—deals with what I call the tough stuff. On that program we handle nitroglycerin, and we handle it every week. We deal with the kind of stories that nobody else deals with that consistently and at that depth. Yes, we make mistakes. At one time or another we have made nearly every mistake that can be made—everything from misspelling names to not editing a piece as we should have. But it's a responsible journalistic enterprise; we do our damndest to make it honest. Nobody wants to be deceptive in the editing, and we aren't. Nobody wants to take anybody out of context, and we don't. We deal with tough journalistic problems.

Now if you're putting out "PM Magazine," for example (which is a good program), you don't open yourself to the kind of criticism "60 Minutes" gets because "PM Magazine" by and large doesn't deal with the tough, nitty-gritty stuff. They deal with so-called good news. There's a place for that. When you put yourself on the cutting edge, when you try to deal with corruption, when you try to deal with some of the deep and abiding problems of society, you are going to get scars. "60 Minutes" has some of those scars. But I take those scars as badges that we've at least been trying to do some of the things that television journalism particularly is often accused of not taking on. On the one hand, people say, "Television journalism is all bland, it's all namby-pamby stuff, they never take on the really tough ones." "60 Minutes" does. But when we take it on, then people say, "Those guys are just showing out." We do make mistakes. And when you handle explosive material, when you make a mistake, if you're lucky, you'll only lose fingers and arms. Not very many people, and increasingly few these days, are willing to handle that kind of journalistic material in any form, television or print. You know the pressure on your average newspapers—"Don't cause trouble, man. Go cover something nice. Go cover the Chamber of Commerce meeting. Don't be out there digging around about why the mayor's built this freeway in the middle of nowhere."

CA: In The Palace Guard, *your 1974 book with Gary P. Gates, and in your later autobiography you described the difficult relationship between the Nixon White House and the press. Would you comment on the current administration's dealings with the press?*

RATHER: As of this date I give President Reagan and his administration high marks in their dealings with the press. We could argue about their policies, domestic and foreign, but I give him high marks in dealing with the press for the following reasons: (1) the president and the main people around him have been accessible; (2) the president has held frequent and regular news conferences, with the exception of the period right after he was shot; (3) President Reagan and his top advisers don't seem to show any hostility toward the press. They seem to be very comfortable around reporters, to understand what their jobs are, what they're trying to do. When you make a mistake they call you and say, "Hey, I think you made a mistake." They don't accuse you of being un-American, of trying to bring down the whole administration. If they continue that way, they may have great difficulties with their other policies, but they're not going to have a lot of difficulty with the press.

CA: You wrote in The Camera Never Blinks *that television coverage of the Vietnam War "changed the way we think about television. And TV changed the way we think about war." Do you agree with the people who believe television coverage helped to end that war sooner than it might have ended otherwise?*

RATHER: I agree with it, but only up to a point. I think television's role in any war is vastly overstated. Keep in mind that television was covering the war early (CBS News, I'm happy to say, led in that). And the majority sentiment in the United States didn't turn against the war until Johnny down the street came home in a body bag and Joe, two blocks over, came home without his legs. That's when people began to say, "Hey, why are we there? What are we doing there? How is this war being fought?" It wasn't in 1964 or '65, '66, '67; it really wasn't until the rank and file of Americans began to *see* the effects of it back in their own neighborhoods that they began to turn against the Johnson-Nixon policies on the war—I really should say Kennedy-Johnson-Nixon, because, as we tend to forget, it was during President Kennedy's time that the nature of that war changed. I was trying to point out in *The Camera Never Blinks* that what television does best is take you there. And for the first time, people at home were actually taken *to* the war on television. Some of those images permeated pretty deeply, and that no doubt had an effect. But I do think it's vastly overstated. A General Westmoreland I think might say, "It was television that really turned the American people against the war." Hogwash! We just don't have that much power.

CA: Do you have any theories on how the role of network television as we know it now will be changed by the continually developing technologies?

RATHER: I don't, and I don't think anyone does. The fabulous thing about this country, without any apology, is that the pace of change is phenomenal—partly because of technology, partly because it's quintessentially American to look for change and to want change and to adapt to change. Whatever network television is or isn't, ten years from now I think it's going to be barely recognizable from what it is today. It's been a rapidly accelerating change, and I think that acceleration will increase, not decrease. But the form it will take, I don't know. My mind boggles at cable, to say nothing of every apartment house having its own dish on the roof and being able to pick up satellite transmissions. I'm fascinated by these dishes. They can go in your backyard, beside your house, and you don't need cable; you just pick up transmissions from everywhere.

Right now, if you have cable, you have maybe forty choices in New York. The day is rapidly coming when you'll have ninety choices or a hundred and fifty—like your radio dial, but even more so.

CA: Do you watch television at all for pleasure?

RATHER: Yes. I watch sports on television for pleasure. I'm a sports nut, and I watch nearly everything from the roller derby to the World Series. Sometimes I watch situation comedies, but my television watching tends to be mostly sports events or news and public affairs.

CA: Do you find time for sports or hobbies yourself?

RATHER: I do. I like to fish. I like to run. I like to walk in the outdoors, observe nature. I like to read and go to the theater. Those are among the things I spend my leisure time doing.

CA: It's amazing that you have any leisure time.

RATHER: I don't have nearly as much as I'd like to have. But also, I like my work so it's not in me to complain.

CA: You credited Hugh Cunningham, your journalism teacher at Sam Houston State Teachers College in Texas, for his strong influence on your career. Do you get a lot of requests for help or advice from aspiring newspeople?

RATHER: I do, and I wish I could respond to more of it. But it would be full-time work to respond to all of the requests I get. I try to help when I can.

CA: Is there any writing in progress that you'd like to talk about?

RATHER: This is a comparatively fallow period for me in writing because of this new challenge that we spoke about earlier; not only does it take a lot of my time, but it takes a lot of my creative and psychic energy. I'm still typing away sporadically on what's left of an idea for a novel. I've learned that dialogue is not as easy to pull off as I thought it might be. When I'm writing down other people's direct quotes, that's one thing, but trying to write dialogue out of your head is another. And I've been working on two nonfiction projects, one of which is something I started much like *The Camera Never Blinks* but taking "60 Minutes" experiences and trying to put those into a book. I don't know if I'll ever finish that or not. The other is on journalism history; it may have the best chance of getting into print. I'd love to get the novel into print, but boy, right now it's tough going!

BIOGRAPHICAL/CRITICAL SOURCES: Newsweek, September 2, 1974, February 25, 1980; *Detroit Free Press,* December 1, 1974; *Newsday,* January 31, 1975; *Authors in the News,* Volume I, Gale, 1976; Dan Rather, *The Camera Never Blinks,* Morrow, 1977; *Publishers Weekly,* May 9, 1977; *Detroit News Magazine,* September 16, 1979; *Time,* February 25, 1980; *People,* March 3, 1980, August 11, 1980; *New Leader,* March 10, 1980.

—Sketch by Deborah A. Straub

—Interview by Jean W. Ross

* * *

RAY, D(avid) Michael 1935-

PERSONAL: Born December 25, 1935, in St. Austell, Cornwall, England; Canadian citizen; son of Fred and Juliette (Gazard) Ray; married Marie Vincent, October 25, 1957; children: Jane, Jonathan, Juliet. *Education:* University of Manchester, B.A. (with honors in geography), 1956, Graduate Certificate in Education, 1957; University of Ottawa, M.A. (cum laude), 1961; University of Chicago, Ph.D., 1965. *Office:* Department of Geography, Carleton University, Ottawa, Ontario, Canada K1S 5B6.

CAREER: Teacher with Montreal Catholic School Commission, Montreal, Quebec, 1957-58; University of Ottawa, Ottawa, Ontario, lecturer, 1958-61, assistant professor of geography, 1961-64; Spartan Air Services Ltd., Ottawa, socioeconomic geographer, 1965-67; University of Waterloo, Waterloo, Ontario, associate professor of geography, 1967-68; State University of New York at Buffalo, associate professor, 1968-71, professor of geography, 1971-73; University of Ottawa, professor of geography, 1973-76; Carleton University, Ottawa, professor of geography, 1976—. Research associate in departments of geography and economics, Carleton University, 1966. Consultant, Ministry of State and Urban Affairs of Canada, 1972-75. *Member:* Canadian Association of Geographers, Association of American Geographers, Regional Science Association.

WRITINGS: Market Potential and Economic Shadow: A Quantitative Analysis of Industrial Location in Southern Ontario, Department of Geography, University of Chicago, 1965; (with others) *Trends, Issues and Possibilities for Urban Development,* Ontario Economic Council, 1970; *Dimensions of Canadian Regionalism,* Department of Energy, Mines, and Resources (Ottawa), 1971; (with B.J.L. Berry and E. C. Conkling) *The Geography of Economic Systems,* Prentice-Hall, 1976; (editor and contributor) *Canadian Urban Trends,* Copp, Volume I: *National Perspective,* 1976, Volume II: *Metropolitan Perspective,* 1977, Volume III: *Neighborhood Perspective,* 1978.

Contributor: R. M. Irving, editor, *Readings in Canadian Geography,* Holt, 1968, 2nd edition, 1972; N. H. Lithwick and G. Paquet, editors, *Urban Growth: A Canadian Perspective,* Methuen, 1968; L. Collins and David Walker, editors, *The Dynamics of Manufacturing Activity,* Wiley, 1975; F.E.I. Hamilton, editor, *Spatial Perspectives on Industrial Organization and Decision Making,* Wiley, 1975; A. Kuklinski, editor, *Regional Development and Planning: International Perspective,* Sijhoff, 1975; Kuklinski, editor, *Regional Development, Regional Policy and Regional Planning,* Sijhoff, 1981; James Lorimer and Carolyn MacGregor, editors, *After the Developers,* Lorimer, 1981.

Contributor to *Economic Geography* and *Canadian Geographer.*

WORK IN PROGRESS: A book with Brian J. L. Berry and Edgar C. Conkling, *Economic Geography: Problems, Approaches, Basic Theory.*

SIDELIGHTS: D. Michael Ray told *CA:* "This writer has a shocking confession to make: he never wanted to write! He was tricked into it by a range of important public policy issues in Canada, including regional disparities, urban growth, foreign ownership, and immigration. Geographers have important contributions which must be made. In essence, these contributions are an integrated, regional view of a country where regionalism is generally an asset, sometimes a problem and always an issue."

RAYMOND, E. V.
See GALLUN, Raymond Z(inke)

* * *

READ, Elfreida 1920-

PERSONAL: Born October 2, 1920, in Vladivostok, Russia; daughter of Albert (an accountant) and Maria (Yacub) Ennock; married George J. Read (a business executive), July 10, 1941; children: Jeananne Patricia, Philip Kendall. *Religion:* Unitarian. *Home:* 2686 West King Edward Ave., Vancouver, British Columbia, Canada V6L 1T6.

CAREER: Writer. *Member:* Writers' Union of Canada. *Awards, honors:* Arts Club top poetry award for British Columbia poetry, 1965; second prize in International Co-operation Year playwriting contest, 1965; first prize for short story for children in national Canadian Centennial contest, 1966.

WRITINGS—All juveniles: *The Dragon and the Jadestone,* Hutchinson, 1958; *The Magic of Light,* Hutchinson, 1959; *The Enchanted Egg,* Hutchinson, 1963, published as *The Magical Egg,* Lippincott, 1965; *The Spell of Chuchuchan,* Hutchinson, 1966, World Publishing, 1967; *Magic for Granny,* Burns & MacEachern, 1967; *Twin Rivers,* Burns & MacEachern, 1968; *No One Need Ever Know,* Ginn, 1971; *Brothers by Choice* (Junior Literary Guild selection), Farrar, Straus, 1974; *The Message of the Mask,* Gage Publishing, 1981; *Kirstine and the Villains,* Gage Publishing, 1982; *Race across Night,* Gage Publishing, in press. Also author of poetry for adults, and plays for children and adults.

SIDELIGHTS: Elfreida Read wrote *CA:* "In writing stories for children and poetry for adults I think I am reaching for the purest kind of writing of which I am capable. There is no room for pretentiousness or anything less than basic truth in either if they are to be successful, and I think that this effort to present experience simply and honestly in turn clarifies my own vision and gives me an occasional brief glimpse into that elusive sense of harmony we all pursue."

* * *

REED, Rex (Taylor) 1938-

PERSONAL: Born October 2, 1938, in Fort Worth, Tex.; son of J. M. (an oil company supervisor) and Jewell (Smith) Reed. *Education:* Louisiana State University, B.A., 1960. *Residence:* New York, N.Y.

CAREER: Worked variously as a jazz singer, television performer, pancake cook, record salesman, and actor, 1960-65; film critic for *Women's Wear Daily,* 1965-69, *Cosmopolitan, Status, Holiday,* beginning 1965; music critic for *Stereo Review,* 1968-75; formerly film critic for *Vogue* and *New York Daily News;* currently film critic for *Gentleman's Quarterly* and the *New York Post;* syndicated columnist for Chicago Tribune syndicate. Member of jury at Berlin, Venice, Atlanta, and U.S.A. Film Festivals; lecturer. Actor in 1970 film "Myra Breckinridge"; cameo appearance in "Superman."

WRITINGS: Do You Sleep in the Nude?, New American Library, 1968; *Conversations in the Raw,* World Publishing, 1970; *Big Screen, Little Screen,* Macmillan, 1971; *People Are Crazy Here,* Delacorte, 1974; *Valentines and Vitriol,* Delacorte, 1977; *Travolta to Keaton,* Morrow, 1979. Contributor to numerous magazines, including *Ladies Home Journal, Esquire, Harper's Bazaar, New York Times, Playboy,* and *Vogue.*

WORK IN PROGRESS: Two screenplays; a novel, *Love in Strawberry Weather.*

SIDELIGHTS: As much a celebrity as many of the entertainers he writes about, critic and journalist Rex Reed is best known for interviews that strip the glamour from Hollywood stars. His incisive writing has earned him a reputation as the "hatchet man" of show business journalism, but Reed asserts that he never goes to interviews with preconceived ideas. "I give people the benefit of the doubt, and if they hang themselves that's their problem," he told a reporter from *Newsweek.* Nonetheless, according to John Simon writing in *National Review,* "clever bitchiness" is a hallmark of Reed's style.

The only child of an oil company supervisor whose work required extensive travel, Reed grew up in a succession of small Southern towns. By the time he graduated from Natchitoches High School in Louisiana, he had attended no less than thirteen public schools. He was, as he told the *Newsweek* reporter, "always the new kid," an experience that he found traumatic: "It was a terrible thing. I withdrew from it all and went to the movies every afternoon. Now when I go to interview movie people they say, 'But when did you see that?'" In college he became a columnist, critic and editorial writer for the campus newspaper and it was there he first established the reputation for controversy that would characterize his career. After attacking segregation in an editorial entitled "The Prince of Prejudice," he was burned in effigy by the Ku Klux Klan.

From the Baton Rouge, Louisiana campus where he graduated with a degree in journalism, Reed moved to New York City. There he perfected his skills as a free-lance writer while working at a number of odd jobs. His first big break came in 1965 when two celebrity interviews he conducted were published in the *New York Times* and *New York* magazine. Since that time, both his film criticism and his interviews have been in national demand.

In 1968, some of Reed's early *New York Times, Esquire* and *Cosmopolitan* articles were compiled in a provocatively entitled best-seller, *Do You Sleep in the Nude?.* The publication was so successful that Reed has compiled his better celebrity interviews into book form ever since. Among those whom Reed has singled out for attention are Paul Newman, Jack Nicholson, Lucille Ball, Barbra Streisand, and such normally reticent stars as Walter Matthau and Geraldine Page. In fact, his reputation is so renown that "the Rex Reed treatment" has become "one of the hallmarks of success for an actor or director," according to Henry Flowers writing in the *New York Times.*

Despite the popularity of his books, many critics disparage Reed's style. "There is panic and fearful insecurity behind this frantic compulsion to mix with the famous and sniff the hem of power. But Rex sees neither the humor nor the mediocrity in a system that elevates his brand of witless ballyhoo to stardom," writes John Lahr in the *New York Times Book Review.* Of Reed's 1977 book, Lahr concludes, "*Valentines and Vitriol* is superficial even in its shallowness. Rex calls himself a 'critic,' as much a misnomer as 'sanitary engineer.'" While Flowers agrees that "Reed's is a severely limited talent," he tempers his assessment by acknowledging that "within his limitations he is excellent." And in the view of Janet Coleman, writing in *Book World,* "Reed brings a rare degree of sophistication and talent to a province of hacks and gossip hounds. He has a storyteller's eye and ear for the revealing, the ironic, the human detail."

BIOGRAPHICAL/CRITICAL SOURCES: Newsweek, January 8, 1968; *Time,* August 23, 1968; *New York Times Book Review,*

November 9, 1969, May 22, 1977; *Cleveland Press,* June 14, 1974; *National Review,* July 5, 1974; *Authors in the News,* Volume I, Gale, 1976; *Film Quarterly,* summer, 1979.

* * *

REES, Barbara (Elizabeth) 1934-

PERSONAL: Born January 9, 1934, in Worcester, England; daughter of Thomas Arthur (an engineer) and Elizabeth (Howells) Rees; married Larry Herman (a photographer), September 1, 1967 (divorced, 1978); children: Melissa Mary. *Education:* Lady Margaret Hall, Oxford, B.A. (with honors), 1956. *Home:* 2B Willes Rd., London NW5 3DS, England.

CAREER: Administrative assistant for United Nations Food and Agriculture Organization in Rome, Italy, 1963-65, and United Nations Development Program, New York, N.Y., 1965-67; University of London, Extra-Mural Department, London, England, teacher of literature, 1971-73; personal assistant, International Planned Parenthood Federation, 1981—. *Awards, honors:* Writer's grant, Arts Council of Great Britain, 1974.

WRITINGS: Try Another Country (three short novels), Harcourt, 1969; *Diminishing Circles* (novel), Secker & Warburg, 1970, Harcourt, 1971; *Prophet of the Wind* (novel), Harcourt, 1973; *George and Anna* (novel), Harper, 1976; *The Victorian Lady* (nonfiction), Gordon & Cremonesi, 1977; *Harriet Dark,* Gordon & Cremonesi, 1978, Warner Books, 1980. Also author of short stories and children's stories.

SIDELIGHTS: According to Edwin H. Kenney, Jr., in his *Nation* review of *Try Another Country,* Barbara Rees writes stories that "capture, illuminate, and preserve the lonely lives of a desperate and articulate underground [of people], cut off from, yet locked within, their social communities." In this particular collection of three short novels, for example, Rees takes as her theme the problem of "choice in a permissive age," where everything one might want to try is available, yet nothing brings satisfaction or has lasting value. As Kenney observes, "In their frenetic quest for freedom [Rees's characters] hunt down and ensnare others as well as themselves. . . . [They] fall prey to one another because each is so trapped by his own desperate needs." Thus, in Rees's eyes, "human life is everywhere the imprisoning of the self by the self."

Diminishing Circles explores a variation of this theme from the point of view of Ruth, a young, well-educated, lower-class girl who seeks to give meaning to her life through marriage to Martin, an upper-class Oxford graduate who is in turn seeking to "better" himself through marriage to a duke's daughter. In this novel, Josephine Hendin remarks in the *Saturday Review,* Rees demonstrates how "class dominates her characters' inner life and controls the workings of passion. . . . [Her] people [attempt to] change their lives and escape despair on the social ladder." For Ruth, the attempt is unsuccessful; when Martin ends their loveless relationship, abruptly destroying Ruth's fantasy of wealth and prestige, she turns to a life of alcoholism and promiscuity, unable to regard herself as anything other than the woman she aspired to be—Martin's wife.

Rees's novel *George and Anna* is also a portrait of people who hope marriage can give meaning to their lives. George and Anna, both in their thirties, both employed by the same company, and both unremarkable in appearance and demeanor, "drift into marriage, have a child, and drift apart," in the words of a *New York Times Book Review* critic. George, a timid, uncomplaining man who enjoys the comfortable confines of marriage and fatherhood, willingly adapts himself to the ever-changing moods of his wife. Anna, who is unhappy in her role of wife and mother, becomes involved with a group of leftist radicals in an attempt to give her life some purpose after George forbids her to return to work following the birth of their son.

The marriage endures despite these differences; in fact, unlike the characters in Rees's other novels, George and Anna do achieve a certain measure of satisfaction in leading separate lives. George, displaying what a *New Yorker* critic calls "a broad capacity for adjusting to all lapses in care and feeding," accepts what his wife says and does and devotes himself to his son. Anna goes about her political activities without interference from her husband and eventually becomes the leader of her political group.

Kenney compares the experience of reading these stories of lonely people to "seeing a fly in amber: one is continually struck by the incongruity of such a mean subject in such a grotesque position enclosed in sure a pure and elegant medium." Concludes the reviewer: "The moments [Rees dramatizes] are not significant or climactic in themselves; but they are the grotesque moments that painfully reveal to the flylike characters and to the reader the terrible vulnerability of our solitary and mean lives."

AVOCATIONAL INTERESTS: Italy, travel, music, the countryside.

BIOGRAPHICAL/CRITICAL SOURCES: Nation, April 14, 1969; *Observer,* September 12, 1969, August 23, 1970; *Times Literary Supplement,* August 28, 1970; *Saturday Review,* February 20, 1971; *New Yorker,* March 15, 1976; *New York Times Book Review,* April 11, 1976.

* * *

REEVES, Thomas C(harles) 1936-

PERSONAL: Born August 25, 1936, in Tacoma, Wash.; son of Clifford (a laborer) and Dorothy L. (Christ) Reeves; married Kathleen Garrison, February 1, 1958; children: Kirsten, Elizabeth, Margaret. *Education:* Pacific Lutheran University, B.A., 1958; University of Washington, Seattle, M.A., 1961; University of California, Santa Barbara, Ph.D., 1966. *Politics:* Democrat. *Home:* 5039 Cynthia Lane, Racine, Wis. 53406. *Office:* Department of History, University of Wisconsin—Parkside, Kenosha, Wis. 53141.

CAREER: Pacific Lutheran University, Tacoma, Wash., instructor in history, 1962-63; University of Colorado, Colorado Springs, assistant professor of history, 1966-70; University of Wisconsin—Parkside, Kenosha, associate professor, 1970-73, professor of history, 1973—. *Military service:* U.S. Marine Corps Reserve, 1954-58. *Awards, honors:* El Pomar Investment Co., research grant, 1968, 1970; American Philosophical Society research grant, 1970, 1975; Stephen Greene Press Award, 1971, for the best article in *Vermont History;* National Endowment for the Humanities research grant, 1976; Wisconsin Creative Writers Council award, 1976.

WRITINGS: Freedom and the Foundation: The Fund for the Republic in the Era of McCarthyism, Knopf, 1969; (editor) *Foundations under Fire,* Cornell University Press, 1970; (editor) *McCarthyism,* Dryden, 1973; (contributor) Harry J. Sievers, editor, *Six Presidents from the Empire State,* Sleepy Hollow Foundation, 1974; *Gentleman Boss: The Life of Chester Alan Arthur,* Knopf, 1975; (editor) *James De Koven, Anglican*

Saint, De Koven Foundation, 1978; *The Life and Times of Joe McCarthy: A Biography,* Stein & Day, 1982. Contributor to *Encyclopaedia Britannica* and *World Book*. Contributor of articles and book reviews to history journals.

WORK IN PROGRESS: America in the Twentieth Century: A Brief History, for Oxford University Press.

SIDELIGHTS: About *The Life and Times of Joe McCarthy: A Biography,* George E. Reedy in the *Chicago Tribune Book World* asserts: "Thomas C. Reeves has almost certainly written the definitive book on Joseph R. McCarthy. But it is not the definitive book on McCarthyism." In the *New York Times Book Review* Eric R. Goldman also applauds the book's scope, terming it "the first full-scale, intensively researched McCarthy biography." Reedy goes on to state that the book, "which can legitimately be described as masterly and exhaustive," demonstrates "meticulous" documentation. He concludes that it is "entitled to a permanent position on the shelf of any student of political history."

Bruce Cook observes in the *Washington Post Book World:* "In a number of ways, Thomas C. Reeves is the ideal biographer for McCarthy. His tenure as professor of history at the University of Wisconsin gave him ample time and opportunity to gather material on the politician's background in his native state, and this portion of the book (its first hundred-plus pages) is the most incisive and revealing of all." Agreeing with Reedy's assessment of the book's failure to treat the phenomenon of McCarthyism, Patrick Diggins comments in the *Los Angeles Times Book Review,* "Thomas Reeves' long-awaited biography deals less with the meaning of the episode than with the man himself." Diggins labels the work "lucid and scholarly" and adds a suggestion, "One wishes Reeves had concluded his otherwise excellent biography by considering the legacy of McCarthyism in American political life."

AVOCATIONAL INTERESTS: Trumpet playing, history of modern jazz, chess, the Episcopal church.

BIOGRAPHICAL/CRITICAL SOURCES: Chicago Tribune Book World, April 11, 1982; *New York Times Book Review,* April 11, 1982; *Washington Post Book World,* April 11, 1982; *Los Angeles Times Book Review,* May 30, 1982.

* * *

REINHARZ, Jehuda 1944-

PERSONAL: Born August 1, 1944, in Haifa, Palestine (now Israel); came to the United States, 1961, naturalized, 1966; son of Fred and Anita (Weigler) Reinharz; married Shulamit Rothschild (an assistant professor). *Education:* Columbia University, B.S., 1967; Jewish Theological Seminary in America, B.R.E., 1967; Harvard University, M.A., 1968; Brandeis University, Ph.D., 1972. *Office:* Department of Near Eastern and Judaic Studies, Brandeis University, Waltham, Mass. 02554.

CAREER: Hebrew College, Brookline, Mass., instructor in Jewish history, 1969-70; Brandeis University, Hiatt Institute, Jerusalem, Israel, instructor in Jewish history, autumn, 1970; University of Michigan, Ann Arbor, assistant professor, 1972-76, associate professor, 1976-80, professor of history, 1980-82, staff member of Center for Near Eastern and North African studies, 1972-82; Brandeis University, Waltham, Mass., Richard Koret Professor of Jewish History, 1982—. Instructor at Boston University, 1969-70, and Clark University, spring, 1972; visiting professor at Hiatt Institute, Brandeis University, 1973; member of Leo Baeck Institute, 1968—.

MEMBER: Association for Jewish Studies (member of board of governors, 1974-84), Leo Baeck Institute, Conference on Jewish Social Studies, World Union of Jewish Studies, American Historical Association. *Awards, honors:* Woodrow Wilson fellowship for research in Germany and Israel, 1970-71, 1973, 1975-76; American Council of Learned Societies fellowship, 1974; National Endowment for the Humanities grant, 1979-80; Leo Baeck Institute fellowship, 1982.

WRITINGS: (Contributor) Herbert A. Strauss, editor, *Conference on Intellectual Policies in American Jewry,* American Federation of Jews from Central Europe, 1972; (contributor) Geoffrey Wigoder, editor, *Zionism,* Keter Publishing House, 1973; (contributor) Michael A. Fishbane and Paul R. Flohr, editors, *Texts and Studies: Essays in Honor of Nahum N. Glatzer,* E. J. Brill, 1975; *Fatherland or Promised Land?: The Dilemma of the German Jew, 1893-1914,* University of Michigan Press, 1975.

(Co-editor) *The Jew in the Modern World,* Oxford University Press, 1980; (editor) *Dokumente zur Geschichte des deutschen Zionismus 1882-1933,* J.C.B. Morh, 1981; (co-editor) *Philosophers, Mystics and Politicians,* Duke University Press, 1982. Editor of *Letters and Papers of Chaim Weizmann,* Volume IX, Oxford University Press.

WORK IN PROGRESS: Editing and translating diaries of Franz Rosenzweig; editing a volume in honor of Alexander Altmann, with Kalman Bland and Daniel Swetschinski, for Duke University Press; editing *Passage to Modernity: A Documentary Study Guide to Modern Jewish History,* with Paul Mendes-Flohr; editing *A Documentary History of German Zionism,* for Leo Baeck Institute; editing documents on Zionism in German-speaking countries for *Documentary History of Zionism,* edited by Israel Kolatt, Michael Heymann, and Gedalia Yogev; coauthor of "From Relativism to Religious Faith: The Testimony of Franz Rosenzweig's Unpublished Diaries," to be included in *Yearbook of the Leo Baeck Institute XXII,* edited by Robert Weltsch and Arnold Paucker.

SIDELIGHTS: Jehuda Reinharz is proficient in Hebrew, German, French, Yiddish, and Aramaic.

* * *

REISS, Albert J(ohn), Jr. 1922-

PERSONAL: Born December 9, 1922, in Cascade, Wis.; son of Albert John and Erma Amanda (Schueler) Reiss; married Emma Lucille Hutto, June, 1953; children: Peter C., Paul Wetherington, Amy. *Education:* Marquette University, Ph.B., 1944; University of Chicago, M.A., 1948, Ph.D., 1949. *Home:* 45 Center Rd., Woodbridge, Conn. 06525. *Office:* Department of Sociology, Yale University, New Haven, Conn. 06520.

CAREER: Illinois Board of Public Welfare Commissioners, Springfield, social research analyst, 1946-47; University of Chicago, Chicago, Ill., instructor, 1947-49, assistant professor, 1949-52, associate director of Chicago Community Inventory, 1947-52; Vanderbilt University, Nashville, Tenn., associate professor, 1952-54, professor of sociology, 1954-58, chairman of department of sociology and anthropology, 1952-58; University of Iowa, Iowa City, professor of sociology, 1958-60, chairman of department of sociology and anthropology, 1959-60, director of Iowa Urban Community Research Center, 1958-60; University of Wisconsin—Madison, professor of sociology and director of Wisconsin Survey Research Laboratory, 1960-61; University of Michigan, Ann Arbor, professor of sociology, 1961-70, chairman of department, 1964-

70, director of Center for Research on Social Organization, 1961-70; Yale University, New Haven, Conn., professor of sociology, 1970-74, William Graham Sumner Professor of Sociology, 1974—, chairman of department, 1972-79, lecturer in law, 1970—, professor of social sciences in Institute for Social and Policy Studies, 1970—.

Member of Mental Health Small Grants Committee, National Institutes of Health, 1960-64; member of advisory panel for sociology and social psychology, National Science Foundation, 1963-65; member of behavioral sciences panel to Wooldridge Committee, Executive Office of the President, Office of Science and Technology, 1964; consultant to President's Commission on Law Enforcement and Administration of Justice, 1966-67, and National Advisory Commission on Civil Disorders, 1967-68; member, National Advisory Committee on Juvenile Justice and Delinquency Prevention, 1975-78. *Military service:* U.S. Army Air Forces, 1943-44.

MEMBER: International Society of Criminology (member of scientific commission), International Association of Chiefs of Police (associate member), American Society of Criminology (member of council, 1979-82; president-elect, 1982-83), American Sociological Association (fellow; member of council, 1962-65; member of executive committee, 1963-65), American Association for the Advancement of Science (fellow), Society for the Study of Social Problems (member of council, 1965-67; vice-president, 1966-67; president, 1969), American Statistical Association, Law and Society Association, Ohio Valley Sociological Association (president, 1966). *Awards, honors:* Bicentennial Medal, Columbia University; M.A. (privatim), Yale University, 1970; Bruce Smith, Sr. Award, Academy of Criminal Justice Sciences, 1981; Edwin H. Sutherland Award, American Society of Criminology, 1981; LL.D. (honoris causa), John Jay College of Criminal Justice of the City University of New York.

WRITINGS: (Editor) *Selected Readings in Social Pathology,* University of Chicago Bookstore, 1947; (with E. W. Burgess, Louis Wirth, and Don T. Blackiston) *Survey of the Chicago Crime Commission,* Chicago Crime Commission, 1948 .

(Editor with Paul K. Hatt) *Reader in Urban Sociology,* Free Press of Glencoe, 1951, revised edition published as *Cities and Society; A Reader in Urban Sociology,* 1957; *Patterns of Occupation Mobility for Workers in Four Cities,* Chicago Community Inventory Publications, 1953; *A Review and Evaluation of Research on the Community: A Memorandum to the Committee on Social Behavior,* Social Science Research Council, 1954; (with Jay W. Artis and Albert L. Rhodes) *Population Handbook: Nashville,* Institute of Research and Training in the Social Sciences, Vanderbilt University, 1955; (with Otis Dudley Duncan) *Social Characteristics of Urban and Rural Communities,* Wiley, 1956, reprinted, Russell, 1976; (editor with Elizabeth Wirth Marvick) *Community Life and Social Policy: Selected Papers by Louis Wirth,* University of Chicago Press, 1956; *A Socio-Psychological Study of Conforming and Deviating Behavior among Adolescents,* University of Iowa Press, 1959.

Occupations and Social Status, Free Press of Glencoe, 1961, reprinted, Arno, 1977, 2nd edition, Free Press, 1965; (editor and author of introduction) *Louis Wirth on Cities and Social Life,* University of Chicago Press, 1964; (editor and author of introduction) *Schools in a Changing Society,* Free Press, 1965; (with Rosemary Sarri and Robert Vinter) *Treating Youthful Offenders in the Community,* Correctional Research Associates, 1966; *Studies in Crime and Law Enforcement in Major Metropolitan Areas,* two volumes, U.S. Government Printing Office, 1967; (editor) *Cooley and Sociological Analysis,* University of Michigan Press, 1968; *The Police and the Public,* Yale University Press, 1971; *Methodological Studies in Crime Classification,* Yale University, 1972; (editor with Stephen E. Frenberg) *Indicators of Crime and Criminal Justice: Quantitive Studies,* Bureau of Justice Statistics, 1980; (with Albert D. Biderman) *Data Sources on White-Collar Law-Breaking,* National Institute of Justice, 1981.

Contributor: R. M. Fisher, editor, *The Metropolis in Modern Life,* Doubleday, 1955; *Juvenile Delinquency and Education,* U.S. Government Printing Office, 1956; Hans Zetterberg, editor, *Sociology in the United States of America,* UNESCO, 1956; William Dobriner, editor, *The Suburban Community,* Putnam, 1958; Hendrick M. Ruitenbeck, *The Problem of Homosexuality in Modern Society,* Dutton, 1963; Ruth S. Caven, editor, *Readings in Juvenile Delinquency,* Lippincott, 1964; Howard S. Becker, editor, *The Other Side: Perspectives on Deviance,* Free Press of Glencoe, 1964; Rose Giallombardo, editor, *Juvenile Delinquency,* Wiley, 1966; David J. Burdua, editor, *The Police: Six Sociological Essays,* Wiley, 1967; John Gagnon and William Simon, editors, *Sexual Deviance,* Harper, 1967; Howard S. Becker and others, editors, *Institutions and the Person,* Aldine, 1968.

Barbara McLennan, editor, *Crime in Urban Society,* Dunellen, 1970; Herbert Costner, editor, *Sociological Methodology,* Jossey-Bass, 1971; Angus Campbell and Philip Converse, editors, *The Human Meaning of Social Change,* Russell Sage, 1972; Daniel Glaser, editor, *Handbook of Criminology,* Rand McNally, 1974; N. J. Demerath III and others, editors, *Social Policy and Sociology,* Academic Press, 1975; A. Wallace Sinarko and L. Broedburg, editors, *Perspectives on Attitude Assessment: Surveys and Their Alternatives,* Smithsonian Institution Press, 1975; Malcolm W. Klein and Katherine S. Teilman, editors, *Handbook of Criminal Justice Evaluation,* Sage Publications, 1980; *Reflections of America: Commemorating the Statistical Abstract Centennial,* U.S. Bureau of the Census, 1980. Also contributor to *Die Psychologie des 20. Jahrhunderts,* Volume XIV.

Author or editor of various other survey reports. Editor, "Arnold and Caroline Rose Monograph" series, American Sociological Association, 1968-71. Contributor to *The Municipal Yearbook,* 1957, *Britannica Book of the Year,* 1959, *Encyclopaedia Britannica,* 1959, *A Dictionary of the Social Sciences,* Free Press of Glencoe, 1964, *Worterbuch der Soziologie,* 1965, *The New Catholic Encyclopedia,* 1967, and to sociology, law, and education journals. Book review editor, *Journal of Marriage and Family Living,* 1949-52; associate editor, *American Journal of Sociology,* 1950-52 and 1961-64, *Social Problems,* 1961-64, and *Social Forces,* 1974-77; sociology editor, *Encyclopedia of Social Sciences,* 1961-67.

* * *

RENFROE, Martha Kay 1938-
(M. K. Wren)

PERSONAL: Born June 5, 1938, in Amarillo, Tex.; daughter of Charles Albert (a geologist) and Katharyn (Miller) Renfroe. *Education:* Attended Amarillo Junior College, 1955, and Oklahoma City University, 1956; University of Oklahoma, B.F.A., 1961; additional study at Kansas City Art Institute, 1962, and University of Washington, Seattle, 1963. *Residence:* Otis, Ore.

CAREER: Hallmark Cards, Inc., Kansas City, Mo., designer, 1961-62; Cascade Artists Gallery, Lincoln City, Ore., permanent exhibitor, 1964-78; novelist. *Member:* Authors Guild, Mystery Writers of America, Science Fiction Writers of America, Portland Art Museum, Willamette Writers.

WRITINGS—All under pseudonym M. K. Wren; mystery novels, except as indicated; published by Doubleday, except as indicated: *Curiosity Didn't Kill the Cat,* 1973; *A Multitude of Sins,* 1975; *Oh, Bury Me Not,* 1976; *Nothing's Certain but Death,* 1978; *Seasons of Death,* 1981; *The Phoenix Legacy* (science fiction trilogy), Berkley Publishing, 1981, Volume I: *Sword of the Lamb,* Volume II: *Shadow of the Swan,* Volume III: *House of the Wolf.*

WORK IN PROGRESS: A mystery novel, *Wake Up, Darlin' Corey.*

SIDELIGHTS: Martha Kay Renfroe writes that she is "an artist for whom writing was a sideline that got out of hand. Began studying painting at age ten, bachelor's degree in fine arts with major in sculpture (too expensive to pursue outside an institution) and painting, by which I still make part of my living. Interest in writing paralleled art, beginning about twelve." Her work has been exhibited at museums and galleries and is included in private collections in Kansas, Missouri, Oklahoma, Texas, Oregon, and Washington.

BIOGRAPHICAL/CRITICAL SOURCES: New Republic, January 27, 1982.

* * *

REYNOLDS, Dallas McCord 1917-
(Mack Reynolds; pseudonyms: Clark Collins, Mark Mallory, Guy McCord, Dallas Ross)

PERSONAL: Born November 11, 1917, in Corcoran, Calif.; son of Verne LaRue and Pauline (McCord) Reynolds; married Helen Jeanette Wooley, September, 1947; children: Emil, LaVerne Reynolds Land, Dallas Mack. *Education:* Attended public schools in Kingston, N.Y. *Politics:* Socialist. *Religion:* Agnostic. *Residence:* San Miguel de Allende, Mexico. *Agent:* Scott Meredith Literary Agency, Inc., 845 Third Ave., New York, N.Y. 10022.

CAREER: Catskill Mountain Star and *Oneonta News,* Oneonta, N.Y., editor, 1937-40; supervisor, California Shipbuilding Corp., San Pedro, and International Business Machine, 1941-44; Socialist Labor Party, New York, N.Y., national organizer and lecturer, 1946-49; free-lance writer, 1946—. Campaigner for Socialist Labor Party in four presidential campaigns. *Wartime service:* U.S. Army Transportation Corps, 1944-46; attended Marine Officer's Cadet School; became navigator in South Pacific with rank equivalent to captain. *Member:* Science Fiction Writers of America.

WRITINGS—Under name Mack Reynolds: *The Case of the Little Green Men,* Phoenix, 1951; (editor with Fredric Brown) *Science-Fiction Carnival: Fun in Science Fiction,* Shasta, 1953; *Episode on the Riviera,* Monarch, 1961; *This Time We Love,* Monarch, 1961; *A Kiss before Loving,* Monarch, 1962; *The Kept Woman,* Monarch, 1963; *The Earth War,* Pyramid Books, 1963; *The Expatriates,* Regency, 1963; *The Jet Set,* Monarch, 1964; *Sweet Dreams, Sweet Princes,* New English Library, 1965, published as *Time Gladiator,* Lancer Books, 1969; *United Planets,* Ace Books, 1965; *Planetary Agent X* (bound with *Behold the Stars* by Kenneth Bulmer), Ace Books, 1965.

Dawnman Planet (also see below; bound with *Space Captain* by William Fitzgerald Jenkins), Ace Books, 1966; *Space Pioneer,* Four Square, 1966; *Of Godlike Power,* Belmont Books, 1966, published as *Earth Unaware,* 1968; *After Some Tomorrow,* Belmont Books, 1967; *The Rival Rigelians* (bound with *Nebula Alert* by A. B. Chandler), Ace Books, 1967; *Computer War,* Ace Books, 1967; *Mercenary from Tomorrow* (also see below; bound with *The Key to Venudine* by Bulmer), Ace Books, 1968; *Star Trek: Mission to Horatius,* Whitman Publishing, 1968; *Code Duello* (bound with *The Age of Ruin* by John M. Faucette), Ace Books, 1968; *The Cosmic Eye,* Belmont Books, 1969; *Puerto Rican Patriot: The Life of Luis Munoz Rivera,* Crowell-Collier, 1969; *The Five Way Secret Agent* (bound with *Mercenary from Tomorrow*), Ace Books, 1969; *The Space Barbarians,* Ace Books, 1969.

Computer World, Curtis Books, 1970; *Once Departed,* Curtis Books, 1970; *Blackman's Burden* [and] *Border, Breed, Nor Birth,* Ace Books, 1972; *Looking Backward, from the Year 2000,* Ace Books, 1973; *Depression or Bust* (bound with *Dawnman Planet*), Ace Books, 1974; *Commune 2000 A.D.,* Bantam, 1974; *Amazon Planet,* Ace Books, 1975; *Tomorrow Might Be Different,* Ace Books, 1975; *The Towers of Utopia,* Bantam, 1975; *Ability Quotient,* Ace Books, 1975; *Satellite City,* Ace Books, 1975.

The Best of Mack Reynolds, Pocket Books, 1976; *Section G: United Planets,* Ace Books, 1976; *Rolltown,* Ace Books, 1976; *Galactic Medal of Honor,* Ace Books, 1976; *Police Patrol: 2000 A.D.,* Ace Books, 1977; *Equality in the Year 2000,* Ace Books, 1977; *Space Visitor,* Ace Books, 1977; *After Utopia,* Ace Books, 1977; *Perchance to Dream,* Ace Books, 1977; *The Best Ye Breed,* Ace Books, 1978; *Brain World,* Nordon, 1978; *The Fracas Factor,* Nordon, 1978; *Trample an Empire Down,* Nordon, 1978; *Lagrange Five,* Bantam, 1979.

Also author of *Night Is for Monsters, Speakeasy, The House in the Kasbah,* and *The Home of the Inquisitor.* Contributor of several hundred stories and articles to science fiction and travel magazines, occasionally under a pseudonym. Foreign editor, *Rogue,* 1955-65.

SIDELIGHTS: Unlike those science-fiction writers who make technology the focus of their work, Mack Reynolds reports that most of his stories and novels consist of "extrapolations in the social sciences"—namely, ethnology, archeology, and socio-economics. Combining observations made during years of traveling throughout the world with insights gained from his study of political, social, and cultural history, "Reynolds has been able to give local color and authenticity to stories that move freely and convincingly in time and space," according to *Dictionary of Literary Biography* critic Anthony Manousos. "His colorful cast of characters often has an international flavor, and Reynolds is superb at animating dialogue through dialect. In his extrapolations of future societies he can be bitingly satiric as well as realistic: he has made the year 2000 his specialty and takes pains to make his future scenarios credible."

Typical targets of Reynolds's scorn are those in positions of power who exploit so-called "lesser breeds" economically, culturally, or politically. Offering his readers a view of "what the world would be like if technocrats, anarchists, socialists, fascists, or other utopian groups were to gain control," the author devises plots whose "twists and intrigues . . . recall the mystery and detective genres with which he began his career," declares Manousos. Thus, satire, political intrigue, and futuristic speculation form the basis of much of Reynolds's fiction.

In Manousos's opinion, Reynolds has not yet written a novel or story of "outstanding or enduring quality." Nevertheless, the critic is quick to point out, "at their best, his works are well crafted, entertaining, and provocative. . . . Reynolds [has proven to be] a penetrating as well as popular social-science-fiction writer who is able to create a cast of memorable characters and plunge them into futuristic scenarios that are both complex and credible. . . . [His works] bear his unmistakable personal stamp."

BIOGRAPHICAL/CRITICAL SOURCES: (Under name Mack Reynolds) *Dictionary of Literary Biography,* Volume VIII: *Twentieth-Century American Science-Fiction Writers,* Gale, 1981.†

* * *

REYNOLDS, David K(ent) 1940-

PERSONAL: Born September 28, 1940, in Dayton, Ohio; son of Charles K. (a security guard) and Marguerite (a secretary; maiden name, Worrell) Reynolds. *Education:* University of California, Los Angeles, B.A., 1964, M.A., 1965, Ph.D., 1969. *Office:* ToDo Institute, 2121 West Ninth St., Suite 317, Los Angeles, Calif. 90006.

CAREER: University of California, Los Angeles, assistant professor of public health, 1970-71; University of Southern California, School of Medicine, Los Angeles, assistant professor of human behavior, 1974-79; University of Houston, Houston, Tex., visiting associate professor, 1979-80; ToDo Institute, Los Angeles, Calif., director, 1980—. Research anthropologist, Veterans Administration Central Research Unit, 1969-75; chief of Behavioral Analysis Division, Deputy Coroner's Branch, Los Angeles County Coroner's Office, 1971-73. *Military service:* U.S. Navy, radioman, 1958-61; served in Pacific Fleet.

MEMBER: American Anthropological Association, American Association of Suicidology, Society for Medical Anthropology, Sigma Xi. *Awards, honors:* Recipient of grants from National Science Foundation, 1967, Japanese NIMH, 1967 and 1968, NDEA, 1967, National Institute of Mental Health, 1972, 1973, and 1975-78, and Tokyo Metropolitan Institute of Gerontology, 1979; Fulbright fellow in Japan, 1973 and 1978.

WRITINGS: Morita Psychotherapy, University of California Press, 1976; (with Norman L. Farberow) *Suicide: Inside and Out,* University of California Press, 1976; (with Richard A. Kalish) *Death and Ethnicity: A Psychocultural Study,* University of Southern California Press, 1976; (with Farberow) *Endangered Hope: Experiences in Psychiatric Aftercare Facilities,* University of California Press, 1977.

The Quiet Therapies: Japanese Pathways to Personal Growth, University Press of Hawaii, 1980; *The Heart of the Japanese People,* Nichieisha Publishers (Tokyo), 1980; (with Farberow) *The Family Shadow: Sources of Suicide and Schizophrenia,* University of California Press, 1981; *Naikan Psychotherapies,* University of Chicago Press, 1983.

Contributor of articles to professional journals, including *International Journal of Social Psychiatry, American Journal of Psychiatry, Journal of Abnormal Psychology, Hospital and Community Psychiatry, Life Threatening Behavior,* and *Journal of Gerontology.*

WORK IN PROGRESS: A Manual for Constructive Living, for University Press of Hawaii; *Situation and Self; Worth Another Look: Eastern Approaches to Christianity; Playing Ball on Running Water: Living Morita Therapy.*

SIDELIGHTS: David K. Reynolds told *CA:* "I see man as much more rational (although not necessarily with awareness), flexible, and situationally responsive than he appears to be in many personality texts. On the mental hospital wards where I have done research this perspective of human nature more closely approximates that which is implicitly held by the nursing assistants rather than that held by the psychiatrists. I think this is because the nursing assistants' perspective is grounded firmly in continuous observation of everyday human behavior.

"My research has been both stimulating and personally rewarding. It has had practical impact on the individuals and institutions that opened themselves to study, and it can be said to have theoretical significance, as well. Although I enjoy the spontaneity and feedback of teaching (and my students seem to, as well), I find teaching most fruitful when sustained by ongoing research interests and activities."

One of Reynolds's main areas of interest and activity is Morita Therapy, a form of psychiatric treatment calling for the patient's total isolation from all interpersonal relations. The patient undergoing Morita Therapy as it is practiced in Japan, the country of its origin, usually is isolated in a single-person hospital room and allowed no contact with other human beings for at least a week. The theory behind this treatment, reports Kenneth Rexroth in a *Los Angeles Times* review of Reynolds's book *The Quiet Therapies: Japanese Pathways to Personal Growth,* is that "most patients, in fact most normal people, become so starved for human contact they tend to fall in love with the first of their captors they see. . . . The patient slowly is reintroduced to a wider range of social contact. . . . The emerging creature is supposed to move along the course of 'therapy' in wonder at the joys of interpersonal relations." Reynolds recommends its use with neurotics and even psychotics, but Rexroth disagrees, concluding: "There is no hint in [this] book that the interpersonal community itself may be sick. . . . [Morita Therapy] certainly makes Japanese squares squarer, but in the course of time its effects wear off."

BIOGRAPHICAL/CRITICAL SOURCES: Washington Post Book World, October 3, 1976; *Los Angeles Times,* September 25, 1980.

* * *

REYNOLDS, Mack
See REYNOLDS, Dallas McCord

* * *

REYNOLDS, Michael Shane 1937-

PERSONAL: Born April 1, 1937, in Kansas City, Mo.; son of Raymond (a geologist) and Theresa (Donnici) Reynolds; married Ann Eubanks, December 30, 1960; children: Dierdre Alisoun, Shauna Iseult. *Education:* Rice University, B.A., 1959; University of North Carolina, M.A., 1960; Duke University, Ph.D., 1970. *Home:* 909 Vance St., Raleigh, N.C. 27608. *Office:* Department of English, North Carolina State University, Raleigh, N.C. 27650.

CAREER: North Carolina State University at Raleigh, instructor, 1965-71, assistant professor, 1971-73, associate professor, 1974-78, professor of English, 1978—. Visiting professor, College of William and Mary, 1978-79. Member of executive board, Theatre in the Park, 1972-75, and Raleigh Little Theatre, 1973-75. *Military service:* U.S. Navy, 1961-65; became lieutenant. *Member:* Modern Language Association of America, Hemingway Society. *Awards, honors:* National Endowment for the Humanities grants, 1974, 1975, and 1981; Primo Vallimbrosa award, 1979.

WRITINGS: Hemingway's First War: The Making of A Farewell to Arms, Princeton University Press, 1976; *Hemingway's Reading: 1910-1940,* Princeton University Press, 1981; *Critical Essays on Hemingway's In Our Time,* G. K. Hall, 1983. Contributor of poetry to *Southern Poetry Review, Georgia Review, Poet Lore,* and *Carolina Quarterly;* contributor of essays to *American Literature, PMLA, Studies in Short Fiction,* and *Hemingway Review.* Member of editorial board, *Hemingway Review,* 1981—.

WORK IN PROGRESS: A literary biography of Hemingway's early years, completion expected in 1984.

SIDELIGHTS: Michael Shane Reynolds told *CA* that important events in his life included "growing up the son of a geologist, who taught me how to see; flunking calculus in 1956, which insured that I would not become an engineer; VA-215 and the flight deck of the *U.S.S. Hancock,* where I first saw courage and more raw fear; the Democratic convention of 1968 and the Vietnam war, which broke my conservative mold. Important people: George Bireline and Hal Hopfenberg, who have kept me honest; my daughters, who set me free. A slow learner, I have finally discovered what I should have known twenty years ago: all writing is fiction—history, biography, the novel—all fiction, all imaginary order. Now I must begin to write as if this were true."

* * *

RHOADES, Jonathan
See OLSEN, John Edward

* * *

RHYMER, Joseph 1927-

PERSONAL: Born September 23, 1927, in Birmingham, England; son of Frank Joseph (a printer) and Kate Rose (Slater) Rhymer. *Education:* University of Leeds, B.A. (with honors in philosophy), 1952; University of Edinburgh, M.Th., 1975. *Home:* 13/1 Whistlefield Ct., 2 Canniesburn Rd., Bearsden, Glasgow, G61 1PX, Scotland. *Agent:* David Bolt, Bolt & Watson Ltd., Cedar House, High St., Ripley, Surrey GU23 6AE, England. *Office:* St. Andrew's College, Bearsden, Glasgow, Scotland.

CAREER: Community of the Resurrection, Mirfield, England, member, 1952-63, ordained Anglican priest, 1956; left Anglican order and was received into Catholic Church, 1963. Codrington College, Barbados, West Indies, vice-principal, 1957-63; Moor Park School, Ludlow, Shropshire, England, deputy headmaster, 1964-66; Christ's College, Liverpool, England, senior lecturer in theology, 1966-68; Notre Dame College, Liverpool, senior lecturer in theology, 1968-75; St. Andrew's College, Bearsden, Glasgow, Scotland, lecturer in religious education, 1975—. Member of religious studies board, Council for National Academic Awards, 1978; secretary of religious studies panel, Scottish Examination Board, 1982. Editorial consultant, Darton, Longman & Todd Ltd. *Military service:* Royal Navy, 1945-48. *Member:* Aristotelian Society, Society for Old Testament Study.

WRITINGS: Way through the Old Testament, Sheed, Volume III: *The Prophets and the Law,* 1964, Volume I: *The Beginnings of a People,* 1966, Volume II: *The Covenant and the Kingdom,* 1968, Volume IV: *The Babylonian Experience,* 1971, Volume V: *The People of the Messiah,* 1972; *The Good News: St. Mark's Insight,* Darton, Longman & Todd, 1965; (editor) H. Gaubert, *The Bible in History,* six volumes, Darton, Longman & Todd, 1968-72; *The Old Testament,* Darton, Longman & Todd, 1969.

(Editor) *The Christian Priesthood,* Darton, Longman & Todd, 1970; (with A. Bullan) *Companion to the Good News,* Collins, 1971; (editor) *The Bible Is for All,* Collins, 1973; *Good News in Romans,* Collins, 1974; *The Bible in Order,* Darton, Longman & Todd, 1975, Doubleday, 1976; *Companion to the Good News Old Testament,* Collins, 1976.

The Good News Bible, Catholic edition, American Bible Society, 1982; *Atlas of the Biblical World,* Greenwich House, 1982.

Contributor: L. Bright, editor, *The People of God,* Sheed, 1965; Bright, editor, *Theology in Modern Education,* Darton, Longman & Todd, 1965; Bright and S. Clements, editors, *The Committed Church,* Darton, Longman & Todd, 1966; Bright, editor, *Prophets,* Sheed, 1971.

WORK IN PROGRESS: Research in the sociology of religious education.

* * *

RICH, Elaine Sommers 1926-

PERSONAL: Born February 8, 1926, in Plevna, Ind.; daughter of Monroe and Effie (Horner) Sommers; married Ronald L. Rich (a chemistry professor), June 14, 1953; children: Jonathan, Andrew, Miriam, Mark. *Education:* Goshen College, B.A., 1947; Michigan State University, M.A., 1950. *Religion:* Mennonite. *Home:* 112 South Spring St., Bluffton, Ohio 45817.

CAREER: Goshen College, Goshen, Ind., instructor in speech and English, 1947-49, 1950-53; Bethel College, North Newton, Kan., instructor in speech, 1953-66; International Christian University, Tokyo, Japan, lecturer, 1971-78; Bluffton College, Bluffton, Ohio, advisor to international students, 1979—. *Member:* National Association for Foreign Student Affairs.

WRITINGS: (Editor) *Breaking Bread Together,* Herald, 1958; *Hannah Elizabeth,* Harper, 1964; (contributor) J. C. Wenger, editor, *They Met God,* Herald, 1964; (contributor) Helen Alderfer, editor, *A Farthing in Her Hand,* Herald, 1964; (contributor) Lisa Sergio, editor, *Prayers of Women,* Harper, 1965; *Tomorrow, Tomorrow, Tomorrow,* Herald, 1966; *Am I This Countryside?* (poems), Pinchpenny Press, 1981; *Mennonite Women, 1683-1983: A Story of God's Faithfulness,* Herald, 1983. Also author of *The Bridge Love Built* and of an unpublished play about Bertha Von Suttner, "Tough Dove." Author of fortnightly column, "Thinking with . . . ," in *Mennonite Weekly Review,* 1973—. Contributor to *Poet, Japan Christian Quarterly,* and other periodicals.

SIDELIGHTS: Elaine Sommers Rich comments on her writing: "C. S. Lewis once said that some of the books he wanted to read did not exist. Therefore he had to write them. I feel that way about my own writing.

"I believe that Jesus Christ is Lord of history. He works in a wonder-inspiring way. (The Pennsylvania Dutch have a saying, 'It wonders me.') Some tremendous things that happen, happen quietly without making big headlines in the world's newspapers. That's exciting to me. Inner growth is exciting. Genuine goodness is exciting, and I'd rather try to portray growth and goodness than to try to write about 'cops 'n robbers and military victories.' *Hannah Elizabeth* tells of how a girl came to glimpse deeply the meaning of her own faith. *Tomorrow, Tomorrow,*

Tomorrow shows a tiny seed of love that grew into a tree, improved treatment of the mentally ill. *The Bridge Love Built,* unfortunately never published, tells about a boy who came to understand that he belonged to two cultures, not just one, as most people do.''

Rich later told *CA:* ''For twenty years I had the privilege of living intimately with our own four children and their many friends, who were in and out of our home in North Newton, Kansas, and on the campus of the International Christian University in Tokyo. I have great respect for the intellect and spiritual sensitivity of these children and of my adult readers.

''I also have great hope for the future. Human beings can learn to use nuclear energy constructively rather than destructively. We could well be on the threshold of a great time in history, a time of worldwide peace when every human being has the good things of life, from food and music to the rights enumerated in the *Universal Declaration of Human Rights.* I hope these values come through in what I write.''

* * *

RICHARDSON, Don(ald MacNaughton) 1935-

PERSONAL: Born June 23, 1935, in Prince Edward Island, Canada; son of Henry George and Harriet Ruth Richardson; married Carol Joy Soderstrom (a registered nurse), August 20, 1960; children: Stephen Laird, Shannon Douglas, Paul Andrew, Valerie Ruth. *Education:* Prairie Bible Institute, diploma, 1957; attended University of Washington, Seattle, summer, 1961. *Home:* 1612 North Hill Ave., Pasadena, Calif. 91104. *Office:* Tribalism Institute, c/o U.S. Center for World Mission, 1605 East Elizabeth St., Pasadena, Calif. 91104; and Regions Beyond Missionary Union, 8102 Elberon Ave., Philadelphia, Pa. 19111.

CAREER: Pastor in Langford, British Columbia, 1957-60; Regions Beyond Missionary Union, Philadelphia, Pa., Protestant missionary, 1960—; U.S. Center for World Mission, Tribalism Institute, Pasadena, Calif., director, 1978—. Lecturer in folk religions, anthropology, theology, and the Stone Age cultures of Irian Jaya, including methods of cross-cultural communication with them.

WRITINGS: A Short Biography of Henry Martyn, privately printed, 1957; *A Dictionary of the Sawi Language,* privately printed, 1974; *The New Testament in Sawi,* privately printed, 1974; *Peace Child,* Regal Books (Glendale, Calif.), 1974; *Lords of the Earth,* Regal Books, 1977; *Eternity in Their Hearts,* Regal Books, 1981; (with Hank Paulsen) *Beyond the Wall,* Regal Books, 1982. Contributor to *Reader's Digest.*

WORK IN PROGRESS: The Seven Thunders of Truth; From Here to Antiquity, a sequel to *Eternity in Their Hearts; Promise Theology.*

SIDELIGHTS: Don Richardson writes: ''My fascination is with the diversity of human cultures, and particularly with solutions to problems of cross-cultural communication. I am especially intrigued by 'redemptive analogies'—elements of pagan cultures which seem to anticipate Christian truth, and if appropriated, facilitate its entrance. On a larger scale, I am fascinated by the way Christian truth, pagan religions, and modern man's scientific discoveries anticipate the existence of a philosophical unified field. I believe I have discovered that unified field. That is what *The Seven Thunders of Truth* is about.''

Following a major earthquake in late summer, 1976, in Irian Jaya, the former Dutch New Guinea, unsympathetic criticism by the press of missionary activity prompted Richardson to write an open letter to the *Washington Post.* Observed the missionary: ''There were other reasons why the missionaries had to go in as soon as they could. History has taught them that even the most isolated minority cultures must eventually be overwhelmed by the commercial and political expansion of majority peoples. Naive academics . . . may protest that the world's remaining miners, hunters, military leaders, roadbuilders, art collectors, tourists, and drug peddlers aren't listening. They are going in anyway. Often to destroy. Cheat. Exploit. Victimize. Corrupt. Taking, and giving little other than diseases for which primitives have no immunity. And no medical help. That is why, since the turn of the century, more than ninety tribes have become extinct in Brazil alone. Many other Latin American, African, and Asian countries also show a similar high extinction rate for their primitive minorities. Primitives are, in fact, vanishing more quickly than the world's endangered animal species. A grim toll of five or six tribes per year is probably a conservative worldwide estimate.

''We missionaries don't want the same fate to befall these magnificent tribes in Irian Jaya. So we risk our lives to get to them first. Because we believe we are more sympathetic agents of change than profit-hungry commercialists. Like our predecessor John Sargent, who in 1796 launched a program which saved the Mohican tribe from extinction, and like our colleagues in Brazil who saved the WaiWai from a similar fate just one generation ago, we believe we know how to precondition tribes in Irian Jaya for survival in the modern world.

''The question 'Should anyone go in?' is obsolete, because obviously someone *will.* It has been replaced by a more practical question: 'Will the most sympathetic persons get there first?' To make the shock of coming out of the Stone Age as easy as possible. To see that tribals gain new ideals to replace those they must lose in order to survive. To teach them the national language so they can defend themselves in civil disputes with 'civilizados.' And yet produce literature in their own language so it will not be forgotten. To teach them the value of money, so that unscrupulous traders cannot easily cheat them. And better yet, set some of them up in business, so that commerce in their areas will not fall entirely into the hands of outsiders. To care for them when epidemics sweep through, or when earthquakes strike. And better yet, train some of them as nurses and doctors to carry on when we are gone.

''We do not go in as parasites. We go in as paracletes. Ombudsmen who help clashing cultures understand each other. Advocates, not only of spiritual truth, but also of physical survival.''

MEDIA ADAPTATIONS: A film version of *Peace Child* is distributed worldwide by Gospel Films. Don Richardson assisted in the script preparation and direction and also performed in the film.

BIOGRAPHICAL/CRITICAL SOURCES: Christian Herald, March, 1976; *Washington Post,* August 3, 1976.

* * *

RICHARDSON, (Stewart) Lee (Jr.) 1940-

PERSONAL: Born July 8, 1940, in Washington, D.C.; son of Stewart Lee (an auditor) and Margaret (Strachan) Richardson; married Maureen Flannigan, January 14, 1981; children: (previous marriage) Lee-Ellen, Stewart III, Lauren, Tiffany Leigh. *Education:* University of Richmond, B.S. in B.A., 1962; Emory University, M.B.A., 1963; University of Colorado, D.B.A.,

1966. *Religion:* Southern Baptist. *Home:* 5651 Lightspun Lane, Columbia, Md. 21045. *Mailing address:* P.O. Box 1106, Columbia, Md. 21044. *Office:* Department of Marketing, University of Baltimore, Charles at Mount Royal, Baltimore, Md. 21201.

CAREER: Louisiana State University, Baton Rouge, beginning 1966, began as assistant professor, became professor of marketing, chairman of department, beginning 1975; University of Baltimore, Baltimore, Md., professor of marketing and Martin Marietta Eminent Scholar, 1982—. Visiting professor, Southern University, 1968-72, University of Pennsylvania, and University of Maryland. Office of Consumer Affairs, U.S. Department of Health, Education, and Welfare, director of consumer education and finance, 1972-74, acting director and director of consumer programs, 1977-79; director of consumer education and finance, Federal Energy Administration, 1974; member of telephone industry advisory group, Federal Communications Commission. Consumer Federation of America, president, 1976-77, currently vice-president; president, Maryland Citizens Consumer Council; chairman of Baltimore area consumer advisory council, C & P Telephone; chairman of consumer affairs advisory board, Howard County, Md. Publisher, "Lee Richardson Letter," 1979—. Consultant to government agencies, consumer organizations, and industry; utility rate expert witness. *Member:* American Marketing Association, Beta Gamma Sigma, Sigma Iota Epsilon.

WRITINGS: (Editor with H. A. Wolf) *Readings in Finance,* Appleton, 1966; (editor with P. R. Cateora) *Readings in Marketing: The Qualitative and Quantitative Areas,* Appleton, 1967; (editor) *Dimensions of Communication,* Appleton, 1969.

(With S. Brown) *Problems of Low Income Consumers,* Louisiana State University, 1973; (contributor) M. Unger and Wolf, editors, *Personal Finance,* 3rd edition, Allyn & Bacon, 1974, 6th edition, 1981; (contributor) *1973 Yearbook of Agriculture,* U.S. Department of Agriculture, 1974; (contributor) P. Sethi, editor, *The Unstable Ground,* Melville Publishing, 1974; (contributor) T. Garman and S. Eckert, editors, *The Consumer's World,* McGraw, 1974; (editor with Norman Kangun) *Consumerism,* American Marketing Association, 1978. Contributor of articles to national publications.

WORK IN PROGRESS: Research on consumerism and U.S. telecommunications policy.

* * *

RICKEY, Don, Jr. 1925-

PERSONAL: Born August 3, 1925, in Chicago, Ill.; son of Don Gladstone and Judith (Sandven) Rickey; married Jean Merriell, January 29, 1949 (divorced December 2, 1964); children: Janet, William, Alec. *Education:* Attended Northern Montana College, 1946-47; University of Kentucky, B.A., 1950; Oklahoma Agricultural and Mechanical College (now Oklahoma State University), M.A., 1951; University of Oklahoma, Ph.D., 1960. *Home:* 29190 Buchanan Dr., Evergreen, Colo. 80439.

CAREER: University of Oklahoma, Norman, librarian and historian of Phillips Collection (Indian and western history), 1953-55; U.S. National Park Service, Custer Battlefield National Monument, Crow Agency, Mont., historian, 1955-60; Jefferson National Expansion Memorial, St. Louis, Mo., chief research historian, 1960-63; U.S. National Park Service, historical master planner for midwest region in Omaha, Neb., 1963-66, and western history research team chief for Division of History in Washington, D.C., 1966-68; Army War College, Carlisle Barracks, Pa., assistant director of U.S. Army military history research collection, 1968-72, member of faculty, 1970-72; U.S. Bureau of Land Management, Denver, Colo., historian, 1972-79; historical researcher, interpretive planner, and consultant, 1979—. Member of advisory committee, Resources Development Internship Program, Western Interstate Commission for Higher Education; vice-chairman, Dominguez-Escalante State/Federal Bicentennial Committee. *Military service:* U.S. Navy, 1943-46 and 1951. *Member:* Western History Association (founding member), Company of Military Historians (fellow), Jefferson County Historical Association, Custer Battlefield Historical and Museum Association (executive secretary, 1956-60), Ft. Laramie Historical Association.

WRITINGS: Forty Miles a Day on Beans and Hay: The Enlisted Soldier Fighting the Indian Wars, University of Oklahoma Press, 1963; (editor with B. F. Cooling III) *Essays in Some Dimensions of Military History,* U.S. Army Military Research Collection, Army War College, 1972; *Ten Dollar Horse, Forty Dollar Saddle: Cowboy Clothing, Arms, Tools, and Horse Gear of the 1880s,* Old Army Press, 1976.

Contributor: M. S. Kennedy, editor, *The Redman's West,* Hastings House, 1965; *Troopers West,* Frontier Heritage Press, 1970; David C. Skaggs, editor, *The Old Northwest in the American Revolution: A Bicentennial Anthology,* State Historical Society of Wisconsin, 1977.

Also author of booklets for the U.S. National Park Service and the Custer Battlefield Historical and Museum Association; editor of song "The Regular Army O!" from original words and music of 1874. Consultant, *The Soldiers,* Time-Life, 1973. Contributor of articles and reviews to historical and military journals.

BIOGRAPHICAL/CRITICAL SOURCES: Omaha World-Herald, May 7, 1963.

* * *

RIEFE, Alan 1925-
(J. D. Hardin, Barbara Riefe; Jake Logan, a house pseudonym)

PERSONAL: Born May 18, 1925, in Waterbury, Conn.; son of B.H.C. (a businessman) and Beatrice (Wise) Riefe; married Martha Daggett, June 10, 1948 (died May 16, 1949); married Barbara Dube, February 9, 1955; children: Martha, Leslie, Sidney, Jordan. *Education:* Colby College, B.A., 1950. *Residence:* Greenwich, Conn. (summer); and Honolulu, Hawaii (winter). *Agent:* Knox Burger Associates Ltd., 39½ Washington Sq. S., New York, N.Y. 10012.

CAREER: Free-lance writer. Wrote twenty-seven network television programs, 1951-65, including "Pulitzer Prize Playhouse," for American Broadcasting Co., "Studio One," for Columbia Broadcasting System, eight years as sole writer of "Masquerade Party," and over two years as chief writer of "Keep Talking." *Military service:* U.S. Army, World War II; served in European theater of operations; received three battle stars. *Member:* Screen Writers Guild, American Civil Liberties Union, National Association for the Advancement of Colored People (member of executive board, Greenwich branch).

WRITINGS: Tales of Horror, Pocket Books, 1965; *Manual for Woman Drivers,* Fawcett, 1966; *I Am Your President* (satire), Curtis Books, 1972; (editor with Dick Harrington) *Sanford and Son,* Curtis Books, 1973.

"Cage" series; all published by Popular Library in 1975: *The Lady Killers; The Conspirators; The Black Widower; The Silver Puma; The Bullet-Proof Man; The Killer with the Golden Touch.*

"Tyger" series; all published by Popular Library in 1976: *Tyger at Bay; Tyger by the Tail; The Smile on the Face of the Tyger; Tyger and the Lady; Hold That Tyger; Tyger, Tyger, Burning Out.*

Western novels; under pseudonym J. D. Hardin; all published by Playboy Press: *The Slick and the Dead,* 1979; *Blood, Sweat and Gold,* 1979; *The Good, the Bad and the Deadly,* 1979; *Bullets, Buzzards, Boxes of Pine,* 1980; *Face Down in a Coffin,* 1980; *The Man Who Bit Snakes,* 1980.

Historical romances; under pseudonym Barbara Riefe; published by Playboy Press, except as indicated: *Barringer House,* Popular Library, 1976; *Rowleston,* Popular Library, 1976; *Auldearn House,* Popular Library, 1976; *This Ravaged Heart,* 1977; *Fire and Flesh,* 1978; *Far beyond Desire,* 1978; *Tempt Not This Flesh,* 1979; *So Wicked the Heart,* 1980; *Black Fire,* 1980; *Olivia,* 1981; *Wildfire,* 1981; *An Extraordinary Woman,* 1983; *Julia,* 1983; *Lucretia,* 1983.

Under house pseudonym Jake Logan; all published by Playboy Press: *Bloody Trail to Texas,* 1976; *White Hell,* 1977; *Iron Mustang,* 1978; *Montana Showdown,* 1978; *See Texas and Die,* 1979.

Also author of "Jazz Milestones," a six-film history of American jazz for New York Times Teaching Resource Films. Contributor of satirical pieces to *True* and science fiction stories to *Boys' Life;* also contributor to numerous other periodicals.

WORK IN PROGRESS: Alexandra's Empire and *The Loves of Alexandra,* both for Playboy Press.

SIDELIGHTS: Alan Riefe told *CA:* "Research is all important to me. Writing fiction may involve some talent; reading fiction is an act of trust. The reader trusts the writer: when he or she offers facts, when he or she is specific regarding any of the myriad touches that enrich the tapestry of the novel—historical names, places, flora, fauna, technical information of the period, etc.—they should be accurate. It's time consuming but when the book is completed and it leaves your hands, it represents quality, at least in this regard. The author has no control over the 'amount' of his gift; he does control his 'homework,' and the quality of it. He's the master of his detail and his thoroughness.

"I began writing at the age of seven. I have two short stories from those tender salad days. I have been writing for fifty years. It is the only thing I've found I can do with any consistent degree of success. One day I hope to write an excellent book, a memorable one, one my great-grandchildren can take down from the shelf and read with pleasure.

"I work nine to five, six days a week. I love it; if I couldn't do it, if I were denied the privilege, I would probably die. Or do something equally tragic, like becoming a registered Republican."

AVOCATIONAL INTERESTS: Travel; gardening; reading.

* * *

RIEFE, Barbara
See RIEFE, Alan

* * *

RIESELBACH, Leroy N(ewman) 1934-

PERSONAL: Born July 11, 1934, in Milwaukee, Wis.; son of L. LeRoy (a lawyer) and Lillian (Newman) Rieselbach; married Helen Funk, June 29, 1957; children: Erik, Kurt, Alice, Karen. *Education:* Harvard University, A.B., 1956; Yale University, M.A., 1958, Ph.D., 1964. *Home:* 108 Glenwood E., Bloomington, Ind. 47401. *Office:* Department of Political Science, Indiana University, Bloomington, Ind. 47405.

CAREER: Indiana University at Bloomington, lecturer, 1964, assistant professor, 1964-66, associate professor, 1966-70, professor of political science, 1970—, chairman of department, 1971-77. Postdoctoral fellow, Mental Health Research Institute, University of Michigan, Ann Arbor, 1964-65; research associate, Center for International Affairs, Harvard University, 1969. *Member:* American Political Science Association, Midwest Political Science Association, Western Political Science Association, Southern Political Science Association.

WRITINGS: The Roots of Isolationism, Bobbs-Merrill, 1967; (editor with George I. Balch) *Psychology and Politics: An Introductory Reader,* Holt, 1969; (editor) *The Congressional System: Notes and Readings,* Duxbury, 1970, 2nd edition, 1979; (contributor) Oliver Walter, editor, *Political Scientists at Work,* Duxbury, 1971; *Congressional Politics,* McGraw, 1973.

(Editor) *People vs. Government: Essays on Institutional Responsiveness,* Indiana University Press, 1975; *Congressional Reform in the Seventies,* General Learning Press, 1977; (editor) *Legislative Reform: The Policy Impact,* Lexington Books, 1978; (contributor) George Bishop, editor, *Presidential Debates of 1976,* Praeger, 1978; (contributor) Dennis Hole, editor, *The U.S. Congress,* Boston University, 1982; (contributor) Stuart Nagel, editor, *Encyclopedia of Policy Studies,* Dekker, 1982. Contributor of articles and reviews to professionsl journals.

WORK IN PROGRESS: Congressional Committee Politics, with Joseph K. Urekis, for Praeger.

* * *

RITSCHL, Dietrich 1929-

PERSONAL: Born January 17, 1929, in Basel, Switzerland; son of Hans and Gertrud (Stoerring) Ritschl; married Rosemarie Courvoisier, April 18, 1952; children: Christian, Lucas, Stephan, Johannes. *Education:* Attended University of Tuebingen, University of Basel, and University of Bern, 1945-50; University of Edinburgh, Ph.D., 1957, D.D., 1976. *Home:* 4418 Reigoldswil, BL, Switzerland. *Office:* Department of Theology, University of Mainz, Mainz, West Germany.

CAREER: Ordained to Presbyterian ministry, 1950; assistant minister in Zyfen, Switzerland, 1950-52; minister in Scotland, 1952-58, and in Wimberly, Tex., 1958-62; Austin Presbyterian Seminary, Austin, Tex., guest professor, 1958-60, associate professor of history of dogma and New Testament, 1960-63; Pittsburgh Theological Seminary, Pittsburgh, Pa., professor of history of doctrine and systematic theology, 1963-69; Union Theological Seminary, New York, N.Y., Harry Emerson Fosdick Professor, 1969-70; University of Mainz, Mainz, West Germany, professor of systematic theology, 1970—. Guest lecturer, Presbyterian College, Montreal, Quebec, 1957, Episcopal Seminary of the Southwest, Austin, 1959-61, and United Theological Faculty, Melbourne, Australia; guest professor, Knox College, Dunedin, New Zealand, 1970, 1972, 1974, 1977, 1979, and 1982. Special lecturer in Hungary, Czechoslovakia, the Soviet Union, India, and Mexico. President of theological commission, National Council of Churches, West Germany and West Berlin, 1979—.

WRITINGS: Vom Leben in der Kirche, [Neukirchen], 1957, translation published as *Christ Our Life,* Oliver & Boyd, 1960; *Die Homiletische Funktion der Geminde,* EvZ (Zurich), 1960; *A Theology of Proclamation,* John Knox, 1960; *The Faith and Mission of the Church,* S.C.M. Press, 1961; *Nur Menschen,* Kathe Vogt Verlag (Berlin), 1962; *Athanasius,* [Zurich], 1963; *Memory and Hope: An Inquiry into the Presence of Christ,* Macmillan, 1967.

Konzepte, Volume I, P. Lang (Bern), 1976; *"Story" als Rohmaterial der Theologie,* Kaiser (Munich), 1976; *Theologie in den neuen Welten,* [Munich], 1981. Contributor of articles on patristics, systematic theology, and medical ethics to theology journals in Switzerland, Germany, Great Britain, and the United States.

* * *

RIVET, A(lbert) L(ionel) F(rederick) 1915-

PERSONAL: Surname is pronounced Reev-ay; born November 30, 1915, in England; son of Albert Robert and Rose (Bulow) Rivet; married Audrey Catherine Webb, April 8, 1947; children: Peter Leo, Anne Catherine. *Education:* Oriel College, Oxford, B.A., 1938, M.A., 1947. *Politics:* Social Democrat. *Religion:* Church of England. *Address:* University of Keele, 7 Springpool, Keele, Staffordshire, England.

CAREER: Teacher in Hitchin, England, 1938-39; civil defense worker in London, England, 1939-40; bookseller in Cambridge, England, Norwich, England, and then Crowborough, England, 1946-51; Ordnance Survey Department, London and Edinburgh, Scotland, assistant archaeology officer, 1951-64; University of Keele, Keele, Staffordshire, England, lecturer, 1964-67, reader in Romano-British studies, 1967-74, professor of Roman provincial studies, 1974-81, Leverhulme Emeritus Fellow, 1981-83. Member of Royal Commission on Historical Monuments, 1979—; member of executive committee, British School at Rome. *Military service:* British Army, Royal Artillery and Royal Signals, 1940-46; became major.

MEMBER: British Academy (fellow), Royal Archaeological Institute (member of council, 1955-59 and 1963-67), Society of Antiquaries (London), Society of Antiquaries of Scotland (member of council, 1960-64), Society for the Promotion of Roman Studies (president, 1977-80), German Archaeological Institute (honorary corresponding fellow).

WRITINGS: (Compiler) *Ordnance Survey Map of Roman Britain,* 3rd edition, Ordnance Survey, 1956; *Town and Country in Roman Britain,* Hutchinson, 1958, revised edition, 1964; (compiler) *Ordnance Survey Map of Southern Britain in the Iron Age,* Ordnance Survey, 1962; (editor) *The Iron Age in Northern Britain,* Edinburgh University Press, 1966; (editor and contributor) *The Roman Villa in Britain,* Praeger, 1969; (with Colin Smith) *The Place-Names of Roman Britain,* Princeton University Press, 1979; *Rudyard Kipling's Roman Britain: Fact and Fiction,* University of Keele, 1980.

Contributor: P. Corder, editor, *Romano-British Villas,* Council for British Archaeology, 1955; S. S. Frere, editor, *Problems of the Iron Age in Southern Britain,* Institute of Archaeology (London), 1960; J. S. Wacher, editor, *The Civitas Capitals of Roman Britain,* Leicester University Press, 1966; M. Jesson and D. Hill, editors, *The Iron Age and Its Hill-Forts,* [Southampton], 1971; R. Chevallier, editor, *Litterature greco-romaine et geographie historique,* [Paris], 1974; H. Temporini, editor, *Aufstieg und Niedergang der Roemischen Welt,* Volume II, Part 3, de Gruyter, 1975; W. Rodwell and T. Rowley, editors, *Small Towns of Roman Britain,* British Archaeological Reports, 1975.

R. Goodburn and P. Bartholomew, editors, *Aspects of the Notitia Dignitatum,* British Archaeological Reports, 1976; M. I. Finley, editor, *Atlas of Classical Archaeology,* McGraw, 1977; P. M. Duval and E. Frezouls, editors, *Themes de recherche sur les villes antiques de l'occident,* CNRS (Paris), 1977; D. Haupt and H. G. Horn, editors, *Studien zu den Militaergrenzen Roms,* Volume II, [Bonn], 1977; N. Coldstream and M.A.R. Colledge, editors, *Acta of the XI International Congress of Classical Archaeology,* [London], 1979; N.G.L. Hammond, editor, *Atlas of the Greek and Roman World in Antiquity,* Noyes Press, 1981.

Editor, *Proceedings* of the Society of Antiquaries of Scotland, 1961-64. Contributor to *Oxford Classical Dictionary* and *Princeton Dictionary of Classical Archaeology.* Contributor to *Britannia* and *Antiquity;* author of reviews on the subject of Roman Britain and Gaul.

WORK IN PROGRESS: The History and Archaeology of Gallia Narbonensis and Alpes Maritimae, for Routledge & Kegan Paul.

BIOGRAPHICAL/CRITICAL SOURCES: Times Literary Supplement, January 11, 1980.

* * *

ROBERTS, (Edward) Adam 1940-

PERSONAL: Born August 29, 1940, in Penrith, England; son of Michael (a teacher and writer) and Janet (a writer; maiden name, Adam-Smith) Roberts; married Frances Dunn, September 16, 1966; children: one son, one daughter. *Education:* Magdalen College, Oxford, B.A., 1962, M.A., 1981; London School of Economics and Political Science, studies in international relations, 1965-68. *Office:* St. Antony's College, Oxford University, Oxford OX2 6JF, England.

CAREER: Peace News (weekly), London, England, assistant editor, 1962-65; University of London, London School of Economics and Political Science, London, lecturer in international relations, 1968-81; Oxford University, St. Antony's College, Oxford, England, Alastair Bucham Reader in International Relations and professorial fellow, 1981—. *Member:* International Institute for Strategic Studies, Royal Institute of International Affairs.

WRITINGS: (Editor) *The Strategy of Civilian Defence: Non-Violent Resistance to Aggression,* Faber, 1967, published as *Civilian Resistance as a National Defense,* Stackpole, 1968; (with Philip Windsor) *Czechoslovakia 1968: Reform, Repression and Resistance,* Columbia University Press, 1969; *Nations in Arms: The Theory and Practice of Territorial Defence,* Praeger, 1976; (with Richard Guelff) *Documents on the Laws of War,* Oxford University Press, 1982; *Occupation, Resistance and Law: International Law on Military Occupations and on Resistance,* Oxford University Press, 1983. Contributor to newspapers and journals, including *New Society, World Today,* and *Survival;* also contributor to British Broadcasting Corp.

* * *

ROBERTS, Edward B(aer) 1935-

PERSONAL: Born November 18, 1935, in Chelsea, Mass.; son of Nathan (a retailer) and Edna (Podradchik) Roberts; married Nancy Helen Rosenthal, June 14, 1959; children: Valerie Jo,

Mitchell Jonathan, Andrea Lynne. *Education:* Massachusetts Institute of Technology, S.B. and S.M. in E.E., 1958, S.M. (industrial management), 1960, Ph.D., 1962. *Politics:* Republican. *Religion:* Judaism. *Home:* 17 Fellsmere Rd., Newton, Mass. 02159. *Office:* Alfred P. Sloan School of Management, Massachusetts Institute of Technology, 50 Memorial Dr., Cambridge, Mass. 02139.

CAREER: Massachusetts Institute of Technology, Alfred P. Sloan School of Management, Cambridge, instructor, 1960-61, assistant professor, 1961-65, associate professor, 1965-70, professor of management, 1970—, David Sarnoff Professor of Management of Technology, 1974—, associate director of M.I.T. Research Program on the Management of Science and Technology, 1963-73, chairman of M.I.T. Technology and Health Management Group, 1974—, and M.I.T. Whitaker College Program in Health Policy and Management, 1979—, director of M.I.T. Program in the Management of Technology, 1980—. President, Pugh-Roberts Associates, Inc., Cambridge, 1963—. Consultant to National Aeronautics and Space Administration, 1961, RAND Corp., 1963-69, and the President's Advisory Council for Management Improvement, 1972-73; member, Air Force Scientific Advisory Board, 1967-70, and Department of Commerce Technical Advisory Board, 1967-72.

MEMBER: Sigma Xi, Tau Beta Pi, Eta Kappa Nu, Tau Kappa Alpha. *Awards, honors:* Named government/defense/space marketing man of the year, American Marketing Association, 1966, for writings on research and development marketing.

WRITINGS: (Contributor) *Problems in Industrial Dynamics,* M.I.T. Press, 1963; *The Dynamics of Research and Development,* Harper, 1964; (co-author) *Systems Simulation for Regional Analysis,* M.I.T. Press, 1968; (co-author) *Persistent Poppy: A Computer-Aided Search for Heroin Policy,* Ballinger, 1975; (co-author) *The Dynamics of Human Service Delivery,* Ballinger, 1976; (editor) *Managerial Applications of System Dynamics,* M.I.T. Press, 1978; (co-editor) *Biomedical Innovation,* M.I.T. Press, 1981; (contributor) *Federal Research on the Biological and Health Effects of Ionizing Radiation,* National Academy Press, 1981. Contributor to engineering, technology, and management journals. Associate editor, *Management Science Bulletin,* 1964-67; *I.E.E.E. Transactions on Engineering Management,* special issue editor, 1967, member of editorial advisory board, 1967—; member of editorial advisory board, *Industrial Marketing Management,* 1975—, and *Technological Forecasting and Social Change,* 1979—.

WORK IN PROGRESS: Research on systems analysis, research and development management, the formation and growth of new enterprise, and health care management.

* * *

ROBERTS, Mervin F(rancis) 1922-

PERSONAL: Born June 7, 1922, in New York, N.Y.; son of Gus R. (an inventor) and Esther N. (a school teacher) Roberts; married Edith May Foster, June, 1949; children: Edith, Robin (deceased), Martha, Nancy, Neel, William. *Education:* Alfred University, B.S., 1944. *Politics:* Republican. *Religion:* Baptist. *Home and office address:* Duck River Lane, Old Lyme, Conn. 06371.

CAREER: Writer; photographer of animal movements; consultant on animal behavior; consultant on fish behavior to Northeast Utilities, 1970—; councillor for marine resources to governor of Connecticut, 1971-72. Chaplain of Old Lyme Fire Department, 1970—. *Military service:* U.S. Naval Reserve, active duty, 1942-46; became lieutenant junior grade. *Member:* National Rifle Association (life member), American Society of Ichthyologists and Herpetologists, Connecticut Association of Conservation Commissioners (past president).

WRITINGS—Published by T.F.H. Publications, except as indicated: *Turtles as Pets,* 1953; *Beginning Your Aquarium,* 1955; *Chameleons,* 1956; *Parakeets in Your Home,* Sterling, 1956; *How to Raise and Train a Pet Hamster,* 1957, reprinted, 1973; *Guinea Pigs,* 1957, published as *Guinea Pigs for Beginners,* 1972; *Snakes,* 1958, published as *All about Boas and Other Snakes,* 1975; *A Camera Is Thrust upon You* (manual), U.S. Navy, 1961; *Pigeons,* 1962.

Tidal Marsh Plants of Connecticut, Connecticut Arboretum, 1970; *Tropical Fish,* 1970; *Your Terrarium,* 1972; *Teddy Bear Hamsters,* 1974; (with daughter, Martha Roberts) *All about Iguanas,* 1976; *All about Salamanders,* 1976; *All about Chameleons and Anoles,* 1977; *All about Ferrets,* 1977; *All about Land Hermit Crabs,* 1978; *Newts and Salamanders,* 1979; *The Tidemarsh Guide,* Dutton, 1979, 2nd edition, Peregrine Press, 1982; *Society Finches,* 1979; *Breeding Society Finches,* 1979; *Breeding Zebra Finches,* 1980; *Turtles,* 1980; *Zebra Finches,* 1981; *The T.F.H. Book of Hamsters,* 1981; *All about Breeding Canaries, 1982.*

Associate editor of *Factory,* 1959.

WORK IN PROGRESS: Rabbits, Gouldian Finches, and *Lovebirds,* all for T.F.H. Publications; *Eels of the Connecticut River* and *Oystering around Long Island,* both for Peregrine Press.

SIDELIGHTS: Mervin F. Roberts told *CA:* "Writing is not much easier than digging ditches but it does keep me out of the cold." *Avocational interests:* Duck hunting, trapshooting, working as a gunsmith, inventing (has invented glass bottle color sorter for the recycling industry and heaters and pumps for aquariums).

* * *

ROBERTSON, D(urant) W(aite), Jr. 1914-

PERSONAL: Born October 11, 1914, in Washington, D.C.; son of Durant Waite and Emma (Jones) Robertson; married Betty McLean Hansen, July 17, 1937; children: Susanna, Durant Waite III, Douglas. *Education:* University of North Carolina at Chapel Hill, B.A., 1935, M.A., 1937, Ph.D., 1945. *Home:* 421 Whitehead Cir., Chapel Hill, N.C. 27514.

CAREER: University of Maryland, College Park, instructor in English, 1938-42; University of North Carolina at Chapel Hill, instructor in English, 1942-44; Yale University, New Haven, Conn., instructor in English, 1945-46; Princeton University, Princeton, N.J., instructor, 1946-47, assistant professor, 1947-55, associate professor, 1955-60, professor of English, 1960-71, Murray Professor of English Literature, 1971-80, professor emeritus, 1980—. *Member:* Mediaeval Academy of America, New Chaucer Society, Renaissance Society of America. *Awards, honors:* American Council of Learned Societies fellow, 1945-46; Guggenheim fellow, 1957; D.Litt. from Villanova University, 1973; Howard T. Behrman Distinguished Achievement in Humanities award, Princeton University, 1978; National Humanities Center fellow, 1980-81; D.H.L. from University of North Carolina at Greensboro, 1982.

WRITINGS: (With Bernard F. Huppe) *Piers Plowman and Scriptural Tradition,* Princeton University Press, 1951; (translator) St. Augustine, *On Christian Doctrine,* Liberal Arts Press, 1958; *A Preface to Chaucer: Studies in Medieval Perspectives,*

Princeton University Press, 1962; (with Huppe) *Fruyt and Chaf: Studies in Chaucer's Allegories,* Princeton University Press, 1963; *Chaucer's London,* Wiley, 1968; (editor) *The Literature of Medieval England,* McGraw, 1970; *Abelard and Heloise,* Dial, 1972; *Essays in Medieval Culture,* Princeton University Press, 1980.

Contributor: Richard J. Schoeck and Jerome Taylor, editors, *Chaucer Criticism,* Volume II, University of Notre Dame Press, 1961; John Mahoney and John Esten Keller, editors, *Mediaeval Studies in Honor of Urban Tigner Holmes, Jr.,* University of North Carolina Press, 1965; F. X. Newman, editor, *The Meaning of Courtly Love,* State University of New York Press, 1968; Beryl Rowland, editor, *Companion to Chaucer Studies,* Oxford University Press, 1968; Ralph Cohen, editor, *New Directions in Literary History,* Routledge & Kegan Paul, 1974; Joseph Gibaldi, editor, *Approaches to Teaching Chaucer's Canterbury Tales,* Modern Language Association of America, 1980; John P. Hermann and John J. Burke, Jr., *Signs and Symbols in Chaucer's Poetry,* University of Alabama Press, 1981; J. P. Van Noppen, editor, *Theolinguistics,* Free University of Brussels, 1981. Contributor of articles and reviews to scholarly journals, including *Speculum, Comparative Literature, Studies in Philology,* and *American Benedictine Review.*

WORK IN PROGRESS: Research for a book, *An Introduction to the Canterbury Tales.*

SIDELIGHTS: D. W. Robertson, Jr. is regarded in the academic world as a leading scholar of medieval literature. He established his reputation with his early works, *Piers Plowman and Scriptural Tradition, A Preface to Chaucer: Studies in Medieval Perspectives,* and *Fruyt and Chaf: Studies in Chaucer's Allegories,* as well as with numerous articles published in critical collections and in scholarly journals.

Two of his more recent books, *Chaucer's London* and *Abelard and Heloise,* exemplify his work and have been cited by critics for their value as historical studies. *Chaucer's London,* which includes prints of illuminated manuscripts from the era, explores the customs and events as well as the physical aspects of the city in the late fourteenth century. The book emphasizes the differences between the medieval perspective and the modern one by outlining the essential features of life in Chaucer's time that shaped the fourteenth-century world view. R. H. Jones, writing in the *American Historical Review,* feels that the book speaks for Robertson's "insight into the relevant historical context." A critic for *Choice* says that although the book's narrative seems somewhat "loose and undisciplined," Robertson's rich background in history compensates for this weakness.

Abelard and Heloise, Robertson's study of the twelfth-century philosopher and theologian Peter Abelard and his legendary lover Heloise, examines the historical facts surrounding these enigmatic figures along with the historical myths that have arisen through the body of literature based on their illicit and passionate affair. Bennett D. Hill, writing in *Library Journal,* feels that the student as well as the general reader will "enjoy the author's fresh insights, his lucid style, and his acerbic wit." Vincent Cronin, in a *Washington Post Book World* review, observes that "the more books like this, the deeper our understanding of the past will be." In the *New York Times Book Review,* David Knowles takes exception to Robertson's thesis that Heloise was actually a fictional creation of Abelard's pen, insisting that Robertson's arguments lack solid support. "When closely examined," says Knowles, they "are in large part simply repeated assertions." Knowles finds that "it must be added that in his chapters on Abelard's early life, [Robertson] gives a fuller and more credible picture than previous historians."

Robertson expresses his basic philosophy of scholarship, telling *CA:* "It has always been my contention that studies of earlier literature, including critical evaluations of that literature, should be based firmly on knowledge gained from primary sources. If we cannot understand literary works in terms that would have been understood by their authors we shall not understand them at all."

BIOGRAPHICAL/CRITICAL SOURCES: Choice, February, 1969; *Booklist,* April 15, 1969; *American Historical Review,* October, 1969; *English Literary Review,* October, 1970; *Speculum,* July, 1971; *Publisher's Weekly,* November 22, 1971; *Library Journal,* February 1, 1972; *New Yorker,* February 12, 1972; *New York Times Book Review,* February 13, 1972; *Washington Post Book World,* February 13, 1972.

* * *

ROBINSON, A(ntony) M(eredith) Lewin 1916-

PERSONAL: Born October 11, 1916, in Swindon, England; son of William Edward (a clergyman) and Margaret (Ostler) Robinson; married Helen Margaret Austin, October 21, 1944; children: Andrew, Dorothea, David. *Education:* Rhodes University, B.A., 1937; University of London, Diploma in Librarianship, 1939; University of Cape Town, Ph.D., 1961. *Home:* 136 Camp Ground Rd., Newlands, Cape Town, South Africa.

CAREER: University of Natal Library, Durban, South Africa, assistant, 1940-43; University of Cape Town, Cape Town, South Africa, assistant, 1943-45; South African Library, Cape Town, deputy librarian, 1945-61, director, 1961-81. Lecturer in bibliocultural studies, University of Cape Town, School of Librarianship. Chairman of organizing committees of Conference of South African Bibliophiles, 1966, 1974, 1981; member of National Library Advisory Council, 1972-81.

MEMBER: Library Association (Great Britain; fellow), South African Institute for Librarianship and Information Science, (honorary secretary, 1946-48; fellow, 1980), English Association, Cape Tercentenary Foundation (member of council, 1961), Rotary Club (Cape Town; president, 1970-71). *Awards, honors:* Carnegie grants for travel in Europe, 1951, and United States, 1965.

WRITINGS: Catalogue of Theses and Dissertations Accepted by South African Universities, 1918-41, privately printed, 1943; *William McDougall, M.B., D.Sc., F.R.S.: A Bibliography,* Duke University Press, 1943; *Bibliography of African Bibliographies,* South African Library, 1950, 3rd edition, 1960.

None Daring to Make Us Afraid: English Periodical Literature in the Cape Colony, 1824-1835, Maskew Miller, 1962; *Systematic Bibliography,* Clive Bingley, 1966; 4th edition, 1979; (editor) *Thomas Pringle's Narrative of a Residence in South Africa, 1834,* C. Struik, 1967; (editor) *The Letters of Lady Anne Barnard to Henry Dundas, 1793-1803,* A. A. Balkema, 1973; (co-editor) *Francois Le Vaillant: Traveller in South Africa and His Collection of 165 Water-colour Paintings,* Library of Parliament, 1973; (editor) *Notes on a Visit to South Africa, 1889, by Stanley Leighton, M.P.,* A. A. Balkema, 1975; *Short Title Catalogue of Early Printed Books in South African Libraries, 1470-1550,* South African Library, 1977; (editor) *Selected Articles from the Cape Monthly Magazine, 1870-76,*

Van Riebeeck Society, 1978; (editor-in-chief) *A South African Bibliography to the Year 1925: Revision and Continuation of Sidney Mendelssohn's South African Bibliography (1910)*, Mansell, 1979; *From Monolith to Microfilm: The Story of the Recorded Word*, South African Library, 1979.

General editor, "Grey Bibliographies" series, 1962-81. Contributor to *Standard Encylopaedia of Southern Africa, Dictionary of South Africa Biography*, and to library journals. Editor, *Quarterly Bulletin of the South African Library*, 1962-81.

WORK IN PROGRESS: The history of St. Paul's Church, Rondebosch, Cape Town, 1834-1984.

SIDELIGHTS: A. M. Lewin Robinson told *CA:* "Having spent the whole of my active professional career in scholarly libraries—principally in a national library—I have been encouraged to undertake bibliographical and historical research on materials close at hand. In this I have been extremely fortunate and my work has been much easier than it might otherwise have been. After all, it has been said that the only person who gets a really first class library service is the librarian!"

* * *

ROBINSON, Halbert B(enefiel) 1925-1981

PERSONAL: Born October 15, 1925, in Winslow, Ariz.; died, 1981; son of Halbert B. and Lois (Eastman) Robinson; married Nancy Lou Mayer, June 24, 1951; children: Christine Louise, Laura Ann, David Merrill, Elizabeth Mayer. *Education:* Attended Pomona College, 1946-49; Stanford University, A.B., 1951, M.A., 1953, Ph.D., 1957. *Home:* 5005 Northeast 45th St., Seattle, Wash. 98105. *Office:* Department of Psychology, University of Washington, Seattle, Wash. 98195.

CAREER: San Francisco State College (now San Francisco State University), San Francisco, Calif., instructor in psychology, 1957-59; University of North Carolina at Chapel Hill, assistant professor, 1959-61, associate professor, 1961-66, professor of psychology, 1966-69, acting chairman of department, 1963-64, director of developmental psychology program, 1964-69, director of Child Development Institute, 1965-68; University of Washington, Seattle, professor of psychology, 1969-81, director of developmental psychology laboratory, 1969-81, director of Child Development Research Group, 1976-81. Director of International Study Group for Early Child Care, 1968-81. Member, President's Task Force on Early Childhood, 1965, and Joint Commission on the Mental Health of Children, 1967-69. Consultant to Veteran's Administration, 1959-69, and Peace Corps; member of advisory committee, North Carolina State Department of Public Health, 1965-69. *Military service:* U.S. Marine Corps, 1942-45. *Member:* American Psychological Association, Society for Research in Child Development, American Association for the Advancement of Science, Sigma Xi.

WRITINGS: (With wife, Nancy Mayer Robinson) *The Mentally Retarded Child: A Psychological Approach*, McGraw, 1965, 2nd edition, 1976; (with N. M. Robinson, M. Walins, U. Bronfenbrenner, and J. Richmond) *Early Child Care in the United States*, Gordon & Breach, 1973; (with Wendy Conklin Roedell and Ronald G. Slaby) *Social Development in Young Children: A Report for Teachers*, National Institute of Education, U.S. Department of Health, Education, and Welfare, 1976; (with Nancy Ewald Jackson) *Cognitive Development in Young Children*, National Institute of Education, U.S. Department of Health Education, and Welfare, 1976; (with Roedell) *Gifted Young Children*, Teachers College Press, 1980.

Editor, with N. M. Robinson, of "International Monograph Series on Early Child Care," Gordon & Breach, 1972-81. Contributor to *Child Development, Pediatrics*, and psychology journals.†

* * *

ROOD, Ronald (N.) 1920-

PERSONAL: Surname rhymes with "food"; born July 7, 1920, in Torrington, Conn.; son of Nellis Frost (a life insurance underwriter) and Bessie (Chamberlain) Rood; married Margaret Bruce (a teacher), December 21, 1942; children: Janice, Thomas Elliot, Alison, Roger Warren. *Education:* University of Connecticut, B.S., 1941, M.S., 1949. *Home and office address:* R.R. 1, Box 131, Lincoln, Vt. 05443.

CAREER: Writer. Long Island Agricultural and Technical Institute, Farmingdale, N.Y., instructor in biology, 1949-53; Grolier Enterprises, New York, N.Y., research editor, 1954-64; Middlebury College, Middlebury, Vt., instructor in biology, 1956-58. Church choir director. *Military service:* U.S. Army Air Forces, fighter pilot, World War II; received Air Medal. *Member:* Forest and Field, American Forestry Association, National Wildlife Federation, Outdoor Writers Association of America, League of Vermont Writers (president, 1965-67, 1975), Vermont Natural Resources Council.

WRITINGS: The How and Why Wonder Book of Insects, Grosset, 1960; *The How and Why Wonder Book of Ants and Bees*, Grosset, 1962; *Land Alive: The World of Nature at One Family's Door*, Stephen Greene, 1962; *The How and Why Wonder Book of Butterflies and Moths*, Grosset, 1963; *The Loon in My Bathtub*, Stephen Greene, 1964; *The Sea and Its Wonderful Creatures*, Whitman Publishing, 1965; *Bees, Bugs and Beetles: The Arrow Book of Insects*, Four Winds, 1965; *Hundred Acre Welcome: The Story of a Chincoteague Pony*, Stephen Greene, 1967; *Vermont Life Book of Nature*, Stephen Greene, 1967; *How Do You Spank a Porcupine?*, Trident, 1969; *Animal Champions*, Grosset, 1969; *Answers about Insects*, Grosset, 1969.

Animals Nobody Loves, Stephen Greene, 1971; *Who Wakes the Groundhog?*, Norton, 1973; *May I Keep This Clam Mother? It Followed Me Home*, Simon & Schuster, 1973; *Good Things Are Happening*,, Stephen Greene, 1975; *It's Going to Sting Me*, Simon & Schuster, 1976; *Possum in the Parking Lot*, Simon & Schuster, 1977; *Elephant Bones and Lonely Hearts*, Stephen Greene, 1977.

Laska, Norton, 1980. Contributor to numerous periodicals, including *Reader's Digest, Coronet, Audubon Magazine, Christian Herald, New York Times, Pageant*, and *Vermont Life*.

* * *

ROONEY, Andrew A(itken) 1919- (Andy Rooney)

PERSONAL: Born January 14, 1919, in Albany, N.Y.; son of Walter Scott and Ellinor (Reynolds) Rooney; married Marguerite Howard (a teacher), April 21, 1942; children: Ellen, Martha, Emily, Brian. *Education:* Attended Albany Academy, Albany, N.Y., and Colgate University, 1942. *Politics:* "Vacillating." *Office:* CBS News, 524 West 57th St., New York, N.Y. 10019.

CAREER: Writer, primarily for television. Worked for Metro-Goldwyn-Mayer, Inc., Hollywood, Calif., one year; free-lance magazine writer, 1947-49; wrote material for Arthur Godfrey, 1949-55, Sam Levenson, Herb Shriner, Victor Borge, and for "Twentieth Century," and "Seven Lively Arts"; Columbia Broadcasting System, Inc., New York City, writer for CBS Radio's "The Garry Moore Show," 1959-65, writer-producer of television essays, documentaries, and specials for CBS News, 1962-70; worked for public television, 1970-71, and for American Broadcasting Companies, Inc. (ABC-TV), 1971-72; Columbia Broadcasting System, Inc., CBS News, writer, producer, and narrator of television essays, documentaries, and specials, 1972—, regular commentator-essayist on CBS News program "60 Minutes," 1978—. *Military service:* U.S. Army, 1942-45, reporter for *Stars and Stripes;* became sergeant; received Air Medal and Bronze Star.

AWARDS, HONORS: Writers Guild of America Award for best television documentary, 1966, for "The Great Love Affair," 1968, for "Black History: Lost, Strayed, or Stolen," 1971, for "An Essay on War," 1975, for "Mr. Rooney Goes to Washington," 1976, for "Mr. Rooney Goes to Dinner," and 1979, for "Happiness: The Elusive Pursuit"; George Foster Peabody Award, University of Georgia, 1975, for "Mr. Rooney Goes to Washington"; recipient of three Emmy Awards, two for "60 Minutes."

WRITINGS: (With Oram C. Hutton) *Air Gunner,* Farrar & Rinehart, 1944; (with Hutton) *The Story of the "Stars and Stripes,"* Farrar & Rinehart, 1946, reprinted, Greenwood Press, 1970; (with Hutton) *Conquerors' Peace: A Report to the American Stockholders,* Doubleday, 1947; (editor and author of notes and comment with Dickson Hartwell) *Off the Record: The Best Stories of Foreign Correspondents,* collected by Overseas Press Club of America, Doubleday, 1952; *The Fortunes of War: Four Great Battles of World War II* (History Book Club selection), Little, Brown, 1962; *A Few Minutes with Andy Rooney* (collection of essays written for television; includes "Hotels," "In Praise of New York City," "Mr. Rooney Goes to Washington," "Mr. Rooney Goes to Dinner," "Mr. Rooney Goes to Work," and "An Essay on War"), Atheneum, 1981; *And More by Andy Rooney* (essays originally published in his syndicated column), Atheneum, 1982.

Author of television essays, documentaries, and specials for CBS-TV, including: "An Essay on Doors"; "An Essay on Bridges"; (with Richard Ellison) "The Great Love Affair," broadcast 1966; "Hotels," broadcast June 28, 1966; "An Essay on Women," broadcast 1967; (with Perry Wolff) "Black History: Lost, Strayed, or Stolen," broadcast 1968; "In Praise of New York City," broadcast February 1, 1974; "Mr. Rooney Goes to Washington," broadcast January 26, 1975; "Mr. Rooney Goes to Dinner," broadcast April 20, 1976; "Mr. Rooney Goes to Work," broadcast July 5, 1977.

Author of documentary "An Essay on War," broadcast by WNET-TV, 1971, as part of "The Great American Dream Machine" series. Co-author of filmscript based on *The Story of the "Stars and Stripes,"* purchased by Metro-Goldwyn-Mayer. Writer, under name Andy Rooney, of column syndicated to over 250 newspapers by Tribune Co. Syndicate, 1979—. Contributor to periodicals.

SIDELIGHTS: Andrew A. Rooney, more affectionately known as Andy, is "the homespun Homer whose celebrations of the commonplace and jeremiads against the degenerating twentieth century are cheered by 40 million viewers of one of the nation's top-rated TV shows," writes Elizabeth Peer in *Newsweek.* A longtime writer and producer for the Columbia Broadcasting System, Rooney became a regular essayist on the CBS newsmagazine "60 Minutes" in 1978 and has evolved into "a one-man institution," notes Anne Chamberlin in the *Washington Post Book World.* His observations on such everyday items as chairs, doors, jeans, and soap not only appear on television but also in a thrice-weekly column syndicated to over 250 newspapers across the country. Moreover, many of these essays have been compiled into two best-sellers, *A Few Minutes with Andy Rooney* and *And More by Andy Rooney.* The multimedia success of these wry, down-to-earth editorials, says Bruce Henstell in the *Los Angeles Times Book Review,* has made Rooney "the most listened-to curmudgeon in recent times."

Admitting in the *Detroit News* that it "makes me mad when people come up to me and don't know I lived before 1979," Rooney has been a writer all his working life. A reporter for the armed forces' *Stars and Stripes* during World War II, he and colleague Oram C. "Bud" Hutton co-authored two books while in the service and one after being discharged. *Air Gunner,* described by the late Edmund Wilson in the *New Yorker* as "an excellent piece of reporting," tells about the American boys who manned the guns on the flying fortresses over Europe, and *The Story of the "Stars and Stripes"* discusses the development of the GI newspaper and its staff over the course of World War II. *Conquerors' Peace* reports the findings of a post-war tour of Europe by Rooney and Hutton, who not only examined the landscape, the American cemeteries, and the displaced persons problem, but also probed into the inhabitants' feelings about the war and the occupation troops.

After being discharged from the army, Rooney went to Hollywood and co-wrote the filmscript of *The Story of the "Stars and Stripes"* for Metro-Goldwyn-Mayer. Then, having finished the script as well as other assignments with Hutton, he became a free-lance writer, publishing pieces in *Reader's Digest, Look, Life, Esquire,* and other magazines. But after spending six weeks on an article for *Harper's* and getting $350 for it, "I realized I was not going to make it as a magazine writer," Rooney says in *Time.* From 1949 to 1955, Rooney was Arthur Godfrey's radio and television writer, "at a more comfortable $625 a week" according to *Time,* and he later crafted clever lines for such personalities as Victor Borge, Sam Levenson, and Herb Shriner.

Rooney began his long affiliation with CBS in 1959, when the network hired him to write for "The Garry Moore Show." Three years later, he teamed up with veteran newsman Harry Reasoner for the first in a series of television essays that focused mainly on such seemingly mundane subjects as bridges, doors, and hotels. During their six-year collaboration from 1962 to 1968, Rooney wrote the words and served as producer of the broadcasts, and Reasoner presented the reports on camera. Susan Slobojan of the *Detroit News* notes that in these specials, "observing life with both eyes open and tongue planted firmly in cheek became a sort of Rooney trademark." She cites the beginning of "An Essay on Women," produced in 1967, as indicative of the approach: "This broadcast was prepared by men, and makes no claim to be fair. Prejudice has saved us a great deal of time in preparation."

But Rooney did not take everything so lightly. In 1970, when CBS wanted to halve and rearrange his philosophical half-hour "An Essay on War," Rooney quit the network in protest and went over to public television—at lower pay, of course. He then bought the essay from CBS to air on "The Great American Dream Machine" series, broadcast by New York's WNET-TV. Unable to use Reasoner's voice for this work, Rooney had to read it himself. "It was the only practical thing to do," he explained to *New York*'s Lewis Grossberger. "We didn't have a star on the 'Dream Machine.' Everybody did their own pieces. So I read it. It wasn't very well read, but the piece was good." Indeed, "An Essay on War" was good enough to win Rooney one of his six Writers Guild of America Awards; perhaps a more important consequence, however, was that it launched him on a career as an on-camera commentator.

Lured back to CBS in 1972, Rooney wrote, produced, and narrated a series of television reports on American life that, like many of his previous essays, "were characterized by the same droll, stubborn sensibility," observes Slobojan. The finest of these reports, according to a *Time* writer, "was probably 'In Praise of New York City' (1974), a journalistic paean that anticipated parts of Woody Allen's 'Manhattan.'" In "Mr. Rooney Goes to Dinner," he examined numerous facets of eating out, noting among other things that a tassel on the menu "can add a couple of dollars per person" to the average bill. "After traveling across the country and visiting more than a hundred factories and other places of business and after seeing a lot of people leaning on their shovels when they should have been shoveling and then hearing people testify that they don't work hard," he concluded in "Mr. Rooney Goes to Work," "I have still become convinced, to my great surprise, that Americans *are* working their tails off." And in the best-known of these reports, "Mr. Rooney Goes to Washington," he wittily surmised that the federal bureaucracy is not "being run by evil people; it's being run by people like you and me. And you know how we have to be watched."

Rooney's reports won several awards and garnered much public attention, but his role at CBS was still somewhat vague. "They have never known exactly what to do with me around here," he told Lewis Grossberger. Rooney felt there was a place for a short essay somewhere around the company, so he requested more air time. The network gave him a chance in 1978 as a summer replacement for the "Point Counterpoint" segment of the CBS newsmagazine "60 Minutes." The move was so successful that "A Few Minutes with Andy Rooney" became a regular feature of the show that fall, alternating with the mini-debates of Shana Alexander and Jack Kilpatrick. One year later, Shana and Jack were gone for good, the frequency of Rooney's appearances increased, and Rooney's popularity soared. "Audiences began wondering where he'd been all these years," writes Slobojan.

Since joining "60 Minutes," Rooney's success has been phenomenal. In addition to prompting comparisons with humorists E. B. White, James Thurber, and Art Buchwald, his deadpan delivery and acerbic wit have made him as popular as Mike Wallace and the rest of the "60 Minutes" crew. A column syndicated to over 250 newspapers, begun in 1979 out of frustration at not having a sufficient outlet for his ideas, earned Rooney $130,000 beyond his $125,000 salary from CBS in 1982, according to Elizabeth Peer. His $10,000 fee per speaking engagement rivals that of Henry Kissinger and William F. Buckley, Jr. Moreover, both his sampling of television essays published as *A Few Minutes with Andy Rooney* and a collection of 127 newspaper columns, *And More by Andy Rooney,* topped the *New York Times*' best-seller list. "In a season when the book business tottered," writes Carolyn See in the *Los Angeles Times,* "[*A Few Minutes with Andy Rooney*] was one of the few titles that booksellers could not keep in stock."

Paradoxically, Rooney's overwhelming success "derives largely from his persona as an ordinary guy," explains Michael Dirda in the *Washington Post Book World*. Described by *Time* as "the Boswell of Stuff" and by CBS colleague Walter Cronkite as "Everyman, articulating all the frustrations with modern life that the rest of us Everymen . . . suffer with silence or mumbled oaths," Rooney told Slobojan he deliberately writes about "subjects of universal interest. Someone suggested I do a piece on telephone answering services. You know those and I know those, but everyone else doesn't. Telephone answering services are not a piece for me to do. Glue is. Doorknobs are." "Rooney appreciates such things," notes Lewis Grossberger, "[because] he believes that the mundane is more important than commonly thought. The pencil, for instance, ultimately has a greater effect on our existence, he figures, than, say, the Vietnam war." Carolyn See maintains that Rooney's attention to the commonplace "puts the rest of those '60 Minutes' in perspective: Crooked union bosses may be one thing, but making good vanilla ice cream, or getting strung out on what shampoo to buy—these are the issues that should, and do, preoccupy America."

Rooney claims to live a normal life and that this helps him in his work. "I'm the all-American consumer," he says in *A Few Minutes with Andy Rooney*. "My idea of a good time is to go out Saturday morning to buy something with some of the money I've made." His tastes, he maintains, are not extravagant. He lives in the same house he bought over thirty years ago, and though he acknowledges "I greatly enjoy the money I make," he adds in the *Detroit News:* "But I spend it on small things. Tools. I'll spend $27 for a chisel that will solve all my problems. It never does."

Though Rooney does not think of himself as a humorist, his wry wit must ultimately be considered part of his appeal. "Rooney's humor is dry," notes Grossberger. "He doesn't do many jokes as such. Instead of 'Ha!' he goes for the 'Huh!'—that grunt of recognition and pleasure evoked when you hit somebody with a homely truth." The preface to *A Few Minutes with Andy Rooney* typifies the Rooney wit. Having expressed an uneasiness over the fact that a book by anyone on a popular television broadcast "will probably sell whether it's any good or not," he deftly admits: "It wasn't hard to talk me into putting this book together. It is unsatisfactory for a writer to have his words said once and then disappear forever into the air. Seeing our names in print leads to the dream all of us have of immortality. You can't ask more from something than immortality and money next week."

CA INTERVIEW

Andrew Rooney, pleading that he could write faster than he could talk, answered *CA*'s questions by mail in November, 1981.

CA: In the preface to A Few Minutes with Andy Rooney, *you said that "television writing in particular has been considered a second-class art form and that's why so much of it isn't any good." Do you think cable and further technological developments are likely to improve this situation?*

ROONEY: No.

CA: When did you first begin to think about being a writer, and how did you get from thinking about it to being one?

ROONEY: I started dreaming of being a writer when I was about twelve. In college I did all the usual things and was editor of a literary-humor magazine. I had worked as a copyboy on an Albany newspaper one summer and after I was drafted and shipped to England with an artillery regiment, I was transferred to the *Stars and Stripes*. The army, in its ignorance, thought I knew something about being a newspaperman. I didn't but I found out in three years with the army paper.

Toward the end of the war Bud Hutton and I wrote a book called *The Story of the "Stars and Stripes."* We were three weeks out of the army as sergeants when MGM bought the book for $55,000 and paid us $1000 a week to go to work in Hollywood. After a year there we returned to Europe on assignment to do ten magazine articles. After that Hutton and I split and I made a living writing magazine articles for several years: *Reader's Digest, Harper's, Look, Life, Esquire,* etc.

In 1949 the free-lance magazine-writing business started to seem like the wrong way to make a decent living. I looked for work at CBS News, did a few reports for them on a free-lance basis, and ran into Arthur Godfrey on the elevator one day. I went to work for him the following Monday and it was a good thing because by then I needed the money again.

*CA: Your first three books—*Air Gunner *in 1944,* The Story of the "Stars and Stripes" *in 1946, and* Conqueror's Peace *in 1947—were collaborations with* [*Oram C.*] *Hutton. How did those collaborations come about, and how did the collaborative process work?*

ROONEY: Hutton and I were both with the *Stars and Stripes*. He was an experienced newspaperman and writer. The collaborative process did not work very well. He wrote his half and I wrote my half. He'd then tell me what was wrong with my half and I'd rewrite it. I learned a lot from Hutton. He was actually such a good editor and so aware of what was wrong with a piece of copy that he eventually found it difficult to write himself. As a writer, he couldn't live up to his own high standards.

CA: In your years with CBS you've won several awards for your documentaries. Is there one that you're proudest of or that you most enjoyed doing?

ROONEY: Awards are spinach. I like to get them but they don't mean anything. Everyone who has worked for very long in broadcasting wins a lot of them whether they're any good or not. "In Praise of New York City" and "Mr. Rooney Goes to Washington" were my best.

CA: Are any long documentaries in the works now?

ROONEY: I'm fighting for time for another—and losing.

CA: When you travel around to get information for a story like the one on working in America or the one on eating out, are you recognized and approached by a lot of people?

ROONEY: Four years ago when I did my last hour documentary, I was not recognized as I traveled around the country. I am now and while I'm hardly offended by people who tell me quickly and briefly that they like my work, I hate the idiots who stop me and want to talk.

CA: You've said you hate giving autographs; how do you handle requests for them?

ROONEY: I don't give autographs and it makes me feel foolish to be asked. Who'd want my name on a piece of paper? I just tell people "I don't do that." They seem to accept it. No one, by the way, ever says they want the autograph for themselves. It's for their wife or their son or their elderly mother.

CA: Do you have complete control over your topics and material for "60 Minutes"?

ROONEY: I have complete control over what subjects I choose to do and the material in them but Don Hewitt, the "60 Minutes" producer, has complete control over whether they get on the air or not.

CA: Do you get a lot of complaints from the people you complain about?

ROONEY: I don't get many complaints. The Kellogg Company, which owns Mrs. Smith's Pies, was angry because I said there was no Mrs. Smith. The druggists were irritated by my portrayal of them in television commercials, but I was kidding commercials, not druggists.

CA: In a "60 Minutes" segment several months ago you talked about women's purses. Did you hear from a lot of women about that?

ROONEY: I was surprised by the reaction I got to the piece on women's purses. Very few women were mad about it. They took it in great good humor. I was really pleased with the reaction to that particular piece.

CA: Do many people write to you offering free ideas for topics?

ROONEY: A lot of people write with ideas. Most of them aren't any good or I've already done them. I don't need ideas anyway. The world is filled with people who have ideas but short of people who know how to do anything with one. Ideas are an overrated commodity.

CA: In the preface to A Few Minutes with Andy Rooney, *you mentioned Bob Forte, your film editor, and Jane Bradford, your associate producer, both of whom you've worked with for over ten years. Can you estimate how much time the three of you spend on an average "60 Minutes" segment?*

ROONEY: I have no idea how much time we spend on a piece. When am I writing? Only when I'm typing? I don't know. Bob Forte spends more time putting it together than I do writing it. He's the one who makes it look the way it does and Jane Bradford keeps both of us from making fools of ourselves with mistakes. Jane also does a lot of research, sets up technical facilities for our pieces, and edits my column.

CA: Don Hewitt said you were "to today's television what H. L. Mencken was to newspapering many years ago." How do you feel about this?

ROONEY: I like it but it's not true. Mencken was an intellectual. I'm not.

CA: What would you like to do that you haven't done yet?

ROONEY: Live to be a hundred.

BIOGRAPHICAL/CRITICAL SOURCES: New Yorker, October 21, 1944, February 16, 1946; *New York Times,* October 29, 1944, February 17, 1946, May 25, 1947; *Saturday Review of Literature,* February 23, 1946, July 26, 1947; *Time,* July 11, 1969, July 21, 1980, November 1, 1982; *New York,* March

17, 1980; Andrew A. Rooney, *A Few Minutes with Andy Rooney,* Atheneum, 1981; *Detroit News,* November 8, 1981; *Los Angeles Times Book Review,* November 29, 1981; *Washington Post Book World,* December 20, 1981; *Virginia Quarterly Review,* spring, 1982; *Washington Post,* November 8, 1982; *Los Angeles Times,* November 11, 1982; *Newsweek,* December 6, 1982; *New York Times Book Review,* December 19, 1982; *Detroit Free Press,* January 19, 1983.

—Sketch by James G. Lesniak

—Interview by Jean W. Ross

* * *

ROONEY, Andy
See ROONEY, Andrew A(itken)

* * *

RORTY, Richard M(cKay) 1931-

PERSONAL: Born October 4, 1931, in New York, N.Y.; son of James (a writer) and Winifred (a writer; maiden name, Raushenbush) Rorty; married Amelie Oksenberg (a college teacher), June 15, 1954 (divorced September 1, 1972); married Mary Rosalind Varney (a college professor), November 4, 1972; children: (first marriage) Jay; (second marriage) Patricia, Kevin. *Education:* University of Chicago, B.A., 1949, M.A., 1952; Yale University, Ph.D., 1956. *Politics:* Democrat. *Religion:* None. *Office:* Department of English, University of Virginia, Charlottesville, Va. 23903.

CAREER: Yale University, New Haven, Conn., instructor in philosophy, 1955-56; Wellesley College, Wellesley, Mass., instructor, 1958-60, assistant professor of philosophy, 1960-61; Princeton University, Princeton, N.J., assistant professor, 1961-65, associate professor, 1965-70, professor of philosophy, 1970-82; University of Virginia, Charlottesville, Kenan Professor of Humanities, 1982—. *Military service:* U.S. Army, 1957-58. *Member:* American Philosophical Association (former president). *Awards, honors:* American Council of Learned Societies fellow, 1969-70; Guggenheim fellow, 1973-74; MacArthur Prize fellow, 1981-86.

WRITINGS: (Editor) *The Linguistic Turn: Recent Essays in Philosophical Method,* University of Chicago Press, 1967; *Philosophy and the Mirror of Nature,* Princeton University Press, 1979; *The Consequences of Pragmatism,* University of Minnesota Press, 1982. Contributor to anthologies and philosophical journals.

BIOGRAPHICAL/CRITICAL SOURCES: Los Angeles Times Book Review, December 19, 1982.

* * *

ROSE, Elizabeth (Jane Pretty) 1933-

PERSONAL: Born June 30, 1933, in Lowestoft, Suffolk, England; daughter of John Harold (a coal merchant) and Dorothy (Easey) Pretty; married Gerald Hembdon Seymour Rose (a lecturer, painter, illustrator, and author), July 27, 1955; children: Martin, Richard. *Education:* Lowestoft Technical College, general certificate of education; Saffron Walden Training College, teacher training course. *Home:* 19 Moorway, Poulton-le-Fylde, Lancashire, England.

CAREER: Author of children's books. Primary school teacher, London, England, 1954-59.

WRITINGS—All juveniles; all illustrated by husband Gerald Rose; published by Faber, except as indicated: *How St. Francis Tamed the Wolf,* 1958; *Wuffles Goes to Town,* 1959.

(Co-author with Gerald Rose) *Old Winkle and the Seagulls,* 1960, reprinted, Penguin, 1976; *Charlie on the Run,* 1961; *The Big River,* 1962, Norton, 1964; (with G. Rose) *Punch and Judy Carry On,* 1962; (with G. Rose) *St. George and the Fiery Dragon,* 1963; (adaptor) *Good King Wenceslas,* 1964, Transatlantic, 1966; (adaptor) *The Sorcerer's Apprentice,* Walker & Co., 1966; *Tim's Giant Marrow,* Benn, 1966; (adaptor) *The Magic Suit,* 1966; (with G. Rose) *Alexander's Flycycle,* 1967, Walker & Co., 1969.

(With G. Rose) *The Great Oak,* 1970; (with G. Rose) *Androcles and the Lion,* 1971; (with G. Rose) *Albert and the Green Bottle,* 1972; (with G. Rose) *Wolf! Wolf!,* Merrimack Book Service, 1974; *Mick Keeps a Secret,* Benn, 1974; (adaptor with G. Rose) *Lucky Hans,* Merrimack Book Service, 1976. Also author of *Beginning to Read Storybook,* Benn, 1977.†

* * *

ROSE, Gerald (Hembdon Seymour) 1935-

PERSONAL: Born July 27, 1935, in Hong Kong; son of Henley Hembdon and Rachel Grace (Law) Rose; married Elizabeth Jane Pretty (an author), July 27, 1955; children: Martin, Richard. *Education:* Attended Lowestoft School of Art; Royal Academy, national diploma in design (honors), 1955. *Home:* 19 Moorway, Poulton-le-Fylde, Lancashire, England.

CAREER: Writer and illustrator.

WRITINGS: All self-illustrated juveniles; published by Merrimack Book Service, except as indicated: *Ironhead,* 1973; *Trouble in the Ark,* Minnow Books, 1975; *Ahhh! Said the Stork,* 1977; *Watch Out!,* Penguin, 1978; *The Tiger-skin Rug,* Prentice-Hall, 1979; *Rabbit Pie,* 1980; *PB Takes a Holiday,* 1980.

All with wife Elizabeth Rose; all self-illustrated juveniles; published by Faber, except as indicated: *Old Winkle and the Seagulls,* 1960, reprinted, Penguin, 1976; *Punch and Judy Carry On,* 1962; *St. George and the Fiery Dragon,* 1963; *Alexander's Flycycle,* 1967, Walker & Co., 1969; *The Great Oak,* 1970; *Androcles and the Lion,* 1971; *Albert and the Green Bottle,* 1972; *Wolf! Wolf!,* Merrimack Book Service, 1974; (adaptor) *Lucky Hans,* Merrimack Book Service, 1976.

Illustrator: E. Rose, *How St. Francis Tamed the Wolf,* Faber, 1958; E. Rose, *Wuffles Goes to Town,* Faber, 1959.

E. Rose, *Charlie on the Run,* Faber, 1961; Carol Odell, *Mark and His Pictures,* Faber, 1962, Walker & Co., 1968; E. Rose, *The Big River,* Faber, 1962, Norton, 1964; Ted Hughes, *Nessie the Mannerless Monster,* Faber, 1964; Irmengarde Eberle, *Pete and the Mouse,* Abelard, 1964; Peter Hughes, *The King Who Loved Candy,* Abelard, 1964; E. Rose, adaptor, *Good King Wenceslas,* Faber, 1964, Transatlantic, 1966; *The Gingerbread Man,* Norton, 1965; E. Rose, adaptor, *The Sorcerer's Apprentice,* Walker & Co., 1966; E. Rose, *Tim's Giant Marrow,* Benn, 1966; E. Rose, adaptor, *The Magic Suit,* Faber, 1966; Leonce Bourliaguet, *The Giant Who Drank from His Shoe,* Abelard, 1966; P. Hughes, *Baron Brandy's Boots,* Abelard, 1966; Bourliaguet, *A Sword to Slice through Mountains,* Abelard, 1968; Charles Lutwidge Dodgson, *Jabberwocky and Other Poems,* Faber, 1968; Dodgson, *The Walrus and the Carpenter and Other Poems,* Dutton, 1968; Edward Lear, *The Dong with a Luminous Nose and Other Poems,* Faber, 1969.

Jeremy Kingston, *The Bird Who Saved the Jungle,* Faber, 1973; Wilma Horsbrugh, *The Bold Bad Bus and Other Rhyming Stories,* British Broadcasting Corp., 1973; Leila Berg, *The Little Cat,* Puffin, 1974; E. Rose, *Mick Keeps a Secret,* Benn, 1974.†

* * *

ROSEN, Joe
See ROSEN, Joseph

* * *

ROSEN, Joseph 1937-
(Joe Rosen)

PERSONAL: Born October 20, 1937, in Kiev, Soviet Union; immigrated to Israel, 1953; son of Nathan (a physicist) and Anna (Belkes) Rosen; married Dalia Musarov (a cell biologist), 1960; children: Laliv. *Education:* Technion—Israel Institute of Technology, B.S., 1960, M.S., 1962; Hebrew University of Jerusalem, Ph.D., 1967. *Home:* 40 Yehuda Hanasi St., Tel-Aviv 69393, Israel. *Office:* Department of Physics and Astronomy, Tel-Aviv University, Tel-Aviv 69978, Israel.

CAREER: Tel-Aviv University, Tel-Aviv, Israel, assistant, 1962-65, senior lecturer in theoretical physics, 1969—. Senior research associate at Boston University, 1965-66; research associate and assistant professor (research) at Brown University, 1966-69; visiting professor at University of North Carolina, 1976-77. *Military service:* Israel Defense Forces, 1960-62; became first lieutenant. *Member:* Israel Physical Society.

WRITINGS—Under name Joe Rosen: *Symmetry Discovered: Concepts and Applications in Nature and Science,* Cambridge University Press, 1975; (editor with Giora Shaviv) *Proceedings of the Seventh International Conference on General Relativity and Gravitation GR7,* Wiley, 1975; *A Symmetry Primer for Scientists,* Wiley, 1983; (editor) *Symmetry and Group Theory in Physics,* American Association of Physics Teachers, 1983. Contributor to physics and mathematical physics journals.

WORK IN PROGRESS: Research on symmetry and conservation laws in theoretical physics and on other fundamental problems such as space, time and spacetime.

AVOCATIONAL INTERESTS: Music (playing, composing, conducting), linguistics, pistol shooting, "tinkering and repairing things," reading, travel, jogging.

SIDELIGHTS: Joseph Rosen writes: "My bibliography might lead one to believe that symmetry has grabbed me hard, and indeed it has. I have met others similarly stricken with the symmetry disease. My guess is that in most cases, as in mine, it is related to a general preference for regularity and to considerations of esthetics. Symptoms usually include interest in the work of the graphic artist M. C. Escher. My conjunction of symmetry and music composition has apparently resulted in tendencies toward strict meter (discrete temporal displacement symmetry, to be technical), especially marches (some twenty-five for wind band), and toward repeated rhythmic figures. I am constantly struggling to counteract these tendencies.

"The two books I authored, *Symmetry Discovered: Concepts and Applications in Nature and Science* and *A Symmetry Primer for Scientists,* were written because in each case: a) I wanted to clarify things for myself by writing them down in an orderly manner; b) I felt that the results of my clarifications should be made public; c) There was a gap in the literature. In both cases I had the first draft finished or almost finished before approaching publishers.

"*Symmetry Discovered* is a semipopular presentation. . . . This being the first book that I ever wrote, it was most encouraging that almost all the reviews were positive, from good to excellent. The only exception was a single review, which worried me at the time but soon stopped bothering me as its true weight became evident. I think now I have the proper attitude toward reviews: Learn what you can from them, but don't take them too seriously. In support of the latter I like to tell about two reviewers' reactions to my extensive use of A. A. Milne quotations in *Symmetry Discovered.* One reviewer, who wrote a very complimentary review, praised the appropriateness of the quotations. The other, the above-mentioned negative one, denounced their irrelevance. In any case, the publisher made a second printing when the first ran out, a science book club offered the book to its members, and a Japanese language edition was published."

BIOGRAPHICAL/CRITICAL SOURCES: Choice, April, 1976.

* * *

ROSENBERG, Jerry M. 1935-

PERSONAL: Born February 5, 1935, in New York, N.Y.; son of Frank (a businessman) and Esther (Gardner) Rosenberg; married Ellen Young, September 11, 1960; children: Lauren Monica, Elizabeth. *Education:* City College (now City College of the City University of New York), B.S., 1956; Ohio State University, M.A., 1957; Sorbonne, University of Paris, Certificate, 1958; New York University, Ph.D., 1962. *Religion:* Hebrew. *Home:* 515 Tulfan Ter., New York, N.Y. 10463. *Office:* Department of Business Administration, Rutgers University, Newark, N.J. 07102.

CAREER: Government Bureau of Automation, Paris, France, research psychologist, 1957-58; State University of New York, School of Industrial and Labor Relations at Cornell University, Ithaca, assistant professor, 1961-64; Columbia University, New York City, assistant professor, 1964-68; Polytechnic Institute of Brooklyn, Brooklyn, N.Y., professor of management and chairman of department, 1974-77; City University of New York, New York City, professor of management, 1977-80; Rutgers University, Newark, N.J., professor in Graduate School of Management and chairman of department of business administration, 1980—. Lecturer, Institute of Productivity, Tel-Aviv, summer, 1962; visiting professor, University of British Columbia, summer, 1967. Former conference director, American Foundation on Automation and Employment. Former member of New York Mayor's Committee on Youth and Work and of National Conference of Christians and Jews advisory committee for labor, management, and public interest. *Member:* Academy of Management. *Awards, honors:* Grants from Fulbright Foundation and French government.

WRITINGS: Automation, Manpower and Education, Random House, 1966; *The Death of Privacy,* Random House, 1969; *The Computer Prophets,* Macmillan, 1969; *Dictionary of Business and Management,* Wiley, 1978; *Dictionary of Banking and Finance,* Wiley, 1982; *Inside the Wall Street Journal,* Macmillan, 1982.

AVOCATIONAL INTERESTS: Tennis, travel, collecting autographed documents and maps.

* * *

ROSENBERG, Stuart E. 1922-

PERSONAL: Born July 5, 1922, in New York, N.Y.; immigrated to Canada in 1956; son of Hyman and Kate (Weissman) Rosenberg; married Hadassa Agassi, February 20, 1944; children: Rachelle, Ronni, Elissa Beth. *Education:* Brooklyn College (now Brooklyn College of the City University of New York), B.A., 1942; Jewish Theological Seminary of America, Rabbi, 1945, M.H.L., 1948; Columbia University, M.A., 1948, Ph.D., 1953.

CAREER: Temple Beth El, Rochester, N.Y., rabbi, 1946-56; Beth Tzedec Congregation, Toronto, Ontario, rabbi, beginning 1956. Lecturer in religion, University of Rochester, Rochester, N.Y., 1951-56; instructor, Graduate Ecumenical Institute of Canada, 1967; visiting lecturer, University of Toronto. Member of rabbinic cabinet and board of overseers, Jewish Theological Seminary of America. Official observer of refugee operations in Iran, North Africa, Austria, Italy, France, and Israel. Trustee, Toronto United Community Fund. *Member:* Rabbinical Assembly of America (member of executive council), National Foundation for Jewish Culture (vice-president), Canadian Foundation for Jewish Culture (president). *Awards, honors:* Citation for leadership, Canadian Mental Health Association, 1963; D.D. from Jewish Theological Seminary of America, 1971.

WRITINGS: The Jewish Community in Rochester, Columbia University Press, 1954; *Man Is Free* (essays), Bloch, 1957; *The Road to Confidence,* Messner, 1959.

A Time to Speak (essays), Bloch, 1960; *Bridge to Brotherhood,* Abelard, 1961; *The Bible Is for You,* McKay, 1961; (editor) *A Humane Society* (essays), University of Toronto Press, 1962; *More Loves Than One: The Bible Confronts Psychiatry,* Ungar, 1963; *America Is Different: The Search for Jewish Identity,* Thomas Nelson, 1964, published as *The Search for Jewish Identity in America,* Doubleday, 1965; *Lines on Life,* Thomas Nelson, 1965; *Judaism,* Paulist Press, 1966, published as *To Understand Jews,* Hodder & Stoughton, 1973; (with Martin E. Marty and Andrew M. Greeley) *What Do We Believe?,* Meredith Press, 1968.

The Jewish Community in Canada, McClelland & Stewart, 1970; *Great Religions of the Holy Land: An Historical Guide to Sacred Places and Sites,* A. S. Barnes, 1971; *When the Bough Breaks,* Berkley Publishing, 1977.

Also author of weekly syndicated column, "Lines on Life," published in United States and Canadian newspapers; contributor to *Chicago Tribune Sunday Magazine,* and to general and scholarly magazines.

WORK IN PROGRESS: Jewish Intellectuals in America.†

* * *

ROSENBERG, Wolfgang 1915-

PERSONAL: Born January 4, 1915, in Berlin, Germany; son of Curt (a solicitor) and Elsa (Stein) Rosenberg; married Ann Eichelbaum (a social worker), February 15, 1946; children: George, William, Vera. *Education:* University of New Zealand, M.Com., 1943, F.C.A., 1945. *Home:* 14 Sherwood Lane, Christchurch, New Zealand. *Office address:* c/o M. J. Knowles, Barrister and Solicitor, Box 2157, Christchurch, New Zealand.

CAREER: University of Canterbury, Christchurch, New Zealand, reader in economics, 1946-80; barrister and solicitor, Christchurch, 1980—.

WRITINGS: Full Employment: Can New Zealand's Economic Miracle Last?, A. H. & A. W. Reed, 1960; *A Guideline to New Zealand's Future,* Caxton Press, 1968; *Money in New Zealand,* Reed Education, 1973; (contributor) Thomson and Trolin, editors, *Contemporary New Zealand,* Hicks, Smith & Wright, 1973; *The Coming Depression,* Caxton, 1978; *C.E.R.: Sanity or Sellout?,* New Zealand Monthly Review Society, 1982.

WORK IN PROGRESS: Research on industrialization, on Korean development in north and south, and on economics of political independence.

SIDELIGHTS: Wolfgang Rosenberg writes: "My main interest is to throw light on the forces which move New Zealand society, a small homogeneous society which nonetheless is split into antagonistic interest groups and subject to the vagaries of the international trading system."

* * *

ROSENBLUM, Richard 1928-

PERSONAL: Born January 24, 1928, in Brooklyn, N.Y.; son of Archie (a retired tailor) and Anna Rosenblum; married Barbara Rhode (a secretary), May 5, 1959; children: Anne. *Education:* Attended Cooper Union, three years, received diploma. *Politics:* "Liberal/Democratic/Independent." *Religion:* Jewish. *Home:* 2 Grace Ct., Brooklyn, N.Y. 11201. *Office:* 392 Fifth Ave., New York, N.Y. 10018.

CAREER: Free-lance illustrator; *New York Herald Tribune,* New York City, art apprentice, 1950-51; CBS-TV News, New York City, staff artist, 1951-52; UPA Films, New York City, animation designer, 1955-57; teacher of illustration at Parsons School of Design. Has had exhibitions at Art Director Club and Society of Illustrators, both New York City. Member of executive board, Grace Court Association. *Military service:* U.S. Army, 1946.

WRITINGS—Self-illustrated: *Tugboats,* Holt, 1976; *Wings,* Four Winds, 1980.

Illustrator: Frank L. Baum, *Kidnapped Santa Claus,* Bobbs-Merrill, 1969; *Ecidujerp-Prejudice,* Watts, 1974; Scott Corbett, *Bridges,* Four Winds, 1978; Judith Herbst, *The Sky Above and Worlds Below,* Atheneum, 1983.

WORK IN PROGRESS: A self-illustrated book, *Wings: The Golden Years,* for Atheneum.

SIDELIGHTS: Richard Rosenblum told *CA:* "Although I do not consider myself a writer, I find that I'm writing more books that I am also illustrating. That's because it's easier to get books to illustrate when you also write them. I do depend on a good editor to make the writing more readable. I'm a terrible grammarian and speller, but my ideas are good! As I write more books I gain more confidence. It will take about 403 more books for me to really believe I'm a writer. An artist, I *know* I am."

BIOGRAPHICAL/CRITICAL SOURCES: New York Times Book Review, January 2, 1977.

* * *

ROSS, Dallas
See REYNOLDS, Dallas McCord

* * *

ROYCE, R(ussell) Joseph 1921-

PERSONAL: Born August 19, 1921, in New York, N.Y.; son

of Alfred and Clara (Andersen) Royce; married Lee Summerlin, April 3, 1944; children: Christopher, Janet. *Education:* Attended City College (now City College of the City University of New York), 1937-38; Denison University, A.B., 1941; Ohio State University, graduate study, 1941-42; University of Chicago, Ph.D., 1951. *Office:* Center for Advanced Study in Theoretical Psychology, University of Alberta, Edmonton, Alberta, Canada T6G 2E9.

CAREER: Drake University, Des Moines, Iowa, assistant professor of psychology, 1949-51; University of Redlands, Redlands, Calif., 1951-60, began as assistant professor, became associate professor of psychology; University of Alberta, Edmonton, professor of psychology and head of department, 1960-67, founder and director of Center for Advanced Study in Theoretical Psychology, 1967—. Visiting professor, University of Hawaii, summer, 1964, and Australian National University, spring, 1975. Lecturer at national and international societies and universities in North America, Europe, United Kingdom, and Australia. Statistical consultant to U.S. Air Force. Psychological consultant to New York City. *Military service:* U.S. Army Air Forces, 1942-46; became first lieutenant.

MEMBER: American Psychological Association (president of division of theoretical and philosophical psychology, 1969-70), Society for Multivariate Experimental Psychology, Behavior Genetics Association, Canadian Psychological Association, Institute on Religion in an Age of Science (member of board of advisors), Alberta Psychological Association, Sigma Xi. *Awards, honors:* Ford Foundation faculty fellow, 1955-60; Canada Council senior research fellow in Europe, 1965-66; received grants from National Institute of Mental Health, American Academy of Arts and Sciences, National Research Council (Canada), Canada Council, and other institutions and foundations.

WRITINGS: The Encapsulated Man: An Interdisciplinary Essay on the Search for Meaning, Van Nostrand, 1964; (editor and contributor) *Psychology and the Symbol: An Interdisciplinary Symposium,* Random House, 1965.

(Editor and contributor) *Toward Unification of Psychology,* University of Toronto Press, 1970; (editor with W. W. Rozeboom) *The Psychology of Knowing,* Gordon & Breach, 1972; (editor and contributor) *Multivariate Analysis and Psychological Theory,* Academic Press, 1973; (editor with L. P. Mos and contributor) *Theoretical Advances in Behavior Genetics,* Sijthoff, 1979.

(With Mos) *The Psycho-Epistemological Profile Manual,* University of Alberta Printing Office, 1980; (editor with Mos and contributor) *Humanistic Psychology: Concepts and Criticisms,* Plenum, 1980; (with A. Powell) *A Theory of Personality and Individual Differences: Factors, Systems, and Processes,* Prentice-Hall, in press.

Contributor: R. S. Daniel, editor, *Contemporary Readings in General Psychology,* Houghton, 1959, 2nd edition, 1965; H. A. Estrin and D. M. Good, editors, *College and University Teaching,* W. C. Brown, 1964; W. A. Fullager, H. G. Lewis, and C. F. Cumber, editors, *Readings for Educational Psychology,* 2nd edition (Royce not associated with previous edition), Crowell, 1964; J. P. Guilford, editor, *Fields of Psychology,* 3rd edition (Royce not associated with previous editions), Van Nostrand, 1966; R. B. Cattell, editor, *Handbook of Multivariate Experimental Psychology,* McNally & Loftin, 1966; D. N. Jackson and S. Messick, editors, *Problems in Human Assessment,* McGraw, 1967; J.F.T. Bugental, editor, *Challenges of Humanistic Psychology,* McGraw, 1967; Joseph Havens, editor, *Psychology and Religion,* Van Nostrand, 1968; M. Manosevitz, G. Lindzey, and D. D. Theissen, editors, *Behavioral Genetics: Method and Research,* Appleton, 1969.

V. S. Sexton and H. Misiak, editors, *Historical Perspectives in Psychology: Readings,* Brooks-Cole, 1971; W. D. Birrell, P.A.R. Hillyard, A. S. Murie and D. D. Roche, editors, *Social Administration: Readings in Applied Social Sciences,* Penguin, 1973; B. B. Wolman, editor, *Handbook of General Psychology,* Prentice-Hall, 1973; E. C. Carterette and M. P. Friedman, editors, *Historical and Philosophical Roots to Perception,* Academic Press, 1974; M. T. Holmes and W. Poley, editors, *Current Problems in Animal Behavior Genetics,* Pavlov Institute of Physiology (Leningrad), 1975; A. Debons and W. Cameron, editors, *NATO Conference on Information Sciences,* International Publishing (Netherlands), 1975; W. J. Arnold, editor, *Nebraska Symposium on the Conceptual Foundations of Theory and Methods in Psychology,* University of Nebraska Press, 1975; J. Christian, editor, *Extra-Terrestrial Intelligence: The Biocosmic Community,* Prometheus Books, 1976; A. Oliverio, editor, *Genetics, Environment and Intelligence,* Elsevier/North Holland, 1977; *Proceedings of the Fifth International Conference on Unity of the Sciences,* International Cultural Foundation Press, 1977; T. S. Krawiec, editor, *The Psychologists,* Clinical Psychology Publishing, 1978; J. M. Scandura and C. J. Brainerd, editors, *NATO Structural Process Theories of Complex Human Behavior,* Sijthoff, 1978.

G. E. Lasker, editor, *Applied Systems in Cybernetics,* Pergamon, 1981; N. Datlof and A. Ugrinsky, editors, *Albert Einstein as an Interdisciplinary and Intercultural Phenomena,* Hofstra University, in press; J. Strelau, F. Farley, and A. Gale, editors, *The Biological Foundations of Personality and Behavior,* Hemisphere Publications, in press.

Contributor of more than 100 articles and reviews to professional journals. Associate editor, *Multivariate Behavioral Research,* 1965-74, *Psychological Record,* 1965-75, *Perspectives: A Journal of General and Liberal Studies,* 1969—, and *Journal of Psycholinguistic Research,* 1970—; editor, *Newsletter of the Philosophical Psychology Division of the American Psychological Association,* 1965-69, and *Theoretical Psychology: Annals,* 1983—.

WORK IN PROGRESS: A book; several theoretical articles; a play, "You're Ill Sam Gill, Take a Pill."

AVOCATIONAL INTERESTS: Sports (skiing and golfing), aficionado of bullfighting, hockey, chess, and theatre.

BIOGRAPHICAL/CRITICAL SOURCES: T. S. Krawiec, *The Psychologists,* Volume III, Ohio University Press, 1975.

* * *

RUBIN, Mark 1946-

PERSONAL: Born May 30, 1946, in New York, N.Y.; son of Murray (a treasury agent) and Edith (an employee of Easter Seals; maiden name, Kasten) Rubin; married Barbara Messenger (a teacher), August 23, 1969. *Education:* Cooper Union, B.F.A., 1967.

CAREER: Mark Rubin Design, New York City, principal designer, 1972-74; Penny Tax Productions, New York City, principal designer, beginning 1974.

WRITINGS: (Self-illustrated) *The Boy Who Painted Wallpaper* (juvenile), F. Watts, 1974; (with Louise Horton) *Art Careers,*

F. Watts, 1975; (with Ralph H. Peck) *Travel Careers,* F. Watts, 1976; (with William Gurney) *Writing Careers,* F. Watts, 1976. Author of filmstrip, "Little Lou and His Strange Little Zoo," Urban Media Materials, 1972.

WORK IN PROGRESS: A magazine, *Penny Tax.*†

* * *

RUDOLF, Anthony 1942-

PERSONAL: Born September 6, 1942, in London, England; son of Henry Cyril (a certified public accountant) and Esther (Rosenberg) Rudolf; married Brenda Marshall (a book designer), March 15, 1970 (divorced, 1981); children: Nathaniel. *Education:* British Institute, Paris, France, certificate (with distinction), 1961; Trinity College, Cambridge, B.A., 1964. *Politics:* Labour Party. *Religion:* Jewish. *Home:* 8 The Oaks, Woodside Avenue, London N12, England.

CAREER: Junior executive with British Travel Association, London, England, and Chicago, Ill., 1964-66; teacher of English and French in London School Service, and private teacher of English as a foreign language, 1967-68; worked in London bookshops including a period as co-proprieter of own business, 1969-71; *European Judaism,* London, literary editor, 1970-72, managing editor, 1972-75. Has broadcast for British Broadcasting Corp. Radio, British Broadcasting Corp. World Service, and French radio, and given poetry readings in Great Britain and Macedonia. *Member:* National Poetry Centre (member of general council, 1970-76).

WRITINGS: (Translator) *Selected Poems of Yves Bonnefoy,* J. Cape, 1968, Grossman, 1969; (translator) Ana Novac, *The Soup Complex* (play), Stand, 1972; (editor with Richard Burns) *An Octave for Paz,* Menard, 1972; (translator) *Tyorkin and the Stovemakers: Selected Verse and Prose of Alexander Tvardovsky,* Carcanet, 1974; (compiler) *Edmund Jabes Bibliography,* Menard, 1974.

(Translator with D. Weisshort) *Selected Verse of Evgeni Vinokurov,* Carcanet, 1975; (translator with Petru Popescu) *Poems of Petru Popescu,* Omphalos, 1975; (editor) *Poems for Shakespeare IV,* Globe Playhouse Trust Publications, 1975; (translator) *The Storm: Verse Play by Eugene Heimler,* Menard, 1976; *The Same River Twice* (poems), Carcanet, 1976; (translator) *Poems of Edmond Jabes,* Menard, 1978; (editor with Howard Schwartz) *Voices within the Ark: The Modern Jewish Poets,* Avon, 1980; *After the Dream* (poems), Cauldron, 1980.

Contributor of poems, articles, and reviews to literary journals, including *Tree, Holy Beggars Gazette, Roy Rogers, Nation,* and *Contemporary Literature in Translation.* London editor of *Stand.* Founder and co-editor of *Journals of Pierre Menard;* advisory editor of *Modern Poetry in Translation* and *Heimler Foundation Newsletter.* Guest editor of *Cambridge Opinion/Circuit,* 1968, *Workshop,* 1971, *Poetry Review,* 1971, *Modern Poetry in Translation,* 1973, *New Linguist,* 1973, *Books,* 1974, and *Roy Rogers,* 1974.

BIOGRAPHICAL/CRITICAL SOURCES: New York Times Book Review, January 4, 1981.

RUTHERFORD, Andrew 1929-

PERSONAL: Born July 23, 1929, in Sutherland, Scotland; son of Thomas Armstrong and Christian (Russell) Rutherford; married Nancy Milroy Browning, 1953; children: Richard, John, Alison. *Education:* University of Edinburgh, M.A. (first class honors), 1951; Oxford University, B.Litt., 1959. *Home:* 150 Hamilton Pl., Aberdeen AB2 4BB, Scotland. *Office:* Department of English Literature, King's College, University of Aberdeen, Aberdeen AB9 2UB, Scotland.

CAREER: University of Edinburgh, Edinburgh, Scotland, assistant lecturer, 1955-56, lecturer in English literature, 1956-64; University of Aberdeen, Aberdeen, Scotland, senior lecturer, 1964-65, professor of English, 1965-68, Regius Professor of English Literature, 1968—, dean of Faculty of Arts and Social Sciences, 1979-82, vice-principal, 1982—. Visiting associate professor of English, University of Rochester, Rochester, N.Y., 1963. *Military service:* British Army, Seaforth Highlanders, 1951-53; served in Somaliland Protectorate; became lieutenant.

WRITINGS: Byron: A Critical Study, Oliver & Boyd, 1961, Stanford University Press, 1962; (editor and contributor) *Kipling's Mind and Art,* Stanford University Press, 1964.

(Editor and compiler) *Byron: The Critical Heritage,* Barnes & Noble, 1970; *Twentieth Century Interpretations of "A Passage to India,"* Prentice-Hall, 1970; (editor) Rudyard Kipling, *Friendly Brook and Other Stories,* Penguin, 1971; (editor) Kipling, *A Sahibs' War and Other Stories,* Penguin, 1971; *The Literature of War: Five Studies in Heroic Virtue,* Macmillan, 1979; (contributor) C. E. Robinson, editor, *Lord Byron and His Contemporaries,* University of Delaware Press, 1982; (contributor) D. Hewitt and M. Spiller, editors, *Literature of the North,* Aberdeen University Press, 1983. Contributor to numerous journals.

WORK IN PROGRESS: A critical edition of Kipling's verse.

SIDELIGHTS: In *The Literature of War: Five Studies in Heroic Virtue,* Andrew Rutherford studies five examples of heroic virtue found in literature and art. A reviewer for *Economist* explains that Rutherford "maintains in this absorbing study of heroism [that] . . . the problems confronting would-be heroes have not essentially changed, but their justification and acceptability have been questioned more searchingly and disturbingly this century than ever before." A critic for *Choice* feels that "Rutherford's subjects 'treat heroic themes and reinvestigate heroic values.'" Finally the reviewer for *Economist* writes in summation: "Rutherford's book is more than literary criticism. It is an elegant, closely argued and encouraging assertion that heroic values survive, and that great heroes can still exist."

BIOGRAPHICAL/CRITICAL SOURCES: Economist, March 24, 1979; *Choice,* April, 1979; *New Statesman,* August 24, 1979.

S

SADIE, Stanley (John) 1930-

PERSONAL: Born October 30, 1930, in Wembley, Middlesex, England; son of David (a textile merchant) and Deborah (Simons) Sadie; married Adele Bloom, December 10, 1953 (died, 1978); married Julie Anne McCornack Vertrees, July 18, 1978; children: (first marriage) Graham Robert, Ursula Joan, Stephen Peter; (second marriage) Celia Kathryn. *Education:* Cambridge University, B.A., 1953, Mus.B., 1953, M.A., 1957, and Ph.D., 1958. *Home:* 1 Carlisle Gardens, Harrow, Middlesex, England. *Office: New Grove Dictionary of Music and Musicians,* Macmillan Publishers Ltd., Little Essex St., London WC2R 3LF, England.

CAREER: Trinity College of Music, London, England, lecturer, 1957-65; *Times,* London, music critic, 1964-81; *Musical Times,* London, associate editor, 1966-67, editor, 1967—; Macmillan Publishers Ltd., London, editor of *New Grove Dictionary of Music and Musicians,* 1970—; J. M. Dent & Sons (publishers), London, editor of "Master Musicians" series, 1976—. *Military service:* Royal Air Force, 1948-49. *Member:* Royal Musical Association, Critics' Circle (honorary secretary, music section, 1965-67; chairman, music section, 1967-70), American Musicological Society.

WRITINGS: Handel, J. Calder, 1962, Crowell, 1968; (with Arthur Jacobs) *Pan Book of Opera,* Pan Books, 1964 (published in England as *The Opera Guide,* Hamish Hamilton, 1964), published as *Great Operas in Synopsis,* Crowell, 1966; *Mozart,* J. Calder, 1966, Grossman, 1970; *Beethoven,* Crowell, 1967; *Handel Concertos,* University of Washington Press, 1972, B.B.C. Publications, 1973; (editor and contributor) *The New Grove Dictionary of Music and Musicans,* Macmillan (London), 1980. Contributor to *Gramophone, Musical Times, Opera,* and other musical publications.

WORK IN PROGRESS: Further studies on Mozart.

SIDELIGHTS: The New Grove Dictionary of Music and Musicians, edited by Stanley Sadie, is "a landmark, a dazzling achievement," exclaims Joseph McLellan in *Washington Post Book World.* "Its appearance is one of the major publishing events of our time." The twenty-volume, twenty million-word compendium of articles on musical movements and genres, composers and performers, instruments and individual works, is "a great achievement, a masterpiece," writes Anthony Burgess in *Times Literary Supplement.* Harold C. Schonberg in *New York Times Book Review* calls the dictionary "the most ambitious and comprehensive musical dictionary and encyclopedia ever attempted, and overall, it is a brilliant success."

Ten years in the making, *The New Grove Dictionary of Music and Musicians* contains thousands of entries examining not only larger aspects of musicology, but also the minutiae. Comments McLellan: "No music scholar, no matter how learned, can read [this dictionary] at random for any length of time without learning something new; . . . no reference library can claim to be adequately well-rounded unless it has a copy." Although reviewers criticize the work for omissions and oversights (Burgess, for instance, cites the absence of entries on harmonica player John Sebastian and composer Stanley Silverman; McLellan laments that while the dictionary contains an entry on birdsong, it lacks one on the music of whales), the dictionary's comprehensive coverage of non-Western, non-classical music "amounts to a revolution," states McLellan. "[This thoroughness is evidenced by] a remarkable fineness of perception," the critic continues. "There is a full page on the Beatles, for example, including some thoughtful musical analysis. There is an entry on Elvis Presley, but none on Dolly Parton—and in terms of their musical importance, this is precisely as it should be. . . . There are special articles on the musical culture of all the world's major cities and virtually every country."

Critics also praise the work's style as well as its content. "The articles on Mozart [written by Sadie], . . . Beethoven, Wagner and the rest can hardly be overpraised," claims Burgess. "They are not merely informative, they are sometimes thrilling in the manner of literature."

The New Grove Dictionary of Music and Musicians is not without its flaws, the critics note. In addition to mentioning the absence of several noteworthy composers, Burgess also questions the amount of space allotted to several entries. Schonberg finds that "a few articles are surprisingly perfunctory and weak," and McLellan points out several errors he attributes to typographical mistakes and careless copy-editing. Furthermore, Burgess, Schonberg, and McLellan all agree that, in Schonberg's words, "there has been no attempt at popularization or easy writing. . . . Some of the articles—the one on Analysis is a good example—are written by experts for experts." The dictionary "does not provide a musical education from scratch. You have to be pretty far gone before you can use [it] at all," says Burgess.

"The flaws [of the dictionary]," comments McLellan, "are present and noticeable." Still, that critic continues, "those [flaws] that I have found so far seem insignificant in relation to the massiveness of the undertaking." *The New Grove Dictionary of Music and Musicians,* concludes Schonberg, is "a heroic effort that leaves its predecessor far behind. Whatever weakness[es] turn up in it will stem from the fallibilities of individual writers rather than from a lack of editorial effort and vision."

AVOCATIONAL INTERESTS: Reading, watching cricket, playing bridge.

BIOGRAPHICAL/CRITICAL SOURCES: New York Times Book Review, December 21, 1980; *Washington Post Book World,* February 1, 1981; *Times Literary Supplement,* February 20, 1981.

* * *

SAGE, Juniper
See HURD, Edith (Thacher)

* * *

SALISBURY, Richard Frank 1926-

PERSONAL: Born December 8, 1926, in London, England; son of Thomas (a contractor) and Marjorie Beatrice (Smith) Salisbury; married Mary Roseborough, August 21, 1954; children: Thomas S., John W., Catherine E. *Education:* St. John's College, Cambridge, B.A., 1949, M.A., 1956; Harvard University, A.M., 1955; Australian National University, Ph.D., 1957. *Home:* 451 Strathcona Ave., Westmount, Quebec, Canada H3Y 2X2. *Office:* Department of Anthropology, McGill University, Montreal, Quebec, Canada.

CAREER: Harvard University, Cambridge, Mass., research associate in public health, 1955-56; Tufts University, Medford, Mass., assistant professor of anthropology, 1956-57; University of California, Berkeley, assistant professor of anthropology, 1957-62; McGill University, Montreal, Quebec, 1962—, began as associate professor, professor of anthropology, 1966—, chairman of department, 1966-70. Visiting professor, University of Papua and New Guinea, 1967. Director, Centre for Developing Area Studies, 1975-78. Member, Social Science Research Council of Canada, 1969, and Canada Council, 1974-78. Consultant to Canadian Department of Agriculture, 1970-72, Administration of Papua and New Guinea, 1971, James Bay Development Corp., 1971-72, Indians of Quebec, 1972-74, and Canadian Department of Communications, 1974-78. Has conducted research in New Guinea and Australia, 1952-54, and 1964-66. *Military service:* Royal Marines, 1945-48; became lieutenant.

MEMBER: Academy of Humanities and Social Sciences (secretary, 1977—), Canadian Ethnological Society, Royal Society of Canada, Canadian Sociology and Anthropology Association (former president), Royal Anthropological Institute, American Anthropological Association, American Ethnological Society, Polynesian Society, English-Speaking Union.

WRITINGS: From Stone to Steel: Economic Consequences of a Technological Change in New Guinea, Cambridge University Press, 1962; *Structures of Custodial Care,* University of California Press, 1962; (with others) *Ethnographic Notes on Amerindian Agriculture,* McGill University, 1968; *Vunamami: Economic Transformation in a Traditional Society,* University of California Press, 1970; (with others) *Development and James Bay,* McGill University, 1972; (editor with M. Silverman) *A House Divided?: Anthropological Studies of Factionalism,* Institute of Social and Economic Research, Memorial University of Newfoundland, 1978. Contributor of over fifty articles to numerous journals, including *Anthropologica, American Anthropologist, Man,* and *Journal of the Polynesian Society.*

* * *

SALTER, Elizabeth 1918-1981

PERSONAL: Born 1918 in Anguston, Australia; died March 14, 1981; daughter of Alfred Fulton and Sarah (Wilkinson) Salter. *Education:* Attended University of Adelaide, 1937-39, and Conservatorium of Adelaide, 1939-41. *Politics:* Liberal. *Religion:* Christian. *Home:* 9 Regina Court, 40 Fitzjohns Ave., London, England. *Agent:* International Famous Agency, 244 East 49th St., New York, N.Y. 10017.

CAREER: Australian Broadcasting Commission, Adelaide, programmer of music, 1941-47; secretary to Dame Edith Sitwell in London, England, 1957-64; writer. *Military service:* Australian Women's Auxiliary Air Force, 1944-46; became entertainments officer.

MEMBER: Crime Writers Association. *Awards, honors:* Commonwealth Literary Award, 1971, for *Daisy Bates,* and 1973-74, for *The Lost Impressionist.*

WRITINGS: Death in a Mist (novel), Bles, 1957, Ace Books, 1958; *Will to Survive,* Bles, 1957, Ace Books, 1958; *There Was a Witness: The Voice of the Peacock* (novel), Bles, 1961, Ace Books, 1963; *Once upon a Tombstone* (novel), Ace Books, 1965; *The Last Years of a Rebel: A Memoir of Edith Sitwell,* Houghton, 1967.

Daisy Bates: "The Great White Queen of the Never Never" (biography), Angus & Robertson, 1971, Coward, 1972; *The Lost Impressionist: A Biography of John Peter Russell,* Angus & Robertson, 1975; (editor with Allanah Harper) Edith Sitwell, *Fire of the Mind* (anthology), M. Joseph, 1976, Vanguard, 1981; *Helpmann: The Authorized Biography of Sir Robert Helpmann,* Angus & Robertson, 1978, Universe, 1981; *Edith Sitwell,* Oresko Books (London), 1979, Hippocrene, 1980. Contributor of poems and short stories to *Woman's Own, Woman's Realm, Woman's Day, Sydney Morning Herald,* and *Woman's Weekly.*

SIDELIGHTS: During the seven years that Australian novelist Elizabeth Salter served as private secretary to Dame Edith Sitwell, she came to know her employer well. In *The Last Years of a Rebel: A Memoir of Edith Sitwell,* Salter gave an intimate account of the poet's last years. Written shortly after Sitwell's death at seventy-seven, the book "is not so much a pre-handling of the life story as a postscript on the broadly-publicized personality and impact of Edith Sitwell," a *Times Literary Supplement* critic observed. Writing in the *New York Times Book Review,* Stanley Weintraub described it as a "gossipy memoir that concerns less Dame Edith's development as celebrated poet and eccentric than her battle to arrest the erosion in health, wealth, reputation and creativity that came with aging."

While Salter's book demonstrated the sharp tongue and acidic wit for which Sitwell was so famous, it also revealed a more vulnerable side of this celebrated personality. In her *Observer Review* critique, Mary Holland wrote that Salter "shows the arrogance, the irritability, the petty bitchery which at times must have made [Sitwell] hell to work for. But she also conveys, vividly, Edith Sitwell's spendthrift generosity in private and professional life, her delight in friendship, [and] her horrified compassion for any suffering.'' Echoing this sentiment, Daniel Hoffman observed in the *Reporter,* ''It is a merit of Miss Salter's story that although Edith Sitwell is shown as proud, impatient, testy, and demanding, the reader is yet won over by her spunk and her own kind of integrity.''

Because Salter's book focused on a period when Sitwell was advanced in age and reduced in circumstances, Weintraub called it ''a tale of decline.'' But the distortions that age had wrought on Sitwell's personality did not cloud Salter's perception of her subject, as Alan Pryce-Jones explained in *Washington Post Book World:* ''She never lost the gift of separating Dame Edith the artist from Dame Edith the difficult old lady, and protecting both. Her awareness of the pathetic is never sentimental, and she writes straightforwardly and with lively ease. Her keen vision makes it the sadder that she only entered Dame Edith's life when it was so far advanced in decline.''

AVOCATIONAL INTERESTS: Music, tennis, swimming, walking, reading, opera, theatre, ballet.

BIOGRAPHICAL/CRITICAL SOURCES: Observer Review, June 11, 1967; *Washington Post Book World,* October 22, 1967; *New York Times Book Review,* October 22, 1967; *Harper's,* November, 1967; *Reporter,* December 28, 1967; *Times Literary Supplement,* December 28, 1967; *National Review,* January 16, 1968.

OBITUARIES: Times (London), March 20, 1981.†

* * *

SANDBERG, Peter Lars 1934-

PERSONAL: Born December 13, 1934, in Winchester, Mass.; son of Lars Josef (a management consultant) and Janice (Whittaker) Sandberg; married Nancy Bell (an English professor), September 8, 1956. *Education:* Florida Southern College, B.S., 1958; University of Colorado, M.A., 1959; graduate study at University of Iowa, 1959-61. *Residence:* Bow Lake, Strafford, N. H.; and Alexandria, Va. *Agent:* McIntosh & Otis, Inc., 475 Fifth Ave., New York, N.Y. 10017.

CAREER: Phoenix College, Phoenix, Ariz., instructor in English, 1961-64; *Phoenix Point West,* Phoenix, editor, 1964-66; National Forge Co., Warren, Pa., writer and researcher, 1966-68; Northeastern University, Boston, Mass., lecturer in English, 1968-76. Guest fiction writer, Holy Cross College, Worcester, Mass., 1978 and 1981.

WRITINGS: (With Robert Parker) *Order and Diversity: The Craft of Prose,* Wiley, 1973; *Wolf Mountain* (novel), Playboy Press, 1975; *King's Point* (novel), Playboy Press, 1978; *Stubb's Run* (novel), Houghton, 1979; (with Mark Berent) *Brass Diamonds* (novel), New American Library, 1980.

Short stories anthologized in *Best Little Magazine Fiction,* edited by Curt Johnson, New York University Press, 1970; *Best American Short Stories,* edited by Martha Foley, Houghton, 1974, and *Playboy's Laughing Lovers,* Playboy Press, 1975. Contributor to *Playboy, McCall's* and literary journals.

WORK IN PROGRESS: A novel, tentatively entitled *Checkmate Caribbean.*

SIDELIGHTS: Peter Lars Sandberg told *CA:* ''I have always been intrigued with the ways in which a man can define his courage and/or cowardice in a confrontation with nature. The first story I wrote had to do with a young man climbing a mountain, and I suspect the last one will have to do with an old man climbing a mountain—though I hasten to add I do write about other things.''

MEDIA ADAPTATIONS: The short story ''Calloway's Climb'' was produced by American Broadcasting Corp. as a television special in 1978.

BIOGRAPHICAL/CRITICAL SOURCES: America, November 15, 1975; *Times Literary Supplement,* April 23, 1976; *New York Times Book Review,* December 2, 1979.

* * *

SANDERSON, Milton W(illiam) 1910-

PERSONAL: Born July 29, 1910, in Pittsburg, Kan.; son of William Calvin and Flora (McKinley) Sanderson; divorced; children: Steven Carl, Joe David. *Education:* University of Kansas, A.B., 1932, M.A., 1933, Ph.D., 1937; additional study at University of Michigan Biological Station, 1935 and 1936. *Home:* 112 Dunnam, Flagstaff, Ariz. 86001. *Agent:* Ruth Cantor, 156 Fifth Ave., New York, N.Y. 10010.

CAREER: University of Arkansas, Fayetteville, instructor and assistant entomologist, 1937-42; Illinois Natural History Survey, Urbana, Ill., assistant entomologist, 1942-47, associate taxonomist, 1947-54, taxonomist in charge of identification service, 1954-75. Cooperating scientist, Systematic Entomology Laboratory, United States Drug Administration. Discoverer of many species of insects new to science. Consultant for graduate students, University of Illinois at Urbana-Champaign, beginning 1942.

MEMBER: Entomological Society of America (fellow; member of editorial board), Coleopterists Society, American Entomological Society, Association of Economic Entomologists, Society of Systematic Zoology, Society for Study of Evolution, American Association for Advancement of Science (fellow), Arizona-Nevada Academy of Science, Illinois State Academy of Science (chairman of zoology section and grants committee), Arkansas Academy of Sciences, Kansas Entomological Society, Entomological Society of Washington, Sigma Xi, Phi Sigma. *Awards, honors:* National Science Foundation grant for scientific investigation in West Indies, 1958-62.

WRITINGS: A Monographic Revision of the North American Species of Stenelmis, University of Kansas Press, 1938; *The Phyllophaga of Hispaniola,* Museum of Comparative Zoology, Harvard University, 1951; (with Melville Harrison Hatch and others) *Staphyliniformia,* University of Washington Press, 1957; (co-author) *Ward and Whipple's Freshwater Biology,* Wiley, 1959.

(With John Mark Kingsolver) *A Selected Biography of Insect-Vascular Plant Associations in the United States and Canada,* Illinois Natural History Survey, 1962, published as *A Selected Bibliography of Insect-Vascular Plant Associational Studies,* Agricultural Research Service, U.S. Department of Agriculture, 1967; (with James Sterling Ayars) *Butterflies, Skippers, and Moths,* Whitman Publishing, 1964; (with Orlando Park and John Wagner) *A Review of the Pselaphid Beetles of the West Indies,* Field Museum of Natural History, 1976; *Gyrinidae and Heteroptera in Aquatic Insects and Oligochaetes of North and South Carolina,* Midwest Aquatic Enterprises, 1981.

Scientific editor for film, ''How to Collect Insects,'' produced by Illinois Natural History Survey in 1960. Contributor to professional journals, and to *Proceedings* of California Academy of Sciences, 1965. Editor of coleoptera section, *Biological Abstracts;* contributing editor, *Coleopterists Bulletin.*

* * *

SANDS, Martin
See BURKE, John (Frederick)

* * *

SARNOFF, Jane 1937-

PERSONAL: Born June 25, 1937, in Brooklyn, N.Y.; daughter of Murray (a jewelry executive) and Teresa (a teacher; maiden name, Rehr) Sarnoff. *Education:* Goucher College, B.A., 1959. *Religion:* Jewish.

CAREER: Sudler & Hennessey Advertising, New York, N.Y., copy supervisor, 1967-71; free-lance writer, 1971—.

WRITINGS—Juvenile books; all published by Scribner; all with illustrator, Reynold Ruffins: *A Great Bicycle Book,* 1973, new edition, 1976; *The Chess Book,* 1973; *What? A Riddle Book,* 1974; *A Riddle Calendar: 1975,* 1974; *The Code and Cipher Book,* 1975; *The Monster Riddle Book,* 1975; *I Know! A Riddle Book,* 1976.

A Great Aquarium Book: The Putting-It-Together Guide for Beginners, 1977; *Giants! A Riddle Book and Mr. Bigperson's Side: A Storybook,* 1977; *Space: A Fact and Riddle Book,* 1978; *Take Warning! A Book of Superstitions,* 1978; *Light the Candles! Beat the Drums! A Book of Holidays,* 1979; *If You Were Really Superstitious,* 1980; *That's Not Fair,* 1980; *Words?! A Book about the Origins of Everyday Words and Phrases,* 1981.

WORK IN PROGRESS: Free-lance pharmaceutical writing.

AVOCATIONAL INTERESTS: Travel (Japan, Hong Kong, Europe, Mexico).†

* * *

SAUER, Carl Ortwin 1889-1975

PERSONAL: Born December 24, 1889, in Warrenton, Mo.; died July 18, 1975, in Berkeley, Calif.; buried in Warrenton, Mo.; son of William Albert and Rosetta J. (Vosholl) Sauer; married Lorena Schowengerdt, December 30, 1913; children: Jonathon, Elizabeth (Mrs. Edward FitzSimmons). *Education:* Central Wesleyan College, A.B., 1908; graduate study at Northwestern University, 1908-09; University of Chicago, Ph.D., 1915.

CAREER: Assistant geologist, Illinois Geographical Survey, 1910-12; Rand McNally Co. (publishers), Chicago, Ill., map editor, 1912-13; State Normal School at Salem (now Salem State College), Salem, Mass., instructor, 1913-14; University of Michigan, Ann Arbor, instructor, 1915-18, assistant professor, 1918-20, associate professor, 1920-22, professor of geography, 1922-23; University of California, Berkeley, professor of geography, 1923-57, chairman of department, 1923-56, acting chairman of department, 1956-57, professor emeritus, 1957-75. Agent in agricultural economics, Office of Farm Management, U.S. Department of Agriculture, 1919-20; founder, Michigan Land Economic Survey, 1922; member of selection board, J. S. Guggenheim Memorial Foundation, 1936-55; member of board of trustees, Air University, 1949-52; co-chairman, Wenner-Gren Princeton Conference, 1955. Senior consultant, Soil Conservation Service.

MEMBER: American Philosophical Society, American Geographical Society, Association of American Geographers (president, 1940; honorary president, 1955), Austrian Geographical Society, Royal Scottish Geographical Society (honorary fellow), Royal Netherlands Geographical Society (honorary member), Finnish Geographical Society (honorary member), Mexican National Academy of Science (honorary member), Geographical Society of Berlin.

AWARDS, HONORS: Guggenheim Memorial fellow, 1931; Charles P. Daly medal from American Geographical Society, 1940; Ph.D. from University of Heidelberg, 1956; Vega Medal from Swedish Society of Anthropology and Geology, 1957; LL.D. from Syracuse University, 1958, University of California, Berkeley, 1960, and University of Glasgow, 1965; Humboldt Medal from Geographical Society of Berlin, 1959; Victoria Medal from Royal Geographical Society, 1975.

WRITINGS: Geography of the Upper Illinois Valley and History of Development, Illinois State Geological Survey, University of Illinois, 1916; (with Gilbert H. Cady and Henry C. Cowles) *Starved Rock State Park and Its Environs,* University of Chicago Press, 1918; *The Geography of the Ozark Highland of Missouri,* University of Chicago Press, 1920, reprinted, Greenwood, 1968; *The Morphology of Landscape,* University of California Press, 1925, reprinted, Johnson Reprint, 1968; (with Pervil Meigs) *Site and Culture at San Fernando de Velicata,* University of California Press, 1927, reprinted, Johnson Reprint, 1968; (with John B. Leighly, Kenneth McMurray, and Clarence W. Newman) *Geography of the Pennroyal: A Study of the Influence of Geology and Physiography upon the Industry, Commerce and Life of the People,* Kentucky Geological Survey, 1927; *Land Forms in the Peninsular Range of California as Developed about Warner's Hot Springs and Mesa Grande,* University of California Press, 1929, reprinted, Johnson Reprint, 1968.

Basin and Range Forms in the Chiricahua Area, University of California Press, 1930, reprinted, Johnson Reprint, 1968; (with Donald Brand) *Pueblo Sites in Southeastern Arizona,* University of California Press, 1930, reprinted, Johnson Reprint, 1968; (with Brand) *Prehistoric Settlements of Sonora, with Special Reference to Cerros de Trincheras,* University of California Press, 1931, reprinted, Johnson Reprint, 1968; *The Road to Cibola,* University of California Press, 1932, reprinted, AMS Press, 1980; (with Brand) *Aztatlan Prehistoric Mexican Frontier on the Pacific Coast,* University of California Press, 1932, reprinted, AMS Press, 1978; *The Distribution of Aboriginal Tribes and Languages in Northwestern Mexico,* University of California Press, 1934; *Aboriginal Population of Northwestern Mexico,* University of California Press, 1935, reprinted, AMS Press, 1978; (with Leo Baisden, Isabel Kelly, Margaret Warthin, and Aileen Corwin) *Man in Nature: America before the Days of the White Men,* Scribner, 1939; *Colima of New Spain in the Sixteenth Century,* University of California Press, 1948, reprinted, Greenwood, 1976.

Agricultural Origins and Dispersals, American Geographical Society, 1952, 2nd edition published as *Agricultural Origins and Dispersals: The Domestication of Animals and Foodstuffs,* M.I.T. Press, 1969, published as *Seeds, Spades, Hearths, and Herbs: The Domestication of Animals and Foodstuff,* 1974; (editor) *Plant and Animal Exchanges between the Old and the New Worlds: Notes from a Seminar,* Los Angeles State College, 1963; *Land and Life: A Selection from the Writings of Carl Ortwin Sauer,* University of California Press, 1963; *The Early Spanish Main,* University of California Press, 1966; *Northern Mists,* University of California Press, 1968.

Sixteenth Century North America: The Land and the People as Seen by the Europeans, University of California Press, 1971; (contributor) James Jerome Parsons, editor, *Fifty Years of Berkeley Geography,* University of California, 1973; *Seventeenth Century North America: French and Spanish Accounts,* Turtle Island Foundation, 1977.

OBITUARIES: Time, August 4, 1975; *AB Bookman's Weekly,* August 25, 1975.†

* * *

SAVARY, Louis M(ichael) 1936-

PERSONAL: First syllable of surname rhymes with "pave"; born January 17, 1936, in Scranton, Pa.; son of Louis Michael and Margaret (Nagy) Savary. *Education:* Fordham University, A.B., 1960; Woodstock College, Ph.L., 1961, S.T.L., 1968; Catholic University of America, M.A., 1963, Ph.D., 1965, S.T.D., 1970. *Home:* 631 17th Ave., South Belmar, N.J. 07719. *Office:* 623 Brielle Ave., Brielle, N.J. 08730.

CAREER: Ordained Roman Catholic priest, member of Society of Jesus (Jesuits), 1954; left priesthood, 1982; Collins Associates, New York, N.Y., writer and senior editor, 1967-74; affiliated with Just for You Books, Brielle, N.J., 1974-80; affiliated with Inner Development Associates (specialists in interpersonal and spiritual growth), Brielle, N.J., 1980—. Currently adjunct member of faculty of St. Joseph College, West Hartford, Conn., Sacred Heart University, Bridgeport, Conn., Biscayne College, Seattle University, and Pacific School of Religion.

MEMBER: Mathematical Association of America, American Statistical Association, American Society of Composers, Authors and Publishers (ASCAP), Institute for Consciousness and Music. *Awards, honors:* Christopher Book Award, 1970, for *Listen to Love.*

WRITINGS: Man: His World and His Work, Paulist Press, 1967; *The Kingdom of Downtown: Finding Teenagers in Their Music,* Paulist Press, 1967; (co-author) *Christian Awareness,* four volumes, Christian Brothers Publications, 1968; (co-author) *Listen to Love,* Regina Press, 1968; (co-author) *Patterns of Promise,* St. Mary's College Press, 1968; (co-author) *Living with Christ,* with teacher's guides, four volumes, St. Mary's College Press, 1968-69; (with Adrianne Blue) *Faces of Freedom,* St. Mary's College Press, 1969; (with Blue) *Horizons of Hope,* St. Mary's College Press, 1969.

(With Maureen P. Collins) *Ritual and Life,* St. Mary's College Press, 1970; (with Collins) *Shaping of a Self,* St. Mary's College Press, 1970; (co-author) *Teaching Your Child about God,* St. Mary's College Press, 1970; (with Thomas J. O'Connor) *Finding Each Other,* Paulist/Newman, 1971; (with O'Connor) *Finding God,* Paulist/Newman, 1971; *Getting High Naturally,* Association Press, 1971; *Love and Hate in America Today,* Association Press, 1971; *Popular Song and Youth Today,* Association Press, 1971; *Touch with Love,* Association Press, 1971; *Cycles,* three volumes, Regina Press, 1971-73.

One Life Together: A Celebration of Love in Marriage, Regina Press, 1972; *A Time for Salvation,* Regina Press, 1972; *Jesus: The Face of Man,* Harper, 1972; (with Marianne S. Andersen) *Passages: A Guide for Pilgrims of the Mind,* Harper, 1972; (with Helen L. Bonny) *Music and Your Mind: Listening with a New Consciousness,* Harper, 1973; *Psychological Themes in the Golden Epistle of William of Saint Thierry,* University of Salzburg, 1973; (with Shirley Linde) *The Sleep Book,* Harper, 1974; (with Muriel James) *The Power at the Bottom of the Well: Transactional Analysis and Religious Experience,* Harper, 1974; *Integrating Values: Theory and Exercises for Clarifying and Integrating Religious Values,* Pflaum/Standard, 1974; (with Bonny) *ASC and Music Experience: A Guide for Facilitators and Leaders,* ICM Press, 1974; *Creativity and Children: Stimulating Imaginative Responses to Music,* ICM Press, 1974.

Who Has Seen the Wind?: The Holy Spirit in the Church and the World, Regina Press, 1975; (with Muriel James) *The Heart of Friendship,* Harper, 1975; (with Mary Paolini and George Lane) *Interpersonal Communication: A Worktext for Self-Understanding and Growth in Personal Relations,* Loyola University Press, 1975; (with Paolini and William E. Frankhauser) *The Storyteller's Bible,* Regina, 1978; (with Margaret Ehlen-Miller) *Mindways: A Guide for Exploring Your Mind,* Harper, 1978.

(With Patricia H. Berne) *Prayerways: For Those Who Feel Discouraged or Distraught, Frightened or Frustrated, Angry or Anxious, Powerless or Purposeless, Over-Extended or Under-Appreciated, Burned Out or Just Plain Worn Out,* Harper, 1980; (with Theresa O'Callaghan Scheihing) *Our Treasured Heritage: Teaching Christian Meditation to Children,* Crossroad, 1981; (with Berne) *Building Self-Esteem in Children,* Continuum, 1981; (with Berne) *What Will the Neighbors Say?,* Continuum, 1982; (with Berne and Stephron K. Williams) *Dreamwork and Spiritual Growth: A Christian Approach,* Crossroad, 1983; *A Spirituality for Relationship,* Crossroad, 1984.

Juveniles; published by Regina Press: *The Life of Jesus for Children,* 1979; *The Friends of Jesus for Children,* 1979; *The Miracles of Jesus for Children,* 1979; *The Prayers of Jesus for Children,* 1980; *The Holy Spirit for Children,* 1980; *The Rosary for Children,* 1981; *The Stations of the Cross for Children,* 1981; *The Mission of Catherine Laboure: The Miraculous Medal,* 1981; *The Seasons of the Church Year for Children,* 1982; *My First Prayer Book,* 1982; *My First Book of Saints,* 1982; *The Life of Mary for Children,* 1982.

Editor: (With Thomas J. O'Connor) *The Heart Has Its Seasons,* Regina Press, 1971; (with Paul Carrico) *Contemporary Film and the New Generation,* Association Press, 1971; (with Maureen P. Collins) *Peace, War and Youth,* Association Press, 1971; (with Thomas P. Collins) *A People of Compassion: The Concerns of Edward Kennedy,* Regina Press, 1972; (with Paolini) *Moments with God: A Book of Prayers for Children,* Regina Press, 1975.

Filmstrip texts; all produced by Thomas S. Klise, except as noted: "Images of Christ," 1971; "Images of Revelation," 1971; "Images of Love," 1971; "Images of the Future," 1971; "Images of the New Man," 1972; "A Time to Grow," Sisters of the Good Shepherd, 1972; "Social Studies," W. H. Sadlier, 1972-73; "Religious Awareness" series, 1973; "A Call to Consecration," Sisters of the Good Shepherd, 1973.

Cassette texts; all produced by NCR Cassettes: "Self-Actualization I," 1975; "Self-Actualization II," 1975; "Biblical Meditations with Music I," 1975; "Biblical Meditations with Music II," 1975; "Meditations with Music: Cycle B," 1976; "Meditations with Music: Cycle C," 1976; "The Inner Me," 1977; "Carrying Out Life Decisions," 1977; 'The Lord's Prayer: Integrating Eastern and Western Prayer," four cassettes, 1977; "You Are Called," twenty cassettes, 1978; "Psalms of Reconciliation," 1978; "Life at the Heart of the World," 1979; "Spiritual Growth through Dreams," six cassettes, 1979;

"Prayers of Power: Mantra Chanting," 1979; "Body/Mind/Spirit Prayers: Twenty Ways to Stay Spiritually Alive," four cassettes, 1980; "Spirituality of Teilhard de Chardin," four cassettes, 1980; "Gift of Life," 1980; "Spirituality for the Eighties," 1980; "The Joyful Mysteries," 1981; "The Sorrowful Mysteries," 1981; "The Glorious Mysteries," 1982; "Healing through Mary," 1982; "Stations of the Cross," 1983; "Praying with the Right Brain," four cassettes, 1983.

Author of two recordings for the Institute for Consciousness and Music, "Creative Listening: Music and Imagination Experiences for Children," and, with M. Trinitas Bochini, "A New Way to Music: Altered States of Consciousness and Music." Co-author of *Religious Awareness Teaching Program,* with teacher's guide and parent/teacher guide, 6 volumes, St. Mary's College Press, 1970; also author of four booklets for Just for You Books, including *Getting to Know You: A Funbook for Families,* 1974, and *Side by Side: Another Funbook for Couples,* 1975. Contributor to *Religious Book Guide, Review for Religious,* and *Sisters Today.*

* * *

SAYLOR, J(ohn) Galen 1902-

PERSONAL: Born December 12, 1902, in Carleton, Neb.; son of John Oliver and Ella (Rothrock) Saylor; married Helen Smith, June 1, 1927; children: John Lowell, Sandra (Mrs. Jim McLean), Sherrill Kay (Mrs. Stephen Lahr). *Education:* McPherson College, A.B., 1922; Columbia University, M.A., 1934, Ph.D., 1941. *Religion:* Presbyterian. *Home:* 3300 South 39th St., Lincoln, Neb. 68506. *Office:* 104 Henzlik Hall, University of Nebraska, Lincoln, Neb. 68508.

CAREER: High school teacher of mathematics in Kansas, 1922-25; high school principal, Waverly, Neb., 1925-29; superintendent of schools, Waterloo, Neb., 1929-35; Nebraska State Education Association, Lincoln, director of research, 1936-38; University of Nebraska, Lincoln, professor of secondary education, 1940-71, professor emeritus, 1971—, chairman of department, 1949-68. Visiting professor at University of Maryland, 1959; Fulbright professor at University of Jyvaskyla, Finland, 1962-63; lecturer at Universities of Rome and Florence, 1963. Consultant on teacher education, Office of U.S. High Commissioner for Germany, 1950; U.S. Department of State representative at International Conference on Programmed Instruction and Teaching Machines, Berlin, 1963; delegate to world assembly of World Confederation of Organizations of the Teaching Profession, Seoul, Korea, 1966. Chairman of board of directors, *PTA Magazine,* 1961-64. Member at various times of Nebraska Governor's committees on safety, employment of the handicapped, beautification, and educational television. *Military service:* U.S. Naval Reserve, active duty, 1943-46; became lieutenant commander.

MEMBER: Association for Supervision and Curriculum Development (executive committee, 1964-67; president, 1965-66), National Association of Secondary School Principals, National Congress of Parents and Teachers (treasurer, 1960-63), National Education Association, Nebraska Congress of Parents and Teachers (president, 1953-56), Kiwanis Club (president of Lincoln chapter, 1942), Phi Delta Kappa. *Awards, honors:* LL.D., McPherson College, 1962; University of Nebraska distinguished teaching award, 1967; Distinguished Contributions to Curriculum Award, American Educational Research Association, Division B, 1983.

WRITINGS: Factors Associated with Participation in Cooperative Curriculum Programs, Teachers College, Columbia University, 1941; (with others) *Junior College Studies,* University of Nebraska Press, 1948; (with William Alexander) *Secondary Education: Basic Principles and Practices,* Rinehart, 1950; (with others) *Better than Rating,* Association for Supervision and Curriculum Development, 1951; (with Alexander) *Curriculum Planning: Basic Principles and Practices,* Rinehart, 1954; (contributor) *La Educacion Secundaria en America,* Division of Education, Pan American Union, 1955; *Course Offerings, Subject Enrollments, Size, and Current Expenditures for Nebraska High Schools,* University of Nebraska Press, 1957; (with Alexander) *Modern Secondary Education,* Rinehart, 1959.

(Contributor) *Becoming an Educator,* edited by Van Cleve Morris, Houghton, 1963; (with Alexander) *Curriculum Planning for Modern Schools,* Holt, 1966; (with Alexander and E. Williams) *The High School: Today and Tomorrow,* Holt, 1971; (with Alexander) *Planning Curriculum for Schools,* Holt, 1974; *Antecedent Developments in the Movement to Performance-Based Programs of Teacher Education,* L & R Center, 1976; *Who Planned the Curriculum?: A Curriculum Plans Reservoir Model with Historical Examples,* Kappa Delta Pi, 1982; *A History of the Department of Secondary Education, University of Nebraska—Lincoln,* Center for Curriculum and Instruction, University of Nebraska, 1982.

Contributor to *Encyclopedia of Educational Research, World Book Encyclopedia, Dictionary of Education, Book of Knowledge,* and to education journals. Special feature editor, *Educational Leadership,* 1947-49; editor of special issue, *Review of Educational Research,* June, 1957; chairman of publications committee, Association for Supervision and Curriculum Development, 1959-62.

AVOCATIONAL INTERESTS: Travel, photography.

* * *

SCANZONI, John H. 1935-

PERSONAL: Born March 25, 1935, in Chicago, Ill.; son of Victor and Ida Scanzoni; married Letha Dawson (a free-lance writer), July 7, 1956; children: Stephen, David. *Education:* Wheaton College, Wheaton, Ill., A.B., 1958; University of Oregon, Ph.D., 1964. *Politics:* Independent. *Religion:* Presbyterian. *Home:* 3905-E Pioneer Way, Greensboro, N.C. 27407. *Office:* Department of Child and Family Science, University of North Carolina, Greensboro, N.C. 27412.

CAREER: Indiana University at Bloomington, assistant professor, 1964-68, associate professor, 1968-72, professor of sociology, 1972-78; University of North Carolina at Greensboro, professor of family relations and sociology, 1978—. *Member:* American Sociological Association, National Council on Family Relations, Southeast Council on Family Relations.

WRITINGS: (Editor) *Readings in Social Problems: Sociology and Social Issues,* Allyn & Bacon, 1967; *Opportunity and the Family,* Free Press, 1970; *The Black Family in Modern Society,* University of Chicago Press, 1971, 2nd edition, 1977; *Sexual Bargaining: Power Politics in American Marriage,* University of Chicago Press, 1972, 2nd edition, 1982; *Sex Roles, Life-Styles and Childbearing: Changing Patterns in Marriage and the Family,* Free Press, 1975.

(With wife, Letha Scanzoni) *Men, Women and Change: A Sociology of Marriage and Family,* McGraw, 1976, 2nd edition, 1981; *Sex Roles, Women's Work, and Marital Conflict,* Lexington Books, 1978; (with L. Scanzoni) *Planning the New*

Office, McGraw, 1978; *Love and Negotiate: Creative Conflict in Marriage,* Word, Inc., 1979; (with Maximiliane Szinovacz) *Family Decision Making: A Developmental Sex Role Model,* Sage Publications, 1980; *Is Family Possible?: Theory and Policy for the Twenty-first Century,* Sage Publications, 1983. Contributor to professional journals and anthologies.

* * *

SCHALLER, George B(eals) 1933-

PERSONAL: Born May 26, 1933, in Berlin, Germany; son of Georg L. (a businessman) and Bettina Byrd (Beals) Schaller; married Kay Morgan, August 26, 1957; children: George Eric, Mark Andrew. *Education:* University of Alaska, B.S. in Zoology, B.A. in Anthropology, 1955; University of Wisconsin, M.S., 1957, Ph.D., 1962. *Office:* Animal Research and Conservation Center, New York Zoological Society, Bronx Park, New York, N.Y. 10460.

CAREER: Center for Advanced Study in the Behavioral Sciences, Stanford, Calif., fellow, 1962-63; Johns Hopkins University, Baltimore, Md., 1963-66, began as research associate, became assistant professor; New York Zoological Society, New York, N.Y., research associate, 1966-79, director of Animal Research and Conservation Center, 1979—. *Awards, honors:* National Book Award, 1973, for *The Serengeti Lion: A Study of Predator-Prey Relations.*

WRITINGS: The Mountain Gorilla: Ecology and Behavior, University of Chicago Press, 1963; *The Year of the Gorilla,* University of Chicago Press, 1964; *The Deer and the Tiger: A Study of Wildlife in India,* University of Chicago Press, 1967; (with M. Selsam) *The Tiger: Its Life in the Wild,* Harper, 1969.

The Serengeti Lion: A Study of Predator-Prey Relations, University of Chicago Press, 1972; *Serengeti: A Kingdom of Predators,* Knopf, 1972; *Golden Shadows, Flying Hooves,* Knopf, 1973; (with wife Kay Schaller) *Wonders of Lions,* Dodd, 1977; *Mountain Monarchs: Wild Sheep and Goats of the Himalaya,* University of Chicago Press, 1977.

Stones of Silence: Journeys in the Himalaya, Viking, 1980. Contributor of articles to zoological journals and to popular magazines, including *Outdoor Life, Animal Kingdom, National Geographic, Natural History, International Wildlife, Ford Times,* and *Life.*

SIDELIGHTS: In 1973 George B. Schaller received the National Book Award for *The Serengeti Lion: A Study of Predator-Prey Relations,* which a *Saturday Review* critic calls "the most comprehensive scientific study of free-living lions." Before writing the book, Schaller spent four years doing intensive research and conducting field studies to examine the role of the lion as an integral part of the African ecological system. J. M. Becker asserts in *Library Journal* that the "great many facts about the large predators [that are presented in *The Serengeti Lion*] add to the understanding of how these animals can best be preserved and managed." A reviewer for *Choice* credits Schaller with "another pioneering investigation of large mammals which will contribute to a growing interest in their study and conservation."

A number of critics praise Schaller's ability to present technical material in a lively, yet detailed and accurate, manner. E. O. Wilson, for example, writes in *Science:* "If you have only enough time to read one book about field biology, this is the one I recommend. Schaller continues the best tradition of Fraser Darling, Paul Errington, and Adolf Murie. . . . The organization and illustrations are sound, and the writing is sometimes delightful. Schaller has the master's ability to enliven his scientific report with brief personal anecdotes and expressions of personal emotion that do not lose objectivity or even noticeably digress from the data." And C. P. Haskins states in the *New York Times Book Review:* "Schaller combines in a most fortunate degree the professional training of a zoologist with the qualities of an exceedingly sensitive and imaginative writer, imbued with a devotion to his subject that illumines his pages. [*The Serengeti Lion* opens] the gates to Schaller's world for the less technically-minded reader, and brings him the methods and results of the author's study."

BIOGRAPHICAL/CRITICAL SOURCES: Sports Illustrated, June 20, 1960; *American Anthropologist,* December, 1963; *Science,* March 3, 1967, February 2, 1973, May 12, 1978; *New York Times Book Review,* April 20, 1969, November 11, 1973; *Saturday Review,* October 28, 1972; *Library Journal,* November 15, 1972, November 15, 1977; *New York Review of Books,* January 25, 1973; *Choice,* March, 1973, June, 1978; *New York Times,* March 18, 1980; *Washington Post Book World,* May 24, 1980.

* * *

SCHIAVONE, James 1933-

PERSONAL: Born January 22, 1933, in New York, N.Y.; son of James P. and Isabel (Bell) Schiavone. *Education:* New York University, B.S., 1955, M.A., 1956; Columbia University, professional diploma, 1957; University of Rome, additional study, 1964-65.

CAREER: Public school teacher in New York City, and Hackensack, N.J., 1955-57; Dade County Board of Public Instruction, Miami, Fla., counselor, 1957-66; G. S. Cook Consultants, Fort Lauderdale, Fla., educational consultant and reading specialist, 1966-68; Monroe County School District, Key West, Fla., coordinator of reading, 1968-70; City University of New York Regional Opportunity Centers, New York City, director of basic education, 1970-71; Borough of Manhattan Community College of the City University of New York, New York City, assistant professor of developmental skills and coordinator for remediation, beginning 1971. Reading consultant to Lindsey Hopkins Adult Education Center, John B. Stetson University, WTHS-TV, Miami, and numerous other institutions, organizations, and universities. *Member:* National Education Association, Florida Education Association, International Reading Association, National Reading Conference.

WRITINGS: You Can Read Faster, Grosset, 1963; *How to Pass Exams,* Grossett, 1964; *Seven Keys to a Richer Vocabulary,* Grossett, 1964; *Help Your Child to Read Better,* Nelson-Hall, 1977; *Springboards: A College Reader,* AMSCO School Publications, 1977. Contributor of book reviews and articles to newspapers and professional journals.†

* * *

SCHISGALL, Oscar 1901-
(Jackson Cole, Stuart Hardy)

PERSONAL: Born February 23, 1901, in Antwerp, Belgium; son of Nathan (a merchant) and Helen (Blumenthal) Schisgall; married Lillian Gelberg (a writer), September 19, 1926; children: Richard, James. *Education:* Attended City College (now City College of the City University of New York), 1919-21, and New York University, 1921-23. *Politics:* Independent. *Home:* 85 East End Ave., New York, N.Y. 10028.

CAREER: Author and speechwriter. Chief of book and magazine bureau, Office of War Information, during World War II. *Member:* Authors League, Authors Guild, American Society of Journalists and Authors, American Society of Composers, Authors, and Publishers, Overseas Press Club. *Awards, honors:* Government citation for work at Office of War Information; Benjamin Franklin Award for magazine writing, 1954.

WRITINGS: *Barron Ixell, Crime Breaker,* Longmans, Green, 1929; *The Devil's Daughter,* Fiction League, 1932; *Swastika,* Knopf, 1939; *The Big Store,* Prentice-Hall, 1955; *Laura Jane Sees Everything at Hess's* (children's book), Public Service Syndicate, 1966; *The Magic of Mergers: The Saga of Meshulam Riklis,* Little, Brown, 1968; *That Remarkable Creature, the Snail* (children's book), Messner, 1970; *My Years with Xerox,* Doubleday, 1972; *Out of One Small Chest: The History of the Bowery Savings Bank,* American Management Association, 1975; *Eyes on Tomorrow: The Evolution of Procter & Gamble,* Doubleday, 1981.

Novels; under pseudonym Jackson Cole: *The Ramblin' Kid,* G. H. Watt, 1933; *Gun Justice,* G. H. Watt, 1933.

Novels; under pseudonym Stuart Hardy: *The Man from Nowhere,* Macaulay Co., 1935; *Arizona Justice,* Green Circle Books, 1936; *Montana Bound,* Green Circle Books, 1936; *The Mountains Are My Kingdom,* Green Circle Books, 1937; *Trouble from Texas,* Macaulay Co., 1938; *Miracle at Gopher Creek,* Green Circle Books, 1938.

Also author of five screenplays and 20 radio and television plays. Contributor to periodicals, including *Reader's Digest, Redbook, Saturday Evening Post,* and *Woman's Day.*

WORK IN PROGRESS: A history of Greyhound Bus Co.

BIOGRAPHICAL/CRITICAL SOURCES: *New York Times Book Review,* March 28, 1982.

* * *

SCHMANDT, Henry J. 1918-

PERSONAL: Born February 21, 1918, in St. Louis, Mo.; married Laura Feuerbacher, 1941; children: David, Richard, Sue Ann. *Education:* Washington University, St. Louis, Mo., B.S., 1946; St. Louis University, Ph.D., 1950; Columbia University, postdoctoral study, 1950-51. *Office:* Center for Urban Programs, St. Louis University, St. Louis, Mo. 63108.

CAREER: University of Detroit, Detroit, Mich., assistant professor of political science, 1951-53; St. Louis University, St. Louis, Mo., associate professor, 1953-59; University of Wisconsin—Milwaukee, professor of political science and chairman of department of urban affairs, 1960-78; St. Louis University, professor of urban affairs, 1978—. Assistant research director, Missouri State Reorganization Commission, 1954-55; associate director, Metropolitan St. Louis Survey, 1956-57; acting director, Metropolitan Community Studies, Dayton, Ohio, 1958. Council, City of Olivette, Mo., 1956-58; chairman, Southeastern Wisconsin Regional Planning Commission, 1960-61. *Military service:* U.S. Army, 1942-45; became first lieutenant. *Member:* American Political Science Association, Midwest Political Science Association.

WRITINGS: (With Paul G. Steinbicker) *Fundamentals of Government,* M. M. Bruce, 1954, 2nd edition, 1963.

A History of Political Philosophy, M. M. Bruce, 1960; (with Steinbicker and George D. Wendel) *Metropolitan Reform in St. Louis,* Holt, 1961; (with John C. Bollens) *The Metropolis: Its People, Politics, and Economic Life,* Harper, 1965, 4th edition, 1981; (with W. H. Standing) *The Milwaukee Metropolitan Study Commission,* Indiana University Press, 1965; (editor with Warner Bloomberg, Jr.) *Power, Poverty and Urban Policy,* Sage Publications, 1968; *Courts in the American Political System,* Dickenson, 1968; (editor with Bloomberg) *The Quality of Urban Life,* Sage Publications, 1969.

(Editor with Bloomberg) *Urban Poverty, Its Social and Political Dimensions,* Sage Publications, 1970; (with John Goldbach and Donald B. Vogel) *Milwaukee: A Contemporary Urban Profile,* Praeger, 1971; (with Harold M. Rose) *Citizen Attitudes in Milwaukee,* Milwaukee Urban Observatory, 1972; (with Bollens) *Political Corruption: Power, Money and Sex,* Palisades, 1979. Contributor to professional journals.

WORK IN PROGRESS: *Urban Theory.*

AVOCATIONAL INTERESTS: Painting, photography.

* * *

SCHMITHALS, Walter 1923-

PERSONAL: Born December 14, 1923, in Wesel, Germany; son of Bernhard and Elisabeth (Indefrey) Schmithals; married Marlene Schubotz, May 19, 1953; children: Gesine, Elisabeth, Barbara, Kathrin, Doerte, Sixta. *Education:* Attended University of Muenster, 1949-50; University of Marburg, Dr.Theol., 1956. *Religion:* Evangelist. *Home:* Landauerstrasse 6, 1 Berlin 33, West Germany.

CAREER: Vicar in Minden, Germany, 1951-53; minister in Raumland, Germany, 1953-63; University of Marburg, Marburg, Germany, lecturer, 1963-68; University of Berlin, Berlin, Germany, professor of New Testament, 1968—.

WRITINGS: *Die Gnosis in Korinth: Eine Untersuchung zu den Korintherbriefen,* Vandenhoeck & Ruprecht (Goettingen), 1956, 3rd edition, 1969, translation by John Steely published as *Gnosticism in Corinth: An Investigation of the Letters to the Corinthians,* Abingdon, 1971; *Das Kirchliche Apostelamt: Eine historische Untersuchung,* Vandenhoeck & Ruprecht, 1961, translation by Steely published as *The Office of Apostle in the Early Church,* Abingdon, 1969; *Paulus and Jakobus,* Vandenhoeck & Ruprecht, 1963, translation by Dorothea Barton published as *Paul and James,* Allenson, 1965; *Paulus und die Gnostiker: Untersuchungen zu den kleinen Paulusbriefen,* Reich (Hamburg-Bergstedt), 1965, translation by Steely published as *Paul and the Gnostics,* Abingdon, 1972; *Die Theologie Rudolf Bultmanns: Eine Einfuehrung,* Mohr (Tuebingen), 1966, 2nd edition, 1967, translation by John Bowden published as *An Introduction to the Theology of Rudolf Bultmann,* Augsburg, 1968.

Wunder und Glaube: Eine Auslegung von Markus 4, 35-6, 6a, Neukirchener (Neukirchen-Vluyn), 1970; *Das Christuszeugnis in der heutigen Gesellschaft: Zur gegenwaertigen Krise von Theologie und Kirche,* Reich, 1970; *Vernunft und Gehorsam: Zur Standortbestimmung der Theologie,* Reich, 1971; *Jesus Christus in der Verkuendigung der Kirche: Aktuelle Beitraege zum notwendigen Streit um Jesus,* Neukirchener, 1972; *Die Apokalyptik: Einfuehrung und Deutung,* Vandenhoeck & Ruprecht, 1973, translation by Steely published as *The Apocalyptic Movement: Introduction and Interpretation,* Abingdon, 1975; *Der Roemerbrief als historisches Problem,* Guetersloher Verlagshaus (Guetersloh), 1975; *Leistung,* Kohlhammer, 1978, translation by David Smith published as *Achievement,* Abingdon, 1981; *Das Evangelium nach Markus,* Mohn, 1979; *Herr-*

schaft, Kohlhammer, 1980, translation by John E. Steely published as *Authority,* Abingdon, 1982; *Die theologische Anthropologie des Paulus: Auslegung van Rom. 7, 17-8, 39,* Kohlhammer, 1980; *Das Evangelium nach Lukas,* Theologischer Verlag Zurich, 1980; *Die Apostelgeschicte des Lukas,* Theologischer Verlag Zurich, 1982.

Contributor of more than three hundred articles to religious journals in Germany.

WORK IN PROGRESS: Neues Testament and *Gnosis.*

SIDELIGHTS: "This book should have been written years ago," comments Royce Gordon Gruenler in his review of *An Introduction to the Theology of Rudolph Bultmann* by Walter Schmithals. "We can be grateful that it has at last appeared. . . . Walter Schmithals was one of Bultmann's pupils—and evidently an apt one, for Bultmann has said that this is the best book on his theology that has ever been written. That is quite an endorsement, and it is borne out in fact. Schmithals has the rare quality of exposing Bultmann's more difficult concepts with remarkable transparency."

BIOGRAPHICAL/CRITICAL SOURCES: Christian Century, November 13, 1968.

* * *

SCHMITT, Martin (Ferdinand) 1917-1978

PERSONAL: Born March 25, 1917, in River Forest, Ill.; died November 22, 1978; son of Ferdinand Henry (a businessman) and Clara Elizabeth (Grauer) Schmitt; married Martha Foster (a librarian), April 9, 1948; children: Sallie (Mrs. Gary Lowenthal). *Education:* University of Illinois, B.S., 1938, B.S., 1939. *Home:* 45 Sunset Dr., Eugene, Ore. 97403. *Office:* University of Oregon Library, Eugene, Ore. 97403.

CAREER: Eureka College, Eureka, Ill., librarian, 1939-40; University of Idaho, Moscow, assistant librarian, 1946-47; University of Oregon Library, Eugene, curator of special collections, beginning 1947. Editor, Champoeg Press, 1953-59. *Military service:* U.S. Army, 1942-45; became sergeant. *Member:* Society of American Archivists, American Library Association, Cannon Hunters Association of Seattle. *Awards, honors:* Waldo Gifford Leland Award from Society of American Archivists, 1972, for *Catalogue of Manuscripts in the University of Oregon Library.*

WRITINGS: (Editor) *General George Crook,* University of Oklahoma Press, 1946; (with Dee Brown) *Fighting Indians of the West,* Scribner, 1948, reprinted, Ballantine, 1974; (with Brown) *Trail Driving Days,* Scribner, 1952, reprinted, 1978; (editor) *Journal of Travel by E. S. McComas,* Champoeg Press, 1954; (with Brown) *Settler's West,* Scribner, 1955; (editor) *Cattle Drives of David Shirk,* Champoeg Press, 1956.

Inventory of the Papers of John T. Flynn, University of Oregon Library, 1966; *List and Index of Pamphlets from the Library of the American Russian Institute,* University of Oregon Library, 1966; *Catalogue of Manuscripts in the University of Oregon Library,* University of Oregon, 1971; *Inventory of the Papers of Senator Wayne L. Morse, 1919-1969,* University of Oregon Library, 1974. Editor of *Call Number,* 1957-68, and *Imprint: Oregon,* beginning 1973.

WORK IN PROGRESS: Cats in Art; editing pioneer diaries and letters.†

SCHREINER, Samuel A(gnew), Jr. 1921-

PERSONAL: Born June 6, 1921, in Mt. Lebanon, Pa.; son of Samuel Agnew (a lawyer) and Mary (Cort) Schreiner; married Doris Moon (an artist and antique dealer and appraiser), September 22, 1945; children: Beverly Ann (Mrs. Jonathan S. Carroll), Carolyn Cort Calder. *Education:* Princeton University, A.B., 1942. *Politics:* Republican. *Religion:* Presbyterian. *Home and office:* 111 Old Kings Highway S., Darien, Conn. 06820. *Agent:* Harold Ober, Inc., 40 East 49th St., New York, N.Y. 10017.

CAREER: McKeesport Daily News, McKeesport, Pa., reporter, 1946; *Pittsburgh Sun-Telegraph,* Pittsburgh, Pa., reporter, 1946-51; *Parade,* New York, N.Y., writer and assistant managing editor, 1951-55; *Reader's Digest,* Pleasantville, N.Y., associate editor, 1955-68, senior editor, 1968-74; full-time writer, 1974—. President of Schreiner Associates. Elder, Noroton Presbyterian Church; secretary, Darien Library Association; former chairman, Darien Youth Advisory Committee and Centre Store. *Military service:* U.S. Army, Office of Strategic Services, cryptographer, 1942-45; served in China-Burma-India theater; became first lieutenant; received Bronze Star and Presidential unit citation.

MEMBER: Authors Guild, Authors League of America, Overseas Press Club, Princeton Club of New York, Noroton Yacht Club.

WRITINGS: Urban Planning and Public Opinion, Bureau of Urban Research, Princeton University, 1942; *Thine Is the Glory* (novel), Arbor House, 1975; *Pleasant Places* (novel), Arbor House, 1976; *The Condensed World of the Reader's Digest,* Stein, 1977; *Angelica* (novel), Arbor House, 1977; *The Possessors and the Possessed* (novel), Arbor House, 1980; *The Van Alens* (novel), Arbor House, 1981.

Contributor of articles and stories to popular magazines, including *McCall's, Saturday Evening Post, Collier's, Redbook, Reader's Digest,* and *National Geographic.*

* * *

SCHWARTZ, Mildred A(nne) 1932-

PERSONAL: Born November 17, 1932, in Toronto, Ontario, Canada; daughter of Max and Rebecca (Silverberg) Schwartz. *Education:* University of Toronto, B.A., 1954, M.A., 1956; Columbia University, Ph.D., 1965. *Religion:* Jewish. *Home:* 5401 South Hyde Park Blvd., No. 704, Chicago, Ill. 60615. *Office address:* University of Illinois at Chicago Circle, Box 4348, Chicago, Ill. 60680.

CAREER: Held research jobs prior to 1962; University of Calgary, Calgary, Alberta, assistant professor of sociology, 1962-64; University of Chicago, Chicago, Ill., research associate, 1964-66; University of Illinois at Chicago Circle, associate professor, 1966-69, professor of sociology, 1969—. Visiting professor, Harvard University, 1973. *Member:* American Sociological Association, American Political Science Association, Canadian Sociology and Anthropology Association, Association for Canadian Studies in the United States, Social Science History Association, Canadian Political Science Association.

WRITINGS: Public Opinion and Canadian Identity, University of California Press, 1967; (with F. C. Engelmann) *Political*

Parties and the Canadian Social Structure, Prentice-Hall, 1967; *Trends in White Attitudes toward Negroes,* National Opinion Research Center, 1967; *Politics and Territory,* McGill-Queen's University Press, 1974; (with Engelmann) *Canadian Political Parties: Origin, Character, Impact,* Prentice-Hall, 1975; *The Environment for Policy-Making in Canada and the United States,* C. D. Howe Institute and National Planning Associates, 1981.

Contributor: B. Blishen, editor, *Canadian Society,* Macmillan, 1961, 2nd edition, 1964; John Meisel, editor, *Papers on the 1962 Election,* University of Toronto Press, 1964; H. Vollmer and D. L. Mills, editors, *Professionalization,* Prentice-Hall, 1966; Richard Preston, editor, *The Influence of the United States on Canadian Development,* Duke University Press, 1972; Richard Rose, editor, *Electoral Behavior,* Free Press, 1974; Dennis Forcese and Stephen Richer, editors, *Issues in Canadian Society: Introduction to Sociology,* Prentice-Hall, 1975; Benjamin Singer, editor, *Communication in Canada,* Copp Clark, 1975; John Redekop, editor, *Approaches to Canadian Politics,* Prentice-Hall, 1978, revised edition, 1982; Harold Clark and Allen Kornberg, editors, *Political Support in Canada,* Duke University Press, 1982.

Contributor to professional journals, including *American Journal of Sociology, American Behavioral Scientist, Transactions of the Royal Society of Canada, Publius,* and *Comparative Social Research.*

WORK IN PROGRESS: Regionalism in Canada and the United States; Integration and Political Party Organization; continuing work with F. C. Engelmann on Austrian politics.

* * *

SCHWERIN, Doris H(alpern) 1922-

PERSONAL: Born June 24, 1922, in Peabody, Mass.; daughter of Harry (a physician) and Mary (a nurse; maiden name, Polivnick) Halpern; married Jules Victor Schwerin (a film director), March 2, 1946; children: Charles Norman. *Education:* Attended New England Conservatory of Music and Boston University, 1939-40; attended Juilliard School, 1941-44. *Home:* 317 West 83rd St., New York, N.Y. 10024.

CAREER: Musical composer, playwright, and author. Member of Eugene O'Neill Memorial Theatre Center. *Member:* American Society of Composers, Authors, and Publishers, Dramatists Guild, Authors League of America. *Awards, honors:* Charles Sergel Drama Prize from University of Chicago, 1973, for "Daddy's in the Cold, Cold Ground."

WRITINGS: Diary of a Pigeon Watcher (memoirs), Morrow, 1976; *Leanna* (novel), Morrow, 1978; *The Tomorrow Book* (juvenile), Pantheon, 1983; *Maxwell Treading* (novel), Ballantine, 1983.

Plays: "Moxie Malone's Two Hundred Days" (two-act), produced at Eugene O'Neill Memorial Theatre Center, 1966; "The Drums Make Me Nervous" (one-act with music), produced at Eugene O'Neill Memorial Theatre Center, 1968; "Where Did You Put It . . . When You Had It?" (one-act with music), first performed in New York City at St. Clement's Church, 1971. Also author of "How Do You Like My Hong Kong Suit?," 1982, and of "Daddy's in the Cold, Cold Ground."

Composer of musical scores, "From Morning 'til Night" (for children), released by RCA Corp., 1962, and "O Oysters," 1961, "Marco's Millions," 1963, "Matty, the Moron, and Madonna," 1965, "Solomon and Ashmedi" (for children), 1968, "The Orchestra," 1969, "Kaboom," 1974, and "The Man Who Stole the Word," 1976.

WORK IN PROGRESS: A novel, *The Rosehill Papers;* a book of short stories, *Foxville Variations.*

SIDELIGHTS: After having a cancerous breast removed, Doris Schwerin had to wait to see if the disease would recur. During that five-year waiting period, Schwerin noticed a nest of pigeons outside her window and began to observe their movements and to keep a diary. That diary became the book *Diary of a Pigeon Watcher,* which records Schwerin's observations of the pigeon family near her window ledge, as well as her thoughts about her own family, her childhood, and the challenges she was facing as an adult. *Diary of a Pigeon Watcher,* writes *New York Times*'s Richard Lingeman, "goes beyond urban natural history, . . . for it is a journey into the sea-caverns of the past—'spiritual spelunking'—in search of meaning, wholeness. . . . Circling around, like birds returning to the nest, the author comes to terms with her past and herself."

Although many of Schwerin's memories are poignant and obviously painful, Anne Roiphe, writing in *New York Times Book Review,* questions whether the author has been able to convey the full impact of her hurt and heartache. "The writing in this book is mostly excellent, evocative and pure," comments Roiphe, "but occasionally it slips into cuteness or sentimentality and there is, despite the hard work of the author in coming to terms with her life experience, a kind of softening of the truth, a turning away from the terror of loneliness and death and pain and making pictures that are more palatable to the mind. . . . Schwerin hovers on the edge of terrible truths and then with a kind of gracious endearing smile backs away." Lingeman also recognizes *Diary of a Pigeon Watcher*'s limitations but finds that in it Schwerin "has awakened the secret inner springs of a discrete-flowing primal love, radiating out through pigeons and parents, home and family, until it glimpses . . . a final, greater whole, the order of the universe."

BIOGRAPHICAL/CRITICAL SOURCES: New York Times Book Review, May 23, 1976; *New York Times,* July 29, 1976; *Washington Post Book World,* June 24, 1978.

* * *

SCOT, Chesman
See BULMER, (Henry) Kenneth

* * *

SCOTT, Peter Dale 1929-
(Adam Greene, John Sproston)

PERSONAL: Born January 11, 1929, in Montreal, Quebec, Canada; son of Francis Reginald (a professor and poet) and Marian Mildred (Dale) Scott; married Mary Elizabeth Marshall (a psychiatric social worker), June 16, 1956; children: Catherine Dale, Thomas, John Daniel. *Education:* McGill University, B.A., 1949, Ph.D., 1955; graduate study at Institut d'Etudes Politiques, University of Paris, 1950, and University College, Oxford, 1950-52. *Home:* 2823 Ashby Ave., Berkeley, Calif. 94705. *Office:* Department of English, University of California, Berkeley, Calif. 94720.

CAREER: Sedbergh School, Montebello, Quebec, teacher, 1952-53; McGill University, Montreal, Quebec, lecturer in political science, 1955-56; Canadian Foreign Service, posts in Ottawa, with United Nations, and in Warsaw, Poland, 1957-61; University of California, Berkeley, assistant professor of speech,

1961-66, assistant professor, 1966-68, associate professor, 1968-80, professor of English, 1980—. *Member:* Foisard Society.

WRITINGS: Poems, Fantasy Press, 1953; (with others) *Education at Berkeley,* University of California Press, 1966; (with Franz Schurmann and Reginald Zelnik) *The Politics of Escalation in Vietnam,* Beacon Press, 1966; (translator with Czeslaw Milosz) Zbigniew Herbert, *Selected Poems,* Penguin, 1968.

The War Conspiracy, Bobbs-Merrill, 1972; (with Paul L. Hoch and Russell Stetler) *The Assassinations: Dallas and Beyond,* Random House, 1976; *Crime and Cover-Up,* Westworks, 1977; *Rumors of No Law* (poems), Thorp Springs Press, 1981; *Prepositions of Jet Travel* (poems), Berkeley Poetry Review Chapbooks, 1981.

Contributor: Mark Selden, editor, *Remaking Asia,* Pantheon, 1974; Steve Weissman, editor, *Big Brother and the Holding Company,* Ramparts, 1974; Malcolm Caldwell, editor, *Ten Years' Military Terror in Indonesia,* Spokesman Books, 1975; Sid Blumenthal and Harvey Yazijian, editors, *Government by Gunplay,* New American Library, 1976; George Levine and U. C. Knoepflmacher, editors, *The Endurance of Frankenstein,* University of California Press, 1979; Margot H. King and Wesley M. Stevens, editors, *Saints, Scholars and Heros,* St. John's Abbey and University Press, 1979; Henrik Krueger, *The Great Heroin Coup,* South End Press, 1980. Also contributor to *Pentagon Papers,* Volume V, edited by Noam Chomsky and H. Zinn, 1973. Contributor of poems, translations of poetry, and articles to journals and periodicals.

WORK IN PROGRESS: A long poem on Indonesia, entitled "Coming to Jakarta"; an analysis of the 1965 coup and massacre in Indonesia; writings on peace studies; translations of Virgil's *Eclogues;* a book-length study on covert U.S. political forces and events.

SIDELIGHTS: Peter Dale Scott told *CA:* "My recent writings, especially the long poem on Indonesia, have aimed at bridging the gap in our globalized and fragmented culture between prose and poetry, politics and the personal, scholarship and imagination, meaning and being. I suspect this concern for integration comes from my Canadian background, and my experience there of a smaller-scale society. (In my long poem I describe sitting in a sleigh en route to a country railway station, on the knee of the local minister of parliament, a country lawyer and storekeeper's brother, who was soon to be Prime Minister.) It also derives from the cultural concerns of [T. S.] Eliot and [Ezra] Pound, especially the former's dictum 'that at the present time the problem of the unification of the world and the problem of the unification of the individual are in the end one and the same.'"

* * *

SCOTT, William Abbott 1926-

PERSONAL: Born April 21, 1926, in Lincoln, Neb.; son of Clarence Kelly (a salesman) and Laura (Duerner) Scott; married Ruth Griggs, June 5, 1957; children: Terry Louise, Vivian Marie, Gregory Bennett, Natalie Elaine. *Education:* Attended Reed College, 1943 and Gonzaga University, 1944; University of New Mexico, B.S., 1950; University of Michigan, M.S., 1951, Ph.D., 1954. *Office:* Department of Psychology, Australian National University, Canberra 2600, Australia.

CAREER: U.S. Military Government in Japan, civil information officer in Matsuyama, Kochi, Yokohama, 1946-49; University of Michigan, Ann Arbor, study director, Survey Research Center, 1951-55; University of Colorado, Boulder, 1955-74, began as assistant professor, became professor of psychology; James Cook University, Townsville, Australia, professor of behavioral science, 1974-77; Australian National University, Canberra, professor of psychology, 1977—. Visiting professor at University of California, Berkeley, spring, 1963, University of Hawaii, summer, 1963, 1974, and Victoria University of Wellington, 1970-71. Research associate, Survey Research Center, University of Michigan, 1956, and International Relations Program, Northwestern University, 1958-65. Consultant to International Studies of Values in Politics, University of Pennsylvania, 1964-67, National Common Causes and Prevention of Violence, 1969-70, and Center for Study of Crime, Delinquency and Correction, Southern Illinois University, 1972. *Military service:* U.S. Naval Reserve, 1944-46; became lieutenant junior grade.

MEMBER: American Psychological Association (fellow), Australian Psychological Society (fellow), Academy of Social Sciences in Australia (fellow), Phi Beta Kappa, Phi Kappa Phi, Sigma Xi. *Awards, honors:* National Institute of Mental Health grants, 1957-60 and 1963-72.

WRITINGS: (With S. B. Withey) *The United States and the United Nations: The Public View,* Manhattan, 1958, reprinted, Greenwood Press, 1974; (with Michael Wertheimer) *Introduction to Psychological Research,* Wiley, 1962; (with wife, Ruth Scott) *Values and Organizations: A Study of Fraternities and Sororities,* Rand McNally, 1965; *Science of Human Behavior* (lecture), James Cook University of North Queensland, 1974; (with others) *Cognitive Structure: Theory and Measurement of Individual Differences,* Halsted Press, 1979.

Contributor: N. F. Washburne, editor, *Decisions, Values, and Groups,* Pergamon, 1962; O. J. Harvey, editor, *Motivation and Social Interaction,* Ronald, 1963; H. C. Kelman, editor, *International Behavior,* Holt, 1965; Harvey, editor, *Flexibility, Adaptability, and Creativity,* Springer Publishing Co., 1966; G. Lindzey and E. Aronson, editors, *Handbook of Social Psychology,* revised edition, Addison-Wesley, 1967; E. F. Borgatta and W. W. Lambert, editors, *Handbook of Personality Theory and Research,* Rand McNally, 1967.

Contributor to professional journals. Consulting and associate editor, *Sociometry,* 1958-63, and *Journal of Personality and Social Psychology,* 1965-76; consulting editor, *Journal of Abnormal and Social Psychology,* 1961-64.

* * *

SCUPHAM, John Peter 1933-

PERSONAL: Born February 24, 1933, in Liverpool, England; son of John (head of educational broadcasting for British Broadcasting Corp.) and Dorothy (Clark) Scupham; married Carola Nance Braunholtz (a teacher), August 10, 1957; children: Kate, Toby, Giles, Roger. *Education:* Emmanuel College, Cambridge, diploma (with honors), 1957. *Home:* 2 Taylor's Hill, Hitchin, Hertfordshire, England. *Office:* St. Christopher School, Barrington Rd., Letchworth, Hertfordshire, England.

CAREER: Taught at grammar school in Lincolnshire, England, 1957-61; St. Christopher School, Letchworth, England, head of English department, 1961—. Co-founder and proprietor of Mandeville Press, 1974—.

WRITINGS—Poems: *The Small Containers* (pamphlet), H. Chambers, 1972; *The Snowing Globe,* E. J. Morten, 1972; *The*

Gift, Keepsake Press, 1973; *Prehistories,* Oxford University Press, 1975; *The Hinterland,* Oxford University Press, 1977; *Summer Palaces,* Oxford University Press, 1980; *Winter Quarters,* Oxford University Press, 1983.

WORK IN PROGRESS: Poems.

SIDELIGHTS: John Peter Scupham writes: "I like poetry of sense, sensibility, and formal elegance and try to write it." The small publishing business he operates prints by hand small editions of new poetry of quality.

* * *

SEIDMAN, Joel 1906-

PERSONAL: Born July 29, 1906, in Baltimore, Md.; son of Alexander (a lawyer) and Rose (Toomim) Seidman; married Evelyn Paulu, August 1, 1938; children: Kathryn A., Barbara R. *Education:* Johns Hopkins University, A.B., 1926, Ph.D., 1932. *Office:* Department of Industrial Relations, University of Chicago, Chicago, Ill. 60637.

CAREER: Editorial Research Reports, Washington, D.C., research worker and writer, 1933-34; Brookwood Labor College, Katonah, N.Y., teacher, 1934-37; League for Industrial Democracy, New York, N.Y., field secretary, 1937-40; National Labor Relations Board, Washington, D.C., field examiner, 1942-46; University of Chicago, Chicago, Ill., 1947—, became professor of industrial relations, professor emeritus, 1971—. Visiting professor, University of Hawaii, 1972. *Member:* American Economic Association, Industrial Relations Research Association. *Awards, honors:* John Dewey Labor research fellowship, 1940-41.

WRITINGS: The Yellow Dog Contract, Johns Hopkins Press, 1932; *The Needle Trades,* Farrar & Rinehart, 1942, reprinted, Johnson Reprint, 1970; *Union Rights and Union Duties,* Harcourt, 1943.

American Labor from Defense to Reconversion, University of Chicago Press, 1953, reprinted, 1974; (co-author) *The Worker Views His Union,* University of Chicago Press, 1958; *The Brotherhood of Railroad Trainmen,* Wiley, 1962; (editor) *Communism in the United States,* Cornell University Press, 1969; *Democracy in the Labor Movement,* New York State School of Industrial and Labor Relations, Cornell University, 1969.

(Editor) *Trade Union Government and Collective Bargaining,* Praeger, 1970; (with Joyce M. Najita) *The Hawaii Law on Collective Bargaining in Public Employment,* Industrial Relations Center, College of Business Administration, University of Hawaii, 1973; (with Jeffrey Sissons, Le Thuy Anh, and Stephen Hutton) *Attitudes of New Zealand Workers,* Victoria University of Wellington Industrial Relations Centre, 1975; *Industrial Relations Systems of the United States and New Zealand: A Comparison,* Industrial Relations Center, College of Business Administration, University of Hawaii, 1975; *A Guide to Discipline in the Public Sector,* Industrial Relations Center, College of Business Administration, University of Hawaii, 1977. Contributor to professional journals.†

* * *

SELZER, Michael (I.) 1940-

PERSONAL: Born October 16, 1940, in Lahore, India; son of Hermann Marcus (a physician) and Kate (a physician; maiden name, Neumann) Selzer; married Miriam Jacobs, 1976; children: Sarah E.J., Abigail D.J. *Education:* Balliol College, Oxford, B.A., 1963, M.A., 1967; City University of New York, Ph.D., 1973. *Home:* 16 Plymouth St., Montclair, N.J. 07042. *Office:* 55 Water St., New York, N.Y. 10041.

CAREER: Brooklyn College of the City University of New York, Brooklyn, N.Y., assistant professor of political science, 1971-78; stockbroker, 1979—, currently first vice president of Lehman Securities Division, Lehman Brothers Kuhn Loeb, Inc., New York, N.Y. Writer and lecturer. *Awards, honors:* National Jewish Book Award, 1979, for *Deliverance Day.*

WRITINGS: Outcasts of Israel: Ethnic Tensions in the Jewish State, Council of the Sephardi Community, 1965; *The Aryanization of the Jewish State: A Polemic,* Black Star Publishing, 1967; *The Wineskin and the Wizard,* Macmillan, 1970; (editor) *Zionism Reconsidered,* Macmillan, 1970; *Politics and Jewish Purpose,* Greenleaf Books, 1972; (editor) *Kike: A Documentary History of Anti-Semitism in America,* World Publishing, 1972; (with Florence Miale) *The Nuremburg Mind: The Psychology of the Nazi Leaders,* Quadrangle, 1975; *Deliverance Day: The Last Hours at Dachau,* Lippincott, 1978; *Terrorist Chic: An Exploration of Violence in the Seventies,* Hawthorn, 1979. General editor of "Ethnic Prejudice in America" series, World Publishing, 1970-72. Contributor to newspapers and scholarly publications.

WORK IN PROGRESS: A psychological biography of Benjamin Disraeli; a translation of La Rochefoucauld's *Maxims.*

SIDELIGHTS: Presented with "apologies to Tom Wolfe," whose essay "Radical Chic" examined the attempts of upper-class New York intellectuals to embrace the liberalism of the early 1970s, Michael Selzer's *Terrorist Chic* demonstrates how "violence, brutality, sadomasochism, evil, and degeneracy in general" have replaced politics as a fashionable pursuit. As defined by the author, terrorist chic is "the outer limit society allows itself in expressing the fantasies which terrorists make explicit." In short, writes Selzer, "what hitherto had existed only in furtive and antisocial behavior" has now become "publicly acceptable and indeed highly fashionable." He then concludes that this bizarre fascination with violence is a product of affluence and boredom and that it could very well culminate in a desire to experience the ultimate "excitement"—world war.

Selzer documents his case with numerous examples of "depravity" encountered in the worlds of music, film, art, and fashion. Much of his material comes from interviews he conducted with the designers, photographers, and "sexual adventurers" who frequent places like the celebrated Studio 54 disco and the less well-known Chateau 19, a club whose brochure invites patrons to attend a special "party" featuring "nonprofessional demonstrations of sexual dominance and submission." Selzer also takes a look at the Dracula revival of the late 1970s as well as the emergence of punk rock, punk fashion, and even punk furniture to help support his contention that terrorism is indeed "in."

For the most part, reviewers agree with the *New York Times*'s Anatole Broyard that Selzer has a "flair for interpreting pop culture." Continues Broyard: "He is a rather good interviewer and, armed with a tape recorder, he has talked to people on the freaky edge of fashion and put together a book that will give us all something to worry or laugh about, according to our respective temperaments." The *New York Times Book Review* critic also finds Selzer's interviews "sharp" in that they reveal, "if nothing else, the vapid minds of his subjects."

Even though they applaud his skills as an interpreter of modern culture, several reviewers take issue with certain parts of *Terrorist Chic*. Broyard, for example, declares that "Selzer's philosophizing . . . is the weakest part of his book. His remarks on political terrorism seem naive. . . . [And] when he coins the phrase 'the anorexia of experience' to explain the vogue for violence, he sounds more chic than scientific himself." The *New York Times Book Review* critic points out that Selzer's reasons for including in the same discussion such diverse people as sadomasochists, readers of thriller novels, and regular patrons of Studio 54 form "the least convincing part of the book." He eventually decides that there are just "too many things . . . mixed together in *Terrorist Chic*."

Grover Sales, commenting in the *Los Angeles Times Book Review*, speculates that the major problem with *Terrorist Chic* may be that "Selzer is both attracted to and repelled by his subject. This ambiguity makes his book at once fascinating and unresolved, provocative and vague. . . . Selzer is more intent on proving his cleverness in argument than in making his case. His ideas are often thought-provoking, even startling, but he has a weakness for tossing out grand theories with no substantiation."

David Speck disagrees with these assessments of the book he describes as "a tour of the American wasteland of depleted values." Writing in *Best Sellers*, Speck admits that Selzer's work may lack the "stylistic brilliance of Wolfe's 'new-wave' journalism" but maintains that *Terrorist Chic* "is of much graver significance." In short, concludes the reviewer, "because Selzer's message is extremely important in a perilously unbalanced and increasingly violent world, *Terrorist Chic* will be read by those who seek to understand this new development in our current predicament at the end (or is it the beginning?) of what Wolfe calls the 'Me Decade.'"

BIOGRAPHICAL/CRITICAL SOURCES: New York Times Book Review, October 8, 1967, July 22, 1979; *Commentary*, December, 1967, January, 1971; *Nation*, June 10, 1968; *Chicago Tribune Book World*, November 26, 1978; Michael Selzer, *Terrorist Chic: An Exploration of Violence in the Seventies*, Hawthorn, 1979; *New York Times*, June 27, 1979; *Los Angeles Times Book Review*, July 15, 1979; *New Yorker*, July 30, 1979; *Best Sellers*, September, 1979.

* * *

SENIOR, Isabel J(anet Couper Syme) (Susan Pleydell)

PERSONAL: Born in Kinross-shire, Scotland; daughter of Colin Couper (a farmer and landowner) and Janet (Reid) Syme; married J.R.M. Senior (a schoolmaster); children: Janet Edith, Alan Murray. *Education:* Royal College of Music, London, England, L.R.A.M. *Religion:* Church of England. *Agent:* A. M. Heath & Co. Ltd., 40-42 William IV St., London WC2N 4DD, England.

CAREER: Writer. Has worked as teacher of piano in girls' boarding school for two years, teacher of piano in boys' schools, and private music teacher, with some concert work. As a student, worked as ballet accompanist.

WRITINGS—Under pseudonym Susan Pleydell, except as indicated: *Summer Term*, Hodder & Stoughton, 1959; *A Festival for Gilbert*, Hodder & Stoughton, 1960; *The Glenvarroch Gathering*, Hodder & Stoughton, 1960; *Good Red Herring*, Jenkins, 1962; *A Young Man's Fancy*, Jenkins, 1962; *Griselda* (first serialized in *Woman's Realm* under title, "In Search of a Name"), Collins, 1964; *The Road to the Harbor*, Collins, 1966.

Jethro's Mill, Collins, 1974; *Pung of Dragons*, Collins, 1975; *Brighouse Hotel*, Collins, 1977; (under name Isabel J. Senior with Ruth Beard) *Motivating Students*, Routledge & Kegan Paul, 1980. Contributor of numerous short stories to periodicals.

SIDELIGHTS: Summer Term was serialized in French and Dutch; extracts from *Good Red Herring* have been broadcast on British Broadcasting Corp. Russian Service. *Avocational interests:* Reading, from theology to thrillers, with particular preference for nineteenth-century novelists, Jane Austen and Anthony Trollope, and for contemporary writers, J. D. Salinger and John Steinbeck.†

* * *

SEWELL, W. R. Derrick 1931-

PERSONAL: Born February 9, 1931, in Rock Ferry, England; son of Wilfred (a company director) and Winifred (Bott) Sewell; married Elizabeth F. Kilgour, May 13, 1961; children: Kirsty, Wendy Anne, Robert. *Education:* University of London, B.Sc. (honors in economics), 1954; University of Washington, Seattle, M.A., 1956, Ph.D., 1964. *Home:* 3926 Woodhaven Ter., Victoria, British Columbia, Canada. *Office:* Department of Geography, University of Victoria, P.O. Box 1700, Victoria, British Columbia, Canada V8W 2Y2.

CAREER: British Columbia Bureau of Economics and Statistics, Victoria, research assistant, 1956-57; Canada Department of Northern Affairs and National Resources, Water Resource Branch, Vancouver, British Columbia, economist, 1957-63; University of Chicago, Chicago, Ill., assistant professor of economics and geography, 1964-66; University of Victoria, Victoria, associate professor, 1966-68, professor of geography and economics, 1969—.

Honorary sessional lecturer on resource economics, University of British Columbia, 1961-62; visiting professor at Utah State University, summer, 1965, University of North Carolina, spring, 1968, University of Hawaii, spring, 1971, and University of Edinburgh, spring, 1972, spring, 1973; distinguished lecturer, National Water Authority, Hungary, 1974; distinguished professor, State University of California at Chico, 1975. Canadian delegate to International Council of Man and the Biosphere Program, 1974, International Symposium on Non-Technical Obstacles to the Use of Solar Energy, Brussels, 1980, and to Scientific Forum of the Conference on Security and Cooperation in Europe, Hamburg, 1980. Organizer of conferences and symposia on various aspects of resources development and environmental management. *Member:* International Association for Water Law, Association of American Geographers, Institute of Public Administration of Canada, Canadian Water Resources Association, Solar Energy Society of Canada.

AWARDS, HONORS: Research grants from U.S. National Science Foundation, 1966, Resources for the Future, 1966, 1969, Canada Department of Energy, Mines and Resources, 1967, National Advisory Committee on Water Resources Research (Canada), 1969-72, Canada Council, 1969, 1973-74, 1977, Canada Department of Fisheries, 1970, Canadian Commission for UNESCO, 1976, Social Sciences and Humanities Research Council, 1978-81; Canadian Association of Geographers' Award for Scholarly Distinction, 1981.

WRITINGS: Water Management and Floods in the Fraser River Basin, Department of Geography, University of Chicago, 1965;

(editor and contributor) *Human Dimensions of Weather Modification,* Department of Geography, University of Chicago, 1966; (editor and contributor) *The Human Use of Atmospheric Resources,* National Science Foundation, 1968; (co-editor and contributor) *Forecasting the Demands for Water,* Queen's Printer, 1969; (co-author) *Water Resources Research in Canada: Social Science Needs and Priorities,* Queen's Printer, 1969.

(Co-author) *Recreational Fishing Evaluation,* Queen's Printer, 1970; (co-editor and contributor) *The Geographer and Society,* Department of Geography, University of Victoria, 1970; (co-editor and contributor) *Resources, Recreation, and Research,* Department of Geography, University of Victoria, 1970; (co-editor and contributor) *Perceptions and Attitudes in Resources Management,* Information Canada, 1971; (editor and contributor) *Modifying the Weather: A Social Assessment,* Department of Geography, University of Victoria, 1973; (editor and contributor) *Environmental Quality,* Sage Publications, 1974; (co-editor) *Natural Resources for a Democratic Society: Public Participation in Decision-Making,* Westview Press, 1976; (co-author) *Images of Canadian Futures: The Role of Renewable Energy Conservation,* Department of the Environment (Ottawa), 1976; (co-editor and contributor) *Spatial Dimensions of Public Policy,* Pergamon, 1976; (co-author) *Solar Home Heating in Canada,* Department of the Environment, 1977; (co-editor and contributor) *Public Participation in Planning,* Wiley, 1977; (co-author) *Canadian Perspectives on U.S. Solar Policies,* Supply and Services (Ottawa), 1978.

(Co-author) *Analysis of U.S. Experience in Modifying Land Use to Conserve Energy,* Environment Canada (Ottawa), 1980; *Accelerating the Acceptance of Solar-Heating: North American Experience and International Implications,* Energy, Mines and Resources Canada (Ottawa), 1980; (co-editor and contributor) *Project Appraisal and Policy Review,* Wiley, 1981; (co-author) *Water, the Emerging Crisis in Canada,* James Lorimer & Sons, 1981; (co-editor and contributor) *Canadian Resource Policies: Problems and Prospects,* Methuen, 1981; (co-author) *An Assessment of Canadian Environmental Policies in Offshore Development,* Environment Canada, 1981.

Contributor: J. G. Jensen, editor, *Spatial Organization of Land Uses,* Oregon State University Press, 1964; Robert M. Brown, editor, *Man Versus Environment,* National Sanitation Foundation, 1966; R. Flaegle, editor, *Weather Modification: Science and Public Policy,* University of Washington Press, 1968; George S. Thompkins, editor, *Geographical Perspectives,* Tantalus Press, 1968; R. J. Chorley, editor, *Water, Earth and Man,* Methuen, 1969; Maynard M. Bufschmidt, editor, *Regional Planning: Challenge and Prospects,* Praeger, 1969; W. J. Maunder and H. D. Foster, editors, *Pollution,* University of Victoria Press, 1969.

F. M. Leversedge, editor, *Priorities in Water Management,* Department of Geography, University of Victoria, 1973; J. T. Coppock and C. B. Wilson, editors, *Environmental Quality,* Scottish Academic Press, 1974; Ian Appleton, editor, *Leisure Research and Policy,* Scottish Academic Press, 1974; Patrick Lavery, editor, *Recreational Geography,* David & Charles, 1975; Gilbert F. White, editor, *Environmental Effects of Complex River Development,* Westview Press, 1977; Charles N. Forward, editor, *Vancouver Island: Land of Contrasts,* Western Geographical Series (Victoria), 1979; Norman Triett, editor, *Environment and Health,* Ann Arbor Science Publishers, 1979.

O. P. Dwivedi, editor, *Resources and Environment: Policy Perspectives for Canada,* McClelland & Stewart, 1980; A. Strub and T. C. Steemers, editors, *Non-Technical Obstacles to the Use of Solar Energy,* Harwood Academic Publishers, 1981.

Contributor to *Annals,* Association of American Geographers, 1960, 1964, and to proceedings; contributor of articles and reviews to geography, conservation, economics, and business journals. Member of editorial board, American Geophysical Union, 1969-79, *Environment and Behaviour,* 1969—, and *Natural Resources Journal,* 1972-80.

* * *

SEYMOUR, John 1914-

PERSONAL: Surname originally Turbayne; surname changed to that of stepfather; born June 12, 1914, in England; son of Albert and Christine (an American; maiden name, Owens) Turbayne; married Sally Medworth (an artist and potter); children: Jane, Anne, Kate. *Home:* Fachongle Isaf, Pembrokeshire, Wales. *Agent:* David Higham Associates Ltd., 5-8 Lower John St., London W1R 4HA, England.

CAREER: Formerly farm manager in southwest Africa, skipper of fishing vessel in southwest Africa and South Africa, miner in Northern Rhodesia (now Zambia), and government livestock officer in Barotseland (now Zambia); operator of a small farm, and free-lance writer. *Military service:* British Army, King's African Rifles, 1940-46; served in Ethiopia and Burma.

WRITINGS: The Hard Way to India, Eyre & Spottiswoode, 1951; *Round about India,* Eyre & Spottiswoode, 1953, published as *Around India,* Day, 1954; *One Man's Africa,* Eyre & Spottiswoode, 1955, Day, 1956; *Boys in the Bundu* (juvenile), Harrap, 1955; *Sailing through England,* Eyre & Spottiswoode, 1956; *The Fat of the Land,* Faber, 1961, reprinted, 1974, Taplinger, 1962, published as *The Fat of the Land: Family Farming on Five Acres,* Schocken Books, 1975; *On My Own Terms,* Faber, 1963, reprinted, 1980. *Willynilly to the Baltic,* W. Blackwood, 1965.

Companion Guide to East Anglia, Collins, 1970, Scribner, 1975; (with wife, Sally Seymour) *Farming for Self-sufficiency: Independence on a Five Acre Farm,* illustrations by S. Seymour, Schocken Books, 1973 (published in England as *Self-sufficiency: The Science and Art of Producing and Preserving Your Own Food,* Faber, 1973); *Companion Guide to the Coast of North-East England,* Collins, 1974; *Companion Guide to the Coast of South-West England,* Collins, 1974; *A Complete Guide to the Coast of South-East England,* Collins, 1975; *The Guide to Self-sufficiency,* Popular Mechanic Books, c. 1976, published in England as *The Complete Book of Self-sufficiency,* Faber, 1976; *Bring Me My Bow,* Turnstone (London), 1977; *The Countryside Explained,* illustrations by S. Seymour, Faber, 1977; *I'm a Stranger Here Myself: The Story of a Welsh Farm,* Faber, 1978; *The Self-sufficient Gardener,* Faber, 1978, published as *The Self-sufficient Gardener: A Complete Guide to Growing and Preserving All Your Own Food,* Doubleday, 1979; *Gardener's Delight,* Harmony Books, 1979. Also author of *Getting It Together,* published by Michael Joseph. Contributor to magazines.

SIDELIGHTS: John Seymour lives on a sixty-two acre farm and grows nine-tenths of his own food. He also raises, kills, and cures his own meat. His books have been translated into Norwegian, Spanish, French, Portuguese, Dutch, German, and

Danish. *Avocational interests:* Cruising in small open boats, travel, topography.

BIOGRAPHICAL/CRITICAL SOURCES: Times Literary Supplement, June 6, 1980.

* * *

SHAW, Alan George Lewers 1916-

PERSONAL: Born February 3, 1916, in Melbourne, Victoria, Australia; son of George (a solicitor) and Ethel (Lewers) Shaw; married Peggy Perrins, May 21, 1956. *Education:* University of Melbourne, B.A. (with honors), 1938; Oxford University, B.A., 1940, M.A., 1944. *Home:* 197 Domain Rd., South Yarra, Victoria, Australia. *Office:* History of Victoria Project, 254 Faraday St., Carlton 3053, Victoria, Australia.

CAREER: Wartime posts with Australian Department of Information, 1940-41, Department of the Army, 1941-42, and Department of Rural Reconstruction, 1943-44; University of Melbourne, Melbourne, Victoria, Australia, lecturer in history, 1941-50, dean of Trinity College, 1946-50; University of Sydney, Sydney, New South Wales, Australia, senior lecturer in history, 1952-64, subwarden of St. Paul's College, 1953-56; Monash University, Melbourne, professor of history, 1964-81, emeritus professor, 1982—. Chairman of History of Victoria Project of Victoria's 150 Anniversary Celebrations.

MEMBER: Australian Academy of the Humanities (fellow), Australian Academy of the Social Sciences (fellow; president, 1978-81), Royal Australian Historical Society (councillor, 1954-64; fellow, 1979), Australian Institute of International Affairs (councillor, 1946-50), New South Wales History Teachers Association (president, 1959; councillor, 1959-63), Royal Historical Society of Victoria (councillor, 1965-72; fellow, 1974). *Awards, honors:* Co-recipient of Harbison-Higinbotham Prize, University of Melbourne, 1945, for *The Australian Coal Industry;* Nuffield traveling scholarship, 1950-51; Smuts visiting fellow at Cambridge University, 1967; Officer of the Order of Australia, 1982.

WRITINGS: (With G. R. Bruns) *The Australian Coal Industry,* Melbourne University Press, 1944; *Economic Development of Australia,* Longmans, Green, 1944, 7th revised edition, Longman, 1980; *The Story of Australia,* Faber, 1955, 5th revised edition, 1983; *Modern World History,* F. W. Cheshire, 1959; *Convicts and the Colonies,* Faber, 1966, revised edition, 1976; (editor) *Great Britain and the Colonies,* Methuen, 1970; (editor) John West, *History of Tasmania,* Angus & Robertson, 1972; *Sir George Arthur, Bart., 1784-1854,* Melbourne University Press, 1980. Contributor to journals in Australia. Editor, *Journal of Royal Australian Historical Society,* 1956-64.

AVOCATIONAL INTERESTS: Golf, bridge.

* * *

SHAW, Peter 1936-

PERSONAL: Born November 25, 1936, in New York, N.Y.; son of Arthur (a builder) and Margaret (a teacher; maiden name, Sandler) Shaw; married Penelope Pugliese (a modern dance teacher), January 12, 1958; children: Jennifer, Steven. *Education:* Cornell University, A.B., 1958; Columbia University, M.A., 1962, Ph.D., 1965. *Politics:* "Former liberal." *Home:* 106 West 69th St., New York, N.Y. 10023. *Agent:* Richard Balkin, 880 West 81st St., New York, N.Y. 10033. *Office:* 155 West 72nd St., New York, N.Y. 10023.

CAREER: State University of New York at Stony Brook, associate professor of English, 1965—. Visiting lecturer at New School for Social Research, 1967. Has appeared on television and radio programs. *Awards, honors:* American Council of Learned Societies grants, summers, 1972, 1976; National Endowment for the Humanities fellowship, 1973; *The Character of John Adams* was chosen as a Vice-President's Library (Washington, D.C.) selection, 1980.

WRITINGS: The Character of John Adams, University of North Carolina Press, 1976; *American Patriots and the Rituals of Revolution,* Harvard University Press, 1981; (editor) *Autobiography and Selected Writings of Benjamin Franklin,* Bantam, 1982. Author of brochures and study guides. Contributor to *Reader's Encyclopedia of American Literature.* Also contributor of articles and reviews to scholarly journals and to popular periodicals, including *Encounter, Harper's, New Republic, Times Literary Supplement, Partisan Review,* and *Sewanee Review.* Editor of *Reader's Encyclopedia of American Literature,* 1962-63; associate editor of *Commentary,* 1968-69; *Early American Literature,* member of board of editors, 1978-81, book review editor, 1981—.

WORK IN PROGRESS: Essays on the decline of contemporary intellectual discourse.

SIDELIGHTS: Peter Shaw told *CA:* "The book, *American Patriots and the Rituals of Revolution,* was a scholarly-historical response to the expressive politics of the 1960s. That era remains a preoccupation whether the ostensible subject be literary criticism, history, or commentary on contemporary culture." *Avocational interests:* Movie reviewing, collecting antique typewriters.

BIOGRAPHICAL/CRITICAL SOURCES: Newsday, May 31, 1976.

* * *

SHELLEY, Bruce L(eon) 1927-

PERSONAL: Born December 20, 1927, in Owensboro, Ky.; son of Leroy and Mabel (Travers) Shelley; married Mary Elizabeth Harrington, August 1, 1952; children: Marshall, David, Karen. *Education:* Columbia Bible College, Columbia, S.C., B.A., 1952; Fuller Theological Seminary, M.Div., 1955; University of Iowa, Ph.D., 1957; Harvard University, postdoctoral study, 1967. *Home:* 3066 South Hurley Cir., Denver, Colo. 80227.

CAREER: Baptist clergyman; Denver Seminary, Denver, Colo., assistant professor, 1957-59, associate professor, 1959-63, professor of church history, 1963—. *Military service:* U.S. Army, 1946-48; became sergeant. *Member:* American Society of Church History, Conference on Faith and History.

WRITINGS: Conservative Baptists: A Story of Twentieth Century Dissent, Conservative Baptist Theological Seminary, 1960, 2nd edition, 1962; *By What Authority?,* Eerdmans, 1965; *Evangelicalism in America,* Eerdmans, 1967; *The Cross and Flame,* Eerdmans, 1967; *Let's Face It,* Moody, 1968; (editor) Earl S. Kalland and others, *A Call to Christian Character: Toward a Recovery of Biblical Piety,* Zondervan, 1970; *The Church: God's People,* Victor Books, 1978; *Four Marks of a Total Christian,* Victor Books, 1978; *A History of Conservative Baptists,* Conservative Baptist Press, 1981; *Church History in Plain Language,* Word, Inc., 1982.

Contributor to *Encyclopedia of Southern Baptists,* 1971, *The New International Dictionary of the Christian Church,* 1974, and *Encyclopedia Americana,* 1974. Contributing editor, *United Evangelical Action,* 1967-77.

* * *

SHERIDAN, L(ionel) A(stor) 1927- (Lee Ang Shoy)

PERSONAL: Born July 21, 1927, in Croydon, England; son of Stanley Frederick (a businessman) and Anne (Quednau) Sheridan; married Margaret Helen Beghin, June 1, 1948; children: Peter Louis. *Education:* University of London, LL.B., 1947; Lincoln's Inn, Barrister-at-Law, 1948; Queen's University of Belfast, Ph.D., 1953. *Religion:* None. *Home:* Cherry Trees, St. Nicholas, South Glamorgan, Wales. *Office:* University College, University of Wales, Cardiff CF1 1XL, Wales.

CAREER: Queen's University of Belfast, Belfast, Northern Ireland, lecturer in law, 1949-56, professor of comparative law, 1963-71; University of Malaya, Singapore, professor of law, 1956-63; University of Wales, University College, Cardiff, professor of law, 1971—. *Member:* Society of Public Teachers of Law, Association of University Teachers, Honourable Society of Cymmrodorion. *Awards, honors:* LL.D., University of Singapore, 1963, and University of London, 1969; University of London, University College fellowship, 1978.

WRITINGS: *Fraud in Equity,* Pitman, 1957; (with B. T. Tan) *Elementary Law,* Donald Moore (Singapore), 1957; (with V.T.H. Delany) *The Cy-Pres Doctrine,* Sweet & Maxwell, 1959, supplement, 1961; *The Federation of Malaya Constitution,* University of Malaya Law Review, 1961, 3rd edition (with H. E. Groves) published as *The Constitution of Malaysia,* Oceana, 1967; (editor and contributor) *Malaya, Singapore, the Borneo Territories: The Development of Their Laws and Constitutions,* Stevens & Sons, 1961; *Constitutional Protection: Expropriation and Restrictions on Property Rights,* Oceana, 1963; (with G. W. Keeton) *Equity,* Pitman, 1969, supplement, 1974, 3rd edition, Professional Books, in press.

(Editor and contributor) *Survey of the Land Law of Northern Ireland,* H.M.S.O., 1971; (with Keeton) *The Modern Law of Charities,* 2nd edition, Northern Ireland Legal Quarterly, 1971, supplement, 1975; (with Keeton) *A Casebook on Equity and Trusts,* 2nd edition, Professional Books, 1974; *Rights in Security,* McDonald & Evans, 1974; (with Keeton) *The Law of Trusts,* 10th edition, Professional Books, 1974, supplement, 1979; (with Keeton) *The Comparative Law of Trusts in the Commonwealth and the Republic of Ireland,* Barry Rose, 1976, supplement, 1981; (with Keeton) *Digest of the English Law of Trusts,* Professional Books, 1981.

Author of Irish supplements: Keeton, *An Introduction to Equity,* 3rd edition, Pitman, 1952, 5th edition, 1961; C. Sweet, *Real Property,* 3rd edition, Butterworth & Co., 1956; Keeton, *Law of Trusts,* 7th edition, Pitman, 1957, 9th edition, 1968.

Contributor: *The United Kingdom: The Development of Its Laws and Constitution,* Stevens & Sons, 1955; *A Bibliographical Guide to United Kingdom Law,* Institute of Advanced Legal Studies, 1956, 2nd edition, 1973; *Studies in Law,* Asia Publishing House (Bombay), 1961; *Report of the Regional Conference on Legal Education, Singapore, 1962,* Faculty of Law, University of Singapore, 1964; *Die moderne Demokratie und ihr Recht,* J.C.B. Mohr, 1966; *Law, Justice and Equity,* Pitman, 1967; *Trusts and Trust-Like Devices,* United Kingdom National Committee of Comparative Law, 1981.

Contributor to *Yearbook of World Affairs* and to more than twenty-five journals in England, Canada, Ireland, Malaya, Australia, Germany, India, and United States. Editor, *University of Malaya Law Review,* 1959-60, *Irish Jurist,* 1964, and *Northern Ireland Legal Quarterly,* 1964-65.

WORK IN PROGRESS: Third edition of *The Modern Law of Charities;* eleventh edition of *The Law of Trusts.*

* * *

SHERWOOD, Frank Persons 1920-

PERSONAL: Born October 11, 1920, in Brunswick, Ga.; son of Clarence M. and Mildred (Persons) Sherwood; married Frances H. Howell, 1948; children: Jeffrey, Robin Ann. *Education:* Dartmouth College, B.A., 1942; St. Catherine's College, Oxford, graduate study, 1945-46; University of Southern California, M.S.P.A., 1949, Ph.D., 1952. *Home:* 913 Gardenia Dr., Tallahassee, Fla. 32312. *Office:* Department of Public Administration, Bellamy Hall, Florida State University, Tallahassee, Fla. 32306.

CAREER: North Shore Publishing Co., San Diego, Calif., president, 1946-49; University of Southern California, Los Angeles, 1951-82, began as assistant professor, professor of public administration, 1959-82, acting dean of administration, 1961-62, director of School of Public Administration, 1967-68, director of Washington Public Affairs Center, 1973-76; Florida State University, Tallahassee, chairman of department of public administration, 1982—. U.S. Civil Service Commission, Federal Executive Institute, director, 1968-73, professor, 1977-82. U.S. Government consultant in Turkey, 1961. Chairman, City of Inglewood (Calif.) Charter Commission, 1959-61. *Military service:* U.S. Army, 1943-46; became lieutenant. *Member:* American Society for Public Administration (president, 1973-74), National Academy of Public Administration.

WRITINGS: *The Management Approach to Budgeting,* International Institute of Administrative Sciences, 1954; (co-author) *Supervisory Techniques in Municipal Administration,* International City Managers Association, 1959; (with John McDonald Pfiffner) *Administrative Organization,* Prentice-Hall, 1960; *A City Manager Tries to Fire His Police Chief,* University of Alabama Press, 1963; *Institutionalizing the Grass Roots in Brazil: A Study in Comparative Local Government,* Chandler Publishing, 1967; (with R. W. Gable) *The California System of Governments,* Dickinson, 1968; *Executive Development and the Federal Executive Institute: Selected Papers,* Federal Executive Institute, U.S. Civil Service Commission, 1971. Also author of *Brazil's Municipalities: A Comparative View,* International Public Administration Center, University of Southern California.

WORK IN PROGRESS: Writings on policy and administration.

* * *

SHERWOOD, Nelson See BULMER, (Henry) Kenneth

* * *

SHIPLEY, Joseph T(wadell) 1893- (Roy Goliard)

PERSONAL: Born August 19, 1893, in Brooklyn, N.Y.; son of Jay R. (a law book salesman) and Jennie (Fragner) Shipley; married Helen Bleet (deceased); married second wife, Anne Ziporkes (deceased); married third wife, Shirley Hector; children: (first marriage) Margaret (Mrs. Leslie Fiedler), Paul David;

(second marriage) John Burke, Howard Thorne. *Education:* City College (now City College of the City University of New York), A.B., 1912; Columbia University, A.M., 1914, Ph.D., 1931. *Religion:* Society of Friends. *Agent:* Shirley Hector Agency, 29 West 46th St., New York, N.Y. 10036.

CAREER: Teacher, drama critic, author. Stuyvesant High School, New York City, instructor in English, 1914-57, senior adviser, 1940-57. Co-organizer of Yeshiva College (now University), New York City, 1926-28, began as assistant professor, became associate professor of English and head of department, 1928-44; lecturer in Graduate Division, City College (now City College of the City University of New York), 1928-38, and Brooklyn College (now Brooklyn College of the City University of New York), 1932-38; conductor of seminar for playwrights, Dramatic Workshop, 1948-52; lecturer on American life and literature on world trip, 1957-58. Chairman, National Committee on Education in the Public Arts; U.S. director, Far East Research Institute; American correspondent, Association pour le Rencontre des Cultures; member of boards of Hwa Kiu University, Macao, and Canton University, Hong Kong. American advisor, Theatre des Nations, Paris, France; member of council of cultural advisors, American College in Paris; editorial advisor, Philosophical Library; vocabulary consultant, Science Research Associates.

MEMBER: Association Internationale des Critiques de Theatre (vice-president for United States), P.E.N., New York Drama Critics Circle (president, 1952-54; secretary, 1968-80), Critics' Circle (London; honorary member), English Association (London; life member), Phi Beta Kappa (honorary member).

WRITINGS: King John (fiction), Greenberg, 1925; *The Art of Eugene O'Neill,* University of Washington Press, 1928; *The Literary Isms,* University of Washington Press, 1931, reprinted, Folcroft, 1969; *The Quest for Literature,* Richard R. Smith, 1931; *Auguste Rodin* (from notes by Rodin's assistant, Victor Frisch), Stokes, 1941; *Dictionary of Word Origins,* Philosophical Library, 1945, revised edition, Greenwood Press, 1969; *Trends in Literature,* Philosophical Library, 1949.

Dictionary of Early English, Philosophical Library, 1955; *Guide to Great Plays,* Public Affairs Press, 1956; *Playing with Words,* Prentice-Hall, 1960; *The Mentally Disturbed Teacher,* Chilton, 1961; *Word Games for Play and Power,* Prentice-Hall, 1962; *Ibsen: Five Major Plays,* American R.D.M., 1965; (under pseudonym Roy Goliard) *A Scholar's Glossary of Sex,* Heinemann, 1968; *Vocabulab,* Science Research Associates, 1970; *Word Play,* Hawthorn, 1972; *In Praise of English,* Times Books, 1977.

Editor: *Dictionary of World Literature: Criticism, Forms, Technique,* Philosophical Library, 1943, new revised edition, Littlefield, 1966, revised and enlarged edition published as *Dictionary of World Literary Terms, Forms, Technique, Criticism,* Writer, 1970; *Encyclopedia of Literature,* two volumes, Philosophical Library, 1946. Also editor of twelve books, and author of seven books, in "Study-Master Guides to Drama" series published by American R.D.M., 1963-65.

Translator from the French: Baudelaire, *Prose Poems and Diaries,* Modern Library, 1919; Paul Geraldy, *You and Me* (poems), Boni & Liveright, 1923; Albert Ades, *A Naked King* (novel), Boni & Liveright, 1924; (and compiler) *Modern French Poetry,* Greenberg, 1926, reprinted, Books for Libraries, 1972; Paul Eluard, *Pablo Picasso,* Philosophical Library, 1947.

Writer of television scripts for "Ford Hour," radio scripts for "Footlight Forum," WMCA, 1938-40, "Word Stories," WOR, 1949-51, and scenarios for forty-eight films of the work of New York City schools, 1938-40.

Author of poems and essays appearing in American, English, French, Indian, and Pakistani magazines, with the poems reprinted in fourteen anthologies in three countries.

Drama critic for *Call,* 1919-21, *Leader,* 1921-22, *New Leader,* 1922-62, and for radio station WEVD, 1940-80. Foreign editor, *Contemporary Verse,* 1919-26; assistant editor, *Journal of the History of Ideas,* 1940-44; editor, *American Bookman,* 1944-50; member of editorial board, *Venture* (Pakistani literary quarterly); former member of editorial board, *Journal of Aesthetics.* Has covered the New York theater for the *Guardian* (Manchester, England) and *Theatre* (Paris, France).

WORK IN PROGRESS: More or Less Me (memoirs); *Where Our Words Began.*

SIDELIGHTS: Reminiscing on his long literary career, Joseph T. Shipley told *CA:* "Graduated from college at eighteen, I knew I would write. How to find publication? I decided it might be well to start with reviewing; but who would trust me, unknown, to discuss a book? And any book I might know of, to ask for, would doubtless already be assigned. So I wrote a review of a novel about a Near-East folk-hero, *Goha le Simple,* not yet translated from the French of Albert Ades. To my delighted surprise, Henry Seidel Canby, editor of the *Saturday Review of Literature,* accepted it. When I called on him, he gave me a book of poetry to review. Soon I was his regular poetry critic. Once a week I took the eight-odd books from the paper's shelf, and decided which to ignore, which to lump in a collective review, and which to emphasize in a separate article.

"In 1918, when a poem of mine was printed by *The Call,* I called upon Ryan Walker there. *The Call*'s drama critic, Anita Bloch, was about to resign. Learning that I had my Master's degree with a thesis on Ibsen and Shaw, they launched me, with a brief trial as Anita's assistant, on my world-record sixty-two years as a professional drama critic. Moral: If you want to learn to write, write. Publication is an added boon."

Various books by Shipley have been translated into Hebrew, Spanish, German, French, and Japanese, and published in English in England and India. Since 1958, Shipley has spent three months annually observing the theater in Europe; on his world trip in 1957-58, he was the guest of eleven governments in Europe and Asia.

During his college days, Shipley was on swimming, tennis, and championship chess teams, and he still plays chess when he can find the time.

BIOGRAPHICAL/CRITICAL SOURCES: Collier's, September 9, 1950; *Saturday Review,* December 5, 1970; *New York Times Book Review,* January 29, 1978; *Christian Science Monitor,* March 29, 1978; *English Journal,* December, 1978.

* * *

SHOEMAKER, Lynn Henry 1939-

PERSONAL: Born March 31, 1939, in Racine, Wis.; son of William (an engineer) and Gretchen (a teacher and poet; maiden name, Gull) Shoemaker; divorced; children: Erica Zoe. *Education:* Harvard University, B.A., 1961; University of South Dakota, M.A., 1962; graduate study at University of California, Davis, 1963-66; State University of New York at Albany, D.A., 1982. *Politics:* "Radical." *Religion:* "Radical Christian." *Office:* Department of English, University of Kansas, Lawrence, Kan. 66045.

CAREER: Yankton College, Yankton, S.D., assistant professor of English, 1962-63; California State College (now University), Los Angeles, lecturer in English, 1966-67; East Los Angeles Junior College, Los Angeles, Calif., lecturer in English, 1970-71; Beverly Hills High School, Beverly Hills, Calif., teacher of English, 1970-71; East Hill School, Ithaca, N.Y., teacher of wood shop, 1973-77; Ithaca College, Ithaca, N.Y., instructor in writing, 1977-78; State University of New York at Albany, teacher of composition, 1979-82; University of Kansas, Lawrence, instructor in English, 1982—. *Member:* Ithaca Community Poets.

WRITINGS: Coming Home (poems), Ithaca House, 1973; *Curses and Blessings* (poems), Ithaca House, 1978; *Hands* (poems), Lynx House Press, 1982.

WORK IN PROGRESS: A book of poems, *Caw.*

* * *

SHOUMATOFF, Alex(ander) 1946-

PERSONAL: Born November 4, 1946, in Mount Kisco, N.Y.; son of Nicholas (an engineer) and Nina (Adamovich) Shoumatoff; married second wife, Ana Dos Santos, April 9, 1977; children: Andre Luis, Nicholas. *Education:* Harvard University, B.A., 1968. *Home:* 86 Huntville Rd., Katonah, N.Y. 10536. *Office: New Yorker,* 25 West 43rd St., New York, N.Y. 10036.

CAREER: Washington Post, Washington, D.C., reporter and book reviewer, 1968-69; variously employed as songwriter, freelance, and instructor in French at New England College, Henniker, N.H., 1969-73; natural history teacher in private school in Bedford, N.Y., 1973-78; currently staff writer, *New Yorker,* New York, N.Y. Executive director and resident naturalist, Marsh Sanctuary, 1973-78; member of board of trustees, Butler Sanctuary. Minister of Universal Life Church. *Military service:* U.S. Marine Corps, 1969-70. *Member:* Bedford Audubon Society (member of board of directors). *Awards, honors:* Woodrow Wilson fellowship, 1968.

WRITINGS: Florida Ramble, Harper, 1974; *The Rivers Amazon,* Sierra Books, 1978; *Westchester: Portrait of a County,* Coward, 1979; *The Capital of Hope,* Coward, 1980; *Russian Blood: A Family Chronicle,* Coward, 1982. Contributor to newspapers and magazines.

SIDELIGHTS: Part naturalist, part journalist, Alex Shoumatoff is, according to a *New York Times Book Review* critic, "a very *New Yorker* kind of writer [who is] civilized, observant to a fault, and low key in style." His portraits of such diverse areas as the Amazon River basin, New York's Westchester County, and Brazil's capital city are testimony to what he terms his "abiding interest in the relationship of man and nature; in the type of writing that conveys the total picture of a place, both its natural and social history."

With his book *Russian Blood: A Family Chronicle,* however, Shoumatoff deviates from this pattern to convey the "total picture" not of a place, but of a people—his Russian ancestors. A blend of personal anecdotes (gathered primarily from the author's two grandmothers), history, and photographs, *Russian Blood* is, in the words of a *Best Sellers* reviewer, "a fascinating story told by a man who has true artistic talent and the storyteller's gift of communicating his own enthusiasm to his readers."

Herbert Gold, on the other hand, comments in the *Los Angeles Times Book Review* that "while the impulse behind the writing is proud and loyal," the book "suffers" in comparison with the memoirs, histories, and reports of other exiles who succumb to "that national nostalgia for the forever lost." Continues the critic: "Generally Shoumatoff is content with a fairly complacent amassing of detail. The dramatic, stagey, eccentric parents and grandparents, uncles, aunts, cousins and connections are reduced to dimensions of cuteness." Nevertheless, Gold concludes, "the resonance of strong autobiographical writing—of strong writing in general—occasionally stirs from the account of Shoumatoff's shimmering, unforgettable characters."

S. Frederick Starr also has words of praise for Shoumatoff's writing. Though he finds a few "plaster props and cliches" in *Russian Blood,* he points out in his *Washington Post* review that "it is not enough just to note that Shoumatoff's memoir displays some of the negative features of the genre. For Shoumatoff is a writer of exceptional sympathy and grace. The world may be full of people like his grandparents, cultured folk uprooted from their cozy environments and thrown into alien and indifferent worlds. But few of them are fortunate enough to have a writer of Shoumatoff's gifts to trace their steps. . . . He achieves just the right balance of objectivity and love."

BIOGRAPHICAL/CRITICAL SOURCES: Washington Post, December 5, 1978, June 25, 1982; *New York Times Book Review,* July 29, 1979, November 2, 1980; *Times Literary Supplement,* May 16, 1980; *Best Sellers,* July, 1982; *Los Angeles Times Book Review,* July 11, 1982.

* * *

SHOY, Lee Ang
See SHERIDAN, L(ionel) A(stor)

* * *

SHULMAN, Neil B(arnett) 1945-

PERSONAL: Born March 18, 1945, in Washington, D.C. *Education:* George Washington University, B.S., 1967; Emory University, M.D., 1971; also attended Harvard University, 1974, and Georgetown University, summer, 1976. *Home:* 2272 Vistamont Dr., Decatur, Ga. 30033. *Office:* Hypertension Program, Emory University School of Medicine, 69 Butler St. S.E., Atlanta, Ga. 30303.

CAREER: Intern at Emory University Hospital, Veterans Administration Hospital, and Grady Memorial Hospital, all Atlanta, Ga., all 1971-72; Grady Memorial Hospital, fellow in nephrology and associate in department of medicine, 1972-74; Emory University School of Medicine, Atlanta, assistant professor of nephrology, 1974-80, associate professor in Division of Hypertension, 1981—; Pine Knoll Nursing Home, Carrollton, Ga., medical director, 1976—; Georgia Department of Human Resources, Atlanta, staff member in Division of Physical Health, 1977-78, primary and rural health care developer, 1977—.

Georgia Heart Association, chairman of state high blood pressure education program, 1973, member of hypertension task force, 1974; National Institutes of Health, conferee for national patient education task force on hypertension, 1973, member of community consultation team for national high blood pressure education program, 1975; member of technical review board, California Regional Medical Program, 1974 and 1976; member of task force to review health care delivery in state prisons, Georgia Department of Human Resources, 1976; reviewer of grants for hypertension education and research, National Heart, Lung and Blood Institute, 1977; chairman of statewide information sharing committee on primary health care, 1977-80; member of board, Georgia Association of Primary Health Care, 1979-81; member of board of directors, Inner City Community Health Center, Atlanta, 1980. Investigator or project director of about a dozen studies on hypertension. Host of daily television program "Health Care U.S.A.," WATL, Atlanta, 1976; host of medical humor shorts, Cable News Network, 1981. Chairman, Georgia 2000 (citizens' health and environmental group), 1977-80; member of board of directors and chairman, Village Writer's Group, 1978—; member of consumer advisory board, Georgia Power Co., 1979—. *Member:* American Heart Association.

AWARDS, HONORS: Medal from Georgia Heart Association, 1974, for volunteer service; Inner City Award of Recognition, 1981, for assisting with the development of the Atlanta Inner City Community Health Center.

WRITINGS: (With B. Corns and S. Heymsfield) *Up and Down: All about Blood Pressure,* Emory University, 1973; (contributor) Fisher, Croole, and McCombs, editors, *Hypertension: Assessment and Management,* Drew Medical-Dental Center, Stanford University, 1975; *Finally I'm a Doctor,* Scribner, 1976; *What? Dead Again?,* Legacy Publishing, 1979; (contributor) J. W. Hurst, *Medicine: The Prevention, Recognition and Treatment of Disease,* Butterworths, 1982.

Contributor to medical journals. Member of editorial board, *Forum* (publication of American College of Physicians), 1979-80, and *Emory Magazine,* 1981—.

WORK IN PROGRESS: Novels on inner-city and rural health care; research on hypertension.

BIOGRAPHICAL/CRITICAL SOURCES: Atlanta, June, 1976; *Chicago Tribune,* August 16, 1976; *Philadelphia Inquirer,* August 23, 1976; *Atlanta Journal and Constitution,* September 19, 1976.

* * *

SHULMAN, Sandra (Dawn) 1944-
(Lisa Montague)

PERSONAL: Born December 15, 1944, in London, England; daughter of Alfred (a textile merchant) and Gladys (Davis) Shulman; married David Montague (a lawyer), 1972. *Education:* St. Godrics College, diploma, 1962. *Politics:* Social Democratic Party. *Religion:* "Jewish/Agnostic and a Freeman of the City of London." *Home and office:* 98 Dudley Ct., Upper Berkeley St., London W1, England. *Agent:* Bolt & Watson, Suite 8, 26 Charing Cross Rd., London WC2H 0DG, England.

CAREER: Writer. Longacre Press, London, England, secretary and personal assistant to fiction editor of children's magazines, 1962-63; free-lance journalist and film researcher; has worked as a broadcaster; lecturer and teacher of workshops on writing. Founding member of Social Democratic Party.

WRITINGS: The Menacing Darkness, Warner Paperback, 1966; *Castlecliff,* Warner Paperback, 1967; *The Brides of Devil's Leap,* Warner Paperback, 1968; *The Daughters of Astaroth,* Warner Paperback, 1968; *The Lady of Arlac,* Warner Paperback, 1969; *The Prisoner of Garve,* Warner Paperback, 1970; *The Temptress,* Warner Paperback, 1971; *The Florentine,* Morrow, 1973; *Madonna of the Shadows,* New English Library, 1973; *Guide to Drugs,* Davis-Poynter, 1975; *Encyclopedia of Astrology,* Hamlyn, 1976; *Nightmare,* David & Charles, 1979; (under pseudonym Lisa Montague) *Lady of Darkness,* Mills & Boon, 1980; (under pseudonym Lisa Montague) *The Emperor's Jewel,* Mills & Boon, 1981; (under pseudonym Lisa Montague) *Fortune's Folly,* Mills & Boon, 1982. Contributor of articles on witchcraft, mythology, and the paranormal to periodicals.

WORK IN PROGRESS: A history of medicine from a feminist viewpoint; a historical novel set in Venice; a modern novel set in Brazil.

SIDELIGHTS: Sandra Shulman told *CA* that she is "an ardent feminist [and] very active in the saner side of the Women's Movement and in local and national politics." She lists her professional interests as English and European history and exploring the role of women in past and present society, particularly in medicine, religion, and magic. She notes that she has been "influenced by Jungian psychology" and "has an abiding curiosity in what makes people 'tick.'" Shulman writes: "[I enjoy] instructing enthusiasts on the techniques of writing, and taking away any romantic notions that it's an activity for the fainthearted or lazy. [I also find] it a way of gaining a perspective on personal reasons for wishing to write."

Shulman has travelled extensively in Europe and Brazil to collect background material for her books. She speaks French, Italian, German, Portuguese, and Spanish. Her books have been translated into Dutch, Norwegian, Swedish, and German.

AVOCATIONAL INTERESTS: Cooking, collecting recipes, crossword puzzles, golf, and weight-lifting.

* * *

SIDEL, Victor W(illiam) 1931-

PERSONAL: Born July 7, 1931, in Trenton, N.Y.; son of Max A. (a pharmacist) and Ida (a pharmacist; maiden name Ring) Sidel; married Ruth Grossman (a professor of sociology and writer), June 3, 1956; children: Mark, Kevin. *Education:* Princeton University, A.B. (cum laude), 1953; Harvard University, M.D. (with honors), 1957; postgraduate study at Harvard University, 1964-66, and University of London, 1967-68. *Home:* 3614 Johnson Ave., Bronx, N.Y. 10463. *Office:* Department of Social Medicine, Montefiore Medical Center, 111 East 210th St., Bronx, N.Y. 10467.

CAREER: Peter Bent Brigham Hospital, Boston, Mass., intern, 1957-58, junior assistant resident in medicine, 1958-59; National Institutes of Health, Bethesda, Md., clinical associate at National Heart Institute and senior assistant surgeon for U.S. Public Health Service, 1959-61; Peter Bent Brigham Hospital, senior assistant resident in medicine, 1961-62, junior associate in medicine, 1962-66; Harvard Medical School, Boston, Mass., instructor in biophysics, 1962-64, associate in preventive medicine, 1964-67, assistant professor of preventive medicine, 1968-69; Massachusetts General Hospital, Boston, chief of preventive medicine unit, 1964-67, chief of community medicine unit, 1968-69; Montefiore Medical Center, Bronx, N.Y., chairman of department of social medicine, 1969—; Albert Einstein College of Medicine, Bronx, professor of social medicine, 1969—, chairman of department of community health, Montefiore Campus, 1972—.

Assistant in medicine, George Washington University School of Medicine, 1960-61; member of Center for Community Health and Medical Care, Harvard Medical School and Harvard School of Public Health. Visiting faculty member, City College of the

City University of New York, 1973—; visiting professor, Scandinavian School of Public Health, 1975, 1976, 1977, and 1981. Advanced research fellow, American Heart Association, 1962-64. Member of Massachusetts Commission on Radiation Protection, 1963-64; member of board of directors and chairman of task force on research of Massachusetts Mental Retardation Planning, 1966-67; member of Citizen's Committee for the Children of New York, 1971-75; project director of the First National House Staff Conference, 1971. Consulting physician in medicine and internist, Family Health Care Program, Children's Hospital Medical Center, Harvard Medical School, 1963-66; consulting physician, Morrisania City Hospital, 1969-76; consultant, World Health Organization, 1969, 1974, 1977, and 1982; current consultant or member of advisory boards, Occupational Health Media Project of the Oil, Chemical and Atomic Workers International Union, Coalition for a National Health Service, Project on Low-Income Consumers of the Consumers Union of the United States, Bronx Community College, New York Botanical Gardens, and National Senior Citizens Education and Research Center. Honorary attending physician, North Central Bronx Hospital, 1976—.

MEMBER: International Epidemiological Association, Physicians for Social Responsibility (vice-chairman, 1966-69; member of national advisory board, 1979—; member of board of directors, 1982—), American Association for the Advancement of Science, American Public Health Association (fellow; member of governing council, 1978—), Association of Teachers of Preventive Medicine, Society for Health and Human Values, Physicians Forum (member of board of directors, 1969—; chairman, 1971-72), New York Academy of Medicine, New York Academy of Sciences, Public Health Association of New York City (member of board of directors, 1979-80; president, 1981-83).

AWARDS, HONORS: Advanced research fellowship from American Heart Association, 1962-64; research fellowship from Medical Foundation, 1964-68; faculty fellowship from Milbank Memorial Fund, 1964-71; Sarah L. Poiley Award from New York Academy of Sciences, 1978, for "outstanding contributions toward improvement in the general health of the population."

WRITINGS: (Editor with Saul Aronow and F. R. Ervin) *The Fallen Sky: Medical Consequences of Thermonuclear War,* Hill & Wang, 1963; (with wife, Ruth Sidel) *Serve the People: Observations on Medicine in the People's Republic of China,* Josiah Macy, Jr., Foundation, 1973; (author of foreword) Bernard Schoenberg and others, editors, *Bereavement: Its Psychosocial Aspects,* Columbia University Press, 1975; (with R. Sidel) *A Healthy State: An International Perspective on the Crisis in U.S. Medical Care,* Pantheon, 1978, revised edition, 1983; (with R. Sidel) *The Health of China: Current Conflicts in Medical and Human Services for One Billion People,* Beacon Press, 1982.

Contributor: Henry Eyring, editor, *Civil Defense,* American Association for the Advancement of Science, 1966; E. F. Torrey, editor, *Ethical Issues in Medicine: The Role of the Physician in Today's Society,* Little, Brown, 1968; Steven Rose, editor, *C.B.W.: Chemical and Biological Warfare,* Harrap, 1968; John Norman, editor, *Medicine in the Ghetto,* Appleton, 1969.

Bonnie Bullough and Vern Bullough, editors, *New Directions for Nurses,* Springer Publishing, 1971; Robert Eilers and Sue Moyerman, editors, *National Health Insurance,* Irwin, 1971; Everett Mendelsohn, Judith P. Swazey, and Irene Taviss, editors, *Human Aspects of Biomedical Innovation,* Harvard University Press, 1971; David Milton and others, editors, *People's China: Social Experimentation, Politics, Entry onto the World Scene, 1966 through 1972,* Vintage Books, 1974; J. R. Quinn, editor, *Medicine and Public Health in the People's Republic of China,* U.S. Department of Health, Education and Welfare, 1972; Michel Oksenberg, editor, *China's Developmental Experience,* Academy of Political Science, Columbia University, 1973; Raymond G. Slavin and others, editors, *Tice's Practice of Medicine,* Harper, 1973, revised edition, 1977; Alan Gartner, Colin Green, and Frank Riessman, editors, *What Nixon Is Doing to Us,* Harper, 1973; John Z. Bowers and Elizabeth Purcell, editors, *Medicine and Society in China,* Josiah Macy, Jr., Foundation, 1974; Quinn, editor, *China Medicine as We Saw It,* U.S. Department of Health, Education and Welfare, 1974.

K. W. Newell, editor, *Health by the People,* World Health Organization, 1975; Ethel Tobach and Harold M. Proshansky, editors, *Genetic Destiny: Scientific Controversy and Social Conflict,* AMS Press, 1975; K. W. Newell, editor, *Health by the People,* World Health Organization (Geneva), 1975; R. M. Veatch and Ray Branson, editors, *Ethics and Health Policy,* Ballinger, 1976; Tobach and H. M. Proshansky, editors, *Genetic Destiny: Scientific Controversy and Social Conflict,* AMS Press, 1976; Elsie Bandman and Bertram Bandman, editors, *Bioethics and Human Rights: A Reader for Health Professionals,* Little, Brown, 1978; *Effects of the Payment Mechanism on the Health Care Delivery System,* National Center for Health Services Research, Department of Health, Education, and Welfare, 1978; Warren T. Reich, editor, *Encyclopedia of Bioethics,* Free Press, 1978; H. D. Schwartz and C. S. Kart, editors, *Dominant Issues in Medical Sociology,* Addison-Wesley, 1978; Samuel Wolfe, editor, *Organization of Health Workers and Labor Conflict,* Baywood, 1978; Neville Maxwell, editor, *China's Road to Development,* Pergamon, 1978, revised edition, 1979; Willoughby Latham, editor, *The Future of Academic Community Medicine in Developing Countries,* Rockefeller Foundation, 1979; Arne J. deKeijzer and Fredric M. Kaplan, editors, *The China Guidebook: A Traveler's Guide to the People's Republic of China,* Eurasia Press, 1979; George K. Chacko, editor, *Health Handbook: An International Reference on Care and Cure,* North-Holland Publishing, 1979.

Mark Reader, editor, *Atom's Eve: Ending the Nuclear Age,* McGraw-Hill, 1980; William Ruddick, editor, *Philosophers in Medical Centers,* Society for Philosophy and Public Affairs, 1980; Walter J. McNerney, editor, *Working for a Healthier America,* Ballinger, 1980; Philip R. Lee, Nancy Brown, and Ida Red, editors, *The Nation's Health,* Boyd & Fraser, 1981; Peter Conrad and Rochelle Kern, editors, *The Sociology of Health and Illness: Critical Perspectives,* St. Martin's, 1981; Ralph A. Straetz, Marvin Lieberman, and Alice Sardell, editors, *Critical Issues in Health Policy,* Lexington Books, 1981; Justin M. Jaffe and George W. Albee, editors, *Prevention through Political Action and Social Change,* University Press of New England, 1981; Kaplan and Julian M. Tobin, editors, *Encyclopedia of China Today,* 3rd edition, Harper, 1981; Ruth Adams and Susan Cullen, editors, *The Final Epidemic: Physicians and Scientists on Nuclear War,* Educational Foundation for Nuclear Science, 1981; Emil Pascarelli, editor, *Hospital-Based Ambulatory Care,* Appleton-Century-Crofts, 1982; *Primary Health Care: More Than Medicine,* Prentice-Hall, 1982; Gartner, Greer, and Riessman, editors, *What Reagan Is Doing to Us,* Harper, 1982; Jane Ives, editor, *Exportation of Hazardous Industries, Products, and Technologies to Developing*

Countries, National Institute for Occupational Safety and Health, 1982.

Also author of scientific abstracts and reports. Contributor to *Encyclopedia Americana* and *Academic American Encyclopedia.* Contributor of over 150 articles and reviews to professional and popular publications. Member of editorial board, *Hospital Practice,* 1966—, *Postgraduate Medicine,* 1969—, *New Physician,* 1971-76, *International Journal of Health Services,* 1971-79, *American Journal of Drug and Alcohol Abuse,* 1973-81, *American Journal of Chinese Medicine,* 1975—, *Forum on Medicine,* 1978-80, *Journal of Prison Health,* 1980—, *Journal of Latin Community Health,* 1980—, and *Journal of Public Health Policy,* 1982—.

SIDELIGHTS: Victor W. Sidel's work centers around community medicine and social medicine. He believes that physicians have to recognize the impact of environmental, political, and social influences upon their patients' health and work with them accordingly. As he remarked to *CA:* "All human beings have a right to social justice, peace, full employment, and humane services. All of us, as human beings, have a duty to fight for changes in control of wealth and power to make this possible. I believe, with Frederick Douglass, 'If there is no struggle, there is no progress.'"

Sidel has traveled and studied in England, Scandinavia, and the Soviet Union. He visited the People's Republic of China at the invitation of the Chinese Medical Association in 1971, 1972, 1977, 1980, and 1982. He has visited Chile twice, the first time in 1973 as a guest of the Ministry of Health and the second time in 1979 as a guest of the Academy of Christian Humanism. He visited Malaysia for the World Health Organization and Vietnam as representative of Medical Aid to Indochina, both in 1974, and in 1978 he was invited to Cuba by the Ministry of Health.

BIOGRAPHICAL/CRITICAL SOURCES: Environment, June, 1972; *Journal of the American Medical Association,* June 4, 1982.

* * *

SIEGEL, Eli 1902-1978

PERSONAL: Born August 16, 1902, in Dvinsk, Latvia (now U.S.S.R.); brought to United States in 1905; died November 8, 1978, in New York, N.Y.; son of Mendel and Sarah (Einhorn) Siegel; married Martha Baird (a writer), 1944 (died October 22, 1981). *Education:* Attended Baltimore City College, 1916-19. *Home:* 67 Jane St., New York, N.Y. 10014. *Address:* c/o Definition Press, 141 Greene St., New York, N.Y. 10012.

CAREER: Associated with V. F. Calverton in founding of *Modern Quarterly,* 1923; columnist, *Baltimore American,* 1925; book reviewer, *Literary Review of New York Evening Post,* 1926, and *Scribner's,* 1931-35; conductor of poetry readings at the Troubadour, Village Mill, Village Vanguard, and other establishments, New York City, 1926-36; founder and teacher of the philosophy of Aesthetic Realism, New York City, 1940-78. Writer and poet. *Awards, honors: Nation* Poetry Prize, 1925, for poem "Hot Afternoons Have Been in Montana"; National Book Award nomination, 1958, for collection *Hot Afternoons Have Been in Montana: Poems.*

WRITINGS—Published by Definition Press, except as indicated: *The Aesthetic Method in Self-Conflict,* 1946, 2nd edition, 1965; *Psychiatry, Economics, Aesthetics,* 1946, reprinted, Aesthetic Analysis, 1964; *Is Beauty the Making One of Opposites?* (broadside), Aesthetic Realism Foundation and Terrain Gallery, 1955; *Hot Afternoons Have Been in Montana: Poems,* 1957; *A Rosary of Evil,* Aesthetic Realism Foundation and Terrain Gallery, 1964; *Damned Welcome: Aesthetic Realism Maxims,* Aesthetic Realism Foundation and Terrain Gallery, 1964, 2nd edition, Definition Press, 1972; *What's There?: Lou Bernstein's Photographs,* Aesthetic Realism Foundation and Terrain Gallery, 1965.

James and the Children: A Consideration of Henry James's "The Turn of the Screw," edited by wife, Martha Baird, 1968; *Hail, American Development* (poems), 1968; *Goodbye Profit System,* edited by Baird, 1970, revised edition published as *Goodbye Profit System: Update,* 1982; *The Williams-Siegel Documentary,* edited by Baird and Ellen Reiss, 1970; *Children's Guide to Parents and Other Matters,* 1971; *The Frances Sanders Lesson and Two Related Works,* 1974; *Self and World: An Explanation of Aesthetic Realism,* edited and introduced by Baird, 1981; *Definitions and Comment: Being a Description of the World,* 1983; *Dear Time* (poems), 1984.

Also author of numerous other works, including booklets published by the Aesthetic Realism Foundation, a free verse translation of the Hebrew Kaddish published in *Commentary* in 1953, and the play "Shakespeare's 'Hamlet': Revisited," 1963, performed in thirteen parts and in a one-evening version for more than a year at the Terrain Gallery.

Work is represented in anthologies, including *City in All Directions,* edited by Arnold Adoff, Macmillan, 1969, *Pith and Vinegar,* edited by William Cole, Simon & Schuster, 1969, *100 American Poems,* edited by Selden Rodman, New American Library, 1972, *Half Serious,* edited by Cole, Eyre Methuen, 1973, and *America: A Prophecy,* edited by Rothenberg and Quasha, Random House, 1973.

Regular contributor, *Right of Aesthetic Realism to Be Known;* contributor of poems, articles, and reviews to *Nation, New Republic, Hound and Horn, Harper's, Poetry, Times Literary Supplement, New Mexico Quarterly, New York Quarterly, Poor Old Tired Horse,* and other publications.

SIDELIGHTS: In 1925, a young, self-educated poet named Eli Siegel was the surprise winner of the prestigious *Nation* Poetry Prize. Cited for his work "Hot Afternoons Have Been in Montana," which Michael Kernan of the *Washington Post* described as "a dazzling 99-line Whitmanesque song to life and the world and the past and the sky," Siegel immediately became the focus of a literary controversy. His innovative technique and unorthodox approach to his material tended to polarize reviewers' reactions to the poem; as Kernan remarked, "some critics loved it, others were outraged. . . . ['Hot Afternoons Have Been in Montana'] was reprinted, anthologized, translated. Then silence."

For the next twenty-five years Siegel worked in relative obscurity, writing more poetry and occasional reviews but devoting most of his time to developing and studying the philosophic principles that were implicit in "Hot Afternoons Have Been in Montana." "Suddenly, in 1951," continued Kernan, "the esteemed poet William Carlos Williams wrote a letter [to Siegel's wife, Martha Baird]. He had read the poem, and it electrified him." In his letter, Williams declared that the poem "is powerful evidence of a new track. The mind that made that mark is a different mind from ours. It is following different incentives. The eyes back of it are new eyes. They are seeing something different from ours. The evidence is technical but it comes out at the non-technical level as either great pleasure to the beholder, a deeper taking of the breath, a feeling of cleanliness, which is the sign of the truly new. The other side of the picture is the extreme resentment that a fixed, sclerotic mind feels confronting this new. It shows itself by the violent opposition Siegel received from the 'authorities' . . . and after that by neglect.''

Despite Williams's enthusiasm, Siegel and his work were ignored until 1957, when his first collection of poems (featuring ''Hot Afternoons Have Been in Montana'' as the title work) was nominated for a National Book Award. He was compared to other poets noted for their unconventionality, including Whitman, Sandburg, Thoreau, and even Gertrude Stein. But Siegel did not win the award, and he was once again forgotten. As Kernan observed, ''It was suggested that Siegel was a one-poem poet. His name was left off lists, he was quoted without acknowledgment, he seemed virtually to vanish from the world of letters.''

Meanwhile, Siegel continued to be preoccupied with studying and teaching the new philosophy of life and art he had begun to develop in the 1920s and 1930s. Known first as Aesthetic Analysis and later as Aesthetic Realism, this philosophy sprang from Siegel's belief that ''what makes a good poem is like what can make a good life . . . , for poetry is a mingling of intensity and calm, emotion and logic.'' Siegel composed ''Hot Afternoons Have Been in Montana'' with this principle in mind, taking ''many things that are thought of usually as being far apart and foreign and [showing], in a beautiful way, that they aren't so separate and that they do have a great deal to do with each other.'' In essence, stated the philosopher, Aesthetic Realism teaches that ''the resolution of conflict in self is like the making one of opposites in art.''

According to the tenets of Aesthetic Realism, life is divided into two parts: oneself and everything that is not oneself (in other words, the outside world). Siegel examined the relationship between these opposites in *Self and World,* a book that offers a new way of looking at such diverse topics as the mind, the family, art, sex, economics, and health. From this discussion emerged four basic principles of the philosophy, now known as the ''Four Statements of Aesthetic Realism.''

The first statement of Aesthetic Realism maintains that ''every person is always trying to put together opposites in himself.'' Though Siegel never intended this principle to become identified with any particular form of self-conflict, it long ago became linked to his position on what he termed the ''H Persuasion''—homosexuality. Because he believed homosexuality arises from contempt for the world that manifests itself as contempt for women, the philosopher reasoned that people could be ''changed from homosexuality'' if they were taught to ''like the world on an honest basis.'' Since 1946, over 100 men and women say they have ''changed from homosexuality'' after attending special question-and-answer consultation sessions conducted by teachers of Aesthetic Realism.

The second and third statements of Aesthetic Realism describe the two opposed purposes in everyone's life. As Siegel once observed, even though ''every person, in order to respect himself, has to see the world as beautiful, or good, or acceptable,'' there is also ''a disposition in every person to think he will be for himself by making less of the outside world.'' According to the philosopher, contempt for the world causes tremendous damage to the self (with effects ranging from boredom to insanity) and, on a larger scale, to the entire world when one nation's contempt for another leads to war. Siegel regarded this emphasis on the attitude of the individual towards the world as the major difference between Aesthetic Realism and other philosophies.

The last statement on Aesthetic Realism discussed in *Self and World* concerns the determination of beauty in life and art. Siegel contended that *all* beauty is the ''making one of opposites, and the making one of opposites is what we are going after in ourselves.'' Health and happiness in life and beauty in art thus depend on how fully, richly, and deeply ''the permanent opposites in reality'' are made one.

Ever since Siegel gave the first Aesthetic Realism lesson in 1941, the movement has faced an uphill struggle to gain recognition and respect among those people who, as the poet-philosopher concluded, preferred to act as if he did not exist. (Many of Siegel's students, for example, wear buttons that proclaim they are ''victims of the press,'' a pointed reference to their belief that newspapers and magazines have deliberately avoided reporting honestly on the philosophy of Aesthetic Realism.) Informing and educating the public has therefore become the primary task of the Aesthetic Realism Foundation, a non-profit organization whose staff members conduct seminars, workshops, and consultation sessions. The foundation's goal is to have Aesthetic Realism become the basis of the American educational system.

Ellen Reiss, an editor at Definition Press (the principal publisher of Siegel's work) and, as she told *CA,* ''the person with the greatest authority to speak on Eli Siegel, Aesthetic Realism, and their history,'' provided the following statement regarding the man Kenneth Rexroth once said should be ''moved up into the ranks of our acknowledged Leading Poets'': ''Eli Siegel's work, which in time became Aesthetic Realism, was the cause of some of the largest praise, the largest love in persons, and also the largest resentment. . . . In writing an entry about [him] for *Contemporary Authors,* you are somewhat in the position you would be writing an entry on the poet John Keats in 1821. That is, if you were to rely on what was said of Keats by most established critics (critics now remembered principally for their injustice to one of the greatest English writers), you would present the author of 'Ode to a Nightingale' as a presumptuous 'Cockney poet' whose works were 'drivelling idiocy.' In writing about Eli Siegel [now], you are writing about a contemporary who is great; who all his life met what William Carlos Williams described him as meeting, 'the extreme resentment that a fixed, sclerotic mind feels confronting this new'; who now, after his death, is *beginning,* just barely beginning, to be seen with something like fairness.''

MEDIA ADAPTATIONS: Eli Siegel's book *Goodbye Profit System* was adapted into a three-act musical play by Siegel's wife, Martha Baird, and Tom Shields. It was produced in New York City at the Terrain Gallery in 1972.

BIOGRAPHICAL/CRITICAL SOURCES: Baltimore Sun, February 2, 1925; Eli Siegel, *Is Beauty the Making One of Opposites?,* Aesthetic Realism Foundation and Terrain Gallery, 1955; *Saturday Review,* August 17, 1957; Karl Shapiro, *In Defense of Ignorance,* Random House, 1960; Howard Nemerov, *Poetry and Fiction,* Rutgers University Press, 1963; *Underground,* November 2, 1966; *Poetry,* November, 1968; *New York Times Book Review,* March 23, 1969; Martha Baird and Ellen Reiss, editors, *The Williams-Siegel Documentary,* Definition Press, 1970; *New Republic,* December 12, 1970; *Right of Aesthetic Realism to Be Known,* October 31, 1973, April 25, 1979; Baird and Reiss, editors, *The Press Boycott of Aesthetic Realism: Documentation,* Definition Press, 1978; *Washington Post,* August 16, 1978; Raymond J. Corsini, editor,

Handbook of Innovative Psychotherapies, Wiley, 1981; Siegel, *Self and World,* Definition Press, 1981; *Smithsonian,* February, 1982.

OBITUARIES: New York Times, November 10, 1978.†

—Sketch by Deborah A. Straub

* * *

SIEGEL, Irving H(erbert) 1914-

PERSONAL: Born February 1, 1914, in New York, N.Y.; son of David and Rebecca (Horowitz) Siegel; married Adelaide Simons (an information specialist), January 2, 1937; children: Judith Adrian Kremen, Ruth Elise Snider. *Education:* City College (now City College of the City University of New York), B.A., 1934; New York University, M.A., 1935; Columbia University, Ph.D., 1951. *Politics:* Independent ("very"). *Religion:* Jewish (unorthodox). *Home and office:* 8312 Bryant Dr., Bethesda, Md. 20034.

CAREER: U.S. Bureau of Labor Statistics, Washington, D.C., assistant chief of Productivity Division, 1941-43; U.S. Veterans Administration, Washington, D.C., chief economist, 1945-49; Johns Hopkins University, Baltimore, Md., director of Soviet Productivity Study in Operations Research Office and university lecturer in political economy, 1949-51; Twentieth Century Fund, Washington, D.C., director of American Technology Study, 1951-53; U.S. Council of Economic Advisers, Washington, D.C., senior staff economist, 1953-60, consultant, 1960-61; Research Analysis Corp., McLean, Va., chief of Economics Division, 1960-63, member of research council, 1963-65; W. E. Upjohn Institute for Employment Research, Washington, D.C., economist, 1965-70; U.S. Department of Commerce, Washington, D.C., economic adviser, 1972-79. Consultant to Patent, Trademark, and Copyright Research Institute of George Washington University, 1955-72, International Business Machines Corp., 1957-65, and American Chemical Society, 1970-73. *Military service:* U.S. Army, 1943-44.

MEMBER: American Statistical Association (fellow), American Economic Association, Econometric Society, Operations Research Society of America, American Association for the Advancement of Science (fellow), Washington Statistical Society (vice-president, 1948-49), New York Academy of Sciences (fellow), Phi Beta Kappa.

WRITINGS: (With H. Magdoff and M. B. Davis) *Production, Employment, and Productivity in Fifty-nine Manufacturing Industries, 1919-36,* three volumes, U.S. Works Progress Administration, 1939; *Concepts and Measurement of Production and Productivity,* U.S. Bureau of Labor Statistics, 1952; *Soviet Labor Productivity,* Johns Hopkins Operations Research Office, 1952; *Strengthening Washington's Technical-Resource Base,* Research Analysis Corp., 1963; (co-editor and contributor) *Dimensions of Manpower Policy: Programs and Research,* Johns Hopkins Press, 1966; (editor and contributor) *Manpower Tomorrow: Prospects and Priorities,* Kelley, 1967; *Aggregation and Averaging,* Upjohn, 1968; (contributor) *Chemistry in the Economy,* American Chemical Society, 1973; *Productivity Measurement: An Evolving Art,* Work in America Institute, 1980; *Company Productivity: Measurement for Improvement,* Upjohn, 1980; *Fuller Employment with Less Inflation,* Upjohn, 1981; (with Edgar Weinberg) Labor-*Management Cooperation: The American Experience,* Upjohn, 1982.

Contributor of scores of articles to professional and technical journals. Member of editorial board, *Idea,* 1957-72.

WORK IN PROGRESS: Books and papers on economic measurement, production and productivity concepts, and statistical methods.

SIDELIGHTS: Reflecting on factual writing, Irving H. Siegel remarked to *CA:* "Remember, in your kindly evening thoughts, the old guy, maid, or mom who counseled you that every paragraph should have a topic sentence. This precept would not make, and could destroy, a Shakespeare (who also would not heed); but it could also improve the output of most of us, who are required merely to tell others what we have in mind. To tell others, we must first find out; and here the topic sentence exerts its discipline, serving as a true instrument of creative research in self-discovery."

Siegel also has some words of advice for the aspiring young writer. "Seek not, or avoid, advice from the bully critic with folded brows who knows in advance ninety-nine reasons why your work is not yet ready for publication," he says. "He may see himself as a gatekeeper of the true culture; but he may be just another of Aesop's bob-tailed foxes, or he may have found that beating another's paper to pulp is easier and cheaper than undergoing psychotherapy. To court his 'avuncular' pre-rejection of your work is far less healthy to you and your career than direct submission to an editor (and his referees), whatever the outcome. Tell the bully critic that, if you are published, you will welcome his critique in the nearest journal. In the unlikely event that he accepts this challenge, you may wish to write a rejoinder—and get another publication to your credit."

* * *

SILVER, Richard
See BULMER, (Henry) Kenneth

* * *

SIMEON, Richard 1943-

PERSONAL: Born March 2, 1943, in England; son of John E. B. (a social worker) and Anne (a writer; maiden name, Dean) Simeon; married Joan Weld, August 6, 1966; children: Stephen, Rachel. *Education:* University of British Columbia, B.A. (with honors), 1964; Yale University, M.A., 1966, Ph.D., 1968. *Home:* 95 Mack St., Kingston, Ontario, Canada. *Office:* Institute of Intergovernmental Relations, Queen's University, Kingston, Ontario, Canada.

CAREER: Queen's University, Kingston, Ontario, assistant professor, 1968-71, associate professor, 1971-76, professor of political studies, 1976—, director of Institute of Intergovernmental Relations, 1976—. Visiting associate professor at University of British Columbia, 1972-73, and University of Essex, 1975-76. Member of advisory Committee on Confederation (Ontario), 1977-82. *Member:* Canadian Political Science Association (member of board of directors, 1973-75), Canadian Tax Foundation, Institute of Public Administration of Canada.

WRITINGS: Federal-Provincial Diplomacy: The Making of Recent Policy in Canada, University of Toronto Press, 1972; (editor) *Must Canada Fail?,* McGill-Queen's University Press, 1977; (editor) *Confrontation or Collaboration,* Institute of Public Administration, 1979; (with David Elkins) *Small Worlds, Provinces and Parties in Canadian Political Life,* Methuen (Toronto), 1980; (editor with Keith Banting) *And No One Cheered: Federalism, Democracy and the Constitution,* Methuen, 1983. Contributor to political science journals. Associate editor of *Canadian Public Policy,* 1974-78.

WORK IN PROGRESS: Research on territorial politics and public policy.

* * *

SIMON, Herbert A(lexander) 1916-

PERSONAL: Born June 15, 1916, in Milwaukee, Wis.; son of Arthur (an engineer) and Edna (Merkel) Simon; married Dorothea Pye (an educational researcher), December 25, 1937; children: Katherine, Peter, Barbara. *Politics:* Democrat. *Religion:* Unitarian. *Education:* University of Chicago, A.B., 1936, Ph.D., 1943. *Home:* 5818 Northumberland St., Pittsburgh, Pa. 15217. *Office:* Carnegie-Mellon University, Pittsburgh, Pa. 15213.

CAREER: International City Managers' Association, Chicago, Ill., staff member and assistant editor of *Public Management and Municipal Year Book,* 1938-39; University of California, Bureau of Public Administration, Berkeley, director of administrative measurement studies, 1939-42; Illinois Institute of Technology, Chicago, 1942-49, began as assistant professor, professor of political science, 1947-49, chairman of department of political and social science, 1946-49; Carnegie-Mellon University, Pittsburgh, Pa., professor of administration, 1949-62, professor of administration and psychology, 1962-65, Richard King Mellon professor of computer science and psychology, 1965—, chairman of department of industrial management, 1949-59, associate dean, 1957-74. Ford Distinguished Visiting Professor, New York University, 1960; distinguished lecturer, Princeton University, Northwestern University, Massachusetts Institute of Technology, Harvard University, University of Michigan, and University of California, Berkeley. Acting director of Management Engineering Branch and consultant, U.S. Economic Cooperation Administration, 1948; chairman of board of directors, Social Science Research Council, 1961-65; chairman, Division of Behavioral Sciences, National Research Council, 1967-69; member, President's Science Advisory Committee, 1968-72. Consultant to several agencies and organizations, including Cowles Foundation for Research in Economics, 1947—, and RAND Corp., 1952—.

MEMBER: Econometric Society (fellow), American Association for the Advancement of Science (fellow), American Academy of Arts and Sciences (fellow), American Psychological Association (fellow), Association for Computing Machinery, American Sociological Association (fellow), National Academy of Sciences (member of council, 1978-81), Institute of Management Sciences (vice-president, 1954), American Philosophical Society, American Political Science Association, American Association of University Professors, Operations Research Society of America, Psychonomic Society, Phi Beta Kappa, Sigma Xi (national lecturer, 1964).

AWARDS, HONORS: Administrator's Award, American College of Hospital Administrators, 1958; recipient of honorary degrees from Yale University, 1963, Case Institute of Technology (now Case Western Reserve University), 1963, University of Chicago, 1964, Lund University, 1967, McGill University, 1971, Erasmus University of Rotterdam, 1974, University of Michigan, 1978, University of Pittsburgh, 1979, and Marquette University, 1981; Distinguished Scientific Contributions Award, American Psychological Association, 1969; Turing Award, Association for Computing Machinery, 1976; Nobel Prize in economics, 1978; named honorary professor at Tianjian University, 1980.

WRITINGS: (With C. E. Ridley) *Measuring Municipal Activities,* International City Managers Association, 1938, 2nd edition, 1943; (with Divine, Cooper, and Chernin) *Determining Work Loads for Professional Staff in a Public Welfare Agency,* Bureau of Public Administration, University of California, 1941; *Fiscal Aspects of Metropolitan Consolidation,* Bureau of Public Administration, University of California, 1943; (with Shepard and Sharp) *Fire Losses and Fire Risks,* Bureau of Public Administration, University of California, 1943; (with others) *Technique of Municipal Administration,* 3rd edition, International City Managers' Association, 1947; *Administrative Behavior,* Macmillan, 1947, 3rd edition, 1976; (editor) *Local Planning Administration,* International City Managers' Association, revised edition, 1948.

(With Smithburg and Thompson) *Public Administration,* Knopf, 1950; (with others) *Fundamental Research in Administration,* Carnegie Institute of Technology Press, 1953; (with Kozmetsky, Guetzkow, and Tyndall) *Centralization vs. Decentralization in Organizing the Controller's Department,* Controllership Foundation, 1954, reprinted, Scholars Book Co., 1978; *Models of Man,* Wiley, 1958; (with J. S. March) *Organizations,* Wiley, 1958; (with Holt, Modigliani, and Muth) *Planning Production, Inventories, and Work Force,* Prentice-Hall, 1960; *The New Science of Management Decision,* Harper, 1960, revised edition, Prentice-Hall, 1977; *The Shape of Automation,* Harper, 1965; *The Sciences of the Artificial,* MIT Press, 1969, 2nd edition, 1981; (with A. Newell) *Human Problem Solving,* Prentice-Hall, 1972; (editor and contributor with L. Silelossy) *Representation and Meaning,* Prentice-Hall, 1972; *Models of Discovery, and Other Topics in the Methods of Science,* Reidel, 1978; *Models of Thought,* Yale University Press, 1979; *Models of Bounded Rationality, and Other Topics in Economics,* two volumes, MIT Press, 1982.

Contributor: *Research Frontiers in Politics and Government,* Brookings Institution, 1955; L. D. White, editor, *The State of the Social Sciences,* University of Chicago Press, 1956; Arensberg and others, editors, *Research in Industrial Human Relations,* Harper, 1957; Mary Jean Bowman, editor, *Expectations, Uncertainty and Business Behavior,* Social Science Research Council, 1958; Henkin, Suppes, and Tarski, editors, *The Axiomatic Method,* North-Holland Publishing, 1959; George P. Schultz and John R. Coleman, *Labor Problems: Cases and Readings,* McGraw, 1959; Warner and Martin, editors, *Industrial Man,* Harper, 1959; Edward H. Bowman and Robert B. Fetter, editors, *Analyses of Industrial Operations,* Irwin, 1959.

Shultz and Whisler, editors, *Management Organization and the Computer,* Free Press of Glencoe, 1960; Melvin Anshen and G. L. Bach, editors, *Management and Corporations, 1985,* McGraw, 1960; Rubenstein and Haberstroh, *Some Theories of Organization,* Irwin, 1960; *Current Trends in Psychological Theory,* University of Pittsburgh Press, 1961; H. Billing, editor, *Lernende Automaten,* R. Oldenbourg, 1961; Harvey S. Perloff, editor, *Planning and the Urban Community,* Carnegie Institute of Technology and University of Pittsburgh Press, 1961; S. M. Farber and Roger H.L. Wilson, editors, *Control of the Mint,* McGraw, 1961; Martin Greenberger, editor, *Management and the Computer of the Future,* Wiley, 1962; William Kessen and Clementina Kuhlman, editors, *Thought in the Young Child,* Society for Research in Child Development, 1962; Morris Philipson, editor, *Automation: Implications for the Future,* Vintage, 1962; *Contemporary Approaches to Creative Thinking,* Atherton, 1962; Sigmund Koch, editor, *Psychology: A Study of a Science,* Volume VI, McGraw, 1963; W. F. Freiberger and William Prager, editors, *Applications of Digital Computers,* Ginn, 1963; Luce and others, editors, *Handbook of Mathematical Psychology,* Volume I, Wiley, 1963; *Essays on the Structure of Social Science Models,* Massachusetts Institute of Technology Press, 1963; Harold Koontz, editor, *Toward a Unified Theory of Management,* McGraw, 1964; Lawrence H. Seltzer, editor, *New Horizons of Economic Progress* (Franklin Memorial Lectures), Wayne State University Press, 1964.

M. A. Sass and W. D. Wilkinson, editors, *Computer Augmentation of Human Reasoning,* Spartan Books, 1965; R. G. Colodny, editor, *Mind and Cosmos,* University of Pittsburgh Press, 1966; D. Easton, editor, *Varieties of Political Theory,* Prentice-Hall, 1966; B. Kleinmuntz, editor, *Problem Solving,* Wiley, 1966; I. de Sola Pool, editor, *Contemporary Political Science,* McGraw, 1967; N. Rescher, editor, *The Logic of Decision and Action,* University of Pittsburgh Press, 1967; Kleinmuntz, editor, *Formal Representation of Human Judgment,* Wiley, 1968; L. W. Gregg, editor, *Cognition in Learning and Memory,* Wiley, 1972; W. R. Close, editor, *Visual Information Processing,* Academic Press, 1973.

Author of foreword; published by Prentice-Hall: Harold Borko, editor, *Computer Applications in the Behavioral Sciences,* 1962; Timothy W. Costello and Sheldon S. Zalkind, *Psychology in Administration: A Research Orientation,* 1963.

Contributor to other books and to published symposia, yearbooks, and conference proceedings. Contributor to economics and sociology journals and other professional publications, including *Public Management, British Journal of Psychology, Science, Management Science, Hospital Administration, Naval War College Review,* and *Connaissance de l'Homme.*

SIDELIGHTS: Among those surprised by the Swedish Academy of Science's choice of Herbert A. Simon for the 1978 Nobel Prize in economics was Simon himself. "It was a little like being struck by lightning," he admitted not long after hearing the news. Cited for his pioneering research on the decision-making process within organizations (conducted during the 1940s and 1950s), Simon is best known not as an economist, but as a computer expert, psychologist, political scientist, and applied mathematician.

As outlined in such books as *Administrative Behavior,* Simon's findings place him at odds with economists who subscribe to the classical theory that man always acts to maximize profits. Based on his own observations of how businessmen make decisions, Simon declares that this classical theory of economics is "an extravagant definition of rationality" that has "little discernible relationship to the actual or possible behavior of flesh-and-blood humans." Instead, he argues, the typical administrator, confronted with a myriad of alternatives and a limited amount of accurate information on which to base his decision, most often rejects the risky yet potentially profitable maneuver in favor of a safer choice that will bring about minimally acceptable gains. Simon calls this "satisficing" behavior—that is, behavior that considers only those solutions that will satisfy reasonable goals with as few complications as possible. Simon thus takes into account the psychological factors involved in decision-making that most classical economists ignore.

Though this discovery was, according to *Newsweek,* one "contemporary businessmen probably regard as obvious," it was (and still is) a source of contention between Simon and traditional economists. But he does have his boosters, especially among academics affiliated with some of the nation's most prestigious programs in business economics and administration. (Simon's theories are also popular in Northern Europe and in several Communist countries.) Professor Joseph Bower of the Harvard Graduate School of Business Administration, for example, credits Simon with changing the way some people regard large corporations. "Economists talk about General Motors as an 'it'—as if 'it' makes a decision," Bower explains. "But Simon says an organization is made up of human beings who, as information processors, make decisions." In short, remarks the Columbia Graduate School of Business's Professor John Farley, "[Simon's] great contribution is the bridge he built between the economic model and the real world."

Since the mid-1950s, however, Simon has devoted less time to economic theory and more time to the creation of artificial intelligence through computer technology. By programming a computer to simulate human reasoning and record the steps it takes to reach a particular decision, Simon believes he can not only gain insights into the thought process itself but also teach people to think more logically, quickly, and efficiently. His developments—including programming computers to play chess, prove mathematical theorems, distinguish between geometrical shapes, and even create abstract art designs—have made him a leader in the field of artificial intelligence.

But Simon has not concentrated solely on research in the decision-making process and artificial intelligence. He has taught graduate level courses in psychology, for example, and in 1977 he took over a freshman history course because he "just wanted to learn about the French Revolution." He has also served in various administrative posts at Carnegie-Mellon University. Yet as Simon points out to *New York Times* reporter Jonathan Williams, "The fact that I've been involved in a number of disciplines results from the fact that decision making is pretty central to psychology, economics, political science and administration. . . . All this business about my wandering here and there isn't true. I've been working on the same problem all my life." His accomplishments in these disciplines, as well as his leisure time interest in such activities as learning foreign languages, playing the piano, sketching, painting, and mountain climbing, make him unusual in this age of specialization, "a thinker of true Nobel Prize dimensions," as Donald Michie states in the *Times Literary Supplement.* Or, as Carnegie-Mellon University president Richard Cyert once described the multitalented Herbert A. Simon: "[He is] the one man in the world who comes closest to the ideal of Aristotle or a Renaissance man."

BIOGRAPHICAL/CRITICAL SOURCES: Herbert A. Simon, *Administrative Behavior,* Macmillan, 1947, 3rd edition, 1976; *Newsweek,* October 30, 1978; *Time,* October 30, 1978; *New York Times,* November 26, 1978; *People,* January 15, 1979; *Times Literary Supplement,* August 22, 1980.

* * *

SIMPSON, James B(easley) 1926-

PERSONAL: Born September 13, 1926, in Mansfield, Ark.; son of E. O. (a business executive) and Ellender (Weaver) Simpson; married Shirley Lee Pick, 1956 (divorced, 1960). *Education:* Northwestern University, B.S. in Journalism, 1949; attended University of Edinburgh, 1950-51. *Home:* Hillspeak, Eureka Springs, Ark. 72632.

CAREER: Southwest American, Fort Smith, Ark., 1943-45, began as reporter, became assistant managing editor; United Press International, New York City, reporter and news editor, 1950-52; affiliated with Associated Press, New York City,

1952-54; Grant Advertising, Inc., New York City, account supervisor, 1954-57; Ellington & Co., New York City, public relations director, 1957-58; Batten, Barton, Durstine & Osborn, New York City, account supervisor, 1959-61; Columbia Gas System, New York City, member of public relations staff, 1962-64; Episcopal priest, 1967—, serving as assistant rector in Rye, N.Y., 1967-70, and as rector in Middletown, N.J., 1970-80. Resident, MacDowell Colony, 1966; resident fellow, Episcopal Seminary of the Southwest, 1982. Director, Episcopal Book Club, 1980—. *Member:* Society of Magazine Writers, Public Relations Society of America, Sigma Delta Chi. *Awards, honors:* Rotary Foundation fellow, 1950-51; Kaltenborn Foundation grant, 1952; Master of Divinity, Nashotah House, 1969.

WRITINGS: (Compiler) *Best Quotes of 1954, 1955,* [and] *1956,* Crowell, 1957; *The Hundredth Archbishop of Canterbury* (Episcopal Book Club selection), Harper, 1962; (compiler) *Contemporary Quotations* (Mid-Century Book Society selection), Crowell, 1964; (with Edward M. Story) *The Long Shadows of Lambeth X: A Critical, Eyewitness Account of the Tenth Decennial Conference of 462 Bishops of the Anglican Communion,* McGraw, 1969; (with Story) *Stars in His Crown: A Centennial History of the Community of St. John Baptist,* Ploughshare Press, 1976; (with Story) *Discerning God's Will: The Complete Eyewitness Report of the Eleventh Lambeth Conference,* Thomas Nelson, 1979. Also author of material for television programs of the National Broadcasting Co. (NBC) and American Broadcasting Co. (ABC).

Contributor to *Reader's Digest, Look, Town and Country, Esquire, Christian Science Monitor,* and *New York Times Sunday Magazine*. Editor, *Anglican Digest*.

* * *

SINGER, Amanda
See BROOKS, Janice Young

* * *

SINGER, Marilyn 1948-

PERSONAL: Born October 3, 1948, in Bronx, N.Y.; daughter of Abraham (a photoengraver) and Shirley (Lax) Singer; married Steven Aronson (an administrator), July 31, 1971. *Education:* Attended University of Reading, 1967-68; Queens College of the City University of New York, B.A. (cum laude), 1969; New York University, M.A., 1979. *Home and office:* 50 Berkeley Pl., Brooklyn, N.Y. 11217.

CAREER: Daniel S. Mead Literary Agency, New York City, editor, 1967; *Where* (magazine), New York City, assistant editor, 1969; teacher of English and speech in New York City, 1969-74; writer, 1974—. *Member:* Society of Children's Book Writers, American Civil Liberties Union, Audubon Society, Phi Beta Kappa.

WRITINGS: The Dog Who Insisted He Wasn't (juvenile), Dutton, 1976; (editor) *A History of Avant-Garde Cinema,* American Federation of Arts, 1976; (editor and contributor) *New American Filmmakers,* American Federation of Arts, 1976; *No Applause, Please* (juvenile), Dutton, 1977; *The Pickle Plan* (juvenile), Dutton, 1978; *It Can't Hurt Forever,* Harper, 1978.

The First Few Friends (young adult novel), Harper, 1981; *Will You Take Me to Town on Strawberry Day?* (picture book), Harper, 1981; *The Fanatic's Ecstatic, Aromatic Guide to Onions, Garlic, Shallots and Leeks* (nonfiction), Prentice-Hall, 1981; *Tarantulas on the Brain,* Harper, 1982; *The Fido Frame-Up,* Warne, in press; *The Course of True Love Never Did Run Smooth* (novel), Harper, in press. Author of scripts for television series "The Electric Company" and of teaching guides. Contributor of poems to magazines, including *Yes, Encore, Corduroy, Tamesis,* and *Gyre*.

WORK IN PROGRESS: Archer Armidillo's Secret Room, a picture book; *Horsemaster,* a fantasy; a sequel to *Tarantulas on the Brain;* a series of short children's mysteries; a nonfiction book on animal mouths, for Western Publishing.

SIDELIGHTS: Marilyn Singer writes: "I write children's books because I want to write children's books. I do not write them in preparation for writing adult novels, nor because they are 'easier' to write. I write them because, corny as it sounds, 'the child is father to the man,' or, in my case, 'mother to the woman'. . . . I draw on a wealth of past and present events and fantasies and people I've known in New York—particularly Long Island where I grew up—England, where I spent a year and many summers, and around the United States where I've travelled."

AVOCATIONAL INTERESTS: Studying Taoist meditation and exercise (Chi Kung, T'ai Chi), practicing Hatha Yoga, learning about herbs and other plants, avant-garde and independent film, bird watching and caring for animals, tap dancing, singing.

* * *

SKINNER, Knute (Rumsey) 1929-

PERSONAL: Born April 25, 1929, in St. Louis, Mo.; son of George Rumsey (a salesman) and Lidi (a civil servant; maiden name, Skjoldvig) Skinner; married Jean Pratt, November, 1953 (divorced, 1954); married Linda Kuhn, March 30, 1961 (divorced September, 1977); married Edna Faye Kiel, March 25, 1978; children: Francis, Dunstan, Morgan. *Education:* Attended Culver-Stockton College, Canton, Mo., 1947-49; Colorado State College (now University of Northern Colorado), A.B., 1951; Middlebury College, M.A., 1954; State University of Iowa, Ph.D., 1958. *Home:* 412 North State St., Bellingham, Wash. 98225; and Killaspuglonane, Labinch, County Clare, Ireland (summer). *Office:* Department of English, Western Washington University, Bellingham, Wash. 98225.

CAREER: Boise Senior High School, Boise, Idaho, teacher of English, 1951-54; State University of Iowa, Iowa City, instructor in English, 1955-56, 1957-58, and 1960-61; Oklahoma College for Women (now University of Science and Arts of Oklahoma), Chickasha, assistant professor of English, 1961-62; Western Washington University, Bellingham, assistant professor, 1962-63, part-time lecturer, 1963-71, associate professor, 1971-73, professor of English, 1973—. Poetry editor, Southern Illinois University Press, 1975-76; editor and publisher, *Bellingham Review* and Signpost Press, 1977—. Has given poetry readings at conferences, colleges, universities, and high schools throughout the United States and Ireland. *Member:* Poetry Society of America, American Committee for Irish Studies, Washington Poets Association. *Awards, honors:* Huntington Hartford Foundation fellowship, 1961; National Endowment for the Arts fellowship in creative writing, 1975; Millay Colony for the Arts fellowship, 1976.

WRITINGS—Poetry: *Stranger with a Watch,* Golden Quill, 1965; *A Close Sky over Killaspuglonane,* Dolmen Press (Dublin), 1968, 2nd edition, Burton International, 1975; *In Dinosaur Country,* Pierian, 1969; *The Sorcerers: A Laotian Tale,*

Goliards Press, 1972; *Hearing of the Hard Times,* Northwoods Press, 1981; *The Flame Room,* Anthelion, 1983.

Contributor to anthologies: *New Campus Writing #3,* Grove, 1959; *Midland,* Random House, 1961; *Doors into Poetry,* Prentice-Hall, 1962; *Flame Annual,* Different Press, 1965; *A Poet's Dozen: Fourteen Poems by Pacific Northwest Poets,* Friends of the Market (Seattle), 1966; *The New Orlando Poetry Anthology,* Volume III, New Orlando Publications, 1967; *Laudamus Te: A Cycle of Poems to the Praise and Glory of God,* Manifold Publications, 1967.

An Introduction to Poetry, 2nd edition, Little, Brown, 1971, 3rd edition, 1974; *New Generation: Poetry Anthology,* Ann Arbor Review Books, 1971; *The Diamond Anthology,* edited by Charles Angoff, A. S. Barnes, 1971; *Our Only Hope Is Humor: Some Public Poems,* Ashland Poetry Press, 1972; *Poetry: An Introduction through Writing,* edited by Lewis Turco, Reston, 1973; *Messages: A Thematic Anthology of Poetry,* edited by X. J. Kennedy, Little, Brown, 1973; *Poets West: Contemporary Poems from the Eleven Western States,* Perivale, 1975; *Literature: An Introduction to Fiction, Poetry and Drama,* Little, Brown, 1976; *A Geography of Poets,* edited by Edward Field, Bantam, 1979.

The Poet's Choice, Tendril, 1980; *Feathers and Bones: Ten Poets of the Irish Earth,* edited by Sevrin Housen, Halcyon Press, 1981; *Tygers of Wrath: Poems of Hate, Anger and Invective,* edited by Kennedy, University of Georgia Press, 1981.

Contributor of poems to numerous periodicals, including *Ohio Review, Colorado Quarterly, New Republic, New Letters, Mid-American Review,* and *Chicago Review;* contributor of short stories and reviews to *Limbo, Quartet, Midwest, Irish Press, Northwest Review,* and *Hibernia.* Guest editor, *Pyramid,* Number 13, 1973.

WORK IN PROGRESS: A book of poetry, *The Back of His Neck.*

SIDELIGHTS: Knute Skinner, who divides his time between homes in Bellingham, Washington, and rural Ireland, told *CA* that life in Ireland "exerts a strong influence on my work." He has recorded his poetry for the British Council, for poetry rooms at Harvard, Leeds, Hull and Durham universities, and for radio programs in the United States and Ireland. His poetry is also the subject of two videotapes, one made at the University of Wisconsin—La Crosse and the other at Triton College in Chicago, and of an educational television film made at the State University of New York College at Brockport.

* * *

SMITH, Elwyn Allen 1919-

PERSONAL: Born September 17, 1919, in Wilmington, Del.; son of H. Framer and Mary (Closson) Smith; married Malvine Rose Maguire, October 5, 1946; children: Paul Framer, Rebecca Morrow, Scott Allen. *Education:* Attended Municipal University of Omaha (now University of Nebraska at Omaha), 1936-38; Wheaton College, Wheaton, Ill., B.A., 1939; Harvard University, M.A., 1941, Ph.D., 1942; Yale Divinity School, B.D., 1943; Princeton Theological Seminary, Th.M., 1944. *Religion:* United Presbyterian. *Home:* 2001 83rd Ave. N., No. 1186, St. Petersburg, Fla. 33702.

CAREER: Presbyterian Church, U.S.A., Westminster Foundation, Washington, D.C., director, 1943-45; Board of Christian Education, Philadelphia, Pa., associate youth editor, 1945-49; Dubuque Theological Seminary, Dubuque, Iowa, dean and professor of church history, 1950-56; Western Theological Seminary, Pittsburgh, Pa., professor of church history, 1957-59; Pittsburgh Theological Seminary, Pittsburgh, Pa., professor of church history, 1959-66; Temple University, Philadelphia, Pa., professor of religion, 1966-70, vice-president for student affairs, 1970-72; Eckerd College, St. Petersburg, Fla., provost and vice-president of academic affairs, 1972-75; executive director, Continuing Education for Church Professionals, 1976-79; Garden Crest United Presbyterian Church, St. Petersburg, senior pastor, 1977-81. Member, Academy for Senior Professionals, Eckerd College. *Member:* American Society of Church History, Presbyterian Historical Society, Society for Reformation Research.

WRITINGS: Men Called Him Master, Westminster, 1948; *The Presbyterian Ministry in American Culture,* Westminster, 1962; *Church and State in Your Community,* Westminster, 1963; (editor) *Church-State Relations in Ecumenical Perspective,* Duquesne University Press, 1966; (editor) *The Religion of the Republic,* Fortress, 1971; (editor) *What the Religious Revolutionaries Are Saying,* Fortress, 1971; *Religious Liberty in the United States: The Development of Church-State Thought since the Revolutionary Era,* Fortress, 1972. Contributor to professional journals. Co-editor, *Journal of Ecumenical Studies,* 1964-74.

WORK IN PROGRESS: Ethics for Clergy.

* * *

SMITH, Hobart M(uir) 1912-

PERSONAL: Born September 26, 1912, in Stanwood, Iowa; son of Charles Henry (a postal clerk) and Frances (Muir) Smith; married Rozella Blood (a research associate), August 26, 1938; children: Bruce Dyfrig, Sally Frances (Mrs. Ronald J. Nadvornik). *Education:* Kansas State University, A.B., 1932; University of Kansas, M.A., 1933, Ph.D., 1936. *Home:* 1393 Northridge Court, Boulder, Colo. 80302. *Office:* Department of Environmental, Population, and Organismic Biology, University of Colorado, Boulder, Colo. 80309.

CAREER: University of Rochester, Rochester, N.Y., instructor in biology, 1941-45; University of Kansas, Lawrence, assistant professor of zoology, 1945-46; Agricultural and Mechanical College of Texas (now Texas A & M University), College Station, associate professor of wildlife management, 1946-47; University of Illinois at Urbana-Champaign, assistant professor, 1947-51, associate professor, 1951-57, professor of zoology, 1957-68, curator of herpetology at Museum of Natural History, 1947-68; University of Colorado, Boulder, professor of environmental, population, and organismic biology, 1968—, chairman of department, 1971-74.

MEMBER: American Society of Ichthyologists and Herpetologists (vice-president, 1938; editor, 1958—), Society for Systematic Zoology (president, 1967), Herpetologists League (president, 1946-58; editor, 1957), Society for Study of Amphibians and Reptiles (editor, 1968—), German Herpetological Society, British Herpetological Society. *Awards, honors:* National Research Council fellow, University of Michigan, 1936-37; assistantship at Chicago Academy of Science, 1937-38, and Chicago Museum of Natural History, 1938; Bacon traveling scholar, Smithsonian Institution, 1938-41.

WRITINGS: Handbook of Lizards of the United States and Canada, Cornell University Press, 1946; (with Herbert S. Zim) *Reptiles and Amphibians Golden Nature Guide,* Simon & Schuster, 1953, revised edition, 1956; *Snakes as Pets,* All-

Pets Books, 1953, 4th edition, T.F.H. Publications, 1977; *Lectures in Comparative Anatomy,* Hutner & Wroughton, 1954; *Pet Turtles,* All-Pets Books, 1954, 2nd edition, 1955; *Evolution of Chordate Structure,* Stipes Publishing, 1957, revised edition, Holt, 1960; *Laboratory Studies of Chordate Structure,* Stipes Publishing, 1957, 7th edition, 1973; *A Golden Stamp Book: Snakes, Turtles, and Lizards* (juvenile), Simon & Schuster, 1958; (with Floyd Boys) *Poisonous Amphibians and Reptiles: Recognition and Bite Treatment,* C. C Thomas, 1959.

Glossary of Terms for Comparative Anatomy, Stipes Publishing, 1961; (with Edward H. Taylor) *Herpetology of Mexico,* Eric Lundberg, 1966; *Turtles in Color,* T.F.H. Publications, 1967; (with wife, Rozella B. Smith) *Early Foundations of Mexican Herpetology: An Annotated and Indexed Bibliography of the Herpetological Publications of Alfredo Duges, 1826-1910,* University of Illinois Press, 1969.

(With Jonathan C. Oldham and Sue Ann Miller) *A Laboratory Perspectus of Snake Anatomy,* Stipes Publishing, 1970; (with R. B. Smith) *Synopsis of the Herpetofauna of Mexico,* Volume I: *Analysis of the Literature on the Mexican Axolotl,* Eric Lundberg, 1971, Volume II: *Analysis of the Literature Exclusive of the Mexican Axolotl,* Eric Lundberg, 1973, Volume III: *Source Analysis and Index for Mexican Reptiles,* J. Johnson, 1976, Volume IV: *Source Analysis and Index for Mexican Amphibians,* J. Johnson, 1976, Volume V: *Guide to Mexican Amphisbaenians and Crocodilians,* J. Johnson, 1977, Volume VI: *Guide to Mexican Turtles,* J. Johnson, 1980; (with Oldham) *Laboratory Anatomy of the Iguana,* W. C. Brown, 1974; *Laboratory Studies of Cat Structure,* Stipes Publishing, 1976; *Amphibians of North America,* Golden Press, 1978; (with Edmund D. Brodie, Jr.) *Reptiles of North America,* Golden Press, 1982. Contributor to more than seventy-five professional journals.

WORK IN PROGRESS: Synopsis of the Herpetofauna of Mexico, Volumes VII-IX.

* * *

SMITH, Karl U(lrich) 1907-

PERSONAL: Born May 1, 1907, in Zanesville, Ohio; son of Harry Howard (a trainmaster) and Katherine (Hoobing) Smith; married Sarah Margaret Foltz, August 3, 1937; children: Thomas Jay, Eric Alan, Joanna Margaret, Sarah Louise, Nicholas Ulrich. *Education:* Attended Ohio University, 1926-27; Miami University, Oxford, Ohio, B.A., 1931; Brown University, M.A., 1933, Ph.D., 1935. *Politics:* Independent Democrat. *Home:* 1001 Tower Blvd., Lake Wales, Fla. 33853. *Office:* Behavioral Cybernetics Laboratory, University of Wisconsin, 918 Conklin Ct., Madison, Wis. 53706.

CAREER: Brown University, Providence, R.I., instructor in psychology, 1935-36; University of Rochester, Rochester, N.Y., instructor, 1936-38, assistant professor of psychology, 1938-42; National Defense Research Council, Washington, D.C., assistant director of a research project at Camp Murphy, Fla., contracted by Yale University, 1943-44, director of a project at Orlando Army Air Forces Tactical Center, Orlando, Fla., 1944, and Laredo Army Air Field, Laredo, Tex., 1944-45; University of Wisconsin—Madison, assistant professor, 1945-47, associate professor, 1947-49, professor of psychology, 1949-77, professor emeritus, 1977—, director of Bureau of Industrial Psychology, 1945-47, director of Behavioral Cybernetics Laboratory, 1964-77, director of Independent House Learning Center and Social Cybernetics Laboratory, 1967. Ford Foundation Distinguished Professor of Business Administration, Indiana University, 1960 and 1961; distinguished visiting professor of psychology, University of South Dakota, 1972; visiting professor, University of Trondheim, 1974. Director of training programs for National Institute of Mental Health, 1959-75; seminar leader, European Association for Humanistic Psychology summer conference, 1980. Consultant in cybernetics.

MEMBER: Society of Experimental Psychologists, American Association for the Advancement of Science (fellow), American Physiological Society, Phi Beta Kappa (honorary member). *Awards, honors:* Citation from U.S. Army and Navy, 1945, for National Defense Research Council work during World War II; Ford Foundation grant, 1959-63; National Science Foundation grants, 1959—; research prize from Television, Inc., 1961; National Institutes of Health grants, 1969—; award for meritorious research from International Congress on Applied Systems Research and Cybernetics, 1980.

WRITINGS: (With W. M. Smith) *The Behavior of Man,* with workbook (with William M. Smith and Janet Hansche), teacher's manual, and test manual, Holt, 1958; *Behavior Organization and Work: A New Approach to Industrial Behavioral Science,* College Printing & Typing, 1962, 3rd edition, 1975; (with W. M. Smith) *Perception and Motion: An Analysis of Space-Structured Behavior,* Saunders, 1962; *Delayed Sensory Feedback and Behavior,* Saunders, 1962; *Work Theory and Economic Behavior* (monograph), Bureau of Business Research, Indiana University, 1962.

(With M. F. Smith) *Cybernetic Principles of Learning and Educational Design,* with instructor's manual and student manual, Holt, 1966; *Review of Principles of Human Factors in Design of the Exoskeleton and Four-Legged Pedipulator,* Behavioral Cybernetics Laboratory, University of Wisconsin, Madison, 1966; *The Human Social Yoke: The Educational Bond between Parent and Child,* Parker Pen Co., 1968; (with T. J. Smith) *Educational Feedback Designs,* George Rainey Harper College, 1968; *Outlook for Development and Application of Behavioral Cybernetics and Educational Feedback Designs in Instructional Technology* (pamphlet), Federal Commission on Instructional Technology, 1968; *New Horizons of Research in Physical Behavior Science and Rehabilitation: Dynamic Feedback Designs in Learning and Training* (pamphlet), National Association of Physical Education of College Women, 1968.

(With Charles Hagberg) *Self-Governed Behavioral Safety Codes for Industry: Management Feedback Control of Accident Prevention in the Work Place* (pamphlet), Department of Industry and Human Relations, Safety Division, State of Wisconsin, and Behavioral Cybernetics Laboratory, University of Wisconsin, Madison, 1970; *Real-Time Computer Analysis of Body Motions: Systems Feedback Analysis and Techniques in Rehabilitation,* Social and Rehabilitation Administration, 1971; (with Larry Schiamberg) *The Infraschool: A Positive Approach to Parent Education for Early Childhood Development,* Behavioral Cybernetics Laboratory, University of Wisconsin, Madison, 1973; *Lectures in Cybernetic Psychology,* Behavioral Cybernetics Laboratory, University of Wisconsin, Madison, 1973; *Ethnic Science: The Alternatives to Academic Racism and Jensenism* (monograph), Behavioral Cybernetics Laboratory, University of Wisconsin, Madison, 1973; *Civil Rights and Psychological Testing: The Psychometric Foundations of Academic Racism* (monograph), Behavioral Cybernetics Laboratory, University of Wisconsin, Madison, 1973; (with M. F. Smith) *Psychology: Introduction to Behavior Science,* with instructor's manual, Little, Brown, 1973.

Industrial Social Cybernetics, Behavioral Cybernetics Laboratory, University of Wisconsin, Madison, 1975; *Human Factors and Systems Principles for Occupational Safety and Health,* Training and Manpower Division, National Institute for Occupational Safety and Health, 1979; (with Schiamberg) *Human Development,* Macmillan, 1982.

Contributor: *Tomorrow's Communications Research,* Television Bureau of Advertising, Inc., 1962; Leon Arons and Mark May, editors, *Television and Human Behavior,* Appleton, 1962; Virgil Herrick, editor, *New Horizons of Handwriting Research,* University of Wisconsin Press, 1963; Edward A. Bilodeau, editor, *Acquisition of Skill,* Academic Press, 1966; E. A. Bilodeau and Ina Bilodeau, editors, *Principles of Skill Acquisition,* Academic Press, 1969.

Charles Wedemeyer, editor, *Report of the William Kellet Commission on Education and the Open School,* Governor's Commission on Education, 1970; Leon Smith, editor, *Motor Skill and Learning,* Athletic Institute, 1970; I. E. Asmussen, editor, *Psychological Aspects of Driver Behavior,* Volume I: *Driver Behavior: NATO Symposium on Psychological Aspects of Driver Behavior,* Institute of Road Safety Research (Voorburg, Netherlands), 1971; R. N. Singer, editor, *The Psychomotor Domain,* Lea & Febriger, 1972; Joanne T. Widner, editor, *Selected Readings in Safety,* Academic Press (Macon, Ga.), 1973; Jack Maser, editor, *Efferent Organization and the Integration of Behavior,* Academic Press, 1973; Henry Gemeinder, editor, *Conference on Defining and Developing a Model Worker Compensation Statistics Program,* Department of Labor, Industry, and Human Relations, State of Wisconsin, 1974.

Gemeinder, editor, *Bureau of Research and Statistics Issue Reports on Industrial Safety and Worker Compensation,* Department of Labor, Industry, and Human Relations, State of Wisconsin, 1975; Gemeinder, editor, *Interservice Conference on New Systems Approaches to Risk Management of Worker's Compensation and Industrial Safety and Health Concepts and Practices,* Numbers 1-16, Bureau of Research and Statistics, Department of Labor, Industry, and Human Relations, State of Wisconsin, 1975.

Also author of fifteen World War II research reports and numerous conference papers. Contributor to *McGraw Hill Encyclopedia of Science and Technology* and to proceedings. Contributor of more than two hundred articles to research journals in his field.

WORK IN PROGRESS: Research on behavioral cybernetics, feedback mechanisms of behavior, theory of biological creationism in human evolution, handwriting and feedback mechanisms of speech, and human development.

SIDELIGHTS: Karl U. Smith told *CA:* "Between the time I entered graduate school in 1931 and World War II, I was dedicated to understanding human and animal vision in terms of its dynamic eye movement tracking mechanisms, an interest which led me into military research in World War II on eye tracking requirements and human-factors requirements of radar and aircraft gun systems. I consider myself as one of the primary creative influences in the original development of the human-factors psychological and engineering fields. My most prized paper (with Dr. John Henry in 1967) I consider to be the application of human-factors principles to rehabilitative design.

"Since World War II I have been dedicated to developing the field of behavioral cybernetics and to systems research on human behavior based on behavioral cybernetics concepts and laboratory methods. My writing in the last decade has played out this interest in presenting the development of the field of hazard management, the study and analysis of social behavior as social tracking, the elucidation of animal and human evolution as a process of biological creationism (i.e., feedback control of selection in evolution as a self-regulatory process), and the study and analysis of human development in terms of its systems aspects and conditions."

* * *

SMOUT, T(homas) C(hristopher) 1933-

PERSONAL: Born December 19, 1933, in Birmingham, England; son of Arthur J. G. (a company director) and A. Hilda (Follows) Smout; married Anne-Marie Schoening, August 15, 1959; children: Pernille Anne, Andrew Michael Christian. *Education:* Clare College, Cambridge, M.A., 1957, Ph.D., 1960. *Office:* Department of Scottish History, University of St. Andrews, Fife, Scotland.

CAREER: University of Edinburgh, Edinburgh, Scotland, assistant, 1959-61, lecturer, 1962-66, reader, 1966-71, professor of economic history, 1971-79; University of St. Andrews, Fife, Scotland, professor of Scottish history, 1980—.

WRITINGS: Scottish Trade on the Eve of Union, 1660-1707, Oliver & Boyd, 1963; *A History of the Scottish People, 1560-1830,* Collins, 1969, Scribner, 1970; (editor with Louis Cullen) *Comparative Aspects of Scottish and Irish Economic and Social History, 1600-1900,* Donald Publishers Ltd., 1976; (with M. W. Flinn and others) *Scottish Population History from the Seventeenth Century to the 1930s,* Cambridge University Press, 1977; (with I. Levitt) *The State of the Scottish Working Class in 1843,* Scottish Academic Press, 1979; (contributor) P. Laslett and others, editors, *Bastardy and Its Comparative History,* Edward Arnold, 1980; (contributor) R. B. Outhwaite, editor, *Marriage and Society,* Europa, 1981.

WORK IN PROGRESS: A book on nineteenth-century Scotland.

AVOCATIONAL INTERESTS: Bird-watching, walking, admiring towns.

BIOGRAPHICAL/CRITICAL SOURCES: Times Literary Supplement, June 20, 1980.

* * *

SNOW, Roslyn 1936-

PERSONAL: Born July 28, 1936, in Chicago, Ill.; daughter of David (a lawyer) and Regina (Kohn) Snow. *Education:* University of Illinois, A.B., 1958, A.M., 1959. *Politics:* Democrat. *Religion:* Jewish. *Office:* Department of English, Orange Coast College, Costa Mesa, Calif. 92626.

CAREER: Orange Coast College, Costa Mesa, Calif., professor of English, 1962—.

WRITINGS: (With Jacob Fuchs) *Man: Alternatives of Experience,* Wadsworth, 1967; *Spelling Rules,* Easy Guides, 1977; *Punctuation Marks,* Easy Guides, 1978; (with Joan Roloff) *Spelling,* Macmillan, 1980; (with Lois Dalla-Riva) *Practical Math,* Easy Guides, 1981; *Preparing the Portfolio for A.P.L.,* Easy Guides, 1981; (contributor with Phyllis A. Bruns) *New Directions in Experiential Learning,* Jossey-Bass, 1982.

* * *

SOBEL, Lester A(lbert) 1919-

PERSONAL: Born October 3, 1919, in New York, N.Y.; son

of David (a baker) and Ray Dorothy (Mendelson) Sobel; married Eileen Lucille Helfer, May 3, 1953; children: Martha Lorraine, Sharon Ruth, Jonathan William. *Education:* City College (now City College of the City University of New York), B.B.A., 1942. *Religion:* Jewish. *Home:* 226 Porterfield Pl., Freeport, N.Y. 11520. *Office:* Leader-Observer, Inc., 80-34 Jamaica Ave., Woodhaven, N.Y. 11421.

CAREER: Facts on File, Inc., New York, N.Y., editor and writer, 1946-80, editor-in-chief, 1960-70, vice-president, 1964-80, senior contributing editor, 1980—; Leader-Observer, Inc., Woodhaven, N.Y., editor of *Realty,* 1975—. *Military service:* U.S. Army, 1942-44; became sergeant; received Bronze Star.

WRITINGS—Editor; all published by Facts on File: *National Issues,* 1956; *Space: From Sputnik to Gemini,* 1965; *South Vietnam: U.S. Communist Confrontation in Southeast Asia,* Volume I, 1966, Volume II, 1969; *Civil Rights, 1960-1966,* 1967.

Russia's Rulers: The Khrushchev Period, 1971; *Inflation and the Nixon Administration,* Volume I, 1974, Volume II, 1975; *Israel and the Arabs: The October 1973 War,* 1974; *Money and Politics: Contributions, Campaign Abuses and the Law,* 1974; *Energy Crisis,* Volume I: *1969-1973,* 1974, Volume II: *1974-1975,* 1975, Volume III: *1975-1977,* 1977, Volume IV: *1977-1979,* 1980; *Chile and Allende,* 1974.

Political Terrorism, Volume I, 1975, Volume II, 1978; *Presidential Succession,* 1975; *Kissinger and Detente,* 1975; *Argentina and Peron, 1970-1975,* 1975; *World Food Crisis,* 1975; *Latin America, 1974,* 1975; *Consumer Protection,* 1976; *Ford and the Economy,* 1976; *Health Care: An American Crisis,* 1976; *Job Bias,* 1976; *New York and the Urban Dilemma,* 1976; *Portuguese Revolution, 1974-1976,* 1976; *War on Privacy,* 1976; *Corruption in Business,* 1977; *Palestinian Impasse: Arab Guerrillas and International Terror,* 1977; *Jobs, Money and Pollution,* 1977; *Medical Science and the Law: The Life and Death Controversy,* 1977; *Welfare and the Poor,* 1977; *Political Prisoners: A World Report,* 1978; *Post-Watergate Morality,* 1978; *Castro's Cuba in the 1970s,* 1978; *Rhodesia/Zimbabwe, 1971-1977,* 1978; *Cancer and the Environment,* 1979; *Refugees: A World Report,* 1979; *Pornography, Obscenity and the Law,* 1979; *The Great American Tax Revolt,* 1979.

Peace-Making in the Middle East, 1980; *Quotas and Affirmative Action,* 1980; *Media Controversies,* 1981; *U.S. Military Dilemma,* 1981.

Editor-in-chief of reference annuals *News Year,* 1960-63, and *News Dictionary,* 1964-73, both published by Facts on File; editor-in-chief of "Interim History" series, Facts on File, 1964-73.

WORK IN PROGRESS: Collecting material for books on the Middle East, Islam's role in world politics, and the arms race.

* * *

SOLBRIG, Otto T(homas) 1930-

PERSONAL: Born December 21, 1930, in Buenos Aires, Argentina; son of Hans Joajim (a businessman) and Rose Mabel (Muggleworth) Solbrig; married Roberta Mae Chittum, August 4, 1956 (divorced, 1969); married Dorothy Jane Crosswhite, June 21, 1969; children: (first marriage) Hans Joseph, Heide Frances. *Education:* Attended Universidad Nacional de La Plata, 1950-54; University of California, Berkeley, Ph.D., 1959. *Politics:* Democrat. *Home:* 16 Pleasant View Rd., Arlington, Mass. 02174. *Office:* Department of Biology, Harvard University, Cambridge, Mass. 02138.

CAREER: Harvard University, Cambridge, Mass., curator of botany, 1959-66; University of Michigan, Ann Arbor, associate professor, 1966-68, professor of botany, 1968-69; Harvard University, professor of biology, 1969—. Member of several botanical expeditions to South America. *Member:* International Association of Plant Biosystematists (secretary general), Botanical Society of America, American Association for the Advancement of Science (fellow), Genetical Society of America, Society for the Study of Evolution (secretary; president, 1982), American Academy of Arts and Sciences (fellow), American Society of Naturalists, American Society of Plant Taxonomists, Phi Beta Kappa, Sigma Xi. *Awards, honors:* Cooley Award for research paper, 1962; M.A., Harvard University, 1969; Willdenow Medal, 1979.

WRITINGS: Evolution and Systematics, Macmillan, 1966; *Plant Biosystematics,* Macmillan, 1969; *Topics in Plant Population Biology,* Columbia University Press, 1979; *Population Biology and Evolution,* Addison-Wesley, 1979; *Plant Demography and Evolution,* Blackwell Scientific Publications, 1980.

Contributor to *Biosystematic Literature Review*; contributor of more than ninety articles on plant genetics and evolution to journals.

WORK IN PROGRESS: Research in plant genetics and evolution.

AVOCATIONAL INTERESTS: Reading history, sailing.

* * *

SOLOMON, Norman 1951-

PERSONAL: Born July 7, 1951, in Washington, D.C.; son of Morris J. (an economist) and Miriam (an economist; maiden name, Abramowitz) Solomon. *Home address:* P.O. Box 42384, Portland, Ore. 97242.

CAREER: Montgomery County Sentinel, Rockville, Md., newspaper reporter, 1968-70; KBOO-FM Radio, Portland, Ore., producer of commentary, 1972-79; free-lance investigative journalist, 1978—. Correspondent, Pacific News Service; associate, Center for Investigative Reporting. *Awards, honors:* Third prize for news reporting, 1970, from Maryland-Delaware Press Association.

WRITINGS—Published by Out of the Ashes Press, except as indicated: *No Title* (novelette), 1971; *The Tragedy of King Lethal* (adaptation of play *King Lear* by William Shakespeare; first produced as a radio play in Portland, Ore., on KBOO-FM, 1972), 1971; *In the Belly of the Dinosaurs: Resisting the Death Convention,* 1972; *Cockroach* (novel), 1974; *Blue Vehicle* (novel), 1978; (with others) *Killing Our Own: The Disaster of America's Experience with Atomic Radiation,* Delacorte, 1982.

Contributor to *Boston Globe, San Francisco Examiner, Progressive, Nation, WIN, New Haven Advocate,* and other publications.

Work is anthologized in *How Old Will You Be in 1984?,* edited by Diane Divoky, Avon, 1969, *High School,* edited by Ronald Gross and Paul Osterman, Simon & Schuster, 1970, *The Soft Revolution,* edited by Neil Postman and Charles Weingartner, Delta Books, 1971, *Radical School Reform,* edited by Beatrice Gross and Ronald Gross, Simon & Schuster, 1971, and *Generation Rap,* edited by Gene Stanford, Dell, 1971.

SIDELIGHTS: "In recent years I have turned my attention to investigative reporting, with particular emphasis on nuclear issues," Norman Solomon told *CA*. "The importance of nuclear technology deserves thorough airing so that citizens can understand choices presently being made regarding atomic energy in its civilian and military applications. Unfortunately, few payrolled 'mainstream' journalists have the time and/or freedom to pursue stories which are intricate or difficult to find quickly; yet it is unacceptable for our media to virtually parrot perspectives offered by governmental public relations machinery on matters as crucial as nuclear weaponry. The need for in-depth investigative journalism has never been greater. I plan to continue to try to do my part in helping meet this need."

BIOGRAPHICAL/CRITICAL SOURCES: Los Angeles Times Book Review, April 4, 1982; *Nation,* May 15, 1982; *Atlantic,* June, 1982; *Washington Post Book World,* July 25, 1982.

* * *

SOURS, John Appling 1931-

PERSONAL: Born January 28, 1931, in Chicago, Ill.; son of William J. (a businessman) and Olive (Appling) Sours; married Angela Dinah Mathews; children: Christopher, Caroline, Jane. *Education:* Yale University, A.B., 1953; Cornell University, M.D., 1957; Columbia Psychoanalytic Clinic, Certificate in Psychoanalytic Medicine, 1967. *Home:* 120 West 88th St., New York, N.Y. 10024. *Office:* The Adams, Suite 207, 2 East 86th St., New York, N.Y. 10028.

CAREER: Columbia University, College of Physicians and Surgeons, New York, N.Y., clinical assistant professor of psychiatry, 1967—, training and supervising psychoanalyst at Center for Training and Research, 1975—. In active practice of general and child psychiatry and psychoanalysis; assistant attending psychiatrist at New York State Psychiatric Institute, Vanderbilt Clinic, and Columbia Presbyterian Medical Center; supervising and clinical psychoanalyst, New York Psychoanalytic Institute, 1976—. *Military service:* U.S. Naval Reserve, Medical Corps, staff psychiatrist at Naval Aerospace Center, Pensacola, Fla., 1961-63; became lieutenant commander.

MEMBER: International Association for Child Psychiatry and Psychology, American College of Psychiatrists, American Psychiatric Association (fellow), Association for Psychoanalytic Medicine, American Psychoanalytic Association, Association for Child Psychoanalysis, Association for Applied Analysis, New York Psychoanalytic Society. *Awards, honors:* Fulbright scholar in London, England, 1958-59; National Institute of Mental Health career teacher grant, 1965-67.

WRITINGS: (With J. D. Goodman) *The Child Mental Status Examination,* Basic Books, 1967; *Starving to Death in a Sea of Objects: The Anorexia Nervosa Syndrome,* Jason Aronson, 1980.

Contributor: Lebovici and Caplan, editors, *Changing Concepts in Adolescence,* Basic Books, 1967; H. F. Conn, editor, *Current Diagnosis,* Saunders, 1971; B. Wolmann, editor, *Manual of Child Psychopathology,* McGraw, 1971; S. Aneti, editor, *American Handbook of Psychiatry,* Volume I, Basic Books, 1974; Jules Glenn, editor, *Child Analysis and Therapy,* Jason Aronson, 1978; J. E. Nospritz, editor, *Basic Handbook of Child Psychiatry,* Basic Books, 1979; J. R. Bemporad, editor, *Child Development in Normality and Psychopathology,* Brunner, 1980; G. P. Sholevar, R. M. Benson, and B. J. Binder, editors, *Treatment of Emotional Disorders in Children and Adolescents,* Spectrum, 1980; M. H. Stone, editor, *Psychiatric Clinics of North America,* Saunders, 1981; M. H. Sachs and M. L. Sachs, editors, *Psychology of Running,* Human Kinetics, 1981. Contributor of over sixty papers in neurology and psychiatry to professional journals.

WORK IN PROGRESS: Two novels, *Dr. Durham's Blindness* and *The Green Mountain Psychiatric Institute;* a book of collected poems, *Vicissitudes of Mental Pain;* editing and contributing to *Child and Adolescent Assessment,* with E. Mahon.

* * *

SPAETH, Gerold 1939-

PERSONAL: Born October 16, 1939, in Rapperswil, Switzerland; son of Josef (an organ builder) and Martha (Ruegg) Spaeth; married Anita Baumann, 1964; children: Veit, Salome. *Education:* Attended commercial schools in Switzerland and England. *Home address:* Sternengraben, Rapperswil 8640, Switzerland. *Agent:* Scott Meredith Literary Agency, Inc., 845 Third Ave., New York, N.Y. 10022.

CAREER: Held various positions in international trade and advertising in Zurich, Switzerland, Vevey, Switzerland, Fribourg, Switzerland, and London, England; free-lance writer, 1968—; part-time employee in family organ-building business, 1975—. *Member:* International P.E.N., Gruppe Olten. *Awards, honors:* Conrad Ferdinand Meyer-Preis und Werkjahr der Stadt Zuerich, 1970; Werkauftrag der Stiftung Pro Helvetia, 1972; Werkjahr der Stiftung der Schweizerischen Landesausstellung, 1973; Werkjahr des Kantons Zuerich, 1975; Anerkennungsgabe der Stadt Zuerich, 1977; Traeger des erstmals verliehenen Alfred Doeblin-Preises, 1979; Stipendiat des DAAD Kuenstlerprogramms Berlin, 1980; Stipendiat des Istituto Svizzero Roma, 1980-82.

WRITINGS: Unschlect (novel), Arche Verlag, 1970, translation by Rita Kimber and Robert Kimber published as *A Prelude to the Long Happy Life of Maximilian Goodman,* Little, Brown, 1975; *Stimmgaenge* (novel), Arche Verlag, 1972; *Zwoelf Geschichten* (short stories), Arche Verlag, 1973; *Die heile Hoelle* (novel; title means "The Hidden Hell"), Arche Verlag, 1974; *Kings Insel* (novel; title means "King's Island"), Arche Verlag, 1976; *Balzapf; oder, Als ich auftauchte* (novel), Arche Verlag, 1977; *Ende der Nacht,* Pfaffenweiler Presse, 1979; *Commedia,* S. Fischer Verlag, 1980.

Radio plays; produced in Switzerland, Germany, and Canada: *Heisser Sonntag,* Schweizerische Werbestelle fuer das Buch des Schweizerischen Buchhaendler- und Verlagsvereins, 1971; "Mein Oktober: Hoellisch," 1972; "Grund-Riss eines grossen Hauses," 1974; "Schattentanz," 1976; "Morgenprozession," 1977; "Heisse Sunntig," 1978; "Lange Leitung," 1978; "In der Ferne eine Stadt," 1979; "Kalter Tag," 1980; "Masken," 1980; "Eine alte Geschichte," 1982.

* * *

SPEIER, Hans 1905-

PERSONAL: Surname rhymes with "buyer"; born February 3, 1905, in Berlin, Germany; came to United States in 1933, naturalized in 1940; son of Adolf and Anna (Person) Speier; married Lisa Griesbach, August 30, 1929; married second wife, Margit Leipnik, February 18, 1967; children: (first marriage) Sybil D. (Mrs. Harvey Barten), Steven W. *Education:* Attended University of Berlin, 1923-25; University of Heidelberg, Ph.D., 1928. *Home:* 167 Concord Ave., Hartsdale, N.Y. 10530.

CAREER: Ullstein Publishing House, Berlin, Germany, book editor, 1929-31; Deutsche Hochschule fuer Politik, Berlin, lecturer in political sociology, 1931-33; New School for Social Research, Graduate Faculty, New York, N.Y., professor of sociology, 1933-42; Federal Communications Commission, Washington, D.C., section chief and later acting chief of Foreign Broadcast Intelligence Service, 1942-44; U.S. Office of War Information, Washington, D.C., adviser to chief of Overseas Branch, 1944-45; U.S. Department of State, Washington, D.C., associate (acting) chief of Occupied Areas Division, 1945-47; New School for Social Research, Graduate Faculty, professor of sociology, 1947; RAND Corp., Santa Monica, Calif., head of Social Science Division, 1948-60, member of Research Council, 1961-69, chairman of Research Council, 1961-62; University of Massachusetts—Amherst, Robert M. MacIver Professor of Sociology and Political Science, 1969-73. Visiting professor, University of Illinois, 1936, and University of Michigan, summer, 1941. Member, U.S. Air Force Scientific Advisory Board, 1948-51; consultant to U.S. Department of State, 1947-51, Research and Development Board, 1948-51, Ford Foundation, 1951, and U.S. Scientific Advisory Board, 1958-62.

MEMBER: World Academy of Art and Science (fellow), American Academy of Arts and Sciences (fellow), American Sociological Association, Deutsche Gesellschaft fuer Soziologie (honorary member). *Awards, honors:* Fellow, Center for Advanced Study in the Behavioral Sciences, 1956-57; senior fellow, Council of Foreign Relations (New York), 1964.

WRITINGS: (Editor with Alfred Kahler and co-author) *War in Our Time,* Norton, 1939; *The Salaried Employee in German Society,* Volume I, Works Progress Administration and Department of Social Sciences, Columbia University, 1939; (editor) Emil Lederer, *State of the Masses,* Norton, 1940; (with Ernst Kris) *German Radio Propaganda,* Oxford University Press, 1944.

Social Order and the Risks of War, George Stewart, 1952, reprinted, MIT Press, 1969; *German Rearmament and Atomic War,* Row, Peterson & Co., 1957; (editor with W. P. Davison) *West German Leadership and Foreign Policy,* Row, Peterson & Co., 1957; *Divided Berlin: The Anatomy of Soviet Political Blackmail,* Praeger, 1961; (translator and author of introduction) Grimmelshausen, *Courage, The Adventuress* [and] *The False Messiah,* Princeton University Press, 1964; *Force and Folly: Essays on Foreign Affairs and the History of Ideas,* MIT Press, 1968.

Witz und Politik: Essay ueber die Macht und das Lachen, Edition Interfrom AG, 1975; *Die Angestellten vor dem Nationalsozialismus: Ein Beitrag zum Verstaendnis der deutschen Sozialstruktur,* Vandenhoeck & Ruprecht, 1977; (editor with Harold D. Lasswell and Daniel Lerner and co-author) *Propaganda and Communication in World History,* University Press of Hawaii, Volume I: *The Symbolic Instrument in Early Times,* 1979, Volume II: *Emergence of Public Opinion in the West,* 1980, Volume III: *A Pluralizing World in Formation,* 1980; *From the Ashes of Disgrace: A Journal from Germany, 1945-1955,* University of Massachusetts Press, 1981.

Contributor: Edward Mead Earle, editor, *Makers of Modern Strategy,* Princeton University Press, 1943; (with Margaret Otis) Paul F. Lazarsfeld and Frank Stanton, editors, *Radio Research, 1942-1943,* Duell, Sloan, & Pearce, 1944; Harry Elmer Barnes, editor, *An Introduction to the History of Ideas,* University of Chicago Press, 1947. Lazarsfeld and Robert K. Merton, editors, *Continuities in Social Research,* Free Press of Glencoe, 1950; Bernard Berelson and Morris Janowitz, editors, *Public Opinion and Communication,* Free Press of Glencoe, 1950; Daniel Lerner, editor, *Propaganda in War and Crisis,* George W. Stewart, 1951; Wilbur Schramm, editor, *The Process and Effects of Mass Communications,* University of Illinois Press, 1954; *Psychological Aspects of Global Conflict,* Industrial College of the Armed Forces, 1955.

Harold K. Jacobson, editor, *American Foreign Policy,* Random House, 1960; J. Cropsey, editor, *Ancients and Moderns: Essays in the History of Political Philosophy in Honor of Leo Strauss,* Basic Books, 1964; R. N. Wilson, editor, *The Arts in Society,* Prentice-Hall, 1964; I. L. Horowitz, editor, *Historia y elementos de la sociologia del concimiento,* Volume I, University of Buenos Aires Press, 1964; Uwe Nerlich and C. Bertelsmann, editors, *Krieg und Frieden im industriellen Zeitalter,* [Gutersloh], 1966; *Congratulatio fuer Joseph C. Witsch,* Kiepenheuer & Witsch, 1966; James R. Roach, editor, *The United States and the Atlantic Community,* University of Texas Press, 1967.

Oskar Schatz, editor, *Der Friede im nuklearen Zeitalter,* Manz Verlag, 1970; Juergen Kocka, editor, *Emil Lederer: Kapitalismus, Klassenstruktur und Probleme der Demokratie in Deutschland, 1910-1940,* Vandenhoeck & Ruprecht, 1979. Contributor of articles to American, Canadian, British, and German journals.

WORK IN PROGRESS: Selected Essays, in German.

* * *

SPRINGER, Marilyn Harris 1931- (Marilyn Harris)

PERSONAL: Born June 4, 1931, in Oklahoma City, Okla.; daughter of John P. (an oil man) and Dora (Veal) Harris; married Edgar V. Springer, Jr. (a professor), February 21, 1953; children: John P., Karen Louise. *Education:* Attended Cottey College, 1949-51; University of Oklahoma, B.A., 1953, M.A., 1955. *Politics:* Independent. *Home:* 1846 Rolling Hills, Norman, Okla. 73069.

CAREER: Writer. *Awards, honors:* University of Oklahoma Literary Award, 1970; Lewis Carroll Shelf Award, 1973, for *The Runaway's Diary;* Oklahoma Federation of Writers Teepee Award, 1974; Women in Communications By-Liner Award, 1975; Oklahoma Writers Hall of Fame Award, 1980; Cottey College Distinguished Alumna Award, 1981.

WRITINGS—Under name Marilyn Harris: *King's Ex* (short stories), Doubleday, 1967; *In the Midst of Earth* (novel), Doubleday, 1969; *The Peppersalt Land,* Four Winds Press, 1970; *The Runaway's Diary,* Four Winds Press, 1971; *Hatter Fox,* Random House, 1973; *The Conjurers,* Random House, 1974; *Bledding Sorrow,* Putnam, 1976; *The Portent,* Putnam, 1980; *The Last Great Love,* Putnam, 1981.

"Eden" series; all published by Putnam: *This Other Eden,* 1977; *The Prince of Eden,* 1978; *The Eden Passion,* 1979; *The Women of Eden,* 1980; *Eden Rising,* 1982.

Also author of *The Diviner,* 1983. Short story is anthologized in *Prize Stories: The O. Henry Awards,* 1968. Contributor to *Red Clay Reader, Malahat Review, Trace,* and *London Weekend Telegraph.*

WORK IN PROGRESS: The American Eden, Volume VI in the "Eden" series of historical romances.

SIDELIGHTS: Marilyn Harris's *Hatter Fox* tells the story of a teenage Navajo girl whose life, reports a *Library Journal* reviewer, "is a series of virtually insufferable physical and mental tortures." Jailed for a minor offense, Hatter Fox stabs Teague Summer, a compassionate young Indian Bureau doctor who tries to break through the wall of hatred and mistrust that surrounds the troubled girl. For this more serious crime she is sent to a New Mexico reformatory, where Dr. Summer continues his efforts to help her. Most of Harris's novel focuses on this rehabilitation process and its tragic (and somewhat inconclusive) result.

Commenting in the *Christian Science Monitor,* Pamela Marsh describes *Hatter Fox* as "a steel trap of a book. Advance a few pages and you'll be stuck fast until [Harris] sees fit to let you go." A *Newsweek* critic, who characterizes the novel as "touching, skillful melodrama," writes that "it worries me to like [*Hatter Fox*], makes me think I'm going soft. . . . Fate conveniently glues a *Love Story* ending onto this romantic fantasy. But the rest of the story works."

Listener critic Sara Maitland is not so sure that Harris's "obvious sincerity and concern" manage to offset the book's "sentimental idealism, sloppy writing and generally inadequate characterisation." But a *Books and Bookmen* reviewer, while agreeing that "the denouement is not free from sentimentality," points out that "the novel raises issues, moral, psychological and social, which are really quite frightening. . . . The final impression [*Hatter Fox*] leaves . . . is of a writer passionately concerned with real issues, to whose further work one will turn eagerly."

MEDIA ADAPTATIONS: Hatter Fox was made into a CBS-TV movie-of-the-week and was broadcast in October, 1978.

BIOGRAPHICAL/CRITICAL SOURCES: Christian Science Monitor, August 22, 1973; *Newsweek,* September 17, 1973; *Listener,* February 13, 1975; *Books and Bookmen,* August, 1975; *Best Sellers,* May, 1977, August, 1978, August, 1979, May, 1980, December, 1980.

* * *

SPROSTON, John
See SCOTT, Peter Dale

* * *

STACK, Frank H(untington) 1937-
(Foolbert Sturgeon)

PERSONAL: Born October 31, 1937, in Houston, Tex.; son of Maurice Z. (a sales manager) and Norma Rose (Huntington) Stack; married Mildred Roberta Powell (a teacher), June 12, 1959; children: Joan Elaine, Robert Huntington. *Education:* University of Texas, B.F.A., 1959; Art Institute of Chicago, graduate study, 1960-61; University of Wyoming, M.A., 1963. *Home:* 409 Thilly Ave., Columbia, Mo. 65201. *Office:* Department of Art, University of Missouri, A-126 Fine Arts Center, Columbia, Mo. 65201.

CAREER: Houston Chronicle, Houston, Tex., assistant fine arts editor, 1959; University of Missouri, Columbia, instructor, 1963-68, assistant professor, 1968-73, associate professor, 1973-78, professor of art, 1978—. Artist with Lakeside Studio (etchings and lithographics), 1974—. Member of board of directors of Columbia Art League, 1975. *Military service:* U.S. Army, 1960, 1961-62. *Member:* College Art Association of America, Columbia Art League.

WRITINGS: (Editor with Robert Bussabarger and Peter Morse) *A Selection of Etchings by John Sloan,* University of Missouri Press, 1968; (editor and illustrator), Sidney Larsen, *Etchings and Lithographs by Frank Stack,* Singing Wind Publications, 1976.

Cartoon books under pseudonym Foolbert Sturgeon; published by Rip Off Press: *New Adventures of Jesus,* Volume I, 1968, Volume II, 1969, Volume III, 1974; *Feel-good Funnies,* 1971; *Amazon Comics,* 1972; *Dorman's Doggie,* 1978; *Collected New Adventures of Jesus,* 1979.

Author of "Between the Lines," an art news column in *Houston Chronicle.* Contributor to art magazines and literary journals, including *Rip Off Review, Sunday Clothes, Help!, Motive, Liberation, National Lampoon,* and *Rip Off Comix.*

WORK IN PROGRESS: A Book of Watercolors by Master Painters; Collected Adventures of Dr. Feelgood; Art Teaching by Aphorism.

SIDELIGHTS: Frank H. Stack writes: "I am primarily a painter and graphic artist and have pursued a career as an artist after some diversion as magazine designer, journalist, art critic, and writer of satirical pieces. I have always felt our society needed good satire on one hand and balanced with serious sympathetic art—a reason I have made a book about John Sloan who was critical without being brutal, and have written and drawn underground comic books criticizing military and academic bureaucracies, cultural and ethical travesties, mechanistic intellectuals, and the appalling ugliness of our drive-in society. By contrast, my figure and landscape paintings celebrate the natural energy and beauty of nature and people."

BIOGRAPHICAL/CRITICAL SOURCES: Mark James Estren, *A History of Underground Comics,* Straight Arrow Books, 1971; *Kansas City Star,* July 29, 1973; *Missouri Historical Review,* October, 1973.

* * *

STECHOW, Wolfgang 1896-1974

PERSONAL: Born June 5, 1896, in Kiel, Germany; came to United States in 1936, naturalized citizen; died October 12, 1974, in Princeton, N.J.; married, 1931; children: three. *Education:* Attended University of Freiburg, 1914, and University of Berlin, 1920; University of Goettingen, Ph.D., 1921. *Home:* 21 Robin Park, Oberlin, Ohio 44074.

CAREER: Kaiser Friedrich Museum, Berlin, Germany, assistant, 1921-22; University of Goettingen, Goettingen, Germany, instructor, 1926-31, assistant professor of art history, 1931-36; University of Wisconsin—Madison, acting assistant professor, 1936, associate professor of fine arts, 1937-40; Oberlin College, Oberlin, Ohio, professor of fine arts, 1940-63, professor emeritus, 1963-74, Charles B. Martin Lecturer, 1966, visiting professor, spring, 1972. Adjunct professor, Case Western Reserve University, beginning 1967. Visiting professor, University of Michigan, 1963-64, Vassar College, 1969-70, Yale University, fall, 1971, University of Goettingen, summer, 1972, University of Delaware, spring, 1973, and Princeton University, 1974; Sterling Clark Professor, Williams College, 1966-67; Mary Flexner Lecturer, Bryn Mawr College, 1967; Neilson Professor, Smith College, spring, 1969; Kress Professor-in-Residence, National Gallery of Art, 1970-71; Regents Professor, University of California, Los Angeles, winter, 1974. Member, National Committee for the History of Art. Fellow, German Institute of Art History (Florence), 1927-28, and Bibliotheca Hertziana (Rome), 1931. Advisory curator on European art, Cleveland Museum of Art, 1964-66.

MEMBER: College Art Association (vice-president, 1945), Archaeological Institute of America, American Society for Aesthetics. *Awards, honors:* L.H.D., University of Michigan, 1966; D.F.A., Oberlin College, 1967, and Baldwin-Wallace College, 1973.

WRITINGS: Apollo und Daphne, B. G. Teubner, 1932, 2nd edition published as *Apollo und Daphne: Mit einem Nachwort und Nachtraegen zum Neudruck,* Wissenschaftliche Buchgesellschaft, 1965; *Salomon van Ruysdael: Eine Einfuehrung in seine Kunst,* Mann, 1938, 2nd edition, 1975; *Dutch Painting in the Seventeenth Century,* Rhode Island Museum Press, 1938; *Pieter Bruegel, the Elder (about 1525-1569),* Abrams, 1954, reprinted, 1970.

Anthony van Dyck's "Betrayal of Christ," privately printed, 1960; (editor) *Northern Renaissance Art, 1400-1600: Sources and Documents,* Prentice-Hall, 1966; *Dutch Landscape Painting of the Seventeenth Century,* Phaidon, 1966, 3rd edition, Cornell University Press, 1981; *Rubens and the Classical Tradition,* Harvard University Press, 1968; *Duerer and America,* National Gallery of Art, 1971; *Landscapes from the Golden Age: An Exhibition of Seventeenth-Century Dutch Paintings* (catalog), [Grand Rapids, Mich.], 1972; (with others) *European Paintings before 1500,* Kent State University Press, 1974; *Catalogue of Drawings and Watercolors in the Allen Memorial Art Museum, Oberlin College,* Oberlin College, 1976.

Also author, with others, of *Studies in the History of Art 1973,* National Gallery of Art. Editor-in-chief, *Art Bulletin,* 1950-52. Consultant to *Art Quarterly* and *California Studies in the History of Art.*

BIOGRAPHICAL/CRITICAL SOURCES: Walter L. Strauss, editor, *Tribute to Wolfgang Stechow,* Pratt Graphics Center, Kennedy Galleries, 1976.

OBITUARIES: New York Times, October 14, 1974.†

* * *

STEELE, Addison II
See LUPOFF, Richard A(llen)

* * *

STEINBERG, Alfred 1917-

PERSONAL: Born December 8, 1917, in St. Paul, Minn.; son of Harry (a salesman) and Libby (Baron) Steinberg; married Florence Louise Schoenberg, September 16, 1940; children: Arne, Lise, Polly. *Education:* University of Minnesota, B.A., 1938, M.A., 1940. *Home and office:* 904 Highland Dr., Silver Spring, Md. 20910.

CAREER: U.S. Government, Washington, D.C., economist with various agencies, 1941-46; United Nations Food and Agricultural Organization, Washington, D.C., economist, 1947; *Economic and Political Weekly News-Letter on Far East,* Washington, D.C., editor and publisher, 1946-47; public relations director, Committee for Equality in Naturalization, 1948; free-lance writer, 1948—.

WRITINGS: (With Senator Tom Connally) *My Name Is Tom Connally,* Crowell, 1954; *Mrs. R.: The Life of Eleanor Roosevelt,* Putnam, 1958; (with Paul Siple) *Ninety Degrees South,* Putnam, 1958; *The Man from Missouri: The Life and Times of Harry S Truman,* Putnam, 1962; *The First Ten: The Founding Presidents and Their Administrations,* Doubleday, 1967; *Sam Johnson's Boy,* Macmillan, 1968; *The Bosses,* Macmillan, 1972; *Sam Rayburn,* Hawthorn, 1975.

Young adult biographies; all published by Putnam: *Eleanor Roosevelt,* 1959; *Daniel Webster,* 1959; *Richard E. Byrd,* 1960; *Douglas MacArthur,* 1961; *Woodrow Wilson,* 1962; *John Marshall,* 1962; *Harry S Truman,* 1963; *James Madison,* 1965; *Herbert Hoover,* 1966; *Dwight D. Eisenhower,* 1967; *John Adams,* 1967; *The Kennedy Brothers,* 1969.

Contributor to encyclopedias. Contributor of over 200 articles on politics, history, and economics to magazines.

WORK IN PROGRESS: Shadow of War: Washington, 1939-1941, for McGraw.

SIDELIGHTS: Throughout his writing career, Alfred Steinberg has made political biography his specialty. His subjects have included more than a dozen presidents of the United States, a world-famous first lady, a senator, a congressman, and several other prominent government officials from various eras of American history. In most instances, reviewers praise Steinberg's attention to detail and somewhat dramatic approach to his material; what they often find distracting, however, is the author's tendency to allow his personal feelings to color his narrative.

Regarding *Mrs. R.: The Life of Eleanor Roosevelt,* for example, several critics make note of the fact that Steinberg had access to the former first lady's papers. To some, this resulted in a biography that, as Frank Freidel states in the *New York Herald Tribune Book Review,* "impressively outlines [Mrs. Roosevelt's] public career and even more effectively portrays her private life." Calling the book "more than a biography," Josephine Ripley of the *Christian Science Monitor* characterizes it as "a dramatic chronicle—a kind of inside story of an epoch." On the other hand, though Arthur Schlesinger, Jr. reports in the *New York Times* that *Mrs. R.* is "competent and interesting," he concludes that "Steinberg's admiration for his subject too often distracts his judgment." *Saturday Review* critic Bess Furman also believes that the author finds Mrs. Roosevelt's papers "all too enchanting"; the story "comes alive," she points out, only in the chapters dealing with Mrs. Roosevelt's life after the White House years, a section in which the author's "descriptions are so true and vivid that they obviously are first-hand telling."

Steinberg's biography of Harry Truman, *The Man from Missouri,* elicits similar responses: critics applaud the "wealth of detail" in the book (especially regarding Truman's pre-White House life) but note a certain "partisan" tone. "From the outset," writes R.J. Donovan in *New York Herald Tribune Books,* "Mr. Steinberg makes it clear that he sides with those who rank Mr. Truman as one of the strong Presidents of the United States." Nevertheless, continues the reviewer, "[*The Man from Missouri*] is an interesting and readable re-telling of the Truman story. . . . In Mr. Steinberg's pages he strides across the stage again as a warm, humorous, industrious, brave and often (but not always) wise man." In his *Saturday Review* article on the biography, Walter Johnson declares that the author "is too disposed toward accepting the ex-President's version of a complex situation." But he, too, concludes that "Steinberg has done well with the difficult task of writing a full-length biography of [a] controversial figure. . . . There are many new and intriguing insights into Mr. Truman as a person and as President."

Sam Johnson's Boy, Steinberg's biography of Lyndon Johnson, strikes critics as being filled with even more personal feeling than the author's previous books. In this instance, however, it is not a question of Steinberg being overtly *pro*-Johnson; on the contrary, writes a *Times Literary Supplement* reviewer, *Sam Johnson's Boy* reads like an "immensely long speech for the prosecution. . . . Steinberg goes over Lyndon Baines Johnson's Texas past with a devotion to detail which only contempt and hatred could inspire." In the *Christian Science Monitor,* William H. Stringer describes the book as "sharply critical throughout" and notes that it ends with a "harsh, unfair verdict." States Larry L. King in the *New Republic:* "Had Johnson sought reelection, Steinberg's *Sam Johnson's Boy* might have come to prominence as the Bible of all who harbor less than love for their President. The many anti-Johnson scenes, stories, moods, and motives will unfailingly please his most severe critics whether of the Left or the Right. . . . There are some truths in Steinberg's book. . . . But there are half-truths; distortions; too much open rancor."

Commenting in the *St. Louis Post-Dispatch,* James Deakin agrees that in *Sam Johnson's Boy* "the Johnson personality and record are treated in immense, less-than-loving detail." Nevertheless, he continues, "those with the stamina to get through this 871-page book will find it a richly rewarding experience. Alfred Steinberg has written what is likely to be the definitive political biography of Lyndon Johnson for some time to come. . . . [He] has immersed himself in Texas political history more deeply than any other Johnson biographer. Through the pages of this disturbing, deeply critical book marches an appalling procession of cheap politicians, scoundrels, rogues, opportunists, demagogues, chauvinists, stumblebums, crooks and out-and-out lunatics who have graced the political leadership of the Lone Star state in the twentieth century. It is always clear that Steinberg . . . considers Lyndon Johnson a product of this shabby environment, with little capacity to rise above it."

Carroll Kilpatrick is similarly impressed by Steinberg's depiction of the young Johnson. As the critic remarks in the *Saturday Review:* "Despite its bias, I found the more than 800 pages of [*Sam Johnson's Boy*] worth the effort because they explore Johnson's early life in great detail. . . . [The author] tells more about LBJ than many readers will want to know, but in Johnson's case the boy is father of the man to an unusual degree."

Patrick Anderson of the *New York Times Book Review* also has words of praise for the first section of the book, which he describes as "a detailed, vivid portrait of a young wheeler-dealer on the make. . . . Steinberg does more than sketch Johnson; he sets him against an equally colorful portrayal of the Texas political world and the U.S. Senate." Though by the end of this first section "the reader is aware that the author has little love for Johnson," continues Anderson, the biography "still seems fair-minded." Then, reports the critic, "suddenly *Sam Johnson's Boy* begins to deteriorate. . . . Much of the book's final section is devoted to a rehash of old material. . . . I don't know why Steinberg let his book fall apart at the end. I would guess that he found Johnson's many sins tolerable as long as he was only a Senator, but he could not control his outrage once his subject became President. His book has many virtues, but in the end it only underscores what a great book remains to be written about Johnson's amazing career. But it will have to be written by someone who, unlike Steinberg, is willing to give the devil his due."

In response to these less-than-flattering appraisals of several of his books, Alfred Steinberg told *CA:* "I have nothing against critics, besotted and pinheaded though they may be. . . . I view biography as the art of the plausible interpretation of a person's existence. The model I strive to rival is Plutarch's *Lives,* still the best in this field after almost 2,000 years. The historical setting, the way of life and the critical judgments through revealing anecdotes are awesome."

BIOGRAPHICAL/CRITICAL SOURCES: New York Times, October 12, 1958; *New York Herald Tribune Book Review,* October 12, 1958; *Christian Science Monitor,* October 15, 1958, April 25, 1962, August 3, 1968; *Saturday Review,* November 8, 1958, April 28, 1962, September 21, 1968; *Chicago Sunday Tribune,* April 29, 1962; *New York Herald Tribune Books,* April 29, 1962; *New York Times Book Review,* April 29, 1962, July 28, 1968, July 6, 1975; *San Francisco Chronicle,* April 29, 1962; *St. Louis Post-Dispatch,* July 7, 1968; *Newsweek,* July 15, 1968; *New Republic,* August 3, 1968; *Times Literary Supplement,* December 12, 1968, March 2, 1973; *Annals of the American Academy of Political and Social Science,* May, 1973; *New Yorker,* September 8, 1975; *Washington Post Book World,* November 21, 1982.

—Sketch by Deborah A. Straub

* * *

STEINBERG, Rafael (Mark) 1927-

PERSONAL: Born June 2, 1927, in Newark, N.J.; son of Isador N. (an artist) and Polly N. (Rifkind) Steinberg; married Tamiko Okamoto (a teacher of Japanese), November 21, 1953 (separated); children: Summer Eve, Joy Nathania. *Education:* Harvard University, A.B. (cum laude), 1950. *Home:* 12 East 75th St., New York, N.Y. 10021. *Office:* 1841 Broadway, New York, N.Y. 10023.

CAREER: Fire Island Reporter, Long Island, N.Y., editor and publisher, summers, 1949-50; International News Service, New York City, war correspondent in Korea, 1951-52; *Time* (magazine), New York City, war correspondent in Korea and Japan, 1952, and in New York City, 1953-55, member of London bureau, 1955-58; *Newsweek* (magazine), New York City, Far Eastern correspondent and bureau chief in Tokyo, Japan, 1959-63; free-lance journalist in Tokyo, serving as correspondent for *Washington Post* and *Saturday Evening Post,* 1963-67, and in the United States, 1968-70; *Newsweek,* general editor, 1970-72, senior editor, 1972-73, managing editor of international edition, 1973; free-lance writer, 1973-75; *Cue* magazine, New York City, editor, 1975-76; free-lance writer, 1976—. Teacher of writing course, School of Continuing Education, New York University, 1981-82. Executive director, Academic and Professional Alliance for a Responsible Congress, 1970. *Military service:* U.S. Naval Reserve, active duty, 1945-46. *Member:* Authors League of America, Authors Guild, Japan Society, Foreign Correspondents Club of Japan, Harvard Club (New York, N.Y.).

WRITINGS: Postscript from Hiroshima, Random House, 1966; *Japan,* Macmillan, 1969; (with Jacob K. Javits) *Javits: The Autobiography of a Public Man,* Houghton, 1981.

With the editors of Time-Life Books; all published by Time-Life: *The Cooking of Japan,* 1969; *Pacific and Southeast Asian Cooking,* 1970; *Man and the Organization,* 1975; *Island Fighting,* 1978; *Return to the Philippines,* 1979.

Also author of scripts for television soap operas. Contributor of articles and stories to newspapers and magazines, including *Playboy, Cosmopolitan, Esquire, New York Times Magazine,*

Saturday Review, Columbia Journalism Review, and *Woman's World.*

SIDELIGHTS: A generation after an atomic bomb virtually flattened the Japanese city of Hiroshima, Rafael Steinberg returned to the scene of the destruction in an effort to discover how Hiroshima and its former and present inhabitants have fared during the intervening years. He reports his findings in *Postscript from Hiroshima,* a book *New Republic* critic Selig S. Harrison finds "powerful . . . yet remarkably free of polemics, sobs and moralizing. Steinberg stands quietly to the side and coaxes his subjects along as they tell their story directly and believably. He immediately disarms the reader who thinks he may already have had quite enough of Hiroshima by focusing not on August 6, 1945, but on what has been happening since in the physical and emotional reconstruction of a city."

"In telling the Hiroshima story," observes a *Newsweek* reviewer, "Steinberg has achieved two very difficult feats of reporting. He has handled a topic that is emotional dynamite calmly, dispassionately, and fairly, without for a moment underestimating the importance and the significance of the issues." As a result, Horace Bristol declares in the *Saturday Review,* "*Postscript from Hiroshima* is just what its title claims. Not that it pretends to be the last word, since it gives no answers to the questions each of us . . . must ask ourselves; its very inconclusiveness forces the reader to search his own heart. . . . In general, a spirit of progressive optimism permeates the book, . . . [but Steinberg makes] no attempt to hide the scars most of us would prefer to forget."

In short, concludes A. M. Rosenthal in the *New York Times,* though *Postscript from Hiroshima* may not be "the work of art that was John Hersey's *Hiroshima,* . . . it is perceptive and warm. . . . Anybody who read Hersey will be intrigued by Steinberg's sequel."

BIOGRAPHICAL/CRITICAL SOURCES: Newsweek, July 18, 1966; *Saturday Review,* July 23, 1966; *New York Times,* July 26, 1966; *New Republic,* March 11, 1967.

* * *

STEPHAN, Leslie (Bates) 1933-

PERSONAL: Born May 1, 1933, in Boston, Mass.; daughter of Leslie Marriner (a dentist) and Ann (Gustafson) Bates; married Richard Allen Stephan (a consultant), January 22, 1955; children: John Eric, Johanna, Anne Christina, Mark David, Martin Jonathan, Maria Alvina. *Education:* Attended Skidmore College, 1951-52, Simmons College, 1952-54; Radcliffe College, B.A. (cum laude), 1957; Lesley College, Cambridge, Mass., elementary teachers certificate, 1981. *Home:* 93 North Main St., Topsfield, Mass. 01983. *Agent:* Oliver G. Swan, Collier Associates, 280 Madison Ave., New York, N.Y. 10016.

CAREER: Director of nursery school in Harrison, N.Y., 1958-59; special education tutor, 1975—.

WRITINGS: A Dam for Nothing, Viking, 1966; *Murder R.F.D.,* Scribner, 1978 (published in England as *Murder in the Family,* R. Hale, 1979); *Murder or Not,* R. Hale, 1981.

WORK IN PROGRESS: Another mystery novel.

SIDELIGHTS: Leslie Stephan lived in Iraq, 1955, in Switzerland, 1960-63, in Mexico, 1966-67, in Algeria, 1968. She speaks German, French, and some Spanish. *Avocational interests:* Reading, gardening, swimming, cross-country skiing, softball, jogging, walking, listening to music.

STEVENS, R(obert) B(ocking) 1933-

PERSONAL: Born June 8, 1933, in Leicester, England; naturalized U.S. citizen, 1971; son of John Skevington and Enid Dorothy (Bocking) Stevens; married Rosemary Anne Wallace (a professor), January 30, 1961; children: Carey Thomasine, Richard Nathaniel. *Education:* Keble College, Oxford, B.A., 1955, B.C.L., 1956, M.A., 1958; Yale University, LL.M., 1958. *Home:* 1 College Cir., Haverford, Pa. 19041. *Office:* Haverford College, Haverford, Pa. 19041.

CAREER: Barrister-at-law, London, England, 1956; Oxford University, Keble College, Oxford, England, tutor in law, 1958-59; Yale University, New Haven, Conn., assistant professor, 1959-61, associate professor, 1961-65, professor of law, 1965-76; Tulane University, New Orleans, La., provost and professor of law and history, 1976-78; Haverford College, Haverford, Pa., president, 1978—. Visiting professor, University of Texas, 1961, University of East Africa, 1962, and Stanford University, 1966. Consultant to United Nations and U.S. Department of State. *Member:* Oxford Club, Cambridge Club, Yale Club. *Awards, honors:* Recipient of grants from Rockefeller Foundation, 1962-64, Ford Foundation, 1962-64 and 1973-74, National Endowment for the Humanities, Nuffield Foundation, and Russell Sage Foundation, 1967-68.

WRITINGS: (With B. S. Yamey) *The Restrictive Practices Court: A Study of the Judicial Process and Economic Policy,* Weidenfeld & Nicolson, 1965; (with B. Abel-Smith) *Lawyers and the Courts: A Sociological Study of the English Legal System, 1750-1965,* Harvard University Press, 1967; (with Abel-Smith) *In Search of Justice: Society and the Legal System,* Penguin, 1969; (editor) *Income Security,* McGraw, 1970; (with wife, Rosemary Stevens) *Welfare Medicine in America,* Free Press, 1974; *Law and Politics: The House of Lords as a Judicial Body,* University of North Carolina Press, 1979; *The Law School: Legal Education from the 1880s to the 1980s,* University of North Carolina Press, 1983.

WORK IN PROGRESS: Research on the English legal system from 1875 to the present and on the concept of law in Connecticut.

* * *

STEVENSON, Anne (Katharine) 1933-

PERSONAL: Born January 3, 1933, in Cambridge, England; daughter of Charles Leslie (a philosopher) and Louise (Destler) Stevenson; married twice; divorced twice; children: (first marriage) Caroline Margaret Hitchcock; (second marriage) John Gawain Elvin, Charles Lionel Elvin. *Education:* University of Michigan, B.A., 1954, M.A., 1962. *Politics:* Democrat. *Home:* 31 Belle Vue Park, Sunderland SR2 75A, England.

CAREER: Poet and critic. Fellow in writing at University of Dundee, Scotland, 1973-75, Lady Margaret Hall, Oxford, 1975-77, and Bulmershe College, Reading, 1977-78; Northern Arts Literary Fellow at University of Newcastle-upon-Tyne and University of Durham, 1981-82. Co-proprietor of The Poetry Bookshop, Hay-on-Wye, Wales, 1978-81. Part-time teacher of cello in Cambridge, England; cellist in string orchestra connected with Cambridge University. *Member:* Royal Society of Literature (fellow), Phi Beta Kappa. *Awards, honors:* Avery and Jules Hopwood Award, University of Michigan, 1950, 1952, 1954; Scottish Arts Council Award, 1974; Welsh Arts Council Award, 1980.

WRITINGS—Poetry, except as indicated: *Living in America,* Generation, 1965; *Elizabeth Bishop* (criticism), Twayne, 1966; *Reversals,* Wesleyan University Press, 1969; *Correspondences: A Family History in Letters,* Wesleyan University Press, 1974; *Travelling behind Glass,* Oxford University Press, 1974; *Enough of Green,* Oxford University Press, 1977; *Minute by Glass Minute,* Oxford University Press, 1982. Contributor to *Times Literary Supplement* and periodicals in United States. Former poetry critic for *Listener*. Co-editor, *Other Poetry Magazine*.

SIDELIGHTS: Anne Stevenson "has what Henry James call[ed] 'sensibility to the scenery of life,'" comments Dorothy Donnelly in *Michigan Quarterly Review*. "Her poems have added considerably to the scenery of our own landscapes." Stevenson's poetry, a *Times Literary Supplement* critic writes, is "remarkable for a fresh, authentic brand of realist observation and an impressive capacity to reflect intelligently on what it sees." Ralph J. Mills, Jr. in *Poetry* calls Stevenson "one of the most promising young women poets."

The landscape that Stevenson creates is a shifting one, built upon the ambiguous borders between England and America, family and self, dependence and independence, tradition and nonconformity. "The landscape created by Anne Stevenson's poems . . . shimmers with the tenuous colors and outlines of reflections in water," Donnelly says of *Reversals*. "The poet hesitates, caught between reality and illusion, moving through a flickering, borderless region, a land behind the land. . . . Stevenson's poems evoke with delicacy the misty, the insubstantial, the indefinite, 'the line between land and water,' the view from which 'there is no end to illusion.'" Nicholas Brooke in *New Review* observes that the poems in *Travelling behind Glass* "characterize America and Europe from no fixed base."

Stevenson herself comments upon the feeling of movement and duality her poetry elicits. "Although I am an American . . . I have lived almost constantly in Great Britain since 1962," she writes *CA*. "This has meant a measure of flexibility and a constant sense of flux . . . [as well as] the sense I have constantly of a divided life between the Old World and the New."

Stevenson has developed this theme of "flux" in much of her work. In many of her poems it takes the form of the narrator questioning her own actions or the direction her life has taken. Stevenson is "given to querying life," states Donnelly, "and the frequent questions asked in these poems [in *Reversals*] indicate their prevailingly tentative tone. Answers are usually avoided, sometimes suggested, often simply not to be had." Kaye Boyd, a principle character in *Correspondences: A Family History in Letters,* questions her decision to become an author—a decision which also entails leaving her family home: "Dear Father, I love you but can't know you. / I've given you all that I can. / Can these pages make amends for what was not said? / Do justice to the living, to the dead?" In "Victory," included in *Reversals,* the narrator is compelled to ask her infant son, "Why do I have to love you?"

Although the "landscape" in which Stevenson moves is "tentative," "flickering," and "borderless," her responses to it are not. *Times Literary Supplement*'s Andrew Motion observes, "The characteristic method of *Enough of Green* is to confront the harsh realities of life, acknowledge the temptation to evade them, and then discover rewards in them as well as disappointments."

Correspondences: A Family History in Letters is Stevenson's most ambitious accomplishment. The book traces the Chandler family from its pre-Revolution, New England roots to the present. "*Correspondences* . . . is an ambitious book," asserts Richard Caram in *Open Places*. "[It] just burns to be an American epic, to combine the insights of history with the characterizations of fiction and the fine aesthetic harmonies of poetry. And it works, in the end, far better than it has a right to—particularly as a very readable form of history, a mythopoetic look backward." Notes Stewart Conn in *Listener:* "With penetrating insight, Anne Stevenson depicts successive generations blighted by drink and estrangement, woe within marriage and a wonderment that man has deserved propagation at all in this wicked world."

Stevenson's characteristic sense of ambiguity is also present in *Correspondences*. Caram concludes that the final section of the book "does most deftly what poetry can do better than history: hold the ambiguities of the lives of the surviving members of the family in lifelike suspension, unwilling to resolve them into finalities, swirling them round and round in a mixture rhetorically rich enough to seem almost a resolution."

Other critics, however, feel that *Correspondences* tries to accomplish too great a task. Douglas Dunn in *Encounter* notes that the work "has been worked hard at, not only as a poem, but as something to hold the reader's attention; unfortunately, the impression is that the clever writer was conjuring with too many gimmicks, for all the weightiness of her critique of America." *New Review*'s Brooke comments that since the poems in *Correspondences* "are not long, it follows they are overloaded, and the story is reduced to familiar types. . . . A novelist would do more than this; a poet should not do less." Concurs Robert Garfitt in *London Magazine:* "Moving as some of [*Correspondences*] is . . . one is left wondering what it has achieved that a novel couldn't have achieved, and, more important, whether a more intimate and telling exploration, accessible only to poetry, hasn't been missed."

Despite these criticisms, Stevenson's reputation remains secure. "Her formal dexterity, her determination to include alternative responses to any given situation, and her ability to write with a detachment which is both objective and engaging prove her a poet of exceptional distinction," states Motion.

AVOCATIONAL INTERESTS: Music, traveling, and reading.

BIOGRAPHICAL/CRITICAL SOURCES: Michigan Quarterly Review, fall, 1966, spring, 1971; *Poetry,* February, 1971, November, 1975; *Times Literary Supplement,* July 19, 1974, November 25, 1977; *Lines Review 50,* September, 1974; *New Review,* October, 1974; *London Magazine,* November, 1974; *New Statesman,* November 28, 1974, February 10, 1978; *Listener,* November 28, 1974; *Encounter,* December, 1974, April, 1978; *Open Places,* spring/summer, 1976; *Contemporary Literary Criticism,* Volume VII, Gale, 1977; *Ploughshares,* autumn, 1978.

—*Sketch by Heidi A. Tietjen*

*   *   *

STINE, G(eorge) Harry 1928-
(Lee Correy)

PERSONAL: Born March 26, 1928, in Philadelphia, Pa.; son of George Haeberle (an eye surgeon) and Rhea Matilda (O'Neil) Stine; married Barbara A. Kauth, June 10, 1952; children: Constance Rhea, Eleanor Ann, George Willard. *Education:* Attended University of Colorado, 1946-50; Colorado College, B.A., 1952. *Home:* 616 West Frier Dr., Phoenix, Ariz. 85021.

Agent: Scott Meredith Literary Agency, Inc., 845 Third Ave., New York, N.Y. 10022.

CAREER: White Sands Proving Ground, White Sands, N.M., chief of controls and instruments section in propulsion branch, 1952-55, chief of range operations division and Navy flight safety engineer, 1955-57; Martin Co., Denver, Colo., design specialist, 1957; Model Missiles, Inc., Denver, president and chief engineer, 1957-59; Stanley Aviation Corp., Denver, design engineer, 1959-60; Huyck Corp., Stamford, Conn., assistant director of research, 1960-65; consulting engineer and science writer in New Canaan, Conn., 1965-73; Flow Technology, Inc., Phoenix, Ariz., marketing manager, 1973-76; science writer and consultant, 1976—.

MEMBER: American Institute of Aeronautics and Astronautics (associate fellow), Instrument Society of America, Academy of Model Aeronautics, National Aeronautic Association, National Association of Rocketry (founder; president, 1957-67; honorary trustee), American Society of Aerospace Education, Science Fiction Writers of America, L-S Society, National Fire Protection Association, British Interplanetary Society (fellow), New York Academy of Sciences, Theta Xi, Explorers Club (New York City; fellow). *Awards, honors:* Special award, American Rocket Society, 1957, for founding and editing *Missile Away!;* Bendix Trophy, National Association of Rocketry, 1964, 1965, 1967, and 1968; Silver Medal, American Space Pioneer, U.S. Army Association, 1965; Silver Medal, payload category, First International Model Rocket Competition, Dubnica, Czechoslovakia, 1966; Special award, National Association of Rocketry, 1967; first recipient of annual award in model rocketry division, Hobby Industry Association of America, 1969.

WRITINGS: Rocket Power and Space Flight, Holt, 1957; *Earth Satellites and the Race for Space Superiority,* Ace Books, 1957; *Man and the Space Frontier,* Knopf, 1962; (contributor) Frederick Pohl, editor, *The Expert Dreamers,* Doubleday, 1962; *The Handbook of Model Rocketry,* Follett, 1965, 5th edition, Arco, 1983; (contributor) George W. Early, editor, *Encounters with Aliens,* Sherbourne, 1969; *The Model Rocket Manual,* Sentinel, 1969.

Model Rocket Safety, Model Products Corp., 1970; (contributor) Ben Bova, editor, *The Analog Science Fact Reader,* Sherbourne, 1974; *The Third Industrial Revolution,* Putnam, 1975; (contributor) Bova, editor, *A New View of the Solar System,* St. Martin's, 1976; *The New Model Rocketry Manual,* Arco, 1977; *Shuttle into Space,* Follett, 1978; *The Space Enterprise,* Ace Books, 1980; *Space Power,* Ace Books, 1981; *Confrontation in Space,* Prentice-Hall, 1981; *The Hopeful Future,* Macmillan, 1983; *Handbook for Space Colonists,* Harcourt, in press.

Under pseudonym Lee Correy: *Starship through Space,* Holt, 1954; *Contraband Rocket,* Ace Books, 1955; *Rocket Man,* Holt, 1956; *Star Driver,* Ballantine, 1980; *Shuttle Down,* Ballantine, 1981; *Space Doctor,* Ballantine, 1981; *The Abode of Life,* Pocket Books, 1982; *Manna,* DAW Books, 1983.

Also author of six technical papers and five filmscripts. Science fiction short stories are represented in anthologies, including *Science Fiction, '58: The Year's Greatest Science Fiction and Fantasy,* edited by Judith Merrill, Gnome, 1958, *The Sixth Annual of the Year's Best Science Fiction,* edited by Merrill, Simon & Schuster, 1961, and *Analog Six,* edited by John W. Campbell, Doubleday, 1968.

Contributor to *Collier's Encyclopedia.* Author of columns "Conquest of Space," *Mechanix Illustrated,* 1956-57, and "The Alternate View," *Analog,* 1980—. Contributor of over 200 science fiction stories, nonfiction articles on science, and articles on model rocketry to magazines, including *Omni, Science Digest, Saturday Evening Post, Astounding, Analog, Science Digest,* and *Magazine of Fantasy and Science Fiction.* Editor, *Missile Away!,* 1953-57, *The Model Rocketeer,* 1958-64, and *Flow Factor,* 1973-76; senior editor, *Aviation/Space,* 1982—.

WORK IN PROGRESS: "Too many authors talk about the stories they are going to do tomorrow. I prefer to discuss only what I have done."

SIDELIGHTS: "I had the good fortune to grow up in Colorado Springs, Colorado, on one of the last physical frontiers on the North American continent, the American West," G. Harry Stine told *CA.* "I also had the good fortune to choose a father who was an eye surgeon, who was an amateur scientist, and who surrounded me with books from as early as I can remember. In concert with my father, a number of men instilled in me a consuming curiosity about the universe around me. Once I asked one of them what I could ever do to repay him. I have been repaying him ever since because he said, 'There is no way that you can repay me directly and personally. The only thing that you can do to repay me is to do the same thing for the next generation. The obligation is always toward the future.'

"I write the sort of thing that I would like to read. I write it the way I would like to read it. I write entertainment. I am competing for the reader's time and money; if he doesn't like what I write, he will not spend his time and plunk down his hard-earned money a second time."

Stine is optimistic about the future; he believes that "the human race is going to survive. We will use the accumulated knowledge of centuries plus our rational minds to solve the problems that seem to beset us at the moment. . . . They are really no worse than the problems that faced other generations in the past. The current problems seem worse because they are current and because we have not yet solved them. What is difficult to us was impossible to our parents and will be commonplace to our children. We will indeed slay the dragons of war, intolerance, and pollution. We will marry the princess of outer space. And we will live happily ever after among the stars. We now have or will soon have the capability to do anything we want to do; we must only be willing to pay for it and to live with all the consequences.

"Like it or not, we live in a technological reality. One can escape it only by regressing through centuries of human history. I have attempted to master or at least understand as much about technology as possible. I have operated or am at least aware of how to operate every possible human transportation machine; for example, I have operated railroad trains, horses, automobiles, boats, and airplanes. I am a licensed pilot, own an airplane, and fly regularly. I hope someday to fly in a rocket-powered space vehicle . . . or in any sort of space vehicle. I greatly admire the fictitious man who, when asked if he could fly a helicopter, replied, 'I don't know; I've never tried.'

"The human race has a long way yet to go, and there are a lot of things left to do. According to a recent U.N. survey, nearly half the people in the world cannot read or write their native language; in the 'literate' United States of America, there are 21,000,000 people who are illiterate. Over 100,000,000 Americans have never been up in an airplane. Ninety per cent of the people on Earth have never been more than 25 miles from their birthplace, nor do they expect to travel beyond their village during their lifetimes."

* * *

STOESSINGER, John G. 1927-

PERSONAL: Born October 14, 1927, in Austria; came to United States in 1947, naturalized in 1956; son of Oscar and Irene (Mestitz) Stoessinger. *Education:* Grinnell College, B.A., 1950; Harvard University, M.A., 1952, Ph.D., 1954. *Home:* 275 Central Park W., New York, N.Y. 10024. *Office:* Department of Political Science, Hunter College of the City University of New York, New York, N.Y. 10021.

CAREER: Wellesley College, Wellesley, Mass., instructor, 1955-56; lecturer, Babson Institute, 1955-57; Massachusetts Institute of Technology, Cambridge, part-time lecturer, 1956-57; Hunter College of the City University of New York, New York, N.Y., assistant professor, 1957-60, associate professor, 1960-63, professor of political science, 1964—. Columbia University, School of International Affairs, visiting associate professor, 1960-63, visiting professor of international relations, beginning 1963; Presidential Professor, Colorado School of Mines, 1978-79. Director of Peace Corps Training Program in World Affairs and American Institutions, 1963-64; acting director of Political Affairs Division, United Nations, 1967-74. Conductor of radio and television courses on international affairs, including one network series; public lecturer on world events. *Member:* Council on Foreign Relations. *Awards, honors:* Bancroft Prize, Columbia University, 1963, for the best book on international relations published in 1962, for *The Might of Nations;* Doctor of Laws, Grinnell College, 1970.

WRITINGS: The Refugee and the World Community, University of Minnesota Press, 1956; *The Might of Nations: World Politics in Our Time,* Random House, 1962, 7th edition, 1982; (with others) *Financing the United Nations System,* Brookings Institution, 1964; (editor with A. F. Westin) *Power and Order,* Harcourt, 1964; *The United Nations and the Superpowers,* Random House, 1965, 4th edition, 1977; *Nations in Darkness: China, Russia, America,* Random House, 1971, 3rd edition, 1978; *Why Nations Go to War,* St. Martin's, 1974, 3rd edition, 1982; *Henry Kissinger: The Anguish of Power,* Norton, 1976; *Night Journey: A Story of Survival and Deliverance* (autobiography), Playboy Press, 1978; *Crusaders and Pragmatists: Movers of Modern American Foreign Policy,* Norton, 1979. Book review editor, *Foreign Affairs,* five years.

SIDELIGHTS: In his study *Henry Kissinger: The Anguish of Power,* John G. Stoessinger attempts to remedy the imbalance he believes exists in most other portraits of the former secretary of state. As a friend of Kissinger for over thirty years, Stoessinger writes with sympathy and undisguised admiration for his subject; as a political scientist, he writes with a desire to clarify the problems involved in making choices that have a direct bearing on world events. Concentrating "less on the outward successes or failures of Kissinger's diplomacy than on the inward motivations and visions," in the words of a *Virginia Quarterly Review* critic, Stoessinger seeks to demonstrate how Kissinger's personal philosophy influenced the decisions he made while serving under Presidents Nixon and Ford.

In general, critics are impressed by what James Burnham of the *National Review* calls Stoessinger's "coherent and useful" summary of major U.S. foreign policy moves during the Kissinger era. What leaves some of them uneasy, however, is the overall tone of the book, a tone the *Washington Post Book World*'s Stanley Karnow declares "borders on the adulatory." In the *New York Times Book Review,* for example, Richard J. Barnet takes issue with Stoessinger's concluding remark that "the world is a safer place today because of [Kissinger's] courage and vision," pointing out that the author presents "no coherent criteria . . . by which to judge [Kissinger's] performance." Observes Stanley Hoffmann in the *New Republic:* "Stoessinger is very critical of Kissinger's policies in Viet Nam, Bangladesh, Cyprus and Portugal. He mentions his subject's long indifference to and belated concern for international economics organizations, and development. He notes the weaknesses of Kissinger's concept of stability. . . . And yet his final judgment is warm and admiring. I have the impression that this tribute owes less to an account that often seems to point the other way, than to Stoessinger's own generous and affectionate feelings toward a man who was a co-student of his at Harvard, with whom he collaborated in the days of the International Seminar, and whom he sees as a fellow refugee and as a friend." According to Burnham, such an approach makes it difficult to regard *Henry Kissinger: The Anguish of Power* as much more than "an apologia, a brief for the defense."

On the other hand, Max Lerner finds Stoessinger "sharp in his analysis, economical in his historical accounts of Kissinger's policies in various world areas, [and] fair-minded in his judgments." As a result, he remarks in the *Saturday Review, Henry Kissinger: The Anguish of Power* is a "close-packed book" that provides a "cohesive" view of its subject; it is a book in which Stoessinger lets us see "the inside of Kissinger's mind—his world view, his self-image, and, above all, his intellectual arsenal of ideas with which he sets out to achieve his effects—without abandoning his critical judgment of Kissinger's policies."

But several reviewers, including Lerner, maintain that a number of years must pass before we can reasonably expect anyone to write a truly balanced, thorough study of Henry Kissinger. As Hoffmann states: "Even a friendly reader cannot help com[ing] to the conclusion that it is still too soon, and that the best one can hope for at present is a very tentative and provisional assessment. . . . Only the future will tell us whether what, today, appears shaky . . . will not go down as genuine diplomatic turning points, or whether some of the most applauded initiatives . . . will not be written off as improvisations without adequate follow-up."

Noting the difficulties involved in writing about a man he describes as "both a culture hero and a culture target," Lerner wonders if nonfiction lends itself to explaining one of the most controversial figures ever to serve as secretary of state. Concludes the critic: "The turmoil over Henry Kissinger rages only in part over his diplomacy, for the legend of his personality and career is deeply embedded in questions of history, tragedy, and myth. . . . Someday a play or novel may capture the Kissinger enigma more imaginatively, and therefore better, than the weightier treatises that are appearing now."

BIOGRAPHICAL/CRITICAL SOURCES: John G. Stoessinger, *Henry Kissinger: The Anguish of Power,* Norton, 1976; *Washington Post Book World,* September 12, 1976; *Saturday Review,* October 16, 1976; *New York Times Book Review,* October 17, 1976; *New Republic,* December 11, 1976; *Best Sellers,* February, 1977; *National Review,* February 18, 1977; *Virginia Quarterly Review,* summer, 1977; Stoessinger, *Night Journey: A Story of Survival and Deliverance* (autobiography), Playboy Press, 1978.

STOKER, Alan 1930-
(Alan Evans)

PERSONAL: Born October 2, 1930, in Sunderland, Durham, England; son of Robert and Edith (Milne) Stoker; married Irene Evans, April 30, 1960; children: Neil Douglas, John Robert. *Education:* Attended schools in Sunderland, England, 1935-47. *Home:* 9 Dale Rd., Walton on Thames, Surrey, England. *Agent:* Murray Pollinger, 4 Garrick St., London WC2E 9BH, England.

CAREER: Civil servant in England, 1951—, currently as an executive officer. *Military service:* British Army, Royal Artillery, 1949-51. Army Reserve, 1951-73; became sergeant.

WRITINGS—Under pseudonym Alan Evans: *The End of the Running,* Cassell, 1966; *Mantrap,* Cassell, 1967; *Bannon,* Cassell, 1968; *Vicious Circle,* R. Hale, 1970; *The Big Deal,* R. Hale, 1971; *Running Scared,* Brokhampton Press, 1975; *Kidnap,* Hodder & Stoughton, 1976; *Thunder at Dawn,* Hodder & Stoughton, 1978; *Escape at the Devil's Gate,* Hodder & Stoughton, 1978; *Ship of Force,* Hodder & Stoughton, 1979; *Dauntless,* Hodder & Stoughton, 1980; *Seek Out and Destroy!,* Hodder & Stoughton, 1982.

WORK IN PROGRESS: Deed of Glory; a naval adventure novel.

AVOCATIONAL INTERESTS: Rugby football, beer ("hate gardening and any kind of work about the house").

* * *

STOLOFF, Carolyn 1927-

PERSONAL: Born January 14, 1927, in New York, N.Y.; daughter of Charles I. (a dentist) and Irma (a sculptor; maiden name, Levy) Stoloff. *Education:* Attended University of Illinois, 1944-46; Columbia University, B.S., 1949; study at Art Students League and Atelier 17; private study of painting with Eric Isenburger, Xavier Gozolez, and Hans Hofman, and of poetry with Stanley Kunitz. *Home:* 24 West 8th St., New York, N.Y. 10011. *Office:* 32 Union Sq. E., Room 911, New York, N.Y. 10003.

CAREER: Painter; has given group and solo shows. Manhattanville College, Purchase, N.Y., assistant professor of painting, 1957-74, chairman of art department, 1960-65, taught seminar in writing poetry. Conducted poetry seminars, 1968-74. Teacher at Baird House (a Quaker halfway house for drug addicts), 1973, and at a women's house of detention. Visiting writer, Stephens College, 1975; has given readings from her works at colleges, universities, libraries, and other public gatherings and on radio programs.

AWARDS, HONORS: Residence grants from MacDowell Colony fellowships, 1961, 1962, 1970, and 1976, Helene Wurlitzer Foundation 1972, 1973, and 1974, Ossabaw Island Project 1976, and Rhode Island Creative Arts Center 1981; Theodore Roethke Award from *Poetry Northwest,* 1967, for four poems; Silver Anniversary Medal, 1967, and Michael Engel Memorial Award, 1982, both from Audubon Artists show; National Council on the Arts grant, 1968; first prize for poetry from *Miscellany,* 1972; travel grant from Manhattanville College, 1972.

WRITINGS—Poems: *Stepping Out,* Unicorn Press, 1971; *In the Red Meadow* (chapbook), New Rivers Press, 1973; *Dying to Survive,* Doubleday, 1973; *Lighter-than-Night* (chapbook), Red Hill Press, 1977; *Swiftly Now,* Ohio University Press, 1982; *A Spool of Blue: New and Selected Poems,* Scarecrow Press, 1983. Also author of poetry broadside, "Triptych," Unicorn Press, 1970.

Contributor to anthologies: *The "New Yorker" Book of Poems,* Viking, 1969; *Our Only Hope Is Humor,* edited by Richard Snyder and Robert McGovern, Ashland Poetry Press, 1972; *Rising Tides,* edited by Laura Chester and Sharon Barba, Washington Square Press, 1973; *Alcatraz,* edited by John Engman, Burning Deck, 1980. Also contributor to *A Carpet of Sparrows,* edited by Sarah Provost, Nocturnal Canary Press.

Contributor of poems to popular magazines and literary journals, including *New Yorker, Nation, Antioch Review, Partisan Review, Chelsea, Kayak,* and *Choice.*

SIDELIGHTS: Carolyn Stoloff, daughter of an artist and musician mother, studied Indian and Spanish dancing and developed a deep interest in the opera, but found the greatest personal satisfaction in painting and, later, in poetry. Travels in Europe and Mexico have enhanced her already broad interest in the arts.

AVOCATIONAL INTERESTS: Ethnic music and dance, ancient history, books on animals and insects, identifying flowers and trees, European and South American poets in translation, conservation, handcrafts, films, travel.

* * *

STORY, G(eorge) M(orley) 1927-

PERSONAL: Born October 13, 1927, in St. John's, Newfoundland; son of George Errington (an accountant) and Dorothy Katherine (White) Story; married Laura Alice Stevenson, May 16, 1968; children: three. *Education:* Attended Memorial University College (now Memorial University of Newfoundland), 1946-48; McGill University, B.A. (with honors in English), 1950; Oxford University, D.Phil., 1954. *Politics:* Liberal Conservative. *Religion:* Methodist. *Home:* 335 Southside Rd., St. John's, Newfoundland, Canada.

CAREER: Memorial University of Newfoundland, St. John's, assistant professor, 1954-58, associate professor, 1959-63, professor of English, 1964—, Henrietta Harvey Professor, 1979—. Chairman, Newfoundland and Labrador Arts Council, 1977-82. Public orator, 1960—. *Member:* Royal Society of Canada (fellow), Royal Historical Society (fellow), Society of Antiquaries (fellow), Bibliographical Society of Great Britain. *Awards, honors:* Rhodes scholarship, 1951-53; Molson Prize, Canada Council, 1977.

WRITINGS: (With E. R. Seary) *Reading English,* Macmillan, 1958, revised edition published as *The Study of English,* St. Martin's, 1960; (editor with Helen Gardner) *The Sonnets of William Alabaster,* Oxford University Press, 1959; (editor) *Lancelot Andrewes: Sermons,* Clarendon Press, 1967; (with Seary and W. J. Kirwin) *The Avalon Peninsula of Newfoundland: An Ethno-linguistic Study,* National Museum of Canada, 1967; (editor with Herbert Halpert) *Christmas Mumming in Newfoundland: Essays in Anthropology, Folklore and History,* University of Toronto Press, 1969; (co-editor) *A Festschrift for Edgar Ronald Seary,* Memorial University of Newfoundland, 1977; (editor) *Early European Settlement and Exploitation in Atlantic Canada,* Memorial University of Newfoundland, 1982; (with W. J. Kirwin and J.D.A. Widdowson) *Dictionary of Newfoundland English,* University of Toronto Press, 1982.

WORK IN PROGRESS: A study of Newfoundland proverbs; textual criticism and bibliography; studies in Tudor literature and Renaissance humanism (especially Erasmus).

AVOCATIONAL INTERESTS: Collecting rare books, especially European humanist works; travel and gardening.

*　*　*

STRATFORD, H. Philip
See BULMER, (Henry) Kenneth

*　*　*

STRATTON, Thomas
See COULSON, Robert S(tratton) and DeWEESE, Thomas Eugene

*　*　*

STRINGFELLOW, (Frank) William 1928-

PERSONAL: Born April 26, 1928, in Johnston, R.I.; son of Frank (an industrial worker) and Margaret Ellen (Abbott) Stringfellow. *Education:* Bates College, A.B. (cum laude), 1949; attended London School of Economics, 1950; Harvard University, LL.B., 1956. *Politics:* Democrat. *Religion:* Episcopalian. *Home:* Penthouse One, 171 West 79th St., New York, N.Y.; and Eschaton, Block Island, R.I. 02807. *Office:* Ellis, Stringfellow & Patton, Suite 300, 41 East 42nd St., New York, N.Y.

CAREER: Admitted to New York State Bar, 1957, U.S. Supreme Court Bar, 1958, and Rhode Island State Bar, 1971; Tufts University, Medford, Mass., instructor, 1954-56; private practice of law in East Harlem, N.Y., 1957-60; Ellis, Stringfellow & Patton (counsellors-at-law), New York City, partner, 1961—. General counsel, George Henry Foundation, Christian Society for Drama, and Foundation for the Arts, Religion and Culture; former special deputy attorney general for New York City. Member of board of directors, George Henry Foundation, Laymen's Academy for Ecumenical Studies, Northern Student Movement, and Church Society of College Work. Member, Faith and Order Commission, World Council of Churches, 1962—; delegate, Synod of the Episcopal Church for the Second Province. Lecturer. *Military service:* U.S. Army, 1950-51, became sergeant.

MEMBER: American Bar Association, New York State Bar Association, Church Club (New York), Phi Beta Kappa. *Awards, honors:* Rotary Foundation fellow, 1950; citation for community service, East Harlem Youth Employment Service.

WRITINGS: A Private and Public Faith, Eerdmans, 1962; *Instead of Death,* Seabury, 1963, new edition, 1976; *My People Is the Enemy: An Autobiographical Polemic,* Holt, 1964; *Free in Obedience,* Seabury, 1964; *Dissenter in a Great Society: A Christian View of America in Crisis,* Holt, 1966; *Count It All Joy: Reflections on Faith, Doubt, and Temptation Seen through the Letter of James,* Eerdmans, 1967; (with Anthony Towne) *The Bishop Pike Affair: Scandals of Conscience and Heresy, Relevance and Solemnity in the Contemporary Church,* Harper, 1967; *Imposters of God: Inquires into Favorite Idols,* Pflaum, 1969.

A Second Birthday (autobiographical), Doubleday, 1970; (with Towne) *Suspect Tenderness: The Ethics of the Berrigan Witness* (autobiographical), Holt, 1971; *An Ethic for Christians and Other Aliens in a Strange Land,* Word, Inc., 1973; (with Towne) *The Death and Life of Bishop Pike,* Doubleday, 1976; *Conscience and Obedience: The Politics of Romans 13 and Revelation 13 in Light of the Second Coming,* Word, Inc., 1977.

Also author of material for cassette "Jerusalem or Babylon: Understanding America Biblically," Word, Inc., 1973. Contributor to law and theology publications.

WORK IN PROGRESS: A trilogy on the book of James, for Eerdmans.

SIDELIGHTS: In collaboration with poet Anthony Towne, lawyer William Stringfellow has written two books that examine in detail the public and private life of James Pike, perhaps the most controversial clergyman of the 1950s and 1960s. To those familiar with his name and reputation, explains Raymond A. Schroth in the *New York Times Book Review,* Pike was a man of many roles: "Columbia University chaplain, Dean of the Cathedral of St. John the Divine, Bishop of California, social activist, gadfly intellectual, TV personality, then, in a final behavior pattern that led some to question his sanity—ex-bishop, 'heretic,' worn-out self-publicist and mystic manque." In *The Bishop Pike Affair* and *The Death and Life of Bishop Pike,* Stringfellow and Towne (both personal friends of Pike's) approach their subject with undisguised affection and admiration, according to most critics. But as Roger Hazelton points out in the *New Republic,* "they do not allow their sympathies to warp their perspective."

Stringfellow and Towne's first joint project, *The Bishop Pike Affair,* focuses on the Episcopal clergyman's widely-publicized confrontations with the church hierarchy. For the most part, these confrontations occurred after Pike began making statements regarding certain points of religious doctrine. An outspoken liberal, he angered many of his fellow Episcopalians by challenging long-held beliefs about such concepts as the virgin birth and the Trinity. He caused further dismay among church members—and among many people outside the church—by taking then-unpopular stands on civil rights issues and the Vietnam War and by "pursuing and promoting" (to use Schroth's words) various intellectual and scientific fads (notably those involving extrasensory perception and other psychic phenomena).

By 1966, tensions had reached the point where some church leaders (led by a conservative Southern bishop) called for Pike to be tried on charges of heresy. For nearly a year, Episcopal officials debated whether or not to risk subjecting the church to the potentially damaging effects of such a trial. Eventually they decided only to censure Pike. As W. W. Bartley III contends in the *New York Review of Books,* however, this was still a victory for Pike; the compromise that had been worked out between those against a trial and those in favor of a trial (which included Pike himself) made "heresy trials virtually impossible within the Episcopal Church. . . . In practice, although not in principle, [it made] virtually any belief doctrinally permissible. . . . To such a free-thinking bishop such a result must have seemed worth a censure."

Though Bartley disagrees with the authors' "decision to cast [Pike] as the underdog in [this] battle for freedom of expression," the critic describes *The Bishop Pike Affair* as an "absorbing study" and "a lucid piece of reportage and analysis." In a *New York Times Book Review* article, E. B. Fiske remarks that it is "plausible" (as the authors maintain) that Pike was "attacked not for his alleged heresies, but for a variety of unstated reasons ranging from opposition to his liberal views on civil rights to personal jealousy"; Fiske believes that "it explains why there has never been a showdown in the church on [Pike's] theological assertions." The *New Republic*'s Hazelton and K. S. Latourette, who writes in the *Saturday Review*, both make note of the informative picture Stringfellow and Towne provide of the inner workings of the Episcopal Church. Hazelton, however, wonders how Pike could have been elected bishop in the first place if the church was as conservative as the authors insist. He suggests that they could have been "more generous in acknowledging this [fact of Pike's election]."

In their second book on Pike, *The Death and Life of Bishop Pike*, Stringfellow and Towne attempt a more comprehensive overview of the clergyman's private and public life. But as Schroth observes, what they have written is "not a formal biography but a virtually unedited, repetitious, loving but frank compilation of interviews, letters, speculation and polemics, as forensic and disconnected as their subject himself. Somehow, through the confusion, Pike comes back to life and reengages us in his cause."

The *New York Times*'s Richard R. Lingeman voices a similar opinion, stating: "[*The Death and Life of Bishop Pike*] is actually a welter of crosscurrents—part apologia, part spiritual brief, part act of homage and part ruthless act of candor. [Stringfellow and Towne] concede right away that their friendship for Bishop Pike disqualifies them from objectivity; further, they reject a conventional chronology, weaving their narrative around recurring threads in Pike's life, and what they call the 'redundancies' that marked his faith. They begin with their subject's death in 1969, while wandering lost in the Judean desert, then jump about among the bizarre and tragic events of Pike's last years. . . . This impressionistic—or associational—continuity is, not surprisingly, confusing to the reader, and implants an esthetic longing for a straightforward narrative in which events flow into their consequences. Still, there is much fascinating reporting in this section, which casts new lights on these events—not always flattering to Pike."

Charles Davis, writing in *Commonweal*, prefaces his remarks on Stringfellow and Towne's biography by saying that since he never met Bishop Pike, he does not feel qualified to judge "how far the personage of their narrative corresponds to the real, historical person." Though Davis does find their account of Pike's fascination with spiritualism "long and tedious," he concludes that on the whole *The Death and Life of Bishop Pike* "is well-written, the documentation without apparent gaps and, judged by internal criteria, the interpretation plausible, consistent and honest."

Perhaps the ultimate compliment to Pike's biographers comes from critic Webster Schott. Observes Schott in his *Washington Post Book World* review: "Part of the literary establishment springing from the new Christianity, William Stringfellow and Anthony Towne loved Pike dearly. They defended him in life. In biography they want Pike whole—and to toss a few grenades at the hypocrites and moneychangers who condemned him. They catch Pike so completely that no one needs to do this job again. He planned to write his autobiography under the title *Nothing to Hide*. They're faithful to his intent."

BIOGRAPHICAL/CRITICAL SOURCES: *Time*, September 22, 1958, January 25, 1963, June 28, 1976; *Presbyterian Life*, February 1, 1961; William Stringfellow, *My People Is the Enemy: An Autobiographical Polemic*, Holt, 1964; *Harper's*, May, 1964; *Best Sellers*, June 1, 1964, October 1, 1970; *Book Week*, July 12, 1964, August 21, 1966; *New York Times Book Review*, July 12, 1964, October 15, 1967, August 1, 1976; *Christian Science Monitor*, August 19, 1966; *Saturday Review*, November 12, 1966, September 16, 1967; *New Republic*, October 7, 1967, November 20, 1971; *New York Review of Books*, November 23, 1967; Stringfellow, *A Second Birthday*, Doubleday, 1970; *Christian Century*, September 23, 1970, February 17, 1971, February 16, 1972; *Commonweal*, December 11, 1970, April 14, 1972, January 21, 1977; *Washington Post*, December 18, 1970; Stringfellow and Anthony Towne, *Suspect Tenderness: The Ethics of the Berrigan Witness*, Holt, 1971; *New York Times*, August 13, 1976; *Washington Post Book World*, August 22, 1976.†

—Sketch by Deborah A. Straub

* * *

STROTHER, Pat Wallace 1929-
(Pat Wallace Latner, Pat Wallace; Patricia Cloud, Vivian Lord, pseudonyms)

PERSONAL: Born March 11, 1929, in Birmingham, Ala.; daughter of Claude Hunter (in insurance) and Gladys Eleanor (English) Wallace; married Lee Levitt (a public relations executive), June, 1951 (divorced, 1957); married David G. Latner, August, 1958 (divorced, 1969); married Robert A. Strother (a building contractor), July, 1980; stepchildren: (third marriage) Robert, Andrea, Douglas. *Education:* Attended University of Tennessee, 1947-51, and Columbia University, 1962. *Politics:* Liberal Democrat. *Religion:* None. *Home:* 117 West 13th St., New York, N.Y. 10011. *Agent:* Jane Rotrosen Agency, 226 East 32nd St., New York, N.Y. 10016.

CAREER: WGNS-Radio, Murfreesboro, Tenn., women's program director, 1951-52; WMAK-Radio, Nashville, Tenn., copy chief and announcer, 1952-54; *Civil Service Leader*, New York City, assistant to editor, 1955-57; International Brotherhood of Teamsters, Local Union 237, New York City, secretary to the president, 1957-76; full-time writer, 1975—. *Member:* American Astrological Association, Authors Guild, Authors League of America.

WRITINGS—Under name Pat Wallace: *House of Scorpio*, Avon, 1975; *The Wand and the Star*, Pocket Books, 1978; *Silver Fire*, Silhouette Romances, 1982; *My Loving Enemy*, Silhouette Romances, 1983.

Under pseudonym Patricia Cloud: *This Willing Passion*, Putnam, 1978.

Under pseudonym Vivian Lord; published by Fawcett: *Traitor in My Arms*, 1979; *The Voyagers*, 1980; *Once More the Sun*, 1982; *Summer Kingdom*, 1983.

Contributor of short stories, under name Pat Wallace Latner, and poems to popular magazines, including *Mademoiselle*, *Beloit Poetry Journal*, and *Canadian Forum*.

SIDELIGHTS: "I started writing poetry at eleven," Pat Wallace Strother told *CA*, "and this was my major interest until 1971, when I began writing novels and invented the astrological novel genre. My interest in astrology goes back to 1963 when Ree Dragonette . . . introduced me to the subject. Though I am not a professional astrologer, my studies and observations have been intense."

In the *Washington Post Book World*, Henry McDonald praises *Traitor in My Arms* for its "inspired treatment of its heroine," and concludes: "Other authors of 'western historical romance novels' would do well to follow [Strother's] lead."

BIOGRAPHICAL/CRITICAL SOURCES: Washington Post Book World, March 4, 1979.

* * *

STUHLMUELLER, Carroll 1923-

PERSONAL: Born April 2, 1923, in Hamilton, Ohio; son of William and Alma (Huesing) Stuhlmueller. *Education:* Attended Passionist seminaries in St. Louis, Mo., Detroit, Mich., Chicago, Ill., and Louisville, Ky., 1936-50; Catholic University of America, S.T.L., 1952; Pontifical Biblical Institute, Rome, Italy, S.S.L., 1954, S.S.D., 1968. *Office:* Catholic Theological Union, 5401 S. Cornell Ave., Chicago, Ill. 60615.

CAREER: Roman Catholic priest of Passionist order; Passionist Seminary, Chicago, Ill., teacher of scripture and Hebrew, 1954-58; Viatorian Seminary, Evanston, Ill., assistant professor of scripture, 1955-58; Passionist Seminary, Louisville, Ky., professor of scripture, 1958-65; Loretto Junior College, Nerinx, Ky., assistant professor of scripture and history, 1959-65; St. Meinrad Seminary, St. Meinrad, Ind., professor of scripture and Hebrew, 1965-68; Catholic Theological Union, Chicago, professor of Old Testament, 1968—. Member of summer faculty, Graduate School of Theology, St. Mary's College, Notre Dame, Ind., 1957-64; member of fall faculty, St. John's University, New York, N.Y., 1970-75. Visiting professor, Ecole Biblique et Archeologique, Jerusalem, 1973, and Winter Theological School, South Africa, summer, 1973. *Member:* Catholic Biblical Association of America (president, 1979), Catholic Theological Society of America, Society of Biblical Literature, National Council of Churches (Catholic member of Faith and Order Commission, 1970-73).

WRITINGS: The Gospel of St. Luke, Liturgical Press, 1960, 2nd edition, 1964; *Leviticus,* Paulist Press, 1960; *Postexilic Prophets,* Paulist Press, 1961; *The Books of Aggai, Zacharia, Malachia, Jona, Joel, Abdia, with a Commentary,* Paulist Press, 1961; *The Prophets and the Word of God,* Fides, 1964, 2nd edition, 1966; (editor) Barnabas Ahern, *New Horizons,* Fides, 1963; *Book of Isaiah,* Liturgical Press, 1964; (contributor) *Jerome Biblical Commentary,* Prentice-Hall, 1968; *Creative Redemption in Deutero-Isaiah,* Biblical Institute Press, 1970; *The Books of Jeremiah and Baruch: Introduction and Commentary,* Liturgical Press, 1971; *Prophets: Charismatic Men,* Argus, 1972; *Biblical Inspiration: Divine-Human Phenomenon,* Argus, 1972; (co-editor) *The Bible Today Reader,* Liturgical Press, 1973; *Reconciliation: A Biblical Call,* Franciscan Herald, 1975; *Isaiah,* Franciscan Herald, 1976; *Thirsting for the Lord: Essays in Biblical Spirituality,* Alba House, 1977, 2nd edition, Doubleday, 1980; *The Psalms,* Franciscan Herald, 1979; *Biblical Meditations for the Easter Season,* Paulist Press, 1980; *Biblical Meditations for Advent and the Christmas Season,* Paulist Press, 1980; (with Donald Senior) *Biblical Foundations of Mission,* Orbis, 1982. Also co-editor of *Old Testament Reading Guide,* Liturgical Press.

Editor, with Martin McNamara, of "Old Testament Message" series, 23 volumes, Michael Glazier. Contributor to *The New Catholic Encyclopedia,* McGraw, 1966. Contributor to Catholic journals. *Bible Today,* member of editorial board, 1965-80, editor, 1980—; member of editorial board, *Catholic Biblical Quarterly,* 1974-78.

WORK IN PROGRESS: A two-volume commentary on Psalms.

STURGEON, Foolbert
See STACK, Frank H(untington)

* * *

STURGILL, Claude C(arol) 1933-

PERSONAL: Surname is pronounced *Stir*-jill; born December 9, 1933, in Glo, Ky.; son of Gomer C. (an attorney) and Luvenia (McComas) Sturgill; married Carrollton Sue Harrison (a teacher of mathematics), September 3, 1956; children: Bonnie Lou, Mary Elizabeth, Virginia Ann, Catherine Elma. *Education:* University of Kentucky, A.B., 1956, M.A., 1959, Ph.D., 1963. *Politics:* Republican. *Religion:* Roman Catholic. *Home:* 630 Northeast Tenth Ave., Gainesville, Fla. 32601. *Office:* Department of History, University of Florida, Gainesville, Fla. 32601.

CAREER: University of Kentucky, Lexington, instructor in history, 1961; Western Kentucky State College (now Western Kentucky University), Bowling Green, instructor, 1962-63, assistant professor of history, 1963-64; Wisconsin State University—Oshkosh (now University of Wisconsin—Oshkosh), assistant professor of French history, 1964-66; East Carolina University, Greenville, N.C., associate professor, 1966-69; University of Florida, Gainesville, associate professor, 1969-77, professor of history, 1977—. Fulbright professor in France, 1980; professor, Centre de Recherches sur la Civilisation de l'Europe Moderne, University of Paris. Member of board of directors, Conference Group for Social and Administrative History, 1971—; member of board of governors, Interuniversity Consortium for the Study of Revolutions: 1750-1850, 1972-77; U.S. Commission on Military History, member of board of trustees, 1973-75, permanent secretary-treasurer, 1973-79. *Military service:* U.S. Army, 1956-58; became first lieutenant.

MEMBER: American Historical Association, French Historical Association, Florida Teachers of College History (secretary-treasurer, 1972-75), Phi Alpha Theta, Phi Sigma Iota, Tau Kappa Delta. *Awards, honors:* Research grants from Kentucky Research Council, 1961, Western Kentucky State College, 1962 and 1963, Wisconsin State University Regents Fund, 1964, and National Endowment for the Humanities, 1968.

WRITINGS: Marshal Villars and the War of the Spanish Succession, University Press of Kentucky, 1965; (author, with Donald W. Hensel, of study guide) S. B. Clough and others, *A History of the Western World,* Heath, 1969, 3rd edition published as *European History in a World Perspective,* 1975; (editor with Lee Kennett) *Proceedings of the Interuniversity Consortium on Revolutionary Europe: 1750-1850,* University of Florida Press, Volume I, 1973, Volume II, 1975, Volume III, 1977; *Claude le Blanc: Civil Servant of the King,* University of Florida Press, 1976; (editor) *Rolle's Petition,* University of Florida Press, 1977; *La Formation de la milice permanente en France, 1726-1730,* Service Historique de l'Armee de Terre et la Faculte des Lettres, Mans, 1977; *L'Organisation et l'administration de la marechaussee et de la justice prevotale,* Service Historique de l'Armee de Terre et la Faculte des Lettres, Mans, 1980; *Le Financement de l'armee de Louis XVe: Les Operations des commissaires des guerres, 1715-1730,* Service Historique de l'Armee de Terre, 1983.

Contributor to proceedings and to professional publications in Europe and the United States. Member of editorial board, *Revue Historique de l'Armee,* 1969-79, and *Societas: A Review of Social History,* 1971—.

WORK IN PROGRESS: Research for *The Little War with Spain, 1718-1720.*

* * *

SUGAR, Bert Randolph 1937-
(John Brooks, Suzanne Davis)

PERSONAL: Born June 7, 1937, in Washington, D.C.; son of Harold Randolph and Anne Edith (Rosensweig) Sugar; married Suzanne Davis (an art teacher and artist), November 22, 1960; children: Jennifer Anne, John-Brooks Randolph. *Education:* Attended Harvard University, 1956; University of Maryland, B.S., 1957; University of Michigan, M.B.A., 1959, LL.B., 1960, J.D., 1960; American University, Ph.D. candidate. *Politics:* Registered Republican. *Religion:* Congregationalist. *Home:* Six Southview Rd., Chappaqua, N.Y. 10514. *Office:* The Ring, 120 West 31st St., New York, N.Y. 10001.

CAREER: Private law practice in Washington, D.C., 1961-63; affiliated with Erickson Advertising Agency, Washington, D.C., 1963-64, J. Walter Thompson (advertising agency), New York City, 1964-65, and Papert Koenig Lois (advertising agency), New York City, 1965-66; McGraw-Hill, *Dimensions in Living* magazine, New York City, editor, 1966; D'Arcy, MacManus & Masius (advertising agency), New York City, director of marketing and vice-president, 1967-70; Champion Sports (publishing firm), New York City, editor and publisher, 1970-73; *Argosy,* New York City, editor-in-chief, 1973-75; Baron, Costello & Fine (advertising agency), New York City, senior vice-president, 1975-77; *The Ring* magazine, New York City, publisher and editor, 1977—. *Member:* American Political Items Collectors Society, Football Writers, Basketball Writers, Boxing Writers, Alpha Delta Sigma.

WRITINGS: (With Jackie Kannon) *Where Were You When the Lights Went Out?,* Kanrom Publishing, 1966; (with Jose Torres and Norman Mailer) *. . . Sting Like a Bee,* Abelard, 1971; (with Floyd Patterson) *Inside Boxing,* Regnery, 1972; *The Sports Collectors Bible,* Wallace-Homestead, 1975; (with Sybil Leek) *The Assassination Chain,* Sterling, 1976; *Who Was Harry Steinfeldt? and Other Baseball Trivia Questions,* Playboy Press, 1976; *The Horseplayers' Guide to Winning Systems,* Corwin, 1976; *Houdini: His Life and Art,* Grosset, 1976; *The Thrill of Victory,* Hawthorn, 1976; *Classic Baseball Cards,* Dover, 1977; *Hit the Sign and Win a Free Suit of Clothes from Harry Finklestein,* Contemporary Books, 1978; *The SEC,* Bobbs-Merrill, 1978; *Nostalgia Collectors Bible,* Putnam, 1980; *Boxing's Greatest Fights,* A. W. Smith, 1981; *505 Boxing Questions,* Walker, 1982; *Boxing's One Hundred Years,* A. W. Smith, 1982. Contributor, sometimes under pseudonyms, to magazines.

WORK IN PROGRESS: Boxing's Greatest; The World's Fair Book; revised edition of *The Sports Collectors Bible.*

SIDELIGHTS: Bert Randolph Sugar told *CA:* "The joy of writing is something no one with an executive mind can understand. It is not delegatable, not something to be decided by committee, nor is it an act to be subjected to the approval of bureaucratic layers of naysayers. Instead, writing is the most fun one can have with his clothes on, although there are times it is so lonely that a writer may have to resort to accepting reverse charge phone calls from heavy breathers."

AVOCATIONAL INTERESTS: Antiques.

SULEIMAN, Michael W(adie) 1934-

PERSONAL: Born February 26, 1934, in Tiberias, Palestine; son of Wadie Michael and Jameeleh (Ailabouny) Suleiman; married Penelope Ann Powers (a bacteriologist), August 31, 1963; children: Suad Michelle, Gibran Michael. *Education:* Bradley University, B.A., 1960; University of Wisconsin, M.S., 1962, Ph.D., 1965. *Home:* 427 Wickham Rd., Manhattan, Kan. 66502. *Office:* Department of Political Science, Kansas State University, Manhattan, Kan. 66506.

CAREER: Kansas State University, Manhattan, assistant professor, 1965-68, associate professor, 1968-72, professor of political science, 1972—, head of department, 1975-82. Member of Midwest Conference of Political Scientists, and American Research Center in Egypt. Traveling fellowship from University of Wisconsin, 1963-64, and from American Philosophical Society, 1974. Research fellowship from Kansas State University, summer, 1966; research associate, University of Denver-Social Science Foundation, summer, 1968. Guest lecturer for various organizations and institutions, including University of Wisconsin, University of California, Berkeley, and Middle East Studies Association. Has reviewed grant proposals for Institute of International Education, Department of Health, Education and Welfare, American Research Center in Egypt, Radcliffe Institute for Independent Study, National Endowment for the Humanities, and National Science Foundation. Member of committee on Middle East images in secondary school texts, 1972-75; chairperson of Middle East Studies Association committee on pre-collegiate education, 1975-78; also member of various academic and administrative committees at Kansas State University.

MEMBER: American Political Science Association, Middle East Institute, Middle East Studies Association of North America (member of board of directors, 1980—), Midwest Political Science Association. *Awards, honors:* Ford Foundation fellowship, 1969-70; American Research Center in Egypt fellowship, 1972-73.

WRITINGS: Political Parties in Lebanon: The Challenge of a Fragmented Political Culture, Cornell University Press, 1967; *American Images of Middle East Peoples: Impact of the High School,* Middle East Studies Association, 1977.

Contributor: Elaine C. Hagopian and Ann Paden, editors, *The Arab-Americans: Studies in Assimilation,* Medina University Press, 1969; T. Y. Ismael, editor, *Governments and Politics of the Contemporary Middle East,* Dorsey, 1970; Ibrahim Abu-Lughod, editor, *The Arab-Israeli Confrontation of June, 1967: An Arab Perspective,* Northwestern University Press, 1970; Michael H. Prosser, editor, *Intercommunication Among Nations and Peoples,* Harper, 1973; Baha Abu-Laban and Faith Zeadey, editors, *Arabs in America: Myths and Realities,* Medina University Press, 1975; Fouad Moughrabi and Naseer Aruri, editors, *Lebanon: Crisis and Challenge in the Arab World,* AAUG, 1977; *Man and Society in the Arab Gulf,* Basrah University, 1979; Michael C. Hudson and Ronald G. Wolfe, editors, *The American Mass Media and the Arabs,* Georgetown University, 1980.

Also author of *Guide to a Correspondence Course in International Relations,* 1966. Contributor to numerous political science journals, including *American Political Science Review, American Journal of Sociology, Arab Studies Quarterly,* and *Western Political Quarterly*. Member of editorial board of *Arab*

Studies Quarterly, 1979—, *Journal of Arab Affairs*, 1980—, and *International Journal of Middle East Studies*, 1982—.

WORK IN PROGRESS: Research on political socialization in the Arab world; a study of values and the process of inculcation of values in the young; a comprehensive study of Arab-Americans.

SIDELIGHTS: Michael W. Suleiman speaks Arabic and has reading knowledge of French. His articles have been translated into Arabic and the main European languages, and he has appeared repeatedly as a guest commentator or panelist on the National Public Radio and many local and regional radio and television stations as well.

* * *

SUSKIND, Richard 1925-

PERSONAL: Born May 2, 1925, in New York, N.Y.; son of Herman R. (a furrier) and Ruth (Raphael) Suskind. *Education:* Attended University of Paris, University of Florence, and Columbia University. *Religion:* Jewish.

CAREER: Merchant seaman, 1950-53; associate editor, *Cavalier*, 1959-60; senior technical writer, 1962; editor-in-chief, *Saga*. *Military service:* U.S. Army, 1943-46; received Combat Infantry Badge.

WRITINGS: The Crusades, Ballantine, 1962; *Do You Want to Live Forever?*, Bantam, 1964; *Cross and Crescent: The Story of the Crusades*, Norton, 1967; *Men in Armor: The Story of Knights and Knighthood* (juvenile), Norton, 1968; *The Battle of Belleau Wood: The Marines Stand Fast*, Macmillan, 1969; *Swords, Spears, and Sandals: The Story of the Roman Legions* (juvenile), Norton, 1969.

The Barbarians: The Story of the European Tribes (juvenile), Norton, 1970; *The Sword of the Prophet: The Story of the Moslem Empire* (juvenile), Grosset, 1971; *By Bullet, Bomb, and Dagger: The Story of Anarchism*, Macmillan, 1971; (with Clifford Irving) *Clifford Irving: What Really Happened, His Untold Story of the Hughes Affair*, Grove, 1972; *The Crusader King: Richard the Lionhearted* (juvenile), Little, Brown, 1973.

SIDELIGHTS: Richard Suskind is fluent in French, Italian, and Spanish.†

* * *

SWETS, John A(rthur) 1928-

PERSONAL: Born June 19, 1928, in Grand Rapids, Mich.; son of John A. and Sara Henrietta (Heyns) Swets; married Maxine Ruth Crawford, July 16, 1949; children: Stephen Arthur, Joel Brian. *Education:* University of Michigan, B.A., 1950, M.A., 1953, Ph.D., 1954. *Home:* 35 Myopia Hill Rd., Winchester, Mass. 01890.

CAREER: University of Michigan, Ann Arbor, instructor in psychology, faculty consultant to Electronic Defense Group, and staff member of Annual Linguistic Institute, 1954-56; Massachusetts Institute of Technology, Cambridge, began as assistant professor of psychology, became associate professor and project supervisor in Research Laboratory of Electronics, 1956-63; Bolt Beranek and Newman, Inc., Cambridge, consultant, 1958-63, supervisory scientist, 1962-64, director of Information Sciences Division and vice-president, 1964-69, senior vice-president, 1969-74, general manager of research, development, and consulting services and director, 1971-74, chief scientist, 1975—. Summer visiting research fellow, Instituut voor Perceptie Onderzoek, Eindhoven, Netherlands, 1958; Regents' Professor, University of California, 1969. National Academy of Sciences-National Research Council, member of Committee on Hearing and Bioacoustics and member of Vision Committee.

MEMBER: Acoustical Society of America (fellow), American Association for the Advancement of Science (fellow), American Psychological Association (fellow), Psychonomic Society, Psychometric Society, Evaluation Research Society, Society for Medical Decision Making, Eastern Psychological Association, Psychonomic Society, Psychometric Society, Sigma Xi.

WRITINGS: (Editor) *Signal Detection and Recognition by Human Observers*, Wiley, 1964; (with D. M. Green) *Signal Detection Theory and Psychophysics*, Wiley, 1966; (editor with L. L. Elliott) *Psychology and the Handicapped Child*, U.S. Government Printing Office, 1974; (with R. M. Pickett) *Evaluation of Diagnostic Systems*, Academic Press, 1982.

Contributor: (With Green) Colin Cherry, editor, *Information Theory*, Buttersworth Scientific Publications (London), 1961; G. A. Miller, editor, *Mathematics and Psychology*, Wiley, 1964; B. F. Lomov, editor, *Detection and Recognition of Signals*, Moscow University Press, 1966; M. Kochen, editor, *The Growth of Knowledge*, Wiley, 1967; W. Edwards and A. Tversky, editors, *Decision Making*, Penguin, 1967; R. N. Haber, editor, *Contemporary Theory and Research in Visual Perception*, Holt, 1968; B. Drake, editor, *Sensory Evaluation of Food: Principles and Methods*, Rydbert, 1969; F. Bresson and M. DeMontmollin, editors, *The Simulation of Human Behavior*, Dunod, 1969.

T. Saracevic, editor, *Introduction to Information Science*, Bowker, 1970; M. H. Appley, editor, *Adaptation-Level Theory: A Symposium*, Academic Press, 1971; W. C. Howell and I. L. Goldstein, editors, *Engineering Psychology: Current Perspectives in Research*, Appleton-Century-Crofts, 1971; W. S. Cain and L. E. Marks, editors, *Stimulus and Sensation: Readings in Psychology*, Little-Brown, 1971; T. W. Christina and L. G. Shaver, editors, *Biological and Psychological Perspectives in the Study of Human Motor Behavior*, Kendall/Hunt, 1972; J. A. Jacquez, editor, *Computer Diagnosis and Diagnostic Methods*, C. C Thomas, 1972; G. M. Murch, editor, *Studies in Perception*, Bobbs-Merrill, 1976; H. G. Geissler and Y. M. Zabrodin, editors, *Advances in Psychophysics*, VEB Deutscher Verlag der Wissenschaften, 1976; R. R. Mackie, editor, *Vigilance: Relationships among Theory, Physiological Coorelates and Operational Performance*, Plenum, 1977; H. L. Pick, Jr., and others, editors, *Psychology: From Research to Practice*, Plenum, 1978; E. D. Schubert, editor, *Psychological Acoustics*, Dowden, 1979.

B. Griffith, editor, *Key Papers in Information Science*, Knowledge Industry Publications, 1980; R. S. Nickerson, editor, *Attention and Performance VIII*, Lawrence Erlbaum, 1980; K. L. Ripley and A. Murray, editors, *Introduction to Automated Arrhythmia Detection*, IEEE Computer Society Press, 1980; D. J. Getty and J. H. Howard, Jr., editors, *Auditory and Visual Pattern Recognition*, Lawrence Erlbaum, 1981; Geissler and P. Petzold, editors, *Psychophysical Judgment and the Process of Perception*, North-Holland Publishing (Amsterdam), 1982; R. Parasuraman, R. Davies, and J. Beatty, editors, *Varieties of Attention*, Academic Press, in press.

Also author of scientific papers and reports for University of Michigan, Massachusetts Institute of Technology, and government scientific groups. Contributor to *Encyclopedia of Science and Technology,* McGraw, 1971, 1982, and to professional journals, including *Science.*

* * *

SZASZ, Thomas (Stephen) 1920-

PERSONAL: Surname is pronounced Sass; born April 15, 1920, in Budapest, Hungary; came to United States in 1938, naturalized in 1944; son of Julius (a businessman) and Lily (Welisch) Szasz; married Rosine Loshkajian, October 19, 1951 (divorced, 1970); children: Margot, Susan. *Education:* University of Cincinnati, A.B. (with honors), 1941, M.D., 1944; Chicago Institute for Psychoanalysis, certificate, 1950. *Home:* 4739 Limberlost Lane, Manlius, N.Y. 13104. *Agent:* McIntosh & Otis, Inc., 475 Fifth Ave., New York, N.Y. 10017. *Office:* Upstate Medical Center, 750 East Adams St., Syracuse, N.Y. 13210.

CAREER: Diplomate, National Board of Medical Examiners, 1945, American Board of Psychiatry and Neurology, 1951; Boston City Hospital, Boston, Mass., intern, 1944-45; Cincinnati General Hospital, Cincinnati, Ohio, assistant resident, 1945-46, clinician, 1946; University of Chicago Clinics, Chicago, Ill., assistant resident in psychiatry, 1946-48; Chicago Institute for Psychoanalysis, Chicago, Ill., staff member, 1951-56; State University of New York, Upstate Medical Center, Syracuse, professor of psychiatry, 1956—; private practice of psychology and psychiatry in Chicago, Ill., 1949-54, Bethesda, Md., 1954-56, Syracuse, N.Y., 1956—.

Fellow, Postgraduate Center for Mental Health, 1962; visiting professor, University of Wisconsin—Madison, 1962, Marquette University, 1968, University of New Mexico, 1981; senior scholar, Eli Lilly Foundation, 1966—; Civil Liberties Carey Lecturer, Cornell University Law School, 1968; C. P. Snow Lecturer, Ithaca University, 1970; Root Tilden Lecturer, New York University School of Law, 1971; Noel Buxton Lectureship, University of Essex, 1975; Robert S. Marx Lectureship, University of Cincinnati College of Law, 1976; Hardy Chair Lectureship, Hartwick College, 1976; E. S. Meyer Memorial Lecturer, University of Queensland Medical School, 1977; delivered Lambie-Dew Oration, Sydney University, 1977. Honorary president, International Commission for Human Rights, London, 1974. Member of board of directors, National Council on Crime and Delinquency; member of research advisory panel, Institute for the Study of Drug Addiction; member of national advisory committee, Living Libraries, Inc.; member of advisory board, corporation for Economic Education, 1977—. *Military service:* U.S. Naval Reserve, 1954-56, became commander.

MEMBER: International Psychoanalytic Association, International Academy of Forensic Psychology (fellow), American Psychiatric Association (fellow), American Psychoanalytic Association, Mark Twain Society (honorary member), Alpha Omega Alpha. *Awards, honors:* Ralph Kharas Award, Central New York Chapter, American Civil Liberties Union, 1967; Holmes-Munsterberg Award from International Academy of Forensic Psychology, 1969; Wisdom Award of Honor, 1970; Academy Prize from Institutum atque Academia Auctorum Internationalis, 1972; Humanist of the Year Award from American Humanist Association, 1973; Second Annual Independence Day Award for the Greatest Public Service Benefiting the Disadvantaged from American Institute for Public Service, 1974; Martin Buber Award, Midway Counseling Center, 1974; honorary doctorate, Allegheny College, 1975, and Universidad Francisco Marroquin, 1979.

WRITINGS: Pain and Pleasure: A Study of Bodily Feelings, Basic Books, 1957; *The Myth of Mental Illness: Foundations of a Theory of Personal Conduct,* Harper, 1961, revised edition, 1974; *Law, Liberty, and Psychiatry: An Inquiry into the Social Uses of Mental Health Practices,* Macmillan, 1963; *Psychiatric Justice,* Macmillan, 1965; *The Ethics of Psychoanalysis: The Theory and Method of Autonomous Psychotherapy,* Basic Books, 1965, reprinted with a new preface, 1974; *Ideology and Insanity: Essays on the Psychiatric Dehumanization of Man,* Doubleday, 1970; *The Manufacture of Madness: A Comparative Study of the Inquisition and the Mental Health Movement,* Harper, 1970; *The Second Sin,* Doubleday, 1973; (editor) *The Age of Madness: A History of Involuntary Mental Hospitalization Presented in Selected Texts,* Doubleday, 1973.

Ceremonial Chemistry: The Ritual Persecution of Drugs, Addicts, and Pushers, Doubleday, 1976; *Heresies,* Doubleday, 1976; *Karl Kraus and the Soul-Doctors: A Pioneer Critic and His Criticism of Psychiatry and Psychoanalysis,* Louisiana State University Press, 1976; *Schizophrenia: The Sacred Symbol of Psychiatry,* Basic Books, 1976; *Psychiatric Slavery: When Confinement and Coercion Masquerade as Cure,* Free Press, 1977; *The Theology of Medicine: The Political-Philosophical Foundations of Medical Ethics,* Louisiana State University Press, 1977; *The Myth of Psychotherapy: Mental Healing as Religion, Rhetoric, and Repression,* Doubleday, 1978; *Sex by Prescription,* Doubleday, 1980 (published in the United Kingdom as *Sex: Facts, Frauds, and Follies,* Blackwell, 1981).

Contributor to professional journals and to popular publications, including *Harper's, New Republic,* and *New York Times.* Member of editorial board, *Contemporary Psychoanalysis, Earth, Free Inquiry, Psychotherapy, Journal of Forensic Psychology, Journal of Humanistic Psychology, Journal of Law and Human Behavior, Psychoanalytic Review, Science Digest, Journal of Libertarian Studies, Children and Youth Services Review, Journal of Mind and Behavior.* Contributing editor, *Reason, Inquiry.*

SIDELIGHTS: Several critics believe that Thomas Szasz has, in effect, started a war on psychiatry as it is currently practiced in the United States. In his book *The Myth of Mental Illness,* Szasz argues, notes Edwin M. Schur in *Atlantic,* "that both our uses of the term 'mental illness' and the activities of the psychiatric profession are often scientifically untenable and morally and socially indefensible." Szasz believes that mental illness differs from organic illness, and he calls the former "problems of living." He believes psychiatrists have glossed over these differences and continue to treat mental disturbances as medical problems. They impose the definition "mentally ill" on a person instead of treating the illness as an objective fact.

Szasz further believes that anyone brought to trial for a criminal offense should be allowed to stand trial instead of, as sometimes happens, being submitted to a pretrial psychiatric examination and then being committed to a mental institution. In fact, he would have the plea of insanity abolished. Nor does he accept dangerousness to oneself as a legitimate basis for institutionalization. He writes: "In a free society, a person must have the right to injure or kill himself." As for dangerousness to others, Schur notes that Szasz expounds on those not incarcerated who are equally as dangerous to others, and cites drunken drivers as one example. Schur writes: "A person's 'dangerousness' becomes a matter for legitimate public control, Szasz argues, only when he actually commits a dangerous act. Then he can be dealt with in accordance with regular criminal law."

Other psychiatrists have called his work "reckless iconoclasm," "reprehensible," and "dangerous." Lawyers, including Arthur Goldberg, praise him. His sole concern, says Schur, is the protection of the individual. Szasz believes that "the poor need jobs and money, not psychoanalysis. The uneducated need knowledge and skills, not psychoanalysis." Though his arguments are often stated in their extreme forms, Schur believes that Szasz "quite probably . . . has done more than any other man to alert the American public to the potential dangers of an excessively psychiatrized society."

Of his own work Szasz says: "I have tried to make two separate and yet connected points. The first point is that not only is mental illness *not* 'like any other illness,' as conventional wisdom now has it, but that mental illness does not exist: the term is a metaphor and belief in it and its implications is a mythology—indeed, it is the central mythology of psychiatry. The second point is that as a profession and as a social enterprise, psychiatry is neither a science nor a healing art but is rather a powerful arm of the modern nation state. The paradigmatic functions of the psychiatrist are inculpating and imprisoning innocent persons, called 'civil commitment,' and exculpating guilty persons and then often imprisoning them too (ostensibly for the 'treatment' of the illness that 'caused' their criminal conduct), called the 'insanity defense' and 'insanity verdict.'

"On conceptual, moral and political grounds I oppose these and all other coercive uses of psychiatry. Involuntary psychiatry is an enemy of liberty and responsibility. Morally and legally the only sexual relations we now regard as legitimate are those between consenting adults. Similarly, we should regard only psychiatric relations between consenting adults as morally and legally legitimate."

BIOGRAPHICAL/CRITICAL SOURCES: New Republic, August 7, 1965; *New York Times Book Review,* August 22, 1965; *Atlantic,* June, 1966; *Toronto Daily Star,* June 20, 1966; *American Journal of Psychiatry,* April, 1969; *New Physician,* June, 1969; *Indiana Legal Forum,* fall, 1969; *Minnesota Mental Health Retardation Newsletter,* October, 1969; *Washington Post,* March 6, 1970; *New Scientist and Science Journal,* June 3, 1971; *New York Times Magazine,* October 3, 1971; *She,* February, 1972; *Human Behavior,* July/August, 1972; *World Medicine,* October 4, 1972; *Penthouse,* October, 1973; *Los Angeles Times Book Review,* October 12, 1980; *Times Literary Supplement,* August 18, 1981.

T

TAHLAQUAH, David
See LeMOND, Alan

* * *

TALBOT, Norman (Clare) 1936-

PERSONAL: Born September 14, 1936, in Gislingham, Suffolk, England; son of Francis Harold (a farm laborer) and Agnes (Rampley) Talbot; married Jean Margaret Perkins (a part-time lecturer), August 17, 1960; children: Clare Elizabeth, Nicholas John, Ruth Catherine. *Education:* Hatfield College, Durham, B.A. (with first class honors), 1959; University of Leeds, Ph.D., 1962; post-doctoral study at Yale University, 1967-68. *Politics:* Pacifist Socialist. *Religion:* Society of Friends. *Home:* 54 Addison Rd., New Lambton, New South Wales, Australia. *Office:* University of Newcastle, New South Wales, Australia.

CAREER: University of Newcastle, New South Wales, Australia, lecturer, 1963-69, senior lecturer, 1969-73, associate professor of English, 1973—. Presented two television series on Shakespeare, Sydney, Australia. Commentator on "The Word This Week," a verbal arts program on Newcastle Community Radio. *Member:* Australian Universities' Languages and Literature Association, Australasian Victorian Studies Association, South Pacific Association for Commonwealth Literature and Language Studies, William Morris Society, Association for the Study of Australian Literature. *Awards, honors:* Gregory Award for poetry, 1965; American Council of Learned Societies fellowship to Yale University, 1967-68.

WRITINGS—Poetry, except as indicated: *The Seafolding of Harri Jones,* Nimrod Publications, 1965; *The Major Poems of John Keats* (criticism), University of Sydney Press, 1968; *Poems for a Female Universe,* South Head Press, 1968; *Son of a Female Universe,* South Head Press, 1971; *The Fishing Boy,* South Head Press, 1973; *Find the Lady: A Female Universe Rides Again,* South Head Press, 1978; *Where Two Rivers Meet,* Nimrod Publications, 1981; *A Glossary of Poetic Terms* (criticism), University of Newcastle, 1982.

Editor: *XI Hunter Valley Poets Plus VII,* Nimrod Publications, 1966; *Hunter Valley Poets 1973,* Nimrod Publications, 1973; *IV Hunter Valley Poets,* Nimrod Publications, 1975; *V Hunter Valley Poets,* Nimrod Publications, 1978; (with Ross Bennett) *The Terrible Echidna?,* New South Wales Education Department, 1979; (with Bennett) *I Is Invulnerable Green,* New South Wales Education Department, 1980; (with Bennett) *The Oak in an Egg,* New South Wales Education Department, 1981; *Book without Barriers* (anthology), Nimrod Publications, 1981; *Under Construction,* Department of Community Programmes, 1981; *The Hawkesbury Vowels,* W.E.A. Metropolitan Region, 1981; (with T. H. Naisby) *Mobile as They Come,* New South Wales Education Department, 1982.

Poetry anthologized, published in numerous Australian journals and in periodicals in England, the United States, and Canada. Editor of "This Place" series, 1980, and "Nimrod's Quarry" series, 1980-82, both published by Nimrod Publications. Contributor of articles and reviews to *Poetry Australia, Southern Review* (Australia), *Quadrant,* and other journals. Founder, president, and editor-in-chief, Nimrod Publications.

WORK IN PROGRESS: Mouse's Footprint: Japanese Haiku, Australian Haiku, with James Fennessy and James Bennett; *The Planet that Was High,* science fiction novel; *Copperlight,* fantasy novel; *Seven Sleepers, Seven Labours,* fantasy short stories; *The Wrath of Tibrogargan,* poetry; *To Eat the Colour of a Blizzard,* anthology, with Naisby and Ross Bennett; an edition of a William Morris story.

SIDELIGHTS: Norman Talbot writes: "In recent years I have lost interest in the national/international poetry scene and establishing a reputation in it. Much of my work involves the encouragement of local writers in the Hunter Valley of New South Wales, the teaching of poetic skills, creative writing for children, and so on. My own tastes in reading and writing have changed, and I am now deeply involved in the writing of science fiction and fantasy novels and short stories, as well as with poetry. Much of my best recent poetry uses the haiku form, as in *Where Two Rivers Meet.* I am now convinced that both the 'traditional' rhymed, stress-syllabic metric verse and 'modernism' need the formal challenge and the imagistic clarity and directness of haiku (though we must make an Australian haiku, not merely employ a Japanese refugee).

"The major influences upon my poetry are Buson, Keats, Browning, Shiki, Emily Dickinson, W. C. Williams, Wallace Stevens, and Gwen Harwood; upon my prose, Dickens, William Morris, Vonnegut, Barth, G. G. Marquez, Borges, Ursula K. Le Guin, and Stoppard. However, such lists are always changing, and I am reading Pynchon, Piers Anthony, and Les

Murray with more relish this week, and Robert Coover and Gene Wolfe are beside my typewriter, waiting to pounce."

AVOCATIONAL INTERESTS: Wine, cricket, the Society of Friends (Quakers), my wife and children.

* * *

TALESE, Gay 1932-

PERSONAL: Given name originally Gaetano; born February 7, 1932, in Ocean City, N.J.; son of Joseph Francis and Catherine (DePaulo) Talese; married Nan Ahearn (a vice president and executive editor at a publishing company), June 10, 1959; children: Pamela, Catherine. *Education:* University of Alabama, B.A., 1953. *Home:* 109 East 61st St., New York, N.Y. 10021; and 154 East Atlantic Blvd., Ocean City, N.J. 08226 (summer).

CAREER: New York Times, New York, N.Y., 1953-65, began as copy boy, became reporter; full-time writer, 1965—. *Military service:* U.S. Army, 1953-55, became first lieutenant. *Member:* P.E.N., Authors League of America, Sigma Delta Chi, Phi Sigma Kappa. *Awards, honors:* Best Sports Stories Award-Magazine Story, E. P. Dutton & Co., 1967, for "The Silent Season of a Hero"; Christopher Book Award, 1970, for *The Kingdom and the Power.*

WRITINGS—Nonfiction: *New York: A Serendipiter's Journey,* Harper, 1961; *The Bridge,* Harper, 1964; *The Overreachers,* Harper, 1965; *The Kingdom and the Power* (Book of the Month Club alternate selection), World Publishing, 1969; *Fame and Obscurity,* World Publishing, 1970; *Honor Thy Father* (Literary Guild selection), World Publishing, 1971; *Thy Neighbor's Wife* (Literary Guild special selection), Doubleday, 1980. Contributor of articles to magazines, including *Reader's Digest, New York Times Magazine,* and *Saturday Evening Post.* Contributing editor, *Esquire,* beginning 1966.

WORK IN PROGRESS: A book on the Italian migration to America at the turn of the century, for Doubleday.

SIDELIGHTS: As a pioneer of the new journalism, Gay Talese was one of the first writers to apply the techniques of fiction to nonfiction. In a *Writer's Digest* interview with Leonard Wallace Robinson, Talese described how and why he began writing in this style while reporting for the *New York Times:* "I found I was leaving the assignment each day, unable with the techniques available to me or permissible to the *New York Times,* to really tell, to report, all that I saw, to communicate through the techniques that were permitted by the archaic copy desk. . . . [So] I started . . . to use the techniques of the short story writer in some of the *Esquire* pieces I did in the early Sixties. . . . It may read like fiction, it may give the impression that it was made up, . . . over-dramatizing incidents for the effect those incidents may cause in the writing, but without question . . . there is reporting. There is reporting that fortifies the whole structure. Fact reporting, leg work."

Now considered classics of the genre, Talese's *Esquire* articles probed the private lives of celebrities such as Frank Sinatra, Joe DiMaggio, and Floyd Patterson. The success of these stories prompted Talese to apply this new technique to larger subjects, and, in 1969, he produced his first bestseller, *The Kingdom and the Power,* a nonfiction work about the *New York Times* written in novelistic style. Since then Talese has explored such controversial topics as the Mafia, in *Honor Thy Father* (1971), and sexuality in America, in *Thy Neighbor's Wife* (1980). Widely respected as a master of his craft, Talese has thought of writing fiction, but, as he explained to the *Los Angeles Times*'s Wayne Warga, nonfiction challenges him more: "I suggest there is art in journalism. I don't want to resort to changing names, to fictionalizing. The reality is more fascinating. My mission is to get deep into the heart and soul of the people in this country."

Talese grew up in Ocean City, New Jersey—a resort town that he describes as "festive and bright in the summertime" and "depressing" the rest of the year. As the son of an Italian immigrant, young Talese was "actually a minority within a minority" according to *Time* magazine's R. Z. Sheppard. He was Catholic in a Protestant community and Italian in a predominately Irish parish. A repressed, unhappy child, Talese remembers himself as a loner who failed most of the classes at his conservative parochial school. Then, when he was thirteen, he made a discovery. "I became involved with the school newspaper," he told Francis Coppola in an *Esquire Film Quarterly* interview, and realized that "you can be shy, as I was, but you can still approach strangers and ask them questions." Throughout high school and college, Talese continued his writing, majoring in journalism at the University of Alabama, contributing sports columns to the campus newspaper, and hoping to someday work for the New York *Herald Tribune* where his literary idol, Red Smith, had a column of his own. After graduation Talese made the rounds of the major New York newspapers, applying for a job and finally being offered one by the paper where he thought his chances were least promising—the *New York Times.* Hired as a copy boy, he was promoted to reporter in just two years.

In 1961 Talese published his first book, *New York: A Serendipiter's Journey.* Composed largely of material from his *New York Times* articles, the book was a critical success and sold about 12,000 copies, mostly in New York. His next venture was *The Bridge,* a book in which, according to *Playboy* magazine, "he took the plunge into the book-length nonfiction novel style." To prepare for this story, Talese spent over a year observing the workers who built the Verrazano-Narrows Bridge connecting Brooklyn and Staten Island. In the *New York Times Book Review* Herbert Mitgang calls the book "a vivid document," noting that Talese "imparts drama and romance to this bridge-building story . . . by concentrating on the boomers, the iron workers who stitch steel and live high in more ways than one." While the publication was not a bestseller, it was critically well-received, and *Playboy* reports that "it was a minor classic in demonstrating how deeply—and subjectively—a reporter could involve himself in the lives of his subjects and bring the flesh and blood of real people to paper in a way that was usually expected only in novels." Furthermore, critics believe it set the scene for the three larger works which would follow in the next sixteen years.

The first of these was *The Kingdom and the Power,* an intimate portrait of the *New York Times* where Talese worked as a reporter for ten years. Published four years after he left the paper, the book is "rich in intimate detail, personal insights and characterizations," according to Ben H. Bagdikian in the *New York Times Book Review.* "In this book," Bagdikian continues, "the men of The Times emerge not as godlike models of intrepid journalism, but as unique individuals who, in addition to other human traits, have trouble with ambitions, alcohol, wives and analysts." In his author's note, Talese describes the book as "a human history of an institution in transition." Specifically, Talese relates the infighting between James ("Scotty") Reston, respected columnist and head of the *New York Times* Washington bureau, and E. Clifton Daniel, managing editor of the paper, for control of the Washington bureau, which had maintained independent status for years. In the end, Reston wins and is appointed executive editor. But "that outcome, of great moment inside the *Times,* is of less than secondary interest to the rest of the world," according to a *Time* critic who adds that "to curry reader excitement, Talese has had to transform the newsroom on the third floor of the *Times* building into a fortress of Machiavellian maneuver. (One wonders, sometimes, how the paper ever got put out at all.)"

Talese's decision to dramatize the story, to relate the process of change at an American institution from the human perspective has been more praised than criticized. Detractors feel that the *New York Times* owners and employees are ultimately unworthy of such elaborate attention, that their petty squabbling diminishes the institution they represent. Supporters argue that Talese's approach is the best way to reveal the inside story and is an example of new journalism at its best.

Among the critics of this approach is John Leo, who writes in *Commonweal*: "The new journalist in Talese is forever trying to capture the real *Times* by a telling scene of explaining what everyone felt at a critical moment. But the effort doesn't amount to much. . . . It is often spectacularly effective in delineating a person, a small group of people or a social event. But for an *institution,* and a ponderous non-dramatic one at that, well, maybe only the boring old journalism will do." Because his focus is on personality rather than issues, some critics believe the perspective is skewed. Among them is Harold E. Fey who writes in the *Christian Century* that Talese "seems unable to understand or to formulate adequately the *Times*'s high purpose, its worthy conceptions of public responsibility, its firm identification of personal with journalistic integrity. These also have something to do with power. And they have much to do with the *New York Times*. They help to explain, as Talese does not, why the *Times,* in his own words, 'influences the world.'"

Fred Powledge in the *Nation,* however, found merit in Talese's approach: "Talese does not attempt to resolve questions [about journalistic procedure and social responsibility,] and some may consider this a fault. I do not think so. If he had entered this vast and relatively unexplored territory . . . the book would have lost some of its timeless, surgically clean quality." And, writing in *Life,* Murray Kempton notes that "by talking about their lives [Talese] has done something for his subjects which they could not do for themselves with their product, and done it superlatively well." Another supporter is David Bernstein. "There are surely criticisms to be made [of the great power the *New York Times* wields over public opinion]," he writes in *New Leader,* "but they are meaningless without an understanding of the private worlds of individual reporters, editors, and publishers and of how these worlds interact. Gay Talese is quite right to place his emphasis upon all this when he describes the kingdom that is the *Times*. What might appear at first glance to be a frivolous book is in fact a serious and important account of one of the few genuinely powerful institutions in our society." Powledge agrees: "The inner conflicts and passions of these men are beautifully documented in *The Kingdom and the Power*. It is no less than a landmark in the field of writing about journalism."

In 1971, Talese produced what many consider to be another landmark—*Honor Thy Father,* an inside look at the life of mafioso Bill Bonanno and a book so popular that it sold more than 300,000 copies within four months of its publication. Like all of Talese's efforts, the story was extensively researched and written in the intimate style of the new journalism. Almost six years elapsed between the day in 1965 when Talese first met Bill Bonanno outside a New York courtroom and the publication of the book. During that time Talese actually lived with the Bonanno family and persuaded them to talk about their business and personal lives, becoming, to use his words, "a source of communication within a family that had long been repressed by a tradition of silence."

While the tone of the book is nonjudgmental. Talese's compassionate portrayal of underworld figures—including Bill and his father, New York boss Joseph Bonanno—incited charges that Talese was giving gangsters moral sanction. Writing in the *New York Times Book Review,* Colin McInnes says that "Gay Talese has become so seduced by his subject and its 'hero,' that he conveys the impression that being a mobster is much the same as being a sportsman, film star or any other kind of public personality." But others, such as the *Times Literary Supplement* critic, defend Talese's treatment, noting that "Mr. Talese's insight will do more to help us understand the criminal than any amount of moral recrimination." And writing in the *New York Review of Books,* Wilfrid Sheed expresses a similar view: "Gay Talese has been criticized for writing what amounts to promotional material for the Bonanno family, but his book is an invaluable document and I don't know how such books can be obtained without some compromise. It is a lot to ask of an author that he betray the confidence of a Mafia family. As with a tapped phone call, one must interpret the message. . . . Talese signals occasionally to his educated audience—dull, aren't they? Almost pathetic. But that's all he can do."

Furthermore, Sheed argues, the technique of new journalism, "an unfortunate strategy for most subjects," is "weirdly right" here: "The prose matches the stiff watchful facade of the Mafia. One is reminded of a touched-up country wedding photo, with the cheeks identically rouged and the eyes glazed, of the kind the Bonanno family might have ordered for themselves back in Sicily."

After the success of *Honor Thy Father,* Doubleday offered Talese a $1.2 million contract for two books. "I was interested in sexual changes and how . . . morality was being defined," Talese told a *Media People* interviewer. To gather material for a chronicle of the American sexual revolution, Talese submerged himself in the subculture of massage parlors, pornographic publishing, blue movies, and, ultimately, Sandstone, the California sexual retreat. He also studied First Amendment decisions in the Supreme Court and law libraries, tracing the effect of Puritanism on American's free rights. As his research stretched from months into years, however, Talese realized that what began as a professional exploration had become a personal odyssey. And because he was asking others to reveal their most intimate sexual proclivities, he felt it would be hypocritical not to reveal his own. Thus, before he had written a word of his book, Talese became the subject of two revealing profiles in *Esquire* and *New York* magazines, the latter entitled "An Evening in the Nude with Gay Talese." The public was titillated, and the resulting publicity virtually guaranteed the book's financial success (and "the critics' wrath," according to Nan Talese in a letter to *CA*). In October, 1979, months before the publication reached bookstores, United Artists bid a record-breaking $2.5 million for film rights to the book Talese entitled *Thy Neighbor's Wife*. Published in 1980, the book became a bestseller and was number one on the *New York Times* bestseller list for three consecutive months.

Despite its popularity, *Thy Neighbor's Wife* received negative reviews from many literary critics. But Nan Talese believes the reasons have less to do with the quality of the book than with its subject matter and the circumstances under which it was written. In her letter to *CA,* she explains: "Because [the] book took so long and was about sex, surely a most intimate and volatile subject, because of the early publicity, the enormous movie sale and the fact that it would be published in fourteen countries abroad, the success was too much and the critics pounced. . . . Writers had a heyday with our marriage, and the book, which is a sociological study as well as a contemporary re-creation, was misrepresented except by serious-minded sociologists and psychologists (who I suppose are less shocked by the human condition)."

Virginia Johnson-Masters, the respected sex researcher, foresaw the ensuing controversy when she wrote an early *Vogue* review saying that Talese "shows us many things about ourselves and the social environment in which we live. Some of them we may not appreciate or want any part of. However, Talese, the author, is fair. Read carefully and perceive that he really does not proselytize, he informs." Johnson-Masters goes on to say: "*Thy Neighbor's Wife* is a scholarly, readable and thoroughly entertaining book. . . . It is a meticulously researched context of people, events, and circumstances through which a reader can identify the process of breakdown in repressive sexual myths dominating our society until quite recently."

Writing in the *New York Times Book Review,* psychiatrist Robert Coles notes that Talese "has a serious interest in watching his fellow human beings, in listening to them, and in presenting honestly what he has seen and heard. He writes clear unpretentious prose. He has a gift, through phrase here, a sentence there, of making important narrative and historical connections. We are given, really, a number of well-told stories, their social message cumulative: A drastically transformed American sexuality has emerged during this past couple of decades."

Despite such praise from sociologists and psychologists, many reviewers criticize the book. Objections range from Ernest van den Haag's charge in the *National Review* that *Thy Neighbor's Wife* is "remarkably shallow" to Robert Sherrill's allegation in the *Washington Post* that it is "constructed mostly of the sort of intellectual plywood you find in most neighborhood bars: part voyeurism, part amateur psychoanalysis, part six-pack philosophy." The most common objections include Talese's apparent lack of analysis, his omission of homosexuality, and his supposed anti-female attitude.

In his *Playboy* review of the book, critic John Leonard articulates each of these objections: "Since Talese parajournalizes so promiscuously—reaching into [his subjects'] minds, reading their thoughts, scratching their itches—one would expect at the very least to emerge from his book, as if from a novel, with some improved comprehension of what they stand for and a different angle on the culture that produced them. One emerges instead, as if from a soft-porn movie in the middle of the afternoon, reproached by sunlight and feeling peripheral to the main business of the universe. . . . If Talese . . . expects us to take his revolutionaries as seriously as he himself takes them, he has to put them in a social context and make them sound interesting. He doesn't." Furthermore, Leonard continues, "Talese almost totally ignores feminism. Gay liberation doesn't interest him. Children, conveniently, do not exist; if they did exist, they would make group sex—Tinkertoys! Erector Sets!—an unseemly hassle. . . . Missing from *Thy Neighbor's Wife* are history and stamina and celebration and mystery, along with birth, blood, death and beauty, not to mention earth, fire, water, politics, and everything else that isn't our urgent plumbing, that refuses to swim in our libidinal pool." The book, responds Nan Talese, "is a sociological study of where we have been in regards to sex and how the sexual revolution changed us. It is fair to say that homosexuality is not represented and the women's movement not annotated, although there are many women in the book and quite a few of them are feminists. But one book cannot do everything and I think now it was a mistake for Doubleday to delete the subtitle *Lust and Longing in America* from the book. Gay had meant it to indicate, along with the title, that it was written very much about men from a man's point of view."

When asked by *Playboy* interviewer Larry DuBois if he were vulnerable to charges that he wrote "only as a reporter telling a series of dramatic stories without understanding and conveying the deeper philosophical meaning of those stories," Talese said he was not. "The characters are described, are understood, are understood in their historical time, and the historical time of the twentieth century is reflected against the background of the nineteenth century. If the book were what you described, I could have done it in six months." It was not, however, only the depth of his research, but also the fact that he refused to change names or use composite characters that made the book eight years in the making. "The book reports fantasy," he told *Washington Post* interviewer Tom Zito. "It reports intimacy. Getting releases from people to use their real names is what took me eight years. I had to develop relationships with these people. I had to convince them that they were typical of their time. And what the book may be able to do is convince other people that what they're doing in private isn't bad, isn't abnormal." Talese considers it the most important story of his life.

The negative reviews, he believes, will not matter in the long run. "Ten years from now this will read as a historical book," he told Clarence Petersen in the *Chicago Tribune*. "The gossip will be forgotten." In the meantime, Talese maintains his composure. "In my personal life certainly there is much that I am willing to apologize for," he told DuBois. "But not in my work. I never apologize for the work I do. That is deliberate, very carefully crafted, done with love and care. I have never been ashamed of anything I have written. Success is marvelous, but all I'm really committed to is writing well."

MEDIA ADAPTATIONS: Honor Thy Father was filmed as a made-for-television movie by Columbia Broadcasting System in 1973.

CA INTERVIEW

CA interviewed Gay Talese by phone on November 4, 1981, at his home in New York City.

CA: Tom Wolfe called you the "real pioneer" in the field of New Journalism with your article on Joe Louis, "The King as a Middle-Aged Man," in the June 1962 Esquire. *Do you accept that tribute?*

TALESE: At the time I was very pleased that a writer I respected as I do Tom Wolfe would give me some recognition for the work I had done. What changes my feeling a little bit now has nothing to do with Tom Wolfe; it has to do with the misunderstanding on the part of many people today about the purpose and goals of the so-called new journalistic movement of the late 1960s, which is when Wolfe made that comment. A lot of people in the 1970s and '80s, following what they believed was something of the style and ambition of Wolfe or me or other people, have created distortions that have been labeled facets of new journalism. Wolfe and I and some others have taken no liberties with fact, but rather have taken a lot of liberty in creative factual writing. That's what I think he was talking about, and what I'm talking about now, that is good. The writing level matches the work of our better fiction writers, except we have remained true to nonfiction and we are responsible for the truth of what we write insofar as we're able to perceive truth in individuals. That aspect of writing remains, for me at least, very challenging.

CA: When you say distortions, do you mean the so-called journalistic fiction?

TALESE: Yes. I think Norman Mailer's recent book, *The Executioner's Song,* should have been categorized as either true fiction or true nonfiction. If fiction, then I don't subscribe to his liberty of giving the real name Gary Gilmore to his character. In *Thy Neighbor's Wife,* even though the book dealt with the private sexual lives of living people, there was not one instance where a name was left out or altered. This was true of the previous books also. Part of the reason it took so much time to do that last book was that I insisted on writing with real names. The book is factual, even though it delves into the most intimate aspects of people's lives, and these people are described as they lived those lives. They're real people, real names, real addresses, real neighborhoods. One of my ambitions is to see how far the writer can go with factual writing. And I think one can see, after reading *Thy Neighbor's Wife,* how far I went.

CA: You've spoken of how you weren't really interested in anything much in your youth except people. Where did the interest begin in observing people so closely as you've learned to do?

TALESE: I don't know why certain people are more curious about life than others are. In my little town of Ocean City, New Jersey (and it was even smaller when I grew up there in the 1930s and 1940s), I had a sense that the people around me appeared to be one thing and were something else. I had a natural curiosity about finding out what they were; I wanted that more incisive view of people. At age fourteen I started writing for the weekly newspaper after school. There was and still is a weekly newspaper called the *Ocean City Sentinel-Ledger*. In 1938, when I was about five, my father had bought the building that used to be the newspaper office; he used it for the ladies' dress business he and my mother had started in 1921 and have been in ever since. So I was reared in a building which had been a newspaper building, and my father always subscribed to out-of-town newspapers, big-city newspapers (the *New York Times* is the one I most remember). During the war years, the emphasis on foreign news and international events aroused in me—in a small town which was certainly not in any way sophisticated—a tendency to look beyond the borders of the town for some answers about what made human nature so unpredictable and fascinating. I was a searching individual, I think, who, had I pursued the academic life, would have become an anthropologist or sociologist. But I didn't. In working first for newspapers and then years later for magazines and still later as a writer of books—and always nonfiction, as I said before—I found my way of establishing something in writing about the way people live and what motivates them.

Each book has been different. The first book was *New York: A Serendipiter's Journey*. I was a young man from a small town coming to the big city, New York, and writing about people who tended to be in the shadows of the skyscrapers, the obscure, the overlooked, the forgotten—individuals who didn't at first glance seem to represent the power and glamour of New York. In the next book, *The Bridge,* I was looking at things a bit differently, at the bridge builders who built magnificent structures but did not necessarily leave any fingerprints or plaque that announced their names and marked the magnificence of their creation.

The major book that followed (after a series of collections), *The Kingdom and the Power,* again dealt with people who would normally not be written about. *The Kingdom and the Power* was the first of the media books, the first of the books that looked at the communicators. But I didn't write about them as part of a major newspaper or network—I wrote about them as a short-story writer or a novelist would write about them, as people. All novelists and short-story writers write about an average person and an average town, a Bartleby the Scrivener working in some large company. Well, I've written about a lot of Bartlebys, but I do it in nonfiction.

With *Honor Thy Father* I went into the Mafia in the same way to look at people: a housewife married to a man who's in the Mafia, the children who see their father's picture in the newspapers and then have to go to school. What is it like to be such a child? What is it like to be such a housewife? How does the public react to them? All of this, which could have been a novel or sections of short stories, I put into a book of nonfiction. In *Thy Neighbor's Wife* I was dealing with the word *obscenity* in a society. What does that word mean? How is it personified? If you have obscenity, who in America is obscene? So I took the personal approach to find out who might be definable by that term, how they live, how they get through the night, what they do that makes them different. It's really taking another look at America.

There's something in my work, as I'm sure many people are aware, of taking the other view, of always taking the somewhat unpopular position, which is the opposite of what Paul Newman might do when he takes movie roles, or Helen Hayes, always the lovable actress. I'm interested in extending the boundaries of knowledge through my nonfiction and giving readers a deeper sense of awareness about other human beings. I do not ever accept a generally accepted view unless I myself explore it, and often when I do explore it as deeply as I do, I find that the presumptions of the past don't hold up. I write about people as being more complex than they are believed to be.

CA: You obviously have excellent interview techniques. Your friend the songwriter Walter Marks called you "the master of the direct question." Did interviewing come naturally to you in the beginning, or did your techniques evolve gradually?

TALESE: I think one thing that cannot be faked is genuine interest in people. There are people who have an interest in other people only up to the point where that other person serves a purpose. Most people in conversations or in transactions are very purposeful. Even when I'm not professionally engaged, I have a genuine curiosity about people. Whether I'm talking to them for the purpose of maybe writing about them or just for the purpose of knowing them a little better, I'm the same person. As for the interview *technique,* that sounds so mannered, studied, learned. It wasn't something I learned; it was something I think I always had. Most people fake listening; they seem to be nodding at you, but they're not really paying attention to what you're saying because they're not interested, because what you're saying does not serve a purpose in their lives.

I'm interested in other people just for the purpose of wanting to know more. I'm probably among the very few in this country who do not know most of what I know from reading books. I don't rely on the written word as much as others who might be considered academicians or serious researchers because I believe most researchers have done a rather superficial job; they've tended, generally speaking, to talk to people who seem to be in power, and used these selected few as representative of the many, so they've left very little in the way of a truly representative record of their lifetime. I believe my own career is one of excursions in many directions; I tend to look at life through the people that historians would normally ignore. And not only historians, but many journalists as well.

I want a personal relationship with the people I write about. That's why I wrote about the Verrazano-Narrows Bridge. If I had been born a hundred years ago, I would have been up on the Brooklyn Bridge, and there would be a book today about the men who were working around the East River in Brooklyn, building this magnificent edifice that has survived more than a century. I would have told you about the sociology, the background of the men, something of the city, something of the politics of the city, something of the funding—how you got funding to build something like the Brooklyn Bridge in that Civil War period. Now when people write about the Brooklyn Bridge they're a hundred years removed from it. I like being there, knowing people, getting the information from them myself and not using secondary sources. I didn't use secondary sources with the Mafia. Rather than be touted off the Mafia book by all the people who were saying the Mafia would not talk to outsiders, I knocked on the door again and again and finally the door was opened and the Mafia did talk to me, they let me in. Anybody could have done that, but so often people are guided by presumptions from the past. I'm not; I find out for myself whether it's true or not.

CA: You've put yourself in various kinds of jeopardy for your books, certainly physically with The Bridge *and* Honor Thy Father. *Were you never afraid when you were spending a lot of time with the Bonannos?*

TALESE: Yes, I was. I was involved for a long period of time with Mafia men—consorting with known criminals, to use the familiar expression—for the purpose of knowing them and writing about them as I believed they are in our society. Again, all in the interest of extending knowlege. With *Thy Neighbor's Wife* I put myself in jeopardy in a social way. You see, it's the willingness to take risks and to be the subject of scorn. That may be a little bit overstated, but I'm not so sure it is. In the last book I dealt with the issue of adultery in America. I dealt with extramarital and lawless sexuality—lawless sexuality meaning pornography, prostitution, mercenary sexuality. I took that subject not because I invented it but because it's there and it's misunderstood. In everything I write I'm trying to get as close as I can to a fuller truth, using real names, real situations, not falsifying or fabricating. And I believe that if I want that from other people, I have to do the same thing myself, so I wrote in *Thy Neighbor's Wife* about my own indiscretions to the degree I thought was essential to the integrity of the work as a whole.

The book focuses on a part of contemporary American life, but I also go back into the history of morality in America, beginning with the religion brought by the early settlers of New England and showing how this puritan state has changed over three hundred years. All my books go back into earlier periods to deal with tradition and change. In *Honor Thy Father* I go back into the sixteenth century to examine old Mafia family life in Sicily; then I show how their traditions were influenced by their resettlement in this country. In *The Kingdom and the Power* I deal with a newspaper family that moved from the South and settled in New York in the 1880s. They bought a bankrupt newspaper called the *New York Times*. They had to change as the economics of big business changed, yet hold on to the diamond-hard traditions of good journalistic practice and a belief in fairness and truth.

CA: In an interview for Media People, *you called* Thy Neighbor's Wife *"an important historical document—the modern story of how, in recent years, morality has been redefined in America." Don't you sense that we are going back to more conservative sexual values?*

TALESE: I know this has often been said by those who might be wishful thinkers, but I don't think that what upset people in the 1970s upsets people in the 1980s. Take homosexuality, for just one small example (and I didn't deal with this in the book because I only wrote about heterosexuality). Homosexuals now not only declare themselves but have become an activist political force wanting equal rights under the law. This is something we cannot underestimate as a sign of change in this country. In universities across the land, in small towns as well as larger cities, there are coed dormitories, fraternity and sorority houses, and apartments where young men and women can sleep together and not be the subject of scandal or be evicted from the student body. That wasn't true in the 1950s. Now are we going back? I wrote in the last chapter of the book, where I am describing my travels through some of the smaller towns in the South and reflecting on that very question, "It would necessitate the outlawing of abortion and contraceptives, the imprisonment of adulterers, the censuring not only of *Playboy* but also *Vogue* and the Maidenform advertisers in the *New York Times* Sunday magazine."

BIOGRAPHICAL/CRITICAL SOURCES: New York Times Book Review, January 17, 1965, June 8, 1969, August 2, 1970, October 31, 1971, May 4, 1980; *New York Times,* May 21, 1969, October 5, 1971, April 30, 1980; *New Leader,* May 26, 1969; *Life,* June 27, 1969; *Time,* July 4, 1969, October 4, 1971; *Newsweek,* July 21, 1969, April 28, 1980; *National Review,* August 12, 1969, March 6, 1981; *Nation,* September 15, 1969; *Christian Century,* October 8, 1969; *Commonweal,* October 17, 1969.

Writer's Digest, January, 1970; *Times Literary Supplement,* May 14, 1971, April 4, 1972, July 4, 1980; *New York Review of Books,* July 20, 1972; *Authors in the News,* Volume I, Gale, 1976; *Washington Post,* October 18, 1979, April 27, 1980, May 7, 1980, May 15, 1980.

People, April 14, 1980; *New York Times Magazine,* April 20, 1980; *Los Angeles Times Book Review,* April 27, 1980; *Media People,* May 1980; *Playboy,* May, 1980; *Los Angeles Times,* May 23, 1980; *Vogue,* June, 1980; *Chicago Tribune,* June 8, 1980; *Esquire Film Quarterly,* July, 1981; *Contemporary Issues Criticism,* Volume I, Gale, 1982; *Publishers Weekly,* January 7, 1983.

—Sketch by Donna Olendorf

—Interview by Jean W. Ross

TATE, Ellalice
See HIBBERT, Eleanor Burford

* * *

TAUBER, Gilbert 1935-

PERSONAL: Born April 20, 1935, in New York, N.Y.; son of Joseph H. and Frances L. Tauber; married Susanne Weil, December 25, 1960 (divorced, 1974); children: Sarah Elizabeth, Katherine Jessica. *Education:* City College (now City College of the City University of New York), B.A., 1956; Hunter College of the City University of New York, M.A. in Urban Planning, 1977. *Home:* 320 Riverside Dr., New York, N.Y. 10025.

CAREER: Dover Publications, Inc. (book publishers), New York City, publicity director, 1958-59; New York Convention and Visitors Bureau, Inc., New York City, assistant promotion director, 1960-65; Hudson River Valley Commission (state agency), Tarrytown, N.Y., information officer, 1965-71; environmental consultant, 1971-77; Ecological Analysts, Inc., Middletown, N.Y., senior scientist, land use studies, 1977-79; Chas-T-Main, Inc., Environmental and Resource Planning Division, Boston, Mass., regional coordinator, 1979—. Lecturer in architectural walking-tour program, Museum of the City of New York, 1959-61. Former chairman of a state advisory committee on preservation of scenic lands along the Hudson. Consultant to business firms on New York City landmarks, history, and ethnic groups. *Military service:* U.S. Army, 1956-58; served in Italy. *Member:* Hudson River Environmental Society (member of board).

WRITINGS: (With Samuel Kaplan) *The New York City Handbook,* Doubleday, 1966, revised edition, 1968; *The Hudson River Tourway,* Doubleday, 1977; (editor with Ralph W. Richardson, Jr.) *The Hudson River Basin: Environmental Problems and Institutional Response,* two volumes, Academic Press, 1979.

WORK IN PROGRESS: A play.

SIDELIGHTS: Gilbert Tauber's idea for *The New York City Handbook* grew out of his interest in architecture and landmarks, as well as his experiences "in coping with the nitty-gritty of life in Manhattan."

* * *

TAUBES, Frederic 1900-1981

PERSONAL: Born April 15, 1900, in Lwow, Poland; came to United States, 1930; died after a long illness, June 20, 1981, in Nyack, N.Y.; son of Louis and Fanny (Taeni) Taubes; married Lili Jacobsen, May 25, 1923; children: Frank Alex. *Education:* Studied at Academy of Art, Vienna, 1916-18, Academy of Art, Munich, 1918-20, Bauhaus, Weimar, 1920-21, and in France and Italy. *Politics:* Conservative. *Religion:* "My own." *Home:* The Studio, Haverstraw, N.Y. 10927.

CAREER: Painter, etcher, and lithographer, exhibiting at more than a hundred one-man shows, and in major museums and galleries throughout America, in Europe and Palestine; art educator and writer on art. Works owned by Metropolitan Museum of Art, San Francisco Museum, San Diego Fine Arts Gallery, William Rockhill Nelson Gallery of Art, High Museum of Atlanta, and some twenty other museums, universities, and corporations. Former head of painting division, Corpus Christi Fine Arts Colony and Ruidoso Art Colony. Had conducted art seminars in Palm Springs and San Antonio. Carnegie Visiting Professor and artist-in-residence at University of Illinois, 1940-41. Visiting professor of art at Mills College, 1938, University of Hawaii, 1939, University of Wisconsin, 1945, University of Alberta, and Colorado State College; instructor at Cooper Union and Art Students' League; lecturer at other art schools in this country, London, and Edinburgh. Formulator of painting materials sold commercially as Taubes Varnishes and Copal Painting Media.

MEMBER: Royal Society of Arts (London; fellow). *Awards, honors:* Named honorary colonel, State of New Mexico, honorary administrator, Leche State of Louisiana, and honorary citizen, San Antonio, Tex., New Iberia, La., and Charlotte, N.C.

WRITINGS: *The Technique of Oil Painting,* Dodd, 1941; *You Don't Know What You Like,* Dodd, 1942; *Studio Secrets,* Watson-Guptill, 1943; *Oil Painting for the Beginner,* Watson-Guptill, 1944, revised and enlarged edition, 1965; *The Amateur Painter's Handbook,* Dodd, 1947; *The Painter's Question and Answer Book,* Watson-Guptill, 1948; *Anatomy of Genius,* Dodd, 1948; *Pictorial Composition and the Art of Drawing,* Dodd, 1949.

Paintings and Essays on Art, Dodd, 1950; *The Quickest Way to Paint Well,* Studio, 1950; *Better Frames for Your Pictures,* Studio, 1952, 3rd revised edition, Viking, 1968; *Oil Painting for the Beginner,* Watson-Guptill, 1953, 2nd revised edition, 1963; *New Essays on Art,* Watson-Guptill, 1955; *Pen and Ink Drawing I,* Watson-Guptill, 1956; *Pictorial Anatomy of the Human Body,* Studio, 1956; *The Art and Technique of Portrait Painting,* Dodd, 1957; *The Mastery of Oil Painting,* Viking, 1957; *The Quickest Way to Draw Well,* Studio, 1958, Penguin, 1977; *Modern Art Sweet and Sour,* Watson-Guptill, 1958.

The Art and Technique of Landscape Painting, Watson, 1960, reprinted as *The Technique of Landscape Painting,* 1966; *New Techniques in Painting,* Dodd, 1962; *Pen and Ink Drawing II,* Pitman, 1962; *Abracadabra and Modern Art,* Dodd, 1963; *Painting Techniques, Ancient and Modern,* Viking, 1963; *A Guide to Traditional and Modern Painting Methods,* Viking and Bonanza Books, 1963; *Painting Materials and Techniques,* Watson-Guptill, 1964; *Oil Painting and Tempera,* Watson-Guptill, 1965; *Taubes' Guide to Oil Painting,* Reinhold, 1965; *The Guide to the Great Art of Europe,* Reinhold, 1966; *The Technique of Portrait Painting,* Watson-Guptill, 1967; *The Technique of Still Life Painting,* Watson-Guptill, 1968; *Anatomy for Artists,* Pitman, 1969; *Restoring and Preserving Antiques,* Watson-Guptill, 1969.

Antiques for the Amateur, Watson-Guptill, 1970; *Acrylic Painting for the Beginner,* Watson-Guptill, 1971; *Antique Finishing for Beginners,* Watson-Guptill, 1972; *The Painter's Dictionary of Arts and Crafts,* Watson-Guptill, 1972; *The Painter's Dictionary of Materials and Methods,* David & Charles, 1973, Watson-Guptill, 1979; *The Human Body: Aspects of Pictorial Anatomy,* C. N. Potter, distributed by Crown, c. 1974; *The Mastery of Alla Prima Printing,* North Light, 1980. Also author of *Basic Enameling,* Grosset, and *Guide to Value Judgements in Art,* C. N. Potter.

American editor of *Artist* and conductor of "Ask Taubes" page in *Illustrator;* former contributing editor, *Encyclopaedia Britannica Yearbooks, American Artist,* and *Pacific Art Review;* contributor to other periodicals.

OBITUARIES: *New York Times,* June 21, 1981; *AB Bookman's Weekly,* July 27, 1981.†

TAYLOR, Elizabeth 1912-1975

PERSONAL: Born July 3, 1912, in Reading, Berkshire, England; died November 19, 1975; daughter of Oliver and Elsie (Fewtrell) Coles; married John William Kendall Taylor, March 11, 1936; children: Renny, Joanna (Mrs. David Routledge). *Education:* Attended the Abbey School, Reading. *Politics:* Labour. *Religion:* None. *Home:* Grove's Barn, Penn, Buckinghamshire, England. *Agent:* Brandt & Brandt, 101 Park Ave., New York, N.Y. 10017.

CAREER: Author. *Member:* P.E.N., Society of Authors.

WRITINGS: At Mrs. Lippincote's, P. Davies, 1945, Knopf, 1946; *Palladian,* P. Davies, 1946, Knopf, 1947, reprinted, Chatto & Windus, 1969; *A View of the Harbour,* Knopf, 1949, reprinted, Chatto & Windus, 1969; *A Wreath of Roses,* Knopf, 1949, reprinted, P. Davies, 1968; *A Game of Hide-and-Seek,* Knopf, 1951; *The Sleeping Beauty,* Viking, 1953, reprinted, Popular Library, 1976; *Hester Lilly: Twelve Short Stories,* Viking, 1954 (published in England as *Hester Lilly and Other Stories,* P. Davies, 1954); *Angel,* Viking, 1957; *The Blush and Other Stories,* P. Davies, 1958, Viking, 1959; *In a Summer Season,* Viking, 1961; *The Soul of Kindness,* Viking, 1964; *A Dedicated Man and Other Stories,* Viking, 1965; *Mossy Trotter* (juvenile), Harcourt, 1967; *The Wedding Group,* Viking, 1968; (contributor) J. Burnley, editor, *Penguin Modern Stories 6,* Penguin, 1970; *Mrs. Palfrey at the Claremont,* Viking, 1971; *The Devastating Boys and Other Stories,* Viking, 1972; *Blaming,* Viking, 1976. Contributor of short stories to the *New Yorker.*

SIDELIGHTS: Shortly before Elizabeth Taylor's death, a *Times Literary Supplement* critic called her one of "the four or five most distinguished living practitioners of the art of the short story in the English-speaking world." Other reviewers wrote similarly of Taylor's talents as a short-story writer and a novelist. In the *New York Times Book Review* Martin Levin referred to the author as "a pastel stylist," and a *Harper's* reviewer noted, "Taylor couldn't write an inelegant sentence if she tried and her prose is a delight." In *Library Journal,* Elizabeth Thalman once listed the "literary qualities that have won . . . Taylor a devoted following." According to Thalman these were "irony, humor, artful structuring and stylistic grace."

Some critics, however, found Taylor's characters insufficiently developed. A *Times Literary Supplement* reviewer, for example, wrote that in *The Wedding Group,* "Taylor . . . left too much unsaid, too many superb opportunities to expand a scene or a character only half explored." And Joyce Carol Oates, writing in the *Washington Post Book World,* remarked: "The people [Taylor] deals with in her fiction are not people, but characters. They are imagined as interior creations, existing within the confines of their particular stories."

Despite such negative criticism, Guy Davenport noted in *National Review* that Taylor's readers "realize that [they] are in the hands of a real novelist, the kind of analytical and unfoolable mind that invented the novel in the first place." Summing up Taylor's work, Alice McCahill wrote in *Best Sellers,* "Elizabeth Taylor . . . has to her credit a list of several novels, . . . all showing the same keen understanding of people, the ability to share that understanding with her readers, a sense of humor, and a gift and feeling for words."

MEDIA ADAPTATIONS: "A Dedicated Man" and *Mrs. Palfrey at the Claremont* were both adapted for television.

AVOCATIONAL INTERESTS: Travel in Greece.

BIOGRAPHICAL/CRITICAL SOURCES: Isis, January 28, 1959; *Review of English Literature* (London), April, 1960; *Harper's,* August, 1964; *New Republic,* August 22, 1964; *Times Literary Supplement,* September 24, 1964, May 9, 1968, August 27, 1971, June 9, 1972; *Library Journal,* February 1, 1968; *New York Times Book Review,* March 31, 1968, April 23, 1972; *Best Sellers,* April 1, 1968; *National Review,* April 23, 1968; *New Statesman,* August 27, 1971; *Washington Post Book World,* April 30, 1972; *Encounter,* September, 1972; *Contemporary Literary Criticism,* Gale, Volume II, 1974, Volume IV, 1975.

OBITUARIES: London Times, November 21, 1975.†

* * *

TAYLOR, (Paul) Kent 1940-

PERSONAL: Born November 8, 1940, in New Castle, Pa.; son of Paul D. Taylor (a salesman) and Goldie (McKee) Mihu; married Joan Czaban, October 5, 1963 (divorced, June 14, 1969); children: Mark Shane. *Education:* Ohio Wesleyan University, B.A., 1962. *Politics:* "Disillusioned radical." *Religion:* None. *Home:* 1450 Tenth Ave., San Francisco. Calif. 94122.

CAREER: Formerly research technician at Case Western Reserve University, Cleveland, Ohio; has worked as merchant seaman and longshoreman; St. Vincent Charity Hospital, Cleveland, Ohio, research technician, 1965-70; University of California, San Francisco, medical research associate, beginning 1970. *Member:* Psi Chi.

WRITINGS—Poetry: *Selected Poems,* Renegade Press, 1963; *Aleatory Letters,* Renegade Press, 1964; (with d. a. levy) *Fortuitous Mother*—, Renegade Press, 1965; *Late Station,* 7 Flowers Press, 1966; (with Carl Woideck and levy) *Three Poems by Cleveland Poets,* Seven Flowers Press, 1967; *Torn Birds,* Black Rabbit Press, 1969; *Poems,* Black Rabbit Press, 1971; *Cleveland Dreams,* Second Aeon Publications, 1971; *Shit Outside When Eating Berries,* Black Rabbit Press, 1971; *Empty Ground,* Black Rabbit Press, 1976; *Driving Like the Sun,* Vagabond Press, 1976.

Contributor to anthologies: *The Living Underground: An Anthology of Contemporary American Poetry,* edited by Hugh Fox, Whitston Publishing Company, 1973; *Vagabond Anthology,* edited by John Bennett, Vagabond Press, 1978; *Planet Detroit Poems Anthology,* edited by Kurt Nimmo and Christine Lahey-Dolega, Planet Detroit Press, 1983.

Author of chapbooks in "Polluted Lake Series" and "Ohio City Series," both 1965. Contributor to *Poetry Review* (Tampa), *Poetmeat, Free Lance input, kauri, Mother, Gooseberry, Marrahwanna Quarterly, Beginning, 15¢, Fine Arts, Radical Voice, Poetry Parade, Melody of the Muse, Silver Cesspool, Ole, Podium,* and other publications.

WORK IN PROGRESS: New poems.

SIDELIGHTS: Kent Taylor told *CA:* "If I were the last person alive, I feel I would still write. Writing poetry is my attempt to hold off the abyss, to pin down some bit of existence, to leave a mark of passage, and, of course, to outwit death. Poems are souvenirs from distant places; places too extreme for long habitation and too remote to find again."

* * *

TAYLOR, Peter (Hillsman) 1917-

PERSONAL: Born January 8, 1917, in Trenton, Tenn.; son of

Matthew Hillsman (a lawyer) and Katherine (Taylor) Taylor; married Eleanor Lilly Ross (a poet), June 4, 1943; children: Katherine Baird, Peter Ross. *Education:* Attended Vanderbilt University, 1936-37, and Southwestern at Memphis, 1937-38; Kenyon College, A.B., 1940. *Home:* 1841 Wayside Pl., Charlottesville, Va. 22903. *Office:* Department of English, Wilson Hall, University of Virginia, Charlottesville, Va. 22901.

CAREER: University of North Carolina at Greensboro, 1946-67, became professor of English; University of Virginia, Charlottesville, professor of English, 1967—. Visiting lecturer, Indiana University, 1949, University of Chicago, 1951, Kenyon College, 1952-57, Oxford University, 1955, Ohio State University, 1957-63, and Harvard University, 1964 and 1972-73. *Military service:* U.S. Army, 1941-45; became sergeant. *Member:* National Academy and Institute of Arts and Letters, American Academy of Arts and Sciences.

AWARDS, HONORS: Guggenheim fellowship in fiction, 1950; National Institute of Arts and Letters grant in literature, 1952; Fulbright fellowship to France, 1955; first prize, O. Henry Memorial Awards, 1959, for short story "Venus, Cupid, Folly and Time"; Ohioana Book Award, 1960, for *Happy Families Are All Alike;* Ford Foundation fellowship, to England, 1961; Rockefeller Foundation grant, 1964; second prize, *Partisan Review-Dial* for short story "The Scoutmaster"; National Academy and Institute of Arts and Letters gold medal for literature, 1979.

WRITINGS: A Long Fourth and Other Stories, introduction by Robert Penn Warren, Harcourt, 1948; *A Woman of Means* (novel), Harcourt, 1950; *The Widows of Thornton* (short stories and a play), Harcourt, 1954; *Tennessee Day in St. Louis* (play), Random House, 1959; *Happy Families Are All Alike: A Collection of Stories,* Astor Honor, 1959; *Miss Leonora When Last Seen and Fifteen Other Stories,* Astor Honor, 1963; (editor with Robert Lowell and Robert Penn Warren) *Randall Jarrell, 1914-1965,* Farrar, Straus, 1967; *The Collected Stories of Peter Taylor,* Farrar, Straus, 1969; "A Stand in the Mountains" (play), first produced in Abingdon, Va., at Barter Theatre, 1971, published in *Kenyon Review,* 1965; *Presences: Seven Dramatic Pieces* (contains "Two Images," "A Father and a Son," "Missing Person," "The Whistler," "Arson," "A Voice through the Door," and "The Sweethearts"), Houghton, 1973; *In the Miro District and Other Stories,* Knopf, 1977; (editor) *The Road and Other Modern Stories,* Cambridge University Press, 1979.

Contributor of stories to numerous anthologies, including: *The Best American Short Stories,* edited by Martha Foley, Houghton, 1945-46, 1950, 1959, 1965, edited by Foley and David Burnett, 1960, 1961; *Prize Stories of 1950: The O. Henry Awards,* edited by Herschell Bricknell, Doubleday, 1950; *The Literature of the South,* edited by R. C. Beatty and others, Scott, Foresman, 1952; *Stories from the Southern Review,* edited by Cleanth Brooks and Robert Penn Warren, Louisiana State University Press, 1953; *Prize Stories 1959: The O. Henry Awards,* edited by Paul Engle, Doubleday, 1959; *Prize Stories 1961: The O. Henry Awards,* edited by Richard Poirier, Doubleday, 1961; *Prize Stories 1965: The O. Henry Awards,* edited by Poirier and William Abrahams, Doubleday, 1965; *The Sense of Fiction,* edited by Robert L. Welker and Herschel Gover, Prentice-Hall, 1966.

Contributor of short stories to *Sewanee Review, Virginia Quarterly Review, Kenyon Review, New Yorker,* and numerous other journals.

WORK IN PROGRESS: A novel; short stories; a play, "The Girl from Forked Deer."

SIDELIGHTS: Although Peter Taylor has received critical acclaim for his novel *A Woman of Means* and for his plays, he is best known for his work in short fiction. Gene Baro, in a *New York Herald Tribune Book Review* article, calls Taylor "one of the most accomplished short-story writers of our time." And John Leonard of the *New York Times* says that "Peter Taylor makes stories the way Mercedes-Benz makes automobiles: to last."

Born in Tennessee and now living in Virginia, Taylor is considered by many critics to be a Southern writer in the tradition of William Faulkner and Flannery O'Connor. A *Village Voice* reviewer notes that Taylor "often writes about the decay of the gentrified South (something he has observed firsthand)." In the *Times Literary Supplement,* Zachary Leader says that Taylor's "roots in the Southern literary tradition are deep, . . . [and an understanding of his] complex relation to the tradition this background fostered is helpful to an appreciation of his stories."

Leader cites Allen Tate (literary critic and poet) and Andrew Lytle (novelist and editor of *Sewanee Review*) as two of Taylor's early influences. As an undergraduate at Vanderbilt University, the author met, and became friends with, several members of the Southern Agrarian movement, including Randall Jarrell and Robert Penn Warren. Later, Taylor, Jarrell, and another friend, Robert Lowell, studied under well-known poet and critic John Crowe Ransom. Ransom was the acknowledged leader of the Agrarians, who advocated, among other things, a return to a non-industrialized South, one free of Northern influence and exploitation. Out of this philosophy, writes Leader, "grew the dream of the 'Old South,' or what Taylor calls 'the old times.' . . . These writings look past the South's supposedly aristocratic origins to the pre-settlement wilderness, an Eden whose native inhabitants were as unspoilt and unspoiling as the surroundings from which they drew their character."

Yet, despite this foundation in Southern literature, Taylor is as often praised for the universality of his stories as for their superior quality. When his first collection, *A Long Fourth and Other Stories,* appeared in 1948, a *New Yorker* critic said that these stories were "particularly notable for a vein of unobtrusive humor and for a complete lack of the regional chauvinism that Southern authors so frequently exhibit when writing about their own." Coleman Rosenberger, in the *New York Herald Tribune Weekly Book Review,* wrote: "These seven short stories by Peter Taylor are a little island of excellence in the flood of books from the South. They have the qualities of permanence: a fine craftmanship, integrity, and the imprint of a subtle and original intelligence."

Critical response to Taylor's next collection, *The Widows of Thornton,* solidified his reputation as a master in his field. Mack Morriss, in a *Saturday Review* article, called the book "as free of ugliness as the lingering nutmeg and as unpretentious as coldwater cornbread. . . . [Taylor] has created a wistful, clinging, but utterly non-depraved image of the Deep South that some of us, his regional contemporaries, have been trying to recall from our childhood." F. H. Lyell of the *New York Times* commented: "The stories in [this book] are outwardly simple but psychologically complex and powerful, and under the surface of events in the regions he knows best the author discloses the universal longings of the human heart." In the *New York Herald Tribune Book Review,* Dan Wickenden declared, "It seems improbable that any American work of fiction more distinguished and enduring than *The Widows of Thornton* will appear this year.''

Through the years, praise for Taylor's work in short fiction has continued, with emphasis on his natural ear for dialogue, his smooth, finely-paced style, and especially his sensitive character portrayal. A *Times Literary Supplement* critic calls him ''a cautious writer with an intellectual respect for his characters. Every change of mood and feeling is something he considers worth recording.'' And, in *Saturday Review,* William Peden writes: ''[Taylor's] stories succeed because his characters and their words are real, moving, and convincing. In each story there is always at least one character who becomes 'finely aware' (the phrase is Henry James's) of the situations in which they find themselves. It is this fine awareness that gives the 'maximum of sense' to what befalls them, which makes these quietly effective stories so meaningful to the reader.''

In *Sewanee Review,* well-respected novelist, editor, and short-story writer George Garrett states: ''There are few American writers, living or dead, who have for so long a time received so much praise—and this from the most honored quarters—for artistic achievement. For thirty years now, . . . [Taylor's] stories have been admired, analyzed, anthologized, preserved as major models of excellence for all other writers.'' Finally, in a *Saturday Review* article, Linda Kuehl concludes, ''I am tempted to say that Peter Taylor is the greatest living short-story writer, but I shall be prudent and suggest he is the greatest one writing in English today.''

CA INTERVIEW

CA interviewed Peter Taylor by phone December 4, 1981, at his home in Charlottesville, Va.

CA: You grew up in a storytelling family. Did that directly inspire your writing?

TAYLOR: I think it did. My theory is that you listen to people talk when you're a child—a Southerner does especially—and they tell stories and stories and stories, and you feel those stories must mean something. So, really, writing becomes an effort to find out what these stories mean in the beginning, and then you want to find out what *all* the stories you hear or think of mean. The story you write is interpretation. People tell the same stories over and over, with the same vocabulary and the same important points, and I don't think it ever crosses their minds what they mean. But they do mean something, and I'm sure that is what influenced me. Then too, you just inherit a storytelling urge.

CA: Anatole Broyard, in a review of In the Miro District *said that you write ''as if [you] came from a place where no one ever interrupts while you are talking.''*

TAYLOR: That is true. That's the only way people can tell stories properly.

CA: Did you have any initial struggle to find your own voice?

TAYLOR: It's very easy after the fact to say, ''Yes, I did this and that.'' If you like to tell stories and you have a certain sensibility, you realize that you have to have the right voice and the right way of telling the stories, and I think you learn from other writers. But I'm always skeptical of people saying this. Hemingway was always said to have been taught so much by Gertrude Stein and Ford and other writers, but if you look at the reports that he wrote for his high-school newspaper in Kansas City, you see they read like pure Hemingway. And then I think in the case of a writer like Hemingway—or maybe this is true with all writers; I hadn't thought of it before—it's a coincidence of the way one tells his stories and what the stories are. It's the right voice for the stories from one's own experience.

CA: Critics often classify your writing as Southern and then go on to show how it differs from other Southern writing. Do you think there's too much critical emphasis on regional distinctions?

TAYLOR: There sometimes is. Everyone wants to be a universal writer, but then that's what art is all about: the relation of the particular to the general. One writes particularly about a place or about a time. Some people are provincial in time, in writing about one period or one kind of experience. And one kind of experience is your relation to a certain place. It's a very complicated thing. I like to think that I write in response to my experience, to discover what I think and what I experience, because I think that's what writing is: a discovery of what you know and a discovery of what you think. Not an *expression* of what you know and what you think, because I think it works the other way for the poet (meaning the literary artist).

I don't think of myself as a regional writer and I don't really like it when people say, ''He writes about the urban South.'' I'm writing about people under certain circumstances, but I'm always concerned with the individual experience and the unique experience of that story. Goodness knows I don't have any political vision for the South, in retrospect or in the future, but I have strong feelings about it. And I think that's the main thing that you have to write about, not only what you have ideas about but what you feel about most keenly. My earliest recollections are a sense of the past in the South, and that's what I think has been responsible for a lot of Southern writing. There was the great turning point: before 1865 is the past; after that, the present. That's dramatic, and it's bound to create stories.

CA: You studied under Allen Tate, John Crowe Ransom, Robert Penn Warren, and Cleanth Brooks. How do you feel they influenced you most strongly?

TAYLOR: It was my great luck to have come along at the time when those people were in the part of the world I was growing up in. And they did influence me very much. Allen Tate was the person who really influenced me most, I suppose, and next John Crowe Ransom. Tate was simply my freshman English teacher, and at once he liked my writing, and he gave me the feeling that writing was important. That's the big thing he did. He was a wonderful teacher in that sense. He made me feel that literature was important. And then he and I became great friends. I learned more from him as a friend than formerly as a teacher. I studied with Ransom, too, for several years, and I think he had a real influence on the form my writing has taken. He made me write poetry and discouraged me from writing fiction. I think that made my fiction more compressed and made me turn to short stories more than to novels, because I did write poetry. And not only was my studying under Ransom an influence in that way, but some other fellow students who became my lifelong friends were poets—Jarrell and Lowell.

CA: You haven't been interested in doing critical writing. Have people pressured you to do any?

TAYLOR: Oh yes, they have. They don't anymore, because they know I'll snap at them. I know if you're editing a literary magazine it's hard to get people to write criticism, so I don't blame them really, but I resolved that if I were to teach school, that would be the limit of my critical exercise. I've taught school off and on for thirty-odd years, and the last review I wrote was of Allen Tate's *The Fathers* when it came out in 1930. I've just refused. It's so hard for me; it's as hard as writing fiction and it takes up just as much time, maybe more time.

I've never learned anything from critics, that is, from people writing about my work. I think one of the difficulties is that literary criticism is in the same medium as its subject. Art criticism is more distinct. But the critic writes with words, which are used in writing stories or poems, and there's really a certain competition. Also, the best criticism is poetry and literature itself. Eliot's essays are literary works of art and so are Tate's and so are Ivor Winters's and Edmund Wilson's, so it's not a distinctly separate thing.

CA: Several of the pieces collected in In the Miro District *are verse narratives. What led you to use that technique?*

TAYLOR: I've always been interested in compression, trying to see how much one could put into a short story and yet have it as good as a longer story. In the end, short stories are not just short novels. They're much more intense, and the words have to do a lot more work. Just as in the lyric poem. You don't say that because something's a sonnet, because it's only fourteen lines, it's not as good as a short story by O. Henry. It's compression; you have to say more in every word. I'd tried for years before I printed these to write stories in formal verse with meter and rhyme, but that was always a failure. When my friends, like Lowell, began writing free verse, I began eyeing it and saying, "Well, why couldn't I do stories in sort of a relaxed way?" But I don't think they are poems. Lowell called them story poems, and he liked them, but I call them broken-line prose. I think the advantage is that you get the two kinds of syntax and, most important, you get the line end. The form doesn't work unless the line end is significant, so that you're saying something by that word, the impact at the end of the line.

CA: The first story of In the Miro District, *"The Captain's Son," is an old favorite of mine. I read it in the* New Yorker *originally.*

TAYLOR: I had fun writing that story. I wrote it first in broken-line prose, but I couldn't sustain it. It's very hard. When those line ends cease to be functional, when I'm just breaking it because it's convenient, then I think, "Well, I've failed." So I went back and put it all in regular prose. I also wrote the title story in that form originally.

CA: Would you like to comment on your long association with the New Yorker*?*

TAYLOR: It's been almost pure joy, because they have treated me very well always. It's *the* magazine that treats its writers well. I have had times, though, when I wasn't published there. I think the differences in editorships entered into that; I don't know. I've only been in the *New Yorker* office about twice. It's all been by correspondence. You hear about the *New Yorker*'s straightening out a writer's style and changing things. Well, they've never changed anything without my consent, not even a comma. I was particularly fond of Katherine White, who was my first editor there. She was so considerate. Then William Maxwell was my editor for a number of years, and I liked him very much. He said in New York last year, "I have only one regret, and that is that I asked you to change certain things in the stories, make them conform more." He said he'd come to think that writers should have their own awkwardnesses, that somehow that's better than having it all just right and conventional. I thought that was a great insight on his part. He's a good writer and he was a fine editor. I feel the *New Yorker* is a real literary magazine, that they select writers and pieces for the work itself and not for the name. They've always played down the name and played up the work, which I think is important. There are criticisms to be made of it, perhaps, because they limit themselves to what sort of thing they will do, but however wrong their judgments, they are *literary* judgments. Most other big, slick magazines primarily follow the trends rather than set them.

CA: How do you approach the teaching of writing?

TAYLOR: I feel that it's a way of teaching literature, a particular way of helping people read literature. If a real writer comes along, you can help him make leaps. But I would feel my class was a great fraud unless I believed that ninety percent of the people I have in it are very literary and want to read better. They want to write, too, but it's mostly immature work. The first six weeks of the term I won't look at anybody's work. I read aloud to them and have them reading the masters. I've had many people tell me that they've never read the same after the writing class. It's like playing tennis: you may not become a champion, but you watch a game with more interest after you've tried to play it. And I think anybody who is going to try to teach literature should discipline himself for a time under a teacher and try to write. We now have one here at Virginia, but I don't really believe in professional schools of writing. I don't believe in degrees in writing unless they are in preparation for teaching.

CA: How is your time divided between teaching and writing?

TAYLOR: I teach rather a good deal in the fall. I do most of my teaching at conferences. I have class meetings also, but that's really to give the students a time to air their opinions and to know each other, the right of young literary people. I have an hour's conference with every student on everything he writes; I think the only way you can teach anything is in a personal confrontation. I have twenty-five or thirty students, and having an hour with them over each of their stories pretty well fills my time. I only teach until Christmas. I teach a full load in the fall, and then after Christmas only my best are allowed to take a course, a sort of correspondence course. I'm gone most of the time. I go to Key West and stay until the first of April. That takes me away from the university. I don't like to be too much inside academia. Being here just in the fall is fun; then I'm in Key West and that's when I do my real writing. I pick up my pencil every day here, but I don't do much work. I don't really worry about it until I get to Key West.

CA: Key West has become quite a writer's colony, hasn't it?

TAYLOR: Yes, there are a lot of writers there. It's wonderful for us because my wife and I have so many old friends who are there just the time we're there.

CA: Do you and your wife [the poet Eleanor Ross Taylor] discuss your work in progress with each other?

TAYLOR: No. We long since came to the notion that it's best not to show each other the work until it's all finished. Then we want to, but we don't even discuss it before; we figure it's sort of bad luck to talk about it while you're doing it.

CA: Is there work under way that you'd like to talk about?

TAYLOR: I'm writing the usual stories. I'm writing some long stories; I have three things going that I'm happy about. Any one of them may turn out to be a couple of hundred pages or all three may, and Knopf will print them. If they're shorter than that, they'll print them together in a book, and if they're not, they'll print them in separate books. I like to work on several things at once.

CA: I've read that you and your wife enjoy buying and restoring old houses. Have you done that recently?

TAYLOR: We've just bought one—don't get me started. It's down in a beautiful little valley with no other house you can see. There's a rock quarry with a place to swim in it and a big spring. The house was built between 1750 and 1800 by some of the Lewises related to Meriwether Lewis, who went west with the Lewis and Clark expedition. It's an amazing house, a very tiny brick end-chimney house. It had no window lights in it. It had a little old English basement with a kitchen in it. We call it "The Ruin" and we're not going to restore it completely; we don't live there. I'm planting fruit trees. I like to say we're going to have an American Sissinghurst.

BIOGRAPHICAL/CRITICAL SOURCES: New Republic, March 8, 1948, June 26, 1950, October 18, 1969, May 7, 1977; *New Yorker,* March 13, 1948; *New York Herald Tribune Weekly Book Review,* March 14, 1948; *New York Times,* March 21, 1948, June 11, 1950, May 2, 1954, October 11, 1969, April 7, 1977; *Saturday Review of Literature,* March 27, 1948; *Chicago Sunday Tribune,* May 14, 1950, December 6, 1959; *Time,* May 15, 1950; *New York Herald Tribune Book Review,* May 2, 1950, May 2, 1954, December 6, 1959; *Saturday Review,* May 8, 1954, November 28, 1959, October 18, 1969, May 14, 1977, March 15, 1980; *San Francisco Chronicle,* May 13, 1954; *New York Times Book Review,* November 22, 1959, March 29, 1964, October 19, 1969, February 12, 1970, April 3, 1977; *New Statesman,* August 6, 1960; *Times Literary Supplement,* August 19, 1960, September 30, 1977, January 22, 1982; Louis D. Rubin, Jr. and Robert D. Jacobs, *South: Modern Southern Literature in Its Cultural Setting,* Doubleday, 1961; *Sewanee Review,* autumn, 1962; Charles E. Eisinger, *Fiction of the Forties,* University of Chicago Press, 1963; *Book Week,* March 8, 1964; *New York Review of Books,* June 11, 1964.

Critique, Volume IX, number 3, 1967; *Newsweek,* October 20, 1969; *Georgia Review,* winter, 1970; Albert Griffith, *Peter Taylor,* Twayne, 1970; *Southern Review,* Volume VII, number 1, 1971, winter, 1979; *Contemporary Literary Criticism,* Gale, Volume I, 1973, Volume IV, 1975, Volume XVIII, 1981; *Shenandoah,* winter, 1973, winter, 1977, summer, 1978; *Virginia Quarterly Review,* spring, 1978; *Washington Post,* March 15, 1980; *Village Voice,* April 28, 1980.

—Sketch by Peter M. Gareffa

—Interview by Jean W. Ross

TAYLOR, Theodore 1921-
(T. T. Lang)

PERSONAL: Born June 23, 1921, in Statesville, N.C.; son of Edward Riley (a molder) and Elnora (Langhans) Taylor; married Gweneth Goodwin, October 25, 1946 (divorced, 1977); married Flora Gray Schoenleber, April 18, 1981; children: (first marriage) Mark, Wendy, Michael. *Education:* Attended U.S. Merchant Marine Academy, 1942-43, and Columbia University; studied with American Theatre Wing, 1947-49. *Politics:* Republican. *Religion:* Protestant. *Home:* 675 Diamond St., Laguna Beach, Calif. *Agent:* Armitage Watkins, A. Watkins, Inc., 77 Park Ave., New York, N.Y. 10016.

CAREER: Portsmouth Star, Portsmouth, Va., reporter, 1941-42; National Broadcasting Co. Radio, New York City, sportswriter, 1942; *Sunset News,* Bluefield, W. Va., sports editor, 1946-47; New York University, New York City, assistant director of public relations, 1947-48; *Orlando Sentinel Star,* Orlando, Fla., reporter, 1949-50; Paramount Pictures, Hollywood, Calif., publicist, 1955-56; Perlberg-Seaton Productions, Hollywood, story editor and associate producer, 1956-61; full-time writer, 1961—. Producer and director of documentary films. *Military service:* U.S. Merchant Marine, 1942-44; U.S. Naval Reserve, active duty, 1944-46, 1950-55, became lieutenant. *Member:* Academy of Motion Picture Arts and Sciences, Writers Guild, Authors League of America, California Writers Guild.

AWARDS, HONORS: California Literature Medal Award, Jane Addam's Children's Book Award, Southern California Council on Literature for Children and Young People Award, Woodward School Award, Lewis Carroll Shelf Award, silver medal from Commonwealth Club, best book award from University of California, Irvine, all 1970, all for *The Cay;* Spur Award from Western Writers of America, 1977, for *A Shepherd Watches, A Shepherd Sings.*

WRITINGS: The Magnificent Mitscher, Norton, 1955; *Fire on the Beaches,* Norton, 1957; *The Body Trade,* Fawcett, 1967; (with Robert Houghton) *Special Unit Senator,* Random House, 1970; (co-author with Kreskin) *The Amazing World of Kreskin,* Random House, 1974; *Jule: The Story of Composer Jule Styne,* Random House, 1979.

Juveniles: *People Who Make Movies,* Doubleday, 1967; *The Cay* (*Horn Book* honor list), Doubleday, 1969; *The Children's War,* Doubleday, 1971; *Air Raid, Pearl Harbor,* Crowell, 1971; *Rebellion Town,* Crowell, 1973; *The Maldonado Miracle,* Doubleday, 1973; *Teetoncey,* Doubleday, 1974; *Teetoncey and Ben O'Neal,* Doubleday, 1975; *Battle in the Arctic Seas,* Crowell, 1976; *The Odyssey of Ben O'Neal,* Doubleday, 1977; *A Shepherd Watches, A Shepherd Sings,* Doubleday, 1977; *The Trouble with Tuck,* Doubleday, 1981; *Battle Off Midway Island,* Avon, 1981; *HMS Hood Versus Bismarck,* Avon, 1982.

Author of two screenplays, "Showdown," Universal, 1973, and "Night without End," and of seventeen documentary films. Also author of books under the pseudonym T. T. Lang. Contributor of short stories and novelettes to magazines, including *Redbook, Argosy,* and *Saturday Evening Post.*

WORK IN PROGRESS: O Break U, for Avon; *Summer Me, Winter Me, Summer Me Again,* with Phyllis Loughton Seaton; *Walking Up a Rainbow,* a novel; *The Book of Islands,* nonfiction.

SIDELIGHTS: Ever since he left home at seventeen to join the *Washington Daily News,* Theodore Taylor has lived a life of adventure. "Dullness is the death of writing, as well as many other things. I love to switch around, to change gears," he told *CA.* In the way of practicing that philosophy, Taylor has been variously employed as a newspaperman, prize-fighter manager, merchant seaman, naval officer, magazine writer, movie publicist, production assistant, and documentary film maker. He has worked in Japan, Taiwan, and Hong Kong, as well as in most of Europe. Some of the background for his award-winning adventure novel *The Cay* came as a result of his living in the Caribbean.

Though he writes both fiction and nonfiction on a variety of subjects, Taylor is perhaps best known for his engrossing accounts of decisive war battles. His 1971 publication for young readers, *Air Raid, Pearl Harbor,* received wide critical acclaim for combining "the values of a documentary with the excitement of a cliff-hanger," in the words of one *Saturday Review* critic. Equally impressive was Taylor's *Battle Off Midway Island,* a children's book that "provided readers of any age with a splendid picture of the naval battles that turned the Pacific War around," according to Drew Middleton in the *New York Times Book Review.* Praising the skill with which Taylor relates his narrative, Middleton concludes: "He does not strain for effect; he does not have to. His depiction of the men, the aircraft and the ships makes the action seem as vivid as it was that day when the Navy took its first step on the long road to victory."

BIOGRAPHICAL/CRITICAL SOURCES: New York Times Book Review, June 26, 1969, July 11, 1971, November 15, 1981; *Saturday Review,* June 28, 1969, August 21, 1971; *Washington Post,* May 26, 1979.

* * *

TENNYSON, G(eorg) B(ernhard) 1930-

PERSONAL: Born July 13, 1930, in Washington, D.C.; son of Georg Bernhard and Emily (Zimmerli) Tennyson; married Elizabeth C. Johnstone, July 13, 1953; children: Cameron Noel Emily, Holly Elizabeth. *Education:* George Washington University, A.B., 1953, M.A., 1959; graduate study at Shakespeare Institute, Stratford on Avon, England, summer, 1952, and University of Freiburg, 1953-54; Princeton University, M.A., 1961, Ph.D., 1963. *Religion:* Anglo-Catholic. *Home:* 4963 Densmore Ave., Encino, Calif. 91436. *Office:* Department of English, University of California, Los Angeles, Calif. 90024.

CAREER: Washington Star, Washington, D.C., reporter, 1956-57; National Security Agency, Washington, D.C., classified work, 1957-59; University of North Carolina at Chapel Hill, assistant professor of English, 1962-64; University of California, Los Angeles, assistant professor, 1964-67, associate professor, 1967-71, professor of English, 1971—. *Military service:* U.S. Army, Signal Corps, 1954-56. *Member:* International Association of University Professors of English, Modern Language Association of America, Philological Association of the Pacific Coast, Victorian Society (London), Carlyle Society (Edinburgh), Conference on Christianity and Literature, Philadelphia Society. *Awards, honors:* Fulbright fellow in Germany, 1953-54; Guggenheim fellow, 1970-71.

WRITINGS: Sartor Called Resartus: The Genesis, Structure, and Style of Thomas Carlyle's First Major Work, Princeton University Press, 1966; *An Introduction to Drama,* Holt, 1967; (editor) *A Carlyle Reader: Selections from the Writings of Thomas Carlyle,* Random House, 1968; *Carlyle and the Modern World,* Carlyle Society, 1972; *Carlyle and His Contemporaries,* Duke University Press, 1975; (editor with Edward E. Ericson, Jr.) *Religion and Modern Literature,* Eerdmans, 1975; (with Donald Gray) *Victorian Literature: Poetry,* Macmillan, 1976; (with Gray) *Victorian Literature: Prose,* Macmillan, 1976; (editor with wife, Elizabeth J. Tennyson) *An Index to "Nineteenth-Century Fiction,"* University of California Press, 1977; (editor and contributor with V. C. Knoepflmacher) *Nature and the Victorian Imagination,* University of California Press, 1977; *Victorian Devotional Poetry: The Tractarian Mode,* Harvard University Press, 1981.

Contributor: *From the Medieval Epic to the Epic Theatre of Bertolt Brecht,* University of Southern California Press, 1967; *Victorian Prose: A Guide to Research,* Modern Language Association of America, 1973; *Evolution of Consciousness: Studies in Polarity,* Wesleyan University Press, 1976; K. J. Fielding and Rodger L. Tarr, editors, *Carlyle Past and Present,* Vision Press, 1976; Owen Barfield, editor, *History, Guilt, and Habit,* Wesleyan University Press, 1979; Richard A. Levine, editor, *The Victorian Experience: The Prose Writers,* Ohio University Press, 1982.

Contributor to *Southern Review, Victorian Poetry, Monatshefte,* and other journals. *Nineteenth-Century Fiction,* editor, 1971-74, member of advisory board, 1974—; member of advisory board of *Victorian Studies,* 1970-73, *Occasional Review,* 1974-77, and *Prose Studies,* 1977—.

WORK IN PROGRESS: A study of the works of Owen Barfield; a study of the prose style of John Henry, Cardinal Newman.

SIDELIGHTS: "In the Academy, it is customary to say that one's writing and research grow out of one's teaching," G. B. Tennyson told *CA.* "This is often but not always true. Sometimes it is the other way around. In recent years, for example, I have been able to offer courses in the Oxford Inklings (C. S. Lewis, Owen Barfield, Charles Williams, Tolkien, et al) because my own reading and research had been quite independently leading in that direction. My particular aim in work on the Inklings is to expand the awareness of the work of Owen Barfield. In that respect I suppose I could be called 'Barfield's Bulldog.' At the same time I continue to write in the area that is my primary teaching responsibility, British Victorian literature, and especially in the work of Thomas Carlyle (who was his own bulldog) and in the writers of the Tractarian Movement. Thus, my writing both grows out of and grows into my teaching. And, like most academic writers, I always hope that what I write will reach not only the professional audience but somehow will also touch one or two of those supposed general readers, opening for them the doors of a larger intellectual life."

AVOCATIONAL INTERESTS: Art, architecture, gardening, Confederate history, ecclesiastical history, Christian mysticism, cartography, iconology, hagiology.

BIOGRAPHICAL/CRITICAL SOURCES: Times Literary Supplement, June 12, 1981.

* * *

TERRACE, Vincent 1948-

PERSONAL: Born May 14, 1948, in Manhattan, N.Y.; son of Vincent (a printer) and Anne (Lauro) Terrace. *Education:* New York Institute of Technology, B.F.A., 1971. *Religion:* Roman

Catholic. *Home and office:* 1830 Delancey Pl., Bronx, N.Y. 10462.

CAREER: Korvette's Department Store, New York, N.Y., salesman, 1971-75; writer, 1975—.

WRITINGS—Published by A. S. Barnes, except as indicated: *The Complete Encyclopedia of Television Programs, 1947-1976,* Volumes I and II, 1976, 2nd edition published as *The Complete Encyclopedia of Television Programs, 1947-1979,* 1979; *Radio's Golden Years, 1930-1960,* 1980; *Television 1970-1980,* A. S. Barnes/Oak Tree, 1981; *Actors' TV Credits, Supplement II, 1977-81,* Scarecrow, 1982.

Contributor: James Robert Parish, *The Great Spy Pictures,* Scarecrow, 1974; Parish, *The Great Gangster Pictures,* Scarecrow, 1976; Parish, *The Great Western Pictures,* Scarecrow, 1976; Parish, *The Great Science Fiction Pictures,* Scarecrow, 1977; Judy Fireman, *The Television Book,* Workman Publishing, 1977; Alvin H. Marill, *Movies Made for Television,* Arlington House, 1980; David Strauss and Fred L. Worth, *Hollywood Trivia,* Warner Books, 1981.

WORK IN PROGRESS: 'Neath the Putty Noses and Fake Hair: The Story of Ross Martin, with Patricia Ann Anders; *Charlie Chan: A Definitive Study,* with Bert Stangler; *Television 1980-1984;* revised edition of *Radio's Golden Years.*

SIDELIGHTS: Vincent Terrace told *CA:* "My television books were the first of their kind and I hope to continue in the future with additional volumes that document, in the most complete detail possible, the countless programs that have and will become a part of American broadcasting history."

* * *

THEMERSON, Stefan 1910-

PERSONAL: Born January 25, 1910, in Poland; married Franciszka Weinles (an artist.). *Education:* Educated in Poland. *Home:* 28 Warrington Crescent, London W.9, England.

CAREER: Writer. *Military service:* Polish Army, 1940-44; served in France and England. *Awards, honors:* Polish Order of Merit, 1976.

WRITINGS—Published by Gaberbocchus, except as indicated: *Dno Nieba* (poems; title means "On the Bottom of the Sky"), [London], 1943; *Croquis dans les tenebres* (poems; title means "Sketches in Darkness"), Hachette, 1944; *The Lay Scripture* (prose-poem), Froshaug, 1947; *Jankel Adler* (essay), 1948; *Bayamus* (novel), Editions Poetry—London, 1949, revised edition, Gaberbocchus, 1965; *Adventures of Peddy Bottom* (juvenile), Editions Poetry—London, 1951, revised edition, Gaberbocchus, 1954; *Wooff Wooff; or, Who Killed Richard Wagner?* (fiction), 1951, revised edition, 1967; *Professor Mmaa's Lecture* (novel), 1953, Overlook Press, 1976; *"Factor T" and "Semantic Sonata"* (essays), 1956, revised edition, 1972; *Kurt Schwitters in England* (essay), 1958.

Cardinal Polatuo (novel), 1961; *Semantic Divertissements* (humor), 1962; *Tom Harris* (novel), 1967, Knopf, 1968; *Appollinaire's Lyrical Ideograms,* 1968; *St. Francis and the Wolf of Gubbio* (opera), 1972; *Special Branch* (essay), 1972; *Logic Labels and Flesh* (philosophical essays), 1974; *On Semantic Poetry,* 1975; *General Piesc; or, The Case of the Forgotten Mission* (fiction), 1976.

The Chair of Decency (the 1981 Johan Huizinga Lecture), Atheaneum (Amsterdam), 1982; *The Urge to Create Visions* (avant-garde film and photography), De Harmonie-Gaberbocchus, 1983.

Avant-garde films, with wife, Franciszka Themerson: "Apteka," 1931; "Europa," 1932; "Moment Musical," 1933; "Zwarcie," 1935; "The Adventures of a Good Citizen," 1937; "Calling Mr. Smith," 1943; "The Eye and the Ear," 1944.

Author of children's books, in Polish, 1930-37.

SIDELIGHTS: "The background of Stefan Themerson as experimental filmmaker, composer, and esthetician naturally arouses expectations of something truly daring from his [1967] novel," Albert Goldman writes in the *New York Times Book Review.* "These expectations are at least partially fulfilled. *Tom Harris* is an epistemological . . . story that poses the question whether any man can truly be known by any other man."

Written as a mystery, arranged in two parts, and told by an unnamed narrator, *Tom Harris* spoofs several conventions of the novel, according to critics who differ widely in their estimations of its success. While *Punch* reviewer Martin Shuttleworth dismisses the book as "incoherent, incompetent, and rather dim," and the *Atlantic*'s Phoebe Adams laments that after a "promising beginning, the book drifts into philosophizing about life," other reviewers cite *Tom Harris*'s redeeming qualities. In his *Books and Bookmen* review, for instance, David Spiller notes the book's close "concern with fundamental human problems; the effects of class, intelligence and physical characteristics upon individuals and society; and notably, an obsession with reality and unreality." And, writing in *Best Sellers,* James A. Phillips allows that Themerson asks some "tricky" questions. "I doubt if this book will gain a wide following, but I, for one, am curious enough to want to see Themerson's next novel," Phillips concludes.

Themerson's books have been published in Polish, Italian, French, German, Swedish, and Dutch.

BIOGRAPHICAL/CRITICAL SOURCES: Punch, May 31, 1967; *Times Literary Supplement,* June 15, 1967; *Books and Bookmen,* August, 1967; *Best Sellers,* April 15, 1968; *Atlantic,* May, 1968; *New York Times Book Review,* May 26, 1968.

* * *

THODY, Philip 1928-

PERSONAL: Born March 21, 1928, in Lincoln, England; son of Thomas Edwin (a teacher) and Florence Ethel (Hart) Thody; married Joyce Elizabeth Woodin, September 18, 1954; children: Peter, Caroline, Sarah, Nicholas. *Education:* King's College, London, B.A. (with first class honors), 1951, M.A. by thesis, 1953. *Politics:* Conservative. *Religion:* Agnostic Anglican. *Home:* 6, The Nook, Leeds, England. *Office:* Department of French, University of Leeds, Leeds LS2 9JT, England.

CAREER: University of Paris, Paris, France, lecteur anglais, 1953-54; University of Birmingham, Birmingham, England, temporary assistant lecturer in French, 1954-55; Queen's University of Belfast, Belfast, Northern Ireland, assistant lecturer, 1955-58, lecturer in French, 1958-65; University of Leeds, Leeds, England, professor of French literature, 1965—. Visiting professor, University of Western Ontario, 1963-64, University of California, Berkeley, summer, 1964, Harvard University, summer, 1968; visiting Centenary Professor, University of Adelaide, 1974; visiting fellow, University of Canterbury, Christchurch, 1977. *Military service:* Royal Air Force, 1946-48.

WRITINGS: Albert Camus: A Study of His Work, Hamish Hamilton, 1957; *Jean-Paul Sartre: A Literary and Political Study,* Hamish Hamilton, 1960; *Albert Camus: 1913-1960,* Hamish Hamilton, 1961; *Jean Genet: A Study of His Novels and Plays,* Hamish Hamilton, 1968, Stein & Day, 1969; *Jean Anouilh,* Oliver & Boyd, 1968; *Four Cases of Literary Censorship* (inaugural lecture), Leeds University Press, 1968.

Laclos: Les Liasons dangereuses, Edward Arnold, 1970; *Jean Paul Sartre: A Biographical Introduction,* Studio Vista, 1971; *Aldous Huxley: A Biographical Introduction,* Studio Vista, 1973; *Roland Barthes: A Conservative Estimate,* Macmillan and Humanities, 1977; *A True Life Reader for Children and Parents,* Wildwood House (London), 1977; *Dog Days in Babel* (novel), Wildwood House, 1979.

Translator: (And author of preface) George Orwell, *Essais choisis,* Gallimard, 1960; (and author of introduction and notes) Albert Camus, *Notebooks, 1935-1942,* Knopf, 1963 (published in England as *Carnets, 1935-1942,* Hamish Hamilton, 1963); Jacqueline de Romilly, *Thucydide et l'imperialisme,* Basil Blackwell, 1963; Jean-Paul Sartre, *Les Sequestres d'Altona,* University of London Press, 1965; Camus, *Carnets, 1942-1951,* Hamish Hamilton, 1966; (and editor) Camus, *Lyrical and Critical Essays,* Hamish Hamilton, 1967.

Also translator of *Le Dieu cache,* by Lucien Goldmann, Routledge & Kegan Paul. Contributor to *Chambers's Encyclopaedia, Concise Encyclopaedia of World Literature,* and of articles and reviews to *Twentieth Century, History Today, London, Revue de Lettres Modernes, Times Literary Supplement,* and *Yorkshire Post.*

WORK IN PROGRESS: Correspondences: Or Where to Change; The Semiology of Everyday Life.

SIDELIGHTS: Jean Genet: A Study of His Novels and Plays has been translated into German, and *Jean-Paul Sartre: A Biographical Introduction* has been translated into Portuguese.

AVOCATIONAL INTERESTS: Cricket, bridge, talk.

BIOGRAPHICAL/CRITICAL SOURCES: Washington Post Book World, April 27, 1969; *Books Abroad,* summer, 1969, winter, 1970.

* * *

THOMAS, G. K.
See DAVIES, L(eslie) P(urnell)

* * *

THOMAS, Gwyn 1913-1981

PERSONAL: Born July 6, 1913, in Cymmer, County of Glamorgan, South Wales; died c. April 14, 1981, in Cardiff, Wales; son of Walter (a miner) and Ziphorah (Davies) Thomas; married Eiluned Thomas (a secretary), May 1, 1938. *Education:* Attended Madrid University, 1933; St. Edmund Hall, Oxford, B.A. (with honors), 1934. *Politics:* Humanist. *Religion:* Humanist. *Home:* Cherry Trees, Wyndham Park, Peterston-Super-Ely, Cardiff CF5 6LR, Wales. *Agent:* Curtis Brown Ltd., 1 Craven Hill, London W2 3EW, England.

CAREER: University of Wales, Cathays Park, extension lecturer, 1934-40; school teacher in modern European languages in Barry, South Wales, 1940-62; full-time playwright and novelist, 1962-81. *Awards, honors: Evening Standard* Newspaper Drama Award-Most Promising Playwright, 1961; *Western Mail* best performer on television award, 1966; Welsh Arts Council award, 1976.

WRITINGS—Novels: *The Dark Philosophers,* Dobson, 1946, Little, Brown, 1947; *The Alone to the Alone,* Nicholson & Watson, 1947, published as *Venus and the Voters,* Little, Brown, 1948; *All Things Betray Thee,* M. Joseph, 1949, published as *Leaves in the Wind,* Little, Brown, 1949; *The World Cannot Hear You: A Comedy of Ancient Desires* (British Book Society selection), Gollancz, 1951, Little, Brown, 1952; *Now Lead Us Home,* Gollancz, 1952; *A Frost on My Frolic,* Gollancz, 1953; *The Stranger at My Side,* Gollancz, 1954; *Point of Order* (British Book Society selection), Gollancz, 1956; *The Love Man* (British Book Society selection), Gollancz, 1958, published as *A Wolf at Dusk,* Macmillan, 1959; *The Sky of Our Lives,* Hutchinson, 1972.

Plays: *The Keep* (first produced in London at Royal Court Theatre, 1961), Elek, 1961; "Loud Organs," first produced in Blackpool, England, 1962; "Jackie the Jumper," first produced in London at Royal Court Theatre, 1963; "The Loot," first produced in schools, 1965; "Sap," first produced in Cardiff at Sherman Theatre, 1974; "The Breakers," first produced in Cardiff at Sherman Theatre, 1976.

Television plays: "The Slip," 1962; "The Dig," 1963; "The Keep," 1970; "Adelphi Terrace," 1975; "Up and Under," 1975.

Radio plays: "Gazooka," 1952; "Forenoon," 1953; "The Deep Sweet Roots," 1953; "The Singers of Meadow Prospect," 1954; "Vive L'Oompa," 1955; "Up the Handling Code," 1955; "To This One Place," 1956; "Merlin's Brow," 1957; "The Long Run," 1958; "Noise," 1960; "The Walk-Out," 1963; "The Entrance," 1964; "The Alderman," 1966; "The Giving Time," 1968; "He Knows, He Knows," 1972.

Other: *Where Did I Put My Pity?* (stories), Progress Publishing, 1946; *Gazooka and Other Stories,* Gollancz, 1957; *Ring Delirium 123* (stories), Gollancz, 1960; *A Welsh Eye* (essays), Stephen Greene, 1964; *A Hatful of Humors* (essays), Schoolmaster Publishing, 1965; *A Few Selected Exits: An Autobiography of Sorts,* Little, Brown, 1968; *The Lust Lobby: Stories,* Hutchinson, 1971; (editor) Saunders Lewis, *Presenting Saunders Lewis,* University of Wales Press, 1973; (with Cyril Batstone) *Old Rhondda in Photographs,* S. Williams, 1974.

Work represented in anthologies, including *Plays of the Year,* Volume 26, edited by J. C. Trewin, Ryerson Press, 1963, and *Eight Plays: Book 2,* edited by Malcolm Stuart Fellows, Cassell, 1965. Contributor to Canadian, British, and U.S. periodicals, including *Atlantic Advocate, Holiday, Travel and Camera, Punch,* and *Listener.*

SIDELIGHTS: Gywn Thomas told *CA:* "My work is based on the humour of astonishment. That has been the prevailing mood of my life, the reaction to multiple shock of a community as sonorously sensitive as a drumskin. I was brought up in South Wales, an area of Britain, pulverised by a long and bitter slump in the years between the wars. The victims of this dislocation were people suckled on evangelical religion and radical politics. To them if any day dawned without the hot promise of heaven upon it, they blamed it on a failure of the post-office. From them I distilled a laughter of ravelling delusions, gallows-humor, scored for a horde of gifted hymn-singers. They lost simultaneously their aboriginal language (Welsh), their major industry (coal) and most of their religion. They recovered from the shock of this only when the Second World War came along with its promise of atomic power and cheaper funerals.

"Yet they remained sweet and, in a sardonic way, serene. That fact has given me my main interest today; the anatomy of those who forswear sweetness and reject serenity. The migrants, the fanatics, the bandits, the aberrants, the lurchers away from stability, courtesy and calm. Will we one day find a social anaesthetic that will keep people from being restless pests? Will it come from philosophic wisdom, lobectomy, overwhelming fear, or pellets in the water-supply?

"In pursuit of this thesis and through sheer physical interest I have paid much attention to the Moorish occupation of Spain. The years when Africa stormed into Europe and the Spanish reconquest made religious and racial violence an essential strand in European policy."

While he was primarily known as a novelist and playwright, Thomas also wrote an autobiography entitled *A Few Selected Exits: An Autobiography of Sorts.* Writing in the *New York Times,* Clive Barnes described the publication as "an engaging book to be warmly recommended to anyone who . . . has an affection for the frantic and untamed Celtic spirit." And, in his *Saturday Review* critique, Philip Burton observed that "Gwyn Thomas transmutes the commonplace into the delightfully grotesque by means of his keen perception, his twinkling compassion, his cartoon comedy, and his deft way with words."

BIOGRAPHICAL/CRITICAL SOURCES: Gwyn Thomas, *A Few Selected Exits: An Autobiography of Sorts,* Little, Brown, 1968; *New York Times,* April 15, 1969; *Saturday Review,* April 26, 1969; *Listener,* February 18, 1971; *Times Literary Supplement,* September 22, 1972.

OBITUARIES: London Times, April 18, 1981; *New York Times,* April 19, 1981; *Detroit Free Press,* April 19, 1981; *Washington Post,* April 20, 1981; *AB Bookman's Weekly,* May 4, 1981; *Publishers Weekly,* May 8, 1981.†

* * *

THOMPSON, William Irwin 1938-

PERSONAL: Born July 16, 1938, in Chicago, Ill.; son of Chester Andrew and Lillian (Fahey) Thompson; married Gail Joan Gordon, February 3, 1960 (divorced, January 30, 1979); married Beatrice Madeleine Rudin, March 1, 1979; children: (first marriage) Evan Timothy, Hilary Joan, Andrew Rhys. *Education:* Pomona College, B.A., 1962; Cornell University, M.A., 1964, Ph.D., 1966. *Home:* Baca Grant Ranch, Crestone, Colo. 81131. *Office address:* Lindisfarne Association, R.F.D. 2, West Stockbridge, Mass. 01266.

CAREER: Massachusetts Institute of Technology, Cambridge, instructor, 1965-66, assistant professor of humanities, 1966-68; York University, Toronto, Ontario, associate professor, 1968-72, professor of humanities, 1972-73; Lindisfarne Association, West Stockbridge, Mass., founder and director, 1973—. Visiting professor, Syracuse University, 1973, University of Hawaii, 1981. *Member:* Society for the Arts, Religion and Contemporary Culture (fellow). *Awards, honors:* Woodrow Wilson fellowship, 1962, dissertation fellowship, 1964; first prize, National Playwriting Contest, University of Santa Clara, 1966; award from the Jasper Whiting Foundation of Boston, 1967; Old Dominion fellowship, 1967; *At the Edge of History* was nominated for a National Book Award, 1972; Threshold Foundation traveling fellowship, 1979.

WRITINGS: The Imagination of an Insurrection: Dublin, Easter 1916, Oxford University Press, 1967; *At the Edge of History,* Harper, 1971; *Passages about Earth: An Exploration of the New Planetary Culture,* Harper, 1974; *Evil and World Order,* Harper, 1976; *Darkness and Scattered Light: Four Talks on the Future,* Doubleday, 1978; *The Time Falling Bodies Take to Light: Mythology, Sexuality, and the Origins of Culture,* St. Martin's, 1981; *From Nation to Emanation: Planetary Culture and World Governance,* [Findhorn, Scotland], 1982; (contributor) Robert O'Driscoll, editor, *The Celtic Consciousness,* Dolmen, 1982.

Also contributor to *Reading Modern Poetry,* edited by Paul Engle, 1967, *Seeing Through Shuck* (anthology), edited by Richard Kostelantz, 1973, and *Tomorrow Is Our Permanent Address,* 1980. Contributor of articles to *Tulane Drama Review, Sewanee Review, Antioch Review,* and other journals.

SIDELIGHTS: William Irwin Thompson "may be classified as a futurist, as a thrower of straws and a reader of tea-cup sludge," observes John Seelye in the *New Republic.* "But he is a particular kind of futurist, enwrapped in myths, primitive rituals, and modern fables: Jung, Tolkein, Pynchon, Chomsky, Marx, N. O. Brown are all grist for his amazing mill." In his National Book Award nominee, *At the Edge of History,* Thompson applies his theory of the future to a study of human history, posing such ambitious questions as: Where is man going? Where has he been?

Unlike those who believe that science will provide the answers, Thompson criticizes technocracy. A teaching stint as a humanities instructor at the Massachusetts Institute of Technology led him to conclude: "M.I.T. needs a large psychiatric clinic because the effect of technological training is to do to the psyche what industry does to the environment." Thompson's alternative to a future rigidly prescribed by technological advancements—"think wild." Specifically, as *Time* reviewer Charles Elliott relates, "Thompson suggests that the seemingly solid fabric of mundane existence has gaps, where 'the millennial imagination of the future is interrupting the daily news of the present.' Spot the gap and you can see forward into history."

Reviewers don't know quite what to make of such assertions. As Elliott puts it, "Thompson's arguments are not always easy to follow (or to swallow); yet they buzz with intelligence and an attractive likelihood." Concludes Seelye, "One comes away from this book as from a magic show, dazzled if not convinced, and . . . you might plan a trip to *The Edge of History* and take a look for yourself. It *is* wild."

AVOCATIONAL INTERESTS: Anthropology, archaeology, and 8mm film-making.

BIOGRAPHICAL/CRITICAL SOURCES: Times Literary Supplement, September 21, 1967; *South Atlantic Quarterly,* summer, 1968; *New York Times,* March 19, 1971; *Time,* April 26, 1971; *New Republic,* June 19, 1971, May 23, 1981; *Best Sellers,* July 15, 1971; *Nation,* January 31, 1981.

* * *

THORNBURG, Newton K(endall) 1930-

PERSONAL: Born May 13, 1930, in Harvey, Ill.; son of Newton Kendall and Rhea (Mattox) Thornburg; married Karin Larson, September 20, 1954; children: Kristen, Mark, Douglas. *Education:* University of Iowa, B.A., 1951, further study at Writers Workshop, 1953. *Politics:* Conservative. *Religion:* Agnostic. *Home:* 10510 Northeast 45th St., Kirkland, Wash. 98033. *Agent:* Don Congdon, Harold Matson Company, 276 Fifth Ave., New York, N.Y. 10001.

CAREER: Advertising copywriter for various agencies, 1960-70; novelist, 1970—.

WRITINGS: Gentlemen Born, Fawcett, 1967; *Knockover,* Fawcett, 1968; *To Die in California,* Little, Brown, 1973; *Cutter and Bone,* Little, Brown, 1976; *Black Angus,* Little, Brown, 1978; *Valhalla,* Little, Brown, 1980; *Beautiful Kate,* Little, Brown, 1982; *Dreamland,* Arbor House, 1983.

SIDELIGHTS: Novelist Newton K. Thornburg writes fast-paced adventure stories that combine cynical humor with a bleak view of modern life. In his second book, *Cutter and Bone,* Thornburg weaves his social commentary into a compelling mystery. As Philip Herrera observes in his *Time* review: "The novel's form—pursuit and confrontation—owes much to the conventional thriller. But *Cutter and Bone* is much more than skillful entertainment. The places and people ring true."

The story concerns Alex Cutter, a disfigured Vietnam veteran, and his friend Rich Bone, a corporate drop-out who bums around Santa Barbara hoping that "something will change." When Bone witnesses a man he later recognizes to be tycoon J. J. Wolfe stuffing a woman's body into a trash can, he and Cutter devise a plan for blackmail. Though the story is told with humor, the *Newsweek* critic suggests that "behind the mordant wise-guy banter that binds Cutter and Bone in a compact of jaundiced alienation, Thornburg spins a serious fable." Their attempt to extort money from Wolfe ultimately leads to their doom.

Writing in the *New York Times Book Review,* Peter Andrews credits the book's success to Thornburg's technique and characterization: "He [has] created one of the few novels in which it is entirely possible for a pair of amateurs to get mixed up in trying to catch a murderer. . . . He tops that by giving a realistic picture of how they are likely to fare, which is not very well. . . . It is a fast, touching, furious and frightening novel that builds to a tremendous climax capped by a shattering last line. I have not read anything better in this genre in the last ten years."

MEDIA ADAPTATIONS: Cutter and Bone was adapted into a movie and released by United Artists in 1981. It was re-released later that year by United Artists Classics under the title "Cutter's Way."

BIOGRAPHICAL/CRITICAL SOURCES: Publishers Weekly, July 19, 1976, November 28, 1980; *New York Times Book Review,* October 24, 1976, November 26, 1978; March 1, 1981; *Newsweek,* October 25, 1976; *Time,* December 6, 1976; *Washington Post,* October 17, 1978; *Los Angeles Times,* January 8, 1981; *Chicago Tribune Book World,* July 19, 1981.

* * *

TICKLE, P(hyllis) A(lexander) 1934-

PERSONAL: Born March 12, 1934, in Johnson City, Tenn.; daughter of Philip Wade (an educator) and Katherine (Porter) Alexander; married Samuel Milton Tickle (a physician), June 17, 1955; children: Nora Katherine (Mrs. Devereaux D. Cannon, Jr.), Mary Gammon (Mrs. David S. Clark), Laura Lee (Mrs. John R. Goodman), John Crockett II, Philip Wade (deceased), Samuel Milton, Jr., Rebecca Rutledge. *Education:* Shorter College, student, 1951-54; East Tennessee State University, B.A., 1955; Furman University, M.A., 1961. *Religion:* Episcopalian. *Home:* 3522 Lucy Road S., Lucy, Tenn. 38053. *Office:* Suite 401, Mid-Memphis Tower, 1407 Union Ave., Memphis, Tenn. 38104.

CAREER: Furman University, Greenville, S.C., instructor in psychology, 1960-62; Southwestern at Memphis, Memphis, Tenn., instructor in English, 1962-65; Memphis Academy of Arts, Memphis, Tenn., teacher and dean of humanities, 1965-71; writer, 1971—. Poet-in-residence, Brooks Memorial, 1977—; poetry co-ordinator for Cumberland Valley Writers' Conference, 1977—. Member of literary panel, Tennessee Arts Commission; member of board of directors of Upward Bound at LeMoyne-Owen College, 1968-70, and Sunshine Day Care Center, 1970-71; member of board of trustees of Grace-St. Luke's Episcopal School, 1970-76.

MEMBER: Tennessee Literary Arts Association (former vice-president for western Tennessee), Committee of Small Magazine Editors and Publishers. *Awards, honors:* Tickle's narrative poem "American Genesis" was selected by Tennessee's American Bicentennial Commission as a bicentennial poem for the state, 1976.

WRITINGS: An Introduction to the Patterns of Indo-European Speech, Memphis Academy of Arts, 1968; *Figs and Fury* (a chancel play; first produced in Memphis, Tenn. at Grace-St. Luke Episcopal Church), St. Luke's Press, 1974, 2nd edition, 1976; *It's No Fun to Be Sick* (juvenile), St. Luke's Press, 1976; *The Story of Two Johns* (for children facing the loss of a loved one), St. Luke's Press, 1976.

On Beyond Koch, Brooks Memorial, 1980; *On Beyond Ais,* Tennessee Arts Commission, 1982; *Puppeteers for Our Lady,* St. Michael's Church, 1982; *The City Essays,* Dixie Flyer Press, 1982.

Contributor to anthologies: *Contemporary Poets of the New South,* Brevity Press, 1977; *The Good People of Gomorrah,* St. Luke's Press, 1979; *Tigris and Euphrates,* St. Luke's Press, 1979; *Windflower Almanac,* Windflower Press, 1980; *Womanblood,* Continuing Saga, 1981.

Columnist for *The Dixie Flyer* and for *The Feminist Digest,* 1975-78; poetry editor, *Chaff,* 1978; founding editor, St. Luke's Press; secretary of the board, Raccoon Books, a tax-exempt sister house to St. Luke's Press. Has contributed poems to periodicals, including *Images, Nexus,* and *Velvet Wings.* Contributor of articles and reviews to magazines.

WORK IN PROGRESS: A nonfiction book on American Christianity.

SIDELIGHTS: Phyllis Tickle writes: "I lecture a great deal in colleges and schools and find this a most satisfying experience. I think of myself as a poetess by trade, but having had seven children has also given me some kind of background for enjoying children's literature and I am finding that rewarding also. Spanish is my language of choice and all things Mexican and/or Spanish are as natural to me as breathing.

"The women's movement comes at a time when being wife, mother, and writer is no longer regarded as natural, but rather as a social statement or a private protest. Within the framework of all these factors, I find myself drawn more and more toward the ancients—to the works and values of Sappho and Catullus—to Cavafy and Rilke in our own time, and always, to Eliot."

* * *

TONEY, Anthony 1913-

PERSONAL: Born June 28, 1913, in Gloversville, N.Y.; son of Michael and Susan (Betor) Toney; married Edna Greenfield (an actress), April 8, 1947; children: Anita Karen, Adele Susan. *Education:* Syracuse University, B.F.A., 1934; attended l'Academie de la Grande Chaumiere and l'Ecole Superieure des Beaux Arts, both in Paris, 1937-38; Columbia University, M.A., 1952, Ed.D., 1955. *Home:* 16 Hampton Pl., Katonah, N.Y. 10536.

CAREER: Painter associated with ACA Gallery, New York, N.Y., graphic artist and illustrator, and instructor in art. Work exhibited at one-man shows at ACA Gallery, 1949—, at Santa Barbara Museum, William Rockhill Nelson Gallery of Art, University of New Mexico, Kansas City Art Institute, Staten Island Museum, and elsewhere, and in group shows at Corcoran Gallery of Art, Carnegie Institute, Whitney Museum of American Art, Pennsylvania Academy, Metropolitan Museum, American Academy of Art, National Academy of Design, and at a number of university and art association exhibitions; paintings in collections of Whitney Museum, Berkshire Museum, University of Illinois, Ohio Wesleyan University, and other public and private collections. Instructor in art at School for Advanced Study, 1934-36, Stevenson School, 1948-52, Hofstra College (now University), 1953-55, and New School for Social Research, 1953—. Has also instructed classes at Rockland Center for the Arts, Bedford Art Center, North Shores Art Center, and Community Arts Council. Director of summer arts workshop, Lenox, Mass., 1955-60. Artist-in-residence, Brandeis University, spring, 1974. *Military service:* U.S. Army Air Forces, 1942-45; served in Southwest Pacific; received Distinguished Flying Cross with two oak leaf clusters and Air Medal with four oak leaf clusters.

MEMBER: Artists Equity Association, National Society of Mural Painters, Audubon Artists, National Academy of Design (academician), Artists Equity Association of New York, Kappa Delta Pi. *Awards, honors:* Purchase prize, University of Illinois, 1950; first prize, Artists Equity Association Show, 1952; Grumbacher Award, 1954, Medal of Honor, 1966, 1975, 1981, all from Audubon Artists; Emily Lowe Award, 1955; first prize, Mickewiecz Art Competition, 1956; purchase prize, Staten Island Museum, 1957; Ranger Fund purchase award, 1966, 1976; Pauline Mintz Memorial Award, 1967, 1975; Childe Hassam purchase award, 1967, 1976; National Institute of Arts and Letters Award, 1968; National Academy Award, 1968; Benjamin Altman 2nd prize for figure painting, from National Academy of Design, 1975, 1981; Judy Brenner Memorial Award.

WRITINGS: (Contributor of drawings with others) *The Tune of the Calliope* (poems and drawings of New York), Yoseloff, 1958; (editor) *150 Masterpieces of Drawing,* Dover, 1963; (author and illustrator) *Creative Painting and Drawing,* Dover, 1966; (contributor) *The Family Creative Workshop,* Time-Life, 1975; *Painting and Drawing,* Prentice-Hall, 1978; (contributor) *Leonardo,* Volume X, Pergamon, 1977; (contributor) *The Palette and the Flame,* International Publishers, 1979. Also contributor to *Funk and Wagnalls Encyclopedia,* 1980. Contributor of articles to art magazines, including *Art Voices* and *Journal of Artists Opinions.*

SIDELIGHTS: Anthony Toney told *CA:* "The search for reality and a more equitable transformation of society motivate whatever I do. Writing has always been a necessity. I outline, but generally rough out whole and then reorganize and refine the work. The art books attempt to develop clear and comprehensive richness on how to paint and draw. Both Dover and Prentice-Hall asked me to do the books. Naturally, I'm influenced by my social context, including its literature. I search for depth, clarity, and, above all, freshness, within the above context. The current scene seems corrupt, dominated by the crassest profit motivations, but good writing persists, most of it unpublished. I advise writers to fight for integrity and discovery. While I'm always involved with some writing and a new work is in process, I'm mainly an easel and mural painter."

* * *

TOPSFIELD, L(eslie) T(homas) 1920-1981

PERSONAL: Born January 6, 1920, in Westcliff-on-Sea, Essex, England; died November 3, 1981; son of Frederick Thomas and Lilian Grace (Cross) Topsfield; married Valerie Green, April 20, 1943; children: David, Andrew. *Education:* St. Catharine's College, Cambridge, B.A., 1946, M.A., 1948, Ph.D., 1951. *Home:* 1 Silver St., Cambridge, England.

CAREER: Cambridge University, Cambridge, England, university assistant lecturer, 1950-55, university lecturer in Provencal and French, 1955-81, St. Catharine's College, fellow, 1953-81, praelector, 1955-60, domestic bursar, 1960-65, tutor, 1966-79. *Military service:* British Army, 1940-46; served in Far East, 1943-45; became major. *Member:* Modern Humanities Research Association (secretary, 1950-56), Society for the Study of Medieval Languages and Literature, Society for French Studies, International Arthurian Society.

WRITINGS: (Contributor) Anthony Thorlby, editor, *Penguin Companion to Literature: European Literature,* Penguin, 1969; *Les Poesies du troubadour Raimon de Miraval,* Nizet (Paris), 1971; *Troubadours and Love,* Cambridge University Press, 1975; *Chretien de Troyes: A Study of the Arthurian Romances,* Cambridge University Press, 1981; (contributor) Bone Ford, editor, *Pelican Guide to English Literature,* Pelican, 1982.

Editor of the *Year's Work in Modern Language Studies,* three volumes, Cambridge University Press, 1957-59; member of executive committee of *Medium Aevum,* 1970-81. Contributor of articles and reviews to journals in his field.

SIDELIGHTS: In his book *Chretien de Troyes: A Study of the Arthurian Romances,* medieval Romance scholar L. T. Topsfield identified the dramatic purposes and underlying themes that he believed characterized de Troyes's texts. Topsfield's thesis, while "rather too tidy" for the *Times Literary Supplement* reviewer D.D.R. Owen was nonetheless acknowledged as being "carefully and elegantly argued," and Owen recommended the book "with the same enthusiasm and cautionary words as when I advance my own very different ideas."

AVOCATIONAL INTERESTS: Archaeological sites of Greek and Roman antiquity.

BIOGRAPHICAL/CRITICAL SOURCES: Times Literary Supplement, September 12, 1975, June 12, 1981; *Yale Review,* December, 1975.

OBITUARIES: London Times, November 12, 1981.

[Revised sketch verified by wife, Valerie Green Topsfield]

* * *

TORRIE, Malcolm
See MITCHELL, Gladys (Maude Winifred)

* * *

TOWNE, Peter
See NABOKOV, Peter (Francis)

TOYNBEE, Polly (Mary Louisa) 1946-

PERSONAL: Born December 27, 1946, on Isle of Wight; daughter of Philip Theodore (a writer) and Anne (Powell) Toynbee; granddaughter of the historian, Arnold Toynbee; married Peter George James Jenkins (a political writer), 1970; children: three daughters. *Education:* Attended St. Anne's College, Oxford. *Politics:* Social Democrat. *Religion:* None. *Home:* 1 Crescent Grove, London S.W. 4, England. *Agent:* A. D. Peters, 10 Buckingham St., London WC2N 6BU, England.

CAREER: Journalist with *Observer,* London, England, 1968-70, *Washington Monthly,* Washington, D.C., 1970-71, *Observer,* 1972-77, *Guardian,* Manchester, England, 1977—.

WRITINGS: Leftovers (novel), Weidenfeld & Nicolson, 1966; *A Working Life* (social reporting), Hodder & Stoughton, 1970; *Hospital,* Hutchinson, 1977; *The Way We Live Now,* Eyre Methuen, 1981. Contributor to *Washington Post, Cosmopolitan, Queen, Observer, New Statesman, Evening Standard, Sunday Times,* and *World Medicine.*

WORK IN PROGRESS: A reporting book on adoption.

BIOGRAPHICAL/CRITICAL SOURCES: Nova, October, 1966; *Private Eye,* April, 1967; *Times Literary Supplement,* December 4, 1981.

* * *

TRAGER, Frank N(ewton) 1905-

PERSONAL: Born October 9, 1905, in New York, N.Y.; son of Benjamin and Eda (Shapiro) Trager; married Helen Gilbson, 1936. *Education:* New York University, B.S., 1927, A.M., 1928, Ph.D., 1951. *Home:* 3024 Santa Lucia Ave., Carmel, Calif. 93923. *Office:* Department of National Securities Affairs, Root Hall, Naval Postgraduate School, Monterey, Calif. 93940.

CAREER: Johns Hopkins University, Baltimore, Md., instructor in philosophy, 1928-34; U.S. Government, Washington, D.C., civil servant, 1934-36; program executive for private social agencies, New York City, 1938-43, 1945-51; Technical Cooperation Administration, director of U.S. aid program, Rangoon, Burma, 1951-53; New York University, New York City, administrator and research professor, 1953-58, professor of international affairs, 1958-81; Naval Postgraduate School, Monterey, Calif., research professor of national security affairs, 1982—. Visiting professor, Yale University, 1960-61; member of faculty, National War College, 1961-63; lecturer at U.S. Department of State Foreign Service Institute and Army, Army Air Forces, and Navy War colleges. Director of studies, National Strategy Information Center, 1966-81; member of Foreign Policy Research Institute. Consultant to U.S. Department of State, RAND Corp., and Hudson Institute. *Military service:* U.S. Army Air Forces, 1943-45.

MEMBER: International Institute for Strategic Studies, Council on Foreign Relations, Association for Asian Studies (board member), Asia Society, Royal Siam Society, Burma Research Society. *Awards, honors:* Research fellow at Center for International Studies, Massachusetts Institute of Technology, 1953-54; Carnegie fellow at Council on Foreign Relations, 1957-58; Air University award, 1966-69.

WRITINGS: Toward a Welfare State in Burma: Economic Reconstruction and Development, 1948-1954, Institute of Pacific Relations, 1954, revised edition published as *Building a Welfare State in Burma: 1948-1956,* 1958; *Burma: Land of Golden Pagodas,* Foreign Policy Association, 1954; (editor and contributor) *Burma,* three volumes, Human Relations Area Files Press, 1956; (with Patricia Wohlgemuth and Lu-Yu Kiang) *Burma's Role in the United Nations: 1948-1955,* Institute of Pacific Relations, 1956; (editor) *Annotated Bibliography of Burma,* Human Relations Area Files Press, 1956, published as *Burma: A Selected and Annotated Bibliography,* 1973; (editor) *Japanese and Chinese Language Sources on Burma: An Annotated Bibliography,* Human Relations Area Files Press, 1957; (editor) *Area Handbook for Burma,* Human Relations Area Files Press, 1958; (editor and author of introduction) *Marxism in Southeast Asia: A Study of Four Countries,* Stanford University Press, 1959.

(Editor and compiler) *Furnivall of Burma: An Annotated Bibliography of the Works of John S. Furnivall,* Southeast Asia Studies, Yale University, 1963; *Burma: From Kingdom to Republic,* Praeger, 1966; *Why Viet Nam?,* Praeger, 1966; (editor) *Communist China, 1949-1969: A Twenty-Year Appraisal,* New York University Press, 1970; (editor and author of introduction) *Burma: Japanese Military Administration,* University of Pennsylvania Press, 1971; (editor with Philip S. Kronenberg) *National Security and American Society: Theory, Process, and Policy,* University Press of Kansas, 1973; (with William Koenig) *Burmese Sittans, 1764-1826: Records of Rural Life and Administration,* University of Arizona Press, 1979.

Contributor: Abshire and Allen, editors, *National Security: Political, Military and Economic Strategies in the Decade Ahead,* Praeger and Hoover Institution, 1963; Jeane J. Kirkpatrick, editor, *The Strategy of Deception,* Farrar, Straus, 1963; William Henderson, editor, *Southeast Asia: Problems of United States Policy,* M.I.T. Press, 1963; Robert K. Sakai, editor, *Studies on Asia, 1965,* University of Nebraska Press, 1965; Marvin E. Gettleman, editor, *Viet Nam: History, Documents, and Opinions on a Major World Crisis,* Fawcett, 1965; *Isolating the Guerrilla, Classic and Basic Studies,* Government Printing Office, 1966; Louis Menashe and Ronald Radosh, editors, *Teach-ins: U.S.A. Reports, Opinions, Documents,* Praeger, 1967; Chonghan Kim, editor, *Communist China,* College of William and Mary, 1967; John G. Kirk, editor, *America Now,* Atheneum, 1968; Thomas M. Franck, editor, *Why Federations Fail: An Inquiry into the Requisites for Successful Federalism,* New York University Press, 1968.

C. C. Van den Heuvel, editor, *Guerrilla Warfare in Asia,* International Documentation and Information Centre, 1971; Witold S. Sworakowski, editor, *World Communism, A Handbook, 1918-1965,* Hoover Institution Press, 1973; Joyce E. Larson, editor, *New Foundations for Asian and Pacific Security,* National Strategy Information Center, 1980; Sam C. Sarkesian and William L. Scully, editors, *Military Struggle in the 1980s: U.S. Policy and Low Intensity Conflict,* Transaction Books, 1980.

Also contributor to *Encyclopedia Year Book 1969, Conference Proceedings: Economic and Political Development in Relation to Sea Power along the Routes from the Indian Ocean, Royal United Services Institute and Brassey's Defence Yearbook, 1975/76,* and *International Encyclopedia of the Social Sciences,* volume XVIII. Contributor of about 150 articles, chiefly on Asian subjects, to journals. Member of editorial board, *Orbis.*

TRECKER, Janice Law 1941-
(Janice Law)

PERSONAL: Born June 10, 1941, in Sharon, Conn.; daughter of James Ord and Janet (Galloway) Law; married Jerrold B. Trecker (a teacher and sportswriter), June 9, 1962; children: James. *Education:* Syracuse University, B.A., 1962; University of Connecticut, M.A., 1967. *Home and office:* 33 Westfield Rd., West Hartford, Conn. 06119.

CAREER: Junior high school English teacher in Windsor, Conn., 1962-66; elementary school mathematics teacher in West Hartford, Conn., 1967; writer, 1967—; University of Hartford, Hartford, Conn., writing instructor, 1981—. *Member:* Authors Guild, Authors League of America, National Organization for Women, Phi Beta Kappa.

WRITINGS—Published under name Janice Law, except as indicated: (Under name Janice Law Trecker), *Women on the Move,* Macmillan, 1975; (under name Janice Law Trecker) *Preachers, Rebels, and Traders,* Pequot Press, 1975; *The Big Payoff* (fiction), Houghton, 1975; *Gemini Trip* (fiction), Houghton, 1976; *Under Orion* (fiction), Houghton, 1978; *The Shadow of the Palms* (fiction), Houghton, 1979; *Death under Par* (fiction), Houghton, 1981. Author of "Women's Work in America," a filmstrip series, Schloat Productions, 1974. Contributor to academic journals and popular magazines, including *Saturday Review, Michigan Quarterly, Northeast Magazine,* and *Take One*. Film reviewer for *West Hartford News,* 1967—.

WORK IN PROGRESS: A historical novel set in the court of Louis XIV; a nonfiction account of the history of chastity; *Time Lapse,* a mystery.

AVOCATIONAL INTERESTS: Art, philosophy, music, bird-watching.

BIOGRAPHICAL/CRITICAL SOURCES: Los Angeles Times Book Review, May 18, 1980; *Washington Post Book World,* January 18, 1981; *Chicago Tribune Book World,* February 15, 1981; *New York Times Book Review,* March 8, 1981.

* * *

TREVINO, Elizabeth B(orton) de 1904-
(Elizabeth Borton)

PERSONAL: Surname given in some sources as de Trevino; born September 2, 1904, in Bakersfield, Calif.; daughter of Fred Ellsworth (a lawyer) and Carrie (Christensen) Borton; married Luis Trevino Gomez (a dealer in insurance and real estate), August 10, 1935; children: Luis Frederico (deceased), Enrique Ricardo. *Education:* Stanford University, B.A., 1925; studied violin at Boston Conservatory of Music. *Religion:* Roman Catholic. *Residence:* Cuernavaca, Mexico. *Agent:* McIntosh & Otis Inc., 475 Fifth Ave., New York, N.Y. 10017.

CAREER: Jamaica Plain Journal, Boston, Mass., reporter, 1927-28; Ginn & Company, Boston, apprentice in production and advertising, 1928-31; *Boston Herald American,* Boston, interviewer, 1930-34; professional writer and journalist. Publicist for Mexico City Tourist Department, National Railways, and National Symphony Orchestra, 1942-52. First violinist in Vivaldi Orchestra, 1962-67. Honorary lecturer, American Institute for Foreign Trade. *Member:* Women in Communications, Pan American Round Tables, Phi Beta Kappa. *Awards, honors:* Honorary citizen of Texas; medal of Kansas City Woman's Organization; Newbery Medal, 1966, for *I, Juan de Pareja;* Headliner award, Women in Communications.

WRITINGS: My Heart Lies South: The Story of My Mexican Marriage, Crowell, 1953, reprinted, 1972; *Even as You Love* (novel), Crowell, 1957; *The Greek of Toledo: A Romantic Narrative about El Greco* (novel), Crowell, 1959; *Where the Heart Is* (memoirs), Doubleday, 1962; *The Fourth Gift* (novel), Doubleday, 1966; *The House on Bittersweet Street* (novel), Doubleday, 1970; *The Music Within* (novel), Doubleday, 1973; *The Hearthstone of My Heart* (memoirs), Doubleday, 1977; *The Heart Possessed* (novel), Doubleday, 1978; *Among the Innocent* (novel), Doubleday, 1981.

Juveniles; under name Elizabeth Borton: *Pollyanna in Hollywood,* L. C. Page, 1931; *Our Little Aztec Cousin of Long Ago, Being the Story of Coyotl and How He Won Honor under His Kings,* L. C. Page, 1934; *Pollyanna's Castle in Mexico,* L. C. Page, 1934; *Our Little Ethiopian Cousin: Children of the Queen of Sheba,* L. C. Page, 1935; *Pollyanna's Door to Happiness,* L. C. Page, 1936; *Pollyanna's Golden Horseshoe,* L. C. Page, 1939.

Juveniles; under name Elizabeth B. de Trevino: *About Bellamy,* Harper, 1940; *Pollyanna and the Secret Mission,* L. C. Page, 1951; *A Carpet of Flowers,* Crowell, 1955, published as *A Carpet of Flowers: Una Alfombra de Flores,* Blaine Ethridge, 1975; *Nacar, the White Deer,* Farrar, Straus, 1963; *I, Juan de Pareja,* Farrar, Straus, 1965; *Casilda of the Rising Moon: A Tale of Magic and of Faith, of Knights and a Saint in Medieval Spain,* Farrar, Straus, 1967; *Turi's Poppa,* Farrar, Straus, 1968 (published in England as *Turi's Pappa,* Gollancz, 1969); *Here Is Mexico,* Farrar, Straus, 1970; *Beyond the Gates of Hercules: A Tale of the Lost Atlantis,* Farrar, Straus, 1971; *Juarez, Man of Law* (biography), Farrar, Straus, 1974.

WORK IN PROGRESS: A new novel, set in Mexico in 1800.

SIDELIGHTS: Many of Elizabeth B. de Trevino's books have been translated into foreign languages.

AVOCATIONAL INTERESTS: Music, history, ecology, Spanish and English literature, the cosmos, modern Catholicism, protection of animals—domestic and wild.

* * *

TRIEM, Eve 1902-

PERSONAL: Born November 2, 1902, in New York, N.Y.; married Paul Ellsworth Triem (a medical writer), September 20, 1924; children: Yvonne Patricia (Mrs. Joseph Prete), Peter Dewey. *Education:* Attended University of California, Berkeley, 1920-24; studied classic Greek at University of Dubuque, 1954-55, and University of Washington, 1961. *Politics:* "Labeled, a Democrat; actually, a Citizen of the Universe." *Religion:* Episcopalian. *Address:* P.O. Box 523, Seattle, Washington 98111.

CAREER: Poet; lecturer on poets; director of poetry workshops, YWCA, Seattle, 1962-64. *Awards, honors:* Award of the League to Support Poetry, 1946; award from National Institute of Arts and Letters, 1966; National Endowment on the Arts grant, 1968; Hart Crane and Alice Crane Memorial Fund prize, 1972; second prize, American Penwomen contest, 1976, for *The Process;* Helen Bullis Prize, from *Poetry Northwest,* 1979, for "Midsummer Rites"; Cortis grant, 1980-81.

WRITINGS: Parade of Doves (poetry), Dutton, 1946; *Poems,* A. Swallow, 1965; (translator) *Heliodora: Translations from the Greek Anthology,* Olivant, 1968; *E. E. Cummings,* University of Minnesota Press, 1969; *The Process* (collection of poetry), illustrations by sculptor Philip McCracken, Querencia Press, 1976; *Dark to Glow,* Querencia Press, 1979; *Midsummer Rites* (poetry), Seal Press, 1981. Contributor to *The Poet* (Scotland), *Botteghe Oscure* (Rome), *Kavita* (India), *Seattle Magazine,* and other publications.

WORK IN PROGRESS: A series of poems using the William Carlos Williams approach to the American language.

SIDELIGHTS: Eve Triem writes: "I have lived a difficult life but not like soldiers or ditch-diggers or engineers or war-correspondents. I have been cloistered within my marriage: perhaps the cloister within the cloister made me a poet. I am always grateful to anything, any incident, that kindles a poem. I envy, I wonder at, the creative ones who have acted in the phenomenal world: I too would have liked to canoe, to fish, to almost drown in waterfalls."

BIOGRAPHICAL/CRITICAL SOURCES: Poetry, May, 1966.

* * *

TRIGGER, Bruce G(raham) 1937-

PERSONAL: Born June 18, 1937, in Preston (now Cambridge), Ontario, Canada; son of John Wesley and Gertrude E. (Graham) Trigger; married Barbara Marian Welch, December, 1968; children: Isabel Marian, Rosalyn Theodora. *Education:* University of Toronto, B.A., 1959; Yale University, Ph.D., 1964. *Politics:* Social Democrat. *Religion:* None. *Home:* 3495 rue de la Montagne, Apt. 603, Montreal, Quebec, Canada H3G 2A5. *Office:* Department of Anthropology, McGill University, Montreal, Quebec, Canada.

CAREER: Chief archaeologist with Pennsylvania-Yale expedition to Egypt, 1962, and Oriental Institute Sudan expedition, 1964; Northwestern University, Evanston, Ill., assistant professor of anthropology, 1963-64; McGill University, Montreal, Quebec, 1964—, began as associate professor, currently professor of anthropology, chairman of department, 1970-75. Social Sciences and Humanities Research Council of Canada fellow, 1983. Member of council of the Institute for American History and Culture, 1980-83, and of board of directors, McCord Museum, 1980—. *Member:* American Anthropological Association (foreign fellow), Royal Anthropological Institute (fellow), Canadian Society for Archaeology Abroad, Royal Society of Canada (fellow), Sigma Xi. *Awards, honors:* Canada Council fellowships, 1968, 1977; Killam Award, 1971; Queen's Silver Jubilee Medal, 1977; Cornplanter Medal, 1979, for Iroquois research.

WRITINGS: History and Settlement in Lower Nubia, Yale University Publications in Anthropology, 1965; *The Late Nubian Settlement at Arminna West,* Publications of the Pennsylvania-Yale Expedition to Egypt, Number 2, 1967; *Beyond History: The Methods of Prehistory,* Holt, 1968; *The Huron: Farmers of the North,* Holt, 1969.

The Meroitic Funerary Inscriptions from Arminna West, Publications of the Pennsylvania-Yale Expedition to Egypt, Number 4, 1970; (with James F. Pendergast) *Cartier's Hochelaga and the Dawson Site,* McGill-Queen's University Press, 1972; *The Children of Aataentsic: A History of the Huron People to 1660,* McGill-Queen's University Press, 1976; *Nubia under the Pharaohs,* Thames & Hudson, 1976; *Time and Traditions: Essays in Archaeological Interpretation,* Columbia University Press, 1978; (editor) *Handbook of North American Indians,* Smithsonian Institution, 1978; *Gordon Childe,* Columbia University Press, 1980.

WORK IN PROGRESS: Preparing a revised edition of *The Children of Aataentsic* for translation into French; writing a book on the implications of archaeological and anthropological research for understanding early Canadian history.

BIOGRAPHICAL/CRITICAL SOURCES: American Anthropologist, April, 1969, April, 1971, August, 1973, December, 1978, September, 1979; *Times Literary Supplement,* November 28, 1980.

* * *

TROST, Lucille W(ood) 1938-

PERSONAL: Born November 4, 1938, in Candor, N.Y.; daughter of Stiles and Alice (Keim) Wood; married Charles H. Trost (a biologist and professor), June 18, 1960 (divorced, 1981); children: Scott Anthony. *Education:* Pennsylvania State University, B.S., 1960; University of Florida, M.S., 1963; Union Graduate School, Ph.D., 1975. *Home:* 225 North Lincoln, Pocatello, Idaho 83201.

CAREER: University of Florida, Gainesville, research associate in biology, 1962-64; free-lance writer, 1964—; Westminster College, Salt Lake City, Utah, assistant professor of behavioral science and director of human relations program, 1976-82. *Member:* National Organization for Women (president of Pocatello chapter), Phi Sigma (honorary member), Sigma Xi (honorary member). *Awards, honors:* Grand prize, Pomona Valley writer's contest, 1965, for the article "A Grain of Sand"; *Lives and Deaths of a Meadow* was selected by the Children's Book Council and the National Science Teachers Association as an outstanding science book for children, 1973.

WRITINGS: Coping with Crib-Sized Campers, Stackpole, 1968; *Broken Ashes,* Branden Press, 1978.

For children: *Biography of a Cottontail,* Putnam, 1971; *A Cycle of Seasons: The Little Brown Bat,* Addison-Wesley, 1971; *The Fence Lizard: A Cycle of Seasons,* Addison-Wesley, 1972; *Lives and Deaths of a Meadow,* Putnam, 1973; *The Wonderful World of American Birds,* Putnam, 1978.

WORK IN PROGRESS: Psychic influences in sickness and health.

* * *

TUCKER, James 1929-
(David Craig)

PERSONAL: Born August 15, 1929, in Cardiff, Wales; son of William Arthur (a company director) and Irene (Bushen) Tucker; married Marian Craig, July 17, 1954; children: Patrick, Catherine, Guy, David. *Education:* University of Wales, B.A., 1951. *Home:* 5 Cefn Coed Rd., Cardiff, Wales. *Agent:* Peter Janson-Smith Ltd., 31 Newington Green, London N. 16, England.

CAREER: Western Mail, Cardiff, Wales, leader writer, 1954-56; *Daily Mirror,* London, England, reporter, 1956-58; has held various jobs with newspapers, 1958—. *Military service:* Royal Air Force, 1951-53; became flying officer. *Member:* Crime Writers Association.

WRITINGS: Equal Partners (novel), Chapman & Hall, 1960; *The Right Hand Man* (novel), Chapman & Hall, 1961; *Honourable Estates* (nonfiction), Gollancz, 1966; *Burster* (novel),

Gollancz, 1966; *The Novels of Anthony Powell* (criticism), Columbia University Press, 1976; *Blaze of Riot* (novel), Hutchinson, 1979; *The King's Friends* (novel), Arrow, 1982.

Under pseudonym David Craig; all novels; all published by Stein & Day: *The Alias Man,* 1968; *Message Ends,* 1969; *Young Men May Die,* 1970; *Contact Lost,* 1970; *Walk at Night,* 1971; *Up from the Grave,* 1971; *Double Take,* 1972; *Bolthole,* 1973; *Whose Little Girl Are You?,* 1974; *The Albin Case,* 1975; *Faith, Hope and Death,* 1976. Writer of television and radio documentaries. Contributor to *Punch, Spectator, New Society,* and *Sunday Times.*

* * *

TYMIENIECKA, Anna-Teresa

PERSONAL: Surname pronounced ''tim-yen-yets-ka''; born in Marianowo, Poland; came to United States, 1954, naturalized citizen, 1959; daughter of Wladyslaw (a country squire) and Maria-Ludwika (de Lanval) Tymieniecka; married Hendrik Houthakker (a professor), 1955; children: Louis, Isabel, John-Nicholas. *Education:* University of Cracow, B.A., 1946; Sorbonne, University of Paris, M.A., 1951; University of Fribourg, Ph.D., 1952. *Home:* 348 Payson Rd., Belmont, Mass. 02178. *Office:* World Phenomenology Institute, 348 Payson Rd., Belmont, Mass. 02178.

CAREER: University of California, Berkeley, teaching assistant in philosophy, 1954-55; Oregon State College (now University), Corvallis, instructor in mathematics, 1955-56; Pennsylvania State University, University Park, assistant professor, 1957; Bryn Mawr College, Bryn Mawr, Pa., lecturer, 1957-58; Radcliffe College, Institute for Independent Study, Cambridge, Mass., associate scholar, 1961-66; St. John's University, Jamaica, N.Y., professor of philosophy, 1970-72; World Institute for Advanced Phenomenological Research and Learning, Belmont, Mass., founder, Roman Ingarden professor of philosophy, and president. Visiting professor, Duquesne University, 1966-68, University of Waterloo, 1969. *Member:* International Society of Philosophy and Literature (founder, 1974; program coordinator), International Husserl and Phenomenological Research Society (founder; secretary-general, 1969—), American Philosophical Association, Society of Phenomenology and Existential Philosophy, Swiss Society for the Philosophy of Science, Societe Europeenne de la Culture.

WRITINGS: Essence et existence: Etude a propos de la philosophie de Roman Ingarden et Nicolai Hartman, Aubier Montaigne (Paris, France), 1957; (with others) *For Roman Ingarden: Nine Essays in Phenomenology,* Nijhoff (The Hague, Netherlands), 1959; *Phenomenology and Science in Contemporary European Thought,* Farrar, Straus, 1962; *Leibniz' Cosmological Synthesis,* Van Gorcum (Assen, Netherlands), 1964; (editor with Charles Parsons and contributor) *Contributions to Logic and Methodology in Honor of J. M. Bochenski,* North-Holland Publishing (Amsterdam), 1965; *Why Is There Something Rather Than Nothing?: Prolegomena to the Phenomenology of Cosmic Creation,* Van Gorcum, 1966; *Eros et Logos,* Nauwelearts (Louvain, Belgium), 1972.

General editor and founder, *Analecta Husserliana: The Yearbook of Phenomenological Research,* D. Reidel, Volume I: *Analecta Husserliana,* 1971, Volume II: *The Later Husserl and the Idea of Phenomenology,* 1972, Volume III: *The Phenomenological Realism of the Possible Worlds,* 1974, (and contributor) Volume IV: *Ingardeniana,* 1976, Volume V: *The Crisis of Culture,* 1976, Volume VI: *The Self and the Other,* 1977, Volume VII: *The Human Being in Action,* 1978, (with Yoshihiro Nitta and Hirotaka Tatematsu) Volume VIII: *Japanese Phenomenology,* 1979, Volume IX: *The Teleologies in Husserlian Phenomenology,* 1979, Volume X: *The Acting Person,* by Karol Wojtyla, in collaboration with Anna-Teresa Tymieniecka, translation by Andrzej Potocki, 1979, (with Angela Ales Bello) Volume XI: *The Great Chain of Being and Italian Phenomenology,* 1981, Volume XIII: *The Unhappy Consciousness,* by Eugene F. Kaelin, 1981, (and contributor) Volume XII: *The Philosophical Reflection of Man in Literature,* 1982, Volume XIV: *The Phenomenology of Man and of the Human Condition,* 1982, (with Calvin C. Schrag and contributor) Volume XV: *Foundations of Morality, Human Rights and the Human Sciences,* 1982.

Also author of *Phenomenologie et creation,* 1972. Contributor of about fifty articles and essays to professional philosophy journals. Also editor and founder of *Phenomenology Information Bulletin: A Review of Philosophical Ideas and Trends,* 1976—.

WORK IN PROGRESS: Phenomenology of Creative Experience; editing *Soul and Body in Husserlian Phenomenology,* volume XVI of *Analecta Husserliana.*

SIDELIGHTS: Anna-Teresa Tymieniecka told *CA:* ''All those who take writing—especially philosophical writing—seriously wonder why they yield to this passion, since writing is actually a constant turmoil and torture. There is, however, a compelling reason to wreck the comfort of everyday life for its sake: my life experience identifies the philosophical urge for seeking the 'ultimate reasons' of all things with that of giving a deeper sense to my most intimately personal life. Indeed, it needs the reflection articulated in writing to *create* my very own and unique 'self-interpretation-in-existence,' as I call it.''

U

UNDERWOOD, Lewis Graham
See WAGNER, C(harles) Peter

* * *

URDANG, Constance (Henriette) 1922-

PERSONAL: Born December 26, 1922, in New York, N.Y.; daughter of Harry Rudman (a teacher) and Annabel (Schafran) Urdang; married Donald Finkel (a writer and poet), August 14, 1956; children: Liza, Thomas Noah, Amy Maria. *Education:* Smith College, A.B., 1943; University of Iowa, M.F.A., 1956. *Home:* 6943 Columbia Pl., St. Louis, Mo. 63130. *Agent:* Georges Borchardt, Inc., 136 East 57th St., New York, N.Y. 10022.

CAREER: Free-lance writer and editor. U.S. Department of the Army, Washington, D.C., military intelligence analyst, 1944-46; National Bellas Hess, Inc., New York City, copy editor, 1947-51; P. F. Collier & Son, New York City, editor, 1952-54. Coordinator of The Writers' Program, Washington University, St. Louis, Mo. *Awards, honors: Carleton Miscellany's* First Centennial Award for prose, for *Natural History;* National Endowment for the Arts fellow, 1976; Delmore Schwartz Memorial Poetry Award, 1981.

WRITINGS: (Editor with Paul Engle) *Prize Short Stories, 1957: The O. Henry Awards,* Doubleday, 1957; (editor with Engle and Curtis Harnack) *Prize Short Stories, 1959: The O. Henry Awards,* Doubleday, 1959; *Charades and Celebrations* (poems), October House, 1965; *Natural History* (novel), Harper, 1969; *The Picnic in the Cemetery* (poems), Braziller, 1975; *The Lone Woman and Others* (poems), University of Pittsburgh Press, 1980; *Only the World* (poems), University of Pittsburgh Press, 1983. Contributor of poetry and prose to anthologies and to numerous periodicals.

SIDELIGHTS: Constance Urdang's poem "The Moon Tree," from her first poetry collection, *Charades and Celebrations,* has been praised by Raymond Roseliep in a *Poetry* article as "the kind of thing Stephen Vincent Benet had in mind when he defined poetry as magic." Roseliep feels that another poem from this collection, "The Old Woman," is "achievement of the same caliber . . . and so is 'In the Junkshop,' which proves that poems can be written about anything." W. T. Scott, writing in *Saturday Review,* says that "by sheer force of style [Urdang] can make mythological figures out of aunts and grandparents, and she can deal with historical figures in exciting livelier ways than we usually get these days. She is a fine poet with a sardonic eye trained to real values."

BIOGRAPHICAL/CRITICAL SOURCES: Poetry, April, 1966; *Saturday Review,* October 9, 1965, July 19, 1969; *New York Times Book Review,* July 20, 1969; *Washington Post Book World,* August 17, 1969; *Virginia Quarterly Review,* autumn, 1969; *Hudson Review,* August, 1981; *Prairie Schooner,* May 13, 1982.

* * *

URIS, Dorothy

PERSONAL: Born in Brooklyn, N.Y.; married Michael Uris (deceased); children: Joseph. *Education:* Attended Cornell University and Columbia University Teachers College. *Home:* 15 West 72nd St., New York, N.Y. 10023. *Agent:* Curtis Brown Ltd., 575 Madison Ave., New York, N.Y. 10022.

CAREER: Began career as stage and film actress; Manhattan School of Music, New York, N.Y., instructor in English diction, 1955—; Mannes College of Music, New York, N.Y., instructor in English diction. English diction coach with Metropolitan Opera Co., Santa Fe Opera Co., Curtis Institute of Music, and the New York City Opera. *Awards, honors:* Grants from the Martha Baird Rockefeller fund for music, 1965, and National Endowment for the Arts, 1980.

WRITINGS: Everybody's Book of Better Speaking, McKay, 1960; *To Sing in English,* Boosey & Hawkes, 1971; *A Woman's Voice,* Stein & Day, 1975; *Say It Again,* Dutton, 1979; (author of introduction) Harry Plunket Greene, *Interpretation in Song,* De Capo, 1979. Contributor to journals in her field.

SIDELIGHTS: Dorothy Uris told *CA:* "I'm a book writer all right, but in my field of speech and communication in song—and that only. Although the description may sound dull and dried, I find much excitement in writing and teaching and coaching. Working with our glorious language on paper or off is an unending source of strength."

* * *

UVEZIAN, Sonia

PERSONAL: Born in Beirut, Lebanon; daughter of Hagop (a

composer, conductor, and violinist) and Satenig (a singer; maiden name, Kibarian) Uvezian; married David Kaiserman (a concert pianist and university professor). *Education:* Attended Academie des Beaux Arts, Beirut, Lebanon, Ecole Superieur de Musique, Beirut, Columbia University, and Queens College of the City University of New York; also studied piano privately. *Residence:* New York, N.Y.

CAREER: Concert pianist. Has taught piano at Iowa State University and in New York City; has worked as a fashion model in New York City. *Awards, honors:* R. T. French Tastemaker Award for best original softcover cookbook, 1977, for *The Book of Salads* and runner-up, 1978, for *The Book of Yogurt.*

WRITINGS: The Cuisine of Armenia, Harper, 1974; *The Best Foods of Russia,* Harcourt, 1976, reissued in paperback as *Cooking from the Caucasus,* 1978; *The Book of Salads* (Book-of-the-Month Club selection), 101 Productions, 1977; *The Book of Yogurt,* 101 Productions, 1978; *The Complete International Sandwich Book,* Stein & Day, 1982.

Contributor: *The International Cooks' Catalogue,* Random House, 1977; *The Whole World Cookbook,* Scribner's, 1979; "The Good Cook: Techniques and Recipes" series; published by Time-Life Books: *Beef and Veal,* 1979, *Vegetables,* 1979, *Classic Desserts,* 1980, *Pasta,* 1980, *Salads,* 1980, *Snacks and Sandwiches,* 1980. Also contributor of articles and recipes to *Vogue, House and Garden, Gourmet, Soviet Armenia* and numerous other magazines and newspapers in the United States and abroad.

WORK IN PROGRESS: Research on foreign cuisine.

SIDELIGHTS: An Armenian born in Lebanon, pianist Sonia Uvezian divides her time between the United States and Europe, giving concert performances and culling gourmet recipes for her international cookbooks. "My books on Armenian and Caucasian cuisine are the first in any language to present comprehensive views of their subjects," Uvezian told *CA.* "A great number of the recipes appearing in both books have never been seen before in the West."

Food critics praise both the authenticity of Uvezian's recipes and the detailed way she presents them. Of her first publication, *The Cuisine of Armenia,* the *Hartford Courant* critic says, "The cookbook is one that a mother would hand down to her daughter and she, in turn, to her daughter." *The Best Foods of Russia,* Uvezian's second volume, also receives the highest praise. "The food is sensationally good," says Mimi Sheraton in the *New York Times Book Review.* "As with her previous book on Armenian cookery, the author writes clear recipes."

Because the recipes in her first two books were so outstanding, some critics now associate her name with quality. "A name can be an immediately recognizable sign of excellence. And so it can be with cookbooks," observes *Seattle Post-Intelligencer*'s Stan Reed. "Such [is] the one I have in hand, titled *The Book of Yogurt,* and bearing an author's name that's a certification of merit—Sonia Uvezian."

The Best Foods of Russia has been translated into Swedish, and *The Book of Yogurt* into German.

BIOGRAPHICAL/CRITICAL SOURCES: Hartford Courant, May 26, 1974, August 4, 1974; *New York,* December 16, 1974; *New York Times Book Review,* December 5, 1976; *Publishers Weekly,* August 15, 1977; *Seattle Post-Intelligencer,* July 12, 1978; *Chicago Sun-Times,* July 27, 1978.

V

van der SMISSEN, Betty
See van der SMISSEN, Margaret Elisabeth

* * *

van der SMISSEN, Margaret Elisabeth 1927-
(Betty van der Smissen)

PERSONAL: Born December 27, 1927, in Great Bend, Kan.; daughter of Theodore Alwin (a minister) and Margaret (Dirks) van der Smissen. *Education:* University of Kansas, A.B., 1949, LL.B., 1952, J.D.; Indiana University, M.S., 1954, Re.D., 1955. *Religion:* Mennonite. *Home:* 224 Baldwin Ave., Bowling Green, Ohio 43402. *Office:* School of Health, Physical Education and Recreation, Bowling Green State University, Bowling Green, Ohio 43403.

CAREER: Ohio District Young Women's Christian Association (Y.W.C.A.), Columbus, program director, 1950-51; Manchester College, North Manchester, Ind., chairman of women's physical education, 1955-56; University of Iowa, Iowa City, beginning 1956, associate professor, 1960-65; National Recreation Association, New York, N.Y., director of research, 1964-65; Pennsylvania State University, University Park, College of Health, Physical Education, and Recreation, associate professor, 1965-68, professor of recreation, 1968-79, associate dean for graduate study and research, 1970-74; Bowling Green State University, Bowling Green, Ohio, School of Health, Physical Education and Recreation, director, 1979—.

WRITINGS—Under name Betty van der Smissen: *The Church Camp Program,* Faith & Life, 1961; (compiler) *A Bibliography of Research (Theses and Dissertations Only) Related to Recreation,* enlarged edition, University of Iowa, 1962; (with Helen Knierim) *Fitness and Fun through Recreational Sports and Games,* Burgess, 1964; (with Oswald Goering) *A Leader's Guide to Nature-Oriented Activities,* Iowa State University Press, 1965, 3rd edition, 1977; (with Dorothy V. Harris) *Campcraft Series One, Instructor's Guide,* Athletic Institute, 1965; (with Harris) *Campcraft Series Two,* Athletic Institute, 1966; *Legal Liability of Cities and Schools for Injuries in Recreation and Parks,* W. H. Anderson, 1968, supplement, 1975, revised edition, Anderson Publishing, 1983.

(Editor with Donald V. Joyce) *Bibliography of Theses and Dissertations in Recreation, Parks, Camping and Outdoor Education,* National Recreation and Park Association, 1970; (editor) *Recreation and Leisure Information Systems: Status and Priorities,* National Recreation and Park Association, 1971; *Evaluation and Self-Study of Public Recreation and Park Agencies,* National Recreation and Park Association, 1972; (compiler) *Indicators of Change in the Recreation Environment: A National Research Symposium,* College of Health, Physical Education and Recreation, Pennsylvania State University, 1975; (compiler) *Research, Camping and Environmental Education,* College of Health, Physical Education and Recreation, Pennsylvania State University, 1976; (with Monty L. Christiansen) *Standards Related to Water-Oriented and Water-Enhanced Recreation in Watersheds,* Pennsylvania State University Institute for Research on Land and Water Resources, Volume I: *Phase I,* 1976, Volume II: *Phases II and III,* 1978; (compiler with A. Hunter) *Compendium of State Laws and Regulations: Youth Camp,* Center for Disease Control, U.S. Department of Health, Education, and Welfare, 1977, revised edition (with Judy Brookhiser) published as *Youth Camp Compendium of State Laws and Regulations,* 1978; *Bibliography of Theses and Dissertations in Recreation and Parks,* National Recreation and Parks Association (Arlington, Va.), 1979.

Legal Liability: Adventure Activities (monograph), New Mexico State University, 1980; *Bibliography of Research in Camping, Interpretive Services and Environmental Education,* American Camping Association, 1982.

Contributor: *Trampoline Safety Manual,* Wagners Printers (Cedar Rapids, Iowa), 1978; *Gymnastics Safety Manual,* Gene Wettstone, editor, 2nd edition, Pennsylvania University Press, 1979; *Fifty Years of Resident Outdoor Education: 1939-1980—Its Impact on American Education,* William M. Hammerman, editor, American Camping Association, 1980; *High Adventure Outdoor Pursuits: Organization and Leadership,* Joel J. Meier, Talmadge W. Marash, and George E. Welton, editors, Brighton Publishing (Salt Lake City), 1980.

* * *

VARDRE, Leslie
See DAVIES, L(eslie) P(urnell)

VAUGHN, Richard C(lements) 1925-

PERSONAL: Born January 17, 1925, in Ionia, Mich.; son of Forrest H. (a designer) and Alice (Haynor) Vaughn; married Frances E. Foreman, March 18, 1947; children: Bonnie, Barbara, Carolyn, Vicki, Elizabeth. *Education:* Michigan State University, B.A., 1948; University of Toledo, M.I.E., 1955. *Home:* 1222 Ridgewood Ave., Ames, Iowa 50010. *Office:* Iowa State University of Science and Technology, Ames, Iowa 50010.

CAREER: Ransom & Randolph Co., Toledo, Ohio, resident associate, 1951; Brown Trailers, Inc., Toledo, time study trainee, 1951-52; Martin-Parry Corp., Toledo, member of time study staff, 1952-53; A. P. Parts Corp., Toledo, industrial engineer, 1953-55; Mather Spring Co., Toledo, chief industrial engineer, 1955; Ford Motor Co., Monroe, Mich., process engineer, 1955-56; Detroit Harvester, Dura Division, Toledo, methods and process supervisor, 1956-57; University of Florida, Gainesville, assistant professor of industrial engineering, 1957-62; Iowa State University of Science and Technology, Ames, associate professor, 1962-67, professor of industrial engineering, 1968—. Instructor in mathematics at evening session, University of Toledo, 1952-57. Consultant to Liberty Bell Manufacturing Co., 1959-61. *Military service:* U.S. Coast Guard Reserve, active duty, 1942-45. U.S. Naval Reserve, 1946-51. *Member:* American Society for Engineering Education, American Society for Quality Control, Institute of Management Science.

WRITINGS: Legal Aspects of Engineering, Prentice-Hall, 1962, 3rd edition, Kendall/Hunt, 1977; *Introduction to Industrial Engineering,* Iowa State University Press, 1967, 2nd edition, 1977; *Quality Control,* Iowa State University Press, 1974; (with Paul Randolph) *Applied Queueing Theory,* Iowa State University, 1981.

SIDELIGHTS: Several of Richard C. Vaughn's books have been translated into Spanish.

* * *

VAYLE, Valerie
See BROOKS, Janice Young

* * *

VERDUIN, John R(ichard), Jr. 1931-

PERSONAL: Born July 6, 1931, in Muskegon, Mich.; son of John Richard (a salesman) and Dorothy (Eckman) Verduin; married Janet M. Falk, January 26, 1963; children: John Richard III, Susan E. *Education:* University of Albuquerque, B.S., 1954; Michigan State University, M.A., 1959, Ph.D., 1962. *Home:* 107 North Lark Lane, Carbondale, Ill. 62901. *Office:* Southern Illinois University, Carbondale, Ill. 62901.

CAREER: Public school teacher in Muskegon, Mich., 1954-56, and Greenville, Mich., 1956-59; State University of New York College at Geneseo, assistant professor, 1962-64, associate professor of education, 1964-67; Southern Illinois University at Carbondale, associate professor, 1967-70, professor in department of educational administration and foundations, 1970—, assistant dean, 1967-73. Member of Teacher Education Committee of Illinois Association of Supervision and Curriculum Development. Member of Carbondale Model Cities Committee and Goals for Carbondale committee; member and chairman of education commission, First United Methodist Church, Carbondale. Special consultant to American Association of Colleges for Teacher Education, 1966-67; State of Illinois Gifted Program, member of advisory council, 1968—, chairman, 1973—. *Military service:* U.S. Marine Corps, 1951. *Member:* Association for Supervision and Curriculum Development, American Educational Research Association, Phi Delta Kappa, Kappa Delta Phi.

WRITINGS: Cooperative Curriculum Improvement, Prentice-Hall, 1967; *Conceptual Models in Teacher Education,* American Association of Colleges for Teacher Education, 1967; (co-author) *Pre-Student Teaching Laboratory Experiences,* Kendall/Hunt, 1970; (contributor) William Joyce, Robert Oana, and W. Robert Houston, editors, *Elementary Education in the Seventies,* Holt, 1970; (co-author) *Project Follow Through,* State of Illinois, 1971; (co-author) *Adults Teaching Adults, Principles and Strategies,* Learning Concepts, 1977; (contributor) James R. Gress and David Purpel, editors, *Curriculum: An Introduction to the Field,* McCutchan, 1978; (co-author) *The Adult Educator: A Handbook for Staff Development,* Gulf Publishing, 1979; *Curriculum Building for Adult Learning,* Southern Illinois University Press, 1980. Also author of reports on educational research and projects for the State of Illinois; contributor of articles to education journals.

WORK IN PROGRESS: Co-authoring *Lifelong Learning for Adults* and *Leisure and Lifelong Learning.*

AVOCATIONAL INTERESTS: Woodworking, gardening, golfing, and tennis.

* * *

von BRAUN, Wernher 1912-1977

PERSONAL: Born March 23, 1912, in Wirsitz, Germany; came to United States in 1945, naturalized U.S. citizen in 1955; died June 16, 1977, of cancer in Alexandria, Va.; son of Magnus (a baron) and Emmy (von Quistorp) von Braun; married Maria Louise von Quistorp, March 1, 1947; children: Iris Careen, Margrit Cecile, Peter Constantine. *Education:* Berlin Institute of Technology, B.S., 1932; University of Berlin, Ph.D., 1934.

CAREER: Assistant to Hermann Oberth in liquid-fuel small rocket motor experiments in Germany, 1930; German Ordnance Department, Kummersdorf Army Proving Grounds, Germany, liquid fuel expert, 1932-37; Liquid Fueled Rocket and Guided Missile Center, Peenemuende, Germany, research and development service, 1937-45; U.S. Army Ordnance Corps, Research and Development Service (Sub-Office Rocket), project director, Fort Bliss, Tex., and technical adviser to White Sands Proving Grounds, 1945-50; Redstone Arsenal, Guided Missile Development Division, Huntsville, Ala., technical director, 1950-52, chief, 1952-56; U.S. Army Ballistic Missile Agency, Development Operations Division, Huntsville, director, 1956-60; George C. Marshall Space Flight Center, Huntsville, director, 1960-70; National Aeronautics and Space Administration, Washington, D.C., deputy associate administrator, 1970-72; Fairchild Industries, Germantown, Md., corporate vice-president of engineering and development, 1972-76.

MEMBER: International Academy of Astronautics, National Academy of Engineering, American Institute of Aeronautics and Astronautics (fellow), American Astronautical Society (fellow), Hermann Oberth Society (honorary member), British Interplanetary Society (honorary fellow), Norwegian Interplanetary Society, German Rocket Society, Hellenic Astronautical Society (honorary member), Rocket City Astronomical Association (president), Explorers Club (New York), Tau Beta Pi (honorary member), Pi Mu Epsilon (honorary member), Omicron Delta Kappa (honorary member).

AWARDS, HONORS: Astronautics Award, 1955; Space Flight Award, 1957; U.S. Department of Defense Distinguished Civilian Service Award, 1957; Department of the Army Decoration for Exceptional Civilian Service, 1957; Award for Great Living Americans, U.S. Chamber of Commerce, 1958; Dr. Robert H. Goddard Memorial Trophy, 1958; first honor award of Nationalities Committee, People-to-People Program, 1958; Americanism Medal of Daughters of American Revolution, 1959; Distinguished Federal Civilian Service Award, 1959; Notre Dame Patriotism Award, 1959; Hamilton Holt Gold Medal, 1959; distinguished service award, Southern Association of Science and Industry, 1959; International Boss of the Year, 1961; gold medal award of British Interplanetary Society, 1961; Greek Fellowship Award, 1961; Hermann Oberth Award, 1961; Order of Merit for Research and Invention, 1962; Elliott Cresson Award, 1962; American Citizen Award, 1963; distinguished service award, National Aeronautics and Space Administration, 1963, 1969; Science and Engineering Award of Drexel Institute of Technology, 1963; American Military Engineers Award, 1963; Louis W. Hill Space Transportation Award, 1965; Diesel Medal in Gold, Diesel Committee of the German Society for Inventions, 1965; Galabert International Astronautical Prize, 1965; National Recognition Award, Freedoms Foundation, 1970; World Citizenship Award, Civitan International, 1970.

Honorary degrees: University of Alabama, 1958; St. Louis University, 1958; University of Chattanooga, 1958; University of Pittsburgh, 1958; Canisius College, 1959; Pennsylvania Military College, 1959; Clark University, 1959; Adelphi College, 1959; Technical University of Berlin, 1963.

WRITINGS: (With others) *Across the Space Frontier,* edited by C. Ryan, Viking, 1952; *Das Marsprojekt: Studie einer interplanetarischen Expedition,* Umschau Verlag, 1952, translation published as *The Mars Project,* University of Illinois Press, 1953, 2nd edition, 1962; (with F. L. Whipple and W. Ley) *Conquest of the Moon,* edited by C. Ryan, Viking, 1953; (with Ley) *Exploration of Mars,* Viking, 1956; *Start in den Weltraum: Ein Buch ueber Raketen, Satelliten und Raumfahrzenge,* S. Fischer, 1958; (with Ley) *Die Eroberung des Weltraums* (based on *Across the Space Frontier* and *Conquest of the Moon*), S. Fischer, 1958.

First Men to the Moon (novel), Holt, 1960; (with C. C. Adams and F. I. Ordway III) *Careers in Astronautics and Rocketry,* McGraw, 1962; (with Ordway) *History of Rocketry and Space Travel,* Crowell, 1966, 3rd revised edition, 1975; *Space Frontier,* Holt, 1967, updated edition, 1971; *Mein Leben fur die Raumfahrt,* Burda Verlag (Offenburg), 1969; (with Ordway) *The Rocket's Red Glare,* Anchor Press, 1976; (with Ordway) *New Worlds: Discoveries from Our Solar System,* Anchor Press, 1979.

Contributor: C. S. White and O. O. Benson, Jr., editors, *Physics and Medicine of the Upper Atmosphere,* University of New Mexico Press, 1952; J. P. Marberger, editor, *Space Medicine,* University of Illinois Press, 1952; H. H. Koelle, editor, *Probleme aus der Astronautischen Grundlagenforschung,* Gesellschaft fuer Weltraumforschung, 1952; J. Logan, editor, *The Complete Book of Outer Space,* Maco Magazine Corp., 1953, 2nd edition published as *The Complete Book of Satellites and Outer Space,* 1957; E. L. Neher, *Menschen zwischen den Planeten: Der Roman der Raumfahrt,* Bechtle, 1953; H. Wright and S. Rappaport, editors, *Great Adventures in Science,* Harper, 1956; K. W. Gatland, editor, *Project Satellite,* British Book Centre, 1958; H.V.H. Bolewski and H. Grottrup, *Der Weltenraum in Menschenhand,* Kreuz-Verlag, 1959; G. B. de Huszur, editor, *National Strategy in an Age of Revolution,* Praeger, 1959; H. J. Luz, editor, *Starten und Fliegen,* Deutsche Verlags-Anstalt, 1959; J. L. Russell, Jr., *History of Rockets,* Popular Mechanics Press, 1959.

Benson and H. Strughold, editors, *Physics and Medicine of the Atmosphere and Space,* Wiley, 1960; *Knut Lundmark och varldsrymdeus erovring,* Varld och ventande Folag, 1961; R. S. Richardson, editor, *Man and the Moon,* World Publishing, 1961; H. Brandon, editor, *As We Are,* Doubleday, 1961; E. Sanger, editor, *Raumfahrt wohin?,* Bechtle, 1962; W. Nichols, editor, *The Third Book of Words to Live By,* Simon & Schuster, 1962; S. T. Butler and H. Messel, editors, *A Journey through Space and the Atom,* Shakespeare Head Press, 1962; G. Lehner, *Griff nach den Sternen,* Ehrenwirth Verlag, 1962; F. E. Kast and J. E. Rosenzweig, editors, *Science, Technology, and Management,* McGraw, 1963; E. E. Emme, editor, *The History of Rocket Technology,* Wayne State University Press, 1964; A. Love and J. S. Childers, editors, *Listen to the Leaders in Engineering,* Holt, 1964.

Author of foreword or introduction: C. C. Adams, *Space Flight,* McGraw, 1958; *Rocket Pioneers on the Road to Space,* edited by B. Williams and S. Epstein, Messner, 1958; E. Bergaust, *Rocket to the Moon,* Van Nostrand, 1958; *Epoche Atom und Automation,* Wilhelm Limpert, 1959; W. Pons, *Steht uns der Himmel Offen?,* Krausskopf-Verlag, 1960; A. C. Clarke, *The Challenge of the Sea,* Holt, 1960; *Aerospace Dictionary,* edited by F. Gaynor, Philosophical Library, 1960; *Die Rakete zu den Planetenraum,* Univerlag, 1960; *Roald Amundsen—Der Letzte Wikinger,* Hoch-Verlag, 1960; A. J. Zaehrenger, *Soviet Space Technology,* Harper, 1961; J. Jensew and others, *Design Guide to Orbital Flight,* McGraw, 1962; D. Huzel, *Peenemunde to Canaveral,* Prentice-Hall, 1962; D. D. Runes, *Treasury of World Science,* Philosophical Library, 1962; *Dictionary of Atomics,* edited by A. Del Vecchio, Philosophical Library, 1964; W. Ley, *Beyond the Solar System,* Viking, 1964; E. Klee and O. Merk, *The Birth of the Missile,* Dutton, 1965.

Contributor to symposia: *Space-Flight Problems: Proceedings of the IV International Astronautical Congress, Zurich, 1953,* Biel-Bienne, 1954; *Proceedings IX International Astronautical Congress, Amsterdam, 1958,* Volume II, Springer-Verlag, 1959; *Proceedings of the Eleventh International Astronautical Congress, Stockholm, 1960,* Springer-Verlag, 1961; *Proceedings of First National Conference on the Peaceful Uses of Space,* U.S. Government Printing Office, 1961 (also contributor to *Proceedings* of Second Conference, 1962, Fourth, 1964, and Fifth, 1965); *Proceedings of the Conference on Space-Age Planning,* U.S. Government Printing Office, 1963.

Also contributor to *Encyclopedia Americana,* 1962, and *Encyclopedia of Science and Technology Year Book,* McGraw, 1962. Articles in *Collier's, This Week, U.S. News and World Report, New York Times, Reader's Digest, Popular Science,* and scientific and space journals.

SIDELIGHTS: Although he wrote many books, German-born Wernher von Braun is best remembered for his scientific contributions. He developed the giant Saturn 5 rocket that launched three American astronauts on man's maiden moon voyage in July, 1969. "While thousands of men have labored to make this mighty machine, it has been the brainchild of only one," observed *Washington Post* staff writer Thomas O'Toole, "the man who sketched its blueprint on yellow note paper . . . just before reaching his 21st birthday.''

Considered the world's foremost rocketeer by the time he was twenty-five, von Braun began his engineering career not in the United States, but in Nazi Germany. There, under orders from Adolf Hitler, he developed the first ballistic missile ever fired. It was this missile, or the V-2 as it was commonly called, that was used to bombard London during the closing months of World War II. When asked how he felt when the first rocket struck London, von Braun was reported by O'Toole to have said: ''Well, it behaved perfectly, but it landed on the wrong planet.''

As the war drew to a close, von Braun and more than 100 of his associates surrendered themselves and their documents to the United States. According to one colleague, there was never even a debate about it. ''We despised the French,'' he told the *Washington Post*'s O'Toole. ''We were afraid of the Russians and we didn't think the British could afford us. That left the Americans.'' Despite such callousness on the part of his coworkers, von Braun reportedly suffered considerable inner turmoil after World War II. ''Thus,'' wrote *Washington Post* staff writer J. Y. Smith, ''he was constantly seeking uses for space technology that he hoped would make the world a less dangerous place. He saw these uses in weather and communications satellites, the development of the computer industry and other spin-offs from space.'' To achieve these ends, von Braun worked first for the government and later for private industry until his retirement on December 31, 1976—just months before his death.

BIOGRAPHICAL/CRITICAL SOURCES—Books: Heinz Gartmann, *Wernher von Braun,* Colloquium, 1959; Erik Bergaust, *Reaching for the Stars,* Doubleday, 1960; Shirley Thomas, *Men of Space,* Volume I, Chilton, 1960; Bergaust, *Wernher von Braun,* Stackpole, 1978.

Articles: *American,* July, 1952; *Aviation Age,* December, 1952; *New York Times,* October 20, 1957, January 28, 1970; *Life,* November, 18, 1957; *American Weekly,* July 20, 1958, July 27, 1958, August 3, 1958; *New Republic,* October 20, 1958; *This Week,* September 13, 1959; *School Arts,* October, 1959; *Guideposts,* October, 1960; *Space World,* November, 1960; *Times Literary Supplement,* December 28, 1967; *Washington Post,* July 16, 1969; *Holiday,* March, 1971.

OBITUARIES: New York Times, June 18, 1977; *Washington Post,* June 18, 1977; *Time,* June 27, 1977; *Newsweek,* June 27, 1977.†

W

WAGGONER, Hyatt H(owe) 1913-

PERSONAL: Born November 19, 1913, in Pleasant Valley, N.Y.; married Louise Feather, June 26, 1937; children: Veronica (Mrs. Edward D. Johnson), Jane. *Education:* Middlebury College, A.B., 1935; University of Chicago, M.A., 1936; Ohio State University, Ph.D., 1942. *Politics:* "Pacifist and Democratic." *Religion:* Episcopalian. *Home address:* R.D. No. 1, Rochester, Vt. 05767.

CAREER: University of Omaha, Omaha, Neb., instructor in English, 1939-42; University of Kansas City, Kansas City, Mo., instructor, 1942-44, assistant professor, 1944-47, associate professor, 1947-50, professor of English, 1950-56, chairman of department, 1952-56; Brown University, Providence, R.I., professor of American literature, 1956-80, chairman of American civilization program, 1960-70. *Member:* Modern Language Association of America, American Studies Association. *Awards, honors:* M.A., Brown University, 1957; Guggenheim fellow, 1963-64 and 1972-73.

WRITINGS: (With Fred A. Dudley, Norbert Fuerst, and Francis R. Johnson) *The Relations of Literature and Science: A Selected Bibliography, 1930-1949,* State College of Washington, 1949; *The Heel of Elohim: Science and Values in Modern American Poetry,* University of Oklahoma Press, 1950; (editor) *Nathaniel Hawthorne: Selected Tales and Sketches,* Rinehart, 1950, revised edition, 1962; *Hawthorne: A Critical Study,* Harvard University Press, 1955, revised and enlarged edition, 1963; *William Faulkner: From Jefferson to the World,* University of Kentucky Press, 1959.

Nathaniel Hawthorne, University of Minnesota Press, 1962; (editor) Nathaniel Hawthorne, *The House of the Seven Gables* (with new text based on the manuscript), Houghton, 1964; (editor with George Monteiro) Hawthorne, *The Scarlet Letter* (facsimile text), Chandler Publishing, 1967; *American Poets from the Puritans to the Present,* Houghton, 1968; *Emerson as Poet,* Princeton University Press, 1975; (editor with Barbara S. Mouffe) *Hawthorne's Lost Notebook, 1835-1941,* Pennsylvania State University Press, 1978; *The Presence of Hawthorne,* Louisiana State University Press, 1979; *American Visionary Poetry,* Louisiana State University Press, 1982.

Contributor: Nathan Scott, editor, *The Tragic Vision and the Christian Faith,* Association Press, 1957; Charles Feidelson and Paul Brodtkorb, editors, *Interpretations of American Literature,* Oxford University Press, 1959; Seymour L. Gross, editor, *A Scarlet Letter Handbook,* Wadsworth, 1960; Edward Sculley Bradley, Richmond Beatty, and E. Hudson Long, editors, *The Scarlet Letter: An Annotated Text* [with] *Backgrounds and Sources* [and] *Essays in Criticism,* Norton, 1962; Agnes Donohue, editor, *A Casebook on the Hawthorne Question,* Crowell, 1962; R. H. Pearce, editor, *Hawthorne Centenary Essays,* Ohio State University Press, 1964.

American Literary Masters, Holt, 1965; A. N. Kaul, editor, *Hawthorne,* Prentice-Hall, 1966; Robert Penn Warren, editor, *Faulkner,* Prentice-Hall, 1966; Malcolm Bradbury, editor, *Forster,* Prentice-Hall, 1966; George A. Panichas, editor, *Mansions of the Spirit,* Hawthorn, 1967; Michael Cowan, editor, *Twentieth-Century Interpretations of "The Sound and the Fury,"* Prentice-Hall, 1968; Richard Foster, editor, *Six American Novelists,* University of Minnesota Press, 1968. Contributor to *American Literary Scholarship: An Annual,* 1963—, and to *Explicator Encyclopedia,* 1966. Contributor of over fifty articles and reviews to literary journals.

WORK IN PROGRESS: Revising *American Poets from the Puritans to the Present.*

SIDELIGHTS: Hyatt H. Waggoner expressed this concern to *CA:* "Now that we have it within our power to destroy all life on earth, can we achieve the wisdom and morality to preserve this beautiful planet for our children and grandchildren to live on and enjoy?"

Waggoner's *American Poets from the Puritans to the Present* attempts "to discover what is American about our poetry," writes a *Virginia Quarterly Review* critic, and "to look at representative poets in terms of their own values." The reviewer adds that Ralph Waldo Emerson's essay "The Poet" emerges as the "central document and Emerson himself as the central figure in our poetry."

AVOCATIONAL INTERESTS: Walking on the back roads of North Hallow, Rochester; gardening; collecting and studying nature books; playing ping-pong with his grandson.

BIOGRAPHICAL/CRITICAL SOURCES: Virginia Quarterly Review, spring, 1968; *Christian Science Monitor,* April 25, 1968; *Carleton Miscellany,* winter, 1969.

WAGNER, C(harles) Peter 1930-
(Epafrodito, Lewis Graham Underwood)

PERSONAL: Born August 15, 1930, in New York, N.Y.; son of C. Graham (a buyer) and Mary (Lewis) Wagner; married Doris Mueller (a missionary), October 15, 1950; children: Karen, Ruth, Rebecca. *Education:* Rutgers University, B.S., 1952; Fuller Theological Seminary, B.D., 1955, M.A., 1968; Princeton Theological Seminary, Th.M., 1962; University of Southern California, Ph.D., 1977. *Home:* 135 North Oakland Ave., Pasadena, Calif. 91101.

CAREER: Congregational clergyman, 1955—; Instituto Biblico del Oriente, San Jose, Bolivia, director, 1956-61; Instituto Biblico Emaus, Cochabamba, Bolivia, professor and director, 1962-71; Andes Evangelical Mission (now S.I.M. International), Cochabamba, associate director, 1964-71; Fuller Theological Seminary, Pasadena, Calif., Professor of church growth, 1971—. Senior field consultant, Fuller Evangelistic Association, Pasadena, 1971—. *Member:* Phi Beta Kappa.

WRITINGS: (With Joseph S. McCullough) *The Condor of the Jungle,* Revell, 1966; *Defeat of the Bird God,* Zondervan, 1967; *Latin American Theology,* Eerdmans, 1969; *The Protestant Movement in Bolivia.* William Carey Library, 1970; (with Ralph Covell) *An Extension Seminary Primer,* William Carey Library, 1971; *A Turned-On Church in an Uptight World,* Zondervan, 1971; *Frontiers in Missionary Strategy,* Moody, 1972; (editor) *Church/Mission Tensions Today,* Moody, 1972; *Look Out! The Pentecostals Are Coming,* Creation House, 1973; *Stop the World, I Want to Get On,* Regal Books, 1974.

Your Church Can Grow: Seven Vital Signs of a Healthy Church, Regal Books, 1976; *Your Church and Church Growth* (includes workbook and six cassette tapes), Fuller Evangelistic Association of Pasadena, 1976, revised edition published as *The Growing Church,* 1982; (editor with Edward R. Dayton) *Unreached Peoples '79,* David C. Cook, 1978; *Your Spiritual Gifts Can Help Your Church Grow,* Regal Books, 1979; *Your Church Can Be Healthy,* Abingdon, 1979; *Our Kind of People: The Ethical Dimensions of Church Growth in America,* John Knox, 1979; (editor with Dayton) *Unreached Peoples '80,* David C. Cook, 1980; (with Bob Waymire) *The Church Growth Survey Handbook,* Global Church Growth Bulletin, 1980; (editor with Dayton) *Unreached Peoples '81,* David C. Cook, 1981; *Church Growth and the Whole Gospel,* Harper, 1981; *Effective Body Building: Biblical Steps to Spiritual Growth,* Here's Life Publishers, 1982; *Helping Your Church Grow* (includes workbook and cassette tapes), David C. Cook, 1982; (editor with Donald A. McGavran and James H. Montgomery) *Church Growth Bulletin: Third Consolidated Volume,* Global Church Growth Bulletin, 1982.

Contributor, sometimes under pseudonyms Epafrodito and Lewis Graham Underwood, to religious periodicals. Former editor of *Vision Evangelica* (Cochabamba, Bolivia), *Pensamiento Cristiano* (Cordova, Argentina), and *Andean Oulook.*

* * *

WAITLEY, Douglas 1927-

PERSONAL: Born November 28, 1927, in Evanston, Ill.; son of Douglas and Marian Waitley; married Mary Avery, April 23, 1960; children: Jeff. *Education:* Northwestern University, B.S., 1949, M.A., 1956. *Home:* 2650 Hillside Lane, Evanston, Ill. 60201. *Office:* Dale's Employment Service, Inc., 1015 Central, Evanston, Ill.

CAREER: Currently president of Dale's Employment Service, Inc., Evanston, Ill. *Military service:* U.S. Navy, 1952-54.

WRITINGS: Portrait of the Midwest, Abelard, 1964; *My Backyard: A Living World of Nature,* David White, 1970; *Roads of Destiny: The Trails that Shaped a Nation,* Luce, 1970; *The War Makers: Twentieth Century Strongmen,* Luce, 1971; *The Roads We Traveled: An Amusing History of the Automobile,* Messner, 1979; (with Bruce Ogilvie) *Rand McNally Picture Atlas of the World,* Rand McNally, 1979; *America at War,* Volume I: *World Wars I and II,* Volume II: *Korea and Vietnam,* Glencoe, 1980; *The Age of the Mad Dragons: Steam Locomotives in North America,* Beaufort Books (New York), 1981.

* * *

WAKOSKI, Diane 1937-
(Diane Wakoski-Sherbell)

PERSONAL: Born August 3, 1937, in Whittier, Calif.; daughter of John Joseph and Marie (Mengel) Wakoski; married S. Shepard Sherbell (a magazine editor), October 22, 1965 (divorced); married Michael Watterlond, February 22, 1973 (divorced, 1975); married Robert J. Turney, February 14, 1982. *Education:* University of California, Berkeley, B.A., 1960. *Home:* 607 Division, East Lansing, Mich. 48823.

CAREER: Poet. Clerk at British Book Centre, New York City, 1960-63; teacher at Junior High School 22, New York City, 1963-66; lecturer at New School for Social Research, 1969; writer-in-residence at California Institute of Technology, 1972, University of Virginia, 1972-73, Williamette University, 1974, University of California, Irvine, 1974, University of Wisconsin—Madison, 1975, Michigan State University, 1975, Whitman College, 1976, University of Washington, 1977, University of Hawaii, 1978, and Emory University, 1980, 1981; member of faculty at Michigan State University, 1976—. *Member:* P.E.N., Authors Guild, Authors League of America. *Awards, honors:* Robert Frost fellowship, Bread Loaf Writers Conference, 1966; Cassandra Foundation award, 1970; New York State Council on the Arts grant, 1971; Guggenheim Foundation grant, 1972; National Endowment for the Arts grant, 1973.

WRITINGS—Poetry, except as indicated: *Coins and Coffins* (also see below), Hawk's Well Press, 1962; (with Rochelle Owens, Barbara Moraff, and Carol Berge) *Four Young Lady Poets,* edited by LeRoi Jones, Totem-Corinth, 1962; *Discrepancies and Apparitions* (also see below), Doubleday, 1966; *The George Washington Poems* (also see below), Riverrun Press, 1967; *The Diamond Merchant,* Sans Souci Press, 1968; *Inside the Blood Factory,* Doubleday, 1968; *The Lament of the Lady Bank Dick,* Sans Souci Press, 1969; *The Moon Has a Complicated Geography,* Odda Tala, 1969; *Poems,* Key Printing Co., 1969; *Some Black Poems for the Buddha's Birthday,* Pierripont Press, 1969; *Thanking My Mother for Piano Lessons,* Perishable Press, 1969.

Love, You Big Fat Snail, Tenth Muse, 1970; *The Motorcycle Betrayal Poems,* Simon & Schuster, 1971; *This Water Baby, for Tony,* Unicorn Press, 1971; *Exorcism,* My Dukes, 1971; *The Purple Finch Song,* Perishable Press, 1972; *Sometimes a Poet Will Hijack the Moon,* Burning Deck, 1972; *Stillife: Michael, Silver Flute and Violets,* University of Connecticut Library, 1973; *The Owl and the Snake: A Fable,* Perishable Press, 1973; (contributor) Karl Malkoff, editor, *Crowell's Handbook of Contemporary American Poetry,* Crowell, 1973; *The Wan-*

dering Tatler, Perishable Press, 1974; *Trilogy* (includes *Coins and Coffins, Discrepancies and Apparitions,* and *The George Washington Poems*), Doubleday, 1974; *Virtuoso Literature for Two and Four Hands,* Doubleday, 1975; *The Fable of the Lion and the Scorpion,* Pentagram Press, 1975; *The Laguna Contract of Diane Wakoski,* Crepuscular Press, 1976; *George Washington's Camp Cups,* Red Ozier Press, 1976; *The Man Who Shook Hands,* Doubleday, 1978; *Toward a New Poetry* (essays), University of Michigan Press, 1979.

Saturn's Rings, Targ Editions, 1982; *Divers,* Barbarian Press, 1982; *The Lady Who Drove Me to the Airport,* Metacom Press, 1982; *Making a Sacher Torte,* Perishable Press, 1982.

All published by Black Sparrow Press: (With Robert Kelly and Ron Loewinsohn) *A Play and Two Poems,* 1968; *Greed,* Parts 1 and 2, 1968, Parts 3 and 4, 1969, Parts 5-7, 1971, Parts 8, 9, 11, 1973; *Black Dream Ditty for Billy "the Kid" M Seen in Dr. Generosity's Bar Recruiting for Hell's Angels the Black Mafia,* 1970; *The Magellanic Clouds,* 1970; *On Barbara's Shore: A Poem,* 1971; (contributor) *The Nest,* 1971; *Smudging,* 1972; *The Pumpkin Pie: Or, Reassurances Are Always False, Tho We Love Them, Only Physics Counts,* 1972; *Form Is an Extension of Content* (essay), 1972; *Winter Sequences,* 1973; *Looking for the King of Spain* (also see below), 1974; *Abalone,* 1974; *Creating a Personal Mythology* (essays), 1975; *Waiting for the King of Spain,* 1976; *The Last Poem,* 1976; *Variations on a Theme* (essay), 1976; *The Ring,* 1977; *Spending Christmas with the Man from Receiving at Sears,* 1977; *Pachelbel's Canon* (also see below), 1978; *Trophies,* 1979; *Cap of Darkness* (includes *Looking for the King of Spain* and *Pachelbel's Canon*), 1980; *The Magician's Feastletters,* 1982.

Author of "Dream Sheet," 1965. Contributor to "Burning Deck Post Cards: The Third Ten," Burning Deck. Regular columnist for *American Poetry Review,* 1972-74; contributor to numerous periodicals. Editor of *Software.*

SIDELIGHTS: Diane Wakoski, described as an "important and moving poet" by Paul Zweig in the *New York Times Book Review,* is frequently named among the foremost contemporary poets by virtue of her experiential vision and her unique voice. Wakoski's poems focus on intensely personal experiences—on her unhappy childhood, on the painful relationships she has had with men, and, perhaps most frequently, on the subject of being Diane Wakoski.

A few critics find her thematic concerns difficult to appreciate, especially the recurring "anti-male rage" theme noted by Peter Schjeldahl in the *New York Times Book Review.* Wakoski's poems, according to Schjeldahl, "are professionally supple and clear . . . but their pervasive unpleasantness makes her popularity rather surprising. One can only conclude that a number of people are angry enough at life to enjoy the sentimental and desolating resentment with which she writes about it."

Many other critics, however, believe that it is through this very rage and resentment that Wakoski makes a significant statement in her work. James F. Mersmann, for example, comments in *Margins* on the body of Wakoski's poetry: "It gives us a moving vision of the terrible last stages of a disintegrating personality and a disintegrating society, and it painfully embodies the schizophrenia, alienation, and lovelessness of our time." Douglas Blazek concludes in *Poetry* that Wakoski's poems have the "substance necessary to qualify them notches above the works of creative 'geniuses', 'stylists', and 'cultural avatars' who have little to say."

The stylistic and structural aspects of Wakoski's poetry are as unique as her poetic statement. Often described as prosy, her poems are usually written in the first person. Rosellen Brown writes in *Parnassus* that Wakoski "is a marvelously abundant woman" who sounds in her poetry "like some friend of yours who's flung herself down in your kitchen to tell you something urgent and makes you laugh and respect her good old-fashioned guts at the same time."

"Diane's style of writing," says David Ignatow in *Margins,* "reminds me of the baroque style of dress . . . : the huge flounces, furbelows, puffed sleeves, trailing skirts, tight waist, heaving bosoms and stylishly protruding buttocks, all carried off with great elegance of movement and poise." In *Mediterranean Review,* critic Robert DeMaria finds that, "stylistically, [Wakoski] has a marvelous and distinctive voice. It lingers in one's mind after one has read her. . . . Her timing is excellent, so excellent that she can convert prose into poetry at times. And most of what she writes is really prose, only slightly transformed, not only because of its arrangement on the page, but because of this music she injects into it."

While the structures of Wakoski's poems appear to be informal and casually built, her artistic control over them is tight. As Hayden Carruth suggests in the *Hudson Review,* "Wakoski has a way of beginning her poems with the most unpromising materials imaginable, then carrying them on, often on and on and on, talkily, until at the end they come into surprising focus, unified works. With her it is a question of thematic and imagistic control, I think; her poems are deeply, rather than verbally, structured." In *Contemporary Literature,* Marjorie G. Perloff speaks of Wakoski's purpose in writing non-traditionally structured poems: "Wakoski strives for a voice that is wholly natural, spontaneous, and direct. Accordingly, she avoids all fixed forms, definite rhythms, or organized image patterns in the drive to tell us the Whole Truth about herself, to be *sincere.*"

"Although her poems are not traditional structures," says Debra Hulbert in *Prairie Schooner,* "she builds them solidly with words which feel chosen, with repetition of images throughout a poem." This repetition, an element that critics mention often, makes its own statement apart from the individual themes of the poems. "Repetition," remarks Gloria Bowles in *Margins,* "has become Wakoski's basic stylistic mode. And since form is an extension of content (et vice versa) Wakoski's poetic themes have become obsessive. Repetition is a formal fact of her poetry and, so she suggests, the basic structure of our lives."

Wakoski's poems often rely on digressions, on tangential wanderings through imagery and fantasy, to present ideas and themes. Blazek observes that "many of her poems sound as if they're constantly in trouble, falling into triteness, clumsiness, or indirection. She is constantly jumping into deep water to save a drowning stanza or into burning buildings to recover disintegrating meaning, always managing to pull these rescues off, sometimes with what appears to be a superhuman determination, drawing gasps from witnesses who never lose that initial impression of disaster." But, he says, these "imaginative excursions and side-journeys (she can get strung-out in just about any poem over a page long) are well-founded in her life—they're not just facile language cyclone-spinning itself to naught. They are doors into her psyche."

Toby Olson, writing in *Margins,* believes that "one of the central forces of [Wakoski's] poems proceeds from a fundamentally serious playfulness, an evident desire to spin out and open the image rather than to close the structure. . . . One of their most compelling qualities is their obsessiveness: the need at every turn to digress, to let the magic of the words take her where they will, because they are so beautiful, because the ability to speak out is not to be taken for granted, is to be wondered at in its foreignness, is to be followed.''

The ''magic'' of Wakoski's words is also wrought through her use of imagery and through her creation of a consistent personal mythology. Commenting on two of the poet's earliest works, *Coins and Coffins* and *Discrepancies and Apparitions,* Sheila Weller writes in *Ms.* that the books ''established [Wakoski] as a poet of fierce imagination. She was at once an eerie imagist (always the swooping gulls, deciduating hands, the hawk that 'pecks out my eyes like two cherries'); and a rapt parablist, reworking Wild West legend and cosmological symbols, transmuting fairy-tale scenes ('three children dancing around an orange tree') into macaberie ('Do you see the round orange tree? . . . glinting through the leaves, / the hanged man'). These poems are vivid landscapes—as diabolic as Dali, as gauzy as Monet.''

In *Poetry,* Sandra M. Gilbert describes Wakoski as ''a fabulist, a weaver of gorgeous webs of imagery and a teller of archetypically glamorous tales [who has] always attempted self-definition through self-mythologizing. 'The poems were a way of inventing myself into a new life,' she has said.'' ''The myth of herself,'' says H. Zinnes in *World Literature Today,* is of ''one 'clothed in fat,' with an ugly face, without wit, brilliance or elegance, but having some 'obsession for truth and history.' This plain seeker after love . . . is of course a poet with a great deal of wit . . . , a poet who in her work and life is not merely searching for a lover,'' although many of her poems touch on this theme.

Wakoski's personal mythology embraces many other archetypal figures as well, including George Washington, the King of Spain, the motorcycle mechanic, the ''man in Receiving at Sears,'' Beethoven, the ''man with the gold tooth,'' and the ''man who shook hands.'' These characters, most of whom appear more than once in Wakoski's canon, serve as symbols, emblematic of emotional states, past experiences, fantasies, and, sometimes, of real people in the poet's life.

George Washington, for example, appears in *The George Washington Poems,* a collection that Weller calls ''witty, caustic takes on the male mystique. In a voice by turns consciously absurdist and tremulously earnest, she takes the first President as her 'mythical father-lover,' romanticizes and barbs 'the militaristic, penalizing, fact-over-feeling male mind that I've always been afraid of and fascinated by.''' Wakoski speaks to George Washington in the poems with various voices—as Martha Washington, as a bitter child whose father has left home, as a lover left behind in the Revolutionary War. As Norman Martien explains in *Partisan Review,* ''the George Washington myths serve to express the failure of a woman's relations to her men, but the myths also give her a means of talking about it. Partly *because* 'George' is so distant, he can be a safe listener . . . [and] he can allow her a voice that can reaffirm human connection, impossible at closer ranges.'' This theme of the failure of relationships, of betrayal by others (especially men), is a central concern of Wakoski's, and many of her mythological figures embody one or more of the facets of human relations in which she sees the possibility of betrayal or loss.

The figure of the motorcycle mechanic in *The Motorcycle Betrayal Poems* symbolizes, as Wakoski says in her dedicatory statement, ''all those men who betrayed me at one time or another.'' According to Zweig, the book is ''haunted by a curious mythology composed of mustached lovers, 'mechanics' who do not understand the engine humming under [the narrator's] skin, the great-grandfatherly warmth of Beethoven and George Washington, to whom she turns with humor but also with a sort of desperation.'' In this book, says Eric Mottram in *Parnassus,* Wakoski ''operates in a world of women as adjuncts to men and the erotics of bikes; the poems are survival gestures.'' According to Weller, the book ''made . . . women start at [Wakoski's] power to personalize the paradox'' of male-female relationships—''their anger at the rejecting male archetype . . . yet their willing glorification of it. . . . The book's theme is the mythology and confusions of . . . love, and the fury at betrayal by symbols, envy, lovers, and self.''

The theme of betrayal, and its resulting pain, also appears in *Inside the Blood Factory*. Here, as Zweig observes, Wakoski writes ''poems of loss. The loss of childhood; the loss of lovers and family; the perpetual loss a woman lives with when she thinks she is not beautiful. These losses [create] a scorched earth of isolation around her, which she [describes] harshly and precisely. . . . From this vulnerable retreat, a stream of liberating images [emerges] to grapple with the world and mythify it.'' Peter D. Zivkovic, writing in *Southwest Review,* believes that *Inside the Blood Factory* is ''significantly more than a memorable reading experience. Perhaps the most remarkable thing about . . . [the book] is the consistent strength of the individual poems. There is not,'' Zivkovic concludes, ''a single weak poem in the volume—an achievement worthy of Frost and other American giants.''

AVOCATIONAL INTERESTS: Astrology; detective fiction; cooking; collecting American Art pottery; growing orchids.

CA INTERVIEW

CA interviewed Diane Wakoski by phone December 15, 1981, at her home in East Lansing, Mich.

CA: In ''Jealousy—A Confessional'' from Greed: Parts 5-7 *you wrote, ''obviously I do believe in exorcism or at least catharsis, and that is my purpose too in writing all this out.'' Was there any such impulse behind the early poems you began writing as a child?*

WAKOSKI: I think so, but in exorcism the idea is getting rid of a devil or some kind of spirit that is invading you, and a magic ritual is needed to get rid of it. I guess I feel that any time I write a poem there's something inside of me that I need to get out, but I don't know if *exorcism* would be the right word, because exorcism is almost always connected with demonic spirits inside of the self that are in some way causing trouble. I don't think everything that's inside of you that wants to get out is necessarily something that's causing trouble, other than in wanting to be out. I've never thought in those terms before, but certainly writing poetry for me is an act of getting something outside that's been inside. When I was a child I suppose I thought mostly of the beautiful things in the world, how overwhelming they were, and felt the need to get that feeling, which was kind of bursting inside of me, outside into something. As I got older, I think it began to encompass both the negative and the positive things.

CA: Was there a great deal of encouragement from family or teachers?

WAKOSKI: I'm not a family person. I never have had close feelings, basically, for my mother and my sister. I grew up without my father. In fact, I think I have had close feelings for my father because I've romanticized him, because he wasn't there. I've always been a very private person, and while I feel the need for other people, I'm very judgmental about them, so I need to choose the people whom I'm involved with.

For me, teachers were extremely important because school was the place where I could be myself, and the teachers were the people who could understand that self. I've had very inspiring encouragement from my teachers all along the way. I don't remember writing poetry in school when I was a child; I don't think that was anything that we ever did. When I started writing poetry, it was on my own, as a result of reading books. And then when I came back to it more actively as a teenager again—this was my sophomore year—it wasn't because my English teacher was encouraging it, but she found out I was writing a lot of poetry and suggested that we have a little after-school group of people to read poetry and talk about it. In a sense poetry has always been a very individual thing for me. I started reading, and as a result of reading wanted to write; and when I wrote, then I think I got a lot of encouragement from teachers, but I don't feel they were ever encouraging me specifically to write.

CA: You studied music for sixteen years, and that background figures very heavily in your poetry. Did you consider a career in music at any time?

WAKOSKI: I wasn't good enough. I fantasized one. But I didn't have any kind of technical background in music when I was young, and I still feel angry that people don't understand that students need technical background in everything they do along with the other parts of it. I don't understand how a music teacher, in all conscience, can let a student study piano for more than two years and not insist she also study theory and harmony. I could have learned that stuff practically by looking at the book. And by the time I was in college, I realized I certainly could never be a performer—I just didn't have the brilliance and the technical competence. So I resent soft-hearted teachers who do not give students strong technical background in whatever they do. I suppose I sort of bent over backwards myself in becoming a teacher by being very stern and requiring technical accomplishment. I wish someone had done that for me in music. I feel I did have that kind of background in literature and writing, maybe because it was easier for my teachers: I never broke down crying, because it was easier for me to do it. I don't blame teachers for not wanting to have crying students on their hands. On the other hand, it seems to me that you can't just cater to the babiness in everybody all along the way, or they never grow up and develop at all.

CA: Your first books were published in 1962: Four Young Lady Poets, *which was written with three other people, and* Coins and Coffins, *which was made up wholly of your own poems. Since then you've produced quite a steady flow of books. When did you first begin to feel established as a poet?*

WAKOSKI: After my second Doubleday book, *Inside the Blood Factory,* was published in 1968. I'd really been serious about poetry in college, and I think I got good attention at Berkeley from Tom Parkinson and a few of the other English faculty. Also, when I was a junior, a group of us Berkeley students were asked to give a reading at the brand new little San Francisco Poetry Center that had just been started. I and three other people gave readings, and my reading was enough of a success that they asked me to come back and read by myself the following year. I felt that was my debut as a public poet. When I went to New York I was included in a series of poetry readings being started at the YMHA Poetry Center. By that time I was beginning to feel that I wasn't just writing and publishing in little magazines and giving ordinary kinds of poetry readings, but I had been invited to read at established places as a new voice, a new poet.

It was the year after that that Jerome Rothenberg published *Coins and Coffins* at Hawk's Well Press. Then I decided it was time for me to have a bigger collection of poems. I sent my poems around and Doubleday accepted my manuscript in one of those lucky flukes. It came out of a slush pile and by accident some senior editor read it and liked it, and it was published in 1966 as *Discrepancies and Apparitions.* Then came *The George Washington Poems,* published by Riverrun Press, then Doubleday did *Inside the Blood Factory.* It got a lot of attention, and if things were the way they should be, probably it would have gotten a prize. I think it was after the publication of *Inside the Blood Factory,* when I got lots and lots of personal responses from people in the more established world of poetry, as well as quite a lot of reviews, that I began to think of myself as an established poet. That's when I really began earning my living giving poetry readings, and I think that was possible because of the good critical attention that book got.

So around 1969 I very much thought of myself as an established poet. A younger poet, yes, and certainly not in the league with Robert Lowell or Allen Ginsberg, my elders whom I admired, but I felt that at least I could hold my own with them, that I was writing my real adult poetry. And in retrospect I think that some of my very best poems are in *Inside the Blood Factory,* and as a collection it shows at least my young work at its most polished and accomplished. It was the turning point in my career from being a young poet, perhaps talented and perhaps accomplished in certain ways, to someone who knew her own voice and had established a real and original voice, different from anyone else, and special.

CA: The Black Sparrow Press books are beautifully designed. Were you involved in any way with their design and production?

WAKOSKI: No, the design is all done by an extremely talented woman, Barbara Martin, who is married to John Martin, the publisher. Actually, I think he sort of employed her as cheap labor. He got a good deal! They *are* beautiful books, and a couple of them, I think, really should have won book-design awards, although those things tend not to go to small presses. It's a pity, because the small presses are often much more concerned about the way books look than trade presses.

CA: You've been teaching and writing for quite a long time now. How do the two activities mesh?

WAKOSKI: For me they mesh rather well, but I'm terribly aware of their limitations for many people and what their limitations are for me. I'm grateful that I didn't become a professor of poetry or teacher of creative writing until I had published half a dozen books and had been writing and publishing for fifteen years, that I came to teaching as a so-called master of the craft. I feel sorry for young people who either think they want to teach or get roped into it because they feel it's the only thing a writer can do. It's even more risk-taking to criticize other people's poetry than to write poetry yourself, and I don't think they're sure enough of their own work to take on other people's. An enormous amount of guilt goes with that position of being the judge; as well as the pleasure of playing God, there is the pain of being God all of the time, and feeling that in fact the only way you can deserve that position is to do the right things for your students. So you constantly have this concern about giving them enough stern disciplinary criticism so that they will develop strength (as I did *not* as a musician) and at the same time not trying to lock them into one way of looking at things—which of course has to be my own point of view; I couldn't have been writing all these years without a very, very strong point of view. And probably one of the things that has stood me in good stead, besides coming to it late in my writing and publishing career, is the fact that I've always associated with a rather wide diversity of poets and been very involved with the avant-garde in both music and the visual arts as well as poetry, so that I tend to have an aesthetic point of view that's much wider than what I practice in my own poetry. Coming to teaching late in your "doing" career, you feel much more like you have something to say, something to teach, than when you yourself are just trying to figure out what it's all about.

When I tell my students this, they don't understand that it's wisdom; they just think I'm trying to keep them away from an easy, good life. I tell them that if they can figure out some way to live their lives as poets or fiction writers or whatever they want to be for fifteen years or so of really serious writing and publishing, they'll have a lot more authority to bring to teaching—they're liable to get hired into better jobs, and they're not going to burn themselves out so easily. Unless they're academics of another sort, unless they really are eighteenth-century scholars and teaching complements their work. But if what they're really interested in doing is being a writer and teaching twentieth-century literature and writing, it's best if they can stay out of the academic world until they're close to forty.

If you're a young M.F.A. graduate in poetry, probably the best job you can hope for is teaching composition with an occasional writing class thrown in, and I can't think of any faster way for a writer to burn himself out than having to read anywhere from fifty to ninety compositions every couple of weeks. A year of that may be good for everyone's soul—a year of any kind of slave labor makes us appreciate our lives—but the burnout it eventually causes is terrible. It makes people not only burned out for their own work, but also embittered and angry. And they make bad academics because they're narrow—they've never had the pleasures of going out and knocking about in the literary world, and at the same time they don't really have any of the excitement of being young academics, because that isn't their world either.

I don't understand why the idea of teaching right away has such enormous appeal, other than the great concern with job security, and that it's a job that people who like to read and write can conceive of doing. When I was an undergraduate at Berkeley, I knew I didn't want to take education courses and I also knew I didn't want to get a graduate degree, and those seem like the two roads to a teaching career. I'm glad I went out and struggled with other jobs.

CA: Your poem "Thanking My Mother For Piano Lessons" touched me very deeply. Have you heard from many other readers who were particularly moved by that poem?

WAKOSKI: Yes, that's probably one of my best poems, and I think it is certainly one of my most appreciated poems. I think of it as a central poem in my work for many reasons, maybe mostly because teaching is a serious subject for me, although I have approached it from lots of different directions. I don't know if I think of school as the primary place where we learn, or the actual schoolteacher as the primary teacher in one's life, but I think the whole idea of teaching and learning is very central to my sense of what life is all about. Probably because school was the only place I was really happy when I was a child, in some way that has become a center for me; perhaps that has become family for me—what most people feel is family. The idea of teaching and learning is that center of all relationships.

CA: James F. Mersmann wrote in "A Symposium on Diane Wakoski" in Margins, *January/February/March 1976, "I am convinced that Wakoski's poetry is a much wiser and more powerful statement about the experience of life in the 1960s and 1970s than most readers have realized." Do you see it from that perspective?*

WAKOSKI: I like that article very much. It's extremely perceptive and well written. When he was writing that essay, Mersmann was also working on *Out of the Vietnam Vortex: A Study of Poets and Poetry against the War*. He knows, both from reading my poetry and from talking to me, that I have never felt that I fit into the politics of the '60s or the '70s because I'm not political. And that while I make no bones about being a woman or writing from the standpoint of being a woman, I've always insisted it is I, Diane Wakoski, speaking; I'm not a spokesman for a group of people and I'm not protesting things that happened to groups of people or lamenting anything except what has happened to me. If other people take that in a political sense, I have no objection to it, but I don't ever want a political point of view imputed to me. One of the problems of people seeing me as a feminist writer or as a woman writer or as one of the protesting writers of the '60s and '70s is that they lose part of what's happening in the poetry, the mythology that's being created. I think that's what Mersmann is getting at in that statement, and for that reason I appreciate it very much. When you look at any kind of literature as representative of a cultural period or a movement or anything group-like, there's a great danger of losing the real value of the literature itself, assuming it has any beyond its cultural moment.

CA: Have you tried to read all the criticism of your work?

WAKOSKI: Well, recently that's been easy—I don't think anybody's been writing about it! No, I really haven't. And as a matter of fact, John Martin is very protective and sheltering of new authors, and he will deliberately not tell me about something because he knows it will upset me. I guess when I do read criticism of my work I take it much too seriously. I never really learned that schoolteacher's lesson of not taking it personally. In a recent issue of the *American Book Review* there is a review by Donna Brooke trashing *Cap of Darkness* and the book of essays and interviews, *Toward New Poetry,* and by my way of looking at it, totally unfairly. It's an extremely well written and intelligent review, which makes it even more painful to read. I am totally trashed because, she says, I don't have a feminist point of view, and at the same time my poems would only appeal to feminists, so there's just nothing there. This is why one's heart warms to the statement you quote from Mersmann, because I feel that I've been caught in that kind of trap so often—that I'm either written off by a critic as just another woman poet lamenting the troubles that women have, or someone like Donna Brooke is saying, "Ultimately, all poetry must be political, and Wakoski totally fails because she refuses to be.''

CA: You've said that you would write novels if you could; you've called yourself ''a novelist in disguise.'' Do you think you'll try doing a novel?

WAKOSKI: I think it's just like my going back to the piano. Each year my hand muscles atrophy more. I think each year it becomes less and less possible for me, if I ever had it in me to be a novelist, to be one. One develops the muscles one uses and, by the same token, loses the ones that he's not using. While I probably read more and more fiction, I think that makes it even less and less likely that I would ever write it. In the same way that I would love to be a pianist, I would love to be a fiction writer. I still don't play the piano, though.

CA: Have you found in your writing that new problems arise as old ones are solved, much like a golfer who develops a slice just as he has perfected his putting?

WAKOSKI: Yes, in one sense, since I think of my poetry as an extension of my life and a kind of organic response to my life through language and imagination. I suppose by definition life is about solving one problem and going on to the next. If nothing else, just our physical existence is going to provide those problems. I've found in retrospect (I didn't realize this at first) that almost all the poems I've written in the past four or five years have tackled the subject of aging and how painful it is in our culture—though I don't talk about it in those terms. All those poems are dealing with a new problem, which obviously wouldn't have been present in the young poems. In a way I see myself as carrying on the same themes, writing about the same things, but the overall meaning of those themes has a whole new set of problems.

I just finished a little group of poems called ''Saturn's Rings.'' One of the poems, which is my favorite, is called ''Joyce Carol Oates Plays the Saturn Piano.'' It's an evolution of that meditation that comes out of ''Thanking My Mother For Piano Lessons.'' A few years ago, when I hadn't been living in East Lansing too long, I got a party invitation from Joyce Carol Oates, who was living in Windsor—a couple of hours from here, across the river from Detroit in Canada. I had met her once, so I was thrilled. Robert and I got in the car and drove there, and when we came into her house I saw this piano covered with all the music that I used to play, and I said, ''I didn't realize you were a pianist.'' She said, ''Oh, I've just started taking piano lessons again.'' This of course brought home all of my memories of my own playing and stopping playing and making my vow to become a poet. I'd been wanting to write about that, but I hadn't known how. Then when I was writing these poems using the image of Saturn and the rings of Saturn in ethereal ways that have nothing to do with astronomy, more to do with mythology, I finally saw how to do it. But of course it really is a meditation on being middle-aged and having failed at many of your younger goals.

It was probably that Donna Brooke review that stimulated my writing it, because I realized that in whatever way my poetry might be successful for some people, or with the world a hundred years from now, to many critics today and to my contemporaries I'm just a failed poet. It is the subject of one's middle age: what one succeeds at, what one fails at, in what ways your children or your works go out in the world and survive. I can talk about it in prose, but I haven't really been able to talk about it in poetry. It seems to me that the more successful in some ways one's worldly life is, the easier it is to confront failure and the more possible it is to talk about failure.

While many people have told me how much they like ''Joyce Carol Oates Plays the Saturn Piano,'' one friend of mine, a poet, said he thought it was self-pitying. He said, ''You have this good job and you're one of the best published poets I know. How can you be sitting there talking about your failure like that?'' And I said, ''I think I can face my failure because my life is not a *total* failure.'' I have a comfortable life with a man I care about, and I do have a good job. This is almost 1982 and the world around us is not an easy world to live in, and I in no way feel like I haven't had my share of good things. But by the same token, the more you've had, the more you can see what you haven't had. I think it would be unrealistic not to talk about it, because those are the things that punish me every day.

When I was young, the thing that punished me was my sense of failure in terms of finding the right man in my life. Now that I'm middle-aged the thing that punishes me is the feeling that I've spent all this time in my career as a poet and haven't made it by my own standards, even though by worldly standards I have a pretty good life. How could we be honest, or really be doing the things that poetry is supposed to do, if we sat around counting our blessings instead of looking at all the discrepancies in the world? I could be ecstatic about the good parts of my life, but I think we're always looking for those cracks, those failures. Probably that's how we grow, that's how we learn, how we change; that's where we get whatever wisdom it is that we have.

BIOGRAPHICAL/CRITICAL SOURCES: Partisan Review, winter, 1971; *New York Times Book Review,* December 12, 1971, August 13, 1978; *Mediterranean Review,* spring, 1972; *Virginia Quarterly Review,* autumn, 1972; *Parnassus,* fall/winter, 1972, spring/summer, 1973; *Prairie Schooner,* spring, 1973; *Contemporary Literary Criticism,* Gale, Volume II, 1974, Volume IV, 1975, Volume VII, 1977, Volume IX, 1978, Volume XI, 1979; *Hudson Review,* summer, 1974; *Poetry,* June, 1974, August, 1976; *Southwest Review,* spring, 1975; *Contemporary Literature,* winter, 1975; *Margins,* January/February/March, 1976; *Ms.,* March, 1976; *World Literature Today,* autumn, 1978; Donald J. Greiner, editor, *Dictionary of Literary Biography,* Volume V: *American Poets after World War II,* Part 2, Gale, 1980.

—Sketch by Kerry L. Lutz

—Interview by Jean W. Ross

* * *

WAKOSKI-SHERBELL, Diane
See WAKOSKI, Diane

* * *

WALKER, Alice 1944-

PERSONAL: Born February 9, 1944, in Eatonton, Ga.; daughter of Willie Lee and Minnie Tallulah (Grant) Walker; married Melvyn Rosenman Leventhal (a civil rights lawyer), March 17, 1967 (divorced, 1976); children: Rebecca Grant. *Education:* Attended Spelman College, 1961-63; Sarah Lawrence College, B.A., 1965. *Residence:* San Francisco, Calif. *Agent:* Wendy Weil, Julian Bach Literary Agency, 747 Third Ave., New York, N.Y. 10017.

CAREER: Writer. Has been a voter registration worker in Georgia, a worker in Head Start program in Mississippi, and on staff of New York City welfare department. Writer-in-residence and teacher of black studies at Jackson State College, 1968-69, and Tougaloo College, 1970-71; lecturer in literature, Wellesley College and University of Massachusetts—Boston, both 1972-73; distinguished writer in Afro-American studies department, University of California, Berkeley, spring, 1982; Fannie Hurst Professor of Literature, Brandeis University, Waltham, Mass., fall, 1982. Lecturer and reader of own poetry at universities and conferences. Member of board of trustees of Sarah Lawrence College. Consultant on black history to Friends of the Children of Mississippi, 1967.

AWARDS, HONORS: Bread Loaf Writer's Conference, scholar, 1966; first prize, *American Scholar* essay contest, 1967; Merrill writing fellowship, 1967; McDowell Colony fellowship, 1967, 1977-78; National Endowment for the Arts grant, 1969; Radcliffe Institute fellowship, 1971-73; National Book Award nomination, 1973, for *Revolutionary Petunias;* Lillian Smith Award, Southern Regional Council, 1973, for *Revolutionary Petunias;* Richard and Hinda Rosenthal Foundation Award, American Academy and Institute of Arts and Letters, 1974, for *In Love and Trouble;* Guggenheim Award, 1977-78; National Book Critics Circle Award nomination, 1982, Pulitzer Prize and American Book Award, 1983, for *The Color Purple.*

WRITINGS—Published by Harcourt, except as indicated; poetry: *Once,* 1968; *Revolutionary Petunias and Other Poems,* 1973; *Goodnight, Willie Lee, I'll See You in the Morning,* Dial, 1979.

Fiction; novels, except as indicated: *The Third Life of Grange Copeland,* 1970; *In Love and Trouble: Stories of Black Women* (short stories), 1973; *Meridian,* 1976; *You Can't Keep a Good Woman Down* (short stories), 1981; *The Color Purple,* 1982.

Other: *Langston Hughes: American Poet* (children's biography), Crowell, 1973; (editor) *I Love Myself When I'm Laughing . . . and then Again When I Am Looking Mean and Impressive: A Zora Neale Hurston Reader,* introduction by Mary Helen Washington, Feminist Press, 1979; (contributor) Dexter Fisher, editor, *The Third Woman: Minority Women Writers of the United States,* 1980.

Work represented in anthologies, including: *Voices of the Revolution,* edited by Helen Haynes, E. & J. Kaplan (Philadelphia), 1967; *The Best Short Stories by Negro Writers from 1899 to the Present: An Anthology,* edited by Langston Hughes, Little, Brown, 1967.

Afro-American Literature: An Introduction, compiled by Robert Hayden, David J. Burrows, and Frederick R. Lapides, Harcourt, 1971; *Tales and Stories for Black Folks,* compiled by Toni Cade Bambara, Zenith Books, 1971; *Black Short Story Anthology,* compiled by Woodie King, New American Library, 1972; *The Poetry of Black America: An Anthology of the Twentieth Century,* compiled by Arnold Adoff, Harper, 1973; *A Rock against the Wind: Black Love Poems,* edited by Lindsay Patterson, Dodd, 1973; *We Would Be Sorcerers: Twenty-five Stories by Black Americans,* edited by Sonia Sanchez, Bantam, 1973; *Images of Women in Literature,* compiled by Mary Anne Ferguson, Houghton, 1973; *Best American Short Stories: 1973,* edited by Margaret Foley, Hart-Davis, 1973; *Best American Short Stories, 1974,* edited by Foley, Houghton, 1974.

Chant of Saints: A Gathering of Afro-American Literature, Art and Scholarship, edited by Michael S. Harper and Robert B. Stepto, University of Illinois Press, 1980; *Midnight Birds: Stories of Contemporary Black Women Authors,* edited by Mary Helen Washington, Anchor Press, 1980.

Contributor to periodicals, including *Negro Digest, Denver Quarterly, Harper's, Black World,* and *Essence.* Contributing editor, *Southern Voices, Freedomways,* and *Ms.*

WORK IN PROGRESS: A collection of essays, *In Search of Our Mothers' Gardens: A Collection of Womanist Prose;* another novel.

SIDELIGHTS: "*The Color Purple,* Alice Walker's third [novel,] could be the kind of popular and literary event that transforms an intense reputation into a national one," according to Gloria Steinem of *Ms.* Judging from the critical enthusiasm for *The Color Purple,* Steinem's words have proved prophetic. "Walker . . . has succeeded," as Andrea Ford notes in the *Detroit Free Press,* "in creating a jewel of a novel." Peter S. Prescott presents a similar opinion in a *Newsweek* review. "I want to say," he comments, "that *The Color Purple* is an American novel of permanent importance, that rare sort of book which (in Norman Mailer's felicitous phrase) amounts to 'a diversion in the fields of dread.'"

Although Walker's other books—novels, volumes of short stories, and poems—have not been completely ignored, they have not received the amount of attention that many critics feel they deserve. For example, William Peden, writing about *In Love and Trouble: Stories of Black Women* in *The American Short Story,* calls the collection of stories "a remarkable book that deserves to be much better known and more widely read." And while Steinem points out that *Meridian,* Walker's second novel, "is often cited as the best novel of the civil rights movement, and is taught as part of some American history as well as literature courses," Steinem maintains that Walker's "visibility as a major American talent has been obscured by a familiar bias that assumes white male writers, and the literature they create, to be the norm. That puts black women (and all women of color) at a double remove."

Jeanne Fox-Alston and Mel Watkins both feel that the appeal of *The Color Purple* is that the novel, as a synthesis of characters and themes found in Walker's earlier works, brings together the best of the author's literary production in one volume. Fox-Alston, in the *Chicago Tribune Book World,* remarks: "Celie, the main character in Walker's third . . . novel, *The Color Purple,* is an amalgam of all those women [characters in Walker's previous books]; she embodies both their desperation and, later, their faith." Watkins states in the *New York Times Book Review:* "Her previous books . . . have elicited praise for Miss Walker as a lavishly gifted writer. *The Color Purple,* while easily satisfying that claim, brings into sharper focus many of the diverse themes that threaded their way through her past work."

Walker's central characters are almost always black women; the themes of sexism and racism are predominant in her work, but her impact is felt across both racial and sexual boundaries. Walker, according to Steinem, "comes at universality through the path of an American black woman's experience. . . . She speaks the female experience more powerfully for being able to pursue it across boundaries of race and class." This fact is also mentioned by Fox-Alston, who notes Walker's "reputation as a provocative writer who writes about blacks in particular, but all humanity in general."

However, many critics see a definite black and female focus in her writings. For example, in her review of *The Color Purple,* Ford suggests that the novel transcends "culture and gender'' lines but also refers to Walker's ''unabashedly feminist viewpoint'' and the novel's ''black . . . texture.'' Walker does not deny this dual bias; the task of revealing the condition of the black woman is particularly important to her. Thadious M. Davis, in his *Dictionary of Literary Biography* article, comments: ''Walker writes best of the social and personal drama in the lives of familiar people who struggle for survival of self in hostile environments. She has expressed a special concern with 'exploring the oppressions, the insanities, the loyalties and the triumph of black women.''' Walker explains in a *Publishers Weekly* interview: ''The black woman is one of America's greatest heroes. . . . Not enough credit has been given to the black woman who has been oppressed beyond recognition.''

Critics reviewing Walker's first collection of short stories, *In Love and Trouble: Stories of Black Women,* respond favorably to the author's rendering of the black experience. In *Ms.* Barbara Smith observes: ''This collection would be an extraordinary literary work, if its only virtue were the fact that the author sets out consciously to explore with honesty the textures and terror of black women's lives. Attempts to penetrate the myths surrounding black women's experiences are so pitifully rare in black, feminist, or American writing that each shred of truth about these experiences constitutes a breakthrough. The fact that Walker's perceptions, style, and artistry are also consistently high makes her work a treasure.'' Mary Helen Washington remarks in a *Black World* review: ''The stories in *In Love and Trouble* . . . constitute a painfully honest, searching examination of the experiences of thirteen Black women. . . . The broad range of these characters is indication of the depth and complexity with which Alice Walker treats a much-abused subject: the Black woman.''

Walker bases her description of black women on what Washington refers to as her ''unique vision and philosophy of the Black woman.'' According to Barbara A. Bannon of *Publishers Weekly,* this philosophy stems from the ''theme of the poor black man's oppression of his family and the unconscious reasons for it.'' Walker, in her interview with the same magazine, asserts: ''The cruelty of the black man to his wife and family is one of the greatest [American] tragedies. It has mutilated the spirit and body of the black family and of most black mothers.'' Through her fiction Walker describes this tragedy. For instance, Smith notes: ''Even as a black woman, I found the cumulative impact of these stories [contained *In Love and Trouble*] devastating. . . . Women love their men, but are neither loved nor understood in return. The affective relationships are [only] between mother and child or between black woman and black woman.'' David Guy's commentary on *The Color Purple* in the *Washington Post Book World* includes this evaluation: ''Accepting themselves for what they are, the women [in the novel] are able to extricate themselves from oppression; they leave their men, find useful work to support themselves.'' Watkins further explains: ''In *The Color Purple* the role of male domination in the frustration of black women's struggle for independence is clearly the focus.''

Some reviewers criticize Walker's fiction for portraying an overly sympathetic view of black women. Katha Pollitt, for example, in the *New York Times Book Review,* calls the stories in *You Can't Keep a Good Woman Down* ''too partisan.'' The critic adds: ''The black woman is *always* the most sympathetic character.'' Guy notes: ''Some readers . . . will object to her overall perspective. Men in [*The Color Purple*] are generally pathetic, weak and stupid, when they are not heartlessly cruel, and the white race is universally bumbling and inept.'' Charles Larson, in his *Detroit News* review of *The Color Purple,* points out: ''I wouldn't go as far as to say that all the male characters [in the novel] are villains, but the truth is fairly close to that.'' However, neither Guy nor Larson feel that this point is a major fault in the novel. Guy, for example, while conceding that ''white men . . . are invisible in Celie's world,'' observes: ''This really is Celie's perspective, however—it is psychologically accurate to her—and Alice Walker might argue that it is only a neat inversion of the view that has prevailed in western culture for centuries.'' Larson also notes that by the end of the novel, ''several of [Walker's] masculine characters have reformed.''

This idea of reformation, this sense of hope even in despair, is at the core of Walker's vision, even though, as John F. Callahan states in *New Republic,* ''There is often nothing but pain, violence, and death for black women [in her fiction].'' In spite of the brutal effects of sexism and racism suffered by the characters of her short stories and novels, critics note what Art Seidenbaum of the *Los Angeles Times* calls Walker's sense of ''affirmation . . . [that] overcomes her anger.'' This is particularly evident in *The Color Purple,* according to reviewers. Ford, for example, asserts: ''Walker's . . . polemics on . . . political and economic issues finally give way to what can only be described as a joyful celebration of human spirit—exulting, uplifting and eminently universal.'' Prescott discovers a similar progression in the novel. He writes: ''[Walker's] story begins at about the point that most Greek tragedies reserve for the climax, then . . . by immeasurable small steps . . . works its way toward acceptance, serenity and joy.'' Walker, according to Ray Anello who quotes the author in *Newsweek,* agrees with this evaluation. Questioned about the novel's importance, she explains: ''Let's hope people can hear Celie's voice. There are so many people like Celie who make it, who come out of nothing. People who triumph.''

Davis refers to this idea as Walker's ''vision of survival'' and offers a summary of its significance in Walker's work. ''At whatever cost, human beings have the capacity to live in spiritual health and beauty; they may be poor, black, and uneducated, but their inner selves can blossom.'' Steinem adds: ''What . . . matters is the knowledge that everybody, no matter how poor or passive on the outside, has . . . possibilities inside.''

BIOGRAPHICAL/CRITICAL SOURCES: Negro Digest, September-October, 1968; *Saturday Review,* August 22, 1970; *Publishers Weekly,* August 31, 1970; *American Scholar,* winter, 1970-71, summer, 1973; *New Leader,* January 25, 1971; *Poetry,* February, 1971, March, 1980; *New Yorker,* February 27, 1971, June 7, 1976; John O'Brien, *Interviews with Black Writers,* Liveright, 1973; *Southern Review,* spring, 1973; *Black World,* September, 1973, October, 1974; *Nation,* November 12, 1973; *Washington Post Book World,* November 18, 1973, October 30, 1979, December 30, 1979, May 31, 1981, July 25, 1982; *Freedomways,* winter, 1973.

Ms., February, 1974, July, 1977, July, 1978, June, 1982; *New York Times Book Review,* March 17, 1974, May 23, 1976, May 29, 1977, December 30, 1979, May 24, 1981, July 25, 1982; *New Republic,* September 14, 1974, December 21, 1974; William Peden, *The American Short Story: Continuity and Change, 1940-1975,* 2nd edition, revised and enlarged, Houghton, 1975; *Contemporary Literary Criticism,* Gale, Volume V, 1976, Volume VI, 1976, Volume IX, 1978, Volume XIX, 1981; *Parnassus: Poetry in Review,* spring-summer, 1976; *Black Scholar,* April, 1976; *Atlantic,* June, 1976; *Yale Review,* autumn, 1976; *Commonweal,* April 29, 1977; *Times Literary Supplement,* August 19, 1977, June 18, 1982.

Dictionary of Literary Biography, Volume VI: *American Novelists since World War II,* 2nd series, Gale, 1980; *Los Angeles Times,* April 29, 1981; *Newsweek,* June 21, 1982; *Chicago Tribune Book World,* August 1, 1982; *Los Angeles Times Book Review,* August 8, 1982; *Detroit Free Press,* August 8, 1982; *Detroit News,* September 15, 1982; *Ann Arbor News,* October 3, 1982; *Washington Post,* October 15, 1982.

—Sketch by Marian Walters

* * *

WALLACE, Pat
See STROTHER, Pat Wallace

* * *

WALLERSTEIN, Immanuel 1930-

PERSONAL: Born September 28, 1930, in New York, N.Y.; son of Lazar and Sally (Guensberg) Wallerstein; married Beatrice Morgenstern, May 25, 1964; children: Katharine Ellen. *Education:* Columbia University, A.B., 1951, M.A., 1954, Ph.D., 1959; Oxford University, graduate study, 1955-56. *Religion:* Jewish. *Office:* Department of Sociology, State University of New York, Binghamton, N.Y. 13401.

CAREER: Columbia University, New York, N.Y., instructor, 1958-59, assistant professor, 1959-63, associate professor of sociology, 1963-71; McGill University, Montreal, Quebec, professor of sociology, 1971-76; State University of New York at Binghamton, distinguished professor of sociology and director of Fernand Braudel Center for the Study of Economies, Historical Systems, and Civilizations, 1976—. *Military service:* U.S. Army, 1951-53. *Member:* International Sociological Association (vice-president, research commission, national movements and imperialism, 1972-86), International African Institute (member of executive council, 1978-84), Social Science Research Council (member of board of directors, 1980-86), African Studies Association (president, 1972-73), American Sociological Association.

WRITINGS: Africa: The Politics of Independence, Random House, 1961; *The Road to Independence: Ghana and the Ivory Coast,* Mouton, 1964; (editor) *Social Change: The Colonial Situation,* Wiley, 1966; *Africa: The Politics of Unity,* Random House, 1967; *University in Turmoil: The Politics of Change,* Atheneum, 1969; (editor with Paul Starr) *The University Crisis: A Reader,* two volumes, Random House, 1970; *The Modern World-System,* Academic Press, Volume I: *Capitalist Agriculture and the Origins of the European World Economy in the Sixteenth Century,* 1974, Volume II: *Mercantilism and the Consolidation of the European World-Economy, 1600-1750,* 1980.

World Inequality, Black Rose Books (Montreal), 1975; (editor with Peter C. Gutkind) *Political Economy of Contemporary Africa,* Sage Publications, 1976; *The Capitalist World-Economy,* Cambridge University Press, 1979; (editor with Terence K. Hopkins) *Processes of the World-System,* Sage Publications, 1980; (with Hopkins and others) *World-Systems Analysis: Theory and Methodology,* Sage Publications, 1982; (with Samir Amin, Giovanni Arrighi, and Andre Gunder Frank) *Dynamics of Global Crisis,* Macmillan, 1982; (editor with Aquino de Braganca) *The African Liberation Reader,* three volumes, Zed Press (London), 1982. Editor, *Political Economy of the World System Annuals.* Contributor to professional journals.

WALLOWER, Lucille

PERSONAL: Born in Waynesboro, Pa.; daughter of Roland C. (in advertising) and Nora Grace (Werdebaugh) Wallower. *Education:* Studied at Pennsylvania Museum School of Art and Traphagen School of Fashion. *Home:* 60 East Main St., Cambridge, N.Y. 12816.

CAREER: Harrisburg Public Library, Harrisburg, Pa., school librarian, 1943-44, assistant children's librarian, 1944-46; fashion artist at Pomeroy's Inc., 1946-49, and at Bowman's, Inc., 1949-52, in Harrisburg; Abington Library, Jenkintown, Pa., children's librarian, 1959-72, librarian, 1972-75; free-lance writer and illustrator, 1975—. Director, Harrisburg Art Association Studio, 1943-48. *Member:* Pennsylvania Library Association, Historical Society of Pennsylvania, Philadelphia Reading Roundtable, Old York Road Historical Society.

WRITINGS—Published by Penns Valley, except as indicated: *Pennsylvania Primer,* 1954, published as *The New Pennsylvania Primer,* 1972; *William Penn,* illustrations by Louis Cary, Follett, 1968; (with Patricia L. Gump) *The Pennsylvania Dutch,* 1971; *Introduction to Pennsylvania,* McRoberts, 1974; (with Marilyn Miller Porter) *African American Workshop,* 1977.

Self-illustrated: *A Conch Shell for Molly* (Junior Literary Guild selection), McKay, 1940; *Chooky,* McKay, 1942; *The Roll of Drums,* Albert Whitman, 1945; *Your Pennsylvania,* 1953, 3rd edition, 1964; *Indians of Pennsylvania,* 1956, 2nd edition, 1965; *Old Satan,* McKay, 1956; *The Hippity Hopper; or, Why There Are No Indians in Pennsylvania,* McKay, 1957; *The Morning Star,* McKay, 1957; *All about Pennsylvania,* 1958; *They Came to Pennsylvania,* 1960; *Your State: Pennsylvania,* 1962; *Pennsylvania A B C,* 1963; *The Lost Prince, Louis XVII of France,* McKay, 1963; *My Book about Abraham Lincoln,* 1967; *Colonial Pennsylvania,* foreword by S. K. Stevens, Thomas Nelson, 1969; (with Annette Brookshire) *Pennsylvania: A Bicentennial Workshop,* 1975; *Indians of Pennsylvania Workshop,* 1976; *They Came to Pennsylvania Workshop,* 1976.

Stories included in: *Uncle Sam's Story Book,* McKay, 1944; *Stories from the East and North,* Silver Burdett, 1945; *With New Friends,* Silver Burdett, 1946; *Shining Hours,* Bobbs-Merrill, 1961.

Illustrator: *Nanka of Old Bohemia,* Albert Whitman, 1937; *The Treasure of Belden Place,* Albert Whitman, 1938; *Ju Ju and His Friends,* Albert Whitman, 1939; *Mystery Mountain,* Albert Whitman, 1940; *Natalie,* Albert Whitman, 1940; *Salute to the Flag,* Albert Whitman, 1941; *Orange on Top,* Harcourt, 1945; *Their Way,* Albert Whitman, 1945; *How Many Friends?,* Judson, 1953; *Kindergarten Songs and Rhythms,* Judson, 1954; *My Bible Story Book,* Judson, 1955; *Mara of Old Babylon,* Abingdon, 1955; *Mara Journeys Home,* Abingdon, 1957.

WORK IN PROGRESS: A novel for teenagers and a picture book.

* * *

WARMKE, Roman F. 1929-

PERSONAL: Born November 23, 1929, in Easton, Minn.; married Dorothy Rose Emmer, 1952 (divorced 1974); married Anna Linea Phillips, 1977; children: (first marriage) Jonathan, James, Jerome, Julie Ann, Joseph, Matthew; (second marriage) Roman; stepchildren: Jennifer, Kristen, Jeffery. *Education:* University of Minnesota, B.S., 1951, M.A., 1952, Ph.D., 1960; postdoctoral study at University of Northern Colorado, University of Minnesota, and Ohio University. *Home:* 399 Beechwood Dr., Athens, Ohio 45701. *Office:* Center for Economic Education, Ohio University, Athens, Ohio 45701.

CAREER: Austin Junior College, Austin, Minn., instructor in marketing and economics, 1952-54; Colorado State College (now University of Northern Colorado), Greeley, assistant professor, 1954-56, associate professor, 1956-60, professor of business and business education, 1960-62, director of Center for Economic Education, 1962; University of Minnesota, Minneapolis, director of economic education, 1962-66; Ohio University, Athens, professor of economic education, 1966—, chairman of department, 1966-72, 1975—, director of Center for Economic Education, 1979—. Visiting lecturer at National University of Mexico, 1960; visiting professor at University of Washington, 1963, Colorado State College (now University of Northern Colorado), 1964, Brigham Young University, 1965, and Mara Institute of Technology, Shah Alam, Malaysia, 1972-73, 1976, 1977, 1979, and 1980. Executive director, Minnesota State Council on Economic Education, 1962-66; Ohio Council on Economic Education, trustee, 1966—, president, 1966-72, member of executive committee, 1978—. Owner of J & W Enterprises (real estate and construction business). Guest lecturer for "The American Economy" television series, Columbia Broadcasting System, 1963, and "Insite" television series, University of Missouri—Columbia, 1975. Member of national advisory committee, Joint Council on Economic Education. Consultant to economics faculty, Mara Institute of Technology, 1972-73; consultant to numerous schools, businesses, and financial institutions.

MEMBER: American Economic Association, American Educational Research Association, National Council for the Social Studies, National Business Education Association, American Council on Consumer Interests, Association for Supervision and Curriculum Development, Academy of National Consumer Education Scholars, Delta Phi Epsilon, Phi Delta Kappa. *Awards, honors:* Distinguished Service Award, Minnesota State Council on Economic Education, 1966.

WRITINGS: (Contributor) *Die Deutsche Berufs—und Fachschule,* Rheininbessische Druckwerkstaette E. Dietl & Co., 1951; (contributor) *Business Education World,* Gregg Publishing Division, McGraw, 1957; *Supervision to Improve Instruction* (monograph), Office of Education, U.S. Department of Health, Education, and Welfare, 1959; *Distributive Education Issues* (monograph), South-Western, 1961; (study director) Harlan M. Smith, editor, *Study Guide for Selected Sixty-Session Series of "The American Economy" TV Films,* Joint Council on Economic Education, 1964; (with Carroll A. Nolan) *Marketing, Sales Promotion, and Advertising,* 7th edition, South-Western, 1965, 8th edition published as *Marketing in Action,* 1976; (editor with Gerald Draager) *Selected Readings in Economic Education,* College of Business Administration, Ohio University, 1969.

(With W. Harmon Wilson) *Life on Paradise Island: Economic Life on an Imaginary Island,* Scott, Foresman, 1970; (with Wyllie, Wilson, and Eyster) *Consumer Economic Problems,* 8th edition, South-Western, 1971, 9th edition, 1977; (contributor with G. Draayer) *Economic Education Experiences of Enterprising Teachers,* Joint Council on Economic Education, 1971; (with Wyllie and Sellers) *Consumer Decision Making: Guides to Better Living,* South-Western, 1972, 2nd edition, 1977; (with Chandriah Appa Rao) *Economics,* Longman (Malaysia), 1974; (with Wyllie) *Free Enterprise in the United States,* South-Western. 1980; *The Study of Economics,* C. E. Merrill, 1980; *The Study and Teaching of Economics,* C. E. Merrill, 1980.

Author of educational films and documentaries for Columbia Broadcasting System, 1963, KTCA-TV, Minneapolis, 1965, National Educational Television, 1971, and Encyclopaedia Britannica, 1981. Contributor to periodicals, including *Business Education Forum, Land Use Survey, National Business Quarterly, Social Education,* and *Journal of Economic Education.* Editor for American Vocational Association, 1959-65, and of special issues of *Business Education Forum,* 1965 and 1966.

WORK IN PROGRESS: Revised editions of *Consumer Economic Problems, Consumer Decision Making,* and *Marketing in Action.*

* * *

WARSH, Lewis 1944-

PERSONAL: Born November 9, 1944, in New York, N.Y.; married Bernadette Mayer (a poet), November, 1975; children: Marie Ray, Sophia Crystal, Max. *Education:* City College of the City University of New York, B.A., 1966, M.A., 1975. *Home and office:* 172 East Fourth St., New York, N.Y. 10009.

CAREER: Poet. *Angel Hair* (magazine) and Angel Hair Books, New York City, co-founder and co-editor, 1966-77; *Boston Eagle,* Boston, Mass., co-editor, 1973-75; *United Artists* (magazine) and United Artists Books, New York City, co-founder and publisher, 1977—. Teacher in St. Marks in the Bowery Poetry Project, 1973-75; lecturer at Kerouac School of Disembodied Poetics, Boulder, Colo., 1978, and New England College, 1979-80. *Awards, honors:* Poet's Foundation Award, 1972; American Society of Composers, Authors, and Publishers grant, 1977; National Endowment for the Arts grant in poetry, 1979; Coordinating Council of Literary Magazines editor's fellowship, 1981.

WRITINGS—Poetry, except as indicated: *The Suicide Rates,* Toad Press, 1967; *Highjacking: Poems,* Boke Press, 1968; *Moving through Air,* Angel Hair Books, 1968; (with Tom Clark) *Chicago,* Angel Hair Books, 1969; *Words, Staring,* Orange Bear Reader, 1971; *Dreaming as One: Poems,* Corinth Books, 1971; *Long Distance,* Ferry Press, 1971; *Part of My History* (autobiography), Coach House Press, 1972; (translator) Robert Desnos, *Night of Loveless Nights,* The Ant's Forefoot, 1973; *Immediate Surrounding,* Other Books, 1974; *Today,* Adventures in Poetry, 1974; *The Maharajah's Son* (autobiography), Angel Hair Books, 1977; *Blue Heaven,* Kulchur, 1978; *Hives,* United Artists Books, 1979; *Methods of Birth Control,* Sun & Moon, 1982. Contributor to *Poetry, Paris Review, Big Sky,* and other publications.

* * *

WARWICK, Dolores

See FRESE, Dolores Warwick

* * *

WASSERMAN, Sheldon 1940-

PERSONAL: Born December 17, 1940, in Boston, Mass.; son of Myer (a laborer) and Florence (Youngstein) Wasserman; married Pauline MacKenzie (a writer), April 13, 1963. *Education:* Attended schools in Providence, R.I. *Home and office:* 16 Rutgers Rd., Piscataway, N.J. 08854.

CAREER: Honeywell Co., programmer analyst in Massachusetts and Colorado, 1963-65; in technical operations in Maryland, 1965, and in computer applications in Massachusetts, 1966-67; RCA Corp., worked in Massachusetts, New Jersey, and Germany as systems designer analyst, systems programmer analyst, and regional systems specialist, 1967-71; Delta Resources, senior programmer analyst in New York, 1972-75; free-lance programmer and systems analyst, 1975—. Lecturer on wine. *Military service:* U.S. Army Reserve, active duty, 1958-61.

MEMBER: Accademia Vitivinicola della Daunia, Commanderie du Bontemps de Medoc, Amici del Vino, New York Wine Writers' Circle, Club Paladini dei Vini di Sicilia. *Awards, honors:* Regione Toscana first prize for foreign journalists (shared with wife, Pauline Wasserman), for "The Wines of Chianti," which appeared in *Vintage,* October, 1981.

WRITINGS—With wife, Pauline Wasserman, except as indicated: (Sole author) *The Wines of Italy: A Consumer's Guide,* Stein & Day, 1976; *The Wines of the Cotes du Rhone,* Stein & Day, 1977; *Don't Ask Your Waiter,* Stein & Day, 1978; *White Wines of the World,* Stein & Day, 1978, revised edition, 1980; *Guide to Fortified Wines,* Marlborough Press, 1982; *Guide to Sparkling Wines,* Marlborough Press, 1983; (contributor) *Il Veronelli, Enciclopedia Mondiale dei Vini e Delle Acquaviti,* Rizzoli Editori, 1983. Contributor to periodicals, including *Italian Wines and Spirits* and *Vintage.*

WORK IN PROGRESS: Pocket Guide to Wine and *Pocket Guide to Italian Wine,* both with wife, Pauline Wasserman; *In Gold We Trust: Causes and Solution to the Current International Monetary Mess.*

SIDELIGHTS: "Economics is still a real interest," Sheldon Wasserman told *CA,* "but wine has become a more compelling one. Speaking on wine to audiences of fellow and future wine-lovers is also a pleasure. Why wine? It is not only a fascination in itself but represents one of the few fields of endeavor today where quality and integrity are still valued over mediocrity."

AVOCATIONAL INTERESTS: Travel "and related research with respect to food, wine, the people and their customs, and history."

* * *

WATERS, Mary-Alice 1942-

PERSONAL: Born January 12, 1942, in the Philippine Islands. *Education:* Carleton College, B.A., 1963; graduate study at University of California, Berkeley, 1963-64. *Politics:* Marxist. *Religion:* Atheist. *Office: Militant,* 14 Charles Lane, New York, N.Y. 10014.

CAREER: Young Socialist, New York City, editor, 1966-67; Young Socialist Alliance, New York City, national chairwoman, 1968; *Militant,* New York City, managing editor, 1970-71, editor, 1971—. National co-chairperson, Socialist Workers Party, 1980—. *Member:* Phi Beta Kappa.

WRITINGS—Published by Pathfinder: (Editor) *Rosa Luxemburg Speaks,* 1970; (with Jack Barnes, George Breitman, Derrick Morrison, and Barry Sheppard) *Towards an American Socialist Revolution,* 1972; *Feminism and Socialism* (pamphlet, 1972; *Feminism and the Marxist Movement,* 1972; (with Tony Thomas, Betsy Stone, Barnes, and Sheppard) *Prospects for Socialism in America,* 1976; *Women and the Socialist Revolution,* 1976; *Proletarian Leadership in Power,* 1980.

WATTS, Franklin (Mowry) 1904-1978

PERSONAL: Born June 11, 1904, in Sioux City, Iowa; died May 21, 1978, in New York, N.Y.; son of John Franklin (a minister) and Amanda (Mowry) Watts; married Helen Hoke (an editor), May 25, 1945. *Education:* Boston University, B.B.A., 1925. *Office:* 200 Park Ave. S., Room 1705, New York, N.Y. 10003.

CAREER: Book buyer for George Innes Co. and L. S. Ayers & Co., 1925-32; sales manager for the New York City publishing firms, Vanguard Press, Inc., 1932-34, Julian Messner, Inc., 1934-50, and Heritage Press, 1936-50; Franklin Watts, Inc. (publishers specializing in children's books), New York City, founder and president, 1942-70, vice-chairman, 1970-78; Franklin Watts Ltd. (a joint venture with Grolier publishers), London, England, founder and managing director, 1970-76; Frank Book Corporation, New York City, founder, 1976. A director, Grolier Enterprises, Inc. Member of American Book Publishers Council and Government Book Program advisory committee; former member, U.S. Department of State international book projects and advisory committee. *Member:* Publishers Lunch Club.

WRITINGS: (Editor) *Voices of History,* F. Watts, 1941, 3rd edition, 1943; (editor) *The Complete Christmas Book,* F. Watts, 1958; *Let's Find Out about Christmas,* F. Watts, 1967; *Let's Find Out about Easter,* F. Watts, 1969.

Published by Childrens Press: *Corn,* 1977; *Rice,* 1977; *Wheat,* 1977; *Oranges,* 1978; *Peanuts,* 1978; *Tomatoes,* 1978.

Editor, *Pocket Book Magazine,* 1954-56.

OBITUARIES: New York Times, May 23, 1978; *Publishers Weekly,* June 5, 1978.†

* * *

WAYLAN, Mildred
See HARRELL, Irene B(urk)

* * *

WEARY, Ogdred
See GOREY, Edward (St. John)

* * *

WEIR, LaVada

PERSONAL: Surname rhymes with "here"; born in Kansas City, Mo.; foster daughter of Manual P. (a building contractor) and Elsie Nestlerode; married Fred J. Weir, July 26, 1950 (divorced, 1973); children: Lucy, Joan and Tracy (twins). *Education:* University of Kansas, B.A., 1941; graduate study at University of Southern California, 1946-50. *Residence:* Redondo Beach, Calif.

CAREER: Writer. Worked as saleswoman, ghost-writer of speeches, and waitress; courier with U.S. Navy shipbuilding program in Kansas and Missouri; underwriter for Prudential Insurance of America; high school English and drama teacher in Kansas, 1943-45, and in California, 1945-51. *Member:* Authors Guild, Authors League of America, Southern California Writers Guild, Southwest Manuscripters, Southern California Council on Literature for Young People and Children, Surf Writers. *Awards, honors:* Awards for best comedy in Southern

California Theatre Tourney and for *Hic Away Henry* in Southern Books Competition.

WRITINGS: (With daughter, Joan Weir) *Hic Away Henry* (juvenile), Steck, 1967; *Little Pup* (juvenile), Steck, 1969; *Howdy!* (juvenile), Steck, 1971; *Skateboards and Skateboarding,* Messner, 1977; *Aviation: A Comprehensive Reading Kit,* Bowmar/Noble, 1978; *Advanced Skateboarding,* Messner, 1979; *The Roller Skating Book,* Messner, 1979; *The First Book of Grass Skiing,* Messner, 1981; (contributor) *Impressions,* Holt, 1983.

"Laurie Newman Adventure" series; published by Children's Press; all 1974: *Breaking Point; Chaotic Kitchen; Edge of Fear; The Horse-Flambeau; Laurie Loves a Horse; A Long Distance; Men!; The New Girl.*

Author of drama reviews and weekly column "Backstage with LaVada," for *Daily Breeze,* Redondo Beach, Calif., 1956-60. Contributor of articles and short stories to periodicals.

WORK IN PROGRESS: "Ghostwriting a series of how-to books in the area of the occult."

* * *

WEISBORD, Marvin R(oss) 1931-

PERSONAL: Born June 11, 1931, in Philadelphia, Pa.; son of William W. (a businessman) and Ida (Rosen) Weisbord; married Dorothy Barclay (an artist), December 23, 1956; children: Joseph, Nina, Robert, Dan. *Education:* Attended University of Arizona, 1949-51; University of Illinois, B.S., 1953; State University of Iowa, M.A., 1955. *Home:* 252 Kent Rd., Wynnewood, Pa. 19096. *Agent:* John Schaffner, 425 East 51st St., New York, N.Y. 10022. *Office:* Block Petrella Weisbord, 119 Sibley Ave., Ardmore, Pa. 19003.

CAREER: Pennsylvania State University, University Park, instructor in journalism, 1957-59; Regent Standard Forms, Philadelphia, Pa., executive vice-president, 1959-68; Block Petrella Associates, Wynnewood, Pa., director of Organization Research and Development Division, 1968-80; Block Petrella Weisbord (management consultants), Ardmore, Pa., senior vice-president, 1980—. Lecturer and adjunct professor at colleges and universities, 1972—. *Military service:* U.S. Navy, journalist, 1955-57. *Member:* International Association of Applied Social Scientists, Certified Consultants International, National Training Laboratories Institute, National Organization Development Network, American Society of Journalists and Authors. *Awards, honors:* Senior fellow, National Health Care Management Center, 1979-81.

WRITINGS: Campaigning for President, Public Affairs Press, 1964; (editor) *A Treasury of Tips for Writers,* Writer's Digest, 1965, reprinted, 1981; *A New Look at the Road to the White House,* Washington Square Press, 1966; *Some Form of Peace: True Stories of the American Friends Service Committee at Home and Abroad,* Viking, 1968; *Basic Photography,* 3rd edition, Amphoto, 1973; (with Howard Lamb and Allan Drexler) *Improving Police Department Management through Problem-Solving Task Forces: A Case Study in Organization Development,* Addison-Wesley, 1974; *Organizational Diagnosis: A Workbook of Theory and Practice,* Addison-Wesley, 1978.

Also author, with Paul R. Lawrence and Martin P. Charns, of *Academic Medical Center Self-Study Guide: Practical Applications of Survey Diagnosis and Data Summaries from Nine Medical Centers, 1974.* Associate editor, *Journal of Applied Behavioral Science,* 1973-79.

WORK IN PROGRESS: Organization Development Consulting: Practice Theories in Action.

SIDELIGHTS: "Over the years," writes Marvin R. Weisbord, "I've metamorphosed from writer to consultant with many institutions, mainly large corporations, medical centers, government agencies and the like. My firm, [Block Petrella Weisbord,] practices a form of collaborative consulting called 'action research,' which is not widely understood, joining with clients to diagnose and resolve situations which have no textbook solutions—reorganizations, mergers, introduction of new technologies, improvement of product and service quality, redesign of work and jobs. The goals are to create enjoyable work and economically sound institutions, and to do both using democratic procedures.

"I think the itch I have been scratching for many years in my writing and consulting is the perpetuation of democratic values in the face of technology, bureaucracy, and super-specialization—forces which tend to work against free choice, free expression, equity, individual growth, mutual support, and personal influence in the workplace. Since there are no 'correct' answers for any of the problems this raises, my field is—always will be—experimental. Consultants and clients join together to study the situation, design solutions, and try them out.

"The . . . interest of Americans in Japanese management, especially participative practices and worker involvement in decisions and problem-solving in factories, has caused a boomlet in my field among people who think the Japanese have 'answers' to problems of product quality, employee motivation, etc. unavailable to Americans. We seek to break out of this thinking—that good results come from using particular techniques. Instead, we are evolving a practice based on trust, more open exchange of information, more cooperation across lines of specialty, function, nationality, color, class, status, and hierarchy, and a better appreciation among all parties of the way in which technical and social systems influence each other.

"Since the early 1970s, I've been writing on this emerging practice for special journals, mainly for other consultants and academics in this country and in Europe. With my work in progress I wish to express some of these abstract ideas more concretely—to support people who want more satisfaction out of work and are willing to experiment with organizational arrangements to get it.

"Much to my surprise (and pleasure), my writings have been widely translated—into Spanish, Portuguese, French, German, Swedish—and I have been invited to do workshops and seminars in Europe and the Far East. I think this is one measure of how much interest is stirring around the world in new ways of organizing work. People everywhere wish to use technology for humane ends in human ways. Nobody wants to be a cog or an extension of a machine or a candidate for heart attacks and ulcers, or 1001 other things it's easy to fall into in large, rapidly-changing institutions."

* * *

WEISS, M(orton) Jerome 1926- (M. Jerry Weiss)

PERSONAL: Born April 16, 1926, in Oxford, N.C.; son of Max I. (a merchant) and Fannie (Cohen) Weiss; married Helen Schwartzbard, October 21, 1950; children: Sharon, Frann, Eileen, Michael. *Education:* University of North Carolina, B.A., 1949; Columbia University, M.A., 1951, Ed.D., 1952. *Reli-*

gion: Jewish. *Office:* Department of English, Jersey City State College, 2039 Kennedy Blvd., Jersey City, N.J. 07305.

CAREER: High school teacher in Chase City, Va., 1949-50; New York Board of Education, New York City, research assistant in Guidance Division, 1951-52; Rhodes Preparatory School, New York City, director of remedial reading, 1952-56; Defiance College, Defiance, Ohio, associate professor of English and director of reading improvement, 1956-58; Pennsylvania State University, University Park, assistant professor of secondary education, 1958-61; Jersey City State College, Jersey City, N.J., professor of English, reading and language arts, 1961-68, Distinguished Service Professor of Communications, 1968—. Visiting professor at University of Toledo, summer, 1957, University of Rhode Island, University of Nevada at Las Vegas, University of Utah, and Western Washington State College. President, Montclair Public Library Board of Trustees, 1976-79. Consultant to McGraw-Hill Book Co., 1967, Dell Publishing Co., Inc., 1968, Odyssey Press, Inc., 1968, Holt, Rinehart & Winston, Inc., 1972, and Paperback Sales, Inc.; principal consultant to "Literature and the Urban Experience" project, Rutgers University, 1981-83. *Military service:* U.S. Naval Reserve, 1944-46.

MEMBER: International Reading Association (chairman of committee on adolescent literature, 1976-78; chairman of committee on reading and the arts, 1978-81), National Council of Teachers of English (president of Assembly on Literature for Adolescents, 1974-75), College Reading Association (president, 1964-65; chairman of media commission, 1982-83), American Personnel and Guidance Association, National Education Association, American Association of University Professors (president of Jersey City State College chapter, 1974-76), Conference on College Composition and Communication, Student Personnel Association for Teacher Education, New Jersey Reading Teachers Association (president, 1974-75), New Jersey Education Association, Phi Delta Kappa, Kappa Delta Pi. *Awards, honors:* Distinguished service awards from College Reading Association, 1973, Assembly on Literature for Adolescents, National Council of Teachers of English, 1976, and New Jersey Reading Association, 1979; Elliott Landau Award, 1977.

WRITINGS: Guidance through Drama, Whiteside, 1954; (co-author) *A Guide to Play Selection,* Appleton, 1958, 3rd edition (with Joseph Mersand and others), National Council of Teachers of English, 1975; (editor) *Reading in the Secondary Schools,* Odyssey, 1961; (editor) *Ten Short Plays,* Dell, 1963; *Books to Grow On: A Paperback Library,* Random House, 1976; (with Bernice Cullinan) *Books I Have Read When I Was Young,* Avon, 1980.

Under name M. Jerry Weiss: (Editor) *An English Teacher's Reader,* Odyssey, 1961; (editor) *Man and War,* Dell, 1963; (compiler with Theresa Oakes) *The Unfinished Journey: Themes from Contemporary Literature,* McGraw, 1967; (editor) *Tales Out of School,* Dell, 1967; (compiler) *Kaleidoscope,* Cummings, 1970; *Man to Himself,* Cummings, 1970; (editor) *New Perspectives on Paperbacks,* College Reading Association, 1972; (compiler with wife, Helen S. Weiss) *The American Way of Laughing,* Bantam, 1977; (editor) *From Writers to Students: The Pleasures and Pains of Writing,* International Reading Association, 1979; (with H. S. Weiss) *More Tales Out of School,* Bantam, 1980.

Contributor to periodicals, including *Journal of the National Association of Deans of Women, Recreation, Journal of Developmental Reading, Studies in the Mass Media, Media and Methods, Midwestern Educational Review, English Journal, New Jersey Journal of Reading, Reading World, Connecticut English Journal,* and *New England Reading Association Journal.*

AVOCATIONAL INTERESTS: Theatre, records.

* * *

WEISS, M. Jerry
See WEISS, M(orton) Jerome

* * *

WELCH, Rowland
See DAVIES, L(eslie) P(urnell)

* * *

WELLS, J. Wellington
See de CAMP, L(yon) Sprague

* * *

WELLS, John Jay
See COULSON, Juanita

* * *

WELLS, Robert
See WELSCH, Roger L(ee)

* * *

WELSCH, Roger L(ee) 1936-
(Robert Wells)

PERSONAL: Born November 6, 1936, in Lincoln, Neb.; son of Christian (a laborer) and Bertha (Flack) Welsch; married Linda Hotovy, April, 1981; children: (previous marriage) Chris, Jennifer, Joyce. *Education:* University of Nebraska, B.A., 1958, M.A., 1960; folklore studies at University of Colorado, 1962, and Indiana University, 1963, 1964. *Home:* 3511 Mohawk, Lincoln, Neb. 68510.

CAREER: Dana College, Blair, Neb., instructor in German, 1960-64; Nebraska Wesleyan University, Lincoln, assistant professor of folklore and German, 1964-73; University of Nebraska, Lincoln, teacher of folklore in Extension Division, 1966—, member of English and anthropology faculties, 1973—. Field operative, Smithsonian Institution, 1974—. Lecturer on folklore and conductor of programs on folklore and folk music; collections from field investigations on deposit with Archives of Traditional Music, Indiana University. *Member:* American Folklore Society (life member), Association of Living History, Farms and Agricultural Museum (member of board of directors), Nebraska State Historical Society, Phi Sigma Iota, Delta Phi Alpha. *Awards, honors:* President's Award for creative young faculty, Nebraska Wesleyan University, 1967.

WRITINGS: A Treasury of Nebraska Pioneer Folklore, University of Nebraska Press, 1966; *An Outline-Guide to Nebraska Folklore* (syllabus), Extension Division, University of Nebraska, 1966; *Sod Walls: The Story of the Nebraska Sod House,* Purcell Publications, 1967; (translator) Kaarle Krohn, *Folklore Methodology,* University of Texas Press, 1971; *Shingling the Fog and Other Plains Lies,* Swallow Press, 1971; *The Tall-tale Postcard: A Pictorial History,* A. S. Barnes, 1976; *Omaha*

Tribal Myths and Trickster Tales, Ohio University Press, 1981; *Mister, You Got Yourself a Horse: Tales of Old-Time Horse Trading,* University of Nebraska Press, 1981; *Catfish at the Pump,* Plains Heritage Press, 1982.

Author of recordings "Songs for Today," Lutheran Records, 1963, and "Sweet Nebraska Land," Folkways, 1965. Regular contributor to *Abstracts of Folklore Studies,* 1963—. Contributor to folklore journals and regional magazines.

WORK IN PROGRESS: Books on regional folklore and folk architecture.

BIOGRAPHICAL/CRITICAL SOURCES: Ray Lawless, *Folksongs and Folksingers,* Duell, 1960.

* * *

WENDLAND, Michael F(letcher) 1946-
(Mike Wendland)

PERSONAL: Born February 8, 1946, in Bay City, Mich.; son of H. R. (a businessman) and Gertrude (Fletcher) Wendland; married Jennifer Jeffrey; children: Wendy, Scott, Jeffrey. *Education:* Attended Delta College, University Center, Mich., 1964-67. *Religion:* Methodist. *Home:* 39775 Spitz Dr., Sterling Heights, Mich. 48078. *Office:* WDIV-TV, 550 West Lafayette Blvd., Detroit, Mich. 48231.

CAREER: WKNX-Radio/Television, Saginaw, Mich., reporter, 1964-67; *Bangor Beacon,* Bay City, Mich., writer, 1967-68; *Bay City Times,* Bay City, reporter, 1968-71; *Detroit News,* Detroit, Mich., reporter, 1971-80; *Toronto Star,* Toronto, Ontario, Canada, foreign correspondent, 1972-81; Washington Post-Newsweek Stations, Inc., WDIV-TV, Detroit, chief reporter for "I-Team" investigative unit, and producer and narrator of news reports and documentaries, 1980—. Has appeared on local and national television and radio; host of television talk show "The Wendland File," Field Communications, Detroit, 1978. *Member:* Detroit Press Club.

AWARDS, HONORS: Associated Press awards, 1970, for boating disaster story and series on bank failures, 1973, for stories on ship sinking, oil spill, and lake flooding, 1976, for investigation of insurance fraud, and 1982, for coverage of riots in Michigan prisons; United Press International awards, 1972, for Lake Erie storm story, 1975, for investigation of Teamsters union and disappearance of James R. Hoffa, and four awards in 1981, for Kalamazoo, Mich. tornado story, for report on adoption law irregularities, for coverage of Ford Motor Co. Pinto trial in Winemac, Ind., and for best documentary of the year, "The People Next Door"; Detroit Press Club medallion, 1972, for work on series, "Voice of Detroit's Blacks"; Advancement of Justice Award, Michigan Bar Association, 1973, for series on prison reform; Odyssey Institute first prize in local news reporting, 1981, for story on hospital bureaucracy, "Babies of Fate"; Midwest Regional Award, Radio-Television News Directors Association, 1981, for series on layoffs in the Detroit Police Department; two Emmy Awards in 1981, for investigative report on adoption law irregularities and for best documentary program, "Land Grab: The Taking of Poletown," and two awards in 1982, for series on life in Poland and for best single feature, "The Search for Santa Claus"; Emmy Award nomination, 1982, for documentary "The People Next Door."

WRITINGS: (Under name Mike Wendland) *CB Update,* Sheed Andrews, 1976; (under name Mike Wendland) *The Wendland CB Glove Compartment Bible,* Sheed Andrews, 1977; *The Arizona Project: How a Team of Investigative Reporters Got Revenge on Deadline,* Sheed Andrews, 1978. Author of documentaries produced by WDIV-TV, including "The People Next Door" and "Land Grab: The Taking of Poletown." Author of "CB Break," a weekly column syndicated by Universal Press Syndicate to about 200 newspapers, 1976-81. Contributor to periodicals, including *CB Digest, MacLeans, Newsday, Chicago Tribune, Harper's, Auto News, Readers Journal, True,* and *Atlantic.*

WORK IN PROGRESS: A novel.

SIDELIGHTS: Michael F. Wendland considers his specialty to be reporting on organized crime and political corruption. From October, 1976, to February, 1977, he was one of forty reporters who, calling themselves the Investigative Reporters and Editors (IRE), formed a task force in Phoenix, Arizona, to investigate the death of Don Bolles. (A reporter for the *Arizona Republic,* Bolles had been fatally wounded when his car was bombed June 2, 1976, as a reprisal for his expose of land fraud activities.) A. L. Miller writes in the *National Review* that despite threats of libel suits, the IRE "pieced together the sordid story of a state beset by the evils . . . of organized crime: land fraud, illegal aliens, drug trafficking, bribery, murder for hire, prostitution, gambling—all with the suggestion of collusion in high places." Through the IRE's efforts, Bolles's killer was eventually convicted, and he implicated the higher-ups involved.

In *The Arizona Project: How a Team of Reporters Got Revenge on Deadline,* Wendland documents the IRE's activity and "provides an objective analysis of its findings," says John Murray in *Best Sellers.* "One of the more significant contributions of this book," adds Murray, "is that it . . . should emerge as a bible for the inexperienced journalist and be an added incentive for the veteran."

AVOCATIONAL INTERESTS: Running, photography, amateur radio, gardening.

BIOGRAPHICAL/CRITICAL SOURCES: Michael F. Wendland, *The Arizona Project: How a Team of Investigative Reporters Got Revenge on Deadline,* Sheed Andrews, 1978; *Best Sellers,* April, 1978; *National Review,* May 12, 1978.

* * *

WENDLAND, Mike
See WENDLAND, Michael F(letcher)

* * *

WESLAGER, C(linton) A(lfred) 1909-

PERSONAL: Surname pronounced Wes-law-ger, with a hard "g"; born April 30, 1909, in Pittsburgh, Pa.; son of Fred H. (a contractor) and Alice (Lowe) Weslager; married Ruth Hurst, June 9, 1933; children: Ann (Mrs. George G. Tatnall), Clinton, Jr., Thomas. *Education:* University of Pittsburgh, B.A., 1933. *Home address:* Old Public Rd., R.D. 2, Box 104, Hockessin, Del. 19707.

CAREER: Life Savers Corp., Port Chester, N.Y., sales promotion manager, 1933-37; E. I. du Pont de Nemours & Co., Inc., Wilmington, Del., 1937—, sales manager, 1959-66, automotive products marketing manager, 1966-68; Brandywine College, Wilmington, Del., visiting professor, 1968—. Member of faculty of history department, Wesley College, 1964, and University of Delaware, 1965, 1967; lecturer to historical, archeological, and other learned societies. President of Richardson Park (Del.) Board of School Trustees, 1953-57. Editor, Archeological Society of Delaware, 1938-53, and Historic Red Clay Valley, Inc., 1960-66. Consultant to Smithsonian Institution on log cabins in the Delaware Valley. *Member:* Chemical Specialties Manufacturers Association (chairman of automotive division, 1959-60), Eastern States Archeological Federation (president, 1954-58), Archeological Society of Delaware (president, 1942-48, 1950-53), New Jersey Archeological Society (fellow), Holland Society of New York (fellow), Sigma Delta Chi. *Awards, honors:* Award of Merit from American Association for State and Local History, 1965, 1968; Lindback Award, 1977; Archibald Crozier Award, Archeological Society of Delaware, 1978.

WRITINGS: Delaware's Forgotten Folk, University of Pennsylvania Press, 1943; *Delaware's Buried Past,* University of Pennsylvania Press, 1944; *Delaware's Forgotten River,* Hambleton, 1947; (contributor) H. Clay Reed, editor, *Delaware: A History of the First State,* three volumes, Lewis Historical Publishing Co., 1947; *The Nanticoke Indians,* Pennsylvania Historical Commission, 1948; *Brandywine Springs,* Knebels, 1949; *Indian Place-Names in Delaware,* Archeological Society of Delaware, 1950; (contributor) Charles B. Clark, editor, *The Eastern Shore of Maryland and Virginia,* three volumes, Lewis Historical Publishing Co., 1950; *Red Men on the Brandywine,* Knebels, 1953; *The Richardsons of Delaware,* Knebels, 1957.

Dutch Explorers, Traders and Settlers in the Delaware Valley, University of Pennsylvania Press, 1961; *The Garrett Snuff Fortune,* Knebels, 1965; *The English on the Delaware,* Rutgers University Press, 1967; *The Log Cabin in America: From Pioneer Days to the Present,* Rutgers University Press, 1969; *History of the Delaware Indians,* Rutgers University Press, 1972; *Magic Medicines of the Indians,* Middle Atlantic Press, 1973; *The Stamp Act Congress,* University of Delaware Press, 1976; *The Delaware Indian Westward Migration,* Middle Atlantic Press, 1978; *The Delaware: A Critical Bibliography,* Indiana University Press, 1978.

Author of six monographs on regional history subjects, 1959-64; also author of historical essays and papers published by Columbia University Press and University of Delaware Press. Contributor of articles and book reviews to historical, archeological, and folklore journals. Editor, *Hole News* (Life Savers Corp.), 1936-37, *F&F Magazine* (Du Pont Co.), 1946-47; contributing editor, *Delaware Today,* 1965.

*   *   *

WESTWOOD, Jennifer
See CHANDLER, Jennifer (Westwood)

*   *   *

WHEATLEY, Dennis (Yeats) 1897-1977

PERSONAL: Born January 8, 1897, in London, England; died November 11, 1977, in London, England; son of Albert David and Florence Baker (Lady Newton) Wheatley; married Nancy Madelaine Leslie Robinson, 1923; married Joan Gwendoline Johnstone, August 8, 1931; children: (first marriage) Anthony Marius. *Education:* Educated at Dulwich College, 1908, aboard H.M.S. *Worcester,* 1909-13, and privately in Germany, 1913. *Politics:* Conservative. *Home and office:* 60 Cadogan Sq., London S.W. 1, England. *Agent:* A. P. Watt Ltd., 26/28 Bedford Row, London WC1R 4HL, England.

CAREER: Wheatley & Son (wine merchants), London, England, 1919-31, became sole owner upon father's death in 1926; free-lance writer, 1932-77. *Wartime service:* British Army, 1914-19; became lieutenant. Member of National Service Recruiting Panel, 1940-41; member of Joint Planning Staff of War Cabinet, 1941-44; wing commander on Sir Winston Churchill's staff, 1945; decorated, awarded U.S. Bronze Star. *Member:* Royal Society of Literature (fellow), Royal Society of Arts (fellow), Old Comrades Association (president, 1960), St. James' Club, Paternoster Club.

WRITINGS—Published by Hutchinson, except as indicated: *The Forbidden Territory* (also see below), 1933, reprinted, Arrow Books, 1978; *Such Power Is Dangerous,* 1933, reprinted, Merrimack Book Service, 1979; *"Old Rowley": A Private Life of Charles II,* 1933, Dutton, 1934, reprinted, Arrow Books, 1969, published as *A Private Life of Charles II,* Hutchinson, 1938, published as *"Old Rowley": A Very Private Life of Charles II,* Arrow Books, 1977; *Black August* (also see below), 1934, reprinted, Edito-Service, 1974; *The Fabulous Valley,* 1934, reprinted, Edito-Service, 1973.

The Devil Rides Out (also see below), 1935, reprinted, Arrow Books, 1979; *The Eunuch of Stamboul,* Little, Brown, 1935, reprinted, Merrimack Book Service, 1979; (editor) *A Century of Horror Stories,* 1935, reprinted, Books for Libraries, 1971; *They Found Atlantis* (also see below), 1936, reprinted, Merrimack Book Service, 1979; (with J. G. Links) *Crimefile Number One: File on Bolitho Blane,* Morrow, 1936 (published in England as *Murder off Miami,* Hutchinson, 1936, reprinted, Mayflower Books, 1979); *Contraband* (also see below), 1936, reprinted, Edito-Service, 1974; *The Secret War,* 1937, reprinted, Arrow Books, 1975; (with Links) *File on Robert Prentice,* Greenberg, 1937 (published in England as *Who Killed Robert Prentice?,* Hutchinson, 1937, reprinted, Mayflower Books, 1980); *Red Eagle: The Story of the Russian Revolution and of Klementy Efremovitch Voroshilov, Marshal and Commissar for Defence of the Union of Socialist Soviet Republics,* 1938, published as *Red Eagle: A Story of the Russian Revolution and of Klementy Efremovitch Voroschilov,* Arrow Books, 1964, published as *Red Eagle: A Story of the Russian Revolution and of Klementy Efremovitch Voroshilov,* Hutchinson, 1967; *Uncharted Seas* (also see below), 1938, reprinted, Arrow Books, 1968; (with Links) *The Malinsay Massacre,* 1938, reprinted, Mayflower Books, 1981; *The Golden Spaniard* (also see below), 1938, reprinted, Edito-Service, 1973; (editor) *A Century of Spy Stories,* 1938; *The Quest of Julian Day,* 1939, reprinted, Heron Books, 1972; (with Links) *Herewith the Clues,* 1939; *Sixty Days to Live,* 1939, reprinted, Arrow Books, 1972; *Those Modern Musketeers* (contains "Three Inquisitive People," *The Forbidden Territory,* and *The Golden Spaniard*), 1939, reprinted, 1954.

Three Inquisitive People (previously published in *Those Modern Musketeers*), 1940, reprinted, Edito-Service, 1973; *The Scarlet Impostor,* 1940, reprinted, Heron Books, 1972; *Faked Passports,* 1940, Macmillan (New York), 1943, reprinted, Ballantine, 1973; *The Black Baroness,* 1940, Ryerson Press, 1941, reprinted, Arrow Books, 1978; *Strange Conflict* (also see below), 1941, reprinted, Merrimack Book Service, 1978; *The Sword of Fate,* 1941, reprinted, Edito-Service, 1973; *Total War: A Paper,* 1941; *V for Vengeance,* 1942, reprinted, 1972; *Mediterranean Nights* (short stories), 1942, revised edition, 1965; *Gunmen, Gallants, and Ghosts* (short stories), 1943, reprinted, 1965, revised edition, Arrow Books, 1968.

The Man Who Missed the War (also see below), 1946, reprinted, Arrow Books, 1973; *Codeword: Golden Fleece,* 1946, reprinted, Edito-Service, 1974; *Come into My Parlor,* 1946, reprinted, Arrow Books, 1975; *The Launching of Roger Brook* (also see below), 1947, reprinted, Heron Books, 1972; *The Shadow of Tyburn Tree* (also see below), 1948, reprinted, Arrow Books, 1979; *The Haunting of Toby Jugg,* 1948, reprinted, Merrimack Book Service, 1976; *The Rising Storm* (also see below), 1949, reprinted, Arrow Books, 1970; *The Seven Ages of Justerini's: 1749-1949,* Riddle Books, 1949, revised edition published as *1749-1965, The Eight Ages of Justerini's,* Dolphin Publishing, 1965.

The Second Seal, 1950, reprinted, 1964; *Early Adventures of Roger Brook* (contains *The Launching of Roger Brook* and *The Shadow of Tyburn Tree*), 1951; *The Man Who Killed the King* (also see below), 1951, Putnam, 1965, reprinted, Arrow Books, 1979; *The Star of Ill-Omen,* 1952, reprinted, Arrow Books, 1979; *Worlds Far from Here* (contains *Uncharted Seas, The Man Who Missed the War,* and *They Found Atlantis*), 1952; *To the Devil—a Daughter* (also see below), 1953, reprinted, Arrow Books, 1974; *Curtain of Fear,* 1953, reprinted, Arrow Books, 1975; *The Island Where Time Stands Still* (also see below), 1954, reprinted, Arrow Books, 1975.

The Dark Secret of Josephine, 1955, reprinted, Arrow Books, 1974; *Secret Missions of Gregory Sallust,* 1955; *Black Magic Omnibus* (contains *The Devil Rides Out, Strange Conflict,* and *To the Devil—a Daughter*), 1956; *The Ka of Gifford Hillary,* 1956, reprinted, Arrow Books, 1974; *The Prisoner in the Mask,* 1957, reprinted, Heron Books, 1972; *Roger Brook in the French Revolution* (contains *The Rising Storm* and *The Man Who Killed the King*), 1957; *Death in the Sunshine,* 1958; *Traitor's Gate,* 1958, reprinted, Edito-Service, 1973; *Plot and Counterplot: Three Adventures of Gregory Sallust* (contains *Black August, Contraband,* and *The Island Where Time Stands Still*), 1959; *Stranger than Fiction,* 1959, reprinted, Arrow Books, 1977; *The Rape of Venice,* 1959, reprinted, Edito-Service, 1974.

The Satanist, 1960, reprinted, Arrow Books, 1979; *Into the Unknown,* 1960; *Selected Works,* 1961; *Saturdays with Bricks, and Other Days under Shell-Fire,* 1961; *Vendetta in Spain,* 1961; *Mayhem in Greece,* 1962; *The Sultan's Daughter,* 1963; *Bill for the Use of a Body,* 1964, new edition, Arrow Books, 1972; *They Used Dark Forces,* 1964.

Dangerous Inheritance, 1965, published as *Dangerous Inheritance: A Duke de Richleau Story,* 1971; (compiler) *Shafts of Fear,* Arrow Books, 1965, published as *Dennis Wheatley's First Book of Horror Stories: Tales of Strange Doings,* Hutchinson, 1968; (compiler) *Quiver of Horror,* Arrow Books, 1965, published as *Dennis Wheatley's Second Book of Horror Stories: Tales of Strange Happenings,* Hutchinson, 1968; *The Wanton Princess,* 1966, published as *The Wanton Princess: A Roger Brook Story,* 1971; *Unholy Crusade,* 1967; *The White Witch of the South Seas,* 1968; *Evil in a Mask,* 1969.

Gateway to Hell, 1970; *The Devil and All His Works,* American Heritage Press, 1971; *The Ravishing of Lady Mary Ware,* 1971; *The Strange Story of Linda Lee,* 1972; *The Irish Witch,* 1973; *Desperate Measures,* 1974; *Uncanny Tales,* Sphere Books, Volumes I-II, 1974, Volume III, 1977.

Satanism and Witches: Essays and Stories, Sphere Books, 1975; *The Time Has Come: The Memoirs of Dennis Wheatley,* Volume I: *The Young Man Said, 1897-1914,* 1977, Volume II: *Officer and Temporary Gentleman, 1914-1919,* 1978, Volume III: *Drink and Ink, 1919-1977,* 1979.

Editor of "Dennis Wheatley's Library of the Occult" series, Sphere Books, 1974-77. Author of personalities page column, *Sunday Graphic,* 1939. Contributor to periodicals, including *Times* (London), *Daily Mail, Daily Express,* and *Cosmopolitan.*

SIDELIGHTS: Dennis Wheatley was a best-selling author of historical thrillers, spy stories, and works on the occult. A writer in the *Washington Post* called him "one of the twentieth century's most prolific and best-selling authors," because his more than sixty books have sold over forty-five million copies and have been translated into twenty-nine languages. His *The Devil and All His Works,* a comprehensive survey of the black arts, "is considered a modern textbook on satanism," according to a *New York Times* writer.

Wheatley once related in the *Writer:* "Numerous distinguished critics said of my first novel, *The Forbidden Territory,* and of its successors, that I had broken every rule in the game, that my punctuation was lamentable and my English appalling—but they praised the story. It was reprinted seven times in seven weeks and within a year translated into a dozen foreign languages." Urging novice authors to be conscientious and persistent, Wheatley wrote that anyone "who is prepared to face hard, hard work can achieve—and maintain—success. In my case it has meant writing two books for each one published: a factual, accurate account of a war or period of history or travel, which will interest the better-educated reader, and a thriller with plenty of throat-cutting and boy jumping into bed with girl, then dovetailing the two. But don't let any pedantic idiot tell you that because, like myself, you haven't the faintest idea what the word 'syntax' means, you can't write a best seller."

MEDIA ADAPTATIONS: J. H. Hoffberg filmed *Forbidden Territory* in 1938 and *The Eunuch of Stamboul*—released as "The Secret of Stamboul"—in 1941. In 1968, Warner Bros. produced "The Lost Continent," a filmed version of *Uncharted Seas,* and Twentieth Century-Fox produced "The Devil's Bride," a filmed version of *The Devil Rides Out.*

AVOCATIONAL INTERESTS: Travel; books; building (Wheatley once estimated he had laid more than sixty thousand bricks in his garden); collecting Georgian furniture, Persian rugs, stamps, and fine wines.

BIOGRAPHICAL/CRITICAL SOURCES: Books and Bookmen, September, 1965; *Writer,* October, 1969; *Los Angeles Times,* November 13, 1980.

OBITUARIES: New York Times, November 12, 1977; *Washington Post,* November 12, 1977; *AB Bookman's Weekly,* February 6, 1978.†

* * *

WHEELER, Michael 1943-

PERSONAL: Born July 25, 1943, in Louisville, Ky.; son of Harry E. (an editor) and Erma (a painter; maiden name, Allen) Wheeler; married Candace Pullman (a planner), June 12, 1971. *Education:* Amherst College, B.A., 1965; Boston University, J.D., 1969; Harvard University, LL.M., 1974. *Agent:* The Otte Co., 9 Goden St., Belmont, Mass. 02178. *Office:* New England School of Law, 154 Stuart St., Boston, Mass. 02116.

CAREER: Private law practice in Boston, Mass., 1969-71; New England School of Law, Boston, assistant professor, 1971-74, associate professor, 1974-76, professor of law, 1976—. Visiting professor, Massachusetts Institute of Technology, 1979—. Research associate, Harvard Negotiation Center, 1982—. *Member:* Authors Guild, Authors League of America.

WRITINGS: No-Fault Divorce, Beacon Press, 1974; *Lies, Damn Lies, and Statistics,* Norton, 1976; (with Ian Tod) *Utopia,*

Harmony, 1978; *Divided Children*, Norton, 1980; (with Andre Mayer) *The Crocodile Man: A Case Study in Brain Chemistry and Criminal Violence*, Houghton, 1982; (with Lawrence Susskind and Lawrence Bacow) *Resolving Environmental Regulatory Disputes*, Schenckman, 1983; (with Bacow) *Environmental Dispute Resolution*, Plenum, 1983. Contributor to law journals, to *Atlantic* and *New Times*, and to newspapers.

SIDELIGHTS: In *The Crocodile Man: A Case Study in Brain Chemistry and Criminal Violence*, Michael Wheeler and co-author Andre Mayer examine the insanity plea. Their book, as Hank Greely explains in the *Los Angeles Times Book Review*, "does not weigh the pros and cons of the current law. More usefully—and much more interestingly—it tells a story, the story of one man's crime and defense."

Written like a mystery, *The Crocodile Man* opens with a description of the deed. One summer evening Charles Decker offered two teenage girls a ride in his convertible. They accepted, and it wasn't until a policeman stopped the car for a minor violation that Decker got mad. When the girls asked to be taken home, he became enraged and, grabbing a stonemason's hammer that was lying under the car seat, fractured their skulls. After a second attack, Decker took the girls to a store where he knew they would find help, called his father, a respected endocrinologist, and turned himself in to the police. Asked what had happened, Decker later replied: "I don't know. I went ape."

When the case came to trial, Decker's lawyers entered an insanity plea, arguing that their defendant was suffering not from an emotional disturbance or psychological pressure, but from an undetectable lesion in the limbic system of his brain. "In humans," explains Tom Wicker in the *New York Times Book Review*, "the cortex system, where the intellectual functions of the brain are centered, ordinarily controls the limbic. But in crocodiles, the limbic dominates the cortex; the defendant's limbic lesion sometimes caused him to act with the same sudden violence as a crocodile lunging at its prey." Hence the name applied to Decker—the "crocodile man."

Because the book is written as a mystery, none of the reviewers reveal the outcome of the trial. But they find much besides the story's suspensefulness that is worth recommending. "For anyone interested in how medicine and the law have developed in the past few centuries to yield the current American version of the insanity defense, their study gives the best available popular summary," observes *Washington Post Book World* reviewer Lincoln Caplan. Tom Wicker also praises the book's "comprehensive review of the insanity defense itself, its origins and development, its necessity and its pitfalls." Concludes Hank Greely: "This book is valuable as well as fascinating."

BIOGRAPHICAL/CRITICAL SOURCES: Washington Post Book World, July 11, 1976, August 29, 1982; *New York Times*, May 20, 1978; *Los Angeles Times Book Review*, August 8, 1982; *New York Times Book Review*, September 19, 1982.

* * *

WHISENHUNT, Donald W(ayne) 1938-

PERSONAL: Born May 16, 1938, in Meadow, Tex.; son of William A. and Beulah (Johnson) Whisenhunt; married Betsy Ann Baker, August 27, 1960; children: Donald Wayne, Jr., William Benton. *Education:* McMurry College, B.A., 1960; graduate study at Eastern New Mexico University, 1961-62; Texas Technological College (now Texas Tech University), M.A., 1962, Ph.D., 1966. *Religion:* Methodist. *Home:* 1407 South Chilton, Tyler, Tex. 75701. *Office:* Office of Academic Affairs, University of Texas at Tyler, Tyler, Tex. 75701.

CAREER: History teacher in public schools in Elida, N.M., 1961-63; Murray State University, Murray, Ky., assistant professor, 1966-68, associate professor of history, 1968-69; Thiel College, Greenville, Pa., associate professor of history and chairman of department, 1969-73; Eastern New Mexico University, Portales, professor of history and dean of College of Liberal Arts and Sciences, 1973-77; University of Texas at Tyler, professor of history and vice-president for academic affairs, 1977—. Visiting professor at Incarnate Word College, summer, 1971, and Allegheny College, summer, 1972; member of commission on archives and history, Texas Conference, United Methodist Church, 1980—. Llano Estacado Heritage, Inc., member of board of directors, 1974-78, book review editor, 1975-77, vice-president, 1975-76, president, 1976-77.

MEMBER: American Historical Association, Organization of American Historians, American Association of University Professors (chapter president, 1970-71), Popular Culture Association, Western History Association, Southern Historical Association, Red River Valley Historical Association (member of board of directors, 1973—), Texas Association of College Teachers, Texas State Historical Association (member of program committee, 1980—), New Mexico Historical Association, West Texas Historical Association (member of executive committee, 1980—), Smith County Historical Society (president and editor, 1980), Mercer County Historical Society (member of board of directors, 1970-73; archivist, 1971-73), Roosevelt County Historical Society, Phi Alpha Theta, Pi Sigma Alpha, Phi Kappa Phi, Pi Delta Epsilon.

AWARDS, HONORS: Research grants from Murray State University, 1967-68 and 1968-69; grant from New Jersey Historical Commission, 1970-71, to edit diaries of John Fell, and 1979, to research the history of Veterans of Future Wars; grant from Lutheran Church in America, 1971-72, to study Texas during the Depression; grant from Thiel College, 1972, to study poetry of the Depression; grant from Eastern New Mexico University, 1973-74, to study the activities of Father James Cox, 1974-75, for pictorial history of New Mexico courthouses, and 1975-76, for a study of Art Names Shows; grant from New Mexico Council on the Humanities, 1974, to present a public conference on water use on the High Plains of eastern New Mexico; grant from New Mexico Arts Commission, 1974-75, for publication of *Liberal Arts Review;* grant from Smith County Historical Society, 1980-81, for a chronology of Smith County, Texas; grant from Mercer County Historical Society, 1980-81, to edit manuscript of John W. Goodsell.

WRITINGS: Fort Richardson: Outpost on the Texas Frontier, Texas Western Press, 1968; (editor and author of introduction) *Delegate from New Jersey: The Journal of John Fell*, Kennikat, 1973; *Teaching Local History*, Media Workshop, 1974; *The Environment and the American Experience: A Historian Looks at the Ecological Crisis*, Kennikat, 1974; *Elias Boudinot*, New Jersey Historical Commission, 1975; (editor) *Proceedings of a Water Symposium*, Eastern New Mexico University, 1975; (editor) Floyd D. Golden, *Eastern New Mexico University: The Golden Years*, Eastern New Mexico University, 1975; (contributor) Jean M. Burroughs, editor, *Roosevelt County: History and Heritage*, Bishop Printing, 1975; *New Mexico Courthouses*, Texas Western Press, 1979; (editor) *The Depression in the Southwest*, Kennikat, 1980; *Chronology of Texas History through 1920*, Eakin Publications, 1982; *A Chronological History of Smith County, Texas*, Eakin Publications, in press.

Also contributor to *Dustbowl and Depression in Oklahoma,* edited by Kenneth E. Hendrickson, Oklahoma Historical Society. Contributor to West Texas Historical Association *Yearbook,* 1977 and 1979, and to *The Encyclopedia of Southern History,* Louisiana State University Press, 1979. Author of "Point of View," a political column in *Murray Democrat,* 1967, and "Bicentennial Notebook," a column appearing in fifteen newspapers in New Mexico and fifteen in Texas, 1974-77. Contributor of over 100 articles and reviews to periodicals, including *Dallas Times-Herald, Civil Rights Digest, American Historical Review, Educational Horizons, Historian, Journal of Southern History, Journal of Popular Culture, New Mexico Historical Review, East Texas Historical Journal, Red River Valley Historical Review,* and *Cresset.* Associate editor, *Mercer County History,* 1971-73; editor of *Liberal Arts Review,* 1974-77, and *Chronicles of Smith County, Texas,* 1980; *New Mexico Historical Review,* member of editorial board, 1975-77, editorial consultant, 1977—; book review editor, *Communal Societies,* 1981—.

WORK IN PROGRESS: Poetry and the Depression, for Bowling Green University; three books for American Press, *The Depression in Texas, History of Higher Education in Texas,* and *A Student's Introduction to History;* editing manuscript of John W. Goodsell, surgeon of Robert Peary's expedition to the North Pole, 1908-09; *An Historical Encyclopedia of Higher Education in Texas.*

* * *

WHITE, Laurence B(arton), Jr. 1935-

PERSONAL: Born September 21, 1935, in Norwood, Mass.; son of Laurence B. (an engineer) and Anna (a teacher; maiden name, Dewhurst) White; married Doris E. Pickard (a teacher aide), September 10, 1961; children: William Oliver, David Laurence. *Education:* University of New Hampshire, B.A., 1958. *Home:* 12 Rockland St., Stoughton, Mass. 02072. *Office:* Needham Science Center, Needham Public Schools, Needham, Mass. 02192.

CAREER: Museum of Science, Boston, Mass., supervisor of programs and courses, 1958-65, acting director of Theatre of Electricity, 1960-65; Needham Public Schools, Needham Science Center, Needham, Mass., assistant director, 1965-79, director, 1979—. *Military service:* U.S. Army, Signal Corps, combat photographer, 1958-59. *Member:* Society of American Magicians, Mycological Society, Beekeepers Association. *Awards, honors:* Child Study Association of America selected *So You Want to Be a Magician?* as one of the children's books of the year, 1972.

WRITINGS—Juveniles; published by Addison-Wesley, except as indicated: *Life in the Shifting Dunes,* Boston Museum of Science, 1960; *Investigating Science with Coins,* 1969; *Investigating Science with Rubber Bands,* 1969; *Investigating Science with Nails,* 1970; *Investigating Science with Paper,* 1970; *So You Want to Be a Magician?,* 1972; *Science Games,* 1975; *Science Puzzles,* 1975; *Science Toys,* 1975; *Science Tricks,* 1975; *The Great Mysto: That's You,* 1975; (with Ray Broekel) *Now You See It,* Little, Brown, 1979; (with Broekel) *The Trick Book,* Doubleday, 1979; (with Broekel) *The Surprise Book,* Doubleday, 1981. Author of material for Eduquip-Macallaster Co. Contributor to children's magazines.

WORK IN PROGRESS: A sourcebook for teachers, detailing many of the "unusual and original" demonstrations and experiments developed at the Needham Science Center for elementary students.

SIDELIGHTS: "The Needham Science Center," Laurence B. White, Jr. told *CA,* "works with all of the elementary schools in [Needham, Massachusetts.] This brings me into direct contact with some 2000 young children each year. It is their curiosity, excitement, and enthusiasm that *makes* me write books for them. Children so enjoy sharing the things they like with me [that] I can do no less than return the favor. . . . I would urge every children's author to visit a local elementary school. As the local 'resident' author in our school system, I am asked to do so regularly. The experience will make you want to rush right home and write another book.

"Children, tomorrow's adults, are a very special audience. Certainly any author could make considerably more money writing adult fiction, but somehow I cannot imagine the effects on the audience to be as far reaching. I would like to think that somewhere I might have planted the seeds deep in a young mind that one day may belong to a world famous scientist or renowned magician. The thought is a delicious one!"

BIOGRAPHICAL/CRITICAL SOURCES: New York Times Book Review, August 20, 1972.

* * *

WHITE, Ray Lewis 1941-

PERSONAL: Born August 11, 1941, in Abingdon, Va.; son of Benjamin Wesley (a farmer) and Maude (Patterson) White. *Education:* Emory and Henry College, B.A., 1962; University of Arkansas, M.A., 1963, Ph.D., 1971. *Office:* Department of English, Illinois State University, Normal, Ill. 61761.

CAREER: North Carolina State University at Raleigh, instructor, 1965-68; Illinois State University, Normal, assistant professor, 1968-70, associate professor, 1970-73, professor of English, 1973—. Fulbright senior professor in Munich, Germany. *Member:* Modern Language Association of America, American Association of University Professors, Society for the Study of Midwestern Literature, Phi Beta Kappa. *Awards, honors:* Woodrow Wilson fellowship; Newberry Library research awards; National Defense Education Act fellowship.

WRITINGS: The Achievement of Sherwood Anderson, University of North Carolina Press, 1966; *Sherwood Anderson: Country Editor,* University of North Carolina Press, 1967; *Gore Vidal,* Twayne, 1968; *A Story Teller's Story: A Critical Text,* Press of Case Western Reserve University, 1968; *Checklist of Sherwood Anderson,* C. E. Merrill, 1969; *The Merrill Studies in Winesburg, Ohio,* C. E. Merrill, 1971; *Marching Men,* Press of Case Western Reserve University, 1972; *Sherwood Anderson: A Reference Bibliography,* G. K. Hall, 1977; *Heinrich Boll in America,* Georg Olms Verlag, 1979; *Par Lagerkvist in America,* Almqvist & Wiksell, 1979; *Gunter Grass in America,* Georg Olms Verlag, 1981.

Editor: Sherwood Anderson, *Return to Winesburg,* University of North Carolina Press, 1967; *Sherwood Anderson's Memoirs: A Critical Edition,* University of North Carolina Press, 1969; Anderson, *Tar: A Midwest Childhood,* Press of Case Western Reserve University, 1969; *Sherwood Anderson-Gertrude Stein: Correspondence and Personal Essays,* University of North Carolina Press, 1972.

* * *

WIEMER, Rudolf Otto 1905-

PERSONAL: Born March 24, 1905, in Friedrichroda, Germany; son of Fritz (a teacher) and Elisabeth (Kretzschmar) Wiemer; married Elisabeth Peinemann, October 12, 1932; children: Wolfgang, Reinhart, Uta. *Education:* Attended teacher's training college in Gotha, Germany, 1923-24. *Religion:* Evangelical Lutheran. *Home:* Nussanger 73, 34 Goettingen, West Germany.

CAREER: Teacher in Czechoslovakia, 1924-25, and then successively in Sondershausen, Hachelbich, Frankenhausen, Othfresen, Salzgitter, and Goettingen, Germany, 1925-67. *Military service:* German Army, 1940-45. *Awards, honors:* Sud-Verlag Konstanz Lyric Prize, 1948.

WRITINGS—Published by Steinkopf, except as indicated: *Die Gitter singen,* J. G. Oncken, 1952; *Der Mann am Feuer,* J. G. Oncken, 1953; *Die Strasse, die du wandern musst,* Deutscher Laienspielverlag, 1955; *Die Nacht der Tiere,* Burckhardthaus, 1957; *Der Ort zu unseren Fussen,* 1958; *Das kleine Rasenstuck,* 1959.

Pit und die Krippenmanner (juvenile), 1960, translation published as *Pete and the Manger Men,* Muhlenberg Press, 1962; *Der Verlorene Sohn* (juvenile), Mohn, 1960; *Machet die Tore weit,* Guetersloher Verlagsanstalt Gerd Mohn, 1960; *Jona und der Grosse Fisch,* Mohn, 1960; *Nicht Stunde noch Tag,* 1961; *Fremde Zimmer,* 1962; *Ernstfall,* 1963; *Nele geht nach Bethlehem,* 1963; *Stier und Taube,* 1964; *Kalle Schneemann* (juvenile), 1964; *Joseph und seine Bruder* (juvenile), Mohn, 1964, translation by Paul T. Martinsen published as *Joseph and His Brothers,* Augsburg, 1967.

Die Weisen aus dem Abendland, 1965; *Liebes altes Lesebuch,* M. von Schroeder, 1966; *Der Gute Rauber Willibald* (juvenile), 1966, reprinted, Loewe, 1981, translation by Barbara Kowal Gollob published as *The Good Robber Willibald,* Atheneum, 1968; *Wir Tiere in dem Stalle,* 1966, translation published as *Animals at the Manger,* Augsburg, 1969; *Helldunkel,* 1967; *Come unto Me* (originally published in German), translation by Martinsen, Augsburg, 1968.

Das Pferd, das in die Schule kam (juvenile), 1970; *Unsereiner* (novel), 1971; *Beispiele zur deutschen grammatik* (poems), Fietkau, 1971; *Geschichten aus dem Raeuberhut,* Schwann, 1972; *Der Kaiser und Der Kleine Mann* (juvenile), 1972; *Wortwechsel* (poems), Fietkau, 1973; *Ein Weihnachtsboum fuer Ludmilla Winzig* (juvenile), Arena, 1974; *Selten wie Sommerschnee* (juvenile),. Schaffstein, 1974; *Bundes deutsch,* Peter Hammer, 1974; *Wo wir Menschen sind,* Schwann, 1974.

Zwischenfaelle (novel), 1975; *Micha moechte gern* (juvenile), Bitter, 1975; *Die Angst vord: Ofensetzer oder Glorreiche Zeiten* (novel), 1975; *Der Engel bei Boltan der Ecke,* Guetersloher Verlagshaus Gerd Mohn, 1976; *Die Schlagzeile,* Braun, 1977; *Er schrieb auf die Erde: Begeguingen mild Mann aus Nazareth,* Herder, 1979; *Reizklina* (novel), Braun, 1979; *Auf und clavon und zurueck* (juvenile), Arena, 1979; *Bethlehem ist ueberall,* Guedersloher Verlagshaus, 1979; *Mahnke: Die Geschichte eines Lueckenbuessers,* Kerle, 1979.

Chance der Baerenraupe (poems), Kerle, 1980; *Lob der Kleinen Schritte* (novel), Reinhardt, 1980; *Johnee faellt auf die Arche,* Kerle, 1981.

* * *

WILLEY, Keith (Greville) 1930-

PERSONAL: Born August 14, 1930, in Boonah, Queensland, Australia; son of Greville Maynard (an accountant) and Eileen May (Kuske) Willey; married Elaine Noreen Fitzgerald, April 25, 1953; children: Joanna Lynette, Patricia Mary, Tanya Dale. *Education:* Australian National University, B.A. (with honors), 1979, graduate study, 1979—. *Politics:* None. *Religion:* Roman Catholic. *Office:* School of Arts, Darling Downs Institute of Advanced Education, P.O. Darling Heights, Toowoomba, Queensland 4350, Australia.

CAREER: Earlier career includes "eighteen years mostly spent as journalist in Australia and New Guinea, also a period as a professional crocodile shooter in the Northern Territory"; *Sun,* Sydney, New South Wales, Australia, feature writer and reporter, 1966-71, with assignments in Israel and Cyprus, 1969, and Vietnam, 1970; *Cairns Post,* Cairns, North Queensland, Australia, assistant editor, 1971-73; Australian Department of Trade and Resources, Canberra, Australian Capital Territory, publicity officer, beginning 1973; Darling Downs Institute of Advanced Education, Darling Heights, Toowoomba, Queensland, lecturer in journalism, 1983—. Reported on the drowning of Australian Prime Minister Harold Holt, the rescue of castaways marooned for thirteen months on Ata Island, 1966, the hanging of Ronald Ryan, 1967, and the salvage of Captain Cook's cannons by an American-led expedition, 1969. *Member:* Australian Journalists' Association, Australian Society of Authors, Canberra Workers Club. *Awards, honors:* Walkley national awards for Australian journalism, 1961, 1962, 1963.

WRITINGS: (With Frank Flynn) *Northern Gateway,* F. P. Leonard, 1963, reprinted, 1979; (with Flynn) *The Living Heart,* F. P. Leonard, 1964; *Eaters of the Lotus,* Jacaranda Press, 1964; *Strange Seeker,* Macmillan, 1965; *Assignment New Guinea,* Jacaranda Press, 1965; *Crocodile Hunt,* Angus & Robertson, 1966; *The Red Centre,* Lansdowne Press, 1967; (with Ian Walsh) *Inside Rugby League,* Horwitz, 1968; (with Flynn) *Northern Frontiers,* F. P. Leonard, 1968; *The First Hundred Years: The Story of Brisbane Grammar School, 1868-1968,* Macmillan, 1968; (with Robin Smith) *New Guinea: A Journey through 10,000 Years,* Lansdowne Press, 1969.

Naked Island and Other South Sea Tales, Hodder & Stoughton, 1970; *Boss Drover,* Rigby, 1971; *Tales of the Big Country,* R. Hale, 1973; *Queensland in Colour,* Lansdowne Press, 1973; *Ghosts of the Big Country,* Rigby, 1975; *Joe Brown's Dog, Bluey* (novel), Rigby, 1978; *When the Sky Fell Down: The Destruction of the Tribes of the Sydney Region, 1788-1850s,* Collins & World, 1979; *The Drovers,* Macmillan, 1982. Author of radio scripts. Contributor of several hundred articles and short stories to magazines and newspapers.

WORK IN PROGRESS: Writing a chapter for *The Stockman,* to be published by Lansdowne Press.

SIDELIGHTS: "I began writing books," Keith Willey told *CA,* "because I felt I had something to say about Australians, particularly about the effect of the country itself, social and geographical, on the development of national character. I like to highlight events with the actions and attitudes of real people, and my background both in the bush and in journalism has helped me gain the necessary experience to do this. I suppose I prefer to *demonstrate* philosophy—my own and that of others—by physical action rather than introspection (as the astronaut said, 'Man's nobility is expressed in action').

"I try to write for several hours a day and have the fortunate knack of being able to 'switch off' and then 'switch on' again, so noise and interruptions seldom bother me. I was a champion swimmer (Queensland State breaststroke champion), surf lifesaver and rugby league footballer in youth, and even today I try to swim for an hour a day or, in winter, take my kayak down to Lake Ginninderra near my home, or another waterway. I find the activity stirs thoughts to the surface.

"Australia is in a sense a prisoner of the English language. It is swamped by all the books on earth written in English, which means its own writers have to compete very hard even for a share of their own national audience. Normally a small edition of most of my works would be published or distributed in England. My book *Crocodile Hunt* . . . coincided with a visit to Brisbane by a representative of the Czech State publishing house, Mlada Fronta, in the brief Dubcek period. This lady for some reason seized on *Crocodile Hunt*—perhaps because Australians and Czechs seem to have in common a love of broad farce—and it sold over 40,000 copies in Czechoslovakia before that country ceased payment of royalties and my contract ceased.

"The writers who have most influenced me were Hemingway (his nihilistic love of action and taut style greatly affected me in my youth), Shakespeare, the poets Tennyson and Byron, 1930s Australian humorist Lennie Lower, and the late Clyde Palmer, an Australian journalist who never published a book but was one of the most incisive writers I ever knew.

"Of the current literary scene I would say that while the written word is under attack, I feel it will survive so long as human intelligence is considered useful. However, authors today should develop communications skills in TV, film, and radio. The writer is a person who has something to say, and he should be capable of putting his message across in any medium."

* * *

WILLIAMS, Vergil L(ewis) 1935-

PERSONAL: Born September 29, 1935, in Crosbyton, Tex.; son of Albert Lewis (a farmer) and Neola Bell (Pinkston) Williams; married Vergnel Campbell Smith, June 6, 1957 (divorced February 10, 1968); married Velma Arlene Minor (a home economics teacher), December 23, 1974; children: (first marriage) Delwin Victor; (second marriage) Colleen Jeffries (stepdaughter). *Education:* West Texas State University, B.S., 1966; graduate study at Southern Illinois University, 1966-68; University of Alabama, Ph.D., 1971. *Religion:* Bahai. *Home:* 49 Woodland Park, Tuscaloosa, Ala. 35404. *Office address:* Department of Criminal Justice, University of Alabama, P.O. Box 6365, University, Ala. 35486.

CAREER: Farmer in Happy, Tex., 1953-60; police patrolman in Amarillo, Tex., 1960-64, patrol sergeant, 1964-66; University of Alabama, University, 1971—, began as assistant professor, professor of criminal justice and chairman of department, 1978—. *Military service:* Texas National Guard, 1953-60. U.S. Army Reserve, Infantry, 1960-66; became captain. *Member:* International Association of Chiefs of Police, American Society of Criminology, National Council on Crime and Delinquency, U.S. Parachute Association, Lambda Alpha Epsilon, Omicron Delta Epsilon.

WRITINGS: (With Mary Fish) *Convicts, Codes, and Contraband: The Prison Life of Men and Women,* Ballinger, 1974; (contributor) Israel Drapkin and Emilio Viano, editors, *Victimology: A New Focus,* Volume II: *Society's Reaction to Victimization,* Lexington Books, 1974; (contributor) Norman Johnston and Leonard D. Savitz, editors, *Justice and Corrections,* Wiley, 1978; (contributor) Nicholas N. Kittrie and Jackwell Susman, editors, *Legality, Morality, and Ethics in Criminal Justice,* Praeger, 1979; *Dictionary of American Penology,* Greenwood Press, 1979. (Contributor) Michael T. Farmer and Raymond O. Sumrall, editors, *Differential Police Response Strategies,* Police Executive Research Forum, 1981; (contributor) Johnston and Savitz, editors, *Legal Process and Corrections,* Wiley, 1982; (with William A. Formby and John C. Watkins, Jr.) *Introduction to Criminal Justice,* Delmar, 1982. Contributor of articles and reviews to *American Journal of Correction, Atlantic Economic Journal, Choice, Corrections Today, Crime and Delinquency, Criminal Justice Review, Journal of Correctional Education, Journal of Criminal Justice, Journal of Police Science and Administration, Midwest Quarterly, Police Chief,* and *World Order.*

WORK IN PROGRESS: Introduction to Law Enforcement, with William A. Formby.

SIDELIGHTS: "Pedantry is the enemy when writing books for a community of scholars," Vergil L. Williams told *CA*. "In the struggle to present well-documented facts in a logical sequence, it is all too easy to create a lifeless manuscript that the reader dreads to approach. I consider my future as an author to be in the writing of texts. My goal is to find ways to bring them alive and make them pleasant to read. I do not claim to have achieved that goal yet, but I believe my writing experience is gradually bringing me closer to that moment."

* * *

WILLIAMSON, Glen 1909-

PERSONAL: Born December 22, 1909, in Masonville, Iowa; son of Andrew Stuart (a farmer) and Rosa Izora (Williams) Williamson; married Corinne Aanas, November 30, 1933; children: Richard, Lorraine (Mrs. Robert Meadows), Anita (Mrs. Gerald Archer), William. *Education:* Attended Coe College, 1928-29; University of Denver, language study, 1968-69; Western Evangelical Seminary, M.A., 1980. *Home:* 20420 Marine Dr. N.W., Stanwood, Wash. 98292.

CAREER: Ordained minister of Free Methodist Church, 1944. Pastor in Des Moines, Iowa, 1941-45; evangelist in the United States and Canada, 1945-52; pastor in Des Moines, 1952-56; Free Methodist Church, Winona, Ind., director of interracial evangelism, 1956-63, director of Rocky Mountain Conference in Denver, Colo., 1963-70; *Sermon Builder,* Golden, Colo., editor, 1970-77; Western Evangelical Seminary, Portland, Ore., member of staff, 1976-81; director of LeSabre Writers Institute, 1982—. Trustee-at-large, Western Evangelical Seminary, 1968-76; vice-president of Church Educational Ministries, 1973—. *Awards, honors:* D.Litt., Western Evangelical Seminary, 1947.

WRITINGS—Published by Light & Life Press, except as indicated: *Julia, Giantess in Generosity,* 1969; *Frank and Hazel, the Adamsons of Kibogora,* 1972; *Repair My House,* Creation House, 1973; *Geneva, Missionary to the Chinese,* 1974; (with Geneva Sayre) *On the Brink,* 1974; *The Doctor and Geraldine,* 1975; *Gonzalo,* 1976; *Brother Kawabe,* 1977. Also author of *Born for Such a Day,* 1974, and a film script, "Land Forming for Irrigation." Contributor of short stories to magazines.

WORK IN PROGRESS: Bishop of Jerusalem, a biographical novel about James, the brother of Jesus.

SIDELIGHTS: Glen Williamson lived in Assisi, Italy, while doing research for *Repair My House,* a biographical novel about St. Francis of Assisi.

WILLKE, John Charles 1925-

PERSONAL: Born April 5, 1925, in Maria Stein, Ohio; son of Gerard T. (a physician) and Marie (Wuennemann) Willke; married Barbara Jean Hiltz (a writer, lecturer, and professor of nursing), June 5, 1948; children: Marie Margaret (Mrs. Robert Meyers), Theresa Ann (Mrs. William Wilka), Charles Gerard, Joseph John, Anne Margaret, Timothy Edward. *Education:* Attended Xavier University, Cincinnati, Ohio, and Oberlin College; University of Cincinnati, M.D., 1948. *Religion:* Roman Catholic. *Home:* 7634 Pineglen Dr., Cincinnati, Ohio 45224. *Office:* National Right to Life Committee, National Press Building, 529 14th St. N.W., Washington, D.C. 20045.

CAREER: Good Samaritan Hospital, Cincinnati, Ohio, intern, 1948-49, resident, 1949-51; private practice in family medicine and counseling, 1950—, and in obstetrics, 1950-65; National Right to Life Committee, Washington, D.C., president, 1980—. Certified sex educator. *Military service:* U.S. Air Force, Medical Corps, 1952-54; became captain.

MEMBER: World Federation of Physicians Who Respect Life (member of founding board of directors), International Birthright (member of founding board of directors), American Medical Association, National Right to Life Committee (member of founding board of directors), American Academy of Family Practice, American Board of Family Practice, American Association of Sex Educators and Counselors, National Alliance for Family Life (founding member), National Institute of Family Relations, Ohio Right to Life Society (past president), Ohio State Medical Association, Academy of Medicine of Cincinnati, Cincinnati Right to Life (co-chairman).

WRITINGS—With wife, Barbara Willke: *The Wonder of Sex,* Hiltz Publishing, 1964; *Sex Education: The How-To for Teachers,* Hiltz Publishing, 1970; *Sex: Should We Wait?,* Hiltz Publishing, 1970; *Handbook on Abortion,* Hayes Publishing, 1971; *Sex and Love,* Silver Burdett, 1972; *Marriage,* Silver Burdett, 1972; *How to Teach the Pro-Life Story,* Hiltz, 1973; *Abortion: How It Is,* Hayes Publishing, 1975; *Abortion: As It Is,* Hayes Publishing, 1981. Contributor to more than fifty magazines and professional journals.

WORK IN PROGRESS: Continued research on fetology, complications of induced abortion, viability and premature baby survival, as well as teaching methods for all these areas.

SIDELIGHTS: John Charles Willke believes in preserving and enhancing family life. In his practice as a physician and counselor, he urges parents to love each other wholeheartedly and to raise responsible children, so as to lead young adults toward mature decisions regarding sex and marriage. As president of the National Right to Life Committee, Willke supports a human life amendment to the U.S. Constitution. He told *CA* he is convinced that if "the war on the unborn [is] won by the pro-abortionists, all other efforts at saving family life in America [are] doomed to failure."

* * *

WILSON, Keith 1927-

PERSONAL: Born December 26, 1927, in Clovis, N.M.; son of Earl C. and Marjorie (Edwards) Wilson; married Heloise Brigham, February 15, 1958; children: Kathy, Kristin, Kevin, Kerrin, Roxanne. *Education:* U.S. Naval Academy, B.S., 1950; University of New Mexico, M.A., 1956, additional study through 1958. *Home:* 1500 Locust, Las Cruces, N.M. 88001. *Office:* Department of English, New Mexico State University, Las Cruces, N.M. 88001.

CAREER: U.S. Navy, midshipman, 1946-50, officer, 1950-54, leaving the service as lieutenant; Sandia Corp., Albuquerque, N.M., technical writer, 1958-60; University of Arizona, Tucson, instructor in English, 1960-65; New Mexico State University, Las Cruces, 1965—, began as assistant professor, became professor of English and poet-in-residence. Has given poetry readings at Folger Shakespeare Library and at universities, including Brown University, Columbia University, Tufts University, and University of Alaska. *Awards, honors:* D. H. Lawrence fellowship in writing, 1972; National Endowment for the Arts creative writing fellowship, 1975-76; Fulbright-Hays senior fellowship, 1975-76.

WRITINGS—Poetry: *Sketches for a New Mexico Hill Town,* Prensa de Lagar-Wine Press, 1966; *II Sequences,* Wine Press Microbook, 1967; *The Shadow of Our Bones,* Prensa de Lagar-Wine Press, 1968; *The Old Car, and Other Black Poems,* Grande Ronde Press, 1968; *Graves Registry, and Other Poems,* Grove, 1969; *Homestead,* Kayak, 1969; *The Old Man and Others,* New Mexico State University, 1971; *Rocks,* Road Runner Press, 1971; *Midwatch,* Sumac Press, 1972; *Thantog: Songs of a Jaguar Priest,* Salt Works Press, 1978; *While Dancing Feet Shatter the Earth,* Utah State University Press, 1978; *Desert Cenote,* Great Raven Press, 1978; *The Streets of San Miguel,* Maguey Press, 1978; *The Shaman Deer,* Salt Works Press, 1978; *Retablos,* San Marcos Press, 1980; *Stone Roses: Poems from Transylvania,* Utah State University Press, 1983.

Work represented in anthologies, including: *Thirty-one New American Poets,* edited by Ronald Schreiber, Hill & Wang, 1968; *Poems Southwest,* edited by Wilbur Stevens, Prescott College Press, 1968; *Some Haystacks Don't Even Have Any Needle,* Scott, Foresman, 1968; *To Play Man Number One,* Atheneum, 1969; *The Wind Is Round,* Atheneum, 1969; *Inside Outer Space,* Doubleday, 1970; *Generation Gap,* Dell, 1971; *The NOW Voices,* Scribner, 1971; *Accent: USA,* Scott, Foresman, 1972; *Moments,* Houghton, 1972; *Reflections,* Houghton, 1972; *Poetry of the Desert Southwest,* Balleen Press, 1973; *From the Belly of the Shark,* Random House, 1973; *Choosing,* Addison-Wesley, 1974; *Active Anthology,* Sumac Press, 1974; *Zero Makes Me Hungry,* Scott, Foresman, 1976; *The Face of Poetry,* Gallimaufry Press, 1976; *The Indian Rio Grande,* San Marcos Press, 1977; *Terpentin on the Rocks,* Marlo Verlag, 1978; *A Geography of Poets,* Bantam, 1979.

Also contributor to *America: A Prophecy,* Random House, and *Voices of the Rio Grande,* Rio Grande Writers Association. Contributor to *Poetry, Descant, New Mexico Quarterly, El Corno Emplumado,* and other periodicals in Mexico, Canada, Japan, Argentina, New Zealand, and the United States.

WORK IN PROGRESS: Martingale, a novel; a collection of short stories.

SIDELIGHTS: Keith Wilson told *CA:* "Primarily I consider myself a poet—I have been heavily influenced by William Carlos Williams, Robert Burns, William Blake, Robert Creeley, Robert Duncan, Charles Olson, and many others. My poems are, in part, descriptions of emotional geography (concerns with the sea, the Southwest, loves and losses, gains)."

Wilson reads and writes Spanish and is especially interested in South American poetry.

BIOGRAPHICAL/CRITICAL SOURCES: Granite, spring, 1974; *San Marcos Review,* Number 3, 1976; *Focus 101,* Heidelberg Graphics, 1979.

* * *

WILSON, Robert L. 1925-

PERSONAL: Born January 19, 1925, in Forty Fort, Pa.; son of Herbert L. and Kathryn C. Wilson; married Betty Berenthien, June 19, 1950; children: Keith Alan, Marian. *Education:* Asbury College, B.A., 1949; Lehigh University, M.A., 1950; Garrett Theological Seminary, B.D., 1955; Northwestern University, Ph.D., 1958. *Home:* 237 Monticello Ave., Durham, N.C. 27707. *Office:* Divinity School, Duke University, Durham, N.C. 27706.

CAREER: Ordained United Methodist clergyman; United Methodist Church, Board of Missions, New York, N.Y., director of research in National Division, 1958-70; Duke University, Divinity School, Durham, N.C., research professor of church and society, 1970—, director of J. M. Ormond Center for Research, Planning, and Development, 1970—, associate dean for curricular affairs, 1980—. Member of research advisory committee of United Methodist Church. *Military service:* U.S. Navy, 1943-46. *Member:* Religious Research Association.

WRITINGS: (With James H. Davis) *The Church in the Racially Changing Community,* Abingdon, 1966; (with Paul A. Mickey) *Conflict and Resolution,* Abingdon, 1973; (with Ezra E. Jones) *What's Ahead for Old First Church,* Harper, 1974; (with Mickey) *What New Creation?: The Agony of Church Restructure,* Abingdon, 1977; (with William H. Willimon) *Preaching and Worship in the Small Church,* Abingdon, 1980; (with Jackson W. Carroll) *Too Many Pastors?: The Clergy Job Market,* Pilgrim Press, 1980; *Shaping the Congregation,* Abingdon, 1981. Contributor of more than ninety articles and research reports to journals.

* * *

WILSON, Robert M(ills) 1929-

PERSONAL: Born March 20, 1929, in Pittsburgh, Pa.; son of C. B. and Helen (Mills) Wilson; married Barbara Stewart, August 11, 1951 (divorced, 1972); married Marcia Mathias Barnes; children: (first marriage) Richard, James, Sharon. *Education:* California State College, California, Pa., B.A., 1950; University of Pittsburgh, M.S., 1956, Ed.D., 1960. *Office:* College of Education, University of Maryland, College Park, Md. 20740.

CAREER: Elementary teacher in West Mifflin, Pa., 1954-59; Edinboro State College, Edinboro, Pa., associate professor, 1960-63, professor of education and director of reading clinic, 1963-65; University of Maryland, College Park, associate professor, 1965-68, professor of education, 1968—, director of Reading Center, 1965—. *Military service:* U.S. Air Force, 1950-54. *Member:* International Reading Association, National Education Association, National Council of Teachers of English, College Reading Association (chairman of research commission, 1967, and ethics commission, 1968-69; president, 1974-75), National Conference on Research in English, Maryland State Education Association, Maryland Corrective Remedial Reading Association, Phi Delta Kappa, Phi Sigma Pi.

WRITINGS: Diagnostic and Remedial Reading, C. E. Merrill, 1967, 4th edition, 1981; *Programmed Word Attack for Teachers,* C. E. Merrill, 1968, 3rd edition, 1979; (co-author) *Reading and the Elementary School Child,* Van Nostrand, 1973; (co-author) *Focusing on the Strengths of Children,* Fearon, 1974; (co-author) *Learning Center,* Instructo Corp., 1975; (co-author) *Programmed Reading,* C. E. Merrill, 1980; *Contract Teaching,* McGraw, 1980; (co-author) *Twenty-eight Ways to Help Your Child Be a Better Reader,* McGraw, 1980; (co-author) *Effecting Change in School Reading Programs,* International Reading Association, 1981; (co-author) *Developing a Successful Tutoring Program,* Teacher's College Press, 1982.

Co-author of "Visual Lingual Reading Program," Tweedy Transparencies, 1967, and "Real Life" reading series, McGraw, 1980. Contributor to education journals. Editor, *Maryland State Newsletter in Reading;* review editor, *Journal of the Reading Specialist,* 1966-68; member of editorial *ERIC-NCTE Topics in Learning and Learning Disabilities.*

WORK IN PROGRESS: Programmed Comprehension for Teachers, for C. E. Merrill.

* * *

WILT, Fred(erick Loren) 1920-

PERSONAL: Born December 14, 1920, in Pendleton, Ind.; son of Jesse and Inez C. (Franklin) Wilt; married Eleanor Christensen, December 23, 1950; children: Barbara. *Education:* Attended Indiana Central College, one year; Indiana University, B.S., 1943; studied law at University of Tennessee, 1946-47; Purdue University, M.S., 1960. *Home:* 2525 Kickapoo Dr., Lafayette, Ind. 47905; and 200 Rideau Terrace, Apt. 1215, Ottawa, Ontario, Canada K1M 0Z3. *Office:* Canadian Track and Field Association, 355 River Rd., Vanier City, Ontario, Canada K1L 8C1.

CAREER: Federal Bureau of Investigation, special agent, 1947-77, with assignments in Pullman, Wash., 1947-48, New York City, beginning 1948, and later in Indiana; currently coordinator of coaching certification, Canadian Track and Field Association, Vanier City, Ontario. Former amateur athlete in national and worldwide competition; member of U.S. Olympic Track Team in 1948 and 1952. Track coach at University of Tennessee, 1946-47; intructor at Royal Canadian Legion National Track and Field Coaching School, summers, 1962-68, St. Joseph's College, 1967-70, International Military Sport-Council Sports School, 1975, and International Amateur Athletic Federation Track and Field Clinic for Oceania Countries, 1978. Director of sports clinics, including Sports International, Inc. Track and Field Clinic, 1963-65, U.S. National Track and Field Clinic, 1970, U.S. National Amateur Athletic Track and Field Clinic, 1972 and 1974, and coaches' clinic at Commonwealth Games in Edmonton, Alberta, 1978. *Military service:* U.S. Navy, 1943-46; became lieutenant.

AWARDS, HONORS: National Collegiate Athletic Association champion in two-mile and four-mile runs while at Indiana University; winner of nine Amateur Athletic Union of the United States national championships in track and field, including 5,000- and 10,000-meter runs in 1949; William O'Dwyer Trophy, 1950; James E. Sullivan Award for top amateur athlete of the year, Amateur Athletic Union of the United States, 1950; set a new world's record (subsequently broken) for the indoor two-mile run, 1952.

WRITINGS: How They Train, Track & Field News, 1959, 2nd edition published in three volumes as *How They Train,* 1974, Volume I: *Middle Distances,* Volume II: *Long Distances,* Volume III: *Sprints and Hurdles;* (with others) *Run-Run-Run,* Track

& Field News, 1964; (with Tom Ecker) *Illustrated Guide to Olympic Track and Field Techniques,* Parker Publishing, 1966; *Sports Illustrated Book of Track and Field,* Lippincott, 1968.

Mechanics without Tears, U.S. Track and Field Federation, 1970; (editor with Ecker) *International Track and Field Coaching Encyclopedia,* Parker Publishing, 1970; (with Ken Bosen) *Motivation and Coaching Psychology,* Tafnews, 1971; *The Jumps: Contemporary Theory, Technique, and Training,* Tafnews, 1972; *The Throws: Contemporary Theory, Technique, and Training,* Tafnews, 1974; (with Ecker) *Olympic Track and Field Techniques: An Illustrated Guide to Developing Champions,* Parker Publishing, 1974; *The Complete Canadian Runner,* Canadian Track and Field Association, 1977; *Championship Track and Field for Women,* Parker Publishing, 1978.

SIDELIGHTS: A former special agent for the Federal Bureau of Investigation, Fred Wilt distinguished himself as a world-class runner during the 1940s and '50s, winning numerous amateur championships and awards. He placed eleventh in the 10,000-meter race at the 1948 Olympic Games in London, and in 1952 he set an American record (subsequently broken) with a time of 4:05.5 for the outdoor mile run. His best known feat came in 1952, when his time of 8:50.7 broke the world's record for the two-mile run set by Greg Rice in 1943. Wilt's time was beaten in 1955 by Sandor Iharos of Hungary, who ran the two miles in 8:33.4.

BIOGRAPHICAL/CRITICAL SOURCES: Time, January 30, 1950; *Christian Science Monitor,* March 12, 1952.

* * *

WISE, Charles C(onrad), Jr. 1913-

PERSONAL: Born April 1, 1913, in Washington, D.C.; son of Charles Conrad (a police detective) and Lorena May (Sweeney) Wise; married Ruth Miles Baxter (a concert dancer), November 19, 1938; children: Gregory Baxter, Charles Conrad III (deceased), Jenifer. *Education:* George Washington University, J.D., 1936, A.B. (cum laude), 1938; Columbus University, M. Fiscal Admin., 1942; American University, graduate study, 1945-46. *Politics:* None. *Religion:* Methodist. *Home:* Solon-Lair, Cross Keys Penn Laird, Va. 22846.

CAREER: Admitted to District of Columbia and Federal Bars, 1935. U.S. Government, Washington, D.C., 1933-73, holding a number of civil service posts, including attorney for Railroad Retirement Board, 1939-41, claims attorney with War Department, 1941-43, assistant counsel in Office of General Counsel, Department of the Navy, 1946-47, counsel with Reconstruction Finance Corp., 1947-53, executive secretary of Subversive Activities Control Board, 1953-61, and security adviser to Department of Defense, 1962-73; Blue Ridge Community College, Weyers Cave, Va., lecturer in religion, philosophy, thanatology, and political science, 1973-81. Instructor in English at George Washington University, 1960, and American University, 1961. *Military service:* U.S. Navy, 1943-46; became lieutenant. *Member:* Federal Bar Association, Phi Beta Kappa, Delta Theta Phi.

WRITINGS: Windows on the Passion, Abingdon, 1967; *Windows on the Master,* Abingdon, 1968; (editor) *Chanticleer: The Poems of Terry Wise,* McClure Press, 1968; *Ruth and Naomi,* McClure Press, 1971; (contributor) John White, editor, *What Is Meditation?,* Doubleday, 1974; *Mind Is It: Meditation, Prayer, Healing, and the Psychic,* Magian Press, 1978; *Picture Windows on the Christ,* Magian Press, 1979; *The Magian Gospel of Brother Yeshua,* Magian Press, 1979.

WORK IN PROGRESS: Thus Saith the Lord, an autobiography of God, psychically inspired.

AVOCATIONAL INTERESTS: Collecting books and records.

BIOGRAPHICAL/CRITICAL SOURCES: Washington Evening Star, January 7, 1967.

* * *

WISEMAN, Ann (Sayre) 1926-
(Ann Wiseman Denzer)

PERSONAL: Born July 20, 1926, in New York, N.Y.; daughter of Mark Huntington (a writer) and Eve Sayre (Norton) Wiseman; married former husband Weyer Vermeer (a physician); married second husband Peter W. Denzer; children: (first marriage) Piet; (second marriage) Erik. *Education:* Attended Art Students League, New York City, and Grande Chaumiere, Paris, France; Lesley College, B.A., M.A. *Residence:* Cambridge, Mass.

CAREER: Museum of Modern Art, New York City, teacher of art classes for children, 1946-50; Lord & Taylor, New York City, display artist, 1946; chairman of art department at country day school in Princeton, N.J., 1964-68; Boston Children's Museum, Boston, Mass., program director, 1969-70; Lesley College, Cambridge, Mass., teacher of methods, materials, and art therapy at Graduate School, 1970—. Artist and writer. Conductor of Metropolitan Museum children's tapestry program, 1967-68, and Boston Bicentennial senior citizens' tapestry program, 1976. Her own tapestry, painting, and kinetic sandfountains have been exhibited in group shows at museums and galleries and are in private collections.

MEMBER: Society of Women Geographers, American Craftsmen's Council, New Jersey Designer-Draftsmen, Boston Visual Artists Union. *Awards, honors:* Karolyi Foundation fellowship in France, 1970.

WRITINGS: (Under name Ann Wiseman Denzer) *Tony's Flower* (children's book), Vanguard, 1959; *Rags, Rugs, and Wool Pictures,* Scribner, 1967; *Rag Tapestries and Wool Mosaics,* Van Nostrand, 1968; *Making Things: Handbook of Creative Discovery* (Book of the Month Club alternate selection; Teachers' Book Club selection), Little, Brown, Book I, 1973, Book II, 1975; *Bread Sculpture: The Edible Art,* 101 Productions, 1975; *Cuts of Cloth: Quick Classics to Sew and Wear,* Little, Brown, 1978; *Making Musical Things,* Scribners, 1979; *Welcome to the World,* Addison-Wesley, 1979; *Finger Paint and Pudding Prints,* Addison-Wesley, 1980; *Rug Hooking and Rag Tapestries,* Van Nostrand, 1981. Also author of *What Are You Doing in My Dreams: A Parents' Primer of Children's Nightmares and Dreams,* as yet unpublished. Author of film "Rag Tapestry of New York City," International Film Foundation, 1968.

WORK IN PROGRESS: Find the Image and Satisfy It, a book about dreams as guides and options for change.

SIDELIGHTS: Ann Wiseman told *CA:* "My books are a sort of depository for all my favorite explorations, which I feel will excite others, confirm and release creativity, enlighten people, help them bypass their shouldn'ts and can'ts, and unblock the inhibitions that keep them from enjoying their birthright of creative improvisation.

"Dreams provide a deeper level from which to create. They are a portable source of originality that lasts a lifetime—a source that our culture tends to inhibit or remove from use by referring us to specialists. Many of us have to fight our way back to our own instinctive wisdom in order to trust in ourselves, in our originality.

"I guess my books speak to right-brain people who read pictures as well as words. One way or another all of my books are in celebration of the creative process."

Making Things: A Handbook of Creative Discovery has been translated into German; *Making Musical Things* has been translated into Afrikaans.

AVOCATIONAL INTERESTS: Travel, including trips to France, Italy, Greece, Portugal, Mexico, the Netherlands, England, and India.

* * *

WODGE, Dreary
See GOREY, Edward (St. John)

* * *

WOLFE, Thomas Kennerly, Jr. 1931-
(Tom Wolfe)

PERSONAL: Born March 2, 1931, in Richmond, Va.; son of Thomas Kennerly (a scientist and business executive) and Helen (Hughes) Wolfe; married Sheila Berger (art director of *Harper's* magazine), 1978; children: Alexandra. *Education:* Washington and Lee University, B.A. (cum laude), 1951; Yale University, Ph.D., 1957. *Residence:* New York, N.Y. *Agent:* International Creative Management, 40 West 57th St., New York, N.Y. 10019.

CAREER: Writer, journalist, social commentator, and artist. *Springfield Union,* Springfield, Mass., reporter, 1956-59; *Washington Post,* Washington, D.C., reporter and Latin American correspondent, 1959-62; *New York Herald Tribune,* New York City, reporter and writer for *New York* Sunday magazine (now *New York* magazine), 1962-66; *New York World Journal Tribune,* New York City, writer, 1966-67; *New York* magazine, New York City, contributing editor, 1968-76; *Esquire* magazine, New York City, contributing editor, 1977—; *Harper's* magazine, New York City, contributing artist, 1978-81. Has exhibited drawings in one-man shows at Maynard Walker Gallery, 1965, and Tunnel Gallery, 1974.

AWARDS, HONORS: Washington Newspaper Guild awards for foreign news reporting and for humor, both 1961; Society of Magazine Writers award for excellence, 1970; D.F.A., Minneapolis College of Art, 1971; Frank Luther Mott research award, 1973; D.Litt., Washington and Lee University, 1974; named Virginia Laureate for literature, 1977; American Book Award and National Book Critics Circle Award, both 1980, for *The Right Stuff;* Harold D. Versell Memorial Award for excellence in literature, American Institute of Arts and Letters, 1980; Columbia Journalism Award, 1980.

WRITINGS—All under name Tom Wolfe; published by Farrar, Straus, except as indicated: (Self-illustrated) *The Kandy-Kolored Tangerine-Flake Streamline Baby* (essays), 1965; (contributor) Alan Rinzler, editor, *The New York Spy,* David White, 1967; *The Electric Kool-Aid Acid Test,* 1968; *The Pump House Gang* (essays), 1968 (published in England as *The Mid-Atlantic Man and Other New Breeds in England and America,* Weidenfeld & Nicolson, 1969); *Radical Chic and Mau Mauing the Flak Catchers* (two essays), 1970; (editor with E. W. Johnson and contributor) *The New Journalism* (anthology), Harper, 1973; (self-illustrated) *The Painted Word,* 1975; (self-illustrated) *Mauve Gloves & Madmen, Clutter & Vine, and Other Short Stories* (essays), 1976; (contributor) Susan Feldman, editor, *Marie Cosindas, Color Photographs,* New York Graphic Society, 1978; *The Right Stuff* (Book-of-the-Month-Club selection), 1979; (self-illustrated) *In Our Time* (essays), 1980; *From Bauhaus to Our House,* 1981; (self-illustrated) *The Purple Decades: A Reader* (collection), 1982. Contributor of numerous articles to periodicals. Co-founder of literary quarterly *Shenandoah.*

WORK IN PROGRESS: A novel; articles.

SIDELIGHTS: "Those of you who are not aware of Tom Wolfe should—really—do your best to acquaint yourselves with him," writes William F. Buckley in the *National Review.* "He is probably the most skilful writer in America. I mean by that he can do more things with words than anyone else." Satirist, caricaturist, social critic, coiner of phrases ("Radical Chic," "The Me Decade"), Wolfe has become known as a leading chronicler of American trends. His painstaking research and detailed accounts have made him a widely-respected reporter; at the same time, his unorthodox style and frequently unpopular opinions have resulted in a great deal of controversy. Leslie Bennetts of the *Philadelphia Bulletin* calls him "a professional rogue," who has "needled and knifed at the mighty of every description, exposing in print the follies and foibles of superstars from Leonard Bernstein to the Hell's Angels. Gleefully ripping off every shred of disguise from anyone's pretensions, Wolfe has performed his dissections in *New York* Magazine, *Esquire,* and *Rolling Stone,* not to mention his earlier years on the *New York Herald Tribune* and the *Washington Post.*"

Wolfe is generally recognized as one of the leaders in the branch of writing known as "New Journalism." Bennetts says that while Wolfe did not invent the movement, "he at least became its stentorian spokesman and most flamboyant practitioner." *Fort Lauderdale Sun-Sentinel* writer Margo Harakas believes that there is "only a handful of standouts among [New Journalists]—Jimmy Breslin, Gay Talese, Hunter Thompson, and of course, Wolfe, with his explosive punctuation, name brand detailing, and kaleidoscopic descriptions." In a *Writer's Digest* article, Wolfe defines New Journalism as "the use by people writing nonfiction of techniques which heretofore had been thought of as confined to the novel or to the short story, to create in one form both the kind of objective reality of journalism and the subjective reality that people have always gone to the novel for." The techniques employed in New Journalism, then, include a number of devices borrowed from traditional fiction writing: extensive dialogue; shifting point of view; scene-by-scene construction; detailed descriptions of setting, clothes, and other physical features; complex character development; and, depending on the reporter and on the subject, varying degrees of innovation in the use of language and punctuation.

Wolfe's association with New Journalism began in 1963, when he wrote his first magazine article, a piece on custom automobiles. He had become intrigued with the strange subculture of West Coast car customizers and was beginning to see these individuals as folk artists worthy of serious study. He convinced *Esquire* magazine to send him to California, where he researched the story, interviewed a number of subjects, and, says Harakas, "racked up a $750 tab at the Beverly Wilshire Hotel (picked up by *Esquire,* of course)." Then, having returned to New York to write the article, he found that standard journalistic techniques, those he had employed so successfully during his years of newspaper work, could not adequately describe the bizarre people and machines he had encountered in California.

Stymied, he put off writing the story until, finally, he called Byron Dobell, his editor at *Esquire,* and admitted that he was unable to finish the project. Dobell told him to type up his notes so that the magazine could get another writer to do the job. In the introduction to *The Kandy-Kolored Tangerine-Flake Streamline Baby,* Wolfe writes: "About 8 o'clock that night I started typing the notes out in the form of a memorandum that began, 'Dear Byron.' I started typing away, starting right with the first time I saw any custom cars in California." In an attempt to provide every possible detail for the writer who was to finish the piece, he wrote in a stream-of-consciousness style, including even some of his most garbled notes and random thoughts. "I wrapped up the memorandum about 6:15 A.M., and by this time it was 49 pages long. I took it over to *Esquire* as soon as they opened up, about 9:30 A.M. About 4 P.M. I got a call from Byron Dobell. He told me they were striking out the 'Dear Byron' at the top of the memorandum and running the rest of it in the magazine."

It is the style developed during the writing of the custom car article—his unique blend of "pop" language and creative punctuation—that for many years remained Wolfe's trademark. He was a pioneer in the use of what several reviewers refer to as an "aural" style of writing, a technique intended to make the reader come as close as possible to experiencing an event first-hand. Wilfrid Sheed, in the *New York Times Book Review,* says that Wolfe tries to find "a language proper to each subject, a special sound to convey its uniqueness"; and *Newsweek*'s Jack Kroll feels that Wolfe is "a genuine poet" among journalists, who is able "to get under the skin of a phenomenon and transmit its metabolic rhythm. . . . He creates the most vivid, most pertinent possible dimension of his subject." F. N. Jones, in a *Library Journal* article, describes Wolfe's prose as "free-flowing colorful Joycean, quote-slang, repetitive, cult or class jargon with literary and other reverberations."

Wolfe's style, combined with solid reporting and a highly critical eye, quickly gained a large audience for his magazine pieces. When his first book, *The Kandy-Kolored Tangerine-Flake Streamline Baby,* a collection of twenty-two of his best essays, was published in 1965, William James Smith wrote in *Commonweal:* "Two years ago [Tom Wolfe] was unknown and today those who are not mocking him are doing their level best to emulate him. Magazine editors are currently flooded with Zonk! articles written, putatively, in the manner of Wolfe and, by common account, uniformly impossible. . . . None of his parodists—and even fewer of his emulators—has successfully captured much of the flavor of Wolfe. . . . They miss the spark of personality that is more arresting than the funny punctuation. Wolfe has it, that magical quality that marks prose as distinctively one's own."

In *The Kandy-Kolored Tangerine-Flake Streamline Baby* Wolfe analyzes, caricaturizes, and satirizes a number of early-sixties American trends and pop culture heroes. His essays zero in on the city of Las Vegas, the Peppermint Lounge, demolition derbies, fashion, art galleries, doormen, nannies, and such personalities as Murray the K, Phil Spector, Baby Jane Holzer, and Muhammed Ali (then Cassius Clay). "He knows everything," writes Kurt Vonnegut in the *New York Times Book Review.* "I do not mean he *thinks* he knows everything. . . . He is loaded with facile junk, as all personal journalists have to be—otherwise, how can they write so amusingly and fast?. . . . Verdict: Excellent book by a genius who will do anything to get attention."

What Wolfe has done, according to *Commonweal*'s Smith, "is simply to describe the brave new world of the 'unconscious avant-garde' who are shaping our future, but he has described this world with a vividness and accuracy that makes it something more than real." In a *New Republic* article, Joseph Epstein expresses the opinion that "Wolfe is perhaps most fatiguing when writing about the lower classes. Here he becomes Dr. Wolfe, Department of American Studies, and what he finds attractive about the lower orders, as has many an intellectual slummer before him, is their vitality. At bottom, what is involved here is worship of the Noble Savage. . . . Wolfe is much better when he writes about New York City. Here he drops his studied spontaneity, eases up on the rococo, slips his doctorate, and takes on the tone of the reasonably feeling New Yorker who has not yet been knocked insensate by the clatter of that city." A *Newsweek* writer concludes that "partly, Wolfe belongs to the old noble breed of poet-journalists, like Ben Hecht, and partly he belongs to a new breed of supereducated hip sensibilities like Jonathan Miller and Terry Southern, who see the complete human comedy in everything from a hair-do to a holocaust. Vulgar? A bit. Sentimental? A tick. But this is the nature of journalism, with its crackling short waves transmitting the living moment."

In *The Electric Kool-Aid Acid Test,* Wolfe applies his distinctive brand of journalism to novelist Ken Kesey and his "Merry Pranksters," a West Coast group dedicated to LSD and the pursuit of the psychedelic experience. Joel Lieber of the *Nation* says that in this book Wolfe "has come as close as seems possible, with words, at re-creating the entire mental atmosphere of a scene in which one's understanding is based on feeling rather than verbalization. . . . [The book] is nonfiction told as experimental fiction; it is a genuine feat and a landmark in reporting style." Lawrence Dietz, in a *National Review* article, calls *The Electric Kool-Aid Acid Test* "the best work Wolfe has done, and certainly the most profound and insightful book that has been written about the psychedelic life. . . . [He] has elicited a history of the spread of LSD from 1960 (when Kesey and others got their first jolts in lab experiments) to 1967, when practically any kid with five dollars could buy some kind of trip or other." Dietz feels that Wolfe displays "a willingness to let accuracy take the place of the hysterical imprecations that have passed for reportage in most magazine articles and books" on this subject.

Wolfe's 1970 book, *Radical Chic and Mau Mauing the Flak Catchers,* was made up of two lengthy essays. The first, "Radical Chic," elicited by far the most critical commentary; it deals with a fund-raising party given by Leonard Bernstein in his Park Avenue apartment on January 14, 1970, to raise money for the Black Panthers. Wolfe was at the party, and he became aware of the incongruity of the scene, distinguished, according to Melvin Maddocks of the *Christian Science Monitor,* by "white liberals nibbling caviar while signing checks for the revolution with their free hand." Thomas R. Edwards writes in the *New York Times Book Review:* "For Wolfe, the scene in the Bernsteins' living room demonstrates his pet sociological thesis, here called *nostalgie de la boue,* the aristocrat's hankering for a proletarian primitivism. He shows us cultivated parvenu Jews, torn between cherished new 'right wing' lifestyles and the 'left wing' politics of their own oppressive history, ludicrously confused about how to take the black revolution. Though there's a touch of ugliness in his determination to let us know, without seeming to do so, that certain socialites with gentile names weren't born that way, 'Radical Chic' is sometimes brilliant and telling in its dramatization of this case."

A *Times Literary Supplement* reviewer says that Wolfe "both defends and exonerates the Bernsteins, that is—their motives were sound, liberal, serious, responsible—while cocking an almighty snook at 'the essential double-track mentality of Radical Chic—*nostalgie de la boue* and high protocol' that can entertain Afro hair-styles with Roquefort cheese savouries in a Park Avenue duplex. . . . The slogan 'Mr. Parlour Panther,' in the end, is inevitably unfurled to flutter in the ironic breeze. Such is this dazzling piece of trapeze work by the most practised social stuntman of them all."

Many readers were not happy with *Radical Chic and Mau Mauing the Flak Catchers.* As William F. Buckley explains in the *National Review,* "[Wolfe] has written a very very controversial book, for which he has been publicly excommunicated from the company of the orthodox by the bishops who preside over the *New York Review of Books.*" Buckley continues: "What Mr. Wolfe did in this book was MAKE FUN of Bernstein et al., and if you have never been told, you MUST NOT MAKE FUN of Bernstein et al., when what hangs in the balance is Bernstein's moral prestige plus the integrity of Black Protest; learn the lesson now." Edwards feels that Wolfe "humiliates and degrades everyone concerned, his pre-potent but child-like and shiftless blacks no less than his gutless, time-serving, sexually-fearful white bureaucrats." Timothy Foote, in a *Time* article, notes: "When a *Time* reporter recently asked a minister of the Panther Party's shadow government about the truthfulness of Wolfe's *Radical Chic* account, the reply was ominous: 'You mean that dirty, blatant, lying, racist dog who wrote that fascist disgusting thing in *New York* magazine?'" Yet, despite the objections to the book, Foote insists, the fact remains that "it is generally so accurate that even some of the irate guests at the Bernsteins later wondered how Wolfe—who in fact used shorthand—managed to smuggle a tape recorder onto the premises."

Christopher Lehmann-Haupt of the *New York Times,* noting that "Radical Chic" first appeared as a magazine article, writes: "When the news got out that it would be published as a book eventually, one began to prepare a mental review of it. One had certain questions—the usual Tom Wolfe questions: Where exactly was Wolfe located when all those things occurred? Just how did he learn Leonard Bernstein's innermost fantasies? At exactly what points did Wolfe's imagination impinge on his inferences, and his inferences on his facts? . . . Still, one was prepared to forget those questions. The vision of the Beautiful People dos-a-dosing with black revolutionaries while white servants passed out 'little Roquefort cheese morsels rolled in crushed nuts' was too outrageous. Shivers of malice ran up and down one's spine. Wolfe's anatomy of radical chic would have to be celebrated." The book, Lehmann-Haupt concludes, "represents Wolfe at his best, worst, and most. It has his uncanny eye for life-styles; his obsessive lists of brand names and artifacts; his wicked, frequently cruel, cartoon of people's physical traits; his perfect mimicry of speech patterns. Once again, Wolfe proves himself the complete chameleon, capable of turning any color. He understands the human animal like no sociologist around."

The Painted Word was another of Wolfe's more controversial works. T. O'Hara, in a *Best Sellers* review, sums up the book's thesis: "About 10,000 people constitute the present art world. Artists, doing what they must to survive, obey orders and follow the gospel as written by the monarchs." Among these monarchs, in Wolfe's opinion, are three of our most influential and well-respected art critics: Clement Greenberg, Harold Rosenberg, and Leo Steinberg (the "kings of cultureburg," he calls them). In a *Time* article, Robert Hughes says that "the New York art world, especially in its present decay, is the easiest target a pop sociologist could ask for. Most of it is a wallow of egotism, social climbing and power brokerage, and the only thing that makes it tolerable is the occasional reward of experiencing a good work of art in all its richness, complexity and difficulty. Take the art from the art world, as Wolfe does, and the matrix becomes fit for caricature. Since Wolfe is unable to show any intelligent response to painting, caricature is what we get. . . . Wolfe seems to know virtually nothing about the history of art, American or European."

New York Times art critic John Russell, writing in the *New York Times Book Review,* states: "If someone who is tone-deaf goes to Carnegie Hall every night of the year, he is, of course, entitled to his opinion of what he has listened to, just as a eunuch is entitled to his opinion of sex. But in the one case, as in the other, we on our side are entitled to discount what they say. Given the range, the variety and the degree of accomplishment represented by the names on Mr. Wolfe's list [including artists such as Pollock, de Kooning, Warhol, Newman, Rauschenberg, and Stella], we are entitled to think that if he got no visual reward from *any* of them, . . . the fault may not lie with the art."

As Ruth Berenson of the *National Review* points out, however, response to the book is generally dependent on the extent to which an individual is involved in the world of modern art. She maintains that *The Painted Word* "will delight those who have long harbored dark suspicions that modern art beginning with Picasso is a put-on, a gigantic hoax perpetrated on a gullible public by a mysterious cabal of artists, critics, dealers, and collectors aided and abetted by *Time* and *Newsweek.* Those who take modern art somewhat more seriously will be disappointed."

In *From Bauhaus to Our House,* published in 1981, Wolfe does to modern architecture what he did to modern art in *The Painted Word,* and the response has been similar: Readers close to the subject tend to resent the intrusion by an "outsider," while those with a more detached point of view often appreciate the author's fresh perspective. *New York Times* architecture critic Paul Goldberger, in a *New York Times Book Review* article, writes: "Mr. Wolfe wants to argue that ideology has gotten in the way of common sense. Beginning half a century ago with the origins of the International Style in Europe, he attempts to trace the development of that style, which for many, including Mr. Wolfe, is a virtual synonym for modern architecture. . . . We are told how the International Style became a 'compound'—a select, private, cult-like group of ideologues [including Walter Gropius, Mies van der Rohe, Marcel Breuer, and Josef Albers] whose great mission, as Mr. Wolfe sees it, was to foist modern design upon an unwilling world. . . . The problem, I think . . . is that Tom Wolfe has no eye. He has a wonderful ear, and he listens hard and long, but he does not seem to see. . . . He does precisely what he warns us against; he has listened to the words, not looked at the architecture."

And in a *Washington Post Book World* review, *Post* architecture critic Benjamin Forgey says that "the book is a case of crying Wolfe for one more time. *Bauhaus* is distinguished by the same total loathing of modern culture that motivated *The Painted Word.* . . . Wolfe's explanation is that modernism has been a conspiracy. In place of the New York critics who foisted abstract art upon us, we have the European giants of architecture . . . and their abject American followers. In Wolfe's view the motivation was pretty much the same, too. They were all playing the hypocritical bohemian game of spitting on the bourgeois.'' Forgey feels that ''there is some truth in this, but it makes for a thin book and a narrow, limited history of architecture in the 20th century.''

On the other hand, *New York Times* literary critic Christopher Lehmann-Haupt makes the point that even many architects have been unhappy with the structures created by proponents of the Bauhaus school. This style of architecture (distinguished by what is often referred to as a ''glass box'' appearance) was, for instance, denigrated by architect Peter Blake in his 1977 book, *Form Follows Fiasco.* According to Lehmann-Haupt, Blake ''anathematized modern architecture for being sterile, functionless and ugly''; thus Wolfe ''has not really come up with anything very startling when he laments the irony that four-fifths of the way into the American Century, when what we ought to be expressing with our building is 'exuberance, power, empire, grandeur, or even high spirits and playfulness,' what we still see inflicted upon us is the anti-bourgeois, socialist, pro-worker ideas that arose from 'the smoking rubble of Europe after the Great War.' But the explication of this notion is done with such verve and hilarity by Mr. Wolfe that its substance almost doesn't seem to matter. . . . It flows with natural rhetorical rhythm. . . . And often enough it is to laugh right out loud.'' John Brooks, in a *Chicago Tribune Book World* review, calls the book ''a readable polemic on how in our architecture over the past few decades things have gone very much as they have in the other visual arts—a triumph of conformity over true innovation, of timidity over uninhibited expression, of irony over straightforwardness, of posing over real accomplishment. . . . *From Bauhaus to Our House* is lucidly and for the most part gracefully written.''

In 1979 Wolfe published the book that many critics consider his finest: *The Right Stuff,* an award-winning study of the early years of the American space program. At one point in the book, Wolfe attempts to define the ''ineffable quality'' from which the title is taken: ''It obviously involved bravery. But it was not bravery in the simple sense of being willing to risk your life . . . any fool could do that. . . . No, the idea . . . seemed to be that a man should have the ability to go up in a hurtling piece of machinery and put his hide on the line and then have the moxie, the reflexes, the experience, the coolness, to pull it back in the last yawning moment—and then to go up again *the next day,* and the next day, and every next day.''

The main characters in the book are, of course, the first U.S. astronaut team: Scott Carpenter, Gordon Cooper, John Glenn, Gus Grissom, Wally Schirra, Alan Shepard, and Deke Slayton. Wolfe assiduously chronicles their early careers as test pilots, their private lives, their selection for the astronaut program and the subsequent medical processing and training. But, as *Commonweal*'s Thomas Powers points out, *The Right Stuff* ''is not a history; it is far too thin in dates, facts and source citations to serve any such purpose. It is a work of literature which must stand or fall as a coherent text, and its subject is not the Mercury program itself but the impulse behind it, the unreflecting competitiveness which drove the original astronauts to the quite extraordinary lengths Wolfe describes so vividly.'' That the author goes beyond mere reportage of historical fact is confirmed by Mort Sheinman in a *Chicago Tribune* article: ''Wolfe tells us what it's like to go 'shooting straight through the top of the sky,' to be 'in a king's solitude, unique and inviolate, above the dome of the world.' He describes what happens when someone is immolated by airplane fuel, and he talks about the nightmares and hallucinations experienced by the wives. . . . [*The Right Stuff*] is a dazzling piece of work, something that reveals much about the nature of bravery and celebrity and—yes—patriotism.''

Time writer R. Z. Sheppard says that the book ''is crammed with inside poop and racy incident that 19 years ago was ignored by what [Wolfe] terms the 'proper Victorian gents' of the press. The fast cars, booze, astro groupies, the envies and injuries of the military caste system were not part of what Americans would have considered the right stuff. Wolfe lays it all out in brilliantly stated Op Lit scenes: the tacky cocktail lounges of Cocoa Beach where one could hear the *Horst Wessel Song* sung by ex-rocket scientists of the Third Reich; Vice President Lyndon Johnson furiously cooling his heels outside the Glenn house because Annie Glenn would not let him in during her husband's countdown; Alan Shepard losing a struggle with his full bladder moments before lift-off; the overeager press terrifying Ham the chimp after his proficient flight; the astronauts surrounded by thousands of cheering Texans waving hunks of raw meat during an honorary barbecue in the Houston Coliseum.''

Christopher Lehmann-Haupt of the *New York Times* writes: ''What fun it is to watch Mr. Wolfe put the antiseptic space program into the traces of his inimitable verbal cadenzas. It's a little like hearing the story of Jesus of Nazareth through the lips of the Chicago nightclub comedian Lord Buckley.'' Lehmann-Haupt says that in this book Wolfe undertakes ''the restoration of the zits and rogue cilia of hair to the face of the American space program'' and reveals a good deal of the gossip that was denied the public by a hero-worshipping press in the early sixties, gossip ''about how the test-pilot fraternity looked down on the early astronauts for being trained monkeys in a capsule ('spam in a can') instead of pilots in control of their craft; about the real feelings of the original seven for one another and the tension that arose between the upright John Glenn and some of the others over their after-hours behavior, particularly with the 'juicy little girls' who materialized wherever they trained; and about what National Aeronautical and Space Administration engineers really felt about the flight of Gus Grissom and Scott Carpenter and the possibility that they had secretly panicked.''

Former test pilot and astronaut Michael Collins (a member of the Gemini 10 flight and command module pilot on the Apollo 11 moon flight), writes in a *Washington Post Book World* review: ''I lived at Edwards [Air Force Base, site of the Air Force Flight Test Center,] for four years, and, improbable as some of Tom's tales seem, I know he's telling it like it was. He is the first gifted writer to explore the relationship between test pilots and astronauts—the obvious similarities and the subtle differences. . . . He's obviously done a lot of homework—too much in some cases. . . . Some of this stuff could only be interesting to Al Shepard's mother. While the first part of the book is a paean to guts, to the 'right stuff,' it is followed by a chronology—but one that might have profited from a little tighter editing. But it's still light-years ahead of the endless drivel [Norman] Mailer has put out about the Apollo program, and in places the Wolfe genius really shines.'' Collins feels that at times Wolfe allows himself to get too close to his subject: ''He's almost one of the boys—and there's too much to admire and not enough to eviscerate.'' As a result ''*The Right Stuff* is not vintage, psychedelic Tom Wolfe, but if you . . . have ever been curious about what the space program was really all about in those halcyon Kennedy and Mercury years, then this is your book.''

In a review of *The Right Stuff* for the *Lone Star Book Review,* Martha Heimberg says that, for the most part, ''Wolfe's reporting, while being marvelously entertaining writing, has also represented a telling and trustworthy point of view. His is one of those finely critical intelligences that can detect the slightest pretention or falsification in an official posture or social pose. And, when he does, he goes after the hypocrisy—whether large or small, left or right—with all the zeal of the dedicated reformer.'' Like Collins, Heimberg feels that *The Right Stuff* ''represents a departure for the satirist whose observant eye and caustic pen have impaled on the page a wide range of American social phenomena'' in that Wolfe ''clearly likes his subjects—none are treated as grist for the satirist's mill, but put down with as great a skill and detail as an observer could possibly muster.'' She concludes that ''the book represents a tremendous accomplishment and a new direction for a writer who figures among the top stylists of his generation.''

Although there can be no question that Tom Wolfe has achieved a reputation as a superb stylist and skillful reporter, no discussion of Wolfe would be complete without some mention of his famous wardrobe. *Philadelphia Bulletin* writer Leslie Bennetts tells of an encounter with the author when he lectured at Villanova University: ''The legendary sartorial splendors were there, of course: the gorgeous three-piece creamy white suit he has been renowned for . . . (how many must he have, do you suppose, to appear in spotless vanilla every day: rows upon rows of them hanging in shadowed closets, a veritable army of Gatsby ghosts waiting to emerge?). Not to mention the navy suede shoes, dark as midnight, or the jaunty matching suede hat, or the sweeping midnight cashmere coat of the exact same hue, or the crisp matching tie on which perched a golden half-moon pin to complement the glittering gold watch chain that swung gracefully from the milky vest. Or the navy silk handkerchief peeking out from the white suit pocket, or the white silk handkerchief peeking out from the navy coat pocket."

Wolfe told Bennetts that he began wearing the white suits in 1962: ''That was when I had a white suit made, started wearing it in January, and found it annoyed people tremendously. Even slight departures in dress at that time really spun people out. So I liked it. It's kind of a harmless form of aggression, I guess.'' But Wolfe's mode of dress has also been an important part of his journalism, serving as a device to distance him from his subject. He told Susan Forrest of the *Fort Lauderdale News:* ''A writer can find out more if he doesn't pretend to be hip. . . . If people see you are an outsider, they will come up and tell you things. If you're trying to be hip, you can't ask a lot of naive questions.'' This technique has been effective for Wolfe in interviewing stock car racers, Hell's Angels, and—particularly—astronauts. He feels that at least part of the success of *The Right Stuff* is due to the fact that he did not try to get too close to that inner circle. Wolfe told Janet Maslin of the *New York Times Book Review:* ''I looked like Ruggles of Red Gap to them, I'm sure. . . . But I've long since given up on the idea of going into a situation trying to act like part of it. . . . Besides, it was useless for me to try to fit into the world of pilots, because I didn't know a thing about flying. I also sensed that pilots, like people in the psychedelic life, really dislike people who presume a familiarity with the Lodge.''

A *Time* reporter says that at one time Wolfe owned nine $600 white suits but notes that more recently the author has been forced to move on to other colors. As Wolfe said in a *Detroit News Magazine* interview with Ron Base: ''I've been put out of business by the Great Gatsby craze and Saturday Night Fever. Now there are white suits all over Sears' basement.'' Base describes a late addition to Wolfe's wardrobe: ''It is canary yellow, almost luminous in the shimmering noonday Manhattan heat, so that he steps into the comparative darkness of the Isle of Capri restaurant, the luminescence is abruptly snuffed out. He is cool and elegant as lemon sherbet. 'My wife won't walk with me when I'm wearing this suit,' Tom Wolfe offers with a soft smile. 'She sends me on ahead. At night I light up the street.'''

Wolfe is a great opponent of what he calls ''funky chic,'' a phenomenon defined by the *New York Times*'s Anatole Broyard as ''the delusion of antifashion, in which the style setters substitute $75 prefaded, artificially aged jeans for slacks from Bendel's.'' Wolfe told Jura Koncius of the *Washington Post:* ''We're still in the funky chic period of the '70s. . . . Most of the clothing experimentation is still in the casual realm. That's why the only fun is to go pretentious. I'm getting my collars stiffer and higher.'' He's also turning to experimentation with socks, which he tells Base are ''the last frontier.'' Koncius says that ''socks are terrifically important to Wolfe. He unearthed the final case of Mary of Holland hand-knit socks last summer in Southampton. 'Mary made the best socks,' says Wolfe. Now there are no more to be found. Where are standards? Tom Wolfe's electric-blue-and-mustard-plaid socks have style.''

The *Time* writer calls Wolfe's form of dress ''a splendiferous advertisement for his individuality. The game requires a lot of reverse spin and body English but it boils down to antichic chic. Exclaims Wolfe proudly: 'I own no summer house, no car, I wear tank tops when I swim, long white pants when I play tennis, and I'm probably the last man in America to still do the Royal Canadian Air Force exercises.'''

AVOCATIONAL INTERESTS: Window shopping.

CA INTERVIEW

CA interviewed Tom Wolfe by phone August 7, 1981, at his office in Southampton, N.Y.

CA: You're credited with creating the nonfiction short story—the New Journalism—which has been criticized for being too personal, too unbelievable. Was this early criticism ever discouraging to you?

WOLFE: Only in the sense that when people referred to it as too personal or too impressionistic, I felt like they had totally missed the point of what I and a number of other writers were doing. Most of the major things that I have written, like *The Right Stuff* and *The Electric Kool-Aid Acid Test,* have not been personal. They've been completely about the lives of other people, with myself hardly intruding into the narrative at all. They were based on reporting, so a lot of it is impersonal and objective. It can be discouraging to see it described as implausible, personal, and unbelievable.

I very seldom use the first person anymore. I think it's a very tricky thing because whether you know it or not, if you use the first person you've turned yourself into a character, and you have to be ready to make that character an important part of the narrative.

CA: In the introduction to The New Journalism, *you wrote about the very few novels that evolved from the 1960s, a period ''the novelists had been kind enough to leave behind'' for the New Journalists. With all that was happening socially and politically then, why do you think novelists shied away from writing about it?*

WOLFE: I think the main reason was because the realistic novel had gone out of fashion. This is part of what I call our colonial complex. In the arts, we're still the most obedient little colonial subjects that Europe could ever ask for. After the Second World War, there was quite a vogue for European fiction as practiced by Kafka, the Soviet writer Evgeny Zamyatin, the South American writer Gabriel Garcia Marquez, and the playwrights Harold Pinter and Samuel Beckett. They were all influential among novelists writing what I think of as the modern fable, in which all of the trappings of realism are scrupulously removed. The realistic novel is considered old-fashioned, old hat. The idea was that after Balzac, Henry James, Proust, and Joyce, what was there left to do with the realistic novel? It had all been done. The flaw there is the fact that realism in prose is not just one technique out of many.

In my opinion, you can't advance the state of the art of literature by turning your back on realism. Due to sheer intellectual fashion you have a generation of young novelists turning their backs on the most potent devices in prose, namely the devices of realism. The only important realists in prose became the journalists. That's why I said that New Journalists had a field day in that period. For example, the three major books written about Vietnam were all by nonfiction writers—Michael Herr's *Dispatches,* C.D.B. Bryan's *Friendly Fire,* and John Sack's *M.* So you have about a thirty-five-year period from 1945 to the present in which the most talented young novelists coming from the universities steered away from the realistic novel. The publishers were dying for the great realistic novels that were going to be written and they just weren't forthcoming. I think the business of intellectual fashion is terribly underrated. I think it plays a much bigger part in the lives and careers of writers than any of the larger issues of the world.

CA: Do you think the events of the 1960s were perhaps too painful for novelists to write about?

WOLFE: I think there are very few things writers find too painful to write about, once they think that's the direction they should go.

CA: In an article in the Los Angeles Times *[19 October 1979] you said, "At the risk of being immodest, I suppose I'm probably the most parodied writer in the last fifteen years." How do you react to the many journalists who try to imitate your style?*

WOLFE: Every now and then somebody will bring me a piece and say, "Here's somebody imitating your style," and I read it and I *like* it, I think it's pretty good. There's always an implied flattery in being parodied, even if the parody is meant to be an attack. That's why I seldom use parody as a weapon, because no matter how vigorous your attack, you're also patting your subject on the back. When I wrote the piece about the *New Yorker* in 1965, I got many people upset. The whole idea was based on a parody that Wolcott Gibbs had done of the *Time* magazine style back in the late 1930s, when *Time* was very new and very lively. I started writing a parody of the *New Yorker* style, but I could see that there had been so many parodies of the *New Yorker* that they were all compliments in a way; they were saying, "Here is a magazine with a recognizable style." If you parody a dull style—and the *New Yorker* style had become very dull—you can get away with it for about a page. For one page, a dull style is funny. For two pages, it just becomes dull and boring. So I opted for the antiparody and took a tone that was as far removed from the *New Yorker* as possible, which was a kind of screaming tabloid style, and I think it worked better.

CA: Do you get many requests from journalists to read their writing and comment on it?

WOLFE: I get a lot of requests from all types of writers, but I've finally reached the point where I just can't accommodate those requests. Once somebody gives you a manuscript, they really want an answer *tomorrow;* they expect it. To tell you the truth, I think I get more requests from novelists than anyone else. One good thing about journalism is that you're being pressured to produce by a deadline and get it out of your system. The manuscripts don't seem to linger around as much, whereas often a novelist or a short-story writer is simply having a hard time getting published at all, and is just looking for any sort of reaction.

CA: What advice would you give aspiring journalists who are just getting started?

WOLFE: I would offer what I think is very practical advice—to somehow understand very early in the game that there is no substitute for reporting. For that reason you should get a job on a newspaper, no matter how miserable it is (this country is mainly full of miserable newspapers) just to get used to the process of reporting and acquaint yourself with a few things that you wouldn't see otherwise, not matter how boring it may seem. I would also suggest that you not be bashful, particularly if you have an idea for a magazine story. You should get up your courage and approach the biggest magazine you can think of that might be interested in the subject. Approach a junior editor rather than the man at the top, because the junior editors are in competition with one another to discover new writers. Even if you've already written it, present the story idea to the editor, because editors like to feel that they're part of the creative process. Wait a decent interval of about two weeks and then send them a manuscript. Magazines will be in a receptive mood if you have approached them ahead of time. They'll want it to be good, they'll want to buy it, and they'll want it to be a success. There's a continual shortage of good writers and good journalists. It's really not an overcrowded field because there's not that much talent to go around. A lot of it is having the determination and perseverance to do the reporting.

CA: You've illustrated most of your own books and have had several one-man shows of your drawings. Do the writing and the art influence each other? Is it hard to separate the two?

WOLFE: They *should* be two very different things because I have the feeling that they are different neurologically. At one point I used to try to illustrate newspaper stories that I had written myself against a daily deadline; so I would do both things in the same day. That was maddening because they're so different. All this business of the two hemispheres of the brain is probably correct. If you're concentrating on a design or a drawing, it's almost impossible to listen to words at the same time. And if you're listening to words for their content, it's almost impossible to draw at the same time. Now I often illustrate the stories after I've written them. Some of the things that I do for *Harper's* magazine, I do the drawing first, just because I've seen something that appealed to me, and then I think of the copy afterwards. I find that the drawings are more successful if they happen that way. If the illustration follows something I've written, I find it more difficult to give the drawing a life or a compelling design of its own. The words that I've already written are influencing the drawing in a bad way. I can't explain that, but I find that if the drawing comes to me first and then the words, it's better.

CA: Reviews of The Right Stuff *were mixed—some critics missed your usual flamboyant stream-of-consciousness style, and others said it was your best book yet. Were you pleased with it?*

WOLFE: I felt that it was my best book. I very consciously tried to make the style fit the particular world I was writing about, mainly the world of military pilots. To have had a prose as wound up as the prose of *The Electric Kool-Aid Acid Test* would have been a stylistic mistake. I've always insisted that there was no set Tom Wolfe style, that I was trying to make the style fit the event. So many of the things that I wrote about in the 1960s were so wild in themselves that a wild style seemed to fit. The world of military pilots was different, a world that seemed to me to require a different tone.

The book was extremely difficult to write. There was no central character, no protagonist. There were seven Mercury astronauts, three or four pilots in the X-series of experimental flights, such as Chuck Yeager and Scott Crossfield. The problem of giving the book a narrative structure, some sort of drive and suspense, was quite tough. I finally adopted the technique of trying to make each chapter, particularly the early ones, like a short story, with the hope that if that chapter was effective, if the story was effective, then you would go on to the next one. It had none of the ordinary structure of the novel, including the nonfiction novel. Yet somehow I had to try to make it work and have a dramatic structure. I think I finally succeeded, but during the writing of it I became tremendously discouraged.

CA: Is The Right Stuff *going to be made into a movie?*

WOLFE: Yes. The project is in the hands of the Alan Ladd, Jr., organization.

CA: Will you have a hand in the production?

WOLFE: No, I will have no part in making the movie; it's out of my hands. I know the producers, and I have every confidence that they'll make a good picture out of it.

CA: Is your work schedule still ten pages a day?

WOLFE: Yes, that's the way I worked on *The Right Stuff.* If you're writing nonfiction, there's no use getting into the schedule until you've done the reporting and you have the material. Once I've done the reporting, I've found that the only way to make myself get the writing done is to adopt the ten-pages-a-day schedule. I always make an outline, but if I try to make myself cover a certain portion of the outline each day, that's very dispiriting. It's psychologically crushing because a part of the outline that you thought would take a page may turn out to take six or seven pages. But if you set a quota, the pain can't last but so long. I do find writing a very painful process—I never understand writers who say it's enjoyable. I think it's the hardest work in the world. It's like having arthritis or something; it's a little pain every day and you have to press on.

I wanted the writing to appear buoyant, free and easy, spontaneous. Creating the effect of spontaneity in writing is one of the most difficult and artificial things you can do. I was much relieved to learn that Celine used to spend four or five years rewriting his novels in order to achieve the effect of someone just sitting down across the table from you, spouting up the story of his life. Writing is an extremely artificial business; it's artificial by its very nature—you're taking sounds and converting them into symbols on a page. To make that transference from one sense to another and reinvest the words with vigor and rhythm and spontaneity is quite a feat.

CA: How much revising do you do?

WOLFE: I tend to do as much revising as editors will let me do. I rewrote most of *The Right Stuff* and I rewrote *Radical Chic* a couple of times. But there was no revision at all with *The Electric Kool-Aid Acid Test.* I was writing against a book deadline and I sent in chapters as I finished them. I did a little bit of last-minute revision when the book was in galley form, but that was it. Sometimes the greatest favor an editor can do a writer is to trick him into yielding up the manuscript.

CA: Has the critical reception of your work—both positive and negative—been helpful to you?

WOLFE: All writers like to say they don't pay any attention to it. I wish I had thought of Arnold Bennett's line, "I don't read my reviews, I only measure them." I don't think Arnold Bennett really meant it. Writers all wear their egos on their sleeves. It's irresistible, the business of reacting to reviews.

I was fortunate in that very early in my career, when I was unknown, I was severely criticized and denounced by very eminent people, particularly in the case of the *New Yorker* article. I was working at the *New York Herald Tribune* at the time and I didn't have a book out or anything—I was just a man who wrote magazine articles for the Sunday supplement. I suddenly found myself denounced by the likes of Joseph Alsop, Walter Lippmann (he called me an ass in print), Murray Kempton, a distinguished columnist for the *New York Post.* Richard Goodwin called up from the White House to denounce me; E. B. White; even J. D. Salinger, whom the press hadn't heard from for years, sent in a telegram denouncing me as a yellow journalist. I really felt that perhaps the world was coming to an end. All these eminent people descended upon me, and I felt the sky was falling in.

Then a few days later I woke up, and nothing had happened. It dawned on me that it's very difficult to get hurt in a literary fight. In a strange way, all the shouting and shooting and the explosions were part of the literary excitement. I took so much abuse at that time that I think it made me fireproof. So now if I am attacked in a review—and it happens quite often—I can't say that I like it, but I know that no matter what it says, the sky really isn't going to fall.

CA: Are you working on a novel now?

WOLFE: I am. I hate people who say they're "working on a novel"; it means they haven't started. But I've begun to do the reporting. The novel depends on it. It's about New York City today. So like anybody else, I have to go out and see what's going on, because you can lose track of things so very quickly. The novel will be about New York, high and low.

CA: Is that a hard transition to make, from journalism into straight fiction?

WOLFE: We'll see. I did one long short story in 1975 called "The Commercial." It's in the collection *Mauve Gloves &*

Madmen, Clutter & Vine. It's about a baseball player making a commercial. I thought I was going to be able to do it in several weekends, but I was quite shocked to see that writing fiction wasn't all that easy. I thought that since you could make up things there was nothing to it, but it's not easy to make up things effectively. The imagination needs material. I had to put everything aside and do some reporting—how commercials are made, what athletes think about, and for that particular story, a little research about class structure in the black community, because the baseball player was black. That story was a good exercise for me because it showed me that I had to approach it with the same kind of reporting that would go into *The Right Stuff* or anything else.

CA: Would you like to comment on the status of New Journalism today?

WOLFE: Fortunately, as a subject that people talk about and write about, it has largely died out except in the case of something like the Janet Cooke fiasco. Then everyone decides they'll blame it on the New Journalism. [Janet Cooke won the Pulitzer Prize for journalism in 1981 for a story she wrote about an eight-year-old heroin addict. She later admitted that the story was a composite, and the prize was relinquished.] That whole business really made me laugh.

It reminded me of when I first went to work on the *New York Herald Tribune* and they were still laughing over the ship-of-sin scandal from prohibition days. An informant had told the *Herald Tribune* that there was a ship of sin operating outside of a three-mile limit off of eastern Long Island. On board you could get liquor and dope and sex. So the *Tribune* sent a reporter out. He didn't find the ship, but he *did* find a saloon in Montauk, and he phoned in about five days' worth of the most lurid stories in the history of drunk newspapermen. Half of New York City gasped and the other half rushed out to eastern Long Island to rent motor launches, until it was discovered he had made up the whole thing. These things happen about every three or four years; some reporter gets caught piping a story out of his skull.

Today, it makes the newspaper industry and publishers and editors feel a lot better if they can blame it on some strange new Legionnaire's Disease, some new strain of bacteria, that is afflicting the young writers. Then all you have to do is develop a vaccine, and the problem is on the way to being cured. Phony stories are going to be written every once in a while, so long as you give reporters the trust that you have to give them. But to blame it on the New Journalism or any other new thing is ludicrous. There's nothing new about sham.

Other than that, the New Journalism was superceded in terms of publicity several years ago by the investigative reporting era, starring Woodward and Bernstein. I think that was all for the good as far as techniques in nonfiction are concerned. I was beginning to feel bad about having touted this thing myself so assiduously. I had the feeling I was beginning to make people self-conscious about the form and the techniques; one of the virtues had been that it had happened without any self-consciousness or tradition. There was a great deal of freedom and a great deal of experimentation with it when it started out. The best thing that could happen is what has happened now. The techniques are all known. The young writers who want to use them will use them because they know what they are. But it's not constantly talked about so that writers will look over their shoulders and wonder if they're doing it correctly.

BIOGRAPHICAL/CRITICAL SOURCES: New York Times Book Review, June 27, 1965, August 18, 1968, November 29, 1970, December 3, 1972, June 15, 1975, December 26, 1976, October 11, 1981, October 10, 1982; *Newsweek,* June 28, 1965, August 26, 1968, June 9, 1975, September 17, 1979; *New Republic,* July 14, 1965, December 19, 1970; *New York Review of Books,* August 26, 1965, December 17, 1970, June 26, 1975, January 20, 1977, October 28, 1979; *Commonweal,* September 17, 1965, December 20, 1968, March 3, 1978, October 12, 1979; *Library Journal,* August, 1968; *National Review,* August 27, 1968, January 26, 1971, August 1, 1975, February 19, 1977; *Time,* September 6, 1968, December 21, 1970, June 23, 1975, December 27, 1976, September 29, 1979; *Partisan Review,* No. 3, 1969, No. 2, 1974.

New York Times, November 25, 1970, May 27, 1975, November 26, 1976, September 14, 1979, October 9, 1981; *Writers Digest,* January, 1970; *Christian Science Monitor,* November 17, 1970; *Harper's,* February, 1971; *Commentary,* March, 1971, May, 1977, February, 1980; *Times Literary Supplement,* October 1, 1971, November 30, 1979, November 26, 1980; *Contemporary Literary Criticism,* Gale, Volume I, 1973, Volume II, 1974, Volume IX, 1978, Volume XV, 1980; Joe David Bellamy, editor, *The New Fiction: Interviews with Innovative American Writers,* University of Illinois Press, 1974; *Philadelphia Bulletin,* February 10, 1975; *Fort Lauderdale Sun-Sentinel,* April 22, 1975; *Fort Lauderdale News,* April 22, 1975; *Best Sellers,* August, 1975; *Authors in the News,* Volume II, Gale, 1976; *New Leader,* January 31, 1977; *America,* February 5, 1977; *Nation,* March 5, 1977, November 3, 1977; *Encounter,* September, 1977; *Washington Post,* September 4, 1979, October 23, 1980; *Chicago Tribune,* September 9, 1979, September 15, 1979; *Washington Post Book World,* September 9, 1979, November 23, 1980, November 15, 1981, November 7, 1982; *Village Voice,* September 10, 1979; *Saturday Review,* September 15, 1979; *Books & Art,* September 28, 1979; *Atlantic,* October, 1979; *Detroit News Magazine,* October 14, 1979; *Los Angeles Times,* October 19, 1979; *Lone Star Book Review,* November, 1979; *Los Angeles Times Book Review,* November 2, 1980, October 25, 1981, October 17, 1982, January 23, 1983; *Detroit News,* November 9, 1980; *Chicago Tribune Book World,* December 7, 1980, October 25, 1981, January 16, 1983.

—Sketch by Peter M. Gareffa

—Interview by Mary V. McLeod

* * *

WOLFE, Tom

See WOLFE, Thomas Kennerly, Jr.

* * *

WOOD, Nancy 1936-

PERSONAL: Born June 20, 1936, in Trenton, N.J.; daughter of Harold William (a businessman) and Eleanor (Green) Clopp; married former husband, Oscar Dull III, 1953; married Myron Gilmore Wood (a photographer), March 1, 1961 (divorced, 1969); married John Brittingham (a rancher), 1977 (divorced, 1982); children: Karin Alison, Christopher Keith, Eleanor Kathryn, India Hart. *Education:* Attended Bucknell University, 1955-56, and University of Colorado, 1958-59. *Politics:* Democrat. *Home:* 825 Paseo, Colorado Springs, Colo. 80907. *Agent:* Curtis Brown Ltd., 575 Madison Ave., New York, N.Y. 10022.

CAREER: Writer and photographer. *Awards, honors:* Carter G. Woodson Award, National Council for the Social Studies,

1980, for *War Cry on a Prayer Feather: Prose and Poetry of the Ute Indians.*

WRITINGS: Clearcut: The Deforestation of America, Sierra Club Books, 1971; *The Last Five Dollar Baby,* Harper, 1972; (with Roy Emerson Stryker) *In This Proud Land: America, 1935-1943, as Seen in the FSA Photographs,* New York Graphic Society, 1973; *Many Winters: Prose and Poetry of the Pueblos,* illustrated by Frank Howell, Doubleday, 1974; *The King of Liberty Bend,* Harper, 1976; *The Man Who Gave Thunder to the Earth: A Taos Way of Seeing and Understanding,* Doubleday, 1976; (self-illustrated with photographs) *The Grass Roots People: An American Requiem,* Harper, 1978; *War Cry on a Prayer Feather: Prose and Poetry of the Ute Indians,* Doubleday, 1979; *When Buffalo Free the Mountains: The Survival of America's Ute Indians,* Doubleday, 1980; *Columbine* (novel), Harper, in press.

Illustrated with photographs by Myron Wood: *Central City: A Ballad of the West,* Chaparral Press, 1963; *West to Durango,* Chaparral Press, 1964; *Little Wrangler,* Doubleday, 1966; *Colorado: Big Mountain Country,* Doubleday, 1969, revised edition, 1972; *Hollering Sun,* Simon & Schuster, 1972.

BIOGRAPHICAL/CRITICAL SOURCES: Washington Post, March 19, 1981.

* * *

WOODMAN, Harold D. 1928-

PERSONAL: Born April 21, 1928, in Chicago, Ill.; son of Joseph B. and Helen (Sollo) Woodman; married Leonora Becker (a professor), October 3, 1954; children: Allan James, David Edward. *Education:* Roosevelt University, B.A., 1957; University of Chicago, M.A., 1959, Ph.D., 1964. *Home:* 1100 North Grant St., West Lafayette, Ind. 47906. *Office:* Department of History, Purdue University, West Lafayette, Ind. 47907.

CAREER: Roosevelt University, Chicago, Ill., lecturer in American history, 1962-63; University of Missouri—Columbia, assistant professor, 1963-66, associate professor of American history, 1966-69, professor of history, 1969-71; Purdue University, West Lafayette, Ind., professor of history, 1971—, chairman of Committee on American Studies, 1981—. Member of editorial board, Wisconsin Historical Society, 1972-76; Purdue University Press, member of editorial board, 1976-80, chairman, 1979-80. Member of Ralph Waldo Emerson Award committee, Phi Beta Kappa, 1977-80; president of Business History Conference, 1980. Member of advisory committee, Eleutherian Mills Hagley Foundation, 1976-79.

MEMBER: American Historical Association, Organization of American Historians (member of membership committee, 1968-70; chairman, 1970-72), Economic History Association (trustee, 1980-83), Agricultural History Society (member of executive committee, 1970-73; president, 1983), Business History Association (president, 1981), American Association of University Professors, Southern Historical Association, Indiana Historical Society.

AWARDS, HONORS: Everett Eugene Edwards Memorial Award of Agricultural History Society, 1962, for article "Chicago Businessmen and the 'Granger Laws,'"; Ramsdell Award of Southern Historical Association, 1964, for article "The Profitability of Slavery: A Historical Perennial"; Social Science Research Council faculty grant, 1969-70; Woodrow Wilson International Center for Scholars fellowship, 1977.

WRITINGS: (Editor with Allen F. Davis) *Conflict or Consensus in American History,* Heath, 1966, expanded two-volume edition, 1968, 5th edition, 1979; *Slavery and the Southern Economy,* Harcourt, 1966; *King Cotton and His Retainers,* University of Kentucky Press, 1968; (author of introduction) J. E. Cairnes, *The Slave Power,* Harper, 1969; *The Legacy of the American Civil War,* Wiley, 1973. General editor, "Topics in American History" series, Forum Press, 1971—; member of editorial advisory board, *Dictionary of Economic History,* Scribner, 1980.

Contributor: Herbert J. Bass, editor, *The State of American History,* Quadrangle, 1970; Stanley L. Engerman and Eugene D. Genovese, editors, *Race and Slavery in the Western Hemisphere: Quantitative Studies,* Princeton University Press, 1974; *Dictionary of American History,* Scribner, 1976; Henry Steele Commager, editor, *The American Destiny,* Danbury Press, 1976; *Research in Economic History,* Volume II, Johnson Associates (Greenwich, Conn.), 1977; *Dictionary of American Economic History,* Scribner, 1980; Clifford Earl Ramsey, editor, *No More Elegies: Essays on the Future of the Humanities,* Federation of Public Programs in the Humanities (Minneapolis, Minn.), 1981; Fred Bateman, editor, *Business in the New South,* University of the South Press, 1981. Also contributor to *Proceedings of the Business History Conference,* 1976.

Contributor of numerous articles to professional journals, including *Agricultural History, Journal of Southern History, American Historical Review,* and *Civil War History.* Member of editorial board, *Business History Review,* 1971-77, *Journal of Southern History,* 1972-75, *Agricultural History,* 1977—, *Plantation Society in the Americas,* 1979—, *Journal of Negro History,* 1980—, and *American Historical Review,* 1981—.

WORK IN PROGRESS: Social and Economic Changes in the American South after the Civil War.

* * *

WOODS, Stockton
See FORREST, Richard S(tockton)

* * *

WORBOYS, Anne(tte Isobel) Eyre
(Annette Eyre; Vicky Maxwell, a pseudonym)

PERSONAL: Born in Aukland, New Zealand; daughter of Thomas Edwardes (a property owner and sheep farmer) and Agnes Helen (Blair) Eyre; married Walter Brindy Worboys (a sales executive), September 20, 1946; children: Carolyn (Mrs. Derek Pretty), Robin. *Home:* The White House, Leigh, Tonbridge, Kent TN11 8RH, England. *Agent:* David Higham Associates, 5-8 Lower John St., Golden Sq., London W1R 4HA, England.

CAREER: Writer. *Military service:* Royal New Zealand Air Force, 1942-45. *Member:* Society of Women Writers and Journalists, Crimewriters Association, Romantic Novelists Association, Tonbridge Wells & District Writers' Circle (chairman), Tonbridge East Theatre. *Awards, honors:* Romantic Novelists Award nomination, 1973, for *The Magnolia Room;* Mary Elgin Prize, 1975, for *The Lion of Delos*; Romantic Novelists Award, 1977, for *Every Man a King.*

WRITINGS—Novels: *The Lion of Delos* (Book-of-the-Month Club selection), Delacourte, 1974; *Every Man a King,* Hodder & Stoughton, 1975, Scribner, 1976; *The Barrancourt Destiny,*

Scribner, 1977, *The Bhunda Jewels,* Severn House, 1980; *Run, Sara, Run* (Detective Book Club selection), Scribner, 1982.

Under name Annette Eyre; published by Hurst & Blackett, except as indicated: *Three Strings to a Fortune,* 1962; *The Valley of Yesterday,* 1965; *A Net to Catch the Wind,* 1966; *Return to Bell Bird Country,* 1966; *The House of Five Pines,* 1967; *The River and Wilderness,* 1967, published as *Give Me Your Love,* New American Library, 1975; *A Wind from the Hill,* 1968; *Thorn-Apple,* 1968; *Tread Softly in the Sun,* 1969; *The Little Millstones,* 1970; *Dolphin Bay,* 1970; *Rainbow Child,* 1971; *The Magnolia Room,* 1972; *Venetian Inheritance,* 1973.

Under pseudonym Vicky Maxwell: *Chosen Child,* Collins, 1973; *Flight to the Villa Mistra,* Collins, 1973; *The Way of the Tamarisk,* Collins, 1974, Delacourte, 1975; *High Hostage,* Collins, 1976; *The Other Side of Summer,* Collins, 1977.

Contributor of short stories to women's magazines.

WORK IN PROGRESS: A "long historical novel making use of the adventures of my own family."

SIDELIGHTS: Anne Eyre Worboys told *CA* she travels extensively to acquire background material for her novels. *Every Man a King,* for instance, "was written after riding a half-Arab, half-Andalusian horse over the Sierra Nevada, sleeping in centuries-old mulemen's posadas [or lodges], crossing the passes at 10,600 feet." Worboys went to Greece for *The Lion of Delos,* Venice for *Venetian Inheritance,* and Spain for *The Other Side of Summer*. She says *Run, Sara, Run* "is one of the few books I have written with an English background."

* * *

WORTH, Douglas 1940-

PERSONAL: Born March 14, 1940, in Philadelphia, Pa.; son of C. Brooke (a naturalist and writer) and Merida (a bookstore operator; maiden name, Grey) Worth; married Karen Weisskopf (an educator), May 2, 1969; children: Colin, Danny. *Education:* Swarthmore College, B.A. (with honors), 1962; Columbia University, M.A., 1964. *Home:* 66 Grove Hill Ave., Newton, Mass. 02160. *Office:* Charles E. Brown Junior High School, Newton, Mass.

CAREER: Teacher of English at private schools in New York City, 1964-68; Meadowbrook Junior High School, Newton, Mass., English teacher, beginning 1969; currently teacher of English at Charles E. Brown Junior High School, Newton, Mass. *Awards, honors:* Artists Foundation fellow, 1979; first prize, International Sri Chinmoy Poetry Awards, 1982, for "Kite."

WRITINGS—Poetry: *Of Earth,* William Bauham, 1974; *Invisibilities,* Apple-Wood, 1977; *Triptych,* Apple-Wood, 1979; *From Dream, from Circumstance,* Apple-Wood, 1983. Work represented in many anthologies, including *New American Poetry,* edited by Richard Monaco, McGraw, 1973. Contributor to periodicals, including *Nation, Prairie Schooner,* and *Massachusetts Review*.

WORK IN PROGRESS: Additional poetry.

SIDELIGHTS: "In my poems," writes Douglas Worth, "I try to express as deeply and as clearly as I can my experience of life and the world around me: the wonders and beauties, the tensions and tragedies, the fears, joys, loves and hopes; most of all, perhaps, the rich combination I feel of all these facets. In particular, I find important and vital the connection between the human species and the rest of nature and often emphasize in my poems that we are a part of the natural world—Nature contemplating itself. I've always drawn this connection in my poems, but I see it more and more as a crucial one to make as human self-centeredness and technology become increasing threats to the natural environment which created us and continues to sustain us, despite our history of war, pollution, greed, and now, of course, the threat of nuclear holocaust.

"Many of my . . . poems have stressed the natural beauties of the world that are still blossoming all around us, . . . that we are intimately a part of, and that may be tragically destroyed by us. I say *may* be because, as 'Nature at its most complex,' we are responsible and have the power to decide whether we will enhance the beauties of our environment through civilization, or end up destroying them as well as ourselves."

* * *

WORTMAN, Richard 1938-

PERSONAL: Born March 24, 1938, in New York, N.Y.; son of Joseph (an attorney) and Ruth (Nacht) Wortman; married Marlene Stein (a historian), June 14, 1960; children: Leonie. *Education:* Cornell University, B.A., 1958; University of Chicago, M.A., 1960, Ph.D., 1964. *Home:* 18 Cameron Ct., Princeton, N.J. 08540. *Office:* Department of History, Princeton University, Princeton, N.J. 08544.

CAREER: University of Chicago, Chicago, Ill., instructor, 1963-64, assistant professor, 1964-69, associate professor, 1969-76, professor of history, 1976-77; Princeton University, Princeton, N.J., professor of history, 1977—. Conducted research in the Soviet Union, 1967-68, 1971; research associate, Institute for Psycho-Social Studies, 1974-75. *Member:* American Association for the Advancement of Slavic Studies, American Association of University Professors, Mid-Atlantic Slavic Association (president, 1982-83). *Awards, honors:* Guggenheim fellow, 1981-82.

WRITINGS: The Crisis of Russian Populism, Cambridge University Press, 1967; *The Development of a Russian Legal Consciousness,* University of Chicago Press, 1976. Contributor to *Slavic Review, Midway,* and *Canadian-American Slavic Studies*.

WORK IN PROGRESS: Research on the symbolism and psychology of Russian autocracy.

SIDELIGHTS: In addition to his work on Russian autocracy, Richard Wortman has a general interest in the use of psychology in history, particularly in the study of the culture and thought of the Russian intelligentsia.

* * *

WREN, M. K.
See RENFROE, Martha Kay

* * *

WRIGHT, Theodore P(aul), Jr. 1926-

PERSONAL: Born April 12, 1926, in Port Washington, N.Y.; son of Theodore Paul (an aeronautical engineer) and Margaret (McCarl) Wright; married Susan J. Standfast (a physician), February 18, 1967; children: Henry Sewall, Margaret Standfast, Catherine Berrian. *Education:* Swarthmore College, B.A. (with high honors), 1949; Yale University, M.A., 1951, Ph.D., 1957. *Politics:* Conservative Democrat. *Religion:* Unitarian.

Office: Graduate School of Public Affairs, State University of New York at Albany, Albany, N.Y. 12222.

CAREER: U.S. Department of Defense, research analyst, 1952-53; Bates College, Lewiston, Me., 1955-65, began as instructor, became associate professor of government; State University of New York at Albany, Graduate School of Public Affairs, associate professor, 1965-1972, professor of political science, 1971—. *Military service:* U.S. Navy, 1944-46. *Member:* American Political Science Association, Association for Asian Studies, American Association of University Professors, Phi Beta Kappa.

AWARDS, HONORS: Carnegie grant in Indian civilization, University of Chicago, 1961-62; Fulbright senior research grant for India, 1963-64; National Defense Foreign Language fellow, University of California, summer, 1967; American Institute of Indian Studies fellow, 1969-70; American Council of Learned Societies South Asia fellow, 1974-75.

WRITINGS: American Support of Free Elections Abroad, Public Affairs, 1964; (contributor) D. E. Smith, editor, *South Asian Politics and Religion,* Princeton University Press, 1966.

Contributor: S. P. Varma and Iqbal Narain, editors, *Fourth General Election in India,* Orient Longmans, 1970; Helen Ullrich, editor, *Competition and Modernization in South Asia,* Abhinav, 1975; Dietmar Rothormund, editor, *Islam in Southern Asia,* Franz Steiner Verlag, 1975; Imtiaz Ahmed, editor, *Family, Kinship, and Marriage among the Muslims,* Manohar, 1976; G. R. Gupta, editor, *Main Currents in Indian Sociology,* Volume III, Carolina Academic Press, 1978; R. V. Weakes, editor, *Ethnographic Survey of the Muslim World,* Greenwood Press, 1978; J. Ross and A. B. Cottrell, editors, *Mobilization of Collective Identity,* University Press of America, 1980. Contributor of articles and reviews to political science journals in the United States and India.

WORK IN PROGRESS: A book on the politics of the Muslim minority in India since independence.

SIDELIGHTS: Theodore P. Wright, Jr. traveled in Europe in 1948, 1951, 1953, and 1974-75; the Middle East in 1958; India in 1961, 1963-64, 1969-70, 1977, and 1979; Southeast Asia in 1961, and the Soviet Union in 1964 and 1969. He has a reading knowledge of French.

* * *

WRYDE, Dogear
See GOREY, Edward (St. John)

* * *

WYLIE, Laurie
See MATTHEWS, Patricia (Anne)

Y

YANEY, Joseph P(aul) 1939-

PERSONAL: Born May 11, 1939, in Scranton, Pa.; son of Alexander and Mary Yaney; married May 30, 1964; wife's name Barbara Ann (a designer); children: Paul, Monica. *Education:* University of Michigan, M.B.A., 1964, J.D., 1964, Ph.D., 1969. *Home:* 3106 42nd St., Lubbock, Tex. 79413. *Office:* College of Business, Texas Tech University, Lubbock, Tex. 79409.

CAREER: University of Michigan, Ann Arbor, program director, 1966-69; Ohio State University, Columbus, associate professor of business, 1969-76; Pennsylvania State University, Middletown, professor of business administration and director of department, 1976-79; Texas Tech University, Lubbock, professor of business administration in College of Business and adjunct professor in School of Medicine, 1979—. Admitted to Bar of State of Michigan. *Military service:* U.S. Army, 1964-66; became captain. *Member:* Academy of Management, Industrial Relations Research Association (president of Ohio chapter, 1972), National Society for Performance and Instruction (treasurer, 1981-83).

WRITINGS: Managing Instructional Progress Effort, University of Michigan Press, 1967; *Labor Relations,* Addison-Wesley, 1968; *Personnel Management,* C. E. Merrill, 1975; (with Stern) *Cases in Labor Law,* Grid Publishing, 1976; *Management by Objectives,* DMD Publishers, 1982.

WORK IN PROGRESS: Research on family systems.

* * *

YARBRO, Chelsea Quinn 1942-

PERSONAL: Born September 15, 1942, in Berkeley, Calif.; daughter of Clarence Elmer (a cartographer) and Lillian (an artist; maiden name, Chatfield) Erickson; married Donald Paul Simpson (an artist and inventor), November 3, 1969 (divorced January, 1982). *Education:* Attended San Francisco State College (now University), 1960-63. *Politics:* Democrat. *Religion:* Atheist. *Address:* c/o Kirby McCauley Ltd., 425 Park Ave. S., New York, N.Y. 10016.

CAREER: C. E. Erickson & Associates, Oakland, Calif., cartographer, 1963-70; program director for Sampo Productions, 1970-71, 1973; Magic Cellar, San Francisco, Calif., tarot reader, 1974—. Voice teacher and composer. Counselor of mentally disturbed children, 1963-64. *Member:* Science Fiction Writers of America (secretary, 1970-72), Mystery Writers of America. *Awards, honors:* Mystery Writers of America scroll, 1973, for "The Ghosts at Iron River."

WRITINGS: (Editor with Thomas N. Scortia and contributor) *Two Views of Wonder* (science fiction anthology), Ballantine, 1973; *Ogilvie, Tallant and Moon,* Putnam, 1976; *Time of the Fourth Horseman,* Doubleday, 1976; *Cautionary Tales* (short stories), Doubleday, 1978; *False Dawn,* Doubleday, 1978; *Messages from Michael on the Nature of the Evolution of the Human Soul* (nonfiction), Playboy Press, 1979; *Music When Sweet Voices Die,* Putnam, 1979; *Ariosto,* Pocket Books, 1980; *Dead and Buried* (novelization of screenplay by Ronald Shusett and Dan O'Bannon), Warner Books, 1980; *Sins of Omission,* Signet, 1980; *A Taste of Wine,* Pocket Books, 1982; *The Godforsaken,* Warner Books, 1983; *Hyacinths to Feed Your Soul,* Doubleday, 1983; *Nomads,* Bantam, 1983. Author, under undisclosed pseudonym, of *The Making of Australia #5,* Richard Gallen, 1983.

"Saint-Germain" series; published by St. Martin's, except as indicated: *Hotel Transylvania* (Literary Guild and Science Fiction Book Club alternate selection), 1978; *The Palace,* 1979; *Blood Games: A Novel of Historical Horror,* 1980; *Path of the Eclipse,* 1981; *Tempting Fate,* 1982; *The Saint-Germain Chronicles* (short stories), Pocket Books, 1983.

Contributor: David Gerrold, editor, *Generation,* Dell, 1972; Robert Hoskins, editor, *Infinity 3,* Lancer, 1972; Scortia, editor, *Strange Bedfellows,* Random House, 1972; Dean Dickensheet, editor, *Men and Malice,* Doubleday, 1973; Carl Mason, editor, *Anthropology through Science Fiction,* St. Martin's, 1974; Roger Elwood, editor, *Vampires, Werewolves, and Other Monsters,* Curtis, 1974; George Zebrowski, editor, *Tomorrow Today,* Unity Press, 1975; Sandra Ley, editor, *Beyond Time,* Pocket Books, 1976; Zebrowski and Jack Dann, editors, *Faster Than Light,* Harper, 1976; Cedric Clute and Nicholas Lewin, editors, *Sleight of Crime,* Regnery, 1977; Bill Pronzini and Barry Malzberg, editors, *Dark Sins, Dark Dreams,* Doubleday, 1978; Alice Laurance, editor, *Cassandra Rising,* Doubleday, 1978; Charles L. Grant, editor, *Nightmares,* Playboy Paperbacks, 1979; Hoskins, editor, *Against Tomorrow,* Fawcett, 1979.

Grant, editor, *Shadows 3,* Doubleday, 1980; Grant, editor, *Horrors,* Playboy Paperbacks, 1981; Grant, editor, *Shadows 4,* Doubleday, 1981; Pronzini, editor, *Ghoul!,* Arbor House, 1982; Grant, editor, *Shadows 5,* Doubleday, 1982; Grant, editor, *The Everest House Gallery of Horror,* Everest House, 1983; Grant, editor, *Fears,* Playboy Paperbacks, 1983.

Author of "The Little-Girl Dragon of Alabaster-on-Fenwick" (satiric fairy tale play), first produced in San Francisco, Calif. at the St. Francis Hotel, July, 1973. Composer of musical works, including "Stabat Mater," "Sayre Cycle," "Alpha and Omega," "Cinque Ritratti," and "Nightpiece for Chamber Orchestra."

SIDELIGHTS: "I've written since I've known how to read," Chelsea Quinn Yarbro told *CA*. "I'm not trying to do anything other than entertain my reader. 'Entertain' is not a dirty word, by the way. Much of my work is quite grim, but that should not be taken as an indication that I am a grim person. Please do not confuse me with my work; it is not me and I am not it. I dislike being categorized as anything beyond writer. For me, clarity of writing is essential. The reader should not be aware of how the words are on the page, or with what pyrotechnics the language is thrown around. Language is not an end in itself, but a means, a channel that a writer must, by the nature of the art, use. Beyond that, the words should not get in the way of the reader building the story in his or her head.

"I have a strong dedication to writing, both words and music, but I don't want to limit it by being too rigorous in my view of my career. I want to branch out in new directions. I want to do historical novels and more suspense and science fiction. How this will work out, I don't know. My music is even more uncertain, though some of this comes from the problem of being a woman composer of serious music. Unfortunately the world of music is still too strongly male-oriented. Finding conductors and groups willing to do my compositions has proved to be difficult, but who knows? Things may improve, but I am not holding my breath."

Susan M. Shwartz writes in the *Washington Post Book World* that Yarbro's "Saint-Germain" series "violates every canon of classic 1950s [science fiction] by breaking taboos and combining fantasy, science, horror, and romance genres into new forms that may appall purists but that are as exciting to read as they are difficult to categorize." *Hotel Transylvania,* says F. Paul Wilson in *Science Fiction Review,* "may be a historical-gothic-horror-love story, but not because the author wanted to try to cash in on multiple markets. All the elements fit. . . . [It is] a tight, well-crafted novel." Shwartz considers *Tempting Fate* "a triumph" and praises the characterization: "Saint-Germain, [the Renaissance man-alchemist who also happens to be a vampire,] is immensely appealing; Madeleine, the eighteenth-century aristocrat turned vampire-archeologist, totally charming. The rest of the characters . . . are well drawn. . . . [A] kind of toughness combined with passion gives Yarbro's characters almost tragic dignity."

BIOGRAPHICAL/CRITICAL SOURCES: Magazine of Fantasy and Science Fiction, January, 1979; *Science Fiction Review,* January-February, 1979; *Washington Post Book World,* March 28, 1982.

* * *

YODER, Glee 1916-

PERSONAL: Born September 15, 1916, in Elkhart, Iowa; daughter of Earl M. (a salesman) and Mary D. (Mathis) Gough-nour; married R. Gordon Yoder (a paralegal), August 20, 1939; children: Marcia (Mrs. Dennis Emmert). *Education:* McPherson College, A.B. (cum laude), 1938. *Religion:* Church of the Brethren. *Home:* 6406 East 15th St., Wichita, Kan. 67206. *Office:* 400 North Woodlawn, Suite 204, Wichita, Kan. 67208.

CAREER: Elementary school teacher in Kansas, 1938-39; survey interviewer for Young & Rubicam, Inc., in Nampa, Idaho, 1943, and McPherson, Kan., 1953; Church of the Brethren, McPherson, children's director for Western region, 1948-58, administrative assistant for Western region, 1954-64, administrative assistant for district of Kansas, 1964-67, curriculum counselor for Midwest region, 1968-78; Henry D. Edwards (attorney), Wichita, Kan., secretary, 1979—. Teacher of Christian education at McPherson College, 1951-52 and 1953-54; church representative at Communications for Laity Conference, University of Denver, 1969, and Third Theological Conference, Bethany Theological Seminary, 1969. Church of the Brethren, Elgin, Ill., member of General Board, 1976-79, vice-chairman of pension board and of general services commission and member of investment committee. Speaker and lecturer. *Member:* National League of Pen Women, Kansas Authors Club, Knife and Fork Club of Wichita (executive secretary, 1979—). *Awards, honors:* Alumni citation of merit, McPherson College, 1978.

WRITINGS: The Church and Infants and Toddlers, Brethren Press, in cooperation with Christian Board of Publication and Warner Press, 1966; *Take It from Here: Suggestions for Creative Activities,* Judson Press, 1973; *Take It from Here, Series Two: Suggestions for Creative Activities,* Judson Press, 1975; *The Unfolding World,* Brethren Press, 1976; *Passing on the Gift: The Story of Dan West* (biography), Brethren Press, 1978.

Church school curriculum courses; published by Warner Press, except as indicated: *Who Is God?,* American Baptist Board of Education and Publication, 1969; *All That Is within Me,* Brethren Press, 1970; *Handle with Care,* Judson Press, 1970; *The Christian Faces Life,* 1970; *The Gospel of Luke,* Christian Board of Publication, 1971; *A World-Wide Fellowship,* 1972; *Why Not Peace?,* Brethren Press, 1972; *Foundations for Life,* 1973, revised edition, 1976; *Christian Sign Language,* 1974, revised edition, 1979; *World of Symbols,* 1975, revised edition, 1978; *To Be Like Jesus,* 1975; *Good News, Everybody,* 1977; *The Lord Is King,* Evangel Press, 1977, revised edition, 1983; *The Ten Commandments,* 1977; *Older Children: A Manual for Christian Education,* Brethren Press, 1977; *Design for Centers for Developing Christian Leadership,* 1978.

Also author of pamphlets published by Brethren Press. Columnist for *Messenger,* 1971-72; contributor to periodicals, including *Gospel Messenger, Leader, Horizons, International Journal of Religious Education, Baptist Leader, Conquest, Friends, Vital Christianity, Bethany Guide, With, Messenger, Reach, Church Advocate,* and *Chorister's Guild.*

WORK IN PROGRESS: A biography.

SIDELIGHTS: Glee Yoder told *CA* that research and the discipline of writing "keep one alert to the world and its people. Ideas are challenged in the process. . . . In 1966 and 1967, I reviewed almost 1,000 books for the Church of the Brethren for their Library of Resources, a punch-card organization of materials for courses of independent study. The books were from all disciplines—history, psychology, education, theology, sociology, etc. I had a great time arguing with, agreeing with, or even discounting some of the ideas of the various authors. It was a most broadening, gratifying, and enjoyable experience!''

AVOCATIONAL INTERESTS: Travel (has been to forty-nine states and over twenty-five countries), bicycling (in six years has ridden over 7,800 miles).

* * *

YOUNG, David P(ollock) 1936-

PERSONAL: Born December 14, 1936, in Davenport, Iowa; son of Cecil T. (a businessman) and Mary (Pollock) Young; married Chloe Hamilton (a museum curator), June 17, 1963; children: Newell Hamilton, Margaret Helen. *Education:* Carleton College, A.B., 1958; Yale University, M.A., 1959, Ph.D., 1965. *Home:* 220 Shipherd Circle, Oberlin, Ohio 44074. *Office:* Department of English, Rice Hall, Oberlin College, Oberlin, Ohio 44074.

CAREER: Oberlin College, Oberlin, Ohio, instructor, 1961-65, assistant professor, 1965-69, associate professor, 1969-73, professor of English, 1973—. *Member:* Modern Language Association of America, American Association of University Professors. *Awards, honors:* Tane Prize for poetry, *Massachusetts Review,* 1965; National Endowment for the Humanities fellow in England, 1967-68; U.S. Award, International Poetry Forum, 1968; Guggenheim fellow, 1978-79; National Endowment for the Arts fellow, 1981-82.

WRITINGS: Something of Great Constancy: The Art of ''A Midsummer Night's Dream,'' Yale University Press, 1966; (editor) *Twentieth-Century Interpretations of ''Henry IV, Part 2,''* Prentice-Hall, 1968; *Sweating Out the Winter* (poetry), University of Pittsburgh Press, 1969; (contributor) *The Major Young Poets,* World Publishing, 1971; (contributor) *Just What the Country Needs: Another Poetry Anthology,* Wadsworth, 1971; *The Heart's Forest: Shakespeare's Pastoral Plays,* Yale University Press, 1972; *Boxcars* (poetry), Ecco Press, 1972; *Work Lights* (prose poems), Cleveland State University Press, 1977; *The Names of a Hare in English* (poetry), University of Pittsburgh Press, 1979; (editor with Stuart Friebert) *A Field Guide to Contemporary Poetry and Poetics,* Longman, 1980; (editor with Friebert and Richard Zipser) *Contemporary East German Poetry: A Special Issue of ''Field,''* Oberlin College, 1980; (editor with Friebert) *Longman's Anthology of Poetry,* Longman, 1982.

Translator: Rainer M. Rilke, *Duino Elegies,* Barn Dream Press, 1975; *Four Tiang Poets,* Field, Oberlin College, 1980; (with Friebert and Walker) *Valuable Nail: Selected Poems of Guenter Eich,* Field, Oberlin College, 1981; Miroslav Holub, *Interferon; or, On Theater,* Field, Oberlin College, 1982.

Contributor to *Criticism* and other periodicals. Editor, *Field: Contemporary Poetry and Poetics,* 1969—.

WORK IN PROGRESS: A new collection of poems; a study of Yeats and Stevens; an anthology of ''magical realist fiction.''

Z

ZABIH, Sepehr 1925-

PERSONAL: Born 1925, in Tehran, Persia (now Iran); naturalized American citizen; married Joan Werner (a psychiatric social worker), June 14, 1959; children: Ramin, Leyla. *Education:* London School of Journalism, diploma, 1954; University of California, B.A., 1957, M.A., 1958, Ph.D., 1963. *Office:* Department of Government, St. Mary's College of California, Moraga, Calif. 94575.

CAREER: Writer in western Europe and the Middle East for Iranian publications, 1949-51; correspondent in Iran for *Times* and *Daily Mail,* both London, England, 1950-53; St. Mary's College of California, Moraga, assistant professor of government, 1963-64; Oberlin College, Oberlin, Ohio, assistant professor of government, 1964-65; St. Mary's College of California, assistant professor, 1965-68, associate professor of government, 1968—. University of California, Berkeley, research fellow, Department of Political Science, 1964—, lecturer in Extension Division, 1966—, research scholar, Institute of International Studies, 1973—. Summer instructor or lecturer at U.S. Army Language School, 1958, 1959, and University of Colorado, 1963; guest scholar, Brookings Institution, Washington, D.C., 1969; visiting associate professor, University of Texas at Austin, 1973. *Member:* American Political Science Association, Middle East Studies Association of North America, Phi Beta Kappa. *Awards, honors:* Senior research fellow at Institute for International Studies, Iran, 1974.

WRITINGS: The Communist Movement in Iran, University of California Press, 1966; (with Chubin Shahram) *The Foreign Relations of Iran: A Small State in a Zone of Great-Power Conflict,* University of California Press, 1975; *Iran's Revolutionary Upheaval,* Alchemy Books, 1979; *The Mussadegh Era,* Lakeview Press, 1982; *Iran since the Revolution,* Johns Hopkins University Press, 1982. Translator into Persian of William Gallagher's *Marxism and the Working Class,* 1945, and Nikolai Lenin's *On Youth,* 1946, both published in Tehran.

* * *

ZAKIA, Richard D(onald) 1925-

PERSONAL: Born December 12, 1925, in Rochester, N.Y.; son of Fuad M. (a tailor) and Rose E. (Karam) Zakia; married Lois Ann Arlidge (a registered nurse and educator), June 21, 1958; children: Renee Arlidge. *Education:* Attended University of Chicago, 1944; Rochester Institute of Technology, B.S., 1956; University of Rochester, Ed.D., 1960. *Politics:* Independent. *Religion:* Roman Catholic. *Home:* 44 Horseshoe Lane N., Henrietta, N.Y. 14467. *Office:* Department of Communications, Rochester Institute of Technology, 1 Lomb Dr., Rochester, N.Y. 14623.

CAREER: Eastman Kodak, Rochester, N.Y., photographic engineer, 1956-58; Rochester Institute of Technology, Rochester, N.Y., assistant professor, 1961-65, associate professor, 1965-69, professor of photography, 1969—, director of instructional development, 1969-75, chairman of fine art photography department and graduate program, 1976—. Member of board of directors of Photographic Sciences Corp., 1970-78. Consultant to Department of Defense, 1973-76. *Military service:* U.S. Navy, 1944-46, 1950-52. *Member:* International Visual Literacy Association, International Visual Sociology Association, International Photo/Therapy Association, International Imagery Association, College Art Association, Friends of Photography, Society for Photographic Education.

WRITINGS: (With Hollis Todd) *Photographic Sensitometry,* Morgan & Morgan, 1967; (with Todd) *One Thousand and One Experiments in Photography,* Morgan & Morgan, 1969; (with John J. Dowdell III) *Zone Systemizer,* Morgan & Morgan, 1973; (with Todd) *Color Primer I and II,* Morgan & Morgan, 1974; *Perception and Photography,* Prentice-Hall, 1975; (with Minor White and Peter Lorenz) *Zone System Manual,* Morgan & Morgan, 1976; (with Leslie Stroebel and Todd) *Visual Concepts for Photographers,* Butterworth, 1980; *Perceptual Quotes for Photographers,* Light Impressions, 1980.

WORK IN PROGRESS: Photographic Materials and Processes, with Stroebel, John Compton, and Ira Current; contributing to *Coping with a Visual World: The Search for Visual Literacy,* edited by Roberts A. Braden.

SIDELIGHTS: Richard D. Zakia told *CA:* "My earlier writings dealt with some of the technical aspects of photography. Recent writing attempts to integrate information from other disciplines and relate it directly to the understanding of photographs in particular and to pictures in general. Each discipline has its own vocabulary in dealing with philosophical issues such as *truth, reality,* and *values,* and the vocabulary used has become a tower of Babel. My interest is to build conceptual linkages among various disciplines by utilizing pictures. We have learned and communicated much by using the written word; we can extend this significantly if we learn how to read pictures. Are there connections to be made between linguistic terms and pictures? What is the visual equivalent of linguistic terms such as metaphor, metonomy, and synocdoche? Does the word onomatopoeia have a visual equivalent?

"In the late 1800's Rudyard Kipling wrote, 'There aren't twelve hundred people in the world who understand pictures. The others pretend and don't care.' "

* * *

ZAWADSKY, Patience 1927-
(Patience Hartman; Becky Lynne, a pseudonym)

PERSONAL: Surname is pronounced Za-*wad*-sky; born March 30, 1927, in Trenton, N.J.; daughter of William C. and Mabel (Leicht) Hartman; married John P. Zawadsky (chairman of philosophy department at University of Wisconsin—Stevens Point), September 8, 1948; children: John, Paul, Rebecca, Elizabeth. *Education:* Douglass College, Rutgers University, B.A., 1948. *Politics:* Democrat. *Religion:* Catholic. *Home:* 3900 Jordan Lane, Stevens Point, Wis. 54481.

CAREER: WTNJ, Trenton, N.J., writer, producer, and actor for radio series, "Teen-Age," 1943-44; Harvard University, Cambridge, Mass., research assistant and secretary, 1949-51; self-employed editor and researcher, Cambridge, 1951-54; Kilmer Job Corps, Edison, N.J., writing consultant, 1966; University of Wisconsin—Stevens Point, lecturer in English, 1967-72, 1980—. Free-lance writer for magazines. President of Children's Art Program, Stevens Point, 1980-81. *Member:* American Association of University Women, Wisconsin Children's Theatre Association (vice-president, 1979-80), Phi Beta Kappa. *Awards, honors:* Author's Award, New Jersey Association of English Teachers, 1968, for *The Mystery of the Old Musket;* plays selected for merit by Wisconsin Children's Theatre Association, 1976-78, 1980.

WRITINGS: (Co-author) *Datebook of Popularity,* Prentice-Hall, 1960; (co-author) *Are These the Wonderful Years?,* Abbey Press, 1965; *The Mystery of the Old Musket* (juvenile), Putnam, 1968; *Welcome to Longfellow,* Transition, 1969; *Stand-In for Murder,* Transition, 1969; *Demon of Raven's Cliff,* Belmont-Tower, 1971; *The Man in the Long Black Cape,* Scholastic Book Services, 1972; *How Much Is That in Rubles?,* University of Wisconsin—Stevens Point, 1973; *From Peacehaven to Peace Haven,* University of Wisconsin—Stevens Point, 1974.

Musicals: "Heavens to Bacchus," first produced at Douglass College, Rutgers University, 1945; "Navy Blues," first produced at Douglass College, Rutgers University, 1946; "Rest Upon the Wind," first produced at Douglass College, Rutgers University, 1948; "Hey, Mr. Time," first produced by University of Florida Sandspurs, 1949.

Juvenile musicals: "Goldilocks and the Three Bears: A Moral Musical," 1973; "The Princess and the Frog," 1974; "The Bunny with the Lopsided Ear," 1975; "The Twelve Dancing Princesses," 1976; "Kitty Cat Blue," 1977; *The Toys in the Haunted Castle* (produced, 1977), I. E. Clark, 1979; "The All New Jack," 1979; "Captain Meano and the Magic Song," 1979; "From Poland with Love," 1980; "The New Cinderella," 1981; "The Little Troll Who Wasn't," 1981; "Sleeping Beauty," 1982; "The Firebird (Chaybarashka)," 1982.

Also author of radio play, "Christmas Fantasy," 1944. Contributor, under pseudonym Becky Lynne, of about forty articles and stories to *Teen;* contributor to *Datebook* under maiden name, Patience Hartman; also contributor to ten other teen and juvenile magazines. In the adult field, has published verse in *Saturday Evening Post, Life Today, Empire, Soviet Life,* and *Laugh Book,* and articles in numerous periodicals, including *Coronet, Discovery, Personal Romances, Chatelaine, Family Digest, Ford Times,* and *Ladies' Home Journal.*

WORK IN PROGRESS: A suspense novel, *Moscow Days and Leningrad Nights.*

SIDELIGHTS: "After decades of writing books and articles for money," writes Patience Zawadsky, "I felt I had paid my dues. I returned to my first love, musical comedy—but this time, musical comedy for children. I found there is little or no money in children's theater. Those who act in it are looked down upon by other actors; those who write for it are looked down upon by other playwrights. But the children's laughter and applause, and sometimes tears, are more of a reward than any other form of writing has to offer. What a shame that America has so little regard, on television and in the theaters, for the enrichment of its children."

* * *

ZETFORD, Tully
See BULMER, (Henry) Kenneth

* * *

ZINK, Lubor Jan 1920-

PERSONAL: Born September 20, 1920, in Klapy, Czechoslovakia; son of Vilem (a teacher) and Bozena (Wohl) Zink; married Zora Nechvile (a librarian), April 1, 1942; children: Alec Guy. *Education:* Attended Prague University, 1937-39, 1945-48. *Politics:* Progressive Conservative. *Religion:* Protestant. *Home:* 47 Queensline Drive, Ottawa, Ontario, Canada K2H 7J3. *Office:* Parliamentary Press Gallery, House of Commons, Ottawa, Ontario, Canada.

CAREER: Czechoslovak Foreign Office, Prague, press officer, 1945-48; British Broadcasting Corp., Foreign Service, Reading, England, monitor and script writer, 1948-58; *Brandon Sun,* Brandon, Manitoba, editor of editorial page, 1958-62; *Toronto Telegram,* Toronto, Ontario, author of daily syndicated political column "Comment," 1962-71; Toronto Sun Syndicate, Toronto, author of syndicated political and economic column "Counterpoint," 1971—. Co-founder of International Union of Students and World Youth Organization, London, 1941-45; Progressive Conservative candidate for Canadian Parliament from Parkdale Riding, 1972 and 1974. Has covered notable news assignments in Europe and the Far East, including Vietnam. *Military service:* British Army, Czechoslovak Armor Brigade, 1940-45; became first lieutenant; received Military Cross, Medal for Bravery, and Medal of Merit. *Awards, honors:* Canadian National Newspaper Award, 1961, for editorial writings in *Brandon Sun;* Bowater Award for Journalism, 1962, for a series of articles titled "The Unfinished Revolution."

WRITINGS—In English: *The Uprooted* (novel), Longmans, Green, 1962; *Under the Mushroom Cloud* (articles previously published in *Brandon Sun*), Brandon Sun, 1962; *Trudeaucracy* (excerpts from columns in *Toronto Telegram* and *Toronto Sun*), Toronto Sun, 1972; *Viva Chairman Pierre* (excerpts from column in *Toronto Sun*), Griffin House (Toronto), 1977; *What Price Freedom?,* Griffin House, 1981. Contributor to periodicals, including *National Review.*

In Czech; poetry, except as indicated: *Dva Roky,* National Union of Czechoslovak Students (London), 1941; *Zhavy Dech,* National Union of Czechoslovak Students, 1942; *17 Listopad* (nonfiction; title means "November 17"), International Union of Students, 1942; *Destiva Noc,* Hradek, 1947. Also author of *Psano na Lafetu,* 1941, and of novels *Cestou Domu* (title means "On the Way Home"), 1948, and *Unor* (title means 'February").

SIDELIGHTS: Lubor Jan Zink has a "consuming concern for survival of responsible freedom," he told *CA,* because he was "deeply influenced" by the Nazi and Communist takeovers of his native Czechoslovakia. A Prague University student at the time of Hitler's invasion, he was forced to flee his homeland in 1939 because of his anti-Nazi activities. Escaping to England, he joined the Czech fighting forces there and served until the war's end. Three years after returning to Czechoslovakia, he was again forced to flee the country when his name appeared on Stalin's enemies-of-the-people list.

Zink says he uses his newspaper column as a "fighting weapon against all forms of totalitarianism," and Peter Worthington, editor-in-chief of the *Toronto Sun,* believes Zink has been particularly effective in writing about Canada under Pierre Trudeau. In the foreword to *Viva Chairman Pierre,* Worthington writes: "Ever since Trudeau first appeared on the Ottawa scene, Zink has been uneasy. He spotted tendencies that his colleagues and other Canadians took years to identify. And he has been a sort of macabre Boswell to Trudeau's years in power—ever recording, analyzing, probing, identifying. . . . In future generations, when historians and social scientists seek to fathom what happened to Canada under Trudeau, Zink's writings will be essential research material. No other Canadian journalist possesses his unique qualifications and insight."

BIOGRAPHICAL/CRITICAL SOURCES: Lubor Jan Zink, *Viva Chairman Pierre,* Griffin House, 1977.

* * *

ZIPES, Jack (David) 1937-

PERSONAL: Born June 7, 1937, in New York, N.Y.; son of Phillip P. (an investor) and Celia (Rifkin) Zipes. *Education:* Dartmouth College, B.A., 1959; Columbia University, M.A., 1960, Ph.D., 1965; graduate study at University of Munich, 1962, and University of Tuebingen, 1963. *Home:* 2847 North Shepard Ave., Milwaukee, Wis. 53211. *Office:* Department of German, University of Wisconsin—Milwaukee, Milwaukee, Wis. 53201.

CAREER: University of Munich, Amerika-Institut, Munich, Germany, instructor in American literature, 1966-67; New York University, New York, N.Y., assistant professor of German, 1967-72; University of Wisconsin—Milwaukee, associate professor of German, 1972-78, professor of German and comparative literature, 1978—. Visiting professor at Paedagogische Hochschule, Berlin, 1978-79; Fulbright professor at University of Frankfurt, 1981-82. *Member:* International Association of Theatre for Children and Young People, International Board on Books for Young People, Modern Language Association of America, American Association of Teachers of German, Children's Literature Association, Europaeische Maerchengesellschaft.

WRITINGS: The Great Refusal: Studies of the Romantic Hero in German and American Literature, Athenaeum, 1970; (translator and author of introduction) Hans Mayer, *Steppenwolf and Everyman,* Crowell, 1971; (with Michael Anderson, Jacques Guicharnaud, and Kristin Morrison) *Crowell's Handbook of Contemporary Drama,* Crowell, 1971; (contributor) Francelia Butler, editor, *Children's Literature: The Great Excluded,* Volumes II and V, Temple University Press, 1973; (editor and author of introduction) Marianne Thalmann, *Romantik in Kritischer Perspektive* (title means "Romanticism in Critical Perspective"), Lothar-Stiehm Verlag, 1976; (editor and translator) *Political Plays for Children,* Telos, 1976; (translator) Mayer, *Richard Wagner in Bayreuth,* Rizzoli, 1976; *Breaking the Magic Spell: Radical Theories of Folk and Fairy Tales,* University of Texas Press, 1979.

Rotkaeppchens Lust und Leid, Eugen Diederichs Verlag, 1982; *The Trials and Tribulations of Little Red Riding Hood,* J. F. Bergin, 1983; (editor and author of introduction), Carl Ewald, *Die Libelle und die Seerose, Maerchen,* Fischer Verlag, 1983; (with Dieter Richter and Bernd Dolle) *Es war—Es wird einmal: Soziale Maerchen aus der Weimarer Republik,* Peter Weismann Verlag, 1983; *Fairy Tales and the Art of Subversion: The Classical Genre for Children and the Process of Civilization,* Wildman Press, 1983. Contributor to *Kindlers Literatur-Lexicon* and *Crowell's Encyclopedia of World Drama.* Contributor of stories, articles, translations, and reviews to journals in the United States and Germany. Co-editor, *New German Critique,* 1973—; contributing editor, *Theater,* 1978—; advisory editor, *Lion and the Unicorn,* 1978—.

WORK IN PROGRESS: A book on "classical children's literature" and a translation "of Ernst Bloch's aesthetical writings."

SIDELIGHTS: "Two major considerations," writes Jack Zipes, "have influenced my critical writings and translations: the need to develop a radical methodology based on critical theory and innovative Marxism and the necessity to study popular forms of culture such as children's theater, film, fairy tales, and best-sellers. As critic and writer I seek to grasp the historical and social forces which form the basis of our everyday experience. If it is true that our experience is preconditioned and framed for us, then writing must be a creative and provocative act, which suggests possibilities for alternative modes of thinking and living."

* * *

ZUMWALT, Eva 1936-

PERSONAL: Born June 8, 1936, in Eunice, N.M.; daughter of Ellis Otto (an oil lease foreman) and Elva (a poet; maiden name, Davidson) Beaty; married Ted L. Zumwalt (a hospital employee), February 21, 1954; children: Karyn Lisa (Mrs. Alan Charles Porter), Kathy Eve. *Education:* Attended high school in Artesia, N.M. *Residence:* Nogal, N.M. 88341. *Agent:* Natalie Carlton, Singer Communications, Inc., 3164 Tyler, Anaheim, Calif. 92801.

CAREER: Free-lance writer.

WRITINGS—Gothic mysteries, except as indicated: *Masquerade of Evil,* Ace Books, 1975; *Briarlea,* Ace Books, 1976; *Sun Dust* (young adult western), McKay, 1976; *The Yearning Years,* Major Books, 1978; *Mansion of Dark Mists,* Tower, 1981; *The Unforgiving,* Tower, 1982; *Love's Sweet Charity* (historical romance), Doubleday, 1982; *The Elusive Heart* (historical romance), Doubleday, 1983. Contributor to *Progressive Farmer.*

WORK IN PROGRESS: The Bloody Sands, a western; *Alexandra's Carousel,* a light historical romance; an untitled romance novel; a saga set in New Mexico's plains, tentatively entitled *Voices in the Wind.*

SIDELIGHTS: Eva Zumwalt writes: "My background has been small town and country. My husband is a fine horseman and cowboy. With him I have ridden a great deal over some of this state's most beautiful country. I am a confirmed nature-lover. I believe in solitude as a healer of troubled spirits, and I value privacy. The social life tempts me not at all. Happiness for me has always been found not among crowds but with my few most beloved people. With no desire to preach, reform or make particular statements, social, political, etc., my purpose is to write what will entertain and give pleasure. I do have a deep belief in the potential beauty of each human spirit, the power of love and concern, and the need for strong family influence on children, and I hope this is reflected in my work."

AVOCATIONAL INTERESTS: Oil painting, horses and dogs, gardening.